DIRECTORY OF NON-GOVERNMENTAL ORGANISATIONS ACTIVE IN SUSTAINABLE DEVELOPMENT

PART I: EUROPE

RÉPERTOIRE DES ORGANISATIONS NON GOUVERNEMENTALES ACTIVES DANS LE DOMAINE DU DÉVELOPPEMENT DURABLE

TOME I : EUROPE

DEVELOPMENT CENTRE
OF THE ORGANISATION FOR ECONOMIC CO-OPERATION AND DEVELOPMENT

CENTRE DE DÉVELOPPEMENT
DE L'ORGANISATION DE COOPÉRATION ET DE DÉVELOPPEMENT ÉCONOMIQUES

ORGANISATION FOR ECONOMIC CO-OPERATION AND DEVELOPMENT

Pursuant to Article 1 of the Convention signed in Paris on 14th December 1960, and which came into force on 30th September 1961, the Organisation for Economic Co-operation and Development (OECD) shall promote policies designed:

- to achieve the highest sustainable economic growth and employment and a rising standard of living in Member countries, while maintaining financial stability, and thus to contribute to the development of the world economy;
- to contribute to sound economic expansion in Member as well as non-member countries in the process of economic development; and
- to contribute to the expansion of world trade on a multilateral, non-discriminatory basis in accordance with international obligations.

The original Member countries of the OECD are Austria, Belgium, Canada, Denmark, France, Germany, Greece, Iceland, Ireland, Italy, Luxembourg, the Netherlands, Norway, Portugal, Spain, Sweden, Switzerland, Turkey, the United Kingdom and the United States. The following countries became Members subsequently through accession at the dates indicated hereafter: Japan (28th April 1964), Finland (28th January 1969), Australia (7th June 1971), New Zealand (29th May 1973), Mexico (18th May 1994) and the Czech Republic (21st December 1995). The Commission of the European Communities takes part in the work of the OECD (Article 13 of the OECD Convention).

The Development Centre of the Organisation for Economic Co-operation and Development was established by decision of the OECD Council on 23rd October 1962 and comprises twenty-two Member countries of the OECD: Austria, Belgium, Canada, the Czech Republic, Denmark, Finland, France, Germany, Greece, Iceland, Ireland, Italy, Japan, Luxembourg, Mexico, the Netherlands, Norway, Portugal, the United States, Spain, Sweden and Switzerland, as well as the Republic of Korea since April 1992 and Argentina and Brazil from March 1994. The Commission of the European Communities also takes part in the Centre's Advisory Board.

The purpose of the Centre is to bring together the knowledge and experience available in Member countries of both economic development and the formulation and execution of general economic policies; to adapt such knowledge and experience to the actual needs of countries or regions in the process of development and to put the results at the disposal of the countries by appropriate means.

The Centre has a special and autonomous position within the OECD which enables it to enjoy scientific independence in the execution of its task. Nevertheless, the Centre can draw upon the experience and knowledge available in the OECD in the development field.

ORGANISATION DE COOPÉRATION
ET DE DÉVELOPPEMENT ÉCONOMIQUES

En vertu de l'article 1ᵉʳ de la Convention signée le 14 décembre 1960, à Paris, et entrée en vigueur le 30 septembre 1961, l'Organisation de Coopération et de Développement Économiques (OCDE) a pour objectif de promouvoir des politiques visant :

- à réaliser la plus forte expansion de l'économie et de l'emploi et une progression du niveau de vie dans les pays Membres, tout en maintenant la stabilité financière, et à contribuer ainsi au développement de l'économie mondiale ;
- à contribuer à une saine expansion économique dans les pays Membres, ainsi que les pays non membres, en voie de développement économique ;
- à contribuer à l'expansion du commerce mondial sur une base multilatérale et non discriminatoire conformément aux obligations internationales.

Les pays Membres originaires de l'OCDE sont : l'Allemagne, l'Autriche, la Belgique, le Canada, le Danemark, l'Espagne, les États-Unis, la France, la Grèce, l'Irlande, l'Islande, l'Italie, le Luxembourg, la Norvège, les Pays-Bas, le Portugal, le Royaume-Uni, la Suède, la Suisse et la Turquie. Les pays suivants sont ultérieurement devenus Membres par adhésion aux dates indiquées ci-après : le Japon (28 avril 1964), la Finlande (28 janvier 1969), l'Australie (7 juin 1971), la Nouvelle-Zélande (29 mai 1973), le Mexique (18 mai 1994) et la République tchèque (21 décembre 1995). La Commission des Communautés européennes participe aux travaux de l'OCDE (article 13 de la Convention de l'OCDE).

Le Centre de Développement de l'Organisation de Coopération et de Développement Économiques a été créé par décision du Conseil de l'OCDE, en date du 23 octobre 1962, et regroupe vingt-deux des pays Membres de l'OCDE : l'Allemagne, l'Autriche, la Belgique, le Canada, le Danemark, la Finlande, l'Espagne, les États-Unis, la France, la Grèce, l'Islande, l'Irlande, l'Italie, le Japon, le Luxembourg, le Mexique, la Norvège, les Pays-Bas, le Portugal, la République tchèque, la Suède et la Suisse, ainsi que la Corée depuis avril 1992 et l'Argentine et le Brésil depuis mars 1994. La Commission des Communautés européennes participe également à la Commission Consultative du Centre.

Il a pour objet de rassembler les connaissances et données d'expériences disponibles dans les pays Membres, tant en matière de développement économique qu'en ce qui concerne l'élaboration et la mise en œuvre de politiques économiques générales ; d'adapter ces connaissances et ces données d'expériences aux besoins concrets des pays et régions en développement et de les mettre à la disposition des pays intéressés, par des moyens appropriés.

Le Centre occupe, au sein de l'OCDE, une situation particulière et autonome qui lui assure son indépendance scientifique dans l'exécution de ses tâches. Il bénéficie pleinement, néanmoins, de l'expérience et des connaissances déjà acquises par l'OCDE dans le domaine du développement.

The Liaison Committee of Development NGOs to the European Union

The Liaison Committee (LC) exists to represent the interests of European Development NGOs to the institutions of the European Union: the Commission, the European Parliament and the Council of Ministers. It seeks to promote the views of European NGDOs on development co-operation and aid policy issues, resource allocations and procedures. It also provides European NGOs with relevant information on the institutions and their work in the fields of development co-operation, humanitarian aid, development education, and a forum for European-level debate on these issues among NGOs.

The LC was established in 1976. It is structured on the basis of NGO "National Platforms" in each Member State of the European Union. Each platform elects one representative to the Liaison Committee itself, as well as representatives to the three standing Working Groups on Development Finance, Development Policy and Development Education, and a delegation to the annual General Assembly. From time to time, other Ad Hoc Groups are set up and specific Seminars and Conferences are organised to deal with particular issues as they arise.

The North-South Centre of the Council of Europe

The European Centre for Global Interdependence and Solidarity (the North-South Centre) was set up in 1990 in Lisbon. The Centre has its roots in the European Public Campaign on North-South Interdependence and Solidarity, launched by the Council of Europe in 1988.

The aims of the Centre are to raise public awareness of issues of global interdependence and solidarity and to advocate pluralist democracy and respect for human rights as fundamental elements of sustainable development. In order to attain its objectives, the Centre organises core projects and partnership projects, where it plays the role of organiser and co-organiser respectively.

The Centre has recently expanded its activities in Central and Eastern Europe in conformity with the all-European constituency of the Council of Europe.

The North-South Centre functions on the basis of a system of quadripartite co-management by parliamentarians, governments, non-governmental organisations and local and regional authorities.

The United Nations Non-Governmental Liaison Service (UN-NGLS)

Established in 1975, NGLS is a voluntarily funded, inter-agency unit of the UN system which seeks to promote enhanced dialogue and co-operation between the UN system and the broad development NGO community on economic and social development issues. NGLS is concerned with the entire UN sustainable development agenda. Current programme priorities are human development, environment and development, the global economy, and African recovery and development. In the pursuit of its mandate and objectives, NGLS executes a wide-ranging programme of information outreach activities, publications and meetings, and supports the participation of NGOs in major UN events and processes. It also supports the development education, information and advocacy work of NGOs. NGLS is supported by the following agencies, programmes and funds of the UN system: UNDP, UNCTAD, UN/DPI, UN/DPCSD, FAO, IFAD, UNCHS-Habitat, UNEP, UNESCO, UNIDO, UNFPA, UNHCR, UNICEF, the World Bank, WFP and WHO. The role and work of NGLS was endorsed by the UN Administrative Committee on Coordination in 1992 and by the General Assembly in 1993.

Le Comité de Liaison des ONG de développement auprès de l'Union européenne

Le Comité de Liaison (CL) est l'organisme qui représente les intérêts des ONG européennes de développement auprès des institutions de l'Union européenne : la Commission, le Parlement européen et le Conseil des ministres. Le CL cherche à promouvoir les points de vue des ONGD européennes sur les questions de coopération au développement et de politique d'aide, des allocations de ressources et des procédures. Le CL fournit aux ONG européennes des informations relatives aux institutions et à leur travail dans les domaines de la coopération au développement, de l'aide humanitaire et de l'éducation au développement, ainsi qu'un Forum au niveau européen pour stimuler le débat sur ces questions parmi les ONG.

Le CL a été établi en 1976. Il se compose de «plates-formes nationales» dans chacun des États membres de l'Union européenne. Chaque plate-forme désigne un représentant auprès du Comité de Liaison, des représentants auprès des trois Groupes de travail (Financement du développement, Politique de développement et Éducation au développement) et une délégation pour l'Assemblée générale annuelle. De temps à autre, des groupes *ad hoc* sont établis ou bien des séminaires spécifiques et des conférences sont organisées sur certains sujets d'ordre ponctuel.

Le Centre Nord-Sud du Conseil de l'Europe

Le Centre européen pour l'interdépendance et la solidarité mondiales (Centre Nord-Sud) a été établi à Lisbonne en 1990. Le Centre trouve son origine dans la campagne publique européenne sur l'interdépendance et la solidarité Nord-Sud, lancée en 1988 par le Conseil de l'Europe.

L'objectif du Centre est de sensibiliser l'opinion publique sur les questions d'indépendance et de solidarité mondiales et de soutenir la démocratie pluraliste et le respect des droits de la personne comme éléments fondamentaux du développement durable. Afin de mener à bien ses objectifs, le Centre organise des projets centraux et en partenariat, au sein desquels il est respectivement organisateur et co-organisateur.

Le Centre a récemment accru ses activités en Europe centrale et orientale conformément à la contribution paneuropéenne du Conseil de l'Europe.

Le Centre Nord-Sud fonctionne sur la base d'un système original de cogestion de parlementaires, gouvernements, organisations non gouvernementales et pouvoirs locaux et régionaux, système intitulé «quadrilogue».

Le Service de Liaison non gouvernemental des Nations Unies

Le SLNG a été créé en 1975. C'est une unité inter-agences du système des Nations Unies reposant sur la base de contributions volontaires et dont le but est de promouvoir une coopération et un dialogue soutenus entre les Nations Unies et l'importante communauté des ONG de développement. Le SLNG s'intéresse à toutes les questions de développement durable traitées par les Nations Unies. Le développement humain, l'environnement et le développement, l'économie mondiale, ainsi que la reprise économique et le développement en Afrique, sont les thèmes prioritaires du programme actuel. Afin de remplir son mandat et d'atteindre ses objectifs, le SLNG a entrepris un programme varié d'activités d'information, de publications et de réunions, et encourage les ONG à participer aux manifestations majeures organisées par les Nations Unies. Il apporte également son soutien aux activités d'éducation au développement, d'information et de promotion des ONG. Le SLNG bénéficie du soutien de 16 agences, programmes et fonds des Nations Unies : le PNUD, CNUCED, UN/DPI, UN/DPCSD, FAO, FIDA, Habitat, PNUE, UNESCO, ONUDI, FNUAP, HCR, UNICEF, la Banque mondiale, WFP et OMS. Le rôle et le travail du SLNG ont reçu l'approbation du Comité administratif des Nations Unies pour la Coordination en 1992, et de l'Assemblée générale en 1993.

Table of Contents

Acknowledgements 8

Preface 9

by Jean Bonvin, President of the OECD Development Centre; Agostinho Jardim Gonçalvez, President of the Liaison Committee of Development NGOs to the European Union; Tony Hill, Co-ordinator of the United Nations Non-Governmental Liaison Service; and Miguel Angel Martinez, President of the Executive Council of the North-South Centre of the Council of Europe

How to Use the Directory: Presentation, Profiles and Indexes 11

Introduction 19

Questionnaire 26

List of Regions and Countries 39

Exchange Rates 42

Profiles of NGOs by Country 43

AUT	Austria	45
BEL	Belgium	59
CHE	Switzerland	106
CYP	Cyprus	168
CZE	Czech Republic	170
DEU	Germany	176
DNK	Denmark	220
ESP	Spain	245
FIN	Finland	266
FRA	France	280
GBR	United Kingdom	372
GRC	Greece	442
HUN	Hungary	446
IRL	Ireland	453
ISL	Iceland	464
ITA	Italy	465
LIE	Liechtenstein	499
LUX	Luxembourg	500
MLT	Malta	512
NLD	Netherlands	515
NOR	Norway	567
POL	Poland	582
PRT	Portugal	588
SVK	Slovak Republic	596
SWE	Sweden	599
TUR	Turkey	630

Sustainable Development Actions Index, by Subject and Regions 633

Information and Educational Activities Index, by Subject and Activities 669

Alphabetical List of NGOs 711

List of Acronyms of NGOs 755

Table des matières

Remerciements 8

Préface 9

par Jean Bonvin, Président du Centre de Développement de l'OCDE ; Agostinho Jardim Gonçalvez, Président du Comité de liaison des ONG pour le développement auprès de l'Union européenne ; Tony Hill, Coordinateur du Service de liaison non gouvernementale des Nations unies ; Miguel Angel Martinez, Président du Conseil exécutif du Centre Nord-Sud du Conseil de l'Europe

Comment utiliser le répertoire : présentation, profils et index 11

Introduction 19

Questionnaire 32

Liste des régions et des pays 39

Taux de change 42

Profils des ONG par pays 43
AUT	Autriche	45
BEL	Belgique	59
CHE	Suisse	106
CYP	Chypre	168
CZE	République tchèque	170
DEU	Allemagne	176
DNK	Danemark	220
ESP	Espagne	245
FIN	Finlande	266
FRA	France	280
GBR	Royaume-Uni	372
GRC	Grèce	442
HUN	Hongrie	446
IRL	Irlande	453
ISL	Islande	464
ITA	Italie	465
LIE	Liechtenstein	499
LUX	Luxembourg	500
MLT	Malte	512
NLD	Pays-Bas	515
NOR	Norvège	567
POL	Pologne	582
PRT	Portugal	588
SVK	République slovaque	596
SWE	Suède	599
TUR	Turquie	630

Index des actions de développement durable dans les régions en développement, par thème et par région 633

Index des activités d'information et d'éducation, par thème et par activité 669

Liste alphabétique des ONG 711

Liste des sigles des ONG 755

Acknowledgements

The four partners gratefully acknowledge the support of the European Commission, the Government of Italy and the Government of the Netherlands for the work on the database and the publication of the Directory.

Remerciements

Les quatre partenaires adressent leurs sincères remerciements à la Commission européenne, et aux autorités italiennes et néerlandaises pour le généreux soutien qu'elles ont apporté au travail sur la base de données et à la publication du répertoire.

The Four Partners / Les quatre partenaires

OECD Development Centre / Centre de Développement de l'OCDE
94 rue Chardon-Lagache, 75016 Paris, France
℡ 33 (1) 45.24.82.19, Fax: 33 (1) 45.24.79.43

Liaison Committee of Development NGOs to the European Union / Comité de liaison des ONG pour le développement auprès de l'Union européenne
Square Ambiorix 10, 1000 Brussels / Bruxelles, Belgium / Belgique
℡ 32 (2) 736.20.30 / 736.40.87, Fax.: 32 (2) 732.19.34

United Nations Non-Governmental Liaison Service / Service de Liaison non gouvernementale des Nations unies
Palais des Nations, 1211 Geneva / Genève 10, Switzerland / Suisse
℡ 41 (22) 798.8400 ext./poste 272, Fax.: 41 (22) 788.7366

North-South Centre of the Council of Europe / Centre Nord-Sud du Conseil de l'Europe
Avenida de Liberdade 229-4, 1250 Lisbon / Lisbonne, Portugal
℡ 351 (1) 352.49.54, Fax.: 351 (1) 353.13.29 / 352.49.66

Preface

In 1995 and 1996, four of the major data-holders on NGOs in Europe joined forces to update their databases, with a view to producing a *Directory of Non-Governmental Organisations Active in Sustainable Development.*

These four organisations are:

* the Liaison Committee of Development NGOs to the European Union (Brussels);
* the North-South Centre of the Council of Europe (Lisbon);
* the Development Centre of the OECD (Paris); and
* the United Nations Non-Governmental Liaison Service (Geneva).

The publication of this Directory is thus the outcome of unprecedented collaboration in this field. The resulting database includes information on 3 900 NGOs from 26 countries in Europe.

These NGOs represent literally millions of citizens who devote time, energy and resources to improving the living conditions of others in developing countries. They also include those who actively seek to broaden public understanding at home of the complex and difficult situations that men and women face in developing regions.

This joint undertaking to update NGO information illustrates how much the activities of NGOs have evolved from individual project support to large-scale mobilisation of public opinion in favour of new approaches to international relations and international development co-operation. Non-Governmental Organisations are currently playing a major role with regard to the four multilateral organisations, namely the Council of Europe, the European Union, the OECD and the United Nations, as well as vis-à-vis the individual Member countries of these organisations.

In this Directory, the field of *Sustainable Development* has been divided into 17 thematic areas of activity reflecting the change in NGO actions from a sectoral,

Préface

En 1995 et 1996, les quatre détenteurs d'information sur les organisations non gouvernementales (ONG) en Europe se sont rassemblés pour mettre à jour les bases de données des ONG dans le but de produire un *Répertoire des ONG actives dans le développement durable.*

Ces quatre organisations sont les suivantes :

* le Comité de liaison des ONG pour le développement auprès de l'Union européenne (Bruxelles) ;
* le Centre Nord-Sud du Conseil de l'Europe (Lisbonne) ;
* le Centre de Développement de l'OCDE (Paris) ;
* le Service de liaison non gouvernementale des Nations unies (Genève).

Ce répertoire a donc pu être publié grâce à la collaboration sans précédent des quatre grands partenaires dans ce domaine. La base de données qui en résulte contient des informations sur 3 900 ONG provenant de 26 pays d'Europe.

Ces ONG représentent littéralement des millions de gens qui consacrent leur temps, leur énergie et toutes leurs ressources afin d'améliorer les conditions de vie des populations des pays en développement. Elles représentent aussi ceux qui cherchent activement à mieux informer l'opinion publique de leur pays des réalités complexes et difficiles auxquelles doivent faire face les femmes et les hommes vivant dans les pays en développement.

Cet effort commun illustre à quel point les activités des ONG ont évolué d'un appui à des micro-projets vers une grande mobilisation de l'opinion publique en faveur de nouvelles approches des relations internationales et de la coopération en matière de développement. A l'heure actuelle, les organisations non gouvernementales et les quatre organisations multilatérales : le Conseil de l'Europe, la Commission des Communautés européennes, l'OCDE, les Nations unies ainsi que chacun des pays Membres de ces organisations travaillent de concert.

Dans ce répertoire, le domaine du *Développement durable* a été divisé en 17 champs d'activités thématiques traduisant l'évolution de l'action des ONG. Celle-ci est

North-South approach in past decades, to a concerted global movement geared towards finding solutions to *global* problems.

We are very grateful to all the NGOs which provided information for this publication. The four partners in this joint project trust that, with this new Directory, they will make a modest contribution to strengthening awareness of NGO initiatives and facilitating communication, both among NGOs themselves, and between NGOs and government policy makers.

passée d'une approche « Nord-Sud » et sectorielle au cours des décennies passées, à une dynamique globale concertée, visant à trouver des solutions aux problèmes *globaux.*

Nous sommes très reconnaissants à toutes les ONG qui ont fourni des informations pour cette publication. Les quatre partenaires de ce projet espèrent, grâce au nouveau répertoire, apporter une contribution, si modeste soit-elle, à une meilleure connaissance des actions des ONG, à un renforcement de la communication non seulement des ONG entre elles, mais aussi entre ONG et responsables gouvernementaux.

Jean Bonvin

President / Président

OECD Development Centre / Centre de Développement de l'OCDE

Paris

Agostinho Jardim Gonçalvez

President / Président

NGDO-EU Liaison Committee / Comité de liaison ONGD-UE

Brussels / Bruxelles

Tony Hill

Co-ordinator / Coordinateur

United Nations NGLS / SLNG des Nations unies

Geneva / Genève

Miguel Angel Martinez

President of the Executive Council / Président du Conseil exécutif

North-South Centre of the Council of Europe / Centre Nord-Sud du Conseil de l'Europe

Lisbon / Lisbonne

April 1996 / avril 1996

How to Use the Directory: Presentation, Profiles and Indexes

The 1996 Directory of Non-Governmental Organisations Active in Sustainable Development contains information on 3 900 NGOs in Europe. Alphabetical lists of NGO names and acronyms have been included to facilitate access to this information, along with two cross-referenced indexes in English and French. Detailed descriptions of NGOs can be found in the Profiles section.

Profiles

The description of each NGO includes information on its aims, structure and major activities. These descriptions, or profiles, are arranged by the country in which the NGO is located. Within country sections, NGOs are listed alphabetically by their official name. Each profile is preceded by a seven figure code, indicating both the country in which it is based and the order in which it appears in the Directory. For example, the NGO AUT0002 is an Austrian NGO whose profile is the second in the Directory.

The profiles are presented in either English or French. This varies according to the language chosen by the NGO when filling out the questionnaire. Information on the NGOs is set out in the categories listed below. In some cases, categories are not included in the profiles as the information was not provided by the NGO.

Name: The official name of the NGO is followed by its acronym in brackets and an English or French translation, when the official name is not in either of these languages. The translation of the NGO's official name is always that provided by the organisation itself.

Address: The address given is the postal address. Telephone, fax and electronic mail numbers are included when available.

Contact: The name of an NGO representative, followed by his/her title.

Comment utiliser le répertoire : présentation, profils et index

Ce répertoire des ONG actives dans le domaine du développement durable contient des informations sur 3 900 ONG en Europe. Des listes alphabétiques des noms des ONG et de leurs sigles, avec deux index croisés en anglais et en français, ont été incluses pour faciliter l'accès à cette information. Une description détaillée des ONG peut être trouvée dans la section « Profils ».

Profils

Les descriptions des ONG contiennent des informations sur leurs objectifs, leur structure et leurs activités principales. Ces descriptions ou profils sont répertoriés selon le pays d'origine des ONG. Pour chaque pays, le classement suit l'ordre alphabétique de leur nom officiel. Chaque profil est précédé d'un code à sept chiffres indiquant à la fois le pays dans lequel se trouve l'ONG et l'ordre dans lequel elle apparaît dans le répertoire. Par exemple, l'ONG AUT0002 est une ONG autrichienne, dont le profil figure en deuxième position dans le répertoire.

Les profils sont, soit en français, soit en anglais, en fonction de la langue dans laquelle les ONG ont rempli le questionnaire. L'information sur chaque ONG est répartie en plusieurs rubriques dont on trouvera la liste ci-dessous. Elles n'apparaissent que si l'information a été fournie par l'ONG.

Nom : Le nom officiel de l'ONG est suivi de son sigle, entre parenthèses, et d'une traduction en anglais ou en français lorsque l'intitulé officiel n'est donné dans aucune de ces deux langues. La traduction du nom officiel de l'ONG est toujours celle qu'elle a elle-même proposée.

Adresse : L'adresse fournie est l'adresse postale. Les numéros de téléphone, de télécopie et de courrier électronique sont indiqués, dans la mesure du possible.

Contact : Il s'agit du nom d'un responsable de l'ONG, suivi éventuellement de son titre.

Objectives

A brief description of the NGO's major aims.

General Information

Creation: Year in which the NGO was founded.

Type of organisation: When applicable, the NGOs are listed under the three following headings: association of NGOs, network or co-ordinating body.

Member organisations: Number of organisations which are members of the NGO.

Affiliations: A list of networks, consortiums, umbrella organisations or federations to which the NGO is affiliated, followed by the countries in which they are located.

Personnel: The figures listed represent staff working for the NGO at the end of 1993. The total number of staff represents the combined total of salaried staff and of volunteers. The numbers of salaried staff and volunteers in developing countries are also indicated when applicable.

Budget: The NGO's budget for 1993 is given at 1993 rates in ECU and US dollars. In converting these amounts from other currencies to ECU and in US dollars, the figures have been rounded off to the closest thousand (for example, 325 650 becomes 326 000 and 325 240 becomes 325 000). A table of exchange rates is included on page 42.

Financial sources: The percentages of funding received by the NGO in 1993 from various sources are indicated, as listed in the following categories:

- *self-financing*, funds raised through the NGO's own activities, such as membership fees, sale of products from developing countries (alternative trade) and endowments;

- *private donations*, received through fund raising, grants, trust funds from the general public/companies/foundations;

- *public funds* from international, national, federal and local authorities.

Publications

Name(s) of the NGO's periodical(s), followed by the number of issues per year.

Objectifs

Brève description des principaux objectifs de l'ONG.

Informations générales

Date de création : Année de création de l'ONG.

Type d'organisation : Les ONG, sauf mention particulière de leur part, sont classées sous trois rubriques : regroupement d'ONG, réseau, ou collectif.

Organisations membres : Nombre des organisations membres lorsque cela a été précisé par l'ONG.

Affiliation : Liste des réseaux, consortiums, collectifs ou fédérations auxquels l'ONG est affiliée, suivie du pays dans lequel ils ont leur siège.

Personnel : Il s'agit de l'effectif du personnel de l'ONG à la fin de l'année 1993. Le total fourni représente la somme de l'effectif des salariés et des bénévoles. L'effectif des salariés et des bénévoles travaillant dans les pays en développement est précisé, le cas échéant.

Budget : Le budget de l'ONG pour l'année 1993 est donné en ÉCU et en dollars. Lors des conversions, les nombres obtenus ont été arrondis au millième supérieur ou inférieur (325 650 devenant, par exemple, 326 000 et 325 240 devenant 325 000). Un tableau des taux de change figure à la page 42.

Sources de financement : Les pourcentages des fonds recueillis par l'ONG en 1993 sont répartis entre les trois catégories suivantes :

- *autofinancement*, c'est-à-dire les fonds obtenus grâce aux activités de l'ONG : cotisations, dotations, vente de produits du tiers monde (commerce solidaire), ou les rémunérations perçues en échange de services ou de conseils ;

- *donations privées* provenant de collectes de fonds, de donations individuelles et fonds fiduciaires provenant d'individus, d'entreprises ou de fondations ;

- *fonds publics* alloués par des administrations internationales, nationales, fédérales ou locales.

Publications

Noms des périodiques publiés par l'ONG, suivis de leur périodicité.

When the NGO publishes an annual report or catalogues and list of available publications and/or educational material, these are mentioned.

Evaluation/Research Activities

When the NGO's evaluation reports on its activities are available, these are mentioned, as are any research activities undertaken.

Planned Activities

A brief description of the most important information campaigns and new activities planned for 1996-97.

Comments

Additional information provided by the NGO. When applicable, the organisation's activities in the Community of Independent States are mentioned.

Activities in Developing Regions

The following information is available in this section:
- the number of countries in which the NGO has worked in 1993, either directly or through local partners;
- the list of activities included in the 17 categories of sustainable development: Children, youth, family; Debt, finance, trade; Democracy, good governance, institution building, participatory development; Ecology, environment, biodiversity; Education, training, literacy; Emergency relief, refugees, humanitarian assistance; Energy, transport; Food, famine; Gender issues, women; Health, sanitation, water; Human rights, peace, conflicts; Population, family planning, demography; Other[1]; Rural development, agriculture; Sending volunteers, experts, technical assistance; Small enterprises, informal sector, handicrafts; Urban development, habitat;

- the geographical regions in which the NGO undertakes its sustainable development activities. The thirteen possible regions are: Caribbean; Central

Évaluation/recherche

Lorsque les rapports d'évaluation des activités de l'ONG sont disponibles, cela est mentionné. Il en va de même lorsqu'elle mène des activités de recherche.

Prévision d'activités

Brève description des principales campagnes d'information et des nouvelles activités envisagées pour la période 1996-97.

Commentaires

Quelques renseignements supplémentaires sur l'ONG. Si cela est mentionné, les activités de l'organisation dans la Communauté des États indépendants sont précisées.

Activités dans les régions en développement

Sous cette rubrique, on trouve les informations suivantes :
- le nombre de pays où l'ONG est intervenue en 1993, soit directement, soit par l'intermédiaire de partenaires locaux ;
- la liste des activités retenues comme caractéristiques d'un développement durable. Celles-ci sont au nombre de 17 : Aliments, famine ; Autres[1] ; Démocratie, bonne gestion publique, création d'institutions, développement participatif ; Dette, finances, commerce ; Développement rural, agriculture ; Développement urbain, habitat ; Droits de l'Homme, paix, conflits ; Écologie, environnement, biodiversité ; Éducation, formation, alphabétisation ; Enfants, jeunesse, famille ; Énergie, transport ; Envoi de volontaires, experts, assistance technique ; Petites entreprises, secteur informel, artisanat ; Population, planning familial, démographie ; Questions relatives aux femmes ; Santé, eau, assainissement ; Secours d'urgence, réfugiés, aide humanitaire ;
- une liste des régions où l'ONG intervient dans le domaine du développement durable a été dressée. Les 13 régions possibles sont les suivantes : Afrique

Africa; Central Asia and South Asia; East Africa; East Asia; Mexico and Central America; the Middle East; North Africa; Oceania; Southern Africa; South America; South East Asia; West Africa.

australe ; Afrique centrale ; Afrique de l'Est ; Afrique de l'Ouest ; Afrique du Nord ; Amérique du Sud ; Asie centrale et du Sud ; Asie de l'Est ; Asie du Sud-Est ; Caraïbes ; Mexique et Amérique centrale ; Moyen-Orient ; Océanie.

Information and Educational Activities

Two lists can be found in this section:
- a list of the themes of NGO activities (20 in total): Children, youth, family; Culture, tradition, religion; Ecology, environment, biodiversity; Education, literacy; Emergency relief, humanitarian assistance, assistance to refugees; Employment, unemployment; Food, famine; Gender issues, women; Health, sanitation, water; Human rights, democracy, politics; International economic relations, trade, debt, finance; International relations, co-operation, development aid; Other[1]; Peace, ethnic, conflicts, armaments, disarmaments; Population, family planning, demography; Poverty, living conditions; Racism, xenophobia, anti-Semitism; Refugees, migrants, ethnic groups; Rural development, agriculture; Urban development, habitat;

- a list of NGO activities (eleven in total): Broadcasting, cultural events; Conferences, seminars, workshops, training; Exchanges, twinning, linking; Formal education; Fund raising; Information campaigns, exhibitions; Information & documentation services, data bases; Lobbying, advocacy; Networking, electronic telecommunication; Other[1]; Publishing, audio-visual materials, educational materials.

NGOs that did not respond to our questionnaire but had been included in one of the four original databases are also included in this Directory, except when they informed us that they did not wish to appear or when we received notice that the NGO ceased to exist or moved without leaving a forwarding address. The NGOs which did not send a response are distinguished by the symbol "§" which follows their name in the alphabetical list of NGO names. In the main text, their names, addresses, year of foundation, and in some cases the name of the contact person are mentioned.

Activités d'information et d'éducation

Dans cette rubrique figurent deux listes :
- la liste des domaines d'activité de l'ONG, au nombre de 20 : Aliments, famine ; Autres[1] ; Culture, tradition, religion ; Droits de l'Homme, paix, conflits ; Développement rural, agriculture ; Développement urbain, habitat ; Écologie, environnement, biodiversité ; Éducation, formation, alphabétisation ; Emploi, chômage ; Enfants, jeunesse, famille ; Paix, conflits ethniques, armement, désarmement ; Pauvreté, conditions de vie ; Population, planning familial, démographie ; Questions relatives aux femmes ; Racisme, xénophobie, antisémitisme ; Réfugiés, migrants, groupes ethniques ; Relations économiques internationales, commerce, dette, finances ; Relations internationales, coopération, aide au développement ; Santé, eau, assainissement ; Secours d'urgence, réfugiés, aide humanitaire ;

- la liste des activités de l'ONG ; celles-ci sont au nombre de onze : Autres[1] ; Campagne d'information, expositions ; Collecte de fonds ; Conférences, séminaires, ateliers, activités de formation ; Échanges, parrainage, jumelage ; Édition, documents audiovisuels, documents éducatifs ; Éducation formelle ; Lobbying, plaidoyer ; Radiodiffusion, manifestations culturelles ; Réseaux, télécommunications électroniques ; Services d'information et de documentation, bases de données.

Même les ONG qui n'ont pas répondu à notre questionnaire, mais qui figuraient dans l'une des quatre bases de données d'origine ont été incluses dans ce répertoire. Seules les ONG ayant cessé d'exister et celles ne désirant pas y apparaître, ou celles dont l'adresse n'est plus valable, n'y figurent pas. Ces ONG se repèrent au symbole « § » qui suit leur nom dans la liste complète des ONG classées par ordre alphabétique. Dans le texte principal, seuls leurs nom et adresse, leur année de création et, éventuellement, le nom de leur responsable sont mentionnés.

14

Indexes

The Directory contains two cross-referenced indexes in English and French. These indexes are presented in the following manner:

Index 1, *Sustainable Development Actions in Developing Regions*: the subjects of sustainable development actions (e.g. Rural development, agriculture; Urban development, habitat) are listed with the respective developing regions in which the NGO carries out its actions (e.g East Africa, West Africa).

Index 2, *Information and Educational Activities*: the topics of information and educational activities undertaken by the NGO in its own country (e.g. Rural development, agriculture; Urban development, habitat) are listed with their respective activities (e.g. Information campaigns, exhibitions; Lobbying, advocacy).

These two cross-referenced indexes have been included to provide users with more detailed information on NGO actions than can be found in the profiles. While both indexes are bi-lingual, the English alphabetical order takes precedence. The NGOs found in each category are indicated by their profile code: the three letter ISO country code and four digit reference number.

The examples below indicate the type of information which can be found in each index and a simple way to find such information.

Index 1 - Examples

A. Which Italian NGOs are active in the field of Human Rights in East Africa?

1. Consult the list of ISO codes (p. 633) at the beginning of Index 1 to find the code for Italy: ITA.
2. Consult the list of Subjects (p. 634) and of Regions (p. 634) to see the categories as they appear in Index 1. Human rights actions are included in the

Index

Le répertoire comporte deux index croisés en anglais et en français qui se présentent de la manière suivante :

Index 1, *Actions de développement durable dans les régions en développement* : aux thèmes des actions de développement durable (par exemple, Développement rural, agriculture ; Développement urbain, habitat), on fait correspondre les régions où elles se déroulent (Afrique de l'Ouest, Afrique de l'Est, etc.).

Index 2, *Activités d'information et d'éducation* : aux thèmes des activités d'information et d'éducation menées par l'ONG dans son propre pays (par exemple, Développement rural, agriculture ; Développement urbain, habitat), on fait correspondre les activités respectives (Campagnes d'information, expositions ; Lobbying, plaidoyer, etc.).

Ces deux index croisés ont été inclus dans ce répertoire afin d'apporter un supplément d'information sur l'action des ONG. Les deux index sont bilingues, mais l'ordre alphabétique suit la version anglaise. Dans chaque catégorie, les ONG peuvent être identifiées grâce au code de leur profil : les trois lettres du code ISO du pays et les quatre chiffres de référence.

Les exemples ci-dessous démontrent le type d'information que l'on peut obtenir par l'usage des index et une méthode simple pour l'obtenir.

Index 1 - Exemples

A. Quelles sont les ONG italiennes qui sont actives dans le domaine des Droits de l'Homme en Afrique de l'Est ?

1. Consultez la liste des codes ISO (p. 633) au début de l'Index 1 pour trouver celui de l'Italie : ITA.
2. Consultez les listes des thèmes (p. 634) et des régions (p. 634) pour voir la façon dont apparaissent les catégories dans l'Index 1. Celles-ci sont répertoriées selon la version alphabétique anglaise, suivie de la traduction française. L'utilisateur francophone doit donc traduire sa recherche en anglais. Par exemple, le thème DROIT DE L'HOMME, PAIX, CONFLITS est

category HUMAN RIGHTS, PEACE, CONFLICT - DROITS DE L'HOMME, PAIX, CONFLITS. East Africa appears as EAST AFRICA - AFRIQUE DE L'EST.

3. Find the category HUMAN RIGHTS, PEACE, CONFLICT - DROITS DE L'HOMME, PAIX, CONFLITS in Index 1.

4. Following each subject is a list of regions, arranged in the alphabetical order of the English name of the region.

5. Under the region EAST AFRICA - AFRIQUE DE L'EST, Italian NGOs can be identified by ITA, followed by four digits forming a unique seven figure code, e.g. ITA2784, ITA2810, etc.

B. In which regions of the developing world does the Dutch NGO NOVIB undertake sustainable development actions in the field of education?

1. Consult the Alphabetical List of Acronyms of NGOs (p. 755) to find this organisation's profile code: NLD3199.

2. In the list of Sustainable Development *Actions* (p. 633), the field of education appears as EDUCATION, TRAINING, LITERACY - EDUCATION, ACTIVITES DE FORMATION, ALPHABETISATION. Find this subject in Index 1.

3. Following each subject is a list of regions arranged in the alphabetical order of the English name of the region.

4. By verifying the presence of the code NLD3199 under each region which follows EDUCATION, TRAINING, LITERACY - EDUCATION, ACTIVITES DE FORMATION, ALPHABETISATION, the user can identify in which regions NOVIB undertakes this action.

traduit par HUMAN RIGHTS, PEACE, CONFLICTS. La région Afrique de l'Est se retrouve sous la catégorie EAST AFRICA - AFRIQUE DE L'EST.

3. Trouvez le thème HUMAN RIGHTS, PEACE, CONFLICTS - DROIT DE L'HOMME, PAIX, CONFLITS dans l'Index 1.

4. Chaque thème est suivi d'une liste des régions, lesquelles sont répertoriées selon l'ordre alphabétique donné par la version anglaise.

5. Trouvez la catégorie EAST AFRICA - AFRIQUE DE L'EST dans la liste des régions. Les ONG italiennes sont identifiées par le code ITA, suivi de leur numéro de profil à quatre chiffres formant ainsi un code unique à sept chiffres, par exemple ITA2784, ITA2810, etc.

B. Dans quelles régions en développement l'ONG hollandaise NOVIB entreprend-elle des activités de développement durable dans le domaine de l'éducation ?

1. Consultez la liste alphabétique des sigles des ONG (p. 755) pour trouver le code du profil de l'organisation : NLD3199.

2. Dans la liste des *Actions* de développement durable (p. 633) qui se trouve au début de l'Index 1, le domaine de l'éducation est classé sous la catégorie EDUCATION, TRAINING, LITERACY - EDUCATION, ACTIVITES DE FORMATION, ALPHABETISATION.

3. Chaque action est suivie d'une liste des régions, lesquelles sont répertoriées selon l'ordre alphabétique donné par la version anglaise.

4. Trouvez le code NLD3199 en vérifiant chaque région qui suit EDUCATION, TRAINING, LITERACY - EDUCATION, ACTIVITES DE FORMATION, ALPHABETISATION. L'utilisateur peut ainsi identifier les régions dans lesquelles NOVIB entreprend cette activité.

Index 2 - Examples

C. Which French NGOs undertake conferences in France on agricultural development in developing countries?

1. Consult the list of ISO codes (p. 669) at the beginning of Index 2 to find the code for France: FRA.

2. Consult the list of Subjects (p. 670) and of Activities (p. 670) at the beginning of Index 2 to see the categories as they appear in Index 2. Agricultural development is included in the category RURAL DEVELOPMENT, AGRICULTURE - DEVELOPPEMENT RURAL, AGRICULTURE. Conferences are found in the category CONFERENCES, SEMINARS, WORKSHOPS, TRAINING ACTIVITIES - CONFERENCES, SEMINAIRES, ATELIERS, ACTIVITES DEFORMATION.

3. Find the subject RURAL DEVELOPMENT, AGRICULTURE - DEVELOPPEMENT RURAL, AGRICULTURE in Index 2.

4. Following each subject is a list of activities arranged in alphabetical order of the English name of the activity.

5. Under the activity CONFERENCES, SEMINARS, WORKSHOPS, TRAINING ACTIVITIES - CONFERENCES, SEMINAIRES, ATELIERS, ACTIVITES DE FORMATION, French NGOs can be identified by FRA, followed by four digits forming a unique seven figure code, e.g. FRA1616, FRA1627, etc.

D. What activities does the Irish NGO, Trocaire, undertake in Ireland on the subject of gender issues?

1. Consult the Alphabetical List of NGOs (p. 711) to find the organisation's profile code: IRL2726.

2. In the list of Subjects (p. 670), the topic of gender issues appears as GENDER ISSUES, WOMEN - QUESTIONS RELATIVES AUX FEMMES. Find this category in Index 2.

3. Following each theme is a list of activities, arranged in the alphabetical order of the English name of the activity.

Index 2 - exemples

C. Quelles sont les ONG françaises qui organisent des conférences en France sur le thème du développement agricole ?

1. Consultez la liste des codes ISO (p. 669) au début de l'Index 2 pour trouver celui de la France : FRA.

2. Consultez les listes des thèmes (p. 670) et des activités (p. 670) qui se trouvent au début de l'Index, pour voir la façon dont apparaissent les catégories dans l'Index 2. Par exemple, le terme de développement agricole est inclus dans la catégorie RURAL DEVELOPMENT, AGRICULTURE - DEVELOPPEMENT RURAL, AGRICULTURE. Le terme de conférence est classé sous la catégorie CONFERENCES, SEMINARS, WORKSHOPS, TRAINING ACTIVITIES - CONFERENCES, SEMINAIRES, ATELIERS, ACTIVITES DE FORMATION.

3. Recherchez la catégorie RURAL DEVELOPMENT, AGRICULTURE - DEVELOPPEMENT RURAL, AGRICULTURE, dans l'Index 2.

4. Chaque thème est suivi d'une liste d'activités, lesquelles sont répertoriées selon l'ordre alphabétique donné par la version anglaise.

5. Sous la catégorie CONFERENCES, SEMINARS, WORKSHOPS, TRAINING ACTIVITIES - CONFERENCE, SEMINAIRES, ATELIERS, ACTIVITES DE FORMATION, les ONG françaises peuvent être identifiées par FRA, suivies de leur numéro de profil à quatre chiffres formant ainsi un code unique à sept chiffres, par exemple FRA1616, FRA1627, etc.

D. Quelles activités l'ONG irlandaise, Trocaire, entreprend-elle en Irlande sur les questions relatives aux femmes ?

1. Consultez la liste alphabétique des ONG (p. 711) pour trouver le code de l'organisation : IRL2726.

2. Dans la liste des thèmes (p. 670), le sujet relatif à la question des femmes se trouve sous la catégorie GENDER ISSUES, WOMEN - QUESTIONS RELATIVES AUX FEMMES. Trouvez ce thème dans l'Index 2.

3. Chaque thème est suivi d'une liste d'activités, selon l'ordre alphabétique donné par la version anglaise.

4. By verifying the presence of the code IRL2726 under each activity which follows the subject GENDER ISSUES, WOMEN - QUESTIONS RELATIVES AUX FEMMES, the user can identify the activities undertaken by Trocaire on this theme.

Note

1. The term "Other" has been used for organisations which specified a category that was not included in the choices available.

4. Trouvez le code IRL2726 en vérifiant chaque activité qui suit le thème GENDER ISSUES, WOMEN - QUESTIONS RELATIVES AUX FEMMES. L'utilisateur peut ainsi identifier les activités entreprises par Trocaire sur ce thème.

Note

1. Le terme « Autres » a été utilisé pour les organisations qui ont mentionné une catégorie non incluse dans les choix proposés.

Introduction

Introduction

The world of Non-Governmental Organisations (NGOs) is dynamic and subject to frequent and rapid change, due to the evolving needs of a developing world to which millions of people working with NGOs devote time and resources. Regular updating is necessary as approximately 20 per cent of the information in data collections on NGOs becomes obsolete each year. The 1996 NGO Directory contains information about European NGOs working in the field of **Sustainable Development**[1].

This directory is comprehensive because it has brought together, for the first time, the four major data holders on NGO activities in Europe: the Liaison Committee of Development NGOs to the European Union (Brussels), the North-South Centre of the Council of Europe (Lisbon), the United Nations Non-Governmental Liaison Service (Geneva) and the OECD Development Centre (Paris).

The profiles of 3 900 NGOs in 26 European countries including all European OECD Member countries and seven other Members of the Council of Europe are listed in this Directory. The inclusion of the additional seven countries was possible because the four collaborating institutions had a sufficient amount of information on them in their original data collections, or had the technical capacity to collect reliable information within the time-span of the project. It is the intention of the partners in this undertaking to include all European countries in future editions of the Directory, whenever technical resources so permit and when more comprehensive information on NGO activities in these countries is available[2].

Presently work has begun on the companion volume of this Directory which will include the OECD Member countries outside Europe.

Le monde des organisations non gouvernementales (ONG) est dynamique et sujet à des changements rapides et fréquents ; cela est dû à la nature évolutive des besoins d'un monde en développement auquel des millions de gens consacrent leur temps et leur énergie. En règle générale, près de 20 pour cent des informations collectées sur les ONG deviennent obsolètes chaque année ; leur mise à jour régulière est donc nécessaire. Le répertoire des ONG de 1996 rassemble un grand nombre d'informations sur les activités des ONG européennes qui agissent en vue d'un **développement durable**[1].

La préparation de ce répertoire fort étendu a réuni, pour la première fois, les quatre grands détenteurs d'informations sur les activités des ONG en Europe : le Comité de liaison des ONG pour le développement auprès de l'Union européenne (Bruxelles), le Centre Nord-Sud du Conseil de l'Europe (Lisbonne), le Service de liaison non gouvernementale des Nations unies (Genève) et le Centre de Développement de l'OCDE (Paris).

Ce répertoire recense 3 900 ONG dans 26 pays européens. Tous les pays européens Membres de l'OCDE y sont inclus. Sept autres membres du Conseil de l'Europe ont été ajoutés. L'inclusion de ces derniers a été possible parce que les quatre institutions concernées disposaient déjà d'informations assez nombreuses sur lesdits membres, ou parce qu'elles avaient la capacité technique de rassembler des informations fiables dans le temps imparti au projet. L'objectif des partenaires est d'inclure tous les pays européens dans l'édition de futurs répertoires, à mesure que les ressources techniques le permettront et à mesure que des informations plus détaillées des ONG seront disponibles[2].

D'ores et déjà, les travaux ont commencé sur le deuxième volume de ce répertoire qui inclura les pays Membres de l'OCDE non européens.

Selection Criteria

The NGOs in each of the countries included in this Directory have their own history and traditions, linked to the development of civil society and its relations with the political and economic structures of its country. Therefore, it is difficult to formulate a definition of NGOs on an international level which is practical and respects their national differences. A flexible "definition" was thus adopted, based on their singular traditions.

The NGOs included in the survey were those which, from the beginning of the project, were present in at least one of the four partners' NGO databases. Questionnaires filled in by the NGOs provided the additional information for this Directory. In general, all organisations were included if they responded positively to the questionnaire. Those excluded were commercial for-profit organisations, research institutes and government departments. Finally, a few organisations sent notice that they did not wish to be included in this Directory, and have subsequently been removed from the database. NGOs that would like to be included in future editions of this publication are requested to inform us accordingly.

While the project partners have used all available expertise to arrive at proper selection decisions, we acknowledge that mistakes could have been made, for which we apologise.

Database Update

The database on NGOs in OECD countries is an inventory which can be continuously updated. Organisations are therefore invited to inform the Development Centre of any corrections, changes or new information, including addresses and contact names.

Sustainable Development

The NGOs included in this Directory are those which undertake sustainable development activities in developing regions, in the following broad thematic areas: Children, youth, family; Debt, finance, trade; Democracy, good governance, institution building, participatory development; Ecology, environment, biodiversity; Education, training, literacy; Emergency

Critères de sélection

Les ONG de chacun des pays figurant dans ce répertoire ont chacune leur histoire, liée au développement de la société civile et à ses relations avec les structures économiques et politiques de son pays. Aussi est-il difficile de donner à un niveau international une définition du terme ONG qui soit commode et respecte les différences locales. Une définition souple a donc été adoptée, basée sur les usages spécifiques des ONG.

Les ONG incluses dans ce répertoire étaient déjà présentes dans au moins l'une des quatre bases de données. Les questionnaires, remplis par les ONG, ont fournit les informations complémentaires pour ce répertoire. En général, toutes les organisations qui ont répondu au questionnaire ont été retenues. Ont été exclus les organisations exerçant des activités à but lucratif, les instituts de recherche et les services publics. Au demeurant, quelques organisations ont signalé qu'elles ne voulaient pas être répertoriées, et ont, par conséquent, été écartées de la base de données. Les ONG qui souhaitent être mentionnées dans les futures éditions du répertoire sont donc invitées à nous en informer.

Bien que les partenaires du projet aient mis à profit toutes leurs compétences pour réaliser une sélection appropriée, le risque d'erreur n'est pas à exclure et nous nous en excusons d'avance.

Mise à jour de la base de données

La base de données sur les ONG des pays de l'OCDE constitue un inventaire qui peut être mis à jour en permanence. Les organisations sont donc invitées à tenir le Centre de Développement informé des corrections, changements ou données nouvelles, même pour ce qui concerne les adresses et les noms des responsables.

Développement durable

Les ONG figurant dans ce répertoire sont celles qui entreprennent des activités de développement durable dans les régions en développement, sur les grands thèmes suivants : Aliments, famine ; Démocratie, bonne gestion publique, création d'institutions, développement participatif ; Dette, finances, commerce ; Développement rural, agriculture ; Développement urbain, habitat ; Droits

relief, refugees, humanitarian assistance; Energy, transport; Food, famine; Gender issues, women; Health, sanitation, water; Human rights, peace, conflicts; Population, family panning, demography; Rural development, agriculture; Sending volunteers, experts, technical assistance; Small enterprises, informal sector, handicrafts; Urban development, habitat.

Furthermore, NGOs were included which carry out information and education activities on sustainable development in their own countries. These activities are classified under the following headings: Children, youth, family; Culture, tradition, religion; Ecology, environment, biodiversity; Education, literacy; Emergency relief, humanitarian assistance, assistance to refugees; Employment, unemployment; Food, famine; Gender issues, women; Health, sanitation, water; Human rights, democracy, politics; International economic relations, trade, debt, finance; International relations, co-operation, development aid; Peace, ethnic, conflicts, armaments, disarmament's; Population, family planning, demography; Poverty, living conditions; Racism, xenophobia, anti-Semitism; Refugees, migrants, ethnic groups; Rural development, agriculture; Urban development, habitat.

The above-mentioned thematic areas were, for the most part, based on practical considerations, such as the way in which information was previously structured in the partners' data collections. A large network of experts from national governments, NGO umbrella organisations and inter-governmental organisations was consulted to ensure that these categories accurately reflect the various activities in sustainable development.

Similarly, the geographical divisions used in defining the regions were based on those commonly used in various multilateral organisations, and adapted to what appeared to be most practical use for data collection purposes.

Neither the thematic areas nor the geographical regions, however, should be considered as formal definitions. The terms employed and the presentation of material throughout this publication do not imply the expression of any opinion whatsoever on the part of the collaborating

de l'Homme, paix, conflits ; Écologie, environnement, biodiversité ; Éducation, formation, alphabétisation ; Enfants, jeunesse, famille ; Énergie, transport ; Envoi de volontaires, experts, assistance technique ; Petites entreprises, secteur informel, artisanat ; Population, planning familial, démographie ; Questions relatives aux femmes ; Santé, assainissement, eau ; Secours d'urgence, réfugiés, aide humanitaire.

En outre, y figurent les ONG exerçant des activités d'informations et d'éducation sur le développement durable dans leur propre pays. Ces activités ont été classées sous les rubriques suivantes : Aliments, famine ; Culture, tradition, religion ; Droits de l'Homme, paix, conflits ; Développement rural, agriculture ; Développement urbain, habitat ; Écologie, environ-nement, biodiversité ; Éducation, formation, alpha-bétisation ; Emploi, chômage ; Enfants, jeunesse, famille ; Paix, conflits ethniques, armement, désarmement ; Pauvreté, conditions de vie ; Population, planning familial, démographie ; Questions relatives aux femmes ; Racisme, xénophobie, antisémitisme ; Réfugiés, migrants, groupes ethniques ; Relations économiques internationales, commerce, dette, finances ; Relations internationales, coopération, aide au développement ; Santé, eau, assainissement ; Secours d'urgence, réfugiés, aide humanitaire.

Les principaux thèmes de développement durable énumérés ci-dessus ont été définis, en grande partie, sur la base de considérations pratiques, notamment la manière selon laquelle les informations ont été préalablement conçues dans les bases de données disponibles chez les partenaires. Un large réseau d'experts de divers gouvernements, de collectifs d'ONG et d'organisations intergouvernementales a été consulté pour refléter aussi fidèlement que possible les activités dans le domaine du développement durable.

De la même manière, les diverses divisions géographiques utilisées pour définir les régions ont été conçues sur les mêmes bases que celles couramment utilisées par les différentes organisations multilatérales ; elles ont été adaptées à ce qui semble le plus conforme aux besoins des bases de données.

Ni les divisions thématiques, ni les régions géographiques ne devraient être perçues comme une définition formelle. Les appellations employées dans cette publication et la présentation des données qui y figurent n'impliquent aucune prise de position de la part des quatre partenaires

partners concerning the legal status of any country, territory, city or area, or of their authorities, or concerning the delimitation of their frontiers or boundaries.

quant au statut juridique des pays, territoires, villes ou zones, ou de leurs autorités, ni quant au tracé de leurs frontières ou limites.

Methodology

This Directory was compiled through a questionnaire survey sent to approximately 4 500 NGOs.

The information contained in the NGO profiles was provided by the NGOs themselves. The purpose of this publication is to make available, rather than to evaluate, the data thus provided.

The names and addresses of NGOs which neither responded to the Questionnaire nor informed us that they did not wish to appear, have been included in the Directory.

Questionnaires were analysed at the Development Centre between October 1994 and September 1995. The information was processed on a microcomputer using Micro CDS/ISIS, a software developed by UNESCO's Division of the General Information Programme.

Keyword indexing was based on the *Macrothesaurus for Information Processing in the Field of Economic and Social Development* (OECD/United Nations, 1991). The Multilingual Thesaurus Management Program (MTM3, OECD Development Centre, 1994) was used for the management of keywords.

Méthodologie

Ce répertoire a été réalisé d'après les résultats d'un questionnaire envoyé à 4 500 ONG.

Les informations contenues dans les profils ont été fournies par les ONG elles-mêmes. L'objectif de cette publication est de rendre disponibles les informations fournies plutôt que de les évaluer.

Les noms et adresses des ONG qui n'ont pas répondu au questionnaire et qui ne nous ont pas informés qu'elles ne souhaitaient pas apparaître dans ce répertoire ont été tout de même inclus.

Les questionnaires ont été analysés au Centre de Développement entre octobre 1994 et septembre 1995. La saisie des informations dans la base de données utilisée pour le projet a été effectuée sur micro-ordinateur sous Micro CDS/ISIS, un logiciel développé par la Division du programme d'information générale de l'UNESCO.

L'indexation des mots clés s'est faite sur la base du *Macrothésaurus pour le traitement de l'information relative au développement économique et social* (OCDE/ Nations unies, 1991) ; la création et la gestion des termes ont été faites à partir du programme du *Logiciel de gestion de thésaurus multilingue* (MTM3, Centre de Développement de l'OCDE, 1994).

Acknowledgements

Many individuals and organisations, both in governmental and non-governmental circles, deserve our gratitude for their support and encouragement during the preparation of this Directory. Sincerest thanks go to all the NGOs that helped make this new publication a reality by responding to our questionnaire survey.

Establishing a list of all the other individuals and organisations that have contributed to such a project would be a long and hazardous process. Let us, nevertheless, address particular thanks to James Mackie and Siegfried Praille of the Liaison Committee of

Remerciements

Nous exprimons notre gratitude aux nombreuses personnes et organisations appartenant aux milieux gouvernementaux ou non gouvernementaux qui nous ont apporté leur soutien et leur encouragement tout au long de ce projet. Nous tenons à remercier sincèrement toutes les ONG qui ont répondu à notre questionnaire : sans elles, cette nouvelle publication n'aurait pu voir le jour.

La liste des personnes et organisations qui ont été sollicitées pour un tel projet serait longue à dresser, et risquerait malgré tout d'être incomplète. Qu'il nous soit néanmoins permis de témoigner une reconnaissance particulière à James Mackie et à Siegfried Praille du

Development NGOs to the European Union, to Jos Lemmers, Suzanne Hana and Susana Nunes of the North-South Centre of the Council of Europe, and last but not least, to Tony Hill and Leyla Alyanak of the United Nations Non-Governmental Liaison Service.

At the Development Centre, Giulio Fossi and Henny Helmich were responsible for the project. Nicole Lallier, Vanda Legrandgérard, Bruno Giret and Ken Smith were actively involved in the conception and distribution of the questionnaires. Alice Watson provided invaluable assistance in the preparation of the text and indexes from the database for publication. Essential data entry programmes for Micro CDS/ISIS were written for this project by André Crisan. Nathalie Laumonerie and Joanne Combes (project co-ordinators), directed the work of the team responsible for the research, compilation and production of the Directory and database. The members of the team included: Fatiha Ammi, Ruth Ben-Artzi, Gia Daniller, Lisa Hayles, Elizabeth Maddison, Vanessa Peat, François Sedogo and Amina Zaarrou, with the help of Ylva Bergström, Muriel Hubert and Jody Kaylor.

Our special thanks go to Catherine Duport, Head of Administration and Colm Foy and his team in the Publications and Information Unit. We would also like to thank all our colleagues from the OECD Secretariat who played an important part in the success of our work.

Comité de liaison des ONG pour le développement auprès de l'Union européenne, à Jos Lemmers, Suzanne Hana et Susana Nunes du Centre Nord-Sud du Conseil de l'Europe, enfin, à Tony Hill et à Leyla Alyanak du Service de liaison non gouvernementale des Nations unies.

Au Centre de Développement, les responsables de ce projet ont été Giulio Fossi et Henny Helmich. Nicole Lallier, Vanda Legrandgérard, Bruno Giret et Ken Smith se sont activement occupés de la conception et de l'envoi des questionnaires. Alice Watson a fourni une aide inestimable pour la préparation des textes et des index provenant de la base de données, en vue de leur publication. Le programme de saisie pour Micro CDS/ISIS a été élaboré par André Crisan. Nathalie Laumonerie et Joanne Combes (coordinatrices du projet), ont dirigé les travaux de l'équipe chargée de l'enquête, de l'analyse de la mise en forme des données du répertoire, à savoir Fatiha Ammi, Ruth Ben-Artzi, Gia Daniller, Lisa Hayles, Elizabeth Maddison, Vanessa Peat, François Sedogo et Amina Zaarrou, avec l'aide de Ylva Bergström, Muriel Hubert et Jody Kaylor.

Nous remercions spécialement Catherine Duport, Responsable des Affaires Administratives ainsi que Colm Foy et son équipe de l'Unité Publications et Information. Nous exprimons aussi toute notre reconnaissance à nos collègues du Secrétariat de l'OCDE pour le rôle très important qu'ils ont joué dans la réussite de nos travaux.

Notes

Notes

1. In 1981, the OECD Development Centre, with the encouragement of the OECD Development Co-operation Directorate, published a revised edition of the first NGO Directory, originally produced in 1967 by the OECD and the International Council of Voluntary Agencies (ICVA).

   Four new directories have been published since then by the Development Centre, in collaboration with various partners. The 1990 Directory contains a broad range of NGOs active in development. The three following directories, on the other hand, concentrated on the work of NGOs in specific areas: Environment and Development, in 1992; Human Rights, Refugees, Migrants and Development, in 1993, and Population and Development, in 1994.

2. For further information about, and addresses of NGOs active in the field of *global interdependence* in the Czech Republic, Hungary, Poland and the Slovak Republic, see the North-South Centre's recent directories compiled by *Dialogue Development,* a Danish NGO. Copies of the directories are available at the following address: The North-South Centre, Avenida da Liberdade 229-4, 1250 Lisbon, Portugal. Tel. 351 (1) 352 4954, Fax: 351 (1) 353 1329/352 4966.

1. Le Centre de Développement, avec l'appui de la Direction de la Coopération pour le Développement de l'OCDE, éditait, en 1981, une nouvelle version du premier répertoire d'ONG initialement élaboré en 1967 par l'OCDE et le CIAB (Conseil international des agences bénévoles).

   Depuis lors, le Centre de Développement a publié quatre nouveaux répertoires, en collaboration avec diverses organisations. Le premier répertoire, celui de 1990, fut le résultat d'une vaste enquête sur les organisations non gouvernementales de développement, quels qu'aient été leurs domaines d'activité. En revanche, les trois autres qui ont suivi furent consacrés à des ONG s'occupant de thèmes spécifiques, à savoir, en 1992 : *L'Environnement et le développement* ; en 1993 : *Droits de l'Homme, réfugiés, migrants et développement* ; en 1994 : *Population et développement.*

2. Pour plus d'information concernant le travail et l'adresse des ONG actives dans le domaine de l'*Interdépendance mondiale* en République tchèque, en Hongrie, en Pologne et en République slovaque, consultez les répertoires publiés par le Centre Nord-Sud. Ces ouvrages ont été préparés par l'ONG danoise, *Dialogue Development.* Des exemplaires de ce répertoire sont disponibles à l'adresse suivante : Centre Nord-Sud, Avenida da Liberdade 229-4, 1250 Lisbonne, Portugal. Téléphone : 351 (1) 352 4954, Télécopie : 351 (1) 353 1329/4966.

QUESTIONNAIRE

SURVEY OF EUROPEAN NON-GOVERNMENTAL ORGANISATIONS (NGOs) ACTIVE IN SUSTAINABLE DEVELOPMENT

The NGDO-EU Liaison Committee, the North-South Centre of the Council of Europe, the United Nations NGLS and the OECD Development Centre would be grateful if you could complete this questionnaire in English or French and return it to the following address:

OECD DEVELOPMENT CENTRE,
Attn. Mr. Henny Helmich, ROOM 807, 94 RUE CHARDON-LAGACHE, 75016 PARIS, FRANCE
Tel: 33 (1) 45 24 82 19 - Fax: 33 (1) 45 24 95 67

I.   GENERAL INFORMATION

1.   *NAME OF NGO* (followed by acronym, if any)

In original language: -

If original language is not English or French, please provide an English or French translation: - - - - - - - - - - - -

- -

2.   *ADDRESS*

Street: -

P.O. Box: -

City, (State/Province), Postal Code: -

Country: -

Telephone: -

Telefax: -

Electronic Mail: -

3.   *YEAR OF FOUNDATION*

- -

4.   *HEAD OF NGO* (name and title)

- -

- -

5. *AIMS* (describe briefly the goals, mandate or mission of your NGO)

----

6. *CONSTITUENCY*

Please describe briefly the support base (members/supporters/donors) of your NGO: - - - - - - - - - - - - - - - - -
----

----

7. *ORGANISATIONAL MEMBERSHIP*

a) Is your NGO:

    an association of NGOs/a network/a co-ordinating body/not applicable?

    (Delete as necessary)

b) If applicable, please indicate the number of NGOs that are members of your NGO: - - - - - - - - - - - - - - - - - -

c) If your NGO is a member of NGO associations, networks, consortiums, umbrella organisations or federations, list their full names and country location

----

----

8. *PERSONNEL* (indicate the number of staff as of 31.12.93 for the following categories)

Salaried staff: - - - - - - - - - -	of which:- - - - - - - - - -	in developing regions
Volunteers: - - - - - - - - - -	of which:- - - - - - - - - -	in developing regions
Total staff: -		

9. *BUDGET* (provide the order of magnitude of the 1993 budget, expressed in national currency)

Total budget (1993): - - - - - - - - - -   Currency:- - - - - - - - - -

10. FINANCIAL SOURCES (indicate the percentage of funding received in 1993 from the following sources)

Self-financing (membership fees, sale of products and services, endowments): -%

Private Donations (fund raising, grants, trust funds from general public, companies, foundations): - - - - - - - -%

Public Funds (international, national, federal and local authorities): -%

II. SUSTAINABLE DEVELOPMENT

11. ACTIVITIES IN DEVELOPING REGIONS

a) Number of developing *countries* in which your NGO worked in 1993: -

b) Does your NGO undertake development activities in developing regions *itself*?

    Yes   ❏   No   ❏

c) Does your NGO maintain *local field presence* in the developing regions in which it works?

    Yes   ❏   No   ❏

d) Does your NGO undertake development activities in developing regions through *local partner/member organisations*?

    Yes   ❏   No   ❏

e) Does your NGO undertake activities in Eastern Europe and/or in the former Soviet Union?

    Yes   ❏   No   ❏

f) Please mark all applicable categories. Use "other" for topics not covered.

    (see list of regions/countries on next page)

Activities \ Regions	West Africa	East Africa	Central Africa	Southern Africa	North Africa	Middle East	Central Asia and South Asia	East Asia	South East Asia	Mexico and Central America	The Caribbean	South America	Oceania
Rural Development/Agriculture	☐	☐	☐	☐	☐	☐	☐	☐	☐	☐	☐	☐	☐
Urban Development/Habitat	☐	☐	☐	☐	☐	☐	☐	☐	☐	☐	☐	☐	☐
Health/Sanitation/Water	☐	☐	☐	☐	☐	☐	☐	☐	☐	☐	☐	☐	☐
Gender Issues/Women	☐	☐	☐	☐	☐	☐	☐	☐	☐	☐	☐	☐	☐
Children/Youth/Family	☐	☐	☐	☐	☐	☐	☐	☐	☐	☐	☐	☐	☐
Population/Family Planning/ Demography	☐	☐	☐	☐	☐	☐	☐	☐	☐	☐	☐	☐	☐
Democracy/Good Governance Institution Building/ Participatory Development	☐	☐	☐	☐	☐	☐	☐	☐	☐	☐	☐	☐	☐
Human Rights/Peace/Conflicts	☐	☐	☐	☐	☐	☐	☐	☐	☐	☐	☐	☐	☐
Ecology/Environment/ Biodiversity	☐	☐	☐	☐	☐	☐	☐	☐	☐	☐	☐	☐	☐
Education/Training/Literacy	☐	☐	☐	☐	☐	☐	☐	☐	☐	☐	☐	☐	☐
Emergency Relief/Refugees/ Humanitarian Assistance	☐	☐	☐	☐	☐	☐	☐	☐	☐	☐	☐	☐	☐
Food/Famine	☐	☐	☐	☐	☐	☐	☐	☐	☐	☐	☐	☐	☐
Energy/Transport	☐	☐	☐	☐	☐	☐	☐	☐	☐	☐	☐	☐	☐
Small Enterprises/Informal Sector/Handicrafts	☐	☐	☐	☐	☐	☐	☐	☐	☐	☐	☐	☐	☐
Debt/Finance/Trade	☐	☐	☐	☐	☐	☐	☐	☐	☐	☐	☐	☐	☐
Sending Volunteers/Experts Technical Assistance	☐	☐	☐	☐	☐	☐	☐	☐	☐	☐	☐	☐	☐
Other:	☐	☐	☐	☐	☐	☐	☐	☐	☐	☐	☐	☐	☐

12. INFORMATION AND EDUCATIONAL ACTIVITIES

a) Please list the periodicals of your NGO

Title	No. per year	Print run
- -	- - - - - - - - - - - - - - - - - - - -	- - - - - - - - -
- -	- - - - - - - - - - - - - - - - - - - -	- - - - - - - - -

b) Does your NGO publish an Annual Report?

    Yes ☐   No ☐

c) Does your NGO produce a list of available publications and/ educational materials?

    Yes ☐   No ☐

d) Does your NGO undertake information and educational activities related to Eastern Europe and/or the former Soviet Union?

Yes ☐   No ☐

e) Please mark all applicable categories. Use "other" for categories not covered.

Topics / Activities	Fund Raising	Lobbying/ Advocacy	Formal Education	Conferences Seminars/ Workshops/ Training	Information & Documentation Services/ Data Bases	Publishing/ Audiovisual Materials/ Educational Materials	Information Campaigns/ Exhibitions	Exchanges Twinning/ Linking	Networking/ Electronic Telecom-munications	Broadcasting/ Cultural Events	Other:
Rural Development/Agriculture	☐	☐	☐	☐	☐	☐	☐	☐	☐	☐	☐
Urban Development/Habitat	☐	☐	☐	☐	☐	☐	☐	☐	☐	☐	☐
Health/Sanitation/Water	☐	☐	☐	☐	☐	☐	☐	☐	☐	☐	☐
Gender Issues/Women	☐	☐	☐	☐	☐	☐	☐	☐	☐	☐	☐
Children/Youth/Family	☐	☐	☐	☐	☐	☐	☐	☐	☐	☐	☐
Population/Family Planning/ Demography	☐	☐	☐	☐	☐	☐	☐	☐	☐	☐	☐
Peace/(Ethnic) Conflicts/ Armament/ Disarmament	☐	☐	☐	☐	☐	☐	☐	☐	☐	☐	☐
Ecology/Environment/ Biodiversity	☐	☐	☐	☐	☐	☐	☐	☐	☐	☐	☐
Food/Famine	☐	☐	☐	☐	☐	☐	☐	☐	☐	☐	☐
International Economic Relations/Trade/Debt/Finance	☐	☐	☐	☐	☐	☐	☐	☐	☐	☐	☐
Poverty/Living Conditions	☐	☐	☐	☐	☐	☐	☐	☐	☐	☐	☐
Refugees/Migrants/ Ethnic Groups	☐	☐	☐	☐	☐	☐	☐	☐	☐	☐	☐
Racism/Xenophobia/ Antisemitism	☐	☐	☐	☐	☐	☐	☐	☐	☐	☐	☐
Culture/Tradition/Religion	☐	☐	☐	☐	☐	☐	☐	☐	☐	☐	☐
Education/Literacy	☐	☐	☐	☐	☐	☐	☐	☐	☐	☐	☐
Employment/Unemployment	☐	☐	☐	☐	☐	☐	☐	☐	☐	☐	☐
Human Rights/Democracy/ Politics	☐	☐	☐	☐	☐	☐	☐	☐	☐	☐	☐
International Relations/ Cooperation/Development Aid	☐	☐	☐	☐	☐	☐	☐	☐	☐	☐	☐
Emergency Relief/ Humanitarian Assistance/ Assistance to Refugees	☐	☐	☐	☐	☐	☐	☐	☐	☐	☐	☐
Other:	☐	☐	☐	☐	☐	☐	☐	☐	☐	☐	☐

III.   EVALUATION AND RESEARCH ACTIVITIES

13.   Does your NGO make available evaluation reports on its activities?

Yes ☐   No ☐

14. Does your NGO undertake research activities?

Yes ☐   No ☐

IV.   PLANNED ACTIVITIES

15.   Please indicate briefly the most important (educational) campaigns, new activities and priorities planned for the period 1995-97

V.   COMMENTS

16.   Please provide any additional information you wish to include

----

Name of Respondent: -
Date: -

THANK YOU FOR TAKING THE TIME TO FILL IN THIS QUESTIONNAIRE
Brochures or other material describing the activities of your NGO would be welcome.

ENQUÊTE SUR LES ORGANISATIONS NON GOUVERNEMENTALES (ONG) EUROPÉENNES ACTIVES DANS LE DOMAINE DU DÉVELOPPEMENT DURABLE

Le Comité de liaison des ONGD, le Centre Nord-Sud du Conseil de l'Europe, le SLNG des Nations unies et le Centre de Développement de l'OCDE vous seraient reconnaissants de bien vouloir compléter ce questionnaire en anglais ou en français et de le retourner à l'adresse ci-dessous :

CENTRE DE DÉVELOPPEMENT DE L'OCDE,
**Attn. M. Henny Helmich, Bureau 807, 94 RUE CHARDON-LAGACHE, 75016 PARIS, FRANCE
Tél. : 33 (1) 45 24 82 19 - Télécopie : 33 (1) 45 24 95 67**

I.   INFORMATIONS GÉNÉRALES

1.   *NOM DE L'ONG* (suivi du sigle, s'il y a lieu)

Dans la langue originale : -
Si la langue originale n'est ni l'anglais ni le français, donner une traduction dans l'une de ces deux langues :
- -

2.   *ADRESSE*

Rue : -
B.P. : -
Ville, (État/Province), Code postal : -
Pays : -
Téléphone : -
Télécopie : -
Courrier électronique : -

3.   *ANNÉE DE FONDATION*

- -

4. RESPONSABLE DE L'ONG (nom et titre)

----

5. OBJECTIFS (décrire brièvement les buts, le mandat ou la mission de votre ONG)

----

6. ADHÉRENTS ET DONATEURS

Décrire brièvement la base de soutien de votre ONG (membres individuels/adhérents/donateurs) : - - - - - - - - - -
----

----

7. AFFILIATIONS DE L'ONG

a) Votre ONG est-elle :

un regroupement d'ONG / un réseau / un collectif / aucun des trois ?

(rayer les mentions inutiles)

b) Le cas échéant, indiquer le nombre d'ONG qui en sont membres : -

c) Si votre ONG est membre de regroupements d'ONG, de réseaux, de consortiums, de collectifs ou de fédérations, indiquer leurs noms en entier et le pays où ils ont leur siège :

----

8. PERSONNEL (indiquer l'effectif du personnel au 31.12.93 pour les catégories suivantes)

Salariés : - - - - - - - - -   dont : - - - - - - - - - -   dans les régions en développement

Bénévoles : - - - - - - - - - -   dont : - - - - - - - - - -   dans les régions en développement

Personnel total -

9. BUDGET (indiquer l'ordre de grandeur de votre budget en 1993, exprimé en monnaie nationale)

Budget total (1993) :- - - - - - - - - -   Monnaie :- - - - - - - - - -

10. SOURCES FINANCIÈRES (indiquer en pourcentages les sources de vos fonds en 1993, selon les catégories ci-dessous)

Autofinancement (cotisations, vente de produits et de services, dotations) : -%
Donations privées (collecte, dons, fonds fiduciaires provenant d'individus, d'entreprises, de fondations) : -%
Fonds publics (administrations internationales, nationales, fédérales et locales) : -%

II. LE DÉVELOPPEMENT DURABLE

11. ACTIVITÉS DANS LES RÉGIONS EN DÉVELOPPEMENT

a) Nombre de *pays* dans lesquels votre ONG est intervenue en 1993 : -

b) Votre ONG intervient-elle *directement* dans les régions en développement ?

   Oui   ☐   Non   ☐

c) Votre ONG maintient-elle une *présence locale sur le terrain* dans les régions en développement où elle intervient ?

   Oui   ☐   Non   ☐

d) Votre ONG intervient-elle dans les régions en développement par l'intermédiaire d'*organisations locales partenaires/membres* ?

   Oui   ☐   Non   ☐

e) Votre ONG intervient-elle en Europe de l'Est et/ou dans l'ex-Union soviétique ?

   Oui   ☐   Non   ☐

f) Prière de cocher toutes les cases appropriées. Utiliser la ligne « autres » pour les domaines non couverts (voir ci-contre la liste des régions et des pays)

Activités \ Régions	Afrique de l'Ouest	Afrique de l'Est	Afrique centrale	Afrique australe	Afrique du Nord	Moyen Orient	Asie centrale et du Sud	Asie de l'Est	Asie du Sud-Est	Mexique et Amérique centrale	Caraïbes	Amérique du Sud	Océanie
Développement rural/Agriculture	☐	☐	☐	☐	☐	☐	☐	☐	☐	☐	☐	☐	☐
Développement urbain/Habitat	☐	☐	☐	☐	☐	☐	☐	☐	☐	☐	☐	☐	☐
Santé/Assainissement/Eau	☐	☐	☐	☐	☐	☐	☐	☐	☐	☐	☐	☐	☐
Questions relatives aux femmes	☐	☐	☐	☐	☐	☐	☐	☐	☐	☐	☐	☐	☐
Enfants/Jeunesse/Famille	☐	☐	☐	☐	☐	☐	☐	☐	☐	☐	☐	☐	☐
Population/Planning familial/Démographie	☐	☐	☐	☐	☐	☐	☐	☐	☐	☐	☐	☐	☐
Démocratie/Bonne gestion publique/Création d'institutions/Développement participatif	☐	☐	☐	☐	☐	☐	☐	☐	☐	☐	☐	☐	☐
Droits de l'Homme/Paix/Conflits	☐	☐	☐	☐	☐	☐	☐	☐	☐	☐	☐	☐	☐
Ecologie/Environnement/Biodiversité	☐	☐	☐	☐	☐	☐	☐	☐	☐	☐	☐	☐	☐
Éducation/Formation Alphabétisation	☐	☐	☐	☐	☐	☐	☐	☐	☐	☐	☐	☐	☐
Secours d'urgence/Réfugiés/Aide humanitaire	☐	☐	☐	☐	☐	☐	☐	☐	☐	☐	☐	☐	☐
Aliments/Famine	☐	☐	☐	☐	☐	☐	☐	☐	☐	☐	☐	☐	☐
Énergie/Transport	☐	☐	☐	☐	☐	☐	☐	☐	☐	☐	☐	☐	☐
Petites entreprises/Secteur informel/Artisanat	☐	☐	☐	☐	☐	☐	☐	☐	☐	☐	☐	☐	☐
Dette/Finances/Commerce	☐	☐	☐	☐	☐	☐	☐	☐	☐	☐	☐	☐	☐
Envoi de volontaires/Experts Assistance technique	☐	☐	☐	☐	☐	☐	☐	☐	☐	☐	☐	☐	☐
Autres :	☐	☐	☐	☐	☐	☐	☐	☐	☐	☐	☐	☐	☐

12. ACTIVITÉS D'INFORMATION ET D'ÉDUCATION

a) Prière d'indiquer les périodiques publiés par votre ONG :

Titre	Périodicité	Tirage
- -	- - - - - - - - - - - -	- - - -
- -	- - - - - - - - - - - -	- - - -

b) Votre ONG publie-t-elle un rapport annuel ?

Oui ☐   Non ☐

c) Avez-vous une liste des publications et/ou du matériel éducatif ?

Oui ☐   Non ☐

d) Avez-vous des activités d'information et d'éducation concernant l'Europe de l'Est et/ou l'ex-Union soviétique ?

Oui ☐   Non ☐

e) Prière de cocher toutes les cases appropriées. Utiliser la ligne « autres » pour les domaines non couverts par la liste ci-après.

Domaines \ Activités	Collecte de fonds	Lobbying/ Plaidoyer	Éducation formelle	Conférences Séminaires/ Ateliers/ Formation	Services d'information & de documentation/ Bases de données	Édition/ Documents audiovisuels Documents éducatifs	Campagnes d'information Expositions	Échanges Parrainage/ Jumelage	Réseaux/ Télécom- munications électroniques	Radiodiffusion/ Manifestations culturelles	Autres :
Développement rural/Agriculture	□	□	□	□	□	□	□	□	□	□	□
Développement urbain/Habitat	□	□	□	□	□	□	□	□	□	□	□
Santé/Assainissement/Eau	□	□	□	□	□	□	□	□	□	□	□
Questions relatives aux femmes	□	□	□	□	□	□	□	□	□	□	□
Enfants/Jeunesse/Famille	□	□	□	□	□	□	□	□	□	□	□
Population/Planning familial Démographie	□	□	□	□	□	□	□	□	□	□	□
Paix/Conflits(ethniques) Armement/Désarmement	□	□	□	□	□	□	□	□	□	□	□
Écologie/Environnement/ Biodiversité	□	□	□	□	□	□	□	□	□	□	□
Aliments/Famine	□	□	□	□	□	□	□	□	□	□	□
Relations écon. internationales Commerce/Dette/Finances	□	□	□	□	□	□	□	□	□	□	□
Pauvreté/Conditions de vie	□	□	□	□	□	□	□	□	□	□	□
Réfugiés/Migrants/ Groupes ethniques	□	□	□	□	□	□	□	□	□	□	□
Racisme/Xénophobie/ Antisémitisme	□	□	□	□	□	□	□	□	□	□	□
Culture/Tradition/Religion	□	□	□	□	□	□	□	□	□	□	□
Éducation/Alphabétisation	□	□	□	□	□	□	□	□	□	□	□
Emploi/Chômage	□	□	□	□	□	□	□	□	□	□	□
Droits de l'Homme/ Démocratie/Politique	□	□	□	□	□	□	□	□	□	□	□
Relations internationales/ Coopération/Aide au développement	□	□	□	□	□	□	□	□	□	□	□
Secours d'urgence/Aide humanitaire/Assistance aux réfugiés	□	□	□	□	□	□	□	□	□	□	□
Autres :	□	□	□	□	□	□	□	□	□	□	□

III. ACTIVITÉS D'ÉVALUATION ET DE RECHERCHE

13. *Les rapports d'évaluation de vos activités sont-ils disponibles ?*

Oui   □   Non   □

14. *Votre ONG a-t-elle des activités de recherche ?*

Oui   □   Non   □

## IV.	PRÉVISION D'ACTIVITÉS

15.	*Veuillez indiquer brièvement les campagnes (d'éducation) les plus importantes ainsi que les priorités et les nouvelles activités envisagées pour la période 1995-97*

V. COMMENTAIRES

16.	*Informations supplémentaires que vous souhaiteriez fournir*

Nom du répondant : -

Date : - - - - - - - - - - - -

MERCI D'AVOIR PRIS LE TEMPS DE REMPLIR CE QUESTIONNAIRE
Prière de joindre toute brochure ou documentation décrivant les activités de votre ONG.

List of Regions and Countries / Liste des régions et des pays

1.   West Africa / Afrique de l'Ouest

Benin / Bénin
Burkina Faso
Cape Verde / Cap Vert
Côte d'Ivoire
Gambia / Gambie
Ghana
Guinea / Guinée
Guinea-Bissau / Guinée-Bissau
Liberia / Libéria
Mali
Mauritania / Mauritanie
Niger
Nigeria
Senegal / Sénégal
Sierra Leone
Togo

2.   East Africa / Afrique de l'Est

Djibouti
Ethiopia / Éthiopie
Kenya
Somalia / Somalie
Sudan / Soudan
Tanzania / Tanzanie
Uganda / Ouganda

3.   Central Africa / Afrique centrale

Burundi
Cameroon / Cameroun
Central African Republic / République centrafricaine
Chad / Tchad
Congo
Equatorial Guinea / Guinée équatoriale

Gabon
Rwanda
Sao Tome & Principe / Sao Tomé-et-Principe
Zaire / Zaïre

4.   Southern Africa / Afrique australe

Angola
Botswana
Comoros / Comores
Lesotho
Madagascar
Malawi
Mauritius / Île Maurice
Mozambique
Namibia /Namibie
Reunion / Île de la Réunion
Saint Helena / Sainte-Hélène
Seychelles
South Africa / Afrique du Sud
Swaziland
Zambia / Zambie
Zimbabwe

5.   North Africa / Afrique du Nord

Algeria / Algérie
Egypt / Égypte
Libya / Libye
Morocco / Maroc
Tunisia / Tunisie

6.   Middle East / Moyen-Orient

Bahrain / Bahreïn
Iran

Iraq
Israel / Israël
Jordan / Jordanie
Kuwait / Koweit
Lebanon / Liban
Oman
Qatar
Saudi Arabia / Arabie saoudite
Syria / Syrie
United Arab Emirates / Émirats arabes unis
Yemen / Yémen

7. Central Asia and South Asia / Asie centrale et Asie du Sud

Afghanistan
Bangladesh
Bhutan / Bhoutan
India / Inde
Kazakhstan
Kyrgyzstan / Kirghizistan
Maldives
Nepal / Népal
Pakistan
Sri Lanka
Tajikistan / Tadjikistan
Turkmenistan / Turkménistan
Uzbekistan / Ouzbékistan

8. East Asia / Asie de l'Est

China / Chine
Hong Kong
Korea / Corée
Macau / Macao
Mongolia / Mongolie
Chinese Taipei / Taipei chinois

9. South East Asia / Asie du Sud-Est

Brunei Darussalam
Cambodia / Cambodge
Indonesia / Indonésie
Laos
Malaysia
Philippines
Singapore / Singapour
Thailand / Thaïlande
Timor
Vietnam

10. Mexico and Central America / Mexique et Amérique centrale

Belize
Costa Rica
El Salvador / Salvador
Guatemala
Honduras
Mexico / Mexique
Nicaragua
Panama

11. The Caribbean / Caraïbes

Anguilla
Antigua & Barbuda
Aruba
Bahamas
Barbados / La Barbade
Cayman Islands/Îles Caïmans
Cuba
Dominican Republic/République dominicaine
Grenada / Grenade
Haiti / Haïti
Jamaica / Jamaïque
Montserrat

Netherlands Antilles / Antilles néerlandaises

Puerto Rico / Porto Rico

Saint Kitts & Nevis

Saint Lucia / Sainte-Lucie

Saint Vincent & the Grenadines / Saint-Vincent-et-les-Grenadines

Trinidad & Tobago / Trinité-et-Tobago

Turks and Caicos Islands / Îles Turks et Caïcos

12. South America / Amérique du Sud

Argentina / Argentine

Bolivia / Bolivie

Brazil / Brésil

Chile / Chili

Colombia / Colombie

Ecuador / Équateur

Falkland Islands / Îles Falkland

Guyana / Guyane

Paraguay

Peru / Pérou

Suriname

Uruguay

Venezuela

13. Oceania / Océanie

Cook Islands / Îles Cook

Fiji / Fidji

Kiribati

Marshall Islands / Îles Marshall

Micronesia / Micronésie

Nauru

New Caledonia / Nouvelle-Calédonie

Niue / Nioué

Pacific Islands / Îles du Pacifique

Papua New Guinea / Papouasie-Nouvelle-Guinée

Polynesia, French / Polynésie française

Samoa

Solomon Islands / Îles Salomon

Tokelau / Tokélaou

Tonga

Tuvalu

Vanuatu

Wallis & Futuna / Wallis-et-Futuna

Exchange Rates
of Countries Covered by the European NGO Survey
National Currency Units for one Ecu and one United States Dollar (1993 average)

Taux de change
des pays inclus dans le répertoire sur les ONG européennes
Unités de monnaie nationale pour un Écu et un dollar des États-Unis
(cours moyen pour 1993)

Country/ Pays	Ecu	$/ Dollar
Austria / Autriche	15.0844	11.632
Belgium / Belgique	40.466	34.597
Cyprus / Chypre	0.6741	0.5198
Czech Republic / République tchèque	37.8056	29.153
Denmark / Danemark	7.5916	6.484
Finland / Finlande	7.4077	5.7123
France	6.6334	5.6632
Germany / Allemagne	1.9368	1.6533
Greece / Grèce	267.99	229.25
Hungary / Hongrie	119.2187	91.933
Iceland / Islande	87.66767	67.603
Ireland / Irlande	0.7991	0.6816
Italy / Italie	1841.6	1573.7
Liechtenstein	1.9162	1.4776
Luxembourg	40.468	34.597
Malta / Malte	0.4955	0.3821
Netherlands / Pays-Bas	2.1723	1.8573
Norway / Norvège	8.3505	7.0941
Poland / Pologne	23491.532	18115
Portugal	187.80	160.80
Slovac Republic / République slovaque	35.30	27.238
Spain / Espagne	165.0308	127.26
Sweden / Suède	9.1146	7.7834
Switzerland / Suisse	1.9162	1.4776
Turkey / Turquie	14244.8293	10984.6
United Kingdom / Royaume-Uni	0.7799	0.6658

PROFILES OF NGOS BY COUNTRY

PROFILS DES ONG PAR PAYS

AUT0001
ACTION 365

Bäckerstrasse 18, 1010 Wien, Austria.

Telephone: 43 (222) 52 79 60. *Contact:* Mag. Hanns Liharzik, President.

AUT0002
AFRO-ASIATISCHES INSTITUT WIEN (AAI) ♦ Afro-Asiatic Institute Vienna

Türkenstrasse 3, 1090 Wien, Austria.

Telephone: 43 (222) 310 51 45 310. *Fax:* 43 (222) 310 51 45 312. *E-mail:* C.Guggenberger@magnet.at. *Contact:* C. Guggenberger, General Secretary.

OBJECTIVES: To promote public relations in Third World matters. To provide scholarships and support for students. To undertake cultural and scientific co-operation with Africa and Asia. To foster cultural and religious dialogue.

GENERAL INFORMATION: *Creation:* 1959. *Affiliated to:* EU Platform of NGOs (Austria) - Koordinierungsstelle der Öst Bischofskonferenz (Austria) - Contact Committee Assistance for Students (Austria). *Budget/Total 1993:* ECU 2231000 (US$ 2893000). *Financial sources:* Private: 10%. Public: 60%. Self-financing: 30%.

PUBLICATIONS: *Periodicals:* AAI-News (11) - Treffpunkt Studienförderung (1). *Annual report.*

PLANNED ACTIVITIES: Holding conferences and seminars on "Women in Africa", "Changes and Constraints of African/Asian Development" and "Tourism and Tradition in Africa and Asia".

ACTIVITIES IN DEVELOPING REGIONS: Active in 2 country(ies). Works through local field partners. Sustainable Development Actions: Education/training/literacy. Regions: Middle East; Southern Africa.

INFORMATION AND EDUCATION ACTIVITIES: Topics: Children/youth/family; Culture/tradition/religion; Gender issues/women; Health/sanitation/water; Human rights/peace/conflicts; Population/family planning/demography; Poverty/living conditions; Racism/xenophobia/antisemitism; Rural development/agriculture; Urban development/habitat. Activities: Conferences/seminars/workshops/training activities; Information and documentation services/data bases; Information campaigns/exhibitions; Lobbying/advocacy.

AUT0003
AKTION BRUDER IN NOT INNSBRUCK ♦ Action People in Need Innsbruck

Wilhelm-Greil Str. 7, P.O. Box 582, 6021 Innsbruck, Austria.

Telephone: 43 (512) 598 47 19. *Fax:* 43 (512) 598 47 72. *Contact:* Bishop Reinhold Stecher.

OBJECTIVES: To support small-scale development projects in rural areas in selected regions of Africa and Latin America. To create political consciousness of development aid policy in Austria.

GENERAL INFORMATION: *Creation:* 1974. *Affiliated to:* Koordinierungsstelle der Österreichischen Bischofskonferenz für Internationale Entwicklung und Mission (Austria) - Kofinanzierungsstelle für Entwicklungszusammenarbeit (Austria) - Österreichischer Entwicklungsdienst (Austria). *Personnel/Total:* 17. Salaried: 2. Volunteers: 15. *Budget/Total 1993:* ECU 1989000 (US$ 2579000). *Financial sources:* Private: 95%. Public: 5%.

PUBLICATIONS: *Annual report. List of publications.*

EVALUATION/RESEARCH: Evaluation reports available.

PLANNED ACTIVITIES: In 1996, work on debt and crisis.

ACTIVITIES IN DEVELOPING REGIONS: Active in 10 country(ies). Works through local field partners. Sustainable Development Actions: Children/youth/family; Democracy/good governance/institution building/participatory development; Ecology/environment/biodiversity; Education/training/literacy; Gender issues/women; Health/sanitation/water; Human rights/peace/conflicts; Rural development/agriculture; Small enterprises/informal sector/handicrafts. Regions: Caribbean; East Africa; Mexico and Central America; South America; West Africa.

INFORMATION AND EDUCATION ACTIVITIES: Topics: Children/youth/family; Ecology/environment/biodiversity; Education/training/literacy; Employment/unemployment; Gender issues/women; Health/sanitation/water; Human rights/peace/conflicts; Peace/ethnic conflicts/armament/disarmament; Poverty/living conditions; Rural development/agriculture. Activities: Fund raising; Lobbying/advocacy.

AUT0004
AKTION DRITTE WELT (A3W) ♦ Third World Action

Kleinbachstrasse 8, 5101 Bergheim, Austria.

Telephone: 43 (662) 52178.

AUT0005
AKTION DRITTE WELT DORNBIRN ♦ Third World Action Group of Dornbirn

Radetzkystrasse 3, 6850 Dornbirn, Austria.

Telephone: 43 (5572) 61 08 34. *Contact:* Peter Niedermair, President.

AUT0006
AKTION DRITTE WELT ST. JOHANN (A3W) ♦ Third World Action - St. Johann

Poststr. 4, 6380 St. Johann, Austria.

Telephone: 43 (5352) 61 890. *Contact:* Eva Novak, Chairwoman.

OBJECTIVES: To encourage a change in the structures of Western societies as a prerequisite to just and equitable development of Third World countries.

GENERAL INFORMATION: *Creation:* 1981. *Personnel/Total:* 6. Salaried: 1. Volunteers: 5. *Budget/Total 1993:* ECU 2000 (US$ 3000). *Financial sources:* Public: 70%. Self-financing: 30%.

INFORMATION AND EDUCATION ACTIVITIES: Topics: Ecology/environment/biodiversity; Refugees/migrants/ethnic groups. Activities: Information campaigns/exhibitions.

AUT0007
AMNESTY INTERNATIONAL, AUSTRIAN SECTION

Wiedner Gürtel 12, A-1040 Vienna, Austria.

Contact: Dr. Wolfgang Aigner.

AUT0008
ARBEITGEMEINSCHAFT ENTWICKLUNGSZUSAMMENARBEIT (AGEZ) ♦ Working Association for Development Cooperation

Berggasse 7, 1090 Wien, Austria.

Telephone: 43 (1) 317 40 16. *Fax:* 43 (1) 317 40 16. *Contact:* Christa Esterhazy, Chairperson.

OBJECTIVES: To improve the qualitative and quantitative standard of Austrian development co-operation and policy. To improve the position of NGOs within Austrian development policy.

GENERAL INFORMATION: *Creation:* 1988. *Type of organisation:* coordinating body. *Member organisations:* 20. *Personnel/Total:* 2. Salaried: 2. *Budget/Total 1993:* ECU 64000 (US$ 83000). *Financial sources:* Self-financing: 100%.

PUBLICATIONS: *Periodicals:* AGEZ information (60). *Annual report.*

PLANNED ACTIVITIES: The priorities of the organisation will be the European Union development policy, especially regarding co-financing programmes for NGOs.

INFORMATION AND EDUCATION ACTIVITIES: Topics: Gender issues/women; Human rights/peace/conflicts; International relations/cooperation/development aid; Racism/xenophobia/antisemitism. Activities: Conferences/seminars/workshops/training activities; Lobbying/advocacy.

Voir : *Comment utiliser le répertoire,* page 11.

AUT0009

ARBEITSGEMEINSCHAFT CHRISTEN FUR CHILE ♦ Working Group of Christians for Chile

Johannesgasse 16/1, 1010 Wien, Austria.

Contact: Jorge Fuentes.

OBJECTIVES: To inform the public about Chile and the issue of liberation theology. To provide financial assistance for self-help projects in Chile.

GENERAL INFORMATION: *Creation:* 1974. *Affiliated to:* Österreichischer Informationsdienst für Entwicklungspolitik (Austria). *Budget/Total 1993:* ECU 7000 (US$ 9000). *Financial sources: Self-financing:* 100%.

PUBLICATIONS: *Periodicals:* Informationen (4).

ACTIVITIES IN DEVELOPING REGIONS: Active in 1 country(ies). Works through local field partners. **Sustainable Development Actions:** Children/youth/family; Education/training/literacy; Human rights/peace/conflicts. **Regions:** South America.

INFORMATION AND EDUCATION ACTIVITIES: Topics: Children/youth/family; Human rights/peace/conflicts. **Activities:** Publishing/audiovisual materials/educational materials.

AUT0010

ARBEITSGEMEINSCHAFT KATHOLISCHER JUGEND OSTERREICHS (AKJÖ) ♦ Austrian Catholic Youth Work Community

Johannesgasse 16, 1010 Wien, Autriche.

Téléphone: 43 (222) 52 16 21. *Fax:* 43 (222) 51 39 460. *Contact:* Mag. Martin Kargl.

OBJECTIFS: Aider les jeunes à développer leur autonomie et leur sens de la responsabilité. Eveiller la responsabilité sociale et politique des jeunes. Contribuer au développement d'une réflexion croyante et critique. Motiver les jeunes à l'action pour une société pacifique, juste et solidaire.

INFORMATIONS GENERALES: *Création:* 1946. *Type d'organisation:* regroupement d'ONG. *Organisations membres:* 3. *Affiliée à:* Österreichischer Bundesjugendring (Austria) - Koordinierungsstelle der Österreichischen Bischofskonferenz für Internationale Entwicklung und Mission (Austria) - Katolische Aktion (Austria). *Personnel/Total:* 2019. *Salariés:* 19. *Bénévoles:* 2000. *Budget/Total 1993:* ECU 663000 (US$ 860000). *Sources financières: Privé:* 25%. *Public:* 70%. *Autofinancement:* 5%.

PUBLICATIONS: *Périodiques:* Jugend & Kirche (4) - Hanna (4) - Aktion (4). *Liste des publications.*

EVALUATION/RECHERCHE: Rapports d'évaluation disponibles.

PREVISIONS D'ACTIVITES: Organisation d'une campagne nationale contre la dette du tiers monde.

COMMENTAIRES: AKJÖ réunit neuf diocèses et trois mouvements nationaux (jeunesse citadine et rurale catholique, jeunesse ouvrière catholique, jeunesse écolière catholique). Activités d'information concernant la Communauté des Etats indépendants.

ACTIVITES D'INFORMATION ET D'EDUCATION: Domaines: Culture/tradition/religion; Développement rural/agriculture; Emploi/chômage; Enfants/jeunesse/famille; Paix/conflits ethniques/armement/désarmement; Pauvreté/conditions de vie; Population/planning familial/démographie; Questions relatives aux femmes; Racisme/xénophobie/antisémitisme; Relations internationales/coopération/aide au développement; Relations économiques internationales/commerce/dette/finances; Réfugiés/migrants/groupes ethniques; Écologie/environnement/biodiversité. **Activités:** Campagnes d'information/expositions; Conférences/séminaires/ateliers/activités de formation; Lobbying/plaidoyer; Radiodiffusion/manifestations culturelles; Réseaux/télécommunications électroniques; Services d'information et de documentation/bases de données; Échanges/parrainage/jumelage; Édition/documents audiovisuels/documents éducatifs.

AUT0011

ARBEITSGEMEINSCHAFT OSTERREICH DRITTE WELT DER SPO

Löwelstrasse 18, 1010 Wien, Austria.

Telephone: 43 (222) 804 65 01. *Fax:* 43 (222) 804 08 74. *Contact:* Albrecht K. Konecny.

OBJECTIVES: To undertake educational work and disseminate information in the fields of development policy and development co-operation.

GENERAL INFORMATION: *Creation:* 1982. *Personnel/Total:* 1. *Salaried:* 1.

PUBLICATIONS: *Periodicals:* Entwicklung und Politik (5).

INFORMATION AND EDUCATION ACTIVITIES: Topics: Ecology/environment/biodiversity; Human rights/peace/conflicts; International economic relations/trade/debt/finance; Population/family planning/demography; Rural development/agriculture. **Activities:** Conferences/seminars/workshops/training activities; Information and documentation services/data bases.

AUT0012

ARBEITSKREIS ENTWICKLUNGSHILFE UND MENSCHENRECHTE (AEM) ♦ Working Group on Development Aid and Human Rights

Hauptstrasse 6, 2353 Guntramsdorf, Austria.

Telephone: 43 (2236) 52 15 25. *Contact:* Dr. Walter Lach.

AUT0013

ARBEITSKREIS WELTKIRCHE DES VIKARIATES SUD ♦ Working Group for World-Church of the Vicar South of the Archdiocese of Vienna

Antonsgasse 20a, 2500 Baden, Austria.

Telephone: 43 (2252) 42 562 / 12. *Contact:* Mrs. Hubert Haschka.

OBJECTIVES: To undertake consciousness raising activities among the Austrian public on problems related to development. To create self-taxation groups to sponsor projects in developing countries. To send volunteers to development work camps in these countries.

GENERAL INFORMATION: *Creation:* 1975. *Type of organisation:* coordinating body. *Personnel/Total:* 9. *Volunteers:* 9. *Financial sources: Private:* 100%.

PUBLICATIONS: *Periodicals:* Impulse fûr eine Welt (4). *Annual report.*

ACTIVITIES IN DEVELOPING REGIONS: Works through local field partners. **Sustainable Development Actions:** Children/youth/family; Education/training/literacy; Food/famine; Gender issues/women; Health/sanitation/water; Rural development/agriculture. **Regions:** Central Africa; Central Asia and South Asia; East Africa; East Asia; Mexico and Central America; North Africa; South America; South East Asia; Southern Africa; West Africa.

AUT0014

ARBEITSKREIS WELTKIRCHE UND ENTWICKLUNGSFORDERUNG DER DIOZESE LINZ (WEKEF) ♦ Working Group of the World Church and Development Aid of the Linz Diocese

Kapuzinerstrasse 84, 4020 Linz, Austria.

Telephone: 43 (732) 27 44 41. *Contact:* Mag. Karl Gstöttenmeier, Chairman.

AUT0015

ASYLKOORDINATION - OSTERREICH ♦ Asylum Co-ordinating Body Austria

Trattnerhof 2/14, 1010 Wien, Austria.

Telephone: 43 (1) 532 12 91. *Fax:* 43 (1) 532 12 91. *Contact:* Anny Knapp.

OBJECTIVES: To provide practical support to and political co-ordination of organisations or initiatives dealing with refugees' and migrants' problems.

GENERAL INFORMATION: *Creation:* 1991. *Type of organisation:* coordinating body. *Member organisations:* 30. *Personnel/Total:* 8. *Salaried:* 4. *Volunteers:* 4. *Budget/Total 1993:* ECU 78000 (US$ 101000). *Financial sources: Private:* 10%. *Public:* 80%. *Self-financing:* 10%.

See: *How to Use the Directory*, page 11.

INFORMATION AND EDUCATION ACTIVITIES: **Topics:** Refugees/migrants/ethnic groups. **Activities:** Information and documentation services/data bases; Information campaigns/exhibitions; Lobbying/advocacy.

AUT0016

AUSSCHUSS DES DIOZESANRATES FUR WELTKIRCHE UND ENTWICKLUNGSFORDERUNG (WEKEF) ♦ Diocesan Council's Commission for the World Church and Development Aid

Waagasse 18, 9013 Klagenfurt, Austria.

Contact: Roman Leitner, Chairman.

AUT0017

AUSTRIAN COMMISSION OF JURISTS

Mariahilfestrasse 17, 1060 Vienna, Austria.

Contact: Dr. Britta Wagner.

AUT0018

AUSTRIAN FEDERATION OF UN AND UNESCO CLUBS

Hofburg/Nordtrakt, 6020 Innsbruck, Austria.

Telephone: 43 (5222) 29 189.

AUT0019

AUSTRIAN INSTITUTE FOR HUMAN RIGHTS

Edmundsburg-Mönchsberg 2, 5020 Salzburg, Austria.

Contact: Prof. Franz Matscher.

AUT0020

BEGEGNUNGSZENTRUM FUR AKTIVE GEWALTLOSIGKEIT (BFAG) ♦ Centre for Active Non-Violence

Wolfgangerstrasse 26, Postfach 504, 4820 Bad Ischl, Austria.

Telephone: 43 (6132) 245 90. *Fax:* 43 (6132) 245 90. *Contact:* Maria Reichl, Secretary General.

OBJECTIVES: To work for non-violent conflict resolution. To defend human/social rights, disarmament, democratic structures, indigenous peoples, religious freedom, ecological systems and all solidarity initiatives of poor and oppressed peoples.

GENERAL INFORMATION: *Creation:* 1980. *Type of organisation:* network. *Affiliated to:* War Resisters International (United Kingdom) - International Fellowship of Reconciliation (the Netherlands) - Anti-Atom-International (Austria). *Personnel/Total:* 4. *Salaried:* 1. *Volunteers:* 3. *Budget/Total 1993:* ECU 13000 (US$ 17000). *Financial sources:* Private: 50%. Self-financing: 50%.

PUBLICATIONS: *Periodicals:* Rundbrief (4). *List of publications.*

EVALUATION/RESEARCH: Undertakes research activities.

COMMENTS: Undertakes activities in the Commonwealth of Independent States. Information activities related to the Commonwealth of Independent States.

INFORMATION AND EDUCATION ACTIVITIES: **Topics:** Children/youth/family; Culture/tradition/religion; Ecology/environment/biodiversity; Education/training/literacy; Emergency relief/refugees/humanitarian assistance; Employment/unemployment; Food/famine; Gender issues/women; Health/sanitation/water; Human rights/peace/conflicts; International economic relations/trade/debt/finance; International relations/cooperation/development aid; Peace/ethnic conflicts/armament/disarmament; Population/family planning/demography; Poverty/living conditions; Racism/xenophobia/antisemitism; Refugees/migrants/ethnic groups; Rural development/agriculture; Urban development/habitat. **Activities:** Broadcasting/cultural events; Conferences/seminars/workshops/training activities; Exchanges/twinning/linking; Formal education; Fund raising; Information and documentation services/data bases; Information campaigns/exhibitions; Lobbying/advocacy; Networking/electronic telecommunications; Publishing/audiovisual materials/educational materials.

AUT0021

BERUFSPADAGOGISCHES INSTITUT - MODLING (BPI) ♦ Professional Teacher Training College and Vocational Training Centre

Guntramsdorferstrasse 10a, 2340 Mödling, Austria.

Telephone: 43 (2236) 232 71. *Fax:* 43 (2236) 232 71. *Contact:* Alois Baumgartner.

OBJECTIVES: To provide aid through education and training. To educate people so that they can be self-sufficient and support their family in their home country.

GENERAL INFORMATION: *Creation:* 1969. *Affiliated to:* Arbeitsgemeinschaft Entwicklungszusammenarbeit (Austria). *Personnel/Total:* 106. *Salaried:* 93 of which: 16 in developing countries. *Volunteers:* 13 of which: 4 in developing countries. *Budget/Total 1993:* ECU 3652000 (US$ 4736000). *Financial sources:* Private: 15%. Public: 70%. Self-financing: 15%.

PUBLICATIONS: *Annual report.*

EVALUATION/RESEARCH: Evaluation reports available.

PLANNED ACTIVITIES: Institution building for local partners in Burkina Faso, Costa Rica, Indonesia and Israel. Training courses in welding technology. Co-operation with vocational training centres in Eastern Europe.

ACTIVITIES IN DEVELOPING REGIONS: Present in developing regions. Active in 10 country(ies). Maintains local field presence. Works through local field partners. **Sustainable Development Actions:** Children/youth/family; Democracy/good governance/institution building/participatory development; Education/training/literacy; Gender issues/women; Sending volunteers/experts/technical assistance. **Regions:** Central Africa; Central Asia and South Asia; East Asia; Mexico and Central America; Middle East; West Africa.

INFORMATION AND EDUCATION ACTIVITIES: **Topics:** Children/youth/family; Education/training/literacy; Employment/unemployment; International relations/cooperation/development aid; Refugees/migrants/ethnic groups. **Activities:** Broadcasting/cultural events; Conferences/seminars/workshops/training activities; Formal education; Fund raising; Lobbying/advocacy.

AUT0022

BROT FUR HUNGERNDE ♦ Pain pour les affamés

Blumengasse 4-6, 1180 Wien, Autriche.

Téléphone: 43 (222) 40 89 605. *Fax:* 43 (222) 40 67 877. *Contact:* Gerhilde Merz, Secrétaire exécutive.

OBJECTIFS: Apporter une aide financière à la population marginale urbaine et à la population rurale pauvre. Lutter contre la violation des droits de l'Homme.

INFORMATIONS GENERALES: *Création:* 1960. *Affiliée à:* EAEZ (Autriche) - AGEZ (Autriche). *Personnel/Total:* var. Salariés: 1. *Bénévoles:* var. *Budget/Total 1993:* ECU 100000 (US$ 129000). *Sources financières:* Privé: 100%.

PREVISIONS D'ACTIVITES: Renforcer l'information envers les membres de l'église protestante, notamment les femmes et les scolaires. Inviter des personnalités du Sud pour parler des problèmes du développement.

ACTIVITES DANS LES REGIONS EN DEVELOPPEMENT: Intervient directement dans les régions en développement. Intervient dans 5 pays. Intervient par l'intermédiaire d'organisations locales partenaires. **Actions de Développement durable:** Droits de l'Homme/paix/conflits; Démocratie/bonne gestion publique/création d'institutions/développement participatif; Développement rural/agriculture; Développement urbain/habitat; Enfants/jeunesse/famille; Petites entreprises/secteur informel/artisanat; Questions relatives aux femmes; Santé/assainissement/eau; Écologie/environnement/biodiversité; Éducation/formation/alphabétisation. **Régions:** Afrique australe; Amérique du Sud; Asie centrale et Asie du Sud.

ACTIVITES D'INFORMATION ET D'EDUCATION: **Domaines:** Droits de l'Homme/paix/conflits; Développement rural/agriculture; Développement urbain/habitat; Enfants/jeunesse/famille; Questions relatives aux femmes; Éducation/formation/alphabétisation. **Activités:** Collecte de fonds.

Voir : *Comment utiliser le répertoire,* page 11.

AUT0023

DIOZESANKOMMISSION FUR WELTKIRCHE UND ENTWICKLUNGSFORDERUNG ♦ Diocesan Committee for World Churches and Development Aid

Leechgasse 22, 8010 Graz, Austria.

Telephone: 43 (316) 31 94 15.

AUT0024

DREIKONIGSAKTION D. KATHOLISCHE JUNGSCHAR OSTERREICHS (KJSÖ) ♦ Austrian Catholic Youth Group

Mittersteig 10, 1050 Wien, Austria.

Telephone: 43 (222) 58 667. *Fax:* 43 (1) 58 667. *Contact:* Ruth Ankerl Vorsitzende, Chairman.

OBJECTIVES: To support the development work of local churches in Africa, Asia and Latin America. To inform the public about the situation and living conditions of people in developing countries.

GENERAL INFORMATION: *Creation:* 1954. *Affiliated to:* Coordinating Office of the Austrian Episcopal Conference for International Development (Austria) - Arbeitgemeinschaft Entwicklungszusammenarbeit (Austria) - KFS Co-financing Office for Development Co-operation (Austria). *Personnel/Total:* 36. *Salaried:* 16. *Volunteers:* 20. *Budget/Total 1993:* ECU 9254000 (US$ 12000000). *Financial sources:* Private: 83%. Public: 17%.

PUBLICATIONS: *Annual report. List of publications.*

ACTIVITIES IN DEVELOPING REGIONS: Active in 69 country(ies). Works through local field partners. **Sustainable Development Actions:** Children/youth/family; Ecology/environment/biodiversity; Education/training/literacy; Gender issues/women; Health/sanitation/water; Human rights/peace/conflicts; Urban development/habitat. **Regions:** Central Africa; Central Asia and South Asia; East Africa; East Asia; Mexico and Central America; Oceania; South America; South East Asia; Southern Africa; West Africa.

INFORMATION AND EDUCATION ACTIVITIES: Topics: Children/youth/family; Culture/tradition/religion; Ecology/environment/biodiversity; Education/training/literacy; Gender issues/women; Human rights/peace/conflicts; Peace/ethnic conflicts/armament/disarmament. **Activities:** Conferences/seminars/workshops/training activities; Formal education; Fund raising; Information and documentation services/data bases; Information campaigns/exhibitions; Lobbying/advocacy; Publishing/audiovisual materials/educational materials.

AUT0025

ENTWICKLUNGSHILFE DER ERZDIOZESEK WIEN - DIOZESEN INFORMATIONSSTELLE DES OED ♦ Development Aid of the Archdiocese of Vienna - Diocesan Information Office of the Austrian Development Service

Stephansplatz 6/5/19, Postfach 977, 1010 Wien, Austria.

Telephone: 43 (222) 53 25 61 ext. 338. *Contact:* Walter Mayr, President.

AUT0026

ENTWICKLUNGSHILFE-KLUB ♦ Development Aid Club

Böcklinstrasse 44, Postfach 250, 1020 Wien, Austria.

Telephone: 43 (1) 26 51 50. *Fax:* 43 (1) 218 37 93. *Contact:* Gerhard Dorffner.

OBJECTIVES: To present development projects to the Austrian public and raise funds for these projects. To create interest in development issues and information services. To give support and counselling to activist groups in Austria.

GENERAL INFORMATION: *Creation:* 1973. *Affiliated to:* Arbeitsgemeinschaft Entwicklungs Zusammenarbeit (Austria). *Personnel/Total:* 36. *Salaried:* 3. *Volunteers:* 33. *Budget/Total 1993:* ECU 875000 (US$ 1135000). *Financial sources:* Private: 96%. Self-financing: 4%.

PUBLICATIONS: *Periodicals:* Unser Projekt (4). *Annual report. List of publications.*

EVALUATION/RESEARCH: Evaluation reports available.

COMMENTS: Undertakes activities in the Commonwealth of Independent States.

ACTIVITIES IN DEVELOPING REGIONS: Active in 26 country(ies). Works through local field partners. **Sustainable Development Actions:** Children/youth/family; Democracy/good governance/institution building/participatory development; Ecology/environment/biodiversity; Education/training/literacy; Gender issues/women; Health/sanitation/water; Human rights/peace/conflicts; Rural development/agriculture; Small enterprises/informal sector/handicrafts; Urban development/habitat. **Regions:** Central Africa; Central Asia and South Asia; East Africa; Mexico and Central America; South America; South East Asia; Southern Africa; West Africa.

INFORMATION AND EDUCATION ACTIVITIES: Topics: Children/youth/family; Culture/tradition/religion; Ecology/environment/biodiversity; Education/training/literacy; Employment/unemployment; Food/famine; Gender issues/women; Health/sanitation/water; Human rights/peace/conflicts; International relations/cooperation/development aid; Peace/ethnic conflicts/armament/disarmament; Population/family planning/demography; Poverty/living conditions; Refugees/migrants/ethnic groups; Rural development/agriculture; Urban development/habitat. **Activities:** Fund raising; Information and documentation services/data bases; Information campaigns/exhibitions; Publishing/audiovisual materials/educational materials.

AUT0027

ENTWICKLUNGSPOLITISCHEN BILDUNGSZENTRUM DES OED UND AAI (EBZ) ♦ ÖED and AAI Development Policy Education Centre

Türkenstrasse 3, 1090 Wien, Austria.

Telephone: 43 (222) 34 46 29. *Contact:* Gerhard Bittner, President.

AUT0028

ENTWICKLUNGSWERKSTATT AUSTRIA (EWA) ♦ Development Workshop Austria

Johann Herbst Strasse 23, 5061 Salzburg-Glasenbach, Austria.

Telephone: 43 (662) 62 71 12. *Fax:* 43 (662) 62 48 12. *Contact:* Rudolf Graf, Director.

OBJECTIVES: To build up rural technical infrastructure together with local self-help groups, especially in West African Sahelian countries.

GENERAL INFORMATION: *Creation:* 1986. *Affiliated to:* Arbeitsgemeinschaft für Entwicklungszusammenarbeit (Austria) - GATE - Deutsche Gesellschaft für Technische Zusammenarbeit (Germany). *Personnel/Total:* 16. *Salaried:* 16 of which: 12 in developing countries. *Budget/Total 1993:* ECU 1147000 (US$ 1487000). *Financial sources:* Private: 9%. Public: 91%.

PUBLICATIONS: *Annual report.*

EVALUATION/RESEARCH: Evaluation reports available.

ACTIVITIES IN DEVELOPING REGIONS: Present in developing regions. Active in 2 country(ies). Maintains local field presence. Works through local field partners. **Sustainable Development Actions:** Democracy/good governance/institution building/participatory development; Ecology/environment/biodiversity; Education/training/literacy; Rural development/agriculture; Sending volunteers/experts/technical assistance; Small enterprises/informal sector/handicrafts. **Regions:** West Africa.

AUT0029

ENTWICKLUNGSZUSAMMENARBEIT MIT DER DRITTEN WELT (EZA) ♦ Development Co-operation with the Third World

Plainbachstrasse 8, 5101 Bergheim, Austria.

Telephone: 43 (662) 52 178. *Fax:* 43 (662) 52 586. *Contact:* Jean-Marie Krier.

OBJECTIVES: To promote just production and living conditions in Third World countries by trading products of NGOs, ecclesiastical or charitable institutions and co-operatives of developing countries. To support projects and activities undertaken by these organisations.

GENERAL INFORMATION: *Creation:* 1975. *Affiliated to:* Arbeitsgemeinschaft Entwicklungszusammenarbeit (Austria) - European Fair Trade Association (the Netherlands) - International Federation for Alternative

See: *How to Use the Directory,* page 11.

Trade. *Personnel/Total:* 36. *Salaried:* 36. *Budget/Total 1993:* ECU 1989000 (US$ 2579000).

PUBLICATIONS: *Periodicals:* EZA-INFO (4) - Aktions-Gruppen-Aktuel (2). *Annual report.*

ACTIVITIES IN DEVELOPING REGIONS: Active in 25 country(ies). Works through local field partners. **Sustainable Development Actions:** Debt/finance/trade; Ecology/environment/biodiversity; Education/training/literacy; Sending volunteers/experts/technical assistance. **Regions:** Caribbean; Central Asia and South Asia; East Africa; Mexico and Central America; South America; South East Asia; Southern Africa; West Africa.

INFORMATION AND EDUCATION ACTIVITIES: **Topics:** Ecology/environment/biodiversity; International economic relations/trade/debt/finance; Rural development/agriculture. **Activities:** Broadcasting/cultural events; Conferences/seminars/workshops/training activities; Exchanges/twinning/linking; Fund raising; Information and documentation services/data bases; Information campaigns/exhibitions; Lobbying/advocacy; Publishing/audiovisual materials/educational materials.

AUT0030

ERKLARUNG VON GRAZ FUR SOLIDARISCHE ENTWICKLUNG (EVG) ♦ Declaration of Graz for Solidarity in Development

Prokopigasse 2, 8010 Graz, Austria.

Telephone: 43 (316) 70 21 53. *Contact:* Mag. Burgi Berhold.

OBJECTIVES: To support projects in the Third World. To raise funds through donations of the members of the NGO.

GENERAL INFORMATION: *Creation:* 1973. *Budget/Total 1993:* ECU 13000 (US$ 17000). *Financial sources: Self-financing:* 100%.

PUBLICATIONS: *Periodicals:* Bunte Blaetter (4).

COMMENTS: The NGO will try to enlarge its support base in 1995.

ACTIVITIES IN DEVELOPING REGIONS: Active in 5 country(ies). Works through local field partners. **Sustainable Development Actions:** Ecology/environment/biodiversity; Education/training/literacy; Gender issues/women; Health/sanitation/water; Rural development/agriculture. **Regions:** East Africa; Mexico and Central America; South America.

INFORMATION AND EDUCATION ACTIVITIES: **Topics:** Education/training/literacy; Gender issues/women; Health/sanitation/water; Rural development/agriculture. **Activities:** Conferences/seminars/workshops/training activities; Fund raising; Information campaigns/exhibitions.

AUT0031

ERZEUGER-VERBRAUCHER INITIATIVEN (EVI) ♦ Producer-Consumer Initiatives

Klostergasse 25, 3100 St. Pölten, Austria.

Telephone: 43 (2742) 39 703. *Contact:* Linda Schletz-Ronniger.

AUT0032

EUROPAHAUS EISENSTADT

Mühlgasse, Eselmühl, 7062 St. Margarethen, Austria.

Telephone: 43 (2680) 29 80. *Fax:* 43 (2680) 29 79. *Contact:* Edith Axmann-Spielberger, Chairman.

OBJECTIVES: To provide information services and political education to European and global politics.

GENERAL INFORMATION: *Creation:* 1967. *Affiliated to:* International Federation of Europe Houses - Osterr.Informadienst für Entwicklungspolitik (Austria). *Personnel/Total:* 4. *Salaried:* 4. *Budget/Total 1993:* ECU 152000 (US$ 198000). *Financial sources: Private:* 10%. *Public:* 89%. *Self-financing:* 1%.

PUBLICATIONS: *Periodicals:* Europahaus Eisenstadt Aktuel (4). *Annual report. List of publications.*

EVALUATION/RESEARCH: Evaluation reports available. Undertakes research activities.

PLANNED ACTIVITIES: Working on "Europe and School" : the European dimension in Education.

COMMENTS: Undertakes activities in the Commonwealth of Independent States. Information activities related to the Commonwealth of Independent States.

INFORMATION AND EDUCATION ACTIVITIES: **Topics:** Ecology/environment/biodiversity; Education/training/literacy; Human rights/peace/conflicts; Refugees/migrants/ethnic groups. **Activities:** Conferences/seminars/workshops/training activities; Information and documentation services/data bases; Information campaigns/exhibitions; Publishing/audiovisual materials/educational materials.

AUT0033

EVANGELISCHER ARBEITSKREIS FUR WELTMISSION IN OSTERREICH (EAWM) ♦ Protestant Association for World Mission in Austria

Postfach 132, Schwarzspanierstr. 13, 1096 Wien, Austria.

Telephone: 43 (1) 408 80 73. *Fax:* 43 (1) 408 06 95 33. *Contact:* Mag Gottfried Mernyi, Secretary.

OBJECTIVES: To undertake mission activities and information campaigns for the development projects of their partner churches and NGOs in Africa. To network among the interested persons of the Protestant Church of Austria.

GENERAL INFORMATION: *Creation:* 1974. *Type of organisation:* coordinating body. *Member organisations:* 2. *Affiliated to:* ÖIE (Austria) - AGEZ (Austria) - EAEZ (Austria) - Basler Mission (Switzerland) - EMS. *Personnel/Total:* 25. *Salaried:* 4 of which: 3 in developing countries. *Volunteers:* 21. *Budget/Total 1993:* ECU 139000 (US$ 180000). *Financial sources: Private:* 10%. *Public:* 10%. *Self-financing:* 80%.

PUBLICATIONS: *Periodicals:* Die Brücke (4). *Annual report.*

PLANNED ACTIVITIES: Undertaking a partnership programme with the Presbyterian Church of Ghana. Organising a youth information campaign.

ACTIVITIES IN DEVELOPING REGIONS: Active in 4 country(ies). Works through local field partners. **Sustainable Development Actions:** Education/training/literacy; Emergency relief/refugees/humanitarian assistance; Gender issues/women; Health/sanitation/water; Human rights/peace/conflicts; Sending volunteers/experts/technical assistance. **Regions:** East Africa; Southern Africa; West Africa.

INFORMATION AND EDUCATION ACTIVITIES: **Topics:** Children/youth/family; Culture/tradition/religion; Education/training/literacy; Emergency relief/refugees/humanitarian assistance; Gender issues/women; Health/sanitation/water; Human rights/peace/conflicts; International economic relations/trade/debt/finance; International relations/cooperation/development aid; Peace/ethnic conflicts/armament/disarmament; Population/family planning/demography; Poverty/living conditions; Racism/xenophobia/antisemitism; Refugees/migrants/ethnic groups. **Activities:** Conferences/seminars/workshops/training activities; Exchanges/twinning/linking; Formal education; Fund raising; Information campaigns/exhibitions; Lobbying/advocacy.

AUT0034

FRAUENSOLIDARITAT - ENTWICKLUNGSPOLITISCHE INITIATIVEN FUR DIE FRAUEN IN DER DRITTEN WELT ♦ Solidarity among Women- Development Initiatives for Women in the "Third World"

Weyrgasse 5/I, 1030 Wien, Austria.

Telephone: 43 (222) 713 35 94. *Fax:* 43 (222) 713 35 94. *Contact:* Sigrun Berger.

OBJECTIVES: To raise awareness of the economical and political needs and demands of women in the Third World. To support initiatives improving the situation of women in Africa, Asia and Latin America. To provide documentation and carry out research on women in the Southern hemisphere.

GENERAL INFORMATION: *Creation:* 1982. *Personnel/Total:* 7. *Salaried:* 5. *Volunteers:* 2.

PUBLICATIONS: *Periodicals:* Frauensolidarität (4). *Annual report. List of publications.*

EVALUATION/RESEARCH: Evaluation reports available. Undertakes research activities.

PLANNED ACTIVITIES: Support of the Europe-wide Committee for the Defense of Women's Rights in Iran.

ACTIVITIES IN DEVELOPING REGIONS: Works through local field partners. **Sustainable Development Actions:** Children/youth/family; Ecology/environment/biodiversity; Education/training/literacy; Gender issues/women. **Regions:** Mexico and Central America; Southern Africa.

INFORMATION AND EDUCATION ACTIVITIES: Topics: Gender issues/women; Refugees/migrants/ethnic groups. **Activities:** Conferences/seminars/workshops/training activities; Exchanges/twinning/linking; Fund raising; Information and documentation services/data bases; Information campaigns/exhibitions; Lobbying/advocacy; Networking/electronic telecommunications; Publishing/audiovisual materials/educational materials.

AUT0035

GESELLSCHAFT FUR OSTERREICHISCH-ARABISCHE BEZIEHUNGEN (GOAB) ♦ Society for Austro-Arab Relations

Lindengasse 61-63/2/V, 1070 Wien, Austria.

Telephone: 43 (1) 526 78 10. **Fax:** 43 (1) 526 77 95. **Contact:** Franz Löschnak, Minister of Interior.

OBJECTIVES: To foster political, cultural and scientific relations between Austria and Arab countries. To develop co-operation with Palestinian Territories. To provide social and legal help for Arabs in need (refugees) in Austria.

GENERAL INFORMATION: Creation: 1982. **Affiliated to:** Parliamentarian Association for European Arab Co-operation - Network of European NGOs in the Occupied Territories.. **Personnel/Total:** 7. Salaried: 7 of which: 2 in developing countries. **Budget/Total 1993:** ECU 861000 (US$ 1118000). **Financial sources:** Private: 10%. Public: 85%. Self-financing: 5%.

PUBLICATIONS: Periodicals: Bulletin der Gesellschaft für Osterreichisch-Arabische Beziehungen (4). Annual report. List of publications.

EVALUATION/RESEARCH: Evaluation reports available. Undertakes research activities.

PLANNED ACTIVITIES: Undertaking research projects about Austrian-Palestinian relations and about economic perspectives in the Middle-East in the light of the peace process. Implementing the Austrian Development Co-operation programme with Palestine.

ACTIVITIES IN DEVELOPING REGIONS: Present in developing regions. Active in 1 country(ies). Maintains local field presence. Works through local field partners. **Sustainable Development Actions:** Ecology/environment/biodiversity; Education/training/literacy; Emergency relief/refugees/humanitarian assistance; Gender issues/women; Health/sanitation/water; Other; Rural development/agriculture; Sending volunteers/experts/technical assistance. **Regions:** Middle East.

INFORMATION AND EDUCATION ACTIVITIES: Topics: Culture/tradition/religion; Emergency relief/refugees/humanitarian assistance; Health/sanitation/water; Human rights/peace/conflicts; International relations/cooperation/development aid; Rural development/agriculture. **Activities:** Broadcasting/cultural events; Conferences/seminars/workshops/training activities; Fund raising; Information and documentation services/data bases; Lobbying/advocacy.

AUT0036

GESELLSCHAFT ÖSTERREICH-VIETNAM ♦ Austrian Vietnamese Society

c/o E. Ringhoffer, Cottagegasse 21, 1180 Wien, Austria.

Telephone: 43 (1) 470 6887. **Fax:** 43 (1) 360 5224. **Contact:** Irma Schwager, President.

OBJECTIVES: To foster the exchange of culture and information with Viet-Nam and provide humanitarian assistance.

GENERAL INFORMATION: Creation: 1975. **Affiliated to:** Association of the Austrian Foreign Societies (Austria). **Personnel/Total:** 5. Volunteers: 5. **Budget/Total 1993:** ECU 2000 (US$ 3000). **Financial sources:** Private: 40%. Self-financing: 60%.

PUBLICATIONS: Periodicals: .

PLANNED ACTIVITIES: Support of an orphanage in Ho Chi Minh city.

ACTIVITIES IN DEVELOPING REGIONS: Present in developing regions. Active in 1 country(ies). Works through local field partners. **Sustainable Development Actions:** Children/youth/family. **Regions:** South East Asia.

AUT0037

HELPING HANDS - KOORDINATIONSBURO FUR FLUCHTLINGSHILFE

Liechtensteinstrasse 13, .070 Wien, Austria.

Telephone: 43 (1) 310 888 010.

AUT0038

HILFE FUR ALLE (HIFA) ♦ Help for All

Staudingergasse 11, 1200 Wien, Austria.

Telephone: 43 (1) 330 04 25. **Fax:** 43 (1) 330 04 25. **E-mail:** 912 211 558 (BTX). **Contact:** Adolf Paster, President.

AUT0039

HUMANA - VEREIN ZUR FORDERUNG NOTLEIDENDER MENSCHEN IN DER DRITTEN WELT (HUMANA) ♦ HUMANA - Association for the Benefit of Needy People in the Third World

Reindorffgasse 35, 1150 Wien, Austria.

Telephone: 43 (1) 869 38 13. **Fax:** 43 (1) 865 34 92. **Contact:** Pelle Christensen, Chairman.

AUT0040

INITIATIVE DRITTE WELT ♦ Third World Initiative

Krankenhausgasse 6, 5280 Braunau am Inn, Austria.

Telephone: 43 (7722) 66470. **Fax:** 43 (7722) 66470. **Contact:** Lizeth Ausserhuber-Camposeco.

OBJECTIVES: To work for global justice. To undertake educational activities in Austria. To sell goods from Third World countries.

GENERAL INFORMATION: Creation: 1978. **Affiliated to:** ARGE Dritte-Welt-Läden. **Personnel/Total:** 17. Salaried: 2. Volunteers: 15. **Budget/Total 1993:** ECU 66000 (US$ 86000). **Financial sources:** Private: 50%. Public: 20%. Self-financing: 30%.

PUBLICATIONS: Periodicals: Rundschrei (2). Annual report.

EVALUATION/RESEARCH: Evaluation reports available.

PLANNED ACTIVITIES: Organising an exhibition about "Women in Islam". Project for the protection of forests in Nicaragua.

ACTIVITIES IN DEVELOPING REGIONS: Active in 2 country(ies). Works through local field partners. **Sustainable Development Actions:** Education/training/literacy; Energy/transport; Health/sanitation/water; Human rights/peace/conflicts; Rural development/agriculture. **Regions:** Central Africa; Mexico and Central America.

AUT0041

INSTITUT FUR INTERNATIONALE ZUSAMMENARBEIT (IIZ) ♦ Institute for International Co-operation

Wipplingerstrasse 32, 1010 Wien, Austria.

Telephone: 43 (1) 533 47 86 - 0. **Fax:** 43 (1) 533 47 86 39. **Contact:** Wolfgang Schindegger, Director.

OBJECTIVES: To support local initiatives in rural areas in Africa and Latin America. To build up integrated development programmes focusing on organic farming, rural crafts, marketing, primary health care and capacity building.

GENERAL INFORMATION: Creation: 1963. **Affiliated to:** Arbeitgemeinschaft Entwicklungszusammenarbeit (Austria) - Koordinierungstelle der Österreichischen Bischofskonferenz für Internationale Entwicklung und Mission - European Conference of Christian Organisations of Interna-

See: *How to Use the Directory,* page 11.

tional Co-operation (Europe). *Personnel/Total:* 107. *Salaried:* 107 of which: 83 in developing countries. *Budget/Total 1993:* ECU 6895000 (US$ 8940000). *Financial sources:* Private: 8%. Public: 92%.

PUBLICATIONS: *Periodicals:* IIZ-Zum Thema (4). *Annual report.*

COMMENTS: IIZ does not send volunteers but employs trained staff (technical advisors) with long- or short-term contracts.

ACTIVITIES IN DEVELOPING REGIONS: Works through local field partners. **Sustainable Development Actions:** Democracy/good governance/institution building/participatory development; Ecology/environment/biodiversity; Education/training/literacy; Gender issues/women; Health/sanitation/water; Human rights/peace/conflicts; Rural development/agriculture; Sending volunteers/experts/technical assistance; Small enterprises/informal sector/handicrafts. **Regions:** Central Africa; East Africa; Mexico and Central America; South America; West Africa.

AUT0042

INSTITUT FUR STAATS- UND VERWALTUNGSRECHT

Schottenbastei 10-16, 1010 Wien, Austria.

Contact: Prof. Felix Ermacora.

AUT0043

INTERNATIONAL FEDERATION OF MEDICAL STUDENTS' ASSOCIATIONS (IFMSA) ♦ Fédération internationale des associations d'étudiants en médecine

Liechtensteinstrasse 13, 1090 Wien, Autriche.

Téléphone: 43 (222) 31 55 66.

AUT0044

INTERNATIONAL HELSINKI FEDERATION FOR HUMAN RIGHTS (IHF)

Rummelhardt Gasse 2/18, 1090 Vienna, Austria.

Telephone: 43 (1) 402 73 87. *Fax:* 43 (1) 408 74 44. *Contact:* Jo Benkow, President.

OBJECTIVES: To monitor compliance with the human rights provisions of the Helsinki Final Act and its follow-up documents.

GENERAL INFORMATION: *Creation:* 1982. *Type of organisation:* coordinating body. *Member organisations:* 28. *Personnel/Total:* 9. *Salaried:* 3. *Volunteers:* 6. *Budget/Total 1993:* ECU 515000 (US$ 668000).

PUBLICATIONS: *Annual report. List of publications.*

EVALUATION/RESEARCH: Undertakes research activities.

COMMENTS: Undertakes activities in the Commonwealth of Independent States. Information activities related to the Commonwealth of Independent States.

INFORMATION AND EDUCATION ACTIVITIES: **Topics:** Human rights/peace/conflicts; Refugees/migrants/ethnic groups. **Activities:** Conferences/seminars/workshops/training activities; Formal education; Fund raising; Information and documentation services/data bases; Information campaigns/exhibitions; Lobbying/advocacy; Publishing/audiovisual materials/educational materials.

AUT0045

INTERNATIONAL SOCIETY OF SOIL SCIENCE (ISSS)

Gregor Mendel- Str. 33, 1180 Vienna, Austria.

Telephone: 43 (1) 310 60 26. *Fax:* 43 (1) 310 60 27. *E-mail:* ISSS@EDV1.BOKU.AC.AT. *Contact:* Winfried E.H. BLUM.

OBJECTIVES: To foster all branches of soil science and its applications. To promote contacts among scientists and other persons engaged in the study and applications of soil science. To stimulate scientific research and to further its application for the benefit of mankind.

GENERAL INFORMATION: *Creation:* 1924. *Affiliated to:* JCSU. *Personnel/Total:* 4. *Salaried:* 1. *Volunteers:* 3. *Budget/Total 1993:* ECU 62000 (US$ 80000). *Financial sources:* Private: 5%. Public: 20%. *Self-financing:* 75%.

PUBLICATIONS: *Periodicals:* Bulletin of ISSS (2). *List of publications.*

EVALUATION/RESEARCH: Evaluation reports available. Undertakes research activities.

COMMENTS: ISSS has individual members in 146 countries and its Bulletin reaches all of them. Undertakes activities in the Commonwealth of Independent States. Information activities related to the Commonwealth of Independent States.

ACTIVITIES IN DEVELOPING REGIONS: Works through local field partners. **Sustainable Development Actions:** Ecology/environment/biodiversity; Rural development/agriculture; Urban development/habitat. **Regions:** Caribbean; Central Africa; Central Asia and South Asia; East Africa; East Asia; Mexico and Central America; Middle East; North Africa; Oceania; South America; South East Asia; Southern Africa; West Africa.

INFORMATION AND EDUCATION ACTIVITIES: **Topics:** Ecology/environment/biodiversity; Rural development/agriculture; Urban development/habitat. **Activities:** Conferences/seminars/workshops/training activities; Information and documentation services/data bases.

AUT0046

INTERNATIONALER VERBAND FORSTLICHER FORSCHUNGSANSTALTEN (IUFRO) ♦ International Union of Forestry Research Organisations

P.O. Box 1131, Seckendorff-Gudent-Weg 8, 1131 Vienna, Austria.

Telephone: 43 (1) 877 01 51. *Fax:* 43 (1) 877 93 55. *E-mail:* X0221DAA@AWIUNI11.BITNET. *Contact:* M.N. Salleh, President.

OBJECTIVES: To promote international co-operation in scientific studies embracing the whole field of research related to forestry. To facilitate exchanges of ideas worldwide among individual research workers and provide development assistance.

GENERAL INFORMATION: *Creation:* 1892. *Type of organisation:* network. *Member organisations:* 720. *Affiliated to:* International Council of Scientific Unions. *Salaried:* 8. *Volunteers:* 8. *Budget/Total 1993:* ECU 1002000 (US$ 1300000). *Financial sources:* Private: 30%. Public: 20%. *Self-financing:* 50%.

PUBLICATIONS: *Periodicals:* IUFRO-News (4) - Information Bulletin for Developing Countries (3). *Annual report. List of publications.*

COMMENTS: Undertakes activities in the Commonwealth of Independent States.

ACTIVITIES IN DEVELOPING REGIONS: Works through local field partners. **Sustainable Development Actions:** Other. **Regions:** South America; South East Asia.

AUT0047

INTERNATIONALER VERSOHNUNGSBUND OSTERREICHISCHER ZWEIG (IVB-ÖZ) ♦ Austrian Branch of International Fellowship of Reconciliation

Lederergasse 23/III/27, 1080 Wien, Austria.

Telephone: 43 (1) 408 53 32. *Fax:* 43 (1) 408 53 32. *Contact:* Irmgard Ehrenberger.

OBJECTIVES: To fight injustice, build friendships and work for human rights. To improve living conditions and foster social and economic structures better adapted to different cultures.

GENERAL INFORMATION: *Creation:* 1920. *Type of organisation:* network. *Affiliated to:* International Fellowship of Reconciliation (the Netherlands). *Personnel/Total:* 4. *Salaried:* 4. *Financial sources:* Private: 70%. Public: 10%. *Self-financing:* 20%.

PUBLICATIONS: *Periodicals:* Spinnrad (4) - Aufbrüche (4).

PLANNED ACTIVITIES: Organising a campaign entitled "Towards a Culture of Non-Violence".

COMMENTS: Undertakes activities in the Commonwealth of Independent States. Information activities related to the Commonwealth of Independent States.

ACTIVITIES IN DEVELOPING REGIONS: Works through local field partners. **Sustainable Development Actions:** Human rights/peace/conflicts. **Regions:** South America.

Voir : *Comment utiliser le répertoire*, page 11.

INFORMATION AND EDUCATION ACTIVITIES: Topics: Human rights/peace/conflicts; Peace/ethnic conflicts/armament/disarmament; Racism/xenophobia/antisemitism; Refugees/migrants/ethnic groups. **Activities:** Conferences/seminars/workshops/training activities; Exchanges/twinning/linking; Information campaigns/exhibitions.

AUT0048

ISLAMIC AFRICAN RELIEF AGENCY

Prater St. 47/3/3, 1020 Vienna, Austria.

AUT0049

ISRAEL-PALASTINA-KOMITEE ♦ Israel-Palestine Committee

Biberstrasse 8/20, 1010 Wien, Austria.

Telephone: 43 (222) 513 67 83. *Contact:* Dr. John Bunzl.

AUT0050

KATHOLISCHE ARBEITNEHMERBEWEGUNG OSTER-REICHS ♦ Austrian Catholic Workers' Movement

Stephansplatz 6/V/34, 1010 Wien, Austria.

Telephone: 43 (222) 53 25 61 (ext. 349).

AUT0051

KATHOLISCHE FRAUENBEWEGUNG OSTERREICHS (KFBÖ) ♦ Catholic Women's Movement of Austria

Spiegelgasse 3, 1010 Wien, Austria.

Telephone: 43 (222) 51 552. *Fax:* 43 (222) 51 670. *Contact:* Ingrid Klein, Chairwoman.

OBJECTIVES: To support and assist woman to better organize their personal daily lives and increase their spiritual development. To encourage active community involvement and promote justice, peace, environmental protection and woman's solidarity.

GENERAL INFORMATION: *Creation:* 1947. *Affiliated to:* World Union of Catholic Women's organizations (Belgium) - Cooperation Internationale pour le Development Solidarité (Belgium) - Women in Development (Austria). *Personnel/Total:* 124. *Salaried:* 4. *Volunteers:* 120. *Budget/Total 1993:* ECU 2389000 (US$ 3098000). *Financial sources:* Private: 100%.

PUBLICATIONS: *Periodicals:* Unser Thema (4). *Annual report. List of publications.*

ACTIVITIES IN DEVELOPING REGIONS: Active in 15 country(ies). Works through local field partners. **Sustainable Development Actions:** Children/youth/family; Democracy/good governance/institution building/participatory development; Ecology/environment/biodiversity; Education/training/literacy; Gender issues/women; Health/sanitation/water; Population/family planning/demography; Rural development/agriculture; Small enterprises/informal sector/handicrafts. **Regions:** Central Africa; Central Asia and South Asia; Mexico and Central America; North Africa; South America; South East Asia; Southern Africa.

INFORMATION AND EDUCATION ACTIVITIES: Topics: Children/youth/family; Culture/tradition/religion; Ecology/environment/biodiversity; Education/training/literacy; Employment/unemployment; Gender issues/women; Health/sanitation/water; Human rights/peace/conflicts; International economic relations/trade/debt/finance; International relations/cooperation/development aid; Population/family planning/demography; Poverty/living conditions; Rural development/agriculture. **Activities:** Conferences/seminars/workshops/training activities; Exchanges/twinning/linking; Fund raising; Information campaigns/exhibitions; Lobbying/advocacy; Networking/electronic telecommunications; Publishing/audiovisual materials/educational materials.

AUT0052

KOFINANZIERUNGSSTELLE FUR ENTWICKLUNGSZUSAM-MENARBEIT (KFS) ♦ Co-financing Office for Development Cooperation

Türkenstrasse 3, 1090 Wien, Austria.

Telephone: 43 (1) 317 67 97. *Fax:* 43 (1) 317 67 96. *Contact:* Hans Bürstmayr, Director.

OBJECTIVES: To co-finance development projects and programmes of member organisations with the Austrian government. To struggle against poverty. To strengthen the ability to achieve self-determination, social justice and the enforcement of human rights.

GENERAL INFORMATION: *Creation:* 1992. *Type of organisation:* association of NGOs. *Member organisations:* 6. *Affiliated to:* Mission KOO (Austria) - AGEZ (Austria). *Personnel/Total:* 1. *Salaried:* 6 of which: 1 in developing countries. *Volunteers:* 6. *Budget/Total 1993:* ECU 3978000 (US$ 5158000). *Financial sources:* Private: 24%. Public: 74%. Self-financing: 2%.

PUBLICATIONS: *Annual report.*

PLANNED ACTIVITIES: Organisation of an educational campaign on "Water" (1993-1995) and one on "Debt-debts relief" (1995).

ACTIVITIES IN DEVELOPING REGIONS: Active in 16 country(ies). Works through local field partners. **Sustainable Development Actions:** Children/youth/family; Democracy/good governance/institution building/participatory development; Ecology/environment/biodiversity; Education/training/literacy; Gender issues/women; Health/sanitation/water; Human rights/peace/conflicts; Rural development/agriculture; Small enterprises/informal sector/handicrafts. **Regions:** Central Asia and South Asia; East Africa; Mexico and Central America; South America; South East Asia; Southern Africa; West Africa.

INFORMATION AND EDUCATION ACTIVITIES: Topics: Children/youth/family; Culture/tradition/religion; Ecology/environment/biodiversity; Health/sanitation/water. **Activities:** Broadcasting/cultural events; Conferences/seminars/workshops/training activities; Formal education; Information campaigns/exhibitions; Publishing/audiovisual materials/educational materials.

AUT0053

KOMITEE FUR MEDIZINISCHE UND SOZIALE HILFE FUR PALASTINENSER ♦ Committee for Medical and Social Help for Palestinians

Mariahilferstrasse 91, 1060 Wien, Austria.

Telephone: 43 (222) 597 43 37. *Contact:* Dr. Franz Mayrhofer.

AUT0054

KOORDINIERUNGSTELLE DER OSTERREICHISCHEN BISCHOFSKONFERENZ FUR INTERNATIONALE ENTWICKLUNG UND MISSION (KOO) ♦ Coordination Office for International Developemnt and Mission Austria

Türkenstrasse 3, 1090 Wien, Autriche.

Téléphone: 43 (1) 34 03 21. *Fax:* 43 (1) 34 03 21. *Contact:* Dr. Helmut Ornauer, Directeur.

OBJECTIFS: To co-ordinate the 34 member organisations in developing countries. To stimulate common project criteria and development policy. To promote co-ordinated development education programmes and computerise the central project registration.

INFORMATIONS GENERALES: *Création:* 1963. *Type d'organisation:* réseau, collectif. *Organisations membres:* 34. *Affiliée à:* CIDSE (Belgium). *Personnel/Total:* 4. *Salariés:* 4. *Budget/Total 1993:* ECU 206000 (US$ 267000). *Sources financières:* Privé: 40%. Autofinancement: 60%.

PUBLICATIONS: *Rapport annuel.*

PREVISIONS D'ACTIVITES: Co-ordinating a campaign on the Third World Debt.

COMMENTAIRES: Intervient dans la Communauté des Etats indépendants. Activités d'information concernant la Communauté des Etats indépendants.

AUT0055

MITTELSCHULERKONGREGATION - JUGENDZEN-TRUM (MK) ♦ Association of Secondary School Pupils

Sillgasse 8A, 6021 Innsbruck, Austria.

Telephone: 43 (5222) 31 311.

See: *How to Use the Directory,* page 11.

AUT0056

THE NATIONAL UNIONS OF STUDENTS IN EUROPE (ESIB)

Liechtensteinstr. 13, 1090 Wien, Austria.

Telephone: 43 (1) 310 88 80 48. *Fax:* 43 (1) 310 88 80 36. *Contact:* Richard Hill, Director.

OBJECTIVES: To facilitate co-operation between national unions of students in Europe. To influence European decision makers on measures concerning students. To co-operate with regional and national student organisations outside Europe.

GENERAL INFORMATION: *Creation:* 1982. *Type of organisation:* association of NGOs. *Member organisations:* 29. *Affiliated to:* Youth Forum of the EC (Belgium). *Personnel/Total:* 2. *Salaried:* 2. *Budget/ Total 1993:* ECU 99000 (US$ 129000). *Financial sources:* Public: 50%. *Self-financing:* 50%.

PUBLICATIONS: *Periodicals:* ESIB News (12) - ESIB Womens News (3). *Annual report. List of publications.*

EVALUATION/RESEARCH: Evaluation reports available. Undertakes research activities.

PLANNED ACTIVITIES: Participation in the Council of Europe's campaign against racism. Starting new activities in the field of North-South co-operation with other regional student organisations.

COMMENTS: Undertakes activities in the Commonwealth of Independent States. Information activities related to the Commonwealth of Independent States.

INFORMATION AND EDUCATION ACTIVITIES: Topics: Children/youth/ family; Education/training/literacy; Employment/unemployment; Gender issues/women; Racism/xenophobia/antisemitism. **Activities:** Conferences/seminars/workshops/training activities; Formal education; Information and documentation services/data bases; Lobbying/advocacy; Publishing/audiovisual materials/educational materials.

AUT0057

NGO PLANNING COMMITTEE

Kirchengasse 26, 1070 Vienna, Austria.

AUT0058

NORD-SUD INSTITUT FUR ENTWICKLUNGSZUSAM-MENARBEIT ♦ Austrian North-South Institute for Dvelopment Co-operation

Möllwaldplatz 4/2, 1040 Wien, Austria.

Telephone: 43 (1) 505 44 92 . *Fax:* 43 (1) 504 46 79. *Contact:* Günter Dietrich, Director.

OBJECTIVES: To implement development co-operation projects together with organisations and institutions in the South. To strengthen democratic structures. To support the implementation of human rights, education, social welfare, equal rights for women and ecology.

GENERAL INFORMATION: *Creation:* 1991. *Personnel/Total:* 15. *Salaried:* 15. *Budget/Total 1993:* ECU 3946000 (US$ 5117000). *Financial sources:* Private: 30%. Public: 69%. Self-financing: 1%.

PUBLICATIONS: *Periodicals:* Nord-Sud Forum (4). *Annual report.*

PLANNED ACTIVITIES: Within the context of the Southern Africa Platform, providing institutional background for Austrian NGOs and strengthening the lobbying for this region.

ACTIVITIES IN DEVELOPING REGIONS: Active in 10 country(ies). Maintains local field presence. Works through local field partners. **Sustainable Development Actions:** Democracy/good governance/institution building/participatory development; Education/training/literacy; Emergency relief/refugees/humanitarian assistance; Gender issues/women; Health/sanitation/water; Human rights/peace/conflicts; Sending volunteers/experts/technical assistance; Small enterprises/informal sector/ handicrafts; Urban development/habitat. **Regions:** East Africa; Mexico and Central America; North Africa; Southern Africa.

INFORMATION AND EDUCATION ACTIVITIES: Topics: Human rights/ peace/conflicts; Refugees/migrants/ethnic groups. **Activities:** Conferences/seminars/workshops/training activities; Lobbying/advocacy.

AUT0059

OSTERREICHISCHE CARITAS-ZENTRALE ♦ Caritas Austria

Nibelungengasse 1, Postfach 114, 1011 Wien, Austria.

Telephone: 43 (222) 587 15 77. *Fax:* 43 (222) 587 15 77/13. *Contact:* Prelat Dr. Leopold Ungar, President.

AUT0060

OSTERREICHISCHE FORSCHUNGSSTIFTUNG FUR ENTWICKLUNGSHILFE (ÖFSE) ♦ Austrian Foundation for Development Research

Berggasse 7, 1090 Wien, Austria.

Telephone: 43 (1) 317 40 10. *Fax:* 43 (1) 317 40 15. *Contact:* Klaus Zapotoczky, President.

OBJECTIVES: To promote and undertake research, documentation and information dissemination on development.

GENERAL INFORMATION: *Creation:* 1967. *Affiliated to:* SATIS (Senegal) - IUEP (Germany) - NORRAG (Switzerland) - ICFO (the Netherlands). *Personnel/Total:* 15. *Salaried:* 15. *Budget/ Total 1993:* ECU 1127000 (US$ 1461000). *Financial sources:* Private: 10%. *Public:* 90%.

PUBLICATIONS: *Periodicals:* Austrian Development Co-operation (1) - Annotated Bibliography (2) -Documentation Services (50). *List of publications.*

PLANNED ACTIVITIES: Establishing an electronic information service. Implementing a European relations department.

COMMENTS: Information activities related to the Commonwealth of Independent States.

INFORMATION AND EDUCATION ACTIVITIES: Topics: Children/youth/ family; Culture/tradition/religion; Ecology/environment/biodiversity; Education/training/literacy; Emergency relief/refugees/humanitarian assistance; Employment/unemployment; Food/famine; Gender issues/ women; Health/sanitation/water; Human rights/peace/conflicts; International economic relations/trade/debt/finance; International relations/ cooperation/development aid; Peace/ethnic conflicts/armament/disarmament; Population/family planning/demography; Poverty/living conditions; Racism/xenophobia/antisemitism; Refugees/migrants/ethnic groups; Rural development/agriculture; Urban development/habitat. **Activities:** Information and documentation services/data bases.

AUT0061

OSTERREICHISCHE GESELLSCHAFT "RETTET DAS KIND" ♦ Austrian Save the Children

Pouthongasse 3, 1150 Wien, Austria.

Telephone: 43 (1) 92 62 16. *Fax:* 43 (1) 92 46 64. *Contact:* Dieter Wesenauer, Secretary General.

OBJECTIVES: To give aid to children irrespective of race, creed, nationality or political ideology.

GENERAL INFORMATION: *Creation:* 1956. *Member organisations:* 7. *Affiliated to:* International Save the Children Alliance (Switzerland). *Personnel/Total:* 54. *Salaried:* 54. *Budget/ Total 1993:* ECU 1279000 (US$ 1500000). *Financial sources:* Private: 30%. Public: 70%.

PUBLICATIONS: *Periodicals:* Mitteilungsblatt (4).

PLANNED ACTIVITIES: Undertaking rural development projects in Mexico and Guatemala and a school project in Tanzania. Establishing an institution for mentally handicapped children in South Africa.

COMMENTS: Undertakes activities in the Commonwealth of Independent States.

ACTIVITIES IN DEVELOPING REGIONS: Works through local field partners. **Sustainable Development Actions:** Education/training/literacy; Rural development/agriculture. **Regions:** East Africa; Mexico and Central America.

Voir : *Comment utiliser le répertoire,* page 11.

AUT0062

OSTERREICHISCHE GESELLSCHAFT DER FREUNDE KENIAS ♦ Austrian Society of the Friends of Kenya

Hohe Warte 7A, 1190 Wien, Austria.

Telephone: 43 (222) 36 51 73. *Contact:* Dr. Karl Kalz, Chairman.

AUT0063

OSTERREICHISCHE GESELLSCHAFT FUR ENTWICKLUNG-SZUSAMMENARBEIT (ADC AUSTRIA) ♦ Austrian Association for Development and Co-operation

Rüdigergasse 3, 1050 Wien, Austria.

Telephone: 43 (1) 587 84 10. *Fax:* 43 (1) 587 84 11. *Contact:* Gerd Kellermann, Director.

OBJECTIVES: To promote sustainable development, mainly in the field of small entreprises, small-scale mining, infrastructure and natural resources management.

GENERAL INFORMATION: *Creation:* 1989. *Affiliated to:* Arbeitsgemeinschaft Entwicklungszusammenarbeit (Austria). *Personnel/Total:* 40. *Salaried:* 40 of which: 20 in developing countries. *Budget/Total 1993:* ECU 7491000 (US$ 11434000). *Financial sources:* Private: 5%. Public: 95%.

PUBLICATIONS: *Annual report.*

ACTIVITIES IN DEVELOPING REGIONS: Present in developing regions. Active in 14 country(ies). Maintains local field presence. Works through local field partners. **Sustainable Development Actions:** Democracy/good governance/institution building/participatory development; Ecology/environment/biodiversity; Education/training/literacy; Emergency relief/refugees/humanitarian assistance; Energy/transport; Health/sanitation/water; Rural development/agriculture; Sending volunteers/experts/technical assistance; Small enterprises/informal sector/handicrafts. **Regions:** Central Africa; Central Asia and South Asia; East Africa; Mexico and Central America; South East Asia; Southern Africa; West Africa.

INFORMATION AND EDUCATION ACTIVITIES: **Topics:** Culture/tradition/religion; Ecology/environment/biodiversity; Refugees/migrants/ethnic groups. **Activities:** Conferences/seminars/workshops/training activities; Formal education; Information campaigns/exhibitions.

AUT0064

OSTERREICHISCHE UNESCO KOMMISSION (ÖUK) ♦ Austrian UNESCO Commission

Mentergasse 11, 1070 Wien, Austria.

Telephone: 43 (222) 93 64 21. *Contact:* Dr. Harald Gardos, General Secretary.

AUT0065

OSTERREICHISCHER AKADEMISCHER AUS-TAUSCHDIENST (ÖAD) ♦ Austrian Academic Exchange Service

Dr Karl Lueger-Ring 1, 1010 Wien, Austria.

Telephone: 43 (1) 42 31 50. *Fax:* 43 (1) 408 17 77. *Contact:* Ludwig Koller, Secretary General.

OBJECTIVES: To promote academic education between Austria and all other countries of the world. To provide scholarships.

GENERAL INFORMATION: *Creation:* 1961. *Affiliated to:* Academic Cooperation Association. *Personnel/Total:* 56. *Salaried:* 56. *Budget/Total 1993:* ECU 15191000 (US$ 19700000). *Financial sources:* Public: 92%. Self-financing: 8%.

PUBLICATIONS: *Annual report.*

EVALUATION/RESEARCH: Evaluation reports available.

PLANNED ACTIVITIES: To organise scholarship-programmes.

COMMENTS: Information activities related to the Commonwealth of Independent States.

INFORMATION AND EDUCATION ACTIVITIES: **Topics:** Ecology/environment/biodiversity; Gender issues/women; Health/sanitation/water; Human rights/peace/conflicts; International economic relations/trade/

debt/finance; International relations/cooperation/development aid; Population/family planning/demography; Rural development/agriculture; Urban development/habitat. **Activities:** Formal education.

AUT0066

OSTERREICHISCHER BUNDESJUGENDRING (ÖBJR) ♦ Austrian Federal Youth Council

Am Modenapark 1-2/326, 1030 Wien, Austria.

Telephone: 43 (1) 715 57 43. *Fax:* 43 (1) 712 85 84. *Contact:* Harald Koller, Secretary General.

OBJECTIVES: To federate twenty-two non-governmental democratic children and youth organisations.

GENERAL INFORMATION: *Creation:* 1953. *Type of organisation:* coordinating body. *Member organisations:* 22. *Personnel/Total:* 26. *Salaried:* 4. *Volunteers:* 22. *Budget/Total 1993:* ECU 199000 (US$ 258000). *Financial sources:* Public: 100%.

PUBLICATIONS: *Annual report.*

EVALUATION/RESEARCH: Evaluation reports available.

COMMENTS: Information activities related to the Commonwealth of Independent States.

ACTIVITIES IN DEVELOPING REGIONS: Active in 1 country(ies). **Sustainable Development Actions:** Children/youth/family. **Regions:** North Africa.

INFORMATION AND EDUCATION ACTIVITIES: **Topics:** Children/youth/family; Racism/xenophobia/antisemitism. **Activities:** Exchanges/twinning/linking; Networking/electronic telecommunications.

AUT0067

OSTERREICHISCHER ENTWICKLUNGSDIENST (ÖED) ♦ Austrian Service for Development Co-operation

Türkenstrasse 3, 1090 Wien, Austria.

Telephone: 43 (1) 310 05 92. *Contact:* Robert Zeiner, Director.

OBJECTIVES: To recruit, train and employ development workers and experts for programmes and projects in developing countries. To support programmes in health and projects in the field of education and vocational training, community development, small enterprises and handicrafts, agriculture and forestry. To plan, implement and evaluate financing programmes and projects.

GENERAL INFORMATION: *Creation:* 1961. *Member organisations:* 14. *Affiliated to:* Co-ordination Office of the Austrian Episcopal Conference for International Development and Mission (Austria) - Co-financing Office for Development Co-operation - Austrian Service for Development Education (Austria) - EZA -Europäisches Forum - SÜDWIND-BUCHWELT Buchandels - AGEZcAustria. *Personnel/Total:* 123. *Salaried:* 123 of which: 108 in developing countries. *Budget/Total 1993:* ECU 5196000 (US$ 6738000). *Financial sources:* Private: 12%. Public: 66%. Self-financing: 22%.

PUBLICATIONS: *Periodicals:* OED-Rundbrief (5). *Annual report. List of publications.*

PLANNED ACTIVITIES: Organisation of workshops on the topic of development education.

COMMENTS: OED has a department for development education to strengthen educational activities in Austria.

ACTIVITIES IN DEVELOPING REGIONS: Present in developing regions. Active in 9 country(ies). Maintains local field presence. Works through local field partners. **Sustainable Development Actions:** Children/youth/family; Education/training/literacy; Health/sanitation/water; Rural development/agriculture; Sending volunteers/experts/technical assistance; Small enterprises/informal sector/handicrafts. **Regions:** East Africa; Mexico and Central America; Oceania; South America; Southern Africa.

INFORMATION AND EDUCATION ACTIVITIES: **Topics:** Culture/tradition/religion; Ecology/environment/biodiversity; Gender issues/women; Health/sanitation/water; Human rights/peace/conflicts; International economic relations/trade/debt/finance; Other; Population/family planning/demography; Racism/xenophobia/antisemitism. **Activities:** Broadcast-

See: *How to Use the Directory,* page 11.

ing/cultural events; Conferences/seminars/workshops/training activities; Information and documentation services/data bases; Information campaigns/exhibitions; Lobbying/advocacy.

AUT0068

OSTERREICHISCHER INFORMATIONSDIENST FUR ENTWICKLUNGSPOLITIK (ÖIE) ♦ Austrian Information Service on Development Policy

Beiggasse 7, 1090 Vienna, Austria.

Telephone: 43 (1) 317 30 90. *Fax:* 43 (1) 317 30 95. *E-mail:* oeie@magnet.at. *Contact:* Franz Bittner, Executive Director.

OBJECTIVES: To undertake information campaigns about such issues as development and the environment, creating sustainable economies, and educational work.

GENERAL INFORMATION: *Creation:* 1979. *Affiliated to:* Alliance of Northern People on Environment and Development - European Network on Debt and Development. *Salaried:* 42. *Volunteers:* 100 of which: 142 in developing countries. *Budget/Total 1993:* ECU 1740000 (US$ 2257000). *Financial sources: Public:* 65%.

PUBLICATIONS: *Periodicals:* Sudwind (10). *Annual report. List of publications.*

INFORMATION AND EDUCATION ACTIVITIES: Topics: Ecology/environment/biodiversity; Gender issues/women; Human rights/peace/conflicts; International economic relations/trade/debt/finance; International relations/cooperation/development aid; Population/family planning/demography; Racism/xenophobia/antisemitism; Rural development/agriculture. **Activities:** Conferences/seminars/workshops/training activities; Formal education; Information campaigns/exhibitions; Lobbying/advocacy; Publishing/audiovisual materials/educational materials.

AUT0069

OSTERREICHISCHES HILFSKOMITEE FUR AFGHANISTAN ♦ Austrian Aid Committee for Afghanistan

C/O Dr. Alfred Janata, Salztorgasse 7/6, 1010 Wien, Austria.

Telephone: 43 (222) 634 08 85. *Contact:* Dr. Alfred Janata, Chairperson.

AUT0070

OSTERREICHISCHES INSTITUT FUR ENTWICKLUNGSHILFE UND TECHNISCHE ZUSAMMENARBEIT MIT DEN ENTWICKLUNGSLANDERN ♦ Austrian Institute for Development Aid for and Technical Co-operation with Developing Countries

Wipplingerstrasse 35, 1010 Wien, Austria.

Telephone: 43 (222) 53444/368. *Fax:* 43 (222) 53444/204. *Contact:* Prof. Kurt Prokop, Director.

AUT0071

OSTERREICHISCHES JUGENDROTKREUZ (ÖJRK) ♦ Austrian Youth Red Cross

Gusshausstrasse 3, 1040 Wien, Austria.

Telephone: 43 (222) 65 36 61. *Contact:* Dr. Kutschera, President.

AUT0072

OSTERREICHISCHES KOMITEE FUR UNICEF ♦ Austrian Committee for UNICEF

Wagramer Strasse 9 - VIC, PO Box 100, 1400 Wien, Austria.

Telephone: 43 (222) 23 60/15 97. *Fax:* 43 (222) 23 98 20. *Contact:* Dr. Martha Kyrle, President.

OBJECTIVES: To disseminate information about UNICEF activities among the Austrian public. To organise fund raising campaigns to support UNICEF projects in developing countries.

GENERAL INFORMATION: *Creation:* 1962. *Personnel/Total:* 10. *Salaried:* 10. *Budget/Total 1993:* ECU 1856000 (US$ 2407000). *Financial sources: Private:* 100%.

PUBLICATIONS: *Periodicals:* Danke (4). *Annual report. List of publications.*

EVALUATION/RESEARCH: Evaluation reports available.

PLANNED ACTIVITIES: Implementation of a project "Medienkoffer" for all Austrian schools of higher education.

COMMENTS: Undertakes activities in the Commonwealth of Independent States. Information activities related to the Commonwealth of Independent States.

INFORMATION AND EDUCATION ACTIVITIES: Topics: Children/youth/family; Education/training/literacy; Human rights/peace/conflicts; Refugees/migrants/ethnic groups. **Activities:** Fund raising.

AUT0073

OSTERREICHISCHES KOMITEE GEGEN DIE FOLTER ♦ AUSTRIAN COMMITTEE AGAINST TORTURE

Institute of International Law and international Relations, Hans-Sachs-Gasse 3/III, 8010 Graz, Austria.

Telephone: 43 (1) 380 3414. *Fax:* 43 (1) 381 1924. *Contact:* Dr. Renate Kicker, Assistant Professor.

AUT0074

OSTERREICHISCHES LATEINAMERIKA-INSTITUT (LAI) ♦ Austrian Institute for Latin America

Schlickgasse 1, 1090 Vienna, Austria.

Telephone: 43 (1) 310 74 65. *Fax:* 43 (1) 310 74 68. *Contact:* Hans Tuppy.

OBJECTIVES: To actively promote and develop relations between Austria and Latin American countries. To organise seminars, discussions, trips and activities concerning Latin America. To serve as the largest language school in Austria for Spanish, Portugese and Indian languages.

GENERAL INFORMATION: *Creation:* 1965. *Type of organisation:* association of NGOs, network. *Affiliated to:* Red Europea de Informacion y Documentacion sobre America Latina (REDIAL) -Austrian Association of Institutions for Information and Documentation of Third World Policy Projects. *Personnel/Total:* 12. *Salaried:* 10. *Volunteers:* 2. *Budget/Total 1993:* ECU 663000 (US$ 860000). *Financial sources: Private:* 15%. *Public:* 40%. *Self-financing:* 45%.

PUBLICATIONS: *Periodicals:* Zeitschrift für Lateinamerika-Wien (2) - Lateinamerika-Pressespiegel (5). *Annual report. List of publications.*

EVALUATION/RESEARCH: Evaluation reports available. Undertakes research activities.

ACTIVITIES IN DEVELOPING REGIONS: Present in developing regions. Maintains local field presence.

INFORMATION AND EDUCATION ACTIVITIES: Topics: Culture/tradition/religion; Ecology/environment/biodiversity; Gender issues/women; Human rights/peace/conflicts; International economic relations/trade/debt/finance; International relations/cooperation/development aid; Peace/ethnic conflicts/armament/disarmament; Population/family planning/demography; Refugees/migrants/ethnic groups; Urban development/habitat. **Activities:** Conferences/seminars/workshops/training activities; Information and documentation services/data bases.

AUT0075

PRIVATINITIATIVE "SAN LUIS", ANCASH - PERU ♦ Private Initiative San Luis

Hildmannplatz 2, 5020 Salzburg, Austria.

Telephone: 43 (662) 84 03 29. *Contact:* Chano Schlachter.

AUT0076

SOS KINDERDORF INTERNATIONAL ♦ SOS-Children's Village International

Hermann-Gmeiner-Strasse 51, 6020 Innsbruck, Austria.

Telephone: 43 (512) 33 10. *Fax:* 43 (512) 33 10 88. *Contact:* Werner Handl, Secretary General.

OBJECTIVES: To provide a caring family environment for orphans and abandonned children through the establishment and running of SOS Children's villages providing them with a permanent home.

GENERAL INFORMATION: *Creation:* 1960. *Type of organisation:* coordinating body. *Member organisations:* 95. *Salaried:* 12300 of which:

Voir : *Comment utiliser le répertoire*, page 11.

var in developing countries. *Volunteers:* var. **Budget/Total 1993:** ECU 140350000 (US$ 182000000). **Financial sources:** *Private:* 86%. *Public:* 1%. *Self-financing:* 13%.

PUBLICATIONS: *Periodicals:* SOS-journal (4) - SOS-Messenger (4) - Magazine of SOS-Children's Village Friends (2). *List of publications.*

EVALUATION/RESEARCH: Undertakes research activities.

COMMENTS: Undertakes activities in the Commonwealth of Independent States. Information activities related to the Commonwealth of Independent States.

ACTIVITIES IN DEVELOPING REGIONS: Present in developing regions. Active in 85 country(ies). Maintains local field presence. Works through local field partners. **Sustainable Development Actions:** Children/youth/family; Education/training/literacy; Emergency relief/refugees/humanitarian assistance; Health/sanitation/water. **Regions:** Caribbean; Central Africa; Central Asia and South Asia; East Africa; East Asia; Mexico and Central America; Middle East; North Africa; South America; South East Asia; Southern Africa; West Africa.

INFORMATION AND EDUCATION ACTIVITIES: Topics: Children/youth/family; Education/training/literacy; Emergency relief/refugees/humanitarian assistance; Food/famine; Health/sanitation/water. **Activities:** Conferences/seminars/workshops/training activities; Formal education; Fund raising; Lobbying/advocacy; Publishing/audiovisual materials/educational materials.

AUT0077
SOS MITMENSCH

Elisabethstrasse 1/20, 1010 Wien, Austria.

Telephone: 43 (1) 586 12 61.

AUT0078
STEIRISCHE ENTWICKLUNGSPOLITISCHE INITIATIVE (SEPI)
♦ Steiermark Initiatives for Development Policies

Mandellstrasse 24, 8010 Graz, Austria.

Telephone: 43 (316) 78 44 15. *Contact:* Eva Pelzl, President.

AUT0079
SUDWIND-BUCHWELT ♦ Third-World Bookshop

Baumgasse 79, 1030 Wien, Austria.

Telephone: 43 (222) 798 83 49. *Fax:* 43 (222) 798 83 75. *Contact:* Rupert Helm, Manager.

OBJECTIVES: To provide information and publications on Third World issues.

GENERAL INFORMATION: Creation: 1984. **Personnel/Total:** 7. **Budget/Total 1993:** ECU 862000 (US$ 1118000). **Financial sources:** *Self-financing:* 100%.

PUBLICATIONS: *Periodicals:* Frischer Südwind-Buchmagazin (4). *Annual report. List of publications.*

INFORMATION AND EDUCATION ACTIVITIES: Topics: Children/youth/family; Culture/tradition/religion; Ecology/environment/biodiversity; Education/training/literacy; Emergency relief/refugees/humanitarian assistance; Employment/unemployment; Food/famine; Gender issues/women; Health/sanitation/water; Human rights/peace/conflicts; International economic relations/trade/debt/finance; International relations/cooperation/development aid; Peace/ethnic conflicts/armament/disarmament; Population/family planning/demography; Poverty/living conditions; Racism/xenophobia/antisemitism; Refugees/migrants/ethnic groups; Rural development/agriculture; Urban development/habitat. **Activities:** Information and documentation services/data bases.

AUT0080
TERRE DES HOMMES, OSTERREICH - HILFE FUR KINDER IN NOT ♦ Terre des Hommes, Austria - Aid for Children in Need

Züglergasse 49, 1070 Wien, Austria.

Telephone: 43 (222) 96 31 20. *Contact:* Friedl Grundei.

AUT0081
UNITED NATIONS ASSOCIATION OF AUSTRIA

Hofburg Schweiserholst, 1010 Vienna, Austria.

Telephone: 43 (222) 713 35 94.

AUT0082
UNTERSTUZUNGSKOMITEE FUR POLITISCH VERFOLGTE AUSLANDERINNEN ♦ Committee to Support Political Percecuted Foreigners

Währingerstrasse 59/II/1.Stock, 1090 Vienna, Austria.

Telephone: 43 (222) 408 42 10/408 55 01. *Fax:* 43 (222) 403 27 37. *Contact:* Karin König, Director.

AUT0083
VEREIN DER FREUNDE UND FORDERER DER OSTERREICHISCHEN ENTWICKLUNGSHELFER (FÖE) ♦
Association of the Friends and Helpers of Austrian Development Personnel

Kirchenplatz 15, 2301 Grossenzersdorf, Austria.

Telephone: 43 (2249) 25 44.

AUT0084
VEREIN GEMEINSAM FUR GERECHTIGKEIT ♦ Together for Justice Association

Stadtplatz 24, 4400 Steyr, Austria.

Telephone: 43 (7252) 23 077. *Contact:* Otto Singhuber.

AUT0085
VEREIN MENSCHEN FUR MENSCHEN ♦ "People for People" Foundation

Capistrangasse 8/6, 1060 Vienna, Austria.

Telephone: 43 (1) 586 69 500. *Fax:* 43 (1) 586 34 49. *Contact:* Karlheinz Böhm, Chairman.

OBJECTIVES: To provide emergency relief and organise long-term relief projects and professional training programmes in Ethiopia in the areas of agriculture, environmental protection, education and medical support. To assist schools and orphanages. To encourage individuals to regain control of their lives and obtain self-sufficiency.

GENERAL INFORMATION: Creation: 1981. **Type of organisation:** association of NGOs. **Personnel/Total:** 442+. *Salaried:* 442 of which: 430 in developing countries. **Budget/Total 1993:** ECU 6629000 (US$ 8597000). **Financial sources:** *Private:* 99%. *Public:* 1%.

PUBLICATIONS: *Periodicals:* Nagaya Letter (4). *Annual report. List of publications.*

EVALUATION/RESEARCH: Evaluation reports available. Undertakes research activities.

ACTIVITIES IN DEVELOPING REGIONS: Present in developing regions. Active in 1 country(ies). Maintains local field presence. Works through local field partners. **Sustainable Development Actions:** Children/youth/family; Ecology/environment/biodiversity; Education/training/literacy; Emergency relief/refugees/humanitarian assistance; Energy/transport; Food/famine; Gender issues/women; Health/sanitation/water; Population/family planning/demography; Rural development/agriculture; Sending volunteers/experts/technical assistance; Small enterprises/informal sector/handicrafts; Urban development/habitat. **Regions:** East Africa.

INFORMATION AND EDUCATION ACTIVITIES: Topics: Children/youth/family; Culture/tradition/religion; Ecology/environment/biodiversity; Education/training/literacy; Emergency relief/refugees/humanitarian assistance; Food/famine; Gender issues/women; Health/sanitation/water; International economic relations/trade/debt/finance; Population/family planning/demography; Poverty/living conditions; Refugees/migrants/ethnic groups; Rural development/agriculture. **Activities:** Conferences/seminars/workshops/training activities; Exchanges/twinning/linking; Formal education; Fund raising; Information and documentation services/

See: How to Use the Directory, page 11.

data bases; Information campaigns/exhibitions; Publishing/audiovisual materials/educational materials.

AUT0086

VEREIN STADTEPARTNERSCHAFT PEDRA BADEJO-LEIBNITZ ♦ Partnership Association Pedra Badejo-Leibnitz

Hauptplatz 1, 8430 Leibnitz, Austria.

Telephone: 43 (3452) 8 64 47. *Fax:* 43 (3452) 7 14 91. *Contact:* Dr. Christl Zach.

OBJECTIVES: To enable the city of Leibnitz to act as a partner city to Pedra Badejo and provide a wide range of direct support and assistance.

GENERAL INFORMATION: *Creation:* 1983. *Affiliated to:* Cabo Verde Network. *Personnel/Total:* 27. *Salaried:* 2. *Volunteers:* 25 of which: 2 in developing countries. *Budget/Total 1993:* ECU 152000 (US$ 198000). *Financial sources:* Private: 5%. Public: 85%. Self-financing: 10%.

PUBLICATIONS: *Periodicals:* Partnership News (4).

EVALUATION/RESEARCH: Evaluation reports available.

ACTIVITIES IN DEVELOPING REGIONS: Present in developing regions. Active in 1 country(ies). Maintains local field presence. Works through local field partners. **Sustainable Development Actions:** Children/youth/family; Democracy/good governance/institution building/participatory development; Education/training/literacy; Energy/transport; Gender issues/women; Health/sanitation/water; Rural development/agriculture; Sending volunteers/experts/technical assistance; Small enterprises/informal sector/handicrafts; Urban development/habitat. **Regions:** West Africa.

INFORMATION AND EDUCATION ACTIVITIES: Topics: Children/youth/family; Education/training/literacy; Health/sanitation/water; International relations/cooperation/development aid; Poverty/living conditions; Rural development/agriculture; Urban development/habitat. **Activities:** Broadcasting/cultural events; Conferences/seminars/workshops/training activities; Exchanges/twinning/linking; Formal education; Fund raising; Information and documentation services/data bases; Information campaigns/exhibitions; Lobbying/advocacy; Publishing/audiovisual materials/educational materials.

AUT0087

VEREIN ZUSAMMENARBEIT DRITTE WELT ♦ Third World Co-operation Association

Litzelhofenstrasse 3, 9800 Spittal, Austria.

Telephone: 43 (4762) 46 584.

AUT0088

VIENNA MALAYALEE ASSOCIATION ♦ Association Malayam de Vienne

Türkenstrasse 3, 1090 Wien, Austria.

Telephone: 43 (222) 34 46 25. *Contact:* Joseph Abraham, President.

AUT0089

VOLKSHILFE OSTERREICH ♦ People' s Aid Austria

Auerspergstrasse 4, 1010 Wien, Austria.

Telephone: 43 (1) 402 62 09. *Fax:* 43 (1) 408 58 01. *Contact:* Wolfgang Sperl, General Secretary.

OBJECTIVES: To support a variety of welfare institutions, including those that provide support to youth and the elderly, and to assist in disaster relief at home and abroad. To lobby for these special groups within Austria.

GENERAL INFORMATION: *Creation:* 1922. *Type of organisation:* association of NGOs. *Member organisations:* 9. *Affiliated to:* International Workers Aid (Germany). *Personnel/Total:* 6. *Salaried:* 6. *Budget/Total 1993:* ECU 1326000 (US$ 1719000). *Financial sources:* Private: 40%. Public: 45%. Self-financing: 15%.

PUBLICATIONS: *Periodicals:* Volkshilfe Magazin (4).

PLANNED ACTIVITIES: Undertaking training in crafts and school programmes in South India.

COMMENTS: Undertakes activities in the Commonwealth of Independent States. Information activities related to the Commonwealth of Independent States.

ACTIVITIES IN DEVELOPING REGIONS: Works through local field partners. **Sustainable Development Actions:** Children/youth/family; Education/training/literacy; Gender issues/women; Health/sanitation/water; Population/family planning/demography. **Regions:** Central Asia and South Asia.

INFORMATION AND EDUCATION ACTIVITIES: Topics: Children/youth/family; Education/training/literacy; Emergency relief/refugees/humanitarian assistance; Food/famine; Gender issues/women; Health/sanitation/water; International relations/cooperation/development aid; Population/family planning/demography; Refugees/migrants/ethnic groups. **Activities:** Conferences/seminars/workshops/training activities; Formal education; Fund raising; Lobbying/advocacy.

AUT0090

WIENER INSTITUT FUR ENTWICKLUNGSFRAGEN UND ZUSAMMENARBEIT ♦ Vienna Institute for Development and Co-operation

Weyrgasse 5, 1030 Vienna, Austria.

Telephone: 43 (1) 713 35 94. *Fax:* 43 (1) 713 35 94 73. *Contact:* Federal Chancellor Franz Vranitzky.

OBJECTIVES: To promote international understanding, tolerance, multiculturalism and North-South co-operation. To assist in the North-South dialogue process. To promote development projects in the South and to establish partnerships between communities in Austria and in Southern countries.

GENERAL INFORMATION: *Creation:* 1987. *Affiliated to:* European Association of Development Research and Training Institutes (Switzerland) - International Coalition for Development action (Belgium). *Personnel/Total:* 25. *Salaried:* 10. *Volunteers:* 15 of which: 15 in developing countries. *Budget/Total 1993:* ECU 1458000 (US$ 1891000). *Financial sources:* Private: 3%. Public: 95%. Self-financing: 2%.

PUBLICATIONS: *Periodicals:* Report Series (6). *Annual report. List of publications.*

EVALUATION/RESEARCH: Undertakes research activities.

PLANNED ACTIVITIES: Organisation of the EADI General Conference and of a festival on "Images of Africa".

ACTIVITIES IN DEVELOPING REGIONS: Present in developing regions. Works through local field partners. **Sustainable Development Actions:** Ecology/environment/biodiversity; Health/sanitation/water; Sending volunteers/experts/technical assistance. **Regions:** East Africa; East Asia; Mexico and Central America; South America.

INFORMATION AND EDUCATION ACTIVITIES: Topics: Culture/tradition/religion; Ecology/environment/biodiversity; Gender issues/women; Human rights/peace/conflicts; International economic relations/trade/debt/finance; International relations/cooperation/development aid; Population/family planning/demography; Urban development/habitat. **Activities:** Broadcasting/cultural events; Conferences/seminars/workshops/training activities; Exchanges/twinning/linking; Lobbying/advocacy; Publishing/audiovisual materials/educational materials.

AUT0091

WORLD VISION OSTERREICH - CHRISTLICHES HILFSWERK ♦ World Vision Austria - Christian Aid Organization

Mariahilfer strasse 10/10, 1070 Wien, Austria.

Telephone: 43 (1) 526 13 33. *Fax:* 43 (1) 523 98 12. *Contact:* Horst Urban, Executive Director.

OBJECTIVES: To support development aid and emergency relief on the grounds of Christian ethics and practical caring. To provide meaningful guidance and support towards independence.

GENERAL INFORMATION: *Creation:* 1981. *Affiliated to:* World Vision International Partnership. *Personnel/Total:* 17. *Salaried:* 17. *Budget/*

Voir : *Comment utiliser le répertoire,* page 11.

Total 1993: ECU 3116000 (US$ 4041000). *Financial sources: Private:* 100%.

PUBLICATIONS: *Periodicals:* Blick in die Welt (5).

EVALUATION/RESEARCH: Evaluation reports available.

PLANNED ACTIVITIES: Organising nationwide slide presentations of our project activities in long-term development. Providing documentation about our projects.

COMMENTS: Undertakes activities in the Commonwealth of Independent States. Information activities related to the Commonwealth of Independent States.

ACTIVITIES IN DEVELOPING REGIONS: Active in 20 country(ies). Maintains local field presence. Works through local field partners. **Sustainable Development Actions:** Children/youth/family; Democracy/good governance/institution building/participatory development; Ecology/environment/biodiversity; Education/training/literacy; Emergency relief/refugees/humanitarian assistance; Food/famine; Gender issues/women; Health/sanitation/water; Population/family planning/demography; Rural development/agriculture; Small enterprises/informal sector/handicrafts; Urban development/habitat. **Regions:** Central Asia and South Asia; East Africa; Mexico and Central America; Middle East; South America; South East Asia; Southern Africa; West Africa.

INFORMATION AND EDUCATION ACTIVITIES: Topics: Children/youth/family; Culture/tradition/religion; Ecology/environment/biodiversity; Education/training/literacy; Emergency relief/refugees/humanitarian assistance; Employment/unemployment; Gender issues/women; Health/sanitation/water; Population/family planning/demography; Poverty/living conditions; Refugees/migrants/ethnic groups; Rural development/agriculture; Urban development/habitat. **Activities:** Fund raising; Information campaigns/exhibitions.

AUT0092

WORLD WIDE FUND FOR NATURE, AUSTRIA (WWF AUSTRIA)

Postfach 1, Ottauringer Strasse 114-116, 1162 Vienna, Austria.

Telephone: 43 (222) 46 12 52/ 400 16 41. *Contact:* Dr. Kurt Harmer, President.

AUT0093

ZENTRUM ZUR SOZIALMEDIZINISCHEN, RECHTLICHEN UND KULTURELLEN BETREUUNG VON AUSLANDERINNEN IN OSTERREICH (ZEBRA) ♦ Centre for Sociomedical, Legal and Cultural Care for Foreigners in Austria

Pestalozzistrasse 59/II, 8010 Graz, Austria.

Telephone: 43 (316) 83 56 30. *Fax:* 43 (316) 81 05 39. *Contact:* Edith Glanzer.

OBJECTIVES: To develop therapeutic programmes. To co-operate with medical doctors and therapists. To provide social care, legal advice, social contacts and cultural programmes for torture victims, refugees and migrants.

GENERAL INFORMATION: *Creation:* 1986. *Affiliated to:* Asylkoordination Osterreich (Austria). *Personnel/Total:* 17. *Salaried:* 7. *Volunteers:* 10. *Budget/Total 1993:* ECU 158000 (US$ 205000). *Financial sources:* Private: 5%. Public: 90%. Self-financing: 5%.

PUBLICATIONS: *Periodicals:* (4). *Annual report.*

EVALUATION/RESEARCH: Undertakes research activities.

PLANNED ACTIVITIES: Research on the frequence of Post Traumatic Stress Disorder among Bosnian war-refugees in 1995.

See: *How to Use the Directory,* page 11.

BEL0094
ACTION MICRO BARRAGES (AMB)
Minderbroedersstraat 42, 3500 Hasselt, Belgique.

Téléphone: 32 (11) 22 24 49. *Contact:* L. Geubels, Secrétaire général.

BEL0095
ACTION NORD SUD
Avenue Claeys 111, 1030 Bruxelles, Belgique.

BEL0096
ACTION VIVRE ENSEMBLE
Rue du Gouvernement provisoire 32, 1000 Bruxelles, Belgique.

Téléphone: 32 (2) 219 19 83. *Fax:* 32 (2) 217 32 59. *Contact:* Daniel Thérasse, Responsable national.

OBJECTIFS: Soutenir financièrement des associations à vocation sociale. Organiser des cours d'éducation permanente, des campagnes de sensibilisation aux problèmatiques sociales et des actions et revendications politiques.

INFORMATIONS GENERALES: *Création:* 1970. *Type d'organisation:* réseau. *Affiliée à:* CARITAS (Belgique) - Confédération Interrégionale des Associations et de leurs Travailleurs (Belgique). *Personnel/Total:* 5. *Salariés:* 5. *Budget/Total 1993:* ECU 494000 (US$ 578000). *Sources financières:* Privé: 95%. Public: 2%. Autofinancement: 3%.

PUBLICATIONS: *Périodiques:* Main à la pâte (4). *Rapport annuel. Liste des publications.*

EVALUATION/RECHERCHE: Rapports d'évaluation disponibles.

PREVISIONS D'ACTIVITES: L'ONG se consacrera plus particulièrement aux problèmes suivants : immigration-réfugiés, pauvreté et développement social, logement-sans-abri, rôle du monde associatif dans la lutte contre l'exclusion sociale.

ACTIVITES D'INFORMATION ET D'EDUCATION: Domaines: Droits de l'Homme/paix/conflits; Développement urbain/habitat; Emploi/chômage; Enfants/jeunesse/famille; Pauvreté/conditions de vie; Racisme/xénophobie/antisémitisme; Réfugiés/migrants/groupes ethniques; Éducation/formation/alphabétisation. **Activités:** Campagnes d'information/expositions; Collecte de fonds; Conférences/séminaires/ateliers/activités de formation; Lobbying/plaidoyer; Édition/documents audiovisuels/documents éducatifs.

BEL0097
ADVENTIST DEVELOPMENT AND RELIEF AGENCY (ADRA-CE)
Rue Ernest Allard 11, 1000 Bruxelles, Belgium.

Telephone: 32 (2) 511 36 80. *Fax:* 32 (2) 513 99 18. *Contact:* Peter Kunze, President.

OBJECTIVES: To help the national ADRA organisations within the EU, by representing them, introducing and keeping track of their proposals and projects.

GENERAL INFORMATION: *Creation:* 1992. *Type of organisation:* association of NGOs, network. *Member organisations:* 10. *Personnel/Total:* 171. *Salaried:* 51 of which: var. in developing countries. *Volunteers:* 120 of which: 120 in developing countries. *Budget/Total 1993:* ECU 1446000 (US$ 16936000). *Financial sources:* Private: 36%. Public: 48%. Self-financing: 16%.

PLANNED ACTIVITIES: Organising a campaign called "Global Village" in different European countries to make the young people aware of the way of life in Third World countries.

COMMENTS: ADRA undertakes activities in developing countries through ADRA International. Undertakes activities in the Commonwealth of Independent States.

ACTIVITIES IN DEVELOPING REGIONS: Active in 67 country(ies). Works through local field partners. **Sustainable Development Actions:** Children/youth/family; Education/training/literacy; Emergency relief/refugees/humanitarian assistance; Food/famine; Gender issues/women; Health/sanitation/water; Rural development/agriculture; Sending volunteers/experts/technical assistance; Small enterprises/informal sector/handicrafts; Urban development/habitat. **Regions:** Caribbean; Central Africa; Central Asia and South Asia; East Africa; East Asia; Mexico and Central America; Middle East; North Africa; South America; South East Asia; Southern Africa; West Africa.

BEL0098
ADVOKATEN ZONDER GRENZEN
Huis van de Advokaat, Gulden Vlieslaan 65, 1060 Bruxelles, Belgique.

BEL0099
AFRICA - EUROPE FAITH & JUSTICE NETWORK (A-EFJN)
174 rue Joseph II, 1040 Bruxelles, Belgium.

Telephone: 32 (2) 230 61 05. *Fax:* 32 (2) 231 14 13. *Contact:* Christel Daun.

OBJECTIVES: To gather and disseminate information on justice issues in Africa and about European policies affecting Africa. To formulate recommendations for advocacy and taking action. To influence in a positive way decisions taken at the European Union which affect people in Africa.

GENERAL INFORMATION: *Creation:* 1989. *Type of organisation:* network. *Personnel/Total:* 2. *Financial sources:* Self-financing: 100%.

PUBLICATIONS: *Periodicals:* Forum For Action (4).

PLANNED ACTIVITIES: Focusing on arms trade and democracy.

COMMENTS: A-EFJN undertakes activities in developing countries through its member organisations. Undertakes activities in the Commonwealth of Independent States.

INFORMATION AND EDUCATION ACTIVITIES: Topics: Ecology/environment/biodiversity; Human rights/peace/conflicts; International economic relations/trade/debt/finance; International relations/cooperation/development aid; Peace/ethnic conflicts/armament/disarmament; Poverty/living conditions; Rural development/agriculture. **Activities:** Information campaigns/exhibitions; Lobbying/advocacy.

BEL0100
AGENCE DE COOPERATION AU DEVELOPPEMENT PAR LES SCIENCES ET LES TECHNIQUES (ACDST)
Place du 20 Août, 32, 4000 Liège, Belgique.

Téléphone: 32 (41) 42 00 80. *Contact:* Mme Dumont.

BEL0101
AGORA - VITRINE DU MONDE
Rue Général Leman 123, 1040 Bruxelles, Belgique.

Téléphone: 32 (2) 736 28 45. *Fax:* 32 (2) 675 38 86. *Contact:* Etienne Niowa, Président.

OBJECTIFS: Faire connaitre la réalité de la vie des PED en Europe et créer une dynamique de développement durable, au niveau socio-économique, par la mise en présence des acteurs Nord/Sud concernés.

INFORMATIONS GENERALES: *Création:* 1992. *Personnel/Total:* 10. *Bénévoles:* 10 dont: 1 dans les pays en développement. *Budget/Total 1993:* ECU 5000 (US$ 5700). *Sources financières:* Autofinancement: 100%.

EVALUATION/RECHERCHE: Entreprend des activités de recherche.

ACTIVITES DANS LES REGIONS EN DEVELOPPEMENT: Intervient dans 1 pays. Maintient une présence locale sur le terrain. Intervient par l'intermédiaire d'organisations locales partenaires.

ACTIVITES D'INFORMATION ET D'EDUCATION: Domaines: Culture/tradition/religion; Développement rural/agriculture; Questions relatives aux femmes; Relations économiques internationales/commerce/dette/finances; Santé/assainissement/eau; Écologie/environnement/biodiversité; Éducation/formation/alphabétisation. **Activités:** Campagnes d'information/expositions; Conférences/séminaires/ateliers/activités de formation; Édition/documents audiovisuels/documents éducatifs.

Voir : *Comment utiliser le répertoire,* page 11.

BEL0102

AIDE AU DEVELOPPEMENT GEMBLOUX

Passage des déportés 2A, 5030 Gembloux, Belgique.

Téléphone: 32 (81) 62 21 04. *Fax:* 32 (81) 61 45 44. *Contact:* Albert Ledent, Président.

OBJECTIFS: Mobiliser parmi la communauté gembloutoise, ainsi qu'au niveau national et international, les moyens humains, scientifiques et techniques utiles à tout projet, programme ou action agronomique ou de développement dans les pays où les circonctances appèlent une aide extérieure en faveur d'un groupe de population. Sélectionner, former et encadrer des coopérants-ONG

INFORMATIONS GENERALES: *Création:* 1986. *Affiliée à:* Association des ONG francophones et germanophones (Belgique). *Personnel/ Total:* 9. *Salariés:* 1 dont: 1 dans les pays en développement. *Bénévoles:* 8. *Budget/Total 1993:* ECU 66000 (US$ 77000). *Sources financières:* Public: 75%. Autofinancement: 25%.

PUBLICATIONS: *Rapport annuel.*

EVALUATION/RECHERCHE: Rapports d'évaluation disponibles.

PREVISIONS D'ACTIVITES: Nouveaux projets au Pérou, en Roumanie, en Croatie et au Burundi.

ACTIVITES DANS LES REGIONS EN DEVELOPPEMENT: Intervient directement dans les régions en développement. Intervient dans 1 pays. Maintient une présence locale sur le terrain. Intervient par l'intermédiaire d'organisations locales partenaires. **Actions de Développement durable:** Développement rural/agriculture. **Régions:** Afrique centrale.

ACTIVITES D'INFORMATION ET D'EDUCATION: Domaines: Développement rural/agriculture. **Activités:** Campagnes d'information/ expositions.

BEL0103

AIDE AU TIERS MONDE (ATM)

Rue de l'Esclinchamps 7, 6470 Sivry, Belgique.

Téléphone: 32 (60) 45 54 61. *Contact:* André Knops.

BEL0104

AIDE AU VOLONTARIAT EN INDE (AVI) ♦ Support for Voluntary Services in India

Rue de Grady 19, 4053 Embourg, Belgique.

Téléphone: 32 (41) 65 00 63. *Contact:* Dominique Dujardin, Président.

OBJECTIFS: Soutenir l'Association de Droit Indien "Volontariat en Inde" à Pondicherry.

INFORMATIONS GENERALES: *Création:* 1963. *Personnel/Total:* 21. *Salariés:* 1. *Bénévoles:* 20. *Budget/Total 1993:* ECU 62000 (US$ 72000). *Sources financières:* Privé: 80%. Autofinancement: 20%.

PUBLICATIONS: *Rapport annuel. Liste des publications.*

EVALUATION/RECHERCHE: Rapports d'évaluation disponibles.

PREVISIONS D'ACTIVITES: Développement des moyens éducatifs.

ACTIVITES DANS LES REGIONS EN DEVELOPPEMENT: Intervient dans 1 pays. Intervient par l'intermédiaire d'organisations locales partenaires. **Actions de Développement durable:** Aliments/famine; Développement rural/agriculture; Enfants/jeunesse/famille; Petites entreprises/secteur informel/artisanat; Questions relatives aux femmes; Santé/assainissement/eau; Éducation/formation/alphabétisation. **Régions:** Asie centrale et Asie du Sud;

ACTIVITES D'INFORMATION ET D'EDUCATION: Domaines: Aliments/ famine; Développement rural/agriculture; Développement urbain/habitat; Emploi/chômage; Enfants/jeunesse/famille; Pauvreté/conditions de vie; Questions relatives aux femmes; Santé/assainissement/eau; Éducation/formation/alphabétisation. **Activités:** Collecte de fonds; Échanges/parrainage/jumelage.

BEL0105

AIDE AUX PERSONNES DEPLACEES (APD) ♦ Aid to Displaced Persons

Rue du Marché 35, 4500 Huy, Belgique.

Téléphone: 32 (85) 21 34 81. *Fax:* 32 (85) 23 01 47. *Contact:* Catherine Noël, Secrétaire générale.

OBJECTIFS: Fournir aide et assistance aux réfugiés en Belgique et, par le biais de parrainages, dans certaines régions du Tiers-Monde.

INFORMATIONS GENERALES: *Création:* 1949. *Affiliée à:* Comité Belge d'Aide aux Réfugiés (Belgique) - Centre d'Initiation pour Réfugiés et Etrangers (Belgique) - European Consultation on Refugees end Exiles. *Personnel/Total:* 2027. *Salariés:* 27. *Bénévoles:* 2000. *Budget/ Total 1993:* ECU 596000 (US$ 697000). *Sources financières:* Privé: 24%. Public: 31%. Autofinancement: 45%.

PUBLICATIONS: *Périodiques:* Réfugiés d'hier et d'aujourd'hui (4). *Rapport annuel.*

EVALUATION/RECHERCHE: Rapports d'évaluation disponibles.

PREVISIONS D'ACTIVITES: Intensification des parrainages pour des jeunes réfugiés ou déplacés dans le tiers-monde.

COMMENTAIRES: Intervient dans la Communauté des Etats indépendants. Activités d'information concernant la Communauté des Etats indépendants.

ACTIVITES DANS LES REGIONS EN DEVELOPPEMENT: Intervient directement dans les régions en développement. Intervient dans 13 pays. **Actions de Développement durable:** Enfants/jeunesse/famille; Secours d'urgence/réfugiés/aide humanitaire; Éducation/formation/ alphabétisation. **Régions:** Afrique centrale; Amérique du Sud; Moyen-Orient.

ACTIVITES D'INFORMATION ET D'EDUCATION: Domaines: Enfants/ jeunesse/famille; Réfugiés/migrants/groupes ethniques; Éducation/formation/alphabétisation. **Activités:** Collecte de fonds; Échanges/parrainage/jumelage.

BEL0106

AIDE ET COOPERATION AU DEVELOPPEMENT D'AREQUIPA (ACDA)

Neuve Chaussée 80, 7600 Peruwelz, Belgique.

Téléphone: 32 (69) 77 43 44. *Fax:* 32 (69) 77 57 72. *Contact:* Christine Dangremont.

BEL0107

AKTIE VOOR SANITAIRE CENTRA IN NOOD (ASN) ♦ Aide aux centres sanitaires en nécessité

Frankryklaan 32, 8450 Bredene, Belgique.

Téléphone: 32 (59) 32 16 37. *Fax:* 32 (59) 32 09 84. *Contact:* J. Pinon, Président.

OBJECTIFS: Fabriquer et fournir gratuitement des antibiotiques.Fournir une formation concernant leur utilisation. Collaborer avec 2 ONG d'ingénieurs pour la création d'infrastructures.

INFORMATIONS GENERALES: *Création:* 1975. *Type d'organisation:* réseau, collectif. *Personnel/Total:* 10. *Bénévoles:* 10. *Budget/ Total 1993:* ECU 32000 (US$ 38000). *Sources financières:* Privé: 25%. Public: 25%.

PUBLICATIONS: *Périodiques:* Circulaire annuelle (1). *Rapport annuel.*

EVALUATION/RECHERCHE: Rapports d'évaluation disponibles. Entreprend des activités de recherche.

COMMENTAIRES: Intervient dans la Communauté des Etats indépendants.

ACTIVITES DANS LES REGIONS EN DEVELOPPEMENT: Intervient directement dans les régions en développement. Intervient dans 20 pays. Maintient une présence locale sur le terrain. Intervient par l'intermédiaire d'organisations locales partenaires. **Actions de Développement durable:** Santé/assainissement/eau; Secours d'urgence/réfugiés/ aide humanitaire; Éducation/formation/alphabétisation. **Régions:** Afrique centrale; Afrique de l'Est; Afrique de l'Ouest; Amérique du Sud; Asie

See: *How to Use the Directory,* page 11.

centrale et Asie du Sud; Asie de l'Est; Asie du Sud-Est; Caraïbes; Mexique et Amerique centrale; Océanie.

ACTIVITES D'INFORMATION ET D'EDUCATION: Domaines: Réfugiés/ migrants/groupes ethniques; Santé/assainissement/eau; Secours d'urgence/réfugiés/aide humanitaire. **Activités:** Collecte de fonds; Conférences/séminaires/ateliers/activités de formation; Réseaux/télé-communications électroniques; Services d'information et de documenta-tion/bases de données.

BEL0108

ALGEMEEN BELGISCH VAK VERBOND/FEDERATION GENERALE DU TRAVAIL DE BELGIQUE (ABVV/FGTB)

Rue Haute 42, 1000 Brussels, Belgium.

Telephone: 32 (2) 506 82 11. *Fax:* 32 (2) 513 47 21. *Contact:* Jos Jan-ssens, Coordinateur.

BEL0109

ALGEMENE STICHTING VOOR ONTWIKKELING (ASO) ♦ Fon-dation pour aide et échanges au développement

Goedheidstraat 4, B11, 1050 Brussels, Belgique.

Téléphone: 32 (2) 537 18 59. *Contact:* Ann Buyssens.

BEL0110

LES AMIS DE GATAGARA

Avenue de Hinnisdael 51, 1150 Bruxelles , Belgique.

Téléphone: 32 (2) 779 21 14. *Fax:* 32 (2) 779 21 14. *Contact:* Julien Nyssens, Président.

OBJECTIFS: Apporter un soutien au home d'enfants handicapés physi-ques de Gatagara au Rwanda.

INFORMATIONS GENERALES: *Création:* 1975. *Personnel/Total:* 700. *Bénévoles:* 700. *Budget/Total 1993:* ECU 258000 (US$ 302000). *Sources financières:* *Privé:* 28%. *Public:* 68%. *Autofinancement:* 4%.

PUBLICATIONS: *Périodiques:* Gatagara (4).

ACTIVITES DANS LES REGIONS EN DEVELOPPEMENT: Intervient directement dans les régions en développement. Intervient dans 1 pays. Maintient une présence locale sur le terrain. Intervient par l'intermédiaire d'organisations locales partenaires. **Actions de Développement dura-ble:** Aliments/famine; Développement rural/agriculture; Enfants/jeu-nesse/famille; Envoi de volontaires/experts/assistance technique; Petites entreprises/secteur informel/artisanat; Questions relatives aux femmes; Santé/assainissement/eau; Éducation/formation/alphabétisa-tion. **Régions:** Afrique centrale.

ACTIVITES D'INFORMATION ET D'EDUCATION: Domaines: Dévelop-pement rural/agriculture; Enfants/jeunesse/famille; Pauvreté/conditions de vie; Questions relatives aux femmes; Santé/assainissement/eau; Éducation/formation/alphabétisation. **Activités:** Collecte de fonds.

BEL0111

LES AMIS DE LA TERRE

Place de la Vingeanne, 5100 Dave, Belgique.

Téléphone: 32 (81) 40 14 78. *Fax:* 32 (81) 40 23 54. *Contact:* Albert Charlier, Président du Conseil d'Administration.

OBJECTIFS: Sensibiliser la population aux problèmes écologiques et les informer sur l'impact des comportements quotidiens.

INFORMATIONS GENERALES: *Création:* 1976. *Type d'organisation:* regroupement d'ONG. *Organisations membres:* 30. *Affiliée à:* Friends of the Earth International (Pays-Bas). *Personnel/Total:* 3. *Salariés:* 3. *Budget/Total 1993:* ECU 111000 (US$ 130000). *Sources finan-cières:* *Privé:* 6%. *Public:* 50%. *Autofinancement:* 44%.

PUBLICATIONS: *Périodiques:* Revue des Amis de la Terre (6). *Liste des publications.*

EVALUATION/RECHERCHE: Entreprend des activités de recherche.

PREVISIONS D'ACTIVITES: Lancement de deux campagnes d'informa-tion : "Emballages" et "Développement durable".

ACTIVITES D'INFORMATION ET D'EDUCATION: Domaines: Dévelop-pement rural/agriculture; Relations économiques internationales/ commerce/dette/finances; Santé/assainissement/eau; Écologie/environ-nement/biodiversité. **Activités:** Campagnes d'information/expositions; Collecte de fonds; Conférences/séminaires/ateliers/activités de forma-tion; Lobbying/plaidoyer; Radiodiffusion/manifestations culturelles; Édi-tion/documents audiovisuels/documents éducatifs; Éducation formelle.

BEL0112

AMITIES BELGIQUE BURUNDI

Rue J.B. Labarre 2, 1180 Uccle/Bruxelles, Belgique.

Téléphone: 32 (2) 377 01 31. *Contact:* Joseph Michel.

BEL0113

AMITIES BELGO-CAMBODGIENNES (ABC)

Avenue Maréchal Foch 86, 1030 Bruxelles, Belgique.

Téléphone: 32 (2) 216 41 69. *Contact:* Philippe Berten, Président.

BEL0114

AMITIES BELGO-CHILIENNES

Rue de la station 69, 1640 Rhode St Genese, Belgique.

Téléphone: 32 (2) 380 77 45. *Contact:* Etienne Van der Rest.

BEL0115

AMNESTY INTERNATIONAL, BELGIAN SECTION

9 Rue Berckmans, 1060 Brussels, Belgique.

Téléphone: 32 (2) 538 81 77. *Fax:* 32 (2) 537 37 29. *Courrier électroni-que:* Amnesty.sn@infoboard.be. *Contact:* Iwan Moxhet, Président.

OBJECTIFS: Empêcher les gouvernements de commettre des violations des droits de l'homme. Obtenir : la libération de tous les prisonniers d'opinion, des procès équitables dans un délai raisonnable pour les prisonniers politiques, l'abolition dela peine de mort, de la torture et de tout traitement cruel, la fin des exécutions extrajudiciaires.

INFORMATIONS GENERALES: *Création:* 1972. *Personnel/Total:* 15. *Salariés:* 15. *Budget/Total 1993:* ECU 1483000 (US$ 1734000). *Sources financières:* *Privé:* 60%. *Public:* 5%. *Autofinancement:* 35%.

PUBLICATIONS: *Rapport annuel. Liste des publications.*

EVALUATION/RECHERCHE: Rapports d'évaluation disponibles. Entre-prend des activités de recherche.

COMMENTAIRES: Ces données ne concernent qu'Amnesty International Belgique francophone.

ACTIVITES D'INFORMATION ET D'EDUCATION: Domaines: Droits de l'Homme/paix/conflits. **Activités:** Campagnes d'information/expositions; Collecte de fonds; Conférences/séminaires/ateliers/activités de forma-tion; Lobbying/plaidoyer; Radiodiffusion/manifestations culturelles; Réseaux/télécommunications électroniques; Services d'information et de documentation/bases de données; Échanges/parrainage/jumelage; Édition/documents audiovisuels/documents éducatifs; Éducation formelle.

BEL0116

AMNESTY INTERNATIONAL, FLEMISH SECTION

Kerkstraat 156, 2060 Antwerpen 6, Belgium.

Telephone: 32 (2) 271 16 16. *Fax:* 32 (2) 235 78 12. *Contact:* Wim Taelman, President.

OBJECTIVES: To campaign in order to free all prisoners of conscience. To ensure fair and prompt trials for political prisoners. To abolish the death penalty, torture and other cruel treatment of prisoners. To end extrajudi-cial executions and disappearences.

GENERAL INFORMATION: *Creation:* 1976. *Affiliated to:* Amnesty Inter-national (United Kingdom). *Personnel/Total:* 48. *Salaried:* 13. *Volun-teers:* 35. *Budget/Total 1993:* ECU 1112000 (US$ 1301000). *Financial sources:* *Private:* 20%. *Self-financing:* 80%.

Voir : *Comment utiliser le répertoire,* page 11.

PUBLICATIONS: *Periodicals:* Amnesty Nieuws (11) - Amnesty in Actie (11). *Annual report. List of publications.*

INFORMATION AND EDUCATION ACTIVITIES: Topics: Emergency relief/refugees/humanitarian assistance; Human rights/peace/conflicts. **Activities:** Broadcasting/cultural events; Conferences/seminars/workshops/training activities; Fund raising; Information and documentation services/data bases; Information campaigns/exhibitions; Lobbying/advocacy; Publishing/audiovisual materials/educational materials.

BEL0117
APPROCHE

1 Voie du Roman Pays, 1348 Louvain-la-Neuve, Belgique.

Téléphone: 32 (10) 47 45 14.

BEL0118
AQUACULTURE ET DEVELOPPEMENT (AQUADEV)

Avenue du Vossegat 43, B46, 1180 Bruxelles, Belgique.

Téléphone: 32 (2) 376 33 72. *Fax:* 32 (2) 376 33 72. *Contact:* Eric Driesen.

OBJECTIFS: Mener des projets visant à l'autosuffisance alimentaire, l'amélioration des revenus, notamment dans le secteur agroalimentaire (production, transformation, commercialisation, formation). Entreprendre, des recherches multidisciplinaires autour de ces projets.

INFORMATIONS GENERALES: *Création:* 1987. *Personnel/Total:* 11. *Salariés:* 3 dont: 1 dans les pays en développement. *Bénévoles:* 8. *Budget/Total 1993:* ECU 136000 (US$ 159000). *Sources financières:* Privé: 20%. Public: 75%. Autofinancement: 5%.

PUBLICATIONS: *Rapport annuel.*

EVALUATION/RECHERCHE: Rapports d'évaluation disponibles. Entreprend des activités de recherche.

ACTIVITES DANS LES REGIONS EN DEVELOPPEMENT: Intervient directement dans les régions en développement. Intervient dans 3 pays. Maintient une présence locale sur le terrain. Intervient par l'intermédiaire d'organisations locales partenaires. **Actions de Développement durable:** Aliments/famine; Dette/finances/commerce; Droits de l'Homme/paix/conflits; Démocratie/bonne gestion publique/création d'institutions/développement participatif; Développement rural/agriculture; Envoi de volontaires/experts/assistance technique; Questions relatives aux femmes; Santé/assainissement/eau; Écologie/environnement/biodiversité; Éducation/formation/alphabétisation. **Régions:** Afrique de l'Ouest; Afrique du Nord.

ACTIVITES D'INFORMATION ET D'EDUCATION: Domaines: Aliments/famine; Développement rural/agriculture; Questions relatives aux femmes; Relations internationales/coopération/aide au développement; Relations économiques internationales/commerce/dette/finances; Écologie/environnement/biodiversité. **Activités:** Collecte de fonds; Lobbying/plaidoyer; Services d'information et de documentation/bases de données; Échanges/parrainage/jumelage.

BEL0119
ASSOCIATION BELGIQUE-BOLIVIE

Avenue de Tervueren 85, 1200 Bruxelles, Belgique.

Téléphone: 32 (2) 733 10 88. *Fax:* 32 (2) 733 10 88. *Contact:* Yves Seghin, Président.

OBJECTIFS: Améliorer la qualité de vie des paysans en Bolivie. Former des Boliviens à la gestion des PME. Faire prendre conscience à ces populations de leur responsabilité dans le processus de développement en les instituant partenaires des projets entrepris.

INFORMATIONS GENERALES: *Création:* 1958. *Type d'organisation:* réseau. *Affiliée à:* CNCD, CODEV, ADO. *Personnel/Total:* 8. *Salariés:* 2. *Bénévoles:* 6. *Budget/Total 1993:* ECU 321000 (US$ 376000). *Sources financières:* Privé: 25%. Public: 75%.

PUBLICATIONS: *Périodiques:* Belgique-Bolivie (4). *Rapport annuel. Liste des publications.*

EVALUATION/RECHERCHE: Entreprend des activités de recherche.

PREVISIONS D'ACTIVITES: Revalorisation du potentiel agricole local (espèces locales, méthodes biologiques). Développement des petites entreprises.

ACTIVITES DANS LES REGIONS EN DEVELOPPEMENT: Intervient dans 1 pays. Intervient par l'intermédiaire d'organisations locales partenaires. **Actions de Développement durable:** Démocratie/bonne gestion publique/création d'institutions/développement participatif; Développement rural/agriculture; Développement urbain/habitat; Enfants/jeunesse/famille; Envoi de volontaires/experts/assistance technique; Petites entreprises/secteur informel/artisanat; Questions relatives aux femmes; Santé/assainissement/eau; Écologie/environnement/biodiversité; Éducation/formation/alphabétisation; Énergie/transport. **Régions:** Amérique du Sud.

ACTIVITES D'INFORMATION ET D'EDUCATION: Domaines: Développement rural/agriculture; Enfants/jeunesse/famille. **Activités:** Campagnes d'information/expositions; Collecte de fonds; Lobbying/plaidoyer.

BEL0120
ASSOCIATION BELGIQUE-RWANDA

Villemont 1, 6730 Tintigny, Belgique.

Téléphone: 32 (0) 63 44 41 54. *Fax:* 32 (0) 63 44 49 04. *Contact:* M. de Jamblinne, Président.

OBJECTIFS: Promouvoir la compréhension mutuelle entre les populations belge et rwandaise et les former à la solidarité internationale. Soutenir des projets d'autodéveloppement souhaités par les rwandais. Diffuser une bonne information sur le Rwanda.

INFORMATIONS GENERALES: *Création:* 1966. *Affiliée à:* Centre National de Coopération au développement (Belgique) - Association des ONG (Belgique.). *Personnel/Total:* 14. *Salariés:* 4 dont: 4 dans les pays en développement. *Bénévoles:* 10. *Budget/Total 1993:* ECU 129000 (US$ 150000). *Sources financières:* Privé: 60%. Public: 39%. Autofinancement: 1%.

PUBLICATIONS: *Périodiques:* Belgique-Rwanda (2). *Rapport annuel.*

EVALUATION/RECHERCHE: Rapports d'évaluation disponibles.

PREVISIONS D'ACTIVITES: Reprise des projets au Rwanda.

COMMENTAIRES: Activités d'information concernant la Communauté des Etats indépendants.

ACTIVITES DANS LES REGIONS EN DEVELOPPEMENT: Intervient directement dans les régions en développement. Intervient dans 1 pays. Maintient une présence locale sur le terrain. Intervient par l'intermédiaire d'organisations locales partenaires. **Actions de Développement durable:** Aliments/famine; Droits de l'Homme/paix/conflits; Démocratie/bonne gestion publique/création d'institutions/développement participatif; Développement rural/agriculture; Enfants/jeunesse/famille; Envoi de volontaires/experts/assistance technique; Petites entreprises/secteur informel/artisanat; Santé/assainissement/eau; Éducation/formation/alphabétisation. **Régions:** Afrique centrale.

ACTIVITES D'INFORMATION ET D'EDUCATION: Domaines: Aliments/famine; Droits de l'Homme/paix/conflits; Développement rural/agriculture; Enfants/jeunesse/famille; Paix/conflits ethniques/armement/désarmement; Pauvreté/conditions de vie; Questions relatives aux femmes; Santé/assainissement/eau; Éducation/formation/alphabétisation. **Activités:** Échanges/parrainage/jumelage; Édition/documents audiovisuels/documents éducatifs.

BEL0121
ASSOCIATION D'AIDE AU DEVELOPPEMENT ECONOMICO-ECOLOGIQUE DE L'EST DE L'AFRIQUE ET DE L'OCEAN INDIEN (ECO-DEV)

Rue de Ménode 216, 1060 Bruxelles, Belgique.

Téléphone: 32 (2) 537 56 13. *Fax:* 32 (2) 539 39 28. *Contact:* Claude Willems, Président.

BEL0122
ASSOCIATION DES CONSOMMATEURS TIERS MONDE (ACTM) ♦ Third World Consumers Union

Rue de Hollande 13, 1060 Bruxelles, Belgique.

See: *How to Use the Directory*, page 11.

Téléphone: 32 (2) 536 64 11. *Fax:* 32 (2) 536 66 20. *Contact:* Yves Genin, Président.

BEL0123

ASSOCIATION DES ETUDIANTS EN SCIENCES ECONOMIQUES ET COMMERCIALES (AIESEC) ◆ International Association of Students in Economics and Management

Rue Washington 40, 1050 Brussels, Belgium.

Telephone: 32 (2) 646 24 20. *Fax:* 32 (2) 646 37 64. *E-mail:* A.1600NA/aisecint@attmail.com. *Contact:* Leonhard Markus Keiper, President.

OBJECTIVES: To contribute to the development of countries and their people, with an overriding commitment to international understanding and co-operation.

GENERAL INFORMATION: *Creation:* 1948. *Type of organisation:* association of NGOs, network. *Personnel/Total:* 50015. *Salaried:* 15 of which: 6 in developing countries. *Volunteers:* 50000 of which: 20000 in developing countries. *Financial sources:* Private: 85%. *Public:* 5%. *Self-financing:* 10%.

PUBLICATIONS: *Periodicals:* The International Link (4) - In Touch (5). *Annual report.*

EVALUATION/RESEARCH: Evaluation reports available. Undertakes research activities.

PLANNED ACTIVITIES: Undertaking educational activities in the fields of development, human rights, and multiculturalism.

COMMENTS: Undertakes activities in the Commonwealth of Independent States. Information activities related to the Commonwealth of Independent States.

ACTIVITIES IN DEVELOPING REGIONS: Present in developing regions. Active in 40 country(ies). Maintains local field presence. Works through local field partners. **Sustainable Development Actions:** Children/youth/family; Debt/finance/trade; Democracy/good governance/institution building/participatory development; Ecology/environment/biodiversity; Education/training/literacy; Gender issues/women; Human rights/peace/conflicts; Population/family planning/demography; Small enterprises/informal sector/handicrafts. **Regions:** Caribbean; Central Africa; Central Asia and South Asia; East Africa; East Asia; Mexico and Central America; North Africa; Oceania; South America; South East Asia; Southern Africa; West Africa.

INFORMATION AND EDUCATION ACTIVITIES: Topics: Children/youth/family; Culture/tradition/religion; Ecology/environment/biodiversity; Education/training/literacy; Emergency relief/refugees/humanitarian assistance; Employment/unemployment; Gender issues/women; Human rights/peace/conflicts; International economic relations/trade/debt/finance; International relations/cooperation/development aid; Peace/ethnic conflicts/armament/disarmament; Population/family planning/demography; Poverty/living conditions; Racism/xenophobia/antisemitism; Refugees/migrants/ethnic groups. **Activities:** Broadcasting/cultural events; Conferences/seminars/workshops/training activities; Exchanges/twinning/linking; Formal education; Fund raising; Information and documentation services/data bases; Information campaigns/exhibitions; Publishing/audiovisual materials/educational materials.

BEL0124

ASSOCIATION EUROPE - TIERS MONDE (ETM) ◆ Europe - Third World Association

Rue de la Loi 170, 1048 Bruxelles, Belgique.

Téléphone: 32 (2) 285 83 77. *Fax:* 32 (2) 285 83 78. *Contact:* Pascal Lejeune, Président.

OBJECTIFS: Financer des micro-projets de développement dans le Tiers-Monde. Informer et sensibiliser des fonctionnaires européens sur la problématique du développement. Réfléchir sur la problématique du développement.

INFORMATIONS GENERALES: *Création:* 1968. *Personnel/Total:* 20. *Bénévoles:* 20. *Budget/Total 1993:* ECU 1483000 (US$ 1734000). *Sources financières:* Privé: 85%. Auto-financement: 15%.

PUBLICATIONS: *Périodiques:* Bulletin d'information.

ACTIVITES DANS LES REGIONS EN DEVELOPPEMENT: Intervient dans 13 pays. Intervient par l'intermédiaire d'organisations locales partenaires. **Actions de Développement durable:** Aliments/famine; Développement rural/agriculture; Développement urbain/habitat; Petites entreprises/secteur informel/artisanat; Questions relatives aux femmes; Santé/assainissement/eau; Secours d'urgence/réfugiés/aide humanitaire; Écologie/environnement/biodiversité. **Régions:** Afrique australe; Afrique centrale; Afrique de l'Est; Afrique de l'Ouest; Afrique du Nord; Amérique du Sud; Asie centrale et Asie du Sud; Asie de l'Est; Asie du Sud-Est; Caraïbes; Mexique et Amerique centrale; Moyen-Orient; Océanie.

BEL0125

ASSOCIATION FEMMES D'EUROPE

Rue Washington 40, 1050 Bruxelles, Belgique.

Téléphone: 32 (2) 640 16 65. *Contact:* Marie Synadino, Présidente.

BEL0126

ASSOCIATION FOR CULTURAL, TECHNICAL AND EDUCATIONAL COOPERATION (ACTEC)

Boulevard A. Reyers 21, b.4., 1040 Bruxelles, Belgique.

Téléphone: 32 (2) 735 10 31. *Fax:* 32 (2) 736 03 77. *Contact:* Stéphane de Lovinfosse.

OBJECTIFS: Développer les ressources locales de formation professionnelle, humaine et culturelle. Encourager les initiatives permettant l'amélioration des conditions de vie. Accentuer la solidarité et l'entraide entre les bénéficiaires et les collectivités locales.

INFORMATIONS GENERALES: *Création:* 1982. *Affiliée à:* Association des ONG - Fédération Envoi Volontaires. *Personnel/Total:* 8. Salariés: 3. *Bénévoles:* 5 dont: 5 dans les pays en développement. *Budget/Total 1993:* ECU 741000 (US$ 867000). *Sources financières:* Privé: 30%. *Public:* 70%.

PUBLICATIONS: *Périodiques:* Students for Development-Stage (1).

PREVISIONS D'ACTIVITES: Organiser des stages de formation et de sensibilisation à la coopération au développement pour étudiants universitaires.

ACTIVITES DANS LES REGIONS EN DEVELOPPEMENT: Intervient dans 7 pays. Intervient par l'intermédiaire d'organisations locales partenaires. **Actions de Développement durable:** Développement rural/agriculture; Petites entreprises/secteur informel/artisanat; Santé/assainissement/eau; Écologie/environnement/biodiversité; Éducation/formation/alphabétisation. **Régions:** Afrique centrale; Amérique du Sud.

BEL0127

ASSOCIATION FOR TEACHER EDUCATION IN EUROPE (ATEE)

60 rue de la Concorde, 1050 Brussels, Belgium.

Telephone: 32 (2) 514 33 40. *Fax:* 32 (2) 514 11 72. *Contact:* A.L. Höstman Tarrou, President.

OBJECTIVES: To help teachers through training and research on teacher education.

GENERAL INFORMATION: *Creation:* 1976. *Personnel/Total:* 3. *Salaried:* 1. *Volunteers:* 2. *Budget/Total 1993:* ECU 247000 (US$ 289000). *Financial sources:* Public: 20%. Self-financing: 80%.

PUBLICATIONS: *Periodicals:* ATEENews (3) - European Journal for Teacher Education (3). *List of publications.*

COMMENTS: The NGO undertakes the information and educational activities mentionned above only in so far as they are related to education. Undertakes activities in the Commonwealth of Independent States. Information activities related to the Commonwealth of Independent States.

INFORMATION AND EDUCATION ACTIVITIES: Topics: Culture/tradition/religion; Education/training/literacy; Gender issues/women; Health/sanitation/water; Human rights/peace/conflicts; Peace/ethnic conflicts/armament/disarmament; Racism/xenophobia/antisemitism; Refugees/migrants/ethnic groups. **Activities:** Conferences/seminars/workshops/

Voir : *Comment utiliser le répertoire,* page 11.

training activities; Information and documentation services/data bases; Publishing/audiovisual materials/educational materials.

BEL0128

ASSOCIATION INTERNATIONALE DE DEVELOPPEMENT ET D'ACTION COMMUNAUTAIRES (AIDAC) ♦ International Association for Community Development

Rue de la Bruyère 157, 6001 Marcinelle, Belgique.

Téléphone: 32 (71) 36 62 73. *Fax:* 32 (71) 47 11 04. *Contact:* Pierre Rozen, Secrétaire général.

OBJECTIFS: Promouvoir le développement communautaire dans le Tiers-monde.

INFORMATIONS GENERALES: *Création:* 1952. *Affiliée à:* Consortium d'ONG (Belgique.). *Personnel/Total:* 8. *Salariés:* 5. *Bénévoles:* 3 dont: 3 dans les pays en développement. *Budget/Total 1993:* ECU 652000 (US$ 762000). *Sources financières:* Privé: 20%. Public: 75%. Autofinancement: 5%.

PUBLICATIONS: *Périodiques:* Newsletter (3). *Rapport annuel.*

EVALUATION/RECHERCHE: Rapports d'évaluation disponibles.

PREVISIONS D'ACTIVITES: Lancement de nouveaux projets en Thailande et aux Philippines.

ACTIVITES DANS LES REGIONS EN DEVELOPPEMENT: Intervient directement dans les régions en développement. Intervient dans 4 pays. Intervient par l'intermédiaire d'organisations locales partenaires. **Actions de Développement durable:** Démocratie/bonne gestion publique/création d'institutions/développement participatif; Développement rural/agriculture; Envoi de volontaires/experts/assistance technique; Petites entreprises/secteur informel/artisanat; Santé/assainissement/eau; Secours d'urgence/réfugiés/aide humanitaire; Écologie/environnement/biodiversité. **Régions:** Afrique centrale; Asie du Sud-Est.

ACTIVITES D'INFORMATION ET D'EDUCATION: Domaines: Développement rural/agriculture; Paix/conflits ethniques/armement/désarmement; Pauvreté/conditions de vie; Relations internationales/coopération/aide au développement; Écologie/environnement/biodiversité. **Activités:** Campagnes d'information/expositions; Collecte de fonds; Conférences/séminaires/ateliers/activités de formation.

BEL0129

ASSOCIATION INTERNATIONALE DES EDUCATEURS POUR LA PAIX DU MONDE

6 rue Moncrabeau, 5000 Namur, Belgique.

Téléphone: 32 (81) 22 06 76. *Contact:* Francis Dessart, Secrétaire général.

OBJECTIFS: Promouvoir l'éducation à la paix. Diffuser le matériel éducatif de l'ONU et d'autres organisations internationales. Entreprendre des recherches et faire de l'éducation en écologie, développement, droit humanitaire.

INFORMATIONS GENERALES: *Création:* 1969. *Personnel/Total:* 80. *Bénévoles:* 80 dont: 50 dans les pays en développement.

PUBLICATIONS: *Périodiques:* Peace Progress (2) - IAEWP News letter (12). *Rapport annuel.*

EVALUATION/RECHERCHE: Entreprend des activités de recherche.

PREVISIONS D'ACTIVITES: Faire de l'éducation à l'oecuménisme et à l'interconfessionnalité. Développer la coopération interuniversitaire en Europe de l'Est et ex-URSS.

COMMENTAIRES: Intervient dans la Communauté des Etats indépendants. Activités d'information concernant la Communauté des Etats indépendants.

ACTIVITES DANS LES REGIONS EN DEVELOPPEMENT: Intervient directement dans les régions en développement. Maintient une présence locale sur le terrain. Intervient par l'intermédiaire d'organisations locales partenaires. **Actions de Développement durable:** Droits de l'Homme/paix/conflits; Démocratie/bonne gestion publique/création d'institutions/développement participatif; Enfants/jeunesse/famille; Envoi de volontaires/experts/assistance technique; Petites entreprises/secteur

informel/artisanat; Questions relatives aux femmes; Secours d'urgence/réfugiés/aide humanitaire; Écologie/environnement/biodiversité; Éducation/formation/alphabétisation. **Régions:** Afrique australe; Afrique centrale; Afrique de l'Est; Afrique de l'Ouest; Afrique du Nord; Amérique du Sud; Asie centrale et Asie du Sud; Asie de l'Est; Asie du Sud-Est; Caraïbes; Mexique et Amerique centrale; Moyen-Orient; Océanie.

ACTIVITES D'INFORMATION ET D'EDUCATION: Domaines: Aliments/famine; Culture/tradition/religion; Droits de l'Homme/paix/conflits; Développement rural/agriculture; Développement urbain/habitat; Emploi/chômage; Enfants/jeunesse/famille; Paix/conflits ethniques/armement/désarmement; Pauvreté/conditions de vie; Population/planning familial/démographie; Questions relatives aux femmes; Racisme/xénophobie/antisémitisme; Relations internationales/coopération/aide au développement; Relations économiques internationales/commerce/dette/finances; Réfugiés/migrants/groupes ethniques; Santé/assainissement/eau; Secours d'urgence/réfugiés/aide humanitaire; Écologie/environnement/biodiversité; Éducation/formation/alphabétisation. **Activités:** Autres; Campagnes d'information/expositions; Collecte de fonds; Conférences/séminaires/ateliers/activités de formation; Lobbying/plaidoyer; Radiodiffusion/manifestations culturelles; Services d'information et de documentation/bases de données; Échanges/parrainage/jumelage; Éducation formelle.

BEL0130

ASSOCIATION INTERNATIONALE DES JURISTES DEMOCRATES ♦ International Association of Democratic Lawyers

263 avenue Albert, 1180 Brussels, Belgium.

Telephone: 32 (2) 345 14 71. *Fax:* 32 (2) 343 35 96. *Contact:* Rene Bridel.

BEL0131

ASSOCIATION OF PROTESTANT DEVELOPMENT ORGANISATIONS IN EUROPE (APRODEV)

174 rue Joseph II, 1040 Brussels, Belgium.

Telephone: 32 (2) 231 01 02. *Fax:* 32 (2) 231 14 13. *E-mail:* GEO2:APRODEV-BRU. *Contact:* CM Bax, General Secretary.

OBJECTIVES: To lobby European institutions on behalf of member organisations and encourage co-operation among members. To raise funds from the public and from governments to fund emergency and development projects to help the poor in developing countries.

GENERAL INFORMATION: *Creation:* 1990. *Type of organisation:* association of NGOs. *Member organisations:* 16. *Personnel/Total:* 3. *Salaried:* 3. *Budget/Total 1993:* ECU 221000 (US$ 258000). *Financial sources:* Self-financing: 100%.

PUBLICATIONS: *Periodicals:* APPRODEV Bulletin (4).

EVALUATION/RESEARCH: Undertakes research activities.

INFORMATION AND EDUCATION ACTIVITIES: Topics: Children/youth/family; Culture/tradition/religion; Ecology/environment/biodiversity; Emergency relief/refugees/humanitarian assistance; Employment/unemployment; Food/famine; Gender issues/women; Health/sanitation/water; Human rights/peace/conflicts; International economic relations/trade/debt/finance; International relations/cooperation/development aid; Peace/ethnic conflicts/armament/disarmament; Population/family planning/demography; Poverty/living conditions; Rural development/agriculture; Urban development/habitat. **Activities:** Lobbying/advocacy.

BEL0132

ASSOCIATION POUR LE DEVELOPPEMENT PAR LA RECHERCHE ET L'ACTION INTEGREES (ADRAI) ♦ Association for the Development by Research and Integrated Actions

Place de l'Université 1, 1348 Louvain-la-Neuve, Belgique.

Téléphone: 32 (10) 47 40 92. *Fax:* 32 (10) 47 88 14. *Courrier électronique:* duque@sco.ucl.ac.be. *Contact:* Stanislas Haumont, Président du Conseil d'Administration.

OBJECTIFS: Favoriser une meilleure articulation entre les projets de développement et la recherche scientifique et technique en s'appuyant sur le potentiel des facultés de l'Université Cathlique de Louvain.

INFORMATIONS GENERALES: *Création:* 1982. *Affiliée à:* Fédération des ONG de Cofinancement Francophone, Fédération Belge des ONG

See: *How to Use the Directory,* page 11.

d'Envoi de Volontaires, Fédération Francophone des ONG d'envoi de Coopérants ONG, Association des ONG, Centre National de Coopération au Développement.. *Personnel/Total:* 37. *Salariés:* 37 dont: 35 dans les pays en développement. *Budget/Total 1993:* ECU 301000 (US$ 352000). *Sources financières:* Privé: 40%. Public: 40%. Autofinancement: 20%.

EVALUATION/RECHERCHE: Entreprend des activités de recherche.

ACTIVITES DANS LES REGIONS EN DEVELOPPEMENT: Intervient directement dans les régions en développement. Intervient dans 20 pays. Maintient une présence locale sur le terrain. Intervient par l'intermédiaire d'organisations locales partenaires. **Actions de Développement durable:** Développement rural/agriculture; Enfants/jeunesse/famille; Envoi de volontaires/experts/assistance technique; Santé/assainissement/eau. **Régions:** Afrique centrale; Afrique de l'Ouest; Afrique du Nord; Amérique du Sud; Mexique et Amerique centrale; Moyen-Orient.

ACTIVITES D'INFORMATION ET D'EDUCATION: **Domaines:** Développement rural/agriculture; Développement urbain/habitat; Enfants/jeunesse/famille; Santé/assainissement/eau. **Activités:** Collecte de fonds.

BEL0133

ASSOCIATION PROTESTANTE DES VOLONTAIRES DE LA COOPERATION (APVC) ♦ Protestant Association of Volunteers for Cooperation

11/13 rue Ernest Allard, 1000 Bruxelles (Sablon), Belgique.

Téléphone: 32 (2) 512 08 81. *Fax:* 32 (2) 502 75 07. *Contact:* Pasteur Antoine Angelini, Administrateur délégué.

OBJECTIFS: Coopérer avec les populations autochtones à leur développement économique et social, notamment en aidant à éliminer la faim, en soignant les malades, en paticipant à la lutte contre l'analphabétisme et en construisant des coopératives agricoles.

INFORMATIONS GENERALES: *Création:* 1966. *Type d'organisation:* réseau. *Affiliée à:* Fédération CODEF-INTERCODEV (Belgique). *Personnel/Total:* 205. *Salariés:* 105. *Bénévoles:* 100 dont: 9 dans les pays en développement. *Budget/Total 1993:* ECU 148000 (US$ 173000). *Sources financières:* Privé: 25%. Public: 75%.

PUBLICATIONS: *Rapport annuel.*

EVALUATION/RECHERCHE: Rapports d'évaluation disponibles.

COMMENTAIRES: Intervient dans la Communauté des Etats indépendants.

ACTIVITES DANS LES REGIONS EN DEVELOPPEMENT: Intervient directement dans les régions en développement. Intervient dans 27 pays. Maintient une présence locale sur le terrain. Intervient par l'intermédiaire d'organisations locales partenaires. **Actions de Développement durable:** Droits de l'Homme/paix/conflits; Développement rural/agriculture; Développement urbain/habitat; Enfants/jeunesse/famille; Envoi de volontaires/experts/assistance technique; Petites entreprises/secteur informel/artisanat; Questions relatives aux femmes; Santé/assainissement/eau; Écologie/environnement/biodiversité; Éducation/formation/alphabétisation; Énergie/transport. **Régions:** Afrique centrale; Afrique de l'Est; Afrique de l'Ouest; Afrique du Nord; Amérique du Sud; Asie centrale et Asie du Sud; Asie de l'Est; Asie du Sud-Est; Mexique et Amerique centrale; Moyen-Orient.

ACTIVITES D'INFORMATION ET D'EDUCATION: **Domaines:** Aliments/famine; Culture/tradition/religion; Enfants/jeunesse/famille; Population/planning familial/démographie; Questions relatives aux femmes; Relations internationales/coopération/aide au développement; Réfugiés/migrants/groupes ethniques; Santé/assainissement/eau; Secours d'urgence/réfugiés/aide humanitaire; Écologie/environnement/biodiversité; Éducation/formation/alphabétisation. **Activités:** Conférences/séminaires/ateliers/activités de formation.

BEL0134

ATD QUART MONDE

Avenue Victor Jacobs 12, 1040 Bruxelles, Belgique.

BEL0135

AVEC VOUS POUR LA DEMOCRATIE CONTRE TOUTES LES EXCLUSIONS

Rue de la Tulipe 34, 1050 Bruxelles, Belgique.

Téléphone: 32 (2) 511 36 99.

BEL0136

BELGIAN INDONESIAN FOUNDATION FOR SOCIAL AIM (BIFOSA)

Avenue de Tervuren 294, 1150 Bruxelles, Belgique.

Contact: Marcel Baukens, Président.

BEL0137

BELGO-INDIAN VILLAGE RECONSTRUCTION ORGANISATION (BIVRO)

Pastorüstraat 16, 9360 Buggenhout, Belgium.

Telephone: 32 (91) 22 09 17. *Contact:* André Arnaut.

BEL0138

BEVRIJDE WERELD

Nieuwstraat 70, 9100 Sint Niklaas, Belgique.

Téléphone: 32 (3) 777 20 15. *Contact:* Jef van den Eeckhout.

BEL0139

BOLIVIACENTRUM ANTWERPEN ♦ Centre Bolivie Anvers/Antwerpen

Lange Lozanastraat 14, 2018 Anvers, Belgique.

Téléphone: 32 (3) 237 74 36. *Fax:* 32 (3) 237 02 25. *Courrier électronique:* bca@antenna.nl. *Contact:* Hugo van Hoecke, Administrateur général.

OBJECTIFS: Promouvoir la solidarité internationale avec la Bolivie à travers des publications, une bibliothèque, des animations de groupe et des projets de développement.

INFORMATIONS GENERALES: *Création:* 1972. *Affiliée à:* NCOS (Belgique) - Asociación de Instituciones de Promoción y Educación (Bolivie) - Procom (Bolivie.). *Personnel/Total:* 10. *Salariés:* 7 dont: 1 dans les pays en développement. *Bénévoles:* 3. *Budget/Total 1993:* ECU 1152000 (US$ 1347000). *Sources financières:* Privé: 22%. Public: 75%. Autofinancement: 3%.

PUBLICATIONS: *Périodiques:* Informatieblad Bolivia (12) - Bulletin d'information Bolivie (6). *Rapport annuel. Liste des publications.*

EVALUATION/RECHERCHE: Rapports d'évaluation disponibles.

PREVISIONS D'ACTIVITES: Lancement de campagnes autour des thèmes suivants: peuples indigènes en Amérique Latine, problèmes de la coca et problèmes des femmes. Organisation d'échanges interculturels.

ACTIVITES DANS LES REGIONS EN DEVELOPPEMENT: Intervient dans 1 pays. Intervient par l'intermédiaire d'organisations locales partenaires. **Actions de Développement durable:** Droits de l'Homme/paix/conflits; Démocratie/bonne gestion publique/création d'institutions/développement participatif; Développement rural/agriculture; Développement urbain/habitat; Enfants/jeunesse/famille; Petites entreprises/secteur informel/artisanat; Questions relatives aux femmes; Santé/assainissement/eau; Écologie/environnement/biodiversité; Éducation/formation/alphabétisation. **Régions:** Amérique du Sud.

ACTIVITES D'INFORMATION ET D'EDUCATION: **Domaines:** Autres; Développement rural/agriculture; Développement urbain/habitat; Pauvreté/conditions de vie; Questions relatives aux femmes; Écologie/environnement/biodiversité. **Activités:** Campagnes d'information/expositions; Services d'information et de documentation/bases de données; Édition/documents audiovisuels/documents éducatifs.

BEL0140

BROEDERLIJK DELEN ♦ Brotherly Sharing

Huidevettersstraat 165, 1000 Brussels, Belgium.

Telephone: 32 (2) 502 57 00. *Fax:* 32 (2) 502 81 01 . *Contact:* J. De Bruyn, Director.

BEL0141

BUREAU D'ETUDES POUR UN DEVELOPPEMENT HARMONISE (BEDH) ♦ Study Centre for Harmonised Development

Avenue des Chênes 23, 1640- Rhode St Genèse, Belgique.

Téléphone: 32 (2) 358 55 40. *Fax:* 32 (2) 358 36 80. *Contact:* P.E. Raymaekers, Président.

OBJECTIFS: Effectuer des recherches appliquées en sciences humaines en vue de la promotion des pays en développement. Réaliser des prospections archéologiques pour approfondir la connaissance du patrimoine culturel africain et d'autres régions en développement (avec association de nationaux et d'étudiants européens). Former des universitaires se destinant à enseigner Outre-Mer.

INFORMATIONS GENERALES: *Création:* 1976. *Personnel/Total:* 39. *Salariés:* 33 dont: 33 dans les pays en développement. *Bénévoles:* 6. *Budget/Total 1993:* ECU 44000 (US$ 52000). *Sources financières:* *Privé:* 100%.

PUBLICATIONS: *Périodiques:* Ngonge Carnets de Sciences Humaines (2). *Rapport annuel. Liste des publications.*

EVALUATION/RECHERCHE: Entreprend des activités de recherche.

COMMENTAIRES: Le BEDH étudie actuellement la possibilité de devenir une Fondation.

ACTIVITES DANS LES REGIONS EN DEVELOPPEMENT: Intervient directement dans les régions en développement. Intervient dans 4 pays. **Actions de Développement durable:** Autres. **Régions:** Afrique de l'Ouest; Asie du Sud-Est.

ACTIVITES D'INFORMATION ET D'EDUCATION: Domaines: Culture/tradition/religion; Développement rural/agriculture; Développement urbain/habitat; Emploi/chômage; Enfants/jeunesse/famille; Population/planning familial/démographie; Relations internationales/coopération/aide au développement; Santé/assainissement/eau. **Activités:** Services d'information et de documentation/bases de données.

BEL0142

BUREAU EUROPEEN DE L'ENVIRONNEMENT (BEE) ♦ European Environmental Bureau

Rue de la Victoire 26, bte 12, 1060 Bruxelles, Belgique.

Téléphone: 32 (2) 539 00 37 . *Fax:* 32 (2) 539 09 21. *Contact:* Raymond van Ermen, Secrétaire général.

OBJECTIFS: Informer, sensibiliser, influencer la politique européenne d'environnement et de développement durable.

INFORMATIONS GENERALES: *Création:* 1974. *Type d'organisation:* regroupement d'ONG. *Organisations membres:* 140. *Personnel/Total:* 12. *Salariés:* 9. *Bénévoles:* 3. *Budget/Total 1993:* ECU 1103000 (US$ 1291000). *Sources financières:* *Privé:* 14%. *Public:* 28%. *Autofinancement:* 58%.

PUBLICATIONS: *Rapport annuel. Liste des publications.*

EVALUATION/RECHERCHE: Rapports d'évaluation disponibles.

PREVISIONS D'ACTIVITES: Projets sur la désertification, les pesticides et agriculture biologique, les marchés régionaux et environnement, l'environnement méditerranéen, l'équité et l'environnement.

COMMENTAIRES: Activités d'information concernant la Communauté des Etats indépendants.

ACTIVITES DANS LES REGIONS EN DEVELOPPEMENT: Intervient par l'intermédiaire d'organisations locales partenaires.

ACTIVITES D'INFORMATION ET D'EDUCATION: Domaines: Relations internationales/coopération/aide au développement; Santé/assainissement/eau; Écologie/environnement/biodiversité. **Activités:** Campagnes d'information/expositions; Collecte de fonds; Conférences/séminaires/ateliers/activités de formation; Lobbying/plaidoyer; Services d'information et de documentation/bases de données; Édition/documents audiovisuels/documents éducatifs.

BEL0143

CAABU

Avenue de Cortenbergh 60, 1040 Bruxelles, Belgique.

Contact: Bernard Mills.

BEL0144

CARE INTERNATIONAL

58/10 boulevard du Régent, 1000 Brussels, Belgium.

Telephone: 32 (2) 502 43 33. *Fax:* 32 (2) 502 82 02. *E-mail:* TCN 206. *Contact:* Tony Eggleton, Secretary General.

OBJECTIVES: To help the poor in developing countries to achieve social and economic well-being. To promote sustainable development. To reach new standards of excellence in offering technical assistance, disaster relief training, food and other materials according to local needs and priorities. To advocate public policies and programmes that support these aims.

GENERAL INFORMATION: *Creation:* 1982. *Affiliated to:* ICVA. *Personnel/Total:* 11000. *Salaried:* 10000 of which: 9500 in developing countries. *Volunteers:* 1000. *Budget/Total 1993:* ECU 14827000 (US$ 17343000).

PUBLICATIONS: *Annual report.*

EVALUATION/RESEARCH: Evaluation reports available.

COMMENTS: C.I. is an organisation of 11 autonomous members. Its office in Brussels acts a co-ordinator for the members. Information activities are undertaken by the members in each country. Undertakes activities in the Commonwealth of Independent States.

ACTIVITIES IN DEVELOPING REGIONS: Present in developing regions. Active in 70 country(ies). Maintains local field presence. Works through local field partners. **Sustainable Development Actions:** Children/youth/family; Ecology/environment/biodiversity; Education/training/literacy; Emergency relief/refugees/humanitarian assistance; Food/famine; Gender issues/women; Health/sanitation/water; Population/family planning/demography; Rural development/agriculture; Sending volunteers/experts/technical assistance; Small enterprises/informal sector/handicrafts; Urban development/habitat. **Regions:** Caribbean; Central Africa; Central Asia and South Asia; East Africa; East Asia; Mexico and Central America; Middle East; North Africa; South America; South East Asia; Southern Africa; West Africa.

BEL0145

CARITATE AEGRORUM SERVI (CARAES)

Stropstraat 119, 9000 Gand, Belgique.

Téléphone: 32 (9) 221 45 45. *Fax:* 32 (9) 221 98 89. *Contact:* Eduard de Parade, Administrateur délégué.

OBJECTIFS: Collaborer à la création et à l'entretien d'établissements pour handicapés mentaux ou physiques. Rassembler et gérer l'argent, le matériel et les médicaments destinés aux œuvres caritatives patronnées par l'association et situées dans les pays en développement.

INFORMATIONS GENERALES: *Création:* 1967. *Personnel/Total:* 3. *Salariés:* 2. *Bénévoles:* 1. *Budget/Total 1993:* ECU 1286000 (US$ 1504000). *Sources financières:* *Privé:* 75%. *Public:* 25%.

PUBLICATIONS: *Rapport annuel.*

EVALUATION/RECHERCHE: Rapports d'évaluation disponibles.

PREVISIONS D'ACTIVITES: Contribuer au redressement de l'éducation agricole, technique et générale au Zaïre et au Rwanda.

ACTIVITES DANS LES REGIONS EN DEVELOPPEMENT: Intervient directement dans les régions en développement. Intervient dans 4 pays. Maintient une présence locale sur le terrain. Intervient par l'intermédiaire d'organisations locales partenaires. **Actions de Développement durable:** Développement rural/agriculture; Santé/assainissement/eau; Éducation/formation/alphabétisation. **Régions:** Afrique centrale; Asie centrale et Asie du Sud; Asie de l'Est.

ACTIVITES D'INFORMATION ET D'EDUCATION: Domaines: Santé/assainissement/eau; Éducation/formation/alphabétisation. **Activités:** Collecte de fonds; Éducation formelle.

See: *How to Use the Directory*, page 11.

BEL0146
CARREFOUR CHANTIERS

Boulevard de l'Empereur 25, 1000 Bruxelles, Belgique.

Téléphone: 32 (2) 511 96 84.

BEL0147
CAUSES COMMUNES

Chaussée de Boendael, 388, 1050 Bruxelles, Belgique.

Téléphone: 32 (2) 640 63 38. *Fax:* 32 (2) 640 29 46. *Contact:* Paul Hermant, Secrétaire général.

OBJECTIFS: Créer des liens durables entre villes et communes d'ex-Yougoslavie et des autres pays d'Europe. Anticiper l'arrivée des réfugiés dans nos pays par un travail concerté avec les communes concernées. Soutenir les médias et les mouvements démocratiques d'ex-Yougoslavie.

INFORMATIONS GENERALES: *Création:* 1992. *Affiliée à:* Opération Villages Roumains (Belgique) - Médecins sans frontières (Belgique.). *Personnel/Total:* 31. *Salariés:* 31 dont: 10 dans les pays en développement. *Budget/Total 1993:* ECU 3353000 (US$ 3921000). *Sources financières:* Privé: 30%. *Public:* 70%.

PUBLICATIONS: *Périodiques:* Via (12) - Causes Communes (1). *Rapport annuel. Liste des publications.*

EVALUATION/RECHERCHE: Rapports d'évaluation disponibles. Entreprend des activités de recherche.

PREVISIONS D'ACTIVITES: Créer des agences de la démocratie locale dans diverses villes et communes d'ex-Yougoslavie.

COMMENTAIRES: Activités d'information concernant la Communauté des Etats indépendants.

ACTIVITES D'INFORMATION ET D'EDUCATION: Domaines: Droits de l'Homme/paix/conflits; Paix/conflits ethniques/armement/désarmement; Relations internationales/coopération/aide au développement; Réfugiés/migrants/groupes ethniques; Secours d'urgence/réfugiés/aide humanitaire. **Activités:** Collecte de fonds; Conférences/séminaires/ateliers/activités de formation; Lobbying/plaidoyer; Radiodiffusion/manifestations culturelles; Échanges/parrainage/jumelage; Édition/documents audiovisuels/documents éducatifs; Éducation formelle.

BEL0148
CENTRE D'AIDE AU DEVELOPPEMENT DANS LA LIBERTE ET LE PROGRES (DELIPRO) ♦ Centre for Development Aid with Liberty and Progress

Rue de Naples 39, 1050 Bruxelles, Belgique.

Téléphone: 32 (2) 512 65 97 . *Fax:* 32 (2) 71 84 56 34. *Contact:* Charles Petitjean, Président.

OBJECTIFS: Réaliser des micro-projets de développement. Envoyer des volontaires sur le terrain. Informer le public belge sur la problématique des pays en développement. Accueillir en Belgique des étudiants du Tiers monde.

INFORMATIONS GENERALES: *Création:* 1962. *Type d'organisation:* regroupement d'ONG. *Affiliée à:* Consortium Liberté Tiers-Monde (Belgique) - CODEF (Belgique). *Personnel/Total:* 100. *Salariés:* 84 dont: 80 dans les pays en développement. *Bénévoles:* 16 dont: 9 dans les pays en développement. *Sources financières:* Privé: 25%. *Public:* 75%.

PUBLICATIONS: *Périodiques:* Liberté (4) - Vrijheid (2). *Rapport annuel.*

EVALUATION/RECHERCHE: Entreprend des activités de recherche.

PREVISIONS D'ACTIVITES: Campagnes nationales sur les solutions libérales contre le sous-développement.

ACTIVITES DANS LES REGIONS EN DEVELOPPEMENT: Intervient directement dans les régions en développement. Intervient dans 25 pays. Maintient une présence locale sur le terrain. Intervient par l'intermédiaire d'organisations locales partenaires. **Actions de Développement durable:** Droits de l'Homme/paix/conflits; Démocratie/bonne gestion publique/création d'institutions/développement participatif; Développement rural/agriculture; Développement urbain/habitat;

Enfants/jeunesse/famille; Envoi de volontaires/experts/assistance technique; Petites entreprises/secteur informel/artisanat; Population/planning familial/démographie; Questions relatives aux femmes; Santé/assainissement/eau; Secours d'urgence/réfugiés/aide humanitaire; Écologie/environnement/biodiversité; Éducation/formation/alphabétisation. **Régions:** Afrique australe; Afrique centrale; Afrique de l'Est; Afrique de l'Ouest; Afrique du Nord; Amérique du Sud; Asie centrale et Asie du Sud; Mexique et Amerique centrale; Moyen-Orient.

ACTIVITES D'INFORMATION ET D'EDUCATION: Domaines: Culture/tradition/religion; Droits de l'Homme/paix/conflits; Développement rural/agriculture; Développement urbain/habitat; Emploi/chômage; Enfants/jeunesse/famille; Paix/conflits ethniques/armement/désarmement; Pauvreté/conditions de vie; Population/planning familial/démographie; Questions relatives aux femmes; Relations internationales/coopération/aide au développement; Réfugiés/migrants/groupes ethniques; Santé/assainissement/eau; Écologie/environnement/biodiversité; Éducation/formation/alphabétisation. **Activités:** Campagnes d'information/expositions; Collecte de fonds; Conférences/séminaires/ateliers/activités de formation; Radiodiffusion/manifestations culturelles; Édition/documents audiovisuels/documents éducatifs; Éducation formelle.

BEL0149
CENTRE D'ETUDE ET DE DOCUMENTATION AFRICAINES (CEDAF) ♦ African Studies and Documentation Centre

Rue Belliard 65, 1040 Bruxelles, Belgique.

Téléphone: 32 (2) 230 75 62. *Fax:* 32 (2) 230 76 05. *Contact:* Gauthier de Villers, Directeur.

OBJECTIFS: Effectuer des recherches, diffuser de la documentation sur les problèmes économiques, politiques et sociaux de l'Afrique et publier les résultats des recherches effectuées par ses chercheurs ou par des chercheurs extérieurs.

INFORMATIONS GENERALES: *Création:* 1970. *Personnel/Total:* 4. *Salariés:* 4. *Budget/Total 1993:* ECU 2310000 (US$ 280000). *Sources financières:* Public: 90%. Autofinancement: 10%.

PUBLICATIONS: *Périodiques:* Cahiers Africains (6). *Liste des publications.*

EVALUATION/RECHERCHE: Entreprend des activités de recherche.

COMMENTAIRES: Le CEDAF est intégré à un établissement d'utilité publique l'"Institut Africain".

ACTIVITES D'INFORMATION ET D'EDUCATION: Domaines: Culture/tradition/religion; Droits de l'Homme/paix/conflits; Développement rural/agriculture; Développement urbain/habitat; Emploi/chômage; Pauvreté/conditions de vie; Questions relatives aux femmes; Relations internationales/coopération/aide au développement; Relations économiques internationales/commerce/dette/finances; Réfugiés/migrants/groupes ethniques; Éducation/formation/alphabétisation. **Activités:** Conférences/séminaires/ateliers/activités de formation; Services d'information et de documentation/bases de données; Édition/documents audiovisuels/documents éducatifs.

BEL0150
CENTRE D'INFORMATION SUR LES PRATIQUES ASSOCIATIVES (CIPA)

Rue de la Sablonnière 18 , 1000 Bruxelles , Belgique.

Téléphone: 32 (2) 217 14 95. *Contact:* Serge Cols, Président.

BEL0151
CENTRE D'INITIATION POUR REFUGIES ET ETRANGERS

1 rue Joseph Stallaert, 1060 Bruxelles, Belgique.

BEL0152
CENTRE INTERNATIONAL D'ETUDES, DE RECHERCHE ET D'ACTIONS POUR LE DEVELOPPEMENT (CINTERAD)

Boulevard Louis Schmidt 14, B.P. 3, 1040 Bruxelles, Belgique.

Téléphone: 32 (2) 736 44 10. *Fax:* 32 (2) 732 17 11. *Contact:* Dayina Mayenga, Administrateur.

Voir : *Comment utiliser le répertoire*, page 11.

OBJECTIFS: Promouvoir les ONG et les communautés villageoises dans les pays d'Afrique, des Caraïbes et du Pacifique. Soutenir la coopération entre ONG du Nord et ONG du Sud.

INFORMATIONS GENERALES: *Création:* 1981. *Affiliée à:* Collectif Stratégies Alimentaires.. *Personnel/Total:* 82. *Salariés:* 22 dont: 20 dans les pays en développement. *Bénévoles:* 60 dont: 50 dans les pays en développement. *Sources financières:* *Privé:* 15%. *Public:* 62%. *Autofinancement:* 23%.

PUBLICATIONS: *Périodiques:* Interdialogue (3).

ACTIVITES DANS LES REGIONS EN DEVELOPPEMENT: Intervient par l'intermédiaire d'organisations locales partenaires. **Actions de Développement durable:** Aliments/famine; Démocratie/bonne gestion publique/création d'institutions/développement participatif; Développement rural/agriculture; Développement urbain/habitat; Questions relatives aux femmes; Santé/assainissement/eau; Secours d'urgence/réfugiés/aide humanitaire; Éducation/formation/alphabétisation. **Régions:** Afrique australe; Afrique centrale; Afrique de l'Ouest.

ACTIVITES D'INFORMATION ET D'EDUCATION: Domaines: Aliments/famine; Développement rural/agriculture; Développement urbain/habitat; Questions relatives aux femmes; Relations internationales/coopération/aide au développement; Réfugiés/migrants/groupes ethniques; Santé/assainissement/eau; Secours d'urgence/réfugiés/aide humanitaire; Éducation/formation/alphabétisation. **Activités:** Conférences/séminaires/ateliers/activités de formation.

BEL0153

CENTRE INTERNATIONAL DE FORMATION DES CADRES DU DEVELOPPEMENT

Avenue Emile de Béco 112, Bte 13, 1050 Bruxelles, Belgique.

Téléphone: 32 (2) 640 23 59. *Fax:* 32 (2) 646 02 84. *Contact:* Philippe Franquin, Président.

OBJECTIFS: Promouvoir des projets d'auto-développement en s'appuyant sur des actions de formation-production avec des artisans, des paysans, des jeunes marginaux et des handicapés dans les pays en développement.

INFORMATIONS GENERALES: *Création:* 1982. *Affiliée à:* Fédération des ONG francophones de co-financement (Belgique) - CODEV (Belgique) - Fédération francophone des ONG d'envoi de coopérants ONG - Comité de liaison des ONG de développement auprès des communautés européennes (Belgique.). *Personnel/Total:* 46. *Salariés:* 33 dont: 30 dans les pays en développement. *Bénévoles:* 13 dont: 13 dans les pays en développement. *Budget/Total 1993:* ECU 1323000 (US$ 1548000). *Sources financières:* *Privé:* 25%. *Public:* 75%.

PUBLICATIONS: *Rapport annuel.*

EVALUATION/RECHERCHE: Rapports d'évaluation disponibles.

ACTIVITES DANS LES REGIONS EN DEVELOPPEMENT: Intervient directement dans les régions en développement. Intervient dans 9 pays. Maintient une présence locale sur le terrain. Intervient par l'intermédiaire d'organisations locales partenaires. **Actions de Développement durable:** Enfants/jeunesse/famille; Envoi de volontaires/experts/assistance technique; Petites entreprises/secteur informel/artisanat; Santé/assainissement/eau; Écologie/environnement/biodiversité; Éducation/formation/alphabétisation. **Régions:** Afrique centrale; Afrique de l'Ouest; Afrique du Nord; Amérique du Sud.

ACTIVITES D'INFORMATION ET D'EDUCATION: Domaines: Santé/assainissement/eau; Écologie/environnement/biodiversité. **Activités:** Collecte de fonds.

BEL0154

CENTRE MEDICO-PSYCHOSOCIAL POUR REFUGIES (EXIL)

52 rue d'Oultremont, 1040 Bruxelles, Belgique.

BEL0155

CENTRE NATIONAL DE COOPERATION AU DEVELOPPEMENT (CNCD)

Quai du Commerce 9, 1000 Bruxelles, Belgique.

Téléphone: 32 (2) 218 47 27. *Fax:* 32 (2) 217 60 78. *Contact:* Jean Ronveaux, Secrétaire général.

OBJECTIFS: Coordonner les ONG actives dans le Tiers-Monde et favoriser la coopération et la communication entre elles. Promouvoir l'amélioration de la politique de la Belgique en matière de coopération au développement. Informer et former l'opinion publique dans ces domaines.

INFORMATIONS GENERALES: *Création:* 1966. *Type d'organisation:* regroupement d'ONG. *Organisations membres:* 85. *Affiliée à:* ICDA - EURO-STEP - Consortium Nicaragua - Consortium Zaïre - Consortium Fonds de survie - Consortium Cap-Vert - Collectif stratégies alimentaires -CCONG - ADO (Belgique.). *Personnel/Total:* 29. *Salariés:* 26. *Bénévoles:* 3. *Budget/Total 1993:* ECU 914000 (US$ 1069000). *Sources financières:* *Privé:* 65%. *Public:* 13%. *Autofinancement:* 22%.

PUBLICATIONS: *Périodiques:* Demain Le Monde (12). *Rapport annuel.* Liste des publications.

EVALUATION/RECHERCHE: Rapports d'évaluation disponibles.

ACTIVITES DANS LES REGIONS EN DEVELOPPEMENT: Intervient directement dans les régions en développement. Intervient dans 3 pays. Intervient par l'intermédiaire d'organisations locales partenaires. **Actions de Développement durable:** Droits de l'Homme/paix/conflits; Démocratie/bonne gestion publique/création d'institutions/développement participatif; Développement rural/agriculture; Développement urbain/habitat; Enfants/jeunesse/famille; Petites entreprises/secteur informel/artisanat; Population/planning familial/démographie; Questions relatives aux femmes; Santé/assainissement/eau; Écologie/environnement/biodiversité; Éducation/formation/alphabétisation. **Régions:** Afrique centrale; Amérique du Sud.

ACTIVITES D'INFORMATION ET D'EDUCATION: Domaines: Aliments/famine; Culture/tradition/religion; Droits de l'Homme/paix/conflits; Développement rural/agriculture; Développement urbain/habitat; Emploi/chômage; Enfants/jeunesse/famille; Pauvreté/conditions de vie; Questions relatives aux femmes; Racisme/xénophobie/antisémitisme; Relations internationales/coopération/aide au développement; Relations économiques internationales/commerce/dette/finances; Réfugiés/migrants/groupes ethniques; Santé/assainissement/eau; Secours d'urgence/réfugiés/aide humanitaire; Écologie/environnement/biodiversité; Éducation/formation/alphabétisation. **Activités:** Campagnes d'information/expositions; Collecte de fonds; Conférences/séminaires/ateliers/activités de formation; Lobbying/plaidoyer; Services d'information et de documentation/bases de données; Édition/documents audiovisuels/documents éducatifs.

BEL0156

CENTRE SCIENTIFIQUE ET MEDICAL DE L'UNIVERSITE LIBRE DE BRUXELLES POUR SES ACTIVITES DE COOPERATION (CEMUBAC)

44 avenue Jeanne, 1050 Bruxelles, Belgique.

Téléphone: 32 (2) 650 34 96. *Fax:* 32 (2) 650 35 21. *Contact:* Baron A. Jaumotte, Président.

OBJECTIFS: Installer des centres médicaux et de recherche scientifique outre-mer.

INFORMATIONS GENERALES: *Création:* 1938. *Type d'organisation:* regroupement d'ONG. *Organisations membres:* 6. *Personnel/Total:* 40. *Salariés:* 25 dont: 20 dans les pays en développement. *Bénévoles:* 15 dont: 3 dans les pays en développement. *Budget/Total 1993:* ECU 1236000 (US$ 1445000). *Sources financières:* *Privé:* 3%. *Public:* 87%. *Autofinancement:* 10%.

PUBLICATIONS: *Rapport annuel.* Liste des publications.

EVALUATION/RECHERCHE: Rapports d'évaluation disponibles. Entreprend des activités de recherche.

PREVISIONS D'ACTIVITES: Lutte contre la drogue en Asie Centrale, Asie du Sud Est, contre le Sida en Région des Grands Lacs.

ACTIVITES DANS LES REGIONS EN DEVELOPPEMENT: Intervient directement dans les régions en développement. Intervient dans 8 pays. Maintient une présence locale sur le terrain. Intervient par l'intermédiaire d'organisations locales partenaires. **Actions de Développement durable:** Aliments/famine; Autres; Développement rural/agriculture; Enfants/

See: How to Use the Directory, page 11.

jeunesse/famille; Envoi de volontaires/experts/assistance technique; Questions relatives aux femmes; Santé/assainissement/eau; Écologie/environnement/biodiversité. **Régions:** Afrique centrale; Afrique de l'Ouest; Asie centrale et Asie du Sud; Asie du Sud-Est.

ACTIVITES D'INFORMATION ET D'EDUCATION: Domaines: Aliments/famine; Culture/tradition/religion; Droits de l'Homme/paix/conflits; Développement rural/agriculture; Enfants/jeunesse/famille; Questions relatives aux femmes; Racisme/xénophobie/antisémitisme; Relations internationales/coopération/aide au développement; Santé/assainissement/eau; Éducation/formation/alphabétisation. **Activités:** Campagnes d'information/expositions; Collecte de fonds; Conférences/séminaires/ateliers/activités de formation; Lobbying/plaidoyer; Radiodiffusion/manifestations culturelles; Services d'information et de documentation/bases de données; Échanges/parrainage/jumelage; Édition/documents audio-visuels/documents éducatifs; Éducation formelle.

BEL0157

CENTRE TRICONTINENTAL (CETRI) ♦ Tricontinental Centre

Avenue Sainte Gertrude 5, 1348 Ottignies-Louvain-la-Neuve, Belgique.

Téléphone: 32 (10) 45 08 22. ***Fax:*** 32 (10) 45 31 52. ***Contact:*** François Houtart, Directeur.

OBJECTIFS: Diffuser de la documentation et des informations sur les problèmes sociaux, économiques et culturels de l'Asie, l'Afrique et l'Amérique Latine. Effectuer des recherches sur la sociologie de la culture de ces pays.

INFORMATIONS GENERALES: *Création:* 1977. ***Personnel/Total:*** 10. *Salariés:* 7. *Bénévoles:* 3. ***Budget/Total 1993:*** ECU 106000 (US$ 124000). ***Sources financières:*** Privé: 25%. Public: 45%. Autofinancement: 30%.

PUBLICATIONS: *Périodiques:* Analyses Nord-Sud (4) - Alternatives Sud (4). *Rapport annuel. Liste des publications.*

EVALUATION/RECHERCHE: Entreprend des activités de recherche.

PREVISIONS D'ACTIVITES: Recherche sur les aspects culturels de l'exclusion dans les pays du Tiers-Monde.

ACTIVITES DANS LES REGIONS EN DEVELOPPEMENT: Intervient directement dans les régions en développement. Intervient dans 5 pays. Intervient par l'intermédiaire d'organisations locales partenaires. **Actions de Développement durable:** Éducation/formation/alphabétisation. **Régions:** Amérique du Sud.

ACTIVITES D'INFORMATION ET D'EDUCATION: Domaines: Culture/tradition/religion. **Activités:** Éducation formelle.

BEL0158

CENTRUM VOOR DORPSINTEGRATIE-BWAMANDA-BEL-GIE (CDI-BWAMANDA) ♦ Centre de Développement Intégral-Bwamanda-Belgique

Bankstraat 71, 3000 Louvain, Belgique.

Téléphone: 32 (16) 20 07 13. ***Fax:*** 32 (16) 20 62 50. ***Contact:*** Jacqueline Vanheers, coordinatrice.

OBJECTIFS: Favoriser le développement intégral de la région de Bwamanda au Zaïre.

INFORMATIONS GENERALES: *Création:* 1971. ***Personnel/Total:*** 8. *Salariés:* 3. *Bénévoles:* 5 dont: 2 dans les pays en développement. ***Budget/Total 1993:*** ECU 2224000 (US$ 2601000). ***Sources financières:*** Privé: 80%. Public: 15%. Autofinancement: 5%.

PUBLICATIONS: *Périodiques:* CDI-Newsbrief (4). *Rapport annuel. Liste des publications.*

EVALUATION/RECHERCHE: Rapports d'évaluation disponibles.

ACTIVITES DANS LES REGIONS EN DEVELOPPEMENT: Intervient directement dans les régions en développement. Intervient dans 2 pays. Maintient une présence locale sur le terrain. Intervient par l'intermédiaire d'organisations locales partenaires. **Actions de Développement durable:** Aliments/famine; Dette/finances/commerce; Démocratie/bonne gestion publique/création d'institutions/développement participatif; Développement rural/agriculture; Développement urbain/habitat; Enfants/jeunesse/famille; Envoi de volontaires/experts/assistance tech-

nique; Petites entreprises/secteur informel/artisanat; Population/planning familial/démographie; Questions relatives aux femmes; Santé/assainissement/eau; Secours d'urgence/réfugiés/aide humanitaire; Éducation/formation/alphabétisation; Énergie/transport. **Régions:** Afrique centrale; Asie centrale et Asie du Sud.

BEL0159

CENTRUM VOOR ONTWIKKELINGSSAMENWERKING KORTRIJK (COK) ♦ Development Co-operation Centre of Kortrijk

Doorniksesteenweg 147, 8500 Kortrijk, Belgium.

Telephone: 32 (56) 21 62 10. ***Contact:*** Rev. O. Tanghe.

BEL0160

CHURCHES COMMISSION FOR MIGRANTS IN EUROPE ♦ Commission des Eglises auprès des Migrants en Europe

174 rue Joseph II, 1040 Brussels, Belgium.

Telephone: 32 (2) 230 20 11. ***Fax:*** 32 (2) 231 14 13. ***Contact:*** Jan Miessen, General Secretary.

OBJECTIVES: To promote and disseminate information on migration issues in Europe. To make the European Institutions aware of the Churches' concern for migrants.

GENERAL INFORMATION: *Creation:* 1964. ***Type of organisation:*** coordinating body. ***Member organisations:*** 18. ***Personnel/Total:*** 3. *Salaried:* 3. ***Financial sources:*** Private: 5%. Public: 5%. Self-financing: 90%.

PUBLICATIONS: *Periodicals:* Migration Newssheet (12) - Briefing Paper Series (4). *List of publications.*

EVALUATION/RESEARCH: Undertakes research activities.

COMMENTS: Undertakes activities in the Commonwealth of Independent States.

INFORMATION AND EDUCATION ACTIVITIES: Topics: Children/youth/family; Gender issues/women; Human rights/peace/conflicts; Poverty/living conditions; Racism/xenophobia/antisemitism; Refugees/migrants/ethnic groups. **Activities:** Conferences/seminars/workshops/training activities; Formal education; Fund raising; Information and documentation services/data bases; Information campaigns/exhibitions; Lobbying/advocacy; Publishing/audiovisual materials/educational materials.

BEL0161

CODEF - FEDERATION FRANCOPHONE DES ONG D'ENVOI DE COOPERANTS-ONG

Quai du Commerce 9, 1000 Bruxelles, Belgique.

Téléphone: 32 (2) 223 03 18. ***Fax:*** 32 (2) 217 60 78. ***Contact:*** Etienne Van Parijs, Secrétaire général.

OBJECTIFS: Représenter, coordonner, défendre et promouvoir ses membres (principalement des ONG d'envoi) vis à vis des pouvoirs publics et de tout autre instance externe nationale ou internationale concernée.

INFORMATIONS GENERALES: *Création:* 1991. ***Type d'organisation:*** collectif. ***Organisations membres:*** 26. ***Affiliée à:*** Centre National de Coopération au développement (Belgique) - Forum Européen pour le Volontariat du Développement (Allemagne.). ***Personnel/Total:*** 4. *Salariés:* 4. ***Budget/Total 1993:*** ECU 148000 (US$ 173000). ***Sources financières:*** Public: 91%. Autofinancement: 9%.

PUBLICATIONS: *Rapport annuel.*

EVALUATION/RECHERCHE: Rapports d'évaluation disponibles.

PREVISIONS D'ACTIVITES: Renforcement de l'image du coopérant-ONG à travers la valorisation des ressources humaines dans la coopération.

COMMENTAIRES: Le CODEF édite une brochure d'information pour les coopérants-ONG.

ACTIVITES DANS LES REGIONS EN DEVELOPPEMENT: Intervient dans 85 pays. Maintient une présence locale sur le terrain. Intervient par l'intermédiaire d'organisations locales partenaires. **Actions de Développement durable:** Envoi de volontaires/experts/assistance technique. **Régions:** Afrique australe; Afrique centrale; Afrique de l'Est; Afrique de l'Ouest; Afrique du Nord; Amérique du Sud; Asie centrale et

Voir : *Comment utiliser le répertoire,* page 11.

Asie du Sud; Asie de l'Est; Asie du Sud-Est; Caraïbes; Mexique et Amerique centrale; Moyen-Orient; Océanie.

BEL0162

COLLABORATION MEDICALE TIERS-MONDE (CMT)

52 rue du Manil, 1301 Bierges, Belgique.

Téléphone: 32 (10) 41 68 19. **Contact:** Charles-Henry Chalant.

BEL0163

COLLECTIF D'ACCUEIL DES REFUGIES DU CHILI (COLARCH-COLOCH)

4 rue Traversière, 1030 Bruxelles, Belgique.

Contact: Pierre Galand.

BEL0164

COLLECTIF D'ECHANGES POUR LA TECHNOLOGIE APPROPRIEE (COTA) ♦ Exchange Group for Appropriate Technology

Rue de la Sablonnière 18, 1000 Bruxelles, Belgique.

Téléphone: 32 (2) 218 18 96. **Fax:** 32 (2) 223 14 95. **Contact:** Francis Douxchamps, Secrétaire général.

OBJECTIFS: Collecter , traiter, classifier et diffuser l'information sur les problèmes techniques rencontrés dans les pays en développement et sur les solutions éventuelles. Réaliser des recherches et des études, organiser des évènements sur ces aspects.

INFORMATIONS GENERALES: Création: 1979. **Type d'organisation:** collectif. **Organisations membres:** 5. **Affiliée à:** SATIS, CNCD (Belgique) - ADO (Belgique) - PRELUDE (Belgique) - CODEF (Belgique.). **Personnel/Total:** 14. Salariés: 8. Bénévoles: 6 dont: 6 dans les pays en développement. **Budget/Total 1993:** ECU 346000 (US$ 405000). **Sources financières:** Public: 13%. Autofinancement: 87%.

PUBLICATIONS: Périodiques: Echos du Cota (4). Rapport annuel. Liste des publications.

EVALUATION/RECHERCHE: Entreprend des activités de recherche.

ACTIVITES DANS LES REGIONS EN DEVELOPPEMENT: Intervient dans 2 pays. Maintient une présence locale sur le terrain. Intervient par l'intermédiaire d'organisations locales partenaires. **Actions de Développement durable:** Développement rural/agriculture; Développement urbain/habitat; Envoi de volontaires/experts/assistance technique; Santé/assainissement/eau; Écologie/environnement/biodiversité. **Régions:** Amérique du Sud; Mexique et Amerique centrale.

ACTIVITES D'INFORMATION ET D'EDUCATION: Domaines: Aliments/famine; Développement rural/agriculture; Développement urbain/habitat; Pauvreté/conditions de vie; Questions relatives aux femmes; Relations internationales/coopération/aide au développement; Relations économiques internationales/commerce/dette/finances; Santé/assainissement/eau; Secours d'urgence/réfugiés/aide humanitaire; Écologie/environnement/biodiversité; Éducation/formation/alphabétisation. **Activités:** Conférences/séminaires/ateliers/activités de formation; Services d'information et de documentation/bases de données; Édition/documents audiovisuels/documents éducatifs.

BEL0165

COLLECTIF STRATEGIES ALIMENTAIRES

Quai du Commerce 9, 1000 Bruxelles, Belgique.

Téléphone: 32 (2) 218 47 27. **Fax:** 32 (2) 217 60 78. **Courrier électronique:** CSA@gn.apc.org. **Contact:** D. van der Steen, Coordinateur.

OBJECTIFS: Sensibiliser le public, les associations spécialisées, les faiseurs d'opinion et les décideurs aux enjeux du développement agricole et paysan dans toutes les régions du monde. Parmi les enjeux: effets des politiques agricoles, commerciales, de coopération.

INFORMATIONS GENERALES: Création: 1984. **Affiliée à:** Centre National de Coopération au développement (Belgique) - ADO (Belgique.). **Personnel/Total:** 4. Salariés: 3. Bénévoles: 1. **Budget/Total 1993:** ECU 124000 (US$ 145000). **Sources financières:** Privé: 15%. Public: 80%. Autofinancement: 5%.

PUBLICATIONS: Périodiques: Les Brèves du CSA (6). Rapport annuel. Liste des publications.

EVALUATION/RECHERCHE: Rapports d'évaluation disponibles. Entreprend des activités de recherche.

PREVISIONS D'ACTIVITES: Exposition sur l'internationalisation agricole. Formation pour les ONG.

COMMENTAIRES: Le CSA développe la recherche et l'échange documentaire sur les enjeux agricoles mondiaux.

ACTIVITES D'INFORMATION ET D'EDUCATION: Domaines: Aliments/famine; Développement rural/agriculture; Relations internationales/coopération/aide au développement; Relations économiques internationales/commerce/dette/finances; Écologie/environnement/biodiversité. **Activités:** Campagnes d'information/expositions; Conférences/séminaires/ateliers/activités de formation; Lobbying/plaidoyer; Radiodiffusion/manifestations culturelles; Réseaux/télécommunications électroniques; Services d'information et de documentation/bases de données; Échanges/parrainage/jumelage; Édition/documents audiovisuels/documents éducatifs.

BEL0166

COMITE BELGE D'AIDE AUX REFUGIES (CBAR)

Rue Defacqz 1, Bte 10, 1050 Bruxelles, Belgique.

Téléphone: 32 (2) 537 82 20. **Contact:** Gilbert Jaeger, Président.

BEL0167

COMITE BELGE DE SECOURS A L'ERYTHREE (CBSE) ♦ Belgian Committee for Assistance to Eritrea

Rue de Mérode 216, 1060 Bruxelles, Belgique.

Téléphone: 32 (2) 539 36 00 . **Fax:** 32 (2) 539 39 28. **Contact:** Richard Leonard, Secrétaire général.

OBJECTIFS: Coopérer au développement en faveur des populations défavorisées. Informer et sensibiliser le public autour des problèmes de ces populations.

INFORMATIONS GENERALES: Création: 1976. **Affiliée à:** Association des ONG francophones et germanophones (Belgique) - COPROGRAM (Belgique) - Centre National de Coopération au Développement (Belgique) -National Centrum voor Ontwikkelingssamenwerking (Belgique) - Comité de Liaison des ONG (Belgique.). **Personnel/Total:** 8. Salariés: 4. Bénévoles: 4. **Budget/Total 1993:** ECU 983000 (US$ 1150000). **Sources financières:** Privé: 15%. Public: 75%. Autofinancement: 10%.

PUBLICATIONS: Périodiques: Bulletin d'information (4). Rapport annuel. Liste des publications.

ACTIVITES DANS LES REGIONS EN DEVELOPPEMENT: Intervient dans 1 pays. Intervient par l'intermédiaire d'organisations locales partenaires. **Actions de Développement durable:** Développement rural/agriculture; Petites entreprises/secteur informel/artisanat; Questions relatives aux femmes; Santé/assainissement/eau. **Régions:** Afrique de l'Est.

ACTIVITES D'INFORMATION ET D'EDUCATION: Domaines: Développement rural/agriculture; Paix/conflits ethniques/armement/désarmement; Questions relatives aux femmes; Santé/assainissement/eau. **Activités:** Campagnes d'information/expositions; Collecte de fonds; Lobbying/plaidoyer; Services d'information et de documentation/bases de données; Édition/documents audiovisuels/documents éducatifs.

BEL0168

COMITE BELGE POUR L'UNICEF

Avenue des Arts, 20, Bte 18, 1040 Bruxelles, Belgique.

Téléphone: 32 (2) 230 59 70. **Fax:** 32 (2) 230 34 62. **Contact:** Dr. Paul Casman, Secrétaire général.

OBJECTIFS: Promouvoir l'UNICEF, récolter des fonds pour l'UNICEF, sensibiliser, informer sur l'UNICEF et la situation des enfants dans le monde.

INFORMATIONS GENERALES: Création: 1952. **Type d'organisation:** regroupement d'ONG. **Affiliée à:** COPROGRAM (Belgique) - VLAAN-

See: *How to Use the Directory*, page 11.

DEREN (Belgique) - ADO (Belgique). *Personnel/Total:* 29. *Salariés:* 24. *Bénévoles:* 5. *Sources financières:* Autofinancement: 100%.

PUBLICATIONS: *Périodiques:* UNICEF-INFO (6). *Rapport annuel. Liste des publications.*

ACTIVITES D'INFORMATION ET D'EDUCATION: Domaines: Aliments/ famine; Enfants/jeunesse/famille; Paix/conflits ethniques/armement/ désarmement; Pauvreté/conditions de vie; Population/planning familial/ démographie; Questions relatives aux femmes; Relations internationa- les/coopération/aide au développement; Relations économiques internationales/commerce/dette/finances; Santé/assainissement/eau; Secours d'urgence/réfugiés/aide humanitaire; Écologie/environnement/ biodiversité. **Activités:** Campagnes d'information/expositions; Collecte de fonds; Conférences/séminaires/ateliers/activités de formation; Lob- bying/plaidoyer; Services d'information et de documentation/bases de données; Édition/documents audiovisuels/documents éducatifs.

BEL0169

COMITE D'AIDE AUX CALAMINOIS DU TIERS MONDE (CACTM)

Rue de l'Eglise 31, 4720 La Calamine, Belgique.

Téléphone: 32 (87) 65 95 10. *Fax:* 32 (87) 65 74 84. *Contact:* W. Schyns.

OBJECTIFS: Aider au développement et à l'investissement pour permet- tre à la population locale de se prendre elle-même en charge.

INFORMATIONS GENERALES: *Création:* 1972. *Personnel/Total:* 7. *Bénévoles:* 7 dont: 4 dans les pays en développement. *Budget/ Total 1993:* ECU 124000 (US$ 145000). *Sources financières:* Privé: 25%. Public: 75%.

PUBLICATIONS: *Rapport annuel.*

PREVISIONS D'ACTIVITES: Projet d'éducation au Zaïre, projet d'éduca- tion, réhabilitation et logement au Rwanda.

ACTIVITES DANS LES REGIONS EN DEVELOPPEMENT: Intervient directement dans les régions en développement. Maintient une pré- sence locale sur le terrain. Intervient par l'intermédiaire d'organisations locales partenaires. **Actions de Développement durable:** Développe- ment rural/agriculture; Enfants/jeunesse/famille; Secours d'urgence/ réfugiés/aide humanitaire; Éducation/formation/alphabétisation. **Régions:** Afrique centrale; Amérique du Sud.

ACTIVITES D'INFORMATION ET D'EDUCATION: Domaines: Dévelop- pement rural/agriculture; Enfants/jeunesse/famille; Secours d'urgence/ réfugiés/aide humanitaire; Éducation/formation/alphabétisation. **Acti- vités:** Collecte de fonds.

BEL0170

COMITE D'AIDE PROFONDEVILLOIS AUX PAYS EN VOIE DE DEVELOPPEMENT

Rue du Cato 32, 5170 Profondeville, Namur, Belgique.

Téléphone: 32 (81) 41 21 10. *Contact:* Jean-Marie Maquet.

BEL0171

COMITE JEAN PAIN (CJP) ◆ Committee Jean Pain

Avenue Princesse Elisabeth 18, 1030 Bruxelles, Belgique.

Téléphone: 32 (52) 30 53 65. *Fax:* 32 (2) 215 00 21. *Contact:* Frederik van den Brande, Président.

OBJECTIFS: Vulgariser les techniques de compostage de broussailles (méthode Jean Pain), d'autres déchets de jardin et de cultures et de déchets ménagers organiques. Informer les stagiaires, les visiteurs ou les coopérants des pays en développement.

INFORMATIONS GENERALES: *Création:* 1978. *Affiliée à:* International Federation of Organisation Agriculture Movement. *Personnel/Total:* 5. *Salariés:* 5. *Budget/Total 1993:* ECU 62000 (US$ 72000). *Sources financières:* Autofinancement: 100%.

PUBLICATIONS: *Périodiques:* Humus News (4).

ACTIVITES DANS LES REGIONS EN DEVELOPPEMENT: Intervient par l'intermédiaire d'organisations locales partenaires.

ACTIVITES D'INFORMATION ET D'EDUCATION: Domaines: Écologie/ environnement/biodiversité. **Activités:** Conférences/séminaires/ateliers/ activités de formation; Services d'information et de documentation/ bases de données;

BEL0172

COMITE NATIONAL POUR LA PAIX ET LE DEVELOPPEMENT (CNADP)

34 rue de la Tulipe, 1050 Bruxelles, Belgique.

Téléphone: 32 (2) 511 36 99. *Fax:* 32 (2) 513 02 55.

BEL0173

COMITE POUR LES RELATIONS INTERNATIONALES DE JEUNESSE DE LA COMMUNAUTE FRANCAISE DE BELGIQUE (CRIJ)

Boulevard A. Max 13, 1000 Bruxelles, Belgique.

Téléphone: 32 (2) 223 15 27. *Fax:* 32 (2) 219 86 12. *Contact:* Véronique Balthasart, Chargée de l'information.

OBJECTIFS: Coordonner les 60 organisations de jeunesse, toutes ten- dances confondues, reconnues par la communauté française de Belgique. Apporter une aide technique à la concrétisation de projets internationaux de nos organisations et de toute personne intéressée, accueillir les délégations étrangères. Fournir une information spécialisée aux jeunes belges qui veulent partir à l'étranger et aux jeunes étrangers qui veulent venir en Belgique.

INFORMATIONS GENERALES: *Création:* 1978. *Type d'organisation:* regroupement d'ONG. *Organisations membres:* 60. *Personnel/Total:* 3. *Salariés:* 3. *Sources financières:* Public: 80%. Autofinancement: 20%.

PUBLICATIONS: *Périodiques:* CRID-Express (30).

PREVISIONS D'ACTIVITES: Maintenir une banque de données d'informa- tion des jeunes au niveau européen.

COMMENTAIRES: Intervient dans la Communauté des Etats indépen- dants. Activités d'information concernant la Communauté des Etats indépendants. **Actions de Développement durable:** Enfants/jeunesse/ famille. **Régions:** Afrique australe; Afrique centrale; Afrique de l'Est; Afrique de l'Ouest; Afrique du Nord; Amérique du Sud; Asie centrale et Asie du Sud; Asie de l'Est; Asie du Sud-Est; Caraïbes; Mexique et Amerique centrale; Moyen-Orient; Océanie.

ACTIVITES D'INFORMATION ET D'EDUCATION: Domaines: Enfants/ jeunesse/famille. **Activités:** Campagnes d'information/expositions; Col- lecte de fonds; Conférences/séminaires/ateliers/activités de formation; Services d'information et de documentation/bases de données.

BEL0174

COMMISSIE RECHTVAARDIGH. EN VREDE ◆ Commission Jus- tice et Paix

Huidevettersstraat 165, 1000 Brussels, Belgium.

Telephone: 32 (2) 502 75 28. *Fax:* 32 (2) 502 75 30. *Contact:* Christine Saval, Secretary general.

OBJECTIVES: To raise awareness of North-South-East relations, human rights, peace and development in the Christian Flemish community. To organise policy lobbying within the Church and State.

GENERAL INFORMATION: *Creation:* 1967. *Type of organisation:* network. *Member organisations:* 30. *Affiliated to:* Conference of European Justice and Peace Commission (Belgium) - National Centre for Development Co-operation (Belgium.). *Personnel/Total:* 4. *Salaried:* 4. *Budget/Total 1993:* ECU 48000 (US$ 73000). *Financial sources:* Private: 35%. Public: 30%. Self-financing: 35%.

PUBLICATIONS: *Periodicals:* KRN Nieuws (12). *Annual report. List of publications.*

EVALUATION/RESEARCH: Undertakes research activities.

COMMENTS: Information activities related to the Commonwealth of Inde- pendent States.

INFORMATION AND EDUCATION ACTIVITIES: Topics: Ecology/envi- ronment/biodiversity; Employment/unemployment; Human rights/peace/

Voir : *Comment utiliser le répertoire,* page 11.

conflicts; International economic relations/trade/debt/finance; International relations/cooperation/development aid; Peace/ethnic conflicts/armament/disarmament; Population/family planning/demography; Poverty/living conditions; Racism/xenophobia/antisemitism; Refugees/migrants/ethnic groups. **Activities:** Conferences/seminars/workshops/training activities; Lobbying/advocacy; Publishing/audiovisual materials/educational materials.

BEL0175

COMMISSION EUROPEENNE IMMIGRES (CEI)

19 avenue Everard, 1190 Bruxelles, Belgique.

Téléphone: 32 (2) 344 44 79. *Contact:* Micheline Six.

BEL0176

COMMISSION JUSTICE ET PAIX

71 rue M. Liétart, 1150 Bruxelles, Belgique.

Téléphone: 32 (2) 231 02 30. *Fax:* 32 (2) 230 56 97. *Contact:* Josette Thibeau, Secrétaire générale.

OBJECTIFS: Entreprendre des travaux d'étude sur la paix, le développement, les droits de l'homme, des travaux d'éducation et d'action auprès de l'opinion publique sur ces questions et les répercuter aux différents niveaux politiques.

INFORMATIONS GENERALES: *Création:* 1967. *Type d'organisation:* regroupement d'ONG. *Affiliée à:* Conférence des commissions Justice et Paix d'Europe (Belgique) - Association des ONG de développement (Belgique). *Personnel/Total:* 14. *Salariés:* 4. *Bénévoles:* 10. *Budget/Total 1993:* ECU 272000 (US\$ 318000). *Sources financières:* Privé: 36%. Public: 52%. Autofinancement: 12%.

PUBLICATIONS: *Périodiques:* La Lettre de Justice et Paix (4) - Bulletin d'information (6). *Rapport annuel. Liste des publications.*

EVALUATION/RECHERCHE: Entreprend des activités de recherche.

PREVISIONS D'ACTIVITES: Organisation d'un colloque européen étudiant les conséquences du sous-emploi sur les relations Est-Ouest-Sud. Campagne d'éducation concernant les populations "Réfugiées".

COMMENTAIRES: Activités d'information concernant la Communauté des Etats indépendants.

ACTIVITES D'INFORMATION ET D'EDUCATION: Domaines: Droits de l'Homme/paix/conflits; Emploi/chômage; Paix/conflits ethniques/armement/désarmement; Pauvreté/conditions de vie; Racisme/xénophobie/antisémitisme; Relations internationales/coopération/aide au développement; Relations économiques internationales/commerce/dette/finances; Réfugiés/migrants/groupes ethniques. **Activités:** Campagnes d'information/expositions; Conférences/séminaires/ateliers/activités de formation; Lobbying/plaidoyer; Édition/documents audiovisuels/documents éducatifs; Éducation formelle.

BEL0177

CONFEDERATION EUROPEENNE DES SYNDICATS (CES) ♦
European Trade Union Confederation (ETUC)

Boulevard Emile Jacqmain, 1210 Bruxelles, Belgique.

Téléphone: 32 (2) 224 04 11. *Fax:* 32 (2) 224 04 54/55. *Contact:* Emilio Gabaglio, Secrétaire général.

OBJECTIFS: Représenter les syndicats affiliés auprès des institutions européennes. Assurer que la dimension sociale soit insérée intégralement dans toute politique économique et géopolitique. Assurer la protection des droits humains, des droits syndicaux et des travailleurs.

INFORMATIONS GENERALES: *Création:* 1973. *Type d'organisation:* collectif. *Organisations membres:* 63. *Affiliée à:* International Confederation of Free Trade Unions. *Personnel/Total:* 48. *Salariés:* 48.

PUBLICATIONS: *Périodiques:* Report (12). *Liste des publications.*

EVALUATION/RECHERCHE: Rapports d'évaluation disponibles. Entreprend des activités de recherche.

PREVISIONS D'ACTIVITES: Séminaires sur l'égalité des chances avec les syndicats maghrébins. Initiatives droits humains et des ethnies en ex-Yougoslavie, campagnes contre l'exclusion sociale.

COMMENTAIRES: Intervient dans la Communauté des Etats indépendants. Activités d'information concernant la Communauté des Etats indépendants.

ACTIVITES D'INFORMATION ET D'EDUCATION: Domaines: Droits de l'Homme/paix/conflits; Emploi/chômage; Enfants/jeunesse/famille; Paix/conflits ethniques/armement/désarmement; Pauvreté/conditions de vie; Questions relatives aux femmes; Racisme/xénophobie/antisémitisme; Relations internationales/coopération/aide au développement; Relations économiques internationales/commerce/dette/finances; Écologie/environnement/biodiversité. **Activités:** Campagnes d'information/expositions; Conférences/séminaires/ateliers/activités de formation; Lobbying/plaidoyer; Radiodiffusion/manifestations culturelles; Réseaux/télécommunications électroniques; Services d'information et de documentation/bases de données; Échanges/parrainage/jumelage; Édition/documents audiovisuels/documents éducatifs; Éducation formelle.

BEL0178

CONFEDERATION INTERNATIONALE DES SYNDICATS LIBRES

37-41 rue Montagne aux Herbes Potagères, 1000 Bruxelles, Belgique.

Contact: J. Vanderveken, Secrétaire Général.

BEL0179

CONFEDERATION MONDIALE DU TRAVAIL (CMT) ♦ World
Confederation of Labour (WCL)

Rue de Trèves 33, 1040 Bruxelles, Belgique.

Téléphone: 32 (2) 230 62 95.

BEL0180

CONSEIL DE LA JEUNESSE CATHOLIQUE (CJC) ♦ Catholic
Youth Council

Rue Belliard 23 A, 1040 Bruxelles, Belgique.

Téléphone: 32 (2) 230 32 83. *Contact:* Stéphan Grawez, Secrétaire général.

BEL0181

CONSEIL EUROPEEN DES COMITES NATIONAUX DE JEUNESSE

8 avenue des Courses, 1050 Bruxelles, Belgique.

Contact: La Rochel Kyte.

BEL0182

COOPERATIE VRIJ TECHNISCH ONDERWIJS WEST-VLAANDEREN ♦ Coopération Education Technique Libre Flandre Occidentale

Boeveriestraat 73, 8000 Bruges, Belgique.

Téléphone: 32 (50) 33 75 14. *Fax:* 32 (50) 33 37 57. *Contact:* Jan Vandenbulcke, Président.

OBJECTIFS: Apporter une aide technique aux pays en développement. Réaliser des projets d'enseignement agronomique et industriel, stimuler la connaissance et la participation dans le domaine du développement.

INFORMATIONS GENERALES: *Création:* 1981. *Budget/Total 1993:* ECU 163000 (US\$ 191000). *Sources financières:* Privé: 100%.

ACTIVITES DANS LES REGIONS EN DEVELOPPEMENT: Intervient par l'intermédiaire d'organisations locales partenaires. **Actions de Développement durable:** Développement rural/agriculture; Éducation/formation/alphabétisation. **Régions:** Amérique du Sud; Mexique et Amérique centrale.

ACTIVITES D'INFORMATION ET D'EDUCATION: Domaines: Développement rural/agriculture; Pauvreté/conditions de vie; Éducation/formation/alphabétisation. **Activités:** Collecte de fonds.

BEL0183

COOPERATION DIALOGUE COMMUNICATION NORD-SUD (CDC N/S)

Square Albert I, 14, bte 10, 1070 Anderlecht, Belgique.

See: *How to Use the Directory,* page 11.

Téléphone: 32 (2) 523 78 92. *Contact:* Yvette Buntinx, Administrateur délégué.

BEL0184
COOPERATION ET PROGRES

Rue de Naples 39, 1050 Bruxelles, Belgique.

Téléphone: 32 (2) 512 30 86. *Fax:* 32 (2) 512 30 86. *Contact:* Chevalier Brassinne, Président.

OBJECTIFS: Exercer une action sociale dans les pays en voie de développement, promouvoir notamment le développement économique et social des pays justifiant la mise en œuvre de projets. Envoyer des volontaires dans ces pays.

INFORMATIONS GENERALES: *Création:* 1972. *Affiliée à:* SLCD (Belgique) - Nord-Sud Coopération (Belgique) - Genagro (Belgique) -CEMUBAC (Belgique) - AADC (Belgique) - Coopération et Progrès (Belgique.). *Personnel/Total:* 22. *Salariés:* 22 dont: 20 dans les pays en développement. *Budget/Total 1993:* ECU 297000 (US$ 347000). *Sources financières:* Privé: 25%. Public: 75%.

PUBLICATIONS: *Périodiques:* Cap Tiers-Monde (4).

ACTIVITES DANS LES REGIONS EN DEVELOPPEMENT: Intervient directement dans les régions en développement. Intervient dans 8 pays. Maintient une présence locale sur le terrain. Intervient par l'intermédiaire d'organisations locales partenaires. **Actions de Développement durable:** Droits de l'Homme/paix/conflits; Développement rural/agriculture; Enfants/jeunesse/famille; Envoi de volontaires/experts/assistance technique; Santé/assainissement/eau; Éducation/formation/alphabétisation. **Régions:** Afrique centrale; Afrique de l'Ouest; Amérique du Sud; Mexique et Amerique centrale.

BEL0185
COOPERATION ET SOLIDARITE

Square Gutenberg 10, 1040 Bruxelles, Belgique.

Téléphone: 32 (2) 230 17 96. *Contact:* M.A. van Istendael.

BEL0186
COOPERATION INTERNATIONALE POUR LE DEVELOPPEMENT ET LA SOLIDARITE (CIDSE) ♦ International Co-operation for Development and Solidarity

16, rue Stévin, 1040 Brussels, Belgium.

Telephone: 32 (2) 230 77 22. *Fax:* 32 (2) 230 70 82. *Contact:* Koenraad Verhagen, Secretary General.

OBJECTIVES: To co-ordinate the actions of its member organisations in the South and lobbying in the North.

GENERAL INFORMATION: *Creation:* 1967. *Type of organisation:* coordinating body. *Member organisations:* 17. *Personnel/Total:* 11. *Salaried:* 11. *Financial sources:* Self-financing: 100%.

PUBLICATIONS: *Periodicals:* EURO-CIDSE News Bulletin (12). *Annual report.*

ACTIVITIES IN DEVELOPING REGIONS: Maintains local field presence. Works through local field partners. **Sustainable Development Actions:** Children/youth/family; Democracy/good governance/institution building/participatory development; Ecology/environment/biodiversity; Education/training/literacy; Gender issues/women; Health/sanitation/water; Human rights/peace/conflicts; Population/family planning/demography; Rural development/agriculture; Small enterprises/informal sector/handicrafts; Urban development/habitat. **Regions:** Caribbean; Central Africa; Central Asia and South Asia; East Africa; East Asia; Mexico and Central America; Middle East; North Africa; Oceania; South America; South East Asia; Southern Africa; West Africa.

INFORMATION AND EDUCATION ACTIVITIES: Topics: Children/youth/family; Ecology/environment/biodiversity; Education/training/literacy; Gender issues/women; Health/sanitation/water; Human rights/peace/conflicts; International economic relations/trade/debt/finance; International relations/cooperation/development aid; Peace/ethnic conflicts/armament/disarmament; Population/family planning/demography; Poverty/living conditions; Rural development/agriculture; Urban development/habitat. **Activities:** Lobbying/advocacy.

BEL0187
COOPERATION PAR L'EDUCATION ET LA CULTURE (CEC)

Rue Joseph II, 18, 1040 Bruxelles, Belgique.

Téléphone: 32 (2) 217 90 71. *Contact:* Ann Gerrard, Administrateur délégué.

BEL0188
COOPERATION TECHNIQUE INTERNATIONALE (ITECO) ♦
International Technical Co-operation

Rue du Boulet 31, 1000 Bruxelles, Belgique.

Téléphone: 32 (2) 511 48 70. *Fax:* 32 (2) 502 36 70. *Contact:* Jacques Bastin, Secrétaire général.

OBJECTIFS: Eduquer au développement. Former les volontaires et les coopérants des ONG. Former des formateurs et des animateurs. Mener des activités de recherche, d'évaluation et de publication sur le développement des rapports Nord-Sud et sur les relations interculturelles. Mener des activités éducatives.

INFORMATIONS GENERALES: *Création:* 1975. *Affiliée à:* Centre National de Coopération au Développement (Belgique) - Association des ONG (Belgique) - Collectif Stratégies Alimentaires (Belgique) - Comité de liaison des ONG-UE (Belgique) - CIRAT. *Personnel/Total:* 8. *Salariés:* 8. *Budget/Total 1993:* ECU 247000 (US$ 289000). *Sources financières:* Privé: 5%. Public: 80%. Autofinancement: 15%.

PUBLICATIONS: *Périodiques:* Antipodes (4). *Liste des publications.*

EVALUATION/RECHERCHE: Rapports d'évaluation disponibles. Entreprend des activités de recherche.

ACTIVITES D'INFORMATION ET D'EDUCATION: Domaines: Culture/tradition/religion; Droits de l'Homme/paix/conflits; Développement urbain/habitat; Emploi/chômage; Paix/conflits ethniques/armement/désarmement; Pauvreté/conditions de vie; Questions relatives aux femmes; Racisme/xénophobie/antisémitisme; Relations internationales/coopération/aide au développement; Relations économiques internationales/commerce/dette/finances; Réfugiés/migrants/groupes ethniques; Santé/assainissement/eau; Écologie/environnement/biodiversité. **Activités:** Conférences/séminaires/ateliers/activités de formation; Édition/documents audiovisuels/documents éducatifs.

BEL0189
COOPIBO PLATTELAND MET TOEKOMST IN NOOR EN ZUID
♦ Coopibo pour un monde rural viable au Nord et au Sud

Naamsesteenweg 573, 3001 Leuven-Heverlee, Belgique.

Téléphone: 32 (16) 40 31 31. *Fax:* 32 (16) 40 55 31. *Contact:* Jan Aertsem, Directeur.

OBJECTIFS: Exécuter des projets de développement qui visent à l'auto-organisation d'une population défavorisée et qui utilisent une méthode participative. Envoyer des coopérants dans les pays en développement. Promouvoir la solidarité internationale par la sensibilisation de l'opinion publique.

INFORMATIONS GENERALES: *Création:* 1962. *Affiliée à:* NCOS - Coprogram/INTERCODEV. *Personnel/Total:* 50. *Salariés:* 50 dont: 38 dans les pays en développement. *Budget/Total 1993:* ECU 3460000 (US$ 4047000). *Sources financières:* Privé: 29%. Public: 70%. Autofinancement: 1%.

PUBLICATIONS: *Périodiques:* WISSEL-STROOM (4) - COURANT ALTERNATIF (4). *Rapport annuel. Liste des publications.*

EVALUATION/RECHERCHE: Rapports d'évaluation disponibles.

PREVISIONS D'ACTIVITES: Promouvoir une agriculture de qualité en Flandre et en Europe.

ACTIVITES DANS LES REGIONS EN DEVELOPPEMENT: Intervient directement dans les régions en développement. Intervient dans 9 pays. Maintient une présence locale sur le terrain. Intervient par l'intermédiaire d'organisations locales partenaires. **Actions de Développement durable:** Développement rural/agriculture; Développement urbain/habitat; Envoi de volontaires/experts/assistance technique; Questions relatives aux femmes; Santé/assainissement/eau. **Régions:** Afrique australe; Afrique centrale; Amérique du Sud; Mexique et Amerique centrale.

Voir : *Comment utiliser le répertoire,* page 11.

ACTIVITES D'INFORMATION ET D'EDUCATION: **Domaines:** Développement rural/agriculture; Développement urbain/habitat; Santé/assainissement/eau. **Activités:** Campagnes d'information/expositions; Lobbying/plaidoyer; Édition/documents audiovisuels/documents éducatifs; Éducation formelle.

BEL0190
COPROGRAM

Vlasfabriekstraat 11, 1060 Bruxelles, Belgique.

Téléphone: 32 (2) 539 35 46. *Fax:* 32 (2) 539 13 43. *Contact:* Mich Roegiers, Secrétaire générale.

OBJECTIFS: Fédérer des ONG pour faire face aux instances officielles belges et européennes. Défendre les intérêts des ONG, améliorer la qualité du travail par des études et par la formation, stimuler la collaboration entre ONG. Promouvoir les ONG.

INFORMATIONS GENERALES: *Création:* 1964. *Type d'organisation:* regroupement d'ONG. *Organisations membres:* 65. *Personnel/Total:* 8. *Salariés:* 8. *Budget/Total 1993:* ECU 346000 (US$ 405000). *Sources financières:* Public: 94%. Autofinancement: 6%.

COMMENTAIRES: Les activités de la fédération sont organisées en fonction des relations Etat-ONG. Elles n'ont donc pas d'impact direct sur l'opinion publique, ni sur des activités de développement.

BEL0191
COUNCIL OF EUROPEAN NATIONAL YOUTH COMMITTEES (CENYC)

Chaussée de Wavre 517-519, 1040 Brussels, Belgium.

Telephone: 32 (2) 648 91 01. *Fax:* 32 (2) 648 96 40. *Contact:* Rosie Dunn, President.

OBJECTIVES: To foster co-operation among young people in Europe and between members of National Youth Councils. To represent National Youth Councils in Europe. To fight for democratic participation. To raise awareness of mutual respect and understanding.

GENERAL INFORMATION: *Creation:* 1964. *Member organisations:* 30. *Affiliated to:* WAY (Denmark). *Personnel/Total:* 3. *Salaried:* 3. *Budget/Total 1993:* ECU 312000 (US$ 365000). *Financial sources:* Private: 1%. Public: 30%. Self-financing: 69%.

PUBLICATIONS: *Periodicals:* CENYC Scene (4) - Youth Opinion (6). *Annual report.*

EVALUATION/RESEARCH: Evaluation reports available.

COMMENTS: The member organisations of CENYC undertake activities in developing countries. Undertakes activities in the Commonwealth of Independent States. Information activities related to the Commonwealth of Independent States.

INFORMATION AND EDUCATION ACTIVITIES: Topics: Children/youth/family; Ecology/environment/biodiversity; Gender issues/women; Human rights/peace/conflicts; International relations/cooperation/development aid; Peace/ethnic conflicts/armament/disarmament; Population/family planning/demography; Racism/xenophobia/antisemitism; Refugees/migrants/ethnic groups. **Activities:** Conferences/seminars/workshops/training activities; Exchanges/twinning/linking; Fund raising; Information and documentation services/data bases; Information campaigns/exhibitions; Lobbying/advocacy; Networking/electronic telecommunications; Publishing/audiovisual materials/educational materials.

BEL0192
CROIX ROUGE DE BELGIQUE ♦ Belgian Red Cross

Chaussée de Vleurgat 98, 1050 Bruxelles, Belgique.

Téléphone: 32 (2) 645 44 11. *Fax:* 32 (2) 640 31 96. *Contact:* Philippe Laurent, Directeur général.

OBJECTIFS: Assister les sociétés nationales de la Croix-Rouge dans les pays en développement.

INFORMATIONS GENERALES: *Création:* 1864. *Affiliée à:* Comité international de la Croix-Rouge (Suisse) - Fédération internationale des Sociétés Croix-Rouge et Croissant-Rouge. *Personnel/Total:* 25300. *Salariés:* 2150 dont: 16 dans les pays en développement. *Béné-*

voles: 23134. *Budget/Total 1993:* ECU 98848000 (US$ 115617000). *Sources financières:* Privé: 45%. Public: 45%. Autofinancement: 10%.

PUBLICATIONS: *Périodiques:* Journal de la Croix-Rouge (4). *Rapport annuel. Liste des publications.*

EVALUATION/RECHERCHE: Rapports d'évaluation disponibles.

COMMENTAIRES: Intervient dans la Communauté des Etats indépendants. Activités d'information concernant la Communauté des Etats indépendants.

ACTIVITES DANS LES REGIONS EN DEVELOPPEMENT: Intervient directement dans les régions en développement. Intervient dans 16 pays. Maintient une présence locale sur le terrain. Intervient par l'intermédiaire d'organisations locales partenaires. **Actions de Développement durable:** Développement rural/agriculture; Enfants/jeunesse/famille; Envoi de volontaires/experts/assistance technique; Petites entreprises/secteur informel/artisanat; Questions relatives aux femmes; Santé/assainissement/eau; Secours d'urgence/réfugiés/aide humanitaire; Écologie/environnement/biodiversité; Éducation/formation/alphabétisation. **Régions:** Afrique australe; Afrique centrale; Afrique de l'Est; Afrique de l'Ouest; Asie centrale et Asie du Sud; Asie du Sud-Est.

ACTIVITES D'INFORMATION ET D'EDUCATION: Domaines: Aliments/famine; Droits de l'Homme/paix/conflits; Développement rural/agriculture; Enfants/jeunesse/famille; Paix/conflits ethniques/armement/désarmement; Pauvreté/conditions de vie; Questions relatives aux femmes; Relations économiques internationales/commerce/dette/finances; Réfugiés/migrants/groupes ethniques; Santé/assainissement/eau; Secours d'urgence/réfugiés/aide humanitaire; Éducation/formation/alphabétisation. **Activités:** Campagnes d'information/expositions; Collecte de fonds; Conférences/séminaires/ateliers/activités de formation; Lobbying/plaidoyer; Radiodiffusion/manifestations culturelles; Services d'information et de documentation/bases de données; Échanges/parrainage/jumelage; Édition/documents audiovisuels/documents éducatifs; Éducation formelle.

BEL0193
CULTURE ET DEVELOPPEMENT

Rue Joseph II 172-174, 1040 Bruxelles, Belgique.

Téléphone: 32 (2) 230 46 37. *Fax:* 32 (2) 231 14 13. *Contact:* Edith Sizoo et Thierry VERHELST.

BEL0194
DAMIAANAKTIE ♦ Fondation Damien

Bld Leopold II, 263, 1080 Bruxelles, Belgique.

Téléphone: 32 (2) 422 59 11. *Fax:* 32 (2) 422 59 00. *Contact:* Rigo Peeters, Secrétaire général.

OBJECTIFS: Participer activement à la lutte contre la lèpre et la tuberculose et dipenser des soins de santé aux lépreux et aux tuberculeux dans les pays en développement. Sensibiliser l'opinion publique belge au problème de la lèpre.

INFORMATIONS GENERALES: *Création:* 1964. *Affiliée à:* International Association of Anti-Leprosy Organisations (Royaume-Uni) - ILEP. *Personnel/Total:* 38. *Salariés:* 38 dont: 20 dans les pays en développement. *Budget/Total 1993:* ECU 7414000 (US$ 8671000). *Sources financières:* Privé: 89%. Public: 5%. Autofinancement: 6%.

PUBLICATIONS: *Périodiques:* DAMIAANAKTIEKRANT (4) - PERSPECTIVES (4). *Rapport annuel. Liste des publications.*

EVALUATION/RECHERCHE: Rapports d'évaluation disponibles. Entreprend des activités de recherche.

ACTIVITES DANS LES REGIONS EN DEVELOPPEMENT: Intervient directement dans les régions en développement. Intervient dans 12 pays. Maintient une présence locale sur le terrain. Intervient par l'intermédiaire d'organisations locales partenaires. **Actions de Développement durable:** Santé/assainissement/eau. **Régions:** Afrique centrale; Afrique de l'Ouest; Asie centrale et Asie du Sud; Caraïbes.

ACTIVITES D'INFORMATION ET D'EDUCATION: Domaines: Santé/assainissement/eau. **Activités:** Campagnes d'information/expositions; Collecte de fonds; Conférences/séminaires/ateliers/activités de forma-

See: *How to Use the Directory,* page 11.

tion; Radiodiffusion/manifestations culturelles; Services d'information et de documentation/bases de données; Édition/documents audiovisuels/documents éducatifs.

BEL0195
DESENVOLVIMENTO INTEGRAL SUDOESTE DO PARANA-BRAZIL (DISOP)

Rue de Spa 32, 1040 Bruxelles, Belgique.

Téléphone: 32 (2) 230 17 92. *Contact:* A.F. Caekelbergh, Président.

BEL0196
DON BOSCO DIENSTBETOON ♦ Entraide de Don Bosco

Verenigde Natieslaan 100, 2710 Antwerpen, Belgium.

Telephone: 32 (2) 827 96 67. *Contact:* A. Boone, President.

BEL0197
DROITS DE L'HOMME SANS FRONTIERES (DHSF)

BP 1, 7090 Braine-le-Comte, Belgique.

Téléphone: 32 (67) 33 39 95. *Fax:* 32 (67) 33 63 45. *Contact:* Willy Fautre.

OBJECTIFS: Défendre les Droits de l'Homme, de la démocratie et de l'Etat de Droit, par l'organisation d'enquêtes, la publication de dossiers, la tenue de conférences de presse. Promouvoir le développement des pays du Tiers-Monde et le droit à l'éducation.

INFORMATIONS GENERALES: *Création:* 1988. *Personnel/Total:* 30. *Bénévoles:* 30. *Budget/Total 1993:* ECU 30000 (US$ 35000). *Sources financières:* Public: 4%. Autofinancement: 96%.

PUBLICATIONS: *Périodiques:* Droits de l'Homme sans Frontières (6). *Liste des publications.*

EVALUATION/RECHERCHE: Rapports d'évaluation disponibles. Entreprend des activités de recherche.

PREVISIONS D'ACTIVITES: L'organisation projette de transformer des prisons en écoles au Burundi.

COMMENTAIRES: L'ONG mène des enquêtes sur le terrain (Grèce, Rwanda, Burundi) et intervient par l'envoi de lettres et la publication de dossiers.

ACTIVITES DANS LES REGIONS EN DEVELOPPEMENT: Intervient dans 45 pays. **Actions de Développement durable:** Droits de l'Homme/paix/conflits. **Régions:** Afrique australe; Afrique centrale; Afrique de l'Est; Afrique de l'Ouest; Afrique du Nord; Moyen-Orient.

ACTIVITES D'INFORMATION ET D'EDUCATION: Domaines: Culture/tradition/religion; Droits de l'Homme/paix/conflits; Paix/conflits ethniques/armement/désarmement; Réfugiés/migrants/groupes ethniques. **Activités:** Campagnes d'information/expositions; Collecte de fonds; Conférences/séminaires/ateliers/activités de formation; Lobbying/plaidoyer; Services d'information et de documentation/bases de données.

BEL0198
EARTH ACTION

Boulevard Brand Whitlock 146, 1200 Brussels, Belgium.

Telephone: 32 (2) 736 80 52. *Fax:* 32 (2) 735 99 50. *Contact:* Nicholas Dunlop, International Co-ordinator.

OBJECTIVES: To generate political will by encouraging our 1000 partners. To take part in our monthly campaigns on environment, development, peace and human rights.

GENERAL INFORMATION: *Creation:* 1991. *Type of organisation:* network. *Member organisations:* 1000. *Personnel/Total:* 9. *Salaried:* 9 of which: 1 in developing countries. *Financial sources:* Private: 20%. Public: 80%.

PUBLICATIONS: Annual report. List of publications.

EVALUATION/RESEARCH: Evaluation reports available.

PLANNED ACTIVITIES: Working on desertification and habitat. Implementing of the decisions taken at the Cairo conference on population and the Social Summit.

COMMENTS: Information activities related to the Commonwealth of Independent States.

ACTIVITIES IN DEVELOPING REGIONS: Active in 50 country(ies). Maintains local field presence. Works through local field partners. **Sustainable Development Actions:** Children/youth/family; Debt/finance/trade; Democracy/good governance/institution building/participatory development; Ecology/environment/biodiversity; Emergency relief/refugees/humanitarian assistance; Energy/transport; Food/famine; Gender issues/women; Health/sanitation/water; Human rights/peace/conflicts; Population/family planning/demography; Rural development/agriculture; Urban development/habitat. **Regions:** Caribbean; Central Africa; Central Asia and South Asia; East Africa; East Asia; Mexico and Central America; Middle East; North Africa; Oceania; South America; South East Asia; Southern Africa; West Africa.

INFORMATION AND EDUCATION ACTIVITIES: Topics: Children/youth/family; Culture/tradition/religion; Ecology/environment/biodiversity; Emergency relief/refugees/humanitarian assistance; Employment/unemployment; Food/famine; Gender issues/women; Health/sanitation/water; Human rights/peace/conflicts; International economic relations/trade/debt/finance; International relations/cooperation/development aid; Peace/ethnic conflicts/armament/disarmament; Population/family planning/demography; Poverty/living conditions; Racism/xenophobia/antisemitism; Refugees/migrants/ethnic groups; Rural development/agriculture; Urban development/habitat. **Activities:** Exchanges/twinning/linking; Fund raising; Information campaigns/exhibitions; Lobbying/advocacy; Networking/electronic telecommunications.

BEL0199
EDUCATION INTERNATIONAL

Maison Syndicale Internationale - Ilot 6 Bloc C, 155 bld Emile Jacqmain, 1210 Brussels, Belgium.

Telephone: 32 (2) 224 06 21. *Fax:* 32 (2) 224 06 06. *Contact:* Fred van Leeuwen, General Secretary.

OBJECTIVES: To promote the status, interests and welfare of teachers and their organisations'rights. To promote the application of the Universal Declaration of Human Rights through the development of education. To promote the International Labour Standards. To encourage the leadership role and involvement of women in society.

GENERAL INFORMATION: *Creation:* 1993. *Type of organisation:* association of NGOs. *Member organisations:* 236. *Personnel/Total:* 29. *Salaried:* 26 of which: 11 in developing countries. *Volunteers:* 3. *Budget/Total 1993:* ECU 3513000 (US$ 4108000). *Financial sources:* Private: 2%. Self-financing: 98%.

PUBLICATIONS: *Periodicals:* Education International (3) - Monitor (12). *Annual report. List of publications.*

EVALUATION/RESEARCH: Evaluation reports available. Undertakes research activities.

COMMENTS: Undertakes activities in the Commonwealth of Independent States. Information activities related to the Commonwealth of Independent States.

ACTIVITIES IN DEVELOPING REGIONS: Present in developing regions. Active in 130 country(ies). Maintains local field presence. Works through local field partners. **Sustainable Development Actions:** Children/youth/family; Democracy/good governance/institution building/participatory development; Education/training/literacy; Gender issues/women; Human rights/peace/conflicts; Sending volunteers/experts/technical assistance. **Regions:** Caribbean; Central Africa; Central Asia and South Asia; East Africa; East Asia; Mexico and Central America; Middle East; North Africa; Oceania; South America; South East Asia; Southern Africa; West Africa.

INFORMATION AND EDUCATION ACTIVITIES: Topics: Children/youth/family; Education/training/literacy; Gender issues/women; Human rights/peace/conflicts; International economic relations/trade/debt/finance; International relations/cooperation/development aid; Other; Peace/ethnic conflicts/armament/disarmament; Racism/xenophobia/antisemitism. **Activities:** Conferences/seminars/workshops/training activities; Fund

Voir : *Comment utiliser le répertoire,* page 11.

raising; Information and documentation services/data bases; Information campaigns/exhibitions; Lobbying/advocacy.

BEL0200

EDUCATION SANITAIRE ET NUTRITIONNELLE EN AFRIQUE CENTRALE (ESNAC)

Rue Brialmont 11, 1030 Bruxelles, Belgique.

Téléphone: 32 (2) 217 04 97. *Contact:* Moeremans d'Emaus, Présidente.

OBJECTIFS: Former et porter assistance aux populations du Zaïre, du Rwanda et du Burundi dans leur lutte contre la malnutrition et les maladies contagieuses.

INFORMATIONS GENERALES: *Création:* 1933. *Personnel/Total:* 126. *Salariés:* 120 dont: 120 dans les pays en développement. *Bénévoles:* 6 dont: 2 dans les pays en développement. *Budget/Total 1993:* ECU 82000 (US$ 96000). *Sources financières:* Privé: 95%. Autofinancement: 5%.

PUBLICATIONS: *Périodiques:* ESNAC (4) - Kontakblad (4).

COMMENTAIRES: L'ESNAC pourrait arrêter ses activités en 1995; l'Organisme MEMISA BELGIQUE prendrait sa relève.

ACTIVITES DANS LES REGIONS EN DEVELOPPEMENT: Intervient directement dans les régions en développement. Intervient dans 3 pays. Maintient une présence locale sur le terrain. Intervient par l'intermédiaire d'organisations locales partenaires. **Actions de Développement durable:** Développement rural/agriculture; Envoi de volontaires/experts/assistance technique; Population/planning familial/démographie; Questions relatives aux femmes; Santé/assainissement/eau; Écologie/environnement/biodiversité; Éducation/formation/alphabétisation. **Régions:** Afrique centrale.

BEL0201

ENFANCE TIERS-MONDE

Rue Rennequin Sualem 13, 4000 Liège, Belgique.

Téléphone: 32 (41) 54 26 71. *Contact:* Christian Modave.

OBJECTIFS: Aider financièrement les familles, les enfants et les populations des bidonvilles. Améliorer leur condition de vie, grâce aux collectes de fonds à travers la vente d'un périodique mensuel. Aider activement sur le terrain, grâce à l'agrément de l'AGCD qui permet d'envoyer des coopérants belges dans les régions déshéritées.

INFORMATIONS GENERALES: *Création:* 1967.

PUBLICATIONS: *Périodiques:* Enfance sans Frontières (12) - Kinderen Zonder Grenzen (12).

ACTIVITES DANS LES REGIONS EN DEVELOPPEMENT: Intervient directement dans les régions en développement. Intervient dans 12 pays. Maintient une présence locale sur le terrain. Intervient par l'intermédiaire d'organisations locales partenaires. **Actions de Développement durable:** Aliments/famine; Démocratie/bonne gestion publique/création d'institutions/développement participatif; Développement rural/agriculture; Développement urbain/habitat; Enfants/jeunesse/famille; Envoi de volontaires/experts/assistance technique; Santé/assainissement/eau; Secours d'urgence/réfugiés/aide humanitaire; Éducation/formation/alphabétisation; Énergie/transport. **Régions:** Afrique centrale; Afrique de l'Ouest; Amérique du Sud; Asie centrale et Asie du Sud; Mexique et Amerique centrale.

ACTIVITES D'INFORMATION ET D'EDUCATION: Domaines: Aliments/famine; Développement urbain/habitat; Enfants/jeunesse/famille; Pauvreté/conditions de vie; Questions relatives aux femmes; Réfugiés/migrants/groupes ethniques; Santé/assainissement/eau; Secours d'urgence/réfugiés/aide humanitaire; Éducation/formation/alphabétisation. **Activités:** Collecte de fonds; Échanges/parrainage/jumelage.

BEL0202

ENTRAIDE ET AMITIE

Rue du Boulet 9, 1000 Bruxelles , Belgique.

Téléphone: 32 (2) 512 36 32. *Contact:* Philippe Dekerck, Coordinateur.

OBJECTIFS: Promouvoir l'engagement gratuit des jeunes au service d'une collectivité où la solidarité active et le sens de l'Autre sont plus que jamais les conditions sine qua non de son développement harmonieux.

INFORMATIONS GENERALES: *Création:* 1962. *Personnel/Total:* 9. *Salariés:* 7. *Bénévoles:* 2. *Budget/Total 1993:* ECU 134000 (US$ 157000). *Sources financières:* Public: 46%. Autofinancement: 54%.

PUBLICATIONS: *Périodiques:* ENTRAM (4). *Rapport annuel. Liste des publications.*

COMMENTAIRES: Intervient dans la Communauté des Etats indépendants. Activités d'information concernant la Communauté des Etats indépendants.

ACTIVITES DANS LES REGIONS EN DEVELOPPEMENT: Intervient directement dans les régions en développement. Intervient dans 30 pays. Intervient par l'intermédiaire d'organisations locales partenaires. **Actions de Développement durable:** Développement urbain/habitat; Enfants/jeunesse/famille; Santé/assainissement/eau; Éducation/formation/alphabétisation. **Régions:** Afrique centrale; Afrique de l'Ouest; Afrique du Nord; Asie centrale et Asie du Sud.

ACTIVITES D'INFORMATION ET D'EDUCATION: Domaines: Enfants/jeunesse/famille; Santé/assainissement/eau. **Activités:** Campagnes d'information/expositions; Conférences/séminaires/ateliers/activités de formation; Éducation formelle.

BEL0203

ENTRAIDE ET FRATERNITE ♦ Inter-AID and Fraternity

Rue du Gouvernement Provisoire 32, 1000 Bruxelles, Belgique.

Téléphone: 32 (2) 219 19 83. *Fax:* 32 (2) 217 32 59. *Contact:* J. Vellut, Coordinateur national.

OBJECTIFS: Soutenir financièrement des projets de développement dans certains pays d'Afrique,d'Amérique Latine et d'Asie, sans discrimination philosophique. Mettre en place des programmes d'éducation au développement et de lobbying dans les communautés francophone et germanophone de Belgique, notamment auprès du public chrétien.

INFORMATIONS GENERALES: *Création:* 1961. *Affiliée à:* Coopération Internationale pour le Développement et la Solidarité - Centre National de Coopération au Développement - Association des ONG francophones et germanophones (Belgique) - Réseau pour l'éducation au développement.. *Personnel/Total:* 32. *Salariés:* 24. *Bénévoles:* 8. *Budget/Total 1993:* ECU 2965000 (US$ 3469000). *Sources financières:* Privé: 80%. Public: 10%. Autofinancement: 10%.

PUBLICATIONS: *Périodiques:* Partenaires (4) - Flash (12) - Voix du Tiers-Monde (4). *Rapport annuel.*

ACTIVITES DANS LES REGIONS EN DEVELOPPEMENT: Intervient directement dans les régions en développement. Intervient dans 30 pays. Intervient par l'intermédiaire d'organisations locales partenaires. **Actions de Développement durable:** Dette/finances/commerce; Droits de l'Homme/paix/conflits; Démocratie/bonne gestion publique/création d'institutions/développement participatif; Développement rural/agriculture; Développement urbain/habitat; Enfants/jeunesse/famille; Petites entreprises/secteur informel/artisanat; Questions relatives aux femmes; Santé/assainissement/eau; Écologie/environnement/biodiversité; Éducation/formation/alphabétisation. **Régions:** Afrique australe; Afrique centrale; Afrique de l'Ouest; Amérique du Sud; Asie centrale et Asie du Sud; Asie du Sud-Est; Mexique et Amerique centrale.

ACTIVITES D'INFORMATION ET D'EDUCATION: Domaines: Droits de l'Homme/paix/conflits; Développement rural/agriculture; Enfants/jeunesse/famille; Pauvreté/conditions de vie; Questions relatives aux femmes; Racisme/xénophobie/antisémitisme; Relations internationales/coopération/aide au développement; Relations économiques internationales/commerce/dette/finances; Réfugiés/migrants/groupes ethniques; Santé/assainissement/eau; Écologie/environnement/biodiversité. **Activités:** Campagnes d'information/expositions; Collecte de fonds; Conférences/séminaires/ateliers/activités de formation; Lobbying/plaidoyer; Radiodiffusion/manifestations culturelles; Services d'information et de documentation/bases de données; Échanges/parrainage/jumelage; Édition/documents audiovisuels/documents éducatifs.

See: *How to Use the Directory,* page 11.

BEL0204

ENVIRONMENT AND DEVELOPMENT RESOURCE CENTRE (EDRC)

Boulevard Brand Whitlock 146, 1200 Brussels, Belgium.

Telephone: 32 (2) 736 80 50. *Fax:* 32 (2) 733 57 08.

BEL0205

EQUILIBRE - BELGIQUE

Boulevard Louis Schmidt 56, 1040 Bruxelles, Belgique.

BEL0206

ESPACE ET COOPERATION

Rue des Echevins 72, 1050 Bruxelles, Belgique.

Téléphone: 32 (2) 647 57 75. *Fax:* 32 (2) 647 57 75. *Contact:* Marc Gosse, Président.

OBJECTIFS: Etablir des programmes de formation pour des cadres africains

INFORMATIONS GENERALES: *Création:* 1986. *Type d'organisation:* réseau. *Affiliée à:* European Group for Local Employment Initiative - Réseau DPH. *Personnel/Total:* 3. *Salariés:* 1. *Bénévoles:* 2. *Budget/ Total 1993:* ECU 30000 (US\$ 35000). *Sources financières:* Autofinancement: 100%.

PUBLICATIONS: *Périodiques:* "Bulletin d'Espace et Coopération" (4).

ACTIVITES DANS LES REGIONS EN DEVELOPPEMENT: Intervient par l'intermédiaire d'organisations locales partenaires. **Actions de Développement durable:** Démocratie/bonne gestion publique/création d'institutions/développement participatif; Éducation/formation/alphabétisation. **Régions:** Afrique de l'Ouest.

ACTIVITES D'INFORMATION ET D'EDUCATION: Domaines: Culture/ tradition/religion; Droits de l'Homme/paix/conflits; Développement urbain/habitat. **Activités:** Campagnes d'information/expositions; Services d'information et de documentation/bases de données; Échanges/ parrainage/jumelage; Édition/documents audiovisuels/documents éducatifs.

BEL0207

EURO CITIZEN ACTION SERVICE (ECAS)

98 rue du Trône, Boîte 8, 1050 Bruxelles, Belgique.

Téléphone: 32 (2) 512 93 60. *Fax:* 32 (2) 512 66 73. *Contact:* Tony Venables, Directeur.

BEL0208

EURO-CARITAS - CARITAS EUROPA (EURO-CARITAS)

Rue du Commerce 70, 1040 Bruxelles, Belgique.

Téléphone: 32 (2) 280 02 80. *Fax:* 32 (2) 230 16 58. *Contact:* Rév. Père Klein, Président.

BEL0209

EURODIAKONIA

Boulevard Charlemagne 28, 1040 Bruxelles, Belgique.

BEL0210

EURONAID

10 Square Ambriorix, 1040 Brussels, Belgium.

BEL0211

EUROPEAN BUREAU FOR CONSERVATION AND DEVELOPMENT

9 rue de la Science, 1040 Brussels, Belgium.

Telephone: 32 (2) 230 30 70. *Fax:* 32 (2) 230 82 72. *Contact:* Despina Symons, Director.

OBJECTIVES: To contribute to the promotion and conservation of European natural species. To work towards the objectives of the World Conservation Strategy.

GENERAL INFORMATION: *Creation:* 1989. *Affiliated to:* IUCN (Switzerland). *Personnel/Total:* 7. *Salaried:* 7. *Budget/ Total 1993:* ECU 247000 (US\$ 289000). *Financial sources:* Private: 20%. Public: 30%. Self-financing: 50%.

PUBLICATIONS: *Periodicals:* EBCD Newsletter (6).

EVALUATION/RESEARCH: Undertakes research activities.

PLANNED ACTIVITIES: Undertaking an information campaign on renewable energy.

ACTIVITIES IN DEVELOPING REGIONS: Active in 5 country(ies). Works through local field partners. **Sustainable Development Actions:** Ecology/environment/biodiversity; Rural development/agriculture. **Regions:** South East Asia; Southern Africa; West Africa.

INFORMATION AND EDUCATION ACTIVITIES: Topics: Ecology/environment/biodiversity; Rural development/agriculture. **Activities:** Conferences/seminars/workshops/training activities; Formal education; Fund raising; Information and documentation services/data bases; Information campaigns/exhibitions; Lobbying/advocacy.

BEL0212

EUROPEAN CONSULTATION ON REFUGEES AND EXILES (ECRE)

Rue Defacqz 1, 1050 Bruxelles, Belgique.

Contact: Peter Sluiter.

BEL0213

EUROPEAN COORDINATION BUREAU

Rue du Marteau 19, 1040 Bruxelles, Belgium.

Telephone: 32 (2) 217 56 32.

BEL0214

EUROPEAN ECUMENICAL ORGANIZATION FOR DEVELOPMENT (EECOD) ♦ Service oecuménique européen pour le développement

Rue Joseph II, 174, 1040 Bruxelles, Belgique.

Téléphone: 32 (2) 230 61 05. *Fax:* 32 (2) 231 14 13. *Contact:* Peter Crossman, Secrétaire général.

OBJECTIFS: Informer les Eglises et organisations chrétiennes membres de la politique de développement des communautés Européennes. Faire du lobbying au nom des membres auprès de la Communauté Européenne afin que celle-ci s'oriente vers une politique globalement plus favorable aux pays en développement. Etablir des contacts avec des ONG d'Europe du Sud.

INFORMATIONS GENERALES: *Création:* 1975. *Type d'organisation:* regroupement d'ONG, réseau. *Organisations membres:* 25. *Personnel/Total:* 3. *Salariés:* 3. *Budget/Total 1993:* ECU 121000 (US\$ 141000). *Sources financières:* Autofinancement: 100%.

PUBLICATIONS: *Rapport annuel. Liste des publications.*

EVALUATION/RECHERCHE: Rapports d'évaluation disponibles. Entreprend des activités de recherche.

ACTIVITES DANS LES REGIONS EN DEVELOPPEMENT: Intervient par l'intermédiaire d'organisations locales partenaires.

ACTIVITES D'INFORMATION ET D'EDUCATION: Domaines: Aliments/ famine; Culture/tradition/religion; Droits de l'Homme/paix/conflits; Développement rural/agriculture; Paix/conflits ethniques/armement/désarmement; Population/planning familial/démographie; Questions relatives aux femmes; Relations internationales/coopération/aide au développement; Relations économiques internationales/commerce/dette/finances; Écologie/environnement/biodiversité. **Activités:** Conférences/séminaires/ateliers/activités de formation; Lobbying/plaidoyer; Services d'information et de documentation/bases de données; Édition/documents audiovisuels/documents éducatifs.

Voir : *Comment utiliser le répertoire,* page 11.

BEL0215

EUROPEAN NETWORK ON DEBT AND DEVELOPMENT (EURODAD)

Square Ambiorix 10, 1040 Bruxelles, Belgium.

Telephone: 32 (2) 732 70 07. *Fax:* 32 (2) 732 19 34. *E-mail:* EURORAD@gn.apc.org. *Contact:* Ted van Hees, Coordinator.

OBJECTIVES: To draw attention to the "debt crisis" in the developing countries. To co-ordinate and support advocacy work of NGOs pressing for reduction in the burden of Third World debt.

GENERAL INFORMATION: *Type of organisation:* network. *Member organisations:* 16. *Affiliated to:* Debt Treaty Movement (Canada). *Personnel/Total:* 3. Salaried: 2. Volunteers: 1. *Budget/Total 1993:* ECU 157000 (US$ 184000). *Financial sources:* Public: 40%. Self-financing: 60%.

PUBLICATIONS: *Periodicals:* Third World Debt in the 1990s (3) - La dette du Tiers-Monde dans les années 90 (3). *Annual report. List of publications.*

EVALUATION/RESEARCH: Undertakes research activities.

ACTIVITIES IN DEVELOPING REGIONS: Works through local field partners.

INFORMATION AND EDUCATION ACTIVITIES: Topics: International economic relations/trade/debt/finance. **Activities:** Conferences/seminars/workshops/training activities; Information and documentation services/data bases; Information campaigns/exhibitions; Lobbying/advocacy.

BEL0216

EUROPEAN SOLIDARITY TOWARDS EQUAL PARTICIPATION OF PEOPLE (EUROSTEP)

Rue Stévin 115, 1040 Bruxelles, Belgium.

Telephone: 32 (2) 231 16 59. *Fax:* 32 (2) 230 37 80. *E-mail:* geo2.EUROSTEP:greenNet:EUROSTEP. *Contact:* Simon Stocker, Director.

OBJECTIVES: To influence official development policies of national governments, the EU and multilateral institutions and to advocate development models based on the perspectives of the NGDOs. To improve the quality and effectiveness of development aid offered by NGDOs.

GENERAL INFORMATION: *Creation:* 1990. *Type of organisation:* network. *Member organisations:* 23. *Personnel/Total:* 5. Salaried: 3. Volunteers: 2. *Budget/Total 1993:* ECU 183000 (US$ 214000). *Financial sources:* Self-financing: 100%.

PUBLICATIONS: *Periodicals:* EUROSTEP News (6). *Annual report.*

EVALUATION/RESEARCH: Evaluation reports available.

PLANNED ACTIVITIES: Specific programmes on: Africa; Peace and Recovery; Gender and Development; Lomé IV Review; Trade and Development; Shadow DAC Report; Monitoring the EC institutions; Bretton Woods institutions.

COMMENTS: Undertakes activities in the Commonwealth of Independent States.

ACTIVITIES IN DEVELOPING REGIONS: Works through local field partners.

INFORMATION AND EDUCATION ACTIVITIES: Topics: Ecology/environment/biodiversity; Emergency relief/refugees/humanitarian assistance; Gender issues/women; International economic relations/trade/debt/finance; International relations/cooperation/development aid; Population/family planning/demography; Poverty/living conditions. **Activities:** Lobbying/advocacy.

BEL0217

THE EUROPEAN YWCAS

Avenue Brugmann 94, 1060 Bruxelles, Belgique.

Téléphone: 32 (2) 344 98 61. *Fax:* 32 (2) 346 59 46. *Contact:* Anita Andersson, Président.

OBJECTIFS: Participer aux rencontres des YWCAs en Europe pour discuter des questions communes et d'intérêt général en Europe et promouvoir le programme de la World YWCA.

INFORMATIONS GENERALES: *Création:* 1971. *Organisations membres:* 19. *Personnel/Total:* var. Salariés: 1. Bénévoles: var. *Budget/Total 1993:* ECU 30000 (US$ 35000). *Sources financières:* Privé: 20%. Public: 50%. Autofinancement: 30%.

PUBLICATIONS: *Périodiques:* Eurinfo (4). *Liste des publications.*

EVALUATION/RECHERCHE: Rapports d'évaluation disponibles.

COMMENTAIRES: Intervient dans la Communauté des Etats indépendants. Activités d'information concernant la Communauté des Etats indépendants.

ACTIVITES DANS LES REGIONS EN DEVELOPPEMENT: Intervient par l'intermédiaire d'organisations locales partenaires.

BEL0218

FEDERATION DES SCOUTS CATHOLIQUES - SCOUTS BADEN POWELL DE BELGIQUE (FSC-SBPB)

Rue de Dublin 21, 1050 Bruxelles, Belgique.

Téléphone: 32 (2) 512 46 91. *Fax:* 32 (2) 511 46 87. *Contact:* Arnaud Gorgemans.

OBJECTIFS: Former de jeunes dans l'esprit du scoutisme et de la solidarité internationale. Contribuer à des actions de développement communautaire, en impliquant dans ces actions les membres de la Fédération.

INFORMATIONS GENERALES: *Création:* 1937. *Type d'organisation:* réseau. *Affiliée à:* World Scout Organisation (Suisse). *Personnel/Total:* 8. Salariés: 3 dont: 2 dans les pays en développement. Bénévoles: 5. *Sources financières:* Public: 50%. Autofinancement: 50%.

PUBLICATIONS: *Périodiques:* Objectifs (6). *Rapport annuel. Liste des publications.*

EVALUATION/RECHERCHE: Rapports d'évaluation disponibles.

PREVISIONS D'ACTIVITES: Thème de l'année 1995-1996: "l'arbre".

COMMENTAIRES: Intervient dans la Communauté des Etats indépendants.

ACTIVITES DANS LES REGIONS EN DEVELOPPEMENT: Intervient directement dans les régions en développement. Intervient dans 7 pays. Maintient une présence locale sur le terrain. Intervient par l'intermédiaire d'organisations locales partenaires. **Actions de Développement durable:** Autres; Droits de l'Homme/paix/conflits; Démocratie/bonne gestion publique/création d'institutions/développement participatif; Développement rural/agriculture; Développement urbain/habitat; Enfants/jeunesse/famille; Envoi de volontaires/experts/assistance technique; Petites entreprises/secteur informel/artisanat; Santé/assainissement/eau; Secours d'urgence/réfugiés/aide humanitaire; Écologie/environnement/biodiversité; Éducation/formation/alphabétisation; Énergie/transport. **Régions:** Afrique centrale; Caraïbes.

ACTIVITES D'INFORMATION ET D'EDUCATION: Domaines: Autres; Culture/tradition/religion; Droits de l'Homme/paix/conflits; Enfants/jeunesse/famille; Paix/conflits ethniques/armement/désarmement; Pauvreté/conditions de vie; Racisme/xénophobie/antisémitisme; Relations internationales/coopération/aide au développement; Relations économiques internationales/commerce/dette/finances; Réfugiés/migrants/groupes ethniques; Secours d'urgence/réfugiés/aide humanitaire; Écologie/environnement/biodiversité; Éducation/formation/alphabétisation. **Activités:** Campagnes d'information/expositions; Conférences/séminaires/ateliers/activités de formation; Lobbying/plaidoyer; Réseaux/télécommunications électroniques; Échanges/parrainage/jumelage; Édition/documents audiovisuels/documents éducatifs; Éducation formelle.

BEL0219

FEDERATION EUROPEENNE DES ASSOCIATIONS NATIONALES TRAVAILLANT AVEC LES SANS-ABRI (FEANTSA) ♦ European Federation of National Organisations Working with the Homeless

1 rue Defacqz, 1050 Brussels, Belgium.

Telephone: 32 (2) 538 66 69. *Fax:* 32 (2) 539 41 74. *Contact:* Brian Harvey, President.

See: *How to Use the Directory,* page 11.

OBJECTIVES: To alert the European institutions and national governments on homelessness as a phenomenon, to promote policies which will help the homeless in the Member States and to encourage the exchange of information between NGOs on that subject.

GENERAL INFORMATION: *Creation:* 1989. *Type of organisation:* network. *Member organisations:* 53. *Affiliated to:* European Anti Poverty Network (Belgium) - Europen Charter for the Right to Housing (France) - Habitat International Coalition (Mexico). *Personnel/Total:* 6. *Salaried:* 4. *Volunteers:* 2. *Budget/Total 1993:* ECU 400000 (US$ 468000). *Financial sources:* Private: 1%. Public: 98%. *Self-financing:* 1%.

PUBLICATIONS: *Annual report. List of publications.*

EVALUATION/RESEARCH: Undertakes research activities.

INFORMATION AND EDUCATION ACTIVITIES: Topics: Poverty/living conditions; Urban development/habitat. **Activities:** Conferences/seminars/workshops/training activities; Exchanges/twinning/linking; Information and documentation services/data bases; Information campaigns/exhibitions; Lobbying/advocacy.

BEL0220
FEDERATION INTERNATIONALE DES JOURNALISTES (FIJ)
♦ International Federation of Journalists

Boulevard Charlemagne 1, Bte 5, 1041 Bruxelles, Belgique.

Téléphone: 32 (2) 238 09 51. *Fax:* 32 (2) 230 36 33. *Contact:* Neal Swancott, Chargé du développement.

BEL0221
FEDERATION INTERNATIONALE DES MOUVEMENTS D'ADULTES RURAUX CATHOLIQUES (FIMARC) ♦ International Federation of Rural Adult Catholic Movements

Rue Jaumain 15, 5330 Assesse, Belgique.

Téléphone: 32 (83) 65 62 36. *Fax:* 32 (83) 65 61 41. *Contact:* Joseph Pirson, Secrétaire général.

OBJECTIFS: Promouvoir les échanges d'expérience, de réflexion entre organisations populaires rurales du Nord et du Sud.

INFORMATIONS GENERALES: *Création:* 1964. *Type d'organisation:* regroupement d'ONG. *Organisations membres:* 45. *Affiliée à:* Conférence des Organisations Internationales Catholiques. *Personnel/Total:* 4. *Salariés:* 2. *Bénévoles:* 2. *Budget/Total 1993:* ECU 114000 (US$ 133000). *Sources financières:* Privé: 75%. Public: 5%. *Autofinancement:* 20%.

PUBLICATIONS: *Périodiques:* Voix du monde rural (4). *Rapport annuel.*

EVALUATION/RECHERCHE: Entreprend des activités de recherche.

COMMENTAIRES: Intervient dans la Communauté des Etats indépendants.

ACTIVITES DANS LES REGIONS EN DEVELOPPEMENT: Intervient directement dans les régions en développement. Intervient dans 45 pays. Maintient une présence locale sur le terrain. Intervient par l'intermédiaire d'organisations locales partenaires. **Actions de Développement durable:** Droits de l'Homme/paix/conflits; Démocratie/bonne gestion publique/création d'institutions/développement participatif; Développement rural/agriculture; Petites entreprises/secteur informel/artisanat; Questions relatives aux femmes; Santé/assainissement/eau; Écologie/environnement/biodiversité; Éducation/formation/alphabétisation. **Régions:** Afrique australe; Afrique centrale; Afrique de l'Est; Afrique de l'Ouest; Afrique du Nord; Amérique du Sud; Asie centrale et Asie du Sud; Asie de l'Est; Asie du Sud-Est; Caraïbes; Mexique et Amerique centrale; Moyen-Orient.

ACTIVITES D'INFORMATION ET D'EDUCATION: Domaines: Culture/tradition/religion; Droits de l'Homme/paix/conflits; Développement rural/agriculture; Emploi/chômage; Paix/conflits ethniques/armement/désarmement; Pauvreté/conditions de vie; Questions relatives aux femmes; Racisme/xénophobie/antisémitisme; Relations internationales/coopération/aide au développement; Relations économiques internationales/commerce/dette/finances; Réfugiés/migrants/groupes ethniques; Santé/assainissement/eau; Écologie/environnement/biodiversité; Éducation/

formation/alphabétisation. **Activités:** Conférences/séminaires/ateliers/activités de formation; Échanges/parrainage/jumelage.

BEL0222
FEDERATION INTERNATIONALE SERV. AMERIQUE LATINE ET ASIE (SELAVIP)

Rue de la Station 69, 1640 Rhode St Genese, Belgique.

Téléphone: 32 (81) 22 90 64. *Contact:* R.P. Mahon.

BEL0223
FEDERATION OF UNESCO CLUBS (FEDUC VZW)

Sparrenweg 110, 3980 Tessenderlo, Belgium.

Telephone: 32 (13) 33 33 20.

BEL0224
FEED THE CHILDREN INTERNATIONAL (FTCI)

18 Lijsterbessenlaan, 3090 Overijse, Brussels, Belgium.

Telephone: 32 (2) 657 55 22. *Fax:* 32 (2) 657 55 22. *Contact:* Larry Jones, President.

OBJECTIVES: To deliver emergency relief and means by which communities can then develop sustainable futures for their children.

GENERAL INFORMATION: *Creation:* 1994. *Type of organisation:* coordinating body. *Member organisations:* 3. *Affiliated to:* Liaison Committee (Belgium) - ICVA (Switzerland) - ECAS (Belgium). *Personnel/Total:* 590. *Salaried:* 340 of which: 185 in developing countries. *Volunteers:* 250 of which: 100 in developing countries. *Budget/Total 1993:* ECU 90396000 (US$ 105888000). *Financial sources:* Private: 69%. Public: 30%. *Self-financing:* 1%.

PUBLICATIONS: *Periodicals:* Connexions (4) - Feed Back (4). *Annual report.*

EVALUATION/RESEARCH: Evaluation reports available.

PLANNED ACTIVITIES: Educational TV programme (30 min/week) in the US. Focus on street children. Focus on integrated rural programmes (development). Income generating projects. Fundamental research regarding the "aid business".

COMMENTS: Feed the Children International has been created this year as the main Switchboard between the three FTC offices (UK, Canada, US) and the 18 FTC field offices. It also aims at the development of a research basis with a more theoretical/philosophical approach to humanitarian aid and development issues. Undertakes activities in the Commonwealth of Independent States. Information activities related to the Commonwealth of Independent States.

ACTIVITIES IN DEVELOPING REGIONS: Present in developing regions. Active in 14 country(ies). Maintains local field presence. Works through local field partners. **Sustainable Development Actions:** Children/youth/family; Education/training/literacy; Emergency relief/refugees/humanitarian assistance; Food/famine; Health/sanitation/water; Population/family planning/demography; Rural development/agriculture; Small enterprises/informal sector/handicrafts. **Regions:** Caribbean; East Africa; Mexico and Central America; South East Asia.

INFORMATION AND EDUCATION ACTIVITIES: Topics: Children/youth/family; Education/training/literacy; Emergency relief/refugees/humanitarian assistance; Food/famine; Health/sanitation/water; International relations/cooperation/development aid; Poverty/living conditions; Refugees/migrants/ethnic groups; Rural development/agriculture. **Activities:** Conferences/seminars/workshops/training activities; Exchanges/twinning/linking; Formal education; Fund raising; Information campaigns/exhibitions; Lobbying/advocacy; Networking/electronic telecommunications; Publishing/audiovisual materials/educational materials.

BEL0225
FLEMISH KOMMISSIE RECHTVAADIGHEID EN VREDE ♦ FLEMISH JUSTICE AND PEACE COMMISSION

Rue Brialmontstraat 11/05, 1030 Brussels, Belgium.

Telephone: 32 (2) 218 63 48. *Fax:* 32 (2) 223 11 59.

Voir : *Comment utiliser le répertoire,* page 11.

BEL0226

FLEMISH ORGANIZATION FOR ASSISTANCE IN DEVELOPMENT (FADO)

Citadellaan 12, 9000 Gent, Belgique.

Téléphone: 32 (9) 220 83 24. *Fax:* 32 (9) 220 84 27. *Contact:* Etienne Bracke.

OBJECTIFS: Financer et soutenir des projets au Sud, en apportant une aide technique et méthodologique, et en fournissant du personnel. Sensibiliser les populations du Nord aux problèmes du développement.

INFORMATIONS GENERALES: *Création:* 1974. *Affiliée à:* NCOS (Belgique) - Coprogramm (Belgique) - Consortium dry land farming (Indonésie). *Personnel/Total:* 11. *Salariés:* 11 dont: 8 dans les pays en développement. *Budget/Total 1993:* ECU 373000 (US$ 437000). *Sources financières: Privé:* 11%. *Public:* 82%. *Autofinancement:* 7%.

PUBLICATIONS: *Périodiques:* SALAM (4). *Rapport annuel. Liste des publications.*

EVALUATION/RECHERCHE: Rapports d'évaluation disponibles.

ACTIVITES DANS LES REGIONS EN DEVELOPPEMENT: Intervient directement dans les régions en développement. Maintient une présence locale sur le terrain. Intervient par l'intermédiaire d'organisations locales partenaires. **Actions de Développement durable:** Développement rural/agriculture; Enfants/jeunesse/famille; Envoi de volontaires/ experts/assistance technique; Petites entreprises/secteur informel/artisanat; Éducation/formation/alphabétisation. **Régions:** Amérique du Sud; Asie du Sud-Est.

ACTIVITES D'INFORMATION ET D'EDUCATION: Domaines: Culture/ tradition/religion; Droits de l'Homme/paix/conflits; Développement rural/ agriculture; Enfants/jeunesse/famille; Paix/conflits ethniques/armement/ désarmement; Pauvreté/conditions de vie; Relations internationales/ coopération/aide au développement; Écologie/environnement/biodiversité. **Activités:** Campagnes d'information/expositions; Radiodiffusion/ manifestations culturelles; Services d'information et de documentation/ bases de données; Édition/documents audiovisuels/documents éducatifs.

BEL0227

FLEMISH PLATFORM FOR INTERNATIONAL YOUTH WORK (JINT)

Grétrystraat 26, 1000 Brussels, Belgium.

Telephone: 32 (2) 218 64 55. *Fax:* 32 (2) 219 46 55. *Contact:* Jan van de Broeck, Project Officer.

BEL0228

FLEMISH SUPPORT GROUP FOR INDIGENOUS PEOPLES (KWIA)

Breughelstraat 31-33, 2018 Antwerpen, Belgium.

Telephone: 32 (3) 218 84 88. *Fax:* 32 (2) 230 45 40. *Contact:* Wendel Trio, Coordinator.

BEL0229

FLORES VRIENDEN

Gebr. Van Eyckstraat 27, 9000 Gent, Belgique.

Téléphone: 32 (51) 23 32 51. *Contact:* M.E. Bracke, Directeur.

BEL0230

FONDATION ANDRE RYCKMANS (FAR)

Avenue du Maréchal Ney 38, 1410 Waterloo, Belgique.

Téléphone: 32 (2) 354 85 03. *Contact:* Geneviève Ryckmans, Présidente.

OBJECTIFS: Contribuer au développement agricole et sanitaire des pays en développement par des micro-projets. Attribuer tous les deux ans un prix à une personnalité marquante en matière de développement.

INFORMATIONS GENERALES: *Création:* 1962. *Type d'organisation:* regroupement d'ONG. *Organisations membres:* 90. *Affiliée à:* Association des ONG Francophones - Centre National de Coopération au

Développement. *Budget/Total 1993:* ECU 205000 (US$ 240000). *Sources financières: Privé:* 80%. *Public:* 10%. *Autofinancement:* 10%.

ACTIVITES DANS LES REGIONS EN DEVELOPPEMENT: Intervient directement dans les régions en développement. Intervient dans 3 pays. Intervient par l'intermédiaire d'organisations locales partenaires. **Actions de Développement durable:** Développement rural/agriculture; Petites entreprises/secteur informel/artisanat. **Régions:** Afrique centrale; Mexique et Amerique centrale.

BEL0231

FONDATION DE SOLIDARITE INTERNATIONALE (FSI)

33 rue de Trèves, 1040 Bruxelles, Belgique.

Téléphone: 32 (2) 230 62 95. *Fax:* 32 (2) 230 87 22. *Contact:* Tran Huu Hai, Directeur.

OBJECTIFS: Promouvoir la solidarité internationale. Aider à la formation et au développement

INFORMATIONS GENERALES: *Création:* 1963. *Personnel/Total:* 6. *Salariés:* 2. *Bénévoles:* 4. *Budget/Total 1993:* ECU 1740000 (US$ 2035000). *Sources financières: Privé:* 24%. *Public:* 51%. *Autofinancement:* 25%.

PUBLICATIONS: *Rapport annuel.*

PREVISIONS D'ACTIVITES: Les projets à venir seront consacrés en priorité à l'Afrique et à l'Asie.

COMMENTAIRES: Intervient dans la Communauté des Etats indépendants.

ACTIVITES DANS LES REGIONS EN DEVELOPPEMENT: Intervient par l'intermédiaire d'organisations locales partenaires. **Actions de Développement durable:** Éducation/formation/alphabétisation. **Régions:** Afrique centrale; Afrique de l'Est; Afrique de l'Ouest; Amérique du Sud; Asie centrale et Asie du Sud; Asie de l'Est; Asie du Sud-Est; Mexique et Amerique centrale.

ACTIVITES D'INFORMATION ET D'EDUCATION: Domaines: Droits de l'Homme/paix/conflits; Développement rural/agriculture; Pauvreté/conditions de vie; Questions relatives aux femmes; Relations internationales/ coopération/aide au développement; Éducation/formation/alphabétisation. **Activités:** Conférences/séminaires/ateliers/activités de formation.

BEL0232

FONDATION DES ROTARY CLUBS BELGES POUR LA COOPERATION AU DEVELOPPEMENT A.S.B.L

Avenue Eugene Plasky, 102 - B.14, 1040 Bruxelles, Belgique.

Téléphone: 32 (2) 734 64 08. *Fax:* 32 (2) 736 89 55 . *Contact:* R. Alexandre, Administrateur.

BEL0233

FONDATION MEDICALE DE L'UNIVERSITE CATHOLIQUE DE LOUVAIN EN AFRIQUE CENTRALE (FOMULAC)

Quartier Campanile, B.P. 20/212, 1200 Bruxelles, Belgique.

Téléphone: 32 (2) 764 73 65. *Fax:* 32 (2) 764 72 35. *Contact:* Dr. M. Kivits, Administrateur-secrétaire.

OBJECTIFS: Dispenser des soins médicaux préventifs et curatifs dans le Kivu, au Zaïre. Former du personnel médical et para-médical. Mener une étude scientifique sur les problèmes de santé de la population de cette région.

INFORMATIONS GENERALES: *Création:* 1926. *Personnel/Total:* 213. *Salariés:* 201 dont: 200 dans les pays en développement. *Bénévoles:* 12 dont: 9 dans les pays en développement. *Budget/Total 1993:* ECU 536000 (US$ 627000). *Sources financières: Privé:* 16%. *Public:* 38%. *Autofinancement:* 46%.

PUBLICATIONS: *Rapport annuel.*

EVALUATION/RECHERCHE: Entreprend des activités de recherche.

ACTIVITES DANS LES REGIONS EN DEVELOPPEMENT: Intervient directement dans les régions en développement. Intervient dans 1 pays. Maintient une présence locale sur le terrain. Intervient par l'intermédiaire

See: *How to Use the Directory,* page 11.

d'organisations locales partenaires. **Actions de Développement durable:** Envoi de volontaires/experts/assistance technique; Santé/assainissement/eau; Éducation/formation/alphabétisation. **Régions:** Afrique centrale.

ACTIVITES D'INFORMATION ET D'EDUCATION: Domaines: Santé/assainissement/eau; Éducation/formation/alphabétisation. **Activités:** Collecte de fonds.

BEL0234
FONDATION PERE DAMIEN POUR LA LUTTE CONTRE LA LEPRE (FOPERDA) ♦ Father Damien Foundation for the Campaign against Leprosy

Boulevard Léopold II, 263, 1080 Bruxelles, Belgique.

Téléphone: 32 (2) 422 59 39. *Fax:* 32 (2) 422 59 00. *Contact:* François Eeckhout, Président.

OBJECTIFS: Dépister la lèpre et la tuberculose, avec application, pour la lèpre, de la polychimiothérapie préconisée. Surveiller attentivement les cas traités et l'évolution de la maladie.

INFORMATIONS GENERALES: *Création:* 1939. *Affiliée à:* International Federation of Anti-Leprosy Associations (Royaume-Uni) - ILEP (Royaume-Uni). *Personnel/Total:* 4. *Salariés:* 2. *Bénévoles:* 2 dont: 2 dans les pays en développement. *Budget/Total 1993:* ECU 300000 (US$ 347000). *Sources financières:* *Privé:* 41%. *Public:* 42%. *Autofinancement:* 17%.

PUBLICATIONS: *Rapport annuel.*

EVALUATION/RECHERCHE: Rapports d'évaluation disponibles. Entreprend des activités de recherche.

ACTIVITES DANS LES REGIONS EN DEVELOPPEMENT: Intervient directement dans les régions en développement. Intervient dans 1 pays. Maintient une présence locale sur le terrain. Intervient par l'intermédiaire d'organisations locales partenaires. **Actions de Développement durable:** Développement rural/agriculture; Développement urbain/habitat; Envoi de volontaires/experts/assistance technique; Santé/assainissement/eau; Éducation/formation/alphabétisation. **Régions:** Afrique centrale.

BEL0235
FONDATION ROGER RIOU D'AIDE AUX PAYS EN VOIE DE DEVELOPPEMENT

Avenue des peupliers 11, 1340 Ottignies, Belgique.

Téléphone: 32 (10) 41 60 43. *Contact:* M. De Coster.

BEL0236
FONDATION ROI BAUDOUIN

Rue Brederode 21, 1000 Bruxelles, Belgique.

Téléphone: 32 (2) 511 18 40. *Fax:* 32 (2) 511 52 21. *Contact:* Eliane Najros.

BEL0237
FONDATION UNIVERSITAIRE POUR LA COOPERATION INTERNATIONALE AU DEVELOPPEMENT (FUCID) ♦ University Foundation for International Cooperation on Development

Rue de Bruxelles 61, 5000 Namur, Belgique.

Téléphone: 32 (81) 72 50 88. *Fax:* 32 (81) 72 50 90. *Contact:* M.E. Jadot, Directeur.

OBJECTIFS: Sensibiliser aux problèmes du Tiers-Monde au sein des Facultés Universitaires Notre-Dame de la Paix.Intervenir dans des projets de développement dans les pays du Sud.

INFORMATIONS GENERALES: *Affiliée à:* Fédération francophone des ONG d'envoi de coopérants (Belgique) - Association des ONG francophones et germanophones (Belgique). *Personnel/Total:* 3. *Salariés:* 2. *Bénévoles:* 1. *Budget/Total 1993:* ECU 210000 (US$ 246000). *Sources financières:* *Privé:* 23%. *Public:* 13%. *Autofinancement:* 64%.

PUBLICATIONS: *Périodiques:* Bulletin de la FUCID (6). *Rapport annuel.*

EVALUATION/RECHERCHE: Rapports d'évaluation disponibles. Entreprend des activités de recherche.

ACTIVITES DANS LES REGIONS EN DEVELOPPEMENT: Intervient directement dans les régions en développement. Intervient dans 3 pays. Maintient une présence locale sur le terrain. Intervient par l'intermédiaire d'organisations locales partenaires. **Actions de Développement durable:** Aliments/famine; Développement rural/agriculture; Envoi de volontaires/experts/assistance technique; Santé/assainissement/eau; Écologie/environnement/biodiversité; Éducation/formation/alphabétisation. **Régions:** Afrique centrale; Afrique de l'Ouest.

ACTIVITES D'INFORMATION ET D'EDUCATION: Domaines: Aliments/famine; Culture/tradition/religion; Droits de l'Homme/paix/conflits; Développement urbain/habitat; Enfants/jeunesse/famille; Paix/conflits ethniques/armement/désarmement; Pauvreté/conditions de vie; Population/planning familial/démographie; Questions relatives aux femmes; Racisme/xénophobie/antisémitisme; Relations internationales/coopération/aide au développement; Relations économiques internationales/commerce/dette/finances; Réfugiés/migrants/groupes ethniques; Santé/assainissement/eau; Secours d'urgence/réfugiés/aide humanitaire; Écologie/environnement/biodiversité; Éducation/formation/alphabétisation. **Activités:** Conférences/séminaires/ateliers/activités de formation; Services d'information et de documentation/bases de données.

BEL0238
FONDS INGRID RENARD

Avenue Emile Max 177, 1040 Bruxelles, Belgique.

Téléphone: 32 (2) 733 67 55. *Contact:* M. Liebaert.

BEL0239
FONDS MEDICAL TROPICAL (FOMETRO) ♦ Medical Tropical Fund

Rue de la Victoire, 94, 1060 Bruxelles, Belgique.

Téléphone: 32 (21) 538 57 17 . *Contact:* Jean Cordy, Président.

BEL0240
FONDS VOOR ONTWIKKELINGSHULP (FOH) ♦ Development Aid Foundation

Sint Jacobcentrum, Stuivenbergbaan 153, 2800 Mechelen, Belgium.

Telephone: 32 (15) 41 12 78. *Contact:* Maria Smets.

BEL0241
FONDS VOOR ONTWIKKELINGSSAMENWERKING (FOS) ♦ Fonds pour la coopération au développement

Grasmarkt 105, boîte 46, 1000 Bruxelles, Belgique.

Téléphone: 32 (2) 513 29 60. *Fax:* 32 (2) 502 52 76. *Contact:* Frans Teuchies, Secrétaire général.

OBJECTIFS: Soutenir des activités dans le Sud qui visent à renforcer des organisations de base. Travailler à l'éducation en milieu socialiste, en Flandre. Influencer politiquement les structures de décision en Belgique et au niveau européen.

INFORMATIONS GENERALES: *Création:* 1963. *Affiliée à:* NCOS (Belgique) - COPROGRAM (Belgique) - Comité de liaison des ONG-CE (Belgique). *Personnel/Total:* 40. *Salariés:* 40 dont: 25 dans les pays en développement. *Budget/Total 1993:* ECU 4720000 (US$ 5521000). *Sources financières:* *Privé:* 22%. *Public:* 78%.

PUBLICATIONS: *Rapport annuel.*

EVALUATION/RECHERCHE: Entreprend des activités de recherche.

ACTIVITES DANS LES REGIONS EN DEVELOPPEMENT: Intervient directement dans les régions en développement. Intervient dans 14 pays. Maintient une présence locale sur le terrain. Intervient par l'intermédiaire d'organisations locales partenaires. **Actions de Développement durable:** Droits de l'Homme/paix/conflits; Démocratie/bonne gestion publique/création d'institutions/développement participatif; Développement rural/agriculture; Développement urbain/habitat; Envoi de volontaires/experts/assistance technique; Petites entreprises/secteur informel/artisanat; Questions relatives aux femmes; Santé/assainissement/eau; Écologie/environnement/biodiversité. **Régions:** Afrique aus-

Voir : Comment utiliser le répertoire, page 11.

trale; Afrique centrale; Amérique du Sud; Asie du Sud-Est; Mexique et Amerique centrale; Moyen-Orient.

ACTIVITES D'INFORMATION ET D'EDUCATION: Domaines: Aliments/famine; Droits de l'Homme/paix/conflits; Développement rural/agriculture; Relations internationales/coopération/aide au développement; Relations économiques internationales/commerce/dette/finances; Écologie/environnement/biodiversité. **Activités:** Campagnes d'information/expositions; Conférences/séminaires/ateliers/activités de formation; Lobbying/plaidoyer; Édition/documents audiovisuels/documents éducatifs.

BEL0242
FOOD AND DISARMAMENT INTERNATIONAL (FDI)
Rue Marché aux Poulets 30, 1000 Brussels, Belgium.

Telephone: 32 (2) 217 82 25. *Fax:* 32 (2) 218 45 69. *Contact:* Michel Clette, Secretary General.

BEL0243
FOODFIRST INFORMATION AND ACTION NETWORK, BELGIUM (FIAN) ♦ Réseau d'Information et d'Action sur les droits des peuples à se nourrir eux-mêmes
9 rue du Château de Jandrain, 1350 Orp-Jauche, Belgique.

Téléphone: 32 (19) 51 10 83. *Fax:* 32 (19) 63 23 73. *Contact:* Cecile Schots-Derave, Présidente.

BEL0244
FOUNDATION FOR DEVELOPMENT (FODEP)
Rue Victor Allard 279, 1180 Bruxelles, Belgique.

Téléphone: 32 (2) 346 25 00. *Contact:* Marc Noël.

BEL0245
FRATERNITE SAINT PAUL POUR L'AIDE AU DEVELOPPEMENT ♦ Saint Paul Brotherhood for Development Aid
Rue de Visé 435, 4020 Liège, Belgique.

Téléphone: 32 (41) 62 72 99. *Contact:* Leo Bonameau, Présidente.

OBJECTIFS: Aider, par des prêts sans intérêts, des groupes de travailleurs pauvres en Asie, en Afrique et en Amérique latine.

INFORMATIONS GENERALES: *Création:* 1960. *Personnel/Total:* 10. *Bénévoles:* 10. *Budget/Total 1993:* ECU 180000 (US$ 211000). *Sources financières:* Privé: 100%.

PUBLICATIONS: *Périodiques:* Bulletin de la Fraternité Saint Paul pour l'aide au développement (6).

EVALUATION/RECHERCHE: Rapports d'évaluation disponibles.

ACTIVITES DANS LES REGIONS EN DEVELOPPEMENT: Intervient directement dans les régions en développement. Intervient dans 12 pays. Intervient par l'intermédiaire d'organisations locales partenaires. **Actions de Développement durable:** Développement rural/agriculture; Développement urbain/habitat; Enfants/jeunesse/famille; Petites entreprises/secteur informel/artisanat; Questions relatives aux femmes; Éducation/formation/alphabétisation. **Régions:** Afrique centrale; Afrique de l'Ouest; Amérique du Sud; Asie centrale et Asie du Sud; Caraïbes; Mexique et Amerique centrale.

ACTIVITES D'INFORMATION ET D'EDUCATION: Domaines: Développement rural/agriculture; Développement urbain/habitat; Enfants/jeunesse/famille; Questions relatives aux femmes; Éducation/formation/alphabétisation. **Activités:** Collecte de fonds; Édition/documents audiovisuels/documents éducatifs.

BEL0246
FRERES DES HOMMES, BELGIQUE (FDH)
Rue de Londres 18, 1050 Bruxelles, Belgique.

Téléphone: 32 (2) 512 97 94. *Fax:* 32 (20) 511 47 61. *Contact:* Eric de Clerck, Secrétaire général.

BEL0247
FRIEDRICH-EBERT-STIFTUNG
Rue Archimède 5, 1040 Bruxelles, Belgium.

Contact: Hermann Bünz.

BEL0248
FRIENDS OF THE EARTH - EUROPE (FOE-E) ♦ Coordination Européenne des Amis de la Terre
29 rue Blanche, 1050 Brussels, Belgium.

Telephone: 32 (2) 537 72 28. *Fax:* 32 (2) 537 55 96.

OBJECTIVES: To promote sustainable development with special emphasis on environmental issues, social justice, democracy and non-discrimination. To co-operate within the global network of FOE International. To support weaker members (Third World, CEE).

GENERAL INFORMATION: *Type of organisation:* association of NGOs, network. *Member organisations:* 27. *Affiliated to:* European Round Table of Environmental NGOs. *Personnel/Total:* 9. *Salaried:* 7. *Volunteers:* 2. *Budget/Total 1993:* ECU 200000 (US$ 234000). *Financial sources:* Private: 5%. Public: 50%. Self-financing: 45%.

PUBLICATIONS: *Periodicals:* FOE Link (4) - FOEE Newsletters (6) - Cleasing house Biotechnology (6). *Annual report. List of publications.*

EVALUATION/RESEARCH: Undertakes research activities.

COMMENTS: FOEE has one member group per country, but in projects/campaigns non-members are invited to participate regularly. Undertakes activities in the Commonwealth of Independent States. Information activities related to the Commonwealth of Independent States.

ACTIVITIES IN DEVELOPING REGIONS: Active in 23 country(ies). Works through local field partners.

INFORMATION AND EDUCATION ACTIVITIES: Topics: Ecology/environment/biodiversity; Employment/unemployment; Human rights/peace/conflicts; International economic relations/trade/debt/finance; Peace/ethnic conflicts/armament/disarmament; Racism/xenophobia/antisemitism; Rural development/agriculture; Urban development/habitat. **Activities:** Conferences/seminars/workshops/training activities; Exchanges/twinning/linking; Formal education; Fund raising; Information and documentation services/data bases; Information campaigns/exhibitions; Lobbying/advocacy; Networking/electronic telecommunications; Publishing/audiovisual materials/educational materials.

BEL0249
GENAGRO
Place Croix du Sud, 3 Sc 15 D, 1348 Louvain-la-Neuve, Belgique.

Téléphone: 32 (10) 47 39 04. *Contact:* B.-P. Louant, Administrateur délégué.

OBJECTIFS: Favoriser la coordination et le dévelopement des initiatives scientifiques et techniques visant à promouvoir la production agricole, notamment dans les pays en développement.

INFORMATIONS GENERALES: *Création:* 1985. *Type d'organisation:* réseau. *Personnel/Total:* 14. *Salariés:* 14. *Budget/Total 1993:* ECU 494000 (US$ 578000). *Sources financières:* Public: 100%.

PUBLICATIONS: *Rapport annuel.*

ACTIVITES DANS LES REGIONS EN DEVELOPPEMENT: Intervient dans 4 pays. Intervient par l'intermédiaire d'organisations locales partenaires. **Actions de Développement durable:** Développement rural/agriculture. **Régions:** Afrique centrale; Afrique de l'Ouest; Afrique du Nord; Amérique du Sud.

ACTIVITES D'INFORMATION ET D'EDUCATION: Domaines: Développement rural/agriculture. **Activités:** Radiodiffusion/manifestations culturelles; Services d'information et de documentation/bases de données; Édition/documents audiovisuels/documents éducatifs; Éducation formelle.

BEL0250
GERNIKA
65 rue du Midi, 1000 Bruxelles, Belgique.

See: *How to Use the Directory*, page 11.

BEL0251

GREENPEACE INTERNATIONAL EC UNIT

Avenue de Tervueren 36, 1040 Bruxelles, Belgique.

Contact: Frank Schwalba-Hoth.

BEL0252

GROUPE DE RECHERCHE POUR UNE STRATEGIE ECONOMIQUE ALTERNATIVE (GRESEA)

Rue Royale 11, 1000 Bruxelles, Belgique.

Téléphone: 32 (2) 219 70 76. *Fax:* 32 (2) 219 64 86. *Courrier électronique:* Geonet:Geo2-Gresea. *Contact:* Jean-luc Iwens, Secrétaire général.

OBJECTIFS: Sensibiliser les organisations syndicales européennes et les ONG aux enjeux des relations Nord-Sud. Publier des analyses sur les problèmes de développement. Organiser et participer à des formations. Organiser des séminaires et des conférences. Mettre à la disposition du public un centre de documentation.

INFORMATIONS GENERALES: *Création:* 1978. *Affiliée à:* National Centrum voor Ontwikkelingssamenwerking (Belgique) - International restructuring Education Network Europe (Pays-Bas) - Comité pour l'annuation de la dette du Tiers-Monde (Belgique). *Personnel/Total:* 9. *Salariés:* 9. *Budget/Total 1993:* ECU 86000 (US$ 101000). *Sources financières:* Privé: 5%. Public: 70%. Autofinancement: 25%.

PUBLICATIONS: *Périodiques:* GRESEA Echos (4). *Liste des publications.*

EVALUATION/RECHERCHE: Entreprend des activités de recherche.

PREVISIONS D'ACTIVITES: Publications, formations et documentations sur l'emploi Nord-Sud. Le développement social. Les technologies de l'informations et de la communication. Les Organisations internationales.

ACTIVITES D'INFORMATION ET D'EDUCATION: Domaines: Droits de l'Homme/paix/conflits; Emploi/chômage; Pauvreté/conditions de vie; Relations internationales/coopération/aide au développement; Relations économiques internationales/commerce/dette/finances. **Activités:** Campagnes d'information/expositions; Conférences/séminaires/ateliers/activités de formation; Lobbying/plaidoyer; Réseaux/télécommunications électroniques; Services d'information et de documentation/bases de données; Édition/documents audiovisuels/documents éducatifs.

BEL0253

GROUPEMENT EUROPEEN DES CAISSES D'EPARGNE (EPARGNEUROP) ♦ European Savings Banks Group

Avenue de la Renaissance 12, 1040 Bruxelles, Belgique.

Téléphone: 32 (2) 739 16 11. *Fax:* 32 (2) 736 09 55. *Contact:* Giampiero Pasquali, Secrétaire.

BEL0254

HABITAT INTERNATIONAL COALITION - EUROPEAN SECTION (HIC)

Place du Levant 1, 1348 Louvain-la-Neuve, Belgium.

Telephone: 32 (10) 47 23 14. *Fax:* 32 (10) 47 30 43. *Contact:* Kirtee Shah, President.

OBJECTIVES: To work for the recognition and implementation of everyone's right to live in a place of peace and dignity.

GENERAL INFORMATION: *Creation:* 1978. *Type of organisation:* association of NGOs. *Member organisations:* 300. *Personnel/Total:* 6. *Salaried:* 6 of which: 6 in developing countries. *Budget/Total 1993:* ECU 276000 (US$ 323000). *Financial sources:* Private: 40%. Public: 45%. Self-financing: 15%.

PUBLICATIONS: *Periodicals:* HIC News (4). *Annual report.*

EVALUATION/RESEARCH: Undertakes research activities.

PLANNED ACTIVITIES: Organising the NGO/CBO involvement in the UN Habitat Conference. Drafting of a Housing Rights Convention. Undertaking human settlements research in co-operation with local governments and NGOs.

COMMENTS: The organisation's headquarters are located: 24 Cordobanes, Col. San José Insurgentes, Mexico D.F. 03900 Undertakes activities in the Commonwealth of Independent States. Information activities related to the Commonwealth of Independent States.

ACTIVITIES IN DEVELOPING REGIONS: Active in 71 country(ies). Works through local field partners. **Sustainable Development Actions:** Education/training/literacy; Gender issues/women; Human rights/peace/conflicts; Other; Urban development/habitat. **Regions:** Caribbean; Central Africa; Central Asia and South Asia; East Africa; East Asia; Mexico and Central America; Middle East; North Africa; South America; South East Asia; Southern Africa; West Africa.

INFORMATION AND EDUCATION ACTIVITIES: Topics: Ecology/environment/biodiversity; Gender issues/women; Human rights/peace/conflicts; Poverty/living conditions; Urban development/habitat. **Activities:** Conferences/seminars/workshops/training activities; Exchanges/twinning/linking; Fund raising; Information and documentation services/data bases; Information campaigns/exhibitions; Lobbying/advocacy; Networking/electronic telecommunications; Publishing/audiovisual materials/educational materials.

BEL0255

HANDICAP INTERNATIONAL, BELGIQUE

Rue de SPA, 67, 1040 Bruxelles, Belgique.

Téléphone: 32 (2) 280 16 01. *Fax:* 32 (2) 230 60 30. *Contact:* Marie-Paule Planchard, Codirecteur.

BEL0256

HANNS SEIDEL STIFTUNG

Rue Montoyer 17-19, 1040 Bruxelles, Belgium.

Contact: Georg M. Regozini.

BEL0257

HELPAGE INTERNATIONAL

Avenue de Tervueren 142-144/5, 1150 Brussels, Belgium.

BEL0258

HULP VAN SINT-ANDRIES AAN DE DERDE WERELD (SATIMO) ♦ Aide de Saint André au Tiers monde

Sint Andriesabdij-Zevenkerke, 8200 Brugge, Belgique.

Téléphone: 32 (50) 38 01 36. *Contact:* Claude Standaert, Président.

OBJECTIFS: Aider le Tiers monde, en particulier le Zaïre, le Rwanda, le Brésil et l'Inde, par la réalisation de projets modestes.

INFORMATIONS GENERALES: *Création:* 1969. *Personnel/Total:* 3. *Bénévoles:* 3. *Budget/Total 1993:* ECU 717000 (US$ 838000). *Sources financières:* Privé: 100%.

PUBLICATIONS: *Périodiques:* Echo-Satimo (4). *Rapport annuel.*

ACTIVITES DANS LES REGIONS EN DEVELOPPEMENT: Intervient dans 8 pays. Maintient une présence locale sur le terrain. **Actions de Développement durable:** Aliments/famine; Développement rural/agriculture; Enfants/jeunesse/famille; Petites entreprises/secteur informel/artisanat; Santé/assainissement/eau; Écologie/environnement/biodiversité; Éducation/formation/alphabétisation. **Régions:** Afrique centrale; Amérique du Sud; Asie centrale et Asie du Sud.

BEL0259

HUMAN RIGHTS WATCH

15 rue van Campenhout, 1040 Bruxelles, Belgium.

Telephone: 32 (2) 732 20 09. *Fax:* 32 (2) 732 04 71.

BEL0260

HUMANA

7 Place Madou, 1030 Bruxelles, Belgium.

Telephone: 32 (2) 218 46 23. *Fax:* 32 (2) 219 44 38. *Contact:* Jytte Nielsen, Chairman.

Voir : *Comment utiliser le répertoire,* page 11.

OBJECTIVES: To provide development aid to the peoples in the Third World.

GENERAL INFORMATION: *Creation:* 1986. *Financial sources:* Self-financing: 100%.

ACTIVITIES IN DEVELOPING REGIONS: Active in 2 country(ies). Works through local field partners. **Sustainable Development Actions:** Children/youth/family; Ecology/environment/biodiversity; Education/training/literacy; Emergency relief/refugees/humanitarian assistance; Food/famine; Health/sanitation/water; Rural development/agriculture; Sending volunteers/experts/technical assistance; Small enterprises/informal sector/handicrafts. **Regions:** Caribbean; Southern Africa.

BEL0261
IEDER VOOR ALLEN ♦ Chacun pour Tous

Minderbroederstraat 8, 3000 Leuven, Belgique.

Téléphone: 32 (16) 24 21 56. *Fax:* 32 (16) 24 20 07. *Contact:* Ir. W. Vandepitte, Président.

OBJECTIFS: Créer des centres de formation et d'enseignement agricole. Lancer des coopératives agricoles. Réaliser des projets horticoles. Améliorer les techniques de production. Promouvoir le rôle de la femme dans le processus de développement.

INFORMATIONS GENERALES: *Création:* 1964. *Affiliée à:* National Centrum voor Ontwikkelingssamenwerking (Belgique) - Coprogram (Belgique). *Personnel/Total:* 17. Salariés: 2. Bénévoles: 15 dont: 6 dans les pays en développement. *Budget/Total 1993:* ECU 618000 (US$ 723000). *Sources financières:* Privé: 30%. Public: 40%. Autofinancement: 30%.

PUBLICATIONS: *Périodiques:* Ieder voor Allen krant (4). *Rapport annuel. Liste des publications.*

EVALUATION/RECHERCHE: Rapports d'évaluation disponibles.

COMMENTAIRES: L'organisation crée, avec le groupe Boerenbond, une cellule "Senior Consultants" à laquelle il pourrait être fait appel pour des missions d'étude et de suivi des projets.

ACTIVITES DANS LES REGIONS EN DEVELOPPEMENT: Intervient directement dans les régions en développement. Intervient dans 7 pays. Maintient une présence locale sur le terrain. Intervient par l'intermédiaire d'organisations locales partenaires. **Actions de Développement durable:** Aliments/famine; Développement rural/agriculture; Envoi de volontaires/experts/assistance technique; Petites entreprises/secteur informel/artisanat; Questions relatives aux femmes; Écologie/environnement/biodiversité. **Régions:** Afrique centrale; Afrique de l'Ouest; Amérique du Sud; Asie centrale et Asie du Sud; Asie du Sud-Est; Mexique et Amerique centrale.

ACTIVITES D'INFORMATION ET D'EDUCATION: Domaines: Aliments/famine; Développement rural/agriculture; Questions relatives aux femmes; Relations internationales/coopération/aide au développement. **Activités:** Campagnes d'information/expositions; Collecte de fonds; Conférences/séminaires/ateliers/activités de formation; Édition/documents audiovisuels/documents éducatifs.

BEL0262
ILES DE PAIX

Rue du Marché 37, 4500 Huy, Belgique.

Téléphone: 32 (85) 23 04 54 . *Contact:* Philippe de Braconier, Secrétaire général.

BEL0263
IMPRESS - DOKUMENTATIONSCENTER OM NARKOTIKA OG UDVIKLING ♦ IMPRESS - Information Centre on Drugs and Development

Tuinbouwstraat 4, 2018 Antwerpen, Belgium.

Telephone: 32 (3) 272 16 82. *Fax:* 32 (2) 733 57 08. *Contact:* Joep Oomen, Coordinator.

OBJECTIVES: To undertake research activities on the links between drug trade and underdevelopment, and to inform the European public about these links.

GENERAL INFORMATION: *Creation:* 1990. *Affiliated to:* European NGO Committee on Drugs (Belgium). *Personnel/Total:* 2. Salaried: 2. *Budget/Total 1993:* ECU 12000 (US$ 14000). *Financial sources:* Private: 20%. Public: 60%. Self-financing: 20%.

PUBLICATIONS: List of publications.

EVALUATION/RESEARCH: Undertakes research activities.

INFORMATION AND EDUCATION ACTIVITIES: Topics: International relations/cooperation/development aid; Other. **Activities:** Broadcasting/cultural events; Conferences/seminars/workshops/training activities; Exchanges/twinning/linking; Information and documentation services/data bases; Information campaigns/exhibitions; Lobbying/advocacy; Publishing/audiovisual materials/educational materials.

BEL0264
IN-MEDIAS

86 rue de la Caserne, 1000 Bruxelles, Belgique.

Téléphone: 32 (2) 514 10 11.

BEL0265
INFEDOP

33 rue de Trèves, 1040 Bruxelles, Belgique.

Téléphone: 32 (2) 230 38 65. *Fax:* 32 (2) 231 14 72. *Contact:* Bert van Caelenberg, Secrétaire général.

OBJECTIFS: Promouvoir l'émancipation économique, sociale et culturelle des travailleurs en général et ceux des services publics en particulier, notamment en créant des installations appropriées et en soutenant le développement des organisations affiliées.

INFORMATIONS GENERALES: *Type d'organisation:* regroupement d'ONG, réseau, collectif. *Affiliée à:* CMT. *Personnel/Total:* 7. *Budget/Total 1993:* ECU 247000 (US$ 289000). *Sources financières:* Public: 10%. Autofinancement: 90%.

PUBLICATIONS: *Périodiques:* SERVUS (6). *Liste des publications.*

EVALUATION/RECHERCHE: Rapports d'évaluation disponibles.

COMMENTAIRES: Intervient dans la Communauté des Etats indépendants. Activités d'information concernant la Communauté des Etats indépendants.

ACTIVITES DANS LES REGIONS EN DEVELOPPEMENT: Intervient directement dans les régions en développement. Intervient dans 31 pays. Maintient une présence locale sur le terrain. Intervient par l'intermédiaire d'organisations locales partenaires. **Actions de Développement durable:** Droits de l'Homme/paix/conflits; Démocratie/bonne gestion publique/création d'institutions/développement participatif; Envoi de volontaires/experts/assistance technique; Questions relatives aux femmes; Santé/assainissement/eau; Énergie/transport. **Régions:** Afrique australe; Afrique centrale; Afrique de l'Est; Afrique de l'Ouest; Afrique du Nord; Amérique du Sud; Asie centrale et Asie du Sud; Asie de l'Est; Caraïbes; Mexique et Amerique centrale.

ACTIVITES D'INFORMATION ET D'EDUCATION: Domaines: Droits de l'Homme/paix/conflits; Emploi/chômage; Questions relatives aux femmes; Relations internationales/coopération/aide au développement; Santé/assainissement/eau. **Activités:** Conférences/séminaires/ateliers/activités de formation; Lobbying/plaidoyer; Réseaux/télécommunications électroniques; Services d'information et de documentation/bases de données; Édition/documents audiovisuels/documents éducatifs; Éducation formelle.

BEL0266
INFO-SOLIDARITE BELGIQUE-TIERS MONDE

Rue Louis Thijs 6, 1150 Bruxelles, Belgique.

Téléphone: 32 (2) 770 25 02. *Contact:* Luc Cabay.

BEL0267
INFO-TURK

38, rue des Eburons, 1040 Brussels, Belgium.

Telephone: 32 (2) 230 34 72. *Fax:* 32 (2) 230 95 42. *Contact:* Dogan Ozgüden, Secretary General.

See: *How to Use the Directory,* page 11.

OBJECTIVES: To defend human rights in Turkey, and draw attention to the specific problems of migrants, refugees and asylum seekers in Belgium.

GENERAL INFORMATION: *Creation:* 1974. *Personnel/Total:* 16. *Salaried:* 10. *Volunteers:* 6. *Budget/Total 1993:* ECU 124000 (US$ 145000). *Financial sources: Public:* 80%. *Self-financing:* 20%.

PUBLICATIONS: *Periodicals:* INFO-TüRK (12). *Annual report. List of publications.*

EVALUATION/RESEARCH: Evaluation reports available. Undertakes research activities.

INFORMATION AND EDUCATION ACTIVITIES: Topics: Children/youth/family; Culture/tradition/religion; Ecology/environment/biodiversity; Education/training/literacy; Employment/unemployment; Gender issues/women; Human rights/peace/conflicts; International economic relations/trade/debt/finance; International relations/cooperation/development aid; Peace/ethnic conflicts/armament/disarmament; Poverty/living conditions; Racism/xenophobia/antisemitism; Refugees/migrants/ethnic groups; Rural development/agriculture; Urban development/habitat. **Activities:** Information and documentation services/data bases; Information campaigns/exhibitions; Lobbying/advocacy.

BEL0268

INSTITUT EUROPEEN DE RECHERCHE ET D'INFORMATION SUR LA PAIX ET LA SECURITE (GRIP)

33 rue Van Hoorde , 1030 Bruxelles, Belgique.

Téléphone: 32 (2) 241 84 20. *Contact:* Bernard Adam, directeur..

OBJECTIFS: Aider les citoyens et les décideurs politiques à prendre des décisions éclairées dans le sens d'une meilleure sécurité internationale basée sur la réduction des armements et l'élaboration de nouveaux concepts de défense.

INFORMATIONS GENERALES: *Création:* 1979. *Personnel/Total:* 17. *Salariés:* 15. *Bénévoles:* 2. *Budget/Total 1993:* ECU 371000 (US$ 434000). *Sources financières: Public:* 50%. *Autofinancement:* 50%.

PUBLICATIONS: *Périodiques:* Grip-Information (1) (12). *Rapport annuel. Liste des publications.*

EVALUATION/RECHERCHE: Entreprend des activités de recherche.

ACTIVITES D'INFORMATION ET D'EDUCATION: Domaines: Culture/tradition/religion; Paix/conflits ethniques/armement/désarmement; Écologie/environnement/biodiversité. **Activités:** Services d'information et de documentation/bases de données; Édition/documents audiovisuels/documents éducatifs.

BEL0269

INSTITUTE OF CULTURAL AFFAIRS

8 rue Amédée Lynen, 1030 Brussels, Belgium.

Telephone: 32 (2) 219 00 87. *Fax:* 32 (2) 219 04 06. *E-mail:* gn:icai. *Contact:* Linda Alton.

OBJECTIVES: To develop and test methods of individual, community and organisational development focusing on participative facilitation methods as the primary process. To develop group skills to further these methods.

GENERAL INFORMATION: *Creation:* 1972. *Type of organisation:* association of NGOs. *Member organisations:* 5. *Affiliated to:* Culture and Development (Belgium) - SIETAR (USA) - Institute of Cultural Affairs International (Belgium). *Personnel/Total:* 4. *Volunteers:* 4. *Budget/Total 1993:* ECU 237000 (US$ 277000). *Financial sources: Private:* 14%. *Public:* 15%. *Self-financing:* 71%.

PUBLICATIONS: *Periodicals:* EDGES (4) - Network Exchange (12). *Annual report. List of publications.*

EVALUATION/RESEARCH: Evaluation reports available. Undertakes research activities.

COMMENTS: ICA Belgium represents ICAs in the UK, Germany, Portugal and the Netherlands, all independenty chartered organisations with sep-

arate boards, with "volunteer" personnel. The Belgian office provides the secretariat function for these other four ICA organisations. Undertakes activities in the Commonwealth of Independent States. Information activities related to the Commonwealth of Independent States.

ACTIVITIES IN DEVELOPING REGIONS: Active in 20 country(ies). Maintains local field presence. Works through local field partners. **Sustainable Development Actions:** Children/youth/family; Democracy/good governance/institution building/participatory development; Education/training/literacy; Gender issues/women; Health/sanitation/water; Population/family planning/demography; Rural development/agriculture; Sending volunteers/experts/technical assistance; Small enterprises/informal sector/handicrafts; Urban development/habitat. **Regions:** Central Asia and South Asia; East Africa; Mexico and Central America; North Africa; Oceania; South America; South East Asia; Southern Africa; West Africa.

BEL0270

INSTITUTE OF CULTURAL AFFAIRS INTERNATIONAL (ICAI)

Rue Amédée Lynen 8, 1030 Brussels, Belgium.

Telephone: 32 (2) 219 49 43. *Fax:* 32 (2) 219 04 06. *E-mail:* gn:icai. *Contact:* Richard H.T. Alton, Secretary General.

OBJECTIVES: To develop and test methods of comprehensive community renewal. To motivate cross-sectoral co-operative actions in support of local development, with special emphasis on the human factor. To catalyse grassroots participation in improving the quality of life through self-development.

GENERAL INFORMATION: *Creation:* 1977. *Type of organisation:* association of NGOs. *Member organisations:* 30. *Affiliated to:* European Association for Development Research and Training Institutes (Switzerland) - International Council of Voluntary Organisations (Switzerland) - Centre for our Common Future (Switzerland) - InterAction (USA). *Personnel/Total:* 300. *Salaried:* 250 of which: 200 in developing countries. *Volunteers:* 50 of which: 25 in developing countries. *Budget/Total 1993:* ECU 40000 (US$ 47000). *Financial sources: Private:* 4%. *Self-financing:* 96%.

PUBLICATIONS: *Periodicals:* The Network Exchange (10) - The Directory (1). *Annual report. List of publications.*

EVALUATION/RESEARCH: Evaluation reports available. Undertakes research activities.

COMMENTS: Undertakes activities in the Commonwealth of Independent States. Information activities related to the Commonwealth of Independent States.

ACTIVITIES IN DEVELOPING REGIONS: Present in developing regions. Active in 10 country(ies). Maintains local field presence. Works through local field partners. **Sustainable Development Actions:** Children/youth/family; Democracy/good governance/institution building/participatory development; Ecology/environment/biodiversity; Education/training/literacy; Food/famine; Gender issues/women; Health/sanitation/water; Rural development/agriculture; Sending volunteers/experts/technical assistance; Small enterprises/informal sector/handicrafts. **Regions:** Central Asia and South Asia; East Africa; Mexico and Central America; Middle East; North Africa; Oceania; South America; South East Asia; West Africa.

INFORMATION AND EDUCATION ACTIVITIES: Topics: Children/youth/family; Culture/tradition/religion; Ecology/environment/biodiversity; Education/training/literacy; Employment/unemployment; Gender issues/women; Health/sanitation/water; Poverty/living conditions; Rural development/agriculture. **Activities:** Conferences/seminars/workshops/training activities; Formal education; Fund raising.

BEL0271

INTERNATIONAL CATHOLIC MIGRATION COMMISSION (ICMC) ♦ Commission internationale catholique pour les Migrations

Rue de Pascale 4, 1040 Bruxelles, Belgium.

Telephone: 32 (2) 230 34 18. *Fax:* 32 (2) 230 34 18.

Voir : *Comment utiliser le répertoire,* page 11.

BEL0272

INTERNATIONAL COALITION FOR DEVELOPMENT ACTION (ICDA)

Rue Stévin 115, 1040 Brussels, Belgium.

Telephone: 32 (2) 230 04 30. *Fax:* 32 (2) 230 03 48. *E-mail:* geo2:ICDA. *Contact:* Pierre Berthelot, Director.

OBJECTIVES: To work for a change in the international economic order through the restructuring of trade and financial relations between developing and developed countries. To support Third World aspirations for increased economic co-operation among developing countries.

GENERAL INFORMATION: *Creation:* 1975. *Type of organisation:* coordinating body. *Member organisations:* 22. *Affiliated to:* Co-ordination for European NGOs Networking on Trade (Belgium). *Personnel/Total:* 8. *Salaried:* 3. *Volunteers:* 5. *Budget/Total 1993:* ECU 60000 (US$ 70000). *Financial sources:* Private: 7%. Public: 87%. Self-financing: 6%.

PUBLICATIONS: *Periodicals:* ICDA Update (4) - ICDA Journal (2). *Annual report.*

EVALUATION/RESEARCH: Evaluation reports available.

PLANNED ACTIVITIES: The organisation will focus on sustainable development and trade, competition policy and regulation of TNCs.

COMMENTS: Programme implementation is heavily dependent on the availability of funding.

INFORMATION AND EDUCATION ACTIVITIES: **Topics:** Ecology/environment/biodiversity; Gender issues/women; Human rights/peace/conflicts; International economic relations/trade/debt/finance; International relations/cooperation/development aid. **Activities:** Conferences/seminars/workshops/training activities; Exchanges/twinning/linking; Fund raising; Information and documentation services/data bases; Information campaigns/exhibitions; Lobbying/advocacy; Networking/electronic telecommunications; Publishing/audiovisual materials/educational materials.

BEL0273

INTERNATIONAL COLLECTIVE IN SUPPORT OF FISHWORKERS (ICSF) ♦ Collectif international d'appui aux travailleurs de la pêche artisanale

Rue Gretry 65, 1000 Brussels, Belgium.

Telephone: 32 (2) 218 15 38. *Fax:* 32 (2) 217 83 05.

OBJECTIVES: To co-ordinate a network of professionals committed to the development of fishery workers' organisations around the world.

GENERAL INFORMATION: *Creation:* 1986. *Affiliated to:* IRED (Switzerland.). *Personnel/Total:* 11. *Salaried:* 4 of which: 3 in developing countries. *Volunteers:* 7 of which: 5 in developing countries. *Budget/Total 1993:* ECU 198000 (US$ 231000). *Financial sources:* Private: 10%. Public: 85%. Self-financing: 5%.

PUBLICATIONS: *Periodicals:* Samudra Report (2) - Samudra Revue (2) - Samudra Revista (2). *Annual report. List of publications.*

EVALUATION/RESEARCH: Evaluation reports available. Undertakes research activities.

PLANNED ACTIVITIES: The organisation will focus on women in fisheries; working conditions of fishworkers on international fishing vends; trawler ban in tropical inshore water.

ACTIVITIES IN DEVELOPING REGIONS: Works through local field partners. **Sustainable Development Actions:** Ecology/environment/biodiversity; Gender issues/women; Other. **Regions:** Central Asia and South Asia; East Africa; East Asia; Mexico and Central America; North Africa; Oceania; South America; South East Asia; Southern Africa; West Africa.

INFORMATION AND EDUCATION ACTIVITIES: **Topics:** Ecology/environment/biodiversity; Gender issues/women; Other. **Activities:** Conferences/seminars/workshops/training activities; Exchanges/twinning/linking; Formal education; Fund raising; Information and documentation services/data bases; Information campaigns/exhibitions; Lobbying/advocacy; Publishing/audiovisual materials/educational materials.

BEL0274

INTERNATIONAL CONFEDERATION OF FREE TRADE UNIONS (ICFTU) ♦ Confédération internationale des syndicats libres

Boulevard Emile Jacqmain 155 B 1, 1210 Brussels, Belgium.

Telephone: 32 (2) 224 02 11. *Fax:* 32 (2) 218 84 15. *E-mail:* GEO2:ICFTU. *Contact:* Enzo Friso, General Secretary.

BEL0275

INTERNATIONAL FALCON MOVEMENT - SOCIALIST EDUCATIONAL INTERNATIONAL (IFM-SEI)

3 rue Quinaux, 1030 Brussels, Belgium.

Telephone: 32 (2) 215 79 27. *Fax:* 32 (2) 245 00 83. *Contact:* Alejandro Moraga, Assistant Secretary General.

OBJECTIVES: To use seminars, camps, symposia, conferences and similar to develop modern methods of socialist education and prepare them for use in teaching by its member organisations.

GENERAL INFORMATION: *Creation:* 1922. *Type of organisation:* coordinating body. *Member organisations:* 53. *Affiliated to:* ECB (Belgium) - Forum de Jeunesse de CE (Belgium) - NGO-Committee of UNICEF (Switzerland). *Personnel/Total:* 6. *Salaried:* 3. *Volunteers:* 3 of which: 3 in developing countries. *Budget/Total 1993:* ECU 169000 (US$ 197000).

PUBLICATIONS: *Periodicals:* IFM-SEI Bulletin (2) - IFM-SEI Flashback (6). *List of publications.*

EVALUATION/RESEARCH: Evaluation reports available. Undertakes research activities.

PLANNED ACTIVITIES: The main topics of the organisation will be the place of the children in our society and in the family.

COMMENTS: Undertakes activities in the Commonwealth of Independent States. Information activities related to the Commonwealth of Independent States.

ACTIVITIES IN DEVELOPING REGIONS: Present in developing regions. Active in 19 country(ies). Maintains local field presence. Works through local field partners. **Sustainable Development Actions:** Children/youth/family; Democracy/good governance/institution building/participatory development; Ecology/environment/biodiversity; Education/training/literacy; Gender issues/women; Health/sanitation/water; Human rights/peace/conflicts; Rural development/agriculture; Small enterprises/informal sector/handicrafts. **Regions:** Central Asia and South Asia; East Africa; East Asia; Mexico and Central America; Middle East; North Africa; South America; South East Asia; Southern Africa; West Africa.

INFORMATION AND EDUCATION ACTIVITIES: **Topics:** Children/youth/family; Culture/tradition/religion; Ecology/environment/biodiversity; Education/training/literacy; Employment/unemployment; Gender issues/women; Human rights/peace/conflicts; International relations/cooperation/development aid; Peace/ethnic conflicts/armament/disarmament; Population/family planning/demography; Poverty/living conditions; Racism/xenophobia/antisemitism. **Activities:** Broadcasting/cultural events; Conferences/seminars/workshops/training activities; Exchanges/twinning/linking; Information and documentation services/data bases; Information campaigns/exhibitions; Lobbying/advocacy; Publishing/audiovisual materials/educational materials.

BEL0276

INTERNATIONAL FEDERATION OF LIBERAL AND RADICAL YOUTH (IFLRY) ♦ Fédération internationale des jeunesses libérales et radicales

P.O. Box 781, 1000 Brussels, Belgium.

Telephone: 32 (2) 512 44 57. *Contact:* Jules Maaten, President.

BEL0277

INTERNATIONAL GRAPHICAL FEDERATION - EDUCATION DEPARTMENT (IGF)

Rue des Fripiers 17, Galerie du Centre, Bloc 2, 1000 Brussels, Belgium.

Telephone: 32 (2) 223 02 20. *Fax:* 32 (2) 223 18 14. *Contact:* Chris Pate, Education Secretary.

See: *How to Use the Directory,* page 11.

BEL0278
INTERNATIONAL LEAGUE OF SOCIETIES FOR PERSONS WITH MENTAL RETARDATION (ILSMH) ♦ Ligue internationale des associations pour les personnes handicapées mentales

Avenue Louise 248, Boîte 17, 1050 Brussels, Belgium.

Telephone: 32 (2) 647 61 80. *Fax:* 32 (2) 647 29 69. *Contact:* Eloisa Garcia Etchegoyhen de Lorenzo, President.

BEL0279
INTERNATIONAL MOVEMENT FOR FRATERNAL UNION AMONG RACES & PEOPLES

Rue Eugène Smits 74, 1030 Brussels, Belgium.

BEL0280
INTERNATIONAL SAVE THE CHILDREN ALLIANCE (ISCA)

Place du Luxembourg 1, 1040 Brussels, Belgium.

BEL0281
INTERNATIONALE VREDESINFORMATIE DIENST (IPIS) ♦ INTERNATIONAL PEACE INFORMATION SERVICE

Italielei 98A, 2000 Antwerpen, Belgium.

Telephone: 32 (3) 225 00 22. *Fax:* 32 (2) 231 01 51. *E-mail:* flemunpeace@gn.apc.org. *Contact:* Mark Heirman, Director.

OBJECTIVES: To collect documentation and information on peace issues and make it accessible to the broader public. To undertake research and edit writings on peace and security problems, international relations, human rights, etc.

GENERAL INFORMATION: *Creation:* 1981. *Personnel/Total:* 8.

PUBLICATIONS: *Periodicals:* IPIS- Information (4). *Annual report. List of publications.*

EVALUATION/RESEARCH: Undertakes research activities.

INFORMATION AND EDUCATION ACTIVITIES: Topics: Human rights/peace/conflicts; International economic relations/trade/debt/finance; International relations/cooperation/development aid; Peace/ethnic conflicts/armament/disarmament. **Activities:** Information and documentation services/data bases; Publishing/audiovisual materials/educational materials.

BEL0282
JAPABEL

Rue Churchill 118, 6180 Courcelles, Belgique.

Téléphone: 32 (71) 45 45 30. *Contact:* Michel André, Président.

OBJECTIFS: Aider au développement du Tiers-Monde par des micro-réalisations.

**INFORMATIONS GENERALES: *Création:* 1976. *Affiliée à:* Association des ONG francophones (Belgique.). *Budget/Total 1993:* ECU 27000 (US$ 31000). *Sources financières:* Privé: 100%.

PUBLICATIONS: *Périodiques:* Revue annuelle (1) - Flash-Infos (1). *Rapport annuel.*

ACTIVITES DANS LES REGIONS EN DEVELOPPEMENT: Intervient directement dans les régions en développement. Intervient dans 1 pays. Intervient par l'intermédiaire d'organisations locales partenaires. **Actions de Développement durable:** Développement rural/agriculture; Développement urbain/habitat; Enfants/jeunesse/famille; Petites entreprises/secteur informel/artisanat; Questions relatives aux femmes; Santé/assainissement/eau; Éducation/formation/alphabétisation. **Régions:** Amérique du Sud.

ACTIVITES D'INFORMATION ET D'EDUCATION: Domaines: Aliments/famine; Développement rural/agriculture; Développement urbain/habitat; Enfants/jeunesse/famille; Pauvreté/conditions de vie; Questions relatives aux femmes; Santé/assainissement/eau; Éducation/formation/alphabétisation. **Activités:** Campagnes d'information/expositions; Collecte de fonds; Conférences/séminaires/ateliers/activités de formation; Lobbying/plaidoyer; Édition/documents audiovisuels/documents éducatifs.

BEL0283
JEKA ONTWIKKELINGSSAMENWERKING

Ambiorix Square 32/28, 1040 Bruxelles, Belgique.

Téléphone: 32 (2) 230 84 55. *Contact:* M. Broekaert.

BEL0284
JESUIT REFUGEE SERVICE - EUROPE (JRS-E)

31 rue M. Liétart, Boite 5, 1150 Brussels, Belgium.

Telephone: 32 (2) 738 08 63. *Fax:* 32 (2) 738 08 64. *Contact:* Eddy Jadot, Regional Director.

OBJECTIVES: To provide legal aid, educational, social, administrative and psychological support to refugees.

GENERAL INFORMATION: *Creation:* 1991. *Type of organisation:* network. *Affiliated to:* European Council on Refugees and Exiles (United Kingdom).

PUBLICATIONS: *Periodicals:* Servir (3). *Annual report.*

EVALUATION/RESEARCH: Evaluation reports available. Undertakes research activities.

PLANNED ACTIVITIES: Undertaking campaign with other international NGOs to ban landmines.

COMMENTS: Undertakes activities in the Commonwealth of Independent States.

ACTIVITIES IN DEVELOPING REGIONS: Present in developing regions. Maintains local field presence. Works through local field partners. **Sustainable Development Actions:** Education/training/literacy; Emergency relief/refugees/humanitarian assistance; Human rights/peace/conflicts. **Regions:** Central Africa; Central Asia and South Asia; East Africa; East Asia; Mexico and Central America; South East Asia.

INFORMATION AND EDUCATION ACTIVITIES: Topics: Education/training/literacy; Emergency relief/refugees/humanitarian assistance; Human rights/peace/conflicts; Peace/ethnic conflicts/armament/disarmament; Racism/xenophobia/antisemitism; Refugees/migrants/ethnic groups. **Activities:** Conferences/seminars/workshops/training activities; Information and documentation services/data bases; Information campaigns/exhibitions; Lobbying/advocacy; Publishing/audiovisual materials/educational materials.

BEL0285
JEUNESSE ET COOPERATION

Boulevard Général Jacques 50, 1050 Bruxelles, Belgique.

Contact: A. Hemlé-Mbeleg, Directeur international.

BEL0286
JEUNESSE ET SANTE

Rue de la Loi 121, 1040 Bruxelles, Belgique.

Téléphone: 32 (2) 237 49 82. *Contact:* Philippe Bodart, Secrétaire général.

BEL0287
JEUNESSE ETUDIANTE CATHOLIQUE INTERNATIONALE - MOUVEMENT INTERNATIONAL D'ETUDIANTS CATHOLIQUES - COORDINATION EUROPEENNE (JECI-MIEC)

19 rue Marteau, 1040 Bruxelles, Belgique.

Téléphone: 32 (2) 218 54 37. *Fax:* 32 (2) 219 83 96. *Contact:* Maria Koutatzi, Secrétaire européenne.

OBJECTIFS: Permettre la collaboration des mouvements et fédérations nationaux d'étudiants catholiques en Europe. Promouvoir des mouvements capables d'éveiller les étudiants à leur responsabilité vis-à-vis de la société.

INFORMATIONS GENERALES: *Création:* 1946. *Type d'organisation:* collectif. *Organisations membres:* 27. *Affiliée à:* BEC - Forum Jeunesse. *Sources financières:* Privé: 5%. Public: 75%. Autofinancement: 20%.

PUBLICATIONS: *Périodiques:* INFORAPID (4). *Rapport annuel. Liste des publications.*

EVALUATION/RECHERCHE: Rapports d'évaluation disponibles.

PREVISIONS D'ACTIVITES: Participation au IV Congrès européen (1996).

COMMENTAIRES: Campagne de sensibilisation des étudiants, en vue de leur faire prendre conscience de leur rôle dans la société. Intervient dans la Communauté des Etats indépendants. Activités d'information concernant la Communauté des Etats indépendants.

ACTIVITES DANS LES REGIONS EN DEVELOPPEMENT: Intervient par l'intermédiaire d'organisations locales partenaires.

ACTIVITES D'INFORMATION ET D'EDUCATION: **Domaines:** Culture/tradition/religion; Enfants/jeunesse/famille; Racisme/xénophobie/antisémitisme; Écologie/environnement/biodiversité; Éducation/formation/alphabétisation. **Activités:** Conférences/séminaires/ateliers/activités de formation.

BEL0288

JEUNESSE OUVRIERE CHRETIENNE EUROPEENNE (JOC EUROPEENNE)

21 rue Vandestichelen, 1210 Bruxelles, Belgique.

Téléphone: 32 (2) 425 97 49.

BEL0289

JEUNESSE OUVRIERE CHRETIENNE INTERNATIO-NALE (JOCI) ♦ International Young Christian Workers (IYCW)

Rue Plantin 11, 1070 Brussels, Belgium.

Telephone: 32 (2) 521 69 83. *Fax:* 32 (2) 521 69 44. *Contact:* Glynn Cloef, President.

OBJECTIVES: To provide education for young workers in the economic, social and political fields with the ultimate goal of contributing to their complete fulfillment as human beings.

GENERAL INFORMATION: *Creation:* 1957. *Type of organisation:* coordinating body. *Member organisations:* 54. *Personnel/Total:* 14. *Salaried:* 6 of which: 2 in developing countries. *Volunteers:* 8 of which: 2 in developing countries. *Budget/Total 1993:* ECU 276000 (US$ 323000). *Financial sources:* Private: 69%. Public: 2%. Self-financing: 29%.

PUBLICATIONS: *Periodicals:* IYCW Info (2) - IYCW Bulletin (4). *Annual report.*

EVALUATION/RESEARCH: Evaluation reports available.

COMMENTS: Undertakes activities in the Commonwealth of Independent States. Information activities related to the Commonwealth of Independent States.

ACTIVITIES IN DEVELOPING REGIONS: Present in developing regions. Active in 38 country(ies). Maintains local field presence. Works through local field partners. **Sustainable Development Actions:** Debt/finance/trade; Democracy/good governance/institution building/participatory development; Education/training/literacy; Gender issues/women; Small enterprises/informal sector/handicrafts. **Regions:** Caribbean; Central Africa; East Africa; East Asia; Mexico and Central America; North Africa; South America; South East Asia; Southern Africa; West Africa.

INFORMATION AND EDUCATION ACTIVITIES: **Topics:** Education/training/literacy; Employment/unemployment; Gender issues/women; Human rights/peace/conflicts; Poverty/living conditions; Racism/xenophobia/antisemitism; Refugees/migrants/ethnic groups. **Activities:** Conferences/seminars/workshops/training activities; Exchanges/twinning/linking; Information campaigns/exhibitions.

BEL0290

JONGEREN EN DE WERELD (JDW) ♦ Youth and World

Vlasfabriekstraat 11, 1060 Brussels, Belgium.

Telephone: 32 (2) 539 26 20. *Fax:* 32 (2) 539 13 43. *Contact:* Steven Vromman, Co-ordinator.

OBJECTIVES: To raise awareness of North-South relations among the youth.

GENERAL INFORMATION: *Creation:* 1990. *Affiliated to:* NCOS (Belgium) - YDC (the Netherlands). *Personnel/Total:* 10. *Salaried:* 4. *Volunteers:* 6. *Budget/Total 1993:* ECU 131000 (US$ 153000). *Financial sources:* Private: 20%. Public: 60%. Self-financing: 20%.

PUBLICATIONS: *Periodicals:* Nieuwsbrief (4) - Knipselkrant (3). *Annual report.*

EVALUATION/RESEARCH: Evaluation reports available.

PLANNED ACTIVITIES: Undertaking the campaigns on the United Nations and sustainable development.

INFORMATION AND EDUCATION ACTIVITIES: **Topics:** Children/youth/family; Food/famine; International economic relations/trade/debt/finance; Racism/xenophobia/antisemitism; Refugees/migrants/ethnic groups. **Activities:** Conferences/seminars/workshops/training activities; Information and documentation services/data bases; Information campaigns/exhibitions; Publishing/audiovisual materials/educational materials.

BEL0291

JUSTICE ET PAIX

12 avenue d'Auderghem, 1040 Bruxelles, Belgique.

Téléphone: 32 (2) 231 02 30.

BEL0292

KAIROS EUROPA - INTERNATIONAL OFFICE

3 avenue du Parc Royal, 1020 Brussels, Belgium.

BEL0293

KATOLIEK BEURZENFONDS VOOR AFRIKANEN (KBA) ♦ Catholic Grant Foundation for Africans

Rue Brialmont 11, bus 2, 1000 Brussels, Belgium.

Telephone: 32 (2) 217 56 10. *Contact:* L. Bonte.

BEL0294

KOMMISSIE RECHTVAARDIGHEID EN VREDE

Brialmontstraat 11/05, 1030 Brussels, Belgique.

Contact: Mr. F. van den Houte.

BEL0295

LIGA VOOR MENSENRECHTEN ♦ League for Human Rights

Universiteitstraat, P.O Box 8, 9000 Gent, Belgium.

Telephone: 32 (91) 64 68 77. *Fax:* 32 (91) 64 69 81. *Contact:* André de Baker, President.

OBJECTIVES: To make the government aware of human rights violations in Flanders.

GENERAL INFORMATION: *Creation:* 1979. *Affiliated to:* Fédération Internationale des Droits de l'Homme (France). *Personnel/Total:* 4. *Salaried:* 4. *Budget/Total 1993:* ECU 25000 (US$ 29000).

PUBLICATIONS: *Periodicals:* Liga Newsbref (Newsbetter) (6) - Fahk. *Annual report. List of publications.*

INFORMATION AND EDUCATION ACTIVITIES: **Topics:** Human rights/peace/conflicts. **Activities:** Lobbying/advocacy.

BEL0296

MEDECINS SANS FRONTIERES INTERNATIONAL

39 rue de la Tourelle, 1040 Bruxelles, Belgique.

Téléphone: 32 (2) 280 18 81. *Fax:* 32 (2) 280 01 73. *Contact:* Docteur Alain Destexhe, Secrétaire général.

OBJECTIFS: Coordonner et représenter les organisations nationales de MSF et leur travail.

See: *How to Use the Directory,* page 11.

INFORMATIONS GENERALES: *Création:* 1991. *Type d'organisation:* réseau. *Organisations membres:* 18. *Personnel/Total:* 1400. *Salariés:* 1400 dont: 1000 dans les pays en développement. *Budget/Total 1993:* ECU 5066000 (US$ 5925000). *Sources financières:* Privé: 40%. *Public:* 60%.

PUBLICATIONS: *Périodiques:* Activity Report (1) - MSF International Newsletter (3) - Populations in Danger (1). *Rapport annuel. Liste des publications.*

COMMENTAIRES: Intervient dans la Communauté des Etats indépendants.

ACTIVITES DANS LES REGIONS EN DEVELOPPEMENT: Intervient directement dans les régions en développement. Intervient dans 72 pays. Maintient une présence locale sur le terrain. Intervient par l'intermédiaire d'organisations locales partenaires.

BEL0297
MEDECINS SANS FRONTIERES, BELGIQUE (MSF-B)

Rue Dupré 94, 1090 Bruxelles, Belgique.

Téléphone: 32 (2) 474 74 74. *Fax:* 32 (2) 474 75 75. *Contact:* Dr. Eric Goemaere, Directeur général.

OBJECTIFS: Porter secours aux populations en détresse, aux victimes de catastrophes écologiques d'origine naturelle ou humaine, de situations de belligérance, sans aucune discrimination raciale, religieuse, philosophique ou politique.

INFORMATIONS GENERALES: *Création:* 1980. *Type d'organisation:* réseau. *Personnel/Total:* 485. *Salariés:* 460 dont: 360 dans les pays en développement. *Bénévoles:* 25. *Budget/Total 1993:* ECU 63016000 (US$ 73706000). *Sources financières:* Privé: 26%. *Public:* 71%. *Autofinancement:* 3%.

PUBLICATIONS: *Périodiques:* Le journal de MSF (4) - Medical News (6). *Rapport annuel. Liste des publications.*

PREVISIONS D'ACTIVITES: Développer auprès des écoliers une "conscience des autres" en leur présentant un outil pédagogique (METEOR) contenant divers supports d'information sur les droits de l'homme.

COMMENTAIRES: Intervient dans la Communauté des Etats indépendants.

ACTIVITES DANS LES REGIONS EN DEVELOPPEMENT: Intervient directement dans les régions en développement. Intervient dans 35 pays. Maintient une présence locale sur le terrain. Intervient par l'intermédiaire d'organisations locales partenaires. **Actions de Développement durable:** Aliments/famine; Droits de l'Homme/paix/conflits; Développement urbain/habitat; Enfants/jeunesse/famille; Envoi de volontaires/experts/assistance technique; Petites entreprises/secteur informel/artisanat; Population/planning familial/démographie; Questions relatives aux femmes; Santé/assainissement/eau; Secours d'urgence/réfugiés/aide humanitaire. **Régions:** Afrique australe; Afrique centrale; Afrique de l'Est; Afrique de l'Ouest; Amérique du Sud; Asie centrale et Asie du Sud; Asie du Sud-Est; Mexique et Amerique centrale; Moyen-Orient.

ACTIVITES D'INFORMATION ET D'EDUCATION: Domaines: Aliments/famine; Droits de l'Homme/paix/conflits; Enfants/jeunesse/famille; Paix/conflits ethniques/armement/désarmement; Pauvreté/conditions de vie; Population/planning familial/démographie; Racisme/xénophobie/antisémitisme; Relations internationales/coopération/aide au développement; Réfugiés/migrants/groupes ethniques; Santé/assainissement/eau; Secours d'urgence/réfugiés/aide humanitaire. **Activités:** Campagnes d'information/expositions; Collecte de fonds; Conférences/séminaires/ateliers/activités de formation; Lobbying/plaidoyer; Services d'information et de documentation/bases de données; Édition/documents audiovisuels/documents éducatifs.

BEL0298
MEDIA ANIMATION

32 avenue Rogier, 1030 Bruxelles, Belgique.

Téléphone: 32 (2) 242 57 93.

BEL0299
MEDICUS MUNDI INTERNATIONAL

Rue du Marteau 19, 1040 Bruxelles, Belgium.

Telephone: 32 (2) 219 95 88. *Fax:* 32 (2) 231 18 52. *Contact:* S.M. Rypkema.

OBJECTIVES: To promote health care in developing countries focusing on the primary health care development at district level, through personnel and financial assistance and professional co-operation.

GENERAL INFORMATION: *Creation:* 1963. *Type of organisation:* coordinating body. *Personnel/Total:* 2. *Salaried:* 1. *Volunteers:* 1. *Budget/Total 1993:* ECU 6000 (US$ 73000).

PUBLICATIONS: *Periodicals:* Newsletter (4) - Survey DHS. *Annual report. List of publications.*

EVALUATION/RESEARCH: Evaluation reports available. Undertakes research activities.

PLANNED ACTIVITIES: International conferences and workshops on health care in developing countries.

ACTIVITIES IN DEVELOPING REGIONS: Present in developing regions. Active in 30 country(ies). Maintains local field presence. Works through local field partners. **Sustainable Development Actions:** Education/training/literacy; Emergency relief/refugees/humanitarian assistance; Health/sanitation/water; Population/family planning/demography; Sending volunteers/experts/technical assistance. **Regions:** Caribbean; Central Africa; Central Asia and South Asia; East Africa; Mexico and Central America; Middle East; South America; South East Asia; Southern Africa; West Africa.

INFORMATION AND EDUCATION ACTIVITIES: Topics: Emergency relief/refugees/humanitarian assistance; Health/sanitation/water. **Activities:** Conferences/seminars/workshops/training activities; Formal education; Fund raising; Information and documentation services/data bases; Information campaigns/exhibitions; Lobbying/advocacy; Publishing/audiovisual materials/educational materials.

BEL0300
MEDICUS MUNDI, BELGIUM (MMB)

Tweekerkenstraat, 64, 1040 Brussels, Belgium.

Telephone: 32 (2) 231 06 05. *Fax:* 32 (2) 231 18 52. *Contact:* Dr. Guy KEGELS, President.

BEL0301
MEMISA BELGIQUE ♦ Medical Mission Action Belgium

Leopold II Laan 195, 1080 Bruxelles, Belgium.

Telephone: 32 (2) 569 03 51. *Fax:* 32 (2) 569 03 51. *Contact:* M. Waals.

OBJECTIVES: To provide medical aid to existing medical projects in the Third World. To send medicines and medical equipment. To help to prepare preventive programmes.

GENERAL INFORMATION: *Creation:* 1988. *Type of organisation:* coordinating body. *Affiliated to:* Coprogram (Belgium) - NGO-CE Liaison Committee. *Personnel/Total:* 8. *Salaried:* 2. *Volunteers:* 6. *Budget/Total 1993:* ECU 29655000 (US$ 34685000). *Financial sources:* Private: 50%. *Public:* 40%. *Self-financing:* 10%.

PUBLICATIONS: *Periodicals:* Memisa Info (4). *Annual report. List of publications.*

EVALUATION/RESEARCH: Evaluation reports available. Undertakes research activities.

PLANNED ACTIVITIES: Starting local groups, increasing the number of exhibitions.

ACTIVITIES IN DEVELOPING REGIONS: Present in developing regions. Active in 36 country(ies). Maintains local field presence. Works through local field partners. **Sustainable Development Actions:** Emergency relief/refugees/humanitarian assistance; Health/sanitation/water. **Regions:** Caribbean; Central Africa; Central Asia and South Asia; East Africa; Mexico and Central America; Middle East; North Africa; South America; South East Asia; Southern Africa; West Africa.

Voir : *Comment utiliser le répertoire,* page 11.

INFORMATION AND EDUCATION ACTIVITIES: Topics: Health/sanitation/water. **Activities:** Conferences/seminars/workshops/training activities; Fund raising; Information and documentation services/data bases; Information campaigns/exhibitions; Lobbying/advocacy; Networking/ electronic telecommunications; Publishing/audiovisual materials/educational materials.

BEL0302

MIGREUROPE

Rue Stévin 115, 1040 Bruxelles, Belgique.

Téléphone: 32 (2) 230 46 21.

BEL0303

MOUVEMENT CHRETIEN POUR LA PAIX INTERNATIONALE (MCPI) ♦ Christian Movement for Peace

3 avenue du Parc Royal, 1020 Brussels, Belgium.

Telephone: 32 (2) 478 94 10. *Fax:* 32 (2) 478 94 32. *Contact:* Teresa Lunha, President.

OBJECTIVES: To promote a just society, peace and human solidarity through youth exchanges and workcamps, seminars and training courses, peace and development education.

GENERAL INFORMATION: Creation: 1923. *Type of organisation:* network. *Member organisations:* 16. *Affiliated to:* Youth Forum - ECB - CCIVS. *Personnel/Total:* 4. *Salaried:* 3. *Volunteers:* 1. *Budget/ Total 1993:* ECU 297000 (US$ 347000). *Financial sources:* Private: 47%. *Public:* 49%. *Self-financing:* 4%.

PUBLICATIONS: *Periodicals:* International Info (6).

EVALUATION/RESEARCH: Evaluation reports available.

COMMENTS: Undertakes activities in the Commonwealth of Independent States. Information activities related to the Commonwealth of Independent States.

ACTIVITIES IN DEVELOPING REGIONS: Present in developing regions. Active in 16 country(ies). Maintains local field presence. Works through local field partners. **Sustainable Development Actions:** Children/ youth/family; Health/sanitation/water; Sending volunteers/experts/technical assistance. **Regions:** Central Asia and South Asia; Middle East; North Africa; South America; Southern Africa.

INFORMATION AND EDUCATION ACTIVITIES: Topics: Children/youth/ family; Culture/tradition/religion; Emergency relief/refugees/humanitarian assistance; Gender issues/women; Health/sanitation/water; Human rights/peace/conflicts; International economic relations/trade/debt/ finance; Peace/ethnic conflicts/armament/disarmament; Poverty/living conditions; Racism/xenophobia/antisemitism; Refugees/migrants/ethnic groups. **Activities:** Broadcasting/cultural events; Conferences/seminars/workshops/training activities; Exchanges/twinning/linking; Formal education; Information and documentation services/data bases; Information campaigns/exhibitions; Networking/electronic telecommunications; Publishing/audiovisual materials/educational materials.

BEL0304

MOUVEMENT CONTRE LE RACISME, L'ANTISEMITISME, LA XENOPHOBIE (MRAX)

Rue de la Poste 37, 1210 Bruxelles, Belgique.

Téléphone: 32 (2) 218 23 71. *Contact:* Vincent Lurquin, Président.

OBJECTIFS: Développer la vigilance à l'égard de toutes les manifestations de racisme. Mener des actions en justice sur la base de la loi de 1981. Accueillir et défendre les droits des travailleurs immigrés et de leurs familles ainsi que des demandeurs d'asile. Contribuer à la construction d'une société démocratique et solidaire par l'éducation.

INFORMATIONS GENERALES: Création: 1946. *Affiliée à:* Réseau Antiraciste européen (Bruxelles.). *Personnel/Total:* 14. *Salariés:* 10. *Bénévoles:* 4. *Budget/Total 1993:* ECU 121000 (US$ 142000). *Sources financières:* Privé: 5%. *Public:* 79%. *Autofinancement:* 16%.

PUBLICATIONS: *Périodiques:* MRAX-Information (4) - Bulletin du MRAX (12). *Rapport annuel.*

PREVISIONS D'ACTIVITES: Projet d'établissement d'antennes du MRAX dans les Provinces francophones du pays. Reprise de la campagne

pour l'obtention du droit de vote et d'elligibilité pour les non-communautaires, pour la reconnaissance de leur citoyenneté, lutte pour leur liberté de circulation en Europe.

ACTIVITES D'INFORMATION ET D'EDUCATION: Domaines: Droits de l'Homme/paix/conflits; Racisme/xénophobie/antisémitisme; Réfugiés/ migrants/groupes ethniques. **Activités:** Campagnes d'information/expositions; Conférences/séminaires/ateliers/activités de formation; Radiodiffusion/manifestations culturelles; Services d'information et de documentation/bases de données; Édition/documents audiovisuels/ documents éducatifs.

BEL0305

MOUVEMENT INTERNATIONAL DE LA JEUNESSE AGRICOLE ET RURALE CATHOLIQUE -EUROPE (MIJARC) ♦ International Movement of Catholic Agricultural and Rural Youth

Rue Vanderstichelen 21, 1210 Brussels, Belgium.

Telephone: 32 (16) 426 28 29. *Fax:* 32 (16) 426 41 72. *Contact:* Jean-Luc Renoux, Secrétaire européen.

BEL0306

NATIONAAL CENTRUM VOOR ONTWIKKELING-SSAMENWERKING (NCOS) ♦ National Centre for Co-operation in Development

Rue de la Linière, 11, 1060 Brussels, Belgium.

Telephone: 32 (2) 539 26 20. *Fax:* 32 (2) 539 13 43. *Contact:* Paul van Steenvoort, Secretary General.

OBJECTIVES: To raise the interest of the Flemish public in development issues through development education campaigns. To collect funds for projects in developing countries. To lobby the Belgian government to improve the quality and quantity of Belgian ODA.

GENERAL INFORMATION: Creation: 1966. *Type of organisation:* association of NGOs. *Member organisations:* 75. *Affiliated to:* International Coalition for Development Action - Agency for Cooperation and Research in Development (United Kingdom) - European Network on Debt and Development (Belgium) - European Solidarity Towards Equal Participation of People (Belgium) - Women in Development Europe (Belgium) - WGNRR (the Netherlands). *Personnel/Total:* 30084. *Salaried:* 84 of which: 4 in developing countries. *Volunteers:* 30000. *Budget/Total 1993:* ECU 6971000 (US$ 8153000). *Financial sources:* Private: 65%. *Public:* 6%. *Self-financing:* 29%.

PUBLICATIONS: *Periodicals:* De Wereld Morgen (The world tomorrow) (11). *Annual report. List of publications.*

EVALUATION/RESEARCH: Evaluation reports available. Undertakes research activities.

ACTIVITIES IN DEVELOPING REGIONS: Active in 20 country(ies). Maintains local field presence. Works through local field partners. **Sustainable Development Actions:** Children/youth/family; Democracy/good governance/institution building/participatory development; Ecology/environment/biodiversity; Education/training/literacy; Emergency relief/refugees/humanitarian assistance; Energy/transport; Food/famine; Gender issues/women; Health/sanitation/water; Human rights/peace/conflicts; Population/family planning/demography; Rural development/agriculture; Sending volunteers/experts/technical assistance; Small enterprises/ informal sector/handicrafts; Urban development/habitat. **Regions:** Caribbean; Central Africa; Central Asia and South Asia; East Africa; Mexico and Central America; Middle East; South America; South East Asia; West Africa.

INFORMATION AND EDUCATION ACTIVITIES: Topics: Children/youth/ family; Culture/tradition/religion; Ecology/environment/biodiversity; Education/training/literacy; Emergency relief/refugees/humanitarian assistance; Employment/unemployment; Food/famine; Gender issues/ women; Health/sanitation/water; Human rights/peace/conflicts; International economic relations/trade/debt/finance; International relations/ cooperation/development aid; Other; Peace/ethnic conflicts/armament/ disarmament; Population/family planning/demography; Poverty/living conditions; Refugees/migrants/ethnic groups; Rural development/agriculture; Urban development/habitat. **Activities:** Conferences/seminars/ workshops/training activities; Exchanges/twinning/linking; Formal education; Fund raising; Information and documentation services/data bases; Information campaigns/exhibitions; Lobbying/advocacy; Publishing/audiovisual materials/educational materials.

See: *How to Use the Directory,* page 11.

BEL0307
NATIONALE VROUWEN RAAD VAN BELGIE
Louiselaan 183, 1050 Brussels, Belgium.

Telephone: 32 (2) 647 09 05. *Contact:* Mme C. Andersen.

BEL0308
NEDERLANDSTALGIE NATIONALE VROUWENRAAD (NVR) ♦
Conseil National des femmes belges - Section Néerlandophone

De Meeussquare 28, 1040 Bruxelles, Belgique.

Téléphone: 32 (2) 511 82 43. *Fax:* 32 (2) 502 44 92. *Contact:* Mieke Van Haegendoren.

OBJECTIFS: Stimuler la participation des femmes à la vie publique, faire prendre conscience aux femmes des problèmes résultant d'une vie socio-économique et politique en évolution, lutter pour l'égalité des chances pour les femmes, surtout dans les domaines de l'éducation, du travail et de la politique.

INFORMATIONS GENERALES: *Création:* 1973. *Type d'organisation:* collectif. *Organisations membres:* 30. *Affiliée à:* Centre Européen du Conseil International des Femmes (Luxembourg) - Conseil International des Femmes (Paris.). *Personnel/Total:* 10. *Salariés:* 10. *Budget/Total 1993:* ECU 167000 (US$ 195000). *Sources financières:* Public: 84%. *Autofinancement:* 16%.

PUBLICATIONS: *Périodiques:* Vrouwenraad (4) - Jaar Boek van de Vrouw Anno (1). *Rapport annuel. Liste des publications.*

EVALUATION/RECHERCHE: Rapports d'évaluation disponibles. Entreprend des activités de recherche.

COMMENTAIRES: Intervient dans la Communauté des Etats indépendants. Activités d'information concernant la Communauté des Etats indépendants.

ACTIVITES D'INFORMATION ET D'EDUCATION: Domaines: Questions relatives aux femmes. **Activités:** Collecte de fonds; Conférences/séminaires/ateliers/activités de formation; Lobbying/plaidoyer; Services d'information et de documentation/bases de données.

BEL0309
NETWORK WOMEN IN DEVELOPMENT EUROPE (WIDE)
Square Ambiorix 10, 1040 Bruxelles, Belgium.

Telephone: 32 (2) 732 44 10. *Fax:* 32 (2) 732 19 34. *E-mail:* WIDE@gn.apc.org. *Contact:* Mieke Van der Veken, Coordinator.

OBJECTIVES: To network and lobby on gender and development issues at the national, European and international levels. To strengthen national platforms. To strengrhen North/South dialogue.

GENERAL INFORMATION: *Creation:* 1985. *Type of organisation:* network. *Member organisations:* 150. *Affiliated to:* Women and Environment network - EURODAD (Belgium). *Personnel/Total:* 2. *Salaried:* 2. *Budget/Total 1993:* ECU 160000 (US$ 187000). *Financial sources:* Private: 50%. Public: 50%.

PUBLICATIONS: *Periodicals:* Wide-Newsletter (6) - Wide-Bulletin (2). *Annual report.*

EVALUATION/RESEARCH: Undertakes research activities.

INFORMATION AND EDUCATION ACTIVITIES: Topics: Employment/unemployment; Gender issues/women; Human rights/peace/conflicts; International economic relations/trade/debt/finance; International relations/cooperation/development aid; Population/family planning/demography; Poverty/living conditions; Refugees/migrants/ethnic groups. **Activities:** Conferences/seminars/workshops/training activities; Exchanges/twinning/linking; Fund raising; Information and documentation services/data bases; Lobbying/advocacy; Networking/electronic telecommunications; Publishing/audiovisual materials/educational materials.

BEL0310
NINAFRI
Burchstraat 9, 9400 Ninove, Belgique.

Téléphone: 32 (54) 32 65 37. *Contact:* Jean Moreau.

BEL0311
NORD-SUD COOPERATION
Boulevard Gendebien 7, 7000 Mons, Belgique.

Téléphone: 32 (65) 33 48 55. *Fax:* 32 9650 34 86 17. *Contact:* Marcel Colart, Président.

BEL0312
NORWEGIAN REFUGEE COUNCIL
Avenue de l'aviation 8B, 1150 Bruxelles, Belgique.

BEL0313
OCIRIZ NATIONAAL
Kap. Cdt. Vinckestraat 11, 8710 Wielsbeke, Belgique.

Téléphone: 32 (56) 66 96 35. *Contact:* Martin Dewitte.

BEL0314
OEUVRE BELGO-COLOMBIENNE DE L'ENFANCE (OBCE)
Boulevard de Waterloo 33, 1000 Bruxelles, Belgique.

Téléphone: 32 (2) 513 88 10. *Fax:* 32 (2) 513 45 74. *Contact:* Nadine de Neve de Rooden, Présidente.

OBJECTIFS: Aider les organisations colombiennes qui fournissent gîte et/ou éducation aux enfants pauvres et abandonnés. Subvenir aux frais médicaux et scolaires des enfants de familles démunies.

INFORMATIONS GENERALES: *Création:* 1975. *Affiliée à:* Association des ONG francophones de Belgique. *Personnel/Total:* 13. *Bénévoles:* 13 dont: 3 dans les pays en développement. *Budget/Total 1993:* ECU 392000 (US$ 459000). *Sources financières:* Privé: 70%. Public: 30%.

PUBLICATIONS: *Périodiques:* Lettre de la présidente (1). *Rapport annuel.*

EVALUATION/RECHERCHE: Rapports d'évaluation disponibles.

COMMENTAIRES: L'ONG pilote des projets en cofinancement avec la CE et l'AGCD

ACTIVITES DANS LES REGIONS EN DEVELOPPEMENT: Intervient dans 1 pays. Maintient une présence locale sur le terrain. Intervient par l'intermédiaire d'organisations locales partenaires. **Actions de Développement durable:** Enfants/jeunesse/famille; Santé/assainissement/eau; Éducation/formation/alphabétisation. **Régions:** Amérique du Sud.

ACTIVITES D'INFORMATION ET D'EDUCATION: Domaines: Aliments/famine; Enfants/jeunesse/famille; Pauvreté/conditions de vie; Éducation/formation/alphabétisation. **Activités:** Collecte de fonds; Conférences/séminaires/ateliers/activités de formation; Édition/documents audiovisuels/documents éducatifs.

BEL0315
OEUVRES SOCIALES ET EDUCATIVES DES JESUITES AU TIERS-MONDE
Rue M/Liétart 31 bte 3, 1150 Bruxelles, Belgique.

Téléphone: 32 (2) 738 08 08. *Fax:* 32 (2) 738 08 09. *Contact:* Louis Hincq, Administrateur-délégué.

OBJECTIFS: Créer et soutenir des œuvres sociales et éducatives pour les territoires en voie de développement telles que les reconnaissent et les patronnent l'ONU et les autorités administratives belges.

INFORMATIONS GENERALES: *Création:* 1966. *Type d'organisation:* regroupement d'ONG. *Bénévoles:* 2. *Budget/Total 1993:* ECU 1582000 (US$ 1850000). *Sources financières:* Privé: 100%.

ACTIVITES DANS LES REGIONS EN DEVELOPPEMENT: Intervient dans 18 pays. Intervient par l'intermédiaire d'organisations locales partenaires. **Actions de Développement durable:** Développement rural/agriculture; Développement urbain/habitat; Santé/assainissement/eau; Secours d'urgence/réfugiés/aide humanitaire; Éducation/formation/alphabétisation. **Régions:** Afrique centrale; Asie centrale et Asie du Sud; Asie du Sud-Est; Mexique et Amerique centrale; Moyen-Orient.

Voir : *Comment utiliser le répertoire,* page 11.

BEL0316

ORBI-PHARMA

Van Trierstraat 40 , 2018 Antwerpen, Belgique.

Téléphone: 32 (3) 216 39 78. *Fax:* 32 (3) 216 98 97. *Contact:* Dr. Jozef Totte, Président.

OBJECTIFS: Procurer des médicaments essentiels, du matériel de laboratoire et du petit matériel chirurgical aux pays en développement et communautés en détresse, à des prix très avantageux, maintenir un bureau de conseil pharmaceutique.

INFORMATIONS GENERALES: *Création:* 1965. *Affiliée à:* CNCD, NCOS. *Personnel/Total:* 27. *Salariés:* 7. *Bénévoles:* 20. *Budget/ Total 1993:* ECU 198000 (US$ 231000). *Sources financières: Public:* 5%. *Autofinancement:* 95%.

PUBLICATIONS: *Périodiques:* Partners (4). *Rapport annuel. Liste des publications.*

EVALUATION/RECHERCHE: Rapports d'évaluation disponibles.

PREVISIONS D'ACTIVITES: Transmission d'informations pharmaceutiques vers les agents sanitaires, implantation des pharmacies-pilotes qui produisent à l'échelle semi-industrielle.

COMMENTAIRES: Intervient dans la Communauté des Etats indépendants.

ACTIVITES DANS LES REGIONS EN DEVELOPPEMENT: Intervient dans 50 pays. Intervient par l'intermédiaire d'organisations locales partenaires. **Actions de Développement durable:** Santé/assainissement/eau; Secours d'urgence/réfugiés/aide humanitaire; Éducation/formation/alphabétisation. **Régions:** Afrique centrale; Afrique de l'Est; Afrique de l'Ouest; Afrique du Nord; Amérique du Sud; Asie du Sud-Est; Caraïbes; Mexique et Amerique centrale; Moyen-Orient.

ACTIVITES D'INFORMATION ET D'EDUCATION: **Domaines:** Santé/assainissement/eau; Secours d'urgence/réfugiés/aide humanitaire. **Activités:** Collecte de fonds; Services d'information et de documentation/bases de données; Édition/documents audiovisuels/documents éducatifs; Éducation formelle.

BEL0317

ORDRE DES CHEVALIERS DU SAINT-SEPULCRE DE JERUSALEM

Rue des Sablons 13, 1000 Bruxelles, Belgique.

Téléphone: 32 (3) 231 96 24. *Fax:* 32 (2) 375 80 43. *Contact:* M. Boelarts.

OBJECTIFS: Aider et soutenir par tous les moyens, financiers ou autres, les séminaires, les œuvres et les écoles confessionnels ou non, situés en Terre Sainte et relevant du Patriarche Latin de Jérusalem ou des autorités ecclésiastiques des divers rites catholiques afin de coopérer au développement du progrès social et de l'instruction.

INFORMATIONS GENERALES: *Création:* 1983. *Personnel/Total:* 4. *Bénévoles:* 4. *Budget/Total 1993:* ECU 156000 (US$ 183000). *Sources financières: Public:* 35%. *Autofinancement:* 65%.

PUBLICATIONS: *Périodiques:* Deus lo vult (3).

PREVISIONS D'ACTIVITES: Soutenir et étendre les centres de formation technique et professionnelle pour filles et jeunes femmes. Agrandir le centre de formation de mécanique pour jeunes gens à Maduba en Jordanie.

ACTIVITES DANS LES REGIONS EN DEVELOPPEMENT: Intervient directement dans les régions en développement. Intervient dans 1 pays. Intervient par l'intermédiaire d'organisations locales partenaires. **Actions de Développement durable:** Petites entreprises/secteur informel/artisanat; Questions relatives aux femmes; Éducation/formation/alphabétisation. **Régions:** Moyen-Orient.

ACTIVITES D'INFORMATION ET D'EDUCATION: **Domaines:** Questions relatives aux femmes; Éducation/formation/alphabétisation. **Activités:** Conférences/séminaires/ateliers/activités de formation; Éducation formelle.

BEL0318

ORDRE DES CHEVALIERS HOSPITALIERS DE SAINT-JEAN DE JERUSALEM (OSJ)

Mechelsestraat 202, 3000 Louvain, Belgium.

Telephone: 32 (2) 759 61 24. *Fax:* 32 (2) 759 61 24. *Contact:* W.J.P.J. Pincket.

OBJECTIVES: To serve the poor of Christ.

GENERAL INFORMATION: *Creation:* 1964. *Type of organisation:* network. *Member organisations:* 19. *Personnel/Total:* 400. *Volunteers:* 400 of which: 15 in developing countries. *Budget/Total 1993:* ECU 1240000 (US$ 1450900). *Financial sources: Private:* 75%. *Public:* 5%. *Self-financing:* 20%.

PUBLICATIONS: *Periodicals:* The Hospitaller (4) - OSJ/UN (9). *Annual report. List of publications.*

EVALUATION/RESEARCH: Evaluation reports available.

COMMENTS: Undertakes activities in the Commonwealth of Independent States. Information activities related to the Commonwealth of Independent States.

ACTIVITIES IN DEVELOPING REGIONS: Present in developing regions. Active in 6 country(ies). Maintains local field presence. Works through local field partners. **Sustainable Development Actions:** Children/youth/family; Emergency relief/refugees/humanitarian assistance; Health/sanitation/water. **Regions:** Central Africa; East Africa; Mexico and Central America; Middle East; South America; South East Asia; West Africa.

INFORMATION AND EDUCATION ACTIVITIES: **Topics:** Children/youth/family; Emergency relief/refugees/humanitarian assistance; Food/famine; Health/sanitation/water; Refugees/migrants/ethnic groups. **Activities:** Conferences/seminars/workshops/training activities; Fund raising; Information and documentation services/data bases; Information campaigns/exhibitions; Lobbying/advocacy; Networking/electronic telecommunications; Publishing/audiovisual materials/educational materials.

BEL0319

ORIENTALIA ♦ International Centre for Co-operation and Research on Development

Rue Marie de Bourgogne 8, 1040 Bruxelles, Belgique.

Téléphone: 32 (2) 512 15 49. *Contact:* Serge Descy, Président.

BEL0320

OVERSEAS MISSION SECRETARIAT

Rue St Boniface 26, 1050 Brussels, Belgium.

Telephone: 32 (2) 513 90 62. *Contact:* R. de Beys.

BEL0321

OXFAM - MAGASINS DU MONDE

Rue F. Michiels 7A, 1180 Bruxelles, Belgique.

BEL0322

OXFAM - WERELDWINKELS ♦ Magasins du Monde - Oxfam

Nieuwland 35-37, 9000 Gand, Belgique.

Téléphone: 32 (9) 223 01 61. *Fax:* 32 (9) 225 04 78. *Contact:* Bontemps Marc, Secrétaire général.

OBJECTIFS: Soutenir des modèles de développement progressifs dans le Tiers-Monde pour parvenir à changer les structures économiques et politiques internationales. Organiser le commerce alternatif.

INFORMATIONS GENERALES: *Création:* 1971. *Type d'organisation:* réseau. *Affiliée à:* EFTA (Europe) - IFAT. *Personnel/Total:* 2012. *Salariés:* 12. *Bénévoles:* 2000. *Budget/Total 1993:* ECU 667000 (US$ 780000). *Sources financières: Privé:* 1%. *Public:* 25%. *Autofinancement:* 74%.

PUBLICATIONS: *Périodiques:* Weeweekrant (12). *Rapport annuel. Liste des publications.*

ACTIVITES DANS LES REGIONS EN DEVELOPPEMENT: Intervient par l'intermédiaire d'organisations locales partenaires. **Actions de Déve-**

See: *How to Use the Directory,* page 11.

loppement durable: Dette/finances/commerce. **Régions:** Afrique australe; Afrique centrale; Afrique de l'Est; Afrique de l'Ouest; Afrique du Nord; Amérique du Sud; Asie de l'Est; Asie du Sud-Est; Caraïbes; Mexique et Amerique centrale; Moyen-Orient.

ACTIVITES D'INFORMATION ET D'EDUCATION: Domaines: Enfants/jeunesse/famille; Racisme/xénophobie/antisémitisme; Relations économiques internationales/commerce/dette/finances; Réfugiés/migrants/groupes ethniques; Écologie/environnement/biodiversité. **Activités:** Campagnes d'information/expositions; Collecte de fonds; Conférences/séminaires/ateliers/activités de formation; Lobbying/plaidoyer; Échanges/parrainage/jumelage; Édition/documents audiovisuels/documents éducatifs; Éducation formelle.

BEL0323
OXFAM BELGIQUE

Rue du Conseil 39 , 1050 Bruxelles, Belgique.

Téléphone: 32 (2) 512 99 90. **Fax:** 32 (2) 514 28 13. **Contact:** Pierre Galand, Secrétaire général.

OBJECTIFS: Promouvoir la coopération et la solidarité par la réalisation de projets de développement. Mobiliser l'opinion publique et les responsables politiques par des actions de sensibilisation à la problématique des relations Nord-Sud, afin de réaliser les objectifs fixés.

INFORMATIONS GENERALES: *Création:* 1964. ***Type d'organisation:*** réseau. ***Organisations membres:*** 4. ***Affiliée à:*** NCOS - CNCD - Coprogram - ADO - VAAK - Consortium Kampuchéa - Consortium belge Sandino Vive - Comité National d'Action pour la Paix et le Développement -EUROSTEP - OXFAM International (Royaume-Uni.). ***Personnel/Total:*** 190. *Salariés:* 80 dont: 35 dans les pays en développement. *Bénévoles:* 110. ***Budget/Total 1993:*** ECU 12109000 (US$ 14163000). ***Sources financières:*** *Privé:* 25%. *Public:* 68%. *Autofinancement:* 7%.

PUBLICATIONS: *Périodiques:* OXFAM Info (4) - OXFAM Nieuws (4). *Rapport annuel. Liste des publications.*

ACTIVITES DANS LES REGIONS EN DEVELOPPEMENT: Intervient directement dans les régions en développement. Intervient dans 36 pays. Maintient une présence locale sur le terrain. Intervient par l'intermédiaire d'organisations locales partenaires. **Actions de Développement durable:** Aliments/famine; Développement rural/agriculture; Développement urbain/habitat; Enfants/jeunesse/famille; Santé/assainissement/eau; Secours d'urgence/réfugiés/aide humanitaire; Éducation/formation/alphabétisation; Énergie/transport. **Régions:** Afrique australe; Afrique centrale; Afrique de l'Est; Afrique de l'Ouest; Afrique du Nord; Amérique du Sud; Asie du Sud-Est; Caraïbes; Mexique et Amerique centrale; Moyen-Orient.

ACTIVITES D'INFORMATION ET D'EDUCATION: Domaines: Aliments/famine; Développement rural/agriculture; Enfants/jeunesse/famille; Paix/conflits ethniques/armement/désarmement; Pauvreté/conditions de vie; Questions relatives aux femmes; Racisme/xénophobie/antisémitisme; Relations internationales/coopération/aide au développement; Relations économiques internationales/commerce/dette/finances; Santé/assainissement/eau; Secours d'urgence/réfugiés/aide humanitaire; Éducation/formation/alphabétisation. **Activités:** Campagnes d'information/expositions; Collecte de fonds; Lobbying/plaidoyer; Édition/documents audiovisuels/documents éducatifs; Éducation formelle.

BEL0324
PAX CHRISTI INTERNATIONAL

Oude Graanmarkt 21, 1000 Brussels, Belgium.

Contact: Mr. E de Jonghe.

BEL0325
PAX CHRISTI WALLONIE-BRUXELLES

Chaussee de Wavre 216, 1040 Bruxelles, Belgique.

Contact: Mr. F. Schiffino.

BEL0326
PHILIPPINE INTERNATIONAL CENTRE FOR HUMAN RIGHTS (PICHR)

Vlasfabriekstraat 11, 1060 Brussels, Belgium.

Telephone: 32 (2) 539 26 20. **Fax:** 32 (2) 539 13 43. **Contact:** Maria L. van der Meer Altamirano, Executive Director.

BEL0327
PLAN INTERNATIONAL, BELGIUM

F. Laurentplein 31, 9000 Gent, Belgium.

Telephone: 32 (9) 224 23 73. **Fax:** 32 (9) 233 10 04. **Contact:** Philippe Vanpeperstraete.

OBJECTIVES: To help needy children, their families and communities by promoting long-term, sustainable grass roots development, built upon people's participation in their own advancement. To foster inter-cultural dialogue and understanding.

GENERAL INFORMATION: *Creation:* 1985. ***Affiliated to:*** Foster Parents Plan International (USA). ***Personnel/Total:*** 47. *Salaried:* 12. *Volunteers:* 35. ***Budget/Total 1993:*** ECU 7908000 (US$ 9249000). ***Financial sources:*** *Private:* 100%.

PUBLICATIONS: *Periodicals:* Plan Magazine (4). *Annual report.*

EVALUATION/RESEARCH: Evaluation reports available. Undertakes research activities.

PLANNED ACTIVITIES: Exhibition on children's toys from Africa.

COMMENTS: Undertakes activities in the Commonwealth of Independent States.

ACTIVITIES IN DEVELOPING REGIONS: Present in developing regions. Active in 30 country(ies). Maintains local field presence. Works through local field partners. **Sustainable Development Actions:** Children/youth/family; Democracy/good governance/institution building/participatory development; Ecology/environment/biodiversity; Education/training/literacy; Gender issues/women; Health/sanitation/water; Population/family planning/demography; Rural development/agriculture; Small enterprises/informal sector/handicrafts; Urban development/habitat. **Regions:** Caribbean; Central Africa; Central Asia and South Asia; East Africa; East Asia; Mexico and Central America; South America; South East Asia; Southern Africa; West Africa.

INFORMATION AND EDUCATION ACTIVITIES: Topics: Children/youth/family; Ecology/environment/biodiversity; Gender issues/women; Health/sanitation/water; Human rights/peace/conflicts; International relations/cooperation/development aid; Population/family planning/demography; Poverty/living conditions; Rural development/agriculture; Urban development/habitat. **Activities:** Broadcasting/cultural events; Exchanges/twinning/linking; Fund raising; Information and documentation services/data bases; Information campaigns/exhibitions; Lobbying/advocacy; Publishing/audiovisual materials/educational materials.

BEL0328
PRIEURE D'AVALTERRE DE L'ORDRE SOUVERAIN DE SAINT-JEAN-DE-JERUSALEM (PRAVOSJ)

Rue de la Régence 23, 7060 Soignies, Belgique.

Téléphone: 32 (67) 33 34 29. **Fax:** 32 (67) 33 34 29. **Contact:** Ernest Foucart, Président.

OBJECTIFS: Pratiquer la charité et agir selon les idéaux de la Déclaration Universelle des Droits de l'Homme, particulièrement dans le domaine de la nutrition et de la santé. Apporter aide sanitaire, soins de santé primaires et éducation à la santé en vue d'aider à l'autosuffisance des régions assistées.

INFORMATIONS GENERALES: *Création:* 1986. ***Personnel/Total:*** 14. *Salariés:* 6 dont: 6 dans les pays en développement. *Bénévoles:* 8 dont: 1 dans les pays en développement. ***Budget/Total 1993:*** ECU 30000 (US$ 35000). ***Sources financières:*** *Privé:* 69%. *Autofinancement:* 31%.

PUBLICATIONS: *Rapport annuel. Liste des publications.*

EVALUATION/RECHERCHE: Rapports d'évaluation disponibles. Entreprend des activités de recherche.

PREVISIONS D'ACTIVITES: Réadaptation de jeunes rwandais dans un cadre socio-professionnel (région de Kigali - structures existantes)

COMMENTAIRES: Intervient dans la Communauté des Etats indépendants.

Voir : *Comment utiliser le répertoire,* page 11.

ACTIVITES DANS LES REGIONS EN DEVELOPPEMENT: Intervient directement dans les régions en développement. Intervient dans 2 pays. Maintient une présence locale sur le terrain. **Actions de Développement durable:** Droits de l'Homme/paix/conflits; Démocratie/bonne gestion publique/création d'institutions/développement participatif; Enfants/jeunesse/famille; Envoi de volontaires/experts/assistance technique; Santé/assainissement/eau; Secours d'urgence/réfugiés/aide humanitaire; Éducation/formation/alphabétisation. **Régions:** Afrique centrale; Afrique de l'Ouest.

ACTIVITES D'INFORMATION ET D'EDUCATION: Domaines: Enfants/jeunesse/famille; Pauvreté/conditions de vie; Santé/assainissement/eau; Secours d'urgence/réfugiés/aide humanitaire. **Activités:** Collecte de fonds.

BEL0329

PROGETTO SUD-UIL

Rue du Gouvernement 34, 1000 Bruxelles, Belgique.

BEL0330

PROGRAMME DE RECHERCHE ET DE LIAISON UNIVERSITAIRES POUR LE DEVELOPPEMENT (PRELUDE)

Facultés Universitaires, Rue des Bruxelles 61, 5000 Namur, Belgique.

Téléphone: 32 (81) 72 41 16 . *Fax:* 32 (81) 72 41 18. *Contact:* Georges Thill, Directeur de la Coordination scientifique.

OBJECTIFS: Concevoir et mettre en œuvre, par des recherches-actions entreprises par des chercheurs volontaires, des pratiques de codéveloppement comme réponse au mal-développement au Nord et au Sud.

INFORMATIONS GENERALES: *Création:* 1985. *Type d'organisation:* réseau.

PUBLICATIONS: *Périodiques:* Bulletin Prélude (4).

BEL0331

PROJECTGROEP VOOR TECHNISCHE ONTWIKKELINGSSA-MENWERKING (PROTOS) ♦ Groupe de projets pour le développement technique en coopération

Groot-Brittanniëlaan 43, 9000 Gand, Belgique.

Téléphone: 32 (9) 225 27 93. *Fax:* 32 (9) 225 66 07. *Contact:* Stef Lambrecht.

OBJECTIFS: Apporter une contribution au développement des populations les plus déshéritées du Tiers monde, grâce à l'étude, l'apport de conseils et la réalisation de projets de développement, en particulier des projets concernant l'eau dans tous les domaines.

INFORMATIONS GENERALES: *Création:* 1977. *Affiliée à:* National Centrum voor Ontwikkelingssamenwerking (Belgique) - Coprogram (Belgique) - Coordination flamande-Haïti (Belgique). *Personnel/Total:* 17. *Salariés:* 17 dont: 7 dans les pays en développement. *Budget/Total 1993:* ECU 1074000 (US$ 1256000). *Sources financières:* Privé: 25%. Public: 75%.

PUBLICATIONS: *Périodiques:* Bonne Nouvelle (4). *Rapport annuel.*

EVALUATION/RECHERCHE: Rapports d'évaluation disponibles.

ACTIVITES DANS LES REGIONS EN DEVELOPPEMENT: Intervient directement dans les régions en développement. Intervient dans 7 pays. Maintient une présence locale sur le terrain. Intervient par l'intermédiaire d'organisations locales partenaires. **Actions de Développement durable:** Aliments/famine; Développement rural/agriculture; Envoi de volontaires/experts/assistance technique; Petites entreprises/secteur informel/artisanat; Santé/assainissement/eau; Éducation/formation/alphabétisation; Énergie/transport. **Régions:** Afrique centrale; Afrique de l'Ouest; Amérique du Sud; Caraïbes.

ACTIVITES D'INFORMATION ET D'EDUCATION: Domaines: Développement rural/agriculture; Santé/assainissement/eau. **Activités:** Campagnes d'information/expositions; Édition/documents audiovisuels/documents éducatifs.

BEL0332

QUAKER COUNCIL FOR EUROPEAN AFFAIRS (QCEA) ♦ Conseil Quaker pour les affaires européennes

50 square Ambiorix, 1040 Brussels, Belgium.

Telephone: 32 (2) 230 49 35. *Fax:* 32 (2) 230 63 70. *Contact:* David Forbes, Representative.

BEL0333

RURALITE-ENVIRONNEMENT-DEVELOPPEMENT (RED)

Rue des Potiers 2, 6717 Attert, Belgique.

Téléphone: 32 (63) 22 37 02. *Fax:* 32 (63) 21 98 70. *Contact:* Patrice Collignon, Directeur.

OBJECTIFS: Promouvoir une politique de développement global en faveur des zones rurales européennes. Echanger et organiser des rencontres. Publier et entreprendre des travaux de recherche appliquée sur des thèmes ruraux.

INFORMATIONS GENERALES: *Création:* 1980. *Type d'organisation:* réseau. *Affiliée à:* Centre Européen d'Intérêt Rural - TASK Force ONG Nature - Bureau Européen de l'Environnement. *Personnel/Total:* 4. *Salariés:* 3. *Bénévoles:* 1. *Budget/Total 1993:* ECU 148000 (US$ 173000). *Sources financières:* Public: 95%. Autofinancement: 5%.

PUBLICATIONS: *Périodiques:* Dossier RED (2) - Bulletin TASK Force (3). *Rapport annuel. Liste des publications.*

COMMENTAIRES: Intervient dans la Communauté des Etats indépendants. Activités d'information concernant la Communauté des Etats indépendants.

ACTIVITES D'INFORMATION ET D'EDUCATION: Domaines: Culture/tradition/religion; Développement rural/agriculture; Écologie/environnement/biodiversité. **Activités:** Conférences/séminaires/ateliers/activités de formation; Lobbying/plaidoyer.

BEL0334

THE SALVATION ARMY, EUROPEAN OFFICE

34 nouveau marché aux grains, 1000 Brussels, Belgium.

Telephone: 32 (2) 512 38 59. *Fax:* 32 (2) 512 38 69. *Contact:* Dirk C. Verpoorte, Director.

BEL0335

SAMEN ANDERS GAAN ONTWIKKELEN (SAGO) ♦ Together Towards an Alternative Development

Lange Lozanastraat 14, 2018 Antwerpen, Belgium.

Telephone: 32 (3) 237 56 30. *Contact:* Yvette Deploige, Co-ordinator.

OBJECTIVES: To sustain and reinforce the process of consciousness raising, autonomy and independence of the popular movement in Latin America. To improve the situation of women and encourage their social development

GENERAL INFORMATION: *Creation:* 1972. *Affiliated to:* NCOS - AQUI NOSOTRAS. *Personnel/Total:* 14. *Salaried:* 13. *Volunteers:* 1. *Financial sources:* Public: 70%. Self-financing: 30%.

PUBLICATIONS: *Periodicals:* America Revista (6) - Boletin Aqui Nosotras (4). *Annual report.*

PLANNED ACTIVITIES: The organisation plans to create a Network of Latin American and European women; linking and exchange programmes between youth and women's groups in Belgium and Latin America; investigation, publication and cultural programmes on Latin American presence in Europe.

ACTIVITIES IN DEVELOPING REGIONS: Active in 4 country(ies). Works through local field partners. **Sustainable Development Actions:** Children/youth/family; Democracy/good governance/institution building/participatory development; Ecology/environment/biodiversity; Education/training/literacy; Gender issues/women; Health/sanitation/water; Human rights/peace/conflicts; Rural development/agriculture; Urban development/habitat. **Regions:** Caribbean; Mexico and Central America; South America.

INFORMATION AND EDUCATION ACTIVITIES: Topics: Children/youth/family; Culture/tradition/religion; Ecology/environment/biodiversity; Education/training/literacy; Employment/unemployment; Food/famine; Gender issues/women; Health/sanitation/water; Human rights/peace/con-

See: *How to Use the Directory,* page 11.

flicts; International economic relations/trade/debt/finance; International relations/cooperation/development aid; Peace/ethnic conflicts/armament/disarmament; Population/family planning/demography; Poverty/living conditions; Racism/xenophobia/antisemitism; Refugees/migrants/ethnic groups; Rural development/agriculture; Urban development/habitat. **Activities:** Conferences/seminars/workshops/training activities; Exchanges/twinning/linking; Fund raising; Information and documentation services/data bases; Information campaigns/exhibitions; Lobbying/advocacy; Networking/electronic telecommunications; Publishing/audiovisual materials/educational materials.

BEL0336

SAMENWERKING LATIJNS AMERIKA (SLA) ♦ Coopération Amérique latine

rue du Collège St. Michel, 38, 1150 Bruxelles, Belgique.

Téléphone: 32 (02) 772 59 48. *Fax:* 32 (02) 772 60 19. *Contact:* Roger de Beir, Président.

OBJECTIFS: Envoyer des coopérants-ONG à la demande de partenaires latino-américains afin d'être insérés dans leurs projets.

INFORMATIONS GENERALES: *Création:* 1958. *Affiliée à:* Fédération des ONG francophones d'envoi de coopérants-ONG - Fédération des ONG neerlandophones d'envoi de coopérants-ONG. *Personnel/Total:* 3. *Salariés:* 2. *Bénévoles:* 1. *Budget/Total 1993:* ECU 178000 (US$ 208000).

PUBLICATIONS: *Périodiques:* Coopération Amérique Latine (4) - Samenwerking Latyns-America (4). *Rapport annuel.*

ACTIVITES DANS LES REGIONS EN DEVELOPPEMENT: Intervient dans 14 pays. Intervient par l'intermédiaire d'organisations locales partenaires. **Actions de Développement durable:** Droits de l'Homme/paix/conflits; Démocratie/bonne gestion publique/création d'institutions/développement participatif; Développement rural/agriculture; Développement urbain/habitat; Enfants/jeunesse/famille; Envoi de volontaires/experts/assistance technique; Petites entreprises/secteur informel/artisanat; Population/planning familial/démographie; Questions relatives aux femmes; Santé/assainissement/eau; Écologie/environnement/biodiversité; Éducation/formation/alphabétisation. **Régions:** Amérique du Sud; Caraïbes; Mexique et Amerique centrale.

BEL0337

SCOTTISH EUROPEAN AID

Rue Vanderkindere 289, 1180 Bruxelles, Belgique.

BEL0338

SECOURS INTERNATIONAL CARITAS CATHOLICA, BELGIQUE (CARITAS)

Rue Guimard 1, 1040 Bruxelles, Belgique.

Téléphone: 32 (2) 511 42 55. *Fax:* 32 (2) 514 48 67. *Contact:* Luc Heymans, Directeur.

OBJECTIFS: Mener des actions humanitaires. Accueillir des réfugiés en Belgique.

INFORMATIONS GENERALES: *Création:* 1949. *Affiliée à:* CARITAS Internationalis (Italie) - VOICE (Belgique). *Personnel/Total:* 45. *Salariés:* 35. *Bénévoles:* 10. *Budget/Total 1993:* ECU 17298000 (US$ 20233000). *Sources financières:* Privé: 40%. *Public:* 60%.

PUBLICATIONS: *Périodiques:* Contacts (4). *Rapport annuel.*

COMMENTAIRES: Intervient dans la Communauté des Etats indépendants. Activités d'information concernant la Communauté des Etats indépendants.

ACTIVITES DANS LES REGIONS EN DEVELOPPEMENT: Intervient dans 2 pays. Intervient par l'intermédiaire d'organisations locales partenaires. **Actions de Développement durable:** Aliments/famine; Secours d'urgence/réfugiés/aide humanitaire. **Régions:** Afrique australe; Afrique centrale; Afrique de l'Est; Afrique de l'Ouest; Afrique du Nord; Amérique du Sud; Asie centrale et Asie du Sud; Asie de l'Est; Asie du Sud-Est; Caraïbes; Mexique et Amerique centrale; Moyen-Orient.

ACTIVITES D'INFORMATION ET D'EDUCATION: Domaines: Secours d'urgence/réfugiés/aide humanitaire. **Activités:** Collecte de fonds;

Conférences/séminaires/ateliers/activités de formation; Services d'information et de documentation/bases de données.

BEL0339

SENSORIAL HANDICAP COOPERATION (SHC)

Chaussée de Waterloo 1504, 1180 Bruxelles, Belgique.

Telephone: 32 (2) 374 90 90. *Contact:* J. Meyers.

BEL0340

SERVICE CIVIL INTERNATIONAL - SOLIDARITY, EXCHANGE, EDUCATION FOR DEVELOPMENT (SCI-SEED)

Draakstraat 37, 2018 Antwerpen, Belgium.

Telephone: 32 (3) 235 94 73. *Fax:* 32 (3) 235 29 73. *Contact:* Owen D. McCarney, Coordinator.

OBJECTIVES: To work for peace, reconciliation and justice through programmes of practical action involving our volunteer membership (SCI). To co-ordinate all SCI's North/South programmes and to support our development education initiatives in Europe (SEEDS).

GENERAL INFORMATION: *Creation:* 1920. *Affiliated to:* Co-ordinating Commitee for International Voluntary Service (France). *Personnel/Total:* 253. *Salaried:* 3 of which: 1 in developing countries. *Volunteers:* 250 of which: 250 in developing countries. *Budget/Total 1993:* ECU 47000 (US$ 61000). *Financial sources:* Private: 10%. Public: 75%. Self-financing: 15%.

PUBLICATIONS: *Periodicals:* Action (4) - Crossing Borders (4) - Long-Term News (4) - Yellow Pages (4). *Annual report.*

EVALUATION/RESEARCH: Evaluation reports available. Undertakes research activities.

PLANNED ACTIVITIES: SCI-SEED has consultative status with UNESCO and the Council of Europe.

COMMENTS: Undertakes activities in the Commonwealth of Independent States. Information activities related to the Commonwealth of Independent States.

ACTIVITIES IN DEVELOPING REGIONS: Present in developing regions. Active in 23 country(ies). Maintains local field presence. Works through local field partners. **Sustainable Development Actions:** Children/youth/family; Democracy/good governance/institution building/participatory development; Ecology/environment/biodiversity; Education/training/literacy; Emergency relief/refugees/humanitarian assistance; Energy/transport; Food/famine; Gender issues/women; Health/sanitation/water; Human rights/peace/conflicts; Population/family planning/demography; Rural development/agriculture; Sending volunteers/experts/technical assistance; Small enterprises/informal sector/handicrafts; Urban development/habitat. **Regions:** Central Asia and South Asia; East Africa; East Asia; Mexico and Central America; Middle East; North Africa; South America; South East Asia; Southern Africa; West Africa.

INFORMATION AND EDUCATION ACTIVITIES: Topics: Culture/tradition/religion; Ecology/environment/biodiversity; Emergency relief/refugees/humanitarian assistance; Gender issues/women; International economic relations/trade/debt/finance; International relations/cooperation/development aid; Peace/ethnic conflicts/armament/disarmament; Racism/xenophobia/antisemitism; Refugees/migrants/ethnic groups; Rural development/agriculture; Urban development/habitat. **Activities:** Broadcasting/cultural events; Conferences/seminars/workshops/training activities; Exchanges/twinning/linking; Information campaigns/exhibitions; Publishing/audiovisual materials/educational materials.

BEL0341

SERVICE DE COOPERATION MISSIONNAIRE AU DEVELOPPEMENT-DMOS (COMIDE-DMOS)

195 boulevard Léopold II, 1080 Bruxelles, Belgique.

Téléphone: 32 (2) 427 47 20. *Fax:* 32 (2) 425 90 31. *Contact:* Constant Provoost.

OBJECTIFS: Aider les missionnaires dans la réalisation de leurs projets de développement en faveur des populations locales et avec elles. Apporter une aide dans les domaines de la formation des adultes, de la formation artisanale, de l'agriculture, des soins préventifs, de l'alimenta-

tion, du développement des ressources humaines et du développement communautaire.

INFORMATIONS GENERALES: *Création:* 1969. *Affiliée à:* Vlaamse Federatie Van Ngo's voor Ontwikkelingssamenwerking (Belgique) - Association des ONG francophones et germanophones (Belgique) - Comité van de Missionerende Instituten (Belgique.). *Personnel/Total:* 19. *Salariés:* 18. *Bénévoles:* 1. *Budget/Total 1993:* ECU 5931000 (US$ 6937000). *Sources financières:* Privé: 32%. *Public:* 58%.

PUBLICATIONS: *Périodiques:* Samen Op Weg (4) (4). *Rapport annuel.*

ACTIVITES DANS LES REGIONS EN DEVELOPPEMENT: Intervient directement dans les régions en développement. Intervient dans 32 pays. Intervient par l'intermédiaire d'organisations locales partenaires. **Actions de Développement durable:** Aliments/famine; Dette/finances/commerce; Droits de l'Homme/paix/conflits; Développement rural/agriculture; Développement urbain/habitat; Enfants/jeunesse/famille; Petites entreprises/secteur informel/artisanat; Population/planning familial/démographie; Questions relatives aux femmes; Santé/assainissement/eau; Écologie/environnement/biodiversité; Éducation/formation/alphabétisation; Énergie/transport. **Régions:** Afrique australe; Afrique centrale; Afrique de l'Est; Afrique de l'Ouest; Amérique du Sud; Asie centrale et Asie du Sud; Asie du Sud-Est; Caraïbes; Mexique et Amerique centrale.

ACTIVITES D'INFORMATION ET D'EDUCATION: Domaines: Développement rural/agriculture; Enfants/jeunesse/famille; Santé/assainissement/eau; Éducation/formation/alphabétisation. **Activités:** Collecte de fonds; Éducation formelle.

BEL0342

SERVICE LAIQUE DE COOPERATION AU DEVELOPPEMENT (SLCD)

Rue des Fripiers 15-17, Galerie du Centre, Bloc 1, 1000 Bruxelles, Belgique.

Téléphone: 32 (2) 217 72 50. *Fax:* 32 (2) 223 02 17. *Contact:* A.M. Hermanus, Président.

OBJECTIFS: Répondre aux demandes des populations les plus démunies des pays en développement en organisant avec elles des actions de coopération, dans le respect des identités et des coutumes locales.

INFORMATIONS GENERALES: *Création:* 1980. *Affiliée à:* CNCD (Belgique) - ADO (Belgique) - COTA (Belgique) - CODEF (Belgique). *Personnel/Total:* 25. *Salariés:* 4. *Bénévoles:* 21 dont: 17 dans les pays en développement. *Budget/Total 1993:* ECU 9885000 (US$ 11562000). *Sources financières:* Privé: 25%. *Public:* 75%.

PUBLICATIONS: *Périodiques:* Service Laïque de Coopération au Développement (4). *Rapport annuel. Liste des publications.*

COMMENTAIRES: L'organisation organise des collectes de fonds et des campagnes d'information sur les projets en cours.

ACTIVITES DANS LES REGIONS EN DEVELOPPEMENT: Intervient directement dans les régions en développement. Intervient dans 13 pays. Maintient une présence locale sur le terrain. Intervient par l'intermédiaire d'organisations locales partenaires. **Actions de Développement durable:** Développement rural/agriculture; Développement urbain/habitat; Enfants/jeunesse/famille; Envoi de volontaires/experts/assistance technique; Petites entreprises/secteur informel/artisanat; Population/planning familial/démographie; Questions relatives aux femmes; Santé/assainissement/eau; Écologie/environnement/biodiversité; Éducation/formation/alphabétisation. **Régions:** Afrique centrale; Afrique de l'Ouest; Afrique du Nord; Asie du Sud-Est; Moyen-Orient.

BEL0343

SERVICE SOCIAL DES ETRANGERS-FORMATION ET AIDE AUX ENTREPRISES-VITROBIO

22, rue de la Croix, 1050 Bruxelles, Belgique.

Téléphone: 32 (2) 649 99 58. *Fax:* 32 (2) 646 43 24. *Contact:* Mauro Sbolgi, Directeur.

OBJECTIFS: Apporter une aide aux pays en développement et aux étrangers vivant en Belgique. Entreprendre des recherches et favoriser les

transferts de technologie dans les domaines du développement rural et de l'agriculture.

INFORMATIONS GENERALES: *Création:* 1962. *Type d'organisation:* regroupement d'ONG. *Organisations membres:* 3. *Personnel/Total:* 70. *Salariés:* 70. *Budget/Total 1993:* ECU 2965000 (US$ 3468000).

PUBLICATIONS: *Rapport annuel.*

EVALUATION/RECHERCHE: Rapports d'évaluation disponibles. Entreprend des activités de recherche.

PREVISIONS D'ACTIVITES: Développer une activitée de recherche agricole et de production de plants

COMMENTAIRES: Intervient dans la Communauté des Etats indépendants.

ACTIVITES DANS LES REGIONS EN DEVELOPPEMENT: Intervient dans 5 pays. Intervient par l'intermédiaire d'organisations locales partenaires. **Actions de Développement durable:** Développement rural/agriculture. **Régions:** Afrique centrale; Afrique de l'Est; Afrique de l'Ouest; Asie centrale et Asie du Sud.

ACTIVITES D'INFORMATION ET D'EDUCATION: Domaines: Développement rural/agriculture. **Activités:** Éducation formelle.

BEL0344

SOBER VOOR ANDEREN ♦ Sobres pour les autres

St. Ritastraat 32, 3900 Lommel, Belgique.

Téléphone: 32 (11) 64 81 29. *Contact:* Jean Claes, Directeur.

BEL0345

SOLIDAR

rue le Titien 28, 1040 Brussels, Belgium.

Telephone: 32 (2) 743 05 70. *Fax:* 32 (2) 743 05 89. *Contact:* Giampiero Alhadeff, Secretary General.

OBJECTIVES: To contribute to the creation of a radical model of economic and social development and to advance practical solutions to alleviate poverty in developed and developing countries.

GENERAL INFORMATION: *Creation:* 1951. *Type of organisation:* association of NGOs. *Member organisations:* 19. *Personnel/Total:* 5. *Salaried:* 3. *Volunteers:* 2. *Budget/Total 1993:* ECU 25000 (US$ 29000). *Financial sources:* Public: 75%. Self-financing: 25%.

PUBLICATIONS: *Annual report. List of publications.*

COMMENTS: Information activities related to the Commonwealth of Independent States.

INFORMATION AND EDUCATION ACTIVITIES: Topics: Emergency relief/refugees/humanitarian assistance; Employment/unemployment; Gender issues/women; Human rights/peace/conflicts; International economic relations/trade/debt/finance; International relations/cooperation/development aid; Peace/ethnic conflicts/armament/disarmament; Poverty/living conditions; Racism/xenophobia/antisemitism; Refugees/migrants/ethnic groups. **Activities:** Conferences/seminars/workshops/training activities; Information and documentation services/data bases; Information campaigns/exhibitions; Lobbying/advocacy; Publishing/audiovisual materials/educational materials.

BEL0346

SOLIDARITE AFGHANISTAN

Rue de Vennes 110, 4020 Liège, Belgique.

Téléphone: 32 (41) 41 40 56. *Fax:* 32 (41) 44 29 10. *Contact:* Benoît Heuchenne, Président.

BEL0347

SOLIDARITE ET COOPERATION MEDICALE AU TIERS MONDE (SCMTM)

1, Avenue Dr. G. Thérasse , 5530 Yvoir, Belgique.

Téléphone: 32 (81) 42 20 87. *Fax:* 32 (81) 42 25 49. *Contact:* Pr. Jacques Prignot, Président.

See: *How to Use the Directory,* page 11.

OBJECTIFS: Lutter contre la tuberculose, dans les pays à haute prévalence exclusivement, comme le Burundi ou la Bolivie.

INFORMATIONS GENERALES: *Création:* 1986. *Type d'organisation:* regroupement d'ONG. *Affiliée à:* ADRAI (Belgique). *Personnel/Total:* 6. *Salariés:* 5 dont: 3 dans les pays en développement. *Bénévoles:* 1. *Budget/Total 1993:* ECU 202000 (US$ 236000).

PUBLICATIONS: *Rapport annuel. Liste des publications.*

EVALUATION/RECHERCHE: Rapports d'évaluation disponibles.

ACTIVITES DANS LES REGIONS EN DEVELOPPEMENT: Intervient directement dans les régions en développement. Intervient dans 2 pays. Maintient une présence locale sur le terrain. Intervient par l'intermédiaire d'organisations locales partenaires. **Actions de Développement durable:** Envoi de volontaires/experts/assistance technique; Santé/assainissement/eau; Éducation/formation/alphabétisation. **Régions:** Afrique centrale; Amérique du Sud.

ACTIVITES D'INFORMATION ET D'EDUCATION: Domaines: Santé/assainissement/eau. **Activités:** Campagnes d'information/expositions; Conférences/séminaires/ateliers/activités de formation; Radiodiffusion/manifestations culturelles; Édition/documents audiovisuels/documents éducatifs; Éducation formelle.

BEL0348
SOLIDARITE INTERNATIONALE DES MAISONS FAMILIALES RURALES

Rue de Spa 32, 1040 Bruxelles, Belgique.

Téléphone: 32 (2) 230 17 92. *Contact:* A. Caeckelbergh.

BEL0349
SOLIDARITE INTERNATIONALE DES TRAVAILLEURS NORD/SUD (SITNS)

Rue Haute 42, 1000 Bruxelles, Belgique.

Téléphone: 32 (2) 513 60 16. *Fax:* 32 (2) 513 49 08. *Contact:* Aimé Lacroix, Administrateur délégué.

BEL0350
SOLIDARITE LIBERALE INTERNATIONALE

Rue de la Samaritaine 56, 1000 Bruxelles, Belgique.

Téléphone: 32 (2) 513 21 34. *Contact:* Dominique Verbrugghe, Secrétaire général.

OBJECTIFS: Collaborer à des opérations d'urgence conjointement avec l'Office Humanitaire de la Communauté Européenne (Echo).

INFORMATIONS GENERALES: *Création:* 1969. *Type d'organisation:* regroupement d'ONG. *Affiliée à:* Comité Belge d'Aide aux Réfugiés - Consortium des ONG belges pour les secours d'urgence - Centre d'initiation pour réfugiés et étrangers.. *Personnel/Total:* 1. *Salariés:* 1. *Budget/Total 1993:* ECU 37000 (US$ 43000).

PUBLICATIONS: *Périodiques:* Cap Tiers-monde (4). *Rapport annuel.*

ACTIVITES DANS LES REGIONS EN DEVELOPPEMENT: Intervient directement dans les régions en développement. Intervient dans 2 pays. Intervient par l'intermédiaire d'organisations locales partenaires. **Actions de Développement durable:** Aliments/famine; Droits de l'Homme/paix/conflits; Envoi de volontaires/experts/assistance technique; Secours d'urgence/réfugiés/aide humanitaire. **Régions:** Afrique centrale.

ACTIVITES D'INFORMATION ET D'EDUCATION: Domaines: Pauvreté/conditions de vie; Réfugiés/migrants/groupes ethniques; Secours d'urgence/réfugiés/aide humanitaire. **Activités:** Campagnes d'information/expositions; Collecte de fonds.

BEL0351
SOLIDARITE MONDIALE (SM) ♦ World Solidarity

Rue de la Loi 103, 1040 Bruxelles, Belgique.

Téléphone: 32 (2) 237 31 11. *Fax:* 32 (2) 237 33 00. *Contact:* Josly Piette, Président.

OBJECTIFS: Mener des projets de développement en Afrique, en Amérique latine et en Asie. Alimenter une banque de médicaments. Sensibiliser l'opinion belge aux problèmes du développement.

INFORMATIONS GENERALES: *Création:* 1974. *Type d'organisation:* collectif. *Affiliée à:* Fondation de Solidarité Internationale. *Personnel/Total:* 5. *Salariés:* 2. *Bénévoles:* 3. *Budget/Total 1993:* ECU 173000 (US$ 202000). *Sources financières:* Privé: 35%. Public: 65%.

PUBLICATIONS: *Périodiques:* Ici et Là-bas (4).

EVALUATION/RECHERCHE: Entreprend des activités de recherche.

ACTIVITES DANS LES REGIONS EN DEVELOPPEMENT: Intervient directement dans les régions en développement. Intervient dans 41 pays. Intervient par l'intermédiaire d'organisations locales partenaires. **Actions de Développement durable:** Droits de l'Homme/paix/conflits; Démocratie/bonne gestion publique/création d'institutions; développement participatif; Développement rural/agriculture; Développement urbain/habitat; Enfants/jeunesse/famille; Petites entreprises/secteur informel/artisanat; Population/planning familial/démographie; Questions relatives aux femmes; Santé/assainissement/eau; Écologie/environnement/biodiversité; Éducation/formation/alphabétisation. **Régions:** Afrique australe; Afrique centrale; Afrique de l'Est; Afrique de l'Ouest; Amérique du Sud; Asie centrale et Asie du Sud; Asie de l'Est; Asie du Sud-Est; Caraïbes; Mexique et Amerique centrale; Moyen-Orient.

ACTIVITES D'INFORMATION ET D'EDUCATION: Domaines: Aliments/famine; Droits de l'Homme/paix/conflits; Développement rural/agriculture; Développement urbain/habitat; Emploi/chômage; Enfants/jeunesse/famille; Pauvreté/conditions de vie; Population/planning familial/démographie; Questions relatives aux femmes; Racisme/xénophobie/antisémitisme; Relations internationales/coopération/aide au développement; Relations économiques internationales/commerce/dette/finances; Réfugiés/migrants/groupes ethniques; Santé/assainissement/eau; Écologie/environnement/biodiversité; Éducation/formation/alphabétisation. **Activités:** Campagnes d'information/expositions; Collecte de fonds; Conférences/séminaires/ateliers/activités de formation; Lobbying/plaidoyer; Édition/documents audiovisuels/documents éducatifs; Éducation formelle.

BEL0352
SOLIDARITE PROTESTANTE (SP)

Rue du Champ de Mars 5, 1050 Bruxelles, Belgique.

Téléphone: 32 (2) 511 70 29. *Fax:* 32 (2) 512 97 68. *Contact:* André Vogel, Secrétaire exécutif.

OBJECTIFS: Organiser des secours d'urgence et cofinancer des projets de développement.

INFORMATIONS GENERALES: *Création:* 1977. *Affiliée à:* Consortium belge des ONG pour les secours d'urgence. *Personnel/Total:* 3. *Salariés:* 3 dont: 1 dans les pays en développement. *Budget/Total 1993:* ECU 762000 (US$ 892000). *Sources financières:* Privé: 30%. Public: 70%.

PUBLICATIONS: *Périodiques:* Info SP (6). *Rapport annuel.*

ACTIVITES DANS LES REGIONS EN DEVELOPPEMENT: Intervient directement dans les régions en développement. Intervient dans 8 pays. Intervient par l'intermédiaire d'organisations locales partenaires. **Actions de Développement durable:** Aliments/famine; Démocratie/bonne gestion publique/création d'institutions/développement participatif; Développement rural/agriculture; Développement urbain/habitat; Enfants/jeunesse/famille; Envoi de volontaires/experts/assistance technique; Petites entreprises/secteur informel/artisanat; Questions relatives aux femmes; Santé/assainissement/eau; Secours d'urgence/réfugiés/aide humanitaire; Écologie/environnement/biodiversité; Éducation/formation/alphabétisation. **Régions:** Afrique centrale; Afrique de l'Ouest; Afrique du Nord; Amérique du Sud; Asie centrale et Asie du Sud.

ACTIVITES D'INFORMATION ET D'EDUCATION: Domaines: Aliments/famine; Développement rural/agriculture; Emploi/chômage; Questions relatives aux femmes; Relations économiques internationales/commerce/dette/finances; Santé/assainissement/eau; Secours d'urgence/réfugiés/aide humanitaire; Éducation/formation/alphabétisa-

Voir : *Comment utiliser le répertoire,* page 11.

tion. **Activités:** Campagnes d'information/expositions; Collecte de fonds; Conférences/séminaires/ateliers/activités de formation.

BEL0353

SOLIDARITE SOCIALISTE - FONDS DE COOPERATION AU DEVELOPPEMENT ♦ Socislist Solidarity - Development Co-operation Fund

Boulevard de l'Empereur 15, boîte 4, 1000 Bruxelles, Belgique.

Téléphone: 32 (2) 513 75 45 . **Fax:** 32 (2) 512 88 16. **Contact:** Marc Bertholome, Administrateur délégué.

OBJECTIFS: Sensibiliser le public socialiste francophone belge aux relations Nord-Sud. Identifier, soutenir et évaluer des projets de développement. Promouvoir le développement de la société civile des pays en voie de développement.

INFORMATIONS GENERALES: *Création:* 1963. **Affiliée à:** Comité National d'Action pour la Paix et le Développement - Action Commune Socialiste - CNCD - ADO - EOI-IWA (Allemagne) - Léo Lagrange Solidarité Internationale.. **Personnel/Total:** 41. *Salariés:* 41 dont: 26 dans les pays en développement. **Budget/Total 1993:** ECU 1717000 (US$ 2009000). **Sources financières:** *Privé:* 15%. *Public:* 70%. *Autofinancement:* 15%.

PUBLICATIONS: *Périodiques:* Solidarité Socialiste (4). *Rapport annuel. Liste des publications.*

EVALUATION/RECHERCHE: Rapports d'évaluation disponibles. Entreprend des activités de recherche.

COMMENTAIRES: L'ONG est prestataire de services auprès de la région wallonne de Belgique, l'Etat belge et le Fonds Européen de Développement dans le domaine de l'assistance technique. Intervient dans la Communauté des Etats indépendants.

ACTIVITES DANS LES REGIONS EN DEVELOPPEMENT: Intervient directement dans les régions en développement. Intervient dans 12 pays. Maintient une présence locale sur le terrain. Intervient par l'intermédiaire d'organisations locales partenaires. **Actions de Développement durable:** Dette/finances/commerce; Droits de l'Homme/paix/conflits; Démocratie/bonne gestion publique/création d'institutions/développement participatif; Développement rural/agriculture; Développement urbain/habitat; Enfants/jeunesse/famille; Envoi de volontaires/experts/assistance technique; Petites entreprises/secteur informel/artisanat; Population/planning familial/démographie; Questions relatives aux femmes; Santé/assainissement/eau; Secours d'urgence/réfugiés/aide humanitaire; Écologie/environnement/biodiversité; Éducation/formation/alphabétisation. **Régions:** Afrique australe; Afrique centrale; Afrique de l'Est; Afrique de l'Ouest; Afrique du Nord; Amérique du Sud; Asie centrale et Asie du Sud; Asie de l'Est; Asie du Sud-Est; Caraïbes; Mexique et Amerique centrale; Moyen-Orient.

ACTIVITES D'INFORMATION ET D'EDUCATION: Domaines: Aliments/famine; Droits de l'Homme/paix/conflits; Développement rural/agriculture; Développement urbain/habitat; Emploi/chômage; Enfants/jeunesse/famille; Paix/conflits ethniques/armement/désarmement; Pauvreté/conditions de vie; Population/planning familial/démographie; Questions relatives aux femmes; Relations internationales/coopération/aide au développement; Relations économiques internationales/commerce/dette/finances; Santé/assainissement/eau; Secours d'urgence/réfugiés/aide humanitaire; Écologie/environnement/biodiversité; Éducation/formation/alphabétisation. **Activités:** Campagnes d'information/expositions; Collecte de fonds; Conférences/séminaires/ateliers/activités de formation; Lobbying/plaidoyer; Radiodiffusion/manifestations culturelles; Services d'information et de documentation/bases de données; Échanges/parrainage/jumelage; Édition/documents audiovisuels/documents éducatifs; Éducation formelle.

BEL0354

SOLIDARITEIT BOLIVIE (SOLBO) ♦ Solidarité Bolivie

Tijl Uilenspiegellaan 12, 2050 Anvers, Belgique.

Téléphone: 32 (3) 219 25 44. **Contact:** Godelieve Scheire, Administrateur délégué.

BEL0355

SOS BOITES DE LAIT

Rue Paradis 64 , 4000 Liège, Belgique.

Téléphone: 32 (41) 52 40 07. **Fax:** 32 (41) 52 05 44. **Contact:** A. Preud'Homme, Administrateur président.

OBJECTIFS: Informer le public de la détresse des pays en développement. Organiser la collecte et l'expédition de produits alimentaires. Collecter des fonds pour soutenir des petits projets de développement dans les pays du Tiers-monde.

INFORMATIONS GENERALES: *Création:* 1962. **Personnel/Total:** 6. *Salariés:* 2. *Bénévoles:* 4. **Budget/Total 1993:** ECU 692000 (US$ 809000). **Sources financières:** *Privé:* 14%. *Public:* 83%. *Autofinancement:* 3%.

EVALUATION/RECHERCHE: Rapports d'évaluation disponibles.

ACTIVITES DANS LES REGIONS EN DEVELOPPEMENT: Intervient par l'intermédiaire d'organisations locales partenaires. **Actions de Développement durable:** Aliments/famine; Développement rural/agriculture; Enfants/jeunesse/famille; Questions relatives aux femmes. **Régions:** Afrique australe; Afrique centrale; Afrique de l'Ouest; Afrique du Nord; Amérique du Sud; Asie centrale et Asie du Sud; Caraïbes.

ACTIVITES D'INFORMATION ET D'EDUCATION: Domaines: Aliments/famine; Développement rural/agriculture; Enfants/jeunesse/famille; Pauvreté/conditions de vie; Questions relatives aux femmes; Réfugiés/migrants/groupes ethniques; Santé/assainissement/eau; Secours d'urgence/réfugiés/aide humanitaire; Éducation/formation/alphabétisation. **Activités:** Collecte de fonds; Échanges/parrainage/jumelage.

BEL0356

SOS FAIM - COMITE BELGE POUR LA CAMPAGNE CONTRE LA FAIM

Rue aux Laines 4, 1000 Bruxelles, Belgique.

Téléphone: 32 (2) 511 22 38. **Fax:** 32 (2) 514 47 77. **Contact:** Michel Falisse, Secrétaire général.

OBJECTIFS: Encourager l'auto-développement des groupes défavorisés en leur permettant de se constituer comme entités socio-économiques à part entière. Uiliser pour cela les formes de financement les plus adaptées: dons, prêts à conditions particulières, investissements dans des réalisations productives ou garanties à des emprunts.

INFORMATIONS GENERALES: *Création:* 1964. **Affiliée à:** Associations des ONG (Belgique). **Personnel/Total:** 12. *Salariés:* 12. **Budget/Total 1993:** ECU 5683000 (US$ 6647000). **Sources financières:** *Privé:* 45%. *Public:* 55%.

PUBLICATIONS: *Périodiques:* Défis-Sud (4). *Rapport annuel. Liste des publications.*

EVALUATION/RECHERCHE: Rapports d'évaluation disponibles. Entreprend des activités de recherche.

ACTIVITES DANS LES REGIONS EN DEVELOPPEMENT: Intervient dans 15 pays. Intervient par l'intermédiaire d'organisations locales partenaires. **Actions de Développement durable:** Démocratie/bonne gestion publique/création d'institutions/développement participatif; Développement rural/agriculture; Petites entreprises/secteur informel/artisanat. **Régions:** Afrique centrale; Afrique de l'Est; Afrique de l'Ouest; Amérique du Sud.

ACTIVITES D'INFORMATION ET D'EDUCATION: Domaines: Développement rural/agriculture. **Activités:** Collecte de fonds; Conférences/séminaires/ateliers/activités de formation; Lobbying/plaidoyer; Services d'information et de documentation/bases de données; Édition/documents audiovisuels/documents éducatifs.

BEL0357

SOS HONGER

Vlasfabriekstraat 11, 1060 Brussels, Belgique.

BEL0358

SOS LAYETTES

Ecole Technique, BP 13, 4040 Herstal, Belgique.

Téléphone: 32 (41) 64 28 75. **Fax:** 32 (41) 64 28 75. **Contact:** M. Droixhe, Présidente.

See: *How to Use the Directory,* page 11.

OBJECTIFS: Informer le public de la détresse des enfants et des mères dans les pays en développement. Répondre aux sollicitations venant de ces pays par la collecte de fonds, le parrainage, la vente de cartes de voeux et la confection de vêtements.

INFORMATIONS GENERALES: *Création:* 1967. *Affiliée à:* Organisation Mondiale de la Presse Périodique - Organisation de la Presse Périodique (Belgique) - Association des ONG (Belgique). *Personnel/Total:* 21. *Salariés:* 1 dont: 1 dans les pays en développement. *Bénévoles:* 20. *Budget/Total 1993:* ECU 1186000 (US$ 1387000). *Sources financières: Privé:* 65%. *Public:* 35%.

PUBLICATIONS: *Périodiques:* Solidarité Maternelle Internationale (2) - Internationale Solidariteit der Moeders (2). *Rapport annuel.*

EVALUATION/RECHERCHE: Rapports d'évaluation disponibles.

COMMENTAIRES: Intervient dans la Communauté des Etats indépendants.

ACTIVITES DANS LES REGIONS EN DEVELOPPEMENT: Intervient directement dans les régions en développement. Intervient par l'intermédiaire d'organisations locales partenaires. **Actions de Développement durable:** Aliments/famine; Développement rural/agriculture; Enfants/jeunesse/famille; Petites entreprises/secteur informel/artisanat; Population/planning familial/démographie; Questions relatives aux femmes; Santé/assainissement/eau; Secours d'urgence/réfugiés/aide humanitaire; Éducation/formation/alphabétisation. **Régions:** Afrique australe; Afrique centrale; Afrique de l'Est; Afrique de l'Ouest; Afrique du Nord; Amérique du Sud; Asie centrale et Asie du Sud; Asie de l'Est; Asie du Sud-Est; Caraïbes; Mexique et Amerique centrale; Moyen-Orient; Océanie.

ACTIVITES D'INFORMATION ET D'EDUCATION: Domaines: Aliments/famine; Développement rural/agriculture; Emploi/chômage; Enfants/jeunesse/famille; Pauvreté/conditions de vie; Population/planning familial/démographie; Réfugiés/migrants/groupes ethniques; Santé/assainissement/eau; Secours d'urgence/réfugiés/aide humanitaire; Éducation/formation/alphabétisation. **Activités:** Campagnes d'information/expositions; Collecte de fonds; Radiodiffusion/manifestations culturelles; Services d'information et de documentation/bases de données; Échanges/parrainage/jumelage.

BEL0359
SOS-PER GENTES PRO GENTIBUS (SOS/PG) ♦ SOS/PG par les peuples, pour les peuples.
Rue de l'Yser 258, 4430 Ans, Belgique.

Téléphone: 32 (41) 46 57 20. *Fax:* 32 (41) 63 04 23. *Contact:* Maurice Lachaussée, Président.

OBJECTIFS: Aider au développement des communautés du Tiers Monde par la réalisation de projets agricoles, artisanaux et médicaux, de projets de formation et d'éducation. Favoriser l'éducation au développement et contribuer à l'information du public belge.

INFORMATIONS GENERALES: *Création:* 1964. *Type d'organisation:* réseau. *Affiliée à:* SOS-Faim (Belgique) - Coordination Amazonie Equatorienne (Belgique) -Rassemblement Ansois pour la Paix (Belgique) - Commission Consultative Communale Solidarité-Liège/Tiers-Monde (Belgique) - CNCD (Belgique) - Coprogram (Belgique). *Personnel/Total:* 610. *Salariés:* 10 dont: 3 dans les pays en développement. *Bénévoles:* 600. *Budget/Total 1993:* ECU 1390000 (US$ 1626000). *Sources financières: Privé:* 50%. *Public:* 35%. *Autofinancement:* 15%.

PUBLICATIONS: *Périodiques:* Peuples et Solidarité (12) - Van Mensen Voor Mensen (6). *Rapport annuel. Liste des publications.*

EVALUATION/RECHERCHE: Rapports d'évaluation disponibles.

ACTIVITES DANS LES REGIONS EN DEVELOPPEMENT: Intervient directement dans les régions en développement. Intervient dans 34 pays. Maintient une présence locale sur le terrain. Intervient par l'intermédiaire d'organisations locales partenaires. **Actions de Développement durable:** Dette/finances/commerce; Démocratie/bonne gestion publique/création d'institutions/développement participatif; Développement rural/agriculture; Développement urbain/habitat; Enfants/jeunesse/famille; Envoi de volontaires/experts/assistance technique; Petites entreprises/secteur informel/artisanat; Questions relatives aux femmes; Santé/assainissement/eau; Secours d'urgence/réfugiés/aide humani-

taire; Écologie/environnement/biodiversité; Éducation/formation/alphabétisation; Énergie/transport. **Régions:** Afrique australe; Afrique centrale; Afrique de l'Est; Afrique de l'Ouest; Afrique du Nord; Amérique du Sud; Asie centrale et Asie du Sud; Asie de l'Est; Asie du Sud-Est; Caraïbes; Mexique et Amerique centrale; Moyen-Orient.

ACTIVITES D'INFORMATION ET D'EDUCATION: Domaines: Culture/tradition/religion; Droits de l'Homme/paix/conflits; Développement rural/agriculture; Développement urbain/habitat; Emploi/chômage; Enfants/jeunesse/famille; Pauvreté/conditions de vie; Population/planning familial/démographie; Questions relatives aux femmes; Racisme/xénophobie/antisémitisme; Relations internationales/coopération/aide au développement; Relations économiques internationales/commerce/dette/finances; Réfugiés/migrants/groupes ethniques; Santé/assainissement/eau; Secours d'urgence/réfugiés/aide humanitaire; Écologie/environnement/biodiversité; Éducation/formation/alphabétisation. **Activités:** Campagnes d'information/expositions; Collecte de fonds; Conférences/séminaires/ateliers/activités de formation; Lobbying/plaidoyer; Radiodiffusion/manifestations culturelles; Services d'information et de documentation/bases de données; Édition/documents audiovisuels/documents éducatifs; Éducation formelle.

BEL0360
SOS-WERELDHANDEL
Blijde Inkomststraat 114, 3000 Leuven, Belgium.

Telephone: 32 (16) 23 62 36. *Contact:* Erik Devogelaere, Co-ordinator.

BEL0361
SOUTH-NORTH NETWORK CULTURES AND DEVELOPMENT
♦ Réseau Sud-Nord Cultures et Développement
174 rue Joseph II , 1040 Bruxelles, Belgium.

Telephone: 32 (2) 230 46 37. *Fax:* 32 (2) 231 74 13. *Contact:* Thierry Verhelst.

OBJECTIVES: To undertake training and research on the role of culture in development. To examine how to help revitalize local skills, values and modes of social organisation as alternatives to Eurocentric development. To act as consultant or evaluator of projects. To offer "custom-made" training to NGOs on the cultural issues in their work and on intercultural misunderstanding.

GENERAL INFORMATION: *Creation:* 1988. *Type of organisation:* network. *Personnel/Total:* 13. *Salaried:* 8 of which: 6 in developing countries. *Volunteers:* 5 of which: 3 in developing countries. *Budget/Total 1993:* ECU 400000 (US$ 468000). *Financial sources: Private:* 50%. *Public:* 45%. *Self-financing:* 5%.

PUBLICATIONS: *Periodicals:* Cultures and Development (4) - Quid Pro Quo. *Annual report.*

EVALUATION/RESEARCH: Evaluation reports available. Undertakes research activities.

ACTIVITIES IN DEVELOPING REGIONS: Maintains local field presence. Works through local field partners. **Sustainable Development Actions:** Children/youth/family; Democracy/good governance/institution building/participatory development; Ecology/environment/biodiversity; Education/training/literacy; Gender issues/women; Health/sanitation/water; Human rights/peace/conflicts; Rural development/agriculture; Sending volunteers/experts/technical assistance; Small enterprises/informal sector/handicrafts; Urban development/habitat. **Regions:** Caribbean; Central Africa; Central Asia and South Asia; East Africa; East Asia; Mexico and Central America; Middle East; North Africa; Oceania; South America; South East Asia; Southern Africa; West Africa.

INFORMATION AND EDUCATION ACTIVITIES: Topics: Culture/tradition/religion; Ecology/environment/biodiversity; Education/training/literacy; Gender issues/women; Health/sanitation/water; Human rights/peace/conflicts; International economic relations/trade/debt/finance; International relations/cooperation/development aid; Peace/ethnic conflicts/armament/disarmament; Racism/xenophobia/antisemitism; Rural development/agriculture; Urban development/habitat. **Activities:** Broadcasting/cultural events; Conferences/seminars/workshops/training activities; Exchanges/twinning/linking; Formal education; Fund raising; Information and documentation services/data bases; Information campaigns/exhibitions; Lobbying/advocacy; Networking/electronic telecommunications; Publishing/audiovisual materials/educational materials.

Voir : *Comment utiliser le répertoire,* page 11.

BEL0362

STEUNFONDS DERDE WERELD ♦ Fonds de Soutien Tiers Monde

Kazernestraat 68, 1000 Bruxelles, Belgique.

Téléphone: 32 (2) 513 72 81. *Fax:* 32 (2) 513 98 31. *Contact:* Pol De Vos, Secrétaire général.

OBJECTIFS: Lutter efficacement, avec la Ligue Anti-Impérialiste, contre l'oppression et l'exploitation dans le Tiers-monde en développant une spécialisation sectorielle sur les "Soins de Santé Libérateurs", basée sur une application conséquente de la déclaration d'Alma Ata.

INFORMATIONS GENERALES: *Affiliée à:* NCOS (Belgique) - CNCD (Belgique) - COPROGRAM (Belgique). *Budget/Total 1993:* ECU 494000 (US$ 578000). *Sources financières:* Privé: 55%. Public: 45%.

PUBLICATIONS: *Périodiques:* Solidarité Internationale (5). *Rapport annuel. Liste des publications.*

EVALUATION/RECHERCHE: Rapports d'évaluation disponibles.

ACTIVITES DANS LES REGIONS EN DEVELOPPEMENT: Intervient dans 5 pays. Maintient une présence locale sur le terrain. **Actions de Développement durable:** Développement rural/agriculture; Enfants/jeunesse/famille; Envoi de volontaires/experts/assistance technique; Questions relatives aux femmes; Santé/assainissement/eau; Secours d'urgence/réfugiés/aide humanitaire; Éducation/formation/alphabétisation. **Régions:** Afrique de l'Ouest; Asie du Sud-Est; Caraïbes; Mexique et Amerique centrale; Moyen-Orient; Océanie.

ACTIVITES D'INFORMATION ET D'EDUCATION: Domaines: Droits de l'Homme/paix/conflits; Développement rural/agriculture; Paix/conflits ethniques/armement/désarmement; Pauvreté/conditions de vie; Racisme/xénophobie/antisémitisme; Relations internationales/coopération/aide au développement; Relations économiques internationales/commerce/dette/finances; Réfugiés/migrants/groupes ethniques; Santé/assainissement/eau; Secours d'urgence/réfugiés/aide humanitaire. **Activités:** Campagnes d'information/expositions; Collecte de fonds; Conférences/séminaires/ateliers/activités de formation; Services d'information et de documentation/bases de données; Édition/documents audiovisuels/documents éducatifs; Éducation formelle.

BEL0363

STICHTING ANTOON SPINOY ♦ Antoon Spinoy Foundation

Grote Markt 20, 2800 Mechelen, Belgium.

Telephone: 32 (15) 29 75 11. *Fax:* 32 (15) 29 75 10. *Contact:* J. Ramaekers, President.

BEL0364

STICHTING EUROPEAN HUMAN RIGHTS FOUNDATION (EHRF)

13 rue van Campenhout, 1040 Bruxelles, Belgium.

Telephone: 32 (2) 734 94 24. *Fax:* 32 (2) 734 68 31. *E-mail:* ehrf@gn.apc.org. *Contact:* Peter Ashman, Director.

OBJECTIVES: To promote human rights and humanitarian aims by providing funds to NGOs and individuals working in these fields.

GENERAL INFORMATION: *Creation:* 1980. *Type of organisation:* association of NGOs. *Personnel/Total:* 11. *Salaried:* 11 of which: 4 in developing countries. *Budget/Total 1993:* ECU 964000 (US$ 1128000). *Financial sources:* Public: 100%.

PUBLICATIONS: *Annual report.*

EVALUATION/RESEARCH: Undertakes research activities.

ACTIVITIES IN DEVELOPING REGIONS: Sustainable Development Actions: Human rights/peace/conflicts. **Regions:** Caribbean; Central Africa; Central Asia and South Asia; East Africa; East Asia; Mexico and Central America; Middle East; Oceania; South America; South East Asia; Southern Africa; West Africa.

BEL0365

STICHTING LEEFMILIEU ♦ Environmental Foundation

Kipdorp 11, 2000 Antwerpen, Belgique.

Téléphone: 32 (3) 231 64 48. *Fax:* 32 (3) 232 63 98. *Contact:* Bavo Rombouts, Secrétaire.

OBJECTIFS: Eduquer et informer le public et les petites et moyennes entreprises sur les problèmes de l'environnement.

INFORMATIONS GENERALES: *Création:* 1970. *Affiliée à:* Bureau Européen de l'Environnement. *Personnel/Total:* 9. *Salariés:* 7. *Bénévoles:* 2. *Sources financières:* Privé: 80%. Autofinancement: 20%.

PUBLICATIONS: *Périodiques:* Leefmilieu (6). *Liste des publications.*

ACTIVITES D'INFORMATION ET D'EDUCATION: Domaines: Aliments/famine; Droits de l'Homme/paix/conflits; Développement rural/agriculture; Développement urbain/habitat; Paix/conflits ethniques/armement/désarmement; Pauvreté/conditions de vie; Population/planning familial/démographie; Questions relatives aux femmes; Relations internationales/coopération/aide au développement; Relations économiques internationales/commerce/dette/finances; Réfugiés/migrants/groupes ethniques; Santé/assainissement/eau; Écologie/environnement/biodiversité. **Activités:** Campagnes d'information/expositions; Services d'information et de documentation/bases de données; Édition/documents audiovisuels/documents éducatifs.

BEL0366

STUDIE EN ORGANISATIE VOOR MEDISCHE AKTIE

Vrijheid 22, 2370 Arendonk, Belgique.

Téléphone: 32 (14) 67 76 61.

BEL0367

STUDIE- EN DOCUMENTATIE CENTRUM VOOR AANGEPASTE TECHNOLOGIE IN ONTWIKKELINGSLANDEN (ATOL) ♦ Centre d'études sur la technologie appropriée dans les pays en développement

Blijde Inkomststraat 9, 3000 Louvain, Belgique.

Téléphone: 32 (16) 22 45 17. *Fax:* 32 (16) 22 22 56. *Contact:* Rob Brusten, Coordinateur.

OBJECTIFS: Promouvoir la technologie appropriée dans les pays en développement grâce à un centre de documentation, des recherches, une assistance technique, des activités de formation.

INFORMATIONS GENERALES: *Création:* 1976. *Affiliée à:* NCOS (Belgique). *Personnel/Total:* 7. *Salariés:* 7. *Budget/Total 1993:* ECU 420000 (US$ 491000). *Sources financières:* Privé: 35%. Public: 30%. Autofinancement: 35%.

PUBLICATIONS: *Périodiques:* Atolberichten (4) (4). *Rapport annuel. Liste des publications.*

EVALUATION/RECHERCHE: Entreprend des activités de recherche.

ACTIVITES DANS LES REGIONS EN DEVELOPPEMENT: Intervient directement dans les régions en développement. Intervient dans 5 pays. Intervient par l'intermédiaire d'organisations locales partenaires. **Actions de Développement durable:** Envoi de volontaires/experts/assistance technique; Petites entreprises/secteur informel/artisanat; Questions relatives aux femmes. **Régions:** Afrique centrale; Afrique de l'Ouest.

BEL0368

TEAR FUND, BELGIUM ♦ The Evangelical Alliance Relief Fund

Groenstraat 19, 1800 Vilvoorde, Belgium.

Telephone: 32 (2) 251 77 10. *Fax:* 32 (2) 251 82 52. *Contact:* Cécil van Maelsaeke, Executive Director.

OBJECTIVES: To finance development projects, child sponsorship and family help programmes in developing countries. To send volunteers and provide emergency relief assistance.

GENERAL INFORMATION: *Creation:* 1979. *Affiliated to:* Conference of Evangelical European Aid Agencies (United Kingdom) - World Evangelical Fellowship (Singapore) - Consortium of Evangelical Relief Organisations (Belgium) - Interchurch Relief and Development Alliance (USA). *Personnel/Total:* 60. *Salaried:* 10 of which: 8 in developing countries. *Volunteers:* 50. *Budget/Total 1993:* ECU 445000 (US$ 520000). *Financial sources:* Private: 100%.

See: *How to Use the Directory,* page 11.

PUBLICATIONS: *Periodicals:* Inzicht (6) - Top-Nieuws (4). *Annual report.*

EVALUATION/RESEARCH: Evaluation reports available.

ACTIVITIES IN DEVELOPING REGIONS: Active in 14 country(ies). Maintains local field presence. Works through local field partners. **Sustainable Development Actions:** Children/youth/family; Education/training/literacy; Emergency relief/refugees/humanitarian assistance; Food/famine; Gender issues/women; Health/sanitation/water; Rural development/agriculture; Sending volunteers/experts/technical assistance; Small enterprises/informal sector/handicrafts. **Regions:** Caribbean; Central Africa; Central Asia and South Asia; East Africa; South America; South East Asia; Southern Africa; West Africa.

INFORMATION AND EDUCATION ACTIVITIES: **Topics:** Children/youth/family; Emergency relief/refugees/humanitarian assistance; Health/sanitation/water; International relations/cooperation/development aid; Peace/ethnic conflicts/armament/disarmament; Population/family planning/demography; Poverty/living conditions; Refugees/migrants/ethnic groups; Rural development/agriculture. **Activities:** Conferences/seminars/workshops/training activities; Formal education; Fund raising; Information campaigns/exhibitions; Publishing/audiovisual materials/educational materials.

BEL0369
TERRE DE DEMAIN

Victor Jacobslaan 12, 1040 Bruxelles, Belgique.

Téléphone: 32 (2) 647 99 00. *Contact:* André Modave.

BEL0370
TERRE DES HOMMES, BELGIQUE

Clos Bel Horizon 17, 1200 Bruxelles, Belgique.

Téléphone: 32 (2) 733 82 18. *Contact:* René Born, Président.

BEL0371
TERRE TIERS-MONDE ET INFORMATION (TTMI)

14 Rue Célestin Demblon, 4683 Vivegnis, Belgique.

Téléphone: 32 (41) 64 97 69. *Fax:* 32 (41) 48 08 84. *Contact:* William Wauters JR., Président et Administrateur délégué.

OBJECTIFS: Réaliser et gérer des projets de développement technique agricole et industriel. Former et envoyer des coopérants ONG dans les pays en de développement. Animer et informer la population européenne sur les problèmes du sous-développement.

INFORMATIONS GENERALES: *Création:* 1982. *Affiliée à:* CODEF - Fédération francophone des ONG d'envoi (Belgique) - Association des ONG (Belgique). *Personnel/Total:* 8. *Salariés:* 5. *Bénévoles:* 3 dont: 3 dans les pays en développement. *Budget/Total 1993:* ECU 618000 (US$ 723000). *Sources financières:* Privé: 25%. Public: 60%. *Autofinancement:* 15%.

PUBLICATIONS: *Périodiques:* Terre (4). *Rapport annuel. Liste des publications.*

PREVISIONS D'ACTIVITES: Réalisation d'un film centré sur la civilisation mondialement solidaire et l'entreprise à but social.

ACTIVITES DANS LES REGIONS EN DEVELOPPEMENT: Intervient directement dans les régions en développement. Intervient dans 5 pays. Maintient une présence locale sur le terrain. Intervient par l'intermédiaire d'organisations locales partenaires. **Actions de Développement durable:** Développement rural/agriculture; Envoi de volontaires/experts/assistance technique; Petites entreprises/secteur informel/artisanat; Santé/assainissement/eau. **Régions:** Afrique de l'Ouest; Amérique du Sud; Mexique et Amerique centrale.

BEL0372
TERRES ET VIE

Rue Laurent Delvaux 13, 1400 Nivelles, Belgique.

Téléphone: 32 (67) 21 71 49. *Contact:* Hugues Dupriez.

BEL0373
TERRES NOUVELLES ♦ New Lands

Avenue Belle-Vue 31, 1310 La Hulpe, Belgique.

Téléphone: 32 (26) 53 46 15. *Contact:* S. Fassin, Présidente.

BEL0374
TILAPIA FOOD AID ORGANIZATION (TFAO)

Avenue Lambeau 3, 1200 Bruxelles, Belgique.

Téléphone: 32 (2) 735 26 64. *Fax:* 32 (2) 733 74 42. *Contact:* Dr. Ernest Tottosy, Secrétaire général.

BEL0375
UN AND UNESCO CENTRE

College Oostende, Vindictivelkan 9, 8400 Oostende, Belgium.

Telephone: 32 (59) 70 10 77.

BEL0376
UNION CATHOLIQUE INTERNATIONALE DE SERVICE SOCIAL (UCISS) ♦ Catholic International Union for Social Service

Rue de la Poste 111, 1030 Brussels, Belgium.

Telephone: 32 (2) 217 79 06. *Contact:* Anne Marie Geleyns, Secretary General.

BEL0377
UNION INTERNATIONALE POUR L'ETUDE SCIENTIFIQUE DE LA POPULATION (UIESP) ♦ International Union for Scientific Study of Population

34 rue des Augustins, 4000 Liège, Belgium.

Telephone: 32 (41) 22 40 80. *Fax:* 32 (41) 22 38 47. *Contact:* Bruno Rekiche, Executive Secretary.

BEL0378
UNIVERSITAIRE STICHTING VOOR ONTWIKKELINGSSAMENWERKING (USOS) ♦ University Foundation for Development Co-operation

Prinsstraat 13, 2000 Antwerpen, Belgium.

Telephone: 32 (3) 220 40 48. *Fax:* 32 (3) 220 44 20. *E-mail:* ddw.bastiaensen.j @alpha.ufsia.ac.be.. *Contact:* Jef Van Gerwen, Chairman.

OBJECTIVES: To organise awareness raising campaigns on Flemish campuses. To undertake applied developmental research and educational support with/for university partners in the South.

GENERAL INFORMATION: *Creation:* 1985. *Personnel/Total:* 14. *Salaried:* 4 of which: 2 in developing countries. *Volunteers:* 10. *Budget/Total 1993:* ECU 247000 (US$ 289000). *Financial sources:* Public: 40%. *Self-financing:* 60%.

PUBLICATIONS: *Annual report. List of publications.*

EVALUATION/RESEARCH: Undertakes research activities.

ACTIVITIES IN DEVELOPING REGIONS: Active in 3 country(ies). Maintains local field presence. Works through local field partners. **Sustainable Development Actions:** Debt/finance/trade; Democracy/good governance/institution building/participatory development; Education/training/literacy; Rural development/agriculture; Sending volunteers/experts/technical assistance; Small enterprises/informal sector/handicrafts; Urban development/habitat. **Regions:** Central Africa; Central Asia and South Asia; Mexico and Central America.

INFORMATION AND EDUCATION ACTIVITIES: **Topics:** International economic relations/trade/debt/finance; International relations/cooperation/development aid; Peace/ethnic conflicts/armament/disarmament; Poverty/living conditions; Rural development/agriculture; Urban development/habitat. **Activities:** Conferences/seminars/workshops/training activities; Exchanges/twinning/linking; Formal education; Publishing/audiovisual materials/educational materials.

BEL0379

UNIVERSITE DE PAIX ♦ University of Peace

Boulevard du Nord 4, 5000 Namur, Belgique.

Téléphone: 32 (81) 22 61 02. *Fax:* 32 (81) 23 18 82. *Contact:* François Bazier, Administrateur délégué.

OBJECTIFS: Former à la gestion positive des conflits: médiation, négociation, coopération, non-violence.

INFORMATIONS GENERALES: *Création:* 1960. *Affiliée à:* International Peace Research Association - Arbeitsgruppe Fridenspädagogik (Allemagne). *Personnel/Total:* 13. *Salariés:* 13. *Budget/Total 1993:* ECU 247000 (US$ 289000). *Sources financières:* Privé: 20%. Public: 50%. Autofinancement: 30%.

PUBLICATIONS: *Périodiques:* Université de Paix (4). *Rapport annuel.* Liste des publications.

ACTIVITES D'INFORMATION ET D'EDUCATION: Domaines: Culture/tradition/religion; Enfants/jeunesse/famille; Paix/conflits ethniques/armement/désarmement; Éducation/formation/alphabétisation. Activités: Conférences/séminaires/ateliers/activités de formation; Services d'information et de documentation/bases de données.

BEL0380

VERENIGING VOOR DE VERENIGDE NATIES (VVN) ♦ Association pour les Nations Unies

Pleinlaan 2, 1050 Bruxelles, Belgique.

Téléphone: 32 (2) 641 24 37. *Contact:* Paul Morren, Président.

BEL0381

VERENIGING VOOR TECHNISCHE SAMENWERKING (ACT) ♦
Agency for Co-operation and Technical Development

Handelsstraat 20 /14, 1040 Bruxelles, Belgium.

Telephone: 32 (2) 513 75 34. *Fax:* 32 (2) 512 05 02. *Contact:* Guido Lamote, General Director.

OBJECTIVES: To share technical know-how, in agricultural projects and small-scale economic activities, from Belgium with local populations of developing countries at the grass-roots level in order to create employment and income generating activities.

GENERAL INFORMATION: *Creation:* 1985. *Affiliated to:* NCOS (Belgium) - Coprogram (Belgium) - UNICOS. *Personnel/Total:* 189. *Salaried:* 79 of which: 64 in developing countries. *Volunteers:* 110 of which: 1 in developing countries. *Budget/Total 1993:* ECU 6493000 (US$ 7594000). *Financial sources:* Private: 18%. Public: 79%. Self-financing: 3%.

PUBLICATIONS: *Annual report.*

EVALUATION/RESEARCH: Evaluation reports available.

ACTIVITIES IN DEVELOPING REGIONS: Present in developing regions. Active in 12 country(ies). Maintains local field presence. Works through local field partners. Sustainable Development Actions: Children/youth/family; Ecology/environment/biodiversity; Gender issues/women; Rural development/agriculture; Sending volunteers/experts/technical assistance; Small enterprises/informal sector/handicrafts; Urban development/habitat. Regions: Central Africa; East Africa; Mexico and Central America; South America; South East Asia; West Africa.

INFORMATION AND EDUCATION ACTIVITIES: Topics: Children/youth/family; Food/famine; Gender issues/women; International economic relations/trade/debt/finance; International relations/cooperation/development aid; Poverty/living conditions; Rural development/agriculture. Activities: Conferences/seminars/workshops/training activities; Exchanges/twinning/linking; Fund raising; Information campaigns/exhibitions; Lobbying/advocacy; Publishing/audiovisual materials/educational materials.

BEL0382

VIE FEMININE - MOUVEMENT CHRETIEN D'ACTION CULTURELLE ET SOCIALE

Rue de la Poste 111, 1210 Bruxelles, Belgique.

Téléphone: 32 (2) 217 29 52. *Fax:* 32 (2) 223 04 42. *Contact:* Mary Malevez, Présidente nationale.

BEL0383

VLAAMS CENTRUM INTEGRATIE MIGRANTEN

Rogierrlaan 106, 1030 Bruxelles, Belgique.

Téléphone: 32 (2) 245 70 50.

BEL0384

VLAAMS INTERNATIONAAL CENTRUM

Laanbrugstraat 11, 1210 Brussels, Belgique.

Téléphone: 32 (2) 245 72 40. *Contact:* Guido Peeters.

BEL0385

VLAAMS OVERLEGCOMITE MIGRANTEN

Poststraat 106, 1030 Bruxelles, Belgique.

Téléphone: 32 (2) 217 11 14.

BEL0386

VLAAMSE VERENIGING VOOR OPLEIDINGSPROGRAMMA'S IN HET BUITENLAND (VVOB) ♦ Association flamande pour les programmes de formation à l'étranger

Maria Theresiastraat 21, 1040 Bruxelles, Belgique.

Téléphone: 32 (2) 217 76 15. *Contact:* W. Blockx, Secrétaire général.

BEL0387

VLAAMSE WERKGROEP INDIANEN ZUID-AMERIKA (VLAAMSE WIZA) ♦ Groupe de travail flamand pour les Indiens d'Amérique du Sud

Rood Kruisstraat 43, 8800 Roeselare, Belgique.

Téléphone: 32 (51) 22 88 49. *Contact:* Stefaan Oplinus, Président.

OBJECTIFS: Soutenir financièrement des projets élaborés et/ou réalisés par des groupes d'indiens d'Amérique du Sud. Diffuser des informations sur la problématique et l'émancipation de ces indiens.

INFORMATIONS GENERALES: *Création:* 1974. *Affiliée à:* NCOS. *Personnel/Total:* 5. *Bénévoles:* 5. *Budget/Total 1993:* ECU 5000 (US$ 6000). *Sources financières:* Privé: 90%. Public: 1%. Autofinancement: 9%.

PUBLICATIONS: *Périodiques:* Wiza-Berichten (4). *Liste des publications.*

EVALUATION/RECHERCHE: Rapports d'évaluation disponibles.

PREVISIONS D'ACTIVITES: Campagne d'information sur les Indiens d'Amazonie surtout par une exposition de photos.

ACTIVITES DANS LES REGIONS EN DEVELOPPEMENT: Intervient dans 3 pays. Intervient par l'intermédiaire d'organisations locales partenaires. Actions de Développement durable: Écologie/environnement/biodiversité; Éducation/formation/alphabétisation. Régions: Amérique du Sud; Mexique et Amerique centrale.

ACTIVITES D'INFORMATION ET D'EDUCATION: Domaines: Culture/tradition/religion; Droits de l'Homme/paix/conflits. Activités: Campagnes d'information/expositions; Collecte de fonds; Édition/documents audiovisuels/documents éducatifs.

BEL0388

VOLONTAIRES POUR L'ENSEIGNEMENT-VOLONTARIAT ET COOPERATION INTERNATIONALE (VOLENS)

Rue du Progrès 333/2, 1210 Bruxelles, Belgique.

Téléphone: 32 (2) 201 02 70. *Fax:* 32 (2) 201 02 93. *Contact:* Jan Kristiaan Fierens, Directeur.

OBJECTIFS: Envoyer des coopérants ONG dans des pays en développement pour des projets nés à partir d'un travail de base, de communautés, de petites ONG, en particulier dans les domaines de l'éducation et de la formation. Informer et sensibiliser la population belge.

INFORMATIONS GENERALES: *Création:* 1959. *Affiliée à:* CODEF - COPROGRAM (Belgique) - CNCD - NCOS. *Personnel/Total:*

See: *How to Use the Directory,* page 11.

215. *Salariés:* 5. *Bénévoles:* 210 dont: 200 dans les pays en développement. ***Budget/Total 1993:*** ECU 198000 (US$ 231000). ***Sources financières:*** *Privé: 40%. Public: 60%.*

PUBLICATIONS: *Périodiques:* Antenne-2 (4). *Rapport annuel.*

ACTIVITES DANS LES REGIONS EN DEVELOPPEMENT: Intervient par l'intermédiaire d'organisations locales partenaires. **Actions de Développement durable:** Envoi de volontaires/experts/assistance technique. **Régions:** Afrique australe; Afrique centrale; Afrique de l'Est; Afrique de l'Ouest; Amérique du Sud; Asie de l'Est; Asie du Sud-Est; Caraïbes; Mexique et Amerique centrale; Océanie.

ACTIVITES D'INFORMATION ET D'EDUCATION: Domaines: Relations internationales/coopération/aide au développement; Éducation/formation/alphabétisation. **Activités:** Conférences/séminaires/ateliers/activités de formation.

BEL0389
VREDE - STUDY AND INFORMATION CENTRE FOR PEACE AND DEVELOPMENT PROBLEMS

Knokkestraat 121, 9000 Gent, Belgium.

Telephone: 32 (91) 21 18 39.

BEL0390
VREDESEILANDEN ♦ Islands of Peace

Ruelensvest 127, 3030 Leuven, Belgium.

Telephone: 32 (16) 22 25 53. *Fax:* 32 (16) 22 23 32. *Contact:* Herman Deprouw, Secretary General.

OBJECTIVES: To establish "Islands of Peace", geographic entities situated in particularly underprivileged areas of the world. To create, with local populations in these areas, the necessary conditions for comprehensive and integrated development.

GENERAL INFORMATION: *Creation:* 1980. *Affiliated to:* COPROGRAM (Belgium) - NCOS (Belgium). *Personnel/Total:* 24. *Salaried:* 22 of which: 3 in developing countries. *Volunteers:* 2. *Budget/Total 1993:* ECU 2045000 (US$ 2392000). *Financial sources:* Private: 65%. Public: 35%.

PUBLICATIONS: *Periodicals:* Vredeseilanden Magazine (5) - Rondom Rwanda (6). *Annual report. List of publications.*

EVALUATION/RESEARCH: Evaluation reports available. Undertakes research activities.

PLANNED ACTIVITIES: An Exchange of artists and journalists between Senegal and Belgium

ACTIVITIES IN DEVELOPING REGIONS: Present in developing regions. Active in 3 country(ies). Maintains local field presence. Works through local field partners. **Sustainable Development Actions:** Children/youth/family; Democracy/good governance/institution building/participatory development; Ecology/environment/biodiversity; Education/training/literacy; Gender issues/women; Health/sanitation/water; Rural development/agriculture; Small enterprises/informal sector/handicrafts; Urban development/habitat. **Regions:** Central Africa; West Africa.

INFORMATION AND EDUCATION ACTIVITIES: Topics: Children/youth/family; Culture/tradition/religion; Ecology/environment/biodiversity; Education/training/literacy; Emergency relief/refugees/humanitarian assistance; Employment/unemployment; Food/famine; Gender issues/women; Health/sanitation/water; Human rights/peace/conflicts; International economic relations/trade/debt/finance; International relations/cooperation/development aid; Other; Peace/ethnic conflicts/armament/disarmament; Population/family planning/demography; Poverty/living conditions; Racism/xenophobia/antisemitism; Refugees/migrants/ethnic groups; Rural development/agriculture; Urban development/habitat. **Activities:** Broadcasting/cultural events; Exchanges/twinning/linking; Formal education; Fund raising; Information and documentation services/data bases; Information campaigns/exhibitions; Publishing/audiovisual materials/educational materials.

BEL0391
WELTLADEN EUPEN ♦ Magasin du Monde Eupen
Rue de la Montagne 45, 4700 Eupen, Belgique.

Téléphone: 32 (87) 74 03 73. *Contact:* Pierre de Dijcker, Administrateur.

BEL0392
WERELDSOLIDARITEIT - SOLIDARITE MONDIALE (WSM)
Wetstraat 121, 1040 Bruxelles, Belgique.

Téléphone: 32 (2) 237 31 11. *Fax:* 32 (2) 237 37 00. *Contact:* Guido Dumon, Secrétaire général.

OBJECTIFS: Contribuer au renforcement des mouvements sociaux dans les pays en voie de développement. Faciliter les relations entre les mouvements sociaux du Sud et du Nord.

INFORMATIONS GENERALES: *Création:* 1971. *Affiliée à:* NCOS (Belgique) - KRV (Belgique) - CLONGD (Europe). *Personnel/Total:* 31. *Salariés:* 31 dont: 1 dans les pays en développement. *Budget/Total 1993:* ECU 6919000 (US$ 8093000). *Sources financières:* Privé: 36%. Public: 64%.

PUBLICATIONS: *Périodiques:* Werelburger (4) - Telex (12). *Rapport annuel. Liste des publications.*

EVALUATION/RECHERCHE: Rapports d'évaluation disponibles. Entreprend des activités de recherche.

ACTIVITES DANS LES REGIONS EN DEVELOPPEMENT: Intervient dans 26 pays. Intervient par l'intermédiaire d'organisations locales partenaires. **Actions de Développement durable:** Droits de l'Homme/paix/conflits; Démocratie/bonne gestion publique/création d'institutions/développement participatif; Développement rural/agriculture; Questions relatives aux femmes; Santé/assainissement/eau; Écologie/environnement/biodiversité; Éducation/formation/alphabétisation. **Régions:** Afrique australe; Afrique centrale; Afrique de l'Est; Afrique de l'Ouest; Amérique du Sud; Asie centrale et Asie du Sud; Asie de l'Est; Asie du Sud-Est; Caraïbes; Mexique et Amerique centrale.

BEL0393
WERELDWIJD ♦ Le Monde Entier
Arthur Goemaerelei 69, 2018 Antwerpen, Belgique.

Téléphone: 32 (3) 216 29 35. *Fax:* 32 (3) 237 77 57. *Contact:* Gie Goris, rédacteur en chef.

OBJECTIFS: Informer et faire de l'animation autour des problèmes du Tiers-Monde.

INFORMATIONS GENERALES: *Création:* 1969. *Affiliée à:* NCOS (Belgique). *Personnel/Total:* 17. *Salariés:* 12. *Bénévoles:* 5.

PUBLICATIONS: *Périodiques:* Wereldwijd (12) - N-2-Cahier (4) - Landenwijrs (12). *Liste des publications.*

ACTIVITES D'INFORMATION ET D'EDUCATION: Domaines: Aliments/famine; Culture/tradition/religion; Droits de l'Homme/paix/conflits; Développement rural/agriculture; Développement urbain/habitat; Emploi/chômage; Enfants/jeunesse/famille; Paix/conflits ethniques/armement/désarmement; Pauvreté/conditions de vie; Population/planning familial/démographie; Questions relatives aux femmes; Racisme/xénophobie/antisémitisme; Relations internationales/coopération/aide au développement; Relations économiques internationales/commerce/dette/finances; Réfugiés/migrants/groupes ethniques; Santé/assainissement/eau; Secours d'urgence/réfugiés/aide humanitaire; Écologie/environnement/biodiversité; Éducation/formation/alphabétisation. **Activités:** Services d'information et de documentation/bases de données; Édition/documents audiovisuels/documents éducatifs.

BEL0394
WERKGROEP BASISPROJEKTEN HAITI ♦ Groupe de projets de base Haïti
Stadsomvaart 94, 3500 Hasselt, Belgique.

Téléphone: 32 (11) 22 78 88. *Contact:* H. Stevens.

OBJECTIFS: Soutenir des projets et des groupements de base en Haïti.

INFORMATIONS GENERALES: *Création:* 1972. *Budget/Total 1993:* ECU 25000 (US$ 29000). *Sources financières:* Privé: 40%. Public: 30%. *Autofinancement:* 30%.

PUBLICATIONS: *Périodiques:* Storing (4). *Liste des publications.*

Voir : *Comment utiliser le répertoire,* page 11.

ACTIVITES DANS LES REGIONS EN DEVELOPPEMENT: Intervient dans 1 pays. Intervient par l'intermédiaire d'organisations locales partenaires. **Actions de Développement durable:** Développement rural/agriculture; Santé/assainissement/eau; Éducation/formation/alphabétisation. **Régions:** Caraïbes.

ACTIVITES D'INFORMATION ET D'EDUCATION: Domaines: Culture/tradition/religion; Développement rural/agriculture; Enfants/jeunesse/famille; Paix/conflits ethniques/armement/désarmement; Pauvreté/conditions de vie. **Activités:** Campagnes d'information/expositions; Conférences/séminaires/ateliers/activités de formation.

BEL0395

WERKGROEP TECHNOLOGIE - DIALOOG ♦ Working Group on Technology - Dialogue

Blijde Inkomststraat 109, 3000 Leuven, Belgium.

Telephone: 32 (16) 23 26 49. *Fax:* 32 (16) 22 87 94. *Contact:* Aerts Ivo.

OBJECTIVES: To organise lectures and workshops on appropriate technology.

GENERAL INFORMATION: *Creation:* 1971. *Personnel/Total:* 5. *Salaried:* 3. *Volunteers:* 2. *Budget/Total 1993:* ECU 50000 (US$ 58000). *Financial sources:* Private: 4%. Public: 95%. Self-financing: 1%.

PUBLICATIONS: *Periodicals:* De Vioevoet (5). *Annual report.*

EVALUATION/RESEARCH: Undertakes research activities.

COMMENTS: Undertakes activities in the Commonwealth of Independent States. Information activities related to the Commonwealth of Independent States.

ACTIVITIES IN DEVELOPING REGIONS: Active in 2 country(ies). Maintains local field presence. Works through local field partners. **Sustainable Development Actions:** Ecology/environment/biodiversity. **Regions:** Central Africa; North Africa; South America; West Africa.

INFORMATION AND EDUCATION ACTIVITIES: Topics: Ecology/environment/biodiversity. **Activities:** Conferences/seminars/workshops/training activities; Exchanges/twinning/linking; Formal education; Information and documentation services/data bases; Information campaigns/exhibitions; Networking/electronic telecommunications; Publishing/audiovisual materials/educational materials.

BEL0396

WITHUIS-VOLONTARIAAT

Peter Benoitlaan 4 , 9820 Merelbeke, Belgique.

Téléphone: 32 (9) 230 85 34. *Fax:* 32 (9) 230 54 54. *Contact:* Frans Ramon, Coordinateur.

OBJECTIFS: Collaborer à un monde plus juste et plus humain par la formation, l'envoi et le suivi de coopérants-ONG, le soutien matériel et financier à des projets de développement et la sensibilisation de la population belge aux problèmes du Tiers-Monde.

INFORMATIONS GENERALES: *Création:* 1977. *Affiliée à:* NCOS - COPROGRAM - INTERCODEV - ITECO - OCCI. *Personnel/Total:* 107. *Salariés:* 7 dont: 1 dans les pays en développement. *Bénévoles:* 100 dont: 80 dans les pays en développement. *Budget/Total 1993:* ECU 1705000 (US$ 1994000). *Sources financières:* Privé: 34%. Public: 62%. Autofinancement: 4%.

PUBLICATIONS: *Périodiques:* LAVALAS (4). *Rapport annuel. Liste des publications.*

EVALUATION/RECHERCHE: Rapports d'évaluation disponibles.

ACTIVITES DANS LES REGIONS EN DEVELOPPEMENT: Intervient directement dans les régions en développement. Intervient dans 40 pays. Maintient une présence locale sur le terrain. Intervient par l'intermédiaire d'organisations locales partenaires. **Actions de Développement durable:** Démocratie/bonne gestion publique/création d'institutions/développement participatif; Développement rural/agriculture; Enfants/jeunesse/famille; Envoi de volontaires/experts/assistance technique; Petites entreprises/secteur informel/artisanat; Santé/assainissement/eau; Écologie/environnement/biodiversité; Éducation/formation/alphabétisation. **Régions:** Afrique centrale; Afrique de l'Ouest; Améri-

que du Sud; Asie centrale et Asie du Sud; Asie du Sud-Est; Caraïbes; Mexique et Amerique centrale.

ACTIVITES D'INFORMATION ET D'EDUCATION: Domaines: Aliments/famine; Culture/tradition/religion; Droits de l'Homme/paix/conflits; Développement rural/agriculture; Emploi/chômage; Enfants/jeunesse/famille; Pauvreté/conditions de vie; Population/planning familial/démographie; Questions relatives aux femmes; Racisme/xénophobie/antisémitisme; Relations internationales/coopération/aide au développement; Relations économiques internationales/commerce/dette/finances; Réfugiés/migrants/groupes ethniques; Écologie/environnement/biodiversité; Éducation/formation/alphabétisation. **Activités:** Campagnes d'information/expositions; Conférences/séminaires/ateliers/activités de formation; Services d'information et de documentation/bases de données; Édition/documents audiovisuels/documents éducatifs.

BEL0397

WORLD WIDE FUND FOR NATURE, BELGIUM

Chaussée de Waterloo 608, 1060 Bruxelles, Belgique.

Téléphone: 32 (2) 347 36 12. *Fax:* 32 (2) 347 43 66. *Contact:* Tony Long.

OBJECTIFS: Préserver la diversité génétique, celle des espèces et des écosystèmes. Veiller à une utilisation durable des ressources naturelles soit durable, dans l'immédiat comme à long terme. Encourager des mesures visant à réduire la pollution et le gaspillage dans l'exploitation et la consommation des ressources et de l'énergie.

INFORMATIONS GENERALES: *Création:* 1961. *Type d'organisation:* réseau. *Affiliée à:* World Wide Fund for Nature. *Personnel/Total:* 7. *Salariés:* 7. *Budget/Total 1993:* ECU 325000 (US$ 421000). *Sources financières:* Public: 25%. Autofinancement: 75%.

PUBLICATIONS: *Périodiques:* WWF News Bulletin (24) - Panda News (12). *Rapport annuel. Liste des publications.*

EVALUATION/RECHERCHE: Rapports d'évaluation disponibles. Entreprend des activités de recherche.

COMMENTAIRES: Intervient dans la Communauté des Etats indépendants. Activités d'information concernant la Communauté des Etats indépendants.

ACTIVITES DANS LES REGIONS EN DEVELOPPEMENT: Intervient directement dans les régions en développement. Maintient une présence locale sur le terrain. Intervient par l'intermédiaire d'organisations locales partenaires. **Actions de Développement durable:** Dette/finances/commerce; Démocratie/bonne gestion publique/création d'institutions/développement participatif; Développement rural/agriculture; Envoi de volontaires/experts/assistance technique; Petites entreprises/secteur informel/artisanat; Population/planning familial/démographie; Écologie/environnement/biodiversité; Énergie/transport. **Régions:** Afrique australe; Afrique centrale; Afrique de l'Est; Afrique de l'Ouest; Afrique du Nord; Amérique du Sud; Asie centrale et Asie du Sud; Asie de l'Est; Asie du Sud-Est; Caraïbes; Mexique et Amerique centrale; Moyen-Orient; Océanie.

ACTIVITES D'INFORMATION ET D'EDUCATION: Domaines: Développement rural/agriculture; Population/planning familial/démographie; Relations internationales/coopération/aide au développement; Relations économiques internationales/commerce/dette/finances; Écologie/environnement/biodiversité. **Activités:** Campagnes d'information/expositions; Conférences/séminaires/ateliers/activités de formation; Lobbying/plaidoyer.

BEL0398

WORLD WIDE FUND FOR NATURE, EUROPEAN POLICY OFFICE (WWF)

608 Chaussée de Waterloo, 1060 Bruxelles, Belgium.

Telephone: 32 (2) 347 36 12. *Fax:* 32 (2) 347 43 66. *Contact:* Tony Long, Director.

OBJECTIVES: To preserve genetic, species and ecosystem diversity. To ensure that use of renewable natural resources is sustainable. To promote actions to reduce pollution, wasteful exploitation and consumption of resources and energy.

GENERAL INFORMATION: *Creation:* 1989. *Type of organisation:* coordinating body. *Member organisations:* 14. *Affiliated to:* World Wide

See: *How to Use the Directory,* page 11.

Fund for Nature (Switzerland). *Personnel/Total:* 7. *Salaried:* 7. *Budget/Total 1993:* ECU 391000 (US$ 508000). *Financial sources:* Public: 25%. *Self-financing:* 75%.

COMMENTS: Undertakes activities in the Commonwealth of Independent States. Information activities related to the Commonwealth of Independent States.

ACTIVITIES IN DEVELOPING REGIONS: Present in developing regions. Maintains local field presence. Works through local field partners.

BEL0399

YOUTH FORUM OF THE EUROPEAN COMMUNITY ♦ Forum
Jeunesse de la Communauté Européenne

Rue Joseph II, 120, 1040 Brussels, Belgium.

Telephone: 32 (2) 230 64 90. *Fax:* 32 (2) 230 21 23. *Contact:* Brian Carty, Secretary General.

OBJECTIVES: To co-operate and work together with young people and youth organisations from African, Caribbean and Pacific countries with which the European Community has signed the Lomé Convention

GENERAL INFORMATION: *Creation:* 1978. *Member organisations:* 75. *Personnel/Total:* 13. *Salaried:* 13. *Budget/Total 1993:* ECU 1532000 (US$ 1792000). *Financial sources:* Public: 100%.

PUBLICATIONS: *Periodicals:* Youth Opinion (4) - ACP-EC Youth Cooperation Bulletin (3). *Annual report.*

EVALUATION/RESEARCH: Evaluation reports available. Undertakes research activities.

COMMENTS: The organisation is a platform of national youth councils and international non-governmental youth organisations towards the institutions of the European Union on all aspects of youth policy.

ACTIVITIES IN DEVELOPING REGIONS: Works through local field partners. **Sustainable Development Actions:** Children/youth/family; Democracy/good governance/institution building/participatory development. **Regions:** Caribbean; Central Africa; East Africa; Middle East; North Africa; Oceania; South America; Southern Africa; West Africa.

INFORMATION AND EDUCATION ACTIVITIES: Topics: Children/youth/family; Ecology/environment/biodiversity; Education/training/literacy; Gender issues/women; International relations/cooperation/development aid; Racism/xenophobia/antisemitism. **Activities:** Conferences/seminars/workshops/training activities; Exchanges/twinning/linking; Information and documentation services/data bases; Information campaigns/exhibitions; Lobbying/advocacy; Publishing/audiovisual materials/educational materials.

BEL0400

YYE ~ ENVIRONMENT POLICY WG

Overzetweg 25, 8510 Kortruk-Marke, Belgium.

BEL0401

ZEBRA - AUDIOVISUAL NETWORK FOR NORTH-SOUTH UNDERSTANDING ♦ ZEBRA - Réseau audiovisuel pour le rapprochement Nord-Sud

Rue Joseph II, 172, 1040 Bruxelles, Belgique.

Téléphone: 32 (2) 231 15 13. *Fax:* 32 (2) 231 14 13. *Contact:* Antoinette Fredericq, Coordinatrice.

CHE0402

ABOKOBI SOCIETY SWITZERLAND

P.O. Box 218, 8029 Zürich, Switzerland.

Telephone: 41 (1) 387 11 22. *Fax:* 41 (1) 387 11 00. *Contact:* Ernst Hofmann, President.

OBJECTIVES: To support agricultural development in Africa. To support mutual co-operation between the local partners and the beneficiaries of such projects.

GENERAL INFORMATION: *Creation:* 1974. *Personnel/Total:* 50. *Salaried:* 50 of which: 50 in developing countries. *Budget/Total 1993:* ECU 104000 (US$ 135000). *Financial sources:* Private: 90%. Public: 10%.

PUBLICATIONS: *Annual report.*

ACTIVITIES IN DEVELOPING REGIONS: Active in 1 country(ies). Works through local field partners. **Sustainable Development Actions:** Children/youth/family; Ecology/environment/biodiversity; Education/training/literacy; Energy/transport; Food/famine; Health/sanitation/water; Population/family planning/demography; Rural development/agriculture; Sending volunteers/experts/technical assistance. **Regions:** West Africa.

INFORMATION AND EDUCATION ACTIVITIES: Topics: Children/youth/family; Ecology/environment/biodiversity; Health/sanitation/water; Poverty/living conditions; Rural development/agriculture. **Activities:** Conferences/seminars/workshops/training activities.

CHE0403

ACADEMIE INTERNATIONALE DE L'ENVIRONNEMENT (AIE)

♦ International Academy of the Environment

4, Chemin de Conches, 1231 Conches (Genève), Suisse.

Téléphone: 41 (22) 789 13 11. *Fax:* 41 (22) 789 25 38. *Courrier électronique:* ide@unige.ch. *Contact:* Bernard Giovannini.

OBJECTIFS: Apporter aux décideurs de haut niveau les éléments de connaissances scientifiques et les principes de gestion qui leur permettent de prendre des décisions compatibles avec un développement durable. Mener des activités de recherche, organiser des séminaires et tenir des tables rondes stratégiques.

INFORMATIONS GENERALES: *Création:* 1991. *Personnel/Total:* 31. *Salariés:* 31. *Budget/Total 1993:* ECU 2609000 (US$ 3384000). *Sources financières:* Privé: 20%. Public: 80%.

PUBLICATIONS: *Périodiques:* Renforcer le potentiel humain pour le développement durable (2). *Rapport annuel. Liste des publications.*

EVALUATION/RECHERCHE: Entreprend des activités de recherche.

COMMENTAIRES: Intervient dans la Communauté des Etats indépendants. Activités d'information concernant la Communauté des Etats indépendants.

ACTIVITES DANS LES REGIONS EN DEVELOPPEMENT: Intervient directement dans les régions en développement. Intervient par l'intermédiaire d'organisations locales partenaires. **Actions de Développement durable:** Dette/finances/commerce; Droits de l'Homme/paix/conflits; Population/planning familial/démographie; Santé/assainissement/eau; Écologie/environnement/biodiversité; Éducation/formation/alphabétisation; Énergie/transport. **Régions:** Afrique australe; Afrique centrale; Afrique de l'Est; Afrique de l'Ouest; Afrique du Nord; Amérique du Sud; Asie centrale et Asie du Sud; Asie de l'Est; Asie du Sud-Est; Caraïbes; Mexique et Amerique centrale; Moyen-Orient; Océanie.

ACTIVITES D'INFORMATION ET D'EDUCATION: Domaines: Paix/conflits ethniques/armement/désarmement; Population/planning familial/démographie; Relations internationales/coopération/aide au développement; Relations économiques internationales/commerce/dette/finances; Santé/assainissement/eau; Écologie/environnement/biodiversité; Éducation/formation/alphabétisation. **Activités:** Autres; Campagnes d'information/expositions; Conférences/séminaires/ateliers/activités de formation; Réseaux/télécommunications électroniques; Services d'information et de documentation/bases de données; Échanges/parrainage/jumelage; Édition/documents audiovisuels/documents éducatifs.

CHE0404

ADOPTION INTERNATIONAL

Postfach P.O.Box, 3063 Ittigen-Bern, Switzerland.

Telephone: 41 (31) 922 18 02. *Contact:* Ueli Wüthvich, President.

CHE0405

ADVENTINISCHE ENTWICKLUNGSUND KATASTROPHENHILFE

Gubelstrasse 23, Postfach 8113, 8052 Zürich, Switzerland.

CHE0406

AFGHANISTAN LIBRE

Avenue Henri-Golay 12B, 1219 Chatelaine-Genève, Suisse.

Téléphone: 41 (22) 796 62 15. *Fax:* 41 (22) 796 62 15. *Contact:* Anna Layla, Président.

OBJECTIFS: Soutenir moralement, politiquement et matériellement la lutte de libération du peuple afghan jusqu'à l'indépendance nationale, la démocratie et la justice sociale.

INFORMATIONS GENERALES: *Création:* 1982. *Affiliée à:* Afghanistan-Libre (Suisse). *Personnel/Total:* 4. *Bénévoles:* 4 dont: 2 dans les pays en développement. *Budget/Total 1993:* ECU 7000 (US$ 9000). *Sources financières:* Privé: 50%. Public: 25%. *Autofinancement:* 25%.

PUBLICATIONS: *Périodiques:* Afghanistan-Libre (1). *Liste des publications.*

ACTIVITES DANS LES REGIONS EN DEVELOPPEMENT: Intervient directement dans les régions en développement. Intervient dans 1 pays. Intervient par l'intermédiaire d'organisations locales partenaires. **Actions de Développement durable:** Autres; Droits de l'Homme/paix/conflits; Développement urbain/habitat; Enfants/jeunesse/famille; Questions relatives aux femmes; Éducation/formation/alphabétisation. **Régions:** Asie centrale et Asie du Sud; Moyen-Orient.

ACTIVITES D'INFORMATION ET D'EDUCATION: Domaines: Culture/tradition/religion; Droits de l'Homme/paix/conflits; Développement urbain/habitat; Enfants/jeunesse/famille; Paix/conflits ethniques/armement/désarmement; Questions relatives aux femmes; Relations internationales/coopération/aide au développement; Éducation/formation/alphabétisation. **Activités:** Campagnes d'information/expositions; Conférences/séminaires/ateliers/activités de formation; Services d'information et de documentation/bases de données; Édition/documents audiovisuels/documents éducatifs.

CHE0407

AFRIKA-KOMITEE BASEL

C.P. 1072, 4001 Basel, Switzerland.

Telephone: 41 (61) 35 24 77.

CHE0408

AGENCE DES CITES POUR LA COOPERATION NORD-SUD (ACUCONS-UTANSCO)

26, rue de l'Athenée, C.P. 370, 1211 Genève 12, Suisse.

Téléphone: 41 (22) 346 71 71. *Fax:* 41 (22) 346 78 81. *Contact:* Henry Bandier, Président.

CHE0409

AIDE AUX ENFANTS DU MAGHREB

Case postale 30, 1211 Genève 4, Suisse.

Contact: Rachid Hadbi, Président.

OBJECTIFS: Venir en aide aux enfants les plus démunis à travers le Maghreb.

INFORMATIONS GENERALES: *Création:* 1990. *Personnel/Total:* 15. *Bénévoles:* 15 dont: 5 dans les pays en développement. *Budget/Total 1993:* ECU 2600 (US$ 3400). *Sources financières:* Privé: 50%. *Autofinancement:* 50%.

PUBLICATIONS: *Rapport annuel.*

See: *How to Use the Directory*, page 11.

COMMENTAIRES: L'Organistion désirerait entrer en contact avec d'autres associations afin de coordonner leurs efforts et multiplier leurs forces.

ACTIVITES DANS LES REGIONS EN DEVELOPPEMENT: Intervient directement dans les régions en développement. Intervient dans 3 pays. Maintient une présence locale sur le terrain. Intervient par l'intermédiaire d'organisations locales partenaires. **Actions de Développement durable:** Enfants/jeunesse/famille; Questions relatives aux femmes; Secours d'urgence/réfugiés/aide humanitaire; Éducation/formation/alphabétisation. **Régions:** Afrique du Nord.

ACTIVITES D'INFORMATION ET D'EDUCATION: Domaines: Enfants/jeunesse/famille; Questions relatives aux femmes; Secours d'urgence/réfugiés/aide humanitaire. **Activités:** Collecte de fonds.

CHE0410
AIDE SANITAIRE SUISSE AUX PALESTINIENS (ASSP)
Rue Kleberg 25, 1201 Genève, Suisse.

Téléphone: 41 (22) 731 32 68. **Fax:** 41 (22) 738 50 49. **Contact:** Jacques Vittori, Directeur.

OBJECTIFS: Répondre aux demandes d'aide de communautés, associations ou groupes de population palestiniens, dans le domaine de la santé et du bien-être social. En Suisse, informer les institutions publiques et privées, et le public en général, des problèmes spécifiques de santé physique et mentale des Palestiniens.

INFORMATIONS GENERALES: Création: 1990. **Affiliée à:** Fédération Genevoise de Coopération (Suisse).

PREVISIONS D'ACTIVITES: Education et formation des paysans à l'utilisation en sécurité des pesticides.

ACTIVITES DANS LES REGIONS EN DEVELOPPEMENT: Intervient dans 1 pays. **Actions de Développement durable:** Enfants/jeunesse/famille; Santé/assainissement/eau; Secours d'urgence/réfugiés/aide humanitaire; Écologie/environnement/biodiversité; Éducation/formation/alphabétisation. **Régions:** Moyen-Orient.

ACTIVITES D'INFORMATION ET D'EDUCATION: Domaines: Réfugiés/migrants/groupes ethniques; Santé/assainissement/eau; Secours d'urgence/réfugiés/aide humanitaire; Écologie/environnement/biodiversité; Éducation/formation/alphabétisation. **Activités:** Campagnes d'information/expositions; Collecte de fonds.

CHE0411
AIDE SUISSE A L'ACTION COMMUNAUTAIRE EN HAITI (ASACH)
C.P. 241, 1211 Genève 16, Suisse.

Téléphone: 41 (22) 757 27 40. **Contact:** Pierre Roehrich, Président.

OBJECTIFS: Assurer une éducation formelle en milieu rural, en Haïti.

INFORMATIONS GENERALES: Création: 1985. **Affiliée à:** Plate-forme Haïti (Suisse) - Fédération genvoise de Coopération (Suisse). **Personnel/Total:** 12. **Bénévoles:** 12. **Budget/Total 1993:** ECU 16000 (US$ 20000). **Sources financières:** Privé: 90%. Autofinancement: 10%.

PUBLICATIONS: *Rapport annuel.*

EVALUATION/RECHERCHE: Rapports d'évaluation disponibles.

ACTIVITES DANS LES REGIONS EN DEVELOPPEMENT: Intervient directement dans les régions en développement. Intervient dans 1 pays. Maintient une présence locale sur le terrain. Intervient par l'intermédiaire d'organisations locales partenaires. **Actions de Développement durable:** Éducation/formation/alphabétisation. **Régions:** Caraïbes.

ACTIVITES D'INFORMATION ET D'EDUCATION: Domaines: Éducation/formation/alphabétisation. **Activités:** Collecte de fonds.

CHE0412
AIDE SUISSE AUX TIBETAINS (AST) ◆ Swiss Aid to Tibetans
p.a. Croix Rouge suisse, Case Postale, 3001 Bern, Suisse.

Téléphone: 41 (31) 387 71 11. **Fax:** 41 (31) 311 27 93.

OBJECTIFS: Aider les réfugiés tibétains vivant en exil dans les pays d'Asie. Apporter une aide aux tibétains qui sont dans le besoin dans leur

pays. Renforcer la culture tibétaine des tibétains vivant en exil, et au Tibet.

INFORMATIONS GENERALES: Création: 1959. **Personnel/Total:** 8. **Budget/Total 1993:** ECU 42000 (US$ 54000). **Sources financières:** Privé: 100%.

PUBLICATIONS: *Rapport annuel.*

PREVISIONS D'ACTIVITES: Etudier les possibilités en vue de promouvoir une caisse de maladie solidaire parmi les tibétains en Inde.

ACTIVITES DANS LES REGIONS EN DEVELOPPEMENT: Intervient directement dans les régions en développement. Intervient dans 2 pays. Intervient par l'intermédiaire d'organisations locales partenaires. **Actions de Développement durable:** Développement urbain/habitat; Enfants/jeunesse/famille; Santé/assainissement/eau; Secours d'urgence/réfugiés/aide humanitaire; Éducation/formation/alphabétisation. **Régions:** Asie centrale et Asie du Sud.

CHE0413
AIUTO MEDICO AL CENTRO AMERICA
Case postale 2536, 6500 Bellinzona, Suisse.

CHE0414
AKTION "KIRCHE WOHIN?" ◆ Eglise, où vas-tu?
Postfach 8631, 3001 Bern, Suisse.

Téléphone: 41 (31) 302 99 79. **Fax:** 41 (31) 302 98 60. **Contact:** Peter Ramser, Président.

OBJECTIFS: Soutenir l'action de l'église en faveur de l'autosuffisance en Afrique du Sud, en particulier dans la région de Sizanani.

INFORMATIONS GENERALES: Création: 1980. **Type d'organisation:** regroupement d'ONG, collectif. **Organisations membres:** 4000. **Personnel/Total:** 8. **Salariés:** 3. **Budget/Total 1993:** ECU 91000 (US$ 118000). **Sources financières:** Privé: 10%. Autofinancement: 90%.

PUBLICATIONS: Périodiques: Mitgliederbrief "Aktion KIRCHE WOHIN?" (8). *Rapport annuel. Liste des publications.*

ACTIVITES DANS LES REGIONS EN DEVELOPPEMENT: Intervient par l'intermédiaire d'organisations locales partenaires. **Actions de Développement durable:** Enfants/jeunesse/famille; Santé/assainissement/eau; Secours d'urgence/réfugiés/aide humanitaire. **Régions:** Afrique australe.

CHE0415
AKTION DER CHRISTEN FUR DIE ABSCHAFFUNG DER FOLTER (ACAT) ◆ Action des Chrétiens pour l'Abolition de la Torture
Speichergasse 29, C.P. 5011, 3001 Bern, Suisse.

Téléphone: 41 (31) 312 20 44. **Fax:** 41 (31) 312 58 11. **Contact:** Jean-Claude Huot, Président.

OBJECTIFS: Lutter pour l'abolition de la torture et de la peine de mort.

INFORMATIONS GENERALES: Création: 1981. **Type d'organisation:** regroupement d'ONG. **Affiliée à:** F.I.C.A.T (France). **Personnel/Total:** 30. **Budget/Total 1993:** ECU 141000 (US$ 183000). **Sources financières:** Privé: 75%. Autofinancement: 20%.

PUBLICATIONS: *Rapport annuel. Liste des publications.*

EVALUATION/RECHERCHE: Rapports d'évaluation disponibles.

PREVISIONS D'ACTIVITES: Améliorer le suivi des appels d'urgence. Réfléchir sur la possibilité de poursuites judiciaires à l'encontre des tortionnaires impliqués dans les guerres et les conflits.

COMMENTAIRES: L'organisation intervient également en Amérique du Nord et en Europe dans la lutte contre la peine de mort. Intervient dans la Communauté des Etats indépendants.

ACTIVITES DANS LES REGIONS EN DEVELOPPEMENT: Intervient directement dans les régions en développement. Intervient dans 56 pays. **Actions de Développement durable:** Droits de l'Homme/paix/conflits. **Régions:** Afrique australe; Afrique centrale; Afrique de l'Est; Afrique de l'Ouest; Afrique du Nord; Amérique du Sud; Asie centrale et

Asie du Sud; Asie de l'Est; Asie du Sud-Est; Caraïbes; Mexique et Amerique centrale; Moyen-Orient; Océanie.

ACTIVITES D'INFORMATION ET D'EDUCATION: Domaines: Droits de l'Homme/paix/conflits. **Activités:** Campagnes d'information/expositions; Collecte de fonds; Conférences/séminaires/ateliers/activités de formation; Lobbying/plaidoyer; Services d'information et de documentation/bases de données; Échanges/parrainage/jumelage.

CHE0416

AKTION FINANZPLATZ SCHWEIZ - DRITTE WELT (AFP) ♦
Action Swiss Financial Centre - Third World

Gerberngasse 21A, 3011 Bern, Switzerland.

Telephone: 41 (31) 311 76 16. **Fax:** 41 (31) 311 77 94. **Contact:** Mascha Madörin, Secretary.

OBJECTIVES: To analyse the relations between financial institutions in Switzerland and the Third World. To organise information and political campaigns on forms of illegal economic activities by the financial sector. To advocate alternative banking and ethical investment. To analyse questions of debt linked to the financial system.

GENERAL INFORMATION: Creation: 1978. **Type of organisation:** association of NGOs. **Personnel/Total:** 2. Salaried: 2. **Budget/Total 1993:** ECU 104000 (US$ 135000). **Financial sources:** Private: 60%. Self-financing: 40%.

PUBLICATIONS: Annual report. List of publications.

EVALUATION/RESEARCH: Undertakes research activities.

PLANNED ACTIVITIES: Co-ordination with the Italian and French parts of Switzerland.

INFORMATION AND EDUCATION ACTIVITIES: Topics: Gender issues/women; International economic relations/trade/debt/finance. **Activities:** Conferences/seminars/workshops/training activities; Information campaigns/exhibitions; Lobbying/advocacy.

CHE0417

ALL INDIA WOMEN'S CONFERENCE (AIWC)
38 chemin du Pont-Céard, 1290 Versoix, Switzerland.

Telephone: 41 (22) 755 11 52. **Contact:** Shobhana Ranade, President.

OBJECTIVES: To work for a society based on the principles of social justice, integrity and equal rights and opportunities. To support the right of every citizen to enjoy basic civil liberties. To raise awareness of the fundamental rights that the Constitution of India offers to women.

GENERAL INFORMATION: Creation: 1927. **Type of organisation:** network. **Personnel/Total:** var.. Salaried: var..

PUBLICATIONS: Periodicals: Roshni (12). Annual report. List of publications.

EVALUATION/RESEARCH: Evaluation reports available. Undertakes research activities.

COMMENTS: The 1993 budget for AIWC was 30 million rupees.

ACTIVITIES IN DEVELOPING REGIONS: Present in developing regions. Maintains local field presence. Works through local field partners. **Sustainable Development Actions:** Children/youth/family; Education/training/literacy; Emergency relief/refugees/humanitarian assistance; Gender issues/women; Health/sanitation/water; Human rights/peace/conflicts; Population/family planning/demography; Rural development/agriculture; Sending volunteers/experts/technical assistance; Small enterprises/informal sector/handicrafts; Urban development/habitat. **Regions:** Central Asia and South Asia.

INFORMATION AND EDUCATION ACTIVITIES: Topics: Children/youth/family; Culture/tradition/religion; Ecology/environment/biodiversity; Education/training/literacy; Emergency relief/refugees/humanitarian assistance; Employment/unemployment; Food/famine; Gender issues/women; Health/sanitation/water; Human rights/peace/conflicts; Peace/ethnic conflicts/armament/disarmament; Population/family planning/demography; Poverty/living conditions; Racism/xenophobia/antisemitism; Refugees/migrants/ethnic groups; Rural development/agriculture; Urban development/habitat. **Activities:** Conferences/seminars/workshops/training activities; Fund raising.

CHE0418

ALLIANCE MISSIONNAIRE INTERNATIONALE
Case postale 24, 1175 Lavigny, Suisse.

CHE0419

ALLIANCE REFORMEE MONDIALE (ARM)
Case postale 2100, Route de Ferney 150, 1211 Genève 2, Suisse.

Téléphone: 41 (22) 791 62 38. **Fax:** 41 (22) 791 65 05.

CHE0420

AMNESTY INTERNATIONAL, SCHWEIZER SEKTION (AI) ♦
Amnesty International, Swiss Section

Monbijoustrasse 26, 3001 Bern, Switzerland.

Telephone: 41 (31) 381 79 66. **Fax:** 41 (31) 382 36 47. **Contact:** Frauke Seidensticker, Secrétaire centrale.

OBJECTIVES: To promote human rights on the basis of the universal declaration of human rights. To work against torture, the death penalty, disappearances and political killings. To support fair trials for political prisoners and the unconditional release of non-violent prisoners of conscience.

GENERAL INFORMATION: Creation: 1971. **Personnel/Total:** 67. Salaried: 17. Volunteers: 50. **Budget/Total 1993:** ECU 2087000 (US$ 2707000).

PUBLICATIONS: Periodicals: Ammnesty Magazin (11) - Liberté (11). Annual report. List of publications.

EVALUATION/RESEARCH: Evaluation reports available. Undertakes research activities.

PLANNED ACTIVITIES: Amnesty International plans a campaign on the UN Conference on Women in Beijing.

COMMENTS: Information activities related to the Commonwealth of Independent States.

ACTIVITIES IN DEVELOPING REGIONS: Sustainable Development Actions: Children/youth/family; Democracy/good governance/institution building/participatory development; Emergency relief/refugees/humanitarian assistance; Gender issues/women; Human rights/peace/conflicts. **Regions:** Caribbean; Central Africa; Central Asia and South Asia; East Africa; East Asia; Mexico and Central America; Middle East; North Africa; Oceania; South America; South East Asia; Southern Africa; West Africa.

INFORMATION AND EDUCATION ACTIVITIES: Topics: Children/youth/family; Emergency relief/refugees/humanitarian assistance; Gender issues/women; Human rights/peace/conflicts; International relations/cooperation/development aid; Peace/ethnic conflicts/armament/disarmament; Refugees/migrants/ethnic groups. **Activities:** Broadcasting/cultural events; Conferences/seminars/workshops/training activities; Exchanges/twinning/linking; Formal education; Fund raising; Information and documentation services/data bases; Information campaigns/exhibitions; Lobbying/advocacy; Networking/electronic telecommunications; Publishing/audiovisual materials/educational materials.

CHE0421

ANTENNA INTERNATIONALE
Rue Grenus 10, 1201 Genève, Suisse.

Téléphone: 41 (22) 731 80 36. **Fax:** 41 (22) 731 97 86. **Courrier électronique:** Antenna-CH. **Contact:** Denis von der Weid, Président.

OBJECTIFS: Faire respecter les Droits de l'Homme dans les pays en développement, avec la collaboration de collectif d'avocats et de juristes. Lutter contre la corruption.

INFORMATIONS GENERALES: Création: 1984. **Personnel/Total:** 15. Bénévoles: 15 dont: 10 dans les pays en développement. **Budget/Total 1993:** ECU 52000 (US$ 68000). **Sources financières:** Privé: 20%. Autofinancement: 80%.

EVALUATION/RECHERCHE: Rapports d'évaluation disponibles. Entreprend des activités de recherche.

See: *How to Use the Directory*, page 11.

PREVISIONS D'ACTIVITES: L'organisation veut intensifier la lutte contre la corruption, en collaboration avec Transparency International. Soutien à des projets en faveur des Droits de l'Homme au Tibet.

ACTIVITES DANS LES REGIONS EN DEVELOPPEMENT: Intervient directement dans les régions en développement. Intervient dans 2 pays. Maintient une présence locale sur le terrain. Intervient par l'intermédiaire d'organisations locales partenaires. **Actions de Développement durable:** Droits de l'Homme/paix/conflits; Enfants/jeunesse/famille. **Régions:** Afrique centrale; Asie centrale et Asie du Sud.

ACTIVITES D'INFORMATION ET D'EDUCATION: Domaines: Droits de l'Homme/paix/conflits. **Activités:** Conférences/séminaires/ateliers/activités de formation; Lobbying/plaidoyer; Services d'information et de documentation/bases de données.

CHE0422
ANTENNA TECHNOLOGY

10, rue Grenus, 1201 Genève, Suisse.

Téléphone: 41 (22) 731 80 36. *Fax:* 41 (22) 731 97 86. *Courrier électronique:* ANTENNACH. *Contact:* Denis von der Weid, Président.

OBJECTIFS: Promouvoir et diffuser des technologies appropriées répondant aux besoins essentiels des populations les plus pauvres.

INFORMATIONS GENERALES: *Création:* 1989. *Organisations membres:* 5. *Personnel/Total:* 52. *Salariés:* 7 dont: 3 dans les pays en développement. *Bénévoles:* 45 dont: 15 dans les pays en développement. *Budget/Total 1993:* ECU 104000 (US$ 135000). *Sources financières:* Privé: 80%. Public: 20%.

EVALUATION/RECHERCHE: Rapports d'évaluation disponibles. Entreprend des activités de recherche.

PREVISIONS D'ACTIVITES: Création de bureaux Antenna Technologie en Belgique, au Brésil et en Afrique. Mise en place de petites unités pharmaceutiques et en Afrique.

COMMENTAIRES: Une fois les projets pilotes aboutis, l'organisation se chargera de la formation et de la réplicabilité des projets dans les pays en voie de développement. Intervient dans la Communauté des Etats indépendants. Activités d'information concernant la Communauté des Etats indépendants.

ACTIVITES DANS LES REGIONS EN DEVELOPPEMENT: Intervient directement dans les régions en développement. Maintient une présence locale sur le terrain. Intervient par l'intermédiaire d'organisations locales partenaires. **Actions de Développement durable:** Aliments/famine; Développement rural/agriculture; Santé/assainissement/eau; Écologie/environnement/biodiversité. **Régions:** Afrique centrale; Asie centrale et Asie du Sud; Asie de l'Est; Asie du Sud-Est.

ACTIVITES D'INFORMATION ET D'EDUCATION: Domaines: Développement rural/agriculture; Développement urbain/habitat; Santé/assainissement/eau; Écologie/environnement/biodiversité. **Activités:** Autres; Collecte de fonds; Conférences/séminaires/ateliers/activités de formation; Éducation formelle.

CHE0423
ANTI-RACISM INFORMATION SERVICE (ARIS)

14 avenue Trembley, 1209 Genève, Suisse.

Téléphone: 41 (22) 735 06 07.

CHE0424
APPOGGIO POPOLAZIONE BIJAGOS (APPOBI)

6950 Campestro di Tessere, Suisse.

CHE0425
ARBEITSGEMEINSCHAFT "BRENNPUNKT WELT"

Neptunstrasse 38, 8032 Zürich, Suisse.

Téléphone: 41 (1) 252 31 60.

CHE0426
ARBEITSGEMEINSCHAFT FUR RUSTUNGSKONTROLLE UND EIN WAFFENAUSFUHRVERBOT (ARW)

Postfach 120, 3000 Bern 6, Switzerland.

Telephone: 41 (31) 311 71 22. *Fax:* 41 (31) 311 77 94. *Contact:* Barbara Haering, Member of Parliament.

OBJECTIVES: To promote the control of arms and disarmament. To fight against the exportation of arms.

GENERAL INFORMATION: *Creation:* 1972. *Affiliated to:* International Peace Bureau (Switzerland).

PUBLICATIONS: *Periodicals:* Friedenspolitik (4). *List of publications.*

PLANNED ACTIVITIES: ARW will organise a referendum in Switzerland for a 50 reduction of the military budget and a total ban on the exportation of arms.

INFORMATION AND EDUCATION ACTIVITIES: Topics: Peace/ethnic conflicts/armament/disarmament. **Activities:** Conferences/seminars/workshops/training activities; Information and documentation services/data bases; Information campaigns/exhibitions; Lobbying/advocacy; Publishing/audiovisual materials/educational materials.

CHE0427
ARBEITSGEMEINSCHAFT GERECHTEN BANANENHANDEL (GEBANA) ♦ Association pour un commerce bananier équitable

Postfach Talbach, 8502 Frauenfeld, Suisse.

Téléphone: 41 (54) 722 45 39. *Contact:* Stefan Bünter.

OBJECTIFS: Commercialiser plus équitablement les bananes des producteurs indépendants, et sensibiliser les consommateurs.

INFORMATIONS GENERALES: *Création:* 1988. *Personnel/Total:* 6. *Salariés:* 3 dont: 1 dans les pays en développement. *Bénévoles:* 3. *Budget/Total 1993:* ECU 148000 (US$ 192000). *Sources financières:* Privé: 75%. Autofinancement: 25%.

PUBLICATIONS: *Rapport annuel. Liste des publications.*

EVALUATION/RECHERCHE: Rapports d'évaluation disponibles. Entreprend des activités de recherche.

ACTIVITES DANS LES REGIONS EN DEVELOPPEMENT: Intervient directement dans les régions en développement. Intervient dans 5 pays. Maintient une présence locale sur le terrain. Intervient par l'intermédiaire d'organisations locales partenaires. **Actions de Développement durable:** Droits de l'Homme/paix/conflits; Questions relatives aux femmes; Santé/assainissement/eau; Écologie/environnement/biodiversité; Éducation/formation/alphabétisation. **Régions:** Mexique et Amerique centrale.

ACTIVITES D'INFORMATION ET D'EDUCATION: Domaines: Droits de l'Homme/paix/conflits; Développement rural/agriculture; Relations internationales/coopération/aide au développement; Relations économiques internationales/commerce/dette/finances. **Activités:** Campagnes d'information/expositions; Conférences/séminaires/ateliers/activités de formation; Lobbying/plaidoyer; Édition/documents audiovisuels/documents éducatifs.

CHE0428
ARBEITSGEMEINSCHAFT SCHWEIZERISCHER ENTWICKLUNGSDIENSTE (UNITE) ♦ Association of Swiss Development Agencies

Schützenmattstrasse 37, 4051 Basel, Switzerland.

Telephone: 41 (61) 271 65 37. *Fax:* 41 (61) 271 65 44. *Contact:* Susy Greuter, Coordinator.

OBJECTIVES: To co-ordinate the activities of member organisations active in the development field, and to promote information exchange between Swiss development agencies.

GENERAL INFORMATION: *Creation:* 1964. *Type of organisation:* association of NGOs. *Member organisations:* 17. *Affiliated to:* European Forum on Development Service.. *Personnel/Total:* 4. *Salaried:* 4. *Budget/Total 1993:* ECU 4071000 (US$ 5278000). *Financial sources:* Self-financing: 100%.

Voir : *Comment utiliser le répertoire*, page 11.

PUBLICATIONS: *Annual report.*

EVALUATION/RESEARCH: Evaluation reports available.

ACTIVITIES IN DEVELOPING REGIONS: Works through local field partners.

CHE0429

ARBEITSGEMEINSCHAFT SWISSAID/FASTENOPFER/BROT FUR ALLE/HELVETAS/CARITAS ♦ Swiss Coalition of Development Organizations Swissaid/Catholic Centre Fund/Bread for All/Helvetas/Caritas

Monbijoustrasse 31, C.P. 6735, 3001 Bern, Suisse.

Téléphone: 41 (31) 381 17 11. *Fax:* 41 (31) 381 17 18. *Contact:* Richard Gerster, Directeur.

OBJECTIFS: Sensibiliser la population suisse sur la situation des pays en développement.

INFORMATIONS GENERALES: *Création:* 1971. *Type d'organisation:* regroupement d'ONG. *Organisations membres:* 5. *Affiliée à:* EUROSTEP (Belgique) - Eurodad (Belgique). *Personnel/Total:* 20. *Salariés:* 20. *Budget/Total 1993:* ECU 2087000 (US\$ 2707000). *Sources financières:* Privé: 48%. Public: 28%. Autofinancement: 24%.

PUBLICATIONS: *Périodiques:* Swiss coalition News (4) - Aktuell (10) - Dokument (4). *Rapport annuel. Liste des publications.*

COMMENTAIRES: Activités d'information concernant la Communauté des Etats indépendants.

ACTIVITES D'INFORMATION ET D'EDUCATION: Domaines: Aliments/famine; Enfants/jeunesse/famille; Paix/conflits ethniques/armement/désarmement; Pauvreté/conditions de vie; Population/planning familial/démographie; Questions relatives aux femmes; Racisme/xénophobie/antisémitisme; Relations internationales/coopération/aide au développement; Relations économiques internationales/commerce/dette/finances; Réfugiés/migrants/groupes ethniques; Écologie/environnement/biodiversité. Activités: Conférences/séminaires/ateliers/activités de formation; Lobbying/plaidoyer; Services d'information et de documentation/bases de données; Édition/documents audiovisuels/documents éducatifs.

CHE0430

ARBEITSGRUPPE FUR ENTWICKLUNGSPOLITISCHE INFORMATION UND BILDUNG (AGIB) ♦ Working Group for Information on Development Policy and Education

Unité, Schützenmattstrasse 37, 4051 Basel, Switzerland.

Telephone: 41 (1) 251 42 15.

CHE0431

ARBEITSGRUPPE LITERATUR AUS AFRIKA, ASIEN UND LATEINAMERIKA/ERKLARUNG VON BERN ♦ Groupe de travail en littérature-"Déclaration de Bern"

Elke Müller, Spechtweg 3, 4125 Riehen, Suisse.

Contact: Elke Müller.

OBJECTIFS: Faire connaître des livres d'auteurs des pays du Tiers monde parus en allemand. Organiser des lectures et des discussions. Publier des critiques.

INFORMATIONS GENERALES: *Création:* 1980. *Affiliée à:* Erklärung von Bern (Suisse). *Personnel/Total:* 14. *Bénévoles:* 14. *Sources financières:* Privé: 100%.

PUBLICATIONS: *Périodiques:* Literatur aus Asien, Afrika und Lateinamerika.

ACTIVITES D'INFORMATION ET D'EDUCATION: Domaines: Culture/tradition/religion. Activités: Campagnes d'information/expositions; Conférences/séminaires/ateliers/activités de formation; Lobbying/plaidoyer; Édition/documents audiovisuels/documents éducatifs.

CHE0432

ARBEITSKREIS SEHEN UND LEBEN ♦ Task Force Sight and Life

c/o Hoffmann-La Roche AG, P.O. Box 2116, 4002 Basel, Switzerland.

Telephone: 41 (61) 691 22 53. *Fax:* 41 (61) 688 19 10. *Contact:* Dr. J. Gmünder, Secretary.

OBJECTIVES: To provide know-how experience to fight against the eye disease xerophthalmia. To provide scientific and technical support and supplies of vitamin A in emergency situations, as well as funds for selected health research programmes.

GENERAL INFORMATION: *Creation:* 1986. *Personnel/Total:* 2. *Salaried:* 2. *Budget/Total 1993:* ECU 574000 (US\$ 744000). *Financial sources:* Private: 100%.

PUBLICATIONS: *Periodicals:* Sight and Life Newsletter (3). *Annual report. List of publications.*

EVALUATION/RESEARCH: Evaluation reports available.

ACTIVITIES IN DEVELOPING REGIONS: Active in 50 country(ies). Works through local field partners. Sustainable Development Actions: Children/youth/family; Education/training/literacy. Regions: Caribbean; Central Africa; Central Asia and South Asia; East Africa; East Asia; Mexico and Central America; North Africa; Oceania; South America; South East Asia; Southern Africa; West Africa.

INFORMATION AND EDUCATION ACTIVITIES: Topics: Children/youth/family; Education/training/literacy. Activities: Formal education; Information and documentation services/data bases; Information campaigns/exhibitions; Publishing/audiovisual materials/educational materials.

CHE0433

ARBEITSKREIS TOURISMUS UND ENTWICKLUNG (AKT+E) ♦ Groupe de travail tourisme et développement

Missionsstrasse 21, 4003 Basel, Suisse.

Téléphone: 41 (61) 261 47 42. *Contact:* Marianne Gujer, ethnologue.

OBJECTIFS: Analyser les problèmes liés à l'activité touristique dans les régions sous-développées. Effectuer un travail de prise de conscience auprès des voyageurs et de l'industrie touristique, en vue d'obtenir un changement de comportement vis-à-vis des populations étrangères visitées.

INFORMATIONS GENERALES: *Création:* 1978. *Organisations membres:* 80. *Affiliée à:* Third World Tourism European Ecumenical Network (Germany). *Personnel/Total:* 3. *Salariés:* 3. *Budget/Total 1993:* ECU 94000 (US\$ 122000).

PUBLICATIONS: *Périodiques:* Kurznachrichten (4). *Rapport annuel. Liste des publications.*

EVALUATION/RECHERCHE: Rapports d'évaluation disponibles. Entreprend des activités de recherche.

COMMENTAIRES: Activités d'information concernant la Communauté des Etats indépendants.

ACTIVITES D'INFORMATION ET D'EDUCATION: Domaines: Autres. Activités: Campagnes d'information/expositions; Conférences/séminaires/ateliers/activités de formation; Lobbying/plaidoyer; Radiodiffusion/manifestations culturelles; Services d'information et de documentation/bases de données; Édition/documents audiovisuels/documents éducatifs; Éducation formelle.

CHE0434

ARMEE DU SALUT

Résidence "Les Fontaines", Chemin de Joran 2A, 1260 Nyon, Suisse.

Téléphone: 41 (22) 362 97 65. *Fax:* 41 (22) 362 97 65. *Contact:* Liselotte Holland-Vogel.

OBJECTIFS: Annoncer l'Evangile de Jésus-Christ et soulager, en son nom, sans distinction aucune, les détresses humaines.

INFORMATIONS GENERALES: *Création:* 1878. *Personnel/Total:* 3576677. *Salariés:* 76677 dont: 11000 dans les pays en développement. *Bénévoles:* 3500000 dont: 50000 dans les pays en développement.

PUBLICATIONS: *Rapport annuel. Liste des publications.*

EVALUATION/RECHERCHE: Rapports d'évaluation disponibles.

See: *How to Use the Directory,* page 11.

COMMENTAIRES: Intervient dans la Communauté des Etats indépendants. Activités d'information concernant la Communauté des Etats indépendants.

ACTIVITES DANS LES REGIONS EN DEVELOPPEMENT: Intervient directement dans les régions en développement. Intervient dans 100 pays. Maintient une présence locale sur le terrain. Intervient par l'intermédiaire d'organisations locales partenaires. **Actions de Développement durable:** Aliments/famine; Droits de l'Homme/paix/conflits; Démocratie/bonne gestion publique/création d'institutions/développement participatif; Développement rural/agriculture; Développement urbain/habitat; Enfants/jeunesse/famille; Envoi de volontaires/experts/assistance technique; Petites entreprises/secteur informel/artisanat; Population/planning familial/démographie; Questions relatives aux femmes; Santé/assainissement/eau; Secours d'urgence/réfugiés/aide humanitaire; Écologie/environnement/biodiversité; Éducation/formation/alphabétisation; Énergie/transport. **Régions:** Afrique australe; Afrique centrale; Afrique de l'Est; Afrique de l'Ouest; Afrique du Nord; Amérique du Sud; Asie centrale et Asie du Sud; Asie de l'Est; Asie du Sud-Est; Caraïbes; Mexique et Amerique centrale; Moyen-Orient; Océanie.

ACTIVITES D'INFORMATION ET D'EDUCATION: Domaines: Aliments/famine; Autres; Culture/tradition/religion; Droits de l'Homme/paix/conflits; Développement rural/agriculture; Développement urbain/habitat; Emploi/chômage; Enfants/jeunesse/famille; Paix/conflits ethniques/armement/désarmement; Pauvreté/conditions de vie; Population/planning familial/démographie; Questions relatives aux femmes; Racisme/xénophobie/antisémitisme; Relations internationales/coopération/aide au développement; Réfugiés/migrants/groupes ethniques; Santé/assainissement/eau; Secours d'urgence/réfugiés/aide humanitaire; Écologie/environnement/biodiversité; Éducation/formation/alphabétisation. **Activités:** Autres; Campagnes d'information/expositions; Collecte de fonds; Conférences/séminaires/ateliers/activités de formation; Lobbying/plaidoyer; Radiodiffusion/manifestations culturelles; Réseaux/télécommunications; Services d'information et de documentation/bases de données; Échanges/parrainage/jumelage; Édition/documents audiovisuels/documents éducatifs; Éducation formelle.

CHE0435
ASSOCIATION 6-S (6S)

3 boulevard James Fazy, 1201 Genève, Suisse.

Téléphone: 41 (22) 73 18 89. **Fax:** 41 (22) 73 18 89. **Contact:** Bernard Lédéa Ouedraugo, Président.

OBJECTIFS: Apporter un soutien aux organisations paysannes par la formation, la mise en place de réseaux et de services de conseils.

INFORMATIONS GENERALES: Création: 1976. **Type d'organisation:** regroupement d'ONG. **Organisations membres:** 100. **Personnel/Total:** 6. Salariés: 6 dont: 6 dans les pays en développement. **Sources financières:** Public: 100%.

ACTIVITES DANS LES REGIONS EN DEVELOPPEMENT: Intervient directement dans les régions en développement. Intervient dans 9 pays. Maintient une présence locale sur le terrain. Intervient par l'intermédiaire d'organisations locales partenaires. **Actions de Développement durable:** Autres; Dette/finances/commerce; Démocratie/bonne gestion publique/création d'institutions/développement participatif; Développement rural/agriculture; Enfants/jeunesse/famille; Petites entreprises/secteur informel/artisanat; Questions relatives aux femmes; Santé/assainissement/eau; Écologie/environnement/biodiversité; Éducation/formation/alphabétisation. **Régions:** Afrique de l'Ouest.

CHE0436
ASSOCIATION ACCUEIL TIERS-MONDE (ATM)

s/c M. Jacques Vittori, Bd Georges-Favon 41, 1204 Genève, Suisse.

Téléphone: 41 (22) 329 81 20. **Fax:** 41 (22) 329 80 16.

CHE0437
ASSOCIATION AFRICAINE D'EDUCATION POUR LE DEVELOPPEMENT (ASAFED)

BP 335, 1211 Genève 4, Suisse.

Téléphone: 41 (22) 328 53 54.

CHE0438
ASSOCIATION ALBORADA

C.P. 1118, 1211 Genève 1, Suisse.

Téléphone: 41 (22) 348 95 09. **Contact:** S. Cuendet, Présidente.

OBJECTIFS: Assurer trois repas par jour aux enfants déshérités, et leur appui scolaire. Organiser des cours d'apprentissage et des cours du soir pour les adultes. Apporter une assistance médicale et dispenser des cours de médecine préventive et d'hygiène aux populations.

INFORMATIONS GENERALES: Création: 1977. **Personnel/Total:** 14. Salariés: 14. **Budget/Total 1993:** ECU 31000 (US$ 40000).

PUBLICATIONS: Rapport annuel.

PREVISIONS D'ACTIVITES: Collecter des fonds en Suisse pour financer les projets d'une fondation chilienne.

ACTIVITES DANS LES REGIONS EN DEVELOPPEMENT: Intervient dans 1 pays. Intervient par l'intermédiaire d'organisations locales partenaires. **Actions de Développement durable:** Enfants/jeunesse/famille; Petites entreprises/secteur informel/artisanat; Questions relatives aux femmes; Santé/assainissement/eau; Secours d'urgence/réfugiés/aide humanitaire; Écologie/environnement/biodiversité; Éducation/formation/alphabétisation. **Régions:** Amérique du Sud.

ACTIVITES D'INFORMATION ET D'EDUCATION: Domaines: Aliments/famine; Développement rural/agriculture; Enfants/jeunesse/famille; Questions relatives aux femmes; Santé/assainissement/eau; Écologie/environnement/biodiversité; Éducation/formation/alphabétisation. **Activités:** Collecte de fonds.

CHE0439
ASSOCIATION ALTER EGO

Avenue Montchoisi 21, BP 151, 1000 Lausanne 19, Suisse.

Téléphone: 41 (21) 701 48 16. **Fax:** 41 (21) 616 41 31. **Contact:** Jacques Barbier, Président.

OBJECTIFS: Exécuter des prestations d'étude, de gestion, de réalisation et de suivi confiées par des mandants. Favoriser une réflexion permanente sur la problématique du développement, alimentée par les expériences du terrain.

INFORMATIONS GENERALES: Création: 1991. **Type d'organisation:** réseau. **Organisations membres:** 3. **Affiliée à:** URBAPLAN (Suisse) - COVE SA (Suisse) - ACADE (Suisse). **Personnel/Total:** 10. Salariés: 10. **Sources financières:** Autofinancement: 100%.

PREVISIONS D'ACTIVITES: L'Organisation veut créer une plate-forme de réflexion sur le lien entre développement et aide d'urgence.

ACTIVITES DANS LES REGIONS EN DEVELOPPEMENT: Intervient directement dans les régions en développement. Intervient dans 2 pays. **Actions de Développement durable:** Démocratie/bonne gestion publique/création d'institutions/développement participatif; Développement rural/agriculture; Développement urbain/habitat; Petites entreprises/secteur informel/artisanat; Questions relatives aux femmes; Écologie/environnement/biodiversité; Éducation/formation/alphabétisation. **Régions:** Afrique de l'Ouest.

ACTIVITES D'INFORMATION ET D'EDUCATION: Domaines: Développement rural/agriculture; Développement urbain/habitat; Questions relatives aux femmes; Écologie/environnement/biodiversité. **Activités:** Autres; Conférences/séminaires/ateliers/activités de formation; Édition/documents audiovisuels/documents éducatifs; Éducation formelle.

CHE0440
ASSOCIATION CARABAYA-PEROU

Case Postale 72, 1211 Genève 29, Suisse.

Contact: M. Torrione, M. Chevallay.

CHE0441
ASSOCIATION COLOMBIE

Case postale 1112, 1211 Genève 1, Suisse.

Téléphone: 41 (22) 758 14 46.

Voir : *Comment utiliser le répertoire,* page 11.

CHE0442

ASSOCIATION COOPERATION COUP DE MAIN - JEUNES POUR L'ENTRAIDE

Case Postale 126, 1211 Genève 28, Suisse.

Téléphone: 41 (22) 45 17 07.

CHE0443

ASSOCIATION D'AMITIE ET DE COOPERATION AVEC L'URUGUAY

Case postale 228, 1217 Meyrin 1, Suisse.

Téléphone: 41 (22) 782 60 07. *Contact:* Christine Meyerhans, Présidente.

OBJECTIFS: Etablir des liens de solidarité avec l'Uruguay. Contribuer à l'organisation des femmes uruguayennes. Sensibiliser et informer le public genevois aux problèmes de l'Urugay.

INFORMATIONS GENERALES: *Création:* 1990. *Personnel/Total:* 10. *Bénévoles:* 10. *Budget/Total 1993:* ECU 5700 (US$ 7400). *Sources financières:* Public: 50%. Autofinancement: 50%.

ACTIVITES DANS LES REGIONS EN DEVELOPPEMENT: Intervient dans 1 pays. Maintient une présence locale sur le terrain. Intervient par l'intermédiaire d'organisations locales partenaires. **Actions de Développement durable:** Enfants/jeunesse/famille; Questions relatives aux femmes; Éducation/formation/alphabétisation. **Régions:** Amérique du Sud.

ACTIVITES D'INFORMATION ET D'EDUCATION: Domaines: Enfants/jeunesse/famille. **Activités:** Collecte de fonds; Échanges/parrainage/jumelage.

CHE0444

ASSOCIATION D'ENTRAIDE POUR LE SAHEL (MORIJA)

En Reutet, BP 114, 1868 Collombey-Le-Grand, Suisse.

Téléphone: 41 (25) 72 80 70. *Fax:* 41 (25) 72 80 93. *Contact:* Michel Raboud, Directeur.

OBJECTIFS: Venir en aide aux orphelins et aux plus déshérités d'Afrique en général, et du Sahel en particulier.

INFORMATIONS GENERALES: *Création:* 1979. *Personnel/Total:* 358. *Salariés:* 108 dont: 100 dans les pays en développement. *Bénévoles:* 250. *Budget/Total 1993:* ECU 1910000 (US$ 2477000). *Sources financières:* Privé: 85%. Public: 13%. Autofinancement: 2%.

PUBLICATIONS: *Périodiques:* Afin qu'ils vivent (12). *Rapport annuel.*

ACTIVITES DANS LES REGIONS EN DEVELOPPEMENT: Intervient directement dans les régions en développement. Intervient dans 5 pays. Maintient une présence locale sur le terrain. Intervient par l'intermédiaire d'organisations locales partenaires. **Actions de Développement durable:** Aliments/famine; Développement rural/agriculture; Enfants/jeunesse/famille; Petites entreprises/secteur informel/artisanat; Population/planning familial/démographie; Questions relatives aux femmes; Santé/assainissement/eau; Écologie/environnement/biodiversité; Éducation/formation/alphabétisation. **Régions:** Afrique centrale; Afrique de l'Ouest.

ACTIVITES D'INFORMATION ET D'EDUCATION: Domaines: Aliments/famine; Développement rural/agriculture; Enfants/jeunesse/famille; Pauvreté/conditions de vie; Questions relatives aux femmes; Santé/assainissement/eau. **Activités:** Campagnes d'information/expositions; Collecte de fonds; Échanges/parrainage/jumelage; Édition/documents audiovisuels/documents éducatifs.

CHE0445

ASSOCIATION DE COOPERATION SUISSE-PEROU

Rue du Rhone 57, 1204 Genève, Suisse.

Téléphone: 41 (22) 28 30 03.

CHE0446

ASSOCIATION DE SOLIDARITE AVEC LE NICARAGUA ET EL SALVADOR (ANS)

Case Postale 1135, 1211 Genève 1, Suisse.

Téléphone: 41 (22) 700 50 84.

OBJECTIFS: Informer le public suisse sur les pays d'Amérique Centrale. Soutenir les organisation populaires et les organisations féminines en Amérique centrale. Promouvoir les coopératives agricoles. Faciliter l'obtention des crédits pour l'économie populaire.

INFORMATIONS GENERALES: *Création:* 1979. *Type d'organisation:* réseau. *Organisations membres:* 8. *Affiliée à:* Fédération Genevoise de Coopération (Suisse). *Personnel/Total:* 6. *Bénévoles:* 6. *Budget/Total 1993:* ECU 78000 (US$ 102000). *Sources financières:* Privé: 17%. Public: 81%. Autofinancement: 2%.

PUBLICATIONS: *Périodiques:* Correos de Centoamérica (5). *Rapport annuel.*

EVALUATION/RECHERCHE: Rapports d'évaluation disponibles.

ACTIVITES DANS LES REGIONS EN DEVELOPPEMENT: Intervient dans 1 pays. Intervient par l'intermédiaire d'organisations locales partenaires. **Actions de Développement durable:** Droits de l'Homme/paix/conflits; Démocratie/bonne gestion publique/création d'institutions/développement participatif; Développement rural/agriculture; Petites entreprises/secteur informel/artisanat; Questions relatives aux femmes; Éducation/formation/alphabétisation. **Régions:** Mexique et Amerique centrale.

ACTIVITES D'INFORMATION ET D'EDUCATION: Domaines: Autres; Droits de l'Homme/paix/conflits; Développement rural/agriculture; Développement urbain/habitat; Paix/conflits ethniques/armement/désarmement; Pauvreté/conditions de vie; Questions relatives aux femmes; Santé/assainissement/eau. **Activités:** Campagnes d'information/expositions; Collecte de fonds; Conférences/séminaires/ateliers/activités de formation.

CHE0447

ASSOCIATION DE SOUTIEN AUX NATIONS AMERINDIENNES

Vieux-Moulin 14, 1018 Lausanne, Suisse.

Téléphone: 41 (21) 647 68 87. *Fax:* 41 (21) 647 68 87. *Contact:* Véra Tchérémissinoff, présidente.

CHE0448

ASSOCIATION DES AMITIES BURUNDI-SUISSE

Postfach 70, Chemin de la Nant 1, 2740 Moutier, Suisse.

Téléphone: 41 (32) 93 18 86. *Fax:* 41 (32) 93 60 60. *Contact:* Pierre Appenzeller, Président.

OBJECTIFS: Créer des liens culturels, économiques, affectifs et humanitaires entre la Suisse et le Burundi.

INFORMATIONS GENERALES: *Personnel/Total:* 25. *Bénévoles:* 25. *Budget/Total 1993:* ECU 18000 (US$ 24000). *Sources financières:* Public: 65%. Autofinancement: 35%.

PUBLICATIONS: *Rapport annuel. Liste des publications.*

ACTIVITES DANS LES REGIONS EN DEVELOPPEMENT: Intervient directement dans les régions en développement. Intervient dans 1 pays. Maintient une présence locale sur le terrain. Intervient par l'intermédiaire d'organisations locales partenaires. **Actions de Développement durable:** Aliments/famine; Droits de l'Homme/paix/conflits; Démocratie/bonne gestion publique/création d'institutions/développement participatif; Développement rural/agriculture; Enfants/jeunesse/famille; Petites entreprises/secteur informel/artisanat; Santé/assainissement/eau; Secours d'urgence/réfugiés/aide humanitaire; Éducation/formation/alphabétisation. **Régions:** Afrique de l'Est.

ACTIVITES D'INFORMATION ET D'EDUCATION: Domaines: Aliments/famine; Autres; Culture/tradition/religion; Droits de l'Homme/paix/conflits; Développement rural/agriculture; Développement urbain/habitat; Emploi/chômage; Enfants/jeunesse/famille; Paix/conflits ethniques/armement/désarmement; Pauvreté/conditions de vie; Population/planning familial/démographie; Questions relatives aux femmes; Racisme/

See: *How to Use the Directory*, page 11.

xénophobie/antisémitisme; Relations internationales/coopération/aide au développement; Relations économiques internationales/commerce/ dette/finances; Réfugiés/migrants/groupes ethniques; Santé/assainissement/eau; Secours d'urgence/réfugiés/aide humanitaire; Écologie/environnement/biodiversité; Éducation/formation/alphabétisation. **Activités:** Collecte de fonds; Conférences/séminaires/ateliers/activités de formation; Lobbying/plaidoyer; Échanges/parrainage/jumelage; Éducation formelle.

CHE0449
ASSOCIATION DES CENTRES MEDICO-EDUCATIFS - CHILI

s/c M. Jean-Pierre Lagnaux, ch. de Sous-le-Clos 10, 1232 Confignon, Suisse.

Téléphone: 41 (22) 757 22 72.

CHE0450
ASSOCIATION EN SUISSE DE DEFENSE DES DROITS DE L'HOMME AU MAGHREB (ASDHM)

Case postale 2041, 1002 Lausanne, Suisse.

Téléphone: 41 (21) 25 29 55.

CHE0451
ASSOCIATION FRATERNELLE INTERNATIONALE (AFI)

Rue de la Servette 91, 1202 Genève, Suisse.

Téléphone: 41 (22) 733 09 07. *Contact:* Anne Brusselmans.

CHE0452
ASSOCIATION INTERNATIONALE DES JURISTES DEMOCRATES

14 chemin de Fantaisie, 1009 Pully/Lausanne, Suisse.

Contact: Renée Bridel, Déléguée.

OBJECTIFS: Faciliter les contacts entre juristes de tous les pays.

INFORMATIONS GENERALES: *Création:* 1948. *Type d'organisation:* réseau. *Organisations membres:* 35. *Affiliée à:* Association Européenne de Juristes Démocrates (France) - Association Française de Juristes Démocrates (France) - Association Suisse Romande de Juristes Démocrates (Etats-Unis) - Association on Haldane Society de Juristes Démocrates (Grande Bretagne).

PUBLICATIONS: *Périodiques:* Revue de Droit Contemporain (12). *Rapport annuel.*

EVALUATION/RECHERCHE: Rapports d'évaluation disponibles. Entreprend des activités de recherche.

COMMENTAIRES: Intervient dans la Communauté des Etats indépendants.

ACTIVITES DANS LES REGIONS EN DEVELOPPEMENT: Intervient directement dans les régions en développement. Maintient une présence locale sur le terrain. **Actions de Développement durable:** Droits de l'Homme/paix/conflits. **Régions:** Afrique australe; Afrique centrale; Afrique de l'Est; Afrique de l'Ouest; Afrique du Nord; Amérique du Sud; Asie centrale et Asie du Sud; Asie de l'Est; Asie du Sud-Est; Caraïbes; Mexique et Amerique centrale; Moyen-Orient; Océanie.

ACTIVITES D'INFORMATION ET D'EDUCATION: Domaines: Droits de l'Homme/paix/conflits. **Activités:** Campagnes d'information/expositions; Collecte de fonds; Conférences/séminaires/ateliers/activités de formation; Lobbying/plaidoyer; Radiodiffusion/manifestations culturelles; Réseaux/télécommunications électroniques; Services d'information et de documentation/bases de données; Échanges/parrainage/jumelage; Édition/documents audiovisuels/documents éducatifs; Éducation formelle.

CHE0453
ASSOCIATION INTERNATIONALE POUR LA DEFENSE DE LA LIBERTE RELIGIEUSE

Schosshaldenstrasse 17, 3006 Bern, Suisse.

Téléphone: 41 (31) 44 62 62. *Fax:* 41 (31) 44 62 66.

CHE0454
ASSOCIATION KOMBIT (HAITI)

s/c M. René Zaugg, Cressonnex 1, 1288 Aire-la-Ville, Suisse.

Téléphone: 41 (22) 757 10 13. *Fax:* 41 (22) 757 38 63. *Contact:* J. Jacques Ingold, Président.

OBJECTIFS: Soutenir des projets de développement élaborés en Haïti, en cherchant des financements. Informer en Suisse sur la situation en Haïti.

INFORMATIONS GENERALES: *Création:* 1986. *Type d'organisation:* réseau. *Affiliée à:* Fédération Genevoise de Coopération (Suisse) - Plate-forme Haïti de Suisse (Suisse). *Personnel/Total:* 7. *Bénévoles:* 7. *Budget/Total 1993:* ECU 80000 (US$ 104000). *Sources financières:* Privé: 40%. Public: 60%.

EVALUATION/RECHERCHE: Rapports d'évaluation disponibles.

ACTIVITES DANS LES REGIONS EN DEVELOPPEMENT: Intervient dans 1 pays. Intervient par l'intermédiaire d'organisations locales partenaires. **Actions de Développement durable:** Autres; Démocratie/ bonne gestion publique/création d'institutions/développement participatif; Développement rural/agriculture; Éducation/formation/alphabétisation. **Régions:** Caraïbes.

CHE0455
ASSOCIATION LA FLORIDA - PEROU

Rue E. Racine 6, 1202 Genève, Suisse.

Téléphone: 41 (22) 733 09 18. *Contact:* Dominique Seydoux.

OBJECTIFS: Aider au développement communautaire. Lutter pour un commerce équitable du café.

INFORMATIONS GENERALES: *Création:* 1982. *Affiliée à:* Fédération Genevoise de Coopération (Suisse). *Personnel/Total:* 14. *Salariés:* 2 dont: 2 dans les pays en développement. *Bénévoles:* 12. *Budget/ Total 1993:* ECU 28000 (US$ 36000). *Sources financières:* Privé: 5%. Public: 5%. Autofinancement: 90%.

PUBLICATIONS: *Périodiques:* Lettre circulaire (3). *Rapport annuel.*

EVALUATION/RECHERCHE: Rapports d'évaluation disponibles.

ACTIVITES DANS LES REGIONS EN DEVELOPPEMENT: Intervient directement dans les régions en développement. Intervient dans 1 pays. Maintient une présence locale sur le terrain. Intervient par l'intermédiaire d'organisations locales partenaires. **Actions de Développement durable:** Dette/finances/commerce; Développement rural/agriculture; Petites entreprises/secteur informel/artisanat; Questions relatives aux femmes; Santé/assainissement/eau; Écologie/environnement/biodiversité; Éducation/formation/alphabétisation. **Régions:** Amérique du Sud.

ACTIVITES D'INFORMATION ET D'EDUCATION: Domaines: Développement rural/agriculture; Questions relatives aux femmes; Relations internationales/coopération/aide au développement; Relations économiques internationales/commerce/dette/finances; Éducation/formation/ alphabétisation. **Activités:** Campagnes d'information/expositions; Collecte de fonds; Conférences/séminaires/ateliers/activités de formation; Lobbying/plaidoyer.

CHE0456
ASSOCIATION MONDIALE POUR L'ECOLE INSTRUMENT DE PAIX (EIP) ♦ World Association for the School as an Instrument of Peace

5 rue du Simplon, 1207 Genève, Suisse.

Téléphone: 41 (22) 735 24 22. *Fax:* 41 (22) 736 48 63. *Contact:* Monique Prindezis, Secrétaire générale.

OBJECTIFS: Promouvoir une éducation relative aux Droits de l'Homme et à la paix.

INFORMATIONS GENERALES: *Création:* 1967. *Type d'organisation:* réseau, collectif. *Organisations membres:* 20. *Personnel/Total:* 31. *Salariés:* 1. *Bénévoles:* 30 dont: 20 dans les pays en développement. *Budget/Total 1993:* ECU 78000 (US$ 102000). *Sources financières:* Privé: 20%. Public: 30%. Autofinancement: 50%.

Voir : *Comment utiliser le répertoire*, page 11.

PUBLICATIONS: *Périodiques:* Bulletin Ecole et Paix (6) - Thématique Droits de l'homme (1). *Rapport annuel. Liste des publications.*

EVALUATION/RECHERCHE: Entreprend des activités de recherche.

COMMENTAIRES: Intervient dans la Communauté des Etats indépendants. Activités d'information concernant la Communauté des Etats indépendants.

ACTIVITES DANS LES REGIONS EN DEVELOPPEMENT: Intervient directement dans les régions en développement. Maintient une présence locale sur le terrain. **Actions de Développement durable:** Droits de l'Homme/paix/conflits; Démocratie/bonne gestion publique/création d'institutions/développement participatif; Éducation/formation/alphabétisation. **Régions:** Afrique centrale; Afrique de l'Ouest; Afrique du Nord; Amérique du Sud; Asie du Sud-Est; Mexique et Amerique centrale; Moyen-Orient.

ACTIVITES D'INFORMATION ET D'EDUCATION: **Domaines:** Droits de l'Homme/paix/conflits; Paix/conflits ethniques/armement/désarmement; Racisme/xénophobie/antisémitisme; Relations internationales/coopération/aide au développement; Éducation/formation/alphabétisation. **Activités:** Campagnes d'information/expositions; Conférences/séminaires/ateliers/activités de formation; Services d'information et de documentation/bases de données; Échanges/parrainage/jumelage; Édition/documents audiovisuels/documents éducatifs; Éducation formelle.

CHE0457
ASSOCIATION ORIENT REALITES

Case postale 2, 1211 Genève 7, Suisse.

Téléphone: 41 (22) 733 77 20.

CHE0458
ASSOCIATION POUR L'UNION ENTRE LES PEUPLES JUIF ET PALESTINIEN

Case postale 43, 1247 Anières, Suisse.

CHE0459
ASSOCIATION POUR LE DEVELOPPEMENT DES ENERGIES RENOUVELABLES (ADER)

1132 Lully, Suisse.

Téléphone: 41 (21) 801 18 94. *Fax:* 41 (21) 802 16 62. *Contact:* Paul Girardet, Président.

OBJECTIFS: Stimuler les études et les applications pratiques concernant la production décentralisée d'énergies renouvelables. Favoriser la réalisation d'installations expérimentales permettant d'accroître l'autonomie énergétique des exploitations de diverses natures, notamment agricoles. Promouvoir les économies d'énergie sous toutes leurs formes.

INFORMATIONS GENERALES: *Création:* 1980. *Personnel/Total:* 70. *Salariés:* 15. *Bénévoles:* 55 dont: 5 dans les pays en développement. *Budget/Total 1993:* ECU 81000 (US$ 106000). *Sources financières:* Privé: 82%. Public: 9%. *Autofinancement:* 9%.

PUBLICATIONS: *Rapport annuel. Liste des publications.*

EVALUATION/RECHERCHE: Rapports d'évaluation disponibles. Entreprend des activités de recherche.

COMMENTAIRES: L'organisation produit 53 rapports d'expériences pilotes Intervient dans la Communauté des Etats indépendants. Activités d'information concernant la Communauté des Etats indépendants.

ACTIVITES DANS LES REGIONS EN DEVELOPPEMENT: Intervient directement dans les régions en développement. Intervient dans 3 pays. Maintient une présence locale sur le terrain. Intervient par l'intermédiaire d'organisations locales partenaires. **Actions de Développement durable:** Énergie/transport. **Régions:** Afrique centrale; Afrique de l'Est.

ACTIVITES D'INFORMATION ET D'EDUCATION: **Domaines:** Autres. **Activités:** Campagnes d'information/expositions; Services d'information et de documentation/bases de données.

CHE0460
ASSOCIATION ROMANDE DES COMMUNAUTES EMMAUS

Case postale 1369, Route de Drize 5, 1227 Carouge, Suisse.

Téléphone: 41 (22) 342 39 59. *Fax:* 41 (22) 300 27 14. *Contact:* Georges Chevieux, Directeur.

OBJECTIFS: Coordonner les activités des six communautés d'Emmaüs en Suisse.

INFORMATIONS GENERALES: *Création:* 1954. *Type d'organisation:* regroupement d'ONG. *Organisations membres:* 6. *Affiliée à:* Emmaüs International (France). *Personnel/Total:* 155. *Salariés:* 35. *Bénévoles:* 120. *Budget/Total 1993:* ECU 2087000 (US$ 2707000). *Sources financières:* Privé: 5%. *Autofinancement:* 95%.

PUBLICATIONS: *Rapport annuel.*

COMMENTAIRES: L'organisation mène des activités dans les régions en développement à travers Emmaüs International.

ACTIVITES D'INFORMATION ET D'EDUCATION: **Domaines:** Aliments/famine; Développement urbain/habitat; Emploi/chômage; Pauvreté/conditions de vie; Relations économiques internationales/commerce/dette/finances. **Activités:** Autres; Campagnes d'information/expositions; Conférences/séminaires/ateliers/activités de formation; Lobbying/plaidoyer; Éducation formelle.

CHE0461
ASSOCIATION ROMANDE DES MAGASINS DU MONDE (MdM)

Montmeillan 15, 1005 Lausanne, Suisse.

Téléphone: 41 (21) 323 57 59. *Contact:* Claire Wermeille, Présidente.

OBJECTIFS: Vendre des produits en provenance des pays en développement pour informer le public suisse sur l'inégalité des relations économiques entre le Nord et le Sud.

INFORMATIONS GENERALES: *Création:* 1974. *Personnel/Total* 805. *Salariés:* 5. *Bénévoles:* 800. *Budget/Total 1993:* ECU 678000 (US$ 880000). *Sources financières:* Autofinancement: 100%.

PUBLICATIONS: *Périodiques:* Forum (4). *Rapport annuel.*

PREVISIONS D'ACTIVITES: Mise sur pied de cycles de formation sur les techniques de vente des MdM. Institution d'une journée européenne des MdM.

ACTIVITES DANS LES REGIONS EN DEVELOPPEMENT: Intervient dans 36 pays. Intervient par l'intermédiaire d'organisations locales partenaires.

ACTIVITES D'INFORMATION ET D'EDUCATION: **Domaines:** Aliments/famine; Culture/tradition/religion; Droits de l'Homme/paix/conflits; Développement rural/agriculture; Développement urbain/habitat; Enfants/jeunesse/famille; Paix/conflits ethniques/armement/désarmement; Pauvreté/conditions de vie; Questions relatives aux femmes; Racisme/xénophobie/antisémitisme; Relations internationales/coopération/aide au développement; Relations économiques internationales/commerce/dette/finances; Réfugiés/migrants/groupes ethniques; Écologie/environnement/biodiversité. **Activités:** Campagnes d'information/expositions; Conférences/séminaires/ateliers/activités de formation.

CHE0462
ASSOCIATION SCOUTISME TIERS-MONDE (ASTM)

C.P. 241, 1211 Genève 4, Suisse.

Téléphone: 41 (22) 320 42 33. *Contact:* Viviane Mouchet Jeannerat, Présidente.

OBJECTIFS: Contribuer à l'amélioration des conditions matérielles et morales des populations du Tiers-Monde à travers le mouvement Scout.

INFORMATIONS GENERALES: *Création:* 1987. *Type d'organisation:* regroupement d'ONG, réseau, collectif. *Affiliée à:* Fédération Genevoise de Coopération (Suisse). *Personnel/Total:* 12. *Bénévoles:* 12.

PUBLICATIONS: *Rapport annuel.*

See: *How to Use the Directory,* page 11.

ACTIVITES DANS LES REGIONS EN DEVELOPPEMENT: Intervient directement dans les régions en développement. Intervient dans 2 pays. Intervient par l'intermédiaire d'organisations locales partenaires. **Actions de Développement durable:** Développement rural/agriculture; Développement urbain/habitat; Enfants/jeunesse/famille; Éducation/formation/alphabétisation. **Régions:** Afrique de l'Est.

ACTIVITES D'INFORMATION ET D'EDUCATION: Domaines: Développement rural/agriculture; Développement urbain/habitat; Enfants/jeunesse/famille; Éducation/formation/alphabétisation. **Activités:** Collecte de fonds; Conférences/séminaires/ateliers/activités de formation.

CHE0463
ASSOCIATION SUISSE D'AIDE A L'HOPITAL ALBERT SCHWEITZER A LAMBARENE

Chemin de la Forêt, 1042 Assens, Suisse.

Téléphone: 41 (21) 881 23 80. *Fax:* 41 (21) 882 10 54. *Contact:* Willy Randin.

OBJECTIFS: Aider l'hôpital créé par le Docteur Albert Schweitzer à Lambaréné, au Gabon. Développer des activités de promotion des énergies douces, surtout dans les pays du Sahel.

INFORMATIONS GENERALES: *Création:* 1959. *Personnel/Total:* 5. *Bénévoles:* 5. *Budget/Total 1993:* ECU 94000 (US$ 122000). *Sources financières:* Privé: 100%.

PUBLICATIONS: *Périodiques:* Nouvelles de Lambaréné et de l'œuvre d'Albert Schweitzer (2).

ACTIVITES DANS LES REGIONS EN DEVELOPPEMENT: Intervient directement dans les régions en développement. Maintient une présence locale sur le terrain. Intervient par l'intermédiaire d'organisations locales partenaires. **Actions de Développement durable:** Développement rural/agriculture; Santé/assainissement/eau; Écologie/environnement/biodiversité. **Régions:** Afrique centrale; Afrique de l'Ouest.

ACTIVITES D'INFORMATION ET D'EDUCATION: Domaines: Développement rural/agriculture; Santé/assainissement/eau; Écologie/environnement/biodiversité. **Activités:** Collecte de fonds.

CHE0464
ASSOCIATION SUISSE DE PLANNING FAMILIAL ET D'EDUCATION SEXUELLE (ASPFES)

Chemin de la Guetta 7, 1073 Savigny, Switzerland.

Telephone: 41 (21) 784 02 46. *Fax:* 41 (21) 784 02 46. *Contact:* C. Magistretti, Executive Secretary.

OBJECTIVES: To promote and defend the right of women and men to decide freely the number and spacing of their children and the right to the highest possible level of sexual and reproductive health. To promote the family planning movement through information, advocacy and services.

GENERAL INFORMATION: *Creation:* 1993. *Affiliated to:* International Planned Parenthood Federation (United Kingdom.). *Personnel/Total:* 10. *Salaried:* 1. *Volunteers:* 9. *Budget/Total 1993:* ECU 2500 (US$ 3200). *Financial sources:* Self-financing: 100%.

PUBLICATIONS: *Periodicals:* News Bulletin (3).

EVALUATION/RESEARCH: Undertakes research activities.

INFORMATION AND EDUCATION ACTIVITIES: Topics: Children/youth/family; Gender issues/women; International relations/cooperation/development aid; Population/family planning/demography; Refugees/migrants/ethnic groups. **Activities:** Conferences/seminars/workshops/training activities; Information and documentation services/data bases; Lobbying/advocacy.

CHE0465
ASSOCIATION SUISSE DE SOLIDARITE AVEC LES PEUPLES INDIGENES "TUPAJ KATARI"/MOUVEMENT INDIEN "TUPAJKATARI"

Case postale 279, 1217 Meyrin 1, Suisse.

Téléphone: 41 (22) 782 60 54. *Contact:* Lararo Pary Anagua, Coordinateur général.

OBJECTIFS: Promouvoir le droit au Développement libre. Défendre l'identité indienne en Amérique Latine. Promouvoir les droits et libertés fondamentaux des peuples et nations autochtones. Promouvoir et protéger le patrimoine culturel. Développer l'esprit de Solidarité à la cause indienne.

INFORMATIONS GENERALES: *Création:* 1978. *Sources financières:* Privé: 10%. Autofinancement: 80%.

PUBLICATIONS: *Périodiques:* Discrimination des peuples autochtones - Bilan de 5 années de dictature en Bolivie - Violations des principes constitutionnels (Bolivie) - 500ans de Résistance indigène, noire et populaire.

EVALUATION/RECHERCHE: Rapports d'évaluation disponibles. Entreprend des activités de recherche.

COMMENTAIRES: Intervient dans la Communauté des Etats indépendants. Activités d'information concernant la Communauté des Etats indépendants.

ACTIVITES DANS LES REGIONS EN DEVELOPPEMENT: Intervient directement dans les régions en développement. Intervient dans 3 pays. Intervient par l'intermédiaire d'organisations locales partenaires. **Actions de Développement durable:** Droits de l'Homme/paix/conflits; Démocratie/bonne gestion publique/création d'institutions/développement participatif; Développement rural/agriculture; Petites entreprises/secteur informel/artisanat; Santé/assainissement/eau; Écologie/environnement/biodiversité; Énergie/transport. **Régions:** Amérique du Sud; Caraïbes; Mexique et Amerique centrale.

CHE0466
ASSOCIATION SUISSE DES AMIS D'HAITI (ASAH)

5 chemin Louis Valencien, 1226 Thonex, Suisse.

Téléphone: 41 (22) 348 62 17. *Contact:* Gérald Gaudin, Président.

OBJECTIFS: Soutenir l'œuvre de scolarisation entreprise par l'Eglise méthodiste d'Haïti.

INFORMATIONS GENERALES: *Création:* 1963. *Type d'organisation:* regroupement d'ONG. *Budget/Total 1993:* ECU 51000 (US$ 66000). *Sources financières:* Privé: 80%. Public: 20%.

PUBLICATIONS: *Périodiques:* Association suisse des amis d'Haïti (4). *Rapport annuel.*

EVALUATION/RECHERCHE: Rapports d'évaluation disponibles.

ACTIVITES DANS LES REGIONS EN DEVELOPPEMENT: Intervient dans 1 pays. Intervient par l'intermédiaire d'organisations locales partenaires. **Actions de Développement durable:** Éducation/formation/alphabétisation. **Régions:** Caraïbes.

ACTIVITES D'INFORMATION ET D'EDUCATION: Domaines: Éducation/formation/alphabétisation. **Activités:** Campagnes d'information/expositions.

CHE0467
ASSOCIATION SUISSE DES AMIS DE L'AFGHANISTAN (ASAA)

En Roseires, 1633 Marsens, Suisse.

Téléphone: 41 (29) 511 57. *Fax:* 41 (27) 510 29. *Contact:* Bernard Repond.

OBJECTIFS: Aider au développement et à la reconstruction. Fournir une aide d'urgence. Etablir des contacts culturels et contribuer à la conservation et à la progation de la culture afghane.

INFORMATIONS GENERALES: *Création:* 1971. *Personnel/Total:* var. *Bénévoles:* 7. *Budget/Total 1993:* ECU 136000 (US$ 176000). *Sources financières:* Privé: 15%. Public: 70%. Autofinancement: 15%.

EVALUATION/RECHERCHE: Rapports d'évaluation disponibles.

ACTIVITES DANS LES REGIONS EN DEVELOPPEMENT: Intervient directement dans les régions en développement. Intervient dans 2 pays. Maintient une présence locale sur le terrain. Intervient par l'intermédiaire d'organisations locales partenaires. **Actions de Développement durable:** Aliments/famine; Démocratie/bonne gestion publique/création d'institutions/développement participatif; Développement rural/agriculture;

Voir : *Comment utiliser le répertoire,* page 11.

Petites entreprises/secteur informel/artisanat; Santé/assainissement/eau; Secours d'urgence/réfugiés/aide humanitaire; Éducation/formation/alphabétisation. **Régions:** Asie centrale et Asie du Sud.

ACTIVITES D'INFORMATION ET D'EDUCATION: Domaines: Aliments/famine; Culture/tradition/religion; Développement rural/agriculture; Réfugiés/migrants/groupes ethniques; Santé/assainissement/eau; Secours d'urgence/réfugiés/aide humanitaire; Éducation/formation/alphabétisation. **Activités:** Campagnes d'information/expositions; Collecte de fonds; Conférences/séminaires/ateliers/activités de formation; Lobbying/plaidoyer.

CHE0468
ASSOCIATION SUISSE RAOUL FOLLEREAU
Rue Louis-Curtat 4, 1005 Lausanne, Suisse.

Téléphone: 41 (21) 312 33 00. **Contact:** Françoise Brunnschweiler, Présidente.

CHE0469
ASSOCIATION SUISSE-CAMEROUN (ASC)
s/c Tschumi & Heurteux, rue des Cordiers 4, 1207 Genève, Suisse.

Téléphone: 41 (22) 735 45 14. **Contact:** Joseph Engamba, Président.

CHE0470
ASSOCIATION SUISSE-CUBA
Case postale 61, 1211 Genève 1, Suisse.

CHE0471
ASSOCIATION SUISSE-PARAGUAY (ASP)
Case postale 1137, 1211 Genève 1, Suisse.

Téléphone: 41 (22) 796 74 81.

CHE0472
ASSOCIAZIONE AMICI DI PADRE MANTOVANI ♦ Association of the Friends of Father Mantovani
Via al Lido 3, 6962 Viganello, Switzerland.

Telephone: 41 (91) 52 27 58. **Contact:** Carlo Tosi, President.

OBJECTIVES: To provide development aid for self-reliance projects in India in the fields of health, food and education.

GENERAL INFORMATION: Creation: 1965. **Type of organisation:** association of NGOs, coordinating body. **Personnel/Total:** 2. Salaried: 2. **Budget/Total 1993:** ECU 157000 (US$ 203000). **Financial sources:** Private: 100%.

PLANNED ACTIVITIES: The Organisation will finance a centre in Madras, India to care for leprosy patients, and will pay for the construction of local schools in Polur, in Covelong and Ahmednagar.

ACTIVITIES IN DEVELOPING REGIONS: Present in developing regions. Active in 1 country(ies). Maintains local field presence. Works through local field partners. **Sustainable Development Actions:** Children/youth/family; Education/training/literacy; Gender issues/women; Health/sanitation/water; Rural development/agriculture; Urban development/habitat. **Regions:** Central Asia and South Asia.

CHE0473
ASSOCIAZIONE MEDAGLIA MIRACOLOS
Via Croci 6, 6850 Mendrisio, Suisse.

Téléphone: 41 (91) 46 28 20.

CHE0474
ATD QUART-MONDE
Rue de St-Jean 61, Ch. Galiffe, 1201 Genève, Suisse.

Téléphone: 41 (22) 344 41 15.

CHE0475
ATELIER DES ENFANTS LIMA
Route de Moudon, 1610 Oron-la-Ville, Suisse.

Téléphone: 41 (21) 907 78 76. **Contact:** Michel Etter, Président.

OBJECTIFS: Intervenir dans les bidonvilles de Lima, dans les centres médicaux et dans les centres de réhabilitation nutrionnelle. Assurer une éducation pré-scolaire (jusqu'à l'âge de 6 ans). Aider les adolescents. Fournir une aide à des écoles de coiffure et de couture. Soutenir des foyers éducatifs: de 6 mois à 3 ans.

INFORMATIONS GENERALES: Création: 1989. **Type d'organisation:** regroupement d'ONG, réseau. **Personnel/Total:** 81. Salariés: 81 dont: 80 dans les pays en développement. **Budget/Total 1993:** ECU 215000 (US$ 279000). **Sources financières:** Privé: 90%. Public: 10%.

PUBLICATIONS: Périodiques: Atelier des enfants Lima (4).

PREVISIONS D'ACTIVITES: L'Organisation projette de collecter des fonds en Suisse.

ACTIVITES DANS LES REGIONS EN DEVELOPPEMENT: Intervient directement dans les régions en développement. Intervient dans 1 pays. Maintient une présence locale sur le terrain. **Actions de Développement durable:** Aliments/famine; Enfants/jeunesse/famille; Population/planning familial/démographie; Questions relatives aux femmes; Santé/assainissement/eau; Secours d'urgence/réfugiés/aide humanitaire; Éducation/formation/alphabétisation. **Régions:** Amérique du Sud.

ACTIVITES D'INFORMATION ET D'EDUCATION: Domaines: Aliments/famine; Enfants/jeunesse/famille; Pauvreté/conditions de vie; Population/planning familial/démographie; Questions relatives aux femmes; Santé/assainissement/eau; Éducation/formation/alphabétisation. **Activités:** Collecte de fonds.

CHE0476
ATELIER PANAFRICAIN DE RECHERCHE-ACTION EN COMMUNICATION (APRACOM)
Case postale 2054, 1002 Lausanne, Suisse.

CHE0477
AUSSATZIGENHILFE EMMAUS-SCHWEIZ ♦ Aide aux lépreux Emmaüs-Suisse
Spitalgasse 9, 3011 Bern, Suisse.

Téléphone: 41 (31) 311 77 97. **Fax:** 41 (31) 318 08 41. **Contact:** Walter Rosenfeld, Président.

OBJECTIFS: Aider les malades de la lèpre et lutter contre cette maladie partout où elle sévit, sur le plan médical, scientifique aussi bien que sur le plan social et humanitaire. Collaborer avec toutes les organisations nationales, internationales ou locales poursuivant un but analogue.

INFORMATIONS GENERALES: Création: 1959. **Affiliée à:** Fédération Internationale des Associations contre la lèpre (Royaume-Uni) -Unité-Communauté de travail des organismes de développement (Suisse) - Fédération Emmaüs (Suisse). **Personnel/Total:** 13. Salariés: 11 dont: 7 dans les pays en développement. **Bénévoles:** 2. **Budget/Total 1993:** ECU 2287000 (US$ 2965000). **Sources financières:** Privé: 99%. Public: 1%.

PUBLICATIONS: Périodiques: "Espoir pour les lépreux" (4) - Campagne nationale (1). *Rapport annuel. Liste des publications.*

PREVISIONS D'ACTIVITES: L'Organisation veut mener une campagne d'information sur la lèpre, et faire des exposés dans les écoles, en Suisse.

ACTIVITES DANS LES REGIONS EN DEVELOPPEMENT: Intervient directement dans les régions en développement. Intervient dans 26 pays. Maintient une présence locale sur le terrain. Intervient par l'intermédiaire d'organisations locales partenaires. **Actions de Développement durable:** Santé/assainissement/eau; Secours d'urgence/réfugiés/aide humanitaire; Éducation/formation/alphabétisation. **Régions:** Afrique centrale; Afrique du Nord; Amérique du Sud; Asie centrale et Asie du Sud; Asie du Sud-Est.

ACTIVITES D'INFORMATION ET D'EDUCATION: Domaines: Santé/assainissement/eau; Secours d'urgence/réfugiés/aide humanitaire.

See: *How to Use the Directory,* page 11.

Activités: Autres; Campagnes d'information/expositions; Collecte de fonds.

CHE0478

BAHA'I INTERNATIONAL COMMUNITY ♦ Communauté Internationale Baha'ie

Route des Morillons 15, 121G Grand-Saconnex, Switzerland.

Telephone: 41 (22) 798 54 00. *Fax:* 41 (22) 798 65 77 . *E-mail:* LAURTURO@BIC.ORG. *Contact:* Lawrence Arturo, Director.

CHE0479

B A S L E R M I S S I O N E V A N G E L I S C H E MISSIONSGESELLSCHAFT IN BASEL ♦ Basel Mission

Missionsstrasse 21, Postfach, 4003 Basel, Switzerland.

Telephone: 41 (61) 268 81 11. *Fax:* 41 (61) 268 82 68. *Contact:* Dr. Wolfgang Schmidt, President.

OBJECTIVES: To proclaim the gospel of Jesus Christ in order to free people from fear and guilt, ignorance and superstition, illness and hunger, oppression and exploitation.

GENERAL INFORMATION: *Creation:* 1815. *Affiliated to:* Cooperation of Evangelical Mission Societies and Churches (Switzerland) -Schweizerischer Evangelischer Missionsrat (Switzerland) - Evangelisches Missionswerk in Südwest Deutschland (Germany). *Personnel/Total:* 139. *Salaried:* 139 of which: 8 in developing countries. *Budget/Total 1993:* ECU 6784000 (US$ 8798000). *Financial sources:* Private: 45%. Public: 55%.

PUBLICATIONS: *Periodicals:* Nachrichten aus der Basler Mission (6). *Annual report.*

ACTIVITIES IN DEVELOPING REGIONS: Active in 12 country(ies). Maintains local field presence. Works through local field partners. **Sustainable Development Actions:** Children/youth/family; Democracy/good governance/institution building/participatory development; Ecology/environment/biodiversity; Education/training/literacy; Emergency relief/refugees/humanitarian assistance; Gender issues/women; Health/sanitation/water; Human rights/peace/conflicts; Population/family planning/demography; Rural development/agriculture; Sending volunteers/experts/technical assistance; Small enterprises/informal sector/handicrafts; Urban development/habitat. **Regions:** South America; South East Asia; West Africa.

INFORMATION AND EDUCATION ACTIVITIES: Topics: Culture/tradition/religion; Ecology/environment/biodiversity; Education/training/literacy; Employment/unemployment; Gender issues/women; Health/sanitation/water; Human rights/peace/conflicts; International economic relations/trade/debt/finance; International relations/cooperation/development aid; Poverty/living conditions; Rural development/agriculture; Urban development/habitat. **Activities:** Conferences/seminars/workshops/training activities; Exchanges/twinning/linking; Formal education; Fund raising; Information and documentation services/data bases; Information campaigns/exhibitions; Lobbying/advocacy; Networking/electronic telecommunications; Publishing/audiovisual materials/educational materials.

CHE0480

BELLERIVE FOUNDATION

4 rue Munier Romilly, C.P. 6, 1211 Geneva 3, Switzerland.

Telephone: 41 (22) 46 88 66. *Fax:* 41 (22) 47 91 59. *Contact:* Prince Sadruddin Aga Khan, President.

CHE0481

BENEDIKTINER MISSIONARE ♦ Benedictine Missionaries

St Otmarsberg, 8730 Uznach, Switzerland.

Telephone: 41 (55) 71 11 61. *Fax:* 41 (55) 72 26 23. *Contact:* Bro. Pius Müller, Procurator.

CHE0482

BEWEGUNG FUR OFFENE, DEMOKRATISCHE UND SOLIDARISCHE SCHWEIZ (BODS)

Postfach 8553, 3001 Bern, Suisse.

Téléphone: 41 (31) 25 39 30. *Fax:* 41 (31) 25 60 14.

CHE0483

BONNE VOLONTE MONDIALE ♦ World Goodwill

1 rue de Varembé, C.P. 31, 1211 Genève 20, Suisse.

Téléphone: 41 (22) 34 12 52. *Contact:* Marianne Hurlimann, Directrice.

OBJECTIFS: Etablir des relations humaines et justes entre les individus, les peuples et les nations.

INFORMATIONS GENERALES: *Création:* 1932. *Personnel/Total:* 11. *Salariés:* 9. *Bénévoles:* 2. *Budget/Total 1993:* ECU 350000 (US$ 305000). *Sources financières:* Privé: 100%.

PUBLICATIONS: *Périodiques:* Bulletin Bonne Volonté Mondiale (4) - Bulletin Triangles (4). *Liste des publications.*

EVALUATION/RECHERCHE: Rapports d'évaluation disponibles.

COMMENTAIRES: Intervient dans la Communauté des Etats indépendants.

ACTIVITES DANS LES REGIONS EN DEVELOPPEMENT: Intervient directement dans les régions en développement. Intervient dans 56 pays. Maintient une présence locale sur le terrain. Intervient par l'intermédiaire d'organisations locales partenaires. **Actions de Développement durable:** Droits de l'Homme/paix/conflits; Éducation/formation/alphabétisation. **Régions:** Afrique australe; Afrique centrale; Afrique de l'Est; Afrique de l'Ouest; Amérique du Sud; Mexique et Amerique centrale.

ACTIVITES D'INFORMATION ET D'EDUCATION: Domaines: Culture/tradition/religion; Éducation/formation/alphabétisation. **Activités:** Édition/documents audiovisuels/documents éducatifs.

CHE0484

BRENNPUNKT WELT (BW) ♦ World Focus

Neptunstrasse 38, 8032 Zürich, Suisse.

Téléphone: 41 (1) 252 31 60. *Contact:* Mani Mezhukanal, Coordinateur.

CHE0485

BRIGADA LATINO-BERNESA

Brunngasse 17, 3011 Bern, Suisse.

Téléphone: 41 (31) 311 62 32. *Contact:* John Schmocker.

OBJECTIFS: Soutenir des œuvres sociales au Nicaragua: écoles, maisons d'enfants, nourriture d'enfant. Financer un projet de médecine populaire.Accorder de petits crédits aux artisans et aux paysans.

INFORMATIONS GENERALES: *Création:* 1984. *Type d'organisation:* collectif. *Personnel/Total:* 12. *Salariés:* 1 dont: 1 dans les pays en développement. *Bénévoles:* 11. *Budget/Total 1993:* ECU 16000 (US$ 20000). *Sources financières:* Privé: 70%. Autofinancement: 30%.

PUBLICATIONS: *Périodiques:* Bulletin der Briglatbern (2).

ACTIVITES DANS LES REGIONS EN DEVELOPPEMENT: Intervient directement dans les régions en développement. Intervient dans 1 pays. Maintient une présence locale sur le terrain. Intervient par l'intermédiaire d'organisations locales partenaires. **Actions de Développement durable:** Aliments/famine; Enfants/jeunesse/famille; Envoi de volontaires/experts/assistance technique; Petites entreprises/secteur informel/artisanat; Santé/assainissement/eau. **Régions:** Mexique et Amerique centrale.

ACTIVITES D'INFORMATION ET D'EDUCATION: Domaines: Aliments/famine; Enfants/jeunesse/famille; Santé/assainissement/eau; Secours d'urgence/réfugiés/aide humanitaire. **Activités:** Collecte de fonds.

CHE0486

BROT FUR ALLE (BFA) ♦ Bread for All

Speichergasse 29, 3000 Bern 7, Switzerland.

Telephone: 41 (31) 312 32 35. *Fax:* 41 (31) 311 54 91. *Contact:* Rev. Dr. Christoph Stückelberger, General Secretary.

Voir : *Comment utiliser le répertoire,* page 11.

OBJECTIVES: To contribute to building a worldwide "multinational corporation of hope" by helping the poor find a voice, power and freedom. To support human rights in developing countries and improve living conditions by fostering self-help projects. To educate the Swiss public on the political, social and economic issues at stake in the South and the implications of these issues in Switzerland.

GENERAL INFORMATION: *Creation:* 1961. *Member organisations:* 18. *Affiliated to:* Swiss Aid Agencies Coalition - Federation of Protestant Churches in Switzerland - APRODEV (Belgium) - EECODC (Belgium). *Personnel/Total:* 16. *Salaried:* 16. *Budget/Total 1993:* ECU 7541000 (US$ 9779000). *Financial sources:* Private: 87%. *Public:* 12%. *Self-financing:* 1%.

PUBLICATIONS: *Annual report. List of publications.*

COMMENTS: BFA does not work directly with partners overseas but rather through Swiss agencies.

ACTIVITIES IN DEVELOPING REGIONS: Works through local field partners. **Sustainable Development Actions:** Children/youth/family; Health/sanitation/water; Human rights/peace/conflicts; Rural development/agriculture. **Regions:** Caribbean; Central Africa; Central Asia and South Asia; East Africa; Mexico and Central America; Middle East; South America; South East Asia; Southern Africa; West Africa.

INFORMATION AND EDUCATION ACTIVITIES: Topics: Children/youth/family; Ecology/environment/biodiversity; Food/famine; Gender issues/women; Health/sanitation/water; Human rights/peace/conflicts; International economic relations/trade/debt/finance; International relations/cooperation/development aid; Peace/ethnic conflicts/armament/disarmament; Population/family planning/demography; Rural development/agriculture. **Activities:** Conferences/seminars/workshops/training activities; Fund raising; Information campaigns/exhibitions; Lobbying/advocacy.

CHE0487

BRUCKE DER BRUDERHILFE ♦ Bridge of Brotherly Help

Ausstellungsstrasse 21, Postfach 349, 8031 Zürich, Switzerland.

Telephone: 41 (1) 271 05 30. *Contact:* Maria Senn, General Secretary.

CHE0488

BUREAU INDEPENDANT SUR LES QUESTIONS HUMANITAIRES ♦ Independent Bureau for Humanitarian Issues

P.O. Box 83, 1211 Genève 20, Suisse.

Contact: Zia Bizvi, Directeur.

CHE0489

BUREAU INTERNATIONAL DE LA PAIX (BIP)

Rue de Zurich 41, 1201 Genève, Suisse.

Téléphone: 41 (22) 731 64 29. *Fax:* 41 (22) 738 94 19.

CHE0490

CAP-VERT GENEVE

C.P. 2001, 1211 Genève 2, Suisse.

Téléphone: 41 (22) 347 75 93. *Fax:* 41 (22) 789 18 33. *Contact:* Gati François, Président.

OBJECTIFS: Promouvoir une coopération internationale en faveur de ceux qui vivent au Cap-Vert des expériences de développement participatif.

INFORMATIONS GENERALES: *Création:* 1978. *Affiliée à:* Fédération Genevoise de Coopération (Suisse). *Personnel/Total:* 10. *Bénévoles:* 10. *Budget/Total 1993:* ECU 34000 (US$ 44000). *Sources financières:* Public: 90%. *Autofinancement:* 10%.

PUBLICATIONS: *Périodiques:* Bulletin d'information (1). *Rapport annuel.*

PREVISIONS D'ACTIVITES: Création d'emplois et de petites entreprises au Cap-Vert.

ACTIVITES DANS LES REGIONS EN DEVELOPPEMENT: Intervient dans 1 pays. Intervient par l'intermédiaire d'organisations locales partenaires. **Actions de Développement durable:** Démocratie/bonne gestion publique/création d'institutions/développement participatif;

Enfants/jeunesse/famille; Santé/assainissement/eau; Éducation/formation/alphabétisation. **Régions:** Afrique de l'Ouest.

CHE0491

CARITAS SCHWEIZ ♦ CARITAS Switzerland

Löwenstrasse 3, 6002 Luzern, Switzerland.

Telephone: 41 (41) 52 22 22. *Fax:* 41 (41) 51 20 64. *Contact:* Jürg Krummenacher, Director.

OBJECTIVES: To assist people who are in need and unable to assist themselves. To promote equality of opportunity and to support local development initiatives.

GENERAL INFORMATION: *Creation:* 1901. *Member organisations:* 53. *Affiliated to:* Swiss Aid Agencies Coalition (Switzerland) - Organisation Suisse d'Aide aux Réfugiés (Switzerland) - Swiss Chain of Solidarity (Switzerland). *Personnel/Total:* 496. *Salaried:* 496 of which: 12 in developing countries. *Budget/Total 1993:* ECU 65494000 (US$ 84935000). *Financial sources:* Private: 42%. *Public:* 51%. *Self-financing:* 8%.

PUBLICATIONS: *Periodicals:* CARITAS-Zeitung (6). *Annual report. List of publications.*

EVALUATION/RESEARCH: Evaluation reports available. Undertakes research activities.

COMMENTS: Undertakes activities in the Commonwealth of Independent States.

ACTIVITIES IN DEVELOPING REGIONS: Present in developing regions. Active in 59 country(ies). Maintains local field presence. Works through local field partners. **Sustainable Development Actions:** Children/youth/family; Democracy/good governance/institution building/participatory development; Ecology/environment/biodiversity; Education/training/literacy; Emergency relief/refugees/humanitarian assistance; Food/famine; Gender issues/women; Health/sanitation/water; Human rights/peace/conflicts; Population/family planning/demography; Rural development/agriculture; Sending volunteers/experts/technical assistance; Small enterprises/informal sector/handicrafts; Urban development/habitat. **Regions:** Caribbean; Central Africa; Central Asia and South Asia; East Africa; Mexico and Central America; Middle East; North Africa; South America; South East Asia; Southern Africa; West Africa.

INFORMATION AND EDUCATION ACTIVITIES: Topics: Ecology/environment/biodiversity; Emergency relief/refugees/humanitarian assistance; Employment/unemployment; Food/famine; Gender issues/women; Human rights/peace/conflicts; International relations/cooperation/development aid; Population/family planning/demography; Racism/xenophobia/antisemitism; Refugees/migrants/ethnic groups; Rural development/agriculture. **Activities:** Broadcasting/cultural events; Conferences/seminars/workshops/training activities; Fund raising; Information and documentation services/data bases; Information campaigns/exhibitions; Lobbying/advocacy; Networking/electronic telecommunications; Publishing/audiovisual materials/educational materials.

CHE0492

CATHOLIC RELIEF SERVICES (CRS)

11 rue de Cornavin, 1201 Geneva, Switzerland.

Contact: Geoffrey P. May, Director of Geneva Office.

CHE0493

CENTRALE SANITAIRE SUISSE (CSS) ♦ Swiss Medical Relief Committee

C.P. 145, 8031 Zürich, Switzerland.

Telephone: 41 (1) 363 39 00. *Fax:* 41 (1) 363 39 00. *Contact:* Emanuela Tognola.

OBJECTIVES: To provide basic health care in developing countries.

GENERAL INFORMATION: *Creation:* 1937. *Personnel/Total:* 63. *Salaried:* 3 of which: 1 in developing countries. *Volunteers:* 60. *Budget/Total 1993:* ECU 365000 (US$ 474000). *Financial sources:* Private: 82%. *Public:* 18%.

PUBLICATIONS: *Periodicals:* CSS-Bulletin (4). *Annual report.*

See: *How to Use the Directory,* page 11.

ACTIVITIES IN DEVELOPING REGIONS: Active in 7 country(ies). Works through local field partners. **Sustainable Development Actions:** Children/youth/family; Education/training/literacy; Gender issues/women; Health/sanitation/water; Human rights/peace/conflicts. **Regions:** East Africa; Mexico and Central America; Middle East; South East Asia.

INFORMATION AND EDUCATION ACTIVITIES: Topics: Gender issues/women; Health/sanitation/water. **Activities:** Fund raising.

CHE0494

CENTRE CATHOLIQUE INTERNATIONAL DE GENEVE (CCIG)

Case postale 43, rue de Varembé 1, 1211 Genève 20, Suisse.

Téléphone: 41 (22) 734 14 65. *Fax:* 41 (22) 733 93 83. *Contact:* Marc Savary, Président.

OBJECTIFS: Contribuer à la qualité de la présence des ONG (et particulièrement des Organisations Internationales Catholiques) dans les instances de l'ONU par un exercice complet et fructueux de leur statut consultatif. Informer sur les activités des Institutions Internationales de Genève. Contribuer à la réflexion sur les enjeux de l'actualité.

INFORMATIONS GENERALES: *Création:* 1950. *Personnel/Total:* 4. *Salariés:* 1. *Bénévoles:* 3. *Budget/Total 1993:* ECU 63000 (US$ 81000). *Sources financières:* Privé: 44%. Autofinancement: 56%.

PUBLICATIONS: *Périodiques:* Informations Internationales de Genève (10).

ACTIVITES D'INFORMATION ET D'EDUCATION: Domaines: Droits de l'Homme/paix/conflits; Paix/conflits ethniques/armement/désarmement; Relations internationales/coopération/aide au développement; Santé/assainissement/eau; Secours d'urgence/réfugiés/aide humanitaire; Écologie/environnement/biodiversité; Éducation/formation/alphabétisation. **Activités:** Conférences/séminaires/ateliers/activités de formation; Services d'information et de documentation/bases de données.

CHE0495

CENTRE D'ETUDES TIBETAINES RABTEN CHOELING

Ch. Derochoz, 1801 Le Mont-Pelerin, Suisse.

Téléphone: 41 (21) 921 36 00. *Fax:* 41 (21) 921 78 68. *Contact:* Gonsar Tulku Rinpoche, Directeur.

OBJECTIFS: Conserver et transmettre la culture et la religion tibétaines et bouddhistes pour ceux qui s'y intéressent en Occident et ailleurs.

INFORMATIONS GENERALES: *Création:* 1977. *Sources financières:* Autofinancement: 95%.

PUBLICATIONS: *Périodiques:* Programme de séminaires et cours (2).

PREVISIONS D'ACTIVITES: Cours d'études permanents au niveau universitaire, séminaires pour laïques et enseignants.

COMMENTAIRES: Activités d'information concernant la Communauté des Etats indépendants. **Actions de Développement durable:** Développement rural/agriculture. **Régions:** Asie centrale et Asie du Sud; Asie de l'Est.

ACTIVITES D'INFORMATION ET D'EDUCATION: Domaines: Développement rural/agriculture. **Activités:** Conférences/séminaires/ateliers/activités de formation; Édition/documents audiovisuels/documents éducatifs; Éducation formelle.

CHE0496

CENTRE D'INFORMATION ET D'ORIENTATION POUR LES PROFESSIONS RELATIVES A LA COOPERATION AU DEVELOPPEMENT ET A L'AIDE HUMANITAIRE

Rue Centrale 121 Case Postale, 2500 Bienne 7, Suisse.

Téléphone: 41 (32) 25 80 02. *Fax:* 41 (32) 25 80 59. *Courrier électronique:* 100632.2216@compuserve.com. *Contact:* Madame Brigit Hagmann, Directrice.

OBJECTIFS: Informer et orienter les personnes qui s'intéressent à la coopération au développement et à l'aide humanitaire, ainsi que les personnes de retour d'une affectation ou sur le point du départ.

INFORMATIONS GENERALES: *Création:* 1990. *Personnel/Total:* 9. *Salariés:* 9. *Budget/Total 1993:* ECU 574000 (US$ 744000). *Sources financières:* Public: 100%.

PUBLICATIONS: *Périodiques:* Cinfoposte (12). *Rapport annuel. Liste des publications.*

EVALUATION/RECHERCHE: Rapports d'évaluation disponibles.

ACTIVITES D'INFORMATION ET D'EDUCATION: Domaines: Culture/tradition/religion; Emploi/chômage; Relations internationales/coopération/aide au développement. **Activités:** Campagnes d'information/expositions; Conférences/séminaires/ateliers/activités de formation; Services d'information et de documentation/bases de données; Édition/documents audiovisuels/documents éducatifs.

CHE0497

CENTRE DE COOPERATION TECHNIQUE ET DE RECHERCHE POUR L'EDUCATION DES TRAVAILLEURS DANS LES PAYS EN VOIE DE DEVELOPPEMENT (CECOTRET)

Route de Ferney 10, 1202 Genève, Suisse.

Téléphone: 41 (22) 734 73 66. *Fax:* 41 (22) 734 56 49. *Contact:* Cynthia Özden-Neutry.

CHE0498

CENTRE ECOLOGIQUE ALBERT SCHWEITZER (CEAS)

Rue de Côte 2, 2000 Neuchâtel, Suisse.

Téléphone: 41 (38) 25 08 36. *Fax:* 41 (38) 25 15 07. *Contact:* Pascal de Pury, Directeur.

OBJECTIFS: Contribuer à la lutte contre la désertification des pays et régions tropicales sèches. Fournir un appui technique aux projets de développement artisanal et agroécologique des partenaires africains.

INFORMATIONS GENERALES: *Création:* 1978. *Affiliée à:* Unité (Suisse) - Technap (France). *Personnel/Total:* 5. *Salariés:* 5 dont: 2 dans les pays en développement. *Budget/Total 1993:* ECU 626000 (US$ 812000). *Sources financières:* Privé: 62%. Public: 30%. Autofinancement: 8%.

PUBLICATIONS: *Périodiques:* "L'Avenir est entre vos mains" (5). *Rapport annuel.*

EVALUATION/RECHERCHE: Entreprend des activités de recherche.

ACTIVITES DANS LES REGIONS EN DEVELOPPEMENT: Intervient directement dans les régions en développement. Intervient dans 2 pays. Maintient une présence locale sur le terrain. Intervient par l'intermédiaire d'organisations locales partenaires. **Actions de Développement durable:** Aliments/famine; Autres; Démocratie/bonne gestion publique/création d'institutions/développement participatif; Développement rural/agriculture; Développement urbain/habitat; Envoi de volontaires/experts/assistance technique; Petites entreprises/secteur informel/artisanat; Santé/assainissement/eau; Écologie/environnement/biodiversité; Éducation/formation/alphabétisation. **Régions:** Afrique australe; Afrique de l'Ouest.

CHE0499

CENTRE EUROPE-TIERS MONDE (CETIM)

Quai Wilson 37, 1201 Genève, Suisse.

Téléphone: 41 (22) 31 59 63. *Fax:* 41 (22) 31 59 63. *Contact:* Micheline Fontolliet, Co-directrice.

OBJECTIFS: Mettre en évidence la part de responsabilité des pays du Nord dans les problèmes rencontrés par la plupart des pays en développement. Montrer comment le mode de vie des pays du Nord menace la survie même de notre planète. Donner la parole aux groupes populaires du Tiers Monde qui luttent pour l'amélioration de leur condition de vie.

INFORMATIONS GENERALES: *Création:* 1970. *Personnel/Total:* 4. *Salariés:* 3. *Bénévoles:* 1. *Budget/Total 1993:* ECU 75000 (US$ 98000). *Sources financières:* Privé: 33%. Public: 37%. Autofinancement: 27%.

PUBLICATIONS: *Rapport annuel. Liste des publications.*

EVALUATION/RECHERCHE: Entreprend des activités de recherche.

Voir : *Comment utiliser le répertoire,* page 11.

ACTIVITES D'INFORMATION ET D'EDUCATION: Domaines: Droits de l'Homme/paix/conflits; Développement rural/agriculture; Emploi/chômage; Enfants/jeunesse/famille; Paix/conflits ethniques/armement/désarmement; Pauvreté/conditions de vie; Questions relatives aux femmes; Racisme/xénophobie/antisémitisme; Relations économiques internationales/commerce/dette/finances; Réfugiés/migrants/groupes ethniques; Écologie/environnement/biodiversité. **Activités:** Édition/documents audiovisuels/documents éducatifs.

CHE0500

CENTRE FOR OUR COMMON FUTURE ♦ Centre pour Notre Avenir à Tous

33 route de Valavran, 1209 Geneva, Switzerland.

Telephone: 41 (22) 774 45 30. **Fax:** 41 (22) 774 45 36. **E-mail:** commonfuture@gn.apc.org. **Contact:** Warren H. Lindner, Executive Director.

OBJECTIVES: To promote and act as a focal point and catalyst in progress towards sustainable development. To encourage public and institutional involvement throughout the world in efforts to achieve sustainable development.

GENERAL INFORMATION: Creation: 1988. **Personnel/Total:** 16. *Salaried:* 13. *Volunteers:* 3. **Budget/Total 1993:** ECU 1566000 (US$ 2030000).

PUBLICATIONS: Periodicals: The Bulletin (4) - The Network (12). *Annual report. List of publications.*

EVALUATION/RESEARCH: Evaluation reports available.

PLANNED ACTIVITIES: The Centre for our Common Future is planning projects for capacity building, funding, referral and partnership projects.

COMMENTS: Undertakes activities in the Commonwealth of Independent States. Information activities related to the Commonwealth of Independent States.

ACTIVITIES IN DEVELOPING REGIONS: Present in developing regions. Works through local field partners.

INFORMATION AND EDUCATION ACTIVITIES: Topics: Ecology/environment/biodiversity. **Activities:** Conferences/seminars/workshops/training activities; Exchanges/twinning/linking; Information and documentation services/data bases; Information campaigns/exhibitions; Networking/electronic telecommunications; Publishing/audiovisual materials/educational materials.

CHE0501

CENTRE HAITIEN DE RECHERCHES ET DE DOCUMENTATION (CHRD)

C.P. 125, 1211 Genève 12, Suisse.

Téléphone: 41 (22) 348 21 94. **Fax:** 41 (22) 348 48 74. **Contact:** Joseph P. Antonio, Responsable Information.

OBJECTIFS: Entreprendre des recherches sur Haïti. Diffuser de l'information et de la documentation sur Haïti. Développer des relations de travail et de solidarité avec Haïti. Promouvoir la justice sociale en Haïti. Réaliser un projet de développemnt communautaire en Haïti.

INFORMATIONS GENERALES: Création: 1980. **Personnel/Total:** 4. *Bénévoles:* 4. **Budget/Total 1993:** ECU 16000 (US$ 20000). **Sources financières:** *Privé:* 40%. *Autofinancement:* 60%.

PUBLICATIONS: Périodiques: Haïti Nouvelles (4) - Haïti Hebdomadaire (52). *Rapport annuel. Liste des publications.*

EVALUATION/RECHERCHE: Entreprend des activités de recherche.

ACTIVITES DANS LES REGIONS EN DEVELOPPEMENT: Intervient directement dans les régions en développement. Intervient dans 1 pays. Maintient une présence locale sur le terrain. Intervient par l'intermédiaire d'organisations locales partenaires. **Actions de Développement durable:** Droits de l'Homme/paix/conflits; Démocratie/bonne gestion publique/création d'institutions/développement participatif; Développement rural/agriculture; Développement urbain/habitat; Santé/assainissement/eau; Éducation/formation/alphabétisation. **Régions:** Caraïbes.

ACTIVITES D'INFORMATION ET D'EDUCATION: Domaines: Culture/tradition/religion; Droits de l'Homme/paix/conflits; Développement rural/agriculture; Développement urbain/habitat; Pauvreté/conditions de vie; Questions relatives aux femmes; Relations internationales/coopération/aide au développement; Relations économiques internationales/commerce/dette/finances; Réfugiés/migrants/groupes ethniques; Santé/assainissement/eau; Écologie/environnement/biodiversité; Éducation/formation/alphabétisation. **Activités:** Campagnes d'information/expositions; Services d'information et de documentation/bases de données; Édition/documents audiovisuels/documents éducatifs.

CHE0502

CENTRE INTERNATIONAL POUR LA PROMOTION ET L'EDUCATION DES DROITS DE L'HOMME (CIPEDH)

Rue Amat 6, 1202 Genève, Suisse.

Téléphone: 41 (22) 731 33 32.

CHE0503

CENTRE MARTIN LUTHER KING POUR LA NON-VIOLENCE

Bethusy 56, 1012 Lausanne, Suisse.

Téléphone: 41 (21) 652 27 27.

OBJECTIFS: Promouvoir la non-violence en Suisse et dans le monde. Fournir de la documentation et publier un bulletin. Organiser des temps de formation, lancer ou relayer des actions, conseiller les objecteurs de conscience.

INFORMATIONS GENERALES: Création: 1968. **Affiliée à:** Conseil Suisse des Activités de jeunesse (Suisse) - Internationale des Résistants à la Guerre (Grande-Bretagne) - Bureau International de la Paix (Suisse). **Personnel/Total:** 23. *Salariés:* 3. *Bénévoles:* 20. **Budget/Total 1993:** ECU 58000 (US$ 75000). **Sources financières:** *Public:* 25%. *Autofinancement:* 75%.

PUBLICATIONS: Périodiques: K comme King (5) - Objecteurs-Info (11). *Rapport annuel. Liste des publications.*

EVALUATION/RECHERCHE: Rapports d'évaluation disponibles.

PREVISIONS D'ACTIVITES: L'organisation projette de fournir au public suisse des informations sur le service civil en Suisse.

ACTIVITES D'INFORMATION ET D'EDUCATION: Domaines: Droits de l'Homme/paix/conflits; Enfants/jeunesse/famille; Paix/conflits ethniques/armement/désarmement; Racisme/xénophobie/antisémitisme. **Activités:** Lobbying/plaidoyer; Services d'information et de documentation/bases de données; Édition/documents audiovisuels/documents éducatifs.

CHE0504

CERCLE DES PROMOTEURS DES RELATIONS AFRIQUE-EUROPE (AEF)

Case postale 739, 1701 Fribourg, Suisse.

CHE0505

CHRISTIAN CHILDREN'S FUND

c/o WCC P.O. Box 2100, 1211 Geneva 2, Switzerland.

Contact: Dr. Eugene Ries, Director.

CHE0506

CHRISTIAN MOVEMENT FOR PEACE

Postfach, 3001 Bern, Switzerland.

Telephone: 41 (31) 26 15 32. **Fax:** 41 (31) 302 87 34.

OBJECTIVES: To support NGOs involved in conflict resolution, human rights and gender issues in developing countries and promote ideas regarding peace and development. To support political demands of overseas projects of partners in Switzerland.

GENERAL INFORMATION: Creation: 1938. **Personnel/Total:** 9. *Salaried:* 9.

PUBLICATIONS: Periodicals: cfd-Zeitung (4) - cfd-Dossier (2). *Annual report. List of publications.*

See: *How to Use the Directory,* page 11.

COMMENTS: Undertakes activities in the Commonwealth of Independent States.

ACTIVITIES IN DEVELOPING REGIONS: Active in 6 country(ies). Works through local field partners. **Sustainable Development Actions:** Children/youth/family; Education/training/literacy; Emergency relief/refugees/humanitarian assistance; Gender issues/women; Health/sanitation/water; Human rights/peace/conflicts; Rural development/agriculture; Small enterprises/informal sector/handicrafts; Urban development/habitat. **Regions:** Middle East; North Africa; Southern Africa.

INFORMATION AND EDUCATION ACTIVITIES: Topics: Children/youth/family; Education/training/literacy; Emergency relief/refugees/humanitarian assistance; Gender issues/women; Health/sanitation/water; Human rights/peace/conflicts; International economic relations/trade/debt/finance; International relations/cooperation/development aid; Peace/ethnic conflicts/armament/disarmament; Racism/xenophobia/antisemitism; Refugees/migrants/ethnic groups; Rural development/agriculture; Urban development/habitat. **Activities:** Broadcasting/cultural events; Conferences/seminars/workshops/training activities; Exchanges/twinning/linking; Fund raising; Information and documentation services/data bases; Information campaigns/exhibitions; Lobbying/advocacy; Networking/electronic telecommunications; Publishing/audiovisual materials/educational materials.

CHE0507
CHRISTIAN SOLIDARITY INTERNATIONAL

P.O. Box 52, Forchstrasse 280, 8029 Zürich, Switzerland.

CHE0508
CHRISTKATHOLISCHES HILFSWERK

Kirchgasse 15, 4600 Olten, Suisse.

Téléphone: 41 (62) 32 23 49.

CHE0509
CHRISTLICHER FRIEDENSDIENST (CFD)

Falkenhöheweg 8, 3001 Bern, Suisse.

Téléphone: 41 (31) 23 60 07. *Fax:* 41 (31) 24 87 34.

CHE0510
CIBA-GEIGY STIFTUNG FUR ZUSAMMENARBEIT MIT ENTWICKLUNGSLANDERN ♦ Fondation Ciba-Geigy pour la coopération avec les pays en développement.

Klybeckstrasse 141, 4002 Basel, Suisse.

Téléphone: 41 (61) 696 22 78. *Fax:* 41 (61) 696 22 39. *Contact:* K.M. Leisinger.

OBJECTIFS: Promouvoir, dans le sens d'une aide à l'auto-assistance, le développpement des pays les plus pauvres du tiers monde, notamment par une coopération dans les domaines de l'agriculture, de la santé et de la formation. Fournir des analyses scientifiques, des conseils et une information sur certains aspects de la politique du développement.

INFORMATIONS GENERALES: *Création:* 1979. *Personnel/Total:* 6. *Salariés:* 6. *Budget/Total 1993:* ECU 2766000 (US$ 3587000). *Sources financières:* Privé: 100%.

PUBLICATIONS: *Rapport annuel. Liste des publications.*

EVALUATION/RECHERCHE: Rapports d'évaluation disponibles.

ACTIVITES DANS LES REGIONS EN DEVELOPPEMENT: Intervient directement dans les régions en développement. Intervient dans 12 pays. Intervient par l'intermédiaire d'organisations locales partenaires. **Actions de Développement durable:** Aliments/famine; Développement rural/agriculture; Enfants/jeunesse/famille; Envoi de volontaires/experts/assistance technique; Petites entreprises/secteur informel/artisanat; Questions relatives aux femmes; Santé/assainissement/eau; Secours d'urgence/réfugiés/aide humanitaire; Écologie/environnement/biodiversité. **Régions:** Afrique australe; Afrique centrale; Afrique de l'Est; Afrique de l'Ouest; Afrique du Nord; Amérique du Sud; Asie centrale et Asie du Sud; Asie de l'Est; Asie du Sud-Est; Caraïbes; Mexique et Amerique centrale; Moyen-Orient; Océanie.

ACTIVITES D'INFORMATION ET D'EDUCATION: Domaines: Développement rural/agriculture; Pauvreté/conditions de vie; Population/planning familial/démographie; Santé/assainissement/eau. **Activités:** Conférences/séminaires/ateliers/activités de formation; Édition/documents audiovisuels/documents éducatifs; Éducation formelle.

CHE0511
CINEDIA

Case Postale 197, 1700 Fribourg 1, Suisse.

Téléphone: 41 (37) 24 85 80. *Fax:* 41 (37) 24 13 77. *Contact:* Yvan Stern.

OBJECTIFS: Promouvoir l'utilisation de produits audiovisuels dans la pastorale, l'éducation et la formation dans les secteurs de l'animation culturelle et des loisirs. Favoriser, par l'audiovisuel, une meilleure connaissance des problèmes humains et sociaux actuels, un plus grand dialogue entre les sociétés, les cultures et les croyances différentes.

INFORMATIONS GENERALES: *Création:* 1981. *Personnel/Total:* 4. *Salariés:* 4. *Budget/Total 1993:* ECU 157000 (US$ 203000). *Sources financières:* Privé: 50%. Autofinancement: 50%.

PUBLICATIONS: *Périodiques:* Ciné-feuilles (6). *Liste des publications.*

ACTIVITES DANS LES REGIONS EN DEVELOPPEMENT: Intervient dans 1 pays. Intervient par l'intermédiaire d'organisations locales partenaires.

ACTIVITES D'INFORMATION ET D'EDUCATION: Domaines: Culture/tradition/religion; Enfants/jeunesse/famille; Paix/conflits ethniques/armement/désarmement. **Activités:** Édition/documents audiovisuels/documents éducatifs.

CHE0512
CLUB INTERNATIONAL DE COOPERATION - GENEVE

Case postale 132, 1211 Genève 28, Suisse.

Téléphone: 41 (22) 28 74 08.

CHE0513
COLLECTIF SUISSE DE SOLIDARITE AVEC LE PEUPLE ALGERIEN (CSSPA)

Case postale 331, 1001 Lausanne, Suisse.

CHE0514
COMITE CHILI

Postfach 113, 2501 Bienne, Suisse.

CHE0515
COMITE COLOMBIE

C.P. 62, 1000 Lausanne 5, Suisse.

OBJECTIFS: Aider les organisations populaires de bienfaisance, de défense des droits de l'homme, des indigènes, et leurs représentants lors de séjours en Suisse. Servir de lien entre ces organismes et les personnes ou les milieux intérssés dans le canton de Vaud.

INFORMATIONS GENERALES: *Création:* 1979. *Personnel/Total:* 12. *Bénévoles:* 12. *Sources financières:* Privé: 100%.

PREVISIONS D'ACTIVITES: L'organisation souhaite désormais concentrer ses efforts sur la Colombie, notamment pour aider les enfants délaissés.

ACTIVITES DANS LES REGIONS EN DEVELOPPEMENT: Intervient directement dans les régions en développement. Intervient dans 1 pays. Intervient par l'intermédiaire d'organisations locales partenaires. **Actions de Développement durable:** Droits de l'Homme/paix/conflits; Développement rural/agriculture; Questions relatives aux femmes; Secours d'urgence/réfugiés/aide humanitaire; Éducation/formation/alphabétisation. **Régions:** Amérique du Sud.

ACTIVITES D'INFORMATION ET D'EDUCATION: Domaines: Droits de l'Homme/paix/conflits; Développement rural/agriculture; Enfants/jeunesse/famille; Pauvreté/conditions de vie; Réfugiés/migrants/groupes ethniques; Éducation/formation/alphabétisation. **Activités:** Campagnes d'information/expositions; Collecte de fonds.

Voir : *Comment utiliser le répertoire,* page 11.

CHE0516

COMITE COMMUN DE LA COOPERATION PEDAGOGIQUE EN AFRIQUE

Postfach 189, 8057 Zürich, Suisse.

Téléphone: 41 (1) 311 83 03.

CHE0517

COMITE DE SOLIDARITE AVEC L'AMERIQUE CENTRALE

Case postale 2475, 1002 Lausanne, Suisse.

Contact: Jean-Charles Delacrétaz.

OBJECTIFS: Développer la solidarité avec l'Amérique centrale.

INFORMATIONS GENERALES: *Création:* 1979. *Type d'organisation:* collectif. *Personnel/Total:* 15. *Salariés:* 2 dont: 1 dans les pays en développement. *Sources financières:* Privé: 20%. Autofinancement: 80%.

PUBLICATIONS: *Périodiques:* Conecs de Centro America (4).

PREVISIONS D'ACTIVITES: L'organisation veut mener une campagne de soutien à l'Amérique centrale.

ACTIVITES DANS LES REGIONS EN DEVELOPPEMENT: Intervient directement dans les régions en développement. Intervient dans 3 pays. Maintient une présence locale sur le terrain. **Actions de Développement durable:** Développement rural/agriculture; Développement urbain/habitat; Enfants/jeunesse/famille; Questions relatives aux femmes; Santé/assainissement/eau; Éducation/formation/alphabétisation. **Régions:** Mexique et Amerique centrale.

ACTIVITES D'INFORMATION ET D'EDUCATION: Domaines: Aliments/ famine; Développement rural/agriculture; Développement urbain/habitat; Relations internationales/coopération/aide au développement; Santé/assainissement/eau. **Activités:** Radiodiffusion/manifestations culturelles; Édition/documents audiovisuels/documents éducatifs.

CHE0518

COMITE DE SOLIDARITE AVEC LE PEUPLE BRESILIEN

Case postale 602, 1212 Grand-Lancy 1, Suisse.

CHE0519

COMITE DE SOUTIEN AU PEUPLE SAHRAOUI

Case postale 177, Rue du Village Suisse 14, 1211 Genève 8, Suisse.

Téléphone: 41 (22) 329 46 46. *Fax:* 41 (22) 312 40 22. *Contact:* Berthier Perregaux, Président.

OBJECTIFS: Soutenir le peuple Sahraoui (en lutte contre le Maroc), dans les camps de réfugiés en Algérie, près de Tindouf, en leur apportant une aide humanitaire et des formations.

INFORMATIONS GENERALES: *Création:* 1976. *Type d'organisation:* réseau. *Personnel/Total:* 25. *Bénévoles:* 25. *Budget/Total 1993:* ECU 146000 (US$ 189000). *Sources financières:* Public: 80%. Autofinancement: 20%.

PUBLICATIONS: *Périodiques:* Nouvelles Sahraouies (4).

ACTIVITES DANS LES REGIONS EN DEVELOPPEMENT: Intervient directement dans les régions en développement. Intervient dans 1 pays. Intervient par l'intermédiaire d'organisations locales partenaires. **Actions de Développement durable:** Droits de l'Homme/paix/conflits; Questions relatives aux femmes; Santé/assainissement/eau; Secours d'urgence/réfugiés/aide humanitaire; Éducation/formation/alphabétisation; Énergie/transport. **Régions:** Afrique de l'Ouest.

ACTIVITES D'INFORMATION ET D'EDUCATION: Domaines: Droits de l'Homme/paix/conflits; Paix/conflits ethniques/armement/désarmement; Questions relatives aux femmes; Santé/assainissement/eau; Secours d'urgence/réfugiés/aide humanitaire; Éducation/formation/alphabétisation. **Activités:** Campagnes d'information/expositions; Collecte de fonds; Conférences/séminaires/ateliers/activités de formation; Lobbying/ plaidoyer.

CHE0520

COMITE EUROPEEN POUR LA DEFENSE DES REFUGIES ET IMMIGRES (CEDRI) ♦ European Committee for the Defense of Refugees and Immigrants

St. Johanns-Vorstadt 13, Postfach 2780 , 4002 Basel, Suisse.

Téléphone: 41 (61) 44 66 19. *Contact:* François Bouchardeau, Président.

CHE0521

COMITE INTER-AFRICAIN SUR LES PRATIQUES TRADITIONNELLES AYANT EFFET SUR LA SANTE DES FEMMES ET DES ENFANTS (CI-AF) ♦ Inter-African Committee on Traditional Practices Affecting the Health of Women and Children

147 rue de Lausanne, 1202 Genève, Suisse.

Téléphone: 41 (22) 731 24 20. *Fax:* 41 (22) 738 18 23. *Contact:* Berhane Ras-Work, President.

OBJECTIFS: Réduire les taux de morbidité et de mortalité chez les femmes et les filles, par l'éradication de pratiques traditionnelles néfastes, notamment les mutilations génitales féminines et le mariage précoce.

INFORMATIONS GENERALES: *Création:* 1984. *Organisations membres:* 24. *Personnel/Total:* 170. *Salariés:* 20 dont: 20 dans les pays en développement. *Bénévoles:* 150 dont: 150 dans les pays en développement. *Budget/Total 1993:* ECU 417000 (US$ 541000). *Sources financières:* Privé: 40%. Public: 60%.

PUBLICATIONS: *Périodiques:* Bulletin du Comité Inter-Africain (2). *Rapport annuel. Liste des publications.*

EVALUATION/RECHERCHE: Entreprend des activités de recherche.

PREVISIONS D'ACTIVITES: Lancement de campagnes d'information et de formation (TIC), et soutenir des projets de formation de formateurs et d'accoucheuses traditionnelles. Etudes sur les aspects socio-économiques du mariage précoce et des mutilations.

ACTIVITES DANS LES REGIONS EN DEVELOPPEMENT: Intervient directement dans les régions en développement. Intervient dans 22 pays. Maintient une présence locale sur le terrain. Intervient par l'intermédiaire d'organisations locales partenaires. **Actions de Développement durable:** Enfants/jeunesse/famille; Questions relatives aux femmes; Santé/assainissement/eau. **Régions:** Afrique centrale; Afrique de l'Est; Afrique de l'Ouest.

ACTIVITES D'INFORMATION ET D'EDUCATION: Domaines: Enfants/ jeunesse/famille; Questions relatives aux femmes; Santé/assainissement/eau. **Activités:** Campagnes d'information/expositions; Collecte de fonds; Conférences/séminaires/ateliers/activités de formation; Lobbying/ plaidoyer; Services d'information et de documentation/bases de données; Édition/documents audiovisuels/documents éducatifs; Éducation formelle.

CHE0522

COMITE INTERNATIONAL DE L'ORDRE DE MALTE POUR L'ASSISTANCE AUX LEPREUX (CIOMAL)

Place Claparede 3, 1205 Genève, Suisse.

Téléphone: 41 (22) 346 86 87. *Fax:* 41 (22) 347 08 61. *Contact:* Philppe de Weck, Président.

OBJECTIFS: Lutter pour la défense et la réhabilitation des lépreux, sur les plans médical et social, sans distinction de race, de langue ou de religion.

INFORMATIONS GENERALES: *Création:* 1958. *Personnel/Total:* 3. *Salariés:* 2. *Bénévoles:* 1. *Budget/Total 1993:* ECU 261000 (US$ 338000). *Sources financières:* Privé: 50%. Autofinancement: 50%.

ACTIVITES DANS LES REGIONS EN DEVELOPPEMENT: Intervient directement dans les régions en développement. Maintient une présence locale sur le terrain. Intervient par l'intermédiaire d'organisations locales partenaires. **Actions de Développement durable:** Santé/assainissement/eau. **Régions:** Afrique centrale; Afrique de l'Est; Afrique de l'Ouest; Afrique du Nord; Amérique du Sud; Asie centrale et Asie du Sud; Asie du Sud-Est.

See: *How to Use the Directory,* page 11.

CHE0523
COMITE INTERNATIONAL DE LA CROIX ROUGE
17 avenue de la Paix, 1202 Genève, Suisse.

Contact: Jean de Courten.

CHE0524
COMITE INTERNATIONAL POUR LA DIGNITE DE L'ENFANT (CIDE)
Avenue de Florimont 24, 1006 Lausanne, Suisse.

Téléphone: 41 (21) 311 51 51. *Fax:* 41 (21) 311 51 52.

OBJECTIFS: Faire respecter les droits élémentaires de l'enfant. Dénoncer publiquement et en toute indépendance les manquements à la "Convention relative aux droits de l'enfant". Offrir une assistance juridique ou ouvrir une action en justice en faveur des enfants victimes de mauvais traitements.

INFORMATIONS GENERALES: *Création:* 1991. *Personnel/Total:* 12. *Salariés:* 2. *Bénévoles:* 10. *Budget/Total 1993:* ECU 46000 (US$ 60000). *Sources financières:* Privé: 64%. Public: 6%. Autofinancement: 30%.

PUBLICATIONS: *Périodiques:* Plaquette du C.I.D.E..

EVALUATION/RECHERCHE: Entreprend des activités de recherche.

COMMENTAIRES: Intervient dans la Communauté des Etats indépendants. Activités d'information concernant la Communauté des Etats indépendants.

ACTIVITES DANS LES REGIONS EN DEVELOPPEMENT: Intervient directement dans les régions en développement. Intervient dans 3 pays. Intervient par l'intermédiaire d'organisations locales partenaires. **Actions de Développement durable:** Droits de l'Homme/paix/conflits; Enfants/jeunesse/famille; Santé/assainissement/eau. **Régions:** Afrique centrale; Asie du Sud-Est.

ACTIVITES D'INFORMATION ET D'EDUCATION: Domaines: Droits de l'Homme/paix/conflits; Enfants/jeunesse/famille; Paix/conflits ethniques/armement/désarmement; Pauvreté/conditions de vie; Relations internationales/coopération/aide au développement; Santé/assainissement/eau; Secours d'urgence/réfugiés/aide humanitaire. **Activités:** Campagnes d'information/expositions; Collecte de fonds; Conférences/séminaires/ateliers/activités de formation; Lobbying/plaidoyer; Radiodiffusion/manifestations culturelles; Réseaux/télécommunications électroniques; Services d'information et de documentation/bases de données; Échanges/parrainage/jumelage.

CHE0525
COMITE NICARAGUA - EL SALVADOR
Case postale 156, 1701 Fribourg, Suisse.

CHE0526
COMITE PAIX
Case postale 242, 1217 Meyrin 1, Suisse.

CHE0527
COMITE PATRICE LUMUMBA
Case postale 623, 1700 Fribourg, Suisse.

CHE0528
COMITE SUISSE CONTRE LA TORTURE
C.P 2267, 1211 Genève 2 Depot, Suisse.

Contact: Francois de Vargas.

CHE0529
COMITE SUISSE DE SOUTIEN AU PEUPLE AFGHAN
Rue du Bourg 24, 3960 Sierre Valais, Suisse.

Téléphone: 41 (27) 55 13 94. *Fax:* 41 (27) 55 14 67. *Contact:* Pierre de Chastonay.

OBJECTIFS: Aider financièrement le peuple afghan, dans les domaines agricole, technique et sanitaire.

INFORMATIONS GENERALES: *Création:* 1985. *Personnel/Total:* 2. *Bénévoles:* 2. *Sources financières:* Privé: 100%.

PUBLICATIONS: *Périodiques:* Revue-Editorial (3).

ACTIVITES DANS LES REGIONS EN DEVELOPPEMENT: Intervient dans 1 pays. Intervient par l'intermédiaire d'organisations locales partenaires. **Actions de Développement durable:** Aliments/famine; Développement rural/agriculture; Développement urbain/habitat; Santé/assainissement/eau. **Régions:** Asie centrale et Asie du Sud; Asie de l'Est.

ACTIVITES D'INFORMATION ET D'EDUCATION: Domaines: Aliments/famine; Développement rural/agriculture; Développement urbain/habitat; Santé/assainissement/eau. **Activités:** Collecte de fonds.

CHE0530
COMITE SUISSE POUR LA DEFENSE DU DROIT D'ASILE
Case postale 543, 1000 Lausanne 17, Suisse.

CHE0531
COMMISSION AFRICAINE DES PROMOTEURS DE LA SANTE ET DES DROITS DE L'HOMME
C.P 2117, Route des Morillons 5, 1211 Genève 2, Suisse.

Téléphone: 41 (22) 788 19 45/791 61 89. *Fax:* 41 (22) 791 03 61. *Contact:* Djely K. Samoura.

CHE0532
COMMISSION ON GLOBAL GOVERNANCE
CP 184, 11 avenue Joli-Mont, 1211 Genève 28, Switzerland.

Telephone: 41 (22) 798 27 13. *Fax:* 41 (22) 798 01 47.

CHE0533
COMMISSION ON THE CHURCHES' PARTICIPATION IN DEVELOPMENT OF THE WORLD COUNCIL OF CHURCHES (CCPD-WCC) ◆ Commission de la participation des églises au développement du Conseil oecuménique des Eglises
150 Route de Ferney, C.P. 66, 1211 Geneva 20, Switzerland.

Telephone: 41 (22) 91 61 11. *Fax:* 41 (22) 91 03 61. *Contact:* Jae Shik Oh.

CHE0534
COMMISSION TIERS-MONDE DE L'EGLISE CATHOLIQUE (COTMEC)
Boulevard du Pont-d'Arve 16, 1205 Genève, Suisse.

Téléphone: 41 (22) 329 26 81. *Fax:* 41 (22) 329 26 81. *Contact:* Dominique Froidevaux, Directeur.

OBJECTIFS: Informer et sensibiliser sur les enjeux de la justice entre le Nord et le Sud. Interpeller les chrétiens et les autorités de l'Eglise quant à leurs responsabilités dans ce domaine, en Suisse, et en particulier à Genève.

INFORMATIONS GENERALES: *Création:* 1968. *Affiliée à:* Fédération Genevoise de Coopération (Suisse) - Action de Carême (Suisse) - Justice et Paix (Suisse) - Pax Christi - ACAT - COTE. *Personnel/Total:* 2. *Salariés:* 1. *Bénévoles:* 1. *Budget/Total 1993:* ECU 13000 (US$ 17000). *Sources financières:* Privé: 40%. Autofinancement: 60%.

PUBLICATIONS: *Périodiques:* COTMEC-Info (12). *Rapport annuel. Liste des publications.*

EVALUATION/RECHERCHE: Entreprend des activités de recherche.

PREVISIONS D'ACTIVITES: Lancement d'une campagne sur le commerce des armes et la politique de paix de la Suisse.

COMMENTAIRES: Le COTMEC a reçu le prix "COURRIER" des droits de l'homme, en 1992. Cette organisation joue surtout un rôle de relais pour de multiples organisme de solidarité, dans l'Eglise et en dehors de l'Eglise.

Voir : *Comment utiliser le répertoire,* page 11.

ACTIVITES D'INFORMATION ET D'EDUCATION: Domaines: Aliments/ famine; Culture/tradition/religion; Droits de l'Homme/paix/conflits; Développement rural/agriculture; Développement urbain/habitat; Emploi/chômage; Enfants/jeunesse/famille; Paix/conflits ethniques/armement/ désarmement; Pauvreté/conditions de vie; Population/planning familial/ démographie; Questions relatives aux femmes; Racisme/xénophobie/ antisémitisme; Relations internationales/coopération/aide au développement; Relations économiques internationales/commerce/dette/finances; Réfugiés/migrants/groupes ethniques; Santé/assainissement/eau; Secours d'urgence/réfugiés/aide humanitaire; Écologie/environnement/ biodiversité; Éducation/formation/alphabétisation. **Activités:** Campagnes d'information/expositions; Conférences/séminaires/ateliers/activités de formation; Lobbying/plaidoyer; Radiodiffusion/manifestations culturelles; Services d'information et de documentation/bases de données; Édition/documents audiovisuels/documents éducatifs.

CHE0535

COMMISSION TIERS-MONDE DE L'EGLISE NATIONALE PROTESTANTE DE GENEVE (COTMEP)

C.P. 230 rue Gourgas 24, 1211 Genève 8, Suisse.

Téléphone: 41 (22) 329 47 64. **Fax:** 41 (22) 320 70 45. **Contact:** Olivier Labarthe.

OBJECTIFS: Permettre à l'Eglise protestante de Genève de rester attentive à la situation d'autres Eglises dans le monde.

INFORMATIONS GENERALES: Création: 1960. **Affiliée à:** Fédération genevoise de coopération (Suisse). **Personnel/Total:** 5. Salariés: 1. Bénévoles: 4. **Sources financières:** Privé: 10%. Public: 90%.

COMMENTAIRES: L'organisation contribue au travail du Département Témoignage et Solidarité de l'Eglise protestante.

ACTIVITES DANS LES REGIONS EN DEVELOPPEMENT: Intervient dans 1 pays. Intervient par l'intermédiaire d'organisations locales partenaires. **Actions de Développement durable:** Développement rural/agriculture; Enfants/jeunesse/famille; Petites entreprises/secteur informel/artisanat; Questions relatives aux femmes; Éducation/formation/alphabétisation. **Régions:** Afrique centrale.

CHE0536

COMMUNAUTE DES MISSIONNAIRES LAIQUES (CMI)

Ch. Cardinal Journet 2, 1752 Villars-sur-Glane, Suisse.

Téléphone: 41 (37) 24 42 81.

CHE0537

COMUNITA DI LAVORO PER I PROBLEMI DEGLI STRANIERI

♦ Communauté de travail pour les problèmes des étrangers dans le canton Tessin

Piazza Collegiata 7, 6500 Bellinzona, Suisse.

Téléphone: 41 (92) 25 23 10. **Fax:** 41 (92) 26 10 93. **Contact:** Stefan R.Ograbek, Secrétaire.

OBJECTIFS: Promouvoir la compréhension réciproque entre Suisses et étrangers, et étudier des mesures visant à faciliter l'intégration de ces derniers Suisse.

INFORMATIONS GENERALES: Création: 1976. **Type d'organisation:** collectif. **Affiliée à:** Communauté des Centres d'information et de Contacts Suisses-Etrangers (Suisse). **Personnel/Total:** 1. Salariés: 1. **Budget/Total 1993:** ECU 37000 (US$ 47000). **Sources financières:** Public: 97%. Autofinancement: 3%.

PUBLICATIONS: Rapport annuel. Liste des publications.

EVALUATION/RECHERCHE: Rapports d'évaluation disponibles. Entreprend des activités de recherche.

ACTIVITES D'INFORMATION ET D'EDUCATION: Domaines: Culture/ tradition/religion; Racisme/xénophobie/antisémitisme; Réfugiés/ migrants/groupes ethniques. **Activités:** Campagnes d'information/expositions; Conférences/séminaires/ateliers/activités de formation; Lobbying/plaidoyer; Services d'information et de documentation/bases de données; Édition/documents audiovisuels/documents éducatifs; Éducation formelle.

CHE0538

CONFERENZA MISSIONARIA DELLA SVIZZERA ITALIANA (CMSI) ♦ Missionary Conference of Italian-speaking Switzerland

Via Moncucco 19, C.P. 112, 6903 Lugano-Besso, Switzerland.

Telephone: 41 (91) 56 72 42. **Contact:** Franco Ferrari.

CHE0539

CONSEIL DES ASSOCIATIONS DES IMMIGRES EN EUROPE

Rue de Genève 44, 1004 Lausanne, Suisse.

Téléphone: 41 (21) 624 62 39.

CHE0540

COOP SUISSE

Postfach 2550, 4002 Basel, Suisse.

Téléphone: 41 (61) 336 66 66. **Fax:** 41 (61) 336 66 48. **Contact:** Louis Chapalay.

OBJECTIFS: Aider au développement et soutenir des projets en faveur de la population béninoise.

INFORMATIONS GENERALES: Création: 1961. **Budget/Total 1993:** ECU 104000 (US$ 135000). **Sources financières:** Privé: 100%.

PUBLICATIONS: Périodiques: Journal COOP (2).

ACTIVITES DANS LES REGIONS EN DEVELOPPEMENT: Intervient directement dans les régions en développement. Intervient dans 1 pays. **Actions de Développement durable:** Développement rural/agriculture; Petites entreprises/secteur informel/artisanat. **Régions:** Afrique de l'Ouest.

CHE0541

COOPERATION POUR LE BIEN-ETRE (CBE)

Case postale 2262, 1211 Genève 2 Dépot, Suisse.

Téléphone: 41 (22) 789 49 05. **Fax:** 41 (22) 789 49 05. **Contact:** Rev. Kabambi Pasinkas, Secrétaire général.

OBJECTIFS: Faire de la recherche, apporter de l'aide et fournir des services aux pays en développement. Mener des opérations en faveur des organisations humanitaires en Afrique.

INFORMATIONS GENERALES: Création: 1986. **Type d'organisation:** regroupement d'ONG. **Organisations membres:** 7. **Personnel/Total:** 43. Salariés: 13 dont: 10 dans les pays en développement. Bénévoles: 30 dont: 25 dans les pays en développement. **Budget/Total 1993:** ECU 154000 (US$ 200000). **Sources financières:** Autofinancement: 100%.

EVALUATION/RECHERCHE: Rapports d'évaluation disponibles. Entreprend des activités de recherche.

PREVISIONS D'ACTIVITES: L'organisation veut s'orienter vers les milieux scolaires de tous les enfants délaissés et orphelins de la province du Ratanga. Encadrement des orpailleurs autochtones à la demande des autorités du Ratanga.

COMMENTAIRES: L'organisation met en vente des billets d'avion à un tarif préférentiel à l'intention de tous les membres des ONG s'occupant du développement dans le monde entier.

ACTIVITES DANS LES REGIONS EN DEVELOPPEMENT: Intervient directement dans les régions en développement. Intervient dans 1 pays. Maintient une présence locale sur le terrain. Intervient par l'intermédiaire d'organisations locales partenaires. **Actions de Développement durable:** Aliments/famine; Dette/finances/commerce; Démocratie/bonne gestion publique/création d'institutions/développement participatif; Développement rural/agriculture; Développement urbain/habitat; Enfants/jeunesse/famille; Petites entreprises/secteur informel/artisanat; Questions relatives aux femmes; Santé/assainissement/eau; Secours d'urgence/réfugiés/aide humanitaire; Éducation/formation/alphabétisation; Énergie/transport. **Régions:** Afrique centrale.

ACTIVITES D'INFORMATION ET D'EDUCATION: Domaines: Aliments/ famine; Culture/tradition/religion; Développement rural/agriculture; Développement urbain/habitat; Emploi/chômage; Enfants/jeunesse/ famille; Pauvreté/conditions de vie; Questions relatives aux femmes; Relations internationales/coopération/aide au développement; Réfugiés/

See: *How to Use the Directory*, page 11.

migrants/groupes ethniques; Santé/assainissement/eau; Secours d'urgence/réfugiés/aide humanitaire; Éducation/formation/alphabétisation. **Activités:** Campagnes d'information/expositions.

CHE0542

COOPERATIVA ESSERE UMANI (CEU) ♦ Coopérative être humain

CP 210, 6904 Lugano 4, Suisse.

Téléphone: 41 (91) 21 30 31. *Contact:* Stefano Cometta, Président.

OBJECTIFS: Mettre en place des services de santé en zone rurale au sein d'un programme de soins de santé primaires et de formation du personnel local. Améliorer la nutrition grâce à une meilleure utilisation des terres agricoles.

INFORMATIONS GENERALES: *Création:* 1979. *Personnel/Total:* 9. *Salariés:* 2 dont: 1 dans les pays en développement. *Bénévoles:* 7. *Budget/Total 1993:* ECU 120000 (US$ 156000). *Sources financières:* Privé: 58%. *Public:* 35%. *Autofinancement:* 7%.

PUBLICATIONS: *Périodiques:* Informazioni CEU (2).

EVALUATION/RECHERCHE: Rapports d'évaluation disponibles.

ACTIVITES DANS LES REGIONS EN DEVELOPPEMENT: Intervient directement dans les régions en développement. Intervient dans 1 pays. Maintient une présence locale sur le terrain. **Actions de Développement durable:** Enfants/jeunesse/famille; Questions relatives aux femmes; Santé/assainissement/eau; Écologie/environnement/biodiversité; Éducation/formation/alphabétisation. **Régions:** Afrique de l'Ouest.

CHE0543

COORDINATION INTERCOMMUNAUTAIRE CONTRE L'ANTISEMITISME ET LA DIFFAMATION (CICAD)

Case postale 30, Rue du Stand 40, 1211 Genève 11, Suisse.

Téléphone: 41 (22) 21 48 78. *Fax:* 41 (22) 21 55 28.

CHE0544

COORDINATION ROMANDE DE "PAYSANS SOLIDAIRES"

Le Taulard, ch. du Boulard 1, 1032 Romanel, Suisse.

Téléphone: 41 (21) 647 85 95. *Fax:* 41 (21) 731 20 79.

OBJECTIFS: Créer des relations entre paysans de Suisse et les paysans d'ailleurs.

INFORMATIONS GENERALES: *Création:* 1984. *Sources financières:* Autofinancement: 100%.

PUBLICATIONS: *Périodiques:* Paysans Solidaires.

ACTIVITES DANS LES REGIONS EN DEVELOPPEMENT: Intervient directement dans les régions en développement. Intervient dans 4 pays. Intervient par l'intermédiaire d'organisations locales partenaires. **Actions de Développement durable:** Développement rural/agriculture. **Régions:** Afrique centrale.

CHE0545

CORPS AFRICAIN DE REFLEXION ET D'ACTION CONTRE LA FAIM (CARAF) ♦ Corps for Africans to Reflect and Act against Famine

Case postale 2123, 1211 Genève 2, Suisse.

CHE0546

COUP DE POUCE SUISSE-HAITI

Rue des Racettes 45, 1213 Onex, Suisse.

Téléphone: 41 (22) 792 59 10. *Contact:* Béatrice Müller.

OBJECTIFS: Soutenir le collège de l'Etoile à Port-au-Prince (Haïti) situé dans un bidonville, en accordant des bourses d'études, des salaires aux enseignants, des repas et des soins médicaux.

INFORMATIONS GENERALES: *Création:* 1982. *Personnel/Total:* 14. *Salariés:* 1 dont: 1 dans les pays en développement. *Bénévoles:* 13. *Budget/Total 1993:* ECU 94000 (US$ 122000). *Sources financières:* Privé: 22%. *Public:* 3%. *Autofinancement:* 75%.

PUBLICATIONS: *Périodiques:* Nouvelles d'Haïti (4). *Rapport annuel.*

EVALUATION/RECHERCHE: Rapports d'évaluation disponibles.

ACTIVITES DANS LES REGIONS EN DEVELOPPEMENT: Intervient directement dans les régions en développement. Intervient dans 1 pays. Maintient une présence locale sur le terrain. Intervient par l'intermédiaire d'organisations locales partenaires. **Actions de Développement durable:** Éducation/formation/alphabétisation. **Régions:** Caraïbes.

ACTIVITES D'INFORMATION ET D'EDUCATION: Domaines: Éducation/formation/alphabétisation. **Activités:** Campagnes d'information/expositions; Collecte de fonds; Échanges/parrainage/jumelage.

CHE0547

CROIX VERTE INTERNATIONALE ♦ Green Cross International

160, route Florissant C.P. 80, 1231 Conches-Genève, Suisse.

Téléphone: 41 (22) 789 16 62. *Fax:* 41 (22) 789 16 95. *Contact:* Andreas Eggenberg, Administrative Director.

OBJECTIFS: Promouvoir le changement de valeur, en vue d'un développement durable. Faciliter la prévention et l'aide en cas de catastrophe écologique. Développer un code international pour l'environnement.

INFORMATIONS GENERALES: *Création:* 1993. *Type d'organisation:* réseau. *Personnel/Total:* 17. *Salariés:* 14. *Bénévoles:* 3. *Sources financières:* Privé: 100%.

PUBLICATIONS: *Rapport annuel.*

COMMENTAIRES: Activités d'information concernant la Communauté des Etats indépendants.

CHE0548

DAENK E MOL LADE

Denkmalstrasse 17, 6000 Luzern 6, Suisse.

Téléphone: 41 (41) 51 31 60.

CHE0549

DECLARATION DE BERNE, SECRETARIAT ROMAND

11 Chemin de Boston, C.P. 81, 1000 Lausanne 9, Suisse.

Téléphone: 41 (21) 624 54 17. *Fax:* 41 (21) 624 54 19. *Contact:* Thierry Pellet.

OBJECTIFS: Promouvoir l'établissement de relations plus justes et une meilleure compréhension entre les peuples. Fournir des éléments d'analyse nécessaires à une prise de conscience individuelle des enjeux et des mécanismes de l'interdépendance mondiale.

INFORMATIONS GENERALES: *Création:* 1968. *Affiliée à:* Fédération Genevoise de Coopération (Suisse) - EURODAD (Belgique) - Health Action International (Pays-Bas). *Personnel/Total:* 15. *Budget/Total 1993:* ECU 209000 (US$ 271000). *Sources financières:* Privé: 86%. *Public:* 7%. *Autofinancement:* 7%.

PUBLICATIONS: *Périodiques:* Vers un développement Solidaire (6) - Med in Switzerland (4). *Rapport annuel. Liste des publications.*

EVALUATION/RECHERCHE: Entreprend des activités de recherche.

PREVISIONS D'ACTIVITES: L'organisation veut mener une campagne sur la dignité de l'emploi au Nord comme au Sud, une campagne sur l'alimentation et une autre sur le désendettement multilatéral.

ACTIVITES DANS LES REGIONS EN DEVELOPPEMENT: Intervient dans 6 pays.

ACTIVITES D'INFORMATION ET D'EDUCATION: Domaines: Aliments/famine; Autres; Emploi/chômage; Enfants/jeunesse/famille; Pauvreté/conditions de vie; Questions relatives aux femmes; Racisme/xénophobie/antisémitisme; Relations internationales/coopération/aide au développement; Relations économiques internationales/commerce/dette/finances; Réfugiés/migrants/groupes ethniques; Santé/assainissement/eau; Écologie/environnement/biodiversité. **Activités:** Campagnes d'information/expositions; Collecte de fonds; Conférences/séminaires/ateliers/activités de formation; Lobbying/plaidoyer; Services d'information et de documentation/bases de données; Édition/documents audiovisuels/documents éducatifs; Éducation formelle.

Voir : *Comment utiliser le répertoire,* page 11.

CHE0550

DEFENCE FOR CHILDREN INTERNATIONAL (DCI) ♦ Défense des Enfants-International

Case Postale 88, Rue de Varembé 1, 1211 Geneve 20, Switzerland.

Telephone: 41 (22) 734 0558. *Fax:* 41 (22) 740 1145. *Contact:* Marc-Alain Berberat, Secretary General.

OBJECTIVES: To promote and project children's rights worldwide.

GENERAL INFORMATION: *Creation:* 1979. *Member organisations:* 50. *Personnel/Total:* 18. Salaried: 10. Volunteers: 8. *Budget/Total 1993:* ECU 771000 (US$ 1000000). *Financial sources:* Private: 40%. Public: 40%. Self-financing: 20%.

PUBLICATIONS: *Periodicals:* International Children's Rights (4) - Monitor. *Annual report. List of publications.*

EVALUATION/RESEARCH: Undertakes research activities.

PLANNED ACTIVITIES: DEI is planning to hold a congress on Children's Rights and the Globalization of Economy.

COMMENTS: Undertakes activities in the Commonwealth of Independent States. Information activities related to the Commonwealth of Independent States.

ACTIVITIES IN DEVELOPING REGIONS: Present in developing regions. Active in 50 country(ies). Maintains local field presence. **Sustainable Development Actions:** Children/youth/family; Gender issues/women; Human rights/peace/conflicts; Sending volunteers/experts/technical assistance. **Regions:** Central Africa; Central Asia and South Asia; East Africa; East Asia; Mexico and Central America; Middle East; North Africa; Oceania; South America; South East Asia; West Africa.

INFORMATION AND EDUCATION ACTIVITIES: Topics: Children/youth/family; Education/training/literacy; Gender issues/women; Human rights/peace/conflicts; International relations/cooperation/development aid; Other; Refugees/migrants/ethnic groups. **Activities:** Conferences/seminars/workshops/training activities; Exchanges/twinning/linking; Fund raising; Information and documentation services/data bases; Information campaigns/exhibitions; Lobbying/advocacy; Networking/electronic telecommunications; Publishing/audiovisual materials/educational materials.

CHE0551

DEPARTEMENT MISSIONNAIRE DES EGLISES PROTESTANTES DE SUISSE ROMANDE

Chemin des Cèdres 5, Case postale 305, 1000 Lausanne 9, Suisse.

Téléphone: 41 (21) 37 34 21. *Fax:* 41 (21) 37 36 01.

CHE0552

DICHIARAZIONE DI BERNA - ASSOCIAZIONE PER UNO SVILUPPO SOLIDARE (DB)

Case postale 1351, 6601 Locarno, Suisse.

CHE0553

DONNE PER LA PACE - GRUPPO TICINO ♦ Femmes pour la paix - Groupe Tessin

Case postale 2469, 6901 Lugano, Suisse.

OBJECTIFS: Attirer l'attention des membres et de l'opinion publique sur les problèmes du moment, et tâcher d'analyser les causes afin de trouver des solutions aux conflits.

INFORMATIONS GENERALES: *Création:* 1982. *Sources financières:* Autofinancement: 100%.

PUBLICATIONS: *Périodiques:* Foglione (4).

ACTIVITES D'INFORMATION ET D'EDUCATION: Domaines: Paix/conflits ethniques/armement/désarmement. **Activités:** Campagnes d'information/expositions; Conférences/séminaires/ateliers/activités de formation; Lobbying/plaidoyer.

CHE0554

ECOPOP

Case Postale 313, 3052 Zollikofen, Suisse.

Téléphone: 41 (31) 911 34 66. *Contact:* Margrit Annen-Ruf, Présidente.

OBJECTIFS: Attirer l'attention du public sur les menaces pour l'environnement de la densité de la population et de la croissance économique, ainsi que sur la nécessité d'une décroissance de la population en Suisse et dans les pays industrialisés.

INFORMATIONS GENERALES: *Création:* 1971. *Personnel/Total:* 8. *Salariés:* 1. *Bénévoles:* 7. *Budget/Total 1993:* ECU 12000 (US$ 16000). *Sources financières:* Privé: 50%. Autofinancement: 50%.

PUBLICATIONS: *Périodiques:* Bulletin de l'ECOPOP (3). *Rapport annuel. Liste des publications.*

EVALUATION/RECHERCHE: Rapports d'évaluation disponibles.

ACTIVITES D'INFORMATION ET D'EDUCATION: Domaines: Emploi/chômage; Population/planning familial/démographie; Questions relatives aux femmes; Relations internationales/coopération/aide au développement; Réfugiés/migrants/groupes ethniques; Écologie/environnement/biodiversité. **Activités:** Campagnes d'information/expositions; Conférences/séminaires/ateliers/activités de formation; Lobbying/plaidoyer; Services d'information et de documentation/bases de données; Édition/documents audiovisuels/documents éducatifs; Éducation formelle.

CHE0555

ECOSOLIDAR

Langstrasse 187, Postfach 162, 8031 Zürich, Switzerland.

Telephone: 41 (1) 272 42 00 . *Fax:* 41 (1) 273 08 80. *Contact:* Diether Grünenfelder, Director.

CHE0556

EDUCATION ET LIBERATION (E&L)

C.P. 61, 1211 Genève 28, Suisse.

Contact: Jean Pierre Langnaux, Secretaire General.

CHE0557

EIRENE - COMITE SUISSE ♦ Service Chrétien International pour la Paix

Case postale 2262, 2300 La Chaux-de-Fonds 2, Suisse.

Téléphone: 41 (39) 28 78 47. *Fax:* 41 (39) 28 78 47. *Contact:* Josiane Huberdeau, Présidente.

OBJECTIFS: Promouvoir la justice sociale et la réconciliation entre les peuples, dans les pays du Sud et du Nord. Mettre à la disposition des partenaires des volontaires qualifiés et engagés. Donner une aide financière à de petits projets sans envoi de volontaires.

INFORMATIONS GENERALES: *Création:* 1966. *Type d'organisation:* réseau. *Affiliée à:* Communauté de travail des organismes de développement (Suisse) - Fédération romande des mouvements non-violents (Suisse) - Eirene International. *Personnel/Total:* 10. *Salariés:* 7 dont: 5 dans les pays en développement. *Bénévoles:* 3. *Budget/Total 1993:* ECU 68000 (US$ 88000). *Sources financières:* Privé: 5%. Public: 85%. Autofinancement: 10%.

PUBLICATIONS: *Périodiques:* Interrogation (8) - Lettre circulaire (4). *Rapport annuel.*

PREVISIONS D'ACTIVITES: L'organisation envisage de mener des actions dans l'ex-Yougoslavie et en Palestine.

COMMENTAIRES: L'organisation collabore avec Frères sans Frontières et GVOM, notamment pour la rédaction du journal "Interrogation".

ACTIVITES DANS LES REGIONS EN DEVELOPPEMENT: Intervient directement dans les régions en développement. Intervient dans 5 pays. Maintient une présence locale sur le terrain. Intervient par l'intermédiaire d'organisations locales partenaires. **Actions de Développement durable:** Développement rural/agriculture; Développement urbain/habitat; Enfants/jeunesse/famille; Envoi de volontaires/experts/assistance technique; Écologie/environnement/biodiversité; Éducation/formation/alphabétisation. **Régions:** Afrique de l'Ouest; Afrique du Nord; Mexique et Amerique centrale.

See: *How to Use the Directory*, page 11.

ACTIVITES D'INFORMATION ET D'EDUCATION: Domaines: Développement rural/agriculture; Enfants/jeunesse/famille; Paix/conflits ethniques/armement/désarmement; Écologie/environnement/biodiversité; Éducation/formation/alphabétisation. **Activités:** Campagnes d'information/expositions; Échanges/parrainage/jumelage.

CHE0558
ENFANTS DU MONDE, SUISSE

Rue Auguste Vilbert 14, C.P. 159, 1218 Grand Saconnex, Suisse.

Téléphone: 41 (22) 798 88 81. **Fax:** 41 (22) 791 00 34. **Contact:** Max Oser, Secrétaire général.

OBJECTIFS: Aider les enfants et les adolescents les plus défavorisés des pays pauvres, tant à la campagne qu'en milieu urbain. Chercher en priorité à satisfaire leurs besoins spécifiques et les aider à sortir durablement de leurs situations de détresse particulières.

INFORMATIONS GENERALES: Création: 1968. **Personnel/Total:** 137. *Salariés:* 135 dont: 130 dans les pays en développement. *Bénévoles:* 2. **Budget/Total 1993:** ECU 2662000 (US$ 3452000). **Sources financières:** *Privé:* 19%. *Public:* 49%. *Autofinancement:* 32%.

PUBLICATIONS: Périodiques: Bulletin d'information (4). *Rapport annuel.*

EVALUATION/RECHERCHE: Rapports d'évaluation disponibles.

PREVISIONS D'ACTIVITES: L'organisation projette d'avoir une présence plus importante en Afrique de l'Ouest et veut aussi mener des programmes par région.

COMMENTAIRES: Intervient dans la Communauté des Etats indépendants.

ACTIVITES DANS LES REGIONS EN DEVELOPPEMENT: Intervient dans 9 pays. Maintient une présence locale sur le terrain. Intervient par l'intermédiaire d'organisations locales partenaires. **Actions de Développement durable:** Développement rural/agriculture; Enfants/jeunesse/famille; Petites entreprises/secteur informel/artisanat; Population/planning familial/démographie; Questions relatives aux femmes; Santé/assainissement/eau; Secours d'urgence/réfugiés/aide humanitaire; Éducation/formation/alphabétisation. **Régions:** Afrique de l'Ouest; Asie centrale et Asie du Sud; Caraïbes; Mexique et Amerique centrale.

ACTIVITES D'INFORMATION ET D'EDUCATION: Domaines: Enfants/jeunesse/famille; Questions relatives aux femmes. **Activités:** Campagnes d'information/expositions; Collecte de fonds.

CHE0559
ENTRAIDE PROTESTANTE SUISSE (EPER)

Stampfenbachstrasse 123, B.P. 168, 8035 Zürich, Suisse.

Téléphone: 41 (1) 361 66 00. **Fax:** 41 (1) 361 78 27. **Contact:** Heinz Kohler, Secrétaire central.

OBJECTIFS: Aider les Eglises européennes. Apporter une aide développement. Apporter une aide en cas de catastrophes. Etre au service des réfugiés. Aider les personnes socialement défavorisées, en Suisse, par des bourses et des parrainages d'enfants.

INFORMATIONS GENERALES: Création: 1946. **Personnel/Total:** 156. *Salariés:* 156 dont: 2 dans les pays en développement. **Budget/Total 1993:** ECU 30790000 (US$ 39930000). **Sources financières:** *Privé:* 40%. *Public:* 45%. *Autofinancement:* 15%.

PUBLICATIONS: Périodiques: Journal HEKS (6). *Rapport annuel.*

COMMENTAIRES: Intervient dans la Communauté des Etats indépendants. Activités d'information concernant la Communauté des Etats indépendants.

ACTIVITES DANS LES REGIONS EN DEVELOPPEMENT: Maintient une présence locale sur le terrain. Intervient par l'intermédiaire d'organisations locales partenaires. **Actions de Développement durable:** Aliments/famine; Dette/finances/commerce; Droits de l'Homme/paix/conflits; Démocratie/bonne gestion publique/création d'institutions/développement participatif; Développement rural/agriculture; Développement urbain/habitat; Enfants/jeunesse/famille; Petites entreprises/secteur informel/artisanat; Population/planning familial/démographie; Questions relatives aux femmes; Santé/assainissement/eau; Secours d'urgence/réfugiés/aide humanitaire; Écologie/environnement/biodiversité; Éducation/formation/alphabétisation. **Régions:** Afrique australe; Afrique cen-

trale; Afrique de l'Est; Afrique de l'Ouest; Amérique du Sud; Asie centrale et Asie du Sud; Asie du Sud-Est; Caraïbes; Mexique et Amerique centrale; Moyen-Orient.

CHE0560
ERKLARUNG VON BERN (EUB) ♦ Déclaration de Berne

Quellenstrasse 25, P.O. Box 177, 8031 Zürich, Switzerland.

Telephone: 41 (1) 271 64 25. **Fax:** 41 (1) 272 60 60. **E-mail:** Bernedecl.gn.apc.org.

OBJECTIVES: To promote the ideal that: "It is less a matter of giving more, but of taking less...". To advocate solidarity with the Third World and modification of trade policies in the North. To disseminate information and carry out activities related to economic relations, food, agriculture, health, pharmaceuticals and culture.

GENERAL INFORMATION: Creation: 1968. **Affiliated to:** Pesticide Action Network (Netherlands) - Seeds Action Network - Eurodad. **Personnel/Total:** 13. *Salaried:* 13. **Budget/Total 1993:** ECU 1044000 (US$ 1354000). **Financial sources:** *Private:* 34%. *Self-financing:* 66%.

PUBLICATIONS: Periodicals: EVB-Magazin (5) - Solidaire (6) - BD-News (2). *Annual report. List of publications.*

EVALUATION/RESEARCH: Undertakes research activities.

INFORMATION AND EDUCATION ACTIVITIES: Topics: Culture/tradition/religion; Ecology/environment/biodiversity; Gender issues/women; Health/sanitation/water; International economic relations/trade/debt/finance; International relations/cooperation/development aid; Population/family planning/demography; Racism/xenophobia/antisemitism; Rural development/agriculture. **Activities:** Broadcasting/cultural events; Conferences/seminars/workshops/training activities; Exchanges/twinning/linking; Formal education; Information campaigns/exhibitions; Lobbying/advocacy; Publishing/audiovisual materials/educational materials.

CHE0561
EVANGELISCH-METHODISTISCHE KIRCHE IN DER SCHWEIZ UND IN FRANKREICH, AUSSERE MISSION (EMK) ♦ United Methodist Church in Switzerland and in France

Badenerstrasse 69, C.P. 136, 8026 Zürich, Switzerland.

Telephone: 41 (1) 242 30 72. **Fax:** 41 (1) 242 01 66. **Contact:** Frédy Schmid, Secretary of Missions.

CHE0562
EVANGELISCHE MISSION IM KWANGO (EMIK) ♦ Mission Evangélique au Kwango

Missionsstrasse 21, 4003 Basel, Suisse.

Téléphone: 41 (61) 268 82 79. **Fax:** 41 (61) 268 82 68. **Contact:** Theo Lüthy, Président.

OBJECTIFS: Annoncer la Bonne Nouvelle par un travail missionnaire au Zaïre. Soutenir l'église partenaire, au Zaïre, dans son travail spirituel et de développement matériel.

INFORMATIONS GENERALES: Création: 1939. **Type d'organisation:** regroupement d'ONG. **Organisations membres:** 2. **Affiliée à:** Kooperation der evangelischen Kirchen und Missionen (Suisse) - Evangelische Hilfswerke und Missionen (Suisse). **Personnel/Total:** 3000. **Budget/Total 1993:** ECU 471000 (US$ 609000). **Sources financières:** *Privé:* 50%. *Public:* 11%. *Autofinancement:* 39%.

PUBLICATIONS: *Rapport annuel.*

EVALUATION/RECHERCHE: Rapports d'évaluation disponibles. Entreprend des activités de recherche.

ACTIVITES DANS LES REGIONS EN DEVELOPPEMENT: Intervient directement dans les régions en développement. Intervient dans 1 pays. Maintient une présence locale sur le terrain. Intervient par l'intermédiaire d'organisations locales partenaires. **Actions de Développement durable:** Aliments/famine; Dette/finances/commerce; Droits de l'Homme/paix/conflits; Démocratie/bonne gestion publique/création d'institutions/développement participatif; Développement rural/agriculture; Développement urbain/habitat; Enfants/jeunesse/famille; Envoi de volontaires/experts/assistance technique; Petites entreprises/secteur informel/arti-

sanat; Population/planning familial/démographie; Questions relatives aux femmes; Santé/assainissement/eau; Secours d'urgence/réfugiés/ aide humanitaire; Écologie/environnement/biodiversité; Éducation/formation/alphabétisation; Énergie/transport. **Régions:** Afrique centrale.

ACTIVITES D'INFORMATION ET D'EDUCATION: Domaines: Aliments/ famine; Culture/tradition/religion; Droits de l'Homme/paix/conflits; Développement rural/agriculture; Développement urbain/habitat; Emploi/chômage; Enfants/jeunesse/famille; Paix/conflits ethniques/armement/ désarmement; Pauvreté/conditions de vie; Population/planning familial/ démographie; Questions relatives aux femmes; Racisme/xénophobie/ antisémitisme; Relations internationales/coopération/aide au développement; Réfugiés/migrants/groupes ethniques; Santé/assainissement/eau; Secours d'urgence/réfugiés/aide humanitaire; Écologie/environnement/ biodiversité; Éducation/formation/alphabétisation. **Activités:** Campagnes d'information/expositions; Collecte de fonds; Conférences/séminaires/ateliers/activités de formation; Lobbying/plaidoyer; Réseaux/télécommunications électroniques; Services d'information et de documentation/bases de données; Échanges/parrainage/jumelage; Édition/documents audiovisuels/documents éducatifs; Éducation formelle.

CHE0563

EVANGLISCHE MISSION IM TSCHAD (EMT)

Grünweg 2, 2502 Biel, Suisse.

Téléphone: 41 (32) 42 38 24. **Fax:** 41 (32) 41 11 76.

CHE0564

EXPERIENCE RURALE ALTERNATIVE (ERA)

C.P. 1450, 1211 Genève 1, Suisse.

Téléphone: 41 (22) 731 05 95. **Contact:** Roger Michel.

OBJECTIFS: Informer sur les types à apporter aux pays en développement. Collecter des fonds pour le financement de projets pilotes. Réaliser des projets de développement rural alternatif, et créer des sociétés rurales de développement.

INFORMATIONS GENERALES: Création: 1983. **Type d'organisation:** réseau. **Personnel/Total:** 20. Salariés: 5 dont: 5 dans les pays en développement. Bénévoles: 15. **Budget/Total 1993:** ECU 28000 (US$ 36000). **Sources financières:** Privé: 30%. Public: 50%. Autofinancement: 20%.

PUBLICATIONS: Rapport annuel. Liste des publications.

EVALUATION/RECHERCHE: Rapports d'évaluation disponibles. Entreprend des activités de recherche.

PREVISIONS D'ACTIVITES: L'organisation veut créer un centre de formation continue en agriculture biologique en Haïti; elle veut aussi faire une campagne sur l'aménagement et la gestion de l'espace agraire.

ACTIVITES DANS LES REGIONS EN DEVELOPPEMENT: Intervient directement dans les régions en développement. Intervient dans 1 pays. Maintient une présence locale sur le terrain. Intervient par l'intermédiaire d'organisations locales partenaires. **Actions de Développement durable:** Démocratie/bonne gestion publique/création d'institutions/développement participatif; Développement rural/agriculture; Développement urbain/habitat; Questions relatives aux femmes; Santé/assainissement/ eau; Écologie/environnement/biodiversité; Éducation/formation/alphabétisation. **Régions:** Caraïbes.

ACTIVITES D'INFORMATION ET D'EDUCATION: Domaines: Développement rural/agriculture; Enfants/jeunesse/famille; Questions relatives aux femmes; Santé/assainissement/eau; Écologie/environnement/biodiversité; Éducation/formation/alphabétisation. **Activités:** Collecte de fonds; Conférences/séminaires/ateliers/activités de formation; Échanges/parrainage/jumelage; Édition/documents audiovisuels/documents éducatifs.

CHE0565

FACHSTELLE DER SCHWEIZERISCHEN ENTWICKLUNGSZUSAMMENARBEIT FUR TECHNOLOGIE MANAGEMENT (SKAT) ♦ Swiss Center for Development Cooperation in Technology and Management

Tigerbergstrasse 2, 9000 St. Gallen, Switzerland.

Fax: 41 (71) 23 75 45. **Contact:** Alex Arter, Director.

OBJECTIVES: To act as an information and documentation centre and a consultancy group. To promote and implement appropriate technology for developing countries.

GENERAL INFORMATION: Creation: 1978. **Type of organisation:** association of NGOs. **Member organisations:** 14. **Affiliated to:** Mini Hydro Power Group (Germany) - Building Advisory Service and Information Network (France) - Handpump Technology Network (Switzerland). **Personnel/Total:** 15. Salaried: 15. **Budget/Total 1993:** ECU 1722000 (US$ 2233000). **Financial sources:** Public: 35%. Selffinancing: 65%.

PUBLICATIONS: Periodicals: SKAT (4) - Basin-News (2). Annual report. List of publications.

EVALUATION/RESEARCH: Evaluation reports available.

COMMENTS: Undertakes activities in the Commonwealth of Independent States.

ACTIVITIES IN DEVELOPING REGIONS: Present in developing regions. Active in 25 country(ies). Works through local field partners. **Sustainable Development Actions:** Energy/transport; Health/sanitation/water; Small enterprises/informal sector/handicrafts; Urban development/ habitat. **Regions:** Central Africa; Central Asia and South Asia; East Africa; East Asia; Mexico and Central America; Middle East; North Africa; Oceania; South America; South East Asia; Southern Africa; West Africa.

INFORMATION AND EDUCATION ACTIVITIES: Topics: Health/sanitation/water; Other; Urban development/habitat. **Activities:** Conferences/ seminars/workshops/training activities; Exchanges/twinning/linking; Information and documentation services/data bases; Networking/electronic telecommunications; Publishing/audiovisual materials/educational materials.

CHE0566

FASTENOPFER KATHOLISCHES HILFSWERK SCHWEIZ ♦
Action de Carême des Catholiques en Suisse

Habsburgerstrasse 44, Postfach 2856, 6002 Lucerne, Suisse.

Téléphone: 41 (41) 23 76 55. **Fax:** 41 (41) 23 13 62 . **Contact:** Ferdinand Luthiger, Directeur.

OBJECTIFS: Réduire les inégalités, combattre les discriminations, libérer l'homme de ses servitudes, le rendre capable d'être lui-même l'agent responsable de son mieux-être matériel, de son progrès social et de son épanouissement spirituel.

INFORMATIONS GENERALES: Création: 1962. **Affiliée à:** Arbeitsgemeinschaft Swissaid (Suisse) - Fastenopfer (Suisse) - Brot für Brüder (Suisse) - Helvetas (Suisse) - Caritas (Suisse) - Coopération Internationale pour le développement et la solidarité (Belgique.). **Personnel/ Total:** 190. Salariés: 40. Bénévoles: 150. **Budget/Total 1993:** ECU 13568000 (US$ 17596000). **Sources financières:** Privé: 80%. Public: 20%.

PUBLICATIONS: Périodiques: Calendrier de Carême (1) - Bulletin (4). Rapport annuel. Liste des publications.

ACTIVITES DANS LES REGIONS EN DEVELOPPEMENT: Intervient directement dans les régions en développement. Intervient par l'intermédiaire d'organisations locales partenaires. **Actions de Développement durable:** Droits de l'Homme/paix/conflits; Développement rural/ agriculture; Enfants/jeunesse/famille; Questions relatives aux femmes; Éducation/formation/alphabétisation. **Régions:** Afrique australe; Afrique centrale; Afrique de l'Est; Afrique de l'Ouest; Amérique du Sud; Asie centrale et Asie du Sud; Asie du Sud-Est; Mexique et Amerique centrale.

ACTIVITES D'INFORMATION ET D'EDUCATION: Domaines: Culture/ tradition/religion; Droits de l'Homme/paix/conflits; Développement rural/ agriculture; Emploi/chômage; Enfants/jeunesse/famille; Paix/conflits ethniques/armement/désarmement; Pauvreté/conditions de vie; Questions relatives aux femmes; Racisme/xénophobie/antisémitisme; Relations internationales/coopération/aide au développement; Relations économiques internationales/commerce/dette/finances; Écologie/environnement/biodiversité; Éducation/formation/alphabétisation. **Activités:** Campagnes d'information/expositions; Collecte de fonds; Conférences/ séminaires/ateliers/activités de formation; Lobbying/plaidoyer; Radiodiffusion/manifestations culturelles; Services d'information et de documen-

tation/bases de données; Échanges/parrainage/jumelage; Édition/documents audiovisuels/documents éducatifs; Éducation formelle.

CHE0567

FEDERATION DES FONDATIONS POUR LA SANTE MONDIALE (FFSM) ♦ Federation of World Health Foundations

Avenue Appia 20, 1211 Genève 27, Suisse.

Téléphone: 41 (22) 3409. ***Contact:*** Milton P. Siegel, Président.

OBJECTIFS: Amener tous les peuples au niveau de santé le plus élevé possible, en coordonnant les activités des fondations nationales et en asssurant la liaison entre les fondations et l'OMS.

INFORMATIONS GENERALES: *Création:* 1965. *Type d'organisation:* regroupement d'ONG. *Organisations membres:* 6. *Personnel/Total:* 4. *Bénévoles:* 4. *Budget/Total 1993:* ECU 16000 (US$ 21000). *Sources financières:* Privé: 100%.

PUBLICATIONS: *Rapport annuel.*

PREVISIONS D'ACTIVITES: L'organisation accorde des Bourses et de l'aide pour les projets de terrain.

ACTIVITES DANS LES REGIONS EN DEVELOPPEMENT: Intervient par l'intermédiaire d'organisations locales partenaires.

CHE0568

FEDERATION GENEVOISE DE COOPERATION (FGC) ♦ Geneva Federation for Co-operation and Development

rue Richemont 10, C.P. 136, 1211 Genève 21, Suisse.

Téléphone: 41 (22) 738 04 88. ***Fax:*** 41 (22) 738 59 59. ***Contact:*** Jean-Pierre Gontard, Président.

OBJECTIFS: Etudier et sélectionner les projets de développement et d'information présentés par les associations membres en vue de leur financement. Informer le public sur les projets en cours, et le sensibiliser aux questions Nord-Sud. Faciliter l'échange d'expériences et d'informations entre les associations membres.

INFORMATIONS GENERALES: *Création:* 1966. *Type d'organisation:* regroupement d'ONG. *Organisations membres:* 50. *Affiliée à:* Coordination Suisse Droit de l'Enfant (Suisse) - Réseau Newspack Femmes et Développement (Suisse). *Personnel/Total:* 38. *Salariés:* 4. *Bénévoles:* 34. *Budget/Total 1993:* ECU 2870000 (US$ 3722000). *Sources financières:* Public: 100%.

PUBLICATIONS: *Périodiques:* Communes genevoises et Tiers-Monde (5).

COMMENTAIRES: Les activités mentionnées sont celles des organisations membres de FGC. **Actions de Développement durable:** Aliments/famine; Dette/finances/commerce; Droits de l'Homme/paix/conflits; Démocratie/bonne gestion publique/création d'institutions/développement participatif; Développement rural/agriculture; Développement urbain/habitat; Enfants/jeunesse/famille; Petites entreprises/secteur informel/artisanat; Population/planning familial/démographie; Questions relatives aux femmes; Santé/assainissement/eau; Écologie/environnement/biodiversité; Éducation/formation/alphabétisation; Energie/transport. **Régions:** Afrique centrale; Afrique de l'Ouest; Afrique du Nord; Amérique du Sud; Asie centrale et Asie du Sud; Asie du Sud-Est; Caraïbes; Mexique et Amerique centrale; Moyen-Orient.

ACTIVITES D'INFORMATION ET D'EDUCATION: Domaines: Culture/tradition/religion; Droits de l'Homme/paix/conflits; Développement rural/agriculture; Développement urbain/habitat; Emploi/chômage; Enfants/jeunesse/famille; Paix/conflits ethniques/armement/désarmement; Pauvreté/conditions de vie; Population/planning familial/démographie; Questions relatives aux femmes; Racisme/xénophobie/antisémitisme; Relations internationales/coopération/aide au développement; Relations économiques internationales/commerce/dette/finances; Réfugiés/migrants/groupes ethniques; Santé/assainissement/eau; Écologie/environnement/biodiversité; Éducation/formation/alphabétisation. **Activités:** Autres; Campagnes d'information/expositions; Conférences/séminaires/ateliers/activités de formation; Lobbying/plaidoyer; Radiodiffusion/manifestations culturelles; Réseaux/télécommunications électroniques; Services d'information et de documentation/bases de données; Édition/documents audiovisuels/documents éducatifs.

CHE0569

FEDERATION INTERNATIONALE DE LA CROIX BLEUE ♦ International Federation of the Blue Cross

Postfach 658, Ländtestrasse 44, 2501 Bienne, Suisse.

Téléphone: 41 (32) 22 75 65. ***Fax:*** 41 (32) 22 75 56. ***Contact:*** Pasteur Raymond Bassin, Président.

OBJECTIFS: Lutter contre l'abus d'alcool et autres drogues.

INFORMATIONS GENERALES: *Création:* 1886. *Type d'organisation:* regroupement d'ONG. *Organisations membres:* 25. *Personnel/Total:* var. *Salariés:* 2. *Bénévoles:* var. *Sources financières:* Privé: 40%. *Public:* 10%. *Autofinancement:* 50%.

PUBLICATIONS: *Périodiques:* Info (2).

COMMENTAIRES: Intervient dans la Communauté des Etats indépendants.

ACTIVITES DANS LES REGIONS EN DEVELOPPEMENT: Intervient dans 22 pays. Intervient par l'intermédiaire d'organisations locales partenaires. **Actions de Développement durable:** Enfants/jeunesse/famille; Santé/assainissement/eau. **Régions:** Afrique australe; Afrique centrale; Afrique de l'Est; Afrique de l'Ouest; Amérique du Sud; Asie centrale et Asie du Sud.

ACTIVITES D'INFORMATION ET D'EDUCATION: Domaines: Enfants/jeunesse/famille; Santé/assainissement/eau. **Activités:** Collecte de fonds; Conférences/séminaires/ateliers/activités de formation; Radiodiffusion/manifestations culturelles; Édition/documents audiovisuels/documents éducatifs.

CHE0570

FEDERATION INTERNATIONALE TERRE DES HOMMES (FITDH) ♦ International Federation Terre des Hommes

31 Chemin Franck-Thomas, 1208 Genève, Suisse.

Téléphone: 41 (22) 736 33 72. ***Fax:*** 41 (22) 736 15 10. ***Contact:*** Hans Vernhout, Président.

OBJECTIFS: Aider les enfants les plus démunis au moyen de projets de développement gérés avec le partenariat des organisations locales. Protéger et promouvoir les droits de l'enfant.

INFORMATIONS GENERALES: *Création:* 1966. *Type d'organisation:* regroupement d'ONG. *Organisations membres:* 9. *Affiliée à:* CONGO - Comité ONG auprès de l'UNICEF - Groupe ONG pour la Convention Relative aux droits de l'enfant. *Personnel/Total:* 12. *Salariés:* 2. *Bénévoles:* 10. *Budget/Total 1993:* ECU 49000 (US$ 64000). *Sources financières:* Autofinancement: 100%.

PREVISIONS D'ACTIVITES: L'organisation veut mener une campagne contre les mines anti-personne.

ACTIVITES DANS LES REGIONS EN DEVELOPPEMENT: Intervient dans 60 pays. Intervient par l'intermédiaire d'organisations locales partenaires. **Actions de Développement durable:** Aliments/famine; Droits de l'Homme/paix/conflits; Démocratie/bonne gestion publique/création d'institutions/développement participatif; Développement rural/agriculture; Développement urbain/habitat; Enfants/jeunesse/famille; Petites entreprises/secteur informel/artisanat; Questions relatives aux femmes; Santé/assainissement/eau; Secours d'urgence/réfugiés/aide humanitaire; Écologie/environnement/biodiversité; Éducation/formation/alphabétisation. **Régions:** Afrique australe; Afrique centrale; Afrique de l'Est; Afrique de l'Ouest; Afrique du Nord; Amérique du Sud; Asie centrale et Asie du Sud; Asie de l'Est; Asie du Sud-Est; Caraïbes; Mexique et Amerique centrale; Moyen-Orient.

ACTIVITES D'INFORMATION ET D'EDUCATION: Domaines: Droits de l'Homme/paix/conflits; Développement rural/agriculture; Enfants/jeunesse/famille; Paix/conflits ethniques/armement/désarmement; Pauvreté/conditions de vie; Questions relatives aux femmes; Relations internationales/coopération/aide au développement; Réfugiés/migrants/groupes ethniques; Éducation/formation/alphabétisation. **Activités:** Campagnes d'information/expositions; Collecte de fonds; Lobbying/plaidoyer; Éducation formelle.

CHE0571

FEDERATION ROMANDE DES CONSOMMATRICES ♦ French-Swiss Women Consumers Association

Voir : *Comment utiliser le répertoire,* page 11.

Rte Genève 7 BP 2820 , 1002 Lausanne, Suisse.

Téléphone: 41 (21) 312 80 06. *Contact:* Tille Marianne, Secrétaire générale.

OBJECTIFS: Informer et défendre les consommateurs

INFORMATIONS GENERALES: *Création:* 1959. *Affiliée à:* Bureau Euro-péen des Unions de consommateurs - Consommateur International. *Salariés:* 12. *Bénévoles:* 300. *Budget/Total 1993:* ECU 626000 (US$ 812000). *Sources financières:* Public: 8%. Autofinancement: 92%.

PUBLICATIONS: *Périodiques:* J'achète mieux (10). *Rapport annuel.* Liste des publications.

ACTIVITES D'INFORMATION ET D'EDUCATION: Domaines: Écologie/ environnement/biodiversité. **Activités:** Campagnes d'information/expositions; Conférences/séminaires/ateliers/activités de formation; Services d'information et de documentation/bases de données.

CHE0572

FEDERATION VAUDOISE DE COOPERATION (FVC)

Case postale 866, 1001 Lausanne, Suisse.

Téléphone: 41 (21) 23 33 73.

CHE0573

FGM - STIFTUNG FUR INTERNATIONALE ZUSAMMENARBEIT ♦ FGM - Foundation for International Co-operation

Oberdorfstrasse 8, 8001 Zürich, Switzerland.

Telephone: 41 (1) 69 42 66. *Fax:* (1) 69 40 75. *Contact:* Dr. Peter Kopa, Executive Secretary.

CHE0574

FLAMANT VERT

Rue Grenus 10, 1201 Genève, Suisse.

Téléphone: 41 (22) 731 80 36. *Fax:* 41 (22) 731 97 86.

CHE0575

FOI ET ECONOMIE - BUREAU INTERCONFESSIONNEL D'INFORMATION

Case postale 28, Impasse de la forêt 5, 1707 Fribourg, Suisse.

Téléphone: 41 (37) 28 11 29.

CHE0576

FONDATION CHRISTOPHE ECKENSTEIN

Case postale 136, rue Rothschild 24, 1211 Genève 21, Suisse.

OBJECTIFS: Faire des études sur les relations entre le Tiers-Monde et la Suisse.

INFORMATIONS GENERALES: *Création:* 1975. *Budget/Total 1993:* ECU 16000 (US$ 20000). *Sources financières:* Privé: 100%.

EVALUATION/RECHERCHE: Entreprend des activités de recherche.

COMMENTAIRES: La fondation exerce principalement ses activités en Suisse, dans le domaine de la recherche. Elle n'accorde pas de bourses d'études et ne finance pas de travaux académiques.

CHE0577

FONDATION FRANZ WEBER

Case postale, 1820 Montreux, Suisse.

CHE0578

FONDATION NESTLE

Place de la Gare 4, C.P. 581, 1001 Lausanne, Switzerland.

Telephone: 41 (21) 320 33 51. *Fax:* 41 (21) 320 33 92. *Contact:* Dr. Beat Schürch, Director.

OBJECTIVES: To initiate and finance research in human nutrition, primarily in developing countries.

GENERAL INFORMATION: *Creation:* 1966. *Personnel/Total:* 25. Salaried: 25 of which: 22 in developing countries. *Budget/Total 1993:* ECU 939000 (US$ 1218000). *Financial sources:* Self-financing: 100%.

PUBLICATIONS: *Annual report. List of publications.*

EVALUATION/RESEARCH: Undertakes research activities.

ACTIVITIES IN DEVELOPING REGIONS: Active in 16 country(ies). Works through local field partners. **Sustainable Development Actions:** Other. **Regions:** Caribbean; Central Asia and South Asia; East Africa; East Asia; Mexico and Central America; Middle East; South America; South East Asia; West Africa.

INFORMATION AND EDUCATION ACTIVITIES: Topics: Other. **Activities:** Conferences/seminars/workshops/training activities; Formal education.

CHE0579

FONDATION OECUMENIQUE POUR L'AIDE AUX EGLISES ♦
Ecumenical Church Loan Fund

150 route de Ferney, P.O. Box 2100, 1211 Genève 2, Suisse.

Téléphone: 41 (22) 91 61 11. *Fax:* 41 (22) 91 03 61.

CHE0580

FONDATION PRO VICTIMIS - GENEVE

4 rue de Rive, 1204 Genève, Suisse.

Téléphone: 41 (22) 781 42 62. *Fax:* 41 (22) 781 42 61. *Contact:* Philippe Grand d'Hauteville, Secrétaire général.

OBJECTIFS: Apporter une aide aux victimes de catostrophes naturelles ou causées par l'homme. Financer des programmes visant à prévenir ou à réparer des dommages, matériels ou autres, causés par la catastrophe dont est victime une communauté. S'occuper prioritairement des victimes ne recevant pas ou peu d'autres secours.

INFORMATIONS GENERALES: *Création:* 1988. *Personnel/Total:* 2. *Salariés:* 2. *Budget/Total 1993:* ECU 1566000 (US$ 2030000). *Sources financières:* Privé: 100%.

COMMENTAIRES: Intervient dans la Communauté des Etats indépendants.

ACTIVITES DANS LES REGIONS EN DEVELOPPEMENT: Intervient dans 20 pays. Intervient par l'intermédiaire d'organisations locales partenaires. **Actions de Développement durable:** Secours d'urgence/ réfugiés/aide humanitaire. **Régions:** Afrique australe; Afrique centrale; Afrique de l'Est; Afrique de l'Ouest; Amérique du Sud; Asie centrale et Asie du Sud; Asie du Sud-Est; Caraïbes; Mexique et Amerique centrale; Moyen-Orient.

CHE0581

FONDATION SIMON I. PATINO

C.P. 182, 1211 Genève 25, Suisse.

Téléphone: 41 (22) 347 02 11. *Fax:* 41 (22) 789 18 29. *Contact:* John Dubouchet, Directeur.

OBJECTIFS: Aider au développement du Tiers monde, et en particulier de la Bolivie, notamment dans les domaines de la santé, de l'éducation et de l'agriculture. Faire connaître les différents aspects de ce continent.

INFORMATIONS GENERALES: *Création:* 1958. *Personnel/Total:* 220. *Salariés:* 220 dont: 200 dans les pays en développement.

PUBLICATIONS: *Rapport annuel.*

EVALUATION/RECHERCHE: Entreprend des activités de recherche.

ACTIVITES DANS LES REGIONS EN DEVELOPPEMENT: Intervient directement dans les régions en développement. Intervient dans 2 pays. Maintient une présence locale sur le terrain. **Actions de Développement durable:** Développement rural/agriculture; Enfants/jeunesse/ famille; Santé/assainissement/eau; Écologie/environnement/biodiversité; Éducation/formation/alphabétisation. **Régions:** Amérique du Sud.

See: *How to Use the Directory,* page 11.

CHE0582

FONDATION SUISSE DU SERVICE SOCIAL INTERNATIO-NAL (SSI-SUISSE)

10 rue Dr. Alfred-Vincent, 1201 Genève, Suisse.

Téléphone: 41 (22) 731 67 00. *Fax:* 41 (22) 731 67 65. *Contact:* Madeleine Duvoisin, Directrice.

OBJECTIFS: Apporter une aide juridique, sur mandat du H.C.R, pour les demandeurs d'asile et réfugiés se trouvant en Suisse francophone. S'occuper de problèmes sociaux internationaux qui impliquent la Suisse et l'étranger.

INFORMATIONS GENERALES: *Création:* 1932. *Type d'organisation:* réseau. *Affiliée à:* Service Social International (Suisse). *Personnel/ Total:* 12. *Salariés:* 12. *Budget/Total 1993:* ECU 522000 (US$ 677000). *Sources financières:* Privé: 20%. Public: 80%.

PUBLICATIONS: *Rapport annuel.*

EVALUATION/RECHERCHE: Rapports d'évaluation disponibles.

ACTIVITES DANS LES REGIONS EN DEVELOPPEMENT: Intervient dans 66 pays. Intervient par l'intermédiaire d'organisations locales partenaires. **Actions de Développement durable:** Enfants/jeunesse/famille. **Régions:** Afrique australe; Afrique centrale; Afrique de l'Est; Afrique de l'Ouest; Afrique du Nord; Amérique du Sud; Asie centrale et Asie du Sud; Asie de l'Est; Asie du Sud-Est; Caraïbes; Mexique et Amerique centrale; Moyen-Orient; Océanie.

ACTIVITES D'INFORMATION ET D'EDUCATION: Domaines: Réfugiés/migrants/groupes ethniques. **Activités:** Services d'information et de documentation/bases de données.

CHE0583

FONDAZIONE ELVETICA OSPEDALE DI MADA - OPERA UMANITARIA DR MAGGI

Case postale 3, 6830 Chiasso, Suisse.

Téléphone: 41 (91) 43 65 75. *Fax:* 41 (91) 42 17 09. *Contact:* Camillo Jelmini, Président.

OBJECTIFS: Gérer l'hôpital de Mada (Extrême Nord du Cameroun), le dernier d'une série d'hôpitaux fondés par le docteur Giuseppe Maggi.

INFORMATIONS GENERALES: *Création:* 1978. *Personnel/Total:* 20. *Salariés:* 11 dont: 11 dans les pays en développement. *Bénévoles:* 9 dont: 1 dans les pays en développement. *Budget/Total 1993:* ECU 104000 (US$ 135000). *Sources financières:* Privé: 100%.

PUBLICATIONS: *Rapport annuel.*

ACTIVITES DANS LES REGIONS EN DEVELOPPEMENT: Intervient directement dans les régions en développement. Intervient dans 1 pays. Maintient une présence locale sur le terrain. **Actions de Développement durable:** Santé/assainissement/eau. **Régions:** Afrique centrale.

ACTIVITES D'INFORMATION ET D'EDUCATION: Domaines: Santé/assainissement/eau. **Activités:** Collecte de fonds.

CHE0584

FONDS FUR ENTWICKLUNG UND PARTNERSCHAFT IN AFRIKA ♦ Foundation for Development and Partnership in Africa

Postfach 151, 4005 Basel, Switzerland.

Telephone: 41 (61) 691 75 16. *Fax:* 41 (61) 691 75 16. *Contact:* Barbara Muller.

OBJECTIVES: To support co-operatives and village self-help schemes in rural areas of Africa.

GENERAL INFORMATION: *Creation:* 1961. *Personnel/Total:* 1. *Salaried:* 1. *Budget/Total 1993:* ECU 83000 (US$ 108000). *Financial sources:* Private: 80%. Public: 20%.

PUBLICATIONS: *Periodicals:* FEPA Mittglungsblatt (2). *Annual report.*

ACTIVITIES IN DEVELOPING REGIONS: Present in developing regions. Active in 3 country(ies). Works through local field partners. **Sustainable Development Actions:** Gender issues/women; Human rights/peace/

conflicts; Rural development/agriculture; Small enterprises/informal sector/handicrafts; Urban development/habitat. **Regions:** Southern Africa.

INFORMATION AND EDUCATION ACTIVITIES: Topics: Culture/tradition/religion; Ecology/environment/biodiversity; Employment/unemployment; Gender issues/women; Human rights/peace/conflicts; International economic relations/trade/debt/finance; International relations/cooperation/development aid; Peace/ethnic conflicts/armament/disarmament; Poverty/living conditions; Rural development/agriculture; Urban development/habitat. **Activities:** Fund raising; Information campaigns/exhibitions.

CHE0585

FONDS POUR L'ENVIRONNEMENT ET LE DEVELOPPEMENT (FED)

10 rue Richemond, 1202 Genève, Suisse.

CHE0586

FOOD FOR THE HUNGRY INTERNATIONAL (FHI)

243 route des Fayards, CP 608, 1290 Versoix/Geneva, Switzerland.

Telephone: 41 (22) 755 14 44. *Fax:* 41 (22) 755 16 86. *Contact:* Tetsunao Yamamori, President.

OBJECTIVES: To work with the poor to overcome hunger and poverty through integrated self-development and relief.

GENERAL INFORMATION: *Creation:* 1971. *Affiliated to:* Federation of International Institutions (Switzerland) - InterAction (USA). *Personnel/ Total:* 1012. *Salaried:* 960 of which: 920 in developing countries. *Volunteers:* 52 of which: 40 in developing countries. *Budget/Total 1993:* ECU 18767000 (US$ 24338000). *Financial sources:* Private: 51%. Public: 49%.

PUBLICATIONS: *Annual report.*

EVALUATION/RESEARCH: Evaluation reports available. Undertakes research activities.

PLANNED ACTIVITIES: FHI plans to work on rural and urban micro-enterprise loan schemes and to support the empowerment of local indigenous institutions.

COMMENTS: Undertakes activities in the Commonwealth of Independent States.

ACTIVITIES IN DEVELOPING REGIONS: Present in developing regions. Active in 16 country(ies). Maintains local field presence. Works through local field partners. **Sustainable Development Actions:** Children/youth/family; Democracy/good governance/institution building/participatory development; Ecology/environment/biodiversity; Education/training/literacy; Emergency relief/refugees/humanitarian assistance; Food/famine; Gender issues/women; Health/sanitation/water; Rural development/agriculture; Sending volunteers/experts/technical assistance; Small enterprises/informal sector/handicrafts; Urban development/habitat. **Regions:** Caribbean; Central Asia and South Asia; East Africa; East Asia; Mexico and Central America; South America; South East Asia; Southern Africa.

INFORMATION AND EDUCATION ACTIVITIES: Topics: Children/youth/family; Ecology/environment/biodiversity; Education/training/literacy; Emergency relief/refugees/humanitarian assistance; Employment/unemployment; Food/famine; Health/sanitation/water; International relations/cooperation/development aid; Other; Poverty/living conditions; Refugees/migrants/ethnic groups; Rural development/agriculture; Urban development/habitat. **Activities:** Conferences/seminars/workshops/training activities; Formal education; Fund raising; Networking/electronic telecommunications.

CHE0587

FORMATION POUR L'AUTOPROMOTION

s/c Mme Gladys D. Rocourt, C.P. 6, rue Fremis 35, 1241 Puplinge, Suisse.

Téléphone: 41 (22) 348 96 31. *Contact:* Marie-Madeleine Beer, Présidente.

OBJECTIFS: Aider à la réalisation de projets dans le cadre éducatif, en visant la formation continue de personnes locales pour amener à une

prise en charge réelle s'appuyant sur des compétences réelles, pouvant conduire à l'autonomie.

INFORMATIONS GENERALES: *Création:* 1992. *Personnel/Total:* 9. *Bénévoles:* 9 dont: 1 dans les pays en développement. *Budget/ Total 1993:* ECU 18000 (US$ 24000). *Sources financières:* Privé: 10%. *Public:* 90%.

COMMENTAIRES: L'organisation travaille uniquement avec des bénévoles, afin de limiter ses charges administratives.

ACTIVITES DANS LES REGIONS EN DEVELOPPEMENT: Intervient dans 1 pays. Intervient par l'intermédiaire d'organisations locales partenaires. **Actions de Développement durable:** Enfants/jeunesse/ famille; Questions relatives aux femmes; Éducation/formation/alphabétisation. **Régions:** Caraïbes.

CHE0588
FORUM CIVIQUE EUROPEEN ♦ European Civic Forum

Postfach, Missionsstrasse 35, 4002 Basel, Suisse.

Téléphone: 41 (61) 44 66 19. *Fax:* 41 (61) 44 66 20.

CHE0589
FORUM SCHULE FUR EINE WELT ♦ Forum École pour un seul monde

Aubrigstr. 23, 8645 Jona, Suisse.

Téléphone: 41 (55) 28 40 82. *Fax:* 41 (55) 28 40 82. *Contact:* Bruno Santini-Amgarten, Président.

OBJECTIFS: Faire valoir à l'école une vision globale du monde qui encourage l'action solidaire et favorise le respect de la paix et de la justice. Inciter les enfants et la jeunesse à prendre une part active dans l'élaboration de l'avenir, et les pousser à défendre des valeurs telles que la dignité, la justice et la solidarité dans le monde.

INFORMATIONS GENERALES: *Création:* 1982. *Type d'organisation:* regroupement d'ONG. *Organisations membres:* 33. *Personnel/Total:* 22. *Salariés:* 2. *Bénévoles:* 20. *Budget/Total 1993:* ECU 157000 (US$ 203000). *Sources financières:* Privé: 25%. Public: 60%. *Autofinancement:* 15%.

PUBLICATIONS: *Périodiques:* Rundbrief (4). *Rapport annuel. Liste des publications.*

EVALUATION/RECHERCHE: Rapports d'évaluation disponibles. Entreprend des activités de recherche.

PREVISIONS D'ACTIVITES: Exposition spéciale sur l'éducation globale à la Worlddidac 1996, à Bâle. Etude "Le monde d'aujourd'hui" sur l'attitude des jeunes envers les problèmes du Tiers-Monde (Répétition de l'étude de 1985).

COMMENTAIRES: L'organisation développe un projet d'apprentissage global qui comprend les formes les plus variées d'information et d'éducation au développement et porte sur toutes les questions de développement durable.

ACTIVITES D'INFORMATION ET D'EDUCATION: Domaines: Autres. **Activités:** Campagnes d'information/expositions; Conférences/séminaires/ateliers/activités de formation; Lobbying/plaidoyer; Services d'information et de documentation/bases de données; Échanges/parrainage/jumelage; Édition/documents audiovisuels/documents éducatifs; Éducation formelle.

CHE0590
F O U N D A T I O N   F O R   E N V I R O N M E N T A L CONSERVATION (FEC)

7 Chemin Taverney, 1218 Grand-Saconnex, Genève, Switzerland.

Telephone: 41 (22) 798 23 83/4. *Fax:* 41 (22) 798 23 44. *Contact:* Nicholas Polunin, President.

CHE0591
FOUNDATION SIMON I. PATINO

Case postale 182, rue Giovanni Gambini 8, 1211 Genève 25, Suisse.

Téléphone: 41 (22) 47 02 11. *Fax:* 41 (22) 789 18 29.

CHE0592
FRANZ JORDAN-VEREIN

Lüssiweg 17, 6300 Zug, Suisse.

Téléphone: 41 (42) 21 08 23.

CHE0593
FRANZ XAVER STIFTUNG ♦ Francis Xaver Foundation

Hirschengraben 74, Postfach 830, 8025 Zürich, Switzerland.

Telephone: 41 (1) 261 27 32. *Fax:* 41 (1) 262 06 71. *Contact:* Dr. Hubert Hänggi.

CHE0594
FRANZISKANER MISSIONSSCHWESTERN VON MARIA HILFE ♦ Aid of the Franciscan Missionary Sisters of Mary

Missionsprokura Acherhof, 6430 Schwyz, Switzerland.

CHE0595
FRAUEN FUR DEN FRIEDEN ♦ Femmes pour la paix

Schafgässlein 8, 4058 Basel, Suisse.

Téléphone: 41 (61) 681 33 12. *Contact:* Monique Bürgen, Déléguée.

OBJECTIFS: Travailler pour la paix. Lutter contre les armes atomiques, biologiques et chimiques, avec les organisations mondiales.

INFORMATIONS GENERALES: *Création:* 1978. *Sources financières:* Privé: 100%.

PREVISIONS D'ACTIVITES: Aide aux femmes en Yougoslavie, par l'envoi de médicaments, de jouets, de vêtements. L'organisation a tenté d'organiser des rencontres entre les trois groupes ethniques de Yougoslavie, en Hongrie.

COMMENTAIRES: L'organisation est surtout constituée d'un petit groupe de femmes oeuvrant pour la paix. Intervient dans la Communauté des Etats indépendants.

ACTIVITES DANS LES REGIONS EN DEVELOPPEMENT: Intervient directement dans les régions en développement. Intervient dans 1 pays. Intervient par l'intermédiaire d'organisations locales partenaires.

ACTIVITES D'INFORMATION ET D'EDUCATION: Domaines: Aliments/ famine; Enfants/jeunesse/famille; Paix/conflits ethniques/armement/ désarmement; Racisme/xénophobie/antisémitisme; Réfugiés/migrants/ groupes ethniques; Santé/assainissement/eau; Secours d'urgence/réfugiés/aide humanitaire. **Activités:** Échanges/parrainage/jumelage.

CHE0596
FRAUENINFORMATIONSZENTRUM DRITTE WELT (FIZ) ♦
Information Centre for Third World Women

Quellenstrasse 25, 8005 Zürich, Switzerland.

Telephone: 41 (1) 271 82 82. *Fax:* 41 (1) 272 50 74. *Contact:* Maud Lebert.

OBJECTIVES: To fight against slavery in collaboration with organisations, authorities and lawyers and to expose all forms of traffic of women in the Third World. To lobby political bodies to improve the situation of women from developing countries in Switzerland. To offer advice to afflicted women and help them to help themselves. To disseminate information on the situation of women from the Third World in Switzerland.

GENERAL INFORMATION: *Creation:* 1985. *Personnel/Total:* 6. *Salaried:* 6. *Budget/Total 1993:* ECU 2323000 (US$ 3012000). *Financial sources:* Private: 20%. Public: 30%. Self-financing: 50%.

PUBLICATIONS: *Periodicals:* Rundbrief (2). *Annual report. List of publications.*

EVALUATION/RESEARCH: Evaluation reports available. Undertakes research activities.

PLANNED ACTIVITIES: All of the activities planned by FIZ will be focusing on "female migration".

COMMENTS: Information activities related to the Commonwealth of Independent States.

See: *How to Use the Directory,* page 11.

ACTIVITIES IN DEVELOPING REGIONS: Present in developing regions. Maintains local field presence. Works through local field partners. **Sustainable Development Actions:** Children/youth/family; Education/training/literacy; Gender issues/women; Health/sanitation/water. **Regions:** South America.

INFORMATION AND EDUCATION ACTIVITIES: Topics: Culture/tradition/religion; Gender issues/women; Human rights/peace/conflicts; International economic relations/trade/debt/finance; Poverty/living conditions; Racism/xenophobia/antisemitism; Refugees/migrants/ethnic groups. **Activities:** Broadcasting/cultural events; Conferences/seminars/workshops/training activities; Exchanges/twinning/linking; Information and documentation services/data bases; Information campaigns/exhibitions; Lobbying/advocacy; Networking/electronic telecommunications; Publishing/audiovisual materials/educational materials.

CHE0597
FREIPLATZAKTION FUR ASYLSUCHENDE

Postfach 2452, c/o BODS, 3001 Bern, Suisse.

Téléphone: 41 (31) 25 39 30.

CHE0598
FRERES DE NOS FRERES

22 rue Michel-Chauvet, 1224 Genève, Suisse.

Téléphone: 41 (22) 735 30 74. ***Fax:*** 41 (22) 735 31 17.

OBJECTIFS: Améliorer les conditions de vie des hommes et des femmes du Tiers-Monde, dans le respect de leur propre culture. Informer le public suisse sur les actions entreprises et collecter des fonds.

INFORMATIONS GENERALES: *Création:* 1965. *Personnel/Total:* 13. *Salariés:* 1. *Bénévoles:* 12. ***Budget/Total 1993:*** ECU 1214000 (US$ 1574000). *Sources financières:* Privé: 70%. Public: 7%. Autofinancement: 23%.

PUBLICATIONS: *Périodiques:* Bulletin (4).

EVALUATION/RECHERCHE: Rapports d'évaluation disponibles.

PREVISIONS D'ACTIVITES: L'organisation veut s'engager dans la lutte contre le Sida.

ACTIVITES DANS LES REGIONS EN DEVELOPPEMENT: Intervient dans 19 pays. Intervient par l'intermédiaire d'organisations locales partenaires. **Actions de Développement durable:** Aliments/famine; Développement rural/agriculture; Développement urbain/habitat; Enfants/jeunesse/famille; Population/planning familial/démographie; Questions relatives aux femmes; Santé/assainissement/eau. **Régions:** Afrique australe; Afrique centrale; Afrique de l'Est; Afrique de l'Ouest; Afrique du Nord; Amérique du Sud; Asie du Sud-Est; Caraïbes.

ACTIVITES D'INFORMATION ET D'EDUCATION: Domaines: Développement rural/agriculture; Développement urbain/habitat; Enfants/jeunesse/famille; Population/planning familial/démographie; Questions relatives aux femmes; Santé/assainissement/eau. **Activités:** Campagnes d'information/expositions; Collecte de fonds; Radiodiffusion/manifestations culturelles.

CHE0599
FREUNDE DES KINDERZENTRUMS MANDIRITUBA (BRASILIEN)

Am Guggenberg 19, 8053 Zürich, Suisse.

Téléphone: 41 (1) 252 39 34.

CHE0600
FREUNDE DES SCHWEIZER KINDERDORFS KIRJATH JEARIM IN ISRAEL ♦ Les amis du village suisse d'enfants Kiriath Yearim en Israel

Postfach, Dufourstrasse 116, 8034 Zürich, Suisse.

Téléphone: 41 (1) 383 07 33. ***Fax:*** 41 (1) 383 02 45. ***Contact:*** Carmen Meyer, Présidente.

OBJECTIFS: Construire, développer, et entretenir le village suisse d'enfants de Kiriath Yearim. Apporter une aide à deux centres communautaires arabes dans la partie Est de Jerusalem, en collaboration avec la "Jerusalem Foundation".

INFORMATIONS GENERALES: *Création:* 1951. ***Personnel/Total:*** 201. *Salariés:* 1. *Bénévoles:* 200. ***Budget/Total 1993:*** ECU 1044000 (US$ 1354000). *Sources financières:* Privé: 100%.

PUBLICATIONS: *Périodiques:* Rapport annnuel (1). *Rapport annuel.* **Actions de Développement durable:** Enfants/jeunesse/famille; Éducation/formation/alphabétisation. **Régions:** Moyen-Orient.

ACTIVITES D'INFORMATION ET D'EDUCATION: Domaines: Enfants/jeunesse/famille; Éducation/formation/alphabétisation. **Activités:** Collecte de fonds; Échanges/parrainage/jumelage; Éducation formelle.

CHE0601
FRIENDS WORLD COMMITTEE FOR CONSULTATION

Quaker House, 13 avenue de Mervelet, 1209 Geneva, Switzerland.

Contact: Joel McClellan, Director.

CHE0602
FUNDES-SUISSE (FUNDES) ♦ Foundation for Sustainable Development in Latin America

Hauptstrasse 10, Postfach, 8872 Weesen, Suisse.

Téléphone: 41 (58) 43 66 50. ***Fax:*** 41 (58) 43 66 51 . ***Contact:*** Ernst A.Brugger.

OBJECTIFS: Contribuer à la stabilisation des économies et au développement durable en Amérique Latine. Faciliter les moyens d'accès au crédit pour les entrepreneurs et améliorer leurs conditions de vie et de travail.

INFORMATIONS GENERALES: *Création:* 1986. ***Type d'organisation:*** réseau. *Organisations membres:* 11. *Personnel/Total:* 159. *Salariés:* 159 dont: 145 dans les pays en développement. ***Budget/Total 1993:*** ECU 2557000 (US$ 3316000).

PUBLICATIONS: *Périodiques:* News/Noticias (2) - Dialogo (2) - Fundes in Short (1). *Rapport annuel. Liste des publications.*

EVALUATION/RECHERCHE: Rapports d'évaluation disponibles. Entreprend des activités de recherche.

PREVISIONS D'ACTIVITES: Création de centres d'entretiens dans les pays FUNDES pour la formation.

ACTIVITES DANS LES REGIONS EN DEVELOPPEMENT: Intervient directement dans les régions en développement. Intervient dans 10 pays. Maintient une présence locale sur le terrain. Intervient par l'intermédiaire d'organisations locales partenaires. **Actions de Développement durable:** Dette/finances/commerce; Démocratie/bonne gestion publique/création d'institutions/développement participatif; Envoi de volontaires/experts/assistance technique; Petites entreprises/secteur informel/artisanat; Santé/assainissement/eau; Écologie/environnement/biodiversité; Éducation/formation/alphabétisation; Énergie/transport. **Régions:** Amérique du Sud; Mexique et Amerique centrale.

ACTIVITES D'INFORMATION ET D'EDUCATION: Domaines: Emploi/chômage; Relations internationales/coopération/aide au développement; Relations économiques internationales/commerce/dette/finances; Écologie/environnement/biodiversité; Éducation/formation/alphabétisation. **Activités:** Collecte de fonds; Conférences/séminaires/ateliers/activités de formation; Lobbying/plaidoyer; Radiodiffusion/manifestations culturelles; Réseaux/télécommunications électroniques; Services d'information et de documentation/bases de données; Édition/documents audiovisuels/documents éducatifs; Éducation formelle.

CHE0603
GENEVA INFANT FEEDING ASSOCIATION (GIFA) ♦ Association Genèvoise pour l'alimentation infantile

C.P. 157, 1211 Geneva 19, Switzerland.

Telephone: 41 (22) 798 91 64. ***Fax:*** 41 (22) 798 44 43. ***Contact:*** Alison Linnecar, Co-ordinator.

OBJECTIVES: To provide better infant health through the protection, promotion and support of breastfeeding and sound weaning practices throughout the world. To help curb the spread of artificial feeding of infants worldwide. To monitor the marketing practices of European babyfood manufacturers in developing countries.

GENERAL INFORMATION: *Creation:* 1979. ***Type of organisation:*** coordinating body. ***Affiliated to:*** International Baby Food Action

Voir : *Comment utiliser le répertoire,* page 11.

Network. **Personnel/Total:** 5. *Salaried:* 3. *Volunteers:* 2. **Financial sources:** *Private:* 4%. *Public:* 90%. *Self-financing:* 6%.

PUBLICATIONS: **Periodicals:** Breastfeeding briefs (2). *Annual report. List of publications.*

EVALUATION/RESEARCH: Evaluation reports available.

COMMENTS: GIFA acts as a co-ordinating body for the International Baby Food Action Network (IBFAN) for their activities in Europe, the Middle East and Africa. GIFA is a member of IBFAN which undertakes activities in 50 developing countries. Undertakes activities in the Commonwealth of Independent States. Information activities related to the Commonwealth of Independent States.

INFORMATION AND EDUCATION ACTIVITIES: **Topics:** Children/youth/family; Emergency relief/refugees/humanitarian assistance; Gender issues/women; Health/sanitation/water. **Activities:** Conferences/seminars/workshops/training activities; Information and documentation services/data bases; Lobbying/advocacy.

CHE0604

GENEVE - TIERS-MONDE (GE-TM)

53, rue de Carouge, 1205 Genève, Suisse.

Téléphone: 41 (22) 329 67 68. **Fax:** 41 (22) 320 33 29. **Contact:** Antoine Droin, Secrétaire général.

OBJECTIFS: Collaborer avec des groupements locaux ayant démontré au préalable leur capacité et leur volonté de maîtiser leur développement.

INFORMATIONS GENERALES: **Création:** 1983. **Personnel/Total:** 13. *Salariés:* 7. *Bénévoles:* 6. **Budget/Total 1993:** ECU 658000 (US$ 853000). **Sources financières:** *Privé:* 21%. *Public:* 59%. *Autofinancement:* 20%.

PUBLICATIONS: **Périodiques:** Le trait d'union (2). *Rapport annuel.*

EVALUATION/RECHERCHE: Rapports d'évaluation disponibles.

ACTIVITES DANS LES REGIONS EN DEVELOPPEMENT: Intervient dans 15 pays. Intervient par l'intermédiaire d'organisations locales partenaires. **Actions de Développement durable:** Autres; Dette/finances/commerce; Démocratie/bonne gestion publique/création d'institutions/développement participatif; Développement rural/agriculture; Développement urbain/habitat; Enfants/jeunesse/famille; Petites entreprises/secteur informel/artisanat; Population/planning familial/démographie; Questions relatives aux femmes; Santé/assainissement/eau; Écologie/environnement/biodiversité; Éducation/formation/alphabétisation; Énergie/transport. **Régions:** Afrique centrale; Afrique de l'Ouest; Amérique du Sud; Asie du Sud-Est.

ACTIVITES D'INFORMATION ET D'EDUCATION: **Domaines:** Autres; Développement rural/agriculture; Développement urbain/habitat; Enfants/jeunesse/famille; Pauvreté/conditions de vie; Questions relatives aux femmes; Relations internationales/coopération/aide au développement; Réfugiés/migrants/groupes ethniques; Santé/assainissement/eau; Écologie/environnement/biodiversité; Éducation/formation/alphabétisation. **Activités:** Campagnes d'information/expositions; Collecte de fonds; Conférences/séminaires/ateliers/activités de formation; Lobbying/plaidoyer; Radiodiffusion/manifestations culturelles; Services d'information et de documentation/bases de données; Échanges/parrainage/jumelage; Édition/documents audiovisuels/documents éducatifs.

CHE0605

GESELLSCHAFT FUR BEDROHTE VOLKER, SCHWEIZ (GFBV) ♦ Société pour les peuples menacés, Suisse

Waisenhausplatz 21, 3011 Bern, Suisse.

Téléphone: 41 (31) 311 90 08. **Fax:** 41 (31) 312 66 62. **Contact:** G. Berweger, Secrétaire. **Actions de Développement durable:** Droits de l'Homme/paix/conflits. **Régions:** Afrique australe; Afrique centrale; Afrique de l'Est; Afrique de l'Ouest; Afrique du Nord; Amérique du Sud; Asie centrale et Asie du Sud; Asie de l'Est; Asie du Sud-Est; Caraïbes; Mexique et Amerique centrale; Moyen-Orient; Océanie.

ACTIVITES D'INFORMATION ET D'EDUCATION: **Domaines:** Culture/tradition/religion; Droits de l'Homme/paix/conflits; Racisme/xénophobie/antisémitisme; Réfugiés/migrants/groupes ethniques. **Activités:** Campagnes d'information/expositions; Conférences/séminaires/ateliers/acti-

vités de formation; Lobbying/plaidoyer; Services d'information et de documentation/bases de données.

CHE0606

GESELLSCHAFT SCHWEIZ-ISRAEL ♦ ASSOCIATION SUISSE-ISRAEL

Postfach 1121, 8036 Zürich, Suisse.

Téléphone: 41 (1) 463 24 25.

CHE0607

GESELLSCHAFT SCHWEIZ-SUDAFRIKA (ASSOCIATION SUISSE-AFRIQUE DU SUD)

Postfach 4357, 8022 Zürich, Suisse.

Téléphone: 41 (1) 234 25 42.

CHE0608

GREENPEACE SCHWEIZ

Postfach 276, Müllerstrasse 37, 8026 Zürich, Suisse.

Téléphone: 41 (1) 241 34 41. **Fax:** 41 (1) 241 38 21.

CHE0609

GROUPE DE REALISATIONS AUDIOVISUELLES POUR LE DEVELOPPEMENT (GRAD)

36, rue des Bains, 1205 Genève, Suisse.

Téléphone: 41 (22) 321 42 40. **Contact:** Benoît Lecomte.

OBJECTIFS: Réaliser de courts montages audiovisuels accompagnés de dossiers explicatifs sur les problèmes du développement, pour informer et faire réfléchir sur les facteurs socio-économiques qui engendrent développement et sous-développement.

INFORMATIONS GENERALES: **Personnel/Total:** 1. *Salariés:* 1. **Budget/Total 1993:** ECU 157000 (US$ 203000). **Sources financières:** *Public:* 80%. *Autofinancement:* 20%.

PUBLICATIONS: *Rapport annuel. Liste des publications.*

ACTIVITES DANS LES REGIONS EN DEVELOPPEMENT: Intervient directement dans les régions en développement. Intervient dans 3 pays. Intervient par l'intermédiaire d'organisations locales partenaires. **Actions de Développement durable:** Éducation/formation/alphabétisation. **Régions:** Afrique de l'Ouest; Mexique et Amerique centrale.

ACTIVITES D'INFORMATION ET D'EDUCATION: **Domaines:** Culture/tradition/religion; Développement rural/agriculture; Réfugiés/migrants/groupes ethniques; Écologie/environnement/biodiversité; Éducation/formation/alphabétisation. **Activités:** Services d'information et de documentation/bases de données; Édition/documents audiovisuels/documents éducatifs.

CHE0610

GROUPE POUR LES DROITS DES MINORITES (CDM)

Case postale 33, 1211 Genève 16, Suisse.

Téléphone: 41 (22) 49 34 95.

CHE0611

GROUPE POUR UNE COORDINATION DE LA DOCUMENTATION DES ONG SUISSES

c/o Arbeitsgemeinschaft Documentation, Postfach Documentation, 3001 Bern, Suisse.

Contact: Walter Eigel, Président.

OBJECTIFS: Agir en tant que réseau suisse d'information et de documentation sur le développement.

INFORMATIONS GENERALES: **Création:** 1984. **Type d'organisation:** réseau. **Organisations membres:** 23.

COMMENTAIRES: Les activités de formation et de documentation sont effectuées par les organisations membres du réseau. Activités d'information concernant la Communauté des Etats indépendants.

See: *How to Use the Directory,* page 11.

CHE0612
GROUPE SOLIDARITE GUATEMALA

Case postale 1135, 1211 Genève 1, Suisse.

CHE0613
GROUPE VOLONTAIRE OUTRE MER (GVOM) ♦ Overseas Voluntary Group

Rue St-Bernard 11, 1510 Moudon, Suisse.

Téléphone: 41 (21) 905 20 43. *Fax:* 41 (21) 905 20 43. *Contact:* Francis Monot, Coordinateur.

OBJECTIFS: Etre un lieu de réflexion, d'imagination et de formation sur les problèmes de développement, auxquels il s'agit d'apporter non pas des solutions miracles, mais des aides pratiques et alternatives. Sélectionner et envoyer des volontaires dans le cadre de la coopération au développement.

INFORMATIONS GENERALES: *Création:* 1962. *Affiliée à:* Plate-Forme Haïti (Suisse). *Personnel/Total:* 17. *Salariés:* 1. *Bénévoles:* 16 dont: 15 dans les pays en développement. *Budget/Total 1993:* ECU 253000 (US$ 329000). *Sources financières:* Privé: 15%. Public: 75%. *Autofinancement:* 10%.

PUBLICATIONS: *Périodiques:* Interrogation (8).

COMMENTAIRES: L'organisation fait également un travail d'accueil et de formation de demandeurs d'asile. Le périodique mentionné est publié en collaboration avec deux autre ONG: FSF et EIRENE.

ACTIVITES DANS LES REGIONS EN DEVELOPPEMENT: Intervient directement dans les régions en développement. Intervient dans 7 pays. Maintient une présence locale sur le terrain. **Actions de Développement durable:** Démocratie/bonne gestion publique/création d'institutions/développement participatif; Développement rural/agriculture; Développement urbain/habitat; Petites entreprises/secteur informel/artisanat; Population/planning familial/démographie; Questions relatives aux femmes; Santé/assainissement/eau; Écologie/environnement/biodiversité; Éducation/formation/alphabétisation. **Régions:** Afrique centrale; Amérique du Sud; Caraïbes; Mexique et Amerique centrale.

ACTIVITES D'INFORMATION ET D'EDUCATION: Domaines: Culture/tradition/religion; Pauvreté/conditions de vie; Relations internationales/coopération/aide au développement; Relations économiques internationales/commerce/dette/finances; Réfugiés/migrants/groupes ethniques. **Activités:** Conférences/séminaires/ateliers/activités de formation; Lobbying/plaidoyer.

CHE0614
GRUPO SOFONIAS

Schatzgutstrasse 9, 8750 Glarus, Switzerland.

Telephone: 41 (58) 61 10 81. *Fax:* 41 (58) 61 10 81. *Contact:* Kurt Rhyner-Pozak, President.

OBJECTIVES: To promote development of housing and construction in rural areas by giving priority to ecological and economical solutions. To support women's development.

GENERAL INFORMATION: *Creation:* 1979. *Personnel/Total:* var. *Salaried:* 26 of which: 24 in developing countries. *Volunteers:* var. *Budget/Total 1993:* ECU 417000 (US$ 541000). *Financial sources:* Private: 40%. Public: 40%. Self-financing: 20%.

PUBLICATIONS: *Periodicals:* Notitejas (4). *Annual report.*

EVALUATION/RESEARCH: Evaluation reports available. Undertakes research activities.

PLANNED ACTIVITIES: The organisation will encourage the production of micro-concrete tiles in Third World countries and conduct related workshops and follow-ups.

ACTIVITIES IN DEVELOPING REGIONS: Present in developing regions. Active in 4 country(ies). Maintains local field presence. Works through local field partners. **Sustainable Development Actions:** Gender issues/women; Health/sanitation/water; Sending volunteers/experts/technical assistance; Small enterprises/informal sector/handicrafts; Urban development/habitat. **Regions:** Caribbean; South America.

INFORMATION AND EDUCATION ACTIVITIES: Topics: Gender issues/women; Urban development/habitat. **Activities:** Conferences/seminars/workshops/training activities.

CHE0615
GRUPPE SCHWEIZ-PHILIPPINEN - REGIONALGRUPPE BERN (GSP)

Postfach 524, 3000 Bern 7, Suisse.

Téléphone: 41 (31) 889 09 01.

CHE0616
GRUPPO NORD-SUD (NS)

Case postale 241, 6962 Viganello, Suisse.

Téléphone: 41 (91) 91 35 31.

CHE0617
GUATEMALA KOMITEE

Postfach 1148, 8036 Zürich, Suisse.

CHE0618
DIE HEILSARMEE - NATIONALES HAUPTQUARTIER MISSIONSABTEILUNG

Laupenstrasse 5, P.O. Box 6575, 3008 Bern, Switzerland.

Telephone: 41 (31) 381 05 91. *Fax:* 41 (31) 382 33 02.

OBJECTIVES: To preach the gospel of Jesus Christ and raise awareness of human needs without discrimination.

GENERAL INFORMATION:

PUBLICATIONS: *Annual report.*

COMMENTS: The Salvation Army works in 63 countries worldwide.

INFORMATION AND EDUCATION ACTIVITIES: Topics: Health/sanitation/water; Poverty/living conditions; Refugees/migrants/ethnic groups. **Activities:** Conferences/seminars/workshops/training activities; Information campaigns/exhibitions; Lobbying/advocacy.

CHE0619
HELVETAS - SCHWEIZER GESELLSCHAFT FUR ENTWICKLUNG UND ZUSAMMENARBEIT (HELVETAS) ♦
Helvetas - Swiss Association for Development and Co-operation

St. Moritzstrasse 15, B.P. 181, 8042 Zürich, Suisse.

Téléphone: 41 (1) 363 50 60. *Fax:* 41 (1) 362 29 53. *Contact:* E. Werner Külling, Secrétaire général.

OBJECTIFS: Apporter une assistance technique à des pays et des régions économiquement peu développées du Tiers-Monde. S'efforcer de collaborer avec d'autres organisations qui poursuivent des buts analogues ainsi qu'avec les autorités officielles. Renseigner le public sur les conditions de vie dans les pays en développement.

INFORMATIONS GENERALES: *Création:* 1955. *Personnel/Total:* 380. *Salariés:* 80 dont: 50 dans les pays en développement. *Bénévoles:* 300. *Budget/Total 1993:* ECU 17222000 (US$ 22333000). *Sources financières:* Privé: 17%. Public: 75%. Autofinancement: 8%.

PUBLICATIONS: *Périodiques:* Partnerschaft (4) - Partenaires (4). *Rapport annuel.*

EVALUATION/RECHERCHE: Rapports d'évaluation disponibles.

COMMENTAIRES: Intervient dans la Communauté des Etats indépendants.

ACTIVITES DANS LES REGIONS EN DEVELOPPEMENT: Intervient directement dans les régions en développement. Intervient dans 20 pays. Maintient une présence locale sur le terrain. Intervient par l'intermédiaire d'organisations locales partenaires. **Actions de Développement durable:** Droits de l'Homme/paix/conflits; Démocratie/bonne gestion publique/création d'institutions/développement participatif; Développement rural/agriculture; Développement urbain/habitat; Envoi de volontaires/experts/assistance technique; Petites entreprises/secteur informel/artisanat; Questions relatives aux femmes; Santé/assainisse-

Voir : *Comment utiliser le répertoire,* page 11.

ment/eau; Écologie/environnement/biodiversité; Éducation/formation/alphabétisation; Énergie/transport. **Régions:** Afrique australe; Afrique centrale; Afrique de l'Est; Afrique de l'Ouest; Amérique du Sud; Asie centrale et Asie du Sud; Asie du Sud-Est; Caraïbes; Mexique et Amerique centrale.

ACTIVITES D'INFORMATION ET D'EDUCATION: Domaines: Culture/tradition/religion; Développement rural/agriculture; Pauvreté/conditions de vie; Questions relatives aux femmes; Relations internationales/coopération/aide au développement; Relations économiques internationales/commerce/dette/finances; Réfugiés/migrants/groupes ethniques; Santé/assainissement/eau; Écologie/environnement/biodiversité; Éducation/formation/alphabétisation. **Activités:** Campagnes d'information/expositions; Collecte de fonds; Conférences/séminaires/ateliers/activités de formation; Lobbying/plaidoyer; Radiodiffusion/manifestations culturelles; Services d'information et de documentation/bases de données; Édition/documents audiovisuels/documents éducatifs.

CHE0620

HILFE FUR TOGO AUF PRIVATER BASIS ♦ Aide au Togo sur base privée

Auf der Halde 13, 8309 Nurensdorf, Suisse.

Téléphone: 41 (1) 836 85 37. *Fax:* 41 (1) 836 85 37. *Contact:* Hans May.

OBJECTIFS: Apporter une aide au Togo dans les domaines de l'éducation(construction d'écoles, scolarisation...), la santé (médicament, construction de dispensaires, maternités), l'économie (développement des petites entreprises), aide aux handicapés.

INFORMATIONS GENERALES: Création: 1983. **Personnel/Total:** 3. *Salariés:* 1 dont: 1 dans les pays en développement. *Bénévoles:* 2 dont: 1 dans les pays en développement. **Budget/Total 1993:** ECU 10000 (US$ 14000). **Sources financières:** Public: 35%. Autofinancement: 65%.

PUBLICATIONS: *Rapport annuel.*

PREVISIONS D'ACTIVITES: Relancer le projet "Développement des petites entreprises" qui fut freiné par les évènements politiques des années 91-94

ACTIVITES DANS LES REGIONS EN DEVELOPPEMENT: Intervient directement dans les régions en développement. Intervient dans 1 pays. Maintient une présence locale sur le terrain. Intervient par l'intermédiaire d'organisations locales partenaires. **Actions de Développement durable:** Enfants/jeunesse/famille; Petites entreprises/secteur informel/artisanat; Questions relatives aux femmes; Santé/assainissement/eau; Secours d'urgence/réfugiés/aide humanitaire; Éducation/formation/alphabétisation. **Régions:** Afrique de l'Est.

CHE0621

HILFSWERK MUTTER TERESA

Postfach, Habsburgerstr. 44/PF 4746, 6002 Luzern, Suisse.

CHE0622

HUMAN RIGHTS INFORMATION AND DOCUMENTATION SYSTEMS INTERNATIONAL (HURIDOCS) ♦ Systèmes d'information et de documentation sur les droits de l'homme

2 rue Jean-Jaquet, 1201 Genève, Switzerland.

Telephone: 41 (22) 741 17 67. *Fax:* 41 (22) 741 17 68. *E-mail:* Huridocs@oln.comlink.apc.org. *Contact:* Kofi Kumado, Chairperson.

OBJECTIVES: To improve access to and dissemination of public information on human rights, through more effective, appropriate and compatible methods and techniques of information handling.

GENERAL INFORMATION: Creation: 1982. **Member organisations:** 500. **Personnel/Total:** 2. *Salaried:* 2. **Budget/Total 1993:** ECU 308000 (US$ 399000). **Financial sources:** Private: 35%. Public: 60%. Self-financing: 5%.

PUBLICATIONS: Periodicals: HURIDOCS News (3). *Annual report. List of publications.*

EVALUATION/RESEARCH: Evaluation reports available.

PLANNED ACTIVITIES: HURIDOCS will organise training courses and workshops on human rights information handling and will develop and

disseminate tools, techniques and software. HURIDOCS plans to decentralise its activities through the organisation of regional meetings and the establishment of regional focal points.

COMMENTS: Undertakes activities in the Commonwealth of Independent States. Information activities related to the Commonwealth of Independent States.

ACTIVITIES IN DEVELOPING REGIONS: Present in developing regions. Maintains local field presence. Works through local field partners. **Sustainable Development Actions:** Democracy/good governance/institution building/participatory development; Education/training/literacy; Human rights/peace/conflicts. **Regions:** Caribbean; Central Africa; Central Asia and South Asia; East Africa; East Asia; Mexico and Central America; Middle East; North Africa; South America; South East Asia; Southern Africa; West Africa.

INFORMATION AND EDUCATION ACTIVITIES: Topics: Human rights/peace/conflicts. **Activities:** Conferences/seminars/workshops/training activities; Exchanges/twinning/linking; Information and documentation services/data bases; Networking/electronic telecommunications; Publishing/audiovisual materials/educational materials.

CHE0623

IAMANEH MUTTER + KIND SCHWEIZ ♦ International Association for Maternal and Neonatal Health

L. Löffler, Geschäftsstelle, Postfach, 4027 Basel, Switzerland.

Telephone: 41 (61) 301 45 61. *Fax:* 41 (61) 301 43 80. *Contact:* Dr. Jean-Léopold Micheli.

GENERAL INFORMATION:

CHE0624

INFOSUD - AGENCE DE PRESSE DOCUMENTATION

10 chemin des Epinettes, 1007 Lausanne, Suisse.

Téléphone: 41 (21) 617 43 53. *Fax:* 41 (21) 617 43 52. *Contact:* Daniel Wermus.

OBJECTIFS: Sensibiliser le public du Nord aux enjeux mondiaux et au développement par une stratégie journalistique efficace, pluraliste, professionnelle. Publier des articles dans les médias francophones. Sensibiliser les journalistes des autres rédactions aux enjeux Nord-Sud. Coopérer avec des jounalistes du Sud.

INFORMATIONS GENERALES: Création: 1982. **Affiliée à:** Infosud - Association Francophone d'Agences d'Information (Belgique.). **Personnel/Total:** 3. *Salariés:* 3. **Budget/Total 1993:** ECU 157000 (US$ 203000). **Sources financières:** Privé: 2%. Autofinancement: 98%.

PUBLICATIONS: *Liste des publications.*

COMMENTAIRES: Activités d'information concernant la Communauté des Etats indépendants.

ACTIVITES DANS LES REGIONS EN DEVELOPPEMENT: Intervient par l'intermédiaire d'organisations locales partenaires. **Actions de Développement durable:** Autres. **Régions:** Afrique de l'Ouest.

ACTIVITES D'INFORMATION ET D'EDUCATION: Domaines: Aliments/famine; Culture/tradition/religion; Droits de l'Homme/paix/conflits; Développement rural/agriculture; Développement urbain/habitat; Emploi/chômage; Enfants/jeunesse/famille; Paix/conflits ethniques/armement/désarmement; Pauvreté/conditions de vie; Questions relatives aux femmes; Racisme/xénophobie/antisémitisme; Relations internationales/coopération/aide au développement; Relations économiques internationales/commerce/dette/finances; Réfugiés/migrants/groupes ethniques; Santé/assainissement/eau; Secours d'urgence/réfugiés/aide humanitaire; Écologie/environnement/biodiversité; Éducation/formation/alphabétisation. **Activités:** Radiodiffusion/manifestations culturelles; Services d'information et de documentation/bases de données.

CHE0625

INGENIEURS DU MONDE - EPFL (IdM)

GC - Ecublens, 1015 Lausanne, Suisse.

Téléphone: 41 (21) 693 20 45. *Fax:* 41 (21) 693 50 60.

See: *How to Use the Directory,* page 11.

CHE0626

INNOVATIONS ET RESEAUX POUR LE DEVELOPPE-MENT (IRED) ♦ Development Innovations and Networks

3 rue de Varembé, C.P. 116, 1211 Genève 20, Suisse.

Téléphone: 41 (22) 734 17 16. *Fax:* 41 (22) 740 00 11. *Courrier électronique:* GEO2:IRED-GVA. *Contact:* Boukary Younoussi, Secrétaire général.

OBJECTIFS: Renforcer la société civile et promouvoir la démocratie et les droits de l'homme. Promouvoir des initiatives éconnmiques des communautés de base en milieu rural et urbain. Parvenir à la maîtrise des techniques de lobbying et de négociation par les leaders des communautés de base.

INFORMATIONS GENERALES: *Création:* 1981. *Type d'organisation:* réseau. *Organisations membres:* 500. *Personnel/Total:* 30. *Salariés:* 30 dont: 26 dans les pays en développement.

PUBLICATIONS: *Périodiques:* IRED-Forum (4). *Rapport annuel. Liste des publications.*

EVALUATION/RECHERCHE: Rapports d'évaluation disponibles. Entreprend des activités de recherche.

ACTIVITES DANS LES REGIONS EN DEVELOPPEMENT: Intervient directement dans les régions en développement. Maintient une présence locale sur le terrain. Intervient par l'intermédiaire d'organisations locales partenaires. **Actions de Développement durable:** Dette/finances/commerce; Droits de l'Homme/paix/conflits; Démocratie/bonne gestion publique/création d'institutions/développement participatif; Petites entreprises/secteur informel/artisanat; Écologie/environnement/biodiversité; Éducation/formation/alphabétisation. **Régions:** Afrique australe; Afrique centrale; Afrique de l'Est; Afrique de l'Ouest; Amérique du Sud; Asie du Sud-Est; Mexique et Amerique centrale.

ACTIVITES D'INFORMATION ET D'EDUCATION: Domaines: Relations économiques internationales/commerce/dette/finances. **Activités:** Conférences/séminaires/ateliers/activités de formation; Lobbying/plaidoyer; Réseaux/télécommunications électroniques; Services d'information et de documentation/bases de données; Échanges/parrainage/jumelage; Édition/documents audiovisuels/documents éducatifs.

CHE0627

INSTITUT INTERNATIONAL DES CAISSES D'EPARGNE (IICE) ♦ International Savings Banks Institute

1-3 rue Albert-Gos, C.P. 355, 1211 Genève 25, Suisse.

Téléphone: 41 (22) 47 74 66. *Fax:* 41 (22) 46 73 56. *Contact:* Jean-Marie Pesant, Directeur général.

CHE0628

INSTITUT MENZINGEN

Mutterhaus, 6313 Menzingen, Switzerland.

Telephone: 41 (42) 52 11 33. *Fax:* 41 (42) 52 35 17. *Contact:* Sister Miguela Müslin, Superior general.

OBJECTIVES: To support programmes in the fields of education, teaching, health, social development and parish work.

GENERAL INFORMATION: *Creation:* 1844. *Personnel/Total:* 2543. *Volunteers:* 2543 of which: 1266 in developing countries. *Budget/Total 1993:* ECU 1252000 (US$ 1624000). *Financial sources:* Private: 59%. Self-financing: 41%.

PUBLICATIONS: *Periodicals:* Coeur en Alerte (6) - Contact (2).

ACTIVITIES IN DEVELOPING REGIONS: Present in developing regions. Active in 7 country(ies). Maintains local field presence. Works through local field partners. **Sustainable Development Actions:** Children/youth/family; Education/training/literacy; Emergency relief/refugees/humanitarian assistance; Gender issues/women; Health/sanitation/water; Population/family planning/demography; Rural development/agriculture; Urban development/habitat. **Regions:** Central Africa; Central Asia and South Asia; South America; Southern Africa.

INFORMATION AND EDUCATION ACTIVITIES: Topics: Children/youth/family; Education/training/literacy; Gender issues/women; Health/sanitation/water; Population/family planning/demography; Rural development/agriculture; Urban development/habitat. **Activities:** Conferences/seminars/workshops/training activities; Formal education.

CHE0629

INSTITUT UNIVERSITAIRE D'ETUDES DU DEVELOPPE-MENT (IUED) ♦ Institute of Development Studies

24 rue Rothschild, C.P. 136, 1211 Genève 21, Suisse.

Téléphone: 41 (22) 906 59 40. *Fax:* 41 (22) 906 59 23. *Contact:* Jean-Luc Maurer, Directeur.

OBJECTIFS: Contribuer par la recherche, l'enseignement et les activités orientées vers la pratique, à une meilleure connaissance des phénomènes de développement dans le monde contemporain. Appréhender ces questions dans leur globalité et dans leur diversité.

INFORMATIONS GENERALES: *Création:* 1961. *Personnel/Total:* 73. *Salariés:* 73 dont: 10 dans les pays en développement. *Budget/Total 1993:* ECU 3914000 (US$ 5076000). *Sources financières:* Public: 84%. Autofinancement: 16%.

PUBLICATIONS: *Périodiques:* Aide suisse aux pays en développement et de l'Europe oriental (1) - Annuaire Suisse-Tiers monde (1) - Horizons-IUED (4) (2). *Rapport annuel. Liste des publications.*

EVALUATION/RECHERCHE: Entreprend des activités de recherche.

ACTIVITES DANS LES REGIONS EN DEVELOPPEMENT: Intervient directement dans les régions en développement. Intervient dans 6 pays. Maintient une présence locale sur le terrain. Intervient par l'intermédiaire d'organisations locales partenaires. **Actions de Développement durable:** Droits de l'Homme/paix/conflits; Développement rural/agriculture; Développement urbain/habitat; Petites entreprises/secteur informel/artisanat; Questions relatives aux femmes; Santé/assainissement/eau; Secours d'urgence/réfugiés/aide humanitaire; Écologie/environnement/biodiversité; Éducation/formation/alphabétisation. **Régions:** Afrique centrale; Afrique de l'Est; Afrique de l'Ouest; Amérique du Sud; Caraïbes.

ACTIVITES D'INFORMATION ET D'EDUCATION: Domaines: Développement rural/agriculture; Développement urbain/habitat; Emploi/chômage; Questions relatives aux femmes; Relations internationales/coopération/aide au développement; Relations économiques internationales/commerce/dette/finances; Réfugiés/migrants/groupes ethniques; Santé/assainissement/eau; Écologie/environnement/biodiversité. **Activités:** Conférences/séminaires/ateliers/activités de formation; Radiodiffusion/manifestations culturelles; Services d'information et de documentation/bases de données.

CHE0630

INTERAID INTERNATIONAL ♦ International Christian Aid

Kornhausstrasse 37, Postfach, 8042 Zürich, Switzerland.

Contact: Maud Lebert, Acting Director.

OBJECTIVES: To carry out social welfare actions in developing countries.

GENERAL INFORMATION: *Creation:* 1981. *Personnel/Total:* 3. *Salaried:* 3. *Budget/Total 1993:* ECU 543000 (US$ 704000). *Financial sources:* Private: 100%.

PUBLICATIONS: *Periodicals:* Bulletin Inter Aid Schweiz (3) - Annual Review Inter Aid Schweiz (1). *Annual report.*

EVALUATION/RESEARCH: Evaluation reports available.

PLANNED ACTIVITIES: INTERAID plans to undertake programmes to further women's causes, child and adult education and rural community development.

ACTIVITIES IN DEVELOPING REGIONS: Present in developing regions. Active in 7 country(ies). Maintains local field presence. Works through local field partners. **Sustainable Development Actions:** Children/youth/family; Ecology/environment/biodiversity; Education/training/literacy; Emergency relief/refugees/humanitarian assistance; Food/famine; Gender issues/women; Health/sanitation/water; Rural development/agriculture; Sending volunteers/experts/technical assistance; Small enterprises/informal sector/handicrafts; Urban development/habitat. **Regions:** Central Africa; East Africa; Mexico and Central America; South East Asia.

Voir : *Comment utiliser le répertoire,* page 11.

INFORMATION AND EDUCATION ACTIVITIES: Topics: Children/youth/family; Ecology/environment/biodiversity; Education/training/literacy; Emergency relief/refugees/humanitarian assistance; Food/famine; Gender issues/women; Health/sanitation/water; Poverty/living conditions; Refugees/migrants/ethnic groups; Rural development/agriculture; Urban development/habitat. **Activities:** Fund raising.

CHE0631

INTERANDES AG ♦ Andean Economies Development Management

Vordergasse 41, 8200 Schaffhausen, Suisse.

Téléphone: 41 (53) 25 43 84. *Fax:* 41 (53) 25 73 50. *Contact:* Conrado A. Surber Devoto, Director.

INFORMATIONS GENERALES: *Création:* 1979.

CHE0632

INTERCOOPERATION - SCHWEIZERISCHE ORGANISATION FUR ENTWICKLUNG UND ZUSAMMENARBEIT (IC) ♦ Intercoopération - Organisation Suisse pour le Développement et la Coopération

Maulbeerstrasse 10, C.P. 6724, 3001 Bern, Suisse.

Téléphone: 41 (31) 382 08 61. *Fax:* 41 (31) 382 14 70. *Contact:* Andreas Schild.

OBJECTIFS: Planifier et gérer des projets de développement rural concernant les forêts, la production animale, l'organisation paysanne, la formation et les ONG locales.

INFORMATIONS GENERALES: *Création:* 1982. *Organisations membres:* 7. *Affiliée à:* IUCN (Suisse) - AGRECOL (Suisse) - WIDE (Belgique). *Salariés:* 105 dont: 72 dans les pays en développement. *Bénévoles:* 105. *Budget/Total 1993:* ECU 19205000 (US$ 24905000). *Sources financières:* Public: 100%.

PUBLICATIONS: *Rapport annuel.*

EVALUATION/RECHERCHE: Rapports d'évaluation disponibles. Entreprend des activités de recherche.

COMMENTAIRES: Intervient dans la Communauté des Etats indépendants.

ACTIVITES DANS LES REGIONS EN DEVELOPPEMENT: Intervient directement dans les régions en développement. Intervient dans 15 pays. Intervient par l'intermédiaire d'organisations locales partenaires. **Actions de Développement durable:** Dette/finances/commerce; Démocratie/bonne gestion publique/création d'institutions/développement participatif; Développement rural/agriculture; Développement urbain/habitat; Envoi de volontaires/experts/assistance technique; Questions relatives aux femmes; Santé/assainissement/eau; Écologie/environnement/biodiversité; Éducation/formation/alphabétisation; Énergie/transport. **Régions:** Afrique australe; Afrique centrale; Afrique de l'Est; Amérique du Sud; Asie centrale et Asie du Sud; Asie du Sud-Est; Mexique et Amerique centrale.

ACTIVITES D'INFORMATION ET D'EDUCATION: Domaines: Développement rural/agriculture; Pauvreté/conditions de vie; Questions relatives aux femmes; Relations internationales/coopération/aide au développement; Relations économiques internationales/commerce/dette/finances; Écologie/environnement/biodiversité. **Activités:** Conférences/séminaires/ateliers/activités de formation; Services d'information et de documentation/bases de données; Échanges/parrainage/jumelage.

CHE0633

INTERNATIONAL ALLIANCE OF WOMEN

Alemannengasse 42, 4058 Basel, Switzerland.

Telephone: 41 (61) 691 30 51.

CHE0634

INTERNATIONAL ASSOCIATION FOR THE EXCHANGE OF STUDENTS FOR TECHNICAL EXPERIENCE (IAESTE)

Rämistrasse 101, Praktikantendienst ETHZ, 8092 Zürich, Switzerland.

Telephone: 41 (1) 632 20 71. *Fax:* 41 (1) 632 12 64. *Contact:* A. Sfier, General Secretary.

OBJECTIVES: To provide students at institutions of higher education with technical experience abroad relative to their studies in the broadest sense. To promote international understanding and goodwill amongst the students of all nations.

GENERAL INFORMATION: *Creation:* 1948. *Type of organisation:* association of NGOs. *Member organisations:* 63. *Personnel/Total:* 2. *Salaried:* 2. *Budget/Total 1993:* ECU 63000 (US$ 81000). *Financial sources:* Public: 100%.

PUBLICATIONS: *Annual report.*

EVALUATION/RESEARCH: Evaluation reports available.

COMMENTS: The IAESTE gives students from developing countries 10 more exchange jobs in order to help them to establish their exchange programme (for developed countries there is a one-to-one exchange policy). Undertakes activities in the Commonwealth of Independent States. Information activities related to the Commonwealth of Independent States.

ACTIVITIES IN DEVELOPING REGIONS: Present in developing regions. Active in 15 country(ies). Works through local field partners. **Sustainable Development Actions:** Education/training/literacy. **Regions:** Central Asia and South Asia; East Africa; Mexico and Central America; Middle East; North Africa; South America; South East Asia; Southern Africa; West Africa.

INFORMATION AND EDUCATION ACTIVITIES: Topics: Education/training/literacy. **Activities:** Exchanges/twinning/linking.

CHE0635

INTERNATIONAL BABY FOOD ACTION NETWORK (IBFAN)

Case postale 157, 1211 Genève 19, Switzerland.

Telephone: 41 (22) 798 91 64. *Fax:* 41 (22) 791 00 34.

CHE0636

INTERNATIONAL CATHOLIC CHILD BUREAU (ICCB) ♦ Bureau International Catholique de l'Enfance

63 rue de Lausanne, 1202 Geneva, Switzerland.

Telephone: 41 (22) 731 32 48. *Fax:* 41 (22) 731 77 93. *Contact:* Dr. François Ruegg, Secretary General.

OBJECTIVES: To collect information and documentation on children's issues. To represent and defend children's interests. To work in areas of non-material needs of refugee children, religious information, spiritual growth and family issues.

GENERAL INFORMATION: *Creation:* 1948. *Type of organisation:* network. *Member organisations:* 146. *Affiliated to:* Conference of International Catholic Organizations - Federation of Semi-Official and Private International Institutions established in Geneva. *Personnel/Total:* 40. *Salaried:* 40 of which: 5 in developing countries. *Budget/Total 1993:* ECU 3131000 (US$ 4060000). *Financial sources:* Private: 100%.

PUBLICATIONS: *Periodicals:* Children Worldwide (2) - Enfants de Partout (4). *Annual report. List of publications.*

EVALUATION/RESEARCH: Evaluation reports available. Undertakes research activities.

COMMENTS: Undertakes activities in the Commonwealth of Independent States. Information activities related to the Commonwealth of Independent States.

ACTIVITIES IN DEVELOPING REGIONS: Maintains local field presence. **Sustainable Development Actions:** Children/youth/family. **Regions:** Central Africa; Central Asia and South Asia; East Asia; Mexico and Central America; South America; South East Asia; West Africa.

INFORMATION AND EDUCATION ACTIVITIES: Topics: Culture/tradition/religion; Refugees/migrants/ethnic groups. **Activities:** Conferences/seminars/workshops/training activities.

See: *How to Use the Directory,* page 11.

CHE0637

INTERNATIONAL CATHOLIC MIGRATION COMMISSION (ICMC)

37-39 rue de Vermont, P.O. Box 96, 1211 Geneva 20, Switzerland.

Telephone: 41 (22) 733 41 50. *Fax:* 41 (22) 734 79 29 . *Contact:* André Van Chau, Secretary General.

OBJECTIVES: To co-operate with local Catholic assistance agencies in over 70 countries, as well as international organisations and governments, in administrating programmes to benefit refugees, migrants and internally displaced persons, and returnees regardless of creed.

GENERAL INFORMATION: *Creation:* 1951. *Type of organisation:* network. *Member organisations:* 73. *Affiliated to:* InterAction (USA). *Personnel/Total:* 868. *Salaried:* 866 of which: 746 in developing countries. *Volunteers:* 2 of which: 1 in developing countries. *Budget/Total 1993:* ECU 18000000 (US$ 23500000). *Financial sources:* Private: 1%. *Public:* 98%. *Self-financing:* 1%.

PUBLICATIONS: *Annual report.*

EVALUATION/RESEARCH: Evaluation reports available.

PLANNED ACTIVITIES: To develop conflict resolution programmes, starting with Rwandan refugees.

COMMENTS: Undertakes activities in the Commonwealth of Independent States. Information activities related to the Commonwealth of Independent States.

ACTIVITIES IN DEVELOPING REGIONS: Present in developing regions. Active in 30 country(ies). Maintains local field presence. Works through local field partners. **Sustainable Development Actions:** Children/youth/family; Education/training/literacy; Emergency relief/refugees/humanitarian assistance; Gender issues/women; Health/sanitation/water; Rural development/agriculture; Sending volunteers/experts/technical assistance; Small enterprises/informal sector/handicrafts. **Regions:** Central Africa; Central Asia and South Asia; East Africa; East Asia; Mexico and Central America; South America; South East Asia; Southern Africa; West Africa.

INFORMATION AND EDUCATION ACTIVITIES: Topics: Education/training/literacy; Emergency relief/refugees/humanitarian assistance; Gender issues/women; Refugees/migrants/ethnic groups. **Activities:** Conferences/seminars/workshops/training activities; Fund raising; Lobbying/advocacy.

CHE0638

INTERNATIONAL CO-OPERATIVE ALLIANCE (ICA) ♦ Alliance Coopérative Internationale (ACI)

15 route des Morillons, 1218 Grand Saconnex, Geneva, Switzerland.

Telephone: 41 (22) 798 41 21. *Fax:* (22) 798 41 22. *E-mail:* icageneva@gn.apc.org. *Contact:* Lars Marcus, President.

OBJECTIVES: To promote and strengthen autonomous co-operatives throughout the world. To facilitate the development of economic relations between its member organisations. To further the economic and social progress of its members and their communities.

GENERAL INFORMATION: *Creation:* 1895. *Type of organisation:* association of NGOs. *Member organisations:* 191. *Affiliated to:* COPAC (Italy) - Conference of Non-Governmental Organisations - Fédération des Institutions Internationales Etablies à Genève. *Personnel/Total:* 78. *Salaried:* 77 of which: 67 in developing countries. *Volunteers:* 1. *Budget/Total 1993:* ECU 4697000 (US$ 6091000).

PUBLICATIONS: *Periodicals:* Review of International Co-operation - ICA News. *Annual report. List of publications.*

EVALUATION/RESEARCH: Evaluation reports available. Undertakes research activities.

COMMENTS: Undertakes activities in the Commonwealth of Independent States. Information activities related to the Commonwealth of Independent States.

ACTIVITIES IN DEVELOPING REGIONS: Present in developing regions. Maintains local field presence. Works through local field partners. **Sustainable Development Actions:** Democracy/good governance/institu-

tion building/participatory development; Ecology/environment/biodiversity; Education/training/literacy; Gender issues/women; Human rights/peace/conflicts; Rural development/agriculture; Small enterprises/informal sector/handicrafts. **Regions:** Central Africa; Central Asia and South Asia; East Africa; East Asia; Mexico and Central America; South America; South East Asia; Southern Africa; West Africa.

INFORMATION AND EDUCATION ACTIVITIES: Topics: Children/youth/family; Ecology/environment/biodiversity; Education/training/literacy; Employment/unemployment; Gender issues/women; Human rights/peace/conflicts; International economic relations/trade/debt/finance; International relations/cooperation/development aid; Poverty/living conditions; Refugees/migrants/ethnic groups; Rural development/agriculture; Urban development/habitat. **Activities:** Conferences/seminars/workshops/training activities; Information and documentation services/data bases; Publishing/audiovisual materials/educational materials.

CHE0639

INTERNATIONAL COMMISSION OF JURISTS (ICJ) ♦ Commission Internationale de Juristes

26 chemin de la Joinville, P.O. Box 160, 1216 Cointrin/Geneve, Switzerland.

Telephone: 41 (22) 788 47 47. *Fax:* 41 (22) 788 48 80. *Contact:* Adama DIENG, Secretary General.

OBJECTIVES: To promote the understanding and observance of the Rule of Law and the legal protection of human rights throughout the world.

GENERAL INFORMATION: *Creation:* 1952. *Personnel/Total:* 17. *Salaried:* 17. *Budget/Total 1993:* ECU 1044000 (US$ 1354000). *Financial sources:* Private: 35%. *Public:* 60%. *Self-financing:* 5%.

PUBLICATIONS: *Periodicals:* Newsletter (4) - ICJ Review (2) - CIJL Yearbook (1). *List of publications.*

EVALUATION/RESEARCH: Undertakes research activities.

PLANNED ACTIVITIES: ICJ will undertake the development of International Law and of regional human rights mechanisms, and will strengthen human rights groups and education.

COMMENTS: Undertakes activities in the Commonwealth of Independent States. Information activities related to the Commonwealth of Independent States.

ACTIVITIES IN DEVELOPING REGIONS: Present in developing regions. Maintains local field presence. Works through local field partners. **Sustainable Development Actions:** Democracy/good governance/institution building/participatory development; Human rights/peace/conflicts. **Regions:** Caribbean; Central Africa; Central Asia and South Asia; East Africa; East Asia; Mexico and Central America; Middle East; North Africa; Oceania; South America; South East Asia; Southern Africa; West Africa.

INFORMATION AND EDUCATION ACTIVITIES: Topics: Culture/tradition/religion; Human rights/peace/conflicts; International relations/cooperation/development aid; Racism/xenophobia/antisemitism. **Activities:** Conferences/seminars/workshops/training activities; Exchanges/twinning/linking; Lobbying/advocacy; Publishing/audiovisual materials/educational materials.

CHE0640

INTERNATIONAL COUNCIL OF JEWISH WOMEN (ICJW)

24 chemin du Pommier, 1218 Geneva, Switzerland.

Telephone: 41 (022) 798 28 82. *Fax:* 41 (022) 733 60 74. *Contact:* Andrée Farhi, Representative.

OBJECTIVES: To promote friendly relations among Jewish women of all countries. To further interests in the fields of international relations, government, social welfare and education. To support the Universal Declaration of Human Rights. To promote equality between men and women.

GENERAL INFORMATION: *Creation:* 1912. *Type of organisation:* association of NGOs, coordinating body. *Member organisations:* 43. *Affiliated to:* World Jewish Congress. *Personnel/Total:* 1. *Salaried:* 1. *Budget/Total 1993:* ECU 15400 (US$ 20000).

Voir : *Comment utiliser le répertoire,* page 11.

PUBLICATIONS: *Periodicals:* Newsletter (3) - Links Around the World (4). *List of publications.*

EVALUATION/RESEARCH: Undertakes research activities.

COMMENTS: Undertakes activities in the Commonwealth of Independent States. Information activities related to the Commonwealth of Independent States.

ACTIVITIES IN DEVELOPING REGIONS: Present in developing regions. Active in 19 country(ies). Works through local field partners. **Sustainable Development Actions:** Children/youth/family; Democracy/good governance/institution building/participatory development; Ecology/environment/biodiversity; Education/training/literacy; Emergency relief/refugees/humanitarian assistance; Gender issues/women; Human rights/peace/conflicts; Population/family planning/demography. **Regions:** Caribbean; Mexico and Central America; Middle East; Oceania; South America; South East Asia; Southern Africa.

INFORMATION AND EDUCATION ACTIVITIES: Topics: Children/youth/family; Culture/tradition/religion; Education/training/literacy; Gender issues/women; Human rights/peace/conflicts; Poverty/living conditions; Racism/xenophobia/antisemitism. **Activities:** Exchanges/twinning/linking; Formal education; Information and documentation services/data bases.

CHE0641

INTERNATIONAL COUNCIL OF SOCIAL WELFARE (ICSW) ♦
Conseil International de l'Action Sociale

Les Crosets, 1873 Val d'Illiez, Suisse.

Contact: Anne Herdt.

CHE0642

INTERNATIONAL COUNCIL OF VOLUNTARY AGENCIES (ICVA) ♦ Conseil International des Agences Bénévoles

13, rue Gautier, Case Postale 216, 1211 Geneva 21, Switzerland.

Telephone: 41 (22) 732 66 00 . **Fax:** 41 (22) 738 99 04. **E-mail:** icva.geneva@cgnet.com. **Contact:** Delmar Blasco, Executive Director.

OBJECTIVES: To provide a global forum for voluntary agencies from the North and South, in order that they may exchange views, share strategies, co-ordinate actions, and forge effective partnerships across cultures and societies with different levels and forms of development. To support the efforts of voluntary agencies in the fields of humanitarian assistance, development co-operation and human rights.

GENERAL INFORMATION: Creation: 1962. **Type of organisation:** association of NGOs. **Member organisations:** 97. **Personnel/Total:** 9. *Salaried:* 9. **Budget/Total 1993:** ECU 1220000 (US$ 1583000). **Financial sources:** Private: 65%. Public: 20%. Self-financing: 15%.

PUBLICATIONS: *Periodicals:* ICVA Forum (10). *Annual report.*

PLANNED ACTIVITIES: ICVA plans to undertake a campaign for debt reduction in Africa.

INFORMATION AND EDUCATION ACTIVITIES: Topics: Children/youth/family; Culture/tradition/religion; Ecology/environment/biodiversity; Education/training/literacy; Emergency relief/refugees/humanitarian assistance; Employment/unemployment; Food/famine; Gender issues/women; Health/sanitation/water; Human rights/peace/conflicts; International economic relations/trade/debt/finance; International relations/cooperation/development aid; Peace/ethnic conflicts/armament/disarmament; Population/family planning/demography; Poverty/living conditions; Racism/xenophobia/antisemitism; Refugees/migrants/ethnic groups; Rural development/agriculture; Urban development/habitat. **Activities:** Conferences/seminars/workshops/training activities; Lobbying/advocacy; Networking/electronic telecommunications.

CHE0643

INTERNATIONAL FEDERATION OF CATHOLIC PAROCHIAL YOUTH COMMUNITIES (FIMCAP)

St. Karliquai 12, 6000 Luzern 5, Switzerland.

Telephone: 41 (41) 52 47 47. **Fax:** 41 (41) 52 47 11. **Contact:** Annette Leimer, General Secretary.

OBJECTIVES: To promote solidarity and mutual friendship through partnership projects, aid, formative activities and inter-cultural exchanges.

GENERAL INFORMATION: Creation: 1962. **Type of organisation:** association of NGOs. **Member organisations:** 35. **Affiliated to:** Youth Forum of the European Union (Belgium) - European Co-ordination Bureau (Belgium) - International Catholic Organisations (Switzerland) - International Catholic Child Bureau (Switzerland). **Personnel/Total:** var. **Budget/Total 1993:** ECU 44000 (US$ 52000). **Financial sources:** Private: 10%. Public: 70%. Self-financing: 20%.

PUBLICATIONS: *Periodicals:* LINK (4).

ACTIVITIES IN DEVELOPING REGIONS: Active in 15 country(ies). Works through local field partners. **Sustainable Development Actions:** Children/youth/family; Democracy/good governance/institution building/participatory development; Education/training/literacy; Emergency relief/refugees/humanitarian assistance; Health/sanitation/water; Human rights/peace/conflicts; Small enterprises/informal sector/handicrafts. **Regions:** Caribbean; Central Africa; Central Asia and South Asia; East Africa; East Asia; South America; South East Asia; Southern Africa; West Africa.

INFORMATION AND EDUCATION ACTIVITIES: Topics: Children/youth/family; Culture/tradition/religion; International relations/cooperation/development aid; Peace/ethnic conflicts/armament/disarmament; Racism/xenophobia/antisemitism; Refugees/migrants/ethnic groups. **Activities:** Exchanges/twinning/linking; Fund raising; Lobbying/advocacy.

CHE0644

INTERNATIONAL FEDERATION OF RED CROSS AND RED CRESCENT SOCIETIES ♦ Fédération Internationale des Societés de la Croix Rouge et du Croissant Rouge

17 chemin des Crêts, C.P. 372, 1211 Geneva 19, Switzerland.

Telephone: 41 (22) 730 42 22. **Fax:** 41 (22) 733 03 95. **Contact:** Head of External Relations.

CHE0645

INTERNATIONAL FEDERATION OF UNIVERSITY WOMEN (IFUW) ♦ Fédération Internationale des Femmes Diplômées des Universités

37 Quai Wilson, 1201 Geneva, Switzerland.

Telephone: 41 (22) 731 23 80. **Fax:** 41 (22) 738 04 40. **Contact:** Dorothy Davies, Secretary General.

OBJECTIVES: To improve the status of women and girls. To protect human rights and to promote peace.

GENERAL INFORMATION: Creation: 1919. **Type of organisation:** association of NGOs. **Member organisations:** 61. **Affiliated to:** CONGO - FIIG. **Personnel/Total:** 10. *Salaried:* 10. *Volunteers:* var.. **Budget/Total 1993:** ECU 339000 (US$ 440000). **Financial sources:** Public: 10%. Self-financing: 90%.

PUBLICATIONS: *Periodicals:* IFUW News (6).

EVALUATION/RESEARCH: Undertakes research activities.

COMMENTS: Undertakes activities in the Commonwealth of Independent States. Information activities related to the Commonwealth of Independent States.

ACTIVITIES IN DEVELOPING REGIONS: Present in developing regions. Works through local field partners. **Sustainable Development Actions:** Children/youth/family; Democracy/good governance/institution building/participatory development; Ecology/environment/biodiversity; Education/training/literacy; Gender issues/women; Human rights/peace/conflicts; Other. **Regions:** Central Africa; Central Asia and South Asia; East Africa; East Asia; Mexico and Central America; Middle East; North Africa; Oceania; South America; South East Asia; Southern Africa; West Africa.

INFORMATION AND EDUCATION ACTIVITIES: Topics: Children/youth/family; Ecology/environment/biodiversity; Education/training/literacy; Gender issues/women; Human rights/peace/conflicts. **Activities:** Broadcasting/cultural events; Conferences/seminars/workshops/training activities; Exchanges/twinning/linking; Formal education; Fund raising; Information and documentation services/data bases; Information campaigns/

See: How to Use the Directory, page 11.

exhibitions; Lobbying/advocacy; Networking/electronic telecommunications; Publishing/audiovisual materials/educational materials.

CHE0646

INTERNATIONAL MOVEMENT AGAINST ALL FORMS OF DISCRIMINATION AND RACISM

P.O. Box 2100, 150 route de Ferney, 1211 Genève, Switzerland.

Telephone: 41 (22) 791 62 63.

CHE0647

INTERNATIONAL PEACE BUREAU

41 rue de Zurich, 1201 Genève, Switzerland.

Telephone: 41 (22) 731 64 29.

CHE0648

INTERNATIONAL SAVE THE CHILDREN ALLIANCE (ISCA) ♦
Alliance internationale des organisations "Save the Children"

147 rue de Lausanne, 1202 Geneva, Switzerland.

Telephone: 41 (22) 31 70 16. *Fax:* 41 (22) 738 08 58. *Contact:* Peter Crowley, Executive Officer.

CHE0649

INTERNATIONAL SCHOOLS ASSOCIATION

CIC Case 20, 1211 Genève 20, Switzerland.

Telephone: 41 (22) 733 67 17. *Fax:* 41 (22) 734 70 82. *Contact:* J. McLellan, President.

OBJECTIVES: To provide advisory and consultative services to international schools. To develop a chain of international and internationally-minded schools.

GENERAL INFORMATION: *Creation:* 1951. *Affiliated to:* Environment Liaison Centre Internaitonal (Nigeria). *Personnel/Total:* 10. *Volunteers:* 10 of which: 1 in developing countries. *Financial sources:* Self-financing: 100%.

PUBLICATIONS: *Periodicals:* Journal (2).

EVALUATION/RESEARCH: Undertakes research activities.

ACTIVITIES IN DEVELOPING REGIONS: Active in 9 country(ies). Works through local field partners. **Sustainable Development Actions:** Children/youth/family; Ecology/environment/biodiversity; Education/training/literacy. **Regions:** East Africa; East Asia; Mexico and Central America; Middle East; South America; South East Asia; West Africa.

INFORMATION AND EDUCATION ACTIVITIES: Topics: Children/youth/family; Ecology/environment/biodiversity; Education/training/literacy; International relations/cooperation/development aid. **Activities:** Conferences/seminars/workshops/training activities; Exchanges/twinning/linking; Formal education; Information and documentation services/data bases; Publishing/audiovisual materials/educational materials.

CHE0650

INTERNATIONAL SERVICE FOR HUMAN RIGHTS ♦ Service
International pour les Droits de l'Homme

P.O. Box 16, 1 rue de Varembé, 1211 Geneva 20, Switzerland.

Telephone: 41 (22) 733 51 23. *Fax:* 41 (22) 733 08 26. *Contact:* Adrien-Claude Zoller, Director.

OBJECTIVES: To provide up-to-date information on human rights work in the United Nations and its specialized agencies. To make better known and facilitate access to the UN procedures, coming to Geneva to testify before the United Nations. To contribute to the promotion of joint NGO initiatives, often through informal meetings.

GENERAL INFORMATION: *Creation:* 1984. *Personnel/Total:* 5. *Budget/Total 1993:* ECU 409000 (US$ 531000). *Financial sources:* Private: 46%. Public: 48%. Self-financing: 6%.

PUBLICATIONS: *Periodicals:* Human Rights Monitor (4) - HR-Documentation-DH (7). *Annual report. List of publications.*

EVALUATION/RESEARCH: Evaluation reports available.

PLANNED ACTIVITIES: The organisation will organise a series of workshops in Geneva on key human rights issues and of training seminars for human rights defenders in their regions of activities, particularly in Africa and the Asia-Pacific region.

ACTIVITIES IN DEVELOPING REGIONS: Present in developing regions. Works through local field partners. **Sustainable Development Actions:** Education/training/literacy; Human rights/peace/conflicts. **Regions:** East Asia; Mexico and Central America; Middle East; North Africa; South America; West Africa.

INFORMATION AND EDUCATION ACTIVITIES: Topics: Human rights/peace/conflicts; Other. **Activities:** Conferences/seminars/workshops/training activities; Exchanges/twinning/linking; Fund raising; Information and documentation services/data bases; Lobbying/advocacy.

CHE0651

INTERNATIONAL SOCIAL SERVICE ♦ Service Social International

32 quai du Seujet, 1201 Genève, Suisse.

Téléphone: 41 (22) 731 74 55. *Fax:* 41 (22) 738 09 49. *Contact:* Damien Ngabonziza, Secrétaire général.

OBJECTIFS: Aider les migrants volontaires ou forcés. Etudier d'un point de vue international les conditions et les conséquences des migrations sur le plan individuel et familial. Formuler les recommandations ou entreprendre toutes les autres actions appropriées en fonction des résultats de ces études. Contribuer à la prévention des problèmes sociaux liés aux migrations ou aux déplacements internationaux.

INFORMATIONS GENERALES: *Création:* 1924. *Type d'organisation:* réseau. *Organisations membres:* 18. *Affiliée à:* CONGO - ICVA - ICSW - FIIG. *Personnel/Total:* 6. *Budget/Total 1993:* ECU 311000 (US$ 403000). *Sources financières:* Privé: 5%. Autofinancement: 95%.

PUBLICATIONS: *Périodiques:* ISS in Brief (3). *Rapport annuel.*

EVALUATION/RECHERCHE: Entreprend des activités de recherche.

PREVISIONS D'ACTIVITES: Mettre au point une banque de données et faire des séminaires sur l'adoption internationale.

COMMENTAIRES: Activités d'information concernant la Communauté des Etats indépendants.

ACTIVITES D'INFORMATION ET D'EDUCATION: Domaines: Enfants/jeunesse/famille; Réfugiés/migrants/groupes ethniques; Secours d'urgence/réfugiés/aide humanitaire. **Activités:** Conférences/séminaires/ateliers/activités de formation; Services d'information et de documentation/bases de données; Édition/documents audiovisuels/documents éducatifs.

CHE0652

INTERNATIONAL YOUTH AND STUDENT MOVEMENT FOR THE UNITED NATIONS

c/- Palais des Nations, 1211 Geneva 10, Switzerland.

CHE0653

INTERNATIONALES KATHOLISCHES MISSIONSWERK (MISSIO)

48 route de la Vignettaz, CP 187, 1704 Fribourg 9, Suisse.

Téléphone: 41 (37) 82 11 20. *Fax:* 41 (37) 82 11 24.

CHE0654

INTERNATIONALES KOMITEE FUR DIE INDIANER AMERIKAS ♦ Incomindios Schweiz

Schützenmattstrasse 37, 4051 Basel, Suisse.

Téléphone: 41 (61) 272 72 49. *Fax:* 41 (61) 272 71 81. *Contact:* Brigitte Vomasch, Helena Nybery, Coordinatrices.

OBJECTIFS: Apporter un soutien politique aux peuples indigènes d'Amérique du Nord, du centre et du Sud, dans le domaine des droits de l'homme et dans leur lutte pour l'obtention de leurs droits politiques, économiques, culturels, religieux et sociaux.

Voir : *Comment utiliser le répertoire,* page 11.

INFORMATIONS GENERALES: *Création:* 1974. *Personnel/Total:* var. *Budget/Total 1993:* ECU 42000 (US$ 54000). *Sources financières:* Privé: 20%. Autofinancement: 80%.

PUBLICATIONS: *Périodiques:* INCOMINDIOS (4). *Rapport annuel.*

COMMENTAIRES: L'organisation agit sur demande des organisations indigènes.

ACTIVITES DANS LES REGIONS EN DEVELOPPEMENT: Intervient directement dans les régions en développement. Intervient par l'intermédiaire d'organisations locales partenaires. **Actions de Développement durable:** Droits de l'Homme/paix/conflits; Écologie/environnement/biodiversité. **Régions:** Amérique du Sud; Mexique et Amerique centrale.

CHE0655

INTERTEAM - ENTWICKLUNGSDIENST DURCH FREIWILLIGEN-EINSATZ (INTERTEAM) ♦ Service de développement par l'envoi de volontaires

Untergeissenstein 10/12, 6000 Luzern 12, Suisse.

Téléphone: 41 (41) 44 67 22. *Fax:* 41 (41) 43 05 80. *Contact:* Luc Bigler, Directeur.

OBJECTIFS: Selectionner et former du personnel qualifié pour travailler dans les pays en développement.

INFORMATIONS GENERALES: *Création:* 1964. *Affiliée à:* Unite (Suisse) - FORUM (Allemagne). *Personnel/Total:* 133. *Salariés:* 8. *Bénévoles:* 125 dont: 125 dans les pays en développement. *Budget/Total 1993:* ECU 1774000 (US$ 2301000). *Sources financières:* Privé: 18%. Public: 82%.

PUBLICATIONS: *Périodiques:* Austausch (7). *Rapport annuel.*

ACTIVITES DANS LES REGIONS EN DEVELOPPEMENT: Intervient dans 19 pays. Maintient une présence locale sur le terrain. Intervient par l'intermédiaire d'organisations locales partenaires. **Actions de Développement durable:** Aliments/famine; Dette/finances/commerce; Droits de l'Homme/paix/conflits; Démocratie/bonne gestion publique/création d'institutions/développement participatif; Développement rural/agriculture; Développement urbain/habitat; Enfants/jeunesse/famille; Envoi de volontaires/experts/assistance technique; Petites entreprises/secteur informel/artisanat; Population/planning familial/démographie; Questions relatives aux femmes; Santé/assainissement/eau; Secours d'urgence/réfugiés/aide humanitaire; Écologie/environnement/biodiversité; Éducation/formation/alphabétisation; Énergie/transport. **Régions:** Afrique australe; Afrique centrale; Afrique de l'Est; Afrique de l'Ouest; Afrique du Nord; Amérique du Sud; Asie centrale et Asie du Sud; Asie de l'Est; Asie du Sud-Est; Caraïbes; Mexique et Amerique centrale; Moyen-Orient; Océanie.

ACTIVITES D'INFORMATION ET D'EDUCATION: **Domaines:** Culture/tradition/religion; Droits de l'Homme/paix/conflits; Développement rural/agriculture; Développement urbain/habitat; Enfants/jeunesse/famille; Paix/conflits ethniques/armement/désarmement; Pauvreté/conditions de vie; Population/planning familial/démographie; Questions relatives aux femmes; Santé/assainissement/eau; Écologie/environnement/biodiversité; Éducation/formation/alphabétisation. **Activités:** Conférences/séminaires/ateliers/activités de formation; Éducation formelle.

CHE0656

INTERTEAM - WALLIS

Rathausstrasse 14, 3930 Visp, Suisse.

Téléphone: 41 (26) 46 48 03.

CHE0657

IRAN DEMOCRATIQUE

Av. Henri-Golay 12B, 1219 Chatelaine, Suisse.

Téléphone: 41 (22) 796 62 15.

CHE0658

ISTITUTO ELVETICO - OPERA DON BOSCO

Via L. Canonica 15, 6900 Lugano, Suisse.

Téléphone: 41 (91) 22 77 33.

CHE0659

LES JARDINS DE COCAGNE SOLIDARITE NORD-SUD

BP 3348, 1211 Genève 3, Suisse.

Téléphone: 41 (22) 794 73 30. *Contact:* Reto Cadotsch.

OBJECTIFS: Apporter un soutien à la structuration des associations paysannes dans la région des trois frontières Mali, Sénégal, Mauritanie.

INFORMATIONS GENERALES: *Création:* 1978. *Affiliée à:* Fédération Genevoise de Coopération (Suisse). *Budget/Total 1993:* ECU 104000 (US$ 135000). *Sources financières:* Privé: 10%. Public: 85%. Autofinancement: 5%.

PUBLICATIONS: *Périodiques:* Bulletin d'information (4). *Rapport annuel.*

EVALUATION/RECHERCHE: Rapports d'évaluation disponibles.

ACTIVITES DANS LES REGIONS EN DEVELOPPEMENT: Intervient directement dans les régions en développement. Intervient dans 2 pays. Intervient par l'intermédiaire d'organisations locales partenaires. **Actions de Développement durable:** Développement rural/agriculture; Questions relatives aux femmes; Santé/assainissement/eau; Écologie/environnement/biodiversité; Éducation/formation/alphabétisation. **Régions:** Afrique de l'Ouest.

ACTIVITES D'INFORMATION ET D'EDUCATION: **Domaines:** Développement rural/agriculture; Questions relatives aux femmes; Santé/assainissement/eau; Écologie/environnement/biodiversité; Éducation/formation/alphabétisation. **Activités:** Campagnes d'information/expositions; Collecte de fonds.

CHE0660

JEMIAT-A-DAWAH ♦ World Islamic Call Society

81 Rue de Lyon, P.O. Box 82, 1203 Geneva, Switzerland.

Telephone: 41 (22) 344 22 68. *Fax:* 41 (22) 344 36 13. *Contact:* Abdul H. Tabibi, Vice President.

OBJECTIVES: To help and provide assistance for refugees and uprooted women. To educate children. To establish schools for needy countries. To implement the aims of the United Nations Charter.

GENERAL INFORMATION: *Creation:* 1970.

PUBLICATIONS: *Periodicals:* Al-Daawa Al-Islamia Watasamou (58). *Annual report. List of publications.*

EVALUATION/RESEARCH: Evaluation reports available. Undertakes research activities.

COMMENTS: The society seeks to strengthen their relations with the humanitarian organisations of the United Nations, particularly with the High Commission of Refugees, UNESCO, WHO, FAO, UNDP and UNICEF. Undertakes activities in the Commonwealth of Independent States. Information activities related to the Commonwealth of Independent States.

ACTIVITIES IN DEVELOPING REGIONS: Present in developing regions. Maintains local field presence. Works through local field partners. **Sustainable Development Actions:** Children/youth/family; Democracy/good governance/institution building/participatory development; Ecology/environment/biodiversity; Education/training/literacy; Emergency relief/refugees/humanitarian assistance; Food/famine; Gender issues/women; Health/sanitation/water; Human rights/peace/conflicts; Rural development/agriculture. **Regions:** Central Africa; Central Asia and South Asia; East Africa; East Asia; Middle East; South America; South East Asia.

INFORMATION AND EDUCATION ACTIVITIES: **Topics:** Children/youth/family; Culture/tradition/religion; Education/training/literacy; Emergency relief/refugees/humanitarian assistance; Food/famine; Gender issues/women; Health/sanitation/water; Human rights/peace/conflicts; International relations/cooperation/development aid; Peace/ethnic conflicts/armament/disarmament; Poverty/living conditions; Racism/xenophobia/antisemitism; Refugees/migrants/ethnic groups. **Activities:** Conferences/seminars/workshops/training activities; Formal education; Information campaigns/exhibitions; Publishing/audiovisual materials/educational materials.

CHE0661

JEUNESSE ETUDIANTE CHRETIENNE (JEC-SUISSE)

30 rue de Candolle, 1205 Genève, Suisse.

Téléphone: 41 (22) 320 96 40. *Fax:* 41 (22) 320 96 40.

OBJECTIFS: Sensibiliser l'opinion publique aux questions de développement. Organiser des échanges avec des mouvements de jeunes du Sud.

INFORMATIONS GENERALES: *Création:* 1937. *Affiliée à:* Jeunesse Etudiante Catholique (France) - Mouvement International des Etudiants Catholiques (France) - Coordination Européenne (Belgique). *Personnel/Total:* 10. *Salariés:* 5. *Bénévoles:* 5. *Budget/Total 1993:* ECU 31000 (US$ 41000). *Sources financières:* Privé: 50%. Public: 30%. Autofinancement: 20%.

PUBLICATIONS: *Périodiques:* Jecris (6). *Rapport annuel.*

COMMENTAIRES: Activités d'information concernant la Communauté des Etats indépendants.

ACTIVITES D'INFORMATION ET D'EDUCATION: Domaines: Droits de l'Homme/paix/conflits; Enfants/jeunesse/famille; Questions relatives aux femmes; Racisme/xénophobie/antisémitisme; Relations économiques internationales/commerce/dette/finances; Réfugiés/migrants/groupes ethniques; Éducation/formation/alphabétisation. **Activités:** Conférences/séminaires/ateliers/activités de formation; Lobbying/plaidoyer; Échanges/parrainage/jumelage.

CHE0662

KINDER IN NOT - HILFSWERK FUR HUNGERNDE KINDER

Forschstrasse 182, 8032 Zürich, Suisse.

CHE0663

KINDER INTERNATIONAL

Jasminweg 15, 8050 Zürich, Suisse.

Téléphone: 41 (1) 311 26 75.

CHE0664

KINDERHILFE BETHLEHEM (KHB) ♦ Caritas Baby Hospital Bethlehem

Wesemlinstrasse 2, P.O Box 6280, 6000 Luzern, Switzerland.

Telephone: 41 (41) 36 57 88. *Fax:* 41 (41) 36 32 50. *Contact:* Klaus Röllin, Managing Director.

OBJECTIVES: To promote mother and child welfare in Israel and the occupied territories. To manage and finance the Caritas Baby Hospital in Bethlehem.

GENERAL INFORMATION: *Creation:* 1963. *Personnel/Total:* 204. *Salaried:* 204 of which: 200 in developing countries. *Budget/Total 1993:* ECU 49577000 (US$ 64293000). *Financial sources:* Private: 67%. Public: 31%. Self-financing: 2%.

PUBLICATIONS: *Annual report.*

EVALUATION/RESEARCH: Evaluation reports available.

ACTIVITIES IN DEVELOPING REGIONS: Present in developing regions. Active in 5 country(ies). Works through local field partners. **Sustainable Development Actions:** Children/youth/family; Education/training/literacy; Food/famine; Gender issues/women; Health/sanitation/water; Sending volunteers/experts/technical assistance. **Regions:** Middle East.

INFORMATION AND EDUCATION ACTIVITIES: Topics: Children/youth/family; Education/training/literacy; Food/famine; Gender issues/women; Health/sanitation/water; Poverty/living conditions. **Activities:** Fund raising; Information and documentation services/data bases; Information campaigns/exhibitions; Publishing/audiovisual materials/educational materials.

CHE0665

KODIS-FACHSTELLE FUR BERUFSBILDUNG IN ENTWICKLUNGSLANDERN (KODIS) ♦ Centre for Technical Education and Vocational Training in Developing Countries

Wartstrasse 6, 8400 Winterthur, Switzerland.

Telephone: 41 (52) 212 51 05. *Fax:* 41 (52) 213 57 17. *Contact:* Rudolf Batliner.

OBJECTIVES: To support project managers and vocational instructors working in developing countries to establish or improve vocational training centres, and to assist them in selecting appropriate teaching and training aids.

GENERAL INFORMATION: *Creation:* 1977. *Type of organisation:* association of NGOs. *Member organisations:* 9. *Personnel/Total:* 4. *Salaried:* 4. *Financial sources:* Public: 55%. Self-financing: 45%.

PUBLICATIONS: *Periodicals:* Kodis-News (2).

COMMENTS: Undertakes activities in the Commonwealth of Independent States. Information activities related to the Commonwealth of Independent States.

ACTIVITIES IN DEVELOPING REGIONS: Present in developing regions. Active in 8 country(ies). Maintains local field presence. Works through local field partners. **Sustainable Development Actions:** Education/training/literacy; Small enterprises/informal sector/handicrafts. **Regions:** Central Asia and South Asia; Mexico and Central America; South America; South East Asia; Southern Africa.

INFORMATION AND EDUCATION ACTIVITIES: Topics: Education/training/literacy; International relations/cooperation/development aid. **Activities:** Conferences/seminars/workshops/training activities; Formal education; Information and documentation services/data bases.

CHE0666

KOMITEE FUR DIE MENSCHENRECHTE IN KUBA

Spalenberg 34, 4051 Basel, Suisse.

Téléphone: 41 (61) 25 55 94.

CHE0667

KOMITEE FUR DIE VERTEIDIGUNG DER CHILENISCHE KULTUR ♦ Comité de défense de la culture chilienne

Postfach 154, 8030 Zürich, Suisse.

Téléphone: 41 (22) 242 64 59. *Fax:* 41 (22) 242 64 59. *Contact:* Humberto Cardenas.

OBJECTIFS: Créer des emplois au Chili. Diffuser la culture chilienne. Organiser des échanges. Offrir des possibilités d'éducation et de formation professionnelle gratuite à des enfants et jeunes au Chili. Informer sur la situation au Chili.

INFORMATIONS GENERALES: *Création:* 1979. *Personnel/Total:* 12. *Bénévoles:* 12. *Budget/Total 1993:* ECU 39000 (US$ 51000). *Sources financières:* Privé: 45%. Public: 5%. Autofinancement: 50%.

PREVISIONS D'ACTIVITES: Promotion d'un projet d'école professionnelle pour la pêche.

ACTIVITES DANS LES REGIONS EN DEVELOPPEMENT: Intervient dans 1 pays. Intervient par l'intermédiaire d'organisations locales partenaires. **Actions de Développement durable:** Éducation/formation/alphabétisation. **Régions:** Amérique du Sud.

ACTIVITES D'INFORMATION ET D'EDUCATION: Domaines: Culture/tradition/religion; Droits de l'Homme/paix/conflits. **Activités:** Campagnes d'information/expositions; Conférences/séminaires/ateliers/activités de formation; Radiodiffusion/manifestations culturelles; Édition/documents audiovisuels/documents éducatifs; Éducation formelle.

CHE0668

KOMITEE GEGEN DIE AUSHOHLUNG DES ASYLRECHTS, ARBEITSSTELLE FUR ASYLFRAGEN ♦ Comité contre le démantèlement du droit d'asile - Bureau pour les questions dans le domaine de l'asile

Postfach 6966, 3001 Bern, Suisse.

Téléphone: 41 (31) 312 40 32. *Fax:* 41 (31) 312 40 45. *Contact:* Jürg Lüdi, Secrétaire.

OBJECTIFS: Montrer un engagement pour les réfugiés et organiser le lobbying au niveau national. Entretenir des archives et une documentation sur les questions d'asile, de racisme et de la migration. Publier un

Voir : *Comment utiliser le répertoire*, page 11.

guide d'adresses des organisations concernées par l'asile, la documentation et les archives pour le public.

INFORMATIONS GENERALES: *Création:* 1986. *Type d'organisation:* réseau. *Affiliée à:* Coordination Suisse Asile - UNITED (Hollande). *Personnel/Total:* 11. *Salariés:* 1. *Bénévoles:* 10. *Budget/Total 1993:* ECU 40000 (US$ 52000). *Sources financières:* Privé: 65%. Autofinancement: 35%.

PUBLICATIONS: *Périodiques:* Mitteilung (4). *Rapport annuel. Liste des publications.*

EVALUATION/RECHERCHE: Rapports d'évaluation disponibles. Entreprend des activités de recherche.

ACTIVITES DANS LES REGIONS EN DEVELOPPEMENT: Intervient par l'intermédiaire d'organisations locales partenaires.

ACTIVITES D'INFORMATION ET D'EDUCATION: Domaines: Culture/tradition/religion; Droits de l'Homme/paix/conflits; Enfants/jeunesse/famille; Paix/conflits ethniques/armement/désarmement; Questions relatives aux femmes; Racisme/xénophobie/antisémitisme; Réfugiés/migrants/groupes ethniques; Secours d'urgence/réfugiés/aide humanitaire. **Activités:** Campagnes d'information/expositions; Lobbying/plaidoyer; Services d'information et de documentation/bases de données; Édition/documents audiovisuels/documents éducatifs.

CHE0669

KOMMISSION FUR ENTWICKLUNGSFRAGEN DER UNIVERSITAT UND ETH ZURICH (KFE) ♦ Commission for Development Questions of the University of Zürich

Leonhardstrasse 15, 8001 Zürich, Switzerland.

Telephone: 41 (1) 632 47 22. *Fax:* 41 (1) 261 05 42. *Contact:* Amanda Weibel.

OBJECTIVES: To raise awareness among the university community and general public of the issues and problems related to development aid.

GENERAL INFORMATION: *Type of organisation:* coordinating body. *Affiliated to:* Erklärung von Bern (Switzerland) - Arbeitkreis Tourismus und Entwicklung -Amnesty International - Helvekas - Lora - Schwiez Arbeiterinnen Hilfswerk -Grouppe Schwiez-Philippinen - CINFO - Terre des Hommes - Unité - Caritas - HEKS - Aktion Finanzplatz. *Personnel/Total:* 20. *Volunteers:* 20. *Budget/Total 1993:* ECU 17000 (US$ 22000).

PUBLICATIONS: *List of publications.*

PLANNED ACTIVITIES: KFE is planning projects on health in Calcutta; ecological agriculture in Ecuador; electricity infrastructure in Ghana.

ACTIVITIES IN DEVELOPING REGIONS: Present in developing regions. Active in 7 country(ies). Works through local field partners. **Sustainable Development Actions:** Children/youth/family; Education/training/literacy; Energy/transport; Gender issues/women; Health/sanitation/water; Human rights/peace/conflicts; Rural development/agriculture; Small enterprises/informal sector/handicrafts. **Regions:** Central Asia and South Asia; South America; South East Asia; West Africa.

INFORMATION AND EDUCATION ACTIVITIES: Topics: Children/youth/family; Culture/tradition/religion; Ecology/environment/biodiversity; Education/training/literacy; Emergency relief/refugees/humanitarian assistance; Employment/unemployment; Food/famine; Gender issues/women; Health/sanitation/water; Human rights/peace/conflicts; International economic relations/trade/debt/finance; International relations/cooperation/development aid; Peace/ethnic conflicts/armament/disarmament; Population/family planning/demography; Poverty/living conditions; Racism/xenophobia/antisemitism; Refugees/migrants/ethnic groups; Rural development/agriculture; Urban development/habitat. **Activities:** Conferences/seminars/workshops/training activities; Information campaigns/exhibitions.

CHE0670

KOOPERATION EVANGELISCHER KIRCHEN UND MISSIONEN DER DEUTSCHEN SCHWEIZ (KEM) ♦ Co-operation of Protestant Churches and Missions of German-speaking Switzerland

Missionstrasse 21, 4003 Basel, Switzerland.

Telephone: 41 (61) 25 37 25. *Contact:* Willy Gysin.

CHE0671

KOORDINATIONSSTELLE FUR OEKUMENE, MISSION UND ENTWICKLUNGSZUSAMMENARBEIT (OEME) ♦ Bureau de coordination pour les questions d'oecuménisme, de mission et de développement

Bürkiweg 8, 3007 Bern, Suisse.

Téléphone: 41 (31) 371 63 27. *Fax:* 41 (31) 371 12 64. *Contact:* Rev. Albrecht Hieber.

OBJECTIFS: Organiser des animations dans les paroisses et auprès des groupes intéressés par dans les questions de développement. Maintenir des contacts avec des églises partenaires d'outre-mer.

INFORMATIONS GENERALES: *Création:* 1972. *Personnel/Total:* 3. *Salariés:* 3. *Sources financières:* Public: 100%.

PUBLICATIONS: *Périodiques:* Rapport annuel (1). *Rapport annuel.*

ACTIVITES DANS LES REGIONS EN DEVELOPPEMENT: Intervient dans 5 pays. Intervient par l'intermédiaire d'organisations locales partenaires. **Actions de Développement durable:** Développement rural/agriculture; Questions relatives aux femmes; Éducation/formation/alphabétisation. **Régions:** Afrique australe; Afrique de l'Ouest; Amérique du Sud; Moyen-Orient.

ACTIVITES D'INFORMATION ET D'EDUCATION: Domaines: Droits de l'Homme/paix/conflits; Développement rural/agriculture; Racisme/xénophobie/antisémitisme. **Activités:** Collecte de fonds; Conférences/séminaires/ateliers/activités de formation.

CHE0672

KOREAN RELIEF ♦ Organisme d'entraide pour les orphelins coréens

Gemeindestrasse 26, 8032 Zürich, Suisse.

Téléphone: 41 (21) 26 20 20.

CHE0673

KULTUR UND ENTWICKLUNG ARBEITSGEMEINSCHAFT ♦ Culture and Development

Postfach 632, Bollwerk 35, 3000 Bern 7, Switzerland.

Telephone: 41 (31) 311 62 60. *Fax:* 41 (31) 312 24 02. *Contact:* Hanna Rutishauser.

OBJECTIVES: To initiate and promote inter-cultural encounters and dialogue to dispel ethnic prejudice. To undertake educational, informational and consciousness-raising activities as part of a comprehensive strategy of development. To collect and disseminate information about art and culture of Africa, Latin America and Asia. To focus on helping unknown artists gain access to the Swiss cultural scene.

GENERAL INFORMATION: *Creation:* 1985. *Type of organisation:* coordinating body. *Member organisations:* 7. *Personnel/Total:* 3. *Salaried:* 3. *Budget/Total 1993:* ECU 185000 (US$ 240000). *Financial sources:* Private: 50%. Public: 50%.

PUBLICATIONS: *Annual report.*

INFORMATION AND EDUCATION ACTIVITIES: Topics: Culture/tradition/religion; Ecology/environment/biodiversity; Education/training/literacy; International economic relations/trade/debt/finance; International relations/cooperation/development aid. **Activities:** Formal education; Information and documentation services/data bases.

CHE0674

KULTURELLE GESELLSCHAFT REPUBLIK KOREA-SCHWEIZ ♦ Société Culturelle République de Corée-Suisse

Postfach, 3001 Bern, Suisse.

Téléphone: 41 (31) 301 28 44. *Fax:* 41 (31) 301 31 19. *Contact:* Lilo Berger-Kirchner.

OBJECTIFS: Développer les échanges culturels, les liens d'amitié (échange d'étudiants, cours de langue...) entre la Suisse et la Corée.

INFORMATIONS GENERALES: *Création:* 1978. *Personnel/Total:* 7. *Bénévoles:* 7. *Budget/Total 1993:* ECU 4000 (US$ 5000). *Sources financières:* Privé: 7%. Autofinancement: 93%.

See: *How to Use the Directory*, page 11.

PUBLICATIONS: *Périodiques:* Bulletin de la Société Culturelle République de Corée-Suisse (2).

PREVISIONS D'ACTIVITES: Echange d'étudiants et d'artistes.

ACTIVITES DANS LES REGIONS EN DEVELOPPEMENT: Intervient dans 1 pays. Intervient par l'intermédiaire d'organisations locales partenaires. **Actions de Développement durable:** Éducation/formation/alphabétisation. **Régions:** Asie de l'Est.

ACTIVITES D'INFORMATION ET D'EDUCATION: Domaines: Culture/ tradition/religion; Enfants/jeunesse/famille; Éducation/formation/alphabétisation. **Activités:** Échanges/parrainage/jumelage.

CHE0675
KURDISTAN INDEPENDANT

Av. Henri-Golay 12B, 1219 Chatelaine, Suisse.

Téléphone: 41 (22) 796 62 15.

CHE0676
LATEINAMERIKA-KOMITEE

Postfach 781, 8401 Winterthur, Suisse.

Téléphone: 41 (52) 25 15 35.

CHE0677
LA LECHE LEAGUE INTERNATIONAL

Alte Landstrasse 89, 8802 Kilchberg, Switzerland.

Telephone: 41 (1) 715 19 46. *Fax:* 41 (1) 202 30 93.

CHE0678
LIGUE INTERNATIONALE DES FEMMES POUR LA PAIX ET LA LIBERTE (LIFPL) ♦ Women International League for Peace and Freedom

Rue de Varembé 1, 1211 Genève 20, Suisse.

Téléphone: 41 (22) 733 62 75.

CHE0679
LIGUE SUISSE DES DROITS DE L'HOMME

Avenue Sainte-Clotilde 9, 1205 Genève, Suisse.

Téléphone: 41 (22) 735 39 38.

CHE0680
LIGUE SUISSE POUR LA PROTECTION DE LA NATURE (LSPN)

Case postale, 4020 Bâle, Suisse.

Téléphone: 41 (61) 317 91 91. *Fax:* 41 (61) 317 91 66. *Contact:* Otto Sieber, Secrétaire général.

OBJECTIFS: Agir pour la protection de la nature et de l'environnement.

INFORMATIONS GENERALES: Création: 1909. *Personnel/Total:* 1080. *Salariés:* 80. *Bénévoles:* 1000. *Budget/Total 1993:* ECU 5219000 (US$ 6768000). *Sources financières:* Privé: 50%. *Public:* 5%. *Autofinancement:* 25%.

PUBLICATIONS: *Périodiques:* Protection de la Nature (8) - Suivez nos Traces (4). *Rapport annuel.*

EVALUATION/RECHERCHE: Rapports d'évaluation disponibles. Entreprend des activités de recherche.

COMMENTAIRES: Intervient dans la Communauté des Etats indépendants.

ACTIVITES DANS LES REGIONS EN DEVELOPPEMENT: Intervient par l'intermédiaire d'organisations locales partenaires.

ACTIVITES D'INFORMATION ET D'EDUCATION: Domaines: Écologie/ environnement/biodiversité. **Activités:** Campagnes d'information/expositions; Conférences/séminaires/ateliers/activités de formation; Lobbying/plaidoyer; Édition/documents audiovisuels/documents éducatifs; Éducation formelle.

CHE0681
LIMMAT FOUNDATION ♦ LIMMAT STIFTUNG

Postfach 564, Rosenbühlstrasse 32, 8044 Zürich, Suisse.

Téléphone: 41 (1) 252 28 38. *Fax:* 41 (1) 252 28 77. *Contact:* François Geinoz, Directeur.

OBJECTIFS: Soutenir des projets à but non lucratif, en particulier dans les domaines de la coopération pour le développement et de la formation.

INFORMATIONS GENERALES: *Création:* 1972. *Personnel/Total:* 6. *Salariés:* 6. *Budget/Total 1993:* ECU 678000 (US$ 880000). *Sources financières:* Privé: 78%. *Public:* 2%. *Autofinancement:* 20%.

PUBLICATIONS: *Périodiques:* Familie und Erziehung (4). *Rapport annuel.*

PREVISIONS D'ACTIVITES: Projets de formation rofessionnelle, en particulier des femmes.

COMMENTAIRES: Intervient dans la Communauté des Etats indépendants.

ACTIVITES DANS LES REGIONS EN DEVELOPPEMENT: Intervient directement dans les régions en développement. Intervient dans 11 pays. Intervient par l'intermédiaire d'organisations locales partenaires. **Actions de Développement durable:** Aliments/famine; Développement rural/agriculture; Enfants/jeunesse/famille; Petites entreprises/secteur informel/artisanat; Questions relatives aux femmes; Éducation/formation/alphabétisation. **Régions:** Afrique centrale; Afrique de l'Est; Amérique du Sud; Asie du Sud-Est.

ACTIVITES D'INFORMATION ET D'EDUCATION: Domaines: Développement rural/agriculture; Emploi/chômage; Enfants/jeunesse/famille; Questions relatives aux femmes; Éducation/formation/alphabétisation. **Activités:** Conférences/séminaires/ateliers/activités de formation; Échanges/parrainage/jumelage; Éducation formelle.

CHE0682
LUTHERAN WORLD FEDERATION - DEPARTMENT FOR WORLD SERVICE (LWF/WS)

Route de Ferney 150, P.O. Box 2100, 1211 Geneva 2, Switzerland.

Telephone: 41 (22) 791 61 11. *Fax:* 41 (22) 791 05 28. *E-mail:* InternetLUTH-SERV@geo2.geonet.de. *Contact:* Brian W. Nelder, Director.

OBJECTIVES: To provide humanitarian assistance and longer term development aid to all those in need regardless of race, sex, religion or political views.

GENERAL INFORMATION: *Creation:* 1947. *Affiliated to:* ICVA - CONGO. *Personnel/Total:* 5100. *Salaried:* 5100 of which: 4998 in developing countries. *Budget/Total 1993:* ECU 75714000 (US$ 98189000). *Financial sources:* Private: 75%. *Public:* 25%.

EVALUATION/RESEARCH: Evaluation reports available. Undertakes research activities.

COMMENTS: Undertakes activities in the Commonwealth of Independent States.

ACTIVITIES IN DEVELOPING REGIONS: Present in developing regions. Active in 22 country(ies). Maintains local field presence. Works through local field partners. **Sustainable Development Actions:** Children/ youth/family; Democracy/good governance/institution building/participatory development; Ecology/environment/biodiversity; Education/ training/literacy; Emergency relief/refugees/humanitarian assistance; Energy/transport; Food/famine; Gender issues/women; Health/sanitation/water; Human rights/peace/conflicts; Population/family planning/ demography; Rural development/agriculture; Small enterprises/informal sector/handicrafts; Urban development/habitat. **Regions:** Caribbean; Central Asia and South Asia; East Africa; Mexico and Central America; Middle East; North Africa; South America; South East Asia; Southern Africa; West Africa.

INFORMATION AND EDUCATION ACTIVITIES: Topics: Culture/tradition/religion; Ecology/environment/biodiversity; Education/training/literacy; Emergency relief/refugees/humanitarian assistance; Food/famine; Gender issues/women; Health/sanitation/water; Human rights/peace/

Voir : *Comment utiliser le répertoire,* page 11.

conflicts; Peace/ethnic conflicts/armament/disarmament; Population/ family planning/demography; Refugees/migrants/ethnic groups; Rural development/agriculture; Urban development/habitat. **Activities:** Conferences/seminars/workshops/training activities; Formal education.

CHE0683

MEDECINS SANS FRONTIERES, SUISSE (MSF-CH)

Clos de la Fonderie 3, 1227 Carouge/Genève, Suisse.

Téléphone: 41 (22) 300 44 45. *Fax:* 41 (21) 300 44 14. *Contact:* Dr. B. Tullen, Directeur.

OBJECTIFS: Venir en aide dans le domaine de la santé, à toute population en situation de détresse ainsi qu'aux victimes de catastrophes naturelles, d'accidents collectifs et de conflits. Apporter une assistance médicale, institutionnelle et une formation de personnel de santé.

INFORMATIONS GENERALES: *Création:* 1981. *Type d'organisation:* réseau. *Organisations membres:* 6. *Personnel/Total:* 84. *Salariés:* 13. *Bénévoles:* 71 dont: 59 dans les pays en développement. *Budget/ Total 1993:* ECU 4227000 (US$ 5482000). *Sources financières:* *Privé:* 45%. *Public:* 52%. *Autofinancement:* 3%.

PUBLICATIONS: *Périodiques:* Journal MSF (4). *Rapport annuel. Liste des publications.*

EVALUATION/RECHERCHE: Rapports d'évaluation disponibles. Entreprend des activités de recherche.

COMMENTAIRES: Intervient dans la Communauté des Etats indépendants. Activités d'information concernant la Communauté des Etats indépendants.

ACTIVITES DANS LES REGIONS EN DEVELOPPEMENT: Intervient directement dans les régions en développement. Intervient dans 11 pays. Maintient une présence locale sur le terrain. **Actions de Développement durable:** Aliments/famine; Questions relatives aux femmes; Santé/assainissement/eau; Secours d'urgence/réfugiés/aide humanitaire. **Régions:** Afrique australe; Afrique centrale; Afrique de l'Est; Amérique du Sud; Asie du Sud-Est; Mexique et Amerique centrale.

ACTIVITES D'INFORMATION ET D'EDUCATION: Domaines: Aliments/ famine; Autres; Enfants/jeunesse/famille; Pauvreté/conditions de vie; Population/planning familial/démographie; Questions relatives aux femmes; Réfugiés/migrants/groupes ethniques; Santé/assainissement/ eau; Secours d'urgence/réfugiés/aide humanitaire. **Activités:** Campagnes d'information/expositions; Conférences/séminaires/ateliers/activités de formation; Lobbying/plaidoyer; Radiodiffusion/manifestations culturelles; Services d'information et de documentation/bases de données; Échanges/parrainage/jumelage; Édition/documents audiovisuels/ documents éducatifs; Éducation formelle.

CHE0684

MEDICAL ENVIRONMENTAL DEVELOPMENT WITH AIR ASSISTANCE (MEDAIR)

77B rue de Genève, 1004 Lausanne, Suisse.

Téléphone: 41 (21) 624 55 33. *Fax:* 41 (21) 625 25 60. *Courrier électronique:* CompuServe 100276,1067. *Contact:* Dr. Erik Volkmar.

OBJECTIFS: Mettre en place une assistance technique qualifiée pour faire face à la souffrance humaine dans des situations d'urgence et de catastrophe.Soutenir l'action médicale, sociale et spirituelle dans les pays sinistrés et promouvoir la formation de personnel national compétent dans ces pays. Former des volontaires de l'urgence en Europe. Mettre à la disposition des pays sinistrés du matériel et des produits de première nécessité.

INFORMATIONS GENERALES: *Création:* 1989. *Personnel/Total:* 186. *Salariés:* 124 dont: 124 dans les pays en développement. *Bénévoles:* 62 dont: 56 dans les pays en développement. *Budget/ Total 1993:* ECU 1200000 (US$ 1557000). *Sources financières:* Privé: 69%. *Public:* 28%. *Autofinancement:* 3%.

PUBLICATIONS: *Périodiques:* Medair News (24). *Rapport annuel.*

COMMENTAIRES: Intervient dans la Communauté des Etats indépendants.

ACTIVITES DANS LES REGIONS EN DEVELOPPEMENT: Intervient directement dans les régions en développement. Intervient dans 5 pays.

Maintient une présence locale sur le terrain. Intervient par l'intermédiaire d'organisations locales partenaires. **Actions de Développement durable:** Aliments/famine; Développement rural/agriculture; Envoi de volontaires/experts/assistance technique; Questions relatives aux femmes; Santé/assainissement/eau; Secours d'urgence/réfugiés/aide humanitaire; Énergie/transport. **Régions:** Afrique centrale; Afrique de l'Est; Afrique de l'Ouest; Moyen-Orient.

ACTIVITES D'INFORMATION ET D'EDUCATION: Domaines: Aliments/ famine; Développement rural/agriculture; Développement urbain/habitat; Paix/conflits ethniques/armement/désarmement; Pauvreté/conditions de vie; Secours d'urgence/réfugiés/aide humanitaire. **Activités:** Campagnes d'information/expositions; Collecte de fonds; Conférences/ séminaires/ateliers/activités de formation; Lobbying/plaidoyer; Édition/ documents audiovisuels/documents éducatifs.

CHE0685

MEDICAL WOMEN'S INTERNATIONAL ASSOCIATION

34 chemin Pont Ceard, 1290 Versoix, Switzerland.

Telephone: 41 (22) 755 29 29.

CHE0686

MEDICAMENTS POUR L'AFRIQUE (MEDAF)

C/ D.Bourgeois , route de Neuchâtel 8, 2022 Bevaix, Suisse.

Téléphone: 41 (38) 46 13 66. *Contact:* Dr. Dominique Bourgeois.

OBJECTIFS: Apporter un soutien à l'action médicale, sociale et spirituelle de l'hôpital de Bébalem au sud du Tchad. Participer à la sélection et à la formation du personnel expatrié et lui apporter un soutien financier. Participer à la formation du personnel indigène local.

INFORMATIONS GENERALES: *Affiliée à:* MEDAF (France) - MEDAF (Allemagne.). *Personnel/Total:* 4. *Salariés:* 3 dont: 3 dans les pays en développement. *Bénévoles:* 1. *Budget/Total 1993:* ECU 21000 (US$ 27000). *Sources financières:* Privé: 100%.

PUBLICATIONS: *Périodiques:* (4).

EVALUATION/RECHERCHE: Rapports d'évaluation disponibles.

PREVISIONS D'ACTIVITES: Aide logistique à la rénovation et à la reconstruction de l'hôpital de Bébalem.

COMMENTAIRES: MEDAF est une petite association liée aux autres MEDAF. La MEDAF France est l'intervenant le plus important.

ACTIVITES DANS LES REGIONS EN DEVELOPPEMENT: Intervient directement dans les régions en développement. Intervient dans 1 pays. Maintient une présence locale sur le terrain. Intervient par l'intermédiaire d'organisations locales partenaires. **Actions de Développement durable:** Aliments/famine; Santé/assainissement/eau; Secours d'urgence/ réfugiés/aide humanitaire. **Régions:** Afrique de l'Ouest.

ACTIVITES D'INFORMATION ET D'EDUCATION: Domaines: Santé/ assainissement/eau. **Activités:** Collecte de fonds.

CHE0687

MEDICUS MUNDI, SCHWEIZ ♦ Medicus Mundi Suisse

Unterer Rheinweg 54, 4057 Basel, Suisse.

Téléphone: 41 (61) 692 42 85. *Fax:* 41 (61) 692 68 38. *Contact:* Dr. N. Lorenz, Président.

OBJECTIFS: Favoriser les échanges d'idées et la coordination entre les membres de l'association afin de promouvoir les soins de santé primaires. Recruter des médecins pour les projets de l'association. Former les futurs médecins du développement. Conseiller le personnel médical envoyé dans le Tiers Monde. Evaluer des projets en cours ou en voie de planification.

INFORMATIONS GENERALES: *Création:* 1973. *Affiliée à:* Medicus Mundi International (Belgique). *Personnel/Total:* 8. *Salariés:* 1. *Bénévoles:* 7. *Budget/Total 1993:* ECU 49000 (US$ 64000).

PUBLICATIONS: *Périodiques:* Bulletin (4). *Rapport annuel.*

PREVISIONS D'ACTIVITES: Lutte contre l'inaccessibilité des services de santé aux pauvres. Développement plus poussé de la santé urbaine dans les bidonvilles.

See: *How to Use the Directory*, page 11.

ACTIVITES DANS LES REGIONS EN DEVELOPPEMENT: Intervient dans 30 pays. **Actions de Développement durable:** Démocratie/bonne gestion publique/création d'institutions/développement participatif; Développement urbain/habitat; Enfants/jeunesse/famille; Envoi de volontaires/experts/assistance technique; Questions relatives aux femmes; Santé/assainissement/eau; Secours d'urgence/réfugiés/aide humanitaire; Éducation/formation/alphabétisation. **Régions:** Afrique australe; Afrique centrale; Afrique de l'Est; Afrique de l'Ouest; Afrique du Nord; Amérique du Sud; Asie centrale et Asie du Sud; Moyen-Orient; Océanie.

ACTIVITES D'INFORMATION ET D'EDUCATION: Domaines: Aliments/famine; Culture/tradition/religion; Développement rural/agriculture; Développement urbain/habitat; Enfants/jeunesse/famille; Paix/conflits ethniques/armement/désarmement; Pauvreté/conditions de vie; Population/planning familial/démographie; Questions relatives aux femmes; Racisme/xénophobie/antisémitisme; Relations internationales/coopération/aide au développement; Relations économiques internationales/commerce/dette/finances; Réfugiés/migrants/groupes ethniques; Santé/assainissement/eau; Secours d'urgence/réfugiés/aide humanitaire; Écologie/environnement/biodiversité; Éducation/formation/alphabétisation. **Activités:** Campagnes d'information/expositions; Collecte de fonds; Conférences/séminaires/ateliers/activités de formation; Lobbying/plaidoyer; Radiodiffusion/manifestations culturelles; Services d'information et de documentation/bases de données; Échanges/parrainage/jumelage; Édition/documents audiovisuels/documents éducatifs; Éducation formelle.

CHE0688
MEDISWISS

Schützenmattstrasse 22, 6020 Emmenbrücke, Suisse.

Téléphone: 41 (41) 55 13 00. **Fax:** 41 (41) 55 13 05. **Contact:** Dr. H.R. Lüssy, Directeur.

OBJECTIFS: Approvisionner des stations de santé situées dans les pays en développement, en médicaments et matériel médical et les assister dans leurs programmes de santé communautaire. Promouvoir la culture des pays du Tiers-Monde en Suisse.

INFORMATIONS GENERALES: Création: 1983. **Personnel/Total:** 4. *Salariés:* 4. **Sources financières:** *Privé:* 40%. *Autofinancement:* 60%.

COMMENTAIRES: Intervient dans la Communauté des Etats indépendants.

ACTIVITES DANS LES REGIONS EN DEVELOPPEMENT: Intervient dans 28 pays. Intervient par l'intermédiaire d'organisations locales partenaires. **Actions de Développement durable:** Santé/assainissement/eau. **Régions:** Afrique centrale; Afrique de l'Est; Afrique de l'Ouest; Afrique du Nord; Amérique du Sud; Asie centrale et Asie du Sud; Asie du Sud-Est.

ACTIVITES D'INFORMATION ET D'EDUCATION: Domaines: Santé/assainissement/eau. **Activités:** Collecte de fonds; Services d'information et de documentation/bases de données; Éducation formelle.

CHE0689
MENNONITE CENTRAL COMMITTEE

52 Grand Rue 114, 2720 Tramelan, Switzerland.

Telephone: 41 (32) 97 57 56. **Fax:** 41 (32) 97 53 35. **E-mail:** CompuServe 100333, 3472. **Contact:** John A. Lapp, Executive Secretary.

OBJECTIVES: To demonstrate God's love through committed women and men who work among people suffering from poverty, conflict, oppression and national disasters.

GENERAL INFORMATION: Creation: 1920. **Type of organisation:** association of NGOs. **Personnel/Total:** 1210. *Salaried:* 275. *Volunteers:* 935 of which: 389 in developing countries. **Budget/Total 1993:** ECU 27145000 (US$ 35202000). **Financial sources:** *Private:* 77%. *Public:* 6%. *Self-financing:* 17%.

PUBLICATIONS: *Annual report. List of publications.*

EVALUATION/RESEARCH: Undertakes research activities.

PLANNED ACTIVITIES: The Mennonite Central Committee will explore new programmes among indigenous peoples in Latin America and Africa.

COMMENTS: Undertakes activities in the Commonwealth of Independent States. Information activities related to the Commonwealth of Independent States.

ACTIVITIES IN DEVELOPING REGIONS: Present in developing regions. Active in 42 country(ies). Maintains local field presence. Works through local field partners. **Sustainable Development Actions:** Children/youth/family; Debt/finance/trade; Democracy/good governance/institution building/participatory development; Ecology/environment/biodiversity; Education/training/literacy; Emergency relief/refugees/humanitarian assistance; Energy/transport; Food/famine; Gender issues/women; Health/sanitation/water; Human rights/peace/conflicts; Population/family planning/demography; Rural development/agriculture; Sending volunteers/experts/technical assistance; Small enterprises/informal sector/handicrafts; Urban development/habitat. **Regions:** Caribbean; Central Africa; Central Asia and South Asia; East Africa; East Asia; Mexico and Central America; Middle East; North Africa; Oceania; South America; South East Asia; Southern Africa; West Africa.

INFORMATION AND EDUCATION ACTIVITIES: Topics: Children/youth/family; Culture/tradition/religion; Ecology/environment/biodiversity; Education/training/literacy; Emergency relief/refugees/humanitarian assistance; Employment/unemployment; Food/famine; Gender issues/women; Health/sanitation/water; Human rights/peace/conflicts; International economic relations/trade/debt/finance; International relations/cooperation/development aid; Peace/ethnic conflicts/armament/disarmament; Population/family planning/demography; Poverty/living conditions; Racism/xenophobia/antisemitism; Refugees/migrants/ethnic groups; Rural development/agriculture; Urban development/habitat. **Activities:** Broadcasting/cultural events; Conferences/seminars/workshops/training activities; Exchanges/twinning/linking; Formal education; Fund raising; Information and documentation services/data bases; Information campaigns/exhibitions; Lobbying/advocacy; Networking/electronic telecommunications; Publishing/audiovisual materials/educational materials.

CHE0690
MISSION BIBLIQUE EN COTE D'IVOIRE

Les Vieux Chemins, 2712 Le Fuet, Suisse.

Téléphone: 41 (32) 91 49 75.

CHE0691
MISSION DER BRUDERGEMEINE - SCHWEIZER ZWEIG ♦
Moravian Mission in Switzerland

Missionsstrasse 21, 4003 Basel, Switzerland.

Telephone: 41 (61) 268 83 11. **Fax:** 41 (61) 268 83 11. **Contact:** Samuel Preiswerk.

OBJECTIVES: To promote the education of the lay people, pastors and children in the Moravian Churches in Tanzania. To train Kimbanguist pastors in Zaire for their work in co-operation with partner churches in their country.

GENERAL INFORMATION: Creation: 1734. **Affiliated to:** KEM (Switzerland). **Personnel/Total:** 3. *Salaried:* 3 of which: 2 in developing countries. **Budget/Total 1993:** ECU 484000 (US$ 628000). **Financial sources:** *Private:* 70%. *Public:* 30%.

PUBLICATIONS: Periodicals: Kommherüber (4). *Annual report.*

COMMENTS: Most of the projects are carried out by the partner churches with the financial support of the Moravian Mission.

ACTIVITIES IN DEVELOPING REGIONS: Present in developing regions. Active in 2 country(ies). Maintains local field presence. Works through local field partners. **Sustainable Development Actions:** Debt/finance/trade; Democracy/good governance/institution building/participatory development; Ecology/environment/biodiversity; Education/training/literacy; Health/sanitation/water; Sending volunteers/experts/technical assistance; Small enterprises/informal sector/handicrafts. **Regions:** Central Africa; East Africa.

INFORMATION AND EDUCATION ACTIVITIES: **Topics:** Children/youth/ family; Education/training/literacy; Gender issues/women; Health/sanitation/water. **Activities:** Fund raising.

CHE0692

MISSION EVANGELIQUE CONTRE LA LEPRE ♦ The Leprosy Mission

Chemin de Réchoz 3, 1027 Lonay, Suisse.

Téléphone: 41 (21) 801 50 81. *Fax:* 41 (21) 803 19 48. *Contact:* Eric Chollet, Directeur.

OBJECTIFS: Soigner les malades de la lèpre, notamment en Asie du Sud, et entreprendre avec ces malades des activités de réadaptation.

INFORMATIONS GENERALES: *Création:* 1905. *Type d'organisation:* regroupement d'ONG. *Organisations membres:* 23. *Affiliée à:* TLM (Royaume-Uni). *Personnel/Total:* 7. *Salariés:* 5 dont: 2 dans les pays en développement. *Bénévoles:* 2. *Budget/Total 1993:* ECU 1044000 (US$ 1353000). *Sources financières:* Privé: 95%. *Public:* 5%.

PUBLICATIONS: *Périodiques:* Associés (2) - En Action (4) - Aktion Lepra (4). *Rapport annuel.*

ACTIVITES DANS LES REGIONS EN DEVELOPPEMENT: Intervient dans 30 pays. **Actions de Développement durable:** Santé/assainissement/eau. **Régions:** Afrique australe; Afrique centrale; Afrique de l'Est; Afrique de l'Ouest; Asie centrale et Asie du Sud; Asie de l'Est; Asie du Sud-Est.

ACTIVITES D'INFORMATION ET D'EDUCATION: Domaines: Santé/ assainissement/eau. **Activités:** Campagnes d'information/expositions; Collecte de fonds; Conférences/séminaires/ateliers/activités de formation; Services d'information et de documentation/bases de données; Édition/documents audiovisuels/documents éducatifs.

CHE0693

MISSIONSGESELLSCHAFT BETHLEHEM (SMB) ♦ Bethlehem Mission Society

Missionshaus Bethlehem, Bethlehemweg 10, 6405 Immensee, Switzerland.

Telephone: 41 (41) 82 81 00 . *Fax:* 41 (41) 82 84 00 . *Contact:* Josef Meili, Superior General.

OBJECTIVES: To undertake mission work, evangelisation, development activities and justice and peace actions in developing countries.

GENERAL INFORMATION: *Creation:* 1921. *Personnel/Total:* 490. *Salaried:* 180. *Volunteers:* 310 of which: 172 in developing countries. *Budget/Total 1993:* ECU 16700000 (US$ 21657000). *Financial sources:* Private: 37%. Public: 2%. Self-financing: 61%.

PUBLICATIONS: *Periodicals:* (11). *List of publications.*

EVALUATION/RESEARCH: Undertakes research activities.

ACTIVITIES IN DEVELOPING REGIONS: Active in 13 country(ies). Maintains local field presence. Works through local field partners. **Sustainable Development Actions:** Children/youth/family; Ecology/environment/biodiversity; Education/training/literacy; Food/famine; Health/ sanitation/water; Human rights/peace/conflicts; Rural development/agriculture; Sending volunteers/experts/technical assistance; Small enterprises/informal sector/handicrafts; Urban development/habitat. **Regions:** Caribbean; Central Africa; East Africa; East Asia; South America; South East Asia; Southern Africa.

INFORMATION AND EDUCATION ACTIVITIES: Topics: Children/youth/ family; Culture/tradition/religion; Ecology/environment/biodiversity; Education/training/literacy; Emergency relief/refugees/humanitarian assistance; Food/famine; Health/sanitation/water; Human rights/peace/conflicts; International economic relations/trade/debt/finance; Peace/ethnic conflicts/armament/disarmament; Population/family planning/demography; Poverty/living conditions; Racism/xenophobia/antisemitism; Refugees/migrants/ethnic groups; Rural development/agriculture; Urban development/habitat. **Activities:** Broadcasting/cultural events; Conferences/seminars/workshops/training activities; Formal education; Fund raising; Information campaigns/exhibitions; Lobbying/advocacy; Publishing/audiovisual materials/educational materials.

CHE0694

MISSIONSKREIS WALLISELLEN ♦ Cercle missionnaire Wallisellen

Glärnischstrasse 8, 8304 Wallisellen, Suisse.

Téléphone: 41 (1) 830 33 31. *Contact:* Ruth Wunderlin, Présidente.

OBJECTIFS: Apporter un soutien financier à diverses missions religieuses à l'œuvre dans les pays en développement.

INFORMATIONS GENERALES: *Création:* 1955. *Personnel/Total:* 23. *Bénévoles:* 23. *Sources financières:* Privé: 20%. *Autofinancement:* 80%.

ACTIVITES DANS LES REGIONS EN DEVELOPPEMENT: Intervient par l'intermédiaire d'organisations locales partenaires.

CHE0695

MOSQUITO

Postfach 5218, 3001 Bern, Suisse.

CHE0696

MOTAMAR AL-ALAM AL-ISLAMI ♦ WORLD MUSLIM CONGRESS

81 rue de Lyon, 1203 Geneva, Switzerland.

Telephone: 41 (22) 344 22 68. *Fax:* 41 (22) 344 36 13. *Contact:* Dr. Abdul Hakim Tabibi.

CHE0697

MOTHER AND CHILD INTERNATIONAL (MCI) ♦ Mère et enfant international

16 chemin de la Grande Gorge, 1255 Veyrier, Switzerland.

Telephone: 41 (22) 784 06 58. *Fax:* 41 (22) 784 06 58. *Contact:* Gerda M. Santschi, Executive Secretary.

CHE0698

MOUVEMENT ANTI-APARTHEID SUISSE, SECTION DE GENEVE (MAAS)

C.P. 2536, 1211 Genève 2 Dépôt, Suisse.

Téléphone: 41 (22) 734 54 82.

CHE0699

MOUVEMENT ATD QUART-MONDE TERRE ET HOMMES DE DEMAIN (ATD)

Rue de St-Jean 61, 1201 Genève, Suisse.

CHE0700

MOUVEMENT INTERNATIONAL POUR L'UNION FRATERNELLE ENTRE LES RACES ET LES PEUPLES (UFER)

Rue de la Servette 91, 1202 Genève, Suisse.

Téléphone: 41 (22) 733 09 07. *Fax:* 41 (22) 733 09 07. *Contact:* Magda Van Malder, Secrétaire générale.

CHE0701

MOUVEMENT POPULAIRE DES FAMILLES (MPF)

Rue Michel Chauvet 22, Case postale 155, 1211 Genève 17, Suisse.

Téléphone: 41 (22) 786 47 02. *Contact:* Renée Sciboz-Revoz.

OBJECTIFS: Permettre aux gens des milieux populaires de se prendre en charge individuellement et collectivement pour construire une société solidaire.

INFORMATIONS GENERALES: *Création:* 1942. *Affiliée à:* Fédération Genevoise de Coopération (Suisse). *Personnel/Total:* 3. *Salariés:* 3. *Budget/Total 1993:* ECU 106000 (US$ 137000). *Sources financières:* Public: 40%. Autofinancement: 60%.

PUBLICATIONS: *Périodiques:* Monde du Travail (11). *Rapport annuel.*

EVALUATION/RECHERCHE: Rapports d'évaluation disponibles.

PREVISIONS D'ACTIVITES: Soutien d'un atelier-école de menuiserie jusqu'à fin 1996.

See: *How to Use the Directory*, page 11.

ACTIVITES DANS LES REGIONS EN DEVELOPPEMENT: Intervient dans 1 pays. Intervient par l'intermédiaire d'organisations locales partenaires. **Actions de Développement durable:** Démocratie/bonne gestion publique/création d'institutions/développement participatif; Enfants/jeunesse/famille; Petites entreprises/secteur informel/artisanat; Éducation/formation/alphabétisation. **Régions:** Amérique du Sud.

ACTIVITES D'INFORMATION ET D'EDUCATION: Domaines: Enfants/jeunesse/famille; Racisme/xénophobie/antisémitisme; Éducation/formation/alphabétisation. **Activités:** Campagnes d'information/expositions; Collecte de fonds; Conférences/séminaires/ateliers/activités de formation.

CHE0702
MOUVEMENT SOS ASILE VAUD (SOS ASILE)

Case postale 3928, 1002 Lausanne, Suisse.

CHE0703
MOUVEMENT SUISSE DE LA PAIX (MSP) ♦ SCHWEIZ. FRIEDENSBEWEGUNG

Rue Amat 6, 1202 Genève, Suisse.

Téléphone: 41 (22) 731 33 32.

CHE0704
MU'ASSAT AL-TA'AWUN ♦ Welfare Association

7 avenue Pictet-de-Rochemont, C.P. 602, 1211 Geneva 6, Switzerland.

Telephone: 41 (22) 786 56 55. *Fax:* (22) 786 53 45. *Contact:* Dr. George T. Abed, Director General.

CHE0705
MUSLIM WORLD LEAGUE

Case postale 212, 34 chemin Colladon, 1211 Geneva 19, Switzerland.

Contact: Yahya Basalamah, Representative.

CHE0706
THE NEW INDEPENDENT COMMISSION

11 avenue Joli-Mont, CP 184, 1211 Genève 28, Switzerland.

CHE0707
NOUVELLE PLANETE

Chemin de la Forêt, 1042 Assens, Suisse.

Téléphone: 41 (21) 881 23 80. *Fax:* 41 (21) 882 10 54. *Contact:* Willy Randin, Directeur.

OBJECTIFS: Développer les énergies alternatives et lutter contre la désertification dans le Tiers monde. Promouvoir les "jumelages solidaires" entre communes, groupes, écoles et familles.

INFORMATIONS GENERALES: *Création:* 1987. *Personnel/Total:* 12. *Salariés:* 9 dont: 5 dans les pays en développement. *Bénévoles:* 3 dont: 3 dans les pays en développement. *Budget/Total 1993:* ECU 929000 (US$ 1205000). *Sources financières:* Privé: 100%.

PUBLICATIONS: *Périodiques:* L'avenir est entre nos mains (5).

ACTIVITES DANS LES REGIONS EN DEVELOPPEMENT: Intervient directement dans les régions en développement. Intervient dans 18 pays. Maintient une présence locale sur le terrain. Intervient par l'intermédiaire d'organisations locales partenaires. **Actions de Développement durable:** Développement rural/agriculture; Enfants/jeunesse/famille; Envoi de volontaires/experts/assistance technique; Petites entreprises/secteur informel/artisanat; Population/planning familial/démographie; Questions relatives aux femmes; Santé/assainissement/eau; Écologie/environnement/biodiversité; Éducation/formation/alphabétisation. **Régions:** Afrique australe; Afrique centrale; Afrique de l'Est; Afrique de l'Ouest.

ACTIVITES D'INFORMATION ET D'EDUCATION: Domaines: Développement rural/agriculture; Enfants/jeunesse/famille; Population/planning familial/démographie; Questions relatives aux femmes; Santé/assainissement/eau; Écologie/environnement/biodiversité; Éducation/formation/alphabétisation. **Activités:** Collecte de fonds.

CHE0708
L'OASIS - ASSOCIATION SUISSE DE SOUTIEN A LA FONDATION DANIEL BALAVOINE

Case postale 268, 1211 Genève 16, Suisse.

Téléphone: 41 (22) 733 21 81.

CHE0709
OEUVRE DE SAINT-PAUL

Case postale 150, 38 Pérolles, 1705 Fribourg, Suisse.

Téléphone: 41 (37) 86 49 50. *Fax:* 41 (37) 86 49 00. *Contact:* Soeur Anne Suter.

OBJECTIFS: Promouvoir la presse catholique sous toutes ses formes (imprimerie, édition, librairie), formation du personnel aux nouvelles techniques, pour une meilleure diffusion de la Parole et le développement de l'homme.

INFORMATIONS GENERALES: *Création:* 1973. *Personnel/Total:* 140. *Budget/Total 1993:* ECU 189000 (US$ 245000). *Sources financières:* Privé: 20%. *Autofinancement:* 80%.

PUBLICATIONS: *Périodiques:* Voix de Saint-Paul (4). *Liste des publications.*

COMMENTAIRES: Le personnel est entièrement composé de religieuses, dont 30 dans les pays en développement.

ACTIVITES DANS LES REGIONS EN DEVELOPPEMENT: Intervient directement dans les régions en développement. Intervient dans 3 pays. Maintient une présence locale sur le terrain. **Actions de Développement durable:** Autres; Éducation/formation/alphabétisation. **Régions:** Afrique australe; Afrique centrale; Moyen-Orient.

ACTIVITES D'INFORMATION ET D'EDUCATION: Domaines: Culture/tradition/religion. **Activités:** Édition/documents audiovisuels/documents éducatifs.

CHE0710
OEUVRE SAINT JUSTIN

Route du Jura 3, 1700 Fribourg, Suisse.

Téléphone: 41 (37) 26 60 99. *Fax:* 41 (37) 26 70 99.

CHE0711
ORGANISATION MONDIALE CONTRE LA TORTURE (OMCT/SOS-TORTURE)

C.P. 119, Rue de Vermont 37-39, 1211 Genève 20 CIC, Suisse.

Téléphone: 41 (22) 733 31 40. *Fax:* 41 (22) 733 10 51. *Courrier électronique:* omct geonet 2.. *Contact:* Eric Sottas, Directeur.

OBJECTIFS: Lutter contre la torture par des interventions urgentes. Animer un réseau d'ONG de défense des droits de l'homme. Apporter une assistance médicale, juridique et sociale d'urgence aux victimes. Elaborer des programmes spécifiques en faveur des enfants.

INFORMATIONS GENERALES: *Création:* 1986. *Type d'organisation:* réseau. *Organisations membres:* 155. *Personnel/Total:* 8. *Salariés:* 5. *Bénévoles:* 3. *Budget/Total 1993:* ECU 626000 (US$ 812000). *Sources financières:* Privé: 26%. *Public:* 53%. *Autofinancement:* 21%.

PUBLICATIONS: *Périodiques:* SOS-Torture (24). *Rapport annuel.*

EVALUATION/RECHERCHE: Entreprend des activités de recherche.

PREVISIONS D'ACTIVITES: Mise en place de mécanismes tendant à anticiper et éviter les violences à grande échelle (travail sur la région des Grands Lacs en Afrique, sur le Pérou et le Mexique entre autres). Campagne contre l'impunité. Projet d'un système international de compensation pour les victimes.

COMMENTAIRES: Intervient dans la Communauté des Etats indépendants.

ACTIVITES DANS LES REGIONS EN DEVELOPPEMENT: Intervient directement dans les régions en développement. Intervient dans 58 pays. Maintient une présence locale sur le terrain. Intervient par l'intermédiaire d'organisations locales partenaires. **Actions de Développe-**

Voir : *Comment utiliser le répertoire,* page 11.

ment durable: Droits de l'Homme/paix/conflits; Démocratie/bonne gestion publique/création d'institutions/développement participatif; Enfants/jeunesse/famille; Questions relatives aux femmes; Secours d'urgence/réfugiés/aide humanitaire. **Régions:** Afrique australe; Afrique centrale; Afrique de l'Est; Afrique de l'Ouest; Afrique du Nord; Amérique du Sud; Asie centrale et Asie du Sud; Asie de l'Est; Asie du Sud-Est; Caraïbes; Mexique et Amerique centrale; Moyen-Orient; Océanie.

ACTIVITES D'INFORMATION ET D'EDUCATION: Domaines: Droits de l'Homme/paix/conflits; Enfants/jeunesse/famille; Paix/conflits ethniques/armement/désarmement; Questions relatives aux femmes; Racisme/xénophobie/antisémitisme; Relations internationales/coopération/aide au développement; Relations économiques internationales/commerce/dette/finances; Réfugiés/migrants/groupes ethniques; Secours d'urgence/réfugiés/aide humanitaire. **Activités:** Campagnes d'information/expositions; Collecte de fonds; Conférences/séminaires/ateliers/activités de formation; Lobbying/plaidoyer; Radiodiffusion/manifestations culturelles; Réseaux/télécommunications électroniques; Services d'information et de documentation/bases de données; Édition/documents audiovisuels/documents éducatifs; Éducation formelle.

CHE0712

ORGANISATION MONDIALE DU MOUVEMENT SCOUT (OMMS)

C.P. 241, Rue Pré-Jérome 5, 1211 Genève 4, Suisse.

Téléphone: 41 (22) 320 42 33. **Fax:** 41 (22) 781 20 53. **Contact:** Jacques Moreillon, Secrétaire général.

OBJECTIFS: Agir comme secrétaire du Mouvement Scout et fournir des services auprès des organisations nationales. Rechercher et collecter des fonds destinés à soutenir l'activité du scoutisme.

INFORMATIONS GENERALES: Création: 1920. **Type d'organisation:** regroupement d'ONG. **Organisations membres:** 136. **Personnel/Total:** var.. **Salariés:** 80 dont: 30 dans les pays en développement. **Bénévoles:** var..

PUBLICATIONS: Périodiques: (6). *Rapport annuel. Liste des publications.*

EVALUATION/RECHERCHE: Rapports d'évaluation disponibles. Entreprend des activités de recherche.

COMMENTAIRES: Les activités de développement mentionnées sont menées par les organisations nationales de l'OMMS. Activités d'information concernant la Communauté des Etats indépendants. **Actions de Développement durable:** Aliments/famine; Droits de l'Homme/paix/conflits; Développement rural/agriculture; Développement urbain/habitat; Enfants/jeunesse/famille; Envoi de volontaires/experts/assistance technique; Petites entreprises/secteur informel/artisanat; Population/planning familial/démographie; Questions relatives aux femmes; Santé/assainissement/eau; Écologie/environnement/biodiversité; Éducation/formation/alphabétisation. **Régions:** Afrique australe; Afrique centrale; Afrique de l'Est; Afrique de l'Ouest; Afrique du Nord; Amérique du Sud; Asie centrale et Asie du Sud; Asie de l'Est; Asie du Sud-Est; Caraïbes; Mexique et Amerique centrale; Moyen-Orient; Océanie.

ACTIVITES D'INFORMATION ET D'EDUCATION: Domaines: Enfants/jeunesse/famille. **Activités:** Campagnes d'information/expositions; Conférences/séminaires/ateliers/activités de formation; Échanges/parrainage/jumelage.

CHE0713

ORGANISATION MONDIALE POUR L'ENFANT (OME)

C.P. 55, Immeuble COE Morillons 5, 1211 Genève 19, Suisse.

Téléphone: 41 (22) 788 08 80. **Fax:** 41 (22) 791 03 61. **Contact:** Eugen F. Mueller, Président.

OBJECTIFS: Mener des projets dans le domaine de l'éducation des enfants et de la formation professionnelle dans le pays et par les autochtones.

INFORMATIONS GENERALES: Création: 1988. *Salariés:* 1. *Bénévoles:* 30 dont: 5 dans les pays en développement. **Budget/Total 1993:** ECU 283000 (US$ 367000). **Sources financières:** *Public:* 50%. *Autofinancement:* 50%.

PUBLICATIONS: *Rapport annuel.*

COMMENTAIRES: Intervient dans la Communauté des Etats indépendants. Activités d'information concernant la Communauté des Etats indépendants.

ACTIVITES DANS LES REGIONS EN DEVELOPPEMENT: Intervient directement dans les régions en développement. Intervient dans 6 pays. Maintient une présence locale sur le terrain. **Actions de Développement durable:** Éducation/formation/alphabétisation. **Régions:** Asie de l'Est; Mexique et Amerique centrale; Moyen-Orient.

ACTIVITES D'INFORMATION ET D'EDUCATION: Domaines: Éducation/formation/alphabétisation. **Activités:** Collecte de fonds; Éducation formelle.

CHE0714

ORGANISATION SUISSE - TIERS MONDE (OS3)

Byfangstrasse 19, Posftach 69, 2552 Orpund, Suisse.

Téléphone: 41 (32) 55 31 55. **Fax:** 41 (32) 55 31 59. **Contact:** Max Leuzinger.

CHE0715

ORGANISATION SUISSE D'AIDE AUX REFUGIES-SECRETARIAT ROMAND (OSAR)

Rue Chaucrau 3, 1003 Lausanne, Suisse.

Téléphone: 41 (21) 320 56 49. **Fax:** 41 (21) 320 11 20. **Contact:** Michel Gönczy, Secrétaire romand.

OBJECTIFS: Sauvegarder et affirmer au sein de la population la disposition à venir en aide aux réfugiés. Coordonner les activités des membres et représenter leurs intérêts auprès des autorités et du public.

INFORMATIONS GENERALES: Création: 1936. **Type d'organisation:** regroupement d'ONG. **Organisations membres:** 5. **Affiliée à:** European Council on Refugees and Exile (Grande-Bretagne.). **Personnel/Total:** 28. *Salariés:* 20. *Bénévoles:* 2. **Budget/Total 1993:** ECU 2609000 (US$ 3384000).

PUBLICATIONS: Périodiques: Osar (6) - Jalons (6). *Rapport annuel. Liste des publications.*

ACTIVITES D'INFORMATION ET D'EDUCATION: Domaines: Droits de l'Homme/paix/conflits; Racisme/xénophobie/antisémitisme; Relations internationales/coopération/aide au développement; Réfugiés/migrants/groupes ethniques. **Activités:** Campagnes d'information/expositions; Collecte de fonds; Conférences/séminaires/ateliers/activités de formation; Lobbying/plaidoyer; Radiodiffusion/manifestations culturelles; Services d'information et de documentation/bases de données; Édition/documents audiovisuels/documents éducatifs.

CHE0716

PAN-PACIFIC SOUTH-EAST ASIAN WOMEN'S ORGANIZATION

145 route de Gy, 1251 Gy, Suisse.

Téléphone: 41 (22) 759 20 25.

CHE0717

THE PATHFINDER FUND

Ch. des Arpillères 30, 1224 Chêne-Bougeries, Switzerland.

CHE0718

PAX CHRISTI SUISSE

15 rue du Valentin, 1004 Lausanne, Suisse.

Téléphone: 41 (21) 312 26 18. **Fax:** 41 (21) 312 38 40. **Contact:** Martin Bernet, Secrétaire .

OBJECTIFS: Eduquer à la paix, faire un travail d'information, exercer un lobby politique (politique nationale et internationale) et dans l'église sur les questions de paix.

INFORMATIONS GENERALES: Affiliée à: CRAL (Suisse) - Pax Christi International (Belgique). **Personnel/Total:** 2. *Salariés:* 2. **Budget/Total 1993:** ECU 63000 (US$ 81000). **Sources financières:** *Privé:* 10%. *Public:* 50%. *Autofinancement:* 40%.

PUBLICATIONS: Périodiques: Si tu veux la paix (n6). *Rapport annuel.*

See: *How to Use the Directory,* page 11.

ACTIVITES D'INFORMATION ET D'EDUCATION: **Domaines:** Culture/tradition/religion; Droits de l'Homme/paix/conflits; Paix/conflits ethniques/armement/désarmement; Pauvreté/conditions de vie; Racisme/xénophobie/antisémitisme; Relations économiques internationales/commerce/dette/finances; Réfugiés/migrants/groupes ethniques. **Activités:** Campagnes d'information/expositions; Conférences/séminaires/ateliers/activités de formation; Lobbying/plaidoyer.

CHE0719

PAX ROMANA - INTERNATIONAL MOVEMENT FOR INTELLECTUAL AND CULTURAL AFFAIRS (ICMICA/MIIC)

rue des Alpes 7, CP 1062, 1701 Fribourg, Switzerland.

Telephone: 41 (22) 733 67 40.

CHE0720

PRODOTTI TERZO MONDO (P3M) ♦ Produits du Tiers monde

Via Vela 21, 6500 Bellinzona, Suisse.

Téléphone: 41 (92) 25 45 77. *Fax:* 41 (92) 25 45 77. *Contact:* Luca Buzzi, Président.

OBJECTIFS: Promouvoir un commerce équitable avec le Sud. Informer sur les rapports Nord-Sud.

INFORMATIONS GENERALES: *Création:* 1979. *Type d'organisation:* regroupement d'ONG. *Organisations membres:* 16. *Affiliée à:* Organisation Suisse Tiers Monde (Suisse) - Association pour un équitable commerce bananier (Suisse). *Personnel/Total:* 18. *Salariés:* 3. *Bénévoles:* 15. *Budget/Total 1993:* ECU 261000 (US$ 338000). *Sources financières:* Autofinancement: 100%.

PUBLICATIONS: *Périodiques:* Informazioni P3M (12). *Rapport annuel.*

PREVISIONS D'ACTIVITES: Campagne d'information sur la musique et les instruments de musique dans le monde. Tournoi de Tiers-Mondopoly.

ACTIVITES DANS LES REGIONS EN DEVELOPPEMENT: Intervient directement dans les régions en développement. Intervient dans 3 pays. Intervient par l'intermédiaire d'organisations locales partenaires. **Actions de Développement durable:** Dette/finances/commerce; Petites entreprises/secteur informel/artisanat; Secours d'urgence/réfugiés/aide humanitaire. **Régions:** Amérique du Sud; Mexique et Amerique centrale.

ACTIVITES D'INFORMATION ET D'EDUCATION: Domaines: Culture/tradition/religion; Pauvreté/conditions de vie; Relations internationales/coopération/aide au développement; Relations économiques internationales/commerce/dette/finances. **Activités:** Campagnes d'information/expositions; Conférences/séminaires/ateliers/activités de formation; Radiodiffusion/manifestations culturelles; Services d'information et de documentation/bases de données.

CHE0721

PROGRAMME TO COMBAT RACISM OF THE WORLD COUNCIL OF CHURCHES

WCC, P.O.Box 2100, 1211 Geneva 2, Switzerland.

Telephone: 41 (22) 791 61 11. *Fax:* 41 (22) 791 03 61. *Contact:* Rev. Konrad Raiser, General Secretary .

OBJECTIVES: To assist WCC member churches to focus on issues of racism and ethnicism. To work with indiginous peoples and support their claims for justice.

GENERAL INFORMATION: *Creation:* 1969. *Personnel/Total:* 6. *Salaried:* 6. *Budget/Total 1993:* ECU 925000 (US$ 1200000). *Financial sources:* Private: 100%.

PUBLICATIONS: *Periodicals:* ECHOES (3). *List of publications.*

EVALUATION/RESEARCH: Evaluation reports available.

PLANNED ACTIVITIES: The WCC is planning a USA campaign on Racism as a Human Rights Violation, the development of SISTERS - Sisters in the Struggle to Eliminate Racism and Sexism. There is also a plan to develop a solidarity programme in India and convene a consultation of indigenous peoples involved in land claims.

COMMENTS: Undertakes activities in the Commonwealth of Independent States.

ACTIVITIES IN DEVELOPING REGIONS: Active in 25 country(ies). Works through local field partners. **Sustainable Development Actions:** Democracy/good governance/institution building/participatory development; Gender issues/women; Human rights/peace/conflicts. **Regions:** Caribbean; Central Africa; Central Asia and South Asia; East Asia; Mexico and Central America; Oceania; South America; South East Asia; Southern Africa; West Africa.

CHE0722

PROGRAMME UNIT ON JUSTICE AND PEACE

WCC, P.O.Box 2100, 1211 Geneva 2, Switzerland.

CHE0723

PROJEKT-SERVICE FUR MISSIONS-, SOZIAL- UND ENTWICKLUNGSHILFE

Postfach 2856, c/o Fastenopfer, Habsburgerstrasse 44, 6002 Luzern, Suisse.

Téléphone: 41 (41) 23 76 55. *Fax:* 41 (41) 23 13 62.

CHE0724

PROJET DE MANILLE - OEUVRE D'ENTRAIDE DU PERE SCHWARTZ

Gemeindestrasse 26, 8032 Zürich, Suisse.

Téléphone: 41 (21) 26 20 20.

CHE0725

LE PROJET FAIM ♦ The Hunger Project

1 rue de Varembé, C.P. 35, 1211 Genève 20, Suisse.

Téléphone: 41 (22) 734 65 19. *Fax:* 41 (22) 733 92 03. *Contact:* Rénata Beguin, Présidente.

CHE0726

QUAKERS UNITED NATIONS OFFICE (QUNO)

13 Avenue du Mervelet, 1209 Geneva, Switzerland.

Telephone: 41 (22) 733 33 97. *Fax:* 41 (22) 734 00 15. *Contact:* Brewster Grace, Representative.

OBJECTIVES: To further Quaker concerns on peace and justice at the United Nations. To organise programmes on disarmament, human rights, refugees, development and trade.

GENERAL INFORMATION: *Creation:* 1926. *Personnel/Total:* 5. *Salaried:* 5. *Budget/Total 1993:* ECU 248000 (US$ 321000). *Financial sources:* Self-financing: 100%.

PUBLICATIONS: *Periodicals:* QUNO Reporter (4). *List of publications.*

EVALUATION/RESEARCH: Undertakes research activities.

COMMENTS: QUNO works with the UN in Geneva and promotes and supports, in Geneva, the activities of its members in developing countries.

ACTIVITIES IN DEVELOPING REGIONS: Works through local field partners.

INFORMATION AND EDUCATION ACTIVITIES: Topics: Ecology/environment/biodiversity. **Activities:** Conferences/seminars/workshops/training activities.

CHE0727

RECHERCHES ET APPLICATIONS DE FINANCEMENTS ALTERNATIFS AU DEVELOPPEMENT (RAFAD) ♦ Research and Applications for Alternative Financing for Development

1 rue de Varembé, C.P. 117, 1211 Genève 20, Suisse.

Téléphone: 41 (22) 733 50 73. *Fax:* 41 (22) 734 70 83. *Contact:* Fernand Vincent, Secrétaire général.

OBJECTIFS: Faciliter l'accès au crédit à des ONG et à des groupes de personnes dans le Tiers monde. Soutenir ces organisations et groupes

Voir : *Comment utiliser le répertoire,* page 11.

dans la gestion de leurs ressources financières. Rechercher et diffuser des formes innovatrices d'appui financier au développement.

INFORMATIONS GENERALES: *Création:* 1985. *Personnel/Total:* 6. *Salariés:* 6 dont: 2 dans les pays en développement. *Budget/ Total 1993:* ECU 375000 (US$ 487000). *Sources financières:* Privé: 20%. Public: 62%. Autofinancement: 18%.

PUBLICATIONS: *Périodiques:* Rafad Info (4). *Rapport annuel.*

EVALUATION/RECHERCHE: Rapports d'évaluation disponibles. Entreprend des activités de recherche.

PREVISIONS D'ACTIVITES: Création d'un fonds international de garanties. Recherche de nouveaux instruments financiers.

ACTIVITES DANS LES REGIONS EN DEVELOPPEMENT: Intervient directement dans les régions en développement. Intervient dans 25 pays. Maintient une présence locale sur le terrain. Intervient par l'intermédiaire d'organisations locales partenaires. **Actions de Développement durable:** Dette/finances/commerce; Développement rural/agriculture; Développement urbain/habitat; Envoi de volontaires/experts/ assistance technique; Petites entreprises/secteur informel/artisanat; Questions relatives aux femmes; Énergie/transport. **Régions:** Afrique australe; Afrique centrale; Afrique de l'Est; Afrique de l'Ouest; Afrique du Nord; Amérique du Sud; Asie centrale et Asie du Sud; Asie du Sud-Est; Mexique et Amerique centrale.

ACTIVITES D'INFORMATION ET D'EDUCATION: Domaines: Développement rural/agriculture; Développement urbain/habitat; Relations internationales/coopération/aide au développement; Relations économiques internationales/commerce/dette/finances. **Activités:** Collecte de fonds; Conférences/séminaires/ateliers/activités de formation; Lobbying/plaidoyer; Services d'information et de documentation/bases de données; Édition/documents audiovisuels/documents éducatifs.

CHE0728

REFUGEE POLICY GROUP

Rue Gautier 7, 1201 Genève, Suisse.

Téléphone: 41 (22) 731 33 60. *Fax:* 41 (22) 738 92 68.

CHE0729

REGARDS AFRICAINS - ASSOCIATION CULTURELLE

Case postale 46, 1211 Genève 46, Suisse.

Téléphone: 41 (22) 43 87 93.

CHE0730

ROTARY INTERNATIONAL

Wtikornerstrasse 15, 8032 Zurichs, Switzerland.

Telephone: 41 (1) 387 71 11. *Fax:* 41 (1) 422 50 41. *Contact:* Herbert A. Pigman, General Secretary.

OBJECTIVES: To encourage and foster the ideal of service as a basis of worthy enterprise by the development of acquaintance as an opportunity for service. To promote high ethical standards in business and professions. To apply the ideal of service to personal, business and community life. To advance international understanding, goodwill and peace through a world fellowship of business and professional persons united in the ideal of service.

GENERAL INFORMATION: *Creation:* 1905. *Type of organisation:* network, coordinating body. *Affiliated to:* World Health Organization. *Personnel/Total:* 535. *Salaried:* 535 of which: 50 in developing countries. *Budget/Total 1993:* ECU 40098000 (US$ 52000000). *Financial sources:* Self-financing: 100%.

PUBLICATIONS: *Periodicals:* The Rotarian Magazine (12). *Annual report. List of publications.*

EVALUATION/RESEARCH: Evaluation reports available.

COMMENTS: Undertakes activities in the Commonwealth of Independent States. Information activities related to the Commonwealth of Independent States.

ACTIVITIES IN DEVELOPING REGIONS: Present in developing regions. Active in 110 country(ies). Maintains local field presence. Works

through local field partners. **Sustainable Development Actions:** Children/youth/family; Ecology/environment/biodiversity; Education/training/ literacy; Emergency relief/refugees/humanitarian assistance; Health/ sanitation/water; Rural development/agriculture; Sending volunteers/ experts/technical assistance; Small enterprises/informal sector/handicrafts; Urban development/habitat. **Regions:** Caribbean; Central Africa; Central Asia and South Asia; East Africa; East Asia; Mexico and Central America; Middle East; North Africa; Oceania; South America; South East Asia; Southern Africa; West Africa.

INFORMATION AND EDUCATION ACTIVITIES: Topics: Children/youth/ family; Culture/tradition/religion; Ecology/environment/biodiversity; Education/training/literacy; Emergency relief/refugees/humanitarian assistance; Employment/unemployment; Food/famine; Health/sanitation/ water; International relations/cooperation/development aid; Peace/ethnic conflicts/armament/disarmament; Poverty/living conditions; Rural development/agriculture; Urban development/habitat. **Activities:** Conferences/seminars/workshops/training activities; Exchanges/twinning/ linking; Formal education; Fund raising; Publishing/audiovisual materials/educational materials.

CHE0731

SAHARA KLEIDERLADEN - SCHWEIZERISCHE ARBEITERHILFSWERK

Heinrichstrasse 87, 8005 Zurich, Suisse.

Téléphone: 41 (1) 44 05 05.

CHE0732

SCHULSTELLE 3. WELT ♦ Service école Tiers monde

Monbijoustrasse 31, Postfach 1686, 3001 Bern, Switzerland.

Telephone: 41 (31) 26 12 34.

CHE0733

SCHWEITZER REDEMPTORISTEN

Bruggerstrasse 143, 5400 Baden, Switzerland.

CHE0734

SCHWEIZER ALLIANZ-MISSION ♦ Swiss Alliance Mission

Wolfensbergstrasse 47, Postfach 28, 8410 Winterthur, Switzerland.

Telephone: 41 (52) 213 13 31. *Fax:* 41 (52) 213 56 81. *Contact:* Martin Voegelin, Director General.

OBJECTIVES: To help fulfil in the name of Christ, the spiritual, physical, educational, social and emotional needs of the people in developing countries.

GENERAL INFORMATION: *Creation:* 1889. *Personnel/Total:* 115. *Salaried:* 115 of which: 56 in developing countries. *Budget/Total 1993:* ECU 1983000 (US$ 2572000). *Financial sources:* Private: 94%. Public: 6%.

PUBLICATIONS: *Periodicals:* SAM-Bote (6) - Gebetsbrief (6). *Annual report.*

EVALUATION/RESEARCH: Evaluation reports available. Undertakes research activities.

ACTIVITIES IN DEVELOPING REGIONS: Present in developing regions. Active in 2 country(ies). Maintains local field presence. Works through local field partners. **Sustainable Development Actions:** Children/ youth/family; Education/training/literacy; Emergency relief/refugees/ humanitarian assistance; Food/famine; Health/sanitation/water; Population/family planning/demography; Rural development/agriculture; Sending volunteers/experts/technical assistance. **Regions:** Southern Africa; West Africa.

INFORMATION AND EDUCATION ACTIVITIES: Topics: Children/youth/ family; Culture/tradition/religion; Education/training/literacy; Food/famine; Health/sanitation/water; Population/family planning/demography; Rural development/agriculture. **Activities:** Conferences/seminars/workshops/training activities; Formal education; Fund raising; Information and documentation services/data bases; Publishing/audiovisual materials/educational materials.

See: *How to Use the Directory*, page 11.

CHE0735

SCHWEIZER INDIANERHILFE ♦ Swiss Support to Ameridians

Gärtnerstrasse 3, 4102 Binningen, Switzerland.

Telephone: 41 (61) 421 26 97. *Contact:* M. Nadolny, President.

OBJECTIVES: To assist Amerindians in need.

GENERAL INFORMATION: *Creation:* 1973. *Affiliated to:* Associación Mexicana Albert Schweitzer (Mexico) - Freundeskreis Indianerhilfe (Germany) - Mazahua Albert Schweitzer Project (USA). *Personnel/ Total:* var.. *Salaried:* 27 of which: 27 in developing countries. *Budget/ Total 1993:* ECU 21000 (US$ 27000). *Financial sources:* Self-financing: 100%.

ACTIVITIES IN DEVELOPING REGIONS: Present in developing regions. Active in 1 country(ies). Works through local field partners. **Sustainable Development Actions:** Children/youth/family; Gender issues/women; Health/sanitation/water; Rural development/agriculture; Small enterprises/informal sector/handicrafts. **Regions:** Mexico and Central America.

CHE0736

SCHWEIZER KOLPINGWERK VERBANDSSEKRETARIAT

St. Karliqaui 12, 6000 Luzern 5, Switzerland.

Telephone: 41 (41) 52 91 39. *Fax:* 41 (41) 51 48 57. *Contact:* Stephan Schmid-Keiser, Dr.theol..

CHE0737

SCHWEIZER MISSIONS VERKEHRS AKTION (MIVA) ♦ Mission Vehicle Agency

Postfach 351, Hubstrasse 32, 9500 Wil 1, Switzerland.

Telephone: 41 (73) 23 85 66. *Fax:* 41 (73) 23 85 90. *Contact:* Peter Eigenmann, Secretary General.

CHE0738

SCHWEIZER NATIONALKOMMISSION JUSTITIA ET PAX ♦

Commission nationale suisse justice et paix

Postfach 6872, Effingerstrasse 11, 3001 Bern, Suisse.

Téléphone: 41 (31) 381 59 55. *Fax:* 41 (31) 381 83 49. *Contact:* Alberto Lepori, Président.

OBJECTIFS: Collaborer, pour l'Eglise catholique en Suisse, dans la recherche de solutions aux problèmes de développement, de politique de paix, de droits de l'homme, de politique sociale, de politique d'asile.

INFORMATIONS GENERALES: *Création:* 1969. *Affiliée à:* Conférence Européenne des commissions Justice et Paix (Belgique). *Personnel/ Total:* 3. *Salariés:* 3. *Budget/Total 1993:* ECU 157000 (US$ 203000). *Sources financières:* Public: 85%. Autofinancement: 15%.

PUBLICATIONS: *Rapport annuel. Liste des publications.*

EVALUATION/RECHERCHE: Entreprend des activités de recherche.

ACTIVITES D'INFORMATION ET D'EDUCATION: Domaines: Culture/ tradition/religion; Droits de l'Homme/paix/conflits; Emploi/chômage; Paix/conflits ethniques/armement/désarmement; Pauvreté/conditions de vie; Racisme/xénophobie/antisémitisme; Relations internationales/ coopération/aide au développement; Relations économiques internationales/commerce/dette/finances; Réfugiés/migrants/groupes ethniques; Écologie/environnement/biodiversité. **Activités:** Édition/documents audiovisuels/documents éducatifs.

CHE0739

SCHWEIZER WIZO-FODERATION (SWF)

Steinenring 5, 4051 Basel, Switzerland.

Telephone: 41 (61) 272 37 10. *Fax:* 41 (61) 272 37 11. *Contact:* Lucie Gideon, President.

OBJECTIVES: To support mothers and children in need in Israel.

GENERAL INFORMATION: *Creation:* 1926. *Personnel/Total:* 2. *Salaried:* 2. *Budget/Total 1993:* ECU 1566000 (US$ 2030000). *Financial sources:* Private: 50%. Self-financing: 50%.

PUBLICATIONS: *Periodicals:* Wizorama (2). *Annual report.*

ACTIVITIES IN DEVELOPING REGIONS: Sustainable Development Actions: Children/youth/family. **Regions:** Middle East.

INFORMATION AND EDUCATION ACTIVITIES: Topics: Children/youth/ family. **Activities:** Formal education; Fund raising.

CHE0740

SCHWEIZERISCH-CHINESISCHE GESELLSCHAFT ♦ Association Suisse-Chine

Igelweid 22, 5000 Aarau, Suisse.

Téléphone: 41 (64) 24 44 64. *Fax:* 41 (64) 24 75 62. *Contact:* Erwin Mosel, Président.

OBJECTIFS: Développer des relations scientifiques, culturelles et amicales avec la Chine.

INFORMATIONS GENERALES: *Création:* 1935. *Budget/Total 1993:* ECU 19000 (US$ 24000). *Sources financières:* Privé: 10%. Autofinancement: 90%.

PUBLICATIONS: *Périodiques:* (4). *Rapport annuel.*

EVALUATION/RECHERCHE: Rapports d'évaluation disponibles.

ACTIVITES D'INFORMATION ET D'EDUCATION: Domaines: Culture/ tradition/religion. **Activités:** Radiodiffusion/manifestations culturelles; Édition/documents audiovisuels/documents éducatifs.

CHE0741

SCHWEIZERISCHE AKADEMIE FUR ENTWICKLUNG (ASD) ♦

Académie Suisse pour le Développement

Postfach 1044, St. Urbangasse 1, 4502 Solothurn, Switzerland.

Telephone: 41 (65) 23 85 43. *Fax:* 41 (65) 23 85 43.

OBJECTIVES: To undertake a research project with the goal of providing practical reference to current conflict points, development disorders, social desintegration and migration movements. To monitore and evaluate activities and operate projects in the refugee sector.

GENERAL INFORMATION: *Creation:* 1990. *Type of organisation:* association of NGOs. *Personnel/Total:* 20. *Salaried:* 20 of which: 15 in developing countries. *Budget/Total 1993:* ECU 193000 (US$ 250000). *Financial sources:* Private: 25%. Public: 25%. Self-financing: 50%.

PUBLICATIONS: *Annual report. List of publications.*

EVALUATION/RESEARCH: Undertakes research activities.

ACTIVITIES IN DEVELOPING REGIONS: Present in developing regions. Active in 1 country(ies). Maintains local field presence. Works through local field partners. **Sustainable Development Actions:** Emergency relief/refugees/humanitarian assistance. **Regions:** Middle East.

INFORMATION AND EDUCATION ACTIVITIES: Topics: Culture/tradition/religion; Emergency relief/refugees/humanitarian assistance; Human rights/peace/conflicts; Racism/xenophobia/antisemitism; Refugees/migrants/ethnic groups. **Activities:** Conferences/seminars/workshops/training activities; Information and documentation services/data bases; Publishing/audiovisual materials/educational materials.

CHE0742

SCHWEIZERISCHE EMMAUS VEREINIGUNG ♦ Fédération Emmaus-Suisse

Spitalgasse 9, 3011 Bern, Suisse.

Téléphone: 41 (31) 311 77 97. *Fax:* 41 (31) 318 08 41. *Contact:* Charles F. Fässler, Président.

OBJECTIFS: Aider, suivant l'exemple et l'œuvre de l'abbé Pierre, les plus souffrants sans distinction confessionnelle, politique ou autre, par des moyens financiers et autres.

INFORMATIONS GENERALES: *Création:* 1958. *Type d'organisation:* regroupement d'ONG. *Organisations membres:* 5. *Personnel/Total:* 10. *Bénévoles:* 10. *Budget/Total 1993:* ECU 104000 (US$ 135000). *Sources financières:* Privé: 1%. Autofinancement: 99%.

Voir : *Comment utiliser le répertoire,* page 11.

EVALUATION/RECHERCHE: Rapports d'évaluation disponibles.

ACTIVITES DANS LES REGIONS EN DEVELOPPEMENT: Intervient dans 3 pays. Maintient une présence locale sur le terrain. Intervient par l'intermédiaire d'organisations locales partenaires. **Actions de Développement durable:** Développement rural/agriculture; Enfants/jeunesse/famille; Envoi de volontaires/experts/assistance technique; Petites entreprises/secteur informel/artisanat; Questions relatives aux femmes; Santé/assainissement/eau; Éducation/formation/alphabétisation. **Régions:** Afrique de l'Ouest; Amérique du Sud; Asie centrale et Asie du Sud.

ACTIVITES D'INFORMATION ET D'EDUCATION: Domaines: Développement rural/agriculture; Développement urbain/habitat; Enfants/jeunesse/famille; Questions relatives aux femmes; Santé/assainissement/eau; Éducation/formation/alphabétisation. **Activités:** Collecte de fonds; Services d'information et de documentation/bases de données.

CHE0743
SCHWEIZERISCHE EVANGELISCHE NILLAND-MISSION

Kreuzhubel 12, 6208 Oberkirch, Suisse.

Téléphone: 41 (45) 21 41 21. **Fax:** 41 (45) 21 01 71.

CHE0744
SCHWEIZERISCHE FLUCHTLINGSHILFE (SFH)

Postfach 279, Kinkelstrasse 2, 8035 Zürich, Suisse.

Téléphone: 41 (1) 368 42 42. **Fax:** 41 (1) 368 42 00. **Contact:** Markus Loosli.

OBJECTIFS: Sauvegarder et affermir au sein de la population la disposition à venir en aide aux réfugiés.

INFORMATIONS GENERALES: Création: 1936. **Type d'organisation:** regroupement d'ONG. **Affiliée à:** European Council on Refugees and Exile. **Personnel/Total:** 25. **Salariés:** 23. **Bénévoles:** 2. **Budget/ Total 1993:** ECU 1566000 (US$ 2030000).

PUBLICATIONS: Rapport annuel. Liste des publications.

ACTIVITES D'INFORMATION ET D'EDUCATION: Domaines: Droits de l'Homme/paix/conflits; Racisme/xénophobie/antisémitisme; Relations internationales/coopération/aide au développement; Réfugiés/migrants/ groupes ethniques. **Activités:** Campagnes d'information/expositions; Collecte de fonds; Conférences/séminaires/ateliers/activités de formation; Lobbying/plaidoyer; Radiodiffusion/manifestations culturelles; Services d'information et de documentation/bases de données; Édition/ documents audiovisuels/documents éducatifs.

CHE0745
SCHWEIZERISCHE FRIEDENSRAT - SEKRETARIAT ♦ Conseil Suisse des Associations pour la Paix

Postfach 6386, 8023 Zürich, Suisse.

Téléphone: 41 (1) 242 93 21. **Fax:** 41 (1) 241 29 26.

CHE0746
SCHWEIZERISCHE KATHOLISCHE ARBEITSGEMEINSCHAFT FUR AUSLANDERFRAGEN (SKAF) ♦ Commission Catholique Suisse pour les Migrants

Neustadtstrasse 7, 6003 Luzern, Suisse.

Téléphone: 41 (41) 23 03 47. **Fax:** 41 (41) 23 58 46. **Contact:** Urs Köppel, Directeur national.

OBJECTIFS: S'occuper de la pastorale des étrangers séjournant en Suisse

INFORMATIONS GENERALES: Création: 1965. **Personnel/Total:** 4. **Salariés:** 4.

PUBLICATIONS: Périodiques: Statistiques de la population étrangère en Suisse (1). Rapport annuel. Liste des publications.

ACTIVITES D'INFORMATION ET D'EDUCATION: Domaines: Réfugiés/ migrants/groupes ethniques. **Activités:** Édition/documents audiovisuels/documents éducatifs.

CHE0747
SCHWEIZERISCHE KINDERSCHUTZBUND (SKSB) ♦ Association Suisse pour la Protection de l'Enfant

Brunnmattstr. 38, B.P. 344, 3000 Bern 14, Suisse.

Téléphone: 41 (31) 382 02 33. **Fax:** 41 (31) 382 45 21. **Contact:** Franz Ziegler.

OBJECTIFS: Renforcer la reconnaissance de la personnalité et de la dignité de l'enfant et de l'adolescent. Faire respecter les droits de l'enfants dans la famille et la société. Favoriser son épanouissement, empêcher les mauvais traitements, aider les parents ayant des difficultés à éduquer leurs enfants.

INFORMATIONS GENERALES: Création: 1982. **Type d'organisation:** réseau. **Personnel/Total:** 26. **Salariés:** 1. **Bénévoles:** 25. **Budget/ Total 1993:** ECU 52000 (US$ 68000). **Sources financières:** Privé: 10%. Public: 40%. Autofinancement: 50%.

PUBLICATIONS: Périodiques: SKSB/ASPE-Bulletin (4). Rapport annuel. Liste des publications.

EVALUATION/RECHERCHE: Rapports d'évaluation disponibles. Entreprend des activités de recherche.

ACTIVITES DANS LES REGIONS EN DEVELOPPEMENT: Intervient dans 1 pays.

ACTIVITES D'INFORMATION ET D'EDUCATION: Domaines: Droits de l'Homme/paix/conflits; Enfants/jeunesse/famille. **Activités:** Campagnes d'information/expositions; Collecte de fonds; Conférences/séminaires/ ateliers/activités de formation; Lobbying/plaidoyer; Réseaux/télécommunications électroniques; Services d'information et de documentation/ bases de données; Édition/documents audiovisuels/documents éducatifs; Éducation formelle.

CHE0748
SCHWEIZERISCHE OEKUMENISCHE FLUCHTLINGSHILFE (SOEF)

Postfach 242, Fellenbergstrasse 18, 3000 Bern 9, Suisse.

Téléphone: 41 (31) 24 35 32.

CHE0749
SCHWEIZERISCHE OSTASIEN-MISSION (SOAM) ♦ Swiss East Asia Mission

Webereistrasse 33, 8134 Adliswil, Switzerland.

Telephone: 41 (1) 710 74 81. **Fax:** 41 (1) 709 12 25. **Contact:** Rev. Adrian Linder M.A., Secretary General.

OBJECTIVES: To co-operate with churches in Japan, Indonesia and South Korea in the fields of development, cultural exchange and inter-religious dialogue. To further the gospel by seeking exchange and co-operation with people of good will in all religions.

GENERAL INFORMATION: Creation: 1884. **Affiliated to:** Co-operation of Evangelical Churches and Missions (Switzerland) - Swiss Evangelical Missionary Council (Switzerland) - European Working Group for Ecumenical Relations with Indonesia. **Personnel/Total:** 24. **Salaried:** 14 of which: 9 in developing countries. **Volunteers:** 10. **Budget/ Total 1993:** ECU 535000 (US$ 694000). **Financial sources:** Private: 50%. Public: 50%.

PUBLICATIONS: Periodicals: Jahresbericht (1). Annual report.

EVALUATION/RESEARCH: Evaluation reports available.

PLANNED ACTIVITIES: Training programmes for trainers in primary health care.

ACTIVITIES IN DEVELOPING REGIONS: Active in 3 country(ies). Maintains local field presence. Works through local field partners. **Sustainable Development Actions:** Children/youth/family; Democracy/good governance/institution building/participatory development; Education/ training/literacy; Population/family planning/demography; Rural development/agriculture; Sending volunteers/ experts/technical assistance; Small enterprises/informal sector/handicrafts. **Regions:** East Asia; South East Asia.

INFORMATION AND EDUCATION ACTIVITIES: Topics: Children/youth/ family; Culture/tradition/religion; Health/sanitation/water; International

See: *How to Use the Directory,* page 11.

relations/cooperation/development aid; Population/family planning/ demography; Rural development/agriculture. **Activities:** Conferences/ seminars/workshops/training activities; Exchanges/twinning/linking; Formal education; Fund raising; Lobbying/advocacy; Publishing/audiovisual materials/educational materials.

CHE0750

SCHWEIZERISCHE PFINGSTMISSION (SPM) ♦ Swiss Pentecostal Mission

Zentralstelle, Postfach 95, 6376 Emmeten, Switzerland.

Telephone: 41 (41) 64 38 94. **Fax:** 41 (41) 64 20 52. **Contact:** Jakob Zopfi, President.

OBJECTIVES: To send missionaries to work in the fields of health, education and agriculture in developing countries.

GENERAL INFORMATION: Creation: 1921. **Affiliated to:** Christoffel Blind-Mission - Bread for the World. **Personnel/Total:** 24. *Salaried:* 20 of which: 18 in developing countries. *Volunteers:* 4 of which: 4 in developing countries. **Budget/Total 1993:** ECU 992000 (US$ 1373000). **Financial sources:** Private: 92%. Public: 6%. *Self-financing:* 2%.

PUBLICATIONS: Periodicals: Wort & Geist (12) - Echo vom Amazonas (12). *Annual report.*

EVALUATION/RESEARCH: Evaluation reports available.

COMMENTS: Undertakes activities in the Commonwealth of Independent States. Information activities related to the Commonwealth of Independent States.

ACTIVITIES IN DEVELOPING REGIONS: Present in developing regions. Active in 3 country(ies). Maintains local field presence. Works through local field partners. **Sustainable Development Actions:** Children/ youth/family; Democracy/good governance/institution building/participatory development; Education/training/literacy; Emergency relief/refugees/humanitarian assistance; Food/famine; Health/sanitation/water; Population/family planning/demography; Rural development/agriculture; Sending volunteers/experts/technical assistance. **Regions:** Central Africa; South America; Southern Africa.

INFORMATION AND EDUCATION ACTIVITIES: Topics: Children/youth/ family; Culture/tradition/religion; Education/training/literacy; Emergency relief/refugees/humanitarian assistance; Food/famine; International relations/cooperation/development aid; Poverty/living conditions. **Activities:** Conferences/seminars/workshops/training activities; Fund raising; Information and documentation services/data bases; Information campaigns/ exhibitions; Publishing/audiovisual materials/educational materials.

CHE0751

SCHWEIZERISCHE STIFTUNG PRO JUVENTUTE - ZENTRAL-SEKRETARIAT ♦ Fondation Suisse Pro Juventute

Postfach, Seefeldstrasse 8, 8022 Zürich, Suisse.

Téléphone: 41 (1) 251 72 44. **Fax:** 41 (1) 252 38 24. **Contact:** Heinz Bruni, Secrétaire général.

OBJECTIFS: S'engager pour le bien-être, la dignité et les droits des enfants, des jeunes et des familles en Suisse.

INFORMATIONS GENERALES: Création: 1912. **Personnel/Total:** 6142. *Salariés:* 142. *Bénévoles:* 6000. **Budget/Total 1993:** ECU 13047000 (US$ 16919000). **Sources financières:** Privé: 80%. *Autofinancement:* 20%.

PUBLICATIONS: Périodiques: Pro Juventute thema (4). *Rapport annuel. Liste des publications.*

ACTIVITES D'INFORMATION ET D'EDUCATION: Domaines: Droits de l'Homme/paix/conflits; Emploi/chômage; Enfants/jeunesse/famille; Santé/assainissement/eau. **Activités:** Campagnes d'information/expositions; Conférences/séminaires/ateliers/activités de formation; Lobbying/plaidoyer; Réseaux/télécommunications électroniques; Services d'information et de documentation/bases de données; Édition/documents audiovisuels/documents éducatifs.

CHE0752

SCHWEIZERISCHE STIFTUNG ZUR FORDERUNG VON KLEININDUSTRIE UND GEWERBE IN DER DRITTEN WELT (FUNDES) ♦ Fondation suisse pour le développement de la petite industrie et de l'artisanat dans le Tiers monde

Bahnhofstrasse, Haus Inseli, 8867 Niederurnen GL, Suisse.

Téléphone: 41 (58) 23 12 70. **Fax:** 41 (58) 21 17 09. **Contact:** Dr. Stéphane Schmidheiny, Président.

CHE0753

SCHWEIZERISCHE UNTERSTUTZUNGSKOMITEE FUR DIE SAHARAOUIS ♦ Comité de soutien de la Suisse alémanique pour les Sahrahouis

Postfach 8205, 3001 Bern, Suisse.

Téléphone: 41 (31) 971 82 51. **Contact:** Elisabeth Baschlin, Présidente.

OBJECTIFS: Apporter une aide en nourriture pour les Saharaouis dans les camps de réfugiés, déployer des activités culturelles et de formation professionnelle à destination des femmes, informer la population suisse de cette situation.

INFORMATIONS GENERALES: Création: 1976. **Type d'organisation:** regroupement d'ONG. **Organisations membres:** 3. **Affiliée à:** Terre des hommes (Suisse) - Mouvement chrétien pour la paix (Suisse) - Schweizevisches ArbeiterInnen Hilfswerk (Suisse). **Personnel/Total:** 6. *Salariés:* 1. *Bénévoles:* 5. **Budget/Total 1993:** ECU 339000 (US$ 440000). **Sources financières:** Privé: 100%.

PUBLICATIONS: Périodiques: Sahara-Info (4). *Rapport annuel. Liste des publications.*

EVALUATION/RECHERCHE: Rapports d'évaluation disponibles.

PREVISIONS D'ACTIVITES: Exposition des dessins d'enfants des camps, information destinées aux écoles suisses.

ACTIVITES DANS LES REGIONS EN DEVELOPPEMENT: Intervient directement dans les régions en développement. Intervient dans 1 pays. Intervient par l'intermédiaire d'organisations locales partenaires. **Actions de Développement durable:** Aliments/famine; Autres; Questions relatives aux femmes; Secours d'urgence/réfugiés/ aide humanitaire; Éducation/formation/alphabétisation. **Régions:** Afrique du Nord.

ACTIVITES D'INFORMATION ET D'EDUCATION: Domaines: Questions relatives aux femmes; Éducation/formation/alphabétisation. **Activités:** Conférences/séminaires/ateliers/activités de formation; Services d'information et de documentation/bases de données; Échanges/parrainage/ jumelage; Éducation formelle.

CHE0754

SCHWEIZERISCHE UNTERSTUTZUNGSKOMITEE FUR ERITREA (SUKE)

Schwyzerstrasse 12, 5430 Wettingen, Switzerland.

Telephone: 41 (56) 27 20 40. **Fax:** 41 (56) 27 10 13. **Contact:** Toni Locher, President.

OBJECTIVES: To provide humanitarian aid to the population of Eritrea and support it with development and reconstruction projects through advice, finances and material. To inform the Swiss public on Eritrea.

GENERAL INFORMATION: Creation: 1977. **Type of organisation:** association of NGOs. **Affiliated to:** CARITAS Switzerland (Switzerland) - Swiss Interchurch Aid (Switzerland) - Terre des Hommes Switzerland (Switzerland). **Personnel/Total:** 27. Salaried: 2. *Volunteers:* 25. **Budget/Total 1993:** ECU 412000 (US$ 5335000). **Financial sources:** Public: 22%. *Self-financing:* 78%.

PUBLICATIONS: Periodicals: Eritrea-Info (2). *Annual report. List of publications.*

ACTIVITIES IN DEVELOPING REGIONS: Active in 1 country(ies). Maintains local field presence. Works through local field partners. **Sustainable Development Actions:** Children/youth/family; Education/training/literacy; Energy/transport; Gender issues/women; Health/sanitation/water. **Regions:** East Africa.

INFORMATION AND EDUCATION ACTIVITIES: Topics: Children/youth/family; Education/training/literacy; Gender issues/women; Health/sanitation/water; International relations/cooperation/development aid; Poverty/living conditions; Urban development/habitat. **Activities:** Conferences/seminars/workshops/training activities; Exchanges/twinning/linking; Fund raising; Information campaigns/exhibitions; Lobbying/advocacy; Networking/electronic telecommunications.

CHE0755

SCHWEIZERISCHES ARBEITERHILFSWERK (SAH) ♦ Oeuvre Suisse d'Entraide Ouvrière

Quellenstrasse 31, Postfach 325, 8031 Zürich, Suisse.

Téléphone: 41 (1) 271 26 00. **Fax:** 41 (1) 272 55 50. **Contact:** Angeline Fankhauser, Conseillère nationale.

OBJECTIFS: Soutenir et appuyer le mouvement ouvrier suisse envers les défavorisés, les proscrits et les opprimés en suisse et à l'étranger

INFORMATIONS GENERALES: Création: 1936. **Type d'organisation:** réseau. **Affiliée à:** Entraide Ouvrière Internationale - Oeuvre Suisse d'Aide aux Réfugiés. **Personnel/Total:** 207. Salariés: 207 dont: 10 dans les pays en développement. **Budget/Total 1993:** ECU 14873000 (US$ 19288000). **Sources financières:** Privé: 15%. Public: 70%. Autofinancement: 15%.

PUBLICATIONS: Périodiques: Solidarité (4). Rapport annuel.

COMMENTAIRES: Intervient dans la Communauté des Etats indépendants. Activités d'information concernant la Communauté des Etats indépendants.

ACTIVITES DANS LES REGIONS EN DEVELOPPEMENT: Intervient directement dans les régions en développement. Intervient dans 10 pays. Maintient une présence locale sur le terrain. Intervient par l'intermédiaire d'organisations locales partenaires. **Actions de Développement durable:** Autres; Droits de l'Homme/paix/conflits; Démocratie/bonne gestion publique/création d'institutions/développement participatif; Développement rural/agriculture; Développement urbain/habitat; Petites entreprises/secteur informel/artisanat; Questions relatives aux femmes; Santé/assainissement/eau; Secours d'urgence/réfugiés/aide humanitaire; Écologie/environnement/biodiversité; Éducation/formation/alphabétisation. **Régions:** Afrique australe; Afrique centrale; Afrique de l'Est; Afrique de l'Ouest; Amérique du Sud; Mexique et Amerique centrale.

ACTIVITES D'INFORMATION ET D'EDUCATION: Domaines: Autres; Droits de l'Homme/paix/conflits; Développement rural/agriculture; Développement urbain/habitat; Emploi/chômage; Paix/conflits ethniques/armement/désarmement; Pauvreté/conditions de vie; Questions relatives aux femmes; Racisme/xénophobie/antisémitisme; Relations internationales/coopération/aide au développement; Relations économiques internationales/commerce/dette/finances; Réfugiés/migrants/groupes ethniques; Santé/assainissement/eau; Secours d'urgence/réfugiés/aide humanitaire; Écologie/environnement/biodiversité; Éducation/formation/alphabétisation. **Activités:** Collecte de fonds; Conférences/séminaires/ateliers/activités de formation; Lobbying/plaidoyer.

CHE0756

SCHWEIZERISCHES KOMITEE FUR UNICEF ♦ Comité suisse pour l'UNICEF

Baumackerstrasse 24, 8050 Zürich, Suisse.

Téléphone: 41 (1) 312 22 66. **Fax:** 41 (1) 312 22 76. **Contact:** Elsbeth Müller, Responsable Communication.

OBJECTIFS: Informer le public suisse sur la situation des enfants dans le monde. Elaborer du matériel d'enseignement pour les écoles sur les problèmes du Tiers-Monde. Collecter des fonds pour financer les projets de l'UNICEF dans les pays en développement.

INFORMATIONS GENERALES: Création: 1959. **Affiliée à:** Forum "Ecole pour un seul monde" (Suisse). **Personnel/Total:** 20. Salariés: 20. **Budget/Total 1993:** ECU 15000 (US$ 20000). **Sources financières:** Privé: 52%. Autofinancement: 48%.

PUBLICATIONS: Rapport annuel. Liste des publications.

COMMENTAIRES: Activités d'information concernant la Communauté des Etats indépendants.

ACTIVITES DANS LES REGIONS EN DEVELOPPEMENT: Intervient par l'intermédiaire d'organisations locales partenaires.

ACTIVITES D'INFORMATION ET D'EDUCATION: Domaines: Aliments/famine; Culture/tradition/religion; Droits de l'Homme/paix/conflits; Développement rural/agriculture; Développement urbain/habitat; Emploi/chômage; Enfants/jeunesse/famille; Paix/conflits ethniques/armement/désarmement; Pauvreté/conditions de vie; Population/planning familial/démographie; Questions relatives aux femmes; Relations internationales/coopération/aide au développement; Réfugiés/migrants/groupes ethniques; Santé/assainissement/eau; Secours d'urgence/réfugiés/aide humanitaire; Écologie/environnement/biodiversité; Éducation/formation/alphabétisation. **Activités:** Campagnes d'information/expositions; Collecte de fonds; Conférences/séminaires/ateliers/activités de formation; Lobbying/plaidoyer; Radiodiffusion/manifestations culturelles; Services d'information et de documentation/bases de données; Édition/documents audiovisuels/documents éducatifs; Éducation formelle.

CHE0757

SCHWEIZERISCHES ROTES KREUZ (SRK) ♦ Swiss Red Cross

IZ/AP, Rainmattstrasse 10, C.P. 2699, 3001 Bern, Switzerland.

Telephone: 41 (31) 387 71 11. **Fax:** 41 (31) 311 27 93. **Contact:** Hubert Bucher, Secretary General.

OBJECTIVES: To relieve distress and to promote human development as defined by the Red Cross principles.

GENERAL INFORMATION: Creation: 1866. **Affiliated to:** International Federation of Red Cross and Red Crescent Societies (Switzerland). Salaried: 62 of which: 40 in developing countries. **Budget/Total 1993:** ECU 13714000 (US$ 17785000). **Financial sources:** Private: 34%. Public: 56%.

PUBLICATIONS: Periodicals: Inter actio (2). Annual report. List of publications.

COMMENTS: The information given refers to the International Co-operation Department of the Swiss Red Cross. Undertakes activities in the Commonwealth of Independent States.

ACTIVITIES IN DEVELOPING REGIONS: Maintains local field presence. Works through local field partners. **Sustainable Development Actions:** Children/youth/family; Democracy/good governance/institution building/participatory development; Education/training/literacy; Emergency relief/refugees/humanitarian assistance; Food/famine; Gender issues/women; Health/sanitation/water; Sending volunteers/experts/technical assistance. **Regions:** Caribbean; Central Africa; Central Asia and South Asia; East Africa; Mexico and Central America; Middle East; South America; South East Asia; Southern Africa; West Africa.

CHE0758

SCHWEIZERISCHES TROPENINSTITUT GESUNDHEITWESEN & EPIDEMIOLOGIE ♦ Swiss Tropical Institute Public Health & Epidemiology

Socinstrasse 57, 4002 Basel, Switzerland.

Telephone: 41 (61) 284 82 83. **Fax:** 41 (61) 271 86 54. **Contact:** Marcel Tanner.

OBJECTIVES: To encourage study, research and information exchange in the field of tropical health. To co-ordinate technical assistance and research support for projects in development co-operation, especially in urban areas and on the district level.

GENERAL INFORMATION: Creation: 1943. **Member organisations:** 28. **Affiliated to:** Association of European Institutes and Schools of Tropical Medicine. **Personnel/Total:** 111. Salaried: 111 of which: 98 in developing countries. **Budget/Total 1993:** ECU 3549000 (US$ 4602000). **Financial sources:** Private: 5%. Public: 80%. Self-financing: 15%.

PUBLICATIONS: Periodicals: ACTA TROPICA (4). Annual report. List of publications.

EVALUATION/RESEARCH: Evaluation reports available. Undertakes research activities.

PLANNED ACTIVITIES: Assistance programmes to local NGO networks in West Africa and regional training courses on public health.

See: *How to Use the Directory,* page 11.

ACTIVITIES IN DEVELOPING REGIONS: Present in developing regions. Active in 8 country(ies). Maintains local field presence. Works through local field partners. **Sustainable Development Actions:** Gender issues/women; Health/sanitation/water; Population/family planning/demography; Sending volunteers/experts/technical assistance. **Regions:** Central Asia and South Asia; East Africa; South East Asia; Southern Africa; West Africa.

INFORMATION AND EDUCATION ACTIVITIES: Topics: Culture/tradition/religion; Gender issues/women; Health/sanitation/water; International relations/cooperation/development aid; Poverty/living conditions; Refugees/migrants/ethnic groups. **Activities:** Conferences/seminars/workshops/training activities; Exchanges/twinning/linking; Information and documentation services/data bases; Publishing/audiovisual materials/educational materials.

CHE0759
SECOURS DENTAIRE INTERNATIONAL (SDI)

En Beau Regard, 1815 Clarens, Suisse.

Téléphone: 41 (21) 964 38 54. *Fax:* 41 (21) 964 38 54. *Contact:* Dr. Jean F. Guignard, Président.

OBJECTIFS: Prévenir et traiter les maladies bucco-dentaires dans le tiers monde, par l'installation de cliniques dentaires sociales, la formation du personnel médico-dentaire, le suivi et la gestion permanente des cliniques, la prévention dans les écoles, l'installation de cliniques dentaires mobiles en brousse.

INFORMATIONS GENERALES: *Création:* 1986. *Type d'organisation:* réseau. *Personnel/Total:* 105. *Salariés:* 80 dont: 80 dans les pays en développement. *Bénévoles:* 25 dont: 25 dans les pays en développement. *Budget/Total 1993:* ECU 261000 (US$ 338000). *Sources financières:* Privé: 50%. Public: 50%.

PUBLICATIONS: *Rapport annuel. Liste des publications.*

ACTIVITES DANS LES REGIONS EN DEVELOPPEMENT: Intervient directement dans les régions en développement. Intervient dans 8 pays. Maintient une présence locale sur le terrain. Intervient par l'intermédiaire d'organisations locales partenaires. **Actions de Développement durable:** Santé/assainissement/eau; Secours d'urgence/réfugiés/aide humanitaire. **Régions:** Afrique australe; Afrique centrale; Afrique de l'Est; Afrique de l'Ouest.

ACTIVITES D'INFORMATION ET D'EDUCATION: Domaines: Enfants/jeunesse/famille; Relations internationales/coopération/aide au développement; Santé/assainissement/eau; Secours d'urgence/réfugiés/aide humanitaire. **Activités:** Services d'information et de documentation/bases de données; Édition/documents audiovisuels/documents éducatifs; Éducation formelle.

CHE0760
SECRETARIADO EUROPEO OSCAR ROMERO DE SOLIDARIDAD CON LOS PUEBLOS CENTROAMERICANOS ♦ Secrétariat européen Oscar Romero de solidarité avec les peuples d'Amérique centrale

c/o Karl Heuberger, Witikonerstrasse 36, 8037 Zürich, Suisse.

Téléphone: 41 (1) 361 66 00. *Fax:* 41 (1) 361 78 27.

CHE0761
SENIOR EXPERT CORPS (SEC)

c/o Swisscontact, Döltschiweg 39, 8055 Zürich, Suisse.

Téléphone: 41 (1) 463 94 11. *Fax:* 41 (1) 462 33 65.

CHE0762
SERVICE CHRETIEN D'ANIMATION RURALE (SCAR) ♦ Christian Service for Rural Development

C.P. 67, 1373 Chavornay, Suisse.

Téléphone: 41 (24) 43 13 42. *Fax:* 41 (24) 43 19 76.

OBJECTIFS: Soutenir les Eglises engagées dans le développement par les évaluations de projets, l'organisation de rencontres et de séminaires, et la diffusion d'informations. Mener des actions de sensibilisation des Chrétiens en Europe.

INFORMATIONS GENERALES: *Création:* 1971. *Type d'organisation:* réseau. *Organisations membres:* 7. *Affiliée à:* Service Chrétien d'Appui à l'Animation Rurale.. *Personnel/Total:* 2. *Salariés:* 2. *Budget/Total 1993:* ECU 115000 (US$ 149000). *Sources financières:* Privé: 100%.

PUBLICATIONS: *Liste des publications.*

PREVISIONS D'ACTIVITES: Renforcement des bureaux de développement des Eglises, renforcement d'échanges commerciaux Sud-Sud et Sud-Nord

COMMENTAIRES: Les activités du SCAR au Sud se font à travers le Service Chrétien d'appui à l'animation rurale qui va bientôt établir son bureau en Afrique. Son adresse actuelle est la même que celle du SCAR.

ACTIVITES DANS LES REGIONS EN DEVELOPPEMENT: Intervient dans 6 pays. Intervient par l'intermédiaire d'organisations locales partenaires. **Actions de Développement durable:** Dette/finances/commerce; Développement rural/agriculture; Enfants/jeunesse/famille; Questions relatives aux femmes; Santé/assainissement/eau; Écologie/environnement/biodiversité; Éducation/formation/alphabétisation. **Régions:** Afrique australe; Afrique centrale; Afrique de l'Ouest.

ACTIVITES D'INFORMATION ET D'EDUCATION: Domaines: Culture/tradition/religion; Développement rural/agriculture; Enfants/jeunesse/famille; Population/planning familial/démographie; Questions relatives aux femmes; Écologie/environnement/biodiversité. **Activités:** Conférences/séminaires/ateliers/activités de formation; Services d'information et de documentation/bases de données; Édition/documents audiovisuels/documents éducatifs;

CHE0763
SERVICE ECOLE DE LA COMMUNAUTE DE TRAVAIL

10 chemin des Epinettes, 1007 Lausanne, Suisse.

Téléphone: 41 (21) 616 84 33. *Fax:* 41 (21) 617 43 52. *Contact:* Pierre Clerici.

OBJECTIFS: Sensibiliser le milieu scolaire suisse à une meilleure connaissance du Tiers Monde et du développement en leur proposant du matériel pédagogique, des animations et des cours de perfectionnement.

INFORMATIONS GENERALES: *Création:* 1982. *Type d'organisation:* regroupement d'ONG. *Affiliée à:* Communauté de travail Swissaid - Action de carême - Pain pour le prochain -Helvetas - Caritas (Suisse). *Personnel/Total:* 3. *Salariés:* 3. *Budget/Total 1993:* ECU 261000 (US$ 338000). *Sources financières:* Privé: 40%. Public: 40%. Autofinancement: 20%.

PUBLICATIONS: *Rapport annuel. Liste des publications.*

COMMENTAIRES: Activités d'information concernant la Communauté des Etats indépendants.

ACTIVITES D'INFORMATION ET D'EDUCATION: Domaines: Aliments/famine; Culture/tradition/religion; Droits de l'Homme/paix/conflits; Développement rural/agriculture; Développement urbain/habitat; Emploi/chômage; Enfants/jeunesse/famille; Paix/conflits ethniques/armement/désarmement; Pauvreté/conditions de vie; Population/planning familial/démographie; Questions relatives aux femmes; Racisme/xénophobie/antisémitisme; Relations internationales/coopération/aide au développement; Relations économiques internationales/commerce/dette/finances; Réfugiés/migrants/groupes ethniques; Santé/assainissement/eau; Secours d'urgence/réfugiés/aide humanitaire; Écologie/environnement/biodiversité; Éducation/formation/alphabétisation. **Activités:** Services d'information et de documentation/bases de données; Édition/documents audiovisuels/documents éducatifs.

CHE0764
SOCIETE INTERNATIONALE MISSIONNAIRE (SIM)

Case postale 60, Rue de Genève 77 bis, 1000 Lausanne 20, Suisse.

Téléphone: 41 (21) 625 51 39. *Fax:* 41 (21) 625 51 69. *Contact:* Claude Brocqueville, Directeur.

OBJECTIFS: Engager, former, envoyer des missionnaires et les soutenir. Aider les pays en voie de développement par une activité sociale sous

forme de dispensaires, hôpitaux, programmes de développement agricole et de formation technique.

INFORMATIONS GENERALES: *Création:* 1977. *Personnel/Total:* 60. *Salariés:* 57 dont: 43 dans les pays en développement. *Bénévoles:* 3 dont: 3 dans les pays en développement. *Budget/Total 1993:* ECU 902000 (US$ 1170000). *Sources financières:* Privé: 100%.

PUBLICATIONS: *Périodiques:* SIM Actualités (4).

EVALUATION/RECHERCHE: Rapports d'évaluation disponibles. Entreprend des activités de recherche.

COMMENTAIRES: Les prévisions d'activité sont à voir avec le siège international à Charlotte aux USA.

ACTIVITES DANS LES REGIONS EN DEVELOPPEMENT: Intervient directement dans les régions en développement. Intervient dans 25 pays. Maintient une présence locale sur le terrain. Intervient par l'intermédiaire d'organisations locales partenaires. **Actions de Développement durable:** Aliments/famine; Développement rural/agriculture; Enfants/jeunesse/famille; Questions relatives aux femmes; Santé/assainissement/eau; Secours d'urgence/réfugiés/aide humanitaire. **Régions:** Afrique de l'Est; Afrique de l'Ouest; Amérique du Sud; Asie centrale et Asie du Sud; Asie de l'Est.

ACTIVITES D'INFORMATION ET D'EDUCATION: Domaines: Aliments/famine; Développement rural/agriculture; Enfants/jeunesse/famille; Questions relatives aux femmes; Réfugiés/migrants/groupes ethniques; Santé/assainissement/eau; Secours d'urgence/réfugiés/aide humanitaire. **Activités:** Collecte de fonds.

CHE0765

SOCIETE INTERNATIONALE POUR LE DEVELOPPEMENT - SECTION SUISSE (SID) ♦ Society for International Development - Swiss Section

Case postale 120, 1218 Grand-Saconnex, Switzerland.

Telephone: 41 (22) 347 52 84. *Fax:* 41 (22) 734 70 82. *Contact:* Cyril Ritchie, President.

OBJECTIVES: To promote new ideas, actions and policy to transform development priorities towards a self reliant world which is sustainable, democratic, just and inclusive.

GENERAL INFORMATION: *Creation:* 1961. *Affiliated to:* SID International. *Personnel/Total:* 7. *Volunteers:* 7. *Financial sources:* Self-financing: 100%.

INFORMATION AND EDUCATION ACTIVITIES: Topics: Children/youth/family; Ecology/environment/biodiversity; Education/training/literacy; Employment/unemployment; Gender issues/women; Health/sanitation/water; Human rights/peace/conflicts; International economic relations/trade/debt/finance; International relations/cooperation/development aid; Population/family planning/demography; Poverty/living conditions; Rural development/agriculture; Urban development/habitat. **Activities:** Conferences/seminars/workshops/training activities; Information campaigns/exhibitions; Lobbying/advocacy.

CHE0766

SOCIETE SUISSE D'ETUDES AFRICAINES (SSEA-SAG)

Dr. C.Savary Musée d'ethnographie, Bd Carl-Vogt 65, 1205 Genève, Suisse.

Téléphone: 41 (22) 328 12 18. *Fax:* 41 (22) 328 52 31. *Contact:* Claude Savary, Président.

OBJECTIFS: Promouvoir et coordonner la recherche, la documentation et l'information sur l'Afrique. Organiser des rencontres sur les questions africaines. Coopérer avec les institutions similaires en Suisse et à l'étranger. Collaborer avec les organisations publiques ou privées de coopération oeuvrant en Afrique.

INFORMATIONS GENERALES: *Création:* 1974. *Type d'organisation:* collectif. *Affiliée à:* Académie suisse des sciences humaines et sociales (Suisse) - Conseil européen des études africaines.. *Personnel/Total:* 7. *Bénévoles:* 7. *Budget/Total 1993:* ECU 14000 (US$ 18000). *Sources financières:* Privé: 5%. Public: 70%. Autofinancement: 25%.

PUBLICATIONS: *Périodiques:* Newsletter (4) - Bibliographie africaine suisse (1). *Liste des publications.*

EVALUATION/RECHERCHE: Entreprend des activités de recherche.

COMMENTAIRES: L'organisation est avant tout une société scientifique réunissant des africanistes appartenant à différentes disciplines.

ACTIVITES D'INFORMATION ET D'EDUCATION: Domaines: Aliments/famine; Culture/tradition/religion; Droits de l'Homme/paix/conflits; Développement rural/agriculture; Développement urbain/habitat; Réfugiés/migrants/groupes ethniques; Écologie/environnement/biodiversité. **Activités:** Conférences/séminaires/ateliers/activités de formation; Services d'information et de documentation/bases de données.

CHE0767

SOCIETE SUISSE POUR LA PROTECTION DE L'ENVIRONNEMENT (SPE)

Rue Saint-Ours 6,, 1205 Genève, Suisse.

Téléphone: 41 (22) 329 99 29. *Fax:* 41 (22) 320 39 77. *Contact:* Longet René, Directeur.

OBJECTIFS: Informer sur la question environnementale, participer aux processus décisionnels, travailler sur l'interface écologie-économie.

INFORMATIONS GENERALES: *Création:* 1964. *Personnel/Total:* 21. *Salariés:* 11. *Bénévoles:* 10. *Budget/Total 1993:* ECU 783000 (US$ 1015000). *Sources financières:* Privé: 30%. Public: 20%. Autofinancement: 50%.

PUBLICATIONS: *Périodiques:* SPE-Info (6) - Bulletin (4). *Rapport annuel. Liste des publications.*

ACTIVITES D'INFORMATION ET D'EDUCATION: Domaines: Aliments/famine; Développement rural/agriculture; Relations économiques internationales/commerce/dette/finances; Santé/assainissement/eau; Écologie/environnement/biodiversité. **Activités:** Campagnes d'information/expositions; Collecte de fonds; Conférences/séminaires/ateliers/activités de formation; Lobbying/plaidoyer; Services d'information et de documentation/bases de données; Édition/documents audiovisuels/documents éducatifs.

CHE0768

SOLARAID ♦ STIFTUNG FUR ENTWICKLUNGSHILFE MIT ANGEPASSTER TECHNOLOGIE

Rotbuchstrasse 6, 8165 Wasen-Schleinikon, Suisse.

Téléphone: 41 (1) 856 06 80. *Fax:* 41 (1) 875 03 02.

CHE0769

SOLIDARIETA MEDICA CON IL NICARAGUA (AMCA)

Case postale 2536, 6500 Bellinzona, Suisse.

Téléphone: 41 (92) 25 03 33.

CHE0770

SOLIDARIETA TERZO MONDO ♦ Solidarité Tiers Monde

Via Maro da Carona 2, 6900 Lugano, Suisse.

Téléphone: 41 (91) 22 77 79. *Contact:* Gabriele Banchini, Président.

CHE0771

SOLIDARITAT MIT MOCAMBIQUE ♦ Solidarité avec le Mozambique

Postfach 259, 9400 Rorschach-ost, Suisse.

Téléphone: 41 (71) 42 74 50. *Contact:* Herbert Schmid, Président.

OBJECTIFS: Collecter de l'information sur le Mozambique et la région et la divulguer en Suisse. Produire du matériel d'information, permettre la diffusion et l'échange de la culture mozambicaine entre les deux pays, organiser des conférences et débats.

INFORMATIONS GENERALES: *Création:* 1986. *Type d'organisation:* collectif. *Affiliée à:* European Solidarity with Mozambique and Angola (Pays-Bas). *Personnel/Total:* 1. *Salariés:* 1. *Budget/Total 1993:* ECU 10000 (US$ 14000). *Sources financières:* Privé: 80%. Autofinancement: 20%.

See: *How to Use the Directory*, page 11.

PUBLICATIONS: *Périodiques:* Mosambik-Rundbrief (4). *Rapport annuel.*

ACTIVITES DANS LES REGIONS EN DEVELOPPEMENT: Intervient dans 1 pays. Maintient une présence locale sur le terrain.

ACTIVITES D'INFORMATION ET D'EDUCATION: Domaines: Culture/tradition/religion; Questions relatives aux femmes. **Activités:** Campagnes d'information/expositions; Conférences/séminaires/ateliers/activités de formation; Services d'information et de documentation/bases de données.

CHE0772
SOLIDARITATSFONDS DES CHRISTLICHNATIONALEN GEWERKSCHAFTSBUNDES DER SCHWEIZ

Postfach 5775, Hopfenweg 21, 3001 Bern, Suisse.

Téléphone: 41 (31) 370 21 11. *Fax:* 41 (31) 370 21 09. *Contact:* Hugo Fasel, Président.

OBJECTIFS: Aider le Tiers-Monde, agir dans l'agriculture, ouvrir des ateliers de couture, des boulangerie, des moulins.

INFORMATIONS GENERALES: *Création:* 1960. *Type d'organisation:* regroupement d'ONG. *Budget/Total 1993:* ECU 60000 (US$ 78000). *Sources financières:* Privé: 100%.

EVALUATION/RECHERCHE: Rapports d'évaluation disponibles. Entreprend des activités de recherche.

ACTIVITES DANS LES REGIONS EN DEVELOPPEMENT: Intervient dans 5 pays. Maintient une présence locale sur le terrain. Intervient par l'intermédiaire d'organisations locales partenaires. **Actions de Développement durable:** Droits de l'Homme/paix/conflits; Développement rural/agriculture; Enfants/jeunesse/famille; Petites entreprises/secteur informel/artisanat; Questions relatives aux femmes; Éducation/formation/alphabétisation. **Régions:** Afrique de l'Est; Afrique de l'Ouest; Amérique du Sud; Mexique et Amerique centrale; Océanie.

ACTIVITES D'INFORMATION ET D'EDUCATION: Domaines: Droits de l'Homme/paix/conflits; Développement rural/agriculture; Emploi/chômage; Enfants/jeunesse/famille; Pauvreté/conditions de vie; Questions relatives aux femmes; Relations internationales/coopération/aide au développement; Éducation/formation/alphabétisation. **Activités:** Collecte de fonds; Conférences/séminaires/ateliers/activités de formation; Édition/documents audiovisuels/documents éducatifs; Éducation formelle.

CHE0773
SOLIDARITATSFONDS FUR DEN SOZIALEN BEFREIUNGSKAMPF IN DER DRITTEN WELT (SOLIFONDS)
♦ Solidarity Fund for the Social Struggle for Liberation in the Third World

Quellenstrasse 31, 8031 Zürich, Switzerland.

Telephone: 41 (1) 272 60 37. *Fax:* 41 (1) 272 55 50. *Contact:* Marco Mona, President.

OBJECTIVES: To support trade unions, human rights organisations and other grassroots groups in developing countries, in their struggle for social freedom.

GENERAL INFORMATION: *Creation:* 1983. *Type of organisation:* coordinating body. *Member organisations:* 14. *Personnel/Total:* 3. *Salaried:* 3. *Budget/Total 1993:* ECU 185000 (US$ 240000). *Financial sources:* Private: 95%. Self-financing: 5%.

PUBLICATIONS: *Annual report.*

COMMENTS: SOLIFONDS is a member of the "Union Syndicale Suisse" and the "Parti Socialiste Suisse."

ACTIVITIES IN DEVELOPING REGIONS: Active in 9 country(ies). Works through local field partners. **Sustainable Development Actions:** Democracy/good governance/institution building/participatory development; Education/training/literacy; Gender issues/women; Human rights/peace/conflicts. **Regions:** Caribbean; Mexico and Central America; Middle East; South America; South East Asia.

INFORMATION AND EDUCATION ACTIVITIES: Topics: Gender issues/women; Human rights/peace/conflicts; International economic relations/trade/debt/finance; International relations/cooperation/development aid; Other; Poverty/living conditions. **Activities:** Conferences/seminars/workshops/training activities; Information campaigns/exhibitions.

CHE0774
SOLIDARITE AFRIQUE DU SUD

Case postale 182, 1211 Genève 12, Suisse.

CHE0775
SOLIDARITE TIERS MONDE ♦ Solidarity with the Third World

C.P. 122, 1800 Vevey 2, Suisse.

Téléphone: 41 (21) 944 51 96. *Contact:* Mauro Tolusso, Secrétaire général.

CHE0776
SOLIDARMED - CHRISTLICHER DIENST FUR MEDIZINISCHE ZUSAMMENARBEIT ♦ Service Chrétien pour la Coopération Médicale

Untergeissenstein 10/12, Postfach 12136, 6000 Luzern 12, Suisse.

Téléphone: 41 (41) 44 66 67. *Fax:* 41 (41) 43 05 80. *Contact:* Hugo Morger, Président.

OBJECTIFS: Promouvoir le service sanitaire et les soins médicaux dans les pays en développement. Recruter des médecins pour les hôpitaux partenaires de ces pays.

INFORMATIONS GENERALES: *Création:* 1926. *Affiliée à:* Medicus Mundi, Unité, MMI (Belgique.). *Personnel/Total:* 16. *Salariés:* 16 dont: 16 dans les pays en développement. *Budget/Total 1993:* ECU 976000 (US$ 1266000). *Sources financières:* Privé: 25%. Public: 71%. Autofinancement: 4%.

PUBLICATIONS: *Périodiques:* Solidarmed-Notizen (3). *Rapport annuel.*

ACTIVITES DANS LES REGIONS EN DEVELOPPEMENT: Intervient directement dans les régions en développement. Intervient dans 3 pays. Maintient une présence locale sur le terrain. **Actions de Développement durable:** Santé/assainissement/eau. **Régions:** Afrique australe; Afrique de l'Est.

CHE0777
SOROPTIMIST INTERNATIONAL

Les Plantées, 1267 Vich, Switzerland.

Telephone: 41 - 64 14 67.

CHE0778
SOS ENVIRONNEMENT A LA BASE

46 route de Vallon, 1224 Chêne-Bougeries, Suisse.

Téléphone: 41 (22) 348 38 50. *Contact:* Jean-Martin Tchaptchet, Coordonnateur général.

OBJECTIFS: Contribuer au développement des ressources humaines et institutionnelles dont les populations ont besoin pour mener de façon intégrée les activités visant à l'amélioration de leurs conditions de vie et à la sauvegarde, la reconstitution et la protection de l'environnement.

INFORMATIONS GENERALES: *Création:* 1991. *Personnel/Total:* 14. *Bénévoles:* 14 dont: 10 dans les pays en développement.

ACTIVITES DANS LES REGIONS EN DEVELOPPEMENT: Intervient directement dans les régions en développement. Intervient par l'intermédiaire d'organisations locales partenaires. **Actions de Développement durable:** Santé/assainissement/eau; Écologie/environnement/biodiversité; Énergie/transport. **Régions:** Afrique australe; Afrique centrale; Afrique de l'Ouest.

ACTIVITES D'INFORMATION ET D'EDUCATION: Domaines: Pauvreté/conditions de vie; Questions relatives aux femmes; Santé/assainissement/eau; Écologie/environnement/biodiversité. **Activités:** Collecte de fonds; Conférences/séminaires/ateliers/activités de formation; Lobbying/plaidoyer; Échanges/parrainage/jumelage.

CHE0779
SOS RACISME VAUD

Case postale 299, 1000 Lausanne 12, Suisse.

Voir : *Comment utiliser le répertoire,* page 11.

CHE0780

STEERING COMMITTEE FOR HUMANITARIAN RESPONSE

17 chemin de Crêts, 1211 Geneva 19, Switzerland.

Telephone: 41 (22) 730 42 22. **Fax:** 41 (22) 733 03 95. **Contact:** Robert Rossborough, Secretary.

OBJECTIVES: To encourage co-operation between member organisations in the execution of international disaster assistance. To clarify policy issues relating to emergency aid. To encourage co-ordinated action by members at headquarters and in the field.

GENERAL INFORMATION: *Creation:* 1972. *Type of organisation:* association of NGOs, coordinating body. *Member organisations:* 7. *Personnel/Total:* 2. *Salaried:* 2. *Budget/Total 1993:* ECU 39000 (US$ 51000). *Financial sources: Self-financing:* 100%.

COMMENTS: The NGO undertakes activities in Eastern Europe through its members.

ACTIVITIES IN DEVELOPING REGIONS: Works through local field partners.

INFORMATION AND EDUCATION ACTIVITIES: Topics: Emergency relief/refugees/humanitarian assistance; Food/famine; Health/sanitation/water. **Activities:** Lobbying/advocacy.

CHE0781

STIFTUNG ENGAGEMENT DRITTE WELT

Untere Waid, 9402 Morschwil, Suisse.

Téléphone: 41 (71) 96 14 24.

CHE0782

STIFTUNG FUR INTERNATIONAL ZUSAMMENARBEIT

Oberdorfstrasse 8, 8024 Zürich 24, Switzerland.

CHE0783

STIFTUNG GERTRUD KURZ

Postfach 8344, 3000 Bern, Suisse.

CHE0784

STIFTUNG KINDERDIREKTHILFE KOLUMBIEN

Postfach 619, Birsigstrasse 119, 4010 Basel, Suisse.

CHE0785

STIFTUNG KINDERDORF PESTALOZZI - ABTEILUNG KINDERHILFE DRITTE WELT   (SKIP) ♦ Pestalozzi Children's Village Foundation - Outreach Programme to Third World Children

Rue Guillimann 12, 1701 Fribourg, Switzerland.

Telephone: 41 (37) 23 26 36. **Fax:** 41 (37) 22 50 43. **Contact:** Peter Meienberger, Programme Director.

OBJECTIVES: To help orphan children and children suffering from neglect. To reunify abandoned children with their families and help distressed youth and families through local foster programmes or alternative solutions within the context of community-based development.

GENERAL INFORMATION: *Creation:* 1982. *Personnel/Total:* 150. *Salaried:* 150 of which: 145 in developing countries. *Budget/Total 1993:* ECU 2124000 (US$ 2755000).

PUBLICATIONS: *Annual report.*

EVALUATION/RESEARCH: Evaluation reports available. Undertakes research activities.

COMMENTS: Undertakes activities in the Commonwealth of Independent States. Information activities related to the Commonwealth of Independent States.

ACTIVITIES IN DEVELOPING REGIONS: Present in developing regions. Active in 8 country(ies). Maintains local field presence. Works through local field partners.

CHE0786

STIFTUNG OFFENE HAND ♦ Foundation Open Hand

Banhaldensrtr. 28, 8307 Effretikon, Suisse.

Contact: Armin Villiger, Président.

OBJECTIFS: Promouvoir la création de petites entreprises en Amérique Latine.

INFORMATIONS GENERALES: *Création:* 1968. *Personnel/Total:* 9. *Bénévoles:* 9. *Budget/Total 1993:* ECU 62000 (US$ 81000). *Sources financières: Privé:* 80%. *Public:* 20%.

PUBLICATIONS: *Rapport annuel.*

ACTIVITES DANS LES REGIONS EN DEVELOPPEMENT: Intervient directement dans les régions en développement. Intervient dans 2 pays. Intervient par l'intermédiaire d'organisations locales partenaires. **Actions de Développement durable:** Petites entreprises/secteur informel/artisanat. **Régions:** Amérique du Sud; Mexique et Amerique centrale.

ACTIVITES D'INFORMATION ET D'EDUCATION: Domaines: Emploi/chômage; Relations internationales/coopération/aide au développement. **Activités:** Collecte de fonds.

CHE0787

STIFTUNG UMWELTBILDUNG SCHWEIZ ♦ Fondation suisse d'éducation pour l'environnement

Rebbergstrasse, 4800 Zofingen, Suisse.

Téléphone: 41 (62) 51 58 55. **Fax:** 41 (62) 51 58 70. **Contact:** Hans C. Selzmann.

OBJECTIFS: Promouvoir et coordonner l'éducation à l'environnement en Suisse

INFORMATIONS GENERALES: *Création:* 1994. *Personnel/Total:* 7. *Salariés:* 7. *Budget/Total 1993:* ECU 522000 (US$ 677000). *Sources financières: Privé:* 10%. *Public:* 80%. *Autofinancement:* 10%.

PUBLICATIONS: *Rapport annuel.*

ACTIVITES D'INFORMATION ET D'EDUCATION: Domaines: Écologie/environnement/biodiversité. **Activités:** Conférences/séminaires/ateliers/activités de formation; Lobbying/plaidoyer; Services d'information et de documentation/bases de données; Éducation formelle.

CHE0788

STIFTUNG UNSERE KLEINEN BRUDER UND SCHWESTERN ♦ Fondation nos petits frères et soeurs

Speerstrasse 18, 9030 Abtwil, Suisse.

Téléphone: 41 (71) 31 55 01. **Contact:** Père W. Wasson.

OBJECTIFS: Aider les orphelins en Amérique latine

INFORMATIONS GENERALES: *Création:* 1985. *Affiliée à:* Our Little Brothers and Sisters (USA). *Personnel/Total:* 4. *Bénévoles:* 4 dont: 2 dans les pays en développement. *Budget/Total 1993:* ECU 444000 (US$ 575000). *Sources financières: Privé:* 100%.

PUBLICATIONS: *Périodiques:* Bulletin d'information (8). *Rapport annuel.*

EVALUATION/RECHERCHE: Rapports d'évaluation disponibles.

ACTIVITES DANS LES REGIONS EN DEVELOPPEMENT: Intervient directement dans les régions en développement. Intervient dans 3 pays. Maintient une présence locale sur le terrain. Intervient par l'intermédiaire d'organisations locales partenaires. **Actions de Développement durable:** Aliments/famine; Développement rural/agriculture; Enfants/jeunesse/famille; Envoi de volontaires/experts/assistance technique; Santé/assainissement/eau; Éducation/formation/alphabétisation. **Régions:** Mexique et Amerique centrale.

ACTIVITES D'INFORMATION ET D'EDUCATION: Domaines: Aliments/famine; Développement rural/agriculture; Enfants/jeunesse/famille; Pauvreté/conditions de vie; Santé/assainissement/eau; Éducation/formation/alphabétisation. **Activités:** Collecte de fonds.

CHE0789

STIFTUNG VIVAMOS MEJOR ◆ Vivamos Mejor Foundation

Spitalackerstrasse 61, 3013 Bern, Switzerland.

Telephone: 41 (31) 331 39 29. *Fax:* 41 (31) 332 03 09. *Contact:* Jürg Meichle, Director.

OBJECTIVES: To improve the health and living conditions of women and children, especially those in the poorest parts of Latin America. To help the target populations develop and fully use their own capabilities and resources. To provide information about health and nutrition, home economics and protection of the environment.

GENERAL INFORMATION: *Creation:* 1981. *Personnel/Total:* 124. *Salaried:* 124 of which: 120 in developing countries. *Budget/Total 1993:* ECU 1148000 (US$ 1489000). *Financial sources:* Private: 59%. Public: 25%. *Self-financing:* 16%.

PUBLICATIONS: *Periodicals:* Intercambio (4). *Annual report.*

ACTIVITIES IN DEVELOPING REGIONS: Present in developing regions. Active in 7 country(ies). Maintains local field presence. Works through local field partners. **Sustainable Development Actions:** Children/youth/family; Ecology/environment/biodiversity; Education/training/literacy; Gender issues/women; Health/sanitation/water; Population/family planning/demography; Small enterprises/informal sector/handicrafts. **Regions:** Mexico and Central America; South America.

INFORMATION AND EDUCATION ACTIVITIES: Topics: Children/youth/family; Ecology/environment/biodiversity; Education/training/literacy; Gender issues/women; Health/sanitation/water; Population/family planning/demography; Poverty/living conditions. **Activities:** Fund raising.

CHE0790

STIFTUNG WIR BAUEN MITEINANDER

Postfach 136, Zugerstrasse 50, 6341 Baar 1, Suisse.

Téléphone: 41 (42) 31 80 71. *Fax:* 41 (42) 31 80 73.

CHE0791

SUDAFRIKA MISSION (SAM)

Missionsstrasse 21, 4003 Basel, Suisse.

Téléphone: 41 (61) 268 82 33. *Fax:* 41 (61) 268 82 68.

CHE0792

SWISS SOCIETY FOR THE PROTECTION OF THE ENVIRONMENT (SGU)

Sandrainstrasse 50, 3007 Bern, Switzerland.

Telephone: 41 (31) 45 62 46.

CHE0793

SWISSCONTACT SCHWEIZERISCHE STIFTUNG FUR TECHNISCHE ENTWICKLUNGSZUSAMMENARBEIT (SWISSCONTACT) ◆ Fondation suisse de coopération au développement technique

Döltschiweg 39, Case postale, 8055 Zürich, Suisse.

Téléphone: 41 (1) 463 94 11. *Fax:* 41 (1) 462 33 65. *Contact:* Robert Jenny, Secrétaire général.

OBJECTIFS: Former des techniciens et des enseignants techniques dans les pays en développement. Promouvoir la petite entreprise et l'écologie.

INFORMATIONS GENERALES: *Création:* 1959. *Affiliée à:* Intercoopération (Suisse) - Kodis (Suisse) - Skat (Suisse). *Personnel/Total:* 77. *Salariés:* 77 dont: 57 dans les pays en développement. *Budget/Total 1993:* ECU 10437000 (US$ 13535000). *Sources financières:* Privé: 12%. Public: 87%. Autofinancement: 1%.

PUBLICATIONS: *Rapport annuel.*

COMMENTAIRES: Intervient dans la Communauté des Etats indépendants.

ACTIVITES DANS LES REGIONS EN DEVELOPPEMENT: Intervient directement dans les régions en développement. Intervient dans 18 pays. Maintient une présence locale sur le terrain. Intervient par l'inter-médiaire d'organisations locales partenaires. **Actions de Développement durable:** Envoi de volontaires/experts/assistance technique; Petites entreprises/secteur informel/artisanat; Écologie/environnement/biodiversité; Éducation/formation/alphabétisation. **Régions:** Afrique australe; Afrique de l'Est; Afrique de l'Ouest; Amérique du Sud; Asie centrale et Asie du Sud; Asie du Sud-Est; Caraïbes; Mexique et Amérique centrale.

ACTIVITES D'INFORMATION ET D'EDUCATION: Domaines: Relations internationales/coopération/aide au développement; Écologie/environnement/biodiversité. **Activités:** Conférences/séminaires/ateliers/activités de formation.

CHE0794

SYNDICAT INTERPROFESSIONNEL DE TRAVAILLEUSES ET TRAVAILLEURS (SIT)

C.P. 343, 1211 Genève 3, Suisse.

Téléphone: 41 (22) 310 50 44. *Fax:* 41 (22) 311 34 64. *Contact:* B. Matthey.

OBJECTIFS: Défendre les intérêts de travailleurs et travailleuses. Lutter pour une société solidaire et démocratique.

INFORMATIONS GENERALES: *Création:* 1921. *Affiliée à:* Fédération Genevoise de Coopération - Confédération Mondiale du Travail. *Personnel/Total:* 53. *Salariés:* 51. *Bénévoles:* 2 dont: 2 dans les pays en développement. *Budget/Total 1993:* ECU 2087000 (US$ 2707000). *Sources financières:* Autofinancement: 100%.

PUBLICATIONS: *Périodiques:* Sit-Info (12). *Rapport annuel. Liste des publications.*

EVALUATION/RECHERCHE: Rapports d'évaluation disponibles. Entreprend des activités de recherche.

ACTIVITES DANS LES REGIONS EN DEVELOPPEMENT: Intervient dans 2 pays. Maintient une présence locale sur le terrain. Intervient par l'intermédiaire d'organisations locales partenaires. **Actions de Développement durable:** Développement rural/agriculture; Éducation/formation/alphabétisation. **Régions:** Asie du Sud-Est; Mexique et Amérique centrale.

ACTIVITES D'INFORMATION ET D'EDUCATION: Domaines: Emploi/chômage; Pauvreté/conditions de vie; Questions relatives aux femmes; Racisme/xénophobie/antisémitisme. **Activités:** Conférences/séminaires/ateliers/activités de formation; Lobbying/plaidoyer; Édition/documents audiovisuels/documents éducatifs.

CHE0795

TECHNOLOGY FOR THE PEOPLE (TFTP) ◆ La technique au service des hommes

9 rue Cornavin, CP 2253, 1211 Geneve, Switzerland.

Telephone: 41 (22) 32 89 26. *Fax:* 41 (22) 738 97 76. *Contact:* David Dichter, Director.

OBJECTIVES: To stimulate economic and social progress in developing regions by supporting the development of small and medium-sized enterprises in both the public and private sectors. To link businesses with development interests and increase productivity, create jobs and raise income levels.

GENERAL INFORMATION: *Creation:* 1978. *Personnel/Total:* 14. *Salaried:* 13 of which: 9 in developing countries. *Volunteers:* 1. *Budget/Total 1993:* ECU 391000 (US$ 508000). *Financial sources:* Public: 93%. *Self-financing:* 7%.

PUBLICATIONS: *Annual report.*

EVALUATION/RESEARCH: Undertakes research activities.

PLANNED ACTIVITIES: Feasibility studies on the productivity of electric vehicles in China and on the possibility of transfering technology from Italy to Albania.

COMMENTS: Most of TFTP's work consists of transfering technologies from Swiss small enterprises to enterprises in seven Asian countries: India, Bangladesh, Thailand, Malaysia, Indonesia, Philippines and China.

Voir : *Comment utiliser le répertoire,* page 11.

ACTIVITIES IN DEVELOPING REGIONS: Active in 7 country(ies). Maintains local field presence. Works through local field partners. **Sustainable Development Actions:** Ecology/environment/biodiversity; Small enterprises/informal sector/handicrafts; Urban development/habitat. **Regions:** East Asia; South East Asia.

INFORMATION AND EDUCATION ACTIVITIES: Topics: Other; Urban development/habitat. **Activities:** Exchanges/twinning/linking; Information and documentation services/data bases.

CHE0796
TERRE DES HOMMES

Case postale, 1000 Lausanne 9, Suisse.

Téléphone: 41 (21) 653 66 66. *Fax:* 41 (21) 653 66 77. *Contact:* Bernard Boeton, Directeur de l'information.

OBJECTIFS: Apporter une aide directe à l'enfance en détresse, sans considération d'ordre politique, confessionnel ou racial.

INFORMATIONS GENERALES: *Création:* 1960. *Budget/Total 1993:* ECU 17222000 (US$ 22333000). *Sources financières:* Privé: 82%. Public: 18%.

PUBLICATIONS: *Périodiques:* "Terre des Hommes" (5) - "Terre des Hommes-Kinderhilfe" (5). *Rapport annuel.*

EVALUATION/RECHERCHE: Rapports d'évaluation disponibles.

COMMENTAIRES: Intervient dans la Communauté des Etats indépendants.

ACTIVITES DANS LES REGIONS EN DEVELOPPEMENT: Intervient directement dans les régions en développement. Intervient dans 42 pays. Maintient une présence locale sur le terrain. Intervient par l'intermédiaire d'organisations locales partenaires. **Actions de Développement durable:** Aliments/famine; Enfants/jeunesse/famille; Envoi de volontaires/experts/assistance technique; Santé/assainissement/eau; Secours d'urgence/réfugiés/aide humanitaire; Éducation/formation/alphabétisation. **Régions:** Afrique australe; Afrique centrale; Afrique de l'Est; Afrique du Nord; Amérique du Sud; Asie centrale et Asie du Sud; Asie de l'Est; Asie du Sud-Est; Mexique et Amerique centrale; Moyen-Orient.

ACTIVITES D'INFORMATION ET D'EDUCATION: Domaines: Aliments/famine; Droits de l'Homme/paix/conflits; Enfants/jeunesse/famille; Pauvreté/conditions de vie; Santé/assainissement/eau; Secours d'urgence/réfugiés/aide humanitaire; Éducation/formation/alphabétisation. **Activités:** Campagnes d'information/expositions; Collecte de fonds; Services d'information et de documentation/bases de données.

CHE0797
TERRE DES HOMMES KINDERHILFE

B.P. 388, 1000 Lausanne 9, Suisse.

Téléphone: 41 (21) 653 66 66. *Fax:* 41 (21) 653 66 67. *Contact:* Richard C. Copeland, Directeur des programmes.

CHE0798
TERRE DES HOMMES, SUISSE - GENEVE (TDHS)

31 ch. Franck Thomas, 1208 Genève, Suisse.

Téléphone: 41 (22) 736 36 36. *Fax:* 41 (22) 736 15 10. *Contact:* Jean-Luc Pittet, Secrétaire général.

OBJECTIFS: Fournir un appui aux groupes qui cherchent un remède aux situations de pauvreté ou d'injustice auxquelles sont confrontés les enfants dans les pays en développement. Soutenir l'organisation des communautés villageoises et des habitants des quartiers pauvres pour accéder à des programmes d'éducation, de santé, de production agricole et artisanale. Accueillir et encadrer des enfants des rues.

INFORMATIONS GENERALES: *Création:* 1965. *Affiliée à:* Terre des Hommes-Suisse - Fédération Internationale de Terre des Hommes - Fédération Genevoise de Coopération (Suisse). *Personnel/Total:* 107. *Salariés:* 7. *Bénévoles:* 100. *Budget/Total 1993:* ECU 1357000 (US$ 1760000). *Sources financières:* Privé: 55%. Public: 30%. *Autofinancement:* 15%.

PUBLICATIONS: *Périodiques:* Journal (4). *Rapport annuel.*

ACTIVITES DANS LES REGIONS EN DEVELOPPEMENT: Intervient directement dans les régions en développement. Intervient dans 23 pays. Maintient une présence locale sur le terrain. **Actions de Développement durable:** Aliments/famine; Droits de l'Homme/paix/conflits; Démocratie/bonne gestion publique/création d'institutions/développement participatif; Développement rural/agriculture; Développement urbain/habitat; Enfants/jeunesse/famille; Petites entreprises/secteur informel/artisanat; Population/planning familial/démographie; Questions relatives aux femmes; Santé/assainissement/eau; Secours d'urgence/réfugiés/aide humanitaire; Écologie/environnement/biodiversité; Éducation/formation/alphabétisation. **Régions:** Afrique australe; Afrique de l'Est; Afrique de l'Ouest; Amérique du Sud; Asie centrale et Asie du Sud; Asie du Sud-Est; Caraïbes.

ACTIVITES D'INFORMATION ET D'EDUCATION: Domaines: Droits de l'Homme/paix/conflits; Développement rural/agriculture; Enfants/jeunesse/famille; Pauvreté/conditions de vie; Questions relatives aux femmes; Santé/assainissement/eau; Éducation/formation/alphabétisation. **Activités:** Campagnes d'information/expositions; Collecte de fonds; Conférences/séminaires/ateliers/activités de formation; Échanges/parrainage/jumelage.

CHE0799
TIBET INSTITUTE

Wildbergstrasse, 8486 Rikon, Switzerland.

Telephone: 41 (52) 35 17 29. *Contact:* Mathilde Kuhn.

OBJECTIVES: To provide a monastic focal point for Tibetans living in exile in Switzerland and other countries by serving their religious needs. To be a place for education and scientific studies in the field of Tibetanistic and Buddhology.

GENERAL INFORMATION: *Creation:* 1967. *Personnel/Total:* 5. *Salaried:* 1. *Volunteers:* 4. *Budget/Total 1993:* ECU 130000 (US$ 169000). *Financial sources:* Private: 100%.

PUBLICATIONS: *Annual report. List of publications.*

EVALUATION/RESEARCH: Evaluation reports available. Undertakes research activities.

INFORMATION AND EDUCATION ACTIVITIES: Topics: Culture/tradition/religion; Education/training/literacy; Refugees/migrants/ethnic groups. **Activities:** Broadcasting/cultural events; Conferences/seminars/workshops/training activities; Formal education; Information and documentation services/data bases; Information campaigns/exhibitions; Publishing/audiovisual materials/educational materials.

CHE0800
TRADITIONS POUR DEMAIN ◆ Traditions For Tomorrow

12 Promenade John Berney, 1180 Rolle, Suisse.

Téléphone: 41 (21) 825 23 31. *Fax:* 41 (21) 825 23 62. *Contact:* Diego Gradis, Président.

OBJECTIFS: Soutenir les efforts de communautés indigènes des pays du Sud, soucieuses de sauvegarder et de consolider leur identité culturelle.

INFORMATIONS GENERALES: *Création:* 1986. *Type d'organisation:* réseau. *Organisations membres:* 3. *Affiliée à:* UNESCO - Fédération Genevoise de Coopération (Suisse) - Fédération Vaudoise de Coopération (Suisse) - ZEWO (Suisse) - Chaîne du Bonheur (Suisse). *Personnel/Total:* 7. *Bénévoles:* 7. *Budget/Total 1993:* ECU 78000 (US$ 101000). *Sources financières:* Privé: 40%. Public: 50%. *Autofinancement:* 10%.

PUBLICATIONS: *Rapport annuel.*

ACTIVITES DANS LES REGIONS EN DEVELOPPEMENT: Intervient directement dans les régions en développement. Intervient dans 10 pays. Intervient par l'intermédiaire d'organisations locales partenaires. **Actions de Développement durable:** Droits de l'Homme/paix/conflits; Enfants/jeunesse/famille; Éducation/formation/alphabétisation. **Régions:** Amérique du Sud; Mexique et Amerique centrale.

ACTIVITES D'INFORMATION ET D'EDUCATION: Domaines: Culture/tradition/religion; Droits de l'Homme/paix/conflits; Enfants/jeunesse/famille; Paix/conflits ethniques/armement/désarmement; Relations internationales/coopération/aide au développement; Éducation/formation/alphabétisation. **Activités:** Campagnes d'information/expositions; Col-

See: *How to Use the Directory,* page 11.

lecte de fonds; Services d'information et de documentation/bases de données.

CHE0801
URUGUAY KOMITEE
Rötelsteig 10, 8037 Zürich, Suisse.

Téléphone: 41 (1) 840 19 29.

CHE0802
VEREIN DER SANDOZ-MITARBEITER FUR BASISHILFE IN DER DRITTEN WELT (BASAID) ♦ Sandoz Employees' Association for Basic Aid in the Third World
c/o Sandoz AG, Lichtstrasse 35, 4002 Basel, Switzerland.

Telephone: 41 (61) 324 53 67. *Fax:* 41 (61) 324 84 55. *Contact:* Luciano Pellegrini, President.

CHE0803
VEREIN SCHWEIZER KINDERHILFE
Grossackerstrasse 15, 9000 St. Gallen, Suisse.

CHE0804
VEREIN STADTEPARTNERSCHAFT BERN-ACHUAPA ♦ Association Jumelage Berne-Achuapa
Postfach 7402, 3001 Bern, Suisse.

Téléphone: 41 (31) 371 67 45. *Contact:* Michael Jordi, Secrétaire.

OBJECTIFS: Soutenir des projets et des ONG (femmes, syndicats, collectifs de production/vente) dans la région d'Achuapa.

INFORMATIONS GENERALES: *Création:* 1985. *Personnel/Total:* 21. *Salariés:* 1 dont: 1 dans les pays en développement. *Bénévoles:* 20 dont: 3 dans les pays en développement. *Budget/Total 1993:* ECU 16000 (US$ 20000). *Sources financières:* Privé: 25%. Public: 5%. *Autofinancement:* 70%.

PUBLICATIONS: *Périodiques:* Flores y espinas (4).

EVALUATION/RECHERCHE: Rapports d'évaluation disponibles.

PREVISIONS D'ACTIVITES: Cours de formation, construction d'un réseau d'eau potable et d'un atelier de couture.

ACTIVITES DANS LES REGIONS EN DEVELOPPEMENT: Intervient dans 1 pays. Maintient une présence locale sur le terrain. Intervient par l'intermédiaire d'organisations locales partenaires. **Actions de Développement durable:** Dette/finances/commerce; Développement rural/agriculture; Petites entreprises/secteur informel/artisanat; Questions relatives aux femmes; Santé/assainissement/eau; Écologie/environnement/biodiversité; Éducation/formation/alphabétisation. **Régions:** Mexique et Amerique centrale.

ACTIVITES D'INFORMATION ET D'EDUCATION: Domaines: Développement rural/agriculture; Questions relatives aux femmes; Relations économiques internationales/commerce/dette/finances; Santé/assainissement/eau; Écologie/environnement/biodiversité; Éducation/formation/alphabétisation. **Activités:** Campagnes d'information/expositions; Collecte de fonds; Échanges/parrainage/jumelage; Édition/documents audiovisuels/documents éducatifs; Éducation formelle.

CHE0805
VEREINIGTE SUDAN MISSION (VSM) ♦ Mission Unie du Soudan
Moosbrunnenstrasse 5, 8426 Lufingen, Suisse.

Téléphone: 41 (1) 813 61 71. *Fax:* 41 (1) 813 61 41. *Contact:* Georg Leimeroth, Secrétaire général.

OBJECTIFS: Apporter l'Evangile aux hommes de la zone sahélienne, fortifier leur foi et les rassembler en églises locales. Mener des projets médicaux et scolaires.

INFORMATIONS GENERALES: *Création:* 1949. *Affiliée à:* Arbeitsgemeinschaft Evangelikaler Missionen. *Personnel/Total:* 57. *Salariés:* 57 dont: 52 dans les pays en développement. *Budget/Total 1993:* ECU 992000 (US$ 1286000). *Sources financières:* Privé: 98%. Public: 2%.

PUBLICATIONS: *Périodiques:* Gehet hin/Je t'enverrai (4) - Gebetsbrief/Bulletin de prières (4). *Rapport annuel. Liste des publications.*

PREVISIONS D'ACTIVITES: Formation de collaborateurs africains dans les domaines ecclésiastique, scolaire, et dans ceux de la santé et de l'alphabétisation.

ACTIVITES DANS LES REGIONS EN DEVELOPPEMENT: Intervient directement dans les régions en développement. Maintient une présence locale sur le terrain. **Actions de Développement durable:** Aliments/famine; Développement rural/agriculture; Enfants/jeunesse/famille; Envoi de volontaires/experts/assistance technique; Petites entreprises/secteur informel/artisanat; Population/planning familial/démographie; Questions relatives aux femmes; Santé/assainissement/eau; Éducation/formation/alphabétisation. **Régions:** Afrique centrale.

ACTIVITES D'INFORMATION ET D'EDUCATION: Domaines: Développement rural/agriculture; Enfants/jeunesse/famille; Pauvreté/conditions de vie; Population/planning familial/démographie; Questions relatives aux femmes; Relations internationales/coopération/aide au développement; Santé/assainissement/eau; Éducation/formation/alphabétisation. **Activités:** Campagnes d'information/expositions; Éducation formelle.

CHE0806
VEREINIGUNG DON BOSCO WERK ♦ Association Oeuvre Don Bosco
Don Boscostrasse, 6215 Beromunster, Suisse.

Téléphone: 41 (45) 51 90 30. *Fax:* 41 (45) 51 31 24. *Contact:* Alfred Fleisch.

OBJECTIFS: Aider aux œuvres des Salésiens de Don Bosco qui travaillent dans 110 pays particulièrement en direction des jeunes pauvres et abandonnés.

INFORMATIONS GENERALES: *Création:* 1975. *Personnel/Total:* 1. *Bénévoles:* 1. *Budget/Total 1993:* ECU 574000 (US$ 744000). *Sources financières:* Privé: 100%.

PUBLICATIONS: *Rapport annuel.*

PREVISIONS D'ACTIVITES: Forage de puits et maisons pour les pauvres dans les Favélas de Manaus; formation professionnelle pour les enfants de la rue au Brésil; projet de bateaux à énergie solaire dans la région amazonienne du Rio Negro.

COMMENTAIRES: L'organisation est au service de la congrégation des Salésiens de Don Bosco qui compte 18000 membres.

ACTIVITES DANS LES REGIONS EN DEVELOPPEMENT: Intervient directement dans les régions en développement. Maintient une présence locale sur le terrain. **Actions de Développement durable:** Aliments/famine; Développement urbain/habitat; Enfants/jeunesse/famille; Petites entreprises/secteur informel/artisanat; Santé/assainissement/eau; Éducation/formation/alphabétisation; Énergie/transport. **Régions:** Afrique centrale; Afrique de l'Ouest; Amérique du Sud.

ACTIVITES D'INFORMATION ET D'EDUCATION: Domaines: Aliments/famine; Enfants/jeunesse/famille; Pauvreté/conditions de vie; Santé/assainissement/eau; Éducation/formation/alphabétisation. **Activités:** Collecte de fonds.

CHE0807
VEREINIGUNG FUR ENTWICKLUNG, GERECHTIGKEIT, SOLIDARITAT (VEGS) ♦ Association for Development, Justice and Solidarity
Fabrikstrasse 26b, 9220 Bischofszell, Switzerland.

Telephone: 41 (71) 81 51 38. *Fax:* 41 (71) 81 51 39.

OBJECTIVES: To organise information sessions on Third World problems. To act as the regional development policy co-ordination centre. To sell food and handicrafts from developing countries to the Swiss public.

GENERAL INFORMATION: *Creation:* 1982. *Personnel/Total:* 5. *Salaried:* 5. *Financial sources:* Private: 30%. Self-financing: 70%.

PUBLICATIONS: *Periodicals:* Vergstrablatt (4) - RL Info (8). *Annual report.*

ACTIVITIES IN DEVELOPING REGIONS: Works through local field partners.

Voir : *Comment utiliser le répertoire,* page 11.

INFORMATION AND EDUCATION ACTIVITIES: Topics: Culture/tradition/religion; Emergency relief/refugees/humanitarian assistance; Food/famine; International relations/cooperation/development aid; Poverty/living conditions; Racism/xenophobia/antisemitism; Refugees/migrants/ethnic groups; Rural development/agriculture; Urban development/habitat. **Activities:** Information campaigns/exhibitions.

CHE0808

VEREINIGUNG SCHWEIZ - ERITREA

Untere Zäune 21, 8001 Zürich, Suisse.

CHE0809

WOMEN'S INTERNATIONAL LEAGUE FOR PEACE AND FREEDOM (WILPF)

Case Postale 28, 1 rue de Varembé, 1211 Genève 20, Switzerland.

Telephone: 41 (22) 733 61 75. *Fax:* 41 (22) 740 10 63. *Contact:* Edith Ballantyne, President.

OBJECTIVES: To strive for political solutions to promote fundamental human rights and the right to development. To promote international peace, disarmament, equal rights for women, economic justice and to end all forms of racism, discrimination and exploitation.

GENERAL INFORMATION: *Creation:* 1915. *Affiliated to:* Conference of Non-Governmental Organisations. *Personnel/Total:* 13. *Salaried:* 3. *Volunteers:* 10. *Budget/Total 1993:* ECU 214000 (US$ 278000). *Financial sources:* Private: 10%. Self-financing: 90%.

PUBLICATIONS: *Periodicals:* International News (4) - Pax et Libertas (4). *Annual report. List of publications.*

EVALUATION/RESEARCH: Evaluation reports available.

PLANNED ACTIVITIES: To undertake a project concerning Arab women and International decision-making.

COMMENTS: Undertakes activities in the Commonwealth of Independent States. Information activities related to the Commonwealth of Independent States.

ACTIVITIES IN DEVELOPING REGIONS: Present in developing regions. Active in 19 country(ies). Maintains local field presence. Works through local field partners. **Sustainable Development Actions:** Gender issues/women; Human rights/peace/conflicts; Rural development/agriculture. **Regions:** Central Asia and South Asia; Mexico and Central America; Middle East; Oceania; South America; South East Asia; Southern Africa.

INFORMATION AND EDUCATION ACTIVITIES: Topics: Ecology/environment/biodiversity; Gender issues/women; Human rights/peace/conflicts; International economic relations/trade/debt/finance; International relations/cooperation/development aid; Peace/ethnic conflicts/armament/disarmament; Poverty/living conditions; Racism/xenophobia/antisemitism; Refugees/migrants/ethnic groups; Rural development/agriculture. **Activities:** Conferences/seminars/workshops/training activities; Exchanges/twinning/linking; Formal education; Fund raising; Information and documentation services/data bases; Information campaigns/exhibitions; Lobbying/advocacy; Networking/electronic telecommunications; Publishing/audiovisual materials/educational materials.

CHE0810

WOMEN'S WORLD SUMMIT FOUNDATION (WWSF)

P.O. Box 2001, 1211 Genève 1, Switzerland.

Telephone: 41 (22) 738 66 19. *Fax:* 41 (22) 738 98 47. *Contact:* Krishna Ahooja-Patel, President.

OBJECTIVES: To support, promote and help implement international objectives for the year 2000, namely the Conventions of Women's and Children's Rights, the reduction of IMR, MMR, malnutrition of children under 5 and adult illiteracy, with an emphasis on female literacy.

GENERAL INFORMATION: *Creation:* 1991. *Type of organisation:* association of NGOs. *Member organisations:* 50. *Affiliated to:* Sewa (India) - Greenbelt (Kenya) - WEDO (USA) - CIVICUS Washington (USA) - RIS (India) - Decade for Human Rights Education (USA) - Voix Libre (Switzerland) -Women for Peace - WILPF (Switzerland) - UK Wise Women (United Kingdom) - NAAM Movement (Burkina Faso) -

International Association 6-S (Burkina Faso) -Yewwu-Yewwi (Senegal) - GREFI (Burkina Faso) - IFAP (France). *Personnel/Total:* 6. *Salaried:* 1. *Volunteers:* 5 of which: 2 in developing countries. *Budget/Total 1993:* ECU 78000 (US$ 101000). *Financial sources:* Private: 50%. Public: 40%. Self-financing: 10%.

PUBLICATIONS: *Periodicals:* Seventy-Five Percent (2). *Annual report. List of publications.*

EVALUATION/RESEARCH: Undertakes research activities.

ACTIVITIES IN DEVELOPING REGIONS: Present in developing regions. Active in 3 country(ies). Maintains local field presence. Works through local field partners. **Sustainable Development Actions:** Gender issues/women; Rural development/agriculture. **Regions:** East Africa; West Africa.

INFORMATION AND EDUCATION ACTIVITIES: Topics: Gender issues/women; Human rights/peace/conflicts; International relations/cooperation/development aid; Poverty/living conditions; Rural development/agriculture. **Activities:** Broadcasting/cultural events; Conferences/seminars/workshops/training activities; Fund raising; Information and documentation services/data bases; Lobbying/advocacy; Publishing/audiovisual materials/educational materials.

CHE0811

WORLD ALLIANCE OF YOUNG MEN'S CHRISTIAN ASSOCIATIONS

37 quai Wilson, 1201 Geneva, Switzerland.

Telephone: 41 (22) 732 31 00. *Fax:* 41 (22) 738 40 15. *Contact:* Joel Kinagwi, Secretary for Refugees and Rehabilitation.

CHE0812

WORLD CONFERENCE ON RELIGION AND PEACE INTERNATIONAL

14 chemin Auguste-Vilbert, 1218 Grand-Saconnex/Geneva, Switzerland.

Contact: Dr. John B. Taylor, Secretary General.

CHE0813

THE WORLD CONSERVATION UNION (IUCN) ♦ Union mondiale pour la nature

28 rue Mauverney, 1196 Gland, Switzerland.

Telephone: 41 (22) 999 00 01. *Fax:* 41 (22) 999 00 02. *E-mail:* mail@hg.iucn.ch.. *Contact:* David McDowell, Director General.

OBJECTIVES: To ensure the conservation of nature, especially of biological diversity. To ensure that the earth's natural resources are used in a sustainable way. To guide the development of human communities towards ways of life that are in enduring harmony with the biosphere.

GENERAL INFORMATION: *Creation:* 1948. *Type of organisation:* network. *Member organisations:* 603. *Personnel/Total:* 500. *Budget/Total 1993:* ECU 28703000 (US$ 37223000). *Financial sources:* Private: 6%. Public: 83%. Self-financing: 11%.

PUBLICATIONS: *Periodicals:* IUCN Bulletin - INTERACT - Red List of Threatened Animals. *Annual report. List of publications.*

EVALUATION/RESEARCH: Evaluation reports available. Undertakes research activities.

COMMENTS: Undertakes activities in the Commonwealth of Independent States. Information activities related to the Commonwealth of Independent States.

ACTIVITIES IN DEVELOPING REGIONS: Present in developing regions. Maintains local field presence. Works through local field partners. **Sustainable Development Actions:** Ecology/environment/biodiversity. **Regions:** Caribbean; Central Africa; Central Asia and South Asia; East Africa; Mexico and Central America; Middle East; North Africa; Oceania; South America; South East Asia; Southern Africa; West Africa.

INFORMATION AND EDUCATION ACTIVITIES: Topics: Ecology/environment/biodiversity. **Activities:** Conferences/seminars/workshops/training activities; Formal education; Information and documentation services/data bases; Networking/electronic telecommunications; Publishing/audiovisual materials/educational materials.

See: *How to Use the Directory,* page 11.

CHE0814
WORLD COUNCIL OF CHURCHES (WCC)

150 route de Ferney, 1211 Geneva 2, Switzerland.

Telephone: 41 (22) 791 61 11. *Fax:* 41 (22) 791 03 61. *Contact:* Konrad Raiser, Secretary General.

OBJECTIVES: To promote the unity of the churches and of humankind.

GENERAL INFORMATION: *Creation:* 1948. *Member organisations:* 324. *Personnel/Total:* 275. *Salaried:* 275.

PUBLICATIONS: *Periodicals:* One World (10) - Ecumenical Press Service (50). *List of publications.*

EVALUATION/RESEARCH: Undertakes research activities.

COMMENTS: Undertakes activities in the Commonwealth of Independent States.

ACTIVITIES IN DEVELOPING REGIONS: Works through local field partners. **Sustainable Development Actions:** Children/youth/family; Debt/finance/trade; Democracy/good governance/institution building/ participatory development; Ecology/environment/biodiversity; Education/ training/literacy; Emergency relief/refugees/humanitarian assistance; Food/famine; Gender issues/women; Health/sanitation/water; Human rights/peace/conflicts; Rural development/agriculture; Small enterprises/ informal sector/handicrafts. **Regions:** Caribbean; Central Africa; Central Asia and South Asia; East Africa; East Asia; Mexico and Central America; Middle East; North Africa; Oceania; South America; South East Asia; Southern Africa; West Africa.

INFORMATION AND EDUCATION ACTIVITIES: Topics: Children/youth/ family; Culture/tradition/religion; Ecology/environment/biodiversity; Education/training/literacy; Emergency relief/refugees/humanitarian assistance; Employment/unemployment; Gender issues/women; Health/sanitation/water; Human rights/peace/conflicts; International economic relations/trade/debt/finance; International relations/cooperation/development aid; Peace/ethnic conflicts/armament/disarmament; Poverty/living conditions; Racism/xenophobia/antisemitism; Refugees/migrants/ethnic groups; Rural development/agriculture. **Activities:** Conferences/seminars/workshops/training activities; Formal education; Fund raising; Information and documentation services/data bases; Information campaigns/ exhibitions; Lobbying/advocacy.

CHE0815
WORLD FEDERATION OF UNITED NATIONS ASSOCIATIONS
♦ Fédération Mondiale des Associations pour les Nations Unies

Rue de Montbrillant 54-56, 1211 Geneva 10, Switzerland.

Telephone: 41 (22) 733 07 30. *Contact:* Dr. Marek Hagmajer, Secretary General.

CHE0816
WORLD JEWISH CONGRESS

Case postale 191, 1202 Geneva, Switzerland.

Contact: Daniel Lack, Legal Advisor.

CHE0817
WORLD ORGANIZATION OF THE SCOUT MOVEMENT (WOSM)

Box 241, 5 rue du Pré-Jérôme, 1211 Geneva 4, Switzerland.

Telephone: 41 (22) 320 42 33. *Fax:* 41 (22) 781 20 53. *E-mail:* asar@scout.gn.apc.org. *Contact:* Jacques Moreillon, Secretary General.

OBJECTIVES: To contribute to the development of young people in achieving their full physical, intellectual, social and spiritual potentials as individuals, as responsible citizens and as members of their local, national and international communities.

GENERAL INFORMATION: *Creation:* 1924. *Member organisations:* 150. *Personnel/Total:* var.. *Salaried:* 55 of which: 15 in developing countries. *Volunteers:* var.. *Budget/Total 1993:* ECU 3253000 (US$ 4221000). *Financial sources:* Private: 33%. Self-financing: 67%.

PUBLICATIONS: *Periodicals:* World Scouting News (4). *Annual report. List of publications.*

EVALUATION/RESEARCH: Evaluation reports available. Undertakes research activities.

COMMENTS: Undertakes activities in the Commonwealth of Independent States. Information activities related to the Commonwealth of Independent States.

ACTIVITIES IN DEVELOPING REGIONS: Present in developing regions. Active in 80 country(ies). Maintains local field presence. Works through local field partners. **Sustainable Development Actions:** Children/ youth/family; Democracy/good governance/institution building/participatory development; Ecology/environment/biodiversity; Emergency relief/refugees/humanitarian assistance; Food/famine; Health/sanitation/ water; Human rights/peace/conflicts; Population/family planning/demography; Rural development/agriculture; Sending volunteers/experts/technical assistance; Small enterprises/informal sector/handicrafts; Urban development/habitat. **Regions:** Caribbean; Central Africa; Central Asia and South Asia; East Africa; East Asia; Mexico and Central America; Middle East; North Africa; Oceania; South America; South East Asia; Southern Africa; West Africa.

INFORMATION AND EDUCATION ACTIVITIES: Topics: Children/youth/ family; Culture/tradition/religion; Ecology/environment/biodiversity; Education/training/literacy; Emergency relief/refugees/humanitarian assistance; Food/famine; Health/sanitation/water; Human rights/peace/conflicts; Peace/ethnic conflicts/armament/disarmament; Population/family planning/demography; Poverty/living conditions; Racism/xenophobia/ antisemitism; Refugees/migrants/ethnic groups; Rural development/ agriculture. **Activities:** Broadcasting/cultural events; Conferences/seminars/workshops/training activities; Information and documentation services/data bases; Lobbying/advocacy; Networking/electronic telecommunications; Publishing/audiovisual materials/educational materials.

CHE0818
WORLD UNIVERSITY SERVICE, SWITZERLAND (WUS-SWITZERLAND) ♦ Entraide Universitaire Mondiale

5 chemin des Iris, 1216 Geneva, Switzerland.

Telephone: 41 (22) 798 87 11. *Fax:* (22) 798 08 29. *Contact:* Nigel Hartley, General Secretary.

CHE0819
WORLD VISION INTERNATIONAL (WVI) ♦ Vision mondiale internationale

Chemin de la Tourelle 6, 1209 Geneva, Switzerland.

Telephone: 41 (22) 798 41 83. *Fax:* 41 (22) 798 65 47. *Contact:* Eric Ram, Director.

OBJECTIVES: To fight poverty through integrated holistic development, emergency relief, health, education, and leadership development for the most needy families and communities.

GENERAL INFORMATION: *Creation:* 1950. *Member organisations:* 65. *Affiliated to:* ICVA (Switzerland) - FIIG (Switzerland) - CONGO. *Personnel/Total:* 5414. *Salaried:* 5414 of which: 3845 in developing countries. *Budget/Total 1993:* ECU 223916000 (US$ 290381000). *Financial sources:* Private: 85%. *Public:* 15%.

PUBLICATIONS: *Periodicals:* Together (6). *Annual report.*

EVALUATION/RESEARCH: Evaluation reports available. Undertakes research activities.

COMMENTS: Undertakes activities in the Commonwealth of Independent States. Information activities related to the Commonwealth of Independent States.

ACTIVITIES IN DEVELOPING REGIONS: Present in developing regions. Active in 95 country(ies). Maintains local field presence. Works through local field partners. **Sustainable Development Actions:** Children/ youth/family; Democracy/good governance/institution building/participatory development; Ecology/environment/biodiversity; Education/ training/literacy; Emergency relief/refugees/humanitarian assistance; Food/famine; Gender issues/women; Health/sanitation/water; Human rights/peace/conflicts; Population/family planning/demography; Rural development/agriculture; Small enterprises/informal sector/handicrafts;

Voir : *Comment utiliser le répertoire,* page 11.

Urban development/habitat. **Regions:** Caribbean; Central Africa; Central Asia and South Asia; East Africa; East Asia; Mexico and Central America; Middle East; Oceania; South America; South East Asia; Southern Africa; West Africa.

INFORMATION AND EDUCATION ACTIVITIES: Topics: Children/youth/family; Culture/tradition/religion; Ecology/environment/biodiversity; Education/training/literacy; Emergency relief/refugees/humanitarian assistance; Employment/unemployment; Food/famine; Gender issues/women; Health/sanitation/water; Human rights/peace/conflicts; International economic relations/trade/debt/finance; International relations/cooperation/development aid; Peace/ethnic conflicts/armament/disarmament; Population/family planning/demography; Poverty/living conditions; Racism/xenophobia/antisemitism; Refugees/migrants/ethnic groups; Rural development/agriculture; Urban development/habitat. **Activities:** Broadcasting/cultural events; Conferences/seminars/workshops/training activities; Exchanges/twinning/linking; Formal education; Fund raising; Information and documentation services/data bases; Information campaigns/exhibitions; Lobbying/advocacy; Networking/electronic telecommunications; Publishing/audiovisual materials/educational materials.

CHE0820

WORLD WIDE FUND FOR NATURE INTERNATIONAL (WWF)

Avenue du Mont-Blanc, 1196 Gland, Switzerland.

Telephone: 41 (22) 364 91 11. **Fax:** 41 (22) 364 58 29. **Contact:** Claude Martin, Director General.

OBJECTIVES: To preserve genetic species and ecosystem diversity. To ensure that the use of renewable natural resources is sustainable. To promote actions to reduce pollution and the wasteful exploitation and consumption of energy and natural resources.

GENERAL INFORMATION: Creation: 1961. **Type of organisation:** network. **Member organisations:** 25. **Personnel/Total:** 1793. Salaried: 1793 of which: 470 in developing countries. **Budget/Total 1993:** ECU 156561000 (US$ 203032000). **Financial sources:** Private: 63%. Public: 21%. Self-financing: 16%.

PUBLICATIONS: Annual report. List of publications.

EVALUATION/RESEARCH: Evaluation reports available.

COMMENTS: Undertakes activities in the Commonwealth of Independent States. Information activities related to the Commonwealth of Independent States.

ACTIVITIES IN DEVELOPING REGIONS: Present in developing regions. Maintains local field presence. Works through local field partners. **Sustainable Development Actions:** Debt/finance/trade; Democracy/good governance/institution building/participatory development; Ecology/environment/biodiversity; Rural development/agriculture. **Regions:** Caribbean; Central Africa; Central Asia and South Asia; East Africa; East Asia; Mexico and Central America; Middle East; North Africa; Oceania; South America; South East Asia; Southern Africa; West Africa.

INFORMATION AND EDUCATION ACTIVITIES: Topics: Culture/tradition/religion; Ecology/environment/biodiversity; International economic relations/trade/debt/finance; International relations/cooperation/development aid; Poverty/living conditions; Rural development/agriculture. **Activities:** Broadcasting/cultural events; Conferences/seminars/workshops/training activities; Formal education; Fund raising; Information and documentation services/data bases; Information campaigns/exhibitions; Lobbying/advocacy; Publishing/audiovisual materials/educational materials.

CHE0821

WORLD WILDLIFE FUND SUISSE (WWF SUISSE)

14 chemin de Poussy, 1214 Vernier, Suisse.

Téléphone: 41 (22) 782 71 51. **Fax:** 41 (22) 41 27 84. **Contact:** Philippe Roch, Directeur.

CHE0822

WORLD YOUNG WOMEN'S CHRISTIAN ASSOCIATION (WYWCA)

37 quai Wilson, 1201 Geneva, Switzerland.

Telephone: 41 (22) 732 31 00. **Fax:** 41 (22) 731 79 38. **Contact:** Amelia Rokotuivuna, Secretary for Advocacy.

CHE0823

YOUTH WITH A MISSION - RELIEF AND DEVELOPMENT SERVICES

77B rue de Genève, 1004 Lausanne, Switzerland.

Telephone: 41 (21) 624 55 33. **Fax:** 41 (21) 625 25 60. **E-mail:** Compusene 1000070, 1445. **Contact:** Scott Morey, Team Leader.

OBJECTIVES: To promote a compassionate Christian response to suffering, through the alleviation of poverty in its various forms, the restoration of human dignity, and the promotion of self-reliance of families and communities.

GENERAL INFORMATION: Personnel/Total: 5. Salaried: 5. **Budget/Total 1993:** ECU 57000 (US$ 74000). **Financial sources:** Private: 99%. Self-financing: 1%.

PUBLICATIONS: Periodicals: JEM Entraide et Développement (4).

EVALUATION/RESEARCH: Undertakes research activities.

COMMENTS: Undertakes activities in the Commonwealth of Independent States.

ACTIVITIES IN DEVELOPING REGIONS: Active in 9 country(ies). Works through local field partners. **Sustainable Development Actions:** Children/youth/family; Democracy/good governance/institution building/participatory development; Ecology/environment/biodiversity; Education/training/literacy; Emergency relief/refugees/humanitarian assistance; Gender issues/women; Health/sanitation/water; Rural development/agriculture; Sending volunteers/experts/technical assistance; Small enterprises/informal sector/handicrafts; Urban development/habitat. **Regions:** East Africa; Middle East; West Africa.

INFORMATION AND EDUCATION ACTIVITIES: Topics: Children/youth/family; Emergency relief/refugees/humanitarian assistance; Food/famine; Gender issues/women; Health/sanitation/water; Poverty/living conditions; Rural development/agriculture; Urban development/habitat. **Activities:** Conferences/seminars/workshops/training activities; Fund raising.

CHE0824

ZENTRALAMERIKA - KOMITEES DER SCHWEIZ (ZAK) ♦
Central America Committees of Switzerland

Baslerstrasse 106, 8048 Zürich, Switzerland.

CHE0825

ZENTRUM FUR ANGEWANDTE OEKOLOGIE SCHATTWEID ♦
Centre pour une écologie appliquée Schattweid

Schattweid, 6114 Steinhuserberg, Suisse.

Téléphone: 41 (41) 71 17 93. **Fax:** 41 (41) 71 40 75. **Contact:** Urs Schori.

OBJECTIFS: Faire de la recherche appliquée et de la formation sur les thèmes suivants: biologie du sol, purification naturelle des eaux usées, compostage et application agronomique des matières fécales humaines, formation du lit des fleuves... Permettre le transfert d'information et de technologie dans les pays en voie de développement.

INFORMATIONS GENERALES: Création: 1984. **Type d'organisation:** collectif. **Affiliée à:** Association des Centres pour l'environnement (Suisse). **Personnel/Total:** 16. Salariés: 13 dont: 3 dans les pays en développement. Bénévoles: 3. **Budget/Total 1993:** ECU 365000 (US$ 474000). **Sources financières:** Privé: 10%. Public: 15%. Autofinancement: 75%.

PUBLICATIONS: Périodiques: Einblick (3). Rapport annuel. Liste des publications.

EVALUATION/RECHERCHE: Rapports d'évaluation disponibles. Entreprend des activités de recherche.

COMMENTAIRES: Intervient dans la Communauté des Etats indépendants. Activités d'information concernant la Communauté des Etats indépendants.

ACTIVITES DANS LES REGIONS EN DEVELOPPEMENT: Maintient une présence locale sur le terrain. Intervient par l'intermédiaire d'organisa-

See: *How to Use the Directory*, page 11.

tions locales partenaires. **Actions de Développement durable:** Santé/assainissement/eau. **Régions:** Amérique du Sud; Asie du Sud-Est; Moyen-Orient.

ACTIVITES D'INFORMATION ET D'EDUCATION: Domaines: Santé/assainissement/eau; Écologie/environnement/biodiversité. **Activités:** Campagnes d'information/expositions; Conférences/séminaires/ateliers/ activités de formation; Services d'information et de documentation/bases de données; Échanges/parrainage/jumelage.

CHE0826
ZONTA INTERNATIONAL

22 avenue du Château, 1008 Prilly, Switzerland.

CYP0827

ASSOCIATION FOR THE PROTECTION OF THE CYPRUS ENVIRONMENT

P.O. Box 3810, Nicosia, Cyprus.

CYP0828

COMMITTEE OF LIMASSOL FOR THE PROTECTION OF THE ENVIRONMENT

P.O. Box 395, Limassol, Cyprus.

Telephone: 357 (5) 363 956. *Fax:* 357 (5) 343 190. *Contact:* Y.D. Potamitis, President.

OBJECTIVES: To preserve and protect the environment.

GENERAL INFORMATION: *Creation:* 1973. *Type of organisation:* association of NGOs. *Member organisations:* 60. *Affiliated to:* Federation of Environmental and Ecological Organisations of Cyprus (Cyprus) -Environment Liaison Office Nairobi (Kenya). *Personnel/Total:* 35. *Volunteers:* 35 of which: 35 in developing countries. *Budget/Total 1993:* ECU 400 (US$ 600). *Financial sources:* Public: 50%. Self-financing: 50%.

PUBLICATIONS: *Annual report.*

EVALUATION/RESEARCH: Evaluation reports available.

INFORMATION AND EDUCATION ACTIVITIES: Topics: Ecology/environment/biodiversity; Health/sanitation/water; Urban development/habitat. **Activities:** Broadcasting/cultural events; Conferences/seminars/workshops/training activities; Formal education; Information and documentation services/data bases; Information campaigns/exhibitions; Lobbying/advocacy; Publishing/audiovisual materials/educational materials.

CYP0829

CYPRUS FORESTRY ASSOCIATION

c/o Department of Forests, Nicosia, Cyprus.

CYP0830

CYPRUS WILDLIFE SOCIETY

PO Box 4281, Nicosia, Cyprus.

Telephone: 357 (2) 30 32 79. *Fax:* 357 (2) 35 03 16. *Contact:* Andreas Demetropoulos, President.

OBJECTIVES: To study and work towards the conservation of the wildlife and habitats of Cyprus.

GENERAL INFORMATION: *Creation:* 1982. *Personnel/Total:* 5. *Volunteers:* 5. *Budget/Total 1993:* ECU 15000 (US$ 19000). *Financial sources:* Private: 4%. Public: 1%. Self-financing: 95%.

PUBLICATIONS: *List of publications.*

EVALUATION/RESEARCH: Undertakes research activities.

PLANNED ACTIVITIES: The Cyprus Wildlife Society plans to promote the conservation of marine turtles and will undertake campaigns for the protection of wetlands, amphibia, fresh water and terrestrial reptiles.

INFORMATION AND EDUCATION ACTIVITIES: Topics: Ecology/environment/biodiversity. **Activities:** Broadcasting/cultural events; Conferences/seminars/workshops/training activities; Fund raising; Information and documentation services/data bases; Information campaigns/exhibitions; Lobbying/advocacy; Publishing/audiovisual materials/educational materials.

CYP0831

THE ECOLOGICAL MOVEMENT OF CYPRUS

P.O. Box 9682, Nicosia, Cyprus.

Telephone: 357 (2) 31 81 63.

OBJECTIVES: To promote the protection of the environment and ecologically correct development. To question modern consumerism, production methods, energy production and usage. To support ecological initiatives by offering technical, scientific and legal advice. To promote sustainable and alternative methods of production and energy use.

GENERAL INFORMATION: *Creation:* 1989. *Personnel/Total:* 10. *Volunteers:* 10. *Budget/Total 1993:* ECU 500 (US$ 700). *Financial sources:* Private: 37%. Self-financing: 63%.

PUBLICATIONS: *Periodicals:* Ecological Update (4). *Annual report.*

EVALUATION/RESEARCH: Evaluation reports available. Undertakes research activities.

INFORMATION AND EDUCATION ACTIVITIES: Topics: Culture/tradition/religion; Ecology/environment/biodiversity; Gender issues/women; Health/sanitation/water; Human rights/peace/conflicts; Peace/ethnic conflicts/armament/disarmament; Population/family planning/demography; Rural development/agriculture; Urban development/habitat. **Activities:** Conferences/seminars/workshops/training activities; Exchanges/twinning/linking; Information and documentation services/data bases; Information campaigns/exhibitions; Lobbying/advocacy; Publishing/audiovisual materials/educational materials.

CYP0832

ENIEA DIMOKRATIKI ORGANOSI NEOLEAS (EDON) ♦ United Democratic Youth Organisation

P.O. Box 1986, Nicosia, Cyprus.

Telephone: 357 (2) 466 459. *Fax:* 357 (2) 365 161. *Contact:* Eleni Mavrou, General Secretary.

OBJECTIVES: To defend youth rights and mobilise the youth to fight for their rights. To carry out solidarity activities and provide youth with alternative forms of recreation.

GENERAL INFORMATION: *Creation:* 1959. *Personnel/Total:* 15. *Salaried:* 15. *Budget/Total 1993:* ECU 237000 (US$ 308000). *Financial sources:* Private: 65%. Public: 20%. Self-financing: 15%.

PUBLICATIONS: *Periodicals:* NEOLEA (52).

EVALUATION/RESEARCH: Undertakes research activities.

COMMENTS: Undertakes activities in the Commonwealth of Independent States. Information activities related to the Commonwealth of Independent States.

ACTIVITIES IN DEVELOPING REGIONS: Works through local field partners. **Sustainable Development Actions:** Children/youth/family; Food/famine; Human rights/peace/conflicts; Sending volunteers/experts/technical assistance. **Regions:** Caribbean; Central Africa; East Africa; Mexico and Central America; Middle East; North Africa; Southern Africa; West Africa.

INFORMATION AND EDUCATION ACTIVITIES: Topics: Children/youth/family; Culture/tradition/religion; Ecology/environment/biodiversity; Education/training/literacy; Emergency relief/refugees/humanitarian assistance; Employment/unemployment; Food/famine; Gender issues/women; Human rights/peace/conflicts; International economic relations/trade/debt/finance; International relations/cooperation/development aid; Peace/ethnic conflicts/armament/disarmament; Population/family planning/demography; Poverty/living conditions; Racism/xenophobia/antisemitism; Refugees/migrants/ethnic groups; Rural development/agriculture; Urban development/habitat. **Activities:** Broadcasting/cultural events; Conferences/seminars/workshops/training activities; Fund raising; Information and documentation services/data bases; Information campaigns/exhibitions; Lobbying/advocacy; Publishing/audiovisual materials/educational materials.

CYP0833

FEDERATION OF ENVIRONMENTAL AND ECOLOGICAL ORGANISATIONS OF CYPRUS

P.O. Box 395, Limassol, Cyprus.

Telephone: 357 (5) 363 956. *Fax:* 357 (5) 477 273. *Contact:* Y.D. Potamitis, President.

OBJECTIVES: To work towards the conservation of nature and the protection of the environment.

GENERAL INFORMATION: *Creation:* 1988. *Type of organisation:* association of NGOs, network, coordinating body. *Member organisations:* 26. *Personnel/Total:* 52. *Volunteers:* 52. *Budget/Total 1993:* ECU 1200 (US$ 1500). *Financial sources:* Self-financing: 100%.

PUBLICATIONS: *Annual report.*

See: *How to Use the Directory,* page 11.

EVALUATION/RESEARCH: Evaluation reports available. Undertakes research activities.

INFORMATION AND EDUCATION ACTIVITIES: Topics: Ecology/environment/biodiversity; Health/sanitation/water; Peace/ethnic conflicts/armament/disarmament; Urban development/habitat. **Activities:** Broadcasting/cultural events; Conferences/seminars/workshops/training activities; Exchanges/twinning/linking; Formal education; Information and documentation services/data bases; Information campaigns/exhibitions; Lobbying/advocacy; Publishing/audiovisual materials/educational materials.

CYP0834
FRIENDS OF THE EARTH, CYPRUS

P.O. Box 3411, Limassol, Cyprus.

CYP0835
INTERNATIONAL ASSOCIATION FOR THE PROTECTION OF HUMAN RIGHTS IN CYPRUS

P.O. Box 5635, Nicosia, Cyprus.

CYP0836
PANCYPRIAN ORGANIZATION OF ARCHITECTURAL HERITAGE

P.O. Box 5380, Nicosia, Cyprus.

Voir : *Comment utiliser le répertoire,* page 11.

CZE0837
AMIGO

Banskobysstricka 168, 621 00 Brno, Czech Republic.

CZE0838
AMNESTY INTERNATIONAL, CZECH SECTION

Palackho 9, 110 00 Praha 1, Czech Republic.

CZE0839
ARCHAIA

Pod Dekankou 19, 147 00 Praha 4- Podolí, Czech Republic.

Telephone: 42 (2) 643 16 72. **Fax:** 42 (2) 643 16 72. **Contact:** Michal Bures, President.

OBJECTIVES: To protect, record and rescue archeological and other historical heritage with strong relations to environment. To provide education in archaeology as an environmental discipline by learning the past to find common roots of European nations and thus support the idea of European unity.

GENERAL INFORMATION: Creation: 1991. **Type of organisation:** network. **Affiliated to:** European Forum of Heritage Associations. **Personnel/Total:** 24. Salaried: 10. Volunteers: 14. **Budget/Total 1993:** ECU 53000 (US$ 69000). **Financial sources:** Private: 15%. Self-financing: 85%.

PUBLICATIONS: Periodicals: Archeologicke Forum (2). Annual report. List of publications.

EVALUATION/RESEARCH: Evaluation reports available. Undertakes research activities.

PLANNED ACTIVITIES: The foundation of an archaeoenvironmental training centre.

COMMENTS: Information activities related to the Commonwealth of Independent States.

INFORMATION AND EDUCATION ACTIVITIES: Topics: Children/youth/family; Culture/tradition/religion; Ecology/environment/biodiversity; Education/training/literacy; International relations/cooperation/development aid. **Activities:** Conferences/seminars/workshops/training activities; Exchanges/twinning/linking; Formal education; Fund raising; Information and documentation services/data bases; Information campaigns/exhibitions; Publishing/audiovisual materials/educational materials.

CZE0840
ASIA FRIENDSHIP ASSOCIATION ♦ CSS-Pratele Asie

Prerovskeho povstani 2, 751 22 Prerov, Czech Republic.

CZE0841
ASSOCIATION FOR EASY CONNECTION (ECONNECT)

Bubenská 6, 170 00 Praha, Czech Republic.

Telephone: 42 (2) 804.521. **Fax:** 42 (2) 804.521. **Contact:** Vojtech Kment, Technical Coordinator.

CZE0842
ASSOCIATION FOR EUROPEAN HOUSE, HELSINKI COMMITTEE

Post. Schranka 7, 119 00 Praha 1 Grad, Czech Republic.

CZE0843
ASSOCIATION FOR THE COOPERATION WITH THE COUNTRIES OF AFRICA, ASIA AND LATIN AMERICA (THE CONTINENTS)

Vitkova 13, 180 00 Prague, Czech Republic.

Telephone: 42 (2) 269.936. **Fax:** 42 (2) 227.581. **Contact:** Dr. Vanicek, Vice-Chairman.

CZE0844
ASSOCIATION OF POLISH YOUTH

Slezka 23, 737 01 Cesky Tesin, Czech Republic.

CZE0845
ASSOCIATION OF WOMEN'S ORGANISATIONS

Husinecka 33, 130 00 Praha 3, Czech Republic.

CZE0846
ASSOCIATION OF YOUNG SCIENTISTS PUGWASH (RAM) ♦
Ostav statu a prava

Narodni 18, 116 91 Praha 1, Czech Republic.

CZE0847
BLOSSOM - ASSOCIATION OF RURAL CHILDREN CLUBS (KVET)

Gorkeho nam 24, 116 47 Praha 1, Czech Republic.

CZE0848
THE BROTHERHOOD FOUNDATION

Slavickova 1678, 356 05 Sokolov, Czech Republic.

CZE0849
CEKOSLOVENSKY USTAV ZAHRANICNI (CSUZ) ♦ Czechoslovak Foreign Institute

Karmelitska 25, P.O. Box 95, 118 31 Praha 1 - Mala Strana, Czech Republic.

Telephone: 42 (24) 51 00 67. **Contact:** Jaromír Slapota, Chairman.

CZE0850
CESKA KATOLICKA CHARITA ♦ Czech Catholic Charity

Vladislavova 12, 111 37 Prague 1, Czech Republic.

Telephone: 42 (2) 24 220 599. **Fax:** 42 (2) 24 220 603. **Contact:** INg P. Roulena, Directeur .

CZE0851
CHAIRNAY'S FUND

Kardasovsk 755, 190 00 Praha 9 - Lehovec, Czech Republic.

CZE0852
CHARLES UNIVERSITY FOUNDATION

Ovocny trh 5, 116 36 Praha 1036, Czech Republic.

CZE0853
CHILDREN OF THE EARTH ♦ Deti Zeme a Nadace Zeme

Decinska 100, 407 21 Ceska Kamenice, Czech Republic.

CZE0854
CIVIC FORUM FOUNDATION

Washingtonova 17, 110 00 Prague 1, Czech Republic.

CZE0855
COMMUNIST YOUTH UNION (KSM)

Politickych vezno 9, 110 00 Praha 1, Czech Republic.

CZE0856
CZECH CULTURE FOUNDATION

Grafick 15, 150 00 Praha 5, Czech Republic.

CZE0857
CZECH HELSINKI COMMITTEE (CHC)

P.O. Box 7, 119 00 Praha 1 - Hrad, Czech Republic.

See: *How to Use the Directory*, page 11.

Telephone: 42 (2) 53 33 61. *Fax:* 42 (2) 55 19 68. *Contact:* Martin Palous.

OBJECTIVES: To monitor the violation of human rights and the improvement of domestic application of international resolutions in the Czech Republic. To provide free legal assistance in human rights cases. To run a human rights documentation centre and counselling centre for refugees.

GENERAL INFORMATION: *Creation:* 1988. *Affiliated to:* International Helsinki Federation for Human Rights (Austria). *Personnel/Total:* 90. *Salaried:* 11. *Volunteers:* 79. *Budget/Total 1993:* ECU 19000 (US$ 25000). *Financial sources:* Private: 100%.

PUBLICATIONS: *Periodicals:* Information Bulletin of CHC (4). *Annual report. List of publications.*

COMMENTS: Undertakes activities in the Commonwealth of Independent States.

INFORMATION AND EDUCATION ACTIVITIES: Topics: Education/training/literacy; Emergency relief/refugees/humanitarian assistance; Human rights/peace/conflicts. **Activities:** Exchanges/twinning/linking; Information and documentation services/data bases; Lobbying/advocacy.

CZE0858
CZECH PEACE SOCIETY

Pansk 7, 116 69 Praha 1, Czech Republic.

CZE0859
CZECH RED CROSS

Thunovska 18, 118 04 Prague 1, Czech Republic.

Telephone: 42 (2) 245 103 47. *Fax:* 42 (2) 245 103 18. *Contact:* Zdenko VLK, President.

OBJECTIVES: To alleviate the suffering of people, to protect life and health and ensure respect for human beings in accordance with the principles and aims of the Red Cross Movement.

GENERAL INFORMATION: *Creation:* 1919. *Type of organisation:* coordinating body. *Affiliated to:* International Federation of Red Cross and Red Crescent Societies. *Personnel/Total:* 370. Salaried: 75. Volunteers: 295 of which: 2 in developing countries. *Budget/Total 1993:* ECU 2910000 (US$ 3773000). *Financial sources:* Private: 7%. Public: 57%. Self-financing: 36%.

PUBLICATIONS: *Periodicals:* Noviny CCK (12) - Zdravi (12). *Annual report.*

EVALUATION/RESEARCH: Evaluation reports available. Undertakes research activities.

PLANNED ACTIVITIES: Courses for medical instructors. A programme to aid the blind and wheelchair users.

COMMENTS: Undertakes activities in the Commonwealth of Independent States. Information activities related to the Commonwealth of Independent States.

ACTIVITIES IN DEVELOPING REGIONS: Active in 5 country(ies). Maintains local field presence. Works through local field partners. **Sustainable Development Actions:** Food/famine; Sending volunteers/experts/technical assistance. **Regions:** Caribbean; Central Asia and South Asia; East Africa.

INFORMATION AND EDUCATION ACTIVITIES: Topics: Children/youth/family; Culture/tradition/religion; Emergency relief/refugees/humanitarian assistance; Food/famine; Health/sanitation/water; Human rights/peace/conflicts; International relations/cooperation/development aid; Peace/ethnic conflicts/armament/disarmament; Population/family planning/demography; Poverty/living conditions; Refugees/migrants/ethnic groups. **Activities:** Broadcasting/cultural events; Conferences/seminars/workshops/training activities; Exchanges/twinning/linking; Formal education; Fund raising; Information and documentation services/data bases; Information campaigns/exhibitions; Networking/electronic telecommunications; Publishing/audiovisual materials/educational materials.

CZE0860
CZECH SOCIETY FOR CHILDREN'S RIGHTS

Gorkho n mest! 24, 116 47 Praha 1, Czech Republic.

CZE0861
CZECHOSLOVAK CHARTA 77 FOUNDATION PRAGUE

Washingtonova 17, 110 00 Prague, Czech Republic.

Telephone: 42 (2) 221.242/2359.364. *Fax:* 42 (2) 235.8784. *Contact:* Tatjana Hlavatá, Executive Director.

CZE0862
CZECHOSLOVAK COMMITTEE FOR EUROPEAN SECURITY AND CO-OPERATION

P.O. Box 7, 119 00 Praha 1 - Hrad, Czech Republic.

CZE0863
CZECHOSLOVAK LATINAMERICAN ASSOCIATION ♦ CS -
Latinskoamecka spo

Vlasitina 846, 160 00 Praha 6, Czech Republic.

CZE0864
DEFENSE FOR CHILDREN INTERNATIONAL (DCI) ♦
Pedagogickl #stav CAV

M chova 7, 120 00 Praha 2, Czech Republic.

CZE0865
EARTHLINKS

Lublanska 18, 120 00 Prague 2, Czech Republic.

Telephone: 42 (2) 29 60 48. *Fax:* 42 (2) 29 60 48. *Contact:* Prokop Verner.

OBJECTIVES: To develop global awareness and individual responsibility through youth environmental education programmes and cultural, social and humanitarian projects.

GENERAL INFORMATION: *Creation:* 1990. *Affiliated to:* Green Circle (Czech Republic) - Earthstewards Network. *Personnel/Total:* 7. *Salaried:* 4. *Volunteers:* 3. *Budget/Total 1993:* ECU 9000 (US$ 12000). *Financial sources:* Private: 80%. Public: 20%.

PUBLICATIONS: *Periodicals:* Newsletter (10). *Annual report. List of publications.*

PLANNED ACTIVITIES: Participation in "Cascadia"-Czech bioregion project. Creation of student's discussion and education clubs.

COMMENTS: The Organisation's activities are mainly supported by the Environmental partnership for Central and Eastern Europe, the PHARE Programme and the Regional Environmental Centrum. Undertakes activities in the Commonwealth of Independent States. Information activities related to the Commonwealth of Independent States.

INFORMATION AND EDUCATION ACTIVITIES: Topics: Culture/tradition/religion; Ecology/environment/biodiversity; Human rights/peace/conflicts; Racism/xenophobia/antisemitism; Refugees/migrants/ethnic groups. **Activities:** Conferences/seminars/workshops/training activities; Exchanges/twinning/linking; Formal education; Fund raising; Information campaigns/exhibitions.

CZE0866
THE EDUCATIONAL PROGRAMME FOUNDATION

Na rybnicku 7, 120 00 Praha 2, Czech Republic.

CZE0867
EDVARD BENES SOCIETY

Prachatick 210, 199 00 Praha 9 Letnany, Czech Republic.

Voir : *Comment utiliser le répertoire,* page 11.

CZE0868

ENVIRONMENTAL SOCIETY ♦ Ekologicka spolecnost

Kamenicka 45, 170 00 Praha 7, Czech Republic.

CZE0869

EUROPEAN ASSOCIATION FOR LEISURE TIME INSTITUTIONS OF CHILDREN AND YOUTH OF GREAT CITIES (EAICY)

Karlinské nàmestí 7, 186 00 Prague, Czech Republic.

Telephone: 42 (2) 235.6562. **Contact:** Oto Maget, Prezident.

CZE0870

EUROPEAN CULTURE CLUB

Valdstejnsk 4, 118 00 Praha 1, Czech Republic.

CZE0871

EUROPEAN HOME IN BRNO ♦ Otakar V cha

Bratislavsk 71, 602 00 Brno, Czech Republic.

CZE0872

EUROPEAN MOVEMENT IN THE CZECH REPUBLIC (FLI-AV CR)

Jilsk 1, 110 00 Praha 1, Czech Republic.

CZE0873

FOR LIFE

P.O. Box 12, 682 01 Vyskov, Czech Republic.

CZE0874

FORUM OF EUROPEAN STUDENTS (AEGEE)

N m. M. Gorkho 24, 116 47 Praha 1, Czech Republic.

CZE0875

FOUNDATION FOR CHILDREN IN DANGER

Legerova 13, 121 45 Praha 2, Czech Republic.

CZE0876

FOUNDATION OF JOSEF PLIVA

N m. Miru 80, 568 02 Svitavy, Czech Republic.

CZE0877

GOOD WILL CENTRE, HUMANITARIAN ASSOCIATION

Hradebni 22, 350 11 Cheb, Czech Republic.

CZE0878

GOTA

Senovazna 2, 110 00 Praha 1, Czech Republic.

CZE0879

GREEN CIRCLE

Lublanskó 18, 120 00 Praha 2, Czech Republic.

Telephone: 42 (2) 29 60 48. **Fax:** 42 (2) 29 60 48. **E-mail:** 2-42429 - ECONNECT. **Contact:** Marie Haisová, Director.

OBJECTIVES: To support NGOs active in the field of nature protection and conservation of natural resources. To help create a healthy living environment. To promote sustainable development of the human community.

GENERAL INFORMATION: *Creation:* 1989. *Member organisations:* 40. *Personnel/Total:* 7. *Salaried:* 4. *Volunteers:* 3. *Budget/Total 1993:* ECU 21000 (US$ 27000). *Financial sources:* Private: 20%. Public: 77%. Self-financing: 3%.

PUBLICATIONS: *Periodicals:* Zpravodan ZK (12). *Annual report.*

EVALUATION/RESEARCH: Evaluation reports available. Undertakes research activities.

INFORMATION AND EDUCATION ACTIVITIES: Topics: Ecology/environment/biodiversity. **Activities:** Conferences/seminars/workshops/training activities; Information and documentation services/data bases; Lobbying/advocacy; Publishing/audiovisual materials/educational materials.

CZE0880

GREEN NET FOUNDATION ♦ Nadace Ceskoslovenske Zelene Site

Soukenicka 30, 110 00 Praha 1, Czech Republic.

CZE0881

GREEN NETWORK FOUNDATION

Soukenická 30, 110 00 Prague 1, Czech Republic.

Telephone: 42 (2) 231.3057. **Fax:** 42 (2) 231.3057. **Contact:** Milan Bunata, Secretary.

CZE0882

HNUTI BRONTOSAURUS ♦ Brontosaurus Movement

Bubenska 6, 170 00 Praha 7, Czech Republic.

Telephone: 42 (2) 667 102 45. **Fax:** 42 (2) 667 102 45. **Contact:** Petr Bartos.

OBJECTIVES: To work for nature conservation. To provide environmental education for youth. To oppose the government's environmental policy.

GENERAL INFORMATION: *Creation:* 1974. *Type of organisation:* network. *Affiliated to:* The World Conservation Union (Suisse) - Youth and Environment Europe (the Netherlands) - European Youth Forest Action (the Netherlands) - Green Circle (Czech Republic) - Circle of Children and Youth (Czech Republic). *Personnel/Total:* 9. *Salaried:* 2. *Volunteers:* 7. *Budget/Total 1993:* ECU 13000 (US$ 17000). *Financial sources:* Private: 70%. Public: 25%. Self-financing: 5%.

PUBLICATIONS: *Periodicals:* Jèster (12). *Annual report.*

COMMENTS: Undertakes activities in the Commonwealth of Independent States. Information activities related to the Commonwealth of Independent States.

ACTIVITIES IN DEVELOPING REGIONS: Maintains local field presence.

INFORMATION AND EDUCATION ACTIVITIES: Topics: Ecology/environment/biodiversity; Rural development/agriculture; Urban development/habitat. **Activities:** Conferences/seminars/workshops/training activities; Exchanges/twinning/linking; Formal education; Fund raising; Information campaigns/exhibitions; Lobbying/advocacy; Publishing/audiovisual materials/educational materials.

CZE0883

HNUTI OBCANSKE SOLIDARITA A TOLERANCE

PB 13, 12800 Prague, Czech Republic.

CZE0884

INDEPENDENT CZECH YOUTH

Ke zderi 1111, 153 00 Praha 5, Czech Republic.

CZE0885

INDIA FRIENDSHIP ASSOCIATION ♦ Sdruzeni pratel Indie

Pricna 8, 110 00 Praha, Czech Republic.

CZE0886

INDONESIA FRIENDSHIP ASSOCIATION ♦ Spolecnost pratel Indonesie

Gothardska 11, 160 00 Praha, Czech Republic.

CZE0887

INSTITUTE FOR DEMOCRACY AND EUROPEAN UNITY

Washingtonova 17, 110 00 Praha 1, Czech Republic.

See: *How to Use the Directory*, page 11.

CZE0888
JAN MASARYK FOUNDATION, UNIVERSITY OF ECONOMICS
n m. W. Churchilla 4, 130 67 Praha 3, Czech Republic.

CZE0889
JOHN HUS EDUCATIONAL FOUNDATION ♦ Vzdelavaci nadace Jana Husa
Radlicka 8, P.O. Box 735, 663 35 Brno, Czech Republic.

CZE0890
KING GEORGE PODEBRADY FOUNDATION FOR EUROPEAN COOPERATION
P.O. Box 7, 119 00 Praha 1 - Hrad, Czech Republic.

CZE0891
KONTINENTY ♦ The Continents, the Association for Co-operation with the Ccountries of Africa, Asia and Latin America
Vítkova 13, 180 00 Praha 8, Czech Republic.

Telephone: 42 (2) 26 34 05. *Contact:* Augustin Palát, President.

OBJECTIVES: To keep the Czech politicians and public aware of the Third World through educative and informative actions.

GENERAL INFORMATION: *Creation:* 1990. *Type of organisation:* coordinating body. *Affiliated to:* North-South Centre - Forum. *Personnel/Total:* 18. *Salaried:* 1. *Volunteers:* 17 of which: 1 in developing countries. *Budget/Total 1993:* ECU 5000 (US$ 7000). *Financial sources:* Self-financing: 100%.

PUBLICATIONS: *Periodicals:* Bulletin Kotinenty/The Continents (2). *Annual report.*

EVALUATION/RESEARCH: Evaluation reports available.

ACTIVITIES IN DEVELOPING REGIONS: Works through local field partners.

INFORMATION AND EDUCATION ACTIVITIES: Topics: Culture/tradition/religion; Ecology/environment/biodiversity; Emergency relief/refugees/humanitarian assistance; Human rights/peace/conflicts; International relations/cooperation/development aid; Population/family planning/demography; Racism/xenophobia/antisemitism; Refugees/migrants/ethnic groups. **Activities:** Broadcasting/cultural events; Conferences/seminars/workshops/training activities; Information campaigns/exhibitions; Lobbying/advocacy.

CZE0892
KRESTANSKE SDRVZENI MLADYCH ZEN - CESKE REPUB-LICE (YWCA) ♦ Young Women Christian Association - Czech Republic
Zitna 12, 129 05 Praha, Czech Republic.

Telephone: 42 (2) 29 12 44. *Fax:* 42 (2) 29 12 44. *Contact:* Daniela Karasová, President.

OBJECTIVES: To support the development of girls and women into independent and responsible citizens and lead them to activities in the spirit of practical Christianity at home and within the society according to the principle of "To live a life of love and service to all human beings".

GENERAL INFORMATION: *Creation:* 1990. *Type of organisation:* network. *Affiliated to:* World YWCA (Switzerland). *Personnel/Total:* 8. *Salaried:* 1. *Volunteers:* 7 of which: 2 in developing countries. *Budget/Total 1993:* ECU 13000 (US$ 17000). *Financial sources:* Private: 45%. Public: 45%. Self-financing: 10%.

PUBLICATIONS: *Periodicals:* Information Bulletin of Prague's YWCA (10). *Annual report.*

EVALUATION/RESEARCH: Evaluation reports available.

PLANNED ACTIVITIES: Development of an environmental educational programme for children and adults and the creation of new branches of YWCA in the country.

COMMENTS: YWCA Czech Republic is fighting for its previous property (after 40 years of break in activities) and has therefore very limited space and financial resources for its activities. The organisation works in the field of development through World YWCA based in Switzerland.

CZE0893
MARIATER HUMANITY FOUNDATION
Cajkovskeho 13, 130 000 Praha 3, Czech Republic.

CZE0894
NADACE EVA - NARODNI STREDISKO EKOL. VYCHOVY ♦ Eva Foundation- National Centre for Environmental Education
Lublanska 18, 120 00 Praha 2, Czech Republic.

Telephone: 42 (2) 29 60 48. *Fax:* 42 (2) 29 60 48. *Contact:* Hana Klonfarova, Director.

OBJECTIVES: To support environment education programmes.

GENERAL INFORMATION: *Creation:* 1991. *Member organisations:* 11. *Affiliated to:* Green Circle (Czech Republic) - Information Centre for Foundations and NGOs (Czech Republic). *Personnel/Total:* 6. *Salaried:* 4. *Volunteers:* 2. *Budget/Total 1993:* ECU 106000 (US$ 137000). *Financial sources:* Private: 30%. Public: 65%. Self-financing: 5%.

PUBLICATIONS: *Periodicals:* Bulletin for Environmental Education (10). *Annual report. List of publications.*

COMMENTS: Undertakes activities in the Commonwealth of Independent States. Information activities related to the Commonwealth of Independent States.

INFORMATION AND EDUCATION ACTIVITIES: Topics: Culture/tradition/religion; Ecology/environment/biodiversity; Employment/unemployment; Human rights/peace/conflicts; International economic relations/trade/debt/finance; International relations/cooperation/development aid. **Activities:** Broadcasting/cultural events; Formal education; Networking/electronic telecommunications; Publishing/audiovisual materials/educational materials.

CZE0895
NADACE HEINRICHE BOLLA PRAZKA KANCELAR
Sokolovska 62, 120 00 Praha 2, Czech Republic.

Telephone: 42 (2) 24 22 78 70. *Fax:* 42 (2) 24 22 20 30. *Contact:* Milan Horacek.

CZE0896
NADACE KRESTANSKA POMOC ♦ Christian Assistance Foundation
Jostova 7, 602 00 Brno, Czech Republic.

Telephone: 42 (5) 21 74 06. *Contact:* Eva Mádrová.

OBJECTIVES: To provide health and social care. To offer consulting services of psychologists, physicians and lawyers. To assist in solving social problems and problems of refugees. To support the elderly and ill people.

GENERAL INFORMATION: *Creation:* 1992. *Affiliated to:* Diakonie of the Church Ceskoslovenska-husitska (Czech Republic). *Personnel/Total:* 12. *Salaried:* 9. *Volunteers:* 3. *Budget/Total 1993:* ECU 22000 (US$ 29000). *Financial sources:* Private: 15%. Public: 50%. Self-financing: 35%.

PUBLICATIONS: *Annual report.*

EVALUATION/RESEARCH: Evaluation reports available.

INFORMATION AND EDUCATION ACTIVITIES: Topics: Children/youth/family; Emergency relief/refugees/humanitarian assistance; Employment/unemployment; Health/sanitation/water; Refugees/migrants/ethnic groups. **Activities:** Formal education; Fund raising; Lobbying/advocacy.

CZE0897
NADACE TOLERANCE ♦ Tolerance Foundation
c/o Libri Prohibiti, Senovazn nam. 2, P.O. Box 8, 111 21 Praha 1, Czech Republic.

E-mail: HELKLI@EARN.CVUT.CZ. *Contact:* Milan Pospísil. President.

OBJECTIVES: To prevent hostility and violence. To work for the prevention of racism, antisemitism, nationalism, xenophobia and ethnocentrism. To support dialogue promote moral values.

GENERAL INFORMATION: *Creation:* 1992. *Personnel/Total:* 52. *Salaried:* 2. *Volunteers:* 50. *Financial sources:* Private: 3%. Public: 97%.

EVALUATION/RESEARCH: Evaluation reports available. Undertakes research activities.

PLANNED ACTIVITIES: Research and campaign in the field of citizenship law. Concerts against racism. Organisation and provision of care (psychotherapy) for the families of the holocaust victims. Publication of booklets to provide education and information on tolerance.

COMMENTS: Undertakes activities in the Commonwealth of Independent States. Information activities related to the Commonwealth of Independent States.

INFORMATION AND EDUCATION ACTIVITIES: Topics: Children/youth/family; Culture/tradition/religion; Ecology/environment/biodiversity; Education/training/literacy; Emergency relief/refugees/humanitarian assistance; Gender issues/women; Human rights/peace/conflicts; International relations/cooperation/development aid; Peace/ethnic conflicts/armament/disarmament; Racism/xenophobia/antisemitism; Refugees/migrants/ethnic groups. **Activities:** Conferences/seminars/workshops/training activities; Information campaigns/exhibitions.

CZE0898

OPEN SOCIETY FOUNDATION

T boritsk 23, 130 87 Praha 3, Czech Republic.

CZE0899

OPUS ARABICUM

P.O. Box 405, 112 1 Prague 1, Czech Republic.

Telephone: 42 (2) 0202.2586. *Contact:* Charif Bahbouh, Chairman.

CZE0900

PIONEER CHILDREN AND YOUTH ORGANIZATION ♦ Pionyr

Senovazne Nam 24, 116 47 Praha 1, Czech Republic.

CZE0901

PIONYR ♦ Pioneer

Gorkeho nam. 24, 116 47 Prague, Czech Republic.

Telephone: 42 (2) 228.883. *Contact:* Tesarkova Radka.

CZE0902

THE PRAGUE FOUNDATION FOR CENTRAL EUROPEAN UNIVERSITY

T boritsk 23, 130 87 Praha 3, Czech Republic.

CZE0903

RURAL YOUTH

Gorkeho nam. 23, 110 00 Praha 1, Czech Republic.

CZE0904

SDRUZENI OBCANU ZABYVAJICICH SE EMIGRANTY (SOZE)
♦ Society of Citizens Assisting Emigrants

Mostecká 16, 614 00 Brno, Czech Republic.

Telephone: 42 (5) 452 136 43. *Fax:* 42 (5) 452 137 46. *Contact:* Cristian Popescu, Director.

OBJECTIVES: To provide social and legal counselling for asylum seekers, refugees and people with temporary refuge. To help in integration of refugees. To organise cultural events and training seminars for a better understanding between Czechs and foreigners.

GENERAL INFORMATION: *Creation:* 1992. *Affiliated to:* European Council for Refugees and Exiles. *Personnel/Total:* 21. Salaried: 9. Volunteers: 12. *Budget/Total 1993:* ECU 34000 (US$ 45000). *Financial sources:* Public: 100%.

PUBLICATIONS: *Periodicals:* People on move. *List of publications.*

EVALUATION/RESEARCH: Evaluation reports available.

COMMENTS: Undertakes activities in the Commonwealth of Independent States. Information activities related to the Commonwealth of Independent States.

INFORMATION AND EDUCATION ACTIVITIES: Topics: Children/youth/family; Emergency relief/refugees/humanitarian assistance; Employment/unemployment; Human rights/peace/conflicts; International relations/cooperation/development aid; Racism/xenophobia/antisemitism; Refugees/migrants/ethnic groups. **Activities:** Broadcasting/cultural events; Conferences/seminars/workshops/training activities; Exchanges/twinning/linking; Formal education; Fund raising; Information and documentation services/data bases; Information campaigns/exhibitions; Lobbying/advocacy; Networking/electronic telecommunications; Publishing/audiovisual materials/educational materials.

CZE0905

SPOLECNOST PRATEL AFRIKY ♦ Africa Friendship Association

Jerevanska 7, 100 00 Praha 10, Czech Republic.

Telephone: 42 (2) 74 05 33. *Contact:* Vladimír Sery.

OBJECTIVES: To promote friendship and cultural co-operation with African countries. To inform the public of various problems in Africa. To organise conferences and seminars.

GENERAL INFORMATION: *Creation:* 1990. *Type of organisation:* association of NGOs. *Member organisations:* 4. *Personnel/Total:* 5. *Volunteers:* 5. *Budget/Total 1993:* ECU 4000 (US$ 5000). *Financial sources:* Private: 40%. Public: 50%. Self-financing: 10%.

PUBLICATIONS: *Periodicals:* Bulletin (4) - Bulletin-Nigeria (2) - Bulletin-Ethiopia (1). *List of publications.*

COMMENTS: Undertakes activities in the Commonwealth of Independent States. Information activities related to the Commonwealth of Independent States.

ACTIVITIES IN DEVELOPING REGIONS: Present in developing regions. Maintains local field presence. Works through local field partners. **Sustainable Development Actions:** Debt/finance/trade; Ecology/environment/biodiversity; Education/training/literacy; Health/sanitation/water; Human rights/peace/conflicts; Rural development/agriculture. **Regions:** Central Africa; East Africa; North Africa; Southern Africa; West Africa.

INFORMATION AND EDUCATION ACTIVITIES: Topics: Culture/tradition/religion; Ecology/environment/biodiversity; Education/training/literacy; Human rights/peace/conflicts; International economic relations/trade/debt/finance; Peace/ethnic conflicts/armament/disarmament; Racism/xenophobia/antisemitism. **Activities:** Broadcasting/cultural events; Conferences/seminars/workshops/training activities; Information campaigns/exhibitions.

CZE0906

SPOLECTNOST CESKO-ARABSKA ♦ Czech-Arab Society

Jerevanska 7, 100 00 Praha 10, Czech Republic.

Telephone: 42 (2) 74 05 33. *Fax:* 42 (2) 421 70 56. *Contact:* Josef Regner, Chairman.

OBJECTIVES: To strengthen mutual understanding and friendly relations between the Czech republic and Arab countries. To disseminate information on important cultural and social events among the Czech Republic and Arab countries and to contribute to better public knowledge about Arab countries.

GENERAL INFORMATION: *Creation:* 1990. *Type of organisation:* coordinating body. *Member organisations:* 15. *Personnel/Total:* 9. *Volunteers:* 9. *Budget/Total 1993:* ECU 5000 (US$ 7000). *Financial sources:* Private: 40%. Public: 50%. Self-financing: 10%.

PUBLICATIONS: *Periodicals:* Bulletin of the Czech-Arab and Czech-African Society (4). *Annual report.*

EVALUATION/RESEARCH: Evaluation reports available.

PLANNED ACTIVITIES: An exhibition on the ancient Egyptian portrait. A campaign in favour of the Arab-Israeli peace talks.

COMMENTS: Undertakes activities in the Commonwealth of Independent States.

See: *How to Use the Directory,* page 11.

ACTIVITIES IN DEVELOPING REGIONS: Works through local field partners. **Sustainable Development Actions:** Debt/finance/trade; Education/training/literacy; Emergency relief/refugees/humanitarian assistance; Human rights/peace/conflicts. **Regions:** Middle East.

INFORMATION AND EDUCATION ACTIVITIES: Topics: Culture/tradition/religion; Human rights/peace/conflicts; International economic relations/trade/debt/finance; Peace/ethnic conflicts/armament/disarmament. **Activities:** Broadcasting/cultural events; Conferences/seminars/workshops/training activities; Information and documentation services/data bases; Information campaigns/exhibitions; Publishing/audiovisual materials/educational materials.

CZE0907

STREDISKO KRESTANSKE POMOCI MLADYM V KRIZI ♦ CENTRE OF CHRISTIAN ASSISTANCE TO YOUNG PEOPLE IN CRISIS

Lidicka 866, 258 01 Vlasim, Czech Republic.

Telephone: 42 (303) 444 28. *Fax:* 42 (303) 444 82. *Contact:* Mgr. Jan Klas.

OBJECTIVES: To maintain an SOS help-line. To provide immediate and life-long help for young people in crisis (former prisoners, drug addicts, homeless and psychologically disturbed individuals) and to educate them on how to prevent their crises. To develop a network of the EXODUS centres at a national level.

GENERAL INFORMATION: *Creation:* 1992. *Affiliated to:* Council for Human Co-operation (Czech Republic). *Personnel/Total:* 31. *Salaried:* 6. *Volunteers:* 25. *Budget/Total 1993:* ECU 32000 (US$ 42000). *Financial sources: Public:* 64%. *Self-financing:* 36%.

PUBLICATIONS: *Annual report.*

EVALUATION/RESEARCH: Evaluation reports available.

INFORMATION AND EDUCATION ACTIVITIES: Topics: Emergency relief/refugees/humanitarian assistance. **Activities:** Formal education.

CZE0908

UNION FOR THE GOOD NEIGHBOURLY RELATIONS WITH THE GERMAN-SPEAKING COUNTRIES

Melantrichova 15, 110 00 Praha 1, Czech Republic.

CZE0909

UNION OF ARAY YOUTH (SVM)

Vitezne nam 4. p.p. 19, 160 00 Praha 6, Czech Republic.

CZE0910

UNION OF YOUTH CLUBS (SKM)

Gorkeho nam 24, 116 47 Praha 1, Czech Republic.

CZE0911

UNIZEM - JUVENA ♦ Union of Agriculture Youth

Gorkeho nam, 24, 116 47 Praha 1, Czech Republic.

CZE0912

VERONICA - THE ECOLOGICAL CENTRE

P.O. Box 91, 601 91 Brno 1, Czech Republic.

CZE0913

YOUNG EUROPEAN FEDERALISTS OF CZECH REPUBLIC

c/o Association for the European Home, P.O. Box 7, 119 00 Praha 1 - Hrad, Czech Republic.

CZE0914

YOUNG SOCIAL DEMOCRATS (MSD)

Hybernska 7, 110 00 Praha 1, Czech Republic.

CZE0915

ZELENY BOD OSTRAVA ♦ The Green Point of Ostrava

Dlouha 8, 702 00 Ostrava, Czech Republic.

Telephone: 42 (69) 23 58 29. *Fax:* 42 (69) 23 45 85. *Contact:* Petr Bielan, Vice-President.

OBJECTIVES: To disseminate information about ecological problems. To increase public interest in the environment. To provide environmental education. To create a platform for negotiations among people and local authorities.

GENERAL INFORMATION: *Creation:* 1991. *Personnel/Total:* 10. *Salaried:* 1. *Volunteers:* 9. *Budget/Total 1993:* ECU 3000 (US$ 4000). *Financial sources: Private:* 32%. *Public:* 58%. *Self-financing:* 10%.

PUBLICATIONS: *Periodicals:* Toulky (10). *Annual report.*

EVALUATION/RESEARCH: Evaluation reports available.

PLANNED ACTIVITIES: A sale exhibition titled "Home Ecology".

COMMENTS: Undertakes activities in the Commonwealth of Independent States. Information activities related to the Commonwealth of Independent States.

INFORMATION AND EDUCATION ACTIVITIES: Topics: Ecology/environment/biodiversity; Urban development/habitat. **Activities:** Conferences/seminars/workshops/training activities; Formal education; Information and documentation services/data bases; Networking/electronic telecommunications; Publishing/audiovisual materials/educational materials.

CZE0916

ZELENY DUM LITVINOV ♦ Green House Litvinov

Rooseweltova 296, 436 00 Litvinov, Czech Republic.

Telephone: 42 (35) 550 82. *Fax:* 42 (35) 523 93. *Contact:* Petr Pakosta, Director.

OBJECTIVES: To promote and support energy efficient technology, research and innovation for alternative, renewable energy sources. To promote sustainable energy policies for the Czech Republic.

GENERAL INFORMATION: *Creation:* 1991. *Personnel/Total:* 5. *Salaried:* 4. *Volunteers:* 1. *Budget/Total 1993:* ECU 26000 (US$ 34000).

PUBLICATIONS: *Periodicals:* Letters from North Bohemia (1).

EVALUATION/RESEARCH: Undertakes research activities.

PLANNED ACTIVITIES: The creation of an ecologicy curriculum in local schools. A PHARE energy study and a campaign to renovate hundreds of homes and schools.

COMMENTS: Undertakes activities in the Commonwealth of Independent States. Information activities related to the Commonwealth of Independent States.

INFORMATION AND EDUCATION ACTIVITIES: Topics: Ecology/environment/biodiversity. **Activities:** Broadcasting/cultural events; Conferences/seminars/workshops/training activities; Formal education; Fund raising; Information and documentation services/data bases; Information campaigns/exhibitions; Lobbying/advocacy; Publishing/audiovisual materials/educational materials.

Voir : *Comment utiliser le répertoire,* page 11.

DEU0917

ADOLF-GRIMME INSTITUT

Eduard-Weitsch Weg 25, 45768 Marl, Germany.

Telephone: 49 (2365) 91890. **Fax:** 49 (2365) 918989. **Contact:** Lutz Hachmeister.

OBJECTIVES: To serve as a forum for the media political debate in Germany and to offer both theoretical and practical education in the different fields of the media.

GENERAL INFORMATION: **Creation:** 1973. **Affiliated to:** German UNESCO Commission - NRW Broadcasting Commission (Germany). **Personnel/Total:** 23. **Salaried:** 11. **Budget/Total 1993:** ECU 1962000 (US$ 2298000). **Financial sources:** Public: 92%. Self-financing: 8%.

PUBLICATIONS: **Periodicals:** Agenda (6) (1). Annual report. List of publications.

EVALUATION/RESEARCH: Evaluation reports available. Undertakes research activities.

INFORMATION AND EDUCATION ACTIVITIES: Topics: Children/youth/family; Culture/tradition/religion; Ecology/environment/biodiversity; Education/training/literacy; Emergency relief/refugees/humanitarian assistance; Employment/unemployment; Food/famine; Gender issues/women; Health/sanitation/water; Human rights/peace/conflicts; International economic relations/trade/debt/finance; International relations/cooperation/development aid; Other; Peace/ethnic conflicts/armament/disarmament; Population/family planning/demography; Poverty/living conditions; Racism/xenophobia/antisemitism; Refugees/migrants/ethnic groups; Urban development/habitat. **Activities:** Broadcasting/cultural events; Conferences/seminars/workshops/training activities; Exchanges/twinning/linking; Information and documentation services/data bases; Information campaigns/exhibitions; Networking/electronic telecommunications; Publishing/audiovisual materials/educational materials.

DEU0918

ADVENTIST DEVELOPMENT AND RELIEF AGENCY (ADRA GERMANY)

Robert-Bosch-Straáe 4, 64331 Weiterstadt, Germany.

Telephone: 49 (6151) 8 11 50. **Fax:** 49 (6151) 81 15 12. **Contact:** E. Lischek, Executive Director.

OBJECTIVES: To reflect the character of God through humanitarian and developmental activities. To actively support communities in need. To actively support sustainable development projects. To build networks which develop indigenous capacity, appropriate technology and skills at all levels.

GENERAL INFORMATION: **Creation:** 1986. **Type of organisation:** network. **Member organisations:** 105. **Affiliated to:** Deutscher Paritätischer Wohlfahrtsverband (Germany) - Bensheimer Kreis (Germany) - Plattform EU (Belgium) - Euronaid - VOICE. **Personnel/Total:** 276. **Salaried:** 26 of which: 10 in developing countries. Volunteers: 250. **Budget/Total 1993:** ECU 4131000 (US$ 4839000). **Financial sources:** Private: 35%. Public: 65%.

PUBLICATIONS: **Periodicals:** ADRA Journal (3). Annual report.

EVALUATION/RESEARCH: Undertakes research activities.

COMMENTS: Undertakes activities in the Commonwealth of Independent States. Information activities related to the Commonwealth of Independent States.

ACTIVITIES IN DEVELOPING REGIONS: Present in developing regions. Maintains local field presence. Works through local field partners. **Sustainable Development Actions:** Democracy/good governance/institution building/participatory development; Ecology/environment/biodiversity; Education/training/literacy; Emergency relief/refugees/humanitarian assistance; Food/famine; Health/sanitation/water; Other; Rural development/agriculture; Sending volunteers/experts/technical assistance; Small enterprises/informal sector/handicrafts; Urban development/habitat. **Regions:** Central Africa; Central Asia and South Asia; East Africa; Middle East; North Africa; South America; South East Asia; Southern Africa; West Africa.

INFORMATION AND EDUCATION ACTIVITIES: Topics: Children/youth/family; Culture/tradition/religion; Emergency relief/refugees/humanitarian assistance; Food/famine; Health/sanitation/water; International relations/cooperation/development aid; Refugees/migrants/ethnic groups; Rural development/agriculture. **Activities:** Broadcasting/cultural events; Conferences/seminars/workshops/training activities; Fund raising; Information and documentation services/data bases; Information campaigns/exhibitions; Publishing/audiovisual materials/educational materials.

DEU0919

AFRIKA-VEREIN (AV) ♦ Africa Association

Neuer Jungfernstieg 21, 20354 Hamburg, Germany.

Telephone: 49 (40) 34 30 51. **Fax:** 49 (40) 35 47 04. **Contact:** Martin Krämer, General Manager.

OBJECTIVES: To undertake evaluations of the economic situation in African countries. To provide advice on export promotion, investment matters and flow of payments. To participate in the formulation of German and European economic policy in relation to Africa.

GENERAL INFORMATION: **Creation:** 1934. **Type of organisation:** coordinating body. **Member organisations:** 348. **Affiliated to:** Europäische Gruppe des privaten Sektors für die Zusammenarbeit (Germany). **Personnel/Total:** 9. **Salaried:** 9. **Budget/Total 1993:** ECU 671200 (US$ 786000). **Financial sources:** Self-financing: 100%.

PUBLICATIONS: **Periodicals:** Afrika-Post (12) - Afrika-Informationen (12). Annual report.

ACTIVITIES IN DEVELOPING REGIONS: Active in 52 country(ies). Works through local field partners. **Sustainable Development Actions:** Energy/transport; Sending volunteers/experts/technical assistance; Small enterprises/informal sector/handicrafts. **Regions:** Central Africa; East Africa; North Africa; Southern Africa; West Africa.

INFORMATION AND EDUCATION ACTIVITIES: Topics: Employment/unemployment; International economic relations/trade/debt/finance; International relations/cooperation/development aid. **Activities:** Conferences/seminars/workshops/training activities; Information and documentation services/data bases; Lobbying/advocacy.

DEU0920

AGENCIA LATINOAMERICANA DE SERVICIOS ESPECIALES DE INFORMACION - INITIATIVE PRO KULTURDIALOG LATEINAMERIKA (ALASEI-Bonn) ♦ Latin-American Agency for Special Information Services - Initiative for Cultural Dialogue with Latin-America

Michaelstrasse 7, 53111 Bonn, Germany.

Telephone: 49 (228) 69 77 22. **Fax:** 49 (228) 1 68 61 84. **Contact:** Gunter Weller, Director.

OBJECTIVES: To provide special information services from and about Latin-America,with emphasis on indigenous peoples. To initiate cultural dialogue between Latin-American citizens and citizens from the German-speaking European countries.

GENERAL INFORMATION: **Creation:** 1990. **Type of organisation:** network. **Member organisations:** 4. **Affiliated to:** One-World-Forum Bonn (Germany) - Europäisches Büro für Kommunale Entwicklungszusammenarbeit der Stadt Mainz (Germany). **Personnel/Total:** 12. Volunteers: 12 of which: 6 in developing countries. **Budget/Total 1993:** ECU 15000 (US$ 18000). **Financial sources:** Private: 20%. Self-financing: 80%.

PUBLICATIONS: **Periodicals:** Lateinamerika Anders Panorama (22) - Nueva Tierra Nuestra (6). List of publications.

EVALUATION/RESEARCH: Evaluation reports available.

ACTIVITIES IN DEVELOPING REGIONS: Active in 4 country(ies). Maintains local field presence. Works through local field partners. **Sustainable Development Actions:** Human rights/peace/conflicts; Other; Small enterprises/informal sector/handicrafts. **Regions:** Caribbean; Mexico and Central America; South America.

INFORMATION AND EDUCATION ACTIVITIES: Topics: Culture/tradition/religion; Human rights/peace/conflicts; Peace/ethnic conflicts/armament/disarmament; Refugees/migrants/ethnic groups. **Activities:** Broadcasting/cultural events; Conferences/seminars/workshops/training

See: *How to Use the Directory*, page 11.

activities; Exchanges/twinning/linking; Information and documentation services/data bases; Information campaigns/exhibitions; Lobbying/advocacy; Publishing/audiovisual materials/educational materials.

DEU0921

AKADEMIE KLAUSENHOF ♦ Academy Klausenhof

Klausenhofstrasse 100, 46499 Hamminkeln, Germany.

Telephone: 49 (2852) 8 90. *Contact:* Alois Becker, Managing Director.

OBJECTIVES: To promote awareness of development issues in the Federal Republic of Germany. To provide training for the staff of local development organisations in developing countries. To promote information exchange between rural youth of developing countries and youth in the Federal Republic of Germany.

GENERAL INFORMATION: *Creation:* 1959. *Affiliated to:* Union of Rural Boarding Schools of Germany (Germany) - Association of Catholic Organizations of Rural Areas. *Personnel/Total:* 5. *Salaried:* 5. *Budget/Total 1993:* ECU 155000 (US$ 181000). *Financial sources:* Public: 100%.

PUBLICATIONS: *Periodicals:* Klausenhof Aktuell (4). *Annual report.*

EVALUATION/RESEARCH: Evaluation reports available.

PLANNED ACTIVITIES: Organisation of training of management staff of non-governmental overseas organisations and a training seminar for Latin-Americans.

COMMENTS: The organisation also promotes the integration of immigrants' children into German society. Information activities related to the Commonwealth of Independent States.

INFORMATION AND EDUCATION ACTIVITIES: Topics: Children/youth/family; Culture/tradition/religion; Ecology/environment/biodiversity; Education/training/literacy; Employment/unemployment; Food/famine; Health/sanitation/water; Human rights/peace/conflicts; International economic relations/trade/debt/finance; International relations/cooperation/development aid; Poverty/living conditions; Racism/xenophobia/antisemitism; Refugees/migrants/ethnic groups; Rural development/agriculture. **Activities:** Broadcasting/cultural events; Conferences/seminars/workshops/training activities; Information and documentation services/data bases; Information campaigns/exhibitions.

DEU0922

AKTION CANCHANABURY, LEPRAHILFE HANS REINHARDT ♦ Action Canchanabury

Alte Banhofstrasse 121, 44892 Bochum, Germany.

Telephone: 49 (234) 28 63 00. *Fax:* 49 (234) 29 20 27. *Contact:* Michael Klüter, President.

OBJECTIVES: To fight leprosy in developing countries. To raise awareness of health and leprosy issues facing developing countries among the German public.

GENERAL INFORMATION: *Creation:* 1961. *Personnel/Total:* 55. *Salaried:* 5. *Volunteers:* 50. *Budget/Total 1993:* ECU 139000 (US$ 848000). *Financial sources:* Private: 90%. Self-financing: 10%.

PUBLICATIONS: *Periodicals:* Mbogi (2). *Annual report. List of publications.*

ACTIVITIES IN DEVELOPING REGIONS: Present in developing regions. Active in 12 country(ies). Maintains local field presence. Works through local field partners. **Sustainable Development Actions:** Children/youth/family; Emergency relief/refugees/humanitarian assistance; Food/famine; Health/sanitation/water; Sending volunteers/experts/technical assistance. **Regions:** Central Africa; Central Asia and South Asia; East Africa; Southern Africa; West Africa.

INFORMATION AND EDUCATION ACTIVITIES: Topics: Children/youth/family; Emergency relief/refugees/humanitarian assistance; Food/famine; Health/sanitation/water; Poverty/living conditions; Refugees/migrants/ethnic groups. **Activities:** Fund raising; Information and documentation services/data bases; Information campaigns/exhibitions; Publishing/audiovisual materials/educational materials.

DEU0923

AKTION COURAGE - SOS RASSISMUS

Postfach 2644, 53016 Bonn, Germany.

Telephone: 49 (228) 21 30 61. *Fax:* 49 (228) 26 29 78. *Contact:* Brigitte Erler.

OBJECTIVES: To work for a peaceful and democratic co-existence of people of different cultures and against the discrimination of minorities.

GENERAL INFORMATION: *Creation:* 1992. *Type of organisation:* association of NGOs. *Affiliated to:* Federation of SOS Racisme (France) - Antiracist Network for Equality in Europe (Belgium). *Personnel/Total:* 5. *Salaried:* 3. *Volunteers:* 2. *Budget/Total 1993:* ECU 124000 (US$ 145000). *Financial sources:* Private: 30%. *Public:* 15%. *Self-financing:* 55%.

PUBLICATIONS: *Periodicals:* Forum Buntes Deutschland (6). *List of publications.*

EVALUATION/RESEARCH: Undertakes research activities.

INFORMATION AND EDUCATION ACTIVITIES: Topics: Racism/xenophobia/antisemitism. **Activities:** Conferences/seminars/workshops/training activities; Fund raising; Information and documentation services/data bases; Information campaigns/exhibitions; Lobbying/advocacy; Networking/electronic telecommunications; Publishing/audiovisual materials/educational materials.

DEU0924

AKTION DER CHRISTEN FUR DIE ABSHAFFUNG DER FOLTER (ACAT) ♦ Action by Christians for the Abolition of Torture

P.O. Box 11 14, 4710 Lüdingshausen, Germany.

Telephone: 49 (25) 91 75 33. *Contact:* Magdalena Marx, Chairwoman.

DEU0925

AKTION DRITTE WELT (ADW)

Kronenstrasse 16HH, Postfach 53 28, 7800 Freiburg, Germany.

Telephone: 49 (761) 74 003. *Fax:* 49 (761) 77 069.

DEU0926

AKTION FAMILIENPLANUNG INTERNATIONAL ♦ Family Planning International

Postfach 110427, 86159 Augsburg, Germany.

Telephone: 49 (821) 57 55 35. *Contact:* Eger-Harsch.

OBJECTIVES: To support the diffusion of family planning in developing countries for health and socio-demographic reasons. To promote studies on family planning and on population in African countries.

GENERAL INFORMATION: *Creation:* 1992. *Personnel/Total:* 4. *Salaried:* 1 of which: 1 in developing countries. *Volunteers:* 3. *Budget/Total 1993:* ECU 9000 (US$ 11000). *Financial sources:* Private: 95%. *Self-financing:* 5%.

PUBLICATIONS: *Annual report.*

EVALUATION/RESEARCH: Evaluation reports available.

ACTIVITIES IN DEVELOPING REGIONS: Present in developing regions. Active in 1 country(ies). Works through local field partners. **Sustainable Development Actions:** Education/training/literacy; Health/sanitation/water; Population/family planning/demography. **Regions:** South America; West Africa.

INFORMATION AND EDUCATION ACTIVITIES: Topics: Health/sanitation/water; Population/family planning/demography. **Activities:** Conferences/seminars/workshops/training activities; Fund raising; Information and documentation services/data bases; Information campaigns/exhibitions; Lobbying/advocacy.

DEU0927

AKTION KINDERHILFE MUNSTER ♦ Action for Children's Assistance

Dürerstrasse 25, 48147 Münster, Germany.

Telephone: 49 (251) 27 48 04. *Contact:* Barbara Hümer, District Council.

Voir : *Comment utiliser le répertoire*, page 11.

OBJECTIVES: To help children in developing countries by regular financial donations. To support actions for children and young people in Africa, Asia and Latin America.

GENERAL INFORMATION: *Creation:* 1968. *Personnel/Total:* 14. *Volunteers:* 14. *Budget/Total 1993:* ECU 168000 (US$ 197000). *Financial sources:* Self-financing: 100%.

ACTIVITIES IN DEVELOPING REGIONS: Active in 15 country(ies). Maintains local field presence. **Sustainable Development Actions:** Children/youth/family. **Regions:** Central Asia and South Asia; Middle East; South America; Southern Africa.

DEU0928

AKTION MISSION UND LEPRAHILFE SCHIEFBAHN ♦ Action Mission and Leprosy Assistance Schiefbahn

Hochstrasse 14, 47877 Willich (Schiefbahn), Germany.

Telephone: 49 (2154) 84 11. *Contact:* Josef Heyes, Chairman.

OBJECTIVES: To grant "first aid" to needy and ill people in developing countries to promote their health and to improve their general living conditions by promoting projects.

GENERAL INFORMATION: *Creation:* 1963. *Type of organisation:* coordinating body. *Personnel/Total:* 803. *Salaried:* 3. *Volunteers:* 800. *Budget/Total 1993:* ECU 365000 (US$ 427000). *Financial sources:* Private: 100%.

PUBLICATIONS: *Annual report.*

EVALUATION/RESEARCH: Evaluation reports available.

ACTIVITIES IN DEVELOPING REGIONS: Active in 20 country(ies). Works through local field partners. **Sustainable Development Actions:** Education/training/literacy; Emergency relief/refugees/humanitarian assistance; Health/sanitation/water; Rural development/agriculture. **Regions:** Central Africa; Central Asia and South Asia; East Africa; South America; South East Asia; West Africa.

INFORMATION AND EDUCATION ACTIVITIES: Topics: Education/training/literacy; Employment/unemployment; Health/sanitation/water; Poverty/living conditions; Rural development/agriculture. **Activities:** Conferences/seminars/workshops/training activities; Formal education; Fund raising.

DEU0929

AKTIONSGEMEINSCHAFT DIENST FUR DEN FRIEDEN (AGDF) ♦ Action Committee Service for Peace

Blücherstrasse 14, 53115 Bonn, Germany.

Telephone: 49 (228) 22 91 92. *Fax:* 49 (228) 21 93 29. *Contact:* Ulrich Frey, Director.

OBJECTIVES: To support the common concerns and projects of member organisations. To advertise and disseminate information about peace service opportunities. To raise awareness about peace issues.

GENERAL INFORMATION: *Creation:* 1968. *Type of organisation:* coordinating body. *Member organisations:* 29. *Affiliated to:* Co-ordinating Committe of International Voluntary Service (France) -Arbeitskreis Lernen und Helfen in Übersee (Germany) - Diakonisches Werk der EKD (Germany). *Personnel/Total:* 4. *Salaried:* 4. *Budget/Total 1993:* ECU 207000 (US$ 242000). *Financial sources:* Private: 75%. Self-financing: 25%.

PUBLICATIONS: *Annual report.*

INFORMATION AND EDUCATION ACTIVITIES: Topics: Culture/tradition/religion; Human rights/peace/conflicts; Peace/ethnic conflicts/armament/disarmament; Racism/xenophobia/antisemitism; Refugees/migrants/ethnic groups. **Activities:** Conferences/seminars/workshops/training activities; Fund raising; Information and documentation services/data bases; Information campaigns/exhibitions; Lobbying/advocacy.

DEU0930

AKTIONSGEMEINSCHAFT FRIEDENSWOCHE MINDEN ♦ Action Community: Freedom Week Minden

Alte Kirchstrasse 1, Postfach 2063, 4950 Minden, Germany.

Telephone: 49 (571) 2 43 39.

DEU0931

AKTIONSGEMEINSCHAFT HUMANE WELT ♦ Action Community for a Humane World

Auf dem Thie 7, 48431 Rheine, Germany.

Telephone: 49 (05971) 1 51 21. *Fax:* 49 (05971) 1 00 06. *Contact:* Michael Seligmann.

OBJECTIVES: To promote international understanding and solidarity.

GENERAL INFORMATION: *Creation:* 1981. *Affiliated to:* Landesarbeitgemeinschaft von 3 Welt Zentrum (Germany) - Bundeskoordination Entwicklungspolitischer Aktionsgruppen (Germany). *Personnel/Total:* 8. *Salaried:* 7. *Volunteers:* 1. *Budget/Total 1993:* ECU 516000 (US$ 605000). *Financial sources:* Private: 3%. Public: 95%. Self-financing: 2%.

PLANNED ACTIVITIES: Exhibition Germany-Zimbabwe (3 artists of each country).

ACTIVITIES IN DEVELOPING REGIONS: Present in developing regions. Active in 2 country(ies). Maintains local field presence. Works through local field partners. **Sustainable Development Actions:** Children/youth/family; Education/training/literacy; Gender issues/women; Rural development/agriculture; Small enterprises/informal sector/handicrafts; Urban development/habitat. **Regions:** South America; Southern Africa.

INFORMATION AND EDUCATION ACTIVITIES: Topics: Culture/tradition/religion; Ecology/environment/biodiversity; International relations/cooperation/development aid; Racism/xenophobia/antisemitism; Refugees/migrants/ethnic groups; Urban development/habitat. **Activities:** Broadcasting/cultural events; Conferences/seminars/workshops/training activities; Fund raising; Information campaigns/exhibitions; Publishing/audiovisual materials/educational materials.

DEU0932

AKTIONSGRUPPE KINDER IN NOT

Hohner Strasse 2, 53578 Windhagen, Germany.

DEU0933

ALFONS GOPPEL-STIFTUNG FONDATION ♦ Fondation Alfons Goppel

Oberanger 32, 80331 München, Allemagne.

Téléphone: 49 (89) 26 40 18. *Fax:* 49 (89) 26 90 00. *Contact:* Ernst Michl.

OBJECTIFS: Réaliser des projets de soutien destinés aux jeunes et aux enfants des pays en développement, particulièrement en Amérique Latine. Améliorer les conditions de vie de ces groupes par des actions de scolarisation et de formation.

INFORMATIONS GENERALES: *Création:* 1981. *Affiliée à:* Bayerisches Landeskomitee für den Kampf gegen den Hunger. *Personnel/Total:* 5. *Salariés:* 3. *Bénévoles:* 2. *Budget/Total 1993:* ECU 1549000 (US$ 1815000). *Sources financières:* Privé: 25%. Public: 75%.

ACTIVITES DANS LES REGIONS EN DEVELOPPEMENT: Intervient directement dans les régions en développement. Intervient dans 5 pays. Maintient une présence locale sur le terrain. Intervient par l'intermédiaire d'organisations locales partenaires. **Actions de Développement durable:** Développement rural/agriculture; Enfants/jeunesse/famille; Santé/assainissement/eau; Éducation/formation/alphabétisation. **Régions:** Afrique de l'Ouest; Amérique du Sud; Mexique et Amerique centrale.

ACTIVITES D'INFORMATION ET D'EDUCATION: Domaines: Développement rural/agriculture; Santé/assainissement/eau; Éducation/formation/alphabétisation. **Activités:** Collecte de fonds; Conférences/séminaires/ateliers/activités de formation; Éducation formelle.

DEU0934

AMALA KREBSHILFE ♦ Amala Aid Against Cancer

Am Stadtwald 64, 5300 Bonn 2, Germany.

Telephone: 49 (228) 31 36 17. *Contact:* Dr. Sudhoff, Secretary.

See: *How to Use the Directory,* page 11.

DEU0935

AMNESTY INTERNATIONAL, GERMAN SECTION

Heerstrasse 178, 5300 Bonn 1, Germany.

DEU0936

AMREF GESELLSCHAFT FUR MEDIZIN UND FORSCHUNG IN AFRIKA (AMREF DEUTSCHLAND) ♦ African Medical and Research Foundation

Mauerkircherstrasse 155, 81925 München 81, Germany.

Telephone: 49 (89) 98 11 29. *Fax:* 49 (89) 98 11 89. *Contact:* Leonore Semler, Vorsitzende.

OBJECTIVES: To identify health needs and develop, implement and evaluate methods and programmes to meet these needs through services, training and research.

GENERAL INFORMATION: *Creation:* 1963. *Personnel/Total:* 7. *Salaried:* 3 of which: 3 in developing countries. *Volunteers:* 4. *Budget/Total 1993:* ECU 1084000 (US$ 1270000). *Financial sources:* Private: 20%. Public: 80%.

PUBLICATIONS: *Annual report. List of publications.*

EVALUATION/RESEARCH: Evaluation reports available. Undertakes research activities.

ACTIVITIES IN DEVELOPING REGIONS: Present in developing regions. Active in 4 country(ies). Maintains local field presence. Works through local field partners. **Sustainable Development Actions:** Children/youth/family; Democracy/good governance/institution building/participatory development; Education/training/literacy; Emergency relief/refugees/humanitarian assistance; Gender issues/women; Health/sanitation/water; Population/family planning/demography; Sending volunteers/experts/technical assistance; Small enterprises/informal sector/handicrafts. **Regions:** East Africa.

DEU0937

ANDHERI-HILFE ♦ Andheri-Help

Mackestrasse 53, 53119 Bonn, Germany.

Telephone: 49 (228) 67 15 86. *Contact:* Rosi Gollmann, President.

DEU0938

ANTIRASSISTISCHE INITIATIVE

Yorckstrasse 59, 10965 Berlin, Germany.

Telephone: 49 (30) 786 99 84.

DEU0939

ARBEITER-SAMARITER-BUND DEUTSCHLAND (ASB) ♦ Workers' Samaritarian Federation

Sülzburgstrasse 140, 5000 Köln 41, Germany.

Telephone: 49 (221) 47 60 50. *Fax:* 49 (221) 47 60 52 88. *Contact:* Wilhelm Müller.

OBJECTIVES: To provide voluntary aid and welfare to anyone who needs it regardless of race, nationality, religious or political affiliations. To advocate co-operation between states and independent associations based on a spirit of mutual trust.

GENERAL INFORMATION: *Creation:* 1888. *Personnel/Total:* 80. *Salaried:* 15 of which: 13 in developing countries. *Budget/Total 1993:* ECU 6196000 (US$ 7258000). *Financial sources:* Private: 05%. Public: 20%. Self-financing: 15%.

PUBLICATIONS: *Annual report.*

EVALUATION/RESEARCH: Evaluation reports available.

PLANNED ACTIVITIES: Development of public health systems in Middle and Eastern Europe.

COMMENTS: The ASB has a total staff of 80. There are however only 15 who work in the field of development. Undertakes activities in the Commonwealth of Independent States.

ACTIVITIES IN DEVELOPING REGIONS: Present in developing regions. Active in 4 country(ies). Maintains local field presence. Works through local field partners. **Sustainable Development Actions:** Emergency relief/refugees/humanitarian assistance; Food/famine; Health/sanitation/water; Rural development/agriculture. **Regions:** East Africa; Middle East; West Africa.

INFORMATION AND EDUCATION ACTIVITIES: Topics: Emergency relief/refugees/humanitarian assistance; Health/sanitation/water. **Activities:** Conferences/seminars/workshops/training activities; Exchanges/twinning/linking.

DEU0940

ARBEITERWOHLFAHRT BUNDESVERBAND (AWO) ♦ National Association of Labour Welfare

Oppelnerstrasse 130, P.O. Box 11 49, 53001 Bonn, Germany.

Telephone: 49 (228) 6 68 50. *Fax:* 49 (228) 6 68 52 09. *Contact:* Ulrich Lottmann.

OBJECTIVES: To organise social work in Germany. To develop social structures in developing countries through financial support for rural and urban projects. To support the creation of local NGOs.

GENERAL INFORMATION: *Creation:* 1919. *Affiliated to:* International Workers Aid (Germany) - International Council of Social Welfare (Germany). *Personnel/Total:* 150. *Salaried:* 150. *Financial sources:* Private: 35%. Public: 65%.

PUBLICATIONS: *Periodicals:* AWO-Magazin (12) - Theoric & Praxis (6).

COMMENTS: The AWO is a social service organization within the FRG. International co-operation is a minor part of activities.

ACTIVITIES IN DEVELOPING REGIONS: Active in 9 country(ies). Works through local field partners. **Sustainable Development Actions:** Education/training/literacy; Gender issues/women; Health/sanitation/water; Rural development/agriculture; Small enterprises/informal sector/handicrafts. **Regions:** Central Asia and South Asia; East Africa; South America; South East Asia; West Africa.

INFORMATION AND EDUCATION ACTIVITIES: Topics: Children/youth/family; Gender issues/women; Health/sanitation/water; Poverty/living conditions; Rural development/agriculture. **Activities:** Information campaigns/exhibitions.

DEU0941

ARBEITGEMEINSCHAFT SPINA BIDIFA UND HYDROCEPHALUS

Münsterstrasse 13, 44145 Dortmund, Germany.

DEU0942

ARBEITSGEMEINSCHAFT DER EVANGELISCHEN JUGEND IN DER BUNDESREPUBLIK DEUTSCHLAND (AEJ) ♦ Federation of Protestant Youth in the Federal Republic of Germany

Otto-Brenner-str.9 PO Box 424, 30004 Hannover, Germany.

Telephone: 49 (511) 1 21 50. *Fax:* 49 (511) 1 21 52 99. *Contact:* Ulrich Fischer, Chairman.

OBJECTIVES: To represent member organisations to the State, Church and society. To promote relations between members and to function as a service organisation. To raise awareness of political, social and economical issues.

GENERAL INFORMATION: *Creation:* 1949. *Type of organisation:* association of NGOs. *Member organisations:* 34. *Personnel/Total:* 38. *Salaried:* 33. *Budget/Total 1993:* ECU 2272000 (US$ 2661000). *Financial sources:* Private: 50%. Public: 40%. Self-financing: 10%.

PUBLICATIONS: *Periodicals:* AEJ Information (6). *List of publications.*

COMMENTS: Undertakes activities in the Commonwealth of Independent States. Information activities related to the Commonwealth of Independent States.

ACTIVITIES IN DEVELOPING REGIONS: Active in 15 country(ies). Works through local field partners. **Sustainable Development Actions:** Children/youth/family. **Regions:** Central Africa; Central Asia and South Asia; East Africa; Mexico and Central America; Middle East; South America; Southern Africa.

Voir : *Comment utiliser le répertoire,* page 11.

INFORMATION AND EDUCATION ACTIVITIES: Topics: Children/youth/family; Culture/tradition/religion; Ecology/environment/biodiversity; Gender issues/women; International economic relations/trade/debt/finance; Peace/ethnic conflicts/armament/disarmament; Poverty/living conditions; Racism/xenophobia/antisemitism; Rural development/agriculture. **Activities:** Conferences/seminars/workshops/training activities; Exchanges/twinning/linking; Fund raising; Information and documentation services/data bases; Information campaigns/exhibitions; Lobbying/advocacy; Publishing/audiovisual materials/educational materials.

DEU0943

ARBEITSGEMEINSCHAFT ENTWICKLUNGSLANDER (AGE) ♦
Working Group Developing Countries

Gustav-Heinemann-Ufer 84-88, Postfach 51 05 48, 50996 Köln, Germany.

Telephone: 49 (221) 3 70 84 15. *Fax:* 49 (221) 3 70 84 20. *Contact:* Hans Singer.

OBJECTIVES: To promote the private sector in developing countries. To support private sector-related development policy of the German government. To offer knowledge of national and international development policy to German companies and business associations.

GENERAL INFORMATION: *Creation:* 1961. ***Type of organisation:*** coordinating body. ***Member organisations:*** 5. ***Affiliated to:*** Bundesverband der Deutschen Industrie (Germany) - Deutscher Industrie und Handelstag (Germany) - Bundesverband Deutscher Banken (Germany) - Bundesverband des Deutschen Grob-und Aubenhandels (Germany) - Arbeitsgemeinschaft Ländervereine (Germany).

DEU0944

ARBEITSGEMEINSCHAFT FUR ENTWICKLUNGSHILFE (AGEH) ♦ Personnel Agency of the German Catholics for International Co-operation

Postfach 21 01 28 Ripuarenstr. 8, 50527 Köln, Germany.

Telephone: 49 (221) 8 89 60. *Fax:* 49 (221) 8 89 61 00. *E-mail:* geod:ageh-contacts. *Contact:* Manfred Sollich.

OBJECTIVES: To promote social justice and sound living conditions for all. To respond to the needs of people in developing countries. To send development co-workers to Africa, Asia and Latin America to work in partner projects.

GENERAL INFORMATION: *Creation:* 1959. ***Member organisations:*** 20. ***Affiliated to:*** Platform-EG (Germany) - OCCI. ***Personnel/Total:*** 370. *Salaried:* 50. *Volunteers:* 320 of which: 320 in developing countries. ***Budget/Total 1993:*** ECU 12392000 (US$ 14516000). ***Financial sources:*** Private: 25%. Public: 75%.

PUBLICATIONS: *Periodicals:* Contacts (4). *Annual report. List of publications.*

COMMENTS: Undertakes activities in the Commonwealth of Independent States. Information activities related to the Commonwealth of Independent States.

ACTIVITIES IN DEVELOPING REGIONS: Active in 60 country(ies). Works through local field partners. Sustainable Development Actions: Children/youth/family; Education/training/literacy; Emergency relief/refugees/humanitarian assistance; Food/famine; Gender issues/women; Health/sanitation/water; Human rights/peace/conflicts; Rural development/agriculture; Sending volunteers/experts/technical assistance. **Regions:** Caribbean; Central Africa; Central Asia and South Asia; East Africa; East Asia; Mexico and Central America; Middle East; North Africa; Oceania; South America; South East Asia; Southern Africa; West Africa.

INFORMATION AND EDUCATION ACTIVITIES: Topics: Children/youth/family; Culture/tradition/religion; Ecology/environment/biodiversity; Education/training/literacy; Emergency relief/refugees/humanitarian assistance; Employment/unemployment; Food/famine; Gender issues/women; Health/sanitation/water; Human rights/peace/conflicts; International economic relations/trade/debt/finance; International relations/cooperation/development aid; Peace/ethnic conflicts/armament/disarmament; Population/family planning/demography; Poverty/living conditions; Racism/xenophobia/antisemitism; Refugees/migrants/ethnic groups; Rural development/agriculture; Urban development/habitat. **Activities:** Conferences/seminars/workshops/training activities; Information and documentation services/data bases; Publishing/audiovisual materials/educational materials.

DEU0945

ARBEITSGEMEINSCHAFT INTERNATIONALE POLITIK

Jaegerhofstrasse 12, 6500 Mainz, Germany.

Telephone: 49 (0 61 31) 68 34 40.

DEU0946

ARBEITSGEMEINSCHAFT KIRCHLICHER ENTWICKLUNGSDIENST - PLANUNGS- UND GRUNDSATZABTEILUNG (AGKED) ♦ Association of the Churches' Development Services - Policy Planning Unit

Kniebisstrasse 29, 70188 Stuttgart, Germany.

Telephone: 49 (711) 9 25 77 10. *Fax:* 49 (711) 9 25 77 25. *E-mail:* geonet:geoo:agked. *Contact:* Helmut Hertel, General Secretary.

OBJECTIVES: To define the churches' principles regarding their contribution to development co-operation and carry out the work of its members as a joint undertaking. To support services that raise awareness of development issues.

GENERAL INFORMATION: *Creation:* 1970. ***Type of organisation:*** coordinating body. ***Member organisations:*** 5. ***Affiliated to:*** European Ecumenical Organisation for Development (Belgium). ***Personnel/Total:*** 10. *Salaried:* 10.

PUBLICATIONS: *Annual report. List of publications.*

ACTIVITIES IN DEVELOPING REGIONS: Works through local field partners.

DEU0947

ARBEITSGEMEINSCHAFT PRIVATER ENTWICKLUNGSDIENSTE (APED) ♦ Association of Private Development Agencies

Argelanderstrasse 50, 53115 Bonn, Germany.

Telephone: 49 (228) 21 59 00. *Contact:* Heribert Handel, Chairman.

OBJECTIVES: To organise development aid and the placement of volunteers abroad. To provide advice on development project preparation and implementation. To represent the interests of its members to the Federal authorities in Bonn. To promote its members' development projects in Bonn and Brussels.

GENERAL INFORMATION: *Creation:* 1967. ***Member organisations:*** 20. ***Affiliated to:*** LHÜ (Germany) - European Forum on Development Service. ***Personnel/Total:*** 1. *Salaried:* 1. ***Financial sources:*** Private: 100%.

ACTIVITIES IN DEVELOPING REGIONS: Maintains local field presence. Works through local field partners. **Sustainable Development Actions:** Children/youth/family; Education/training/literacy; Health/sanitation/water; Rural development/agriculture. **Regions:** East Africa; Mexico and Central America; South America; South East Asia.

INFORMATION AND EDUCATION ACTIVITIES: Topics: Children/youth/family. **Activities:** Conferences/seminars/workshops/training activities.

DEU0948

ARBEITSGEMEINSCHAFT REGENWALD UND ARTENSCHUTZ (ARA) ♦ Working Group on Rainforests and Biodiversity

Klasingstrasse 17, P.O. Box 100466, 33602 Bielefeld, Germany.

Telephone: 49 (521) 6 59 43. *Fax:* 49 (521) 6 49 75. *E-mail:* araoffice@gu.apc.org. *Contact:* Monika Nolle.

OBJECTIVES: To form and co-ordinate joint iniatives of German NGOs in the fields of Biodiversity and Forest Use and Conservation. To formulate project criteria for ecologically and socially sound German development aid.

GENERAL INFORMATION: *Creation:* 1987. ***Type of organisation:*** coordinating body. ***Affiliated to:*** Deutsche Naturshutsring - DNR - European Rainforest Movement (the Netherlands). ***Personnel/Total:*** 9. *Salaried:* 2. *Volunteers:* 7. ***Budget/Total 1993:*** ECU 232000 (US$ 272000). ***Financial sources:*** Private: 10%. Public: 50%. *Self-financing:* 40%.

See: *How to Use the Directory,* page 11.

PUBLICATIONS: *Periodicals:* ARA-aktuell (3). *Annual report. List of publications.*

EVALUATION/RESEARCH: Evaluation reports available. Undertakes research activities.

ACTIVITIES IN DEVELOPING REGIONS: Active in 3 country(ies). Works through local field partners. **Sustainable Development Actions:** Ecology/environment/biodiversity; Health/sanitation/water; Human rights/peace/conflicts. **Regions:** Mexico and Central America; South America; South East Asia.

INFORMATION AND EDUCATION ACTIVITIES: Topics: Ecology/environment/biodiversity. **Activities:** Conferences/seminars/workshops/training activities; Fund raising; Information and documentation services/data bases; Information campaigns/exhibitions; Lobbying/advocacy; Publishing/audiovisual materials/educational materials.

DEU0949

ARBEITSKREIS "LERNEN UND HELFEN IN UBERSEE" (LHÜ)
♦ Association "apprendre et aider Outremer"

Thomas-Mann-Strasse 52, 53111 Bonn, Allemagne.

Téléphone: 49 (228) 63 44 24. *Fax:* 49 (228) 65 04 14. *Contact:* Götz Hünemörder, Président.

OBJECTIFS: Fournir des informations sur les problèmes du développement. Renseigner sur les moyens de participer aux actions sur le terrain. Servir d'intermédiaire pour les citoyens allemands qui veulent participer au programme des Volontaires des Nations Unies.

INFORMATIONS GENERALES: *Création:* 1961. *Type d'organisation:* regroupement d'ONG. *Organisations membres:* 33. *Affiliée à:* Conseil d'Administration du DED (Allemagne) - Forum Européen du Développement. *Personnel/Total:* 4. *Salariés:* 4.

PUBLICATIONS: *Périodiques:* LHÜ Info-Dienst (12). *Rapport annuel. Liste des publications.*

EVALUATION/RECHERCHE: Rapports d'évaluation disponibles. Entreprend des activités de recherche.

PREVISIONS D'ACTIVITES: Des recherches sur la réintégration des volontaires á leurs retour et sur la possibilité qu'ils ont de faire du lobbying. Promouvoir l'anti-racisme et le financement par le ministère allemand pour la coopération.

ACTIVITES DANS LES REGIONS EN DEVELOPPEMENT: Intervient dans 1 pays.

DEU0950

ARBEITSKREIS ENTWICKLUNGSPOLITIK (AKE) ♦ Association for Development Studies

Horstweg 11, 4973 Vlotho, Germany.

Telephone: 49 (5733) 68 00 / 29 77. *Contact:* Andreas Schüssler, President.

DEU0951

ARBEITSKREIS MEDIZINISCHE ENTWICKLUNG-SHILFE (AKME) ♦ Working Group on Medical Development Aid

Deutsche Stiftung für Internationale Entwicklung - Zentralstelle für Gesundheit, 10178 Berlin, Germany.

Telephone: 49 (30) 23 11 91 01. *Fax:* 49 (30) 23 11 91 11. *Contact:* Dr. Walter Seidel, Secretary.

OBJECTIVES: To harmonize the German development aid policy in the health sector. To encourage the exchange of technical information among member organisations.

GENERAL INFORMATION: *Creation:* 1972. *Type of organisation:* association of NGOs. *Member organisations:* 47. *Personnel/Total:* 1. *Volunteers:* 1.

INFORMATION AND EDUCATION ACTIVITIES: Topics: Health/sanitation/water; Population/family planning/demography. **Activities:** Exchanges/twinning/linking; Lobbying/advocacy; Networking/electronic telecommunications.

DEU0952

ARBEITSSTELLE FRIEDENSFORSCHUNG BONN ♦ Information Unit Peace Research Bonn

Beethovenallee 4, 5300 Bonn 2, Germany.

Telephone: 49 (228) 35 60 32.

DEU0953

ARCHIV FUR POLITIK UND ZEITGESCHICHTE / DRITTE-WELT-ARCHIV GYMNASIUM WERTINGEN/SCHWABEN ♦
Third World Archive at the High School Wertingen

Pestalozzistrasse 12, 8857 Wertingen, Germany.

Telephone: 49 (8272) 27 73. *Contact:* Dr. Wolfgang Pfaffenberger.

DEU0954

ARTZE FUR DIE DRITTE WELT ♦ German Doctors for Developing Countries

Elsheimerstrasse 9, 60322 Frankfurt, Germany.

Telephone: 49 (69) 71 91 14 56. *Fax:* 49 (69) 71 91 14 50. *Contact:* Dr. Lothar Watrinet.

OBJECTIVES: To provide medical, social and humanitarian assistance to sick and destitute peoples in the Third World.

GENERAL INFORMATION: *Creation:* 1983. *Personnel/Total:* 240. *Salaried:* 190 of which: 185 in developing countries. *Volunteers:* 50 of which: 40 in developing countries. *Budget/Total 1993:* ECU 3779000 (US$ 4427000). *Financial sources:* Private: 85%. Public: 15%.

PUBLICATIONS: *Annual report.*

ACTIVITIES IN DEVELOPING REGIONS: Present in developing regions. Active in 5 country(ies). Maintains local field presence. Works through local field partners. **Sustainable Development Actions:** Children/youth/family; Education/training/literacy; Food/famine; Gender issues/women; Health/sanitation/water; Human rights/peace/conflicts; Population/family planning/demography; Sending volunteers/experts/technical assistance. **Regions:** Central Asia and South Asia; Mexico and Central America; South East Asia.

INFORMATION AND EDUCATION ACTIVITIES: Topics: Children/youth/family; Education/training/literacy; Emergency relief/refugees/humanitarian assistance; Employment/unemployment; Food/famine; Gender issues/women; Health/sanitation/water; Human rights/peace/conflicts; Population/family planning/demography; Poverty/living conditions; Refugees/migrants/ethnic groups. **Activities:** Conferences/seminars/workshops/training activities; Formal education; Fund raising; Lobbying/advocacy.

DEU0955

ASSOCIATION FOR PROGRESSIVE COMMUNICA-TIONS (APC/ComLink)

Au der Lutherkirche 6, 30167 Hannover, Germany.

Telephone: 49 (511) 1 61 78 11. *Fax:* 49 (511) 1 65 26 11. *E-mail:* support@oln.comlink.apc.org.

OBJECTIVES: To provide e-mail services for NGOs world-wide. To provide communication training for NGOs.

GENERAL INFORMATION: *Creation:* 1989. *Type of organisation:* network. *Affiliated to:* Association for Progressive Communications (Brazil). *Personnel/Total:* 5. *Salaried:* 3. *Volunteers:* 2. *Budget/Total 1993:* ECU 15000 (US$ 18000). *Financial sources:* Private: 15%. Public: 10%. Self-financing: 75%.

PUBLICATIONS: *List of publications.*

COMMENTS: Undertakes activities in the Commonwealth of Independent States. Information activities related to the Commonwealth of Independent States.

ACTIVITIES IN DEVELOPING REGIONS: Active in 60 country(ies). Works through local field partners.

INFORMATION AND EDUCATION ACTIVITIES: Topics: Children/youth/family; Culture/tradition/religion; Ecology/environment/biodiversity; Education/training/literacy; Emergency relief/refugees/humanitarian assis-

tance; Employment/unemployment; Food/famine; Gender issues/women; Health/sanitation/water; Human rights/peace/conflicts; International economic relations/trade/debt/finance; International relations/cooperation/development aid; Peace/ethnic conflicts/armament/disarmament; Population/family planning/demography; Poverty/living conditions; Racism/xenophobia/antisemitism; Refugees/migrants/ethnic groups; Rural development/agriculture; Urban development/habitat. **Activities:** Information campaigns/exhibitions; Networking/electronic telecommunications.

DEU0956

AUSBILDUNGSSTATTE FUR AUSLANDISCHE FERNSEHKRAFTE BEIM SENDER FREIES BERLIN

Masurenallee 8-14, 14046 Berlin, Germany.

Telephone: 49 (30) 30 31 40 50. *Fax:* 49 (30) 30 31 40 59. *Contact:* Dietrich Berwanger.

OBJECTIVES: To provide advanced training for journalistic, editorial, managerial and engineering staff of television stations in developing countries. To offer consultancy and project management.

GENERAL INFORMATION: Creation: 1970. **Personnel/Total:** 14. *Salaried:* 14. **Budget/Total 1993:** ECU 2582000 (US$ 3024000). **Financial sources:** *Public:* 100%.

PUBLICATIONS: Periodicals: TTC Newsletter (1).

EVALUATION/RESEARCH: Undertakes research activities.

COMMENTS: Undertakes activities in the Commonwealth of Independent States. Information activities related to the Commonwealth of Independent States.

ACTIVITIES IN DEVELOPING REGIONS: Present in developing regions. Active in 10 country(ies). Works through local field partners. **Sustainable Development Actions:** Other. **Regions:** Central Africa; Central Asia and South Asia; East Africa; East Asia; Middle East; North Africa; Oceania; South East Asia; Southern Africa; West Africa.

INFORMATION AND EDUCATION ACTIVITIES: Topics: Other. **Activities:** Broadcasting/cultural events; Information and documentation services/data bases; Networking/electronic telecommunications; Publishing/audiovisual materials/educational materials.

DEU0957

AUSSCHUSS FUR ENTWICKLUNGSBEZOGENE BILDUNG UND PUBLIZISTIK (ABP) ♦ Committee for Development Education and Publications

Kniebisstrasse 29, 70188 Stuttgart, Germany.

Telephone: 49 (711) 9 25 77 40. *Fax:* 49 (711) 9 25 77 49. *Contact:* Klaus Seitz, Executive Secretary.

OBJECTIVES: To promote, fund and co-ordinate programmes for development education in Germany.

GENERAL INFORMATION: Creation: 1977. **Type of organisation:** coordinating body. **Personnel/Total:** 6. *Salaried:* 6. **Budget/Total 1993:** ECU 5473000 (US$ 6411000). **Financial sources:** Self-financing: 100%.

PUBLICATIONS: *Annual report.*

INFORMATION AND EDUCATION ACTIVITIES: Topics: Children/youth/family; Culture/tradition/religion; Ecology/environment/biodiversity; Education/training/literacy; Emergency relief/refugees/humanitarian assistance; Employment/unemployment; Food/famine; Gender issues/women; Health/sanitation/water; Human rights/peace/conflicts; International economic relations/trade/debt/finance; International relations/cooperation/development aid; Peace/ethnic conflicts/armament/disarmament; Population/family planning/demography; Poverty/living conditions; Racism/xenophobia/antisemitism; Refugees/migrants/ethnic groups; Rural development/agriculture; Urban development/habitat. **Activities:** Fund raising.

DEU0958

AUSSENSTELLE DES EKD KIRCHENAMTS

Auguststrasse 80, 1040 Berlin, Germany.

DEU0959

AUXILIUM GESELSCHAFT FUR ENTWICKLUNGSHILFE

Höllstrasse 8, 78315 Radolfzell, Germany.

DEU0960

AYUDAME-HILFE FUR PERU

Beudenstrasse 18, 72768 Reutlingen, Germany.

DEU0961

BECKER MOBIL

Hasenweg 8, 26188 Edewecht, Germany.

DEU0962

BEHANDLUNGSZENTRUM FUR FOLTEROPFER (BZFO) ♦
Treatment Centre for Torture Victims

Spandauer Damm 130, Haus 6, 1000 Berlin 19, Germany.

Telephone: 49 (30) 30 35 35 91. *Fax:* 49 (30) 30 35 34 82. *Contact:* Dr. Christian Pross.

DEU0963

BENSHEIMER KREIS ♦ Bensheim Circle

c/o Kübel-Stiftung, Darmstädter Strasse 100, Postfach 1563, 6140 Bensheim, Germany.

Telephone: 49 (6251) 7 00 50. *Contact:* Burkhard Gnärig.

OBJECTIVES: To foster co-operation among member organisations and the exchange of experiences in the fields of development co-operation and education policy. To provide information and represent NGO's interests at public, parliamentary and governmental levels.

GENERAL INFORMATION: Creation: 1976. **Type of organisation:** association of NGOs. **Member organisations:** 40. **Personnel/Total:** 30. *Volunteers:* 30. **Budget/Total 1993:** ECU 10000 (US$ 12000). **Financial sources:** Self-financing: 100%.

INFORMATION AND EDUCATION ACTIVITIES: Topics: International relations/cooperation/development aid; Poverty/living conditions. **Activities:** Conferences/seminars/workshops/training activities; Information campaigns/exhibitions; Lobbying/advocacy.

DEU0964

BERLINER MISSIONSWERK (BMW) ♦ World Mission of the Protestant Church in Berlin

Handjerystrasse 19, 1000 Berlin 41, Germany.

Telephone: 49 (30) 85 10 21. *Contact:* Rev. Klaus Gruhn, Director.

DEU0965

BESCHAFFUNGSGESELLSCHAFT MIT BESCHRANKTER HAFTUNG FUR KIRCHLICHE, CARITATIVE UND SOZIALE EINRICHTUNGEN (BEGECA) ♦ Procurement Agency for Church-related and Charitable Projects

Franzstrasse 109, Postfach 287, 52003 Aachen, Germany.

Telephone: 49 (241) 47 79 80. *Fax:* 49 (241) 4 77 98 40. *Contact:* Horst Neckenig, Executive Director.

OBJECTIVES: To help church-related, charitable and social institutions to purchase the equipment, goods and materials they need.

GENERAL INFORMATION: Creation: 1968. **Personnel/Total:** 32. *Salaried:* 32. **Budget/Total 1993:** ECU 16522000 (US$ 19355000). **Financial sources:** Private: 100%.

PUBLICATIONS: *Annual report.*

PLANNED ACTIVITIES: Offferring advice on matters of transport, shipment and importation.

COMMENTS: Undertakes activities in the Commonwealth of Independent States.

ACTIVITIES IN DEVELOPING REGIONS: Active in 54 country(ies). Works through local field partners. **Sustainable Development Actions:** Children/youth/family; Education/training/literacy; Emergency relief/refu-

gees/humanitarian assistance; Energy/transport; Gender issues/women; Health/sanitation/water; Rural development/agriculture; Urban development/habitat. **Regions:** Caribbean; Central Africa; Central Asia and South Asia; East Africa; South America; Southern Africa; West Africa.

DEU0966

BILDUNGS - UND AKTIONS - ZENTRUM DRITTE WELT (BAZ)
♦ Third World Education and Project Centre

Oranienstrasse 159, 1000 Berlin 21, Germany.

Telephone: 49 (30) 6 14 50 98. *Contact:* Dr. Ilse Schimpf-Herken.

DEU0967

BISCHOFLICHE AKTION ADVENIAT

Postfach 10 01 52, 45001 Essen 1, Germany.

Telephone: 49 (201) 1 75 60. *Fax:* 49 (201) 1 75 61 11. *E-mail:* Telekom-Telebox 400 - 1005840. *Contact:* Dieter Spelthahn, Director.

OBJECTIVES: To finance aid to the pastoral work of the Catholic Church in Latin America.

GENERAL INFORMATION: *Creation:* 1961. *Personnel/Total:* 90. *Salaried:* 90. *Budget/Total 1993:* ECU 92937000 (US$ 108873000). *Financial sources:* Private: 100%.

PUBLICATIONS: *Periodicals:* Aktions mappe (1) - Aktions Zeitüng (1). *Annual report. List of publications.*

ACTIVITIES IN DEVELOPING REGIONS: Active in 30 country(ies). **Sustainable Development Actions:** Children/youth/family; Other. **Regions:** Caribbean; Mexico and Central America; South America.

DEU0968

BISCHOFLICHES HILFSWERK MISEREOR ♦ Bishops' Relief
Fund - Misereor

Mozartstrasse 9, 52064 Aachen, Germany.

Telephone: 49 (241) 44 20. *Fax:* 49 (241) 44 21 88. *Contact:* Msgr. Norbert Herkenrath, Executive Director.

OBJECTIVES: To promote long-term solutions to problems in developing countries by financing projects which emphasize self-help.

GENERAL INFORMATION: *Creation:* 1959. *Affiliated to:* International Cooperation for Development and Solidarity (Belgium). *Personnel/Total:* 260. *Salaried:* 260. *Budget/Total 1993:* ECU 183140000 (US$ 214540000). *Financial sources:* Private: 49%. Public: 46%. Self-financing: 5%.

PUBLICATIONS: *Periodicals:* MISEREOR Aktuell (6). *Annual report. List of publications.*

EVALUATION/RESEARCH: Undertakes research activities.

COMMENTS: Undertakes activities in the Commonwealth of Independent States.

ACTIVITIES IN DEVELOPING REGIONS: Active in 97 country(ies). Works through local field partners. **Sustainable Development Actions:** Children/youth/family; Education/training/literacy; Emergency relief/refugees/humanitarian assistance; Energy/transport; Food/famine; Gender issues/women; Health/sanitation/water; Human rights/peace/conflicts; Population/family planning/demography; Rural development/agriculture; Sending volunteers/experts/technical assistance; Small enterprises/informal sector/handicrafts; Urban development/habitat. **Regions:** Caribbean; Central Africa; Central Asia and South Asia; East Africa; East Asia; Mexico and Central America; Middle East; North Africa; Oceania; South America; South East Asia; Southern Africa; West Africa.

INFORMATION AND EDUCATION ACTIVITIES: Topics: Children/youth/family; Culture/tradition/religion; Ecology/environment/biodiversity; Education/training/literacy; Emergency relief/refugees/humanitarian assistance; Employment/unemployment; Food/famine; Gender issues/women; Health/sanitation/water; Human rights/peace/conflicts; International economic relations/trade/debt/finance; International relations/cooperation/development aid; Peace/ethnic conflicts/armament/disarmament; Population/family planning/demography; Poverty/living conditions; Racism/xenophobia/antisemitism; Refugees/migrants/ethnic groups; Rural development/agriculture; Urban development/habitat.

Activities: Conferences/seminars/workshops/training activities; Fund raising; Information and documentation services/data bases; Lobbying/advocacy; Publishing/audiovisual materials/educational materials.

DEU0969

BOLIVIANISCHES KINDERHILFSWERK

Danziger Strasse 13, 73240 Wendlingen, Germany.

DEU0970

BRASILIENWERK DES MARTIN-LUTHER-BUNDES ♦ Brazil
Society of the Martin Luther Federation

Haagerstrasse 10, 8806 Neuendettelsau, Allemagne.

Téléphone: 49 (9874) 92 71. *Contact:* Hans Roser.

DEU0971

BREMER ARBEITSGEMEINSCHAFT FUR UBERSEEFORSCHUNG UND ENTWICKLUNG (BORDA) ♦
Bremen Overseas Research and Development Association

Breitenweg 55, 28195 Bremen, Germany.

Telephone: 49 (421) 1 37 18. *Fax:* 49 (421) 1 65 53 23. *Contact:* Ulrich Reeps, Director.

OBJECTIVES: To develop and disseminate appropriate technologies, mainly related to biogas and hydropower. To support integrated rural development and slum development projects with an emphasis on women's development and vocational training. To develop and disseminate waste water treatment systems with low maintenance and capital.

GENERAL INFORMATION: *Creation:* 1977. *Personnel/Total:* 25. *Salaried:* 8 of which: 2 in developing countries. *Volunteers:* 15. *Budget/Total 1993:* ECU 2065000 (US$ 2419000). *Financial sources:* Private: 1%. Public: 80%. Self-financing: 19%.

PUBLICATIONS: *Periodicals:* Biogas-Forum (4). *List of publications.*

EVALUATION/RESEARCH: Evaluation reports available. Undertakes research activities.

PLANNED ACTIVITIES: The development of strategies in waste water treatment.

ACTIVITIES IN DEVELOPING REGIONS: Present in developing regions. Active in 9 country(ies). Maintains local field presence. Works through local field partners. **Sustainable Development Actions:** Children/youth/family; Democracy/good governance/institution building/participatory development; Ecology/environment/biodiversity; Education/training/literacy; Energy/transport; Gender issues/women; Health/sanitation/water; Other; Rural development/agriculture; Sending volunteers/experts/technical assistance; Urban development/habitat. **Regions:** Central Asia and South Asia; East Asia; South East Asia; West Africa.

DEU0972

BROT FUR DIE WELT ♦ Bread for the World

Stafflenbergstrasse 76, Postfach 10 11 42, 70010 Stuttgart, Germany.

Telephone: 49 (711) 2 15 90. *Fax:* 49 (711) 2 15 92 88. *Contact:* Hans-Otto Hahn, Director.

OBJECTIVES: To provide constructive forms of assistance in accordance with the principle "help people to help themselves".

GENERAL INFORMATION: *Creation:* 1959. *Affiliated to:* AGKED. *Personnel/Total:* 60. *Salaried:* 60. *Budget/Total 1993:* ECU 84676000 (US$ 99196000). *Financial sources:* Private: 100%.

PUBLICATIONS: *Annual report. List of publications.*

ACTIVITIES IN DEVELOPING REGIONS: Active in 80 country(ies). Works through local field partners. **Sustainable Development Actions:** Children/youth/family; Democracy/good governance/institution building/participatory development; Ecology/environment/biodiversity; Education/training/literacy; Gender issues/women; Health/sanitation/water; Human rights/peace/conflicts; Rural development/agriculture; Small enterprises/informal sector/handicrafts; Urban development/habitat. **Regions:** Caribbean; Central Africa; Central Asia and South Asia; East Africa; East Asia; Mexico and Central America; Middle East; North Africa; Oceania; South America; South East Asia; Southern Africa; West Africa.

Voir : *Comment utiliser le répertoire*, page 11.

INFORMATION AND EDUCATION ACTIVITIES: **Topics:** Ecology/environment/biodiversity; Gender issues/women; Health/sanitation/water; Human rights/peace/conflicts; International economic relations/trade/debt/finance; Rural development/agriculture. **Activities:** Fund raising; Information campaigns/exhibitions; Lobbying/advocacy; Publishing/audiovisual materials/educational materials.

DEU0973
BRUDERHILFE RUMANIEN
Robert-Koch-Strasse 18/320, 37075 Göttingen, Germany.

DEU0974
BUKO PHARMA-KAMPAGNE ♦ Buko-Pharma Campaign
August Bebel Strasse 62, 33602 Bielefeld, Germany.

Telephone: 49 (521) 6 05 50. **Fax:** 49 (521) 6 37 89. **Contact:** Annette Will.

OBJECTIVES: To monitor the business of German pharmaceutical companies in Third World countries. To organise public campaigns against certain products or companies. To inform the press and health workers in the Thirld World.

GENERAL INFORMATION: Creation: 1980. **Type of organisation:** coordinating body. **Member organisations:** 250. **Affiliated to:** BUKO (Germany) - Health Action International. **Personnel/Total:** 6. Salaried: 5. Volunteers: 1. **Financial sources:** Private: 20%. Public: 75%. Self-financing: 5%.

PUBLICATIONS: Periodicals: Pharma-Brief (10). List of publications.

EVALUATION/RESEARCH: Undertakes research activities.

PLANNED ACTIVITIES: International campaign to stop research on "vaccines" against pregnancy. Birth control methods and their risks.

INFORMATION AND EDUCATION ACTIVITIES: Topics: Health/sanitation/water; Other; Population/family planning/demography. **Activities:** Conferences/seminars/workshops/training activities; Information campaigns/exhibitions; Lobbying/advocacy; Networking/electronic telecommunications; Publishing/audiovisual materials/educational materials.

DEU0975
BUND DER DEUTSCHEN KATHOLISCHEN JUGEND (BDKJ) ♦
Federation of German Catholic Youth
Carl-Mosterts-Platz 1, Postfach 320520, 4000 Düsseldorf 30, Germany.

Telephone: 49 (211) 4 69 30. **Fax:** 49 (211) 4 69 31 20. **Contact:** Karin Kortmann.

OBJECTIVES: To undertake educational activities in the Federal Republic of Germany in order to raise awareness of problems existing in developing countries. To support alternative trade activities with developing countries.

GENERAL INFORMATION: Creation: 1947. **Member organisations:** 17. **Affiliated to:** Gesellschaft zur Förderung der Partnerschaft mit der 3. Welt (Forum on "Environment and Development") (Germany.). **Personnel/Total:** 2. Salaried: 2.

PUBLICATIONS: Periodicals: BDKJ Journal (10). Annual report. List of publications.

EVALUATION/RESEARCH: Undertakes research activities.

COMMENTS: Information activities related to the Commonwealth of Independent States.

INFORMATION AND EDUCATION ACTIVITIES: Topics: Children/youth/family; Ecology/environment/biodiversity; Education/training/literacy; Food/famine; International economic relations/trade/debt/finance; International relations/cooperation/development aid; Poverty/living conditions; Racism/xenophobia/antisemitism; Refugees/migrants/ethnic groups; Rural development/agriculture. **Activities:** Broadcasting/cultural events; Conferences/seminars/workshops/training activities; Exchanges/twinning/linking; Formal education; Fund raising; Information and documentation services/data bases; Information campaigns/exhibitions; Lobbying/advocacy; Networking/electronic telecommunications; Publishing/audiovisual materials/educational materials.

DEU0976
BUND FUR UMWELT UND NATURSCHUTZ DEUTSCHLAND (BUND) ♦ Friends of the Earth - Germany
Im Rheingarten 7, 53225 Bonn, Germany.

Telephone: 49 (228) 40 09 70. **Fax:** 49 (228) 4 00 97 40. **Contact:** Jens Katzek, International Coordinator.

DEU0977
BUNDESKONGRESS ENTWICKLUNGSPOLITISCHER AKTIONSGRUPPEN (BUKO) ♦ Federal Congress of Development Action Groups
Nernstweg 32-34, 22765 Hamburg, Germany.

Telephone: 49 (40) 39 31 56. **Fax:** 49 (40) 3 90 75 20.

OBJECTIVES: To engage in development education activities and campaigns on specific issues. To promote human rights issues, cultural understanding and exchanges between Germany and the Third World. To protect Third World countries against exploitation from multinational companies. To fight against arms exportation from the Federal Republic of Germany.

GENERAL INFORMATION: Creation: 1977. **Type of organisation:** association of NGOs. **Member organisations:** 200. **Affiliated to:** ICDA (Belgium) - HAI (the Netherlands). **Personnel/Total:** 66. Salaried: 16. Volunteers: 50. **Budget/Total 1993:** ECU 620000 (US$ 726000). **Financial sources:** Private: 10%. Public: 75%. Self-financing: 15%.

PUBLICATIONS: Periodicals: Forum Entwidelungspolitischer Aktionsgruppen (8). Annual report. List of publications.

EVALUATION/RESEARCH: Undertakes research activities.

INFORMATION AND EDUCATION ACTIVITIES: Topics: Ecology/environment/biodiversity; Gender issues/women; International economic relations/trade/debt/finance; International relations/cooperation/development aid; Peace/ethnic conflicts/armament/disarmament; Population/family planning/demography; Racism/xenophobia/antisemitism; Refugees/migrants/ethnic groups; Rural development/agriculture. **Activities:** Conferences/seminars/workshops/training activities; Information and documentation services/data bases; Information campaigns/exhibitions; Publishing/audiovisual materials/educational materials.

DEU0978
CARE DEUTSCHLAND ♦ Care Germany
Herbert-Rabius strasse 26, 53225 Bonn, Germany.

Telephone: 49 (228) 97 56 30. **Fax:** 49 (228) 9 75 63 51. **Contact:** Peter Molt, Director General.

OBJECTIVES: To improve living conditions in developing countries through support for self-help projects and social and economic aid. To provide emergency relief when needed. To carry out development education activities in the Federal Republic of Germany.

GENERAL INFORMATION: Creation: 1979. **Affiliated to:** Care International (Belgium). **Personnel/Total:** 78. Salaried: 32 of which: 8 in developing countries. Volunteers: 46. **Budget/Total 1993:** ECU 10575000 (US$ 12389000). **Financial sources:** Private: 70%. Public: 30%.

PUBLICATIONS: Periodicals: CARE-Report (2). Annual report.

EVALUATION/RESEARCH: Evaluation reports available.

COMMENTS: Undertakes activities in the Commonwealth of Independent States. Information activities related to the Commonwealth of Independent States.

ACTIVITIES IN DEVELOPING REGIONS: Present in developing regions. Active in 6 country(ies). Maintains local field presence. Works through local field partners. **Sustainable Development Actions:** Children/youth/family; Education/training/literacy; Emergency relief/refugees/humanitarian assistance; Gender issues/women; Health/sanitation/water; Rural development/agriculture; Small enterprises/informal sector/handicrafts. **Regions:** Central Africa; East Africa; South East Asia.

See: *How to Use the Directory*, page 11.

INFORMATION AND EDUCATION ACTIVITIES: Topics: Children/youth/family; Emergency relief/refugees/humanitarian assistance; Health/sanitation/water; Rural development/agriculture. **Activities:** Fund raising.

DEU0979

CARITAS KONFERENZEN DEUTSCHLANDS (CKD) ♦ Conférences Caritas d'Allemagne

Karlstrasse 40, Postfach 420, 79004 Freiburg/Breisgau, Allemagne.

Téléphone: 49 (761) 20 00. *Fax:* 49 (761) 2 05 72. *Contact:* Elisabeth Freifrau von Lüninck, Présidente.

OBJECTIFS: Participer, dans le cadre de l'Association Internationale des Charités à Bruxelles, à des projets sociaux et á de projets de formation. Attribuer des moyens financiers à ces, projets en provenance d'autres organismes humanitaires.

INFORMATIONS GENERALES: *Création:* 1931. *Organisations membres:* 140. *Affiliée à:* Association Internationale des Charités (Belgique). *Personnel/Total:* 71011. *Salariés:* 11. *Bénévoles:* 71000. *Budget/Total 1993:* ECU 258000 (US$ 302000). *Sources financières:* Privé: 20%. Public: 60%. Autofinancement: 20%.

PUBLICATIONS: *Périodiques:* Begegnen und Helfen (4) (1). *Rapport annuel. Liste des publications.*

PREVISIONS D'ACTIVITES: Campagnes d'information. Travailler avec la presse sur les thèmes comme la pauvreté et la situation des femmes volontaires.

COMMENTAIRES: Intervient dans la Communauté des Etats indépendants. Activités d'information concernant la Communauté des Etats indépendants.

ACTIVITES DANS LES REGIONS EN DEVELOPPEMENT: Intervient par l'intermédiaire d'organisations locales partenaires.

ACTIVITES D'INFORMATION ET D'EDUCATION: Domaines: Culture/tradition/religion; Enfants/jeunesse/famille. **Activités:** Conférences/séminaires/ateliers/activités de formation.

DEU0980

CARL DUISBERG CENTREN GEMINNUTZIGE GESELLSCHAFT MBH (CDC)

Hansaring 49-51, 50670 Köln, Germany.

Telephone: 49 (221) 1 62 60. *Fax:* 49 (221) 1 62 62 22. *Contact:* Johannes Schlaghecke.

OBJECTIVES: To provide the means for cultural exchanges, international transfer of knowledge and training. To organise foreign exchange programmess for experts and executives worldwide.

GENERAL INFORMATION: *Creation:* 1962. *Personnel/Total:* 190. *Salaried:* 190. *Budget/Total 1993:* ECU 15489000 (US$ 18146000). *Financial sources:* Self-financing: 100%.

PUBLICATIONS: *Periodicals:* Transfer (4) - CD-Intern (4). *Annual report.*

PLANNED ACTIVITIES: The foundation of a German language centre in Malaysia.

COMMENTS: Undertakes activities in the Commonwealth of Independent States. Information activities related to the Commonwealth of Independent States.

ACTIVITIES IN DEVELOPING REGIONS: Present in developing regions. Active in 3 country(ies). Maintains local field presence. Works through local field partners. **Sustainable Development Actions:** Education/training/literacy. **Regions:** Central Asia and South Asia; East Africa; East Asia; Mexico and Central America; Middle East; North Africa; South America; South East Asia; Southern Africa; West Africa.

INFORMATION AND EDUCATION ACTIVITIES: Topics: Education/training/literacy. **Activities:** Conferences/seminars/workshops/training activities; Exchanges/twinning/linking; Formal education; Information and documentation services/data bases; Information campaigns/exhibitions; Publishing/audiovisual materials/educational materials.

DEU0981

CARL DUISBERG GESELLSCHAFT (CDG)

Hohenstaufenring 30-32, Postfach 26 01 20, 5000 Köln, Germany.

Telephone: 49 (2 21) 2 09 80. *Fax:* 49 (2 21) 2 09 81 11. *Contact:* Dr Norbert Schneider.

DEU0982

CARL DUISBERG GESELLSCHAFT, ASA-PROGRAMM ♦ Programme for Research and Co-operation Short Term Stays in the Third World-Carl Duisberg Society

Lützowufer 6-9, 10785 Berlin, Germany.

Telephone: 49 (30) 2 54 82 0. *Fax:* 49 (30) 2 54 82 1 05. *Contact:* Peter Müller-Rockstroh, Executive Director.

GENERAL INFORMATION: *Creation:* 1960.

DEU0983

CCF KINDERHILFSWERK (CCF GERMANY) ♦ Christian Children's Fund

Postfach 1105, 72601 Nuertingen, Germany.

Telephone: 49 (7022) 3 30 19. *Fax:* 49 (7022) 84 42. *Contact:* Cornelia Wolf, National Director.

OBJECTIVES: To aid the development of children and their families where local resources are limited. To provide children with services to meet their needs and to offer them the opportunity to exchange correspondence with sponsors worldwide.

GENERAL INFORMATION: *Creation:* 1978. *Member organisations:* 10. *Affiliated to:* World Alliance of CCF's. *Personnel/Total:* 14. *Salaried:* 14. *Budget/Total 1993:* ECU 6017000 (US$ 7048000). *Financial sources:* Private: 100%.

PUBLICATIONS: *Periodicals:* Unsere Kinder in aller Welt (2). *Annual report.*

EVALUATION/RESEARCH: Evaluation reports available.

COMMENTS: Undertakes activities in the Commonwealth of Independent States.

ACTIVITIES IN DEVELOPING REGIONS: Present in developing regions. Active in 40 country(ies). Works through local field partners. **Sustainable Development Actions:** Children/youth/family; Democracy/good governance/institution building/participatory development; Ecology/environment/biodiversity; Education/training/literacy; Emergency relief/refugees/humanitarian assistance; Food/famine; Gender issues/women; Health/sanitation/water; Human rights/peace/conflicts; Population/family planning/demography; Rural development/agriculture; Sending volunteers/experts/technical assistance; Small enterprises/informal sector/handicrafts; Urban development/habitat. **Regions:** Caribbean; Central Asia and South Asia; East Africa; Mexico and Central America; Middle East; South America; South East Asia; West Africa.

INFORMATION AND EDUCATION ACTIVITIES: Topics: Children/youth/family; Culture/tradition/religion; Ecology/environment/biodiversity; Education/training/literacy; Emergency relief/refugees/humanitarian assistance; Employment/unemployment; Food/famine; Gender issues/women; Health/sanitation/water; Human rights/peace/conflicts; International relations/cooperation/development aid; Peace/ethnic conflicts/armament/disarmament; Population/family planning/demography; Poverty/living conditions; Racism/xenophobia/antisemitism; Refugees/migrants/ethnic groups; Rural development/agriculture; Urban development/habitat. **Activities:** Conferences/seminars/workshops/training activities; Exchanges/twinning/linking; Formal education; Fund raising; Information campaigns/exhibitions; Lobbying/advocacy.

DEU0984

CENTRUM FUR TECHNOLOGIETRANSFER CLAUSTHAL E.V. (CTTC)

Burgstädter Strasse 6, 3392 Clausthal-Zellerfeld, Germany.

Telephone: 49 (53 23) 52 49. *Fax:* 49 (53 23) 7 86 76. *Contact:* Paul Funke.

DEU0985

CEYLON-DIREKTHILFE ♦ Ceylon Direct Help Organisation

Felder Weg 7, 42799 Leichlingen, Germany.

Telephone: 49 (2174) 35 55. **Fax:** 49 (2174) 3 83 65. **Contact:** Carl-Heinz Beier, President.

OBJECTIVES: To support self-help projects among the poorest people in Sri Lanka. To assist in upgrading the health care system and to provide care for the disabled.

GENERAL INFORMATION: Creation: 1981. **Affiliated to:** DPWV (Germany). **Personnel/Total:** 9. Salaried: 2. Volunteers: 7. **Budget/Total 1993:** ECU 774000 (US$ 907000). **Financial sources:** Private: 20%. Public: 80%.

PUBLICATIONS: Periodicals: Aktiv-Ceylon Direkt Helfen (3).

EVALUATION/RESEARCH: Undertakes research activities.

ACTIVITIES IN DEVELOPING REGIONS: Active in 1 country(ies). Works through local field partners. **Sustainable Development Actions:** Children/youth/family; Education/training/literacy; Emergency relief/refugees/humanitarian assistance; Health/sanitation/water; Rural development/agriculture; Small enterprises/informal sector/handicrafts. **Regions:** Central Asia and South Asia.

DEU0986

CHRISTLICHE FACHKRAFTE INTERNATIONAL (CFI)

Hohenheimer Strasse 60, 70184 Stuttgart, Germany.

Telephone: 49 (711) 23 35 64. **Fax:** 49 (711) 23 39 22. **Contact:** Winrich Scheffbuch.

OBJECTIVES: To provide professional training in medicine, agriculture, technical assistance and vocational training.

GENERAL INFORMATION: Creation: 1984. **Affiliated to:** Arbeitskreis Lernen und Helfen (Germany) - Arbeitsgemeinschaft der Dienste (Germany.). Volunteers: 41 of which: 34 in developing countries. **Budget/Total 1993:** ECU 1837000 (US$ 2152000). **Financial sources:** Private: 25%. Public: 75%.

PUBLICATIONS: Periodicals: Christliche Fachkräfte International (4). Annual report.

EVALUATION/RESEARCH: Evaluation reports available.

PLANNED ACTIVITIES: The promotion of preventive medicine programmes. Supporting church planting and development work in war countries, such as Mozambique, Angola, Cambodia and Vietnam.

ACTIVITIES IN DEVELOPING REGIONS: Active in 32 country(ies). Works through local field partners. **Sustainable Development Actions:** Education/training/literacy; Health/sanitation/water; Rural development/agriculture; Sending volunteers/experts/technical assistance; Urban development/habitat. **Regions:** Caribbean; Central Africa; East Africa; South America; South East Asia; Southern Africa; West Africa.

DEU0987

CHRISTLICHER FRIEDENSDIENST (CFD) ♦ Christian Movement for Peace

Rendelerstrasse 9-11, 60385 Frankfurt/Main 60, Germany.

Telephone: 49 (69) 45 90 72. **Fax:** 49 (69) 46 12 13. **Contact:** Ursula Pohl.

DEU0988

CHRISTLICHES INITIATIV- UND STUDIENZENTRUM DORTMUND (CIS) ♦ Christian Centre for Initiative and Study in Dortmund

Luisenstrasse 17, 4600 Dortmund 1, Germany.

Telephone: 49 (231) 14 35 85.

DEU0989

CHRISTOFFEL-BLINDENMISSION (CBM) ♦ Christian Blind Mission International

Nibelungenstrasse 124, 64625 Bensheim, Germany.

Telephone: 49 (6251) 13 10. **Fax:** 49 (6251) 13 11 65. **Contact:** Christian Garms, Executive Director.

OBJECTIVES: To assist aid organisations in providing funds, experts and professional knowledge to prevent and cure blindness. To educate and rehabilitate blind and other handicapped, sick and poor people.

GENERAL INFORMATION: Creation: 1908. **Member organisations:** 3. **Affiliated to:** CBMI (Switzerland) - DW (Germany) - AEM (Germany) - EMW (Germany) - Bensheimer Kreis (Germany) - IAPB - ICEVI (Malaysia) - European Partners for Blindness Prevention (United Kingdom) - ERP (France). **Personnel/Total:** 279. Salaried: 279 of which: 106 in developing countries. **Budget/Total 1993:** ECU 41563000 (US$ 48690000). **Financial sources:** Private: 100%.

PUBLICATIONS: Periodicals: Christoffel-Blindenmission Berichtsheft (6) - Christoffel-Blindenmission Freundesbrief (6). Annual report. List of publications.

EVALUATION/RESEARCH: Undertakes research activities.

COMMENTS: Undertakes activities in the Commonwealth of Independent States. Information activities related to the Commonwealth of Independent States.

ACTIVITIES IN DEVELOPING REGIONS: Active in 102 country(ies). Maintains local field presence. Works through local field partners. **Sustainable Development Actions:** Children/youth/family; Education/training/literacy; Emergency relief/refugees/humanitarian assistance; Gender issues/women; Health/sanitation/water; Rural development/agriculture; Sending volunteers/experts/technical assistance; Small enterprises/informal sector/handicrafts; Urban development/habitat. **Regions:** Caribbean; Central Africa; Central Asia and South Asia; East Africa; East Asia; Mexico and Central America; Middle East; North Africa; Oceania; South America; South East Asia; Southern Africa; West Africa.

INFORMATION AND EDUCATION ACTIVITIES: Topics: Children/youth/family; Culture/tradition/religion; Education/training/literacy; Emergency relief/refugees/humanitarian assistance; Employment/unemployment; Health/sanitation/water; International relations/cooperation/development aid; Poverty/living conditions; Refugees/migrants/ethnic groups; Rural development/agriculture; Urban development/habitat. **Activities:** Broadcasting/cultural events; Conferences/seminars/workshops/training activities; Formal education; Fund raising; Information and documentation services/data bases; Lobbying/advocacy; Publishing/audiovisual materials/educational materials.

DEU0990

CLEARINGHOUSE FOR APPLIED FUTURES (CAF)

c/o Wuppertal Institute, Döppersberg 19, 42103 Wuppertal, Germany.

Telephone: 49 (202) 2 49 21 82 14. **Fax:** 49 (202) 2 49 22 10. **Contact:** Peter Moll.

OBJECTIVES: To encourage and provide for "learning from practical experience" to those working in the field of development, by means of workshops and an international network of institutions.

GENERAL INFORMATION: Creation: 1993. **Member organisations:** 16. **Personnel/Total:** 18. Salaried: 2. Volunteers: 16 of which: 7 in developing countries. **Budget/Total 1993:** ECU 77000 (US$ 91000). **Financial sources:** Public: 60%. Self-financing: 40%.

EVALUATION/RESEARCH: Undertakes research activities.

COMMENTS: Undertakes activities in the Commonwealth of Independent States.

ACTIVITIES IN DEVELOPING REGIONS: Active in 7 country(ies). Maintains local field presence. Works through local field partners. **Sustainable Development Actions:** Debt/finance/trade; Democracy/good governance/institution building/participatory development; Ecology/environment/biodiversity; Education/training/literacy; Energy/transport; Health/sanitation/water; Human rights/peace/conflicts; Population/family planning/demography; Rural development/agriculture; Small enterprises/informal sector/handicrafts; Urban development/habitat. **Regions:** Central Asia and South Asia; North Africa; South America; South East Asia.

See: *How to Use the Directory*, page 11.

INFORMATION AND EDUCATION ACTIVITIES: Topics: Children/youth/ family; Culture/tradition/religion; Ecology/environment/biodiversity; Education/training/literacy; Emergency relief/refugees/humanitarian assistance; Employment/unemployment; Food/famine; Gender issues/ women; Health/sanitation/water; Human rights/peace/conflicts; International economic relations/trade/debt/finance; International relations/ cooperation/development aid; Peace/ethnic conflicts/armament/disarmament; Population/family planning/demography; Poverty/living conditions; Racism/xenophobia/antisemitism; Refugees/migrants/ethnic groups; Rural development/agriculture; Urban development/habitat. **Activities:** Conferences/seminars/workshops/training activities; Exchanges/twinning/linking; Information and documentation services/ data bases; Networking/electronic telecommunications.

DEU0991

CVJM - GESAMTVERBAND IN DEUTSCHLAND ♦ YMCA National Council of Germany

Im Druseltal 8, Postfach 41 01 54, 34114 Kassel, Germany.

Telephone: 49 (561) 3 08 72 50. **Fax:** 49 (561) 3 08 72 37. **Contact:** Walter E. Sommer, President.

OBJECTIVES: To promote justice, peace and Christian values in the world through educational programmes. To strengthen other YMCA movements and foster co-operation.

GENERAL INFORMATION: Creation: 1882. **Type of organisation:** coordinating body. **Member organisations:** 13. **Affiliated to:** European Alliance of YMCAs (Switzerland) - World Alliance of YMCAs (Switzerland). **Personnel/Total:** 12. **Salaried:** 10 of which: 3 in developing countries. **Volunteers:** 2 of which: 2 in developing countries. **Budget/ Total 1993:** ECU 1757000 (US$ 2059000). **Financial sources:** Private: 96%. Public: 1%. Self-financing: 3%.

PUBLICATIONS: Periodicals: Aktion Hoffnungszeichen Aktuell (3). Annual report. List of publications.

EVALUATION/RESEARCH: Evaluation reports available.

PLANNED ACTIVITIES: Assisting refugees and asylum workers and working for the integration of young foreigners in Germany.

COMMENTS: Undertakes activities in the Commonwealth of Independent States. Information activities related to the Commonwealth of Independent States.

ACTIVITIES IN DEVELOPING REGIONS: Active in 30 country(ies). Works through local field partners. **Sustainable Development Actions:** Children/youth/family; Democracy/good governance/institution building/participatory development; Ecology/environment/biodiversity; Education/ training/literacy; Emergency relief/refugees/humanitarian assistance; Health/sanitation/water; Population/family planning/demography; Rural development/agriculture; Sending volunteers/experts/technical assistance; Small enterprises/informal sector/handicrafts; Urban development/habitat. **Regions:** Caribbean; Central Africa; Central Asia and South Asia; East Africa; Mexico and Central America; Middle East; South America; Southern Africa; West Africa.

INFORMATION AND EDUCATION ACTIVITIES: Topics: Children/youth/ family; Culture/tradition/religion; Emergency relief/refugees/humanitarian assistance; Employment/unemployment; Food/famine; Health/sanitation/water; International relations/cooperation/development aid; Poverty/living conditions; Racism/xenophobia/antisemitism; Refugees/ migrants/ethnic groups; Rural development/agriculture. **Activities:** Conferences/seminars/workshops/training activities; Exchanges/twinning/ linking; Fund raising; Publishing/audiovisual materials/educational materials.

DEU0992

DEUTSCH PAZIFISCHE GESELLSCHAFT (DPG) ♦ German Pacific Society

Feichtmayrstrasse 25, 80992 München, Germany.

Telephone: 49 (89) 15 11 58. **Fax:** 49 (89) 15 18 33. **Contact:** Friedrich Steinbauer, President.

OBJECTIVES: To promote understanding and co-operation between the inhabitants of the Pacific and German-speaking countries. To support scientific, educational and cultural activities.

GENERAL INFORMATION: Creation: 1974. **Budget/Total 1993:** ECU 18000 (US$ 21000). **Financial sources:** Private: 40%. Public: 20%. Self-financing: 40%.

PUBLICATIONS: Periodicals: News Bulletin G-series (6) - News Bulletin P-series (4) - News Bulletin S-series (4).

EVALUATION/RESEARCH: Undertakes research activities.

ACTIVITIES IN DEVELOPING REGIONS: Sustainable Development Actions: Children/youth/family; Ecology/environment/biodiversity; Education/training/literacy; Emergency relief/refugees/humanitarian assistance; Food/famine; Gender issues/women; Health/sanitation/water; Human rights/peace/conflicts; Population/family planning/demography; Rural development/agriculture; Urban development/habitat. **Regions:** Oceania.

INFORMATION AND EDUCATION ACTIVITIES: Topics: Children/youth/ family; Culture/tradition/religion; Ecology/environment/biodiversity; Education/training/literacy; Gender issues/women; Peace/ethnic conflicts/ armament/disarmament. **Activities:** Conferences/seminars/workshops/ training activities.

DEU0993

DEUTSCHE AFGHANISTAN STIFTUNG (DAS) ♦ German Afghanistan Foundation

Adenauerallee 11, 53111 Bonn, Germany.

Telephone: 49 (228) 22 14 04. **Fax:** 49 (228) 22 05 59. **Contact:** Kakojan Niazi, Chairman.

OBJECTIVES: To promote and develop relations between Germans and Afghans. To promote understanding and tolerance in all areas of culture. To provide services for political, racial or religious victims of persecution, refugees, displaced persons and war victims.

GENERAL INFORMATION: Creation: 1985. **Affiliated to:** Agency Coordinating Body for Afghan Relief (Pakistan). **Personnel/Total:** 231. **Salaried:** 226 of which: 225 in developing countries. **Volunteers:** 5. **Budget/ Total 1993:** ECU 2014000 (US$ 2359000). **Financial sources:** Private: 20%. Public: 80%.

PUBLICATIONS: Periodicals: Zukunft für Afghanistan (4). Annual report.

PLANNED ACTIVITIES: Setting up a vocational training programme in Afghanistan.

ACTIVITIES IN DEVELOPING REGIONS: Present in developing regions. Active in 1 country(ies). Maintains local field presence. **Sustainable Development Actions:** Children/youth/family; Emergency relief/refugees/humanitarian assistance; Food/famine; Health/sanitation/water; Rural development/agriculture; Urban development/habitat. **Regions:** Central Asia and South Asia.

INFORMATION AND EDUCATION ACTIVITIES: Topics: Children/youth/ family; Education/training/literacy; Emergency relief/refugees/humanitarian assistance; Employment/unemployment; Food/famine; Gender issues/women; Health/sanitation/water; Peace/ethnic conflicts/armament/disarmament; Poverty/living conditions; Refugees/migrants/ethnic groups. **Activities:** Fund raising.

DEU0994

DEUTSCHE ARZTEGEMEINSCHAFT FUR MEDIZINISCHE ZUSAMMENARBEIT (DÄZ) ♦ Association allemande de médecins pour la coopération médicale

Prenzlauer Allee 90, 10409 Berlin, Allemagne.

Téléphone: 49 (30) 4 21 38 28/29. **Fax:** 49 (30) 4 21 38 28/29. **Contact:** Dr. Reimann, Président.

OBJECTIFS: Soutenir des projets de développement sanitaire et d'assistance humanitaire, sous forme d'envoi de médicaments, d'équipement, etc., dans les pays en voie de développement et dans les pays de l'Europe centrale et de l'Est. Soutenir la formation continue du personnel médical originaire des pays cités ci-dessus.

INFORMATIONS GENERALES: Création: 1951. **Affiliée à:** Bensheimer Kreis (Allemagne) - Arbeitskreis Medizinische Entwicklungshilfe (Allemagne). **Personnel/Total:** 16. **Salariés:** 11. **Bénévoles:** 5. **Budget/ Total 1993:** ECU 2047000 (US$ 2398000). **Sources financières:** Privé: 59%. Public: 41%.

PUBLICATIONS: *Rapport annuel.*

COMMENTAIRES: Intervient dans la Communauté des Etats indépendants. Activités d'information concernant la Communauté des Etats indépendants.

ACTIVITES DANS LES REGIONS EN DEVELOPPEMENT: Intervient dans 14 pays. Intervient par l'intermédiaire d'organisations locales partenaires. **Actions de Développement durable:** Santé/assainissement/eau; Secours d'urgence/réfugiés/aide humanitaire; Éducation/formation/alphabétisation. **Régions:** Afrique de l'Est; Afrique de l'Ouest; Amérique du Sud; Asie de l'Est; Asie du Sud-Est.

ACTIVITES D'INFORMATION ET D'EDUCATION: Domaines: Relations internationales/coopération/aide au développement; Santé/assainissement/eau; Secours d'urgence/réfugiés/aide humanitaire. **Activités:** Collecte de fonds.

DEU0995

DEUTSCHE ENTWICKLUNGSHILFE FUR SOZIALES WOHNUNGS- UND SIEDLUNGSWESEN (DESWOS) ♦ Aide allemande au développement de l'habitat social

Bismarckstrasse 7, 50672 Köln, Allemagne.

Téléphone: 49 (221) 57 98 90. **Fax:** 49 (221) 579 89 99. **Contact:** Dieter Baldeaux, Secrétaire général.

OBJECTIFS: Répandre l'idée d'autoassistance solidaire dans le secteur du logement, pour les couches sociales à faible revenu, dans les pays en voie de développement. Apporter une solidarité matérielle directe et soutenir des organisations de base dans le Tiers monde.

INFORMATIONS GENERALES: Création: 1969. **Personnel/Total:** 59. *Salariés:* 9. *Bénévoles:* 50. **Budget/Total 1993:** ECU 4673000 (US$ 5474000). **Sources financières:** *Privé:* 20%. *Public:* 80%.

PUBLICATIONS: Périodiques: DESWOS-Brief (6) (var). *Rapport annuel.*

PREVISIONS D'ACTIVITES: Campagne européenne, afin de faire prendre conscience de la situation du logement dans le Tiers monde.

COMMENTAIRES: Activités d'information concernant la Communauté des Etats indépendants.

ACTIVITES DANS LES REGIONS EN DEVELOPPEMENT: Intervient dans 23 pays. Intervient par l'intermédiaire d'organisations locales partenaires. **Actions de Développement durable:** Développement rural/agriculture; Développement urbain/habitat; Petites entreprises/secteur informel/artisanat; Santé/assainissement/eau; Éducation/formation/alphabétisation. **Régions:** Afrique australe; Afrique centrale; Afrique de l'Est; Afrique de l'Ouest; Afrique du Nord; Amérique du Sud; Asie centrale et Asie du Sud; Asie de l'Est; Asie du Sud-Est; Mexique et Amerique centrale; Moyen-Orient; Océanie.

DEU0996

DEUTSCHE GESELLSCHAFT FUR DIE VEREINTEN NATIONEN (DGVN) ♦ German Association for the United Nations

Poppelsdorfer Allee 55, 53115 Bonn, Germany.

Telephone: 49 (228) 21 36 46. **Fax:** 49 (228) 21 74 92. **Contact:** Joachim Krause, Secretary General.

OBJECTIVES: To build public awareness and to provide information concerning the United Nations and other UN-specialized agencies.

GENERAL INFORMATION: Creation: 1952. **Type of organisation:** coordinating body. **Affiliated to:** Forum Menschenrechte (Germany) - Komitee 50 Jahre Vereinte Nationen (Germany) -Arbeitskreis Entwicklungs Politische Öffentlichkeitsarbeit (Germany) - WFUNA. **Personnel/Total:** 10. *Salaried:* 10. **Budget/Total 1993:** ECU 671000 (US$ 746000). **Financial sources:** *Private:* 10%. *Public:* 85%. *Self-financing:* 5%.

PUBLICATIONS: Periodicals: Vereinte Nationen (6) - Dritte Welt Presse (1) - UNFPA Informationsdienst (4) -Informationen Aus Unserer Arbeit (3). *Annual report. List of publications.*

EVALUATION/RESEARCH: Undertakes research activities.

COMMENTS: Information activities related to the Commonwealth of Independent States.

INFORMATION AND EDUCATION ACTIVITIES: Topics: Ecology/environment/biodiversity; Human rights/peace/conflicts; International economic relations/trade/debt/finance; International relations/cooperation/development aid; Peace/ethnic conflicts/armament/disarmament; Population/family planning/demography; Racism/xenophobia/antisemitism; Refugees/migrants/ethnic groups. **Activities:** Conferences/seminars/workshops/training activities; Information and documentation services/data bases; Information campaigns/exhibitions; Lobbying/advocacy; Networking/electronic telecommunications.

DEU0997

DEUTSCHE GESELLSCHAFT ZUR RETTUNG SCHIFFBRUCHIGER

Werderstrasse 2, 28199 Bremen, Germany.

DEU0998

DEUTSCHE KOMMISSION JUSTITIA ET PAX ♦ German Commission for Justice and Peace

Adenauerallee 134, 53113 Bonn, Germany.

Telephone: 49 (228) 10 32 17. **Fax:** 49 (228) 10 33 18. **Contact:** Bishop Leo Schwarz, President.

OBJECTIVES: To make Christians aware of their duty to seek global justice. To further human and social development. To defend human rights. To promote co-operation between the churches and foster dialogue within the political sphere and the community at large.

GENERAL INFORMATION: Creation: 1967. **Personnel/Total:** 5. *Salaried:* 5. **Budget/Total 1993:** ECU 310000 (US$ 363000). **Financial sources:** *Private:* 95%. *Self-financing:* 5%.

PUBLICATIONS: *Annual report. List of publications.*

PLANNED ACTIVITIES: The promotion of the participation of women in the process of development.

INFORMATION AND EDUCATION ACTIVITIES: Topics: Ecology/environment/biodiversity; Employment/unemployment; Human rights/peace/conflicts; International economic relations/trade/debt/finance; International relations/cooperation/development aid; Peace/ethnic conflicts/armament/disarmament; Poverty/living conditions; Racism/xenophobia/antisemitism; Refugees/migrants/ethnic groups. **Activities:** Conferences/seminars/workshops/training activities; Information and documentation services/data bases; Information campaigns/exhibitions; Lobbying/advocacy.

DEU0999

DEUTSCHE LANDWIRTSCHAFTS-GESELLSCHAFT (DLG) ♦ German Agricultural Society

Eschbower Landstrasse 122, 60489 Frankfurt am Main, Germany.

Telephone: 49 (69) 24 788-0. **Fax:** 49 (69) 247 88 113. **Contact:** Günter Flessner, President.

OBJECTIVES: To promote biological, technical, economic and social progress in agriculture and related industries. To control the quality of agricultural machinery, products etc. To organise fairs, conferences, exhibitions.

GENERAL INFORMATION: Creation: 1885. **Personnel/Total:** 2660. *Salaried:* 160. *Volunteers:* 2500. **Budget/Total 1993:** ECU 14457000 (US$ 16936000). **Financial sources:** *Public:* 30%. *Self-financing:* 70%.

PUBLICATIONS: Periodicals: DLG-Mitteilungen (12). *Annual report. List of publications.*

EVALUATION/RESEARCH: Evaluation reports available.

PLANNED ACTIVITIES: Organisation of agricultural fairs (in 1995, 1996).

COMMENTS: DLG also undertakes agricultural activities and sends technical experts and volunteers to Eastern Europe. DLG works closely with a subsidiairy company, DLG-Agriservice, in providing the knowledge for technical assistance.DLG is a member organisation of the German Central Committee for Agriculture. Undertakes activities in the Commonwealth of Independent States.

See: *How to Use the Directory,* page 11.

ACTIVITIES IN DEVELOPING REGIONS: Present in developing regions. Active in 5 country(ies). Works through local field partners. **Sustainable Development Actions:** Rural development/agriculture; Sending volunteers/experts/technical assistance. **Regions:** North Africa.

INFORMATION AND EDUCATION ACTIVITIES: Topics: International relations/cooperation/development aid; Rural development/agriculture. **Activities:** Conferences/seminars/workshops/training activities; Exchanges/twinning/linking; Fund raising; Information and documentation services/data bases; Information campaigns/exhibitions; Lobbying/advocacy; Publishing/audiovisual materials/educational materials.

DEU1000

DEUTSCHE STIFTUNG FUR INTERNATIONALE ENTWICKLUNG (DSE)

Rauchstr. 25, 1000 Berlin, Germany.

Telephone: 49 (30) 2 60 61. *Fax:* 49 (30) 2 60 63 75. *Contact:* Annette Hornung, Press officer.

DEU1001

DEUTSCHE STIFTUNG FUR UNO-FLUCHTLINGSHILFE ♦ German Foundation for UN Refugee Aid

Ludwig-Erhard-Platz 1, 53179 Bonn, Germany.

Telephone: 49 (228) 8 31 26 83. *Fax:* 49 (228) 8 31 26 55. *Contact:* Gustav Koch.

OBJECTIVES: To raise funds in support of UNHCR, UNWRA and national refugee projects. To promote the idea of international and national aid for refugees.

GENERAL INFORMATION: *Creation:* 1980. *Member organisations:* 1. *Personnel/Total:* 8. *Volunteers:* 8. *Budget/Total 1993:* ECU 2272000 (US$ 2661000). *Financial sources:* Private: 97%. Self-financing: 3%.

INFORMATION AND EDUCATION ACTIVITIES: Topics: Children/youth/family; Ecology/environment/biodiversity; Education/training/literacy; Emergency relief/refugees/humanitarian assistance; Health/sanitation/water; Human rights/peace/conflicts; Peace/ethnic conflicts/armament/disarmament; Racism/xenophobia/antisemitism; Refugees/migrants/ethnic groups. **Activities:** Formal education; Fund raising; Information and documentation services/data bases.

DEU1002

DEUTSCHE STIFTUNG WELTBEVOLKERUNG (DSW) ♦ German World Population Foundation

Goettinger Chaussee 115, 30459 Hannover, Germany.

Telephone: 49 (511) 2 34 50 50. *Fax:* 49 (511) 2 34 50 51. *Contact:* Hans Fleisch.

OBJECTIVES: To provide financial assistance and support research for charitable organisations undertaking family planning or population growth projects in developing countries. To disseminate information and promote co-operation worldwide on population issues.

GENERAL INFORMATION: *Creation:* 1991. *Personnel/Total:* 5. *Salaried:* 5. *Financial sources:* Private: 90%. Self-financing: 10%.

PUBLICATIONS: *Periodicals:* ICPD-Newsletter (12). *Annual report. List of publications.*

EVALUATION/RESEARCH: Evaluation reports available. Undertakes research activities.

COMMENTS: The budget for 1994 was 454,000 $ (39000 ECU).

ACTIVITIES IN DEVELOPING REGIONS: Active in 5 country(ies). Works through local field partners. **Sustainable Development Actions:** Children/youth/family; Education/training/literacy; Health/sanitation/water; Population/family planning/demography. **Regions:** East Africa; Mexico and Central America.

INFORMATION AND EDUCATION ACTIVITIES: Topics: Children/youth/family; Culture/tradition/religion; Ecology/environment/biodiversity; Education/training/literacy; Emergency relief/refugees/humanitarian assistance; Employment/unemployment; Food/famine; Gender issues/women; Health/sanitation/water; Human rights/peace/conflicts; Interna-

tional economic relations/trade/debt/finance; International relations/cooperation/development aid; Peace/ethnic conflicts/armament/disarmament; Population/family planning/demography; Poverty/living conditions; Racism/xenophobia/antisemitism; Refugees/migrants/ethnic groups; Rural development/agriculture; Urban development/habitat. **Activities:** Conferences/seminars/workshops/training activities; Formal education; Fund raising; Information and documentation services/data bases; Information campaigns/exhibitions; Lobbying/advocacy; Networking/electronic telecommunications; Publishing/audiovisual materials/educational materials.

DEU1003

DEUTSCHE TECHNISCHE AKADEMIE

Bötticherstrasse 2, Postfach 16 70, 3330 Helmstedt, Germany.

Telephone: 49 (53 51) 1 20 40. *Fax:* 49 (53 51) 12 04 40. *Contact:* Michael Jischa.

DEU1004

DEUTSCHE UNESCO-KOMMISSION (DUK) ♦ German Commission for UNESCO

Colmantstr. 15, 53115 Bonn, Germany.

Telephone: 49 (228) 69 20 91/69 20 92. *Fax:* 49 (228) 63 69 12. *Contact:* Peter Canisius, President.

OBJECTIVES: To advise the federal government and the Laender ministeries on all matters concerning UNESCO. To organise and implement UNESCO's programmes in Germany. To promote international collaboration and establish co-operation between UNESCO and German organisations and institutions.

GENERAL INFORMATION: *Creation:* 1950. *Type of organisation:* coordinating body. *Member organisations:* 63. *Personnel/Total:* 23. *Salaried:* 21. *Volunteers:* 2. *Budget/Total 1993:* ECU 2582000 (US$ 3024000). *Financial sources:* Private: 50%. Public: 45%. Self-financing: 5%.

PUBLICATIONS: *Periodicals:* UNESCO Heute (4) - UNESCO Kurier (12). *Annual report. List of publications.*

COMMENTS: Information activities related to the Commonwealth of Independent States.

INFORMATION AND EDUCATION ACTIVITIES: Topics: Children/youth/family; Culture/tradition/religion; Ecology/environment/biodiversity; Education/training/literacy; Emergency relief/refugees/humanitarian assistance; Gender issues/women; Human rights/peace/conflicts; Peace/ethnic conflicts/armament/disarmament; Racism/xenophobia/antisemitism; Refugees/migrants/ethnic groups; Urban development/habitat. **Activities:** Broadcasting/cultural events; Conferences/seminars/workshops/training activities; Exchanges/twinning/linking; Fund raising; Information and documentation services/data bases; Information campaigns/exhibitions; Lobbying/advocacy; Networking/electronic telecommunications; Publishing/audiovisual materials/educational materials.

DEU1005

DEUTSCHE WELLE - AUSBILDUNGSZENTRUM (DWAZ)

Raderberggürtel 50, 50588 Köln, Germany.

Telephone: 49 (221) 3 89 20 31. *Fax:* 49 (221) 3 89 35 50. *Contact:* W.I. Graff, Director.

OBJECTIVES: To assist broadcasting organisations in developing countries and Eastern Europe in their efforts to improve their programmes and technical standards.

GENERAL INFORMATION: *Creation:* 1965. *Affiliated to:* International Association of Media and Communication Researchers. *Personnel/Total:* 18. *Salaried:* 18. *Budget/Total 1993:* ECU 2582000 (US$ 3024000). *Financial sources:* Self-financing: 100%.

PUBLICATIONS: *Periodicals:* DWAZ Dialogue (1). *Annual report. List of publications.*

COMMENTS: Undertakes activities in the Commonwealth of Independent States. Information activities related to the Commonwealth of Independent States.

ACTIVITIES IN DEVELOPING REGIONS: Present in developing regions. Active in 15 country(ies). Works through local field. **Sustainable Development Actions:** Education/training/literacy. **Regions:** Central Africa; Central Asia and South Asia; East Africa; East Asia; Mexico and Central America; Middle East; North Africa; South America; South East Asia; Southern Africa; West Africa.

INFORMATION AND EDUCATION ACTIVITIES: Topics: Other. **Activities:** Broadcasting/cultural events; Conferences/seminars/workshops/ training activities; Exchanges/twinning/linking; Publishing/audiovisual materials/educational materials.

DEU1006

DEUTSCHE WELTHUNGERHILFE (DW) ♦ German Agro Action

Adenauer Allee 134, 53113 Bonn, Germany.

Telephone: 49 (228) 2 28 80. **Fax:** 49 (228) 22 07 10. **Contact:** Volker Hausmann, Secretary General.

OBJECTIVES: To promote awareness of developmental problems and opportunities of the Third World in Germany. To support self-help projects and programmes in developing countries in the field of food security, rural development and agriculture.

GENERAL INFORMATION: Creation: 1962. **Affiliated to:** Bensheimer Kreis (Germany) - ACORD (United Kingdom) - Eurostiep (Belgium). **Personnel/Total:** 128. **Salaried:** 128 of which: 30 in developing countries. **Budget/Total 1993:** ECU 60673000 (US$ 71077000). **Financial sources:** Private: 34%. Public: 43%. Self-financing: 23%.

PUBLICATIONS: Periodicals: Welternährung (4) - Spenderbrief (4). Annual report. List of publications.

COMMENTS: Undertakes activities in the Commonwealth of Independent States.

ACTIVITIES IN DEVELOPING REGIONS: Present in developing regions. Active in 51 country(ies). Maintains local field presence. Works through local field partners. **Sustainable Development Actions:** Children/ youth/family; Democracy/good governance/institution building/participatory development; Ecology/environment/biodiversity; Emergency relief/refugees/humanitarian assistance; Food/famine; Gender issues/ women; Rural development/agriculture; Sending volunteers/experts/ technical assistance; Small enterprises/informal sector/handicrafts. **Regions:** Central Africa; Central Asia and South Asia; East Africa; East Asia; South America; South East Asia; Southern Africa; West Africa.

INFORMATION AND EDUCATION ACTIVITIES: Topics: Children/youth/ family; Ecology/environment/biodiversity; Emergency relief/refugees/ humanitarian assistance; Food/famine; Gender issues/women; Health/ sanitation/water; Human rights/peace/conflicts; International relations/ cooperation/development aid; Poverty/living conditions; Rural development/agriculture. **Activities:** Conferences/seminars/workshops/training activities; Fund raising; Information campaigns/exhibitions; Lobbying/ advocacy.

DEU1007

DEUTSCHER BUNDESJUGENDRING

Haager Weg 44, 5300 Bonn, Germany.

Telephone: 49 (2 28) 28 50 25. **Fax:** 49 (2 28) 28 56 20. **Contact:** Ronald Berthelmann.

DEU1008

DEUTSCHER CARITASVERBAND (DCV) ♦ German Caritas Association

Karlstrasse 40, Postfach 420, 79104 Freiburg , Germany.

Telephone: 49 (761) 20 00. **Fax:** 49 (761) 20 05 83. **Contact:** Karl Ammann.

DEU1009

DEUTSCHER ENTWICKLUNGSDIENST (DED) ♦ German Volunteer Service

Kladower Damm 299, Postfach 22 00 35, 1000 Berlin 22, Germany.

Telephone: 49 (30) 3 65 09-0. **Fax:** 49 (30) 36 50 92 71. **Contact:** Dr. Hans-Dietrich Pallmann, Director.

DEU1010

DEUTSCHER FRAUENRAT - LOBBY DER FRAUEN (DF) ♦ National Council of German Women's Organizations

Simrockstrasse 5, 53113 Bonn, Germany.

Telephone: 49 (228) 22 30 08. **Fax:** 49 (228) 21 88 19. **Contact:** Irmgard Falowy, President.

OBJECTIVES: To lobby for equal opportunities for women and for the protection of the environmnet.

GENERAL INFORMATION: Creation: 1951. **Type of organisation:** coordinating body. **Member organisations:** 80. **Personnel/Total:** 7. **Financial sources:** Public: 100%.

PUBLICATIONS: Periodicals: Informationen Für Die Frau (10). Annual report.

INFORMATION AND EDUCATION ACTIVITIES: Topics: Gender issues/ women; Human rights/peace/conflicts. **Activities:** Conferences/seminars/workshops/training activities; Information campaigns/exhibitions; Lobbying/advocacy.

DEU1011

DEUTSCHER FRAUENRING (DFR) ♦ German Women's Organisation

Brüder Bonhoefferstr. 11, 51377 Leverkusen, Germany.

Telephone: 49 (431) 9 72 22. **Contact:** Inge Heyl.

DEU1012

DEUTSCHER FREIWILLIGENDIENST IN UBERSEE (DFU) ♦ German Overseas Volunteer Service

Argelanderstrasse 50, 53115 Bonn, Germany.

Telephone: 49 (228) 41 59 00. **Contact:** Heribert Handel, Chairman.

OBJECTIVES: To prepare development workers for volunteer work in developing countries, assisting the local populations in their community development, agriculture and education activities.

GENERAL INFORMATION: Creation: 1970. **Affiliated to:** APED - LHÜ. **Personnel/Total:** 11. **Salaried:** 1. **Volunteers:** 10 of which: 10 in developing countries. **Financial sources:** Private: 100%.

ACTIVITIES IN DEVELOPING REGIONS: Present in developing regions. Maintains local field presence. Works through local field partners. **Sustainable Development Actions:** Children/youth/family; Health/sanitation/water; Rural development/agriculture. **Regions:** East Africa; Mexico and Central America; South America.

INFORMATION AND EDUCATION ACTIVITIES: Topics: Children/youth/ family. **Activities:** Conferences/seminars/workshops/training activities.

DEU1013

DEUTSCHER GEWERKSCHAFTSBUND (DGB) ♦ German Trade Union Federation

Hans-Böckler-Strasse 39, 40001 Düsseldorf, Germany.

Telephone: 49 (211) 4 30 10. **Fax:** 49 (211) 4 30 13 24. **Contact:** Dieter Schulte, Chairman.

OBJECTIVES: To represent the social, economic and cultural interests of German Trade Union members' workers. To support the democratic foundation of Germany. To defend and strengthen the social welfare state. To support the strengthening of the European unification.

GENERAL INFORMATION: Creation: 1949. **Member organisations:** 16. **Affiliated to:** ICFTU (Belgium). **Personnel/Total:** 3. **Salaried:** 3. **Financial sources:** Self-financing: 100%.

PUBLICATIONS: Periodicals: Die Quelle (12). List of publications.

EVALUATION/RESEARCH: Evaluation reports available. Undertakes research activities.

COMMENTS: The budget for 1992 was 350,837,000 DM. Undertakes activities in the Commonwealth of Independent States.

ACTIVITIES IN DEVELOPING REGIONS: Works through local field partners.

See: *How to Use the Directory*, page 11.

INFORMATION AND EDUCATION ACTIVITIES: Topics: Employment/ unemployment; Gender issues/women; Human rights/peace/conflicts; International economic relations/trade/debt/finance; Poverty/living conditions; Refugees/migrants/ethnic groups. **Activities:** Conferences/seminars/workshops/training activities; Information and documentation services/data bases; Information campaigns/exhibitions; Lobbying/advocacy; Publishing/audiovisual materials/educational materials.

DEU1014

DEUTSCHER HILFSVEREIN FUR DAS ALBERT-SCHWEITZER-SPITAL IN LAMBARENE ♦ Association allemande d'aide à l'hôpital du Docteur Albert Schweitzer à Lambaréné

Neue Schlesingergasse 22-24, 6000 Frankfurt 1, Allemagne.

Téléphone: 49 (69) 28 49 51. *Contact:* Dr. Claus Günzler.

DEU1015

DEUTSCHER INDUSTRIE- UND HANDELSTAG (DIHT)

Adenauerallee 148, 53113 Bonn, Germany.

Telephone: 49 (228) 10 40. *Fax:* 49 (228) 10 41 58. *Contact:* Hans Peter Stihl, President.

OBJECTIVES: To represent the economical interests of their members by carrying out economic and legal assessments, acting as experts and assessors and undertaking vocational training programmes and administrative tasks.

GENERAL INFORMATION: *Type of organisation:* association of NGOs. *Member organisations:* 83.

PUBLICATIONS: *Annual report. List of publications.*

COMMENTS: Undertakes activities in the Commonwealth of Independent States. Information activities related to the Commonwealth of Independent States.

ACTIVITIES IN DEVELOPING REGIONS: Present in developing regions. Active in 15 country(ies). Maintains local field presence. Works through local field partners. **Sustainable Development Actions:** Education/training/literacy; Small enterprises/informal sector/handicrafts. **Regions:** Central Asia and South Asia; East Asia; Mexico and Central America; Middle East; Oceania; South America; South East Asia; Southern Africa.

INFORMATION AND EDUCATION ACTIVITIES: Topics: Education/training/literacy; Employment/unemployment; International economic relations/trade/debt/finance; International relations/cooperation/development aid. **Activities:** Conferences/seminars/workshops/training activities; Exchanges/twinning/linking; Information and documentation services/data bases; Lobbying/advocacy.

DEU1016

DEUTSCHER VOLKSHOCHSCHUL-VERBAND (DVV) ♦ German Adult Education Association

Obere Wilhelmstr. 32, 53225 Bonn, Germany.

Telephone: 49 (228) 97 56 90. *Fax:* 49 (228) 9 75 69 55. *Contact:* Rita Süssmuth, President.

OBJECTIVES: To provide co-operation and support the reinforcement of adult education by training teachers, producing learning materials and supporting community development projects.

GENERAL INFORMATION: *Creation:* 1953. *Type of organisation:* coordinating body. *Member organisations:* 16. *Affiliated to:* European Adult Education Association. *Personnel/Total:* 140. *Salaried:* 140 of which: 12 in developing countries. *Financial sources: Public:* 100%.

PUBLICATIONS: *Periodicals:* Adult Education and Development (2). *Annual report. List of publications.*

EVALUATION/RESEARCH: Evaluation reports available. Undertakes research activities.

COMMENTS: Undertakes activities in the Commonwealth of Independent States. Information activities related to the Commonwealth of Independent States.

ACTIVITIES IN DEVELOPING REGIONS: Present in developing regions. Maintains local field presence. Works through local field partners. **Sustainable Development Actions:** Education/training/literacy; Sending

volunteers/experts/technical assistance. **Regions:** Caribbean; Central Africa; Central Asia and South Asia; East Africa; East Asia; Mexico and Central America; Middle East; Oceania; South America; South East Asia; Southern Africa; West Africa.

INFORMATION AND EDUCATION ACTIVITIES: Topics: Education/training/literacy. **Activities:** Conferences/seminars/workshops/training activities; Publishing/audiovisual materials/educational materials.

DEU1017

DEUTSCHES AUSSATZIGEN-HILFSWERK (DAHW) ♦ German Leprosy Relief Association

Dominikanerplatz 4, 97070 Würzburg, Germany.

Telephone: 49 (931) 3 52 10. *Fax:* 49 (931) 3 52 11 60. *Contact:* Dr. Helmut Müller, President.

OBJECTIVES: To initiate and support measures to combat leprosy. To conduct combined leprosy and TB programs. To foster medical and social rehabilitation. To support leprosy and TB research and training.

GENERAL INFORMATION: *Creation:* 1957. *Affiliated to:* International Federation of Anti-Leprosy Association (United kingdom). *Personnel/Total:* 100. *Salaried:* 100 of which: 40 in developing countries. *Budget/Total 1993:* ECU 16729000 (US$ 19597000). *Financial sources:* Private: 99%. *Public:* 1%.

PUBLICATIONS: *Periodicals:* Miteinander (3) - Hoffnung auf Partnerschaft (7). *Annual report. List of publications.*

EVALUATION/RESEARCH: Undertakes research activities.

COMMENTS: Undertakes activities in the Commonwealth of Independent States.

ACTIVITIES IN DEVELOPING REGIONS: Present in developing regions. Active in 46 country(ies). Maintains local field presence. Works through local field partners. **Sustainable Development Actions:** Education/training/literacy; Emergency relief/refugees/humanitarian assistance; Food/famine; Health/sanitation/water; Sending volunteers/experts/technical assistance. **Regions:** Central Africa; Central Asia and South Asia; East Africa; East Asia; Middle East; North Africa; Oceania; South America; South East Asia; West Africa.

INFORMATION AND EDUCATION ACTIVITIES: Topics: Education/training/literacy; Health/sanitation/water. **Activities:** Conferences/seminars/workshops/training activities; Formal education; Fund raising; Information and documentation services/data bases; Information campaigns/exhibitions; Publishing/audiovisual materials/educational materials.

DEU1018

DEUTSCHES BLINDENHILFSWERK

Grabensstrasse 179, 47003 Duisberg, Germany.

DEU1019

DEUTSCHES INSTITUT FUR ARZTLICHE MISSION ♦ German Institute for Medical Mission

Paul-Lechler-Strasse 24, Postfach 1307, 72003 Tüebingen, Germany.

Telephone: 49 (7071) 20 65 12. *Fax:* 49 (7071) 2 71 25. *Contact:* Dr. Rainward Bastian.

OBJECTIVES: To advise and support doctors and nurses working with churches in Africa, Asia and Latin America. To provide them with medical equipment for the free treatment of patients unable to afford medical care.

GENERAL INFORMATION: *Creation:* 1906. *Type of organisation:* coordinating body. *Affiliated to:* Diakon. Werk der EKD (Germany) - Ev. Missionswerk in Deutschland (Germany). *Personnel/Total:* n.a.. *Salaried:* 10. *Financial sources: Private:* 99%. *Self-financing:* 1%.

PUBLICATIONS: *Periodicals:* Nachrichten aus der ärztlichen Mission (4). *Annual report. List of publications.*

PLANNED ACTIVITIES: To concentrate on the on-going debate on justice and health. Role of the Church in health, communally and congregationally based activities; pharmaceutical issues.

COMMENTS: Information activities related to the Commonwealth of Independent States.

Voir : *Comment utiliser le répertoire,* page 11.

INFORMATION AND EDUCATION ACTIVITIES: Topics: Children/youth/family; Culture/tradition/religion; Education/training/literacy; Gender issues/women; Health/sanitation/water; Human rights/peace/conflicts; International economic relations/trade/debt/finance; Other; Population/family planning/demography; Poverty/living conditions; Refugees/migrants/ethnic groups. **Activities:** Conferences/seminars/workshops/training activities; Exchanges/twinning/linking; Formal education; Fund raising; Information and documentation services/data bases; Information campaigns/exhibitions; Lobbying/advocacy; Networking/electronic telecommunications; Publishing/audiovisual materials/educational materials.

DEU1020

DEUTSCHES INSTITUT FUR ENTWICKLUNGSPOLITIK GMBH (DIE) ♦ German Development Institute

Hallerstrasse 3, 10587 Berlin, Germany.

Telephone: 49 (30) 39 07 30. **Fax:** 49 (30) 3 90 73 30. **Contact:** Hans-Helmut Taake, Director.

OBJECTIVES: To provide consultancy and training on the basis of independent research. To study development policy issues for public institutions in the FRG and abroad. To offer advice on current aspects of cooperation between industrialized and developing countries.

GENERAL INFORMATION: Creation: 1964. **Personnel/Total:** 47. Salaried: 47. **Budget/Total 1993:** ECU 3911000 (US$ 4581000). **Financial sources:** Public: 100%.

PUBLICATIONS: List of publications.

EVALUATION/RESEARCH: Undertakes research activities.

PLANNED ACTIVITIES: Studies on democracy and human rights, international trade policy and the environment, transfer of technology, competitiveness among semi-industrialized states, the exportation from developing countries to the European Union and the problem of ecological product requirements.

COMMENTS: Information activities related to the Commonwealth of Independent States.

INFORMATION AND EDUCATION ACTIVITIES: Topics: Ecology/environment/biodiversity; Education/training/literacy; Employment/unemployment; Food/famine; Gender issues/women; Health/sanitation/water; Human rights/peace/conflicts; International economic relations/trade/debt/finance; International relations/cooperation/development aid; Population/family planning/demography; Poverty/living conditions; Refugees/migrants/ethnic groups; Rural development/agriculture; Urban development/habitat. **Activities:** Conferences/seminars/workshops/training activities; Exchanges/twinning/linking; Information and documentation services/data bases; Publishing/audiovisual materials/educational materials.

DEU1021

DEUTSCHES KATOLISCHES BLINDENWERK

Eschstrasse 12, 52351 Düren, Germany.

DEU1022

DEUTSCHES KOMITEE FUR UNICEF ♦ German Committee for UNICEF

Höninger Weg 104, 50969 Köln, Germany.

Telephone: 49 (221) 93 65 00. **Fax:** 49 (221) 93 65 02 79. **Contact:** Reinhard Schlagintweit, Chairman.

OBJECTIVES: To support the tasks, projects and aims of UNICEF. To inform the German public of the UN's objectives (as stated in the UN Charter). To encourage cooperation and support in the field of child welfare in Germany.

GENERAL INFORMATION: Creation: 1953. **Type of organisation:** network. **Member organisations:** 7. **Affiliated to:** Trans-Fair (Germany) - Eine Welt für Alle (Germany) - AEBÖ (Germany). **Personnel/Total:** 8062. Salaried: 62. Volunteers: 8000. **Budget/Total 1993:** ECU 57931000 (US$ 67864000). **Financial sources:** Private: 98%. Public: 2%.

PUBLICATIONS: Periodicals: UNICEF-Nachrichten (4). Annual report. List of publications.

COMMENTS: Information activities related to the Commonwealth of Independent States.

INFORMATION AND EDUCATION ACTIVITIES: Topics: Children/youth/family; Ecology/environment/biodiversity; Education/training/literacy; Emergency relief/refugees/humanitarian assistance; Food/famine; Gender issues/women; Health/sanitation/water; Human rights/peace/conflicts; International economic relations/trade/debt/finance; International relations/cooperation/development aid; Other; Peace/ethnic conflicts/armament/disarmament; Population/family planning/demography; Poverty/living conditions; Racism/xenophobia/antisemitism; Urban development/habitat. **Activities:** Broadcasting/cultural events; Conferences/seminars/workshops/training activities; Fund raising; Information and documentation services/data bases; Information campaigns/exhibitions; Publishing/audiovisual materials/educational materials.

DEU1023

DEUTSCHES MEDIKAMENTEN-HILFSWERK (ACTION MEDEOR) ♦ German Medical Welfare Organisation Action Medeor

Töniser Strasse 21, Postfach 2140, Tönisvorst 47913, Germany.

Telephone: 49 (215) 69 78 80. **Fax:** 49 (215) 68 06 32. **Contact:** Hans Hochbruck, Board Chairman.

OBJECTIVES: To promote health as a basis for development. To supply hospitals, primary health care services and missionary stations, in developing countries, with essential medecinal drugs.

GENERAL INFORMATION: Creation: 1964. **Affiliated to:** Bensheimer Kreis (Germany) - MMI (Belgium). **Personnel/Total:** 42. **Budget/Total 1993:** ECU 11100000 (US$ 13004000). **Financial sources:** Private: 19%. Self-financing: 81%.

PUBLICATIONS: Periodicals: Medeor Report (2) - Mailings (6). Annual report. List of publications.

EVALUATION/RESEARCH: Evaluation reports available.

COMMENTS: Undertakes activities in the Commonwealth of Independent States. Information activities related to the Commonwealth of Independent States.

ACTIVITIES IN DEVELOPING REGIONS: Active in 123 country(ies). Works through local field partners. **Sustainable Development Actions:** Health/sanitation/water. **Regions:** Caribbean; Central Africa; Central Asia and South Asia; East Africa; East Asia; Mexico and Central America; Middle East; North Africa; Oceania; South America; South East Asia; Southern Africa; West Africa.

INFORMATION AND EDUCATION ACTIVITIES: Topics: Health/sanitation/water. **Activities:** Conferences/seminars/workshops/training activities; Exchanges/twinning/linking; Fund raising; Information and documentation services/data bases; Information campaigns/exhibitions; Lobbying/advocacy; Publishing/audiovisual materials/educational materials.

DEU1024

DEUTSCHES ROTES KREUZ (DRK) ♦ German Red Cross

Friedrich-Ebert-Allee 71, Postfach 1460, 5300 Bonn 1, Germany.

Telephone: 49 (228) 54 11. **Fax:** 49 (228) 54 12 90. **Contact:** Botho Prins zu Sayn-Wittgenstein, President.

DEU1025

DGB-BUIDINGSWERK NORD-SUD-NETZ

Hans-Böckler-Strasse 39, 40476 Düsseldorf, Germany.

Telephone: 49 (211) 4 30 13 84. **Fax:** 49 (211) 4 30 15 00. **Contact:** Werner Oesterheld, Department Officer.

OBJECTIVES: To promote co-operation between the North and South among German Trade Unions. To develop education.

GENERAL INFORMATION: Creation: 1987. **Member organisations:** 70. **Personnel/Total:** 3. Salaried: 2. Volunteers: 1. **Budget/Total 1993:** ECU 336000 (US$ 393000). **Financial sources:** Public: 55%. Self-financing: 45%.

PUBLICATIONS: List of publications.

See: *How to Use the Directory*, page 11.

PLANNED ACTIVITIES: Supporting education centres in Brazil. The promotion of democracy in South Africa. Supporting gender issues and education in South Korea.

COMMENTS: DGB has about 20 publications.

ACTIVITIES IN DEVELOPING REGIONS: Present in developing regions. Active in 1 country(ies). Maintains local field presence. Works through local field partners. **Sustainable Development Actions:** Education/training/literacy. **Regions:** Mexico and Central America.

INFORMATION AND EDUCATION ACTIVITIES: Topics: Children/youth/family; Ecology/environment/biodiversity; Employment/unemployment; Gender issues/women; Human rights/peace/conflicts; International economic relations/trade/debt/finance; International relations/cooperation/development aid; Poverty/living conditions; Racism/xenophobia/antisemitism; Refugees/migrants/ethnic groups. **Activities:** Conferences/seminars/workshops/training activities; Fund raising; Information and documentation services/data bases; Information campaigns/exhibitions; Publishing/audiovisual materials/educational materials.

DEU1026

DIAKONISCHES WERK DER EVANGELISCHEN KIRCHE IN DEUTSCHLAND

Stafflenbergstasse 76, 70184 Stuttgart, Germany.

Fax: 49 (0711) 2 15 92 88. *Contact:* Rev. Karl Heinz Neukamm, President.

OBJECTIVES: To co-ordinate all activities of the Evangelical Church in Germany.

GENERAL INFORMATION: *Type of organisation:* coordinating body.

DEU1027

DIALOG INTERNATIONAL, FORDERGEMEINSCHAFT FUR DEMOKRATISCHE FRIEDENS ENTWICKLUNG ♦ Dialog International, Association pour la promotion de la paix et le développement

Postfach 26 01 24, 40094 Düsseldorf, Germany.

Telephone: 49 (211) 31 26 08. *Contact:* Etienne R. Mbaya.

OBJECTIVES: To work for peace between Europe and Africa. To organise development projects in Zaire. To inform Europeans of the situation of Zaire.

GENERAL INFORMATION: *Creation:* 1992. *Affiliated to:* International Peace Bureau (Switzerland). *Personnel/Total:* 10. *Volunteers:* 10 of which: 2 in developing countries.

PUBLICATIONS: *Periodicals:* Der Pazifist (12). *List of publications.*

EVALUATION/RESEARCH: Evaluation reports available. Undertakes research activities.

ACTIVITIES IN DEVELOPING REGIONS: Present in developing regions. Maintains local field presence. Works through local field partners. **Sustainable Development Actions:** Democracy/good governance/institution building/participatory development; Education/training/literacy; Health/sanitation/water; Human rights/peace/conflicts; Rural development/agriculture. **Regions:** Central Africa.

INFORMATION AND EDUCATION ACTIVITIES: Topics: Health/sanitation/water; Human rights/peace/conflicts; Peace/ethnic conflicts/armament/disarmament; Racism/xenophobia/antisemitism; Refugees/migrants/ethnic groups; Rural development/agriculture. **Activities:** Conferences/seminars/workshops/training activities; Fund raising; Information and documentation services/data bases; Publishing/audiovisual materials/educational materials.

DEU1028

DIALOG-BILDUNGSWERK ♦ Society for Dialogue and Education

Teigelhügel 6, 4402 Greven 1, Germany.

Telephone: 49 (2571) 25 87. *Contact:* Wilfried Rehfeld.

DEU1029

DIENSTE IN UBERSEE - ARBEITSGEMEINSCHAFT EVANGELISCHER KIRCHEN IN DEUTSCHLAND (DU) ♦ Committee of Protestant Churches in Germany for Service Overseas

P.O. Box 100340, 70747 Leinfelden-Echterdingen, Germany.

Telephone: 49 (711) 7 98 90. *Fax:* 49 (711) 7 98 91 23. *Contact:* Gertraude Kaiser, General Secretary.

OBJECTIVES: To recruit and sponsor skilled personnel for, limited periods of service in developing countries. To organise and encourage participation in educational programmes for development in Germany.

GENERAL INFORMATION: *Creation:* 1960. *Type of organisation:* association of NGOs. *Member organisations:* 35. *Affiliated to:* Arbeitsgemeinschaft Kirchlicher Entwicklungsdienst (Germany) - Arbeitskreis Lernen und Helfen in Übersee (Germany) - Arbeitsgemeinschaft der Entwicklungs Dienste (Germany). *Personnel/Total:* n.a.. *Salaried:* 77. *Volunteers:* 295 of which: 267 in developing countries. *Budget/Total 1993:* ECU 15696000 (US$ 18387000). *Financial sources:* Private: 70%. Public: 30%.

PUBLICATIONS: *Periodicals:* Der Überblick (4) - Texte zum Kirchlichen Entwicklungsdienst (3). *Annual report. List of publications.*

ACTIVITIES IN DEVELOPING REGIONS: Active in 58 country(ies). Works through local field partners. **Sustainable Development Actions:** Sending volunteers/experts/technical assistance. **Regions:** Caribbean; Central Africa; Central Asia and South Asia; East Africa; East Asia; Mexico and Central America; Middle East; North Africa; Oceania; South America; South East Asia; Southern Africa; West Africa.

INFORMATION AND EDUCATION ACTIVITIES: Topics: Other. **Activities:** Conferences/seminars/workshops/training activities.

DEU1030

DOKUMENTATIONS UND INFORMATIONSZENTRUM MENSCHENRECHTE IN LATEINAMERIKA (DIML) ♦ Documentation and Information Center for Human Rights in Latin America

Fürther Straáe 22, 90429 Nürnberg, Germany.

Telephone: 49 (911) 26 79 42. *Fax:* 49 (911) 26 59 74. *E-mail:* diml@link-N.nbg.sub.org. *Contact:* Siegfried König.

OBJECTIVES: To provide documentation of work done on human rights and their violations in Latin America. To create a collection of documents, literature, etc., which are accessible to the public and NGOs in Latin America.

GENERAL INFORMATION: *Creation:* 1989. *Affiliated to:* REDIAL (France). *Personnel/Total:* 9. *Salaried:* 1. *Volunteers:* 8. *Budget/Total 1993:* ECU 41000 (US$ 48000). *Financial sources:* Private: 10%. Public: 85%. Self-financing: 5%.

PUBLICATIONS: *Periodicals:* Memoria (1). *List of publications.*

EVALUATION/RESEARCH: Undertakes research activities.

INFORMATION AND EDUCATION ACTIVITIES: Topics: Human rights/peace/conflicts. **Activities:** Conferences/seminars/workshops/training activities; Fund raising; Information and documentation services/data bases; Networking/electronic telecommunications.

DEU1031

DRITTE WELT HAUS ♦ Third World House

August Bebel Strasse 62, 33602 Bielefeld, Germany.

Telephone: 49 (521) 6 28 02. *Fax:* 49 (521) 6 37 89. *E-mail:* jenke.gn.apc.org. *Contact:* R. Jenke.

OBJECTIVES: To help reduce hunger, poverty and repression in developing countries. To demonstrate how the FDR and other industrialized countries are maintaining Third World nations in a state of dependency.

GENERAL INFORMATION: *Creation:* 1980. *Affiliated to:* Platform for German NGOs cooperating with the EU - BUKO (Bundeskongreb Entwicklungspolitischer Aktionsgruppen) (Germany). *Personnel/Total:* 133. *Salaried:* 13 of which: 1 in developing countries. *Volunteers:* 120. *Budget/Total 1993:* ECU 413000 (US$ 484000). *Financial sources:* Private: 20%. Public: 70%. Self-financing: 10%.

PUBLICATIONS: *Periodicals:* DWH-Info (4). *Annual report. List of publications.*

ACTIVITIES IN DEVELOPING REGIONS: Present in developing regions. Active in 9 country(ies). Maintains local field presence. Works through local field partners. **Sustainable Development Actions:** Children/

youth/family; Democracy/good governance/institution building/participatory development; Ecology/environment/biodiversity; Education/training/literacy; Health/sanitation/water; Rural development/agriculture; Small enterprises/informal sector/handicrafts; Urban development/habitat. **Regions:** Caribbean; East Africa; Mexico and Central America; South America; Southern Africa.

INFORMATION AND EDUCATION ACTIVITIES: Topics: Children/youth/family; Culture/tradition/religion; Ecology/environment/biodiversity; Food/famine; Gender issues/women; International economic relations/trade/debt/finance; International relations/cooperation/development aid; Population/family planning/demography; Poverty/living conditions; Racism/xenophobia/antisemitism; Refugees/migrants/ethnic groups; Rural development/agriculture. **Activities:** Broadcasting/cultural events; Conferences/seminars/workshops/training activities; Information and documentation services/data bases; Information campaigns/exhibitions; Publishing/audiovisual materials/educational materials.

DEU1032

ECOLOGY AGRICULTURE DEVELOPMENT (EcoAgriDev)

Botzenstrasse 47, 79219 Staufen, Germany.

Telephone: 49 (7633) 55 69. *Fax:* 49 (7633) 50 05 83. *Contact:* Rüdiger Stegemann.

OBJECTIVES: To support ecological sustainability. To guarantee fair opportunities for peasant farmers to sustain themselves. To support non-profit consultancy, advocacy and educational campaigns, aimed at global, national and social justice.

GENERAL INFORMATION: *Creation:* 1993. ***Personnel/Total:*** 2. *Volunteers:* 2 of which: 2 in developing countries.

EVALUATION/RESEARCH: Undertakes research activities.

PLANNED ACTIVITIES: Implementation of the Convention on Biodiversity. Political framework of genetic ressources. Plant breeding and seed industry.

ACTIVITIES IN DEVELOPING REGIONS: Present in developing regions. Active in 1 country(ies). Works through local field partners. **Sustainable Development Actions:** Ecology/environment/biodiversity; Food/famine; Gender issues/women; Rural development/agriculture. **Regions:** East Africa.

INFORMATION AND EDUCATION ACTIVITIES: Topics: Ecology/environment/biodiversity; Food/famine; Gender issues/women; International economic relations/trade/debt/finance; International relations/cooperation/development aid; Rural development/agriculture. **Activities:** Conferences/seminars/workshops/training activities; Lobbying/advocacy.

DEU1033

ECUMENICAL HEARING ON THE INTERNATIONAL FINANCIAL SYSTEM

Roseggerstrasse 13, 5600 Wuppertal 2, Germany.

Telephone: 49 (202) 63673.

DEU1034

EINE WELT FUR ALLE ♦ One World

Adenauerallee 37, 53113 Bonn, Germany.

Telephone: 49 (228) 2 67 98 18. *Fax:* 49 (228) 2 67 98 78. *Contact:* Ulrich Schmid, Chairman.

OBJECTIVES: To raise awareness in the general public about the interrelatedness of global development and environmental problems. To encourage the change of the way of life based on overconsumption of natural resources.

GENERAL INFORMATION: *Creation:* 1989. ***Type of organisation:*** coordinating body. ***Member organisations:*** 32. ***Personnel/Total:*** 2. *Salaried:* 2. ***Budget/Total 1993:*** ECU 155000 (US$ 181000). ***Financial sources:*** Public: 50%. Self-financing: 50%.

PUBLICATIONS: *Periodicals:* One World Reporter (12). *Annual report. List of publications.*

EVALUATION/RESEARCH: Evaluation reports available.

INFORMATION AND EDUCATION ACTIVITIES: Topics: Ecology/environment/biodiversity; Peace/ethnic conflicts/armament/disarmament; Population/family planning/demography; Poverty/living conditions; Racism/xenophobia/antisemitism. **Activities:** Conferences/seminars/workshops/training activities; Information campaigns/exhibitions; Publishing/audiovisual materials/educational materials.

DEU1035

EINE-WELT TEAM VERSAND ♦ One World Team mail order shop

Leyer Strasse 26, Postfach 4006, 49030 Osnabrück, Germany.

Telephone: 49 (541) 91 70 20. *Fax:* 49 (541) 91 70 14. *Contact:* Ludwig Flatau, General Manager.

OBJECTIVES: To import consumer goods from selected producers in developing countries for distribution in Germany by mail-order catalogue. To inform the public of development issues, including the economic situation of developing countries.

GENERAL INFORMATION: *Creation:* 1978. ***Affiliated to:*** International Federation for Alternative Trade. ***Personnel/Total:*** 46. *Salaried:* 46. ***Financial sources:*** Self-financing: 100%.

PUBLICATIONS: *Periodicals:* Catalogue Einkaufen mit Herz und Verstand (2).

PLANNED ACTIVITIES: Importation of handicrafts from small producer groups on devleoping countries and their sale in Germany through a mail-order catalogue.

ACTIVITIES IN DEVELOPING REGIONS: Sustainable Development Actions: Debt/finance/trade. **Regions:** Central Africa; Central Asia and South Asia; East Africa; East Asia; Mexico and Central America; South America; South East Asia; West Africa.

DEU1036

EJF HEIMBETRIEBSGESELLSCHAFT GEMEINNUTZIGE GMBH

Königsberger Strasse 28a, 12207 Berlin, Germany.

DEU1037

ENTWICKLUNGSPOLITISCHE BILDUNGSARBEIT AUF DEM LANDE IN DER EVANGELISCHEN KIRCHE IN DEUTSCHLAND ♦ Rural Development Education of the German Protestant Council of Churches

Hohebuch, Ev. Bauernwerk in Würt, 74638 Waldenburg, Germany.

Telephone: 49 (7942) 1 07 74. *Fax:* 49 (7942) 1 07 77. *E-mail:* ebw@link.cr.comlink.apc.org. *Contact:* Rudolf Buntzel.

OBJECTIVES: To make German farmers aware of the worldwide state of agriculture. To contribute to future forums and dialogues between farmers worldwide.

GENERAL INFORMATION: *Creation:* 1977. ***Affiliated to:*** Agrarbündnis (Germany) - Forum Umwelt und Entwichlung (Germany). ***Personnel/Total:*** 2. *Salaried:* 2. ***Budget/Total 1993:*** ECU 26000 (US$ 30000). ***Financial sources:*** Private: 100%.

PUBLICATIONS: *Annual report. List of publications.*

EVALUATION/RESEARCH: Undertakes research activities.

PLANNED ACTIVITIES: Commodity campaigns and the creation of a new international network of farmers.

COMMENTS: Undertakes activities in the Commonwealth of Independent States. Information activities related to the Commonwealth of Independent States.

ACTIVITIES IN DEVELOPING REGIONS: Works through local field partners. **Sustainable Development Actions:** Ecology/environment/biodiversity; Rural development/agriculture. **Regions:** South East Asia; West Africa.

INFORMATION AND EDUCATION ACTIVITIES: Topics: Ecology/environment/biodiversity; Food/famine; International economic relations/trade/debt/finance; Rural development/agriculture. **Activities:** Conferences/seminars/workshops/training activities; Exchanges/twinning/linking; Information and documentation services/data bases; Information

See: *How to Use the Directory,* page 11.

campaigns/exhibitions; Lobbying/advocacy; Publishing/audiovisual materials/educational materials.

DEU1038

ENTWICKLUNGSPOLITISCHEN GESELLSCHAFT BERLIN (EPOG)

Treskowallee 8, 10313 Berlin, Germany.

Telephone: 49 (30) 5 19 28 92. *Fax:* 49 (30) 5 19 28 43. *Contact:* Peter Stier, Chairman.

OBJECTIVES: To inform the public of conditions in developing countries as well as of development policy issues. To organise educational programmes in schools and universities. To co-operate with NGOs in developing countries.

GENERAL INFORMATION: *Creation:* 1990. *Affiliated to:* German Platform of the Liaison Committee of Development NGOs to the European Community (Belgium) - Bensheimer Kreis (Germany). *Personnel/Total:* 40. *Salaried:* 5. *Volunteers:* 35 of which: 3 in developing countries. *Financial sources:* Private: 5%. Public: 94%. Self-financing: 1%.

PUBLICATIONS: *Periodicals:* Trialogue-Information-Service for East-West-South-Relations (4). *Annual report. List of publications.*

PLANNED ACTIVITIES: The promotion of development co-operation between the municipalities of Berlin and those of Mozambique and Uzbekistan.

COMMENTS: Undertakes activities in the Commonwealth of Independent States. Information activities related to the Commonwealth of Independent States.

ACTIVITIES IN DEVELOPING REGIONS: Present in developing regions. Active in 5 country(ies). Works through local field partners. **Sustainable Development Actions:** Children/youth/family; Education/training/literacy; Gender issues/women; Rural development/agriculture; Small enterprises/informal sector/handicrafts. **Regions:** Central Asia and South Asia; South America; Southern Africa; West Africa.

INFORMATION AND EDUCATION ACTIVITIES: Topics: Children/youth/family; Culture/tradition/religion; Education/training/literacy; Employment/unemployment; Gender issues/women; Human rights/peace/conflicts; International economic relations/trade/debt/finance; International relations/cooperation/development aid; Peace/ethnic conflicts/armament/disarmament; Poverty/living conditions. **Activities:** Conferences/seminars/workshops/training activities; Exchanges/twinning/linking; Fund raising; Information campaigns/exhibitions; Lobbying/advocacy; Publishing/audiovisual materials/educational materials.

DEU1039

ERITREA-HILFSWERK IN DEUTSCHLAND (EHD)

Markstrasse 8, 50968 Köln, Germany.

DEU1040

EUROPAISCHE BILDUNGS- UND AKTIONSGEMEINSCHAFT (EBAG)

Bertha-von-Suttner-Platz 13, 5300 Bonn, Germany.

Telephone: 49 (2 28) 65 77 02. *Fax:* 49 (2 28) 65 76 85. *Contact:* Dr Otto Schmuck.

DEU1041

EUROPEAN ACADEMY FOR THE ENVIRONMENT

Probstingerallee 14, 46325 Borken, Germany.

DEU1042

EUROPEAN FORUM ON DEVELOPMENT SERVICE ♦ Forum européen du Volontariat pour le Développement

Thomas Mannsstrasse 52, 53111 Bonn, Germany.

Telephone: 49 (228) 65 41 60. *Fax:* 49 (228) 65 04 14. *Contact:* Paul Jubin, Chairman.

OBJECTIVES: To promote international voluntary services in development co-operation. To represent agencies concerned with sending out qualified personnel to developing countries. To provide them with a forum for discussion at a European level.

GENERAL INFORMATION: *Creation:* 1964. *Type of organisation:* network, coordinating body. *Member organisations:* 24. *Personnel/Total:* 2. *Salaried:* 2. *Budget/Total 1993:* ECU 170000 (US$ 200000). *Financial sources:* Private: 40%. Public: 45%. Self-financing: 15%.

EVALUATION/RESEARCH: Evaluation reports available. Undertakes research activities.

COMMENTS: FORUM is an umbrella organization of some 300 NGOs based in 19 countries and has, at any given time, more than 13000 volunteers overseas. Undertakes activities in the Commonwealth of Independent States.

ACTIVITIES IN DEVELOPING REGIONS: Maintains local field presence. Works through local field partners.

DEU1043

EUROPEAN MIGRATION CENTRE

Postfach 301125, 10722 Berlin, Germany.

Telephone: 49 (30) 44 83 671.

DEU1044

EUROPEAN SUPPORT ASSOCIATIONS OF THE ECUMENICAL DEVELOPMENT CO-OPERATIVE SOCIETY

Auf der Brück 48, 51645 Gummersbach, Germany.

Telephone: 49 (2261) 7 25 86. *Fax:* 49 (2261) 70 09 59. *Contact:* Ulrike Chini.

OBJECTIVES: To provide loans for development projects in poor regions. To carry out development education in the North. To encourage churches to invest their capital in development via EDCS.

GENERAL INFORMATION: *Creation:* 1983. *Type of organisation:* association of NGOs, coordinating body. *Member organisations:* 18. *Affiliated to:* EDCS (the Netherlands). *Personnel/Total:* 66. *Salaried:* 6. *Volunteers:* 60. *Financial sources:* Private: 10%. Self-financing: 90%.

PUBLICATIONS: *Annual report. List of publications.*

EVALUATION/RESEARCH: Evaluation reports available.

PLANNED ACTIVITIES: To network with institutions involved in alternative trade, debt, international trade and finance, ethical investment.

INFORMATION AND EDUCATION ACTIVITIES: Topics: Ecology/environment/biodiversity; Education/training/literacy; Employment/unemployment; Gender issues/women; International economic relations/trade/debt/finance; International relations/cooperation/development aid; Poverty/living conditions; Rural development/agriculture; Urban development/habitat. **Activities:** Conferences/seminars/workshops/training activities; Fund raising; Lobbying/advocacy; Publishing/audiovisual materials/educational materials.

DEU1045

DAS EVANGELISCHE JUGENDWERK AN DER SAAR ♦ Evangelical Youth Council of the Saar

Grossherzog-Friedrich-Strasse 44, 6600 Saarbrücken 3, Germany.

Telephone: 49 (6) 8 13 04 41. *Contact:* Martin Keiper, Advisor.

DEU1046

EVANGELISCHE STUDENTENGEMEINDE

Kniebisstrasse 29, c/o Evangelische Akademikerschaft, 7000 Stuttgart, Germany.

Telephone: 49 (711) 28 10 34.

DEU1047

EVANGELISCHE ZENTRALSTELLE FUR ENTWICKLUNGSHILFE (EZE) ♦ Protestant Association for Co-operation in Development

Mittelstrasse 35-37, 53175 Bonn, Germany.

Voir : *Comment utiliser le répertoire,* page 11.

Telephone: 49 (228) 8 10 10. *Fax:* 49 (228) 8 10 11 60. *Contact:* Hartmut Bauer, Director.

OBJECTIVES: To support church-based development programmes, giving primary attention to the poorest groups in society. To promote the active participation of the people involved and help create and strengthen their self-reliance.

GENERAL INFORMATION: *Creation:* 1962. *Affiliated to:* Association of Churches Development Services (Germany) - Association of Protestant Development Organisations in Europe (Belgium). *Personnel/Total:* 92. *Salaried:* 92 of which: 72 in developing countries. *Budget/ Total 1993:* ECU 1006000 (US$ 1178000). *Financial sources:* Public: 90%. *Self-financing:* 10%.

PUBLICATIONS: *Annual report.*

COMMENTS: Undertakes activities in the Commonwealth of Independent States.

ACTIVITIES IN DEVELOPING REGIONS: Active in 70 country(ies). Works through local field partners. **Sustainable Development Actions:** Debt/finance/trade; Democracy/good governance/institution building/participatory development; Education/training/literacy; Gender issues/women; Rural development/agriculture; Sending volunteers/experts/technical assistance; Small enterprises/informal sector/handicrafts; Urban development/habitat. **Regions:** Caribbean; Central Africa; Central Asia and South Asia; East Africa; East Asia; Mexico and Central America; Middle East; North Africa; Oceania; South America; South East Asia; Southern Africa; West Africa.

INFORMATION AND EDUCATION ACTIVITIES: Topics: Gender issues/women; Human rights/peace/conflicts; International economic relations/trade/debt/finance; International relations/cooperation/development aid; Rural development/agriculture. **Activities:** Conferences/seminars/workshops/training activities; Exchanges/twinning/linking; Publishing/audiovisual materials/educational materials.

DEU1048

FOODFIRST INFORMATION AND ACTION NETWORK, GERMANY (FIAN) ♦ Pour le Droit à se Nourrir

Postfach 10 22 43, 69012 Heidelberg, Germany.

Telephone: 49 (622) 5 01 08. *Fax:* 49 (6222) 5 01 07. *Contact:* Dr. Rolf Knnemann, Secretary General.

DEU1049

FORDERKREIS "HOSPITAL ANDINO" PERU ♦ Patronage Circle "Andino Hospital" Peru

Wiesbadener Strasse 26, 61462 Koenigstein/Ts, Germany.

Telephone: 49 (61) 74 57 78. *Fax:* 49 (69) 66 44 91 13. *Contact:* Werner von Sengbusch, President.

DEU1050

FORDERKREIS-KREBSKRANKE KINDER

Büchsenstrasse 22, 70174 Stuttgart, Germany.

DEU1051

FORDERVEREIN BASISGESUNDHEITSDIENST IN DER PARTNERDIOZESE JABALPUR/INDIEN

Hegerskamp 71, 48115 Münster, Germany.

DEU1052

FORDERVEREIN FUR HUMANITARE WOHLTATIGKEIT IN KOSOVO "MUTTER THERESA"

Landrat-Dengler-Strasse 5, 64646 Heppenheim, Germany.

DEU1053

FRIEDENSDORF INTERNATIONAL ♦ Peace Village International

P.O. Box 14 01 62, 46131 Oberhausen, Germany.

Telephone: 49 (208) 99 61 80. *Fax:* 49 (208) 67 54 45. *Contact:* Ronald Gegenfurtner, Director.

OBJECTIVES: To provide medical aid and assistance for children who are victims of war and crisis.

GENERAL INFORMATION: *Creation:* 1967. *Personnel/Total:* 263. *Salaried:* 43. *Volunteers:* 220. *Budget/Total 1993:* ECU 4766000 (US$ 5583000). *Financial sources:* Private: 43%. Public: 52%. *Self-financing:* 5%.

PUBLICATIONS: *Periodicals:* Friedensdorf International Report (2) - Bildungswerk Programme (2). *List of publications.*

EVALUATION/RESEARCH: Undertakes research activities.

COMMENTS: The organisation's street address is Pfeilstrasse 35, 46147 Oberhausen. Undertakes activities in the Commonwealth of Independent States.

ACTIVITIES IN DEVELOPING REGIONS: Present in developing regions. Active in 13 country(ies). Works through local field partners. **Sustainable Development Actions:** Children/youth/family; Emergency relief/refugees/humanitarian assistance; Health/sanitation/water. **Regions:** Caribbean; Central Africa; Central Asia and South Asia; East Africa; Mexico and Central America; South East Asia; West Africa.

INFORMATION AND EDUCATION ACTIVITIES: Topics: Children/youth/family; Emergency relief/refugees/humanitarian assistance; Health/sanitation/water. **Activities:** Broadcasting/cultural events; Conferences/seminars/workshops/training activities; Information campaigns/exhibitions.

DEU1054

FRIEDENSZENTRUM MARTIN-NIEMOLLER-HAUS ♦ Martin-Niemöller-Haus Peace Centre

Pacelliallee 1, 1000 Berlin 33, Germany.

Telephone: 49 (30) 8 32 54 97. *Fax:* 49 (30) 8 31 61 53. *E-mail:* M. HEIMBACH@TELEMAIL.BERLINET.IN-BERLINDE.

OBJECTIVES: To undertake development education activities, solidarity work, anti-apartheid actions and refugee assistance. To sell products from developing countries in the Federal Republic of Germany.

GENERAL INFORMATION: *Creation:* 1980. *Member organisations:* 21. *Affiliated to:* AGDF (Germany). *Personnel/Total:* 5. *Volunteers:* 5. *Budget/Total 1993:* ECU 36000 (US$ 42000). *Financial sources:* Private: 90%. Public: 5%. *Self-financing:* 5%.

PUBLICATIONS: *Periodicals:* Martin-Niemoeller Haus-Info (6).

COMMENTS: Undertakes activities in the Commonwealth of Independent States. Information activities related to the Commonwealth of Independent States.

ACTIVITIES IN DEVELOPING REGIONS: Works through local field partners.

INFORMATION AND EDUCATION ACTIVITIES: Topics: Emergency relief/refugees/humanitarian assistance; Human rights/peace/conflicts; Peace/ethnic conflicts/armament/disarmament; Racism/xenophobia/antisemitism; Refugees/migrants/ethnic groups. **Activities:** Conferences/seminars/workshops/training activities; Fund raising; Information and documentation services/data bases; Lobbying/advocacy.

DEU1055

FRIEDRICH-EBERT-STIFTUNG ♦ Friedrich-Ebert-Foundation

Godesberger Allee 149, 53170 Bonn, Germany.

Telephone: 49 (228) 88 30. *Fax:* 49 (228) 88 36 96. *Contact:* Holger Börner, President.

OBJECTIVES: To further a political culture based on democracy and pluralism by means of education. To contribute to international understanding and co-operation. To improve social and political conditions of development.

GENERAL INFORMATION: *Creation:* 1925. *Salaried:* 690 of which: 130 in developing countries. *Budget/Total 1993:* ECU 108426000 (US$ 127019000). *Financial sources:* Private: 2%. *Public:* 90%. *Self-financing:* 8%.

PUBLICATIONS: *Periodicals:* International Politics and Society (4). *Annual report. List of publications.*

                                                 See: *How to Use the Directory,* page 11.

EVALUATION/RESEARCH: Evaluation reports available. Undertakes research activities.

COMMENTS: Undertakes activities in the Commonwealth of Independent States. Information activities related to the Commonwealth of Independent States.

ACTIVITIES IN DEVELOPING REGIONS: Present in developing regions. Active in 80 country(ies). Maintains local field presence. Works through local field partners. **Sustainable Development Actions:** Debt/finance/trade; Democracy/good governance/institution building/participatory development; Ecology/environment/biodiversity; Education/training/literacy; Gender issues/women; Human rights/peace/conflicts; Sending volunteers/experts/technical assistance; Small enterprises/informal sector/handicrafts. **Regions:** Caribbean; Central Africa; Central Asia and South Asia; East Africa; East Asia; Mexico and Central America; Middle East; North Africa; Oceania; South America; South East Asia; Southern Africa; West Africa.

INFORMATION AND EDUCATION ACTIVITIES: Topics: Culture/tradition/religion; Ecology/environment/biodiversity; Education/training/literacy; Employment/unemployment; Gender issues/women; Human rights/peace/conflicts; International economic relations/trade/debt/finance; International relations/cooperation/development aid; Peace/ethnic conflicts/armament/disarmament; Poverty/living conditions; Racism/xenophobia/antisemitism; Refugees/migrants/ethnic groups. **Activities:** Conferences/seminars/workshops/training activities; Exchanges/twinning/linking; Lobbying/advocacy; Networking/electronic telecommunications; Publishing/audiovisual materials/educational materials.

DEU1056

FRIEDRICH-NAUMANN-STIFTUNG (FNST) ♦ Friedrich Naumann Foundation

Margarethenhof, 53639 Königswinter, Germany.

Telephone: 49 (22) 23 70 10. *Fax:* 49 (22) 23 70 11 88. *Contact:* Fritz Fliszar, Executive Chairman.

OBJECTIVES: To promote liberal values and policies.

GENERAL INFORMATION: *Creation:* 1958. *Personnel/Total:* 270. *Salaried:* 270 of which: 80 in developing countries. *Budget/Total 1993:* ECU 52664000 (US$ 61695000). *Financial sources:* Private: 3%. Public: 97%.

PUBLICATIONS: *Periodicals:* Liberal (4). *Annual report. List of publications.*

PLANNED ACTIVITIES: Promotion of liberal values and policies in Germany.

COMMENTS: Undertakes activities in the Commonwealth of Independent States. Information activities related to the Commonwealth of Independent States.

ACTIVITIES IN DEVELOPING REGIONS: Present in developing regions. Active in 75 country(ies). Maintains local field presence. Works through local field partners. **Sustainable Development Actions:** Democracy/good governance/institution building/participatory development; Human rights/peace/conflicts; Other. **Regions:** Caribbean; Central Africa; Central Asia and South Asia; East Africa; East Asia; Mexico and Central America; Middle East; North Africa; South America; South East Asia; Southern Africa; West Africa.

INFORMATION AND EDUCATION ACTIVITIES: Topics: Human rights/peace/conflicts; International relations/cooperation/development aid; Peace/ethnic conflicts/armament/disarmament; Racism/xenophobia/antisemitism. **Activities:** Conferences/seminars/workshops/training activities; Exchanges/twinning/linking; Lobbying/advocacy.

DEU1057

FRIEDRICH-THIEDING-STIFTUNG

Godesberger Allee 54, 53175 Bonn, Germany.

DEU1058

GEMEINSAN IST ES MOGLICH

Siegstrasse 17, 56410 Montabaur, Germany.

DEU1059

GEMEINSCHAFT DER VINZENZ-KONFERENZEN DEUTSCH-LANDS ♦ Society of Saint Vincent de Paul

Blumenstrasse 20, 50670 Köln, Germany.

Telephone: 49 (221) 13 11 31. *Fax:* 49 (221) 13 89 53. *Contact:* Erich Schmitz, President.

DEU1060

GEMEINSCHAFT ZUR FORDERUNG SOZIAL-MEDIZINISCHER STIFTUNGEN AMBERG ♦ Association for the Promotion of Socio-medical Foundations

Schlottstrasse 3, 8450 Amberg/Opf., Germany.

Telephone: 49 (9621) 6 43 75. *Contact:* Dr. Dietrich W. Luppa.

DEU1061

GERMAN EMERGENCY DOCTORS

Kupferstrasse 7, 5210 Troisdorf 22, Germany.

Contact: Dr. Rupert Neudeck, Chairman.

DEU1062

GERMANWATCH - NORD-SUD INITIATIVE

Adenauerallee 37, 53113 Bonn, Germany.

Telephone: 49 (228) 2 67 98 15. *Fax:* 49 (228) 2 67 98 19. *Contact:* Holger Baum, Chairperson.

OBJECTIVES: To advocate the organisation of countries in the South and change the policies of developed countries.

GENERAL INFORMATION: *Creation:* 1991. *Affiliated to:* Climate Action Network - Bensheimer Kreis (Germany) - Forum Umwelt und Entwicklung (Germany). *Personnel/Total:* 6. Salaried: 4. Volunteers: 2. *Budget/Total 1993:* ECU 258000 (US$ 302000). *Financial sources:* Private: 25%. Public: 50%. Self-financing: 25%.

PUBLICATIONS: *Periodicals:* Membership Newsletter (6) - Action Newsletter (3). *Annual report. List of publications.*

EVALUATION/RESEARCH: Undertakes research activities.

INFORMATION AND EDUCATION ACTIVITIES: Topics: Ecology/environment/biodiversity; Gender issues/women; Human rights/peace/conflicts; International economic relations/trade/debt/finance; International relations/cooperation/development aid; Peace/ethnic conflicts/armament/disarmament; Population/family planning/demography; Poverty/living conditions; Racism/xenophobia/antisemitism; Refugees/migrants/ethnic groups. **Activities:** Conferences/seminars/workshops/training activities; Exchanges/twinning/linking; Fund raising; Information and documentation services/data bases; Information campaigns/exhibitions; Lobbying/advocacy; Networking/electronic telecommunications; Publishing/audiovisual materials/educational materials.

DEU1063

GESELLSCHAFT DER FREUNDE DES SAHRAUISCHEN VOLKES (GFSV) ♦ Association of Friends of the Sahrawi People

Lange Reihe 22, 20099 Hamburg, Germany.

Telephone: 49 (40) 2 80 35 67. *Contact:* Martin Schaedel, President.

OBJECTIVES: To spread information and news of the conflict in Western Sahara and the situation of refugee camps located there. To organise humanitarian aid to refugee camps near Tindouf in Algeria. To reinforce the friendship between the German and Sahrawi people.

GENERAL INFORMATION: *Creation:* 1981. *Affiliated to:* European Committees Coordination for Help to the Sahrawi People. *Personnel/Total:* 103. *Volunteers:* 103. *Budget/Total 1993:* ECU 238000 (US$ 278000). *Financial sources:* Private: 15%. Public: 80%. Self-financing: 5%.

PUBLICATIONS: *Periodicals:* Sahara Info (6).

ACTIVITIES IN DEVELOPING REGIONS: Present in developing regions. Active in 1 country(ies). Works through local field partners. **Sustainable Development Actions:** Education/training/literacy; Emergency relief/refugees/humanitarian assistance; Health/sanitation/water; Human

rights/peace/conflicts; Sending volunteers/experts/technical assistance; Small enterprises/informal sector/handicrafts. **Regions:** North Africa.

INFORMATION AND EDUCATION ACTIVITIES: Topics: Education/training/literacy; Emergency relief/refugees/humanitarian assistance; Health/sanitation/water; Human rights/peace/conflicts. **Activities:** Conferences/seminars/workshops/training activities; Formal education; Fund raising; Information and documentation services/data bases; Information campaigns/exhibitions; Lobbying/advocacy; Publishing/audiovisual materials/educational materials.

DEU1064

GESELLSCHAFT FUR BEDROHTE VOLKER (GFBV) ♦ Association pour les Peuples Menacés

Postfach 2024, 37010 Göttingen, Allemagne.

Téléphone: 49 (551) 49 90 60. *Fax:* 49 (551) 5 80 28. *Contact:* Tilman Zülch, Président.

OBJECTIFS: Organiser des campagnes et services d'information et de documentation, afin de soutenir les peuples et minorités menacés.

INFORMATIONS GENERALES: *Création:* 1968. *Type d'organisation:* réseau. *Organisations membres:* 6. *Personnel/Total:* 320. *Salariés:* 20. *Bénévoles:* 300 dont: 10 dans les pays en développement. *Budget/Total 1993:* ECU 1807000 (US$ 2117000). *Sources financières:* Privé: 70%. Public: 5%. Autofinancement: 25%.

PUBLICATIONS: *Périodiques:* Pogrom-Zeitschrift für bedrohte Völker (6) - Vierte Welt Aktuell (4). *Rapport annuel. Liste des publications.*

COMMENTAIRES: Activités d'information concernant la Communauté des Etats indépendants.

ACTIVITES DANS LES REGIONS EN DEVELOPPEMENT: Intervient dans 25 pays. **Actions de Développement durable:** Droits de l'Homme/paix/conflits. **Régions:** Afrique australe; Afrique centrale; Afrique de l'Est; Afrique de l'Ouest; Afrique du Nord; Amérique du Sud; Asie centrale et Asie du Sud; Asie de l'Est; Asie du Sud-Est; Caraïbes; Mexique et Amerique centrale; Moyen-Orient; Océanie.

ACTIVITES D'INFORMATION ET D'EDUCATION: Domaines: Aliments/famine; Culture/tradition/religion; Droits de l'Homme/paix/conflits; Paix/conflits ethniques/armement/désarmement; Pauvreté/conditions de vie; Racisme/xénophobie/antisémitisme; Réfugiés/migrants/groupes ethniques; Secours d'urgence/réfugiés/aide humanitaire. **Activités:** Campagnes d'information/expositions; Collecte de fonds; Conférences/séminaires/ateliers/activités de formation; Lobbying/plaidoyer; Services d'information et de documentation/bases de données; Édition/documents audiovisuels/documents éducatifs.

DEU1065

GESELLSCHAFT FUR EUROPAISCHE KOMMUNIKATION (EUROCOM) ♦ Society for European Communication

Hallesches Ufer 30, 10963 Berlin, Germany.

Telephone: 49 (30) 2 51 39 02. *Fax:* 49 (30) 2 51 44 25. *Contact:* M. Ernst-Pörksen.

OBJECTIVES: To extend a dialogue for co-operation on economic and financial problems to NGOs in developing countries.

GENERAL INFORMATION: *Creation:* 1989. *Personnel/Total:* 27. *Salaried:* 7 of which: 1 in developing countries. *Volunteers:* 20. *Budget/Total 1993:* ECU 88000 (US$ 103000). *Financial sources:* Private: 10%. Public: 85%. Self-financing: 5%.

EVALUATION/RESEARCH: Evaluation reports available. Undertakes research activities.

PLANNED ACTIVITIES: Youth and cultural exchanges between Palestinians, Israelis, Germans; North-South-West NGOs and Russia-Ukraine-Israel-Germany.

COMMENTS: EUROCOM also organises three offices for Information and Training centres for NGOs in Kiev, Saint Petersburg and Ternopol, Western Ukraine. Undertakes activities in the Commonwealth of Independent States. Information activities related to the Commonwealth of Independent States.

ACTIVITIES IN DEVELOPING REGIONS: Present in developing regions. Active in 5 country(ies). Maintains local field presence. Works through

local field partners. **Sustainable Development Actions:** Children/youth/family; Debt/finance/trade; Democracy/good governance/institution building/participatory development; Ecology/environment/biodiversity; Education/training/literacy; Energy/transport; Gender issues/women; Health/sanitation/water; Human rights/peace/conflicts; Sending volunteers/experts/technical assistance; Small enterprises/informal sector/handicrafts; Urban development/habitat. **Regions:** Middle East; Southern Africa.

INFORMATION AND EDUCATION ACTIVITIES: Topics: Children/youth/family; Culture/tradition/religion; Ecology/environment/biodiversity; Education/training/literacy; Employment/unemployment; Gender issues/women; Human rights/peace/conflicts; International economic relations/trade/debt/finance; International relations/cooperation/development aid; Peace/ethnic conflicts/armament/disarmament; Urban development/habitat. **Activities:** Conferences/seminars/workshops/training activities; Exchanges/twinning/linking; Formal education; Fund raising; Information campaigns/exhibitions; Networking/electronic telecommunications.

DEU1066

GESELLSCHAFT FUR SOLIDARISCHE ENTWICKLUNGSZUSAMMENARBEIT (GSE) ♦ Society for Solidarity Development Cooperation

Georgenkirchstr. 70, 10249 Berlin, Germany.

Telephone: 49 (30) 24 06 32 97. *Fax:* 49 (30) 24 06 32 52. *Contact:* Ramesh Arennamaneni, President of the Board.

OBJECTIVES: To promote an understanding of the world as a global community. To encourage the adoption of alternative attitudes and behavior which can assure a sustainable future.

GENERAL INFORMATION: *Creation:* 1990. *Type of organisation:* association of NGOs, network. *Affiliated to:* Bensheim Cirde (Germany) - Learning and Helping Overseas (Germany) - Forum Appropriate Technology (Germany). *Personnel/Total:* 20. *Volunteers:* 20. *Budget/Total 1993:* ECU 413000 (US$ 484000). *Financial sources:* Private: 7%. Public: 91%. Self-financing: 1%.

PUBLICATIONS: *Periodicals:* GSE INFO-BLATT (2). *Annual report. List of publications.*

EVALUATION/RESEARCH: Evaluation reports available.

ACTIVITIES IN DEVELOPING REGIONS: Active in 3 country(ies). Works through local field partners. **Sustainable Development Actions:** Children/youth/family; Democracy/good governance/institution building/participatory development; Ecology/environment/biodiversity; Education/training/literacy; Emergency relief/refugees/humanitarian assistance; Gender issues/women; Health/sanitation/water; Rural development/agriculture; Sending volunteers/experts/technical assistance; Small enterprises/informal sector/handicrafts; Urban development/habitat. **Regions:** Central Asia and South Asia; East Africa; South America.

INFORMATION AND EDUCATION ACTIVITIES: Topics: Children/youth/family; Culture/tradition/religion; Ecology/environment/biodiversity; Emergency relief/refugees/humanitarian assistance; Gender issues/women; Health/sanitation/water; International economic relations/trade/debt/finance; Poverty/living conditions; Racism/xenophobia/antisemitism; Rural development/agriculture; Urban development/habitat. **Activities:** Conferences/seminars/workshops/training activities; Exchanges/twinning/linking; Fund raising; Information campaigns/exhibitions; Lobbying/advocacy; Publishing/audiovisual materials/educational materials.

DEU1067

GESELLSCHAFT ZUR FORDERUNG INTERDISZIPLINARER PROJEKTE IN LATEINAMERIKA (GELAT) ♦ Society for the Promotion of Interdisciplinary Projects in Latin America

Dominicusstrasse 3, 1000 Berlin 62, Germany.

Telephone: 49 (30) 7 82 31 12. *Contact:* H. Calderon.

DEU1068

GESELLSCHAFT ZUR FORDERUNG KONKRETER ENTWICKLUNGPROJEKTE

Kölner Strasse 20, 58135 Hagen, Germany.

See: *How to Use the Directory*, page 11.

DEU1069

GHANA-AKTION

Chauny Ring 11, 50126 Bergheim, Germany.

Telephone: 49 (227) 16 62 63. *Fax:* 49 (227) 16 62 63. *Contact:* Walter J. Zielniok.

OBJECTIVES: To help the blind and visually handicapped in Africa by providing equipment, medical help, educational work and project partnership.

GENERAL INFORMATION: *Creation:* 1983. *Personnel/Total:* 16. *Salaried:* 1. *Volunteers:* 15. *Budget/Total 1993:* ECU 62000 (US$ 73000). *Financial sources:* Private: 60%. Public: 40%.

PUBLICATIONS: *Periodicals:* Weiter Sehen (2) - Info intern (4). *Annual report.*

PLANNED ACTIVITIES: Opening an eye clinic in Dodi-Papase (Ghana), centres for unemployed youth in Volta-Region (Ghana) and a rehabilitation centre for war disabled children in Bomnanga (Niger). Providing primary health care services in Bomnanga (Niger).

ACTIVITIES IN DEVELOPING REGIONS: Active in 6 country(ies). Works through local field partners. **Sustainable Development Actions:** Children/youth/family; Education/training/literacy; Gender issues/women; Health/sanitation/water; Rural development/agriculture; Sending volunteers/experts/technical assistance; Small enterprises/informal sector/handicrafts. **Regions:** East Africa; Southern Africa; West Africa.

DEU1070

THE GRAIL - INTERNATIONAL MOVEMENT OF CHRISTIAN WOMEN

International Secretariat, Duisburgerstrasse 470, 4330 Mülheim/Ruhr, Germany.

Telephone: 49 (208) 5 16 47.

DEU1071

GREENPEACE GERMANY

Vorsetzallee 53, 2000 Hamburg 11, Germany.

Telephone: 49 (40) 311 86 143. *Fax:* 49 (40) 311 86 141.

DEU1072

HANNS-SEIDEL-STIFTUNG - INSTITUT FUR INTERNATIONALE BEGEGNUNGEN UND ZUSAMMENARBEIT ♦ Fondation Hanns Seidel - Institut des rencontres internationales et de la coopération

Fritz-Schäffer-Str. 7, 53113 Bonn, Allemagne.

Téléphone: 49 (89) 1 25 80. *Fax:* 49 (89) 125 83 38. *Contact:* Karl-Peter Schönfisch.

DEU1073

HAUS DER KULTUREN DER WELT

Ehemalige Kongresshalle, John-Foster-Dulles-Allee 10, 1000 Berlin, Germany.

Telephone: 49 (30) 39 78 70. *Fax:* 49 (30) 3 94 86 79. *Contact:* Günter Coenen.

DEU1074

HEINRICH BOLL STIFTUNG ♦ Heinrich Böll Foudation

Brückenstrasse 5-11, 50667 Köln, Germany.

Telephone: 49 (221) 20 71 10. *Fax:* 49 (221) 2 07 11 51. *E-mail:* hbs-koeln@oln.comlink.apc.org. *Contact:* Frieder Wolf, General Manager.

OBJECTIVES: To promote issues of ecology, participatory democracy and the respect for multi-culturalism at the social and political level.

GENERAL INFORMATION: *Creation:* 1987. *Affiliated to:* Stiftungsverband Regenbogen (Germany) - Bündnis 90 (Germany) - Die Grünen (Germany). *Personnel/Total:* 84. *Salaried:* 34 of which: 2 in developing countries. *Volunteers:* 50. *Budget/Total 1993:*

ECU 5163000 (US$ 6049000). *Financial sources:* Private: 5%. Public: 90%. *Self-financing:* 5%.

PUBLICATIONS: *Annual report. List of publications.*

COMMENTS: Undertakes activities in the Commonwealth of Independent States. Information activities related to the Commonwealth of Independent States.

ACTIVITIES IN DEVELOPING REGIONS: Active in 24 country(ies). Maintains local field presence. Works through local field partners. **Sustainable Development Actions:** Debt/finance/trade; Democracy/good governance/institution building/participatory development; Ecology/environment/biodiversity; Education/training/literacy; Gender issues/women; Human rights/peace/conflicts; Rural development/agriculture; Sending volunteers/experts/technical assistance; Urban development/habitat. **Regions:** Caribbean; Central Asia and South Asia; East Africa; Mexico and Central America; South America; South East Asia; Southern Africa; West Africa.

INFORMATION AND EDUCATION ACTIVITIES: Topics: Children/youth/family; Culture/tradition/religion; Ecology/environment/biodiversity; Education/training/literacy; Employment/unemployment; Gender issues/women; Human rights/peace/conflicts; International economic relations/trade/debt/finance; International relations/cooperation/development aid; Peace/ethnic conflicts/armament/disarmament; Racism/xenophobia/antisemitism; Refugees/migrants/ethnic groups; Rural development/agriculture. **Activities:** Broadcasting/cultural events; Conferences/seminars/workshops/training activities; Exchanges/twinning/linking; Formal education; Information and documentation services/data bases; Lobbying/advocacy; Publishing/audiovisual materials/educational materials.

DEU1075

HELP-HILFE ZUR SELBSTHILFE

Kaiserplatz 3, 53113 Bonn, Germany.

DEU1076

HEPD - ENTWICKLUNGSPOLITIK ♦ Development Policy (Protestant Press Agency)

P.O. Box 500550, 60394 Frankfurt, Germany.

Telephone: 49 (69) 58 09 80. *Fax:* 49 (69) 58 09 81 22. *Contact:* K. Friedrich Schade, Editor in Chief.

OBJECTIVES: To raise the level of consciousness, mainly in the Federal Republic of Germany, regarding issues related to developing countries, through the publication of news, information and documentary analyses of events and trends in these countries.

GENERAL INFORMATION: *Creation:* 1970. *Personnel/Total:* 4. *Salaried:* 4. *Budget/Total 1993:* ECU 258000 (US$ 302000). *Financial sources:* Private: 80%. *Self-financing:* 20%.

PUBLICATIONS: *Periodicals:* EPD-Dritte Welt-Information (12).

EVALUATION/RESEARCH: Evaluation reports available. Undertakes research activities.

INFORMATION AND EDUCATION ACTIVITIES: Topics: Children/youth/family; Culture/tradition/religion; Ecology/environment/biodiversity; Education/training/literacy; Emergency relief/refugees/humanitarian assistance; Employment/unemployment; Food/famine; Gender issues/women; Health/sanitation/water; Human rights/peace/conflicts; International economic relations/trade/debt/finance; International relations/cooperation/development aid; Peace/ethnic conflicts/armament/disarmament; Population/family planning/demography; Poverty/living conditions; Racism/xenophobia/antisemitism; Refugees/migrants/ethnic groups; Rural development/agriculture; Urban development/habitat. **Activities:** Information and documentation services/data bases; Publishing/audiovisual materials/educational materials.

DEU1077

HERBERT-THEIS-STIFTUNG

BischofsgrünerWeg 104, 12247 Berlin, Germany.

DEU1078

HERMANN-GMEINER-FONDS DEUTSCHLAND ♦ Hermann-Gmeiner-Fonds Germany

Voir : *Comment utiliser le répertoire,* page 11.

Menzinger Strasse 23, 80638 München, Germany.

Telephone: 49 (89) 17 91 40. *Fax:* 49 (89) 17 91 41 00. *Contact:* Helmut Kutin, President.

OBJECTIVES: To support the construction and maintenance of SOS-Children's villages which includes projects such as: building schools, training workshops, hospitals, medical centers, nursery schools for orphaned, abandoned children all over the world.

GENERAL INFORMATION: *Creation:* 1963. *Affiliated to:* SOS-Kinderdorf International (Austria) - Deutscher Paritätischer Wohlfahrtsverband (Germany) - Bensheimer Kreis (Germany). *Personnel/Total:* 120. *Salaried:* 120 of which: 70 in developing countries. *Budget/Total 1993:* ECU 103263000 (US$ 120970000). *Financial sources: Private:* 99%.

PUBLICATIONS: *Periodicals:* Zeitschrift der Freunde der SOS-Kinderdörfer in aller Welt (4). *List of publications.*

COMMENTS: Undertakes activities in the Commonwealth of Independent States.

ACTIVITIES IN DEVELOPING REGIONS: Present in developing regions. Active in 122 country(ies). Maintains local field presence. Works through local field partners. **Sustainable Development Actions:** Children/youth/family. **Regions:** Caribbean; Central Africa; Central Asia and South Asia; East Africa; East Asia; Mexico and Central America; Middle East; North Africa; Oceania; South America; South East Asia; Southern Africa; West Africa.

INFORMATION AND EDUCATION ACTIVITIES: Topics: Children/youth/family. **Activities:** Fund raising.

DEU1079

HILFE FUR KINDER IN NOT

Hildsheimer Strasse 139, 30173 Hannover, Germany.

DEU1080

HILFE FUR OSTEEUROPA TODTNAU SEELSCHEID

Meinrad-Thoma-Strasse 19, 79614 Todtnau, Germany.

DEU1081

HILFSWERK DER DEUTSCHEN LIONS ♦ Aid Service of the Lions Club of Germany

St Michael Str. 6, 57072 Siegen, Germany.

Telephone: 49 (271) 4 56 59. *Fax:* 49 (271) 4 29 11. *Contact:* Thomas Wegner.

OBJECTIVES: To help the poor world wide. To support various kinds of projects in developing countries.

GENERAL INFORMATION: *Creation:* 1972. *Type of organisation:* association of NGOs. *Affiliated to:* Bensheimer Kreis (Germany). *Personnel/Total:* 4. *Volunteers:* 4. *Budget/Total 1993:* ECU 1291000 (US$ 1512000). *Financial sources: Private:* 5%. *Public:* 55%. *Self-financing:* 40%.

PUBLICATIONS: *Periodicals:* Lion (12).

PLANNED ACTIVITIES: Building three eye-clinics in South India.

COMMENTS: Undertakes activities in the Commonwealth of Independent States.

ACTIVITIES IN DEVELOPING REGIONS: Present in developing regions. Active in 10 country(ies). Works through local field partners. **Sustainable Development Actions:** Education/training/literacy; Health/sanitation/water. **Regions:** East Africa; Mexico and Central America; South East Asia; Southern Africa; West Africa.

DEU1082

HUMANA KLEIDERHANDEL (HUMANA)

Gross Berliner Damm 82, 12487 Berlin, Germany.

Telephone: 49 (30) 6 31 09 86. *Fax:* 49 (30) 6 31 09 87. *Contact:* Per Knudsen, Executive Director.

OBJECTIVES: To provide development aid to the people of the Third World.

GENERAL INFORMATION: *Creation:* 1989. *Financial sources: Self-financing:* 100%.

ACTIVITIES IN DEVELOPING REGIONS: Active in 3 country(ies). Works through local field partners. **Sustainable Development Actions:** Children/youth/family; Ecology/environment/biodiversity; Education/training/literacy; Emergency relief/refugees/humanitarian assistance; Food/famine; Health/sanitation/water; Rural development/agriculture; Sending volunteers/experts/technical assistance; Small enterprises/informal sector/handicrafts. **Regions:** South East Asia; Southern Africa.

DEU1083

IBERO-AMERIKA VEREIN (IAV) ♦ Ibero-America Association

Alsterglacis 8, 20354 Hamburg, Germany.

Telephone: 49 (40) 41 47 82 02. *Fax:* 49 (40) 45 79 60. *Contact:* Albrecht C. Rädecke.

OBJECTIVES: To support the activities of the private sector in Latin America, the Caribbean abd the Iberian Peninsula. To promote the strengthening of economic, social and cultural ties within these regions.

GENERAL INFORMATION: *Creation:* 1916. *Personnel/Total:* 9. *Salaried:* 9. *Financial sources: Self-financing:* 100%.

PUBLICATIONS: *Periodicals:* Wirtschaftliche Miteilungen (10). *Annual report.*

EVALUATION/RESEARCH: Undertakes research activities.

ACTIVITIES IN DEVELOPING REGIONS: Works through local field partners. **Sustainable Development Actions:** Debt/finance/trade; Other; Small enterprises/informal sector/handicrafts. **Regions:** Caribbean; Mexico and Central America; South America.

INFORMATION AND EDUCATION ACTIVITIES: Topics: International economic relations/trade/debt/finance. **Activities:** Conferences/seminars/workshops/training activities; Information and documentation services/data bases; Information campaigns/exhibitions; Lobbying/advocacy.

DEU1084

IMPORTE AUS AFRIKA, ASIEN, SUD- UND CENTRALAMERIKA (AFRASSCA) ♦ Imports from Africa, Asia, South and Central America

Plinganser Strasse 23, 8000 München 70, Germany.

Telephone: 49 (89) 5 95 04. *Contact:* Bernhard Baier.

DEU1085

INDEPENDENT INSTITUTE FOR PEACE AND CONFLICT RESEARCH

Gundermannstrasse 9, 7072 Leipzig, Germany.

DEU1086

INDIENHILFE - VEREIN FUR DEUTSCH-INDISCHE ENTWICKLUNGSZUSAMMENARBEIT ♦ Association for Indo-German Development Co-operation

Luitpoldstrasse 20, 82211 Herrsching, Germany.

Telephone: 49 (81) 52 12 31. *Contact:* Elisabeth Kreuz.

OBJECTIVES: To co-operate with social movements and project partners in India by means of financial assistance and exchange of information. To publish information in Germany about Indian social movements in order to promote development action.

GENERAL INFORMATION: *Creation:* 1980. *Affiliated to:* Bensheimer Kreis (Germany) - DPWV - IFOAM - Eine Welt für Alle (Germany) -EG-Solar Altötting (Germany). *Personnel/Total:* 18. *Salaried:* 3. *Volunteers:* 15. *Budget/Total 1993:* ECU 207000 (US$ 242000). *Financial sources: Private:* 50%. *Public:* 40%. *Self-financing:* 10%.

PUBLICATIONS: *Annual report. List of publications.*

ACTIVITIES IN DEVELOPING REGIONS: Active in 1 country(ies). Works through local field partners. **Sustainable Development Actions:** Chil-

See: *How to Use the Directory,* page 11.

dren/youth/family; Democracy/good governance/institution building/participatory development; Ecology/environment/biodiversity; Education/training/literacy; Emergency relief/refugees/humanitarian assistance; Energy/transport; Gender issues/women; Health/sanitation/water; Human rights/peace/conflicts; Population/family planning/demography; Rural development/agriculture; Sending volunteers/experts/technical assistance; Small enterprises/informal sector/handicrafts. **Regions:** Central Asia and South Asia.

INFORMATION AND EDUCATION ACTIVITIES: Topics: Children/youth/family; Culture/tradition/religion; Ecology/environment/biodiversity; Education/training/literacy; Emergency relief/refugees/humanitarian assistance; Food/famine; Gender issues/women; Health/sanitation/water; Human rights/peace/conflicts; International economic relations/trade/debt/finance; International relations/cooperation/development aid; Peace/ethnic conflicts/armament/disarmament; Population/family planning/demography; Poverty/living conditions; Refugees/migrants/ethnic groups; Rural development/agriculture; Urban development/habitat. **Activities:** Fund raising; Information and documentation services/data bases; Information campaigns/exhibitions; Publishing/audiovisual materials/educational materials.

DEU1087

INDIENHILFE - VEREIN ZUR UNTERSTUTZUNG UND FORDERUNG NOTLEINDER KINDER

Römerstrasse 90, 50996 Köln, Germany.

DEU1088

INFORMATIONS-, DOKUMENTATIONS- UND AKTIONSZENTRUM GEGEN AUSLAENDERFEINDLICHKEIT FUR EINE MULTIKULTURELLE ZUKUNFT ♦ Information, Documentation and Activity Center against Xenophobia for a Multicultural Future

Charlottenstrasse 55, 40210 Düsseldorf, Germany.

Telephone: 49 (211) 1 64 94 32. *Fax:* 49 (211) 35 13 26. *Contact:* Volker Robocha, Chairman of the Board.

OBJECTIVES: To offer information on anti-foreign development and to call attention to racist tendencies in Germany. To provide youth organisations and interested individuals with information and an overall view of the problem of xenophobia.

GENERAL INFORMATION: *Creation:* 1990. ***Type of organisation:*** association of NGOs. ***Member organisations:*** 22. ***Personnel/Total:*** 3. *Salaried:* 3. ***Budget/Total 1993:*** ECU 155000 (US$ 181000). ***Financial sources:*** Public: 90%. Self-financing: 10%.

PUBLICATIONS: *List of publications.*

INFORMATION AND EDUCATION ACTIVITIES: Topics: Children/youth/family; Racism/xenophobia/antisemitism; Refugees/migrants/ethnic groups. **Activities:** Information and documentation services/data bases.

DEU1089

INFORMATIONSSTELLE LATEINAMERIKA (ILA) ♦ Bureau d'informations Amérique latine

Heerstrasse 205, 5300 Bonn 1, Allemagne.

Téléphone: 49 (228) 65 86 13.

DEU1090

INFORMATIONSSTELLE SUDLICHES AFRIKA (ISSA) ♦ Information Centre on Southern Africa

Königswinterer Strasse 116, 53227 Bonn, Germany.

Telephone: 49 (228) 46 43 69. *Fax:* 49 (228) 46 81 77. *Contact:* Hein Möllers.

OBJECTIVES: To research the conditions in Southern Africa, in particular the scientific analysis of the social, political, economic and racist causes of conflict.To make the results of this research available to the public.

GENERAL INFORMATION: *Creation:* 1971. ***Personnel/Total:*** 4. *Salaried:* 4. ***Budget/Total 1993:*** ECU 114000 (US$ 133000). ***Financial sources:*** Private: 20%. Public: 30%. Self-financing: 50%.

PUBLICATIONS: *Periodicals:* Afrika Süd (6). *List of publications.*

EVALUATION/RESEARCH: Undertakes research activities.

INFORMATION AND EDUCATION ACTIVITIES: Topics: Children/youth/family; Culture/tradition/religion; Ecology/environment/biodiversity; Education/training/literacy; Employment/unemployment; Food/famine; Gender issues/women; Health/sanitation/water; Human rights/peace/conflicts; International economic relations/trade/debt/finance; International relations/cooperation/development aid; Peace/ethnic conflicts/armament/disarmament; Population/family planning/demography; Poverty/living conditions; Racism/xenophobia/antisemitism; Refugees/migrants/ethnic groups; Rural development/agriculture; Urban development/habitat. **Activities:** Conferences/seminars/workshops/training activities; Information and documentation services/data bases.

DEU1091

INFORMATIONSZENTRUM DRITTE WELT (iz3w) ♦ Information Centre for the Third World

Postfach 5328, 79020 Freiburg, Germany.

Telephone: 49 (761) 7 40 03. *Fax:* 49 (761) 70 98 66.

OBJECTIVES: To disseminate information on the problems in developing countries, including those resulting from global trade, racism, nationalism and ecological mismanagement.

GENERAL INFORMATION: *Creation:* 1968. ***Type of organisation:*** coordinating body. ***Affiliated to:*** Bundeskonferenz Entwicklungspolitischer Aktionsgruppen (Germany). ***Personnel/Total:*** 9. *Salaried:* 8. *Volunteers:* 1. ***Budget/Total 1993:*** ECU 26000 (US$ 30000). ***Financial sources:*** Private: 10%. Public: 60%. Self-financing: 30%.

PUBLICATIONS: *Periodicals:* Blätter des iz3w (8). *List of publications.*

EVALUATION/RESEARCH: Undertakes research activities.

COMMENTS: Information activities related to the Commonwealth of Independent States.

ACTIVITIES IN DEVELOPING REGIONS: Maintains local field presence.

INFORMATION AND EDUCATION ACTIVITIES: Topics: Children/youth/family; Culture/tradition/religion; Ecology/environment/biodiversity; Education/training/literacy; Emergency relief/refugees/humanitarian assistance; Employment/unemployment; Food/famine; Gender issues/women; Health/sanitation/water; Human rights/peace/conflicts; International economic relations/trade/debt/finance; International relations/cooperation/development aid; Peace/ethnic conflicts/armament/disarmament; Population/family planning/demography; Poverty/living conditions; Racism/xenophobia/antisemitism; Refugees/migrants/ethnic groups; Rural development/agriculture; Urban development/habitat. **Activities:** Information and documentation services/data bases.

DEU1092

INFORMATIONSZENTRUM DRITTE WELT DORTMUND ♦ Third World Information Centre Dortmund

Luisenstrasse 17, 4600 Dortmund 1, Germany.

Telephone: 49 (231) 14 52 34.

DEU1093

INFORMATIONSZENTRUM DRITTE WELT HANNOVER ♦ Third World Information Centre Hannover

Herzberger Strasse, Postfach 29, 3411 Kattenburg, Germany.

Telephone: 49 (5552) 322. *Contact:* Pastor Martin Weskott.

DEU1094

INKOTA OKUMENISCHES NETZWERK E.V. (INKOTA)

Georgenkirchstr. 70, 10249 Berlin, Germany.

Telephone: 49 (30) 4 38 32 07. *Fax:* 49 (30) 4 38 32 77. *Contact:* Hans-Joachim Döring, Managing Director.

DEU1095

INSTITUT FUR AFRIKA-KUNDE (IAK) ♦ Institute of African Affairs

Neuer Jungfernstieg 21, 20354 Hamburg, Germany.

Telephone: 49 (40) 3 56 25 23. *Fax:* 49 (40) 3 56 25 47. *Contact:* Rolf Hofmeier, Director.

Voir : *Comment utiliser le répertoire,* page 11.

OBJECTIVES: To carry out research and to disseminate information on contemporary social, economic and political developments in Sub-saharan Africa. To provide consultancy services related to development activities.

GENERAL INFORMATION: *Creation:* 1963. *Affiliated to:* Member of Deutsches Übersee-Institut (Germany) - VAD (Germany) - ADAF (Germany) . *Personnel/Total:* 16. *Salaried:* 16. *Budget/Total 1993:* ECU 774000 (US$ 907000). *Financial sources:* Public: 90%. *Self-financing:* 10%.

PUBLICATIONS: *Periodicals:* Afrika Spectrum (3) - Aktneller Informationsdienst Afrika (25). *Annual report. List of publications.*

EVALUATION/RESEARCH: Undertakes research activities.

COMMENTS: IAK focuses on research, documentation. IAK offers limited consultancy and work to policy-making and public institutions. There is not an emphasis on public campaigns and projects.

INFORMATION AND EDUCATION ACTIVITIES: Topics: Culture/tradition/religion; Education/training/literacy; Employment/unemployment; Food/famine; Human rights/peace/conflicts; International economic relations/trade/debt/finance; International relations/cooperation/development aid; Peace/ethnic conflicts/armament/disarmament; Poverty/living conditions; Refugees/migrants/ethnic groups. **Activities:** Publishing/audiovisual materials/educational materials.

DEU1096

INSTITUT FUR ASIENKUNDE IM VERBAND DER STIFTUNG DEUTSCHES UBERSEE-INSTITUT (IFA)

Rothenbaumschaussee 32, 2000 Hamburg, Germany.

Telephone: 49 (40) 44 30 01. *Fax:* 49 (40) 4 10 79 45. *Contact:* Dr Werner Draguhn.

DEU1097

INSTITUT FUR INTERNATIONALE ZUSAMMENARBEIT DES DEUTSCHEN VOLKSHOCHSCHUL-VERBANDES (IIZ-DVV)
♦ Institute for International Co-operation of the German Adult Education Association

Obere Wilhelmstrasse 32, 53225 Bonn, Germany.

Telephone: 49 (228) 97 56 90. *Fax:* 49 (228) 9 75 69 55. *Contact:* Heribert Hinzen, Director.

OBJECTIVES: To promote international co-operation in the field of adult education with partners worldwide, especially with NGOs in developing countries. To increase development work in Eastern Europe. To co-operate with adult education institutions in the European Union.

GENERAL INFORMATION: *Creation:* 1969. *Type of organisation:* association of NGOs. *Member organisations:* 16. *Affiliated to:* European Association for the Education of Adults (Spain) - Bensheimer Kreis (Germany) - Eine Welt für Alle (Germany). *Personnel/Total:* 100. *Salaried:* 100 of which: 80 in developing countries. *Budget/Total 1993:* ECU 7745000 (US$ 9073000). *Financial sources:* Public: 100%.

PUBLICATIONS: *Periodicals:* Adult Education and Development (2) - International Perspectives on ADEP (4) -Volkshodsdulen u.d. Themenbereich Afrika, Asia und Lateinamerika (2). *Annual report. List of publications.*

EVALUATION/RESEARCH: Evaluation reports available. Undertakes research activities.

COMMENTS: Undertakes activities in the Commonwealth of Independent States. Information activities related to the Commonwealth of Independent States.

ACTIVITIES IN DEVELOPING REGIONS: Present in developing regions. Active in 30 country(ies). Maintains local field presence. Works through local field partners. **Sustainable Development Actions:** Democracy/good governance/institution building/participatory development; Ecology/environment/biodiversity; Education/training/literacy; Gender issues/women; Human rights/peace/conflicts; Rural development/agriculture; Sending volunteers/experts/technical assistance; Urban development/habitat. **Regions:** Caribbean; Central Africa; Central Asia and South Asia; East Africa; East Asia; Mexico and Central America; Middle

East; Oceania; South America; South East Asia; Southern Africa; West Africa.

INFORMATION AND EDUCATION ACTIVITIES: Topics: Ecology/environment/biodiversity; Education/training/literacy; Gender issues/women; International relations/cooperation/development aid; Peace/ethnic conflicts/armament/disarmament; Poverty/living conditions; Racism/xenophobia/antisemitism; Refugees/migrants/ethnic groups; Rural development/agriculture; Urban development/habitat. **Activities:** Conferences/seminars/workshops/training activities; Exchanges/twinning/linking; Information and documentation services/data bases; Lobbying/advocacy; Networking/electronic telecommunications; Publishing/audiovisual materials/educational materials.

DEU1098

INSTITUT FUR KULTURELLE WEITERBILDUNG ♦ Institute for Cultural Education

Postfach 102018, Stammstrasse 90, 50458 Köln, Germany.

Telephone: 49 (221) 51 95 00. *Fax:* 49 (221) 52 58 82. *Contact:* Rose Haferkamp.

OBJECTIVES: To promote cultural exchanges and education related to matters of development. To co-operate with self-help organisations.

GENERAL INFORMATION: *Creation:* 1981. *Member organisations:* 7. *Affiliated to:* Organisation for Cultural Policy. *Personnel/Total:* 7. *Salaried:* 1. *Volunteers:* 6. *Budget/Total 1993:* ECU 87000 (US$ 102000). *Financial sources:* Private: 10%. Public: 80%. *Self-financing:* 10%.

PUBLICATIONS: *List of publications.*

EVALUATION/RESEARCH: Undertakes research activities.

ACTIVITIES IN DEVELOPING REGIONS: Active in 1 country(ies). Works through local field partners. **Sustainable Development Actions:** Education/training/literacy. **Regions:** South America; West Africa.

INFORMATION AND EDUCATION ACTIVITIES: Topics: Culture/tradition/religion; Education/training/literacy; Racism/xenophobia/antisemitism; Refugees/migrants/ethnic groups. **Activities:** Conferences/seminars/workshops/training activities; Information campaigns/exhibitions; Publishing/audiovisual materials/educational materials.

DEU1099

INSTITUT FUR WISSENSCHAFTLICHE ZUSAM-MENARBEIT (IWZE) ♦ Institute for Scientific Cooperation

Landhausstrasse 18, 72074 Tübingen, Germany.

Telephone: 49 (071) 50 66. *Fax:* 49 (071) 2 67 53. *Contact:* J. Hohnholz.

OBJECTIVES: To maintain the educational systems of developing countries. To integrate rural development in South and South-East Asia. To study fields such as tropical fish-breeding, aquaculture and ecophysiology. To examine the economic and social problems of the Islamic Orient. To support regional policy and development planning.

GENERAL INFORMATION: *Creation:* 1966. *Personnel/Total:* 315. *Salaried:* 15 of which: 1 in developing countries. *Volunteers:* 300 of which: 100 in developing countries. *Budget/Total 1993:* ECU 774000 (US$ 907000). *Financial sources:* Private: 5%. Public: 90%. *Self-financing:* 5%.

PUBLICATIONS: *List of publications.*

EVALUATION/RESEARCH: Undertakes research activities.

PLANNED ACTIVITIES: The establishment of a centre of horticulture in Sindl, Pakistan.

ACTIVITIES IN DEVELOPING REGIONS: Present in developing regions. Active in 128 country(ies). Maintains local field presence. Works through local field partners. **Sustainable Development Actions:** Rural development/agriculture. **Regions:** Central Africa; Central Asia and South Asia; South East Asia.

DEU1100

INSTITUT FUR WISSENSCHAFTLICHE ZUSAMMENARBEIT MIT ENTWICKLUNGSLANDERN (IWZE)

Landhausstrasse 18, 72074 Tübingen, Germany.

See: *How to Use the Directory,* page 11.

Telephone: 49 (7071) 50 66. **Fax:** 49 (7071) 2 67 53. **Contact:** Wolfgang Voelter, President.

OBJECTIVES: To maintain scientific co-operation with developing countries. To organise programmes with and in developing nations. To provide consultancy to ministries and universities. To transfer technology.

GENERAL INFORMATION: Creation: 1968. **Affiliated to:** AGID - SID. **Personnel/Total:** 14. **Salaried:** 14. **Budget/Total 1993:** ECU 774000 (US$ 907000). **Financial sources:** *Private: 5%. Public: 93%. Self-financing: 2%.*

PUBLICATIONS: *List of publications.*

EVALUATION/RESEARCH: Undertakes research activities.

ACTIVITIES IN DEVELOPING REGIONS: Present in developing regions. Active in 3 country(ies). Maintains local field presence. Works through local field partners. **Sustainable Development Actions:** Rural development/agriculture; Sending volunteers/experts/technical assistance. **Regions:** Central Asia and South Asia; East Asia.

INFORMATION AND EDUCATION ACTIVITIES: Topics: Culture/tradition/religion; Ecology/environment/biodiversity; International economic relations/trade/debt/finance; International relations/cooperation/development aid; Poverty/living conditions; Refugees/migrants/ethnic groups; Rural development/agriculture; Urban development/habitat. **Activities:** Conferences/seminars/workshops/training activities; Formal education; Fund raising; Lobbying/advocacy.

DEU1101
INSTITUTE OF CULTURAL AFFAIRS

Boockholtzstr. 30, 22880 Wedel, Germany.

Contact: Mrs U. Winteler.

DEU1102
INTEGRRAVE SCHULE FRANKFURT AM MAIN GRUND-UND SONDERSCHULE GMBH

Praunheimer Weg 44, 60439 Frankfurt am Main, Germany.

DEU1103
INTER NATIONES (IN)

Kennedyallee 91-103, 53175 Bonn, Germany.

Telephone: 49 (228) 88 00. **Fax:** 49 (228) 88 04 57. **Contact:** Dieter W. Benecke.

OBJECTIVES: To arouse and deepen interest and understanding abroad towards the Federal Republic of Germany by means of realistic and objective information on culture, society, economy and politics.

GENERAL INFORMATION: Creation: 1952. **Affiliated to:** Vereinigung für Internationale Zusammenarbeit (Germany). **Personnel/Total:** 158. *Salaried: 158.* **Budget/Total 1993:** ECU 28914000 (US$ 33872000). **Financial sources:** *Public: 100%.*

PUBLICATIONS: Periodicals: Kultur-Chronile (6) - Humboldt (3) - Fikrun wa Fann (2). *Annual report. List of publications.*

PLANNED ACTIVITIES: German language television course. The purchase of books for German libraries.

COMMENTS: Undertakes activities in the Commonwealth of Independent States. Information activities related to the Commonwealth of Independent States.

ACTIVITIES IN DEVELOPING REGIONS: Sustainable Development Actions: Education/training/literacy. **Regions:** Caribbean; Central Africa; Central Asia and South Asia; East Africa; East Asia; Mexico and Central America; Middle East; North Africa; Oceania; South America; South East Asia; Southern Africa; West Africa.

INFORMATION AND EDUCATION ACTIVITIES: Topics: Culture/tradition/religion; Education/training/literacy. **Activities:** Information and documentation services/data bases; Publishing/audiovisual materials/educational materials.

DEU1104
INTEREG

Postfach 34 01 61, 8000 München 34, Germany.

DEU1105
INTERMEDICA-MEDIKAMENTENHILFE FUR ENTWICKLUNG-SLANDER ♦ Intermedica - Medical Aid for Developing Countries

Im Kalten Tale 33, 38304 Wolfenbüttel, Germany.

Telephone: 49 (5331) 4 68 80. **Contact:** Dr. Ortwin Hantelmann, Chairman.

OBJECTIVES: To provide medicine and medical equipment to hospitals, dispensaries and SOS Chidlren's villages in developing countries.

GENERAL INFORMATION: Creation: 1964. **Affiliated to:** Bensheimer Kreis (Germany). **Personnel/Total:** 10. *Salaried: 2. Volunteers: 8.* **Budget/Total 1993:** ECU 112000 (US$ 131000). **Financial sources:** *Private: 100%.*

PUBLICATIONS: Periodicals: Intermedica-Post (2). *Annual report.*

COMMENTS: Undertakes activities in the Commonwealth of Independent States.

ACTIVITIES IN DEVELOPING REGIONS: Active in 30 country(ies). **Sustainable Development Actions:** Health/sanitation/water. **Regions:** Caribbean; Central Africa; Central Asia and South Asia; East Africa; South America; South East Asia; West Africa.

DEU1106
INTERNATIONAL ALLIANCE OF WOMEN (IAW)

Neue Strasse 10, 79194 Gundelfingen, Germany.

Telephone: 49 (761) 55 22 90. **Fax:** 49 (761) 5 63 15. **Contact:** Marieluise Weber, Convenor for Europe.

OBJECTIVES: To secure all reforms that are necessary to establish equality of liberties, status and opportunities between men and women. To urge women to accept their responsibilities and use their rights and influence in public life. To promote a better quality of life and understanding among people.

GENERAL INFORMATION: Creation: 1902. **Member organisations:** 73. **Personnel/Total:** 48. *Volunteers: 48 of which: 9 in developing countries.* **Budget/Total 1993:** ECU 11000 (US$ 13000). **Financial sources:** *Self-financing: 100%.*

PUBLICATIONS: Periodicals: International Women's News (4).

EVALUATION/RESEARCH: Evaluation reports available. Undertakes research activities.

PLANNED ACTIVITIES: Triennial Congress in India in 1996.

COMMENTS: Undertakes activities in the Commonwealth of Independent States. Information activities related to the Commonwealth of Independent States.

ACTIVITIES IN DEVELOPING REGIONS: Present in developing regions. Active in 28 country(ies). Maintains local field presence. Works through local field partners. **Sustainable Development Actions:** Children/youth/family; Debt/finance/trade; Democracy/good governance/institution building/participatory development; Ecology/environment/biodiversity; Education/training/literacy; Food/famine; Gender issues/women; Health/sanitation/water; Human rights/peace/conflicts; Population/family planning/demography; Rural development/agriculture; Sending volunteers/experts/technical assistance; Small enterprises/informal sector/handicrafts; Urban development/habitat. **Regions:** Caribbean; Central Africa; Central Asia and South Asia; East Africa; East Asia; Mexico and Central America; Middle East; North Africa; Oceania; South East Asia; Southern Africa; West Africa.

INFORMATION AND EDUCATION ACTIVITIES: Topics: Children/youth/family; Ecology/environment/biodiversity; Education/training/literacy; Emergency relief/refugees/humanitarian assistance; Employment/unemployment; Gender issues/women; Health/sanitation/water; Human rights/peace/conflicts; International economic relations/trade/debt/finance; International relations/cooperation/development aid; Other; Peace/ethnic conflicts/armament/disarmament; Population/family planning/demography; Poverty/living conditions; Rural development/agricul-

ture; Urban development/habitat. **Activities:** Conferences/seminars/ workshops/training activities; Exchanges/twinning/linking; Fund raising; Other.

DEU1107

INTERNATIONAL FEDERATION OF ORGANIC AGRICULTURE MOVEMENTS

Ökozentrum, 6695 Tholey-Theley, Germany.

Telephone: 49 (6853) 51 90. *Fax:* 49 (6853) 51 90. *E-mail:* ifoam.secretary@oln.comlink.apc.org.

OBJECTIVES: To represent internationally the organic movement in parliamentary, administrative and policy-making forums. To set and regularly revise international production, processing and trading standards. To co-ordinate a network of the organic movement around the world.

GENERAL INFORMATION: *Creation:* 1972. *Member organisations:* 350. *Personnel/Total:* 22. *Salaried:* 2. *Volunteers:* 20 of which: 8 in developing countries. *Budget/Total 1993:* ECU 165000 (US$ 194000). *Financial sources:* Private: 15%. Public: 5%. *Self-financing:* 80%.

PUBLICATIONS: *Periodicals:* Ecology and Farming (3) - Okologic und Landbau (4). *List of publications.*

COMMENTS: Undertakes activities in the Commonwealth of Independent States. Information activities related to the Commonwealth of Independent States.

ACTIVITIES IN DEVELOPING REGIONS: Active in 50 country(ies). Works through local field partners. **Sustainable Development Actions:** Ecology/environment/biodiversity; Rural development/agriculture. **Regions:** Caribbean; Central Africa; Central Asia and South Asia; East Africa; East Asia; Mexico and Central America; Middle East; North Africa; Oceania; South America; South East Asia; Southern Africa; West Africa.

DEU1108

INTERNATIONAL REFUGEE DOCUMENTATION NETWORK (IRDN)

Schliemannstrasse 23, PO Box 30 11 25, 10722 Berlin, Germany.

Telephone: 49 (30) 4 44 10 88. *Fax:* 49 (30) 4 44 10 85. *E-mail:* bivscomm@combox.de. *Contact:* Co-ordinating Board.

OBJECTIVES: To link institutions that support refugees world wide. To offer information on current migratory movements and regions in crisis.

GENERAL INFORMATION: *Creation:* 1986. *Type of organisation:* network. *Member organisations:* 350. *Personnel/Total:* 2. *Volunteers:* 2. *Budget/Total 1993:* ECU 15000 (US$ 18000). *Financial sources:* Private: 50%. Public: 50%.

PUBLICATIONS: *Periodicals:* IRDN Circular (4). *Annual report. List of publications.*

EVALUATION/RESEARCH: Evaluation reports available. Undertakes research activities.

PLANNED ACTIVITIES: Supporting documentation centers in developing countries, in Eastern and South-Eastern Europe. Providing infrastructural and financial support and training for documentation technologies.

COMMENTS: Undertakes activities in the Commonwealth of Independent States. Information activities related to the Commonwealth of Independent States.

ACTIVITIES IN DEVELOPING REGIONS: Active in 3 country(ies). Maintains local field presence. Works through local field partners. **Sustainable Development Actions:** Emergency relief/refugees/humanitarian assistance; Human rights/peace/conflicts. **Regions:** Caribbean; Central Africa; Central Asia and South Asia; East Africa; East Asia; Mexico and Central America; Middle East; North Africa; Oceania; South America; South East Asia; Southern Africa; West Africa.

INFORMATION AND EDUCATION ACTIVITIES: Topics: Refugees/ migrants/ethnic groups. **Activities:** Conferences/seminars/workshops/ training activities; Fund raising; Information and documentation services/ data bases; Networking/electronic telecommunications.

DEU1109

INTERNATIONAL WORKERS AID (IWA)

Oppelner Strasse 130, 53119 Bonn, Germany.

Telephone: 49 (228) 66 81 40. *Fax:* 49 (228) 6 68 52 09. *Contact:* Rainers Brückers, Secretary General.

OBJECTIVES: To promote the ideas of development co-operation, social welfare, humanitarian aid, development education and international solidarity.

GENERAL INFORMATION: *Creation:* 1951. *Member organisations:* 33. *Affiliated to:* International Confederation of Free Trade Unions. *Personnel/Total:* 3. *Salaried:* 3. *Budget/Total 1993:* ECU 516000 (US$ 605000). *Financial sources:* Private: 40%. Public: 50%. *Self-financing:* 10%.

PLANNED ACTIVITIES: An educational campaign on "Violence against Women: a Block to Development".

COMMENTS: Undertakes activities in the Commonwealth of Independent States.

ACTIVITIES IN DEVELOPING REGIONS: Present in developing regions. Active in 5 country(ies). Works through local field partners. **Sustainable Development Actions:** Democracy/good governance/institution building/participatory development; Emergency relief/refugees/humanitarian assistance; Urban development/habitat. **Regions:** East Africa; Mexico and Central America; South America; Southern Africa; West Africa.

INFORMATION AND EDUCATION ACTIVITIES: Topics: Gender issues/ women. **Activities:** Broadcasting/cultural events; Conferences/seminars/workshops/training activities; Information and documentation services/data bases; Information campaigns/exhibitions; Lobbying/advocacy; Publishing/audiovisual materials/educational materials.

DEU1110

INTERNATIONALE GESELLSCHAFT FUR MENSCHENRECHTE (IGFM) ♦ International Society for Human Rights

Kaiserstrasse 72, 60329 Frankfurt/Main 1, Germany.

Telephone: 49 (69) 23 69 71 / 23 69 72. *Fax:* 49 (69) 23 41 00. *Contact:* Robert Chambers, Secretary General.

OBJECTIVES: To advocate and to provide information and support for human rights movements. To provide concrete help to victims of human rights violations, racism, xenophobia and discrimination. To support democracy and human rights education.

GENERAL INFORMATION: *Creation:* 1982. *Affiliated to:* Earthaction (USA) - Forum Menschenrechte (Germany). *Personnel/Total:* 20. *Salaried:* 20 of which: 4 in developing countries. *Volunteers:* var. of which: var. in developing countries. *Budget/Total 1993:* ECU 1756000 (US$ 2056000). *Financial sources:* Private: 80%. Public: 10%. *Self-financing:* 10%.

PUBLICATIONS: *Periodicals:* Human Rights Worldwide (4) - Menschenrechte (6). *Annual report. List of publications.*

EVALUATION/RESEARCH: Evaluation reports available. Undertakes research activities.

COMMENTS: Undertakes activities in the Commonwealth of Independent States. Information activities related to the Commonwealth of Independent States.

ACTIVITIES IN DEVELOPING REGIONS: Present in developing regions. Active in 8 country(ies). Maintains local field presence. Works through local field partners. **Sustainable Development Actions:** Children/ youth/family; Democracy/good governance/institution building/participatory development; Emergency relief/refugees/humanitarian assistance; Gender issues/women; Human rights/peace/conflicts; Sending volunteers/experts/technical assistance. **Regions:** Caribbean; Central Africa; Central Asia and South Asia; Mexico and Central America; Oceania; South America; South East Asia; Southern Africa; West Africa.

INFORMATION AND EDUCATION ACTIVITIES: Topics: Children/youth/ family; Emergency relief/refugees/humanitarian assistance; Gender issues/women; Human rights/peace/conflicts; International relations/ cooperation/development aid; Peace/ethnic conflicts/armament/disarmament; Racism/xenophobia/antisemitism; Refugees/migrants/ethnic groups. **Activities:** Broadcasting/cultural events; Conferences/semi-

See: *How to Use the Directory,* page 11.

nars/workshops/training activities; Exchanges/twinning/linking; Formal education; Fund raising; Information and documentation services/data bases; Information campaigns/exhibitions; Lobbying/advocacy; Networking/electronic telecommunications; Publishing/audiovisual materials/educational materials.

DEU1111

INTERNATIONALE JUGENDGEMEINSCHAFTSDIENSTE ♦
International Youth Community Services

Tempelhofer Damm 2, 12101 Berlin, Germany.

Telephone: 49 (30) 7 85 20 48. *Fax:* 49 (30) 7 85 90 99. *Contact:* Lourens de Jong, Coordinator for International Exchange.

OBJECTIVES: To undertake educational activities that promote inter-cultural understanding and solidarity with the weaker sectors of society, including those in developing countries. To organise international voluntary workcamps.

GENERAL INFORMATION: *Creation:* 1948. *Affiliated to:* AKLHÜ (Germany) - Deutscher Paritätischer Wohlfahrtsverband (Germany) -Arbeitsgemeinschaft für Jugendhilfe (Germany) - Arbeitskreis Deutscher Bildungsstätten (Germany) - CCIVS (France). *Personnel/Total:* 25. *Salaried:* 25. *Budget/Total 1993:* ECU 2840000 (US$ 3327000). *Financial sources:* Public: 65%. Self-financing: 35%.

PUBLICATIONS: *Periodicals:* IJGD-Rundbrief (4). *Annual report.*

EVALUATION/RESEARCH: Evaluation reports available.

COMMENTS: Undertakes activities in the Commonwealth of Independent States. Information activities related to the Commonwealth of Independent States.

ACTIVITIES IN DEVELOPING REGIONS: Active in 10 country(ies). Maintains local field presence. Works through local field partners. **Sustainable Development Actions:** Ecology/environment/biodiversity; Health/sanitation/water; Rural development/agriculture; Sending volunteers/experts/technical assistance; Urban development/habitat. **Regions:** Central Asia and South Asia; East Africa; Mexico and Central America; North Africa; South America; Southern Africa; West Africa.

INFORMATION AND EDUCATION ACTIVITIES: Topics: Culture/tradition/religion; Ecology/environment/biodiversity; International relations/cooperation/development aid; Racism/xenophobia/antisemitism; Refugees/migrants/ethnic groups. **Activities:** Conferences/seminars/workshops/training activities; Exchanges/twinning/linking; Fund raising; Information and documentation services/data bases; Information campaigns/exhibitions.

DEU1112

INTERNATIONALER ARBEITSKREIS (IAK) ♦ International Study Group

c/o BAZ, Oranienstrasse 159, 1000 Berlin 61, Germany.

Telephone: 49 (30) 6 14 50 98. *Contact:* Theresa Endres.

DEU1113

INTERNATIONALER BUND FUR SOZIALARBEIT - JUGEND-SOZIALWERK (IB-JSW) ♦ International Federation for Social Work - Social Youth Service Association

Ludolfusstrasse 2-4, Postfach 900520, 6000 Frankfurt/Main 90, Germany.

Telephone: 49 (69) 7 95 40. *Fax:* 49 (69) 7954 203. *Contact:* Dr. Georg Leber.

DEU1114

INTERNATIONALER CHRISTLICHER FRIEDENS-DIENST (EIRENE) ♦ Service Chrétien International pour la Paix

Engerserstrasse 74 B, 56564 Neuwied, Allemagne.

Téléphone: 49 (2631) 8 37 90. *Fax:* 49 (2631) 3 11 60. *Contact:* Anne Dietrich.

OBJECTIFS: Travailler pour la justice et la paix en soutenant financièrement des partenaires en Amérique Latine et en Afrique. Soutenir le développement et le changement écologique au Nord. Envoyer des volontaires en Amérique Latine, en Afrique, en Europe et en Amérique du Nord.

INFORMATIONS GENERALES: *Création:* 1957. *Type d'organisation:* regroupement d'ONG. *Affiliée à:* Mouvement International pour la Reconciliation - Brethren Service - Mennonite Central Committee. *Personnel/Total:* 128. *Salariés:* 20 dont: 8 dans les pays en développement. *Bénévoles:* 70 dont: 30 dans les pays en développement. *Budget/Total 1993:* ECU 2169000 (US$ 2540000). *Sources financières:* Privé: 35%. *Public:* 35%. *Autofinancement:* 30%.

PUBLICATIONS: *Périodiques:* EIRENE Rundbrief (4). *Rapport annuel. Liste des publications.*

PREVISIONS D'ACTIVITES: Travailler pour le développement et contre la violence au Sud et au Nord. La commercialisation dans la coopération entre les ONG du Nord et du Sud.

COMMENTAIRES: Intervient dans la Communauté des Etats indépendants.

ACTIVITES DANS LES REGIONS EN DEVELOPPEMENT: Intervient directement dans les régions en développement. Intervient dans 28 pays. Maintient une présence locale sur le terrain. Intervient par l'intermédiaire d'organisations locales partenaires. **Actions de Développement durable:** Droits de l'Homme/paix/conflits; Démocratie/bonne gestion publique/création d'institutions/développement participatif; Développement rural/agriculture; Développement urbain/habitat; Enfants/jeunesse/famille; Envoi de volontaires/experts/assistance technique; Petites entreprises/secteur informel/artisanat; Questions relatives aux femmes; Écologie/environnement/biodiversité; Éducation/formation/alphabétisation. **Régions:** Afrique centrale; Afrique de l'Ouest; Amérique du Sud; Mexique et Amerique centrale.

ACTIVITES D'INFORMATION ET D'EDUCATION: Domaines: Culture/tradition/religion; Droits de l'Homme/paix/conflits; Développement rural/agriculture; Développement urbain/habitat; Enfants/jeunesse/famille; Paix/conflits ethniques/armement/désarmement; Pauvreté/conditions de vie; Écologie/environnement/biodiversité; Éducation/formation/alphabétisation. **Activités:** Campagnes d'information/expositions; Collecte de fonds; Conférences/séminaires/ateliers/activités de formation; Lobbying/plaidoyer; Radiodiffusion/manifestations culturelles; Services d'information et de documentation/bases de données; Échanges/parrainage/jumelage; Éducation formelle.

DEU1115

INTERNATIONALER VERBAND WESTFALISCHER KINDERDORFER ♦ International Association of Westphalian Children's Villages

Von Dript Weg 2, 33098 Paderborn, Germany.

Telephone: 49 (525) 2 15 12 50. *Fax:* 49 (525) 2 15 30 11. *Contact:* Friedhelm Bertling, President.

OBJECTIVES: To provide homes, school education and an apprenticeship to homeless children.

GENERAL INFORMATION: *Creation:* 1977. *Type of organisation:* association of NGOs. *Affiliated to:* Deutscher Spendenrat (Germany). *Salaried:* 8 of which: 3 in developing countries. *Budget/Total 1993:* ECU 415000 (US$ 486000). *Financial sources:* Private: 100%.

PUBLICATIONS: *Annual report.*

EVALUATION/RESEARCH: Evaluation reports available.

PLANNED ACTIVITIES: Building a new family house in the Children's Village Peru.

ACTIVITIES IN DEVELOPING REGIONS: Active in 3 country(ies). Works through local field partners. **Sustainable Development Actions:** Children/youth/family. **Regions:** Central Asia and South Asia; South America; West Africa.

INFORMATION AND EDUCATION ACTIVITIES: Topics: Children/youth/family. **Activities:** Fund raising; Publishing/audiovisual materials/educational materials.

DEU1116

INTERNATIONALES INSTITUT FUR JOURNALISMUS IN BERLIN (IIJ)

Budapester Strasse 41, 10781 Berlin, Germany.

Telephone: 49 (30) 2 62 20 25. *Fax:* 49 (30) 2 62 56 94. *Contact:* Robert H. Lochner, Director.

OBJECTIVES: To organise 3 advanced three-months training courses in Berlin for print journalists from Africa and Asia; and 3 two-week overseas seminars each year.

GENERAL INFORMATION: *Creation:* 1964. *Personnel/Total:* 5. *Salaried:* 5. *Budget/Total 1993:* ECU 929000 (US$ 1089000). *Financial sources:* Public: 100%.

PLANNED ACTIVITIES: A yearly course for journalists from Eastern European countries.

COMMENTS: IIJ also has about 30 free-lance lecturers as part of the staff. Undertakes activities in the Commonwealth of Independent States. Information activities related to the Commonwealth of Independent States.

ACTIVITIES IN DEVELOPING REGIONS: Present in developing regions. Active in 54 country(ies). **Sustainable Development Actions:** Ecology/environment/biodiversity; Education/training/literacy. **Regions:** Central Africa; Central Asia and South Asia; East Africa; East Asia; Middle East; North Africa; South East Asia; Southern Africa; West Africa.

INFORMATION AND EDUCATION ACTIVITIES: Topics: International economic relations/trade/debt/finance; International relations/cooperation/development aid. **Activities:** Conferences/seminars/workshops/training activities; Formal education.

DEU1117

IPS-DRITTE WELT NACHRICHTENAGENTUR ♦ IPS - Third World News Agency

Pressehaus II, Zimmer 205/8, Heussallee 2-10, 5300 Bonn, Germany.

Telephone: 49 (228) 21 91 38. *Fax:* 49 (228) 26 12 05. *Contact:* Ramesh Jaura, Director.

DEU1118

JUGEND DRITTE WELT ♦ Youth Third World

Strässchensweg 3, 53113 Bonn, Germany.

Telephone: 49 (228) 23 10 84. *Fax:* 49 (228) 23 44 88. *Contact:* Hubertus Kribken, President.

OBJECTIVES: To support projects in the sector of education, schools and professional formation in collaboration with the Society of the Salesians of Don Bosco.

GENERAL INFORMATION: *Creation:* 1979. *Type of organisation:* network. *Affiliated to:* Comide International (Belgium). *Personnel/Total:* 6. *Salaried:* 4. *Volunteers:* 2. *Financial sources:* Private: 38%. *Public:* 60%. *Self-financing:* 2%.

PUBLICATIONS: *Periodicals:* Don Bosco Telex (4). *Annual report.*

EVALUATION/RESEARCH: Evaluation reports available.

COMMENTS: Undertakes activities in the Commonwealth of Independent States. Information activities related to the Commonwealth of Independent States.

ACTIVITIES IN DEVELOPING REGIONS: Works through local field partners. **Sustainable Development Actions:** Education/training/literacy; Food/famine; Rural development/agriculture; Small enterprises/informal sector/handicrafts. **Regions:** Central Africa; Central Asia and South Asia; East Africa; East Asia; Mexico and Central America; South America; South East Asia; West Africa.

DEU1119

JUGEND-BILDUNG-HILFE IN BOLIVIEN (JBH) ♦ Aide à l'éducation de la jeunesse en Bolivie

Eicheneck 1, 8970 Immenstadt, Allemagne.

Téléphone: 49 (8323) 84 23. *Contact:* Richard Stängl, Président.

DEU1120

JURGEN-WAHN-STIFTUNG

Aldergreverwall 31, 59494 Soest, Germany.

DEU1121

KARL KUBEL STIFTUNG FUR KIND UND FAMILIE (KKS) ♦ Karl Kübel Foundation for Child and Family

Postfach 1563, 64605 Bensheim, Germany.

Telephone: 49 (625) 17 00 50. *Fax:* 49 (625) 1 70 05 55. *Contact:* George Arickal.

OBJECTIVES: To improve the living conditions of people in developing countries and to encourage self-help capacities. To enable parents in developing countries to promote the mental and spiritual development of their children.

GENERAL INFORMATION: *Creation:* 1966. *Affiliated to:* Bensheimer Kreis (Germany). *Personnel/Total:* 37. *Salaried:* 37 of which: 4 in developing countries.

PUBLICATIONS: *Annual report.*

COMMENTS: Undertakes activities in the Commonwealth of Independent States.

ACTIVITIES IN DEVELOPING REGIONS: Active in 3 country(ies). Works through local field partners. **Sustainable Development Actions:** Children/youth/family; Democracy/good governance/institution building/participatory development; Ecology/environment/biodiversity; Education/training/literacy; Emergency relief/refugees/humanitarian assistance; Gender issues/women; Health/sanitation/water; Rural development/agriculture. **Regions:** Central Asia and South Asia; East Africa.

DEU1122

KARTEI DER NOT-HILFSWERK DER AUGSBURGER ALLGEMEINEN UND DER ALLGAUER ZEITUNG MIT IHREN HEIMATBLATTERN

Curt Frenzel Strasse 2, 86167 Augsburg, Germany.

DEU1123

KATHOLISCHE ZENTRALSTELLE FUR ENTWICKLUNGSHILFE ♦ Catholic Central Agency for Development Aid

Mozartstrasse 9, Postfach 14 50, 5100 Aachen, Germany.

Telephone: 49 (241) 4420. *Fax:* 49 (241) 44 21 88. *Contact:* Paul Bocklet, Chairman.

DEU1124

KATHOLISCHER AKADEMISCHER AUSLANDER-DIENST (KAAD) ♦ Catholic Service for Foreign Students

Hausdorffstrasse 151, 53129 Bonn, Germany.

Telephone: 49 (228) 91 75 80. *Fax:* 49 (228) 9 17 58 58. *Contact:* Peter Hünermann.

OBJECTIVES: To provide scholarships for students and scientists. To hold cultural events and seminars for foreign students.

GENERAL INFORMATION: *Creation:* 1958. *Personnel/Total:* 20. *Salaried:* 20. *Budget/Total 1993:* ECU 5060000 (US$ 5928000). *Financial sources:* Public: 100%.

PUBLICATIONS: *Periodicals:* Jahresakademic (1). *Annual report. List of publications.*

COMMENTS: Information activities related to the Commonwealth of Independent States.

INFORMATION AND EDUCATION ACTIVITIES: Topics: Culture/tradition/religion; International economic relations/trade/debt/finance; Racism/xenophobia/antisemitism; Refugees/migrants/ethnic groups. **Activities:** Conferences/seminars/workshops/training activities; Lobbying/advocacy.

See: *How to Use the Directory,* page 11.

DEU1125
KINDER- UND LEPRAHILFE ANDHERI

Markstrasse 27, 48249 Dülmen, Germany.

DEU1126
KINDERDORF RIO ♦ Children's Village Rio

Brücktorstrasse 139 A, 46047 Oberhausen, Germany.

Telephone: 49 (208) 87 45 30.

DEU1127
KINDERHILFSWERK FUR DIE DRITTE WELT ♦ Oeuvre d'aide à l'enfance du Tiers monde

Hamburger Strasse 11, 22083 Hamburg, Allemagne.

Téléphone: 49 (40) 2 27 99 96. *Fax:* 49 (40) 2 27 98 69. *Contact:* Hans-Georg Graichen, Président .

OBJECTIFS: Aider les enfants et adolescents en détresse dans les pays en voie de développement. Faciliter le développement socio-sanitaire de ces pays.

INFORMATIONS GENERALES: *Création:* 1975. *Affiliée à:* Bensheimer Kreis (Allemagne) - Deutscher Paritätischer Wohlfahrtsverband (Allemagne). *Personnel/Total:* 4. *Salariés:* 4 dont: 3 dans les pays en développement. *Budget/Total 1993:* ECU 294000 (US$ 345000). *Sources financières:* Privé: 47%. Public: 53%.

PUBLICATIONS: *Périodiques:* Circulaire à l'adresse des donateurs (4). *Rapport annuel.*

PREVISIONS D'ACTIVITES: Construction de centres de santé pour les mères et enfants de la région francophone de l'Afrique.

ACTIVITES DANS LES REGIONS EN DEVELOPPEMENT: Intervient directement dans les régions en développement. Intervient dans 6 pays. Maintient une présence locale sur le terrain. **Actions de Développement durable:** Développement rural/agriculture; Enfants/jeunesse/famille; Santé/assainissement/eau; Éducation/formation/alphabétisation. **Régions:** Afrique australe; Afrique de l'Ouest; Amérique du Sud; Asie centrale et Asie du Sud; Caraïbes.

DEU1128
KINDERMISSIONSWERK ♦ Holy Childhood

Stephanstrasse 35, 52064 Aachen, Germany.

Telephone: 49 (241) 2 10 67. *Fax:* 49 (241) 2 10 60. *Contact:* Arnold Poll, President.

OBJECTIVES: To help children live a fuller life in their society. To disseminate information on this theme in Germany and to support projects for children and youth in developing countries.

GENERAL INFORMATION: *Creation:* 1846. *Affiliated to:* Pontifical Mission Aid Services. *Personnel/Total:* 80045. *Salaried:* 45. *Volunteers:* 80000. *Financial sources:* Private: 93%. Public: 6%. *Self-financing:* 1%.

PUBLICATIONS: *Periodicals:* Die Sternsinger-Mission (4) - Schule und Mission (4) - Kindergarten und Mission (2). *Annual report. List of publications.*

ACTIVITIES IN DEVELOPING REGIONS: Active in 101 country(ies). Works through local field partners. **Sustainable Development Actions:** Children/youth/family; Education/training/literacy; Food/famine; Health/sanitation/water; Rural development/agriculture; Small enterprises/informal sector/handicrafts; Urban development/habitat. **Regions:** Caribbean; Central Africa; Central Asia and South Asia; East Africa; East Asia; Mexico and Central America; Middle East; North Africa; Oceania; South America; South East Asia; Southern Africa; West Africa.

INFORMATION AND EDUCATION ACTIVITIES: Topics: Children/youth/family. **Activities:** Fund raising; Lobbying/advocacy; Publishing/audiovisual materials/educational materials.

DEU1129
KINDERNOTHILFE ♦ Help for Children in Need

p.o. bOX 281143, 47249 Duisburg, Germany.

Telephone: 49 (203) 7 78 90. *Fax:* 49 (203) 7 78 91 18. *Contact:* Rev. Hanns P. Keiling, Director.

OBJECTIVES: To support poor children and youth. To provide the German public with development-related information and education.

GENERAL INFORMATION: *Creation:* 1959. *Affiliated to:* Bensheimer Kreis - Platform EU - Arbeitsgemeinschaft Entwicklungsbezog Bildung und Offenteichtreitanbeit - Initiative "Entwicklung Braucht Entschulding". *Personnel/Total:* 140. *Salaried:* 140 of which: 4 in developing countries. *Budget/Total 1993:* ECU 38104000 (US$ 44638000). *Financial sources:* Private: 99%. Public: 1%.

PUBLICATIONS: *Periodicals:* Zeitschrift Kindernothilfe - Jugendzeitschrift WAOW. *Annual report. List of publications.*

COMMENTS: The organisation's street address is Düseldorfer Landstrasse 180, 47241 Duisburg.

ACTIVITIES IN DEVELOPING REGIONS: Active in 27 country(ies). Maintains local field presence. Works through local field partners. **Sustainable Development Actions:** Children/youth/family; Democracy/good governance/institution building/participatory development; Education/training/literacy; Emergency relief/refugees/humanitarian assistance; Energy/transport; Gender issues/women; Health/sanitation/water; Human rights/peace/conflicts; Rural development/agriculture; Small enterprises/informal sector/handicrafts; Urban development/habitat. **Regions:** Central Asia and South Asia; East Africa; East Asia; Mexico and Central America; South America; South East Asia; Southern Africa.

INFORMATION AND EDUCATION ACTIVITIES: Topics: Children/youth/family; Ecology/environment/biodiversity; Education/training/literacy; Employment/unemployment; Gender issues/women; Health/sanitation/water; International economic relations/trade/debt/finance; Poverty/living conditions; Refugees/migrants/ethnic groups. **Activities:** Conferences/seminars/workshops/training activities; Formal education; Information and documentation services/data bases; Information campaigns/exhibitions; Publishing/audiovisual materials/educational materials.

DEU1130
KIRCHE IN NOT-OSTPRIESTERHILFE DEUTSCHLAND

Albert Rosshaupter Strasse 16, 81169 München, Germany.

DEU1131
KIRCHLICHER ENTWICKLUNGSDIENST DER EVANGELISCHEN KIRCHE IN DEUTSCHLAND (KED) ♦ The Churches' Development Service

Herrenhäuserstrasse 12, 30419 Hannover, Germany.

Telephone: 49 (511) 2 79 6 0. *Fax:* 49 (511) 2 79 67 17. *Contact:* Warner Conring.

OBJECTIVES: To support development projects in health, agriculture, social work and community development. To help structure local churches to carry out development projects in these fields. To increase awareness of the Church's policy on development issues.

GENERAL INFORMATION: *Creation:* 1968. *Member organisations:* 25. *Affiliated to:* Arbeitsgemeinschaft Kirchlicher Entwicklungsdienst (Germany). *Personnel/Total:* 7. *Salaried:* 7. *Budget/Total 1993:* ECU 68154000 (US$ 79840000). *Financial sources:* Private: 100%.

COMMENTS: Undertakes activities in the Commonwealth of Independent States.

ACTIVITIES IN DEVELOPING REGIONS: Works through local field partners. **Sustainable Development Actions:** Children/youth/family; Democracy/good governance/institution building/participatory development; Ecology/environment/biodiversity; Education/training/literacy; Emergency relief/refugees/humanitarian assistance; Energy/transport; Food/famine; Gender issues/women; Health/sanitation/water; Human rights/peace/conflicts; Population/family planning/demography; Rural development/agriculture; Sending volunteers/experts/technical assistance; Small enterprises/informal sector/handicrafts; Urban develop-

Voir : *Comment utiliser le répertoire*, page 11.

ment/habitat. **Regions:** Caribbean; Central Africa; Central Asia and South Asia; East Africa; East Asia; Mexico and Central America; Middle East; North Africa; Oceania; South America; Southern Africa; West Africa.

INFORMATION AND EDUCATION ACTIVITIES: Topics: Culture/tradition/religion; Food/famine; Gender issues/women; Human rights/peace/conflicts; International economic relations/trade/debt/finance; Peace/ethnic conflicts/armament/disarmament; Population/family planning/demography; Poverty/living conditions; Racism/xenophobia/antisemitism; Refugees/migrants/ethnic groups. **Activities:** Conferences/seminars/workshops/training activities; Lobbying/advocacy.

DEU1132

KOMITEE ARZTE FUR DIE DRITTE WELT ♦ German Doctors for Developing Countries

Elsheimerstrasse 9, 60322 Frankfurt, Germany.

Telephone: 49 (69) 71 91 14 56. *Fax:* 49 (69) 71 91 14 50. *Contact:* P. Bernhard Ehlen.

OBJECTIVES: To provide voluntary medical assistance in slums and rural areas in developing countries. To help train local doctors and health workers. To educate the public in Germany about development issues.

GENERAL INFORMATION: *Creation:* 1983. *Personnel/Total:* 250. *Salaried:* 205 of which: 200 in developing countries. *Volunteers:* 45 of which: 35 in developing countries. *Budget/Total 1993:* ECU 4544000 (US$ 5323000). *Financial sources:* Private: 60%. Public: 40%.

PUBLICATIONS: *Periodicals:* Rundbrief (3).

ACTIVITIES IN DEVELOPING REGIONS: Present in developing regions. Active in 13 country(ies). Maintains local field presence. Works through local field partners. **Sustainable Development Actions:** Children/youth/family; Debt/finance/trade; Ecology/environment/biodiversity; Education/training/literacy; Emergency relief/refugees/humanitarian assistance; Food/famine; Gender issues/women; Health/sanitation/water; Human rights/peace/conflicts; Population/family planning/demography; Rural development/agriculture; Sending volunteers/experts/technical assistance; Small enterprises/informal sector/handicrafts; Urban development/habitat. **Regions:** Central Asia and South Asia; Mexico and Central America; South America; South East Asia.

INFORMATION AND EDUCATION ACTIVITIES: Topics: Children/youth/family; Emergency relief/refugees/humanitarian assistance; Food/famine; Gender issues/women; Health/sanitation/water; Population/family planning/demography; Poverty/living conditions; Refugees/migrants/ethnic groups; Rural development/agriculture; Urban development/habitat. **Activities:** Conferences/seminars/workshops/training activities; Formal education; Fund raising; Information campaigns/exhibitions; Lobbying/advocacy.

DEU1133

KOMITEE CAP ANAMUR

Kupferstr. 7, 5210 Troisdorf, Germany.

Telephone: 49 (22 41) 4 60 20. *Fax:* 49 (22 41) 40 11 91. *Contact:* Dr Rupert Neudeck.

DEU1134

KOMMUNALES KINO ♦ Communal Cinema

Im Alten Wiehrebahnhof, Urachstrasse 40, 7800 Freiburg, Germany.

Contact: W. Karow, Chairman.

DEU1135

KONRAD-ADENAUER-STIFTUNG

Rathausallee 12, 53757 St Augustin, Germany.

Contact: Mr Nobert.

DEU1136

KULTURBURO 3. WELT - KULTUR-COOPERATION AFRIKA, ASIEN, LATEIN AMERIKA ♦ Third World Culture Office - Culture Co-operation Africa, Asia, Latin America

Nernstweg 32-34, 2000 Hamburg 50, Germany.

Telephone: 49 (40) 39 41 33/ 390 94 63. *Contact:* Judy Engelhardt.

DEU1137

LANDESGEMEINSCHAFT NATURSCHUTZ UND UMWELT NORDRHEIN WESTFALEN ♦ North-Rhemish-Westphalian Society for Conservation of Nature and Environment

Postfach 420606, 50900 Köln, Germany.

Telephone: 49 (221) 41 69 24. *Fax:* 49 (221) 0 29 32. *Contact:* Hermann-Josef Roth.

GENERAL INFORMATION: *Creation:* 1976. *Member organisations:* 73. *Affiliated to:* Deutscher Naturschutzring (Germany). *Personnel/Total:* 8. *Salaried:* 3. *Volunteers:* 5. *Budget/Total 1993:* ECU 258000 (US$ 302000). *Financial sources:* Private: 20%. Public: 20%. *Self-financing:* 60%.

PUBLICATIONS: *Periodicals:* Natur und Umweltschutz (4) - Arnsberger Gespräche (1). *Annual report. List of publications.*

EVALUATION/RESEARCH: Evaluation reports available. Undertakes research activities.

ACTIVITIES IN DEVELOPING REGIONS: Active in 5 country(ies). Works through local field partners. **Sustainable Development Actions:** Ecology/environment/biodiversity. **Regions:** South America.

INFORMATION AND EDUCATION ACTIVITIES: Topics: Ecology/environment/biodiversity. **Activities:** Information and documentation services/data bases; Information campaigns/exhibitions; Publishing/audiovisual materials/educational materials.

DEU1138

LATEINAMERIKA-ZENTRUM (LAZ) ♦ Latin America Centre

Argelanderstrasse 59, 53113 Bonn, Germany.

Telephone: 49 (228) 21 07 88. *Fax:* 49 (228) 24 16 58. *Contact:* Helmut Hoffmann, Vice President.

OBJECTIVES: To improve the living conditions of the needy population in Latin America through educational projects for children and adolescents, professional training projects, rural development and medical care.

GENERAL INFORMATION: *Creation:* 1961. *Affiliated to:* Deutche EU-Plattform (Germany). *Personnel/Total:* 9. *Salaried:* 6 of which: 1 in developing countries. *Volunteers:* 3 of which: 3 in developing countries. *Budget/Total 1993:* ECU 1859000 (US$ 2177000). *Financial sources:* Private: 8%. Public: 85%. *Self-financing:* 7%.

PUBLICATIONS: *Periodicals:* Deutsch-Brasilianisches Heft (4). *Annual report.*

ACTIVITIES IN DEVELOPING REGIONS: Active in 5 country(ies). Maintains local field presence. Works through local field partners. **Sustainable Development Actions:** Children/youth/family; Ecology/environment/biodiversity; Education/training/literacy; Gender issues/women; Health/sanitation/water; Rural development/agriculture; Urban development/habitat. **Regions:** Mexico and Central America; South America.

INFORMATION AND EDUCATION ACTIVITIES: Topics: Children/youth/family; Culture/tradition/religion; Ecology/environment/biodiversity; Education/training/literacy; Employment/unemployment; Gender issues/women; Health/sanitation/water; Poverty/living conditions; Rural development/agriculture; Urban development/habitat. **Activities:** Fund raising; Information and documentation services/data bases.

DEU1139

LATEINAMERIKAKREIS DER KATHOLISCHEN STUDENTINNENGEMEINDE BERLIN ♦ Latin America Circle of the Catholic Students' Community Berlin

Klopstockstrasse 31, 1000 Berlin 21, Germany.

Telephone: 49 (30) 3 91 70 71.

DEU1140

LEBENSHILFE FUR GEISTIG BEHINDERTE KREISVEREINIGUNG EHEMALIGER DILLKREIS

Am Forstdenkmal 9, 35683 Dillenburg, Germany.

DEU1141

MALTESER AUSLANDSDIENST ♦ Maltese Cross Foreign Service

Steinfelder Giasse 9, 50670 Köln, Germany.

Telephone: 49 (221) 1 60 29 02. *Fax:* 49 (221) 1 60 29 63. *Contact:* Johannes Freiherr Heereman von Zuydtwyck.

OBJECTIVES: To support disaster relief, emergency and development aid.

GENERAL INFORMATION: *Creation:* 1953. *Affiliated to:* Order of Malta (Italy) - VOICE (Belgium). *Personnel/Total:* 65. *Salaried:* 35 of which: 20 in developing countries. *Volunteers:* 30 of which: 25 in developing countries. *Budget/Total 1993:* ECU 7848000 (US$ 9194000). *Financial sources:* Private: 40%. Public: 31%. Self-financing: 29%.

PUBLICATIONS: *Periodicals:* Malteser-Mitteilüngen (6) - Malteser-Aüslandsinfo (4). *Annual report.*

EVALUATION/RESEARCH: Evaluation reports available.

COMMENTS: Undertakes activities in the Commonwealth of Independent States. Information activities related to the Commonwealth of Independent States.

ACTIVITIES IN DEVELOPING REGIONS: Present in developing regions. Active in 10 country(ies). Maintains local field presence. Works through local field partners. **Sustainable Development Actions:** Children/youth/family; Emergency relief/refugees/humanitarian assistance; Food/famine; Health/sanitation/water; Population/family planning/demography; Sending volunteers/experts/technical assistance. **Regions:** Central Africa; Central Asia and South Asia; East Africa; Mexico and Central America; Middle East; South America; South East Asia; Southern Africa.

INFORMATION AND EDUCATION ACTIVITIES: Topics: Children/youth/family; Culture/tradition/religion; Emergency relief/refugees/humanitarian assistance; Food/famine; Health/sanitation/water; Population/family planning/demography; Poverty/living conditions; Refugees/migrants/ethnic groups. **Activities:** Conferences/seminars/workshops/training activities; Exchanges/twinning/linking; Formal education; Fund raising; Information and documentation services/data bases; Information campaigns/exhibitions; Lobbying/advocacy; Publishing/audiovisual materials/educational materials.

DEU1142

MEDICAL WOMEN'S INTERNATIONAL ASSOCIATION (MWIA)

Herbert-Lewin-Strasse 1, 50931 Köln, Germany.

Telephone: 49 (221) 40 05 58. *Fax:* 49 (221) 4 00 45 57. *Contact:* Carolyn Motzel, Secretary General.

OBJECTIVES: To encourage the entry of women into the medical field. To foster friendship and understanding among medical women everywhere. To aid such women in developing countries by offering scholarships and fellowships to study abroad.

GENERAL INFORMATION: *Creation:* 1919. *Personnel/Total:* 2. *Salaried:* 2. *Financial sources:* Self-financing: 100%.

PUBLICATIONS: *Periodicals:* Circular Letter (4) - Newsletter Letter (2).

EVALUATION/RESEARCH: Evaluation reports available. Undertakes research activities.

COMMENTS: Undertakes activities in the Commonwealth of Independent States. Information activities related to the Commonwealth of Independent States.

ACTIVITIES IN DEVELOPING REGIONS: Present in developing regions. Active in 20 country(ies). Maintains local field presence. Works through local field partners. **Sustainable Development Actions:** Children/youth/family; Education/training/literacy; Gender issues/women; Health/sanitation/water; Human rights/peace/conflicts; Population/family planning/demography; Sending volunteers/experts/technical assistance. **Regions:** Caribbean; Central Asia and South Asia; East Africa; East Asia; Mexico and Central America; North Africa; Oceania; South America; Southern Africa; West Africa.

INFORMATION AND EDUCATION ACTIVITIES: Topics: Children/youth/family; Culture/tradition/religion; Gender issues/women; Health/sanitation/water; Human rights/peace/conflicts; International relations/cooperation/development aid; Population/family planning/demography; Poverty/living conditions; Refugees/migrants/ethnic groups. **Activities:** Broadcasting/cultural events; Conferences/seminars/workshops/training activities; Information campaigns/exhibitions; Lobbying/advocacy; Publishing/audiovisual materials/educational materials;

DEU1143

MEDICO INTERNATIONAL

Obermainanlage 7, 60314 Frankfurt/Main, Germany.

Telephone: 49 (69) 9 44 38 20. *Fax:* 49 (69) 43 60 02. *Contact:* Hans Branscheidt.

OBJECTIVES: To improve living conditions in developing countries through the development of primary health care services. To inform the public about the socio-economic background of North-South relations and Third World development. To promote international solidarity and human rights.

GENERAL INFORMATION: *Creation:* 1968. *Affiliated to:* BUKO (United Kingdom) - HAI (the Netherlands). *Personnel/Total:* 18. *Salaried:* 18 of which: 3 in developing countries. *Budget/Total 1993:* ECU 5163000 (US$ 6049000). *Financial sources:* Private: 59%. Public: 38%. Self-financing: 3%.

PUBLICATIONS: *Periodicals:* Medico Rundschreiben (4). *Annual report. List of publications.*

EVALUATION/RESEARCH: Evaluation reports available. Undertakes research activities.

ACTIVITIES IN DEVELOPING REGIONS: Present in developing regions. Active in 12 country(ies). Maintains local field presence. Works through local field partners. **Sustainable Development Actions:** Children/youth/family; Debt/finance/trade; Emergency relief/refugees/humanitarian assistance; Energy/transport; Food/famine; Health/sanitation/water; Human rights/peace/conflicts; Population/family planning/demography; Rural development/agriculture; Small enterprises/informal sector/handicrafts. **Regions:** East Asia; Mexico and Central America; Middle East; South America; Southern Africa; West Africa.

INFORMATION AND EDUCATION ACTIVITIES: Topics: Education/training/literacy; Food/famine; Health/sanitation/water; Human rights/peace/conflicts; International economic relations/trade/debt/finance; International relations/cooperation/development aid; Refugees/migrants/ethnic groups; Rural development/agriculture. **Activities:** Broadcasting/cultural events; Conferences/seminars/workshops/training activities; Fund raising; Information and documentation services/data bases; Information campaigns/exhibitions; Lobbying/advocacy; Publishing/audiovisual materials/educational materials.

DEU1144

MEDIENPLANUNG FUR ENTWICKLUNGSLANDER ♦ Catholic Media Council

Anton-Kurze-Allee 2, Postfach 1912, 52074 Aachen, Germany.

Telephone: 49 (241) 7 30 81. *Fax:* 49 (241) 7 34 62. *Contact:* Hans Peter Gohla, Executive Director.

OBJECTIVES: To evaluate and co-ordinate communication projects from developing countries submitted to church funding agencies in industrialised countries. To promote co-operation and co-ordination with other Christian media and funding organisations on an ecumenical basis.

GENERAL INFORMATION: *Creation:* 1969. *Personnel/Total:* 10. *Salaried:* 10.

PUBLICATIONS: *Periodicals:* Information Bulletin (4).

INFORMATION AND EDUCATION ACTIVITIES: Topics: Other. **Activities:** Broadcasting/cultural events; Conferences/seminars/workshops/training activities; Formal education; Information and documentation services/data bases; Information campaigns/exhibitions; Networking/electronic telecommunications.

DEU1145

MENSCHEN FUR MENSCHEN ♦ People for People

Nussbaumstraáe 8, 80336 München, Germany.

Telephone: 49 (89) 59 66 22. *Fax:* 49 (89) 59 48 78. *Contact:* Karlheinz Böhm, Chairman.

OBJECTIVES: To help others help themselves. To provide emergency relief to drought victims. To support an overall development programme in four regions of Ethiopia. To raise funds and promote greater awareness of the organisation's programmes.

GENERAL INFORMATION: *Creation:* 1981. *Personnel/Total:* 16. *Salaried:* 16 of which: 7 in developing countries. *Financial sources:* Private: 100%.

PUBLICATIONS: *Annual report.*

ACTIVITIES IN DEVELOPING REGIONS: Present in developing regions. Active in 1 country(ies). Maintains local field presence. Works through local field partners. **Sustainable Development Actions:** Children/youth/family; Education/training/literacy; Emergency relief/refugees/humanitarian assistance; Food/famine; Gender issues/women; Health/sanitation/water; Population/family planning/demography; Rural development/agriculture; Small enterprises/informal sector/handicrafts. **Regions:** East Africa.

DEU1146

MISSIO INTERNATIONALES KATHOLISCHES MISSIONSWERK - PAPSTLICHES WERK DER GLAUBENSVERBREITUNG ♦ International Catholic Missionary Aid Association - Papal Society for the Propagation of Faith

Goethestrasse 43, Postfach 1110, 520164 Aachen, Germany.

Telephone: 49 (241) 75 07 00. *Fax:* 49 (241) 75 07 00 335. *Contact:* Mgr. Bernd Kaut, President.

OBJECTIVES: To develop and strengthen church structures, through education and training of personnel and pastoral work. To provide equipment to organisations in developing countries.

GENERAL INFORMATION: *Creation:* 1832. *Personnel/Total:* 150. *Salaried:* 150. *Financial sources:* Private: 94%. Self-financing: 6%.

PUBLICATIONS: *Periodicals:* Missio Aktuell (6). *Annual report.*

ACTIVITIES IN DEVELOPING REGIONS: Works through local field partners. **Sustainable Development Actions:** Education/training/literacy; Emergency relief/refugees/humanitarian assistance; Gender issues/women; Human rights/peace/conflicts; Other. **Regions:** Central Africa; Central Asia and South Asia; East Africa; East Asia; Middle East; North Africa; Oceania; South East Asia; Southern Africa; West Africa.

INFORMATION AND EDUCATION ACTIVITIES: Topics: Culture/tradition/religion; Human rights/peace/conflicts; Peace/ethnic conflicts/armament/disarmament; Population/family planning/demography; Poverty/living conditions; Refugees/migrants/ethnic groups. **Activities:** Conferences/seminars/workshops/training activities; Exchanges/twinning/linking; Formal education; Fund raising; Information and documentation services/data bases; Information campaigns/exhibitions; Lobbying/advocacy; Publishing/audiovisual materials/educational materials.

DEU1147

MISSIONSARZTLICHES INSTITUT - ARBEITSGRUPPE AIDS UND INTERNATIONALE GESUNDHEIT ♦ Medical Mission Institute in Würzburg

Salvatorstrasse 22, 8700 Würzburg, Germany.

Telephone: 49 (931) 80 94 41. *Fax:* 49 (931) 80 94 53.

DEU1148

MISSIONSWERK DER EVANGELISCHE-LUTHERISCHE KIRCHE IN BAYERN ♦ World Mission Department of the Evangelical Lutheran Church in Bavaria

Hauptstrasse 2, Postfach 68, 8806 Neuendettelsau, Germany.

Telephone: 49 (9874) 90. *Fax:* 49 (9874) 93 30. *Contact:* Rev. Herman Vorländer, Director.

DEU1149

MISSIONSZENTRALE DER FRANZISKANER (MZF) ♦ Mission Centre of the Franciscans

Albertus-Magnus-Strasse 39, Postfach 20 09 53, 53139 Bonn , Germany.

Telephone: 49 (228) 95 35 40. *Fax:* 49 (228) 95 35 40. *Contact:* Andreas Müller, Director.

OBJECTIVES: To further integral human development, to aid pastoral work and to enhance Franciscan life.

GENERAL INFORMATION: *Creation:* 1969. *Affiliated to:* Franciscan International (USA) - AG der Missionswissenschaftler -Internationales Institut für Missionswissenschaftliche Forschungen. *Personnel/Total:* 23. *Salaried:* 23. *Budget/Total 1993:* ECU 8519000 (US$ 9980000). *Financial sources:* Private: 85%. Public: 10%. Self-financing: 5%.

PUBLICATIONS: *Periodicals:* Missionsbrief (4) - Information (12) - Kalenderbrief (6) - Grüne Reihe (4) -Pressedienst (12). *Annual report.*

COMMENTS: Undertakes activities in the Commonwealth of Independent States. Information activities related to the Commonwealth of Independent States.

ACTIVITIES IN DEVELOPING REGIONS: Active in 34 country(ies). Works through local field partners. **Sustainable Development Actions:** Children/youth/family; Democracy/good governance/institution building/participatory development; Ecology/environment/biodiversity; Education/training/literacy; Emergency relief/refugees/humanitarian assistance; Energy/transport; Food/famine; Gender issues/women; Health/sanitation/water; Human rights/peace/conflicts; Population/family planning/demography; Rural development/agriculture; Small enterprises/informal sector/handicrafts; Urban development/habitat. **Regions:** Central Africa; Central Asia and South Asia; East Africa; East Asia; Mexico and Central America; Oceania; South America; South East Asia; Southern Africa; West Africa.

INFORMATION AND EDUCATION ACTIVITIES: Topics: Children/youth/family; Culture/tradition/religion; Ecology/environment/biodiversity; Education/training/literacy; Emergency relief/refugees/humanitarian assistance; Employment/unemployment; Food/famine; Gender issues/women; Health/sanitation/water; Human rights/peace/conflicts; International economic relations/trade/debt/finance; International relations/cooperation/development aid; Peace/ethnic conflicts/armament/disarmament; Population/family planning/demography; Poverty/living conditions; Racism/xenophobia/antisemitism; Refugees/migrants/ethnic groups; Rural development/agriculture; Urban development/habitat. **Activities:** Broadcasting/cultural events; Conferences/seminars/workshops/training activities; Exchanges/twinning/linking; Formal education; Fund raising; Information and documentation services/data bases; Information campaigns/exhibitions; Lobbying/advocacy; Networking/electronic telecommunications; Publishing/audiovisual materials/educational materials.

DEU1150

NAH - UND MITTELOST-VEREIN (NUMOV) ♦ Near and Middle East Association

Mittelweg 151, 20148 Hamburg, Germany.

Telephone: 49 (40) 44 02 51. *Fax:* 49 (40) 41 82 14. *Contact:* Otto Plassmann.

OBJECTIVES: To promote Germany's economic co-operation with the Near and Middle East. To provide information and bring companies and individuals into contact.

GENERAL INFORMATION: *Creation:* 1934. *Personnel/Total:* 7. *Salaried:* 3. *Volunteers:* 4. *Budget/Total 1993:* ECU 207000 (US$ 242000). *Financial sources:* Private: 5%. Self-financing: 95%.

PUBLICATIONS: *Periodicals:* Kurznachrichten (10). *List of publications.*

EVALUATION/RESEARCH: Undertakes research activities.

ACTIVITIES IN DEVELOPING REGIONS: Active in 17 country(ies). Works through local field partners. **Sustainable Development Actions:** Debt/finance/trade; Ecology/environment/biodiversity; Education/training/literacy; Energy/transport; Rural development/agriculture; Sending volunteers/experts/technical assistance; Small enterprises/informal sector/handicrafts; Urban development/habitat. **Regions:** Middle East.

See: *How to Use the Directory,* page 11.

INFORMATION AND EDUCATION ACTIVITIES: Topics: International economic relations/trade/debt/finance; International relations/cooperation/development aid. **Activities:** Conferences/seminars/workshops/training activities; Information campaigns/exhibitions; Publishing/audiovisual materials/educational materials.

DEU1151

NATURSCHUTZBUND DEUTSCHLAND (NABU)

Richard-Strauss-Strasse 35, 47800 Krefeld, Germany.

Telephone: 49 (2841) 10 32 65. *Fax:* 49 (2151) 59 52 11. *Contact:* Jochin Flasbarth.

OBJECTIVES: To organise campaigns and conferences on ecological issues.

GENERAL INFORMATION: *Creation:* 1899. *Affiliated to:* Birdlife International - Deutscher Naturschutzring (Germany) - Forum Umwelt und Entwichlung (Germany). *Personnel/Total:* 10150. *Salaried:* 150 of which: 1 in developing countries. *Volunteers:* 10000 of which: 3 in developing countries. ***Budget/Total 1993:*** ECU 5163000 (US$ 6049000). *Financial sources: Private:* 30%. *Public:* 20%. *Self-financing:* 40%.

PUBLICATIONS: *Periodicals:* Naturschutz Hurte (4). *Annual report. List of publications.*

EVALUATION/RESEARCH: Undertakes research activities.

PLANNED ACTIVITIES: Campaigning for the ecological management of forests and rivers. Conference on Taiga problems. Regional sustainable development using as models the biosphere reserves of Kazakhstan, Uzbekistan and the Kyrgyz Republic.

COMMENTS: Undertakes activities in the Commonwealth of Independent States. Information activities related to the Commonwealth of Independent States.

ACTIVITIES IN DEVELOPING REGIONS: Present in developing regions. Active in 3 country(ies). Maintains local field presence. Works through local field partners. **Sustainable Development Actions:** Democracy/good governance/institution building/participatory development; Ecology/environment/biodiversity; Energy/transport; Health/sanitation/water; Rural development/agriculture; Small enterprises/informal sector/handicrafts. **Regions:** Central Asia and South Asia; North Africa; West Africa.

INFORMATION AND EDUCATION ACTIVITIES: Topics: Ecology/environment/biodiversity; Health/sanitation/water; International economic relations/trade/debt/finance; Poverty/living conditions; Rural development/agriculture; Urban development/habitat. **Activities:** Broadcasting/cultural events; Conferences/seminars/workshops/training activities; Formal education; Fund raising; Information and documentation services/data bases; Information campaigns/exhibitions; Lobbying/advocacy; Publishing/audiovisual materials/educational materials.

DEU1152

NORD-SUD-FORUM

c/o Dritte Welt Café, Daiserstr. 9, 8000 München, Germany.

Telephone: 49 (89) 7 47 07 44. *Fax:* 49 (89) 7 47 05 85. *Contact:* Trudi Schulze.

DEU1153

NOTHELFERGEMEINSCHAFT DER FREUNDE ♦ Friends Service Association

Auf der Körnerwiese 5, 6000 Frankfurt/Main 1, Germany.

Telephone: 49 (69) 59 95 57. *Contact:* Paul Krahé, President.

DEU1154

OEKUMENISCHE GESELLSCHAFT FUR GERECHTIGKEIT, FRIEDEN UND BEWAHRUNG DER SCHOPFUNG GEM.

Mittelstrasse 4, 3549 Wethen, Germany.

DEU1155

OIEW

Laurentinshof, 3543 Diemelstadt, Germany.

DEU1156

OIKOS EINE WELT

Oranienburger Strasse 46, 1040 Berlin, Germany.

Telephone: 49 (30) 2 82 39 31. *Fax:* 49 (30) 2 82 39 31. *Contact:* Kathrin Buhl.

DEU1157

OKOMEDIA INSTITUT - INSTITUT FUR OKOLOGISCHE MEDIENARBEIT (OKOMEDIA) ♦ Okomedia Institute - Institute for Ecological Media

Habsburgerstrasse 9a, 79104 Freiburg i. Br., Germany.

Telephone: 49 (761) 5 20 24. *Fax:* 49 (761) 55 57 24. *Contact:* Heidi Knoff.

OBJECTIVES: To promote ecological media in the fields of education, culture, science and research. To raise and expand ecological awareness.

GENERAL INFORMATION: *Creation:* 1984. *Affiliated to:* EEB. *Personnel/Total:* 8. *Salaried:* 6. *Volunteers:* 2. ***Budget/Total 1993:*** ECU 413000 (US$ 484000). *Financial sources: Private:* 50%. *Public:* 47%. *Self-financing:* 3%.

PUBLICATIONS: *List of publications.*

PLANNED ACTIVITIES: The establishment of an environmental media center in Eastern Europe. Increasing the availability of media data and catalogues.

COMMENTS: OKOMEDIA publishes every two years a media catalogue for Germany. Undertakes activities in the Commonwealth of Independent States. Information activities related to the Commonwealth of Independent States.

ACTIVITIES IN DEVELOPING REGIONS: Works through local field partners.

INFORMATION AND EDUCATION ACTIVITIES: Topics: Ecology/environment/biodiversity. **Activities:** Broadcasting/cultural events; Conferences/seminars/workshops/training activities; Information and documentation services/data bases; Publishing/audiovisual materials/educational materials.

DEU1158

OKUMENISCHES STUDIENWERK (ÖSW)

Girondelle 80, 44799 Bochum, Germany.

Telephone: 49 (234) 3 86 84/5. *Fax:* 49 (234) 38 47 00. *Contact:* Rudolf Ficker.

OBJECTIVES: To distribute resources in education. To contribute to human resources development, predominantly in churches and church-related organisations in developing countries. To sponsor post-graduates from developing countries for advanced studies.

GENERAL INFORMATION: *Creation:* 1970. *Personnel/Total:* 16. *Salaried:* 16. ***Budget/Total 1993:*** ECU 1859000 (US$ 2177000).

PUBLICATIONS: *Periodicals:* ÖSW News (3). *Annual report.*

COMMENTS: ÖSW's budget is financed by the Churches Development Service.

INFORMATION AND EDUCATION ACTIVITIES: Topics: Other. **Activities:** Formal education.

DEU1159

ORT DEUTSCHLAND ♦ Organisation for Rehabilitation through Training Germany

Hebelstrasse 6, 60318 Frankfurt/Main, Germany.

Telephone: 49 (69) 44 90 81. *Fax:* 49 (69) 496 00 85. *Contact:* Yissakhar Ben-Yaacov, Director.

DEU1160

OSTASIATISCHER VEREIN E.V. (OAV)

Neuer Jungfernstieg 21, 2000 Hamburg, Germany.

Voir : *Comment utiliser le répertoire,* page 11.

Telephone: 49 (40) 34 04 15. *Fax:* 49 (40) 34 18 15. *Contact:* Edgar E. Nordmann.

DEU1161

PAULO FREIRE GESELLSCHAFT ♦ Association Paulo Freire

Adlzreiterstrasse 23, 80337 München, Germany.

Telephone: 49 (89) 77 40 77. *Contact:* Heinz Schulze.

OBJECTIVES: To promote awareness in Germany about issues concerning developing countries. To support other groups involved in projects in these countries. To organise discussions on how to "learn from the Third World".

GENERAL INFORMATION: *Creation:* 1994. *Personnel/Total:* 5. *Salaried:* 5. *Budget/Total 1993:* ECU 17000 (US$ 20000). *Financial sources:* Private: 10%. Public: 50%. Self-financing: 40%.

PUBLICATIONS: *List of publications.*

COMMENTS: Undertakes activities in the Commonwealth of Independent States.

ACTIVITIES IN DEVELOPING REGIONS: Active in 4 country(ies). Works through local field partners. **Sustainable Development Actions:** Children/youth/family; Democracy/good governance/institution building/participatory development; Education/training/literacy; Gender issues/women; Human rights/peace/conflicts. **Regions:** Caribbean; Mexico and Central America; South America; Southern Africa.

DEU1162

PAX CHRISTI DEUTSCHLAND

P. O. Box 1345, 6368 Bad Vilbel, Germany.

Contact: Mr. J. Garstgecki.

DEU1163

PESTIZID AKTIONS NETZWERK (PAN) ♦ Pesticide Action Network

Nernstweg 32, 22765 Hamburg, Germany.

Telephone: 49 (40) 39 39 78. *Fax:* 49 (40) 3 90 75 20. *Contact:* Bödeker, Chairman.

OBJECTIVES: To work for the reduction and phasing-out of the use of pesticides.

GENERAL INFORMATION: *Creation:* 1984. *Member organisations:* 25. *Affiliated to:* PAN International. *Personnel/Total:* 4. *Salaried:* 3. *Volunteers:* 1.

PUBLICATIONS: *Periodicals:* PAN Pestizid-Brief (12). *List of publications.*

EVALUATION/RESEARCH: Undertakes research activities.

PLANNED ACTIVITIES: Supporting sustainable cotton production.

ACTIVITIES IN DEVELOPING REGIONS: Works through local field partners. **Sustainable Development Actions:** Rural development/agriculture. **Regions:** Mexico and Central America; South America; South East Asia; West Africa.

INFORMATION AND EDUCATION ACTIVITIES: Topics: Ecology/environment/biodiversity; Food/famine; Rural development/agriculture. **Activities:** Conferences/seminars/workshops/training activities; Exchanges/twinning/linking; Information and documentation services/data bases; Information campaigns/exhibitions.

DEU1164

PETER-HESSE-STIFTUNG - SOLIDARITAT IN PARTNERSCHAFT ♦ Fondation Peter Hesse - Solidarité dans le partenariat

Otto-Hahn-Strasse 2, 40699 Erkrath, Allemagne.

Téléphone: 49 (211) 2 50 94 40. *Fax:* 49 (211) 2 50 94 61. *Contact:* Peter Hesse, Directeur.

OBJECTIFS: Apporter une aide financière aux populations démunies du Tiers monde, notamment dans les cas de secours d'urgence. Soutenir les projets d'autosuffisance. Promouvoir la tolérance et la compréhension entre les peuples des pays en voie de développement et les européens.

INFORMATIONS GENERALES: *Création:* 1983. *Affiliée à:* Deutscher Paritätischer Wohlfahrtsverband (Allemagne). *Personnel/Total:* 2. *Salariés:* 1 dont: 1 dans les pays en développement. *Bénévoles:* 1 dont: 1 dans les pays en développement. *Budget/Total 1993:* ECU 129000 (US$ 151000). *Sources financières:* Privé: 85%. Autofinancement: 15%.

PUBLICATIONS: *Périodiques:* Projektberichte (3). *Rapport annuel.*

ACTIVITES DANS LES REGIONS EN DEVELOPPEMENT: Intervient directement dans les régions en développement. Intervient dans 1 pays. Maintient une présence locale sur le terrain. Intervient par l'intermédiaire d'organisations locales partenaires. **Actions de Développement durable:** Enfants/jeunesse/famille; Éducation/formation/alphabétisation. **Régions:** Caraïbes.

ACTIVITES D'INFORMATION ET D'EDUCATION: Domaines: Droits de l'Homme/paix/conflits; Enfants/jeunesse/famille; Racisme/xénophobie/antisémitisme; Éducation/formation/alphabétisation. **Activités:** Campagnes d'information/expositions; Lobbying/plaidoyer.

DEU1165

PRO ASYL, ARBEITSGEMEINSCHAFT FUR FLUCHTLINGE ♦ Pro Asylum, Association For Refugees

Neue Schlesingergasse 22, 6000 Frankfurt am Main, Germany.

Telephone: 49 (69) 29 31 60. *Fax:* 49 (69) 28 3 70. *Contact:* Herbert Leuninger, Spokesman.

DEU1166

PRO FAMILIA: DEUTSCHE GESELLSCHAFT FUR SEXUELBERATUNG UND FAMILIENPLANNUNG

Bundesverband, Cronsterrenstasse 30, Frankfurt am Main, Germany.

DEU1167

PRO REGENWALD

Frohschammerstrasse 14, 80807 München, Germany.

Telephone: 49 (89) 3 59 86 50. *Fax:* 49 (89) 3 59 66 22. *E-mail:* prmunic@gn.apc.org. *Contact:* Hermann Edelmann.

OBJECTIVES: To conserve forests of all types. To support indigenous people in their fight for the right to land and self-determined development. To protect bio- and cultural diversity. To establish the sustainable use of resources. To facilitate the co-operation among NGOs.

GENERAL INFORMATION: *Creation:* 1988. *Member organisations:* 15. *Affiliated to:* Regenwälder Kampagne (Germany) - Taiga Rescue Network (Sweden) - Forest Movement Europe (the Netherlands) - Nord-Sud Forum (Germany). *Personnel/Total:* 26. Salaried: 4. Volunteers: 22 of which: 2 in developing countries. *Budget/Total 1993:* ECU 207000 (US$ 242000). *Financial sources:* Private: 30%. Public: 45%. Self-financing: 25%.

PUBLICATIONS: *Periodicals:* Yanomami-Rundbrief (4). *Annual report. List of publications.*

EVALUATION/RESEARCH: Undertakes research activities.

ACTIVITIES IN DEVELOPING REGIONS: Present in developing regions. Active in 10 country(ies). Maintains local field presence. Works through local field partners. **Sustainable Development Actions:** Debt/finance/trade; Ecology/environment/biodiversity; Education/training/literacy; Human rights/peace/conflicts; Rural development/agriculture; Sending volunteers/experts/technical assistance; Small enterprises/informal sector/handicrafts. **Regions:** Central Africa; Central Asia and South Asia; East Asia; Mexico and Central America; South America; South East Asia.

INFORMATION AND EDUCATION ACTIVITIES: Topics: Culture/tradition/religion; Ecology/environment/biodiversity; Education/training/literacy; Human rights/peace/conflicts; International economic relations/trade/debt/finance; International relations/cooperation/development aid; Refugees/migrants/ethnic groups; Rural development/agriculture. **Activities:** Conferences/seminars/workshops/training activities; Exchanges/twinning/linking; Formal education; Fund raising; Information and documentation services/data bases; Information campaigns/exhibitions; Lobbying/advocacy; Networking/electronic telecommunications; Publishing/audiovisual materials/educational materials.

See: *How to Use the Directory,* page 11.

DEU1168

PUERTO MORAZAN - OBERHAUSENER BURGER HELFEN NICARAGUA ♦ Puerto Morazan - Citizens of Oberhausen Help Nicaragua

Werrastrasse 2-4, 42 Oberhausen, Germany.

Telephone: 49 (208) 66 92 93. *Contact:* Dieter Linka.

DEU1169

RAPHAELS-WERK ♦ St. Raphael's Association

Adenauerallee 41, 20097 Hamburg, Germany.

Telephone: 49 (40) 2 48 44 20. *Fax:* 49 (40) 24 84 42 26. *Contact:* Christopher Layden, Secretary General.

OBJECTIVES: To counsel people "on the move" in cases of emigration, repatriation and of marriages of mixed nationality.

GENERAL INFORMATION: *Creation:* 1871. *Affiliated to:* International Catholic Migration Commission (Switzerland) - Deutscher Caritasverband (Germany). *Personnel/Total:* 50. *Salaried:* 50. *Budget/Total 1993:* ECU 516000 (US$ 605000). *Financial sources:* Private: 80%. *Public:* 20%.

PUBLICATIONS: *Annual report.*

EVALUATION/RESEARCH: Evaluation reports available.

PLANNED ACTIVITIES: Setting up counselling centers for migrants in Poland, Czech Republic and the Republic of Slovak.

COMMENTS: Undertakes activities in the Commonwealth of Independent States. Information activities related to the Commonwealth of Independent States.

INFORMATION AND EDUCATION ACTIVITIES: Topics: Refugees/migrants/ethnic groups. **Activities:** Conferences/seminars/workshops/training activities; Fund raising; Information and documentation services/data bases; Information campaigns/exhibitions; Lobbying/advocacy; Other.

DEU1170

RELACIONES - VEREIN ZUR FORDERUNG ENTWICKLUNGSPOLITISCHER INITIATIVEN UND ENTWICKLUNGSZUSAMMENARBEIT IN NIEDERSACHSEN (VEN)

Bahnhofstr. 16, 2847 Bamsdorf, Germany.

Telephone: 49 (5442) 24 14. *Fax:* 49 (5442) 22 41. *Contact:* Klaus Schmelz.

DEU1171

RUDOLF WALTHER STIFTUNG

Rabenhaustrasse 25a, 63584 Gründau, Germany.

DEU1172

SEEDS ACTION NETWORK (SAN-FRG)

Wohlersallee 18, 2000 Hamburg 50, Germany.

Telephone: 49 (40) 4390122. *Fax:* 49 (40) 4398829.

DEU1173

SEKRETARIAT FUR ENTWICKLUNGSBEZOGENE BILDUNG UND PUBLIZISTIK (ABP)

Haussmannstrasse 16, 70188 Stuttgart, Germany.

Telephone: 49 (711) 23 69 515. *Fax:* 49 (711) 26 23 391.

DEU1174

SENIOR EXPERTEN SERVICE (SES)

Postfach 22 62, 53012 Bonn, Germany.

Telephone: 49 (228) 26 09 00. *Fax:* 49 (228) 2 60 90 77. *Contact:* Heinrich Nordsieck, Executive Director.

OBJECTIVES: To recruit and assign retired but highly motivated managers and qualified personnel in order to teach and promote special knowledge and skills to local personnel in small and medium-sized enterprises.

GENERAL INFORMATION: *Creation:* 1983. *Affiliated to:* European Senior Services Consortium (the Netherlands). *Personnel/Total:* 91. *Salaried:* 32. *Volunteers:* 59. *Budget/Total 1993:* ECU 2995000 (US$ 3508000). *Financial sources:* Private: 5%. *Public:* 17%. *Self-financing:* 78%.

PUBLICATIONS: *Periodicals:* SES Aktuel (4). *Annual report.*

EVALUATION/RESEARCH: Evaluation reports available.

COMMENTS: Undertakes activities in the Commonwealth of Independent States. Information activities related to the Commonwealth of Independent States.

ACTIVITIES IN DEVELOPING REGIONS: Present in developing regions. Active in 72 country(ies). Maintains local field presence. **Sustainable Development Actions:** Education/training/literacy; Energy/transport; Rural development/agriculture; Sending volunteers/experts/technical assistance; Small enterprises/informal sector/handicrafts. **Regions:** Caribbean; Central Africa; Central Asia and South Asia; East Africa; East Asia; Mexico and Central America; Middle East; North Africa; South America; South East Asia; Southern Africa; West Africa.

INFORMATION AND EDUCATION ACTIVITIES: Topics: International economic relations/trade/debt/finance; International relations/cooperation/development aid. **Activities:** Conferences/seminars/workshops/training activities.

DEU1175

SERVICE CIVIL INTERNATIONAL (SCI)

Blücherstrasse 14, 53115 Bonn, Germany.

Telephone: 49 (228) 21 20 86/87. *Fax:* 49 (228) 21 93 29. *Contact:* Uli Hanke, General Secretary.

OBJECTIVES: To promote international peace, understanding and reconciliation by organising international workcamps in Germany and in 20 other European and Asian countries. To encourage the exchange of volunteers between the East and West. To carry out solidarity work.

GENERAL INFORMATION: *Creation:* 1947. *Type of organisation:* coordinating body. *Personnel/Total:* 15. *Salaried:* 9 of which: 1 in developing countries. *Volunteers:* 6. *Budget/Total 1993:* ECU 774000 (US$ 907000). *Financial sources:* Private: 15%. *Public:* 70%. *Self-financing:* 15%.

PUBLICATIONS: *Periodicals:* Amitiés (4) - SCI-Action (4) - SCI-East Europe "Yellow Pages" (2).

EVALUATION/RESEARCH: Evaluation reports available.

COMMENTS: Undertakes activities in the Commonwealth of Independent States. Information activities related to the Commonwealth of Independent States.

ACTIVITIES IN DEVELOPING REGIONS: Active in 23 country(ies). Works through local field partners. **Sustainable Development Actions:** Sending volunteers/experts/technical assistance. **Regions:** Central Asia and South Asia; East Africa; Mexico and Central America; North Africa; South America; South East Asia; Southern Africa; West Africa.

INFORMATION AND EDUCATION ACTIVITIES: Topics: Children/youth/family; Culture/tradition/religion; International relations/cooperation/development aid; Peace/ethnic conflicts/armament/disarmament; Racism/xenophobia/antisemitism; Refugees/migrants/ethnic groups. **Activities:** Conferences/seminars/workshops/training activities; Exchanges/twinning/linking; Fund raising; Information campaigns/exhibitions.

DEU1176

SOLIDARITATSDIENST-INTERNATIONAL (SODI) ♦ Solidarity Service International

Grevesmühlener Strasse 16, 13059 Berlin, Germany.

Telephone: 49 (30) 9 21 60 47. *Fax:* 49 (30) 9 21 60 03. *Contact:* Carl Ordnung.

OBJECTIVES: To organise programmes to overcome illiteracy and for re-integration and creation of jobs. To support and implement development

projects in the Third World. To provide assistance for primary medical care and curative treatment for victims of disasters, war, torture, etc. To help disadvantaged and destitute children.

GENERAL INFORMATION: *Creation:* 1990. *Personnel/Total:* 7. *Salaried:* 7. *Budget/Total 1993:* ECU 1652000 (US$ 1936000). *Financial sources:* Private: 99%. Self-financing: 1%.

PUBLICATIONS: *Periodicals:* SODI-Report (6). *List of publications.*

PLANNED ACTIVITIES: Training of 60 individuals from developing countries in Germany. Donation of medical equipment and medicine to hospitals and orphanages in Romania and in the Chernobyl region.

COMMENTS: Undertakes activities in the Commonwealth of Independent States. Information activities related to the Commonwealth of Independent States.

ACTIVITIES IN DEVELOPING REGIONS: Present in developing regions. Active in 20 country(ies). Works through local field partners. **Sustainable Development Actions:** Children/youth/family; Food/famine; Gender issues/women; Health/sanitation/water; Small enterprises/informal sector/handicrafts. **Regions:** East Africa; Mexico and Central America; Middle East; North Africa; South East Asia; Southern Africa.

INFORMATION AND EDUCATION ACTIVITIES: Topics: Children/youth/family; Ecology/environment/biodiversity; Emergency relief/refugees/humanitarian assistance; Health/sanitation/water; International relations/cooperation/development aid; Population/family planning/demography; Racism/xenophobia/antisemitism; Refugees/migrants/ethnic groups. **Activities:** Formal education; Fund raising; Information campaigns/exhibitions; Lobbying/advocacy; Publishing/audiovisual materials/educational materials.

DEU1177

SOLIDARITATSFONDS DRITTE WELT ♦ Fund for Solidarity with the Third World

Rosenbach 10, 53129 Bonn, Germany.

Contact: Roland Röscheisen, President.

OBJECTIVES: To support development education in Germany and activities in the Third World. To generate support for self-reliant, basic needs' projects and political participation.

GENERAL INFORMATION: *Creation:* 1980. *Type of organisation:* network. *Member organisations:* 80. *Budget/Total 1993:* ECU 21000 (US$ 24000). *Financial sources:* Public: 75%. Self-financing: 25%.

PUBLICATIONS: *Annual report.*

ACTIVITIES IN DEVELOPING REGIONS: Active in 4 country(ies). Works through local field partners. **Sustainable Development Actions:** Children/youth/family; Gender issues/women; Small enterprises/informal sector/handicrafts. **Regions:** Mexico and Central America; North Africa; South America; South East Asia.

INFORMATION AND EDUCATION ACTIVITIES: Topics: Human rights/peace/conflicts; International relations/cooperation/development aid. **Activities:** Information campaigns/exhibitions; Lobbying/advocacy.

DEU1178

SOZIAL- UND ENTWICKLUNGSHILFE DES KOLPINGWERKES ♦ Aide sociale et aide au développement de la société Kolping

Kolpingplatz 5-11, Postfach 100428, 50448 Köln, Allemagne.

Téléphone: 49 (221) 20 70 10. *Fax:* 49 (221) 2 07 01 46. *Contact:* Hubert Tintelott, Secrétaire général.

OBJECTIFS: Travailler pour le développement. Promouvoir les associations Kolping dans le Tiers monde et en Europe de l'Est.

INFORMATIONS GENERALES: *Création:* 1972. *Type d'organisation:* regroupement d'ONG. *Organisations membres:* 21. *Personnel/Total:* 11. *Salariés:* 11. *Budget/Total 1993:* ECU 6196000 (US$ 7258000). *Sources financières:* Privé: 35%. Public: 65%.

PUBLICATIONS: *Périodiques:* Dialogue (4). *Rapport annuel.*

PREVISIONS D'ACTIVITES: Education professionnelle. Renforcement de l'atisanat et de la famille.

COMMENTAIRES: Intervient dans la Communauté des Etats indépendants. Activités d'information concernant la Communauté des Etats indépendants.

ACTIVITES DANS LES REGIONS EN DEVELOPPEMENT: Intervient dans 20 pays. Intervient par l'intermédiaire d'organisations locales partenaires. **Actions de Développement durable:** Droits de l'Homme/paix/conflits; Démocratie/bonne gestion publique/création d'institutions/développement participatif; Développement rural/agriculture; Enfants/jeunesse/famille; Envoi de volontaires/experts/assistance technique; Petites entreprises/secteur informel/artisanat; Questions relatives aux femmes; Santé/assainissement/eau; Écologie/environnement/biodiversité; Éducation/formation/alphabétisation. **Régions:** Afrique de l'Est; Afrique de l'Ouest; Amérique du Sud; Asie centrale et Asie du Sud; Asie du Sud-Est; Mexique et Amerique centrale.

ACTIVITES D'INFORMATION ET D'EDUCATION: Domaines: Culture/tradition/religion; Droits de l'Homme/paix/conflits; Développement rural/agriculture; Enfants/jeunesse/famille; Questions relatives aux femmes; Relations internationales/coopération/aide au développement; Santé/assainissement/eau; Écologie/environnement/biodiversité; Éducation/formation/alphabétisation. **Activités:** Campagnes d'information/expositions; Collecte de fonds; Conférences/séminaires/ateliers/activités de formation; Lobbying/plaidoyer; Services d'information et de documentation/bases de données; Échanges/parrainage/jumelage; Éducation formelle.

DEU1179

SOZIALWISSENSCHAFTLICHER STUDIENKREIS FUR INTERNATIONALE PROBLEME (SSIP) ♦ Society for the Study of International Problems

Gierolstrasse 45, 53127 Bonn, Germany.

Telephone: 49 (228) 28 30 75. *Fax:* 49 (228) 28 30 85. *Contact:* Dieter Danckwortt, Secr..

OBJECTIVES: To advocate co-operation and co-ordination among social scientists in Germany training and doing research in International Relations. To organise working groups on the academic exchange on individuals, migration and refugees, development education, history of German cultural relations. To promote tourism and cultural understanding.

GENERAL INFORMATION: *Creation:* 1959. *Type of organisation:* coordinating body. *Budget/Total 1993:* ECU 2600 (US$ 3000). *Financial sources:* Self-financing: 100%.

PUBLICATIONS: *Periodicals:* SSIP-Newsletter (12) - SSIP-Bulletin. *Annual report. List of publications.*

EVALUATION/RESEARCH: Undertakes research activities.

COMMENTS: The staff is formed solely by volunteers. Undertakes activities in the Commonwealth of Independent States. Information activities related to the Commonwealth of Independent States.

INFORMATION AND EDUCATION ACTIVITIES: Topics: Culture/tradition/religion; International relations/cooperation/development aid; Peace/ethnic conflicts/armament/disarmament; Refugees/migrants/ethnic groups. **Activities:** Conferences/seminars/workshops/training activities; Information and documentation services/data bases; Lobbying/advocacy.

DEU1180

STIFTUNG ENTWICKLUNG UND FRIEDEN ♦ Development and Peace Foundation

Gotenstrasse 152, 53175 Bonn, Germany.

Telephone: 49 (228) 95 92 50. *Fax:* 49 (228) 9 59 25 99. *Contact:* Kurt H. Biedenkopf, President.

OBJECTIVES: To foster understanding and equity between peoples and states. To facilitate co-operation and development. To raise awareness of global interconnections between the world economy, the environment and international security.

GENERAL INFORMATION: *Creation:* 1986. *Affiliated to:* Forum Environment and Development (Germany) - German Working Group on Biodiversity (Germany). *Personnel/Total:* 5. Salaried: 5. *Budget/Total 1993:* ECU 516000 (US$ 605000). *Financial sources:* Public: 100%.

See: *How to Use the Directory,* page 11.

PUBLICATIONS: *Periodicals:* EINE Welt (4) - Interdependenz (7). *Annual report. List of publications.*

COMMENTS: The foundation publishes, every two years, a periodical entitled "Global Trends". Information activities related to the Commonwealth of Independent States.

ACTIVITIES IN DEVELOPING REGIONS: Active in 1 country(ies).

INFORMATION AND EDUCATION ACTIVITIES: Topics: Children/youth/family; Culture/tradition/religion; Ecology/environment/biodiversity; Education/training/literacy; Employment/unemployment; Food/famine; Gender issues/women; Health/sanitation/water; Human rights/peace/conflicts; International economic relations/trade/debt/finance; International relations/cooperation/development aid; Peace/ethnic conflicts/armament/disarmament; Population/family planning/demography; Poverty/living conditions; Racism/xenophobia/antisemitism; Refugees/migrants/ethnic groups; Rural development/agriculture; Urban development/habitat. Activities: Conferences/seminars/workshops/training activities; Exchanges/twinning/linking; Information and documentation services/data bases; Networking/electronic telecommunications; Publishing/audiovisual materials/educational materials.

DEU1181
STIFTUNG KINDER IN AFRIKA ♦ Foundation "Children in Africa"
Holsteiner Strasse 12 C, 21465 Reinbek, Germany.

Telephone: 49 (40) 7 22 11 05. *Fax:* 49 (40) 7 22 11 05. *Contact:* Horst W. Zillmer.

OBJECTIVES: To help needy children in Africa by granting medical aid to health units. To provide assistance to refugee camps, day-care and vocational training centres and to help with the co-financing of pre-schools.

GENERAL INFORMATION: *Creation:* 1984. *Budget/Total 1993:* ECU 3207000 (US$ 3757000).

PUBLICATIONS: *Annual report.*

COMMENTS: Undertakes activities in the Commonwealth of Independent States.

ACTIVITIES IN DEVELOPING REGIONS: Active in 21 country(ies). Works through local field partners. Sustainable Development Actions: Children/youth/family; Education/training/literacy; Emergency relief/refugees/humanitarian assistance; Health/sanitation/water. Regions: East Africa; Southern Africa; West Africa.

DEU1182
STIFTUNG WIR FUR KINDER IN NOT
Oberer Laubenheimer Weg 58, 55131 Mainz, Germany.

DEU1183
STRAFFALLIGEN-UND BEWAHRUNGSHILFE BERLIN
Bundesallee 42, 10715 Berlin, Germany.

DEU1184
SUDOSTASIEN-INFORMATIONSSTELLE ♦ South East Asia Information Centre
Josephinenstrasse 71, 44807 Bochum 1, Germany.

Telephone: 49 (234) 50 27 48. *Fax:* 49 (234) 50 27 90. *E-mail:* Seainfo@geod.geonet.de. *Contact:* Peter Franke, Managing Director.

OBJECTIVES: To inform the German-speaking public on current social, cultural, environmental and political events and developments in South-East Asia. To create a network between German social action groups and their counterparts in developing countries.

GENERAL INFORMATION: *Creation:* 1984. *Affiliated to:* BUKO (Germany) - European Committee on Human Rights in Malaysia and Singapore -German Association for Asian Studies (Germany) - German Asia Foundation (Germany). *Personnel/Total:* 7. *Salaried:* 5. *Volunteers:* 3. *Budget/Total 1993:* ECU 208000 (US$ 244000). *Financial sources:* Private: 27%. Public: 58%. Self-financing: 15%.

PUBLICATIONS: *Periodicals:* Südostasien Informationen (4). *List of publications.*

EVALUATION/RESEARCH: Evaluation reports available. Undertakes research activities.

INFORMATION AND EDUCATION ACTIVITIES: Topics: Children/youth/family; Culture/tradition/religion; Ecology/environment/biodiversity; Education/training/literacy; Employment/unemployment; Food/famine; Gender issues/women; Health/sanitation/water; Human rights/peace/conflicts; International economic relations/trade/debt/finance; International relations/cooperation/development aid; Peace/ethnic conflicts/armament/disarmament; Population/family planning/demography; Poverty/living conditions; Racism/xenophobia/antisemitism; Refugees/migrants/ethnic groups; Rural development/agriculture; Urban development/habitat. Activities: Conferences/seminars/workshops/training activities; Information and documentation services/data bases; Lobbying/advocacy; Publishing/audiovisual materials/educational materials.

DEU1185
TECHNOLOGIE TRANSFER MARBURG IN DIE DRITTE WELT
♦ Technology Transfer for the Third World Marburg
Siegenerstrasse 33, 35094 Lahntal-Gossfelden, Germany.

Telephone: 49 (6423) 30 36. *Fax:* 49 (6423) 45 24. *Contact:* Wolfram Aeckersberg, Managing Director.

OBJECTIVES: To acquire and repair used medical apparatus that is suitable for use in developing countries. To adapt the equipment to its place of operation and ship it to its destination. To help interested parties find financial sponsors. To provide supplies of new medical technical equipment and medical consumables at wholesale prices.

GENERAL INFORMATION: *Creation:* 1983. *Personnel/Total:* 20. *Salaried:* 20. *Budget/Total 1993:* ECU 2065000 (US$ 2419000). *Financial sources: Public:* 10%. *Self-financing:* 90%.

EVALUATION/RESEARCH: Undertakes research activities.

COMMENTS: Undertakes activities in the Commonwealth of Independent States.

ACTIVITIES IN DEVELOPING REGIONS: Present in developing regions. Works through local field partners. Sustainable Development Actions: Health/sanitation/water; Sending volunteers/experts/technical assistance. Regions: Caribbean; Central Africa; Central Asia and South Asia; East Africa; East Asia; Mexico and Central America; Middle East; North Africa; Oceania; South America; South East Asia; Southern Africa; West Africa.

DEU1186
TERRE DES FEMMES, HUMAN RIGHTS FOR WOMEN ♦ Land of Women
Postfach 2531, 72015 Tübingen, Germany.

Telephone: 49 (7071) 2 42 89. *Fax:* 49 (7071) 55 03 52. *Contact:* Christa Stolle.

OBJECTIVES: To fight against every form of human rights' violation against women. To give practical and discrete aid to women who are victims of maltreatment, persecution and exploitation. To achieve refugee status for women who are persecuted on account of their gender.

GENERAL INFORMATION: *Creation:* 1981. *Member organisations:* 6. *Affiliated to:* Women's Forum (Germany) - Agisra-Frankfurt (Germany) - BUKO (Germany) -International Campaign against Child Prostitution and the Exploitation of Flower Workers (Thailand) - European Women's Lobby (Belgium) - Women in Development Europe (Belgium) - Frauen Austittung (Germany). *Personnel/Total:* 39. *Salaried:* 9. *Volunteers:* 30 of which: 2 in developing countries. *Budget/Total 1993:* ECU 155000 (US$ 181000). *Financial sources: Private:* 20%. *Public:* 65%. *Self-financing:* 15%.

PUBLICATIONS: *Periodicals:* Terre des Femmes Rundbrief (4). *List of publications.*

EVALUATION/RESEARCH: Evaluation reports available.

ACTIVITIES IN DEVELOPING REGIONS: Works through local field partners. Sustainable Development Actions: Children/youth/family; Education/training/literacy; Gender issues/women; Health/sanitation/

water; Rural development/agriculture. **Regions:** Central Asia and South Asia; South America; South East Asia; West Africa.

INFORMATION AND EDUCATION ACTIVITIES: Topics: Gender issues/ women; Human rights/peace/conflicts; Refugees/migrants/ethnic groups. **Activities:** Conferences/seminars/workshops/training activities; Exchanges/twinning/linking; Fund raising; Information and documentation services/data bases; Information campaigns/exhibitions; Lobbying/ advocacy; Networking/electronic telecommunications; Publishing/audiovisual materials/educational materials.

DEU1187

TERRE DES HOMMES, BUNDESREPUBLIK DEUTSCHLAND
♦ TERRE DES HOMMES, GERMANY

Ruppenkampstrasse 11a, Postfach 41 26, 49031 Osnabrück, Germany.

Telephone: 49 (541) 7 10 10. **Fax:** 49 (541) 70 72 33. **Contact:** Burkhard Gnärig, Director.

OBJECTIVES: To undertake development-oriented projects for children. To provide assistance for abandoned, sick and handicapped children. To disseminate information and undertake projects in Germany.

GENERAL INFORMATION: Creation: 1967. **Affiliated to:** Bensheimer Kreis (Germany) - EUROSTEP (Belgium) - Forum Menschenrechte (Germany) - Federation Internationale Terre des Hommes (Switzerland) - Pro Agyl (Germany) - Trägerkreis Teppichkampagne (Germany) - Towns and Development (Germany) - Transfair (Germany). **Personnel/Total:** 75. Salaried: 75. **Budget/ Total 1993:** ECU 13527000 (US$ 15847000). **Financial sources:** Private: 68%. Public: 18%.

PUBLICATIONS: Periodicals: Die Zeitung (5) - Intern (6). Annual report. List of publications.

EVALUATION/RESEARCH: Evaluation reports available. Undertakes research activities.

PLANNED ACTIVITIES: Campaigning on the rights of the child.

ACTIVITIES IN DEVELOPING REGIONS: Active in 20 country(ies). Maintains local field presence. Works through local field partners. **Sustainable Development Actions:** Children/youth/family; Debt/finance/trade; Democracy/good governance/institution building/participatory development; Ecology/environment/biodiversity; Education/training/literacy; Emergency relief/refugees/humanitarian assistance; Food/famine; Gender issues/women; Health/sanitation/water; Human rights/peace/conflicts; Population/family planning/demography; Rural development/agriculture; Small enterprises/informal sector/handicrafts; Urban development/habitat. **Regions:** Central Asia and South Asia; Mexico and Central America; South America; South East Asia; Southern Africa; West Africa.

INFORMATION AND EDUCATION ACTIVITIES: Topics: Children/youth/ family; Education/training/literacy; Employment/unemployment; Gender issues/women; Health/sanitation/water; Human rights/peace/conflicts; International economic relations/trade/debt/finance; International relations/cooperation/development aid; Peace/ethnic conflicts/armament/ disarmament; Poverty/living conditions; Racism/xenophobia/antisemitism; Refugees/migrants/ethnic groups; Rural development/agriculture; Urban development/habitat. **Activities:** Conferences/seminars/workshops/training activities; Fund raising; Information campaigns/exhibitions; Lobbying/advocacy; Networking/electronic telecommunications; Publishing/audiovisual materials/educational materials.

DEU1188

TIERRA NUEVA ♦ New Home, New Land to Settle

Lindemannstrasse 84, 4600 Dortmund, Germany.

Telephone: 49 (231) 13 67 26. **Contact:** Detlev Brum.

DEU1189

TOLSTOY FOUNDATION

Thierschstrasse 11/v, 8002 München 22, Germany.

Contact: Alexander Koltschak, Director for Europe and the Middle East.

DEU1190

TRANSFAIR INTERNATIONAL

Am Ochsenberg 16, 73614 Schorndorf, Germany.

Telephone: 49 (7181) 6 54 17. **Fax:** 49 (7181) 6 55 46. **E-mail:** tfi@link.s.cl.sub.de. **Contact:** Martin Kunz, General Secretary.

OBJECTIVES: To support sustainable development in international commercial relations. To provide financial stability and decent living conditions to disadvantaged producers by organising fairs.

GENERAL INFORMATION: Type of organisation: association of NGOs. **Member organisations:** 7. **Affiliated to:** IFAT - IFOAM. **Personnel/Total:** 3. Salaried: 3. **Financial sources:** Self-financing: 100%.

EVALUATION/RESEARCH: Undertakes research activities.

PLANNED ACTIVITIES: Introduction of Transfair-labelled products in member countries. Development of Fair Trade criteria for new products.

ACTIVITIES IN DEVELOPING REGIONS: Sustainable Development Actions: Other. **Regions:** Caribbean; Central Asia and South Asia; East Africa; Mexico and Central America; South America; South East Asia; Southern Africa; West Africa.

DEU1191

EIN TROPFCHEN MILCH ♦ La Goutte de Lait allemandee

Südhang 3, 65719 Hofheim, Germany.

Telephone: 49 (61) 98 90 26. **Fax:** 49 (61) 9 83 41 43. **Contact:** Christel Jeschke, President.

OBJECTIVES: To provide developing countries with structural aid, including small hospitals and ambulances, schools, waterworks, solar energy systems, lorrys, workshops for women, orphanages and help for the handicapped.

GENERAL INFORMATION: Creation: 1984. **Personnel/Total:** 6. Salaried: 1. Volunteers: 5. **Budget/Total 1993:** ECU 258000 (US$ 302000). **Financial sources:** Private: 50%. Public: 40%. Self-financing: 10%.

PUBLICATIONS: Periodicals: Nur gemeinsam kommen wir zum Ziel (2) - Meine Zukunft liegt hier. Annual report. List of publications.

EVALUATION/RESEARCH: Undertakes research activities.

PLANNED ACTIVITIES: The construction of a tourist centre in Saharan Nigeria.

ACTIVITIES IN DEVELOPING REGIONS: Present in developing regions. Active in 1 country(ies). Works through local field partners. **Sustainable Development Actions:** Children/youth/family; Democracy/good governance/institution building/participatory development; Emergency relief/ refugees/humanitarian assistance; Energy/transport; Gender issues/ women; Health/sanitation/water; Population/family planning/demography; Small enterprises/informal sector/handicrafts. **Regions:** North Africa.

DEU1192

UBERSEE-DOKUMENTATION IM DEUTSCHEN UBERSEE-INSTITUT ♦ German Overseas Institute/Section Overeas Documentation Centre

Neuer Jungfernstieg 21, 20354 Hamburg, Germany.

Telephone: 49 (40) 3 56 25 98. **Fax:** 49 (40) 3 56 25 47. **Contact:** Gottfried Reinknecht.

OBJECTIVES: To act as an information centre referring users to the literature on contemporary area studies on the regions of Africa, Asia and the South Pacific, Latin America and the Near and Middle East.

GENERAL INFORMATION: Creation: 1985. **Personnel/Total:** 17. Salaried: 15. Volunteers: 2. **Budget/Total 1993:** ECU 904000 (US$ 1058000). **Financial sources:** Public: 100%.

PUBLICATIONS: Periodicals: Select-a selected bibliography of recent literature (4). Annual report.

COMMENTS: Nine major institutions co-operate with the Institute in setting up the common database and network in Germany.

See: *How to Use the Directory,* page 11.

INFORMATION AND EDUCATION ACTIVITIES: Topics: Children/youth/family; Culture/tradition/religion; Ecology/environment/biodiversity; Education/training/literacy; Employment/unemployment; Food/famine; Gender issues/women; Health/sanitation/water; Human rights/peace/conflicts; International economic relations/trade/debt/finance; International relations/cooperation/development aid; Peace/ethnic conflicts/armament/disarmament; Population/family planning/demography; Poverty/living conditions; Racism/xenophobia/antisemitism; Refugees/migrants/ethnic groups; Rural development/agriculture; Urban development/habitat. **Activities:** Information and documentation services/data bases.

DEU1193

VERBAND BI NATIONALER FAMILIEN UND PARTNER-SCHAFTEN (IAF) ♦ Association of Binational Marriages, Families and Partnerships

Kasseler Strasse 1a, 60486 Frankfurt, Germany.

Telephone: 49 (69) 7 07 50 87. *Fax:* 49 (69) 7 07 50 92. *Contact:* Sabine Kriechhammer-Yagmur, Federal Manager.

OBJECTIVES: To represent the interests of bi-national families and couples and secure their legal rights. To provide counselling and a forum for bi-nationals to meet and exchange opinions. To work against racism in all forms. To promote the idea of a multi-national society and among the general public.

GENERAL INFORMATION: *Creation:* 1972. *Type of organisation:* network. *Affiliated to:* Deutscher Paritätischer Wohlfahrtsverband (Germany) - Deutscher Frauenrat (Germany) - Verband Initiativen in der Ausländerarbeit (Germany) - European Conference of Binational/Bi-cultural Relationships - Nord-Süd-Forum (Germany). *Personnel/Total:* 361. *Salaried:* 31. *Volunteers:* 330. *Budget/Total 1993:* ECU 1807000 (US$ 2117000). *Financial sources:* Private: 1%. Public: 89%. Self-financing: 10%.

PUBLICATIONS: *Periodicals:* IAF-Informationen (4). *Annual report. List of publications.*

EVALUATION/RESEARCH: Evaluation reports available.

INFORMATION AND EDUCATION ACTIVITIES: Topics: Children/youth/family; Culture/tradition/religion; Gender issues/women; Human rights/peace/conflicts; Peace/ethnic conflicts/armament/disarmament; Racism/xenophobia/antisemitism; Refugees/migrants/ethnic groups. **Activities:** Conferences/seminars/workshops/training activities; Exchanges/twinning/linking; Fund raising; Information and documentation services/data bases; Information campaigns/exhibitions; Lobbying/advocacy; Publishing/audiovisual materials/educational materials.

DEU1194

VERBAND UNABHANGIG BERATENDER INGENIEURFIRMEN E.V. (VUBI)

Winston-Churchill-Strase 1, Postfach 12 04 64, 5300 Bonn, Germany.

Telephone: 49 (2 28) 21 70 63. *Fax:* 49 (2 28) 21 70 62. *Contact:* Heinrich Els.

DEU1195

VEREIN FUR AFGHANISTAN-FORDERUNG

Oxforstrasse 2, 53113 Bonn, Germany.

DEU1196

VEREIN FUR STADTEPARTNERSCHAFT FREIBURG-WIWILI
♦ Organisation for the Development of Twinning between Freiburg and Wiwili

Habsburgerstrasse 9, 7800 Freiburg, Germany.

Telephone: 49 (761) 5 75 20. *Contact:* Reinold Seidelmann.

DEU1197

VEREIN ZUR UNTERSTUTZUNG DER HUNGERNDEN, VERLASSEN UND KRANKEN KINDER INDIENS

Blumenstrasse 3, 30159 Hannover, Germany.

DEU1198

VEREINIGUNG EHEMALIGER ENTWICKLUNGSHELFERINNEN UND ENTWICKLUNGSHELFER (VEHEMENT) ♦ Organisation of Ex-volunteers

Remiginstrasse 21, 50937 Köln, Germany.

Telephone: 49 (221) 4 20 04 71. *Fax:* 49 (221) 4 20 05 75. *Contact:* Hans-Werner Emrich, President.

OBJECTIVES: To encourage solidarity among all people. To collaborate with various organisations, institutions and individuals, in the search for a common reflection of the attitudes and relationships between the North and South.

GENERAL INFORMATION: *Creation:* 1988. *Personnel/Total:* 2. *Salaried:* 2. *Budget/Total 1993:* ECU 166000 (US$ 194000). *Financial sources:* Private: 15%. Public: 50%. Self-financing: 35%.

PUBLICATIONS: *Periodicals:* EKI (2) - Standpunkte (1) - Literaturhefte (2). *List of publications.*

PLANNED ACTIVITIES: Dessimenation of information about the effects of tourism in Latin America, Africa and Asia. Evaluation of development cooperation of municipalities.

INFORMATION AND EDUCATION ACTIVITIES: Topics: Children/youth/family; Ecology/environment/biodiversity; Education/training/literacy; Emergency relief/refugees/humanitarian assistance; Employment/unemployment; Gender issues/women; Human rights/conflicts; International economic relations/trade/debt/finance; International relations/cooperation/development aid; Peace/ethnic conflicts/armament/disarmament; Population/family planning/demography; Poverty/living conditions; Racism/xenophobia/antisemitism; Refugees/migrants/ethnic groups; Rural development/agriculture. **Activities:** Conferences/seminars/workshops/training activities; Exchanges/twinning/linking; Information campaigns/exhibitions; Publishing/audiovisual materials/educational materials.

DEU1199

VEREINIGUNG FUR INTERNATIONALE ZUSAM-MENARBEIT (VIZ) ♦ Association for International Co-operation

Wissenschaftszentrum, Ahrstrasse 45, 5300 Bonn 2, Germany.

Contact: Martin L. Mruck.

DEU1200

WELTFRIEDENSDIENST (WFD) ♦ Community Services

Hedemannstrasse 72, 10969 Berlin, Germany.

Telephone: 49 (30) 2 53 99 00. *Fax:* 49 (30) 2 51 18 87. *Contact:* Walter Spellmeyer, Director of the Board of Directors.

OBJECTIVES: To support grass-root and self-help groups in developing countries which are working towards reducing their economic, social and political dependence. To provide financial and professional assistance for rural development projects.

GENERAL INFORMATION: *Creation:* 1959. *Affiliated to:* Bensheimer Kreis (Germany). *Personnel/Total:* 26. *Salaried:* 11. *Volunteers:* 15 of which: 15 in developing countries. *Budget/Total 1993:* ECU 1549000 (US$ 1814000). *Financial sources:* Private: 5%. Public: 75%. Self-financing: 10%.

PUBLICATIONS: *Periodicals:* Querbrief (4). *Annual report. List of publications.*

EVALUATION/RESEARCH: Evaluation reports available. Undertakes research activities.

ACTIVITIES IN DEVELOPING REGIONS: Active in 7 country(ies). Works through local field partners. **Sustainable Development Actions:** Gender issues/women; Rural development/agriculture; Sending volunteers/experts/technical assistance; Small enterprises/informal sector/handicrafts. **Regions:** Middle East; Southern Africa; West Africa.

INFORMATION AND EDUCATION ACTIVITIES: Topics: Ecology/environment/biodiversity; Gender issues/women; Racism/xenophobia/antisemitism; Rural development/agriculture. **Activities:** Broadcasting/cultural events; Conferences/seminars/workshops/training activities; Exchanges/twinning/linking; Fund raising; Information and documenta-

Voir : *Comment utiliser le répertoire,* page 11.

tion services/data bases; Information campaigns/exhibitions; Lobbying/advocacy; Publishing/audiovisual materials/educational materials.

DEU1201

WELTWEITE PARTNERSCHAFT (WWP)

Normannenweg 17-21, 20537 Hamburg, Germany.

Telephone: 49 (40) 250 18 99. *Fax:* 49 (40) 250 18 44. *Contact:* Renate Kuhlmann-Wetter, Director.

DEU1202

WERKHOF DARMSTADT ♦ Workgroup Darmstadt

Rundeturmstrasse 16, 64283 Darmstadt, Germany.

Telephone: 49 (6151) 2 66 64. *Fax:* 49 (6151) 2 02 85.

OBJECTIVES: To provide technical assistance in the fields of radio equipment and machinery. To raise consciousness among the German population about problems in developing countries and particularly, about their dependency on the industrialized world. To foster international solidarity.

GENERAL INFORMATION: *Creation:* 1983. *Affiliated to:* DPWV - KKM. *Personnel/Total:* 9. *Salaried:* 6 of which: 1 in developing countries. *Volunteers:* 3 of which: 3 in developing countries. *Budget/Total 1993:* ECU 1291000 (US$ 1512000). *Financial sources:* Private: 10%. *Public:* 90%.

PUBLICATIONS: *Periodicals:* Rundumschau (4). *Annual report.*

EVALUATION/RESEARCH: Evaluation reports available. Undertakes research activities.

ACTIVITIES IN DEVELOPING REGIONS: Maintains local field presence. Works through local field partners. **Sustainable Development Actions:** Ecology/environment/biodiversity; Education/training/literacy; Energy/transport; Health/sanitation/water; Rural development/agriculture; Sending volunteers/experts/technical assistance; Small enterprises/informal sector/handicrafts; Urban development/habitat. **Regions:** East Africa; Mexico and Central America; Southern Africa.

INFORMATION AND EDUCATION ACTIVITIES: Topics: Ecology/environment/biodiversity; Employment/unemployment; Refugees/migrants/ethnic groups; Urban development/habitat. **Activities:** Fund raising; Information campaigns/exhibitions.

DEU1203

WERKSTATT OKONOMIE

Obere Seegasse 18, 69124 Heidelberg, Germany.

Telephone: 49 (6221) 72 02 96. *Fax:* 49 (6221) 78 11 83. *Contact:* Kristian Hungar.

OBJECTIVES: To organise political and development education programmes and campaigns on behalf of trade unions and churches. To focus on transnational corporations, the countries of South Africa and Brazil and on the theme of child labour in the carpet industry.

GENERAL INFORMATION: *Creation:* 1983. *Personnel/Total:* 5. *Salaried:* 4. *Volunteers:* 1. *Budget/Total 1993:* ECU 140000 (US$ 164000). *Financial sources:* Private: 51%. *Self-financing:* 48%.

PUBLICATIONS: *Periodicals:* Werkstaff-Berichte (2) - Werkstaff-Rundbrief (2). *List of publications.*

EVALUATION/RESEARCH: Undertakes research activities.

INFORMATION AND EDUCATION ACTIVITIES: Topics: Children/youth/family; Employment/unemployment; International economic relations/trade/debt/finance; Racism/xenophobia/antisemitism. **Activities:** Broadcasting/cultural events; Conferences/seminars/workshops/training activities; Exchanges/twinning/linking; Formal education; Information and documentation services/data bases; Information campaigns/exhibitions; Lobbying/advocacy; Networking/electronic telecommunications; Publishing/audiovisual materials/educational materials.

DEU1204

WORLD UNIVERSITY SERVICE, DEUTSCHES KOMITEE (WUS) ♦ Entraide Universitaire Mondiale, Comité allemand

Goebenstrasse 35, 6200 Wiesbaden, Germany.

Telephone: 49 (6121) 44 66 48. *Contact:* Dr. Kambiz Ghawami, Chairman.

DEU1205

WORLD VISION INTERNATIONAL

Postfach 1848, 6370 Oberursel, Germany.

Telephone: 49 (6171) 56074. *Fax:* 49 (6171) 56078.

DEU1206

WORT & TAT, ALLGEMEINE MISSIONSGESELLSCHAFT

Boehnertweg 9, 45359 Essen, Germany.

DEU1207

ZENTRALE DOKUMENTATIONSSTELLE DER FREIEN WOHLFAHRTSPFLEGE FUR FLUCHTLINGE (ZDWF) ♦ Information and Documentation Centre of Welfare Organizations for Refugees

Cecilenstrasse 8, 53721 Siegburg, Germany.

Telephone: 49 (2241) 5 00 01. *Fax:* 49 (2241) 5 00 03. *Contact:* Karsten Lüthke, Director.

OBJECTIVES: To provide information and documentation on asylum law concerning recognized refugees, quota refugees and asylum seekers. To disseminate information on the situation in refugees' countries of origin.

GENERAL INFORMATION: *Creation:* 1980. *Type of organisation:* association of NGOs. *Member organisations:* 6. *Affiliated to:* HURIDOCS (Norway) - IRDN - European Council on Refugees and Exiles (United Kingdom) - European Legal Network on Asylum (United Kingdom). *Personnel/Total:* 12. *Salaried:* 6. *Volunteers:* 6. *Budget/Total 1993:* ECU 413000 (US$ 484000). *Financial sources:* Public: 92%. *Self-financing:* 8%.

PUBLICATIONS: *Annual report. List of publications.*

INFORMATION AND EDUCATION ACTIVITIES: Topics: Emergency relief/refugees/humanitarian assistance; Human rights/peace/conflicts; Peace/ethnic conflicts/armament/disarmament; Racism/xenophobia/antisemitism; Refugees/migrants/ethnic groups. **Activities:** Information and documentation services/data bases.

DEU1208

ZENTRALSTELLE FUR UMWELTERZIEHUNG

Universitätstrasse 5, Fachbereich 9, 4300 Essen 1, Germany.

DEU1209

ZENTRALVERBAND DES DEUTSCHEN HANDWERKS (ZDH) ♦ German Confederation of Skilled Crafts

Johanniterstrasse 1, 53113 Bonn, Germany.

Telephone: 49 (228) 54 52 80. *Fax:* 49 (228) 54 52 05. *Contact:* Hanns-Eberhard Schleyer, Secretary General.

OBJECTIVES: To represent the interests of the sector of skilled crafts as a whole vis-à-vis the German government and all central authorities. To arrive at a consensus within the craft organisation on all major issues of craft policy.

GENERAL INFORMATION: *Creation:* 1949. *Type of organisation:* association of NGOs. *Member organisations:* 120. *Affiliated to:* SEQUA. *Personnel/Total:* 130. *Salaried:* 130. *Budget/Total 1993:* ECU 10326000 (US$ 12097000). *Financial sources:* Self-financing: 100%.

PUBLICATIONS: *Periodicals:* ZDH-Jahresbericht "Das Handwerk" (1) - Handwerksfsltblatt (1) - ZDH-Politik (12) - ZDH-Politik-Brüssel (12) - DHKT-Info (10) - EURO INFO Service (12) -Konjunkturbericht (2) - ZDH-Aktuell (var). *Annual report. List of publications.*

See: How to Use the Directory, page 11.

EVALUATION/RESEARCH: Evaluation reports available. Undertakes research activities.

COMMENTS: Undertakes activities in the Commonwealth of Independent States. Information activities related to the Commonwealth of Independent States.

ACTIVITIES IN DEVELOPING REGIONS: Present in developing regions. Active in 30 country(ies). Maintains local field presence. Works through local field partners. **Sustainable Development Actions:** Democracy/good governance/institution building/participatory development; Education/training/literacy; Small enterprises/informal sector/handicrafts. **Regions:** Caribbean; Central Africa; Central Asia and South Asia; East Africa; East Asia; Mexico and Central America; North Africa; South America; South East Asia; Southern Africa; West Africa.

INFORMATION AND EDUCATION ACTIVITIES: Topics: Other. **Activities:** Conferences/seminars/workshops/training activities; Exchanges/twinning/linking; Formal education; Fund raising; Information and documentation services/data bases; Information campaigns/exhibitions; Lobbying/advocacy; Publishing/audiovisual materials/educational materials.

DEU1210

ZENTRUM FUR ENTWICKLUNGSBEZOGENE BILDUNG ♦ Centre for Development Education

Kniebisstrasse 29, 70188 Stuttgart, Germany.

Telephone: 49 (711) 9 25 77 60. **Fax:** 49 (711) 9 25 77 49. **Contact:** K.H. Rudersdorf.

OBJECTIVES: To support regional (Ba-Wü) development education.

GENERAL INFORMATION: Creation: 1975. **Affiliated to:** Dienste in Übersee/Service Overseas and Association of Protestant Church Development Service (Germany). **Personnel/Total:** 2. **Salaried:** 2. **Budget/Total 1993:** ECU 26000 (US$ 30000). **Financial sources:** Private: 100%.

EVALUATION/RESEARCH: Undertakes research activities.

PLANNED ACTIVITIES: Project on injustice and peace. Campaigns against children working in the carpet industry and for the promotion of fair trade. Training foreign students in development issues.

INFORMATION AND EDUCATION ACTIVITIES: Topics: Culture/tradition/religion; Ecology/environment/biodiversity; Education/training/literacy; Employment/unemployment; Food/famine; Human rights/peace/conflicts; International economic relations/trade/debt/finance; Peace/ethnic conflicts/armament/disarmament; Population/family planning/demography; Poverty/living conditions; Racism/xenophobia/antisemitism; Refugees/migrants/ethnic groups. **Activities:** Conferences/seminars/workshops/training activities; Exchanges/twinning/linking; Networking/electronic telecommunications.

DEU1211

ZENTRUM FUR HANDELSFORUDERUNG GMBH ♦ Centre for Trade Development

Neuer Jungfernstieg 21, 20354 Hamburg, Germany.

Telephone: 49 (40) 34 30 95. **Fax:** 49 (40) 35 47 04. **Contact:** Uwe Waltsgott, Managing Director.

OBJECTIVES: To provide assistance for private sector companies, their associations and chambers. To promote investment, trade development, technology transfers and institution-building.

GENERAL INFORMATION: Personnel/Total: 112. **Salaried:** 12 of which: 7 in developing countries. **Volunteers:** 100.

EVALUATION/RESEARCH: Undertakes research activities.

ACTIVITIES IN DEVELOPING REGIONS: Present in developing regions. Active in 4 country(ies). Maintains local field presence. Works through local field partners. **Sustainable Development Actions:** Debt/finance/trade; Sending volunteers/experts/technical assistance; Small enterprises/informal sector/handicrafts. **Regions:** East Africa; East Asia; South America; Southern Africa; West Africa.

INFORMATION AND EDUCATION ACTIVITIES: Topics: Ecology/environment/biodiversity; International economic relations/trade/debt/finance. **Activities:** Conferences/seminars/workshops/training activities; Exchanges/twinning/linking; Information and documentation services/data bases; Information campaigns/exhibitions; Lobbying/advocacy.

DEU1212

ZIMBABWE HILFSAKTION (ZIHA) ♦ Zimbabwe Relief Organisation

Graffring 47, 4630 Bochum 1, Germany.

Telephone: 49 (234) 31 27 72. **Contact:** Saul Binya Masuka, Chairman.

DNK1213

ABEN AV-RADGIVNING OM U-LANDSSPORGSMAL

c/o Fønix Film, Troensevej 13, 4700 Næstved, Denmark.

Telephone: 45 (53) 72 71 46. **Fax:** 45 (53) 72 71 76. **Contact:** Finn Brasen.

DNK1214

ADVENTIST DEVELOPMENT AND RELIEF AGENCY (ADRA DENMARK)

Concordiavej 16 - P.O. Box 15, 2850 Naerum , Denmark.

Telephone: 45 (45) 80 56 00. **Fax:** 45 (45) 80 70 75. **Contact:** Helge Andersen, General Secretary.

OBJECTIVES: To provide disaster relief and support for development projects.

GENERAL INFORMATION: Creation: 1987. **Personnel/Total:** 33. *Salaried:* 31 of which: 27 in developing countries. *Volunteers:* 2 of which: 2 in developing countries. **Budget/Total 1993:** ECU 3246000 (US$ 3800000). **Financial sources:** *Private:* 17%. *Public:* 80%. *Self-financing:* 3%.

PUBLICATIONS: Periodicals: ADRA-Nyt (4). *Annual report.*

EVALUATION/RESEARCH: Evaluation reports available. Undertakes research activities.

PLANNED ACTIVITIES: AIDS educational project in Malawi. Construction of 30 schools and teacher training programme in Uganda. Maintenance instruction and installation of wells and handpumps in desert villages in Sudan.

COMMENTS: ADRA Denmark is part of an international network of ADRA organisations existing in nearly all industrial countries and in 70 developing countries. Undertakes activities in the Commonwealth of Independent States.

ACTIVITIES IN DEVELOPING REGIONS: Active in 16 country(ies). Maintains local field presence. Works through local field partners. **Sustainable Development Actions:** Education/training/literacy; Emergency relief/refugees/humanitarian assistance; Energy/transport; Health/sanitation/water; Rural development/agriculture. **Regions:** Central Africa; East Africa; West Africa.

INFORMATION AND EDUCATION ACTIVITIES: Topics: Children/youth/family; Education/training/literacy; Emergency relief/refugees/humanitarian assistance; Health/sanitation/water; Refugees/migrants/ethnic groups. **Activities:** Formal education; Fund raising; Information campaigns/exhibitions; Publishing/audiovisual materials/educational materials.

DNK1215

AGORO I DANMARK ♦ AGORO in Denmark

Amtsgymnasiet i Roskilde, Domkirkepladsen, 4000 Roskilde, Denmark.

Telephone: 45 (42) 35 34 44. **Fax:** 45 (42) 35 14 10. **Contact:** Hanne Tofte Jespersen.

OBJECTIVES: To develop cultural co-operation between Ghana and Denmark in the areas of music, dance and drama. To act as a supportive link in providing equipment, students and guest teachers to the centre in Ghana. To serve as an information centre and programme organiser in Denmark on Ghanian music and culture.

GENERAL INFORMATION: Creation: 1993. **Personnel/Total:** 11. *Volunteers:* 11 of which: 1 in developing countries. **Budget/Total 1993:** ECU 4000 (US$ 4500). **Financial sources:** *Private:* 7%. *Public:* 85%. *Self-financing:* 8%.

PUBLICATIONS: *List of publications.*

EVALUATION/RESEARCH: Evaluation reports available. Undertakes research activities.

PLANNED ACTIVITIES: Exchange of cultural instructors and musical cultural groups from the Cape Coast, Ghana to Denmark. Promotion and sale of musical cassettes on environmental issues, produced in Ghana. Development of a centre of renovated musical instruments to support the AGORO centre in Ghana.

ACTIVITIES IN DEVELOPING REGIONS: Active in 1 country(ies). Maintains local field presence. Works through local field partners. **Sustainable Development Actions:** Children/youth/family; Democracy/good governance/institution building/participatory development; Ecology/environment/biodiversity; Education/training/literacy; Sending volunteers/experts/technical assistance; Small enterprises/informal sector/handicrafts; Urban development/habitat. **Regions:** West Africa.

INFORMATION AND EDUCATION ACTIVITIES: Topics: Children/youth/family; Culture/tradition/religion; Ecology/environment/biodiversity; Education/training/literacy; International relations/cooperation/development aid. **Activities:** Broadcasting/cultural events; Conferences/seminars/workshops/training activities; Exchanges/twinning/linking; Fund raising; Information and documentation services/data bases; Information campaigns/exhibitions; Networking/electronic telecommunications; Publishing/audiovisual materials/educational materials.

DNK1216

AKTION BøRNEHJAELP ♦ Action Children Aid

Ryparken 98, 2100 København ø, Denmark.

Telephone: 45 (31) 20 36 10. **Fax:** 45 (31) 20 36 10. **Contact:** Grete Lauritzen, Chairman.

OBJECTIVES: To support poor children and their families in India and Bangladesh.

GENERAL INFORMATION: Creation: 1965. **Affiliated to:** Emmaus International (France). **Personnel/Total:** 12. *Salaried:* 2. *Volunteers:* 10. **Budget/Total 1993:** ECU 1102000 (US$ 1290000). **Financial sources:** *Private:* 60%. *Public:* 40%.

PUBLICATIONS: Periodicals: Orientering (1) - Newsletter (4). *Annual report. List of publications.*

ACTIVITIES IN DEVELOPING REGIONS: Active in 1 country(ies). Works through local field partners. **Sustainable Development Actions:** Children/youth/family; Education/training/literacy; Food/famine; Health/sanitation/water; Rural development/agriculture; Urban development/habitat. **Regions:** Central Asia and South Asia.

INFORMATION AND EDUCATION ACTIVITIES: Topics: Children/youth/family; Education/training/literacy; Food/famine; Health/sanitation/water; Poverty/living conditions; Rural development/agriculture; Urban development/habitat. **Activities:** Fund raising; Publishing/audiovisual materials/educational materials.

DNK1217

AMNESTY INTERNATIONAL, DANSK AFDELING (AI)

Dyrkøb 3, 1166 København K, Denmark.

Telephone: 45 (33) 11 75 41. **Fax:** 45 (33) 93 37 46. **Contact:** Lars Christensen.

DNK1218

APOSTOLSK KIRKES MISSION (AKM) ♦ Apostolic Church Mission

Lykkegaardsvej 100, 6000 Kolding, Denmark.

Telephone: 45 (75) 54 12 01. **Fax:** 45 (75) 52 11 64. **Contact:** Jens Erik Jacobsen, Missionary Secretary.

OBJECTIVES: To evangelize, build churches and train leaders. To provide self-help techniques, social and medical aid. To organise training in farming, nursing, literacy. To provide Bible translation programmes, prison missions and humanitarian aid to Eastern Europe.

GENERAL INFORMATION: Creation: 1924. **Affiliated to:** Danish Missionary Council (Denmark). **Personnel/Total:** 49. *Salaried:* 21 of which: 19 in developing countries. *Volunteers:* 28 of which: 28 in developing countries. **Budget/Total 1993:** ECU 399000 (US$ 467000). **Financial sources:** *Private:* 100%.

PUBLICATIONS: Periodicals: Evangeliebladet (11) - Newsletter (11).

PLANNED ACTIVITIES: To organise self-help programmes for the mothers and children who lost their husbands and fathers to AIDS.

COMMENTS: Undertakes activities in the Commonwealth of Independent States.

See: *How to Use the Directory*, page 11.

ACTIVITIES IN DEVELOPING REGIONS: Present in developing regions. Active in 5 country(ies). Maintains local field presence. **Sustainable Development Actions:** Children/youth/family; Education/training/literacy; Gender issues/women; Health/sanitation/water; Other; Rural development/agriculture; Sending volunteers/experts/technical assistance. **Regions:** Central Africa; Central Asia and South Asia; East Africa; South America; Southern Africa; West Africa.

INFORMATION AND EDUCATION ACTIVITIES: Topics: Children/youth/family; Education/training/literacy; Emergency relief/refugees/humanitarian assistance; Health/sanitation/water; Other; Rural development/agriculture. **Activities:** Conferences/seminars/workshops/training activities; Exchanges/twinning/linking; Formal education; Fund raising; Information and documentation services/data bases; Information campaigns/exhibitions; Publishing/audiovisual materials/educational materials.

DNK1219
ARBEJDERBEVAEGELSENS INTERNATIONALE FORUM (AIF) ♦ Labour Movement International Forum

Teglværksgade 27, 3, 2100 København O, Denmark.

Telephone: 45 (31) 29 60 66. *Fax:* 45 (31) 20 10 19. *Contact:* Ib Wistisen, President.

DNK1220
ARBEJDERBEVAEGELSENS U-LANDSUDVALG (AOF) ♦ Third World Committee of the Danish Labour Movement

Teglvaerksgade 27.3, 2100 København O, Denmark.

Telephone: 45 (1) 29 60 66. *Contact:* Mogens Jensen.

DNK1221
ARHUS-KLUNSERNE

Poppelgårdsvej 1, Lading, 8471 Sabro, Denmark.

Telephone: 45 (86) 94 86 11.

DNK1222
ASF-DANSK FOLKEHJAELP ♦ Danish People's Relief Association

Jernbanevej 12, P.O. Box 206, 4960 Holeby, Denmark.

Telephone: 45 (53) 90 74 00. *Fax:* 45 (53) 90 73 99. *Contact:* Ib. Jensen, Chairman.

OBJECTIVES: To provide emergency relief and development aid to developing countries. To undertake first aid education and social activities in Denmark.

GENERAL INFORMATION: *Creation:* 1907. *Affiliated to:* Dansk Flygtningehjalp - IAH (Germany) - VOICE. *Personnel/Total:* 4026. *Salaried:* 26 of which: 14 in developing countries. *Volunteers:* 4000. *Financial sources:* Private: 40%. Public: 40%. Self-financing: 20%.

PUBLICATIONS: *Periodicals:* Folkehjoelpsbladet (4). *List of publications.*

EVALUATION/RESEARCH: Evaluation reports available. Undertakes research activities.

COMMENTS: Undertakes activities in the Commonwealth of Independent States. Information activities related to the Commonwealth of Independent States.

ACTIVITIES IN DEVELOPING REGIONS: Active in 5 country(ies). **Sustainable Development Actions:** Children/youth/family; Education/training/literacy; Food/famine; Gender issues/women; Health/sanitation/water; Rural development/agriculture. **Regions:** Central Asia and South Asia; East Africa; Southern Africa.

INFORMATION AND EDUCATION ACTIVITIES: Topics: Children/youth/family; Ecology/environment/biodiversity; Education/training/literacy; Emergency relief/refugees/humanitarian assistance; Food/famine; Gender issues/women; Health/sanitation/water; Human rights/peace/conflicts; International relations/cooperation/development aid; Peace/ethnic conflicts/armament/disarmament; Population/family planning/demography; Poverty/living conditions; Refugees/migrants/ethnic groups; Rural development/agriculture. **Activities:** Formal education; Fund raising.

DNK1223
ASSOCIATION INTERNATIONALE DE DEFENSE DES ARTISTES (AIDA)

Postboks 316, 1503 København V, Denmark.

Téléphone: 45 (35) 26 16 24. *Fax:* 45 (64) 82 64 68. *Contact:* Lars Sidenius.

DNK1224
ASSOCIATION OF WORLD EDUCATION (AWE)

Ostbanagade 7, 2100 København 0, Denmark.

Telephone: 45 (31) 42 24 13. *Contact:* Michel AAbling.

DNK1225
AZ-INTERNATIONAL TECHNICAL TEAM (AZITT)

c/o Erik Gregersen, Sjællandsgade 95A, 8000 Århus C, Denmark.

DNK1226
BISU ♦ Construction, International Co-operation, Development

Strandboulevarden 116, 2100 København O, Denmark.

Telephone: 45 (35) 43 60 03. *Fax:* 45 (31) 38 56 16. *Contact:* Mogens Sigersdal, Constructor.

OBJECTIVES: To assist and consult governmental and private organisations in and outside Denmark on projects for development, low-cost human settlement, and construction and emergency aid. To co-operate with poor communities and minority groups. To prioritise support for projects concerning the protection of the environment.

GENERAL INFORMATION: *Creation:* 1991. *Affiliated to:* EU NGO Platform. *Personnel/Total:* 11. *Salaried:* 1 of which: 1 in developing countries. *Volunteers:* 10 of which: 10 in developing countries. *Budget/Total 1993:* ECU 132000 (US$ 154000). *Financial sources:* Private: 95%. Self-financing: 5%.

PUBLICATIONS: *Periodicals:* BISU NYT (5). *Annual report.*

EVALUATION/RESEARCH: Evaluation reports available. Undertakes research activities.

PLANNED ACTIVITIES: Human settlement project in Nicaragua and in the Philippines. Environmental project in Brazil. Ecotourism project in Nicaragua.

COMMENTS: Members of the European Union NGO Platform.

ACTIVITIES IN DEVELOPING REGIONS: Present in developing regions. Active in 2 country(ies). Maintains local field presence. Works through local field partners. **Sustainable Development Actions:** Democracy/good governance/institution building/participatory development; Ecology/environment/biodiversity; Education/training/literacy; Emergency relief/refugees/humanitarian assistance; Health/sanitation/water; Rural development/agriculture; Sending volunteers/experts/technical assistance; Small enterprises/informal sector/handicrafts; Urban development/habitat. **Regions:** Mexico and Central America.

INFORMATION AND EDUCATION ACTIVITIES: Topics: Ecology/environment/biodiversity; Poverty/living conditions; Urban development/habitat. **Activities:** Conferences/seminars/workshops/training activities; Formal education; Fund raising; Information and documentation services/data bases; Information campaigns/exhibitions; Lobbying/advocacy.

DNK1227
BORNEFONDEN ♦ Children's Fund

Blegdamsvej 29, 2100 København O, Denmark.

Telephone: 45 (35) 43 63 63. *Fax:* 45 (35) 43 01 25. *Contact:* Søren Stenum, Director.

OBJECTIVES: To provide healthcare and education to underprivileged children in combination with community development activities.

GENERAL INFORMATION: *Creation:* 1972. *Type of organisation:* coordinating body. *Member organisations:* 75. *Personnel/Total:* 1650. *Salaried:* 500 of which: 485 in developing countries. *Volunteers:* 1150 of which: 1137 in developing countries. *Budget/Total 1993:*

ECU 8167000 (US$ 9562000). *Financial sources:* Private: 97%. Public: 1%. Self-financing: 2%.

PUBLICATIONS: *Periodicals:* Fra Os Til Jer (4). *Annual report.*

PLANNED ACTIVITIES: Begin work in Benin.

COMMENTS: BøRNEfonden is the chair organisation for the World Alliance of CCFs.

ACTIVITIES IN DEVELOPING REGIONS: Present in developing regions. Active in 3 country(ies). Maintains local field presence. **Sustainable Development Actions:** Children/youth/family; Democracy/good governance/institution building/participatory development; Education/training/literacy; Emergency relief/refugees/humanitarian assistance; Gender issues/women; Health/sanitation/water; Population/family planning/demography; Rural development/agriculture; Small enterprises/informal sector/handicrafts; Urban development/habitat. **Regions:** Central Africa; West Africa.

INFORMATION AND EDUCATION ACTIVITIES: Topics: Children/youth/family; Education/training/literacy; Emergency relief/refugees/humanitarian assistance; Employment/unemployment; Gender issues/women; Health/sanitation/water; Human rights/peace/conflicts; International relations/cooperation/development aid; Peace/ethnic conflicts/armament/disarmament; Population/family planning/demography; Poverty/living conditions; Rural development/agriculture; Urban development/habitat. **Activities:** Conferences/seminars/workshops/training activities; Formal education; Fund raising; Lobbying/advocacy.

DNK1228

BRODREMENIGHEDENS DANSKE MISSION (BDM) ♦ The Danish Moravian Mission

Norregade 14, P.O. Box 30, 6070 Christiansfeld, Denmark.

Telephone: 45 (74) 56 22 33. *Fax:* 45 (74) 56 13 34. *Contact:* Rev. Georg C. Sørensen, Chairman of the Board.

DNK1229

BUTIK PAPAYA ♦ Shop Papaya

Brandstrupsgade 4, 9000 Aalborg, Denmark.

Telephone: 45 (98) 11 30 44. *Contact:* Else Bro.

OBJECTIVES: To promote the idea of fair trade with Third World countries and ensure the living conditions of their producers. To disseminate knowledge about the living and working conditions in developing countries.

GENERAL INFORMATION: *Creation:* 1991. *Affiliated to:* International Solidarity(umbrella organisation) (Denmark). *Personnel/Total:* 22. *Salaried:* 2. *Volunteers:* 20. *Budget/Total 1993:* ECU 40000 (US$ 46000). *Financial sources:* Self-financing: 100%.

PUBLICATIONS: *Periodicals:* Butik Papaya Nyhedsbrev (4).

ACTIVITIES IN DEVELOPING REGIONS: Active in 22 country(ies). **Sustainable Development Actions:** Children/youth/family; Debt/finance/trade; Education/training/literacy; Gender issues/women; Small enterprises/informal sector/handicrafts. **Regions:** Central Asia and South Asia; East Africa; Mexico and Central America; South East Asia; Southern Africa.

INFORMATION AND EDUCATION ACTIVITIES: Topics: Human rights/peace/conflicts; International economic relations/trade/debt/finance; International relations/cooperation/development aid; Poverty/living conditions. **Activities:** Conferences/seminars/workshops/training activities; Information and documentation services/data bases; Information campaigns/exhibitions.

DNK1230

BUTIK SALAM ♦ Boutique Salam

Brandts Passage 34, 5000 Odense C, Denmark.

Telephone: 45 (66) 13 00 45. *Fax:* 45 (66) 13 90 45. *Contact:* Mette Mark, Chairman.

OBJECTIVES: To practice alternative trade and guarantee fair prices.

GENERAL INFORMATION: *Creation:* 1987. *Affiliated to:* International Federation of Alternative Trade. *Personnel/Total:* 32. *Salaried:* 2. *Vol-*

unteers: 30. *Budget/Total 1993:* ECU 395000 (US$ 463000). *Financial sources:* Public: 5%. Self-financing: 95%.

ACTIVITIES IN DEVELOPING REGIONS: Active in 20 country(ies). **Sustainable Development Actions:** Debt/finance/trade. **Regions:** Central Africa; Central Asia and South Asia; East Africa; East Asia; Mexico and Central America; North Africa; South America; South East Asia; Southern Africa.

INFORMATION AND EDUCATION ACTIVITIES: **Topics:** International economic relations/trade/debt/finance. **Activities:** Conferences/seminars/workshops/training activities; Information and documentation services/data bases; Information campaigns/exhibitions.

DNK1231

CAFE CIKADEN

Griffenfeldsgade 35, 2200 København N, Denmark.

Telephone: 45 (31) 35 34 23. *Fax:* 45 (35) 37 19 80.

DNK1232

CARE DANMARK ♦ CARE Denmark

Borgergade 14, 1., 1300 København K, Denmark.

Telephone: 45 (33) 15 00 07. *Fax:* 45 (33) 15 39 07. *Contact:* Niels Tofte, Secretary General.

OBJECTIVES: To improve living conditions in developing countries by organising projects that create balance between an increased agricultural production and a suitable utilization of the natural resources.

GENERAL INFORMATION: *Creation:* 1987. *Type of organisation:* association of NGOs. *Affiliated to:* CARE International (Belgium) - Danish Refugee Council (Denmark) - The Daniish EC-NGO Platform (Denmark) - Forum for Energy and Development. *Personnel/Total:* 15. *Salaried:* 6 of which: 1 in developing countries. *Volunteers:* 9. *Budget/Total 1993:* ECU 3520000 (US$ 4121000). *Financial sources:* Private: 2%. Public: 90%. Self-financing: 2%.

PUBLICATIONS: *Periodicals:* CARE NYT (4). *Annual report. List of publications.*

EVALUATION/RESEARCH: Evaluation reports available.

ACTIVITIES IN DEVELOPING REGIONS: Present in developing regions. Active in 5 country(ies). Maintains local field presence. **Sustainable Development Actions:** Rural development/agriculture. **Regions:** Central Africa; Central Asia and South Asia; Mexico and Central America; South America; South East Asia.

INFORMATION AND EDUCATION ACTIVITIES: **Topics:** Rural development/agriculture. **Activities:** Fund raising; Information campaigns/exhibitions; Publishing/audiovisual materials/educational materials.

DNK1233

CARIBIENKOMITEEN ♦ The Caribbean Committee

c/o Susanne Pascal, Lerhus Allé 56, 1., 8270 Højbjerg, Denmark.

Telephone: 45 (86) 27 97 15.

DNK1234

CARITAS DANMARK ♦ Caritas Denmark

Bredgade 69, 1260 København K, Denmark.

Telephone: 45 (33) 12 72 61. *Fax:* 45 (33) 32 47 11. *Contact:* Anne Lise Timmermann, President.

OBJECTIVES: To fund development and emergency projects in developing countries, irrespective of race, creed and political affiliation.

GENERAL INFORMATION: *Creation:* 1947. *Affiliated to:* Caritas Internationalis (Italy) - International Catholic Migration Commission (Switzerland) - Danish Refugee Council (Denmark) - Caritas Europe (Belgium) -Danish EC-NGO Liaison Committee (Denmark). *Personnel/Total:* 7. *Salaried:* 6. *Volunteers:* 1. *Budget/Total 1993:* ECU 9682000 (US$ 11336000). *Financial sources:* Private: 6%. Public: 94%.

PUBLICATIONS: *Periodicals:* Caritas-Nyt (2). *Annual report.*

PLANNED ACTIVITIES: Lenten campaign.

See: *How to Use the Directory,* page 11.

COMMENTS: Undertakes activities in the Commonwealth of Independent States.

ACTIVITIES IN DEVELOPING REGIONS: Active in 21 country(ies). Works through local field partners.

DNK1235
CENTER FOR ALTERNATIV SAMFUNDSANALYSE (CASA)

Linnésgade 25, 3., 1361 København K, Denmark.

Telephone: 45 (33) 32 05 55. *Fax:* 45 (33) 33 05 54.

DNK1236
CHILD CARE INTERNATIONAL - DENMARK

Godthaabsvaenget 23, 2000 Frederiksberg, Denmark.

Telephone: 45 (38) 88 04 18. *Fax:* 45 (38) 88 28 11. *Contact:* Vivi Labo, Secretary.

DNK1237
CHILDHOPE - DEN INTERNATIONALE BEVEGELSE FOR GADEBORN

Postboks 306, 2730 Herlev, Denmark.

DNK1238
CO-OPERATIVE CENTRE DENMARK (CCD)

Ahlefeldtsgade 18, 1359 København K, Denmark.

Telephone: 45 (33) 91 86 86. *Fax:* 45 (33) 91 80 05. *Contact:* Ole Baekgaard, Secretary General.

OBJECTIVES: To establish development collaboration between the Danish and Third World co-operative movements.

GENERAL INFORMATION: *Creation:* 1986. *Type of organisation:* coordinating body. *Member organisations:* 60. *Affiliated to:* International Co-operative Alliance (Switzerland) - Den Danske NGO Platform (Denmark). *Personnel/Total:* 15. *Salaried:* 11 of which: 7 in developing countries. *Volunteers:* 4. *Financial sources:* Private: 40%. Public: 60%.

PUBLICATIONS: *Periodicals:* (var). *Annual report.*

EVALUATION/RESEARCH: Evaluation reports available.

PLANNED ACTIVITIES: To support co-operatives and agriculture in Indonesia. To increase co-operation between movements among the Baltic states.

COMMENTS: Undertakes activities in the Commonwealth of Independent States. Information activities related to the Commonwealth of Independent States.

ACTIVITIES IN DEVELOPING REGIONS: Present in developing regions. Active in 5 country(ies). Maintains local field presence. Works through local field partners. **Sustainable Development Actions:** Debt/finance/trade; Democracy/good governance/institution building/participatory development; Education/training/literacy; Gender issues/women; Rural development/agriculture; Sending volunteers/experts/technical assistance; Small enterprises/informal sector/handicrafts. **Regions:** Central Africa; Central Asia and South Asia; East Africa; South America; South East Asia; Southern Africa; West Africa.

INFORMATION AND EDUCATION ACTIVITIES: Topics: Gender issues/women; International economic relations/trade/debt/finance; International relations/cooperation/development aid; Rural development/agriculture. **Activities:** Conferences/seminars/workshops/training activities; Exchanges/twinning/linking; Fund raising; Information and documentation services/data bases; Lobbying/advocacy; Publishing/audiovisual materials/educational materials.

DNK1239
COMORER KOMITEEN

c/o Jørgen Sprogøe Petersen, Gasværksvej 33, 4. tv, 1656 København V, Denmark.

Telephone: 45 (31) 22 13 53.

DNK1240
DANISH COMMITTEE FOR AID TO AFGHAN REFUGEES (DACAAR)

Postboks 53, Borgergade 10, 3 sal, 1002 København K, Denmark.

Telephone: 45 (33) 91 27 00. *Fax:* 45 (33) 32 84 48. *Contact:* Programme Consultant.

DNK1241
DANISH RESOURCE MANAGEMENT CENTRE (RENDAN A/S)

Gladsaxevej 382, 2860 Soborg, Denmark.

Telephone: 45 (39) 66 12 00. *Fax:* 45 (39) 66 16 00. *Contact:* Dorte Kardel, Superviser.

DNK1242
DANSK - TANZANIANSK VENSKABSFORENING (DANTAN) ♦
Danish - Tanzanian Friendship Association

P.O. Box 257, 1502 København V, Denmark.

Telephone: 45 (31) 10 01 10. *Fax:* 45 (31) 10 01 10. *Contact:* Jesper Kirknæs, Chairman.

OBJECTIVES: To promote contact, understanding and co-operation between the people of Denmark and Tanzania by supporting economic projects.

GENERAL INFORMATION: *Creation:* 1980. *Member organisations:* 4. *Affiliated to:* DANTAN Solidarity (Denmark) - Msitu wa Kesho (Tanzania) - Pambazuka (Tanzania). *Personnel/Total:* 17. *Volunteers:* 17 of which: 2 in developing countries. *Budget/Total 1993:* ECU 32000 (US$ 37000). *Financial sources:* Private: 50%. Public: 40%. *Self-financing:* 10%.

PUBLICATIONS: *Periodicals:* Kumekucha (4). *Annual report.*

EVALUATION/RESEARCH: Evaluation reports available. Undertakes research activities.

PLANNED ACTIVITIES: The initiation of street kids' project. Supporting women's groups.

ACTIVITIES IN DEVELOPING REGIONS: Present in developing regions. Active in 1 country(ies). Maintains local field presence. Works through local field partners. **Sustainable Development Actions:** Health/sanitation/water; Sending volunteers/experts/technical assistance; Small enterprises/informal sector/handicrafts. **Regions:** East Africa.

INFORMATION AND EDUCATION ACTIVITIES: Topics: Health/sanitation/water; Rural development/agriculture. **Activities:** Conferences/seminars/workshops/training activities; Exchanges/twinning/linking; Fund raising; Information and documentation services/data bases; Lobbying/advocacy; Publishing/audiovisual materials/educational materials.

DNK1243
DANSK AFS

Nordre Fasanvej 111, 2000 Frederiksberg, Denmark.

Telephone: 45 (38) 34 33 00. *Fax:* 45 (38) 34 66 00. *Contact:* Ina Groth.

OBJECTIVES: To promote peace and global understanding. To support international youth and adult exchange programmes.

GENERAL INFORMATION: *Creation:* 1957. *Affiliated to:* Danish Youth Council (Denmark) - Mellemfolkeligt Samvirke (Denmark) - UN Association (Denmark) - North/South Coalition (Denmark). *Personnel/Total:* var. *Salaried:* 10. *Volunteers:* var.

PUBLICATIONS: *Periodicals:* Forum (4) - Medlemsnyt (12). *Annual report.*

EVALUATION/RESEARCH: Evaluation reports available. Undertakes research activities.

PLANNED ACTIVITIES: Partnership development in African countries.

COMMENTS: Undertakes activities in the Commonwealth of Independent States. Information activities related to the Commonwealth of Independent States.

ACTIVITIES IN DEVELOPING REGIONS: Present in developing regions. Active in 4 country(ies). Maintains local field presence. Works through

Voir : *Comment utiliser le répertoire,* page 11.

local field partners. **Sustainable Development Actions:** Democracy/ good governance/institution building/participatory development; Education/training/literacy. **Regions:** Southern Africa.

INFORMATION AND EDUCATION ACTIVITIES: Topics: Culture/tradition/religion; Education/training/literacy; Gender issues/women; International relations/cooperation/development aid. **Activities:** Conferences/seminars/workshops/training activities; Exchanges/twinning/linking; Formal education; Fund raising; Publishing/audiovisual materials/educational materials.

DNK1244

DANSK BORNEFOND ♦ The Danish Children's Fund

Vemmetoftevej 6, 4640 Fakse, Denmark.

Telephone: 45 (53) 71 00 78. *Fax:* 45 (53) 71 01 30. *Contact:* Inger Mortensen.

OBJECTIVES: To support the education of children in the Third World.

GENERAL INFORMATION: *Creation:* 1981. *Member organisations:* 1768. *Personnel/Total:* 13. *Salaried:* 3 of which: 2 in developing countries. *Volunteers:* 10 of which: 8 in developing countries. *Budget/Total 1993:* ECU 316000 (US$ 370000). *Financial sources:* Private: 2%. *Self-financing:* 98%.

PUBLICATIONS: *Periodicals:* Nyt Fra Dansk Børnefond (3). *Annual report.*

EVALUATION/RESEARCH: Undertakes research activities.

ACTIVITIES IN DEVELOPING REGIONS: Present in developing regions. Active in 11 country(ies). Works through local field partners. **Sustainable Development Actions:** Children/youth/family; Education/training/literacy; Food/famine; Health/sanitation/water; Small enterprises/informal sector/handicrafts. **Regions:** Central Asia and South Asia; East Africa; East Asia; South America; West Africa.

DNK1245

DANSK ETHIOPER MISSION (DEM) ♦ Danish Evangelical Mission

Norregade 14, P.O. Box 24, 6070 Christiansfeld, Denmark.

Telephone: 45 (74) 56 22 33. *Fax:* 45 (74) 56 13 34. *Contact:* Keld Kobborg Andersen , Secretary General.

OBJECTIVES: To meet the spiritual and physical needs of people in co-operation with partner churches in Ethiopia, Liberia and Botswana.

GENERAL INFORMATION: *Creation:* 1948. *Affiliated to:* Dansk Missionråd (Denmark). *Personnel/Total:* 33. *Salaried:* 31 of which: 24 in developing countries. *Volunteers:* 2 of which: 2 in developing countries. *Budget/Total 1993:* ECU 962000 (US$ 1126000). *Financial sources:* Private: 97%. Public: 3%.

PUBLICATIONS: *Periodicals:* DEM-Bladet (6) - Magasinet (4).

ACTIVITIES IN DEVELOPING REGIONS: Active in 2 country(ies). Maintains local field presence. Works through local field partners. **Sustainable Development Actions:** Children/youth/family; Education/training/literacy; Emergency relief/refugees/humanitarian assistance; Energy/transport; Food/famine; Health/sanitation/water; Rural development/agriculture; Sending volunteers/experts/technical assistance; Urban development/habitat. **Regions:** East Africa; Southern Africa.

INFORMATION AND EDUCATION ACTIVITIES: Topics: Children/youth/family; Education/training/literacy; Emergency relief/refugees/humanitarian assistance; Food/famine; Health/sanitation/water; Peace/ethnic conflicts/armament/disarmament; Poverty/living conditions; Rural development/agriculture. **Activities:** Fund raising; Information campaigns/exhibitions.

DNK1246

DANSK FILIPPINSK GRUPPE (DFG)

c/o Viggo Brun, Grøndalsvæenge Allé 7, 2400 København NV, Denmark.

Telephone: 45 (31) 19 62 64.

DNK1247

DANSK FILIPPINSK KVINDEGRUPPE

c/o Nina Ellinger, Grøndalsvaenge Allé 7, 2400 København NV, Denmark.

Telephone: 45 (31) 19 62 64.

DNK1248

DANSK FLYGTNINGEHJALP ♦ Danish Refugee Council

Borgergade 10,3 P.O. Box 53, 1002 København K, Denmark.

Telephone: 45 (33) 91 27 00. *Fax:* 45 (33) 32 84 48. *Contact:* Arne Piel Christensen, Secretary General.

OBJECTIVES: To raise funds for refugee self-help projects. To promote humanitarian refugee legislation. To encourage the integration of refugees in Denmark. To represent member organisations in negotiations with public authorities and international refugee organisations. To aid in asylum counselling. To assist with the repatriation of migrants to their country of origin.

GENERAL INFORMATION: *Creation:* 1956. *Member organisations:* 18. *Affiliated to:* International Council of Voluntary Agencies (Switzerland) - European Council on Refugees in Exile (United Kingdom). *Personnel/Total:* 1615. *Salaried:* 1615 of which: 126 in developing countries. *Budget/Total 1993:* ECU 90231000 (US$ 105640000). *Financial sources:* Private: 2%. Public: 98%.

PUBLICATIONS: *Periodicals:* Exil (4) - Refugee News (6) - Refugees (1). *List of publications.*

EVALUATION/RESEARCH: Evaluation reports available.

COMMENTS: Undertakes activities in the Commonwealth of Independent States. Information activities related to the Commonwealth of Independent States.

ACTIVITIES IN DEVELOPING REGIONS: Active in 6 country(ies). Maintains local field presence. Works through local field partners. **Sustainable Development Actions:** Children/youth/family; Democracy/good governance/institution building/participatory development; Education/training/literacy; Emergency relief/refugees/humanitarian assistance; Energy/transport; Gender issues/women; Health/sanitation/water; Rural development/agriculture; Small enterprises/informal sector/handicrafts; Urban development/habitat. **Regions:** Central Africa; Central Asia and South Asia; South America; South East Asia; Southern Africa; West Africa.

INFORMATION AND EDUCATION ACTIVITIES: Topics: Children/youth/family; Culture/tradition/religion; Education/training/literacy; Emergency relief/refugees/humanitarian assistance; Employment/unemployment; Gender issues/women; Human rights/peace/conflicts; International relations/cooperation/development aid; Other; Racism/xenophobia/antisemitism; Refugees/migrants/ethnic groups. **Activities:** Conferences/seminars/workshops/training activities; Fund raising; Information and documentation services/data bases; Information campaigns/exhibitions; Lobbying/advocacy; Networking/electronic telecommunications; Publishing/audiovisual materials/educational materials.

DNK1249

DANSK FOLKEOPLYSNINGS SAMRAD ♦ Danish Council for Adult Education

Romersgade 7, 1362 København K, Denmark.

DNK1250

DANSK INDISK FORENING ♦ Danish Indian Society

c/o Finn Norring, Rytterager 44, 2791 Dragør, Denmark.

Telephone: 45 (32) 53 24 75. *Contact:* Finn Norring, Chairman.

OBJECTIVES: To encourage cultural, commercial and economic co-operation between Denmark and India. To disseminate information on India and provide a meeting place for Danes and Indians, notably on festive occasions.

GENERAL INFORMATION: *Creation:* 1948. *Personnel/Total:* 7. *Volunteers:* 7. *Budget/Total 1993:* ECU 2600 (US$ 3000). *Financial sources:* Public: 10%. *Self-financing:* 90%.

INFORMATION AND EDUCATION ACTIVITIES: **Topics:** Culture/tradition/religion; International economic relations/trade/debt/finance; International relations/cooperation/development aid; Poverty/living conditions. **Activities:** Broadcasting/cultural events; Exchanges/twinning/linking.

DNK1251
DANSK INTERNATIONAL BOSAETNINGSSERVICE (DIB) ♦
Danish International Human Settlement Service

Klostertorvet 9, 4., 8000 Århus C, Denmark.

Telephone: 45 (86) 13 19 07. *Fax:* 45 (86) 19 27 97. *Contact:* Gitte Strøier, President.

OBJECTIVES: To limit the use of economical and ecological unsustainable materials. To raise the level of consciousness regarding the importance of an integrated human settlement policy, which considers health and income-generating activitiesand to create solutions for low-income families.

GENERAL INFORMATION: *Creation:* 1989. *Type of organisation:* coordinating body. *Personnel/Total:* 26. *Salaried:* 6 of which: 4 in developing countries. *Volunteers:* 20 of which: 5 in developing countries. *Budget/Total 1993:* ECU 432000 (US$ 505000). *Financial sources:* Private: 5%. Public: 90%. Self-financing: 5%.

PUBLICATIONS: *Periodicals:* DIB-Nyt (4). *List of publications.*

EVALUATION/RESEARCH: Evaluation reports available. Undertakes research activities.

PLANNED ACTIVITIES: Integrated development and settlement in Bolivia. Low-cost housing and the gener0tion of income in Sri Lanka. Preliminary investigatory missions in Ethiopia and Vietnam.

ACTIVITIES IN DEVELOPING REGIONS: Present in developing regions. Active in 3 country(ies). Maintains local field presence. **Sustainable Development Actions:** Ecology/environment/biodiversity; Education/training/literacy; Sending volunteers/experts/technical assistance; Small enterprises/informal sector/handicrafts; Urban development/habitat. **Regions:** East Asia; South America.

INFORMATION AND EDUCATION ACTIVITIES: Topics: Poverty/living conditions; Refugees/migrants/ethnic groups; Rural development/agriculture; Urban development/habitat. **Activities:** Fund raising; Information and documentation services/data bases; Information campaigns/exhibitions; Publishing/audiovisual materials/educational materials.

DNK1252
DANSK INTERNATIONAL CHRISTIAN YOUTH EXCHANGE (ICYE)
Sønderport 7, Postboks 642, 8100 Århus C, Denmark.

Telephone: 45 (86) 11 60 33.

DNK1253
DANSK KURDISK KULTUR OG SOLIDARITETS FORENING (DKKSF)
Ny Munkegade 13 A, 8000 Århus C, Denmark.

Contact: N. Yigen.

DNK1254
DANSK KVINDESAMFUND (DK)
Niels Hemmingsensgade 10, 3., 1153 København K, Denmark.

Telephone: 45 (33) 15 78 37. *Fax:* 45 (33) 15 79 37. *Contact:* Lori Ottensteen.

DNK1255
DANSK MISSIONSRADS PROJEKTAFDELING (DMR-P) ♦ Danish Missionary Council Development Office
Skt. Lukas Vej 13, 2900 Hellerup, Denmark.

Telephone: 45 (31) 62 65 82. *Fax:* 45 (31) 62 74 82. *Contact:* Svend Bernhard, Chairman.

OBJECTIVES: To support and assist member organisations and their partners in the Third World in their social and humanitarian development

work. To contribute to the social, physical, spiritual development of men and women. To support democratic institutions worldwide.

GENERAL INFORMATION: *Creation:* 1986. *Type of organisation:* association of NGOs. *Member organisations:* 15. *Affiliated to:* Council of International Development Co-operation Advisory to the Ministry of Foreign Affairs (Denmark) - Danish EC-NGO Platform (Denmark) - Danish Organisation for International Co-operation (Denmark). *Personnel/Total:* 12. *Salaried:* 12 of which: 7 in developing countries. *Budget/Total 1993:* ECU 948000 (US$ 1110000). *Financial sources:* Private: 100%.

PUBLICATIONS: *List of publications.*

ACTIVITIES IN DEVELOPING REGIONS: Present in developing regions. Maintains local field presence. Works through local field partners. **Sustainable Development Actions:** Democracy/good governance/institution building/participatory development; Ecology/environment/biodiversity; Education/training/literacy; Energy/transport; Gender issues/women; Health/sanitation/water; Human rights/peace/conflicts; Rural development/agriculture; Sending volunteers/experts/technical assistance; Small enterprises/informal sector/handicrafts. **Regions:** Central Africa; Central Asia and South Asia; East Africa; North Africa; Southern Africa; West Africa.

INFORMATION AND EDUCATION ACTIVITIES: Topics: Health/sanitation/water; Other; Rural development/agriculture. **Activities:** Publishing/audiovisual materials/educational materials.

DNK1256
DANSK MONGOLSK SELSKAB ♦ Danish Mongolian Society
Fuglebo 2, 2000 Frederiksberg, Denmark.

Telephone: 45 (38) 33 21 06. *Fax:* 45 (33) 47 33 20. *Contact:* Rolf Gilberg, Chairman.

OBJECTIVES: To spread information about the Mongols, their culture and history, to the people in Denmark, by means of a member magazine and lectures.

GENERAL INFORMATION: *Personnel/Total:* 7. *Volunteers:* 7. *Budget/Total 1993:* ECU 1600 (US$ 2000). *Financial sources:* Self-financing: 100%.

PUBLICATIONS: *Periodicals:* GER (3). *List of publications.*

PLANNED ACTIVITIES: Seminar in 1996 to celebrate the 100-year anniversary of the birth of Mr. Haslund-Christensen who spent many years in Mongolia.

INFORMATION AND EDUCATION ACTIVITIES: Topics: Culture/tradition/religion. **Activities:** Broadcasting/cultural events; Information and documentation services/data bases.

DNK1257
DANSK PALAESTINENSISK VENSKABSFORENING
c/o Katja Klerk, Søllerød Park 5016, 2840 Holte, Denmark.

Telephone: 45 (42) 80 66 38. *Contact:* Søren Højmark.

DNK1258
DANSK POLYNESISK SELSKAB
c/o Sydjysk Universitetscenter, Niels Bohrs Vej 9, 6700 Esbjerg, Denmark.

Telephone: 45 (75) 14 11 11. *Fax:* 45 (79) 14 11 99. *Contact:* Jan Hjarnø.

DNK1259
DANSK RODE KORS (DRK) ♦ Danish Red Cross
P.O. Box 2600, 27, Blegdamsvej, 2100 København O, Denmark.

Telephone: 45 (31) 38 14 44. *Fax:* 45 (31) 42 11 86. *Contact:* Eigil Pedersen, Secretary General.

OBJECTIVES: To undertake humanitarian, relief and educational activities. To assist and work directly with Danish authorities in carrying out emergency aid relief. To participate in the general development of Red Cross/Red Crescent Societies in developing countries. To develop their

community services in health, education and protection of the environment.

GENERAL INFORMATION: *Creation:* 1876. *Type of organisation:* network. *Member organisations:* 161. *Affiliated to:* International Federation of Red Cross and Red Crescent Societies (Switzerland) - Danish Centre for Human Rights (Denmark) - Danish Refugee Council (Denmark). *Personnel/Total:* 15500. *Salaried:* 3500 of which: 30 in developing countries. *Volunteers:* 12000. *Budget/Total 1993:* ECU 223930000 (US$ 262180000). *Financial sources:* Private: 4%. Public: 92%. Self-financing: 4%.

PUBLICATIONS: *Periodicals:* HJÆLP (12) - DIALOG (6). *Annual report. List of publications.*

EVALUATION/RESEARCH: Evaluation reports available. Undertakes research activities.

COMMENTS: Undertakes activities in the Commonwealth of Independent States.

ACTIVITIES IN DEVELOPING REGIONS: Present in developing regions. Active in 15 country(ies). Maintains local field presence. Works through local field partners. **Sustainable Development Actions:** Children/youth/family; Democracy/good governance/institution building/participatory development; Ecology/environment/biodiversity; Education/training/literacy; Emergency relief/refugees/humanitarian assistance; Food/famine; Gender issues/women; Health/sanitation/water; Human rights/peace/conflicts; Population/family planning/demography; Rural development/agriculture; Sending volunteers/experts/technical assistance; Urban development/habitat. **Regions:** Central Asia and South Asia; East Africa; South East Asia; Southern Africa; West Africa.

INFORMATION AND EDUCATION ACTIVITIES: Topics: Children/youth/family; Ecology/environment/biodiversity; Emergency relief/refugees/humanitarian assistance; Food/famine; Health/sanitation/water; International relations/cooperation/development aid; Population/family planning/demography; Poverty/living conditions; Refugees/migrants/ethnic groups. **Activities:** Exchanges/twinning/linking; Fund raising; Information and documentation services/data bases; Information campaigns/exhibitions; Lobbying/advocacy; Publishing/audiovisual materials/educational materials.

DNK1260

DANSK SANTALMISSION ♦ Danish Santal Mission

Kobmagergade 67, 5, 1150 København K, Denmark.

Telephone: 45 (33) 93 80 95. *Fax:* 45 (33) 93 03 95. *Contact:* Rev. Thorkild Schousboe Laursen, Chairman.

OBJECTIVES: To support and further evangelism and inter-church cooperation. To assist local Lutheran Churches in developing countries along with other development activities.

GENERAL INFORMATION: *Creation:* 1867. *Affiliated to:* Danish Missionary Council (Denmark). *Personnel/Total:* 40. *Salaried:* 35 of which: 23 in developing countries. *Volunteers:* 5 of which: 5 in developing countries. *Budget/Total 1993:* ECU 1976000 (US$ 2313000). *Financial sources:* Private: 54%. Public: 46%.

PUBLICATIONS: *Periodicals:* Sidste Santal Nyt (4) - Dansk Mission (4) - Santal Posten (4) - Orienterings Brevet (6). *Annual report. List of publications.*

EVALUATION/RESEARCH: Evaluation reports available. Undertakes research activities.

ACTIVITIES IN DEVELOPING REGIONS: Present in developing regions. Maintains local field presence. Works through local field partners. **Sustainable Development Actions:** Children/youth/family; Education/training/literacy; Emergency relief/refugees/humanitarian assistance; Health/sanitation/water; Rural development/agriculture; Small enterprises/informal sector/handicrafts; Urban development/habitat. **Regions:** Central Asia and South Asia; East Asia; South East Asia.

INFORMATION AND EDUCATION ACTIVITIES: Topics: Children/youth/family; Culture/tradition/religion; Education/training/literacy; Food/famine; Gender issues/women; Health/sanitation/water; Poverty/living conditions; Rural development/agriculture. **Activities:** Information campaigns/exhibitions; Publishing/audiovisual materials/educational materials.

DNK1261

DANSK SELSKAB FOR TIBETANSK KULTUR ♦ Danish Tibetan Cultural Society

Store Søhøj, Hørsholm Kongevej 40, 2970 Hørsholm, Denmark.

Telephone: 45 (42) 86 57 15. *Contact:* Tarab Tulku, President.

DNK1262

DANSK UNICEF KOMITE ♦ Danish Committee for UNICEF

Billedvej 8, 2100 København O, Denmark.

Telephone: 45 (39) 29 51 11. *Fax:* 45 (39) 27 05 77. *Contact:* Arne Stinus, Secretary General.

OBJECTIVES: To disseminate information about, and raise funds for, UNICEF projects in developing countries.

GENERAL INFORMATION: *Creation:* 1954. *Member organisations:* 78. *Personnel/Total:* 913. *Salaried:* 13. *Volunteers:* 900. *Budget/Total 1993:* ECU 2503000 (US$ 2930000). *Financial sources:* Self-financing: 100%.

PUBLICATIONS: *Periodicals:* UNICEF Nyt (4). *Annual report. List of publications.*

INFORMATION AND EDUCATION ACTIVITIES: Topics: Children/youth/family; Emergency relief/refugees/humanitarian assistance; Gender issues/women; Health/sanitation/water; Human rights/peace/conflicts; International relations/cooperation/development aid; Peace/ethnic conflicts/armament/disarmament; Population/family planning/demography; Poverty/living conditions. **Activities:** Formal education; Fund raising; Information and documentation services/data bases; Information campaigns/exhibitions; Lobbying/advocacy; Publishing/audiovisual materials/educational materials.

DNK1263

DANSK VIETNAMESISK FORENING ♦ Association Danemark Vietnam

Kulturhuset Cikaden, Griffenfeldsgade 35, 1052 København N, Danemark.

Téléphone: 45 (35) 36 07 01. *Fax:* 45 (35) 37 19 80. *Contact:* Kirsten Vagn Jensen, President.

DNK1264

DANSK-ARABISK UDVALG ♦ Danish-Arab Committee

Mølle Allé 1, 2., 2500 Valby, Denmark.

Telephone: 45 (36) 30 90 29. *Contact:* Kuno Malinowski, Président.

DNK1265

DANSK-CUBANSK FORENING

Griffenfeldsgade 35, 2200 København N, Denmark.

Telephone: 45 (31) 35 10 50. *Fax:* 45 (35) 37 19 80.

DNK1266

DANSK-GAMBIANSK FORENING, GAMBIAS VENNER ♦ Danish-Gambian Friendship Society, Gambia's Friends

Klovervej 8, 8450 Hammel, Denmark.

Telephone: 45 (86) 96 32 91. *Fax:* 45 (86) 96 94 82. *Contact:* Per Hausmann Andersen, Chairman.

OBJECTIVES: To provide better health for people and education for children in Gambia.

GENERAL INFORMATION: *Creation:* 1975. *Personnel/Total:* 30. *Volunteers:* 30 of which: 9 in developing countries. *Budget/Total 1993:* ECU 66000 (US$ 78000). *Financial sources:* Private: 10%. Public: 50%. Self-financing: 40%.

PUBLICATIONS: *Periodicals:* Gambia News (2). *Annual report.*

EVALUATION/RESEARCH: Evaluation reports available. Undertakes research activities.

ACTIVITIES IN DEVELOPING REGIONS: Present in developing regions. Active in 1 country(ies). Works through local field partners. **Sustainable

See: *How to Use the Directory*, page 11.

Development Actions: Children/youth/family; Education/training/literacy; Emergency relief/refugees/humanitarian assistance; Health/sanitation/water. **Regions:** West Africa.

INFORMATION AND EDUCATION ACTIVITIES: Topics: Children/youth/family; Education/training/literacy; Emergency relief/refugees/humanitarian assistance; Health/sanitation/water. **Activities:** Fund raising.

DNK1267
DANSK-KURDISK VENSKABSFORENING (DKV)

Dronningensgade 14, Postboks 1926, 1023 København K, Denmark.
Telephone: 45 (31) 71 05 72. *Contact:* Christian Jørgensen.

DNK1268
DANSK-SRI LANKA FORENING ♦ Danish-Sri Lanka Society

Sindalsvej 7, 8900 Randers, Denmark.
Telephone: 45 (86) 43 94 19. *Contact:* Peter Staugård.

DNK1269
DANSK-UGANDISK VENSKABSFORENING (DUWA) ♦ Danish-Ugandan Wanainchi Association

c/o Kellen Ajule, Egedalsveange 23, 1 th., 2980 Kokkedal, Denmark.
Telephone: 45 (42) 24 10 36. *Contact:* Kellen Ajule, President.

DNK1270
DEN DANSKE AFGHANISTAN KOMITE

c/o N-A Rye Andersen, Dalgas Boulevard 91, 2000 Frederiksberg, Denmark.
Telephone: 45 (31) 87 19 51. *Contact:* Viggo Fischer, President.

DNK1271
DEN DANSKE BANGLADESHFORENING

c/o Lis Rasmussen, Oehlenschlaegersgade 10 A, 4 th., 1663 København V, Denmark.
Telephone: 45 (31) 21 90 48. *Contact:* Lis Rasmussen, President.

DNK1272
DET DANSKE BAPTISTSAMFUND - YDRE MISSION ♦ Danish Baptist Union - Department of Foreign Missions

Laerdalsgade 5.1, 2300 København S, Denmark.
Telephone: 45 (31) 59 07 08. *Fax:* 45 (31) 59 01 33. *Contact:* Jorgen Krabbe-Sorensen, Foreign Missions Secretary.

OBJECTIVES: To support independent projects in developing countries in the fields of health, education and agriculture.

GENERAL INFORMATION: *Creation:* 1916. *Affiliated to:* European Baptist Federation - Baptist World Alliance (USA). *Personnel/Total:* 13. *Salaried:* 13 of which: 12 in developing countries. *Budget/Total 1993:* ECU 319000 (US$ 373000). *Financial sources:* Private: 50%. Public: 50%.

PUBLICATIONS: *Periodicals:* Baptist (40). *Annual report. List of publications.*

COMMENTS: Undertakes activities in the Commonwealth of Independent States.

ACTIVITIES IN DEVELOPING REGIONS: Active in 2 country(ies). Maintains local field presence. Works through local field partners. **Sustainable Development Actions:** Children/youth/family; Democracy/good governance/institution building/participatory development; Education/training/literacy; Emergency relief/refugees/humanitarian assistance; Food/famine; Gender issues/women; Health/sanitation/water; Population/family planning/demography; Rural development/agriculture; Sending volunteers/experts/technical assistance; Small enterprises/informal sector/handicrafts. **Regions:** Central Africa.

INFORMATION AND EDUCATION ACTIVITIES: Topics: Children/youth/family; Gender issues/women; Health/sanitation/water; Population/family planning/demography; Rural development/agriculture. **Activities:**

Conferences/seminars/workshops/training activities; Formal education; Information campaigns/exhibitions.

DNK1273
DET DANSKE CENTER FOR MENNESKERET-TIGHEDER (DCMR) ♦ Danish Centre for Human Rights

38 Studiestraede, 2nd floor, 1455 København K, Denmark.
Telephone: 45 (33) 91 12 99. *Fax:* 45 (33) 91 02 99. *Contact:* Morten Kjaerum, Director.

OBJECTIVES: To facilitate Danish research efforts in human rights' law. To organise and promote human rights' education. To promote the coordination of NGO work and international human rights' co-operation.

GENERAL INFORMATION: *Creation:* 1987. *Affiliated to:* HURIDOCS (Norway) - Organisation Mondiale Contre la Torture (Switzerland). *Personnel/Total:* 38. *Salaried:* 33. *Volunteers:* 5. *Budget/Total 1993:* ECU 1968000 (US$ 2304000). *Financial sources:* Private: 1%. Public: 97%. Self-financing: 2%.

PUBLICATIONS: *Annual report. List of publications.*

EVALUATION/RESEARCH: Undertakes research activities.

COMMENTS: Undertakes activities in the Commonwealth of Independent States. Information activities related to the Commonwealth of Independent States.

ACTIVITIES IN DEVELOPING REGIONS: Present in developing regions. Active in 8 country(ies). Works through local field partners. **Sustainable Development Actions:** Democracy/good governance/institution building/participatory development; Education/training/literacy; Human rights/peace/conflicts; Sending volunteers/experts/technical assistance. **Regions:** East Africa; Southern Africa.

INFORMATION AND EDUCATION ACTIVITIES: Topics: Culture/tradition/religion; Education/training/literacy; Gender issues/women; Human rights/peace/conflicts; International relations/cooperation/development aid; Peace/ethnic conflicts/armament/disarmament; Racism/xenophobia/antisemitism; Refugees/migrants/ethnic groups. **Activities:** Conferences/seminars/workshops/training activities; Formal education; Fund raising; Information campaigns/exhibitions; Publishing/audiovisual materials/educational materials.

DNK1274
DANSKE GYMNASTIK- OG IDRAETSFORENINGER (DGI) ♦ Danish Gymnastics and Sorts Associations

Vingsted Skovvej 1, P.O. Box 569, 7100 Vejle, Denmark.
Telephone: 45 (79) 40 40 40. *Fax:* 45 (79) 40 40 80. *Contact:* Leif Mikkelsen, President.

OBJECTIVES: To strengthen the actions of voluntary organisations to promote education by doing sports and other cultural activities.

GENERAL INFORMATION: *Creation:* 1992. *Type of organisation:* association of NGOs. *Member organisations:* 6000. *Affiliated to:* Mellemfolkeligt Samvirke (Denmark). *Personnel/Total:* 60. *Salaried:* 60 of which: 4 in developing countries. *Budget/Total 1993:* ECU 23710000 (US$ 27761000). *Financial sources:* Public: 100%.

PUBLICATIONS: *Periodicals:* Dansk Ungdom og Idræt (39) - Krumspring (9).

EVALUATION/RESEARCH: Evaluation reports available. Undertakes research activities.

PLANNED ACTIVITIES: Training programmes in gymnastics, sports and body culture in Zimbabwe and Tanzania. "Grassroots and Club Democracy" seminars for participants from Eastern and Central Europe and Africa.

COMMENTS: Undertakes activities in the Commonwealth of Independent States. Information activities related to the Commonwealth of Independent States.

ACTIVITIES IN DEVELOPING REGIONS: Present in developing regions. Active in 7 country(ies). Maintains local field presence. Works through local field partners. **Sustainable Development Actions:** Democracy/good governance/institution building/participatory development; Education/training/literacy; Other; Rural development/agriculture; Small enter-

prises/informal sector/handicrafts. **Regions:** East Africa; Mexico and Central America; South East Asia; Southern Africa.

INFORMATION AND EDUCATION ACTIVITIES: Topics: Human rights/ peace/conflicts; Other. **Activities:** Broadcasting/cultural events; Conferences/seminars/workshops/training activities; Exchanges/twinning/linking; Publishing/audiovisual materials/educational materials.

DNK1275
DET DANSKE MISSIONSSELSKAB ♦ Danish Missionary Society

Strandagervej 24, 2900 Hellerup, Denmark.

Telephone: 45 (31) 62 99 11. **Fax:** 45 (31) 62 02 06. **Contact:** Anders Mielke, Secretary General.

OBJECTIVES: To send missionaries, pastors, teachers, doctors, nurses and other skilled personnel to work in developing countries depending on the needs and requests of local partner churches.

GENERAL INFORMATION: Creation: 1821. **Affiliated to:** Det Mellemkirkelige Råd - Det økumeniske Fællesråd - MS - Folkekirkens Nødhjælp - United Evangelical Lutheran Churches (India) - Lutheran Co-ordination Service (Tanzania) - Dansk Missionråd (Denmark). **Personnel/Total:** 97. Salaried: 77 of which: 56 in developing countries. Volunteers: 20 of which: 18 in developing countries. **Budget/Total 1993:** ECU 2282000 (US$ 2672000). **Financial sources:** Private: 94%. Self-financing: 6%.

PUBLICATIONS: Periodicals: Dansk Missionsblad (8) - En Hel Verdew (4). Annual report. List of publications.

EVALUATION/RESEARCH: Evaluation reports available. Undertakes research activities.

ACTIVITIES IN DEVELOPING REGIONS: Present in developing regions. Active in 10 country(ies). Maintains local field presence. Works through local field partners. **Sustainable Development Actions:** Children/ youth/family; Debt/finance/trade; Democracy/good governance/institution building/participatory development; Ecology/environment/biodiversity; Education/training/literacy; Emergency relief/refugees/humanitarian assistance; Energy/transport; Gender issues/women; Health/sanitation/ water; Other; Rural development/agriculture; Sending volunteers/ experts/technical assistance; Small enterprises/informal sector/handicrafts. **Regions:** Central Asia and South Asia; East Africa; East Asia; Middle East; North Africa; Southern Africa.

INFORMATION AND EDUCATION ACTIVITIES: Topics: Children/youth/ family; Ecology/environment/biodiversity; Education/training/literacy; Gender issues/women; Health/sanitation/water; International economic relations/trade/debt/finance; Refugees/migrants/ethnic groups; Rural development/agriculture. **Activities:** Conferences/seminars/workshops/ training activities; Exchanges/twinning/linking; Formal education; Information campaigns/exhibitions; Lobbying/advocacy; Publishing/audiovisual materials/educational materials.

DNK1276
DANSKE OG SYDAMERIKANSKE VENNER (DOSV)

c/o Susanne Gottfredsen, Gavlhusvej 49 st. tv., 2700 Brønshøj, Denmark.

Telephone: 45 (31) 28 64 32. **Contact:** Alfonso Guzmán, President.

DNK1277
DE DANSKE PALAESTINEGRUPPER

H.C. Orstedsvej 17, 3 th., 1879 Frederiksberg C, Denmark.

Telephone: 45 (31) 22 84 72. **Contact:** Søren Højmark.

DNK1278
DEN DANSKE PALAESTINEKOMITE (DDP)

Guldsmedegade 25, 2., Postboks 641, 8100 Århus C, Denmark.

Telephone: 45 (86) 15 15 64. **Contact:** Karin Busk.

DNK1279
DEN DANSKE STOTTEGRUPPE FOR MENNESKERETTIGHEDSKOMMISSIONEN I CHILE

c/o Hanne Rädeker, A.F. Beyers Vej 22, 1. th., 2720 Vanløse, Denmark.

Telephone: 45 (31) 19 84 81. **Contact:** Ninja Fagerholt.

DNK1280
DEN DANSKE STOTTEKOMITE FOR KOREAS GENFORENING ♦ Danish Supporting Committee for the Reunification of Korea

c/o Anders Kristensen, Tordenskjoldsgade 14, 1 th., 1055 København K, Denmark.

Telephone: 45 (33) 14 15 26. **Contact:** Anders Kristensen, Secretary.

DNK1281
DANSKE STUDERENDES FELLESRAD (DSF) ♦ National Union of Danish Students

Knabrostraede 25, kld., 1210 København K, Denmark.

Telephone: 45 (33) 11 82 60. **Fax:** 45 (33) 14 30 76.

OBJECTIVES: To support the activities of students in developing countries through the dissemination of information and fund raising among Danish students.

GENERAL INFORMATION: Creation: 1932. **Type of organisation:** association of NGOs. **Member organisations:** 23. **Affiliated to:** WUS (Denmark) - National Unions of Students in Europe (Austria) - Danish Youth Council (Denmark). **Personnel/Total:** 11. Salaried: 2. Volunteers: 9. **Budget/Total 1993:** ECU 224000 (US$ 262000). **Financial sources:** Private: 98%. Public: 2%.

PUBLICATIONS: Periodicals: Studenter Bladet (8). Annual report. List of publications.

COMMENTS: Information activities related to the Commonwealth of Independent States.

INFORMATION AND EDUCATION ACTIVITIES: Topics: Education/training/literacy; Gender issues/women; International relations/cooperation/ development aid; Poverty/living conditions. **Activities:** Conferences/ seminars/workshops/training activities; Formal education; Information and documentation services/data bases; Information campaigns/exhibitions; Lobbying/advocacy; Networking/electronic telecommunications; Publishing/audiovisual materials/educational materials.

DNK1282
DEMOS' DOKUMENTATIONSGRUPPE (IIC)

Elmegade 27, st., 2200 København N, Denmark.

Telephone: 45 (31) 35 12 12.

DNK1283
DVI- LEG OG VIRKE (DVI) ♦ DVI- PLAY AND WORK

Torveporten 2, 2500 Valby, Denmark.

Telephone: 45 (36) 17 72 00. **Fax:** 45 (36) 44 27 76. **Contact:** Helle Christensen, President.

OBJECTIVES: To help integrate socially disabled children and young adults in a democratic society.

GENERAL INFORMATION: Creation: 1905. **Affiliated to:** International Falcon Movement - Socialist Educational International (Belgium) - Dansk Ungdoms Fællesråd (Denmark). **Personnel/Total:** 1810. Salaried: 10 of which: 1 in developing countries. Volunteers: 1800 of which: 4 in developing countries. **Budget/Total 1993:** ECU 1317000 (US$ 1542000). **Financial sources:** Private: 32%. Public: 23%. Self-financing: 45%.

PUBLICATIONS: Periodicals: Regnbvebørn (4) - MB-Leg Og Virke (6). List of publications.

EVALUATION/RESEARCH: Evaluation reports available.

PLANNED ACTIVITIES: Supporting education and activities for children of unemployed parents in Denmark. Organising educational programmes for street children in Nicaragua, El Salvador and Albania. Exchange tours with Eastern Europe.

COMMENTS: Undertakes activities in the Commonwealth of Independent States. Information activities related to the Commonwealth of Independent States.

ACTIVITIES IN DEVELOPING REGIONS: Present in developing regions. Active in 1 country(ies). Maintains local field presence. Works through local field partners. **Sustainable Development Actions:** Children/youth/family; Democracy/good governance/institution building/participatory development; Ecology/environment/biodiversity; Education/training/literacy; Gender issues/women; Health/sanitation/water; Sending volunteers/experts/technical assistance. **Regions:** Mexico and Central America.

INFORMATION AND EDUCATION ACTIVITIES: Topics: Children/youth/family; Culture/tradition/religion; Ecology/environment/biodiversity; Education/training/literacy; Employment/unemployment; Gender issues/women; Human rights/peace/conflicts; International relations/cooperation/development aid; Peace/ethnic conflicts/armament/disarmament; Poverty/living conditions; Racism/xenophobia/antisemitism; Refugees/migrants/ethnic groups; Urban development/habitat. **Activities:** Broadcasting/cultural events; Conferences/seminars/workshops/training activities; Exchanges/twinning/linking; Formal education; Fund raising; Information and documentation services/data bases; Information campaigns/exhibitions; Lobbying/advocacy; Networking/electronic telecommunications; Publishing/audiovisual materials/educational materials.

DNK1284
EMMAUS DANMARK

c/o Svalerne, Rosensgade 24, 8000 Aarhus C, Denmark.

DNK1285
EMMAUS-SAMFUNDET I AALBORG - ABBE PIERRES KLUNSERE ♦ Communauté d'Emmaüs Aalborg - Les chiffonniers de l'Abbé Pierre

'Vesterholt" Ajstrup Hjallerupvej 70, 9382 Tylstrup, Danemark.

Téléphone: 45 (98) 26 16 97. *Contact:* Roger Depoilly.

OBJECTIFS: Promouvoir le développement, non par charité, mais dans l'espoir que les projets seront repris par la population locale afin d'obtenir leur autonomie.

INFORMATIONS GENERALES: *Création:* 1970. *Affiliée à:* Emmaüs International (France) - Emmaüs Samfundet (Aalborg). *Personnel/Total:* 4. *Bénévoles:* 4. *Budget/Total 1993:* ECU 46000 (US$ 54000). *Sources financières:* Autofinancement: 100%.

PREVISIONS D'ACTIVITES: Campagne d'information sur le 25ème anniversaire de la communauté Emmaüs d'Aalborg.

ACTIVITES DANS LES REGIONS EN DEVELOPPEMENT: Intervient directement dans les régions en développement. Intervient dans 1 pays. Intervient par l'intermédiaire d'organisations locales partenaires. **Actions de Développement durable:** Dette/finances/commerce; Démocratie/bonne gestion publique/création d'institutions/développement participatif; Développement rural/agriculture; Enfants/jeunesse/famille; Petites entreprises/secteur informel/artisanat; Questions relatives aux femmes; Santé/assainissement/eau; Éducation/formation/alphabétisation; Énergie/transport. **Régions:** Afrique de l'Est.

ACTIVITES D'INFORMATION ET D'EDUCATION: Domaines: Développement rural/agriculture; Enfants/jeunesse/famille; Questions relatives aux femmes; Santé/assainissement/eau; Éducation/formation/alphabétisation. **Activités:** Campagnes d'information/expositions.

DNK1286
DEN ERITREANSKE HJAELPEORGANISATION I DANMARK (ERA) ♦ Eritrean Aid Organisation in Denmark

P.O. Box 2072, 1013 København K, Denmark.

Telephone: 45 (1) 39 75 70. *Contact:* Tekle Yigzaw.

DNK1287
FAGBEVAEGELSENS U-LANDSSEKRETARIAT ♦ Danish Trade Union Council for International Development Co-operation

Nyropsgade 14, 6., 1602 København V, Denmark.

Telephone: 45 (33) 14 11 22. *Fax:* 45 (33) 12 27 02. *Contact:* Jørgen Diemer Petersen.

OBJECTIVES: To strengthen trade unions through workers' education.

GENERAL INFORMATION: *Type of organisation:* association of NGOs. *Personnel/Total:* 8. *Salaried:* 8. *Budget/Total 1993:* ECU 4215000 (US$ 4935000). *Financial sources:* Public: 85%. Self-financing: 15%.

PUBLICATIONS: *Periodicals:* Yearbook (1) - Human and Trade Union Rights (1). *Annual report.*

EVALUATION/RESEARCH: Evaluation reports available. Undertakes research activities.

ACTIVITIES IN DEVELOPING REGIONS: Active in 40 country(ies). Maintains local field presence. Works through local field partners. **Sustainable Development Actions:** Education/training/literacy; Human rights/peace/conflicts; Sending volunteers/experts/technical assistance. **Regions:** Central Africa; Central Asia and South Asia; East Africa; East Asia; Mexico and Central America; South America; South East Asia; West Africa.

INFORMATION AND EDUCATION ACTIVITIES: Topics: Education/training/literacy; Human rights/peace/conflicts. **Activities:** Conferences/seminars/workshops/training activities; Information and documentation services/data bases; Information campaigns/exhibitions.

DNK1288
FEDERATIONEN FOR PROJEKTER, KNYTTET TIL DEN INTERNATIONALE FRA FOLK TIL FOLK BEVEGELSE ♦ The Federation for Projects Connected to the International People to People Movement

Niels Finsenvej 11, 7100 Vejle, Denmark.

Telephone: 45 (75) 83 60 11. *Fax:* 45 (75) 84 02 44. *Contact:* Poul Jørgensen, Chairman.

OBJECTIVES: To provide development aid to the people of the Third World.

GENERAL INFORMATION: *Financial sources:* Self-financing: 100%.

ACTIVITIES IN DEVELOPING REGIONS: Works through local field partners. **Sustainable Development Actions:** Children/youth/family; Ecology/environment/biodiversity; Education/training/literacy; Emergency relief/refugees/humanitarian assistance; Food/famine; Health/sanitation/water; Rural development/agriculture; Sending volunteers/experts/technical assistance; Small enterprises/informal sector/handicrafts. **Regions:** Caribbean; South America; South East Asia; Southern Africa.

DNK1289
FIU-CENTRET ♦ Trade Union Internal Training

Buddinge Hovedgade, Postboks 80, 2860 Søborg, Denmark.

Telephone: 45 (31) 67 53 33. *Fax:* 45 (31) 66 10 33. *Contact:* Kjeld Aakjær.

OBJECTIVES: To carry out educational activities for the trade unions in Central and Eastern Europe and in developing countries.

GENERAL INFORMATION: *Type of organisation:* network, coordinating body. *Member organisations:* 30. *Personnel/Total:* 85. *Salaried:* 85. *Budget/Total 1993:* ECU 19759000 (US$ 23134000). *Financial sources:* Public: 5%. Self-financing: 95%.

EVALUATION/RESEARCH: Undertakes research activities.

COMMENTS: FIU-CENTRET is part of the Danish NGO Network. Undertakes activities in the Commonwealth of Independent States. Information activities related to the Commonwealth of Independent States.

ACTIVITIES IN DEVELOPING REGIONS: Present in developing regions. Works through local field partners. **Sustainable Development Actions:** Democracy/good governance/institution building/participatory development; Human rights/peace/conflicts. **Regions:** South America; Southern Africa.

INFORMATION AND EDUCATION ACTIVITIES: Topics: Employment/unemployment; Gender issues/women; Human rights/peace/conflicts; International relations/cooperation/development aid; Peace/ethnic conflicts/armament/disarmament; Poverty/living conditions; Racism/xenophobia/antisemitism; Refugees/migrants/ethnic groups. **Activities:** Conferences/seminars/workshops/training activities; Exchanges/twinning/linking; Formal education; Information and documentation services/data

Voir : *Comment utiliser le répertoire,* page 11.

bases; Information campaigns/exhibitions; Lobbying/advocacy; Publishing/audiovisual materials/educational materials.

DNK1290

FN - FORBUNDET ♦ Danish United Nations Association

Skindergade 26, 1., 1159 København K, Denmark.

Telephone: 45 (33) 12 39 39. *Fax:* 45 (33) 12 10 58. *Contact:* Erik Hundewadt, General Secretary.

DNK1291

FOLKECENTRE FOR RENEWABLE ENERGY

P.O. Box 208, 7760 Hurup Thy, Denmark.

Telephone: 45 (97) 95 66 00. *Fax:* 45 (97) 95 65 65. *E-mail:* foenergy@inet.uni.c.dk. *Contact:* Preben Maegaard, Executive Director.

OBJECTIVES: To develop, test and disseminate information on renewable and ecological technologies especially for use in rural areas. To conduct training programmes on new energy solutions and sustainable technologies.

GENERAL INFORMATION: *Creation:* 1983. *Type of organisation:* coordinating body. *Affiliated to:* European Solar Energy Association (Germany) - Forum for Energy and Development (Denmark) - Global Renewable Energy and Ecology Centres for Action (Denmark) - Danish Renewable Energy Association (Denmark) - European Renewable Energy Centres Agency (Belgium). *Personnel/Total:* 34. *Salaried:* 22. *Volunteers:* 12. *Budget/Total 1993:* ECU 1794000 (US$ 2100000). *Financial sources:* Private: 5%. Public: 90%. *Self-financing:* 5%.

PUBLICATIONS: *Periodicals:* FC-Revue (4). *Annual report. List of publications.*

EVALUATION/RESEARCH: Undertakes research activities.

COMMENTS: Undertakes activities in the Commonwealth of Independent States.

ACTIVITIES IN DEVELOPING REGIONS: Present in developing regions. Maintains local field presence. Works through local field partners. **Sustainable Development Actions:** Ecology/environment/biodiversity; Energy/transport; Rural development/agriculture; Sending volunteers/experts/technical assistance; Small enterprises/informal sector/handicrafts. **Regions:** Caribbean; Central Asia and South Asia; East Africa; South America; West Africa.

INFORMATION AND EDUCATION ACTIVITIES: Topics: Ecology/environment/biodiversity; Rural development/agriculture. **Activities:** Conferences/seminars/workshops/training activities; Exchanges/twinning/linking; Fund raising; Lobbying/advocacy; Publishing/audiovisual materials/educational materials.

DNK1292

FOLKEKIRKENS NODHJELP (FKN) ♦ Danchurchaid

Norregade 13, 1165 København K, Denmark.

Telephone: 45 (33) 15 28 00. *Fax:* 45 (33) 15 38 60. *E-mail:* Geo2:Danchurchaid. *Contact:* Christian Balslev-Olesen, Secretary General.

OBJECTIVES: To alleviate human suffering by providing humanitarian assistance. To educate the public on the root causes of that suffering.

GENERAL INFORMATION: *Creation:* 1922. *Affiliated to:* International Ecumenical Network - Lutheran World Federation - World Council of Churches - Association of Protestant Development Organisations in Europe -Danish Refugee Council. *Personnel/Total:* 2917. *Salaried:* 117 of which: 40 in developing countries. *Volunteers:* 2800 of which: 6 in developing countries. *Budget/Total 1993:* ECU 53704000 (US$ 62878000). *Financial sources:* Private: 18%. *Public:* 82%.

PUBLICATIONS: *Periodicals:* NøD (12). *Annual report. List of publications.*

EVALUATION/RESEARCH: Evaluation reports available.

COMMENTS: Undertakes activities in the Commonwealth of Independent States. Information activities related to the Commonwealth of Independent States.

ACTIVITIES IN DEVELOPING REGIONS: Present in developing regions. Active in 80 country(ies). Maintains local field presence. Works through local field partners. **Sustainable Development Actions:** Children/youth/family; Democracy/good governance/institution building/participatory development; Ecology/environment/biodiversity; Education/training/literacy; Emergency relief/refugees/humanitarian assistance; Food/famine; Gender issues/women; Health/sanitation/water; Human rights/peace/conflicts; Population/family planning/demography; Rural development/agriculture; Sending volunteers/experts/technical assistance; Small enterprises/informal sector/handicrafts. **Regions:** Caribbean; Central Africa; Central Asia and South Asia; East Africa; East Asia; Mexico and Central America; Middle East; Oceania; South America; South East Asia; Southern Africa; West Africa.

INFORMATION AND EDUCATION ACTIVITIES: Topics: Children/youth/family; Culture/tradition/religion; Ecology/environment/biodiversity; Education/training/literacy; Emergency relief/refugees/humanitarian assistance; Food/famine; Gender issues/women; Health/sanitation/water; Human rights/peace/conflicts; International economic relations/trade/debt/finance; International relations/cooperation/development aid; Peace/ethnic conflicts/armament/disarmament; Poverty/living conditions; Racism/xenophobia/antisemitism; Refugees/migrants/ethnic groups; Rural development/agriculture; Urban development/habitat. **Activities:** Fund raising; Information and documentation services/data bases; Information campaigns/exhibitions; Lobbying/advocacy; Networking/electronic telecommunications; Publishing/audiovisual materials/educational materials.

DNK1293

FOLKELIGT OPLYSNINGS FORBUND (FOF) ♦ Popular Education Association

Kongensgade 883, 1264 København K, Denmark.

Telephone: 45 (1) 14 09 38. *Contact:* Aage Hastrup, President.

DNK1294

FOLKETEKNIK, DANSKE ABGEJDERES U-LANDSGRUPPER
♦ Peoples' Technology - Danish Workers' Developing Country Group

Dr. Tvaergade 29, 6, 1302 København K, Denmark.

Telephone: 45 (1) 32 30 55. *Contact:* Erik Hannerik.

DNK1295

FOR INDIAN - INUIT - INDIGENOUS RIGHTS EVERYWHERE (FIRE)

c/o Arthur Krasilnikoff, Stendyssevej 12, 3540 Lynge, Denmark.

Telephone: 45 (42) 18 90 06.

DNK1296

FORENINGEN AF ZANZIBARIER I SKANDINAVIEN ♦ Union of Zanzibari in Scandinavia

Postboks 545, 2620 Albertslund, Denmark.

Telephone: 45 (43) 62 06 63. *Contact:* Hamed Hilal.

DNK1297

FORENINGEN ECUADORGRUPPEN

c/o Birgitta Feiring, HF Kalvebod 5, 2450 København SV, Denmark.

Telephone: 45 (36) 30 36 82. *Contact:* Birgitte Feiring, Jakob Kronik.

DNK1298

FORENINGEN FOR FAMILIEPLANLAEGNING, SEX OG SAMFUND (FF) ♦ Danish Family Planning Association, Sex and Society

Aurehøjvej 2, 2900 Hellerup, Denmark.

Telephone: 45 (31) 62 56 88. *Fax:* 45 (31) 62 02 82. *Contact:* Hanne Risør, President.

OBJECTIVES: To advocate the right to family planning and sexual education irrespective of age, sex, religion. To contribute to the creation of the

See: *How to Use the Directory*, page 11.

best possible conditions for the reproductive and sexual well-being and autonomy of all individuals.

GENERAL INFORMATION: *Creation:* 1956. *Type of organisation:* association of NGOs. *Member organisations:* 19. *Affiliated to:* International Planned Parenthood Federation (United Kingdom) - IAMANEH (Switzerland) - ICOMP (Malaysia) - Danish Women's National Council (Denmark) -KULU-Women and Development (Denmark) - European Society of Contraception. *Personnel/Total:* 22. *Salaried:* 7. *Volunteers:* 15. *Budget/Total 1993:* ECU 659000 (US$ 771000). *Financial sources: Private:* 1%. *Public:* 50%. *Self-financing:* 49%.

PUBLICATIONS: *Periodicals:* Sex og Samfund (4) - Information og Debat (4).

EVALUATION/RESEARCH: Evaluation reports available. Undertakes research activities.

COMMENTS: FF operates mainly in Denmark but participates in international activities via its membership of the IPPF and in co-operation with DANIDA. FF is a member of the National committees for UNICEF, UNESCO and the UN.

ACTIVITIES IN DEVELOPING REGIONS: Active in 1 country(ies). Works through local field partners. **Sustainable Development Actions:** Gender issues/women. **Regions:** South East Asia.

INFORMATION AND EDUCATION ACTIVITIES: Topics: Gender issues/ women; Population/family planning/demography. **Activities:** Conferences/seminars/workshops/training activities; Formal education; Information and documentation services/data bases; Information campaigns/ exhibitions; Lobbying/advocacy; Publishing/audiovisual materials/educational materials.

DNK1299

FORENINGEN TIL STOTTE FOR KULTUREN I NICARAGUA

c/o Jens Bertelsen, Agnetevej 13, 2840 Holte, Denmark.

Telephone: 45 (45) 41 00 80. *Fax:* 45 (420 42 46 22. *Contact:* Jens Erik Ohrt, President.

DNK1300

FORUM FOR ENERGI OG UDVIKLING (FEU) ♦ Forum for Energy and Development

Borgergade 14, 5., 1300 København K, Denmark.

Telephone: 45 (33) 12 13 07. *Fax:* 45 (33) 12 13 08. *E-mail:* inforse@pns.apc.org. *Contact:* René Karottki.

OBJECTIVES: To promote global co-operation for sustainable development with an emphasis on renewable energy, energy conservation and efficiency.

GENERAL INFORMATION: *Creation:* 1987. *Type of organisation:* association of NGOs. *Member organisations:* 9. *Personnel/Total:* 6. *Salaried:* 5. *Volunteers:* 1. *Budget/Total 1993:* ECU 329000 (US$ 386000). *Financial sources: Public:* 100%.

PUBLICATIONS: *Periodicals:* Sustainable Energy News (4). *Annual report.*

EVALUATION/RESEARCH: Undertakes research activities.

COMMENTS: FEU is an association/umbrella organisation of the major Danish NGOs involved in sustainable energy development and other development activities. FEU also works with INforSE (International Network for Sustainable Energy). Undertakes activities in the Commonwealth of Independent States. Information activities related to the Commonwealth of Independent States.

ACTIVITIES IN DEVELOPING REGIONS: Active in 25 country(ies). Works through local field partners. **Sustainable Development Actions:** Democracy/good governance/institution building/participatory development; Ecology/environment/biodiversity; Energy/transport; Small enterprises/informal sector/handicrafts. **Regions:** Caribbean; Central Africa; Central Asia and South Asia; East Africa; East Asia; Mexico and Central America; Middle East; North Africa; Oceania; South America; South East Asia; Southern Africa; West Africa.

INFORMATION AND EDUCATION ACTIVITIES: Topics: Ecology/environment/biodiversity; International relations/cooperation/development aid; Other. **Activities:** Conferences/seminars/workshops/training activi-

ties; Information and documentation services/data bases; Information campaigns/exhibitions; Lobbying/advocacy; Networking/electronic telecommunications.

DNK1301

FOUNDATION FOR ENVIRONMENTAL EDUCATION IN EUROPE (FEEE)

Friluftsrådet, Olof Palmesgade 10, 2100 København O, Denmark.

Telephone: 45 (31) 42 32 22. *Fax:* 45 (31) 42 34 78. *Contact:* Jan Eriksen, Director.

DNK1302

FREMTIDSSKOVEN - MSITU WA KESHO ♦ Forest of the Future

Postboks 128, 2000 Frederiksberg, Denmark.

Telephone: 45 (31) 10 01 10. *Fax:* 45 (31) 10 01 10. *Contact:* Jesper Kirknaes, Co-ordinator.

OBJECTIVES: To promote sustainable development in rural areas of Tanzania.

GENERAL INFORMATION: *Creation:* 1986. *Affiliated to:* Pambazuka (Tanzania) - Msitu Wa Kesho (Tanzania). *Personnel/Total:* 51. *Salaried:* 1 of which: 1 in developing countries. *Volunteers:* 50 of which: 45 in developing countries. *Budget/Total 1993:* ECU 2600 (US$ 3000). *Financial sources: Private:* 10%. *Self-financing:* 90%.

PUBLICATIONS: *Annual report. List of publications.*

ACTIVITIES IN DEVELOPING REGIONS: Present in developing regions. Active in 1 country(ies). Maintains local field presence. Works through local field partners. **Sustainable Development Actions:** Democracy/ good governance/institution building/participatory development; Ecology/environment/biodiversity; Gender issues/women. **Regions:** East Africa.

INFORMATION AND EDUCATION ACTIVITIES: Topics: Ecology/environment/biodiversity; Rural development/agriculture. **Activities:** Exchanges/twinning/linking; Fund raising; Information and documentation services/data bases; Lobbying/advocacy; Publishing/audiovisual materials/educational materials.

DNK1303

FRILUFTSRADET ♦ The Open Air Council

Olof Palmesgade 10, 2100 København O, Denmark.

Telephone: 45 (31) 42 32 22. *Fax:* 45 (31) 42 34 78. *Contact:* Jan Eriksen, Director.

DNK1304

FRIVILLIGT DRENGE - OG PIGE-FORBUND (FDF) ♦ Voluntary Christian Boys' and Girls' Association

Rysensteensgade 3, 1564 København V, Denmark.

Telephone: 45 (33) 13 68 88. *Fax:* 45 (33) 91 91 65. *Contact:* Tage Kleinbeck, Secretary General.

OBJECTIVES: To raise funds for development projects. To undertake campaigns to raise awareness and youth exchange programmes in cooperation with Danish development NGOs, churches and organisations in developing countries.

GENERAL INFORMATION: *Creation:* 1902. *Affiliated to:* Danish Youth Council (Denmark) - Ecumenical Council of Denmark (Denmark) - European Fellowship - World Conference. *Personnel/Total:* 6030. *Salaried:* 30. *Volunteers:* 6000 of which: 12 in developing countries. *Budget/Total 1993:* ECU 2634000 (US$ 3085000). *Financial sources: Private:* 25%. *Public:* 50%. *Self-financing:* 25%.

PUBLICATIONS: *Periodicals:* Lederen (10) - Seniorbladet (4) - Glimt (9). *Annual report. List of publications.*

EVALUATION/RESEARCH: Evaluation reports available.

PLANNED ACTIVITIES: Training of leaders and financial support for new Christian Youth organisations in Bangladesh and India. Seminars for training youth leaders in Central and Southern Africa. Visits to Denmark by groups of Middle Eastern and Baltic youth leaders.

Voir : *Comment utiliser le répertoire,* page 11.

COMMENTS: Undertakes activities in the Commonwealth of Independent States. Information activities related to the Commonwealth of Independent States.

ACTIVITIES IN DEVELOPING REGIONS: Active in 8 country(ies). Works through local field partners. **Sustainable Development Actions:** Children/youth/family; Democracy/good governance/institution building/participatory development; Ecology/environment/biodiversity; Education/training/literacy; Emergency relief/refugees/humanitarian assistance; Human rights/peace/conflicts; Sending volunteers/experts/technical assistance. **Regions:** Central Asia and South Asia; Middle East; North Africa; South America; West Africa.

INFORMATION AND EDUCATION ACTIVITIES: Topics: Children/youth/family; Education/training/literacy; Emergency relief/refugees/humanitarian assistance; Human rights/peace/conflicts; International economic relations/trade/debt/finance; Poverty/living conditions; Refugees/migrants/ethnic groups. **Activities:** Broadcasting/cultural events; Conferences/seminars/workshops/training activities; Exchanges/twinning/linking; Fund raising; Information campaigns/exhibitions; Lobbying/advocacy; Publishing/audiovisual materials/educational materials.

DNK1305

DET FYNSKE U-LANDSKAB (DFU) ♦ The Funen NGO Landscape

Klostervej 28, 5000 Odense C, Denmark.

Telephone: 45 (66) 12 90 48. **Fax:** 45 (66) 13 90 45. **Contact:** Niels Jørgen Jensen.

OBJECTIVES: To promote development education co-operation between Funen NGOs and humanitarian organisations. To increase international understanding and the availability of development education to the general population and to raise a global consciousness.

GENERAL INFORMATION: Creation: 1993. **Type of organisation:** association of NGOs. **Member organisations:** 21. **Budget/Total 1993:** ECU 19000 (US$ 22000). **Financial sources:** Private: 2%. Public: 91%. Self-financing: 7%.

PUBLICATIONS: Periodicals: Det Fynske U-Landskab (10). Annual report.

EVALUATION/RESEARCH: Evaluation reports available.

INFORMATION AND EDUCATION ACTIVITIES: Topics: Children/youth/family; Culture/tradition/religion; Emergency relief/refugees/humanitarian assistance; Gender issues/women; Human rights/peace/conflicts; International relations/cooperation/development aid; Peace/ethnic conflicts/armament/disarmament; Population/family planning/demography; Poverty/living conditions; Racism/xenophobia/antisemitism; Refugees/migrants/ethnic groups. **Activities:** Conferences/seminars/workshops/training activities; Fund raising; Information and documentation services/data bases; Information campaigns/exhibitions.

DNK1306

GENVEJ TIL UDVIKLING (GTU) ♦ Short Cut to Development

Poste Restante, 8000 Arhus C, Denmark.

Telephone: 45 (86) 44 72 88. **Contact:** Per A. Christensen, Chairman.

OBJECTIVES: To support self-confidence, self-supply and self-determination of people in developing countries. To support a plaster factory in Northern Mali and in Tessalit. To support a project of recycling household waste in Benin.

GENERAL INFORMATION: Creation: 1978. **Affiliated to:** Emmaüs International (Denmark) - Mellemfolkeligt Samvirke (Denmark) -FN-Forbundet (Denmark) - Oplysningscenter om den 3. Verden (Denmark) -Nord-Syd-Koalitionen (Denmark). **Personnel/Total:** 30. *Volunteers:* 30. *Budget/Total 1993:* ECU 11000 (US$ 12000). **Financial sources:** Private: 15%. Public: 65%. Self-financing: 20%.

PUBLICATIONS: Periodicals: Projekt og Kultur (3). Annual report.

ACTIVITIES IN DEVELOPING REGIONS: Works through local field partners. **Sustainable Development Actions:** Ecology/environment/biodiversity; Education/training/literacy; Rural development/agriculture; Small enterprises/informal sector/handicrafts. **Regions:** West Africa.

INFORMATION AND EDUCATION ACTIVITIES: Topics: Culture/tradition/religion; Ecology/environment/biodiversity; International economic relations/trade/debt/finance; International relations/cooperation/development aid; Rural development/agriculture. **Activities:** Exchanges/twinning/linking; Fund raising; Information and documentation services/data bases; Information campaigns/exhibitions; Lobbying/advocacy.

DNK1307

GHANA VENSKABSGRUPPERNE I DANMARK/GHANAIAN DANISH COMMUNITIES ASSOCIATION ♦ Ghana-Friendship Groups in Denmark/Ghanaian Danish Communities Association

Nygade 30, 8600 Silkeborg, Denmark.

Telephone: 45 (86) 80 33 01. **Fax:** 45 (86) 80 53 01. **Contact:** Thomas Ravn-Pedersen, Chairman.

OBJECTIVES: To establish relations of friendship and promote interaction between people in the rural areas of Northern Ghana and Denmark. To help Ghanaian communities implement their development plans.

GENERAL INFORMATION: Creation: 1979. **Type of organisation:** association of NGOs. **Member organisations:** 5. **Affiliated to:** Nord/Syd Koalitionen (Denmark). **Personnel/Total:** 36. Salaried: 27 of which: 26 in developing countries. Volunteers: 9 of which: 2 in developing countries. **Budget/Total 1993:** ECU 323000 (US$ 378000). **Financial sources:** Public: 99%. Self-financing: 1%.

PUBLICATIONS: Periodicals: Håndslag (4). Annual report. List of publications.

ACTIVITIES IN DEVELOPING REGIONS: Present in developing regions. Active in 1 country(ies). Maintains local field presence. Works through local field partners. **Sustainable Development Actions:** Democracy/good governance/institution building/participatory development; Education/training/literacy; Emergency relief/refugees/humanitarian assistance; Gender issues/women; Health/sanitation/water; Human rights/peace/conflicts; Rural development/agriculture; Sending volunteers/experts/technical assistance; Small enterprises/informal sector/handicrafts. **Regions:** West Africa.

INFORMATION AND EDUCATION ACTIVITIES: Topics: Children/youth/family; Culture/tradition/religion; Education/training/literacy; Emergency relief/refugees/humanitarian assistance; Gender issues/women; Health/sanitation/water; Human rights/peace/conflicts; International relations/cooperation/development aid; Peace/ethnic conflicts/armament/disarmament; Refugees/migrants/ethnic groups; Rural development/agriculture. **Activities:** Broadcasting/cultural events; Conferences/seminars/workshops/training activities; Exchanges/twinning/linking; Information campaigns/exhibitions; Networking/electronic telecommunications.

DNK1308

GRON BURKINA FASO ♦ Green Burkina Faso

Kirkedalsvej 8, 9690 Fjerritslev, Denmark.

Telephone: 45 (98) 21 51 47. **Contact:** Arne Bjerregaard.

OBJECTIVES: To support the agricultural project run by Jacques Nignan. To support the general development of farming in the South of Burkina Faso.

GENERAL INFORMATION: Creation: 1988. **Budget/Total 1993:** ECU 5600 (US$ 6600). **Financial sources:** Private: 10%. Self-financing: 90%.

ACTIVITIES IN DEVELOPING REGIONS: Active in 1 country(ies). Works through local field partners. **Sustainable Development Actions:** Ecology/environment/biodiversity; Energy/transport; Health/sanitation/water; Rural development/agriculture. **Regions:** West Africa.

DNK1309

GRUPO CULTURAL LOS ANDES DEL PERU

c/o Fina Villarreal de Berger, Værebrovej 86, st 07, 2880 Bagsværd, Denmark.

Telephone: 45 (44) 98 32 23.

See: *How to Use the Directory,* page 11.

DNK1310

HANDICAP INTERNATIONAL, DANMARK

c/o IMCC, Panum Instituttet 9.2.2., Blegdamsvej 3B, 2200 København N, Denmark.

Telephone: 45 (31) 21 51 54. *Fax:* 45 (33) 25 24 27. *Contact:* Otto Rungby, President.

OBJECTIVES: To support the physically disabled in the Third World with the aim that they will become self-reliant in their communities.

GENERAL INFORMATION: *Creation:* 1990. *Personnel/Total:* 12. *Volunteers:* 12. *Budget/Total 1993:* ECU 6600 (US$ 7700). *Financial sources:* Private: 80%. Self-financing: 20%.

PUBLICATIONS: *Periodicals:* Handicap International (4). *Annual report.*

EVALUATION/RESEARCH: Evaluation reports available. Undertakes research activities.

COMMENTS: Handicap International-DK is a full member of Handicap International and independent organisations in France and Belgium. Undertakes activities in the Commonwealth of Independent States.

ACTIVITIES IN DEVELOPING REGIONS: Present in developing regions. Active in 31 country(ies). Maintains local field presence. Works through local field partners. **Sustainable Development Actions:** Health/sanitation/water. **Regions:** Central Africa; Central Asia and South Asia; East Africa; East Asia; Mexico and Central America; Middle East; North Africa; Oceania; South America; South East Asia; West Africa.

INFORMATION AND EDUCATION ACTIVITIES: Topics: Health/sanitation/water. **Activities:** Broadcasting/cultural events; Conferences/seminars/workshops/training activities; Formal education; Fund raising; Information and documentation services/data bases; Information campaigns/exhibitions; Lobbying/advocacy; Publishing/audiovisual materials/educational materials.

DNK1311

HEALTH ACTION INTERNATIONAL, DANMARK (HAI-DK)

c/o Mellemfolkeligt Samvirke, Konsolenttjenesten Borgergade 10-14, 1300 København K, Denmark.

Telephone: 45 (1) 32 62 44.

DNK1312

IBIS

Noerrebrogade 68B, 2 sal, 2200 København N, Denmark.

Telephone: 45 (31) 35 87 88. *Fax:* 45 (31) 35 06 96. *Contact:* Frans Mikael Jansen, Secretary General.

OBJECTIVES: To support oppressed people in developing countries. To disseminate information about developing countries in Denmark. To promote ecologically sustainable growth. To promote a change of the present economic world order. To create debate on Danish foreign aid policy.

GENERAL INFORMATION: *Creation:* 1966. *Affiliated to:* Eurostep (Belgium) - Interfund (South Africa). *Personnel/Total:* 156. *Salaried:* 156 of which: 130 in developing countries. *Budget/Total 1993:* ECU 22393000 (US$ 26218000). *Financial sources:* Public: 99%. Self-financing: 1%.

PUBLICATIONS: *Periodicals:* Zig Zag (9). *Annual report.*

EVALUATION/RESEARCH: Evaluation reports available. Undertakes research activities.

ACTIVITIES IN DEVELOPING REGIONS: Present in developing regions. Active in 9 country(ies). Maintains local field presence. Works through local field partners. **Sustainable Development Actions:** Children/youth/family; Democracy/good governance/institution building/participatory development; Ecology/environment/biodiversity; Education/training/literacy; Gender issues/women; Health/sanitation/water; Human rights/peace/conflicts; Population/family planning/demography; Rural development/agriculture; Sending volunteers/experts/technical assistance; Small enterprises/informal sector/handicrafts; Urban development/habitat. **Regions:** Mexico and Central America; South America; Southern Africa.

INFORMATION AND EDUCATION ACTIVITIES: Topics: Children/youth/family; Culture/tradition/religion; Ecology/environment/biodiversity; Education/training/literacy; Employment/unemployment; Gender issues/women; Health/sanitation/water; Human rights/peace/conflicts; International economic relations/trade/debt/finance; International relations/cooperation/development aid; Peace/ethnic conflicts/armament/disarmament; Population/family planning/demography; Poverty/living conditions; Refugees/migrants/ethnic groups; Rural development/agriculture; Urban development/habitat. **Activities:** Conferences/seminars/workshops/training activities; Formal education; Information campaigns/exhibitions; Lobbying/advocacy; Publishing/audiovisual materials/educational materials.

DNK1313

IND-SAM, DE ETNISKE MINDRETAL I DANMARK ♦ Federation of Ethnic Minorities in Denmark

Blegdamsvej 4, st., 2200 Københav N, Denmark.

Telephone: 45 (31) 39 21 43. *Fax:* 45 (35) 36 24 10.

DNK1314

INDUSTRIALISERINGSFONDEN FOR UDVIKLINGSLANDENE (IFU) ♦ The Industrialization Fund for Developing Countries

Postboks 2155, Bremerholm 4, 1016 København K, Denmark.

Telephone: 45 (33) 14 25 75. *Fax:* 45 (33) 32 25 24. *Contact:* Henry Petersen, Chairman.

OBJECTIVES: To invest in developing countries in collaboration with Danish companies in order to promote economic activity. To participate in projects within all types of industry and trade, agriculture, consulting engineering, transport and other services.

GENERAL INFORMATION: *Creation:* 1967. *Personnel/Total:* 57. *Salaried:* 57 of which: 13 in developing countries. *Budget/Total 1993:* ECU 21076000 (US$ 24676000). *Financial sources:* Self-financing: 100%.

PUBLICATIONS: *Annual report.*

COMMENTS: IFU acts as a shareholder in joint venture companies. IFU may operate in developing countries with a GNP per capita no greater than 4715 US$ (1994).

ACTIVITIES IN DEVELOPING REGIONS: Active in 49 country(ies). Maintains local field presence. **Sustainable Development Actions:** Debt/finance/trade; Ecology/environment/biodiversity; Energy/transport; Health/sanitation/water; Rural development/agriculture; Sending volunteers/experts/technical assistance; Small enterprises/informal sector/handicrafts; Urban development/habitat. **Regions:** Caribbean; Central Africa; Central Asia and South Asia; East Africa; East Asia; Mexico and Central America; Middle East; North Africa; Oceania; South America; South East Asia; Southern Africa; West Africa.

DNK1315

INDVANDRERNES FELLESRAD I DANMARK (IFD)

Vesterbrogade 40, 1 tv, 1620 København V, Denmark.

Telephone: 45 (31) 24 63 30. *Fax:* 45 (31) 24 34 05. *Contact:* Aydin Tasbent, Secretary General.

DNK1316

INTERNATIONAL BORNEHJAELP ♦ International Child Welfare Service

174 Granvaenget 6, 5700 Svendborg, Denmark.

Telephone: 45 (62) 20 84 93. *Fax:* 45 (62) 20 81 13. *Contact:* Bjørn Johansen, President.

OBJECTIVES: To provide support for orphans and destitute children.

GENERAL INFORMATION: *Creation:* 1974. *Personnel/Total:* 7. *Volunteers:* 7. *Budget/Total 1993:* ECU 527000 (US$ 617000). *Financial sources:* Private: 70%. Public: 20%. Self-financing: 10%.

PUBLICATIONS: *Periodicals:* Verdens Børn (4). *Annual report.*

COMMENTS: Undertakes activities in the Commonwealth of Independent States.

ACTIVITIES IN DEVELOPING REGIONS: Active in 5 country(ies). Maintains local field presence. Works through local field partners. **Sustainable Development Actions:** Children/youth/family; Education/training/literacy; Food/famine; Gender issues/women; Health/sanitation/water; Population/family planning/demography; Rural development/agriculture; Small enterprises/informal sector/handicrafts; Urban development/habitat. **Regions:** East Africa; South East Asia.

INFORMATION AND EDUCATION ACTIVITIES: Topics: Culture/tradition/religion; Education/training/literacy; Health/sanitation/water; Population/family planning/demography; Poverty/living conditions; Refugees/migrants/ethnic groups; Rural development/agriculture; Urban development/habitat. **Activities:** Fund raising; Publishing/audiovisual materials/educational materials.

DNK1317

INTERNATIONAL FORUM ♦ Forum International

Griffenfeldsgade 35, 2200 København, Denmark.

Telephone: 45 (35) 37 18 88. **Fax:** 45 (35) 37 19 80. **E-mail:** inforum@pns.apc.org. **Contact:** Albert Jensen, Secretary General.

OBJECTIVES: To promote solidarity work and development education activities in relation to developing countries. To support national liberation movements and popular organisations fighting for self-determination. To organise human rights' campaigns in Denmark.

GENERAL INFORMATION: Creation: 1970. **Affiliated to:** International Students and Youth Movement for the UN - EC-NGDO Network of Development NGOs in the EC - Danish Youth Federation (Denmark). **Personnel/Total:** 95. *Salaried:* 5 of which: 1 in developing countries. *Volunteers:* 90 of which: 3 in developing countries. **Budget/Total 1993:** ECU 263000 (US$ 308000). **Financial sources:** *Private:* 50%. *Public:* 15%. *Self-financing:* 35%.

PUBLICATIONS: *Periodicals:* GAIA (4). *Annual report. List of publications.*

EVALUATION/RESEARCH: Evaluation reports available. Undertakes research activities.

ACTIVITIES IN DEVELOPING REGIONS: Active in 11 country(ies). Maintains local field presence. Works through local field partners. **Sustainable Development Actions:** Children/youth/family; Democracy/good governance/institution building/participatory development; Ecology/environment/biodiversity; Education/training/literacy; Emergency relief/refugees/humanitarian assistance; Food/famine; Gender issues/women; Health/sanitation/water; Human rights/peace/conflicts; Sending volunteers/experts/technical assistance; Urban development/habitat. **Regions:** Caribbean; East Asia; Mexico and Central America; Middle East; South America; South East Asia.

INFORMATION AND EDUCATION ACTIVITIES: Topics: Children/youth/family; Culture/tradition/religion; Education/training/literacy; Employment/unemployment; Human rights/peace/conflicts; International economic relations/trade/debt/finance; International relations/cooperation/development aid; Poverty/living conditions; Racism/xenophobia/antisemitism; Refugees/migrants/ethnic groups. **Activities:** Information and documentation services/data bases; Information campaigns/exhibitions; Networking/electronic telecommunications; Publishing/audiovisual materials/educational materials.

DNK1318

INTERNATIONAL KONTAKT (IK)

Postboks 114, 4450 Jyderup, Denmark.

Telephone: 45 (59) 29 31 15. **Fax:** 45 (59) 29 44 35. **Contact:** Anette Sonne, President.

OBJECTIVES: To reinforce international education and to develop an educational system which encourages global interactions. To promote global solidarity.

GENERAL INFORMATION: Creation: 1982. **Affiliated to:** Mellemfolkeligt Samvirke (Denmark) - Samrådet for Ungdomsudveksling (Denmark). **Personnel/Total:** 30. *Volunteers:* 30. **Financial sources:** *Self-financing:* 100%.

PUBLICATIONS: *List of publications.*

EVALUATION/RESEARCH: Evaluation reports available.

ACTIVITIES IN DEVELOPING REGIONS: Active in 2 country(ies). **Sustainable Development Actions:** Education/training/literacy. **Regions:** North Africa; West Africa.

INFORMATION AND EDUCATION ACTIVITIES: Topics: Culture/tradition/religion; International relations/cooperation/development aid; Racism/xenophobia/antisemitism. **Activities:** Exchanges/twinning/linking; Information and documentation services/data bases; Information campaigns/exhibitions; Publishing/audiovisual materials/educational materials.

DNK1319

INTERNATIONAL MEDICAL COOPERATION COMMITTEE (IMCC)

Panum Instituttet 9.2.2. Blegdamsvej 3B, 2200 København N, Denmark.

Telephone: 45 (35) 32 64 11. **Fax:** 45 (35) 32 64 10. **Contact:** Natalia Nielsen.

OBJECTIVES: To contribute to the improvement of people's health and to development in the project regions.

GENERAL INFORMATION: Personnel/Total: 23. *Salaried:* 8 of which: 7 in developing countries. *Volunteers:* 15. **Budget/Total 1993:** ECU 329000 (US$ 386000). **Financial sources:** *Public:* 100%.

PUBLICATIONS: *Annual report.*

EVALUATION/RESEARCH: Evaluation reports available.

PLANNED ACTIVITIES: Training of village health-care workers in Bolivia.

ACTIVITIES IN DEVELOPING REGIONS: Present in developing regions. Active in 1 country(ies). Maintains local field presence. Works through local field partners. **Sustainable Development Actions:** Democracy/good governance/institution building/participatory development; Education/training/literacy; Health/sanitation/water; Population/family planning/demography; Sending volunteers/experts/technical assistance. **Regions:** South America.

INFORMATION AND EDUCATION ACTIVITIES: Topics: Health/sanitation/water; Population/family planning/demography; Poverty/living conditions. **Activities:** Conferences/seminars/workshops/training activities; Information campaigns/exhibitions; Publishing/audiovisual materials/educational materials.

DNK1320

INTERNATIONAL SOLID WASTES ASSOCIATION (ISWA)

Bremerholm 1, 1069 København K, Denmark.

Telephone: 45 (33) 91 44 91. **Fax:** 45 (33) 91 91 88. **Contact:** Jeanne Moller, General Secretary.

OBJECTIVES: To promote and develop professional solid waste management worldwide.

GENERAL INFORMATION: Creation: 1972. **Type of organisation:** coordinating body. **Member organisations:** 20. **Personnel/Total:** 4. *Salaried:* 4. **Budget/Total 1993:** ECU 356000 (US$ 416000). **Financial sources:** *Self-financing:* 100%.

PUBLICATIONS: *Periodicals:* Waste Management and Research (6) - ISWA Times (4). *Annual report. List of publications.*

COMMENTS: Undertakes activities in the Commonwealth of Independent States. Information activities related to the Commonwealth of Independent States.

ACTIVITIES IN DEVELOPING REGIONS: Maintains local field presence. Works through local field partners. **Sustainable Development Actions:** Education/training/literacy. **Regions:** Caribbean; Middle East; West Africa.

INFORMATION AND EDUCATION ACTIVITIES: Topics: Other. **Activities:** Conferences/seminars/workshops/training activities.

DNK1321

INTERNATIONAL SOLIDARITET ♦ International Solidarity

Brandstrupsgade 4, st. th., 9000 Ålborg, Denmark.

Telephone: 45 (98) 11 30 44. **Contact:** Helle Rasmussen.

See: *How to Use the Directory,* page 11.

OBJECTIVES: To act as the co-ordinating body for the Third World organisations in Ålborg.

GENERAL INFORMATION: *Creation:* 1983. *Type of organisation:* coordinating body. *Member organisations:* 5.

ACTIVITIES IN DEVELOPING REGIONS: Present in developing regions. Active in 1 country(ies). Maintains local field presence. **Sustainable Development Actions:** Education/training/literacy. **Regions:** Mexico and Central America.

INFORMATION AND EDUCATION ACTIVITIES: Topics: Poverty/living conditions; Refugees/migrants/ethnic groups. **Activities:** Publishing/audiovisual materials/educational materials.

DNK1322

INTERNATIONAL WORK GROUP FOR INDIGENOUS AFFAIRS (IWGIA)

Internationalt Sekretariat, Fiolstræde 10, 1171 København K, Denmark.

Telephone: 45 (33) 12 47 24. *Fax:* 45 (33) 14 77 49. *Contact:* Rene Fuerst, Chairman.

DNK1323

DEN INTERNATIONALE FOLKEHOJSKOLE ♦ International People's College

1 Montebello Allé, 3000 Elsinore, Denmark.

Telephone: 45 (2) 21 33 61. *Contact:* Erik Hogsbro Holm, Principal.

DNK1324

DEN INTERNATIONALE HOJSKOLE ♦ The International People's College

Montebello Alle 1, 3000 Helsingør, Denmark.

Telephone: 45 (49) 21 33 61. *Fax:* 45 (49) 21 21 28. *Contact:* Kristof Kristiansen, Principal.

OBJECTIVES: To promote peace and international understanding. To offer innovative adult educational programmes in order to promote cross-cultural dialogue and co-operation. To provide inter-disciplinary, multi-cultural and creative education to students from all over the world.

GENERAL INFORMATION: *Creation:* 1921. *Affiliated to:* Danish Association of Folk High Schools. *Personnel/Total:* 21. *Salaried:* 19. *Budget/Total 1993:* ECU 1186000 (US$ 1388000). *Financial sources:* Private: 10%. Public: 50%. Self-financing: 40%.

PUBLICATIONS: *Periodicals:* 7PC Report (3).

EVALUATION/RESEARCH: Evaluation reports available. Undertakes research activities.

COMMENTS: IPC was officially designated "Peace Messenger" by the United Nations in 1988. Information activities related to the Commonwealth of Independent States.

INFORMATION AND EDUCATION ACTIVITIES: Topics: Culture/tradition/religion; Other. **Activities:** Conferences/seminars/workshops/training activities.

DNK1325

INTERNATIONALT HUS

Klostervej 28, 5000 Odense C, Denmark.

Telephone: 45 (66) 19 13 44. *Fax:* 45 (66) 13 90 45. *Contact:* Claus Riis, President.

DNK1326

INTERNATIONALT LANDSBY SAMARBEJDE ♦ International Village Co-operation

Skovhusevej 31, 9574 Baelum, Denmark.

Telephone: 45 (8) 33 73 53. *Contact:* Finn Olesen.

DNK1327

KALAHARI-GRUPPEN

c/o Vibeke Cramer, Bjørnsonsvej 84, 2500 Valby, Denmark.

Telephone: 45 (31) 17 78 02.

DNK1328

KENYANSK DANSK VENSKABSFORENING ♦ Kenyan Danish Friendship Association

Kenya Airways, Trommesalen 5, 4., 1614 København V, Denmark.

Telephone: 45 (42) 65 93 12. *Contact:* Joseph Karuri, President.

OBJECTIVES: To maintain a friendly relationship and social and cultural ties between the people of Kenya and Denmark. To serve as a medium of communication.

GENERAL INFORMATION: *Personnel/Total:* 7. *Salaried:* 1. *Volunteers:* 6. *Budget/Total 1993:* ECU 1500 (US$ 1700). *Financial sources:* Self-financing: 100%.

PUBLICATIONS: *Annual report.*

PLANNED ACTIVITIES: Cultural education evening classes.

ACTIVITIES IN DEVELOPING REGIONS: Maintains local field presence. **Sustainable Development Actions:** Children/youth/family. **Regions:** East Africa.

DNK1329

KIRKERNES RACEPROGRAM ♦ Programme to Combat Racism

Kløvermarksvej 4, 8200 Århus N, Denmark.

Telephone: 45 (86) 16 26 55. *Fax:* 45 (86) 16 34 22. *Contact:* Poul Abildgaard, President.

DNK1330

KIRKERNES U-LANDSOPLYSNING ♦ Churches' Third World Information

Skindergade 24, 1., 1159 København K, Denmark.

Telephone: 45 (33) 15 59 27. *Fax:* 45 (33) 11 32 14. *Contact:* Birthe Juel Christensen.

DNK1331

KOGE OG OMEGNS GHANA VENSKABSFORENING

Tinggården 111, 4681 Herfølge, Denmark.

Telephone: 45 (56) 27 51 38. *Contact:* Morten Ledskov.

DNK1332

KOMITEEN FOR SOLIDARITET MED BURUNDIS FOLK (BURUNDIKOMITEEN) ♦ Danish Committee for Solidarity with the People of Burundi

Postboks 56, 8310 Tranbjerg, Denmark.

Telephone: 45 (86) 29 36 36. *Fax:* 45 (86) 29 52 25. *Contact:* Etienne Karatasi, Chairman.

DNK1333

KVINDERNES U-LANDSUDVALG (KULU) ♦ Women and Development

Landgreven 7, 3 tv., 1301 København K, Denmark.

Telephone: 45 (33) 15 78 70. *Fax:* 45 (33) 32 53 30. *Contact:* Ruth Ejdrup Olsen.

DNK1334

LAERERNES MISSIONS FORENING (LMF) ♦ Teachers' Missions Association

Klaksvej 17, 4262 Sandved, Denmark.

Telephone: 45 (3) 75 60 82. *Fax:* 45 (3) 75 60 48. *Contact:* Tove Høst, Chairman of the Board.

OBJECTIVES: To support teachers from different mission organisations working abroad, both financially and spiritually.

GENERAL INFORMATION: *Creation:* 1902. *Type of organisation:* association of NGOs. *Affiliated to:* Danish Missionary Council (Denmark). *Personnel/Total:* 1. *Salaried:* 1. *Budget/Total 1993:* ECU 112000 (US$ 131000). *Financial sources:* Private: 100%.

Voir : *Comment utiliser le répertoire,* page 11.

PUBLICATIONS: *Periodicals:* LMF (10).

DNK1335

LANDSORGANISATIONEN I DANMARK (LO) ♦ The Danish Confederation of Trade Unions

Rosenors Alle 12, 1634 København V, Denmark.

Telephone: 45 (31) 35 35 41. *Fax:* 45 (35) 37 37 41. *Contact:* Finn Thorgrimson, President.

OBJECTIVES: To bring together the national trade unions in order to protect the interests of wage earners and to support the implementation of industrial and economic democracy.

GENERAL INFORMATION: *Creation:* 1898. *Type of organisation:* association of NGOs. *Member organisations:* 25. *Personnel/Total:* 130. *Salaried:* 130. *Financial sources: Self-financing:* 100%.

PUBLICATIONS: *Periodicals:* LO-Bladet (52). *Annual report. List of publications.*

EVALUATION/RESEARCH: Evaluation reports available.

COMMENTS: Undertakes activities in the Commonwealth of Independent States. Information activities related to the Commonwealth of Independent States.

INFORMATION AND EDUCATION ACTIVITIES: Topics: Children/youth/family; Culture/tradition/religion; Ecology/environment/biodiversity; Education/training/literacy; Emergency relief/refugees/humanitarian assistance; Employment/unemployment; Gender issues/women; Human rights/peace/conflicts; International economic relations/trade/debt/finance; International relations/cooperation/development aid; Poverty/living conditions; Racism/xenophobia/antisemitism; Refugees/migrants/ethnic groups. **Activities:** Conferences/seminars/workshops/training activities; Formal education; Information and documentation services/data bases; Information campaigns/exhibitions; Lobbying/advocacy; Publishing/audiovisual materials/educational materials.

DNK1336

LATINAMERIKA INFORMATION (LA-INFO) ♦ Latin American Information and Consultancy Agency for Cultural Exchange and Development Projects

Bækvangen 22, 8530 Hjortshøj, Denmark.

Telephone: 45 (86) 74 15 20. *Fax:* 45 (86) 74 15 20. *Contact:* Jacob B. Melbye, President.

DNK1337

LEGER UDEN GRENSER ♦ Médecins Sans Frontières

Strandveien 171, 1., 2900 Hellerup, Denmark.

Telephone: 45 (31) 62 63 01. *Fax:* 45 (39) 40 14 92. *Contact:* Jean-Pierre Luxen.

DNK1338

LIONS CLUB INTERNATIONAL

Hvidklovervej 3, Tune, 4000 Roskilde, Denmark.

Contact: Harely Jensen.

DNK1339

MELLEMFOLKELIGT SAMVIRKE (MS) ♦ Danish Association for International Co-operation

Borgergade 10-14, 1300 København K, Denmark.

Telephone: 45 (33) 32 62 44. *Fax:* 45 (33) 15 62 43. *Contact:* Knud Vilby, President.

OBJECTIVES: To further international understanding and solidarity. To bridge the gap between national and cultural differences. To support the development process by sending workers to developing countries and by influencing Danish development aid policy.

GENERAL INFORMATION: *Creation:* 1944. *Member organisations:* 120. *Personnel/Total:* 467. *Salaried:* 107 of which: 27 in developing countries. *Volunteers:* 360 of which: 360 in developing countries. *Budget/Total 1993:* ECU 24237000 (US$ 28378000). *Financial sources: Private:* 10%. *Public:* 90%.

PUBLICATIONS: *Periodicals:* MS-REVY (8) - Kontakt (8) - Zapp (6). *Annual report. List of publications.*

EVALUATION/RESEARCH: Evaluation reports available.

PLANNED ACTIVITIES: Cultural Festival, 1996, on the Images of Africa.

COMMENTS: Undertakes activities in the Commonwealth of Independent States. Information activities related to the Commonwealth of Independent States.

ACTIVITIES IN DEVELOPING REGIONS: Maintains local field presence. Works through local field partners. **Sustainable Development Actions:** Children/youth/family; Democracy/good governance/institution building/participatory development; Ecology/environment/biodiversity; Education/training/literacy; Emergency relief/refugees/humanitarian assistance; Gender issues/women; Health/sanitation/water; Human rights/peace/conflicts; Rural development/agriculture; Sending volunteers/experts/technical assistance; Small enterprises/informal sector/handicrafts; Urban development/habitat. **Regions:** Central Asia and South Asia; East Africa; Mexico and Central America; Southern Africa.

INFORMATION AND EDUCATION ACTIVITIES: Topics: Children/youth/family; Culture/tradition/religion; Ecology/environment/biodiversity; Emergency relief/refugees/humanitarian assistance; Food/famine; Gender issues/women; Health/sanitation/water; Human rights/peace/conflicts; International economic relations/trade/debt/finance; International relations/cooperation/development aid; Peace/ethnic conflicts/armament/disarmament; Population/family planning/demography; Poverty/living conditions; Racism/xenophobia/antisemitism; Refugees/migrants/ethnic groups; Rural development/agriculture; Urban development/habitat. **Activities:** Broadcasting/cultural events; Conferences/seminars/workshops/training activities; Exchanges/twinning/linking; Formal education; Information and documentation services/data bases; Information campaigns/exhibitions; Lobbying/advocacy; Publishing/audiovisual materials/educational materials.

DNK1340

MENNESKERETTIGHEDSGRUPPEN SOL

c/o Cikaden, Griffenfeldsgade 35, 2200 København N, Denmark.

Telephone: 45 (31) 85 67 65. *Fax:* 45 (35) 37 19 80.

DNK1341

MODRENE FRA PLAZA DE MAYO, STOTTEGRUPPE I DK

Peter Sabroesgade 32, 3 tv., 2450 København SV, Denmark.

Telephone: 45 (31) 22 36 27. *Fax:* 45 (35) 37 19 80. *Contact:* Rut Hernandez, President.

DNK1342

MORSO U-LANDSFORENING ♦ Morso Third World Association

Norregade 3, P.O. Box 35, 7900 Nykobing Mors, Denmark.

Telephone: 45 (97) 72 48 00. *Fax:* 45 (97) 72 07 80. *Contact:* John Tousig, Chairman.

OBJECTIVES: To increase the knowledge and understanding of problems in developing countries. To support projects of benefit to developing countries, regardless of the political or religious affiliation of the recipient country or organisation.

GENERAL INFORMATION: *Creation:* 1980. *Personnel/Total:* 9. *Volunteers:* 9. *Budget/Total 1993:* ECU 13000 (US$ 15000). *Financial sources: Private:* 14%. *Public:* 69%. *Self-financing:* 17%.

EVALUATION/RESEARCH: Evaluation reports available.

PLANNED ACTIVITIES: Sending Danish volunteers to Tanzania and exchange study tours.

ACTIVITIES IN DEVELOPING REGIONS: Present in developing regions. Active in 1 country(ies). Maintains local field presence. Works through local field partners. **Sustainable Development Actions:** Children/youth/family; Education/training/literacy; Energy/transport; Gender issues/women; Health/sanitation/water; Small enterprises/informal sector/handicrafts. **Regions:** East Africa.

INFORMATION AND EDUCATION ACTIVITIES: Topics: Children/youth/family; Culture/tradition/religion; Education/training/literacy; Gender issues/women; Health/sanitation/water. **Activities:** Exchanges/twinning/

See: *How to Use the Directory,* page 11.

linking; Formal education; Information campaigns/exhibitions; Publishing/audiovisual materials/educational materials.

DNK1343
NAIROBI - KLUBBEN, SAMMENSLUTNINGEN AF DANSKE U-LANDSJOURNALISTER
c/o Erik Lyngsø-Petersen, Folkevej 4, 2820 Gentofte, Denmark.

DNK1344
NICARAGUA KOMITEEN
Griffenfeldsgade 35, 2200 København N, Denmark.
Telephone: 45 (35) 37 14 30. *Fax:* 45 (35) 37 19 80.

DNK1345
NOAH - FRIENDS OF THE EARTH, DANMARK
Nørrebrogade 39, 2200 København N, Denmark.
Telephone: 45 (35) 36 12 12. *Fax:* 45 (35) 36 12 17. *Contact:* Pia Jørgensen.

OBJECTIVES: To campaign and raise awareness in Denmark about global and local environmental issues.

GENERAL INFORMATION: *Creation:* 1969. *Affiliated to:* Friends of the Earth International (the Netherlands). *Personnel/Total:* 102. *Salaried:* 2. *Volunteers:* 100. *Budget/Total 1993:* ECU 105000 (US$ 123000). *Financial sources:* Public: 50%. Self-financing: 50%.

PUBLICATIONS: *Periodicals:* NOAH-Bladet (6).

EVALUATION/RESEARCH: Undertakes research activities.

COMMENTS: Information activities related to the Commonwealth of Independent States.

INFORMATION AND EDUCATION ACTIVITIES: Topics: Ecology/environment/biodiversity. **Activities:** Conferences/seminars/workshops/training activities; Formal education; Information campaigns/exhibitions; Lobbying/advocacy; Publishing/audiovisual materials/educational materials.

DNK1346
NORD/SYD-KOALITITONEN
c/o Mellemfolkeligt Samvirke, Borgergade 10, 1300 København K, Denmark.
Telephone: 45 (33) 32 62 44. *Contact:* Ellen Farr.

DNK1347
NORDVESTJYSK FOLKECENTER FOR VEDVARENDE ENERGI ♦ Danish Centre for Renewable Energy
Asgaard, Sdr. Ydby., 7760 Hurup Thy, Denmark.
Telephone: 45 (97) 95 65 55. *Fax:* 45 (97) 95 65 65.

DNK1348
OASIS - BEHANDLING OG RADGIVNING FOR FLYGTNINGE ♦ OASIS - Treatment and Counselling for Refugees
Strandboulevarden 96, 2, 2100 København O, Denmark.
Telephone: 45 (35) 26 57 26. *Fax:* 45 (35) 26 55 33. *Contact:* Birgitte Holst, leader.

DNK1349
DET OKUMENISKE CENTER ♦ Ecumenical Centre
Kløvermarksvej 4, 8200 Aarhus N, Denmark.
Telephone: 45 (6) 16 26 55. *Contact:* Erik Jørgensen, Chairperson.

DNK1350
DET OKUMENISKE FELLESRAD I DANMARK (DOF) ♦ Ecumenical Council of Denmark
Skindergade 24/1, 1159 København K, Denmark.

Telephone: 45 (33) 15 59 27. *Fax:* 45 (33) 11 32 14. *Contact:* Jørgen Thomsen, General Secretary.

DNK1351
OPERATION DAGSVERK (OD) ♦ Operation Daywork Denmark
Godthåbsvej 26 C, 2., 2000 Frederiksberg, Denmark.
Telephone: 45 (38) 88 48 22. *Fax:* 45 (38) 88 48 33. *Contact:* Lars Borking.

OBJECTIVES: To initiate and carry out a nationwide collection of funds for a selected educational project in developing countries. To help secondary students have a better understanding of the Third World by producing educational materials, slideshows, videos and newspapers.

GENERAL INFORMATION: *Creation:* 1984. *Type of organisation:* coordinating body. *Personnel/Total:* 13. *Salaried:* 3. *Volunteers:* 10 of which: 2 in developing countries. *Budget/Total 1993:* ECU 303000 (US$ 355000). *Financial sources:* Private: 13%. Public: 63%. Self-financing: 24%.

PUBLICATIONS: *Periodicals:* DAGSVÆRKAVISEN (6) - DAGSVÆRK NEWS (10). *Annual report.*

EVALUATION/RESEARCH: Evaluation reports available.

COMMENTS: "Operation Daywork" is initiated by students.

ACTIVITIES IN DEVELOPING REGIONS: Active in 4 country(ies). Maintains local field presence. Works through local field partners. **Sustainable Development Actions:** Democracy/good governance/institution building/participatory development; Education/training/literacy; Emergency relief/refugees/humanitarian assistance. **Regions:** East Africa; Mexico and Central America; South America; Southern Africa.

INFORMATION AND EDUCATION ACTIVITIES: Topics: Children/youth/family; Culture/tradition/religion; Education/training/literacy; Human rights/peace/conflicts; Population/family planning/demography; Poverty/living conditions; Rural development/agriculture; Urban development/habitat. **Activities:** Fund raising; Information campaigns/exhibitions; Publishing/audiovisual materials/educational materials.

DNK1352
OPLYSNINGSCENTER OM DEN 3. VERDEN (O3V) ♦ Center for Development Education
Guldsmedegade 25, 3., 8000 Århus C, Denmark.
Telephone: 45 (86) 12 20 78. *Contact:* Valborg Fogh Pedersen, President.

DNK1353
ORGANISATIONEN FOR VEDVARENDE ENERGI (OVE) ♦ Danish Organisation for Renewable Energy
Skovvangsvej 191, 8200 Arhus N, Denmark.
Telephone: 45 (86) 10 64 11. *Fax:* 45 (86) 10 61 88. *E-mail:* OVE@NS.apc.org. *Contact:* Hans Bjerregaard, Chairman.

OBJECTIVES: To promote the use of sustainable energy and support environmental policy.

GENERAL INFORMATION: *Creation:* 1975. *Affiliated to:* Forum for Energy and Development (Denmark) - Climate Network Europe (Belgium) -Eurosolar (Germany) - INforSE (Denmark). *Personnel/Total:* 5. *Salaried:* 3. *Volunteers:* 2. *Budget/Total 1993:* ECU 224000 (US$ 262000). *Financial sources:* Private: 10%. Public: 70%. Self-financing: 20%.

PUBLICATIONS: *Periodicals:* Vedvarende Energi Amiljø (6) - Sustainable Energy News (4). *Annual report. List of publications.*

COMMENTS: Undertakes activities in the Commonwealth of Independent States. Information activities related to the Commonwealth of Independent States.

INFORMATION AND EDUCATION ACTIVITIES: Topics: Ecology/environment/biodiversity; Rural development/agriculture; Urban development/habitat. **Activities:** Conferences/seminars/workshops/training activities.

Voir : *Comment utiliser le répertoire,* page 11.

DNK1354

OSTTIMOR-KOMITEEN ◆ East Timor Committee in Denmark

c/o Torben Retbøll, Falstergade 3, 8000 Århus C, Denmark.

Telephone: 45 (86) 12 67 53. *Contact:* Torben Retbøll, Chairman.

DNK1355

PALESTINAKAMPAGNEN

Griffenfeldsgade 35, st., 2200 København N, Denmark.

Telephone: 45 (35) 37 18 88. *Fax:* 45 (35) 37 19 80.

DNK1356

PAX CHRISTI DANMARK ◆ Pax Christi Denmark

Vesterbrogade 28, 3, 1620 København V, Denmark.

Telephone: 45 (1) 31 24 26 30. *Contact:* Jan Orsted.

DNK1357

PORTO NOVO MISSIONEN ◆ Danish Porto Novo Mission

Olsted Praestegård, 8723 Losning, Denmark.

Telephone: 45 (5) 65 21 91. *Contact:* Rev. Johs Bonlokke.

DNK1358

RED BARNET ◆ Save the Children-Denmark

Brogårdsvaenget 4, 2820 Gentofte, Denmark.

Telephone: 45 (31) 68 08 88. *Fax:* 45 (31) 68 05 10. *Contact:* Niels-Christian Andersen, Secretary General.

OBJECTIVES: To protect children's rights to survival, development, protection and participation in a democratic society.

GENERAL INFORMATION: *Creation:* 1945. *Affiliated to:* International Save the Children Alliance (Switzerland). *Personnel/Total:* 46. *Salaried:* 46 of which: 2 in developing countries. *Budget/Total 1993:* ECU 42216000 (US$ 49428000). *Financial sources:* Private: 8%. Public: 91%. Self-financing: 1%.

PUBLICATIONS: *Periodicals:* Projekt (11). *Annual report.*

COMMENTS: Undertakes activities in the Commonwealth of Independent States. Information activities related to the Commonwealth of Independent States.

ACTIVITIES IN DEVELOPING REGIONS: Active in 17 country(ies). Maintains local field presence. Works through local field partners. **Sustainable Development Actions:** Children/youth/family; Education/training/literacy; Emergency relief/refugees/humanitarian assistance; Food/famine; Gender issues/women; Health/sanitation/water; Rural development/agriculture; Sending volunteers/experts/technical assistance; Urban development/habitat. **Regions:** Central Africa; Central Asia and South Asia; East Africa; East Asia; Mexico and Central America; North Africa; South America; Southern Africa.

INFORMATION AND EDUCATION ACTIVITIES: Topics: Children/youth/family; Emergency relief/refugees/humanitarian assistance; Gender issues/women; Health/sanitation/water; Human rights/peace/conflicts; International economic relations/trade/debt/finance; International relations/cooperation/development aid; Peace/ethnic conflicts/armament/disarmament; Population/family planning/demography; Poverty/living conditions; Refugees/migrants/ethnic groups. **Activities:** Conferences/seminars/workshops/training activities; Information and documentation services/data bases; Information campaigns/exhibitions; Lobbying/advocacy; Publishing/audiovisual materials/educational materials.

DNK1359

REGNSKOVSGRUPPEN NEPENTHES

Nepenthes Århus, Odensegade 4, 8000 Århus, Denmark.

Telephone: 45 (86) 19 68 61. *Fax:* 45 (31) 83 28 44. *Contact:* Jan Peter Feil, President.

OBJECTIVES: To encourage sustainable development of forests in the world.

GENERAL INFORMATION: *Creation:* 1982. *Type of organisation:* association of NGOs. *Personnel/Total:* 32. *Salaried:* 2. *Volunteers:* 30. *Budget/Total 1993:* ECU 659000 (US$ 771000). *Financial sources:* Private: 8%. Public: 90%. Self-financing: 2%.

PUBLICATIONS: *Periodicals:* Regnskov (4). *Annual report. List of publications.*

EVALUATION/RESEARCH: Evaluation reports available. Undertakes research activities.

ACTIVITIES IN DEVELOPING REGIONS: Present in developing regions. Active in 1 country(ies). Maintains local field presence. Works through local field partners. **Sustainable Development Actions:** Ecology/environment/biodiversity; Education/training/literacy; Health/sanitation/water; Rural development/agriculture. **Regions:** Mexico and Central America.

INFORMATION AND EDUCATION ACTIVITIES: Topics: Ecology/environment/biodiversity; Rural development/agriculture. **Activities:** Networking/electronic telecommunications.

DNK1360

REHABILITERINGS-OG FORSKNINGSCENTRET FOR TORTUROFRE & INTERNATIONAL REHABILITATION COUNCIL FOR TORTURE VICTIMS (IRCT) ◆ Rehabilitation and Research Centre for Torture victims and International Centre for Torture Victims

Borgergade 13, P.O. Box 2107, 1014 København K, Denmark.

Telephone: 45 (1) 33 76 06 00. *Fax:* 45 (1) 33 76 05 00. *Contact:* Inge Genefke, Medical Director.

OBJECTIVES: To rehabilitate torture victims and their families. To train Danish health workers in the examination and treatment of torture victims. To research torture, its nature and consequences. To disseminate information on torture, torture methods and rehabilitation possibilities.

GENERAL INFORMATION: *Creation:* 1982. *Personnel/Total:* 62. *Salaried:* 61. *Volunteers:* 1. *Budget/Total 1993:* ECU 4352000 (US$ 5095000). *Financial sources:* Private: 19%. Public: 79%. Self-financing: 2%.

PUBLICATIONS: *Periodicals:* Torture (6). *Annual report. List of publications.*

EVALUATION/RESEARCH: Evaluation reports available. Undertakes research activities.

COMMENTS: Undertakes activities in the Commonwealth of Independent States. Information activities related to the Commonwealth of Independent States.

ACTIVITIES IN DEVELOPING REGIONS: Present in developing regions. Active in 37 country(ies). Works through local field partners. **Sustainable Development Actions:** Children/youth/family; Education/training/literacy; Human rights/peace/conflicts; Sending volunteers/experts/technical assistance. **Regions:** Central Africa; Central Asia and South Asia; East Africa; Mexico and Central America; Middle East; North Africa; South America; South East Asia; Southern Africa; West Africa.

INFORMATION AND EDUCATION ACTIVITIES: Topics: Children/youth/family; Human rights/peace/conflicts; Refugees/migrants/ethnic groups. **Activities:** Conferences/seminars/workshops/training activities; Formal education; Fund raising; Information and documentation services/data bases; Networking/electronic telecommunications; Publishing/audiovisual materials/educational materials.

DNK1361

SAMARBEJDET FOR INTERNATIONALT MILJO OG UDVIKLING (SIMU) ◆ Danish Coalition for Environment and Development

c/o Organisationen for Vedvarende Energi, Blegdamsvej 4, 2200 København N, Denmark.

Telephone: 45 (35) 37 35 65. *Fax:* 45 (35) 37 36 76. *E-mail:* OVE@PNS.APC.ORG. *Contact:* Jørgen Martinus, Biologist.

OBJECTIVES: To co-ordinate environmental and development activities of members of Danish organisations and institutions. To disseminate information regarding these activities to the general public.

GENERAL INFORMATION: *Creation:* 1990. *Type of organisation:* network. *Member organisations:* 40. *Personnel/Total:* 1. *Volunteers:*

See: *How to Use the Directory*, page 11.

1. *Budget/Total 1993:* ECU 53000 (US$ 62000). *Financial sources:* Public: 95%. Self-financing: 5%.

INFORMATION AND EDUCATION ACTIVITIES: Topics: Children/youth/ family; Ecology/environment/biodiversity; Food/famine; Gender issues/ women; Health/sanitation/water; Human rights/peace/conflicts; International economic relations/trade/debt/finance; International relations/ cooperation/development aid; Population/family planning/demography; Rural development/agriculture; Urban development/habitat. **Activities:** Conferences/seminars/workshops/training activities.

DNK1362
SAMF. OG HJEM FOR VANFORE

Borgervænget 7, 2100 København O, Denmark.

Contact: I. Skov Mikkelsen.

DNK1363
SAMRADET FOR UNGDOMSUDVEKSLING (SAFU)

Nordre Fasanvej 111, 2000 Frederiksberg, Denmark.

Fax: 45 (38) 34 66 00. *Contact:* Niels Lund, President.

DNK1364
SCT. GEORGS GILDERNE

Mikkel Bryggersgade 1, 1460 København K, Denmark.

DNK1365
SELSKABET FOR NORD-SYD SAMARBEJDE ♦ Society for North-South Co-operation

Fibigerstraede 2, 9220 Aalborg ø, Denmark.

Telephone: 45 (8) 15 85 22 ext 2226. *Fax:* 45 (8) 15 69 50. *Contact:* D.V.M. Jorgen Baltzer.

DNK1366
SOS-BORNEBYERNE, DANMARK ♦ SOS-Childrens Villages

Poul Ankers Gade 2, 2. sal, 1271 København K, Denmark.

Telephone: 45 (33) 13 02 33. *Fax:* 45 (33) 13 40 15. *Contact:* Bjørn Henriksen.

OBJECTIVES: To fundraise for and raise awareness of SOS Children's Villages and other SOS institutions primarily in the Third World.

GENERAL INFORMATION: *Creation:* 1964. *Affiliated to:* SOS Kinderdorf International (Austria). *Salaried:* 7. *Budget/Total 1993:* ECU 4242000 (US$ 4966000). *Financial sources:* Private: 52%. Public: 4%. Self-financing: 44%.

PUBLICATIONS: *Periodicals:* SOS Børneby NYT (4). *Annual report.*

COMMENTS: Undertakes activities in the Commonwealth of Independent States.

ACTIVITIES IN DEVELOPING REGIONS: Active in 70 country(ies). Works through local field partners. **Sustainable Development Actions:** Children/youth/family; Democracy/good governance/institution building/participatory development; Education/training/literacy; Emergency relief/refugees/humanitarian assistance; Food/famine; Health/sanitation/water; Small enterprises/informal sector/handicrafts. **Regions:** Caribbean; Central Africa; Central Asia and South Asia; East Africa; East Asia; Mexico and Central America; Middle East; North Africa; South America; South East Asia; Southern Africa; West Africa.

INFORMATION AND EDUCATION ACTIVITIES: Topics: Children/youth/ family; Education/training/literacy; Emergency relief/refugees/humanitarian assistance; Food/famine; Health/sanitation/water; Refugees/ migrants/ethnic groups. **Activities:** Broadcasting/cultural events; Conferences/seminars/workshops/training activities; Fund raising; Information campaigns/exhibitions; Lobbying/advocacy.

DNK1367
SPECIALARBEJDERFORBUNDET I DANMARK (SID) ♦ General Workers' Union in Denmark

Nyropsgade 30, Postboks 392, 1790 København V, Denmark.

Telephone: 45 (31) 14 21 40. *Fax:* 45 (33) 32 14 50. *Contact:* Claus Larsen-Jensen, International Secretary.

OBJECTIVES: To work for peace, development and freedom through closer international co-operation and solidarity.

GENERAL INFORMATION: *Creation:* 1873. *Affiliated to:* Danish Trade Union Congress (Denmark) - Fagbevægeisens Ulandssekretariat (Denmark) - Arbejderbevægelsens Internationale Forum (Denmark) - ASF-Dansk Folkehjælp (Denmark) - MS (Denmark) - Dansk Flygtningehopelp (Denmark) - UNICEF (Denmark). *Personnel/Total:* 17650. *Salaried:* 650 of which: 2 in developing countries. *Volunteers:* 17000. *Budget/Total 1993:* ECU 52690000 (US$ 61690000). *Financial sources:* Public: 1%. Self-financing: 99%.

PUBLICATIONS: *Periodicals:* Fagbladet (45).

EVALUATION/RESEARCH: Undertakes research activities.

PLANNED ACTIVITIES: New development activities will start in Honduras, Guatemala, Palestinian territories, South Korea.

COMMENTS: Undertakes activities in the Commonwealth of Independent States. Information activities related to the Commonwealth of Independent States.

ACTIVITIES IN DEVELOPING REGIONS: Active in 5 country(ies). Maintains local field presence. Works through local field partners. **Sustainable Development Actions:** Democracy/good governance/institution building/participatory development; Other. **Regions:** Mexico and Central America; Middle East; South America; Southern Africa.

DNK1368
SRI LANKA INFORMATIONSGRUPPE (SLIG) ♦ Sri Lanka Information Group

c/o Mazanti, Hyllinge Station, 4700 Naestved, Denmark.

Telephone: 45 (3) 74 41 42. *Fax:* 45 (3) 64 70 77. *Contact:* Ivan Mazanti.

DNK1369
STORSTROMS AMTS U AND K FORVALTNINGEN U-LAND-SPROJEKTET ♦ Storstroms County's Development Aid Project

Parkvej 37, 4800 Nykobing E, Denmark.

Telephone: 45 (54) 82 32 32. *Fax:* 45 (54) 82 21 83. *Contact:* Arne Kjarsgaard.

OBJECTIVES: To employ long-term unemployed individuals in collecting and restoring old articles, such as hospital equipment, typewriters and sewing machines, which are sent free of charge to developing countries. To undertake development education activities.

**GENERAL INFORMATION: *Creation:* 1984. *Personnel/Total:* 15. *Salaried:* 15. *Budget/Total 1993:* ECU 211000 (US$ 247000). *Financial sources:* Public: 100%.

PUBLICATIONS: *Periodicals:* SABU INFO (4). *Annual report.*

EVALUATION/RESEARCH: Evaluation reports available.

COMMENTS: Undertakes activities in the Commonwealth of Independent States.

ACTIVITIES IN DEVELOPING REGIONS: Active in 20 country(ies). Works through local field partners. **Sustainable Development Actions:** Education/training/literacy; Health/sanitation/water; Small enterprises/informal sector/handicrafts. **Regions:** Central Asia and South Asia; East Africa; Mexico and Central America; South America; West Africa.

INFORMATION AND EDUCATION ACTIVITIES: Topics: Employment/ unemployment; International relations/cooperation/development aid. **Activities:** Conferences/seminars/workshops/training activities.

DNK1370
STOTTEGRUPPE FOR BEDSTEMODRENE PA PLAZA DE MAYO, ARGENTINA

c/o Det økumeniske Fællesråd, Skindergade 24, 1., 1159 København K, Denmark.

Telephone: 45 (33) 15 59 27. *Fax:* 45 (33) 11 32 14. *Contact:* Harriet Armstrong-See, President.

Voir : *Comment utiliser le répertoire,* page 11.

DNK1371

STOTTEGRUPPEN FOR ANDES

c/o Knud Dal, Enghavevej 35, 9000 Ålborg, Denmark.

Telephone: 45 (98) 11 75 46. *Contact:* Knud Dal, President.

DNK1372

STOTTEKOMITEEN FOR GHASSAN KANAFANIS KULTURFOND ♦ Ghassan Kanafani Cultural Foundation (Danish Committee)

Saettedammen 16, 3400 Hillerød, Denmark.

Telephone: 45 (42) 26 15 24. *Contact:* Vagn Andersen.

OBJECTIVES: To establish and operate kindergartens, a school for kindergarten teachers and health clinics for Palestinians and Lebanese in the refugee camps of Lebanon.

GENERAL INFORMATION: *Creation:* 1974. *Personnel/Total:* 10. *Volunteers:* 10. *Budget/Total 1993:* ECU 3000 (US$ 3900). *Financial sources:* Private: 100%.

PUBLICATIONS: *Annual report.*

ACTIVITIES IN DEVELOPING REGIONS: Present in developing regions. Active in 1 country(ies). Maintains local field presence. Works through local field partners. **Sustainable Development Actions:** Children/youth/family; Education/training/literacy; Health/sanitation/water. **Regions:** Middle East.

INFORMATION AND EDUCATION ACTIVITIES: **Topics:** Education/training/literacy; Health/sanitation/water. **Activities:** Fund raising; Information campaigns/exhibitions.

DNK1373

STOTTEKOMITEEN FOR TIBET, DANMARK ♦ The Tibet Support Committee, Denmark

c/o Henrik Schmith, H.C. Orstedsvej 22 G, 2 th., 1879 Frederiksberg C, Denmark.

Telephone: 45 (33) 32 54 16. *Fax:* 45 (31) 23 14 26. *Contact:* Mikkel Bohm, President.

DNK1374

SUDAN MISSIONEN ♦ Sudan United Mission - Danish Branch

Norregade 14, 6070 Christiansfeld, Denmark.

Telephone: 45 (74) 56 22 33. *Fax:* 45 (74) 56 13 34. *Contact:* Mogens S. Mogensen, Secretary General.

OBJECTIVES: To support missions and development projects in Nigeria, Sierra Leone and the Central African Republic.

GENERAL INFORMATION: *Creation:* 1911. *Affiliated to:* Sudan United Mission. *Personnel/Total:* 70. *Salaried:* 50 of which: 45 in developing countries. *Volunteers:* 20 of which: 20 in developing countries. *Budget/Total 1993:* ECU 1673000 (US$ 1959000). *Financial sources:* Private: 80%. *Public:* 4%. *Self-financing:* 16%.

PUBLICATIONS: *Annual report. List of publications.*

ACTIVITIES IN DEVELOPING REGIONS: Present in developing regions. Active in 3 country(ies). Maintains local field presence. Works through local field partners. **Sustainable Development Actions:** Children/youth/family; Education/training/literacy; Emergency relief/refugees/humanitarian assistance; Food/famine; Gender issues/women; Health/sanitation/water; Population/family planning/demography; Rural development/agriculture; Sending volunteers/experts/technical assistance; Urban development/habitat. **Regions:** West Africa.

DNK1375

SYDAFRIKA KONTAKT (SAK) ♦ South Africa Contact

Wesselsgade 4, kld., 2200 København N, Denmark.

Telephone: 45 (31) 35 92 32. *Fax:* 45 (31) 35 43 32. *Contact:* Gorm Gunnarsen, Chairman.

OBJECTIVES: To support mass movements and others working for the democratization of South Africa and her neighbouring countries, by way of political, economic and humanitarian assistance. To help strengthen the contact and dialogue between the Danish and South African people.

GENERAL INFORMATION: *Creation:* 1978. *Member organisations:* 5. *Affiliated to:* Liaison Group of AAM Countries of the EU - Nordic Anti-Apartheid Forum. *Personnel/Total:* 14. *Salaried:* 2. *Volunteers:* 12. *Budget/Total 1993:* ECU 112000 (US$ 131000). *Financial sources:* Private: 20%. Public: 40%. Self-financing: 40%.

PUBLICATIONS: *Periodicals:* Amandla (4). *Annual report. List of publications.*

EVALUATION/RESEARCH: Evaluation reports available.

PLANNED ACTIVITIES: A "raise awareness" campaign on South Africa. Education and democratization of the police and prison services in South Africa.

ACTIVITIES IN DEVELOPING REGIONS: Active in 1 country(ies). Works through local field partners. **Sustainable Development Actions:** Children/youth/family; Democracy/good governance/institution building/participatory development; Education/training/literacy; Energy/transport; Gender issues/women; Human rights/peace/conflicts; Sending volunteers/experts/technical assistance; Urban development/habitat. **Regions:** Southern Africa.

INFORMATION AND EDUCATION ACTIVITIES: **Topics:** Children/youth/family; Culture/tradition/religion; Education/training/literacy; Employment/unemployment; Gender issues/women; Human rights/peace/conflicts; International relations/cooperation/development aid; Peace/ethnic conflicts/armament/disarmament; Poverty/living conditions; Racism/xenophobia/antisemitism; Refugees/migrants/ethnic groups; Urban development/habitat. **Activities:** Broadcasting/cultural events; Conferences/seminars/workshops/training activities; Exchanges/twinning/linking; Formal education; Fund raising; Information and documentation services/data bases; Information campaigns/exhibitions; Lobbying/advocacy; Networking/electronic telecommunications; Publishing/audiovisual materials/educational materials.

DNK1376

TAMILSK DANSK VENSKABSFORENING ♦ Tamil- Danish Friendship Association

Porsvaenget 7-2, 7400 Herning, Denmark.

Telephone: 45 (97) 12 55 93. *Fax:* 45 (97) 12 55 93. *Contact:* T. Selvakumar.

OBJECTIVES: To develop friendship and understanding between Tamils and Danes.

GENERAL INFORMATION: *Creation:* 1986. *Affiliated to:* Ethnic Minority Federation (Denmark) - Federation of Tamil Danish Organisations - Migrants Forum (Belgium) - International Tamil Refugee Network (United Kingdom). *Budget/Total 1993:* ECU 5000 (US$ 5900). *Financial sources:* Private: 30%. Public: 40%. Self-financing: 30%.

INFORMATION AND EDUCATION ACTIVITIES: **Topics:** Culture/tradition/religion; Education/training/literacy; Emergency relief/refugees/humanitarian assistance; Health/sanitation/water; Human rights/peace/conflicts; Peace/ethnic conflicts/armament/disarmament; Racism/xenophobia/antisemitism; Refugees/migrants/ethnic groups. **Activities:** Broadcasting/cultural events; Conferences/seminars/workshops/training activities; Exchanges/twinning/linking; Formal education; Fund raising; Information and documentation services/data bases; Information campaigns/exhibitions; Lobbying/advocacy; Publishing/audiovisual materials/educational materials.

DNK1377

TAN-DAN FORENING

Postboks 2641, 8200 Århus N, Denmark.

Telephone: 45 (86) 13 59 68. *Fax:* 45 (86) 18 03 03. *Contact:* Rogers Mfaume, Chairman.

OBJECTIVES: To maintain good relations between Tanzania, Denmark and Europe. To promote African culture and co-operation among Africans and Europeans. To spread information on, and promote development in Europe and Africa.

See: *How to Use the Directory,* page 11.

GENERAL INFORMATION: *Creation:* 1991. *Affiliated to:* Ethnic Minority Federation in Denmark (Denmark) - West Gambia Culture Association (Denmark) - Swahili Culture Association (Denmark). *Personnel/Total:* 12. *Volunteers:* 12. *Budget/Total 1993:* ECU 81000 (US$ 95000). *Financial sources:* Private: 50%. Public: 25%. Self-financing: 25%.

PUBLICATIONS: *Periodicals:* Kunduchi Production School (12) - Afro-News Magazine (12). *Annual report. List of publications.*

EVALUATION/RESEARCH: Evaluation reports available. Undertakes research activities.

PLANNED ACTIVITIES: Working with the Ministry of Health in order to send hospital equipment for Tanzania.

ACTIVITIES IN DEVELOPING REGIONS: Present in developing regions. Active in 1 country(ies). Maintains local field presence. Works through local field partners. **Sustainable Development Actions:** Children/youth/family; Ecology/environment/biodiversity; Education/training/literacy; Gender issues/women; Health/sanitation/water; Sending volunteers/experts/technical assistance; Urban development/habitat. **Regions:** East Africa.

INFORMATION AND EDUCATION ACTIVITIES: Topics: Children/youth/family; Culture/tradition/religion; Health/sanitation/water; International relations/cooperation/development aid; Rural development/agriculture. **Activities:** Broadcasting/cultural events; Exchanges/twinning/linking; Formal education; Fund raising.

DNK1378

TERRE DES HOMMES, DENMARK (TDH)

Himmelev Bygade 44, Himmelev, 4000 Roskilde, Denmark.

Telephone: 45 (42) 35 56 09. *Contact:* Elin Sørensen.

DNK1379

DEN ; 3.=TRE VERDENS AFTENHOJSKOLE ♦ Third World Night School

Marathonvej 18, 2300 København S, Denmark.

Telephone: 45 (1) 58 92 29. *Contact:* P. Mutahi.

DNK1380

TREDJE VERDEN INFORMATION

Skt. Marcus Kirkeplads 24, 8000 Århus C, Denmark.

Telephone: 45 (86) 12 96 71. *Fax:* 45 (86) 12 25 83. *Contact:* Jette Eistrup.

DNK1381

TREDJE VERDENS STEMME (TVS) ♦ Third World Voice

Kingosgade 15, kld. th., 1818 Frederiksberg C, Denmark.

Telephone: 45 (38) 88 19 77. *Contact:* Bashy Quraishy, President.

DNK1382

U-LANDSDEBAT 1980 (ULD-80) ♦ Developing Country Debate 1980

c/o Sonja Eeg Petersen, Jævndøgnsvej 18, 8200 Århus N, Denmark.

Telephone: 45 (86) 16 51 25. *Contact:* Sonja Eeg Petersen, Secretary.

DNK1383

U-LANDSFONDEN AF 1962 ♦ Developing Countries Foundation of 1962

Århus Statsgymnasium, Fenrisvej 33, 8210 Århus V, Denmark.

Telephone: 45 (86) 15 99 62. *Fax:* 45 (86) 75 29 00. *Contact:* Henning Munk, Secretary.

DNK1384

U-LANDSFORENINGEN SVALERNE ♦ The Swallows in Denmark

Osterbrogade 49, 2100 København O, Denmark.

Telephone: 45 (35) 26 17 47. *Fax:* 45 (31) 38 17 46. *Contact:* Niels Jørgen Jensen, Chairman.

OBJECTIVES: To improve the living conditions of the poorest people in the Third World according to the principles of Abbé Pierre.

GENERAL INFORMATION: *Creation:* 1963. *Affiliated to:* Emmaus International - KULU (Denmark) - MS (Denmark) - EU-NGO-Platform (Denmark) - Emmaus Norden. *Personnel/Total:* 101. *Salaried:* 1. *Volunteers:* 100. *Budget/Total 1993:* ECU 154000 (US$ 180000). *Financial sources:* Public: 36%. Self-financing: 64%.

PUBLICATIONS: *Periodicals:* The Swallows Magazine (1). *Annual report.*

EVALUATION/RESEARCH: Evaluation reports available.

ACTIVITIES IN DEVELOPING REGIONS: Active in 2 country(ies). Works through local field partners. **Sustainable Development Actions:** Children/youth/family; Democracy/good governance/institution building/participatory development; Ecology/environment/biodiversity; Education/training/literacy; Gender issues/women; Health/sanitation/water; Human rights/peace/conflicts; Rural development/agriculture; Small enterprises/informal sector/handicrafts. **Regions:** Central Asia and South Asia.

DNK1385

U-LANDSGRUPPEN FOR FREDERIKSBORG AMT ♦ Development Group of Frederiksborg County

Vinkelvej 9, 3200 Helsinge, Denmark.

Telephone: 45 (2) 29 61 29. *Contact:* Leo H. Knudsen, Chairman.

DNK1386

U-LANDSGRUPPEN PA KUL ♦ Students' Third World Group of the Royal Veterinary and Agricultural University of Copenhagen

c/o De Studerendes Råd, Bülowsvey 13 (KUL), P.O. Box 1870, Frederiksberg C, Denmark.

Telephone: 45 (1) 35 17 88. *Contact:* Ole Quist Sorensen.

DNK1387

U-LANDSGRUPPEN PA LANDBOHOJSKOLEN

Bellowsv. 13, 1870 Frederiksberg C, Denmark.

Telephone: 45 (1) 37 28 12.

DNK1388

U-LANDSHJELP FRA FOLK TIL FOLK (UFF) ♦ Development Aid from People to People

Energivg 2, 2750 Ballerup, Denmark.

Telephone: 45 (44) 66 40 16. *Fax:* 45 (44) 66 40 36. *Contact:* Bolette Knigge-Olsen, Chairman.

OBJECTIVES: To provide development aid to the people of the Third World.

GENERAL INFORMATION: *Creation:* 1977. *Financial sources:* Self-financing: 100%.

ACTIVITIES IN DEVELOPING REGIONS: Active in 6 country(ies). Works through local field partners. **Sustainable Development Actions:** Children/youth/family; Ecology/environment/biodiversity; Education/training/literacy; Emergency relief/refugees/humanitarian assistance; Food/famine; Health/sanitation/water; Rural development/agriculture; Sending volunteers/experts/technical assistance; Small enterprises/informal sector/handicrafts. **Regions:** Southern Africa.

DNK1389

U-LANDSIMPORTEN ♦ Third World Import

Postboks 7, Rostrupbakken 6, 7900 Nykøbing M, Denmark.

Telephone: 45 (97) 72 57 88. *Fax:* 45 (97) 72 53 54. *Contact:* Gunhild Thingaard, Chairman.

OBJECTIVES: To practice trade in commodity goods from developing countries in accordance with sustainable trade principles. To spread information about trade relations between the North and South.

GENERAL INFORMATION: *Creation:* 1984. *Affiliated to:* Mellemfolkeligt Samvirke (Denmark) - International Federation for Alternative Trade (USA). *Salaried:* 4. *Budget/Total 1993:* ECU 847000 (US$ 992000). *Financial sources:* Self-financing: 100%.

Voir : *Comment utiliser le répertoire,* page 11.

PUBLICATIONS: *Periodicals:* Trade Fair (4).

ACTIVITIES IN DEVELOPING REGIONS: Active in 8 country(ies). Works through local field partners. **Sustainable Development Actions:** Rural development/agriculture. **Regions:** Caribbean; Central Asia and South Asia; East Africa; Mexico and Central America; South America; Southern Africa.

INFORMATION AND EDUCATION ACTIVITIES: **Topics:** International economic relations/trade/debt/finance; Rural development/agriculture. **Activities:** Broadcasting/cultural events; Conferences/seminars/workshops/training activities; Information and documentation services/data bases; Information campaigns/exhibitions; Lobbying/advocacy; Networking/electronic telecommunications; Publishing/audiovisual materials/educational materials.

DNK1390

U-LANDSTV (UTV)

c/o Mediehuset København, Roskildevej 160, 2500 Valby, Denmark.

Telephone: 45 (31) 74 80 51. *Contact:* Sidsel Dyekjær.

DNK1391

UNGDOMMENS RODE KORS ♦ Danish Red Cross Youth

Postboks 2668, Blegdamsvej 27, 2100 København 0, Denmark.

Telephone: 45 (35) 26 14 20. *Fax:* 45 (35) 26 30 33. *Contact:* Lisbeth Nielsen, Chairman.

OBJECTIVES: To inspire young people to think and act according to the humanitarian principles of the Red Cross/Red Crescent Movement. To promote international understanding and friendship among children and youth across the world.

GENERAL INFORMATION: *Creation:* 1988. *Affiliated to:* Danish Youth Council (Denmark) - International Federation of the Red Cross and Red Crescent (Switzerland). *Personnel/Total:* 8. *Salaried:* 4. *Volunteers:* 4. *Budget/Total 1993:* ECU 711000 (US$ 833000). *Financial sources:* Private: 8%. Public: 70%. Self-financing: 22%.

PUBLICATIONS: *Periodicals:* Action (4). *List of publications.*

COMMENTS: Undertakes activities in the Commonwealth of Independent States. Information activities related to the Commonwealth of Independent States.

ACTIVITIES IN DEVELOPING REGIONS: Present in developing regions. Active in 3 country(ies). Works through local field partners. **Sustainable Development Actions:** Children/youth/family; Education/training/literacy; Health/sanitation/water; Sending volunteers/experts/technical assistance. **Regions:** East Africa; Southern Africa.

INFORMATION AND EDUCATION ACTIVITIES: **Topics:** Children/youth/family; Health/sanitation/water; International relations/cooperation/development aid; Refugees/migrants/ethnic groups. **Activities:** Conferences/seminars/workshops/training activities; Exchanges/twinning/linking; Fund raising; Information campaigns/exhibitions; Publishing/audiovisual materials/educational materials.

DNK1392

UNIFEM-DANMARK, DEN DANSKE FORENING FOR FN'S UDVIKLINGSFOND FOR KVINDER ♦ UNIFEM-Denmark, the Danish Association for UNs Developmnent Fund for Women

Hostrups Have 58, 1954 Frederiksberg C, Denmark.

Telephone: 45 (35) 37 60 07. *Contact:* Grete Kjerldgaard Ejler, Chairman.

OBJECTIVES: To promote and support better economic and social conditions for women in developing countries by spreading information and collecting funds.

GENERAL INFORMATION: *Personnel/Total:* 15. *Volunteers:* 15. *Budget/Total 1993:* ECU 20000 (US$ 23000). *Financial sources:* Private: 33%. Self-financing: 66%.

PUBLICATIONS: *Periodicals:* UNIFEM-NYT (4).

PLANNED ACTIVITIES: Family development project in Ethiopia.

ACTIVITIES IN DEVELOPING REGIONS: Works through local field partners. **Sustainable Development Actions:** Children/youth/family; Debt/finance/trade; Education/training/literacy; Gender issues/women; Rural development/agriculture; Small enterprises/informal sector/handicrafts; Urban development/habitat. **Regions:** Central Africa; East Africa.

INFORMATION AND EDUCATION ACTIVITIES: **Topics:** Children/youth/family; Gender issues/women; Rural development/agriculture. **Activities:** Fund raising.

DNK1393

UNION OF UGANDANS

c/o Rødovre Parkvej 243, 2., 2610 Rødovre, Denmark.

Telephone: 45 (36 72 73 15. *Contact:* John Eric Moli.

DNK1394

UTAMADUNI CENTRE FOR CULTURAL EXCHANGE

c/o Rex Jensen, Emmelev Kærvej 9, 8500 Grenå, Denmark.

Telephone: 45 (86) 38 72 75.

DNK1395

VENSKABSFORBUNDET DANMARK-KINA

Griffenfeldsgade 10, 2200 København N, Denmark.

Telephone: 45 (31) 35 88 11. *Contact:* Kjeld A. Larsen, Chairman.

DNK1396

VENSKABSFORENINGEN DANMARK-BHUTAN ♦ Danish-Bhutanese Friendship Association

c/o Huus-Bruun, Smedebakken 22, Mygind, 8544 Mørke, Denmark.

Telephone: 45 (86) 97 45 67. *Contact:* Hans-Christian Køie Poulsen, Chairman.

DNK1397

VENSKABSFORENINGEN DANMARK-BURKINA FASO ♦ Association d'amitié Danmark-Burkina Faso

Overdrevet 3, 8382 Hinnerup, Denmark.

Telephone: 45 (86) 91 21 04. *Fax:* 45 (86) 91 21 04. *Contact:* Thyge Christensen, President.

OBJECTIVES: To foster ties between the people of Burkina Faso and Denmark. To inform the Danish public of the realities of Burkina Faso.

GENERAL INFORMATION: *Creation:* 1987. *Member organisations:* 2. *Affiliated to:* FN-Forbundet (Denmark) - Mellemfolkeligt Samvirke (Denmark). *Personnel/Total:* 1. *Salaried:* 1. *Budget/Total 1993:* ECU 962000 (US$ 1126000). *Financial sources:* Public: 99%. Self-financing: 1%.

PUBLICATIONS: *Periodicals:* Burkina Kontakt (4). *Annual report. List of publications.*

ACTIVITIES IN DEVELOPING REGIONS: Present in developing regions. Active in 1 country(ies). Maintains local field presence. **Sustainable Development Actions:** Education/training/literacy. **Regions:** West Africa.

INFORMATION AND EDUCATION ACTIVITIES: **Topics:** Culture/tradition/religion; Education/training/literacy. **Activities:** Conferences/seminars/workshops/training activities; Publishing/audiovisual materials/educational materials.

DNK1398

VENSKABSFORENINGEN DANMARK-DEN DEMOKRATISKE FOLKEREPUBLIK KOREA ♦ Denmark - The Democratic People's Republic of Korea Friendship Association

Tordenskjoldsgade 14, 1.th., 1055 København K, Denmark.

Telephone: 45 (33) 14 15 26. *Contact:* Anders Kristensen, Chairman.

OBJECTIVES: To disseminate knowledge about the Democratic People's Republic of Korea and about the policy of the Workers' Party of Korea. To promote solidarity for the struggle for reunification of the entire Korean population and for the suppressed South Koreans. To support

See: *How to Use the Directory*, page 11.

the conversion of the Korean peninsula into a nuclear weapon free peace zone.

GENERAL INFORMATION: *Creation:* 1968. *Affiliated to:* International Liaison Committee for Reunification and Peace in Korea (France). *Personnel/Total:* 10. *Volunteers:* 10. *Budget/Total 1993:* ECU 1900 (US$ 2200). *Financial sources:* Self-financing: 100%.

PUBLICATIONS: *Periodicals:* Korea Bulletin (4). *Annual report.*

EVALUATION/RESEARCH: Undertakes research activities.

INFORMATION AND EDUCATION ACTIVITIES: Topics: Children/youth/family; Culture/tradition/religion; Ecology/environment/biodiversity; Education/training/literacy; Emergency relief/refugees/humanitarian assistance; Employment/unemployment; Food/famine; Gender issues/women; Health/sanitation/water; Human rights/peace/conflicts; International economic relations/trade/debt/finance; International relations/cooperation/development aid; Peace/ethnic conflicts/armament/disarmament; Poverty/living conditions; Racism/xenophobia/antisemitism; Refugees/migrants/ethnic groups; Rural development/agriculture; Urban development/habitat. **Activities:** Conferences/seminars/workshops/training activities; Information and documentation services/data bases; Information campaigns/exhibitions.

DNK1399

VENSKABSFORENINGEN DANMARK-NIGER ♦ Friendship Association Denmark-Niger

Thorshavnsgade 10, 2.TV, 2300 København S, Denmark.

Telephone: 45 (31) 57 80 35. *Contact:* Claudia Heim, President.

OBJECTIVES: To spread knowledge about the social, cultural, political and economic conditions in Niger among the Danish population. To lobby decision makers for the support of Niger.

GENERAL INFORMATION: *Creation:* 1992. *Budget/Total 1993:* ECU 3300 (US$ 3900). *Financial sources:* Private: 40%. Public: 40%. Self-financing: 20%.

PUBLICATIONS: *Periodicals:* Noget om Niger (4).

PLANNED ACTIVITIES: Two publications concerning Niger. Participation of a Nigerien guest to discuss Danish-Nigerien development cooperation.

INFORMATION AND EDUCATION ACTIVITIES: Topics: Culture/tradition/religion; Ecology/environment/biodiversity; Gender issues/women; Health/sanitation/water; Human rights/peace/conflicts; Population/family planning/demography; Rural development/agriculture. **Activities:** Fund raising; Lobbying/advocacy; Publishing/audiovisual materials/educational materials.

DNK1400

VENSKABSFORENINGEN DANMARK-ZAMBIA ♦ Danish Zambian Friendship Society

c/o Kell Kaare Sørensen, Ved Bellahøj 23A, 8.th., 2700 Brønshøj, Denmark.

Telephone: 45 (31) 28 03 47. *Contact:* Kell Kaare Sørensen, Chairman.

DNK1401

VERDENSVERKSTEDET

Anholtsgade 4, st., 8000 Århus C, Denmark.

Telephone: 45 (86) 13 08 86. *Fax:* 45 (86) 13 08 86.

DNK1402

WORLD ASSEMBLY OF YOUTH (WAY)

4 Ved Bellahøj, 2700 Brønshøj, København, Denmark.

Telephone: 45 (31) 60 77 70. *Fax:* 45 (31) 60 57 97. *Contact:* Datuk Ali Rustam, President.

OBJECTIVES: To foster international understanding, co-operation and the exchange of ideas. To promote the collection and dissemination of information about the needs and problems of youth and the activities of youth organisations.

GENERAL INFORMATION: *Creation:* 1949. *Type of organisation:* association of NGOs. *Member organisations:* 70. *Affiliated to:* Geneva Informal Meeting of International Youth NGOs (Switzerland) - Co-ordinating Committee of NGOs with UN Status - International Union for Conservation of Nature - CHILDHOPE. *Personnel/Total:* 25. *Salaried:* 6. *Volunteers:* 19 of which: 13 in developing countries. *Budget/Total 1993:* ECU 269000 (US$ 316000). *Financial sources:* Private: 6%. Public: 82%. Self-financing: 12%.

PUBLICATIONS: *Periodicals:* WAY Information (6) - The Youth Round Up (6) (4). *Annual report.*

EVALUATION/RESEARCH: Evaluation reports available. Undertakes research activities.

PLANNED ACTIVITIES: Preparing a World Youth Programme for the year 2000.

ACTIVITIES IN DEVELOPING REGIONS: Present in developing regions. Active in 8 country(ies). Works through local field partners. **Sustainable Development Actions:** Children/youth/family; Health/sanitation/water; Population/family planning/demography; Sending volunteers/experts/technical assistance. **Regions:** Caribbean; Central Africa; Central Asia and South Asia; East Africa; East Asia; Mexico and Central America; Middle East; North Africa; Oceania; South America; South East Asia; Southern Africa; West Africa.

DNK1403

WORLD WIDE FUND FOR NATURE, DENMARK (WWF DENMARK)

Ryesgade 3F, 2200 København N, Denmark.

Telephone: 45 (35) 36 36 35. *Fax:* 45 (31) 39 20 62. *Contact:* Lene Wirbe, Secretary General.

OBJECTIVES: To conserve nature and ecological processes by preserving genetic integrity, species and diversity, ensuring the sustainability of renewable natural resources. To promote the reduction of pollution and the wasteful exploitation and consumption of resources and energy.

GENERAL INFORMATION: *Creation:* 1972. *Type of organisation:* network. *Member organisations:* 28. *Affiliated to:* WWF International (Switzerland) - Danish Nordic South Coalition (Denmark). *Personnel/Total:* 23. *Salaried:* 20. *Volunteers:* 3 of which: 1 in developing countries. *Budget/Total 1993:* ECU 1745000 (US$ 2043000). *Financial sources:* Private: 34%. Public: 29%. Self-financing: 37%.

PUBLICATIONS: *Periodicals:* Living Nature (4) - Panda Club (6). *Annual report. List of publications.*

EVALUATION/RESEARCH: Evaluation reports available. Undertakes research activities.

PLANNED ACTIVITIES: Campaigns on conservation and sustainable use of rain forests in West and Central Africa, in the Baltic States and European Russia and on sustainable forest management in Denmark.

COMMENTS: Undertakes activities in the Commonwealth of Independent States.

ACTIVITIES IN DEVELOPING REGIONS: Present in developing regions. Active in 7 country(ies). Maintains local field presence. Works through local field partners. **Sustainable Development Actions:** Debt/finance/trade; Democracy/good governance/institution building/participatory development; Ecology/environment/biodiversity; Education/training/literacy; Energy/transport; Gender issues/women; Health/sanitation/water; Human rights/peace/conflicts; Rural development/agriculture; Sending volunteers/experts/technical assistance; Small enterprises/informal sector/handicrafts. **Regions:** East Africa; South America; South East Asia; Southern Africa; West Africa.

INFORMATION AND EDUCATION ACTIVITIES: Topics: Ecology/environment/biodiversity; Gender issues/women; Human rights/peace/conflicts; International economic relations/trade/debt/finance; International relations/cooperation/development aid; Population/family planning/demography; Poverty/living conditions; Refugees/migrants/ethnic groups; Rural development/agriculture. **Activities:** Broadcasting/cultural events; Conferences/seminars/workshops/training activities; Formal education; Fund raising; Information and documentation services/data bases; Information campaigns/exhibitions; Lobbying/advocacy; Publishing/audiovisual materials/educational materials.

Voir : *Comment utiliser le répertoire*, page 11.

DNK1404

YOUTH AND ENVIRONMENT EUROPE (YEE)

Klostermollevej 48A, 8660 Skanderborg, Denmark.

Telephone: 45 (5) 78 20 44. *Fax:* 45 (5) 78 20 44. *Contact:* Adelheid Byttebier, Chairperson.

DNK1405

ZANZIBAR DEMOCRATIC ALTERNATIVE (HAMAKI)

Offenbachsvej 35, 2. th., 2450 København SV, Denmark.

Telephone: 45 (31) 16 62 26. *Contact:* Yussuf S. Salim, Secretary General.

OBJECTIVES: To promote respect for the principles of equal rights, self-determination, equality and justice. To support development and a higher standard of living. To help the people of Zanzibar realise the right to self-determination.

GENERAL INFORMATION: *Creation:* 1988. *Type of organisation:* association of NGOs. *Member organisations:* 3. *Affiliated to:* Unrepresented Nations and Peoples Organisation (the Netherlands). *Personnel/Total:* 50. *Volunteers:* 50 of which: 30 in developing countries. *Budget/Total 1993:* ECU 1300 (US$ 1500). *Financial sources:* Self-financing: 100%.

PUBLICATIONS: *Periodicals:* HAMAKI (12).

EVALUATION/RESEARCH: Undertakes research activities.

PLANNED ACTIVITIES: Literacy campaign for peasants. Health education for young mothers. Anti-narcotic campaign for the youth.

ACTIVITIES IN DEVELOPING REGIONS: Present in developing regions. Active in 1 country(ies). Maintains local field presence. Works through local field partners. **Sustainable Development Actions:** Children/youth/family; Democracy/good governance/institution building/participatory development; Education/training/literacy; Gender issues/women; Health/sanitation/water; Human rights/peace/conflicts; Rural development/agriculture; Small enterprises/informal sector/handicrafts. **Regions:** East Africa.

INFORMATION AND EDUCATION ACTIVITIES: **Topics:** Children/youth/family; Culture/tradition/religion; Education/training/literacy; Gender issues/women; Health/sanitation/water; Human rights/peace/conflicts; International relations/cooperation/development aid; Peace/ethnic conflicts/armament/disarmament; Poverty/living conditions; Refugees/migrants/ethnic groups; Rural development/agriculture. **Activities:** Broadcasting/cultural events; Conferences/seminars/workshops/training activities; Formal education; Fund raising; Information and documentation services/data bases; Information campaigns/exhibitions; Lobbying/advocacy; Publishing/audiovisual materials/educational materials.

See: *How to Use the Directory,* page 11.

ESP1406
ACADEMIA REMEMBER

Apartado 507, 11701 Ceuta, Spain.

Telephone: 34 (56) 51 84 71. **Fax:** 34 (56) 50 05 83. **Contact:** Martin A. Merki, Director.

OBJECTIVES: To undertake and promote development education and cultural exchanges.

GENERAL INFORMATION: *Creation:* 1985. *Personnel/Total:* 4. *Salaried:* 2 of which: 2 in developing countries. *Volunteers:* 2 of which: 2 in developing countries. ***Budget/Total 1993:*** ECU 48000 (US$ 63000). *Financial sources:* Private: 50%. Self-financing: 50%.

ACTIVITIES IN DEVELOPING REGIONS: Present in developing regions. Active in 2 country(ies). Maintains local field presence. **Sustainable Development Actions:** Children/youth/family; Debt/finance/trade; Education/training/literacy; Small enterprises/informal sector/handicrafts; Urban development/habitat. **Regions:** North Africa.

INFORMATION AND EDUCATION ACTIVITIES: Topics: Children/youth/family; Culture/tradition/religion; Education/training/literacy; Employment/unemployment; International economic relations/trade/debt/finance; Urban development/habitat. **Activities:** Broadcasting/cultural events; Conferences/seminars/workshops/training activities; Exchanges/twinning/linking; Formal education.

ESP1407
ACCION SOLIDARIA ARAGONESA ♦ Action solidaire aragonaise

Carmen 28, principal Dcha., 50005 Zaragoza, Espagne.

Téléphone: 34 (76) 21 09 76. **Contact:** Francisco Javier Altuna, Vice-Président.

OBJECTIFS: Encourager la solidarité avec les pays pauvres et la coopération pour le partage des biens et des cultures. Organiser des projets de développement et d'éducation. Sensibiliser à la situation du Tiers monde.

INFORMATIONS GENERALES: *Création:* 1985. *Type d'organisation:* collectif. *Organisations membres:* 4. *Affiliée à:* Fédération aragonaise de solidarité (Espagne) - Coordination d'ONG pour le développement (Espagne) - Comité de liaisons ONG-CE (Belgique). *Personnel/Total:* 250. *Bénévoles:* 250. ***Budget/Total 1993:*** ECU 273000 (US$ 354000). *Sources financières:* Privé: 30%. Public: 50%. Autofinancement: 20%.

PUBLICATIONS: *Périodiques:* ?Y el sur? (4). *Rapport annuel. Liste des publications.*

EVALUATION/RECHERCHE: Entreprend des activités de recherche.

ACTIVITES DANS LES REGIONS EN DEVELOPPEMENT: Intervient directement dans les régions en développement. Intervient dans 10 pays. Intervient par l'intermédiaire d'organisations locales partenaires. **Actions de Développement durable:** Aliments/famine; Droits de l'Homme/paix/conflits; Démocratie/bonne gestion publique/création d'institutions/développement participatif; Développement rural/agriculture; Développement urbain/habitat; Enfants/jeunesse/famille; Petites entreprises/secteur informel/artisanat; Santé/assainissement/eau. **Régions:** Afrique de l'Ouest; Amérique du Sud; Mexique et Amerique centrale.

ACTIVITES D'INFORMATION ET D'EDUCATION: Domaines: Aliments/famine; Culture/tradition/religion; Droits de l'Homme/paix/conflits; Développement rural/agriculture; Développement urbain/habitat; Enfants/jeunesse/famille; Paix/conflits ethniques/armement/désarmement; Pauvreté/conditions de vie; Population/planning familial/démographie; Questions relatives aux femmes; Racisme/xénophobie/antisémitisme; Relations internationales/coopération/aide au développement; Relations économiques internationales/commerce/dette/finances; Réfugiés/migrants/groupes ethniques; Santé/assainissement/eau; Écologie/environnement/biodiversité; Éducation/formation/alphabétisation. **Activités:** Campagnes d'information/expositions; Conférences/séminaires/ateliers/activités de formation; Lobbying/plaidoyer; Services d'information et de documentation/bases de données; Édition/documents audiovisuels/documents éducatifs; Éducation formelle.

ESP1408
ALIMENTACION Y DESARME (FDI) ♦ Food and Disarmament International

Eustasio Amilibia 4-41, 20011 San Sebastian, Espagne.

Téléphone: 34 (943) 47 02 72. **Fax:** 34 (943) 47 02 72. **Contact:** Juantxo Dominguez.

ESP1409
ALTERNATIVA SOLIDARIA - PLENTY ♦ Plenty Spain

Apartado de Correos 5409, 08080 Barcelona, Spain.

Telephone: 34 (93) 340 43 62. **Fax:** 34 (93) 830 12 53. **Contact:** Mario Edoardo Rimoldi, Manager.

OBJECTIVES: To contribute to world peace, through the development of the poorest areas of developing countries. To encourage a more equitable distribution of material resources and knowledge between the various peoples, cultures and ethnic affiliations of the world.

GENERAL INFORMATION: *Creation:* 1986. *Member organisations:* 1. *Affiliated to:* Federación de ONGs Catalanas - Anped (Alianza de los Pueblos del Norte). *Personnel/Total:* 19. *Salaried:* 5. *Volunteers:* 14 of which: 1 in developing countries. *Budget/Total 1993:* ECU 176000 (US$ 228000). *Financial sources:* Private: 75%. Self-financing: 25%.

PUBLICATIONS: *Periodicals:* Alternativa Solideria - Plenty (4).

EVALUATION/RESEARCH: Evaluation reports available.

ACTIVITIES IN DEVELOPING REGIONS: Present in developing regions. Active in 3 country(ies). Maintains local field presence. Works through local field partners. **Sustainable Development Actions:** Debt/finance/trade; Democracy/good governance/institution building/participatory development; Ecology/environment/biodiversity; Education/training/literacy; Energy/transport; Health/sanitation/water; Rural development/agriculture; Small enterprises/informal sector/handicrafts. **Regions:** Mexico and Central America; South America.

INFORMATION AND EDUCATION ACTIVITIES: Topics: Culture/tradition/religion; Ecology/environment/biodiversity; Health/sanitation/water; International economic relations/trade/debt/finance; International relations/cooperation/development aid; Peace/ethnic conflicts/armament/disarmament; Poverty/living conditions; Refugees/migrants/ethnic groups; Rural development/agriculture. **Activities:** Conferences/seminars/workshops/training activities; Formal education; Fund raising; Information campaigns/exhibitions; Publishing/audiovisual materials/educational materials.

ESP1410
AMIGOS DE LA TIERRA ♦ Friends of the Earth - Spain

c/San Bernardo 24, 3°, 28015 Madrid, Spain.

Telephone: 34 (1) 523 07 50. **Fax:** 34 (1) 523 09 15. **Contact:** Sandy Hemingway.

OBJECTIVES: To protect the environment.

GENERAL INFORMATION: *Creation:* 1979. *Member organisations:* 20. *Affiliated to:* Friends of the Earth International (the Netherlands) - International Union for the Conservation of Nature (Switzerland). *Personnel/Total:* 21. *Salaried:* 6. *Volunteers:* 15.

PUBLICATIONS: *Periodicals:* Amigos de la Tierra (4) - Boletín "Proyecto Foei Humedales (3) - Newsletter (3) . *Annual report. List of publications.*

EVALUATION/RESEARCH: Evaluation reports available. Undertakes research activities.

ACTIVITIES IN DEVELOPING REGIONS: Present in developing regions. Maintains local field presence. Works through local field partners. **Sustainable Development Actions:** Democracy/good governance/institution building/participatory development; Education/training/literacy; Human rights/peace/conflicts; Urban development/habitat. **Regions:** South America.

INFORMATION AND EDUCATION ACTIVITIES: Topics: Ecology/environment/biodiversity; Health/sanitation/water; International economic relations/trade/debt/finance; International relations/cooperation/development aid; Other; Rural development/agriculture; Urban development/

Voir : *Comment utiliser le répertoire,* page 11.

habitat. **Activities:** Broadcasting/cultural events; Conferences/seminars/workshops/training activities; Fund raising; Information campaigns/exhibitions; Lobbying/advocacy; Publishing/audiovisual materials/educational materials.

ESP1411
AMNESTY INTERNATIONAL, SPANISH SECTION
Gran Via 6, 5° piso, 28080 Madrid, Spain.

ESP1412
ANESVAD
Teófilo Guiard 2, 48011 Bilbao, Espagne.

Téléphone: 34 (94) 441 80 08. *Fax:* 34 (94) 441 07 39. *Contact:* José Miguel Sustacha.

ESP1413
ASOCIACION ANDALUZA POR LA SOLIDARIDAD Y LA PAZ (ASPA) ♦ Association andalouse pour la solidarité et la paix
Avenida de Barcelona 1, 14010 Cordoba, Espagne.

Téléphone: 34 (957) 43 72 51. *Fax:* 34 (957) 43 73 77. *Contact:* Carlos Javier Moreno Garcia, Président.

OBJECTIFS: Contribuer à la construction d'un monde plus juste et au développement de la solidarité à travers de projets d'éducation et d'aide au développement.

INFORMATIONS GENERALES: *Création:* 1987. *Affiliée à:* Fédération des ONG de l'Andalousie (Espagne) - Fédération des ONG d'Espagne (Espagne). *Personnel/Total:* 29. *Salariés:* 3 dont: 1 dans les pays en développement. *Bénévoles:* 26. *Budget/Total 1993:* ECU 360000 (US$ 467000). *Sources financières:* Privé: 25%. Public: 65%. Autofinancement: 10%.

PUBLICATIONS: *Périodiques:* Cahiers pour la solidarité - De Sur a Sur (4). *Rapport annuel. Liste des publications.*

EVALUATION/RECHERCHE: Rapports d'évaluation disponibles.

PREVISIONS D'ACTIVITES: Campagnes d'appui au peuple cubain, saharien et de Chiapas.

ACTIVITES DANS LES REGIONS EN DEVELOPPEMENT: Intervient directement dans les régions en développement. Intervient dans 6 pays. Intervient par l'intermédiaire d'organisations locales partenaires. **Actions de Développement durable:** Développement rural/agriculture; Développement urbain/habitat; Enfants/jeunesse/famille; Envoi de volontaires/experts/assistance technique; Questions relatives aux femmes; Santé/assainissement/eau; Écologie/environnement/biodiversité; Éducation/formation/alphabétisation; Énergie/transport. **Régions:** Amérique du Sud; Mexique et Amerique centrale.

ACTIVITES D'INFORMATION ET D'EDUCATION: Domaines: Développement rural/agriculture; Développement urbain/habitat; Enfants/jeunesse/famille; Pauvreté/conditions de vie; Questions relatives aux femmes; Racisme/xénophobie/antisémitisme; Relations internationales/coopération/aide au développement; Réfugiés/migrants/groupes ethniques; Secours d'urgence/réfugiés/aide humanitaire; Écologie/environnement/biodiversité; Éducation/formation/alphabétisation. **Activités:** Campagnes d'information/expositions; Collecte de fonds; Conférences/séminaires/ateliers/activités de formation; Radiodiffusion/manifestations culturelles; Services d'information et de documentation/bases de données; Échanges/parrainage/jumelage; Édition/documents audiovisuels/documents éducatifs.

ESP1414
ASOCIACION CATALANA DE PROFESIONALES PARA LA COOPERACION CON NICARAGUA
Diputación 185 1° 1a, 08011 Barcelona, Espagne.
Contact: Montserrat Segarra.

ESP1415
ASOCIACION DE AMIGOS DE LA REPUBLICA ARABE SAHARAUI DEMOCRATICA DE ARAGON
Cedena 5, 50001 Zaragoza, Espagne.

Contact: Júlian Herrero .

ESP1416
ASOCIACION DE COLABORACION Y AMISTAD CON MOZAMBIQUE
c/Junta de Comercio 24, pral., 1a, 08001 Barcelona, Espagne.

Téléphone: 34 (93) 412 38 80. *Fax:* 34 (93) 318 63 22. *Contact:* Natalia Calsina I Albareda.

ESP1417
ASOCIACION DE INVESTIGACION Y ESPECIALIZACION SOBRE TEMAS IBEROAMERICANOS (AIETI)
Claudio Coello 101, bajo Izq., 28006 Madrid, Spain.

Telephone: 34 (91) 577 06 40. *Fax:* 34 (91) 576 30 70. *Contact:* Guadalupe Ruiz-Giménez.

OBJECTIVES: To promote co-operation and joint research between academics and specialists from Latin America and Spain on current issues of interest in Latin America.

GENERAL INFORMATION: *Creation:* 1981. *Affiliated to:* EADI - CEISAL - Coordinadora de ONGs de España (Spain). *Personnel/Total:* 4. *Financial sources:* Private: 80%. Public: 15%. Self-financing: 5%.

PUBLICATIONS: *Periodicals:* Sintesis (2). *Annual report.*

EVALUATION/RESEARCH: Undertakes research activities.

INFORMATION AND EDUCATION ACTIVITIES: Topics: Culture/tradition/religion; Ecology/environment/biodiversity; International economic relations/trade/debt/finance; International relations/cooperation/development aid; Racism/xenophobia/antisemitism; Refugees/migrants/ethnic groups. **Activities:** Conferences/seminars/workshops/training activities; Information and documentation services/data bases; Publishing/audiovisual materials/educational materials.

ESP1418
ASOCIACION DE TRABAJADORES INMIGRANTES EN ESPANA (ATIME)
c/ Jesús 14, 3§, 28014 Madrid, Spain.

ESP1419
ASOCIACION ECOLOGISTA DE DEFENSA DE LA NATURALEZA (AEDENAT) ♦ Ecologist Association for the Defense of Nature
Calle Campomanes 13,2, 28013 Madrid, Spain.

Telephone: 34 (1) 541 10 71. *Fax:* 34 (1) 571 71 08. *E-mail:* aedenat@nodo50.gn.apc.org. *Contact:* Jose Luis Garcia Lano, President.

OBJECTIVES: To work on issues such as energy-efficient transport, pollution and environmental waste and overall conservation of the environment.

GENERAL INFORMATION: *Creation:* 1976. *Type of organisation:* association of NGOs. *Member organisations:* 30. *Affiliated to:* European Federation for Transport and Environment - Climate Action Network (Belgium) - EEB - ANPED. *Personnel/Total:* 53. *Salaried:* 3. *Volunteers:* 50. *Budget/Total 1993:* ECU 61000 (US$ 79000). *Financial sources:* Public: 10%. Self-financing: 90%.

PUBLICATIONS: *Periodicals:* Hiedra (6) - Informes (10). *List of publications.*

ACTIVITIES IN DEVELOPING REGIONS: Present in developing regions. Active in 2 country(ies). **Sustainable Development Actions:** Ecology/environment/biodiversity; Energy/transport; Health/sanitation/water. **Regions:** Caribbean; South America.

ESP1420
ASOCIACION HUMANA (HUMANA)
Poligono Industrial con Volart, CTRA N152, Km 22, 08150 Parets de Valles, Spain.

Telephone: 34 (3) 573 1210. *Fax:* 34 (3) 426 6154. *Contact:* Elisabeth Molnar, Chairman.

OBJECTIVES: To provide development aid to the peoples in the Third World.

GENERAL INFORMATION: *Creation:* 1987. *Affiliated to:* International People to People Movement (Denmark). *Financial sources:* Self-financing: 100%.

ACTIVITIES IN DEVELOPING REGIONS: Active in 4 country(ies). Works through local field partners. **Sustainable Development Actions:** Children/youth/family; Ecology/environment/biodiversity; Education/training/literacy; Emergency relief/refugees/humanitarian assistance; Food/famine; Health/sanitation/water; Rural development/agriculture; Sending volunteers/experts/technical assistance; Small enterprises/informal sector/handicrafts. **Regions:** South East Asia; Southern Africa.

ESP1421

ASOCIACION MALAGUENA PARA LA PROTECCION DE LA VIDA SILVESTRE

Apdo. Correos 4046, 29080 Malaga, Espagne.

Téléphone: 34 (952) 22 95 95. *Fax:* 34 (952) 22 95 95. *Contact:* Saturnino Morelo Borrell, President.

ESP1422

ASOCIACION PARA LA COOPERACION CON EL SUR - LAS SEGOVIAS (ACSUR - LAS SEGOVIAS) ♦ Association pour la coopération avec le Sud - Las Segovias

Fernanflor, 6, 4° Centro isq., 28014 Madrid, Espagne.

Téléphone: 34 (1) 429 14 70. *Fax:* 34 (1) 429 15 26. *Contact:* Miguel Nuñez, Présidente.

ESP1423

ASOCIACION PARA LA COOPERACION CON LOS PUEBLOS DE AMERICA CENTRAL

c/. Nunoz de Balboa 21, 28902 Getafe, Espagne.

Téléphone: 34 (91) 682 13 63. *Fax:* 34 (91) 682 13 63. *Contact:* Jesús Béjar.

ESP1424

ASOCIACION PARA LA DEFENSA DE LA SALUD PUBLICA

Barrenkale 40, 1° , 48005 Bilbao, Espagne.

Téléphone: 34 (94) 416 22 02. *Contact:* Juan Luis Urla.

ESP1425

ASOCIACION PARA REFUGIADOS AFRICANOS (KARIBU)

c/ Santa Engracia 140, 28003 Madrid, Spain.

ESP1426

ASOCIACION PRO DERECHOS HUMANOS (APDH)

Jose Ortega y Gasset 77,2.A, 28006 Madrid, Spain.

ESP1427

ASOCIACION RUBEN DARIO ♦ Ruben Dario Asociation

Escorial 16 3° Isq., 28004 Madrid, Spain.

Telephone: 34 (91) 522 87 56. *Fax:* 34 (91) 523 27 95. *Contact:* José Torres, President.

OBJECTIVES: To raise funds for development projects. To manage the material and human resources to promote the cultures of Nicaragua and Latin America. To sensitize public opinion to the problems of the developing world.

GENERAL INFORMATION: *Affiliated to:* Coordinadora Estatal de ONG - Federacion de ONG de Madrid - CIFCA. *Personnel/Total:* 32. Salaried: 2. Volunteers: 30. *Budget/Total 1993:* ECU 71000 (US$ 92000). *Financial sources:* Public: 47%. Self-financing: 53%.

PUBLICATIONS: *Periodicals:* Baletin"Ruben Dario" (2) - Lineas del Sur (4). *Annual report.*

EVALUATION/RESEARCH: Undertakes research activities.

ACTIVITIES IN DEVELOPING REGIONS: Active in 1 country(ies). Works through local field partners. **Sustainable Development Actions:** Ecology/environment/biodiversity; Education/training/literacy; Emergency relief/refugees/humanitarian assistance; Gender issues/women; Health/sanitation/water; Rural development/agriculture; Sending volunteers/experts/technical assistance; Small enterprises/informal sector/handicrafts; Urban development/habitat. **Regions:** Mexico and Central America.

INFORMATION AND EDUCATION ACTIVITIES: Topics: Children/youth/family; Culture/tradition/religion; Ecology/environment/biodiversity; Education/training/literacy; Food/famine; Gender issues/women; Health/sanitation/water; International economic relations/trade/debt/finance; International relations/cooperation/development aid; Peace/ethnic conflicts/armament/disarmament; Racism/xenophobia/antisemitism; Refugees/migrants/ethnic groups; Rural development/agriculture. **Activities:** Formal education.

ESP1428

ASOCIACION UNICEF-ESPANA

Apartado 12021, Mauricio Legendre 36, Madrid 16, Spain.

ESP1429

ASSOCIACIO CATALANA DE PROFESSIONALS PER LA COOPERACIO AMB NICARAGUA ♦ Catalan Association of Professionals for Co-operation with Nicaragua

Diputació 185 3° 1a, 08024 Barcelona, Spain.

Telephone: 34 (3) 253 64 42. *Contact:* Dr. Antoni Puigvert, President.

ESP1430

ASSOCIACIO PER A LES NACIONS UNIDES A ESPANYA ♦ Association pour les Nations Unies en Espagne

Fontanella, 14, 1er, 08010 Barcelona, Espagne.

Téléphone: 34 (3) 301 39990. *Fax:* 34 (3) 317 57 68. *Contact:* Francesco Noguero, Secrétaire général.

OBJECTIFS: Défendre et promouvoir les principes établis dans la Charte des Nations Unies.

INFORMATIONS GENERALES: *Création:* 1963. *Affiliée à:* World Federation of United Nations Associations (Suisse). *Personnel/Total:* 10. *Salariés:* 7. *Bénévoles:* 3. *Budget/Total 1993:* ECU 151000 (US$ 196000). *Sources financières:* Public: 93%. Autofinancement: 7%.

PUBLICATIONS: *Périodiques:* La revista NU (24) - Dossiers NU (4). *Rapport annuel. Liste des publications.*

EVALUATION/RECHERCHE: Rapports d'évaluation disponibles.

PREVISIONS D'ACTIVITES: Organisation d'une campagne pour l'enseignement des droits de l'homme à l'école.

ACTIVITES DANS LES REGIONS EN DEVELOPPEMENT: Intervient directement dans les régions en développement. Intervient dans 1 pays. Intervient par l'intermédiaire d'organisations locales partenaires. **Actions de Développement durable:** Développement rural/agriculture; Développement urbain/habitat. **Régions:** Afrique de l'Ouest.

ACTIVITES D'INFORMATION ET D'EDUCATION: Domaines: Aliments/famine; Culture/tradition/religion; Droits de l'Homme/paix/conflits; Développement rural/agriculture; Développement urbain/habitat; Emploi/chômage; Enfants/jeunesse/famille; Paix/conflits ethniques/armement/désarmement; Pauvreté/conditions de vie; Population/planning familial/démographie; Questions relatives aux femmes; Racisme/xénophobie/antisémitisme; Relations internationales/coopération/aide au développement; Relations économiques internationales/commerce/dette/finances; Réfugiés/migrants/groupes ethniques; Santé/assainissement/eau; Secours d'urgence/réfugiés/aide humanitaire; Écologie/environnement/biodiversité; Éducation/formation/alphabétisation. **Activités:** Conférences/séminaires/ateliers/activités de formation; Radiodiffusion/manifestations culturelles; Services d'information et de documentation/bases de données; Édition/documents audiovisuels/documents éducatifs.

Voir : *Comment utiliser le répertoire,* page 11.

ESP1431

ATELIER - ASOCIACION PARA LA COOPERACION INTERNACIONAL AL DESARROLLO ♦ Association pour la coopération internationale au développement

La Nave 7, 1° F, 46003 Valencia, Espagne.

Téléphone: 34 (96) 394 29 03. *Fax:* 34 (96) 392 27 64. *Contact:* Liduvina Calatayud.

OBJECTIFS: Promouvoir la coopération avec les pays en voie de développement ainsi que la communication, l'échange culturel et la coopération technique et économique entre l'Europe et l'Amérique Latine et les pays arabes du bassin méditerranéen.

INFORMATIONS GENERALES: *Création:* 1989. *Personnel/Total:* 29. *Salariés:* 4 dont: 4 dans les pays en développement. *Bénévoles:* 25 dont: 25 dans les pays en développement. *Budget/Total 1993:* ECU 93000 (US$ 121000). *Sources financières:* *Privé:* 30%. *Public:* 50%. *Autofinancement:* 20%.

PUBLICATIONS: *Rapport annuel. Liste des publications.*

EVALUATION/RECHERCHE: Entreprend des activités de recherche.

ACTIVITES DANS LES REGIONS EN DEVELOPPEMENT: Intervient directement dans les régions en développement. Intervient par l'intermédiaire d'organisations locales partenaires. **Actions de Développement durable:** Développement rural/agriculture; Envoi de volontaires/experts/assistance technique; Petites entreprises/secteur informel/artisanat; Questions relatives aux femmes; Éducation/formation/alphabétisation. **Régions:** Amérique du Sud; Mexique et Amerique centrale.

ACTIVITES D'INFORMATION ET D'EDUCATION: Domaines: Aliments/famine; Droits de l'Homme/paix/conflits; Développement rural/agriculture; Développement urbain/habitat; Emploi/chômage; Paix/conflits ethniques/armement/désarmement; Pauvreté/conditions de vie; Population/planning familial/démographie; Questions relatives aux femmes; Relations internationales/coopération/aide au développement; Relations économiques internationales/commerce/dette/finances; Réfugiés/migrants/groupes ethniques; Santé/assainissement/eau; Secours d'urgence/réfugiés/aide humanitaire; Écologie/environnement/biodiversité; Éducation/formation/alphabétisation. **Activités:** Campagnes d'information/expositions; Collecte de fonds; Conférences/séminaires/ateliers/activités de formation; Lobbying/plaidoyer; Radiodiffusion/manifestations culturelles; Services d'information et de documentation/bases de données; Édition/documents audiovisuels/documents éducatifs; Éducation formelle.

ESP1432

AYUDA EN ACCION ♦ ActionAid

Barquillo 8-1° DCHA, 28004 Madrid, Spain.

Telephone: 34 (91) 523 21 90. *Fax:* 34 (91) 523 25 29. *E-mail:* ANTONIO.FERNANDEZ@SCB.REIDRIS.ES. *Contact:* Marisa Alvarez, Director.

OBJECTIVES: To promote development programmes in rural areas in Africa, Asia and Latin America, designed to improve the living conditions in poor communities. To carry out development education activities and awareness-raising activities in Spain.

GENERAL INFORMATION: *Creation:* 1981. *Affiliated to:* Coordinadora de ONGs (Spain). *Personnel/Total:* 47. *Salaried:* 32. *Volunteers:* 15. *Budget/Total 1993:* ECU 5454000 (US$ 7072000). *Financial sources:* *Private:* 8%. *Public:* 7%. *Self-financing:* 85%.

PUBLICATIONS: *Periodicals:* Ayuda en Acción Boletin (10). *Annual report.*

EVALUATION/RESEARCH: Undertakes research activities.

ACTIVITIES IN DEVELOPING REGIONS: Present in developing regions. Active in 10 country(ies). Maintains local field presence. Works through local field partners. **Sustainable Development Actions:** Children/youth/family; Democracy/good governance/institution building/participatory development; Ecology/environment/biodiversity; Education/training/literacy; Emergency relief/refugees/humanitarian assistance; Food/famine; Gender issues/women; Health/sanitation/water; Rural development/agriculture; Small enterprises/informal sector/handicrafts; Urban development/habitat. **Regions:** East Africa; East Asia; Mexico and Central America; South America.

ESP1433

AYUDA FRATERNA - VOLUNTARIADO INTERNACIONAL Y CRISTIANO ♦ Aide fraternelle - Volontariat international et chrétien

Alcala 155, 4 dcha, 28009 Madrid, Espagne.

Téléphone: 34 (1) 275 26 53. *Contact:* Maria Dolores Bustamante.

ESP1434

BOLETIN ONG (RED GRROUND!)

c/ Monterra 11-4° , 28013 Madrid, Spain.

Telephone: 34 (1) 531 31 41. *Fax:* 34 (1) 522 13 73. *E-mail:* grround@.gn.apc.org. *Contact:* J.C. Devs, Chairman.

OBJECTIVES: To act as a network of communication and database of the alternative social sphere of Spain. To support a positive evolution in humanity by integrating six waves of human activity in the fields of social transformation, personal growth, art and communication, ecology, spirituality and science.

GENERAL INFORMATION: *Creation:* 1992. *Type of organisation:* network. *Personnel/Total:* 5. *Volunteers:* 5. *Budget/Total 1993:* ECU 12000 (US$ 16000). *Financial sources:* *Self-financing:* 100%.

PUBLICATIONS: *Periodicals:* Boletín ONG (10).

EVALUATION/RESEARCH: Undertakes research activities.

PLANNED ACTIVITIES: Publishing an electronic version of Boletín ONG.

INFORMATION AND EDUCATION ACTIVITIES: Topics: Children/youth/family; Culture/tradition/religion; Ecology/environment/biodiversity; Education/training/literacy; Emergency relief/refugees/humanitarian assistance; Employment/unemployment; Food/famine; Gender issues/women; Health/sanitation/water; Human rights/peace/conflicts; International economic relations/trade/debt/finance; International relations/cooperation/development aid; Other; Peace/ethnic conflicts/armament/disarmament; Population/family planning/demography; Poverty/living conditions; Racism/xenophobia/antisemitism; Refugees/migrants/ethnic groups; Rural development/agriculture; Urban development/habitat. **Activities:** Information and documentation services/data bases; Networking/electronic telecommunications; Publishing/audiovisual materials/educational materials.

ESP1435

CARITAS ESPANOLA ♦ CARITAS Espagne

San Bernardo 99 bis 7° , 28015 Madrid, Espagne.

Téléphone: 34 (1) 445 53 00. *Fax:* 34 (1) 593 48 82. *Contact:* Luis Franco Martinez-Osorio, Président.

OBJECTIFS: Réaliser les actions caritatives et sociales de l'Eglise espagnole. Encourager la communication chrétienne sous toutes ses formes et aider à la promotion et au développement de tous les hommes. Aider les pays en développement par le biais des Caritas locales et leur fournir un secours en cas d'urgence. Appuyer des programmes de réhabilitation et sensibiliser l'opinion publique.

INFORMATIONS GENERALES: *Création:* 1942. *Type d'organisation:* réseau. *Organisations membres:* 69. *Affiliée à:* Caritas Internationalis (Cité du Vatican) - Caritas Europe (Belgique) -EURONAID (Pays Bas) - EURODAD (Belgique) - VOICE (Belgique) - Coordinadora ONGD (Espagne). *Personnel/Total:* 58. *Salariés:* 53 dont: 1 dans les pays en développement. *Bénévoles:* 5. *Budget/Total 1993:* ECU 6637000 (US$ 8607000). *Sources financières:* *Privé:* 49%. *Public:* 51%.

PUBLICATIONS: *Périodiques:* Red Solidaria (4). *Rapport annuel.*

ACTIVITES DANS LES REGIONS EN DEVELOPPEMENT: Intervient dans 43 pays. Intervient par l'intermédiaire d'organisations locales partenaires. **Actions de Développement durable:** Aliments/famine; Démocratie/bonne gestion publique/création d'institutions/développement participatif; Développement rural/agriculture; Développement urbain/habitat; Enfants/jeunesse/famille; Envoi de volontaires/experts/assistance technique; Petites entreprises/secteur informel/artisanat; Questions relatives aux femmes; Santé/assainissement/eau; Secours d'urgence/réfugiés/aide humanitaire; Écologie/environnement/biodiversité; Éducation/formation/alphabétisation. **Régions:** Afrique australe; Afrique centrale; Afrique de l'Est; Afrique de l'Ouest; Afrique du Nord;

See: *How to Use the Directory*, page 11.

Amérique du Sud; Asie centrale et Asie du Sud; Asie de l'Est; Asie du Sud-Est; Caraïbes; Mexique et Amerique centrale; Moyen-Orient.

ACTIVITES D'INFORMATION ET D'EDUCATION: Domaines: Aliments/famine; Culture/tradition/religion; Droits de l'Homme/paix/conflits; Développement rural/agriculture; Développement urbain/habitat; Emploi/chômage; Enfants/jeunesse/famille; Paix/conflits ethniques/armement/désarmement; Pauvreté/conditions de vie; Population/planning familial/démographie; Questions relatives aux femmes; Racisme/xénophobie/antisémitisme; Relations internationales/coopération/aide au développement; Réfugiés/migrants/groupes ethniques; Santé/assainissement/eau; Secours d'urgence/réfugiés/aide humanitaire; Écologie/environnement/biodiversité; Éducation/formation/alphabétisation. **Activités:** Campagnes d'information/expositions; Collecte de fonds; Conférences/séminaires/ateliers/activités de formation; Radiodiffusion/manifestations culturelles; Services d'information et de documentation/bases de données; Édition/documents audiovisuels/documents éducatifs.

ESP1436

CENTRE UNESCO DE CATALUNYA (CUC)

Mallorca 285, 08037 Barcelona, Spain.

Telephone: 34 (3) 207 17 16. **Fax:** 34 (3) 457 58 51. **E-mail:** CUNESCO@WELL.SF.CA.US/EDUCO@CC.UAB.ES. **Contact:** Felix Marti, Director.

OBJECTIVES: To disseminate information, mainly in Catalan-speaking areas, on the ideals and activities of UNESCO and the UN. To inform the Catalan scientific and intellectual community of the possibilities of contributing and participating in the tasks and programmes of UNESCO. To promote Catalan culture abroad. To assist the UNESCO Secretariat, particularly in their activities regarding Latin America and the Mediterranean.

GENERAL INFORMATION: Creation: 1984. **Affiliated to:** Catalan Federation of UNESCO Associations & Clubs (Spain) - Catalan Federation of NGOs for Human Rights (Spain) - Catalan Federation of NGOs for Development (Spain). **Personnel/Total:** 12. **Salaried:** 12. **Budget/Total 1993:** ECU 1024000 (US$ 1328000). **Financial sources:** Private: 30%. Public: 70%.

PUBLICATIONS: Periodicals: All of Us (12) - Sources (12) - Catalonia (4). Annual report. List of publications.

EVALUATION/RESEARCH: Undertakes research activities.

PLANNED ACTIVITIES: Undertaking peace and disarmament research. Contributing to UNESCO's Culture of Peace programme. Promoting and reinforcing the LINGUAPAX project in Latin America and Eastern Europe.

COMMENTS: CUC is associated with the United Nations Department of Public Information. Information activities related to the Commonwealth of Independent States.

INFORMATION AND EDUCATION ACTIVITIES: Topics: Children/youth/family; Culture/tradition/religion; Ecology/environment/biodiversity; Education/training/literacy; Human rights/peace/conflicts; International relations/cooperation/development aid; Peace/ethnic conflicts/armament/disarmament; Refugees/migrants/ethnic groups. **Activities:** Broadcasting/cultural events; Conferences/seminars/workshops/training activities; Exchanges/twinning/linking; Formal education; Information and documentation services/data bases; Information campaigns/exhibitions; Lobbying/advocacy; Publishing/audiovisual materials/educational materials.

ESP1437

CENTRO DE COMUNICACION, INVESTIGACION Y DOCUMENTACION ENTRE EUROPA, ESPANA Y AMERICA LATINA (CIDEAL) ♦ Centre de communication, recherche et documentation entre l'Europe, l'Espagne et l'Amérique Latine

Paseo de la Habana 150, 3° Dcha, 28036 Madrid, Espagne.

Téléphone: 34 (1) 457 70 65. **Fax:** 34 (1) 457 50 80. **Contact:** Alfonso Lasso de la Vega, Directeur.

OBJECTIFS: Réaliser des études et des recherches dans le domaine des relations internationales et de l'aide au développement. Promouvoir des initiatives de coopération internationale. Entreprendre des actions d'éducation au développement en Espagne et des projets de dévelop-

pement dans les pays du sud. Organiser des cours de formation sur la coopération et le développement.

INFORMATIONS GENERALES: Création: 1983. **Affiliée à:** Coordinadora de ONG para el Desarrollo (Espagne) - Consejo Español de Estudios Iberoamericanos (Espagne) - Federación Internacional de Estudios sobre América Latina y el Caribe (Espagne). **Personnel/Total:** 18. Salariés: 12 dont: 2 dans les pays en développement. Bénévoles: 6. **Budget/Total 1993:** ECU 487000 (US$ 631000). **Sources financières:** Privé: 2%. Public: 76%. Autofinancement: 22%.

PUBLICATIONS: Rapport annuel. Liste des publications.

EVALUATION/RECHERCHE: Entreprend des activités de recherche.

PREVISIONS D'ACTIVITES: Coopération avec les institutions publiques de la Palestine.

ACTIVITES DANS LES REGIONS EN DEVELOPPEMENT: Intervient directement dans les régions en développement. Intervient dans 5 pays. Maintient une présence locale sur le terrain. Intervient par l'intermédiaire d'organisations locales partenaires. **Actions de Développement durable:** Dette/finances/commerce; Démocratie/bonne gestion publique/création d'institutions/développement participatif; Développement rural/agriculture; Développement urbain/habitat; Petites entreprises/secteur informel/artisanat; Questions relatives aux femmes; Écologie/environnement/biodiversité; Éducation/formation/alphabétisation. **Régions:** Amérique du Sud; Mexique et Amerique centrale.

ACTIVITES D'INFORMATION ET D'EDUCATION: Domaines: Culture/tradition/religion; Droits de l'Homme/paix/conflits; Développement urbain/habitat; Emploi/chômage; Pauvreté/conditions de vie; Questions relatives aux femmes; Racisme/xénophobie/antisémitisme; Relations internationales/coopération/aide au développement; Relations économiques internationales/commerce/dette/finances; Écologie/environnement/biodiversité; Éducation/formation/alphabétisation. **Activités:** Campagnes d'information/expositions; Conférences/séminaires/ateliers/activités de formation; Lobbying/plaidoyer; Radiodiffusion/manifestations culturelles; Services d'information et de documentation/bases de données; Édition/documents audiovisuels/documents éducatifs; Éducation formelle.

ESP1438

CENTRO DE ESTUDIOS Y DESARROLLO RURAL (CEIDER) ♦
Centre d'études et développement rural

c/Pascual y Genis, 21 pta 10, 46002 Valencia, Espagne.

Téléphone: 34 (6) 394 37 89. **Fax:** 34 (6) 394 06 61. **Contact:** Francisco Garcia Lopez, Coordinateur.

OBJECTIFS: Etudier les questions sociales en rapport avec l'agriculture et le milieu rural. Analyser et faire des recherches sur les problèmes intéressant la population agricole. Collaborer avec d'autres organisations dans le domaine du développement rural. Sensibiliser la population espagnole à la situation des pays en développement.

INFORMATIONS GENERALES: Création: 1986. **Affiliée à:** Colectivos de Acción Solidaria. **Personnel/Total:** 4. Bénévoles: 4. **Sources financières:** Autofinancement: 100%.

PUBLICATIONS: Périodiques: Semillas (4).

EVALUATION/RECHERCHE: Entreprend des activités de recherche.

ACTIVITES D'INFORMATION ET D'EDUCATION: Domaines: Culture/tradition/religion; Développement rural/agriculture; Relations internationales/coopération/aide au développement; Relations économiques internationales/commerce/dette/finances; Écologie/environnement/biodiversité. **Activités:** Campagnes d'information/expositions; Conférences/séminaires/ateliers/activités de formation; Lobbying/plaidoyer; Services d'information et de documentation/bases de données; Édition/documents audiovisuels/documents éducatifs.

ESP1439

CENTRO DE ESTUDIOS Y SOLIDARIDAD CON AMERICA LATINA ♦ Centre d'études et de solidarité avec l'Amérique Latine

Pensamiento 27, 7° ap.1, 28020 Madrid, Espagne.

Téléphone: 34 (91) 570 36 62. **Fax:** 34 (91) 570 39 09. **Contact:** Javier Restán, Directeur.

Voir : *Comment utiliser le répertoire,* page 11.

OBJECTIFS: Elaborer, formuler et réaliser des projets de coopération au développement et de solidarité en Amérique Latine. Entreprendre des activités de recherche et diffuser l'information sur des sujets culturels et sociopolitiques relatifs à l'Amérique Latine.

INFORMATIONS GENERALES: *Création:* 1988. *Affiliée à:* Coordinadora de ONG de España (Espagne) - Groupe SYNERGY (Italie) - Comision Latinoamericana por los derechos humanos y las libertades de los pueblos (Venezuela). *Personnel/Total:* 8. *Salariés:* 2. *Bénévoles:* 6. *Budget/Total 1993:* ECU 232000 (US$ 301000). *Sources financières: Privé:* 14%. *Public:* 76%. *Autofinancement:* 10%.

PUBLICATIONS: *Rapport annuel. Liste des publications.*

EVALUATION/RECHERCHE: Entreprend des activités de recherche.

PREVISIONS D'ACTIVITES: Réalisation d'un projet de recherches sur le développement urbain au Pérou et sur l'histoire du mouvement ouvrier en Amérique Latine.

ACTIVITES DANS LES REGIONS EN DEVELOPPEMENT: Intervient dans 3 pays. Intervient par l'intermédiaire d'organisations locales partenaires. **Actions de Développement durable:** Développement rural/agriculture; Santé/assainissement/eau. **Régions:** Afrique centrale; Amérique du Sud; Mexique et Amerique centrale.

ACTIVITES D'INFORMATION ET D'EDUCATION: Domaines: Aliments/ famine; Culture/tradition/religion; Développement rural/agriculture; Développement urbain/habitat; Pauvreté/conditions de vie; Relations internationales/coopération/aide au développement. **Activités:** Campagnes d'information/expositions; Collecte de fonds; Conférences/séminaires/ateliers/activités de formation; Radiodiffusion/manifestations culturelles.

ESP1440

CENTRO DE INFORMACION EDUCACION Y AUDIOVISUALES PARA EL DESARROLLO (CINADE) ♦ Centre for Information, Education and Audiovisuals for Development

General Vives 76, P.O. Box 2494, 35007 Las Palmas de Gran Canaria, Spain.

Telephone: 34 (28) 22 07 77. *Contact:* Casiano Manrique, President.

ESP1441

CENTRO DE INFORMACION Y DOCUMENTACION INTERNACIONALES EN BARCELONA (CIDOB) ♦ Centre d'information et de documentation internationales à Barcelone

Elisabets 12, 08001 Barcelona, Espagne.

Téléphone: 34 (3) 302 64 95. *Fax:* 34 (3) 302 21 18. *Courrier électronique:* josepribera@cidob.es.. *Contact:* Josep Ribera, Directeur.

OBJECTIFS: Faire de la recherche sur les relations internationales, notamment dans les domaines suivants: politique internationale, études stratégiques, coopération et recherches sur la paix.

INFORMATIONS GENERALES: *Création:* 1979. *Affiliée à:* Coordinadora ONGD (Espagne) - European Association of Development Research and Training Institutions (the Netherlands) - International Peace Research Association - Red Europea de Documentacion e Informacion sobre America Latina (Espagne). *Personnel/Total:* 27. *Salariés:* 22 dont: 1 dans les pays en développement. *Bénévoles:* 5. *Budget/Total 1993:* ECU 927000 (US$ 1202000). *Sources financières: Public:* 60%. *Autofinancement:* 40%.

PUBLICATIONS: *Périodiques:* Afers Internacionals (4) - Anuario Internacional CIDOB (1) - DCIDOB (24). *Rapport annuel.*

EVALUATION/RECHERCHE: Entreprend des activités de recherche.

COMMENTAIRES: Activités d'information concernant la Communauté des Etats indépendants.

ACTIVITES D'INFORMATION ET D'EDUCATION: Domaines: Aliments/ famine; Droits de l'Homme/paix/conflits; Développement rural/agriculture; Développement urbain/habitat; Enfants/jeunesse/famille; Paix/ conflits ethniques/armement/désarmement; Pauvreté/conditions de vie; Population/planning familial/démographie; Questions relatives aux femmes; Racisme/xénophobie/antisémitisme; Relations internationales/ coopération/aide au développement; Relations économiques internationales/commerce/dette/finances; Réfugiés/migrants/groupes ethniques;

Santé/assainissement/eau; Secours d'urgence/réfugiés/aide humanitaire; Écologie/environnement/biodiversité. **Activités:** Campagnes d'information/expositions; Conférences/séminaires/ateliers/activités de formation; Services d'information et de documentation/bases de données.

ESP1442

CENTRO DE INVESTIGACIONES Y PROMOCION IBEROAMERICA-EUROPA (CIPIE) ♦ Research and Promotion Center for IberoAmerica and Europe

Puerto Del Sol, 4, 28013 Madrid, Spain.

Telephone: 34 (1) 532 28 28. *Fax:* 34 (1) 532 26 99. *Contact:* Hector Casanueva Ojeda, Director.

OBJECTIVES: To undertake co-operation and development projects. To sensitize the Spanish public to the problems of racism and xenophobia.

GENERAL INFORMATION: *Creation:* 1981. *Personnel/Total:* 37. *Salaried:* 19 of which: 5 in developing countries. *Volunteers:* 18. *Budget/Total 1993:* ECU 1578000 (US$ 2046000). *Financial sources: Private:* 10%. *Public:* 72%. *Self-financing:* 18%.

PUBLICATIONS: *Periodicals:* Analisis Prensa Sobre Racismo y Xenofobia (4).

EVALUATION/RESEARCH: Evaluation reports available. Undertakes research activities.

ACTIVITIES IN DEVELOPING REGIONS: Present in developing regions. Active in 14 country(ies). Maintains local field presence. Works through local field partners. **Sustainable Development Actions:** Children/ youth/family; Democracy/good governance/institution building/participatory development; Ecology/environment/biodiversity; Education/ training/literacy; Energy/transport; Gender issues/women; Health/sanitation/water; Human rights/peace/conflicts; Population/family planning/ demography; Rural development/agriculture; Sending volunteers/ experts/technical assistance; Small enterprises/informal sector/handicrafts; Urban development/habitat. **Regions:** Caribbean; Mexico and Central America; North Africa; South America.

INFORMATION AND EDUCATION ACTIVITIES: Topics: Children/youth/ family; Ecology/environment/biodiversity; Education/training/literacy; Employment/unemployment; Gender issues/women; Health/sanitation/ water; Human rights/peace/conflicts; Peace/ethnic conflicts/armament/ disarmament; Population/family planning/demography; Poverty/living conditions; Racism/xenophobia/antisemitism; Refugees/migrants/ethnic groups; Rural development/agriculture; Urban development/habitat. **Activities:** Conferences/seminars/workshops/training activities; Fund raising; Information and documentation services/data bases; Information campaigns/exhibitions; Publishing/audiovisual materials/educational materials.

ESP1443

CENTRO PARA EL DESARROLLO DE LA MUJER IBEROAMERICANA (CEDEMI)

Nunez Morgado 4, of. 92, 28036 Madrid, Espagne.

Téléphone: 34 (91) 314 51 93. *Fax:* 34 (91) 323 37 89. *Contact:* Yvonne David Allende.

OBJECTIFS: Aider les femmes étrangères vivant en Espagne à s'intégrer dans la société et défendre leurs droits. Réaliser des programmes d'information et d'orientation afin de faciliter leur intégration dans la vie active en Espagne. Promouvoir la coopération au développement et les échanges culturels.

INFORMATIONS GENERALES: *Création:* 1991. *Personnel/Total:* 25. *Salariés:* 5. *Bénévoles:* 20. *Budget/Total 1993:* ECU 25000 (US$ 32000). *Sources financières: Public:* 95%. *Autofinancement:* 5%.

PUBLICATIONS: *Rapport annuel.*

EVALUATION/RECHERCHE: Rapports d'évaluation disponibles.

ACTIVITES D'INFORMATION ET D'EDUCATION: Domaines: Questions relatives aux femmes; Relations internationales/coopération/aide au développement; Secours d'urgence/réfugiés/aide humanitaire. **Activités:** Campagnes d'information/expositions; Conférences/séminaires/ ateliers/activités de formation; Services d'information et de documenta-

See: *How to Use the Directory*, page 11.

tion/bases de données; Édition/documents audiovisuels/documents éducatifs.

ESP1444

CHILE-AMERIKA CENTRO DE ESTUDIOS, DOCUMENTACION Y PROMOCION DE AMERICA LATINA Y EL CARIBE, CILE-AMERICA

Arhabán 7 Desp 64-65, 28014 Madrid, Espagne.

Contact: Fernando Murillo.

ESP1445

CIRUJANOS Y ENFERMERAS EN ACCION ♦ CHIRURGIENS ET INFIRMIERES EN ACTION

Bertrand i Serra 6 - 10, Bajos 1a, 08022 Barcelona, Espagne.

Téléphone: 34 (93) 418 48 78. *Fax:* 32 (93) 418 64 28. *Contact:* Dr. Ricardo Riad Cortés Ocariz, Président.

OBJECTIFS: Apporter une aide, notamment en chirurgie, aux hôpitaux de campagne en situation de guerre.

INFORMATIONS GENERALES: *Création:* 1993. *Affiliée à:* Coordinadora de ONG para el desarrolla (Espagne) - Federació Catalana de ONG per al desenvolupament (Catalogne). *Personnel/Total:* 26. *Salariés:* 20 dont: 2 dans les pays en développement. *Bénévoles:* 6 dont: 4 dans les pays en développement. *Budget/Total 1993:* ECU 121000 (US$ 157000). *Sources financières:* Privé: 18%. Public: 72%. *Autofinancement:* 10%.

PUBLICATIONS: *Périodiques:* Chirurgie de guerre. *Liste des publications.*

EVALUATION/RECHERCHE: Entreprend des activités de recherche.

PREVISIONS D'ACTIVITES: Mise au point de projets de lutte contre les-sequelles de guerre au Mozambique et en Angola.

COMMENTAIRES: Intervient dans la Communauté des Etats indépendants.

ACTIVITES DANS LES REGIONS EN DEVELOPPEMENT: Intervient directement dans les régions en développement. Intervient dans 2 pays. Maintient une présence locale sur le terrain. **Actions de Développement durable:** Droits de l'Homme/paix/conflits; Envoi de volontaires/experts/assistance technique; Santé/assainissement/eau; Éducation/formation/alphabétisation. **Régions:** Afrique australe.

ACTIVITES D'INFORMATION ET D'EDUCATION: Domaines: Droits de l'Homme/paix/conflits; Paix/conflits ethniques/armement/désarmement; Racisme/xénophobie/antisémitisme; Réfugiés/migrants/groupes ethniques; Secours d'urgence/réfugiés/aide humanitaire. **Activités:** Collecte de fonds; Conférences/séminaires/ateliers/activités de formation; Échanges/parrainage/jumelage.

ESP1446

COLECTIVOS DE ACCION SOLIDARIA

Modesto Lafuente 8, 1° izq., 34002 Palencia, Espagne.

Téléphone: 34 (988) 72 94 18. *Fax:* 34 (988) 72 97 48. *Contact:* Jerónimo Aguado Martinez.

ESP1447

COMISION CATOLICA ESPANOLA DE MIGRACION ♦ Commission Catholique Espagnole pour les Migrants

Valenzuela 10, 28014 Madrid, Espagne.

Téléphone: 34 (1) 532 74 78. *Fax:* 34 (1) 532 20 59. *Contact:* Ramon de Marcos, Directeur.

OBJECTIFS: Aider les réfugiés et faciliter leur insertion sociale et professionnelle.

INFORMATIONS GENERALES: *Création:* 1955. *Affiliée à:* Commission Espagnole d'Aide aux Réfugiés. *Personnel/Total:* 32. *Salariés:* 25. *Bénévoles:* 7. *Budget/Total 1993:* ECU 1212000 (US$ 1572000). *Sources financières:* Privé: 5%. Public: 80%. *Autofinancement:* 15%.

PUBLICATIONS: *Rapport annuel. Liste des publications.*

EVALUATION/RECHERCHE: Entreprend des activités de recherche.

COMMENTAIRES: Intervient dans la Communauté des Etats indépendants. Activités d'information concernant la Communauté des Etats indépendants.

ACTIVITES DANS LES REGIONS EN DEVELOPPEMENT: Intervient par l'intermédiaire d'organisations locales partenaires.

ACTIVITES D'INFORMATION ET D'EDUCATION: Domaines: Développement rural/agriculture; Relations internationales/coopération/aide au développement; Réfugiés/migrants/groupes ethniques. **Activités:** Collecte de fonds; Services d'information et de documentation/bases de données; Échanges/parrainage/jumelage.

ESP1448

COMISION DERECHOS HUMANOS GUATEMALA

Embajadores 216-3A, 28045 Madrid, Spain.

ESP1449

COMISION ESPANOLA DE "JUSTICIA Y PAZ" ♦ Commission espagnole "Justice et Paix"

Francisco Silvela 77 bis, 1 dcha, 28028 Madrid, Espagne.

Téléphone: 34 (1) 261 12 14. *Contact:* Javier Anso, Secrétaire général.

ESP1450

COMISION ESPANOLA DE AYUDA AL REFUGIADO (CEAR) ♦ Commission espagnole d'aide aux réfugiés

Gran Vía 6, 6p, 28020 Madrid, Espagne.

Téléphone: 34 (1) 555 06 98. *Fax:* 34 (1) 555 54 16. *Contact:* Maria Jesus Arsuaga, Secrétaire général.

OBJECTIFS: Apporter une assistance juridique et sociale aux réfugiés et aux demandeurs d'asile en Espagne. Sensibiliser l'opinion publique sur les conditions des réfugiés en Espagne et lutter contre le racisme et la xénophobie. Réaliser des projets de réhabilitation et de développement dans le Tiers monde.

INFORMATIONS GENERALES: *Création:* 1979. *Affiliée à:* Coordinadora de ONG para el Desarrollo (Espagne) - European Council on Refugees and Exiles. *Personnel/Total:* 129. *Salariés:* 29 dont: 2 dans les pays en développement. *Bénévoles:* 100. *Budget/Total 1993:* ECU 3272000 (US$ 4243000). *Sources financières:* Privé: 3%. *Public:* 96%. *Autofinancement:* 1%.

PUBLICATIONS: *Rapport annuel. Liste des publications.*

EVALUATION/RECHERCHE: Rapports d'évaluation disponibles. Entreprend des activités de recherche.

COMMENTAIRES: Intervient dans la Communauté des Etats indépendants. Activités d'information concernant la Communauté des Etats indépendants.

ACTIVITES DANS LES REGIONS EN DEVELOPPEMENT: Intervient directement dans les régions en développement. Intervient dans 4 pays. Maintient une présence locale sur le terrain. Intervient par l'intermédiaire d'organisations locales partenaires. **Actions de Développement durable:** Développement rural/agriculture; Développement urbain/habitat; Envoi de volontaires/experts/assistance technique; Petites entreprises/secteur informel/artisanat; Questions relatives aux femmes; Santé/assainissement/eau; Secours d'urgence/réfugiés/aide humanitaire; Écologie/environnement/biodiversité; Éducation/formation/alphabétisation. **Régions:** Afrique australe; Amérique du Sud; Mexique et Amerique centrale; Moyen-Orient.

ACTIVITES D'INFORMATION ET D'EDUCATION: Domaines: Droits de l'Homme/paix/conflits; Développement rural/agriculture; Développement urbain/habitat; Paix/conflits ethniques/armement/désarmement; Pauvreté/conditions de vie; Questions relatives aux femmes; Racisme/xénophobie/antisémitisme; Relations internationales/coopération/aide au développement; Réfugiés/migrants/groupes ethniques; Secours d'urgence/réfugiés/aide humanitaire. **Activités:** Campagnes d'information/expositions; Collecte de fonds; Conférences/séminaires/ateliers/activités de formation; Services d'information et de documentation/bases de données; Édition/documents audiovisuels/documents éducatifs; Éducation formelle.

Voir : *Comment utiliser le répertoire,* page 11.

ESP1451

COMITE DE DEFENSA DE LOS REFUGIADOS, ASILADOS E IMMIGRANTES (COMRADE) ♦ Committee for Defense of Refugees, Asylum Seekers and Migrants in Spain

c/Guttierez de Cetina 88 - Local 3, 28017 Madrid, Spain.

Telephone: 34 (1) 377 44 43. *Contact:* Rafael L. Guardo Polo, President of the Commission of the Directorate.

OBJECTIVES: To transform society into a multicultural and democratic community. To raise awareness of antiracist and multicultural issues among Spanish citizens. To provide social services for refugees, asylum seekers and migrants. To develop new projects and services through intercultural and antiracist education and solidarity programmes.

GENERAL INFORMATION: *Creation:* 1987. *Affiliated to:* United for Intercultural Action (the Netherlands). *Personnel/Total:* 74. *Salaried:* 7 of which: in developing countries. *Volunteers:* 67. *Budget/Total 1993:* ECU 115000 (US$ 149000). *Financial sources:* Private: 10%. Public: 80%. Self-financing: 10%.

PUBLICATIONS: *Periodicals:* Sin fronteras (24). *Annual report. List of publications.*

EVALUATION/RESEARCH: Evaluation reports available. Undertakes research activities.

COMMENTS: Undertakes activities in the Commonwealth of Independent States. Information activities related to the Commonwealth of Independent States.

ACTIVITIES IN DEVELOPING REGIONS: Active in 11 country(ies). Works through local field partners. **Sustainable Development Actions:** Emergency relief/refugees/humanitarian assistance. **Regions:** Caribbean; Central Africa; Central Asia and South Asia; East Africa; East Asia; Mexico and Central America; Middle East; North Africa; Oceania; South America; South East Asia; Southern Africa; West Africa.

INFORMATION AND EDUCATION ACTIVITIES: **Topics:** Emergency relief/refugees/humanitarian assistance; Human rights/peace/conflicts; Refugees/migrants/ethnic groups. **Activities:** Conferences/seminars/workshops/training activities; Exchanges/twinning/linking; Formal education; Fund raising; Information and documentation services/data bases; Information campaigns/exhibitions; Lobbying/advocacy; Publishing/audiovisual materials/educational materials.

ESP1452

COMMISSION PRO-AMAZONIA ♦ Pro-Amazonia Commission

Calle Campomanes 13,2, Madrid 28013, Spain.

Telephone: 34 (1) 541 10 71. *Fax:* 34 (1) 559 78 97. *Contact:* Jose Santamarta, Chairman.

OBJECTIVES: To promote sustainable development in the Amazon region and protect the region's biodiversity and indigenous peoples.

GENERAL INFORMATION: *Creation:* 1987. *Affiliated to:* Coordinadora de Organizaciones de Defensa Ambiental (Spain) - European Working Group on Amazonia (Belgium) - Alliance of Northern People for Environment and Development (Germany). *Personnel/Total:* 13. *Salaried:* 4. *Volunteers:* 9. *Budget/Total 1993:* ECU 58000 (US$ 75000). *Financial sources:* Private: 37%. Public: 35%. Self-financing: 28%.

PUBLICATIONS: *Periodicals:* Amazonia Urgente (4). *Annual report. List of publications.*

EVALUATION/RESEARCH: Evaluation reports available. Undertakes research activities.

ACTIVITIES IN DEVELOPING REGIONS: Present in developing regions. Active in 4 country(ies). Works through local field partners. **Sustainable Development Actions:** Children/youth/family; Debt/finance/trade; Democracy/good governance/institution building/participatory development; Ecology/environment/biodiversity; Energy/transport; Gender issues/women; Health/sanitation/water; Human rights/peace/conflicts; Population/family planning/demography; Rural development/agriculture; Sending volunteers/experts/technical assistance. **Regions:** South America.

INFORMATION AND EDUCATION ACTIVITIES: **Topics:** Ecology/environment/biodiversity; Human rights/peace/conflicts; International relations/cooperation/development aid; Poverty/living conditions; Rural

development/agriculture. **Activities:** Broadcasting/cultural events; Conferences/seminars/workshops/training activities; Exchanges/twinning/linking; Formal education; Fund raising; Information and documentation services/data bases; Information campaigns/exhibitions; Lobbying/advocacy; Networking/electronic telecommunications; Publishing/audiovisual materials/educational materials.

ESP1453

CONCERTACIO N/S

Junta del Comerç 24, princ 1°, 08001 Barcelona, Espagne.

Téléphone: 34 (93) 412 38 80. *Fax:* 34 (93) 318 63 22. *Courrier électronique:* CONCERTA@PANGEA.UPC.ES. *Contact:* Josep Miguel Alegret, Secrétaire général.

OBJECTIFS: Promouvoir la coopération au développement en collaborant avec des ONG du sud.

INFORMATIONS GENERALES: *Création:* 1988. *Affiliée à:* Frères des Hommes-Europe. *Personnel/Total:* 10. *Salariés:* 5. *Bénévoles:* 5. *Budget/Total 1993:* ECU 303000 (US$ 393000). *Sources financières:* Privé: 20%. Public: 70%. Autofinancement: 10%.

PUBLICATIONS: *Périodiques:* Interdependencias (24) - Bulletin (4). *Rapport annuel. Liste des publications.*

ACTIVITES DANS LES REGIONS EN DEVELOPPEMENT: Intervient dans 5 pays. Intervient par l'intermédiaire d'organisations locales partenaires. **Actions de Développement durable:** Développement rural/agriculture; Développement urbain/habitat; Santé/assainissement/eau; Écologie/environnement/biodiversité. **Régions:** Afrique australe; Afrique centrale; Amérique du Sud; Mexique et Amerique centrale.

ACTIVITES D'INFORMATION ET D'EDUCATION: **Domaines:** Autres. **Activités:** Conférences/séminaires/ateliers/activités de formation; Lobbying/plaidoyer; Services d'information et de documentation/bases de données; Édition/documents audiovisuels/documents éducatifs.

ESP1454

CONSEJO INTERHOSPITALARIO DE COOPERACION

Sabino Arana s/n, 08028 Barcelona, Espagne.

Téléphone: 34 (93) 330 85 11. *Fax:* 34 (93) 201 65 15. *Contact:* Angel Amilibia.

OBJECTIFS: Promouvoir le développement sanitaire à long terme dans les pays en développement.

INFORMATIONS GENERALES: *Création:* 1982. *Affiliée à:* Coordinadora de ONG para el Desarrollo (Espagne). *Personnel/Total:* 22. *Salariés:* 20 dont: 16 dans les pays en développement. *Bénévoles:* 2. *Budget/Total 1993:* ECU 848000 (US$ 1100000). *Sources financières:* Privé: 12%. Public: 78%. Autofinancement: 10%.

EVALUATION/RECHERCHE: Rapports d'évaluation disponibles. Entreprend des activités de recherche.

ACTIVITES DANS LES REGIONS EN DEVELOPPEMENT: Intervient directement dans les régions en développement. Intervient dans 1 pays. Maintient une présence locale sur le terrain. **Actions de Développement durable:** Enfants/jeunesse/famille; Envoi de volontaires/experts/assistance technique; Petites entreprises/secteur informel/artisanat; Santé/assainissement/eau. **Régions:** Afrique australe.

ESP1455

COOPERACION AL DESARROLLO Y PROMOCION DE ACTIVIDADES ASISTENCIALES (CODESPA) ♦ Co-operation for the Promotion and Development of Welfare Activities

Ibiza 33, 28009 Madrid, Spain.

Telephone: 34 (1) 504 01 98. *Fax:* 34 (1) 409 79 78. *Contact:* Laureano López Rodó, President.

OBJECTIVES: To promote co-operation for the economic and social development of developing countries, especially those in Latin America.

GENERAL INFORMATION: *Creation:* 1985. *Affiliated to:* Coordinadora de ONG para el Desarrollo (Spain) - Centro de Fundaciones (Spain) - Consorcio de Fundaciones Americanas de Desarrollo (Dominican Republic). *Personnel/Total:* 13. *Salaried:* 5. *Volunteers:* 8 of which: 5 in developing countries. *Budget/Total 1993:*

See: *How to Use the Directory,* page 11.

ECU 3568000 (US$ 4626000). *Financial sources:* Private: 79%. Public: 21%.

PUBLICATIONS: *Periodicals:* Boletín (4) - Memoria de Actividades (1). *Annual report.*

EVALUATION/RESEARCH: Evaluation reports available. Undertakes research activities.

ACTIVITIES IN DEVELOPING REGIONS: Present in developing regions. Active in 41 country(ies). Maintains local field presence. Works through local field partners. **Sustainable Development Actions:** Children/youth/family; Debt/finance/trade; Ecology/environment/biodiversity; Education/training/literacy; Food/famine; Gender issues/women; Health/sanitation/water; Population/family planning/demography; Rural development/agriculture; Sending volunteers/experts/technical assistance; Small enterprises/informal sector/handicrafts; Urban development/habitat. **Regions:** Caribbean; Mexico and Central America; Middle East; North Africa; South America.

INFORMATION AND EDUCATION ACTIVITIES: Topics: Children/youth/family; Ecology/environment/biodiversity; Education/training/literacy; Employment/unemployment; Food/famine; Gender issues/women; Health/sanitation/water; International economic relations/trade/debt/finance; International relations/cooperation/development aid; Population/family planning/demography; Poverty/living conditions; Racism/xenophobia/antisemitism; Rural development/agriculture; Urban development/habitat. **Activities:** Broadcasting/cultural events; Conferences/seminars/workshops/training activities; Formal education; Fund raising; Information and documentation services/data bases; Lobbying/advocacy; Publishing/audiovisual materials/educational materials.

ESP1456

COORDINADORA DE ONG PARA EL DESARROLLO

Cartagena 22-2º izq., 28028 Madrid, Spain.

Telephone: 34 (1) 361 10 96. *Fax:* 34 (1) 361 11 45. *E-mail:* CONGDE@NODO50.gn.apc.org. *Contact:* Teresa Serrano Oñate.

OBJECTIVES: To serve as an umbrella organisation for NGOs and represent the interests of the NGO community in Spain. To provide information and training services for member NGOs. To facilitate relations between NGOs and the public.

GENERAL INFORMATION: *Creation:* 1986. *Type of organisation:* network. *Affiliated to:* WIDE (Belgium) - European Forum on Development Service (Germany). *Personnel/Total:* 3. *Budget/Total 1993:* ECU 164000 (US$ 212000). *Financial sources:* Public: 50%. Self-financing: 50%.

PUBLICATIONS: *Periodicals:* Punto de Encuentro (3). *Annual report.*

ACTIVITIES IN DEVELOPING REGIONS: Works through local field partners.

INFORMATION AND EDUCATION ACTIVITIES: Topics: Emergency relief/refugees/humanitarian assistance; Gender issues/women; International economic relations/trade/debt/finance; International relations/cooperation/development aid; Population/family planning/demography. **Activities:** Conferences/seminars/workshops/training activities; Information campaigns/exhibitions; Lobbying/advocacy; Publishing/audiovisual materials/educational materials.

ESP1457

COORDINADORA DE ORGANIZACIONES DE DEFENSA AMBIENTAL (CODA) ♦ Environmental Defense Network

Pza. Santo Domingo 7 - 7 piso B, 28013 Madrid, Spain.

Telephone: 34 (1) 559 60 25. *Fax:* 34 (1) 559 78 97. *Contact:* José Santamarta Flórez, Executive Director.

OBJECTIVES: To provide information on climate change, biodiversity, forests, energy, pollution, waste, recycling, transportation, trade, water, acid rain and the environment.

GENERAL INFORMATION: *Creation:* 1982. *Type of organisation:* network. *Member organisations:* 170. *Affiliated to:* IUCN (Switzerland) - ANPED (the Netherlands) - EEB (Belgium) - Earthaction (USA). *Personnel/Total:* 41. *Salaried:* 13. *Volunteers:* 28. *Budget/Total 1993:* ECU 321000 (US$ 416000). *Financial sources:* Private: 12%. Public: 27%. Self-financing: 61%.

PUBLICATIONS: *Periodicals:* GAIA (6). *Annual report. List of publications.*

EVALUATION/RESEARCH: Evaluation reports available. Undertakes research activities.

COMMENTS: Information activities related to the Commonwealth of Independent States.

ACTIVITIES IN DEVELOPING REGIONS: Present in developing regions. Active in 6 country(ies). Maintains local field presence. Works through local field partners. **Sustainable Development Actions:** Debt/finance/trade; Ecology/environment/biodiversity; Education/training/literacy; Human rights/peace/conflicts; Rural development/agriculture; Sending volunteers/experts/technical assistance; Small enterprises/informal sector/handicrafts; Urban development/habitat. **Regions:** Mexico and Central America; South America.

INFORMATION AND EDUCATION ACTIVITIES: Topics: Culture/tradition/religion; Ecology/environment/biodiversity; Education/training/literacy; Employment/unemployment; Gender issues/women; Health/sanitation/water; Human rights/peace/conflicts; International economic relations/trade/debt/finance; International relations/cooperation/development aid; Peace/ethnic conflicts/armament/disarmament; Population/family planning/demography; Poverty/living conditions; Racism/xenophobia/antisemitism; Refugees/migrants/ethnic groups; Rural development/agriculture; Urban development/habitat. **Activities:** Broadcasting/cultural events; Conferences/seminars/workshops/training activities; Exchanges/twinning/linking; Formal education; Fund raising; Information and documentation services/data bases; Information campaigns/exhibitions; Lobbying/advocacy; Networking/electronic telecommunications; Publishing/audiovisual materials/educational materials.

ESP1458

CRUZ ROJA ESPANOLA ♦ Croix Rouge espagnole

Rafael Villa s/n, 28023 El Plantio-Madrid, Espagne.

Téléphone: 34 (91) 335 44 44. *Fax:* 34 (91) 335 44 55. *Contact:* José Ramón Bronnet.

ESP1459

DIRECCION DE SERVICIOS DE COOPERACION INTERNACIONAL I AYUDA HUMANITARIA

Ajuntamiento de Barcelona, Plaza Sant Jaime 3er, 08002 Barcelona, Espagne.

Téléphone: 34 (93) 402 74 41. *Contact:* Manuel Vila i Motllo.

ESP1460

EDIFICANDO-COMUNIDAD DE NAZARET

Joaquin Costa, 21, Bajo Izda, 28002 Madrid, Espagne.

Téléphone: 34 (91) 563 58 39. *Contact:* Juan Antonio Lascurain.

ESP1461

EDUCACION SIN FRONTERAS (ESF) ♦ Education sans frontières

Josep Ansel m Clavé 6, 1º, 1a, 08002 Barcelona, Espagne.

Téléphone: 34 (93) 412 72 17. *Fax:* 34 (93) 412 40 36. *Contact:* Rosa López.

OBJECTIFS: Appuyer des programmes de développement et d'éducation, visant en particulier les enfants, dans les pays en développement.

INFORMATIONS GENERALES: *Création:* 1988. *Affiliée à:* Coordinadora de ONG para el Desarrollo (Espagne) - Fédération Catalane d'ONGD (Espagne) - Coordinadora Andaluzada de ONGD para el Desarrollo (Espagne). *Budget/Total 1993:* ECU 111000 (US$ 144000). *Sources financières:* Privé: 15%. Public: 75%. Autofinancement: 10%.

PUBLICATIONS: *Périodiques:* Bulletin (4). *Rapport annuel. Liste des publications.*

EVALUATION/RECHERCHE: Rapports d'évaluation disponibles. Entreprend des activités de recherche.

ACTIVITES DANS LES REGIONS EN DEVELOPPEMENT: Intervient directement dans les régions en développement. Intervient dans 4 pays. Intervient par l'intermédiaire d'organisations locales partenaires. **Actions de Développement durable:** Droits de l'Homme/

Voir : *Comment utiliser le répertoire,* page 11.

paix/conflits; Démocratie/bonne gestion publique/création d'institutions/ développement participatif; Développement rural/agriculture; Enfants/ jeunesse/famille; Envoi de volontaires/experts/assistance technique; Petites entreprises/secteur informel/artisanat; Questions relatives aux femmes; Secours d'urgence/réfugiés/aide humanitaire; Éducation/formation/alphabétisation. **Régions:** Amérique du Sud; Caraïbes; Mexique et Amerique centrale.

ACTIVITES D'INFORMATION ET D'EDUCATION: Domaines: Développement rural/agriculture; Enfants/jeunesse/famille; Paix/conflits ethniques/armement/désarmement; Pauvreté/conditions de vie; Racisme/ xénophobie/antisémitisme; Réfugiés/migrants/groupes ethniques; Éducation/formation/alphabétisation. **Activités:** Campagnes d'information/ expositions; Collecte de fonds; Conférences/séminaires/ateliers/activités de formation; Services d'information et de documentation/bases de données; Édition/documents audiovisuels/documents éducatifs.

ESP1462
EKUMENE
Av. Federico Rubió y Galí 98, 28040 Madrid, Espagne.

Téléphone: 34 (1) 450 38 28.

ESP1463
ENTREPUEBLOS
Feliu Casanova 19, 1º , 08028 Barcelona, Espagne.

Téléphone: 34 (93) 422 85 62. *Fax:* 34 (93) 422 85 62. *Contact:* Gabriela Serra Frediani, Secrétaire général.

ESP1464
EQUIPO DE COMUNICACION EDUCATIVA (ECOE) ♦ Equipe de communication éducative
Teniente Muñoz Diaz, 13, bajo, 28018 Madrid, Espagne.

Téléphone: 34 (91) 477 13 42. *Fax:* 34 (91) 477 63 81. *Contact:* Martin Valmaseda, Président.

ESP1465
FE Y ALEGRIA ♦ Faith and Joy
Almagro 6, 28010 Madrid, Spain.

Telephone: 34 (1) 319 05 56. *Fax:* 34 (1) 319 05 56. *Contact:* Cesareo Garcia.

ESP1466
FEDERACION DE ORGANIZACIONES PARA REFUGIADOS Y ASILADOS (FEDORA)
c/ Arlabán 7, 28014 Madrid, Spain.

Telephone: 34 (91) 523 16 18. *Fax:* 34 (91) 523 34 91. *Contact:* Bushra Razzak, Présidente.

ESP1467
FEDERACION ESPANOLA DE RELIGIOSAS SANITARIAS (FERS) ♦ Fédération espagnole des religieuses agissant dans le domaine de la santé
Santa Engracia, 131 2º Izq., 28003 Madrid, Espagne.

Téléphone: 34 (1) 441 14 33. *Fax:* 34 (1) 441 97 26. *Contact:* Rosario Sanchez Benito.

OBJECTIFS: Encourager les activités missionnaires des religieuses dans le domaine de la santé. Favoriser la collaboration entre les institutions religieuses et les associations nationales et internationales travaillant dans le domaine de santé.

INFORMATIONS GENERALES: *Création:* 1952. *Affiliée à:* CONFER - CICIAMS - Caritas. *Personnel/Total:* 34. *Bénévoles:* 34 dont: 34 dans les pays en développement. *Sources financières:* Autofinancement: 100%.

PUBLICATIONS: *Rapport annuel.*

ACTIVITES DANS LES REGIONS EN DEVELOPPEMENT: Intervient directement dans les régions en développement. Intervient dans 1 pays. Maintient une présence locale sur le terrain. **Actions de Développe-**

ment durable: Aliments/famine; Population/planning familial/démographie; Santé/assainissement/eau. **Régions:** Afrique centrale.

ESP1468
FEDERACION ESPANOLA DE RELIGIOSOS DE ENSENANZA (FERE) ♦ Education Religious Spanish Federation
Conde de Penalver 45, 4a planta, B.P. 53052, 28006 Madrid, Spain.

Telephone: 34 (91) 402 13 00. *Fax:* 34 (91) 309 17 40. *Contact:* Angel Astorgano Ruiz, General Secretary.

OBJECTIVES: To promote the development and education of women and children of all ages. To support local communities in West Africa through developing co-operatives, associations, farms, workshops and improved health standards.

GENERAL INFORMATION: *Creation:* 1957. *Type of organisation:* coordinating body. *Affiliated to:* National Federation of Spanish DNGOs - Madrid Federation of NGOs. *Personnel/Total:* 140. *Salaried:* 95 of which: 92 in developing countries. *Volunteers:* 45 of which: 45 in developing countries. *Financial sources:* Private: 15%. Public: 80%. Self-financing: 5%.

EVALUATION/RESEARCH: Evaluation reports available.

ACTIVITIES IN DEVELOPING REGIONS: Present in developing regions. Active in 1 country(ies). Maintains local field presence. Works through local field partners. **Sustainable Development Actions:** Children/ youth/family; Education/training/literacy; Food/famine; Gender issues/ women; Health/sanitation/water; Rural development/agriculture; Sending volunteers/experts/technical assistance; Small enterprises/informal sector/handicrafts. **Regions:** West Africa.

INFORMATION AND EDUCATION ACTIVITIES: Topics: Children/youth/ family; Culture/tradition/religion; Education/training/literacy; Gender issues/women. **Activities:** Formal education; Publishing/audiovisual materials/educational materials.

ESP1469
FONDACION PABLO IGLESIAS
Monte Esquinza No. 30-2º dcha., 28010 Madrid, Spain.

Telephone: 34 (91) 410 45 60.

ESP1470
FONS DE DOCUMENTACIO DEL MEDI AMBIENT ♦ Environmental Information Center
Portal de Valldigna, 15-baix, La Casa Verde, 46003 Valencia, Espagne.

Téléphone: 34 (96) 391 78 64. *Fax:* 34 (96) 391 78 64. *Contact:* Alejandro de la Cueva Martin, Président.

OBJECTIFS: Apporter une à l'information et la consultation bibliographiques dans le domaine du développement.

INFORMATIONS GENERALES: *Création:* 1982. *Personnel/Total:* 6. *Salariés:* 1. *Bénévoles:* 5. *Budget/Total 1993:* ECU 3000 (US$ 4000). *Sources financières:* Privé: 60%. Public: 30%. Autofinancement: 10%.

PUBLICATIONS: *Liste des publications.*

ACTIVITES D'INFORMATION ET D'EDUCATION: Domaines: Aliments/ famine; Développement rural/agriculture; Développement urbain/habitat; Santé/assainissement/eau; Écologie/environnement/biodiversité. **Activités:** Collecte de fonds; Services d'information et de documentation/bases de données.

ESP1471
FUNDACION ESPANOLA PARA LA COOPERACION
7 Glorieta Quevedo 6D, 28015 Madrid, Espagne.

Contact: A. Yanez- Barnuveo, Directrice.

ESP1472
FUNDACION HUMANISMO Y DEMOCRACIA ♦ Fondation Humanisme et Démocratie
Velázquez, 78, 1º , 28001 Madrid, Espagne.

See: *How to Use the Directory,* page 11.

Téléphone: 34 (1) 435 06 29. *Fax:* 34 (1) 435 10 57. *Contact:* Carlos Moro, Directeur.

OBJECTIFS: Effectuer des études et analyser les problèmes du développement avec les ONG du Sud. Réaliser des projets dans les domaines de l'assainissement, du traitement des déchets, de la santé et de l'environnement.

INFORMATIONS GENERALES: *Création:* 1977. *Affiliée à:* Centro de Fundaciones (Espagne) - Coordinadora de Organizaciones no Gubernamentales (Espagne) - Centro Europeo para Asuntos de los Trabajadores. *Personnel/Total:* 18. *Salariés:* 5. *Bénévoles:* 13 dont: 3 dans les pays en développement. *Budget/Total 1993:* ECU 27000 (US$ 35000). *Sources financières:* Privé: 50%. Public: 50%.

PUBLICATIONS: *Rapport annuel. Liste des publications.*

EVALUATION/RECHERCHE: Rapports d'évaluation disponibles. Entreprend des activités de recherche.

PREVISIONS D'ACTIVITES: Appui aux campagnes d'éducation et de sensibilisation et en rapport avec les objectifs de l'organisation. Organisation de séminaires sur: le dialogue Nord-Sud, l'aide aux personnes âgées, la formation professionnelle, le dialogue social européen.

COMMENTAIRES: Intervient dans la Communauté des Etats indépendants. Activités d'information concernant la Communauté des Etats indépendants.

ACTIVITES DANS LES REGIONS EN DEVELOPPEMENT: Intervient directement dans les régions en développement. Intervient par l'intermédiaire d'organisations locales partenaires. **Actions de Développement durable:** Aliments/famine; Droits de l'Homme/paix/conflits; Démocratie/bonne gestion publique/création d'institutions/développement participatif; Développement rural/agriculture; Petites entreprises/secteur informel/artisanat; Questions relatives aux femmes; Santé/assainissement/eau; Écologie/environnement/biodiversité. **Régions:** Afrique de l'Ouest; Amérique du Sud; Caraïbes; Mexique et Amerique centrale.

ACTIVITES D'INFORMATION ET D'EDUCATION: Domaines: Droits de l'Homme/paix/conflits; Développement rural/agriculture; Emploi/chômage; Enfants/jeunesse/famille; Paix/conflits ethniques/armement/désarmement; Questions relatives aux femmes; Racisme/xénophobie/antisémitisme; Relations internationales/coopération/aide au développement; Réfugiés/migrants/groupes ethniques; Santé/assainissement/eau; Écologie/environnement/biodiversité. **Activités:** Conférences/séminaires/ateliers/activités de formation; Éducation formelle.

ESP1473

FUNDACION LARGO CABALLERO

Depart. de Cooperacion, San Bernardo 20, 5° , 28015 Madrid, Espagne.

Téléphone: 34 (91) 532 73 64. *Fax:* 34 (91) 532 93 79. *Contact:* José Carpio Martin.

ESP1474

FUNDACION PARA EL DESARROLLO DEL COOPERATIVISMO Y LA ECONOMIA SOCIAL (FUNDESCOOP)

San Bernardo 20 - 5° Planta, 28015 Madrid, Espagne.

Téléphone: 34 (1) 522 31 55. *Fax:* 34 (1) 532 93 79. *Contact:* Rafael Gimenez, Directeur.

OBJECTIFS: Promouvoir la coopération et l'économie sociale afin de créer de l'emploi. Développer l'idée du travail autonome par les communautés dans les pays en voie de développement.

INFORMATIONS GENERALES: *Création:* 1985. *Affiliée à:* Asociación Latinoamericana de Centros de Educación Cooperativa (Argentine) - Coordinadora Española de Organizaciones no Gubernamentales (Espagne). *Personnel/Total:* 53. *Salariés:* 53 dont: 4 dans les pays en développement. *Budget/Total 1993:* ECU 4423000 (US$ 5736000). *Sources financières:* Public: 2%. Autofinancement: 98%.

PUBLICATIONS: *Rapport annuel. Liste des publications.*

EVALUATION/RECHERCHE: Rapports d'évaluation disponibles. Entreprend des activités de recherche.

PREVISIONS D'ACTIVITES: Organisation de campagnes pour le développement des coopératives en Amérique du Sud et à Cuba. Aide à la formation en gestion des coopératives au Venezuela ainsi que dans les pays sus-cités.

ACTIVITES DANS LES REGIONS EN DEVELOPPEMENT: Intervient directement dans les régions en développement. Intervient dans 8 pays. Maintient une présence locale sur le terrain. Intervient par l'intermédiaire d'organisations locales partenaires. **Actions de Développement durable:** Dette/finances/commerce; Développement rural/agriculture; Développement urbain/habitat; Enfants/jeunesse/famille; Envoi de volontaires/experts/assistance technique; Petites entreprises/secteur informel/artisanat; Écologie/environnement/biodiversité. **Régions:** Afrique centrale; Amérique du Sud; Caraïbes; Mexique et Amerique centrale.

ACTIVITES D'INFORMATION ET D'EDUCATION: Domaines: Développement rural/agriculture; Développement urbain/habitat; Emploi/chômage; Enfants/jeunesse/famille; Questions relatives aux femmes; Relations internationales/coopération/aide au développement; Relations économiques internationales/commerce/dette/finances. **Activités:** Conférences/séminaires/ateliers/activités de formation; Édition/documents audiovisuels/documents éducatifs.

ESP1475

FUNDACION PAZ Y SOLIDARIDAD ♦ Peace and Solidarity Foundation

Fernandez de la Hoz 12, 28010 Madrid, Spain.

Telephone: 34 (91) 308 36 48. *Fax:* 34 (91) 308 36 70. *Contact:* Andres Mellado, Director.

OBJECTIVES: To promote international development co-operation, international trade union co-operation and trade union development education.

GENERAL INFORMATION: *Creation:* 1989. *Affiliated to:* Coordinadora de ONG para el Desarrolla (Spain) - Grupo Sur. *Personnel/Total:* 46. *Salaried:* 6. *Volunteers:* 40 of which: 2 in developing countries. *Budget/Total 1993:* ECU 1194000 (US$ 1548000). *Financial sources:* Private: 23%. Public: 71%. Self-financing: 6%.

PUBLICATIONS: *Periodicals:* Cuadernos Paz y Solidaridad (6). *Annual report.*

EVALUATION/RESEARCH: Evaluation reports available.

PLANNED ACTIVITIES: Raising awareness of development education among teachers.

COMMENTS: Information activities related to the Commonwealth of Independent States.

ACTIVITIES IN DEVELOPING REGIONS: Present in developing regions. Active in 18 country(ies). Works through local field partners. **Sustainable Development Actions:** Children/youth/family; Democracy/good governance/institution building/participatory development; Ecology/environment/biodiversity; Education/training/literacy; Emergency relief/refugees/humanitarian assistance; Energy/transport; Food/famine; Gender issues/women; Health/sanitation/water; Human rights/peace/conflicts; Population/family planning/demography; Rural development/agriculture; Sending volunteers/experts/technical assistance; Small enterprises/informal sector/handicrafts. **Regions:** Caribbean; Central Africa; Mexico and Central America; North Africa; South America.

INFORMATION AND EDUCATION ACTIVITIES: Topics: Culture/tradition/religion; Ecology/environment/biodiversity; Education/training/literacy; Emergency relief/refugees/humanitarian assistance; Human rights/peace/conflicts; International economic relations/trade/debt/finance; International relations/cooperation/development aid; Peace/ethnic conflicts/armament/disarmament; Population/family planning/demography; Poverty/living conditions; Refugees/migrants/ethnic groups. **Activities:** Broadcasting/cultural events; Conferences/seminars/workshops/training activities; Exchanges/twinning/linking; Information campaigns/exhibitions; Lobbying/advocacy; Publishing/audiovisual materials/educational materials.

ESP1476

GIPZUZKOA BIDE LAGUNTZA ELKARTEA (DYA)

Casino de Liborioene 30 Bajo, Donostia, Gipuzkoa, Spain.

Voir : *Comment utiliser le répertoire,* page 11.

Telephone: 34 (43) 464 622.

ESP1477

GRUPO ECOLOGISTA HELICA

c/Mayor 35, 2° , 44600 Alcaniz, Espagne.

Téléphone: 34 (974) 83 10 67. *Contact:* Amor Pascual Carceller.

ESP1478

GRUPS DE RECERIA I ACTUACIO SOBRE MINORIES CULTURALS I TREBALLADORS ESTRANGERS (GRAMC) ♦ GROUPES DE RECHERCHE ET D'ACTION SUR LES MINORITES CULTURELLES ET TRAVAILLEURS ETRANGERS

Plaça Luis Companys, 12, 17003 Girona, Espagne.

Téléphone: 34 (72) 21 96 00. *Fax:* 34 (72) 21 37 17 . *Courrier électronique:* (19) 3472. *Contact:* Josep Ma Terricabras, Président.

OBJECTIFS: Promouvoir la solidarité, l'hospitalité et le respect mutuel tant pour la majorité de la population que pour les minorités culturelles vivant en Espagne. Former des moniteurs et agents sociaux au sein des minorités culturelles. Sensibiliser sur les problèmes réels de l'immigration et lutter contre l'exclusion, le racisme, la discrimination et la xénophobie.

INFORMATIONS GENERALES: *Création:* 1989. *Personnel/Total:* 304. *Salariés:* 4. *Bénévoles:* 300. *Budget/Total 1993:* ECU 39000 (US$ 51000). *Sources financières:* Privé: 15%. Public: 80%. Autofinancement: 5%.

PUBLICATIONS: *Périodiques:* Bulletin GRAMC (4). *Rapport annuel. Liste des publications.*

EVALUATION/RECHERCHE: Rapports d'évaluation disponibles. Entreprend des activités de recherche.

COMMENTAIRES: L'organisation est en train de renseigner et de conseiller des associations d'immigrés du Sénégal et de la Gambie, afin qu'elles puissent former et constituer des associations de développement dans leur pays d'origine.

ACTIVITES D'INFORMATION ET D'EDUCATION: Domaines: Culture/tradition/religion; Droits de l'Homme/paix/conflits; Enfants/jeunesse/famille; Racisme/xénophobie/antisémitisme; Relations internationales/coopération/aide au développement; Réfugiés/migrants/groupes ethniques; Santé/assainissement/eau. **Activités:** Campagnes d'information/expositions; Conférences/séminaires/ateliers/activités de formation; Radiodiffusion/manifestations culturelles; Services d'information et de documentation/bases de données; Édition/documents audiovisuels/documents éducatifs.

ESP1479

HEGOA CENTRO DE DOCUMENTACION E INVESTIGACIONES SOBRE PAISES EN DESARROLLO (HEGOA) ♦ Centre de documentation et de recherche sur les pays en développement

Avda. Lehendakari Aguirre 83, 48015 Bilbao, Espagne.

Téléphone: 34 (4) 447 35 12. *Fax:* 34 (4) 476 26 53. *Courrier électronique:* GEO2HEGOA y GreenNet HEGOA. *Contact:* Alfonso Dubois, Directeur.

OBJECTIFS: Diffuser des informations sur le développement et les relations Nord-Sud. Encourager la coopération au développement, à travers un travail d'étude et de recherche.

INFORMATIONS GENERALES: *Création:* 1987. *Type d'organisation:* collectif. *Affiliée à:* WIDE (Belgique) – EADI (Suisse) – ASERCCA (Pays-Bas) – Red Europea de Documentación e Información sobre America Latina – Concertación para las Relaciones entre Europa y America Latina – Society for International Development – Coordinadora de ONG's del Pais Vasco – Coordinadora Estatal de ONGD. *Personnel/Total:* 20. *Salariés:* 8. *Bénévoles:* 12. *Budget/Total 1993:* ECU 527000 (US$ 684000). *Sources financières:* Privé: 25%. Public: 55%. Autofinancement: 20%.

PUBLICATIONS: *Périodiques:* Working Papers (4) – Monographiques (2). *Rapport annuel. Liste des publications.*

EVALUATION/RECHERCHE: Entreprend des activités de recherche.

ACTIVITES D'INFORMATION ET D'EDUCATION: Domaines: Aliments/famine; Culture/tradition/religion; Droits de l'Homme/paix/conflits; Développement rural/agriculture; Enfants/jeunesse/famille; Paix/conflits ethniques/armement/désarmement; Pauvreté/conditions de vie; Population/planning familial/démographie; Questions relatives aux femmes; Racisme/xénophobie/antisémitisme; Relations internationales/coopération/aide au développement; Relations économiques internationales/commerce/dette/finances; Réfugiés/migrants/groupes ethniques; Santé/assainissement/eau; Secours d'urgence/réfugiés/aide humanitaire; Écologie/environnement/biodiversité; Éducation/formation/alphabétisation. **Activités:** Conférences/séminaires/ateliers/activités de formation; Lobbying/plaidoyer; Radiodiffusion/manifestations culturelles; Réseaux/télécommunications électroniques; Services d'information et de documentation/bases de données; Édition/documents audiovisuels/documents éducatifs; Éducation formelle.

ESP1480

HERMANDADES DEL TRABAJO

Presidente Juan de Austria 6, 28010 Madrid, Espagne.

Téléphone: 34 (91) 447 30 00 ext. 269. *Fax:* 34 (91) 446 42 92. *Contact:* Piedad Lopez.

ESP1481

INSTITUTO DE ESTUDIOS POLITICOS PARA AMERICA LATINA Y AFRICA (IEPALA) ♦ Institute of Political Studies on Latin America and Africa

Hermanos Garcia Noblejas, 41 - Piso 8, P.O. Box 35154, 28037 Madrid, Spain.

Telephone: 34 (91) 408 41 12. *Fax:* 34 (91) 408 70 47. *Contact:* Carmelo Garcia, Secretary General.

ESP1482

INSTITUTO INTERCULTURAL PARA LA AUTOGESTION Y LA ACCION COMUNAL (FLAPE-INAUCO) ♦ Institut interculturel pour l'autogestion et l'action commune

Facultad de Derecho-U.A.M., Ciudad Universitaria de Cantoblanco, 28049 Madrid, Espagne.

Téléphone: 34 (91) 397 50 00. *Fax:* 34 (91) 397 41 23. *Contact:* Antonio Colomer Viodel, Directeur.

OBJECTIFS: Former des cadres capables de gérer des projets d'autogestion dans les pays en développement, en les dotant d'une solide base technique en économie sociale et développement alternatif.

INFORMATIONS GENERALES: *Création:* 1978. *Affiliée à:* Coordinadora de ONG para el Desarrollo (Espagne). *Personnel/Total:* 15.

PUBLICATIONS: *Périodiques:* Revista Iberoamericana de Autogestión y Acción Comunal (2).

ACTIVITES D'INFORMATION ET D'EDUCATION: Domaines: Développement rural/agriculture; Développement urbain/habitat; Emploi/chômage; Population/planning familial/démographie; Questions relatives aux femmes; Relations internationales/coopération/aide au développement; Relations économiques internationales/commerce/dette/finances; Écologie/environnement/biodiversité. **Activités:** Conférences/séminaires/ateliers/activités de formation; Services d'information et de documentation/bases de données; Éducation formelle.

ESP1483

INSTITUTO PARA LA PROMOCION Y APOYO AL DESARROLLO (IPADE)

Plaza Espana, 10, 5° izq., 28008 Madrid, Espagne.

Téléphone: 34 (91) 541 56 77. *Fax:* 34 (91) 541 41 84. *Contact:* Isidoro Vicente.

ESP1484

INSTITUTO SINDICAL DE COOPERACION AL DESARROLLO (ISCOD) ♦ TRADE UNION INSTITUTE OF CO-OPERATION FOR DEVELOPMENT

San Bernardo, 20-5° , 28015 Madrid, Spain.

See: *How to Use the Directory,* page 11.

Telephone: 34 (1) 522 31 55. *Fax:* 34 (1) 532 93 79. *Contact:* Maite Nuñez Gascon, Director.

OBJECTIVES: To develop the cultural, social and economic level of workers. To strengthen the trade union movement.

GENERAL INFORMATION: *Creation:* 1990. *Personnel/Total:* 16. *Salaried:* 4. *Volunteers:* 12. *Budget/Total 1993:* ECU 703000 (US$ 912000). *Financial sources:* Private: 20%. Public: 75%. Self-financing: 5%.

PUBLICATIONS: *Periodicals:* Informacion ISCOD (2). *Annual report.*

EVALUATION/RESEARCH: Evaluation reports available.

PLANNED ACTIVITIES: Organising training courses for trade union leaders. Preparing educational materials for campaigns on co-operation for development.

COMMENTS: Undertakes activities in the Commonwealth of Independent States.

ACTIVITIES IN DEVELOPING REGIONS: Works through local field partners. **Sustainable Development Actions:** Ecology/environment/ biodiversity; Education/training/literacy; Gender issues/women; Health/ sanitation/water; Rural development/agriculture; Small enterprises/informal sector/handicrafts. **Regions:** Caribbean; Mexico and Central America; South America.

INFORMATION AND EDUCATION ACTIVITIES: Topics: Human rights/ peace/conflicts. **Activities:** Conferences/seminars/workshops/training activities.

ESP1485
INTER-ACCION

Ríos Rosas 30, 4° D, 28003 Madrid, Spain.

Telephone: 34 (91) 442 85 42. *Fax:* 34 (91) 442 85 42. *Contact:* Ana Vera.

OBJECTIVES: To investigate and research autochthonous materials, building techniques and mixed systems for conservation and restoration of artistic and social heritage as well as contemporary housing, bioclimatic architecture and low cost housing for developing countries.

GENERAL INFORMATION: *Affiliated to:* Coordinadora española de ONGs para el Desarrollo (Spain) - ICOMOS - CYTED. *Budget/ Total 1993:* ECU 59000 (US$ 77000). *Financial sources:* Private: 3%. Public: 80%.

PUBLICATIONS: *Annual report. List of publications.*

ACTIVITIES IN DEVELOPING REGIONS: Present in developing regions. Active in 2 country(ies). Works through local field partners. **Sustainable Development Actions:** Ecology/environment/biodiversity; Education/ training/literacy; Energy/transport; Health/sanitation/water; Sending volunteers/experts/technical assistance; Urban development/habitat. **Regions:** Mexico and Central America; South America.

INFORMATION AND EDUCATION ACTIVITIES: Topics: Ecology/environment/biodiversity; International relations/cooperation/development aid; Rural development/agriculture; Urban development/habitat. **Activities:** Conferences/seminars/workshops/training activities; Information campaigns/exhibitions; Publishing/audiovisual materials/educational materials.

ESP1486
INTERMON

Roger de Llúria 15, 08010 Barcelona, Espagne.

Téléphone: 34 (3) 482 07 00. *Fax:* 34 (3) 482 07 07. *Contact:* Ignasi Carreras, Directeur général.

OBJECTIFS: Sensibiliser la population espagnole à la solidarité avec les pays les plus pauvres. Promouvoir la coopération technique et financière avec les ONG du Sud. Appuyer l'éducation aux problèmes de développement.

INFORMATIONS GENERALES: *Création:* 1956. *Type d'organisation:* collectif. *Affiliée à:* EUROSTEP (Belgique). *Personnel/Total:* 305. *Salariés:* 95 dont: 17 dans les pays en développement. *Bénévoles:* 210. *Budget/Total 1993:* ECU 20602000 (US$ 26717000). *Sources financières:* Privé: 54%. Public: 41%. Autofinancement: 5%.

PUBLICATIONS: *Périodiques:* Boletin Intermon (6). *Rapport annuel. Liste des publications.*

EVALUATION/RECHERCHE: Rapports d'évaluation disponibles. Entreprend des activités de recherche.

PREVISIONS D'ACTIVITES: Organisation d'une campagne sur l'Afrique subsaharienne.

ACTIVITES DANS LES REGIONS EN DEVELOPPEMENT: Intervient dans 30 pays. Maintient une présence locale sur le terrain. Intervient par l'intermédiaire d'organisations locales partenaires. **Actions de Développement durable:** Aliments/famine; Droits de l'Homme/paix/ conflits; Démocratie/bonne gestion publique/création d'institutions/développement participatif; Développement rural/agriculture; Développement urbain/habitat; Enfants/jeunesse/famille; Envoi de volontaires/experts/ assistance technique; Petites entreprises/secteur informel/artisanat; Questions relatives aux femmes; Santé/assainissement/eau; Secours d'urgence/réfugiés/aide humanitaire; Écologie/environnement/biodiversité; Éducation/formation/alphabétisation. **Régions:** Afrique australe; Afrique centrale; Afrique de l'Est; Afrique de l'Ouest; Afrique du Nord; Amérique du Sud; Asie centrale et Asie du Sud; Caraïbes; Mexique et Amerique centrale.

ACTIVITES D'INFORMATION ET D'EDUCATION: Domaines: Aliments/ famine; Autres; Culture/tradition/religion; Droits de l'Homme/paix/ conflits; Développement rural/agriculture; Développement urbain/habitat; Emploi/chômage; Enfants/jeunesse/famille; Paix/conflits ethniques/ armement/désarmement; Pauvreté/conditions de vie; Population/planning familial/démographie; Questions relatives aux femmes; Racisme/ xénophobie/antisémitisme; Relations internationales/coopération/aide au développement; Relations économiques internationales/commerce/ dette/finances; Réfugiés/migrants/groupes ethniques; Santé/assainissement/eau; Secours d'urgence/réfugiés/aide humanitaire; Écologie/environnement/biodiversité; Éducation/formation/alphabétisation. **Activités:** Campagnes d'information/expositions; Collecte de fonds; Conférences/ séminaires/ateliers/activités de formation; Lobbying/plaidoyer; Radiodiffusion/manifestations culturelles; Réseaux/télécommunications électroniques; Services d'information et de documentation/bases de données; Échanges/parrainage/jumelage; Édition/documents audiovisuels/documents éducatifs; Éducation formelle.

ESP1487
INTERNATIONAL RESCUE COMMITTEE

Luchana No. 36, 4 Piso, Buzon 11, 28010 Madrid, Spain.

Contact: Margaret Hussman, Director.

ESP1488
JOVENES DEL TERCER MUNDO (JTM) ♦ Third World Youth

Lisboa 6, 28008 Madrid, Spain.

Telephone: 34 (1) 544 76 20. *Fax:* 34 (1) 549 83 34. *Contact:* Enrique Sanchez Beltran, President.

OBJECTIVES: To provide financial, technical and material resources to development projects in developing countries, especially those focused on children. To provide volunteers for such projects and raise awareness in Spain about development issues.

GENERAL INFORMATION: *Creation:* 1988. *Type of organisation:* association of NGOs. *Affiliated to:* Cordinadora Nacional de ONGs Españolas (Spain) - Comite de Enlace de ONGs Europeas. *Personnel/ Total:* 73. *Salaried:* 3. *Volunteers:* 70 of which: 15 in developing countries. *Budget/Total 1993:* ECU 808000 (US$ 1048000). *Financial sources:* Private: 35%. Public: 50%. Self-financing: 15%.

PUBLICATIONS: *Periodicals:* Jovenes Tercer Mundo Boletin Informativo (6). *Annual report. List of publications.*

EVALUATION/RESEARCH: Evaluation reports available.

PLANNED ACTIVITIES: Holding an international volunteer meeting and a summer workshop for volunteers.

ACTIVITIES IN DEVELOPING REGIONS: Present in developing regions. Active in 12 country(ies). Maintains local field presence. Works through local field partners. **Sustainable Development Actions:** Children/ youth/family; Ecology/environment/biodiversity; Education/training/literacy; Energy/transport; Food/famine; Health/sanitation/water; Rural development/agriculture; Sending volunteers/experts/technical assis-

Voir : *Comment utiliser le répertoire,* page 11.

tance; Urban development/habitat. **Regions:** Caribbean; Mexico and Central America; South America; West Africa.

INFORMATION AND EDUCATION ACTIVITIES: Topics: Children/youth/family; Education/training/literacy; Food/famine; Health/sanitation/water; Poverty/living conditions; Rural development/agriculture. **Activities:** Conferences/seminars/workshops/training activities; Information campaigns/exhibitions; Publishing/audiovisual materials/educational materials.

ESP1489

JUSTICIA I PAU ♦ Justice et Paix

Rivadeneyra 6, 10e, 08002 Barcelona, Espagne.

Téléphone: 34 (3) 317 61 77. **Fax:** 34 (3) 412 83 54. **Contact:** Joan Gomis, Président.

OBJECTIFS: Promouvoir et défendre les droits de l'homme, en priorité dans le cadre des relations nord-sud. Exercer des pressions sur les pouvoirs publics, dans une inspiration chrétienne.

INFORMATIONS GENERALES: Création: 1968. **Affiliée à:** Fédération Catalane d'ONGD (Espagne). **Personnel/Total:** 58. Salariés: 4. Bénévoles: 54. **Budget/Total 1993:** ECU 139000 (US$ 181000). **Sources financières:** Privé: 20%. Public: 40%. Autofinancement: 40%.

PUBLICATIONS: Périodiques: Justicia i Pau (4) - Papers (6).

EVALUATION/RECHERCHE: Rapports d'évaluation disponibles.

ACTIVITES DANS LES REGIONS EN DEVELOPPEMENT: Intervient directement dans les régions en développement. Intervient dans 10 pays. Intervient par l'intermédiaire d'organisations locales partenaires. **Actions de Développement durable:** Droits de l'Homme/paix/conflits; Éducation/formation/alphabétisation. **Régions:** Afrique centrale; Afrique de l'Est; Amérique du Sud; Asie centrale et Asie du Sud; Asie du Sud-Est; Caraïbes; Mexique et Amerique centrale.

ESP1490

JUSTICIA Y PAZ ♦ Justice et Paix

Francisco Silvela 77 bis, 1° D., 28028 Madrid, Espagne.

Telephone: 34 (91) 561 12 14. **Fax:** 34 (91) 561 12 14. **Contact:** Javier Anso, Secrétaire Général.

OBJECTIVES: Promouvoir l'éducation au développement et la solidarité Nord-Sud. Défendre les droits humains.

GENERAL INFORMATION: Creation: 1968. **Personnel/Total:** 103. Salaried: 3. Volunteers: 100. **Budget/Total 1993:** ECU 303000 (US$ 393000). **Financial sources:** Private: 30%. Public: 10%. Self-financing: 60%.

PUBLICATIONS: Periodicals: Bulletin Justice et Paix (6). List of publications.

ACTIVITIES IN DEVELOPING REGIONS: Active in 2 country(ies). Works through local field partners. **Actions de Développement durable:** Droits de l'Homme/paix/conflits. **Régions:** Afrique australe; Afrique centrale; Afrique de l'Est; Afrique de l'Ouest; Afrique du Nord; Amérique du Sud; Asie centrale et Asie du Sud; Asie de l'Est; Asie du Sud-Est; Caraïbes; Mexique et Amerique centrale; Moyen-Orient; Océanie.

ACTIVITES D'INFORMATION ET D'EDUCATION: Domaines: Droits de l'Homme/paix/conflits; Emploi/chômage; Paix/conflits ethniques/armement/désarmement; Pauvreté/conditions de vie; Racisme/xénophobie/antisémitisme; Relations internationales/coopération/aide au développement; Relations économiques internationales/commerce/dette/finances; Réfugiés/migrants/groupes ethniques; Écologie/environnement/biodiversité. **Activités:** Campagnes d'information/expositions; Conférences/séminaires/ateliers/activités de formation; Lobbying/plaidoyer; Radiodiffusion/manifestations culturelles; Services d'information et de documentation/bases de données; Édition/documents audiovisuels/documents éducatifs; Éducation formelle.

ESP1491

MADRESELVA

María Auxiliadora 9, 28040 Madrid, Spain.

Telephone: 34 (1) 450 04 72. **Fax:** 34 (1) 450 04 19. **Contact:** Pilar Andrés.

OBJECTIVES: To carry out social and development programmes and sanitary projects in developing countries.

GENERAL INFORMATION: Creation: 1984. **Affiliated to:** Coordinadora de ONGs para Desarrollo (Spain) - VIDES (Italy). **Personnel/Total:** 24. Volunteers: 23. **Budget/Total 1993:** ECU 496000 (US$ 643000). **Financial sources:** Private: 21%. Public: 73%. Self-financing: 6%.

EVALUATION/RESEARCH: Evaluation reports available.

ACTIVITIES IN DEVELOPING REGIONS: Present in developing regions. Maintains local field presence. Works through local field partners. **Sustainable Development Actions:** Children/youth/family; Education/training/literacy; Food/famine; Gender issues/women; Health/sanitation/water; Sending volunteers/experts/technical assistance. **Regions:** Caribbean; Central Africa; Central Asia and South Asia; East Africa; Mexico and Central America; North Africa; South America; Southern Africa; West Africa.

INFORMATION AND EDUCATION ACTIVITIES: Topics: Children/youth/family; Culture/tradition/religion; Education/training/literacy; Emergency relief/refugees/humanitarian assistance; Gender issues/women; Health/sanitation/water; Poverty/living conditions; Refugees/migrants/ethnic groups. **Activities:** Conferences/seminars/workshops/training activities; Fund raising; Information campaigns/exhibitions; Publishing/audiovisual materials/educational materials.

ESP1492

MANOS UNIDAS - COMITE CATOLICO DE LA CAMPANA CONTRA EL HAMBRE ♦ Joint Hands - Catholic Committee of the Campaign Against Hunger

Barquillo 38, 2° , 28004 Madrid, Spain.

Telephone: 34 (91) 308 20 20. **Fax:** 34 (91) 308 42 08. **Contact:** Ana de Felipe, President.

OBJECTIVES: To raise awareness about the realities of developing countries. To finance projects for the improvement of living conditions and support self-sufficiency in those regions.

GENERAL INFORMATION: Creation: 1960. **Affiliated to:** Coordinadora Española de ONGD (Spain) - CIDSE y Cor Unum. **Personnel/Total:** 10040. Salaried: 40. Volunteers: 10000. **Budget/Total 1993:** ECU 33768000 (US$ 43790000). **Financial sources:** Public: 14%. Self-financing: 86%.

PUBLICATIONS: Periodicals: Boletin (5). Annual report. List of publications.

EVALUATION/RESEARCH: Evaluation reports available. Undertakes research activities.

PLANNED ACTIVITIES: To hold an educational programme on equality in 1995-6, and an educational programme on health in 1996-7.

ACTIVITIES IN DEVELOPING REGIONS: Active in 58 country(ies). Works through local field partners. **Sustainable Development Actions:** Children/youth/family; Ecology/environment/biodiversity; Education/training/literacy; Energy/transport; Gender issues/women; Health/sanitation/water; Rural development/agriculture; Small enterprises/informal sector/handicrafts; Urban development/habitat. **Regions:** Caribbean; Central Africa; Central Asia and South Asia; East Africa; East Asia; Mexico and Central America; North Africa; Oceania; South America; South East Asia; West Africa.

INFORMATION AND EDUCATION ACTIVITIES: Topics: Ecology/environment/biodiversity; Health/sanitation/water; Racism/xenophobia/antisemitism. **Activities:** Formal education.

ESP1493

MEDICOS SIN FRONTERAS (MSF) ♦ Médecins sans frontières

Nou de la Rambla, 26, 08001 Barcelona, Espagne.

Téléphone: 34 (93) 302 61 00. **Fax:** 34 (93) 302 61 02. **Contact:** Dr. Pilar Carrasco Rodriguez, Président.

OBJECTIFS: Apporter de l'aide aux pays en développement en situation d'urgence en cas de catastrophe d'origine naturelle et humaine. Appuyer la réhabilitation et l'organisation des services sanitaires.

See: *How to Use the Directory*, page 11.

INFORMATIONS GENERALES: *Création:* 1986. *Personnel/Total:* 117. *Salariés:* 57. *Bénévoles:* 60 dont: 140 dans les pays en développement. *Budget/Total 1993:* ECU 27874000 (US$ 36146000). *Sources financières:* Privé: 51%. *Public:* 48%. *Autofinancement:* 1%.

PUBLICATIONS: *Périodiques:* Revue MSF (3). *Rapport annuel. Liste des publications.*

EVALUATION/RECHERCHE: Rapports d'évaluation disponibles. Entreprend des activités de recherche.

COMMENTAIRES: Intervient dans la Communauté des Etats indépendants.

ACTIVITES DANS LES REGIONS EN DEVELOPPEMENT: Intervient directement dans les régions en développement. Intervient dans 16 pays. Maintient une présence locale sur le terrain. Intervient par l'intermédiaire d'organisations locales partenaires. **Actions de Développement durable:** Aliments/famine; Droits de l'Homme/paix/conflits; Envoi de volontaires/experts/assistance technique; Population/planning familial/démographie; Santé/assainissement/eau; Secours d'urgence/réfugiés/aide humanitaire. **Régions:** Afrique australe; Afrique centrale; Afrique de l'Est; Afrique de l'Ouest; Afrique du Nord; Amérique du Sud; Mexique et Amerique centrale.

ACTIVITES D'INFORMATION ET D'EDUCATION: Domaines: Aliments/famine; Droits de l'Homme/paix/conflits; Paix/conflits ethniques/armement/désarmement; Pauvreté/conditions de vie; Racisme/xénophobie/antisémitisme; Relations internationales/coopération/aide au développement; Réfugiés/migrants/groupes ethniques; Secours d'urgence/réfugiés/aide humanitaire. **Activités:** Campagnes d'information/expositions; Conférences/séminaires/ateliers/activités de formation; Services d'information et de documentation/bases de données.

ESP1494
MEDICUS MUNDI, CATALOGNE

Elisa 14, 08023 Barcelona, Espagne.

Téléphone: 34 (3) 418 47 62. *Fax:* 34 (3) 418 48 66. *Contact:* Dr. Alfons Sancho, Président.

ESP1495
MEDICUS MUNDI, ESPANA

c/ Juan de Urbieta, 5 esc. dcha 1° B, 28007 Madrid, Spain.

Telephone: 34 (91) 552 54 38. *Fax:* 34 (91) 552 01 59. *Contact:* Rapael Rodriguez-Contreras Pelayo, President.

OBJECTIVES: To promote and organise the technical management of development projects. To train local personnel in developing countries. To educate the industrialised world about the health and social problems of countries in the developing world.

GENERAL INFORMATION: *Creation:* 1963. *Type of organisation:* network. *Member organisations:* 17. *Affiliated to:* Coordinadora ONGD Española - Medicus Mundi Internacional. *Personnel/Total:* 203. *Salaried:* 53 of which: 20 in developing countries. *Volunteers:* 150. *Budget/Total 1993:* ECU 5613000 (US$ 7279000). *Financial sources:* Public: 53%. Self-financing: 47%.

PUBLICATIONS: *Periodicals:* Boletin Medicus Mundi (4). *Annual report. List of publications.*

EVALUATION/RESEARCH: Evaluation reports available. Undertakes research activities.

PLANNED ACTIVITIES: Medicus Mundi plans to expand its contacts with the developing world through an interactive exposition with games, videos, music, computers etc.

ACTIVITIES IN DEVELOPING REGIONS: Present in developing regions. Active in 18 country(ies). Maintains local field presence. Works through local field partners. **Sustainable Development Actions:** Health/sanitation/water; **Regions:** Central Africa; Mexico and Central America; North Africa; South America; Southern Africa; West Africa.

INFORMATION AND EDUCATION ACTIVITIES: Topics: Health/sanitation/water. **Activities:** Conferences/seminars/workshops/training activities; Exchanges/twinning/linking; Formal education; Fund raising; Information and documentation services/data bases; Information campaigns/exhibitions; Publishing/audiovisual materials/educational materials.

ESP1496
MISION AMERICA

Colegio Vasco de Quiroga, Camino de las Moreras s/n., 28040 Madrid, Espagne.

Téléphone: 34 (91) 549 88 96. *Contact:* Juan Quesada Aguilera, Directeur.

OBJECTIFS: Soutenir, promouvoir et financer des projets de développement destinés aux pays d'Amérique centrale et du sud.

INFORMATIONS GENERALES: *Création:* 1993. *Personnel/Total:* var.. *Salariés:* 1. *Bénévoles:* var..

PUBLICATIONS: *Périodiques:* Carta de casa (12).

ACTIVITES DANS LES REGIONS EN DEVELOPPEMENT: Intervient directement dans les régions en développement. Intervient dans 18 pays. Maintient une présence locale sur le terrain. **Actions de Développement durable:** Enfants/jeunesse/famille; Envoi de volontaires/experts/assistance technique; Santé/assainissement/eau; Éducation/formation/alphabétisation. **Régions:** Amérique du Sud; Caraïbes; Mexique et Amerique centrale.

ESP1497
MOVIMIENTO 0.7

Rocafort 244, 1° 1a, 08029 Barcelona, Espagne.

Téléphone: 34 (93) 322 15 80. *Fax:* 34 (93) 439 46 16. *Contact:* Luis Garcia Ramos.

ESP1498
MOVIMIENTO POR LA PAZ, EL DESARME Y LA LIBERTAD (MPDL)

Santa Catalina 8, 2§, 28014 Madrid, Espagne.

Téléphone: 34 (91) 429 76 44. *Fax:* 34 (91) 429 73 73. *Contact:* Esteban Tomás.

ESP1499
NOUS CAMINS ♦ New Paths

Clot 97, 08018 Barcelona, Spain.

Telephone: 34 (93) 231 07 12. *Fax:* 34 (93) 447 23 50. *Contact:* Ma Angels Fornaguera.

ESP1500
OBRA COOPERACION APOSTOLICA SEGLAR HISPA-NOAMERICANA (OCASHA) ♦ Apostolic and Lay Co-operative Action in Latin America

José Marañon 3, 28010 Madrid, Spain.

Telephone: 34 (91) 445 40 22. *Fax:* 34 (91) 594 26 65. *Contact:* Angeles Vlios Blanco.

ESP1501
OBRA DE COOPERACION SACERDOTAL HISPANO AMERI-CANA (OCSHA) ♦ Oeuvre de coopération sacerdotale avec l'Amérique latine

c/ Añastro 1, B.P. 29075, 28033 Madrid, Espagne.

Téléphone: 34 (1) 766 55 00. *Fax:* 34 (1) 766 79 81. *Contact:* D. Jose Luis Irizar Artiach.

ESP1502
ONG PARA LA PROMOCION DE LA SALUD EN PAISES EN DESARROLLO (PROSALUS)

María Panes 4, 28003 Madrid, Spain.

Telephone: 34 (91) 553 35 91. *Fax:* 34 (91) 535 06 65. *Contact:* Mercedes Alonso, Director.

Voir : *Comment utiliser le répertoire,* page 11.

OBJECTIVES: To promote health in developing countries through the provision of medical and technical personnel, health supplies and equipment. To support hospitals and health centres in developing countries.

GENERAL INFORMATION: *Creation:* 1985. *Affiliated to:* Coordinadora de ONG para el Desarrollo (Spain) - EuronAid (the Netherlands) -Union Internationale d'Education pour la Santé (France). *Personnel/Total:* 45. *Salaried:* 5 of which: 1 in developing countries. *Volunteers:* 40 of which: 4 in developing countries. *Budget/Total 1993:* ECU 87000 (US$ 113000). *Financial sources:* Private: 20%. Public: 75%. Self-financing: 5%.

PUBLICATIONS: *Periodicals:* Prosalus Informativo (4) - Amigos de Prosalus (12). *Annual report.*

ACTIVITIES IN DEVELOPING REGIONS: Present in developing regions. Active in 8 country(ies). Maintains local field presence. Works through local field partners. **Sustainable Development Actions:** Children/ youth/family; Education/training/literacy; Food/famine; Gender issues/ women; Health/sanitation/water; Population/family planning/demography; Rural development/agriculture; Sending volunteers/experts/technical assistance; Urban development/habitat. **Regions:** South America; Southern Africa; West Africa.

INFORMATION AND EDUCATION ACTIVITIES: Topics: Children/youth/ family; Culture/tradition/religion; Food/famine; Health/sanitation/water; Population/family planning/demography; Poverty/living conditions. **Activities:** Conferences/seminars/workshops/training activities; Formal education; Fund raising; Information and documentation services/data bases; Information campaigns/exhibitions; Lobbying/advocacy.

ESP1503

ORGANIZACION DE COOPERACION Y SOLIDARIDAD INTERNACIONAL (OCSI/AMS) ♦ Organisation de coopération et de solidarité internationales

Ercilla 48, 1° b, 28005 Madrid, Espagne.

Téléphone: 34 (91) 474 57 02. *Fax:* 34 (91) 474 57 02. *Contact:* Santiago Matute.

OBJECTIFS: Promouvoir la coopération et la solidarité avec les peuples défavorisés en encourageant le volontariat. Sensibiliser le publique aux problèmes de développement. Collecter des fonds pour réaliser des projets de développement.

INFORMATIONS GENERALES: *Création:* 1947. *Affiliée à:* Coordinadora de ONGs para el Desarrollo en España (Espagne). *Sources financières:* Autofinancement: 100%.

PUBLICATIONS: *Périodiques:* Hoja Informativa OCIS/AMS (2). *Liste des publications.*

ACTIVITES DANS LES REGIONS EN DEVELOPPEMENT: Intervient directement dans les régions en développement. Intervient dans 5 pays. Maintient une présence locale sur le terrain. Intervient par l'intermédiaire d'organisations locales partenaires. **Actions de Développement durable:** Droits de l'Homme/paix/conflits; Développement rural/agriculture; Envoi de volontaires/experts/assistance technique; Questions relatives aux femmes; Santé/assainissement/eau; Éducation/formation/alphabétisation. **Régions:** Amérique du Sud; Mexique et Amerique centrale.

ACTIVITES D'INFORMATION ET D'EDUCATION: Domaines: Droits de l'Homme/paix/conflits; Pauvreté/conditions de vie; Racisme/xénophobie/ antisémitisme; Réfugiés/migrants/groupes ethniques. **Activités:** Campagnes d'information/expositions; Édition/documents audiovisuels/documents éducatifs.

ESP1504
PAS

C/Pacerro 5, 28004 Madrid, Spain.

Contact: Frederica Carraro.

ESP1505

PAZ Y COOPERACION ♦ Peace and Co-operation

Meléndez Valdés 68, 4° , 28015 Madrid, Spain.

Telephone: 34 (1) 543 52 82. *Fax:* 34 (1) 543 52 82. *Contact:* Joaquín Antuña.

OBJECTIVES: To promote disarmament, human rights and sustainable development through peace and development education, and to undertake development projects in developing countries.

GENERAL INFORMATION: *Creation:* 1982. *Affiliated to:* Coordinadora de ONG para el Desarrollo (Spain) - Federacion de Asociaciones de Defensa y Promoción de los Derechos Humanos (Spain) - Spanish Committee of NGOs on the Palestinian Question (Spain) - International Peace Bureau (Switzerland) - FMJV (France) - World Future Studies Federation (USA). *Personnel/Total:* 228. *Salaried:* 8 of which: 4 in developing countries. *Volunteers:* 220 of which: 2 in developing countries. *Budget/Total 1993:* ECU 321000 (US$ 416000). *Financial sources:* Private: 20%. Public: 60%. Self-financing: 20%.

PUBLICATIONS: *Periodicals:* Premio Escolar Paz y Cooperacion (2). *Annual report. List of publications.*

EVALUATION/RESEARCH: Evaluation reports available.

PLANNED ACTIVITIES: Holding a world campaign for street children in 1996.

ACTIVITIES IN DEVELOPING REGIONS: Present in developing regions. Maintains local field presence. Works through local field partners. **Sustainable Development Actions:** Children/youth/family; Education/training/literacy; Gender issues/women; Health/sanitation/water; Human rights/peace/conflicts; Rural development/agriculture; Sending volunteers/experts/technical assistance; Urban development/habitat. **Regions:** Mexico and Central America; North Africa; South America.

INFORMATION AND EDUCATION ACTIVITIES: Topics: Children/youth/ family; Education/training/literacy; Health/sanitation/water; Human rights/peace/conflicts; International relations/cooperation/development aid; Peace/ethnic conflicts/armament/disarmament; Racism/xenophobia/antisemitism; Refugees/migrants/ethnic groups; Rural development/ agriculture. **Activities:** Conferences/seminars/workshops/training activities; Fund raising; Information campaigns/exhibitions; Lobbying/advocacy; Publishing/audiovisual materials/educational materials.

ESP1506

PAZ Y TERCER MUNDO (PTM) ♦ Peace and Third World

Zumarraga 5, bajo dcha., 48006 Bilbao, Spain.

Telephone: 34 (4) 416 23 25. *Fax:* 34 (4) 415 26 76. *Contact:* Inaki Markiegi, Projects Coordinator.

OBJECTIVES: To undertake development projects in Central America. To sensitize the Spanish population to the problems of the developing world.

GENERAL INFORMATION: *Creation:* 1988. *Personnel/Total:* 42. *Salaried:* 17 of which: 11 in developing countries. *Volunteers:* 25 of which: 15 in developing countries. *Budget/Total 1993:* ECU 568000 (US$ 736000). *Financial sources:* Public: 73%. Self-financing: 27%.

PUBLICATIONS: *Periodicals:* Memory of Activities in the Year (1). *Annual report.*

EVALUATION/RESEARCH: Evaluation reports available. Undertakes research activities.

ACTIVITIES IN DEVELOPING REGIONS: Present in developing regions. Active in 4 country(ies). Maintains local field presence. Works through local field partners. **Sustainable Development Actions:** Children/ youth/family; Debt/finance/trade; Democracy/good governance/institution building/participatory development; Ecology/environment/biodiversity; Education/training/literacy; Emergency relief/refugees/humanitarian assistance; Energy/transport; Food/famine; Gender issues/women; Health/sanitation/water; Human rights/peace/conflicts; Rural development/agriculture; Sending volunteers/experts/technical assistance; Small enterprises/informal sector/handicrafts; Urban development/ habitat. **Regions:** Mexico and Central America.

INFORMATION AND EDUCATION ACTIVITIES: Topics: Children/youth/ family; Ecology/environment/biodiversity; Emergency relief/refugees/ humanitarian assistance; Food/famine; Gender issues/women; Health/ sanitation/water; Human rights/peace/conflicts; International economic relations/trade/debt/finance; International relations/cooperation/development aid; Peace/ethnic conflicts/armament/disarmament; Poverty/living conditions; Racism/xenophobia/antisemitism; Refugees/migrants/ethnic groups; Rural development/agriculture; Urban development/habitat.

See: *How to Use the Directory,* page 11.

Activities: Broadcasting/cultural events; Conferences/seminars/workshops/training activities; Formal education; Fund raising; Information and documentation services/data bases; Information campaigns/exhibitions; Lobbying/advocacy; Publishing/audiovisual materials/educational materials.

ESP1507
PERSONAS ♦ Personnes

Juan XXIII 4, 2° a, 10001 Caceres, Espagne.

Téléphone: 34 (927) 22 36 53. *Fax:* 34 (927) 22 36 53. *Contact:* José Ignacio Urquijo Valdivielso, Président.

OBJECTIFS: Promouvoir la coopération avec le Tiers monde en réalisant des projets de développement.

INFORMATIONS GENERALES: *Création:* 1990. *Affiliée à:* Coordinadora Española de ONGD (Espagne). *Personnel/Total:* 11. *Bénévoles:* 11 dont: 6 dans les pays en développement. *Budget/Total 1993:* ECU 14000 (US$ 18000). *Sources financières:* Privé: 70%. Public: 5%. *Autofinancement:* 25%.

PUBLICATIONS: *Périodiques:* Personas Informa (4) - Memoria Anual (1). *Rapport annuel. Liste des publications.*

EVALUATION/RECHERCHE: Rapports d'évaluation disponibles. Entreprend des activités de recherche.

ACTIVITES DANS LES REGIONS EN DEVELOPPEMENT: Intervient directement dans les régions en développement. Intervient dans 3 pays. Maintient une présence locale sur le terrain. Intervient par l'intermédiaire d'organisations locales partenaires. **Actions de Développement durable:** Développement rural/agriculture; Développement urbain/habitat; Enfants/jeunesse/famille; Envoi de volontaires/experts/assistance technique; Questions relatives aux femmes; Santé/assainissement/eau; Éducation/formation/alphabétisation. **Régions:** Afrique centrale; Afrique de l'Ouest; Amérique du Sud; Caraïbes.

ACTIVITES D'INFORMATION ET D'EDUCATION: Domaines: Culture/tradition/religion; Droits de l'Homme/paix/conflits; Développement rural/agriculture; Développement urbain/habitat; Enfants/jeunesse/famille; Pauvreté/conditions de vie; Racisme/xénophobie/antisémitisme; Relations économiques internationales/commerce/dette/finances; Réfugiés/migrants/groupes ethniques; Santé/assainissement/eau; Éducation/formation/alphabétisation. **Activités:** Campagnes d'information/expositions; Collecte de fonds; Conférences/séminaires/ateliers/activités de formation; Radiodiffusion/manifestations culturelles; Services d'information et de documentation/bases de données; Édition/documents audiovisuels/documents éducatifs.

ESP1508
PROMOCION CLARETIANA DE DESARROLLO (PROCLADE)

Clara del Rey 6, 28002 Madrid, Spain.

Telephone: 34 (91) 415 23 61. *Fax:* 34 (91) 519 62 87. *Contact:* Mikel Burgos.

OBJECTIVES: To promote and provide education for development projects. To send volunteers to developing countries.

GENERAL INFORMATION: *Creation:* 1987. *Type of organisation:* association of NGOs. *Personnel/Total:* 130. *Volunteers:* 130 of which: 120 in developing countries. *Financial sources:* Private: 65%. Public: 25%. Self-financing: 10%.

PUBLICATIONS: *Periodicals:* Claret Gaur (3) - En Familia (3).

ACTIVITIES IN DEVELOPING REGIONS: Present in developing regions. Active in 3 country(ies). Maintains local field presence. Works through local field partners. **Sustainable Development Actions:** Children/youth/family; Ecology/environment/biodiversity; Education/training/literacy; Emergency relief/refugees/humanitarian assistance; Energy/transport; Food/famine; Gender issues/women; Health/sanitation/water; Human rights/peace/conflicts; Rural development/agriculture; Sending volunteers/experts/technical assistance. **Regions:** East Asia; South America.

INFORMATION AND EDUCATION ACTIVITIES: Topics: Children/youth/family; Culture/tradition/religion; Ecology/environment/biodiversity; Health/sanitation/water; Human rights/peace/conflicts; International relations/cooperation/development aid; Peace/ethnic conflicts/armament/

disarmament; Poverty/living conditions; Racism/xenophobia/antisemitism; Rural development/agriculture. **Activities:** Conferences/seminars/workshops/training activities; Formal education; Fund raising; Information and documentation services/data bases; Information campaigns/exhibitions.

ESP1509
PROPAGE

c/o Estación Phoenix, Hort del Gat, 03203 Elche, Spain.

Telephone: 34 (65) 45 74 96. *Fax:* 34 (65) 42 37 06. *Contact:* Michel Ferry, President.

OBJECTIVES: To protect and promote arid land plant resources.

GENERAL INFORMATION: *Creation:* 1987. *Personnel/Total:* 12. Salaried: 2. Volunteers: 10 of which: 4 in developing countries. *Budget/Total 1993:* ECU 75000 (US$ 88000). *Financial sources:* Private: 10%. Public: 80%. Self-financing: 10%.

EVALUATION/RESEARCH: Evaluation reports available. Undertakes research activities.

ACTIVITIES IN DEVELOPING REGIONS: Present in developing regions. Active in 4 country(ies). Maintains local field presence. Works through local field partners. **Sustainable Development Actions:** Ecology/environment/biodiversity; Education/training/literacy; Rural development/agriculture. **Regions:** East Africa; Southern Africa.

INFORMATION AND EDUCATION ACTIVITIES: Topics: Ecology/environment/biodiversity; Rural development/agriculture. **Activities:** Conferences/seminars/workshops/training activities; Information and documentation services/data bases.

ESP1510
PROYDE - PROMOCION Y DESARROLLO

Marqués de Mondejar 32, 28028 Madrid, Espagne.

Téléphone: 34 (1) 356 06 07. *Fax:* 34 (1) 725 35 22. *Contact:* Pedro Arrambide, Vice Président.

OBJECTIFS: Réaliser des projets de développement dans les domaines de l'alphabétisation, l'agriculture, la femme et l'enfant ainsi que la santé.

INFORMATIONS GENERALES: *Création:* 1988. *Affiliée à:* Education et Développement (France) - Promozione e Sviluppo (Italie) - Promoció e Desenvolupament (Espagne). *Personnel/Total:* 179. *Bénévoles:* 179 dont: 51 dans les pays en développement. *Budget/Total 1993:* ECU 49000 (US$ 64000). *Sources financières:* Privé: 36%. Public: 55%. *Autofinancement:* 9%.

PUBLICATIONS: *Périodiques:* PROYDE (4).

EVALUATION/RECHERCHE: Entreprend des activités de recherche.

PREVISIONS D'ACTIVITES: Sensibilisation aux problèmes de développement en distribuant des calendriers avec des images et textes éducatifs.

COMMENTAIRES: Intervient dans la Communauté des Etats indépendants.

ACTIVITES DANS LES REGIONS EN DEVELOPPEMENT: Intervient directement dans les régions en développement. Intervient dans 12 pays. Maintient une présence locale sur le terrain. Intervient par l'intermédiaire d'organisations locales partenaires. **Actions de Développement durable:** Démocratie/bonne gestion publique/création d'institutions/développement participatif; Développement rural/agriculture; Enfants/jeunesse/famille; Envoi de volontaires/experts/assistance technique; Petites entreprises/secteur informel/artisanat; Questions relatives aux femmes; Santé/assainissement/eau; Secours d'urgence/réfugiés/aide humanitaire; Éducation/formation/alphabétisation. **Régions:** Afrique de l'Est; Afrique de l'Ouest; Amérique du Sud; Asie centrale et Asie du Sud; Asie de l'Est; Asie du Sud-Est; Mexique et Amerique centrale.

ACTIVITES D'INFORMATION ET D'EDUCATION: Domaines: Aliments/famine; Culture/tradition/religion; Développement rural/agriculture; Enfants/jeunesse/famille; Pauvreté/conditions de vie; Questions relatives aux femmes; Relations internationales/coopération/aide au développement; Santé/assainissement/eau; Secours d'urgence/réfugiés/aide humanitaire; Éducation/formation/alphabétisation. **Activités:** Campagnes d'information/expositions; Collecte de fonds; Conférences/séminaires/ateliers/activités de formation; Radiodiffusion/manifestations

Voir : *Comment utiliser le répertoire,* page 11.

culturelles; Édition/documents audiovisuels/documents éducatifs; Éducation formelle.

ESP1511

PROYECTO CULTURA Y SOLIDARIDAD ♦ Projet culture et solidarité

Sierpe 3, 3° d, 28005 Madrid, Espagne.

Téléphone: 34 (91) 364 08 05. ***Contact:*** Maria Angustias Aguilar.

OBJECTIFS: Sensibiliser l'opinion publique à la question des droits de l'homme et du développement. Soutenir les organisations qui travaillent pour la solidarité et la justice. Appuyer les programmes de coopération internationale.

INFORMATIONS GENERALES: *Création:* 1990. *Affiliée à:* Coordinadora Española de ONG de Desarrollo (Espagne). *Personnel/Total:* 15. *Bénévoles:* 15. *Budget/Total 1993:* ECU 69000 (US$ 89000). *Sources financières:* Privé: 41%. Public: 33%. Autofinancement: 26%.

PUBLICATIONS: *Rapport annuel. Liste des publications.*

EVALUATION/RECHERCHE: Rapports d'évaluation disponibles.

COMMENTAIRES: Intervient dans la Communauté des Etats indépendants. Activités d'information concernant la Communauté des Etats indépendants.

ACTIVITES DANS LES REGIONS EN DEVELOPPEMENT: Intervient par l'intermédiaire d'organisations locales partenaires. **Actions de Développement durable:** Autres; Droits de l'Homme/paix/conflits; Développement rural/agriculture; Enfants/jeunesse/famille; Éducation/formation/alphabétisation. **Régions:** Amérique du Sud; Mexique et Amerique centrale.

ACTIVITES D'INFORMATION ET D'EDUCATION: Domaines: Autres; Droits de l'Homme/paix/conflits; Paix/conflits ethniques/armement/désarmement; Pauvreté/conditions de vie; Racisme/xénophobie/antisémitisme; Relations internationales/coopération/aide au développement; Relations économiques internationales/commerce/dette/finances; Réfugiés/migrants/groupes ethniques; Écologie/environnement/biodiversité; Éducation/formation/alphabétisation. **Activités:** Campagnes d'information/expositions; Conférences/séminaires/ateliers/activités de formation; Services d'information et de documentation/bases de données.

ESP1512

PROYECTO LOCAL

124, bajos la, 08009 Barcelona, Espagne.

Téléphone: 34 (93) 457 38 30. ***Fax:*** 34 (93) 207 66 36. ***Contact:*** Fernando Barreiro Cavestany.

OBJECTIFS: Promouvoir des actions solidaires et de coopération avec des pays en voie de développement. Participer activement à des projets qui mettent en action le développement local dans les pays en voie de développement. Sensibiliser et divulguer la problématique des pays en voie de développement en Catalogne et en Espagne.

INFORMATIONS GENERALES: *Création:* 1989. *Personnel/Total:* 6. *Salariés:* 1. *Bénévoles:* 5. *Budget/Total 1993:* ECU 61000 (US$ 79000).

PUBLICATIONS: *Rapport annuel.*

COMMENTAIRES: Intervient dans la Communauté des Etats indépendants.

ACTIVITES DANS LES REGIONS EN DEVELOPPEMENT: Intervient directement dans les régions en développement. Intervient dans 2 pays. Intervient par l'intermédiaire d'organisations locales partenaires. **Actions de Développement durable:** Envoi de volontaires/experts/assistance technique; Petites entreprises/secteur informel/artisanat; Questions relatives aux femmes. **Régions:** Afrique du Nord; Amérique du Sud.

ACTIVITES D'INFORMATION ET D'EDUCATION: Domaines: Emploi/chômage; Racisme/xénophobie/antisémitisme; Réfugiés/migrants/groupes ethniques. **Activités:** Campagnes d'information/expositions; Conférences/séminaires/ateliers/activités de formation; Éducation formelle.

ESP1513

PUEBLOS HERMANOS ♦ Peuples frères

P° de las Delicias, 47 - 6° C, 28045 Madrid, Espagne.

Téléphone: 34 (91) 528 74 26. ***Fax:*** 34 (91) 517 41 78. ***Contact:*** Paz Almazan Hernandez.

OBJECTIFS: Promouvoir des rapports culturels, sociaux et humains entre le Nord et le Sud.

INFORMATIONS GENERALES: *Création:* 1986. *Affiliée à:* Coordinadora des ONG (Espagne). *Personnel/Total:* 63. Salariés: 6 dont: 6 dans les pays en développement. Bénévoles: 57 dont: 31 dans les pays en développement. *Budget/Total 1993:* ECU 142000 (US$ 184000). *Sources financières:* Privé: 38%. Public: 6%. Autofinancement: 56%.

PUBLICATIONS: *Périodiques:* Pueblos Hermanos (4).

ACTIVITES DANS LES REGIONS EN DEVELOPPEMENT: Intervient directement dans les régions en développement. Intervient dans 6 pays. Maintient une présence locale sur le terrain. Intervient par l'intermédiaire d'organisations locales partenaires. **Actions de Développement durable:** Droits de l'Homme/paix/conflits; Développement rural/agriculture; Enfants/jeunesse/famille; Envoi de volontaires/experts/assistance technique; Petites entreprises/secteur informel/artisanat; Questions relatives aux femmes; Santé/assainissement/eau; Secours d'urgence/réfugiés/aide humanitaire; Éducation/formation/alphabétisation. **Régions:** Afrique centrale; Amérique du Sud; Asie centrale et Asie du Sud.

ACTIVITES D'INFORMATION ET D'EDUCATION: Domaines: Pauvreté/conditions de vie; Questions relatives aux femmes; Relations internationales/coopération/aide au développement. **Activités:** Campagnes d'information/expositions; Conférences/séminaires/ateliers/activités de formation; Radiodiffusion/manifestations culturelles; Éducation formelle.

ESP1514

RESEAU PALMIER DATTIER ET OASIS (RESOPALM)

c/o Estación Phoenix, Hort del Gat, 03203 Elche, Espagne.

Téléphone: 34 (65) 45 74 96. ***Fax:*** 34 (65) 42 37 06. ***Contact:*** Michel Ferry, Président.

OBJECTIFS: Animer un réseau de chercheurs et de développeurs concernés par la culture du palmier dattier (Phoenix Dactylifera L.) et par l'agronomie oasienne.

INFORMATIONS GENERALES: *Création:* 1988. *Type d'organisation:* regroupement d'ONG. *Organisations membres:* 2. *Personnel/Total:* 8. Bénévoles: 5 dont: 3 dans les pays en développement. *Sources financières:* Privé: 20%. Public: 80%.

EVALUATION/RECHERCHE: Rapports d'évaluation disponibles. Entreprend des activités de recherche.

PREVISIONS D'ACTIVITES: Création d'une base de données informatisées.

ACTIVITES DANS LES REGIONS EN DEVELOPPEMENT: Intervient directement dans les régions en développement. Intervient dans 20 pays. **Actions de Développement durable:** Développement rural/agriculture; Écologie/environnement/biodiversité; Éducation/formation/alphabétisation. **Régions:** Afrique de l'Est; Afrique de l'Ouest; Moyen-Orient.

ESP1515

SECRETARIADO LATINOAMERICANO DE LA COMPANIA DE JESUS ♦ Latin American Bureau of the Society of Jesus

Almagro 6, 28010 Madrid, Spain.

Telephone: 34 (1) 319 75 81. ***Fax:*** 34 (1) 319 05 56. ***Contact:*** Cesareo Garcia del Cerro.

ESP1516

SERVICIO DE REFUGIADOS Y MIGRANTES

C/Valenzuela 10, 1o Izda, 28014 Madrid, Espagne.

Contact: Ramon de Marcos Sanz, Directeur.

See: *How to Use the Directory,* page 11.

ESP1517

SETEM - SERVICIO TERCER MUNDO ♦ Service Tiers Monde

Gaztambide 65, 28015 Madrid, Espagne.

Téléphone: 34 (1) 549 91 28. *Fax:* 34 (1) 549 91 28. *Contact:* Javier Agudo Garcia.

OBJECTIFS: Envoyer des volontaires vers les pays en développement. Sensibiliser la jeunesse européenne à la solidarité internationale.

INFORMATIONS GENERALES: *Création:* 1968. *Affiliée à:* Coordination espagnole d'ONG pour le Développement - Forum européen volontariat pour le Développement - O.C.C.I.. *Personnel/Total:* 72. *Salariés:* 7. *Bénévoles:* 65 dont: 6 dans les pays en développement. *Budget/Total 1993:* ECU 1065000 (US$ 1381000). *Sources financières:* Public: 13%. Autofinancement: 87%.

PUBLICATIONS: *Périodiques:* SETEM (6). *Rapport annuel. Liste des publications.*

EVALUATION/RECHERCHE: Rapports d'évaluation disponibles. Entreprend des activités de recherche.

COMMENTAIRES: Intervient dans la Communauté des Etats indépendants. Activités d'information concernant la Communauté des Etats indépendants.

ACTIVITES DANS LES REGIONS EN DEVELOPPEMENT: Intervient directement dans les régions en développement. Intervient dans 21 pays. Maintient une présence locale sur le terrain. Intervient par l'intermédiaire d'organisations locales partenaires. **Actions de Développement durable:** Droits de l'Homme/paix/conflits; Démocratie/bonne gestion publique/création d'institutions/développement participatif; Développement rural/agriculture; Développement urbain/habitat; Enfants/jeunesse/famille; Envoi de volontaires/experts/assistance technique; Petites entreprises/secteur informel/artisanat; Questions relatives aux femmes; Écologie/environnement/biodiversité; Éducation/formation/alphabétisation. **Régions:** Afrique centrale; Afrique de l'Ouest; Amérique du Sud; Asie centrale et Asie du Sud; Caraïbes; Mexique et Amérique centrale.

ACTIVITES D'INFORMATION ET D'EDUCATION: Domaines: Culture/tradition/religion; Droits de l'Homme/paix/conflits; Développement rural/agriculture; Développement urbain/habitat; Emploi/chômage; Enfants/jeunesse/famille; Paix/conflits ethniques/armement/désarmement; Pauvreté/conditions de vie; Questions relatives aux femmes; Racisme/xénophobie/antisémitisme; Relations internationales/coopération/aide au développement; Relations économiques internationales/commerce/dette/finances; Réfugiés/migrants/groupes ethniques; Santé/assainissement/eau; Écologie/environnement/biodiversité; Éducation/formation/alphabétisation. **Activités:** Campagnes d'information/expositions; Collecte de fonds; Conférences/séminaires/ateliers/activités de formation; Échanges/parrainage/jumelage; Édition/documents audiovisuels/documents éducatifs; Éducation formelle.

ESP1518

7 CAMPAIGN

c/o Justicia y Paz, Francisco Silvela, 77 bis dcha, 28028 Madrid, Spain.

Telephone: 34 (1) 261 12 14. *Contact:* Juan Romani.

ESP1519

SOCIEDAD INTERNACIONAL PARA EL DESARROLLO (SID)

Santa Catalina 6, 28014 Madrid, Spain.

Telephone: 34 (91) 429 44 77. *Fax:* 34 (91) 537 85 57. *Contact:* Lorenzo Diez.

ESP1520

SOLIDARIDAD DEMOCRATICA ♦ Democratic Solidarity

Paseo de las Delicias 59, 28045 Madrid, Spain.

Telephone: 34 (1) 239 34 96. *Contact:* Pedro del Pozo Anton, Chairman.

ESP1521

SOLIDARIDAD INTERNACIONAL - FUNDUCION ESPANOLA PARA LA COOPERACION (SI) ♦ International Solidarity

Glorieta de Quevedo 7, 6° dcha, 28015 Madrid, Spain.

Telephone: 34 (1) 593 11 13. *Fax:* 34 (1) 448 44 69. *Contact:* Angeles Yánes-Barnuevo, Executive Director.

OBJECTIVES: To provide urgent humanitarian aid. To undertake education and awareness-raising campaigns in Spain. To finance and manage development projects directed towards the most needy populations in the following areas: infrastructure, production, health, education and training.

GENERAL INFORMATION: *Creation:* 1986. *Affiliated to:* Coordinadora Española de ONGD (Spain) - International Workers' Aid (Germany). *Personnel/Total:* 33. *Salaried:* 11 of which: 3 in developing countries. *Volunteers:* 22. *Budget/Total 1993:* ECU 2937000 (US$ 3808000). *Financial sources:* Private: 3%. Public: 90%. Self-financing: 7%.

PUBLICATIONS: *Periodicals:* Solidaridad Internacional (3). *Annual report. List of publications.*

EVALUATION/RESEARCH: Evaluation reports available. Undertakes research activities.

ACTIVITIES IN DEVELOPING REGIONS: Present in developing regions. Active in 14 country(ies). Maintains local field presence. Works through local field partners. **Sustainable Development Actions:** Children/youth/family; Democracy/good governance/institution building/participatory development; Ecology/environment/biodiversity; Education/training/literacy; Emergency relief/refugees/humanitarian assistance; Gender issues/women; Health/sanitation/water; Rural development/agriculture; Sending volunteers/experts/technical assistance; Small enterprises/informal sector/handicrafts. **Regions:** Mexico and Central America; North Africa; South America.

INFORMATION AND EDUCATION ACTIVITIES: Topics: Ecology/environment/biodiversity; Emergency relief/refugees/humanitarian assistance; Gender issues/women; International relations/cooperation/development aid. **Activities:** Conferences/seminars/workshops/training activities; Exchanges/twinning/linking; Formal education; Information and documentation services/data bases; Information campaigns/exhibitions; Lobbying/advocacy; Publishing/audiovisual materials/educational materials.

ESP1522

SOLIDARIDAD PARA EL DESARROLLO Y LA PAZ (SODEPAZ) ♦ Solidarity for Development and Peace

Pizarro 5, 28004 Madrid, Spain.

Telephone: 34 (91) 522 80 91. *Fax:* 34 (91) 523 38 32. *Contact:* Mbuyi Kabunda, President.

OBJECTIVES: To promote solidarity between the popular movements in the South that organise co-operation projects between grassroots organisations and local communities and individuals.

GENERAL INFORMATION: *Creation:* 1987. *Affiliated to:* Coordinadora Española de ONGO - Coordinadora de ONG de Castilla y Leon -Federacion de ONG Catalana - Coordinadora Valenciana de ONGD - Coordinadora Gallega de ONGD - Federacion de ONGD de la CAM. *Personnel/Total:* 36. *Salaried:* 6. *Volunteers:* 30 of which: 5 in developing countries. *Budget/Total 1993:* ECU 606000 (US$ 786000). *Financial sources:* Private: 13%. Public: 84%. Self-financing: 3%.

PUBLICATIONS: *Periodicals:* Cuadernos Africa-America Latina (4). *Annual report. List of publications.*

EVALUATION/RESEARCH: Evaluation reports available. Undertakes research activities.

ACTIVITIES IN DEVELOPING REGIONS: Active in 13 country(ies). Works through local field partners. **Sustainable Development Actions:** Debt/finance/trade; Ecology/environment/biodiversity; Education/training/literacy; Energy/transport; Gender issues/women; Health/sanitation/water; Human rights/peace/conflicts; Rural development/agriculture. **Regions:** Caribbean; Mexico and Central America; Middle East; South America.

INFORMATION AND EDUCATION ACTIVITIES: Topics: Culture/tradition/religion; Ecology/environment/biodiversity; Gender issues/women; Health/sanitation/water; Human rights/peace/conflicts; International economic relations/trade/debt/finance; International relations/cooperation/development aid; Peace/ethnic conflicts/armament/disarmament; Poverty/living conditions; Racism/xenophobia/antisemitism; Refugees/migrants/ethnic groups; Rural development/agriculture; Urban develop-

Voir : *Comment utiliser le répertoire,* page 11.

ment/habitat. **Activities:** Conferences/seminars/workshops/training activities; Exchanges/twinning/linking; Formal education; Information and documentation services/data bases; Information campaigns/exhibitions; Lobbying/advocacy; Networking/electronic telecommunications; Publishing/audiovisual materials/educational materials.

ESP1523

SOS RACISMO ESPANA ♦ SOS Racism - Spain

Escudellers Blancs 12, 08002 Barcelona, Espagne.

Téléphone: 34 (3) 30 10 597. ***Fax:*** 34 (3) 301 01 47. ***Contact:*** HamiD Hilal, membre de la Commission permanente.

OBJECTIFS: Lutter contre le racisme. Promouvoir l'égalité, la paix sociale des rapports harmonieux entre les ethnies.

INFORMATIONS GENERALES: *Création:* 1988. ***Organisations membres:*** 7. ***Affiliée à:*** Fédération Internationale de SOS Racisme - Réseau Antiraciste pour l'Egalité en Europe. ***Personnel/Total:*** 804. *Salariés:* 4. *Bénévoles:* 800. ***Budget/Total 1993:*** ECU 424000 (US$ 550000). ***Sources financières:*** *Privé:* 10%. *Public:* 70%. *Autofinancement:* 20%.

PUBLICATIONS: *Périodiques:* Etnopolis (6). *Rapport annuel. Liste des publications.*

EVALUATION/RECHERCHE: Rapports d'évaluation disponibles. Entreprend des activités de recherche.

PREVISIONS D'ACTIVITES: Organisation d'une rencontre des ONG européennes, du Magreb et de l'Afrique du Sud.

COMMENTAIRES: Intervient dans la Communauté des Etats indépendants.

ACTIVITES DANS LES REGIONS EN DEVELOPPEMENT: Intervient par l'intermédiaire d'organisations locales partenaires. **Actions de Développement durable:** Droits de l'Homme/paix/conflits; Éducation/formation/alphabétisation. **Régions:** Afrique australe; Afrique du Nord; Amérique du Sud; Asie centrale et Asie du Sud; Mexique et Amerique centrale.

ACTIVITES D'INFORMATION ET D'EDUCATION: Domaines: Droits de l'Homme/paix/conflits; Paix/conflits ethniques/armement/désarmement; Racisme/xénophobie/antisémitisme; Relations internationales/coopération/aide au développement. **Activités:** Campagnes d'information/expositions; Collecte de fonds; Conférences/séminaires/ateliers/activités de formation; Radiodiffusion/manifestations culturelles; Services d'information et de documentation/bases de données; Échanges/parrainage/jumelage; Édition/documents audiovisuels/documents éducatifs; Éducation formelle.

ESP1524

SUR ♦ Sud

Paseo Imperial 19, 3° IZDA, 28005 Madrid, Espagne.

Téléphone: 34 (91) 365 99 70. ***Fax:*** 34 (91) 364 08 77. ***Contact:*** Angela Uriarte Rodriguez, Présidente.

OBJECTIFS: Coopérer avec le Tiers monde, dans les domaines de l'éducation et du développement, grâce à l'information, aux conseils techniques, etc.

INFORMATIONS GENERALES: *Création:* 1987. ***Affiliée à:*** D.U.G.D. (Espagne). ***Personnel/Total:*** 5. *Bénévoles:* 5 dont: 1 dans les *pays en développement.* ***Budget/Total 1993:*** ECU 240000 (US$ 311000). ***Sources financières:*** *Privé:* 2%. *Public:* 96%. *Autofinancement:* 2%.

PUBLICATIONS: *Rapport annuel. Liste des publications.*

EVALUATION/RECHERCHE: Rapports d'évaluation disponibles. Entreprend des activités de recherche.

ACTIVITES DANS LES REGIONS EN DEVELOPPEMENT: Intervient dans 5 pays. Maintient une présence locale sur le terrain. Intervient par l'intermédiaire d'organisations locales partenaires. **Actions de Développement durable:** Droits de l'Homme/paix/conflits; Démocratie/bonne gestion publique/création d'institutions/développement participatif; Développement rural/agriculture; Développement urbain/habitat; Enfants/jeunesse/famille; Envoi de volontaires/experts/assistance technique; Questions relatives aux femmes; Santé/assainissement/eau;

Secours d'urgence/réfugiés/aide humanitaire; Éducation/formation/alphabétisation; Énergie/transport. **Régions:** Afrique de l'Est; Afrique de l'Ouest; Caraïbes; Mexique et Amerique centrale; Moyen-Orient.

ACTIVITES D'INFORMATION ET D'EDUCATION: Domaines: Droits de l'Homme/paix/conflits; Développement urbain/habitat; Enfants/jeunesse/famille; Questions relatives aux femmes; Réfugiés/migrants/groupes ethniques; Santé/assainissement/eau; Éducation/formation/alphabétisation. **Activités:** Campagnes d'information/expositions; Conférences/séminaires/ateliers/activités de formation; Éducation formelle.

ESP1525

UNION DE CIUDADES CAPITALES IBEROAMERI-CANAS (UCCI) ♦ Union of Iberio-American Capital Cities

C/ Recoletos, 5. 4° Izquierda, 28001 Madrid, Spain.

Telephone: 34 (91) 578 38 80. ***Fax:*** 34 (91) 578 34 74. ***Contact:*** José María de Alvarez del Manzano, President.

OBJECTIVES: To promote the development of balanced and harmonious relationships between Ibero-American capital cities and co-operation among the various communities. To encourage citizen participation in public affairs and work to strengthen neighbourhood rights.

GENERAL INFORMATION: *Creation:* 1982. ***Type of organisation:*** network. ***Member organisations:*** 26. ***Personnel/Total:*** 9. *Salaried:* 9. ***Budget/Total 1993:*** ECU 415000 (US$ 538500).

PUBLICATIONS: *Periodicals:* Ciudades Iberoamericanas (2). *Annual report.*

EVALUATION/RESEARCH: Evaluation reports available.

ACTIVITIES IN DEVELOPING REGIONS: Present in developing regions. Active in 20 country(ies). Maintains local field presence. Works through local field partners. **Sustainable Development Actions:** Children/youth/family; Democracy/good governance/institution building/participatory development; Ecology/environment/biodiversity; Education/training/literacy; Energy/transport; Health/sanitation/water; Human rights/peace/conflicts; Sending volunteers/experts/technical assistance; Small enterprises/informal sector/handicrafts; Urban development/habitat. **Regions:** Caribbean; Mexico and Central America; South America.

INFORMATION AND EDUCATION ACTIVITIES: Topics: Culture/tradition/religion; Ecology/environment/biodiversity; Education/training/literacy; Employment/unemployment; Health/sanitation/water; Human rights/peace/conflicts; International relations/cooperation/development aid; Population/family planning/demography; Poverty/living conditions; Urban development/habitat. **Activities:** Broadcasting/cultural events; Conferences/seminars/workshops/training activities; Exchanges/twinning/linking; Information and documentation services/data bases; Lobbying/advocacy; Publishing/audiovisual materials/educational materials.

ESP1526

UNION DE ESCUELAS FAMILIARES AGRARIAS (UNEFA) ♦ Union des écoles familiales agraires

General Oraa 29, 28006 Madrid, Espagne.

Téléphone: 34 (91) 411 32 11. ***Fax:*** 34 (91) 411 69 02. ***Contact:*** Juan Cano Ruano, Président.

ESP1527

UNION SOLIDARIA (UNIS)

Paseo Juan XXIII, 15, 28040 Madrid, Espagne.

Téléphone: 34 (91) 553 66 03. ***Contact:*** Carmen de Villa.

ESP1528

UNIVERSITARIS PEL TERCER MON (MON-3) ♦ Universitaires pour le Tiers monde

Av. Diagonal 690, 08034 Barcelona, Espagne.

Téléphone: 34 (3) 402 43 25. ***Fax:*** 34 (3) 280 23 78. ***Contact:*** Lorenzo Albandiaz, Président.

OBJECTIFS: Réaliser des actions de sensibilisation et d'information sur les réalités du Tiers monde. Mener des activités de formation et de

See: *How to Use the Directory,* page 11.

recherche en matière de développement. Fournir une assistance technique aux coopérants.

INFORMATIONS GENERALES: *Création:* 1985. *Type d'organisation:* collectif. *Affiliée à:* Universitarios Solidarios (Espagne) - Coordinadora Estatal de ONG (Espagne) -Federación Catalana de ONG (Espagne) - EADI (Suisse) - Youth for Development and Cooperation (Pays-Bas). *Personnel/Total:* 35. *Salariés:* 5. *Bénévoles:* 30. *Budget/ Total 1993:* ECU 149000 (US$ 193000). *Sources financières:* Privé: 4%. *Public:* 81%. *Autofinancement:* 15%.

PUBLICATIONS: *Périodiques:* Informes (2) - Boletín informativo de la asociación (12) - Boletín de la oficina de coperación universitaria (12). *Rapport annuel.*

EVALUATION/RECHERCHE: Rapports d'évaluation disponibles.

COMMENTAIRES: Activités d'information concernant la Communauté des Etats indépendants.

ACTIVITES DANS LES REGIONS EN DEVELOPPEMENT: Intervient directement dans les régions en développement. Maintient une présence locale sur le terrain. Intervient par l'intermédiaire d'organisations locales partenaires. **Actions de Développement durable:** Développement rural/agriculture; Développement urbain/habitat; Secours d'urgence/réfugiés/aide humanitaire. **Régions:** Afrique centrale; Afrique de l'Est; Afrique de l'Ouest; Amérique du Sud; Mexique et Amerique centrale.

ACTIVITES D'INFORMATION ET D'EDUCATION: Domaines: Aliments/ famine; Droits de l'Homme/paix/conflits; Développement rural/agriculture; Paix/conflits ethniques/armement/désarmement; Pauvreté/conditions de vie; Population/planning familial/démographie; Questions relatives aux femmes; Racisme/xénophobie/antisémitisme; Relations internationales/coopération/aide au développement; Relations économiques internationales/commerce/dette/finances; Réfugiés/migrants/ groupes ethniques; Secours d'urgence/réfugiés/aide humanitaire; Écologie/environnement/biodiversité. **Activités:** Campagnes d'information/ expositions; Collecte de fonds; Conférences/séminaires/ateliers/activités de formation; Lobbying/plaidoyer; Édition/documents audiovisuels/ documents éducatifs; Éducation formelle.

ESP1529

VETERINARIOS SIN FRONTERAS (VETERMON) ♦ Veterinarians without Borders

Josep Anselm Clavé 6, 1° , 1a, 08002 Barcelona, Spain.

Telephone: 34 (3) 412 71 08. *Fax:* 34 (3) 412 40 36. *Contact:* Xavier Such Marti.

OBJECTIVES: To implement development projects, teaching programmes, and exchange information and documentation with developing countries. To raise awareness of the problems of developing countries and to promote the education and training of veterinarians in tropical medicine.

GENERAL INFORMATION: *Creation:* 1987. *Affiliated to:* DJO (the Netherlands) - VET AID (United Kingdom). *Personnel/Total:* 24. *Salaried:* 9 of which: 5 in developing countries. *Volunteers:* 15. *Budget/ Total 1993:* ECU 608000 (US$ 793000). *Financial sources:* Private: 2%. *Public:* 90%. *Self-financing:* 8%.

PUBLICATIONS: *Periodicals:* Circular de VETERMON (6) - Gacetilla de VETERMON (4). *Annual report. List of publications.*

EVALUATION/RESEARCH: Evaluation reports available.

ACTIVITIES IN DEVELOPING REGIONS: Present in developing regions. Active in 7 country(ies). Works through local field partners. **Sustainable Development Actions:** Ecology/environment/biodiversity; Education/ training/literacy; Rural development/agriculture; Sending volunteers/ experts/technical assistance; Small enterprises/informal sector/handicrafts. **Regions:** Caribbean; Central Africa; Mexico and Central America; South America.

INFORMATION AND EDUCATION ACTIVITIES: Topics: Rural development/agriculture. **Activities:** Conferences/seminars/workshops/training activities; Formal education; Fund raising; Information and documentation services/data bases; Information campaigns/exhibitions; Publishing/ audiovisual materials/educational materials.

ESP1530

WORLD FEDERATION OF DEVELOPMENT FINANCING INSTITUTIONS (WFDFI)

c/o Instituto de Credito Oficial, Paseo del Prado 4, 28014 Madrid, Spain.

Telephone: 34 (1) 221 36 39. *Contact:* J.E. Gallegos Romero, Secretary General.

Voir : *Comment utiliser le répertoire,* page 11.

FIN1531

AFRIKAN TAHTI RY ♦ Star of African Association

Mannerheimintie 5 B, 5th Floor, 00100 Helsinki, Finland.

Telephone: 358 (0) 635 889. *Fax:* 358 (0) 13 11 42 16.

OBJECTIVES: To increase awareness of development issues, especially among students of Helsinki University and Helsinki School of Economics. To raise awareness of "fair trade" among Finnish consumers.

GENERAL INFORMATION: *Creation:* 1988. *Type of organisation:* coordinating body. *Member organisations:* 1. *Affiliated to:* Federation of Finnish Alternative Trade Organisations (Finland) - Service Centre for Development Cooperation/Finnish Volunteer Service - cFinland. *Personnel/Total:* 8. *Salaried:* 1. *Volunteers:* 7. *Budget/Total 1993:* ECU 18000 (US$ 23000). *Financial sources:* Private: 40%. Public: 52%. Self-financing: 8%.

PUBLICATIONS: *Periodicals:* Afrikan Tahti (2) (8). *Annual report.*

EVALUATION/RESEARCH: Evaluation reports available. Undertakes research activities.

PLANNED ACTIVITIES: Campaign on fair trade/alternative consumption in Finland.

ACTIVITIES IN DEVELOPING REGIONS: Sustainable Development Actions: Debt/finance/trade; Education/training/literacy; Small enterprises/informal sector/handicrafts. **Regions:** Central Africa; East Africa; North Africa; South America; Southern Africa; West Africa.

INFORMATION AND EDUCATION ACTIVITIES: Topics: Culture/tradition/religion; Food/famine; International relations/cooperation/development aid. **Activities:** Broadcasting/cultural events; Conferences/seminars/workshops/training activities; Information campaigns/exhibitions; Lobbying/advocacy; Networking/electronic telecommunications; Publishing/audiovisual materials/educational materials.

FIN1532

AMNESTY INTERNATIONAL, SUOMEN OSASTO ♦ Amnesty International, Finnish Section

Ruoholahdenkatu 24 D, 00180 Helsinki, Finland.

Telephone: 358 (0) 69 31 488. *Fax:* 358 (0) 69 31 975. *Contact:* Taina Järvinen, Section Chair.

OBJECTIVES: To free all prisoners of conscience. To ensure fair and prompt trials for political prisoners. To abolish the death penalty, torture and other cruel treatment of prisoners. To end extrajudicial executions and "disappearances".

GENERAL INFORMATION: *Creation:* 1967. *Affiliated to:* Amnesty International (United Kingdom). *Personnel/Total:* 3. *Salaried:* 3. *Financial sources:* Private: 50%. Self-financing: 50%.

PUBLICATIONS: *Periodicals:* Amnesty Tiedote-Bulletinen (5). *List of publications.*

COMMENTS: Information activities related to the Commonwealth of Independent States.

ACTIVITIES IN DEVELOPING REGIONS: Sustainable Development Actions: Human rights/peace/conflicts. **Regions:** Caribbean; Central Africa; Central Asia and South Asia; East Africa; East Asia; Mexico and Central America; Middle East; North Africa; Oceania; South America; South East Asia; Southern Africa; West Africa.

INFORMATION AND EDUCATION ACTIVITIES: Topics: Human rights/peace/conflicts. **Activities:** Broadcasting/cultural events; Conferences/seminars/workshops/training activities; Fund raising; Information and documentation services/data bases; Information campaigns/exhibitions; Lobbying/advocacy; Publishing/audiovisual materials/educational materials.

FIN1533

AUTO-JA KULJGTUSALAN TYONTEKIJALUTTO (AKT) ♦ Finnish Transport Workers' Union

Haapaniemenk 7-9 B-talo, PL 313, 00531 Helsinki, Finland.

Telephone: 358 (0) 70 911. *Fax:* 358 (0) 739 287. *Contact:* Risto Kuisma, President.

FIN1534

FINLANDS SVENSKA MARTHAFORBUND ♦ The Swedish Finnish Martha Organisation

Lilla Robertsgatan 5B 15, 00130 Helsingfors, Finland.

FIN1535

FINLANDS SVENSKA PINGSTMISSION - FILADELFIAFORSAMLINGEN I HELSINGFORS ♦ Finland's Swedish Pentecostal Mission

Albertsgatan 31, 00180 Helsingfors, Finland.

Telephone: 358 (0) 69 40 400. *Contact:* Rev. Arne Herberts.

FIN1536

FINLANDS SVENSKA SKOLUNGDOMSFORBUND (FSS) ♦ Finnish - Swedish Secondary School Youth Organisation

Stora Robertsgatan 3-5 B33, 00120 Helsingfors, Finland.

Telephone: 358 (90) 644 881. *Contact:* Johanna Koljonen.

OBJECTIVES: To work for the rights of Swedish speaking students in Finland. To help disseminate the opinions and views of the students. To arrange seminars and courses and to distribute information on the environment, sustainable development etc.

GENERAL INFORMATION: *Creation:* 1921. *Type of organisation:* network, coordinating body. *Affiliated to:* Allianssi ry (Finland) - Aktiv Ungdom (Finland). *Personnel/Total:* 5. *Volunteers:* 5.

PUBLICATIONS: *Periodicals:* Elevbadet Ebl (4).

COMMENTS: FSS is a grass-roots organisation run by secondary school students.

INFORMATION AND EDUCATION ACTIVITIES: Topics: Children/youth/family; Culture/tradition/religion; Ecology/environment/biodiversity; Education/training/literacy; Emergency relief/refugees/humanitarian assistance; Food/famine; Gender issues/women; Health/sanitation/water; Human rights/peace/conflicts; International economic relations/trade/debt/finance; International relations/cooperation/development aid; Other; Peace/ethnic conflicts/armament/disarmament; Poverty/living conditions; Racism/xenophobia/antisemitism; Refugees/migrants/ethnic groups; Urban development/habitat. **Activities:** Broadcasting/cultural events; Conferences/seminars/workshops/training activities; Other; Publishing/audiovisual materials/educational materials.

FIN1537

FINNWID

Aitanavain 4 H 31, 01660 Vanytaa, Finland.

FIN1538

FOLKHASAN

Topeliuksenkatu 20, 00250 Helsinki, Finland.

FIN1539

HENGITYD JA TERVEIS RY ♦ Finnish Lung Health Association

Sibeliuksenkatu 11 A 1, 00250 Helsinki, Finland.

Telephone: 358 (0) 447 668. *Fax:* 358 (0) 447 739. *Contact:* Dr. Eljas Brander, President.

OBJECTIVES: To work for the elimination of tuberculosis and lung diseases in Finland throughout the world.

GENERAL INFORMATION: *Creation:* 1907. *Affiliated to:* International Union Against Tuberculosis and Lung Disease (France). *Personnel/Total:* 8. *Salaried:* 8. *Budget/Total 1993:* ECU 840000 (US$ 1090000). *Financial sources:* Private: 1%. Public: 5%. Self-financing: 94%.

PUBLICATIONS: *Periodicals:* Tuberkuloosi ja Keuhosairaudet Vuosikirja (1). *Annual report. List of publications.*

EVALUATION/RESEARCH: Evaluation reports available. Undertakes research activities.

PLANNED ACTIVITIES: Education concerning important infectious diseases other than tuberculosis. Participation in rehabilitation of disabled persons.

COMMENTS: Undertakes activities in the Commonwealth of Independent States. Information activities related to the Commonwealth of Independent States.

ACTIVITIES IN DEVELOPING REGIONS: Active in 1 country(ies). Sustainable Development Actions: Education/training/literacy. Regions: East Africa.

INFORMATION AND EDUCATION ACTIVITIES: Topics: Health/sanitation/water. Activities: Conferences/seminars/workshops/training activities.

FIN1540

IHMISOIKEUSLIITTO ♦ Finish League for Human Rights

P.O. Box 245, Mariankatu 28, 00171 Helsinki, Finland.

Telephone: 358 (0) 13 51 470. Fax: 358 (0) 13 51 101. Contact: Taina Dahlgren, Secretary General.

OBJECTIVES: To promote and publicize human rights issues.

GENERAL INFORMATION: Creation: 1979. Personnel/Total: 1. Salaried: 1.

PUBLICATIONS: Periodicals: Ihmisoikeusraportti (4) - Ihmisoikeudet (var.). Annual report. List of publications.

EVALUATION/RESEARCH: Undertakes research activities.

PLANNED ACTIVITIES: Organisation of a civic education programme in Estonia together with several partner organisations and institutes.

COMMENTS: Undertakes activities in the Commonwealth of Independent States. Information activities related to the Commonwealth of Independent States.

ACTIVITIES IN DEVELOPING REGIONS: Present in developing regions. Works through local field partners.

INFORMATION AND EDUCATION ACTIVITIES: Topics: Human rights/peace/conflicts; Racism/xenophobia/antisemitism; Refugees/migrants/ethnic groups. Activities: Conferences/seminars/workshops/training activities; Formal education; Fund raising; Information and documentation services/data bases; Information campaigns/exhibitions; Lobbying/advocacy; Publishing/audiovisual materials/educational materials.

FIN1541

INSTITUTE FOR HUMAN RIGHTS

PO Box 696, 00101 Helsinki, Finland.

FIN1542

INTERPEDIA

Koulukatu 10 B, 65100 Vaasa, Finland.

Telephone: 358 (61) 31 77 812. Fax: 358 (61) 31 77 813.

FIN1543

KANSAINVALINEN KRISTILLINEN NUORISOVAIH-TORY (ICYE) ♦ International Christian Youth Exchange

Lönnrotin Katu 18C, 00120 Helsinki, Finland.

Telephone: 358 (0) 69 49 638. Fax: 358 (0) 68 53 316. Contact: Anni Koskela, Secretary General.

OBJECTIVES: To increase understanding among different cultures, organisations and religions.

GENERAL INFORMATION: Creation: 1958. Affiliated to: Finnish NGO Development Cooperation (Finland) - National Youth Committee Alliance (Finland) - Parish Work Association of the Lutheran Church of Finalnd (Finland) - International Christian Youth Exchange (Germany). Personnel/Total: 2. Salaried: 2. Financial sources: Private: 5%. Public: 5%. Self-financing: 80%.

PUBLICATIONS: Periodicals: ICYE Info (4). Annual report. List of publications.

EVALUATION/RESEARCH: Evaluation reports available.

ACTIVITIES IN DEVELOPING REGIONS: Works through local field partners.

INFORMATION AND EDUCATION ACTIVITIES: Topics: Culture/tradition/religion; Human rights/peace/conflicts; Peace/ethnic conflicts/armament/disarmament; Racism/xenophobia/antisemitism. Activities: Conferences/seminars/workshops/training activities; Exchanges/twinning/linking; Information campaigns/exhibitions; Lobbying/advocacy; Networking/electronic telecommunications.

FIN1544

KANSAINVALINEN SOLIDAARISUUSSAATIO ♦ International Solidarity Foundation

Agricolankatu 4, 00530 Helsinki, Finland.

Telephone: 358 (0) 70 11 200. Fax: 358 (0) 77 31 702. Contact: Jari Luoto, Director.

OBJECTIVES: To support development that strengthens democracy, equality and human rights internationally. To support development cooperation projects and to provide humanitarian assistance.

GENERAL INFORMATION: Creation: 1970. Affiliated to: International Workers' Aid - Service Centre for Development/Finnish Volunteer Service. Personnel/Total: 9. Salaried: 9 of which: 6 in developing countries. Budget/Total 1993: ECU 1012000 (US$ 1313000). Financial sources: Private: 30%. Public: 70%.

PUBLICATIONS: Periodicals: Apuraporth (2).

ACTIVITIES IN DEVELOPING REGIONS: Present in developing regions. Active in 4 country(ies). Maintains local field presence. Works through local field partners. Sustainable Development Actions: Children/youth/family; Democracy/good governance/institution building/participatory development; Ecology/environment/biodiversity; Education/training/literacy; Food/famine; Gender issues/women; Rural development/agriculture; Sending volunteers/experts/technical assistance; Small enterprises/informal sector/handicrafts; Urban development/habitat. Regions: East Africa; Mexico and Central America; Southern Africa.

INFORMATION AND EDUCATION ACTIVITIES: Topics: Children/youth/family; Ecology/environment/biodiversity; Education/training/literacy; Food/famine; Gender issues/women; Human rights/peace/conflicts; International economic relations/trade/debt/finance; International relations/cooperation/development aid; Poverty/living conditions; Refugees/migrants/ethnic groups; Rural development/agriculture; Urban development/habitat. Activities: Conferences/seminars/workshops/training activities; Fund raising; Information campaigns/exhibitions; Lobbying/advocacy; Publishing/audiovisual materials/educational materials.

FIN1545

KANSAN SIVISTYSTYON LIITTO (KSL) ♦ People's Educational and Cultural Association

Kumpulantie 7, 00520 Helsinki, Finland.

Telephone: 358 (0) 27 87 100. Fax: 358 (0) 278 050. E-mail: jtainio@katto.kaapeli.fi. Contact: Jukka Tainio, General Secretary.

OBJECTIVES: To build up networks and bridges between peoples and ideas, and to maintain educational centres. To promote radical left-wing ideas and culture.

GENERAL INFORMATION: Creation: 1964. Type of organisation: association of NGOs. Affiliated to: Nordic Umbrella Organisation of Socialist Adult Education (Denmark). Salaried: 24. Budget/Total 1993: ECU 1566000 (US$ 2031000). Financial sources: Private: 11%. Public: 74%. Self-financing: 14%.

PUBLICATIONS: Annual report. List of publications.

EVALUATION/RESEARCH: Undertakes research activities.

COMMENTS: Undertakes activities in the Commonwealth of Independent States. Information activities related to the Commonwealth of Independent States.

ACTIVITIES IN DEVELOPING REGIONS: Works through local field partners.

Voir : *Comment utiliser le répertoire,* page 11.

INFORMATION AND EDUCATION ACTIVITIES: Topics: Culture/tradition/religion; Ecology/environment/biodiversity; Education/training/literacy; Employment/unemployment; Food/famine; Gender issues/women; Human rights/peace/conflicts; International economic relations/trade/debt/finance; International relations/cooperation/development aid; Peace/ethnic conflicts/armament/disarmament; Poverty/living conditions; Racism/xenophobia/antisemitism; Refugees/migrants/ethnic groups; Rural development/agriculture; Urban development/habitat. Activities: Broadcasting/cultural events; Conferences/seminars/workshops/training activities; Exchanges/twinning/linking; Formal education; Fund raising; Information and documentation services/data bases; Information campaigns/exhibitions; Lobbying/advocacy; Networking/electronic telecommunications; Publishing/audiovisual materials/educational materials.

FIN1546

KEHITYSYHTEISTYON PALVELUKESKUS   (KEPA) ♦ Service Centre for Development Co-operation - Finnish Volunteer Service

Fredrikinkatu 63 A 8, 00100 Helsinki, Finland.

Telephone: 358 (0) 69 44 233. **Fax:** 358 (0) 69 41 786. **E-mail:** Kepa@nordnet.se. **Contact:** Folke Sundman, Executive Secretary.

OBJECTIVES: To administer the Finnish Volunteer Programme. To provide services to Finnish NGOs engaged in development activities and to provide a platform for NGO co-operation and advocacy work in North-South issues.

GENERAL INFORMATION: Creation: 1985. **Type of organisation:** association of NGOs. **Member organisations:** 155. **Affiliated to:** European Forum on Development Service (Germany) - Eurostop (Belgium) - El Taller (Tunisia) - Towns and Development (the Netherlands) - European Centre for Global Interdependence and Solidarity (Portugal) - Alliance of Northern People for Environment and Development (Germany). **Personnel/Total:** 102. **Salaried:** 27 of which: 14 in developing countries. **Volunteers:** 75 of which: 75 in developing countries. **Budget/Total 1993:** ECU 3442000 (US$ 4464000). **Financial sources:** Private: 1%. Public: 95%. Self-financing: 4%.

PUBLICATIONS: Periodicals: Kehitystyön Kumppani (4) - Joukkoleikkaus (6). Annual report. List of publications.

EVALUATION/RESEARCH: Evaluation reports available.

PLANNED ACTIVITIES: Campaign on Finnish ODA. Participation in the European Campaign against Racism and Xenophobia.

COMMENTS: Information activities related to the Commonwealth of Independent States.

ACTIVITIES IN DEVELOPING REGIONS: Present in developing regions. Active in 3 country(ies). Maintains local field presence. Works through local field partners. **Sustainable Development Actions:** Children/youth/family; Democracy/good governance/institution building/participatory development; Ecology/environment/biodiversity; Education/training/literacy; Gender issues/women; Health/sanitation/water; Other; Rural development/agriculture; Sending volunteers/experts/technical assistance; Small enterprises/informal sector/handicrafts. **Regions:** Mexico and Central America; Southern Africa.

INFORMATION AND EDUCATION ACTIVITIES: Topics: Culture/tradition/religion; Ecology/environment/biodiversity; Education/training/literacy; Emergency relief/refugees/humanitarian assistance; Gender issues/women; Health/sanitation/water; Human rights/peace/conflicts; International economic relations/trade/debt/finance; International relations/cooperation/development aid; Poverty/living conditions; Racism/xenophobia/antisemitism; Refugees/migrants/ethnic groups; Rural development/agriculture. **Activities:** Broadcasting/cultural events; Conferences/seminars/workshops/training activities; Exchanges/twinning/linking; Fund raising; Information and documentation services/data bases; Information campaigns/exhibitions; Lobbying/advocacy; Networking/electronic telecommunications; Publishing/audiovisual materials/educational materials.

FIN1547

KEMIANLIITTO - KEMIFACKET RY ♦ Chemical Workers Union

Haapaniemenkatu 7-9B Talo, Box 324, 00531 Helsinki, Finland.

Telephone: 358 (0) 773 971. **Fax:** 358 (0) 75 38 040. **Contact:** Hilkka Häkkilä, President.

OBJECTIVES: To develop international solidarity among trade unions in industrialized and developing countries.

GENERAL INFORMATION: Creation: 1993. **Member organisations:** 250. **Affiliated to:** Central Organisation of Finnish Trade Unions (Finland). **Personnel/Total:** 38. Salaried: 38. **Budget/Total 1993:** ECU 3105000 (US$ 4026000). **Financial sources:** Self-financing: 100%.

PUBLICATIONS: Periodicals: Reaktio (16). Annual report.

EVALUATION/RESEARCH: Evaluation reports available.

COMMENTS: Undertakes activities in the Commonwealth of Independent States. Information activities related to the Commonwealth of Independent States.

ACTIVITIES IN DEVELOPING REGIONS: Present in developing regions. Active in 1 country(ies). Works through local field partners. **Sustainable Development Actions:** Education/training/literacy; Human rights/peace/conflicts. **Regions:** East Africa; Southern Africa.

INFORMATION AND EDUCATION ACTIVITIES: Topics: Ecology/environment/biodiversity; Employment/unemployment; International economic relations/trade/debt/finance; International relations/cooperation/development aid. **Activities:** Conferences/seminars/workshops/training activities; Exchanges/twinning/linking; Information and documentation services/data bases; Information campaigns/exhibitions; Publishing/audiovisual materials/educational materials.

FIN1548

KIHITYSMAANTIETEEN YHDISTYS ♦ The Finnish Association for Development Geography

University of Helsinki,Department of Geography, Hallitusk 11-13, P.O. Box 4, 00014 Helsinki , Finland.

Telephone: 358 (0) 62 21 609. **Contact:** Anita Toro.

OBJECTIVES: To organise workshops and publish periodicals on development geography.

GENERAL INFORMATION: Creation: 1979. **Affiliated to:** The Nordic Association for Development Geography - The Finnish Volunteer Service (Finland). **Personnel/Total:** 9. Volunteers: 9. **Budget/Total 1993:** ECU 3000 (US$ 4000). **Financial sources:** Public: 70%. Self-financing: 30%.

PUBLICATIONS: Periodicals: Maapallo (4). List of publications.

EVALUATION/RESEARCH: Evaluation reports available. Undertakes research activities.

COMMENTS: Undertakes activities in the Commonwealth of Independent States. Information activities related to the Commonwealth of Independent States.

INFORMATION AND EDUCATION ACTIVITIES: Topics: Children/youth/family; Culture/tradition/religion; Ecology/environment/biodiversity; Education/training/literacy; Food/famine; Gender issues/women; Health/sanitation/water; Human rights/peace/conflicts; International economic relations/trade/debt/finance; International relations/cooperation/development aid; Peace/ethnic conflicts/armament/disarmament; Population/family planning/demography; Poverty/living conditions; Refugees/migrants/ethnic groups; Rural development/agriculture; Urban development/habitat. **Activities:** Conferences/seminars/workshops/training activities; Information and documentation services/data bases; Publishing/audiovisual materials/educational materials.

FIN1549

KIRKON ULKOMAANAPU (KUA) ♦ Finnchurchaid

Luotsikatu 1 a, 5 Floor, P.O. Box 185, 00161 Helsinki, Finland.

Telephone: 358 (0) 18 021 . **Fax:** 358 (0) 18 02 207. **Contact:** Tapio Saraneva, Executive Director.

OBJECTIVES: To carry out development and relief work on behalf of the Evangelical Lutheran Church of Finland, striving to relieve distress and destitution and to promote self-determination, human rights, equality and democracy.

GENERAL INFORMATION: Creation: 1964. **Affiliated to:** Evangelical Lutheran Church of Finland for International Diaconia (Switzerland) -

                                                      See: *How to Use the Directory*, page 11.

World Council of Churches (Switzerland) - Emergrncy Relief Desk (Eritrea) -Sudan Emergency Consortium (Sudan) - Finnish Volunteer Service (Finland). *Personnel/Total:* 26. *Salaried:* 25. *Volunteers:* 1. *Budget/Total 1993:* ECU 6750000 (US$ 8753000). *Financial sources: Private:* 56%. *Public:* 43%. *Self-financing:* 1%.

PUBLICATIONS: *Periodicals:* Tule Ja Auta (4). *Annual report.*

COMMENTS: Undertakes activities in the Commonwealth of Independent States. Information activities related to the Commonwealth of Independent States.

ACTIVITIES IN DEVELOPING REGIONS: Present in developing regions. Active in 55 country(ies). Maintains local field presence. Works through local field partners. **Sustainable Development Actions:** Children/ youth/family; Debt/finance/trade; Democracy/good governance/institution building/participatory development; Ecology/environment/biodiversity; Education/training/literacy; Emergency relief/refugees/humanitarian assistance; Food/famine; Health/sanitation/water; Human rights/peace/ conflicts; Rural development/agriculture; Sending volunteers/experts/ technical assistance; Small enterprises/informal sector/handicrafts; Urban development/habitat. **Regions:** Central Africa; Central Asia and South Asia; East Africa; East Asia; Mexico and Central America; Middle East; South America; South East Asia; Southern Africa; West Africa.

INFORMATION AND EDUCATION ACTIVITIES: **Topics:** Children/youth/ family; Culture/tradition/religion; Ecology/environment/biodiversity; Education/training/literacy; Emergency relief/refugees/humanitarian assistance; Employment/unemployment; Food/famine; Gender issues/ women; Health/sanitation/water; Human rights/peace/conflicts; International economic relations/trade/debt/finance; International relations/ cooperation/development aid; Peace/ethnic conflicts/armament/disarmament; Poverty/living conditions; Racism/xenophobia/antisemitism; Refugees/migrants/ethnic groups; Rural development/agriculture. **Activities:** Broadcasting/cultural events; Conferences/seminars/workshops/ training activities; Fund raising; Information campaigns/exhibitions; Lobbying/advocacy; Publishing/audiovisual materials/educational materials.

FIN1550

KUNTA-ALAN AMMATTILIITTO KTV ♦ Trade Union for Municipal Sector KTV

Kolmas Linja 4, PL 101, 00530 Helsinki, Finland.

Telephone: 358 (0) 77 031. *Fax:* 358 (0) 77 03 397. *E-mail:* KTV-FINLAND. *Contact:* Jouni Riskilä, President.

FIN1551

LAAKARIN SOSIAALINEN VASTUU (LSV) ♦ Physicians for Social Responsibility

KTL, Mannerheimintie 166, 00300 Helsinki, Finland.

Telephone: 358 (0) 47 44 230. *Fax:* 358 (0) 47 44 238. *Contact:* Dr. Pirjo Makela, Chairman.

OBJECTIVES: To support health care projects in developing countries. To undertake development education activities in Finland for physicians and the general public. To contribute to a greater understanding of health care, environment and peace issues throughout the world.

GENERAL INFORMATION: *Creation:* 1982. *Affiliated to:* International Physicians for the Prevention of Nuclear War - North-South Collaboration of Health Workers for Social and Environmental Responsibility - Health Action Internaitonal. *Personnel/Total:* 10. *Volunteers:* 10. *Budget/Total 1993:* ECU 135000 (US$ 175000). *Financial sources: Private:* 15%. *Public:* 75%. *Self-financing:* 10%.

PUBLICATIONS: *Periodicals:* LSV-Tiedote (8). *List of publications.*

EVALUATION/RESEARCH: Evaluation reports available.

COMMENTS: Undertakes activities in the Commonwealth of Independent States. Information activities related to the Commonwealth of Independent States.

ACTIVITIES IN DEVELOPING REGIONS: Present in developing regions. Active in 4 country(ies). Maintains local field presence. Works through local field partners. **Sustainable Development Actions:** Health/sanitation/water. **Regions:** East Africa; South America; South East Asia.

INFORMATION AND EDUCATION ACTIVITIES: **Topics:** Ecology/environment/biodiversity; Employment/unemployment; Health/sanitation/

water; International relations/cooperation/development aid; Peace/ethnic conflicts/armament/disarmament; Refugees/migrants/ethnic groups. **Activities:** Conferences/seminars/workshops/training activities; Exchanges/twinning/linking; Fund raising; Information campaigns/exhibitions; Lobbying/advocacy; Publishing/audiovisual materials/educational materials.

FIN1552

LASTENSUOJELUN KESKUSLIITTO ♦ Central Union for Child Welfare in Finland

Armfeltintie 1, 00150 Helsinki, Finland.

Telephone: 358 (90) 625 901. *Fax:* 358 (90) 627 990. *Contact:* Mauri Upanne, Executive Director.

OBJECTIVES: To safeguard the rights of children and families and to promote their well-being. To co-ordinate co-operation in the field of child welfare between NGOs, local authorities and the state. To promote the implementation of the UN convention on the Rights of the Child.

GENERAL INFORMATION: *Creation:* 1937. *Type of organisation:* coordinating body. *Member organisations:* 80. *Affiliated to:* End Physical Punishment of Children Worldwide - European Association for Children in Hospital - European Citizen Action Service - European Consumer Safety Association - Fédération Internationale des Communautés Educatives -International Forum on Child Welfare - International Society for the Prevention of Child Abuse and Neglect - Organisation Mondiale pour l'Education Préscolaire . *Personnel/Total:* 15. *Salaried:* 15. *Budget/ Total 1993:* ECU 1080000 (US$ 1400000). *Financial sources: Private:* 70%. *Self-financing:* 30%.

PUBLICATIONS: *Periodicals:* Lapsen Maailma (12). *Annual report. List of publications.*

EVALUATION/RESEARCH: Undertakes research activities.

PLANNED ACTIVITIES: Radio broadcasts for adults with news and information about children and their living conditions.

COMMENTS: Information activities related to the Commonwealth of Independent States.

INFORMATION AND EDUCATION ACTIVITIES: **Topics:** Children/youth/ family; Human rights/peace/conflicts; International relations/cooperation/ development aid. **Activities:** Conferences/seminars/workshops/training activities; Exchanges/twinning/linking; Information and documentation services/data bases; Information campaigns/exhibitions; Lobbying/advocacy; Networking/electronic telecommunications; Publishing/audiovisual materials/educational materials.

FIN1553

LATINALAISEN AMERIKAN KULTTUURIKESKUS ♦ Latinamerican Cultural Center

PL 254, 00121 Helsinki, Finland.

Telephone: 358 (0) 607 836. *Fax:* 358 (0) 607 846. *Contact:* Viveca Hedengren, President.

OBJECTIVES: To collect and distribute information on the countries of Latin America and the Caribbean among members and in Finland. To support artistic, literary and scientific projects concerning these countries.

GENERAL INFORMATION: *Type of organisation:* association of NGOs. *Affiliated to:* Service Centre for Development Cooperation (Finland) - Ulkomaanyhdiztysten Yhteiztyoparperto (Finland). *Personnel/Total:* 6. *Volunteers:* 6. *Budget/Total 1993:* ECU 3000 (US$ 4000). *Financial sources: Private:* 1%. *Public:* 10%. *Self-financing:* 89%.

PUBLICATIONS: *Annual report. List of publications.*

INFORMATION AND EDUCATION ACTIVITIES: **Topics:** Children/youth/ family; Culture/tradition/religion; Ecology/environment/biodiversity; Education/training/literacy; Emergency relief/refugees/humanitarian assistance; Food/famine; Gender issues/women; Health/sanitation/water; Human rights/peace/conflicts; International economic relations/trade/ debt/finance; International relations/cooperation/development aid; Peace/ethnic conflicts/armament/disarmament; Population/family planning/demography; Poverty/living conditions; Racism/xenophobia/ antisemitism; Refugees/migrants/ethnic groups; Rural development/

Voir : *Comment utiliser le répertoire,* page 11.

agriculture; Urban development/habitat. **Activities:** Broadcasting/cultural events; Conferences/seminars/workshops/training activities; Information campaigns/exhibitions.

FIN1554

LIIKEALAN AMMATTILIITTO ♦ Union of Commercial Employees

Paasivuorenkatu 4-6 A, 00530 Helsinki, Finland.

Telephone: 358 (0) 77 571. *Fax:* 358 (0) 70 11 119. *Contact:* Maj-Len Remahl, President.

OBJECTIVES: To improve the welfare of workers in Finland and in developing countries and to increase solidarity between Finnish and developing country trade unions.

GENERAL INFORMATION: *Creation:* 1906. *Type of organisation:* association of NGOs. *Member organisations:* 160. *Affiliated to:* SASK (Finland) - FIET (Switzerland). *Personnel/Total:* 168. *Salaried:* 168. *Financial sources:* Self-financing: 100%.

PUBLICATIONS: *Periodicals:* puntari/Pyndaren (20). *Annual report.*

EVALUATION/RESEARCH: Evaluation reports available. Undertakes research activities.

COMMENTS: Undertakes activities in the Commonwealth of Independent States. Information activities related to the Commonwealth of Independent States.

ACTIVITIES IN DEVELOPING REGIONS: Present in developing regions. Active in 2 country(ies). Works through local field partners. **Sustainable Development Actions:** Democracy/good governance/institution building/participatory development; Education/training/literacy; Gender issues/women; Human rights/peace/conflicts; Small enterprises/informal sector/handicrafts. **Regions:** Southern Africa.

INFORMATION AND EDUCATION ACTIVITIES: **Topics:** Children/youth/family; Education/training/literacy; Human rights/peace/conflicts; International relations/cooperation/development aid. **Activities:** Conferences/seminars/workshops/training activities; Fund raising.

FIN1555

LUONTO-LIITTO ♦ THE NATURE LEAGUE

Perämiehenkatu 11 A PL 226, 00151 Helsinki, Finland.

Telephone: 358 (90) 630 300. *Fax:* 358 (90) 630 414. *Contact:* Rauna Mannermaa, Chairperson.

OBJECTIVES: To encourage children and young people to love and respect nature through environmental education. To help encourage young people to take part in local and national decision-making.

GENERAL INFORMATION: *Creation:* 1943. *Type of organisation:* coordinating body. *Member organisations:* 8. *Affiliated to:* Finnish Association for the Conservation of Nature (Finland). *Personnel/Total:* 6. *Salaried:* 6. *Volunteers:* var.. *Financial sources:* Private: 33%. Public: 33%. Self-financing: 33%.

PUBLICATIONS: *Periodicals:* Nuoren Luonto (8) - Sieppo (6). *Annual report. List of publications.*

COMMENTS: Undertakes activities in the Commonwealth of Independent States. Information activities related to the Commonwealth of Independent States.

INFORMATION AND EDUCATION ACTIVITIES: **Topics:** Children/youth/family; Ecology/environment/biodiversity; International relations/cooperation/development aid. **Activities:** Broadcasting/cultural events; Conferences/seminars/workshops/training activities; Exchanges/twinning/linking; Formal education; Fund raising; Information and documentation services/data bases; Information campaigns/exhibitions; Lobbying/advocacy; Networking/electronic telecommunications; Other; Publishing/audiovisual materials/educational materials.

FIN1556

MANNERHEIMIN LASTENSUOJELULIITTO ♦ Mannerheim League For Child Welfare

Toinen linja 17, P.O. Box 141, 00531 Helsinki, Finland.

Telephone: 358 (0) 34 811 500. *Fax:* 358 (0) 34 811 509. *Contact:* Kauko Kouvalainen, Chairman.

OBJECTIVES: To promote the interests of children, young people and families through services, education, training, research and information.

GENERAL INFORMATION: *Creation:* 1920. *Type of organisation:* association of NGOs. *Affiliated to:* Central Union for Child Welfare (Finland) - Finnish Federation for Social Welfare (Finland) - International Council on Social Welfare (Austria) -International Forum for Child Welfare - Internaitonal Association for the Child's Right to Play (USA) - International Children's Community (USA). *Personnel/Total:* 21100. *Salaried:* 1100 of which: 30 in developing countries. *Volunteers:* 20000 of which: 10000 in developing countries. *Budget/Total 1993:* ECU 5400000 (US$ 7002000). *Financial sources:* Private: 20%. Public: 3%. Self-financing: 77%.

PUBLICATIONS: *Periodicals:* Lapsemme (4) - Neuvola (4). *Annual report. List of publications.*

EVALUATION/RESEARCH: Undertakes research activities.

COMMENTS: The organisation is affiliated to 14 organisation throughout the world. Undertakes activities in the Commonwealth of Independent States. Information activities related to the Commonwealth of Independent States.

ACTIVITIES IN DEVELOPING REGIONS: Present in developing regions. Active in 2 country(ies). Maintains local field presence. Works through local field partners. **Sustainable Development Actions:** Children/youth/family; Education/training/literacy; Health/sanitation/water; Population/family planning/demography; Sending volunteers/experts/technical assistance. **Regions:** East Africa; Southern Africa.

INFORMATION AND EDUCATION ACTIVITIES: **Topics:** Children/youth/family; Health/sanitation/water. **Activities:** Conferences/seminars/workshops/training activities; Exchanges/twinning/linking; Information campaigns/exhibitions; Publishing/audiovisual materials/educational materials.

FIN1557

MARTTALIITTO ♦ The Martha Organization

P.O. Box PL 292, 00121 Helsinki, Finland.

Telephone: 358 (0) 646 217. *Fax:* 358 (0) 646 560. *Contact:* Maija Riihijärvi-Samuel, Executive Director.

OBJECTIVES: To improve the well being of homes by promoting the presuppositions for home economics as well as by providing cultural and civic education.

GENERAL INFORMATION: *Creation:* 1899. *Affiliated to:* The National Council of Women of Finland (Finland) - Service Centre for Development Cooperation-Finish Volunteer Service (Finland) - The Nordic Housewives' Association - The Associated Country Women of the World (United Kingdom). *Personnel/Total:* 60. *Salaried:* 16. *Volunteers:* 44. *Budget/Total 1993:* ECU 437000 (US$ 566000). *Financial sources:* Private: 3%. Public: 46%. Self-financing: 51%.

PUBLICATIONS: *Periodicals:* Emäntälehti (12). *Annual report. List of publications.*

EVALUATION/RESEARCH: Evaluation reports available.

COMMENTS: Undertakes activities in the Commonwealth of Independent States. Information activities related to the Commonwealth of Independent States.

ACTIVITIES IN DEVELOPING REGIONS: Active in 1 country(ies). Maintains local field presence. Works through local field partners. **Sustainable Development Actions:** Children/youth/family; Democracy/good governance/institution building/participatory development; Ecology/environment/biodiversity; Education/training/literacy; Food/famine; Gender issues/women; Rural development/agriculture; Small enterprises/informal sector/handicrafts. **Regions:** Southern Africa.

INFORMATION AND EDUCATION ACTIVITIES: **Topics:** Children/youth/family; Culture/tradition/religion; Ecology/environment/biodiversity; Education/training/literacy; Food/famine; Gender issues/women; International relations/cooperation/development aid; Other; Population/family planning/demography; Refugees/migrants/ethnic groups. **Activities:** Conferences/seminars/workshops/training activities; Fund raising; Information campaigns/exhibitions; Publishing/audiovisual materials/educational materials.

See: *How to Use the Directory*, page 11.

FIN1558

NAISASIALIITTO SUOMESSA RY (UNIONI) ♦ The League of Finnish Feminists

Bulevardi 11 A 1, 00120 Helsinki, Finland.

Telephone: 358 (0) 643 158. *Fax:* 358 (0) 643 193.

OBJECTIVES: To promote women's empowerment through the recognition of women's economic, physical and intellectual independence. To promote equal pay for equal work. To work for the criminalisation of all violence towards women. To provide crisis services to women.

GENERAL INFORMATION: *Creation:* 1892. *Affiliated to:* N4TAS (Finland) - IAW. *Salaried:* 4. *Budget/Total 1993:* ECU 297000 (US$ 385000). *Financial sources:* Self-financing: 100%.

PUBLICATIONS: *Annual report.*

ACTIVITIES IN DEVELOPING REGIONS: Present in developing regions. Active in 1 country(ies). Works through local field partners. **Sustainable Development Actions:** Children/youth/family; Education/training/literacy; Gender issues/women; Health/sanitation/water; Population/family planning/demography. **Regions:** South America.

FIN1559

NAKOVAMMAISTEN KESKUSLIITTO (NKL) ♦ Finnish Federation of the Visually Handicapped

Mäkelänkatu 50, 00510 Helsinki, Finland.

Telephone: 358 (0) 396 041. *Fax:* 358 (0) 39 604 200. *E-mail:* FFVH@NKL.FI. *Contact:* Pentti Lappalainen, Executive Director.

OBJECTIVES: To provide information and services for the blind, including rehabilitation, employment assistance and leisure time activities.

GENERAL INFORMATION: *Creation:* 1928. *Type of organisation:* association of NGOs, coordinating body. *Member organisations:* 25. *Affiliated to:* World Blind Union - European Blind Union - International Blind Sports Association - International Agency for the Prevention of Blindness -Sosiaaliturvan Keskusliitto (Finland) - Raha-automaattiyhdistys (Finland) - YTY (Finland). *Personnel/Total:* 300. *Salaried:* 300 of which: 2 in developing countries. *Budget/Total 1993:* ECU 10125000 (US$ 13130000). *Financial sources:* Private: 10%. Public: 40%. Self-financing: 50%.

PUBLICATIONS: *Periodicals:* Näkövammaisen Airut (33) - Manteli (8) - Nyöri (11). *Annual report. List of publications.*

EVALUATION/RESEARCH: Evaluation reports available. Undertakes research activities.

COMMENTS: Undertakes activities in the Commonwealth of Independent States. Information activities related to the Commonwealth of Independent States.

ACTIVITIES IN DEVELOPING REGIONS: Present in developing regions. Active in 3 country(ies). Maintains local field presence. Works through local field partners. **Sustainable Development Actions:** Democracy/good governance/institution building/participatory development; Education/training/literacy; Health/sanitation/water; Other; Sending volunteers/experts/technical assistance. **Regions:** South America; Southern Africa.

INFORMATION AND EDUCATION ACTIVITIES: Topics: Culture/tradition/religion; Education/training/literacy; Health/sanitation/water; Other. **Activities:** Broadcasting/cultural events; Conferences/seminars/workshops/training activities; Formal education; Fund raising; Information and documentation services/data bases; Information campaigns/exhibitions; Lobbying/advocacy; Publishing/audiovisual materials/educational materials.

FIN1560

NUORTEN KOTKAIN KESKUSLIITTO ♦ Finnish Falcon Movement

Sturenkatn 27 B, 00510 Helsinki, Finland.

Telephone: 358 (0) 765 199. *Fax:* 358 (0) 730 383. *Contact:* Saara-Maria Paakkinen.

OBJECTIVES: To help children to develop the ability to think critically. To encourage feelings of responsibility and the desire to work on behalf of society.

GENERAL INFORMATION: *Creation:* 1943. *Salaried:* 25. *Volunteers:* 1300. *Budget/Total 1993:* ECU 715000 (US$ 928000). *Financial sources:* Private: 24%. Public: 25%. Self-financing: 51%.

PUBLICATIONS: *Periodicals:* Kotkaviesti (6) - Ohjaajalehti (4).

EVALUATION/RESEARCH: Evaluation reports available. Undertakes research activities.

PLANNED ACTIVITIES: Undertaking research on the effects of parents' unemployment on children. Campaigning against racism and xenophobia.

COMMENTS: Information activities related to the Commonwealth of Independent States.

INFORMATION AND EDUCATION ACTIVITIES: Topics: Children/youth/family; Ecology/environment/biodiversity; Human rights/peace/conflicts; International relations/cooperation/development aid; Peace/ethnic conflicts/armament/disarmament; Racism/xenophobia/antisemitism; Refugees/migrants/ethnic groups. **Activities:** Broadcasting/cultural events; Conferences/seminars/workshops/training activities; Formal education; Information and documentation services/data bases; Information campaigns/exhibitions; Lobbying/advocacy; Publishing/audiovisual materials/educational materials.

FIN1561

NUORTEN NAISTEN KRISTILLISTEN YHDISTYSTEN LIITTO ♦ YWCA of Finland

P. Rautatiekatu 19 C, 00100 Helsinki, Finland.

Telephone: 358 (0) 448 066. *Fax:* (0) 441 087. *Contact:* Aila Niinikoski, National President.

FIN1562

OPETTAJIEN AMMATTIJARJESTO (OAJ) ♦ Teachers' Trade Union in Finland

Rautatieläisenkatu 6, 00520 Helsinki, Finland.

Telephone: 358 (0) 15 021. *Fax:* 358 (0) 15 02 281. *Contact:* Voitto Ranne, President.

FIN1563

OPINTOTOIMINNAN KESKUSLIITTO ♦ Central Association for Adult Education

Mariankatu 12 A 13, 00170 Helsinki , Finland.

Telephone: 358 (0) 176 633. *Fax:* 358 (0) 626 507. *Contact:* H. Voitto Häkipää, Executive Director.

OBJECTIVES: To organise adult education activities.

GENERAL INFORMATION: *Creation:* 1943. *Member organisations:* 57. *Affiliated to:* Nordic Association of Adult Education (Sweden) - The Association of Finnish Adult Education Organizations (Finland). *Personnel/Total:* 24. *Salaried:* 24. *Budget/Total 1993:* ECU 2025000 (US$ 2626000). *Financial sources:* Public: 70%. Self-financing: 30%.

PUBLICATIONS: *Periodicals:* Opintokenholainen (4). *Annual report. List of publications.*

COMMENTS: Undertakes activities in the Commonwealth of Independent States. Information activities related to the Commonwealth of Independent States.

ACTIVITIES IN DEVELOPING REGIONS: Present in developing regions. **Sustainable Development Actions:** Children/youth/family; Education/training/literacy; Health/sanitation/water; Population/family planning/demography. **Regions:** West Africa.

INFORMATION AND EDUCATION ACTIVITIES: Topics: Culture/tradition/religion; Ecology/environment/biodiversity; Education/training/literacy; Gender issues/women; International relations/cooperation/development aid; Refugees/migrants/ethnic groups. **Activities:** Broadcasting/cultural events; Conferences/seminars/workshops/training activities; Publishing/audiovisual materials/educational materials.

Voir : *Comment utiliser le répertoire,* page 11.

FIN1564

PAKOLAISNEUVONTA ♦ Refugee Advice Center

Ludviginkatu 3-5 B 42, 4th Floor, 00130 Helsinki, Finland.

Telephone: 358 (0) 644 104. *Fax:* 358 (0) 644 109. *Contact:* Leena-Kaisa Åberg, Information Officer.

OBJECTIVES: To provide legal aid, as well as improve the legal status of asylum seekers, refugees and other foreigners living in Finland.

GENERAL INFORMATION: *Creation:* 1988. *Type of organisation:* association of NGOs. *Affiliated to:* European Consultation on Refugees and Exiles (United Kingdom). *Personnel/Total:* 7. *Salaried:* 7. *Budget/Total 1993:* ECU 189000 (US$ 245000). *Financial sources:* Private: 30%. Public: 70%.

PUBLICATIONS: *Annual report.*

EVALUATION/RESEARCH: Evaluation reports available. Undertakes research activities.

PLANNED ACTIVITIES: Organising an education campaign for NGOs in Russia on refugee law.

COMMENTS: Undertakes activities in the Commonwealth of Independent States. Information activities related to the Commonwealth of Independent States.

INFORMATION AND EDUCATION ACTIVITIES: Topics: Racism/xenophobia/antisemitism; Refugees/migrants/ethnic groups. **Activities:** Conferences/seminars/workshops/training activities; Information and documentation services/data bases; Lobbying/advocacy.

FIN1565

PARASTA LAPSILLE RY ♦ the Best of Children

Vilppulantie 2 talo 1, 00700 Helsinki, Finland.

FIN1566

PEHMEAN TEKNOLIGIAN SEURA / PEHMEAN KEHITYKSEN RAHASTO (PTS/PKR) ♦ Finnish Society for Soft Technology / Finnish Fund for Appropriate Technology

Mannerheimintie 13 a, 00100 Helsinki, Finland.

Telephone: 358 (0) 409 227. *Contact:* Ola Poikela .

FIN1567

PELASTAKAA LAPSET RY ♦ The Finnish Child Welfare Association

Lapinrinne 2, P.O. Box 177, 00181 Helsinki, Finland.

Telephone: 358 (0) 69 40 422. *Fax:* 358 (0) 69 44 688. *Contact:* Mirja Winter-Heikkilä, Executive Director.

OBJECTIVES: To protect and nurture children who are in danger of not receiving adequate care. To promote the interests of children in accordance with the UN Convention on the Rights of the Child.

GENERAL INFORMATION: *Creation:* 1922. *Type of organisation:* association of NGOs, coordinating body. *Member organisations:* 120. *Affiliated to:* Association of Special Care Organisations (Finland) - Central Union of Child Welfare (Finland) - Association for Cooperation between Social Welfare and Health Organisations (Finland) - The Finnish Committee of ICSW - International Foster Care Organisation (United Kingdom) - International Social Service (Switzerland). *Personnel/Total:* 10072. *Salaried:* 72. *Volunteers:* 10000. *Budget/Total 1993:* ECU 4995000 (US$ 6477000). *Financial sources:* Private: 24%. Public: 54%. Self-financing: 22%.

PUBLICATIONS: *Periodicals:* Pelastakaa Lapset (4). *Annual report. List of publications.*

EVALUATION/RESEARCH: Evaluation reports available. Undertakes research activities.

PLANNED ACTIVITIES: A project in preventive child welfare work, opening a new regional office in Finland, establishing a new children's family group home.

COMMENTS: Undertakes activities in the Commonwealth of Independent States.

ACTIVITIES IN DEVELOPING REGIONS: Active in 24 country(ies). Works through local field partners. **Sustainable Development Actions:** Children/youth/family; Education/training/literacy. **Regions:** Caribbean; Central Asia and South Asia; East Africa; East Asia; Mexico and Central America; Middle East; North Africa; Oceania; South East Asia; Southern Africa; West Africa.

INFORMATION AND EDUCATION ACTIVITIES: Topics: Children/youth/family. **Activities:** Broadcasting/cultural events; Conferences/seminars/workshops/training activities; Exchanges/twinning/linking; Fund raising; Information and documentation services/data bases; Information campaigns/exhibitions; Lobbying/advocacy; Publishing/audiovisual materials/educational materials.

FIN1568

RAITTIUDEN YSTAVAT (RY) ♦ Friends of Temperance

Annankatu 29 A 9, 00100 Helsinki, Finland.

Telephone: 358 (0) 69 44 177. *Fax:* 358 (0) 69 44 407. *Contact:* Matti Jääskinen, Secretary general.

OBJECTIVES: To encourage member organisations, including those in developing countries, to become involved in temperance activities.

GENERAL INFORMATION: *Creation:* 1853. *Type of organisation:* association of NGOs. *Affiliated to:* Raittiusjärjestöjen RY (Finland). *Personnel/Total:* 11. *Salaried:* 11 of which: 1 in developing countries. *Budget/Total 1993:* ECU 270000 (US$ 350000). *Financial sources:* Public: 80%. Self-financing: 20%.

PUBLICATIONS: *Periodicals:* Ystäview Kesken (6).

ACTIVITIES IN DEVELOPING REGIONS: Active in 1 country(ies). Maintains local field presence. Works through local field partners. **Sustainable Development Actions:** Health/sanitation/water. **Regions:** Southern Africa.

INFORMATION AND EDUCATION ACTIVITIES: Topics: Health/sanitation/water. **Activities:** Publishing/audiovisual materials/educational materials.

FIN1569

RAKENNUSLIITTO ♦ Construction Trade Union

Siltasaarenkatu 4, P.O. Box 307, 00530 Helsinki, Finland.

Telephone: 358 (0) 77 021. *Fax:* 358 (0) 77 02 241. *Contact:* Pekka Hynönen, Chairman.

OBJECTIVES: To develop solidarity with workers and trade unions in developing countries.

GENERAL INFORMATION: *Creation:* 1925. *Affiliated to:* International Federation of Building and Wood Workers - International Federation of Chemical, Energy and General Workers' Unions. *Personnel/Total:* 2180. *Salaried:* 180. *Volunteers:* 2000. *Financial sources:* Self-financing: 100%.

PUBLICATIONS: *Periodicals:* Rakentaja (36). *List of publications.*

COMMENTS: Undertakes activities in the Commonwealth of Independent States. Information activities related to the Commonwealth of Independent States.

ACTIVITIES IN DEVELOPING REGIONS: Present in developing regions. Active in 4 country(ies). Works through local field partners. **Sustainable Development Actions:** Education/training/literacy. **Regions:** South America; Southern Africa.

INFORMATION AND EDUCATION ACTIVITIES: Topics: Other. **Activities:** Conferences/seminars/workshops/training activities; Formal education; Information and documentation services/data bases; Publishing/audiovisual materials/educational materials.

FIN1570

SADANKOMITEALIITTO ♦ Committee of 100 in Finland

Peace Station Veturitori 3, 00520 Helsinki, Finland.

Telephone: 358 (0) 141 336. *Fax:* 358 (0) 147 297. *Contact:* Folke Sundman, Chair.

See: *How to Use the Directory,* page 11.

OBJECTIVES: To work towards disarmament and the abolishment of general conscription. To lobby for changes in Finnish security policy based on citizens' security and global responsibility.

GENERAL INFORMATION: *Creation:* 1963. *Affiliated to:* Peace Union of Finland (Finland) - International Peace Bureau (Finland) -Helsinki Citizen's Assembly (Czech Republic) - Warresisters International (United Kingdom). *Personnel/Total:* 6. *Salaried:* 2. *Volunteers:* 4. *Budget/Total 1993:* ECU 58000 (US$ 75000). *Financial sources: Public:* 71%. *Self-financing:* 29%.

PUBLICATIONS: *Periodicals:* PAX Magazine (4). *Annual report. List of publications.*

EVALUATION/RESEARCH: Evaluation reports available.

COMMENTS: Information activities related to the Commonwealth of Independent States.

ACTIVITIES IN DEVELOPING REGIONS: Present in developing regions. Active in 1 country(ies). Works through local field partners. **Sustainable Development Actions:** Children/youth/family; Education/training/literacy; Emergency relief/refugees/humanitarian assistance; Human rights/peace/conflicts. **Regions:** Middle East.

INFORMATION AND EDUCATION ACTIVITIES: Topics: Education/training/literacy; Human rights/peace/conflicts; International relations/cooperation/development aid; Peace/ethnic conflicts/armament/disarmament; Racism/xenophobia/antisemitism; Refugees/migrants/ethnic groups. **Activities:** Conferences/seminars/workshops/training activities; Fund raising; Information campaigns/exhibitions; Lobbying/advocacy; Networking/electronic telecommunications; Publishing/audiovisual materials/educational materials.

FIN1571

SOCIETY FOR INTERNATIONAL DEVELOPMENT, FINNISH CHAPTER (SID-FINLAND)

Hiihtomäentie 27B 18, 00800 Helsinki, Finland.

Contact: Helena Tapper.

FIN1572

SUOMEN 4H-LIITTO ♦ Finnish 4H Federation

Bulevardi 28, 00120 Helsinki 12, Finland.

Telephone: 358 (0) 645 133. *Fax:* 358 (0) 604 612. *Contact:* Timo Lilja, General Secretary.

OBJECTIVES: To promote "learning by doing" and preliminary vocational training for the young in the fields of agriculture, forestry, gardening, housekeeping, handicrafts, environmental protection etc.

GENERAL INFORMATION: *Creation:* 1928. *Affiliated to:* The European Committee for Young Farmers Clubs and 4H Clubs - The Nordic Youth Cooperation Organisation. *Personnel/Total:* 1350. *Salaried:* 350 of which: 1 in developing countries. *Volunteers:* 1000. *Budget/Total 1993:* ECU 2835000 (US$ 3676000). *Financial sources: Private:* 10%. *Public:* 85%. *Self-financing:* 5%.

PUBLICATIONS: *Periodicals:* Nuorten Sarka (9). *Annual report. List of publications.*

EVALUATION/RESEARCH: Evaluation reports available.

COMMENTS: Undertakes activities in the Commonwealth of Independent States. Information activities related to the Commonwealth of Independent States.

ACTIVITIES IN DEVELOPING REGIONS: Present in developing regions. Active in 1 country(ies). Maintains local field presence. Works through local field partners. **Sustainable Development Actions:** Children/youth/family; Democracy/good governance/institution building/participatory development; Ecology/environment/biodiversity; Food/famine; Gender issues/women; Rural development/agriculture; Sending volunteers/experts/technical assistance; Small enterprises/informal sector/handicrafts. **Regions:** East Africa.

INFORMATION AND EDUCATION ACTIVITIES: Topics: Children/youth/family; Culture/tradition/religion; Ecology/environment/biodiversity; Emergency relief/refugees/humanitarian assistance; Employment/unemployment; Human rights/peace/conflicts; International relations/cooperation/development aid; Peace/ethnic conflicts/armament/dis-

armament; Racism/xenophobia/antisemitism; Rural development/agriculture; Urban development/habitat. **Activities:** Conferences/seminars/workshops/training activities; Exchanges/twinning/linking; Fund raising; Information and documentation services/data bases; Information campaigns/exhibitions; Lobbying/advocacy; Networking/electronic telecommunications; Publishing/audiovisual materials/educational materials.

FIN1573

SUOMEN ADVENTTIKIRKKO ♦ Seventh Day Adventist Church in Finland

Uudenmaantie 50, P.O. Box 2, 20720 Turku, Finland.

Telephone: 358 (21) 365 100. *Fax:* 358 (21) 365 507. *Contact:* Pastor Olavi Rouhe.

FIN1574

SUOMEN AMMATTILIITTOJEN SOLIDAARISUUSKES-KUS (SASK) ♦ Trade Union Solidarity Centre of Finland

Unioninkatu 45 H 115, 00170 Helsinki, Finland.

Telephone: 358 (0) 13 51 833. *Fax:* 358 (0) 13 55 703. *E-mail:* geo2:sask-finland. *Contact:* Dave Seligson, Director.

OBJECTIVES: To support the trade union movement in developing countries through organisational and material aid. To promote occupational health and safety. To promote equality, democracy and human rights.

GENERAL INFORMATION: *Creation:* 1986. *Type of organisation:* association of NGOs. *Member organisations:* 32. *Affiliated to:* KePa (Finland) - Finnish Voluntary Service (Finland). *Personnel/Total:* 5. *Salaried:* 5 of which: 5 in developing countries. *Budget/Total 1993:* ECU 1269000 (US$ 1646000). *Financial sources: Public:* 70%. *Self-financing:* 30%.

PUBLICATIONS: *Annual report.*

EVALUATION/RESEARCH: Evaluation reports available.

COMMENTS: Undertakes activities in the Commonwealth of Independent States. Information activities related to the Commonwealth of Independent States.

ACTIVITIES IN DEVELOPING REGIONS: Active in 15 country(ies). Works through local field partners. **Sustainable Development Actions:** Democracy/good governance/institution building/participatory development; Education/training/literacy; Human rights/peace/conflicts; Other; Small enterprises/informal sector/handicrafts. **Regions:** Caribbean; Central Asia and South Asia; Mexico and Central America; South America; Southern Africa.

INFORMATION AND EDUCATION ACTIVITIES: Topics: Employment/unemployment; Gender issues/women; Health/sanitation/water; Human rights/peace/conflicts; Other; Poverty/living conditions. **Activities:** Conferences/seminars/workshops/training activities; Information and documentation services/data bases; Information campaigns/exhibitions; Lobbying/advocacy.

FIN1575

SUOMEN DEMOKRATIAN PIONEERIEN LIITTO (SDPL) ♦ Democratic Union of Finnish Pioneers

Elimäenkatu 14-16 B, 00510 Helsinki, Finland.

Telephone: 358 (0) 765 166. *Fax:* 358 (0) 77 33 544. *Contact:* Paula Gekelä, Chairman.

OBJECTIVES: To instruct children and youth on class consciousness so that they will grow into fully developed human beings who display initiative, independence and the capability for co-operation. To co-operate with all individuals and organisations who work with children.

GENERAL INFORMATION: *Creation:* 1945. *Personnel/Total:* 3014. *Salaried:* 14. *Volunteers:* 3000. *Budget/Total 1993:* ECU 297000 (US$ 385000). *Financial sources: Public:* 55%. *Self-financing:* 45%.

PUBLICATIONS: *Periodicals:* Punos (4). *Annual report. List of publications.*

EVALUATION/RESEARCH: Evaluation reports available.

Voir : *Comment utiliser le répertoire,* page 11.

PLANNED ACTIVITIES: Themes of the year: 1996-"Friends Everywhere", 1997-"Naturally SDPL".

COMMENTS: Undertakes activities in the Commonwealth of Independent States.

ACTIVITIES IN DEVELOPING REGIONS: Works through local field partners.

INFORMATION AND EDUCATION ACTIVITIES: Topics: Children/youth/family; Health/sanitation/water. **Activities:** Fund raising; Information campaigns/exhibitions.

FIN1576

SUOMEN KATILOLITTO ♦ Federation of Finnish Midwives

Asemamiehenkatu 4, 00520 Helsinki, Finland.

FIN1577

SUOMEN KIRJASTOSEURA ♦ Finnish Library Association

Kansakouluk 10 A 19, 00100 Helsinki, Finland.

Telephone: 358 (0) 69 41 858. *Fax:* 358 (0) 69 41 859. *Contact:* Mirja Ryynànen, President.

OBJECTIVES: To unite libraries and librarians in Finland. To inform the public about libraries. To maintain domestic and international relations.

GENERAL INFORMATION: *Creation:* 1910. *Type of organisation:* network. *Affiliated to:* Finnish Reading Center (Finland) - Peace Education Institute (Finland) -International Federation of Library Associations and Institutions (the Netherlands) - European Bureau of Library Documentation and Archives (the Netherlands). *Personnel/Total:* 6. *Salaried:* 6. *Budget/Total 1993:* ECU 391000 (US$ 508000). *Financial sources:* Private: 6%. Public: 35%. Self-financing: 59%.

PUBLICATIONS: *Periodicals:* Kirjastolehti (11).

EVALUATION/RESEARCH: Evaluation reports available.

COMMENTS: Undertakes activities in the Commonwealth of Independent States. Information activities related to the Commonwealth of Independent States.

ACTIVITIES IN DEVELOPING REGIONS: Active in 2 country(ies). Works through local field partners. **Sustainable Development Actions:** Democracy/good governance/institution building/participatory development; Education/training/literacy. **Regions:** Southern Africa.

INFORMATION AND EDUCATION ACTIVITIES: Topics: Children/youth/family; Culture/tradition/religion; Ecology/environment/biodiversity; Education/training/literacy; Gender issues/women; International relations/cooperation/development aid; Peace/ethnic conflicts/armament/disarmament; Refugees/migrants/ethnic groups. **Activities:** Broadcasting/cultural events; Conferences/seminars/workshops/training activities; Exchanges/twinning/linking; Information and documentation services/data bases; Information campaigns/exhibitions; Lobbying/advocacy; Publishing/audiovisual materials/educational materials.

FIN1578

SUOMEN KRISTILLINEN YLIOPPILASLASLIITTO ♦ Student Christian Movement in Finland

Siltasaarenkatu 11 C 47, 00530 Helsinki, Finland.

Telephone: 358 (90) 719 286. *Fax:* 358 (90) 719 633. *Contact:* Tuula Helppi, Chairperson.

OBJECTIVES: To promote Christian values in higher education. To organise Christian activities among students.

GENERAL INFORMATION: *Creation:* 1897. *Type of organisation:* association of NGOs. *Member organisations:* 7. *Personnel/Total:* 26. *Salaried:* 1. *Volunteers:* 25. *Budget/Total 1993:* ECU 54000 (US$ 70000). *Financial sources:* Private: 5%. Public: 80%. Self-financing: 1%.

PUBLICATIONS: *Periodicals:* Etsifà (4) - Ad Lucem (6). *Annual report.*

EVALUATION/RESEARCH: Evaluation reports available.

COMMENTS: Undertakes activities in the Commonwealth of Independent States. Information activities related to the Commonwealth of Independent States.

ACTIVITIES IN DEVELOPING REGIONS: Active in 1 country(ies). Works through local field partners. **Sustainable Development Actions:** Democracy/good governance/institution building/participatory development; Education/training/literacy; Sending volunteers/experts/technical assistance. **Regions:** Mexico and Central America.

INFORMATION AND EDUCATION ACTIVITIES: Topics: Children/youth/family; Culture/tradition/religion; Ecology/environment/biodiversity; Education/training/literacy; Emergency relief/refugees/humanitarian assistance; Employment/unemployment; Food/famine; Gender issues/women; Health/sanitation/water; Human rights/peace/conflicts; International economic relations/trade/debt/finance; International relations/cooperation/development aid; Peace/ethnic conflicts/armament/disarmament; Population/family planning/demography; Poverty/living conditions; Racism/xenophobia/antisemitism; Refugees/migrants/ethnic groups; Rural development/agriculture; Urban development/habitat. **Activities:** Conferences/seminars/workshops/training activities; Information and documentation services/data bases.

FIN1579

SUOMEN LAAKARILIITTO ♦ Finnish Medical Association

Mäkelänkatu 2, P.O. Box 49, 00501 Helsinki, Finland.

Telephone: 358 (0) 393 091. *Fax:* 358 (0) 39 30 795. *Contact:* Dr. Markku Äärimaa, Secretary General.

OBJECTIVES: To represent the interests of physicians in Finland. To promote health care in developing countries and encourage Finnish physicians to work in developing countries.

GENERAL INFORMATION: *Creation:* 1910.

PUBLICATIONS: *Periodicals:* Finnish Medical Journal (36). *Annual report. List of publications.*

EVALUATION/RESEARCH: Evaluation reports available. Undertakes research activities.

COMMENTS: Undertakes activities in the Commonwealth of Independent States. Information activities related to the Commonwealth of Independent States.

ACTIVITIES IN DEVELOPING REGIONS: Present in developing regions. Active in 1 country(ies). Works through local field partners. **Sustainable Development Actions:** Education/training/literacy; Health/sanitation/water; Sending volunteers/experts/technical assistance. **Regions:** Southern Africa.

INFORMATION AND EDUCATION ACTIVITIES: Topics: Health/sanitation/water. **Activities:** Broadcasting/cultural events; Conferences/seminars/workshops/training activities; Information and documentation services/data bases; Information campaigns/exhibitions; Networking/electronic telecommunications; Publishing/audiovisual materials/educational materials.

FIN1580

SUOMEN LAHETYSSEURA ♦ Finnish Evangelical Lutheran Mission

Tahtitorninkatu 18, P.O. Box 154, 00141 Helsinki, Finland.

Telephone: 358 (0) 12 971. *Fax:* 358 (0) 12 97 268. *Contact:* Leo Huostila, Development Co-ordinator.

OBJECTIVES: To participate with indigenous protestant church bodies in the development of communities in developing countries.

GENERAL INFORMATION: *Creation:* 1859. *Affiliated to:* Finnish Volunteer Service. *Personnel/Total:* 430. *Salaried:* 430 of which: 320 in developing countries. *Budget/Total 1993:* ECU 18899000 (US$ 24509000). *Financial sources:* Private: 75%. Public: 20%. Self-financing: 5%.

PUBLICATIONS: *Periodicals:* Mission (12) - Lähetyssandmat (12). *Annual report.*

EVALUATION/RESEARCH: Evaluation reports available.

PLANNED ACTIVITIES: Integration of Diocesan school system in Pakistan. Establishment of vocational training in a high school in Ethiopia.

COMMENTS: Undertakes activities in the Commonwealth of Independent States.

See: *How to Use the Directory*, page 11.

ACTIVITIES IN DEVELOPING REGIONS: Active in 22 country(ies). Maintains local field presence. Works through local field partners. **Sustainable Development Actions:** Children/youth/family; Education/training/literacy; Energy/transport; Food/famine; Gender issues/women; Health/sanitation/water; Population/family planning/demography; Rural development/agriculture; Sending volunteers/experts/technical assistance; Small enterprises/informal sector/handicrafts. **Regions:** Central Asia and South Asia; East Africa; Mexico and Central America; South East Asia; Southern Africa; West Africa.

INFORMATION AND EDUCATION CO-ACTIVITIES: Topics: Children/youth/family; Education/training/literacy; Emergency relief/refugees/humanitarian assistance; Food/famine; Gender issues/women; Health/sanitation/water; Population/family planning/demography. **Activities:** Conferences/seminars/workshops/training activities; Formal education; Fund raising; Publishing/audiovisual materials/educational materials.

FIN1581

SUOMEN LEPRALAHETYS RY ♦ THE FINNISH LEPROSY MISSION

P.O. Box 160 , 00211 Helsinki, Finland.

Telephone: 358 (0) 69 23 690. *Fax:* 358 (0) 69 24 323. *Contact:* Eeva-Liisa Moilanen, National Director.

OBJECTIVES: To support the work of Leprosy Mission International. To raise public awareness in Finland about the leprosy situation in the world.

GENERAL INFORMATION: *Creation:* 1981. *Type of organisation:* association of NGOs. *Affiliated to:* The Leprosy Mission International (United Kingdom). *Personnel/Total:* 5. *Volunteers:* 5. *Budget/Total 1993:* ECU 102000 (US$ 133000). *Financial sources:* Private: 46%. Public: 54%.

PUBLICATIONS: *Periodicals:* Kädestä Käteen (3) - Från Hand till Hand (3). *Annual report.*

ACTIVITIES IN DEVELOPING REGIONS: Active in 3 country(ies). Works through local field partners. **Sustainable Development Actions:** Health/sanitation/water; Sending volunteers/experts/technical assistance. **Regions:** Central Asia and South Asia.

INFORMATION AND EDUCATION ACTIVITIES: Topics: Health/sanitation/water; Poverty/living conditions. **Activities:** Conferences/seminars/workshops/training activities; Fund raising; Information campaigns/exhibitions; Publishing/audiovisual materials/educational materials.

FIN1582

SUOMEN NUORISOYHTEIDSTHYO ALLIANSI ♦ Finnish Youth Co-operation Alliance

Olympiastadion, 00250 Helsinki, Finland.

Telephone: 358 (0) 34 82 422. *Fax:* 358 (0) 491 290. *Contact:* Olli Sarekoski, Secretary General.

OBJECTIVES: To help young people become responsible citizens. To promote their participation in decision-making and international activities.

GENERAL INFORMATION: *Creation:* 1992. *Type of organisation:* coordinating body. *Member organisations:* 100. *Affiliated to:* European Youth Information and Counselling Association (France) - Council of European National Youth Committees (Belgium) - Youth Forum of the European Union (Belgium) - World Assembly of Youth (Denmark) - Centre for Development Co-operation (Finland) - Pohjola-Norden (Finland) - The Finnish Library Association (Finland) - The Finnish Scientific Library Association (Finland). *Personnel/Total:* 24. *Salaried:* 24. *Budget/Total 1993:* ECU 1166000 (US$ 1513000). *Financial sources:* Private: 2%. Public: 63%. Self-financing: 35%.

PUBLICATIONS: *Periodicals:* Nuorisotyo (8) - Allianssiex-press (26). *Annual report. List of publications.*

EVALUATION/RESEARCH: Evaluation reports available.

COMMENTS: Undertakes activities in the Commonwealth of Independent States.

ACTIVITIES IN DEVELOPING REGIONS: Works through local field partners. **Sustainable Development Actions:** Sending volunteers/

experts/technical assistance. **Regions:** Central Asia and South Asia; Mexico and Central America; Middle East; South America.

INFORMATION AND EDUCATION ACTIVITIES: Topics: Children/youth/family; Ecology/environment/biodiversity; Employment/unemployment; Gender issues/women; Human rights/peace/conflicts; International relations/cooperation/development aid; Poverty/living conditions; Racism/xenophobia/antisemitism; Refugees/migrants/ethnic groups. **Activities:** Broadcasting/cultural events; Conferences/seminars/workshops/training activities; Exchanges/twinning/linking; Information and documentation services/data bases; Information campaigns/exhibitions; Lobbying/advocacy; Networking/electronic telecommunications; Publishing/audiovisual materials/educational materials.

FIN1583

SUOMEN NUORTEN JA OPISKELIJOIDEN YK-LUITO (UNSAF)
♦ United Nations Youth and Student Association of Finland

P.O. Box 93, 00101 Helsinki, Finland.

Telephone: 358 (0) 625 398. *Fax:* 358 (0) 625 398. *Contact:* Tuija Hellakoski.

OBJECTIVES: To promote the principles of the United Nations Declaration of Human Rights. To provide a forum for discussion among members. To foster the creation of international links and exchanges of views and ideas.

GENERAL INFORMATION: *Creation:* 1963. *Type of organisation:* coordinating body. *Member organisations:* 5. *Salaried:* 0. *Budget/Total 1993:* ECU 4000 (US$ 6000). *Financial sources:* Public: 80%. *Self-financing:* 20%.

PUBLICATIONS: *Periodicals:* Sininen Plsneetia (4).

COMMENTS: Undertakes activities in the Commonwealth of Independent States. Information activities related to the Commonwealth of Independent States.

INFORMATION AND EDUCATION ACTIVITIES: Topics: Children/youth/family; Culture/tradition/religion; Ecology/environment/biodiversity; Gender issues/women; International economic relations/trade/debt/finance; International relations/cooperation/development aid; Peace/ethnic conflicts/armament/disarmament; Poverty/living conditions; Refugees/migrants/ethnic groups; Rural development/agriculture. **Activities:** Conferences/seminars/workshops/training activities; Fund raising; Information campaigns/exhibitions; Networking/electronic telecommunications.

FIN1584

SUOMEN OSUUSTOIMINNAN KEHITYSYHTEISTYOKEK-SUS (FCC) ♦ Finnish Cooperative Development Centre

Annankatu 29 A 17, 00100 Helsinki, Finland.

Telephone: 358 (0) 69 44 199. *Fax:* 358 (0) 69 46 860. *Contact:* Harri Porvali, Managing Director.

OBJECTIVES: To promote co-operatives in developing countries.

GENERAL INFORMATION: *Creation:* 1990. *Type of organisation:* association of NGOs. *Member organisations:* 3. *Salaried:* 2. *Budget/Total 1993:* ECU 270000 (US$ 350000). *Financial sources:* Self-financing: 100%.

EVALUATION/RESEARCH: Evaluation reports available. Undertakes research activities.

COMMENTS: Undertakes activities in the Commonwealth of Independent States.

ACTIVITIES IN DEVELOPING REGIONS: Present in developing regions. Active in 8 country(ies). Maintains local field presence. Works through local field partners. **Sustainable Development Actions:** Ecology/environment/biodiversity; Gender issues/women; Rural development/agriculture; Small enterprises/informal sector/handicrafts. **Regions:** Caribbean; East Africa; South East Asia; Southern Africa.

INFORMATION AND EDUCATION ACTIVITIES: Topics: Rural development/agriculture. **Activities:** Conferences/seminars/workshops/training activities; Lobbying/advocacy.

FIN1585

SUOMEN PAKOLAISAPU ♦ Finnish Refugee Council

Ludviginkatu 3-5 B 42, 00130 Helsinki, Finland.

Telephone: 358 (0) 644 100. *Fax:* 358 (0) 644 109. *Contact:* Arja Rämö-Touray, Secretary General.

OBJECTIVES: To raise money on behalf of UNHCR and UNRWA to assist refugees from developing countries. To provide information in Finland on all aspects of the refugee issue. To maintain refugee assistance projects in developing countries.

GENERAL INFORMATION: *Creation:* 1965. *Type of organisation:* association of NGOs. *Member organisations:* 30. *Affiliated to:* The Finnish Volunteer Service (Finland) - European Consultaion on Refugees and Exiles (United Kingdom) - Refugee Advice Centre. *Personnel/Total:* 33. *Salaried:* 13 of which: 9 in developing countries. *Volunteers:* 20. *Financial sources:* Private: 25%. Public: 70%. Self-financing: 5%.

PUBLICATIONS: *Periodicals:* Pakolainen (4). *Annual report. List of publications.*

EVALUATION/RESEARCH: Evaluation reports available.

ACTIVITIES IN DEVELOPING REGIONS: Present in developing regions. Active in 1 country(ies). Maintains local field presence. **Sustainable Development Actions:** Children/youth/family; Gender issues/women; Health/sanitation/water. **Regions:** East Africa.

INFORMATION AND EDUCATION ACTIVITIES: Topics: Children/youth/family; Culture/tradition/religion; Education/training/literacy; Emergency relief/refugees/humanitarian assistance; Gender issues/women; Health/sanitation/water; Human rights/peace/conflicts; International relations/cooperation/development aid; Racism/xenophobia/antisemitism; Refugees/migrants/ethnic groups. **Activities:** Conferences/seminars/workshops/training activities; Formal education; Fund raising; Information and documentation services/data bases; Information campaigns/exhibitions; Lobbying/advocacy; Publishing/audiovisual materials/educational materials.

FIN1586

SUOMEN PARTIOLAISET - FINLANDS SCOUTER ♦ Guides and Scouts of Finland

Kylänvanhimmantie 29, 00640 Helsinki, Finland.

Telephone: 358 (0) 72 82 811. *Fax:* 358 (0) 75 22 681. *Contact:* Kirsti Vaalikivi, Chief Executive.

FIN1587

SUOMEN PUNAINEN RISTI ♦ Finnish Red Cross

Tehtaankatu 1 a, P.O. Box 168, 00141 Helsinki, Finland.

Telephone: 358 (0) 12 931. *Fax:* 358 (0) 654 149. *Contact:* Markku Niskala, Secretary General.

OBJECTIVES: To prevent and alleviate human suffering and to safeguard life, health and human dignity.

GENERAL INFORMATION: *Creation:* 1877. *Type of organisation:* network. *Affiliated to:* International Federation of Red Cross and Red Crescent Societies (Switzerland). *Personnel/Total:* 30250. *Salaried:* 250. *Volunteers:* 30000. *Budget/Total 1993:* ECU 24300000 (US$ 31511000). *Financial sources:* Private: 20%. Public: 30%. Self-financing: 20%.

PUBLICATIONS: *Periodicals:* Punainen Risti, Röda Korset (5) - Katastrofirahasto, Katastroffonden (6). *Annual report. List of publications.*

EVALUATION/RESEARCH: Evaluation reports available.

COMMENTS: Most of the international activities are executed through the ICRC or the Federation of the RC. Undertakes activities in the Commonwealth of Independent States. Information activities related to the Commonwealth of Independent States.

ACTIVITIES IN DEVELOPING REGIONS: Present in developing regions. Active in 50 country(ies). Maintains local field presence. Works through local field partners. **Sustainable Development Actions:** Democracy/good governance/institution building/participatory development; Emergency relief/refugees/humanitarian assistance; Food/famine; Gender

issues/women; Health/sanitation/water; Population/family planning/demography; Rural development/agriculture; Sending volunteers/experts/technical assistance. **Regions:** Caribbean; Central Africa; Central Asia and South Asia; East Africa; Mexico and Central America; Middle East; North Africa; South America; South East Asia; Southern Africa; West Africa.

INFORMATION AND EDUCATION ACTIVITIES: Topics: International relations/cooperation/development aid; Other; Poverty/living conditions; Racism/xenophobia/antisemitism; Refugees/migrants/ethnic groups. **Activities:** Conferences/seminars/workshops/training activities; Exchanges/twinning/linking; Publishing/audiovisual materials/educational materials.

FIN1588

SUOMEN RAUHANLIITTO - YK - YHDISTYS ♦ PEACE UNION OF FINLAND - ASSOCIATION FOR THE UN

Peace Station, Veturitori 3, 00520 Helsinki, Finland.

Telephone: 358 (0) 141 314. *Fax:* 358 (0) 147 297. *Contact:* Kalevi Suomela, Chair.

OBJECTIVES: To promote peaceful international exchanges regardless of political, linguistic, religious or other differences.

GENERAL INFORMATION: *Creation:* 1920. *Type of organisation:* association of NGOs. *Member organisations:* 10. *Affiliated to:* International Peace Bureau (Geneva). *Personnel/Total:* 2. *Salaried:* 2. *Budget/Total 1993:* ECU 74000 (US$ 96000). *Financial sources:* Public: 88%. Self-financing: 12%.

PUBLICATIONS: *Periodicals:* PAX Magazine (4) - Fredsposten (6). *Annual report. List of publications.*

EVALUATION/RESEARCH: Evaluation reports available.

COMMENTS: Information activities related to the Commonwealth of Independent States.

ACTIVITIES IN DEVELOPING REGIONS: Present in developing regions. Active in 1 country(ies). Works through local field partners. **Sustainable Development Actions:** Children/youth/family; Education/training/literacy; Food/famine; Human rights/peace/conflicts. **Regions:** Middle East.

INFORMATION AND EDUCATION ACTIVITIES: Topics: Education/training/literacy; Human rights/peace/conflicts; International relations/cooperation/development aid; Peace/ethnic conflicts/armament/disarmament; Racism/xenophobia/antisemitism; Refugees/migrants/ethnic groups. **Activities:** Conferences/seminars/workshops/training activities; Fund raising; Information and documentation services/data bases; Information campaigns/exhibitions; Lobbying/advocacy; Networking/electronic telecommunications; Publishing/audiovisual materials/educational materials.

FIN1589

SUOMEN UNICEF-YHDISTYS ♦ Finnish National Committee for UNICEF

Perttulantie 6, P.O. Box 148, 00211 Helsinki, Finland.

Telephone: 358 (90) 69 27 500. *Fax:* 358 (90) 69 23 932. *Contact:* U.B. Lindström, Executive Secretary.

OBJECTIVES: To support and promote in Finland the work of UNICEF, by distributing information and educational materials, by raising private funds and selling greeting cards and by lobbying government on behalf of the needs of children.

GENERAL INFORMATION: *Creation:* 1968. *Salaried:* 20.

INFORMATION AND EDUCATION ACTIVITIES: Topics: Children/youth/family; Population/family planning/demography. **Activities:** Conferences/seminars/workshops/training activities.

FIN1590

SUOMEN UNIFEM ♦ UNIFEM Finland

PL 996, Salomonkatu 17 A 4th floor, 00101 Helsinki, Finland.

Telephone: 358 (0) 69 40 944. *Fax:* 358 (0) 69 40 990. *Contact:* Ms. Eila Alanko, Executive Director.

See: *How to Use the Directory,* page 11.

FIN1591

SUOMEN WORLD VISION (SWV) ♦ World Vision Finland

Yrjonkatu 30, 5 KRS, 00100 Helsinki, Finland.

Telephone: 358 (0) 603 422. **Fax:** 358 (0) 603 058. **Contact:** Ulla Tervo, Director.

OBJECTIVES: To enable people to change their condition and reach self-reliance in a sustainable manner. To alleviate poverty and encourage solidarity.

GENERAL INFORMATION: Creation: 1983. **Affiliated to:** World Vision's Worldwide Partnership - Kepa (Finland) - EC-Liaison Committee (Belgium). **Personnel/Total:** 14. Salaried: 4. Volunteers: 10. **Budget/Total 1993:** ECU 508000 (US$ 658000). **Financial sources:** Private: 70%. Public: 30%.

PUBLICATIONS: Periodicals: Katse Maailmalle (2). Annual report. List of publications.

EVALUATION/RESEARCH: Evaluation reports available.

COMMENTS: SWV works closely with other Finnish NGOs and World Vision sister organisations in Europe. Undertakes activities in the Commonwealth of Independent States. Information activities related to the Commonwealth of Independent States.

ACTIVITIES IN DEVELOPING REGIONS: Works through local field partners. **Sustainable Development Actions:** Children/youth/family; Ecology/environment/biodiversity; Education/training/literacy; Gender issues/women; Health/sanitation/water; Rural development/agriculture; Small enterprises/informal sector/handicrafts; Urban development/habitat. **Regions:** Central Asia and South Asia; East Africa; Mexico and Central America.

INFORMATION AND EDUCATION ACTIVITIES: Topics: Children/youth/family; Culture/tradition/religion; Ecology/environment/biodiversity; Education/training/literacy; Emergency relief/refugees/humanitarian assistance; Employment/unemployment; Food/famine; Gender issues/women; Health/sanitation/water; International relations/cooperation/development aid; Population/family planning/demography; Poverty/living conditions; Refugees/migrants/ethnic groups; Rural development/agriculture; Urban development/habitat. **Activities:** Fund raising; Information and documentation services/data bases; Information campaigns/exhibitions; Networking/electronic telecommunications; Publishing/audiovisual materials/educational materials.

FIN1592

SUOMEN YK-LIITTO RY ♦ Finnish UN Association

Unioninkatu 45 B, 00170 Helsinki, Finland.

Telephone: 358 (0) 13 51 402. **Fax:** 358 (0) 13 52 173. **E-mail:** irporane@freenet.hut.fi. **Contact:** Juha Eskelinen, Secretary General.

OBJECTIVES: To disseminate information and material about the UN, its goals and activities. To raise awareness of general international issues and to take an active part in development education in Finland.

GENERAL INFORMATION: Creation: 1954. **Member organisations:** 85. **Affiliated to:** The World Federation of UN Assocaitions. **Personnel/Total:** 4. Salaried: 4. **Budget/Total 1993:** ECU 134000 (US$ 175000). **Financial sources:** Public: 75%. Self-financing: 25%.

PUBLICATIONS: Periodicals: Mkailmanpyörä (4). Annual report. List of publications.

INFORMATION AND EDUCATION ACTIVITIES: Topics: Children/youth/family; Culture/tradition/religion; Ecology/environment/biodiversity; Gender issues/women; Human rights/peace/conflicts; International relations/cooperation/development aid; Peace/ethnic conflicts/armament/disarmament; Population/family planning/demography; Poverty/living conditions; Racism/xenophobia/antisemitism; Refugees/migrants/ethnic groups; Urban development/habitat. **Activities:** Conferences/seminars/workshops/training activities; Information and documentation services/data bases; Information campaigns/exhibitions; Publishing/audiovisual materials/educational materials.

FIN1593

SUOMI-NICARAGUA-SEURA

Tarkk'ampujankatu 10, 00150 Helsinki, Finland.

Telephone: 358 (90) 179 421.

FIN1594

SVENSK UNGDOM - SVENSKA FOLKPARTIETS UNGDOM-SORGANISATION ♦ Svensk Ungdom-The Youth Organisation of the Swedish People's Party in Finland

Gräsviksgatan 14, P.O. Box 282, 00181 Helsingfors, Finland.

Telephone: 358 (0) 69 31 895. **Fax:** 358 (0) 69 31 968. **Contact:** Orn Witting, Chairman.

OBJECTIVES: To motivate the Swedish-speaking youth in political affairs. To inform the public about the problems of the Swedish speaking people in Finland. To promote human and cultural rights. To encourage the Finnish to become more involved in development projects.

GENERAL INFORMATION: Creation: 1943. **Type of organisation:** association of NGOs. **Member organisations:** 56. **Affiliated to:** National Committee of Finnish Youth Organizations (Finland) - Nordic Centre Youth - International Federation of Liberal and Radical Youth. **Personnel/Total:** 208. Salaried: 8. Volunteers: 200. **Budget/Total 1993:** ECU 243000 (US$ 315000). **Financial sources:** Private: 25%. Public: 55%. Self-financing: 20%.

PUBLICATIONS: Periodicals: Svensk Framtid (7). Annual report.

EVALUATION/RESEARCH: Evaluation reports available.

COMMENTS: Undertakes activities in the Commonwealth of Independent States. Information activities related to the Commonwealth of Independent States.

ACTIVITIES IN DEVELOPING REGIONS: Sustainable Development Actions: Children/youth/family; Democracy/good governance/institution building/participatory development; Energy/transport; Human rights/peace/conflicts; Rural development/agriculture. **Regions:** Central Africa; Central Asia and South Asia; South America.

INFORMATION AND EDUCATION ACTIVITIES: Topics: Children/youth/family; Culture/tradition/religion; Ecology/environment/biodiversity; Emergency relief/refugees/humanitarian assistance; Employment/unemployment; Human rights/peace/conflicts; International relations/cooperation/development aid; Peace/ethnic conflicts/armament/disarmament; Racism/xenophobia/antisemitism; Refugees/migrants/ethnic groups; Rural development/agriculture. **Activities:** Conferences/seminars/workshops/training activities; Fund raising; Information campaigns/exhibitions; Lobbying/advocacy.

FIN1595

TAKSVARKKITOIMIKUNTA-85 ♦ Finnish Operation Dayswork Committee-85

Viherniemenkatu 5 A 13, 00530 Helsinki 53, Finland.

Telephone: 358 (0) 70 14 114. **Contact:** Tarja Halonen.

FIN1596

TAMPEREEN KEHITYSMAAKAUPPAVHDISTYS ♦ Tamprere Alternative Trade Organisation

Possijarvenkatu 12, 33400 Tampere, Finland.

Telephone: 358 (31) 34 46 770. **Fax:** 358 (31) 34 50 521. **Contact:** Erkki Aunola, Chairman.

OBJECTIVES: To promote fair trade between developed and developing countries. To offer technical assistance to partners in developing countries to develop and market their products.

GENERAL INFORMATION: Creation: 1983. **Affiliated to:** Suomen Kehitysmaa Kauppayhdistystenliitto ry (Finland) - Internaitonal Federation for Alternative Trade (USA). **Personnel/Total:** 46. Salaried: 5 of which: 2 in developing countries. Volunteers: 41. **Budget/Total 1993:** ECU 287000 (US$ 372000). **Financial sources:** Private: 3%. Public: 16%. Self-financing: 81%.

EVALUATION/RESEARCH: Undertakes research activities.

ACTIVITIES IN DEVELOPING REGIONS: Present in developing regions. Active in 8 country(ies). Works through local field partners. **Sustainable Development Actions:** Debt/finance/trade; Sending volunteers/experts/ technical assistance; Small enterprises/informal sector/handicrafts. **Regions:** Central Asia and South Asia; East Africa; Mexico and Central America; South America; West Africa.

INFORMATION AND EDUCATION ACTIVITIES: **Topics:** International economic relations/trade/debt/finance. **Activities:** Conferences/seminars/workshops/training activities; Fund raising; Information campaigns/exhibitions; Lobbying/advocacy; Publishing/audiovisual materials/educational materials.

FIN1597

TERVEYSKASVATUKSEN KESKUS RY ♦ Finnish Council for Health Education

Karjalankatu 2 C 63, 00520 Helsinki, Finland.

FIN1598

THIRD WORLD TRADE ASSOCIATION OF TURKU

Eerikinkatu 5, 20110 Turku, Finland.

FIN1599

U-LANDSFORENINGEN SVALORNA ♦ Swallows of Finland

Fabriksgatan 40 D, 00150 Helsingfors, Finland.

Telephone: 358 (0) 626 202. *Fax:* 358 (0) 626 202. *Contact:* Johan von Bonsdorff.

OBJECTIVES: To work for international justice and solidarity by supporting local development initiatives in developing countries and by working for this goal in Finland.

GENERAL INFORMATION: *Creation:* 1964. *Affiliated to:* The Finnish Volunteer Service (Finland) - Emmaus International (France) -Prosenttiliike (Finland). *Personnel/Total:* 5. *Salaried:* 3. *Volunteers:* 2. *Budget/ Total 1993:* ECU 66000 (US$ 85000). *Financial sources:* Private: 54%. Public: 15%. Self-financing: 31%.

PUBLICATIONS: *Periodicals:* Svalakvitter (4). *Annual report.*

EVALUATION/RESEARCH: Evaluation reports available.

PLANNED ACTIVITIES: Holding international solidarity campaigns in schools.

ACTIVITIES IN DEVELOPING REGIONS: Active in 2 country(ies). Works through local field partners. **Sustainable Development Actions:** Children/youth/family; Ecology/environment/biodiversity; Education/training/ literacy; Food/famine; Gender issues/women. **Regions:** Mexico and Central America; South East Asia.

INFORMATION AND EDUCATION ACTIVITIES: **Topics:** Children/youth/ family; Culture/tradition/religion; Ecology/environment/biodiversity; Education/training/literacy; Food/famine; Gender issues/women; International economic relations/trade/debt/finance; International relations/ cooperation/development aid; Poverty/living conditions; Rural development/agriculture. **Activities:** Conferences/seminars/workshops/training activities; Fund raising; Information and documentation services/data bases; Information campaigns/exhibitions; Lobbying/advocacy; Networking/electronic telecommunications.

FIN1600

THE UNION OF HEALTH AND SOCIAL CARE SERVICES (TEHY)

Asemamiehenkatu 4, 00520 Helsinki, Finland.

FIN1601

UNITED NATIONS YOUTH AND STUDENT ASSOCIATION OF FINLAND (UNSAF)

P.O. Box 93, 00100 Helsinki, Finland.

Telephone: 358 (0) 62 53 98. *Contact:* Tvija Hellakoski.

FIN1602

VAESTOLIITTO ♦ The Family Federation of Finland

Kalevankatu 16, 00100 Helsinki, Finland.

Telephone: 358 (0) 640 235. *Fax:* 358 (0) 61 21 211. *E-mail:* VL–UMM@cc.helsinki.fi. *Contact:* Jouko Hulkko, Managing Director.

OBJECTIVES: To promote balanced population development throughout the world. To promote the rights of access to information, skills and guidance in family life and family planning

GENERAL INFORMATION: *Creation:* 1941. *Member organisations:* 22. *Affiliated to:* IUFO (France) - IPPF (United Kingdom) - International Council of Homehelp Service (the Netherlands). *Personnel/Total:* 240. *Salaried:* 240. *Budget/Total 1993:* ECU 3915000 (US$ 5077000). *Financial sources:* Private: 36%. Public: 9%. Self-financing: 55%.

PUBLICATIONS: *Periodicals:* Yearbook of Population Research in Finland (1). *Annual report. List of publications.*

EVALUATION/RESEARCH: Evaluation reports available. Undertakes research activities.

PLANNED ACTIVITIES: To raise awareness among parliamentarians, other decision makers and general public on family planning and population issues.

COMMENTS: Undertakes activities in the Commonwealth of Independent States. Information activities related to the Commonwealth of Independent States.

ACTIVITIES IN DEVELOPING REGIONS: Active in 1 country(ies). Works through local field partners. **Sustainable Development Actions:** Children/youth/family; Gender issues/women; Population/family planning/ demography. **Regions:** Mexico and Central America.

INFORMATION AND EDUCATION ACTIVITIES: **Topics:** Children/youth/ family; Gender issues/women; International relations/cooperation/development aid; Population/family planning/demography; Refugees/ migrants/ethnic groups. **Activities:** Conferences/seminars/workshops/ training activities; Exchanges/twinning/linking; Formal education; Information and documentation services/data bases; Information campaigns/ exhibitions; Lobbying/advocacy; Publishing/audiovisual materials/educational materials.

FIN1603

VAMMAISJARJESTOJEN KEHITYSYHTEIST-TOYHDISTTS (FIDIDA) ♦ Finnish Disabled People's International Development Association

Kumpulanme 1 A, 00520 Helsinki, Finland.

Telephone: 358 (0) 613 191. *Fax:* 358 (0) 14 61 443. *Contact:* Arvo Karvinen, Chairman.

OBJECTIVES: To provide service and collaborate with member organisations on issues concerning the disabled, and to implement projects in this field.

GENERAL INFORMATION: *Creation:* 1989. *Type of organisation:* association of NGOs. *Member organisations:* 7. *Affiliated to:* Finnish Volunteer Service (Finland). *Personnel/Total:* 1. *Salaried:* 1. *Budget/ Total 1993:* ECU 135000 (US$ 175000). *Financial sources:* Public: 90%. Self-financing: 10%.

PUBLICATIONS: *Annual report.*

EVALUATION/RESEARCH: Evaluation reports available.

PLANNED ACTIVITIES: Rehabilitation project in Nicaragua.

COMMENTS: FIDIDA's information activities focus on disability issues.

ACTIVITIES IN DEVELOPING REGIONS: Present in developing regions. Works through local field partners. **Sustainable Development Actions:** Democracy/good governance/institution building/participatory development; Education/training/literacy; Gender issues/women; Health/sanitation/water; Other; Sending volunteers/experts/technical assistance; Small enterprises/informal sector/handicrafts. **Regions:** Mexico and Central America; South East Asia; Southern Africa.

INFORMATION AND EDUCATION ACTIVITIES: **Topics:** Health/sanitation/water. **Activities:** Conferences/seminars/workshops/training activi-

ties; Exchanges/twinning/linking; Information and documentation services/data bases; Information campaigns/exhibitions; Lobbying/advocacy; Publishing/audiovisual materials/educational materials.

FIN1604

WORLD FEDERATION OF THE DEAF (WFD)

Ilkantie 4. P.O. Box 65, 00401 Helsinki, Finland.

Telephone: 358 (0) 58 031. *Fax:* 358 (0) 58 03 770. *Contact:* Yerker Anderson, President.

OBJECTIVES: To promote the human and linguistic rights of deaf people in society. To provide support to deaf people to set up and run their own organisations, especially in developing countries.

GENERAL INFORMATION: *Creation:* 1951. *Member organisations:* 103. *Personnel/Total:* 6. *Salaried:* 6. *Budget/Total 1993:* ECU 202000 (US$ 263000). *Financial sources:* Private: 3%. Public: 90%. *Self-financing:* 7%.

PUBLICATIONS: *Periodicals:* WFD News (4). *Annual report. List of publications.*

EVALUATION/RESEARCH: Evaluation reports available. Undertakes research activities.

COMMENTS: Undertakes activities in the Commonwealth of Independent States. Information activities related to the Commonwealth of Independent States.

ACTIVITIES IN DEVELOPING REGIONS: Present in developing regions. Works through local field partners. **Sustainable Development Actions:** Democracy/good governance/institution building/participatory development; Education/training/literacy; Human rights/peace/conflicts; Other; Sending volunteers/experts/technical assistance. **Regions:** Caribbean; Central Africa; Central Asia and South Asia; East Africa; East Asia; Mexico and Central America; Middle East; North Africa; Oceania; South America; South East Asia; Southern Africa; West Africa.

INFORMATION AND EDUCATION ACTIVITIES: Topics: Children/youth/family; Culture/tradition/religion; Education/training/literacy; Employment/unemployment; Gender issues/women; Human rights/peace/conflicts; International relations/cooperation/development aid; Other. **Activities:** Broadcasting/cultural events; Conferences/seminars/workshops/training activities; Exchanges/twinning/linking; Fund raising; Information and documentation services/data bases; Information campaigns/exhibitions; Lobbying/advocacy; Networking/electronic telecommunications; Publishing/audiovisual materials/educational materials.

FIN1605

WORLD FUTURES STUDIES FEDERATION (WFSF)

President's Office, Finland Futures Research Centre, Lemminkäisenkatu 14-18c, P.O. Box 110, 20521 Turku, Finland.

Telephone: 358 (21) 263 83 529. *Fax:* 358 (21) 23 30 755. *E-mail:* Malaska@utu.fi. *Contact:* Pentti Malaska, President.

OBJECTIVES: To serve as a forum for the exchange of information and opinions, thus stimulating co-operative research activities in all fields of future studies. To plan and hold regional and global future studies and conferences. To encourage the democratization of future-oriented thinking and acting.

GENERAL INFORMATION: *Creation:* 1973. *Type of organisation:* network. *Member organisations:* 58. *Personnel/Total:* var.. *Salaried:* 4. *Volunteers:* var.. *Budget/Total 1993:* ECU 25000 (US$ 33000).

PUBLICATIONS: *Periodicals:* Futures Bulletin (4).

EVALUATION/RESEARCH: Evaluation reports available. Undertakes research activities.

PLANNED ACTIVITIES: WFSF 15th world conference, in Australia 1997, on the theme of "Globally netweaving visions of the 22nd century". The establishment of introductory futures courses in South and Central America

COMMENTS: WSF is a network of scholars, planners and policy makers. It does not undertake development activities itself. Individual members in developing regions may support some of the activities listed. Information activities related to the Commonwealth of Independent States.

INFORMATION AND EDUCATION ACTIVITIES: Topics: Culture/tradition/religion; Ecology/environment/biodiversity; Human rights/peace/conflicts; Other; Peace/ethnic conflicts/armament/disarmament. **Activities:** Conferences/seminars/workshops/training activities; Exchanges/twinning/linking; Information and documentation services/data bases; Networking/electronic telecommunications.

FIN1606

YMPARISTO JA KEHITYS ♦ Coalition for Environment and Development

Ympäristökeskus, Hietaniemenkatu 10, 00100 Helsinki, Finland.

Telephone: 358 (0) 746 399. *Contact:* Meri Koivusalo, Chairman.

Voir : *Comment utiliser le répertoire*, page 11.

FRA1607

ACAUPED-MISSION MEDICALE

BP 2, 59932 La Chapelle d'Armentières cedex, France.

Téléphone: 33 - 20 35 77 00. *Fax:* 33 - 20 35 91 74. *Contact:* Armand Marzynski, Président.

OBJECTIFS: Coordonner des projets de développement, apporter un appui technique, matériel, médical et des médicaments à des micro projets. Former et recycler du personnel de santé en même temps que la création de centres de soins de santé primaire, de préférence dans des zones enclavées.

INFORMATIONS GENERALES: *Création:* 1984. *Personnel/Total:* var.. *Salariés:* 2. *Bénévoles:* 350 dont: 350 dans les pays en développement. *Budget/Total 1993:* ECU 150000 (US$ 176000). *Sources financières: Privé:* 2%. *Public:* 8%. *Autofinancement:* 90%.

PUBLICATIONS: *Rapport annuel.*

EVALUATION/RECHERCHE: Rapports d'évaluation disponibles. Entreprend des activités de recherche.

PREVISIONS D'ACTIVITES: Projets de formation et recyclage du personnel de santé, formation à l'échographie et l'endoscopie en Afrique de l'Ouest.

COMMENTAIRES: Intervient dans la Communauté des Etats indépendants.

ACTIVITES DANS LES REGIONS EN DEVELOPPEMENT: Intervient directement dans les régions en développement. Intervient dans 3 pays. Intervient par l'intermédiaire d'organisations locales partenaires. **Actions de Développement durable:** Démocratie/bonne gestion publique/création d'institutions/développement participatif; Enfants/jeunesse/famille; Population/planning familial/démographie; Questions relatives aux femmes; Santé/assainissement/eau; Éducation/ formation/alphabétisation. **Régions:** Afrique de l'Ouest.

ACTIVITES D'INFORMATION ET D'EDUCATION: Domaines: Aliments/ famine; Enfants/jeunesse/famille; Population/planning familial/démographie; Questions relatives aux femmes; Relations internationales/coopération/aide au développement; Santé/assainissement/eau. **Activités:** Campagnes d'information/expositions; Collecte de fonds; Échanges/ parrainage/jumelage; Édition/documents audiovisuels/documents éducatifs; Éducation formelle.

FRA1608

ACCUEIL SANS FRONTIERES (ASF)

Maison pour tous Léo Lagrange, La Paillade, 34100 Montpellier, France.

Téléphone: 33 - 67 44 74 21. *Contact:* Yves Moxin-Wolyung, Président.

FRA1609

ACTEURS ICI ET LA-BAS

8 rue Gustave Rouanet, 75018 Paris, France.

Téléphone: 33 (1) 42 58 36 64. *Contact:* Geneviève Petauton, Présidente.

FRA1610

ACTION D'URGENCE INTERNATIONALE (AUI)

10, rue Félix Ziem, 75018 Paris, France.

Téléphone: 33 (1) 42 64 75 88. *Fax:* 33 (1) 42 54 00 73. *Contact:* José

OBJECTIFS: Tavailler avec les populations sinistrées lors de catastrophes naturelles. Mener des actions dans les domaines de la prévention, de la reconstruction et de la formation.

INFORMATIONS GENERALES: *Création:* 1977. *Affiliée à:* Comité de Coordination du Service Volontaire Internationale - Comité de Liaison des ONG Européennes - Centre de Recherche et d'Information sur le Développement - COTRAVAUX. *Personnel/Total:* 83. *Salariés:* 3. *Bénévoles:* 80. *Budget/Total 1993:* ECU 226000 (US$ 265000). *Sources financières: Privé:* 39%. *Public:* 46%. *Autofinancement:* 15%.

PUBLICATIONS: *Périodiques:* Action S.U.D (4). *Rapport annuel.*

EVALUATION/RECHERCHE: Entreprend des activités de recherche.

COMMENTAIRES: L'action de l'organisation est "thématique" et non "géographique". Les volontaires de l'association interviennent en phase d'urgence et, bien qu'il n'y ait pas de règles précises, l'action se prolonge par un soutien des initiatives locales. Intervient dans la Communauté des Etats indépendants.

ACTIVITES DANS LES REGIONS EN DEVELOPPEMENT: Intervient directement dans les régions en développement. Maintient une présence locale sur le terrain. Intervient par l'intermédiaire d'organisations locales partenaires. **Actions de Développement durable:** Développement urbain/habitat; Envoi de volontaires/experts/assistance technique; Santé/assainissement/eau; Secours d'urgence/réfugiés/aide humanitaire; Écologie/environnement/biodiversité; Éducation/formation/alphabétisation. **Régions:** Afrique australe; Afrique centrale; Afrique de l'Est; Afrique de l'Ouest; Afrique du Nord; Amérique du Sud; Asie centrale et Asie du Sud; Asie de l'Est; Asie du Sud-Est; Caraïbes; Mexique et Amerique centrale; Moyen-Orient; Océanie.

ACTIVITES D'INFORMATION ET D'EDUCATION: Domaines: Développement urbain/habitat; Pauvreté/conditions de vie; Relations internationales/coopération/aide au développement; Santé/assainissement/eau; Secours d'urgence/réfugiés/aide humanitaire; Écologie/environnement/ biodiversité. **Activités:** Campagnes d'information/expositions; Collecte de fonds; Conférences/séminaires/ateliers/activités de formation; Services d'information et de documentation/bases de données; Édition/ documents audiovisuels/documents éducatifs.

FRA1611

ACTION DES CHRETIENS POUR L'ABOLITION DE LA TORTURE, FRANCE (ACAT FRANCE) ♦ Action of Christians Against Torture, France

252 Rue Saint-Jacques, 75005 Paris, France.

Téléphone: 33 (1) 43 29 88 52. *Fax:* 33 (1) 40 46 01 83. *Contact:* André Jacques, Président.

OBJECTIFS: Aider tous ceux qui sont torturés, détenus dans des conditions inhumaines, exécutés ou qui ont disparu, quels que soient leur pays, leur race, leurs opinions politiques et religieuses.

INFORMATIONS GENERALES: *Création:* 1974. *Type d'organisation:* regroupement d'ONG. *Affiliée à:* Fédération Internationale de l'Action des Chrétiens pour l'Abolition de la Torture (France.). *Personnel/Total:* 93. *Salariés:* 13. *Bénévoles:* 80. *Budget/Total 1993:* ECU 840000 (US$ 954000). *Sources financières: Privé:* 10%. *Autofinancement:* 90%.

PUBLICATIONS: *Périodiques:* Le "Courrier" de l'Acat (9). *Liste des publications.*

EVALUATION/RECHERCHE: Entreprend des activités de recherche.

COMMENTAIRES: Activités d'information concernant la Communauté des Etats indépendants.

ACTIVITES DANS LES REGIONS EN DEVELOPPEMENT: Intervient dans 71 pays. **Actions de Développement durable:** Droits de l'Homme/paix/conflits; Enfants/jeunesse/famille. **Régions:** Afrique australe; Afrique centrale; Afrique de l'Est; Afrique de l'Ouest; Afrique du Nord; Amérique du Sud; Asie centrale et Asie du Sud; Asie de l'Est; Asie du Sud-Est; Caraïbes; Mexique et Amerique centrale; Moyen-Orient.

ACTIVITES D'INFORMATION ET D'EDUCATION: Domaines: Droits de l'Homme/paix/conflits; Enfants/jeunesse/famille. **Activités:** Collecte de fonds; Conférences/séminaires/ateliers/activités de formation; Édition/ documents audiovisuels/documents éducatifs.

FRA1612

ACTION ET PARTAGE HUMANITAIRE (ACPAHU)

10 rue Eugène Dischert, 67230 Benfeld, France.

Téléphone: 33 - 88 74 04 06. *Contact:* Jacky Wolfarth, Président.

OBJECTIFS: Apporter une aide aux pays en développement par l'envoi d'équipes de volontaires travaillant avec les populations locales et le financement de divers projets.

INFORMATIONS GENERALES: *Création:* 1986. *Personnel/Total:* 22. *Bénévoles:* 22 dont: 2 dans les pays en développement. *Budget/*

See: *How to Use the Directory,* page 11.

Total 1993: ECU 9000 (US$ 11000). *Sources financières:* Privé: 43%. *Public:* 5%. *Autofinancement:* 52%.

PUBLICATIONS: *Périodiques:* L'Acpahucien (6).

EVALUATION/RECHERCHE: Rapports d'évaluation disponibles.

PREVISIONS D'ACTIVITES: Développement du périodique "Acpahucien", organisation d'expositions sur l'Afrique, conférences, festival achat/vente BD et CD.

ACTIVITES DANS LES REGIONS EN DEVELOPPEMENT: Intervient directement dans les régions en développement. Intervient dans 2 pays. Maintient une présence locale sur le terrain. Intervient par l'intermédiaire d'organisations locales partenaires. **Actions de Développement durable:** Aliments/famine; Développement rural/agriculture; Petites entreprises/secteur informel/artisanat; Santé/assainissement/eau; Éducation/formation/alphabétisation. **Régions:** Afrique de l'Ouest.

ACTIVITES D'INFORMATION ET D'EDUCATION: Domaines: Aliments/famine; Développement rural/agriculture; Santé/assainissement/eau; Éducation/formation/alphabétisation. **Activités:** Collecte de fonds; Radiodiffusion/manifestations culturelles; Édition/documents audiovisuels/documents éducatifs.

FRA1613
ACTION ET SOLIDARITE AVEC LES PEUPLES D'AFRIQUE CENTRALE (ASPAC)

BP 30, 77542 Savigny-le-Temple, France.

Téléphone: 33 (1) 64 41 69 70. *Contact:* Albert Jerry Mahele, Président.

FRA1614
ACTION INTERNATIONALE CONTRE LA FAIM (AICF)

9 rue Dareau, 75014 Paris, France.

Téléphone: 33 (1) 45 65 40 40. *Fax:* 33 (1) 45 65 92 50. *Contact:* Nathalie Duhamel, Directeur général.

OBJECTIFS: Lutter contre la faim en mettant en œuvre des programmes d'urgence et de réhabilitation dans les domaines de la nutrition, la santé, l'eau et la relance agricole. Secourir de façon rapide et durable la population des régions les plus défavorisées du monde en privilégiant l'action directe sur le terrain.

INFORMATIONS GENERALES: *Création:* 1979. *Affiliée à:* Coordination d'Agen. *Personnel/Total:* 199. *Salariés:* 29. *Bénévoles:* 170. *Budget/Total 1993:* ECU 18088000 (US$ 21189000). *Sources financières:* Privé: 25%. Public: 75%.

PUBLICATIONS: *Périodiques:* Interventions (4). *Rapport annuel.*

EVALUATION/RECHERCHE: Rapports d'évaluation disponibles. Entreprend des activités de recherche.

COMMENTAIRES: Intervient dans la Communauté des Etats indépendants.

ACTIVITES DANS LES REGIONS EN DEVELOPPEMENT: Intervient directement dans les régions en développement. Intervient dans 16 pays. Maintient une présence locale sur le terrain. Intervient par l'intermédiaire d'organisations locales partenaires. **Actions de Développement durable:** Aliments/famine; Développement rural/agriculture; Développement urbain/habitat; Santé/assainissement/eau; Secours d'urgence/réfugiés/aide humanitaire; Éducation/formation/alphabétisation. **Régions:** Afrique australe; Afrique centrale; Afrique de l'Est; Afrique de l'Ouest; Asie du Sud-Est; Caraïbes.

ACTIVITES D'INFORMATION ET D'EDUCATION: Domaines: Aliments/famine; Pauvreté/conditions de vie; Population/planning familial/démographie; Santé/assainissement/eau; Secours d'urgence/réfugiés/aide humanitaire; Éducation/formation/alphabétisation. **Activités:** Collecte de fonds; Conférences/séminaires/ateliers/activités de formation; Lobbying/plaidoyer; Radiodiffusion/manifestations culturelles; Services d'information et de documentation/bases de données; Édition/documents audiovisuels/documents éducatifs.

FRA1615
ACTION INTERNATIONALE POUR LES DROITS DE L'ENFANT (AIDE) ♦ International Action for the Rights of the Child

BP 427, 75870 Paris cedex 18, France.

Fax: 33 (1) 42 05 55 52. *Contact:* Luc Chaumont, Président.

OBJECTIFS: Aider l'enfance en détresse par des actes inspirés d'un esprit de tolérance, d'amour et de justice, par des interventions approrpiées.

INFORMATIONS GENERALES: *Création:* 1986. *Personnel/Total:* 87. *Salariés:* 5 dont: 4 dans les pays en développement. *Bénévoles:* 82 dont: 49 dans les pays en développement. *Budget/Total 1993:* ECU 106000 (US$ 124000). *Sources financières:* Privé: 90%. *Autofinancement:* 10%.

PUBLICATIONS: *Périodiques:* Lettre d'information (4). *Rapport annuel.*

EVALUATION/RECHERCHE: Entreprend des activités de recherche.

ACTIVITES DANS LES REGIONS EN DEVELOPPEMENT: Intervient directement dans les régions en développement. Intervient dans 5 pays. Maintient une présence locale sur le terrain. Intervient par l'intermédiaire d'organisations locales partenaires. **Actions de Développement durable:** Droits de l'Homme/paix/conflits; Démocratie/bonne gestion publique/création d'institutions/développement participatif; Enfants/jeunesse/famille; Envoi de volontaires/experts/assistance technique; Secours d'urgence/réfugiés/aide humanitaire; Éducation/formation/alphabétisation. **Régions:** Afrique de l'Ouest; Amérique du Sud; Asie du Sud-Est.

ACTIVITES D'INFORMATION ET D'EDUCATION: Domaines: Culture/tradition/religion; Enfants/jeunesse/famille; Pauvreté/conditions de vie; Réfugiés/migrants/groupes ethniques; Secours d'urgence/réfugiés/aide humanitaire. **Activités:** Campagnes d'information/expositions; Collecte de fonds; Conférences/séminaires/ateliers/activités de formation; Radiodiffusion/manifestations culturelles; Services d'information et de documentation/bases de données; Édition/documents audiovisuels/documents éducatifs; Éducation formelle.

FRA1616
ACTION LOCALE POUR UN DEVELOPPEMENT INTERNATIONAL SOLIDAIRE (ALDIS)

12 rue Souchu Servinière, 53000 Laval, France.

Téléphone: 33 (1) 43 56 24 72. *Fax:* 33 (1) 43 49 38 61. *Contact:* Vincent Restif, Président.

OBJECTIFS: Susciter des échanges directs avec les agriculteurs du Tiers monde. Réfléchir avec des groupes d'agriculteurs pour promouvoir des exploitations agricoles durables, respectueuses de l'environnement et assurant l'harmonie entre le Nord et Sud.

INFORMATIONS GENERALES: *Création:* 1984. *Type d'organisation:* réseau. *Affiliée à:* Fédération Départementale des Centres d'Initiatives pour Valoriser l'Agriculture et le Milieu rural (France.). *Personnel/Total:* 9. *Salariés:* 5. *Bénévoles:* 4. *Sources financières:* Privé: 5%. Public: 90%. *Autofinancement:* 5%.

PUBLICATIONS: *Périodiques:* Lettre ALDIS (4). *Rapport annuel. Liste des publications.*

EVALUATION/RECHERCHE: Rapports d'évaluation disponibles. Entreprend des activités de recherche.

ACTIVITES DANS LES REGIONS EN DEVELOPPEMENT: Maintient une présence locale sur le terrain. **Actions de Développement durable:** Développement rural/agriculture; Écologie/environnement/biodiversité; Éducation/formation/alphabétisation. **Régions:** Afrique centrale; Amérique du Sud.

ACTIVITES D'INFORMATION ET D'EDUCATION: Domaines: Développement rural/agriculture; Relations internationales/coopération/aide au développement; Santé/assainissement/eau; Écologie/environnement/biodiversité. **Activités:** Conférences/séminaires/ateliers/activités de formation; Échanges/parrainage/jumelage.

FRA1617
ACTION NORD SUD (ANS)

14, avenue Berthelot,BP ERAC, 69361 Lyon cedex 07, France.

Voir : *Comment utiliser le répertoire,* page 11.

Téléphone: 33 - 78 69 79 91. *Fax:* 33 - 78 69 79 90. *Contact:* Claude Isakov, Directrice.

OBJECTIFS: Promouvoir une intervention pluridisciplinaire dans différents domaines, en s'appuyant sur la mise en commun, avec nos partenaires du Sud et du Nord, par des moyens humains, techniques et logistiques, en évitant le cloisonnement traditionnel des interventions.

INFORMATIONS GENERALES: *Création:* 1989. *Type d'organisation:* regroupement d'ONG. *Organisations membres:* 5. *Affiliée à:* Coordination Sud (France) - Coordination d'Agen (France) - France-Pays du Mékong (France) - Comité Urgence-Réhabiliation-Développement (France). *Personnel/Total:* 61. *Salariés:* 8. *Bénévoles:* 53 dont: 50 dans les pays en développement. *Budget/Total 1993:* ECU 5050000 (US$ 5915000). *Sources financières:* Privé: 12%. Public: 85%. Autofinancement: 3%.

PUBLICATIONS: *Périodiques:* Nouvelles d'Action Nord Sud (4). *Rapport annuel.*

EVALUATION/RECHERCHE: Rapports d'évaluation disponibles.

PREVISIONS D'ACTIVITES: Renforcement de l'action autour de la prévention du Sida

COMMENTAIRES: Intervient dans la Communauté des Etats indépendants. Activités d'information concernant la Communauté des Etats indépendants.

ACTIVITES DANS LES REGIONS EN DEVELOPPEMENT: Intervient directement dans les régions en développement. Intervient dans 7 pays. Maintient une présence locale sur le terrain. Intervient par l'intermédiaire d'organisations locales partenaires. **Actions de Développement durable:** Aliments/famine; Développement rural/agriculture; Développement urbain/habitat; Enfants/jeunesse/famille; Envoi de volontaires/experts/assistance technique; Population/planning familial/démographie; Santé/assainissement/eau; Secours d'urgence/réfugiés/aide humanitaire. **Régions:** Afrique centrale; Afrique de l'Est; Amérique du Sud; Asie du Sud-Est; Moyen-Orient.

ACTIVITES D'INFORMATION ET D'EDUCATION: Domaines: Développement rural/agriculture; Développement urbain/habitat; Population/planning familial/démographie; Relations internationales/coopération/aide au développement; Santé/assainissement/eau; Secours d'urgence/réfugiés/aide humanitaire. **Activités:** Collecte de fonds; Conférences/séminaires/ateliers/activités de formation; Services d'information et de documentation/bases de données; Édition/documents audiovisuels/documents éducatifs.

FRA1618
ACTION POUR LES ENFANTS DES LEPREUX DE CALCUTTA

26 avenue Kléber, 75116 Paris, France.

Téléphone: 33 (1) 45 00 85 56. *Contact:* Dominique Lapierre.

FRA1619
ACTION SCOLAIRE ET SANITAIRE POUR L'AFRIQUE FRANCOPHONE (ASSAF)

41 rue Molière, 59650 Villeneuve-d'Ascq, France.

Téléphone: 33 - 20 47 31 57. *Contact:* Siradiou Bah, Président.

OBJECTIFS: Promouvoir l'éducation en Afrique. Etablir des échanges entre des écoles françaises et africaines. Contribuer au développement de la santé publique en Afrique par l'envoi de médicaments essentiels, de matériel médical et par l'organisaion de missions médicales.

INFORMATIONS GENERALES: *Création:* 1986. *Affiliée à:* Maison des Droits de l'Homme (France). *Personnel/Total:* 14. *Bénévoles:* 14. *Budget/Total 1993:* ECU 13000 (US$ 15000). *Sources financières:* Public: 30%. Autofinancement: 70%.

PUBLICATIONS: *Rapport annuel. Liste des publications.*

PREVISIONS D'ACTIVITES: Achat et collecte de livres et fournitures scolaires pour l'Afrique, construction d'une bibliothèque àLabe (Guinée), conférences sur les thèmes "Education pour tous", "l'école, base du développement".

ACTIVITES DANS LES REGIONS EN DEVELOPPEMENT: Intervient directement dans les régions en développement. Intervient dans 2 pays. Intervient par l'intermédiaire d'organisations locales

partenaires. **Actions de Développement durable:** Enfants/jeunesse/famille; Santé/assainissement/eau; Éducation/formation/alphabétisation. **Régions:** Afrique de l'Ouest.

ACTIVITES D'INFORMATION ET D'EDUCATION: Domaines: Aliments/famine; Culture/tradition/religion; Droits de l'Homme/paix/conflits; Enfants/jeunesse/famille; Pauvreté/conditions de vie; Racisme/xénophobie/antisémitisme; Relations internationales/coopération/aide au développement; Santé/assainissement/eau; Secours d'urgence/réfugiés/aide humanitaire; Écologie/environnement/biodiversité; Éducation/formation/alphabétisation. **Activités:** Campagnes d'information/expositions; Conférences/séminaires/ateliers/activités de formation; Radiodiffusion/manifestations culturelles.

FRA1620
AFRANE

B.P. 254, 75524 Paris cedex, France.

FRA1621
AFRIQUE CA NOUS INTERESSE (ACNI)

BP 54, 67033 Strasbourg cedex, France.

Téléphone: 33 - 88 78 70 71. *Fax:* 33 - 88 78 70 44. *Contact:* Albin Feliho, Président.

OBJECTIFS: Promouvoir le partenariat d'entreprises Nord-Sud. Aider à la réinsertion des migrants dans leur pays d'origine. Informer et sensibiliser aux problèmes du développement.

INFORMATIONS GENERALES: *Création:* 1990. *Type d'organisation:* réseau. *Affiliée à:* Collectif des Associations d'Afrique Noire d'Alsace (France). *Bénévoles:* 40 dont: 2 dans les pays en développement. *Sources financières:* Privé: 20%. Public: 30%. Autofinancement: 50%.

PUBLICATIONS: *Rapport annuel.*

COMMENTAIRES: Nous produisons et animons une émission hebdomadaire sur l'Afrique le dimanche de 17h à 21h sur FM

ACTIVITES DANS LES REGIONS EN DEVELOPPEMENT: Intervient directement dans les régions en développement. Intervient dans 2 pays. Intervient par l'intermédiaire d'organisations locales partenaires. **Actions de Développement durable:** Petites entreprises/secteur informel/artisanat; Éducation/formation/alphabétisation. **Régions:** Afrique de l'Ouest.

ACTIVITES D'INFORMATION ET D'EDUCATION: Domaines: Aliments/famine; Culture/tradition/religion; Droits de l'Homme/paix/conflits; Emploi/chômage; Enfants/jeunesse/famille; Paix/conflits ethniques/armement/désarmement; Pauvreté/conditions de vie; Population/planning familial/démographie; Questions relatives aux femmes; Racisme/xénophobie/antisémitisme; Relations internationales/coopération/aide au développement; Relations économiques internationales/commerce/dette/finances; Réfugiés/migrants/groupes ethniques; Santé/assainissement/eau; Écologie/environnement/biodiversité; Éducation/formation/alphabétisation. **Activités:** Conférences/séminaires/ateliers/activités de formation; Radiodiffusion/manifestations culturelles.

FRA1622
AFRIQUE 2000

16 rue des Ecoles, 75005 Paris, France.

Téléphone: 33 (1) 43 29 86 20. *Contact:* Denis Pryen, Président.

FRA1623
AFRIQUE PARTENAIRES SERVICES

115 boulevard Lefèbvre, 75015 Paris, France.

Téléphone: 33 (1) 45 33 21 38. *Contact:* Claudette Bodin, Coordinatrice Projets.

FRA1624
AFRIQUE VERTE

49 rue de la Glacière, 75013 Paris, France.

Téléphone: 33 (1) 43 36 00 33. *Fax:* 33 (1) 43 36 67 07. *Contact:* Alain Pecqueur, Directeur.

See: *How to Use the Directory,* page 11.

OBJECTIFS: Contribuer à l'autosuffisance du Sahel en aidant les organisations paysannes à commercialiser leurs céréales, à se forger à la gestion et à se concerter au niveau régional et national. Sensibiliser en France le grand public et les décideurs.

INFORMATIONS GENERALES: *Création:* 1990. *Type d'organisation:* regroupement d'ONG. *Organisations membres:* 5. *Personnel/Total:* 2. *Salariés:* 12 dont: 3 dans les pays en développement. *Bénévoles:* 10. *Budget/Total 1993:* ECU 362000 (US$ 424000). *Sources financières:* *Privé:* 5%. *Public:* 60%. *Autofinancement:* 35%.

PUBLICATIONS: *Liste des publications.*

EVALUATION/RECHERCHE: Rapports d'évaluation disponibles. Entreprend des activités de recherche.

PREVISIONS D'ACTIVITES: Extension d'Afrique Verte au Tchad.

ACTIVITES DANS LES REGIONS EN DEVELOPPEMENT: Intervient directement dans les régions en développement. Intervient dans 2 pays. Maintient une présence locale sur le terrain. **Actions de Développement durable:** Aliments/famine; Dette/finances/commerce; Développement rural/agriculture; Envoi de volontaires/experts/assistance technique; Éducation/formation/alphabétisation. **Régions:** Afrique de l'Ouest.

ACTIVITES D'INFORMATION ET D'EDUCATION: Domaines: Aliments/famine; Développement rural/agriculture; Relations économiques internationales/commerce/dette/finances. **Activités:** Campagnes d'information/expositions; Collecte de fonds; Lobbying/plaidoyer; Édition/documents audiovisuels/documents éducatifs.

FRA1625
AGENCE D'INFORMATION ET DE PRESSE HUMANITAIRE (AIPH)

56 boulevard Foch, 93800 Epinay-sur-Seine, France.

Téléphone: 33 (1) 42 35 23 25. *Fax:* 33 (1) 40 70 00 28. *Contact:* Nicolas Gros.

FRA1626
AGENCE ENVIRONNEMENT DEVELOPPEMENT

30 rue Rambuteau, 75003 Paris, France.

Téléphone: 33 (1) 48 04 99 01. *Fax:* 33 (1) 48 04 99 02.

FRA1627
AGENCE EUROPEENNE DE PROMOTION ET DE REALISATIONS TIERS MONDE (AGEP TIERS MONDE)

28 rue Jacob, 75006 Paris, France.

Téléphone: 33 (1) 46 33 01 90. *Fax:* 33 (1) 64 24 62 14. *Contact:* Geneviève Laporte de Pierrebourg, Présidente.

OBJECTIFS: Sensibiliser les opinions publiques occidentales aux problèmes du Tiers monde par la réalisation de documentaires montrant les réalités quotidiennes dans les pays d'Afrique francophone

INFORMATIONS GENERALES: *Création:* 1983. *Personnel/Total:* 15. *Bénévoles:* 15. *Sources financières:* *Privé:* 20%. *Public:* 60%. *Autofinancement:* 20%.

PUBLICATIONS: *Périodiques:* Programme Action (2). *Liste des publications.*

EVALUATION/RECHERCHE: Rapports d'évaluation disponibles.

PREVISIONS D'ACTIVITES: Opération destinée à alimenter des bibliothèques et des centres culturels au Bénin.

ACTIVITES DANS LES REGIONS EN DEVELOPPEMENT: Intervient directement dans les régions en développement. Intervient dans 2 pays. Intervient par l'intermédiaire d'organisations locales partenaires. **Actions de Développement durable:** Autres. **Régions:** Afrique centrale; Afrique de l'Ouest.

ACTIVITES D'INFORMATION ET D'EDUCATION: Domaines: Aliments/famine; Culture/tradition/religion; Développement rural/agriculture; Développement urbain/habitat; Enfants/jeunesse/famille; Pauvreté/conditions de vie; Population/planning familial/démographie; Questions relatives aux femmes; Réfugiés/migrants/groupes ethniques; Santé/assainissement/eau; Écologie/environnement/biodiversité; Éducation/

formation/alphabétisation. **Activités:** Conférences/séminaires/ateliers/activités de formation; Radiodiffusion/manifestations culturelles; Échanges/parrainage/jumelage; Édition/documents audiovisuels/documents éducatifs; Éducation formelle.

FRA1628
AGENCE EUROPEENNE POUR DES ACTIONS DE COOPERATION TECHNIQUE (EUROPACT)

44 rue de la Paroisse, 78000 Versailles, France.

Téléphone: 33 (1) 30 21 21 01. *Fax:* 33 (1) 39 53 11 28. *Contact:* Marc Giordan, Directeur.

OBJECTIFS: Appuyer l'action des ONG par une aide au recrutement, par une évaluation des projets, et par des études préalables. Appuyer l'action des partenaires du Sud, notamment pour le compte d'organisations internationales.

INFORMATIONS GENERALES: *Création:* 1989. *Organisations membres:* 10. *Salariés:* 5 dont: 2 dans les pays en développement. *Budget/Total 1993:* ECU 241000 (US$ 283000). *Sources financières:* *Privé:* 50%. *Public:* 50%.

EVALUATION/RECHERCHE: Rapports d'évaluation disponibles.

ACTIVITES DANS LES REGIONS EN DEVELOPPEMENT: Intervient directement dans les régions en développement. Intervient dans 4 pays. Maintient une présence locale sur le terrain. Intervient par l'intermédiaire d'organisations locales partenaires. **Actions de Développement durable:** Développement rural/agriculture; Envoi de volontaires/experts/assistance technique; Population/planning familial/démographie; Éducation/formation/alphabétisation. **Régions:** Afrique de l'Est; Asie du Sud-Est; Caraïbes; Moyen-Orient.

ACTIVITES D'INFORMATION ET D'EDUCATION: Domaines: Développement rural/agriculture; Population/planning familial/démographie; Santé/assainissement/eau. **Activités:** Éducation formelle.

FRA1629
AGENCE FRANCOPHONE POUR L'ENSEIGNEMENT SUPERIEUR ET LA RECHERCHE

Bureau Europe, 4 Place de la Sorbonne, 75005 Paris, France.

Téléphone: 33 (1) 44 41 18 18. *Fax:* 33 (1) 44 41 18 19. *Contact:* Michel Guillou, Directeur général-Recteur.

OBJECTIFS: Mailler et consolider l'espace scientifique francophone. Promouvoir la science en français; relancer la recherche au Sud. Créer un espace de mobilité pour les étudiants et les chercheurs. Jouer le rôle d'opérateur du sommet des chefs d'Etat francophones pour l'enseignement supérieur et la recherche.

INFORMATIONS GENERALES: *Création:* 1961. *Type d'organisation:* réseau. *Salariés:* 100 dont: 50 dans les pays en développement. *Budget/Total 1993:* ECU 22613000 (US$ 26487000). *Sources financières:* *Privé:* 2%. *Public:* 90%. *Autofinancement:* 8%.

PUBLICATIONS: *Périodiques:* Universités (4) - Uref-Actualités (6) - Info-Ficu (4) - Le Français (4). *Rapport annuel. Liste des publications.*

EVALUATION/RECHERCHE: Entreprend des activités de recherche.

PREVISIONS D'ACTIVITES: Mise en place d'Ecoles doctorales régionales, de laboratoires associés à l'UREF. Développement de classes bilingues en Asie du Sud-Est. Développement de l'université audiovisuelle francophone. Consolidation du Réseau électronique francophone au sein d'INTERNET.

COMMENTAIRES: Intervient dans la Communauté des Etats indépendants. Activités d'information concernant la Communauté des Etats indépendants.

ACTIVITES DANS LES REGIONS EN DEVELOPPEMENT: Intervient directement dans les régions en développement. Intervient dans 20 pays. Maintient une présence locale sur le terrain. **Actions de Développement durable:** Dette/finances/commerce; Droits de l'Homme/paix/conflits; Démocratie/bonne gestion publique/création d'institutions/développement participatif; Développement rural/agriculture; Envoi de volontaires/experts/assistance technique; Petites entreprises/secteur informel/artisanat; Population/planning familial/démographie; Santé/assainissement/eau; Écologie/environnement/biodiversité; Éducation/

Voir : *Comment utiliser le répertoire*, page 11.

formation/alphabétisation. **Régions:** Afrique centrale; Afrique de l'Ouest; Afrique du Nord; Asie du Sud-Est; Caraïbes; Moyen-Orient.

ACTIVITES D'INFORMATION ET D'EDUCATION: Domaines: Développement rural/agriculture; Enfants/jeunesse/famille; Population/planning familial/démographie; Relations économiques internationales/commerce/dette/finances; Santé/assainissement/eau; Écologie/environnement/biodiversité; Éducation/formation/alphabétisation. **Activités:** Autres; Conférences/séminaires/ateliers/activités de formation; Réseaux/télécommunications électroniques; Services d'information et de documentation/bases de données; Édition/documents audiovisuels/documents éducatifs.

FRA1630
AGENCE INTERNATIONALE POUR LE DEVELOPPEMENT (AIDE)

32 rue Traversière, 75012 Paris, France.

Téléphone: 33 (1) 43 41 50 80. **Fax:** (1) 43 44 38 40. **Contact:** Abdelkbir El-Hakkaoui, Président.

FRA1631
AGENCE PERISCOOP

Parc scientifique Agropolis, 34397 Montpellier cedex 5, France.

Téléphone: 33 (1) 67 61 13 61 . **Fax:** 33 (1) 67 52 39 11. **Contact:** Christophe Naigeon, Directeur.

OBJECTIFS: Recueillir, traiter et diffuser l'information susceptible de favoriser le développement économique et social des pays du Sud.

INFORMATIONS GENERALES: Création: 1983. **Type d'organisation:** regroupement d'ONG. **Personnel/Total:** 47. **Salariés:** 12. **Bénévoles:** 35. **Budget/Total 1993:** ECU 1357000 (US$ 1589000). **Sources financières:** Public: 70%. Autofinancement: 30%.

PUBLICATIONS: Périodiques: Bulletin de presse SYFIA (12) - SPORE (24).

PREVISIONS D'ACTIVITES: Formation en stages de longue durée de journalistes africains. Sensibilisation du Nord aux problèmes du Sud.

COMMENTAIRES: L'organisation emploie des pigistes dans les régions en développement.

ACTIVITES DANS LES REGIONS EN DEVELOPPEMENT: Intervient dans 25 pays.

ACTIVITES D'INFORMATION ET D'EDUCATION: Domaines: Aliments/famine; Développement rural/agriculture; Paix/conflits ethniques/armement/désarmement; Pauvreté/conditions de vie; Réfugiés/migrants/groupes ethniques; Secours d'urgence/réfugiés/aide humanitaire; Écologie/environnement/biodiversité. **Activités:** Autres; Radiodiffusion/manifestations culturelles; Services d'information et de documentation/bases de données; Édition/documents audiovisuels/documents éducatifs.

FRA1632
AGIR AVEC LE TIERS MONDE

83 rue des Haies, 75020 Paris, France.

Téléphone: 33 (1) 43 79 34 49. **Contact:** Laure Herbert, Présidente.

OBJECTIFS: Contribuer à la réalisation de projets de développement. Sensibiliser les jeunes à la question des droits de l'homme.

INFORMATIONS GENERALES: Création: 1982. **Affiliée à:** Fédération Française des Clubs Uresco (France). **Personnel/Total:** 10. **Bénévoles:** 10. **Budget/Total 1993:** ECU 11000 (US$ 13000). **Sources financières:** Privé: 5%. Autofinancement: 95%.

PUBLICATIONS: Périodiques: Blim (4). *Rapport annuel.*

EVALUATION/RECHERCHE: Rapports d'évaluation disponibles.

PREVISIONS D'ACTIVITES: Envoi de manuels scolaires au Burkina Faso.

ACTIVITES DANS LES REGIONS EN DEVELOPPEMENT: Intervient dans 2 pays. Intervient par l'intermédiaire d'organisations locales partenaires. **Actions de Développement durable:** Développement

rural/agriculture; Santé/assainissement/eau; Éducation/formation/alphabétisation. **Régions:** Afrique de l'Ouest.

ACTIVITES D'INFORMATION ET D'EDUCATION: Domaines: Droits de l'Homme/paix/conflits; Développement rural/agriculture; Santé/assainissement/eau. **Activités:** Campagnes d'information/expositions; Collecte de fonds; Conférences/séminaires/ateliers/activités de formation.

FRA1633
AGIR ICI POUR UN MONDE SOLIDAIRE ♦ Act Here

14 passage Dubail, 75010 Paris, France.

Téléphone: 33 (1) 40 35 07 00. **Fax:** 33 (1) 40 35 06 20. **Contact:** Jean-Marie Fardeau, Secrétaire National.

OBJECTIFS: Mener des actions de lobbying auprès des décideurs politiques et économiques (France, CEE) pour l'établissement de relations Nord-Sud plus équitables et plus favorables au développement des peuples.

INFORMATIONS GENERALES: Création: 1988. **Personnel/Total:** 13. *Salariés:* 3. *Bénévoles:* 10. **Budget/Total 1993:** ECU 256000 (US$ 300000). **Sources financières:** Privé: 80%. Autofinancement: 20%.

PUBLICATIONS: Périodiques: La Lettre des Signataires (5) - Documents de campagne (4) - Citoyens et Entreprises (4). *Rapport annuel. Liste des publications.*

PREVISIONS D'ACTIVITES: Campagne contre le tourisme sexuel. Campagne pour l'appui aux mouvements démocratiques en Afrique. Campagne contre la corruption internationale.

ACTIVITES D'INFORMATION ET D'EDUCATION: Domaines: Autres; Droits de l'Homme/paix/conflits; Développement rural/agriculture; Enfants/jeunesse/famille; Paix/conflits ethniques/armement/désarmement; Population/planning familial/démographie; Relations internationales/coopération/aide au développement; Relations économiques internationales/commerce/dette/finances; Réfugiés/migrants/groupes ethniques; Santé/assainissement/eau; Écologie/environnement/biodiversité. **Activités:** Campagnes d'information/expositions; Conférences/séminaires/ateliers/activités de formation; Lobbying/plaidoyer.

FRA1634
AGRICULTEURS FRANCAIS ET DEVELOPPEMENT INTERNATIONAL (AFDI)

11 rue de la Baume, 75008 Paris, France.

Téléphone: 33 (1) 45 62 25 54. **Fax:** 33 (1) 42 89 58 16. **Contact:** Henry Jouve, Président.

OBJECTIFS: Appuyer les agriculteurs du Sud dans leurs démarches d'organisation professionnelle. Développer les échanges entre agriculteurs du Sud et du Nord. Contribuer à un développement rural durable.

INFORMATIONS GENERALES: Création: 1975. **Type d'organisation:** réseau. **Organisations membres:** 73. **Personnel/Total:** 50. *Salariés:* 35 dont: 15 dans les pays en développement. *Bénévoles:* 15. **Budget/Total 1993:** ECU 2789000 (US$ 3267000). **Sources financières:** Privé: 8%. Public: 34%. Autofinancement: 58%.

PUBLICATIONS: *Rapport annuel.*

EVALUATION/RECHERCHE: Rapports d'évaluation disponibles.

PREVISIONS D'ACTIVITES: Formation à la gestion des exploitations et des organisations professionnelles. Formation à la prise de responsabilités de leaders agricoles.

ACTIVITES DANS LES REGIONS EN DEVELOPPEMENT: Intervient directement dans les régions en développement. Intervient dans 12 pays. Maintient une présence locale sur le terrain. Intervient par l'intermédiaire d'organisations locales partenaires. **Actions de Développement durable:** Développement rural/agriculture; Envoi de volontaires/experts/assistance technique; Santé/assainissement/eau; Écologie/environnement/biodiversité; Éducation/formation/alphabétisation. **Régions:** Afrique centrale; Afrique de l'Ouest; Amérique du Sud; Asie du Sud-Est.

ACTIVITES D'INFORMATION ET D'EDUCATION: Domaines: Développement rural/agriculture; Relations internationales/coopération/aide au développement; Santé/assainissement/eau; Écologie/environnement/

See: *How to Use the Directory,* page 11.

biodiversité. **Activités:** Campagnes d'information/expositions; Conférences/séminaires/ateliers/activités de formation; Lobbying/plaidoyer; Échanges/parrainage/jumelage.

FRA1635

AGRICULTURE ET PAYS DU TIERS MONDE (AGPTM)

293 chemin des Micocoules, 84140 Montfavet, France.

Téléphone: 33 - 90 87 56 92. *Contact:* Roland Lichière, Président.

FRA1636

AGRICULTURE SANS FRONTIERES (ASF)

Palais de l'Agriculture, 113 promenade des Anglais, 06200 Nice, France.

Téléphone: 33 - 93 86 58 44. *Contact:* Pierre Canard, Président.

OBJECTIFS: Contribuer à l'amélioration des productions végétales et animales par l'utilisation rationnelle des ressources. Promouvoir la recherche et l'accroissement de débouchés les plus valorisants pour les producteurs.

INFORMATIONS GENERALES: *Création:* 1985. *Personnel/Total:* 47. *Bénévoles:* 47 dont: 5 dans les pays en développement. *Sources financières:* *Privé:* 20%. *Autofinancement:* 80%.

EVALUATION/RECHERCHE: Entreprend des activités de recherche.

ACTIVITES DANS LES REGIONS EN DEVELOPPEMENT: Intervient directement dans les régions en développement. Intervient dans 16 pays. **Actions de Développement durable:** Autres; Dette/finances/commerce; Démocratie/bonne gestion publique/création d'institutions/développement participatif; Développement rural/agriculture; Envoi de volontaires/experts/assistance technique; Petites entreprises/secteur informel/artisanat; Écologie/environnement/biodiversité; Éducation/formation/alphabétisation. **Régions:** Afrique centrale; Afrique de l'Est; Afrique de l'Ouest; Afrique du Nord; Amérique du Sud; Mexique et Amerique centrale; Moyen-Orient.

ACTIVITES D'INFORMATION ET D'EDUCATION: Domaines: Développement rural/agriculture; Pauvreté/conditions de vie; Relations internationales/coopération/aide au développement; Relations économiques internationales/commerce/dette/finances; Écologie/environnement/biodiversité. **Activités:** Collecte de fonds; Conférences/séminaires/ateliers/activités de formation; Lobbying/plaidoyer; Services d'information et de documentation/bases de données.

FRA1637

AGRONOMES SANS FRONTIERES (ASF)

49 rue de la Glacière, 75013 Paris, France.

Téléphone: 33 (1) 43 36 03 62. *Contact:* Marcel Mazoyer, Président.

FRA1638

AIDE A L'ENFANCE DU VIET NAM (AEVN)

92 avenue du Général Leclerc, BP 5, 91192 Gif-sur-Yvette, France.

Téléphone: 33 (1) 69 07 00 44. *Contact:* Tran-Thanh-Van, Présidente.

OBJECTIFS: Venir en aide aux enfants vietnamiens en détresse.

INFORMATIONS GENERALES: *Création:* 1970. *Affiliée à:* Fédération Internationale des Village d'Enfants SOS (Autriche). *Personnel/Total:* 43. *Salariés:* 23 dont: 20 dans les pays en développement. *Bénévoles:* 20. *Budget/Total 1993:* ECU 301000 (US$ 353000). *Sources financières:* *Privé:* 50%. *Autofinancement:* 50%.

PUBLICATIONS: *Périodiques:* Le Lien (4).

PREVISIONS D'ACTIVITES: Créer de nouveaux villages d'enfants, de nouveaux centres socio-éducatifs et médicaux au Vietnam.

ACTIVITES DANS LES REGIONS EN DEVELOPPEMENT: Intervient directement dans les régions en développement. Intervient dans 2 pays. Maintient une présence locale sur le terrain. Intervient par l'intermédiaire d'organisations locales partenaires. **Actions de Développement durable:** Enfants/jeunesse/famille; Santé/assainissement/eau; Secours d'urgence/réfugiés/aide humanitaire; Éducation/formation/alphabétisation. **Régions:** Asie du Sud-Est.

ACTIVITES D'INFORMATION ET D'EDUCATION: Domaines: Culture/tradition/religion; Enfants/jeunesse/famille; Secours d'urgence/réfugiés/aide humanitaire. **Activités:** Campagnes d'information/expositions; Échanges/parrainage/jumelage; Édition/documents audiovisuels/documents éducatifs.

FRA1639

AIDE A L'ENFANT REFUGIE (AER)

5 rue Gassendi, 75014 Paris, France.

Téléphone: 33 (1) 43 27 81 88. *Contact:* Yvonne Clarens, Présidente.

FRA1640

AIDE A L'EQUIPEMENT MEDICAL DANS LE TIERS MONDE

69 rue Saint Laurent, 38000 Grenoble, France.

Téléphone: 33 - 76 51 84 91. *Fax:* 33 - 76 44 71 27. *Contact:* Jean Chung Minh, Président.

OBJECTIFS: Collecter, remettre en état et envoyer du matériel médical dans les pays en développement. Effectuer des missions d'enseignement médical et des missions d'urgence.

INFORMATIONS GENERALES: *Création:* 1986. *Affiliée à:* Collectif Tiers-Monde (France). *Personnel/Total:* 63. *Salariés:* 3. *Bénévoles:* 60 dont: 10 dans les pays en développement. *Budget/Total 1993:* ECU 75000 (US$ 88000). *Sources financières:* *Privé:* 80%. *Public:* 10%. *Autofinancement:* 10%.

PUBLICATIONS: *Périodiques:* Action Humanitaire (4). *Rapport annuel.*

EVALUATION/RECHERCHE: Rapports d'évaluation disponibles.

PREVISIONS D'ACTIVITES: Equipements hospitaliers pour la Bosnie et l'Europe de l'Est.

COMMENTAIRES: Intervient dans la Communauté des Etats indépendants.

ACTIVITES DANS LES REGIONS EN DEVELOPPEMENT: Intervient directement dans les régions en développement. Intervient par l'intermédiaire d'organisations locales partenaires. **Actions de Développement durable:** Envoi de volontaires/experts/assistance technique; Santé/assainissement/eau; Secours d'urgence/réfugiés/aide humanitaire; Éducation/formation/alphabétisation. **Régions:** Asie du Sud-Est.

ACTIVITES D'INFORMATION ET D'EDUCATION: Domaines: Aliments/famine; Relations internationales/coopération/aide au développement; Santé/assainissement/eau; Secours d'urgence/réfugiés/aide humanitaire. **Activités:** Conférences/séminaires/ateliers/activités de formation.

FRA1641

AIDE ASSISTANCE RETOUR CREATIF PLUS (AARC+)

c/o M. Imele, 256 Les Erables, 17ème rue, 69009 Lyon, France.

Téléphone: 33 - 78 66 10 26. *Fax:* 33 - 78 43 87 70. *Contact:* M. Aletanou, Président.

FRA1642

AIDE AU VOLONTARIAT EN INDE

9 rue Sesquières, B.P. 58, 31012 Toulouse Cedex, France.

Téléphone: 33 - 61 25 15 37. *Fax:* 33 - 61 55 17 70. *Contact:* André Seguela, Président.

OBJECTIFS: Venir en aide à l'association Volontariat de Pondichéry (Inde), notamment par un système de parrainage, par la vente de tissage fabriqués par des lépreux guéris et par une information auprès des écoles sur le Tiers-Monde.

INFORMATIONS GENERALES: *Création:* 1973. *Affiliée à:* CIDES (France) - Fédération des Associations Volontariat Inde. *Personnel/Total:* 30. *Bénévoles:* 30. *Budget/Total 1993:* ECU 151000 (US$ 177000). *Sources financières:* *Privé:* 60%. *Autofinancement:* 40%.

PUBLICATIONS: *Périodiques:* Volontariat (4). *Liste des publications.*

PREVISIONS D'ACTIVITES: Mise en œuvre d'un centre d'apprentissage. Construction de logements solides pour des familles pauvres. Dévelop-

Voir : *Comment utiliser le répertoire,* page 11.

per l'emploi. Action dans le domaine de l'hygiène, notamment le problème de l'eau.

ACTIVITES DANS LES REGIONS EN DEVELOPPEMENT: Intervient dans 1 pays. Intervient par l'intermédiaire d'organisations locales partenaires. **Actions de Développement durable:** Développement rural/agriculture; Développement urbain/habitat; Enfants/jeunesse/famille; Petites entreprises/secteur informel/artisanat; Population/planning familial/démographie; Questions relatives aux femmes; Santé/assainissement/eau; Écologie/environnement/biodiversité; Éducation/formation/alphabétisation. **Régions:** Asie centrale et Asie du Sud.

ACTIVITES D'INFORMATION ET D'EDUCATION: Domaines: Développement rural/agriculture; Développement urbain/habitat; Emploi/chômage; Enfants/jeunesse/famille; Pauvreté/conditions de vie; Questions relatives aux femmes; Santé/assainissement/eau; Éducation/formation/alphabétisation. **Activités:** Campagnes d'information/expositions; Collecte de fonds; Conférences/séminaires/ateliers/activités de formation; Échanges/parrainage/jumelage; Édition/documents audiovisuels/documents éducatifs.

FRA1643

AIDE AUX DISPENSAIRES DE KOUDOUGOU ET BOASSA (ADKB)

127 boulevard Raspail, 75006 Paris, France.

Téléphone: 33 (1) 45 48 70 79. *Contact:* Dr. Flahault, Président.

FRA1644

AIDE ET ACTION

67 boulevard Soult, 75592 Paris cedex 12, France.

Téléphone: 33 (1) 40 19 04 14. *Fax:* 33 (1) 40 19 06 62. *Contact:* Jean-Claude Buchet, Directeur général.

OBJECTIFS: Améliorer les conditions de scolarisation des enfants dans les pays du Tiers-Monde grâce aux actions de développement en milieu scolaire et dans l'environnement social.

INFORMATIONS GENERALES: *Création:* 1981. *Affiliée à:* Coordinatio d'Agen (France, Fédération de la Voix de l'Enfant) - Comité de la Charte de Déontologie des Organisations Sociales et Humanitaires.. *Personnel/Total:* 700. Salariés: 200 dont: 175 dans les pays en développement. Bénévoles: 500. *Budget/Total 1993:* ECU 11065000 (US$ 12961000). *Sources financières:* Privé: 88%. Public: 2%. Autofinancement: 10%.

PUBLICATIONS: *Périodiques:* Aide et Action (4). *Rapport annuel.*

EVALUATION/RECHERCHE: Rapports d'évaluation disponibles.

PREVISIONS D'ACTIVITES: L'organisation prévoit d'étendre son activité aux projets d'appui pédagogique, y compris les contenus des programmes scolaires. Elle prévoit aussi des actions au bénéfice des exclus du système scolaire et des parrainages de classes.

COMMENTAIRES: Pour la période 1995-2005, en cours d'étude, l'organisation prévoit une plus forte implantation en Afrique et une intervention en Amérique centrale.

ACTIVITES DANS LES REGIONS EN DEVELOPPEMENT: Intervient directement dans les régions en développement. Intervient dans 9 pays. Maintient une présence locale sur le terrain. Intervient par l'intermédiaire d'organisations locales partenaires. **Actions de Développement durable:** Aliments/famine; Développement rural/agriculture; Enfants/jeunesse/famille; Petites entreprises/secteur informel/artisanat; Questions relatives aux femmes; Santé/assainissement/eau; Secours d'urgence/réfugiés/aide humanitaire; Écologie/environnement/biodiversité; Éducation/formation/alphabétisation. **Régions:** Afrique de l'Est; Afrique de l'Ouest; Asie centrale et Asie du Sud; Caraïbes.

ACTIVITES D'INFORMATION ET D'EDUCATION: Domaines: Développement rural/agriculture; Enfants/jeunesse/famille; Pauvreté/conditions de vie; Santé/assainissement/eau; Secours d'urgence/réfugiés/aide humanitaire; Écologie/environnement/biodiversité; Éducation/formation/alphabétisation. **Activités:** Collecte de fonds; Conférences/séminaires/ateliers/activités de formation; Radiodiffusion/manifestations culturelles; Réseaux/télécommunications électroniques; Échanges/parrainage/jumelage; Édition/documents audiovisuels/documents éducatifs.

FRA1645

AIDE INTER-MONASTERES (AIM)

7 rue d'Issy, 92170 Vanves, France.

Téléphone: 33 (1) 46 44 60 05. *Fax:* 33 (1) 41 08 85 38. *Contact:* Père Bernard de Soos, Président.

OBJECTIFS: Apporter une aide aux monastères des ordres bénédictin et cistercien récemment fondés dans le Tiers-Monde, afin qu'ils puissent assurer leurs propres charges matérielles et aider les populations locales, souvent démunies, qui les accueillent.

INFORMATIONS GENERALES: *Création:* 1960. *Personnel/Total:* 3. *Bénévoles:* 3. *Budget/Total 1993:* ECU 377000 (US$ 441000). *Sources financières:* Privé: 100%.

PUBLICATIONS: *Périodiques:* Bulletin de l'AIM (2) - Lettre (4). *Liste des publications.*

EVALUATION/RECHERCHE: Entreprend des activités de recherche.

PREVISIONS D'ACTIVITES: Ouverture de trois studium de théologie.

ACTIVITES DANS LES REGIONS EN DEVELOPPEMENT: Intervient directement dans les régions en développement. Intervient dans 24 pays. Intervient par l'intermédiaire d'organisations locales partenaires. **Actions de Développement durable:** Développement rural/agriculture; Envoi de volontaires/experts/assistance technique; Éducation/formation/alphabétisation. **Régions:** Afrique australe; Afrique centrale; Afrique de l'Est; Afrique de l'Ouest; Amérique du Sud; Asie centrale et Asie du Sud; Asie du Sud-Est; Mexique et Amerique centrale; Moyen-Orient.

ACTIVITES D'INFORMATION ET D'EDUCATION: Domaines: Culture/tradition/religion; Développement rural/agriculture; Éducation/formation/alphabétisation. **Activités:** Collecte de fonds; Conférences/séminaires/ateliers/activités de formation; Édition/documents audiovisuels/documents éducatifs; Éducation formelle.

FRA1646

AIDE MEDICALE ET SANITAIRE AU NEPAL (AMS) ♦ French Medical and Sanitary Aid for Nepal

144 rue de Grenelle, 75007 Paris, France.

Téléphone: 33 (1) 45 55 85 93. *Contact:* Dr. Sylvie Besson, Présidente.

FRA1647

AIDE MEDICALE INTERNATIONALE (AMI)

119 rue des Amandiers, 75020 Paris, France.

Téléphone: 33 (1) 46 36 04 04 . *Fax:* 33 (1) 46 36 66 10. *Contact:* Edith Leroux, Présidente.

OBJECTIFS: Porter secours, sans discrimination, aux populations menacées ou délaissées sur le plan sanitaire. Aider ces populations à se prendre en charge.

INFORMATIONS GENERALES: *Création:* 1979. *Type d'organisation:* réseau. *Affiliée à:* Coordination d'Agen (France). *Personnel/Total:* 102. *Salariés:* 2. *Bénévoles:* 100 dont: 15 dans les pays en développement. *Budget/Total 1993:* ECU 422000 (US$ 494000). *Sources financières:* Privé: 51%. Public: 46%. Autofinancement: 3%.

PUBLICATIONS: *Périodiques:* La Chronique (4). *Rapport annuel.*

ACTIVITES DANS LES REGIONS EN DEVELOPPEMENT: Intervient directement dans les régions en développement. Intervient dans 5 pays. Maintient une présence locale sur le terrain. Intervient par l'intermédiaire d'organisations locales partenaires. **Actions de Développement durable:** Développement rural/agriculture; Questions relatives aux femmes; Secours d'urgence/réfugiés/aide humanitaire; Éducation/formation/alphabétisation. **Régions:** Afrique centrale; Amérique du Sud; Asie centrale et Asie du Sud; Asie du Sud-Est.

ACTIVITES D'INFORMATION ET D'EDUCATION: Domaines: Questions relatives aux femmes; Relations économiques internationales/commerce/dette/finances; Santé/assainissement/eau; Secours d'urgence/réfugiés/aide humanitaire; Éducation/formation/alphabétisation. **Activités:** Campagnes d'information/expositions; Collecte de fonds; Conférences/séminaires/ateliers/activités de formation; Services

d'information et de documentation/bases de données; Échanges/parrainage/jumelage; Édition/documents audiovisuels/documents éducatifs; Éducation formelle.

FRA1648

AIDE ODONTOLOGIQUE INTERNATIONALE (AOI)

115 rue Lamarck, 75018 Paris, France.

Téléphone: 33 (1) 42 26 52 90. *Fax:* 33 (1) 42 26 07 92. *Contact:* Dr. Jacques Abellard, Président.

OBJECTIFS: Analyser la situation bucco-dentaire, mettre en place et gérer des services dentaires. Faire de la prévention. Former des prothésistes et des infirmiers pour les soins de premier secours.

INFORMATIONS GENERALES: *Création:* 1983. *Affiliée à:* CLONG (France). *Personnel/Total:* 10. *Salariés:* 3. *Bénévoles:* 7 dont: 7 dans les pays en développement. *Budget/Total 1993:* ECU 271000 (US$ 318000). *Sources financières:* Privé: 20%. Public: 40%. Autofinancement: 40%.

PUBLICATIONS: *Périodiques:* Lettre de l'AOI (4). *Liste des publications.*

EVALUATION/RECHERCHE: Rapports d'évaluation disponibles. Entreprend des activités de recherche.

COMMENTAIRES: Intervient dans la Communauté des Etats indépendants.

ACTIVITES DANS LES REGIONS EN DEVELOPPEMENT: Intervient directement dans les régions en développement. Intervient dans 9 pays. Maintient une présence locale sur le terrain. **Actions de Développement durable:** Santé/assainissement/eau. **Régions:** Afrique de l'Ouest; Asie du Sud-Est.

ACTIVITES D'INFORMATION ET D'EDUCATION: Domaines: Santé/assainissement/eau. **Activités:** Campagnes d'information/expositions; Collecte de fonds; Conférences/séminaires/ateliers/activités de formation; Édition/documents audiovisuels/documents éducatifs.

FRA1649

AIR SECOURS INTERNATIONAL (ASI)

5 rue Lebon, 75017 Paris, France.

Téléphone: 33 (1) 45 74 77 66. *Fax:* 33 (1) 31 83 24 55. *Contact:* Dr. Jean-Luc Condamine, Président.

OBJECTIFS: Mettre au point des projets de développement intégrés à deux volets: santé et économie, avec des objectifs de formation et d'autonomie financière, en utilisant des moyens logistiques aériens.

INFORMATIONS GENERALES: *Création:* 1983. *Personnel/Total:* 17. *Salariés:* 8 dont: 8 dans les pays en développement. *Bénévoles:* 9 dont: 9 dans les pays en développement. *Budget/Total 1993:* ECU 300000 (US$ 353000). *Sources financières:* Privé: 20%. Public: 60%. Autofinancement: 20%.

PUBLICATIONS: *Périodiques:* ASI Info (4). *Rapport annuel.*

EVALUATION/RECHERCHE: Rapports d'évaluation disponibles.

ACTIVITES DANS LES REGIONS EN DEVELOPPEMENT: Intervient directement dans les régions en développement. Intervient dans 2 pays. Maintient une présence locale sur le terrain. Intervient par l'intermédiaire d'organisations locales partenaires. **Actions de Développement durable:** Démocratie/bonne gestion publique/création d'institutions/développement participatif; Développement rural/agriculture; Petites entreprises/secteur informel/artisanat; Santé/assainissement/eau. **Régions:** Afrique centrale; Afrique de l'Ouest.

ACTIVITES D'INFORMATION ET D'EDUCATION: Domaines: Développement rural/agriculture; Relations internationales/coopération/aide au développement; Santé/assainissement/eau. **Activités:** Collecte de fonds; Éducation formelle.

FRA1650

ALERTE AUX REALITES INTERNATIONALES

9 bis rue de Valence, 75009 Paris, France.

Téléphone: 33 (1) 47 07 10 23. *Fax:* 33 (1) 47 07 10 33. *Contact:* Jacques Bourdillon, Président.

OBJECTIFS: Aider à la prise de conscience des mutations et des enjeux internationaux et contribuer à rendre chacun plus lucide, plus responsable et soucieux du respect de l'autre.

INFORMATIONS GENERALES: *Création:* 1983. *Type d'organisation:* réseau. *Personnel/Total:* 62. *Salariés:* 2. *Bénévoles:* 60. *Budget/Total 1993:* ECU 48000 (US$ 57000). *Sources financières:* Public: 25%. Autofinancement: 75%.

PUBLICATIONS: *Périodiques:* La Lettre d'Alerte aux Réalités Internationales (12). *Liste des publications.*

PREVISIONS D'ACTIVITES: Cycles de formation aux réalités internationales, conférences-débat, journées d'études, voyages d'études.

COMMENTAIRES: Activités d'information concernant la Communauté des Etats indépendants.

FRA1651

ALLIANCE DES UNIONS CHRETIENNES DE JEUNES GENS DE FRANCE (UCJG)

5 place de Vénétie, 75643 Paris cedex 13, France.

Téléphone: 33 (1) 45 86 84 32. *Fax:* 33 (1) 45 86 64 92. *Contact:* François Seidenbinder, Secrétaire général.

OBJECTIFS: Sensibiliser l'opinion publique, en France, aux problèmes de développement afin de créer des réseaux de solidarité Nord-Sud. Soutenir des actions de formation pour les acteurs de développement, notamment les jeunes et les femmes, dans les pays en développement.

INFORMATIONS GENERALES: *Création:* 1844. *Affiliée à:* Alliance Universelle Y.M.C.A. (Suisse). *Personnel/Total:* 17. *Salariés:* 17. *Budget/Total 1993:* ECU 2261000 (US$ 2649000). *Sources financières:* Privé: 25%. Public: 15%. Autofinancement: 60%.

PUBLICATIONS: *Périodiques:* Triangle (4). *Liste des publications.*

PREVISIONS D'ACTIVITES: Déployer l'activité autour des drois des enfants et de la formation des femmes.

ACTIVITES DANS LES REGIONS EN DEVELOPPEMENT: Intervient dans 5 pays. Intervient par l'intermédiaire d'organisations locales partenaires. **Actions de Développement durable:** Droits de l'Homme/paix/conflits; Développement rural/agriculture; Enfants/jeunesse/famille; Secours d'urgence/réfugiés/aide humanitaire; Écologie/environnement/biodiversité; Éducation/formation/alphabétisation. **Régions:** Afrique australe; Afrique centrale; Afrique de l'Est; Afrique de l'Ouest; Afrique du Nord; Amérique du Sud; Asie centrale et Asie du Sud; Asie de l'Est; Asie du Sud-Est; Caraïbes; Mexique et Amerique centrale; Moyen-Orient; Océanie.

ACTIVITES D'INFORMATION ET D'EDUCATION: Domaines: Droits de l'Homme/paix/conflits; Développement rural/agriculture; Enfants/jeunesse/famille; Pauvreté/conditions de vie; Racisme/xénophobie/antisémitisme; Réfugiés/migrants/groupes ethniques; Secours d'urgence/réfugiés/aide humanitaire; Écologie/environnement/biodiversité; Éducation/formation/alphabétisation. **Activités:** Campagnes d'information/expositions; Collecte de fonds; Conférences/séminaires/ateliers/activités de formation; Lobbying/plaidoyer; Radiodiffusion/manifestations culturelles; Échanges/parrainage/jumelage; Éducation formelle.

FRA1652

ALLIANCE INTERNATIONALE DE LA COOPERATION SCOLAIRE (AICS)

101 bis rue du Ranelagh, 75016 Paris, France.

Téléphone: 33 (1) 45 25 46 07. *Contact:* Madeleine Alary, Présidente.

FRA1653

ALTAIR

14 avenue Berthelot, 69007 Lyon, France.

Téléphone: 33 - 78 92 93 64. *Contact:* Christèle Morel, Présidente.

OBJECTIFS: Prendre part à des projets de développement rural dans les zones les plus défavorisées du monde en coopérant avec les organisations qui y travaillent. Favoriser l'éducation au développement rural. Permettre aux étudiants d'acquérir une connaissance et une expérience du développement rural.

Voir : *Comment utiliser le répertoire,* page 11.

INFORMATIONS GENERALES: *Création:* 1989. *Type d'organisation:* collectif. *Affiliée à:* Action Nord-Sud (France) - Associations de Développement du Rhône (France). *Personnel/Total:* 20. *Bénévoles:* 20. *Budget/Total 1993:* ECU 15000 (US$ 18000). *Sources financières:* Autofinancement: 100%.

PUBLICATIONS: *Périodiques:* Action Développement (4).

COMMENTAIRES: ALTAIR est une association d'étudiants de l'ISARA (Institut Supérieur d'Agriculture Rhône-Alpes), et est entièrement gérée par ces étudiants.

ACTIVITES DANS LES REGIONS EN DEVELOPPEMENT: Intervient dans 2 pays. Intervient par l'intermédiaire d'organisations locales partenaires. **Actions de Développement durable:** Développement rural/agriculture. **Régions:** Afrique de l'Est; Asie du Sud-Est.

ACTIVITES D'INFORMATION ET D'EDUCATION: **Domaines:** Développement rural/agriculture. **Activités:** Campagnes d'information/expositions; Conférences/séminaires/ateliers/activités de formation; Radiodiffusion/manifestations culturelles.

FRA1654

ALTERNATIVES TECHNIQUES ET SYSTEMES ALIMENTAIRES (ALTERSIAL)

1 avenue des Olympiades, 91305 Massy, France.

Téléphone: 33 (1) 69 20 05 23. *Contact:* José Muchnik.

FRA1655

LES AMIS D'UN COIN DE L'INDE ET DU MONDE (LACIM)

42540 Croizet-sur-Gand, France.

Téléphone: 33 - 77 63 21 07. *Contact:* Claude Charlat, Présidente.

OBJECTIFS: Effectuer des jumelages entre des groupes français et des villages du Tiers monde. Apporter de l'aide, notamment pour le forage de puits et l'achat d'animaux. Fournir une assistance aux écoles, aux dispensaires et aux maternités.

INFORMATIONS GENERALES: *Création:* 1966. *Personnel/Total:* VAR. *Salariés:* 17 dont: 13 dans les pays en développement. *Bénévoles:* VAR. *Budget/Total 1993:* ECU 1609000 (US$ 1884000). *Sources financières:* Privé: 94%. Public: 16%.

PUBLICATIONS: *Rapport annuel.*

EVALUATION/RECHERCHE: Rapports d'évaluation disponibles. Entreprend des activités de recherche.

ACTIVITES DANS LES REGIONS EN DEVELOPPEMENT: Intervient directement dans les régions en développement. Intervient dans 26 pays. Maintient une présence locale sur le terrain. Intervient par l'intermédiaire d'organisations locales partenaires. **Actions de Développement durable:** Développement rural/agriculture; Petites entreprises/secteur informel/artisanat; Santé/assainissement/eau; Éducation/formation/alphabétisation. **Régions:** Afrique de l'Ouest; Amérique du Sud; Asie centrale et Asie du Sud.

ACTIVITES D'INFORMATION ET D'EDUCATION: **Domaines:** Développement rural/agriculture; Pauvreté/conditions de vie; Santé/assainissement/eau; Éducation/formation/alphabétisation. **Activités:** Échanges/parrainage/jumelage.

FRA1656

LES AMIS DE LA TERRE ♦ Friends of the Earth

38 rue Meslay, 75003 Paris, France.

Téléphone: 33 (1) 48 87 33 44. *Fax:* 33 (1) 48 87 28 23. *Contact:* Philippe Lequenne, Président.

OBJECTIFS: Contribuer à la protection de l'environnement dans tous les domaines: air, eau, déchets, littoral, mers, forêts, énergie. Travailler autour du thème de l'économie durable. Rendre la science et le progrès compatibles avec un monde solidaire. Promouvoir les biotechnologies et la bioéthique.

INFORMATIONS GENERALES: *Création:* 1970. *Type d'organisation:* réseau. *Affiliée à:* Fédération Mondiale des Amis de la Terre (Pays-Bas). *Personnel/Total:* 27. *Salariés:* 5. *Bénévoles:* 22. *Budget/*

Total 1993: ECU 226000 (US$ 265000). *Sources financières:* Privé: 46%. Public: 22%. Autofinancement: 30%.

PUBLICATIONS: *Périodiques:* Courrier de la Baleine (12). *Rapport annuel. Liste des publications.*

COMMENTAIRES: Intervient dans la Communauté des Etats indépendants.

ACTIVITES DANS LES REGIONS EN DEVELOPPEMENT: Intervient par l'intermédiaire d'organisations locales partenaires.

ACTIVITES D'INFORMATION ET D'EDUCATION: **Domaines:** Écologie/environnement/biodiversité. **Activités:** Campagnes d'information/expositions; Conférences/séminaires/ateliers/activités de formation; Services d'information et de documentation/bases de données; Édition/documents audiovisuels/documents éducatifs.

FRA1657

LES AMIS DE TOPAZA

16460 Aunac, France.

Téléphone: 33 - 45 22 24 07. *Fax:* 33 - 45 22 56 70. *Contact:* Marie-Thérèse Miremont, Présidente.

OBJECTIFS: Réaliser des actions dans les domaines de la santé, de l'éducation et du développement agricole, à Madagascar.

INFORMATIONS GENERALES: *Création:* 1986. *Personnel/Total:* 29. *Salariés:* 1. *Bénévoles:* 28 dont: 3 dans les pays en développement. *Budget/Total 1993:* ECU 38000 (US$ 44000). *Sources financières:* Privé: 45%. Autofinancement: 55%.

ACTIVITES DANS LES REGIONS EN DEVELOPPEMENT: Intervient dans 1 pays. Intervient par l'intermédiaire d'organisations locales partenaires. **Actions de Développement durable:** Développement rural/agriculture; Enfants/jeunesse/famille; Santé/assainissement/eau; Secours d'urgence/réfugiés/aide humanitaire; Éducation/formation/alphabétisation. **Régions:** Afrique australe.

ACTIVITES D'INFORMATION ET D'EDUCATION: **Domaines:** Pauvreté/conditions de vie. **Activités:** Campagnes d'information/expositions.

FRA1658

LES AMIS DES ENFANTS DU MONDE (AEM) ♦ Friends of the Children of the World

9 rue Delerue, 92120 Montrouge, France.

Téléphone: 33 (1) 42 53 98 16. *Fax:* 33 (1) 42 53 80 08. *Contact:* M.J. Gallozzi-Ulmann, Présidente.

OBJECTIFS: Apporter une aide à l'enfance malheureuse.

INFORMATIONS GENERALES: *Création:* 1975. *Salariés:* 2. *Bénévoles:* 250. *Sources financières:* Privé: 50%. Autofinancement: 50%.

PUBLICATIONS: *Périodiques:* Le Toit (2). *Rapport annuel.*

COMMENTAIRES: Intervient dans la Communauté des Etats indépendants.

ACTIVITES DANS LES REGIONS EN DEVELOPPEMENT: Intervient dans 14 pays. Intervient par l'intermédiaire d'organisations locales partenaires. **Actions de Développement durable:** Enfants/jeunesse/famille; Petites entreprises/secteur informel/artisanat; Santé/assainissement/eau; Éducation/formation/alphabétisation. **Régions:** Afrique australe; Afrique de l'Est; Afrique de l'Ouest; Amérique du Sud; Asie centrale et Asie du Sud; Asie de l'Est; Mexique et Amerique centrale.

ACTIVITES D'INFORMATION ET D'EDUCATION: **Domaines:** Enfants/jeunesse/famille; Éducation/formation/alphabétisation. **Activités:** Échanges/parrainage/jumelage.

FRA1659

LES AMIS DES PECHEURS MALGACHES (APM)

26 Résidence Germinal, 91700 Sainte-Geneviève-des-Bois, France.

Téléphone: 33 (1) 69 04 34 90. *Contact:* Jean-François Dumay, Président.

See: *How to Use the Directory,* page 11.

OBJECTIFS: Apporter une aide technique au développement et une assistance matérielle aux jeunes côtiers de Madagascar pour les former à la pêche artisanale leur permettant de mieux améliorer leurs besoins alimentaires et de devenir progressivement autonomes.

INFORMATIONS GENERALES: *Création:* 1990. *Personnel/Total:* 17. *Bénévoles:* 17 dont: 1 dans les pays en développement. *Budget/Total 1993:* ECU 300 (US$ 400). *Sources financières:* Privé: 5%. Autofinancement: 95%.

PUBLICATIONS: *Rapport annuel.*

EVALUATION/RECHERCHE: Rapports d'évaluation disponibles. Entreprend des activités de recherche.

ACTIVITES DANS LES REGIONS EN DEVELOPPEMENT: Intervient directement dans les régions en développement. Intervient dans 1 pays. Maintient une présence locale sur le terrain. Intervient par l'intermédiaire d'organisations locales partenaires. **Actions de Développement durable:** Aliments/famine; Démocratie/bonne gestion publique/création d'institutions/développement participatif; Développement rural/agriculture; Enfants/jeunesse/famille; Petites entreprises/secteur informel/artisanat; Éducation/formation/alphabétisation. **Régions:** Afrique australe.

FRA1660
LES AMIS DU CESO

7 boulevard de la Victoire, 67000 Strasbourg, France.

Téléphone: 33 - 88 36 27 21. *Contact:* René Tardy, Président.

FRA1661
LES AMIS DU PERE GUEZOU ET DE DON BOSCO EN INDE

42/47 rue de Barbieux, 59100 Roubaix, France.

Téléphone: 33 - 20 36 62 01. *Fax:* 33 - 20 24 18 40. *Contact:* Léon Duhayon, Président.

OBJECTIFS: Apporter une aide au développement en Inde, en particulier dans les domaines de l'éducation, de la santé, de la formation, des cultures de subsistance...

INFORMATIONS GENERALES: *Création:* 1953. *Personnel/Total:* 29. *Bénévoles:* 29 dont: 25 dans les pays en développement. *Budget/Total 1993:* ECU 693000 (US$ 812000). *Sources financières:* Privé: 100%.

PUBLICATIONS: *Périodiques:* Les Amis du Père Guezou et de Don Bosco en Inde (1) - Lettre d'information (2) . *Rapport annuel.*

EVALUATION/RECHERCHE: Rapports d'évaluation disponibles.

COMMENTAIRES: Le père Guézou permanent en Inde depuis 1952 est maintenant le seul salésien missionnaire français oeuvrant dans ce pays.

ACTIVITES DANS LES REGIONS EN DEVELOPPEMENT: Intervient directement dans les régions en développement. Intervient dans 1 pays. Maintient une présence locale sur le terrain. Intervient par l'intermédiaire d'organisations locales partenaires. **Actions de Développement durable:** Aliments/famine; Dette/finances/commerce; Développement rural/agriculture; Développement urbain/habitat; Enfants/jeunesse/famille; Petites entreprises/secteur informel/artisanat; Questions relatives aux femmes; Santé/assainissement/eau; Secours d'urgence/réfugiés/aide humanitaire; Écologie/environnement/biodiversité; Éducation/formation/alphabétisation. **Régions:** Asie centrale et Asie du Sud.

ACTIVITES D'INFORMATION ET D'EDUCATION: Domaines: Aliments/famine; Développement rural/agriculture; Développement urbain/habitat; Enfants/jeunesse/famille; Pauvreté/conditions de vie; Population/planning familial/démographie; Questions relatives aux femmes; Santé/assainissement/eau; Secours d'urgence/réfugiés/aide humanitaire; Écologie/environnement/biodiversité; Éducation/formation/alphabétisation. **Activités:** Collecte de fonds; Conférences/séminaires/ateliers/activités de formation; Lobbying/plaidoyer; Échanges/parrainage/jumelage; Édition/documents audiovisuels/documents éducatifs; Éducation formelle.

FRA1662
LES AMIS DU TOGO

38 rue Edouard Herriot, 21240 Talant, France.

Téléphone: 33 - 80 57 11 57. *Contact:* Bernard Ehret, Secrétaire.

FRA1663
LES AMIS SEINE ET MARNAIS DU BURKINA FASO

24 rue de Crécy, 77580 Bouleurs, France.

Téléphone: 33 - 64 63 79 38. *Contact:* René Bellisson, Président.

OBJECTIFS: Aider les paysans du Burkina Faso dans le domaine de la terre et de l'eau.

INFORMATIONS GENERALES: *Création:* 1968. *Personnel/Total:* 10. *Bénévoles:* 10. *Budget/Total 1993:* ECU 15000 (US$ 18000). *Sources financières:* Privé: 80%. Autofinancement: 20%.

PUBLICATIONS: *Périodiques:* Bulletin des S et M (2). *Liste des publications.*

COMMENTAIRES: Cette association s'appelait Les amis du Burkina Faso "Maurice Colas"

ACTIVITES DANS LES REGIONS EN DEVELOPPEMENT: Intervient directement dans les régions en développement. Intervient dans 1 pays. Maintient une présence locale sur le terrain. Intervient par l'intermédiaire d'organisations locales partenaires. **Actions de Développement durable:** Développement rural/agriculture; Santé/assainissement/eau; Écologie/environnement/biodiversité; Éducation/formation/alphabétisation. **Régions:** Afrique de l'Ouest.

ACTIVITES D'INFORMATION ET D'EDUCATION: Domaines: Développement rural/agriculture; Santé/assainissement/eau; Écologie/environnement/biodiversité; Éducation/formation/alphabétisation. **Activités:** Campagnes d'information/expositions; Collecte de fonds.

FRA1664
AMITIE ET DEVELOPPEMENT

44, rue saint Charles, 75015 Paris, France.

Téléphone: 33 (1) 45 79 24 20. *Contact:* Emmanuel Lamy, Président.

OBJECTIFS: Aider au développement et à la formation dans divers pays d'Afrique, principalement le Burkina Faso, et subsidiairement la Côte d'Ivoire et la Guinée.

INFORMATIONS GENERALES: *Création:* 1974. *Personnel/Total:* 3. *Bénévoles:* 3. *Budget/Total 1993:* ECU 93000 (US$ 109000). *Sources financières:* Privé: 25%. Autofinancement: 75%.

PUBLICATIONS: *Périodiques:* Compte-rendu d'activité (1). *Rapport annuel.*

EVALUATION/RECHERCHE: Rapports d'évaluation disponibles.

ACTIVITES DANS LES REGIONS EN DEVELOPPEMENT: Intervient dans 3 pays. Maintient une présence locale sur le terrain. Intervient par l'intermédiaire d'organisations locales partenaires. **Actions de Développement durable:** Aliments/famine; Développement rural/agriculture; Enfants/jeunesse/famille; Petites entreprises/secteur informel/artisanat; Questions relatives aux femmes; Santé/assainissement/eau; Secours d'urgence/réfugiés/aide humanitaire; Éducation/formation/alphabétisation. **Régions:** Afrique de l'Ouest.

ACTIVITES D'INFORMATION ET D'EDUCATION: Domaines: Aliments/famine; Développement rural/agriculture; Enfants/jeunesse/famille; Pauvreté/conditions de vie; Questions relatives aux femmes; Relations internationales/coopération/aide au développement; Santé/assainissement/eau; Secours d'urgence/réfugiés/aide humanitaire; Éducation/formation/alphabétisation. **Activités:** Collecte de fonds; Éducation formelle.

FRA1665
AMITIE EURO-KHMERE

23 allée Edouard Lalo, 42000 Saint-Etienne, France.

Fax: 33 - 77 41 00 25. *Contact:* Jean-Jacques Point.

FRA1666
AMITIE FRANCO-AFGHANE (AFRANE)

B.P. 254, 75524 Paris cedex 11, France.

Téléphone: 33 (1) 43 26 04 14.

Voir : *Comment utiliser le répertoire,* page 11.

FRA1667

AMITIES FRANCO-KHMERES

14 rue Mouraud, 75020 Paris, France.

Téléphone: 33 (1) 43 71 60 84/ 01 01. *Contact:* Guy Evin, Président.

OBJECTIFS: Apporter une aide multiforme au Kampuchéa, en France et sur place.

INFORMATIONS GENERALES: *Création:* 1975. *Personnel/Total:* 5. *Salariés:* 1. *Bénévoles:* 4. *Budget/Total 1993:* ECU 15000 (US$ 18000). *Sources financières:* *Privé:* 10%. *Public:* 80%. *Autofinancement:* 10%.

PUBLICATIONS: *Rapport annuel.*

ACTIVITES DANS LES REGIONS EN DEVELOPPEMENT: Intervient directement dans les régions en développement. Intervient dans 1 pays. **Actions de Développement durable:** Santé/assainissement/eau; Secours d'urgence/réfugiés/aide humanitaire; Éducation/formation/alphabétisation. **Régions:** Asie du Sud-Est.

ACTIVITES D'INFORMATION ET D'EDUCATION: Domaines: Emploi/chômage; Secours d'urgence/réfugiés/aide humanitaire; Éducation/formation/alphabétisation. **Activités:** Collecte de fonds; Édition/documents audiovisuels/documents éducatifs.

FRA1668

AMITIES FRANCO-TANZANIENNES (AFT)

20 rue de Rochechouart, 75009 Paris, France.

Téléphone: 33 (1) 48 78 55 54. *Contact:* Jean-Paul Desgranges, Président.

OBJECTIFS: Favoriser une meilleure connaissance mutuelle entre francophones et tanzaniens. Informer sur tout ce qui concerne la Tanzanie. Soutenir les initiatives qui contribuent au développement de ce pays.

INFORMATIONS GENERALES: *Création:* 1978. *Personnel/Total:* 10. *Bénévoles:* 10 dont: 2 dans les pays en développement. *Budget/Total 1993:* ECU 1800 (US$ 2000). *Sources financières:* *Privé:* 20%. *Autofinancement:* 80%.

PUBLICATIONS: *Périodiques:* Urafiki Tanzania (4). *Rapport annuel.*

ACTIVITES DANS LES REGIONS EN DEVELOPPEMENT: Maintient une présence locale sur le terrain. **Actions de Développement durable:** Développement rural/agriculture; Questions relatives aux femmes; Santé/assainissement/eau. **Régions:** Afrique de l'Est.

ACTIVITES D'INFORMATION ET D'EDUCATION: Domaines: Culture/tradition/religion; Droits de l'Homme/paix/conflits; Développement rural/agriculture; Enfants/jeunesse/famille; Paix/conflits ethniques/armement/désarmement; Questions relatives aux femmes; Relations internationales/coopération/aide au développement; Relations économiques internationales/commerce/dette/finances; Réfugiés/migrants/groupes ethniques; Santé/assainissement/eau; Écologie/environnement/biodiversité; Éducation/formation/alphabétisation. **Activités:** Édition/documents audiovisuels/documents éducatifs.

FRA1669

ANIMATION ET DEVELOPPEMENT (ANIDEVELOP)

168bis rue Cardinet, 75017 Paris, France.

Téléphone: 33 (1) 46 27 79 74. *Fax:* 33 (1) 42 28 87 46. *Contact:* Lucien Trichaud.

FRA1670

ANTHROPOLOGIE MEDICALE APPLIQUEE AU DEVELOPPEMENT ET A LA SANTE (AMADES)

36 avenue des Cottages, 31400 Toulouse, France.

Téléphone: 33 - 61 34 21 50. *Contact:* Alice Desclaux.

OBJECTIFS: Promouvoir l'approche interdisciplinaire santé publique et anthropologie dans les projets de développement sanitaires.

INFORMATIONS GENERALES: *Création:* 1988. *Bénévoles:* 10 dont: 1 dans les pays en développement. *Budget/Total 1993:* ECU 9000 (US$ 10000). *Sources financières:* *Public:* 10%. *Autofinancement:* 40%.

PUBLICATIONS: *Périodiques:* Bulletin de l'Amades (4).

PREVISIONS D'ACTIVITES: Publication des actes du colloque "Anthropologie et Sida"

ACTIVITES DANS LES REGIONS EN DEVELOPPEMENT: Intervient dans 20 pays. Intervient par l'intermédiaire d'organisations locales partenaires. **Actions de Développement durable:** Santé/assainissement/eau. **Régions:** Afrique de l'Ouest; Amérique du Sud; Asie centrale et Asie du Sud; Asie du Sud-Est; Caraïbes; Océanie.

ACTIVITES D'INFORMATION ET D'EDUCATION: Domaines: Santé/assainissement/eau. **Activités:** Conférences/séminaires/ateliers/activités de formation; Services d'information et de documentation/bases de données; Édition/documents audiovisuels/documents éducatifs.

FRA1671

APPEL AIDE AUX ENFANTS VICTIMES DE CONFLITS DANS LES PAYS EN VOIE DE DEVELOPPEMENT

89 rue de Flandre, 75019 Paris, France.

Téléphone: 33 (1) 42 02 77 78. *Fax:* 33 (1) 40 36 57 10. *Contact:* Dr. Jacques Lalande, Président.

OBJECTIFS: Venir en aide aux enfants victimes de conflits, surtout dans le domaine de la sant,é dans les pays en voie de développement.

INFORMATIONS GENERALES: *Création:* 1969. *Personnel/Total:* 30. *Salariés:* 5 dont: 2 dans les pays en développement. *Bénévoles:* 25 dont: 1 dans les pays en développement. *Budget/Total 1993:* ECU 432000 (US$ 506000). *Sources financières:* *Privé:* 7%. *Public:* 68%. *Autofinancement:* 25%.

PUBLICATIONS: *Périodiques:* L'Appel (4).

COMMENTAIRES: Intervient dans la Communauté des Etats indépendants.

ACTIVITES DANS LES REGIONS EN DEVELOPPEMENT: Intervient directement dans les régions en développement. Intervient dans 9 pays. Intervient par l'intermédiaire d'organisations locales partenaires. **Actions de Développement durable:** Enfants/jeunesse/famille; Population/planning familial/démographie; Questions relatives aux femmes; Santé/assainissement/eau. **Régions:** Afrique australe; Afrique centrale; Asie du Sud-Est; Mexique et Amerique centrale.

ACTIVITES D'INFORMATION ET D'EDUCATION: Domaines: Population/planning familial/démographie; Santé/assainissement/eau. **Activités:** Campagnes d'information/expositions; Conférences/séminaires/ateliers/activités de formation; Échanges/parrainage/jumelage; Édition/documents audiovisuels/documents éducatifs.

FRA1672

APPEL DETRESSE (AD)

83 rue de la Garde, 44300 Nantes, France.

Téléphone: 33 - 40 49 50 88. *Fax:* 33 - 40 50 15 61. *Contact:* Mme Tournemine, Présidente.

OBJECTIFS: Permettre aux plus démunis de parvenir à l'autonomie, en créant des moyens de développement (dispensaires, écoles, coopératives, etc.).

INFORMATIONS GENERALES: *Création:* 1974. *Type d'organisation:* regroupement d'ONG, réseau. *Personnel/Total:* 2000. *Bénévoles:* 2000 dont: 50 dans les pays en développement. *Budget/Total 1993:* ECU 724000 (US$ 848000). *Sources financières:* *Privé:* 90%. *Public:* 2%. *Autofinancement:* 8%.

PUBLICATIONS: *Périodiques:* Circulaire AD (6). *Rapport annuel.*

EVALUATION/RECHERCHE: Entreprend des activités de recherche.

COMMENTAIRES: Tous les membres d'AD en poste à l'étranger doivent avoir exercéun métier afin de l'enseigner, et avoir participé à l'animation d'une section AD en France pendant un an. Tous sont bénévoles.

ACTIVITES DANS LES REGIONS EN DEVELOPPEMENT: Intervient directement dans les régions en développement. Intervient dans 16 pays. Maintient une présence locale sur le terrain. **Actions de Développement durable:** Aliments/famine; Développement rural/agriculture; Enfants/jeunesse/famille; Envoi de volontaires/experts/assistance technique; Petites entreprises/secteur informel/artisanat; Population/plan-

See: *How to Use the Directory,* page 11.

ning familial/démographie; Questions relatives aux femmes; Santé/assainissement/eau; Éducation/formation/alphabétisation. **Régions:** Afrique australe; Afrique de l'Est; Afrique de l'Ouest; Amérique du Sud; Asie de l'Est; Asie du Sud-Est; Caraïbes; Mexique et Amerique centrale; Océanie.

ACTIVITES D'INFORMATION ET D'EDUCATION: Domaines: Aliments/famine; Développement rural/agriculture; Emploi/chômage; Enfants/jeunesse/famille; Pauvreté/conditions de vie; Population/planning familial/démographie; Questions relatives aux femmes; Relations internationales/coopération/aide au développement; Santé/assainissement/eau; Éducation/formation/alphabétisation. **Activités:** Campagnes d'information/expositions; Collecte de fonds; Conférences/séminaires/ateliers/activités de formation; Radiodiffusion/manifestations culturelles; Services d'information et de documentation/bases de données; Échanges/parrainage/jumelage; Édition/documents audiovisuels/documents éducatifs; Éducation formelle.

FRA1673
APPUI MUTUEL POUR UN USAGE SOCIAL DE L'INFORMATION (L'AMI)

61, rue Victor Hugo, 93500 Pantin, France.

Téléphone: 33 (1) 48 44 09 52. *Fax:* 33 (1) 48 44 09 52. *Courrier électronique:* CRISAN@LAMI.ORSTOM>FR. *Contact:* LARREGLE ANA, Chargée de Projet.

OBJECTIFS: Fournir un appui technique, méthodologique et de formation en matière de gestion de l'information: développement logiciel, Hot Line, rédaction d'outils pédagogiques. Constituer des bases de données.

INFORMATIONS GENERALES: *Création:* 1993. *Affiliée à:* Dialogue pour le progrès de l'humanité (France). *Personnel/Total:* 23. *Salariés:* 2. *Bénévoles:* 21 dont: 14 dans les pays en développement. *Budget/Total 1993:* ECU 57000 (US$ 67000). *Sources financières:* Privé: 78%. Autofinancement: 22%.

PUBLICATIONS: *Liste des publications.*

EVALUATION/RECHERCHE: Entreprend des activités de recherche.

PREVISIONS D'ACTIVITES: Préparation d'une étude sur les expériences innovantes d'appui pour l'emploi des plus défavorisés.

ACTIVITES DANS LES REGIONS EN DEVELOPPEMENT: Intervient directement dans les régions en développement. Intervient par l'intermédiaire d'organisations locales partenaires. **Actions de Développement durable:** Envoi de volontaires/experts/assistance technique; Éducation/formation/alphabétisation. **Régions:** Amérique du Sud; Mexique et Amerique centrale.

ACTIVITES D'INFORMATION ET D'EDUCATION: Domaines: Autres; Emploi/chômage; Relations internationales/coopération/aide au développement. **Activités:** Réseaux/télécommunications électroniques; Services d'information et de documentation/bases de données; Édition/documents audiovisuels/documents éducatifs.

FRA1674
L'ARCHE

Rue Trosly-Breuil, B.P. 35, 60350 Cuise-La-Motte, France.

Téléphone: 33 - 44 85 61 02. *Contact:* Jean Vanier.

FRA1675
L'ARCHE DE LA FRATERNITE

Toit de la Grande Arche, 92044 Paris la Défense, France.

Téléphone: 33 (1) 49 07 27 27. *Fax:* 33 (1) 49 07 27 21. *Contact:* Marc Agi, Directeur Général.

OBJECTIFS: Sensibiliser le public aux actions positives menées dans le domaine des droits de l'homme. Accueillir les personnes et les associations désirant s'exprimer sous la forme d'expositions, de débats, de colloques.

INFORMATIONS GENERALES: *Création:* 1989. *Personnel/Total:* 8. *Salariés:* 6. *Bénévoles:* 2. *Budget/Total 1993:* ECU 226000 (US$ 265000). *Sources financières:* Privé: 10%. Public: 20%. Autofinancement: 70%.

PUBLICATIONS: *Rapport annuel. Liste des publications.*

EVALUATION/RECHERCHE: Rapports d'évaluation disponibles. Entreprend des activités de recherche.

PREVISIONS D'ACTIVITES: Universités d'été internationales (annuelles) de formation de formateurs en droits de l'homme et citoyenneté démocratique. Fête des libertés (annuelle).

COMMENTAIRES: Intervient dans la Communauté des Etats indépendants. Activités d'information concernant la Communauté des Etats indépendants.

ACTIVITES DANS LES REGIONS EN DEVELOPPEMENT: Intervient directement dans les régions en développement. Intervient dans 40 pays. Intervient par l'intermédiaire d'organisations locales partenaires. **Actions de Développement durable:** Droits de l'Homme/paix/conflits; Démocratie/bonne gestion publique/création d'institutions/développement participatif; Enfants/jeunesse/famille; Éducation/formation/alphabétisation. **Régions:** Afrique australe; Afrique de l'Est; Afrique de l'Ouest; Afrique du Nord; Amérique du Sud; Asie du Sud-Est; Caraïbes; Mexique et Amerique centrale; Moyen-Orient.

ACTIVITES D'INFORMATION ET D'EDUCATION: Domaines: Culture/tradition/religion; Droits de l'Homme/paix/conflits; Enfants/jeunesse/famille; Paix/conflits ethniques/armement/désarmement; Racisme/xénophobie/antisémitisme; Relations internationales/coopération/aide au développement; Réfugiés/migrants/groupes ethniques; Éducation/formation/alphabétisation. **Activités:** Campagnes d'information/expositions; Conférences/séminaires/ateliers/activités de formation; Radiodiffusion/manifestations culturelles; Services d'information et de documentation/bases de données; Éducation formelle.

FRA1676
ARCHITECTES ET INGENIEURS DU MONDE (AIM)

42, Rue Sala, 69002 Lyon, France.

Téléphone: 33 - 78 37 12 11. *Fax:* 33 - 78 37 11 10. *Contact:* Xavier Pangaud, Président.

OBJECTIFS: Assister bénévolement en matière d'habitat, d'équipement et d'aménagement les personnes victimes de crises de développement ou de situations d'urgence; actions menées par des équipes pluridisciplinaires du bâtiment et des travaux publics.

INFORMATIONS GENERALES: *Création:* 1987. *Affiliée à:* CLONG. *Personnel/Total:* 22. *Salariés:* 4 dont: 1 dans les pays en développement. *Bénévoles:* 18 dont: 11 dans les pays en développement. *Budget/Total 1993:* ECU 1809000 (US$ 2119000). *Sources financières:* Privé: 7%. Public: 90%. Autofinancement: 3%.

EVALUATION/RECHERCHE: Entreprend des activités de recherche.

COMMENTAIRES: Intervient dans la Communauté des Etats indépendants. Activités d'information concernant la Communauté des Etats indépendants.

ACTIVITES DANS LES REGIONS EN DEVELOPPEMENT: Intervient directement dans les régions en développement. Intervient dans 2 pays. Maintient une présence locale sur le terrain. Intervient par l'intermédiaire d'organisations locales partenaires. **Actions de Développement durable:** Développement urbain/habitat; Envoi de volontaires/experts/assistance technique; Petites entreprises/secteur informel/artisanat; Santé/assainissement/eau; Secours d'urgence/réfugiés/aide humanitaire. **Régions:** Caraïbes.

ACTIVITES D'INFORMATION ET D'EDUCATION: Domaines: Culture/tradition/religion; Développement urbain/habitat; Santé/assainissement/eau; Secours d'urgence/réfugiés/aide humanitaire. **Activités:** Campagnes d'information/expositions; Radiodiffusion/manifestations culturelles.

FRA1677
ARCHITECTES SANS FRONTIERES (ASF)

144 rue de Flandre, 75019 Paris, France.

Téléphone: 33 (1) 42 05 98 78. *Fax:* 33 (1) 42 05 95 75. *Contact:* Micheline Baussard, Directeur.

OBJECTIFS: Aider à l'amélioration des conditions de vie des plus défavorisés, en transformant leur environnement naturel ou bâti, et leur apprendre les techniques qui leur permettront d'être autonomes dans

Voir : *Comment utiliser le répertoire,* page 11.

tous les domaines relevant de l'art de bâtir, de l'urbanisme et de l'environnement.

INFORMATIONS GENERALES: *Création:* 1979. *Personnel/Total:* 47. *Salariés:* 2. *Bénévoles:* 45 dont: 15 dans les pays en développement. *B u d g e t / T o t a l   1 9 9 3 :* ECU 973000 (US$ 1140000). *Sources financières:* Privé: 15%. Public: 80%. Autofinancement: 5%.

PUBLICATIONS: *Périodiques:* ASF Info (1).

COMMENTAIRES: Intervient dans la Communauté des Etats indépendants.

ACTIVITES DANS LES REGIONS EN DEVELOPPEMENT: Intervient directement dans les régions en développement. Intervient dans 9 pays. Maintient une présence locale sur le terrain. **Actions de Développement durable:** Développement urbain/habitat; Enfants/jeunesse/famille; Envoi de volontaires/experts/assistance technique; Petites entreprises/secteur informel/artisanat; Santé/assainissement/eau; Éducation/formation/alphabétisation. **Régions:** Afrique australe; Afrique centrale; Afrique de l'Est; Afrique de l'Ouest; Amérique du Sud; Asie centrale et Asie du Sud; Mexique et Amerique centrale; Moyen-Orient.

FRA1678
ARDESCO

7 rue Olivier de Serres, 07270 Lamastre, France.

Téléphone: 33 - 75 06 46 27. *Contact:* Nicole Julien, Coordinatrice.

FRA1679
ARMOR DEVELOPPEMENT - SAHEL

B.P. 404, 22004 Saint-Brieuc cedex 1, France.

Téléphone: 33 - 96 62 20 40. *Contact:* Jean Stalaven.

OBJECTIFS: Soutenir les objectifs de développement communautaire en éducation et nutrition, en Afrique Subsaharienne.

INFORMATIONS GENERALES: *Création:* 1990. *Personnel/Total:* 6. *Bénévoles:* 6. *Budget/Total 1993:* ECU 55000 (US$ 65000). *Sources financières:* Privé: 6%. Public: 92%. Autofinancement: 2%.

PUBLICATIONS: *Rapport annuel.*

EVALUATION/RECHERCHE: Rapports d'évaluation disponibles. Entreprend des activités de recherche.

PREVISIONS D'ACTIVITES: Plantation d'arbres; mise au point de produits à base de fruits du néré; mise en place d'unités pilotes de fabrication et de distribution dans les zones concernées.

ACTIVITES DANS LES REGIONS EN DEVELOPPEMENT: Intervient dans 1 pays. Intervient par l'intermédiaire d'organisations locales partenaires. **Actions de Développement durable:** Aliments/famine; Développement rural/agriculture; Enfants/jeunesse/famille; Écologie/environnement/biodiversité; Éducation/formation/alphabétisation. **Régions:** Afrique de l'Ouest.

ACTIVITES D'INFORMATION ET D'EDUCATION: Domaines: Aliments/famine; Développement rural/agriculture; Enfants/jeunesse/famille; Écologie/environnement/biodiversité. **Activités:** Collecte de fonds; Conférences/séminaires/ateliers/activités de formation.

FRA1680
ART CULTURE COMMUNICATION (ACC)

3 rue Claude Debussy, 77720 Mormant, France.

Téléphone: 33 (1) 64 06 93 50. *Fax:* 33 (1) 64 39 59 02. *Contact:* Renaud Barillet, Secrétaire général.

FRA1681
ARTISANAT SERVICE

BP 2, 45701 Villemandeur cedex, France.

Téléphone: 33 (1) 38 89 21 00. *Fax:* 33 (1) 38 85 14 09. *Contact:* Gauthier de Smidt.

OBJECTIFS: Contribuer à la création de coopératives d'artisanat dans les pays en voie de développement.

INFORMATIONS GENERALES: *Création:* 1981. *Type d'organisation:* réseau. *Affiliée à:* GOED WERK (pays-Bas) - TEAR CRAFT (Grande Bretagne). *Personnel/Total:* 254. *Salariés:* 4 dont: 1 dans les pays en développement. *Bénévoles:* 250. *Budget/Total 1993:* ECU 603000 (US$ 706000). *Sources financières:* Privé: 4%. Autofinancement: 96%.

PUBLICATIONS: *Périodiques:* SEL-Information (4). *Rapport annuel. Liste des publications.*

PREVISIONS D'ACTIVITES: Projet de développement de l'artisanat en Arménie.

ACTIVITES DANS LES REGIONS EN DEVELOPPEMENT: Intervient directement dans les régions en développement. Intervient dans 13 pays. Maintient une présence locale sur le terrain. Intervient par l'intermédiaire d'organisations locales partenaires. **Actions de Développement durable:** Petites entreprises/secteur informel/artisanat. **Régions:** Afrique australe; Afrique de l'Ouest; Amérique du Sud; Asie centrale et Asie du Sud; Asie de l'Est; Asie du Sud-Est.

FRA1682
ARTS ET OCEANS

123 boulevard Voltaire, 75011 Paris, France.

Téléphone: 33 (1) 44 64 92 00. *Contact:* Fabrice Roger.

FRA1683
ASMAE-LES AMIS DE SOEUR EMMANUELLE (ASMAE)

15, rue Chapon, 75003 Paris, France.

Téléphone: 33 (1) 42 78 38 96. *Fax:* 33 (1) 42 78 38 97. *Contact:* Catherine Alvarez, Directrice.

OBJECTIFS: Soutenir, mettre en œuvre, imaginer et encourager toutes les initiaves qui sont propres à l'ASMAE, ou qui lui sont suggérées par des partenaires, en direction des milieux les plus défavorisés, et plus particulièrement des enfants du Tiers monde, en matière de relations humaines, d'éducation, de formation, de santé, d'hygiène, de travail et de loisirs.

INFORMATIONS GENERALES: *Création:* 1988. *Affiliée à:* CLONG (France). *Personnel/Total:* 304. *Salariés:* 4. *Bénévoles:* 300 dont: 200 dans les pays en développement. *Budget/Total 1993:* ECU 2533000 (US$ 2967000). *Sources financières:* Privé: 95%. Public: 5%.

PUBLICATIONS: *Périodiques:* La Lettre de soeur Emmanuelle (4). *Rapport annuel.*

ACTIVITES DANS LES REGIONS EN DEVELOPPEMENT: Intervient directement dans les régions en développement. Intervient dans 7 pays. Maintient une présence locale sur le terrain. Intervient par l'intermédiaire d'organisations locales partenaires. **Actions de Développement durable:** Aliments/famine; Développement urbain/habitat; Envoi de volontaires/experts/assistance technique; Petites entreprises/secteur informel/artisanat; Questions relatives aux femmes; Santé/assainissement/eau; Éducation/formation/alphabétisation. **Régions:** Afrique de l'Est; Afrique de l'Ouest; Afrique du Nord; Amérique du Sud; Asie du Sud-Est; Moyen-Orient.

FRA1684
ASSISTANCE MEDICALE INTER-SANITAIRE (AMIS)

B.P. 49, 01400 Châtillon sur Chalaronne, France.

Téléphone: 33 - 74 55 03 34. *Contact:* Jean Couturier, Président.

OBJECTIFS: Approvisionner régulièrement en médicaments et en matériel de soin les différents dispensaires et hôpitaux d'Afrique Noire.

INFORMATIONS GENERALES: *Création:* 1978. *Personnel/Total:* 3. *Budget/Total 1993:* ECU 18000 (US$ 21000). *Sources financières:* Privé: 10%. Autofinancement: 90%.

PUBLICATIONS: *Périodiques:* AMIS-T.M (4).

COMMENTAIRES: L'organisation approvisionne depuis 15 ans les mêmes centres de soins, et cela sur ses propres fonds. Intervient dans la Communauté des Etats indépendants.

See: *How to Use the Directory,* page 11.

ACTIVITES DANS LES REGIONS EN DEVELOPPEMENT: Intervient directement dans les régions en développement. **Actions de Développement durable:** Santé/assainissement/eau. **Régions:** Afrique centrale; Afrique de l'Ouest.

ACTIVITES D'INFORMATION ET D'EDUCATION: Domaines: Santé/assainissement/eau. **Activités:** Collecte de fonds.

FRA1685

ASSISTANCE TECHNIQUE INTERNATIONALE (ATI) ♦ International Technical Assistance

26 Cité Poiriers, B.P. 305, 97203 Fort de France , France.

Téléphone: 19 (596) - 61 32 08. *Fax:* 19 (596) - 61 33 93. *Contact:* Dominique Bruch, Président.

OBJECTIFS: Apporter une assistance technique lors de la deuxième phase des secours d'urgence, à la suite de catastrophes naturelles. Effectuer des recherches au niveau technique, dans le cadre de l'aide au développement. Réaliser des actions de sensibilisation et de formation au secours d'urgence.

INFORMATIONS GENERALES: *Création:* 1983. *Type d'organisation:* réseau. *Affiliée à:* OHI (France) - AFS (France) - Association Française de solidarité - Handicap International - Association Urgence internationale - Médecins Sans Frontières. *Personnel/Total:* 22. *Bénévoles:* 22 dont: 10 dans les pays en développement. *Budget/Total 1993:* ECU 3000 (US\$ 4000). *Sources financières:* Privé: 100%.

PUBLICATIONS: *Rapport annuel. Liste des publications.*

PREVISIONS D'ACTIVITES: Reprise du bulletin de formation et d'information sur la vulgarisation des problèmes liés à l'aide humanitaire.

ACTIVITES DANS LES REGIONS EN DEVELOPPEMENT: Intervient directement dans les régions en développement. Maintient une présence locale sur le terrain. **Actions de Développement durable:** Aliments/famine; Développement rural/agriculture; Enfants/jeunesse/famille; Envoi de volontaires/experts/assistance technique; Santé/assainissement/eau; Secours d'urgence/réfugiés/aide humanitaire. **Régions:** Amérique du Sud; Caraïbes; Mexique et Amerique centrale.

ACTIVITES D'INFORMATION ET D'EDUCATION: Domaines: Aliments/famine; Pauvreté/conditions de vie; Santé/assainissement/eau; Secours d'urgence/réfugiés/aide humanitaire. **Activités:** Campagnes d'information/expositions; Collecte de fonds; Conférences/séminaires/ateliers/activités de formation; Lobbying/plaidoyer; Échanges/parrainage/jumelage; Édition/documents audiovisuels/documents éducatifs.

FRA1686

ASSOCIATION ARC EN CIEL

31 rue Commanderie, 60330 Lagny le Sec, France.

Téléphone: 33 - 44 60 52 31. *Fax:* 33 - 44 60 11 44. *Contact:* Evelyne Babault, Présidente.

FRA1687

ASSOCIATION ASSISTANCE EN FRANCE (ASA-FRANCE)

13 rue Georges Lebeuf, 91080 Courcouronnes, France.

Téléphone: 33 (1) 60 86 23 01. *Contact:* Blandine Cavelot.

FRA1688

ASSOCIATION AUBE-GUINEE

La Renardière, Saint Phal, 10130 Ervy-le-Chatel, France.

Téléphone: 33 - 25 42 17 28. *Contact:* Josiane Witzer, Présidente.

FRA1689

ASSOCIATION BANCAIRE POUR L'ENTREPRISE ET LE DEVELOPPEMENT (ABED)

18 rue La Fayette, 75009 Paris, France.

Téléphone: 33 (1) 48 00 52 01. *Fax:* 33 (1) 42 46 76 40. *Contact:* Georges Bernard, Secrétaire exécutif.

FRA1690

ASSOCIATION CHAMPENOISE DE COOPERATION INTER-REGIONALE (ACCIR)

6, rue Eustache Deschamps, 51000 Châlons sur Marne, France.

Téléphone: 33 - 26 64 28 58. *Contact:* Vianney Danet, Secrétaire général.

OBJECTIFS: Soutenir les actions de formation et la mise en place d'organisations paysannes en Afrique de l'Ouest. Travailler en collaboraton étroite avec celles-ci et les ONG africaines. Mener des actions d'information et de sensibilisation de l'opinion publique française à la problématique du développement.

INFORMATIONS GENERALES: *Création:* 1968. *Personnel/Total:* 1. *Salariés:* 1. *Bénévoles:* var. *Budget/Total 1993:* ECU 279000 (US\$ 327000). *Sources financières:* Privé: 90%. Autofinancement: 10%.

PUBLICATIONS: *Périodiques:* Coopération Inter Régionale (4). *Liste des publications.*

PREVISIONS D'ACTIVITES: Information sur les problèmes économiques, notamment après la dévaluation du Franc CFA.

ACTIVITES DANS LES REGIONS EN DEVELOPPEMENT: Intervient dans 4 pays. Intervient par l'intermédiaire d'organisations locales partenaires. **Actions de Développement durable:** Démocratie/bonne gestion publique/création d'institutions/développement participatif; Développement rural/agriculture; Enfants/jeunesse/famille; Petites entreprises/secteur informel/artisanat; Population/planning familial/démographie; Questions relatives aux femmes; Santé/assainissement/eau; Écologie/environnement/biodiversité; Éducation/formation/alphabétisation. **Régions:** Afrique de l'Ouest.

ACTIVITES D'INFORMATION ET D'EDUCATION: Domaines: Culture/tradition/religion; Développement rural/agriculture; Enfants/jeunesse/famille; Population/planning familial/démographie; Questions relatives aux femmes; Relations internationales/coopération/aide au développement; Relations économiques internationales/commerce/dette/finances; Santé/assainissement/eau; Écologie/environnement/biodiversité; Éducation/formation/alphabétisation. **Activités:** Campagnes d'information/expositions; Collecte de fonds; Conférences/séminaires/ateliers/activités de formation; Radiodiffusion/manifestations culturelles.

FRA1691

ASSOCIATION CONTRE L'EXCLUSION, POUR LA SANTE ET LE DEVELOPPEMENT COMMUNAUTAIRE (AESDC)

162, Avenue Lacassagne, 69424 Lyon cedex 03, France.

Téléphone: 33 - 72 11 57 69. *Contact:* Mamadou Wade, Président.

OBJECTIFS: Aider toutes les populations à travers le monde, dans le cadre de projets de développement à moyen et long termes; quelles que soient leurs convictions, leur religion ou leur nationalité; que leur détresse soit d'origine naturelle, politique ou sociale. Promouvoir le développement communautaire: santé, éducation, formation, agriculture et élevage.

INFORMATIONS GENERALES: *Création:* 1994. *Affiliée à:* E.S.P.O.I.R. (France). *Personnel/Total:* 10. *Salariés:* 8 dont: 4 dans les pays en développement. *Bénévoles:* 2 dont: 1 dans les pays en développement. *Sources financières:* Privé: 20%. Autofinancement: 80%.

PUBLICATIONS: *Rapport annuel.*

PREVISIONS D'ACTIVITES: L'organisation veut étendre ses activités à d'autres secteurs tels que le Projet Sénégal et le Projet Madagascar.

ACTIVITES DANS LES REGIONS EN DEVELOPPEMENT: Intervient directement dans les régions en développement. Maintient une présence locale sur le terrain. **Actions de Développement durable:** Aliments/famine; Démocratie/bonne gestion publique/création d'institutions/développement participatif; Développement rural/agriculture; Enfants/jeunesse/famille; Population/planning familial/démographie; Questions relatives aux femmes; Santé/assainissement/eau; Éducation/formation/alphabétisation. **Régions:** Afrique australe; Afrique de l'Ouest.

ACTIVITES D'INFORMATION ET D'EDUCATION: Domaines: Emploi/chômage; Enfants/jeunesse/famille; Pauvreté/conditions de vie; Popula-

Voir : *Comment utiliser le répertoire,* page 11.

tion/planning familial/démographie; Santé/assainissement/eau; Secours d'urgence/réfugiés/aide humanitaire; Éducation/formation/alphabétisation. **Activités:** Collecte de fonds; Échanges/parrainage/jumelage.

FRA1692

ASSOCIATION CULTURELLE ET AMICALE DES FAMILLES D'OUTRE-MER ET MIGRANTS (ACAFOM)

42 rue des Sept Arpents, 93500 Pantin, France.

Téléphone: 33 (1) 48 44 48 08. *Contact:* Suzanne Gueydon de Dives, Directrice.

FRA1693

ASSOCIATION D'ACCUEIL AUX MEDECINS ET PERSONNELS DE SANTE REFUGIES EN FRANCE (AMPSRF)

Pavillon Benjamin Ball, Hôpital Sainte Anne, 1 Rue Cabanis, 75014 Paris , France.

Téléphone: 33 (1) 45 65 87 50. *Contact:* Dr. Claire Hatzfeld, Secrétaire Générale.

OBJECTIFS: Accueillir les médecins et personnels de santé réfugiés en France pour les aider à trouver une insertion professionnelle.

INFORMATIONS GENERALES: *Création:* 1973. *Affiliée à:* Commission de Sauvegarde du Droit d'Asile (France). *Personnel/Total:* 8. *Bénévoles:* 8. *Budget/Total 1993:* ECU 14000 (US$ 16000). *Sources financières:* Autofinancement: 100%.

PUBLICATIONS: *Rapport annuel.*

EVALUATION/RECHERCHE: Rapports d'évaluation disponibles.

ACTIVITES D'INFORMATION ET D'EDUCATION: Domaines: Réfugiés/migrants/groupes ethniques. **Activités:** Autres.

FRA1694

ASSOCIATION D'ALSACE DES OEUVRES HOSPITALIERES DE SAINT LAZARE (OSL)

15, avenue du Général de Gaulle, 67000 Strasbourg, France.

Téléphone: 33 - 88 61 32 72. *Contact:* Jean Bezaut, Président.

OBJECTIFS: Apporter une aide médicale aux lépreux et assurer une meilleure protection maternelle et infantile dans quatre dispensaires du Nord-Cameroun. Dispenser une formation médicale aux femmes et aux agents de santé.

INFORMATIONS GENERALES: *Création:* 1968. *Affiliée à:* Emmaüs (Suisse). *Personnel/Total:* 7. *Salariés:* 6 dont: 6 dans les pays en développement. *Bénévoles:* 1 dont: 1 dans les pays en développement. *Budget/Total 1993:* ECU 45000 (US$ 53000). *Sources financières:* Privé: 100%.

PUBLICATIONS: *Périodiques:* Informations (2). *Rapport annuel.*

EVALUATION/RECHERCHE: Rapports d'évaluation disponibles.

ACTIVITES DANS LES REGIONS EN DEVELOPPEMENT: Intervient directement dans les régions en développement. Intervient dans 1 pays. Maintient une présence locale sur le terrain. **Actions de Développement durable:** Santé/assainissement/eau. **Régions:** Afrique centrale.

ACTIVITES D'INFORMATION ET D'EDUCATION: Domaines: Santé/assainissement/eau. **Activités:** Campagnes d'information/expositions; Collecte de fonds; Éducation formelle.

FRA1695

ASSOCIATION D'AMITIE FRANCO-VIETNAMIENNE (AAFV)

44 rue Alexis Lepere, 93100 Montreuil, France.

Téléphone: 33 (1) 42 87 44 34. *Contact:* Charles Fourniau, Secrétaire général.

FRA1696

ASSOCIATION D'ECHANGES CULTURELS EN MEDITERRANEE (ECUME)

13, rue Mazagran, 13001 Marseille, France.

Téléphone: 33 - 91 42 72 74. *Fax:* 33 - 91 47 95 12. *Contact:* Omar Daniel Belli, Secrétaire général.

OBJECTIFS: Concevoir et réaliser des manifestations culturelles pour le développement de la coopération en Méditerranée.

INFORMATIONS GENERALES: *Création:* 1983. *Personnel/Total:* 9. *Salariés:* 4. *Bénévoles:* 5. *Budget/Total 1993:* ECU 226000 (US$ 265000). *Sources financières:* Privé: 5%. Public: 65%. Autofinancement: 30%.

ACTIVITES DANS LES REGIONS EN DEVELOPPEMENT: Intervient directement dans les régions en développement. Intervient dans 7 pays. Intervient par l'intermédiaire d'organisations locales partenaires. **Actions de Développement durable:** Éducation/formation/alphabétisation. **Régions:** Afrique du Nord; Moyen-Orient.

ACTIVITES D'INFORMATION ET D'EDUCATION: Domaines: Culture/tradition/religion. **Activités:** Campagnes d'information/expositions; Conférences/séminaires/ateliers/activités de formation; Radiodiffusion/manifestations culturelles; Échanges/parrainage/jumelage.

FRA1697

ASSOCIATION DE DEFENSE DES DROITS DE L'HOMME AU MAROC

269 bis rue du Faubourg Saint Antoine, 75011 Paris, France.

FRA1698

ASSOCIATION DE FORMATION ET D'INFORMATION POUR LE DEVELOPPEMENT D'INITIATIVES RURALES (AFIP)

2 rue Paul Escudier, 75009 Paris, France.

Téléphone: 33 (1) 48 74 52 88. *Fax:* 33 (1) 42 80 49 27. *Contact:* Jean Claude Colmagne, Président.

OBJECTIFS: Aider des groupes d'agriculteurs et de ruraux à s'organiser pour mener à bien les projets qu'ils se sont donnés.

INFORMATIONS GENERALES: *Création:* 1981. *Affiliée à:* CELAVAR (France) - VIRGILE.

PUBLICATIONS: *Périodiques:* Trans Rural Initiatives (26).

COMMENTAIRES: Intervient dans la Communauté des Etats indépendants.

ACTIVITES D'INFORMATION ET D'EDUCATION: Domaines: Développement rural/agriculture. **Activités:** Services d'information et de documentation/bases de données.

FRA1699

ASSOCIATION DE LIAISON D'AGNAM (ALDA)

122, rue Falguière, 75015 Paris, France.

Téléphone: 33 (1) 45 67 47 11. *Contact:* Samba Diallo, Président.

OBJECTIFS: Promouvoir le développement économique et social des villages d'Agnom(Département de Matam), au Sénégal.

INFORMATIONS GENERALES: *Création:* 1980. *Budget/Total 1993:* ECU 8000 (US$ 9000). *Sources financières:* Autofinancement: 100%.

PUBLICATIONS: *Rapport annuel.*

EVALUATION/RECHERCHE: Rapports d'évaluation disponibles.

PREVISIONS D'ACTIVITES: Adduction d'eau et élargissement du réseau existant. Alphabétisation (construction, formation d'alphabétiseurs). Reboisement (plantation de haies et d'un bois, formation agroforestière de plusieurs personnes).

ACTIVITES DANS LES REGIONS EN DEVELOPPEMENT: Intervient directement dans les régions en développement. Intervient dans 1 pays. Maintient une présence locale sur le terrain. Intervient par l'intermédiaire d'organisations locales partenaires. **Actions de Développement durable:** Développement rural/agriculture; Petites entreprises/secteur informel/artisanat; Santé/assainissement/eau; Écologie/environnement/biodiversité; Éducation/formation/alphabétisation. **Régions:** Afrique de l'Ouest.

See: *How to Use the Directory,* page 11.

ACTIVITES D'INFORMATION ET D'EDUCATION: **Domaines:** Développement rural/agriculture; Emploi/chômage; Santé/assainissement/eau; Éducation/formation/alphabétisation. **Activités:** Échanges/parrainage/jumelage; Éducation formelle.

FRA1700
ASSOCIATION DE PARTENAIRES DES ARTISANS DU SAHEL (APAS)

83 bis, rue Joliot Curie, 69005 Lyon, France.

Téléphone: 33 - 78 25 54 55. *Contact:* Jacques Porte, Président.

OBJECTIFS: Développer la production des artisans de la région d'Agadez, au Niger. Acheter, diffuser et commercialiser cette production artisanale, en France et en Europe.

INFORMATIONS GENERALES: *Création:* 1986. *Affiliée à:* Collectif des Associations de Développement Rhône-Alpes (France). *Bénévoles:* 12. *Budget/Total 1993:* ECU 39000 (US$ 46000). *Sources financières:* Autofinancement: 100%.

PUBLICATIONS: *Périodiques:* Bulletin (2).

ACTIVITES DANS LES REGIONS EN DEVELOPPEMENT: Intervient directement dans les régions en développement. Intervient dans 1 pays. Intervient par l'intermédiaire d'organisations locales partenaires. **Actions de Développement durable:** Petites entreprises/secteur informel/artisanat. **Régions:** Afrique de l'Ouest.

ACTIVITES D'INFORMATION ET D'EDUCATION: Domaines: Développement rural/agriculture; Emploi/chômage; Pauvreté/conditions de vie; Questions relatives aux femmes; Relations internationales/coopération/aide au développement; Relations économiques internationales/commerce/dette/finances. **Activités:** Autres.

FRA1701
ASSOCIATION DE RECHERCHE COOPERATIVE INTERNATIONALE (ARCI)

1, rue du 11 Novembre, 92120 Montrouge, France.

Téléphone: 33 (1) 47 46 97 88/40 92 01 02. *Fax:* 33 (1) 46 54 01 32. *Contact:* Colette Berger-Forestier, Présidente.

OBJECTIFS: Assurer la coopération scientifique, sur le plan international, de chercheurs spécialistes, dans l'étude des transformations sociales et de la demande culturelle, dans les sociétés contemporaines.

INFORMATIONS GENERALES: *Création:* 1985. *Type d'organisation:* réseau. *Personnel/Total:* 9. *Salariés:* 2. *Bénévoles:* 7. *Budget/Total 1993:* ECU 75000 (US$ 88000). *Sources financières:* Privé: 60%. Autofinancement: 40%.

PUBLICATIONS: *Périodiques:* Bulletin de liaison de l'ARCI (4). *Liste des publications.*

EVALUATION/RECHERCHE: Entreprend des activités de recherche.

ACTIVITES DANS LES REGIONS EN DEVELOPPEMENT: Intervient dans 12 pays. Intervient par l'intermédiaire d'organisations locales partenaires. **Actions de Développement durable:** Démocratie/bonne gestion publique/création d'institutions/développement participatif; Développement urbain/habitat; Questions relatives aux femmes; Santé/assainissement/eau. **Régions:** Afrique du Nord; Amérique du Sud; Asie du Sud-Est; Mexique et Amerique centrale.

ACTIVITES D'INFORMATION ET D'EDUCATION: Domaines: Culture/tradition/religion; Droits de l'Homme/paix/conflits; Développement rural/agriculture; Développement urbain/habitat; Pauvreté/conditions de vie; Questions relatives aux femmes; Éducation/formation/alphabétisation. **Activités:** Conférences/séminaires/ateliers/activités de formation; Services d'information et de documentation/bases de données.

FRA1702
ASSOCIATION DE RECHERCHE EN AMENAGEMENT DU TERRITOIRE DANS LES PVD (ARAT)

11 bis rue Quinault, 75015 Paris, France.

Téléphone: 33 (1) 43 06 04 83. *Contact:* Nseke Bollo, Secrétaire général.

FRA1703
ASSOCIATION DE SOLIDARITE AVEC LES PAYSANS D'AMERIQUE LATINE (ASPAL)

La Croix Guillaud, 16440 Mouthiers-sur-Boeme, France.

Téléphone: 33 - 45 67 88 47 . *Fax:* 33 - 45 67 81 29. *Contact:* Geneviève Despres, Présidente.

OBJECTIFS: Diffuser en France des produits artisanaux fabriqués par des organisations populaires, dont les paysans d'Amérique latine, et informer sur la vie concrète de ces populations. Réaliser des actions en faveur de la défense des droits de l'Homme dans cette partie du monde.

INFORMATIONS GENERALES: *Création:* 1979. *Organisations membres:* 50. *Affiliée à:* Centre de Recherche et d'Information sur le Développement (France). *Personnel/Total:* 5. *Salariés:* 3. *Bénévoles:* 2. *Budget/Total 1993:* ECU 181000 (US$ 212000). *Sources financières:* Privé: 10%. Public: 5%. Autofinancement: 85%.

PUBLICATIONS: *Périodiques:* ASPAL infos, un autre regard sur l'Amérique (4). *Liste des publications.*

EVALUATION/RECHERCHE: Rapports d'évaluation disponibles.

PREVISIONS D'ACTIVITES: L'organisation travaille à renforcer l'éducation et à promouvoir le commerce équitable international à plus grande échelle.

ACTIVITES DANS LES REGIONS EN DEVELOPPEMENT: Intervient directement dans les régions en développement. Intervient dans 3 pays. Maintient une présence locale sur le terrain. Intervient par l'intermédiaire d'organisations locales partenaires. **Actions de Développement durable:** Droits de l'Homme/paix/conflits; Démocratie/bonne gestion publique/création d'institutions/développement participatif; Développement rural/agriculture; Petites entreprises/secteur informel/artisanat; Questions relatives aux femmes; Écologie/environnement/biodiversité; Éducation/formation/alphabétisation. **Régions:** Amérique du Sud; Mexique et Amerique centrale.

ACTIVITES D'INFORMATION ET D'EDUCATION: Domaines: Culture/tradition/religion; Droits de l'Homme/paix/conflits; Développement rural/agriculture; Paix/conflits ethniques/armement/désarmement; Pauvreté/conditions de vie; Questions relatives aux femmes; Relations internationales/coopération/aide au développement; Relations économiques internationales/commerce/dette/finances; Écologie/environnement/biodiversité; Éducation/formation/alphabétisation. **Activités:** Campagnes d'information/expositions; Collecte de fonds; Conférences/séminaires/ateliers/activités de formation; Lobbying/plaidoyer; Radiodiffusion/manifestations culturelles; Services d'information et de documentation/bases de données; Édition/documents audiovisuels/documents éducatifs.

FRA1704
ASSOCIATION DE SOUTIEN DES MISSIONS DES ASSEMBLEES DE FRANCE (ASMAF)

11, rue de la Brasserie, 67340 Ingwiller, France.

Téléphone: 33 - 88 89 46 32. *Contact:* Jean-Pierre Bory, Président.

OBJECTIFS: Fournir aux églises évangéliques du Tchad une aide en personnel et en moyens matériels pour leur permettre de former leurs cadres, et de participer au développement du pays sur le plan sanitaire, agricole et social.

INFORMATIONS GENERALES: *Création:* 1967. *Affiliée à:* Fédération des Missions Evangéliques Francophones.. *Personnel/Total:* 9. *Salariés:* 4 dont: 3 dans les pays en développement. *Bénévoles:* 5 dont: 1 dans les pays en développement. *Budget/Total 1993:* ECU 68000 (US$ 79000). *Sources financières:* Privé: 100%.

PUBLICATIONS: *Périodiques:* Circulaire de nouvelles ASMAF (3).

ACTIVITES DANS LES REGIONS EN DEVELOPPEMENT: Intervient directement dans les régions en développement. Intervient dans 1 pays. Maintient une présence locale sur le terrain. Intervient par l'intermédiaire d'organisations locales partenaires. **Actions de Développement durable:** Aliments/famine; Développement rural/agriculture; Enfants/jeunesse/famille; Envoi de volontaires/experts/assistance technique; Questions relatives aux femmes; Santé/assainissement/eau; Éducation/formation/alphabétisation. **Régions:** Afrique centrale.

ACTIVITES D'INFORMATION ET D'EDUCATION: Domaines: Aliments/famine; Culture/tradition/religion; Développement rural/agriculture;

Voir : *Comment utiliser le répertoire,* page 11.

Enfants/jeunesse/famille; Pauvreté/conditions de vie; Questions relatives aux femmes; Relations internationales/coopération/aide au développement; Santé/assainissement/eau; Secours d'urgence/réfugiés/aide humanitaire. **Activités:** Campagnes d'information/expositions; Collecte de fonds; Conférences/séminaires/ateliers/activités de formation; Radio-diffusion/manifestations culturelles; Échanges/parrainage/jumelage; Édition/documents audiovisuels/documents éducatifs; Éducation formelle.

FRA1705

ASSOCIATION DES AMIS DE CHARLES DE FOUCAULD

33 rue Lionnois, 54000 Nancy, France.

Téléphone: 33 - 83 51 14 34. *Fax:* 33 - 83 32 67 26. *Contact:* Jean-Claude Piloy.

FRA1706

ASSOCIATION DES AMIS DE LA MAISON FAMILIALE DE FORMATION RURALE D'HAHOMEGBE

Mairie, 73330 Le Pont de Beauvoisin, France.

Téléphone: 33 - 76 37 07 16. *Contact:* Raymond Ferraud, Président.

FRA1707

ASSOCIATION DES ANALYSTES DE PROJETS INDUSTRIELS ET AGRICOLES (APIA)

7 place Hoche, Faculté des Sciences Economiques, 35000 Rennes, France.

Téléphone: 33 - 99 25 35 00. *Contact:* Marielle Criscuolo.

FRA1708

ASSOCIATION DES CENTRES DE PREFORMATION MEDITERRANEENS (ACPM)

48 boulevard Marcel Delprat, 13013 Marseille, France.

Téléphone: 33 - 91 05 73 52. *Fax:* 33 - 91 05 34 44. *Contact:* Roland Bourglan, Directeur général.

FRA1709

ASSOCIATION DES CONSTRUCTEURS POUR LA REHABILITATION ET L'OPTIMALISATION DE LA TERRE (ACROTERRE)

60, place des Géants, 38100 Grenoble, France.

Téléphone: 33 - 76 33 08 34. *Fax:* 33 - 76 33 30 54. *Contact:* Bernard Mottuel, Président.

OBJECTIFS: Développer l'habitat à faible coût à travers l'amélioration des matériaux locaux. Soutenir les projets d'auto-construction. Aider d'autres ONG dans la réalisation d'équipements collectifs.

INFORMATIONS GENERALES: *Création:* 1985. *Affiliée à:* Collectif des associations de développement Rhône-Alpes.. *Personnel/Total:* 9. *Salariés:* 1. *Bénévoles:* 8. *Budget/Total 1993:* ECU 76000 (US\$ 89000). *Sources financières:* Public: 35%. Autofinancement: 65%.

PUBLICATIONS: *Rapport annuel. Liste des publications.*

EVALUATION/RECHERCHE: Rapports d'évaluation disponibles.

PREVISIONS D'ACTIVITES: Elargissement du programme d'éducation au développement "Maison Racontée", en collaboration avec d'autres ONG européennes. Le projet "Maison Racontée" a pour thèmes principaux l'habitat et l'environnement, et pour objectif de faire découvrir et comprendre d'autres modes de vie et d'autres cultures.

COMMENTAIRES: L'organisation est en phase de restructuration. Les objectifs visés sont les suivants: ouverture de l'association à d'autres catégories professionnelles (sciences sociales, sociologie); élargissement des domaines d'activité au niveau géographique et sectoriel; construction d'un réseau habitat-construction en France et à l'étranger.

ACTIVITES DANS LES REGIONS EN DEVELOPPEMENT: Intervient directement dans les régions en développement. **Actions de Développement durable:** Développement urbain/habitat; Petites entreprises/secteur informel/artisanat. **Régions:** Afrique australe; Afrique centrale;

Afrique de l'Est; Afrique de l'Ouest; Afrique du Nord; Amérique du Sud; Asie centrale et Asie du Sud; Asie de l'Est; Asie du Sud-Est; Caraïbes; Mexique et Amerique centrale; Moyen-Orient; Océanie.

ACTIVITES D'INFORMATION ET D'EDUCATION: Domaines: Culture/tradition/religion; Développement rural/agriculture; Relations internationales/coopération/aide au développement. **Activités:** Campagnes d'information/expositions; Conférences/séminaires/ateliers/activités de formation; Services d'information et de documentation/bases de données; Édition/documents audiovisuels/documents éducatifs.

FRA1710

ASSOCIATION DES FEMMES URUGUAYENNES LOURDES PINTOS (AMULP)

15, rue Paul Cézanne, 93600 Aulnay-sous-Bois, France.

Téléphone: 33 (1) 48 68 47 46. *Fax:* 33 (1) 48 68 47 80. *Contact:* Corina Devitta, Secrétaire.

OBJECTIFS: Mener en Uruguay des actions pour la promotion de la femme, l'éducation et la santé. Sensibiliser la population et informer sur le travail d'AMULP. Rechercher des financements. Présenter des projets. Organiser des ventes d'objets artisanaux.

INFORMATIONS GENERALES: *Création:* 1984. *Type d'organisation:* réseau. *Personnel/Total:* 1. *Salariés:* 1. *Budget/Total 1993:* ECU 36000 (US\$ 42000). *Sources financières:* Privé: 15%. Autofinancement: 85%.

PUBLICATIONS: *Périodiques:* Bulletin (3).

EVALUATION/RECHERCHE: Rapports d'évaluation disponibles.

ACTIVITES DANS LES REGIONS EN DEVELOPPEMENT: Intervient dans 1 pays. Intervient par l'intermédiaire d'organisations locales partenaires. **Actions de Développement durable:** Développement rural/agriculture; Enfants/jeunesse/famille; Petites entreprises/secteur informel/artisanat; Questions relatives aux femmes; Santé/assainissement/eau; Éducation/formation/alphabétisation. **Régions:** Amérique du Sud.

ACTIVITES D'INFORMATION ET D'EDUCATION: Domaines: Relations internationales/coopération/aide au développement. **Activités:** Collecte de fonds.

FRA1711

ASSOCIATION DES FOYERS INTERNATIONAUX (AFI)

28 rue de la Grange aux Belles, 75010 Paris, France.

Téléphone: 33 (1) 42 00 11 28. *Contact:* Jean Arthuys, Directeur.

FRA1712

ASSOCIATION DES JOURNALISTES-ECRIVAINS POUR LA NATURE ET L'ECOLOGIE (JNE)

8, rue de la Harpe, 75005 Paris, France.

Téléphone: 33 (1) 46 33 00 56. *Fax:* 33 (1) 43 29 81 34. *Contact:* Nicole Lauroy, Présidente.

OBJECTIFS: Grouper ceux qui, par leur professsion (presse écrite et audio-visuelle, cinéastes,etc.), contribuent à la connaissance et à la sauvegarde du "patrimoine Nature" et à la prise de conscience des problèmes de l'environnement pour un développement harmonieux et respectueux du maintien des équilibres naturels.

INFORMATIONS GENERALES: *Création:* 1969. *Affiliée à:* Fédération internationale des journalistes de l'environnement - France Nature Environnement. *Personnel/Total:* 8. *Bénévoles:* 8. *Budget/Total 1993:* ECU 23000 (US\$ 26000). *Sources financières:* Public: 50%. Autofinancement: 50%.

PUBLICATIONS: *Périodiques:* Canard Sauvage (6).

COMMENTAIRES: Intervient dans la Communauté des Etats indépendants. Activités d'information concernant la Communauté des Etats indépendants.

ACTIVITES D'INFORMATION ET D'EDUCATION: Domaines: Écologie/environnement/biodiversité. **Activités:** Conférences/séminaires/ateliers/activités de formation; Services d'information et de documentation/

bases de données; Édition/documents audiovisuels/documents éducatifs.

FRA1713
ASSOCIATION DES TROIS MONDES (ATM)

63 bis, rue du Cardinal Lemoine, 75005 Paris, France.

Téléphone: 33 (1) 43 54 78 69. *Fax:* 33 (1) 46 34 70 19. *Contact:* Dominique Sentilhes, Président.

OBJECTIFS: Promouvoir les œuvres cinématographiques en provenance des pays en développement, pour aider le public français à comprendre l'histoire, la culture et les problèmes socio-économiques de ces pays.

INFORMATIONS GENERALES: *Création:* 1981. *Type d'organisation:* collectif. *Affiliée à:* CRID - RITIMO (France). *Personnel/Total:* 4. *Salariés:* 2. *Bénévoles:* 2. *Budget/Total 1993:* ECU 106000 (US$ 124000). *Sources financières:* *Privé:* 10%. *Public:* 70%. *Autofinancement:* 20%.

PUBLICATIONS: *Périodiques:* Images Nord-Sud (4). *Liste des publications.*

EVALUATION/RECHERCHE: Entreprend des activités de recherche.

PREVISIONS D'ACTIVITES: L'organisation projette de mener un travail thématique, sur les problèmes de l'immigration, la rencontre des cultures auprès des scolaires.

ACTIVITES DANS LES REGIONS EN DEVELOPPEMENT: Intervient par l'intermédiaire d'organisations locales partenaires.

ACTIVITES D'INFORMATION ET D'EDUCATION: Domaines: Aliments/famine; Culture/tradition/religion; Droits de l'Homme/paix/conflits; Développement rural/agriculture; Développement urbain/habitat; Emploi/chômage; Enfants/jeunesse/famille; Paix/conflits ethniques/armement/désarmement; Pauvreté/conditions de vie; Population/planning familial/démographie; Questions relatives aux femmes; Racisme/xénophobie/antisémitisme; Relations internationales/coopération/aide au développement; Relations économiques internationales/commerce/dette/finances; Réfugiés/migrants/groupes ethniques; Santé/assainissement/eau; Secours d'urgence/réfugiés/aide humanitaire; Écologie/environnement/biodiversité; Éducation/formation/alphabétisation. **Activités:** Édition/documents audiovisuels/documents éducatifs.

FRA1714
ASSOCIATION DU VOLONTARIAT EN EUROPE (AVE)

333 route de Fabregas, 83500 La Seyne sur Mer, France.

Contact: Jean Guinamant.

FRA1715
ASSOCIATION ENFANTS DU MONDE

24, rue Jean Martin, 13005 Marseille, France.

Téléphone: 33 - 91 48 29 19. *Fax:* 33 -91 48 98 50. *Contact:* Alain Delsanti, Président.

OBJECTIFS: Soutenir des projets qui ont pour but d'améliorer les conditions de vie des enfants en France et dans le monde.

INFORMATIONS GENERALES: *Création:* 1980. *Personnel/Total:* 95. *Salariés:* 12. *Bénévoles:* 83. *Budget/Total 1993:* ECU 724000 (US$ 848000). *Sources financières:* *Privé:* 58%. *Public:* 2%. *Autofinancement:* 40%.

PUBLICATIONS: *Périodiques:* Enfants du Monde Actions (4). *Rapport annuel.*

EVALUATION/RECHERCHE: Rapports d'évaluation disponibles.

COMMENTAIRES: Intervient dans la Communauté des Etats indépendants.

ACTIVITES DANS LES REGIONS EN DEVELOPPEMENT: Intervient directement dans les régions en développement. Intervient dans 16 pays. Intervient par l'intermédiaire d'organisations locales partenaires. **Actions de Développement durable:** Aliments/famine; Développement rural/agriculture; Développement urbain/habitat; Enfants/jeunesse/famille; Envoi de volontaires/experts/assistance technique; Population/planning familial/démographie; Questions relatives aux femmes; Santé/assainissement/eau; Secours d'urgence/réfugiés/aide humanitaire; Éducation/formation/alphabétisation. **Régions:** Afrique australe; Afrique centrale; Afrique de l'Est; Afrique de l'Ouest; Afrique du Nord; Amérique du Sud; Asie centrale et Asie du Sud; Asie du Sud-Est; Moyen-Orient.

ACTIVITES D'INFORMATION ET D'EDUCATION: Domaines: Aliments/famine; Enfants/jeunesse/famille; Pauvreté/conditions de vie; Relations internationales/coopération/aide au développement; Réfugiés/migrants/groupes ethniques; Secours d'urgence/réfugiés/aide humanitaire; Éducation/formation/alphabétisation. **Activités:** Échanges/parrainage/jumelage; Édition/documents audiovisuels/documents éducatifs.

FRA1716
ASSOCIATION EURO-AFRICAINE POUR L'ANTHROPOLOGIE DU CHANGEMENT SOCIAL ET DU DEVELOPPEMENT (APAD)

2 rue de la Charité, 13002 Marseille, France.

Téléphone: 33 - 91 91 92 62. *Fax:* 33 - 91 91 34 01. *Contact:* Jean-Pierre Olivier de Sardan, Président.

FRA1717
ASSOCIATION EUROPEENNE POUR L'ETUDE DE L'ALIMENTATION ET DU DEVELOPPEMENT DE L'ENFANT (ADE) ♦ European Association for Studies on Nutrition and Child Development

9, boulevard des Capucines, 75002 Paris, France.

Téléphone: 33 (1) 44 73 67 39. *Fax:* 33 (1) 44 73 67 39. *Contact:* Dr. Zygmunt L. Ostrowski, Président.

OBJECTIFS: Mener des études sur l'état nutritionnel et le développement de l'enfant. Promouvoir des actions humanitaires en faveur des enfants.

INFORMATIONS GENERALES: *Création:* 1976. *Personnel/Total:* 7. *Salariés:* 2 dont: 1 dans les pays en développement. *Bénévoles:* 5 dont: 3 dans les pays en développement. *Budget/Total 1993:* ECU 599000 (US$ 702000). *Sources financières:* *Privé:* 15%. *Public:* 80%. *Autofinancement:* 5%.

PUBLICATIONS: *Liste des publications.*

EVALUATION/RECHERCHE: Entreprend des activités de recherche.

COMMENTAIRES: Intervient dans la Communauté des Etats indépendants. Activités d'information concernant la Communauté des Etats indépendants.

ACTIVITES DANS LES REGIONS EN DEVELOPPEMENT: Intervient directement dans les régions en développement. Intervient dans 5 pays. Maintient une présence locale sur le terrain. **Actions de Développement durable:** Aliments/famine; Droits de l'Homme/paix/conflits; Enfants/jeunesse/famille; Envoi de volontaires/experts/assistance technique; Santé/assainissement/eau; Éducation/formation/alphabétisation. **Régions:** Afrique de l'Est.

ACTIVITES D'INFORMATION ET D'EDUCATION: Domaines: Santé/assainissement/eau. **Activités:** Conférences/séminaires/ateliers/activités de formation.

FRA1718
ASSOCIATION FORAGES MALI

Hôtel de Ville - Place Foch, 61000 Alençon, France.

Téléphone: 33 - 33 32 40 00. *Fax:* 33 - 33 32 13 22. *Contact:* Pierre Mauger.

OBJECTIFS: Réaliser des forages de puits dans les villages afin d'éviter les déplacements des populations rurales vers les villes. Améliorer l'état sanitaire des habitants et développer le maraîchage et la petite agriculture.

INFORMATIONS GENERALES: *Création:* 1984. *Type d'organisation:* réseau. *Personnel/Total:* var. *Bénévoles:* var. *Budget/Total 1993:* ECU 80000 (US$ 94000). *Sources financières:* *Privé:* 5%. *Public:* 80%. *Autofinancement:* 15%.

PUBLICATIONS: *Périodiques:* Terrya Dji (2). *Liste des publications.*

EVALUATION/RECHERCHE: Rapports d'évaluation disponibles.

Voir : *Comment utiliser le répertoire,* page 11.

PREVISIONS D'ACTIVITES: Assistance aux initiatives de développement avec un partenaire malien.

ACTIVITES DANS LES REGIONS EN DEVELOPPEMENT: Intervient directement dans les régions en développement. Intervient dans 1 pays. Maintient une présence locale sur le terrain. Intervient par l'intermédiaire d'organisations locales partenaires. **Actions de Développement durable:** Santé/assainissement/eau. **Régions:** Afrique de l'Ouest.

ACTIVITES D'INFORMATION ET D'EDUCATION: Domaines: Santé/assainissement/eau. **Activités:** Campagnes d'information/expositions; Collecte de fonds.

FRA1719

ASSOCIATION FORET MEDITERRANEENNE

14, rue Louis Astouin, 13002 Marseille, France.

Téléphone: 33 - 91 56 06 91. *Fax:* 33 - 91 91 93 97. *Contact:* Jean Bonnier, Secrétaire Général.

OBJECTIFS: Rassembler toutes les personnes qui s'intéressent, à quelque titre que ce soit, à la forêt méditerranéenne.

INFORMATIONS GENERALES: *Création:* 1978. *Type d'organisation:* regroupement d'ONG. *Personnel/Total:* 3. *Salariés:* 3. *Budget/Total 1993:* ECU 151000 (US$ 177000). *Sources financières:* Privé: 8%. *Public:* 64%. *Autofinancement:* 28%.

PUBLICATIONS: *Périodiques:* Forêt Méditerranéenne (4) - La feuille et l'Aiguille (4). *Liste des publications.*

EVALUATION/RECHERCHE: Rapports d'évaluation disponibles.

PREVISIONS D'ACTIVITES: Projet de création d'une association Forêt Méditerranéenne Internationale.

ACTIVITES DANS LES REGIONS EN DEVELOPPEMENT: Intervient dans 2 pays. Intervient par l'intermédiaire d'organisations locales partenaires. **Actions de Développement durable:** Développement rural/agriculture; Écologie/environnement/biodiversité. **Régions:** Afrique du Nord.

ACTIVITES D'INFORMATION ET D'EDUCATION: Domaines: Développement rural/agriculture; Écologie/environnement/biodiversité. **Activités:** Conférences/séminaires/ateliers/activités de formation; Services d'information et de documentation/bases de données; Édition/documents audiovisuels/documents éducatifs.

FRA1720

ASSOCIATION FRANCAISE D'AMITIE ET DE SOLIDARITE AVEC LES PEUPLES D'AFRIQUE (AFASPA)

21 rue Marceau, 93100 Montreuil, France.

Téléphone: 33 (1) 48 58 71 20. *Fax:* 33 (1) 48 70 91 26. *Contact:* François Lançon.

FRA1721

ASSOCIATION FRANCAISE D'ENTRAIDE

7 rue Frochot, 75009 Paris, France.

Téléphone: 33 (1) 42 85 10 67. *Contact:* Roger Parmelau.

FRA1722

ASSOCIATION FRANCAISE DE FORMATION, COOPERATION, PROMOTION ET ANIMATION D'ENTREPRISES (AFCOPA)

12 avenue Marceau, 75008 Paris, France.

Téléphone: 33 (1) 47 20 70 40. *Contact:* Henri Denque.

FRA1723

ASSOCIATION FRANCAISE DE SOLIDARITE (AFS)

Rue des Déportés, 29260 Lesneven, France.

Téléphone: 33 - 98 83 24 78. *Contact:* Jean-Louis Ollivier, Président.

FRA1724

ASSOCIATION FRANCAISE DE SOLIDARITE INTERNATIONALE (AFSI)

9 rue de Dantzig, 75015 Paris, France.

Téléphone: 33 (1) 45 33 54 64. *Fax:* 33 (1) 45 33 65 45. *Contact:* Marie-Sylvie Buisson, Présidente.

OBJECTIFS: Promouvoir l'éducation.

INFORMATIONS GENERALES: *Création:* 1988. *Personnel/Total:* 62. *Salariés:* 12 dont: 12 dans les pays en développement. *Bénévoles:* 50 dont: 30 dans les pays en développement. *Budget/Total 1993:* ECU 459000 (US$ 530000). *Sources financières:* Privé: 10%. *Public:* 5%. *Autofinancement:* 85%.

PUBLICATIONS: *Rapport annuel.*

EVALUATION/RECHERCHE: Rapports d'évaluation disponibles.

PREVISIONS D'ACTIVITES: Scolarisation au Liban, au Viet Nam, en Arménie et au Rwanda.

COMMENTAIRES: Intervient dans la Communauté des Etats indépendants. Activités d'information concernant la Communauté des Etats indépendants.

ACTIVITES DANS LES REGIONS EN DEVELOPPEMENT: Intervient directement dans les régions en développement. Intervient dans 4 pays. Maintient une présence locale sur le terrain. Intervient par l'intermédiaire d'organisations locales partenaires. **Actions de Développement durable:** Aliments/famine; Enfants/jeunesse/famille; Envoi de volontaires/experts/assistance technique; Petites entreprises/secteur informel/artisanat; Questions relatives aux femmes; Éducation/formation/alphabétisation. **Régions:** Moyen-Orient.

ACTIVITES D'INFORMATION ET D'EDUCATION: Domaines: Culture/tradition/religion; Questions relatives aux femmes; Éducation/formation/alphabétisation. **Activités:** Collecte de fonds; Échanges/parrainage/jumelage; Éducation formelle.

FRA1725

ASSOCIATION FRANCAISE DES EXPERTS DE LA COOPERATION TECHNIQUE INTERNATIONALE (AFECTI)

Bourse du Travail - Place Benoit Frachon, 93100 Montreuil-sous-Bois, France.

Téléphone: 33 (1) 48 70 12 80. *Contact:* Paul Fenonjoie, Président.

FRA1726

ASSOCIATION FRANCAISE DES VILLAGES D'ENFANTS SOS DANS LE MONDE (VESOS MONDE)

6 cité Monthiers, 75009 Paris, France.

Téléphone: 33 (1) 45 26 71 79. *Fax:* 33 (1) 49 95 02 85. *Contact:* Bernard Bouygues, Président.

OBJECTIFS: Construire des villages d'enfants SOS pour permettre l'accueil dans un cadre familial d'enfants orphelins ou de cas sociaux. Aider et soutenir les villages SOS déjà existants, grâce à des parrainages et des aides diverses.

INFORMATIONS GENERALES: *Création:* 1979. *Affiliée à:* SOS Kinderdorf International (Autriche). *Personnel/Total:* 10. *Salariés:* 7 dont: 2 dans les pays en développement. *Bénévoles:* 3 dont: 3 dans les pays en développement. *Budget/Total 1993:* ECU 3626000 (US$ 4248000). *Sources financières:* Privé: 94%. *Autofinancement:* 6%.

PUBLICATIONS: *Périodiques:* Revue des villages d'Enfants SOS (4). *Rapport annuel.*

EVALUATION/RECHERCHE: Rapports d'évaluation disponibles.

COMMENTAIRES: Intervient dans la Communauté des Etats indépendants.

ACTIVITES DANS LES REGIONS EN DEVELOPPEMENT: Intervient directement dans les régions en développement. Intervient dans 20 pays. Maintient une présence locale sur le terrain. Intervient par l'intermédiaire d'organisations locales partenaires. **Actions de Développement durable:** Enfants/jeunesse/famille. **Régions:** Afrique australe;

See: *How to Use the Directory*, page 11.

Afrique de l'Ouest; Afrique du Nord; Amérique du Sud; Asie du Sud-Est; Caraïbes.

ACTIVITES D'INFORMATION ET D'EDUCATION: Domaines: Enfants/jeunesse/famille. **Activités:** Campagnes d'information/expositions; Collecte de fonds; Radiodiffusion/manifestations culturelles; Services d'information et de documentation/bases de données; Échanges/parrainage/jumelage.

FRA1727
ASSOCIATION FRANCAISE DES VOLONTAIRES DU PROGRES (AFVP)

B.P. 207, 91311 Montlhéry cedex, France.

Téléphone: 33 (1) 69 01 10 95. *Fax:* 33 (1) 69 80 75 34. *Contact:* Guy Philippoteaux, Délégué Général.

OBJECTIFS: Permettre à des jeunes de participer à des actions de développement économique et social dans les pays du Tiers Monde.

INFORMATIONS GENERALES: *Création:* 1963. ***Organisations membres:*** 16. ***Affiliée à:*** Commission Nationale de la jeunesse pour le Développement - Comité Français contre la Faim - Comité de liaison ONG de volontariat - Forum Européen du Volontariat pour le Développement (Allemagne). ***Personnel/Total:*** 563. ***Salariés:*** 119 dont: 56 dans les pays en développement. *Bénévoles:* 444 dont: 444 dans les pays en développement. ***Budget/Total 1993:*** ECU 27514000 (US\$ 32228000). ***Sources financières:*** *Privé:* 28%. *Public:* 70%. *Autofinancement:* 2%.

PUBLICATIONS: *Périodiques:* Volontaires (3) - VP Infos (6). *Rapport annuel. Liste des publications.*

EVALUATION/RECHERCHE: Rapports d'évaluation disponibles. Entreprend des activités de recherche.

PREVISIONS D'ACTIVITES: Actions en faveur du développement rural et de l'environnement. Promotion du champ urbain (réhabilitation de quartiers de villes moyennes).

ACTIVITES DANS LES REGIONS EN DEVELOPPEMENT: Intervient directement dans les régions en développement. Intervient dans 24 pays. Maintient une présence locale sur le terrain. Intervient par l'intermédiaire d'organisations locales partenaires. **Actions de Développement durable:** Démocratie/bonne gestion publique/création d'institutions/développement participatif; Développement rural/agriculture; Développement urbain/habitat; Enfants/jeunesse/famille; Envoi de volontaires/experts/assistance technique; Petites entreprises/secteur informel/artisanat; Questions relatives aux femmes; Santé/assainissement/eau; Écologie/environnement/biodiversité; Éducation/formation/alphabétisation. **Régions:** Afrique australe; Afrique centrale; Afrique de l'Est; Afrique de l'Ouest.

ACTIVITES D'INFORMATION ET D'EDUCATION: Domaines: Développement rural/agriculture; Développement urbain/habitat; Santé/assainissement/eau; Écologie/environnement/biodiversité. **Activités:** Campagnes d'information/expositions; Conférences/séminaires/ateliers/activités de formation; Services d'information et de documentation/bases de données; Édition/documents audiovisuels/documents éducatifs.

FRA1728
ASSOCIATION FRANCAISE RAOUL FOLLEREAU

31 rue de Dantzig, B.P. 19, 75722 Paris cedex 15, France.

Téléphone: 33 (1) 48 28 72 42. *Fax:* (1) 48 56 22 22. *Contact:* André Récipon, Président.

FRA1729
ASSOCIATION FRANCE TCHAD ESPOIR

18, Allée de la Duchesse Anne, 35230 Châtillon-sur-Seiche, France.

Téléphone: 33 - 99 52 29 78. *Fax:* 33 - 99 52 29 78. *Contact:* Dr. N'Deikoundam Ngaugro Mosurel Ngaugro Mosurel.

FRA1730
ASSOCIATION FRANCE-PALESTINE

B.P. 184-04, 75160 Paris Cedex 04, France.

Téléphone: 33 (1) 45 21 07 49. *Contact:* Francis Blanchet, Secrétaire général.

FRA1731
ASSOCIATION GENERALE DES INTERVENANTS RETRAITES - ACTIONS DE BENEVOLES POUR LA COOPERATION ET LE DEVELOPPEMENT (AGIR-ABCD)

8 rue Ambroise-Thomas, B.P. 41, 75430 Paris cedex 09, France.

Téléphone: 33 (1) 47 70 18 90. *Fax:* 33 (1) 47 70 36 26. *Contact:* Jacques Michel, Président.

OBJECTIFS: Susciter dans les pays en développppement et dans les pays d'Europe centrale et orientale, des actions d'intérêt général, grâce au concours volontaire et bénévole de retraités apportant leur expérience et leur compétence professionnelles.

INFORMATIONS GENERALES: *Création:* 1983. ***Affiliée à:*** CFCF - Coordination d'Agen. ***Personnel/Total:*** 2500. *Bénévoles:* 2500. ***Budget/Total 1993:*** ECU 543000 (US\$ 836000). ***Sources financières:*** *Privé:* 15%. *Public:* 73%. *Autofinancement:* 12%.

PUBLICATIONS: *Périodiques:* Lettre d'Agir (4). *Rapport annuel.*

EVALUATION/RECHERCHE: Rapports d'évaluation disponibles.

COMMENTAIRES: Intervient dans la Communauté des Etats indépendants. Activités d'information concernant la Communauté des Etats indépendants.

ACTIVITES DANS LES REGIONS EN DEVELOPPEMENT: Intervient directement dans les régions en développement. Intervient dans 52 pays. Intervient par l'intermédiaire d'organisations locales partenaires. **Actions de Développement durable:** Développement rural/agriculture; Développement urbain/habitat; Santé/assainissement/eau; Éducation/formation/alphabétisation; Énergie/transport. **Régions:** Afrique australe; Afrique centrale; Afrique de l'Est; Afrique de l'Ouest; Afrique du Nord; Amérique du Sud; Asie du Sud-Est; Moyen-Orient.

ACTIVITES D'INFORMATION ET D'EDUCATION: Domaines: Développement rural/agriculture; Développement urbain/habitat; Enfants/jeunesse/famille; Pauvreté/conditions de vie; Population/planning familial/démographie; Questions relatives aux femmes; Relations internationales/coopération/aide au développement; Santé/assainissement/eau; Éducation/formation/alphabétisation. **Activités:** Conférences/séminaires/ateliers/activités de formation; Éducation formelle.

FRA1732
ASSOCIATION INDUSTRIES ET TECHNOLOGIES POUR LE DEVELOPPEMENT (AITD-TIERS MONDE)

4/1270 rue d'Alembert, 02100 Saint Quentin, France.

Téléphone: 33 - 23 68 61 95. *Contact:* Pascal Beaumont.

FRA1733
ASSOCIATION INTERNATIONALE DE TECHNICIENS, EXPERTS ET CHERCHEURS (AITEC)

14 place de Rungis, 75013 Paris, France.

Téléphone: 33 (1) 45 31 18 08. *Fax:* 33 (1) 45 31 64 37. *Contact:* Gustave Massiah, Président.

FRA1734
ASSOCIATION INTERNATIONALE DES MAISONS FAMILIALES RURALES (AIMFR)

36 allée Vivaldi, 75012 Paris, France.

Téléphone: 33 (1) 40 01 12 12. *Fax:* 33 (1) 40 04 93 56. *Contact:* Aimé Caekelbergh, Secrétaire Général.

OBJECTIFS: Encourager les actions des organisations des Maisons Familiales Rurales dans le monde. Défendre les intérêts des organisations membres auprès des instances internationales. Faire connaitre le but de l'organisation, qui est de fournir aux jeunes une formation agricole et rurale.

INFORMATIONS GENERALES: *Création:* 1975. ***Type d'organisation:*** collectif. ***Organisations membres:*** 22. ***Personnel/Total:*** 36. *Salariés:* 1. *Bénévoles:* 35 dont: 25 dans les pays en développement. ***Budget/***

Voir : Comment utiliser le répertoire, page 11.

Total 1993: ECU 14000 (US$ 17000). *Sources financières: Privé:* 50%. *Autofinancement:* 50%.

PUBLICATIONS: *Périodiques:* INFODOC (3).

EVALUATION/RECHERCHE: Entreprend des activités de recherche.

COMMENTAIRES: Intervient dans la Communauté des Etats indépendants.

ACTIVITES D'INFORMATION ET D'EDUCATION: **Domaines:** Développement rural/agriculture. **Activités:** Lobbying/plaidoyer.

FRA1735
ASSOCIATION INTERNATIONALE POUR LA RECHERCHE ET LE DEVELOPPEMENT EN AFRIQUE (ARDA)

15 Courdimanche, BP 207, 91941 Les Ulis cedex, France.

Téléphone: 33 (1) 69 07 59 39. *Contact:* Mamadou Traore, Président.

FRA1736
ASSOCIATION JEUNES TIERS MONDE (AJTM)

3 impasse du Château Silhal, 30000 Nîmes, France.

Téléphone: 33 - 66 26 34 39. *Contact:* Claude Figueras.

FRA1737
ASSOCIATION JEUNESSE D'ACTIONS POUR LA COOPERATION ET LA SOLIDARITE (AJACS)

77 rue Bressigny, 49100 Angers, France.

Téléphone: 33 - 41 86 03 76. *Contact:* Brigitte Pecqueur, Présidente.

OBJECTIFS: Faire de l'animation rurale dans le Centre-Est du Burkina Faso. Mener, en France, des actions de sensibilisation aux problèmes de développement auprès d'écoles, de collèges et de comités d'entreprise.

INFORMATIONS GENERALES: *Création:* 1967. *Affiliée à:* Réseau d'informations Tiers-Monde (France) - Comité Français Contre la Faim (France) - Coordination Tiers-Monde de Maine et Loire (France). *Personnel/Total:* 1. *Bénévoles:* 1 dont: 1 dans les pays en développement. *Budget/Total 1993:* ECU 79000 (US$ 93000). *Sources financières: Privé:* 9%. *Public:* 87%. *Autofinancement:* 4%.

PUBLICATIONS: *Rapport annuel.*

EVALUATION/RECHERCHE: Rapports d'évaluation disponibles.

PREVISIONS D'ACTIVITES: Réouverture du centre de Documentation qui sera accessible au public. Participation à la campagne du CFCF sur le thème de l'eau et l'environnement.

COMMENTAIRES: L'organisation souhaite désormais s'orienter vers l'éducation au développement en France.

ACTIVITES DANS LES REGIONS EN DEVELOPPEMENT: Intervient directement dans les régions en développement. Intervient dans 1 pays. Maintient une présence locale sur le terrain. Intervient par l'intermédiaire d'organisations locales partenaires. **Actions de Développement durable:** Développement rural/agriculture; Questions relatives aux femmes; Santé/assainissement/eau; Écologie/environnement/biodiversité; Éducation/formation/alphabétisation. **Régions:** Afrique de l'Ouest.

ACTIVITES D'INFORMATION ET D'EDUCATION: **Domaines:** Aliments/famine; Culture/tradition/religion; Droits de l'Homme/paix/conflits; Développement rural/agriculture; Développement urbain/habitat; Enfants/jeunesse/famille; Paix/conflits ethniques/armement/désarmement; Pauvreté/conditions de vie; Population/planning familial/démographie; Questions relatives aux femmes; Racisme/xénophobie/antisémitisme; Relations internationales/coopération/aide au développement; Relations économiques internationales/commerce/dette/finances; Réfugiés/migrants/groupes ethniques; Santé/assainissement/eau; Secours d'urgence/réfugiés/aide humanitaire; Écologie/environnement/biodiversité; Éducation/formation/alphabétisation. **Activités:** Campagnes d'information/expositions; Collecte de fonds; Conférences/séminaires/ateliers/activités de formation; Radiodiffusion/manifestations culturelles; Services d'information et de documentation/bases de données; Édition/documents audiovisuels/documents éducatifs.

FRA1738
ASSOCIATION LANGUEDOC-COMORES

29 boulevard du Monument, BP 46, 11210 Port-la-Nouvelle, France.

Téléphone: 33 - 68 48 00 70. *Fax:* 33 - 68 48 43 77. *Contact:* Dr. Yves Chavernac, Président.

OBJECTIFS: Aider au fonctionnement de différents hôpitaux comoriens, en améliorant notamment l'infrastructure hospitalière. Apporter une aide matérielle aux établissemnts scolaires de Domoni et de ses environs.

INFORMATIONS GENERALES: *Création:* 1982. *Type d'organisation:* collectif. *Personnel/Total:* 52. *Salariés:* 2 dont: 2 dans les pays en développement. *Bénévoles:* 50 dont: 10 dans les pays en développement. *Budget/Total 1993:* ECU 188000 (US$ 221000). *Sources financières: Privé:* 100%.

EVALUATION/RECHERCHE: Rapports d'évaluation disponibles.

PREVISIONS D'ACTIVITES: Campagnes d'hygiène et de nutrition.

ACTIVITES DANS LES REGIONS EN DEVELOPPEMENT: Intervient directement dans les régions en développement. Intervient dans 1 pays. Maintient une présence locale sur le terrain. Intervient par l'intermédiaire d'organisations locales partenaires. **Actions de Développement durable:** Aliments/famine; Démocratie/bonne gestion publique/création d'institutions/développement participatif; Développement urbain/habitat; Enfants/jeunesse/famille; Envoi de volontaires/experts/assistance technique; Questions relatives aux femmes; Santé/assainissement/eau; Écologie/environnement/biodiversité; Éducation/formation/alphabétisation; Énergie/transport. **Régions:** Afrique australe.

ACTIVITES D'INFORMATION ET D'EDUCATION: **Domaines:** Aliments/famine; Développement urbain/habitat; Enfants/jeunesse/famille; Questions relatives aux femmes; Santé/assainissement/eau; Écologie/environnement/biodiversité; Éducation/formation/alphabétisation. **Activités:** Campagnes d'information/expositions; Collecte de fonds; Éducation formelle.

FRA1739
ASSOCIATION LANGUEDOCIENNE D'AIDE AU DEVELOPPEMENT (ALAD)

12 Grand'Rue, 30000 Nîmes, France.

Téléphone: 33 - 66 21 90 01. *Contact:* Paul Regnier-Vigouroux.

OBJECTIFS: Promouvoir toutes les actions de développement, notamment l'éducation, la scolarisation, l'alphabétisation, la formation, la santé, l'hygiène, la nutrition, l'économie, la gestion, la culture et l'animation.

INFORMATIONS GENERALES: *Création:* 1985. *Organisations membres:* 100. *Personnel/Total:* 15. *Bénévoles:* 15 dont: 14 dans les pays en développement. *Budget/Total 1993:* ECU 75000 (US$ 88000). *Sources financières: Privé:* 90%. *Autofinancement:* 10%.

PUBLICATIONS: *Rapport annuel.*

ACTIVITES DANS LES REGIONS EN DEVELOPPEMENT: Intervient directement dans les régions en développement. Intervient dans 1 pays. Maintient une présence locale sur le terrain. **Actions de Développement durable:** Aliments/famine; Démocratie/bonne gestion publique/création d'institutions/développement participatif; Développement rural/agriculture; Enfants/jeunesse/famille; Petites entreprises/secteur informel/artisanat; Population/planning familial/démographie; Questions relatives aux femmes; Santé/assainissement/eau; Secours d'urgence/réfugiés/aide humanitaire; Écologie/environnement/biodiversité; Éducation/formation/alphabétisation. **Régions:** Afrique de l'Ouest.

ACTIVITES D'INFORMATION ET D'EDUCATION: **Domaines:** Aliments/famine; Culture/tradition/religion; Développement rural/agriculture; Emploi/chômage; Enfants/jeunesse/famille; Pauvreté/conditions de vie; Population/planning familial/démographie; Questions relatives aux femmes; Santé/assainissement/eau; Secours d'urgence/réfugiés/aide humanitaire; Écologie/environnement/biodiversité; Éducation/formation/alphabétisation. **Activités:** Campagnes d'information/expositions; Collecte de fonds; Éducation formelle.

See: *How to Use the Directory,* page 11.

FRA1740

ASSOCIATION LASER PRODUCTIONS - CAISSE PHARMACEUTIQUE D'ASSISTANCE SOCIALE

31 rue de la Liberté, 77680 Roissy-en-Brie, France.

Téléphone: 33 - 60 29 31 95. *Contact:* Placide Mutombo Tshikuku, Président.

OBJECTIFS: Fabriquer des produits pharmaceutiques et les distribuer aux populations. Promouvoir la caisse pharmaceutique d'assistance sociale. Créer des centres de formation professionnelle pour les enfants défavorisés.

INFORMATIONS GENERALES: *Création:* 1994. *Type d'organisation:* réseau. *Organisations membres:* 2. *Affiliée à:* Maison des clubs UNESCO (France). *Personnel/Total:* 17. *Salariés:* 7 dont: 4 dans les pays en développement. *Bénévoles:* 10 dont: 6 dans les pays en développement. *Budget/Total 1993:* ECU 176000 (US$ 207000). *Sources financières:* Autofinancement: 100%.

PUBLICATIONS: *Rapport annuel. Liste des publications.*

EVALUATION/RECHERCHE: Rapports d'évaluation disponibles. Entreprend des activités de recherche.

PREVISIONS D'ACTIVITES: Création d'un centre de formation professionnelle pour les jeunes défavorisés.

ACTIVITES DANS LES REGIONS EN DEVELOPPEMENT: Intervient directement dans les régions en développement. Intervient dans 1 pays. Maintient une présence locale sur le terrain. Intervient par l'intermédiaire d'organisations locales partenaires. **Actions de Développement durable:** Développement rural/agriculture; Enfants/jeunesse/famille; Petites entreprises/secteur informel/artisanat; Population/planning familial/démographie; Santé/assainissement/eau; Secours d'urgence/réfugiés/aide humanitaire; Écologie/environnement/biodiversité; Éducation/formation/alphabétisation. **Régions:** Afrique centrale.

ACTIVITES D'INFORMATION ET D'EDUCATION: Domaines: Développement rural/agriculture; Santé/assainissement/eau; Secours d'urgence/réfugiés/aide humanitaire. **Activités:** Lobbying/plaidoyer; Éducation formelle.

FRA1741

ASSOCIATION LORRAINE POUR LE DEVELOPPEMENT DES PEUPLES (ASSAJVCO)

8 rue du Prel, 57260 Dieuze, France.

Téléphone: 33 - 87 86 84 98. *Contact:* Michel Liegey, Président.

OBJECTIFS: Lutter contre le gaspillage en récupérant,en recyclant et en vendant tout ce qui peut encore servir. Se former et s'informer sur les réalités internationales, les besoins et les combats d'autres peuples. Apporter une aide financière aux petits projets de développement.

INFORMATIONS GENERALES: *Création:* 1971. *Affiliée à:* Artisans du monde - Peuples solidaires - Cicda. *Personnel/Total:* 125. *Salariés:* 1. *Bénévoles:* 124. *Budget/Total 1993:* ECU 130000 (US$ 153000). *Sources financières:* Privé: 8%. Public: 2%. Autofinancement: 70%.

PUBLICATIONS: *Périodiques:* Change échange (4). *Rapport annuel.*

COMMENTAIRES: Intervient dans la Communauté des Etats indépendants.

ACTIVITES DANS LES REGIONS EN DEVELOPPEMENT: Intervient directement dans les régions en développement. Intervient dans 3 pays. Intervient par l'intermédiaire d'organisations locales partenaires. **Actions de Développement durable:** Droits de l'Homme/paix/conflits; Développement rural/agriculture; Enfants/jeunesse/famille; Santé/assainissement/eau; Éducation/formation/alphabétisation. **Régions:** Amérique du Sud.

ACTIVITES D'INFORMATION ET D'EDUCATION: Domaines: Développement rural/agriculture; Enfants/jeunesse/famille; Santé/assainissement/eau; Secours d'urgence/réfugiés/aide humanitaire. **Activités:** Campagnes d'information/expositions; Collecte de fonds.

FRA1742

ASSOCIATION MEDICALE ENGHIENNOISE (AME)

41 bis rue des Thermes, 95880 Enghien-les-Bains, France.

Téléphone: 33 - 34 12 35 59. *Contact:* Jean-Michel Blanche.

FRA1743

ASSOCIATION MEDICALE FRANCO-PALESTINIENNE

14 rue de Nanteuil, 75015 Paris, France.

Téléphone: 33 (1) 45 30 12 08. *Contact:* Jean-Marie Gaubert.

FRA1744

ASSOCIATION MONDIALE DES GRANDES METROPOLES (METROPOLIS)

Secrétariat général IAURIF - 251 rue de Vaugirard, 75740 Paris cedex 15, France.

Téléphone: 33 (1) 40 43 78 00. *Fax:* 33 (1) 40 43 79 85. *Contact:* Michel Giraud, Président.

OBJECTIFS: Promouvoir la planification et la gestion urbaines.Sensibiliser à la question de l'environnement, de l'écologie urbaine et de la santé. Favoriser les échanges d'informations et d'expériences. Organiser des sessions de formation.

INFORMATIONS GENERALES: *Création:* 1985. *Type d'organisation:* réseau. *Personnel/Total:* 4. *Salariés:* 4.

PUBLICATIONS: *Périodiques:* Bulletin de l'Association (3).

EVALUATION/RECHERCHE: Entreprend des activités de recherche.

FRA1745

ASSOCIATION NATIONALE POUR LE DEVELOPPEMENT AGRICOLE (ANDA)

25-27 avenue de Villiers, 75017 Paris, France.

Téléphone: 33 (1) 47 66 55 50. *Fax:* 33 (1) 42 27 50 32. *Contact:* Michel Fau, Président.

OBJECTIFS: Favoriser le développement agricole, en France et à l'étranger.

INFORMATIONS GENERALES: *Création:* 1967. *Personnel/Total:* 27. *Salariés:* 27. *Budget/Total 1993:* ECU 105527000 (US$ 123605000). **Actions de Développement durable:** Développement rural/agriculture. **Régions:** Afrique centrale; Afrique de l'Ouest; Afrique du Nord; Asie du Sud-Est.

FRA1746

ASSOCIATION NIORTAISE POUR LE JUMELAGE ET LA COOPERATION AVEC ATAKPAME (ANJCA)

22 rue du Côteau St. Hubert, 79000 Niort, France.

Téléphone: 33 - 49 73 46 57. *Contact:* André Pineau, Président.

OBJECTIFS: Multiplier les échanges et contribuer au développement de la ville d'Atakpamé, au Togo.

INFORMATIONS GENERALES: *Création:* 1986. *Affiliée à:* F.M.C.U - C.U.F.. *Budget/Total 1993:* ECU 68000 (US$ 79000). *Sources financières:* Privé: 40%. Public: 30%. Autofinancement: 30%.

PUBLICATIONS: *Périodiques:* "Atakpamé" (5). *Rapport annuel.*

EVALUATION/RECHERCHE: Rapports d'évaluation disponibles.

ACTIVITES DANS LES REGIONS EN DEVELOPPEMENT: Intervient directement dans les régions en développement. Intervient dans 1 pays. **Actions de Développement durable:** Démocratie/bonne gestion publique/création d'institutions/développement participatif; Développement rural/agriculture; Développement urbain/habitat; Enfants/jeunesse/famille; Petites entreprises/secteur informel/artisanat; Questions relatives aux femmes; Santé/assainissement/eau; Éducation/formation/alphabétisation. **Régions:** Afrique de l'Ouest.

ACTIVITES D'INFORMATION ET D'EDUCATION: Domaines: Aliments/famine; Culture/tradition/religion; Droits de l'Homme/paix/conflits; Développement rural/agriculture; Développement urbain/habitat; Emploi/chômage; Enfants/jeunesse/famille; Paix/conflits ethniques/armement/

Voir : *Comment utiliser le répertoire,* page 11.

désarmement; Pauvreté/conditions de vie; Population/planning familial/démographie; Questions relatives aux femmes; Racisme/xénophobie/antisémitisme; Relations internationales/coopération/aide au développement; Relations économiques internationales/commerce/dette/finances; Réfugiés/migrants/groupes ethniques; Santé/assainissement/eau; Secours d'urgence/réfugiés/aide humanitaire; Écologie/environnement/biodiversité; Éducation/formation/alphabétisation. **Activités:** Échanges/parrainage/jumelage.

FRA1747

ASSOCIATION POUR COMBATTRE LA MALNUTRITION PAR ALGOCULTURE (ACMA)

La Roquette Saint-Bauzille de Putois, 34190 Ganges, France.

Téléphone: 33 - 67 73 70 60. *Fax:* 33 - 67 73 33 22. *Contact:* Denise Fox, Présidente.

OBJECTIFS: Lutter contre la malnutrition par l'introduction dans les pays développement de la culture de la microalgue spiruline, riche en protéines et vitamines, fer et éléments capables de renforcer le système immunitaire.

INFORMATIONS GENERALES: *Création:* 1971. *Affiliée à:* Comité Français de Solidarité Internationale (France) - Technap (France). *Personnel/Total:* 4. *Bénévoles:* 4 dont: 1 dans les pays en développement. *Budget/Total 1993:* ECU 15000 (US$ 18000). *Sources financières:* Privé: 94%. Autofinancement: 6%.

EVALUATION/RECHERCHE: Entreprend des activités de recherche.

PREVISIONS D'ACTIVITES: Collaboration avec d'autres ONG ou universités. Recherche de gisements naturels de spiruline.

COMMENTAIRES: Intervient dans la Communauté des Etats indépendants.

ACTIVITES DANS LES REGIONS EN DEVELOPPEMENT: Intervient directement dans les régions en développement. Intervient dans 4 pays. Maintient une présence locale sur le terrain. Intervient par l'intermédiaire d'organisations locales partenaires. **Actions de Développement durable:** Aliments/famine. **Régions:** Afrique centrale; Afrique de l'Ouest; Amérique du Sud; Asie centrale et Asie du Sud; Asie de l'Est; Asie du Sud-Est; Mexique et Amerique centrale.

ACTIVITES D'INFORMATION ET D'EDUCATION: Domaines: Aliments/famine. **Activités:** Conférences/séminaires/ateliers/activités de formation; Services d'information et de documentation/bases de données.

FRA1748

ASSOCIATION POUR L'ETABLISSEMENT DES REFUGIES

21 bis rue de la Pérouse, 75116 Paris, France.

Contact: Jean-Paul Angles, Président.

FRA1749

ASSOCIATION POUR LA COOPERATION ET LE DEVELOPPEMENT DES STRUCTURES SANITAIRES (ACODESS)

11, rue Rondelet, 75012 Paris, France.

Téléphone: 33 (1) 44 68 98 33. *Fax:* 33 (1) 44 68 98 34. *Contact:* Patrick Mordelet, Président.

OBJECTIFS: Apporter une assistance technique aux Ministères de la Santé et aux hôpitaux des pays en développement. Rechercher les technologies et les modes de gestion les plus appropriés pour répondre aux besoins de santé des populations.

INFORMATIONS GENERALES: *Création:* 1986. *Personnel/Total:* 53. *Salariés:* 3. *Bénévoles:* 50. *Budget/Total 1993:* ECU 452000 (US$ 530000). *Sources financières:* Public: 95%. Autofinancement: 5%.

PUBLICATIONS: *Périodiques:* "Hémisphères" (4). *Liste des publications.*

EVALUATION/RECHERCHE: Rapports d'évaluation disponibles. Entreprend des activités de recherche.

COMMENTAIRES: Intervient dans la Communauté des Etats indépendants. Activités d'information concernant la Communauté des Etats indépendants.

ACTIVITES DANS LES REGIONS EN DEVELOPPEMENT: Intervient directement dans les régions en développement. Intervient dans 12 pays. Intervient par l'intermédiaire d'organisations locales partenaires. **Actions de Développement durable:** Envoi de volontaires/experts/assistance technique; Santé/assainissement/eau; Éducation/formation/alphabétisation. **Régions:** Afrique du Nord; Amérique du Sud; Asie de l'Est; Asie du Sud-Est; Moyen-Orient.

FRA1750

ASSOCIATION POUR LA DEFENSE DES DROITS DE L'HOMME EN AFRIQUE (ADDHA)

BP.8375, 95805 Cergy Pontoise cedex, France.

Téléphone: 33 (1) 30 30 40 34. *Fax:* 33 (1) 34 24 92 64. *Contact:* Matre Lembelembe N'Kaschama, Président Exécutif.

FRA1751

ASSOCIATION POUR LA FORMATION EN MILIEU RURAL (AFMR)

Rue Etcharry, 64120 Saint-Palais, France.

Téléphone: 33 - 59 65 72 82. *Fax:* 33 - 59 65 83 96. *Contact:* Franz Dubosq.

FRA1752

ASSOCIATION POUR LA GERANCE DES LYCEES ET DES ECOLES DE FORMATION MARITIME ET AQUACOLE (AGEMA) ♦ Sea Training Schools Association

51 bis rue Sainte-Anne, 75002 Paris, France.

Téléphone: 33 (1) 44 77 80 30. *Fax:* 33 (1) 42 86 85 53. *Contact:* Jean-Claude Lanos, Secrétaire général.

OBJECTIFS: Promouvoir et centraliser les activités tendant à assurer et à développer la formation professionnelle, le perfectionnement et la promotion sociale dans les secteurs de la marine de commerce, de la pêche maritime et des cultures marines. Gérer et faire fonctionner les lycées et écoles maritimes et aquacoles qui sont confiés à l'association.

INFORMATIONS GENERALES: *Création:* 1941. *Type d'organisation:* réseau. *Personnel/Total:* 430. *Salariés:* 430 dont: 5 dans les pays en développement. *Budget/Total 1993:* ECU 15075000 (US$ 17658000). *Sources financières:* Privé: 20%. *Public:* 80%.

PUBLICATIONS: *Rapport annuel. Liste des publications.*

EVALUATION/RECHERCHE: Rapports d'évaluation disponibles. Entreprend des activités de recherche.

COMMENTAIRES: Projet d'association de l'AGEMA avec l'ensemble des écoles de pêche francophones: échange de programmes d'enseignement, de logiciels, de didacticiels, voire d'enseignements.

ACTIVITES DANS LES REGIONS EN DEVELOPPEMENT: Intervient directement dans les régions en développement. Intervient par l'intermédiaire d'organisations locales partenaires. **Actions de Développement durable:** Envoi de volontaires/experts/assistance technique; Éducation/formation/alphabétisation. **Régions:** Afrique de l'Ouest.

ACTIVITES D'INFORMATION ET D'EDUCATION: Domaines: Éducation/formation/alphabétisation. **Activités:** Services d'information et de documentation/bases de données; Édition/documents audiovisuels/documents éducatifs; Éducation formelle.

FRA1753

ASSOCIATION POUR LA MEDECINE ET LA RECHERCHE EN AFRIQUE (AMREF FRANCE)

66 bis rue Saint-Didier, 75116 Paris, France.

Téléphone: 33 (1) 45 53 27 84/29. *Contact:* Dominique Gautheron, Secrétaire générale.

See: *How to Use the Directory,* page 11.

FRA1754

ASSOCIATION POUR LA PREPARATION AU VOLONTARIAT (PREDEP)

BP 4, 34390 Olargues, France.

Contact: Pierre Micheletti.

FRA1755

ASSOCIATION POUR LA PROMOTION DE LA MEDECINE PREVENTIVE (APMP)

5 boulevard Montparnasse, 75006 Paris, France.

Téléphone: 33 (1) 47 34 52 94. *Fax:* 33 (1) 47 83 56 22. *Contact:* Philippe Stoeckel, Directeur.

FRA1756

ASSOCIATION POUR LA PROMOTION DES RECHERCHES ET ETUDES FONCIERES EN AFRIQUE (APREFA)

Université de Paris I - Laboratoire d'anthropologie juridique de Paris - 14 rue Cujas, 75231 Paris cedex 05, France.

Téléphone: 33 (1) 40 46 28 32. *Fax:* 33 (1) 40 46 28 29. *Contact:* E. Le Roy, Président.

OBJECTIFS: Organiser le monde de la recherche internationale sur le foncier en Afrique pour faire prévaloir, par des interventions sur le terrain, des évaluations ou des consultations, des publications scientifiques et des interventions auprès des décideurs.

INFORMATIONS GENERALES: *Création:* 1987. *Personnel/Total:* 1. *Bénévoles:* 1. *Budget/Total 1993:* ECU 1500 (US$ 1700). *Sources financières:* Autofinancement: 100%.

PUBLICATIONS: *Liste des publications.*

EVALUATION/RECHERCHE: Rapports d'évaluation disponibles. Entreprend des activités de recherche.

ACTIVITES DANS LES REGIONS EN DEVELOPPEMENT: Intervient directement dans les régions en développement. Intervient dans 3 pays. Maintient une présence locale sur le terrain. Intervient par l'intermédiaire d'organisations locales partenaires. **Actions de Développement durable:** Autres; Démocratie/bonne gestion publique/création d'institutions/développement participatif; Développement rural/agriculture; Développement urbain/habitat; Écologie/environnement/biodiversité. **Régions:** Afrique australe; Afrique centrale; Afrique de l'Est; Afrique de l'Ouest.

ACTIVITES D'INFORMATION ET D'EDUCATION: Domaines: Autres; Développement rural/agriculture; Développement urbain/habitat; Écologie/environnement/biodiversité. **Activités:** Conférences/séminaires/ateliers/activités de formation; Lobbying/plaidoyer; Services d'information et de documentation/bases de données; Édition/documents audiovisuels/documents éducatifs.

FRA1757

ASSOCIATION POUR LA PROTECTION DES ANIMAUX SAUVAGES ET DU PATRIMOINE NATUREL (ASPAS)

B.P. 34, 26270 Loriol, France.

Téléphone: 33 - 75 62 64 86. *Fax:* 33 - 75 62 66 00. *Contact:* Alain Clément, Président.

OBJECTIFS: Protéger la faune, la flore et le milieu naturel.

INFORMATIONS GENERALES: *Création:* 1980. *Organisations membres:* 500. *Affiliée à:* France Nature Environnement (France) - Bureau européen de l'Environnement (Belgique). *Personnel/Total:* 206. Salariés: 6. Bénévoles: 200 dont: 5 dans les pays en développement.

PUBLICATIONS: *Périodiques:* ASPAS Mag (4). *Rapport annuel. Liste des publications.*

EVALUATION/RECHERCHE: Entreprend des activités de recherche.

PREVISIONS D'ACTIVITES: Réhabilitation du loup, du renard et des mustélidés. Développement de la lutte biologique par les auxiliaires de l'agriculture.

ACTIVITES DANS LES REGIONS EN DEVELOPPEMENT: Intervient dans 30 pays. Intervient par l'intermédiaire d'organisations locales partenaires. **Actions de Développement durable:** Écologie/environnement/biodiversité. **Régions:** Afrique centrale; Afrique du Nord; Asie centrale et Asie du Sud; Asie de l'Est; Mexique et Amerique centrale.

ACTIVITES D'INFORMATION ET D'EDUCATION: Domaines: Écologie/environnement/biodiversité. **Activités:** Campagnes d'information/expositions; Collecte de fonds; Conférences/séminaires/ateliers/activités de formation; Lobbying/plaidoyer; Édition/documents audiovisuels/documents éducatifs; Éducation formelle.

FRA1758

ASSOCIATION POUR LA VALORISATION ET LA PERFORMANCE DE L'ENCADREMENT AFRICAIN (AVP)

41 rue de la Frégate B., 77380 Combs-la-ville, France.

Téléphone: 33 (1) 64 88 42 47. *Contact:* Roger-Etienne Tape, Président.

FRA1759

ASSOCIATION POUR LE CONSEIL A LA CREATION D'ENTREPRISES ET LA COOPERATION INTERNATIONALE (A3CI)

14, rue des Dominicaines, 13001 Marseille, France.

Téléphone: 33 - 91 56 08 05. *Fax:* 33 - 91 56 14 07. *Contact:* Tahar Rahmani, Directeur.

OBJECTIFS: Promouvoir la création d'entreprises pour un public démuni au Magrehb.

INFORMATIONS GENERALES: *Création:* 1984. *Type d'organisation:* réseau. *Personnel/Total:* 35. *Salariés:* 35. *Budget/Total 1993:* ECU 905000 (US$ 1059000). *Sources financières:* Privé: 5%. Public: 80%. Autofinancement: 15%.

PUBLICATIONS: *Périodiques:* Mouvements (2). *Rapport annuel. Liste des publications.*

EVALUATION/RECHERCHE: Rapports d'évaluation disponibles. Entreprend des activités de recherche.

ACTIVITES DANS LES REGIONS EN DEVELOPPEMENT: Intervient directement dans les régions en développement. Intervient dans 3 pays. Intervient par l'intermédiaire d'organisations locales partenaires. **Actions de Développement durable:** Démocratie/bonne gestion publique/création d'institutions/développement participatif; Envoi de volontaires/experts/assistance technique; Petites entreprises/secteur informel/artisanat; Éducation/formation/alphabétisation. **Régions:** Afrique du Nord.

ACTIVITES D'INFORMATION ET D'EDUCATION: Domaines: Emploi/chômage. **Activités:** Échanges/parrainage/jumelage; Édition/documents audiovisuels/documents éducatifs; Éducation formelle.

FRA1760

ASSOCIATION POUR LE DEVELOPPEMENT AGRO-INDUSTRIEL DU SAHEL (ADAIS)

01150 Vaux-en-Bugey, France.

Téléphone: 33 - 74 35 83 42. *Fax:* 33 - 42 45 55 98. *Contact:* François Escoffier, Président.

OBJECTIFS: Favoriser l'autosuffisance alimentaire au Burkina Faso par le développement conjoint de l'agriculture et de la petite industrie.

INFORMATIONS GENERALES: *Création:* 1983. *Affiliée à:* Peuples solidaires. *Personnel/Total:* 16. *Salariés:* 2 dont: 2 dans les pays en développement. Bénévoles: 14. *Budget/Total 1993:* ECU 60000 (US$ 71000). *Sources financières:* Privé: 10%. Public: 80%. Autofinancement: 10%.

PUBLICATIONS: *Périodiques:* Adaïs-Informations (2). *Rapport annuel.*

EVALUATION/RECHERCHE: Rapports d'évaluation disponibles.

ACTIVITES DANS LES REGIONS EN DEVELOPPEMENT: Intervient directement dans les régions en développement. Intervient dans 1 pays. Maintient une présence locale sur le terrain. Intervient par l'intermédiaire d'organisations locales partenaires. **Actions de Développement durable:** Dette/finances/commerce; Démocratie/bonne gestion publique/création d'institutions/développement participatif; Développement rural/agriculture; Petites entreprises/secteur informel/artisanat; Population/planning familial/démographie; Questions relatives aux femmes; Santé/

Voir : *Comment utiliser le répertoire,* page 11.

assainissement/eau; Écologie/environnement/biodiversité; Éducation/ formation/alphabétisation. **Régions:** Afrique de l'Ouest.

ACTIVITES D'INFORMATION ET D'EDUCATION: Domaines: Développement rural/agriculture; Population/planning familial/démographie; Questions relatives aux femmes; Santé/assainissement/eau; Écologie/ environnement/biodiversité; Éducation/formation/alphabétisation. **Activités:** Collecte de fonds; Radiodiffusion/manifestations culturelles.

FRA1761

ASSOCIATION POUR LE DEVELOPPEMENT DE MELGA (ADM)

25, rue Emile Zola, 78360 Montesson, France.

Téléphone: 33 (1) 39 52 06 19. **Contact:** Pierrette Hirschauer, Présidente.

OBJECTIFS: Soutenir la communauté villageoise de Melga, au Mali, dans sa volonté de prendre en mains son développement et de parvenir à l'autosuffisance alimentaire.

INFORMATIONS GENERALES: Création: 1986. **Budget/Total 1993:** ECU 6000 (US$ 7000). **Sources financières:** Privé: 10%. Public: 20%. Autofinancement: 70%.

PUBLICATIONS: Périodiques: Journal de l'ADM (4).

PREVISIONS D'ACTIVITES: Construction de puits à Melga. Aide à l'organisation du groupe de femmes de Melga vivant là-bas ou en France. Mise en place d'un jardin maraîcher à Melga. Aide au fonctionnement de la caisse à pharmacie villageoise. Aide à l'éducation des villageois.

COMMENTAIRES: L'originalité de l'association est d'être composée de migrants originaires de Melga (Mali). Elle permet un partenariat total entre les membres actifs en France et les villageois au Mali.

ACTIVITES DANS LES REGIONS EN DEVELOPPEMENT: Intervient directement dans les régions en développement. Intervient dans 1 pays. Maintient une présence locale sur le terrain. **Actions de Développement durable:** Développement rural/agriculture; Questions relatives aux femmes; Santé/assainissement/eau; Éducation/formation/alphabétisation. **Régions:** Afrique de l'Ouest.

ACTIVITES D'INFORMATION ET D'EDUCATION: Domaines: Développement rural/agriculture; Questions relatives aux femmes; Santé/assainissement/eau; Éducation/formation/alphabétisation. **Activités:** Campagnes d'information/expositions; Collecte de fonds; Services d'information et de documentation/bases de données; Échanges/parrainage/jumelage; Éducation formelle.

FRA1762

ASSOCIATION POUR LE DEVELOPPEMENT DES ACTIVITES MARITIMES (CEASM)

28, rue Godefroy Cavaignac, 75011 Paris, France.

Téléphone: 33 (1) 40 09 28 08. **Fax:** 33 (1) 40 09 00 89. **Contact:** Philippe Prigent, Directeur.

OBJECTIFS: Réaliser des études de faisabilité, mettre en œuvre et gérer des projets, fournir une assistance technique, former des cadres professionnels et administratifs dans le domaine de la pêche artisanale, en Afrique.

INFORMATIONS GENERALES: Création: 1960. **Personnel/Total:** 5. Salariés: 5. **Budget/Total 1993:** ECU 524000 (US$ 614000). **Sources financières:** Autofinancement: 100%.

PUBLICATIONS: Rapport annuel.

EVALUATION/RECHERCHE: Rapports d'évaluation disponibles. Entreprend des activités de recherche.

PREVISIONS D'ACTIVITES: Valorisation des produits de la pêche artisanale.

COMMENTAIRES: L'organisation fait des enquêtes et des études à caractère socio-économique.

ACTIVITES DANS LES REGIONS EN DEVELOPPEMENT: Intervient directement dans les régions en développement. Maintient une présence locale sur le terrain. Intervient par l'intermédiaire d'organisations

locales partenaires. **Actions de Développement durable:** Autres; Envoi de volontaires/experts/assistance technique; Petites entreprises/ secteur informel/artisanat; Questions relatives aux femmes. **Régions:** Afrique de l'Est; Afrique de l'Ouest; Afrique du Nord.

ACTIVITES D'INFORMATION ET D'EDUCATION: Domaines: Autres. **Activités:** Autres; Services d'information et de documentation/bases de données.

FRA1763

ASSOCIATION POUR LE DEVELOPPEMENT DES ECHANGES EN TECHNOLOGIE ECONOMIQUE ET FINANCIERE (ADETEF)

120 rue de Bercy Teledoc 711, 75572 Paris cedex 12, France.

Téléphone: 33 (1) 40 04 32 86. **Fax:** 33 (1) 40 04 32 76. **Contact:** Régis Gouze, Délégué.

FRA1764

ASSOCIATION POUR LE DEVELOPPEMENT DES ECHANGES INTERNATIONAUX DE PRODUITS ET TECHNIQUES AGROALIMENTAIRES (ADEPTA)

3 rue Barbet de Jouy, 75007 Paris, France.

Téléphone: 33 (1) 49 55 49 81. **Fax:** 33 (1) 49 55 59 42. **Contact:** Yves Jacques, Président.

FRA1765

ASSOCIATION REGIONALE POUR LE DEVELOPPEMENT DE LA COOPERATION INDUSTRIELLE INTERNATIONALE (ADECI)

2, rue Henri Barbusse, immeuble CMCI, 13001 Marseille, France.

Téléphone: 33 - 91 91 92 48. **Fax:** 33 - 91 91 85 37 . **Contact:** Jean-Claude Sitbon, Directeur.

OBJECTIFS: Aider les PME-PMI de la région Provence-Alpes-Côte d'Azur dans la réalisation d'accords de coopération industrielle inter-entreprises avec des partenaires potentiels des pays en développement et de l'Europe.

INFORMATIONS GENERALES: Création: 1980. **Type d'organisation:** regroupement d'ONG. **Affiliée à:** Réseau BC-NET. **Personnel/Total:** 3. Salariés: 3. **Budget/Total 1993:** ECU 332000 (US$ 388000). **Sources financières:** Public: 70%. Autofinancement: 30%.

PUBLICATIONS: Périodiques: Bulletin d'information de l'ADECI (2). Rapport annuel.

ACTIVITES DANS LES REGIONS EN DEVELOPPEMENT: Intervient directement dans les régions en développement. Intervient dans 10 pays. Intervient par l'intermédiaire d'organisations locales partenaires. **Actions de Développement durable:** Petites entreprises/ secteur informel/artisanat. **Régions:** Afrique centrale; Afrique de l'Ouest; Afrique du Nord.

ACTIVITES D'INFORMATION ET D'EDUCATION: Domaines: Relations internationales/coopération/aide au développement. **Activités:** Échanges/parrainage/jumelage.

FRA1766

ASSOCIATION SOLIDARITE SANTE

Centre social de Pen-ar-Créac'h, 13 rue Pr. Chrétien, 29200 Brest, France.

Téléphone: 33 - 98 02 18 56. **Contact:** Denis Calvez, Président.

OBJECTIFS: Collecter, trier et expédier des médicaments de première nécessité vers les populations démunies. Acheter, selon nos possibilités financières, des médicaments génériques, notamment à la centrale d'achat PSF, ou auprès de laboratoires. Collecter du petit matériel "médico-chirurgical".

INFORMATIONS GENERALES: Création: 1984. **Personnel/Total:** 40. Bénévoles: 40. **Budget/Total 1993:** ECU 21000 (US$ 25000). **Sources financières:** Public: 100%.

PUBLICATIONS: Rapport annuel.

                    See: *How to Use the Directory,* page 11.

COMMENTAIRES: Intervient dans la Communauté des Etats indépendants.

ACTIVITES DANS LES REGIONS EN DEVELOPPEMENT: Intervient directement dans les régions en développement. Intervient dans 13 pays. Intervient par l'intermédiaire d'organisations locales partenaires. **Actions de Développement durable:** Santé/assainissement/eau. **Régions:** Afrique australe; Afrique de l'Ouest; Afrique du Nord; Amérique du Sud; Asie du Sud-Est.

ACTIVITES D'INFORMATION ET D'EDUCATION: Domaines: Santé/assainissement/eau. **Activités:** Campagnes d'information/expositions.

FRA1767

ASSOCIATION TECHNIQUE AFRICAINE (ATA) ♦ African Technical Association

23 rue du Rocher, 75008 Paris, France.

Téléphone: 33 (1) 42 94 22 75. **Fax:** 33 (1) 42 94 27 82. **Contact:** Pierre Bousez, Délégué général.

FRA1768

ASSOCIATION TECHNIQUE DE RECHERCHES ET D'INFORMATIONS AUDIOVISUELLES (ATRIA)

16, boulevard Jules Ferry, 75011 Paris, France.

Téléphone: 33 (1) 43 57 17 32. **Fax:** 33 (1) 43 57 01 33. **Contact:** Andrée Davanture, Déléguée générale.

OBJECTIFS: Promouvoir, au plan économique et social, les populations des pays en développement, principalement dans les domaines culturel et technique, par tous les moyens audiovisuels. Susciter et soutenir l'éclosion des nouvelles cinématographies en Afrique, en apportant une aide technique aux cinéastes africains.

INFORMATIONS GENERALES: Création: 1980. **Affiliée à:** Fondation de France (France) - Bureau de Liaison du Cinéma de l'Espace Francophone (Belgique). **Personnel/Total:** 3. **Salariés:** 3. **Budget/Total 1993:** ECU 117000 (US$ 136000). **Sources financières:** Privé: 10%. Public: 70%. Autofinancement: 10%.

PUBLICATIONS: Rapport annuel. Liste des publications.

EVALUATION/RECHERCHE: Rapports d'évaluation disponibles. Entreprend des activités de recherche.

ACTIVITES DANS LES REGIONS EN DEVELOPPEMENT: Intervient directement dans les régions en développement. Intervient dans 20 pays. Intervient par l'intermédiaire d'organisations locales partenaires. **Actions de Développement durable:** Autres; Droits de l'Homme/paix/conflits; Enfants/jeunesse/famille; Population/planning familial/démographie; Questions relatives aux femmes. **Régions:** Afrique australe; Afrique de l'Ouest; Afrique du Nord.

ACTIVITES D'INFORMATION ET D'EDUCATION: Domaines: Culture/tradition/religion; Droits de l'Homme/paix/conflits; Enfants/jeunesse/famille; Questions relatives aux femmes; Relations internationales/coopération/aide au développement; Réfugiés/migrants/groupes ethniques. **Activités:** Radiodiffusion/manifestations culturelles; Édition/documents audiovisuels/documents éducatifs.

FRA1769

ASSOCIATION TEMO

283, rue Frédéric Sévène, 33400 Talence, France.

Téléphone: 33 - 56 80 60 51. **Contact:** David Afonso, Président.

OBJECTIFS: Réfléchir et créer des entreprises communautaires en Afrique. Faire naître la solidarité communautaire entre les peuples par le développement des milieux ruraux. Assurer la formation des agents de développement. Venir en aide aux entreprises, grâce au fonds TEMO de développement.

INFORMATIONS GENERALES: Création: 1985. **Type d'organisation:** réseau. **Affiliée à:** Famille Coop (Zaïre) - Angolada (Angola) - Cruz-Amarela (Angola). **Personnel/Total:** 10. Bénévoles: 10 dont: 5 dans les pays en développement. **Sources financières:** Privé: 80%. Autofinancement: 20%.

PUBLICATIONS: Liste des publications.

EVALUATION/RECHERCHE: Rapports d'évaluation disponibles. Entreprend des activités de recherche.

PREVISIONS D'ACTIVITES: Mobiliser l'opinion internationale sur la situation des enfants angolais victimes de la guerre. Organiser des collectes de produits de première nécessité avec les écoles et les institutions. Impliquer les ONG et envoyer sur place du matériel et des volontaires.

ACTIVITES DANS LES REGIONS EN DEVELOPPEMENT: Intervient directement dans les régions en développement. Maintient une présence locale sur le terrain. Intervient par l'intermédiaire d'organisations locales partenaires. **Actions de Développement durable:** Aliments/famine; Développement rural/agriculture; Développement urbain/habitat; Enfants/jeunesse/famille; Envoi de volontaires/experts/assistance technique; Petites entreprises/secteur informel/artisanat; Population/planning familial/démographie; Santé/assainissement; Éducation/formation/alphabétisation. **Régions:** Afrique australe; Afrique centrale.

ACTIVITES D'INFORMATION ET D'EDUCATION: Domaines: Aliments/famine; Développement rural/agriculture; Développement urbain/habitat; Pauvreté/conditions de vie; Relations internationales/coopération/aide au développement; Réfugiés/migrants/groupes ethniques; Santé/assainissement/eau; Secours d'urgence/réfugiés/aide humanitaire; Éducation/formation/alphabétisation. **Activités:** Campagnes d'information/expositions; Collecte de fonds; Échanges/parrainage/jumelage; Édition/documents audiovisuels/documents éducatifs; Éducation formelle.

FRA1770

ASSOCIATION TERRA-BRASIL (AT-B)

174 route d'Albi, 31000 Toulouse, France.

Téléphone: 33 - 61 48 77 09. **Contact:** Jean-Michel Sirven, Président.

FRA1771

ASSOCIATION TERRE D'AMITIE

306 rue André Philip, 69003 Lyon, France.

Téléphone: 33 - 78 95 30 47. **Fax:** 33 - 78 62 04 00. **Contact:** Anne-Marie Machon, Présidente.

OBJECTIFS: Apporter une aide d'urgence, collecter quotidiennement des médicaments inutilisés (pharmacies, répartiteurs). Trier, classer et expédier par conteneurs des médicaments et du matériel médical, à destination de l'Afrique, de Madagascar, du Liban et de l'Europe de l'Est, en collaboration avec d'autres associations. Apporter une aide nutritionnelle.

INFORMATIONS GENERALES: Création: 1966. **Personnel/Total:** 753. Salariés: 3. Bénévoles: 750. **Budget/Total 1993:** ECU 362000 (US$ 424000). **Sources financières:** Public: 2%. Autofinancement: 98%.

PUBLICATIONS: Rapport annuel.

EVALUATION/RECHERCHE: Rapports d'évaluation disponibles.

PREVISIONS D'ACTIVITES: L'organisation souhaiterait intensifier sa participation au projet de réhabilitation de l'hôpital d'Antalaha, à Madagascar, en coordination avec le centre hospitalier Félix Guyon de la Réunion; cela dépendra des moyens dont elle disposera.

COMMENTAIRES: Intervient dans la Communauté des Etats indépendants.

ACTIVITES DANS LES REGIONS EN DEVELOPPEMENT: Intervient directement dans les régions en développement. Intervient par l'intermédiaire d'organisations locales partenaires. **Actions de Développement durable:** Aliments/famine; Santé/assainissement/eau; Secours d'urgence/réfugiés/aide humanitaire. **Régions:** Afrique australe; Afrique centrale; Afrique de l'Ouest; Moyen-Orient.

ACTIVITES D'INFORMATION ET D'EDUCATION: Domaines: Aliments/famine; Santé/assainissement/eau; Secours d'urgence/réfugiés/aide humanitaire; Éducation/formation/alphabétisation. **Activités:** Campagnes d'information/expositions; Collecte de fonds; Radiodiffusion/manifestations culturelles.

FRA1772

ASSOCIATION TIERS-MONDE (ATM)

41 rue Saint Gervais, 17500 Jonzac, France.

Voir : *Comment utiliser le répertoire,* page 11.

Téléphone: 33 - 46 48 47 32. *Contact:* Lucienne Laroche, Présidente.

FRA1773

ASSOCIATION TIERS-MONDE DE LA REGION DE QUINTIN

Mairie, 22800 Quintin, France.

Téléphone: 33 - 96 74 84 01. *Contact:* Jean Verdier, Président.

FRA1774

ASSOCIATION TOKOMBERE

28, rue Godefroy Cavaignac, 75011 Paris, France.

Téléphone: 33 (1) 40 09 23 89. *Fax:* 33 (1) 40 09 23 89. *Contact:* François Beaufils, Président.

OBJECTIFS: Soutenir toute activité dans le domaine de la santé à Tokambéré, au Cameroun. Agir dans le sens d'un partage équitable des richesses entre le Nord et le Sud.

INFORMATIONS GENERALES: *Personnel/Total:* 10. *Salariés:* 2. *Bénévoles:* 8. *Budget/Total 1993:* ECU 74000 (US$ 87000). *Sources financières:* Privé: 58%. Public: 5%. Autofinancement: 37%.

PUBLICATIONS: *Périodiques:* Liaison et échange avec le Centre de Promotion de la santé de *Rapport annuel. Liste des publications.*

EVALUATION/RECHERCHE: Rapports d'évaluation disponibles.

PREVISIONS D'ACTIVITES: Conférences auprès des différentes facultés de médecine.

ACTIVITES DANS LES REGIONS EN DEVELOPPEMENT: Intervient directement dans les régions en développement. Intervient dans 1 pays. Maintient une présence locale sur le terrain. **Actions de Développement durable:** Développement rural/agriculture; Enfants/jeunesse/famille; Envoi de volontaires/experts/assistance technique; Petites entreprises/secteur informel/artisanat; Population/planning familial/démographie; Questions relatives aux femmes; Santé/assainissement/eau; Éducation/formation/alphabétisation. **Régions:** Afrique centrale.

ACTIVITES D'INFORMATION ET D'EDUCATION: Domaines: Santé/assainissement/eau. Activités: Campagnes d'information/expositions; Collecte de fonds; Conférences/séminaires/ateliers/activités de formation; Radiodiffusion/manifestations culturelles; Édition/documents audiovisuels/documents éducatifs.

FRA1775

ASSOCIATION VITROLLES-KIFFA

Le Bosquet, Bât. B, 13127 Vitrolles, France.

Téléphone: 33 - 42 75 26 02. *Contact:* René Calot, Président.

FRA1776

ATELIER POUR LES INITIATIVES DE DEVELOPPEMENT (AID) ♦ Workshop for Development Initiatives

30, rue de la Solidarité, 94300 Vincennes, France.

Téléphone: 33 (1) 43 74 58 47. *Fax:* 33 (1) 43 74 12 86. *Contact:* Michel Barnaud, Président.

OBJECTIFS: Promouvoir des actions de développement local en Afrique subsaharienne. Repérer les initiatives de base auprès des acteurs ruraux, formaliser en partenariat le montage d'actions de développement, appuyer l'exécution de projets délégant aux organisations rurales la maîtrise des actions de développement.

INFORMATIONS GENERALES: *Création:* 1986. *Personnel/Total:* 5. *Salariés:* 2. *Bénévoles:* 3 dont: 3 dans les pays en développement. *Budget/Total 1993:* ECU 68000 (US$ 79000). *Sources financières:* Public: 90%. Autofinancement: 10%.

EVALUATION/RECHERCHE: Entreprend des activités de recherche.

PREVISIONS D'ACTIVITES: Formation et accompagnement d'un groupe de Rwandais et de Burundais réfugiés en France, afin de les réinsérer dans une logique professessionelle postérieure à la crise actuelle. Favoriser un retour au dialogue au sein d'une population traumatisée.

ACTIVITES DANS LES REGIONS EN DEVELOPPEMENT: Intervient directement dans les régions en développement. Intervient dans 2 pays.

Maintient une présence locale sur le terrain. **Actions de Développement durable:** Démocratie/bonne gestion publique/création d'institutions/développement participatif; Développement rural/agriculture; Envoi de volontaires/experts/assistance technique. **Régions:** Afrique centrale; Afrique de l'Ouest.

ACTIVITES D'INFORMATION ET D'EDUCATION: Domaines: Développement rural/agriculture; Relations internationales/coopération/aide au développement. **Activités:** Conférences/séminaires/ateliers/activités de formation; Échanges/parrainage/jumelage.

FRA1777

ATELIERS VARAN

6 impasse Mont-Louis, 75011 Paris, France.

Téléphone: 33 (1) 43 56 64 04. *Fax:* 33 (1) 43 46 29 02. *Contact:* Chantal Roussel, Administratrice.

FRA1778

ATLIK

06390 Coaraze, France.

Téléphone: 33 - 93 79 35 08. *Fax:* 33- 93 79 37 54. *Contact:* Maguy Vautier, Présidente.

OBJECTIFS: Aider les tribus nomades, au Niger et au Mali, sous forme d'une aide économique, sanitaire et scolaire, pour maintenir leurs traditions.

INFORMATIONS GENERALES: *Création:* 1984. *Affiliée à:* Aminata (France) - Cyrav (France) - Touaregs (France). *Personnel/Total:* 32. *Salariés:* 2 dont: 2 dans les pays en développement. *Bénévoles:* 30 dont: 2 dans les pays en développement. *Budget/Total 1993:* ECU 69000 (US$ 81000). *Sources financières:* Privé: 50%. Public: 10%. Autofinancement: 40%.

PUBLICATIONS: *Périodiques:* Bulletin "ATLIK" (4).

PREVISIONS D'ACTIVITES: Création d'écoles à Niamey, à Buré et à Bagga, au Niger, et à Ebangue, au Mali. Création d'un centre d'alphabétisation.

COMMENTAIRES: Préoccupations majeures: rapatriement des réfugiés, urgences et vivres des réfugiés, mise en valeur de terres cultivables, au Niger et au Mali, pour produire des céréales, avec création de coopératives.

ACTIVITES DANS LES REGIONS EN DEVELOPPEMENT: Intervient directement dans les régions en développement. Intervient dans 2 pays. Maintient une présence locale sur le terrain. **Actions de Développement durable:** Aliments/famine; Droits de l'Homme/paix/conflits; Développement rural/agriculture; Développement urbain/habitat; Enfants/jeunesse/famille; Envoi de volontaires/experts/assistance technique; Petites entreprises/secteur informel/artisanat; Questions relatives aux femmes; Santé/assainissement/eau; Secours d'urgence/réfugiés/aide humanitaire; Écologie/environnement/biodiversité; Éducation/formation/alphabétisation; Énergie/transport. **Régions:** Afrique de l'Ouest.

ACTIVITES D'INFORMATION ET D'EDUCATION: Domaines: Développement rural/agriculture; Développement urbain/habitat; Questions relatives aux femmes; Relations internationales/coopération/aide au développement; Réfugiés/migrants/groupes ethniques; Santé/assainissement/eau; Secours d'urgence/réfugiés/aide humanitaire; Éducation/formation/alphabétisation. **Activités:** Collecte de fonds; Conférences/séminaires/ateliers/activités de formation; Radiodiffusion/manifestations culturelles; Échanges/parrainage/jumelage; Édition/documents audiovisuels/documents éducatifs.

FRA1779

AUVERGNE MALI 87 (AM87)

11 boulevard Charles de Gaulle, 63000 Clermont-Ferrand, France.

FRA1780

AUX QUATRE COINS DU MONDE

8 rue Mi-Carême, 42000 Saint-Etienne, France.

Téléphone: 33 - 77 34 09 08.

                                See: *How to Use the Directory,* page 11.

FRA1781

AVIATION SANS FRONTIERES (ASF)

Orly Fret 768, 94398 Orly Aérogare Cedex, France.

Téléphone: 33 (1) 49 75 74 37. **Fax:** 33 (1) 49 75 74 33. **Contact:** Marcel Poulet, Président.

OBJECTIFS: Venir au secours des victimes des calamités naturelles, des conflits humains et des drames de l'isolement géographique et acheminer des médicaments et des malades, grâce à l'utilisation de l'avion. Agir comme conseiller technique auprès des organisations humanitaires pour résoudre leurs problèmes de transport.

INFORMATIONS GENERALES: *Création:* 1980. *Personnel/Total:* 13. *Salariés:* 3. *Bénévoles:* 10 dont: 5 dans les pays en développement. *Budget/Total 1993:* ECU 1206000 (US$ 1413000). *Sources financières:* Privé: 85%. Autofinancement: 15%.

PUBLICATIONS: *Périodiques:* Bulletin d'information (2). *Rapport annuel.*

EVALUATION/RECHERCHE: Rapports d'évaluation disponibles.

PREVISIONS D'ACTIVITES: L'organisation prévoit de mettre un ou deux avions à la disposition des ONG en Tanzanie.

ACTIVITES DANS LES REGIONS EN DEVELOPPEMENT: Intervient directement dans les régions en développement. Intervient dans 3 pays. Maintient une présence locale sur le terrain. **Actions de Développement durable:** Énergie/transport. **Régions:** Afrique australe; Afrique centrale; Asie du Sud-Est.

FRA1782

AVICEN

17 rue de Paradis, 13001 Marseille, France.

Téléphone: 33 - 91 55 67 51. **Fax:** 33 - 91 54 11 47. **Contact:** Philippe Tourny.

FRA1783

BAMTARE - ASSOCIATION POUR LE DEVELOPPEMENT D'OUROSSOGUI

3 square de Verdun, 75010 Paris, France.

Téléphone: 33 (1) 42 40 46 49. **Contact:** Elhadji Dia, Président.

FRA1784

BENEVOLES FRANCO-MALIENS POUR L'AIDE AU DEVELOPPEMENT DE L'ARRONDISSEMENT DE MOURDIAH

Studio No.56, AFTAM, 56 rue des Fillettes, 93300 Aubervilliers, France.

Téléphone: 33 (1) 48 39 93 81. **Contact:** Mamadou Doucouré, Président.

FRA1785

BENEVOLES FRANCO-MALIENS POUR L'AIDE AU DEVELOPPEMENT DE L'ARRONDISSEMENT DE OUSSOU-BIDIAGNA (MALI) (BFM-ADAO)

70, rue de la Villette, 75019 Paris, France.

Téléphone: 33 (1) 42 41 23 27. **Contact:** Yéra Dembélé, Président.

OBJECTIFS: Procéder à l'approvisionnement en eau potable, à la création d'abreuvoirs, à l'assainissement rural et à l'aménagement hydroagricole. Fournir du matériel agricole, médical et scolaire, ainsi que des médicaments, à l'arrondissement de Oussoubidiagna, au Mali. Créer un centre de santé à Oussoubidiagna, grâce au jumelage.

INFORMATIONS GENERALES: *Création:* 1991. *Type d'organisation:* réseau. *Organisations membres:* 3. *Affiliée à:* LIACOFA - Réseau des Associations de la Vallée du Fleuve Sénégal - Fédération des Associations franco-africaines de Développement.. *Personnel/Total:* 860. *Salariés:* 1 dont: 1 dans les pays en développement. *Bénévoles:* 859 dont: 305 dans les pays en développement. *Budget/Total 1993:* ECU 9000 (US$ 11000). *Sources financières:* Privé: 30%. Autofinancement: 70%.

PUBLICATIONS: *Rapport annuel. Liste des publications.*

EVALUATION/RECHERCHE: Rapports d'évaluation disponibles.

ACTIVITES DANS LES REGIONS EN DEVELOPPEMENT: Intervient directement dans les régions en développement. Intervient dans 2 pays. Maintient une présence locale sur le terrain. Intervient par l'intermédiaire d'organisations locales partenaires. **Actions de Développement durable:** Aliments/famine; Dette/finances/commerce; Démocratie/bonne gestion publique/création d'institutions/développement participatif; Développement rural/agriculture; Développement urbain/habitat; Enfants/jeunesse/famille; Envoi de volontaires/experts/assistance technique; Petites entreprises/secteur informel/artisanat; Population/planning familial/démographie; Questions relatives aux femmes; Santé/assainissement/eau; Secours d'urgence/réfugiés/aide humanitaire; Écologie/environnement/biodiversité; Éducation/formation/alphabétisation; Énergie/transport. **Régions:** Afrique de l'Ouest.

ACTIVITES D'INFORMATION ET D'EDUCATION: Domaines: Aliments/famine; Culture/tradition/religion; Développement rural/agriculture; Développement urbain/habitat; Enfants/jeunesse/famille; Pauvreté/conditions de vie; Population/planning familial/démographie; Questions relatives aux femmes; Relations internationales/coopération/aide au développement; Relations économiques internationales/commerce/dette/finances; Réfugiés/migrants/groupes ethniques; Santé/assainissement/eau; Secours d'urgence/réfugiés/aide humanitaire; Écologie/environnement/biodiversité; Éducation/formation/alphabétisation. **Activités:** Autres; Campagnes d'information/expositions; Collecte de fonds; Conférences/séminaires/ateliers/activités de formation; Lobbying/plaidoyer; Radiodiffusion/manifestations culturelles; Réseaux/télécommunications électroniques; Services d'information et de documentation/bases de données; Échanges/parrainage/jumelage; Édition/documents audiovisuels/documents éducatifs; Éducation formelle.

FRA1786

BENEVOLES FRANCO-MALIENS POUR L'AIDE AU DEVELOPPEMENT DE SAMANTARA (MALI)

Résidence Charles de Gaulle, 16 route de Montreuil, 93230 Romainville, France.

Téléphone: 33 (1) 48 58 39 67. **Contact:** Djimé Cisse, Président.

OBJECTIFS: Encourager et développer la francophonie en apportant une aide matérielle éducative et culturelle à l'enseignement laïque francophone, et à l'alphabétisation des adultes. Oeuvrer dans le domaine de la santé (prévention, information, éducation familiale, nutritionnelle et ménagère).

INFORMATIONS GENERALES: *Création:* 1990. *Affiliée à:* Fédération des associations franco-africaines de développement (France) -Liaison et Action contre la Faim (France). *Personnel/Total:* 13. *Bénévoles:* 13. *Budget/Total 1993:* ECU 600 (US$ 700). *Sources financières:* Autofinancement: 100%.

PUBLICATIONS: *Rapport annuel.*

EVALUATION/RECHERCHE: Rapports d'évaluation disponibles.

ACTIVITES DANS LES REGIONS EN DEVELOPPEMENT: Intervient directement dans les régions en développement. Intervient dans 1 pays. Maintient une présence locale sur le terrain. Intervient par l'intermédiaire d'organisations locales partenaires. **Actions de Développement durable:** Enfants/jeunesse/famille; Santé/assainissement/eau; Éducation/formation/alphabétisation. **Régions:** Afrique de l'Ouest.

ACTIVITES D'INFORMATION ET D'EDUCATION: Domaines: Enfants/jeunesse/famille; Santé/assainissement/eau; Éducation/formation/alphabétisation. **Activités:** Collecte de fonds.

FRA1787

BENEVOLES FRANCO-MALIENS POUR L'AIDE AU DEVELOPPEMENT DES LOCALITES DE MOUSSALA ET MADIHAWAYA

12/14, rue Henri Matisse / Chambre 462, 93600 Aulnay-Sous-Bois, France.

Téléphone: 33 (1) 48 91 91 34/48 69 78 01. **Contact:** Bakary Sissoko, Président.

OBJECTIFS: Créer un vaste réseau d'intérêts et de solidarité pour le développement humanitaire multiforme des localités déshéritées de Moussala et de Madihawaya, au Mali.

INFORMATIONS GENERALES: *Création:* 1990. **Organisations membres:** 2. **Affiliée à:** LIA.CO.FA. **Personnel/Total:** 274. *Salariés:* 4 dont: 4 dans les pays en développement. *Bénévoles:* 270 dont: 250 dans les pays en développement. **Budget/Total 1993:** ECU 4000 (US$ 4000). **Sources financières:** *Public:* 5%. *Autofinancement:* 90%.

PUBLICATIONS: *Rapport annuel.*

EVALUATION/RECHERCHE: Rapports d'évaluation disponibles.

PREVISIONS D'ACTIVITES: Sensibilsation à la prévention sanitaire et aux soins de santé de base. Aménagement hydro-agricole. Soutien à la mise en place de projets individuels des migrants et à l'épargne-projet.

COMMENTAIRES: Le centre de santé communautaire, créé à Madiawaya (Mali), sera entièrement pris en charge par la population locale pour ce qui concerne la couverture des coûts de fonctionnement.

ACTIVITES DANS LES REGIONS EN DEVELOPPEMENT: Intervient directement dans les régions en développement. Intervient dans 3 pays. Maintient une présence locale sur le terrain. Intervient par l'intermédiaire d'organisations locales partenaires. **Actions de Développement durable:** Aliments/famine; Dette/finances/commerce; Démocratie/bonne gestion publique/création d'institutions/développement participatif; Développement rural/agriculture; Développement urbain/habitat; Enfants/jeunesse/famille; Envoi de volontaires/experts/assistance technique; Petites entreprises/secteur informel/artisanat; Population/planning familial/démographie; Questions relatives aux femmes; Santé/assainissement/eau; Secours d'urgence/réfugiés/aide humanitaire; Écologie/environnement/biodiversité; Éducation/formation/alphabétisation; Énergie/transport. **Régions:** Afrique centrale; Afrique de l'Ouest.

ACTIVITES D'INFORMATION ET D'EDUCATION: Domaines: Aliments/famine; Culture/tradition/religion; Développement rural/agriculture; Développement urbain/habitat; Enfants/jeunesse/famille; Pauvreté/conditions de vie; Population/planning familial/démographie; Questions relatives aux femmes; Relations internationales/coopération/aide au développement; Relations économiques internationales/commerce/dette/finances; Réfugiés/migrants/groupes ethniques; Santé/assainissement/eau; Secours d'urgence/réfugiés/aide humanitaire; Écologie/environnement/biodiversité; Éducation/formation/alphabétisation. **Activités:** Campagnes d'information/expositions; Collecte de fonds; Conférences/séminaires/ateliers/activités de formation; Lobbying/plaidoyer; Radiodiffusion/manifestations culturelles; Services d'information et de documentation/bases de données; Échanges/parrainage/jumelage; Édition/documents audiovisuels/documents éducatifs; Éducation formelle.

FRA1788

BIOFORCE DEVELOPPEMENT ♦ Bioforce Development

44, boulevard Lénine, 69200 Vénissieux, France.

Téléphone: 33 - 78 67 32 32. **Fax:** 33 - 78 70 27 12. **Contact:** Patrice Blanc, Directeur.

OBJECTIFS: Former des logisticiens qui vont travailler dans les ONG. Assurer l'ingénierie pédagogique pour des formations en logistique, en assainissement, maintenance hospitalière. Organiser des stages spécifiques pour la préparation au départ dans les pays en voie de développement.

INFORMATIONS GENERALES: *Création:* 1983. **Affiliée à:** Centre collaborateur de l'Organisation Mondiale de la Santé (OMS). **Personnel/Total:** 38. *Salariés:* 35. *Bénévoles:* 3. **Budget/Total 1993:** ECU 1658000 (US$ 1942000). **Sources financières:** *Privé:* 9%. *Public:* 88%. *Autofinancement:* 3%.

COMMENTAIRES: L'association n'intervient pas directement dans les pays en développement; elle assure une formation polyvalente de départ de 10 mois à des formateurs en communication interculturelle; formation technique et administrative, urgence et aptitude physique.

ACTIVITES D'INFORMATION ET D'EDUCATION: Domaines: Autres; Relations économiques internationales/commerce/dette/finances; Santé/assainissement/eau; Secours d'urgence/réfugiés/aide humanitaire. **Activités:** Conférences/séminaires/ateliers/activités de formation.

FRA1789

BURKINA-87 (B87)

B.P. 44, 87202 Saint-Junien Cedex, France.

Téléphone: 33 - 55 02 69 48. **Fax:** 33 - 55 02 95 00. **Contact:** Guy Courbarien, Président.

OBJECTIFS: Aider le village de Donse et la province d'Oubritenga (Burkina Faso) à se développer, ceci en coopération étroite avec la population locale afin que celle-ci reste maître de son avenir et conserve sa dignité.

INFORMATIONS GENERALES: *Création:* 1986. **Affiliée à:** FLAD (France). **Personnel/Total:** 80. *Bénévoles:* 80. **Budget/Total 1993:** ECU 30000 (US$ 35000). **Sources financières:** *Privé:* 40%. *Public:* 50%. *Autofinancement:* 10%.

PUBLICATIONS: *Périodiques:* Burkina 87 Infos (var). *Rapport annuel.*

EVALUATION/RECHERCHE: Rapports d'évaluation disponibles.

ACTIVITES DANS LES REGIONS EN DEVELOPPEMENT: Intervient directement dans les régions en développement. Intervient dans 1 pays. Intervient par l'intermédiaire d'organisations locales partenaires. **Actions de Développement durable:** Développement rural/agriculture; Enfants/jeunesse/famille; Envoi de volontaires/experts/assistance technique; Petites entreprises/secteur informel/artisanat; Questions relatives aux femmes; Santé/assainissement/eau; Éducation/formation/alphabétisation. **Régions:** Afrique de l'Ouest.

ACTIVITES D'INFORMATION ET D'EDUCATION: Domaines: Culture/tradition/religion; Développement rural/agriculture; Enfants/jeunesse/famille; Questions relatives aux femmes; Santé/assainissement/eau; Éducation/formation/alphabétisation. **Activités:** Collecte de fonds; Conférences/séminaires/ateliers/activités de formation; Éducation formelle.

FRA1790

CAISSE NATIONALE DU CREDIT AGRICOLE (CNCA)

91-93 boulevard Pasteur, 75015 Paris, France.

Téléphone: 33 (1) 43 23 43 27. **Contact:** Christian Bosseno, Directeur.

FRA1791

LES CAMIONS DE L'ESPERANCE

Allée des Vignères, 13300 Salon de Provence, France.

Téléphone: 33 - 90 53 52 43. **Fax:** 33 - 90 53 52 50. **Contact:** Jean-Claude Gozzi, Directeur.

OBJECTIFS: Créer des emplois, en France, pour les personnes de milieux défavorisés, en les mettant au service de l'aide humanitaire internationale. Apporter un soutien ponctuel aux peuples en voie de développement, surtout dans le domaine sanitaire.

INFORMATIONS GENERALES: *Création:* 1992. **Personnel/Total:** 28. *Salariés:* 10. *Bénévoles:* 18 dont: 6 dans les pays en développement. **Budget/Total 1993:** ECU 151000 (US$ 177000). **Sources financières:** *Privé:* 40%. *Autofinancement:* 60%.

PUBLICATIONS: *Rapport annuel. Liste des publications.*

PREVISIONS D'ACTIVITES: L'Organisation contribue au développement économique, social et culturel des pays en voie de développement.

COMMENTAIRES: Intervient dans la Communauté des Etats indépendants. Activités d'information concernant la Communauté des Etats indépendants.

ACTIVITES DANS LES REGIONS EN DEVELOPPEMENT: Intervient directement dans les régions en développement. Intervient dans 7 pays. Maintient une présence locale sur le terrain. Intervient par l'intermédiaire d'organisations locales partenaires. **Actions de Développement durable:** Aliments/famine; Droits de l'Homme/paix/conflits; Démocratie/bonne gestion publique/création d'institutions/développement participatif; Enfants/jeunesse/famille; Population/planning familial/démographie; Questions relatives aux femmes; Santé/assainissement/eau; Secours d'urgence/réfugiés/aide humanitaire; Écologie/environnement/biodiversité; Éducation/formation/alphabétisation. **Régions:** Moyen-Orient.

ACTIVITES D'INFORMATION ET D'EDUCATION: Domaines: Aliments/famine; Droits de l'Homme/paix/conflits; Emploi/chômage; Paix/conflits ethniques/armement/désarmement; Pauvreté/conditions de vie; Questions relatives aux femmes; Racisme/xénophobie/antisémitisme; Relations internationales/coopération/aide au développement; Réfugiés/

See: *How to Use the Directory,* page 11.

migrants/groupes ethniques; Santé/assainissement/eau; Secours d'urgence/réfugiés/aide humanitaire. **Activités:** Campagnes d'information/expositions; Collecte de fonds; Conférences/séminaires/ateliers/activités de formation; Lobbying/plaidoyer; Radiodiffusion/manifestations culturelles; Échanges/parrainage/jumelage.

FRA1792
CARE FRANCE

40 rue de Paradis, 75010 Paris, France.

Téléphone: 33 (1) 45 23 22 55. *Fax:* 33 (1) 45 23 22 56. *Contact:* Marina de Brantes, Présidente.

FRA1793
CARITAS UNIVERSALIS

Centre Michel Colucci, Allée des Vignères, 13300 Salon de Provence, France.

Téléphone: 33 - 90 53 52 43. *Fax:* 33 - 90 53 52 50. *Contact:* Nicole de Portal, Présidente.

OBJECTIFS: Créer des emplois, en France, et, par ce travail, apporter aux peuples dans les pays en voie de développement une aide constructive et ponctuelle.

INFORMATIONS GENERALES: *Création:* 1982. *Personnel/Total:* 85. *Salariés:* 20 dont: 5 dans les pays en développement. *Bénévoles:* 65 dont: 35 dans les pays en développement. *Budget/Total 1993:* ECU 452000 (US$ 530000). *Sources financières:* Privé: 58%. Public: 2%. Autofinancement: 40%.

PUBLICATIONS: *Rapport annuel. Liste des publications.*

PREVISIONS D'ACTIVITES: Préparation de convois humanitaires au profit des pays en voie de développement (aide alimentaire, vestimentaire, médicale).L'organisation intervient également dans des pays en situation conflictuelle.

COMMENTAIRES: Intervient dans la Communauté des Etats indépendants. Activités d'information concernant la Communauté des Etats indépendants.

ACTIVITES DANS LES REGIONS EN DEVELOPPEMENT: Intervient directement dans les régions en développement. Intervient dans 7 pays. Maintient une présence locale sur le terrain. Intervient par l'intermédiaire d'organisations locales partenaires. **Actions de Développement durable:** Aliments/famine; Droits de l'Homme/paix/conflits; Démocratie/bonne gestion publique/création d'institutions/développement participatif; Enfants/jeunesse/famille; Population/planning familial/démographie; Questions relatives aux femmes; Santé/assainissement/eau; Secours d'urgence/réfugiés/aide humanitaire; Éducation/formation/alphabétisation. **Régions:** Moyen-Orient.

ACTIVITES D'INFORMATION ET D'EDUCATION: Domaines: Aliments/famine; Droits de l'Homme/paix/conflits; Emploi/chômage; Paix/conflits ethniques/armement/désarmement; Pauvreté/conditions de vie; Questions relatives aux femmes; Racisme/xénophobie/antisémitisme; Relations internationales/coopération/aide au développement; Réfugiés/migrants/groupes ethniques; Santé/assainissement/eau; Secours d'urgence/réfugiés/aide humanitaire. **Activités:** Campagnes d'information/expositions; Collecte de fonds; Conférences/séminaires/ateliers/activités de formation; Lobbying/plaidoyer; Radiodiffusion/manifestations culturelles; Échanges/parrainage/jumelage.

FRA1794
CARREFOUR INTERNATIONAL D'ECHANGES DE PRATIQUES APPLIQUEES AU DEVELOPPEMENT (CIEPAD)

Le Triol BP 3, 34380 Viols-Le-Fort, France.

Téléphone: 33 - 67 55 07 97. *Fax:* 33 - 67 55 75 78. *Contact:* Pierre Rbhi, Président.

OBJECTIFS: Faire un travail d'éducation et de formation à l'agroécologie et au développement durable. Faire des expérimentations agricoles, apporter un soutien aux initiatives en matière d'agroécologie et de développement durable, sur le plan international.

INFORMATIONS GENERALES: *Création:* 1988. *Organisations membres:* 12. *Affiliée à:* ALLIANCE (France) - Alliance Maghreb-Machrek sur l'eau (France) - EULEISA -Ecole et Nature (France) - FORMA-

BIO (France) - Ligue de l'enseignement (France) . *Personnel/Total:* 15. *Salariés:* 7. *Bénévoles:* 8 dont: 2 dans les pays en développement. *Sources financières:* Privé: 10%. Public: 40%. Autofinancement: 50%.

PUBLICATIONS: *Périodiques:* Lettre d'Information du CIEPAD (4) - ACACIA (3). *Liste des publications.*

EVALUATION/RECHERCHE: Entreprend des activités de recherche.

PREVISIONS D'ACTIVITES: Action d'accueil de classes de découverte et de formation des enseignants.

COMMENTAIRES: Intervient dans la Communauté des Etats indépendants.

ACTIVITES DANS LES REGIONS EN DEVELOPPEMENT: Intervient directement dans les régions en développement. Intervient dans 5 pays. Intervient par l'intermédiaire d'organisations locales partenaires. **Actions de Développement durable:** Développement rural/agriculture; Envoi de volontaires/experts/assistance technique; Questions relatives aux femmes; Santé/assainissement/eau; Écologie/environnement/biodiversité; Éducation/formation/alphabétisation. **Régions:** Afrique de l'Ouest; Afrique du Nord; Moyen-Orient.

ACTIVITES D'INFORMATION ET D'EDUCATION: Domaines: Droits de l'Homme/paix/conflits; Développement rural/agriculture; Emploi/chômage; Pauvreté/conditions de vie; Relations internationales/coopération/aide au développement; Relations économiques internationales/commerce/dette/finances; Écologie/environnement/biodiversité. **Activités:** Conférences/séminaires/ateliers/activités de formation; Lobbying/plaidoyer; Radiodiffusion/manifestations culturelles; Services d'information et de documentation/bases de données; Édition/documents audiovisuels/documents éducatifs; Éducation formelle.

FRA1795
CE QU'IL FAUDRAIT DEVELOPPER (CQFD)

110 boulevard Sébastopol, 75003 Paris, France.

Téléphone: 33 (1) 43 49 04 65. *Fax:* 33 (1) 43 49 46 54. *Contact:* Emmanuel Justin.

OBJECTIFS: Promouvoir par les moyens de communication appropriés toutes les initiatives culturelles et humanitaires.

INFORMATIONS GENERALES: *Budget/Total 1993:* ECU 9000 (US$ 11000). *Sources financières:* Autofinancement: 100%.

PUBLICATIONS: *Liste des publications.*

PREVISIONS D'ACTIVITES: L'organisation veut réaliser une série de films sur les médecines traditionnelles.

ACTIVITES DANS LES REGIONS EN DEVELOPPEMENT: Intervient directement dans les régions en développement. Intervient par l'intermédiaire d'organisations locales partenaires. **Actions de Développement durable:** Autres; Envoi de volontaires/experts/assistance technique. **Régions:** Afrique australe; Afrique centrale; Afrique de l'Ouest; Asie centrale et Asie du Sud; Mexique et Amerique centrale.

ACTIVITES D'INFORMATION ET D'EDUCATION: Domaines: Culture/tradition/religion; Développement rural/agriculture; Enfants/jeunesse/famille; Paix/conflits ethniques/armement/désarmement; Réfugiés/migrants/groupes ethniques; Santé/assainissement/eau; Écologie/environnement/biodiversité; Éducation/formation/alphabétisation. **Activités:** Édition/documents audiovisuels/documents éducatifs.

FRA1796
CEMEA-CLED

76 boulevard de la Villette, 75940 Paris cedex 19, France.

Téléphone: 33 (1) 42 02 43 15. *Fax:* 33 (1) 40 40 43 06. *Contact:* Joël Chanoir.

OBJECTIFS: Agir au Nord et au Sud pour appuyer le développement de la société civile et son implication dans les domaines de la culture, de l'éducation formelle et non formelle, de la santé et de l'action sociale.

INFORMATIONS GENERALES: *Création:* 1936. *Affiliée à:* Fédération internationale des CEMEA (Belgique) - Statut B des ONG de l'UNESCO. *Personnel/Total:* 160. *Salariés:* 10. *Bénévoles:* 150. *Bud-*

Voir : *Comment utiliser le répertoire,* page 11.

get/**Total** *1993:* ECU 754000 (US$ 883000). ***Sources financières:*** *Public:* 75%. *Autofinancement:* 25%.

PUBLICATIONS: *Rapport annuel.*

EVALUATION/RECHERCHE: Rapports d'évaluation disponibles. Entreprend des activités de recherche.

COMMENTAIRES: Intervient dans la Communauté des Etats indépendants.

ACTIVITES DANS LES REGIONS EN DEVELOPPEMENT: Intervient directement dans les régions en développement. Intervient dans 20 pays. Maintient une présence locale sur le terrain. Intervient par l'intermédiaire d'organisations locales partenaires. **Actions de Développement durable:** Développement urbain/habitat; Enfants/jeunesse/famille; Envoi de volontaires/experts/assistance technique; Écologie/environnement/biodiversité; Éducation/formation/alphabétisation. **Régions:** Afrique australe; Afrique centrale; Afrique de l'Est; Afrique de l'Ouest; Afrique du Nord; Caraïbes.

FRA1797

CENTRE AUVERGNE POUR UNE SOLIDARITE INTERNATIONALE (CASI)

Local du Mazet, 11 rue des deux Marches, 63000 Clermont-Ferrand, France.

Téléphone: 33 - 73 91 47 51. ***Fax:*** 33 - 73 91 47 51. ***Contact:*** Frédérique Louault, Présidente.

OBJECTIFS: Organiser des animations et participer aux débats portant sur les problèmes du développement et les relations Nord-Sud. Animer et gérer un lieu d'échanges et de rencontres, le centre de documentation tiers-monde.

INFORMATIONS GENERALES: *Création:* 1982. *Type d'organisation:* collectif. *Organisations membres:* 5. *Affiliée à:* Réseau d'Information Tiers-Monde (France). *Personnel/Total:* 12. *Salariés:* 2. *Bénévoles:* 10. *Budget/Total 1993:* ECU 11000 (US$ 13000). *Sources financières:* Public: 85%. Autofinancement: 15%.

ACTIVITES D'INFORMATION ET D'EDUCATION: Domaines: Aliments/famine; Culture/tradition/religion; Droits de l'Homme/paix/conflits; Développement rural/agriculture; Développement urbain/habitat; Emploi/chômage; Enfants/jeunesse/famille; Paix/conflits ethniques/armement/désarmement; Pauvreté/conditions de vie; Population/planning familial/démographie; Questions relatives aux femmes; Racisme/xénophobie/antisémitisme; Relations internationales/coopération/aide au développement; Relations économiques internationales/commerce/dette/finances; Réfugiés/migrants/groupes ethniques; Santé/assainissement/eau; Secours d'urgence/réfugiés/aide humanitaire; Écologie/environnement/biodiversité; Éducation/formation/alphabétisation. **Activités:** Campagnes d'information/expositions; Conférences/séminaires/ateliers/activités de formation; Lobbying/plaidoyer; Services d'information et de documentation/bases de données.

FRA1798

CENTRE CATHOLIQUE INTERNATIONAL POUR L'UNESCO (CCIC)

9 rue Cler, 75007 Paris, France.

Téléphone: 33 (1) 47 05 17 59. ***Fax:*** 33 (1) 45 56 90 92. ***Contact:*** Jean Larnaud, Secrétaire général.

FRA1799

CENTRE D'ECHANGES ET PROMOTION DES ARTISANS EN ZONES A EQUIPER (CEPAZE)

18 rue de Varenne, 75007 Paris, France.

Téléphone: 33 (1) 45 44 68 75. ***Fax:*** 33 (1) 45 44 04 18. ***Contact:*** Bernard Clamagirand, Président.

OBJECTIFS: Promouvoir et appuyer les technologies villageoises et des quartiers urbains, à la demande des paysans des pays à faible revenu, et avec leur concours. Sensibiliser l'opinion publique française aux problèmes auxquels sont confrontés les groupements villageois ou les groupements d'artisans de ces pays. Participer à l'organisation des actions de développement depuis le village jusqu'à l'Etat.

INFORMATIONS GENERALES: *Création:* 1975. *Affiliée à:* Technap (France) - CFCF (France) - GRAT (Mali). *Personnel/Total:* 2. *Bénévoles:* 2. *Budget/Total 1993:* ECU 15000 (US$ 18000). *Sources financières:* Privé: 90%. Autofinancement: 10%.

PUBLICATIONS: *Périodiques:* Echanges (3). *Rapport annuel. Liste des publications.*

EVALUATION/RECHERCHE: Rapports d'évaluation disponibles. Entreprend des activités de recherche.

ACTIVITES DANS LES REGIONS EN DEVELOPPEMENT: Intervient directement dans les régions en développement. Intervient dans 1 pays. Maintient une présence locale sur le terrain. Intervient par l'intermédiaire d'organisations locales partenaires. **Actions de Développement durable:** Démocratie/bonne gestion publique/création d'institutions/développement participatif; Développement rural/agriculture; Développement urbain/habitat; Petites entreprises/secteur informel/artisanat; Questions relatives aux femmes; Éducation/formation/alphabétisation. **Régions:** Afrique de l'Ouest.

ACTIVITES D'INFORMATION ET D'EDUCATION: Domaines: Droits de l'Homme/paix/conflits; Développement rural/agriculture; Développement urbain/habitat; Emploi/chômage; Pauvreté/conditions de vie; Questions relatives aux femmes; Relations internationales/coopération/aide au développement; Relations économiques internationales/commerce/dette/finances. **Activités:** Campagnes d'information/expositions; Conférences/séminaires/ateliers/activités de formation; Lobbying/plaidoyer; Édition/documents audiovisuels/documents éducatifs.

FRA1800

CENTRE D'ECHANGES INTERNATIONAUX DU NORD

219 bis boulevard de la Liberté, BP 200 1, 59011 Lille, France.

Téléphone: 33 - 20 52 72 07. ***Fax:*** 33 - 20 52 25 01. ***Contact:*** Daniel Zielinski, Directeur.

OBJECTIFS: Susciter, organiser et coordonner les échanges entre le Nord de la France et le reste de l'Europe. Fournir tous les renseignements et les moyens nécessaires au développement de ces échanges.

INFORMATIONS GENERALES: *Création:* 1953. *Personnel/Total:* 43. *Salariés:* 13. *Bénévoles:* 30. *Budget/Total 1993:* ECU 1207000 (US$ 1413000). *Sources financières:* Public: 10%. Autofinancement: 90%.

PUBLICATIONS: *Rapport annuel.*

EVALUATION/RECHERCHE: Rapports d'évaluation disponibles.

COMMENTAIRES: Cette organisation travaille principalement avec les pays d'Europe Centrale et Orientale. Intervient dans la Communauté des Etats indépendants. Activités d'information concernant la Communauté des Etats indépendants.

ACTIVITES DANS LES REGIONS EN DEVELOPPEMENT: Intervient dans 15 pays.

ACTIVITES D'INFORMATION ET D'EDUCATION: Domaines: Développement rural/agriculture; Enfants/jeunesse/famille; Racisme/xénophobie/antisémitisme; Relations économiques internationales/commerce/dette/finances; Réfugiés/migrants/groupes ethniques; Éducation/formation/alphabétisation. **Activités:** Conférences/séminaires/ateliers/activités de formation; Services d'information et de documentation/bases de données.

FRA1801

CENTRE D'EDUCATION ET DE FORMATION PROFESSIONNELLE DU MARANHAO (CEPROMAR)

B.P. 34, 53020 Laval cedex, France.

Téléphone: 33 (1) 45 06 55 76. ***Contact:*** Marc Dumaire, Président.

FRA1802

CENTRE D'ETUDE DU DEVELOPPEMENT EN AMERIQUE LATINE (CEDAL)

49 rue de la Glacière, 75013 Paris, France.

Téléphone: 33 (1) 45 43 57 64. ***Fax:*** 33 (1) 45 42 88 60. ***Contact:*** Sebastien Cox.

FRA1803

CENTRE D'ETUDE ET DE DEVELOPPEMENT DES RESSOURCES ECOLOGIQUES (CEDRE)

42bis avenue de Saxe, 75007 Paris, France.

Téléphone: 33 (1) 45 27 17 27. *Fax:* 33 (1) 54 74 20 80. *Contact:* Jean-Philippe Beau.

FRA1804

CENTRE D'ETUDE RECHERCHE-ACTION POUR LE DEVELOPPEMENT DE LA ZONE SOUDANO-SAHELIENNE (CERADS)

13 rue Gandon, 75013 Paris, France.

Téléphone: 33 (1) 46 66 02 48. *Fax:* 33 (1) 46 66 53 58. *Contact:* Jacques Dubreuil, Secrétaire général.

FRA1805

CENTRE D'ETUDES CONFLITS ET TIERS MONDE

15 rue Buffon, 75005 Paris, France.

Téléphone: 33 (1) 43 36 11 78. *Contact:* Janine Luben, Présidente.

OBJECTIFS: Organiser des colloques, faire de la recherche et publier des études, des ouvrages et des articles sur les conflits dans le monde et leurs conséquences.

INFORMATIONS GENERALES: *Création:* 1985.

EVALUATION/RECHERCHE: Entreprend des activités de recherche. **Actions de Développement durable:** Droits de l'Homme/paix/conflits. **Régions:** Afrique australe; Afrique centrale; Afrique de l'Est; Afrique de l'Ouest; Afrique du Nord; Amérique du Sud; Asie centrale et Asie du Sud; Asie de l'Est; Asie du Sud-Est; Caraïbes; Mexique et Amerique centrale; Moyen-Orient; Océanie.

FRA1806

CENTRE D'ETUDES ET D'INITIATIVES DE SOLIDARITE INTERNATIONALE (CEDETIM)

14 rue de Nanteuil, 75015 Paris, France.

Téléphone: 33 (1) 45 31 43 38. *Fax:* 33 (1) 45 31 64 37. *Contact:* Gustave Massiah, Président.

FRA1807

CENTRE D'INFORMATION ET D'ETUDES SUR LES MIGRATIONS INTERNATIONALES (CIEMI)

46 rue de Montreuil, 75011 Paris, France.

Téléphone: 33 (1) 43 70 01 40. *Fax:* 33 (1) 43 72 06 42. *Contact:* Philippe Farine.

FRA1808

CENTRE D'INFORMATION ET DE DOCUMENTATION - MAISON DES ASSOCIATIONS HUMANITAIRES DE TOURAINE (CID-MAHT)

10 rue Jourdan, 37000 Tours, France.

Téléphone: 33 - 47 66 43 38. *Contact:* Vincent Pitois, Président.

OBJECTIFS: Agir auprès du public, au moyen de l'information et de l'éducation sur les thèmes du respect des droits de l'Homme, la participation au développement des pays du Sud, la lutte contre la précarité en France, et l'exclusion d'une façon générale.

INFORMATIONS GENERALES: *Création:* 1981. *Type d'organisation:* collectif. *Organisations membres:* 19. *Affiliée à:* Réseau d'informations Tiers-Monde (France). *Personnel/Total:* 22. *Salariés:* 2. *Bénévoles:* 20. *Budget/Total 1993:* ECU 38000 (US$ 44000). *Sources financières:* Public: 95%. Autofinancement: 5%.

EVALUATION/RECHERCHE: Rapports d'évaluation disponibles.

COMMENTAIRES: Activités d'information concernant la Communauté des Etats indépendants.

ACTIVITES D'INFORMATION ET D'EDUCATION: Domaines: Aliments/famine; Culture/tradition/religion; Droits de l'Homme/paix/conflits; Développement rural/agriculture; Enfants/jeunesse/famille; Paix/conflits eth-niques/armement/désarmement; Pauvreté/conditions de vie; Population/planning familial/démographie; Racisme/xénophobie/antisémitisme; Relations internationales/coopération/aide au développement; Relations économiques internationales/commerce/dette/finances; Réfugiés/migrants/groupes ethniques; Santé/assainissement/eau; Secours d'urgence/réfugiés/aide humanitaire; Écologie/environnement/biodiversité; Éducation/formation/alphabétisation. **Activités:** Campagnes d'information/expositions; Collecte de fonds; Conférences/séminaires/ateliers/activités de formation; Lobbying/plaidoyer; Radiodiffusion/manifestations culturelles; Services d'information et de documentation/bases de données.

FRA1809

CENTRE DE CULTURE ET D'INFORMATION SUR LE MONDE ARABE

13 rue St Savournin, 13005 Marseille, France.

Téléphone: 33 - 91 48 43 61. *Contact:* Victoria Roger, Directrice.

FRA1810

CENTRE DE DOCUMENTATION INTERNATIONALE POUR LE DEVELOPPEMENT, LES LIBERTES ET LA PAIX (CEDIDELP)

21 ter rue Voltaire, 75011 Paris, France.

Téléphone: 33 (1) 44 64 74 14. *Fax:* 33 (1) 44 64 74 14. *Contact:* Suzanne Humberset.

OBJECTIFS: Fournir l'information et la documentation sur le développement, les libertés, la paix, l'environnement, la coopération dans/ou avec les pays du Tiersmonde.

INFORMATIONS GENERALES: *Création:* 1981. *Affiliée à:* Réseau d'Information sur le Tiers-Monde (France) - Centre de Recherche et d'Information sur le Développement (France) - Dialogues et Documents pour le progrès de l'Homme (France) - Centre International de Culture Populaire (France). *Personnel/Total:* 5. *Salariés:* 2. *Bénévoles:* 3. *Budget/Total 1993:* ECU 223000 (US$ 261000). *Sources financières:* Privé: 40%. Public: 15%. Autofinancement: 45%.

PUBLICATIONS: *Périodiques:* Le Bibliotin (4) - Passerelles (4). *Liste des publications.*

EVALUATION/RECHERCHE: Rapports d'évaluation disponibles. Entreprend des activités de recherche.

ACTIVITES D'INFORMATION ET D'EDUCATION: Domaines: Droits de l'Homme/paix/conflits; Développement rural/agriculture; Développement urbain/habitat; Paix/conflits ethniques/armement/désarmement; Pauvreté/conditions de vie; Questions relatives aux femmes; Racisme/xénophobie/antisémitisme; Relations internationales/coopération/aide au développement; Relations économiques internationales/commerce/dette/finances; Réfugiés/migrants/groupes ethniques; Santé/assainissement/eau; Écologie/environnement/biodiversité; Éducation/formation/alphabétisation. **Activités:** Services d'information et de documentation/bases de données; Édition/documents audiovisuels/documents éducatifs.

FRA1811

CENTRE DE DOCUMENTATION TIERS MONDE PEUPLES SOLIDAIRES

20, rue Bastion St. Nicolas, 17000 La Rochelle, France.

Téléphone: 33 - 46 41 01 48. *Fax:* 33 - 46 50 50 81. *Contact:* Jeanne Du Portal, Présidente.

OBJECTIFS: Informer et sensibiliser l'opinion publique aux problèmes des pays en voie de développement.

INFORMATIONS GENERALES: *Création:* 1981. *Type d'organisation:* réseau. *Affiliée à:* RITIMO (France) - Peuples Solidaires (France). *Personnel/Total:* 21. *Salariés:* 1. *Bénévoles:* 20. *Budget/Total 1993:* ECU 35000 (US$ 41000). *Sources financières:* Privé: 11%. Public: 17%. Autofinancement: 72%.

PUBLICATIONS: *Rapport annuel. Liste des publications.*

EVALUATION/RECHERCHE: Rapports d'évaluation disponibles.

ACTIVITES D'INFORMATION ET D'EDUCATION: Domaines: Aliments/famine; Culture/tradition/religion; Droits de l'Homme/paix/conflits; Déve-

loppement rural/agriculture; Emploi/chômage; Enfants/jeunesse/famille; Paix/conflits ethniques/armement/désarmement; Pauvreté/conditions de vie; Population/planning familial/démographie; Questions relatives aux femmes; Racisme/xénophobie/antisémitisme; Relations internationales/coopération/aide au développement; Relations économiques internationales/commerce/dette/finances; Réfugiés/migrants/groupes ethniques; Santé/assainissement/eau; Secours d'urgence/réfugiés/aide humanitaire; Écologie/environnement/biodiversité; Éducation/formation/alphabétisation. **Activités:** Campagnes d'information/expositions; Collecte de fonds; Conférences/séminaires/ateliers/activités de formation; Services d'information et de documentation/bases de données.

FRA1812

CENTRE DE FORMATION AUX REALITES INTERNATIONALES (CEFRI)

30 rue Cabanis, 75014 Paris, France.

Téléphone: 33 (1) 45 65 25 00. *Fax:* 33 (1) 45 81 63 91. *Contact:* Irène Dupoux-Couturier, Directrice.

FRA1813

CENTRE DE FORMATION ET D'ECHANGES INTERNATIO-NAUX (CFEI) ♦ International Training and Exchange Center

246 boulevard Saint-Denis - BP 36, 92403 Courbevoie, France.

Téléphone: 33 (1) 43 33 97 60. *Fax:* 33 (1) 47 88 90 46. *Contact:* Lise Neault, Responsable.

OBJECTIFS: Former les jeunes et les responsables des associatons de jeunes aux problèmes de développement.

INFORMATIONS GENERALES: *Création:* 1959. *Affiliée à:* CRID (France). *Personnel/Total:* 2. *Salariés:* 2. *Sources financières:* *Privé:* 30%. *Public:* 50%. *Autofinancement:* 20%.

PUBLICATIONS: *Périodiques:* Inter-Peuples (5). *Liste des publications.*

EVALUATION/RECHERCHE: Rapports d'évaluation disponibles.

PREVISIONS D'ACTIVITES: Organiser des stages de sensibilisation sur le thème "Immigration et développement". Réalisation d'un jeu sur la Corée du Sud. Edition d'un numéro spécial sur l'Asie (Inter-Peuples)

COMMENTAIRES: Activités d'information concernant la Communauté des Etats indépendants.

ACTIVITES D'INFORMATION ET D'EDUCATION: Domaines: Aliments/famine; Culture/tradition/religion; Développement rural/agriculture; Développement urbain/habitat; Emploi/chômage; Enfants/jeunesse/famille; Paix/conflits ethniques/armement/désarmement; Pauvreté/conditions de vie; Racisme/xénophobie/antisémitisme; Relations internationales/coopération/aide au développement; Relations économiques internationales/commerce/dette/finances; Réfugiés/migrants/groupes ethniques; Santé/assainissement/eau; Secours d'urgence/réfugiés/aide humanitaire; Écologie/environnement/biodiversité. **Activités:** Campagnes d'information/expositions; Conférences/séminaires/ateliers/activités de formation; Édition/documents audiovisuels/documents éducatifs.

FRA1814

CENTRE DE FORMATION ET DE COOPERATION INTERNATIONALE (CFCI)

13 rue des Ecluses Saint-Martin, 75010 Paris, France.

Téléphone: 33 (1) 42 45 22 95. *Fax:* 33 (1) 42 00 44 04. *Contact:* Armel Gourmelon.

FRA1815

CENTRE DE FORMATION POUR LE DEVELOPPEMENT (CEFODE)

3 rue St. Léon, 67082 Strasbourg cedex, France.

Téléphone: 33 - 88 32 60 02. *Fax:* 33 - 88 32 68 22. *Contact:* Roger Lehmann, Président.

OBJECTIFS: Apporter un soutien aux programmes de développement en Afrique et en Amérique Latine par l'envoi de coopérants volontaires. Contribuer à la formation de publics acteurs de la coopération internationale.

INFORMATIONS GENERALES: *Création:* 1963. *Affiliée à:* Comité de Liaison des ONG de Volontariat - Comité de liaison des organismes chrétiens de Coopération Internationale - Forum Européen du Volontariat.. *Salariés:* 2. *Bénévoles:* 18. *Budget/Total 1993:* ECU 81000 (US$ 95000). *Sources financières:* Privé: 80%. Public: 5%. Autofinancement: 15%.

PUBLICATIONS: *Périodiques:* Entreprises Solidaires (1). *Rapport annuel.*

EVALUATION/RECHERCHE: Entreprend des activités de recherche.

ACTIVITES DANS LES REGIONS EN DEVELOPPEMENT: Intervient directement dans les régions en développement. Intervient dans 16 pays. Maintient une présence locale sur le terrain. Intervient par l'intermédiaire d'organisations locales partenaires. **Actions de Développement durable:** Démocratie/bonne gestion publique/création d'institutions/développement participatif; Développement rural/agriculture; Développement urbain/habitat; Enfants/jeunesse/famille; Envoi de volontaires/experts/assistance technique; Petites entreprises/secteur informel/artisanat; Questions relatives aux femmes; Santé/assainissement/eau; Écologie/environnement/biodiversité; Éducation/formation/alphabétisation. **Régions:** Afrique centrale; Afrique de l'Ouest; Afrique du Nord; Amérique du Sud; Mexique et Amerique centrale.

ACTIVITES D'INFORMATION ET D'EDUCATION: Domaines: Culture/tradition/religion; Droits de l'Homme/paix/conflits; Développement rural/agriculture; Développement urbain/habitat; Enfants/jeunesse/famille; Pauvreté/conditions de vie; Questions relatives aux femmes; Relations internationales/coopération/aide au développement; Relations économiques internationales/commerce/dette/finances; Santé/assainissement/eau; Éducation/formation/alphabétisation. **Activités:** Conférences/séminaires/ateliers/activités de formation; Services d'information et de documentation/bases de données.

FRA1816

CENTRE DE RECHERCHE ET D'INFORMATION POUR LE DEVELOPPEMENT (CRID) ♦ Centre for Research and Information on Development

14 Passage Dubail, 75010 Paris, France.

Téléphone: 33 (1) 44 72 07 71. *Fax:* 33 (1) 44 72 06 84. *Courrier électronique:* CRID@globenet.gn.apc.org. *Contact:* Denise de Leiris, Déléguée générale.

OBJECTIFS: Promouvoir des solutions politiques à l'échelon national et international pour rééquilibrer les relations entre les pays du Nord et ceux du Sud. Promouvoir un développement décentralisé et participatif qui s'appuie sur les capacités d'information des populations et favorise l'appropriation des programmes de développement au niveau local.

INFORMATIONS GENERALES: *Création:* 1976. *Type d'organisation:* collectif. *Organisations membres:* 37. *Affiliée à:* Coordination Sud Solidarité.Urgence.Développement (France) - Commission Coopération Développement (France) - Alliance des gens du Nord pour l'Environnement et le Développement (France) - ICVA (Suisse). *Personnel/Total:* 4. *Salariés:* 4. *Budget/Total 1993:* ECU 754000 (US$ 883000). *Sources financières:* Public: 85%. Autofinancement: 15%.

PUBLICATIONS: *Périodiques:* Un Monde à venir (4) (4). *Rapport annuel. Liste des publications.*

PREVISIONS D'ACTIVITES: Campagne Environnement/Développement "Un Monde à Venir; étude sur le partenariat.

ACTIVITES D'INFORMATION ET D'EDUCATION: Domaines: Population/planning familial/démographie; Relations internationales/coopération/aide au développement; Relations économiques internationales/commerce/dette/finances; Écologie/environnement/biodiversité. **Activités:** Campagnes d'information/expositions; Conférences/séminaires/ateliers/activités de formation; Lobbying/plaidoyer; Réseaux/télécommunications électroniques; Services d'information et de documentation/bases de données; Édition/documents audiovisuels/documents éducatifs.

FRA1817

CENTRE DE RECHERCHE ET DE COOPERATION INTERNATIONALE (CERCI)

263 rue de Paris, 93516 Montreuil cedex, France.

See: *How to Use the Directory,* page 11.

Téléphone: 33 (1) 48 18 81 28. *Fax:* 33 (1) 48 18 84 43. *Contact:* Alphonse Veronese, Président.

OBJECTIFS: Contribuer à des recherches sur le développement en coopération avec des syndicats. Participer à la formation syndicale dans les pays du Tiers-Monde.

INFORMATIONS GENERALES: *Création:* 1975. *Type d'organisation:* regroupement d'ONG.

PUBLICATIONS: *Liste des publications.*

COMMENTAIRES: Intervient dans la Communauté des Etats indépendants. Activités d'information concernant la Communauté des Etats indépendants.

ACTIVITES DANS LES REGIONS EN DEVELOPPEMENT: Intervient directement dans les régions en développement. Intervient par l'intermédiaire d'organisations locales partenaires. **Actions de Développement durable:** Droits de l'Homme/paix/conflits; Démocratie/bonne gestion publique/création d'institutions/développement participatif; Envoi de volontaires/experts/assistance technique; Questions relatives aux femmes; Éducation/formation/alphabétisation. **Régions:** Afrique australe; Afrique centrale; Afrique de l'Est; Afrique de l'Ouest; Afrique du Nord; Amérique du Sud; Asie centrale et Asie du Sud; Asie de l'Est; Asie du Sud-Est; Caraïbes; Mexique et Amerique centrale; Moyen-Orient; Océanie.

FRA1818
CENTRE DE RECHERCHE, D'INFORMATION ET DE SOLIDARITE AVEC LES PEUPLES D'AFRIQUE, D'AMERIQUE LATINE ET D'ASIE (CRISLA)

1 avenue de la Marne, 56100 Lorient, France.

Téléphone: 33 - 97 64 64 32. *Fax:* 33 - 97 64 24 57. *Contact:* Jacques Cherel, Président.

OBJECTIFS: Réfléchir et informer sur les relations Nord-Sud et les pays du Sud, contribuer à l'éducation au développement et à l'organisation du partenariat avec des associations des pays du Sud.

INFORMATIONS GENERALES: *Création:* 1979. *Affiliée à:* RITIMO (France) - CRID (France) - Coordination Régionale des Associations de Solidarité Internationale (France.). *Personnel/Total:* 12. *Salariés:* 2. *Bénévoles:* 10. *Budget/Total 1993:* ECU 52000 (US$ 61000). *Sources financières:* Privé: 44%. Public: 42%. Autofinancement: 14%.

PUBLICATIONS: *Périodiques:* Pêche et Développement (4). *Liste des publications.*

EVALUATION/RECHERCHE: Rapports d'évaluation disponibles. Entreprend des activités de recherche.

PREVISIONS D'ACTIVITES: Déployer notre activité autour de la pêche, la consommation et de développement durable, la mondialisation économique et l'exclusion.

ACTIVITES DANS LES REGIONS EN DEVELOPPEMENT: Intervient dans 1 pays. Intervient par l'intermédiaire d'organisations locales partenaires. **Actions de Développement durable:** Autres; Démocratie/bonne gestion publique/création d'institutions/développement participatif; Développement rural/agriculture. **Régions:** Afrique de l'Ouest.

ACTIVITES D'INFORMATION ET D'EDUCATION: Domaines: Aliments/famine; Autres; Culture/tradition/religion; Droits de l'Homme/paix/conflits; Développement rural/agriculture; Développement urbain/habitat; Emploi/chômage; Enfants/jeunesse/famille; Paix/conflits ethniques/armement/désarmement; Pauvreté/conditions de vie; Questions relatives aux femmes; Racisme/xénophobie/antisémitisme; Relations internationales/coopération/aide au développement; Relations économiques internationales/commerce/dette/finances; Réfugiés/migrants/groupes ethniques; Santé/assainissement/eau; Secours d'urgence/réfugiés/aide humanitaire; Écologie/environnement/biodiversité; Éducation/formation/alphabétisation. **Activités:** Campagnes d'information/expositions; Conférences/séminaires/ateliers/activités de formation; Lobbying/plaidoyer; Services d'information et de documentation/bases de données; Échanges/parrainage/jumelage; Édition/documents audiovisuels/documents éducatifs.

FRA1819
CENTRE DE RECHERCHE-INFORMATION ACTION POUR LE DEVELOPPEMENT EN AFRIQUE (CRIAA)

69, avenue du Maine, 75014 Paris, France.

Téléphone: 33 (1) 43 20 29 61. *Fax:* 33 (1) 43 20 83 39. *Contact:* Jacques Marchand, Secrétaire général.

OBJECTIFS: Mener des programmes de développement économique et social, des opérations d'aide humanitaire (réfugiés), principalement en Afrique australe.

INFORMATIONS GENERALES: *Création:* 1977. *Affiliée à:* CRID. *Personnel/Total:* 13. *Salariés:* 13 dont: 6 dans les pays en développement. *Budget/Total 1993:* ECU 3899000 (US$ 4566000). *Sources financières:* Privé: 3%. Public: 80%. Autofinancement: 17%.

PUBLICATIONS: *Rapport annuel.*

EVALUATION/RECHERCHE: Entreprend des activités de recherche.

COMMENTAIRES: Le CRIAA travaille soit avec des partenaires locaux privés (ONG du Sud, groupes de base, etc.), soit avec les autorités et administrations gouvernementales. Compte tenu de sa spécialisation géographique et sectorielle, le CRIAA est en mesure d'opérer sur l'ensemble des phases d'un projet, de l'identification à l'exécution, en passant par le montage financier et la mise en place de l'assistance technique.

ACTIVITES DANS LES REGIONS EN DEVELOPPEMENT: Intervient directement dans les régions en développement. Intervient dans 5 pays. Maintient une présence locale sur le terrain. Intervient par l'intermédiaire d'organisations locales partenaires. **Actions de Développement durable:** Aliments/famine; Démocratie/bonne gestion publique/création d'institutions/développement participatif; Développement rural/agriculture; Développement urbain/habitat; Envoi de volontaires/experts/assistance technique; Petites entreprises/secteur informel/artisanat; Santé/assainissement/eau; Secours d'urgence/réfugiés/aide humanitaire. **Régions:** Afrique australe; Afrique centrale.

FRA1820
CENTRE DE RECHERCHES ET D'ETUDES POUR LE DEVELOPPEMENT DE LA SANTE (CREDES)

53 rue de Turbigo, 75003 Paris, France.

Téléphone: 33 (1) 42 74 23 25. *Fax:* 33 (1) 42 74 11 20. *Contact:* Jean-Daniel Rainhorn, Président.

OBJECTIFS: Réaliser des études et des recherches dans le domaine de la santé.Apporter une assistance technique et un suivi des projets de développement dans le domaine sanitaire, avec une compétence particulière pour les politiques pharmaceutiques.

INFORMATIONS GENERALES: *Création:* 1983. *Type d'organisation:* regroupement d'ONG. *Affiliée à:* Réseau Médicament (France) - Commission Mixte Franco-Burkinabé (France). *Personnel/Total:* 6. *Salariés:* 2. *Bénévoles:* 4. *Budget/Total 1993:* ECU 110000 (US$ 129000). *Sources financières:* Privé: 40%. Public: 50%. Autofinancement: 10%.

PUBLICATIONS: *Liste des publications.*

EVALUATION/RECHERCHE: Rapports d'évaluation disponibles. Entreprend des activités de recherche.

PREVISIONS D'ACTIVITES: Contacts privilégiés de formation avec les centres de mise au point de médicaments à partir de la pharmacopée traditionnelle dans plusieurs pays d'Afrique et d'Asie du Sud-Est: apport scientifique, technique et de gestion, formation de chercheurs et de laborantins.

ACTIVITES DANS LES REGIONS EN DEVELOPPEMENT: Intervient directement dans les régions en développement. Intervient dans 12 pays. Intervient par l'intermédiaire d'organisations locales partenaires. **Actions de Développement durable:** Envoi de volontaires/experts/assistance technique; Petites entreprises/secteur informel/artisanat; Santé/assainissement/eau; Éducation/formation/alphabétisation. **Régions:** Afrique australe; Afrique centrale; Afrique de l'Ouest; Asie du Sud-Est.

Voir : *Comment utiliser le répertoire,* page 11.

FRA1821

CENTRE DE RELATIONS INTERNATIONALES ENTRE AGRICULTEURS POUR LE DEVELOPPEMENT (CRIAD)

36 rue Vaubecour, 69002 Lyon, France.

Téléphone: 33 - 78 42 45 24. *Contact:* Laurent Barras.

FRA1822

CENTRE EUROPEEN DE FORMATION DES STATISTICIENS ECONOMISTES DES PAYS EN VOIE DE DEVELOPPE-MENT (CESD) ♦ European Training Centre for Economic Statisticians of Developing Countries

3 Avenue Pierre Larousse, 92240 Malakoff, France.

Telephone: 33 (1) 45 40 10 07. *Fax:* 33 (1) 42 53 45 35. *Contact:* Jean-Pierre Behmoiras, Président.

FRA1823

CENTRE FRANCAIS DE PROMOTION INDUSTRIELLE EN AFRIQUE (CEPIA) ♦ French Centre for Industrial Promotion in Africa

11 rue Marbeuf, 75008 Paris, France.

Téléphone: 33 (1) 47 20 22 03. *Fax:* 33 (1) 47 23 44 71. *Contact:* Jean-Louis Vilgrain.

FRA1824

CENTRE FRANCAIS DE PROTECTION DE L'ENFANCE (CFPE)

97 boulevard Berthier, 75017 Paris, France.

Téléphone: 33 (1) 43 80 26 53. *Fax:* 33 (1) 43 80 86 62. *Contact:* Xavier Besson, Président.

OBJECTIFS: Venir en aide aux enfants dans la détresse. Améliorer les conditions de la protection de l'enfance. Contribuer au développement tant moral que physique de l'enfant.

INFORMATIONS GENERALES: *Création:* 1947. *Personnel/Total:* 370. *Salariés:* 170. *Bénévoles:* 200. *Budget/Total 1993:* ECU 6332000 (US$ 7416000). *Sources financières:* Privé: 30%. Public: 60%. Autofinancement: 10%.

PUBLICATIONS: *Périodiques:* La lettre du CFPE (4). *Rapport annuel.*

EVALUATION/RECHERCHE: Rapports d'évaluation disponibles.

ACTIVITES DANS LES REGIONS EN DEVELOPPEMENT: Intervient directement dans les régions en développement. Intervient dans 22 pays. Maintient une présence locale sur le terrain. Intervient par l'intermédiaire d'organisations locales partenaires. **Actions de Développement durable:** Aliments/famine; Enfants/jeunesse/famille; Secours d'urgence/réfugiés/aide humanitaire; Éducation/formation/alphabétisation. **Régions:** Afrique australe; Afrique centrale; Afrique de l'Est; Afrique de l'Ouest; Amérique du Sud; Asie centrale et Asie du Sud; Asie du Sud-Est; Caraïbes; Mexique et Amerique centrale; Moyen-Orient.

ACTIVITES D'INFORMATION ET D'EDUCATION: Domaines: Aliments/famine; Enfants/jeunesse/famille; Pauvreté/conditions de vie; Réfugiés/migrants/groupes ethniques; Secours d'urgence/réfugiés/aide humanitaire; Éducation/formation/alphabétisation. **Activités:** Collecte de fonds; Lobbying/plaidoyer; Radiodiffusion/manifestations culturelles; Échanges/parrainage/jumelage.

FRA1825

CENTRE FRANCE-ASIE

16 rue Royer-Collard, 75005 Paris, France.

Téléphone: 33 (1) 43 25 77 64. *Contact:* Joseph Parais, Directeur.

OBJECTIFS: Déployer une activité d'assistance et de bienfaisance envers les Asiatiques d'Extrême-Orient en France particulièrement les étudiants, les réfugiés demandeurs d'asile.

INFORMATIONS GENERALES: *Création:* 1975. *Type d'organisation:* regroupement d'ONG. *Salariés:* 5. *Bénévoles:* 60. *Budget/Total 1993:* ECU 271000 (US$ 320000). *Sources financières:* Privé: 56%. Public: 11%. Autofinancement: 33%.

PUBLICATIONS: *Rapport annuel.*

ACTIVITES D'INFORMATION ET D'EDUCATION: Domaines: Autres; Emploi/chômage; Réfugiés/migrants/groupes ethniques; Secours d'urgence/réfugiés/aide humanitaire; Éducation/formation/alphabétisation. **Activités:** Autres; Collecte de fonds; Services d'information et de documentation/bases de données; Éducation formelle.

FRA1826

CENTRE FRANCO-BENINOIS D'ECHANGES CULTURELS (CFBEC)

B.P. 124, 75966 Paris cedex 20, France.

Téléphone: 33 (1) 43 32 98 21. *Contact:* Léonard Gbohounon, Président.

FRA1827

CENTRE INTERNATIONAL D'ETUDES POUR LE DEVELOPPEMENT LOCAL (CIEDEL)

30 rue Sainte-Hélène, 69002 Lyon, France.

Téléphone: 33 - 78 37 83 24. *Fax:* 33 - 72 41 99 88.

OBJECTIFS: Déployer une activité de formation à l'ingénierie de développement.

INFORMATIONS GENERALES: *Création:* 1991. *Affiliée à:* Centre de Recherche d'Information pour le Développement - Groupe Initiatives. *Personnel/Total:* 17. *Salariés:* 16. *Bénévoles:* 1. *Budget/Total 1993:* ECU 678000 (US$ 795000). *Sources financières:* Public: 15%. Autofinancement: 85%.

PUBLICATIONS: *Périodiques:* Histoires de Développement (4). *Liste des publications.*

EVALUATION/RECHERCHE: Rapports d'évaluation disponibles. Entreprend des activités de recherche.

ACTIVITES DANS LES REGIONS EN DEVELOPPEMENT: Intervient directement dans les régions en développement. Intervient dans 20 pays. Intervient par l'intermédiaire d'organisations locales partenaires. **Actions de Développement durable:** Démocratie/bonne gestion publique/création d'institutions/développement participatif; Développement rural/agriculture; Développement urbain/habitat; Petites entreprises/secteur informel/artisanat; Population/planning familial/démographie; Questions relatives aux femmes; Écologie/environnement/biodiversité; Éducation/formation/alphabétisation. **Régions:** Afrique australe; Afrique centrale; Afrique de l'Ouest; Amérique du Sud; Caraïbes; Mexique et Amerique centrale; Moyen-Orient.

ACTIVITES D'INFORMATION ET D'EDUCATION: Domaines: Culture/tradition/religion; Développement rural/agriculture; Développement urbain/habitat; Population/planning familial/démographie; Questions relatives aux femmes; Relations internationales/coopération/aide au développement; Relations économiques internationales/commerce/dette/finances; Écologie/environnement/biodiversité; Éducation/formation/alphabétisation. **Activités:** Services d'information et de documentation/bases de données; Édition/documents audiovisuels/documents éducatifs; Éducation formelle.

FRA1828

CENTRE INTERNATIONAL DE COOPERATION POUR LE DEVELOPPEMENT AGRICOLE (CICDA)

67 rue Robespierre, CAP 122, 93100 Montreuil cedex, France.

Téléphone: 33 (1) 48 51 67 90. *Fax:* 33 (1) 48 51 52 73. *Contact:* Jean-Jacques Boutrou, Directeur.

OBJECTIFS: Réaliser des programmes d'action et de coopération avec des institutions nationales, publiques ou privées, ayant pour fonction de promouvoir le développement socio-économique d'une région rurale considérée.

INFORMATIONS GENERALES: *Création:* 1977. *Affiliée à:* CFCF - CRID - Groupe Amérique Transversales et d'Evaluations - Groupe Initiatives - Max Howelaar - France (France). *Personnel/Total:* 31. *Salariés:* 29 dont: 25 dans les pays en développement. *Bénévoles:* 2. *Budget/Total 1993:* ECU 1485000 (US$ 1740000). *Sources financières:* Privé: 15%. Public: 72%. Autofinancement: 13%.

PUBLICATIONS: *Périodiques:* Communiquer (4) - RURALTER (2). *Rapport annuel. Liste des publications.*

See: *How to Use the Directory,* page 11.

EVALUATION/RECHERCHE: Rapports d'évaluation disponibles.

PREVISIONS D'ACTIVITES: Réactivation de la coopération avec coopératives de producteurs au Pérou. Structuration d'un service expertise.

COMMENTAIRES: Intervient dans la Communauté des Etats indépendants.

ACTIVITES DANS LES REGIONS EN DEVELOPPEMENT: Intervient directement dans les régions en développement. Intervient dans 5 pays. Maintient une présence locale sur le terrain. Intervient par l'intermédiaire d'organisations locales partenaires. **Actions de Développement durable:** Dette/finances/commerce; Développement rural/agriculture; Envoi de volontaires/experts/assistance technique; Questions relatives aux femmes; Écologie/environnement/biodiversité. **Régions:** Amérique du Sud.

ACTIVITES D'INFORMATION ET D'EDUCATION: Domaines: Développement rural/agriculture; Questions relatives aux femmes; Écologie/ environnement/biodiversité. **Activités:** Collecte de fonds; Conférences/ séminaires/ateliers/activités de formation; Services d'information et de documentation/bases de données; Échanges/parrainage/jumelage; Édition/documents audiovisuels/documents éducatifs.

FRA1829
CENTRE INTERNATIONAL DE CULTURE POPULAIRE (CICP)

21 Ter rue Voltaire, 75015 Paris, France.

Téléphone: 33 (1) 43 72 15 73. **Fax:** 33 (1) 43 72 15 77. **Contact:** François Della Sudda, Président.

OBJECTIFS: Promouvoir et défendre la culture populaire de tous les pays en fournissant aux adhérents du CICP les moyens matériels et, en général, tout moyen d'expression utile à son développement.

INFORMATIONS GENERALES: Création: 1976. **Type d'organisation:** réseau. **Personnel/Total:** 3. **Salariés:** 3. **Budget/Total 1993:** ECU 90000 (US$ 106000). **Sources financières:** Autofinancement: 100%.

COMMENTAIRES: L'association est une association de prestation de services d'ONG et d'associations (loi de 1901) oeuvrant dans le secteur de la solidarité internationale et de l'action sociale.

FRA1830
CENTRE INTERNATIONAL DE DEVELOPPEMENT ET DE RECHERCHE (CIDR) ♦ International Centre for Development and Research

17 rue de l'Hermitage, 60350 Autrèches, France.

Téléphone: 33 - 44 42 11 06. **Fax:** 33 - 44 42 94 52. **Contact:** Nicolas Beroff, Président.

OBJECTIFS: Etudier, formuler et mettre en œuvre des programmes de développement local ou régional, en France et à l'étranger, basés sur la création et/ou l'appui à des activités économiques et financières, dans le respect de l'équilibre socio-culturel des populations partenaires.

INFORMATIONS GENERALES: Création: 1961. **Affiliée à:** Coordination d'Agen. **Personnel/Total:** 36. **Salariés:** 36 dont: 25 dans les pays en développement. **Budget/Total 1993:** ECU 2367000 (US$ 2770000). **Sources financières:** Privé: 24%. Public: 24%. Autofinancement: 52%.

EVALUATION/RECHERCHE: Rapports d'évaluation disponibles. Entreprend des activités de recherche.

ACTIVITES DANS LES REGIONS EN DEVELOPPEMENT: Intervient directement dans les régions en développement. Intervient dans 12 pays. Maintient une présence locale sur le terrain. Intervient par l'intermédiaire d'organisations locales partenaires. **Actions de Développement durable:** Dette/finances/commerce; Développement rural/agriculture; Envoi de volontaires/experts/assistance technique; Petites entreprises/secteur informel/artisanat. **Régions:** Afrique australe; Afrique centrale; Afrique de l'Est; Afrique de l'Ouest; Asie centrale et Asie du Sud.

FRA1831
CENTRE INTERNATIONAL DE L'EAU (NAN.C.IE) ♦ International Water Centre

BP 290 - Rue Gabriel Péri, 54515 Vandœuvre-Les-Nancy Cedex, France.

Téléphone: 33 - 83 15 87 87. **Fax:** 33 - 83 15 87 99. **Contact:** Patrick Faivre, Directeur général.

OBJECTIFS: Apporter le savoir-faire dans les domaines de l'eau et de l'assainissement dans des projets de coopération décentralisés.

INFORMATIONS GENERALES: Création: 1984. **Type d'organisation:** réseau. **Personnel/Total:** 28. **Salariés:** 24 dont: 2 dans les pays en développement. **Bénévoles:** 4. **Budget/Total 1993:** ECU 4221000 (US$ 4944000). **Sources financières:** Public: 17%. Autofinancement: 83%.

PUBLICATIONS: Périodiques: Hydroscopie (5). **Rapport annuel. Liste des publications.**

EVALUATION/RECHERCHE: Rapports d'évaluation disponibles. Entreprend des activités de recherche.

COMMENTAIRES: Intervient dans la Communauté des Etats indépendants. Activités d'information concernant la Communauté des Etats indépendants.

ACTIVITES DANS LES REGIONS EN DEVELOPPEMENT: Intervient directement dans les régions en développement. Intervient dans 4 pays. Maintient une présence locale sur le terrain. Intervient par l'intermédiaire d'organisations locales partenaires. **Actions de Développement durable:** Envoi de volontaires/experts/assistance technique; Santé/assainissement/eau; Éducation/formation/alphabétisation. **Régions:** Afrique du Nord; Amérique du Sud; Asie centrale et Asie du Sud; Mexique et Amerique centrale.

ACTIVITES D'INFORMATION ET D'EDUCATION: Domaines: Questions relatives aux femmes. **Activités:** Collecte de fonds; Conférences/séminaires/ateliers/activités de formation; Lobbying/plaidoyer; Services d'information et de documentation/bases de données; Échanges/parrainage/jumelage.

FRA1832
CENTRE INTERNATIONAL DE L'ENFANCE (CIE)

Château de Longchamp, Carrefour de Longchamp, Bois de Boulogne, 75016 Paris, France.

Téléphone: 33 (1) 44 30 20 00. **Fax:** 33 (1) 45 25 73 67. **Contact:** Michèle Puybasset, Directeur général.

OBJECTIFS: Réfléchir et agir pour la santé et le développement des enfants et des adolescents dans le monde. Déployer des actions de formation. Diffuser des connaissances en vue du renforcement des capacités des acteurs locaux dans les pays en développement.

INFORMATIONS GENERALES: Création: 1949. **Personnel/Total:** 76. **Salariés:** 76. **Budget/Total 1993:** ECU 6030000 (US$ 7063000). **Sources financières:** Privé: 1%. Public: 89%. Autofinancement: 10%.

PUBLICATIONS: Périodiques: L'enfant en milieu tropical (6). **Rapport annuel. Liste des publications.**

EVALUATION/RECHERCHE: Entreprend des activités de recherche.

ACTIVITES DANS LES REGIONS EN DEVELOPPEMENT: Intervient directement dans les régions en développement. Intervient dans 25 pays. Intervient par l'intermédiaire d'organisations locales partenaires. **Actions de Développement durable:** Développement rural/agriculture; Développement urbain/habitat; Enfants/jeunesse/ famille; Santé/assainissement/eau. **Régions:** Afrique centrale; Afrique de l'Ouest; Afrique du Nord; Amérique du Sud; Asie du Sud-Est; Moyen-Orient.

ACTIVITES D'INFORMATION ET D'EDUCATION: Domaines: Aliments/ famine; Développement rural/agriculture; Développement urbain/habitat; Enfants/jeunesse/famille; Réfugiés/migrants/groupes ethniques; Santé/assainissement/eau. **Activités:** Conférences/séminaires/ateliers/ activités de formation; Services d'information et de documentation/ bases de données; Édition/documents audiovisuels/documents éducatifs.

Voir : *Comment utiliser le répertoire,* page 11.

FRA1833

CENTRE INTERNATIONAL DE LA CONSTRUCTION EN TERRE (CRATERRE-EAG)

Maison Leurat, Rue du Lac, BP 53, 38092 Villefontaine cedex, France.

Téléphone: 33 - 74 96 60 56. *Fax:* 33 - 74 96 04 63. *Contact:* Patrice Doat, Président.

OBJECTIFS: Améliorer les conditions d'habitat des populations les plus défavorisées. Promouvoir la prise en charge des problèmes d'aménagement de l'espace par les collectivités locales. Favoriser la production et le contrôle de son cadre de vie par l'usager lui-même. Conseiller et former

INFORMATIONS GENERALES: *Création:* 1979. *Type d'organisation:* réseau. *Affiliée à:* Conseil International du Bâtiment (Pays-Bas) - CLEDTIERRA (Pérou) -International Association for Housing Science (Etats-Unis) - RILEM - ICCROM -ICCOMOS - IFEC - REII - BASIN. *Personnel/Total:* 34. *Salariés:* 9. *Bénévoles:* 25 dont: 8 dans les pays en développement. *Sources financières: Public:* 40%. *Autofinancement:* 60%.

PUBLICATIONS: *Périodiques:* Bulletin d'Information CRATERRE-EAG (3) - BASIN-NEWS (3). *Rapport annuel. Liste des publications.*

EVALUATION/RECHERCHE: Rapports d'évaluation disponibles. Entreprend des activités de recherche.

PREVISIONS D'ACTIVITES: Formation en France et à l'étranger, lancement de petites filières de fabrication, lancement de cours sur la construction en terre dans certains pays, édition.

COMMENTAIRES: Intervient dans la Communauté des Etats indépendants. Activités d'information concernant la Communauté des Etats indépendants.

ACTIVITES DANS LES REGIONS EN DEVELOPPEMENT: Intervient directement dans les régions en développement. Intervient dans 21 pays. Maintient une présence locale sur le terrain. Intervient par l'intermédiaire d'organisations locales partenaires. **Actions de Développement durable:** Développement urbain/habitat; Petites entreprises/secteur informel/artisanat; Éducation/formation/alphabétisation. **Régions:** Afrique australe; Afrique centrale; Afrique de l'Est; Afrique de l'Ouest; Afrique du Nord; Asie de l'Est; Mexique et Amerique centrale.

ACTIVITES D'INFORMATION ET D'EDUCATION: Domaines: Développement urbain/habitat; Secours d'urgence/réfugiés/aide humanitaire; Écologie/environnement/biodiversité. **Activités:** Conférences/séminaires/ateliers/activités de formation; Services d'information et de documentation/bases de données; Édition/documents audiovisuels/documents éducatifs.

FRA1834

CENTRE INTERNATIONAL DE RECHERCHES ET D'ETUDES SUR LE DEVELOPPEMENT ECONOMIQUE ET COMMERCIAL NORD-SUD

24 rue Joannes Masset, 69009 Lyon, France.

Téléphone: 33 - 78 83 00 54. *Contact:* Francis Oyegbola, Directeur.

FRA1835

CENTRE INTERNATIONAL DU CREDIT MUTUEL (CICM)

88-90 rue Cardinet, 75017 Paris, France.

Téléphone: 33 (1) 44 01 11 90. *Fax:* 33 (1) 44 01 12 75. *Contact:* Yann Gauthier, Directeur.

OBJECTIFS: Aider les pays en développement qui en font la demande, à mobiliser leur propre épargne au niveau des villes , villages et dans les zones rurales, en marge des institutions financières classiques qui ne peuvent, pour des raisons d'organisation et de coût, rentabiliser un réseau bancaire traditionnel.

INFORMATIONS GENERALES: *Création:* 1979. *Personnel/Total:* 29. *Salariés:* 29 dont: 25 dans les pays en développement. *Budget/ Total 1993:* ECU 5276000 (US$ 6180000).

ACTIVITES DANS LES REGIONS EN DEVELOPPEMENT: Intervient directement dans les régions en développement. Maintient une pré-

sence locale sur le terrain. **Actions de Développement durable:** Dette/finances/commerce; Éducation/formation/alphabétisation. **Régions:** Afrique centrale; Afrique de l'Est; Afrique de l'Ouest.

FRA1836

CENTRE INTERNATIONAL POUR L'EDUCATION PERMANENTE ET L'AMENAGEMENT CONCERTE (CIEPAC)

663 avenue de la Pompignane, 34170 Castelnau-le-lez, France.

Téléphone: 33 - 67 79 60 11. *Fax:* 33 - 67 72 99 76. *Contact:* Jacques Berthome, Secrétaire général.

OBJECTIFS: Soutenir des projets de développement dans lesquels sont impliquées des structures populaires. Assurer la formation des partenaires, paysans et agents de développement. Effectuer des échanges de coopération décentralisée.

INFORMATIONS GENERALES: *Création:* 1979. *Affiliée à:* CRID (France) - Groupe Initiatives (France). *Personnel/Total:* 15. *Salariés:* 12 dont: 4 dans les pays en développement. *Bénévoles:* 3 dont: 1 dans les pays en développement. *Budget/Total 1993:* ECU 528000 (US$ 618000). *Sources financières: Privé:* 69%. *Public:* 30%. *Autofinancement:* 1%.

PUBLICATIONS: *Liste des publications.*

EVALUATION/RECHERCHE: Rapports d'évaluation disponibles. Entreprend des activités de recherche.

ACTIVITES DANS LES REGIONS EN DEVELOPPEMENT: Intervient directement dans les régions en développement. Intervient dans 9 pays. Intervient par l'intermédiaire d'organisations locales partenaires. **Actions de Développement durable:** Démocratie/bonne gestion publique/création d'institutions/développement participatif; Développement rural/agriculture; Développement urbain/habitat; Petites entreprises/secteur informel/artisanat; Écologie/environnement/biodiversité; Éducation/formation/alphabétisation. **Régions:** Afrique centrale; Afrique de l'Ouest; Afrique du Nord; Amérique du Sud.

ACTIVITES D'INFORMATION ET D'EDUCATION: Domaines: Aliments/famine; Culture/tradition/religion; Développement rural/agriculture; Développement urbain/habitat; Enfants/jeunesse/famille; Population/planning familial/démographie; Questions relatives aux femmes; Relations internationales/coopération/aide au développement; Relations économiques internationales/commerce/dette/finances; Santé/assainissement/eau; Écologie/environnement/biodiversité; Éducation/formation/alphabétisation. **Activités:** Échanges/parrainage/jumelage; Édition/documents audiovisuels/documents éducatifs.

FRA1837

CENTRE INTERNATIONAL POUR LA FORMATION ET LES ECHANGES GEOLOGIQUES (CIFEG) ♦ International Centre for Training and Exchanges in the Geosciences

Avenue de Concyr, BP 6517, 45065 Orléans cedex 2, France.

Téléphone: 33 - 38 64 33 67. *Fax:* 33 - 38 64 34 72. *Contact:* Jean-Claude Napias, Directeur général.

OBJECTIFS: Favoriser les échanges Nord-Sud dans le domaine des sciences de la terre.

INFORMATIONS GENERALES: *Création:* 1980. *Personnel/Total:* 5. *Salariés:* 5. *Sources financières: Public:* 50%. *Autofinancement:* 50%.

PUBLICATIONS: *Périodiques:* Bulletin Bibliographique de Géologie Africaine (4) - Pangea (2). *Liste des publications.*

ACTIVITES DANS LES REGIONS EN DEVELOPPEMENT: Intervient par l'intermédiaire d'organisations locales partenaires. **Actions de Développement durable:** Autres. **Régions:** Afrique australe; Afrique centrale; Afrique de l'Est; Afrique de l'Ouest; Afrique du Nord; Amérique du Sud; Mexique et Amerique centrale.

ACTIVITES D'INFORMATION ET D'EDUCATION: Domaines: Autres. **Activités:** Conférences/séminaires/ateliers/activités de formation; Réseaux/télécommunications électroniques; Services d'information et de documentation/bases de données; Édition/documents audiovisuels/documents éducatifs.

See: *How to Use the Directory,* page 11.

FRA1838

CENTRE LEBRET (CL)

43ter rue de la Glacière, 75013 Paris, France.

Téléphone: 33 (1) 47 07 10 07. *Fax:* 33 (1) 47 07 68 66. *Contact:* Eric Sottas, Président.

OBJECTIFS: Rechercher, vérifier et proposer des alternatives en relation avec les principales organisations internationales non-gouvernementales pour assurer une formation garante d'un développement centré sur l'homme. Etre un lieu de recherche et de réflexion sur "l'économie humaine".

INFORMATIONS GENERALES: *Création:* 1972. *Type d'organisation:* réseau. *Affiliée à:* CRID - CFSI. *Personnel/Total:* 26. *Salariés:* 1. *Bénévoles:* 25. *Budget/Total 1993:* ECU 102000 (US$ 119000). *Sources financières:* Privé: 50%. Autofinancement: 50%.

PUBLICATIONS: *Périodiques:* Foi et Développement (10). *Liste des publications.*

EVALUATION/RECHERCHE: Entreprend des activités de recherche.

PREVISIONS D'ACTIVITES: Colloques prévus en 1995-96-97 et travaillés par le réseau sur les thèmes: aménagement du territoire et développement humain, instruments d'économie sociale et développement humain, relations économiques internationales et développement humain.

ACTIVITES D'INFORMATION ET D'EDUCATION: Domaines: Culture/tradition/religion; Droits de l'Homme/paix/conflits; Relations internationales/coopération/aide au développement; Relations économiques internationales/commerce/dette/finances; Écologie/environnement/biodiversité. **Activités:** Conférences/séminaires/ateliers/activités de formation; Services d'information et de documentation/bases de données.

FRA1839

CENTRE LORRAIN D'INFORMATION POUR LE DEVELOPPEMENT (CLID)

1 rue de la Ravinelle, 54000 Nancy, France.

Téléphone: 33 (1) 83 37 44 86. *Fax:* 33 (1) 83 37 44 86. *Contact:* Hubert Gérardin, Président.

OBJECTIFS: Favoriser les actions d'animation et d'information sur les problèmes des pays en développement. Gérer un centre de documentation ouvert au public sur les réalités internationales. Soutenir les initiatives des associations membres.

INFORMATIONS GENERALES: *Création:* 1981. *Type d'organisation:* collectif. *Organisations membres:* 10. *Affiliée à:* Réseau d'Information Tiers-Monde (France). *Personnel/Total:* 12. *Salariés:* 1. *Bénévoles:* 11. *Budget/Total 1993:* ECU 30000 (US$ 36000). *Sources financières:* Privé: 28%. Public: 45%. Autofinancement: 27%.

PUBLICATIONS: *Périodiques:* CLID-INFO (!). *Rapport annuel. Liste des publications.*

ACTIVITES D'INFORMATION ET D'EDUCATION: Domaines: Aliments/famine; Autres; Culture/tradition/religion; Droits de l'Homme/paix/conflits; Développement rural/agriculture; Développement urbain/habitat; Emploi/chômage; Enfants/jeunesse/famille; Paix/conflits ethniques/armement/désarmement; Pauvreté/conditions de vie; Population/planning familial/démographie; Questions relatives aux femmes; Racisme/xénophobie/antisémitisme; Relations internationales/coopération/aide au développement; Relations économiques internationales/commerce/dette/finances; Réfugiés/migrants/groupes ethniques; Santé/assainissement/eau; Secours d'urgence/réfugiés/aide humanitaire; Écologie/environnement/biodiversité. **Activités:** Campagnes d'information/expositions; Services d'information et de documentation/bases de données; Édition/documents audiovisuels/documents éducatifs;

FRA1840

CENTRE NORD-SUD DE L'INSTITUT DE L'ENTREPRISE

6 rue Clément Marot, 75008 Paris, France.

Téléphone: 33 (1) 47 23 63 28. *Fax:* 33 (1) 47 23 79 01. *Contact:* René Lapautre.

FRA1841

CENTRE RENNAIS D'INFORMATION POUR LE DEVELOPPEMENT ET LA LIBERATION DES PEUPLES (CRIDEV)

41 avenue Janvier, 35000 Rennes, France.

Téléphone: 33 - 99 30 27 20. *Fax:* 33 - 99 30 27 20. *Contact:* Sophie Ronco.

OBJECTIFS: Informer, documenter et former le public rennais sur le thème du développement économique et politique.

INFORMATIONS GENERALES: *Création:* 1974. *Affiliée à:* Réseau national des centres d'information Tiers-Monde - CRID (France) - Réseau Solidarité - Mouvement anti-apartheid.. *Personnel/Total:* 19. *Salariés:* 4. *Bénévoles:* 15. *Budget/Total 1993:* ECU 90000 (US$ 106000). *Sources financières:* Privé: 10%. Public: 45%. Autofinancement: 45%.

PUBLICATIONS: *Périodiques:* Bulletin CRIDEV (12). *Rapport annuel. Liste des publications.*

EVALUATION/RECHERCHE: Rapports d'évaluation disponibles.

ACTIVITES D'INFORMATION ET D'EDUCATION: Domaines: Aliments/famine; Culture/tradition/religion; Droits de l'Homme/paix/conflits; Développement rural/agriculture; Développement urbain/habitat; Emploi/chômage; Enfants/jeunesse/famille; Paix/conflits ethniques/armement/désarmement; Pauvreté/conditions de vie; Population/planning familial/démographie; Questions relatives aux femmes; Racisme/xénophobie/antisémitisme; Relations internationales/coopération/aide au développement; Relations économiques internationales/commerce/dette/finances; Réfugiés/migrants/groupes ethniques; Santé/assainissement/eau; Secours d'urgence/réfugiés/aide humanitaire; Écologie/environnement/biodiversité; Éducation/formation/alphabétisation. **Activités:** Campagnes d'information/expositions; Conférences/séminaires/ateliers/activités de formation; Lobbying/plaidoyer; Services d'information et de documentation/bases de données; Éducation formelle.

FRA1842

CHILI FLASH ESPACE LATINO-AMERICAIN

17 bis rue Louis Adam, 69100 Villeurbanne, France.

Téléphone: 33 - 78 68 93 77. *Contact:* Januario Espinosa, Directeur.

FRA1843

CIMADE - SERVICE OECUMENIQUE D'ENTRAIDE (CIMADE)

176 rue de Grenelle, 75007 Paris, France.

Téléphone: 33 (1) 44 18 60 50. *Fax:* 33 (1) 45 55 72 53. *Courrier électronique:* Geonet:Geo2:CIMADE. *Contact:* Geneviève Jacques, Secrétaire générale.

OBJECTIFS: Manifester une solidarité active avec ceux qui souffrent, qui sont opprimés et exploités, et assurer leur défense, quelles que soient leur nationalité, leur race, leur position politique ou religieuse. En particulier, combattre le racisme et collaborer avec divers organismes, notamment au service des réfugiés, des travailleurs migrants, des détenus et des peuples des pays en voie de développement.

INFORMATIONS GENERALES: *Création:* 1939. *Affiliée à:* Centre de Recherche et d'Information pour le Développement - Comité Français de Solidarité Internationale - Réseau européen des Agences de Développement Protestantes - Groupe de Recherche et d'Echanges Technologiques - Agence d'Images du Monde/Groupe de Communications Internationales . *Personnel/Total:* 134. *Salariés:* 134. *Budget/Total 1993:* ECU 6030000 (US$ 7063000). *Sources financières:* Privé: 25%. Public: 65%. Autofinancement: 10%.

PUBLICATIONS: *Périodiques:* Cimade-Information (6) - Interventions (6). *Rapport annuel. Liste des publications.*

EVALUATION/RECHERCHE: Entreprend des activités de recherche.

ACTIVITES DANS LES REGIONS EN DEVELOPPEMENT: Intervient directement dans les régions en développement. Intervient dans 30 pays. Maintient une présence locale sur le terrain. Intervient par l'intermédiaire d'organisations locales partenaires. **Actions de Développement durable:** Dette/finances/commerce; Droits de l'Homme/paix/conflits; Démocratie/bonne gestion publique/création d'institutions/développement participatif; Développement rural/agriculture; Développement

Voir : *Comment utiliser le répertoire,* page 11.

urbain/habitat; Enfants/jeunesse/famille; Questions relatives aux femmes; Santé/assainissement/eau; Éducation/formation/alphabétisation. **Régions:** Afrique australe; Afrique centrale; Afrique de l'Est; Afrique de l'Ouest; Afrique du Nord; Amérique du Sud; Asie centrale et Asie du Sud; Asie du Sud-Est; Caraïbes; Mexique et Amerique centrale; Moyen-Orient.

ACTIVITES D'INFORMATION ET D'EDUCATION: Domaines: Culture/tradition/religion; Droits de l'Homme/paix/conflits; Développement rural/agriculture; Développement urbain/habitat; Enfants/jeunesse/famille; Paix/conflits ethniques/armement/désarmement; Pauvreté/conditions de vie; Questions relatives aux femmes; Racisme/xénophobie/antisémitisme; Relations internationales/coopération/aide au développement; Relations économiques internationales/commerce/dette/finances; Réfugiés/migrants/groupes ethniques; Santé/assainissement/eau; Éducation/formation/alphabétisation. **Activités:** Campagnes d'information/expositions; Collecte de fonds; Lobbying/plaidoyer; Édition/documents audiovisuels/documents éducatifs.

FRA1844
CINEMAS D'AFRIQUE ANGERS

3 bis quai Gambetta, 49100 Angers, France.

Téléphone: 33 - 41 20 08 22. *Fax:* 33 - 41 20 08 27. *Contact:* Gérard Moreau, Directeur.

OBJECTIFS: Développer les échanges culturels avec l'Afrique. Organiser à Angers, tous les deux ans, le festival Cinémas d'Afrique ainsi que des expositions et conférences, des stages en entreprises pour des professionnels africains.

INFORMATIONS GENERALES: *Création:* 1992. *Personnel/Total:* 29. *Salariés:* 2. *Bénévoles:* 27. *Budget/Total 1993:* ECU 143000 (US$ 168000). *Sources financières:* Public: 85%. Autofinancement: 15%.

EVALUATION/RECHERCHE: Rapports d'évaluation disponibles.

COMMENTAIRES: L'organisation publie un catalogue tous les deux ans et des documents du festival.

ACTIVITES DANS LES REGIONS EN DEVELOPPEMENT: Intervient par l'intermédiaire d'organisations locales partenaires. **Actions de Développement durable:** Éducation/formation/alphabétisation. **Régions:** Afrique de l'Ouest.

ACTIVITES D'INFORMATION ET D'EDUCATION: Domaines: Culture/tradition/religion. **Activités:** Campagnes d'information/expositions; Conférences/séminaires/ateliers/activités de formation; Radiodiffusion/manifestations culturelles.

FRA1845
CITES UNIES DEVELOPPEMENT

22 rue d'Alsace, 92532 Levallois Perret cedex, France.

Téléphone: 33 (1) 47 39 36 86. *Fax:* 33 (1) 42 70 37 99. *Contact:* Jean-Marie Tetart, Directeur général.

FRA1846
CITES UNIES FRANCE - VILLES JUMELEES

10 cité Vaneau, 75007 Paris, France.

Téléphone: 33 (1) 45 61 24 54. *Fax:* 33 (1) 45 63 26 10. *Contact:* Michel Bescond, Directeur.

OBJECTIFS: Promouvoir la coopération décentralisée entre les collectivités locales françaises et leurs homologues étrangères et favoriser dans les pays en développement des projets de développement.

INFORMATIONS GENERALES: *Création:* 1975. *Type d'organisation:* réseau. *Affiliée à:* Fédération mondiale des cités unies. *Personnel/Total:* 12. *Salariés:* 9. *Bénévoles:* 3. *Budget/Total 1993:* ECU 754000 (US$ 883000).

PUBLICATIONS: *Périodiques:* Le Journal de Cités Unies France (4). *Rapport annuel.*

COMMENTAIRES: Intervient dans la Communauté des Etats indépendants.

ACTIVITES DANS LES REGIONS EN DEVELOPPEMENT: Intervient par l'intermédiaire d'organisations locales partenaires. **Actions de Développement durable:** Démocratie/bonne gestion publique/création d'institutions/développement participatif; Développement rural/agriculture; Développement urbain/habitat; Enfants/jeunesse/famille; Envoi de volontaires/experts/assistance technique; Petites entreprises/secteur informel/artisanat; Population/planning familial/démographie; Questions relatives aux femmes; Santé/assainissement/eau; Éducation/formation/alphabétisation; Énergie/transport. **Régions:** Afrique de l'Ouest; Afrique du Nord; Amérique du Sud; Asie du Sud-Est; Caraïbes; Mexique et Amerique centrale; Moyen-Orient.

ACTIVITES D'INFORMATION ET D'EDUCATION: Domaines: Aliments/famine; Droits de l'Homme/paix/conflits; Développement rural/agriculture; Développement urbain/habitat; Emploi/chômage; Enfants/jeunesse/famille; Pauvreté/conditions de vie; Population/planning familial/démographie; Questions relatives aux femmes; Relations internationales/coopération/aide au développement; Réfugiés/migrants/groupes ethniques; Santé/assainissement/eau; Écologie/environnement/biodiversité; Éducation/formation/alphabétisation. **Activités:** Conférences/séminaires/ateliers/activités de formation; Services d'information et de documentation/bases de données; Échanges/parrainage/jumelage.

FRA1847
CITOYENS ET DEVELOPPEMENT

B.P. 14, 32700 Lectoure, France.

Téléphone: 33 - 62 28 67 43. *Fax:* 33 - 62 28 60 95. *Contact:* Christian Ponticelli, Président.

FRA1848
CLAIR-LOGIS AFRIQUE

59 rue de l'Ourcq, 75019 Paris, France.

Téléphone: 33 (1) 40 35 40 31. *Fax:* 33 (1) 40 36 93 04. *Contact:* Christiane Muller, Secrétaire générale.

OBJECTIFS: Contribuer à la formation des jeunes filles et jeunes femmes africaines les plus défavorisées, autour de la vie familiale et domestique, sociale et civique, ainsi que par l'organisation de cours d'alphabétisation.

INFORMATIONS GENERALES: *Création:* 1961. *Personnel/Total:* 33. *Salariés:* 32 dont: 32 dans les pays en développement. *Bénévoles:* 1. *Budget/Total 1993:* ECU 276000 (US$ 323000). *Sources financières:* Privé: 37%. Public: 46%. Autofinancement: 17%.

PUBLICATIONS: *Rapport annuel.*

EVALUATION/RECHERCHE: Rapports d'évaluation disponibles.

PREVISIONS D'ACTIVITES: Formation professionnelle des jeunes et des aînées en vue de leur réinsertion sociale et économique dans leur milieu.

ACTIVITES DANS LES REGIONS EN DEVELOPPEMENT: Intervient directement dans les régions en développement. Intervient dans 4 pays. Maintient une présence locale sur le terrain. Intervient par l'intermédiaire d'organisations locales partenaires. **Actions de Développement durable:** Enfants/jeunesse/famille; Envoi de volontaires/experts/assistance technique; Petites entreprises/secteur informel/artisanat; Questions relatives aux femmes; Santé/assainissement/eau; Éducation/formation/alphabétisation. **Régions:** Afrique de l'Ouest.

ACTIVITES D'INFORMATION ET D'EDUCATION: Domaines: Enfants/jeunesse/famille; Questions relatives aux femmes; Santé/assainissement/eau; Éducation/formation/alphabétisation. **Activités:** Campagnes d'information/expositions; Conférences/séminaires/ateliers/activités de formation; Éducation formelle.

FRA1849
CLUB TIERS MONDE DE SAINT-ADRIEN (CTM)

15 rue Jean-Baptiste de la Salle, B.P. 167, 59653 Villeneuve d'Ascq cedex, France.

Téléphone: 33 - 20 91 18 32. *Fax:* 33 - 20 91 98 59. *Contact:* Etienne Verbaere, Trésorier.

OBJECTIFS: Faire prendre conscience de la solidarité nécessaire et réaliser des actions en faveur du quart monde et du tiers monde. S'informer,

See: *How to Use the Directory,* page 11.

informer, agir et faire de l'animation agricole et rurale. Promouvoir des actions dans les domaines de l'animation agricole et rurale, de la santé et de l'enseignement technique et professionnel.

INFORMATIONS GENERALES: *Création:* 1983. *Affiliée à:* Lia.Co.Fa (France). *Personnel/Total:* 15. *Bénévoles:* 15 dont: 4 dans les pays en développement. *Budget/Total 1993:* ECU 42000 (US$ 49000). *Sources financières:* Privé: 40%. Public: 50%. *Autofinancement:* 10%.

PUBLICATIONS: *Périodiques:* Bulletin du Club Tiers-Monde (4). *Rapport annuel. Liste des publications.*

EVALUATION/RECHERCHE: Rapports d'évaluation disponibles.

ACTIVITES DANS LES REGIONS EN DEVELOPPEMENT: Intervient directement dans les régions en développement. Intervient dans 3 pays. Maintient une présence locale sur le terrain. Intervient par l'intermédiaire d'organisations locales partenaires.

ACTIVITES D'INFORMATION ET D'EDUCATION: Domaines: Culture/tradition/religion; Droits de l'Homme/paix/conflits; Développement rural/agriculture; Emploi/chômage; Enfants/jeunesse/famille; Pauvreté/conditions de vie; Questions relatives aux femmes; Relations internationales/coopération/aide au développement; Santé/assainissement/eau; Éducation/formation/alphabétisation. **Activités:** Campagnes d'information/expositions; Collecte de fonds; Conférences/séminaires/ateliers/activités de formation; Services d'information et de documentation/bases de données; Édition/documents audiovisuels/documents éducatifs; Éducation formelle.

FRA1850

CODEV-VIET-PHAP (CVP) ◆ Coopération Développement franco-vietnamien

Route de Sens - Ecuelles - BP 1, 77250 Moret-sur-Loing, France.

Téléphone: 33 (1) 60 73 73 80. *Fax:* 33 (1) 60 73 73 81. *Contact:* Michel Detot, Président.

OBJECTIFS: Participer à l'équipement et au fonctionnement de structures scolaires et médicales. Organiser et commercialiser des voyages culturels au Vietnam. Former du personnel. Développer les échanges culturels. Aider au développement de la fabrication de produits artisanaux et à leur commercialisation. Faciliter le développement des relations industrielles et commerciales entre les partenaires français et vietnamiens.

INFORMATIONS GENERALES: *Création:* 1990. *Affiliée à:* Comité France-Pays du Mekong (France) - CODEV (France). *Personnel/Total:* 2. *Bénévoles:* 2 dont: 1 dans les pays en développement. *Budget/Total 1993:* ECU 633000 (US$ 742000). *Sources financières:* Privé: 6%. Public: 25%. Autofinancement: 69%.

PUBLICATIONS: *Périodiques:* Le Lien (3).

EVALUATION/RECHERCHE: Entreprend des activités de recherche.

ACTIVITES DANS LES REGIONS EN DEVELOPPEMENT: Intervient directement dans les régions en développement. Intervient dans 1 pays. Maintient une présence locale sur le terrain. **Actions de Développement durable:** Aliments/famine; Démocratie/bonne gestion publique/création d'institutions/développement participatif; Développement urbain/habitat; Enfants/jeunesse/famille; Envoi de volontaires/experts/assistance technique; Petites entreprises/secteur informel/artisanat; Santé/assainissement/eau; Secours d'urgence/réfugiés/aide humanitaire; Éducation/formation/alphabétisation; Énergie/transport. **Régions:** Asie du Sud-Est.

ACTIVITES D'INFORMATION ET D'EDUCATION: Domaines: Culture/tradition/religion; Développement urbain/habitat; Enfants/jeunesse/famille; Relations internationales/coopération/aide au développement; Santé/assainissement/eau; Secours d'urgence/réfugiés/aide humanitaire; Éducation/formation/alphabétisation. **Activités:** Campagnes d'information/expositions; Collecte de fonds; Conférences/séminaires/ateliers/activités de formation; Lobbying/plaidoyer; Radiodiffusion/manifestations culturelles; Échanges/parrainage/jumelage.

FRA1851

COLLECTIF ENVIRONNEMENT DEVELOPPEMENT INTERNATIONAL (CEDI)

3, Place de Thorigny, 75003 Paris, France.

Téléphone: 33 (1) 42 78 15 00. *Contact:* Eric de Romain, Président.

OBJECTIFS: Développer la présence des associations françaises s'occupant des questions d'environnement sur la scène internationale. Faire respecter les engagements pris au sommet de Rio.

INFORMATIONS GENERALES: *Création:* 1991. *Type d'organisation:* collectif. *Organisations membres:* 30. *Personnel/Total:* 8. *Salariés:* 3. *Bénévoles:* 5. *Budget/Total 1993:* ECU 151000 (US$ 177000). *Sources financières:* Public: 90%. Autofinancement: 10%.

PUBLICATIONS: *Rapport annuel.*

EVALUATION/RECHERCHE: Rapports d'évaluation disponibles. Entreprend des activités de recherche.

COMMENTAIRES: Intervient dans la Communauté des Etats indépendants.

ACTIVITES DANS LES REGIONS EN DEVELOPPEMENT: Intervient directement dans les régions en développement. Maintient une présence locale sur le terrain. Intervient par l'intermédiaire d'organisations locales partenaires.

FRA1852

COMITE AMERIQUE CENTRALE DE CHABLAIS

Les Bolliets 124, 74140 Douvaine, France.

Téléphone: 33 - 50 94 13 41. *Contact:* Joël Perroud, Président.

OBJECTIFS: Faire connaître les réalités de l'Amérique centrale, favoriser les actions de solidarité dans cette région, participer à des opérations de développement.

INFORMATIONS GENERALES: *Création:* 1983. *Type d'organisation:* collectif. *Organisations membres:* 5. *Affiliée à:* Partage et Développement (France). *Personnel/Total:* 3. *Bénévoles:* 3. *Budget/Total 1993:* ECU 15000 (US$ 18000). *Sources financières:* Privé: 51%. Public: 7%. Autofinancement: 42%.

PREVISIONS D'ACTIVITES: Sensibilisation des scolaires principalement, aux problèmes du sous-développement, appui aux organisations de promotion des droits de l'homme au Guatémala

ACTIVITES DANS LES REGIONS EN DEVELOPPEMENT: Intervient dans 2 pays. Intervient par l'intermédiaire d'organisations locales partenaires. **Actions de Développement durable:** Dette/finances/commerce; Droits de l'Homme/paix/conflits; Développement rural/agriculture; Développement urbain/habitat; Questions relatives aux femmes; Éducation/formation/alphabétisation. **Régions:** Mexique et Amerique centrale.

ACTIVITES D'INFORMATION ET D'EDUCATION: Domaines: Culture/tradition/religion; Droits de l'Homme/paix/conflits; Développement rural/agriculture; Développement urbain/habitat; Pauvreté/conditions de vie; Questions relatives aux femmes; Relations internationales/coopération/aide au développement. **Activités:** Campagnes d'information/expositions; Collecte de fonds; Conférences/séminaires/ateliers/activités de formation; Échanges/parrainage/jumelage; Édition/documents audiovisuels/documents éducatifs.

FRA1853

COMITE CATHOLIQUE CONTRE LA FAIM ET POUR LE DEVELOPPEMENT (CCFD)

4 rue Jean Lantier, 75001 Paris, France.

Téléphone: 33 (1) 42 61 51 60. *Fax:* 33 (1) 40 26 11 23. *Contact:* Claude Baehrel, Secrétaire général.

FRA1854

COMITE CHRETIEN D'AIDE AU TIERS-MONDE (CCATM)

17 rue Saint Nicolas, 62290 Noeux-les-Mines, France.

Téléphone: 33 - 21 26 34 24. *Contact:* Michel Huart, Président.

FRA1855

COMITE D'ACTION SOCIALE ET CULTURELLE JEUNESSE D'ETHIOPIE ET DE FRANCE (CASC)

46 avenue du général Billotte, 94000 Créteil, France.

Voir : *Comment utiliser le répertoire,* page 11.

Téléphone: 33 (1) 43 39 26 94. *Fax:* 33 (1) 43 39 26 94. *Contact:* Anne-Marie Maillot, Présidente.

OBJECTIFS: Agir dans les domaines humanitaire, de la santé, de l'éducation et du sport.

INFORMATIONS GENERALES: *Création:* 1988. *Type d'organisation:* regroupement d'ONG. *Personnel/Total:* 50. *Bénévoles:* 50 dont: 50 dans les pays en développement.

PUBLICATIONS: *Rapport annuel. Liste des publications.*

EVALUATION/RECHERCHE: Rapports d'évaluation disponibles.

ACTIVITES DANS LES REGIONS EN DEVELOPPEMENT: Intervient directement dans les régions en développement. Maintient une présence locale sur le terrain. Intervient par l'intermédiaire d'organisations locales partenaires. **Actions de Développement durable:** Aliments/famine; Droits de l'Homme/paix/conflits; Développement urbain/habitat; Enfants/jeunesse/famille; Questions relatives aux femmes; Secours d'urgence/réfugiés/aide humanitaire; Éducation/formation/alphabétisation. **Régions:** Afrique de l'Est.

ACTIVITES D'INFORMATION ET D'EDUCATION: Domaines: Aliments/famine; Culture/tradition/religion; Droits de l'Homme/paix/conflits; Enfants/jeunesse/famille; Paix/conflits ethniques/armement/désarmement; Pauvreté/conditions de vie; Réfugiés/migrants/groupes ethniques; Santé/assainissement/eau; Secours d'urgence/réfugiés/aide humanitaire; Éducation/formation/alphabétisation. **Activités:** Collecte de fonds; Radiodiffusion/manifestations culturelles; Échanges/parrainage/jumelage.

FRA1856

COMITE DE COOPERATION SCIENTIFIQUE ET TECHNIQUE FRANCE-NICARAGUA (CCSTF-N)

2 rue de Sébastopol, 92400 Courbevoie, France.

Téléphone: 33 (1) 47 88 64 28. *Contact:* Michel Picquart, Secrétaire.

OBJECTIFS: Renforcer la coopération scientifique et technique dans les domaines universitaire et de la recherche. Réaliser des projets de développement dans différents secteurs scientifiques au Nicaragua.

INFORMATIONS GENERALES: *Création:* 1981. *Personnel/Total:* 11. *Salariés:* 6. *Bénévoles:* 5 dont: 5 dans les pays en développement. *Budget/Total 1993:* ECU 75000 (US$ 88000). *Sources financières:* Privé: 40%. Public: 50%. Autofinancement: 10%.

COMMENTAIRES: L'organisation n'a pas de titre de publication propre, mais elle participe à "Volcans" revue du COSOPAC (ex-CSN).

ACTIVITES DANS LES REGIONS EN DEVELOPPEMENT: Intervient directement dans les régions en développement. Intervient dans 1 pays. **Actions de Développement durable:** Développement rural/agriculture; Envoi de volontaires/experts/assistance technique; Santé/assainissement/eau; Éducation/formation/alphabétisation. **Régions:** Mexique et Amerique centrale.

ACTIVITES D'INFORMATION ET D'EDUCATION: Domaines: Développement rural/agriculture; Santé/assainissement/eau; Éducation/formation/alphabétisation. **Activités:** Éducation formelle.

FRA1857

COMITE DE JUMELAGE - COMMISSION COOPERATION EPERNAY FADA N'GOURMA

19 rue de l'Arquebuse, 51200 Epernay, France.

Téléphone: 33 - 26 51 92 54. *Contact:* Philippe Paillotin, Vice-président.

FRA1858

COMITE DE LIAISON DES ORGANISATIONS DE SOLIDARITE INTERNATIONALE (CLOSI)

49 rue de la Glacière, 75013 Paris, France.

Téléphone: 33 (1) 40 56 97 78. *Fax:* 33 (1) 43 06 67 07. *Contact:* Bernard Holzer.

FRA1859

COMITE DE LIAISON DES ORGANISATIONS NON GOUVERNEMENTALES DE VOLONTARIAT (CLONG-VOLONTARIAT)

49 rue de la Glacière, 75013 Paris, France.

Téléphone: 33 (1) 43 36 61 18. *Fax:* 33 (1) 43 36 67 07. *Contact:* Annette Irunberry, Secrétaire exécutive.

FRA1860

COMITE DE LIAISON ENERGIES RENOUVELABLES (CLER)

28, rue Bosfoi, 75011 Paris, France.

Téléphone: 33 (1) 46 59 04 44. *Fax:* 33 (1) 46 59 03 92. *Contact:* Liliane Battais, Déléguée générale.

OBJECTIFS: Oeuvrer pour le développement des énergies renouvelables, en vue de préserver l'environnement et de promouvoir l'économie sociale et le développement local.

INFORMATIONS GENERALES: *Création:* 1984. *Type d'organisation:* réseau. *Organisations membres:* 75. *Affiliée à:* Fédération Européenne Energies Renouvelables (France). *Personnel/Total:* 158. *Salariés:* 6. *Budget/Total 1993:* ECU 3769000 (US$ 4414000). *Sources financières:* Public: 80%. Autofinancement: 20%.

PUBLICATIONS: *Rapport annuel. Liste des publications.*

EVALUATION/RECHERCHE: Entreprend des activités de recherche.

COMMENTAIRES: Intervient dans la Communauté des Etats indépendants. Activités d'information concernant la Communauté des Etats indépendants.

ACTIVITES DANS LES REGIONS EN DEVELOPPEMENT: Intervient directement dans les régions en développement. Intervient dans 2 pays. Intervient par l'intermédiaire d'organisations locales partenaires. **Actions de Développement durable:** Développement rural/agriculture; Développement urbain/habitat; Envoi de volontaires/experts/assistance technique; Santé/assainissement/eau; Écologie/environnement/biodiversité; Énergie/transport. **Régions:** Asie du Sud-Est; Caraïbes.

ACTIVITES D'INFORMATION ET D'EDUCATION: Domaines: Développement rural/agriculture; Développement urbain/habitat; Emploi/chômage; Relations internationales/coopération/aide au développement; Santé/assainissement/eau; Écologie/environnement/biodiversité. **Activités:** Conférences/séminaires/ateliers/activités de formation; Services d'information et de documentation/bases de données; Échanges/parrainage/jumelage; Édition/documents audiovisuels/documents éducatifs.

FRA1861

COMITE DE SAINT PIERRE ET MIQUELON D'AIDE AU DEVELOPPEMENT ET DE LUTTE CONTRE LA FAIM DANS LE MONDE ♦ St Pierre et Miquelon F.F.H.C. Committee

28 rue Balzac, 92600 Asnières, France.

Téléphone: 33 (1) 58 41 33 50. *Contact:* Françoise Claireaux, Présidente.

OBJECTIFS: Sensibiliser l'opinion publique et les instances de décision nationales et internationales à la question des pêches traditionnelles dans les pays du Sud. Soutenir des projets de développement pour la modernisation des pêches traditionnelles, le développement agricole et l'action sanitaire.

INFORMATIONS GENERALES: *Création:* 1967. *Personnel/Total:* 10. *Bénévoles:* 10. *Sources financières:* Privé: 90%. Autofinancement: 10%.

PUBLICATIONS: *Rapport annuel.*

ACTIVITES DANS LES REGIONS EN DEVELOPPEMENT: Intervient directement dans les régions en développement. Intervient dans 1 pays. Intervient par l'intermédiaire d'organisations locales partenaires. **Actions de Développement durable:** Développement rural/agriculture; Petites entreprises/secteur informel/artisanat; Questions relatives aux femmes; Santé/assainissement/eau. **Régions:** Afrique centrale; Afrique de l'Ouest.

                                                                   See: *How to Use the Directory*, page 11.

ACTIVITES D'INFORMATION ET D'EDUCATION: **Domaines:** Développement rural/agriculture; Questions relatives aux femmes; Relations internationales/coopération/aide au développement; Santé/assainissement/eau. **Activités:** Campagnes d'information/expositions; Collecte de fonds; Conférences/séminaires/ateliers/activités de formation.

FRA1862

COMITE DE SOUTIEN AU PEUPLE TIBETAIN (CSPT)

2 rue d'Agnou, 78580 Maule, France.

Fax: 33 (1) 30 90 88 25. *Contact:* J.P. Ribes, Président.

OBJECTIFS: Défendre l'identité culturelle et les droits du peuple Tibétain, par des actions d'information et de solidarité mobilisant les responsables politiques, les média et l'opinion publique.

INFORMATIONS GENERALES: *Création:* 1987. *Type d'organisation:* regroupement d'ONG. *Personnel/Total:* 15. *Bénévoles:* 15. *Budget/Total 1993:* ECU 15000 (US$ 18000). *Sources financières:* Autofinancement: 100%.

PUBLICATIONS: *Périodiques:* Le Bulletin du CSPT (4) - La Lettre du Tibet (12). *Liste des publications.*

ACTIVITES DANS LES REGIONS EN DEVELOPPEMENT: Intervient directement dans les régions en développement. Intervient dans 3 pays. Maintient une présence locale sur le terrain. Intervient par l'intermédiaire d'organisations locales partenaires. **Actions de Développement durable:** Droits de l'Homme/paix/conflits; Démocratie/bonne gestion publique/création d'institutions/développement participatif; Questions relatives aux femmes; Secours d'urgence/réfugiés/aide humanitaire; Écologie/environnement/biodiversité. **Régions:** Asie centrale et Asie du Sud.

ACTIVITES D'INFORMATION ET D'EDUCATION: Domaines: Culture/tradition/religion; Droits de l'Homme/paix/conflits; Paix/conflits ethniques/armement/désarmement; Population/planning familial/démographie; Questions relatives aux femmes; Racisme/xénophobie/antisémitisme; Relations économiques internationales/commerce/dette/finances; Réfugiés/migrants/groupes ethniques; Secours d'urgence/réfugiés/aide humanitaire; Écologie/environnement/biodiversité. **Activités:** Campagnes d'information/expositions; Conférences/séminaires/ateliers/activités de formation; Lobbying/plaidoyer; Radiodiffusion/manifestations culturelles; Réseaux/télécommunications électroniques; Échanges/parrainage/jumelage; Édition/documents audiovisuels/documents éducatifs.

FRA1863

COMITE ECHANGES ISERE-KIVU (CEIK) ♦ Isère-Kivu Exchange Committee

1 place des Tilleuls, 38000 Grenoble, France.

Contact: O. Cazaillet, Président.

OBJECTIFS: Développer les échanges culturels et techniques entre les populations de l'Isère, en France, et celle du Kivu, au Zaïre. Etre solidaire de ceux qui, au Kivu, luttent pour leur propre développement et soutenir leurs efforts.

INFORMATIONS GENERALES: *Création:* 1981. *Organisations membres:* 6. *Budget/Total 1993:* ECU 35000 (US$ 40000). *Sources financières:* Privé: 23%. Public: 72%. Autofinancement: 5%.

PUBLICATIONS: *Périodiques:* L'Echange (1).

COMMENTAIRES: Le CEIK cherche des associations au Kivu et en Europe susceptibles de prendre sa succession, car lui-même arrive en bout de course.

ACTIVITES DANS LES REGIONS EN DEVELOPPEMENT: Intervient directement dans les régions en développement. Intervient dans 1 pays. Intervient par l'intermédiaire d'organisations locales partenaires. **Actions de Développement durable:** Démocratie/bonne gestion publique/création d'institutions/développement participatif; Envoi de volontaires/experts/assistance technique; Santé/assainissement/eau; Éducation/formation/alphabétisation. **Régions:** Afrique centrale.

FRA1864

COMITE EUROPEEN DE L'ASSOCIATION MONDIALE DES GUIDES ET DES ECLAIREUSES

7 rue de Wissembourg, 67000 Strasbourg, France.

Contact: Catherine Mies-Schaller.

FRA1865

COMITE FRANCAIS CONTRE LA FAIM (CFCF)

8 rue du Dobropol, 75017 Paris, France.

Téléphone: 33 (1) 40 55 09 33. *Fax:* 33 (1) 45 74 22 48. *Contact:* Bernard Husson, Délégué Général.

OBJECTIFS: Informer l'opinion publique sur les problèmes de la faim et du développement. Soutenir les projets favorisant la capacité d'organisation des communautés dans les pays en développement. Coopérer pour cela avec les organisations membres, associations, organisations professionnelles, collectivités locales, entreprises, centres de recherche... qui gèrent la plupart des opérations.

INFORMATIONS GENERALES: *Création:* 1960. *Organisations membres:* 30. *Affiliée à:* CECCM (Mali) - Plate-forme Européenne des ONG - Institut Belleville (France). *Personnel/Total:* 25. *Salariés:* 15. *Bénévoles:* 10. *Budget/Total 1993:* ECU 2231000 (US$ 2613000). *Sources financières:* Privé: 60%. Public: 35%. Autofinancement: 5%.

PUBLICATIONS: *Périodiques:* Nations Solidaires (4). *Liste des publications.*

EVALUATION/RECHERCHE: Rapports d'évaluation disponibles.

PREVISIONS D'ACTIVITES: Coordination de la campagne "Demain le Monde...l'Eau"

ACTIVITES DANS LES REGIONS EN DEVELOPPEMENT: Intervient par l'intermédiaire d'organisations locales partenaires. **Actions de Développement durable:** Aliments/famine; Développement urbain/habitat; Enfants/jeunesse/famille; Petites entreprises/secteur informel/artisanat; Questions relatives aux femmes; Santé/assainissement/eau; Écologie/environnement/biodiversité; Éducation/formation/alphabétisation; Énergie/transport. **Régions:** Afrique australe; Afrique centrale; Afrique de l'Ouest; Amérique du Sud; Asie de l'Est; Asie du Sud-Est; Caraïbes; Moyen-Orient.

FRA1866

COMITE FRANCAIS DE SOUTIEN GK-SAVAR BANGLADESH

23 esplanade Raoul Follereau, 92130 Issy-les-Moulineaux, France.

Téléphone: 33 (1) 46 45 39 57. *Fax:* 33 (1) 60 26 22 92. *Contact:* Lucien Bigeault, Président.

OBJECTIFS: Soutenir humainement et matériellement G.K-Savar Bangladesh qui est une organisation non gouvernementale de développement intégré animé par une équipe pluridisciplinaire bangalaises. Les activités portent sur la santé, l'éducation des enfants et des adultes, la formation paramédicale et artisanale, le développement agricole, le crédit rural, les secours d'urgence et l'assistance des populations sinistrées lors de catastrophes naturelles.

INFORMATIONS GENERALES: *Création:* 1972. *Personnel/Total:* 28. *Budget/Total 1993:* ECU 53000 (US$ 62000).

PUBLICATIONS: *Liste des publications.*

PREVISIONS D'ACTIVITES: Soutien aux écoles primaires installées dans les abris anti-cyclone de la zone de Coxs Baza

ACTIVITES DANS LES REGIONS EN DEVELOPPEMENT: Intervient dans 1 pays. Intervient par l'intermédiaire d'organisations locales partenaires. **Actions de Développement durable:** Développement rural/agriculture; Enfants/jeunesse/famille; Questions relatives aux femmes; Santé/assainissement/eau; Secours d'urgence/réfugiés/aide humanitaire; Éducation/formation/alphabétisation. **Régions:** Asie centrale et Asie du Sud.

ACTIVITES D'INFORMATION ET D'EDUCATION: Domaines: Développement rural/agriculture; Enfants/jeunesse/famille; Questions relatives aux femmes; Santé/assainissement/eau; Secours d'urgence/réfugiés/aide humanitaire. **Activités:** Collecte de fonds.

FRA1867

COMITE FRANCAIS POUR L'ENVIRONNEMENT (CFE)

B.P. 43, 92204 Neuilly-sur-Seine cedex, France.

Téléphone: 33 (1) 47 45 42 58. *Fax:* 33 (1) 47 38 20 18. *Contact:* Jean-Marc Proust, Chargé de mission.

FRA1868

COMITE FRANCAIS POUR L'UNICEF

3 rue Duguay-Trouin, 75282 Paris cedex 06, France.

Téléphone: 33 (1) 44 39 77 77. *Fax:* 33 (1) 44 39 77 20. *Contact:* François Rémy, Président.

FRA1869

COMITE LAIQUE POUR L'EDUCATION AU DEVELOPPEMENT - EDUCATEURS SANS FRONTIERES (CLED-ESF)

28 boulevard Bonne-Nouvelle, 75010 Paris, France.

Téléphone: 33 (1) 45 23 10 81. *Fax:* 33 (1) 48 01 08 69. *Contact:* Alain Roux, Délégué Général.

OBJECTIFS: Sensibiliser en France comme à l'étranger, l'opinion publique aux problèmes du développement. Promouvoir dans les milieux scolaires et associatifs l'éducation au développement. Promouvoir des actions de solidarité avec nos partenaires homologues du Tiers Monde.

INFORMATIONS GENERALES: *Création:* 1983. *Type d'organisation:* collectif. *Organisations membres:* 16. *Affiliée à:* Comité de Liaison des Organisations de Solidarité Internationale (France). *Personnel/ Total:* 100. *Bénévoles:* 100 dont: 20 dans les pays en développement. *Budget/Total 1993:* ECU 94000 (US$ 110000). *Sources financières:* Privé: 30%. Public: 50%. *Autofinancement:* 20%.

PUBLICATIONS: *Périodiques:* CLED Nouvelles (2). *Liste des publications.*

EVALUATION/RECHERCHE: Rapports d'évaluation disponibles.

COMMENTAIRES: Intervient dans la Communauté des Etats indépendants.

ACTIVITES DANS LES REGIONS EN DEVELOPPEMENT: Intervient directement dans les régions en développement. Intervient dans 8 pays. Intervient par l'intermédiaire d'organisations locales partenaires. **Actions de Développement durable:** Éducation/formation/alphabétisation. **Régions:** Afrique de l'Ouest; Amérique du Sud; Asie du Sud-Est.

ACTIVITES D'INFORMATION ET D'EDUCATION: Domaines: Éducation/ formation/alphabétisation. **Activités:** Campagnes d'information/expositions; Conférences/séminaires/ateliers/activités de formation; Échanges/parrainage/jumelage; Édition/documents audiovisuels/documents éducatifs; Éducation formelle.

FRA1870

COMITE MEDICAL POUR LES EXILES (COMEDE)

78 rue du Général Leclerc, B.P. 31, 94270 Le Kremlin Bicêtre, France.

Téléphone: 33 (1) 45 21 38 40. *Contact:* Patrick August, Directeur.

FRA1871

COMITE NATIONAL DE SOLIDARITE LAIQUE

62 boulevard Garibaldi, 75015 Paris, France.

Téléphone: 33 (1) 47 83 66 66. *Fax:* 33 (1) 40 61 96 38. *Contact:* Guy Georges, Président.

OBJECTIFS: Venir en aide , en France et dans le monde, aux personnes victimes de catastrophes, de la misère, de la maladie, de la guerre et du racisme.

INFORMATIONS GENERALES: *Création:* 1981. *Type d'organisation:* regroupement d'ONG. *Organisations membres:* 55. *Personnel/Total:* 172. *Salariés:* 2. *Bénévoles:* 170 dont: 120 dans les pays en développement. *Budget/Total 1993:*

ECU 377000 (US$ 441000). *Sources financières:* Privé: 27%. Public: 52%. *Autofinancement:* 5%.

PUBLICATIONS: *Périodiques:* Contact (2).

COMMENTAIRES: Intervient dans la Communauté des Etats indépendants. Activités d'information concernant la Communauté des Etats indépendants.

ACTIVITES DANS LES REGIONS EN DEVELOPPEMENT: Intervient par l'intermédiaire d'organisations locales partenaires. **Actions de Développement durable:** Démocratie/bonne gestion publique/création d'institutions/développement participatif; Enfants/jeunesse/famille; Éducation/formation/alphabétisation. **Régions:** Afrique australe; Afrique de l'Ouest; Afrique du Nord; Asie de l'Est; Asie du Sud-Est.

ACTIVITES D'INFORMATION ET D'EDUCATION: Domaines: Droits de l'Homme/paix/conflits; Enfants/jeunesse/famille; Secours d'urgence/ réfugiés/aide humanitaire; Éducation/formation/alphabétisation. **Activités:** Collecte de fonds; Conférences/séminaires/ateliers/activités de formation; Radiodiffusion/manifestations culturelles; Services d'information et de documentation/bases de données; Échanges/parrainage/ jumelage.

FRA1872

COMITE NATIONAL POUR L'INDEPENDANCE ET LE DEVELOPPEMENT (CNID) ♦ National Committee for Independence and Development

139 boulevard Victor Hugo, 93400 Saint-Ouen, France.

Téléphone: 33 (1) 40 12 09 12.

FRA1873

COMITE POUR LERE

14 avenue Berthelot, 69007 Lyon, France.

Téléphone: 33 - 78 69 79 55. *Fax:* 33 - 78 69 79 52. *Contact:* Alain Hattet, Président.

FRA1874

COMITE POUR LES RELATIONS NATIONALES ET INTERNATIONALES DES ASSOCIATIONS DE JEUNESSE ET D'EDUCATION POPULAIRE (CNAJEP)

15 rue Martel, 75010 Paris, France.

Téléphone: 33 (1) 47 70 71 31. *Contact:* Alain Goze, Président.

FRA1875

COMITE TOULOUSE-BAURU/FRANCE-BRESIL (CTB)

11 boulevard Carnot, 31000 Toulouse, France.

Téléphone: 33 - 61 33 09 41. *Fax:* 33 - 61 33 09 41. *Contact:* Oswaldo Penna, Président.

FRA1876

COMMISSION LUTHERIENNE DES RELATIONS AVEC LES EGLISES D'OUTRE-MER (COLUREOM)

16, rue Chauchat, 75009 Paris, France.

Contact: Jean-Georges Barth, Secrétaire général.

OBJECTIFS: Apporter une aide financière et en personnel pour réaliser des projets d'assistance sanitaire et d'éducation des populations, ceci à la demande des partenaires africains.

INFORMATIONS GENERALES: *Création:* 1968. *Type d'organisation:* regroupement d'ONG. *Affiliée à:* Alliance Nationale des Eglises Luthériennes de France (France) - Fédération Protestante de France (France) - Fédération Luthérienne Mondiale (Suisse). *Personnel/Total:* 30. *Bénévoles:* 30 dont: 10 dans les pays en développement. *Budget/Total 1993:* ECU 106000 (US$ 124000). *Sources financières:* Privé: 100%.

PUBLICATIONS: *Périodiques:* "Eglise Missionnaire" (4). *Rapport annuel.*

ACTIVITES DANS LES REGIONS EN DEVELOPPEMENT: Intervient directement dans les régions en développement. Intervient dans 10 pays. Maintient une présence locale sur le terrain. Intervient par l'intermédiaire d'organisations locales partenaires. **Actions de Développe-**

ment durable: Droits de l'Homme/paix/conflits; Développement rural/agriculture; Enfants/jeunesse/famille; Envoi de volontaires/experts/assistance technique; Questions relatives aux femmes; Santé/assainissement/eau; Secours d'urgence/réfugiés/aide humanitaire; Éducation/formation/alphabétisation. **Régions:** Afrique australe; Afrique centrale; Afrique de l'Ouest.

ACTIVITES D'INFORMATION ET D'EDUCATION: Domaines: Aliments/famine; Culture/tradition/religion; Droits de l'Homme/paix/conflits; Développement rural/agriculture; Enfants/jeunesse/famille; Paix/conflits ethniques/armement/désarmement; Pauvreté/conditions de vie; Questions relatives aux femmes; Racisme/xénophobie/antisémitisme; Relations internationales/coopération/aide au développement; Santé/assainissement/eau; Secours d'urgence/réfugiés/aide humanitaire; Écologie/environnement/biodiversité; Éducation/formation/alphabétisation. **Activités:** Campagnes d'information/expositions; Collecte de fonds; Lobbying/plaidoyer; Échanges/parrainage/jumelage.

FRA1877

COMMISSION NATIONALE DE LA JEUNESSE POUR LE DEVELOPPEMENT (CNJD)

5 place de Vénétie, 75643 Paris cedex 13, France.

Téléphone: 33 (1) 45 86 84 32. *Fax:* 33 (1) 45 86 64 92. *Contact:* Claude Cournot, Président.

FRA1878

COMPAGNONS BATISSEURS (CB)

5 rue des Immeubles Industriels, 75011 Paris, France.

Téléphone: 33 (1) 43 73 70 63. *Fax:* 33 (1) 43 73 72 26. *Contact:* Tom Roberts, Délégué international.

FRA1879

CONFERENCE PERMANENTE DES COMPAGNIES CONSULAIRES AFRICAINES ET FRANCAISES (CPCCA & F)

2, rue de Viarmes, 75001 Paris, France.

Téléphone: 33 (1) 45 08 35 28/45 08 35 67. *Fax:* 33 (1) 45 08 39 40. *Contact:* Jean Secheresse, Secrétaire général Rémy Poliwa, Conseiller Technique.

OBJECTIFS: Favoriser les relations internationales euro-africaines et l'assistance dans les missions de représentation, de formation, d'information économique et de gestion des équipements.

INFORMATIONS GENERALES: *Création:* 1973. *Type d'organisation:* réseau. *Personnel/Total:* 3. *Salariés:* 2. *Bénévoles:* 1. *Budget/Total 1993:* ECU 168000 (US$ 197000). *Sources financières:* Public: 50%. *Autofinancement:* 50%.

PUBLICATIONS: *Périodiques:* Bulletin de liaison interconsulaire Franco africain (2).

PREVISIONS D'ACTIVITES: Elargissement du réseau aux compagnies consulaires non francophones et aux membres associés.

ACTIVITES DANS LES REGIONS EN DEVELOPPEMENT: Intervient directement dans les régions en développement. Intervient dans 10 pays. Maintient une présence locale sur le terrain. Intervient par l'intermédiaire d'organisations locales partenaires. **Actions de Développement durable:** Dette/finances/commerce; Démocratie/bonne gestion publique/création d'institutions/développement participatif; Développement rural/agriculture; Envoi de volontaires/experts/assistance technique; Petites entreprises/secteur informel/artisanat; Éducation/formation/alphabétisation; Énergie/transport. **Régions:** Afrique australe; Afrique centrale; Afrique de l'Est; Afrique de l'Ouest.

ACTIVITES D'INFORMATION ET D'EDUCATION: Domaines: Relations internationales/coopération/aide au développement; Relations économiques internationales/commerce/dette/finances; Éducation/formation/alphabétisation. **Activités:** Conférences/séminaires/ateliers/activités de formation; Lobbying/plaidoyer; Éducation formelle.

FRA1880

CONGREGATION DES MISSIONS AFRICAINES PROVINCE DE LYON (SMA)

36, rue Miguel Hidalgo, 75019 Paris, France.

Téléphone: 33 (1) 42 06 22 48. *Fax:* 33 (1) 40 40 04 51. *Contact:* François Feneon, Provincial.

OBJECTIFS: Soutenir temporellement et spirituellement l'Afrique, grâce à l'Eglise. Aider les populations africaines dans leur pays d'origine ou hors d'Afrique.

INFORMATIONS GENERALES: *Création:* 1856. *Affiliée à:* Missions africaines (Italie). *Personnel/Total:* 294. *Bénévoles:* 254 dont: 154 dans les pays en développement. *Budget/Total 1993:* ECU 1809000 (US$ 2119000). *Sources financières:* Privé: 100%.

PUBLICATIONS: *Périodiques:* L'Appel de l'Afrique (4).

ACTIVITES DANS LES REGIONS EN DEVELOPPEMENT: Intervient directement dans les régions en développement. Intervient dans 11 pays. Maintient une présence locale sur le terrain. Intervient par l'intermédiaire d'organisations locales partenaires. **Actions de Développement durable:** Dette/finances/commerce; Droits de l'Homme/paix/conflits; Développement rural/agriculture; Enfants/jeunesse/famille; Envoi de volontaires/experts/assistance technique; Petites entreprises/secteur informel/artisanat; Questions relatives aux femmes; Santé/assainissement/eau; Secours d'urgence/réfugiés/aide humanitaire; Écologie/environnement/biodiversité; Éducation/formation/alphabétisation. **Régions:** Afrique centrale; Afrique de l'Ouest.

ACTIVITES D'INFORMATION ET D'EDUCATION: Domaines: Culture/tradition/religion; Droits de l'Homme/paix/conflits; Pauvreté/conditions de vie; Relations internationales/coopération/aide au développement; Réfugiés/migrants/groupes ethniques; Secours d'urgence/réfugiés/aide humanitaire; Éducation/formation/alphabétisation. **Activités:** Collecte de fonds; Radiodiffusion/manifestations culturelles.

FRA1881

CONSEIL DES INVESTISSEURS FRANCAIS EN AFRIQUE (CIAN)

190 boulevard Haussmann, 75008 Paris, France.

Téléphone: 33 (1) 45 62 55 76. *Contact:* Jean-Pierre Ranchon.

FRA1882

CONSEIL EUROPEEN DES ETUDES AFRICAINES

3 rue de l'Argonne, 67083 Strasbourg cedex, France.

Contact: Jean-Pierre Blanck.

FRA1883

CONSEIL INTERNATIONAL DES UNIONS SCIENTIFIQUES (ICSU) ♦ International Council of Scientific Unions

51, boulevard de Montmorency, 75016 Paris, France.

Téléphone: 33 - 45 25 03 29. *Fax:* 33 - 42 88 94 31. *Contact:* Julia Marton-Lefevre.

OBJECTIFS: Promouvoir l'activité scientifique internationale dans les différentes branches de la science et leurs applications pour le bénéfice de l'humanité.

INFORMATIONS GENERALES: *Création:* 1931.

PUBLICATIONS: *Périodiques:* The ICSU Yearbook (1) - Science International (4). *Rapport annuel.*

EVALUATION/RECHERCHE: Entreprend des activités de recherche.

ACTIVITES D'INFORMATION ET D'EDUCATION: Domaines: Autres; Écologie/environnement/biodiversité. **Activités:** Conférences/séminaires/ateliers/activités de formation; Édition/documents audiovisuels/documents éducatifs.

FRA1884

CONSEIL INTERNATIONAL DU CINEMA, DE LA TELEVISION ET DE LA COMMUNICATION AUDIOVISUELLE

1 rue Miollis, 75732 Paris cedex 15, France.

Contact: Gérard Bolla.

Voir : *Comment utiliser le répertoire,* page 11.

FRA1885

CONTRIBUTION A LA COMMUNICATION ET A L'ECHANGE D'EXPERIENCES POUR UN MEILLEUR DEVELOPPEMENT (CONCED)

5, Les Aulnes, 77680 Roissy-en-Brie, France.

Téléphone: 33 (1) 60 29 53 96. *Contact:* Jacques Nsoumbi.

OBJECTIFS: Rechercher, étudier et valoriser, à l'échelle de la Planète, des domaines de compétences intellectuelles humaines favorisant le développement international. Renforcer le jumelage Nord/Sud. Diffuser par tous les moyens les expériences des membres pouvant susciter le développement.

INFORMATIONS GENERALES: *Création:* 1991. *Personnel/Total:* 2. *Bénévoles:* 2 dont: 1 dans les pays en développement. *Budget/ Total 1993:* ECU 4500 (US$ 5000). *Sources financières:* Privé: 70%. *Autofinancement:* 30%.

EVALUATION/RECHERCHE: Entreprend des activités de recherche.

ACTIVITES DANS LES REGIONS EN DEVELOPPEMENT: Intervient directement dans les régions en développement. Intervient par l'intermédiaire d'organisations locales partenaires. **Actions de Développement durable:** Démocratie/bonne gestion publique/création d'institutions/développement participatif; Enfants/jeunesse/famille; Éducation/ formation/alphabétisation. **Régions:** Afrique centrale; Afrique de l'Ouest.

ACTIVITES D'INFORMATION ET D'EDUCATION: Domaines: Développement rural/agriculture; Développement urbain/habitat; Enfants/jeunesse/famille; Relations internationales/coopération/aide au développement. **Activités:** Campagnes d'information/expositions; Conférences/ séminaires/ateliers/activités de formation; Échanges/parrainage/ jumelage.

FRA1886

COOPERATION DEVELOPPEMENT INDUSTRIEL ET FORMATION (CODIFOR)

13, rue Blaise Pascal, 54320 Maxeville, France.

Téléphone: 33 - 83 95 35 11. *Fax:* 33 - 83 98 09 00. *Contact:* Jean-Luc Martin.

OBJECTIFS: Réaliser des opérations d'ingénierie pédagogique au niveau international, avec notamment la mise en place de programmes de formation professionnelle et la conception d'équipements adaptés. Mener des études et des audits liés au développement économique et industriel. Promouvoir le partenariat d'entreprises.

INFORMATIONS GENERALES: *Création:* 1981. *Personnel/Total:* 12. *Salariés:* 12 dont: 3 dans les pays en développement. *Budget/ Total 1993:* ECU 1357000 (US$ 1589000). *Sources financières:* Public: 20%. *Autofinancement:* 80%.

PUBLICATIONS: *Rapport annuel. Liste des publications.*

COMMENTAIRES: Intervient dans la Communauté des Etats indépendants. Activités d'information concernant la Communauté des Etats indépendants.

ACTIVITES DANS LES REGIONS EN DEVELOPPEMENT: Intervient directement dans les régions en développement. Intervient dans 10 pays. Maintient une présence locale sur le terrain. Intervient par l'intermédiaire d'organisations locales partenaires. **Actions de Développement durable:** Envoi de volontaires/experts/assistance technique; Petites entreprises/secteur informel/artisanat; Éducation/formation/ alphabétisation. **Régions:** Afrique centrale; Afrique de l'Est; Afrique de l'Ouest; Afrique du Nord; Amérique du Sud; Asie centrale et Asie du Sud; Asie du Sud-Est; Moyen-Orient.

ACTIVITES D'INFORMATION ET D'EDUCATION: Domaines: Emploi/ chômage; Relations internationales/coopération/aide au développement; Éducation/formation/alphabétisation. **Activités:** Conférences/ séminaires/ateliers/activités de formation; Services d'information et de documentation/bases de données; Échanges/parrainage/jumelage; Édition/documents audiovisuels/documents éducatifs; Éducation formelle.

FRA1887

COORDINATING COMMITTEE FOR INTERNATIONAL VOLUNTARY SERVICE (CCIVS) ♦ Comité de Coordination du Service Volontaire International

Maison de l'UNESCO, 1 rue Miollis, 75015 Paris, France.

Téléphone: 33 (1) 45 68 27 31. *Fax:* 33 (1) 42 73 05 21. *Contact:* Nigel Watt, Directeur.

OBJECTIFS: Coordonner les activités des organismes de service volontaire. Promouvoir le volontariat,la compréhension internationale et la solidarité dans le monde.

INFORMATIONS GENERALES: *Création:* 1948. *Organisations membres:* 130. *Personnel/Total:* 3. *Salariés:* 2. *Bénévoles:* 1 dont: 1 dans les pays en développement. *Budget/Total 1993:* ECU 33000 (US$ 39000). *Sources financières:* Privé: 25%. Public: 50%. *Autofinancement:* 25%.

PUBLICATIONS: *Périodiques:* CCIVS News (3). *Liste des publications.*

EVALUATION/RECHERCHE: Rapports d'évaluation disponibles. Entreprend des activités de recherche.

COMMENTAIRES: Intervient dans la Communauté des Etats indépendants.

ACTIVITES DANS LES REGIONS EN DEVELOPPEMENT: Intervient directement dans les régions en développement. Intervient dans 2 pays. Intervient par l'intermédiaire d'organisations locales partenaires. **Actions de Développement durable:** Développement rural/agriculture; Développement urbain/habitat; Enfants/jeunesse/ famille; Questions relatives aux femmes; Santé/assainissement/eau; Secours d'urgence/réfugiés/aide humanitaire; Écologie/environnement/ biodiversité; Éducation/formation/alphabétisation. **Régions:** Afrique australe; Afrique centrale; Afrique de l'Est; Afrique de l'Ouest; Afrique du Nord; Asie centrale et Asie du Sud.

ACTIVITES D'INFORMATION ET D'EDUCATION: Domaines: Paix/ conflits ethniques/armement/désarmement; Racisme/xénophobie/antisémitisme; Relations internationales/coopération/aide au développement; Réfugiés/migrants/groupes ethniques; Secours d'urgence/réfugiés/aide humanitaire; Écologie/environnement/biodiversité. **Activités:** Conférences/séminaires/ateliers/activités de formation; Échanges/parrainage/jumelage.

FRA1888

COORDINATION D'AGEN POUR LES MISSIONS D'URGENCE ET DE COOPERATION VOLONTAIRE

11, rue de Vaugirard, 75006 Paris, France.

Téléphone: 33 (1) 43 26 97 52. *Fax:* 33 (1) 46 34 75 45. *Contact:* Jean Claude Buchet, Président.

OBJECTIFS: Coordonner les activités des ONG membres. Harmoniser leurs rapports avec les partenaires publics ou privés.

INFORMATIONS GENERALES: *Création:* 1988. *Type d'organisation:* réseau. *Organisations membres:* 17. *Affiliée à:* Solidarité Urgence Développement (France). *Personnel/Total:* 5. *Salariés:* 1. *Bénévoles:* 4. *Budget/Total 1993:* ECU 75000 (US$ 88000). *Sources financières:* Privé: 100%.

PUBLICATIONS: *Périodiques:* France-pays du Mékong Info (6). *Rapport annuel.*

EVALUATION/RECHERCHE: Rapports d'évaluation disponibles.

PREVISIONS D'ACTIVITES: La prévention des crises humanitaires. Le partenariat entre coopération publique et privée. Zones d'activité: Rwanda et la Péninsule Indochinoise.

ACTIVITES DANS LES REGIONS EN DEVELOPPEMENT: Intervient par l'intermédiaire d'organisations locales partenaires.

ACTIVITES D'INFORMATION ET D'EDUCATION: Domaines: Autres; Relations internationales/coopération/aide au développement; Secours d'urgence/réfugiés/aide humanitaire. **Activités:** Campagnes d'information/expositions; Collecte de fonds; Conférences/séminaires/ateliers/ activités de formation; Lobbying/plaidoyer.

See: *How to Use the Directory,* page 11.

FRA1889
COORDINATION INFORMATION TIERS-MONDE (CITIM)

70, rue de Bayeux, 14000 Caen, France.

Téléphone: 33 - 31 85 20 78. *Contact:* Pierre Morice, Président.

OBJECTIFS: Informer le public de Basse Normandie sur les problèmes de développement des pays du Tiers monde et sur l'immigration.

INFORMATIONS GENERALES: *Création:* 1979. *Affiliée à:* CRID (France) - RITIMO. *Personnel/Total:* 3. *Salariés:* 2. *Bénévoles:* 1. *Budget/Total 1993:* ECU 19000 (US$ 22000). *Sources financières:* Privé: 9%. Public: 6%. Autofinancement: 85%.

PUBLICATIONS: *Périodiques:* Bulletin CITIM (4).

ACTIVITES D'INFORMATION ET D'EDUCATION: Domaines: Aliments/famine; Culture/tradition/religion; Droits de l'Homme/paix/conflits; Développement rural/agriculture; Développement urbain/habitat; Emploi/chômage; Enfants/jeunesse/famille; Paix/conflits ethniques/armement/désarmement; Pauvreté/conditions de vie; Population/planning familial/démographie; Questions relatives aux femmes; Racisme/xénophobie/antisémitisme; Relations internationales/coopération/aide au développement; Relations économiques internationales/commerce/dette/finances; Réfugiés/migrants/groupes ethniques; Santé/assainissement/eau; Secours d'urgence/réfugiés/aide humanitaire; Écologie/environnement/biodiversité; Éducation/formation/alphabétisation. **Activités:** Campagnes d'information/expositions; Collecte de fonds; Conférences/séminaires/ateliers/activités de formation; Lobbying/plaidoyer; Radiodiffusion/manifestations culturelles; Réseaux/télécommunications électroniques; Services d'information et de documentation/bases de données; Échanges/parrainage/jumelage; Édition/documents audiovisuels/documents éducatifs; Éducation formelle.

FRA1890
CORPS MONDIAL DE SECOURS (CMS)

11 bis rue Lord Byron, 75008 Paris, France.

Téléphone: 33 (1) 45 63 86 24. *Fax:* 33 (1) 40 84 28 90. *Contact:* Pierre Micheleau, Délégué général.

FRA1891
LES COUREURS DU MONDE ♦ World Runners

8, rue de la Mare, 75020 Paris, France.

Téléphone: 33 (1) 46 36 50 89. *Contact:* Claude Lupu, Président.

OBJECTIFS: Contribuer à l'élimination de la faim dans le monde d'ici à l'an 2000, en utilisant la course à pied pour susciter l'engagement des individus. Financer, avec d'autres associations, des projets dans les pays en développement et dans le Quart Monde, qui soient créateurs d'avenir et d'autonomie.

INFORMATIONS GENERALES: *Création:* 1983. *Type d'organisation:* réseau. *Organisations membres:* 30. *Affiliée à:* World Runners Europe - World Runners International. *Personnel/Total:* 170. *Bénévoles:* 170. *Budget/Total 1993:* ECU 8000 (US$ 9000). *Sources financières:* Privé: 20%. Autofinancement: 80%.

PUBLICATIONS: *Périodiques:* Journal des Coureurs du Monde (6).

EVALUATION/RECHERCHE: Rapports d'évaluation disponibles.

PREVISIONS D'ACTIVITES: Création d'un collectif Sport Solidarité: réseau d'associations humanitaires et/ou sportives pour mettre en place des moyens d'entraides entre ces associations, notamment en matière d'information.

ACTIVITES DANS LES REGIONS EN DEVELOPPEMENT: Intervient dans 1 pays. Intervient par l'intermédiaire d'organisations locales partenaires. **Actions de Développement durable:** Aliments/famine; Enfants/jeunesse/famille; Éducation/formation/alphabétisation. **Régions:** Asie du Sud-Est.

ACTIVITES D'INFORMATION ET D'EDUCATION: Domaines: Aliments/famine; Enfants/jeunesse/famille; Pauvreté/conditions de vie; Éducation/formation/alphabétisation. **Activités:** Collecte de fonds.

FRA1892
CROIX ROUGE FRANCAISE (CRF)

1 place Henry Dunant, 75008 Paris , France.

Téléphone: 33 (1) 44 43 11 00. *Fax:* 33 (1) 44 43 11 01. *Contact:* André Delaude, Président.

FRA1893
CULTURE ET DEVELOPPEMENT (CED)

9, rue de la Poste, 38000 Grenoble, France.

Téléphone: 33 (16) 76 46 80 29. *Fax:* 33 (16) 76 46 06 05. *Contact:* François-Noël Simoneau, Président.

OBJECTIFS: Promouvoir des projets de coopération pour le développement culturel en Afrique, au niveau des villes et du monde rural, dans les domaines de l'écrit (livres, lecture), du patrimoine culturel et des rapports entre l'éducation et la culture: information-conseil, formation, publication de guides et d'ouvrages de réflexion, inventaires des actions, études.

INFORMATIONS GENERALES: *Création:* 1962. *Affiliée à:* "Lire au-delà des Mers" (France). *Personnel/Total:* 28. *Salariés:* 25. *Bénévoles:* 3. *Budget/Total 1993:* ECU 226000 (US$ 265000). *Sources financières:* Privé: 5%. Public: 90%. Autofinancement: 5%.

PUBLICATIONS: *Périodiques:* Guide des échanges culturels France-Afrique - Bulletin Territoires-Culture (2). *Liste des publications.*

ACTIVITES DANS LES REGIONS EN DEVELOPPEMENT: Intervient dans 5 pays. Intervient par l'intermédiaire d'organisations locales partenaires. **Actions de Développement durable:** Éducation/formation/alphabétisation. **Régions:** Afrique centrale; Afrique de l'Ouest.

ACTIVITES D'INFORMATION ET D'EDUCATION: Domaines: Culture/tradition/religion; Relations internationales/coopération/aide au développement; Éducation/formation/alphabétisation. **Activités:** Conférences/séminaires/ateliers/activités de formation; Radiodiffusion/manifestations culturelles; Édition/documents audiovisuels/documents éducatifs.

FRA1894
CULTURE ET LIBERTE

9 rue Louis David, BP 92, 93172 Bagnolet cedex, France.

Téléphone: 33 (1) 43 60 74 90. *Fax:* 33 (1) 43 60 97 99.

FRA1895
DAKSA DEVELOPPEMENT

41 boulevard Gergovia, Faculté des Sciences Economiques, B.P. 54, 63002 Clermont-Ferrand Cedex, France.

Téléphone: 33 - 73 93 84 20. *Contact:* Florian Marsaud et Nathalie Mielbach, Présidents.

FRA1896
DATA FOR DEVELOPMENT (DFD) ♦ Données pour le développement

122 avenue de Hambourg, 13008 Marseille, France.

Telephone: 33 - 91 73 90 18. *Fax:* 33 - 91 73 01 38. *Contact:* Jean Salmona, Director General.

FRA1897
DATAFRO

180, avenue Henri Ravera, Boîte 8, 92220 Bagneux, France.

Téléphone: 33 - 49 65 50 76. *Contact:* Aubert Passy, Président.

OBJECTIFS: Valoriser le patrimoine culturel de l'Afrique. Promouvoir les échanges Nord-Sud en matière d'éducation, de recherche, de culture et de transfert de technologies. Publier les recherches et les études par le biais des éditions dénommées DATAFRO.

INFORMATIONS GENERALES: *Création:* 1987. *Personnel/Total:* 10. *Bénévoles:* 10 dont: 3 dans les pays en développement. *Budget/Total 1993:* ECU 23000 (US$ 26000). *Sources financières:* Privé: 20%. Public: 30%. Autofinancement: 50%.

Voir : *Comment utiliser le répertoire,* page 11.

PUBLICATIONS: *Périodiques:* Alternatives Africaines (4) - Gorée (4). *Rapport annuel. Liste des publications.*

EVALUATION/RECHERCHE: Entreprend des activités de recherche.

PREVISIONS D'ACTIVITES: Campagne de sensibilisation sur l'Ile de Gorée.

ACTIVITES DANS LES REGIONS EN DEVELOPPEMENT: Intervient directement dans les régions en développement. Intervient dans 5 pays. Maintient une présence locale sur le terrain. **Actions de Développement durable:** Développement rural/agriculture. **Régions:** Afrique centrale; Afrique de l'Ouest.

ACTIVITES D'INFORMATION ET D'EDUCATION: **Domaines:** Culture/tradition/religion; Développement urbain/habitat; Emploi/chômage; Relations internationales/coopération/aide au développement; Réfugiés/migrants/groupes ethniques; Écologie/environnement/biodiversité; Éducation/formation/alphabétisation. **Activités:** Conférences/séminaires/ateliers/activités de formation; Édition/documents audiovisuels/documents éducatifs.

FRA1898

DELEGATION CATHOLIQUE POUR LA COOPERATION (DCC)

9-11, rue Guyton de Morveau, 75013 Paris, France.

Téléphone: 33 (1) 45 65 96 65. *Fax:* 33 (1) 45 81 30 81. *Contact:* Père Joseph Hardy, Président.

OBJECTIFS: Sélectionner, former, et envoyer des volontaires au nom de l'Eglise de France dans des projets de développement initiés par des Eglises partenaires dans les pays en développement.

INFORMATIONS GENERALES: *Création:* 1967. *Affiliée à:* CLONG-Volontariat (France) - Organisation catholique de Coopération Internationale (France) - Forum européen de Développement (Allemagne) - CLONG-Europe-Institut Belleville (Belgique). *Personnel/Total:* 653. *Salariés:* 30 dont: 1 dans les pays en développement. *Bénévoles:* 623. *Budget/Total 1993:* ECU 5065000 (US$ 5933000). *Sources financières:* Privé: 1%. Public: 60%. Autofinancement: 39%.

PUBLICATIONS: *Périodiques:* Volontaires en Eglise (4). *Rapport annuel.*

PREVISIONS D'ACTIVITES: Organisation d'assises pour les volontaires de retour, dans les dix dernières années.

COMMENTAIRES: Intervient dans la Communauté des Etats indépendants.

ACTIVITES DANS LES REGIONS EN DEVELOPPEMENT: Intervient directement dans les régions en développement. Intervient dans 61 pays. Maintient une présence locale sur le terrain. Intervient par l'intermédiaire d'organisations locales partenaires. **Actions de Développement durable:** Envoi de volontaires/experts/assistance technique. **Régions:** Afrique australe; Afrique centrale; Afrique de l'Est; Afrique de l'Ouest; Afrique du Nord; Amérique du Sud; Asie centrale et Asie du Sud; Asie de l'Est; Asie du Sud-Est; Caraïbes; Mexique et Amerique centrale; Moyen-Orient; Océanie.

ACTIVITES D'INFORMATION ET D'EDUCATION: **Domaines:** Relations internationales/coopération/aide au développement. **Activités:** Conférences/séminaires/ateliers/activités de formation.

FRA1899

DELTA 7

24 rue Marc Seguin, 75018 Paris, France.

Téléphone: 33 (1) 46 07 42 22. *Fax:* 33 (1) 40 38 91 80. *Contact:* Mr. Jacques Bernard, Président.

FRA1900

DEMAIN, HOPITAUX SANS FRONTIERES (DHSF)

10 avenue du Général de Gaulle, BP 609, 03006 Moulins, France.

Téléphone: 33 - 70 44 21 21. *Contact:* Christian Beligon.

FRA1901

DEMOCRATIE POUR L'AFRIQUE

217 avenue Général Frere, 69008 Lyon, France.

Téléphone: 33 - 78 01 32 38. *Contact:* Antoine Sery.

FRA1902

DENTISTES SANS FRONTIERES ♦ Dentists Overseas Humanitarian Organization

33 rue Gambetta, 93100 Montreuil, France.

Contact: Dr. C. Samuel, Président.

FRA1903

DEPARTEMENT EVANGELIQUE FRANCAIS D'ACTION APOSTOLIQUE (DEFAP)

102, boulevard Arago, 75014 Paris, France.

Téléphone: 33 (1) 43 20 70 95. *Fax:* 33 (1) 43 35 00 55. *Contact:* Marthe Westphal, Présidente.

OBJECTIFS: Réaliser des projets de développement, notamment grâce à l'envoi de volontaires, en collaboration avec les églises des pays concernés. Faire connaître ces projets au public français.

INFORMATIONS GENERALES: *Création:* 1971. *Affiliée à:* Fédération Protestante de France - Communauté Evangélique d'Action Apostolique - CLONG-Volontariat - COE (Suisse). *Personnel/Total:* 165. *Salariés:* 25. *Bénévoles:* 140 dont: 140 dans les pays en développement. *Budget/Total 1993:* ECU 2864000 (US$ 3355000). *Sources financières:* Privé: 84%. Public: 6%. Autofinancement: 10%.

PUBLICATIONS: *Périodiques:* Mission (10) - Info-DEFAP (4). *Rapport annuel. Liste des publications.*

EVALUATION/RECHERCHE: Rapports d'évaluation disponibles.

COMMENTAIRES: Intervient dans la Communauté des Etats indépendants.

ACTIVITES DANS LES REGIONS EN DEVELOPPEMENT: Maintient une présence locale sur le terrain. Intervient par l'intermédiaire d'organisations locales partenaires. **Actions de Développement durable:** Développement rural/agriculture; Envoi de volontaires/experts/assistance technique; Petites entreprises/secteur informel/artisanat; Santé/assainissement/eau; Éducation/formation/alphabétisation. **Régions:** Afrique australe; Afrique centrale; Afrique de l'Est; Afrique de l'Ouest; Amérique du Sud; Caraïbes.

FRA1904

DETACHEMENT D'INTERVENTION CONTRE LES CATASTROPHES ET DE FORMATION DE LA FEDERATION FRANCAISE DE SAUVETAGE ET DE SECOURISME (DICAF/FFSS)

Centre Jean Mermoz, 91170 Viry-Chatillon, France.

Téléphone: 33 (1) 69 45 11 49. *Fax:* 33 (1) 69 44 23 95. *Contact:* Pierre Bansard, Directeur.

OBJECTIFS: Intervenir contre les catastrophes naturelles ou technologiques. Résoudre les problèmes sociaux. Apporter une aide matérielle aux populations. Former dans les domaines médical et para-médical, et dans ceux du sauvetage et de la protection civile.

INFORMATIONS GENERALES: *Création:* 1982. *Type d'organisation:* regroupement d'ONG. *Organisations membres:* 52. *Personnel/Total:* 210003. *Salariés:* 3. *Bénévoles:* 210000. *Budget/Total 1993:* ECU 23000 (US$ 26000). *Sources financières:* Privé: 30%. Autofinancement: 70%.

PUBLICATIONS: *Périodiques:* La revue du D.I.CA.F (1). *Rapport annuel. Liste des publications.*

COMMENTAIRES: Intervient dans la Communauté des Etats indépendants. Activités d'information concernant la Communauté des Etats indépendants.

ACTIVITES DANS LES REGIONS EN DEVELOPPEMENT: Intervient directement dans les régions en développement. Intervient dans 5 pays. Maintient une présence locale sur le terrain. Intervient par l'intermédiaire d'organisations locales partenaires. **Actions de Développement durable:** Aliments/famine; Développement urbain/habitat; Envoi de volontaires/experts/assistance technique; Santé/assainissement/eau; Secours d'urgence/réfugiés/aide humanitaire; Éducation/formation/alphabétisation. **Régions:** Afrique centrale; Amérique du Sud; Asie cen-

trale et Asie du Sud; Caraïbes; Mexique et Amerique centrale; Moyen-Orient.

ACTIVITES D'INFORMATION ET D'EDUCATION: Domaines: Aliments/famine; Développement urbain/habitat; Relations internationales/coopération/aide au développement; Santé/assainissement/eau; Secours d'urgence/réfugiés/aide humanitaire. **Activités:** Campagnes d'information/expositions; Collecte de fonds; Conférences/séminaires/ateliers/activités de formation; Lobbying/plaidoyer; Radiodiffusion/manifestations culturelles; Réseaux/télécommunications électroniques; Services d'information et de documentation/bases de données; Échanges/parrainage/jumelage; Édition/documents audiovisuels/documents éducatifs; Éducation formelle.

FRA1905
DIALOGUE ET COOPERATION

140, avenue Daumesnil, 75012 Paris, France.

Téléphone: 33 (1) 43 44 05 06. *Contact:* Jacqueline Crette, Présidente.

OBJECTIFS: Fournir un soutien matériel, moral et spirituel aux enseignants chrétiens travaillant dans des écoles non confessionnelles et collaborant à la recherche d'un système éducatif démocratique adapté aux besoins de la population.

INFORMATIONS GENERALES: *Création:* 1964. *Affiliée à:* CCFD (France). *Personnel/Total:* 1. *Salariés:* 1. *Sources financières:* Privé: 5%. Autofinancement: 95%.

EVALUATION/RECHERCHE: Rapports d'évaluation disponibles.

PREVISIONS D'ACTIVITES: L'organisation milite pour la défense de la vie en Amérique latine; elle contribue aussi à une éducation à la paix.

ACTIVITES DANS LES REGIONS EN DEVELOPPEMENT: Intervient par l'intermédiaire d'organisations locales partenaires. **Actions de Développement durable:** Droits de l'Homme/paix/conflits; Enfants/jeunesse/famille; Éducation/formation/alphabétisation. **Régions:** Afrique centrale; Afrique de l'Ouest; Amérique du Sud; Asie centrale et Asie du Sud; Asie du Sud-Est; Caraïbes; Mexique et Amerique centrale.

FRA1906
DIALOGUES

71 rue Beaubourg, 75003 Paris, France.

Téléphone: 33 (1) 48 04 98 76. *Fax:* 33 (1) 42 72 21 32.

FRA1907
DIAPANTE

34, rue Baussenque, 13002 Marseille, France.

Téléphone: 33 - 91 91 29 59. *Fax:* 33 - 91 90 88 76. *Contact:* Alain Kasriel, Délégué.

OBJECTIFS: Favoriser tous les échanges Nord-Sud dans les domaines économique, social et culturel. Contribuer à l'amélioration des conditions socio-économiques des sénégalais ruraux ou des habitants de la région du Fleuve Sénégal. Contribuer à optimiser le transfert des compétences.

INFORMATIONS GENERALES: *Création:* 1987. *Affiliée à:* Réseau Recherche-Développement (France) - Réseau groupements, association et organisation villageoise (France) - Réseau stratégies alimentaires (France) -Réseau transformation des produits alimentaires (France) - Réseau Femmes et développement (France) - Programme Solidarité-eau (France). *Personnel/Total:* 15. *Salariés:* 5 dont: 5 dans les pays en développement. *Bénévoles:* 10 dont: 6 dans les pays en développement. *Budget/Total 1993:* ECU 226000 (US$ 265000). *Sources financières:* Privé: 10%. Public: 30%. Autofinancement: 60%.

PUBLICATIONS: *Rapport annuel. Liste des publications.*

EVALUATION/RECHERCHE: Rapports d'évaluation disponibles. Entreprend des activités de recherche.

ACTIVITES DANS LES REGIONS EN DEVELOPPEMENT: Intervient directement dans les régions en développement. Intervient dans 2 pays. Maintient une présence locale sur le terrain. Intervient par l'intermédiaire d'organisations locales partenaires. **Actions de Développement durable:** Démocratie/bonne gestion publique/création d'institutions/développement participatif; Développement rural/agriculture; Enfants/jeunesse/famille; Envoi de volontaires/experts/assistance technique; Petites entreprises/secteur informel/artisanat; Questions relatives aux femmes; Écologie/environnement/biodiversité; Éducation/formation/alphabétisation. **Régions:** Afrique de l'Ouest.

ACTIVITES D'INFORMATION ET D'EDUCATION: Domaines: Développement rural/agriculture; Enfants/jeunesse/famille; Questions relatives aux femmes; Relations internationales/coopération/aide au développement; Écologie/environnement/biodiversité; Éducation/formation/alphabétisation. **Activités:** Conférences/séminaires/ateliers/activités de formation; Services d'information et de documentation/bases de données; Échanges/parrainage/jumelage; Édition/documents audiovisuels/documents éducatifs.

FRA1908
DOCUMENTATION-REFUGIES (DR)

11, rue Ferdinand Gambon, 75020 Paris, France.

Téléphone: 33 (1) 43 48 15 66. *Fax:* 33 (1) 43 48 17 22. *Contact:* Philippe Texier, Président.

OBJECTIFS: Recueillir des documents et des informations relatifs au droit d'asile et aux réfugiés. Effectuer des études et des recherches. Diffuser les résultats et informations obtenus.

INFORMATIONS GENERALES: *Création:* 1986. *Type d'organisation:* regroupement d'ONG. *Organisations membres:* 6. *Affiliée à:* Amnesty Internationale - CIMADE - Croix-Rouge - France Tere d'Asile (France) - Ligue des Droits de l'Homme - Service d'Aide aux Immigrants - Réseau international de Documentation sur les Réfugiés - Réseau INFODOC du Conseil Européen sur les Réfugiés et Exilés - Réseau REMISIS - Réseau HINARME. *Personnel/Total:* 15. *Salariés:* 5. *Bénévoles:* 10. *Budget/Total 1993:* ECU 362000 (US$ 424000). *Sources financières:* Privé: 66%. Public: 33%. Autofinancement: 1%.

PUBLICATIONS: *Périodiques:* Documentation-Réfugiés (24). *Rapport annuel.*

EVALUATION/RECHERCHE: Entreprend des activités de recherche.

COMMENTAIRES: Activités d'information concernant la Communauté des Etats indépendants.

ACTIVITES D'INFORMATION ET D'EDUCATION: Domaines: Culture/tradition/religion; Droits de l'Homme/paix/conflits; Paix/conflits ethniques/armement/désarmement; Racisme/xénophobie/antisémitisme; Réfugiés/migrants/groupes ethniques; Secours d'urgence/réfugiés/aide humanitaire. **Activités:** Réseaux/télécommunications électroniques; Services d'information et de documentation/bases de données; Édition/documents audiovisuels/documents éducatifs.

FRA1909
DOUAR NEVEZ-TERRE NOUVELLE

36 rue Richemont, 56000 Vannes, France.

Téléphone: 33 - 97 63 01 44. *Contact:* Yves Roger-Machart.

FRA1910
DROIT DE PAROLE

56, rue de la Glacière, 75013 Paris, France.

Téléphone: 33 (1) 44 08 75 00. *Fax:* 33 (1) 44 08 74 99. *Contact:* Dr. Michel Bonnot, Président.

OBJECTIFS: Agir pour la liberté d'expression, là où elle n'existe pas, en s'appuyant sur l'article 19 de la Déclaration Universelle des Droits de l'Homme. Apporter une aide concrète en matériel ou en compétences humaines.

INFORMATIONS GENERALES: *Création:* 1992. *Affiliée à:* Collectif pour la paix en ex-Yougoslavie. *Personnel/Total:* 22. *Salariés:* 21 dont: 17 dans les pays en développement. *Bénévoles:* 1. *Budget/Total 1993:* ECU 5578000 (US$ 6533000). *Sources financières:* Privé: 15%. Public: 80%. Autofinancement: 5%.

PREVISIONS D'ACTIVITES: Priorité et nouvelles activités envisagées dans le domaine de la liberté d'expression: région Caraïbes et Asie du Sud.

Voir : *Comment utiliser le répertoire,* page 11.

COMMENTAIRES: Intervient dans la Communauté des Etats indépendants.

ACTIVITES DANS LES REGIONS EN DEVELOPPEMENT: Intervient directement dans les régions en développement. Intervient dans 2 pays. Maintient une présence locale sur le terrain. Intervient par l'intermédiaire d'organisations locales partenaires. **Actions de Développement durable:** Autres; Droits de l'Homme/paix/conflits; Démocratie/bonne gestion publique/création d'institutions/développement participatif. **Régions:** Asie centrale et Asie du Sud.

ACTIVITES D'INFORMATION ET D'EDUCATION: Domaines: Autres; Droits de l'Homme/paix/conflits; Paix/conflits ethniques/armement/désarmement; Réfugiés/migrants/groupes ethniques; Secours d'urgence/réfugiés/aide humanitaire. **Activités:** Campagnes d'information/expositions; Collecte de fonds; Lobbying/plaidoyer; Radiodiffusion/manifestations culturelles; Réseaux/télécommunications électroniques.

FRA1911
DROITS DE L'HOMME ET SOLIDARITE
127 rue Notre Dame des Champs, 75006 Paris, France.

FRA1912
EAU POUR LA VIE ♦ WATER FOR LIFE
Appt. 390, Tour IV, Résidence Serge Formanoir, 33600 Pessac, France.

Téléphone: 33 - 56 46 20 33. *Contact:* Francis Gay.

FRA1913
EAU VIVE
12, rue Rochambeau, 75009 Paris, France.

Téléphone: 33 (1) 48 78 30 33. *Fax:* (1) 48 74 14 10. *Contact:* Laurent Chabert d'Hieres, Délégué général.

OBJECTIFS: Financer des actions de développement villageois au Sahel: eau, santé, instruction, production, organisation. Aider les associations et les entreprises locales.

INFORMATIONS GENERALES: *Création:* 1978. ***Affiliée à:*** CRID - Plateforme des ONG françaises auprès de l'Union Européenne. ***Personnel/Total:*** 10. *Salariés:* 10 dont: 6 dans les pays en développement. ***Budget/Total 1993:*** ECU 980000 (US$ 1148000). ***Sources financières:*** Privé: 60%. Public: 40%.

PUBLICATIONS: *Périodiques:* Eau vive Actualités (1). *Rapport annuel.*

EVALUATION/RECHERCHE: Rapports d'évaluation disponibles. Entreprend des activités de recherche.

COMMENTAIRES: Ouverture de l'action à d'autres pays.

ACTIVITES DANS LES REGIONS EN DEVELOPPEMENT: Intervient directement dans les régions en développement. Intervient dans 5 pays. Maintient une présence locale sur le terrain. Intervient par l'intermédiaire d'organisations locales partenaires. **Actions de Développement durable:** Démocratie/bonne gestion publique/création d'institutions/développement participatif; Développement rural/agriculture; Enfants/jeunesse/famille; Petites entreprises/secteur informel/artisanat; Questions relatives aux femmes; Santé/assainissement/eau; Écologie/environnement/biodiversité; Éducation/formation/alphabétisation. **Régions:** Afrique de l'Ouest.

ACTIVITES D'INFORMATION ET D'EDUCATION: Domaines: Développement rural/agriculture; Enfants/jeunesse/famille; Questions relatives aux femmes; Santé/assainissement/eau; Écologie/environnement/biodiversité. **Activités:** Collecte de fonds; Échanges/parrainage/jumelage; Édition/documents audiovisuels/documents éducatifs.

FRA1914
EAU, AGRICULTURE ET SANTE EN MILIEU TROPICAL (EAST)
s/c Docteur Monjour, 35 rue Broca, 75005 Paris, France.

Téléphone: 33 (1) 43 26 12 08. *Fax:* 33 (1) 43 29 70 93. *Contact:* Loïc Monjour.

OBJECTIFS: Promouvoir le développement intersectoriel en milieux villageois et péri-urbain. Faire de l'éducation sanitaire. Procurer de l'eau potable. Promouvoir la santé, l'hygiène et l'assainissement.

INFORMATIONS GENERALES: *Création:* 1986. ***Personnel/Total:*** 13. *Salariés:* 6 dont: 5 dans les pays en développement. *Bénévoles:* 7. ***Budget/Total 1993:*** ECU 151000 (US$ 177000). ***Sources financières:*** Privé: 30%. Public: 65%. Autofinancement: 5%.

PUBLICATIONS: *Rapport annuel. Liste des publications.*

EVALUATION/RECHERCHE: Rapports d'évaluation disponibles. Entreprend des activités de recherche.

COMMENTAIRES: EAST participe à la gestion des laboratoires de contrôle de l'eau de la ville de Ouagadougou, au Burkina Faso, et de Cotonou, au Bénin. L'organisation a débuté des programmes similaires dans le Sud-Est Asiatique.

ACTIVITES DANS LES REGIONS EN DEVELOPPEMENT: Intervient directement dans les régions en développement. Intervient dans 2 pays. Maintient une présence locale sur le terrain. Intervient par l'intermédiaire d'organisations locales partenaires. **Actions de Développement durable:** Enfants/jeunesse/famille; Envoi de volontaires/experts/assistance technique; Questions relatives aux femmes; Santé/assainissement/eau; Écologie/environnement/biodiversité; Éducation/formation/alphabétisation. **Régions:** Afrique de l'Ouest.

ACTIVITES D'INFORMATION ET D'EDUCATION: Domaines: Enfants/jeunesse/famille; Questions relatives aux femmes; Santé/assainissement/eau; Écologie/environnement/biodiversité; Éducation/formation/alphabétisation. **Activités:** Collecte de fonds.

FRA1915
ECHANGE COOPERATION EN MILIEU RURAL (ECMR-CIVAM)
Domaine de Puechlong, 30610 Saint Nazaire des Gardies, France.

Téléphone: 33 - 66 77 11 12. *Fax:* 33 - 66 77 10 83. *Contact:* Jean-Paul Cabanis, Président.

FRA1916
ECHANGE FRANCE-COLOMBIE
11 rue d'Argentan, 61000 Alençon, France.

Téléphone: 33 - 33 32 04 75. *Contact:* Paul Vannier, Président.

FRA1917
ECHANGES ET CONSULTATIONS TECHNIQUES INTERNATIONAUX (ECTI)
3, rue de Logelbach, 75847 Paris cedex 17, France.

Téléphone: 33 (1) 46 22 20 19. *Fax:* (1) 43 80 51 14. *Contact:* Henri Dhavernas, Président.

OBJECTIFS: Mener des missions d'assistance multifonction de courte durée, grâce à des organisations (associations, entreprises, collectivités locales) et à des consultants en retraite.

INFORMATIONS GENERALES: *Création:* 1975. ***Affiliée à:*** Coordination d'Agen (France) - CLONG-D (France) - Comité de Liaison Solidarité Europe de l'Est - Consortium "Seniors" (Belgique) - EUROLINK AGE (Royaume Uni). ***Personnel/Total:*** 4206. *Salariés:* 6. *Bénévoles:* 4200 dont: 30 dans les pays en développement. ***Budget/Total 1993:*** ECU 2488000 (US$ 2914000). ***Sources financières:*** Autofinancement: 98%.

PUBLICATIONS: *Périodiques:* ECTI-Informations (6). *Rapport annuel.*

COMMENTAIRES: ECTI est une agence de mise en relation de demandeurs de missions et de consultants expérimentés. L'organisation a créé une délégation à l'économie sociale (contact: Jean Claude Buchotte). Intervient dans la Communauté des Etats indépendants. Activités d'information concernant la Communauté des Etats indépendants.

ACTIVITES DANS LES REGIONS EN DEVELOPPEMENT: Intervient directement dans les régions en développement. Intervient dans 81 pays. Maintient une présence locale sur le terrain. Intervient par l'intermédiaire d'organisations locales partenaires. **Actions de Développement durable:** Dette/finances/commerce; Démocratie/bonne gestion publique/création d'institutions/développement participatif; Développement rural/agriculture; Développement urbain/habitat; Envoi de volon-

See: *How to Use the Directory,* page 11.

taires/experts/assistance technique; Petites entreprises/secteur informel/artisanat; Population/planning familial/démographie; Santé/assainissement/eau; Éducation/formation/alphabétisation; Énergie/transport. **Régions:** Afrique australe; Afrique centrale; Afrique de l'Est; Afrique de l'Ouest; Afrique du Nord; Amérique du Sud; Asie centrale et Asie du Sud; Asie de l'Est; Asie du Sud-Est; Caraïbes; Mexique et Amerique centrale; Moyen-Orient; Océanie.

ACTIVITES D'INFORMATION ET D'EDUCATION: Domaines: Développement rural/agriculture; Développement urbain/habitat; Emploi/chômage; Paix/conflits ethniques/armement/désarmement; Population/planning familial/démographie; Relations internationales/coopération/aide au développement; Relations économiques internationales/commerce/dette/finances; Santé/assainissement/eau; Écologie/environnement/biodiversité; Éducation/formation/alphabétisation. **Activités:** Conférences/séminaires/ateliers/activités de formation.

FRA1918
ECHANGES ET SOLIDARITE

120 rue du Marais, 91210 Draveil, France.

Téléphone: 33 (1) 69 42 42 02. *Contact:* Berthe Le Goff, Secrétaire.

FRA1919
ECLAIREUSES ET ECLAIREURS DE FRANCE (EEDF)

12 place Georges Pompidou, 93167 Noisy-le-grand, France.

Téléphone: 33 (1) 48 15 17 66. *Fax:* 33 (1) 48 15 17 60. *Contact:* Daniel Goux, Président.

FRA1920
ECOLES SANS FRONTIERES (ESF)

Cité St Jean, Bât. H2, bd de Stalingrad, 83500 La Seyne-sur-Mer, France.

Téléphone: 33 - 94 30 09 10. *Fax:* 33 - 94 30 10 25. *Contact:* Dr. Phat Nguyen, Président.

OBJECTIFS: Développer le niveau d'éducation des populations défavorisées, et contribuer à la sauvegarde de leur culture d'origine. Faciliter, par l'enseignement, la recherche de solutions durables au problème des réfugiés.

INFORMATIONS GENERALES: *Création:* 1980. *Personnel/Total:* 21. *Salariés:* 3. *Bénévoles:* 18 dont: 18 dans les pays en développement. *Budget/Total 1993:* ECU 377000 (US$ 441000). *Sources financières:* Privé: 27%. Public: 71%. Autofinancement: 2%.

PUBLICATIONS: *Périodiques:* Echos sans Frontières (4). *Rapport annuel. Liste des publications.*

EVALUATION/RECHERCHE: Rapports d'évaluation disponibles. Entreprend des activités de recherche.

ACTIVITES DANS LES REGIONS EN DEVELOPPEMENT: Intervient directement dans les régions en développement. Intervient dans 4 pays. Maintient une présence locale sur le terrain. Intervient par l'intermédiaire d'organisations locales partenaires. **Actions de Développement durable:** Éducation/formation/alphabétisation. **Régions:** Asie du Sud-Est; Mexique et Amerique centrale.

ACTIVITES D'INFORMATION ET D'EDUCATION: Domaines: Aliments/famine; Culture/tradition/religion; Développement rural/agriculture; Enfants/jeunesse/famille; Pauvreté/conditions de vie; Population/planning familial/démographie; Questions relatives aux femmes; Réfugiés/migrants/groupes ethniques; Santé/assainissement/eau; Éducation/formation/alphabétisation. **Activités:** Campagnes d'information/expositions; Radiodiffusion/manifestations culturelles; Échanges/parrainage/jumelage; Édition/documents audiovisuels/documents éducatifs.

FRA1921
ECONOMIE ET HUMANISME

14, rue Antoine Dumont, 69008 Lyon , France.

Téléphone: 33 - 78 61 32 23. *Fax:* 33 - 78 69 86 96. *Contact:* Philippe Blancher, Directeur général.

OBJECTIFS: Promouvoir une économie au service de l'homme. Développer les solidarités internationales.

INFORMATIONS GENERALES: *Création:* 1941. *Affiliée à:* Réseau Solidarité (France). *Personnel/Total:* 15. *Salariés:* 10. *Bénévoles:* 5. *Budget/Total 1993:* ECU 407000 (US$ 477000). *Sources financières:* Privé: 5%. Public: 90%. Autofinancement: 5%.

PUBLICATIONS: *Périodiques:* Economie et Humanisme (4). *Liste des publications.*

EVALUATION/RECHERCHE: Rapports d'évaluation disponibles. Entreprend des activités de recherche.

COMMENTAIRES: Intervient dans la Communauté des Etats indépendants. Activités d'information concernant la Communauté des Etats indépendants.

ACTIVITES DANS LES REGIONS EN DEVELOPPEMENT: Intervient directement dans les régions en développement. Intervient dans 2 pays. **Actions de Développement durable:** Démocratie/bonne gestion publique/création d'institutions/développement participatif; Développement urbain/habitat; Santé/assainissement/eau; Écologie/environnement/biodiversité. **Régions:** Asie centrale et Asie du Sud; Asie de l'Est; Asie du Sud-Est.

ACTIVITES D'INFORMATION ET D'EDUCATION: Domaines: Droits de l'Homme/paix/conflits; Développement urbain/habitat; Emploi/chômage; Relations internationales/coopération/aide au développement; Relations économiques internationales/commerce/dette/finances; Santé/assainissement/eau; Écologie/environnement/biodiversité. **Activités:** Conférences/séminaires/ateliers/activités de formation; Échanges/parrainage/jumelage.

FRA1922
ECOROPA

42 rue Sorbier, 75020 Paris, France.

FRA1923
EDITIONS FRANCOPHONES D'AMNESTY INTERNATIONAL (EFAI)

17 rue du Pont-aux-Choux, 75003 Paris, France.

Téléphone: 33 (1) 44 59 29 89. *Fax:* 33 (1) 44 59 29 80. *Contact:* Maitre Bochra Bel Haj Hmida.

OBJECTIFS: Traduire, fabriquer, éditer et diffuser aux sections et au secrétariat international d'Amnesty International, du matériel du mouvement en langue française.

INFORMATIONS GENERALES: *Création:* 1986. *Organisations membres:* 10. *Affiliée à:* Amnesty International (Belgique) - AI Limited - AI (France) - AI (Tunisie) - AI (Luxembourg) - AI (Suisse) - AI (Canada) - AI (Côte d'Ivoire) - AI (Ile Maurice) - AI (Algérie). *Salariés:* 12. *Budget/Total 1993:* ECU 482000 (US$ 565000). *Sources financières:* Autofinancement: 100%.

PUBLICATIONS: *Rapport annuel. Liste des publications.*

COMMENTAIRES: Activités d'information concernant la Communauté des Etats indépendants.

ACTIVITES DANS LES REGIONS EN DEVELOPPEMENT: Intervient dans 15 pays. Intervient par l'intermédiaire d'organisations locales partenaires. **Actions de Développement durable:** Droits de l'Homme/paix/conflits. **Régions:** Afrique australe; Afrique centrale; Afrique de l'Est; Afrique de l'Ouest; Afrique du Nord; Amérique du Sud; Asie centrale et Asie du Sud; Asie du Sud-Est; Caraïbes; Mexique et Amerique centrale; Moyen-Orient; Océanie.

ACTIVITES D'INFORMATION ET D'EDUCATION: Domaines: Droits de l'Homme/paix/conflits; Paix/conflits ethniques/armement/désarmement. **Activités:** Campagnes d'information/expositions; Radiodiffusion/manifestations culturelles; Édition/documents audiovisuels/documents éducatifs.

FRA1924
EDUCATION ET ECHANGES (EE)

108, rue Saint-Maur, 75011 Paris, France.

Voir : *Comment utiliser le répertoire*, page 11.

Téléphone: 33 (1) 43 14 09 02. **Fax:** 33 (1) 48 07 05 76 pour EE. **Contact:** Jean-Paul Vigier, Président.

OBJECTIFS: Développer les échanges culturels, l'information et la formation sur le plan international. Susciter et soutenir financièrement des actions innovatrices dans le domaine du développement au sens large.

INFORMATIONS GENERALES: *Création:* 1949. *Personnel/Total:* 2. *Salariés:* 1. *Bénévoles:* 1. *Budget/Total 1993:* ECU 193000 (US$ 225000). *Sources financières:* Privé: 45%. Public: 50%. Autofinancement: 5%.

PUBLICATIONS: *Rapport annuel.*

PREVISIONS D'ACTIVITES: L'organisation va poursuivre le concours CREA (aide à la création d'entreprises) en Afrique francophone, avec une extension probable à d'autres continents.

COMMENTAIRES: L'organisation concentre essentiellement ses activités autour de l'organisation d'un concours d'aide à la création d'entreprises (CREA) et au soutien de ses lauréats.

ACTIVITES DANS LES REGIONS EN DEVELOPPEMENT: Intervient directement dans les régions en développement. Intervient par l'intermédiaire d'organisations locales partenaires. **Actions de Développement durable:** Petites entreprises/secteur informel/artisanat. **Régions:** Afrique australe; Afrique de l'Ouest.

FRA1925

EIRENE FRANCE-SERVICE CHRETIEN INTERNATIONAL POUR LA PAIX (EIRENE-FRANCE)

c/o Irène Ponsoye, 19 rue Guyton de Morveau, 75013 Paris, France.

Téléphone: 33 (1) 45 65 23 08. **Contact:** Marlin Friesen, Président.

FRA1926

EMMAUS INTERNATIONAL (EI)

183 bis rue Vaillant Couturier, BP 91, 94140 Alfortville, France.

Téléphone: 33 (1) 48 93 29 50. **Fax:** 33 (1) 43 53 19 26. **Contact:** Francesco Bettoli, Président.

OBJECTIFS: Aider les personnes exclues ou marginalisées à œuvrer en faveur de leur réinsertion sociale. Oeuvrer pour des rapports internationaux plus équitables et respectueux des besoins fondamentaux de tout homme. Lutter contre le gaspillage des ressources humaines et naturelles, grâce au recyclage des produits rejetés par les pays nantis.

INFORMATIONS GENERALES: *Création:* 1949. *Type d'organisation:* regroupement d'ONG. *Organisations membres:* 345. *Affiliée à:* CFSI - Centre de Recherche et d'information sur le développement (France) - European Anti Poverty Network. *Personnel/Total:* 9. *Salariés:* 7. *Bénévoles:* 2. *Budget/Total 1993:* ECU 2135000 (US$ 2500000). *Sources financières:* Privé: 2%. Public: 21%. Autofinancement: 77%.

PUBLICATIONS: *Périodiques:* (6).

COMMENTAIRES: Statut consultatif (catégorie II) auprès de l'ECOSOC des Nations Unies. Intervient dans la Communauté des Etats indépendants.

ACTIVITES DANS LES REGIONS EN DEVELOPPEMENT: Intervient dans 17 pays. Intervient par l'intermédiaire d'organisations locales partenaires. **Actions de Développement durable:** Développement rural/agriculture; Développement urbain/habitat; Enfants/jeunesse/famille; Petites entreprises/secteur informel/artisanat; Santé/assainissement/eau; Secours d'urgence/réfugiés/aide humanitaire; Ecologie/environnement/biodiversité; Education/formation/alphabétisation. **Régions:** Afrique centrale; Afrique de l'Ouest; Afrique du Nord; Amérique du Sud; Asie centrale et Asie du Sud; Moyen-Orient.

FRA1927

ENERGIE & ENVIRONNEMENT - SOLUTIONS ADAPTEES POUR UN ENVIRONNEMENT DURABLE (SOLAGRO)

219, avenue de Muret, 31300 Toulouse, France.

Téléphone: 33 - 61 59 56 16. **Fax:** 33 - 61 59 98 41. **Contact:** Madeleine Charru, Directrice.

OBJECTIFS: Favoriser l'émergence et le dévelopement dans les domaines de l'énergie, de l'environnement, de l'agriculture, de pratiques et de procédés participant à une gestion économe, solidaire et de long terme des ressources naturelles.

INFORMATIONS GENERALES: *Création:* 1981. *Affiliée à:* Comité de Liaison Energies Renouvelables (France). *Personnel/Total:* 9. *Salariés:* 7. *Budget/Total 1993:* ECU 452000 (US$ 530000). *Sources financières:* Public: 40%. Autofinancement: 60%.

PUBLICATIONS: *Périodiques:* Les nouvelles de SOLAGRO (4). *Rapport annuel.*

EVALUATION/RECHERCHE: Entreprend des activités de recherche.

ACTIVITES DANS LES REGIONS EN DEVELOPPEMENT: Intervient par l'intermédiaire d'organisations locales partenaires. **Actions de Développement durable:** Ecologie/environnement/biodiversité; Energie/transport. **Régions:** Afrique de l'Ouest; Afrique du Nord; Amérique du Sud; Asie centrale et Asie du Sud.

ACTIVITES D'INFORMATION ET D'EDUCATION: Domaines: Ecologie/environnement/biodiversité. **Activités:** Conférences/séminaires/ateliers/activités de formation; Services d'information et de documentation/bases de données.

FRA1928

ENFANCE ESPOIR (EE)

30, rue de l'Epargne, 94600 Choisy-le-Roi, France.

Téléphone: 33 (1) 48 90 95 71. **Fax:** 33 (1) 48 92 01 59. **Contact:** Claude Daniel, Présidente.

OBJECTIFS: Améliorer les conditions de vie des enfants, dans les domaines de l'éducation, de la santé et de la formation pré-professionnelle.

INFORMATIONS GENERALES: *Création:* 1982. *Personnel/Total:* 36. *Salariés:* 1. *Bénévoles:* 35 dont: 7 dans les pays en développement. *Budget/Total 1993:* ECU 251000 (US$ 293000). *Sources financières:* Privé: 45%. Public: 31%. Autofinancement: 24%.

PUBLICATIONS: *Périodiques:* Enfance Espoir-Bulletin de liaison (2). *Rapport annuel.*

EVALUATION/RECHERCHE: Rapports d'évaluation disponibles.

PREVISIONS D'ACTIVITES: Construction de 2 écoles primaires, à Dacca (Bangla Desh). Construction de 3 ateliers de formation professionnelle, au Chili, pour les enfants accidentés de la rue. Ouverture d'un gîte rural en France pour les R.M.I. Mise en place d'une pharmacopée pour enfants leucémiques, à Bucarest, en Roumanie

ACTIVITES DANS LES REGIONS EN DEVELOPPEMENT: Intervient directement dans les régions en développement. Intervient dans 9 pays. Maintient une présence locale sur le terrain. **Actions de Développement durable:** Envoi de volontaires/experts/assistance technique; Santé/assainissement/eau; Secours d'urgence/réfugiés/aide humanitaire; Education/formation/alphabétisation. **Régions:** Afrique centrale; Afrique de l'Ouest; Amérique du Sud; Asie du Sud-Est; Mexique et Amerique centrale.

ACTIVITES D'INFORMATION ET D'EDUCATION: Domaines: Enfants/jeunesse/famille; Relations internationales/coopération/aide au développement; Santé/assainissement/eau; Education/formation/alphabétisation. **Activités:** Campagnes d'information/expositions; Collecte de fonds; Echanges/parrainage/jumelage.

FRA1929

ENFANCE ET PARTAGE

40, rue de la République, 61200 Argentan, France.

Téléphone: 33 - 33 67 11 95. **Fax:** 33 - 33 39 34 72. **Contact:** Jean Mazière, Président.

OBJECTIFS: Aider l'enfance en détresse en France et dans le monde.

INFORMATIONS GENERALES: *Création:* 1977. *Personnel/Total:* 52. *Salariés:* 2. *Bénévoles:* 50 dont: 15 dans les pays en développement. *Budget/Total 1993:* ECU 452000 (US$ 530000). *Sources financières:* Privé: 70%. Autofinancement: 30%.

PUBLICATIONS: *Périodiques:* Enfance et Partage (4). *Rapport annuel.*

See: *How to Use the Directory*, page 11.

EVALUATION/RECHERCHE: Rapports d'évaluation disponibles.

COMMENTAIRES: Intervient dans la Communauté des Etats indépendants.

ACTIVITES DANS LES REGIONS EN DEVELOPPEMENT: Intervient directement dans les régions en développement. Intervient dans 9 pays. Maintient une présence locale sur le terrain. Intervient par l'intermédiaire d'organisations locales partenaires. **Actions de Développement durable:** Aliments/famine; Autres; Enfants/jeunesse/famille; Population/planning familial/démographie; Questions relatives aux femmes; Santé/assainissement/eau; Secours d'urgence/réfugiés/aide humanitaire; Éducation/formation/alphabétisation. **Régions:** Afrique de l'Ouest; Asie centrale et Asie du Sud; Asie de l'Est; Caraïbes.

ACTIVITES D'INFORMATION ET D'EDUCATION: Domaines: Aliments/famine; Emploi/chômage; Enfants/jeunesse/famille; Pauvreté/conditions de vie; Population/planning familial/démographie; Réfugiés/migrants/groupes ethniques; Secours d'urgence/réfugiés/aide humanitaire; Éducation/formation/alphabétisation. **Activités:** Campagnes d'information/expositions; Collecte de fonds; Échanges/parrainage/jumelage; Édition/documents audiovisuels/documents éducatifs.

FRA1930
ENFANCE ET PARTAGE

10, rue des Bluets, 75011 Paris, France.

Téléphone: 33 (1) 43 55 85 85. *Fax:* 33 (1) 43 38 68 76. *Contact:* Sylvie Vay, Présidente.

OBJECTIFS: Aider l'enfant en détresse et en danger, en France et dans le monde. Défendre et protéger les droits de l'enfant; prévenir les dangers auxquels il est exposé.

INFORMATIONS GENERALES: *Création:* 1977. *Type d'organisation:* réseau. *Affiliée à:* Coordination d'Agen pour les missions d'urgence et de coopération volontaire (France). *Personnel/Total:* 503. *Salariés:* 3. *Bénévoles:* 500. *Budget/Total 1993:* ECU 980000 (US$ 1148000). *Sources financières:* Privé: 95%. Autofinancement: 5%.

PUBLICATIONS: *Périodiques:* "Enfance et partage" (4). *Rapport annuel.*

COMMENTAIRES: L'association possède deux volets d'actions dont "Action Internationale": soutien de programmes pour l'enfance (14 pays), et "Action France": défense et protection de l'Enfant victime de maltraitance et/ou d'abus sexuels. Intervient dans la Communauté des Etats indépendants.

ACTIVITES DANS LES REGIONS EN DEVELOPPEMENT: Intervient dans 14 pays. Intervient par l'intermédiaire d'organisations locales partenaires. **Actions de Développement durable:** Démocratie/bonne gestion publique/création d'institutions/développement participatif; Développement rural/agriculture; Développement urbain/habitat; Enfants/jeunesse/famille; Petites entreprises/secteur informel/artisanat; Santé/assainissement/eau; Secours d'urgence/réfugiés/aide humanitaire; Éducation/formation/alphabétisation. **Régions:** Afrique australe; Afrique de l'Est; Afrique de l'Ouest; Amérique du Sud; Asie du Sud-Est.

ACTIVITES D'INFORMATION ET D'EDUCATION: Domaines: Développement rural/agriculture; Développement urbain/habitat; Enfants/jeunesse/famille; Pauvreté/conditions de vie; Questions relatives aux femmes; Éducation/formation/alphabétisation. **Activités:** Campagnes d'information/expositions; Collecte de fonds; Conférences/séminaires/ateliers/activités de formation; Services d'information et de documentation/bases de données; Éducation formelle.

FRA1931
ENFANCE ET VIE

109 rue Calmette, 59120 Loos lez Lille, France.

Téléphone: 33 - 20 07 82 20. *Contact:* Claude Fondeur.

FRA1932
ENFANCE MEURTRIE : UN SOURIRE RETOUVE (EM)

37, rue Le Bourblanc, 78590 Noisy-le-Roi, France.

Téléphone: 33 (1) 34 62 09 98. *Contact:* Marie-Anne Dupin de Lacoste, Présidente.

OBJECTIFS: Répondre aux besoins des enfants qui vivent dans des conditions critiques en France et à l'étranger.

INFORMATIONS GENERALES: *Création:* 1981. *Personnel/Total:* 25. *Bénévoles:* 25. *Budget/Total 1993:* ECU 151000 (US$ 177000). *Sources financières:* Privé: 50%. Autofinancement: 50%.

PUBLICATIONS: *Périodiques:* Lettre d'information (1).

ACTIVITES DANS LES REGIONS EN DEVELOPPEMENT: Intervient directement dans les régions en développement. Intervient dans 3 pays. Maintient une présence locale sur le terrain. **Actions de Développement durable:** Aliments/famine; Enfants/jeunesse/famille; Questions relatives aux femmes; Santé/assainissement/eau; Éducation/formation/alphabétisation. **Régions:** Afrique de l'Ouest; Amérique du Sud.

FRA1933
ENFANT D'EL SALVADOR ♦ Child of El Salvador

7 passage Cottin, 75018 Paris, France.

Téléphone: 33 (1) 42 59 06 59. *Contact:* Jean-Claude Ponsin, Président.

FRA1934
UN ENFANT PAR LA MAIN ♦ A child by the hand

6, rue Paul Cézanne, 93364 Neuilly-Plaisance cedex, France.

Téléphone: 33 (1) 49 44 66 33. *Fax:* 33 (1) 49 44 66 30. *Contact:* Jean-Pierre Cabouat, Président.

OBJECTIFS: Prendre en charge la santé, la croissance et l'éducation des enfants les plus démunis, et ce, dans le plus grand respect de leur culture, grâce une action concrète et durable à travers 176 projets communautaires.

INFORMATIONS GENERALES: *Création:* 1990. *Type d'organisation:* regroupement d'ONG. *Organisations membres:* 12. *Affiliée à:* Christian Children's Fund. *Personnel/Total:* 16. *Salariés:* 6. Bénévoles: 10. *Budget/Total 1993:* ECU 1599000 (US$ 1872000). *Sources financières:* Privé: 34%. Public: 1%. Autofinancement: 62%.

PUBLICATIONS: *Périodiques:* Le Journal des Parrains (3). *Rapport annuel.*

COMMENTAIRES: Les projets de l'association sont répartis dans 22 pays, sur les quatre continents: Europe, Afrique, Asie et Amérique. Intervient dans la Communauté des Etats indépendants.

ACTIVITES DANS LES REGIONS EN DEVELOPPEMENT: Intervient directement dans les régions en développement. Intervient dans 22 pays. Maintient une présence locale sur le terrain. Intervient par l'intermédiaire d'organisations locales partenaires. **Actions de Développement durable:** Aliments/famine; Enfants/jeunesse/famille; Petites entreprises/secteur informel/artisanat; Santé/assainissement/eau; Secours d'urgence/réfugiés/aide humanitaire; Écologie/environnement/biodiversité; Éducation/formation/alphabétisation. **Régions:** Afrique centrale; Afrique de l'Est; Afrique de l'Ouest; Amérique du Sud; Asie centrale et Asie du Sud; Asie du Sud-Est; Caraïbes; Mexique et Amerique centrale.

FRA1935
L'ENFANT POUR L'ENFANT (ISD)

15, rue de l'Ecole de Médecine, 75270 Paris cedex 06, France.

Téléphone: 33 (1) 43 26 59 78. *Fax:* 33 (1) 43 29 70 93. *Contact:* Dr. Elisabeth Dumurgier, Présidente.

OBJECTIFS: Agir pour préserver la santé de l'enfant et celle de son entourage, par la stimulation et l'éveil du jeune enfant, la prévention des accidents, la préservation de l'environnement, la prise en compte des problèmes spécifiques des enfants en grande difficulté.

INFORMATIONS GENERALES: *Création:* 1985. *Type d'organisation:* réseau. *Personnel/Total:* 9. *Salariés:* 1. Bénévoles: 8. *Budget/Total 1993:* ECU 75000 (US$ 88000). *Sources financières:* Privé: 40%. Public: 40%. Autofinancement: 20%.

PUBLICATIONS: *Liste des publications.*

EVALUATION/RECHERCHE: Rapports d'évaluation disponibles. Entreprend des activités de recherche.

COMMENTAIRES: "L'Enfant pour l'Enfant" est un groupe de recherche au sein de l'association "Santé et Développement" qui comprend d'autres groupes travaillant dans d'autres domaines (SIDA, etc.) touchant à la santé et au développement.

ACTIVITES DANS LES REGIONS EN DEVELOPPEMENT: Intervient par l'intermédiaire d'organisations locales partenaires. **Actions de Développement durable:** Enfants/jeunesse/famille; Population/planning familial/démographie; Questions relatives aux femmes; Santé/assainissement/eau; Éducation/formation/alphabétisation. **Régions:** Afrique de l'Ouest.

ACTIVITES D'INFORMATION ET D'EDUCATION: **Domaines:** Enfants/jeunesse/famille; Population/planning familial/démographie; Questions relatives aux femmes; Santé/assainissement/eau; Éducation/formation/alphabétisation. **Activités:** Conférences/séminaires/ateliers/activités de formation; Services d'information et de documentation/bases de données; Édition/documents audiovisuels/documents éducatifs; Éducation formelle.

FRA1936
ENFANTS DE LA TERRE (EDLT)
BP 30, 78860 Saint-Nom-la-Bretèche, France.

Téléphone: 33 (1) 34 62 07 07. *Fax:* 33 (1) 30 56 71 35. *Contact:* Marie-Claire Noah.

FRA1937
ENFANTS DU MEKONG (EDM)
5, rue de la Comète, 92600 Asnières, France.

Téléphone: 33 (1) 47 91 00 84. *Fax:* 33 (1) 47 33 40 44. *Courrier électronique:* EPHATA EDM 3615. *Contact:* Yves Meaudre des Gouttes, Directeur général.

OBJECTIFS: Apporter une aide aux enfants des 4 pays du Sud-Est asiatique traversés par le Mékong: Laos, Thaïlande, Cambodge et Viet Nam. Aider les réfugiés à se réinserrer socialement.

INFORMATIONS GENERALES: *Création:* 1958. *Type d'organisation:* réseau. *Affiliée à:* Solidarité Mékong - Guilde du Raid. *Personnel/Total:* 47. *Salariés:* 19. *Bénévoles:* 28 dont: 9 dans les pays en développement. *Budget/Total 1993:* ECU 2412000 (US$ 2825000). *Sources financières:* Privé: 96%. Public: 3%. Autofinancement: 1%.

PUBLICATIONS: *Périodiques:* Enfants du Mékong (6). *Rapport annuel.*

EVALUATION/RECHERCHE: Rapports d'évaluation disponibles.

ACTIVITES DANS LES REGIONS EN DEVELOPPEMENT: Intervient directement dans les régions en développement. Intervient dans 4 pays. Maintient une présence locale sur le terrain. **Actions de Développement durable:** Aliments/famine; Développement rural/agriculture; Enfants/jeunesse/famille; Envoi de volontaires/experts/assistance technique; Petites entreprises/secteur informel/artisanat; Secours d'urgence/réfugiés/aide humanitaire; Éducation/formation/alphabétisation. **Régions:** Asie du Sud-Est.

ACTIVITES D'INFORMATION ET D'EDUCATION: **Domaines:** Aliments/famine; Développement rural/agriculture; Enfants/jeunesse/famille; Secours d'urgence/réfugiés/aide humanitaire; Éducation/formation/alphabétisation. **Activités:** Campagnes d'information/expositions; Collecte de fonds; Conférences/séminaires/ateliers/activités de formation; Radiodiffusion/manifestations culturelles; Échanges/parrainage/jumelage; Éducation formelle.

FRA1938
ENFANTS DU MONDE - DROITS DE L'HOMME
13, rue Payenne, 75003 Paris, France.

Téléphone: 33 (1) 42 72 71 78. *Fax:* 33 (1) 42 72 64 06. *Contact:* Yves Buannic, Président.

OBJECTIFS: Défendre les droits de l'enfant en conformité avec la convention internationale des droits de l'enfant signée à l'ONU en novembre 1989.

INFORMATIONS GENERALES: *Création:* 1986. *Affiliée à:* Conseil Français des Associations pour les Droits (France) - La Voix de l'Enfant (France). *Personnel/Total:* 16. *Salariés:* 1. *Bénévoles:* 15 dont: 2 dans les pays en développement. *Budget/Total 1993:* ECU 146000 (US$ 171000). *Sources financières:* Privé: 49%. Public: 37%. Autofinancement: 14%.

PUBLICATIONS: *Périodiques:* Enfants du Monde-Droits de l'Homme (4). *Rapport annuel. Liste des publications.*

EVALUATION/RECHERCHE: Rapports d'évaluation disponibles.

PREVISIONS D'ACTIVITES: Réalisation d'une malette pédagogique destinée à tout enseignant ou personne souhaitant participer à la convention des droits de l'enfant.

ACTIVITES DANS LES REGIONS EN DEVELOPPEMENT: Intervient directement dans les régions en développement. Intervient dans 3 pays. Maintient une présence locale sur le terrain. Intervient par l'intermédiaire d'organisations locales partenaires. **Actions de Développement durable:** Aliments/famine; Droits de l'Homme/paix/conflits; Développement rural/agriculture; Enfants/jeunesse/famille; Envoi de volontaires/experts/assistance technique; Santé/assainissement/eau; Secours d'urgence/réfugiés/aide humanitaire; Éducation/formation/alphabétisation. **Régions:** Afrique du Nord; Amérique du Sud; Asie du Sud-Est; Mexique et Amerique centrale; Moyen-Orient.

ACTIVITES D'INFORMATION ET D'EDUCATION: **Domaines:** Aliments/famine; Culture/tradition/religion; Droits de l'Homme/paix/conflits; Enfants/jeunesse/famille; Paix/conflits ethniques/armement/désarmement; Pauvreté/conditions de vie; Santé/assainissement/eau; Secours d'urgence/réfugiés/aide humanitaire; Éducation/formation/alphabétisation. **Activités:** Campagnes d'information/expositions; Collecte de fonds; Conférences/séminaires/ateliers/activités de formation; Radiodiffusion/manifestations culturelles; Services d'information et de documentation/bases de données; Échanges/parrainage/jumelage; Édition/documents audiovisuels/documents éducatifs; Éducation formelle.

FRA1939
ENFANTS DU MONDE, FRANCE
126, boulevard Vauban, 59800 Lille, France.

Téléphone: 33 - 78 83 77 51. *Fax:* 33 - 78 83 97 38. *Contact:* Guy Mine, Président.

OBJECTIFS: Oeuvrer en faveur du partage des richessses et de cultures avec les pays du Tiers-Monde, en soutenant des projets de développement. Sensibiliser l'opinion publique française aux problèmes du développement.

INFORMATIONS GENERALES: *Création:* 1975. *Personnel/Total:* 80. *Bénévoles:* 80. *Budget/Total 1993:* ECU 302000 (US$ 353000). *Sources financières:* Privé: 95%. Autofinancement: 5%.

PUBLICATIONS: *Périodiques:* Enfants du Monde (4).

EVALUATION/RECHERCHE: Rapports d'évaluation disponibles.

COMMENTAIRES: L'association est agréée au plan national par l'adoption internationale.

ACTIVITES DANS LES REGIONS EN DEVELOPPEMENT: Intervient dans 18 pays. Intervient par l'intermédiaire d'organisations locales partenaires. **Actions de Développement durable:** Développement rural/agriculture; Développement urbain/habitat; Petites entreprises/secteur informel/artisanat; Questions relatives aux femmes; Santé/assainissement/eau; Éducation/formation/alphabétisation. **Régions:** Afrique centrale; Afrique de l'Est; Afrique de l'Ouest; Amérique du Sud; Asie centrale et Asie du Sud; Asie du Sud-Est; Caraïbes; Mexique et Amerique centrale.

ACTIVITES D'INFORMATION ET D'EDUCATION: **Domaines:** Culture/tradition/religion; Développement rural/agriculture; Développement urbain/habitat; Enfants/jeunesse/famille; Pauvreté/conditions de vie; Questions relatives aux femmes; Réfugiés/migrants/groupes ethniques; Santé/assainissement/eau; Écologie/environnement/biodiversité; Éducation/formation/alphabétisation. **Activités:** Campagnes d'information/expositions; Collecte de fonds.

FRA1940
LES ENFANTS DU SOLEIL
25 ter avenue du Cep, 78300 Poissy, France.

See: *How to Use the Directory*, page 11.

Téléphone: 33 (1) 30 65 84 66. *Contact:* Robert Richard.

FRA1941
ENFANTS ET DEVELOPPEMENT

13, rue Jules Simon, Esc. 6, 75015 Paris, France.

Téléphone: 33 (1) 48 42 23 03. *Fax:* 33 (1) 48 42 41 75. *Contact:* Danièle Cheysson, Présidente.

OBJECTIFS: Apporter une aide aux enfants particulièrement défavorisés, afin d'améliorer leur état de santé, leurs conditions de vie et leur formation.

INFORMATIONS GENERALES: *Création:* 1984. *Affiliée à:* Fédération de la Voix de l'Enfant - International Save the Children Alliance. *Personnel/Total:* 31. *Salariés:* 23 dont: 17 dans les pays en développement. *Bénévoles:* 8. *Budget/Total 1993:* ECU 1427000 (US$ 1672000). *Sources financières:* Privé: 34%. Public: 60%. Autofinancement: 6%.

PUBLICATIONS: *Périodiques:* Enfants et développement (4). *Liste des publications.*

EVALUATION/RECHERCHE: Rapports d'évaluation disponibles.

ACTIVITES DANS LES REGIONS EN DEVELOPPEMENT: Intervient directement dans les régions en développement. Intervient dans 4 pays. Maintient une présence locale sur le terrain. Intervient par l'intermédiaire d'organisations locales partenaires. **Actions de Développement durable:** Aliments/famine; Enfants/jeunesse/famille; Envoi de volontaires/experts/assistance technique; Population/planning familial/démographie; Questions relatives aux femmes; Santé/assainissement/eau; Éducation/formation/alphabétisation. **Régions:** Asie du Sud-Est.

ACTIVITES D'INFORMATION ET D'EDUCATION: Domaines: Santé/assainissement/eau. **Activités:** Échanges/parrainage/jumelage; Édition/documents audiovisuels/documents éducatifs; Éducation formelle.

FRA1942
ENFANTS REFUGIES DU MONDE (ERM)

Cap Gaillard, 34, rue Gaston Lauriau, 93100 Montreuil, France.

Téléphone: 33 (1) 48 59 60 29. *Fax:* 33 (1) 48 59 64 88. *Contact:* Dr. Mireille Szatan, Présidente.

OBJECTIFS: Intervenir auprès d'enfants réfugiés ou déplacés dans le Tiers-Monde en envoyant des équipes pluridisciplinaires pour la mise en œuvre de programmes à moyen et long terme dans les domaines de la santé, de l'éducation et de l'animation. Former du personnel local.

INFORMATIONS GENERALES: *Création:* 1981. *Affiliée à:* Fédération de la Voix de l'Enfant - ICCB/BICE (Suisse) - CLONG-Volontariat. *Personnel/Total:* 102. *Salariés:* 75 dont: 67 dans les pays en développement. *Bénévoles:* 27 dont: 17 dans les pays en développement. *Budget/Total 1993:* ECU 1269000 (US$ 1487000). *Sources financières:* Privé: 24%. Public: 67%. Autofinancement: 9%.

PUBLICATIONS: *Périodiques:* Bulletin d'ERM (4).

EVALUATION/RECHERCHE: Rapports d'évaluation disponibles.

COMMENTAIRES: Intervient dans la Communauté des Etats indépendants.

ACTIVITES DANS LES REGIONS EN DEVELOPPEMENT: Intervient directement dans les régions en développement. Intervient dans 5 pays. Maintient une présence locale sur le terrain. **Actions de Développement durable:** Enfants/jeunesse/famille; Envoi de volontaires/experts/assistance technique; Petites entreprises/secteur informel/artisanat; Secours d'urgence/réfugiés/aide humanitaire; Éducation/formation/alphabétisation. **Régions:** Afrique du Nord; Mexique et Amerique centrale; Moyen-Orient.

ACTIVITES D'INFORMATION ET D'EDUCATION: Domaines: Culture/tradition/religion; Droits de l'Homme/paix/conflits; Enfants/jeunesse/famille; Paix/conflits ethniques/armement/désarmement; Réfugiés/migrants/groupes ethniques; Secours d'urgence/réfugiés/aide humanitaire; Éducation/formation/alphabétisation. **Activités:** Campagnes d'information/expositions; Collecte de fonds; Services d'information et de documentation/bases de données; Échanges/parrainage/jumelage; Édition/documents audiovisuels/documents éducatifs.

FRA1943
ENSEIGNANTS FRANCAIS ET DEVELOPPEMENT INTERNATIONAL (EFDI)

13 rue Marceau, 37000 Tours, France.

Téléphone: 33 - 47 20 55 75. *Contact:* Gilbert Passot, Secrétaire.

FRA1944
ENTRAIDE MEDICALE INTERNATIONALE (EMI)

70, allée Jacques Prévert, 14790 Verson, France.

Téléphone: 33 - 31 26 20 30. *Fax:* 33 - 31 26 22 00. *Contact:* Dr. Pierre Lobry, Président.

OBJECTIFS: Mener des actions de santé publique.

INFORMATIONS GENERALES: *Création:* 1972. *Personnel/Total:* 45. *Salariés:* 9 dont: 7 dans les pays en développement. *Bénévoles:* 36 dont: 16 dans les pays en développement. *Budget/Total 1993:* ECU 573000 (US$ 671000). *Sources financières:* Public: 75%.

PUBLICATIONS: *Périodiques:* Les Nouvelles d'E.M.I (4). *Rapport annuel.*

EVALUATION/RECHERCHE: Rapports d'évaluation disponibles. Entreprend des activités de recherche.

ACTIVITES DANS LES REGIONS EN DEVELOPPEMENT: Intervient directement dans les régions en développement. Intervient dans 3 pays. Maintient une présence locale sur le terrain. Intervient par l'intermédiaire d'organisations locales partenaires. **Actions de Développement durable:** Envoi de volontaires/experts/assistance technique; Santé/assainissement/eau. **Régions:** Afrique de l'Ouest.

ACTIVITES D'INFORMATION ET D'EDUCATION: Domaines: Santé/assainissement/eau. **Activités:** Collecte de fonds; Conférences/séminaires/ateliers/activités de formation.

FRA1945
ENTREPRISE ET DEVELOPPEMENT - RESEAU D'INITIATIVES DECENTRALISEES POUR LE PARTENARIAT INDUSTRIEL NORD-SUD

12 rue Henri Barbusse, 13001 Marseille, France.

Téléphone: 33 - 91 08 60 84. *Contact:* Jean-Claude Sitbon.

FRA1946
ENVIRONNEMENT ET DEVELOPPEMENT DU TIERS MONDE - DELEGATION EN EUROPE (ENDA-TM) ♦ Environment and Development of the Third World - European Delegation

5, rue des Immeubles Industriels, 75011 Paris, France.

Téléphone: 33 (1) 43 72 09 09. *Fax:* (1) 43 72 16 81. *Courrier électronique:* Endaparis@globenet.gn.apc.org. *Contact:* Henri de Reboul, délégué général.

OBJECTIFS: Engager des campagnes de sensibilisation sur les thèmes de l'environnement. Faire le lien entre les équipes et les antennes d'ENDA au Sud et les partenaires du Nord.

INFORMATIONS GENERALES: *Création:* 1990. *Affiliée à:* ENDA Tiers Monde (Sénégal). *Personnel/Total:* 23. *Salariés:* 8 dont: 1 dans les pays en développement. *Bénévoles:* 15. *Budget/Total 1993:* ECU 302000 (US$ 353000). *Sources financières:* Privé: 40%. Public: 50%. Autofinancement: 10%.

PUBLICATIONS: *Périodiques:* Vivre autrement (4). *Rapport annuel. Liste des publications.*

EVALUATION/RECHERCHE: Rapports d'évaluation disponibles. Entreprend des activités de recherche.

ACTIVITES DANS LES REGIONS EN DEVELOPPEMENT: Intervient dans 15 pays. Intervient par l'intermédiaire d'organisations locales partenaires. **Actions de Développement durable:** Droits de l'Homme/paix/conflits; Démocratie/bonne gestion publique/création d'institutions/développement participatif; Développement rural/agriculture; Développement urbain/habitat; Enfants/jeunesse/famille; Petites entreprises/secteur informel/artisanat; Population/planning familial/démographie; Questions relatives aux femmes; Santé/assainissement/eau; Écologie/environnement/biodiversité; Éducation/formation/alphabétisation; Éner-

Voir : *Comment utiliser le répertoire*, page 11.

gie/transport. **Régions:** Afrique australe; Afrique centrale; Afrique de l'Ouest; Afrique du Nord; Amérique du Sud; Asie du Sud-Est; Caraïbes.

ACTIVITES D'INFORMATION ET D'EDUCATION: Domaines: Autres; Droits de l'Homme/paix/conflits; Développement rural/agriculture; Développement urbain/habitat; Emploi/chômage; Enfants/jeunesse/famille; Paix/conflits ethniques/armement/désarmement; Pauvreté/conditions de vie; Population/planning familial/démographie; Questions relatives aux femmes; Racisme/xénophobie/antisémitisme; Relations internationales/coopération/aide au développement; Réfugiés/migrants/groupes ethniques; Santé/assainissement/eau; Écologie/environnement/biodiversité; Éducation/formation/alphabétisation. **Activités:** Campagnes d'information/expositions; Collecte de fonds; Conférences/séminaires/ateliers/activités de formation; Lobbying/plaidoyer; Services d'information et de documentation/bases de données; Échanges/parrainage/jumelage; Édition/documents audiovisuels/documents éducatifs; Éducation formelle.

FRA1947
EPARGNE SANS FRONTIERE (ESF)

32, rue Le Peletier, 75009 Paris, France.

Téléphone: 33 (1) 48 00 96 82. **Fax:** 33 (1) 48 00 96 59. **Contact:** Guy Dupasquier, Président.

OBJECTIFS: Etudier les problèmes liés au financement du développement. Favoriser la synergie entre les différents intervenants dans les projets de développement. Coupler l'épargne du Nord et du Sud, pour la rendre plus productive. Promouvoir la création de nouveaux produits financiers. Diffuser l'information relative à ces questions.

INFORMATIONS GENERALES: Création: 1985. **Type d'organisation:** réseau. **Affiliée à:** Collectif ONG France/ Afrique du Sud (France). **Personnel/Total:** 3. Salariés: 3 dont: 1 dans les pays en développement. **Budget/Total 1993:** ECU 151000 (US$ 177000).

PUBLICATIONS: Périodiques: "Techniques Financières et Développement" (4).

EVALUATION/RECHERCHE: Entreprend des activités de recherche.

PREVISIONS D'ACTIVITES: Epargne sans Frontière lance avec le soutien de l'Union Européenne une Campagne de vulgarisation, éclaircissement et approfondissement des nouveaux mécanismes et nouvelles logiques de financement du développement.

COMMENTAIRES: Intervient dans la Communauté des Etats indépendants. Activités d'information concernant la Communauté des Etats indépendants. **Actions de Développement durable:** Dette/finances/commerce; Développement rural/agriculture; Développement urbain/habitat; Petites entreprises/secteur informel/artisanat; Questions relatives aux femmes. **Régions:** Afrique australe; Afrique centrale; Afrique de l'Est; Afrique de l'Ouest; Afrique du Nord; Amérique du Sud; Mexique et Amerique centrale.

ACTIVITES D'INFORMATION ET D'EDUCATION: Domaines: Développement rural/agriculture; Développement urbain/habitat; Questions relatives aux femmes; Relations économiques internationales/commerce/dette/finances. **Activités:** Campagnes d'information/expositions; Conférences/séminaires/ateliers/activités de formation; Services d'information et de documentation/bases de données.

FRA1948
EQUILIBRE

23 allée du Mens, B.P. 1613, 69606 Villeurbanne Cedex (Lyon), France.

Téléphone: 33 - 78 79 33 33. **Fax:** 33- 78 79 50 02. **Courrier électronique:** 3615 Equilibre. **Contact:** Alain Michel, Président.

OBJECTIFS: Acheminer des produits de première nécessité de la France vers les pays qui en manquent. Résoudre les problèmes des pays en détresse par une aide d'urgence associée à un programme de développement. Réinserrer socialement, en France, par l'humanitaire et la formation, les gens en difficulté.

INFORMATIONS GENERALES: Création: 1984. **Personnel/Total:** 745. Salariés: 245 dont: 160 dans les pays en développement. Bénévoles: 500. **Budget/Total 1993:** ECU 13030000 (US$ 15262000). **Sources financières:** Privé: 16%. Public: 81%. Autofinancement: 3%.

PUBLICATIONS: Périodiques: Présence dans le monde (4). *Rapport annuel.*

COMMENTAIRES: Intervient dans la Communauté des Etats indépendants.

ACTIVITES DANS LES REGIONS EN DEVELOPPEMENT: Intervient directement dans les régions en développement. Intervient dans 9 pays. Maintient une présence locale sur le terrain. Intervient par l'intermédiaire d'organisations locales partenaires. **Actions de Développement durable:** Développement rural/agriculture; Développement urbain/habitat; Enfants/jeunesse/famille; Envoi de volontaires/experts/assistance technique; Petites entreprises/secteur informel/artisanat; Questions relatives aux femmes; Santé/assainissement/eau; Secours d'urgence/réfugiés/aide humanitaire; Éducation/formation/alphabétisation; Énergie/transport. **Régions:** Afrique australe; Afrique centrale; Afrique de l'Ouest; Moyen-Orient.

FRA1949
EQUILIBRES ET POPULATIONS

140 rue Jules Guesde, 92300 Levallois-Perret, France.

Téléphone: 33 (1) 47 30 76 62. **Fax:** 33 (1) 47 30 76 93. **Contact:** Marie-Claude Tesson-Millet, Présidente.

OBJECTIFS: Développer l'aide aux pays en développement, promouvoir la réflexion et l'action internationales dans le domaine de la démographie. Contribuer à la mise en place et au soutien de programmes d'aide à la santé, l'information et l'éducation.

INFORMATIONS GENERALES: Création: 1993. Salariés: 1. Bénévoles: 3. **Budget/Total 1993:** ECU 226000 (US$ 265000).

PUBLICATIONS: Périodiques: Lettre mensuelle d'information (12).

ACTIVITES DANS LES REGIONS EN DEVELOPPEMENT: Intervient directement dans les régions en développement. **Actions de Développement durable:** Population/planning familial/démographie. **Régions:** Afrique de l'Ouest.

ACTIVITES D'INFORMATION ET D'EDUCATION: Domaines: Aliments/famine; Pauvreté/conditions de vie; Population/planning familial/démographie; Questions relatives aux femmes; Relations internationales/coopération/aide au développement; Écologie/environnement/biodiversité. **Activités:** Conférences/séminaires/ateliers/activités de formation; Lobbying/plaidoyer.

FRA1950
ESPOIR POUR UN ENFANT

27, bd Louis Blanc, Maison des Tiers-Mondes, 34090 Montpellier, France.

Téléphone: 33 - 67 27 66 75. **Contact:** Chantal Duplissy, Présidente.

FRA1951
ETUDIANTS POUR LE DEVELOPPEMENT (EPDE)

Rue Pierre Waguet, BP 585, 60005 Beauvais, France.

Téléphone: 33 - 44 48 22 57. **Contact:** Bertrand Dayot, Président.

FRA1952
FASSODEMIN

12 rue des Bapaumes, 95130 Le Plessis-Bouchard, France.

Téléphone: 33 - 34 15 92 97. **Contact:** Kaba Djiba, Président.

FRA1953
FEDERATION ABOLITIONISTE MONDIALE

29 rue Henri Laurain, 21000 Dijon, France.

Contact: José Dillenseger.

FRA1954
FEDERATION ARTISANS DU MONDE (FAM)

4 rue Franklin, 75019 Saint Denis, France.

Téléphone: 33 (1) 40 35 17 22. **Contact:** Jean-Luc Duret, Président.

See: *How to Use the Directory,* page 11.

FRA1955

FEDERATION DES ASSOCIATIONS DE RECHERCHE ET D'EDUCATION POUR LA PAIX (FAREP)

16 rue Giono, 91000 Evry, France.

Téléphone: 33 (1) 64 97 83 46. **Fax:** 33 (1) 60 78 28 61.

OBJECTIFS: Coordonner l'action de centres de recherches, d'initiatives et de formation sur les questions de conflits et de leur résolution.

INFORMATIONS GENERALES: *Création:* 1980. *Type d'organisation:* regroupement d'ONG. *Organisations membres:* 5. *Personnel/Total:* 315. *Salariés:* 15. *Bénévoles:* 300. *Budget/Total 1993:* ECU 45000 (US$ 53000).

EVALUATION/RECHERCHE: Entreprend des activités de recherche.

ACTIVITES DANS LES REGIONS EN DEVELOPPEMENT: Intervient dans 4 pays. Intervient par l'intermédiaire d'organisations locales partenaires. **Actions de Développement durable:** Droits de l'Homme/paix/conflits. **Régions:** Afrique centrale; Afrique de l'Ouest; Afrique du Nord; Moyen-Orient.

ACTIVITES D'INFORMATION ET D'EDUCATION: Domaines: Paix/conflits ethniques/armement/désarmement. **Activités:** Campagnes d'information/expositions; Conférences/séminaires/ateliers/activités de formation; Services d'information et de documentation/bases de données; Échanges/parrainage/jumelage; Édition/documents audiovisuels/documents éducatifs.

FRA1956

FEDERATION DES ASSOCIATIONS FRANCO-AFRICAINES DE DEVELOPPEMENT (FAFRAD)

9 boulevard Saint Martin, 75003 Paris, France.

Téléphone: 33 (1) 48 91 91 34. **Fax:** 33 (1) 40 26 34 67. **Contact:** Yéra Dembélé, Président.

OBJECTIFS: Procéder à l'approvisionnement en eau potable, à la création d'abreuvoirs, à l'assainissement rural et à l'aménagement hydroagricole. Fournir du matériel agricole, médical et scolaire, ainsi que des médicaments.

INFORMATIONS GENERALES: *Création:* 1992. *Type d'organisation:* regroupement d'ONG. *Organisations membres:* 75. *Affiliée à:* LIACOFA - Comité Inter-ONG pour les Jeunes de la Rue. *Personnel/Total:* 69. *Salariés:* 4. *Bénévoles:* 65 dont: 55 dans les pays en développement. *Budget/Total 1993:* ECU 28000 (US$ 33000). *Sources financières:* Privé: 5%. Autofinancement: 95%.

PUBLICATIONS: *Périodiques:* Liaison Franco-Africaine (6). *Rapport annuel. Liste des publications.*

EVALUATION/RECHERCHE: Rapports d'évaluation disponibles. Entreprend des activités de recherche.

ACTIVITES DANS LES REGIONS EN DEVELOPPEMENT: Intervient directement dans les régions en développement. Intervient dans 7 pays. Maintient une présence locale sur le terrain. Intervient par l'intermédiaire d'organisations locales partenaires. **Actions de Développement durable:** Aliments/famine; Dette/finances/commerce; Droits de l'Homme/paix/conflits; Démocratie/bonne gestion publique/création d'institutions/développement participatif; Développement rural/agriculture; Développement urbain/habitat; Enfants/jeunesse/famille; Envoi de volontaires/experts/assistance technique; Petites entreprises/secteur informel/artisanat; Population/planning familial/démographie; Questions relatives aux femmes; Santé/assainissement/eau; Secours d'urgence/réfugiés/aide humanitaire; Écologie/environnement/biodiversité; Éducation/formation/alphabétisation; Énergie/transport. **Régions:** Afrique australe; Afrique centrale; Afrique de l'Est; Afrique de l'Ouest; Afrique du Nord.

ACTIVITES D'INFORMATION ET D'EDUCATION: Domaines: Aliments/famine; Culture/tradition/religion; Droits de l'Homme/paix/conflits; Développement rural/agriculture; Développement urbain/habitat; Enfants/jeunesse/famille; Paix/conflits ethniques/armement/désarmement; Pauvreté/conditions de vie; Population/planning familial/démographie; Questions relatives aux femmes; Racisme/xénophobie/antisémitisme; Relations internationales/coopération/aide au développement; Relations économiques internationales/commerce/dette/finances; Réfugiés/migrants/groupes ethniques; Santé/assainissement/eau; Secours d'urgence/réfugiés/aide humanitaire; Écologie/environnement/biodiver-

sité; Éducation/formation/alphabétisation. **Activités:** Autres; Campagnes d'information/expositions; Conférences/séminaires/ateliers/activités de formation; Lobbying/plaidoyer; Radiodiffusion/manifestations culturelles; Réseaux/télécommunications électroniques; Services d'information et de documentation/bases de données; Échanges/parrainage/jumelage; Édition/documents audiovisuels/documents éducatifs; Éducation formelle.

FRA1957

FEDERATION DES TRAVAILLEURS AFRICAINS (FETAF)

Esplanade Benoit Frachon, 93100 Montreuil, France.

Téléphone: 33 (1) 48 58 28 84. **Contact:** Guèye Sidi Tidiane.

OBJECTIFS: Organiser la solidarité entre les travailleurs africains immigrés en France; défendre les intérêts matériels et moraux de ses adhérents; assurer une assistance sur tous les plans, aux travailleurs migrants africains en France et en Europe.

INFORMATIONS GENERALES: *Création:* 1981. *Type d'organisation:* regroupement d'ONG. *Organisations membres:* 16. *Personnel/Total:* 20. *Salariés:* 8. *Bénévoles:* 12. *Budget/Total 1993:* ECU 53000 (US$ 62000). *Sources financières:* Public: 90%. Autofinancement: 10%.

PUBLICATIONS: *Périodiques:* Flash Info (4). *Liste des publications.*

EVALUATION/RECHERCHE: Rapports d'évaluation disponibles.

ACTIVITES D'INFORMATION ET D'EDUCATION: Domaines: Droits de l'Homme/paix/conflits; Emploi/chômage; Racisme/xénophobie/antisémitisme; Réfugiés/migrants/groupes ethniques; Secours d'urgence/réfugiés/aide humanitaire; Éducation/formation/alphabétisation. **Activités:** Campagnes d'information/expositions; Collecte de fonds; Conférences/séminaires/ateliers/activités de formation; Lobbying/plaidoyer; Radiodiffusion/manifestations culturelles; Édition/documents audiovisuels/documents éducatifs; Éducation formelle.

FRA1958

FEDERATION EUROPEENNE DE PROFESSIONNELS DE L'ENVIRONNEMENT

55 rue de Varenne, 75007 Paris, France.

FRA1959

FEDERATION FRANCAISE DES CLUBS UNESCO (FFCU) ♦
French Federation of Unesco Clubs

2 rue Lapeyrère, 75018 Paris, France.

Téléphone: 33 (1) 42 58 68 06. **Fax:** 33 (1) 46 06 28 08. **Contact:** Bruno Granozio, Délégué Général.

FRA1960

FEDERATION INTERNATIONALE DE L'ACTION DES CHRETIENS POUR L'ABOLITION DE LA TORTURE (FIACAT)

27 rue de Maubeuge, 75009 Paris, France.

Téléphone: 33 (1) 42 80 01 60. **Fax:** 33 (1) 42 80 20 89. **Contact:** Guy Aurenche, Président.

OBJECTIFS: Faciliter la coordination entre les associations affiliées aux organisations internationales où la FIACAT a le statut consultatif (ONU, Conseil de l'Europe, Commission Africaine des droits de l'homme et des peuples), assurer une formation aux membres des ACAT en organisant des séminaires.

INFORMATIONS GENERALES: *Création:* 1987. *Type d'organisation:* regroupement d'ONG. *Organisations membres:* 26. *Personnel/Total:* 9. *Bénévoles:* 9. *Budget/Total 1993:* ECU 80000 (US$ 94000). *Sources financières:* Privé: 34%. Public: 52%. Autofinancement: 14%.

PUBLICATIONS: *Périodiques:* FIACAT Information (4).

PREVISIONS D'ACTIVITES: Colloque international et séminaire de réflexion à Munster (Allemagne) 7-11 Juin 95 sur "paroles chrétiennes sur un chemin de réconciliation". Séminaire de formation aux droits de l'homme Bucarest sept.95

Voir : *Comment utiliser le répertoire,* page 11.

COMMENTAIRES: La FIACAT lance des campagnes qui sont reprises par toutes les ACAT membres, en 1995: peine de mort. Intervient dans la Communauté des Etats indépendants. Activités d'information concernant la Communauté des Etats indépendants.

ACTIVITES DANS LES REGIONS EN DEVELOPPEMENT: Intervient directement dans les régions en développement. Maintient une présence locale sur le terrain. Intervient par l'intermédiaire d'organisations locales partenaires. **Actions de Développement durable:** Droits de l'Homme/paix/conflits. **Régions:** Afrique centrale; Afrique de l'Ouest; Amérique du Sud; Asie du Sud-Est; Mexique et Amerique centrale.

ACTIVITES D'INFORMATION ET D'EDUCATION: Domaines: Droits de l'Homme/paix/conflits. **Activités:** Campagnes d'information/expositions; Collecte de fonds; Conférences/séminaires/ateliers/activités de formation; Lobbying/plaidoyer; Échanges/parrainage/jumelage; Éducation formelle.

FRA1961

FEDERATION INTERNATIONALE DES CENTRES D'ENTRAINEMENT AUX METHODES D'EDUCATION ACTIVES (FICEMEA)

76 boulevard de la Villette, 75940 Paris cedex 19, France.

Téléphone: 33 (1) 40 40 43 43. *Fax:* 33 (1) 40 40 43 19. *Contact:* Claude Vercautere.

FRA1962

FEDERATION INTERNATIONALE DES LIGUES DES DROITS DE L'HOMME (FIDH)

14 passage Dubail, 75010 Paris, France.

Téléphone: 33 (1) 40 37 54 26. *Fax:* 33 (1) 44 72 05 86. *Contact:* Mr. P.Y Chenivesse-Bernadac, Secrétaire administratif.

FRA1963

FEDERATION INTERNATIONALE POUR L'ECONOMIE FAMILIALE (FIEF)

5 avenue de la Porte Brancion, 75015 Paris, France.

Téléphone: 33 (1) 48 42 34 74. *Fax:* 33 (1) 42 50 09 89. *Contact:* Odette Goncet.

FRA1964

FEDERATION MONDIALE DES CITES UNIES ET VILLES JUMELEES (FMVJ)

22 rue d'Alsace, 92300 Levallois-Perret cedex, France.

Téléphone: 33 (1) 47 39 36 86. *Fax:* 33 (1) 47 39 36 85. *Contact:* Hubert Lesire-Ogrel, Secrétaire général.

OBJECTIFS: Développer les relations et la coopération internationale entre les villes et les collectivités territoriales. Promouvoir la mise en place de pouvoirs locaux démocratiques, basés sur la participation des citoyens. Défendre les droits de l'homme et les libertés individuelles et collectives. Agir pour la paix par les échanges entre les peuples. Contribuer à un développement durable par la coopération.

INFORMATIONS GENERALES: *Création:* 1957. *Personnel/Total:* 23. *Salariés:* 20. *Bénévoles:* 3. *Budget/Total 1993:* ECU 1477000 (US$ 1730000). *Sources financières:* Privé: 25%. Public: 15%. Autofinancement: 60%.

PUBLICATIONS: *Périodiques:* Lettre Des Cités Unies (6). *Rapport annuel.*

EVALUATION/RECHERCHE: Rapports d'évaluation disponibles.

PREVISIONS D'ACTIVITES: La priorité sera donnée à la question de l'autonomie et la démocratie locales

COMMENTAIRES: La FMCU a créé depuis 1989 une Agence (Cités Unies Développement- CUD) chargée de mettre en œuvre les projets de coopération décentralisée menés dans le cadre de la Fédération (même adresse). Intervient dans la Communauté des Etats indépendants. Activités d'information concernant la Communauté des Etats indépendants.

ACTIVITES DANS LES REGIONS EN DEVELOPPEMENT: Intervient directement dans les régions en développement. Maintient une pré-

sence locale sur le terrain. **Actions de Développement durable:** Droits de l'Homme/paix/conflits; Démocratie/bonne gestion publique/création d'institutions/développement participatif; Développement urbain/habitat; Santé/assainissement/eau; Écologie/environnement/biodiversité. **Régions:** Afrique de l'Ouest; Afrique du Nord; Amérique du Sud; Asie du Sud-Est; Caraïbes; Mexique et Amerique centrale; Moyen-Orient.

ACTIVITES D'INFORMATION ET D'EDUCATION: Domaines: Droits de l'Homme/paix/conflits; Développement urbain/habitat; Racisme/xénophobie/antisémitisme; Relations internationales/coopération/aide au développement; Santé/assainissement/eau; Écologie/environnement/biodiversité. **Activités:** Conférences/séminaires/ateliers/activités de formation; Échanges/parrainage/jumelage.

FRA1965

FEMMES SOUS LOIS MUSULMANES

BP 23, 34790 Grabels (Montpellier), France.

Contact: Ms. Marie-Aimee Helie-Luca.

FRA1966

FIDESCO

BP 137, 92223 Bagneux Cedex, France.

Téléphone: 33 (1) 41 17 48 20. *Fax:* 33 (1) 46 55 71 29. *Contact:* Christian You, Délégué général.

OBJECTIFS: Promouvoir le développement intégral de l'homme par la coopération technique

INFORMATIONS GENERALES: *Création:* 1981. *Affiliée à:* Délégation catholique de coopération (France). *Personnel/Total:* 66. *Salariés:* 6. *Bénévoles:* 60 dont: 55 dans les pays en développement. *Budget/Total 1993:* ECU 784000 (US$ 918000). *Sources financières:* Privé: 94%. Autofinancement: 6%.

PUBLICATIONS: *Périodiques:* Le Courrier de Fidesco (4). *Rapport annuel.*

EVALUATION/RECHERCHE: Entreprend des activités de recherche.

PREVISIONS D'ACTIVITES: Développement en Asie (Vietnam, Philippines, Thaïlande), en Amérique du Sud (Pérou, Nicaragua, Brésil). Augmenter le nombre de volontaires.

COMMENTAIRES: Intervient dans la Communauté des Etats indépendants. Activités d'information concernant la Communauté des Etats indépendants.

ACTIVITES DANS LES REGIONS EN DEVELOPPEMENT: Intervient directement dans les régions en développement. Intervient dans 12 pays. Maintient une présence locale sur le terrain. Intervient par l'intermédiaire d'organisations locales partenaires. **Actions de Développement durable:** Aliments/famine; Développement rural/agriculture; Enfants/jeunesse/famille; Envoi de volontaires/experts/assistance technique; Santé/assainissement/eau; Éducation/formation/alphabétisation. **Régions:** Afrique australe; Afrique centrale; Afrique de l'Est; Afrique de l'Ouest; Afrique du Nord; Asie centrale et Asie du Sud; Asie de l'Est; Asie du Sud-Est.

ACTIVITES D'INFORMATION ET D'EDUCATION: Domaines: Culture/tradition/religion; Développement rural/agriculture; Enfants/jeunesse/famille; Relations internationales/coopération/aide au développement; Santé/assainissement/eau; Éducation/formation/alphabétisation. **Activités:** Autres; Collecte de fonds; Éducation formelle.

FRA1967

FONDATION DE FRANCE

40 avenue Hoche, 75008 Paris, France.

Téléphone: 33 (1) 42 25 66 66. *Fax:* 33 (1) 45 63 92 59. *Contact:* Anne-Marie Seydoux, Directeur des programmes.

OBJECTIFS: Apporter un soutien financier à des projets de développement menés par des ONG, de préférence des ONG du Sud, dans des domaines prioritaires (l'épargne, le crédit, la création d'entreprises, les initiatives urbaines, les échanges Sud-Sud et le transfert des compétences), ainsi qu'à des programmes menés dans des régions prioritaires (le fleuve Sénégal, Madagascar, Asie du Sud-Est).

See: *How to Use the Directory,* page 11.

INFORMATIONS GENERALES: *Création:* 1969. *Personnel/Total:* 57. *Salariés:* 57. *Sources financières:* *Privé:* 100%.

PUBLICATIONS: *Périodiques:* Journal de la Fondation de Franc (12). *Rapport annuel. Liste des publications.*

EVALUATION/RECHERCHE: Rapports d'évaluation disponibles. Entreprend des activités de recherche.

COMMENTAIRES: Intervient dans la Communauté des Etats indépendants. Activités d'information concernant la Communauté des Etats indépendants.

ACTIVITES DANS LES REGIONS EN DEVELOPPEMENT: Intervient dans 12 pays. Intervient par l'intermédiaire d'organisations locales partenaires. **Actions de Développement durable:** Développement rural/agriculture; Développement urbain/habitat; Enfants/jeunesse/famille; Petites entreprises/secteur informel/artisanat; Questions relatives aux femmes; Santé/assainissement/eau; Secours d'urgence/réfugiés/aide humanitaire; Écologie/environnement/biodiversité; Éducation/formation/alphabétisation. **Régions:** Afrique de l'Est; Afrique de l'Ouest; Asie du Sud-Est; Caraïbes; Mexique et Amerique centrale; Moyen-Orient; Océanie.

FRA1968
FONDATION DE L'EAU (FDE) ♦ Water Foundation

Rue Edouard Chamberland, 87065 Limoges cedex, France.

Téléphone: 33 - 55 79 77 99. *Fax:* 33 - 55 77 71 15. *Contact:* Patrick R. Philip, Directeur.

FRA1969
FONDATION INTERNATIONALE POUR LE DEVELOPPEMENT (FID)

39 rue de la Rochefoucauld, 92200 Boulogne, France.

Téléphone: 33 (1) 48 25 27 23. *Contact:* Philippe de la Roche.

FRA1970
FONDATION LEILA FODIL

37 Boulevard de Bury, 16000 Angoulème, France.

Téléphone: 33 - 45 95 28 52. *Fax:* 33 - 45 94 62 45. *Contact:* Dr. Jean Bernard Joly, Président.

OBJECTIFS: Apporter une aide dans le domaine de la santé des enfants, dans les pays en développement.

INFORMATIONS GENERALES: *Création:* 1992. *Personnel/Total:* 2. *Bénévoles:* 2. *Budget/Total 1993:* ECU 19000 (US$ 23000). *Sources financières:* *Autofinancement:* 100%.

PUBLICATIONS: *Rapport annuel.*

EVALUATION/RECHERCHE: Rapports d'évaluation disponibles.

COMMENTAIRES: Intervient dans la Communauté des Etats indépendants.

ACTIVITES DANS LES REGIONS EN DEVELOPPEMENT: Intervient directement dans les régions en développement. Intervient dans 4 pays. **Actions de Développement durable:** Population/planning familial/démographie; Santé/assainissement/eau. **Régions:** Afrique de l'Ouest; Afrique du Nord; Asie du Sud-Est.

ACTIVITES D'INFORMATION ET D'EDUCATION: Domaines: Population/planning familial/démographie; Santé/assainissement/eau. **Activités:** Conférences/séminaires/ateliers/activités de formation; Édition/documents audiovisuels/documents éducatifs.

FRA1971
FONDATION LIBANAISE POUR LA PAIX CIVILE PERMANENTE

58 Rue d'Issy, 92170 Vanves, France.

Téléphone: 33 (1) 46 42 87 97/44 27 16 25. *Contact:* Georges Dagher, Représentant en France.

FRA1972
FONDATION POUR LE MECENAT HUMANITAIRE (FMH)

14 rue de Londres, 75009 Paris, France.

Téléphone: 33 (1) 40 82 16 02. *Contact:* Jean-Jacques Guicheney.

FRA1973
FONDS DE SOLIDARITE POUR LE LIBAN

33 rue de Dantzig, 75015 Paris, France.

Téléphone: 33 (1) 48 28 72 42. *Contact:* André Récipon.

FRA1974
FOYER D'ECHANGES ET DE RENCONTRES ADMINISTRATIFS MONDIAUX (FERAM)

56 rue Gay-Lussac, 75005 Paris, France.

Téléphone: 33 (1) 46 33 95 99. *Contact:* Jean Mouton-Brady, Président.

OBJECTIFS: Accueillir des administrateurs étrangers en stage de formation en France. Créer un réseau mondial entre les anciens stagiaires dans un esprit d'amitié et de paix.

INFORMATIONS GENERALES: *Création:* 1965. *Personnel/Total:* 15. *Bénévoles:* 15. *Budget/Total 1993:* ECU 29000 (US$ 34000). *Sources financières:* *Privé:* 15%. *Public:* 60%. *Autofinancement:* 25%.

PUBLICATIONS: *Périodiques:* Le Courrier du Feram (4). *Rapport annuel.*

COMMENTAIRES: Intervient dans la Communauté des Etats indépendants. Activités d'information concernant la Communauté des Etats indépendants.

ACTIVITES DANS LES REGIONS EN DEVELOPPEMENT: Intervient dans 87 pays. Intervient par l'intermédiaire d'organisations locales partenaires. **Actions de Développement durable:** Droits de l'Homme/paix/conflits; Démocratie/bonne gestion publique/création d'institutions/développement participatif. **Régions:** Afrique centrale; Afrique de l'Ouest; Afrique du Nord; Amérique du Sud; Asie du Sud-Est; Mexique et Amerique centrale; Moyen-Orient.

ACTIVITES D'INFORMATION ET D'EDUCATION: Domaines: Droits de l'Homme/paix/conflits; Relations internationales/coopération/aide au développement. **Activités:** Conférences/séminaires/ateliers/activités de formation; Radiodiffusion/manifestations culturelles; Échanges/parrainage/jumelage.

FRA1975
FRANCE AMERIQUE LATINE (FAL)

37 boulevard Saint Jacques, 75014 Paris, France.

Téléphone: 33 (1) 45 88 20 00. *Fax:* 33 (1) 45 65 20 87. *Contact:* Gérard Fenoy, Secrétaire général.

OBJECTIFS: Réaliser des actions d'alphabétisation. Participer à des constructions d'écoles. Apporter une aide d'urgence à l'enfance. Aider au développement sanitaire de l'Amérique Latine. Former des animateurs culturels.

INFORMATIONS GENERALES: *Création:* 1970. *Affiliée à:* Plate-forme Française ONG-CEE - Commission Coopération Développement (France). *Personnel/Total:* 23. *Salariés:* 6 dont: 1 dans les pays en développement. *Bénévoles:* 17 dont: 7 dans les pays en développement. *Budget/Total 1993:* ECU 1019000 (US$ 1194000). *Sources financières:* *Privé:* 10%. *Public:* 25%. *Autofinancement:* 65%.

PUBLICATIONS: *Périodiques:* France-Amérique Latine Magazine (24). *Rapport annuel.*

EVALUATION/RECHERCHE: Rapports d'évaluation disponibles.

ACTIVITES DANS LES REGIONS EN DEVELOPPEMENT: Intervient directement dans les régions en développement. Intervient dans 10 pays. Intervient par l'intermédiaire d'organisations locales partenaires. **Actions de Développement durable:** Droits de l'Homme/paix/conflits; Démocratie/bonne gestion publique/création d'institutions/développement participatif; Enfants/jeunesse/famille; Envoi de volontaires/experts/assistance technique; Population/planning familial/démographie; Questions relatives aux femmes; Secours d'urgence/réfugiés/

aide humanitaire; Éducation/formation/alphabétisation. **Régions:** Amérique du Sud; Caraïbes; Mexique et Amerique centrale.

ACTIVITES D'INFORMATION ET D'EDUCATION: Domaines: Culture/tradition/religion; Enfants/jeunesse/famille; Paix/conflits ethniques/armement/désarmement; Questions relatives aux femmes. **Activités:** Conférences/séminaires/ateliers/activités de formation.

FRA1976
LA FRANCE AVEC VOUS

2 rue Neuve Saint Pierre, 75004 Paris, France.

Téléphone: 33 (1) 48 87 92 23. **Contact:** Anne Bolliet.

FRA1977
FRANCE TERRE D'ASILE (FTDA)

4/6 passage Louis-Philippe, 75011 Paris, France.

Téléphone: 33 (1) 48 07 10 10. **Fax:** 33 (1) 48 07 26 50. **Contact:** Mr. G. Millet, Directeur.

FRA1978
FRANCE-LIBERTES FONDATION DANIELLE MITTERRAND

Palais de Chaillot, 1 place du Trocadéro, 75116 Paris, France.

Téléphone: 33 (1) 47 55 81 81. **Fax:** 33 (1) 47 04 37 07. **Contact:** Danielle Mitterrand, Présidente.

OBJECTIFS: Favoriser l'épanouissement ainsi que le renforcement des libertés individuelles et collectives dans le monde, en soutenant, notamment, les plus démunis.

INFORMATIONS GENERALES: Création: 1981. **Type d'organisation:** collectif. **Affiliée à:** Collectif Rwanda-Afrique du Sud-Haïti-Algérie - Collectif ex-Yougoslavie -Réseau Passeport Européen contre le Racisme (France). *Salariés:* 10. *Bénévoles:* 100 dont: 50 dans les pays en développement. **Budget/Total 1993:** ECU 3784000 (US$ 4432000). **Sources financières:** *Privé:* 85%. *Public:* 10%. *Autofinancement:* 5%.

PUBLICATIONS: Périodiques: Lettre de la Fondation (4). *Rapport annuel.*

COMMENTAIRES: Intervient dans la Communauté des Etats indépendants.

ACTIVITES DANS LES REGIONS EN DEVELOPPEMENT: Intervient directement dans les régions en développement. Intervient dans 40 pays. Maintient une présence locale sur le terrain. Intervient par l'intermédiaire d'organisations locales partenaires. **Actions de Développement durable:** Aliments/famine; Droits de l'Homme/paix/conflits; Développement rural/agriculture; Développement urbain/habitat; Enfants/jeunesse/famille; Questions relatives aux femmes; Santé/assainissement/eau; Secours d'urgence/réfugiés/aide humanitaire; Éducation/formation/alphabétisation. **Régions:** Afrique australe; Afrique centrale; Afrique de l'Est; Afrique de l'Ouest; Afrique du Nord; Amérique du Sud; Asie centrale et Asie du Sud; Asie de l'Est; Asie du Sud-Est; Caraïbes; Mexique et Amerique centrale; Moyen-Orient.

ACTIVITES D'INFORMATION ET D'EDUCATION: Domaines: Aliments/famine; Culture/tradition/religion; Droits de l'Homme/paix/conflits; Développement rural/agriculture; Développement urbain/habitat; Enfants/jeunesse/famille; Paix/conflits ethniques/armement/désarmement; Pauvreté/conditions de vie; Questions relatives aux femmes; Racisme/xénophobie/antisémitisme; Relations internationales/coopération/aide au développement; Réfugiés/migrants/groupes ethniques; Santé/assainissement/eau; Éducation/formation/alphabétisation. **Activités:** Collecte de fonds; Conférences/séminaires/ateliers/activités de formation.

FRA1979
FRATERNITE EUROPE-ASIE (FEA)

18 rue du Cardinal-Lemoine, 75005 Paris, France.

Téléphone: 33 (1) 43 26 27 78. **Fax:** 33 (1) 46 34 72 75. **Contact:** Nguyen Dinh Thi.

OBJECTIFS: Promouvoir des relations fraternelles et des échanges socioculturels et technologiques. Poursuivre des actions d'aide humanitaire en faveur des populations vietnamiennes.

INFORMATIONS GENERALES: Création: 1967. **Type d'organisation:** réseau. **Affiliée à:** France-Pays du Mékong (France). **Personnel/Total:** 48. *Salariés:* 23 dont: 20 dans les pays en développement. *Bénévoles:* 25 dont: 20 dans les pays en développement.

ACTIVITES DANS LES REGIONS EN DEVELOPPEMENT: Intervient directement dans les régions en développement. Intervient dans 2 pays. Maintient une présence locale sur le terrain. **Actions de Développement durable:** Aliments/famine; Développement rural/agriculture; Développement urbain/habitat; Enfants/jeunesse/famille; Envoi de volontaires/experts/assistance technique; Questions relatives aux femmes; Santé/assainissement/eau; Secours d'urgence/réfugiés/aide humanitaire; Écologie/environnement/biodiversité; Éducation/formation/alphabétisation. **Régions:** Asie du Sud-Est.

ACTIVITES D'INFORMATION ET D'EDUCATION: Domaines: Enfants/jeunesse/famille. **Activités:** Échanges/parrainage/jumelage.

FRA1980
FRERES DES HOMMES, FRANCE

9 rue de Savoie, 75006 Paris, France.

Téléphone: 33 (1) 43 25 18 18. **Fax:** 33 (1) 43 29 99 77. **Contact:** Philippe Blancher, Président.

OBJECTIFS: Soutenir des initiatives locales de développement en milieu urbain ou rural dans le Tiers-Monde. Etre actif dans le domaine de l'éducation au développement en Europe et exercer une pression auprès des décideurs économiques et politiques.

INFORMATIONS GENERALES: Création: 1965. **Affiliée à:** CRID - CLONG-Volontariat - Eurostep. **Personnel/Total:** 15. *Salariés:* 4. *Bénévoles:* 10 dont: 1 dans les pays en développement. **Budget/Total 1993:** ECU 1809000 (US$ 2119000). **Sources financières:** *Privé:* 65%. *Public:* 15%. *Autofinancement:* 20%.

PUBLICATIONS: Périodiques: Témoignages et dossiers (4) - Une Seule Terre (4). *Rapport annuel.*

EVALUATION/RECHERCHE: Rapports d'évaluation disponibles.

PREVISIONS D'ACTIVITES: La priorité sera donnée à la consolidation de la démocratie, l'économie sociale, le crédit et l'épargne.

ACTIVITES DANS LES REGIONS EN DEVELOPPEMENT: Intervient dans 17 pays. Intervient par l'intermédiaire d'organisations locales partenaires. **Actions de Développement durable:** Droits de l'Homme/paix/conflits; Démocratie/bonne gestion publique/création d'institutions/développement participatif; Développement rural/agriculture; Développement urbain/habitat; Enfants/jeunesse/famille; Envoi de volontaires/experts/assistance technique; Petites entreprises/secteur informel/artisanat; Écologie/environnement/biodiversité; Éducation/formation/alphabétisation. **Régions:** Afrique australe; Afrique centrale; Afrique de l'Ouest; Amérique du Sud; Asie centrale et Asie du Sud; Asie du Sud-Est; Caraïbes; Mexique et Amerique centrale.

ACTIVITES D'INFORMATION ET D'EDUCATION: Domaines: Droits de l'Homme/paix/conflits; Développement rural/agriculture; Développement urbain/habitat; Emploi/chômage; Pauvreté/conditions de vie; Écologie/environnement/biodiversité; Éducation/formation/alphabétisation. **Activités:** Collecte de fonds; Conférences/séminaires/ateliers/activités de formation; Lobbying/plaidoyer; Échanges/parrainage/jumelage.

FRA1981
FRONTIERES OUVERTES ISERE-FERKESSEDOUGOU

Mairie, 38870 St. Pierre de Bressieux, France.

Téléphone: 33 - 74 20 00 81. **Contact:** Gilbert Cadat, Président.

FRA1982
GEOMETRES SANS FRONTIERES (GSF)

285 rue Alfred Nobel, 34036 Montpellier cedex, France.

Téléphone: 33 - 67 69 75 16. **Fax:** 33 - 67 64 20 19. **Contact:** Bernard Espeut.

FRA1983
GRENOBLE PARTAGE

11 boulevard Jean Pain, 38000 Grenoble, France.

See: How to Use the Directory, page 11.

Téléphone: 33 - 76 76 39 85. *Fax:* 33 - 76 51 10 59. *Contact:* Bruno Dardelet, Président.

OBJECTIFS: Coordonner et soutenir les différentes actions menées par les associations humanitaires oeuvrant pour le Tiers monde et dans les zones du monde en difficulté et qui ont besoin d'une aide extérieure.

INFORMATIONS GENERALES: *Création:* 1989. *Type d'organisation:* collectif. *Organisations membres:* 70. *Salariés:* 1. *Bénévoles:* 2. *Budget/Total 1993:* ECU 15000 (US$ 18000). *Sources financières:* Public: 100%.

PUBLICATIONS: *Périodiques:* La Lettre de Grenoble Partage (12).

COMMENTAIRES: Intervient dans la Communauté des Etats indépendants. Activités d'information concernant la Communauté des Etats indépendants.

ACTIVITES DANS LES REGIONS EN DEVELOPPEMENT: Intervient directement dans les régions en développement. Intervient dans 6 pays. Maintient une présence locale sur le terrain. Intervient par l'intermédiaire d'organisations locales partenaires. **Actions de Développement durable:** Envoi de volontaires/experts/assistance technique; Éducation/formation/alphabétisation. **Régions:** Asie du Sud-Est.

FRA1984
GROUPE D'ETUDES ET DE FORMATION SUR LES OUTILS SOLAIRES ET LES ALTERNATIVES TECHNOLOGIQUES (GEFOSAT)

Domaine de Grammont - Route de Mauguio, 34000 Montpellier, France.

Téléphone: 33 - 67 65 94 06. *Fax:* 33 - 67 20 29 62. *Courrier électronique:* Calva Com Tsrio. *Contact:* Thierry Salomon, Délégué général.

OBJECTIFS: Participer à la réalisation de projets de développement dans les pays du Sud. Déployer des activités productives dans les domaines de la petite entreprise agroalimentaire, de l'habitat, de l'artisanat, de l'utilisation des énergies renouvelables.

INFORMATIONS GENERALES: *Création:* 1978. *Affiliée à:* Technologies Appropriées (France) - Comité Français Contre la Faim (France). *Personnel/Total:* 7. *Salariés:* 3. *Bénévoles:* 4. *Budget/Total 1993:* ECU 106000 (US$ 1240000). *Sources financières:* Public: 70%. Autofinancement: 30%.

PUBLICATIONS: *Rapport annuel.*

EVALUATION/RECHERCHE: Rapports d'évaluation disponibles. Entreprend des activités de recherche.

ACTIVITES DANS LES REGIONS EN DEVELOPPEMENT: Intervient directement dans les régions en développement. Intervient dans 4 pays. Intervient par l'intermédiaire d'organisations locales partenaires. **Actions de Développement durable:** Développement rural/agriculture; Développement urbain/habitat; Envoi de volontaires/experts/assistance technique; Petites entreprises/secteur informel/artisanat; Énergie/transport. **Régions:** Afrique centrale; Afrique de l'Est; Afrique de l'Ouest.

FRA1985
GROUPE D'ETUDES ET DE SERVICES POUR L'ECONOMIE DES RESSOURCES (GEYSER)

Rue Grande, 04870 St. Michel l'Observatoire, France.

Téléphone: 33 - 92 76 62 44. *Fax:* 33 - 92 76 65 50. *Courrier électronique:* geyser.phi@globenet.gn.apc.org. *Contact:* Philippe Barret, chargé de programmes.

OBJECTIFS: Participer par des études, des réalisations, des activités de formation et d'information, au développement endogène des zones rurales, à l'économie des ressources naturelles, à l'autonomie des groupes de base et au développement durable.

INFORMATIONS GENERALES: *Création:* 1983. *Affiliée à:* Comité Français pour la Solidarité Internationale (France) - Commission Coopération Développement (France) - Collectif Environnement Développement International (France) - Patrimoine Génétique Provence (France) - REMERGE (France) - AgriBioMéditerranéo (France). *Personnel/Total:* 7. *Salariés:* 7. *Budget/Total 1993:* ECU 206000 (US$ 241000). *Sources financières:* Privé: 30%. Public: 30%. Autofinancement: 40%.

PUBLICATIONS: *Périodiques:* Alter Agri (4). *Liste des publications.*

PREVISIONS D'ACTIVITES: Action prévue dans les domaines de l'agriculture écologique, la gestion durable des forêts et ressources hydriques, la démocratie et la lutte contre l'exclusion, la gestion de territoires abandonnés, le réseau européen de développement durable.

ACTIVITES DANS LES REGIONS EN DEVELOPPEMENT: Intervient directement dans les régions en développement. Intervient dans 3 pays. Intervient par l'intermédiaire d'organisations locales partenaires. **Actions de Développement durable:** Droits de l'Homme/paix/conflits; Démocratie/bonne gestion publique/création d'institutions/développement participatif; Développement rural/agriculture; Envoi de volontaires/experts/assistance technique; Écologie/environnement/biodiversité. **Régions:** Afrique du Nord; Mexique et Amerique centrale.

ACTIVITES D'INFORMATION ET D'EDUCATION: Domaines: Droits de l'Homme/paix/conflits; Développement rural/agriculture; Paix/conflits ethniques/armement/désarmement; Relations internationales/coopération/aide au développement; Écologie/environnement/biodiversité. **Activités:** Campagnes d'information/expositions; Conférences/séminaires/ateliers/activités de formation; Lobbying/plaidoyer; Réseaux/télécommunications électroniques; Services d'information et de documentation/bases de données; Échanges/parrainage/jumelage; Édition/documents audiovisuels/documents éducatifs.

FRA1986
GROUPE DE REALISATIONS AUDIOVISUELLES POUR LE DEVELOPPEMENT (GRAD)

228 rue Manet, 74130 Bonneville, France.

Téléphone: 33 - 50 97 08 85. *Fax:* 33 - 50 25 69 81. *Contact:* Renée Lecomte, Secrétaire générale.

OBJECTIFS: Informer et former en France sur tout ce qui concerne le développement. Aider à la communication entre groupements paysans en Afrique de l'Ouest.

INFORMATIONS GENERALES: *Création:* 1981. *Personnel/Total:* 6. *Salariés:* 4. *Bénévoles:* 2. *Budget/Total 1993:* ECU 145000 (US$ 170000). *Sources financières:* Public: 50%. Autofinancement: 50%.

PUBLICATIONS: *Liste des publications.*

PREVISIONS D'ACTIVITES: La priorité sera donnée aux problèmes féminins en Afrique et à l'éducation des enfants du primaire en Europe.

ACTIVITES DANS LES REGIONS EN DEVELOPPEMENT: Intervient par l'intermédiaire d'organisations locales partenaires. **Actions de Développement durable:** Autres; Éducation/formation/alphabétisation. **Régions:** Afrique de l'Ouest.

ACTIVITES D'INFORMATION ET D'EDUCATION: Domaines: Aliments/famine; Culture/tradition/religion; Droits de l'Homme/paix/conflits; Développement rural/agriculture; Développement urbain/habitat; Enfants/jeunesse/famille; Paix/conflits ethniques/armement/désarmement; Pauvreté/conditions de vie; Population/planning familial/démographie; Questions relatives aux femmes; Relations internationales/coopération/aide au développement; Relations économiques internationales/commerce/dette/finances; Santé/assainissement/eau; Écologie/environnement/biodiversité; Éducation/formation/alphabétisation. **Activités:** Édition/documents audiovisuels/documents éducatifs.

FRA1987
GROUPE DE RECHERCHE ET D'APPUI POUR L'AUTOPROMOTION PAYSANNE (GRAAP)

c/o Geneviève Jacquot, 29 bd Maréchal Foch, 38100 Grenoble, France.

Téléphone: 33 - 76 87 92 56. *Contact:* Alain Husson.

FRA1988
GROUPE DE RECHERCHE ET D'ECHANGES TECHNOLOGIQUES (GRET) ♦ Technological Research and Exchange Group

213 rue Lafayette, 75010 Paris, France.

Téléphone: 33 (1) 40 05 61 61. *Fax:* 33 (1) 40 05 61 10. *Contact:* Jean-Luc Gonneau, Directeur.

Voir : *Comment utiliser le répertoire,* page 11.

OBJECTIFS: Promouvoir des alternatives technologiques pour un développement autocentré. S'appuyer pour cela sur des savoir-faire populaires et sur des techniques appropriées au milieu et appropriables par les bénéficiaires. Développer les échanges technologiques au service des populations les plus défavorisées. Mobiliser et diffuser les informations scientifiques et techniques et les compétences professionnelles spécialisées.

INFORMATIONS GENERALES: *Création:* 1976. *Affiliée à:* CRID (France) - CFSI (France) - Groupe Initiatives (France) - ATO (Pays-Bas) -TECHNAP (France.). *Personnel/Total:* 72. *Salariés:* 54 dont: 9 dans les pays en développement. *Bénévoles:* 18 dont: 18 dans les pays en développement. *Budget/Total 1993:* ECU 6784000 (US$ 7946000). *Sources financières:* Public: 15%. *Autofinancement:* 85%.

PUBLICATIONS: *Périodiques:* CHRONIQUES (4). *Rapport annuel. Liste des publications.*

EVALUATION/RECHERCHE: Rapports d'évaluation disponibles. Entreprend des activités de recherche.

COMMENTAIRES: Intervient dans la Communauté des Etats indépendants.

ACTIVITES DANS LES REGIONS EN DEVELOPPEMENT: Intervient directement dans les régions en développement. Intervient dans 25 pays. Maintient une présence locale sur le terrain. Intervient par l'intermédiaire d'organisations locales partenaires. **Actions de Développement durable:** Démocratie/bonne gestion publique/création d'institutions/développement participatif; Développement rural/agriculture; Développement urbain/habitat; Envoi de volontaires/experts/assistance technique; Petites entreprises/secteur informel/artisanat; Écologie/environnement/biodiversité; Énergie/transport. **Régions:** Afrique australe; Afrique centrale; Afrique de l'Est; Afrique de l'Ouest; Afrique du Nord; Amérique du Sud; Asie centrale et Asie du Sud; Asie du Sud-Est; Mexique et Amerique centrale; Moyen-Orient.

ACTIVITES D'INFORMATION ET D'EDUCATION: Domaines: Développement rural/agriculture; Développement urbain/habitat; Relations internationales/coopération/aide au développement; Santé/assainissement/eau; Écologie/environnement/biodiversité; Éducation/formation/alphabétisation. **Activités:** Conférences/séminaires/ateliers/activités de formation; Radiodiffusion/manifestations culturelles; Services d'information et de documentation/bases de données.

FRA1989
GROUPE DE RECHERCHE ET DE REALISATIONS POUR LE DEVELOPPEMENT RURAL DANS LE TIERS MONDE (GRDR)

20 rue Voltaire, 93100 Montreuil, France.

Téléphone: 33 (1) 48 57 75 80. *Fax:* 33 (1) 48 57 59 75. *Contact:* Paul Schrumpf, Président.

FRA1990
GROUPE DE SOUTIEN AUX MOUVEMENTS D'EDUCATION POPULAIRE ET DE DEVELOPPEMENT EN INDE (SME)

11 rue de la Plaine de France, 95570 Bouffemont, France.

Téléphone: 33 (1) 39 91 20 05. *Contact:* Andrée Courel, Présidente.

OBJECTIFS: Soutenir l'action sur le terrain d'une ONG indienne (actuellement Mass Education, association bengalie de la région de Calcutta), en lui fournissant un apport financier, et en faisant connaître en France les raisons du sous-développement en Inde.

INFORMATIONS GENERALES: *Création:* 1985. *Personnel/Total:* 15. *Bénévoles:* 15. *Budget/Total 1993:* ECU 38000 (US$ 44000). *Sources financières:* Privé: 90%. Public: 2%. *Autofinancement:* 8%.

ACTIVITES DANS LES REGIONS EN DEVELOPPEMENT: Intervient dans 1 pays. Intervient par l'intermédiaire d'organisations locales partenaires. **Actions de Développement durable:** Aliments/famine; Droits de l'Homme/paix/conflits; Démocratie/bonne gestion publique/création d'institutions/développement participatif; Développement rural/agriculture; Enfants/jeunesse/famille; Petites entreprises/secteur informel/artisanat; Population/planning familial/démographie; Questions relatives aux femmes; Santé/assainissement/eau; Écologie/environnement/

biodiversité; Éducation/formation/alphabétisation. **Régions:** Asie centrale et Asie du Sud.

ACTIVITES D'INFORMATION ET D'EDUCATION: Domaines: Aliments/famine; Culture/tradition/religion; Droits de l'Homme/paix/conflits; Développement rural/agriculture; Enfants/jeunesse/famille; Pauvreté/conditions de vie; Population/planning familial/démographie; Questions relatives aux femmes; Relations internationales/coopération/aide au développement; Relations économiques internationales/commerce/dette/finances; Santé/assainissement/eau; Écologie/environnement/biodiversité; Éducation/formation/alphabétisation. **Activités:** Campagnes d'information/expositions; Collecte de fonds; Conférences/séminaires/ateliers/activités de formation; Radiodiffusion/manifestations culturelles; Services d'information et de documentation/bases de données; Édition/documents audiovisuels/documents éducatifs.

FRA1991
GROUPE DEVELOPPEMENT

Bât. 106 BP 07, 93352 Le Bourget cedex, France.

Téléphone: 33 (1) 49 34 83 13. *Fax:* 33 (1) 49 34 83 10. *Contact:* Jean-François Dewitte, Secrétaire général.

OBJECTIFS: Promouvoir les iniiatives locales de développement socio-économique par un appui technique et financier. Favoriser le dialogue entre acteurs du développement au Nord et au Sud. Promouvoir le respect des droits de l'homme à travers des actions spécifiques.

INFORMATIONS GENERALES: *Création:* 1981. *Affiliée à:* CRID (France) - EUROSTEP (Belgique) - ACORD (Grande-Bretagne). *Personnel/Total:* 6. *Salariés:* 6. *Bénévoles:* 2. *Budget/Total 1993:* ECU 1055000 (US$ 1236000). *Sources financières:* Privé: 2%. Public: 98%.

PUBLICATIONS: *Périodiques:* Lettre "TRANSFAIRE" (4). *Rapport annuel. Liste des publications.*

PREVISIONS D'ACTIVITES: Instauration d'une journée mondiale des droits de l'homme. Lutte contre le tourisme sexuel.

ACTIVITES DANS LES REGIONS EN DEVELOPPEMENT: Intervient directement dans les régions en développement. Maintient une présence locale sur le terrain. Intervient par l'intermédiaire d'organisations locales partenaires. **Actions de Développement durable:** Droits de l'Homme/paix/conflits; Démocratie/bonne gestion publique/création d'institutions/développement participatif; Développement rural/agriculture; Développement urbain/habitat; Enfants/jeunesse/famille; Petites entreprises/secteur informel/artisanat; Questions relatives aux femmes; Santé/assainissement/eau; Secours d'urgence/réfugiés/aide humanitaire; Éducation/formation/alphabétisation. **Régions:** Afrique centrale; Afrique de l'Est; Afrique de l'Ouest; Afrique du Nord; Amérique du Sud; Asie centrale et Asie du Sud; Asie du Sud-Est; Mexique et Amerique centrale; Moyen-Orient.

ACTIVITES D'INFORMATION ET D'EDUCATION: Domaines: Droits de l'Homme/paix/conflits; Développement rural/agriculture; Développement urbain/habitat; Emploi/chômage; Enfants/jeunesse/famille; Paix/conflits ethniques/armement/désarmement; Questions relatives aux femmes; Relations internationales/coopération/aide au développement; Santé/assainissement/eau; Secours d'urgence/réfugiés/aide humanitaire; Écologie/environnement/biodiversité. **Activités:** Campagnes d'information/expositions; Collecte de fonds; Lobbying/plaidoyer; Radiodiffusion/manifestations culturelles; Services d'information et de documentation/bases de données; Édition/documents audiovisuels/documents éducatifs.

FRA1992
GROUPE ENERGIES RENOUVELABLES ET ENVIRONNEMENT (GERES)

73 avenue Corot, 13013 Marseille, France.

Téléphone: 33 - 91 70 92 93. *Fax:* 33 - 91 06 19 46. *Contact:* Alain Guinebault, Délégué général.

OBJECTIFS: Etre un trait d'union entre utilisateurs, acteurs et décideurs du développement et favoriser l'innovation en matière d'énergie. Evaluer les besoins énergétiques d'une zone géographique et choisir les systèmes de production énergétique les plus adaptés, utilisant en priorité des ressources locales et des énergies renouvelables.

See: *How to Use the Directory,* page 11.

INFORMATIONS GENERALES: *Création:* 1976. *Affiliée à:* Comité de Liaison Energies Renouvelables - Technap. *Personnel/Total:* 8. Salariés: 6. Bénévoles: 2. *Budget/Total 1993:* ECU 407000 (US$ 477000). *Sources financières:* Privé: 15%. Public: 80%. Autofinancement: 5%.

PUBLICATIONS: *Périodiques:* Echo du GERES (3). *Rapport annuel.* Liste des publications.

EVALUATION/RECHERCHE: Rapports d'évaluation disponibles. Entreprend des activités de recherche.

COMMENTAIRES: Intervient dans la Communauté des Etats indépendants.

ACTIVITES DANS LES REGIONS EN DEVELOPPEMENT: Intervient directement dans les régions en développement. Intervient dans 8 pays. Maintient une présence locale sur le terrain. Intervient par l'intermédiaire d'organisations locales partenaires. **Actions de Développement durable:** Aliments/famine; Développement rural/agriculture; Développement urbain/habitat; Envoi de volontaires/experts/assistance technique; Petites entreprises/secteur informel/artisanat; Questions relatives aux femmes; Santé/assainissement/eau; Écologie/environnement/biodiversité; Éducation/formation/alphabétisation; Énergie/transport. **Régions:** Afrique centrale; Afrique de l'Est; Afrique de l'Ouest; Afrique du Nord; Asie de l'Est; Asie du Sud-Est.

ACTIVITES D'INFORMATION ET D'EDUCATION: **Domaines:** Aliments/famine; Autres; Développement rural/agriculture; Développement urbain/habitat; Questions relatives aux femmes; Santé/assainissement/eau; Écologie/environnement/biodiversité; Éducation/formation/alphabétisation. **Activités:** Campagnes d'information/expositions; Conférences/séminaires/ateliers/activités de formation; Radiodiffusion/manifestations culturelles; Édition/documents audiovisuels/documents éducatifs; Éducation formelle.

FRA1993
GROUPEMENT DES ASSOCIATIONS DENTAIRES FRANCOPHONES (GADEF)

22 avenue de Villiers, 75017 Paris, France.

Téléphone: 33 (1) 47 66 02 32. *Contact:* Dr. Paulette Perrein, Présidente.

OBJECTIFS: Défendre la langue française pour la science dentaire. Promouvoir la prévention bucco-dentaire dans les pays en développement. Favoriser la mise en place ou le renforcement des structures des associations professionnelles.

INFORMATIONS GENERALES: *Création:* 1971. *Affiliée à:* ACCT - AFAL. *Bénévoles:* 6. *Budget/Total 1993:* ECU 6000 (US$ 7000).

PUBLICATIONS: *Périodiques:* Bulletin du Gadef (3).

COMMENTAIRES: Intervient dans la Communauté des Etats indépendants. Activités d'information concernant la Communauté des Etats indépendants.

ACTIVITES DANS LES REGIONS EN DEVELOPPEMENT: Intervient directement dans les régions en développement. Maintient une présence locale sur le terrain. Intervient par l'intermédiaire d'organisations locales partenaires. **Actions de Développement durable:** Santé/assainissement/eau; Éducation/formation/alphabétisation. **Régions:** Afrique australe; Afrique centrale; Afrique de l'Ouest; Afrique du Nord; Caraïbes.

FRA1994
LES GUIDES DE FRANCE

65 rue de la Glacière, 75013 Paris, France.

FRA1995
GUILDE EUROPEENNE DU RAID

11 rue de Vaugirard, 75006 Paris, France.

Téléphone: 33 (1) 43 26 97 52. *Fax:* 33 (1) 46 34 75 45. *Contact:* Patrick Edel, Délégué général.

FRA1996
HANDICAP INTERNATIONAL, FRANCE

14 Avenue Berthelot, 69361 Lyon cedex 07, France.

Téléphone: 33 - 78 69 79 79. *Fax:* 33 - 78 69 79 94. *Contact:* Dr. Richardier, Directeur.

FRA1997
HOMEOPATHES SANS FRONTIERES (HSF)

19 avenue de l'Ecole d'Agriculture, 34000 Montpellier, France.

Téléphone: 33 - 67 72 93 48. *Contact:* Catherine Gaucher.

FRA1998
HOPITAL SANS FRONTIERE

Hôpital Rothschild, 33 boulevard de Picpus, 75012 Paris, France.

Téléphone: 33 (1) 43 44 24 24. *Fax:* 33 (1) 43 44 80 39. *Contact:* Jean-Claude Lafeuillade, Président.

FRA1999
HUMAN RIGHTS ADVOCATES - GENEVA OFFICE

86 Pre de Planche, 01280 Prevessin, France.

Contact: Mr. Hrair Balian.

FRA2000
IMAGES ET SOLIDARITE

16 Mail des Garennes, 78280 Guyancourt, France.

Téléphone: 33 (1) 30 43 13 06. *Contact:* André Deharbe, Président.

FRA2001
THE INDEPENDENT COMMISSION FOR POPULATION AND QUALITY OF LIFE ♦ La commission indépendante pour la population et la qualité de la vie

1 Rue Miollis, 75732 Paris cedex 15, France.

Telephone: 33 (1) 45 68 45 72. *Fax:* 33 (1) 40 61 91 36. *Contact:* Nadia Khouri Dagher, Communication Specialist.

OBJECTIVES: To promote a fresh vision on population and quality of life that engages, inspires and commits actions on a broader scale worldwide.

GENERAL INFORMATION: *Creation:* 1992. *Personnel/Total:* 8. Salaried: 8 of which: 4 in developing countries. *Budget/Total 1993:* ECU 2561000 (US$ 3000000). *Financial sources:* Private: 50%. Public: 50%.

PUBLICATIONS: *Periodicals:* Newsletter of the Independent Commission for Population and Quality of Life (4) .

EVALUATION/RESEARCH: Undertakes research activities.

COMMENTS: Undertakes activities in the Commonwealth of Independent States. Information activities related to the Commonwealth of Independent States.

ACTIVITIES IN DEVELOPING REGIONS: Active in 4 country(ies). Works through local field partners.

INFORMATION AND EDUCATION ACTIVITIES: **Topics:** Children/youth/family; Ecology/environment/biodiversity; Gender issues/women; Human rights/peace/conflicts; Population/family planning/demography. **Activities:** Publishing/audiovisual materials/educational materials.

FRA2002
INFORMATION ACTION TIERS MONDE EN AQUITAINE (IATMA)

14 rue Charles Gounod, 33400 Talence, France.

Téléphone: 33 - 56 04 49 16. *Contact:* Jacky Scuiller, Président.

OBJECTIFS: Informer le public aquitain de la situation des pays du Tiers-Monde et des actions de solidarité qui y sont menées. Diffuser de la documentation et organiser des manifestations (conférences, expositions,etc.).

INFORMATIONS GENERALES: *Création:* 1981. *Affiliée à:* Réseau d'Information Tiers-Monde (France) - Réseau Aquitain de Développement et de Solidarité Internationale (France). *Personnel/Total:* 5. Béné-

voles: 5. **Budget/Total 1993:** ECU 23000 (US$ 26000). **Sources financières:** Privé: 10%. Public: 30%. Autofinancement: 60%.

PUBLICATIONS: **Périodiques:** Latitudes (6). Rapport annuel. Liste des publications.

EVALUATION/RECHERCHE: Rapports d'évaluation disponibles. Entreprend des activités de recherche.

COMMENTAIRES: Lieu de stage pour étudiants en formation en "techniques de développement, en documentation et en animation. L'ONG publie un répertoire aquitain des organismes de solidarité internationale.

ACTIVITES D'INFORMATION ET D'EDUCATION: **Domaines:** Aliments/famine; Culture/tradition/religion; Droits de l'Homme/paix/conflits; Développement rural/agriculture; Développement urbain/habitat; Enfants/jeunesse/famille; Paix/conflits ethniques/armement/désarmement; Pauvreté/conditions de vie; Population/planning familial/démographie; Questions relatives aux femmes; Racisme/xénophobie/antisémitisme; Relations internationales/coopération/aide au développement; Relations économiques internationales/commerce/dette/finances; Réfugiés/migrants/groupes ethniques; Santé/assainissement/eau; Secours d'urgence/réfugiés/aide humanitaire; Écologie/environnement/biodiversité; Éducation/formation/alphabétisation. **Activités:** Campagnes d'information/expositions; Conférences/séminaires/ateliers/activités de formation; Lobbying/plaidoyer; Radiodiffusion/manifestations culturelles; Services d'information et de documentation/bases de données; Édition/documents audiovisuels/documents éducatifs; Éducation formelle.

FRA2003

INFORMATION PRESSE HUMANITAIRE (IPH)

56 boulevard Foch, 93800 Epinay sur Seine, France.

Téléphone: 33 (1) 42 35 23 25. **Contact:** Nicolas Gros.

FRA2004

INFORMATION-FOI-DEVELOPPEMENT (INFODEV)

21 rue du Faubourg de Saverne, 67000 Strasbourg, France.

Téléphone: 33 - 88 32 95 79. **Fax:** 33 - 88 75 60 02. **Contact:** Edouard Brucker, Directeur.

OBJECTIFS: Informer le public le plus large possible sur le mal-développement et ses causes. Faire connaître les pays du Tiers-Monde. Promouvoir et participer à des actions pour que changent les relations Nord-Sud.

INFORMATIONS GENERALES: **Création:** 1986. **Type d'organisation:** réseau. **Organisations membres:** 20. **Affiliée à:** Réseau Informationm Tiers-Monde. **Personnel/Total:** 4. Salariés: 1. Bénévoles: 3. **Budget/Total 1993:** ECU 39000 (US$ 46000). **Sources financières:** Privé: 10%. Public: 30%. Autofinancement: 60%.

EVALUATION/RECHERCHE: Rapports d'évaluation disponibles.

ACTIVITES D'INFORMATION ET D'EDUCATION: **Domaines:** Aliments/famine; Culture/tradition/religion; Droits de l'Homme/paix/conflits; Développement rural/agriculture; Développement urbain/habitat; Emploi/chômage; Enfants/jeunesse/famille; Paix/conflits ethniques/armement/désarmement; Pauvreté/conditions de vie; Questions relatives aux femmes; Racisme/xénophobie/antisémitisme; Relations internationales/coopération/aide au développement; Relations économiques internationales/commerce/dette/finances; Réfugiés/migrants/groupes ethniques; Santé/assainissement/eau; Secours d'urgence/réfugiés/aide humanitaire; Écologie/environnement/biodiversité; Éducation/formation/alphabétisation. **Activités:** Conférences/séminaires/ateliers/activités de formation; Lobbying/plaidoyer; Services d'information et de documentation/bases de données; Édition/documents audiovisuels/documents éducatifs; Éducation formelle.

FRA2005

INGENIEURS SANS FRONTIERES (ISF)

1 place Valhubert, 75013 Paris, France.

Téléphone: 33 (1) 44 24 06 82. **Fax:** 33 (1) 44 24 26 94. **Contact:** Michel Salem, Président.

OBJECTIFS: Offrir un appui technique aux projets de développement initiés par les populations les plus démunies des pays du Sud. Sensibiliser les ingénieurs européens à l'interdépendance du Nord et du Sud et aux problèmes de ces pays.

INFORMATIONS GENERALES: **Création:** 1982. **Affiliée à:** CRID (France) - CFCF (France). **Personnel/Total:** 60. Salariés: 3. Bénévoles: 57. **Budget/Total 1993:** ECU 603000 (US$ 706000). **Sources financières:** Privé: 50%. Public: 30%. Autofinancement: 20%.

PUBLICATIONS: **Périodiques:** Ingénieurs Sans Frontières (3).

EVALUATION/RECHERCHE: Rapports d'évaluation disponibles.

ACTIVITES DANS LES REGIONS EN DEVELOPPEMENT: Intervient directement dans les régions en développement. Intervient dans 15 pays. Intervient par l'intermédiaire d'organisations locales partenaires. **Actions de Développement durable:** Aliments/famine; Démocratie/bonne gestion publique/création d'institutions/développement participatif; Développement rural/agriculture; Développement urbain/habitat; Petites entreprises/secteur informel/artisanat; Questions relatives aux femmes; Santé/assainissement/eau; Écologie/environnement/biodiversité; Éducation/formation/alphabétisation; Énergie/transport. **Régions:** Afrique australe; Afrique centrale; Afrique de l'Ouest; Amérique du Sud; Asie du Sud-Est.

ACTIVITES D'INFORMATION ET D'EDUCATION: **Domaines:** Culture/tradition/religion; Développement rural/agriculture; Développement urbain/habitat; Population/planning familial/démographie; Questions relatives aux femmes; Relations internationales/coopération/aide au développement; Relations économiques internationales/commerce/dette/finances; Écologie/environnement/biodiversité. **Activités:** Campagnes d'information/expositions; Collecte de fonds; Conférences/séminaires/ateliers/activités de formation; Services d'information et de documentation/bases de données; Édition/documents audiovisuels/documents éducatifs; Éducation formelle.

FRA2006

INSERMEDIA

83 rue de Ségur, 33000 Bordeaux, France.

Téléphone: 33 - 56 96 29 23. **Fax:** 33 - 56 96 47 95. **Contact:** Mokrane Ait Ali, Directeur général.

OBJECTIFS: Alphabétiser, développer l'utilisation de la méthode d'apprentissage de la lecture par la couleur.

INFORMATIONS GENERALES: **Création:** 1987. **Personnel/Total:** 13. Salariés: 9. Bénévoles: 4. **Budget/Total 1993:** ECU 528000 (US$ 618000). **Sources financières:** Public: 75%. Autofinancement: 25%.

PUBLICATIONS: **Rapport annuel.**

ACTIVITES DANS LES REGIONS EN DEVELOPPEMENT: Intervient dans 1 pays. **Actions de Développement durable:** Éducation/formation/alphabétisation. **Régions:** Afrique de l'Ouest.

ACTIVITES D'INFORMATION ET D'EDUCATION: **Domaines:** Éducation/formation/alphabétisation. **Activités:** Conférences/séminaires/ateliers/activités de formation.

FRA2007

INSTITUT AFRICAIN POUR LE DEVELOPPEMENT ECONOMIQUE ET SOCIAL - FRANCE (INADES-FORMATION)

Chez M. Yves Tortrat, 44 rue Albert Sarrault, 78000 Versailles, France.

Téléphone: 33 (1) 39 51 44 02. **Contact:** Yves Tortrat.

FRA2008

INSTITUT BELLEVILLE

4 Boulevard de la Villette, 75955 Paris cedex 19, France.

Téléphone: 33 (1) 42 03 80 60. **Fax:** 33 (1) 42 03 80 61. **Contact:** Bernard Thoreau, Délégué général.

FRA2009

INSTITUT DE FORMATION ET DE COOPERATION DECENTRALISEE (IFCOD)

16 rue d'Armaillé, 75017 Paris, France.

Téléphone: 33 (1) 45 72 50 39. *Fax:* 33 (1) 45 72 50 39. *Contact:* Adolphe Memevegni, Directeur.

OBJECTIFS: Agir pour le renforcement des pouvoirs locaux en Afrique à travers des sessions de formation des élus locaux et des responsables des associations de développement. Promouvoir des échanges d'expériences entre les collectivités du Nord et du Sud

INFORMATIONS GENERALES: *Création:* 1990. *Affiliée à:* Fédération des Organisations non Gouvernementales du Benin.. *Personnel/Total:* 24. *Salariés:* 6 dont: 4 dans les pays en développement. *Bénévoles:* 18 dont: 15 dans les pays en développement. *Budget/Total 1993:* ECU 60000 (US$ 71000). *Sources financières:* Privé: 20%. Public: 75%. Autofinancement: 5%.

PUBLICATIONS: *Rapport annuel.*

EVALUATION/RECHERCHE: Rapports d'évaluation disponibles.

PREVISIONS D'ACTIVITES: Vulgarisation de la loi de décentralisation au Bénin

ACTIVITES DANS LES REGIONS EN DEVELOPPEMENT: Intervient directement dans les régions en développement. Intervient dans 1 pays. Maintient une présence locale sur le terrain. **Actions de Développement durable:** Démocratie/bonne gestion publique/création d'institutions/développement participatif; Enfants/jeunesse/famille; Petites entreprises/secteur informel/artisanat; Éducation/formation/alphabétisation. **Régions:** Afrique de l'Ouest.

ACTIVITES D'INFORMATION ET D'EDUCATION: Domaines: Droits de l'Homme/paix/conflits; Emploi/chômage; Enfants/jeunesse/famille; Relations internationales/coopération/aide au développement. **Activités:** Conférences/séminaires/ateliers/activités de formation; Services d'information et de documentation/bases de données; Échanges/parrainage/jumelage.

FRA2010
INSTITUT DE L'ENVIRONNEMENT INTERNATIONAL (IEI)

2 boulevard de la Roche du Roi, BP 1298, 73106 Aix-les-Bains cedex, France.

Téléphone: 33 - 79 88 20 00. *Fax:* 33 - 79 88 22 12. *Contact:* Catherine Soubrier, Chargée de mission.

FRA2011
INSTITUT DE RECHERCHE ET D'APPUI AU DEVELOPPEMENT INTERCONTINENTAL ENDOGENE (IRADIE)

Le Jonchier Aubres, 26110 Nyons, France.

Téléphone: 33 - 75 26 05 05 . *Fax:* 33 - 75 26 32 54. *Contact:* Wouendeu Pierre.

OBJECTIFS: Promouvoir, sur le plan national et international, la recherche et les activités susceptibles d'entrainer un développement endogène.

INFORMATIONS GENERALES: *Création:* 1989. *Type d'organisation:* réseau. *Affiliée à:* EADI (Suisse). *Personnel/Total:* 11. *Salariés:* 5 dont: 4 dans les pays en développement. *Bénévoles:* 6. *Budget/Total 1993:* ECU 121000 (US$ 141000). *Sources financières:* Privé: 5%. Autofinancement: 95%.

EVALUATION/RECHERCHE: Rapports d'évaluation disponibles. Entreprend des activités de recherche.

ACTIVITES DANS LES REGIONS EN DEVELOPPEMENT: Intervient directement dans les régions en développement. Intervient dans 10 pays. Maintient une présence locale sur le terrain. Intervient par l'intermédiaire d'organisations locales partenaires. **Actions de Développement durable:** Démocratie/bonne gestion publique/création d'institutions/développement participatif; Développement rural/agriculture; Développement urbain/habitat; Questions relatives aux femmes; Santé/assainissement/eau; Éducation/formation/alphabétisation. **Régions:** Afrique centrale.

FRA2012
INSTITUT DE RECHERCHES ET D'APPLICATIONS DES METHODES DE DEVELOPPEMENT (IRAM)

49 rue de la Glacière, 75013 Paris, France.

Téléphone: 33 (1) 43 36 03 62. *Fax:* 33 (1) 43 31 66 31. *Contact:* Annette Correze, Présidente.

OBJECTIFS: Renforcer la maîtrise des organisations rurales sur leurs environnements. Accompagner les initiatives de développement à travers 4 thèmes essentiels: développement local et gestion des terroirs, financement local (épargne et crédit), appui à la définition des politiques agricoles, appui aux organisations paysannes.

INFORMATIONS GENERALES: *Création:* 1956. *Personnel/Total:* 40. *Salariés:* 40 dont: 13 dans les pays en développement. *Budget/Total 1993:* ECU 3317000 (US$ 3885000). *Sources financières:* Public: 99%. Autofinancement: 1%.

PUBLICATIONS: *Rapport annuel. Liste des publications.*

EVALUATION/RECHERCHE: Entreprend des activités de recherche.

ACTIVITES DANS LES REGIONS EN DEVELOPPEMENT: Intervient directement dans les régions en développement. Intervient dans 25 pays. Maintient une présence locale sur le terrain. Intervient par l'intermédiaire d'organisations locales partenaires. **Actions de Développement durable:** Autres; Dette/finances/commerce; Démocratie/bonne gestion publique/création d'institutions/développement participatif; Développement rural/agriculture; Développement urbain/habitat; Envoi de volontaires/experts/assistance technique; Petites entreprises/secteur informel/artisanat; Questions relatives aux femmes; Secours d'urgence/réfugiés/aide humanitaire; Écologie/environnement/biodiversité; Éducation/formation/alphabétisation. **Régions:** Afrique australe; Afrique centrale; Afrique de l'Est; Afrique de l'Ouest; Afrique du Nord; Amérique du Sud; Asie du Sud-Est; Caraïbes; Mexique et Amerique centrale.

ACTIVITES D'INFORMATION ET D'EDUCATION: Domaines: Développement rural/agriculture; Développement urbain/habitat; Questions relatives aux femmes; Relations internationales/coopération/aide au développement; Relations économiques internationales/commerce/dette/finances; Écologie/environnement/biodiversité. **Activités:** Autres; Conférences/séminaires/ateliers/activités de formation.

FRA2013
INSTITUT DES DROITS DE L'HOMME, UNIVERSITE CATHOLIQUE DE LYON

10-12 rue A. Fochier, 69002 Lyon, France.

Téléphone: 33 - 72 32 50 50. *Fax:* 33 - 72 32 50 50. *Contact:* Pascale Boucaud, Directrice.

OBJECTIFS: Assurer l'enseignement, la formation et la recherche sur les droits de l'homme. Délivrer des diplômes universitaires dans ce domaine.

INFORMATIONS GENERALES: *Création:* 1985. *Personnel/Total:* 6. *Salariés:* 6. *Budget/Total 1993:* ECU 143000 (US$ 168000). *Sources financières:* Privé: 30%. Public: 5%. Autofinancement: 65%.

PUBLICATIONS: *Périodiques:* Revue de l'Insitut des Droits de l'Homme de Lyon (4). *Rapport annuel. Liste des publications.*

EVALUATION/RECHERCHE: Entreprend des activités de recherche.

PREVISIONS D'ACTIVITES: Sessions de formation en Europe de l'Est, en Afrique Centrale et en Afrique du Nord.

COMMENTAIRES: Intervient dans la Communauté des Etats indépendants. Activités d'information concernant la Communauté des Etats indépendants.

ACTIVITES DANS LES REGIONS EN DEVELOPPEMENT: Intervient directement dans les régions en développement. Intervient dans 9 pays. Maintient une présence locale sur le terrain. Intervient par l'intermédiaire d'organisations locales partenaires. **Actions de Développement durable:** Droits de l'Homme/paix/conflits. **Régions:** Afrique centrale; Afrique de l'Est; Afrique de l'Ouest; Afrique du Nord; Amérique du Sud; Asie du Sud-Est; Mexique et Amerique centrale; Moyen-Orient; Océanie.

ACTIVITES D'INFORMATION ET D'EDUCATION: Domaines: Culture/tradition/religion; Droits de l'Homme/paix/conflits; Racisme/xénophobie/antisémitisme; Réfugiés/migrants/groupes ethniques. **Activités:** Conférences/séminaires/ateliers/activités de formation; Services d'information et de documentation/bases de données; Édition/documents audiovisuels/documents éducatifs.

FRA2014

INSTITUT DES SCIENCES ET DES TECHNIQUES DE L'EQUIPEMENT ET DE L'ENVIRONNEMENT POUR LE DEVELOPPEMENT (ISTED)

la Grande Arche-Paroi Sud, 92055 Paris-La Défense Cedex 04 , France.

Téléphone: 33 (1) 40 81 24 06. *Fax:* 33 (1) 40 81 23 31. *Contact:* Jean Baudoin, Président.

OBJECTIFS: Contribuer à la diffusion, au partage des connaissances et aux transferts de compétences dans les domaines de l'équipement et de l'environnement.

INFORMATIONS GENERALES: *Création:* 1981. *Organisations membres:* 21. *Personnel/Total:* 13. *Salariés:* 13. *Budget/Total 1993:* ECU 488000 (US$ 572000). *Sources financières:* Public: 60%. Autofinancement: 40%.

PUBLICATIONS: *Périodiques:* Villes en Développement" (4) - Equipement et Développement (6). *Rapport annuel. Liste des publications.*

EVALUATION/RECHERCHE: Rapports d'évaluation disponibles.

PREVISIONS D'ACTIVITES: Organiser des colloques, séminaires, expositions et congrès, dans les domaines routiers, urbains et des transports (PVD, Europe, Amérique du Nord) ainsi que des actions de coopération, dans les PVD, dans ces mêmes domaines.

ACTIVITES DANS LES REGIONS EN DEVELOPPEMENT: Intervient directement dans les régions en développement. Intervient dans 1 pays. Intervient par l'intermédiaire d'organisations locales partenaires. **Actions de Développement durable:** Autres; Développement urbain/habitat; Énergie/transport. **Régions:** Afrique australe; Afrique centrale; Afrique de l'Ouest.

ACTIVITES D'INFORMATION ET D'EDUCATION: Domaines: Développement urbain/habitat; Relations internationales/coopération/aide au développement. **Activités:** Conférences/séminaires/ateliers/activités de formation; Réseaux/télécommunications électroniques; Services d'information et de documentation/bases de données; Échanges/parrainage/jumelage; Édition/documents audiovisuels/documents éducatifs.

FRA2015

INSTITUT EUROPE-AFRIQUE (IEA)

1 place d'Athènes, BP 66, 67045 Strasbourg cedex, France.

Téléphone: 33 - 88 45 70 07. *Fax:* 33 - 88 31 22 44. *Contact:* Simon Tiebey-Dalou, Secrétaire général.

OBJECTIFS: Contribuer, au niveau universitaire, à la coopération Nord-Sud, par le renforcement des relations culturelles, scientifiques et socio-économiques entre l'Europe et l'Afrique. Intervenir dans la formation au développement, dans l'enseignement, la recherche scientifique, la documentation universitaire, le financement d'opérations, le soutien logistique et le parrainage.

INFORMATIONS GENERALES: *Création:* 1989. *Personnel/Total:* 3. *Bénévoles:* 2 dont: 1 dans les pays en développement. *Budget/Total 1993:* ECU 38000 (US$ 44000). *Sources financières:* Privé: 70%. Public: 15%. Autofinancement: 15%.

PUBLICATIONS: *Rapport annuel.*

EVALUATION/RECHERCHE: Rapports d'évaluation disponibles. Entreprend des activités de recherche.

PREVISIONS D'ACTIVITES: Organiser des conférences thématiques sur le cinéma colonial et contemporain.

COMMENTAIRES: Activités d'information concernant la Communauté des Etats indépendants.

ACTIVITES DANS LES REGIONS EN DEVELOPPEMENT: Intervient directement dans les régions en développement. Intervient dans 1 pays. Maintient une présence locale sur le terrain. Intervient par l'intermédiaire d'organisations locales partenaires. **Actions de Développement durable:** Autres; Développement rural/agriculture; Éducation/formation/alphabétisation. **Régions:** Afrique centrale; Afrique de l'Ouest; Afrique du Nord.

ACTIVITES D'INFORMATION ET D'EDUCATION: Domaines: Culture/tradition/religion; Droits de l'Homme/paix/conflits; Développement rural/agriculture; Emploi/chômage; Relations internationales/coopération/aide au développement. **Activités:** Collecte de fonds; Conférences/séminaires/ateliers/activités de formation; Services d'information et de documentation/bases de données; Éducation formelle.

FRA2016

INSTITUT EUROPEEN DE COOPERATION ET DE DEVELOPPEMENT (IECD) ♦ European Institute for Co-operation and Development

12 rue Rosenwald, 75015 Paris, France.

Téléphone: 33 (1) 45 33 40 50. *Fax:* 33 (1) 45 33 40 38. *Contact:* Xavier Boutin, Directeur éxécutif.

OBJECTIFS: Financer et/ou réaliser des opérations de développement. Faire des évaluations et donner des conseils dans le domaine du développement.

INFORMATIONS GENERALES: *Création:* 1988. *Affiliée à:* Association pour la Conversion de la Dette pour le Développement et l'Environnement (France). *Personnel/Total:* 14. *Salariés:* 4 dont: 2 dans les pays en développement. *Bénévoles:* 10 dont: 3 dans les pays en développement. *Budget/Total 1993:* ECU 482000 (US$ 565000). *Sources financières:* Privé: 49%. Public: 48%. Autofinancement: 3%.

PUBLICATIONS: *Rapport annuel.*

ACTIVITES DANS LES REGIONS EN DEVELOPPEMENT: Intervient dans 11 pays. Intervient par l'intermédiaire d'organisations locales partenaires. **Actions de Développement durable:** Développement rural/agriculture; Développement urbain/habitat; Enfants/jeunesse/famille; Envoi de volontaires/experts/assistance technique; Questions relatives aux femmes; Santé/assainissement/eau; Éducation/formation/alphabétisation. **Régions:** Afrique centrale; Afrique de l'Ouest; Amérique du Sud; Asie du Sud-Est; Mexique et Amerique centrale; Moyen-Orient.

ACTIVITES D'INFORMATION ET D'EDUCATION: Domaines: Développement rural/agriculture; Développement urbain/habitat; Enfants/jeunesse/famille; Questions relatives aux femmes; Relations internationales/coopération/aide au développement; Santé/assainissement/eau; Éducation/formation/alphabétisation. **Activités:** Collecte de fonds; Conférences/séminaires/ateliers/activités de formation; Échanges/parrainage/jumelage; Éducation formelle.

FRA2017

INSTITUT INTERNATIONAL DE LA DEMOCRATIE (IID) ♦ International Institute for Democracy

Palais de l'Europe, B.P. 431 R 6, 67075 Strasbourg Cedex, France.

Téléphone: 33 - 88 41 25 41. *Fax:* 33 - 88 41 27 81. *Contact:* Mme. Enie Wesseldijk, Secrétaire Exécutif.

OBJECTIFS: Encourager la coopération à l'échelle mondiale entre les organisations gouvernementales, non gouvernementales et inter-parlementaires, ainsi qu'entre parlements nationaux, en vue de promouvoir et de renforcer la démocratie.

INFORMATIONS GENERALES: *Création:* 1989. *Personnel/Total:* 2. *Salariés:* 2. *Budget/Total 1993:* ECU 90000 (US$ 106000). *Sources financières:* Public: 100%.

PUBLICATIONS: *Périodiques:* Bulletin "Informations d'activité" (6) - Démocratie (4). *Rapport annuel.*

EVALUATION/RECHERCHE: Rapports d'évaluation disponibles. Entreprend des activités de recherche.

COMMENTAIRES: Intervient dans la Communauté des Etats indépendants. Activités d'information concernant la Communauté des Etats indépendants.

ACTIVITES DANS LES REGIONS EN DEVELOPPEMENT: Intervient directement dans les régions en développement. Intervient dans 3 pays. Intervient par l'intermédiaire d'organisations locales partenaires.

ACTIVITES D'INFORMATION ET D'EDUCATION: Domaines: Droits de l'Homme/paix/conflits. **Activités:** Collecte de fonds; Conférences/séminaires/ateliers/activités de formation; Lobbying/plaidoyer; Services d'information et de documentation/bases de données; Éducation formelle.

See: How to Use the Directory, page 11.

FRA2018

INSTITUT INTERNATIONAL DE RECHERCHE ET DE FORMATION: EDUCATION ET DEVELOPPEMENT (IRFED)

49 rue de la Glacière, 75013 Paris, France.

Téléphone: 33 (1) 43 31 98 90. *Fax:* 33 (1) 43 37 54 33. *Contact:* Roland Colin, Vice-Président.

OBJECTIFS: Ouvrir des voies nouvelles dans la recherche, l'action, la formation afin de donner au développement son caractère global. Valoriser la dimension humaine du développement. Eclairer les rapports entre économie, technologie et culture. Analyser l'impact des projets de développement sur le mouvement social.

INFORMATIONS GENERALES: *Création:* 1958. *Affiliée à:* CRID (France) - RITIMO (France) - CFCF (France) - DHP - EADI (Pays-Bas). *Personnel/Total:* 20. *Salariés:* 13 dont: 2 dans les pays en développement. *Bénévoles:* 7. *Budget/Total 1993:* ECU 603000 (US$ 706000). *Sources financières:* Public: 20%. Autofinancement: 80%.

PUBLICATIONS: *Périodiques:* Bulletin bibliographique (4). *Liste des publications.*

EVALUATION/RECHERCHE: Rapports d'évaluation disponibles. Entreprend des activités de recherche.

PREVISIONS D'ACTIVITES: L'organisation projette la création d'instruments de formation en vue d'accroître la capacité de gestion participative et démocratique dans les actions de développement.

COMMENTAIRES: Intervient dans la Communauté des Etats indépendants. Activités d'information concernant la Communauté des Etats indépendants.

ACTIVITES DANS LES REGIONS EN DEVELOPPEMENT: Intervient directement dans les régions en développement. Intervient dans 6 pays. Maintient une présence locale sur le terrain. Intervient par l'intermédiaire d'organisations locales partenaires. **Actions de Développement durable:** Démocratie/bonne gestion publique/création d'institutions/développement participatif; Développement rural/agriculture; Développement urbain/habitat; Enfants/jeunesse/famille; Envoi de volontaires/experts/assistance technique; Petites entreprises/secteur informel/artisanat; Population/planning familial/démographie; Écologie/environnement/biodiversité; Éducation/formation/alphabétisation. **Régions:** Afrique australe; Afrique de l'Ouest; Afrique du Nord; Amérique du Sud; Asie du Sud-Est.

ACTIVITES D'INFORMATION ET D'EDUCATION: Domaines: Aliments/famine; Autres; Culture/tradition/religion; Droits de l'Homme/paix/conflits; Développement rural/agriculture; Développement urbain/habitat; Emploi/chômage; Enfants/jeunesse/famille; Paix/conflits ethniques/armement/désarmement; Pauvreté/conditions de vie; Population/planning familial/démographie; Questions relatives aux femmes; Relations internationales/coopération/aide au développement; Relations économiques internationales/commerce/dette/finances; Réfugiés/migrants/groupes ethniques; Santé/assainissement/eau; Écologie/environnement/biodiversité; Éducation/formation/alphabétisation. **Activités:** Conférences/séminaires/ateliers/activités de formation; Réseaux/télécommunications électroniques; Services d'information et de documentation/bases de données; Édition/documents audiovisuels/documents éducatifs; Éducation formelle.

FRA2019

INSTITUT INTERNATIONAL DES DROITS DE L'HOMME ♦
International Institute of Human Rights

1 Quai Lezay Marnesia, 67000 Strasbourg, France.

Téléphone: 33 - 88 35 05 50. *Fax:* 33 - 88 36 38 55. *Contact:* Jean-Bernard Marie, Secrétaire général.

OBJECTIFS: Promouvoir le développement des droits de l'Homme à travers l'enseignement et la recherche.

INFORMATIONS GENERALES: *Création:* 1969. *Affiliée à:* HURIDOCS - Suisse (Suisse). *Personnel/Total:* 9. *Salariés:* 8. *Bénévoles:* 1. *Budget/Total 1993:* ECU 905000 (US$ 1059000). *Sources financières:* Privé: 3%. Public: 72%. Autofinancement: 25%.

PUBLICATIONS: *Périodiques:* Journal de l'IIDH (4). *Liste des publications.*

EVALUATION/RECHERCHE: Entreprend des activités de recherche.

PREVISIONS D'ACTIVITES: Session annuelle d'enseignement. Sessions extérieures de formation.

COMMENTAIRES: Intervient dans la Communauté des Etats indépendants. Activités d'information concernant la Communauté des Etats indépendants.

ACTIVITES DANS LES REGIONS EN DEVELOPPEMENT: Intervient directement dans les régions en développement. Intervient dans 2 pays. Intervient par l'intermédiaire d'organisations locales partenaires.

ACTIVITES D'INFORMATION ET D'EDUCATION: Domaines: Droits de l'Homme/paix/conflits; Enfants/jeunesse/famille; Paix/conflits ethniques/armement/désarmement; Population/planning familial/démographie; Questions relatives aux femmes; Racisme/xénophobie/antisémitisme; Réfugiés/migrants/groupes ethniques. **Activités:** Conférences/séminaires/ateliers/activités de formation; Services d'information et de documentation/bases de données; Éducation formelle.

FRA2020

INSTITUT PANOS

53 rue Turbigo, 75003 Paris, France.

Téléphone: 33 (1) 42 71 20 21. *Fax:* 33 (1) 42 71 21 55. *Contact:* Charles Condamines, Directeur.

OBJECTIFS: Appuyer les capacités locales de production et de circulation d'informations pluralistes dans les pays en développement. Développer des circuits d'information du Sud vers le Nord, notamment sur les thèmes liés à l'environnement et au développement, ainsi que les migrations et la coopération internationale.

INFORMATIONS GENERALES: *Création:* 1987. *Affiliée à:* Panos International. *Personnel/Total:* 20. *Budget/Total 1993:* ECU 1206000 (US$ 1413000). *Sources financières:* Privé: 50%. Public: 50%.

PUBLICATIONS: *Rapport annuel. Liste des publications.*

EVALUATION/RECHERCHE: Entreprend des activités de recherche.

ACTIVITES DANS LES REGIONS EN DEVELOPPEMENT: Intervient directement dans les régions en développement. Intervient dans 24 pays. Maintient une présence locale sur le terrain. Intervient par l'intermédiaire d'organisations locales partenaires. **Actions de Développement durable:** Écologie/environnement/biodiversité. **Régions:** Afrique centrale; Afrique de l'Ouest.

ACTIVITES D'INFORMATION ET D'EDUCATION: Domaines: Réfugiés/migrants/groupes ethniques; Écologie/environnement/biodiversité. **Activités:** Campagnes d'information/expositions; Conférences/séminaires/ateliers/activités de formation; Services d'information et de documentation/bases de données; Édition/documents audiovisuels/documents éducatifs.

FRA2021

INSTITUT POUR LA RENOVATION INDUSTRIELLE DANS LES PAYS ACP - INSTITUT POUR LA RENOVATION INDUSTRIELLE EN AFRIQUE NOIRE (IRIACP-IRIAN)

20-22 rue Beccaria, 75012 Paris, France.

Téléphone: 33 (1) 43 87 48 06. *Fax:* 33 (1) 43 87 48 06. *Contact:* S. Atta Diouf, President.

OBJECTIFS: Contribuer à la multiplication des créateurs d'entreprises par la formation. Développer des activités de recherche scientifique en vue d'aider et d'encadrer les inventeurs et porteurs de projets dans le domaine de l'énergie solaire.

INFORMATIONS GENERALES: *Organisations membres:* 3. *Affiliée à:* Observatoire des Pratiques Comptables en Afrique - Société Africaine de Mathématiques et de Physique et leurs applications - Observatoire Socio-économique Panafricain.. *Sources financières:* Autofinancement: 100%.

PUBLICATIONS: *Rapport annuel. Liste des publications.*

EVALUATION/RECHERCHE: Entreprend des activités de recherche.

PREVISIONS D'ACTIVITES: Bibliothèque économique et Scientifique Africaine pour l'Afrique Noire à Paris.

Voir : *Comment utiliser le répertoire,* page 11.

ACTIVITES DANS LES REGIONS EN DEVELOPPEMENT: Intervient directement dans les régions en développement. Intervient dans 5 pays. Maintient une présence locale sur le terrain. **Actions de Développement durable:** Petites entreprises/secteur informel/artisanat; Éducation/formation/alphabétisation; Énergie/transport. **Régions:** Afrique centrale; Afrique de l'Ouest.

ACTIVITES D'INFORMATION ET D'EDUCATION: Domaines: Emploi/chômage; Relations économiques internationales/commerce/dette/finances; Éducation/formation/alphabétisation. **Activités:** Campagnes d'information/expositions; Conférences/séminaires/ateliers/activités de formation; Services d'information et de documentation/bases de données; Édition/documents audiovisuels/documents éducatifs; Éducation formelle.

FRA2022

INSTITUT POUR LE DEVELOPPEMENT ECONOMIQUE, SOCIAL ET CULTUREL

198 avenue du Maine, 75014 Paris, France.

Téléphone: 33 (1) 45 39 22 03. **Fax:** 33 (1) 45 45 54 52. **Contact:** Jacques Pé, Secrétaire confédéral.

FRA2023

INTER AIDE

44 rue de la paroisse, 78000 Versailles, France.

Téléphone: 33 (1) 39 02 38 59 . **Fax:** 33 (1) 39 53 11 28. **Contact:** Paul Lesaffre, Directeur.

OBJECTIFS: Réaliser, depuis la conception jusqu'au suivi, des programmes concrets de développement.

INFORMATIONS GENERALES: Création: 1980. **Affiliée à:** Comité Français contre la Faim (France). **Personnel/Total:** 90. *Salariés:* 48 dont: 38 dans les pays en développement. *Bénévoles:* 42. **Budget/Total 1993:** ECU 6030000 (US$ 7063000). **Sources financières:** *Privé:* 60%. *Public:* 40%.

ACTIVITES DANS LES REGIONS EN DEVELOPPEMENT: Intervient directement dans les régions en développement. Intervient dans 10 pays. Maintient une présence locale sur le terrain. Intervient par l'intermédiaire d'organisations locales partenaires. **Actions de Développement durable:** Développement rural/agriculture; Développement urbain/habitat; Enfants/jeunesse/famille; Petites entreprises/secteur informel/artisanat; Population/planning familial/démographie; Questions relatives aux femmes; Santé/assainissement/eau; Éducation/formation/alphabétisation. **Régions:** Afrique australe; Afrique de l'Est; Amérique du Sud; Asie centrale et Asie du Sud; Asie du Sud-Est; Caraïbes.

FRA2024

INTER MED ASSISTANCE

66 rue René Boulanger, B.P. 281, 75010 Paris cedex, France.

Contact: Nacer Kettane.

FRA2025

INTERFERENCES CULTURELLES

12 rue Guy de la Brosse, 75005 Paris, France.

Téléphone: 33 (1) 47 07 11 58. **Fax:** 33 (1) 43 37 18 53. **Contact:** Bernard Zoegger, Président.

OBJECTIFS: Sensibiliser le public français (Ile de France) aux problèmes des immigrés et du Tiers-Monde. Favoriser le dialogue et les contacts entre des personnes et des groupes de cultures différentes.

INFORMATIONS GENERALES: Création: 1986. **Personnel/Total:** 20. *Bénévoles:* 20. **Budget/Total 1993:** ECU 18000 (US$ 22000). **Sources financières:** *Privé:* 33%. *Public:* 19%. *Autofinancement:* 48%.

PUBLICATIONS: *Rapport annuel.*

EVALUATION/RECHERCHE: Rapports d'évaluation disponibles.

PREVISIONS D'ACTIVITES: Sensibilisation aux problèmes de l'Europe de l'Est par des films.

ACTIVITES D'INFORMATION ET D'EDUCATION: Domaines: Culture/tradition/religion; Racisme/xénophobie/antisémitisme; Réfugiés/migrants/groupes ethniques. **Activités:** Collecte de fonds; Conférences/séminaires/ateliers/activités de formation; Radiodiffusion/manifestations culturelles.

FRA2026

INTERNATIONAL ASSOCIATION FOR THE EXCHANGE OF STUDENTS FOR TECHNICAL EXPERIENCE (IAESTE)

B.P. 3672, 54096 Nancy cedex, France.

Telephone: 33 - 83 37 41 11. **Fax:** 33 - 83 57 97 94. **E-mail:** sfeir@mines.u-nancy.fr. **Contact:** Prof. A. Sfeir.

OBJECTIVES: To provide technical experience abroad to students at institutions of higher learning. To promote international understanding and goodwill amongst students of all nations.

GENERAL INFORMATION: Creation: 1948. **Type of organisation:** network. **Member organisations:** 63. **Personnel/Total:** 2. **Budget/Total 1993:** ECU 73000 (US$ 95000). **Financial sources:** *Private:* 100%.

PUBLICATIONS: *Annual report.*

EVALUATION/RESEARCH: Evaluation reports available.

PLANNED ACTIVITIES: Expansion of membership in South-East Asia

COMMENTS: Undertakes activities in the Commonwealth of Independent States.

ACTIVITIES IN DEVELOPING REGIONS: Present in developing regions. Maintains local field presence. Works through local field partners. **Sustainable Development Actions:** Education/training/literacy. **Regions:** Caribbean; Central Asia and South Asia; East Asia; Mexico and Central America; Middle East; North Africa; Oceania; South America; South East Asia; Southern Africa; West Africa.

FRA2027

INTERNATIONAL CHAMBER OF COMMERCE - COMMISSION ON ENVIRONMENT (ICC) ♦ Chambre de Commerce International - Commission de l'Environnement

38 cours Albert Premier, 75008 Paris, France.

Telephone: 33 (1) 49 53 28 28. **Fax:** 33 (1) 42 25 86 63. **Contact:** Torvild Aakvaag, Chairman.

FRA2028

INTERNATIONAL COUNCIL OF JEWISH WOMEN ♦ Conseil international des femmes juives

19 rue de Téhéran, 75008 Paris, France.

Telephone: 33 (1) 46 24 78 34. **Contact:** Stella Rozan, President.

FRA2029

INTERNATIONAL FEDERATION OF AGRICULTURAL PRODUCERS (IFAP) ♦ Fédération internationale des producteurs agricoles (FIPA)

21 rue Chaptal, 75009 Paris, France.

Telephone: 33 (1) 45 26 05 53. **Fax:** (1) 48 74 72 12. **Contact:** Graham Blight, President.

OBJECTIVES: To reinforce the self-help efforts of farmers' organisations from the grass roots to the national levels. To effectively serve and represent their members, especially small farmers and women producers.

GENERAL INFORMATION: Creation: 1946. **Type of organisation:** association of NGOs. **Member organisations:** 86. **Personnel/Total:** 10. **Budget/Total 1993:** ECU 754000 (US$ 883000). **Financial sources:** *Private:* 10%. *Self-financing:* 90%.

PUBLICATIONS: Periodicals: IFAP Neewsletter (6) (4).

EVALUATION/RESEARCH: Evaluation reports available.

PLANNED ACTIVITIES: Undertaking actions for the promotion of women farmers.

                                    See: *How to Use the Directory,* page 11.

COMMENTS: The member organisations of IFAP carry out development activities in 25 countries all over the world. Undertakes activities in the Commonwealth of Independent States.

ACTIVITIES IN DEVELOPING REGIONS: Present in developing regions. Active in 25 country(ies). Works through local field partners.

INFORMATION AND EDUCATION ACTIVITIES: Topics: Children/youth/family; Ecology/environment/biodiversity; Food/famine; Gender issues/women; International economic relations/trade/debt/finance; International relations/cooperation/development aid; Rural development/agriculture. **Activities:** Conferences/seminars/workshops/training activities; Exchanges/twinning/linking; Information and documentation services/data bases.

FRA2030

INTERNATIONAL ORGANIZATION OF CONSUMERS UNIONS (IOCU)

Champs de la Croix, 01710 Thoiry, France.

FRA2031

INTERNATIONAL UNION AGAINST TUBERCULOSIS AND LUNG DISEASE (IUATLD) ♦ Union internationale contre la tuberculose et les maladies respiratoires

68 boulevard Saint-Michel, 75006 Paris, France.

Telephone: 33 (1) 46 33 08 30. *Fax:* 33 (1) 43 29 90 87. *Contact:* Brett Ridgway, Director.

FRA2032

JEUNESSE ETUDIANTE CATHOLIQUE INTERNATIONALE ♦
International Young Catholic Students

171 rue de Rennes, 75006 Paris, France.

Téléphone: 33 (1) 45 48 14 72. *Fax:* 33 (1) 42 84 04 53. *Contact:* Lazare Animako Kabran, Secrétaire général.

OBJECTIFS: Etre responsable, sur le plan apostolique, du milieu étudiant dans tous les pays du monde, en relation avec les autres organisations apostoliques. Rendre compte des expériences vécues par les mouvements de jeunes. Coopérer au travail des organisations internationales pour la jeunesse.

INFORMATIONS GENERALES: Création: 1946. **Type d'organisation:** collectif. **Organisations membres:** 88. **Affiliée à:** Conférence des Organisations Catholiques Internationales. **Personnel/Total:** 21. Salariés: 3 dont: 1 dans les pays en développement. Bénévoles: 18 dont: 12 dans les pays en développement. **Budget/Total 1993:** ECU 121000 (US$ 141000). **Sources financières:** Privé: 70%. Public: 10%. Autofinancement: 20%.

PUBLICATIONS: Périodiques: Nouvelles Internationales (4). *Rapport annuel.*

COMMENTAIRES: Intervient dans la Communauté des Etats indépendants. Activités d'information concernant la Communauté des Etats indépendants.

ACTIVITES DANS LES REGIONS EN DEVELOPPEMENT: Maintient une présence locale sur le terrain. Intervient par l'intermédiaire d'organisations locales partenaires. **Actions de Développement durable:** Droits de l'Homme/paix/conflits; Démocratie/bonne gestion publique/création d'institutions/développement participatif; Développement rural/agriculture; Enfants/jeunesse/famille; Questions relatives aux femmes; Éducation/formation/alphabétisation. **Régions:** Afrique australe; Afrique centrale; Afrique de l'Est; Afrique de l'Ouest; Amérique du Sud; Asie centrale et Asie du Sud; Asie de l'Est; Asie du Sud-Est; Caraïbes; Mexique et Amerique centrale; Moyen-Orient; Océanie.

ACTIVITES D'INFORMATION ET D'EDUCATION: Domaines: Droits de l'Homme/paix/conflits; Enfants/jeunesse/famille; Paix/conflits ethniques/armement/désarmement; Racisme/xénophobie/antisémitisme; Réfugiés/migrants/groupes ethniques; Écologie/environnement/biodiversité. **Activités:** Conférences/séminaires/ateliers/activités de formation; Lobbying/plaidoyer; Échanges/parrainage/jumelage; Édition/documents audiovisuels/documents éducatifs; Éducation formelle.

FRA2033

JUMELAGE ET RENCONTRE POUR L'ENTRAIDE MEDICALE INTERNATIONALE (JEREMI)

Centre municipal des Associations, 2 rue des Corroyeurs, 21068 Dijon cedex, France.

Téléphone: 33 - 80 42 82 59. *Contact:* Philippe Maupetit.

FRA2034

JURISTES-SOLIDARITES

49 rue de la Glacière, 75013 Paris, France.

Téléphone: 33 (1) 43 37 87 08. *Fax:* 33 (1) 43 37 87 18. *Contact:* Jean Designe, Coordinateur général.

OBJECTIFS: Etre un réseau international d'information et de formation à l'action juridique et judiciaire. Soutenir les actions qui permettent aux personnes de vivre au quotidien leurs droits individuels et collectifs.

INFORMATIONS GENERALES: Création: 1989. **Type d'organisation:** réseau. **Affiliée à:** CRID (France) - Commission Coopération Développement -Groupe Amérique Latine-France-. **Personnel/Total:** 10. Salariés: 3. Bénévoles: 7. **Budget/Total 1993:** ECU 106000 (US$ 124000). **Sources financières:** Privé: 55%. Public: 44%. Autofinancement: 1%.

PUBLICATIONS: Périodiques: Le Courrier de Juristes-Solidarités (4). *Liste des publications.*

EVALUATION/RECHERCHE: Rapports d'évaluation disponibles. Entreprend des activités de recherche.

PREVISIONS D'ACTIVITES: Mise en place d'une école juridique alternative mobile pour l'Amérique du Sud et les Caraïbes, d'un collectif d'organisations et de réseaux thématiques pour l'Asie. Organisation d'une rencontre intercontinentale pour 1996.

ACTIVITES DANS LES REGIONS EN DEVELOPPEMENT: Intervient dans 12 pays. Intervient par l'intermédiaire d'organisations locales partenaires. **Actions de Développement durable:** Droits de l'Homme/paix/conflits; Démocratie/bonne gestion publique/création d'institutions/développement participatif; Développement rural/agriculture; Développement urbain/habitat; Enfants/jeunesse/famille; Population/planning familial/démographie; Questions relatives aux femmes; Éducation/formation/alphabétisation. **Régions:** Afrique centrale; Afrique de l'Ouest; Afrique du Nord; Amérique du Sud; Asie centrale et Asie du Sud; Asie du Sud-Est; Caraïbes; Mexique et Amerique centrale.

ACTIVITES D'INFORMATION ET D'EDUCATION: Domaines: Droits de l'Homme/paix/conflits; Paix/conflits ethniques/armement/désarmement. **Activités:** Conférences/séminaires/ateliers/activités de formation; Services d'information et de documentation/bases de données; Échanges/parrainage/jumelage; Édition/documents audiovisuels/documents éducatifs.

FRA2035

JUSTICE ET PAIX ♦ Justice and Peace

17 rue Notre-Dame Des Champs, 75006 Paris, France.

Téléphone: 33 (1) 45 44 26 14. *Fax:* 33 (1) 45 44 25 77. *Contact:* Mgr Jacques Delaporte, Président.

OBJECTIFS: Informer, former et développer la vigilance en matière de droits de l'Homme, du développement, de la sécurité et de la paix.

INFORMATIONS GENERALES: Création: 1967. **Affiliée à:** Justice et Paix. **Personnel/Total:** 3. Salariés: 3. **Budget/Total 1993:** ECU 113000 (US$ 132000). **Sources financières:** Privé: 80%. Autofinancement: 20%.

PUBLICATIONS: Périodiques: La Lettre de Justice et Paix (12). *Liste des publications.*

COMMENTAIRES: Intervient dans la Communauté des Etats indépendants. Activités d'information concernant la Communauté des Etats indépendants.

ACTIVITES DANS LES REGIONS EN DEVELOPPEMENT: Intervient par l'intermédiaire d'organisations locales partenaires. **Actions de Développement durable:** Droits de l'Homme/paix/conflits. **Régions:** Afrique australe; Afrique centrale; Afrique de l'Est; Afrique de l'Ouest; Afrique du

Voir : *Comment utiliser le répertoire,* page 11.

Nord; Amérique du Sud; Asie centrale et Asie du Sud; Asie de l'Est; Asie du Sud-Est; Caraïbes; Mexique et Amerique centrale; Moyen-Orient; Océanie.

ACTIVITES D'INFORMATION ET D'EDUCATION: Domaines: Droits de l'Homme/paix/conflits; Population/planning familial/démographie; Questions relatives aux femmes; Relations internationales/coopération/aide au développement. **Activités:** Campagnes d'information/expositions; Conférences/séminaires/ateliers/activités de formation; Lobbying/plaidoyer; Services d'information et de documentation/bases de données.

FRA2036
LIAISON ET ACTION CONTRE LA FAIM (LIA.CO.FA)
4 square du Nouveau Belleville, 75020 Paris, France.

Téléphone: 33 (1) 47 97 13 74. **Contact:** Louis Garnier, Président.

OBJECTIFS: Apporter aux ONG membres un soutien logistique dans les affaires administratives et la recherche d'informations.

INFORMATIONS GENERALES: Création: 1981. **Type d'organisation:** collectif. **Organisations membres:** 30. **Budget/Total 1993:** ECU 600 (US$ 710). **Sources financières:** Autofinancement: 100%.

FRA2037
LIENS-SAHEL
19 rue La Fontaine, 92350 Le Plessis-Robinson, France.

Téléphone: 33 (1) 43 50 68 52. **Contact:** Natacha Seailles, Présidente.

OBJECTIFS: Coopérer, à la demande des populations locales, à des projets ponctuels de développement dans la zone sahélienne de l'Afrique de l'Ouest.

INFORMATIONS GENERALES: Création: 1987. **Personnel/Total:** 5. **Bénévoles:** 5. **Budget/Total 1993:** ECU 12000 (US$ 14000). **Sources financières:** Privé: 75%. Autofinancement: 25%.

PUBLICATIONS: Rapport annuel.

ACTIVITES DANS LES REGIONS EN DEVELOPPEMENT: Intervient directement dans les régions en développement. Intervient dans 1 pays. Intervient par l'intermédiaire d'organisations locales partenaires. **Actions de Développement durable:** Développement rural/agriculture; Enfants/jeunesse/famille; Questions relatives aux femmes; Santé/assainissement/eau. **Régions:** Afrique de l'Ouest.

ACTIVITES D'INFORMATION ET D'EDUCATION: Domaines: Développement rural/agriculture; Enfants/jeunesse/famille; Questions relatives aux femmes; Santé/assainissement/eau. **Activités:** Collecte de fonds.

FRA2038
LIGUE DES DROITS DE L'HOMME
27 rue Jean-Dolent, 75014 Paris, France.

FRA2039
LIGUE FRANCAISE DE L'ENSEIGNEMENT ET DE L'EDUCATION PERMANENTE (LA LIGUE)
3 rue Récamier, 75341 Paris cedex 07, France.

Téléphone: 33 (1) 43 58 97 01. **Fax:** 33 (1) 43 58 97 02. **Contact:** Claude Julien, Président.

OBJECTIFS: Développer un programme de formation à la citoyenneté. Fédérer des associations oeuvrant dans l'ensemble des domaines de l'éducation populaire.

INFORMATIONS GENERALES: Création: 1866. **Type d'organisation:** regroupement d'ONG. **Affiliée à:** EFYSO - CLOSI - UNAT - CNAJEP - CELAVAR - JPA - CECOREL - CEDAG - CLAMCA -UNESCO. **Personnel/Total:** 10000.

PUBLICATIONS: Périodiques: Les Idées en Mouvement (12). Rapport annuel. Liste des publications.

EVALUATION/RECHERCHE: Rapports d'évaluation disponibles. Entreprend des activités de recherche.

COMMENTAIRES: Intervient dans la Communauté des Etats indépendants. Activités d'information concernant la Communauté des Etats indépendants.

ACTIVITES DANS LES REGIONS EN DEVELOPPEMENT: Intervient directement dans les régions en développement. Intervient par l'intermédiaire d'organisations locales partenaires. **Actions de Développement durable:** Développement rural/agriculture; Enfants/jeunesse/famille; Envoi de volontaires/experts/assistance technique; Écologie/environnement/biodiversité; Éducation/formation/alphabétisation. **Régions:** Afrique centrale; Afrique de l'Est; Afrique de l'Ouest; Asie centrale et Asie du Sud; Asie du Sud-Est.

ACTIVITES D'INFORMATION ET D'EDUCATION: Domaines: Droits de l'Homme/paix/conflits; Développement rural/agriculture; Développement urbain/habitat; Enfants/jeunesse/famille; Relations internationales/coopération/aide au développement; Écologie/environnement/biodiversité; Éducation/formation/alphabétisation. **Activités:** Campagnes d'information/expositions; Conférences/séminaires/ateliers/activités de formation; Lobbying/plaidoyer; Services d'information et de documentation/bases de données; Échanges/parrainage/jumelage; Édition/documents audiovisuels/documents éducatifs; Éducation formelle.

FRA2040
LIGUE INTERNATIONALE CONTRE LE RACISME ET L'ANTISEMITISME (LICRA)
40 rue de Paradis, 75010 Paris, France.

Téléphone: 33 (1) 47 70 13 28. **Fax:** 33 (1) 48 00 03 99. **Contact:** Pierre Didenbaum, Président.

OBJECTIFS: Lutter contre toutes les formes de racisme et d'exclusion.

INFORMATIONS GENERALES: Création: 1927. **Personnel/Total:** 5. Salariés: 5. **Sources financières:** Public: 20%. Autofinancement: 80%.

PUBLICATIONS: Périodiques: Droit de Vivre (6). Liste des publications.

COMMENTAIRES: Intervient dans la Communauté des Etats indépendants.

ACTIVITES DANS LES REGIONS EN DEVELOPPEMENT: Intervient directement dans les régions en développement. Maintient une présence locale sur le terrain. Intervient par l'intermédiaire d'organisations locales partenaires.

ACTIVITES D'INFORMATION ET D'EDUCATION: Domaines: Droits de l'Homme/paix/conflits; Enfants/jeunesse/famille; Questions relatives aux femmes; Racisme/xénophobie/antisémitisme. **Activités:** Campagnes d'information/expositions; Conférences/séminaires/ateliers/activités de formation; Radiodiffusion/manifestations culturelles; Édition/documents audiovisuels/documents éducatifs.

FRA2041
LIGUE INTERNATIONALE DE FEMMES POUR LA PAIX ET LA LIBERTE - SECTION FRANCAISE (LIFPL)
114 rue de Vaugirard, 75006 Paris, France.

Téléphone: 33 - 42 22 24 54. **Contact:** Simone Landry, Secrétaire générale.

OBJECTIFS: Contribuer à l'éducation dans le domaine de la paix et la compréhension internationale, le désarmement, la suppression de toute discrimination, la condition de la femme, le respect des Droits de la personne, le développement, l'environnement.

INFORMATIONS GENERALES: Création: 1918. **Personnel/Total:** 12. Bénévoles: 12. **Budget/Total 1993:** ECU 6000 (US$ 7000).

PUBLICATIONS: Périodiques: Paix et Liberté. Rapport annuel.

COMMENTAIRES: Intervient dans la Communauté des Etats indépendants.

ACTIVITES DANS LES REGIONS EN DEVELOPPEMENT: Intervient dans 3 pays. **Actions de Développement durable:** Droits de l'Homme/paix/conflits; Enfants/jeunesse/famille; Envoi de volontaires/experts/assistance technique; Questions relatives aux femmes; Secours d'urgence/réfugiés/aide humanitaire; Écologie/environnement/biodiversité; Éducation/formation/alphabétisation. **Régions:** Afrique australe;

See: *How to Use the Directory*, page 11.

Afrique de l'Est; Amérique du Sud; Asie centrale et Asie du Sud; Asie du Sud-Est; Mexique et Amerique centrale; Moyen-Orient; Océanie.

ACTIVITES D'INFORMATION ET D'EDUCATION: Domaines: Droits de l'Homme/paix/conflits; Développement rural/agriculture; Enfants/jeunesse/famille; Paix/conflits ethniques/armement/désarmement; Questions relatives aux femmes; Racisme/xénophobie/antisémitisme; Réfugiés/migrants/groupes ethniques; Secours d'urgence/réfugiés/aide humanitaire. **Activités:** Collecte de fonds; Conférences/séminaires/ateliers/activités de formation; Lobbying/plaidoyer; Services d'information et de documentation/bases de données; Édition/documents audiovisuels/documents éducatifs.

FRA2042
LIGUE INTERNATIONALE DE L'ENSEIGNEMENT, DE L'EDUCATION ET DE LA CULTURE POPULAIRE (LIEECP)

3 rue Récamier, 75007 Paris, France.

Téléphone: 33 (1) 43 58 97 30. **Fax:** 33 (1) 42 84 13 34. **Contact:** François Coursin, Secrétaire général.

OBJECTIFS: Regrouper les organismes nationaux qui ont pour objet de développer la connaissance, la culture et les institutions publiques d'éducation laïque, pour permettre aux hommes et aux citoyens de défendre la liberté de conscience, l'idéal démocratique, les droits de l'Homme et la paix.

INFORMATIONS GENERALES: Création: 1889. **Type d'organisation:** regroupement d'ONG. **Organisations membres:** 52. **Personnel/Total:** 3. **Salariés:** 3. **Budget/Total 1993:** ECU 226000 (US$ 265000). **Sources financières:** Public: 31%. Autofinancement: 69%.

PUBLICATIONS: Périodiques: EUROLIG (6). Rapport annuel. Liste des publications.

EVALUATION/RECHERCHE: Rapports d'évaluation disponibles. Entreprend des activités de recherche.

COMMENTAIRES: Intervient dans la Communauté des Etats indépendants. Activités d'information concernant la Communauté des Etats indépendants.

ACTIVITES DANS LES REGIONS EN DEVELOPPEMENT: Intervient directement dans les régions en développement. Intervient dans 50 pays. Maintient une présence locale sur le terrain. Intervient par l'intermédiaire d'organisations locales partenaires. **Actions de Développement durable:** Droits de l'Homme/paix/conflits; Enfants/jeunesse/famille; Questions relatives aux femmes; Santé/assainissement/eau; Éducation/formation/alphabétisation. **Régions:** Afrique centrale; Afrique de l'Ouest; Amérique du Sud; Asie centrale et Asie du Sud; Mexique et Amerique centrale.

ACTIVITES D'INFORMATION ET D'EDUCATION: Domaines: Culture/tradition/religion; Droits de l'Homme/paix/conflits; Enfants/jeunesse/famille; Paix/conflits ethniques/armement/désarmement; Racisme/xénophobie/antisémitisme; Relations internationales/coopération/aide au développement; Éducation/formation/alphabétisation. **Activités:** Conférences/séminaires/ateliers/activités de formation; Édition/documents audiovisuels/documents éducatifs.

FRA2043
LA MAIN TENDUE

118 avenue de Beaumont, 60260 Lamorlaye , France.

Téléphone: 33 - 44 21 42 68. **Contact:** Elisabeth Nicot.

OBJECTIFS: Susciter le dynamisme en Europe à partir de l'étude d'un dynamisme vécu en Afrique. Sensibiliser la jeunesse et soutenir des projets intégrés.

INFORMATIONS GENERALES: Création: 1982. **Type d'organisation:** réseau. **Affiliée à:** ENDA - EARTH ACTION - RAIC. **Personnel/Total:** 80. Bénévoles: 80 dont: 20 dans les pays en développement. **Sources financières:** Privé: 50%. Public: 25%. Autofinancement: 25%.

PUBLICATIONS: Rapport annuel. Liste des publications.

EVALUATION/RECHERCHE: Rapports d'évaluation disponibles. Entreprend des activités de recherche.

COMMENTAIRES: Intervient dans la Communauté des Etats indépendants.

ACTIVITES DANS LES REGIONS EN DEVELOPPEMENT: Intervient directement dans les régions en développement. Intervient dans 3 pays. Intervient par l'intermédiaire d'organisations locales partenaires. **Actions de Développement durable:** Droits de l'Homme/paix/conflits; Démocratie/bonne gestion publique/création d'institutions/développement participatif; Développement rural/agriculture; Développement urbain/habitat; Enfants/jeunesse/famille; Petites entreprises/secteur informel/artisanat; Santé/assainissement/eau; Éducation/formation/alphabétisation. **Régions:** Afrique de l'Ouest.

FRA2044
DES MAINS SANS FRONTIERE

BP 105, 78470 Saint-Rémy-les-Chevreuse, France.

Téléphone: 33 (1) 30 52 40 73. **Fax:** 33 (1) 30 52 40 73. **Contact:** Philippe Battesti, Président.

OBJECTIFS: Se mettre au service des causes humanitaires et sociales afin de répondre aux besoins de formation, d'éducation et de développement, et cela dans un esprit d'universalité.

INFORMATIONS GENERALES: Création: 1990. **Affiliée à:** Membre du CLONG-Volontariat (France). **Personnel/Total:** 56. Salariés: 50 dont: 48 dans les pays en développement. Bénévoles: 6. **Budget/Total 1993:** ECU 422000 (US$ 494000). **Sources financières:** Privé: 5%. Public: 90%. Autofinancement: 5%.

PUBLICATIONS: Périodiques: (2). Rapport annuel.

EVALUATION/RECHERCHE: Rapports d'évaluation disponibles.

COMMENTAIRES: Intervient dans la Communauté des Etats indépendants. Activités d'information concernant la Communauté des Etats indépendants.

ACTIVITES DANS LES REGIONS EN DEVELOPPEMENT: Intervient directement dans les régions en développement. Maintient une présence locale sur le terrain. Intervient par l'intermédiaire d'organisations locales partenaires. **Actions de Développement durable:** Dette/finances/commerce; Développement rural/agriculture; Développement urbain/habitat; Envoi de volontaires/experts/assistance technique; Santé/assainissement/eau; Éducation/formation/alphabétisation. **Régions:** Afrique australe; Afrique de l'Ouest; Amérique du Sud; Asie centrale et Asie du Sud; Asie du Sud-Est; Mexique et Amerique centrale; Moyen-Orient.

ACTIVITES D'INFORMATION ET D'EDUCATION: Domaines: Aliments/famine; Culture/tradition/religion; Droits de l'Homme/paix/conflits; Développement urbain/habitat; Emploi/chômage; Enfants/jeunesse/famille; Paix/conflits ethniques/armement/désarmement; Pauvreté/conditions de vie; Questions relatives aux femmes; Racisme/xénophobie/antisémitisme; Relations internationales/coopération/aide au développement; Relations économiques internationales/commerce/dette/finances; Santé/assainissement/eau; Secours d'urgence/réfugiés/aide humanitaire; Écologie/environnement/biodiversité. **Activités:** Conférences/séminaires/ateliers/activités de formation; Échanges/parrainage/jumelage; Éducation formelle.

FRA2045
MAIRES SANS FRONTIERES

Hôtel de Ville, 56 grande Rue, 91160 Longjumeau, France.

Téléphone: 33 (1) 69 34 13 13. **Fax:** 33 (1) 69 09 43 65. **Contact:** Roobun Marimootoo.

FRA2046
MARINS SANS FRONTIERES

51 rue Léon David, 85100 Les Sables d'Olonne, France.

Téléphone: 33 - 51 21 55 37. **Fax:** 33 - 51 21 55 00. **Contact:** Martine Le Fur, Présidente.

OBJECTIFS: Aider les populations en détresse dépendant, par leur approvisionnement, de la mer ou de voies navigables. Améliorer leur santé et leurs conditions de vie.

Voir : *Comment utiliser le répertoire,* page 11.

INFORMATIONS GENERALES: *Création:* 1984. *Personnel/Total:* 8. *Salariés:* 3. *Bénévoles:* 5 dont: 5 dans les pays en développement. *Budget/Total 1993:* ECU 260000 (US$ 304000). *Sources financières:* *Privé:* 30%. *Public:* 64%. *Autofinancement:* 6%.

ACTIVITES DANS LES REGIONS EN DEVELOPPEMENT: Intervient directement dans les régions en développement. Intervient dans 1 pays. Maintient une présence locale sur le terrain. **Actions de Développement durable:** Aliments/famine; Population/planning familial/démographie; Santé/assainissement/eau; Secours d'urgence/réfugiés/aide humanitaire. **Régions:** Afrique de l'Est.

FRA2047
MEDECINS DU MONDE (MDM-F)
67 avenue de la République, 75011 Paris, France.

Téléphone: 33 (1) 49 29 15 15 . *Fax:* 33 (1) 49 29 14 69. *Contact:* Dr. Bernard Granjon, Président.

OBJECTIFS: Aider, soigner, témoigner.

INFORMATIONS GENERALES: *Création:* 1980. *Type d'organisation:* réseau. *Organisations membres:* 10. *Personnel/Total:* 4120. *Salariés:* 120. *Bénévoles:* 4000 dont: 600 dans les pays en développement. *Budget/Total 1993:* ECU 45226000 (US$ 52974000). *Sources financières:* *Privé:* 51%. *Public:* 43%. *Autofinancement:* 6%.

PUBLICATIONS: *Périodiques:* Les Nouvelles (4) - Ingérence (3). *Rapport annuel. Liste des publications.*

EVALUATION/RECHERCHE: Rapports d'évaluation disponibles. Entreprend des activités de recherche.

COMMENTAIRES: Intervient dans la Communauté des Etats indépendants. Activités d'information concernant la Communauté des Etats indépendants.

ACTIVITES DANS LES REGIONS EN DEVELOPPEMENT: Intervient directement dans les régions en développement. Intervient dans 63 pays. Maintient une présence locale sur le terrain. Intervient par l'intermédiaire d'organisations locales partenaires. **Actions de Développement durable:** Aliments/famine; Droits de l'Homme/paix/conflits; Envoi de volontaires/experts/assistance technique; Petites entreprises/secteur informel/artisanat; Santé/assainissement/eau; Secours d'urgence/réfugiés/aide humanitaire; Éducation/formation/alphabétisation. **Régions:** Afrique australe; Afrique centrale; Afrique de l'Est; Afrique de l'Ouest; Afrique du Nord; Amérique du Sud; Asie centrale et Asie du Sud; Asie de l'Est; Asie du Sud-Est; Caraïbes; Mexique et Amerique centrale; Moyen-Orient; Océanie.

ACTIVITES D'INFORMATION ET D'EDUCATION: **Domaines:** Aliments/famine; Droits de l'Homme/paix/conflits; Enfants/jeunesse/famille; Paix/conflits ethniques/armement/désarmement; Pauvreté/conditions de vie; Racisme/xénophobie/antisémitisme; Relations internationales/coopération/aide au développement; Réfugiés/migrants/groupes ethniques; Santé/assainissement/eau; Secours d'urgence/réfugiés/aide humanitaire. **Activités:** Campagnes d'information/expositions; Collecte de fonds; Conférences/séminaires/ateliers/activités de formation; Lobbying/plaidoyer; Radiodiffusion/manifestations culturelles; Réseaux/télécommunications électroniques; Services d'information et de documentation/bases de données; Échanges/parrainage/jumelage; Édition/documents audiovisuels/documents éducatifs.

FRA2048
MEDECINS DU SECOURS POPULAIRE FRANCAIS
9/11 rue Froissart, 75140 Paris cedex 03, France.

Téléphone: 33 (1) 42 78 50 48. *Fax:* 33 (1) 42 74 71 01. *Contact:* Julien Laupretre.

FRA2049
MEDECINS POUR TOUS LES HOMMES
33 rue Espiot, 33200 Bordeaux, France.

Téléphone: 33 - 56 98 68 00. *Contact:* Jacques Dupoux.

FRA2050
MEDECINS SANS FRONTIERES, FRANCE (MSF)
8 rue Saint-Sabin, 75544 Paris cedex 11, France.

Téléphone: 33 (1) 40 21 29 29. *Fax:* 33 (1) 48 06 68 68. *Contact:* Dr. Brigitte Vasset, Directeur des opérations.

FRA2051
MEDICO-LIONS CLUBS DE FRANCE
17 rue Madame Lafayette, 76600 Le Havre, France.

Téléphone: 33 - 35 41 38 55. *Fax:* 33 - 35 42 18 11. *Contact:* Jean Behar, Président.

OBJECTIFS: Aider les pays en voie de développement, dans les domaines de la santé et de l'éducation.

INFORMATIONS GENERALES: *Création:* 1978. *Salariés:* 4. *Bénévoles:* 5. *Budget/Total 1993:* ECU 151000 (US$ 177000). *Sources financières:* *Privé:* 50%. *Autofinancement:* 50%.

PUBLICATIONS: *Rapport annuel.*

COMMENTAIRES: Cette organisation agit en liaison avec les Lions clubs des pays en voie de développement qui contrôlent l'utilisation des dons et produits qui sont adressés à destination des pays où ils résident.

ACTIVITES DANS LES REGIONS EN DEVELOPPEMENT: Intervient directement dans les régions en développement. Intervient dans 23 pays. Maintient une présence locale sur le terrain. Intervient par l'intermédiaire d'organisations locales partenaires. **Actions de Développement durable:** Santé/assainissement/eau; Éducation/formation/alphabétisation. **Régions:** Afrique centrale; Afrique de l'Est; Afrique de l'Ouest.

FRA2052
MIGRATIONS SANTE - COMITE MEDICO-SOCIAL POUR LA SANTE DES MIGRANTS
23 rue du Louvre, 75001 Paris, France.

Contact: Dr. P. Lombrail, Secrétaire Général.

FRA2053
MISSION ENFANCE
33 rue Galilée, 75116 Paris, France.

Téléphone: 33 (1) 44 43 53 86. *Fax:* 33 (1) 47 23 68 14. *Contact:* Patricia Husson, Présidente.

OBJECTIFS: Porter secours, dans le monde, aux enfants en détresse.

INFORMATIONS GENERALES: *Création:* 1991. *Affiliée à:* Mission Enfance (Monaco.). *Personnel/Total:* 90. *Salariés:* 10 dont: 7 dans les pays en développement. *Bénévoles:* 80 dont: 10 dans les pays en développement. *Budget/Total 1993:* ECU 620000 (US$ 726000). *Sources financières:* *Privé:* 90%. *Autofinancement:* 10%.

PUBLICATIONS: *Périodiques:* Mission Enfance (2). *Rapport annuel.*

EVALUATION/RECHERCHE: Rapports d'évaluation disponibles.

COMMENTAIRES: Intervient dans la Communauté des Etats indépendants.

ACTIVITES DANS LES REGIONS EN DEVELOPPEMENT: Intervient directement dans les régions en développement. Intervient dans 8 pays. Intervient par l'intermédiaire d'organisations locales partenaires. **Actions de Développement durable:** Droits de l'Homme/paix/conflits; Développement urbain/habitat; Santé/assainissement/eau; Éducation/formation/alphabétisation. **Régions:** Asie centrale et Asie du Sud; Asie du Sud-Est; Mexique et Amerique centrale; Moyen-Orient.

ACTIVITES D'INFORMATION ET D'EDUCATION: **Domaines:** Aliments/famine; Paix/conflits ethniques/armement/désarmement; Pauvreté/conditions de vie; Relations internationales/coopération/aide au développement; Relations économiques internationales/commerce/dette/finances; Secours d'urgence/réfugiés/aide humanitaire; Éducation/formation/alphabétisation. **Activités:** Campagnes d'information/expositions; Collecte de fonds; Conférences/séminaires/ateliers/activités de formation; Édition/documents audiovisuels/documents éducatifs.

See: *How to Use the Directory*, page 11.

FRA2054

MISSION EVANGELIQUE CONTRE LA LEPRE ◆ The Leprosy Mission

BP 186, 63204 Riom cedex, France.

Téléphone: 33 - 73 38 76 60. *Contact:* Jean Clavaud, Directeur.

OBJECTIFS: Secourir les victimes de la lèpre physiquement, moralement et spirituellement.

INFORMATIONS GENERALES: *Création:* 1978. *Personnel/Total:* 85. *Salariés:* 85 dont: 85 dans les pays en développement. *Budget/ Total 1993:* ECU 241000 (US$ 283000). *Sources financières:* Privé: 100%.

PUBLICATIONS: *Périodiques:* En Action (4). *Rapport annuel. Liste des publications.*

EVALUATION/RECHERCHE: Rapports d'évaluation disponibles. Entreprend des activités de recherche.

COMMENTAIRES: Les informations données ici revêtent une dimension internationale; l'action spécifique de l'organisation n'ayant pas été fournie.

ACTIVITES DANS LES REGIONS EN DEVELOPPEMENT: Intervient directement dans les régions en développement. Intervient dans 33 pays. Maintient une présence locale sur le terrain. **Actions de Développement durable:** Envoi de volontaires/experts/assistance technique; Santé/assainissement/eau; Éducation/formation/alphabétisation. **Régions:** Afrique australe; Afrique centrale; Afrique de l'Est; Afrique de l'Ouest; Asie centrale et Asie du Sud; Asie de l'Est; Asie du Sud-Est.

ACTIVITES D'INFORMATION ET D'EDUCATION: Domaines: Santé/ assainissement/eau. **Activités:** Campagnes d'information/expositions; Collecte de fonds; Conférences/séminaires/ateliers/activités de formation; Radiodiffusion/manifestations culturelles; Services d'information et de documentation/bases de données; Édition/documents audiovisuels/ documents éducatifs.

FRA2055

MISSION PROTESTANTE FRANCO SUISSE DU TCHAD (MPFST)

39 Grande Rue Charles de Gaulle, 94130 Nogent sur Marne, France.

Téléphone: 33 (1) 48 73 16 60. *Contact:* Bernard Huck.

OBJECTIFS: Développer les contacts avec la population, par l'accueil des orphelins, les soins de santé maternelle, l'enseignement pré-scolaire.

INFORMATIONS GENERALES: *Création:* 1952. *Type d'organisation:* regroupement d'ONG. *Affiliée à:* Alliance Evangélique Française. *Personnel/Total:* 14. *Salariés:* 12 dont: 10 dans les pays en développement. *Bénévoles:* 2 dont: 2 dans les pays en développement. *Budget/Total 1993:* ECU 181000 (US$ 212000). *Sources financières:* Privé: 70%. Public: 30%.

PUBLICATIONS: *Périodiques:* OBEIR (4).

EVALUATION/RECHERCHE: Rapports d'évaluation disponibles.

ACTIVITES DANS LES REGIONS EN DEVELOPPEMENT: Intervient directement dans les régions en développement. Intervient dans 1 pays. Maintient une présence locale sur le terrain. Intervient par l'intermédiaire d'organisations locales partenaires. **Actions de Développement durable:** Aliments/famine; Développement rural/agriculture; Enfants/jeunesse/famille; Santé/assainissement/eau; Éducation/formation/alphabétisation. **Régions:** Afrique centrale.

FRA2056

MISSIONS ET DEVELOPPEMENT

7bis rue Gay-Lussac, 21300 Chenove, France.

Téléphone: 33 - 80 51 44 67. *Contact:* Pierre Piroelle, Président.

OBJECTIFS: Apporter une aide matérielle et/ou morale aux bénévoles qui travaillent dans les pays en développement ou en situation de crise, particulièrement en Afrique occidentale, en Afrique centrale et à Madagascar.

INFORMATIONS GENERALES: *Création:* 1971. *Personnel/Total:* 247. *Bénévoles:* 247 dont: 132 dans les pays en développement. *Budget/Total 1993:* ECU 47000 (US$ 55000). *Sources financières:* Privé: 84%. *Public:* 5%. *Autofinancement:* 11%.

COMMENTAIRES: Intervient dans la Communauté des Etats indépendants.

ACTIVITES DANS LES REGIONS EN DEVELOPPEMENT: Intervient directement dans les régions en développement. Intervient dans 16 pays. Maintient une présence locale sur le terrain. Intervient par l'intermédiaire d'organisations locales partenaires. **Actions de Développement durable:** Aliments/famine; Santé/assainissement/eau. **Régions:** Afrique australe; Afrique centrale; Afrique de l'Ouest; Amérique du Sud; Asie du Sud-Est; Caraïbes; Moyen-Orient.

ACTIVITES D'INFORMATION ET D'EDUCATION: Domaines: Aliments/ famine; Santé/assainissement/eau. **Activités:** Autres; Collecte de fonds.

FRA2057

MOUVEMENT CHRETIEN POUR LA PAIX (MCP)

38 rue du Faubourg Saint Denis, 75010 Paris, France.

Téléphone: 33 (1) 48 00 09 05. *Fax:* 33 (1) 47 70 68 27. *Contact:* Thierry Picquart, Secrétaire général.

OBJECTIFS: Agir contre l'exclusion des plus défavorisés, pour un développement local soucieux de l'individu, de l'environnement, du patrimoine culturel, pour un décloisonnement inter-générations, inter-culturel et international. Agir en faveur d'une construction concrète de la paix.

INFORMATIONS GENERALES: *Création:* 1923. *Affiliée à:* MCP International (Belgique) - CCSVI (France) - COTRAVAUX (France) - CNAJEP (France.). *Salariés:* 20. *Bénévoles:* 600 dont: 100 dans les pays en développement. *Budget/Total 1993:* ECU 1508000 (US$ 1766000). *Sources financières:* Public: 62%. *Autofinancement:* 38%.

PUBLICATIONS: *Périodiques:* Dialogue (4). *Rapport annuel.*

EVALUATION/RECHERCHE: Rapports d'évaluation disponibles. Entreprend des activités de recherche.

COMMENTAIRES: Intervient dans la Communauté des Etats indépendants. Activités d'information concernant la Communauté des Etats indépendants.

ACTIVITES DANS LES REGIONS EN DEVELOPPEMENT: Intervient dans 50 pays. Intervient par l'intermédiaire d'organisations locales partenaires. **Actions de Développement durable:** Droits de l'Homme/ paix/conflits; Démocratie/bonne gestion publique/création d'institutions/ développement participatif; Développement rural/agriculture; Développement urbain/habitat; Enfants/jeunesse/famille; Envoi de volontaires/ experts/assistance technique; Petites entreprises/secteur informel/artisanat; Questions relatives aux femmes; Santé/assainissement/eau; Secours d'urgence/réfugiés/aide humanitaire; Écologie/environnement/ biodiversité; Éducation/formation/alphabétisation. **Régions:** Afrique de l'Ouest; Afrique du Nord; Amérique du Sud; Asie centrale et Asie du Sud; Asie du Sud-Est; Mexique et Amerique centrale; Moyen-Orient.

ACTIVITES D'INFORMATION ET D'EDUCATION: Domaines: Culture/ tradition/religion; Droits de l'Homme/paix/conflits; Développement rural/ agriculture; Développement urbain/habitat; Emploi/chômage; Enfants/ jeunesse/famille; Paix/conflits ethniques/armement/désarmement; Pauvreté/conditions de vie; Questions relatives aux femmes; Racisme/xénophobie/antisémitisme; Relations internationales/coopération/aide au développement; Relations économiques internationales/commerce/ dette/finances; Réfugiés/migrants/groupes ethniques; Santé/assainissement/eau; Secours d'urgence/réfugiés/aide humanitaire; Écologie/environnement/biodiversité. **Activités:** Campagnes d'information/expositions; Conférences/séminaires/ateliers/activités de formation; Lobbying/ plaidoyer; Radiodiffusion/manifestations culturelles; Échanges/parrainage/jumelage; Édition/documents audiovisuels/documents éducatifs; Éducation formelle.

FRA2058

MOUVEMENT CONTRE LE RACISME ET POUR L'AMITIE ENTRE LES PEUPLES (MRAP) ◆ Movement against Racism and for Friendship between Peoples

Voir : *Comment utiliser le répertoire,* page 11.

89 rue Oberkampf, 75543 Paris cedex 11, France.

Téléphone: 33 (1) 48 06 88 00. *Fax:* 33 (1) 48 06 88 01. *Contact:* Mouloud Aounit, Secrétaire général.

FRA2059

MOUVEMENT D'ENTRAIDE POUR LE TIERS MONDE ET LA COOPERATION (ETM)

36 rue René Boulanger, 75010 Paris, France.

Téléphone: 33 (1) 42 39 40 59. *Contact:* Pierre Max.

FRA2060

MOUVEMENT INTERNATIONAL ATD - AIDE A TOUTE DETRESSE - QUART MONDE (ATD)

107, avenue du Général Leclerc, 95480 Pierrelaye, France.

Téléphone: 33 (1) 30 37 11 11 . *Fax:* 33 (1) 30 37 65 12. *Contact:* E. Band, Secrétaire général.

OBJECTIFS: Lutter contre l'ignorance, la faim, l'aumône et l'exclusion. Apporter sa contribution pour la destruction de la misère, de l'extrême pauvreté dans le monde, conformément à la pensée du père Joseph Wresinski.

INFORMATIONS GENERALES: *Création:* 1957. *Organisations membres:* 20. *Budget/Total 1993:* ECU 75000 (US$ 88000). *Sources financières:* Privé: 50%. Public: 40%. Autofinancement: 10%.

PUBLICATIONS: *Périodiques:* Lettre aux Amis du Monde (3). *Rapport annuel. Liste des publications.*

EVALUATION/RECHERCHE: Entreprend des activités de recherche.

COMMENTAIRES: Le Mouvement entretient des rapports avec les comités d'ONG auprès des instances de l'ONU (Ecosos, Unicef, Unesco) et du Conseil de l'Europe. Il repose sur un groupe de personnes réunies au sein du volontariat international ATD Quart Monde. Intervient dans la Communauté des Etats indépendants. Activités d'information concernant la Communauté des Etats indépendants.

ACTIVITES DANS LES REGIONS EN DEVELOPPEMENT: Intervient directement dans les régions en développement. Intervient dans 25 pays. Maintient une présence locale sur le terrain. Intervient par l'intermédiaire d'organisations locales partenaires. **Actions de Développement durable:** Autres; Enfants/jeunesse/famille; Santé/assainissement/eau; Éducation/formation/alphabétisation. **Régions:** Afrique australe; Afrique centrale; Afrique de l'Est; Afrique de l'Ouest; Afrique du Nord; Amérique du Sud; Asie centrale et Asie du Sud; Asie de l'Est; Asie du Sud-Est; Caraïbes; Mexique et Amerique centrale; Moyen-Orient; Océanie.

ACTIVITES D'INFORMATION ET D'EDUCATION: Domaines: Enfants/jeunesse/famille; Pauvreté/conditions de vie. **Activités:** Campagnes d'information/expositions; Collecte de fonds; Conférences/séminaires/ateliers/activités de formation; Lobbying/plaidoyer; Radiodiffusion/manifestations culturelles; Réseaux/télécommunications électroniques; Échanges/parrainage/jumelage; Édition/documents audiovisuels/documents éducatifs.

FRA2061

MOUVEMENT MONDIAL DES MERES (MMM) ♦ World Movement of Mothers

56 rue de Passy, 75016 Paris, France.

Téléphone: 33 (1) 45 20 55 80 . *Contact:* Monique de Vaublanc, Secrétaire générale.

OBJECTIFS: Représenter les mères dans la vie internationale et nationale. Aider les mères à assumer leurs responsabilités familiales, sociales et civiques. Faire reconnaître l'importance du rôle de la mère.

INFORMATIONS GENERALES: *Création:* 1947. *Type d'organisation:* regroupement d'ONG. *Organisations membres:* 60. *Personnel/Total:* 8. *Bénévoles:* 8. *Budget/Total 1993:* ECU 5000 (US$ 6000). *Sources financières:* Privé: 50%. Autofinancement: 50%.

PUBLICATIONS: *Rapport annuel.*

EVALUATION/RECHERCHE: Entreprend des activités de recherche.

ACTIVITES DANS LES REGIONS EN DEVELOPPEMENT: Intervient directement dans les régions en développement. Intervient par l'intermédiaire d'organisations locales partenaires. **Actions de Développement durable:** Enfants/jeunesse/famille; Questions relatives aux femmes; Éducation/formation/alphabétisation. **Régions:** Afrique centrale; Afrique de l'Ouest; Afrique du Nord.

ACTIVITES D'INFORMATION ET D'EDUCATION: Domaines: Culture/tradition/religion; Enfants/jeunesse/famille; Questions relatives aux femmes. **Activités:** Conférences/séminaires/ateliers/activités de formation.

FRA2062

MOUVEMENT RURAL DE LA JEUNESSE CHRETIENNE (MRJC)

53 rue des Renaudes, 75017 Paris, France.

Téléphone: 33 (1) 42 27 74 18. *Fax:* 33 (1) 47 66 38 67. *Contact:* Patrice Coutagny.

OBJECTIFS: Intervenir sur toutes les questions qui touchent les jeunes en milieu rural. Agir en faveur d'une transformation sociale et d'un mouvement d'éducation populaire.

INFORMATIONS GENERALES: *Création:* 1929. *Affiliée à:* MIJARC - CCFD. *Personnel/Total:* 1080. *Salariés:* 80. *Bénévoles:* 1000. *Budget/Total 1993:* ECU 2412000 (US$ 2825000). *Sources financières:* Public: 70%. Autofinancement: 30%.

PUBLICATIONS: *Périodiques:* MRJC INFO (6) - MIJARC (4). *Rapport annuel. Liste des publications.*

EVALUATION/RECHERCHE: Rapports d'évaluation disponibles. Entreprend des activités de recherche.

PREVISIONS D'ACTIVITES: Campagne avec les de l'Est sur la citoyenneté.

COMMENTAIRES: Intervient dans la Communauté des Etats indépendants. Activités d'information concernant la Communauté des Etats indépendants.

ACTIVITES DANS LES REGIONS EN DEVELOPPEMENT: Intervient directement dans les régions en développement. Intervient dans 45 pays. Maintient une présence locale sur le terrain. Intervient par l'intermédiaire d'organisations locales partenaires. **Actions de Développement durable:** Droits de l'Homme/paix/conflits; Démocratie/bonne gestion publique/création d'institutions/développement participatif; Développement rural/agriculture; Enfants/jeunesse/famille; Petites entreprises/secteur informel/artisanat; Population/planning familial/démographie; Questions relatives aux femmes; Santé/assainissement/eau; Secours d'urgence/réfugiés/aide humanitaire; Écologie/environnement/biodiversité; Éducation/formation/alphabétisation; Énergie/transport. **Régions:** Afrique australe; Afrique centrale; Afrique de l'Est; Afrique de l'Ouest; Afrique du Nord; Amérique du Sud; Asie centrale et Asie du Sud; Asie de l'Est; Asie du Sud-Est; Caraïbes; Mexique et Amerique centrale.

ACTIVITES D'INFORMATION ET D'EDUCATION: Domaines: Culture/tradition/religion; Droits de l'Homme/paix/conflits; Développement rural/agriculture; Emploi/chômage; Enfants/jeunesse/famille; Paix/conflits ethniques/armement/désarmement; Pauvreté/conditions de vie; Population/planning familial/démographie; Questions relatives aux femmes; Racisme/xénophobie/antisémitisme; Relations internationales/coopération/aide au développement; Relations économiques internationales/commerce/dette/finances; Réfugiés/migrants/groupes ethniques; Santé/assainissement/eau; Écologie/environnement/biodiversité; Éducation/formation/alphabétisation. **Activités:** Campagnes d'information/expositions; Conférences/séminaires/ateliers/activités de formation; Lobbying/plaidoyer; Radiodiffusion/manifestations culturelles; Services d'information et de documentation/bases de données; Échanges/parrainage/jumelage; Édition/documents audiovisuels/documents éducatifs; Éducation formelle.

FRA2063

NATURE ET PROGRES

40 route de Rouen, 80500 Montdidier, France.

See: *How to Use the Directory,* page 11.

FRA2064

NON AU DROIT D'AFFAMER - OPINION PUBLIQUE ET FAIM DANS LE MONDE (NODAF) ♦ No to the Right to Starve People - Public Opinion and Hunger in the World

49 rue Gaston Baratte, 59493 Villeneuve d'Ascq, France.

Téléphone: 33 - 20 92 43 93. *Contact:* Etienne Verbaere, Président.

FRA2065

OEUVRES DU SAHEL-ASIE (OSA)

182 rue Pourquoi Pas, 83100 Toulon, France.

Téléphone: 33 - 94 41 38 05. *Fax:* 33- 94 46 32 58. *Contact:* Monique Biessy, Présidente.

OBJECTIFS: Mettre en place des structures sanitaires. Former des agents de santé et construire des écoles primaires en Afrique de l'Ouest avec la participation des populations locales. Apporter une aide alimentaire aux enfants de trois centres au Vietnam du Sud, ainsi qu'une aide financière pour la réalisation de garderie et une aide aux adoptants dans leurs démarches administratives.

INFORMATIONS GENERALES: *Création:* 1984. *Organisations membres:* 4. *Bénévoles:* 6 dont: 1 dans les pays en développement. *Budget/Total 1993:* ECU 30000 (US$ 35000). *Sources financières:* Privé: 45%. Autofinancement: 45%.

ACTIVITES DANS LES REGIONS EN DEVELOPPEMENT: Intervient directement dans les régions en développement. Intervient dans 3 pays. **Actions de Développement durable:** Aliments/famine; Enfants/ jeunesse/famille; Santé/assainissement/eau. **Régions:** Afrique de l'Ouest; Asie du Sud-Est.

ACTIVITES D'INFORMATION ET D'EDUCATION: Domaines: Enfants/ jeunesse/famille; Santé/assainissement/eau. **Activités:** Radiodiffusion/ manifestations culturelles; Échanges/parrainage/jumelage.

FRA2066

OEUVRES HOSPITALIERES FRANCAISES DE L'ORDRE DE MALTE (OHFOM)

92 rue du Ranelagh, 75016 Paris , France.

Téléphone: 33 (1) 45 20 80 20. *Fax:* 33 (1) 45 20 48 04. *Contact:* Arnold de Waresquiel, Président.

FRA2067

OEUVRES PONTIFICALES MISSIONNAIRES

5 rue Monsieur, 75007 Paris, France.

Téléphone: 33 (1) 47 83 67 95. *Contact:* Maurice Delorme.

FRA2068

OFFICE FRANCAIS DE LA FONDATION POUR L'EDUCATION A L'ENVIRONNEMENT EN EUROPE (OF-FEEE)

127 rue de Flandre, 75019 Paris, France.

Téléphone: 33 (1) 40 35 02 31. *Fax:* 33 (1) 40 35 02 33. *Contact:* Thomas Joly, Directeur.

OBJECTIFS: Sensibiliser les différents publics (collectivités locales, scolaires et lycéens) au respect de l'environnement, au moyen de "labels" de qualité tels Pavillon Bleu d'Europe, Eco Ecole, etc.

INFORMATIONS GENERALES: *Création:* 1981. *Type d'organisation:* collectif. *Organisations membres:* 13. *Affiliée à:* FEEE/European Office (Danemark). *Personnel/Total:* 8. *Salariés:* 5 dont: 1 dans les pays en développement. *Bénévoles:* 3. *Budget/Total 1993:* ECU 705000 (US$ 826000).

PUBLICATIONS: *Périodiques:* Bleu Blanc Vert (4). *Rapport annuel. Liste des publications.*

EVALUATION/RECHERCHE: Rapports d'évaluation disponibles. Entreprend des activités de recherche.

COMMENTAIRES: Activités d'information concernant la Communauté des Etats indépendants.

ACTIVITES DANS LES REGIONS EN DEVELOPPEMENT: Intervient dans 13 pays. Intervient par l'intermédiaire d'organisations locales partenaires.

ACTIVITES D'INFORMATION ET D'EDUCATION: Domaines: Développement urbain/habitat; Emploi/chômage; Relations internationales/ coopération/aide au développement; Santé/assainissement/eau; Écologie/environnement/biodiversité; Éducation/formation/alphabétisation. **Activités:** Campagnes d'information/expositions; Réseaux/télécommunications électroniques; Échanges/parrainage/jumelage; Édition/documents audiovisuels/documents éducatifs.

FRA2069

OFFICE INTERNATIONAL DE L'EAU (O.I.EAU) ♦ International Office for Water

21 rue de Madrid, 75008 Paris, France.

Téléphone: 33 (1) 45 22 14 67. *Fax:* 33 (1) 40 08 01 45. *Contact:* Jean-François Donzier, Directeur général.

OBJECTIFS: Gérer un centre de formation professionnelle aux métiers de l'eau et de l'assainissement (assistance technique et ingéniérie pédagogique). Fournir un service national d'information et de documentation sur l'eau, avec un réseau national de données. Animer et promouvoir des programmes d'études et de recherche sur l'eau. Apporter une expertise et une assitance institutionnelle dans le domaine international.

INFORMATIONS GENERALES: *Création:* 1977. *Type d'organisation:* réseau. *Affiliée à:* Secrétariat International de l'Eau (Canada). *Personnel/Total:* 90. *Salariés:* 90. *Budget/Total 1993:* ECU 7085000 (US$ 8299000). *Sources financières:* Autofinancement: 100%.

PUBLICATIONS: *Périodiques:* Les Nouvelles/News (3) (11) (3). *Rapport annuel. Liste des publications.*

EVALUATION/RECHERCHE: Rapports d'évaluation disponibles. Entreprend des activités de recherche.

COMMENTAIRES: Intervient dans la Communauté des Etats indépendants. Activités d'information concernant la Communauté des Etats indépendants.

ACTIVITES DANS LES REGIONS EN DEVELOPPEMENT: Intervient directement dans les régions en développement. Intervient dans 33 pays. Intervient par l'intermédiaire d'organisations locales partenaires. **Actions de Développement durable:** Démocratie/bonne gestion publique/création d'institutions/développement participatif; Développement rural/agriculture; Santé/assainissement/eau; Écologie/ environnement/biodiversité; Éducation/formation/alphabétisation. **Régions:** Afrique centrale; Afrique de l'Est; Afrique de l'Ouest; Afrique du Nord; Amérique du Sud; Asie du Sud-Est; Caraïbes; Mexique et Amerique centrale; Moyen-Orient.

ACTIVITES D'INFORMATION ET D'EDUCATION: Domaines: Développement rural/agriculture; Développement urbain/habitat; Pauvreté/ conditions de vie; Relations internationales/coopération/aide au développement; Santé/assainissement/eau; Écologie/environnement/biodiversité. **Activités:** Campagnes d'information/expositions; Collecte de fonds; Conférences/séminaires/ateliers/activités de formation; Lobbying/ plaidoyer; Radiodiffusion/manifestations culturelles; Réseaux/télécommunications électroniques; Services d'information et de documentation/ bases de données; Échanges/parrainage/jumelage; Édition/documents audiovisuels/documents éducatifs; Éducation formelle.

FRA2070

OFFICE TECHNIQUE D'ETUDES ET DE COOPERATION INTERNATIONALE (OTECI)

61 rue d'Anjou, 75008 Paris, France.

Téléphone: 33 (1) 47 42 18 71. *Fax:* 33 (1) 42 66 27 44. *Contact:* Philippe Duseigneur, Président.

OBJECTIFS: Promouvoir la coopération industrielle avec les pays du Tiers monde. Aider au développement d'un tissu industriel de petites et moyennes entreprises.

INFORMATIONS GENERALES: *Création:* 1979. *Personnel/Total:* 306. *Bénévoles:* 306. *Budget/Total 1993:* ECU 116000 (US$ 136000). *Sources financières:* Privé: 75%. Public: 20%. Autofinancement: 5%.

Voir : *Comment utiliser le répertoire,* page 11.

EVALUATION/RECHERCHE: Rapports d'évaluation disponibles.

COMMENTAIRES: Intervient dans la Communauté des Etats indépendants. Activités d'information concernant la Communauté des Etats indépendants.

ACTIVITES DANS LES REGIONS EN DEVELOPPEMENT: Intervient directement dans les régions en développement. Intervient dans 10 pays. Intervient par l'intermédiaire d'organisations locales partenaires. **Actions de Développement durable:** Dette/finances/commerce; Développement rural/agriculture; Envoi de volontaires/experts/assistance technique; Petites entreprises/secteur informel/artisanat; Santé/assainissement/eau. **Régions:** Afrique australe; Afrique centrale; Afrique de l'Est; Afrique de l'Ouest; Afrique du Nord; Amérique du Sud; Asie centrale et Asie du Sud; Asie de l'Est; Asie du Sud-Est; Caraïbes; Moyen-Orient.

ACTIVITES D'INFORMATION ET D'EDUCATION: Domaines: Développement rural/agriculture; Relations internationales/coopération/aide au développement; Santé/assainissement/eau; Secours d'urgence/réfugiés/aide humanitaire. **Activités:** Conférences/séminaires/ateliers/activités de formation.

FRA2071

OPHTALMO SANS FRONTIERES (OSF)

Le Rondos, Chasnais, 85400 Luçon, France.

Téléphone: 33 - 51 97 72 22. *Fax:* 33 - 51 97 73 95. *Contact:* Marcel Jouandet, Président.

FRA2072

ORCHIDEES

23 rue Pierre Curie, 94200 Ivry-sur-Seine, France.

Téléphone: 33 (1) 46 71 82 53. *Fax:* 33 (1) 46 72 51 01. *Contact:* Ho Thuy Tien, Directrice.

OBJECTIFS: Produire et distribuer des films documentaires sur les pays du Tiers-Monde en vue de sensibiliser l'opinion publique.

INFORMATIONS GENERALES: *Création:* 1981. *Type d'organisation:* réseau. *Organisations membres:* 5. *Affiliée à:* CIMADE (France) - Comité Catholique contre la Faim et pour le Développement -Terre des Hommes - Frères des Hommes - Ligue Française de l'Enseignement. *Personnel/Total:* 9. *Salariés:* 4. *Bénévoles:* 5. *Budget/Total 1993:* ECU 113000 (US$ 132000). *Sources financières:* Public: 50%. Autofinancement: 50%.

PUBLICATIONS: *Périodiques:* Le Pavé dans le Marigot (4). *Liste des publications.* **Actions de Développement durable:** Autres. **Régions:** Afrique de l'Est; Afrique de l'Ouest; Amérique du Sud; Asie de l'Est; Asie du Sud-Est; Mexique et Amerique centrale.

ACTIVITES D'INFORMATION ET D'EDUCATION: Domaines: Culture/tradition/religion; Développement rural/agriculture; Développement urbain/habitat; Enfants/jeunesse/famille; Population/planning familial/démographie; Questions relatives aux femmes; Écologie/environnement/biodiversité. **Activités:** Édition/documents audiovisuels/documents éducatifs.

FRA2073

ORGANISATION DES TRAVAILLEURS MALIENS DU CERCLE DE DIEMA EN FRANCE (OTMCDF)

23 rue du Retrait, 75020 Paris, France.

Téléphone: 33 (1) 43 58 75 05. *Contact:* Sacko Mamadou, Président.

FRA2074

ORGANISATION INTERNATIONALE DE COOPERATION POUR LA SANTE MEDICUS MUNDI, FRANCE (MEDICUS MUNDI) ♦ International Organisation for Co-operation in Health Care Medicus Mundi, France

153 rue de Charonne, 75011 Paris, France.

Téléphone: 33 (1) 43 70 87 57. *Fax:* 33 (1) 43 70 34 85. *Contact:* Serge Gottot, Président.

OBJECTIFS: Soutenir les projets d'initiative locale ou nationale dans le domaine de la santé. Collaborer à la mise en place de systèmes de soins et de prévention adéquats, par la formation des personnels de santé, l'appui à l'organisation et à la gestion, ainsi que la mobilisation des populations et des compétences locales.

INFORMATIONS GENERALES: *Création:* 1963. *Affiliée à:* CLONG-Volontariat - CFCF - CRID - MMI. *Personnel/Total:* 39. *Salariés:* 9 dont: 5 dans les pays en développement. *Bénévoles:* 30 dont: 20 dans les pays en développement. *Budget/Total 1993:* ECU 1658000 (US$ 1942000). *Sources financières:* Privé: 20%. Public: 70%. Autofinancement: 10%.

PUBLICATIONS: *Périodiques:* Objectif Santé (4).

EVALUATION/RECHERCHE: Rapports d'évaluation disponibles. Entreprend des activités de recherche.

ACTIVITES DANS LES REGIONS EN DEVELOPPEMENT: Intervient directement dans les régions en développement. Intervient dans 12 pays. Maintient une présence locale sur le terrain. Intervient par l'intermédiaire d'organisations locales partenaires. **Actions de Développement durable:** Enfants/jeunesse/famille; Envoi de volontaires/experts/assistance technique; Population/planning familial/démographie; Santé/assainissement/eau. **Régions:** Afrique australe; Afrique centrale; Afrique de l'Ouest; Amérique du Sud; Asie centrale et Asie du Sud; Asie du Sud-Est; Mexique et Amerique centrale.

ACTIVITES D'INFORMATION ET D'EDUCATION: Domaines: Relations internationales/coopération/aide au développement; Santé/assainissement/eau. **Activités:** Conférences/séminaires/ateliers/activités de formation.

FRA2075

ORGANISATION POUR LA PREVENTION DE LA CECITE (OPC)

9 rue Mathurin Régnier, 75015 Paris, France.

Téléphone: 33 (1) 40 61 99 05. *Fax:* 33 (1) 40 61 01 99. *Contact:* Jean Langlois, Président.

OBJECTIFS: Participer aux programmes nationaux de lutte contre la cécité en Afrique francophone. Apporter un soutien et participer à l'équipement des services d'ophtalmologie des hôpitaux en Afrique francophone et au Vietnam. Fournir des bourses de formation d'ophtalmologistes et d'infirmiers spécialisés en ophtalmologie.

INFORMATIONS GENERALES: *Création:* 1978. *Affiliée à:* International Agency for the Prevention of Blindness (Grande Bretagne) -Christoffel Blindenmission (Allemagne) - Oeil Sous les Tropiques (Belgique) - SBO (Hollande) - Helen Keller International (Etats-Unis) - ONCE (Espagne). *Personnel/Total:* 17. *Salariés:* 2 dont: 1 dans les pays en développement. *Bénévoles:* 15 dont: 10 dans les pays en développement. *Budget/Total 1993:* ECU 845000 (US$ 990000). *Sources financières:* Privé: 75%. Public: 9%. Autofinancement: 16%.

ACTIVITES DANS LES REGIONS EN DEVELOPPEMENT: Intervient directement dans les régions en développement. Intervient dans 15 pays. Maintient une présence locale sur le terrain. **Actions de Développement durable:** Santé/assainissement/eau. **Régions:** Afrique australe; Afrique de l'Est; Afrique de l'Ouest; Afrique du Nord; Asie de l'Est; Asie du Sud-Est.

FRA2076

ORGANISATION POUR LA RECHERCHE, LA COMMUNICATION ET L'ACTION EN FAVEUR D'UN DEVELOPPEMENT SOLIDAIRE ENTRE LE NORD ET LE SUD (ORCADES)

12 rue des Carmélites, 86000 Poitiers, France.

Téléphone: 33 - 49 41 49 11. *Fax:* 33 - 49 52 22 66. *Contact:* Benoît Theau.

OBJECTIFS: Eduquer, former, informer et sensibiliser l'opinion publique sur les problèmes du développement, de l'environnement et des relations Nord-Sud.

INFORMATIONS GENERALES: *Création:* 1974. *Affiliée à:* RITIMO (France) - Peuples Solidaires (France). *Personnel/Total:* 41. *Salariés:* 6 dont: 2 dans les pays en développement. *Bénévoles:* 35 dont: 5 dans les pays en développement. *Budget/Total 1993:*

See: *How to Use the Directory,* page 11.

ECU 362000 (US$ 424000). *Sources financières:* Privé: 1%. Public: 22%. *Autofinancement:* 77%.

PUBLICATIONS: *Rapport annuel. Liste des publications.*

EVALUATION/RECHERCHE: Rapports d'évaluation disponibles.

ACTIVITES DANS LES REGIONS EN DEVELOPPEMENT: Intervient directement dans les régions en développement. Intervient dans 1 pays. Maintient une présence locale sur le terrain. **Actions de Développement durable:** Éducation/formation/alphabétisation. **Régions:** Asie du Sud-Est.

ACTIVITES D'INFORMATION ET D'EDUCATION: Domaines: Aliments/famine; Droits de l'Homme/paix/conflits; Développement rural/agriculture; Développement urbain/habitat; Emploi/chômage; Enfants/jeunesse/famille; Pauvreté/conditions de vie; Questions relatives aux femmes; Relations économiques internationales/commerce/dette/finances; Santé/assainissement/eau; Écologie/environnement/biodiversité; Éducation/formation/alphabétisation. **Activités:** Campagnes d'information/expositions; Conférences/séminaires/ateliers/activités de formation; Services d'information et de documentation/bases de données; Édition/documents audiovisuels/documents éducatifs.

FRA2077
ORTHOPEDIE SANS FRONTIERES

1, Allée des Troënes, 44100 Nantes, France.

Téléphone: 33 - 40 94 32 87. *Fax:* 33 - 40 59 62 93. *Contact:* Maxime Audrain, Président.

OBJECTIFS: Permettre la réhabilitation fonctionnelle orthopédique de personnes amputées. Récupérer en France du matériel usagé et le recycler en Afrique. Approvisionner les petits ateliers africains de fabrication de matériel orthopédique. Former des personnes sur le terrain capables d'appareiller ceux qui en ont besoin.

INFORMATIONS GENERALES: *Création:* 1986. *Type d'organisation:* réseau, collectif. *Affiliée à:* OSF (Burkina Faso). *Personnel/Total:* 25. *Bénévoles:* 25 dont: 1 dans les pays en développement. *Budget/Total 1993:* ECU 32000 (US$ 38000). *Sources financières:* Privé: 20%. *Public:* 75%. *Autofinancement:* 5%.

PUBLICATIONS: *Rapport annuel.*

EVALUATION/RECHERCHE: Rapports d'évaluation disponibles.

ACTIVITES DANS LES REGIONS EN DEVELOPPEMENT: Intervient dans 3 pays. **Actions de Développement durable:** Autres; Santé/assainissement/eau; Secours d'urgence/réfugiés/aide humanitaire; Éducation/formation/alphabétisation. **Régions:** Afrique de l'Ouest.

ACTIVITES D'INFORMATION ET D'EDUCATION: Domaines: Secours d'urgence/réfugiés/aide humanitaire. **Activités:** Collecte de fonds.

FRA2078
OUAGA-BORDEAUX PARTAGE (OBP)

Le Peychon, 33370 Tresses, France.

Téléphone: 33 - 56 21 96 38. *Contact:* Joseph Ceccato, Président.

FRA2079
PARI DU COEUR - ANITOU

100 boulevard Daloz, 62520 Le Touquet, France.

Téléphone: 33 - 21 94 00 61. *Contact:* Michel Nollevalle.

FRA2080
PARRAINS DE L'ESPOIR

9, rue du Bon Voisin, 67404 Illkirch cedex, France.

Téléphone: 33 - 88 66 07 82. *Fax:* 33 - 88 67 24 67. *Contact:* André Gasser, Directeur.

OBJECTIFS: Parrainer des enfants. Promouvoir le développement. Promouvoir la scolarisation. Fournir une aide médicale.

INFORMATIONS GENERALES: *Création:* 1978. *Personnel/Total:* 25. *Salariés:* 10. *Bénévoles:* 15. *Budget/Total 1993:* ECU 3166000 (US$ 3708000). *Sources financières:* Privé: 100%.

PUBLICATIONS: *Rapport annuel.*

COMMENTAIRES: Intervient dans la Communauté des Etats indépendants. Activités d'information concernant la Communauté des Etats indépendants.

ACTIVITES DANS LES REGIONS EN DEVELOPPEMENT: Intervient directement dans les régions en développement. Intervient dans 15 pays. Intervient par l'intermédiaire d'organisations locales partenaires. **Actions de Développement durable:** Aliments/famine; Développement rural/agriculture; Enfants/jeunesse/famille; Population/planning familial/démographie; Questions relatives aux femmes; Santé/assainissement/eau; Secours d'urgence/réfugiés/aide humanitaire; Éducation/formation/alphabétisation. **Régions:** Afrique australe; Afrique centrale; Afrique de l'Est; Asie du Sud-Est; Mexique et Amerique centrale.

ACTIVITES D'INFORMATION ET D'EDUCATION: Domaines: Aliments/famine; Développement rural/agriculture; Enfants/jeunesse/famille; Pauvreté/conditions de vie; Questions relatives aux femmes; Santé/assainissement/eau; Secours d'urgence/réfugiés/aide humanitaire; Éducation/formation/alphabétisation. **Activités:** Collecte de fonds.

FRA2081
PARTAGE AVEC LES ENFANTS DU MONDE ♦ Share with Third World Children

11, rue du Change, B.P. 311, 60200 Compiègne, France.

Téléphone: 33 - 44 20 92 92. *Fax:* 33 - 44 20 94 95. *Contact:* Pierre Marchand, Directeur.

OBJECTIFS: Soutenir, dans les pays en développemnet, des organismes locaux au service des enfants de leur communauté.

INFORMATIONS GENERALES: *Création:* 1973. *Affiliée à:* International Felowship of Reconciliation (Pays Bas) - La Fédération de "la Voix de l'Enfant" (France). *Personnel/Total:* 20. *Salariés:* 20. *Budget/Total 1993:* ECU 8845000 (US$ 10360000). *Sources financières:* Privé: 84%. *Public:* 13%. *Autofinancement:* 3%.

PUBLICATIONS: *Périodiques:* Bulletin trimestriel (4). *Rapport annuel.*

EVALUATION/RECHERCHE: Rapports d'évaluation disponibles. Entreprend des activités de recherche.

COMMENTAIRES: L'organisation travaille également en Croatie Intervient dans la Communauté des Etats indépendants.

ACTIVITES DANS LES REGIONS EN DEVELOPPEMENT: Maintient une présence locale sur le terrain. Intervient par l'intermédiaire d'organisations locales partenaires. **Actions de Développement durable:** Développement rural/agriculture; Enfants/jeunesse/famille; Questions relatives aux femmes; Santé/assainissement/eau; Éducation/formation/alphabétisation. **Régions:** Afrique centrale; Afrique de l'Est; Amérique du Sud; Asie centrale et Asie du Sud; Asie du Sud-Est; Caraïbes; Mexique et Amerique centrale; Moyen-Orient.

ACTIVITES D'INFORMATION ET D'EDUCATION: Domaines: Droits de l'Homme/paix/conflits; Développement rural/agriculture; Enfants/jeunesse/famille; Pauvreté/conditions de vie; Population/planning familial/démographie; Questions relatives aux femmes; Santé/assainissement/eau; Secours d'urgence/réfugiés/aide humanitaire; Éducation/formation/alphabétisation. **Activités:** Collecte de fonds; Échanges/parrainage/jumelage.

FRA2082
PARTENAIRES DU MONDE

15 rue Royale, 75008 Paris, France.

Téléphone: 33 (1) 42 65 27 37. *Contact:* Michel Giraud, Président.

FRA2083
PATRIMUNDIA

4 rue Eugène Labiche, 75016 Paris, France.

Téléphone: 33 (1) 42 72 60 60. *Fax:* 33 (1) 42 72 18 35. *Contact:* Antoine Dousse, Président.

Voir : *Comment utiliser le répertoire,* page 11.

FRA2084

PAX ROMANA - MOUVEMENT INTERNATIONAL DES JURISTES CATHOLIQUES (MIJC)

4, Square La Bruyère, 75009 Paris, France.

Téléphone: 33 (1) 42 80 49 54. *Fax:* 33 (1) 48 74 15 00. *Contact:* Louis Pettiti.

OBJECTIFS: Promouvoir l'enseignement et la recherche sur les droits de l'Homme et ceux de la famille.

INFORMATIONS GENERALES: *Création:* 1948. *Type d'organisation:* regroupement d'ONG. *Budget/Total 1993:* ECU 8000 (US$ 9000). *Sources financières:* Privé: 20%. Autofinancement: 80%.

PUBLICATIONS: *Périodiques:* (1).

EVALUATION/RECHERCHE: Rapports d'évaluation disponibles. Entreprend des activités de recherche.

COMMENTAIRES: Intervient dans la Communauté des Etats indépendants. Activités d'information concernant la Communauté des Etats indépendants.

ACTIVITES DANS LES REGIONS EN DEVELOPPEMENT: Intervient directement dans les régions en développement. Intervient dans 10 pays. Intervient par l'intermédiaire d'organisations locales partenaires. **Actions de Développement durable:** Droits de l'Homme/paix/conflits; Enfants/jeunesse/famille; Questions relatives aux femmes; Éducation/formation/alphabétisation. **Régions:** Afrique centrale; Afrique de l'Ouest; Amérique du Sud; Asie du Sud-Est.

ACTIVITES D'INFORMATION ET D'EDUCATION: Domaines: Droits de l'Homme/paix/conflits. **Activités:** Conférences/séminaires/ateliers/activités de formation; Éducation formelle.

FRA2085

PEUPLE ET CULTURE

108 rue Saint Maur, 75011 Paris, France.

Téléphone: 33 (1) 43 38 49 00. *Contact:* Marc Vignal, Président.

FRA2086

PEUPLES SOLIDAIRES (PSO)

4, rue Franklin, 93200 Saint Denis, France.

Téléphone: 33 (1) 48 09 30 90. *Fax:* 33 (1) 48 09 30 85. *Contact:* Pierre Laronche, Président.

OBJECTIFS: Etablir des relations d'amitié entre des organisations populaires des pays du Sud et des groupes français. Participer à des campagnes de pression sur les décideurs des pays du Nord et à des actions de sensibilisation sur les problèmes de développement.

INFORMATIONS GENERALES: *Création:* 1983. *Type d'organisation:* regroupement d'ONG. *Organisations membres:* 100. *Affiliée à:* CRID (France). *Personnel/Total:* 4013. Salariés: 13 dont: 4 dans les pays en développement. *Bénévoles:* 4000. *Budget/Total 1993:* ECU 498000 (US$ 583000). *Sources financières:* Privé: 26%. Public: 25%. Autofinancement: 49%.

PUBLICATIONS: *Périodiques:* Peuples en Marche (12). *Rapport annuel.* Liste des publications.

EVALUATION/RECHERCHE: Rapports d'évaluation disponibles.

PREVISIONS D'ACTIVITES: Campagne "Environnement et Développement"; campagne "Pour une économie au service de l'homme; campagne "Politiques de développement et développement durable"

ACTIVITES DANS LES REGIONS EN DEVELOPPEMENT: Intervient directement dans les régions en développement. Intervient dans 14 pays. Maintient une présence locale sur le terrain. Intervient par l'intermédiaire d'organisations locales partenaires. **Actions de Développement durable:** Aliments/famine; Dette/finances/commerce; Droits de l'Homme/paix/conflits; Démocratie/bonne gestion publique/création d'institutions/développement participatif; Développement rural/agriculture; Développement urbain/habitat; Enfants/jeunesse/famille; Envoi de volontaires/experts/assistance technique; Petites entreprises/secteur informel/artisanat; Questions relatives aux femmes; Santé/assainissement/eau; Écologie/environnement/biodiversité; Éducation/formation/

alphabétisation. **Régions:** Afrique centrale; Afrique de l'Ouest; Amérique du Sud; Asie centrale et Asie du Sud; Caraïbes; Océanie.

ACTIVITES D'INFORMATION ET D'EDUCATION: Domaines: Droits de l'Homme/paix/conflits; Développement rural/agriculture; Développement urbain/habitat; Emploi/chômage; Enfants/jeunesse/famille; Paix/conflits ethniques/armement/désarmement; Pauvreté/conditions de vie; Questions relatives aux femmes; Racisme/xénophobie/antisémitisme; Relations internationales/coopération/aide au développement; Relations économiques internationales/commerce/dette/finances; Réfugiés/migrants/groupes ethniques; Santé/assainissement/eau; Secours d'urgence/réfugiés/aide humanitaire; Écologie/environnement/biodiversité; Éducation/formation/alphabétisation. **Activités:** Campagnes d'information/expositions; Collecte de fonds; Conférences/séminaires/ateliers/activités de formation; Lobbying/plaidoyer; Échanges/parrainage/jumelage; Édition/documents audiovisuels/documents éducatifs.

FRA2087

PHARMACIENS SANS FRONTIERES (PSF)

4, Voie Militaire des Gravanches, 63100 Clermont-Ferrand, France.

Téléphone: 33 - 73 98 24 98. *Fax:* 33 - 73 98 24 90. *Contact:* Jean-Louis Machuron, Président.

OBJECTIFS: Promouvoir la santé publique. Collecter et distribuer des médicaments non utilisés. Protéger l'environnement en détruisant les médicaments non utilisés et les films de radiographies devenus inutiles. Créer et réhabiliter des laboratoires de biologie médicale. Réhabiliter des hôpitaux.

INFORMATIONS GENERALES: *Création:* 1985. *Affiliée à:* Voice - Coordination d'Agen (France). *Personnel/Total:* 188. Salariés: 95. Bénévoles: 93. *Budget/Total 1993:* ECU 12506000 (US$ 14648000). *Sources financières:* Privé: 5%. Public: 85%. Autofinancement: 10%.

PUBLICATIONS: *Périodiques:* Pharmacies Sans Frontières. *Rapport annuel.*

EVALUATION/RECHERCHE: Entreprend des activités de recherche.

COMMENTAIRES: Intervient dans la Communauté des Etats indépendants.

ACTIVITES DANS LES REGIONS EN DEVELOPPEMENT: Intervient directement dans les régions en développement. Intervient dans 50 pays. Maintient une présence locale sur le terrain. Intervient par l'intermédiaire d'organisations locales partenaires. **Actions de Développement durable:** Envoi de volontaires/experts/assistance technique; Santé/assainissement/eau; Secours d'urgence/réfugiés/aide humanitaire. **Régions:** Afrique centrale; Afrique de l'Est; Afrique de l'Ouest; Afrique du Nord; Amérique du Sud; Asie de l'Est; Asie du Sud-Est; Caraïbes.

FRA2088

PLANETE SANS FRONTIERES (PSF)

14, rue Ménard, 78000 Versailles, France.

Téléphone: 33 (1) 39 20 15 64. *Contact:* Houndomou Gbetondji, Secrétaire général.

OBJECTIFS: Eduquer et sensiliser des jeunes au développement et à la solidarité internationale, notamment par des actions liées à l'environnement et à l'écologie.

INFORMATIONS GENERALES: *Création:* 1988. *Affiliée à:* Fédération des Jeunes pour la Nature (France). *Personnel/Total:* 11. Salariés: 1. Bénévoles: 10 dont: 3 dans les pays en développement. *Budget/Total 1993:* ECU 38000 (US$ 44000). *Sources financières:* Public: 60%. Autofinancement: 40%.

ACTIVITES DANS LES REGIONS EN DEVELOPPEMENT: Intervient directement dans les régions en développement. Intervient dans 1 pays. Maintient une présence locale sur le terrain. Intervient par l'intermédiaire d'organisations locales partenaires. **Actions de Développement durable:** Autres; Écologie/environnement/biodiversité. **Régions:** Afrique de l'Ouest.

ACTIVITES D'INFORMATION ET D'EDUCATION: Domaines: Autres; Écologie/environnement/biodiversité. **Activités:** Autres; Campagnes d'information/expositions; Éducation formelle.

See: *How to Use the Directory*, page 11.

FRA2089
PLEIN-CHAMP

10 rue du Plâtre, 75004 Paris, France.

Téléphone: 33 (1) 42 71 76 22. *Fax:* 33 (1) 42 71 76 23. *Contact:* Johnny Egg.

FRA2090
PRANAMAYA

07360 Saint-Michel-de-Chabrillanoux, France.

Téléphone: 33 - 75 66 30 32. *Contact:* Marie-Dominique Gyss-Mendez, Présidente.

OBJECTIFS: Découvrir la région de Pranamaya, au Guatemala, à travers des rendonnées en groupes, pour mieux connaître les réalités de ce pays. Participer au développement de la communauté paysanne, en séjournant sur le site d'un centre expérimental pour la protection de l'environnement. Améliorer les techniques de production et la formation des jeunes agriculteurs de Pranamaya. Dynamiser les différents postes de travail à la ferme.

INFORMATIONS GENERALES: *Création:* 1989. *Personnel/Total:* 8. *Salariés:* 1. *Bénévoles:* 7 dont: 1 dans les pays en développement. *Budget/Total 1993:* ECU 15000 (US$ 18000). *Sources financières:* Privé: 1%. Public: 40%. Autofinancement: 59%.

ACTIVITES DANS LES REGIONS EN DEVELOPPEMENT: Intervient directement dans les régions en développement. Intervient dans 1 pays. Maintient une présence locale sur le terrain. Intervient par l'intermédiaire d'organisations locales partenaires. **Actions de Développement durable:** Développement rural/agriculture; Enfants/jeunesse/famille; Envoi de volontaires/experts/assistance technique; Écologie/environnement/biodiversité; Éducation/formation/alphabétisation. **Régions:** Mexique et Amerique centrale.

ACTIVITES D'INFORMATION ET D'EDUCATION: Domaines: Culture/tradition/religion; Développement rural/agriculture; Relations internationales/coopération/aide au développement. **Activités:** Radiodiffusion/manifestations culturelles; Échanges/parrainage/jumelage; Éducation formelle.

FRA2091
PREMIERE URGENCE

B.P. 53, 92404 Courbevoie, France.

Téléphone: 33 (1) 41 16 84 00. *Fax:* 33 (1) 41 16 84 10. *Contact:* Thierry Mauricet, Directeur.

OBJECTIFS: Venir en aide, à l'étranger, aux victimes de catostrophes naturelles, de guerres civiles et de conflits.

INFORMATIONS GENERALES: *Création:* 1992. *Type d'organisation:* regroupement d'ONG. *Organisations membres:* 42. *Affiliée à:* La Voix de l'Enfant (France). *Personnel/Total:* 130. *Salariés:* 10. *Bénévoles:* 120 dont: 115 dans les pays en développement. *Budget/Total 1993:* ECU 6030000 (US$ 7063000). *Sources financières:* Privé: 30%. *Public:* 60%. Autofinancement: 10%.

COMMENTAIRES: Intervient dans la Communauté des Etats indépendants.

ACTIVITES DANS LES REGIONS EN DEVELOPPEMENT: Intervient directement dans les régions en développement. Intervient dans 2 pays. Maintient une présence locale sur le terrain. **Actions de Développement durable:** Secours d'urgence/réfugiés/aide humanitaire. **Régions:** Afrique centrale.

ACTIVITES D'INFORMATION ET D'EDUCATION: Domaines: Aliments/famine; Enfants/jeunesse/famille; Paix/conflits ethniques/armement/désarmement; Secours d'urgence/réfugiés/aide humanitaire. **Activités:** Collecte de fonds.

FRA2092
PRO-NATURA INTERNATIONAL

134, Rue Danton, 92300 Levallois-Perret, France.

Téléphone: (33) 47 59 10 09. *Fax:* (33) 47 59 10 60. *Contact:* Guy F. Reinaud, Président.

OBJECTIFS: Mettre en œuvre, en zone de forêt tropicale, des projets d'éco-développement, en utilisant principalement des techniques d'agroforesterie. Aider d'autres ONG locales à réaliser des projets ayant la même philosophie, dans le domaine de l'agroforesterie et du marketing.

INFORMATIONS GENERALES: *Création:* 1992. *Type d'organisation:* réseau. *Organisations membres:* 17. *Personnel/Total:* 436. *Salariés:* 26 dont: 25 dans les pays en développement. *Bénévoles:* 410 dont: 340 dans les pays en développement. *Budget/Total 1993:* ECU 473000 (US$ 554000). *Sources financières:* Privé: 46%. Public: 24%. Autofinancement: 30%.

PUBLICATIONS: *Périodiques:* Newsletter Pro-Natura International (24) - Lettre d'Information Pro-Natura International (24). *Rapport annuel.*

EVALUATION/RECHERCHE: Rapports d'évaluation disponibles. Entreprend des activités de recherche.

ACTIVITES DANS LES REGIONS EN DEVELOPPEMENT: Intervient directement dans les régions en développement. Intervient dans 17 pays. Maintient une présence locale sur le terrain. Intervient par l'intermédiaire d'organisations locales partenaires. **Actions de Développement durable:** Démocratie/bonne gestion publique/création d'institutions/développement participatif; Développement rural/agriculture; Envoi de volontaires/experts/assistance technique; Petites entreprises/secteur informel/artisanat; Écologie/environnement/biodiversité; Éducation/formation/alphabétisation. **Régions:** Afrique centrale; Afrique de l'Ouest; Amérique du Sud; Mexique et Amerique centrale.

ACTIVITES D'INFORMATION ET D'EDUCATION: Domaines: Aliments/famine; Culture/tradition/religion; Développement rural/agriculture; Emploi/chômage; Pauvreté/conditions de vie; Relations internationales/coopération/aide au développement; Écologie/environnement/biodiversité; Éducation/formation/alphabétisation. **Activités:** Collecte de fonds; Radiodiffusion/manifestations culturelles; Échanges/parrainage/jumelage.

FRA2093
PROGRAMME SOLIDARITE - EAU (PS-EAU) ♦ Water Network

213, rue Lafayette, 75010 Paris, France.

Téléphone: 33 (1) 40 05 61 23. *Fax:* (1) 40 05 61 10. *Contact:* M. Hessel, Président.

OBJECTIFS: Rassembler les collectivités locales et les ONG européennes autour d'un même programme pour apporter, de façon coordonnée, une aide pour une meilleure maîtrise de l'eau dans les pays en développement.

INFORMATIONS GENERALES: *Création:* 1984. *Type d'organisation:* réseau. *Organisations membres:* 13. *Personnel/Total:* 2. *Salariés:* 2. *Budget/Total 1993:* ECU 181000 (US$ 212000). *Sources financières:* Public: 100%.

PUBLICATIONS: *Périodiques:* Lettre du P Seau (4). *Rapport annuel.* Liste des publications.

EVALUATION/RECHERCHE: Rapports d'évaluation disponibles.

ACTIVITES DANS LES REGIONS EN DEVELOPPEMENT: Intervient par l'intermédiaire d'organisations locales partenaires. **Actions de Développement durable:** Développement rural/agriculture; Envoi de volontaires/experts/assistance technique; Santé/assainissement/eau. **Régions:** Afrique centrale; Afrique de l'Est; Afrique de l'Ouest; Afrique du Nord; Amérique du Sud; Asie du Sud-Est; Mexique et Amerique centrale.

ACTIVITES D'INFORMATION ET D'EDUCATION: Domaines: Développement rural/agriculture; Santé/assainissement/eau. **Activités:** Campagnes d'information/expositions; Conférences/séminaires/ateliers/activités de formation; Lobbying/plaidoyer; Services d'information et de documentation/bases de données; Édition/documents audiovisuels/documents éducatifs.

FRA2094
PROJET TOMORROW

Route d'Aubussargues, 30700 Serviers, France.

Téléphone: 33 (1) 66 22 53 93. *Fax:* 33 (1) 66 03 01 70. *Contact:* Yvette Pierpaoli, Secrétaire générale.

Voir : *Comment utiliser le répertoire,* page 11.

FRA2095

PROMOPIC INTERNATIONAL

11 Mail Albert 1er, 80026 Amiens, France.

Téléphone: 33 - 22 97 37 37. *Contact:* Elisabeth Begue.

FRA2096

PUBLIC SERVICES INTERNATIONAL (PSI) ♦ Internationale des services publics

45, avenue Voltaire, BP 9, 0121 Ferney-Voltaire cedex, France.

Telephone: 33 - 50 40 64 64. *Fax:* 33 - 50 40 73 20. *E-mail:* PSI@GEO2.GEONET.DE. *Contact:* Hans Engelberts.

OBJECTIVES: To represent and defend the interests of affiliated organisations and their members before international authorities. To ensure the universal and unrestricted recognition and application of the rights of individuals working in public services and trade unions. To develop and implement trade union education and training programmes with the main priority in the Third World.

GENERAL INFORMATION: *Creation:* 1907. *Personnel/Total:* 55. *Salaried:* 55 of which: 17 in developing countries. *Budget/Total 1993:* ECU 2240000 (US$ 2624000). *Financial sources:* Public: 18%. *Self-financing:* 82%.

PUBLICATIONS: *Periodicals:* "FOCUS" (4) - "FLASH" (20). *Annual report. List of publications.*

EVALUATION/RESEARCH: Evaluation reports available. Undertakes research activities.

COMMENTS: Undertakes activities in the Commonwealth of Independent States. Information activities related to the Commonwealth of Independent States.

ACTIVITIES IN DEVELOPING REGIONS: Present in developing regions. Active in 88 country(ies). Maintains local field presence. Works through local field partners. **Sustainable Development Actions:** Children/youth/family; Debt/finance/trade; Democracy/good governance/institution building/participatory development; Ecology/environment/biodiversity; Education/training/literacy; Emergency relief/refugees/humanitarian assistance; Energy/transport; Gender issues/women; Health/sanitation/water; Human rights/peace/conflicts; Sending volunteers/experts/technical assistance. **Regions:** Caribbean; Central Africa; Central Asia and South Asia; East Africa; East Asia; Mexico and Central America; Middle East; North Africa; Oceania; South America; South East Asia; Southern Africa; West Africa.

INFORMATION AND EDUCATION ACTIVITIES: **Topics:** Children/youth/family; Ecology/environment/biodiversity; Education/training/literacy; Employment/unemployment; Food/famine; Gender issues/women; Health/sanitation/water; Human rights/peace/conflicts; International economic relations/trade/debt/finance; International relations/cooperation/development aid; Peace/ethnic conflicts/armament/disarmament; Poverty/living conditions; Racism/xenophobia/antisemitism; Refugees/migrants/ethnic groups. **Activities:** Conferences/seminars/workshops/training activities; Fund raising; Information and documentation services/data bases; Information campaigns/exhibitions; Lobbying/advocacy; Networking/electronic telecommunications; Publishing/audiovisual materials/educational materials.

FRA2097

LES RAMEAUX VERTS

25, rue Pauline Borghèse, 92200 Neuilly-sur-Seine, France.

Téléphone: 33 (1) 47 22 78 71. *Contact:* Louis Coignard.

OBJECTIFS: Sauver les enfants en détresse dans les pays du Tiers Monde, par la voie du développement communautaire. Parrainer des enfants. Apporter du secours d'urgence.

INFORMATIONS GENERALES: *Création:* 1976. *Personnel/Total:* 15. *Bénévoles:* 15. *Budget/Total 1993:* ECU 75376 (US$ 88000). *Sources financières:* Privé: 75%. Autofinancement: 25%.

ACTIVITES DANS LES REGIONS EN DEVELOPPEMENT: Intervient dans 3 pays. Intervient par l'intermédiaire d'organisations locales partenaires. **Actions de Développement durable:** Aliments/famine; Développement rural/agriculture; Développement urbain/habitat;

Enfants/jeunesse/famille; Petites entreprises/secteur informel/artisanat; Questions relatives aux femmes; Santé/assainissement/eau; Secours d'urgence/réfugiés/aide humanitaire; Éducation/formation/alphabétisation; Énergie/transport. **Régions:** Afrique centrale; Asie du Sud-Est.

FRA2098

REGARDS CROISES DIALOGUE DES CULTURES (A COMME AFRIQUE)

17 lotissement de la Chartreuse, 56400 Auray, France.

Téléphone: 33 - 97 56 33 32. *Contact:* Yvon Dupré, Président.

FRA2099

RENCONTRES AFRICAINES

2 rue de Viarmes, 75001 Paris, France.

Téléphone: 33 (1) 45 08 35 00. *Contact:* Jean-Paul Benoit, Président.

FRA2100

RENCONTRES AFRICAINES - MAISON DES ASSOCIATIONS

6, rue Berthe de Boissieux, 38000 Grenoble, France.

Téléphone: 33 - 76 87 91 90. *Contact:* Hervé Gay, Président.

OBJECTIFS: Aider les travailleurs immigrés africains, dans le domaine du logement et de l'alphabétisation. Apporter du soutien aux travailleurs africains, en vue de leur retour au pays. Promouvoir le développement des villages d'origine des travailleurs africains.

INFORMATIONS GENERALES: *Création:* 1974. *Budget/Total 1993:* ECU 3000 (US$ 4000). *Sources financières:* Public: 30%.

COMMENTAIRES: Les actions de développement en Afrique sont autofinancées par les membres de l'association. Celle-ci fait un emprunt auprès des banques qui est remboursé par les membres des villages.

ACTIVITES DANS LES REGIONS EN DEVELOPPEMENT: Intervient directement dans les régions en développement. Intervient dans 2 pays. Intervient par l'intermédiaire d'organisations locales partenaires. **Actions de Développement durable:** Aliments/famine; Développement rural/agriculture; Santé/assainissement/eau. **Régions:** Afrique de l'Ouest.

ACTIVITES D'INFORMATION ET D'EDUCATION: **Domaines:** Développement rural/agriculture; Réfugiés/migrants/groupes ethniques; Éducation/formation/alphabétisation. **Activités:** Campagnes d'information/expositions; Radiodiffusion/manifestations culturelles; Échanges/parrainage/jumelage; Éducation formelle.

FRA2101

REPORTERS SANS FRONTIERES

5, rue Geoffroy Marie, 75009 Paris, France.

Téléphone: 33 (1) 44 83 84 84. *Fax:* 33 (1) 45 23 11 51. *Contact:* Robert Ménard, Directeur.

OBJECTIFS: Défendre la liberté de la presse dans le monde.

INFORMATIONS GENERALES: *Création:* 1985. *Type d'organisation:* réseau. *Organisations membres:* 7. *Personnel/Total:* 7. *Salariés:* 7. *Budget/Total 1993:* ECU 1055000 (US$ 1236000). *Sources financières:* Privé: 16%. Public: 46%. Autofinancement: 38%.

PUBLICATIONS: *Périodiques:* La Lettre de Reporters sans Frontières (12). *Rapport annuel.*

COMMENTAIRES: Intervient dans la Communauté des Etats indépendants.

ACTIVITES DANS LES REGIONS EN DEVELOPPEMENT: Intervient par l'intermédiaire d'organisations locales partenaires. **Actions de Développement durable:** Droits de l'Homme/paix/conflits; Démocratie/bonne gestion publique/création d'institutions/développement participatif. **Régions:** Afrique australe; Afrique centrale; Afrique de l'Est; Afrique de l'Ouest; Afrique du Nord; Amérique du Sud; Asie centrale et Asie du Sud; Asie de l'Est; Asie du Sud-Est; Caraïbes; Mexique et Amerique centrale; Moyen-Orient.

ACTIVITES D'INFORMATION ET D'EDUCATION: **Domaines:** Droits de l'Homme/paix/conflits. **Activités:** Collecte de fonds; Conférences/sémi-

                              See: *How to Use the Directory*, page 11.

naires/ateliers/activités de formation; Échanges/parrainage/jumelage; Édition/documents audiovisuels/documents éducatifs.

FRA2102

RESCUE INTERNATIONAL ASSISTANCE LEAGUE (RIAL)

Centre Jean Mermoz, avenue Jean Mermoz, 91170 Viry-Châtillon, France.

Téléphone: 33 - 69 45 11 49. *Fax:* 33 - 69 44 23 95. *Contact:* Pierre Bansard, Président.

OBJECTIFS: Apporter une aide en cas de catastrophes naturelles, technologiques, ou en cas d'événements sociaux. Former dans le domaine médical et paramédical, dans le domaine du sauvetage ou de la protection civile.

INFORMATIONS GENERALES: *Création:* 1982. *Type d'organisation:* regroupement d'ONG. *Organisations membres:* 52. *Personnel/Total:* 210003. *Salariés:* 3. *Bénévoles:* 210000. *Budget/Total 1993:* ECU 30000 (US$ 35000). *Sources financières:* Privé: 30%. Autofinancement: 70%.

PUBLICATIONS: *Périodiques:* The Times of Rescue International Assistance League (1). *Rapport annuel. Liste des publications.*

COMMENTAIRES: Intervient dans la Communauté des Etats indépendants. Activités d'information concernant la Communauté des Etats indépendants.

ACTIVITES DANS LES REGIONS EN DEVELOPPEMENT: Intervient directement dans les régions en développement. Intervient dans 5 pays. Intervient par l'intermédiaire d'organisations locales partenaires. **Actions de Développement durable:** Aliments/famine; Envoi de volontaires/experts/assistance technique; Questions relatives aux femmes; Santé/assainissement/eau; Secours d'urgence/réfugiés/ aide humanitaire; Éducation/formation/alphabétisation. **Régions:** Afrique centrale; Amérique du Sud; Asie centrale et Asie du Sud; Caraïbes; Mexique et Amerique centrale.

ACTIVITES D'INFORMATION ET D'EDUCATION: Domaines: Aliments/famine; Développement urbain/habitat; Relations internationales/coopération/aide au développement; Santé/assainissement/eau; Secours d'urgence/réfugiés/aide humanitaire. **Activités:** Campagnes d'information/expositions; Collecte de fonds; Conférences/séminaires/ateliers/ activités de formation; Lobbying/plaidoyer; Radiodiffusion/manifestations culturelles; Réseaux/télécommunications électroniques; Services d'information et de documentation/bases de données; Échanges/parrainage/jumelage; Édition/documents audiovisuels/documents éducatifs; Éducation formelle.

FRA2103

RESEAU D'APPUI AUX FORMATIONS POUR LE DEVELOPPEMENT (RAFOD)

30, rue Sainte-Hélène, 69002 Lyon, France.

Téléphone: 33 - 78 37 83 24. *Fax:* 33 - 72 41 99 88. *Contact:* Gilbert Graugnard.

OBJECTIFS: Favoriser la mise en place de formations professionnalisées pour des Instituts de formation au développement du Nord et du Sud. Accorder des bourses d'études pour des acteurs de développement non-gouvernementaux des pays en développement.

INFORMATIONS GENERALES: *Création:* 1990. *Type d'organisation:* réseau. *Organisations membres:* 2. *Personnel/Total:* 8. *Bénévoles:* 8. *Budget/Total 1993:* ECU 377000 (US$ 441000). *Sources financières:* Privé: 50%. Public: 49%. Autofinancement: 1%.

PUBLICATIONS: *Périodiques:* Lettre du Réseau (2). *Liste des publications.*

EVALUATION/RECHERCHE: Rapports d'évaluation disponibles. Entreprend des activités de recherche.

ACTIVITES DANS LES REGIONS EN DEVELOPPEMENT: Intervient directement dans les régions en développement. Intervient dans 16 pays. Intervient par l'intermédiaire d'organisations locales partenaires. **Actions de Développement durable:** Démocratie/bonne gestion publique/création d'institutions/développement participatif; Développement rural/agriculture; Développement urbain/habitat; Petites entreprises/secteur informel/artisanat; Population/planning familial/

démographie; Questions relatives aux femmes; Écologie/environnement/biodiversité; Éducation/formation/alphabétisation. **Régions:** Afrique australe; Afrique centrale; Afrique de l'Ouest; Amérique du Sud; Caraïbes; Mexique et Amerique centrale; Moyen-Orient.

ACTIVITES D'INFORMATION ET D'EDUCATION: Domaines: Aliments/famine; Autres; Culture/tradition/religion; Développement rural/agriculture; Développement urbain/habitat; Enfants/jeunesse/famille; Paix/conflits ethniques/armement/désarmement; Population/planning familial/démographie; Questions relatives aux femmes; Relations internationales/coopération/aide au développement; Relations économiques internationales/commerce/dette/finances; Santé/assainissement/eau; Écologie/environnement/biodiversité; Éducation/formation/alphabétisation. **Activités:** Collecte de fonds; Services d'information et de documentation/bases de données; Édition/documents audiovisuels/documents éducatifs; Éducation formelle.

FRA2104

RESEAU D'INFORMATION TIERS MONDE DES CENTRES DE DOCUMENTATION POUR LE DEVELOPPEMENT (RITIMO) ♦
Third World Information Network of Development Documentation Centres

21ter rue Voltaire, 75011 Paris, France.

Téléphone: 33 (1) 43 72 12 45. *Fax:* 33 (1) 40 24 08 52. *Contact:* Emmanuel Charles, Président.

OBJECTIFS: Informer un public aussi large que possible sur le mal-développement et ses causes. Participer à des actions dans le but de transformer les relations Nord-Sud.

INFORMATIONS GENERALES: *Création:* 1985. *Type d'organisation:* réseau. *Organisations membres:* 37. *Affiliée à:* CRID (France). *Personnel/Total:* 10. *Salariés:* 10. *Budget/Total 1993:* ECU 302000 (US$ 353000). *Sources financières:* Public: 60%. Autofinancement: 40%.

PUBLICATIONS: *Périodiques:* Passerelles (4) - Ritimo'thèque (4). *Liste des publications.*

PREVISIONS D'ACTIVITES: De 1994 à 1996 le réseau s'occupera des questions de l'environnement, du développement social et de l'exclusion.

ACTIVITES D'INFORMATION ET D'EDUCATION: Domaines: Aliments/famine; Culture/tradition/religion; Droits de l'Homme/paix/conflits; Développement rural/agriculture; Développement urbain/habitat; Emploi/chômage; Enfants/jeunesse/famille; Paix/conflits ethniques/armement/désarmement; Pauvreté/conditions de vie; Population/planning familial/démographie; Questions relatives aux femmes; Racisme/xénophobie/antisémitisme; Relations internationales/coopération/aide au développement; Relations économiques internationales/commerce/dette/finances; Réfugiés/migrants/groupes ethniques; Santé/assainissement/eau; Secours d'urgence/réfugiés/aide humanitaire; Écologie/environnement/biodiversité; Éducation/formation/alphabétisation. **Activités:** Campagnes d'information/expositions; Services d'information et de documentation/bases de données; Édition/documents audiovisuels/documents éducatifs.

FRA2105

RESEAU DES ONG EUROPEENNES SUR LES QUESTIONS AGRO-ALIMENTAIRES ET LE DEVELOPPEMENT (RONGEAD) ♦ European NGOs Network on Agriculture, Food and Development

14, rue Antoine Dumont, 69372 Lyon cedex 08, France.

Téléphone: 33 - 78 61 32 23. *Fax:* 33 - 78 69 86 96. *Contact:* Joseph Rocher, Coordinateur.

OBJECTIFS: Inciter les gouvernements et les acteurs économiques du Nord à mettre en place, dans le cadre des négociations du GATT, des règles du commerce international et des politiques agricoles nationales qui tiennent plus compte des besoins réels du développement.

INFORMATIONS GENERALES: *Création:* 1983. *Type d'organisation:* réseau. *Personnel/Total:* 7. *Salariés:* 4. *Bénévoles:* 3. *Budget/Total 1993:* ECU 226000 (US$ 265000). *Sources financières:* Privé: 10%. Public: 70%. Autofinancement: 20%.

Voir : *Comment utiliser le répertoire,* page 11.

PUBLICATIONS: *Périodiques:* "Gatt Briefing" (3). *Rapport annuel. Liste des publications.*

EVALUATION/RECHERCHE: Rapports d'évaluation disponibles. Entreprend des activités de recherche.

COMMENTAIRES: Intervient dans la Communauté des Etats indépendants. Activités d'information concernant la Communauté des Etats indépendants.

ACTIVITES DANS LES REGIONS EN DEVELOPPEMENT: Intervient directement dans les régions en développement. Intervient dans 15 pays. Intervient par l'intermédiaire d'organisations locales partenaires. **Actions de Développement durable:** Dette/finances/commerce; Démocratie/bonne gestion publique/création d'institutions/développement participatif; Envoi de volontaires/experts/assistance technique; Écologie/environnement/biodiversité; Éducation/formation/alphabétisation. **Régions:** Afrique centrale; Afrique de l'Ouest.

ACTIVITES D'INFORMATION ET D'EDUCATION: **Domaines:** Développement rural/agriculture; Relations internationales/coopération/aide au développement; Relations économiques internationales/commerce/dette/finances; Écologie/environnement/biodiversité. **Activités:** Conférences/séminaires/ateliers/activités de formation; Lobbying/plaidoyer; Réseaux/télécommunications électroniques; Services d'information et de documentation/bases de données; Édition/documents audiovisuels/documents éducatifs; Éducation formelle.

FRA2106
R E S E A U   E N S E I G N E M E N T   T E C H N I Q U E   E T DEVELOPPEMENT INDUSTRIEL (ETDI)

GRET, 213 rue Lafayette, 75010 Paris, France.

Téléphone: 33 (1) 40 05 61 61. *Fax:* 33 (1) 40 05 61 10. *Contact:* André Delluc, Coordinateur.

OBJECTIFS: Promouvoir une meilleure adéquation des formations techniques et professionnelles au développement des entreprises artisanales et industrielles africaines.

INFORMATIONS GENERALES: *Création:* 1987. *Type d'organisation:* réseau. *Personnel/Total:* 2. *Salariés:* 2. *Budget/Total 1993:* ECU 90000 (US$ 106000). *Sources financières:* Privé: 10%. Public: 85%. Autofinancement: 5%.

PUBLICATIONS: *Périodiques:* Courrier du réseau ETDI (4). *Rapport annuel. Liste des publications.*

EVALUATION/RECHERCHE: Rapports d'évaluation disponibles. Entreprend des activités de recherche.

ACTIVITES DANS LES REGIONS EN DEVELOPPEMENT: Intervient directement dans les régions en développement. Intervient dans 21 pays. Maintient une présence locale sur le terrain. Intervient par l'intermédiaire d'organisations locales partenaires. **Actions de Développement durable:** Développement rural/agriculture; Envoi de volontaires/experts/assistance technique; Petites entreprises/secteur informel/artisanat; Éducation/formation/alphabétisation. **Régions:** Afrique centrale; Afrique de l'Est; Afrique de l'Ouest; Caraïbes.

ACTIVITES D'INFORMATION ET D'EDUCATION: **Domaines:** Développement rural/agriculture; Emploi/chômage; Relations internationales/coopération/aide au développement; Éducation/formation/alphabétisation. **Activités:** Campagnes d'information/expositions; Conférences/séminaires/ateliers/activités de formation; Lobbying/plaidoyer; Radiodiffusion/manifestations culturelles; Réseaux/télécommunications électroniques; Services d'information et de documentation/bases de données; Échanges/parrainage/jumelage; Édition/documents audiovisuels/documents éducatifs; Éducation formelle.

FRA2107
RESEAU FEMMES ET DEVELOPPEMENT

s/c GRDR, 8 rue Paul Bert, 93300 Aubervilliers, France.

Téléphone: 33 (1) 48 34 95 94. *Fax:* 33 (1) 48 34 01 67. *Contact:* Sadika Benslimane, Coordinatrice.

OBJECTIFS: Promouvoir le rôle de la femme dans tous les types de projets de développement. Rendre les femmes actrices et bénéficiaires des projets.

INFORMATIONS GENERALES: *Création:* 1983. *Type d'organisation:* réseau. *Personnel/Total:* 31. *Salariés:* 1. *Bénévoles:* 30. *Sources financières:* Public: 100%.

PUBLICATIONS: *Périodiques:* Lettre d'Information (4) - Bulletin thétique annuel (1).

EVALUATION/RECHERCHE: Entreprend des activités de recherche.

ACTIVITES DANS LES REGIONS EN DEVELOPPEMENT: Intervient par l'intermédiaire d'organisations locales partenaires. **Actions de Développement durable:** Développement rural/agriculture; Développement urbain/habitat; Enfants/jeunesse/famille; Population/planning familial/démographie; Questions relatives aux femmes; Santé/assainissement/eau; Éducation/formation/alphabétisation. **Régions:** Afrique australe; Afrique centrale; Afrique de l'Est; Afrique de l'Ouest; Afrique du Nord; Amérique du Sud.

ACTIVITES D'INFORMATION ET D'EDUCATION: **Domaines:** Questions relatives aux femmes. **Activités:** Campagnes d'information/expositions; Conférences/séminaires/ateliers/activités de formation; Services d'information et de documentation/bases de données; Échanges/parrainage/jumelage; Éducation formelle.

FRA2108
RESEAU GROUPEMENTS - ASSOCIATIONS VILLAGEOISES - ORGANISATIONS PAYSANNES (Réseau GAO)

16, rue Claude Bernard, I.N.A. P-G, Chaire de Sociologie rurale, 75231 Paris cedex 05, France.

Téléphone: 33 (1) 44 08 16 36. *Fax:* 33 (1) 44 08 18 55. *Contact:* D. Pesche, Secrétaire technique.

OBJECTIFS: Echanger des informations et animer des réflexions sur les organisations paysannes et rurales au Sud, principalement en Afrique sub-saharienne.

INFORMATIONS GENERALES: *Création:* 1987. *Personnel/Total:* 1. *Salariés:* 1. *Budget/Total 1993:* ECU 75000 (US$ 88000). *Sources financières:* Public: 100%.

PUBLICATIONS: *Périodiques:* Lettre du Réseau GAO (4). *Rapport annuel.*

EVALUATION/RECHERCHE: Rapports d'évaluation disponibles. Entreprend des activités de recherche. **Actions de Développement durable:** Éducation/formation/alphabétisation. **Régions:** Afrique centrale; Afrique de l'Ouest.

ACTIVITES D'INFORMATION ET D'EDUCATION: **Domaines:** Développement rural/agriculture. **Activités:** Conférences/séminaires/ateliers/activités de formation; Édition/documents audiovisuels/documents éducatifs.

FRA2109
RESEAU RECHERCHE DEVELOPPEMENT

213, rue Lafayette, 75010 Paris, France.

Téléphone: 33 (1) 40 35 13 14. *Fax:* 33 (1) 40 35 08 39. *Contact:* Dominique Gentil, Président.

OBJECTIFS: Favoriser le décloisonnement de la réflexion entre personnes appartenant à des institutions et de compétences différentes. Faire de la recherche autour des thèmes de la formation, de l'irrigation, de la gestion du terroir et de l'agriculture en zone tropicale humide.

INFORMATIONS GENERALES: *Création:* 1982. *Type d'organisation:* réseau. *Personnel/Total:* 2. *Salariés:* 2. *Budget/Total 1993:* ECU 249000 (US$ 291000). *Sources financières:* Public: 100%.

PUBLICATIONS: *Périodiques:* Lettre du réseau Recherche Développement (3). *Rapport annuel. Liste des publications.*

EVALUATION/RECHERCHE: Rapports d'évaluation disponibles.

ACTIVITES DANS LES REGIONS EN DEVELOPPEMENT: Intervient dans 81 pays. Maintient une présence locale sur le terrain. Intervient par l'intermédiaire d'organisations locales partenaires. **Actions de Développement durable:** Développement rural/agriculture; Écologie/environnement/biodiversité. **Régions:** Afrique australe; Afrique centrale; Afrique de l'Est; Afrique de l'Ouest; Afrique du Nord; Amérique du Sud;

See: *How to Use the Directory,* page 11.

Asie centrale et Asie du Sud; Asie de l'Est; Asie du Sud-Est; Caraïbes; Mexique et Amerique centrale; Moyen-Orient; Océanie.

ACTIVITES D'INFORMATION ET D'EDUCATION: Domaines: Développement rural/agriculture; Relations internationales/coopération/aide au développement; Écologie/environnement/biodiversité. **Activités:** Conférences/séminaires/ateliers/activités de formation; Réseaux/télécommunications électroniques; Services d'information et de documentation/bases de données; Édition/documents audiovisuels/documents éducatifs.

FRA2110
RESEAU SOLIDARITE

5, rue François Bizette, 35000 Rennes, France.

Téléphone: 33 - 99 38 82 40. **Fax:** 33 - 99 38 01 50. **Contact:** Myriam Cruls, Secrétaire exécutive.

OBJECTIFS: Mettre à la disposition des ONG du Sud, qui luttent pour leurs droits économiques et sociaux, un réseau d'opinion publique susceptible d'appuyer leur action.

INFORMATIONS GENERALES: Création: 1981. **Type d'organisation:** regroupement d'ONG, réseau. **Affiliée à:** Fédération Peuples Solidaires (France). **Personnel/Total:** 6. **Salariés:** 1. **Bénévoles:** 5. **Budget/ Total 1993:** ECU 61000 (US$ 71000). **Sources financières:** Privé: 90%. Public: 5%. Autofinancement: 5%.

PUBLICATIONS: Périodiques: Solidarité (4). *Rapport annuel. Liste des publications.*

EVALUATION/RECHERCHE: Rapports d'évaluation disponibles.

ACTIVITES D'INFORMATION ET D'EDUCATION: Domaines: Droits de l'Homme/paix/conflits; Développement rural/agriculture; Développement urbain/habitat; Emploi/chômage; Enfants/jeunesse/famille; Pauvreté/conditions de vie; Questions relatives aux femmes; Relations économiques internationales/commerce/dette/finances; Réfugiés/migrants/groupes ethniques; Santé/assainissement/eau; Écologie/environnement/biodiversité. **Activités:** Lobbying/plaidoyer.

FRA2111
ROUE LIBRE VOYAGES

72, chemin Morillon, Fleurieux s/Arbresle, B.P. 2, 69591 L'Arbresle cedex, France.

Téléphone: 33 - 74 01 07 40. **Fax:** 33 - 74 01 19 82. **Contact:** Daniel Deze, Président.

OBJECTIFS: Sensibiliser les Européens aux modes de vie des sociétés du Sud et favoriser les échanges. Pratiquer un tourisme d'aventure en petits groupes, basé sur la rencontre et la découverte des habitants.

INFORMATIONS GENERALES: Création: 1980. **Personnel/Total:** 6. Salariés: 1. Bénévoles: 5. **Budget/Total 1993:** ECU 302000 (US$ 353000). **Sources financières:** Autofinancement: 100%.

PUBLICATIONS: Périodiques: Carnet de Route (4). *Rapport annuel. Liste des publications.*

EVALUATION/RECHERCHE: Rapports d'évaluation disponibles.

PREVISIONS D'ACTIVITES: Programme de santé pour les Berbères du Maroc.

ACTIVITES DANS LES REGIONS EN DEVELOPPEMENT: Intervient directement dans les régions en développement. Intervient dans 2 pays. Intervient par l'intermédiaire d'organisations locales partenaires. **Actions de Développement durable:** Enfants/jeunesse/famille; Éducation/formation/alphabétisation. **Régions:** Afrique du Nord; Amérique du Sud.

ACTIVITES D'INFORMATION ET D'EDUCATION: Domaines: Enfants/jeunesse/famille; Éducation/formation/alphabétisation. **Activités:** Autres.

FRA2112
SAHEL INTER ACTIONS SERVICES (SIAS)

12 rue de Paris, 92190 Meudon, France.

Téléphone: 33 (1) 46 26 92 19. **Contact:** Walick Diop, Délégué général.

FRA2113
SANABEL FRANCE

101 rue Boucicaut, B.P. 45, 92263 Fontenay-aux-Roses Cedex, France.

Téléphone: 33 (1) 46 60 47 10. **Contact:** Victor Gohargui, Secrétaire général.

FRA2114
SANTE SUD

200, boulevard National, Bât. N, 13003 Marseille, France.

Téléphone: 33 - 91 95 63 45. **Fax:** 33 - 91 95 68 05. **Contact:** Dr. H. Alexis, Coordinateur général.

OBJECTIFS: Réaliser des projets de développement à long terme (aide financière, technique et matérielle), essentiellement dans le domaine de la santé.

INFORMATIONS GENERALES: Création: 1986. **Personnel/Total:** 116. **Salariés:** 6. **Bénévoles:** 110 dont: 73 dans les pays en développement. **Budget/Total 1993:** ECU 1050000 (US$ 1230000). **Sources financières:** Privé: 39%. Public: 59%. Autofinancement: 2%.

PUBLICATIONS: Périodiques: Santé-Sud (4).

EVALUATION/RECHERCHE: Rapports d'évaluation disponibles. Entreprend des activités de recherche.

ACTIVITES DANS LES REGIONS EN DEVELOPPEMENT: Intervient dans 14 pays. Maintient une présence locale sur le terrain. Intervient par l'intermédiaire d'organisations locales partenaires. **Actions de Développement durable:** Enfants/jeunesse/famille; Envoi de volontaires/experts/assistance technique; Questions relatives aux femmes; Santé/assainissement/eau; Éducation/formation/alphabétisation. **Régions:** Afrique australe; Afrique centrale; Afrique de l'Ouest; Afrique du Nord; Amérique du Sud; Asie de l'Est; Asie du Sud-Est; Moyen-Orient.

ACTIVITES D'INFORMATION ET D'EDUCATION: Domaines: Santé/assainissement/eau. **Activités:** Conférences/séminaires/ateliers/activités de formation; Échanges/parrainage/jumelage; Édition/documents audiovisuels/documents éducatifs.

FRA2115
SCOUTS DE FRANCE

54 avenue Jean Jaurès, 75940 Paris cedex 19, France.

Téléphone: 33 (1) 42 38 37 37. **Fax:** 33 (1) 42 38 09 87. **Contact:** Bertrand Chanzy.

FRA2116
SECOURS CATHOLIQUE - CARITAS FRANCE

106, rue du Bac, 75341 Paris cedex 07, France.

Téléphone: 33 (1) 43 20 14 14. **Fax:** 33 (1) 45 49 94 50. **Contact:** Michel Durel, Conseiller technique.

OBJECTIFS: Venir en aide à toute personne en difficulté, dans le respect de son projet et en l'aidant à devenir l'acteur de son propre redressement. Favoriser, par la réalisation de micro-projets, la volonté des populations du tiers-Monde de prendre en main leur développppement. Participer, en cas de catastrophes nationales, avec les Caritas concernés, à l'aide d'urgence et aux actions de réhabilitation qui s'ensuivent.

INFORMATIONS GENERALES: Création: 1946. **Affiliée à:** Caritas Internationalis (Italie) - C.F.C.F - C.N.J.D. - U.N.I.O.P.S.. **Personnel/Total:** 71457. **Salariés:** 757. **Bénévoles:** 70700 dont: 75 dans les pays en développement. **Budget/Total 1993:** ECU 108240000 (US$ 126783000). **Sources financières:** Privé: 78%. Public: 5%. Autofinancement: 17%.

PUBLICATIONS: Périodiques: "Messages" (12) - Les Cahiers du Secours Catholique (12). *Rapport annuel. Liste des publications.*

EVALUATION/RECHERCHE: Rapports d'évaluation disponibles.

Voir : *Comment utiliser le répertoire*, page 11.

COMMENTAIRES: Intervient dans la Communauté des Etats indépendants. Activités d'information concernant la Communauté des Etats indépendants.

ACTIVITES DANS LES REGIONS EN DEVELOPPEMENT: Intervient directement dans les régions en développement. Intervient dans 80 pays. Maintient une présence locale sur le terrain. Intervient par l'intermédiaire d'organisations locales partenaires. **Actions de Développement durable:** Aliments/famine; Dette/finances/commerce; Développement rural/agriculture; Développement urbain/habitat; Enfants/jeunesse/famille; Envoi de volontaires/experts/assistance technique; Petites entreprises/secteur informel/artisanat; Questions relatives aux femmes; Santé/assainissement/eau; Secours d'urgence/réfugiés/aide humanitaire; Éducation/formation/alphabétisation. **Régions:** Afrique australe; Afrique centrale; Afrique de l'Est; Afrique de l'Ouest; Afrique du Nord; Amérique du Sud; Asie centrale et Asie du Sud; Asie de l'Est; Asie du Sud-Est; Caraïbes; Mexique et Amerique centrale; Moyen-Orient; Océanie.

ACTIVITES D'INFORMATION ET D'EDUCATION: Domaines: Aliments/famine; Droits de l'Homme/paix/conflits; Développement rural/agriculture; Développement urbain/habitat; Emploi/chômage; Enfants/jeunesse/famille; Pauvreté/conditions de vie; Questions relatives aux femmes; Relations internationales/coopération/aide au développement; Relations économiques internationales/commerce/dette/finances; Réfugiés/migrants/groupes ethniques; Santé/assainissement/eau; Secours d'urgence/aide humanitaire; Éducation/formation/alphabétisation. **Activités:** Campagnes d'information/expositions; Collecte de fonds; Lobbying/plaidoyer; Services d'information et de documentation/bases de données; Édition/documents audiovisuels/documents éducatifs.

FRA2117
SECOURS POPULAIRE FRANCAIS (SPF)

9, rue Froissart, 75003 Paris, France.

Téléphone: 33 (1) 44 78 21 00. **Fax:** 33 (1) 42 74 71 01. **Contact:** Julien Laupretre, Secrétaire général.

OBJECTIFS: Soutenir, dans l'esprit de la Déclaration Universelle des Droits de l'Homme, au plan matériel, sanitaire, médical, moral et juridique, les personnes et leurs familles victimes de l'arbitraire, de l'injustice sociale, des calamités naturellles, de la misère, de la faim, du sous-développement et des conflits armés.

INFORMATIONS GENERALES: Création: 1946. **Affiliée à:** UNI-OPS (France) - CNVA (France) - Fonda (France) - CNAJEP - CFSI (France) -EURONAID (Pays-Bas) - Voice (Belgique) - Clong-Développement (Belgique) - ESAN (France) - Réeau européen de lutte contre la pauvreté (France) - CEDAG (France) - ICVA (Suisse). **Personnel/Total:** 66000. Salariés: 145 dont: 8 dans les pays en développement. Bénévoles: 65855 dont: 200 dans les pays en développement. **Budget/Total 1993:** ECU 33165000 (US$ 38847000). **Sources financières:** Privé: 51%. Public: 34%. Autofinancement: 15%.

PUBLICATIONS: Périodiques: Convergence (12) - Copain du Monde (4). *Rapport annuel.*

EVALUATION/RECHERCHE: Rapports d'évaluation disponibles.

COMMENTAIRES: Intervient dans la Communauté des Etats indépendants. Activités d'information concernant la Communauté des Etats indépendants.

ACTIVITES DANS LES REGIONS EN DEVELOPPEMENT: Intervient dans 64 pays. Intervient par l'intermédiaire d'organisations locales partenaires. **Actions de Développement durable:** Droits de l'Homme/paix/conflits; Développement rural/agriculture; Enfants/jeunesse/famille; Petites entreprises/secteur informel/artisanat; Population/planning familial/démographie; Questions relatives aux femmes; Santé/assainissement/eau; Secours d'urgence/réfugiés/aide humanitaire; Écologie/environnement/biodiversité; Éducation/formation/alphabétisation. **Régions:** Afrique australe; Afrique centrale; Afrique de l'Est; Afrique de l'Ouest; Afrique du Nord; Amérique du Sud; Asie centrale et Asie du Sud; Asie du Sud-Est; Caraïbes; Mexique et Amerique centrale; Moyen-Orient; Océanie.

ACTIVITES D'INFORMATION ET D'EDUCATION: Domaines: Droits de l'Homme/paix/conflits; Développement rural/agriculture; Emploi/chô-

mage; Enfants/jeunesse/famille; Pauvreté/conditions de vie; Questions relatives aux femmes; Racisme/xénophobie/antisémitisme; Relations internationales/coopération/aide au développement; Réfugiés/migrants/groupes ethniques; Santé/assainissement/eau; Secours d'urgence/réfugiés/aide humanitaire; Écologie/environnement/biodiversité; Éducation/formation/alphabétisation. **Activités:** Campagnes d'information/expositions; Collecte de fonds; Conférences/séminaires/ateliers/activités de formation; Lobbying/plaidoyer; Radiodiffusion/manifestations culturelles; Échanges/parrainage/jumelage.

FRA2118
SERVICE CIVIL INTERNATIONAL, BRANCHE FRANCAISE (SCI)

2 rue Eugène Fournière, 75018 Paris, France.

Téléphone: 33 (1) 42 54 62 43. **Contact:** Véronique Busson-Landos.

FRA2119
SERVICE D'ENTRAIDE ET DE LIAISON (SEL)

9, rue de la Gare, 94230 Cachan, France.

Téléphone: 33 (1) 46 65 83 03. **Fax:** 33 (1) 46 63 23 77. **Contact:** Patrick Guiborat, Directeur administratif.

OBJECTIFS: Venir en aide aux personnes en difficulté, et plus particulièrement aux enfants dans les pays pauvres du Tiers-Monde. Aider au financement et à la réalisation des secours d'urgence, et des projets de développement dans le domaine de l'éducation, de la santé, de l'agriculture et de toute autre action d'assistance et de bienfaisance.

INFORMATIONS GENERALES: Création: 1980. **Type d'organisation:** regroupement d'ONG. **Affiliée à:** Inter Church Relief a Development Alliance (Pays Bas) - Conference of European Evangelical Aid Agencies (France). **Personnel/Total:** 79. Salariés: 9. Bénévoles: 70. **Budget/Total 1993:** ECU 1598000 (US$ 1872000). **Sources financières:** Privé: 69%. Autofinancement: 1%.

PUBLICATIONS: Périodiques: SEL Informations (4). *Liste des publications.*

COMMENTAIRES: Intervient dans la Communauté des Etats indépendants.

ACTIVITES DANS LES REGIONS EN DEVELOPPEMENT: Intervient dans 35 pays. Intervient par l'intermédiaire d'organisations locales partenaires. **Actions de Développement durable:** Aliments/famine; Développement rural/agriculture; Enfants/jeunesse/famille; Questions relatives aux femmes; Santé/assainissement/eau; Secours d'urgence/réfugiés/aide humanitaire; Éducation/formation/alphabétisation. **Régions:** Afrique australe; Afrique centrale; Afrique de l'Est; Afrique de l'Ouest; Amérique du Sud; Asie centrale et Asie du Sud; Asie du Sud-Est; Caraïbes; Mexique et Amerique centrale.

ACTIVITES D'INFORMATION ET D'EDUCATION: Domaines: Aliments/famine; Développement rural/agriculture; Enfants/jeunesse/famille; Questions relatives aux femmes; Réfugiés/migrants/groupes ethniques; Santé/assainissement/eau; Secours d'urgence/réfugiés/aide humanitaire; Éducation/formation/alphabétisation. **Activités:** Collecte de fonds; Échanges/parrainage/jumelage; Édition/documents audiovisuels/documents éducatifs.

FRA2120
SERVICE DE COOPERATION AU DEVELOPPEMENT (SCD)

42 montée St. Barthélemy, 69005 Lyon, France.

Téléphone: 33 - 78 25 41 65. **Fax:** 33 - 78 36 60 00. **Contact:** Ya Mutuale-Balume, Délégué général.

FRA2121
SERVICE INTERNATIONAL D'APPUI AU DEVELOPPEMENT (SIAD)

40 rue Mortinat, 92600 Asnières, France.

Téléphone: 33 (1) 47 33 14 72. **Contact:** Didier François, Secrétaire exécutif.

See: *How to Use the Directory,* page 11.

FRA2122
SERVICE INTERNATIONAL DE LIAISON D'ORGANISATION POUR UN DEVELOPPEMENT SOLIDAIRE (SILO)

1, place de l'Eglise. La Rochette, 77000 Melun, France.

Téléphone: 33 (1) 64 37 49 30. *Fax:* 33 (1) 64 37 62 37. *Contact:* Evelyne Engel, Secrétaire générale.

OBJECTIFS: Former et informer dans les pays du Tiers-Monde.

INFORMATIONS GENERALES: *Création:* 1982. *Type d'organisation:* collectif. *Personnel/Total:* 6. *Salariés:* 5. *Bénévoles:* 1. *Budget/ Total 1993:* ECU 302000 (US$ 353000). *Sources financières: Privé:* 8%. *Public:* 2%. *Autofinancement:* 90%.

PUBLICATIONS: *Périodiques:* . *Liste des publications.*

COMMENTAIRES: Activités d'information concernant la Communauté des Etats indépendants.

ACTIVITES DANS LES REGIONS EN DEVELOPPEMENT: Intervient directement dans les régions en développement. Intervient dans 2 pays. **Actions de Développement durable:** Éducation/formation/alpha-bétisation. **Régions:** Afrique centrale; Afrique de l'Ouest.

ACTIVITES D'INFORMATION ET D'EDUCATION: **Domaines:** Aliments/ famine; Culture/tradition/religion; Droits de l'Homme/paix/conflits; Dé-veloppement rural/agriculture; Développement urbain/habitat; Enfants/jeu-nesse/famille; Paix/conflits ethniques/armement/désarmement; Pau-vreté/conditions de vie; Population/planning familial/démographie; Questions relatives aux femmes; Racisme/xénophobie/antisémitisme; Relations internationales/coopération/aide au développement; Relations économiques internationales/commerce/dette/finances; Réfugiés/ migrants/groupes ethniques; Santé/assainissement/eau; Écologie/envi-ronnement/biodiversité; Éducation/formation/alphabétisation. **Activités:** Campagnes d'information/expositions; Conférences/séminaires/ateliers/ activités de formation; Radiodiffusion/manifestations culturelles; Ser-vices d'information et de documentation/bases de données; Édition/ documents audiovisuels/documents éducatifs.

FRA2123
SERVICE MISSIONNAIRE DES JEUNES (SMJ)

5, rue Monsieur, 75007 Paris, France.

Téléphone: 33 (1) 47 83 67 95. *Fax:* 33 (1) 47 34 26 63. *Contact:* Claude Lenga, Animateur national.

OBJECTIFS: Appeler les jeunes Chrétiens à partager leur foi avec d'autres et à développer une solidarité entre les peuples. Soutenir la mission le monde.

INFORMATIONS GENERALES: *Création:* 1951. *Type d'organisation:* réseau. *Affiliée à:* Oeuvres Pontificales Missionnnaires (France) - Coopération Missionnaire (France). *Salariés:* 1.

PUBLICATIONS: *Périodiques:* Partage sans Frontière (36c500) - Soli-daires (12). *Liste des publications.*

ACTIVITES DANS LES REGIONS EN DEVELOPPEMENT: Intervient directement dans les régions en développement. Intervient dans 160 pays. Intervient par l'intermédiaire d'organisations locales partenaires. **Actions de Développement durable:** Droits de l'Homme/ paix/conflits; Enfants/jeunesse/famille; Envoi de volontaires/experts/ assistance technique; Santé/assainissement/eau; Éducation/formation/ alphabétisation. **Régions:** Afrique australe; Afrique centrale; Afrique de l'Est; Afrique de l'Ouest; Amérique du Sud; Asie centrale et Asie du Sud; Asie de l'Est; Asie du Sud-Est; Mexique et Amerique centrale; Moyen-Orient.

ACTIVITES D'INFORMATION ET D'EDUCATION: **Domaines:** Culture/ tradition/religion; Droits de l'Homme/paix/conflits; Enfants/jeunesse/ famille; Pauvreté/conditions de vie; Relations internationales/coopéra-tion/aide au développement; Réfugiés/migrants/groupes ethniques. **Activités:** Conférences/séminaires/ateliers/activités de formation; Lob-bying/plaidoyer; Services d'information et de documentation/bases de données; Édition/documents audiovisuels/documents éducatifs; Éduca-tion formelle.

FRA2124
SERVICE SOCIAL D'AIDE AUX EMIGRANTS

72 rue Regnault, 75013 Paris, France.

Téléphone: 33 (1) 40 77 94 00. *Fax:* 33 (1) 45 84 43 05. *Contact:* Marie Annik Frere, Service Communication.

FRA2125
SERVICE TECHNIQUE D'INFORMATION ET DE RECHERCHE D'EQUIPEMENTS POUR LE DEVELOPPEMENT

35 rue Madame, 75016 Paris, France.

Téléphone: 33 (1) 45 44 00 08. *Fax:* 33 (1) 45 44 35 02.

FRA2126
SILVA, ARBRES, FORETS ET SOCIETES ♦ Silva, Trees, Forests and Communities

21, rue Paul Bert, 94130 Nogent-sur-Marne, France.

Téléphone: 33 (1) 48 75 59 44. *Fax:* 33 (1) 48 76 31 93. *Contact:* Jean Gadant, Président.

OBJECTIFS: Diffuser des informations pour le grand public sur tout ce qui a trait aux arbres et aux forêts. Donner des cours de formation techni-que en foresterie. Fournir une assistance technique et effectuer des expertises, dans les zones tropicales.

INFORMATIONS GENERALES: *Création:* 1986. *Affiliée à:* Réseau Arbres tropicaux et Collectif des associations d'environnement à dimen-sion internationale (France) - Réseau Forêts, Arbres et Communautés Rurales (Italie) - Entente des Associations Forestières Françai-ses (France). *Personnel/Total:* 63. *Salariés:* 4. *Bénévoles:* 59 dont: 35 dans les pays en développement. *Budget/Total 1993:* ECU 241000 (US$ 283000). *Sources financières: Privé:* 5%. *Public:* 75%. *Autofinancement:* 20%.

PUBLICATIONS: *Périodiques:* La Feuille de SILVA (4) - Le Flam-boyant (4) - Arbres Forêts et Communautés rurales (4). *Rapport annuel. Liste des publications.*

EVALUATION/RECHERCHE: Rapports d'évaluation disponibles.

COMMENTAIRES: L'Association SILVA assure le secrétariat technique du réseau Arbres Tropicaux qui a des membres dans 85 pays et dont la langue de communication est le français.

ACTIVITES DANS LES REGIONS EN DEVELOPPEMENT: Intervient directement dans les régions en développement. Intervient dans 35 pays. Maintient une présence locale sur le terrain. Intervient par l'inter-médiaire d'organisations locales partenaires. **Actions de Développe-ment durable:** Autres; Démocratie/bonne gestion publique/création d'institutions/développement participatif; Développement rural/agricul-ture; Questions relatives aux femmes; Écologie/environnement/biodiver-sité; Éducation/formation/alphabétisation. **Régions:** Afrique australe; Afrique centrale; Afrique de l'Est; Afrique de l'Ouest; Afrique du Nord; Asie du Sud-Est; Caraïbes; Océanie.

ACTIVITES D'INFORMATION ET D'EDUCATION: **Domaines:** Autres; Culture/tradition/religion; Développement rural/agriculture; Questions relatives aux femmes; Relations internationales/coopération/aide au développement; Écologie/environnement/biodiversité; Éducation/forma-tion/alphabétisation. **Activités:** Campagnes d'information/expositions; Conférences/séminaires/ateliers/activités de formation; Lobbying/plai-doyer; Radiodiffusion/manifestations culturelles; Réseaux/télécommuni-cations électroniques; Services d'information et de documentation/ bases de données; Échanges/parrainage/jumelage; Édition/documents audiovisuels/documents éducatifs.

FRA2127
SOCIETE D'INVESTISSEMENT ET DE DEVELOPPEMENT INTERNATIONAL (SIDI)

rue St Maur, 75007 Paris, France.

Téléphone: 33 (1) 42 33 35 22. *Fax:* 33 (1) 40 26 11 23.

Voir : *Comment utiliser le répertoire,* page 11.

FRA2128

SOCIETE DE SAINT-VINCENT DE PAUL/CONSEIL GENERAL INTERNATIONAL ♦ Society of Saint Vincent de Paul

5 rue du Pré-aux-Clercs, 75007 Paris, France.

Téléphone: 33 (1) 42 61 50 25. *Fax:* 33 (1) 42 61 72 56. *Contact:* César Augusto Nunes-Viana, Président Général International.

FRA2129

SOCIETE INTERNATIONALE POUR LE DEVELOPPEMENT, FRANCE (SID-FRANCE) ♦ Society for International Development, France

58, boulevard Arago, 75013 Paris, France.

Téléphone: 33 (1) 44 08 73 07. *Fax:* 33 (1) 47 07 81 75. *Contact:* Jean Masini, Président.

OBJECTIFS: Organiser un forum où les personnes professionnellement intéressées par le développement économique et social du Tiers-Monde peuvent échanger leurs idées et faire connaître leurs expériences.

INFORMATIONS GENERALES: *Création:* 1973. *Type d'organisation:* regroupement d'ONG. *Affiliée à:* Society for International Development (Italie). *Personnel/Total:* 3. *Bénévoles:* 3. *Budget/Total 1993:* ECU 26000 (US$ 31000). *Sources financières:* Privé: 10%. Public: 40%. Autofinancement: 50%.

PUBLICATIONS: *Rapport annuel.*

COMMENTAIRES: Activités d'information concernant la Communauté des Etats indépendants.

ACTIVITES DANS LES REGIONS EN DEVELOPPEMENT: Intervient directement dans les régions en développement. Intervient dans 2 pays. Intervient par l'intermédiaire d'organisations locales partenaires. **Actions de Développement durable:** Éducation/formation/alphabétisation. **Régions:** Afrique du Nord.

ACTIVITES D'INFORMATION ET D'EDUCATION: Domaines: Questions relatives aux femmes; Relations internationales/coopération/aide au développement; Relations économiques internationales/commerce/dette/finances; Écologie/environnement/biodiversité; Éducation/formation/alphabétisation. **Activités:** Conférences/séminaires/ateliers/activités de formation.

FRA2130

SOCIETE POUR LA PROMOTION ET LA GESTION INDUSTRIELLE (SOPROGI)

c/o J.P. Gardinier, "Le France", 4 square Léon Blum, 92800 Puteaux, France.

Téléphone: 33 (1) 47 74 80 50. *Fax:* 33 (1) 60 11 11 21. *Contact:* Jean-Pierre Maurus, Secrétaire général.

OBJECTIFS: Assurer la promotion industrielle des pays en développement, par la création d'entreprises et d'emplois. Créer des usines dans les pays en développement pour leur permettre de créer des emplois productifs.

INFORMATIONS GENERALES: *Création:* 1972. *Personnel/Total:* 3. *Salariés:* 3. *Budget/Total 1993:* ECU 75000 (US$ 89000). *Sources financières:* Public: 60%. Autofinancement: 40%.

PUBLICATIONS: *Périodiques:* Investir à Madagascar (1).

ACTIVITES DANS LES REGIONS EN DEVELOPPEMENT: Intervient directement dans les régions en développement. Intervient dans 2 pays. **Actions de Développement durable:** Petites entreprises/secteur informel/artisanat. **Régions:** Afrique australe.

ACTIVITES D'INFORMATION ET D'EDUCATION: Domaines: Relations internationales/coopération/aide au développement. **Activités:** Conférences/séminaires/ateliers/activités de formation; Services d'information et de documentation/bases de données.

FRA2131

SOLIDARITE

52, rue du Château du Roi, 81600 Gaillac, France.

Téléphone: 33 - 63 41 01 14. *Fax:* 33 - 63 57 60 05. *Contact:* Jean-Louis Bato, Secrétaire général.

OBJECTIFS: Participer, dans un véritable esprit de solidarité, à la réduction du chômage rural et à la satisfaction des besoins essentiels des paysanneries les plus défavorisées.

INFORMATIONS GENERALES: *Création:* 1980. *Affiliée à:* Centre d'Information pour un Développement Solidaire - CFCF - CIDDEV - EARTHACTION (Royaume Uni) - Coordination Amazonie Equatorienne (Belgique). *Personnel/Total:* 35. *Salariés:* 14 dont: 9 dans les pays en développement. *Bénévoles:* 21 dont: 3 dans les pays en développement. *Budget/Total 1993:* ECU 905000 (US$ 1059000). *Sources financières:* Privé: 80%. Public: 15%. Autofinancement: 5%.

PUBLICATIONS: *Périodiques:* Solidarité (4). *Rapport annuel. Liste des publications.*

EVALUATION/RECHERCHE: Rapports d'évaluation disponibles. Entreprend des activités de recherche.

ACTIVITES DANS LES REGIONS EN DEVELOPPEMENT: Intervient directement dans les régions en développement. Maintient une présence locale sur le terrain. Intervient par l'intermédiaire d'organisations locales partenaires. **Actions de Développement durable:** Droits de l'Homme/paix/conflits; Développement rural/agriculture; Développement urbain/habitat; Enfants/jeunesse/famille; Envoi de volontaires/experts/assistance technique; Petites entreprises/secteur informel/artisanat; Population/planning familial/démographie; Questions relatives aux femmes; Santé/assainissement/eau; Écologie/environnement/biodiversité; Éducation/formation/alphabétisation. **Régions:** Afrique de l'Ouest; Amérique du Sud; Asie centrale et Asie du Sud.

ACTIVITES D'INFORMATION ET D'EDUCATION: Domaines: Aliments/famine; Culture/tradition/religion; Droits de l'Homme/paix/conflits; Développement rural/agriculture; Développement urbain/habitat; Emploi/chômage; Enfants/jeunesse/famille; Paix/conflits ethniques/armement/désarmement; Pauvreté/conditions de vie; Population/planning familial/démographie; Questions relatives aux femmes; Racisme/xénophobie/antisémitisme; Relations internationales/coopération/aide au développement; Relations économiques internationales/commerce/dette/finances; Réfugiés/migrants/groupes ethniques; Santé/assainissement/eau; Secours d'urgence/réfugiés/aide humanitaire; Écologie/environnement/biodiversité; Éducation/formation/alphabétisation. **Activités:** Campagnes d'information/expositions; Collecte de fonds; Conférences/séminaires/ateliers/activités de formation; Lobbying/plaidoyer; Services d'information et de documentation/bases de données; Échanges/parrainage/jumelage; Édition/documents audiovisuels/documents éducatifs; Éducation formelle.

FRA2132

SOLIDARITE FRANCE BRESIL (SFB)

17 rue Robert Lindet, 75015 Paris, France.

Téléphone: 33 (1) 45 33 57 80. *Contact:* Hélène Blondet, Présidente.

FRA2133

SOLIDARITE INTERNATIONALE ET DEVELOPPEMENT RURAL (SOLIDER)

1, rue Joutx-Aigues, 31000 Toulouse, France.

Téléphone: 33 - 61 25 88 09. *Fax:* 33 - 62 26 12 18. *Contact:* Kriemild Keltsh, Président.

OBJECTIFS: Mettre en relation, coordonner et représenter les ONG françaises cherchant à metttre en place, au Nord comme au Sud, les bases d'un développement rural durable plus et plus solidaire.

INFORMATIONS GENERALES: *Création:* 1984. *Type d'organisation:* réseau. *Organisations membres:* 3. *Affiliée à:* Centre de Recherche et d'Information sur le Développement. *Personnel/Total:* 3. *Bénévoles:* 3. *Budget/Total 1993:* ECU 3000 (US$ 4000). *Sources financières:* Autofinancement: 100%.

FRA2134

SOLIDARITE-VILLES

48, rue du Bourdon Blanc, 45000 Orléans, France.

Téléphone: 33 - 38 77 95 18. *Contact:* Gérard Gasselin, Secrétaire général.

See: *How to Use the Directory*, page 11.

OBJECTIFS: Contribuer au développement économique et social pour le soutien à des politiques de développement.

INFORMATIONS GENERALES: *Création:* 1987. *Type d'organisation:* réseau. *Personnel/Total:* 1. *Salariés:* 1. *Budget/Total 1993:* ECU 30000 (US$ 35000). *Sources financières:* Public: 90%. Autofinancement: 10%.

ACTIVITES DANS LES REGIONS EN DEVELOPPEMENT: Intervient directement dans les régions en développement. Intervient dans 2 pays. Intervient par l'intermédiaire d'organisations locales partenaires. **Actions de Développement durable:** Développement urbain/habitat; Envoi de volontaires/experts/assistance technique; Santé/assainissement/eau. **Régions:** Afrique de l'Ouest; Asie du Sud-Est.

FRA2135
SOLIDARITES AGRO-ALIMENTAIRES (SOLAGRAL)

11 passage Penel, 75018 Paris, France.

Téléphone: 33 (1) 42 51 06 00. *Fax:* 33 (1) 42 51 18 29. *Contact:* Laurence Tubiana, Présidente.

FRA2136
SOLIDARITES INTERNATIONALES (SI)

12 Cité Malesherbes, 75009 Paris, France.

Téléphone: 33 (1) 42 85 12 27. *Contact:* Philippe Farine, Président.

FRA2137
SOS ENFANTS SANS FRONTIERES

56, rue de Tocqueville, 75017 Paris, France.

Téléphone: 33 (1) 43 80 80 80. *Fax:* 33 (1) 43 80 80 00. *Contact:* Jacqueline Bonheur, Présidente.

OBJECTIFS: Apporter une aide à l'enfance en détresse. Mener des actions nutrionnelles, éducatives et médicales.

INFORMATIONS GENERALES: *Création:* 1974. *Personnel/Total:* 54. *Salariés:* 4. *Bénévoles:* 50 dont: 3 dans les pays en développement. *Budget/Total 1993:* ECU 1292000 (US$ 1514000). *Sources financières:* Privé: 99%. Public: 1%.

PUBLICATIONS: *Périodiques:* SOS Info (4).

ACTIVITES DANS LES REGIONS EN DEVELOPPEMENT: Intervient directement dans les régions en développement. Intervient dans 7 pays. Maintient une présence locale sur le terrain. Intervient par l'intermédiaire d'organisations locales partenaires. **Actions de Développement durable:** Aliments/famine; Enfants/jeunesse/famille; Envoi de volontaires/experts/assistance technique; Population/planning familial/démographie; Santé/assainissement/eau; Éducation/formation/alphabétisation. **Régions:** Afrique centrale; Afrique de l'Ouest; Amérique du Sud; Asie du Sud-Est; Caraïbes; Moyen-Orient.

ACTIVITES D'INFORMATION ET D'EDUCATION: Domaines: Aliments/famine; Enfants/jeunesse/famille; Santé/assainissement/eau; Secours d'urgence/réfugiés/aide humanitaire; Éducation/formation/alphabétisation. **Activités:** Collecte de fonds.

FRA2138
SOS SAHEL INTERNATIONAL, FRANCE

94, rue Saint-Lazare, 75442 Paris cedex 09, France.

Téléphone: 33 (1) 42 85 08 44. *Fax:* 33 (1) 45 96 07 15. *Contact:* Hubert Dubois, Président.

OBJECTIFS: Aider au développpement des villages du Sahel pour atteindre l'autosuffisance alimentaire. Soulager le travail des femmes et enrayer l'exode rural, en agissant dans trois domaines essentiels: l'eau, la végétation et la santé.

INFORMATIONS GENERALES: *Création:* 1978. *Type d'organisation:* réseau. *Organisations membres:* 10. *Personnel/Total:* 15. *Salariés:* 7. *Bénévoles:* 9. *Budget/Total 1993:* ECU 3219000 (US$ 3770000). *Sources financières:* Privé: 80%. Public: 20%.

PUBLICATIONS: *Périodiques:* La Lettre du Sahel (4). *Rapport annuel.*

ACTIVITES DANS LES REGIONS EN DEVELOPPEMENT: Intervient dans 5 pays. Maintient une présence locale sur le terrain. Intervient par l'intermédiaire d'organisations locales partenaires. **Actions de Développement durable:** Aliments/famine; Développement rural/agriculture; Enfants/jeunesse/famille; Petites entreprises/secteur informel/artisanat; Population/planning familial/démographie; Questions relatives aux femmes; Santé/assainissement/eau; Éducation/formation/alphabétisation. **Régions:** Afrique de l'Ouest.

ACTIVITES D'INFORMATION ET D'EDUCATION: Domaines: Aliments/famine; Développement rural/agriculture; Population/planning familial/démographie; Questions relatives aux femmes; Santé/assainissement/eau. **Activités:** Campagnes d'information/expositions; Collecte de fonds; Édition/documents audiovisuels/documents éducatifs.

FRA2139
SOS-CECITE

24 boulevard Gambetta, 38000 Grenoble, France.

Téléphone: 33 - 76 87 29 21. *Contact:* Dr. Michel Istre, Président.

FRA2140
SOUTIEN A L'INITIATIVE PRIVEE POUR L'AIDE A LA RECONSTRUCTION DES PAYS DU SUD-EST ASIATIQUE (SIPAR)

42, bis rue St. Charles, 78000 Versailles, France.

Téléphone: 33 (1) 39 02 32 52. *Fax:* 33 (1) 30 21 92 64. *Contact:* Magali Petitmengin, Présidente.

OBJECTIFS: Créer des groupes d'accueil en France pouvant participer à l'insertion de réfugiés indochinois. Former des instituteurs dans quatre provinces du Cambodge.

INFORMATIONS GENERALES: *Création:* 1983. *Type d'organisation:* regroupement d'ONG. *Organisations membres:* 25. *Affiliée à:* France Pays du Mékong (France). *Personnel/Total:* 41. *Salariés:* 14 dont: 11 dans les pays en développement. *Bénévoles:* 27 dont: 18 dans les pays en développement. *Budget/Total 1993:* ECU 898000 (US$ 1052000). *Sources financières:* Privé: 15%. Public: 85%.

PUBLICATIONS: *Périodiques:* "Par Sipar La" (4). *Rapport annuel. Liste des publications.*

EVALUATION/RECHERCHE: Rapports d'évaluation disponibles. Entreprend des activités de recherche.

ACTIVITES DANS LES REGIONS EN DEVELOPPEMENT: Intervient directement dans les régions en développement. Intervient dans 1 pays. Maintient une présence locale sur le terrain. Intervient par l'intermédiaire d'organisations locales partenaires. **Actions de Développement durable:** Aliments/famine; Démocratie/bonne gestion publique/création d'institutions/développement participatif; Développement rural/agriculture; Développement urbain/habitat; Enfants/jeunesse/famille; Envoi de volontaires/experts/assistance technique; Santé/assainissement/eau; Secours d'urgence/réfugiés/aide humanitaire; Écologie/environnement/biodiversité; Éducation/formation/alphabétisation. **Régions:** Asie du Sud-Est.

ACTIVITES D'INFORMATION ET D'EDUCATION: Domaines: Aliments/famine; Culture/tradition/religion; Développement rural/agriculture; Développement urbain/habitat; Enfants/jeunesse/famille; Pauvreté/conditions de vie; Relations internationales/coopération/aide au développement; Réfugiés/migrants/groupes ethniques; Santé/assainissement/eau; Secours d'urgence/réfugiés/aide humanitaire; Éducation/formation/alphabétisation. **Activités:** Campagnes d'information/expositions; Collecte de fonds; Conférences/séminaires/ateliers/activités de formation; Lobbying/plaidoyer; Services d'information et de documentation/bases de données; Échanges/parrainage/jumelage; Édition/documents audiovisuels/documents éducatifs; Éducation formelle.

FRA2141
STATION INTERNATIONALE DE RECHERCHE CONTRE LA FAIM DANS LE MONDE (SIRCOFAM)

31 allées Jules Guesde, 31000 Toulouse, France.

Téléphone: 33 - 61 55 32 02. *Contact:* Jean-Jacques Conté.

Voir : *Comment utiliser le répertoire,* page 11.

FRA2142
SURVIE

57, avenue du Maine, 75014 Paris, France.

Téléphone: 33 (1) 43 27 03 25. **Fax:** 33 (1) 43 20 55 58. **Contact:** Jean Carbonare, Président.

OBJECTIFS: Coordonner en France, la campagne internationale d'action du Manifeste de 120 prix Nobel contre la faim et pour le développement. Faire du lobbying auprès des élus et décideurs pour que la France "donne valeur de loi au devoir de sauver les vivants", en concevant et en se dotant des lois, budgets et institutions nécessaires.

INFORMATIONS GENERALES: *Création:* 1984. *Type d'organisation:* réseau. *Affiliée à:* Forum Européen pour un contrat de génération Nord-Sud (Belgique). *Personnel/Total:* 6. *Salariés:* 1. *Bénévoles:* 5. *Budget/Total 1993:* ECU 53000 (US$ 62000). *Sources financières:* Privé: 70%. *Public:* 10%. *Autofinancement:* 20%.

PUBLICATIONS: *Périodiques:* Le Point sur la Loi pour la survie et le développement (12) - Billets d'Afrique (12).

ACTIVITES DANS LES REGIONS EN DEVELOPPEMENT: Intervient dans 1 pays. Intervient par l'intermédiaire d'organisations locales partenaires. **Actions de Développement durable:** Développement rural/agriculture; Santé/assainissement/eau. **Régions:** Afrique de l'Ouest.

ACTIVITES D'INFORMATION ET D'EDUCATION: Domaines: Droits de l'Homme/paix/conflits; Développement rural/agriculture; Paix/conflits ethniques/armement/désarmement; Pauvreté/conditions de vie; Relations internationales/coopération/aide au développement; Relations économiques internationales/commerce/dette/finances. **Activités:** Campagnes d'information/expositions; Conférences/séminaires/ateliers/activités de formation; Lobbying/plaidoyer; Édition/documents audiovisuels/documents éducatifs.

FRA2143
SURVIVAL INTERNATIONAL FRANCE

45, rue du Faubourg du Temple, 75010 Paris, France.

Telephone: 33 (1) 42 41 47 62. **Fax:** 33 (1) 42 45 34 51. **Contact:** Jean Patrick Razon, Director.

OBJECTIVES: To support the rights of threatened tribal peoples.

GENERAL INFORMATION: *Creation:* 1979. *Affiliated to:* Survival International (United Kingdom). *Personnel/Total:* 18. *Salaried:* 3. *Volunteers:* 15. *Budget/Total 1993:* ECU 60000 (US$ 71000). *Financial sources:* Private: 25%. *Public:* 5%. *Self-financing:* 70%.

PUBLICATIONS: *Periodicals:* Ethnies-Droits de l'homme et peuples autochtones (2) - Les Nouvelles de Survival (4). *Annual report. List of publications.*

EVALUATION/RESEARCH: Undertakes research activities.

COMMENTS: Undertakes activities in the Commonwealth of Independent States. Information activities related to the Commonwealth of Independent States.

ACTIVITIES IN DEVELOPING REGIONS: Maintains local field presence. **Sustainable Development Actions:** Human rights/peace/conflicts. **Regions:** Central Africa; Central Asia and South Asia; East Africa; Mexico and Central America; North Africa; Oceania; South America; South East Asia; Southern Africa; West Africa.

INFORMATION AND EDUCATION ACTIVITIES: Topics: Culture/tradition/religion; Human rights/peace/conflicts; Peace/ethnic conflicts/armament/disarmament; Racism/xenophobia/antisemitism; Refugees/migrants/ethnic groups. **Activities:** Conferences/seminars/workshops/training activities; Formal education; Information and documentation services/data bases; Information campaigns/exhibitions; Lobbying/advocacy; Publishing/audiovisual materials/educational materials.

FRA2144
SYNOPSIS

Route d'Olmet, 34700 Lodève, France.

Téléphone: 33 - 67 44 04 10. **Fax:** 33 - 67 44 06 01. **Contact:** Michael Grupp, Coordinateur.

OBJECTIFS: Etre actif dans la recherche et la mise en œuvre d'appareils fonctionnant à base d'énergie solaire thermique. Effectuer des missions de conseil dans les pays en développement sur les technologies appropriées. Démarrer des projets de production locale.

INFORMATIONS GENERALES: *Création:* 1977. *Personnel/Total:* 6. *Salariés:* 5. *Bénévoles:* 1. *Sources financières:* Autofinancement: 100%.

PUBLICATIONS: *Périodiques:* Rapport annuel (1). *Rapport annuel. Liste des publications.*

EVALUATION/RECHERCHE: Entreprend des activités de recherche.

ACTIVITES DANS LES REGIONS EN DEVELOPPEMENT: Intervient directement dans les régions en développement. Intervient par l'intermédiaire d'organisations locales partenaires. **Actions de Développement durable:** Énergie/transport. **Régions:** Afrique de l'Est; Afrique de l'Ouest; Asie centrale et Asie du Sud.

ACTIVITES D'INFORMATION ET D'EDUCATION: Domaines: Autres. **Activités:** Conférences/séminaires/ateliers/activités de formation.

FRA2145
TAM-TAM DE NKOL EKONG

4, rue du Maréchal de Lattre de Tassigny, 59100 Roubaix, France.

Téléphone: 33 - 20 73 14 50. **Fax:** 33- 20 75 82 78. **Contact:** Paul Delétoille, Président.

OBJECTIFS: Collecter des médicaments et du matériel sanitaire en France, afin de les envoyer à l'Action Sanitaire dans le Sud du Cameroun. Apporter un soutien, dans ce pays, à des dispensaires, à des hôpitaux et à l'Ecole d'Enfants Sourds de Yaoundé.

INFORMATIONS GENERALES: *Création:* 1969. *Personnel/Total:* 26. *Bénévoles:* 26 dont: 6 dans les pays en développement. *Budget/Total 1993:* ECU 81000 (US$ 94000). *Sources financières:* Privé: 100%.

PUBLICATIONS: *Périodiques:* Appel Annuel (1). *Rapport annuel.*

EVALUATION/RECHERCHE: Rapports d'évaluation disponibles.

PREVISIONS D'ACTIVITES: Formation de médecins camerounais pour relayer les médecins coopérants, à la disposition de l'Hôpital de Pouma. Mise sur pieds de soins de santé primaire dans les villages. Formation de professeurs, et développement du langage des signes, pour l'Ecole des Enfants Sourds.

COMMENTAIRES: Intervient dans la Communauté des Etats indépendants.

ACTIVITES DANS LES REGIONS EN DEVELOPPEMENT: Intervient directement dans les régions en développement. Intervient dans 3 pays. Maintient une présence locale sur le terrain. Intervient par l'intermédiaire d'organisations locales partenaires. **Actions de Développement durable:** Enfants/jeunesse/famille; Envoi de volontaires/experts/assistance technique; Santé/assainissement/eau; Éducation/formation/alphabétisation. **Régions:** Afrique centrale; Moyen-Orient.

ACTIVITES D'INFORMATION ET D'EDUCATION: Domaines: Enfants/jeunesse/famille; Relations internationales/coopération/aide au développement; Santé/assainissement/eau; Éducation/formation/alphabétisation. **Activités:** Collecte de fonds; Échanges/parrainage/jumelage; Édition/documents audiovisuels/documents éducatifs; Éducation formelle.

FRA2146
TCHAD, PAYS DE LA SERRE, SOLIDAIRES

2 rue des Etangs, Marcy-sous-Marle, 02250 Marle, France.

Téléphone: 33 - 23 20 00 04. **Contact:** François Braillon, Président.

FRA2147
TECHNAP

4, rue Le Bouvier, 92340 Bourg-la-Reine, France.

Téléphone: 33 (1) 46 61 60 00. **Fax:** 33 (1) 46 61 50 00. **Contact:** Pierre Labat, Président.

OBJECTIFS: Travailler dans le domaine de la technologie appropriée. Coordonner l'action des ONG par la mise en commun de leurs moyens

                                    See: *How to Use the Directory,* page 11.

et de leurs compétences et une meilleure transmission de leur savoir-faire.

INFORMATIONS GENERALES: *Création:* 1965. *Type d'organisation:* collectif. *Organisations membres:* 14. *Affiliée à:* CFCF - Plate-forme nationale. *Personnel/Total:* 3. *Bénévoles:* 3. *Budget/Total 1993:* ECU 75000 (US$ 88000). *Sources financières:* Public: 83%. Autofinancement: 17%.

PUBLICATIONS: *Périodiques:* Bulletin de liaison TECHNAP (3). *Rapport annuel.*

PREVISIONS D'ACTIVITES: Développer un véritable partenariat avec les ONG africaines. Participation aux programmes qui seraient mis en place dans les pays africains, à la suite des commissions mixtes franco-africaines. Développement de la fabrication et de la commercialisation de la spiruline dans certains pays africains.

ACTIVITES DANS LES REGIONS EN DEVELOPPEMENT: Intervient directement dans les régions en développement. Intervient dans 6 pays. Intervient par l'intermédiaire d'organisations locales partenaires. **Actions de Développement durable:** Aliments/famine; Développement rural/agriculture; Développement urbain/habitat; Petites entreprises/secteur informel/artisanat. **Régions:** Afrique centrale; Afrique de l'Est; Afrique de l'Ouest.

ACTIVITES D'INFORMATION ET D'EDUCATION: Domaines: Développement rural/agriculture; Développement urbain/habitat. **Activités:** Conférences/séminaires/ateliers/activités de formation.

FRA2148
TERRE D'AMITIE

306, rue André Philip, 69003 Lyon, France.

Téléphone: 33 - 78 95 30 47. *Fax:* 33 - 78 62 04 00. *Contact:* Anne-Marie Machon, Présidente.

OBJECTIFS: Informer sur les problèmes de santé dans le monde, notamment en Afrique. Apporter une aide médicale à dix pays africains, à Madagascar, au Liban et à l'Europe de l'Est. Lutter contre la malnutrition. Promouvoir l'éducation.

INFORMATIONS GENERALES: *Création:* 1966. *Personnel/Total:* 1003. *Salariés:* 3. *Bénévoles:* 1000. *Budget/Total 1993:* ECU 377000 (US$ 441000). *Sources financières:* Privé: 43%. Public: 2%. Autofinancement: 55%.

PUBLICATIONS: *Rapport annuel.*

EVALUATION/RECHERCHE: Rapports d'évaluation disponibles.

COMMENTAIRES: Intervient dans la Communauté des Etats indépendants.

ACTIVITES DANS LES REGIONS EN DEVELOPPEMENT: Intervient directement dans les régions en développement. Intervient dans 10 pays. Intervient par l'intermédiaire d'organisations locales partenaires. **Actions de Développement durable:** Aliments/famine; Enfants/jeunesse/famille; Santé/assainissement/eau; Secours d'urgence/réfugiés/aide humanitaire. **Régions:** Afrique centrale; Afrique de l'Ouest.

ACTIVITES D'INFORMATION ET D'EDUCATION: Domaines: Aliments/famine; Secours d'urgence/réfugiés/aide humanitaire. **Activités:** Collecte de fonds.

FRA2149
TERRE DE VIE

26, rue de Bégueneau, 44320 St Père en Retz, France.

Téléphone: 33 - 40 21 15 16. *Fax:* 33 - 40 21 18 24. *Contact:* Michel Duret, Directeur.

OBJECTIFS: Porter secours aux enfants et soutenir des projets de développement dans les pays du Tiers-Monde. Diffuser des informationss auprès du public français dans le cadre de l'éducation au développement.

INFORMATIONS GENERALES: *Création:* 1976. *Affiliée à:* La Voix de l'Enfant (France). *Personnel/Total:* 204. *Salariés:* 24 dont: 21 dans les pays en développement. *Bénévoles:* 180 dont: 20 dans les pays en développement. *Budget/Total 1993:*

ECU 302000 (US$ 353000). *Sources financières:* Privé: 97%. Public: 2%. Autofinancement: 1%.

PUBLICATIONS: *Périodiques:* Terre de Vie (4). *Rapport annuel.*

ACTIVITES DANS LES REGIONS EN DEVELOPPEMENT: Intervient directement dans les régions en développement. Intervient dans 13 pays. Intervient par l'intermédiaire d'organisations locales partenaires. **Actions de Développement durable:** Développement rural/agriculture; Enfants/jeunesse/famille; Population/planning familial/démographie; Santé/assainissement/eau; Secours d'urgence/réfugiés/aide humanitaire; Éducation/formation/alphabétisation. **Régions:** Afrique centrale; Afrique de l'Ouest; Amérique du Sud; Asie de l'Est; Mexique et Amerique centrale; Moyen-Orient.

ACTIVITES D'INFORMATION ET D'EDUCATION: Domaines: Enfants/jeunesse/famille; Santé/assainissement/eau; Secours d'urgence/réfugiés/aide humanitaire; Éducation/formation/alphabétisation. **Activités:** Collecte de fonds; Édition/documents audiovisuels/documents éducatifs.

FRA2150
TERRE DES HOMMES, FRANCE (TDHF)

4, rue Franklin, 93200 Saint-Denis, France.

Téléphone: 33 (1) 48 09 09 76. *Fax:* 33 (1) 48 09 15 75. *Contact:* Hervé Riols, Directeur.

OBJECTIFS: Agir ici pour que ça change là-bas. Aider des ONG du Sud à créer les conditions pour un développement global.

INFORMATIONS GENERALES: *Création:* 1963. *Type d'organisation:* collectif. *Affiliée à:* Fédération Internationale Terre des Hommes - Centre de Recherche et d'Information pour le Développement. *Personnel/Total:* 215. *Salariés:* 15. *Bénévoles:* 200. *Budget/Total 1993:* ECU 1884000 (US$ 2207000). *Sources financières:* Privé: 37%. Public: 6%. Autofinancement: 57%.

PUBLICATIONS: *Périodiques:* Peuples en marche (12) - Défi (4). *Rapport annuel.*

EVALUATION/RECHERCHE: Rapports d'évaluation disponibles.

ACTIVITES DANS LES REGIONS EN DEVELOPPEMENT: Intervient par l'intermédiaire d'organisations locales partenaires. **Actions de Développement durable:** Dette/finances/commerce; Droits de l'Homme/paix/conflits; Démocratie/bonne gestion publique/création d'institutions/développement participatif; Développement rural/agriculture; Développement urbain/habitat; Enfants/jeunesse/famille; Petites entreprises/secteur informel/artisanat; Questions relatives aux femmes; Santé/assainissement/eau; Secours d'urgence/réfugiés/aide humanitaire; Écologie/environnement/biodiversité; Éducation/formation/alphabétisation. **Régions:** Afrique centrale; Afrique de l'Ouest; Afrique du Nord; Amérique du Sud; Asie centrale et Asie du Sud; Asie du Sud-Est; Caraïbes; Mexique et Amerique centrale; Moyen-Orient.

ACTIVITES D'INFORMATION ET D'EDUCATION: Domaines: Droits de l'Homme/paix/conflits; Développement rural/agriculture; Développement urbain/habitat; Enfants/jeunesse/famille; Pauvreté/conditions de vie; Questions relatives aux femmes; Relations internationales/coopération/aide au développement; Relations économiques internationales/commerce/dette/finances; Réfugiés/migrants/groupes ethniques; Écologie/environnement/biodiversité; Éducation/formation/alphabétisation. **Activités:** Campagnes d'information/expositions; Conférences/séminaires/ateliers/activités de formation; Lobbying/plaidoyer; Échanges/parrainage/jumelage; Éducation formelle.

FRA2151
TOXICOMANIES-COOPERATION

Route de Publier, Moruel, 74200 Marin, France.

Téléphone: 33 - 50 26 22 69. *Fax:* 33 - 50 26 22 69. *Contact:* Detlef Servas, Secrétaire général.

OBJECTIFS: Organiser des campagnes de prévention et de formation relatives à l'usage des drogues, sous forme de séminaires, de conférences, de débats, et en utilisant des moyens audiovisuels. Réaliser des projets de téléenseignement.

INFORMATIONS GENERALES: *Création:* 1991. *Type d'organisation:* réseau. *Personnel/Total:* 5. *Salariés:* 3 dont: 1 dans les pays en

développement. *Bénévoles:* 2. **Budget/Total 1993:** ECU 151000 (US$ 177000). *Sources financières:* Privé: 80%. Public: 10%. *Autofinancement:* 10%.

PUBLICATIONS: *Rapport annuel. Liste des publications.*

EVALUATION/RECHERCHE: Entreprend des activités de recherche.

COMMENTAIRES: Intervient dans la Communauté des Etats indépendants. Activités d'information concernant la Communauté des Etats indépendants.

ACTIVITES DANS LES REGIONS EN DEVELOPPEMENT: Intervient dans 7 pays. Maintient une présence locale sur le terrain. Intervient par l'intermédiaire d'organisations locales partenaires. **Actions de Développement durable:** Santé/assainissement/eau. **Régions:** Afrique australe; Afrique de l'Ouest; Asie centrale et Asie du Sud; Océanie.

ACTIVITES D'INFORMATION ET D'EDUCATION: Domaines: Culture/tradition/religion; Enfants/jeunesse/famille; Santé/assainissement/eau. **Activités:** Campagnes d'information/expositions; Collecte de fonds; Conférences/séminaires/ateliers/activités de formation; Lobbying/plaidoyer; Radiodiffusion/manifestations culturelles; Services d'information et de documentation/bases de données; Échanges/parrainage/jumelage; Édition/documents audiovisuels/documents éducatifs; Éducation formelle.

FRA2152
TRADITIONS POUR DEMAIN ♦ Traditions for Tomorrow

B.P. 477-07, 75327 Paris cedex 07, France.

Téléphone: 33 (1) 47 05 16 24. **Fax:** 33 (1) 45 56 05 51. **Contact:** Diégo Gradis, Président.

OBJECTIFS: Diffuser et soutenir les initiatives provenant de communautés indigènes d'Amérique latine dans le domaine de la valorisation de leur environnement et de identité culturelle.

INFORMATIONS GENERALES: *Création:* 1986. **Type d'organisation:** réseau. **Organisations membres:** 3. **Affiliée à:** UNESCO - Commission Coopération et Développement (France). **Personnel/Total:** 6. *Bénévoles:* 6. **Budget/Total 1993:** ECU 90000 (US$ 106000). *Sources financières:* Privé: 40%. Public: 50%. *Autofinancement:* 10%.

PUBLICATIONS: *Rapport annuel.*

ACTIVITES DANS LES REGIONS EN DEVELOPPEMENT: Intervient directement dans les régions en développement. Intervient dans 10 pays. Intervient par l'intermédiaire d'organisations locales partenaires. **Actions de Développement durable:** Droits de l'Homme/paix/conflits; Enfants/jeunesse/famille; Éducation/formation/alphabétisation. **Régions:** Amérique du Sud; Mexique et Amerique centrale.

ACTIVITES D'INFORMATION ET D'EDUCATION: Domaines: Culture/tradition/religion; Droits de l'Homme/paix/conflits; Enfants/jeunesse/famille; Paix/conflits ethniques/armement/désarmement; Relations internationales/coopération/aide au développement; Éducation/formation/alphabétisation. **Activités:** Campagnes d'information/expositions; Collecte de fonds; Services d'information et de documentation/bases de données.

FRA2153
TRANS-AFRICA ASSOCIATION (TAA)

174 avenue du Maine, 75014 Paris, France.

Téléphone: 33 (1) 45 43 85 26. **Fax:** 33 (1) 45 43 51 59. **Contact:** Claude Landez.

FRA2154
TRANSFERTS D'URGENCE DE L'INDUSTRIE PHARMACEUTIQUE

25, rue de Montévidéo, 75116 Paris, France.

Téléphone: 33 (1) 47 12 08 97. **Fax:** 33 (1) 46 84 04 06. **Contact:** Sebbag, Président.

OBJECTIFS: Distribuer des produits pharmaceutiques dans le monde entier, en réponse aux projets proposés par les organisations humanitaires.

INFORMATIONS GENERALES: *Création:* 1982. **Type d'organisation:** collectif. **Personnel/Total:** 25. *Salariés:* 3. *Bénévoles:* 20. **Budget/Total 1993:** ECU 151000 (US$ 177000). *Sources financières:* Privé: 100%.

PUBLICATIONS: *Périodiques:* TULIPE Info (4). *Rapport annuel.*

EVALUATION/RECHERCHE: Rapports d'évaluation disponibles. Entreprend des activités de recherche.

COMMENTAIRES: Intervient dans la Communauté des Etats indépendants.

ACTIVITES DANS LES REGIONS EN DEVELOPPEMENT: Intervient par l'intermédiaire d'organisations locales partenaires. **Actions de Développement durable:** Santé/assainissement/eau; Secours d'urgence/réfugiés/aide humanitaire. **Régions:** Afrique australe; Afrique centrale; Afrique de l'Est; Afrique de l'Ouest; Afrique du Nord; Amérique du Sud; Asie centrale et Asie du Sud; Asie de l'Est; Asie du Sud-Est; Caraïbes; Mexique et Amerique centrale; Moyen-Orient; Océanie.

FRA2155
TRANSSAHARA - CARAVANES SANS FRONTIERES

9 rue de Septèmes, 13015 Marseille, France.

Téléphone: 33 - 91 55 14 37. **Contact:** Loïc Fauchon, Président.

FRA2156
UNION EUROPEENNE FEMININE

5 avenue Monge, 44100 Nantes, France.

Contact: Nelly Monjouste.

FRA2157
UNION INTERNATIONALE DE PROMOTION DE LA SANTE ♦
International Union for Health Promotion

15-21 rue de L'Ecole de Médecine, 75270 Paris cedex 06, France.

Telephone: 33 (1) 43 26 90 82. **Fax:** 33 (1) 43 29 33 15. **Contact:** Marie Claude Lamarre, Directeur Exécutif.

FRA2158
UNION INTERNATIONALE DES ASSOCIATIONS ET ORGANISMES TECHNIQUES (UATI) ♦ International Union of Technical Associations and Organizations (UATI)

1, rue Miollis, 75732 Paris cedex 15, France.

Téléphone: 33 (1) 45 66 94 10. **Fax:** 33 (1) 43 06 29 27. **Contact:** Michel Saillard, Président.

OBJECTIFS: Participer à l'élaboration des programmes annuels et pluriannuels des organismes des Nations Unies. Faire bénéficier les associations membres de tous les systèmes d'aide dont dispose l'ONU, pour leurs actions en faveur des pays en développement. Représenter et défendre les intérêts des associations membres auprès des Nations Unies.

INFORMATIONS GENERALES: *Création:* 1951. **Type d'organisation:** regroupement d'ONG. **Organisations membres:** 30. **Personnel/Total:** 7. *Salariés:* 2. *Bénévoles:* 5. **Budget/Total 1993:** ECU 151000 (US$ 177000). *Sources financières:* Public: 55%. *Autofinancement:* 45%.

PUBLICATIONS: *Périodiques:* Bulletin UATI (2).

PREVISIONS D'ACTIVITES: Préparation d'un congrès mondial "Doyens d'Université / Dirigeants d'Industrie" (Paris, Juillet 1996).

COMMENTAIRES: Intervient dans la Communauté des Etats indépendants.

ACTIVITES DANS LES REGIONS EN DEVELOPPEMENT: Intervient directement dans les régions en développement. Intervient dans 6 pays. Intervient par l'intermédiaire d'organisations locales partenaires. **Actions de Développement durable:** Écologie/environnement/biodiversité; Éducation/formation/alphabétisation. **Régions:** Afrique de l'Ouest; Afrique du Nord; Amérique du Sud; Asie centrale et Asie du Sud; Caraïbes; Mexique et Amerique centrale; Moyen-Orient.

See: *How to Use the Directory*, page 11.

ACTIVITES D'INFORMATION ET D'EDUCATION: **Domaines:** Écologie/
environnement/biodiversité; Éducation/formation/alphabétisation. **Activités:** Campagnes d'information/expositions; Conférences/séminaires/
ateliers/activités de formation.

FRA2159
UNION INTERNATIONALE DES ORGANISMES FAMILIAUX (UIOF)

28, place Saint-Georges, 75009 Paris, France.

Téléphone: 33 (1) 48 78 07 59. *Fax:* 33 (1) 42 82 95 24. *Contact:* Maria
Teresa da Costa Macedo, Présidente.

OBJECTIFS: Oeuvrer pour le mieux-être et la solidarité entre les familles
en établissant des liens entre tous les organismes qui, dans le monde,
s'y intéressent. Promouvoir et favoriser la coordination de tous les organismes privés ou publics partageant les buts de l'union. Représenter les
intérêts des familles. Organiser des rencontres internationales.

INFORMATIONS GENERALES: *Création:* 1947. *Organisations membres:* 300. *Personnel/Total:* 20. *Salariés:* 7. *Budget/Total 1993:*
ECU 452000 (US$ 530000). *Sources financières:* Autofinancement:
100%.

PUBLICATIONS: *Rapport annuel.*

EVALUATION/RECHERCHE: Rapports d'évaluation disponibles. Entreprend des activités de recherche.

COMMENTAIRES: L'organisation regroupe des institutions gouvernementales de tous les continents ainsi que des membres non-gouvernementaux. Intervient dans la Communauté des Etats indépendants. Activités
d'information concernant la Communauté des Etats indépendants.

ACTIVITES DANS LES REGIONS EN DEVELOPPEMENT: Intervient
directement dans les régions en développement. Maintient une présence locale sur le terrain. Intervient par l'intermédiaire d'organisations
locales partenaires. **Actions de Développement durable:** Droits de
l'Homme/paix/conflits; Démocratie/bonne gestion publique/création
d'institutions/développement participatif; Développement rural/agricul-
ture; Développement urbain/habitat; Enfants/jeunesse/famille; Envoi de
volontaires/experts/assistance technique; Population/planning familial/
démographie; Questions relatives aux femmes; Santé/assainissement/
eau; Éducation/formation/alphabétisation. **Régions:** Afrique australe;
Afrique centrale; Afrique de l'Est; Afrique de l'Ouest; Afrique du Nord;
Amérique du Sud; Asie centrale et Asie du Sud; Asie de l'Est; Asie du
Sud-Est; Caraïbes; Mexique et Amerique centrale; Moyen-Orient;
Océanie.

ACTIVITES D'INFORMATION ET D'EDUCATION: **Domaines:** Culture/
tradition/religion; Droits de l'Homme/paix/conflits; Développement rural/
agriculture; Développement urbain/habitat; Enfants/jeunesse/famille;
Paix/conflits ethniques/armement/désarmement; Pauvreté/conditions de
vie; Population/planning familial/démographie; Questions relatives aux
femmes; Racisme/xénophobie/antisémitisme; Relations internationales/
coopération/aide au développement; Santé/assainissement/eau;
Secours d'urgence/réfugiés/aide humanitaire; Éducation/formation/
alphabétisation. **Activités:** Campagnes d'information/expositions; Collecte de fonds; Conférences/séminaires/ateliers/activités de formation;
Lobbying/plaidoyer; Radiodiffusion/manifestations culturelles; Réseaux/
télécommunications électroniques; Services d'information et de docu-
mentation/bases de données; Échanges/parrainage/jumelage; Édition/
documents audiovisuels/documents éducatifs; Éducation formelle.

FRA2160
UNION MONDIALE DES ENSEIGNANTS CATHOLIQUES

5 rue Saint-Paul, 594320 Mouvaux, France.

Contact: Geneviève Lingelser.

FRA2161
UNION NATIONALE DES CENTRES PERMANENTS D'INITIATION A L'ENVIRONNEMENT (UNCPIE)

2, rue Washington, 75008 Paris, France.

Téléphone: 33 (1) 45 63 63 67. *Fax:* 33 (1) 42 89 55 18. *Contact:* Jean-
François Legrand, Président.

OBJECTIFS: Soutenir et promouvoir l'action des Centres Permanents
d'Initiation à l'Environnement. Participer au développement local et

durable des pays. Former, éduquer, conseiller, sensibiliser à l'environnement naturel et humain, à la gestion des milieux et à l'aménagement.

INFORMATIONS GENERALES: *Création:* 1977. *Type d'organisation:*
réseau. *Organisations membres:* 40. *Affiliée à:* Réseau européen
Virgile (Belgique) - Fédération des Parcs Naturels de France (France) -
Fondation pour l'Education à l'Environnement en Europe (France) -
Réseau du Comité d'Etudes et de liaison des Associations à vocation
agricole et rurale (France). *Personnel/Total:* 30. *Salariés:* 5. *Bénévoles:*
25. *Budget/Total 1993:* ECU 588000 (US$ 689000). *Sources finan-
cières:* Privé: 5%. Public: 45%. Autofinancement: 50%.

PUBLICATIONS: *Périodiques:* Info UNCPIE (12) - Réseau (12). *Rapport
annuel.*

EVALUATION/RECHERCHE: Rapports d'évaluation disponibles. Entreprend des activités de recherche.

COMMENTAIRES: Intervient dans la Communauté des Etats
indépendants.

ACTIVITES DANS LES REGIONS EN DEVELOPPEMENT: Intervient
directement dans les régions en développement. Intervient dans 2
pays. **Actions de Développement durable:** Démocratie/bonne gestion
publique/création d'institutions/développement participatif; Développement urbain/habitat; Envoi de volontaires/experts/assistance technique;
Petites entreprises/secteur informel/artisanat; Écologie/environnement/
biodiversité; Éducation/formation/alphabétisation. **Régions:** Afrique de
l'Ouest; Caraïbes.

ACTIVITES D'INFORMATION ET D'EDUCATION: **Domaines:** Culture/
tradition/religion; Développement rural/agriculture; Développement
urbain/habitat; Écologie/environnement/biodiversité. **Activités:** Confé-
rences/séminaires/ateliers/activités de formation; Échanges/parrainage/
jumelage; Édition/documents audiovisuels/documents éducatifs.

FRA2162
UNIVERSITE SANS FRONTIERE (USF)

86, rue Hameaux de la Plaine, 86000 Poitiers, France.

Téléphone: 33 - 49 01 28 14. *Fax:* 33 - 49 01 28 14. *Contact:* Claude
Agbangla, Président.

OBJECTIFS: Promouvoir et diffuser l'enseignement des techniques, de la
recherche universitaire et para universitaire en les adaptant aux besoins
locaux.

INFORMATIONS GENERALES: *Création:* 1990. *Personnel/Total:*
120. *Bénévoles:* 120 dont: 10 dans les pays en développement. *Bud-
get/Total 1993:* ECU 19000 (US$ 22000). *Sources financières:* Privé:
3%. Public: 84%. Autofinancement: 13%.

PUBLICATIONS: *Rapport annuel. Liste des publications.*

COMMENTAIRES: L'organisation publie tous les deux ans une revue inti-
tulée "Afrique-Université-Universalité." Elle fait aussi des dons de livres
à la demande des bibliothèques universitaires des pays francophones
d'Afrique et du Viet-Nam.

ACTIVITES DANS LES REGIONS EN DEVELOPPEMENT: Intervient
directement dans les régions en développement. Intervient dans 3 pays.
Maintient une présence locale sur le terrain. Intervient par l'intermédiaire
d'organisations locales partenaires. **Actions de Développement durable:** Développement urbain/habitat; Santé/assainissement/eau; Écolo-
gie/environnement/biodiversité; Éducation/formation/alphabétisation.
Régions: Afrique australe; Afrique centrale; Afrique de l'Ouest; Asie du
Sud-Est.

ACTIVITES D'INFORMATION ET D'EDUCATION: **Domaines:** Développement urbain/habitat; Racisme/xénophobie/antisémitisme; Santé/
assainissement/eau; Écologie/environnement/biodiversité. **Activités:**
Conférences/séminaires/ateliers/activités de formation.

FRA2163
VETERINAIRES SANS FRONTIERES (VSF)

Espace Rhône Alpes Coopération, 14 avenue Berthelot, 69361 Lyon
cedex 07, France.

Téléphone: 33 - 78 69 79 59. *Fax:* 33 - 78 69 79 56. *Contact:* Bruno
Rebelle, Directeur général.

OBJECTIFS: Apporter une aide vétérinaire aux pays les plus démunis. Participer à des actions de formation et de vulgarisation des techniques d'élevage et de prévention des maladies animales. Accompagner les processus d'organisation du monde rural pour la conduite d'actions de développement durable.

INFORMATIONS GENERALES: *Création:* 1983. *Personnel/Total:* 70. *Salariés:* 20 dont: 2 dans les pays en développement. *Bénévoles:* 60 dont: 55 dans les pays en développement. *Budget/Total 1993:* ECU 3769000 (US$ 4414000). *Sources financières:* *Privé:* 20%. *Public:* 70%. *Autofinancement:* 10%.

PUBLICATIONS: *Périodiques:* Habbanae (4). *Rapport annuel.*

EVALUATION/RECHERCHE: Rapports d'évaluation disponibles.

COMMENTAIRES: Intervient dans la Communauté des Etats indépendants.

ACTIVITES DANS LES REGIONS EN DEVELOPPEMENT: Intervient directement dans les régions en développement. Intervient dans 17 pays. Maintient une présence locale sur le terrain. Intervient par l'intermédiaire d'organisations locales partenaires. **Actions de Développement durable:** Développement rural/agriculture; Envoi de volontaires/experts/assistance technique; Questions relatives aux femmes; Santé/assainissement/eau; Écologie/environnement/biodiversité. **Régions:** Afrique australe; Afrique centrale; Afrique de l'Est; Afrique de l'Ouest; Amérique du Sud; Asie centrale et Asie du Sud; Asie du Sud-Est; Caraïbes; Mexique et Amerique centrale; Moyen-Orient.

ACTIVITES D'INFORMATION ET D'EDUCATION: Domaines: Développement rural/agriculture; Relations internationales/coopération/aide au développement; Réfugiés/migrants/groupes ethniques; Écologie/environnement/biodiversité. **Activités:** Campagnes d'information/expositions; Collecte de fonds; Conférences/séminaires/ateliers/activités de formation; Lobbying/plaidoyer; Services d'information et de documentation/bases de données; Échanges/parrainage/jumelage.

FRA2164
VIE ET LIBERTE

BP 56, 78193 Trappes cedex, France.

Téléphone: 33 - 30 69 93 86. *Fax:* 33 - 30 69 93 86. *Contact:* Ndualu Maurice Nsiangani, Président.

OBJECTIFS: Apporter une aide, dans le domaine de la santé et de la médecine, à la population démunie de l'Afrique francophone, par la collecte et la distribution de matériels médicaux. Assurer une éducation sanitaire en Afrique, particulièrement dans les villages.

INFORMATIONS GENERALES: *Création:* 1994.

ACTIVITES DANS LES REGIONS EN DEVELOPPEMENT: Intervient directement dans les régions en développement. Maintient une présence locale sur le terrain. Intervient par l'intermédiaire d'organisations locales partenaires. **Actions de Développement durable:** Santé/assainissement/eau; Secours d'urgence/réfugiés/aide humanitaire. **Régions:** Afrique centrale.

ACTIVITES D'INFORMATION ET D'EDUCATION: Domaines: Santé/assainissement/eau; Secours d'urgence/réfugiés/aide humanitaire. **Activités:** Collecte de fonds.

FRA2165
LA VIE NOUVELLE

74 boulevard Beaumarchais, 75011 Paris, France.

Téléphone: 33 (1) 43 55 64 58. *Fax:* 33 (1) 43 38 94 74. *Contact:* Jean-Louis Joliot, Président.

OBJECTIFS: Développer une éducation populaire pour former des citoyens acteurs de la société.

INFORMATIONS GENERALES: *Création:* 1947. *Type d'organisation:* regroupement d'ONG. *Personnel/Total:* 1002. *Salariés:* 2. *Bénévoles:* 1000. *Budget/Total 1993:* ECU 271000 (US$ 318000). *Sources financières:* *Public:* 10%. *Autofinancement:* 90%.

PUBLICATIONS: *Périodiques:* Vers la Vie Nouvelle (6) - Citoyens (6). *Rapport annuel. Liste des publications.*

EVALUATION/RECHERCHE: Rapports d'évaluation disponibles. Entreprend des activités de recherche. **Actions de Développement durable:** Démocratie/bonne gestion publique/création d'institutions/développement participatif. **Régions:** Mexique et Amerique centrale.

ACTIVITES D'INFORMATION ET D'EDUCATION: Domaines: Culture/tradition/religion; Droits de l'Homme/paix/conflits; Emploi/chômage; Relations internationales/coopération/aide au développement. **Activités:** Conférences/séminaires/ateliers/activités de formation; Échanges/parrainage/jumelage; Édition/documents audiovisuels/documents éducatifs.

FRA2166
VIVRE ENSEMBLE AVEC NOS DIFFERENCES

24 rue de la Chine, 75020 Paris, France.

Contact: Roland Merieux.

FRA2167
WORLD INDUSTRY COUNCIL FOR THE ENVIRONMENT (WICE)

40, cours Albert 1er, 75008 Paris, France.

Téléphone: 33 (1) 49 53 28 91. *Fax:* 33 (1) 49 53 28 89. *Contact:* Jan-Olaf Willums, Directeur exécutif.

OBJECTIFS: Agir, à l'échelle nationale et internationale, sur les politiques gouvernementales concernant l'environnement. Faire connaître les progrès accomplis par les sociétés dans la gestion des problèmes de l'environneent.

INFORMATIONS GENERALES: *Création:* 1993. *Personnel/Total:* 6. *Salariés:* 6. *Budget/Total 1993:* ECU 1365984 (US$ 1600000). *Sources financières:* Autofinancement: 100%.

PUBLICATIONS: *Périodiques:* WICE Newsletter (4).

EVALUATION/RECHERCHE: Entreprend des activités de recherche.

PREVISIONS D'ACTIVITES: Trois thèmes de recherche et de réflexion: 1) Comment les entreprises peuvent-elles répondre aux défis lancés par le Sommet de Rio? 2) Le commerce et l'environnement. 3) Les outils de la gestion de l'environnement.

COMMENTAIRES: Intervient dans la Communauté des Etats indépendants.

ACTIVITES D'INFORMATION ET D'EDUCATION: Domaines: Écologie/environnement/biodiversité. **Activités:** Conférences/séminaires/ateliers/activités de formation; Lobbying/plaidoyer; Échanges/parrainage/jumelage; Édition/documents audiovisuels/documents éducatifs.

FRA2168
WORLD UNION OF CATHOLIC WOMEN'S ORGANIZATIONS (UMOFC-WUCWO)

20 rue Notre-Dame-des-Champs, 75006 Paris, France.

Telephone: 33 (1) 45 44 27 65. *Fax:* 33 (1) 42 84 04 80. *Contact:* Marie-Thérèse van Heteren-Hogenhuis, President .

OBJECTIVES: To study and encourage women's participation in the Church's mission of evangelization. To study in a Christian spirit problems of general interest in international affairs. To promote action to enable women to better fulfill their vocation in the Church and in the world.

GENERAL INFORMATION: *Creation:* 1910. *Type of organisation:* association of NGOs. *Member organisations:* 93. *Affiliated to:* International Catholic Organisations - Conference of International Non Governmental Organisations - European Women's Lobby.. *Salaried:* 3. *Volunteers:* var. *Budget/Total 1993:* ECU 3703000 (US$ 4337000). *Financial sources:* Private: 66%. Self-financing: 34%.

PUBLICATIONS: *Periodicals:* Newsletter (4).

COMMENTS: Undertakes activities in the Commonwealth of Independent States.

 See: *How to Use the Directory*, page 11.

ACTIVITIES IN DEVELOPING REGIONS: Works through local field partners. **Sustainable Development Actions:** Children/youth/family; Ecology/environment/biodiversity; Education/training/literacy; Food/famine; Gender issues/women; Health/sanitation/water; Human rights/peace/conflicts; Rural development/agriculture; Small enterprises/informal sector/handicrafts. **Regions:** Caribbean; Central Africa; Central Asia and South Asia; East Africa; East Asia; Mexico and Central America; Oceania; South America; South East Asia; Southern Africa; West Africa.

FRA2169
YAKA

29 bis avenue de la Motte Picquet, 75007 Paris, France.

Téléphone: 33 (1) 45 55 82 37. *Contact:* Didier Biau, Président.

FRA2170
ZONTA INTERNATIONAL COMMITTEE

c/o Ndiaye Janine, Lycée Jean de la Fontaine, 75016 Paris, France.

Téléphone: 33 - 46 51 38 71. *Contact:* Folake Solanke, Président.

OBJECTIFS: Améliorer le statut juridique, politique, économique et professionel de la femme. Développer les valeurs morales dans les affaires et les professions libérales. Travailler à l'avènement de la compréhension mutuelle et de la paix. Apporter une aide personnelle et financière aux œuvres nationales et internationales. Fonder de mouveaux clubs ZONTA.

INFORMATIONS GENERALES: *Création:* 1919. *Salariés:* 20. **Budget/Total 1993:** ECU 21343000 (US$ 25000000). *Sources financières:* Privé: 9%. Public: 1%. Autofinancement: 90%.

PUBLICATIONS: *Périodiques:* ZONTIAN (3). *Rapport annuel.*

EVALUATION/RECHERCHE: Rapports d'évaluation disponibles.

PREVISIONS D'ACTIVITES: Sensibilisation à la santé. Alphabétisation. Actions en faveur de l'environnement.

COMMENTAIRES: Intervient dans la Communauté des Etats indépendants. Activités d'information concernant la Communauté des Etats indépendants.

ACTIVITES DANS LES REGIONS EN DEVELOPPEMENT: Intervient directement dans les régions en développement. Maintient une présence locale sur le terrain. Intervient par l'intermédiaire d'organisations locales partenaires. **Actions de Développement durable:** Droits de l'Homme/paix/conflits; Questions relatives aux femmes; Écologie/environnement/biodiversité; Éducation/formation/alphabétisation. **Régions:** Afrique australe; Afrique centrale; Afrique de l'Est; Afrique de l'Ouest; Afrique du Nord; Amérique du Sud; Asie centrale et Asie du Sud; Asie de l'Est; Asie du Sud-Est; Caraïbes; Mexique et Amerique centrale; Moyen-Orient; Océanie.

ACTIVITES D'INFORMATION ET D'EDUCATION: Domaines: Questions relatives aux femmes; Racisme/xénophobie/antisémitisme; Éducation/formation/alphabétisation. **Activités:** Campagnes d'information/expositions; Collecte de fonds; Conférences/séminaires/ateliers/activités de formation; Lobbying/plaidoyer; Radiodiffusion/manifestations culturelles; Réseaux/télécommunications électroniques; Services d'information et de documentation/bases de données; Échanges/parrainage/jumelage; Édition/documents audiovisuels/documents éducatifs; Éducation formelle.

Voir : *Comment utiliser le répertoire,* page 11.

GBR2171
ACET

P.O. Box 1323, London W5 5TF, United Kingdom.

Contact: Sara Cole.

GBR2172
ACTION HEALTH

The Gate House, 25 Gwydir Street, Cambridge CB1 2LG, United Kingdom.

Telephone: 44 (1223) 480853. *Fax:* 44 (1223) 480853. *Contact:* Philippa Young, Director.

OBJECTIVES: To develop primary health care and training programmes in partnership with communities across the world.

GENERAL INFORMATION: *Creation:* 1984. *Type of organisation:* network. *Member organisations:* 250. *Affiliated to:* EC NGO Network (United Kingdom) - UK NGO AIDS Consortium (United Kingdom) - FORUM (United Kingdom) - British Overseas NGOs for Development (United Kingdom) . *Personnel/Total:* 205. *Salaried:* 5. *Volunteers:* 200 of which: 35 in developing countries. *Budget/Total 1993:* ECU 191050 (US$ 224000). *Financial sources:* Private: 64%. Self-financing: 36%.

PUBLICATIONS: *Periodicals:* Action for Health (4). *Annual report.*

EVALUATION/RESEARCH: Evaluation reports available. Undertakes research activities.

ACTIVITIES IN DEVELOPING REGIONS: Present in developing regions. Active in 4 country(ies). Maintains local field presence. Works through local field partners. **Sustainable Development Actions:** Children/youth/family; Education/training/literacy; Gender issues/women; Health/sanitation/water; Population/family planning/demography; Sending volunteers/experts/technical assistance. **Regions:** Central Asia and South Asia; East Africa.

INFORMATION AND EDUCATION ACTIVITIES: Topics: Children/youth/family; Gender issues/women; Health/sanitation/water; Other; Population/family planning/demography. **Activities:** Conferences/seminars/workshops/training activities; Fund raising; Information campaigns/exhibitions.

GBR2173
ACTION ON DISABILITY AND DEVELOPMENT (ADD)

23, Lower Keyford, Frome, Somerset BA11 4AP, United Kingdom.

Telephone: 44 (1373) 473064. *Fax:* 44 (1373) 452075. *E-mail:* ADD@gn.apc.org. *Contact:* Chris Underhill, Director.

OBJECTIVES: To support disabled people in the development process. To work with associations of disabled people in order to achieve development in income generation, social programmes and community-based rehabilitation.

GENERAL INFORMATION: *Creation:* 1985. *Affiliated to:* Charity Commission in the UK (United Kingdom). *Personnel/Total:* 50. *Salaried:* 40 of which: 30 in developing countries. *Volunteers:* 10 of which: 3 in developing countries. *Budget/Total 1993:* ECU 1096694 (US$ 1284638). *Financial sources:* Private: 40%. Public: 50%. Self-financing: 10%.

PUBLICATIONS: *Annual report.*

EVALUATION/RESEARCH: Evaluation reports available. Undertakes research activities.

PLANNED ACTIVITIES: The organisation plans to focus on the development of programmes in Zambia, Ghana, Cambodia, Bangladesh.

ACTIVITIES IN DEVELOPING REGIONS: Present in developing regions. Active in 15 country(ies). Maintains local field presence. Works through local field partners. **Sustainable Development Actions:** Democracy/good governance/institution building/participatory development; Gender issues/women; Health/sanitation/water; Rural development/agriculture; Small enterprises/informal sector/handicrafts; Urban development/habitat. **Regions:** Central Africa; Central Asia and South Asia; East Africa; Southern Africa; West Africa.

GBR2174
ACTIONAID

Hamlyn House, Macdonald Road, London N19 5PG, United Kingdom.

Telephone: 44 (171) 281 4101. *Fax:* 44 (171) 263 7599. *E-mail:* actionaid@aaukion.demon.co.uk. *Contact:* John Batten.

OBJECTIVES: To create conditions under which poverty can be reduced through integrated, long-term development programmes. To ensure access to vital services such as clean water, primary health care, education and local economic development.

GENERAL INFORMATION: *Creation:* 1972. *Personnel/Total:* 3727. *Salaried:* 3727 of which: 3500 in developing countries. *Budget/Total 1993:* ECU 40556000 (US$ 47507000).

PUBLICATIONS: *Periodicals:* Education Action (4) - Common Cause (2). *Annual report. List of publications.*

EVALUATION/RESEARCH: Evaluation reports available. Undertakes research activities.

ACTIVITIES IN DEVELOPING REGIONS: Present in developing regions. Maintains local field presence. Works through local field partners. **Sustainable Development Actions:** Children/youth/family; Debt/finance/trade; Democracy/good governance/institution building/participatory development; Ecology/environment/biodiversity; Education/training/literacy; Emergency relief/refugees/humanitarian assistance; Food/famine; Gender issues/women; Health/sanitation/water; Human rights/peace/conflicts; Population/family planning/demography; Rural development/agriculture; Sending volunteers/experts/technical assistance; Small enterprises/informal sector/handicrafts; Urban development/habitat. **Regions:** Central Africa; Central Asia and South Asia; East Africa; Mexico and Central America; South America; Southern Africa; West Africa.

INFORMATION AND EDUCATION ACTIVITIES: Topics: Children/youth/family; Ecology/environment/biodiversity; Education/training/literacy; Emergency relief/refugees/humanitarian assistance; Food/famine; Gender issues/women; Health/sanitation/water; Peace/ethnic conflicts/armament/disarmament; Population/family planning/demography; Poverty/living conditions; Rural development/agriculture; Urban development/habitat. **Activities:** Conferences/seminars/workshops/training activities; Formal education; Fund raising; Information and documentation services/data bases; Information campaigns/exhibitions; Lobbying/advocacy; Networking/electronic telecommunications; Publishing/audiovisual materials/educational materials.

GBR2175
ADVENTIST DEVELOPMENT AND RELIEF AGENCY (ADRA)

119 St. Peter's Street,, St. Albans, Herts AL1 3EY, United Kingdom.

Telephone: 44 (1727) 860331. *Fax:* 44 (1727) 866312. *Contact:* W.J. Arthur.

OBJECTIVES: To help the poor regardless of race, religion, gender, ethnicity or political persuasion. To offer assistance in the form of relief supplies in the short-term to be followed by developmental projects leading to long-term self-sufficiency.

GENERAL INFORMATION: *Creation:* 1975. *Type of organisation:* network. *Member organisations:* 124. *Affiliated to:* CLONG (Belgium) - VOICE (Belgium). *Personnel/Total:* 540. *Salaried:* 500 of which: 400 in developing countries. *Volunteers:* 40 of which: 40 in developing countries. *Budget/Total 1993:* ECU 17073983 (US$ 20000000). *Financial sources:* Private: 5%. Public: 75%. Self-financing: 20%.

PUBLICATIONS: *Periodicals:* ADRA Today (4) - ADRA Advertiser (2). *Annual report. List of publications.*

EVALUATION/RESEARCH: Evaluation reports available. Undertakes research activities.

COMMENTS: Undertakes activities in the Commonwealth of Independent States. Information activities related to the Commonwealth of Independent States.

ACTIVITIES IN DEVELOPING REGIONS: Present in developing regions. Active in 121 country(ies). Maintains local field presence. Works through local field partners. **Sustainable Development Actions:** Children/youth/family; Ecology/environment/biodiversity; Education/training/

See: How to Use the Directory, page 11.

literacy; Emergency relief/refugees/humanitarian assistance; Food/famine; Gender issues/women; Health/sanitation/water; Population/family planning/demography; Rural development/agriculture; Sending volunteers/experts/technical assistance; Small enterprises/informal sector/handicrafts; Urban development/habitat. **Regions:** Caribbean; Central Africa; Central Asia and South Asia; East Africa; East Asia; Mexico and Central America; Middle East; North Africa; Oceania; South America; South East Asia; Southern Africa; West Africa.

INFORMATION AND EDUCATION ACTIVITIES: Topics: Children/youth/family; Culture/tradition/religion; Education/training/literacy; Emergency relief/refugees/humanitarian assistance; Employment/unemployment; Food/famine; Gender issues/women; Health/sanitation/water; Poverty/living conditions; Refugees/migrants/ethnic groups; Rural development/agriculture; Urban development/habitat. **Activities:** Broadcasting/cultural events; Conferences/seminars/workshops/training activities; Formal education; Fund raising; Information campaigns/exhibitions; Lobbying/advocacy; Publishing/audiovisual materials/educational materials.

GBR2176
AFGHANAID

292 Pentonville Road, London NI 9NR, United Kingdom.

Telephone: 44 (171) 278 2832. *Fax:* 44 (171) 837 8155. *Contact:* Prudence Lambert, Director.

OBJECTIVES: To provide humanitarian assistance to the people of Afghanistan. To contribute towards rural rehabilitation. To provide assistance to the war affected and destitute.

GENERAL INFORMATION: *Creation:* 1983. *Affiliated to:* British Agencies Afghan Group (United Kingdom) - Agencies Co-ordinating Body for Afghan Relief (Pakistan) - British Overseas NGOs for Development (United Kingdom). *Personnel/Total:* 134. *Salaried:* 130 of which: 124 in developing countries. *Volunteers:* 4. *Budget/Total 1993:* ECU 1923324 (US$ 2252929). *Financial sources:* Private: 5%. Public: 95%.

PUBLICATIONS: *Periodicals:* Jahrchi (3). *Annual report.*

EVALUATION/RESEARCH: Evaluation reports available. Undertakes research activities.

PLANNED ACTIVITIES: Small scale, income-generating programmes targeting women. Reforestation and social forestry in arid mountain communities.

ACTIVITIES IN DEVELOPING REGIONS: Present in developing regions. Active in 1 country(ies). Maintains local field presence. **Sustainable Development Actions:** Democracy/good governance/institution building/participatory development; Ecology/environment/biodiversity; Education/training/literacy; Emergency relief/refugees/humanitarian assistance; Food/famine; Gender issues/women; Rural development/agriculture; Sending volunteers/experts/technical assistance; Small enterprises/informal sector/handicrafts; Urban development/habitat. **Regions:** Central Asia and South Asia.

INFORMATION AND EDUCATION ACTIVITIES: Topics: Ecology/environment/biodiversity; Emergency relief/refugees/humanitarian assistance; Food/famine; Gender issues/women; Poverty/living conditions; Refugees/migrants/ethnic groups; Rural development/agriculture; Urban development/habitat. **Activities:** Conferences/seminars/workshops/training activities; Fund raising.

GBR2177
AFRICA CENTRE

38 King Street, London WC2E 8JT, United Kingdom.

Telephone: 44 (171) 836 1973. *Fax:* 44 (171) 836 1975.

GBR2178
AFRICA EDUCATIONAL TRUST (AET)

38 King Street, London WC2E 8JT, United Kingdom.

Telephone: 44 (171) 836 1973. *Fax:* 44 (171) 379 0090. *Contact:* Michael Brophy, Director.

OBJECTIVES: To further the study and dissemination of knowledge concerning African affairs. To help support education for all people in Africa and for those of African descent outside Africa.

GENERAL INFORMATION: *Creation:* 1958. *Personnel/Total:* 9. *Salaried:* 9. *Budget/Total 1993:* ECU 2100269 (US$ 2460198). *Financial sources:* Private: 4%. Public: 96%.

PUBLICATIONS: *Annual report. List of publications.*

EVALUATION/RESEARCH: Evaluation reports available. Undertakes research activities.

PLANNED ACTIVITIES: Training programmes in Somaliland and establishing a Gender Studies Institute at the University of Cape Town. Surveying educational needs of women in Ethiopia and Eritrea.

ACTIVITIES IN DEVELOPING REGIONS: Works through local field partners. **Sustainable Development Actions:** Children/youth/family; Education/training/literacy; Gender issues/women; Sending volunteers/experts/technical assistance. **Regions:** Central Africa; East Africa; Southern Africa; West Africa.

INFORMATION AND EDUCATION ACTIVITIES: Topics: Children/youth/family; Education/training/literacy; Gender issues/women; Human rights/peace/conflicts; Other; Refugees/migrants/ethnic groups; Urban development/habitat. **Activities:** Conferences/seminars/workshops/training activities; Formal education; Fund raising; Information and documentation services/data bases; Lobbying/advocacy; Publishing/audiovisual materials/educational materials.

GBR2179
AFRICA INLAND MISSION INTERNATIONAL (AIM)

2 Vorley Road, London N19 5HE, United Kingdom.

Telephone: 44 (171) 281 1184. *Fax:* 44 (171) 281 4479. *Contact:* Rev. Timothy Alford, Secretary General.

OBJECTIVES: To take the gospel of Jesus Christ to people who have no viable church of their own. To help churches become more mature, especially by the training of national leaders. To demonstrate the love of Christ by various works of compassion.

GENERAL INFORMATION: *Creation:* 1895. *Personnel/Total:* 185. *Salaried:* 185 of which: 160 in developing countries. *Budget/Total 1993:* ECU 1846391 (US$ 2162812). *Financial sources:* Private: 100%.

PUBLICATIONS: *Periodicals:* AIM International (4).

ACTIVITIES IN DEVELOPING REGIONS: Present in developing regions. Active in 14 country(ies). Maintains local field presence. Works through local field partners. **Sustainable Development Actions:** Children/youth/family; Education/training/literacy; Emergency relief/refugees/humanitarian assistance; Health/sanitation/water; Other; Population/family planning/demography; Rural development/agriculture; Sending volunteers/experts/technical assistance; Small enterprises/informal sector/handicrafts; Urban development/habitat. **Regions:** East Africa.

GBR2180
AFRICA NOW

Bovis House, Townmead Road, London SW6 2RH, United Kingdom.

Telephone: 44 (171) 371 5603. *Fax:* 44 (171) 371 7104. *Contact:* Shala Kaussari, Executive Director.

OBJECTIVES: To respond to requests from local groups for financial and technical assistance. To support grassroot initiatives with a mixture of grants, low-interest loans, technical and management training. To create long-term income generating and employment opportunities. To encourage self-sufficiency.

GENERAL INFORMATION: *Creation:* 1982. *Affiliated to:* British Overseas NGOs for Development (United Kingdom) - EC-NGO Network. *Personnel/Total:* 8. *Salaried:* 6 of which: 2 in developing countries. *Volunteers:* 2 of which: 2 in developing countries. *Budget/Total 1993:* ECU 319272 (US$ 374000). *Financial sources:* Private: 70%. Public: 30%.

PUBLICATIONS: *Annual report.*

PLANNED ACTIVITIES: Concentrating on replication and expansion of enterprise development projects. Focusing on rural communities and women.

ACTIVITIES IN DEVELOPING REGIONS: Present in developing regions. Active in 4 country(ies). Maintains local field presence. Works through

Voir : *Comment utiliser le répertoire*, page 11.

local field partners. **Sustainable Development Actions:** Debt/finance/trade; Education/training/literacy; Food/famine; Gender issues/women; Health/sanitation/water; Population/family planning/demography; Rural development/agriculture; Sending volunteers/experts/technical assistance; Urban development/habitat. **Regions:** Central Africa; East Africa; West Africa.

INFORMATION AND EDUCATION ACTIVITIES: Topics: Children/youth/family; Education/training/literacy; Food/famine; Gender issues/women; Health/sanitation/water; Population/family planning/demography; Poverty/living conditions; Rural development/agriculture. **Activities:** Fund raising.

GBR2181

AFRICA RESOURCES TRUST   (ART)

The Old Lodge, Christchurch Road, Epsom, Surrey KT19 8NE, United Kingdom.

Telephone: 44 (1372) 741237. *Fax:* 44 (1372) 725604. *Contact:* K.A. Madders, Chief Executive Director.

OBJECTIVES: To help relieve poverty. To promote sustainable development. To advocate awareness education and training in husbanding natural resources. To collect, analyse and disseminate information regarding the work of governments and NGOs in the areas mentioned above.

GENERAL INFORMATION: *Creation:* 1991. *Affiliated to:* World Conservation Union - Campfire Collaborative Group (Zimbabwe) - Zimbabwe National Environment Trust (Zimbabwe) - Community Action Network - British Overseas NGOs for Development (United Kingdom) - Outreach Network. *Personnel/Total:* 14. *Salaried:* 11 of which: 11 in developing countries. *Volunteers:* 3. *Budget/Total 1993:* ECU 450058 (US$ 527000). *Financial sources:* Private: 80%. Public: 18%. Self-financing: 2%.

PUBLICATIONS: *Periodicals:* Action Magazine (3) - Research Papers (3). *Annual report. List of publications.*

EVALUATION/RESEARCH: Evaluation reports available. Undertakes research activities.

ACTIVITIES IN DEVELOPING REGIONS: Present in developing regions. Active in 8 country(ies). Maintains local field presence. Works through local field partners. **Sustainable Development Actions:** Children/youth/family; Democracy/good governance/institution building/participatory development; Ecology/environment/biodiversity; Education/training/literacy; Gender issues/women; Human rights/peace/conflicts; Other; Rural development/agriculture; Urban development/habitat. **Regions:** Southern Africa.

INFORMATION AND EDUCATION ACTIVITIES: Topics: Children/youth/family; Culture/tradition/religion; Ecology/environment/biodiversity; Education/training/literacy; Food/famine; Gender issues/women; Health/sanitation/water; Human rights/peace/conflicts; Other; Population/family planning/demography; Poverty/living conditions; Rural development/agriculture; Urban development/habitat. **Activities:** Conferences/seminars/workshops/training activities; Exchanges/twinning/linking; Formal education; Fund raising; Information campaigns/exhibitions; Lobbying/advocacy; Networking/electronic telecommunications; Publishing/audiovisual materials/educational materials.

GBR2182

AFRICA WOMEN'S SUPPORT GROUP

Southwark Training Centre, Copperfield Street, London SE1 OEN, United Kingdom.

Contact: Mary Alhassan.

GBR2183

AFRICAN MEDICAL AND RESEARCH FOUNDATION - UNITED KINGDOM   (AMREF UK)

2nd Floor, 8 Bourdon Street, London W1X 9HX, United Kingdom.

Telephone: 44 (171) 409 32 30. *Fax:* 44 (171) 629 20 06. *Contact:* Alexander Heroys, Director.

OBJECTIVES: To support primary health care actions in Africa.

GENERAL INFORMATION: *Creation:* 1967. *Type of organisation:* association of NGOs. *Member organisations:* 13. *Personnel/Total:* 3. *Salaried:* 3. *Budget/Total 1993:* ECU 64000 (US$ 571000). *Financial sources:* Private: 75%. Public: 20%. Self-financing: 5%.

PUBLICATIONS: *Periodicals:* Educational Publications. *Annual report. List of publications.*

EVALUATION/RESEARCH: Evaluation reports available. Undertakes research activities.

ACTIVITIES IN DEVELOPING REGIONS: Present in developing regions. Active in 20 country(ies). Maintains local field presence. Works through local field partners. **Sustainable Development Actions:** Children/youth/family; Education/training/literacy; Emergency relief/refugees/humanitarian assistance; Gender issues/women; Health/sanitation/water; Population/family planning/demography; Sending volunteers/experts/technical assistance; Small enterprises/informal sector/handicrafts. **Regions:** Central Africa; East Africa; Southern Africa; West Africa.

INFORMATION AND EDUCATION ACTIVITIES: Topics: Children/youth/family; Emergency relief/refugees/humanitarian assistance; Gender issues/women; Health/sanitation/water; Population/family planning/demography. **Activities:** Conferences/seminars/workshops/training activities; Fund raising; Publishing/audiovisual materials/educational materials.

GBR2184

AFRICAN REFUGEE HOUSING ACTION GROUP   (ARHAG)

25 Leighton Road, St. Margarets, Kentish Town, London NW5 2QD, United Kingdom.

Telephone: 44 (171) 482 3829. *Contact:* Ronnie Moodley, Director.

GBR2185

AFRICAN SOCIETY OF INTERNATIONAL AND COMPARATIVE LAW

Aberdeen House, 22 Highbury Grove, London N5 2EA, United Kingdom.

Telephone: 44 (171) 704 0610. *Fax:* 44 (171) 704 0973. *Contact:* Emile Yakpo, Secretary General.

OBJECTIVES: To educate the public on civil liberties. To provide each African country with comprehensive legal aid systems. To organise workshops for law enforcement of civil liberties. To promote the African contribution to the development of International Law.

GENERAL INFORMATION: *Creation:* 1986. *Type of organisation:* coordinating body. *Member organisations:* 15. *Personnel/Total:* 15. *Salaried:* 5 of which: 3 in developing countries. *Volunteers:* 10 of which: 6 in developing countries. *Budget/Total 1993:* ECU 232081 (US$ 272000). *Financial sources:* Private: 75%. Public: 5%. Self-financing: 20%.

PUBLICATIONS: *Periodicals:* African Journal of International and Comparative Law (4) - Proceedings of Annual Conferences (1). *Annual report. List of publications.*

EVALUATION/RESEARCH: Evaluation reports available. Undertakes research activities.

PLANNED ACTIVITIES: Establishing of an "African Research Library", an African Academy of International Law and a School for Diplomacy.

ACTIVITIES IN DEVELOPING REGIONS: Present in developing regions. Active in 54 country(ies). Maintains local field presence. Works through local field partners. **Sustainable Development Actions:** Children/youth/family; Debt/finance/trade; Democracy/good governance/institution building/participatory development; Ecology/environment/biodiversity; Education/training/literacy; Emergency relief/refugees/humanitarian assistance; Energy/transport; Gender issues/women; Health/sanitation/water; Human rights/peace/conflicts; Population/family planning/demography; Rural development/agriculture; Sending volunteers/experts/technical assistance; Small enterprises/informal sector/handicrafts; Urban development/habitat. **Regions:** Central Africa; East Africa; North Africa; Southern Africa; West Africa.

INFORMATION AND EDUCATION ACTIVITIES: Topics: Children/youth/family; Culture/tradition/religion; Ecology/environment/biodiversity; Education/training/literacy; Emergency relief/refugees/humanitarian assis-

See: *How to Use the Directory*, page 11.

tance; Employment/unemployment; Food/famine; Gender issues/women; Health/sanitation/water; Human rights/peace/conflicts; International economic relations/trade/debt/finance; International relations/cooperation/development aid; Other; Peace/ethnic conflicts/armament/disarmament; Population/family planning/demography; Poverty/living conditions; Racism/xenophobia/antisemitism; Refugees/migrants/ethnic groups; Rural development/agriculture; Urban development/habitat. **Activities:** Broadcasting/cultural events; Conferences/seminars/workshops/training activities; Formal education; Fund raising; Information and documentation services/data bases; Lobbying/advocacy; Publishing/audiovisual materials/educational materials.

GBR2186

AGA KHAN FOUNDATION (AKF-UK)

33 Thurloe Square, London SW7 2SD, United Kingdom.

Telephone: 44 (171) 225 2001. *Fax:* 44 (171) 589 0641. *Contact:* Firoze Manji, Chief Executive Officer.

OBJECTIVES: To promote social development, primarily in low income countries of Asia and Africa by funding programmes in health, education and rural development. To select grantees and beneficiaries regardless of race, religion or political persuasion.

GENERAL INFORMATION: *Creation:* 1973. *Affiliated to:* UK NGO Education Forum - British Overseas NGOs for Development - UK NGO/EC Network. *Personnel/Total:* 10. *Salaried:* 7. *Volunteers:* 3. *Budget/Total 1993:* ECU 4872420 (US$ 5707000). *Financial sources:* Private: 20%. *Public:* 80%.

PUBLICATIONS: *Periodicals:* AKF Information Bulletin (1) - AKF Annual Review (1). *Annual report. List of publications.*

EVALUATION/RESEARCH: Evaluation reports available. Undertakes research activities.

COMMENTS: Undertakes activities in the Commonwealth of Independent States. Information activities related to the Commonwealth of Independent States.

ACTIVITIES IN DEVELOPING REGIONS: Present in developing regions. Active in 7 country(ies). Maintains local field presence. Works through local field partners. **Sustainable Development Actions:** Children/youth/family; Democracy/good governance/institution building/participatory development; Ecology/environment/biodiversity; Education/training/literacy; Emergency relief/refugees/humanitarian assistance; Energy/transport; Food/famine; Gender issues/women; Health/sanitation/water; Rural development/agriculture; Sending volunteers/experts/technical assistance; Small enterprises/informal sector/handicrafts. **Regions:** Central Asia and South Asia; East Africa.

INFORMATION AND EDUCATION ACTIVITIES: Topics: Children/youth/family; Culture/tradition/religion; Ecology/environment/biodiversity; Education/training/literacy; Emergency relief/refugees/humanitarian assistance; Food/famine; Gender issues/women; Health/sanitation/water; International relations/cooperation/development aid; Poverty/living conditions; Racism/xenophobia/antisemitism; Refugees/migrants/ethnic groups; Rural development/agriculture. **Activities:** Broadcasting/cultural events; Conferences/seminars/workshops/training activities; Exchanges/twinning/linking; Formal education; Fund raising; Information campaigns/exhibitions; Lobbying/advocacy; Publishing/audiovisual materials/educational materials.

GBR2187

AGENCY FOR CO-OPERATION AND RESEARCH IN DEVELOPMENT (ACORD)

Francis House (3rd Floor), Francis Street, London SW1P 1DQ, United Kingdom.

Telephone: 44 (171) 828 7611. *Fax:* 44 (171) 976 6113. *E-mail:* ACORD@GN.APC.ORG. *Contact:* Idriss Jazairy, Executive Director.

OBJECTIVES: To respond to development needs, when collective action is deemed appropriate, in the most marginalised parts of Africa. To facilitate the emergence of non-governmental organisational structures or to strengthen those structures that are weak.

GENERAL INFORMATION: *Creation:* 1976. *Type of organisation:* association of NGOs. *Member organisations:* 13. *Personnel/Total:* 575. *Salaried:* 575 of which: 550 in developing countries. *Budget/*

Total 1993: ECU 9916656 (US$ 11616000). *Financial sources:* Private: 65%. *Public:* 35%.

PUBLICATIONS: *Annual report.*

EVALUATION/RESEARCH: Evaluation reports available. Undertakes research activities.

ACTIVITIES IN DEVELOPING REGIONS: Present in developing regions. Active in 15 country(ies). Maintains local field presence. **Sustainable Development Actions:** Ecology/environment/biodiversity; Education/training/literacy; Emergency relief/refugees/humanitarian assistance; Gender issues/women; Health/sanitation/water; Rural development/agriculture; Small enterprises/informal sector/handicrafts; Urban development/habitat. **Regions:** Central Africa; East Africa; Southern Africa; West Africa.

GBR2188

AID FOR DESTITUTE VICTIMS OF OPPRESSION (ADVO)

330 Copley Close, Hanwell, London W7 1QF, United Kingdom.

Telephone: 44 (181) 575 6591. *Contact:* Matilda Nantogmah, Director.

GBR2189

AKINA MAMA WA AFRIKA ♦ London's Women's Centre

4 Wild Course, Wesley House, London WC2B 5AU, United Kingdom.

Telephone: 44 (171) 405 0678. *Fax:* 44 (171) 831 3947.

GBR2190

THE AKLETON TRUST

Coulnakyle, Nethy Bridge, Inverness-shire PH25 3EA, United Kingdom.

Telephone: 44 (1479) 821393. *Fax:* 44 (1479) 821441. *E-mail:* jbryden@.aberdeen.ac.uk. *Contact:* John M. Bryden, Programme Director.

OBJECTIVES: To study new approaches to rural development and education. To improve understanding between-policy makers, researchers and practitioners.

GENERAL INFORMATION: *Creation:* 1977. *Type of organisation:* network. *Affiliated to:* EADI (Switzerland) - EAAE (The Netherlands) - AARG (Canada) - CRRF (Canada) -REAPER. *Personnel/Total:* 8. *Salaried:* 5. *Volunteers:* 3 of which: 3 in developing countries. *Budget/Total 1993:* ECU 256443 (US$ 300000). *Financial sources:* Private: 10%. *Public:* 80%. *Self-financing:* 10%.

PUBLICATIONS: *Periodicals:* Newsletter (1). *List of publications.*

EVALUATION/RESEARCH: Undertakes research activities.

PLANNED ACTIVITIES: Planning the creation of two networks of rural social scientists. Holding a seminar on rural development and the Information Highway.

ACTIVITIES IN DEVELOPING REGIONS: Active in 2 country(ies). Works through local field partners. **Sustainable Development Actions:** Rural development/agriculture. **Regions:** Central Africa; Central Asia and South Asia; East Africa; Mexico and Central America; South America; Southern Africa; West Africa.

INFORMATION AND EDUCATION ACTIVITIES: Topics: Rural development/agriculture. **Activities:** Conferences/seminars/workshops/training activities; Exchanges/twinning/linking; Fund raising; Information and documentation services/data bases; Networking/electronic telecommunications; Other; Publishing/audiovisual materials/educational materials.

GBR2191

ALTERNATIVE FOR INDIA DEVELOPMENT

Laurel Works, Laurel Road, Handsworth, Birmingham B21 9PG, United Kingdom.

Contact: Ravi Kumar.

GBR2192

AMANI CHRISTIAN COMMUNITY

33 Cornwallis Road, Oxford OX4 3NW, United Kingdom.

Contact: Isabel Allen.

GBR2193

AMNESTY INTERNATIONAL, BRITISH SECTION (AI)

1 Easton Street, London WC1X 8DJ, United Kingdom.

Telephone: 44 (171) 413 5500. *Fax:* 44 (171) 956 1157. *E-mail:* (GreenNet)amnestyis@gn.apc.org. *Contact:* Pierre Sané, Secretary General.

OBJECTIVES: To campaign for freedom for all prisoners of conscience, fair and prompt trials for political prisoners, and the abolition of the death penalty and other cruel treatment of prisoners. To oppose abuses by opposition groups and arbitrary killings.

GENERAL INFORMATION: *Creation:* 1961. *Personnel/Total:* 350. *Salaried:* 280. *Volunteers:* 70. *Budget/Total 1993:* ECU 16355558 (US$ 19158000).

PUBLICATIONS: *Periodicals:* Amnesty International Newsletter (12). *Annual report. List of publications.*

EVALUATION/RESEARCH: Undertakes research activities.

COMMENTS: Undertakes activities in the Commonwealth of Independent States. Information activities related to the Commonwealth of Independent States.

ACTIVITIES IN DEVELOPING REGIONS: Present in developing regions. Maintains local field presence. Works through local field partners. **Sustainable Development Actions:** Human rights/peace/conflicts. **Regions:** Caribbean; Central Africa; Central Asia and South Asia; East Africa; East Asia; Mexico and Central America; Middle East; North Africa; Oceania; South America; South East Asia; Southern Africa; West Africa.

INFORMATION AND EDUCATION ACTIVITIES: Topics: Human rights/peace/conflicts; Refugees/migrants/ethnic groups. **Activities:** Broadcasting/cultural events; Conferences/seminars/workshops/training activities; Formal education; Fund raising; Information and documentation services/data bases; Information campaigns/exhibitions; Lobbying/advocacy; Networking/electronic telecommunications; Other; Publishing/audiovisual materials/educational materials.

GBR2194

ANTI-RACIST ALLIANCE

P.O. Box 150, London WC1X 9NQ, United Kingdom.

Telephone: 44 (171) 278 6869. *Fax:* 44 (171) 278 6886. *Contact:* Marc Wadsworth, National Secretary.

OBJECTIVES: To fight against racism, anti-semitism and fascism.

GENERAL INFORMATION: *Creation:* 1991. *Personnel/Total:* 8. *Salaried:* 4. *Volunteers:* 4. *Budget/Total 1993:* ECU 128222 (US$ 150000). *Financial sources:* Private: 30%. Self-financing: 70%.

PUBLICATIONS: *Annual report. List of publications.*

EVALUATION/RESEARCH: Evaluation reports available. Undertakes research activities.

PLANNED ACTIVITIES: Campaign for asylum rights and for new legislation to make racial harassment a specific criminal offence. Campaign for the closing down of racist and fascist organisations.

COMMENTS: The ARA has actitivies in Britain and Europe only. Undertakes activities in the Commonwealth of Independent States. Information activities related to the Commonwealth of Independent States.

INFORMATION AND EDUCATION ACTIVITIES: Topics: Children/youth/family; Culture/tradition/religion; Gender issues/women; Human rights/peace/conflicts; Racism/xenophobia/antisemitism; Refugees/migrants/ethnic groups. **Activities:** Broadcasting/cultural events; Conferences/seminars/workshops/training activities; Formal education; Fund raising; Information and documentation services/data bases; Information campaigns/exhibitions; Lobbying/advocacy; Other; Publishing/audiovisual materials/educational materials.

GBR2195

ANTI-SLAVERY INTERNATIONAL (ASI)

The Stableyard, Broomgrove Road, London SW9 9TL, United Kingdom.

Telephone: 44 (171) 924 9555. *Fax:* 44 (171) 738 4110. *Contact:* Lesley Roberts, Director.

OBJECTIVES: To work for the abolition of all forms of slavery, slave trade and all forms of forced labour, and the protection and advancement of peoples and groups who are not strong enough to protect themselves.

GENERAL INFORMATION: *Creation:* 1839. *Affiliated to:* Human Rights Fund for Indigenous Peoples (United Kingdom) - European Alliance with Indigenous Peoples (Belgium) - Coalition on Child Prostitution and Tourism (United Kingdom). *Personnel/Total:* 16. *Salaried:* 8. *Volunteers:* 8. *Budget/Total 1993:* ECU 333376 (US$ 391000). *Financial sources:* Private: 63%. Public: 12%. Self-financing: 25%.

PUBLICATIONS: *Periodicals:* Anti-Slavery Newsletter (3) - Anti-Slavery Reporter (1). *Annual report. List of publications.*

EVALUATION/RESEARCH: Evaluation reports available. Undertakes research activities.

PLANNED ACTIVITIES: Research, lobbying and campaign on children working as domestic servants. Research and awareness raising on servile forms of marriage, particularly child marriage.

ACTIVITIES IN DEVELOPING REGIONS: Sustainable Development Actions: Debt/finance/trade; Human rights/peace/conflicts. **Regions:** Central Africa; Central Asia and South Asia; Mexico and Central America; North Africa; South America; South East Asia; Southern Africa; West Africa.

INFORMATION AND EDUCATION ACTIVITIES: Topics: Children/youth/family; Gender issues/women; Human rights/peace/conflicts; International economic relations/trade/debt/finance. **Activities:** Conferences/seminars/workshops/training activities; Information and documentation services/data bases; Information campaigns/exhibitions; Lobbying/advocacy; Publishing/audiovisual materials/educational materials.

GBR2196

APPROPRIATE HEALTH RESOURCES AND TECHNOLOGIES ACTION GROUP (AHRTAG)

1 London Bridge Street, London SEI 9SG, United Kingdom.

Telephone: 44 (171) 378 1403 . *Fax:* 44 (171) 403 6003. *Contact:* Kathy Attawell, Abdul Jetha, Suzanne Fustukian, Co-Directors.

OBJECTIVES: To promote information sharing and awareness building as a strategy for expanding the support base for primary health care in developing countries. To provide technical support and resources to organisations in developing countries involved in health.

GENERAL INFORMATION: *Creation:* 1977. *Affiliated to:* UK NGO AIDS Consortium - EC NGO Network - Hand in Hand Network - British Overseas NGOs for Development (United Kingdom) - Consortium for Street Youth (United Kingdom) - Health and Environment in the Cities - European Association of Development Institutions. *Personnel/Total:* 25. *Salaried:* 25. *Financial sources:* Public: 100%.

PUBLICATIONS: *Annual report. List of publications.*

EVALUATION/RESEARCH: Undertakes research activities.

ACTIVITIES IN DEVELOPING REGIONS: Works through local field partners. **Sustainable Development Actions:** Health/sanitation/water. **Regions:** Caribbean; Central Africa; Central Asia and South Asia; East Africa; East Asia; Mexico and Central America; Middle East; North Africa; South America; South East Asia; Southern Africa; West Africa.

INFORMATION AND EDUCATION ACTIVITIES: Topics: Health/sanitation/water. **Activities:** Conferences/seminars/workshops/training activities; Information and documentation services/data bases; Publishing/audiovisual materials/educational materials.

GBR2197

APPROPRIATE TECHNOLOGY FOR TIBETANS TRUST (APTT)

6 Rockhall Road, London NW2 6DT, United Kingdom.

Telephone: 44 (181) 452 2820. *Fax:* 44 (181) 450 9705. *Contact:* Greta Jensen, Executive Director.

OBJECTIVES: To assist Tibetan refugees in India and, where appropriate, the local communities, with projects to facilitate sustainable develop-

                                    See: *How to Use the Directory,* page 11.

ment. To build skills and capabilities within the Tibetan refugee community and promote the principles of ecological development and the use of appropriate technologies.

GENERAL INFORMATION: *Creation:* 1984. *Affiliated to:* British Overseas NGOs for Development (United Kingdom) - EC-NGO Network. *Personnel/Total:* 4. *Salaried:* 2. *Volunteers:* 2 of which: 1 in developing countries. *Budget/Total 1993:* ECU 125657 (US$ 147000). *Financial sources:* Private: 20%. Public: 70%. *Self-financing:* 10%.

PUBLICATIONS: *Periodicals:* APTT Newsletter (1).

EVALUATION/RESEARCH: Evaluation reports available. Undertakes research activities.

PLANNED ACTIVITIES: Strengthening co-operation between Tibetan and local Indian communities. Furthering awareness of gender issues. Developing a women's training project. Producing an educational documentary on the situation of Tibetan refugees.

ACTIVITIES IN DEVELOPING REGIONS: Present in developing regions. Active in 1 country(ies). Maintains local field presence. Works through local field partners. **Sustainable Development Actions:** Children/youth/family; Democracy/good governance/institution building/participatory development; Ecology/environment/biodiversity; Education/training/literacy; Emergency relief/refugees/humanitarian assistance; Energy/transport; Gender issues/women; Health/sanitation/water; Rural development/agriculture; Sending volunteers/experts/technical assistance; Small enterprises/informal sector/handicrafts; Urban development/habitat. **Regions:** Central Asia and South Asia.

INFORMATION AND EDUCATION ACTIVITIES: Topics: Children/youth/family; Culture/tradition/religion; Ecology/environment/biodiversity; Education/training/literacy; Emergency relief/refugees/humanitarian assistance; Employment/unemployment; Gender issues/women; Health/sanitation/water; Poverty/living conditions; Refugees/migrants/ethnic groups; Rural development/agriculture; Urban development/habitat. **Activities:** Conferences/seminars/workshops/training activities; Fund raising; Information and documentation services/data bases.

GBR2198
APT DESIGN AND DEVELOPMENT

29 Northwick Business Centre, Moreton-in-Marsh GL56 9RF, Gloucestershire, United Kingdom.

Telephone: 44 (1386) 700130. *Fax:* 44 (1386) 701010. *Contact:* Michael Walsby, Chief Executive.

OBJECTIVES: To help alleviate poverty and promote the growth of local economies in less developed countries, by providing specialist support for the training and development of small-scale enterprises.

GENERAL INFORMATION: *Creation:* 1984. *Affiliated to:* Liaison Committee of Development NGOs to the European Communities - British Overseas NGOs for Development (United Kingdom). *Personnel/Total:* 25. *Salaried:* 25 of which: 19 in developing countries. *Budget/Total 1993:* ECU 769329 (US$ 901000). *Financial sources:* Private: 28%. Public: 70%. *Self-financing:* 2%.

PUBLICATIONS: *Annual report. List of publications.*

EVALUATION/RESEARCH: Undertakes research activities.

COMMENTS: APT is affiliated with over 600 professionals, who are skilled and experienced in all areas of Small Enterprise Development. Undertakes activities in the Commonwealth of Independent States. Information activities related to the Commonwealth of Independent States.

ACTIVITIES IN DEVELOPING REGIONS: Present in developing regions. Active in 8 country(ies). Maintains local field presence. Works through local field partners. **Sustainable Development Actions:** Democracy/good governance/institution building/participatory development; Education/training/literacy; Gender issues/women; Rural development/agriculture; Sending volunteers/experts/technical assistance; Small enterprises/informal sector/handicrafts; Urban development/habitat. **Regions:** Caribbean; East Africa; South East Asia; Southern Africa; West Africa.

INFORMATION AND EDUCATION ACTIVITIES: Topics: Other. **Activities:** Fund raising; Publishing/audiovisual materials/educational materials.

GBR2199
ARTICLE 19, THE INTERNATIONAL CENTRE AGAINST CENSORSHIP

Lancaster House, 33 Islington High Street, London N1 9HL, United Kingdom.

Telephone: 44 (171) 278 9292. *Fax:* 44 (171) 713 1356. *Contact:* Frances D'Souza, Executive Director.

OBJECTIVES: To promote the right to freedom of expression and to defend victims of censorship worldwide through publication campaigns and education.

GENERAL INFORMATION: *Creation:* 1986. *Personnel/Total:* 12. *Salaried:* 12. *Volunteers:* 6.

PUBLICATIONS: *Periodicals:* The Article 19 Bulletin (3) - Censorship News Series (10). *List of publications.*

EVALUATION/RESEARCH: Undertakes research activities.

COMMENTS: Undertakes activities in the Commonwealth of Independent States. Information activities related to the Commonwealth of Independent States.

ACTIVITIES IN DEVELOPING REGIONS: Active in 15 country(ies). Works through local field partners. **Sustainable Development Actions:** Democracy/good governance/institution building/participatory development; Gender issues/women; Human rights/peace/conflicts; Population/family planning/demography. **Regions:** Central Africa; East Africa; East Asia; Mexico and Central America; Middle East; North Africa; South East Asia; Southern Africa.

INFORMATION AND EDUCATION ACTIVITIES: Topics: Gender issues/women; Human rights/peace/conflicts; Population/family planning/demography. **Activities:** Conferences/seminars/workshops/training activities; Exchanges/twinning/linking; Formal education; Information and documentation services/data bases; Information campaigns/exhibitions; Lobbying/advocacy; Networking/electronic telecommunications; Publishing/audiovisual materials/educational materials.

GBR2200
ARTISAN TRUST

The Ford, North Hinksey Village, Oxford OX2 6HU, United Kingdom.

Contact: John Pirie.

GBR2201
ASHOKA UK TRUST

7th Floor, Windsor House, 83 Kingsway, London WC2B 6SD, United Kingdom.

Telephone: 44 (171) 405 3477. *Fax:* 44 (171) 240 0503. *Contact:* Susan H. Gillie, Chairman of the Trustees.

OBJECTIVES: To enable Third World "social entrepreneurs" to develop their own projects to a level where they can attract funding according to the standards set by Ashoka.

GENERAL INFORMATION: *Creation:* 1989. *Personnel/Total:* 8. *Volunteers:* 8. *Budget/Total 1993:* ECU 230800 (US$ 270000). *Financial sources:* Private: 100%.

PUBLICATIONS: *Annual report.*

COMMENTS: Undertakes activities in the Commonwealth of Independent States.

ACTIVITIES IN DEVELOPING REGIONS: Works through local field partners. **Sustainable Development Actions:** Children/youth/family; Debt/finance/trade; Democracy/good governance/institution building/participatory development; Ecology/environment/biodiversity; Education/training/literacy; Energy/transport; Gender issues/women; Health/sanitation/water; Human rights/peace/conflicts; Rural development/agriculture; Small enterprises/informal sector/handicrafts; Urban development/habitat. **Regions:** Central Asia and South Asia; Mexico and Central America; South America; South East Asia; Southern Africa; West Africa.

INFORMATION AND EDUCATION ACTIVITIES: Topics: Children/youth/family; Culture/tradition/religion; Ecology/environment/biodiversity; Education/training/literacy; Gender issues/women; Health/sanitation/water; Human rights/peace/conflicts; Peace/ethnic conflicts/armament/dis-

armament; Poverty/living conditions; Racism/xenophobia/antisemitism; Rural development/agriculture; Urban development/habitat. **Activities:** Fund raising.

GBR2202

ASSOCIATED COUNTRY WOMEN OF THE WORLD (ACWW) ♦
Union mondiale des femmes rurales

Vincent House, Vincent Square, London SW1P 2NB, United Kingdom.

Telephone: 44 (171) 834 8635. *Contact:* Valerie Fisher, World President.

OBJECTIVES: To improve the conditions of rural women and raise the standard of living of women and their families all over the world. To work together to relieve poverty and promote education for the preservation of health.

GENERAL INFORMATION: *Creation:* 1930. *Type of organisation:* coordinating body. *Member organisations:* 500. *Personnel/Total:* 9. *Salaried:* 9. *Budget/Total 1993:* ECU 437236 (US$ 512000). *Financial sources:* Private: 74%. Self-financing: 26%.

PUBLICATIONS: *Periodicals:* The Country Woman (4). *Annual report.*

COMMENTS: ACWW is an umbrella organisation. Undertakes activities in the Commonwealth of Independent States. Information activities related to the Commonwealth of Independent States.

ACTIVITIES IN DEVELOPING REGIONS: Active in 18 country(ies). Works through local field partners. **Sustainable Development Actions:** Children/youth/family; Education/training/literacy; Health/sanitation/water; Population/family planning/demography; Rural development/agriculture; Small enterprises/informal sector/handicrafts. **Regions:** Central Africa; Central Asia and South Asia; East Africa; East Asia; Mexico and Central America; Oceania; South America; South East Asia; Southern Africa; West Africa.

INFORMATION AND EDUCATION ACTIVITIES: **Topics:** Children/youth/family; Ecology/environment/biodiversity; Education/training/literacy; Food/famine; Gender issues/women; Health/sanitation/water; Human rights/peace/conflicts; Population/family planning/demography; Poverty/living conditions; Rural development/agriculture. **Activities:** Conferences/seminars/workshops/training activities; Lobbying/advocacy.

GBR2203

ASSOCIATED HOUSING ADVISORY SERVICES FOR ALTERNATIVES IN HOUSING FOR ANOTHER SOCIETY (AHAS)

51 St. Mary's Terrace, West Hill, Shastings, East Sussex TN34 3LR, United Kingdom.

Contact: John Turner.

GBR2204

ASSOCIATION OF UNGANDAN YOUTH AND STUDENTS

23 Bevenden Street, London N1 6BH, United Kingdom.

Telephone: 44 (171) 253 4186.

GBR2205

BABY MILK ACTION

23 St. Andrews Street, Cambridge CB2 3AX, United Kingdom.

Telephone: 44 (1223) 464420. *Fax:* 44 (1223) 464417. *Contact:* Patti Rundall, International Co-ordinator.

OBJECTIVES: To halt the commercial promotion of bottle feeding and to promote good and appropriate infant nutrition.

GENERAL INFORMATION: *Creation:* 1979. *Affiliated to:* International Baby Food Action Network (Switzerland). *Personnel/Total:* 137. *Salaried:* 7. *Volunteers:* 130. *Budget/Total 1993:* ECU 184639 (US$ 216281). *Financial sources:* Private: 33%. Public: 33%. Self-financing: 33%.

PUBLICATIONS: *Periodicals:* Baby Milk Action 'Update' (4). *Annual report. List of publications.*

COMMENTS: Baby Milk Action is a member of 140 groups in over 70 countries. Information activities related to the Commonwealth of Independent States.

INFORMATION AND EDUCATION ACTIVITIES: **Topics:** Food/famine; Gender issues/women; Health/sanitation/water. **Activities:** Conferences/seminars/workshops/training activities; Information and documentation services/data bases; Information campaigns/exhibitions; Lobbying/advocacy; Networking/electronic telecommunications; Publishing/audiovisual materials/educational materials.

GBR2206

BAM

8 St. Michael's Road, London SW9 0SL, United Kingdom.

Contact: Richard Kemball-Cook.

GBR2207

BERTRAND RUSSELL PEACE FOUNDATION

Bertrand Russell House, Gamble Street, Nottingham NG7 4ET, United Kingdom.

GBR2208

BICTIN OVERSEAS AGRICULTURAL TRUST

Middle Woodbeer Farm, Plymptee, Cullompton, Devon EX15 2LN, United Kingdom.

Contact: Bill Vellacott.

GBR2209

BIRMINGHAM ONE WORLD COMMITTEE

One World Desk, Carrs Lane Church Centre, Birmingham B4 7SX, United Kingdom.

Telephone: 44 (21) 643 2249.

GBR2210

BOOK AID INTERNATIONAL (RLS)

39-41 Coldharbour Lane, Camberwell, London SE5 9NR, United Kingdom.

Telephone: 44 (171) 733 3577. *Fax:* 44 (171) 978 8006. *E-mail:* rls@gn.apc.org. *Contact:* Sara Harrity, Director.

OBJECTIVES: To support education and literacy programmes, mainly in developing countries, through the provision of appropriate books. To strengthen publishing in Africa through the purchase and distribution of locally published books.

GENERAL INFORMATION: *Creation:* 1953. *Affiliated to:* UK NGO AIDS Consortium (United Kingdom) - International Debt Crisis Network - BOND. *Personnel/Total:* 37. *Salaried:* 22. *Volunteers:* 15. *Budget/Total 1993:* ECU 769000 (US$ 900000). *Financial sources:* Private: 85%. Public: 15%.

PUBLICATIONS: *Annual report.*

EVALUATION/RESEARCH: Undertakes research activities.

COMMENTS: Undertakes activities in the Commonwealth of Independent States.

ACTIVITIES IN DEVELOPING REGIONS: Present in developing regions. Active in 72 country(ies). Works through local field partners. **Sustainable Development Actions:** Education/training/literacy. **Regions:** Caribbean; Central Africa; Central Asia and South Asia; East Africa; East Asia; North Africa; Oceania; South East Asia; Southern Africa; West Africa.

INFORMATION AND EDUCATION ACTIVITIES: **Topics:** Education/training/literacy. **Activities:** Fund raising; Information campaigns/exhibitions; Lobbying/advocacy.

GBR2211

BOY'S BRIGADE

Church House, Fisherwick Place, Belfast NR6 5NU, United Kingdom.

Contact: Stewart Mccullough.

See: *How to Use the Directory*, page 11.

GBR2212
BRIDGE PROGRAMME OF OXFAM TRADING

274 Murdock Road, Bicestor Oxon OX6 7RF, United Kingdom.

Telephone: 44 (1869) 245011. *Fax:* 44 (1869) 247987.

OBJECTIVES: To improve the lives of Third World producers by marketing their crafts. To promote the small industry sectors in developing countries, providing employment and increasing incomes by buying directly from producers.

GENERAL INFORMATION: *Creation:* 1975. *Affiliated to:* European Fair Trade association - International Federation for Alternative Trade (United States). *Personnel/Total:* var.. *Salaried:* 32 of which: 16 in developing countries. *Volunteers:* var.. *Budget/Total 1993:* ECU 468000 (US$ 548000). *Financial sources:* Private: 1%. Self-financing: 99%.

PUBLICATIONS: *Periodicals:* Bridge News (3). *Annual report. List of publications.*

EVALUATION/RESEARCH: Evaluation reports available. Undertakes research activities.

ACTIVITIES IN DEVELOPING REGIONS: Present in developing regions. Active in 38 country(ies). Maintains local field presence. Works through local field partners. **Sustainable Development Actions:** Debt/finance/trade; Democracy/good governance/institution building/participatory development; Education/training/literacy; Gender issues/women; Sending volunteers/experts/technical assistance; Small enterprises/informal sector/handicrafts. **Regions:** Caribbean; Central Asia and South Asia; East Africa; Mexico and Central America; South America; South East Asia; Southern Africa.

GBR2213
BRITAIN - NEPAL MEDICAL TRUST (BNMT)

16 East Street, Tonbridge, Kent TN9 1HG, United Kingdom.

Telephone: 44 (1732) 360284. *Fax:* 44 (1732) 363876. *Contact:* I.A. Baker, Chairman.

OBJECTIVES: To help the people of Nepal improve their health. To assist the government with its health delivery services through the training of health workers, the provision of essential drugs and supply of materials.

GENERAL INFORMATION: *Creation:* 1968. *Affiliated to:* British Overseas NGOs for Development (United Kingdom). *Personnel/Total:* 153. *Salaried:* 153 of which: 151 in developing countries. *Budget/Total 1993:* ECU 589000 (US$ 689000). *Financial sources:* Private: 19%. Public: 63%. Self-financing: 18%.

PUBLICATIONS: *Annual report. List of publications.*

PLANNED ACTIVITIES: Evaluation of the effectiveness of different types of drug schemes, short-course chemotherapy for the treatment of TB in Nepal and of microscopy camps for the identification of TB sufferers. To work with the government of Nepal to develop an effective national TB programme.

ACTIVITIES IN DEVELOPING REGIONS: Present in developing regions. Active in 1 country(ies). Maintains local field presence. Works through local field partners. **Sustainable Development Actions:** Democracy/good governance/institution building/participatory development; Education/training/literacy; Gender issues/women; Health/sanitation/water; Rural development/agriculture; Sending volunteers/experts/technical assistance. **Regions:** Central Asia and South Asia.

INFORMATION AND EDUCATION ACTIVITIES: Topics: Education/training/literacy; Emergency relief/refugees/humanitarian assistance; Gender issues/women; Health/sanitation/water; Rural development/agriculture. **Activities:** Conferences/seminars/workshops/training activities; Fund raising; Networking/electronic telecommunications.

GBR2214
BRITAIN TANZANIA SOCIETY (BTS UK)

13 Highfield Drive, Uxbridge, Middlesex UB10 8AL, United Kingdom.

Telephone: 44 (1895) 235983. *Contact:* Trevor Jaggar, Secretary.

OBJECTIVES: To increase mutual knowledge, understanding and respect between the citizens of Tanzania and the United Kingdom.

GENERAL INFORMATION: *Creation:* 1975. *Type of organisation:* association of NGOs. *Budget/Total 1993:* ECU 44000 (US$ 52000). *Financial sources:* Private: 60%. Public: 40%.

PUBLICATIONS: *Periodicals:* Bulletin of Tanzanian Affairs (3). *Annual report.*

ACTIVITIES IN DEVELOPING REGIONS: Active in 1 country(ies). Works through local field partners. **Sustainable Development Actions:** Education/training/literacy; Energy/transport; Health/sanitation/water; Rural development/agriculture; Small enterprises/informal sector/handicrafts; Urban development/habitat. **Regions:** East Africa.

INFORMATION AND EDUCATION ACTIVITIES: Topics: Culture/tradition/religion; Ecology/environment/biodiversity; Education/training/literacy; Health/sanitation/water; International economic relations/trade/debt/finance; International relations/cooperation/development aid; Poverty/living conditions; Rural development/agriculture; Urban development/habitat. **Activities:** Conferences/seminars/workshops/training activities; Exchanges/twinning/linking; Lobbying/advocacy.

GBR2215
BRITISH AFRO-ASIAN SOLIDARITY ORGANIZATION

9 Galveston Road, London SW15 2RZ, United Kingdom.

Telephone: 44 (181) 788 7706. *Fax:* 44 (181) 789 6503. *Contact:* Mohammed Arif.

OBJECTIVES: To develop solidarity with the people of Asia, Africa and Latin America. To campaign for the establishment of equal and just political and economic relations between the North and South. To encourage sustainable development in the Third World.

GENERAL INFORMATION: *Creation:* 1984. *Type of organisation:* association of NGOs. *Personnel/Total:* 21. *Salaried:* 1. *Volunteers:* 20. *Budget/Total 1993:* ECU 6400 (US$ 7600). *Financial sources:* Private: 90%. Self-financing: 10%.

PUBLICATIONS: *Periodicals:* Solidarity Newsletter (3). *Annual report.*

EVALUATION/RESEARCH: Undertakes research activities.

ACTIVITIES IN DEVELOPING REGIONS: Active in 4 country(ies).

INFORMATION AND EDUCATION ACTIVITIES: Topics: Ecology/environment/biodiversity; Education/training/literacy; Gender issues/women; Human rights/peace/conflicts; Peace/ethnic conflicts/armament/disarmament; Poverty/living conditions; Racism/xenophobia/antisemitism; Refugees/migrants/ethnic groups. **Activities:** Broadcasting/cultural events; Conferences/seminars/workshops/training activities; Lobbying/advocacy.

GBR2216
BRITISH AIRWAYS TRUST

Tristar House No. 27, Pob 6, Heathrow Airport, Hounslow, Middlesex TW6 2JR, United Kingdom.

Contact: Pat Kerr.

GBR2217
BRITISH ALL PARTY PARLIAMENTARY GROUP ON POPULATION AND DEVELOPMENT

Room 301, Norman Shaw South, House of Commons, London SW1A 0AA, United Kingdom.

Telephone: 44 (171) 219 2492. *Fax:* 44 (171) 219 2641. *Contact:* Trudy Davies, Administrator.

OBJECTIVES: To assess how the UK might best respond to the global demand for family planning and to encourage the British Parliament and other governing bodies to help meet this demand. To keep under review population policies. To consult with international institutions and independent organisations on population policy and activities.

GENERAL INFORMATION: *Creation:* 1979. *Affiliated to:* UK NGO Forum ICPD (Egypt). *Personnel/Total:* 2. *Salaried:* 2. *Budget/Total 1993:* ECU 77000 (US$ 90000). *Financial sources:* Private: 100%.

PUBLICATIONS: *Annual report.*

EVALUATION/RESEARCH: Evaluation reports available. Undertakes research activities.

INFORMATION AND EDUCATION ACTIVITIES: Topics: Children/youth/ family; Gender issues/women; International relations/cooperation/development aid; Population/family planning/demography. **Activities:** Conferences/seminars/workshops/training activities; Lobbying/advocacy.

GBR2218

BRITISH EXECUTIVE SERVICE OVERSEAS (BESO)

164 Vauxhall Bridge Road, London SW1V 2RB, United Kingdom.

Telephone: 44 (171) 630 0644. *Fax:* 44 (171) 630 0624. *Contact:* Timothy Bellers, Director.

OBJECTIVES: To work overseas with people in their own communities. To make use of volunteer experts with considerable experience by providing hands-on advice and training on assignments lasting between two weeks and six months.

GENERAL INFORMATION: *Creation:* 1972. *Affiliated to:* British Overseas NGOs for Development (United Kingdom) - European Senior Services Consortium. *Personnel/Total:* 130. *Salaried:* 10. *Volunteers:* 120 of which: 90 in developing countries. *Budget/Total 1993:* ECU 1667000 (US$ 1953000). *Financial sources:* *Private:* 30%. *Public:* 70%.

PUBLICATIONS: *Periodicals:* BESO News (4). *Annual report.*

COMMENTS: Undertakes activities in the Commonwealth of Independent States. Information activities related to the Commonwealth of Independent States.

ACTIVITIES IN DEVELOPING REGIONS: Present in developing regions. Active in 90 country(ies). Maintains local field presence. Works through local field partners. **Sustainable Development Actions:** Children/ youth/family; Debt/finance/trade; Ecology/environment/biodiversity; Education/training/literacy; Energy/transport; Food/famine; Gender issues/ women; Health/sanitation/water; Population/family planning/demography; Rural development/agriculture; Sending volunteers/experts/technical assistance; Small enterprises/informal sector/handicrafts; Urban development/habitat. **Regions:** Caribbean; Central Africa; Central Asia and South Asia; East Africa; East Asia; Mexico and Central America; Middle East; North Africa; Oceania; South America; South East Asia; Southern Africa; West Africa.

GBR2219

BRITISH LEPROSY RELIEF ASSOCIATION (LEPRA)

Fairfax House, Causton Road, Colchester CO1 1PU, United Kingdom.

Telephone: 44 (1206) 562286. *Fax:* 44 (1206) 762151. *Contact:* T. Vasey, Director.

OBJECTIVES: To help eradicate leprosy.

GENERAL INFORMATION: *Creation:* 1924. *Affiliated to:* International Federation of Anti-Leprosy Associations (United Kingdom). *Personnel/ Total:* 90. *Salaried:* 75 of which: 49 in developing countries. *Volunteers:* 15. *Budget/Total 1993:* ECU 1949000 (US$ 2283000). *Financial sources:* *Private:* 80%. *Public:* 20%.

PUBLICATIONS: *Periodicals:* "Leprosy Review" (4). *Annual report.*

EVALUATION/RESEARCH: Evaluation reports available. Undertakes research activities.

ACTIVITIES IN DEVELOPING REGIONS: Maintains local field presence. Works through local field partners. **Sustainable Development Actions:** Health/sanitation/water; Sending volunteers/experts/technical assistance. **Regions:** Central Asia and South Asia; East Africa; South America;

GBR2220

BRITISH OVERSEAS AID GROUP (BOAG)

Parnell House, Wilton Road, London SW1, United Kingdom.

GBR2221

BRITISH PHOTOVOLTAICS ASSOCIATION (PV-UK)

Bramshill Road, The Warren, Eversley, Hants. RG27 OPR, United Kingdom.

Telephone: 44 (1734) 730373. *Fax:* 44 (1734) 730820. *Contact:* Jenny Gregory, Secretary General.

OBJECTIVES: To raise awareness about the potential for and many uses of solar photovoltaic technologies. To promote photovoltaic technologies to the government and within the industry, both in the United Kingdom and worldwide.

GENERAL INFORMATION: *Creation:* 1992. *Type of organisation:* coordinating body. *Personnel/Total:* 5. *Salaried:* 1. *Volunteers:* 4. *Financial sources:* *Public:* 20%. *Self-financing:* 80%.

PUBLICATIONS: *Periodicals:* PV Newsletter (3). *List of publications.*

EVALUATION/RESEARCH: Undertakes research activities.

PLANNED ACTIVITIES: To undertake analysis for the photovoltaic industry. To highlight priority areas of need in developing countries.

COMMENTS: PV-UK is associated with the other renewable energy NGOs based in the UK.

ACTIVITIES IN DEVELOPING REGIONS: Sustainable Development Actions: Energy/transport; Health/sanitation/water; Rural development/ agriculture. **Regions:** Caribbean; Central Africa; Central Asia and South Asia; East Africa; East Asia; Mexico and Central America; Middle East; North Africa; Oceania; South America; South East Asia; Southern Africa; West Africa.

GBR2222

BRITISH RED CROSS SOCIETY (BRCS) ♦ Croix Rouge Britannique

9 Grosvenor Crescent, London SW1X 7EJ, United Kingdom.

Telephone: 44 (171) 235 5454. *Fax:* 44 (171) 245 6315. *Contact:* Michael R. Whitlam, Director General.

OBJECTIVES: To work for the improvement of health and to furnish aid to the sick and wounded in time of war. To help in the prevention of diseases and the mitigation of suffering throughout the world.

GENERAL INFORMATION: *Creation:* 1870. *Affiliated to:* International Red Cross and Red Crescent Movement (Switzerland) - International Federation of Red Cross and Red Crescent Societies (Switzerland). *Personnel/Total:* 101500. *Salaried:* 1500 of which: 88 in developing countries. *Volunteers:* 100000. *Budget/Total 1993:* ECU 75266000 (US$ 88165000). *Financial sources:* *Private:* 42%. *Public:* 25%. *Self-financing:* 33%.

PUBLICATIONS: *Periodicals:* Dignity for All (2) - In Contact (4) - Networking (6). *Annual report. List of publications.*

EVALUATION/RESEARCH: Evaluation reports available. Undertakes research activities.

COMMENTS: Undertakes activities in the Commonwealth of Independent States.

ACTIVITIES IN DEVELOPING REGIONS: Present in developing regions. Active in 30 country(ies). Maintains local field presence. Works through local field partners. **Sustainable Development Actions:** Children/ youth/family; Debt/finance/trade; Democracy/good governance/institution building/participatory development; Ecology/environment/biodiversity; Emergency relief/refugees/humanitarian assistance; Food/famine; Health/sanitation/water; Sending volunteers/experts/technical assistance. **Regions:** Central Africa; Central Asia and South Asia; East Africa; East Asia; North Africa; South East Asia; Southern Africa; West Africa.

INFORMATION AND EDUCATION ACTIVITIES: Topics: Emergency relief/refugees/humanitarian assistance; Food/famine; Health/sanitation/ water; Human rights/peace/conflicts; International relations/cooperation/ development aid; Peace/ethnic conflicts/armament/disarmament; Refugees/migrants/ethnic groups; Rural development/agriculture. **Activities:** Broadcasting/cultural events; Conferences/seminars/workshops/training activities; Fund raising; Information and documentation services/data bases; Information campaigns/exhibitions; Publishing/audiovisual materials/educational materials.

See: *How to Use the Directory,* page 11.

GBR2223

BRITISH REFUGEE COUNCIL (BRC)

Bondway House, 3-9 Bondway, London SW8 1SJ, United Kingdom.

Telephone: 44 (171) 582 6922. *Fax:* 44 (171) 582 9929. *Contact:* Alf Dubs, Director.

OBJECTIVES: To provide settlements, housing and training services for refugees in the United Kingdom. To monitor the protection and assistance given to refugees overseas. To organise advocacy on the above and other issues related to refugees.

GENERAL INFORMATION: *Creation:* 1981. *Type of organisation:* association of NGOs. *Member organisations:* 126. *Affiliated to:* European Consultation on Refugees and Exiles (United Kingdom) - International Council of Voluntary Agencies (Switzerland). *Personnel/Total:* 175. *Salaried:* 175. *Budget/Total 1993:* ECU 7693294 (US$ 9012000). *Financial sources:* Private: 10%. Public: 60%. Self-financing: 30%.

PUBLICATIONS: *Periodicals:* Exile (10) - Sri Lanka Monitor (12) - Gulf Newsletter (4). *Annual report. List of publications.*

EVALUATION/RESEARCH: Evaluation reports available.

PLANNED ACTIVITIES: "Refugees in the New Europe", a three-year development education programme targetting schools and the general public. Campaign on anti-personnel landmines.

INFORMATION AND EDUCATION ACTIVITIES: Topics: Emergency relief/refugees/humanitarian assistance; Racism/xenophobia/antisemitism; Refugees/migrants/ethnic groups. **Activities:** Conferences/seminars/workshops/training activities; Formal education; Fund raising; Information and documentation services/data bases; Information campaigns/exhibitions; Lobbying/advocacy; Publishing/audiovisual materials/educational materials.

GBR2224

BUSOGA TRUST

St. Margaret Pattens, Eastcheap, London EC3 M1HS, United Kingdom.

Telephone: 44 (171) 283 2304. *Fax:* 44 (171) 283 2304. *Contact:* Roy Giles.

OBJECTIVES: To create partnerships between countries of the North and South to improve human well being. To advance rural development through clean water and sanitation initiatives.

GENERAL INFORMATION: *Creation:* 1983. *Personnel/Total:* 30. *Salaried:* 26 of which: 24 in developing countries. *Volunteers:* 4 of which: 2 in developing countries. *Budget/Total 1993:* ECU 324000 (US$ 380000). *Financial sources:* Private: 25%. Public: 75%.

PUBLICATIONS: *Periodicals:* The Busoga Bugle (1). *Annual report.*

EVALUATION/RESEARCH: Evaluation reports available.

ACTIVITIES IN DEVELOPING REGIONS: Active in 1 country(ies). Maintains local field presence. Works through local field partners. **Sustainable Development Actions:** Children/youth/family; Health/sanitation/water. **Regions:** East Africa.

INFORMATION AND EDUCATION ACTIVITIES: Topics: Children/youth/family; Health/sanitation/water. **Activities:** Conferences/seminars/workshops/training activities; Exchanges/twinning/linking; Fund raising; Information and documentation services/data bases; Lobbying/advocacy; Publishing/audiovisual materials/educational materials.

GBR2225

CAMBODIA TRUST

The Rookery, Adderbury, Oxon OX17 3NA, United Kingdom.

Contact: Stan Windass.

GBR2226

CARE BRITAIN

36-38 Southampton Street, London WC2E 7HE, United Kingdom.

Telephone: 44 (171) 379 5247. *Fax:* 44 (171) 379 0543. *Contact:* Charles Tapp, Chief Executive.

OBJECTIVES: To help the world's poor improve their circumstances through active programmes in primary health care, agriculture, income generation, conservation of the environment, education and training. To provide relief aid during emergencies.

GENERAL INFORMATION: *Creation:* 1985. *Type of organisation:* network. *Member organisations:* 11. *Affiliated to:* British Overseas NGOs for Development (United Kingdom) - EC-NGO Liaison Committee - Institute for Charity Fundraising Managers - United Nations Environment and Development (United Kingdom). *Personnel/Total:* 36. *Salaried:* 32. *Volunteers:* 4. *Budget/Total 1993:* ECU 28209000 (US$ 33043000). *Financial sources:* Private: 11%. Public: 89%.

PUBLICATIONS: *Periodicals:* CARE News (4). *Annual report.*

EVALUATION/RESEARCH: Evaluation reports available.

COMMENTS: Undertakes activities in the Commonwealth of Independent States.

ACTIVITIES IN DEVELOPING REGIONS: Present in developing regions. Maintains local field presence. Works through local field partners. **Sustainable Development Actions:** Ecology/environment/biodiversity; Emergency relief/refugees/humanitarian assistance; Food/famine; Gender issues/women; Health/sanitation/water; Population/family planning/demography; Rural development/agriculture; Sending volunteers/experts/technical assistance; Small enterprises/informal sector/handicrafts; Urban development/habitat. **Regions:** Central Asia and South Asia; East Africa; East Asia; Mexico and Central America; Middle East; North Africa; South America; South East Asia; Southern Africa; West Africa.

INFORMATION AND EDUCATION ACTIVITIES: Topics: Ecology/environment/biodiversity; Education/training/literacy; Emergency relief/refugees/humanitarian assistance; Food/famine; Gender issues/women; Health/sanitation/water; International relations/cooperation/development aid; Population/family planning/demography; Poverty/living conditions; Rural development/agriculture; Urban development/habitat. **Activities:** Broadcasting/cultural events; Conferences/seminars/workshops/training activities; Fund raising; Information and documentation services/data bases; Networking/electronic telecommunications; Publishing/audiovisual materials/educational materials.

GBR2227

CARE FOR THE WILD

1 Ashfolds Horsham Road, Rusper, West Sussex RH12 4QX, United Kingdom.

Telephone: 44 (1293) 871596. *Fax:* 44 (1293) 871022. *Contact:* Bill Jordan.

OBJECTIVES: To protect wildlife from cruelty and exploitation. To inform the public about the suffering and abuse caused by human beings.

GENERAL INFORMATION: *Creation:* 1984. *Affiliated to:* Wildlife Link. *Personnel/Total:* 6. *Salaried:* 6. *Budget/Total 1993:* ECU 513000 (US$ 601000). *Financial sources:* Private: 95%. Self-financing: 5%.

PUBLICATIONS: *Periodicals:* Care for the Wild News (3). *Annual report.*

EVALUATION/RESEARCH: Evaluation reports available. Undertakes research activities.

PLANNED ACTIVITIES: Establishing various animal sanctuaries and undertaking protection projects in Kenya, Thailand and Sri Lanka.

ACTIVITIES IN DEVELOPING REGIONS: Present in developing regions. Active in 2 country(ies). Maintains local field presence. Works through local field partners. **Sustainable Development Actions:** Ecology/environment/biodiversity. **Regions:** Central Asia and South Asia; East Africa.

INFORMATION AND EDUCATION ACTIVITIES: Topics: Ecology/environment/biodiversity. **Activities:** Broadcasting/cultural events; Fund raising; Publishing/audiovisual materials/educational materials.

GBR2228

CATHOLIC FUND FOR OVERSEAS DEVELOPMENT (CAFOD)

Romero Close, Stockwell Road, London SW9 9TY, United Kingdom.

Voir : *Comment utiliser le répertoire,* page 11.

Telephone: 44 (171) 733 7900. *Fax:* 44 (171) 274 9630. *Contact:* Julian Filochowski, Director.

OBJECTIVES: To promote human development and social justice according to Christian faith and gospel values.

GENERAL INFORMATION: *Creation:* 1962. *Affiliated to:* Caritas Internationalis (Italy) - CIDSE (Belgium) - Asia Partnership for Human Development - Pacific Partnership for Human Development. *Personnel/ Total:* 110. *Salaried:* 100. *Volunteers:* 10. *Budget/Total 1993:* ECU 25645000 (US$ 30039000). *Financial sources:* Private: 70%. Public: 30%.

PUBLICATIONS: *Periodicals:* CAFOD Magazine (4). *Annual report. List of publications.*

COMMENTS: Undertakes activities in the Commonwealth of Independent States.

ACTIVITIES IN DEVELOPING REGIONS: Active in 75 country(ies). Works through local field partners. **Sustainable Development Actions:** Children/youth/family; Democracy/good governance/institution building/participatory development; Ecology/environment/biodiversity; Education/training/literacy; Emergency relief/refugees/humanitarian assistance; Food/famine; Gender issues/women; Health/sanitation/water; Human rights/peace/conflicts; Rural development/agriculture; Small enterprises/informal sector/handicrafts; Urban development/habitat. **Regions:** Caribbean; Central Asia and South Asia; East Africa; East Asia; Mexico and Central America; Middle East; Oceania; South America; South East Asia; Southern Africa; West Africa.

INFORMATION AND EDUCATION ACTIVITIES: Topics: Children/youth/family; Education/training/literacy; Emergency relief/refugees/humanitarian assistance; Food/famine; Gender issues/women; Health/sanitation/water; Human rights/peace/conflicts; International economic relations/trade/debt/finance; International relations/cooperation/development aid; Poverty/living conditions; Refugees/migrants/ethnic groups; Rural development/agriculture; Urban development/habitat. **Activities:** Conferences/seminars/workshops/training activities; Formal education; Fund raising; Information campaigns/exhibitions; Lobbying/advocacy; Publishing/audiovisual materials/educational materials.

GBR2229

CATHOLIC INSTITUTE FOR INTERNATIONAL RELATIONS (CIIR)

Unit 3 Canonbury Yard, 190A New North Road, Islington, London N1 7BJ, United Kingdom.

Telephone: 44 (171) 354 0883. *Fax:* 44 (171) 359 0017. *E-mail:* (Poptel)geo2:ciir. *Contact:* Ian Linden, General Secretary .

OBJECTIVES: To promote social justice and development in response to demands from developing countries with particular emphasis on international economic justice, human rights and democracy.

GENERAL INFORMATION: *Creation:* 1940. *Affiliated to:* Copenhagen Initiative for Central America (Denmark) - South African Working Group (Belgium). *Personnel/Total:* 45 of which: 8 in developing countries. *Volunteers:* 105 of which: 105 in developing countries. *Budget/Total 1993:* ECU 4103000 (US$ 4806000). *Financial sources:* Private: 30%. Public: 68%. Self-financing: 2%.

PUBLICATIONS: *Periodicals:* CIIR News (4) - Comment (5) - Briefing Papers (5). *Annual report. List of publications.*

EVALUATION/RESEARCH: Evaluation reports available. Undertakes research activities.

PLANNED ACTIVITIES: Undertaking programmes on the control of transnational corporations and on narcotics production and development and on the impact of newly industrialised countries on the marginalised in South East Asia.

COMMENTS: CIIR does not fund projects or offer grants.

ACTIVITIES IN DEVELOPING REGIONS: Present in developing regions. Active in 9 country(ies). Maintains local field presence. Works through local field partners. **Sustainable Development Actions:** Children/youth/family; Democracy/good governance/institution building/participatory development; Ecology/environment/biodiversity; Education/training/literacy; Emergency relief/refugees/humanitarian assistance;

Gender issues/women; Health/sanitation/water; Human rights/peace/conflicts; Rural development/agriculture; Sending volunteers/experts/technical assistance; Urban development/habitat. **Regions:** Caribbean; East Africa; Mexico and Central America; Middle East; North Africa; South America; Southern Africa.

INFORMATION AND EDUCATION ACTIVITIES: Topics: Culture/tradition/religion; Ecology/environment/biodiversity; Food/famine; Gender issues/women; Health/sanitation/water; Human rights/peace/conflicts; International economic relations/trade/debt/finance; International relations/cooperation/development aid; Other; Poverty/living conditions; Refugees/migrants/ethnic groups; Rural development/agriculture; Urban development/habitat. **Activities:** Broadcasting/cultural events; Conferences/seminars/workshops/training activities; Exchanges/twinning/linking; Fund raising; Information and documentation services/data bases; Information campaigns/exhibitions; Lobbying/advocacy; Networking/electronic telecommunications; Publishing/audiovisual materials/educational materials.

GBR2230

CENTRAL BRITISH FUND FOR WORLD JEWISH RELIEF

Drayton House, 30 Gordon Street, London WC1H OAN, United Kingdom.

Telephone: 44 (171) 387 3925. *Fax:* 44 (171) 383 4810. *Contact:* C. Mariner, Executive Director.

OBJECTIVES: To help Jewish refugees seeking sanctuary in the United Kingdom. To support Holocaust survivor communities in Eastern Europe and all other Jews in beleaguered situations worldwide.

GENERAL INFORMATION: *Creation:* 1933. *Affiliated to:* International Council of Jewish Welfare Organisations (United Kingdom). *Personnel/ Total:* 18. *Salaried:* 15. *Volunteers:* 3. *Budget/Total 1993:* ECU 2503000 (US$ 3004000). *Financial sources:* Private: 100%.

PUBLICATIONS: *Annual report.*

COMMENTS: Undertakes activities in the Commonwealth of Independent States. Information activities related to the Commonwealth of Independent States.

ACTIVITIES IN DEVELOPING REGIONS: Sustainable Development Actions: Education/training/literacy; Emergency relief/refugees/humanitarian assistance. **Regions:** Middle East.

INFORMATION AND EDUCATION ACTIVITIES: Topics: Culture/tradition/religion; Education/training/literacy; Emergency relief/refugees/humanitarian assistance; Food/famine; Refugees/migrants/ethnic groups. **Activities:** Fund raising.

GBR2231

THE CENTRAL BUREAU FOR EDUCATIONAL VISITS AND EXCHANGES (CBEVE)

Seymour Mews House, Seymour Mews, London W1H 9PE, United Kingdom.

Telephone: 44 (171) 486 5101. *Fax:* 44 (171) 935 5741. *E-mail:* CAMPUS 2000 01:YNK 330. *Contact:* A.H. Male, Director.

OBJECTIVES: To provide information and advice on all forms of educational visits and exchanges through information and advisory services and an extended range of publications.

GENERAL INFORMATION: *Creation:* 1948. *Type of organisation:* coordinating body. *Affiliated to:* UK Centre for European Education (United Kingdom) - IAESTE - LINGUA and PETRA EU PROGRAMMES - EURODESK. *Personnel/Total:* 100. *Salaried:* 100. *Budget/Total 1993:* ECU 10001000 (US$ 11715000). *Financial sources:* Private: 1%. Public: 64%. Self-financing: 35%.

PUBLICATIONS: *Periodicals:* School Unit News (3) - European Education News (2) - Link Up (3). *Annual report. List of publications.*

EVALUATION/RESEARCH: Evaluation reports available. Undertakes research activities.

PLANNED ACTIVITIES: Organising regional workshops for teacher and student gatherings. Preparing for European Union Socrates and Leonardo programmes.

See: *How to Use the Directory*, page 11.

COMMENTS: Undertakes activities in the Commonwealth of Independent States. Information activities related to the Commonwealth of Independent States.

ACTIVITIES IN DEVELOPING REGIONS: Active in 20 country(ies). **Sustainable Development Actions:** Education/training/literacy. **Regions:** Mexico and Central America; North Africa; South America.

INFORMATION AND EDUCATION ACTIVITIES: Topics: Children/youth/family; Education/training/literacy; Employment/unemployment; International relations/cooperation/development aid; Racism/xenophobia/antisemitism. **Activities:** Broadcasting/cultural events; Conferences/seminars/workshops/training activities; Exchanges/twinning/linking; Formal education; Information and documentation services/data bases; Information campaigns/exhibitions; Networking/electronic telecommunications; Publishing/audiovisual materials/educational materials.

GBR2232
CENTRE FOR ENVIRONMENTAL MANAGEMENT AND PLANNING (CEMP)

23 St Machar Drive, Aberdeen AB2 1RY, United Kingdom.

Telephone: 44 (1224) 272353. *Fax:* 44 (1224) 487658. *Contact:* Brian D. Clark, Executive Director.

OBJECTIVES: To help strengthen institutions and encourage capacity building in all environmental subjects. To promote environmental management, research, development. To disseminate information on the environment.

GENERAL INFORMATION: *Creation:* 1972. *Personnel/Total:* 10. *Salaried:* 10. *Budget/Total 1993:* ECU 641000 (US$ 751000). *Financial sources:* Private: 10%. Public: 10%. Self-financing: 80%.

PUBLICATIONS: *List of publications.*

EVALUATION/RESEARCH: Undertakes research activities.

COMMENTS: Undertakes activities in the Commonwealth of Independent States. Information activities related to the Commonwealth of Independent States.

ACTIVITIES IN DEVELOPING REGIONS: Present in developing regions. Active in 5 country(ies). **Sustainable Development Actions:** Democracy/good governance/institution building/participatory development; Ecology/environment/biodiversity; Education/training/literacy; Health/sanitation/water; Rural development/agriculture. **Regions:** Caribbean; Central Africa; Central Asia and South Asia; East Africa; East Asia; Mexico and Central America; Middle East; North Africa; Oceania; South America; South East Asia; Southern Africa; West Africa.

INFORMATION AND EDUCATION ACTIVITIES: Topics: Ecology/environment/biodiversity; Health/sanitation/water; Rural development/agriculture. **Activities:** Conferences/seminars/workshops/training activities; Information and documentation services/data bases; Publishing/audiovisual materials/educational materials.

GBR2233
CENTRE FOR GLOBAL EDUCATION

Univ. Coll. of Ripon & York St. John, Lord Mayor's Walk, York Y03 7EX, United Kingdom.

Telephone: 44 (1904) 616839. *Fax:* 44 (1904) 612512. *Contact:* Margot Brown, National Coordinator.

OBJECTIVES: To support teachers for students of all ages in developing countries and to adopt a curicula to include a global perspective. To encourage an understanding of multi ethnic society.

GENERAL INFORMATION: *Creation:* 1982. *Affiliated to:* Development Education Association (United Kingdom) - Education in Human Rights Network (United Kingdom) - World Studies Project (United Kingdom). *Personnel/Total:* 1. *Salaried:* 1. *Financial sources:* Public: 75%. Self-financing: 25%.

PUBLICATIONS: *Periodicals:* Human Rights Education (3). *Annual report. List of publications.*

PLANNED ACTIVITIES: Preparing a teaching kit for Spanish classrooms in the UK, based on development issues.

COMMENTS: Undertakes activities in the Commonwealth of Independent States.

INFORMATION AND EDUCATION ACTIVITIES: Topics: Education/training/literacy; Gender issues/women; Human rights/peace/conflicts; Peace/ethnic conflicts/armament/disarmament; Racism/xenophobia/antisemitism. **Activities:** Formal education.

GBR2234
CENTRE FOR INTERNATIONAL STUDIES

Meadowlea House, 86 Littleham Road, Exmouth, Devon EX8 2QT, United Kingdom.

Telephone: 44 (1395) 264902. *Fax:* 44 (1395) 268031. *E-mail:* eurokom-Brian.Champness.C.I.S.. *Contact:* Roger W. R. Morgan.

GBR2235
CHANGE INTERNATIONAL REPORTS ♦ Femmes et Changement

P.O. Box 824, London SE24 9JS, United Kingdom.

Telephone: 44 (171) 277 6187. *Fax:* 44 (171) 277 6187. *Contact:* Georgina Ashworth, Director.

OBJECTIVES: To educate and alert public opinion to the unequal status of women as imposed by law, practice and custom by disseminating information on their present situation. To advance the recognition of the inalienable human rights and dignity of women.

GENERAL INFORMATION: *Creation:* 1979. *Personnel/Total:* 10. *Volunteers:* 10. *Financial sources:* Private: 5%. Self-financing: 95%.

PUBLICATIONS: *Periodicals:* Changing the World (4). *List of publications.*

EVALUATION/RESEARCH: Undertakes research activities.

COMMENTS: Information activities related to the Commonwealth of Independent States.

ACTIVITIES IN DEVELOPING REGIONS: Present in developing regions. Active in 5 country(ies). **Sustainable Development Actions:** Gender issues/women. **Regions:** Caribbean; Central Africa; Central Asia and South Asia; East Africa; East Asia; Oceania; South America; South East Asia; Southern Africa; West Africa.

INFORMATION AND EDUCATION ACTIVITIES: Topics: Gender issues/women; Human rights/peace/conflicts; Poverty/living conditions. **Activities:** Broadcasting/cultural events; Conferences/seminars/workshops/training activities; Information and documentation services/data bases; Information campaigns/exhibitions; Lobbying/advocacy; Publishing/audiovisual materials/educational materials.

GBR2236
CHILDHOPE

40 Rosebery Avenue, London EC1R 4RN, United Kingdom.

Telephone: 44 (171) 833 0868. *Fax:* 44 (171) 833 2500. *E-mail:* gn:chuk. *Contact:* Nicolas Fenton.

OBJECTIVES: To defend the rights and improve the lives of street children.

GENERAL INFORMATION: *Creation:* 1989. *Affiliated to:* UNICEF (United Kingdom) - BOND (United Kingdom) - Consortium for Street Children (United Kingdom). *Personnel/Total:* 11. *Salaried:* 3. *Volunteers:* 8. *Budget/Total 1993:* ECU 192000 (US$ 225000). *Financial sources:* Private: 25%. Public: 75%.

PUBLICATIONS: *Periodicals:* Annual Review (1). *Annual report.*

EVALUATION/RESEARCH: Undertakes research activities.

PLANNED ACTIVITIES: Developing projects and establishing a network in Eastern Europe for street children.

COMMENTS: Undertakes activities in the Commonwealth of Independent States. Information activities related to the Commonwealth of Independent States.

ACTIVITIES IN DEVELOPING REGIONS: Present in developing regions. Active in 7 country(ies). Works through local field partners. **Sustainable**

Development Actions: Children/youth/family; Human rights/peace/conflicts. **Regions:** Central Asia and South Asia; Mexico and Central America; South America; South East Asia; Southern Africa.

GBR2237

CHILDREN'S INTERNATIONAL SUMMER VILLAGES (CISV)

MEA House, Ellison Place, Newcastle upon Tyne NE1 8XS, United Kingdom.

Telephone: 44 (191) 232 4998. *Fax:* (91) 261 4710. *Contact:* Joseph G. Banks, Secretary General.

GBR2238

CHRISTIAN AID

P.O. Box 100, 35 Lower Marsh, London SE1 7RT, United Kingdom.

Telephone: 44 (171) 620 4444. *Fax:* 44 (171) 620 0719. *Contact:* Michael Taylor, Director.

OBJECTIVES: To help the poor through relief, development and public education campaigning for change.

GENERAL INFORMATION: *Creation:* 1946. *Affiliated to:* Disasters Emergency Committee (United Kingdom) - APRODEV (Belgium) - British Overseas Aid Group (United Kingdom) - EURONAID (Holland) - EECOD (Belgium) -VOICE (Belgium) - EC-NGO Network (United Kingdom) - Liaison Committee of Development NGOs.. *Personnel/ Total:* 320. *Salaried:* 200. *Volunteers:* 120. *Budget/Total 1993:* ECU 61426000 (US$ 71953000). *Financial sources:* *Private:* 70%. *Public:* 30%.

PUBLICATIONS: *Periodicals:* Christian Aid News (4). *Annual report.* List of publications.

EVALUATION/RESEARCH: Evaluation reports available. Undertakes research activities.

PLANNED ACTIVITIES: Undertaking a campaign on international financial institutions.

COMMENTS: Undertakes activities in the Commonwealth of Independent States. Information activities related to the Commonwealth of Independent States.

ACTIVITIES IN DEVELOPING REGIONS: Active in 70 country(ies). Works through local field partners. **Sustainable Development Actions:** Children/youth/family; Debt/finance/trade; Democracy/good governance/ institution building/participatory development; Ecology/environment/ biodiversity; Education/training/literacy; Emergency relief/refugees/ humanitarian assistance; Energy/transport; Food/famine; Gender issues/women; Health/sanitation/water; Human rights/peace/conflicts; Population/family planning/demography; Rural development/agriculture; Sending volunteers/experts/technical assistance; Small enterprises/ informal sector/handicrafts; Urban development/habitat. **Regions:** Caribbean; Central Africa; Central Asia and South Asia; East Africa; East Asia; Mexico and Central America; Middle East; North Africa; South America; South East Asia; Southern Africa; West Africa.

INFORMATION AND EDUCATION ACTIVITIES: Topics: Children/youth/ family; Culture/tradition/religion; Ecology/environment/biodiversity; Education/training/literacy; Emergency relief/refugees/humanitarian assistance; Employment/unemployment; Food/famine; Gender issues/ women; Health/sanitation/water; Human rights/peace/conflicts; International economic relations/trade/debt/finance; International relations/ cooperation/development aid; Peace/ethnic conflicts/armament/disarmament; Population/family planning/demography; Poverty/living conditions; Racism/xenophobia/antisemitism; Refugees/migrants/ethnic groups; Rural development/agriculture; Urban development/habitat. **Activities:** Broadcasting/cultural events; Conferences/seminars/workshops/training activities; Formal education; Fund raising; Information and documentation services/data bases; Information campaigns/exhibitions; Lobbying/advocacy; Publishing/audiovisual materials/educational materials.

GBR2239

CHRISTIAN CONCERN FOR ONE WORLD (CCOW)

The Knowle, Philcote Street, Deddington, Banbury, Oxon 0x15 0TB, United Kingdom.

Telephone: 44 (1869) 338225. *Fax:* 44 (1869) 338225. *Contact:* Rev. Hugh Cross.

OBJECTIVES: To raise awareness of issues of justice, peace and the environment primarily among church members in the counties of Berkshire, Buckinghamshire and Oxfordshire.

GENERAL INFORMATION: *Creation:* 1989. *Type of organisation:* network. *Affiliated to:* Development Education Association (United Kingdom). *Personnel/Total:* 1. *Salaried:* 1. *Budget/Total 1993:* ECU 31000 (US$ 36000). *Financial sources:* Private: 100%.

PUBLICATIONS: *Periodicals:* Newsletter (3).

INFORMATION AND EDUCATION ACTIVITIES: Topics: Culture/tradition/religion; Ecology/environment/biodiversity; Food/famine; Gender issues/women; Health/sanitation/water; International economic relations/trade/debt/finance; International relations/cooperation/development aid; Peace/ethnic conflicts/armament/disarmament; Poverty/living conditions; Refugees/migrants/ethnic groups. **Activities:** Information and documentation services/data bases; Information campaigns/exhibitions; Lobbying/advocacy; Publishing/audiovisual materials/educational materials.

GBR2240

CHRISTIAN OUTREACH

1 New Street, Leamington Spa, Warwicks CV31 1HP, United Kingdom.

Telephone: 44 (1926) 315301 . *Fax:* 44 (1926) 885786. *Contact:* Martin Lee, Director.

OBJECTIVES: To show the love of Jesus, with God's guidance, by practical care of vulnerable and disadvantaged people in developing countries, especially unaccompanied children and refugees.

GENERAL INFORMATION: *Creation:* 1967. *Budget/Total 1993:* ECU 2777000 (US$ 3253000). *Financial sources:* Private: 31%. Public: 68%. Self-financing: 1%.

PUBLICATIONS: *Periodicals:* Companion in Action (4). *Annual report.*

EVALUATION/RESEARCH: Evaluation reports available.

PLANNED ACTIVITIES: Providing assistance in repatriation of refugees to Mozambique, Eritrea and Rwanda.

ACTIVITIES IN DEVELOPING REGIONS: Present in developing regions. Active in 9 country(ies). Maintains local field presence. Works through local field partners. **Sustainable Development Actions:** Children/ youth/family; Democracy/good governance/institution building/participatory development; Education/training/literacy; Emergency relief/refugees/humanitarian assistance; Food/famine; Gender issues/women; Health/sanitation/water; Population/family planning/demography; Rural development/agriculture; Sending volunteers/experts/technical assistance; Small enterprises/informal sector/handicrafts. **Regions:** Central Africa; East Africa; South East Asia; Southern Africa.

INFORMATION AND EDUCATION ACTIVITIES: Topics: Children/youth/ family; Culture/tradition/religion; Education/training/literacy; Emergency relief/refugees/humanitarian assistance; Employment/unemployment; Food/famine; Gender issues/women; Health/sanitation/water; Population/family planning/demography; Poverty/living conditions; Refugees/ migrants/ethnic groups; Rural development/agriculture. **Activities:** Conferences/seminars/workshops/training activities; Fund raising; Other.

GBR2241

CHRISTIANS ABROAD

1 Stockwell Green, London SW9 9HP, United Kingdom.

Telephone: 44 (171) 737 7811. *Fax:* 44 (171) 737 3237. *Contact:* Colin South.

OBJECTIVES: To share skills and resources and promote development co-operation with developing countries.

GENERAL INFORMATION: *Creation:* 1972. *Type of organisation:* network, coordinating body. *Member organisations:* 30. *Affiliated to:* Council of Churches of Britain and Ireland - Churches Commission on Mission -National Association of Christian Communities and Networks - British Overseas NGOs for Development (United Kingdom). *Personnel/ Total:* 10. *Salaried:* 6. *Volunteers:* 4. *Budget/Total 1993:*

See: How to Use the Directory, page 11.

ECU 167000 (US$ 195000). *Financial sources: Private:* 65%. *Public:* 20%. *Self-financing:* 15%.

PUBLICATIONS: *Periodicals:* (10) (2) - World Service Enquiry (1). *Annual report. List of publications.*

COMMENTS: Information activities related to the Commonwealth of Independent States.

ACTIVITIES IN DEVELOPING REGIONS: Present in developing regions. Active in 8 country(ies). Works through local field partners. **Sustainable Development Actions:** Children/youth/family; Debt/finance/trade; Democracy/good governance/institution building/participatory development; Education/training/literacy; Gender issues/women; Health/sanitation/water; Rural development/agriculture; Sending volunteers/experts/technical assistance. **Regions:** Caribbean; Central Africa; Central Asia and South Asia; East Africa; Middle East; West Africa.

INFORMATION AND EDUCATION ACTIVITIES: Topics: Other; Rural development/agriculture; Urban development/habitat. **Activities:** Broadcasting/cultural events; Conferences/seminars/workshops/training activities; Information and documentation services/data bases; Information campaigns/exhibitions; Lobbying/advocacy; Publishing/audiovisual materials/educational materials.

GBR2242
CHURCH OF SCOTLAND-WORLD MISSION

121 George Street, Edinburgh EH2 4YN, United Kingdom.

Telephone: 44 (131) 225 5722. *Fax:* 44 (131) 226 6121. *E-mail:* KIRKWRKDLINK@GN.APC.ORG. *Contact:* Rev. Chris Wigglesworth.

OBJECTIVES: To maximize the number of people in Scotland concerned with cultural, ecological, political, economic and religious issues, especially in the Third World and in relation to the role of churches.

GENERAL INFORMATION: *Creation:* 1560. *Affiliated to:* Action of Churches Together in Scotland (Scotland) - Council of Churches for Britain and Ireland (United Kingdom) - Conference of European Churches (Switzerland) - European Ecumenical Commission for Church and Society (Belgium) - World Alliance of Reformed Churches (Switzerland) - World Council of Churches (Switzerland). *Personnel/Total:* 115. *Salaried:* 115 of which: 95 in developing countries. *Budget/Total 1993:* ECU 4103000 (US$ 4806000). *Financial sources: Private:* 100%.

PUBLICATIONS: *Annual report.*

COMMENTS: Undertakes activities in the Commonwealth of Independent States. Information activities related to the Commonwealth of Independent States.

ACTIVITIES IN DEVELOPING REGIONS: Present in developing regions. Maintains local field presence. Works through local field partners. **Sustainable Development Actions:** Children/youth/family; Democracy/good governance/institution building/participatory development; Education/training/literacy; Food/famine; Gender issues/women; Health/sanitation/water; Human rights/peace/conflicts; Population/family planning/demography; Rural development/agriculture; Sending volunteers/experts/technical assistance; Urban development/habitat. **Regions:** Caribbean; Central Asia and South Asia; East Africa; Mexico and Central America; South East Asia; Southern Africa; West Africa.

INFORMATION AND EDUCATION ACTIVITIES: Topics: Children/youth/family; Culture/tradition/religion; Ecology/environment/biodiversity; Education/training/literacy; Emergency relief/refugees/humanitarian assistance; Food/famine; Gender issues/women; Health/sanitation/water; International economic relations/trade/debt/finance; International relations/cooperation/development aid; Peace/ethnic conflicts/armament/disarmament; Population/family planning/demography; Poverty/living conditions; Rural development/agriculture; Urban development/habitat. **Activities:** Conferences/seminars/workshops/training activities; Exchanges/twinning/linking; Formal education; Fund raising; Information and documentation services/data bases; Information campaigns/exhibitions; Lobbying/advocacy; Networking/electronic telecommunications.

GBR2243
CLIMATE ACTION NETWORK UK

21 Tower Street, London WC2H 9NS, United Kingdom.

Telephone: 44 (171) 240 4936. *Fax:* 44 (171) 497 2712.

GBR2244
CO-OPERATION FOR DEVELOPMENT ♦ Coopération pour le développement

118 Broad Street, Chesham, Bucks HP5 3ED, United Kingdom.

Telephone: 44 (1494) 775 557. *Fax:* 44 (1494) 791 376. *Contact:* Terry Lacey, Managing Director.

OBJECTIVES: To relieve poverty anywhere in the world and to promote development projects. To promote self-sustaining income-generating projects so that future aid subsidies to projects will not be necessary.

GENERAL INFORMATION: *Creation:* 1983. *Affiliated to:* British Overseas NGOs for Development (United Kingdom) - EEC NGO Network (Belgium) - British Refugee Council (United Kingdom). *Personnel/Total:* 38. *Salaried:* 36 of which: 30 in developing countries. *Volunteers:* 2 of which: 2 in developing countries. *Budget/Total 1993:* ECU 4076000 (US$ 4775000). *Financial sources: Private:* 15%. *Public:* 85%.

PUBLICATIONS: *Periodicals:* Whats New (1). *Annual report. List of publications.*

EVALUATION/RESEARCH: Evaluation reports available. Undertakes research activities.

ACTIVITIES IN DEVELOPING REGIONS: Present in developing regions. Active in 25 country(ies). Maintains local field presence. Works through local field partners. **Sustainable Development Actions:** Democracy/good governance/institution building/participatory development; Ecology/environment/biodiversity; Emergency relief/refugees/humanitarian assistance; Gender issues/women; Rural development/agriculture; Sending volunteers/experts/technical assistance; Small enterprises/informal sector/handicrafts. **Regions:** Caribbean; Mexico and Central America; Middle East; South America; Southern Africa; West Africa.

INFORMATION AND EDUCATION ACTIVITIES: Topics: Ecology/environment/biodiversity; Emergency relief/refugees/humanitarian assistance; Gender issues/women; Other; Refugees/migrants/ethnic groups; Rural development/agriculture. **Activities:** Conferences/seminars/workshops/training activities; Fund raising; Publishing/audiovisual materials/educational materials.

GBR2245
THE CO-OPERATIVE BANK ♦ La banque coopérative

9 Prescot Street, London E1 8BE, United Kingdom.

Telephone: 44 (171) 480 5171. *Contact:* T.I. Peat, International Department.

GBR2246
CODA INTERNATIONAL TRAINING (CIT)

7B Broad Street, Nottingham NG1 3AJ, United Kingdom.

Contact: Peter Benjamin.

GBR2247
CODE EUROPE

The Jam Factory, 27 Park End Street, Oxford OX1 1HU, United Kingdom.

Telephone: 44 (1865) 202438. *Fax:* 44 (1865) 202439. *Contact:* Kelvin Smith, Director.

OBJECTIVES: To support local publishing, literacy and library development programmes in developing countries. To engage in development education efforts in Europe.

GENERAL INFORMATION: *Creation:* 1993. *Type of organisation:* association of NGOs. *Affiliated to:* CODE (Canada) - Bellagio Publishing Network (United Kingdom) - British Overseas NGOs for Development (United Kingdom). *Personnel/Total:* 2. *Salaried:* 2. *Budget/Total 1993:* ECU 78000 (US$ 91000). *Financial sources: Private:* 77%. *Public:* 23%.

PUBLICATIONS: *Periodicals:* NGOMA (2). *Annual report.*

EVALUATION/RESEARCH: Evaluation reports available. Undertakes research activities.

Voir : *Comment utiliser le répertoire,* page 11.

PLANNED ACTIVITIES: Supporting CODE Children's Book Projects in Zambia, Kenya and Mali.

ACTIVITIES IN DEVELOPING REGIONS: Present in developing regions. Active in 15 country(ies). Maintains local field presence. Works through local field partners. **Sustainable Development Actions:** Children/ youth/family; Democracy/good governance/institution building/participatory development; Education/training/literacy; Other. **Regions:** Caribbean; East Africa; Mexico and Central America; Oceania; Southern Africa; West Africa.

INFORMATION AND EDUCATION ACTIVITIES: Topics: Children/youth/ family; Culture/tradition/religion; Education/training/literacy; International relations/cooperation/development aid; Other. **Activities:** Conferences/ seminars/workshops/training activities; Fund raising; Information campaigns/exhibitions; Publishing/audiovisual materials/educational materials.

GBR2248
COMIC RELIEF - CHARITY PROJECTS

74 New Oxford Street, 1st Floor, London WC1A 1EF, United Kingdom.

Telephone: 44 (171) 436 1122. **Fax:** 44 (171) 436 1541. **Contact:** Jane Tewson, Executive Director.

OBJECTIVES: To raise funds and allocate them in an effective way. To inform the public of the issues surrounding the work of Comic Relief.

GENERAL INFORMATION: Creation: 1984. **Personnel/Total:** 26. *Salaried:* 26. **Budget/Total 1993:** ECU 7693294 (US$ 9012000). **Financial sources:** *Private:* 100%.

PUBLICATIONS: *Annual report. List of publications.*

EVALUATION/RESEARCH: Undertakes research activities.

INFORMATION AND EDUCATION ACTIVITIES: Topics: Education/training/literacy; Emergency relief/refugees/humanitarian assistance; Food/ famine; Gender issues/women; Health/sanitation/water; International economic relations/trade/debt/finance; International relations/cooperation/development aid; Population/family planning/demography; Poverty/ living conditions; Refugees/migrants/ethnic groups; Rural development/ agriculture; Urban development/habitat. **Activities:** Broadcasting/cultural events; Conferences/seminars/workshops/training activities; Fund raising; Information campaigns/exhibitions; Lobbying/advocacy; Publishing/audiovisual materials/educational materials.

GBR2249
COMITE EXTERIOR MAPUCHE, ENGLISH SECTION ♦ External Mapuche Committee

6 Lodge Street, Bristol BS1 5LR, United Kingdom.

Telephone: 44 (272) 279391. **Fax:** 44 (272) 279391. **Contact:** Reynaldo Mariqueo, Executive Secretary.

GBR2250
COMMISSION FOR RACIAL EQUALITY

Elliot House, 10/12 Allington Street, London SW1E 5EH, United Kingdom.

Telephone: 44 (171) 828 7022. **Fax:** 44 (171) 630 7605. **Contact:** Chris Myant.

GBR2251
COMMONWEAL

41 George IV Bridge, Edinburgh EH1 1EL, Scotland, United Kingdom.

Telephone: 44 (131) 225 1772. **Contact:** Kathy Gallonay, Convenor.

OBJECTIVES: To offer a focus and a resource for Scottish churches and others in tackling questions of poverty, injustice and conflict in the world. To be committed to international solidarity with other faith movements working for justice.

GENERAL INFORMATION: Creation: 1977. **Personnel/Total:** 4. *Salaried:* 2. *Volunteers:* 2. **Budget/Total 1993:** ECU 19000 (US$ 22000). **Financial sources:** *Private:* 95%. *Self-financing:* 5%.

PUBLICATIONS: *Periodicals:* Commonweal Newsletter (3). *Annual report.*

INFORMATION AND EDUCATION ACTIVITIES: Topics: Culture/tradition/religion; Gender issues/women; International economic relations/ trade/debt/finance; International relations/cooperation/development aid; Other; Peace/ethnic conflicts/armament/disarmament; Poverty/living conditions; Racism/xenophobia/antisemitism. **Activities:** Broadcasting/ cultural events; Conferences/seminars/workshops/training activities; Lobbying/advocacy; Publishing/audiovisual materials/educational materials.

GBR2252
COMMONWEALTH ASSOCIATION OF ARCHITECTS (CAA)

66 Portland Place, London W1N 4AD, United Kingdom.

Telephone: 44 (171) 636 8276/636 7596. **Fax:** 44 (171) 255 1541. **Contact:** Wale Odeleye, President.

GBR2253
COMMONWEALTH HUMAN ECOLOGY COUNCIL (CHEC)

57/58 Stanhope Gardens, London SW7 5RF, United Kingdom.

Telephone: 44 (171) 373 6761. **Fax:** 44 (171) 244 7470. **Contact:** Zena Daysh, Executive Vice-Chairman.

OBJECTIVES: To promote understanding and action in the development of resources for the wholeness of human life and well-being, through ecologically satisfactory policies and programmes in the countries of the Commonwealth and elsewhere.

GENERAL INFORMATION: Creation: 1969. **Type of organisation:** coordinating body. **Member organisations:** 24. **Personnel/Total:** 525. *Salaried:* 5. *Volunteers:* 520 of which: 500 in developing countries. **Budget/ Total 1993:** ECU 128000 (US$ 150000). **Financial sources:** *Private:* 40%. *Public:* 50%. *Self-financing:* 10%.

PUBLICATIONS: *Periodicals:* The CHEC Journal (1) - CHEC Points Newsletter (3). *Annual report. List of publications.*

COMMENTS: National CHECs carry out activities in Asia, Africa and the Caribbean.

ACTIVITIES IN DEVELOPING REGIONS: Present in developing regions. Maintains local field presence. Works through local field partners.

GBR2254
COMMONWEALTH HUMAN RIGHTS INITIATIVE

27-28 Russell Square, London WC1B 5DS, United Kingdom.

Telephone: M4 (171) 580 5876. **Fax:** 44 (171) 255 2160. **Contact:** Richard Bourne, director.

GBR2255
COMMONWEALTH INSTITUTE (CI)

Kensington High Street, London W8 6NQ, United Kingdom.

Telephone: 44 (171) 603 4535. **Fax:** 44 (171) 602 7374. **Contact:** Hilary Sewell, Head of Marketing and Publicity.

GBR2256
COMMONWEALTH MEDICAL ASSOCIATION (CMA)

BMA House, Tavistock Square, London WC1H 9JP, United Kingdom.

Telephone: 44 (171) 383 6095. **Fax:** 44 (171) 383 6195. **Contact:** Dr. J.D.J. Havard.

OBJECTIVES: To strengthen the capacity of national medical associations in developing countries in order to improve the health and wellbeing of their communities.

GENERAL INFORMATION: Creation: 1962. **Type of organisation:** network. **Member organisations:** 38. **Personnel/Total:** 4. *Salaried:* 4. **Budget/Total 1993:** ECU 161600 (US$ 189000). **Financial sources:** *Public:* 84%. *Self-financing:* 16%.

PUBLICATIONS: *Periodicals:* Commonhealth (3) - Advocacy for Women's Health (var) - AIDS Newsletter (var). *Annual report. List of publications.*

PLANNED ACTIVITIES: Undertaking a series of regional workshops in developing countries for national medical and nursing associations on various themes: medical ethics, human rights, reproductive and adolescent health and sexuality and AIDS.

ACTIVITIES IN DEVELOPING REGIONS: Present in developing regions. Works through local field partners. **Sustainable Development Actions:** Children/youth/family; Democracy/good governance/institution building/participatory development; Gender issues/women; Health/sanitation/water; Human rights/peace/conflicts; Population/family planning/demography; Sending volunteers/experts/technical assistance. **Regions:** Caribbean; Central Asia and South Asia; East Africa; Mexico and Central America; Oceania; South East Asia; Southern Africa; West Africa.

INFORMATION AND EDUCATION ACTIVITIES: Topics: Children/youth/family; Gender issues/women; Health/sanitation/water; Human rights/peace/conflicts; Population/family planning/demography. **Activities:** Conferences/seminars/workshops/training activities; Lobbying/advocacy.

GBR2257
COMMONWEALTH SOCIETY FOR THE DEAF
105 Gower Street, London WC1E 6AH, United Kingdom.

Telephone: 44 (171) 387 8033. *Contact:* Elisabeth Lubienska.

GBR2258
COMMONWEALTH TRADE UNION COUNCIL (CTUC)
Congress House, 23 Great Russell Street, London WC1B 3LS, United Kingdom.

Telephone: 44 (171) 631 0728. *Fax:* (71) 436 0301. *Contact:* Patrick Quinn, Director.

GBR2259
CONCERN UNIVERSAL
14 Manor Road, Chatham, Kent ME4 6AN, United Kingdom.

Telephone: 44 (1634) 813942. *Fax:* 44 (1634) 402942. *Contact:* Alo Donnelly, Executive Director.

OBJECTIVES: To work for social justice through short-term relief activities and sustainable development programmes in partnership with the under-privileged people of the developing world.

GENERAL INFORMATION: Creation: 1976. *Type of organisation:* association of NGOs. *Member organisations:* 3. *Affiliated to:* AID-LINK (Ireland) - VEGFAM (United Kingdom) - CONCERN AMERICA (USA) - Refugee Trust (Ireland). *Personnel/Total:* 23. *Salaried:* 9. *Volunteers:* 14 of which: 13 in developing countries. *Budget/Total 1993:* ECU 1795000 (US$ 2103000). *Financial sources: Private:* 7%. *Public:* 93%.

PUBLICATIONS: *Periodicals:* Concern Universal News (2).

EVALUATION/RESEARCH: Evaluation reports available. Undertakes research activities.

PLANNED ACTIVITIES: Organising a campaign entitled "Change for Children".

ACTIVITIES IN DEVELOPING REGIONS: Present in developing regions. Active in 19 country(ies). Maintains local field presence. Works through local field partners. **Sustainable Development Actions:** Children/youth/family; Debt/finance/trade; Democracy/good governance/institution building/participatory development; Ecology/environment/biodiversity; Education/training/literacy; Emergency relief/refugees/humanitarian assistance; Food/famine; Gender issues/women; Health/sanitation/water; Human rights/peace/conflicts; Population/family planning/demography; Rural development/agriculture; Sending volunteers/experts/technical assistance; Small enterprises/informal sector/handicrafts; Urban development/habitat. **Regions:** Central Africa; Central Asia and South Asia; East Africa; Mexico and Central America; South America; Southern Africa; West Africa.

INFORMATION AND EDUCATION ACTIVITIES: Topics: Children/youth/family; Ecology/environment/biodiversity; Education/training/literacy; Emergency relief/refugees/humanitarian assistance; Employment/unemployment; Food/famine; Gender issues/women; Health/sanitation/

water; Refugees/migrants/ethnic groups; Rural development/agriculture; Urban development/habitat. **Activities:** Fund raising; Information campaigns/exhibitions.

GBR2260
CONCORD VIDEO AND FILM COUNCIL
201 Felixstowe Road, Ipswich, Suffolk IP3 9BJ, United Kingdom.

Telephone: 44 (1473) 726012/715754. *Fax:* 44 (1473) 274531. *Contact:* Roy Carter, General Manager.

OBJECTIVES: To distribute videos and films on developing countries, focusing on such issues as health, population, economic development and aid.

GENERAL INFORMATION: Creation: 1959. *Type of organisation:* association of NGOs. *Personnel/Total:* 15. *Salaried:* 15. *Budget/Total 1993:* ECU 256000 (US$ 300000). *Financial sources: Self-financing:* 100%.

PUBLICATIONS: *Periodicals:* Video and Film Catalogues (1). *Annual report. List of publications.*

PLANNED ACTIVITIES: Promoting all educational, ethical, social, environmental and medical programmes.

COMMENTS: Undertakes activities in the Commonwealth of Independent States.

ACTIVITIES IN DEVELOPING REGIONS: Active in 5 country(ies). **Sustainable Development Actions:** Children/youth/family; Ecology/environment/biodiversity; Education/training/literacy; Food/famine; Gender issues/women; Health/sanitation/water; Human rights/peace/conflicts; Population/family planning/demography; Urban development/habitat. **Regions:** Central Asia and South Asia; East Asia; Middle East; South East Asia; Southern Africa.

INFORMATION AND EDUCATION ACTIVITIES: Topics: Gender issues/women; Health/sanitation/water; Human rights/peace/conflicts; Peace/ethnic conflicts/armament/disarmament; Racism/xenophobia/antisemitism. **Activities:** Conferences/seminars/workshops/training activities.

GBR2261
CONFEDERATION OF REFUGEE GROUPS AND ETHNIC MINORITIES
190 Walm Lane, London NW2, United Kingdom.

Telephone: 44 (181) 450 3812.

GBR2262
CONSERVATION FOUNDATION
1 Kensington Gore, London SW7 2AR, United Kingdom.

Telephone: 44 (171) 823 8842. *Fax:* 44 (171) 823 8791. *E-mail:* conservef@gn.apc.org. *Contact:* David Shreeve, Executive Director.

OBJECTIVES: To provide a means for governments, corporations, institutions and organisations, to collaborate on environmental causes. To create and manage a wide range of projects and programmes.

GENERAL INFORMATION: Creation: 1982. *Personnel/Total:* var. *Salaried:* 4. *Volunteers:* var. *Budget/Total 1993:* ECU 320000 (US$ 375000). *Financial sources: Private:* 8%. *Public:* 30%. *Self-financing:* 62%.

PUBLICATIONS: *Periodicals:* Network 21 (2). *Annual report.*

EVALUATION/RESEARCH: Undertakes research activities.

COMMENTS: Undertakes activities in the Commonwealth of Independent States. Information activities related to the Commonwealth of Independent States.

ACTIVITIES IN DEVELOPING REGIONS: Active in 2 country(ies). Works through local field partners. **Sustainable Development Actions:** Children/youth/family; Ecology/environment/biodiversity; Education/training/literacy; Rural development/agriculture. **Regions:** East Africa.

INFORMATION AND EDUCATION ACTIVITIES: Topics: Ecology/environment/biodiversity; International relations/cooperation/development aid. **Activities:** Conferences/seminars/workshops/training activities; Exchanges/twinning/linking; Networking/electronic telecommunications.

GBR2263

CONSORTIUM FOR STREET CHILDREN

House of Commons, Room 301, Norman Shaw South, Victoria Embankment, London SW1A 2H2, United Kingdom.

Telephone: 44 (171) 219 2492. *Fax:* 44 (171) 219 2641.

GBR2264

CONSUMERS' INTERNATIONAL

24 Highbury Crescent, London N5 5RX, United Kingdom.

Telephone: 44 (171) 226 6663. *Fax:* 44 (171) 354 0607. *E-mail:* sharon@iocu.dircon.co.uk. *Contact:* James Firebrace.

OBJECTIVES: To build the international consumer movement to enable it to protect and promote consumer rights and interests. To represent consumer concerns on international policy-making bodies.

GENERAL INFORMATION: *Creation:* 1960. *Member organisations:* 203. *Affiliated to:* CONGO - NGO Committee on Ageing - NGO Committee on the Status of Women - NGO Committee on the Family. *Personnel/Total:* 70. *Salaried:* 70 of which: 48 in developing countries. *Budget/Total 1993:* ECU 2845379 (US$ 3333000). *Financial sources:* Private: 4%. Public: 52%. Self-financing: 44%.

PUBLICATIONS: *Periodicals:* World Consumer (6) - Consumer Currents (10) - Consumidores y Desarrollo (10) -Africa Circular Newsletter (6) - Kontakt (6). *Annual report. List of publications.*

EVALUATION/RESEARCH: Undertakes research activities.

PLANNED ACTIVITIES: The education of consumers about the effects of GATT and the promotion of sustainable consumption and production.

COMMENTS: Undertakes activities in the Commonwealth of Independent States. Information activities related to the Commonwealth of Independent States.

ACTIVITIES IN DEVELOPING REGIONS: Present in developing regions. Active in 47 country(ies). Maintains local field presence. Works through local field partners. **Sustainable Development Actions:** Children/youth/family; Debt/finance/trade; Democracy/good governance/institution building/participatory development; Ecology/environment/biodiversity; Education/training/literacy; Food/famine; Gender issues/women; Health/sanitation/water; Urban development/habitat. **Regions:** Central Asia and South Asia; East Africa; East Asia; Mexico and Central America; Oceania; South America; South East Asia; Southern Africa; West Africa.

INFORMATION AND EDUCATION ACTIVITIES: **Topics:** Children/youth/family; Ecology/environment/biodiversity; Education/training/literacy; Food/famine; Gender issues/women; Health/sanitation/water; International economic relations/trade/debt/finance; International relations/cooperation/development aid; Poverty/living conditions; Urban development/habitat. **Activities:** Conferences/seminars/workshops/training activities; Exchanges/twinning/linking; Formal education; Fund raising; Information and documentation services/data bases; Information campaigns/exhibitions; Lobbying/advocacy; Networking/electronic telecommunications; Publishing/audiovisual materials/educational materials.

GBR2265

COUNCIL FOR EDUCATION IN WORLD CITIZENSHIP (CEWC)

Seymour Mews House, Seymour Mews, London W1H 9PE, United Kingdom.

Telephone: 44 (171) 935 1752. *Fax:* 44 (171) 935 5741. *Contact:* Patricia Rogers, Director.

OBJECTIVES: To prepare young people for their responsibilities as citizens in an internationally interdependent world. To encourage the study and understanding of world affairs.

GENERAL INFORMATION: *Creation:* 1939. *Affiliated to:* Inter Agency Committee on Development Education - Council of Europe North-South Quadrilogue - NGO Constituency of the EEC - All Party Parliamentary Group on Overseas Development - Development Education Association - Human Rights Education Network - National Peace Council - Environmental Information Forum -Saferworld. *Personnel/Total:* 37. *Salaried:* 7. *Volunteers:* 30. *Budget/Total 1993:*

ECU 205155 (US$ 240000). *Financial sources:* Private: 5%. Public: 75%. Self-financing: 20%.

PUBLICATIONS: *Annual report. List of publications.*

EVALUATION/RESEARCH: Undertakes research activities.

PLANNED ACTIVITIES: The publishing of workshop material on various themes related to homelessness. The development of a support pack for the Model United Nations General Assemblies.

COMMENTS: Information activities related to the Commonwealth of Independent States.

INFORMATION AND EDUCATION ACTIVITIES: **Topics:** Children/youth/family; Culture/tradition/religion; Ecology/environment/biodiversity; Education/training/literacy; Emergency relief/refugees/humanitarian assistance; Employment/unemployment; Food/famine; Gender issues/women; Health/sanitation/water; Human rights/peace/conflicts; International economic relations/trade/debt/finance; International relations/cooperation/development aid; Peace/ethnic conflicts/armament/disarmament; Population/family planning/demography; Poverty/living conditions; Racism/xenophobia/antisemitism; Refugees/migrants/ethnic groups; Rural development/agriculture; Urban development/habitat. **Activities:** Conferences/seminars/workshops/training activities; Formal education; Information and documentation services/data bases; Information campaigns/exhibitions; Networking/electronic telecommunications; Publishing/audiovisual materials/educational materials.

GBR2266

THE COUNCIL FOR WORLD MISSION (CWM)

11 Carteret Street Livingstone House, London SW1H 9DL, United Kingdom.

Telephone: 44 (171) 222 4214. *Fax:* 44 (171) 233 1747. *Contact:* D.P. Niles, General Secretary.

OBJECTIVES: To spread the knowledge of Christ throughout the world. To undertake development programmes.

GENERAL INFORMATION: *Creation:* 1977. *Affiliated to:* World Council of Churches (Switzerland). *Personnel/Total:* 20. *Salaried:* 20. *Budget/Total 1993:* ECU 3014489 (US$ 3531000). *Financial sources:* Private: 3%. Self-financing: 97%.

PUBLICATIONS: *Periodicals:* News Share (6) - Insaka (4). *Annual report. List of publications.*

EVALUATION/RESEARCH: Undertakes research activities.

PLANNED ACTIVITIES: Acting as a partner in the Mission Conference and undertaking awareness raising on various themes such as bars to women in the Church and society in Southern Africa and the Pacific.

ACTIVITIES IN DEVELOPING REGIONS: Works through local field partners. **Sustainable Development Actions:** Children/youth/family; Debt/finance/trade; Democracy/good governance/institution building/participatory development; Ecology/environment/biodiversity; Education/training/literacy; Emergency relief/refugees/humanitarian assistance; Energy/transport; Food/famine; Gender issues/women; Health/sanitation/water; Human rights/peace/conflicts; Rural development/agriculture; Sending volunteers/experts/technical assistance; Small enterprises/informal sector/handicrafts; Urban development/habitat. **Regions:** Caribbean; Central Asia and South Asia; East Asia; Oceania; South America; South East Asia; Southern Africa.

INFORMATION AND EDUCATION ACTIVITIES: **Topics:** Children/youth/family; Culture/tradition/religion; Ecology/environment/biodiversity; Education/training/literacy; Emergency relief/refugees/humanitarian assistance; Food/famine; Gender issues/women; Health/sanitation/water; Human rights/peace/conflicts; International economic relations/trade/debt/finance; International relations/cooperation/development aid; Peace/ethnic conflicts/armament/disarmament; Poverty/living conditions; Racism/xenophobia/antisemitism; Refugees/migrants/ethnic groups; Rural development/agriculture; Urban development/habitat. **Activities:** Conferences/seminars/workshops/training activities; Exchanges/twinning/linking; Formal education; Fund raising; Information and documentation services/data bases; Lobbying/advocacy; Publishing/audiovisual materials/educational materials.

See: *How to Use the Directory*, page 11.

GBR2267

COUNCIL OF CHURCHES FOR BRITAIN AND IRELAND

Inter-Church House, 35-41 Lower Marsh, London SE1 7RL, United Kingdom.

Telephone: 44 (171) 620 4444. *Fax:* 44 (171) 928 0010. *Contact:* Reud Keith Clements, Coordinating Secretary for International Affairs.

OBJECTIVES: To co-ordinate the work of all the major churches in Britain and Ireland, including in the areas of public and international affairs.

GENERAL INFORMATION: *Creation:* 1990. *Type of organisation:* network. *Member organisations:* 35. *Personnel/Total:* 50. *Salaried:* 50.

PUBLICATIONS: *List of publications.*

EVALUATION/RESEARCH: Undertakes research activities.

COMMENTS: CCBI finds the resources for member churches working on Africa, former Yugoslavia, arms trade, human rights and nuclear non-proliferation. Most of the work in development undertaken on behalf of CCBI is carried out by the aid agencies Christian Aid, CAFOD and SCIAF. One World Week is a body in association with CCBI. Information activities related to the Commonwealth of Independent States.

GBR2268

CUSICHACA PROJECT TRUST

Springfields, 62 High Street, Belbroughton, Stourbridge, West Midland DY9 9SU, United Kingdom.

Contact: Ann Kendall.

GBR2269

CYFANFYD ♦ Whole World

27 Church Road, Whitchurch, Cardiff CF4 2DX, Wales, United Kingdom.

Telephone: 44 (1222) 614435. *Contact:* Elenid Jones, Secretary.

OBJECTIVES: To promote through conferences and exhibitions a wider interest in development education in Welsh colleges.

GENERAL INFORMATION: *Creation:* 1991. *Type of organisation:* association of NGOs. *Personnel/Total:* 8. *Volunteers:* 8. *Financial sources:* Private: 100%.

INFORMATION AND EDUCATION ACTIVITIES: Topics: Children/youth/family; Culture/tradition/religion; Ecology/environment/biodiversity; Education/training/literacy; Emergency relief/refugees/humanitarian assistance; Employment/unemployment; Food/famine; Gender issues/women; Health/sanitation/water; Human rights/peace/conflicts; International economic relations/trade/debt/finance; International relations/cooperation/development aid; Peace/ethnic conflicts/armament/disarmament; Population/family planning/demography; Poverty/living conditions; Racism/xenophobia/antisemitism; Refugees/migrants/ethnic groups; Rural development/agriculture; Urban development/habitat. **Activities:** Conferences/seminars/workshops/training activities; Formal education; Information campaigns/exhibitions; Lobbying/advocacy.

GBR2270

DERRY DEVELOPMENT EDUCATION CENTRE (DDEC) ♦ Centre de Derry pour l'éducation au développement

13a Pump Street, Derry BT48 6JG, United Kingdom.

Telephone: 44 (1504) 269183. *Contact:* Martin Walsh.

GBR2271

DEVELOPMENT EDUCATION ASSOCIATION (DEA)

3rd floor, 29-31 Cowper Street, London EC2A 4AP, United Kingdom.

Telephone: 44 (171) 490 8108. *Fax:* 44 (171) 490 8123. *Contact:* Doug Bourn, Co-ordinator.

OBJECTIVES: To promote development education in the United Kingdom. To provide information and support to development education practitioners. To facilitate networking and co-operation at local, national and international levels.

GENERAL INFORMATION: *Creation:* 1993. *Type of organisation:* network. *Member organisations:* 40. *Personnel/Total:* 7. Salaried:

7. *Budget/Total 1993:* ECU 256443 (US$ 300000). *Financial sources:* Private: 33%. Public: 34%. Self-financing: 33%.

PUBLICATIONS: *Periodicals:* DEA Monthly Bulletin (12) - The development education journal (2). *Annual report. List of publications.*

EVALUATION/RESEARCH: Evaluation reports available. Undertakes research activities.

INFORMATION AND EDUCATION ACTIVITIES: Topics: Children/youth/family; Culture/tradition/religion; Ecology/environment/biodiversity; Education/training/literacy; Employment/unemployment; Food/famine; Gender issues/women; Health/sanitation/water; Human rights/peace/conflicts; International economic relations/trade/debt/finance; International relations/cooperation/development aid; Peace/ethnic conflicts/armament/disarmament; Population/family planning/demography; Poverty/living conditions; Racism/xenophobia/antisemitism; Refugees/migrants/ethnic groups; Rural development/agriculture. **Activities:** Publishing/audiovisual materials/educational materials.

GBR2272

DEVELOPMENT INITIATIVES

258 Pentonville Road, London N1 9JY, United Kingdom.

Telephone: 44 (171) 278 3833.

GBR2273

DEVELOPMENT PLANNING UNIT (DPU)

9 Endsleigh Gardens, London WC1H 0ED, United Kingdom.

Telephone: 44 (171) 388 7581. *Fax:* 44 (171) 387 4541. *Contact:* Patrick Wakely, Director.

OBJECTIVES: To enhance the capacity of developing countries to cope with the problems of accelerated urbanisation through training, educational programmes and consultancy in London and overseas, in the fields of urban and regional planning, city management, transportation and housing.

GENERAL INFORMATION: *Creation:* 1971. *Personnel/Total:* 20. *Salaried:* 20 of which: 2 in developing countries. *Budget/Total 1993:* ECU 1093730 (US$ 1281000). *Financial sources:* Self-financing: 100%.

PUBLICATIONS: *Periodicals:* DPU Working Papers (var) - DPU News (2). *List of publications.*

EVALUATION/RESEARCH: Evaluation reports available. Undertakes research activities.

COMMENTS: Undertakes activities in the Commonwealth of Independent States. Information activities related to the Commonwealth of Independent States.

ACTIVITIES IN DEVELOPING REGIONS: Present in developing regions. Active in 9 country(ies). Works through local field partners. **Sustainable Development Actions:** Democracy/good governance/institution building/participatory development; Gender issues/women; Urban development/habitat. **Regions:** Caribbean; Central Asia and South Asia; East Africa; Mexico and Central America; Middle East; South America; South East Asia; Southern Africa; West Africa.

INFORMATION AND EDUCATION ACTIVITIES: Topics: Gender issues/women; Urban development/habitat. **Activities:** Formal education.

GBR2274

DEVON AID

14 South Avenue,, Exeter, Devon EX1 2DZ, United Kingdom.

Telephone: 44 (1392) 77520. *Contact:* Richard King.

OBJECTIVES: To promote community links between towns and villages in Devon (England) and communities in Africa and Asia for education, community development and mutual understanding.

GENERAL INFORMATION: *Creation:* 1986. *Type of organisation:* network. *Affiliated to:* UK One World Links Association. *Personnel/Total:* 10. *Volunteers:* 10. *Budget/Total 1993:* ECU 1300 (US$ 1500). *Financial sources:* Private: 50%. Self-financing: 50%.

PUBLICATIONS: *Periodicals:* Devon Aid News (1).

EVALUATION/RESEARCH: Evaluation reports available.

ACTIVITIES IN DEVELOPING REGIONS: Active in 10 country(ies). Works through local field partners. **Sustainable Development Actions:** Children/youth/family; Education/training/literacy; Gender issues/women; Health/sanitation/water; Rural development/agriculture; Sending volunteers/experts/technical assistance. **Regions:** Central Africa; Central Asia and South Asia; East Africa; West Africa.

INFORMATION AND EDUCATION ACTIVITIES: Topics: Children/youth/family; Education/training/literacy; Gender issues/women; Health/sanitation/water; Rural development/agriculture; Urban development/habitat. **Activities:** Conferences/seminars/workshops/training activities; Exchanges/twinning/linking; Fund raising.

GBR2275
DHAMMANAT FOUNDATION

Nettlecombe Studios, Williton, Taunton, Somerset TA4 4HS, United Kingdom.

Contact: Pat Wolsey.

GBR2276
DISASTERS EMERGENCY COMMITTEE ♦ Comité d'urgence pour les désastres

c/o SCF, Grove Lane, London SE5 8RD, United Kingdom.

Telephone: 44 (171) 703 5400. *Fax:* 44 (171) 252 4805. *Contact:* Baroness Shreela Flather, Chairman.

OBJECTIVES: To raise funds nationally on television, radio and via the press for Committee members involved in relief measures during an overseas disaster.

GENERAL INFORMATION: *Creation:* 1963. *Type of organisation:* coordinating body. *Member organisations:* 7. *Personnel/Total:* 8. *Salaried:* 3. *Volunteers:* 5. *Budget/Total 1993:* ECU 192000 (US$ 225000). *Financial sources: Public:* 40%. *Self-financing:* 60%.

PUBLICATIONS: *Annual report.*

INFORMATION AND EDUCATION ACTIVITIES: Topics: Emergency relief/refugees/humanitarian assistance. **Activities:** Fund raising; Information campaigns/exhibitions.

GBR2277
DURHAM - LESOTHO DIOCESAN LINK

26 Allergate, Durham DH1 4ET, United Kingdom.

Telephone: 44 (191) 384 8385. *Contact:* Reverend G.S. Pedley.

OBJECTIVES: To support the exchange of ideas, information and personnel between the two Anglican dioceses and to generate self-help schemes at the community level in Lesotho.

GENERAL INFORMATION: *Creation:* 1986. *Type of organisation:* association of NGOs. *Member organisations:* 1. *Volunteers:* 78 of which: 12 in developing countries. *Budget/Total 1993:* ECU 295000 (US$ 345000). *Financial sources: Private:* 50%. *Public:* 50%.

PUBLICATIONS: *Periodicals:* MOHO-TOGETHER (2). *Annual report.*

EVALUATION/RESEARCH: Evaluation reports available.

ACTIVITIES IN DEVELOPING REGIONS: Present in developing regions. Active in 1 country(ies). Maintains local field presence. Works through local field partners. **Sustainable Development Actions:** Children/youth/family; Democracy/good governance/institution building/participatory development; Ecology/environment/biodiversity; Education/training/literacy; Energy/transport; Food/famine; Gender issues/women; Health/sanitation/water; Rural development/agriculture; Sending volunteers/experts/technical assistance; Small enterprises/informal sector/handicrafts. **Regions:** Southern Africa.

INFORMATION AND EDUCATION ACTIVITIES: Topics: Children/youth/family; Ecology/environment/biodiversity; Education/training/literacy; Food/famine; Gender issues/women; Health/sanitation/water; International relations/cooperation/development aid; Poverty/living conditions; Rural development/agriculture. **Activities:** Conferences/seminars/workshops/training activities; Formal education; Fund raising; Information campaigns/exhibitions.

GBR2278
EARTHWATCH EUROPE

Belsyre Court, 57 Woodstock Road , Oxford OX2 6HU, United Kingdom.

Telephone: 44 (1865) 311600. *Fax:* 44 (1865) 311383. *Contact:* Brian W. Walker, Executive Director.

OBJECTIVES: To improve human understanding of the planet, the diversity of its inhabitants and the processes which affect the quality of life on earth. To support high quality field-based research on the earth, life and human sciences and humanities.

GENERAL INFORMATION: *Creation:* 1985. *Type of organisation:* association of NGOs. *Member organisations:* 5. *Personnel/Total:* 22. *Salaried:* 16. *Volunteers:* 6. *Budget/Total 1993:* ECU 1538658 (US$ 1802000). *Financial sources: Private:* 35%. *Public:* 5%. *Self-financing:* 60%.

PUBLICATIONS: *Periodicals:* Earthwatch (6) - Earthwatch Europe Bulletin (6). *Annual report.*

EVALUATION/RESEARCH: Evaluation reports available. Undertakes research activities.

PLANNED ACTIVITIES: The preparation of a teachers' resource pack and carrying out various programmes: a teacher fellowship programme for Africa and Asia and a European-based events programme and "discovery trips".

COMMENTS: Undertakes activities in the Commonwealth of Independent States. Information activities related to the Commonwealth of Independent States.

ACTIVITIES IN DEVELOPING REGIONS: Present in developing regions. Active in 40 country(ies). Maintains local field presence. Works through local field partners. **Sustainable Development Actions:** Children/youth/family; Democracy/good governance/institution building/participatory development; Ecology/environment/biodiversity; Education/training/literacy; Energy/transport; Health/sanitation/water; Population/family planning/demography; Rural development/agriculture; Sending volunteers/experts/technical assistance. **Regions:** Caribbean; Central Africa; Central Asia and South Asia; East Africa; East Asia; Mexico and Central America; Middle East; North Africa; Oceania; South America; South East Asia; Southern Africa; West Africa.

INFORMATION AND EDUCATION ACTIVITIES: Topics: Culture/tradition/religion; Ecology/environment/biodiversity; Education/training/literacy; Health/sanitation/water; Poverty/living conditions; Rural development/agriculture. **Activities:** Broadcasting/cultural events; Conferences/seminars/workshops/training activities; Exchanges/twinning/linking; Formal education; Fund raising; Information and documentation services/data bases; Information campaigns/exhibitions; Networking/electronic telecommunications; Publishing/audiovisual materials/educational materials.

GBR2279
EARTHWISE

Exmoor House, Methuen Street, Southampton S02 0FQ, United Kingdom.

Telephone: 44 (1703) 336446. *Fax:* 44 (1703) 230440. *Contact:* Sue Johnson, Director.

OBJECTIVES: To raise environmental and ethical awareness through consultancy, research, education, training and information services. To foster North-South Relations in order to diminish the existing social, political, economic and environmental inequities.

GENERAL INFORMATION: *Creation:* 1991. *Personnel/Total:* 3. *Salaried:* 3.

PUBLICATIONS: *Annual report. List of publications.*

EVALUATION/RESEARCH: Evaluation reports available. Undertakes research activities.

See: *How to Use the Directory,* page 11.

INFORMATION AND EDUCATION ACTIVITIES: **Topics:** Children/youth/family; Culture/tradition/religion; Ecology/environment/biodiversity; Education/training/literacy; Emergency relief/refugees/humanitarian assistance; Employment/unemployment; Food/famine; Gender issues/women; Health/sanitation/water; Human rights/peace/conflicts; International economic relations/trade/debt/finance; International relations/cooperation/development aid; Peace/ethnic conflicts/armament/disarmament; Population/family planning/demography; Poverty/living conditions; Racism/xenophobia/antisemitism; Refugees/migrants/ethnic groups; Rural development/agriculture; Urban development/habitat. **Activities:** Conferences/seminars/workshops/training activities; Information and documentation services/data bases; Information campaigns/exhibitions; Networking/electronic telecommunications; Publishing/audiovisual materials/educational materials.

GBR2280
ECHO INTERNATIONAL HEALTH SERVICES LIMITED

Ullswater Crescent, Coulsdon, Surrey CR5 2HR, United Kingdom.

Telephone: 44 (181) 660 2220. **Fax:** 44 (181) 668 0751. **Contact:** Keith Slatter, Chief Executive.

OBJECTIVES: To supply low cost medical equipment, pharmaceuticals and other items on demand to mission, charity and government hospitals in developing countries. To provide specialised medical, pharmaceutical, and technical advisory services without cost to mission and charity medical units.

GENERAL INFORMATION: Creation: 1966. **Member organisations:** 26. **Affiliated to:** EC NGO Network (United Kingdom) - British Overseas NGOs for Development - UK NGO AIDS Consortium for the Third World. **Personnel/Total:** 70. Salaried: 70. **Budget/Total 1993:** ECU 8975510 (US$ 10514000). **Financial sources:** Private: 4%. Self-financing: 96%.

PUBLICATIONS: Periodicals: ECHO Around the World Newsletter (2). *Annual report.*

COMMENTS: Undertakes activities in the Commonwealth of Independent States.

ACTIVITIES IN DEVELOPING REGIONS: Active in 120 country(ies). Works through local field partners. **Sustainable Development Actions:** Children/youth/family; Democracy/good governance/institution building/participatory development; Emergency relief/refugees/humanitarian assistance; Health/sanitation/water. **Regions:** Caribbean; Central Africa; Central Asia and South Asia; East Africa; East Asia; Mexico and Central America; Middle East; North Africa; Oceania; South America; South East Asia; Southern Africa; West Africa.

INFORMATION AND EDUCATION ACTIVITIES: Topics: Health/sanitation/water; Poverty/living conditions; Refugees/migrants/ethnic groups. **Activities:** Fund raising.

GBR2281
EDUCATION FOR DEVELOPMENT

Woodmans, Westwood Row, Tilehurst, Reading RG3 6LT, United Kingdom.

Telephone: 44 (1734) 426772. **Fax:** 44 (1734) 852080. **E-mail:** emsroyal@reading.ac.uk. **Contact:** Alan Rogers, Executive Director.

OBJECTIVES: To promote the use of modern approaches to adult learning in development programmes in developing countries. To provide opportunities for those engaged in adult education and development in the West to learn from Third World development programmes.

GENERAL INFORMATION: Creation: 1985. **Personnel/Total:** 2. Salaried: 2. **Budget/Total 1993:** ECU 38470 (US$ 45000). **Financial sources:** Private: 10%. Public: 80%. Self-financing: 10%.

PUBLICATIONS: *Annual report. List of publications.*

EVALUATION/RESEARCH: Evaluation reports available. Undertakes research activities.

PLANNED ACTIVITIES: Various literacy projects and training programmes in Havana, South Africa, India, China (adult education) and agricultural training in Jamaica.

COMMENTS: Information activities related to the Commonwealth of Independent States.

ACTIVITIES IN DEVELOPING REGIONS: Active in 7 country(ies). Maintains local field presence. Works through local field partners. **Sustainable Development Actions:** Democracy/good governance/institution building/participatory development; Education/training/literacy; Gender issues/women; Human rights/peace/conflicts; Population/family planning/demography; Rural development/agriculture; Sending volunteers/experts/technical assistance; Small enterprises/informal sector/handicrafts. **Regions:** Caribbean; Central Asia and South Asia; East Africa; Middle East; North Africa; Southern Africa.

INFORMATION AND EDUCATION ACTIVITIES: Topics: Education/training/literacy; Gender issues/women; Health/sanitation/water; Population/family planning/demography; Rural development/agriculture. **Activities:** Conferences/seminars/workshops/training activities; Exchanges/twinning/linking; Formal education; Information and documentation services/data bases; Information campaigns/exhibitions; Lobbying/advocacy; Publishing/audiovisual materials/educational materials.

GBR2282
ETHIOPIAID

114 Peascod Street, Windsor, Berks SL4 1DT, United Kingdom.

Telephone: 44 (1753) 868277. **Fax:** 44 (1753) 841688. **Contact:** Tom Lovell, Administrator.

OBJECTIVES: To raise money in Britain to support projects in Ethiopia, particularly long-term indigenous projects in and around Addis Ababa.

GENERAL INFORMATION: Creation: 1989. **Personnel/Total:** 2. Salaried: 1. Volunteers: 1. **Budget/Total 1993:** ECU 769000 (US$ 900000). **Financial sources:** Private: 100%.

EVALUATION/RESEARCH: Evaluation reports available.

ACTIVITIES IN DEVELOPING REGIONS: Active in 1 country(ies). Works through local field partners. **Sustainable Development Actions:** Children/youth/family; Education/training/literacy; Emergency relief/refugees/humanitarian assistance; Food/famine; Gender issues/women; Health/sanitation/water; Population/family planning/demography; Small enterprises/informal sector/handicrafts; Urban development/habitat. **Regions:** East Africa.

INFORMATION AND EDUCATION ACTIVITIES: Topics: Emergency relief/refugees/humanitarian assistance; Urban development/habitat. **Activities:** Fund raising.

GBR2283
EUROPEAN CONSULTATION ON REFUGEES AND EXILES (ECRE) ♦ Consultation Européenne sur les Réfugiés et les Exilés

Bondway House, 3/9 Bondway, Wauxhall, London SW8 1SJ, United Kingdom.

Telephone: 44 (71) 582 9928. **Fax:** 44 (71) 820 9725. **E-mail:** (GEONET) NCR 1: ECRE.. **Contact:** Philip Rudge, General Secretary.

GBR2284
EUROPEAN CONTACT GROUP ON URBAN INDUSTRIAL MISSION (ECG) ♦ Communauté Européenne de Travail Eglise et Société Industrielle

48 Peveril Crescent, Manchester M21 9WS, United Kingdom.

Telephone: 44 (161) 881 6031/275 6534. **Fax:** 44 (161) 881 6031. **Contact:** Rev. A.J. Addy.

OBJECTIVES: To co-ordinate the actions of church related organisations involved in improving living and working conditions. To provide information, training and development. To facilitate common actions and networking by those affected by economic or social policy.

GENERAL INFORMATION: Creation: 1966. **Type of organisation:** coordinating body. **Member organisations:** 20. **Affiliated to:** European Ecumenical Commission on Church and Society (Belgium) - Conference of European Churches (Switzerland). **Personnel/Total:** 2. Salaried: 2. **Budget/Total 1993:** ECU 128222 (US$ 150000). **Financial sources:** Private: 70%. Public: 10%. Self-financing: 20%.

Voir : *Comment utiliser le répertoire*, page 11.

PUBLICATIONS: *Periodicals:* ECG News (3). *List of publications.*

EVALUATION/RESEARCH: Undertakes research activities.

PLANNED ACTIVITIES: Carrying out a programme on economic literacy for women and on new ways of organising for marginalised workers.

COMMENTS: Information activities related to the Commonwealth of Independent States.

INFORMATION AND EDUCATION ACTIVITIES: Topics: Culture/tradition/religion; Education/training/literacy; Employment/unemployment; Gender issues/women; Poverty/living conditions; Racism/xenophobia/antisemitism; Refugees/migrants/ethnic groups; Urban development/habitat. Activities: Conferences/seminars/workshops/training activities; Exchanges/twinning/linking; Information and documentation services/data bases; Lobbying/advocacy; Networking/electronic telecommunications.

GBR2285

EUROPEAN DEVELOPMENT EDUCATION NETWORK (EDEN)

♦ Réseau Européen de l'Education au Développement

41 Derby Road, Melbourne, Derbyshire DE73 1FE, United Kingdom.

Telephone: 44 (1332) 864794. *Fax:* 44 (1332) 864794. *E-mail:* eden@gn.apc.org. *Contact:* Pat Gerrard, Networker.

OBJECTIVES: To maintain and build contacts in Europe between churches and church-related agencies involved in development education.

GENERAL INFORMATION: *Creation:* 1990. *Type of organisation:* network. *Member organisations:* 170. *Affiliated to:* ARENA Network - World Council of Churches (Switzerland). *Personnel/Total:* 1. *Salaried:* 1. *Budget/Total 1993:* ECU 9000 (US$ 11000). *Financial sources:* Public: 7%. Self-financing: 93%.

PUBLICATIONS: *Periodicals:* EDEN News (3). *Annual report.*

PLANNED ACTIVITIES: Partaking in a campaign on "Fortress Europe" and on Southern perspectives of theological education. A conference on "Theology of Hope" for educators.

COMMENTS: Information activities related to the Commonwealth of Independent States.

INFORMATION AND EDUCATION ACTIVITIES: Topics: Children/youth/family; Culture/tradition/religion; Ecology/environment/biodiversity; Education/training/literacy; Emergency relief/refugees/humanitarian assistance; Employment/unemployment; Food/famine; Gender issues/women; Health/sanitation/water; Human rights/peace/conflicts; International economic relations/trade/debt/finance; International relations/cooperation/development aid; Peace/ethnic conflicts/armament/disarmament; Population/family planning/demography; Poverty/living conditions; Racism/xenophobia/antisemitism; Refugees/migrants/ethnic groups; Rural development/agriculture; Urban development/habitat. Activities: Networking/electronic telecommunications.

GBR2286

EUROPEAN DIALOGUE (ED)

11 Goodwin Street, London 3HQ, United Kingdom.

Telephone: 44 (71) 272 9092. *Fax:* 44 (71) 272 9092. *Contact:* Jeanette Bvirski, Co-ordinator.

GBR2287

EUROPEAN HUMAN RIGHTS FOUNDATION

95a Chancery Lane, London WC2 1DT, United Kingdom.

GBR2288

FARMERS' WORLD NETWORK (FWN)

The Arthur Rank Centre, National Agricultural Centre, Kenilworth, Warwickshire CV8 2LZ, United Kingdom.

Telephone: 44 (1203) 696969 ext 338. *Fax:* 44 (1203) 696900. *Contact:* Adrian Friggens, Co-ordinator.

OBJECTIVES: To raise awareness in the United Kingdom farming community about farming and policies in developing countries and the effects of European farm practices.

GENERAL INFORMATION: *Creation:* 1985. *Type of organisation:* network. *Personnel/Total:* 6. Salaried: 6. *Budget/Total 1993:* ECU 128000 (US$ 150000). *Financial sources:* Private: 45%. Public: 50%. Self-financing: 5%.

PUBLICATIONS: *Periodicals:* Landmark (6) - Agri-Repère (6). *List of publications.*

EVALUATION/RESEARCH: Evaluation reports available.

INFORMATION AND EDUCATION ACTIVITIES: Topics: Rural development/agriculture. Activities: Conferences/seminars/workshops/training activities; Exchanges/twinning/linking; Information campaigns/exhibitions.

GBR2289

FEED THE CHILDREN EUROPE

82 Caversham road, Reading, Berkshire, RG1 8AE, United Kingdom.

Telephone: 44 (1734) 584000. *Fax:* 44 (1734) 588988. *Contact:* David Grobb, Executive Director.

OBJECTIVES: To relieve those who are suffering hardship or distress anywhere in the world as a result of famine, drought, flood, war or any other calamity.

GENERAL INFORMATION: *Creation:* 1990. *Personnel/Total:* 120. Salaried: 40 of which: 15 in developing countries. Volunteers: 80. *Budget/Total 1993:* ECU 4549000 (US$ 5328000). *Financial sources:* Private: 49%. Public: 51%.

PUBLICATIONS: *Periodicals:* Annual Review (1) - Feedback (4). *Annual report.*

COMMENTS: Feed the Children Europe will soon have programmes in Armenia and Haiti. Undertakes activities in the Commonwealth of Independent States. Information activities related to the Commonwealth of Independent States.

ACTIVITIES IN DEVELOPING REGIONS: Present in developing regions. Active in 5 country(ies). Maintains local field presence. Sustainable Development Actions: Children/youth/family; Emergency relief/refugees/humanitarian assistance; Food/famine; Gender issues/women; Health/sanitation/water. Regions: Central Africa.

INFORMATION AND EDUCATION ACTIVITIES: Topics: Children/youth/family; Culture/tradition/religion; Education/training/literacy; Emergency relief/refugees/humanitarian assistance; Food/famine; Gender issues/women; Health/sanitation/water; Poverty/living conditions; Refugees/migrants/ethnic groups. Activities: Fund raising; Information campaigns/exhibitions; Publishing/audiovisual materials/educational materials.

GBR2290

FEED THE MINDS

Robertson House, Leas Road, Guildford, Surrey GU1 4QW, United Kingdom.

Telephone: 44 (1483) 577877. *Fax:* 44 (1483) 301387. *Contact:* Alwyn Marriage.

OBJECTIVES: To contribute to the production and distribution of literature and promote literacy in developing countries by giving grants to projects set up by regionally-based churches and Christian organisations.

GENERAL INFORMATION: *Creation:* 1964. *Type of organisation:* coordinating body. *Member organisations:* 18. *Personnel/Total:* 9. Salaried: 5. Volunteers: 4. *Budget/Total 1993:* ECU 428000 (US$ 501000). *Financial sources:* Private: 88%. Public: 7%. Self-financing: 5%.

PUBLICATIONS: *Periodicals:* Theological Book Review (3). *Annual report. List of publications.*

COMMENTS: Undertakes activities in the Commonwealth of Independent States. Information activities related to the Commonwealth of Independent States.

ACTIVITIES IN DEVELOPING REGIONS: Active in 30 country(ies). Works through local field partners. Sustainable Development Actions: Children/youth/family; Education/training/literacy; Gender issues/women;

See: *How to Use the Directory,* page 11.

Rural development/agriculture. **Regions:** Central Asia and South Asia; South America; Southern Africa.

INFORMATION AND EDUCATION ACTIVITIES: Topics: Culture/tradition/religion; Education/training/literacy. **Activities:** Conferences/seminars/workshops/training activities; Fund raising; Information campaigns/exhibitions.

GBR2291
FIND YOUR FEET (FYF)

Fenner Brockway House, 37-39 Great Guildford Street, London SE1 OES, United Kingdom.

Telephone: 44 (171) 794 6435. *Contact:* Jenni Sindfield.

GBR2292
FOOD AND AGRICULTURAL RESEARCH MANAGEMENT AFRICA (FARM-AFRICA)

9-10 Southampton Place, London WC1A 2DA, United Kingdom.

Telephone: 44 (171) 430 0440. *Fax:* 44 (171) 430 0460. *E-mail:* FarmAfrica@gn.apc.org. *Contact:* David Campbell, Executive Director.

OBJECTIVES: To provide long-term assistance to enable the people of Africa to feed themselves and provide marketable surpluses, and so break the cycle of famine. To develop sustainable systems of agriculture and to preserve and maintain the African environment.

GENERAL INFORMATION: *Creation:* 1985. *Personnel/Total:* 136. *Salaried:* 130 of which: 120 in developing countries. *Volunteers:* 6 of which: 2 in developing countries. *Budget/Total 1993:* ECU 1795000 (US$ 2103000). *Financial sources:* Private: 10%. Public: 90%.

PUBLICATIONS: *Periodicals:* FARM-Africa Newsletter (4). *Annual report.*

ACTIVITIES IN DEVELOPING REGIONS: Present in developing regions. Active in 4 country(ies). Maintains local field presence. Works through local field partners. **Sustainable Development Actions:** Children/youth/family; Ecology/environment/biodiversity; Education/training/literacy; Emergency relief/refugees/humanitarian assistance; Food/famine; Gender issues/women; Health/sanitation/water; Population/family planning/demography; Rural development/agriculture; Sending volunteers/experts/technical assistance; Small enterprises/informal sector/handicrafts. **Regions:** East Africa; Southern Africa.

INFORMATION AND EDUCATION ACTIVITIES: Topics: Children/youth/family; Ecology/environment/biodiversity; Education/training/literacy; Emergency relief/refugees/humanitarian assistance; Food/famine; Gender issues/women; Health/sanitation/water; Population/family planning/demography; Poverty/living conditions; Rural development/agriculture. **Activities:** Conferences/seminars/workshops/training activities; Fund raising.

GBR2293
FOOD FOR THE HUNGRY

6 Galtres Avenue, Stockton Lane, York Y03 0JT, United Kingdom.

Telephone: 44 (1904) 424136. *Fax:* 44 (1904) 424136. *Contact:* Nigel J.Poulton.

OBJECTIVES: To work with the poor in Africa, Asia and Latin America, and help them overcome hunger and poverty through: sustainable food production, water resource development, primary health care and microenterprise development.

GENERAL INFORMATION: *Creation:* 1989. *Personnel/Total:* 1. *Salaried:* 1. *Budget/Total 1993:* ECU 2308000 (US$ 2704000). *Financial sources:* Private: 35%. Public: 65%.

PUBLICATIONS: *Annual report.*

EVALUATION/RESEARCH: Evaluation reports available. Undertakes research activities.

COMMENTS: Undertakes activities in the Commonwealth of Independent States.

ACTIVITIES IN DEVELOPING REGIONS: Present in developing regions. Active in 16 country(ies). Maintains local field presence. Works through local field partners. **Sustainable Development Actions:** Children/

youth/family; Ecology/environment/biodiversity; Education/training/literacy; Emergency relief/refugees/humanitarian assistance; Food/famine; Health/sanitation/water; Rural development/agriculture; Sending volunteers/experts/technical assistance; Urban development/habitat. **Regions:** Caribbean; Central Africa; East Africa; Mexico and Central America; South America; South East Asia; Southern Africa.

GBR2294
FOUNDATION FOR INTERNATIONAL ENVIRONMENTAL LAW AND DEVELOPMENT (FIELD)

SOAS, University of London, 46-47 Russell Square, London WC1B 4JP, United Kingdom.

Telephone: 44 (171) 637 7950. *Fax:* 44 (171) 637 7951. *E-mail:* field@gn.apc.org. *Contact:* Roger Wilson, Managing Director.

OBJECTIVES: To contribute to the progressive development of international law including the law of the European Community for the protection of the environment and the attainment of sustainable development. To achieve this through research, consultancy, training and assistance.

GENERAL INFORMATION: *Creation:* 1989. *Affiliated to:* IUCN - World Conservation Council. *Personnel/Total:* 20. *Salaried:* 12. *Volunteers:* 8. *Budget/Total 1993:* ECU 551353 (US$ 646000). *Financial sources:* Private: 75%. Self-financing: 25%.

PUBLICATIONS: *Periodicals:* RECIEL (4). *Annual report. List of publications.*

EVALUATION/RESEARCH: Undertakes research activities.

COMMENTS: FIELD also undertakes development activities alongside inter-governmental organisations as well as with NGOs and governments in specific countries. Undertakes activities in the Commonwealth of Independent States.

ACTIVITIES IN DEVELOPING REGIONS: Present in developing regions. Works through local field partners. **Sustainable Development Actions:** Debt/finance/trade; Democracy/good governance/institution building/participatory development; Ecology/environment/biodiversity; Energy/transport. **Regions:** Caribbean; East Asia; Oceania; South America; South East Asia; Southern Africa; West Africa.

INFORMATION AND EDUCATION ACTIVITIES: Topics: Ecology/environment/biodiversity; International economic relations/trade/debt/finance. **Activities:** Conferences/seminars/workshops/training activities; Formal education; Lobbying/advocacy; Publishing/audiovisual materials/educational materials.

GBR2295
FOUNDATION FOR WOMEN'S HEALTH

The Africa Centre, 38 King Street, Covent Garden, London WC2E 8JT, United Kingdom.

Contact: Efua Dorkendoo.

GBR2296
FREEDOM FROM HUNGER CAMPAIGN

Welsh Centre for International Affairs, Temple of Peace, Cathays PCF1 3AP, United Kingdom.

Contact: W.R. Davies.

GBR2297
FRIENDS OF ASSEFA

Fenner Brockway House, 37-39 Great Guildford Street, London SE1 OES, United Kingdom.

Telephone: 44 (171) 620 0761. *Fax:* 44 (171) 261 9291. *Contact:* Gordan Peters.

OBJECTIVES: To support community-based rural development projects in India. To learn from and disseminate information about rural development initiatives in India.

GENERAL INFORMATION: *Creation:* 1988. *Affiliated to:* India-UK Association (United Kingdom). *Personnel/Total:* 42. *Salaried:* 2. *Volunteers:* 40. *Budget/Total 1993:* ECU 100013 (US$ 117000). *Financial sources:* Private: 50%. Public: 45%. Self-financing: 5%.

Voir : *Comment utiliser le répertoire,* page 11.

PUBLICATIONS: *Periodicals:* Village Matters (2). *Annual report. List of publications.*

EVALUATION/RESEARCH: Evaluation reports available. Undertakes research activities.

PLANNED ACTIVITIES: The dissemination of audio visual materials on rural development, most importantly the video "Bonds of Hope".

ACTIVITIES IN DEVELOPING REGIONS: Active in 1 country(ies). Works through local field partners. **Sustainable Development Actions:** Debt/finance/trade; Democracy/good governance/institution building/participatory development; Ecology/environment/biodiversity; Education/training/literacy; Gender issues/women; Health/sanitation/water; Human rights/peace/conflicts; Rural development/agriculture; Small enterprises/informal sector/handicrafts. **Regions:** Central Asia and South Asia.

INFORMATION AND EDUCATION ACTIVITIES: Topics: Education/training/literacy; Employment/unemployment; Gender issues/women; Health/sanitation/water; Poverty/living conditions; Rural development/agriculture. **Activities:** Broadcasting/cultural events; Fund raising; Information campaigns/exhibitions; Publishing/audiovisual materials/educational materials.

GBR2298

FRIENDS OF CONSERVATION

Sloane Square House, Holbein Place, London SW1W 8NS, United Kingdom.

Telephone: 44 (171) 730 7904. *Contact:* Jonathan Knocker.

OBJECTIVES: To protect and preserve wildlife and its habitat in East Africa. To provide education on the benefits of wildlife conservation to indigenous populations. To promote tourist education in East African national parks and reserves.

GENERAL INFORMATION: *Personnel/Total:* 22. *Salaried:* 22 of which: 18 in developing countries. *Budget/Total 1993:* ECU 539000 (US$ 631000). *Financial sources:* Private: 61%. Public: 31%. Self-financing: 8%.

PUBLICATIONS: *Periodicals:* Survivor (4). *Annual report.*

EVALUATION/RESEARCH: Undertakes research activities.

PLANNED ACTIVITIES: The undertaking of a community conservation education programme and the establishment of an education resource centre in Kenya.

ACTIVITIES IN DEVELOPING REGIONS: Present in developing regions. Active in 3 country(ies). Maintains local field presence. Works through local field partners. **Sustainable Development Actions:** Ecology/environment/biodiversity; Education/training/literacy; Rural development/agriculture. **Regions:** Central Africa; East Africa.

INFORMATION AND EDUCATION ACTIVITIES: Topics: Ecology/environment/biodiversity; Rural development/agriculture. **Activities:** Conferences/seminars/workshops/training activities; Fund raising; Information and documentation services/data bases.

GBR2299

FRIENDS OF THE CENTRE FOR REHABILITATION AND PARALYSED (FCRP)

The Old Rectory , Fulmer Village, Buckinghamshire SL3 6HD, United Kingdom.

Telephone: 44 (1753) 662913. *Contact:* J.A. Morrell.

OBJECTIVES: To support the work of the Centre for the Rehabilitation of the Paralysed in Bangladesh and to provide the running costs of the Centre for six months of every year.

GENERAL INFORMATION: *Creation:* 1989. *Personnel/Total:* 11. *Salaried:* 1. *Volunteers:* 10. *Budget/Total 1993:* ECU 103000 (US$ 120000). *Financial sources:* Private: 93%. Self-financing: 7%.

PUBLICATIONS: *Periodicals:* FCRP Newsletter (2). *Annual report.*

ACTIVITIES IN DEVELOPING REGIONS: **Sustainable Development Actions:** Other. **Regions:** Central Asia and South Asia.

GBR2300

FRIENDS OF THE JAIROS JIRI ASSOCIATION

Beechings, 14 Bordyke, Tonbridge, Kent TN9 1NN, United Kingdom.

Contact: Alastair Association.

GBR2301

FRIENDS OF URAMBO AND MWANHALA

Gulworthy Farm, Tavistock, Devon PL19 8JQ, United Kingdom.

Telephone: 44 (1822) 832346. *Contact:* John Gillett, Secretary.

GBR2302

FRIENDS OF VELLORE ♦ Les amis de Vellore

Highfield House, Upper Court Road, Woldingham, Surrey CR3 7BE, United Kingdom.

Telephone: 44 (188) 365 3176. *Contact:* E.C. Howes, Director.

OBJECTIVES: To support medical programmes at the Vellore Christian Medical College Hospital, as well as community primary health care and socio-economic programmes in South India.

GENERAL INFORMATION: *Creation:* 1940. *Type of organisation:* coordinating body. *Personnel/Total:* 2. *Salaried:* 2. *Budget/Total 1993:* ECU 128222 (US$ 150000). *Financial sources:* Private: 93%. Public: 5%. Self-financing: 2%.

PUBLICATIONS: *Periodicals:* Vellore Newsletter (2).

ACTIVITIES IN DEVELOPING REGIONS: Present in developing regions. Active in 1 country(ies). Maintains local field presence. Works through local field partners. **Sustainable Development Actions:** Children/youth/family; Democracy/good governance/institution building/participatory development; Education/training/literacy; Gender issues/women; Health/sanitation/water; Population/family planning/demography; Rural development/agriculture; Sending volunteers/experts/technical assistance; Small enterprises/informal sector/handicrafts. **Regions:** Central Asia and South Asia.

INFORMATION AND EDUCATION ACTIVITIES: Topics: Children/youth/family; Education/training/literacy; Gender issues/women; Health/sanitation/water; International relations/cooperation/development aid; Population/family planning/demography; Poverty/living conditions; Rural development/agriculture. **Activities:** Conferences/seminars/workshops/training activities; Exchanges/twinning/linking; Fund raising.

GBR2303

FRIENDS WORLD COMMITTEE FOR CONSULTATION

4 Byng Place, London WC1E 7JH, United Kingdom.

Telephone: 44 (171) 388 0497. *Fax:* 44 (171) 383 3722. *Contact:* Thomas F. Taylor, General Secretary.

OBJECTIVES: To co-ordinate Quaker activities in accordance with their principles of peace, social justice and right principles with all of God's creation. To sponsor the Quaker UN offices in Geneva and New York.

GENERAL INFORMATION: *Creation:* 1937. *Type of organisation:* coordinating body. *Affiliated to:* Conference of NGOs (USA) - International Council of Voluntary Agencies (Switzerland). *Personnel/Total:* 18. *Salaried:* 17 of which: 3 in developing countries. *Volunteers:* 1. *Budget/Total 1993:* ECU 192332 (US$ 225000). *Financial sources:* Private: 100%.

PUBLICATIONS: *Periodicals:* In and Around the UN (5) - Quno Reporter (4). *Annual report. List of publications.*

PLANNED ACTIVITIES: The implementation of a new programme focusing on the Korean peninsula, the expansion of programmes into the Andes region and the beginning of peace-making and peace-building efforts in Africa.

COMMENTS: Undertakes activities in the Commonwealth of Independent States. Information activities related to the Commonwealth of Independent States.

ACTIVITIES IN DEVELOPING REGIONS: Present in developing regions. Active in 33 country(ies). Maintains local field presence. Works through local field partners. **Sustainable Development Actions:** Children/youth/family; Democracy/good governance/institution building/par-

See: How to Use the Directory, page 11.

ticipatory development; Education/training/literacy; Emergency relief/refugees/humanitarian assistance; Food/famine; Gender issues/women; Health/sanitation/water; Human rights/peace/conflicts; Rural development/agriculture; Sending volunteers/experts/technical assistance; Small enterprises/informal sector/handicrafts; Urban development/habitat. **Regions:** Central Asia and South Asia; East Africa; Mexico and Central America; Middle East; North Africa; South America; South East Asia; Southern Africa; West Africa.

INFORMATION AND EDUCATION ACTIVITIES: Topics: Children/youth/family; Ecology/environment/biodiversity; Education/training/literacy; Emergency relief/refugees/humanitarian assistance; Food/famine; Gender issues/women; Health/sanitation/water; Human rights/peace/conflicts; International economic relations/trade/debt/finance; International relations/cooperation/development aid; Peace/ethnic conflicts/armament/disarmament; Refugees/migrants/ethnic groups; Rural development/agriculture; Urban development/habitat. **Activities:** Conferences/seminars/workshops/training activities; Information campaigns/exhibitions; Lobbying/advocacy; Publishing/audiovisual materials/educational materials.

GBR2304
FUND FOR WOMEN

UK Committee of the UN Development, 3 Whitehall Court, London SW1A 2EL, United Kingdom.

Telephone: 44 (171) 839 1790.

GBR2305
GAIA FOUNDATION

18 Well Walk, Hampstead, London NW3 1LD, United Kingdom.

Contact: Helena Paul.

GBR2306
GAP ACTIVITY PROJECTS (GAP)

44 Queens Road, Reading, Berkshire RG1 4BB, United Kingdom.

Telephone: 44 (1491) 594914. *Fax:* 44 (1491) 576634. *Contact:* Brigadier John Cornell, Director.

OBJECTIVES: To arrange work opportunities for UK students overseas and for Commonwealth and foreign students.

GENERAL INFORMATION: *Creation:* 1972. ***Type of organisation:*** association of NGOs. ***Personnel/Total:*** 112. *Salaried:* 12. *Volunteers:* 100 of which: 20 in developing countries. ***Budget/Total 1993:*** ECU 740000 (US$ 866000). ***Financial sources:*** Private: 27%. *Self-financing:* 73%.

PUBLICATIONS: *Periodicals:* Network (1). *Annual report.*

EVALUATION/RESEARCH: Evaluation reports available. Undertakes research activities.

PLANNED ACTIVITIES: Planning new activities for Bangladesh, Fiji, Morocco and Zambia in the fields of education, conservation and animal welfare.

COMMENTS: Undertakes activities in the Commonwealth of Independent States. Information activities related to the Commonwealth of Independent States.

ACTIVITIES IN DEVELOPING REGIONS: Present in developing regions. Active in 15 country(ies). Maintains local field presence. **Sustainable Development Actions:** Children/youth/family; Education/training/literacy; Health/sanitation/water; Rural development/agriculture. **Regions:** Central Asia and South Asia; East Asia; Mexico and Central America; Oceania; South America; South East Asia; Southern Africa.

INFORMATION AND EDUCATION ACTIVITIES: Topics: Education/training/literacy. **Activities:** Exchanges/twinning/linking; Formal education.

GBR2307
GATEWAY

117 Golden Lane, London EC1Y 0RT, United Kingdom.

Telephone: 44 (171) 454 0454. *Fax:* 44 (171) 608 3254. *Contact:* Robert Hunter.

OBJECTIVES: To advance the personal development of people with learning disabilities through greater leisure opportunities, by promoting personal choice and independence and encouraging their full participation, integration and involvement in the community.

GENERAL INFORMATION: *Type of organisation:* association of NGOs. ***Member organisations:*** 700. ***Affiliated to:*** NCVYS (United Kingdom) - NYA (United Kingdom) - Sports Council (United Kingdom) . ***Personnel/Total:*** 715. *Salaried:* 15. *Volunteers:* 700. ***Budget/Total 1993:*** ECU 1522000 (US$ 1783000). ***Financial sources:*** Private: 12%. *Public:* 22%. *Self-financing:* 66%.

PUBLICATIONS: *Periodicals:* Gatepost (4) - Mencap News (12). *Annual report. List of publications.*

EVALUATION/RESEARCH: Evaluation reports available. Undertakes research activities.

PLANNED ACTIVITIES: Developing family support and educational services in India for disabled people.

COMMENTS: Undertakes activities in the Commonwealth of Independent States. Information activities related to the Commonwealth of Independent States.

ACTIVITIES IN DEVELOPING REGIONS: Present in developing regions. Active in 4 country(ies). Works through local field partners. **Sustainable Development Actions:** Children/youth/family; Education/training/literacy; Health/sanitation/water; Sending volunteers/experts/technical assistance. **Regions:** Central Asia and South Asia; East Africa.

INFORMATION AND EDUCATION ACTIVITIES: Topics: Children/youth/family. **Activities:** Conferences/seminars/workshops/training activities; Exchanges/twinning/linking; Information and documentation services/data bases; Information campaigns/exhibitions; Lobbying/advocacy; Publishing/audiovisual materials/educational materials.

GBR2308
GEORGE ADAMSON WILDLIFE PRESERVATION TRUST

2 Marchmont Gardens, Richmond, Surrey TW10 6ET, United Kingdom.

Contact: Lucy Mellotte.

GBR2309
GLOBAL INK

23 Adria Road, Didsbury, Manchester M20 6SQ, United Kingdom.

Telephone: 44 (161) 445 1489. *Fax:* 44 (161) 445 1489. *Contact:* Bob Kirby.

OBJECTIVES: To provide support to development education NGOs and small charities in the form of management, evaluation, research, writing, editing and fundraising.

GENERAL INFORMATION: *Creation:* 1993. ***Affiliated to:*** Development Education Association (United Kingdom). ***Personnel/Total:*** 1. *Salaried:* 1. ***Budget/Total 1993:*** ECU 25644 (US$ 30000). ***Financial sources:*** Private: 25%. *Self-financing:* 75%.

EVALUATION/RESEARCH: Evaluation reports available. Undertakes research activities.

PLANNED ACTIVITIES: Evaluating the promotion of development education throughout Scotland.

COMMENTS: The work of the organisation is not topic-specific. Global Ink undertakes educational activities on most of the topics listed in this survey.

GBR2310
GORDON BARCLAY VIETNAM FUND (GBVF)

77 Maze Hill, Greenwich, London SE10 8XG, United Kingdom.

Telephone: 44 (181) 858 4968. *Contact:* Reginald Norton, Chairman.

OBJECTIVES: To provide healthcare and education in South East Asia. To support a blind school project in Haipaong and a toy-making programme in Thai Binh.

GENERAL INFORMATION: *Creation:* 1968. ***Personnel/Total:*** 2. *Volunteers:* 2. ***Budget/Total 1993:*** ECU 35000 (US$ 41000). ***Financial sources:*** Private: 26%. *Public:* 46%.

PUBLICATIONS: *Annual report.*

COMMENTS: GBVF originally started to give medical relief and child care in Saigon.

ACTIVITIES IN DEVELOPING REGIONS: Present in developing regions. Active in 1 country(ies). Works through local field partners. **Sustainable Development Actions:** Children/youth/family; Education/training/literacy; Health/sanitation/water. **Regions:** South East Asia.

INFORMATION AND EDUCATION ACTIVITIES: Topics: Children/youth/family; Education/training/literacy; Emergency relief/refugees/humanitarian assistance; Health/sanitation/water. **Activities:** Fund raising.

GBR2311

GREATER LONDON ACTION FOR RACIAL EQUALITY (GLARE)

London Voluntary Sector Resource Centre, 356 Holloway Road, London N7 6PA, United Kingdom.

Telephone: 44 (171) 700 8135. **Fax:** 44 (171) 700 0099. **Contact:** Patrick Edwards, Director.

OBJECTIVES: To promote the development and advocacy of policies and practice for the achievement of racial equality. To encourage the implementation of such policies by lobbying the government, parliament, employers and commercial institutions. To disseminate information and undertake policy research.

GENERAL INFORMATION: *Creation:* 1981. *Type of organisation:* coordinating body. *Member organisations:* 32. *Personnel/Total:* 4. *Salaried:* 4 of which: 4 in developing countries. *Budget/Total 1993:* ECU 119000 (US$ 139000). *Financial sources:* Private: 19%. Public: 80%. Self-financing: 1%.

PUBLICATIONS: *Periodicals:* GLARE Journal (4) - Policy/Research Documents (6). *Annual report.*

EVALUATION/RESEARCH: Evaluation reports available. Undertakes research activities.

PLANNED ACTIVITIES: Carrying out a statistical study on racial harassment in the Greater London area. Undertaking research on policing and criminal justice and on careers and education.

INFORMATION AND EDUCATION ACTIVITIES: Topics: Other; Racism/xenophobia/antisemitism; Refugees/migrants/ethnic groups. **Activities:** Broadcasting/cultural events; Conferences/seminars/workshops/training activities; Fund raising; Information and documentation services/data bases; Information campaigns/exhibitions; Lobbying/advocacy; Publishing/audiovisual materials/educational materials.

GBR2312

GREEN LIGHT TRUST

Lawshall Green, Bury St. Edmunds, Suffolk, United Kingdom.

Telephone: 44 (1284) 828754. **Contact:** Nigel Hughes, Richard Edmunds.

OBJECTIVES: To undertake environmental education through creative action.

GENERAL INFORMATION: *Creation:* 1990. *Personnel/Total:* 52. *Salaried:* 2. *Volunteers:* 50 of which: 20 in developing countries. *Budget/Total 1993:* ECU 42000 (US$ 49000). *Financial sources:* Private: 25%. Self-financing: 75%.

PUBLICATIONS: *Periodicals:* Newsletters (4). *Annual report. List of publications.*

PLANNED ACTIVITIES: Planning to publish a pre-school education book and organising an educational, awareness-raising theatre tour.

ACTIVITIES IN DEVELOPING REGIONS: Present in developing regions. Active in 1 country(ies). Works through local field partners. **Sustainable Development Actions:** Children/youth/family; Democracy/good governance/institution building/participatory development; Ecology/environment/biodiversity; Education/training/literacy; Gender issues/women; Human rights/peace/conflicts; Population/family planning/demography; Rural development/agriculture; Sending volunteers/experts/technical

assistance; Small enterprises/informal sector/handicrafts. **Regions:** Oceania.

INFORMATION AND EDUCATION ACTIVITIES: Topics: Children/youth/family; Culture/tradition/religion; Ecology/environment/biodiversity; Education/training/literacy; Gender issues/women; Human rights/peace/conflicts; Peace/ethnic conflicts/armament/disarmament; Rural development/agriculture. **Activities:** Broadcasting/cultural events; Conferences/seminars/workshops/training activities; Exchanges/twinning/linking; Fund raising; Information campaigns/exhibitions; Publishing/audiovisual materials/educational materials.

GBR2313

GREENNET

393-395 City Road, London EC1V 1NE, United Kingdom.

Telephone: 44 (171) 713 1941. **Fax:** 44 (171) 833 1169. **E-mail:** Support n.apc.org.. **Contact:** Viv Kendon, Co-ordinator.

OBJECTIVES: To provide a global computer communications network for environment, peace and human rights groups. To provide services to countries poorly served by commercial communications services.

GENERAL INFORMATION: *Creation:* 1986. *Type of organisation:* network. *Member organisations:* 1000. *Affiliated to:* Association for Progressive Communications (Brazil). *Personnel/Total:* 8. *Salaried:* 4. *Volunteers:* 4. *Financial sources:* Self-financing: 100%.

PUBLICATIONS: *Periodicals:* GREENNET Newsletter (4).

COMMENTS: Undertakes activities in the Commonwealth of Independent States. Information activities related to the Commonwealth of Independent States.

ACTIVITIES IN DEVELOPING REGIONS: Present in developing regions. Works through local field partners. **Sustainable Development Actions:** Other. **Regions:** Central Africa; Central Asia and South Asia; East Africa; East Asia; Mexico and Central America; Middle East; North Africa; South East Asia; Southern Africa; West Africa.

INFORMATION AND EDUCATION ACTIVITIES: Topics: Children/youth/family; Culture/tradition/religion; Ecology/environment/biodiversity; Education/training/literacy; Emergency relief/refugees/humanitarian assistance; Employment/unemployment; Food/famine; Gender issues/women; Health/sanitation/water; Human rights/peace/conflicts; International economic relations/trade/debt/finance; International relations/cooperation/development aid; Peace/ethnic conflicts/armament/disarmament; Population/family planning/demography; Poverty/living conditions; Racism/xenophobia/antisemitism; Refugees/migrants/ethnic groups; Rural development/agriculture; Urban development/habitat. **Activities:** Networking/electronic telecommunications.

GBR2314

HALO TRUST

804 Drake House, Dolphin Square, London SW1V 8NS, United Kingdom.

Contact: Susan Mitchell.

GBR2315

HAMPSHIRE DEVELOPMENT EDUCATION CENTRE

Professionnal Centre, Falcon House, Romsey Road, Winchester SO22 5PL, United Kingdom.

Telephone: 44 (1962) 856106. **Contact:** Pat Francis, Co-ordinator.

OBJECTIVES: To further the promotion of an understanding of social, economic and political change. To promote sustainable development through education.

GENERAL INFORMATION: *Creation:* 1979. *Affiliated to:* Development Education Association (United Kingdom). *Personnel/Total:* 3. *Salaried:* 2. *Volunteers:* 1. *Budget/Total 1993:* ECU 15000 (US$ 17300). *Financial sources:* Private: 75%. Public: 25%.

INFORMATION AND EDUCATION ACTIVITIES: Topics: Ecology/environment/biodiversity; Rural development/agriculture; Urban development/habitat. **Activities:** Formal education.

See: How to Use the Directory, page 11.

GBR2316
HAND IN HAND

Mere Fish Farm, Ivy Mead, Mere, Near Warminster, Wilts BA12 6EN, United Kingdom.

Contact: Ian Tew.

GBR2317
HAROLD MACMILLAN TRUST

Room 114 Temple Chambers, Temple Avenue, London EC4Y 0DT, United Kingdom.

Contact: James Houston.

GBR2318
HARVEST HELP

3-4 Old Bakery Row, Wellington, Telford TF1 1PS, United Kingdom.

Telephone: 44 (1952) 260699. *Fax:* 44 (1952) 247158. *Contact:* David White, Director.

OBJECTIVES: To support Third World groups in their efforts to become more self-reliant by enhancing ecologically sustainable food production and other economic activities.

GENERAL INFORMATION: *Creation:* 1985. *Affiliated to:* British Overseas NGOs for Development (United Kingdom) - EC-NGO Network. *Personnel/Total:* 20. *Salaried:* 10 of which: 6 in developing countries. *Volunteers:* 10 of which: 5 in developing countries. *Budget/Total 1993:* ECU 289000 (US$ 338000). *Financial sources:* Private: 70%. *Public:* 30%.

PUBLICATIONS: *Periodicals:* Harvest Helper (4). *Annual report.*

EVALUATION/RESEARCH: Evaluation reports available.

ACTIVITIES IN DEVELOPING REGIONS: Active in 2 country(ies). Maintains local field presence. Works through local field partners. **Sustainable Development Actions:** Children/youth/family; Debt/finance/trade; Ecology/environment/biodiversity; Education/training/literacy; Energy/transport; Food/famine; Gender issues/women; Health/sanitation/water; Population/family planning/demography; Rural development/agriculture; Sending volunteers/experts/technical assistance; Small enterprises/informal sector/handicrafts. **Regions:** Central Asia and South Asia; Southern Africa.

INFORMATION AND EDUCATION ACTIVITIES: Topics: Children/youth/family; Ecology/environment/biodiversity; Education/training/literacy; Food/famine; Gender issues/women; Health/sanitation/water; Population/family planning/demography; Poverty/living conditions; Rural development/agriculture. **Activities:** Fund raising; Publishing/audiovisual materials/educational materials.

GBR2319
HEALTH AID MOYO

6 Frobisher Close, Pinner, Middlesex HA5 1NN, United Kingdom.

Telephone: 44 (181) 866 6009. *Fax:* 44 (181) 866 6009. *Contact:* Bishop Donald Arden, Chairman.

OBJECTIVES: To aid church health services in Malawi.

GENERAL INFORMATION: *Creation:* 1990. *Personnel/Total:* 1. *Volunteers:* 1. *Budget/Total 1993:* ECU 271000 (US$ 317000). *Financial sources:* Private: 51%. *Public:* 46%. *Self-financing:* 3%.

PUBLICATIONS: *Annual report.*

ACTIVITIES IN DEVELOPING REGIONS: Present in developing regions. Active in 1 country(ies). Works through local field partners. **Sustainable Development Actions:** Children/youth/family; Gender issues/women; Health/sanitation/water; Population/family planning/demography. **Regions:** Southern Africa.

INFORMATION AND EDUCATION ACTIVITIES: Topics: Children/youth/family; Gender issues/women; Health/sanitation/water. **Activities:** Fund raising; Lobbying/advocacy.

GBR2320
HEALTH PROJECTS ABROAD

Hms President (1918), Victoria Embankment, London EC4Y 0HJ, United Kingdom.

Telephone: 44 (171) 583 5725. *Fax:* 44 (171) 583 2840. *Contact:* Simon Headington, Director.

OBJECTIVES: To protect and preserve good health in developing countries.

GENERAL INFORMATION: *Creation:* 1989. *Personnel/Total:* 28. *Salaried:* 3 of which: 1 in developing countries. *Volunteers:* 25 of which: 25 in developing countries. *Budget/Total 1993:* ECU 256000 (US$ 300000). *Financial sources:* Private: 45%. *Public:* 5%. *Self-financing:* 50%.

PUBLICATIONS: *Annual report.*

PLANNED ACTIVITIES: Establishing a new health programme in the Singida region of Tanzania.

ACTIVITIES IN DEVELOPING REGIONS: Present in developing regions. Active in 1 country(ies). Maintains local field presence. **Sustainable Development Actions:** Health/sanitation/water; Sending volunteers/experts/technical assistance. **Regions:** East Africa.

INFORMATION AND EDUCATION ACTIVITIES: Topics: Culture/tradition/religion. **Activities:** Conferences/seminars/workshops/training activities.

GBR2321
HEALTH UNLIMITED

3 Stamford Street, London SE1 9NT, United Kingdom.

Telephone: 44 (171) 928 8105 . *Fax:* 44 (171) 928 7736. *E-mail:* healthunltd@gn.apc.org.. *Contact:* Clive Nettleton, Director.

OBJECTIVES: To improve health care in communities affected by conflict. To establish long term development projects and primary health care services in partnership with local communities and organisations.

GENERAL INFORMATION: *Creation:* 1984. *Affiliated to:* British Overseas NGOs for Development (United Kingdom) - National Council for Voluntary Organisations (United Kingdom) - EC-NGO Liaison Group (United Kingdom) - Refugee Council (United Kingdom) - British Agencies Afghan Group (United Kingdom). *Personnel/Total:* 36. *Salaried:* 31 of which: 20 in developing countries. *Volunteers:* 5. *Budget/Total 1993:* ECU 1780000 (US$ 2085000). *Financial sources:* Private: 18%. *Public:* 80%. *Self-financing:* 2%.

PUBLICATIONS: *Periodicals:* Health Outpost (4). *Annual report.*

EVALUATION/RESEARCH: Evaluation reports available. Undertakes research activities.

PLANNED ACTIVITIES: Developing models for radio broadcasting, as a medium for health education in conflict situations.

ACTIVITIES IN DEVELOPING REGIONS: Present in developing regions. Active in 13 country(ies). Maintains local field presence. Works through local field partners. **Sustainable Development Actions:** Children/youth/family; Democracy/good governance/institution building/participatory development; Education/training/literacy; Gender issues/women; Health/sanitation/water; Human rights/peace/conflicts; Population/family planning/demography; Rural development/agriculture; Sending volunteers/experts/technical assistance; Small enterprises/informal sector/handicrafts. **Regions:** Central Asia and South Asia; East Africa; Mexico and Central America; South America; South East Asia; Southern Africa.

INFORMATION AND EDUCATION ACTIVITIES: Topics: Children/youth/family; Culture/tradition/religion; Education/training/literacy; Gender issues/women; Health/sanitation/water; Peace/ethnic conflicts/armament/disarmament; Population/family planning/demography; Poverty/living conditions; Refugees/migrants/ethnic groups; Rural development/agriculture. **Activities:** Conferences/seminars/workshops/training activities; Fund raising; Information campaigns/exhibitions; Networking/electronic telecommunications; Publishing/audiovisual materials/educational materials.

Voir : *Comment utiliser le répertoire,* page 11.

GBR2322

HEDLEY ROBERTS TRUST

18 Rotherfield Road, Henley-on-Thames, Oxon RG9 1NN, United Kingdom.

Contact: Project Officer.

GBR2323

THE HEKIMA TRUST

23 Bevenden Street, London N1 6BH, United Kingdom.

Telephone: 44 (71) 251 1503. *Contact:* Ben Turok, Executive Secretary.

GBR2324

HELPAGE INTERNATIONAL

St. James's Walk, Clerkenwell Green, London EC1R OBE, United Kingdom.

Telephone: 44 (171) 253 0253. *Fax:* 44 (171) 253 4814. *E-mail:* helpage@gn.apc.org. *Contact:* Dr. Christopher Beer, Chief Executive.

OBJECTIVES: To work with and for older people worldwide to achieve lasting improvement in the quality of their lives.

GENERAL INFORMATION: *Creation:* 1983. *Type of organisation:* network. *Member organisations:* 19. *Affiliated to:* International Association of Gerontology - International Federation on Aging -International Institute on Aging - International Council of Voluntary Agencies - International Council on Social Welfare. *Personnel/Total:* 309. *Salaried:* 176 of which: 144 in developing countries. *Volunteers:* 133. *Budget/Total 1993:* ECU 2358000 (US$ 2762000). *Financial sources:* Private: 46%. Public: 22%. Self-financing: 32%.

PUBLICATIONS: *Periodicals:* AGEWAYS (4) - Side By Side (4) - HelpAge International News (4) (1). *Annual report. List of publications.*

EVALUATION/RESEARCH: Undertakes research activities.

COMMENTS: HAI was designated a Patron of the UN International Year of the Family in 1994. Undertakes activities in the Commonwealth of Independent States.

ACTIVITIES IN DEVELOPING REGIONS: Present in developing regions. Active in 40 country(ies). Maintains local field presence. Works through local field partners. **Sustainable Development Actions:** Education/training/literacy; Emergency relief/refugees/humanitarian assistance; Gender issues/women; Health/sanitation/water; Other; Rural development/agriculture; Small enterprises/informal sector/handicrafts; Urban development/habitat. **Regions:** Caribbean; Central Asia and South Asia; East Africa; Mexico and Central America; South America; South East Asia; Southern Africa; West Africa.

INFORMATION AND EDUCATION ACTIVITIES: Topics: Emergency relief/refugees/humanitarian assistance; Food/famine; Gender issues/women; Health/sanitation/water; Other; Poverty/living conditions; Refugees/migrants/ethnic groups; Rural development/agriculture; Urban development/habitat. **Activities:** Conferences/seminars/workshops/training activities; Fund raising; Information and documentation services/data bases; Information campaigns/exhibitions; Lobbying/advocacy; Networking/electronic telecommunications; Publishing/audiovisual materials/educational materials.

GBR2325

HOMELESS INTERNATIONAL

5 The Butts, Coventry CV1 3GH, United Kingdom.

Telephone: 44 (1203) 632802. *Fax:* 44 (1203) 632911. *Contact:* Ruth McLeod, Chief Executive.

OBJECTIVES: To provide assistance and support to community-based and non-governmental agencies working to improve the shelter conditions of the poor in Africa, Asia, Latin America and the Caribbean.

GENERAL INFORMATION: *Creation:* 1989. *Affiliated to:* Habitat International Coalition (Mexico) - British Overseas NGOs for Development (United Kingdom) - EC-NGO Network (United Kingdom). *Personnel/Total:* 8. *Salaried:* 5. *Volunteers:* 3. *Budget/Total 1993:* ECU 1301000 (US$ 1001000). *Financial sources:* Private: 48%. Public: 50%. Self-financing: 2%.

PUBLICATIONS: *Periodicals:* Bulletin (1) - HI Newsletter (2). *Annual report.*

EVALUATION/RESEARCH: Evaluation reports available. Undertakes research activities.

PLANNED ACTIVITIES: Launching and implementing a new funding initiative and carrying out a development education activity, "landgrab".

ACTIVITIES IN DEVELOPING REGIONS: Active in 9 country(ies). Works through local field partners. **Sustainable Development Actions:** Health/sanitation/water; Sending volunteers/experts/technical assistance; Urban development/habitat. **Regions:** Caribbean; Central Asia and South Asia; East Africa; South America; Southern Africa.

INFORMATION AND EDUCATION ACTIVITIES: Topics: Emergency relief/refugees/humanitarian assistance; Employment/unemployment; Gender issues/women; Health/sanitation/water; Other; Poverty/living conditions; Rural development/agriculture; Urban development/habitat. **Activities:** Conferences/seminars/workshops/training activities; Exchanges/twinning/linking; Fund raising; Information and documentation services/data bases; Information campaigns/exhibitions; Lobbying/advocacy; Networking/electronic telecommunications; Publishing/audiovisual materials/educational materials.

GBR2326

HOUSEWIVES IN DIALOGUE (HinD)

P.O. Box 287, London NW6 5QU, United Kingdom.

Telephone: 44 (171) 837 7509 . *Fax:* 44 (171) 833 4817. *Contact:* Wilmette Brown and Solveig Francis, joint Co-ordinators.

OBJECTIVES: To advance the education of the public by undertaking research on the race and community relations in industrialised and Third World countries with particular reference to women as unwaged workers.

GENERAL INFORMATION: *Creation:* 1976. *Type of organisation:* network. *Personnel/Total:* 10. *Salaried:* 0. *Volunteers:* 10. *Budget/Total 1993:* ECU 12000 (US$ 14000). *Financial sources:* Private: 25%. Public: 5%. Self-financing: 70%.

PUBLICATIONS: *List of publications.*

EVALUATION/RESEARCH: Undertakes research activities.

PLANNED ACTIVITIES: Acting as consultants for the Pilot Study on Unwaged Work in Trinidad and Tobago and will do research on solar cookers.

ACTIVITIES IN DEVELOPING REGIONS: Sustainable Development Actions: Gender issues/women. **Regions:** Caribbean; Central Asia and South Asia; South East Asia.

INFORMATION AND EDUCATION ACTIVITIES: Topics: Children/youth/family; Ecology/environment/biodiversity; Gender issues/women; International economic relations/trade/debt/finance; International relations/cooperation/development aid; Poverty/living conditions; Racism/xenophobia/antisemitism; Refugees/migrants/ethnic groups. **Activities:** Conferences/seminars/workshops/training activities; Fund raising; Information and documentation services/data bases; Information campaigns/exhibitions; Other; Publishing/audiovisual materials/educational materials.

GBR2327

HUMAN RIGHTS NETWORK

c/o UNA, 3 Whitehall Court, London SW1A 2EL, United Kingdom.

Telephone: 44 (171) 930 2931. *Fax:* 44 (171) 930 5893. *Contact:* Suzanne Long, Co-ordinator.

OBJECTIVES: To co-ordinate the work of human rights organisations and to organise conferences and seminars on human rights related issues.

GENERAL INFORMATION: *Creation:* 1975. *Type of organisation:* network. *Member organisations:* 80. *Personnel/Total:* 1. *Salaried:* 1. *Volunteers:* var. *Budget/Total 1993:* ECU 1025 (US$ 1200). *Financial sources:* Self-financing: 100%.

INFORMATION AND EDUCATION ACTIVITIES: Topics: Human rights/peace/conflicts; International relations/cooperation/development aid;

                                        See: *How to Use the Directory,* page 11.

Racism/xenophobia/antisemitism. **Activities:** Conferences/seminars/ workshops/training activities.

GBR2328
HUMAN RIGHTS WATCH

33 Islington High Street, London N1 9HL, United Kingdom.

Telephone: 44 (171) 713 1995. *Fax:* 44 (171) 713 1800. *E-mail:* hrwatchuk@gn.apc.org.. *Contact:* Kenneth Roth, Executive Director.

OBJECTIVES: To monitor human rights practices of governments and violations of the law by governments and rebel groups. To lobby and campaign for the respect of human rights.

GENERAL INFORMATION: *Creation:* 1979. *Personnel/Total:* 90. *Salaried:* 90 of which: 3 in developing countries. *Budget/Total 1993:* ECU 6825400 (US$ 7995000).

PUBLICATIONS: *Annual report. List of publications.*

EVALUATION/RESEARCH: Undertakes research activities.

COMMENTS: Undertakes activities in the Commonwealth of Independent States.

ACTIVITIES IN DEVELOPING REGIONS: Present in developing regions. Maintains local field presence. **Sustainable Development Actions:** Human rights/peace/conflicts. **Regions:** Caribbean; Central Africa; Central Asia and South Asia; East Africa; East Asia; Mexico and Central America; Middle East; South America; South East Asia; Southern Africa; West Africa.

INFORMATION AND EDUCATION ACTIVITIES: Topics: Children/youth/ family; Gender issues/women; Human rights/peace/conflicts; Peace/ethnic conflicts/armament/disarmament; Refugees/migrants/ethnic groups. **Activities:** Conferences/seminars/workshops/training activities; Fund raising; Information and documentation services/data bases; Information campaigns/exhibitions; Lobbying/advocacy; Networking/electronic telecommunications; Publishing/audiovisual materials/educational materials.

GBR2329
IDEALS AID INTERNATIONAL

89 Burnham Way, London W13 9YB, United Kingdom.

Contact: Wendy Barber.

GBR2330
IMPACT FOUNDATION

151 Western Road, Haywards Heath, West Sussex RH16 3LH, United Kingdom.

Telephone: 44 (1444) 457080. *Fax:* 44 (1444) 457877. *Contact:* Claire Hicks, Director.

OBJECTIVES: To help prevent avoidable disability.

GENERAL INFORMATION: *Creation:* 1985. *Personnel/Total:* 4. *Salaried:* 4. *Budget/Total 1993:* ECU 280000 (US$ 330000). *Financial sources:* Private: 88%. Public: 7%. Self-financing: 5%.

PUBLICATIONS: *Annual report.*

EVALUATION/RESEARCH: Evaluation reports available.

ACTIVITIES IN DEVELOPING REGIONS: Present in developing regions. Active in 6 country(ies). Works through local field partners. **Sustainable Development Actions:** Children/youth/family; Health/sanitation/water. **Regions:** Central Africa; Central Asia and South Asia; East Africa; South East Asia.

GBR2331
INCA

Gabb & Co., 2 Bank Buildings, Crickhowell, Powys NP8 1AD, United Kingdom.

Contact: Carol Sahley.

GBR2332
INDEX ON CENSORSHIP ♦ Index sur la Censure

33 Islington High Street, London N1 9LH, United Kingdom.

Telephone: 44 (171) 278 2313. *Fax:* 44 (171) 278 1878. *E-mail:* Indexoncenso@gn.apc.org. *Contact:* Ursula Owen, Editor & Chief Executive.

OBJECTIVES: To defend and promote the freedom of expression and access to information.

GENERAL INFORMATION: *Creation:* 1972. *Affiliated to:* International Freedom of Expression Exchange (Canada). *Personnel/Total:* 19. *Salaried:* 11 of which: 1 in developing countries. *Volunteers:* 8. *Budget/ Total 1993:* ECU 501000 (US$ 600000). *Financial sources:* Private: 50%. Public: 25%. Self-financing: 25%.

PUBLICATIONS: *Periodicals:* Index on Censorship (6). *Annual report. List of publications.*

EVALUATION/RESEARCH: Undertakes research activities.

PLANNED ACTIVITIES: Co-operating with Russia on education and with African partners.

COMMENTS: Undertakes activities in the Commonwealth of Independent States. Information activities related to the Commonwealth of Independent States.

ACTIVITIES IN DEVELOPING REGIONS: Present in developing regions. Maintains local field presence. Works through local field partners. **Sustainable Development Actions:** Democracy/good governance/institution building/participatory development; Gender issues/women; Human rights/peace/conflicts. **Regions:** Caribbean; Central Africa; Central Asia and South Asia; East Africa; East Asia; Mexico and Central America; Middle East; North Africa; Oceania; South America; South East Asia; Southern Africa; West Africa.

INFORMATION AND EDUCATION ACTIVITIES: Topics: Human rights/ peace/conflicts. **Activities:** Broadcasting/cultural events; Conferences/ seminars/workshops/training activities; Exchanges/twinning/linking; Formal education; Fund raising; Information and documentation services/ data bases; Information campaigns/exhibitions; Lobbying/advocacy; Networking/electronic telecommunications; Publishing/audiovisual materials/educational materials.

GBR2333
INDIA DEVELOPMENT GROUP UK (IDG)

68 Downlands Road, Purley, Surrey CR8 4JF, United Kingdom.

Telephone: 44 (181) 668 3161. *Fax:* 44 (181) 660 85 41. *Contact:* Surur Hoda, Chairman.

OBJECTIVES: To encourage rural development and employment through the use of appropriate technology. To provide training to improve health care and the environment in rural areas.

GENERAL INFORMATION: *Creation:* 1970. *Type of organisation:* coordinating body. *Member organisations:* 2. *Personnel/Total:* 24. *Salaried:* 21 of which: 20 in developing countries. *Volunteers:* 3. *Budget/ Total 1993:* ECU 85000 (US$ 99000). *Financial sources:* Private: 8%. Public: 92%.

PUBLICATIONS: *Periodicals:* APTECH (var). *Annual report.*

EVALUATION/RESEARCH: Evaluation reports available. Undertakes research activities.

PLANNED ACTIVITIES: Organising a project, "Wealth from Waste", producing electricity from agricultural, animal and human waste. Undertaking a training programme for women in order to generate self-employment in social forestry.

ACTIVITIES IN DEVELOPING REGIONS: Active in 1 country(ies). Works through local field partners. **Sustainable Development Actions:** Ecology/environment/biodiversity; Education/training/literacy; Energy/transport; Gender issues/women; Health/sanitation/water; Population/family planning/demography; Rural development/agriculture; Sending volunteers/experts/technical assistance; Small enterprises/informal sector/ handicrafts. **Regions:** Central Asia and South Asia.

INFORMATION AND EDUCATION ACTIVITIES: Topics: Ecology/environment/biodiversity; Education/training/literacy; Employment/unem-

Voir : *Comment utiliser le répertoire,* page 11.

ployment; Gender issues/women; Health/sanitation/water; International relations/cooperation/development aid; Population/family planning/demography; Rural development/agriculture. **Activities:** Broadcasting/cultural events; Conferences/seminars/workshops/training activities; Formal education; Fund raising; Information and documentation services/data bases.

GBR2334

INDIAN VOLUNTEERS FOR COMMUNITY SERVICE (IVCS)

12 Eastleigh Avenue, S. Harrow, Middlesex HA2 0UF, United Kingdom.

Telephone: 44 (181) 864 4740. *Contact:* Jyoti Singh, General Secretary.

OBJECTIVES: To relieve poverty in India by assisting village development schemes and to help Indian ethnic minorities through voluntary work. To educate the public in the United Kingdom about Indian culture, traditions and other aspects of Indian life.

GENERAL INFORMATION: *Creation:* 1981. *Personnel/Total:* 27. *Salaried:* 1 of which: 1 in developing countries. *Volunteers:* 26 of which: 1 in developing countries. *Budget/Total 1993:* ECU 11000 (US$ 13000). *Financial sources: Private:* 25%. *Self-financing:* 75%.

PUBLICATIONS: *Periodicals:* Vikas Seva (2) - International Journal of Rural Studies (2). *Annual report.*

EVALUATION/RESEARCH: Evaluation reports available.

ACTIVITIES IN DEVELOPING REGIONS: Active in 1 country(ies). Maintains local field presence. Works through local field partners. **Sustainable Development Actions:** Children/youth/family; Democracy/good governance/institution building/participatory development; Ecology/environment/biodiversity; Education/training/literacy; Health/sanitation/water; Human rights/peace/conflicts; Population/family planning/demography; Rural development/agriculture; Sending volunteers/experts/technical assistance; Small enterprises/informal sector/handicrafts. **Regions:** Central Asia and South Asia.

INFORMATION AND EDUCATION ACTIVITIES: Topics: Children/youth/family; Culture/tradition/religion; Poverty/living conditions; Rural development/agriculture. **Activities:** Conferences/seminars/workshops/training activities; Exchanges/twinning/linking; Formal education; Fund raising; Publishing/audiovisual materials/educational materials.

GBR2335

INDIGENOUS MINORITIES RESEARCH COUNCIL

6 Lodge Street, Bristol BS1 5LR, United Kingdom.

GBR2336

INFOLIFE

23 New Mount Street, Manchester M4 4DE, United Kingdom.

Telephone: 44 (61) 953 4049. *Contact:* J. Gomling, Coordinator.

GBR2337

INSTITUTE FOR AFRICAN ALTERNATIVES

23 Bevenden Street, London N1 6BH, United Kingdom.

Telephone: 44 (171) 251 1503. *Fax:* 44 (171) 253 0801. *E-mail:* ifaanetuk@gn.apc.org. *Contact:* Mohamed Suliman.

OBJECTIVES: To undertake research, publish reports and arrange conferences, workshops and seminars on alternative development policies for Africa. To maintain ongoing contact with the official bodies concerned with Africa, development policies and Third World problems.

GENERAL INFORMATION: *Creation:* 1986. *Type of organisation:* network. *Member organisations:* 6. *Personnel/Total:* 50. *Salaried:* 20 of which: 16 in developing countries. *Volunteers:* 30 of which: 26 in developing countries. *Budget/Total 1993:* ECU 512000 (US$ 600000). *Financial sources: Private:* 10%. *Public:* 60%. *Self-financing:* 30%.

PUBLICATIONS: *Periodicals:* IFAA News (4). *Annual report. List of publications.*

EVALUATION/RESEARCH: Evaluation reports available. Undertakes research activities.

PLANNED ACTIVITIES: Planning to train middle-ranking personnel from the NGO movement in South Africa. Undertaking research in the United Kingdom entitled "Ecology, Development and Armed Conflict" and in Nigeria, "Beyond Structural Adjustment".

ACTIVITIES IN DEVELOPING REGIONS: Present in developing regions. Active in 5 country(ies). Maintains local field presence. Works through local field partners. **Sustainable Development Actions:** Debt/finance/trade; Democracy/good governance/institution building/participatory development; Ecology/environment/biodiversity; Education/training/literacy; Gender issues/women; Human rights/peace/conflicts; Rural development/agriculture. **Regions:** Central Africa; East Africa; Southern Africa; West Africa.

INFORMATION AND EDUCATION ACTIVITIES: Topics: Ecology/environment/biodiversity; Human rights/peace/conflicts; International economic relations/trade/debt/finance; International relations/cooperation/development aid; Peace/ethnic conflicts/armament/disarmament; Poverty/living conditions; Rural development/agriculture. **Activities:** Conferences/seminars/workshops/training activities; Formal education; Fund raising; Lobbying/advocacy; Networking/electronic telecommunications; Publishing/audiovisual materials/educational materials.

GBR2338

INSTITUTE OF CULTURAL AFFAIRS, UNITED KINGDOM (ICA-UK)

P.O. Box 133, Bristol BS99 1HR, United Kingdom.

Contact: Alan Berresford, Secretary.

OBJECTIVES: To provide orientation for individuals seeking to volunteer in the United Kingdom or abroad. To raise funds through a sponsorship programme to support community development workers in Kenya.

GENERAL INFORMATION: *Creation:* 1976. *Affiliated to:* ICA International (Belgium). *Personnel/Total:* 15. *Volunteers:* 15. *Budget/Total 1993:* ECU 5000 (US$ 6000). *Financial sources: Private:* 100%.

PUBLICATIONS: *Periodicals:* Village Volunteers Newsletter (4).

ACTIVITIES IN DEVELOPING REGIONS: Active in 1 country(ies). Works through local field partners. **Sustainable Development Actions:** Children/youth/family; Debt/finance/trade; Education/training/literacy; Gender issues/women; Health/sanitation/water; Rural development/agriculture. **Regions:** East Africa.

GBR2339

INTERMEDIATE TECHNOLOGY DEVELOPMENT GROUP (ITDG) ♦ Groupe pour le développement de la technologie appropriée

Myson House, Railway Terrace, Rugby, Warks CV21 3HT, United Kingdom.

Telephone: 44 (1788) 560631. *Fax:* 44 (1788) 540270. *E-mail:* itdgcru@gn.apc.org. *Contact:* Jackie Taylor, Chief Executive .

OBJECTIVES: To enable poor people in developing countries to develop and use skills and technologies which give them more control over their lives and which contribute to the sustainable development of their communities.

GENERAL INFORMATION: *Creation:* 1965. *Personnel/Total:* 250. *Salaried:* 250 of which: 150 in developing countries. *Budget/Total 1993:* ECU 9076000 (US$ 10631000). *Financial sources: Private:* 60%. *Public:* 40%.

PUBLICATIONS: *Periodicals:* Appropriate Technology - Waterlines (3) - Food Chain (3) - Small Enterprise Development (3). *Annual report. List of publications.*

ACTIVITIES IN DEVELOPING REGIONS: Present in developing regions. Active in 6 country(ies). Maintains local field presence. Works through local field partners. **Sustainable Development Actions:** Democracy/good governance/institution building/participatory development; Energy/transport; Food/famine; Rural development/agriculture; Small enterprises/informal sector/handicrafts; Urban development/habitat. **Regions:** Central Asia and South Asia; East Africa; South America; South East Asia; Southern Africa.

INFORMATION AND EDUCATION ACTIVITIES: Topics: Ecology/environment/biodiversity; Gender issues/women; International economic

See: *How to Use the Directory,* page 11.

relations/trade/debt/finance; Rural development/agriculture. **Activities:** Information and documentation services/data bases; Information campaigns/exhibitions.

GBR2340

INTERNATIONAL AFRICAN INSTITUTE (IAI) ♦ Institut Africain International

School of Oriental and African Studies, Thornhaugh Street, Russell Square, London WC1H OXG, United Kingdom.

Telephone: 44 (171) 323 6035. *Fax:* 44 (171) 323 6118. *E-mail:* intafrin@clus1.ulcc.ac.uk. *Contact:* William Shack, Chairman.

OBJECTIVES: To promote the education of the public in the study of Africa and its languages and cultures. To act as an association of academic institutions and scholarly associations subscribing to its objectives.

GENERAL INFORMATION: *Creation:* 1926. *Type of organisation:* network, coordinating body. *Personnel/Total:* 4. *Salaried:* 4. *Budget/Total 1993:* ECU 449000 (US$ 526000). *Financial sources:* Private: 40%. *Public:* 53%. *Self-financing:* 7%.

PUBLICATIONS: *Periodicals:* Africa (4). *List of publications.*

EVALUATION/RESEARCH: Undertakes research activities.

ACTIVITIES IN DEVELOPING REGIONS: Present in developing regions. Works through local field partners. **Sustainable Development Actions:** Education/training/literacy. **Regions:** Central Africa; East Africa; Southern Africa; West Africa.

INFORMATION AND EDUCATION ACTIVITIES: Topics: Education/training/literacy. **Activities:** Conferences/seminars/workshops/training activities; Information and documentation services/data bases; Networking/electronic telecommunications; Publishing/audiovisual materials/educational materials.

GBR2341

INTERNATIONAL AGRICULTURAL TRAINING PROGRAMME (IATP)

East Close, Ditcheat, Shepton Mallet, Somerset BA4 6PS, United Kingdom.

Telephone: 44 (1749) 860358. *Fax:* 44 (1749) 860358. *Contact:* Jeremy St. John Groome, Executive Director.

OBJECTIVES: To conduct training projects overseas and to provide expertise for the design, conduct and evaluation of training programmes for teachers.

GENERAL INFORMATION: *Creation:* 1986. *Affiliated to:* British Overseas NGOs for Development (United Kingdom). *Personnel/Total:* 5. *Salaried:* 5 of which: 2 in developing countries. *Budget/Total 1993:* ECU 385000 (US$ 450000). *Financial sources:* Public: 70%. *Self-financing:* 30%.

PUBLICATIONS: *Periodicals:* Train the Trainer Newsletter (3). *Annual report. List of publications.*

EVALUATION/RESEARCH: Evaluation reports available.

PLANNED ACTIVITIES: Establishing a resource centre in co-operation with Southern NGOs in selected countries.

COMMENTS: IATP is currently the only UK NGO capable of offering internationally recognised accreditation in teaching skills.

ACTIVITIES IN DEVELOPING REGIONS: Present in developing regions. Active in 6 country(ies). Maintains local field presence. Works through local field partners. **Sustainable Development Actions:** Education/training/literacy; Rural development/agriculture; Sending volunteers/experts/technical assistance. **Regions:** Caribbean; Central Asia and South Asia; East Africa; Southern Africa; West Africa.

INFORMATION AND EDUCATION ACTIVITIES: Topics: Education/training/literacy; Gender issues/women; Rural development/agriculture. **Activities:** Conferences/seminars/workshops/training activities; Formal education; Publishing/audiovisual materials/educational materials.

GBR2342

INTERNATIONAL ALERT ♦ Alerte Internationale

1 Glyn Street, London SE11 5HT, United Kingdom.

Telephone: 44 (171) 793 8383. *Fax:* 44 (171) 793 7975. *E-mail:* GEO2:Intl-Alert.. *Contact:* Kumar Rupesinghe, Secretary General.

GBR2343

INTERNATIONAL ALLIANCE OF WOMEN

50 Priory Gardens, London NW1 8EE, United Kingdom.

Telephone: 44 (171) 7437. *E-mail:* ALLINTER LONDON NW1.

GBR2344

INTERNATIONAL ASSOCIATION ON WATER QUALITY (IAWQ)

1 Queen Anne's Gate, London SW1H 9BT, United Kingdom.

Telephone: 44 (171) 222 3848. *Fax:* 44 (171) 233 1197. *Contact:* A. Milburn, Executive Director.

OBJECTIVES: To advance the science and practice of water pollution control and water quality management worldwide, with a focus on domestic and industrial waste water treatment, hazardous waste management, the impact of pollution on receiving waters and environmental restoration.

GENERAL INFORMATION: *Creation:* 1965. *Affiliated to:* International Council of Scientific Unions (France). *Personnel/Total:* 9. *Salaried:* 9. *Budget/Total 1993:* ECU 833000 (US$ 976000). *Financial sources:* Self-financing: 100%.

PUBLICATIONS: *Periodicals:* Water Research (12) - Water Science and Technology (24) - Water Quality International (4). *Annual report. List of publications.*

COMMENTS: Undertakes activities in the Commonwealth of Independent States.

ACTIVITIES IN DEVELOPING REGIONS: Active in 1 country(ies). Works through local field partners. **Sustainable Development Actions:** Health/sanitation/water. **Regions:** Oceania; South America; South East Asia.

INFORMATION AND EDUCATION ACTIVITIES: Topics: Health/sanitation/water. **Activities:** Conferences/seminars/workshops/training activities; Publishing/audiovisual materials/educational materials.

GBR2345

INTERNATIONAL BROADCASTING TRUST (IBT)

2 Ferdinand Place, London NW1 8EE, United Kingdom.

Telephone: 44 (171) 482 2847. *Fax:* 44 (171) 284 3374. *Contact:* Paddy Coulter, Director.

OBJECTIVES: To produce television films and printed materials on Third World development issues. To promote a wider understanding of these issues through the use of media.

GENERAL INFORMATION: *Creation:* 1982. *Type of organisation:* association of NGOs. *Member organisations:* 65. *Affiliated to:* Development Education Association (United Kingdom) - EC/NGO Assembly (United Kingdom). *Personnel/Total:* 6. *Salaried:* 6. *Volunteers:* 2. *Budget/Total 1993:* ECU 487000 (US$ 571000). *Financial sources:* Private: 2%. *Public:* 23%. *Self-financing:* 75%.

PUBLICATIONS: *Periodicals:* Fast Forward (2). *Annual report. List of publications.*

EVALUATION/RESEARCH: Evaluation reports available. Undertakes research activities.

PLANNED ACTIVITIES: Disseminating, in Africa, several major schools' TV series and a printed backup providing authentic imagery. Producing a television drama on aid and development issues.

INFORMATION AND EDUCATION ACTIVITIES: Topics: Culture/tradition/religion; Ecology/environment/biodiversity; Emergency relief/refugees/humanitarian assistance; Food/famine; Gender issues/women; Health/sanitation/water; Human rights/peace/conflicts; International economic relations/trade/debt/finance; International relations/cooperation/

development aid; Other; Peace/ethnic conflicts/armament/disarmament; Poverty/living conditions; Racism/xenophobia/antisemitism; Refugees/migrants/ethnic groups; Rural development/agriculture; Urban development/habitat. **Activities:** Broadcasting/cultural events; Formal education; Information campaigns/exhibitions; Publishing/audiovisual materials/educational materials.

GBR2346

INTERNATIONAL CENTRE FOR CONSERVATION EDUCATION (ICCE)

Greenfield House, Gutting Power, Cheltenham, Gloucestershire GL54 5TZ, United Kingdom.

Telephone: 44 (1451) 850777. **Fax:** 44 (1451) 850705. **E-mail:** icce.demon.co.uk. **Contact:** Mark Boulton, Director.

OBJECTIVES: To promote greater understanding of conservation and the environment worldwide and to encourage sustainable development.

GENERAL INFORMATION: Creation: 1984. **Affiliated to:** IUCN's Commission on Education and Communication (Switzerland) - Fauna and Flora Preservation Society (United Kingdom). **Personnel/Total:** 10. *Salaried:* 10. **Budget/Total 1993:** ECU 256400 (US$ 300000). **Financial sources:** *Private:* 15%. *Self-financing:* 85%.

PUBLICATIONS: Periodicals: Annual Review (1). *Annual report. List of publications.*

EVALUATION/RESEARCH: Evaluation reports available.

PLANNED ACTIVITIES: Completing of a research programme on Environmental Education in Africa and presentation of proposals for targetting DGVIII funding from 1995. Developing a series of specific training modules. Promoting the use of technology (CD Rom) in environmental education.

COMMENTS: Undertakes activities in the Commonwealth of Independent States. Information activities related to the Commonwealth of Independent States.

ACTIVITIES IN DEVELOPING REGIONS: Present in developing regions. Active in 10 country(ies). Works through local field partners. **Sustainable Development Actions:** Ecology/environment/biodiversity; Education/training/literacy. **Regions:** Caribbean; Central Africa; Central Asia and South Asia; East Africa; South East Asia; Southern Africa; West Africa.

INFORMATION AND EDUCATION ACTIVITIES: Topics: Culture/tradition/religion; Ecology/environment/biodiversity; Education/training/literacy; Food/famine; Gender issues/women; Poverty/living conditions. **Activities:** Conferences/seminars/workshops/training activities; Fund raising; Information and documentation services/data bases; Networking/electronic telecommunications; Publishing/audiovisual materials/educational materials.

GBR2347

INTERNATIONAL CENTRE FOR THE LEGAL PROTECTION OF HUMAN RIGHTS (INTERIGHTS) ♦ Le Centre International pour la Protection des Droits de l'Homme

33 Islington High Street, London N1 9LH, United Kingdom.

Telephone: 44 (171) 278 3230. **Fax:** 44 (171) 278 4334. **Contact:** Emma Playfair, Executive Director.

OBJECTIVES: To provide leadership in the development of legal protection of human rights and freedoms through the effective use of international and comparative human rights law. To help judges, lawyers, practitioners, NGOs and victims protect and promote rights through the use of international human rights standards.

GENERAL INFORMATION: Creation: 1982. **Personnel/Total:** 14. *Salaried:* 10. *Volunteers:* 4. **Budget/Total 1993:** ECU 437200 (US$ 512000). **Financial sources:** *Private:* 56%. *Public:* 44%.

PUBLICATIONS: Periodicals: INTERIGHTS Bulletin (4). *Annual report. List of publications.*

EVALUATION/RESEARCH: Evaluation reports available. Undertakes research activities.

PLANNED ACTIVITIES: Undertaking strategic litigation which aims to promote the development of interpretation and use of human rights norms.

COMMENTS: Undertakes activities in the Commonwealth of Independent States. Information activities related to the Commonwealth of Independent States.

ACTIVITIES IN DEVELOPING REGIONS: Present in developing regions. Active in 12 country(ies). Works through local field partners. **Sustainable Development Actions:** Human rights/peace/conflicts. **Regions:** Caribbean; Central Africa; Central Asia and South Asia; East Africa; Middle East; North Africa; Southern Africa; West Africa.

INFORMATION AND EDUCATION ACTIVITIES: Topics: Human rights/peace/conflicts; Racism/xenophobia/antisemitism; Refugees/migrants/ethnic groups. **Activities:** Conferences/seminars/workshops/training activities; Exchanges/twinning/linking; Formal education; Information and documentation services/data bases; Lobbying/advocacy; Publishing/audiovisual materials/educational materials.

GBR2348

INTERNATIONAL CHILDCARE TRUST (ICT)

D16 Peabody Estate, Wild Street, London WC2B 4AG, United Kingdom.

Telephone: 44 (171) 379 4947. **Fax:** 44 (171) 379 4947. **Contact:** David Lamont, President.

OBJECTIVES: To improve the lives and environment of the most deprived and poorest children, youths, and families irrespective of other factors.

GENERAL INFORMATION: Creation: 1982. **Type of organisation:** network. **Member organisations:** 9. **Personnel/Total:** 12. *Salaried:* 6 of which: 4 in developing countries. *Volunteers:* 6 of which: 4 in developing countries. **Budget/Total 1993:** ECU 640300 (US$ 750000). **Financial sources:** *Private:* 51%. *Public:* 49%.

PUBLICATIONS: *Annual report. List of publications.*

EVALUATION/RESEARCH: Undertakes research activities.

ACTIVITIES IN DEVELOPING REGIONS: Present in developing regions. Active in 4 country(ies). Maintains local field presence. Works through local field partners. **Sustainable Development Actions:** Children/youth/family; Ecology/environment/biodiversity; Education/training/literacy; Emergency relief/refugees/humanitarian assistance; Food/famine; Gender issues/women; Health/sanitation/water; Rural development/agriculture; Sending volunteers/experts/technical assistance; Small enterprises/informal sector/handicrafts. **Regions:** Central Asia and South Asia; East Africa; Southern Africa.

INFORMATION AND EDUCATION ACTIVITIES: Topics: Children/youth/family; Ecology/environment/biodiversity; Education/training/literacy; Emergency relief/refugees/humanitarian assistance; Employment/unemployment; Food/famine; Gender issues/women; Health/sanitation/water; Poverty/living conditions; Refugees/migrants/ethnic groups; Rural development/agriculture. **Activities:** Conferences/seminars/workshops/training activities; Formal education; Fund raising; Information and documentation services/data bases; Lobbying/advocacy; Networking/electronic telecommunications.

GBR2349

INTERNATIONAL CHILDRENS TRUST

50 Willesden Avenue, Peterborough, Cambridgeshire PE4 6EA, United Kingdom.

Telephone: 44 (1733) 576597. **Fax:** 44 (1733) 571236. **Contact:** J. Strover, Director of Fundraising.

OBJECTIVES: To improve the health and quality of life of poor children through education and the relief of poverty in the community in which they live.

GENERAL INFORMATION: Creation: 1967. **Personnel/Total:** 4. *Salaried:* 4 of which: 1 in developing countries. **Budget/Total 1993:** ECU 349000 (US$ 409000). **Financial sources:** *Private:* 51%. *Public:* 16%. *Self-financing:* 33%.

PUBLICATIONS: *Annual report.*

PLANNED ACTIVITIES: Setting-up a new project working with street children in Ecuador.

　　　　See: How to Use the Directory, page 11.

ACTIVITIES IN DEVELOPING REGIONS: Present in developing regions. Active in 5 country(ies). Maintains local field presence. Works through local field partners. **Sustainable Development Actions:** Children/youth/family; Education/training/literacy; Rural development/agriculture; Sending volunteers/experts/technical assistance. **Regions:** Central Asia and South Asia; Mexico and Central America; South East Asia; Southern Africa.

INFORMATION AND EDUCATION ACTIVITIES: Topics: Children/youth/family; Education/training/literacy; Rural development/agriculture. **Activities:** Formal education; Fund raising.

GBR2350

INTERNATIONAL CHRISTIAN RELIEF (ICR)

16 St. John's Hill, Sevenoaks, Kent TN13 3NP, United Kingdom.

Telephone: 44 (1732) 450250. *Fax:* 44 (1732) 741190. *Contact:* Rudi van den Hurk, National Director.

OBJECTIVES: To raise funds to assist Third World countries through affiliates. To establish awareness of Third World related issues.

GENERAL INFORMATION: *Creation:* 1978. *Type of organisation:* association of NGOs. *Personnel/Total:* 14. *Salaried:* 14.

PUBLICATIONS: *Periodicals:* ICR Annual Review (1) - ICR News (3) - Appeals (7). *Annual report.*

EVALUATION/RESEARCH: Evaluation reports available.

ACTIVITIES IN DEVELOPING REGIONS: Active in 6 country(ies). **Sustainable Development Actions:** Children/youth/family; Ecology/environment/biodiversity; Education/training/literacy; Emergency relief/refugees/humanitarian assistance; Food/famine; Health/sanitation/water; Rural development/agriculture. **Regions:** Caribbean; Central Africa; East Africa; South East Asia.

INFORMATION AND EDUCATION ACTIVITIES: Topics: Children/youth/family; Ecology/environment/biodiversity; Education/training/literacy; Emergency relief/refugees/humanitarian assistance; Food/famine; Health/sanitation/water; Poverty/living conditions; Refugees/migrants/ethnic groups; Rural development/agriculture; Urban development/habitat. **Activities:** Conferences/seminars/workshops/training activities; Formal education; Fund raising; Information campaigns/exhibitions.

GBR2351

INTERNATIONAL COMMMUNITY EDUCATION ASSOCIATION (ICEA)

Lyng Hall, Blackberry Lane, Coventry CV2 3JS, United Kingdom.

Telephone: 44 (01203) 638670. *Fax:* 44 (01203) 681161. *Contact:* Alan Blackhurst, Secretary General.

OBJECTIVES: To promote the concept and practice of community education at local, national, regional and international levels and develop a world-wide network of members who are actively involved. To motivate and educate people to transform their local communities.

GENERAL INFORMATION: *Creation:* 1974. *Type of organisation:* network. *Personnel/Total:* 3. *Salaried:* 3. *Volunteers:* 24 of which: 24 in developing countries. *Budget/Total 1993:* ECU 85000 (US$ 10000). *Financial sources:* Private: 95%. Self-financing: 5%.

PUBLICATIONS: *Periodicals:* ICEA News (3) - Comm Education International (3). *Annual report.*

EVALUATION/RESEARCH: Evaluation reports available.

COMMENTS: Undertakes activities in the Commonwealth of Independent States. Information activities related to the Commonwealth of Independent States.

ACTIVITIES IN DEVELOPING REGIONS: Present in developing regions. Active in 85 country(ies). Maintains local field presence. Works through local field partners. **Sustainable Development Actions:** Children/youth/family; Democracy/good governance/institution building/participatory development; Ecology/environment/biodiversity; Education/training/literacy; Gender issues/women; Health/sanitation/water; Human rights/peace/conflicts; Population/family planning/demography; Rural development/agriculture; Small enterprises/informal sector/handicrafts; Urban development/habitat. **Regions:** Caribbean; Central Africa;

Central Asia and South Asia; East Africa; East Asia; Mexico and Central America; Middle East; North Africa; Oceania; South America; South East Asia; Southern Africa; West Africa.

INFORMATION AND EDUCATION ACTIVITIES: Topics: Culture/tradition/religion; Ecology/environment/biodiversity; Education/training/literacy; Gender issues/women; Human rights/peace/conflicts; International relations/cooperation/development aid; Population/family planning/demography; Poverty/living conditions; Racism/xenophobia/antisemitism; Refugees/migrants/ethnic groups; Rural development/agriculture. **Activities:** Broadcasting/cultural events; Conferences/seminars/workshops/training activities; Fund raising; Information campaigns/exhibitions; Lobbying/advocacy; Networking/electronic telecommunications; Publishing/audiovisual materials/educational materials.

GBR2352

INTERNATIONAL COUNCIL FOR BIRD PRESERVATION (ICBP)

32 Cambridge Road, Girton, Cambridge CB3 0PJ, United Kingdom.

Telephone: 44 (1223) 277318. *Fax:* 44 (1223) 277200. *Contact:* Dr Christoph Imboden, Director-General.

GBR2353

INTERNATIONAL EXTENSION COLLEGE (IEC)

Dales Brewery, Gwydir Street, Cambridge CB1 2LJ, United Kingdom.

Telephone: 44 (1223) 353321. *Fax:* 44 (1223) 464734. *Contact:* Tony Dodds, Executive Director.

OBJECTIVES: To promote development and improvement in the quality of life through the expansion of education opportunities, using distance education techniques.

GENERAL INFORMATION: *Creation:* 1971. *Affiliated to:* EC NGDO Forum (Belgium) - UK Section (United Kingdom) - British Overseas NGOs for Development (United Kingdom) - UK NGO Education Forum (United Kingdom) -IMAGE (Finland) - EDEN (Finland) - ICDE (Finland) - Refugee Council (United Kingdom). *Personnel/Total:* 21. *Salaried:* 21 of which: 7 in developing countries. *Budget/Total 1993:* ECU 1300000 (US$ 1500000). *Financial sources:* Private: 5%. Public: 75%. *Self-financing:* 20%.

PUBLICATIONS: *Periodicals:* IEC News (4). *Annual report. List of publications.*

EVALUATION/RESEARCH: Undertakes research activities.

ACTIVITIES IN DEVELOPING REGIONS: Active in 16 country(ies). Maintains local field presence. Works through local field partners. **Sustainable Development Actions:** Education/training/literacy; Emergency relief/refugees/humanitarian assistance; Gender issues/women; Sending volunteers/experts/technical assistance. **Regions:** Central Asia and South Asia; East Africa; Mexico and Central America; South East Asia; Southern Africa; West Africa.

INFORMATION AND EDUCATION ACTIVITIES: Topics: Education/training/literacy; Gender issues/women; Health/sanitation/water; Human rights/peace/conflicts; Refugees/migrants/ethnic groups; Rural development/agriculture. **Activities:** Conferences/seminars/workshops/training activities; Fund raising; Information and documentation services/data bases; Information campaigns/exhibitions; Publishing/audiovisual materials/educational materials.

GBR2354

INTERNATIONAL FEDERATION OF FREE JOURNALISTS (IFFJ)

4 Overton Road, London N14 4SY, United Kingdom.

Telephone: 44 (181) 360 2991. *Contact:* L. Sirc.

OBJECTIVES: To uphold the principles of freedom of the press. To promote human and national rights. To raise standards and ethics of journalism and propagate honesty of news.

GENERAL INFORMATION: *Creation:* 1942. *Personnel/Total:* 3. *Volunteers:* 3. *Financial sources:* Self-financing: 100%.

COMMENTS: Information activities related to the Commonwealth of Independent States.

Voir : *Comment utiliser le répertoire,* page 11.

INFORMATION AND EDUCATION ACTIVITIES: **Topics:** Human rights/ peace/conflicts. **Activities:** Information campaigns/exhibitions.

GBR2355

INTERNATIONAL FEDERATION OF SETTLEMENTS AND NEIGHBOURHOOD CENTRES (IFS)

Derwent Centre, Clarke Street, Derby DE1 2BU, United Kingdom.

Telephone: 44 (1332) 204219. **Fax:** 44 (1332) 371355. **Contact:** Emily Menlo Marks, President.

OBJECTIVES: To strengthen communities in our society.

GENERAL INFORMATION: *Creation:* 1926. ***Type of organisation:*** association of NGOs. ***Member organisations:*** 44. ***Affiliated to:*** International Council of Social Welfare (Canada) - European Anti-Poverty Network (Belgium). ***Personnel/Total:*** 1. *Salaried:* 1. ***Budget/ Total 1993:*** ECU 38500 (US$ 45000). ***Financial sources:*** *Private:* 10%. *Self-financing:* 90%.

PUBLICATIONS: *Periodicals:* IFS Newsletter (4).

EVALUATION/RESEARCH: Undertakes research activities.

PLANNED ACTIVITIES: Organising in 1996 a Conference and Linking Process to strengthen communities in our society. Setting-up a network of East-West co-operation and extending the links with organisations in the southern hemisphere, specifically in the Americas.

COMMENTS: Undertakes activities in the Commonwealth of Independent States. Information activities related to the Commonwealth of Independent States.

ACTIVITIES IN DEVELOPING REGIONS: Works through local field partners.

INFORMATION AND EDUCATION ACTIVITIES: Topics: Children/youth/ family; Culture/tradition/religion; Education/training/literacy; Employment/unemployment; Gender issues/women; Human rights/peace/conflicts; International relations/cooperation/development aid; Other; Population/family planning/demography; Poverty/living conditions; Racism/ xenophobia/antisemitism; Refugees/migrants/ethnic groups; Urban development/habitat. **Activities:** Broadcasting/cultural events; Conferences/seminars/workshops/training activities; Exchanges/twinning/linking; Formal education; Fund raising; Information and documentation services/data bases; Information campaigns/exhibitions; Lobbying/advocacy; Networking/electronic telecommunications; Publishing/audiovisual materials/educational materials.

GBR2356

INTERNATIONAL HEALTH EXCHANGE (IHE) ♦ Bureau des services médicaux outre-mer

Africa Centre, 38 King Street, London WC2E 8JT, United Kingdom.

Telephone: 44 (171) 836 5833. **Fax:** 44 (171) 379 1239. **Contact:** Isobel McConnan, Director.

OBJECTIVES: To run a database of health professionals interested in working in developing countries. To provide recruitment services to agencies and hold courses and workshops.

GENERAL INFORMATION: *Creation:* 1979. ***Type of organisation:*** coordinating body. ***Affiliated to:*** NCVO (United Kingdom) - UK NGO AIDS Consortium for the Third World (United Kingdom) - International Health consortium. ***Personnel/Total:*** 4. *Salaried:* 4. ***Budget/Total 1993:*** ECU 205000 (US$ 240000). ***Financial sources:*** *Private:* 37%. *Public:* 25%. *Self-financing:* 38%.

PUBLICATIONS: *Periodicals:* The Health Exchange (6). *Annual report. List of publications.*

PLANNED ACTIVITIES: Lobbying the UK National Health Service to improve release and re-entry and recognition of experience gained by those working in developing countries.

INFORMATION AND EDUCATION ACTIVITIES: Topics: Emergency relief/refugees/humanitarian assistance; Health/sanitation/water. **Activities:** Conferences/seminars/workshops/training activities; Information and documentation services/data bases; Lobbying/advocacy.

GBR2357

INTERNATIONAL INSTITUTE FOR ENVIRONMENT AND DEVELOPMENT (IIED)

3 Endsleigh Street, London WC1H 0DD, United Kingdom.

Telephone: 44 (171) 388 2117. **Fax:** (71) 388 2826. **Contact:** Richard Sandbrook, Executive Director.

GBR2358

INTERNATIONAL NEPAL FELLOWSHIP (INF)

69 Wentworth Road, Harborne, Birmingham B17 9SS, United Kingdom.

Telephone: 44 (121) 427 8833. **Fax:** 44 (121) 428 3110. **Contact:** John Putman, Chairman.

OBJECTIVES: To provide medical aid and other development projects to the people of Nepal.

GENERAL INFORMATION: *Creation:* 1940. ***Type of organisation:*** association of NGOs, network. ***Personnel/Total:*** 61. *Salaried:* 60 of which: 57 in developing countries. *Volunteers:* 1. ***Budget/Total 1993:*** ECU 563300 (US$ 660000). ***Financial sources:*** *Private:* 83%. *Public:* 16%. *Self-financing:* 1%.

PUBLICATIONS: *Periodicals:* Today in Nepal (4). *Annual report. List of publications.*

EVALUATION/RESEARCH: Evaluation reports available. Undertakes research activities.

PLANNED ACTIVITIES: Medical and technical assistance to government district hospitals in the western region of Nepal, and the development of Leprosy TB services in West and mid-West regions of Nepal.

ACTIVITIES IN DEVELOPING REGIONS: Present in developing regions. Active in 1 country(ies). Maintains local field presence. Works through local field partners. **Sustainable Development Actions:** Children/ youth/family; Democracy/good governance/institution building/participatory development; Ecology/environment/biodiversity; Education/ training/literacy; Emergency relief/refugees/humanitarian assistance; Energy/transport; Food/famine; Gender issues/women; Health/sanitation/water; Other; Rural development/agriculture; Sending volunteers/ experts/technical assistance; Small enterprises/informal sector/handicrafts. **Regions:** Central Asia and South Asia.

INFORMATION AND EDUCATION ACTIVITIES: Topics: Children/youth/ family; Ecology/environment/biodiversity; Education/training/literacy; Food/famine; Gender issues/women; Health/sanitation/water; Poverty/ living conditions; Rural development/agriculture. **Activities:** Conferences/seminars/workshops/training activities; Fund raising; Information campaigns/exhibitions; Other; Publishing/audiovisual materials/educational materials.

GBR2359

INTERNATIONAL PLANNED PARENTHOOD FEDERATION (IPPF)

Regents College, Inner Circle, Regents Park, London NW1 4NS, United Kingdom.

Telephone: 44 (171) 486 0741. **Fax:** 44 (171) 487 7950 . **Contact:** Dr. Halfdan Mahler, Secretary General.

OBJECTIVES: To provide family planning and reproductive health services and information.

GENERAL INFORMATION: *Creation:* 1952. ***Type of organisation:*** network. ***Member organisations:*** 112. ***Personnel/Total:*** 340. *Salaried:* 340 of which: 220 in developing countries. ***Budget/Total 1993:*** ECU 97300000 (US$ 114000000). ***Financial sources:*** *Private:* 4%. *Public:* 96%.

PUBLICATIONS: *Periodicals:* IPPF OPLW File Newsletter (11). *Annual report. List of publications.*

EVALUATION/RESEARCH: Evaluation reports available.

COMMENTS: Undertakes activities in the Commonwealth of Independent States.

ACTIVITIES IN DEVELOPING REGIONS: Present in developing regions. Maintains local field presence. Works through local field partners. **Sustainable Development Actions:** Children/youth/family; Democracy/

See: *How to Use the Directory,* page 11.

good governance/institution building/participatory development; Gender issues/women; Population/family planning/demography; Sending volunteers/experts/technical assistance. **Regions:** Caribbean; Central Africa; Central Asia and South Asia; East Africa; East Asia; Mexico and Central America; Middle East; North Africa; Oceania; South America; South East Asia; Southern Africa; West Africa.

INFORMATION AND EDUCATION ACTIVITIES: Topics: Children/youth/family; Gender issues/women; Population/family planning/demography. **Activities:** Broadcasting/cultural events; Conferences/seminars/workshops/training activities; Exchanges/twinning/linking; Formal education; Fund raising; Information and documentation services/data bases; Information campaigns/exhibitions; Lobbying/advocacy; Networking/electronic telecommunications; Publishing/audiovisual materials/educational materials.

GBR2360

INTERNATIONAL PRESS INSTITUTE

Dilke House, 1 Malet Street, London WC1 7JA, United Kingdom.

GBR2361

INTERNATIONAL RESCUE CORPS (IRC)

8 Kings Road, Grangemouth, Stirlingshire FK3 9BB, United Kingdom.

Telephone: 44 (1324) 665011. *Fax:* 44 (1324) 666130. *Contact:* Margaret or Willier McMartin, National Officers.

OBJECTIVES: To provide humanitarian aid in the form of quick response search and rescue teams to disasters worldwide upon request, and to aid other organisations with specific tasks.

GENERAL INFORMATION: *Creation:* 1981. *Affiliated to:* New Pathfinders (United Kingdom). *Personnel/Total:* 60. *Volunteers:* 60. *Budget/Total 1993:* ECU 90000 (US$ 105000). *Financial sources:* Private: 100%.

PUBLICATIONS: *Annual report. List of publications.*

COMMENTS: Undertakes activities in the Commonwealth of Independent States.

ACTIVITIES IN DEVELOPING REGIONS: Active in 2 country(ies). **Sustainable Development Actions:** Emergency relief/refugees/humanitarian assistance; Energy/transport; Food/famine; Health/sanitation/water; Sending volunteers/experts/technical assistance. **Regions:** Caribbean; Central Africa; Central Asia and South Asia; East Africa; East Asia; Mexico and Central America; Middle East; North Africa; Oceania; South America; South East Asia; Southern Africa; West Africa.

GBR2362

INTERNATIONAL SOCIAL SERVICE GREAT BRITAIN

Cranmer House, 39 Brixton Road, London SW9 6DD, United Kingdom.

Contact: David Harrison, Director.

GBR2363

INTERNATIONAL SOLAR ENERGY SOCIETY - UK SECTION (UK-ISES)

192 Franklin Road, Birmingham B30 2HE, United Kingdom.

Telephone: 44 (121) 459 4826. *Fax:* 44 (121) 459 8206. *Contact:* Bernard McNelis, Chairperson.

OBJECTIVES: To promote the integration of sustainable and renewable energy technologies into all energy planning. To lobby decision-makers at all levels and to involve and educate the NGO community on renewable energy.

GENERAL INFORMATION: *Creation:* 1973. *Personnel/Total:* 11. *Salaried:* 1. *Volunteers:* 10. *Financial sources:* Private: 10%. *Self-financing:* 90%.

PUBLICATIONS: *Periodicals:* Sunworld (4) - Solar Energy (4) - Solar World (2). *List of publications.*

COMMENTS: UK-ISES is the national section of the International Solar Energy Society (ISES), which undertakes activities in developing countries either through its Director or through national sections or regional offices. Undertakes activities in the Commonwealth of Independent States. Information activities related to the Commonwealth of Independent States.

INFORMATION AND EDUCATION ACTIVITIES: Topics: Other. **Activities:** Conferences/seminars/workshops/training activities; Information and documentation services/data bases; Information campaigns/exhibitions; Lobbying/advocacy.

GBR2364

INTERNATIONAL TASK FORCE FOR THE RURAL POOR (INTAF)

12 Eastleigh Avenue, South Harrow, HA2 0UF, United Kingdom.

Telephone: 44 (181) 864 4740. *Contact:* Mukat Singh.

OBJECTIVES: To identify and publicize policies, programmes and projects of integrated education and development which contribute most to all around development of the rural poor.

GENERAL INFORMATION: *Creation:* 1989. *Type of organisation:* network, coordinating body. *Member organisations:* 49. *Personnel/Total:* 265. *Volunteers:* 265 of which: 255 in developing countries. *Budget/Total 1993:* ECU 5800 (US$ 6800). *Financial sources:* Private: 50%. *Self-financing:* 50%.

PUBLICATIONS: *Periodicals:* International Journal of Rural Studies (2) - VIKAS SEVA (2).

EVALUATION/RESEARCH: Undertakes research activities.

PLANNED ACTIVITIES: Linking organisations in developing countries to exchange their experiences.

ACTIVITIES IN DEVELOPING REGIONS: Active in 3 country(ies). Works through local field partners. **Sustainable Development Actions:** Democracy/good governance/institution building/participatory development; Education/training/literacy; Rural development/agriculture; Sending volunteers/experts/technical assistance. **Regions:** Central Africa; Central Asia and South Asia; Southern Africa.

INFORMATION AND EDUCATION ACTIVITIES: Topics: Poverty/living conditions; Rural development/agriculture. **Activities:** Conferences/seminars/workshops/training activities; Lobbying/advocacy; Networking/electronic telecommunications.

GBR2365

INTERNATIONAL TREE PLANTING COMMITTEE (ITPC) ♦
Comité pour la Plantation des Arbres

International Tree Foundation, Sandy Lane, Crawley Down, West Sussex RH10 4HS, United Kingdom.

Telephone: 44 (1342) 712536. *Fax:* 44 (1342) 718282. *Contact:* Donald Palmer, Chairman.

OBJECTIVES: To help the provision of tree planting and related research, especially in developing countries, so as to arrest desertification, prevent land erosion, sustain tropical rainforests, secure water-table improvement, and provide timber, fuelwood, edible produce and shade.

GENERAL INFORMATION: *Creation:* 1922. *Affiliated to:* The Parliamentary Environmental Group (United Kingdom) - The UK Forest Network (United Kingdom). *Personnel/Total:* 3497. *Salaried:* 4. *Volunteers:* 3493. *Budget/Total 1993:* ECU 16000 (US$ 18000). *Financial sources:* Private: 100%.

PUBLICATIONS: *Periodicals:* Trees are News (3) - International Tree Foundation Journal and Yearbook (1). *Annual report.*

EVALUATION/RESEARCH: Evaluation reports available.

ACTIVITIES IN DEVELOPING REGIONS: Active in 34 country(ies). Works through local field partners. **Sustainable Development Actions:** Ecology/environment/biodiversity. **Regions:** Caribbean; Central Africa; East Africa; Middle East; North Africa; South America; Southern Africa; West Africa.

INFORMATION AND EDUCATION ACTIVITIES: Topics: Ecology/environment/biodiversity. **Activities:** Broadcasting/cultural events; Conferences/seminars/workshops/training activities; Exchanges/twinning/linking; Fund raising; Information and documentation services/data bases; Information campaigns/exhibitions; Lobbying/advocacy; Networking/

electronic telecommunications; Publishing/audiovisual materials/educational materials.

GBR2366

INTERNATIONAL UNION OF PURE AND APPLIED CHEMISTRY (IUPAC)

Bank Court Chambers, 2-3 Pound Way, Templars Square, Cowley, Oxford OX4 3YF, United Kingdom.

Telephone: 44 (1865) 747744. *Fax:* 44 (1865) 747510. *E-mail:* IUPAC@vax.oxford.ac.uk. *Contact:* K.I. Zamaraev, President.

OBJECTIVES: To study topics of international importance to pure and applied chemistry which need regulation, standardization or codification. To co-operate with other international organisations which deal with topics of a chemical nature.

GENERAL INFORMATION: *Creation:* 1919. *Type of organisation:* association of NGOs. *Member organisations:* 41. *Affiliated to:* International Council of Scientific Unions (France). *Personnel/Total:* 10. *Salaried:* 10. *Budget/Total 1993:* ECU 807000 (US$ 946000). *Financial sources:* Self-financing: 71%.

PUBLICATIONS: *Periodicals:* Pure and Applied Chemistry (12) - Chemistry International (6). *List of publications.*

EVALUATION/RESEARCH: Evaluation reports available.

COMMENTS: Undertakes activities in the Commonwealth of Independent States. Information activities related to the Commonwealth of Independent States.

ACTIVITIES IN DEVELOPING REGIONS: Present in developing regions. Works through local field partners.

INFORMATION AND EDUCATION ACTIVITIES: Topics: Ecology/environment/biodiversity. **Activities:** Conferences/seminars/workshops/training activities; Lobbying/advocacy; Publishing/audiovisual materials/educational materials.

GBR2367

INTERNATIONAL VOLUNTARY SERVICE - UNITED KINGDOM (IVS) ♦ Service Civil International - Section britannique

162 Upper New Walk, Leicester LE1 7QA, United Kingdom.

Telephone: 44 (1533) 549430. *Contact:* Malcolm Goldsmith, General Secretary.

GBR2368

INTERNATIONAL WAGES FOR HOUSEWORK CAMPAIGN

King's Cross Women's Centre, 71 Tonbridge Street, London WC1H 9DZ, United Kingdom.

Telephone: 44 (171) 837 7509. *Fax:* 44 (171) 833 4817. *Contact:* Anne Neale.

GBR2369

INTERNATIONAL WATER SUPPLY ASSOCIATION

1 Queen Annes Gate, London SW1H 9BT, United Kingdom.

Telephone: 44 (171) 222 8111. *Fax:* 44 (171) 222 7243. *Contact:* L.R. Bays, Secretary General.

OBJECTIVES: To exchange information with other organisations engaged in water supply worldwide.

GENERAL INFORMATION: *Creation:* 1947. *Personnel/Total:* 6. *Salaried:* 6. *Budget/Total 1993:* ECU 577000 (US$ 676000). *Financial sources:* Self-financing: 100%.

PUBLICATIONS: *Periodicals:* Aqua (6) - Water Supply (4) - Year Book (1).

COMMENTS: Undertakes activities in the Commonwealth of Independent States. Information activities related to the Commonwealth of Independent States.

ACTIVITIES IN DEVELOPING REGIONS: Active in 32 country(ies). **Sustainable Development Actions:** Education/training/literacy; Health/sanitation/water. **Regions:** Central Africa; Central Asia and South Asia;

East Africa; East Asia; Middle East; North Africa; Oceania; South America; South East Asia; Southern Africa; West Africa.

INFORMATION AND EDUCATION ACTIVITIES: Topics: Health/sanitation/water. **Activities:** Conferences/seminars/workshops/training activities; Information and documentation services/data bases.

GBR2370

INTERNATIONAL WATERFOWL AND WETLANDS RESEARCH BUREAU (IWRB) ♦ Bureau International de Recherches sur les Oiseaux d'Eau et les Zones Humides

Slimbridge, Goucester, GL2 7BX, United Kingdom.

Telephone: 44 (1453) 890643. *Fax:* 44 (1453) 890697. *Contact:* Michael Moser.

OBJECTIVES: To stimulate international co-operation for the conservation of migratory waterfowl and their wetland habitats.

GENERAL INFORMATION: *Creation:* 1954. *Type of organisation:* coordinating body. *Member organisations:* 38. *Personnel/Total:* 13. *Salaried:* 13. *Budget/Total 1993:* ECU 577000 (US$ 676000). *Financial sources:* Private: 60%. Public: 35%. Self-financing: 5%.

PUBLICATIONS: *Periodicals:* IWRB News (2). *Annual report. List of publications.*

EVALUATION/RESEARCH: Evaluation reports available. Undertakes research activities.

COMMENTS: Undertakes activities in the Commonwealth of Independent States. Information activities related to the Commonwealth of Independent States.

ACTIVITIES IN DEVELOPING REGIONS: Active in 17 country(ies). Maintains local field presence. Works through local field partners. **Sustainable Development Actions:** Ecology/environment/biodiversity. **Regions:** Central Africa; Central Asia and South Asia; East Africa; East Asia; North Africa; Oceania; South East Asia; Southern Africa; West Africa.

INFORMATION AND EDUCATION ACTIVITIES: Topics: Ecology/environment/biodiversity. **Activities:** Conferences/seminars/workshops/training activities; Exchanges/twinning/linking; Fund raising; Information and documentation services/data bases; Networking/electronic telecommunications; Publishing/audiovisual materials/educational materials.

GBR2371

IRISH METHODIST WORLD DEVELOPMENT FUND

3 Strathmore Park South, Belfast BT1S 5HJ, United Kingdom.

Telephone: 44 (1648) 33691. *Fax:* 44 (1648) 33691. *Contact:* Rev. Frederick Munce.

OBJECTIVES: To challenge Methodists to contribute one percent of their income to development and relief activities.

GENERAL INFORMATION: *Creation:* 1970. *Type of organisation:* network. *Affiliated to:* Methodist International Development and Relief Association (United Kingdom). *Personnel/Total:* 10. *Salaried:* 1. *Volunteers:* 9. *Budget/Total 1993:* ECU 1600900 (US$ 1950000). *Financial sources:* Private: 90%. Self-financing: 10%.

PUBLICATIONS: *Periodicals:* Funds in Focus (6). *Annual report. List of publications.*

EVALUATION/RESEARCH: Evaluation reports available. Undertakes research activities.

COMMENTS: Undertakes activities in the Commonwealth of Independent States. Information activities related to the Commonwealth of Independent States.

ACTIVITIES IN DEVELOPING REGIONS: Present in developing regions. Active in 25 country(ies). Maintains local field presence. Works through local field partners. **Sustainable Development Actions:** Children/youth/family; Debt/finance/trade; Ecology/environment/biodiversity; Education/training/literacy; Emergency relief/refugees/humanitarian assistance; Energy/transport; Food/famine; Gender issues/women; Health/sanitation/water; Human rights/peace/conflicts; Population/family planning/demography; Rural development/agriculture; Sending volunteers/experts/technical assistance; Small enterprises/informal sector/handi-

See: *How to Use the Directory,* page 11.

crafts; Urban development/habitat. **Regions:** Caribbean; Central Africa; Central Asia and South Asia; East Africa; East Asia; Mexico and Central America; Middle East; North Africa; Oceania; South America; South East Asia; Southern Africa; West Africa.

INFORMATION AND EDUCATION ACTIVITIES: Topics: Children/youth/family; Culture/tradition/religion; Ecology/environment/biodiversity; Education/training/literacy; Emergency relief/refugees/humanitarian assistance; Employment/unemployment; Food/famine; Gender issues/women; Health/sanitation/water; Human rights/peace/conflicts; International economic relations/trade/debt/finance; International relations/cooperation/development aid; Peace/ethnic conflicts/armament/disarmament; Population/family planning/demography; Poverty/living conditions; Racism/xenophobia/antisemitism; Refugees/migrants/ethnic groups; Rural development/agriculture; Urban development/habitat. **Activities:** Broadcasting/cultural events; Conferences/seminars/workshops/training activities; Exchanges/twinning/linking; Formal education; Fund raising; Information and documentation services/data bases; Information campaigns/exhibitions; Lobbying/advocacy; Networking/electronic telecommunications; Other; Publishing/audiovisual materials/educational materials.

GBR2372
JALCHATRA PROJECT

138 Freiston Road, Boston, Lincs PE21 0JP, United Kingdom.

Telephone: 44 (1205) 350221. **Contact:** Carmella Riddell, Project Organiser.

OBJECTIVES: To promote development among the Yaro tribal people of Bangladesh which includes work in modern farming water supply, health care, fish farming and simple sanitation. To provide education for children and adults.

GENERAL INFORMATION: Creation: 1974. **Personnel/Total:** 13. *Volunteers:* 13 of which: 1 in developing countries. **Budget/Total 1993:** ECU 18000 (US$ 21000). **Financial sources:** *Private:* 100%.

PUBLICATIONS: Periodicals: Newsletter (2).

ACTIVITIES IN DEVELOPING REGIONS: Present in developing regions. Active in 1 country(ies). Maintains local field presence. **Sustainable Development Actions:** Children/youth/family; Ecology/environment/biodiversity; Education/training/literacy; Food/famine; Gender issues/women; Health/sanitation/water; Human rights/peace/conflicts; Population/family planning/demography; Rural development/agriculture; Small enterprises/informal sector/handicrafts. **Regions:** Central Asia and South Asia.

INFORMATION AND EDUCATION ACTIVITIES: Topics: Ecology/environment/biodiversity; Education/training/literacy; Emergency relief/refugees/humanitarian assistance; Food/famine; Gender issues/women; Health/sanitation/water; Human rights/peace/conflicts; Population/family planning/demography; Poverty/living conditions; Rural development/agriculture. **Activities:** Broadcasting/cultural events; Fund raising.

GBR2373
JOSPICE INTERNATIONAL

Ince Road, La Casa de San Jose, Thornton, Liverpool L23 4UE, United Kingdom.

Telephone: 44 (151) 924 7871. **Fax:** 44 (151) 931 5727. **Contact:** Father Francis O'Leary, Director.

OBJECTIVES: To build and administer hospices.

GENERAL INFORMATION: Creation: 1962. **Personnel/Total:** 210. *Salaried:* 180 of which: 40 in developing countries. *Volunteers:* 30 of which: 15 in developing countries. **Budget/Total 1993:** ECU 1701000 (US$ 1953000). **Financial sources:** *Private:* 90%. *Public:* 10%.

PUBLICATIONS: Annual report. List of publications.

EVALUATION/RESEARCH: Evaluation reports available.

PLANNED ACTIVITIES: Carrying out new hospice work in Central America.

ACTIVITIES IN DEVELOPING REGIONS: Present in developing regions. Active in 4 country(ies). Maintains local field presence. Works through local field partners. **Sustainable Development Actions:** Emergency relief/refugees/humanitarian assistance; Gender issues/women; Health/sanitation/water; Rural development/agriculture; Urban development/habitat. **Regions:** Caribbean; Mexico and Central America; South America.

INFORMATION AND EDUCATION ACTIVITIES: Topics: Food/famine; Gender issues/women; Health/sanitation/water; Rural development/agriculture. **Activities:** Fund raising.

GBR2374
JUSTICE

59 Carer Lane, London EC4V 5AQ, United Kingdom.

Telephone: 44 (171) 353 51 00. **Fax:** 44 (171) 353 50 55. **Contact:** Anne Owers, Director.

OBJECTIVES: To promote the rule of law in the United Kingdom and the territories for which the United Kingdom is responsible.

GENERAL INFORMATION: Creation: 1957. **Affiliated to:** International Commission of Jurists. **Personnel/Total:** var. *Salaried:* 7. *Volunteers:* 6-20. **Budget/Total 1993:** ECU 154000 (US$ 180000). **Financial sources:** *Private:* 20%. *Public:* 10%. *Self-financing:* 70%.

PUBLICATIONS: Periodicals: Bulletin (3). Annual report. List of publications.

EVALUATION/RESEARCH: Undertakes research activities.

INFORMATION AND EDUCATION ACTIVITIES: Topics: Human rights/peace/conflicts; Racism/xenophobia/antisemitism; Refugees/migrants/ethnic groups. **Activities:** Conferences/seminars/workshops/training activities; Information campaigns/exhibitions; Lobbying/advocacy; Publishing/audiovisual materials/educational materials.

GBR2375
THE KARUNA TRUST

186 Cowley Road, Oxford OX4 1UE, United Kingdom.

Telephone: 44 (1865) 728794. **Fax:** 44 (1865) 792941. **Contact:** Peter Joseph, Director.

OBJECTIVES: To promote among the poorest people in India the development of self-confidence, a sense of dignity and an ability to create the conditions for self-reliance. To support projects in education, health, social development and vocational training.

GENERAL INFORMATION: Creation: 1980. **Affiliated to:** EEC-NGO Liason Group - British Overseas NGO for Development - India UK Association. **Personnel/Total:** 11. *Salaried:* 9 of which: 1 in developing countries. *Volunteers:* 2. **Financial sources:** *Private:* 95%. *Public:* 5%.

PUBLICATIONS: Annual report.

COMMENTS: The Karuna Trust is a Buddhist charity whose social programmes are open to all.

ACTIVITIES IN DEVELOPING REGIONS: Active in 1 country(ies). Maintains local field presence. Works through local field partners. **Sustainable Development Actions:** Children/youth/family; Democracy/good governance/institution building/participatory development; Education/training/literacy; Gender issues/women; Health/sanitation/water; Small enterprises/informal sector/handicrafts; Urban development/habitat. **Regions:** Central Asia and South Asia.

INFORMATION AND EDUCATION ACTIVITIES: Topics: Children/youth/family; Culture/tradition/religion; Education/training/literacy; Gender issues/women; Health/sanitation/water; Poverty/living conditions; Urban development/habitat. **Activities:** Fund raising.

GBR2376
KATHMANDU ENVIRONMENTAL EDUCATION PROJECT (KEEP-UK)

72 Newhaven Road, Edinburgh EH6 5QG, United Kingdom.

Telephone: 44 (131) 332 7990. **Fax:** 44 (131) 554 8656. **Contact:** John Woods, Director.

OBJECTIVES: To help minimize the negative impacts of tourism on the environment and culture of Nepal while maximizing the economic benefits available to the locals.

GENERAL INFORMATION: *Creation:* 1991. ***Affiliated to:*** Kathmandu Environmental Education Project (Nepal). ***Personnel/Total:*** 1. *Salaried:* 1. ***Budget/Total 1993:*** ECU 12000 (US$ 14000). ***Financial sources:*** *Private:* 76%. *Self-financing:* 24%.

PUBLICATIONS: *Periodicals:* Newsletter (2). *Annual report. List of publications.*

EVALUATION/RESEARCH: Undertakes research activities.

ACTIVITIES IN DEVELOPING REGIONS: Active in 1 country(ies). Works through local field partners. **Sustainable Development Actions:** Ecology/environment/biodiversity; Education/training/literacy; Small enterprises/informal sector/handicrafts. **Regions:** Central Asia and South Asia.

INFORMATION AND EDUCATION ACTIVITIES: Topics: Ecology/environment/biodiversity; Education/training/literacy; International economic relations/trade/debt/finance; Poverty/living conditions. **Activities:** Fund raising; Lobbying/advocacy.

GBR2377
KING MAHENDRA TRUST
26 Little Chester Street, London SW1X 7AP, United Kingdom.
Contact: David Newbigging.

GBR2378
KURDISTAN WORKERS ASSOCIATION (KWA)
Fairfax Hall, Portland Gardens, London N4 1HU, United Kingdom.
Telephone: 44 (181) 880 1804. ***Fax:*** 44 (181) 802 9963. ***Contact:*** Sheri Laizer, Co-ordinator.

OBJECTIVES: To advance education. To relieve poverty and promote racial harmony. To assist in the provision of facilities for recreation and leisure for all persons in the United Kingdom, particularly Kurdish people, who find themselves in disadvantaged social and economic circumstances.

GENERAL INFORMATION: *Creation:* 1989. ***Affiliated to:*** National Council of Voluntary Organisations (United Kingdom). ***Personnel/Total:*** 16. *Salaried:* 6. *Volunteers:* 10. ***Budget/Total 1993:*** ECU 185000 (US$ 216000). ***Financial sources:*** *Private:* 70%. *Public:* 20%. *Self-financing:* 10%.

PUBLICATIONS: *Periodicals:* Kurdistan Report (10). *Annual report. List of publications.*

EVALUATION/RESEARCH: Evaluation reports available. Undertakes research activities.

PLANNED ACTIVITIES: Raising the public awareness of the Kurdish question and helping preserve the Kurdish heritage.

ACTIVITIES IN DEVELOPING REGIONS: Active in 2 country(ies). Works through local field partners. **Sustainable Development Actions:** Children/youth/family; Education/training/literacy; Emergency relief/refugees/humanitarian assistance; Gender issues/women; Human rights/peace/conflicts; Sending volunteers/experts/technical assistance. **Regions:** Middle East.

INFORMATION AND EDUCATION ACTIVITIES: Topics: Children/youth/family; Culture/tradition/religion; Education/training/literacy; Emergency relief/refugees/humanitarian assistance; Employment/unemployment; Gender issues/women; Human rights/peace/conflicts; International relations/cooperation/development aid; Peace/ethnic conflicts/armament/disarmament; Racism/xenophobia/antisemitism; Refugees/migrants/ethnic groups. **Activities:** Broadcasting/cultural events; Conferences/seminars/workshops/training activities; Formal education; Fund raising; Information and documentation services/data bases; Information campaigns/exhibitions; Lobbying/advocacy; Networking/electronic telecommunications; Other; Publishing/audiovisual materials/educational materials.

GBR2379
LANCASHIRE DEVELOPMENT EDUCATION GROUP
Global Education Centre, 37 St Peter's Square, Preston PR1 7BX, United Kingdom.
Telephone: 44 (1772) 252299. ***Contact:*** Willy McCourt, Chairperson.

OBJECTIVES: To enable people in Lancashire to understand the links between their own lives and those of people around the world by providing resources in support of development education.

GENERAL INFORMATION: *Creation:* 1982. ***Affiliated to:*** Development Education Association. ***Personnel/Total:*** 11. *Salaried:* 5. *Volunteers:* 6. ***Budget/Total 1993:*** ECU 32000 (US$ 38000). ***Financial sources:*** *Private:* 60%. *Public:* 20%. *Self-financing:* 20%.

PUBLICATIONS: *Periodicals:* Development Education (3) - Lancashire Global Education Network Bulletin (6). *Annual report. List of publications.*

COMMENTS: Information activities related to the Commonwealth of Independent States.

INFORMATION AND EDUCATION ACTIVITIES: Topics: Children/youth/family; Culture/tradition/religion; Ecology/environment/biodiversity; Education/training/literacy; Emergency relief/refugees/humanitarian assistance; Employment/unemployment; Food/famine; Gender issues/women; Health/sanitation/water; Human rights/peace/conflicts; International economic relations/trade/debt/finance; International relations/cooperation/development aid; Peace/ethnic conflicts/armament/disarmament; Population/family planning/demography; Poverty/living conditions; Racism/xenophobia/antisemitism; Refugees/migrants/ethnic groups; Rural development/agriculture; Urban development/habitat. **Activities:** Exchanges/twinning/linking; Formal education; Information and documentation services/data bases.

GBR2380
LEEDS DEVELOPMENT EDUCATION CENTRE (LEEDS DEC)
151-153 Cardigan Road, Leeds LS6 1LJ, United Kingdom.
Telephone: 44 (113) 278 4030. ***Fax:*** 44 (113) 274 4759. ***E-mail:*** leedsdec@gn.apc.org.. ***Contact:*** Nigel West, Co-ordinator.

OBJECTIVES: To promote a critical awareness towards personal, local and world development. To encourage participation in decision-making at all levels of society. To challenge attitudes and structures that contribute to poverty and inequality in all countries of the world.

GENERAL INFORMATION: *Creation:* 1978. ***Affiliated to:*** Development Education Association (United Kingdom). ***Personnel/Total:*** 27. *Salaried:* 7. *Volunteers:* 20. ***Budget/Total 1993:*** ECU 121000 (US$ 141000). ***Financial sources:*** *Private:* 55%. *Public:* 30%. *Self-financing:* 15%.

PUBLICATIONS: *Periodicals:* Newsletter (3). *Annual report. List of publications.*

EVALUATION/RESEARCH: Evaluation reports available.

PLANNED ACTIVITIES: Publishing educational materials on street children for school use and to work with local black communities to increase their input in the geography curriculum in local schools.

COMMENTS: Leeds DEC has a wide array of publications on development issues.

INFORMATION AND EDUCATION ACTIVITIES: Topics: Children/youth/family; Ecology/environment/biodiversity; Education/training/literacy; Gender issues/women; International economic relations/trade/debt/finance; Racism/xenophobia/antisemitism. **Activities:** Conferences/seminars/workshops/training activities; Formal education; Publishing/audiovisual materials/educational materials.

GBR2381
LEONARD CHESHIRE FOUNDATION INTERNATIONAL ◆
Fondation internationale Leonard Cheshire
26-29 Maunsel Street, London SW1P 2QN, United Kingdom.
Telephone: 44 (171) 828 1822. ***Fax:*** (71) 828 0699. ***Contact:*** Sir Henry Marking, Chairman.

See: *How to Use the Directory*, page 11.

GBR2382

THE LEPROSY MISSION INTERNATIONAL (TLM) ◆ Mission évangelique contre la lèpre

80 Windmill Road, Brentford, Middlesex TW8 0QH, United Kingdom.

Telephone: 44 (181) 569 7292. *Fax:* 44 (181) 569 7808. *Contact:* T.D. Durston, General Director.

OBJECTIVES: To bring physical, spiritual, social and psychological healing to those affected by leprosy worldwide and to work towards the eradication of the disease. To enable cured patients to become economically independent.

GENERAL INFORMATION: *Creation:* 1874. *Affiliated to:* International Federation of Anti-Leprosy Organisations (ILEP). *Personnel/Total:* 1820. *Salaried:* 1820 of which: 1650 in developing countries. *Budget/Total 1993:* ECU 8100 (US$ 9500). *Financial sources:* Private: 88%. Public: 5%. Self-financing: 7%.

PUBLICATIONS: *Annual report. List of publications.*

EVALUATION/RESEARCH: Undertakes research activities.

ACTIVITIES IN DEVELOPING REGIONS: Present in developing regions. Active in 32 country(ies). Maintains local field presence. Works through local field partners. **Sustainable Development Actions:** Education/training/literacy; Health/sanitation/water; Sending volunteers/experts/technical assistance; Small enterprises/informal sector/handicrafts. **Regions:** Central Africa; Central Asia and South Asia; East Africa; East Asia; Oceania; South East Asia; Southern Africa; West Africa.

INFORMATION AND EDUCATION ACTIVITIES: Topics: Education/training/literacy; Health/sanitation/water. **Activities:** Broadcasting/cultural events; Conferences/seminars/workshops/training activities; Formal education; Fund raising; Information and documentation services/data bases; Information campaigns/exhibitions; Publishing/audiovisual materials/educational materials.

GBR2383

LIVING EARTH

Warwick House, 106 Harrow Road, London W2 1XD, United Kingdom.

Telephone: 44 (171) 258 1823. *Fax:* 44 (171) 258 1824. *Contact:* Roger Hammond, Chief Executive Director.

OBJECTIVES: To help people take responsibility for their impact on the environment through environmental education.

GENERAL INFORMATION: *Creation:* 1988. *Type of organisation:* association of NGOs, coordinating body. *Member organisations:* 3. *Affiliated to:* Living Earth - Cameroon Environmental Education Programme (Cameroon) - Tierra Viva (Venezuela) - Vivens a Terra (Brazil). *Personnel/Total:* 30. *Salaried:* 23 of which: 17 in developing countries. *Volunteers:* 7. *Budget/Total 1993:* ECU 641000 (US$ 751000). *Financial sources:* Private: 20%. Public: 40%. Self-financing: 40%.

PUBLICATIONS: *List of publications.*

EVALUATION/RESEARCH: Evaluation reports available.

PLANNED ACTIVITIES: Environmental education in Hungary, Columbia, Nigeria and sustainable tourism education in the Baltic states.

COMMENTS: Undertakes activities in the Commonwealth of Independent States. Information activities related to the Commonwealth of Independent States.

ACTIVITIES IN DEVELOPING REGIONS: Present in developing regions. Maintains local field presence. Works through local field partners. **Sustainable Development Actions:** Children/youth/family; Democracy/good governance/institution building/participatory development; Ecology/environment/biodiversity; Education/training/literacy; Energy/transport; Health/sanitation/water; Rural development/agriculture; Small enterprises/informal sector/handicrafts. **Regions:** East Africa; South America; West Africa.

INFORMATION AND EDUCATION ACTIVITIES: Topics: Children/youth/family; Ecology/environment/biodiversity; Education/training/literacy; Health/sanitation/water; International relations/cooperation/development aid; Poverty/living conditions; Urban development/habitat. **Activities:** Broadcasting/cultural events; Conferences/seminars/workshops/training

activities; Exchanges/twinning/linking; Formal education; Fund raising; Information and documentation services/data bases; Information campaigns/exhibitions; Lobbying/advocacy; Networking/electronic telecommunications; Publishing/audiovisual materials/educational materials.

GBR2384

MARGARET PYKE MEMORIAL TRUST

73-75 Charlotte Street, London WI, United Kingdom.

Contact: Jean Medawar, Director.

OBJECTIVES: To make family planning education and reproductive health services available to all men and women of London. To conduct biomedical research and train doctors and nurses in these fields.

GENERAL INFORMATION: *Creation:* 1969. *Personnel/Total:* 115. *Salaried:* 100. *Volunteers:* 15. *Budget/Total 1993:* ECU 128000 (US$ 150000). *Financial sources:* Private: 15%. Public: 80%. Self-financing: 5%.

EVALUATION/RESEARCH: Undertakes research activities.

COMMENTS: Undertakes activities in the Commonwealth of Independent States. Information activities related to the Commonwealth of Independent States.

INFORMATION AND EDUCATION ACTIVITIES: Topics: Other; Population/family planning/demography. **Activities:** Broadcasting/cultural events; Conferences/seminars/workshops/training activities; Exchanges/twinning/linking; Formal education; Fund raising; Information and documentation services/data bases; Information campaigns/exhibitions; Lobbying/advocacy; Other; Publishing/audiovisual materials/educational materials.

GBR2385

MARIE STOPES INTERNATIONAL

62 Grafton Way, London W1P 5LD, United Kingdom.

Telephone: 44 (171) 388 3740. *Fax:* (171) 388 1946. *Contact:* Timothy R.L. Black, Chief Executive.

OBJECTIVES: To provide reproductive healthcare/family planning services and information to enable individuals all over the world to have children by choice, not by chance.

GENERAL INFORMATION: *Creation:* 1971. *Type of organisation:* association of NGOs. *Member organisations:* 23. *Personnel/Total:* 30. *Salaried:* 30. *Financial sources:* Private: 44%. Public: 56%.

PUBLICATIONS: *Periodicals:* First People (2).

EVALUATION/RESEARCH: Undertakes research activities.

COMMENTS: Undertakes activities in the Commonwealth of Independent States. Information activities related to the Commonwealth of Independent States.

ACTIVITIES IN DEVELOPING REGIONS: Present in developing regions. Active in 24 country(ies). Works through local field partners. **Sustainable Development Actions:** Children/youth/family; Education/training/literacy; Emergency relief/refugees/humanitarian assistance; Gender issues/women; Health/sanitation/water; Population/family planning/demography. **Regions:** Caribbean; Central Asia and South Asia; East Africa; Mexico and Central America; Middle East; North Africa; South East Asia; Southern Africa; West Africa.

INFORMATION AND EDUCATION ACTIVITIES: Topics: Children/youth/family; Education/training/literacy; Emergency relief/refugees/humanitarian assistance; Gender issues/women; Health/sanitation/water; Human rights/peace/conflicts; Population/family planning/demography; Poverty/living conditions; Refugees/migrants/ethnic groups. **Activities:** Conferences/seminars/workshops/training activities; Fund raising; Information and documentation services/data bases; Information campaigns/exhibitions.

GBR2386

MARINE CONSERVATION SOCIETY

9 Gloucester Road, Ross-on-Wye, herefordshire HR9SBU, United Kingdom.

Telephone: 44 (1989) 566017. *Fax:* 44 (1989) 567815. *Contact:* Robin Duchesne, Chairman.

OBJECTIVES: To protect the marine environment for wildlife and for future generations.

GENERAL INFORMATION: *Creation:* 1982. *Personnel/Total:* 7. *Salaried:* 7. *Budget/Total 1993:* ECU 321000 (US$ 376000). *Financial sources:* Private: 15%. Public: 60%. Self-financing: 25%.

PUBLICATIONS: *Periodicals:* Marine Conservation (3). *Annual report. List of publications.*

EVALUATION/RESEARCH: Undertakes research activities.

PLANNED ACTIVITIES: An ocean survey for yachtsmen worldwide, beach monitoring project for UK schools and UK marine debris survey.

ACTIVITIES IN DEVELOPING REGIONS: Present in developing regions. Active in 1 country(ies). Works through local field partners. **Sustainable Development Actions:** Ecology/environment/biodiversity. **Regions:** Caribbean.

INFORMATION AND EDUCATION ACTIVITIES: Topics: Ecology/environment/biodiversity; Health/sanitation/water. Activities: Conferences/seminars/workshops/training activities; Formal education; Fund raising; Information and documentation services/data bases; Information campaigns/exhibitions; Lobbying/advocacy; Publishing/audiovisual materials/educational materials.

GBR2387
MEDIA NATURA

21 Tower Street, London WC2H 9NS, United Kingdom.

Telephone: 44 (171) 240 4936. *Fax:* 44 (171) 240 2291. *E-mail:* medianatura@gn.apc.org. *Contact:* Michael Keating, Director.

OBJECTIVES: To raise awareness of environment/development problems and solutions by mobilising the skills, talents and resources of the media industry.

GENERAL INFORMATION: *Creation:* 1988. *Personnel/Total:* 17. *Salaried:* 10. *Volunteers:* 4. *Financial sources:* Self-financing: 100%.

EVALUATION/RESEARCH: Undertakes research activities.

INFORMATION AND EDUCATION ACTIVITIES: Topics: Children/youth/family; Ecology/environment/biodiversity; Education/training/literacy; Emergency relief/refugees/humanitarian assistance; Food/famine; Gender issues/women; Health/sanitation/water; Human rights/peace/conflicts; International economic relations/trade/debt/finance; International relations/cooperation/development aid; Peace/ethnic conflicts/armament/disarmament; Population/family planning/demography; Poverty/living conditions; Refugees/migrants/ethnic groups; Rural development/agriculture; Urban development/habitat. Activities: Conferences/seminars/workshops/training activities; Information and documentation services/data bases; Information campaigns/exhibitions; Networking/electronic telecommunications; Other; Publishing/audiovisual materials/educational materials.

GBR2388
MEDICAL ACTION FOR GLOBAL SECURITY (MEDACT)

601 Holloway Road, London N19 4DJ, United Kingdom.

Telephone: 44 (171) 272 2020. *Fax:* 44 (171) 281 5717. *E-mail:* medact@gn.apc.org. *Contact:* Dr. Martin Hartos, Chairman.

OBJECTIVES: To prevent war and promote peace to make the world safer and healthier and to bring together the expertise of health professionals to do so.

GENERAL INFORMATION: *Creation:* 1992. *Affiliated to:* International Physicians for the Prevention of Nuclear War (USA) -International Peace Bureau (Switzerland) - United Nations Association (United Kingdom) - Professions for Social Responsibility (United Kingdom) - World Court Project UK (United Kingdom) - CAMDUN (United Kingdom) - British Nuclear Test Ban Coalition - National Council for Voluntary Organisations (United Kingdom) -National Peace Council (United Kingdom). *Personnel/Total:* 4. *Salaried:* 4. *Budget/Total 1993:* ECU 97000 (US$ 11400). *Financial sources:* Private: 35%. Self-financing: 59%.

PUBLICATIONS: *Periodicals:* Global Security (3) - Medicin and War (4). *Annual report. List of publications.*

EVALUATION/RESEARCH: Undertakes research activities.

PLANNED ACTIVITIES: Campaign to achieve test ban treaty and extension of Nuclear Non Proliferation Treaty; psychosocial support in former Yugoslavia and a debt project in Uganda.

COMMENTS: Undertakes activities in the Commonwealth of Independent States. Information activities related to the Commonwealth of Independent States.

ACTIVITIES IN DEVELOPING REGIONS: Works through local field partners. **Sustainable Development Actions:** Debt/finance/trade. **Regions:** East Africa.

INFORMATION AND EDUCATION ACTIVITIES: Topics: Emergency relief/refugees/humanitarian assistance; International economic relations/trade/debt/finance; Peace/ethnic conflicts/armament/disarmament; Refugees/migrants/ethnic groups. Activities: Conferences/seminars/workshops/training activities; Fund raising; Information and documentation services/data bases; Information campaigns/exhibitions; Lobbying/advocacy; Publishing/audiovisual materials/educational materials.

GBR2389
MEDICAL AID FOR PALESTINIANS

3rd floor, 9 Cavendish Square, London W1M 9DD, United Kingdom.

Contact: Teresa Hanley.

GBR2390
MEDICAL MISSION SISTERS (MMS)

41 Chatsworth Gardens, Acton, London W3 9LP, United Kingdom.

Telephone: 44 (181) 992 6444. *Fax:* 44 (181) 896 2397. *Contact:* Sister Rita Syron, Society Co-ordinator.

OBJECTIVES: To promote the One World of God's wholeness by the ministry of healing and the promotion of health, especially for the poor and for women. To protect the environment and promote peace and justice.

GENERAL INFORMATION: *Creation:* 1925. *Affiliated to:* United Nations Association (United Kingdom) - PAX CHRISTI (United Kingdom) - Friends of the Earth (United Kingdom) - Third World First (United Kingdom) -Women's International League for Peace and Freedom - Africa-Europe Faith and Justice Network (Belgium) - World Court Project (United Kingdom). *Budget/Total 1993:* ECU 228000 (US$ 267350). *Financial sources:* Private: 100%.

PUBLICATIONS: *Periodicals:* Intercontinent (6).

EVALUATION/RESEARCH: Evaluation reports available. Undertakes research activities.

COMMENTS: Work mainly in association and collaboration with other groups.

ACTIVITIES IN DEVELOPING REGIONS: Present in developing regions. Active in 14 country(ies). Maintains local field presence. Works through local field partners. **Sustainable Development Actions:** Children/youth/family; Debt/finance/trade; Education/training/literacy; Emergency relief/refugees/humanitarian assistance; Food/famine; Gender issues/women; Health/sanitation/water; Population/family planning/demography; Rural development/agriculture; Sending volunteers/experts/technical assistance; Small enterprises/informal sector/handicrafts; Urban development/habitat. **Regions:** Central Africa; Central Asia and South Asia; East Africa; Mexico and Central America; South America; South East Asia; Southern Africa; West Africa.

INFORMATION AND EDUCATION ACTIVITIES: Topics: Children/youth/family; Culture/tradition/religion; Ecology/environment/biodiversity; Education/training/literacy; Emergency relief/refugees/humanitarian assistance; Employment/unemployment; Food/famine; Gender issues/women; Health/sanitation/water; Human rights/peace/conflicts; International economic relations/trade/debt/finance; International relations/cooperation/development aid; Peace/ethnic conflicts/armament/disarmament; Population/family planning/demography; Poverty/living conditions; Racism/xenophobia/antisemitism; Refugees/migrants/ethnic groups; Rural development/agriculture; Urban development/habitat.

See: *How to Use the Directory,* page 11.

Activities: Broadcasting/cultural events; Conferences/seminars/workshops/training activities; Exchanges/twinning/linking; Formal education; Fund raising; Information and documentation services/data bases; Lobbying/advocacy; Publishing/audiovisual materials/educational materials.

GBR2391

METHODIST CHURCH, OVERSEAS DIVISION (MCOD)

25 Marylebone Road, London NW1 5JR, United Kingdom.

Telephone: 44 (171) 486 5502. *Fax:* 44 (171) 935 1507. *Contact:* Rev. John R. Pritchard, General Secretary.

OBJECTIVES: To work with churches overseas in a wide variety of evangelistic and social projects. To provide co-operative aid in personnel and money for educational, medical, rehabilitation and rural health projects, urban and agricultural development projects.

GENERAL INFORMATION: *Creation:* 1786. *Personnel/Total:* 49. *Salaried:* 49. *Budget/Total 1993:* ECU 6411000 (US$ 7510000). *Financial sources:* Private: 100%.

PUBLICATIONS: *Periodicals:* Facets (4). *Annual report. List of publications.*

PLANNED ACTIVITIES: Education and fund-raising activities in South India. The preparation of a video information pack on China.

COMMENTS: Undertakes activities in the Commonwealth of Independent States.

ACTIVITIES IN DEVELOPING REGIONS: Works through local field partners. **Sustainable Development Actions:** Sending volunteers/experts/technical assistance. **Regions:** Caribbean; Central Africa; Central Asia and South Asia; East Africa; East Asia; Mexico and Central America; Middle East; North Africa; Oceania; South America; South East Asia; Southern Africa; West Africa.

INFORMATION AND EDUCATION ACTIVITIES: Topics: Culture/tradition/religion. **Activities:** Conferences/seminars/workshops/training activities; Exchanges/twinning/linking; Fund raising; Information and documentation services/data bases; Lobbying/advocacy; Publishing/audiovisual materials/educational materials.

GBR2392

METHODIST RELIEF AND DEVELOPMENT FUND

1 Central Buildings, Westminster, London SW1H 9NH, United Kingdom.

Telephone: 44 (171) 222 8010. *Fax:* 44 (171) 799 2153. *Contact:* Rachel E. Stephens.

OBJECTIVES: To tackle the root causes of poverty and injustice through raising awareness, channelling grants for relief, rehabilitation and development. To work with other organisations to represent the needs of developing countries and those who are suffering from poverty, oppression or exploitation.

GENERAL INFORMATION: *Creation:* 1945. *Affiliated to:* World Methodist Council - World Council of Churches (Switzerland) - European Ecumenical Commission on Development (Belgium) - Conference of European Churches - Council of Churches in Britain and Ireland. *Personnel/Total:* var.. *Salaried:* 8 of which: 1 in developing countries. *Volunteers:* var.. *Budget/Total 1993:* ECU 1360000 (US$ 1592000). *Financial sources:* Private: 97%. Public: 3%.

PUBLICATIONS: *Periodicals:* Funds in Focus (6) - Annual Report (1). *Annual report.*

COMMENTS: Undertakes activities in the Commonwealth of Independent States. Information activities related to the Commonwealth of Independent States.

ACTIVITIES IN DEVELOPING REGIONS: Active in 47 country(ies). Works through local field partners. **Sustainable Development Actions:** Children/youth/family; Ecology/environment/biodiversity; Education/training/literacy; Emergency relief/refugees/humanitarian assistance; Food/famine; Gender issues/women; Health/sanitation/water; Human rights/peace/conflicts; Rural development/agriculture; Small enterprises/informal sector/handicrafts; Urban development/habitat. **Regions:** Caribbean; Central Africa; Central Asia and South Asia; East Africa; East Asia; Mexico and Central America; Middle East; North Africa; Oceania; South America; South East Asia; Southern Africa; West Africa.

INFORMATION AND EDUCATION ACTIVITIES: Topics: Emergency relief/refugees/humanitarian assistance; Food/famine; Gender issues/women; Health/sanitation/water; Human rights/peace/conflicts; International economic relations/trade/debt/finance; Peace/ethnic conflicts/armament/disarmament; Poverty/living conditions; Racism/xenophobia/antisemitism; Refugees/migrants/ethnic groups; Rural development/agriculture. **Activities:** Conferences/seminars/workshops/training activities; Formal education; Fund raising; Information and documentation services/data bases; Information campaigns/exhibitions; Lobbying/advocacy; Networking/electronic telecommunications; Publishing/audiovisual materials/educational materials.

GBR2393

METHODIST WORLD DEVELOPMENT AND RELIEF COMMITTEE (MWDRC)

3 Strathmore Park South, Belfast BT15 5HJ, United Kingdom.

Telephone: 353 (1232) 778749. *Contact:* Rev. Fred Munce.

OBJECTIVES: To fund raise for development activities and to promote development education.

GENERAL INFORMATION: *Creation:* 1971. *Personnel/Total:* 4. *Salaried:* 2. *Volunteers:* 2. *Budget/Total 1993:* ECU 250000 (US$ 293000). *Financial sources:* Private: 100%.

COMMENTS: The organisation undertakes fundraising campaigns for projects undertaken by the Methodist Church.

GBR2394

MINES ADVISORY GROUP (MAG-UK)

54A Main Street, Cockermouth, Cumbria CA13 9LU, United Kingdom.

Telephone: 44 (1900) 828580/828688. *Fax:* 44 (1900) 827088. *Contact:* Rae McGrath, Director.

OBJECTIVES: To remove land mines from developing countries in order to protect the lives of rural dwellers, refugees and displaced persons. To campaign for a complete ban on the manufacture, sale, transfer and stockpiling of mines.

GENERAL INFORMATION: *Creation:* 1990. *Personnel/Total:* 632. *Salaried:* 632 of which: 626 in developing countries. *Budget/Total 1993:* ECU 2600000 (US$ 3001000). *Financial sources:* Private: 2%. Public: 98%.

PUBLICATIONS: *Annual report. List of publications.*

EVALUATION/RESEARCH: Evaluation reports available.

PLANNED ACTIVITIES: New projects in Mozambique, Croatia and Afghanistan.

ACTIVITIES IN DEVELOPING REGIONS: Present in developing regions. Active in 4 country(ies). Maintains local field presence. **Sustainable Development Actions:** Other. **Regions:** Middle East; South East Asia; Southern Africa.

INFORMATION AND EDUCATION ACTIVITIES: Topics: Other. **Activities:** Conferences/seminars/workshops/training activities; Information and documentation services/data bases; Information campaigns/exhibitions; Lobbying/advocacy; Publishing/audiovisual materials/educational materials.

GBR2395

MINEWATCH

218 Liverpool Road, London N1 1LE, United Kingdom.

Telephone: 44 (171) 609 1852. *Fax:* 44 (171) 700 6189. *Contact:* Christine Lancaster and Roger Moody, Co-ordinators.

GBR2396

MINORITY RIGHTS GROUP - INTERNATIONAL SECRETARIAT

379 Brixton Road, London SW9 7DE, United Kingdom.

Telephone: 44 (171) 978 9498. *Fax:* 44 (171) 738 6265. *Contact:* Alan Phillips, Director.

OBJECTIVES: To secure justice for minority and non-dominant majority groups suffering from discrimination through fostering understanding of the factions which create prejudicial treatment and group tension.

GENERAL INFORMATION: *Creation:* 1969. *Affiliated to:* Euro-Citizen Action Service (Belgium) - National Council for Voluntary Organisations (United Kingdom). *Personnel/Total:* 26. *Salaried:* 24. *Volunteers:* 2. *Budget/Total 1993:* ECU 901000 (US$ 1050000). *Financial sources: Private:* 30%. *Public:* 50%. *Self-financing:* 20%.

PUBLICATIONS: *Periodicals:* Outsider (4) - Reports (6). *Annual report. List of publications.*

EVALUATION/RESEARCH: Undertakes research activities.

COMMENTS: Undertakes activities in the Commonwealth of Independent States. Information activities related to the Commonwealth of Independent States.

ACTIVITIES IN DEVELOPING REGIONS: Works through local field partners. **Sustainable Development Actions:** Children/youth/family; Democracy/good governance/institution building/participatory development; Education/training/literacy; Gender issues/women; Human rights/ peace/conflicts. **Regions:** Central Africa; Central Asia and South Asia; East Africa; Mexico and Central America; Middle East; South East Asia; West Africa.

INFORMATION AND EDUCATION ACTIVITIES: Topics: Children/youth/ family; Culture/tradition/religion; Education/training/literacy; Emergency relief/refugees/humanitarian assistance; Employment/unemployment; Gender issues/women; Health/sanitation/water; Human rights/peace/ conflicts; International relations/cooperation/development aid; Peace/ ethnic conflicts/armament/disarmament; Poverty/living conditions; Racism/xenophobia/antisemitism; Refugees/migrants/ethnic groups. **Activities:** Conferences/seminars/workshops/training activities; Exchanges/twinning/linking; Formal education; Fund raising; Information and documentation services/data bases; Information campaigns/exhibitions; Lobbying/advocacy; Publishing/audiovisual materials/educational materials.

GBR2397
MONEY FOR MADAGASCAR

29 Queens Road, Sketty, Swansea SA2 0SB, United Kingdom.

Contact: Allan Prys-Williams.

GBR2398
NAIROBI HOSPICE CHARITABLE TRUST

Hunterston, Donhead St. Andrew, Shaftesbury, Dorset SP7 8EB, United Kingdom.

Contact: Gillian Hunter.

GBR2399
NAMIBIA SUPPORT COMMITTEE

37-39 Great Guildford Street, London SE1 0ES, United Kingdom.

Contact: J. Barker.

GBR2400
NATIONAL COUNCIL FOR VOLUNTARY ORGANISATIONS (NCVO)

Regents Wharf, 8 All Saints Street, London N1 9RL, United Kingdom.

Telephone: 44 (171) 713 6161. *Fax:* 44 (171) 713 6300. *Contact:* Simon Hedbitch, Acting Director.

OBJECTIVES: To provide professional advisory services to national voluntary organisations, protect their interests and promote new social action. To work with voluntary organisations on issues of immediate concern and create projects to strengthen the effectiveness of voluntary action.

GENERAL INFORMATION: *Creation:* 1919. *Type of organisation:* coordinating body. *Member organisations:* 650. *Affiliated to:* CEPAG (France). *Personnel/Total:* 100. *Budget/Total 1993:* ECU 5200600 (US$ 6101000). *Financial sources: Private:* 54%. *Public:* 28%. *Self-financing:* 18%.

PUBLICATIONS: *Periodicals:* NCVO News (10). *Annual report. List of publications.*

EVALUATION/RESEARCH: Undertakes research activities.

INFORMATION AND EDUCATION ACTIVITIES: Topics: Ecology/environment/biodiversity; Employment/unemployment; Other. **Activities:** Conferences/seminars/workshops/training activities; Fund raising; Information and documentation services/data bases; Lobbying/advocacy; Networking/electronic telecommunications; Publishing/audiovisual materials/educational materials.

GBR2401
NATIONAL PEACE COUNCIL (NPC)

88 Islington High Street, London N1 8EG, United Kingdom.

Telephone: 44 (171) 354 5200. *Fax:* 44 (171) 354 0033. *E-mail:* NPC.@GN.APC.ORG. *Contact:* Archbishop Trevor Huddleston.

OBJECTIVES: To provide a network of local, regional and national organisations concerned with peace, justice and a safer environment.

GENERAL INFORMATION: *Creation:* 1908. *Type of organisation:* network. *Member organisations:* 220. *Affiliated to:* Special NGO Committee for Disarmament (Switzerland) - International Peace Bureau. *Personnel/Total:* 14. *Salaried:* 4. *Volunteers:* 10. *Budget/ Total 1993:* ECU 151000 (US$ 180000). *Financial sources: Private:* 25%. *Public:* 10%. *Self-financing:* 5%.

PUBLICATIONS: *Periodicals:* National Peace Council Newsletter (10). *Annual report. List of publications.*

PLANNED ACTIVITIES: Setting-up an education network of Peace Education for children.

COMMENTS: Information activities related to the Commonwealth of Independent States.

INFORMATION AND EDUCATION ACTIVITIES: Topics: Human rights/ peace/conflicts; International relations/cooperation/development aid; Peace/ethnic conflicts/armament/disarmament. **Activities:** Conferences/seminars/workshops/training activities; Lobbying/advocacy; Networking/electronic telecommunications; Publishing/audiovisual materials/educational materials.

GBR2402
NATIONAL UNION OF STUDENTS (NUS)

461 Holloway Road, London N7 6LJ, United Kingdom.

Telephone: 44 (171) 272 8900. *Fax:* 44 (171) 263 5713. *Contact:* Shrupi Shah, Vice President.

OBJECTIVES: To represent the students of the United Kingdom locally, nationally and internationally. To promote and maintain the educational, social, cultural and general interests of students.

GENERAL INFORMATION: *Creation:* 1922. *Type of organisation:* network. *Member organisations:* 850. *Affiliated to:* National Union of Students in Europe (Austria). *Personnel/Total:* 90. *Salaried:* 90. *Budget/Total 1993:* ECU 3850650 (US$ 4501000). *Financial sources: Public:* 94%. *Self-financing:* 6%.

PUBLICATIONS: *Periodicals:* NUS Action (12). *Annual report. List of publications.*

EVALUATION/RESEARCH: Evaluation reports available. Undertakes research activities.

COMMENTS: Undertakes activities in the Commonwealth of Independent States.

ACTIVITIES IN DEVELOPING REGIONS: Works through local field partners. **Sustainable Development Actions:** Children/youth/family; Debt/finance/trade; Democracy/good governance/institution building/ participatory development; Education/training/literacy; Gender issues/ women; Human rights/peace/conflicts; Sending volunteers/experts/technical assistance. **Regions:** Central Africa; Central Asia and South Asia; East Africa; East Asia; Mexico and Central America; Middle East; North Africa; South America; South East Asia; Southern Africa; West Africa.

INFORMATION AND EDUCATION ACTIVITIES: Topics: Education/training/literacy; Gender issues/women; Health/sanitation/water; Human rights/peace/conflicts; Peace/ethnic conflicts/armament/disarmament; Poverty/living conditions; Racism/xenophobia/antisemitism. **Activities:** Conferences/seminars/workshops/training activities; Exchanges/twin-

See: How to Use the Directory, page 11.

ning/linking; Information and documentation services/data bases; Information campaigns/exhibitions; Networking/electronic telecommunications; Publishing/audiovisual materials/educational materials.

GBR2403
NCH EDUCATION FOR CHILDREN

85 Highbury Park, London N5 1UD, United Kingdom.

Telephone: 44 (171) 226 2033. *Fax:* 44 (171) 226 2537. *Contact:* Tom White, Chief Executive.

OBJECTIVES: To enhance the lives of children and young people in society. To offer specialized services to help sustain natural family units and provide alternative care when necessary. To advocate the interests of children, young people and families.

GENERAL INFORMATION: *Creation:* 1869. *Affiliated to:* International Foundation for Child Welfare (Switzerland) - European Forum for Child Welfare (Belgium). *Personnel/Total:* 3690. *Salaried:* 2165 of which: 50 in developing countries. *Volunteers:* 1525 of which: 25 in developing countries. *Budget/Total 1993:* ECU 64100800 (US$ 75101000). *Financial sources: Private:* 23%. *Public:* 70%. *Self-financing:* 7%.

PUBLICATIONS: *Annual report.*

EVALUATION/RESEARCH: Undertakes research activities.

COMMENTS: Information activities related to the Commonwealth of Independent States.

ACTIVITIES IN DEVELOPING REGIONS: Present in developing regions. Active in 7 country(ies). Works through local field partners. **Sustainable Development Actions:** Children/youth/family; Education/training/literacy. **Regions:** Caribbean; Central Africa.

INFORMATION AND EDUCATION ACTIVITIES: Topics: Children/youth/family. **Activities:** Conferences/seminars/workshops/training activities.

GBR2404
NEPALWATCH - UK

6 School Terrace, Reading, Berkshire, United Kingdom.

Telephone: 44 (173) 466 3781. *Contact:* Dave Richards.

GBR2405
NEW AGE ACCESS

3 Orchard Place, Hexham NE46 1QQ, United Kingdom.

Contact: Nick Murgatroyd.

GBR2406
NEW ECONOMICS FOUNDATION (NEF)

Vine Court, 1st Floor, 112-116 Whitechapel Road, London E1 1JE, United Kingdom.

Telephone: 44 (171) 377 5696. *Fax:* 44 (171) 377 5720. *E-mail:* neweconomics@gn.apc.org. *Contact:* Ed Mayo, Director.

OBJECTIVES: To work for a just and sustainable economy. To undertake research and educational projects focusing on new economics for development.

GENERAL INFORMATION: *Creation:* 1986. *Personnel/Total:* 6. *Salaried:* 6. *Budget/Total 1993:* ECU 321000 (US$ 376000). *Financial sources: Private:* 80%. *Public:* 5%. *Self-financing:* 15%.

PUBLICATIONS: *Periodicals:* New Economics (4). *Annual report. List of publications.*

EVALUATION/RESEARCH: Evaluation reports available. Undertakes research activities.

COMMENTS: Information activities related to the Commonwealth of Independent States.

INFORMATION AND EDUCATION ACTIVITIES: Topics: Culture/tradition/religion; Ecology/environment/biodiversity; Employment/unemployment; International economic relations/trade/debt/finance; International

relations/cooperation/development aid. **Activities:** Broadcasting/cultural events; Conferences/seminars/workshops/training activities; Exchanges/twinning/linking; Formal education; Fund raising; Information and documentation services/data bases; Information campaigns/exhibitions; Lobbying/advocacy; Networking/electronic telecommunications; Publishing/audiovisual materials/educational materials.

GBR2407
THE NEW REFUGEE UNIT

2nd floor, County House, 190 Great Dover Street, London SE1 4YB, United Kingdom.

Telephone: 44 (171) 357 7421. *Fax:* 44 (171) 378 1979.

GBR2408
NORFOLK EDUCATION AND ACTION FOR DEVELOPMENT (NEAD)

Development and Environment Centre, 38-40 Exchange Street, Norwich NR2 1AX, United Kingdom.

Telephone: 44 (1603) 610993. *Fax:* 44 (1603) 761645.

OBJECTIVES: To raise awareness about inequalities in our world and increase understanding of their causes. To show how all people can act together to build a more sustainable future.

GENERAL INFORMATION: *Creation:* 1973. *Affiliated to:* Development Education Association. *Personnel/Total:* 19. *Salaried:* 4. *Volunteers:* 15. *Budget/Total 1993:* ECU 65000 (US$ 77000). *Financial sources: Private:* 35%. *Public:* 45%. *Self-financing:* 20%.

PUBLICATIONS: *Annual report.*

EVALUATION/RESEARCH: Evaluation reports available.

PLANNED ACTIVITIES: Trade campaigns.

INFORMATION AND EDUCATION ACTIVITIES: Topics: Children/youth/family; Culture/tradition/religion; Ecology/environment/biodiversity; Emergency relief/refugees/humanitarian assistance; Employment/unemployment; Food/famine; Gender issues/women; Health/sanitation/water; Human rights/peace/conflicts; International economic relations/trade/debt/finance; International relations/cooperation/development aid; Peace/ethnic conflicts/armament/disarmament; Population/family planning/demography; Poverty/living conditions; Racism/xenophobia/antisemitism; Refugees/migrants/ethnic groups; Rural development/agriculture; Urban development/habitat. **Activities:** Conferences/seminars/workshops/training activities; Formal education; Information and documentation services/data bases; Information campaigns/exhibitions; Publishing/audiovisual materials/educational materials.

GBR2409
OASIS CHARITABLE TRUST

87 Blackfriars Road, London SE1 8HA, United Kingdom.

Telephone: 44 (171) 928 9422. *Fax:* 44 (171) 928 6770. *Contact:* Graham Mungeam.

OBJECTIVES: To communicate the Christian faith, train youth in leadership and provide for the needs of the poor, especially the homeless.

GENERAL INFORMATION: *Creation:* 1985. *Personnel/Total:* 68. *Salaried:* 65 of which: 9 in developing countries. *Volunteers:* 3 of which: 2 in developing countries. *Budget/Total 1993:* ECU 1501000 (US$ 1800000).

PUBLICATIONS: *Periodicals:* Backchat (3). *Annual report.*

ACTIVITIES IN DEVELOPING REGIONS: Present in developing regions. Active in 2 country(ies). Maintains local field presence. Works through local field partners. **Sustainable Development Actions:** Children/youth/family; Education/training/literacy; Sending volunteers/experts/technical assistance; Small enterprises/informal sector/handicrafts. **Regions:** Central Asia and South Asia; East Africa.

INFORMATION AND EDUCATION ACTIVITIES: Topics: Culture/tradition/religion; Employment/unemployment. **Activities:** Conferences/seminars/workshops/training activities; Fund raising.

GBR2410
THE OCKENDEN VENTURE

Ockenden, Constitution Hill, Woking, Surrey GU22 7UU, United Kingdom.

Telephone: 44 (1483) 772012. **Fax:** 44 (1483) 750774. **Contact:** Ailsa Moore, Chief Executive.

OBJECTIVES: To assist refugees, displaced persons and others in need around the world. To provide for their rehabilitation and care in Great Britain or elsewhere in the world.

GENERAL INFORMATION: Creation: 1955. **Affiliated to:** Refugee Council (United Kingdom) - ICVA (Geneva) - British Overseas NGOs for Development (United Kingdom). **Personnel/Total:** 43. Salaried: 40 of which: 7 in developing countries. Volunteers: 3. **Budget/Total 1993:** ECU 1990000 (US$ 2300000).

PUBLICATIONS: Periodicals: Newsletter (3). Annual report.

EVALUATION/RESEARCH: Undertakes research activities.

COMMENTS: Undertakes activities in the Commonwealth of Independent States.

ACTIVITIES IN DEVELOPING REGIONS: Present in developing regions. Active in 4 country(ies). Maintains local field presence. **Sustainable Development Actions:** Children/youth/family; Education/training/literacy; Emergency relief/refugees/humanitarian assistance; Gender issues/women; Small enterprises/informal sector/handicrafts. **Regions:** Central Asia and South Asia; East Africa; South East Asia.

GBR2411
OMEGA FOUNDATION

6 Mount Street, Manchester M2 5NS, United Kingdom.

Telephone: 44 (161) 834 8223. **Contact:** Steve Wright.

OBJECTIVES: To research companies that manufacture or supply paramilitary and security equipment and to monitor the impact of such trade on human rights violations.

GENERAL INFORMATION: Creation: 1989. **Personnel/Total:** 2. Salaried: 2. **Budget/Total 1993:** ECU 32000 (US$ 38000). **Financial sources:** Private: 90%. Self-financing: 10%.

PUBLICATIONS: List of publications.

EVALUATION/RESEARCH: Undertakes research activities.

PLANNED ACTIVITIES: The collection of new data on light weapons trade. The production of a consumer guide on industries profiting from paramilitary tradeing up with human rights groups to improve pressure on legislation to halt this trade.

COMMENTS: Undertakes activities in the Commonwealth of Independent States. Information activities related to the Commonwealth of Independent States.

ACTIVITIES IN DEVELOPING REGIONS: Present in developing regions. Active in 2 country(ies). Works through local field partners. **Sustainable Development Actions:** Education/training/literacy; Human rights/peace/conflicts. **Regions:** Caribbean; Central Africa; Central Asia and South Asia; East Africa; East Asia; Mexico and Central America; Middle East; North Africa; Oceania; South America; South East Asia; Southern Africa; West Africa.

INFORMATION AND EDUCATION ACTIVITIES: Topics: Human rights/peace/conflicts; Peace/ethnic conflicts/armament/disarmament. **Activities:** Broadcasting/cultural events; Conferences/seminars/workshops/training activities; Formal education; Fund raising; Information and documentation services/data bases; Information campaigns/exhibitions; Lobbying/advocacy; Networking/electronic telecommunications; Publishing/audiovisual materials/educational materials.

GBR2412
ONE VILLAGE

Charlbury, Oxford OX7 3SQ, United Kingdom.

Telephone: 44 (1608) 811811. **Fax:** 44 (1608) 811911.

GBR2413
ONE WORLD ACTION

5th floor, Weddel House, 13-14 West Smithfield, London EC1A 9HY, United Kingdom.

Telephone: 44 (171) 324 8111. **Fax:** 44 (171) 329 6238. **E-mail:** owa@gn.apc.org. **Contact:** Jane Wendel, Director.

OBJECTIVES: To take bold, innovative steps to end poverty, inequality and discrimination and to support those who challenge the unequal distribution of the world's resources.

GENERAL INFORMATION: Creation: 1989. **Affiliated to:** International Workers Aid (Germany) - Saharah Agricultural Constorium (United Kingdom) - Women in Development Europe (Belgium) - NGO-EC Liaison Committee (Belgium). **Personnel/Total:** 22. Salaried: 10 of which: 1 in developing countries. Volunteers: 12. **Budget/Total 1993:** ECU 1400000 (US$ 1650000). **Financial sources:** Private: 38%. Public: 60%. Self-financing: 2%.

PUBLICATIONS: Periodicals: Action Report (2) - Interaction (6). Annual report. List of publications.

EVALUATION/RESEARCH: Undertakes research activities.

ACTIVITIES IN DEVELOPING REGIONS: Active in 12 country(ies). Works through local field partners. **Sustainable Development Actions:** Children/youth/family; Debt/finance/trade; Democracy/good governance/institution building/participatory development; Ecology/environment/biodiversity; Education/training/literacy; Emergency relief/refugees/humanitarian assistance; Gender issues/women; Health/sanitation/water; Human rights/peace/conflicts; Rural development/agriculture; Small enterprises/informal sector/handicrafts; Urban development/habitat. **Regions:** Central Asia and South Asia; East Africa; Mexico and Central America; North Africa; South East Asia; Southern Africa; West Africa.

INFORMATION AND EDUCATION ACTIVITIES: Topics: Education/training/literacy; Gender issues/women; Health/sanitation/water; Human rights/peace/conflicts; International economic relations/trade/debt/finance; International relations/cooperation/development aid; Poverty/living conditions; Refugees/migrants/ethnic groups; Rural development/agriculture; Urban development/habitat. **Activities:** Conferences/seminars/workshops/training activities; Fund raising; Information and documentation services/data bases; Lobbying/advocacy; Networking/electronic telecommunications; Publishing/audiovisual materials/educational materials.

GBR2414
ONE WORLD BROADCASTING TRUST

93 Ashmill Street, London NW1A 6RA, United Kingdom.

Telephone: 44 (171) 487 7437. **Contact:** Johnny Wilkinson, Director.

GBR2415
ONE WORLD CENTRE FOR NORTHERN IRELAND

4 Lower Crescent, Belfast BT7 1NR, United Kingdom.

Telephone: 44 (1232) 241879. **E-mail:** belfastdec@gn.apc.org.. **Contact:** Stephen McCloskey, Centre Co-ordinator.

OBJECTIVES: To promote development education in both the formal and informal educational sectors. To contribute to a mutual understanding of social, cultural, economic, political and environmental conditions in a local and global context.

GENERAL INFORMATION: Creation: 1987. **Affiliated to:** Development Education Association (United Kingdom) - Irish Development Educators Association (Ireland) - Northern Ireland Development Education Forum (Ireland). **Personnel/Total:** 8. Salaried: 5. Volunteers: 3. **Budget/Total 1993:** ECU 63000 (US$ 73000). **Financial sources:** Private: 84%. Self-financing: 16%.

PUBLICATIONS: Periodicals: Guide to Ireland in a Developing World (1). Annual report. List of publications.

EVALUATION/RESEARCH: Evaluation reports available. Undertakes research activities.

PLANNED ACTIVITIES: Publishing a primary school resource pack focusing on Ireland and India.

                                                    See: *How to Use the Directory*, page 11.

COMMENTS: Information activities related to the Commonwealth of Independent States.

INFORMATION AND EDUCATION ACTIVITIES: Topics: Children/youth/family; Culture/tradition/religion; Ecology/environment/biodiversity; Education/training/literacy; Employment/unemployment; Food/famine; Gender issues/women; Health/sanitation/water; Human rights/peace/conflicts; International economic relations/trade/debt/finance; International relations/cooperation/development aid; Peace/ethnic conflicts/armament/disarmament; Population/family planning/demography; Poverty/living conditions; Racism/xenophobia/antisemitism; Refugees/migrants/ethnic groups; Rural development/agriculture; Urban development/habitat. **Activities:** Broadcasting/cultural events; Conferences/seminars/workshops/training activities; Exchanges/twinning/linking; Formal education; Information and documentation services/data bases; Information campaigns/exhibitions; Networking/electronic telecommunications; Publishing/audiovisual materials/educational materials.

GBR2416
ONE WORLD QUILT 2000

c/o The Apple Loft, 9B West Street, Olney, Bucks MK46 5MJ, United Kingdom.

Telephone: 44 (1234) 711286. *Contact:* Deidre Hancock, Co-ordinator.

OBJECTIVES: To promote sustainable development through an interchange of ideas and information between people of all ages, ethnicity, and social background.

GENERAL INFORMATION: *Creation:* 1991. *Type of organisation:* network. *Affiliated to:* The Milton Keynes Environmental Network (United Kingdom). *Personnel/Total:* 7. *Salaried:* 7. *Volunteers:* var.. *Budget/Total 1993:* ECU 3800 (US$ 4500). *Financial sources:* Private: 10%. Public: 90%.

PUBLICATIONS: *Annual report. List of publications.*

EVALUATION/RESEARCH: Evaluation reports available.

ACTIVITIES IN DEVELOPING REGIONS: Works through local field partners.

INFORMATION AND EDUCATION ACTIVITIES: Topics: Children/youth/family; Culture/tradition/religion; Ecology/environment/biodiversity; Food/famine; Gender issues/women; Human rights/peace/conflicts; International economic relations/trade/debt/finance; International relations/cooperation/development aid; Peace/ethnic conflicts/armament/disarmament; Poverty/living conditions; Racism/xenophobia/antisemitism; Refugees/migrants/ethnic groups. **Activities:** Broadcasting/cultural events; Conferences/seminars/workshops/training activities; Exchanges/twinning/linking; Information and documentation services/data bases; Information campaigns/exhibitions; Networking/electronic telecommunications; Publishing/audiovisual materials/educational materials.

GBR2417
ONE WORLD WEEK

35 Lower Marsh, P.O. Box 100, London SE1 7RT, United Kingdom.

Telephone: 44 (171) 620 4444. *Fax:* 44 (171) 620 0719. *Contact:* Tany Alexander.

OBJECTIVES: To raise consciousness on issues of justice, peace and sustainable development by undertaking a development education week, held each October around United Nations Day.

GENERAL INFORMATION: *Creation:* 1977. *Type of organisation:* network, coordinating body. *Affiliated to:* ARENA Network (Switzerland) - EDEN. *Personnel/Total:* 4. *Salaried:* 3. *Volunteers:* 1. *Financial sources:* Private: 75%. Self-financing: 25%.

PUBLICATIONS: *Periodicals:* One World Week Study Guide (1). *Annual report. List of publications.*

EVALUATION/RESEARCH: Evaluation reports available.

INFORMATION AND EDUCATION ACTIVITIES: Topics: Rural development/agriculture. **Activities:** Broadcasting/cultural events; Conferences/seminars/workshops/training activities; Exchanges/twinning/linking; Formal education; Information campaigns/exhibitions; Publishing/audiovisual materials/educational materials.

GBR2418
OPERATION CHRISTMAS CHILD (OCC)

P.O. Box 732, Wrexham, Clwyd LL11 1 RQ, United Kingdom.

Telephone: 44 (1978) 660465. *Fax:* 44 (1978) 660294.

GBR2419
OPPORTUNITY TRUST

103 High Street, Oxford OX1 4BW, United Kingdom.

Telephone: 44 (1865) 794411. *Fax:* 44 (1865) 791343. *Contact:* William Day, Director.

OBJECTIVES: To assist entrepreneurs in poor countries through the provision of small loans and training programmes.

GENERAL INFORMATION: *Creation:* 1992. *Type of organisation:* network. *Member organisations:* 45. *Personnel/Total:* 6. *Salaried:* 4. *Volunteers:* 2. *Budget/Total 1993:* ECU 718000 (US$ 841000). *Financial sources:* Private: 80%. Public: 20%.

PUBLICATIONS: *Periodicals:* (3). *Annual report.*

EVALUATION/RESEARCH: Evaluation reports available. Undertakes research activities.

PLANNED ACTIVITIES: Launching of a social investment fund.

COMMENTS: Undertakes activities in the Commonwealth of Independent States.

ACTIVITIES IN DEVELOPING REGIONS: Active in 21 country(ies). Works through local field partners. **Sustainable Development Actions:** Democracy/good governance/institution building/participatory development; Gender issues/women; Rural development/agriculture; Sending volunteers/experts/technical assistance; Small enterprises/informal sector/handicrafts; Urban development/habitat. **Regions:** Caribbean; Central Asia and South Asia; East Africa; Mexico and Central America; South America; South East Asia; Southern Africa; West Africa.

INFORMATION AND EDUCATION ACTIVITIES: Topics: Emergency relief/refugees/humanitarian assistance; Employment/unemployment; Gender issues/women; Poverty/living conditions; Refugees/migrants/ethnic groups; Rural development/agriculture; Urban development/habitat. **Activities:** Broadcasting/cultural events; Conferences/seminars/workshops/training activities; Fund raising; Information campaigns/exhibitions; Lobbying/advocacy; Publishing/audiovisual materials/educational materials.

GBR2420
THE ORDER OF ST. JOHN

1 Grosvenor Crescent, London SW1X 7EF, United Kingdom.

Telephone: 44 (171) 235 5231. *Fax:* 44 (171) 235 0796.

GBR2421
OUTWARD BOUND INTERNATIONAL SECRETARIAT

Outward Bound Trust, Chestnut Field, Regent Place, Rugby CV21 2PJ, United Kingdom.

Telephone: 44 (1788) 60423. *Fax:* 44 (1788) 541069. *Contact:* Ian Fothergill, Director.

GBR2422
OVERSEAS DEVELOPMENT INSTITUTE (ODI) ♦ Institut pour le Développement Outremer

Regent's College, Inner Circle, Regent's Park, London NW1 4NS , United Kingdom.

Telephone: 44 (171) 487 7413. *Fax:* 44 (171) 487 7545. *E-mail:* 72: MAG 100474. *Contact:* John Howell, Director.

OBJECTIVES: To research and provide a forum for the discussion of development issues.

GENERAL INFORMATION: *Creation:* 1960. *Affiliated to:* Relief and Rehabilitation Network - Agriculture Research and Extension Network - Rural Development Forestry Network - Pastoral Development Network. *Personnel/Total:* 48. *Salaried:* 48 of which: 1 in developing

countries. **Budget/Total 1993:** ECU 3600000 (US$ 4200000). **Financial sources:** *Private: 25%. Public: 60%. Self-financing: 15%.*

PUBLICATIONS: Periodicals: Disasters (4) - Developpment Research Insights (4) - Development Policy Review (4) - Briefing Papers (6). *Annual report. List of publications.*

EVALUATION/RESEARCH: Undertakes research activities.

ACTIVITIES IN DEVELOPING REGIONS: Present in developing regions. Active in 50 country(ies). Works through local field partners. **Sustainable Development Actions:** Debt/finance/trade; Democracy/good governance/institution building/participatory development; Ecology/environment/biodiversity; Emergency relief/refugees/humanitarian assistance; Food/famine; Health/sanitation/water; Rural development/agriculture; Sending volunteers/experts/technical assistance. **Regions:** Caribbean; Central Africa; Central Asia and South Asia; East Africa; East Asia; Mexico and Central America; Middle East; North Africa; Oceania; South America; South East Asia; Southern Africa; West Africa.

INFORMATION AND EDUCATION ACTIVITIES: Topics: Ecology/environment/biodiversity; Emergency relief/refugees/humanitarian assistance; Food/famine; International economic relations/trade/debt/finance; International relations/cooperation/development aid; Rural development/agriculture. **Activities:** Conferences/seminars/workshops/training activities; Information and documentation services/data bases; Networking/electronic telecommunications; Publishing/audiovisual materials/educational materials.

GBR2423
OXFAM UK

274 Banbury Road, Oxford OX2 7DZ, United Kingdom.

Telephone: 44 (1865) 311311. **Fax:** 44 (1865) 312600. **E-mail:** 0865312550. **Contact:** David Bryer, Director.

OBJECTIVES: To relieve poverty, distress and suffering throughout the world. To educate the public concerning the nature, cause and effects of poverty. To work with the poor regardless of their race or religion, through relief, development, research overseas and public education at home.

GENERAL INFORMATION: Creation: 1942. **Type of organisation:** association of NGOs. **Affiliated to:** British Overseas Aid Group (United Kingdom) - Disasters Emergency Committee (United Kingdom) - ACORD (United Kingdom) - CONGO (United Kingdom) - ICVA (Switzerland) - Steering Committee for Humanitarian Response (Switzerland) -EUROSTEP (Belgium). **Personnel/Total:** 28988. *Salaried:* 1988 of which: 1020 in developing countries. *Volunteers:* 27000. **Budget/Total 1993:** ECU 100201000 (US$ 118500000). **Financial sources:** *Private: 40%. Public: 17%. Self-financing: 30%.*

PUBLICATIONS: Periodicals: Development in Practice (4) - Focus on Gender (3) - Boobab (3) - Oxfam News (4) . *Annual report. List of publications.*

EVALUATION/RESEARCH: Evaluation reports available. Undertakes research activities.

PLANNED ACTIVITIES: Campaign based on Sustainable Livelihood and Basic Rights, starting from 1995-1999: Influence the influencial, attract more people to Oxfam and work with international Oxfams.

COMMENTS: Undertakes activities in the Commonwealth of Independent States. Information activities related to the Commonwealth of Independent States.

ACTIVITIES IN DEVELOPING REGIONS: Present in developing regions. Active in 80 country(ies). Maintains local field presence. Works through local field partners. **Sustainable Development Actions:** Debt/finance/trade; Democracy/good governance/institution building/participatory development; Ecology/environment/biodiversity; Education/training/literacy; Emergency relief/refugees/humanitarian assistance; Food/famine; Gender issues/women; Health/sanitation/water; Human rights/peace/conflicts; Population/family planning/demography; Rural development/agriculture; Sending volunteers/experts/technical assistance; Small enterprises/informal sector/handicrafts. **Regions:** Caribbean; Central Africa; Central Asia and South Asia; East Africa; East Asia; Mexico and Central America; Middle East; North Africa; Oceania; South America; South East Asia; Southern Africa; West Africa.

INFORMATION AND EDUCATION ACTIVITIES: Topics: Culture/tradition/religion; Ecology/environment/biodiversity; Education/training/literacy; Emergency relief/refugees/humanitarian assistance; Food/famine; Gender issues/women; Health/sanitation/water; Human rights/peace/conflicts; International economic relations/trade/debt/finance; International relations/cooperation/development aid; Peace/ethnic conflicts/armament/disarmament; Population/family planning/demography; Poverty/living conditions; Refugees/migrants/ethnic groups; Rural development/agriculture; Urban development/habitat. **Activities:** Broadcasting/cultural events; Conferences/seminars/workshops/training activities; Exchanges/twinning/linking; Formal education; Fund raising; Information and documentation services/data bases; Information campaigns/exhibitions; Lobbying/advocacy; Publishing/audiovisual materials/educational materials.

GBR2424
OXFORD DEVELOPMENT EDUCATION CENTRE (ODEC)

East Oxford Community Centre, Princes Street, Oxford OX4 1HU, United Kingdom.

Telephone: 44 (1865) 790490. **Fax:** 44 (1865) 724317. **E-mail:** odec@gn.apc.org. **Contact:** Alison Norris, Centre and Project Worker.

OBJECTIVES: To promote development education to increase effective participation for social change.

GENERAL INFORMATION: Creation: 1978. **Affiliated to:** Development Education Association (United KIngdom). **Personnel/Total:** 7. *Salaried:* 2. *Volunteers:* 5. **Budget/Total 1993:** ECU 51000 (US$ 60000). **Financial sources:** *Private: 85%. Public: 5%. Self-financing: 10%.*

PUBLICATIONS: Periodicals: Interchange (3). *Annual report. List of publications.*

INFORMATION AND EDUCATION ACTIVITIES: Topics: Ecology/environment/biodiversity; Education/training/literacy; Employment/unemployment; Food/famine; Gender issues/women; Health/sanitation/water; Human rights/peace/conflicts; International economic relations/trade/debt/finance; International relations/cooperation/development aid; Peace/ethnic conflicts/armament/disarmament; Population/family planning/demography; Poverty/living conditions; Racism/xenophobia/antisemitism; Refugees/migrants/ethnic groups; Rural development/agriculture; Urban development/habitat. **Activities:** Conferences/seminars/workshops/training activities; Exchanges/twinning/linking; Formal education; Fund raising; Networking/electronic telecommunications; Publishing/audiovisual materials/educational materials.

GBR2425
PACE-UK INTERNATIONAL AFFAIRS

73 Spencer Road, Isleworth, Middx TW7 4BN, United Kingdom.

GBR2426
PANOS LONDON ♦ L'Institut Panos

9 White Lion Street, London N1 9PD, United Kingdom.

Telephone: 44 (171) 278 1111. **Fax:** 44 (171) 278 0345. **E-mail:** Panoslondon.apc.org. **Contact:** Liz Carlile, Deputy Director.

OBJECTIVES: To promote socially, environmentally and economically sustainable development. To combine careful research with imaginative and forceful dissemination of information.

GENERAL INFORMATION: Creation: 1986. **Personnel/Total:** 28. *Salaried:* 25. *Volunteers:* 3.

PUBLICATIONS: Periodicals: Eco-Reports (2) - Media Briefings (12) - Panoscope (4) - SIDAmerica (2) -WorldAIDS (6) - Panos Features (12). *Annual report. List of publications.*

COMMENTS: Information activities related to the Commonwealth of Independent States.

ACTIVITIES IN DEVELOPING REGIONS: Present in developing regions. Active in 12 country(ies). Works through local field partners. **Sustainable Development Actions:** Health/sanitation/water; Other. **Regions:** East Africa; East Asia; South East Asia; Southern Africa.

INFORMATION AND EDUCATION ACTIVITIES: Topics: Ecology/environment/biodiversity; Health/sanitation/water; Other. **Activities:** Confer-

                    See: *How to Use the Directory,* page 11.

ences/seminars/workshops/training activities; Publishing/audiovisual materials/educational materials.

GBR2427
PARLIAMENTARY HUMAN RIGHTS GROUP

House of Lords, Palace of Westminister, London SW1A OPW, United Kingdom.

GBR2428
THE PARNHAM TRUST

Parnham House, Beaminster, Dorset DT8 3NA, United Kingdom.

Telephone: 44 (1308) 862204. *Fax:* 44 (1308) 863494. *Contact:* John Makepeace, Director.

OBJECTIVES: To support sustainable development through research.

GENERAL INFORMATION: *Creation:* 1977. *Personnel/Total:* 15. *Salaried:* 15. *Budget/Total 1993:* ECU 641000 (US$ 751000). *Financial sources:* Private: 40%. Public: 10%. Self-financing: 50%.

PUBLICATIONS: *Periodicals:* Parnham Review (1). *Annual report.*

EVALUATION/RESEARCH: Undertakes research activities.

PLANNED ACTIVITIES: Developing low cost housing systems. Information campaign for enterprises in industrialised and developing countries.

ACTIVITIES IN DEVELOPING REGIONS: Works through local field partners.

INFORMATION AND EDUCATION ACTIVITIES: Topics: Ecology/environment/biodiversity; Education/training/literacy; Employment/unemployment; Rural development/agriculture. **Activities:** Conferences/seminars/workshops/training activities; Formal education; Fund raising.

GBR2429
PASSE-PARTOUT

72 St. John Street, London EC1M 4DT, United Kingdom.

Contact: Susan Morris.

GBR2430
PEACE BRIDGES INTERNATIONAL, INTERNATIONAL OFFICE (PBI)

5 Caledonian Road, London N19 DK, United Kingdom.

GBR2431
PEACE PLEDGE UNION

6 Endleigh Street, London WC1H ODX, United Kingdom.

Telephone: 44 (171) 387 5501.

GBR2432
PESTALOZZI CHILDREN'S VILLAGE TRUST

Sedlescombe, Battle, Sussex TN33 0RR, United Kingdom.

Telephone: 44 (142) 487444. *Fax:* 44 (142) 487 0655. *Contact:* Maurice Phillips.

OBJECTIVES: To sponsor the secondary and higher education of bright, poor children from developing countries.

GENERAL INFORMATION: *Creation:* 1959. *Personnel/Total:* 140. *Salaried:* 40 of which: 4 in developing countries. *Volunteers:* 100. *Budget/Total 1993:* ECU 1026000 (US$ 1201000). *Financial sources:* Private: 90%. Public: 8%. Self-financing: 2%.

PUBLICATIONS: *Periodicals:* The Village News (4). *Annual report.*

PLANNED ACTIVITIES: The establishment of a second trust and a new U.K based further education programme, for young people from the age of 16 whose secondary education has been sponsored in their native country.

ACTIVITIES IN DEVELOPING REGIONS: Active in 4 country(ies). Maintains local field presence. **Sustainable Development Actions:** Education/training/literacy. **Regions:** Central Asia and South Asia; Southern Africa.

INFORMATION AND EDUCATION ACTIVITIES: Topics: Children/youth/family. **Activities:** Formal education.

GBR2433
PESTICIDES ACTION NETWORK - EUROPE (PAN-EUROPE)

23 Beehive Place, Brixton, London SW9 7QR, United Kingdom.

Telephone: 44 (171) 9260386.

GBR2434
THE PESTICIDES TRUST

Ewolink Centre, 49 Ettra Road, London SW2 1B2, United Kingdom.

Telephone: 44 (171) 274 8895. *Fax:* 44 (171) 274 9084. *E-mail:* gn:pesttrust. *Contact:* Barbara Dinham.

OBJECTIVES: To reduce and eliminate the hazards of pesticides and to promote sustainable agriculture.

GENERAL INFORMATION: *Creation:* 1987. *Type of organisation:* association of NGOs, coordinating body. *Affiliated to:* Pesticide Action Network - European Environment Bureau. *Personnel/Total:* 6. Salaried: 6. *Budget/Total 1993:* ECU 192000 (US$ 225000).

PUBLICATIONS: *Periodicals:* Pesticides News (4). *Annual report. List of publications.*

EVALUATION/RESEARCH: Evaluation reports available. Undertakes research activities.

COMMENTS: Information activities related to the Commonwealth of Independent States.

ACTIVITIES IN DEVELOPING REGIONS: Works through local field partners. **Sustainable Development Actions:** Ecology/environment/biodiversity; Health/sanitation/water; Rural development/agriculture; Urban development/habitat. **Regions:** Caribbean; Central Africa; Central Asia and South Asia; East Africa; East Asia; Mexico and Central America; Middle East; North Africa; Oceania; South America; South East Asia; Southern Africa; West Africa.

INFORMATION AND EDUCATION ACTIVITIES: Topics: Ecology/environment/biodiversity; Health/sanitation/water; Rural development/agriculture; Urban development/habitat. **Activities:** Information and documentation services/data bases; Information campaigns/exhibitions; Lobbying/advocacy; Networking/electronic telecommunications; Publishing/audiovisual materials/educational materials.

GBR2435
PHILIPPINE RESOURCE CENTRE

84 Long Lane, London SE1 4AU, United Kingdom.

Telephone: 44 (171) 378 0296. *Fax:* 44 (171) 403 3997. *E-mail:* GEO2.PRC. *Contact:* Mara Stankovitch, Co-ordinator.

OBJECTIVES: To inform and educate groups and individuals in Britain on issues of political, social, economic and cultural importance to the Philippines and Filipinos. To enhance the activities of development, environment and solidarity organisations in Britain working on the Philippines, including those of the Filipino community.

GENERAL INFORMATION: *Creation:* 1984. *Affiliated to:* Alliance for the Rights of Indigenous Peoples (United Kingdom) - SAPs Working Group (United Kingdom) - Debt Crisis Network (United Kingdom) - Aid and Environment Group (United Kingdom) - Philippines Solidarity Conference in Europe (Netherlands) - Development Education Association (United Kingdom). *Personnel/Total:* 8. *Salaried:* 5 of which: 1 in developing countries. *Volunteers:* 3 of which: 1 in developing countries. *Budget/Total 1993:* ECU 147000 (US$ 173000). *Financial sources:* Private: 62%. Public: 29%. Self-financing: 9%.

PUBLICATIONS: *Periodicals:* Common Ground (4) - Philippines Information Exchange (6). *Annual report. List of publications.*

EVALUATION/RESEARCH: Undertakes research activities.

PLANNED ACTIVITIES: Education campaign on human environmental impact of "Pacific Ruin" development model. To develop an education pack on migration from the Philippines to Britain.

Voir : *Comment utiliser le répertoire,* page 11.

ACTIVITIES IN DEVELOPING REGIONS: Present in developing regions. Active in 1 country(ies). Maintains local field presence. Works through local field partners. **Sustainable Development Actions:** Education/ training/literacy. **Regions:** South East Asia.

INFORMATION AND EDUCATION ACTIVITIES: Topics: Children/youth/ family; Culture/tradition/religion; Ecology/environment/biodiversity; Education/training/literacy; Emergency relief/refugees/humanitarian assistance; Employment/unemployment; Food/famine; Gender issues/ women; Health/sanitation/water; Human rights/peace/conflicts; International economic relations/trade/debt/finance; International relations/ cooperation/development aid; Other; Peace/ethnic conflicts/armament/ disarmament; Population/family planning/demography; Poverty/living conditions; Racism/xenophobia/antisemitism; Refugees/migrants/ethnic groups; Rural development/agriculture; Urban development/habitat. **Activities:** Conferences/seminars/workshops/training activities; Exchanges/twinning/linking; Information and documentation services/ data bases; Information campaigns/exhibitions; Lobbying/advocacy; Networking/electronic telecommunications; Other; Publishing/audiovisual materials/educational materials.

GBR2436

PLAN INTERNATIONAL, UK ♦ Plan International Grande-Bretagne

5-6 Underhill Street, London NW1 7HS, United Kingdom.

Telephone: 44 (171) 485 6612. **Fax:** 44 (171) 485 2107. **E-mail:** cgi 378. **Contact:** Stephen Bingham, National Director.

OBJECTIVES: To enable children, families and communities to escape poverty and improve their quality of life. To foster communication and understanding between people of different cultures.

GENERAL INFORMATION: Creation: 1971. **Personnel/Total:** 46. *Salaried:* 26. *Volunteers:* 20. **Budget/Total 1993:** ECU 7450000 (US$ 8700000). **Financial sources:** *Private:* 89%. *Public:* 11%.

PUBLICATIONS: Periodicals: Organizational Overview (1) - World Family (2). *Annual report.*

EVALUATION/RESEARCH: Evaluation reports available. Undertakes research activities.

COMMENTS: Undertakes activities in the Commonwealth of Independent States. Information activities related to the Commonwealth of Independent States.

ACTIVITIES IN DEVELOPING REGIONS: Present in developing regions. Active in 32 country(ies). Maintains local field presence. Works through local field partners. **Sustainable Development Actions:** Children/ youth/family; Democracy/good governance/institution building/participatory development; Ecology/environment/biodiversity; Education/ training/literacy; Emergency relief/refugees/humanitarian assistance; Food/famine; Gender issues/women; Health/sanitation/water; Population/family planning/demography; Rural development/agriculture; Small enterprises/informal sector/handicrafts; Urban development/habitat. **Regions:** Caribbean; Central Asia and South Asia; East Africa; Mexico and Central America; South America; South East Asia; Southern Africa; West Africa.

INFORMATION AND EDUCATION ACTIVITIES: Topics: Children/youth/ family; Ecology/environment/biodiversity; Education/training/literacy; Emergency relief/refugees/humanitarian assistance; Employment/ unemployment; Food/famine; Gender issues/women; Health/sanitation/ water; Peace/ethnic conflicts/armament/disarmament; Population/family planning/demography; Poverty/living conditions; Rural development/ agriculture; Urban development/habitat. **Activities:** Broadcasting/cultural events; Conferences/seminars/workshops/training activities; Formal education; Fund raising; Publishing/audiovisual materials/educational materials.

GBR2437

PLUNKETT FOUNDATION ♦ Fondation Plunkett

23 Hanborough Business Park, Long Hanborough, Oxford OX8 8LH, United Kingdom.

Telephone: 44 (1993) 883636. **Fax:** 44 (1993) 883576. **Contact:** Edgar Parnell, Director.

OBJECTIVES: To provide a source of information, advice and support to assist the development of co-operative forms of business.

GENERAL INFORMATION: Creation: 1919. **Affiliated to:** International Co-operative Alliance (Switzerland). **Personnel/Total:** 20. *Salaried:* 20. **Budget/Total 1993:** ECU 970000 (US$ 1101000). **Financial sources:** *Private:* 3%. *Public:* 69%. *Self-financing:* 28%.

PUBLICATIONS: Periodicals: World of Co-operative Enterprise (1) - Newsletters (3). *Annual report. List of publications.*

EVALUATION/RESEARCH: Evaluation reports available. Undertakes research activities.

PLANNED ACTIVITIES: Promoting the development of farmer co-operatives using local Farmers' Enterprise Development Centres. Promoting "People Centred Businesses" as a mainstream form of enterprise to increase economic activity.

COMMENTS: Undertakes activities in the Commonwealth of Independent States. Information activities related to the Commonwealth of Independent States.

ACTIVITIES IN DEVELOPING REGIONS: Present in developing regions. Active in 3 country(ies). Works through local field partners. **Sustainable Development Actions:** Democracy/good governance/institution building/participatory development; Education/training/literacy; Rural development/agriculture; Small enterprises/informal sector/handicrafts. **Regions:** Caribbean; Central Africa; Central Asia and South Asia; East Africa; Mexico and Central America; North Africa; Oceania; South America; South East Asia; Southern Africa; West Africa.

INFORMATION AND EDUCATION ACTIVITIES: Topics: Gender issues/ women; International economic relations/trade/debt/finance; Other; Rural development/agriculture. **Activities:** Conferences/seminars/workshops/training activities; Exchanges/twinning/linking; Information and documentation services/data bases; Information campaigns/exhibitions; Networking/electronic telecommunications; Publishing/audiovisual materials/educational materials.

GBR2438

POPTEL-SOFT SOLUTION

30 Naples Street, Manchester M4 4DB, United Kingdom.

Telephone: 44 (161) 839 4212. **Fax:** 44 (161) 839 4214. **E-mail:** poptel.admin@geo2.poptel.org.uk. **Contact:** Shaun Fensom.

OBJECTIVES: To assist social and economic development in "technology poor" communities by helping to make advanced telematics services available. To encourage people who work for social change to use telematics and to develop and adapt sources to meet their needs.

GENERAL INFORMATION: Creation: 1983. **Affiliated to:** GEONET Association of Telematics Service Providers - European Telematics Partnership - Internet Services Provider. **Personnel/Total:** 14. *Salaried:* 14. **Budget/Total 1993:** ECU 917000 (US$ 1001000). **Financial sources:** *Public:* 30%. *Self-financing:* 70%.

PUBLICATIONS: Periodicals: Poptel News (2). *List of publications.*

EVALUATION/RESEARCH: Evaluation reports available. Undertakes research activities.

PLANNED ACTIVITIES: Developing the use of telematics and providing communications and on-line information services to labour movements internationally, UK voluntary sector, agencies and Third World development bodies.

COMMENTS: Undertakes activities in the Commonwealth of Independent States. Information activities related to the Commonwealth of Independent States.

ACTIVITIES IN DEVELOPING REGIONS: Active in 40 country(ies). **Sustainable Development Actions:** Other. **Regions:** Caribbean; Central Africa; Central Asia and South Asia; East Africa; East Asia; Mexico and Central America; Middle East; North Africa; Oceania; South America; South East Asia; Southern Africa; West Africa.

INFORMATION AND EDUCATION ACTIVITIES: Topics: Children/youth/ family; Culture/tradition/religion; Ecology/environment/biodiversity; Education/training/literacy; Emergency relief/refugees/humanitarian assistance; Employment/unemployment; Food/famine; Gender issues/ women; Health/sanitation/water; Human rights/peace/conflicts; Interna-

tional economic relations/trade/debt/finance; International relations/cooperation/development aid; Peace/ethnic conflicts/armament/disarmament; Population/family planning/demography; Poverty/living conditions; Racism/xenophobia/antisemitism; Refugees/migrants/ethnic groups; Rural development/agriculture; Urban development/habitat. **Activities:** Information and documentation services/data bases; Networking/electronic telecommunications.

GBR2439
POPULATION CONCERN

178-202 Great Portland Street, London WIN 5TB, United Kingdom.

Telephone: 44 (171) 631 1546. *Fax:* 44 (171) 436 2143. *Contact:* Wendy Thomas, Director.

OBJECTIVES: To raise awareness and create a better understanding of the interrelated issues of population, development and the environment. To promote population and development programmes around the world, which encourage human welfare, personal freedom and the quality of life.

GENERAL INFORMATION: *Creation:* 1977. *Type of organisation:* coordinating body. *Affiliated to:* EC-NGO Network (United Kingdom) - National Council of Women in Great Britain (United Kingdom) - Consortium for Street Children (United Kingdom) - Public Information Group (United Kingdom) - Action for Safe Motherhood (United Kingdom) - Development Education Association (United Kingdom) - BOND (United Kingdom) - Working Group on Population (United Kingdom) - UK NGO AIDS Consortium (United Kingdom). *Personnel/Total:* 18. *Salaried:* 15. *Volunteers:* 3. *Budget/Total 1993:* ECU 1371000 (US$ 1601000). *Financial sources:* Private: 37%. Public: 57%. Self-financing: 2%.

PUBLICATIONS: *Periodicals:* Newsletter (1). *Annual report. List of publications.*

PLANNED ACTIVITIES: To hold two youth conferences annually for students aged 16-19. New information and education publications and resources including country profiles and information factsheets. The production of a population teaching aid for schoolteachers.

ACTIVITIES IN DEVELOPING REGIONS: Present in developing regions. Active in 16 country(ies). Works through local field partners. **Sustainable Development Actions:** Children/youth/family; Education/training/literacy; Gender issues/women; Health/sanitation/water; Population/family planning/demography. **Regions:** Caribbean; Central Asia and South Asia; East Africa; Mexico and Central America; South America; West Africa.

INFORMATION AND EDUCATION ACTIVITIES: Topics: Children/youth/family; Ecology/environment/biodiversity; Gender issues/women; Population/family planning/demography; Poverty/living conditions. **Activities:** Broadcasting/cultural events; Conferences/seminars/workshops/training activities; Exchanges/twinning/linking; Formal education; Fund raising; Information and documentation services/data bases; Information campaigns/exhibitions; Lobbying/advocacy; Publishing/audiovisual materials/educational materials.

GBR2440
PROJECT MALA

1 Bredume, Off Church Road, Kenley, Surrey CR8 5DU, United Kingdom.

Telephone: 44 (181) 660 1929. *Fax:* 44 (171) 630 0624. *Contact:* Jack Phillips, Director.

OBJECTIVES: To assist in the removal of child labour from the Indian carpet looms by providing a curriculum of non-formal education and vocational training appropriate to the needs of the local communities.

GENERAL INFORMATION: *Creation:* 1989. *Type of organisation:* association of NGOs. *Personnel/Total:* 41. *Salaried:* 27 of which: 27 in developing countries. *Volunteers:* 14 of which: 7 in developing countries. *Budget/Total 1993:* ECU 55000 (US$ 64000). *Financial sources:* Private: 15%. Public: 85%.

PUBLICATIONS: *Annual report.*

ACTIVITIES IN DEVELOPING REGIONS: Present in developing regions. Active in 1 country(ies). Maintains local field presence. Works through local field partners. **Sustainable Development Actions:** Children/

youth/family; Education/training/literacy. **Regions:** Central Asia and South Asia.

INFORMATION AND EDUCATION ACTIVITIES: Topics: Education/training/literacy. **Activities:** Conferences/seminars/workshops/training activities.

GBR2441
THE PROJECT TRUST

The Hebridean Centre, Isle of Coll - Scotland PA78 6TB, United Kingdom.

Telephone: 44 (187) 93444. *Fax:* 44 (187) 93357. *Contact:* Nicholas MacLean-Bristol.

OBJECTIVES: To educate a new generation in the United Kingdom through service with peoples overseas, particularly in developing countries.

GENERAL INFORMATION: *Creation:* 1967. *Personnel/Total:* 14. *Salaried:* 14. *Financial sources:* Private: 100%.

PUBLICATIONS: *Periodicals:* Project Trust Post (2). *Annual report.*

PLANNED ACTIVITIES: The expansion of activities to Horn of Africa and Indochina.

ACTIVITIES IN DEVELOPING REGIONS: Active in 19 country(ies). Maintains local field presence. Works through local field partners. **Sustainable Development Actions:** Education/training/literacy; Sending volunteers/experts/technical assistance. **Regions:** Caribbean; East Africa; East Asia; Mexico and Central America; Middle East; South America; South East Asia; Southern Africa.

GBR2442
QUAKER PEACE AND SERVICE (QPS)

Friends House, Euston Road, London NW1 2BJ, United Kingdom.

Telephone: 44 (121) 387 3601. *Fax:* 44 (121) 388 1977. *Contact:* Mary Hogan, General Secretary.

GBR2443
READING INTERNATIONAL SUPPORT CENTRE (RISC)

103 London Street, Reading RG1 4QA, United Kingdom.

Telephone: 44 (1734) 586692. *Contact:* Martin Mikhail.

GBR2444
REFUGEE ACTION

The Offices, The Cedars, Oakwood, Derby DE2 4FY, United Kingdom.

Telephone: 44 (1332) 833310. *Fax:* 44 (1332) 834946. *Contact:* Yan Ji (Jack) Shieh, Director.

GBR2445
REFUGEE COUNCIL

Bondway House, 3-9 Bondway, London SW8 1SJ, United Kingdom.

Telephone: 44 (171) 582 6922. *Fax:* 44 (171) 582 9929. *Contact:* Alf Dubs, Director.

OBJECTIVES: To give practical help to refugees and to promote their rights in the UK and abroad by providing information and advice services, lobbying decision makers, vocational training courses and employment preparation courses.

GENERAL INFORMATION: *Creation:* 1950. *Member organisations:* 150. *Affiliated to:* International Council of Voluntary Organisations - National Council of Voluntary Organisations.. *Personnel/Total:* 350. *Salaried:* 300 of which: 180 in developing countries. *Volunteers:* 50 of which: 47 in developing countries. *Budget/Total 1993:* ECU 1300000 (US$ 1501000). *Financial sources:* Private: 7%. Public: 86%. *Self-financing:* 7%.

PUBLICATIONS: *Periodicals:* (12). *Annual report. List of publications.*

EVALUATION/RESEARCH: Evaluation reports available. Undertakes research activities.

Voir : *Comment utiliser le répertoire,* page 11.

COMMENTS: Information activities related to the Commonwealth of Independent States.

ACTIVITIES IN DEVELOPING REGIONS: Active in 10 country(ies). Maintains local field presence. Works through local field partners. **Sustainable Development Actions:** Children/youth/family; Education/training/literacy; Gender issues/women; Health/sanitation/water; Human rights/peace/conflicts; Population/family planning/demography; Sending volunteers/experts/technical assistance. **Regions:** Caribbean; Central Africa; Central Asia and South Asia; East Africa; East Asia; Mexico and Central America; Middle East; North Africa; Oceania; South America; South East Asia; Southern Africa; West Africa.

INFORMATION AND EDUCATION ACTIVITIES: Topics: Children/youth/family; Culture/tradition/religion; Ecology/environment/biodiversity; Education/training/literacy; Emergency relief/refugees/humanitarian assistance; Employment/unemployment; Food/famine; Gender issues/women; Health/sanitation/water; Human rights/peace/conflicts; International economic relations/trade/debt/finance; International relations/cooperation/development aid; Other; Peace/ethnic conflicts/armament/disarmament; Population/family planning/demography; Poverty/living conditions; Racism/xenophobia/antisemitism; Refugees/migrants/ethnic groups; Rural development/agriculture; Urban development/habitat. **Activities:** Conferences/seminars/workshops/training activities; Exchanges/twinning/linking; Formal education; Fund raising; Information and documentation services/data bases; Information campaigns/exhibitions; Lobbying/advocacy; Publishing/audiovisual materials/educational materials.

GBR2446
REFUGEE HEALTH GROUP

London School of Hygiene and Tropical Medicine, Keppel Street, London WC1E 7HT, United Kingdom.

Contact: Stephanie P. Simmonds, Head.

GBR2447
REFUGEE LEGAL CENTRE

Sussex House, 39/45 Bermondsey Street, London SE1 3XF, United Kingdom.

Telephone: 44 (171) 827 9090. *Fax:* 44 (171) 378 1979. *Contact:* Barry Stoyle, Director.

OBJECTIVES: To provide legal advice and representation to asylum seekers and refugees.

GENERAL INFORMATION: Creation: 1992. **Affiliated to:** British Refugee Council (United Kingdom) - European Council on Refugees and Exiles (United Kingdom) - Amnesty International-British Section (United Kingdom). **Personnel/Total:** 107. *Salaried:* 107. **Budget/Total 1993:** ECU 3981000 (US$ 4660000). **Financial sources:** *Public:* 100%.

PUBLICATIONS: *Annual report.*

EVALUATION/RESEARCH: Evaluation reports available.

PLANNED ACTIVITIES: Campaign on asylum laws and procedures in the United Kingdom and Europe.

INFORMATION AND EDUCATION ACTIVITIES: Topics: Refugees/migrants/ethnic groups. **Activities:** Conferences/seminars/workshops/training activities; Lobbying/advocacy.

GBR2448
REFUGEE STUDIES PROGRAMME (RSP)

Queen Elizabeth House, Oxford University, 21 St Giles, Oxford OX1 3LA, United Kingdom.

Telephone: 44 (1865) 270722. *Fax:* 44 (1865) 270721. *E-mail:* RSP@VAX.OXFORD.AC.UK. *Contact:* B.E. Harrell-Bond, Director.

OBJECTIVES: To increase understanding of the causes, consequences and experiences of forced migration through interdisciplinary research, teaching and information provision on forced migration issues.

GENERAL INFORMATION: Creation: 1982. **Affiliated to:** International Council of Voluntary Agencies (United Kingdom) - European Consultation on Refugees and Exiles (United Kingdom). **Personnel/Total:** 26. *Salaried:* 21. *Volunteers:* 5. **Budget/Total 1993:**

ECU 1000600 (US$ 1200000). **Financial sources:** *Private:* 43%. *Public:* 41%. *Self-financing:* 16%.

PUBLICATIONS: *Periodicals:* Refugee Participation Network (3) - Journal of Refugee Studies (4). *Annual report. List of publications.*

EVALUATION/RESEARCH: Evaluation reports available. Undertakes research activities.

PLANNED ACTIVITIES: Offering courses on Psycho-Social issues and on health and a one month summer school.

COMMENTS: The RSP provides courses for humanitarian workers, including host government officials and NGOs. Undertakes activities in the Commonwealth of Independent States. Information activities related to the Commonwealth of Independent States.

ACTIVITIES IN DEVELOPING REGIONS: Sustainable Development Actions: Sending volunteers/experts/technical assistance. **Regions:** Central Africa; Central Asia and South Asia; East Africa; East Asia; Middle East; North Africa; South East Asia; Southern Africa; West Africa.

INFORMATION AND EDUCATION ACTIVITIES: Topics: Culture/tradition/religion; Emergency relief/refugees/humanitarian assistance; Food/famine; Human rights/peace/conflicts; International relations/cooperation/development aid; Poverty/living conditions; Racism/xenophobia/antisemitism; Refugees/migrants/ethnic groups. **Activities:** Conferences/seminars/workshops/training activities; Exchanges/twinning/linking; Formal education; Information and documentation services/data bases; Networking/electronic telecommunications; Publishing/audiovisual materials/educational materials.

GBR2449
REGISTER OF ENGINEERS FOR DISASTER RELIEF (RedR)

1-7 Great Georges Street, London SW1P 3AA, United Kingdom.

Telephone: 44 (171) 233 3116. *Fax:* 44 (171) 222 7500. *Contact:* Jon Lane, Director.

GBR2450
RELIEF SOCIETY OF TIGRAY - UK SUPPORT COMMITTEE

211 Clapham Road, London SW9 OGH, United Kingdom.

GBR2451
RESOURCES FOR LEARNING DEVELOPMENT UNIT

Bishpston, Bishop Road, Bristol BS7 8LS, United Kingdom.

Telephone: 44 (272) 428208.

GBR2452
RESULTS EDUCATION

Cross Street, Venture House, Macslesfield, Cheshire SK11 7PG, United Kingdom.

Telephone: 44 (1625) 611437. *Fax:* 44 (171) 611493. *Contact:* Sheila Davie, National Director.

OBJECTIVES: To educate members of the community, parliamentarians and the media about hunger and poverty.

GENERAL INFORMATION: Creation: 1986. **Personnel/Total:** 101. *Salaried:* 1. *Volunteers:* 100. **Financial sources:** *Private:* 100%.

PUBLICATIONS: *Annual report. List of publications.*

EVALUATION/RESEARCH: Evaluation reports available.

INFORMATION AND EDUCATION ACTIVITIES: Topics: Children/youth/family; Education/training/literacy; Food/famine; Gender issues/women; Health/sanitation/water; International economic relations/trade/debt/finance; International relations/cooperation/development aid; Population/family planning/demography; Poverty/living conditions; Rural development/agriculture; Urban development/habitat. **Activities:** Conferences/seminars/workshops/training activities; Formal education; Information and documentation services/data bases; Information campaigns/exhibitions; Publishing/audiovisual materials/educational materials.

See: How to Use the Directory, page 11.

GBR2453
RETURNED VOLUNTEER ACTION (RVA)

1 Amwell Street, London EC1R 1UL, United Kingdom.

Telephone: 44 (171) 278 0804. *Contact:* Mark Stacey, Chairperson.

OBJECTIVES: To provide advice and information to people interested in overseas development work. To encourage and support returned volunteer involvement in development education work. To monitor and evaluate the effectiveness of agency programmes and the support they provide to their volunteers.

GENERAL INFORMATION: *Creation:* 1960. *Affiliated to:* Development Education Association (United Kingdom) - EC NGO Network (United Kingdom) - British Overseas NGOs in Development (United Kingdom) - Ex-Volunteers International (the Netherlands). *Personnel/Total:* 6. *Salaried:* 3. *Volunteers:* 3. *Budget/Total 1993:* ECU 47000 (US$ 56000). *Financial sources:* Private: 49%. Public: 37%. Self-financing: 14%.

PUBLICATIONS: *Periodicals:* Comeback (4) - Development Action (12). *Annual report. List of publications.*

EVALUATION/RESEARCH: Undertakes research activities.

INFORMATION AND EDUCATION ACTIVITIES: Topics: Gender issues/women; International economic relations/trade/debt/finance; International relations/cooperation/development aid; Other; Racism/xenophobia/antisemitism. **Activities:** Conferences/seminars/workshops/training activities; Information and documentation services/data bases; Lobbying/advocacy; Publishing/audiovisual materials/educational materials.

GBR2454
THE RICHMOND FELLOWSHIP INTERNATIONAL

8 Addison Road, Kensington, London W14 8DL, United Kingdom.

Telephone: 44 (171) 603 2442. *Fax:* 44 (171) 602 0199. *Contact:* Elly Jansen, Chief Executive Officer.

OBJECTIVES: To rehabilitate people with mental health and addiction problems throughout the world by helping them to reintegrate into their communities. To promote good practices in the management of mental illness.

GENERAL INFORMATION: *Creation:* 1981. *Type of organisation:* coordinating body. *Member organisations:* 32. *Personnel/Total:* 7. *Salaried:* 4 of which: 1 in developing countries. *Volunteers:* 3. *Budget/Total 1993:* ECU 319000 (US$ 371000). *Financial sources:* Private: 100%.

PUBLICATIONS: *Annual report.*

EVALUATION/RESEARCH: Undertakes research activities.

PLANNED ACTIVITIES: Opening a day care and residential centre for the treatment of abused children in Costa Rica, a day care and vocational centre for the rehabilitation of the mentally ill in India and in Zimbabwe.

ACTIVITIES IN DEVELOPING REGIONS: Present in developing regions. Works through local field partners. **Sustainable Development Actions:** Children/youth/family; Education/training/literacy; Health/sanitation/water; Sending volunteers/experts/technical assistance. **Regions:** Caribbean; Central Africa; South America.

INFORMATION AND EDUCATION ACTIVITIES: Topics: Children/youth/family; Health/sanitation/water. **Activities:** Conferences/seminars/workshops/training activities; Information campaigns/exhibitions.

GBR2455
RIGHTS AND HUMANITY

65 A Swinton Street, London WC1X 9NT, United Kingdom.

Telephone: 44 (171) 837 4188. *Fax:* 44 (171) 278 4576. *Contact:* Julia Häusermann.

OBJECTIVES: To focus attention on international humanitarian concerns, work for global concensus and promote practical strategies for action based on respect for human rights and responsibilities.

GENERAL INFORMATION: *Creation:* 1986. *Affiliated to:* Human Rights Network (United Kingdom). *Personnel/Total:* 7. *Salaried:* 1. *Volunteers:*

6. *Budget/Total 1993:* ECU 128000 (US$ 150000). *Financial sources:* Private: 70%. Public: 30%.

PUBLICATIONS: *List of publications.*

EVALUATION/RESEARCH: Undertakes research activities.

COMMENTS: Undertakes activities in the Commonwealth of Independent States. Information activities related to the Commonwealth of Independent States.

ACTIVITIES IN DEVELOPING REGIONS: Active in 1 country(ies). **Sustainable Development Actions:** Education/training/literacy; Human rights/peace/conflicts. **Regions:** Middle East.

INFORMATION AND EDUCATION ACTIVITIES: Topics: Culture/tradition/religion; Education/training/literacy; Gender issues/women; Health/sanitation/water; Human rights/peace/conflicts; International relations/cooperation/development aid; Peace/ethnic conflicts/armament/disarmament; Refugees/migrants/ethnic groups. **Activities:** Conferences/seminars/workshops/training activities; Formal education; Information and documentation services/data bases; Information campaigns/exhibitions; Lobbying/advocacy; Networking/electronic telecommunications; Publishing/audiovisual materials/educational materials.

GBR2456
RIO MAZAN

38-40 Exchange Street, Norwich NR2 1AX, United Kingdom.

Telephone: 44 (1603) 611953. *Fax:* 44 (1603) 761645. *Contact:* Clive Sexton.

OBJECTIVES: To empower Ecuadorians to act in defence of their environment and to promote the conservation of Andean forests.

GENERAL INFORMATION: *Creation:* 1983. *Personnel/Total:* 1. *Salaried:* 1. *Budget/Total 1993:* ECU 26000 (US$ 30000). *Financial sources:* Private: 34%. Public: 50%. Self-financing: 16%.

PUBLICATIONS: *Periodicals:* Rio Mazan Update (4). *Annual report. List of publications.*

EVALUATION/RESEARCH: Evaluation reports available. Undertakes research activities.

PLANNED ACTIVITIES: Rio Mazan is planning the construction of a visitors' center in a reserve in Cloudforest.

ACTIVITIES IN DEVELOPING REGIONS: Active in 1 country(ies). Works through local field partners. **Sustainable Development Actions:** Ecology/environment/biodiversity; Education/training/literacy; Rural development/agriculture; Sending volunteers/experts/technical assistance. **Regions:** South America.

INFORMATION AND EDUCATION ACTIVITIES: Topics: Ecology/environment/biodiversity; Education/training/literacy; Rural development/agriculture. **Activities:** Fund raising; Information and documentation services/data bases; Publishing/audiovisual materials/educational materials.

GBR2457
ROYAL BOTANIC GARDENS

Kew, Richmond, Surrey TW9 3AB, United Kingdom.

Contact: Roger M. Polhill.

GBR2458
THE ROYAL SOCIETY

6 Carlton House Terrace, London SW1Y 5AG, United Kingdom.

Telephone: 44 (171) 837 4188. *Fax:* 44 (171) 278 4576. *Contact:* P.T. Warren, Executive Secretary.

OBJECTIVES: To promote the natural and applied sciences nationally and internationally through fellowships and grants, international scientific exchange, promoting science education and advice.

GENERAL INFORMATION: *Creation:* 1660. *Affiliated to:* National Academies Policy Advisory Group - European Science Foundation -International Council of Scientific Unions - General Assembly of the European Academies of Science and Humanities. *Personnel/Total:* 126. *Salaried:*

Voir : *Comment utiliser le répertoire,* page 11.

126. **Budget/Total 1993:** ECU 30800000 (US$ 36001000). **Financial sources:** Public: 78%. Self-financing: 22%.

PUBLICATIONS: Periodicals: Philosophical Translations A (12) - Philosophical Translations B (12) -PROCEEDINGS A (12) - PROCEEDINGS B (12) - Notes and Records (3) - Yearbook (1). *Annual report. List of publications.*

EVALUATION/RESEARCH: Evaluation reports available. Undertakes research activities.

COMMENTS: Undertakes activities in the Commonwealth of Independent States. Information activities related to the Commonwealth of Independent States.

ACTIVITIES IN DEVELOPING REGIONS: Active in 36 country(ies). Works through local field partners. **Sustainable Development Actions:** Population/family planning/demography; Sending volunteers/experts/technical assistance. **Regions:** Caribbean; Central Africa; Central Asia and South Asia; East Africa; East Asia; Mexico and Central America; Middle East; North Africa; Oceania; South America; South East Asia; Southern Africa; West Africa.

INFORMATION AND EDUCATION ACTIVITIES: Topics: Ecology/environment/biodiversity; Health/sanitation/water; Population/family planning/demography. **Activities:** Conferences/seminars/workshops/training activities; Information and documentation services/data bases; Information campaigns/exhibitions; Publishing/audiovisual materials/educational materials.

GBR2459
RUFIJI LEPROSY TRUST

N2, 47 Sussex Square, Brighton, East Sussex BN2 1GE, United Kingdom.

Telephone: 44 (1273) 607456. **Fax:** 44 (1273) 727229. **Contact:** Dr. Alexander de Waal.

OBJECTIVES: To assist the Tanzanian government health services in the national campaign against leprosy in the Refiji district in Tanzania.

GENERAL INFORMATION: Creation: 1982. **Affiliated to:** Britain Tanzania Society. *Personnel/Total:* 10. *Salaried:* 3 of which: 2 in developing countries. *Volunteers:* 7 of which: 1 in developing countries. *Financial sources:* Private: 15%. Public: 85%.

PUBLICATIONS: Periodicals: The Rufiji Leprosy Trust Quarterly (4).

EVALUATION/RESEARCH: Evaluation reports available.

PLANNED ACTIVITIES: To hold a disability prevention programme.

ACTIVITIES IN DEVELOPING REGIONS: Active in 1 country(ies). Maintains local field presence. Works through local field partners. **Sustainable Development Actions:** Children/youth/family; Democracy/good governance/institution building/participatory development; Education/training/literacy; Emergency relief/refugees/humanitarian assistance; Health/sanitation/water; Rural development/agriculture. **Regions:** East Africa.

GBR2460
RURAL DEVELOPMENT COUNSELLORS FOR CHRISTIAN CHURCHES IN AFRICA (RURCON) ♦ Agence de développement rural pour les églises chrétiennes en Afrique

4 Churchfield, Wincanton BA9 9AJ, United Kingdom.

Telephone: 44 (1963) 33043. **Fax:** 44 (1963) 31129. **Contact:** Barnaba Dusu, Chairman.

OBJECTIVES: To promote the holistic development of African people with the help of their leaders, focusing on agriculture, health, community development, appropriate technology and Christian teaching.

GENERAL INFORMATION: Creation: 1971. **Personnel/Total:** 15. *Salaried:* 5 of which: 3 in developing countries. *Volunteers:* 10 of which: 10 in developing countries. **Budget/Total 1993:** ECU 112000 (US$ 131000). **Financial sources:** Private: 82%. Public: 16%. Self-financing: 2%.

PUBLICATIONS: Periodicals: RURCON Newsletter (4). *Annual report. List of publications.*

EVALUATION/RESEARCH: Evaluation reports available.

ACTIVITIES IN DEVELOPING REGIONS: Present in developing regions. Active in 10 country(ies). Maintains local field presence. Works through local field partners. **Sustainable Development Actions:** Children/youth/family; Democracy/good governance/institution building/participatory development; Ecology/environment/biodiversity; Education/training/literacy; Energy/transport; Food/famine; Gender issues/women; Health/sanitation/water; Rural development/agriculture; Sending volunteers/experts/technical assistance; Small enterprises/informal sector/handicrafts; Urban development/habitat. **Regions:** Central Africa; East Africa; Southern Africa; West Africa.

INFORMATION AND EDUCATION ACTIVITIES: Topics: Children/youth/family; Culture/tradition/religion; Ecology/environment/biodiversity; Education/training/literacy; Food/famine; Gender issues/women; Health/sanitation/water; Human rights/peace/conflicts; Poverty/living conditions; Rural development/agriculture; Urban development/habitat. **Activities:** Conferences/seminars/workshops/training activities.

GBR2461
SAINT JOSEPH'S HOSPICE ASSOCIATION - HOSPICE INTERNATIONAL

La Casa de San Jose, Ince Road, Thornton, Liverpool L23 4UE, United Kingdom.

Telephone: 44 (151) 924 3812. **Contact:** Rev. Francis O'Leary, Director.

GBR2462
SALTLIC

West House Farm, Birstwirth, Harrogate, N. Yorkshire HG3 3AW, United Kingdom.

Contact: Ivan Holmes.

GBR2463
THE SALVATION ARMY ♦ L'Armée du Salut

101 Queen Victoria Street, P.O. Box 249, London EC4P 4EP, United Kingdom.

Telephone: 44 (171) 236 5222. **Fax:** 44 (171) 236 4981.

OBJECTIVES: To raise the quality of life of communities and individuals, within the context of the Christian Gospel.

GENERAL INFORMATION: Creation: 1865.

PUBLICATIONS: *Annual report.*

COMMENTS: Undertakes activities in the Commonwealth of Independent States.

ACTIVITIES IN DEVELOPING REGIONS: Present in developing regions. Active in 38 country(ies). Maintains local field presence. **Sustainable Development Actions:** Children/youth/family; Education/training/literacy; Emergency relief/refugees/humanitarian assistance. **Regions:** Caribbean; Central Asia and South Asia; East Africa; Mexico and Central America; South America; Southern Africa; West Africa.

INFORMATION AND EDUCATION ACTIVITIES: Topics: Children/youth/family; Culture/tradition/religion; Education/training/literacy; Emergency relief/refugees/humanitarian assistance; International relations/cooperation/development aid; Rural development/agriculture. **Activities:** Broadcasting/cultural events; Conferences/seminars/workshops/training activities; Formal education; Fund raising; Publishing/audiovisual materials/educational materials.

GBR2464
THE SAVE THE CHILDREN FUND (SCF)

17 Grove Lane, London SE5 8RD, United Kingdom.

Telephone: 44 (171) 703 5400. **Fax:** 44 (171) 703 2278. **Contact:** Nicholas Hinton, Director General.

OBJECTIVES: To achieve lasting benefits for children within the communities in which they live by influencing policy and practice, based on experience and study in different parts of the world. To lobby on behalf of children's rights.

GENERAL INFORMATION: Creation: 1919. **Affiliated to:** International Save the Children Alliance (WSwitzerland) - British Overseas NGOs for Development (United Kingdom) - The EC-NGO Network (United

                    See: How to Use the Directory, page 11.

Kingdom) -Disasters Emergency Committee (United Kingdom) - Voluntary Organisations in Co-operation in Emergencies. **Personnel/Total:** 24550. *Salaried:* 4550 of which: 3750 in developing countries. *Volunteers:* 20000. **Budget/Total 1993:** ECU 111500000 (US$ 130571000). **Financial sources:** *Private:* 8%. *Public:* 49%. *Self-financing:* 41%.

PUBLICATIONS: *Periodicals:* Development Policy News (2) - SCF Overseas Research News (2) - Learning from Experience (2). *Annual report. List of publications.*

EVALUATION/RESEARCH: Evaluation reports available. Undertakes research activities.

COMMENTS: Undertakes activities in the Commonwealth of Independent States.

ACTIVITIES IN DEVELOPING REGIONS: Present in developing regions. Active in 56 country(ies). Maintains local field presence. Works through local field partners. **Sustainable Development Actions:** Children/youth/family; Democracy/good governance/institution building/participatory development; Education/training/literacy; Emergency relief/refugees/humanitarian assistance; Energy/transport; Food/famine; Gender issues/women; Health/sanitation/water; Human rights/peace/conflicts; Population/family planning/demography; Rural development/agriculture; Sending volunteers/experts/technical assistance; Small enterprises/informal sector/handicrafts; Urban development/habitat. **Regions:** Caribbean; Central Africa; Central Asia and South Asia; East Africa; East Asia; Mexico and Central America; Middle East; North Africa; South America; South East Asia; Southern Africa; West Africa.

INFORMATION AND EDUCATION ACTIVITIES: **Topics:** Children/youth/family; Education/training/literacy; Emergency relief/refugees/humanitarian assistance; Food/famine; Gender issues/women; Health/sanitation/water; Human rights/peace/conflicts; International economic relations/trade/debt/finance; International relations/cooperation/development aid; Peace/ethnic conflicts/armament/disarmament; Population/family planning/demography; Poverty/living conditions; Refugees/migrants/ethnic groups. **Activities:** Broadcasting/cultural events; Conferences/seminars/workshops/training activities; Formal education; Fund raising; Information and documentation services/data bases; Information campaigns/exhibitions; Lobbying/advocacy; Networking/electronic telecommunications; Publishing/audiovisual materials/educational materials.

GBR2465
SCHOOL LINKS INTERNATIONAL (SLI)

School House, Bishop Road, Bishopston, Bristol BS1 8LS, United Kingdom.

Contact: Ray Harris, Co-ordinator.

GBR2466
SCOPE

12 Park Crescent, London W1N 4EQ, United Kingdom.

Telephone: 44 (171) 636 5020. **Fax:** 44 (171) 436 2601. **Contact:** Anthony Hewson, Chairman.

OBJECTIVES: To enable men, women and children with cerebral palsy and associated disabilities to claim their rights, lead fulfilling and rewarding lives and play a full part in society.

GENERAL INFORMATION: *Creation:* 1952.

PUBLICATIONS: *Annual report. List of publications.*

ACTIVITIES IN DEVELOPING REGIONS: Maintains local field presence. Works through local field partners.

INFORMATION AND EDUCATION ACTIVITIES: **Topics:** Children/youth/family; Education/training/literacy; Human rights/peace/conflicts; Other; Poverty/living conditions. **Activities:** Broadcasting/cultural events; Conferences/seminars/workshops/training activities; Formal education; Fund raising; Information and documentation services/data bases; Information campaigns/exhibitions; Lobbying/advocacy; Publishing/audiovisual materials/educational materials.

GBR2467
SCOTTISH CATHOLIC INTERNATIONAL AID FUND (SCIAF)

5 Oswald Street, Glasgow G1 4QR, Scoltland, United Kingdom.

Telephone: 44 (141) 221 4447. **Fax:** 44 (141) 221 2373. **E-mail:** (GEONET)GEO2:SCIAF.SCOTLAND. **Contact:** Duncan MacLaren, Executive Director.

OBJECTIVES: To support the poor in developing countries in their efforts to liberate themselves from poverty, underdevelopment and oppression. To educate Scots, especially the Scottish Catholic Community, about the causes of world injustice and their role in changing the structures which cause injustice.

GENERAL INFORMATION: *Creation:* 1965. *Type of organisation:* network. **Member organisations:** 17. **Affiliated to:** CIDSE (Belgium). **Personnel/Total:** 21. *Salaried:* 16. *Volunteers:* 5. **Budget/Total 1993:** ECU 2701000 (US$ 3150000). **Financial sources:** *Private:* 88%. *Public:* 10%. *Self-financing:* 2%.

PUBLICATIONS: *Periodicals:* SCIAF Review (4). *Annual report. List of publications.*

EVALUATION/RESEARCH: Evaluation reports available.

PLANNED ACTIVITIES: SCIAF is planning an 18 month to 2 year long campaign on Conflict Resolution and a partnership consultation in Brazil.

COMMENTS: Undertakes activities in the Commonwealth of Independent States.

ACTIVITIES IN DEVELOPING REGIONS: Active in 29 country(ies). Works through local field partners. **Sustainable Development Actions:** Children/youth/family; Democracy/good governance/institution building/participatory development; Education/training/literacy; Emergency relief/refugees/humanitarian assistance; Food/famine; Gender issues/women; Health/sanitation/water; Human rights/peace/conflicts; Rural development/agriculture; Small enterprises/informal sector/handicrafts; Urban development/habitat. **Regions:** Central Africa; Central Asia and South Asia; East Africa; East Asia; Mexico and Central America; South America; South East Asia; Southern Africa.

INFORMATION AND EDUCATION ACTIVITIES: **Topics:** Children/youth/family; Culture/tradition/religion; Ecology/environment/biodiversity; Education/training/literacy; Emergency relief/refugees/humanitarian assistance; Food/famine; Gender issues/women; Health/sanitation/water; Human rights/peace/conflicts; International economic relations/trade/debt/finance; International relations/cooperation/development aid; Peace/ethnic conflicts/armament/disarmament; Poverty/living conditions; Racism/xenophobia/antisemitism; Refugees/migrants/ethnic groups; Rural development/agriculture; Urban development/habitat. **Activities:** Broadcasting/cultural events; Conferences/seminars/workshops/training activities; Formal education; Information campaigns/exhibitions; Lobbying/advocacy; Publishing/audiovisual materials/educational materials.

GBR2468
SCOTTISH DEVELOPMENT EDUCATION CENTRE

Old Playhouse Close, Moray House Institute of Education, Holyrood Road, Edinburgh EH8 8AQ, United Kingdom.

Telephone: 44 (131) 557 3810. **Fax:** 44 (131) 556 8239. **Contact:** Linda Cracknell, Co-ordinator.

OBJECTIVES: To promote the acceptance of a development education focus in the Scotish school curriculum to increase people's understanding and enable them to become active in shaping a more just world.

GENERAL INFORMATION: *Creation:* 1984. *Type of organisation:* association of NGOs. **Member organisations:** 5. **Affiliated to:** Scottish Forum for Development Education in Schools (United Kingdom) -International Development Education Association for Scotland (United Kingdom) -Development Education Association (United Kingdom) - Scottish Environmental Education Council (United Kingdom). **Personnel/Total:** 3. *Salaried:* 3. **Budget/Total 1993:** ECU 90000 (US$ 105000). **Financial sources:** *Private:* 62%. *Public:* 8%. *Self-financing:* 30%.

PUBLICATIONS: *Periodicals:* Newsletter (3) - Resources Catalogue (1). *Annual report. List of publications.*

EVALUATION/RESEARCH: Evaluation reports available.

PLANNED ACTIVITIES: The production of materials for early secondary schools' curriculum in Scotland on Southern Africa.

Voir : *Comment utiliser le répertoire,* page 11.

COMMENTS: Information activities related to the Commonwealth of Independent States.

INFORMATION AND EDUCATION ACTIVITIES: Topics: Children/youth/family; Culture/tradition/religion; Ecology/environment/biodiversity; Education/training/literacy; Emergency relief/refugees/humanitarian assistance; Employment/unemployment; Food/famine; Gender issues/women; Health/sanitation/water; Human rights/peace/conflicts; International economic relations/trade/debt/finance; International relations/cooperation/development aid; Peace/ethnic conflicts/armament/disarmament; Population/family planning/demography; Poverty/living conditions; Racism/xenophobia/antisemitism; Refugees/migrants/ethnic groups; Rural development/agriculture; Urban development/habitat. **Activities:** Formal education.

GBR2469

SCOTTISH EDUCATION AND ACTION FOR DEVELOPMENT (SEAD)

23 Castle Street, Edinburgh EH2 3DN, United Kingdom.

Telephone: 44 (131) 225 6550. *Fax:* 44 (131) 226 6384. *Contact:* Linda Gray, Director.

OBJECTIVES: To research, publish materials, campaign and organise events on the links between poverty and underdevelopment in Scotland and the developing world.

GENERAL INFORMATION: *Creation:* 1978. *Affiliated to:* Scottish Anti-Poverty Network (United Kingdom) - Women's Forum Scotland (United Kingdom) - International Development Education Association of Scotland (United Kingdom). *Personnel/Total:* 10. *Salaried:* 7. *Volunteers:* 3. *Budget/Total 1993:* ECU 89000 (US$ 104000). *Financial sources:* Private: 90%. Public: 5%. Self-financing: 5%.

PUBLICATIONS: *Periodicals:* SEAD News (4) - Action for Development Network Bulletin (6). *Annual report. List of publications.*

EVALUATION/RESEARCH: Undertakes research activities.

INFORMATION AND EDUCATION ACTIVITIES: Topics: Gender issues/women; Poverty/living conditions. **Activities:** Broadcasting/cultural events; Conferences/seminars/workshops/training activities; Exchanges/twinning/linking; Fund raising; Information and documentation services/data bases; Information campaigns/exhibitions; Lobbying/advocacy; Networking/electronic telecommunications; Publishing/audiovisual materials/educational materials.

GBR2470

SCOTTISH EDUCATIONAL TRUST FOR UNITED NATIONS AND INTERNATIONAL AFFAIRS

Conference Room, Stirling's Library, Queen Street, Glasgow G1 3AZ, United Kingdom.

Telephone: 44 (141) 248 3244.

GBR2471

SCRIPTURE UNION, SCOTLAND

9 Canal Street, Glasgow G4 0AB, United Kingdom.

Telephone: 44 (141) 332 1162. *Fax:* 44 (141) 332 5925. *Contact:* Graham Wilson, Director.

OBJECTIVES: To provide Christian education to young people.

GENERAL INFORMATION: *Creation:* 1868. *Type of organisation:* network. *Personnel/Total:* 3052. *Salaried:* 52 of which: 2 in developing countries. *Volunteers:* 3000 of which: 4 in developing countries. *Budget/Total 1993:* ECU 962000 (US$ 1101000). *Financial sources:* Private: 88%. Public: 2%. Self-financing: 10%.

PUBLICATIONS: *Periodicals:* TELL (4).

PLANNED ACTIVITIES: Scripture Union-Scotland is planning an AIDS education programme for secondary schools in Zimbabwe and possibly Mozambique, Tanzania and Kenya.

COMMENTS: Undertakes activities in the Commonwealth of Independent States. Information activities related to the Commonwealth of Independent States.

ACTIVITIES IN DEVELOPING REGIONS: Present in developing regions. Active in 2 country(ies). Works through local field partners. **Sustainable Development Actions:** Children/youth/family; Education/training/literacy; Rural development/agriculture; Sending volunteers/experts/technical assistance. **Regions:** East Africa; Southern Africa.

INFORMATION AND EDUCATION ACTIVITIES: Topics: Children/youth/family; Culture/tradition/religion; Education/training/literacy; Rural development/agriculture. **Activities:** Conferences/seminars/workshops/training activities; Formal education; Information campaigns/exhibitions; Publishing/audiovisual materials/educational materials.

GBR2472

SDB TRUSTEES

Salesian Provincial House, 266 Wellington Road North, Stockport, Cheshire SK4 2QR, United Kingdom.

Telephone: 44 (161) 431 6633. *Contact:* Michael Cunningham.

OBJECTIVES: To work for the moral, spiritual and physical needs of young people.

GENERAL INFORMATION: *Creation:* 1890. *Type of organisation:* coordinating body. *Personnel/Total:* 8. *Volunteers:* 8 of which: 8 in developing countries. *Budget/Total 1993:* ECU 128000 (US$ 150000). *Financial sources:* Private: 100%.

ACTIVITIES IN DEVELOPING REGIONS: Present in developing regions. Active in 1 country(ies). Maintains local field presence. **Sustainable Development Actions:** Children/youth/family; Education/training/literacy; Emergency relief/refugees/humanitarian assistance; Food/famine. **Regions:** West Africa.

GBR2473

SELLY OAK DEVELOPMENT EDUCATION CENTRE

Gillette Centre, Selly Oak College, Bristol Road, Birmingham B29 6LF, United Kingdom.

Telephone: 44 (121) 472 4231. *Contact:* S. Sinclair.

GBR2474

SEND A COW

Unit 4, Priston Mill, Priston, Bath BA2 9EQ, United Kingdom.

Telephone: 44 (1225) 447041. *Fax:* 44 (1225) 317627. *Contact:* Anthony Herbert, Chairman.

OBJECTIVES: To overcome poverty and malnutrition through development of dairy cattle, aiming to reach sustainability by working through local institutions.

GENERAL INFORMATION: *Creation:* 1988. *Personnel/Total:* 56. *Salaried:* 6 of which: 3 in developing countries. *Volunteers:* 50. *Budget/Total 1993:* ECU 269000 (US$ 315000). *Financial sources:* Private: 80%. Public: 20%.

PUBLICATIONS: *Periodicals:* Newsletter (4). *Annual report. List of publications.*

EVALUATION/RESEARCH: Evaluation reports available. Undertakes research activities.

ACTIVITIES IN DEVELOPING REGIONS: Present in developing regions. Active in 2 country(ies). Maintains local field presence. Works through local field partners. **Sustainable Development Actions:** Children/youth/family; Democracy/good governance/institution building/participatory development; Ecology/environment/biodiversity; Education/training/literacy; Gender issues/women; Rural development/agriculture. **Regions:** East Africa.

INFORMATION AND EDUCATION ACTIVITIES: Topics: Children/youth/family; Health/sanitation/water; International economic relations/trade/debt/finance; Poverty/living conditions; Rural development/agriculture. **Activities:** Conferences/seminars/workshops/training activities; Formal education; Fund raising; Information campaigns/exhibitions; Lobbying/advocacy; Publishing/audiovisual materials/educational materials.

GBR2475
SERVE

Samarkand Camden Park, Tunbridge Wells, Kent TN2 4TW, United Kingdom.

Fax: 44 (1892) 528313. *Contact:* Howard Harper.

OBJECTIVES: To undertake relief and development activities among refugees and in Afghanistan.

GENERAL INFORMATION: *Creation:* 1980. *Personnel/Total:* 55. *Salaried:* 15 of which: 15 in developing countries. *Volunteers:* 40 of which: 40 in developing countries. *Budget/Total 1993:* ECU 640000 (US$ 750000). *Financial sources:* Private: 75%. Public: 15%. *Self-financing:* 10%.

PUBLICATIONS: List of publications.

EVALUATION/RESEARCH: Undertakes research activities.

ACTIVITIES IN DEVELOPING REGIONS: Present in developing regions. Active in 2 country(ies). Maintains local field presence. **Sustainable Development Actions:** Ecology/environment/biodiversity; Education/training/literacy; Emergency relief/refugees/humanitarian assistance; Energy/transport; Food/famine; Health/sanitation/water; Rural development/agriculture; Sending volunteers/experts/technical assistance; Small enterprises/informal sector/handicrafts; Urban development/habitat. **Regions:** Central Asia and South Asia.

INFORMATION AND EDUCATION ACTIVITIES: Topics: Emergency relief/refugees/humanitarian assistance; Employment/unemployment; Food/famine; Health/sanitation/water; Poverty/living conditions; Refugees/migrants/ethnic groups; Rural development/agriculture; Urban development/habitat. **Activities:** Conferences/seminars/workshops/training activities; Formal education; Fund raising; Information and documentation services/data bases; Information campaigns/exhibitions; Publishing/audiovisual materials/educational materials.

GBR2476
SID VALE AFRICA LINK

Coombe Bank, Coombe Cross, Tipton St. John, Sidmouth, Devon EX10 0AX, United Kingdom.

Contact: Roger Cozens.

GBR2477
SIGHT SAVERS, THE ROYAL COMMONWEALTH SOCIETY FOR THE BLIND

Grosvenor Hall, Bolnore Road, Haywards Heath, West Sussex RH16 4BX, United Kingdom.

Telephone: 44 (1444) 412424. *Fax:* 44 (1444) 415866. *Contact:* Dick Parker, Executive Director.

OBJECTIVES: To prevent and cure blindness in developing countries and to provide integrated education and community rehabilitation for incurably blind people.

GENERAL INFORMATION: *Creation:* 1950. *Affiliated to:* World Health Organization - PBL Partnership Committee - World Blind Union -International Council for Education of People with Visual Impairment - European Partners for Blindness Prevention - National Council of Voluntary Organisations (United Kingdom) - BOND (United Kingdom) - WHO/PBL Consultative Group. *Personnel/Total:* 128. *Salaried:* 90 of which: 20 in developing countries. *Volunteers:* 38. *Budget/Total 1993:* ECU 10771000 (US$ 12600000). *Financial sources:* Private: 88%. Public: 9%. Self-financing: 3%.

PUBLICATIONS: *Periodicals:* Horizons (4). Annual report.

EVALUATION/RESEARCH: Undertakes research activities.

ACTIVITIES IN DEVELOPING REGIONS: Present in developing regions. Active in 28 country(ies). Maintains local field presence. Works through local field partners. **Sustainable Development Actions:** Education/training/literacy; Health/sanitation/water; Other. **Regions:** Caribbean; Central Africa; Central Asia and South Asia; East Africa; East Asia; Oceania; South East Asia; Southern Africa; West Africa.

INFORMATION AND EDUCATION ACTIVITIES: Topics: Children/youth/family; Education/training/literacy; Health/sanitation/water; International relations/cooperation/development aid; Other. **Activities:** Conferences/seminars/workshops/training activities; Fund raising; Information and documentation services/data bases; Information campaigns/exhibitions; Publishing/audiovisual materials/educational materials.

GBR2478
SKILLSHARE AFRICA

3 Belvoir Street, Leicester LE1 6SL, United Kingdom.

Telephone: 44 (116) 254 1862. *Fax:* 44 (116) 254 2614. *Contact:* C.G. Allum, Director.

OBJECTIVES: To develop and transfer people's skills and strengthen local institutions in communities of southern Africa.

GENERAL INFORMATION: *Creation:* 1990. *Affiliated to:* British Overseas NGOs for Development (United Kingdom) - National Council for Voluntary Organisations (United Kingdom) - British Volunteers Agencies Liason Group (United Kingdom). *Personnel/Total:* 110. *Salaried:* 39 of which: 26 in developing countries. *Volunteers:* 71 of which: 71 in developing countries. *Budget/Total 1993:* ECU 2301000 (US$ 2701000). *Financial sources:* Private: 10%. Public: 90%.

PUBLICATIONS: *Annual report.*

EVALUATION/RESEARCH: Undertakes research activities.

ACTIVITIES IN DEVELOPING REGIONS: Present in developing regions. Active in 4 country(ies). Maintains local field presence. Works through local field partners. **Sustainable Development Actions:** Democracy/good governance/institution building/participatory development; Education/training/literacy; Gender issues/women; Health/sanitation/water; Rural development/agriculture; Sending volunteers/experts/technical assistance; Small enterprises/informal sector/handicrafts. **Regions:** Southern Africa.

GBR2479
SOCIETY FOR INTERNATIONAL DEVELOPMENT, UK CHAPTER (SID UK)

29 Wellington Road, Parkstone, Poole, Dorset BH14 9LF, United Kingdom.

Telephone: 44 (1202) 743968.

GBR2480
SOIL ASSOCIATION

86 Colston Street, Bristol BS1 5BB, United Kingdom.

Telephone: 44 (1272) 290661. *Fax:* 44 (1272) 252504. *Contact:* Francis Blake, General Secretary.

OBJECTIVES: To research, develop and promote sustainable relationships between soils, plants, animals, people and the biosphere in order to produce healthy food and products whilst protecting and enhancing the environment.

GENERAL INFORMATION: *Creation:* 1946. *Affiliated to:* International Federation of Organic Agriculture Movements (Germany) -International Federation of Organic Agriculture Movements-EU Group (United Kingdom) - Safe Alliance (United Kingdom). *Personnel/Total:* 15. *Salaried:* 12. *Volunteers:* 3. *Budget/Total 1993:* ECU 641000 (US$ 751000). *Financial sources:* Private: 40%. Self-financing: 60%.

PUBLICATIONS: *Periodicals:* The Living Earth (4) - Symbol News (4). Annual report. List of publications.

EVALUATION/RESEARCH: Evaluation reports available. Undertakes research activities.

PLANNED ACTIVITIES: The establishment of an organic farming centre to develop indigenous organic certification schemes and infrastructures in Poland, Iceland, Uganda and Venezuela. Also planned are a Forestry Programme and a "Go Organic" campaign.

COMMENTS: Undertakes activities in the Commonwealth of Independent States. Information activities related to the Commonwealth of Independent States.

Voir : *Comment utiliser le répertoire,* page 11.

ACTIVITIES IN DEVELOPING REGIONS: Present in developing regions. Active in 9 country(ies). Works through local field partners. **Sustainable Development Actions:** Ecology/environment/biodiversity; Rural development/agriculture. **Regions:** Central Asia and South Asia; East Africa; Mexico and Central America; Oceania; South America; Southern Africa.

INFORMATION AND EDUCATION ACTIVITIES: **Topics:** Ecology/environment/biodiversity; Rural development/agriculture. **Activities:** Conferences/seminars/workshops/training activities; Fund raising; Information and documentation services/data bases; Publishing/audiovisual materials/educational materials.

GBR2481

SOROPTIMIST INTERNATIONAL, UNITED KINGDOM (SI)

87 Glisson Road, Cambridge CB1 2HG, United Kingdom.

Telephone: 44 (1223) 311833. **Fax:** 44 (1223) 467951. **Contact:** Janet Bilton, Executive Officer.

OBJECTIVES: To promote human rights for all and, in particular, to advance the status of women. To contribute to international understanding and universal friendship. To maintain high ethical standards in business, the professions and other aspects of life.

GENERAL INFORMATION: *Creation:* 1921. *Member organisations:* 4. *Personnel/Total:* 3. *Financial sources: Self-financing:* 100%.

PUBLICATIONS: *Periodicals:* The International Soroptimist (4) - World Span (4).

COMMENTS: Undertakes activities in the Commonwealth of Independent States. Information activities related to the Commonwealth of Independent States.

ACTIVITIES IN DEVELOPING REGIONS: Maintains local field presence. Works through local field partners. **Sustainable Development Actions:** Children/youth/family; Ecology/environment/biodiversity; Education/training/literacy; Gender issues/women; Health/sanitation/water; Small enterprises/informal sector/handicrafts. **Regions:** Caribbean; Central Africa; Central Asia and South Asia; East Africa; East Asia; Mexico and Central America; Oceania; South America; South East Asia; Southern Africa; West Africa.

INFORMATION AND EDUCATION ACTIVITIES: **Topics:** Children/youth/family; Ecology/environment/biodiversity; Education/training/literacy; Emergency relief/refugees/humanitarian assistance; Employment/unemployment; Gender issues/women; Health/sanitation/water; Human rights/peace/conflicts; Refugees/migrants/ethnic groups. **Activities:** Conferences/seminars/workshops/training activities; Exchanges/twinning/linking; Formal education; Fund raising; Lobbying/advocacy.

GBR2482

SOS CHILDREN'S VILLAGES UNITED KINGDOM (SOS-UK)

32 Bridge Street, Cambridge CB2 1UJ, United Kingdom.

Telephone: 44 (1223) 65589. **Fax:** 44 (1223) 322613. **Contact:** Daniel Fox, Director.

OBJECTIVES: To help fund the worldwide work of SOS Children's Villages in providing orphaned and abandoned children with a mother, a family, a home and a secure future.

GENERAL INFORMATION: *Creation:* 1968. *Personnel/Total:* 6. *Salaried:* 6. *Budget/Total 1993:* ECU 630000 (US$ 738000). *Financial sources: Private:* 100%.

PUBLICATIONS: *Periodicals:* SOS Children World (4). *Annual report.*

COMMENTS: SOS-UK carries out activities through its members which worked in 114 developing countries in 1993.

ACTIVITIES IN DEVELOPING REGIONS: Works through local field partners.

GBR2483

SOS SAHEL INTERNATIONAL, UNITED KINGDOM

1 Tolpuddle Street, London N1 0XT, United Kingdom.

Telephone: 44 (171) 837 9129. **Fax:** 44 (171) 837 0856. **E-mail:** sossaheluk@gn.apc.org. **Contact:** Nigel Cross, Director.

OBJECTIVES: To assist people to design and implement small-scale, sustainable agriculture projects in the Sahel region and adjacent areas and to conserve and improve their physical environment.

GENERAL INFORMATION: *Creation:* 1983. *Affiliated to:* CCA-ONG (Mali) - CRDA (Ethiopia). *Personnel/Total:* 300. *Salaried:* 300 of which: 285 in developing countries. *Budget/Total 1993:* ECU 2201000 (US$ 2601000). *Financial sources: Private:* 36%. *Public:* 64%.

PUBLICATIONS: *Periodicals:* Newsletter (1). *Annual report. List of publications.*

EVALUATION/RESEARCH: Evaluation reports available. Undertakes research activities.

ACTIVITIES IN DEVELOPING REGIONS: Present in developing regions. Active in 6 country(ies). Maintains local field presence. Works through local field partners. **Sustainable Development Actions:** Democracy/good governance/institution building/participatory development; Ecology/environment/biodiversity; Education/training/literacy; Emergency relief/refugees/humanitarian assistance; Food/famine; Gender issues/women; Health/sanitation/water; Other; Rural development/agriculture; Sending volunteers/experts/technical assistance; Small enterprises/informal sector/handicrafts. **Regions:** East Africa; Southern Africa; West Africa.

INFORMATION AND EDUCATION ACTIVITIES: **Topics:** Culture/tradition/religion; Ecology/environment/biodiversity; Education/training/literacy; Emergency relief/refugees/humanitarian assistance; Food/famine; Gender issues/women; Health/sanitation/water; Refugees/migrants/ethnic groups; Rural development/agriculture. **Activities:** Conferences/seminars/workshops/training activities; Fund raising; Information and documentation services/data bases; Information campaigns/exhibitions; Lobbying/advocacy; Publishing/audiovisual materials/educational materials.

GBR2484

SOUTH AFRICAN TOWNSHIPS

37 Inverness Street, London NW1 7HB, United Kingdom.

Contact: Mary Hope.

GBR2485

SOUTH AMERICAN MISSIONARY SOCIETY (SAMS)

Allen Gardiner House, Pembury Road, Tunbridge Wells, Kent TN2 3QV, United Kingdom.

Telephone: 44 (1892) 538647. **Fax:** 44 (1892) 525797. **Contact:** Bishop David Evans, General Secretary.

OBJECTIVES: To work in partnership with the Anglican Church in South America, Spain and Portugal. To teach and apply the Christian Gospel at every level of society, support the Anglican Church by training national leadership, and work for the relief of human suffering and indignity in accordance with the Scriptures.

GENERAL INFORMATION: *Creation:* 1844. *Personnel/Total:* 195. *Salaried:* 90 of which: 70 in developing countries. *Volunteers:* 105 of which: 5 in developing countries. *Budget/Total 1993:* ECU 1400000 (US$ 1650000). *Financial sources: Private:* 80%. *Public:* 10%. *Self-financing:* 10%.

PUBLICATIONS: *Periodicals:* SHARE (4). *Annual report. List of publications.*

ACTIVITIES IN DEVELOPING REGIONS: Active in 4 country(ies). Maintains local field presence. Works through local field partners. **Sustainable Development Actions:** Children/youth/family; Education/training/literacy; Food/famine; Health/sanitation/water; Rural development/agriculture; Sending volunteers/experts/technical assistance; Small enterprises/informal sector/handicrafts. **Regions:** South America.

INFORMATION AND EDUCATION ACTIVITIES: **Topics:** Children/youth/family; Culture/tradition/religion; Education/training/literacy; Poverty/living conditions; Rural development/agriculture; Urban development/habitat. **Activities:** Publishing/audiovisual materials/educational materials.

See: *How to Use the Directory*, page 11.

GBR2486
SOUTHEAST-ASIAN OUTREACH

90 Windmill Street, Gravesend, Kent DA12 1LH, United Kingdom.

Telephone: 44 (1474) 534101. *Fax:* 44 (1474) 323461. *Contact:* John Heard.

OBJECTIVES: To promote the Christian faith and relieve poverty and distress among the peoples of South East Asia particularly by helping explain, practice and disseminate the teachings of Jesus Christ amongst the Cambodian people.

GENERAL INFORMATION: *Creation:* 1973. *Affiliated to:* Cambodia Christian Services (Cambodia) - Evangelical Missionary Alliance (United Kingdom). *Personnel/Total:* 13. *Salaried:* 3. *Volunteers:* 10 of which: 10 in developing countries. *Budget/Total 1993:* ECU 342000 (US$ 400000). *Financial sources: Private:* 85%. *Public:* 12%. *Self-financing:* 3%.

PUBLICATIONS: *Periodicals:* Vision (4). *Annual report.*

EVALUATION/RESEARCH: Evaluation reports available.

ACTIVITIES IN DEVELOPING REGIONS: Present in developing regions. Active in 1 country(ies). Maintains local field presence. **Sustainable Development Actions:** Education/training/literacy; Health/sanitation/water; Rural development/agriculture; Sending volunteers/experts/technical assistance. **Regions:** South East Asia.

GBR2487
SPANA

15 Buckingham Gate, London SW1E 6LB, United Kingdom.

Contact: W.B. Teasdale.

GBR2488
SPICMA

49 Gainsborough Street, Sudbury, Surrey CO10 6ET, United Kingdom.

Contact: Patrick J. Phelan.

GBR2489
ST. JOHN AMBULANCE

Order of St. John, Overseas Department, 1 Grosvenor Crescent, London SW1X 7EF, United Kingdom.

Telephone: 44 (171) 235 5231. *Fax:* 44 (171) 235 4574. *Contact:* M. Keith Batt, Deputy Director Overseas Relations.

OBJECTIVES: To provide first aid and health-orientated caring services in local communities without regard to race, religion or gender.

GENERAL INFORMATION: *Creation:* 1113. *Type of organisation:* network. *Member organisations:* 41. *Personnel/Total:* 281600. *Salaried:* 1350 of which: 400 in developing countries. *Volunteers:* 280250 of which: 168800 in developing countries. *Budget/Total 1993:* ECU 366715 (US$ 429560). *Financial sources: Private:* 30%. *Self-financing:* 70%.

PUBLICATIONS: *Periodicals:* Overseas Newsletter (1). *Annual report.* List of publications.

COMMENTS: St. John Ambulance is an international NGO which is largely Commonwealth-based. Each of its worldwide organisations is independently constituted within the Most Venerable Order of St. John of Jerusalem.

ACTIVITIES IN DEVELOPING REGIONS: Active in 33 country(ies). Maintains local field presence. Works through local field partners. **Sustainable Development Actions:** Children/youth/family; Emergency relief/refugees/humanitarian assistance; Health/sanitation/water. **Regions:** Caribbean; East Africa; Middle East; Oceania; South America; Southern Africa; West Africa.

INFORMATION AND EDUCATION ACTIVITIES: Topics: Children/youth/family; Health/sanitation/water. **Activities:** Exchanges/twinning/linking; Fund raising; Publishing/audiovisual materials/educational materials.

GBR2490
STATES OF EMERGENCY DATABASE CENTRE

Queen's University of Belfast, Belfast BT7 1NN, United Kingdom.

Telephone: 44 (232) 245133 ext. 3866. *Fax:* 44 (232) 247895. *E-mail:* JPG005@qub.ac.uk. *Contact:* K.S. Venkateswaran.

OBJECTIVES: To provide information on states of emergency and their impact on human rights. To provide training and consultancy services on human rights documentation. To undertake research and publication projects jointly with NGOs and other academic institutions.

GENERAL INFORMATION: *Creation:* 1990. *Personnel/Total:* 3. *Salaried:* 3. *Budget/Total 1993:* ECU 46160 (US$ 54070). *Financial sources: Private:* 100%.

PUBLICATIONS: *Periodicals:* Country studies (4). *List of publications.*

EVALUATION/RESEARCH: Evaluation reports available. Undertakes research activities.

PLANNED ACTIVITIES: States of Emergency Database Centre plans to carry out human rights training programmes in different parts of the world and to undertake publication work on human rights. They will make their database available on INTERNET via Mosaic/Cello.

COMMENTS: Undertakes activities in the Commonwealth of Independent States. Information activities related to the Commonwealth of Independent States.

ACTIVITIES IN DEVELOPING REGIONS: Active in 6 country(ies). Maintains local field presence. Works through local field partners. **Sustainable Development Actions:** Democracy/good governance/institution building/participatory development; Human rights/peace/conflicts. **Regions:** Central Asia and South Asia; East Asia; Mexico and Central America; North Africa; Oceania; South America; South East Asia; Southern Africa; West Africa.

INFORMATION AND EDUCATION ACTIVITIES: Topics: Human rights/peace/conflicts. **Activities:** Conferences/seminars/workshops/training activities; Exchanges/twinning/linking; Information and documentation services/data bases; Networking/electronic telecommunications; Publishing/audiovisual materials/educational materials.

GBR2491
SUDAN HUMAN RIGHTS ORGANIZATION (SHRO)

BM Box 8238, London WC1 N3XX, United Kingdom.

Telephone: 44 (171) 378 8008. *Fax:* 44 (171) 378 8029. *Contact:* Dr. A. Sinada, President.

GBR2492
SUE RYDER FOUNDATION

Cavendish, Sudbury, Suffolk C010 8AY, United Kingdom.

Telephone: 44 (1787) 280252. *Fax:* 44 (1787) 280548. *Contact:* Vaughan Stone.

OBJECTIVES: To run a programme of community health care in Malawi. To improve the quality of life and help attain economic independence.

GENERAL INFORMATION: *Creation:* 1953. *Personnel/Total:* 7095. *Salaried:* 2095 of which: 25 in developing countries. *Volunteers:* 5000 of which: 200 in developing countries. *Budget/Total 1993:* ECU 24750760 (US$ 28990680). *Financial sources: Private:* 48%. *Public:* 34%. *Self-financing:* 18%.

PUBLICATIONS: *Periodicals:* Remembrance Magazine (1). *Annual report.*

EVALUATION/RESEARCH: Evaluation reports available.

COMMENTS: Undertakes activities in the Commonwealth of Independent States.

ACTIVITIES IN DEVELOPING REGIONS: Present in developing regions. Active in 3 country(ies). Maintains local field presence. Works through local field partners. **Sustainable Development Actions:** Children/youth/family; Education/training/literacy; Health/sanitation/water; Small enterprises/informal sector/handicrafts. **Regions:** Central Asia and South Asia; Southern Africa.

Voir : *Comment utiliser le répertoire,* page 11.

INFORMATION AND EDUCATION ACTIVITIES: Topics: Children/youth/family; Education/training/literacy; Health/sanitation/water; Poverty/living conditions. **Activities:** Conferences/seminars/workshops/training activities; Fund raising.

GBR2493

SURVIVAL INTERNATIONAL

310 Edgware Road, London W2 1DY, United Kingdom.

Telephone: 44 (171) 723 5535. *Fax:* 44 (171) 723 4059. *E-mail:* GN:SURVIVAL. *Contact:* Stephen Corry, Director General.

OBJECTIVES: To support tribal peoples, in standing for their right to decide their own future and to help them protect their lands, environment and way of life.

GENERAL INFORMATION: *Creation:* 1969. *Personnel/Total:* 69. *Salaried:* 19. *Volunteers:* 50. *Budget/Total 1993:* ECU 512890 (US$ 600780). *Financial sources:* Private: 33%. Self-financing: 65%.

PUBLICATIONS: *Periodicals:* Survival International Newsletter (2) - Urgent Action Bulletins (10). *List of publications.*

EVALUATION/RESEARCH: Evaluation reports available.

COMMENTS: Undertakes activities in the Commonwealth of Independent States. Information activities related to the Commonwealth of Independent States.

ACTIVITIES IN DEVELOPING REGIONS: Present in developing regions. Active in 23 country(ies). Works through local field partners. **Sustainable Development Actions:** Human rights/peace/conflicts. **Regions:** Central Africa; Central Asia and South Asia; East Africa; Mexico and Central America; South America; South East Asia; Southern Africa.

INFORMATION AND EDUCATION ACTIVITIES: Topics: Emergency relief/refugees/humanitarian assistance; Human rights/peace/conflicts; International relations/cooperation/development aid; Refugees/migrants/ethnic groups. **Activities:** Broadcasting/cultural events; Fund raising; Information and documentation services/data bases; Information campaigns/exhibitions; Lobbying/advocacy; Publishing/audiovisual materials/educational materials.

GBR2494

SUSSEX ALLIANCE FOR NUCLEAR DISARMAMENT (SAND)

187 Eastern Road, Brighton BN2 5BB, United Kingdom.

Telephone: 44 (273) 681 181. *Contact:* Eileen Daffern, Secretary.

GBR2495

SUSTAINABLE AGRICULTURE FOOD AND ENVIRONMENT ALLIANCE (SAFE)

38 Ebury Street, London SWIW OLU, United Kingdom.

Telephone: 44 (171) 823 5660. *Fax:* 44 (171) 823 5673. *E-mail:* safe@gn.apc.org.. *Contact:* Hugh Raven, Co-ordinator.

OBJECTIVES: To research and promote issues affecting sustainability in agriculture and food economy.

GENERAL INFORMATION: *Creation:* 1991. *Type of organisation:* association of NGOs. *Member organisations:* 60. *Personnel/Total:* 2. *Salaried:* 2. *Budget/Total 1993:* ECU 76930 (US$ 90120). *Financial sources:* Private: 100%.

PUBLICATIONS: *Periodicals:* SAFE News (6). *Annual report. List of publications.*

EVALUATION/RESEARCH: Undertakes research activities.

PLANNED ACTIVITIES: SAFE plans to research common agricultural policy reform, rural policy and the implications of long-distance food transport.

INFORMATION AND EDUCATION ACTIVITIES: Topics: Ecology/environment/biodiversity; Food/famine; Human rights/peace/conflicts; International economic relations/trade/debt/finance; International relations/cooperation/development aid; Poverty/living conditions; Rural development/agriculture. **Activities:** Conferences/seminars/workshops/training activities; Information and documentation services/data bases; Informa-

tion campaigns/exhibitions; Lobbying/advocacy; Networking/electronic telecommunications.

GBR2496

TAMIL INFORMATION CENTRE

Thamil House, 720 Romford Road, London E12 6BT, United Kingdom.

Contact: Ms. V. Shyla.

GBR2497

TANZANIA DEVELOPMENT TRUST

Battle Hill, Austwick, Lancaster LA2 88W, United Kingdom.

Telephone: 44 (1524) 251484. *Contact:* Roger Carter.

OBJECTIVES: To promote friendship and understanding by giving support to villagers and other groups in order to promote development through the implementation of development projects.

GENERAL INFORMATION: *Creation:* 1975. *Affiliated to:* Britain-Tanzania Society. *Personnel/Total:* 6. *Volunteers:* 6 of which: 3 in developing countries. *Budget/Total 1993:* ECU 38470 (US$ 45060). *Financial sources:* Private: 13%. Public: 43%. Self-financing: 42%.

PUBLICATIONS: *Annual report.*

ACTIVITIES IN DEVELOPING REGIONS: Present in developing regions. Active in 1 country(ies). Maintains local field presence. Works through local field partners. **Sustainable Development Actions:** Democracy/good governance/institution building/participatory development; Education/training/literacy; Energy/transport; Health/sanitation/water; Rural development/agriculture. **Regions:** East Africa.

GBR2498

TAPOL INDONESIA HUMAN RIGHTS CAMPAIGN

111 Northwood Road Thornton Heath, Surrey CR7 8HW, United Kingdom.

Telephone: 44 (181) 771 2904. *Fax:* 44 (181) 653 0322. *E-mail:* gn:tapol.. *Contact:* Carmel Budiardjo, Organising Secretary.

OBJECTIVES: To monitor and disseminate information on human rights violations by the Indonesian government. To lobby Members of Parliament in the UK and elsewhere to pressure the Indonesian regime to stop their human rights abuses.

GENERAL INFORMATION: *Creation:* 1973. *Affiliated to:* Campaign Against Arms Trade (United Kingdom) - British Coalitiom for East Timor . *Personnel/Total:* 7. *Salaried:* 4. *Volunteers:* 3. *Budget/Total 1993:* ECU 62000 (US$ 72000). *Financial sources:* Private: 84%. Self-financing: 16%.

PUBLICATIONS: *Periodicals:* TAPOL-The Indonesia Human Rights Campaign Bulletin (6). *List of publications.*

EVALUATION/RESEARCH: Evaluation reports available. Undertakes research activities.

PLANNED ACTIVITIES: TAPOL will undertake a major project on "Labour Conditions in Indonesia".

ACTIVITIES IN DEVELOPING REGIONS: Active in 1 country(ies). **Sustainable Development Actions:** Debt/finance/trade; Democracy/good governance/institution building/participatory development; Education/training/literacy; Emergency relief/refugees/humanitarian assistance; Human rights/peace/conflicts; Small enterprises/informal sector/handicrafts; Urban development/habitat. **Regions:** South East Asia.

INFORMATION AND EDUCATION ACTIVITIES: Topics: Culture/tradition/religion; Education/training/literacy; Emergency relief/refugees/humanitarian assistance; Employment/unemployment; Gender issues/women; Human rights/peace/conflicts; International economic relations/trade/debt/finance; International relations/cooperation/development aid; Peace/ethnic conflicts/armament/disarmament; Population/family planning/demography; Poverty/living conditions; Refugees/migrants/ethnic groups; Rural development/agriculture; Urban development/habitat. **Activities:** Broadcasting/cultural events; Conferences/seminars/workshops/training activities; Fund raising; Information and documentation services/data bases; Information campaigns/exhibitions; Lobbying/advo-

cacy; Networking/electronic telecommunications; Publishing/audiovisual materials/educational materials.

GBR2499

TEACHING AIDS AT LOW COST (TALC)

P.O. Box 49, St Albans, Herts AL1 4AX, United Kingdom.

Telephone: 44 (1727) 853869. *Fax:* 44 (1727) 846852. *Contact:* Barbara Harvey, Administrator.

OBJECTIVES: To supply low cost health care teaching aids to Third World countries.

GENERAL INFORMATION: *Creation:* 1965. *Personnel/Total:* 26. *Salaried:* 20. *Volunteers:* 6. *Financial sources:* Private: 5%. Self-financing: 95%.

PUBLICATIONS: List of publications.

INFORMATION AND EDUCATION ACTIVITIES: Topics: Education/training/literacy; Health/sanitation/water; Rural development/agriculture. **Activities:** Publishing/audiovisual materials/educational materials.

GBR2500

TEAR FUND

100 Church Road, Teddington, Middlesex TW11 8QE, United Kingdom.

Telephone: 44 (181) 977 9144. *Fax:* 44 (181) 943 3594. *Contact:* David Adeney, Executive Director.

OBJECTIVES: To serve Jesus Christ by enabling those who share evangelical Christian beliefs to bring good news to the poor.

GENERAL INFORMATION: *Creation:* 1968. *Affiliated to:* Evangelical Missionary Alliance (United Kingdom) - Interchurch Relief and Development Alliance - World Evangelical Feloowship - Euronaid - British Overseas NGOs in Development - Voluntary Organisations in Co-operation in Emergencies. *Personnel/Total:* 721. *Salaried:* 245 of which: 83 in developing countries. *Volunteers:* 450. *Budget/Total 1993:* ECU 25640310 (US$ 30040050). *Financial sources:* Private: 95%. *Public:* 5%.

PUBLICATIONS: *Periodicals:* Tear Times (4) - Footsteps (4). *Annual report.* List of publications.

EVALUATION/RESEARCH: Evaluation reports available. Undertakes research activities.

COMMENTS: Undertakes activities in the Commonwealth of Independent States. Information activities related to the Commonwealth of Independent States.

ACTIVITIES IN DEVELOPING REGIONS: Present in developing regions. Works through local field partners. **Sustainable Development Actions:** Children/youth/family; Democracy/good governance/institution building/participatory development; Ecology/environment/biodiversity; Education/training/literacy; Emergency relief/refugees/humanitarian assistance; Energy/transport; Food/famine; Gender issues/women; Health/sanitation/water; Human rights/peace/conflicts; Population/family planning/demography; Rural development/agriculture; Sending volunteers/experts/technical assistance; Small enterprises/informal sector/handicrafts; Urban development/habitat. **Regions:** Caribbean; Central Africa; Central Asia and South Asia; East Africa; East Asia; Mexico and Central America; Middle East; North Africa; South America; South East Asia; Southern Africa; West Africa.

INFORMATION AND EDUCATION ACTIVITIES: Topics: Children/youth/family; Culture/tradition/religion; Ecology/environment/biodiversity; Education/training/literacy; Emergency relief/refugees/humanitarian assistance; Food/famine; Gender issues/women; Health/sanitation/water; Human rights/peace/conflicts; International economic relations/trade/debt/finance; International relations/cooperation/development aid; Peace/ethnic conflicts/armament/disarmament; Population/family planning/demography; Poverty/living conditions; Refugees/migrants/ethnic groups; Rural development/agriculture; Urban development/habitat. **Activities:** Conferences/seminars/workshops/training activities; Fund raising; Lobbying/advocacy; Publishing/audiovisual materials/educational materials.

GBR2501

TELEVISION TRUST FOR THE ENVIRONMENT (TVE)

Prince Albert Road, London NW1 4RZ, United Kingdom.

Telephone: 44 (171) 586 5526. *Fax:* 44 (171) 586 4866. *E-mail:* GEO NET TVE-UK. *Contact:* Robert Lamb, Director.

OBJECTIVES: To promote environment and development issues through the production of audiovisual materials. To help with funding and co-production of films providing special support to film-makers in the South.

GENERAL INFORMATION: *Creation:* 1984. *Type of organisation:* coordinating body. *Affiliated to:* IUCN (Switzerland). *Personnel/Total:* 16. *Salaried:* 10. *Volunteers:* 6. *Financial sources:* Private: 45%. Public: 45%. *Self-financing:* 10%.

PUBLICATIONS: *Periodicals:* Moving Pictures Catalogue (1) - Moving Pictures Bulletin (4). List of publications.

EVALUATION/RESEARCH: Undertakes research activities.

COMMENTS: Undertakes activities in the Commonwealth of Independent States. Information activities related to the Commonwealth of Independent States.

ACTIVITIES IN DEVELOPING REGIONS: Maintains local field presence. Works through local field partners. **Sustainable Development Actions:** Children/youth/family; Debt/finance/trade; Democracy/good governance/institution building/participatory development; Ecology/environment/biodiversity; Education/training/literacy; Emergency relief/refugees/humanitarian assistance; Energy/transport; Food/famine; Gender issues/women; Health/sanitation/water; Human rights/peace/conflicts; Population/family planning/demography; Rural development/agriculture; Sending volunteers/experts/technical assistance; Small enterprises/informal sector/handicrafts; Urban development/habitat. **Regions:** Caribbean; Central Africa; Central Asia and South Asia; East Africa; East Asia; Mexico and Central America; Middle East; North Africa; Oceania; South America; South East Asia; Southern Africa; West Africa.

INFORMATION AND EDUCATION ACTIVITIES: Topics: Children/youth/family; Culture/tradition/religion; Ecology/environment/biodiversity; Education/training/literacy; Emergency relief/refugees/humanitarian assistance; Employment/unemployment; Food/famine; Gender issues/women; Health/sanitation/water; Human rights/peace/conflicts; International economic relations/trade/debt/finance; International relations/cooperation/development aid; Peace/ethnic conflicts/armament/disarmament; Population/family planning/demography; Poverty/living conditions; Racism/xenophobia/antisemitism; Refugees/migrants/ethnic groups; Rural development/agriculture; Urban development/habitat. **Activities:** Broadcasting/cultural events; Publishing/audiovisual materials/educational materials.

GBR2502

TESO DEVELOPMENT TRUST

1 Broadway, Jaywick Sands, Clacton-on-Sea, Essex CO15 2EA, United Kingdom.

Telephone: 44 (1255) 424282. *Fax:* 44 (1255) 424282. *Contact:* Neil Stedman, General Secretary.

OBJECTIVES: To assist in relief, rehabilitation and development in the Teso districts of Uganda, in co-operation with the Church of Uganda and other organisations.

GENERAL INFORMATION: *Creation:* 1988. *Affiliated to:* EC-NGO Network. *Personnel/Total:* 3. *Salaried:* 2 of which: 1 in developing countries. *Volunteers:* 1. *Budget/Total 1993:* ECU 53000 (US$ 62000). *Financial sources:* Private: 20%. Self-financing: 80%.

PUBLICATIONS: *Periodicals:* Teso Newsletter (3). *Annual report.*

ACTIVITIES IN DEVELOPING REGIONS: Active in 1 country(ies). Maintains local field presence. Works through local field partners. **Sustainable Development Actions:** Children/youth/family; Emergency relief/refugees/humanitarian assistance; Food/famine; Health/sanitation/water; Rural development/agriculture; Sending volunteers/experts/technical assistance. **Regions:** East Africa.

Voir : *Comment utiliser le répertoire,* page 11.

GBR2503

THIRD WORLD FIRST (3W1)

217 Cowley Road, Oxford OX4 1XG, United Kingdom.

Telephone: 44 (1865) 245678. *Fax:* 44 (1865) 200179. *Contact:* L.A. Reveco, Director.

OBJECTIVES: To create awareness about the root causes of poverty and underdevelopment. To educate, campaign and raise funds among students and young people.

GENERAL INFORMATION: *Creation:* 1969. *Affiliated to:* YDC (Netherlands) - EURODAD (Belgium) - Debt Crisis Network (United Kingdom) -Development Education Association (United Kingdom) - National Council of Voluntary Organisations (United Kingdom). *Personnel/Total:* 11. *Salaried:* 6. *Volunteers:* 5. *Budget/Total 1993:* ECU 321000 (US$ 375000). *Financial sources:* Private: 60%. *Self-financing:* 40%.

PUBLICATIONS: *Annual report. List of publications.*

EVALUATION/RESEARCH: Evaluation reports available. Undertakes research activities.

PLANNED ACTIVITIES: Third World First will focus on the impact of the European Union the Third World Debt, Trade and Aid, and on Women and the Environment.

COMMENTS: Information activities related to the Commonwealth of Independent States.

INFORMATION AND EDUCATION ACTIVITIES: Topics: Children/youth/family; Culture/tradition/religion; Ecology/environment/biodiversity; Education/training/literacy; Emergency relief/refugees/humanitarian assistance; Food/famine; Gender issues/women; Health/sanitation/water; Human rights/peace/conflicts; International economic relations/trade/debt/finance; International relations/cooperation/development aid; Peace/ethnic conflicts/armament/disarmament; Population/family planning/demography; Poverty/living conditions; Racism/xenophobia/antisemitism; Refugees/migrants/ethnic groups; Rural development/agriculture. **Activities:** Conferences/seminars/workshops/training activities; Fund raising; Information campaigns/exhibitions; Lobbying/advocacy; Publishing/audiovisual materials/educational materials.

GBR2504

THIRD WORLD MEDIA (TWM)

New Zealand House, 13th floor, 80 Haymarket, London SW1Y 4TS, United Kingdom.

Telephone: 44 (171) 839 6167.

GBR2505

THIRD WORLD NETWORK - EUROPE

336 Pinner Road, North Harrow, Middlesex, United Kingdom.

Telephone: 44 (181) 861 2012. *Fax:* 44 (181) 861 3113.

GBR2506

TIBET SOCIETY AND TIBET RELIEF FUND OF THE UNITED KINGDOM

Olympia Bridge Quay, 70 Russell Road, London W14, United Kingdom.

Telephone: 44 (171) 603 7764. *Contact:* Yangchmen Yeshi, General Secretary.

OBJECTIVES: To support Tibet's right to self determination and independence and to draw the attention of the world to Tibet's plight. To assist Tibetan refugees and to finance a variety of projects in Tibetan refugee settlements in India and Nepal.

GENERAL INFORMATION: *Creation:* 1959. *Personnel/Total:* 6. *Salaried:* 2. *Volunteers:* 4. *Financial sources:* Private: 70%. *Self-financing:* 30%.

PLANNED ACTIVITIES: The Tibet Society will campaign for the inclusion of Tibetan women at the Fourth World Conference in Beijing and will work for human rights in Tibet.

ACTIVITIES IN DEVELOPING REGIONS: Active in 3 country(ies). Works through local field partners. **Sustainable Development Actions:** Children/youth/family; Education/training/literacy; Emergency relief/refu-

gees/humanitarian assistance; Gender issues/women; Human rights/peace/conflicts; Rural development/agriculture; Small enterprises/informal sector/handicrafts. **Regions:** Central Asia and South Asia.

INFORMATION AND EDUCATION ACTIVITIES: Topics: Peace/ethnic conflicts/armament/disarmament; Refugees/migrants/ethnic groups. **Activities:** Fund raising; Publishing/audiovisual materials/educational materials.

GBR2507

TIVERTON KABALE LINK

12 Marguerite Road, Lowman Park, Tiverton, Devon EX16 6TD, United Kingdom.

Contact: David Davies.

GBR2508

TIVERTON SUNDARBAN LINK

Lower Beer, Uplowman, Tiverton, Devon EX16 7PF, United Kingdom.

Telephone: 44 (1884) 821239. *Fax:* 44 (1884) 821239. *Contact:* Robert Hodgson, Secretary.

OBJECTIVES: To assist Chetonar Dak NGO in the task of relieving poverty in the city of Sundarban in Bangladesh. To foster understanding and co-operation between Tiverton, the United Kingdom, and Sundarban.

GENERAL INFORMATION: *Creation:* 1990. *Affiliated to:* Devon Aid (United Kingdom) - UK One World Link Association. *Personnel/Total:* 9. *Volunteers:* 9. *Budget/Total 1993:* ECU 4000 (US$ 5000). *Financial sources:* Private: 50%. Self-financing: 50%.

PUBLICATIONS: *Periodicals:* Newsletter (3). *Annual report.*

ACTIVITIES IN DEVELOPING REGIONS: Active in 1 country(ies). Works through local field partners. **Sustainable Development Actions:** Children/youth/family; Democracy/good governance/institution building/participatory development; Education/training/literacy; Gender issues/women; Population/family planning/demography; Rural development/agriculture; Sending volunteers/experts/technical assistance; Small enterprises/informal sector/handicrafts. **Regions:** South East Asia.

INFORMATION AND EDUCATION ACTIVITIES: Topics: Children/youth/family; Education/training/literacy; Gender issues/women; Population/family planning/demography; Rural development/agriculture. **Activities:** Fund raising.

GBR2509

TOC H

1 Forest Close, Wendover, Aylesbury, Bucks HP22 6BT, United Kingdom.

Telephone: 44 (1296) 623911. *Fax:* 44 (1296) 696137. *Contact:* Ian Pearce.

OBJECTIVES: To help overcome divisions in society by bringing together a diversity of people and promoting community service. To provide opportunities for people to develop fellowship, to work together, and to discover a faith to live by.

GENERAL INFORMATION: *Creation:* 1915. *Personnel/Total:* 2080. *Salaried:* 80. *Volunteers:* 2000. *Budget/Total 1993:* ECU 2560000 (US$ 3001000). *Financial sources:* Private: 30%. Public: 5%. Self-financing: 65%.

PUBLICATIONS: *Periodicals:* Friends of Khasdobir Newsletter (4).

COMMENTS: Undertakes activities in the Commonwealth of Independent States.

ACTIVITIES IN DEVELOPING REGIONS: Active in 4 country(ies). Works through local field partners. **Sustainable Development Actions:** Children/youth/family; Education/training/literacy; Emergency relief/refugees/humanitarian assistance; Health/sanitation/water; Population/family planning/demography; Small enterprises/informal sector/handicrafts. **Regions:** Central Asia and South Asia; Southern Africa.

INFORMATION AND EDUCATION ACTIVITIES: Topics: Children/youth/family; Education/training/literacy; Health/sanitation/water; Poverty/living conditions; Urban development/habitat. **Activities:** Fund raising.

See: *How to Use the Directory,* page 11.

GBR2510

TOOLS FOR SELF RELIANCE (TFSR)

Netley Marsh Workshops, Southampton SO40 7GY, United Kingdom.
Telephone: 44 (1703) 869697. *Fax:* 44 (1703) 868544. *E-mail:* tools@gn.apc.org. *Contact:* Mark Smith, Coordinator.

OBJECTIVES: To provide refurbished tools to co-operative and communal work projects in developing countries and to refugee communities in other countries. To promote the local production of tools in developing countries and to undertake development education in the United Kingdom.

GENERAL INFORMATION: *Creation:* 1978. *Affiliated to:* NADEC - World Development Movement. *Personnel/Total:* 807. *Salaried:* 7. *Volunteers:* 800. *Budget/Total 1993:* ECU 295000 (US$ 345000). *Financial sources:* Private: 65%. Public: 20%. Self-financing: 15%.

PUBLICATIONS: *Periodicals:* Elbow Grease (4) - Forging Links (3). *Annual report. List of publications.*

EVALUATION/RESEARCH: Evaluation reports available.

PLANNED ACTIVITIES: TFSR will organise an exhibition, a tool-making competition and seminar in Zimbabwe. TFSR will undertake a workshop for all European tool-sending organisations.

ACTIVITIES IN DEVELOPING REGIONS: Active in 7 country(ies). Works through local field partners. Sustainable Development Actions: Other; Rural development/agriculture; Small enterprises/informal sector/handicrafts. Regions: East Africa; Mexico and Central America; Southern Africa; West Africa.

INFORMATION AND EDUCATION ACTIVITIES: Topics: Children/youth/family; Employment/unemployment; International economic relations/trade/debt/finance; International relations/cooperation/development aid; Rural development/agriculture. Activities: Conferences/seminars/workshops/training activities; Information campaigns/exhibitions; Lobbying/advocacy; Other; Publishing/audiovisual materials/educational materials.

GBR2511

TOURISM CONCERN

Southlands College, Roehampton Institute, Wimbledon Parkside, London SW19 5NN, United Kingdom.
Telephone: 44 (181) 944 0464. *Fax:* 44 (181) 944 6583. *Contact:* Patricia Barnett, Co-ordinator.

OBJECTIVES: To campaign for just tourism. To support the rights of residents to be involved in the development and management of tourism. To promote sustainable tourism.

GENERAL INFORMATION: *Creation:* 1989. *Type of organisation:* network. *Affiliated to:* European Tourism Network (Germany) - Centre for Responsible Tourism (USA) -Ecumenical Coalition on Third World Tourism (Thailand). *Personnel/Total:* 16. *Salaried:* 6. *Volunteers:* 10. *Budget/Total 1993:* ECU 64000 (US$ 75000).

PUBLICATIONS: *Periodicals:* In Focus (4). *Annual report. List of publications.*

EVALUATION/RESEARCH: Undertakes research activities.

PLANNED ACTIVITIES: Tourism Concern will organise an international youth conference and will campaign about the displacement of people for tourism development.

INFORMATION AND EDUCATION ACTIVITIES: Topics: Ecology/environment/biodiversity; Gender issues/women; Health/sanitation/water; Human rights/peace/conflicts; International relations/cooperation/development aid; Other; Rural development/agriculture; Urban development/habitat. Activities: Broadcasting/cultural events; Conferences/seminars/workshops/training activities; Formal education; Fund raising; Information and documentation services/data bases; Information campaigns/exhibitions; Lobbying/advocacy; Publishing/audiovisual materials/educational materials.

GBR2512

TOWER HAMLETS INTERNATIONAL SOLIDARITY (THIS)

Oxford House, Derbyshire Street , London E2 6HG, United Kingdom.

Telephone: 44 (171) 739 1786. *Contact:* Helen Attewell.

GBR2513

TRADE UNION INTERNATIONAL RESEARCH AND EDUCATION GROUP (TUIREG)

Ruskin College, Walton Street, Oxford OX1 2HE, United Kingdom.
Telephone: 44 (1865) 54599/56564. *Fax:* 44 (1865) 511313. *Contact:* Jimmy Browne, Director.

OBJECTIVES: To establish links between trade unions in Europe and countries in the South. To use established trade union education and organisational structures to promote development.

GENERAL INFORMATION: *Creation:* 1976. *Type of organisation:* association of NGOs. *Affiliated to:* British Overseas NGOs for Development (United Kingdom) - EC-NGO Network (United Kingdom) - Development Education Association (United Kingdom). *Personnel/Total:* 5. *Salaried:* 4 of which: 1 in developing countries. *Budget/Total 1993:* ECU 181000 (US$ 210000). *Financial sources:* Private: 25%. Public: 45%. Self-financing: 30%.

PUBLICATIONS: *Periodicals:* TUIREG Newsletter (4). *Annual report. List of publications.*

EVALUATION/RESEARCH: Evaluation reports available. Undertakes research activities.

PLANNED ACTIVITIES: TUIREG will conduct a study of North-South industries and on the single European market and its effects on developing countries. TUIREG will carry out a health care training programme and will make available on E-mail the diary of trade union visitors from developing countries.

COMMENTS: Information activities related to the Commonwealth of Independent States.

ACTIVITIES IN DEVELOPING REGIONS: Present in developing regions. Works through local field partners. Sustainable Development Actions: Education/training/literacy; Gender issues/women; Health/sanitation/water. Regions: Caribbean; East Africa; Mexico and Central America; Southern Africa; West Africa.

INFORMATION AND EDUCATION ACTIVITIES: Topics: Education/training/literacy; Employment/unemployment; Gender issues/women; Health/sanitation/water; Human rights/peace/conflicts; International economic relations/trade/debt/finance; Poverty/living conditions. Activities: Conferences/seminars/workshops/training activities; Fund raising; Information and documentation services/data bases; Publishing/audiovisual materials/educational materials.

GBR2514

TRAIDCRAFT EXCHANGE

Kingsway, Team Valley Trading Estate, Gateshead NE11 0NE, United Kingdom.
Telephone: 44 (191) 491 0591. *Fax:* 44 (191) 482 2690. *Contact:* Graham Young, Director.

OBJECTIVES: To raise awareness and concern about issues of justice in trade. To encourage and support small business enterprises in developing countries whose aims and practices reflect concern for the needs of the workers.

GENERAL INFORMATION: *Creation:* 1986. *Affiliated to:* European Fair Trade Association (Netherlands). *Personnel/Total:* 24. *Salaried:* 24. *Budget/Total 1993:* ECU 961000 (US$ 1130000). *Financial sources:* Private: 65%. Public: 35%.

PUBLICATIONS: *Periodicals:* Traidcraft Exchange Magazine (3). *Annual report. List of publications.*

EVALUATION/RESEARCH: Evaluation reports available. Undertakes research activities.

ACTIVITIES IN DEVELOPING REGIONS: Active in 7 country(ies). Works through local field partners. Sustainable Development Actions: Small enterprises/informal sector/handicrafts. Regions: Central Asia and South Asia; East Africa; South East Asia; Southern Africa.

INFORMATION AND EDUCATION ACTIVITIES: Topics: International economic relations/trade/debt/finance. Activities: Conferences/semi-

nars/workshops/training activities; Formal education; Fund raising; Information and documentation services/data bases; Publishing/audiovisual materials/educational materials.

GBR2515

TRAX PROGRAMME SUPPORT

22 Warren Hill Road, Woodbridge, Ipswich IPIZ 4D4, United Kingdom.

Telephone: 44 (1394) 380518. *Fax:* 44 (1394) 380518. *Contact:* Christine Richardson.

OBJECTIVES: To relieve poverty in rural areas of Africa, by addressing the problems of environmental degradation and the consequent decreasing agricultural productivity. To provide technical and educational support for locally initiated development programmes.

GENERAL INFORMATION: *Creation:* 1987. *Personnel/Total:* 6. *Salaried:* 3 of which: 2 in developing countries. *Volunteers:* 3 of which: 3 in developing countries. *Budget/Total 1993:* ECU 45000 (US$ 53000). *Financial sources:* Private: 50%. Public: 50%.

PUBLICATIONS: *Annual report.*

EVALUATION/RESEARCH: Evaluation reports available.

PLANNED ACTIVITIES: Trax Programme Support will establish a training programme for other NGOs and government departments working in the region, will develop a resource centre to accommodate the needs of the community, and will expand their watershed management project into a larger area.

ACTIVITIES IN DEVELOPING REGIONS: Present in developing regions. Active in 1 country(ies). Maintains local field presence. Works through local field partners. **Sustainable Development Actions:** Democracy/good governance/institution building/participatory development; Ecology/environment/biodiversity; Education/training/literacy; Food/famine; Gender issues/women; Rural development/agriculture; Sending volunteers/experts/technical assistance; Small enterprises/informal sector/handicrafts. **Regions:** West Africa.

INFORMATION AND EDUCATION ACTIVITIES: Topics: Ecology/environment/biodiversity; Education/training/literacy; Food/famine; Gender issues/women; Health/sanitation/water; Rural development/agriculture; Urban development/habitat. **Activities:** Broadcasting/cultural events; Conferences/seminars/workshops/training activities; Exchanges/twinning/linking; Fund raising; Information and documentation services/data bases; Information campaigns/exhibitions; Publishing/audiovisual materials/educational materials.

GBR2516

TREE TRUST

Wellspring Cottage, Deerfold, Lingen, Bucknell, Shropshire SY7 0EE, United Kingdom.

Contact: Paul Caton-O'Grady.

GBR2517

TROPICAL HEALTH AND EDUCATION TRUST (THET)

21 Edenhurst Avenue, London SW6 3PD, United Kingdom.

Telephone: 44 (171) 927 2411. *Fax:* 44 (171) 637 4314. *Contact:* Professor Eldryd Parry.

OBJECTIVES: To enable training institutions for health care in poorer tropical countries to develop in a relevant and appropriate fashion.

GENERAL INFORMATION: *Creation:* 1989. *Affiliated to:* British Overseas NGOs for Development (United Kingdom). *Personnel/Total:* 2. *Salaried:* 2. *Budget/Total 1993:* ECU 192000 (US$ 225000). *Financial sources:* Private: 100%.

PUBLICATIONS: *Annual report.*

EVALUATION/RESEARCH: Evaluation reports available.

PLANNED ACTIVITIES: THET plans to strengthen links between tropical and European health care training institutions, to develop a programme for students' intervention in primary health care in Ethiopia and to undertake distance education projects.

ACTIVITIES IN DEVELOPING REGIONS: Present in developing regions. Active in 10 country(ies). Works through local field partners. **Sustainable Development Actions:** Education/training/literacy; Health/sanitation/water; Population/family planning/demography; Sending volunteers/experts/technical assistance. **Regions:** Central Africa; Central Asia and South Asia; East Africa; West Africa.

INFORMATION AND EDUCATION ACTIVITIES: Topics: Education/training/literacy; Health/sanitation/water. **Activities:** Conferences/seminars/workshops/training activities; Exchanges/twinning/linking; Fund raising; Lobbying/advocacy; Publishing/audiovisual materials/educational materials.

GBR2518

TWIN - DEVELOPMENT THROUGH TRADE ♦ TWIN -Développement par le Commerce

5-11 Worship Street, London EC2A 2BH, United Kingdom.

Telephone: 44 (171) 628 6878. *Fax:* 44 (171) 628 1859. *E-mail:* GreenNet:twin@gn.apc. *Contact:* Pauline Tiffen, Director.

OBJECTIVES: To overcome obstacles to independent trade in partnership with producing organisations. To ensure that more benefits of production remain in the hands of producers. To enable producers to implement social and economic development programmes on their own.

GENERAL INFORMATION: *Creation:* 1985. *Personnel/Total:* 18. *Salaried:* 16 of which: 1 in developing countries. *Volunteers:* 2. *Budget/Total 1993:* ECU 256000 (US$ 300000). *Financial sources:* Private: 25%. Public: 30%. Self-financing: 45%.

PUBLICATIONS: *Periodicals:* The Network (4). *Annual report. List of publications.*

EVALUATION/RESEARCH: Evaluation reports available. Undertakes research activities.

PLANNED ACTIVITIES: TWIN plans to compile a directory of minor commodities.

COMMENTS: TWIN produces a bi-monthly fax report, called TWINcafé Bulletin, for farmers and NGOs in 21 countries active in support of farmers who grow coffee. Undertakes activities in the Commonwealth of Independent States. Information activities related to the Commonwealth of Independent States.

ACTIVITIES IN DEVELOPING REGIONS: Present in developing regions. Active in 10 country(ies). Works through local field partners. **Sustainable Development Actions:** Debt/finance/trade; Ecology/environment/biodiversity; Education/training/literacy; Rural development/agriculture; Small enterprises/informal sector/handicrafts. **Regions:** Caribbean; East Africa; Mexico and Central America; South America; West Africa.

INFORMATION AND EDUCATION ACTIVITIES: Topics: International economic relations/trade/debt/finance. **Activities:** Broadcasting/cultural events; Conferences/seminars/workshops/training activities; Exchanges/twinning/linking; Formal education; Fund raising; Information and documentation services/data bases; Information campaigns/exhibitions; Lobbying/advocacy; Networking/electronic telecommunications; Other; Publishing/audiovisual materials/educational materials.

GBR2519

TZEDEK

26 Goodwyns Vale, London N10 2HA, United Kingdom.

GBR2520

UGANDA DEVELOPMENT SERVICES (UDS)

Castle View Cottage, Smithy Lane, Mouldsworth, Cheshire CH3 8AR, United Kingdom.

Telephone: 44 (1928) 740660. *Fax:* 44 (1928) 740660. *Contact:* John Maitland, Executive Secretary.

OBJECTIVES: To promote and protect the physical and mental well-being of disabled children in Uganda.

GENERAL INFORMATION: *Creation:* 1994. *Personnel/Total:* 2. *Salaried:* 1. *Volunteers:* 1. *Financial sources:* Self-financing: 100%.

PUBLICATIONS: *Annual report.*

See: *How to Use the Directory,* page 11.

PLANNED ACTIVITIES: UDS plans to establish a base in Uganda and to accumulate information useful to NGOs and about NGOs in Uganda. UDS will begin to offer facilitation to the smaller indigenous and foreign NGOs working in Uganda.

COMMENTS: Uganda Development Services is a newly established NGO which has not yet developed any programme of activities.

GBR2521

UGANDA SOCIETY FOR DISABLED CHILDREN (USDC)

Chichester House, 145A London Road, Kingston-upon-Thames, Surrey KT2 6NH, United Kingdom.

Telephone: 44 (181) 541 3736. **Fax:** 44 (181) 541 3736. **Contact:** Jonathan Hett.

OBJECTIVES: To advance the education and welfare of disabled children in Uganda by providing the equipment and tools needed to assist them to develop their physical and mental capacities and to improve their conditions of life.

GENERAL INFORMATION: Creation: 1984. **Affiliated to:** EEC-NGO Network (United Kingdom) - British Overseas NGOs for Development. **Personnel/Total:** 30. Salaried: 30 of which: 28 in developing countries. **Budget/Total 1993:** ECU 610000 (US$ 713000). **Financial sources:** Private: 35%. Public: 65%.

PUBLICATIONS: Periodicals: USDC News (1). Annual report.

PLANNED ACTIVITIES: USDC will investigate fund raising through East African donors and will develop a programme into four new districts of Uganda.

ACTIVITIES IN DEVELOPING REGIONS: Present in developing regions. Active in 1 country(ies). Maintains local field presence. Works through local field partners. **Sustainable Development Actions:** Children/youth/family; Gender issues/women; Health/sanitation/water; Rural development/agriculture. **Regions:** East Africa.

INFORMATION AND EDUCATION ACTIVITIES: Topics: Children/youth/family; Gender issues/women. **Activities:** Broadcasting/cultural events; Fund raising.

GBR2522

UK COMMITTEE FOR THE UNITED NATIONS CHILDREN'S FUND

55 Lincoln's Inn Fields, London WC2A 3NB, United Kingdom.

Telephone: 44 (171) 405 5592. **Fax:** 44 (171) 405 2332. **Contact:** Robert D. Smith, Director.

OBJECTIVES: To support the work of UNICEF throughout the world by fundraising and advocacy. To represent UNICEF in the United Kingdom.

GENERAL INFORMATION: Creation: 1956. **Personnel/Total:** 2060. Salaried: 60. Volunteers: 2000. **Budget/Total 1993:** ECU 17950000 (US$ 21030000). **Financial sources:** Private: 50%. Public: 50%.

PUBLICATIONS: Periodicals: Children First (3). Annual report. List of publications.

EVALUATION/RESEARCH: Evaluation reports available. Undertakes research activities.

PLANNED ACTIVITIES: The UK Committee for UNICEF plans to work in issues such as conflict, landmines, discrimination, children's rights, promotion of breastfeeding and debt.

COMMENTS: Information activities related to the Commonwealth of Independent States.

INFORMATION AND EDUCATION ACTIVITIES: Topics: Children/youth/family; Education/training/literacy; Emergency relief/refugees/humanitarian assistance; Food/famine; Gender issues/women; Health/sanitation/water; Human rights/peace/conflicts; International economic relations/trade/debt/finance; International relations/cooperation/development aid; Peace/ethnic conflicts/armament/disarmament; Population/family planning/demography; Poverty/living conditions; Racism/xenophobia/antisemitism; Refugees/migrants/ethnic groups. **Activities:** Conferences/seminars/workshops/training activities; Formal education; Fund

raising; Information and documentation services/data bases; Information campaigns/exhibitions; Lobbying/advocacy; Networking/electronic telecommunications; Publishing/audiovisual materials/educational materials.

GBR2523

UK JEWISH AID

33 Seymour Place, London W1H 6AT, United Kingdom.

Telephone: 44 (171) 7233442. **Fax:** 44 (171) 7233445. **Contact:** Michael Harris, Director.

OBJECTIVES: To relieve poverty, sickness and distress arising in any part of the world and amongst people of all races and religions. To initiate and maintain relief and development work in emergencies and other adversities.

GENERAL INFORMATION: Creation: 1989. **Personnel/Total:** 6. Salaried: 1. Volunteers: 5. **Budget/Total 1993:** ECU 282000 (US$ 330000). **Financial sources:** Private: 25%. Public: 75%.

PUBLICATIONS: Periodicals: UKJAID Newsletter (3). Annual report.

EVALUATION/RESEARCH: Evaluation reports available. Undertakes research activities.

PLANNED ACTIVITIES: UKJAID plans to support an agricultural project in Eritrea and educational projects in South Africa.

COMMENTS: Undertakes activities in the Commonwealth of Independent States.

ACTIVITIES IN DEVELOPING REGIONS: Works through local field partners. **Sustainable Development Actions:** Emergency relief/refugees/humanitarian assistance; Health/sanitation/water; Sending volunteers/experts/technical assistance. **Regions:** East Africa; Southern Africa.

INFORMATION AND EDUCATION ACTIVITIES: Topics: Emergency relief/refugees/humanitarian assistance; Refugees/migrants/ethnic groups. **Activities:** Fund raising; Lobbying/advocacy.

GBR2524

UNITED KINGDOM FOUNDATION FOR THE PEOPLES OF THE SOUTH PACIFIC (UKFSP)

32 Howe Park, Edinburgh EH10 7HF, United Kingdom.

Telephone: 44 (131) 445 5010. **Fax:** 44 (131) 445 5255. **Contact:** Dorothy McIntosh, Director.

OBJECTIVES: To assist the peoples of the South Pacific in economic and human development, in education and in the sustainable use of local resources.

GENERAL INFORMATION: Creation: 1981. **Personnel/Total:** 41. Salaried: 31 of which: 27 in developing countries. Volunteers: 10 of which: 9 in developing countries. **Budget/Total 1993:** ECU 385000 (US$ 451000). **Financial sources:** Private: 25%. Public: 70%. Self-financing: 5%.

PUBLICATIONS: Periodicals: UKFSP Newsletter (4). Annual report.

EVALUATION/RESEARCH: Evaluation reports available. Undertakes research activities.

PLANNED ACTIVITIES: UKFSP plans to begin activities into peripheral countries of South East Asia, to organise a seminar and a development education campaign on sustainable forestry.

ACTIVITIES IN DEVELOPING REGIONS: Active in 6 country(ies). Maintains local field presence. Works through local field partners. **Sustainable Development Actions:** Children/youth/family; Democracy/good governance/institution building/participatory development; Ecology/environment/biodiversity; Education/training/literacy; Emergency relief/refugees/humanitarian assistance; Food/famine; Gender issues/women; Health/sanitation/water; Human rights/peace/conflicts; Population/family planning/demography; Rural development/agriculture; Sending volunteers/experts/technical assistance; Small enterprises/informal sector/handicrafts. **Regions:** Oceania.

INFORMATION AND EDUCATION ACTIVITIES: Topics: Children/youth/family; Ecology/environment/biodiversity; Education/training/literacy;

Voir : *Comment utiliser le répertoire,* page 11.

Emergency relief/refugees/humanitarian assistance; Food/famine; Gender issues/women; Health/sanitation/water; Peace/ethnic conflicts/armament/disarmament; Population/family planning/demography; Poverty/living conditions; Refugees/migrants/ethnic groups; Rural development/agriculture. **Activities:** Conferences/seminars/workshops/training activities; Fund raising; Information campaigns/exhibitions; Publishing/audiovisual materials/educational materials.

GBR2525

UNITED NATIONS ASSOCIATION INTERNATIONAL SERVICE (UNAIS)

Suite 3A, Hunter House, 57 Goodramgate, York, N. Yorks YO1 2LS, United Kingdom.

Telephone: 44 (1904) 647799. **Fax:** 44 (1904) 652353. **Contact:** Jane Carter, General Secretary.

OBJECTIVES: To promote long-term development by providing skilled and experienced technicians to locally organised initiatives in Latin America, West Africa and the Middle East.

GENERAL INFORMATION: Creation: 1953. **Affiliated to:** British Volunteer Agencies Liaison Group - British Overseas NGOs for Development. **Personnel/Total:** 15. Salaried: 15 of which: 5 in developing countries. **Budget/Total 1993:** ECU 1541000 (US$ 1800000). **Financial sources:** Private: 25%. Public: 75%.

PUBLICATIONS: Periodicals: VIVA (3). Annual report.

ACTIVITIES IN DEVELOPING REGIONS: Active in 5 country(ies). Maintains local field presence. Works through local field partners. **Sustainable Development Actions:** Children/youth/family; Democracy/good governance/institution building/participatory development; Ecology/environment/biodiversity; Education/training/literacy; Gender issues/women; Health/sanitation/water; Human rights/peace/conflicts; Rural development/agriculture; Sending volunteers/experts/technical assistance; Small enterprises/informal sector/handicrafts; Urban development/habitat. **Regions:** Middle East; South America; West Africa.

INFORMATION AND EDUCATION ACTIVITIES: Topics: Children/youth/family; Ecology/environment/biodiversity; Education/training/literacy; Gender issues/women; Health/sanitation/water; Human rights/peace/conflicts; Poverty/living conditions; Rural development/agriculture; Urban development/habitat. **Activities:** Fund raising; Publishing/audiovisual materials/educational materials.

GBR2526

UNITED NATIONS ASSOCIATION OF GREAT BRITAIN AND NORTHERN IRELAND (UNA-UK) ♦ L'Association pour les Nations Unies du Royaume-Uni

3 Whitehall Court, London SW1A 2EL, United Kingdom.

Telephone: 44 (171) 930 2931. **Fax:** 44 (171) 930 5893. **E-mail:** UNA@MCRI.Poptel.org.uk. **Contact:** Malcolm Harper, Director.

OBJECTIVES: To encourage a better understanding and use of the United Nations, its agencies, of programmes by the government, parliament and action at local and national levels.

GENERAL INFORMATION: Creation: 1945. **Affiliated to:** World Federation of UNAs - Human Rights Network. **Personnel/Total:** 16. Salaried: 16. Volunteers: var. **Budget/Total 1993:** ECU 705000 (US$ 826000). **Financial sources:** Private: 50%. Public: 8%. Self-financing: 42%.

PUBLICATIONS: Periodicals: New World (4). Annual report. List of publications.

EVALUATION/RESEARCH: Undertakes research activities.

PLANNED ACTIVITIES: UNA-UK will launch campaigns on refugees, conflict and the role of the United Nations in sustainable development.

INFORMATION AND EDUCATION ACTIVITIES: Topics: Children/youth/family; Ecology/environment/biodiversity; Emergency relief/refugees/humanitarian assistance; Human rights/peace/conflicts; International relations/cooperation/development aid; Peace/ethnic conflicts/armament/disarmament; Racism/xenophobia/antisemitism; Refugees/migrants/ethnic groups. **Activities:** Conferences/seminars/workshops/

training activities; Fund raising; Information campaigns/exhibitions; Lobbying/advocacy; Publishing/audiovisual materials/educational materials.

GBR2527

UNITED NATIONS ENVIRONMENT AND DEVELOPMENT UK COMMITTEE

c/o UNA, 3 Whitehall Court, London SWIA 2EL, United Kingdom.

Telephone: 44 (171) 930 2931. **Fax:** 44 (171) 930 5843. **E-mail:** UNA@MCRI.poptel.org.uk.. **Contact:** Felix Dodds, Director.

OBJECTIVES: To promote global environmental protection and sustainable development, particularly through support of UN and inter-governmental institutions.

GENERAL INFORMATION: Creation: 1993. **Type of organisation:** coordinating body. **Personnel/Total:** 4. Salaried: 2. Volunteers: 2. **Budget/Total 1993:** ECU 90000 (US$ 105000). **Financial sources:** Private: 10%. Public: 45%. Self-financing: 45%.

PUBLICATIONS: Periodicals: Connections (4) - Reports (4). Annual report. List of publications.

INFORMATION AND EDUCATION ACTIVITIES: Topics: Ecology/environment/biodiversity; Employment/unemployment; Health/sanitation/water; International economic relations/trade/debt/finance; International relations/cooperation/development aid; Poverty/living conditions; Rural development/agriculture; Urban development/habitat. **Activities:** Conferences/seminars/workshops/training activities; Information campaigns/exhibitions; Lobbying/advocacy; Publishing/audiovisual materials/educational materials.

GBR2528

UNITED WORLD COLLEGES INTERNATIONAL (UWC) ♦ Collèges du Monde Uni

London House, Mecklenburgh Square, London WC1N 2AB, United Kingdom.

Telephone: 44 (171) 833 2626. **Fax:** 44 (171) 837 3102. **Contact:** Mr. Jeremy R. Varcoe, Director General.

GBR2529

URBANAID

79 Amsterdam Road, London Yard, London E14 3UU, United Kingdom.

Telephone: 44 (1342) 870 270. **Fax:** 44 (1342) 870 898. **Contact:** Ian Eiloart, Honorary Treasurer.

OBJECTIVES: To provide health care and health education for women and children in West Africa.

GENERAL INFORMATION: Creation: 1988. **Personnel/Total:** 39. Salaried: 38 of which: 38 in developing countries. Volunteers: 1 of which: 1 in developing countries. **Financial sources:** Private: 57%. Public: 29%. Self-financing: 14%.

PUBLICATIONS: Periodicals: Newsletter (2). Annual report.

EVALUATION/RESEARCH: Evaluation reports available.

ACTIVITIES IN DEVELOPING REGIONS: Present in developing regions. Active in 1 country(ies). Maintains local field presence. **Sustainable Development Actions:** Children/youth/family; Gender issues/women; Health/sanitation/water; Population/family planning/demography. **Regions:** West Africa.

INFORMATION AND EDUCATION ACTIVITIES: Topics: Children/youth/family; Gender issues/women; Health/sanitation/water; Population/family planning/demography. **Activities:** Lobbying/advocacy.

GBR2530

VETAID

Center for Tropical Veterinary Medicine, Easter Bush, Roslin, Midlothian EH25 9RG, Scotland, United Kingdom.

Telephone: 44 (131) 445 3129. **Fax:** 44 (131) 445 3129. **Contact:** Jeremy Cosmo Davies, National Coordinator.

OBJECTIVES: To prevent suffering and hunger by active promotion of animal health, welfare and improved husbandry. To enhance the envi-

                      See: *How to Use the Directory,* page 11.

ronment within which animals live and that of people who depend upon livestock for their survival.

GENERAL INFORMATION: *Creation:* 1989. *Affiliated to:* Vétérinaires Sans Frontières. *Personnel/Total:* 14. *Salaried:* 13 of which: 10 in developing countries. *Volunteers:* 1. *Budget/Total 1993:* ECU 256000 (US$ 300000).

PUBLICATIONS: *Periodicals:* VETAID News (2) - VETAID Programme News (1). *List of publications.*

EVALUATION/RESEARCH: Evaluation reports available. Undertakes research activities.

PLANNED ACTIVITIES: VETAID plans to undertake several institutional programmes in Somaliland, Somalia and Tanzania, a restocking programme in Mozambique and an ethno-veterinary development in Tanzania.

ACTIVITIES IN DEVELOPING REGIONS: Present in developing regions. Active in 4 country(ies). Maintains local field presence. Works through local field partners. **Sustainable Development Actions:** Democracy/good governance/institution building/participatory development; Gender issues/women; Other; Sending volunteers/experts/technical assistance; Small enterprises/informal sector/handicrafts. **Regions:** Central Africa; Central Asia and South Asia; East Africa; Southern Africa; West Africa.

INFORMATION AND EDUCATION ACTIVITIES: Topics: Emergency relief/refugees/humanitarian assistance; International relations/cooperation/development aid; Other; Poverty/living conditions. **Activities:** Fund raising; Lobbying/advocacy; Networking/electronic telecommunications; Publishing/audiovisual materials/educational materials.

GBR2531
VIETNAMESE REFUGEES COMMUNITY IN LONDON
Community Hall, North Peckham Estate, Hordle Promenade East, London SE15 6JB, United Kingdom.
Telephone: 44 (171) 703 0036. *Contact:* Tran Van Tong, Chairman.

GBR2532
VILLAGE SERVICE TRUST
68 High Street, Hail Weston, Huntingdon, Cambridgeshire PE19 4JW, United Kingdom.
Telephone: 44 (1480) 473437. *Contact:* Tony Huckle, Secretary.

OBJECTIVES: To provide assistance for medical and development projects in India.

GENERAL INFORMATION: *Creation:* 1977. *Affiliated to:* India-UK Association (United Kingdom). *Personnel/Total:* 3. *Salaried:* 1 of which: 1 in developing countries. *Volunteers:* 2. *Budget/Total 1993:* ECU 64000 (US$ 75000). *Financial sources:* Private: 80%. Public: 20%.

PUBLICATIONS: *Periodicals:* VST News (2). *Annual report.*

EVALUATION/RESEARCH: Evaluation reports available.

ACTIVITIES IN DEVELOPING REGIONS: Active in 1 country(ies). Maintains local field presence. Works through local field partners. **Sustainable Development Actions:** Children/youth/family; Democracy/good governance/institution building/participatory development; Education/training/literacy; Gender issues/women; Health/sanitation/water; Rural development/agriculture; Small enterprises/informal sector/handicrafts. **Regions:** Central Asia and South Asia.

INFORMATION AND EDUCATION ACTIVITIES: Topics: Children/youth/family; Education/training/literacy; Employment/unemployment; Gender issues/women; Health/sanitation/water; International relations/cooperation/development aid; Poverty/living conditions; Rural development/agriculture. **Activities:** Fund raising.

GBR2533
VISION AID OVERSEAS (VAO)
56-66 Highlands Road, Leatherhead, Surrey KT22 8NR, United Kingdom.
Telephone: 44 (1372) 360822. *Fax:* 44 (1372) 360822. *Contact:* Helen Brooke, Chairman.

OBJECTIVES: To provide eyecare, spectacles and training in refraction and optical workshop techniques in developing countries.

GENERAL INFORMATION: *Creation:* 1985. *Personnel/Total:* 45. *Salaried:* 2. *Volunteers:* 43 of which: 43 in developing countries. *Budget/Total 1993:* ECU 208000 (US$ 243000). *Financial sources:* Private: 60%. Public: 30%. *Self-financing:* 10%.

PUBLICATIONS: *Periodicals:* Outlook (2). *Annual report.*

PLANNED ACTIVITIES: Vision Aid Overseas will set up a spectacle workshop and training programme in Uganda, Sierra Leone and Malawi.

COMMENTS: The collection and analysis of second-hand spectacles is carried out via the prison service. Prisoners are trained by volunteers of Vision Aid Overseas to clean and analyse spectacles for use in developing countries.

ACTIVITIES IN DEVELOPING REGIONS: Present in developing regions. Active in 6 country(ies). Works through local field partners. **Sustainable Development Actions:** Education/training/literacy; Health/sanitation/water; Sending volunteers/experts/technical assistance; Small enterprises/informal sector/handicrafts. **Regions:** East Africa; South East Asia; West Africa.

INFORMATION AND EDUCATION ACTIVITIES: Topics: Health/sanitation/water. **Activities:** Conferences/seminars/workshops/training activities; Formal education; Publishing/audiovisual materials/educational materials.

GBR2534
VISION INTERNATIONAL HEALTHCARE
Samarkand, Camden Park, Tunbridge Wells, Kent TN2 4WT, United Kingdom.
Contact: Howard F. Harper, Chairman.

GBR2535
VOLUNTARY SERVICE OVERSEAS (VSO)
317 Putney Bridge Road, London SW15 2PN, United Kingdom.
Telephone: 44 (181) 780 2266. *Fax:* 44 (181) 780 1326. *Contact:* David Green, Director.

OBJECTIVES: To enable men and women to work alongside people in poorer countries in order to share skills, build capabilities and promote international understanding and action, in the pursuit of a more equitable world.

GENERAL INFORMATION: *Creation:* 1958. *Affiliated to:* British Volunteer Agencies Liaison Group (United Kingdom) - British Overseas NGOs for Development (United Kingdom) - European Forum on Development Service (Germany) - National Council for Voluntary Organisations (United Kingdom). *Personnel/Total:* 2050. *Salaried:* 300 of which: 150 in developing countries. *Volunteers:* 1750 of which: 1750 in developing countries. *Budget/Total 1993:* ECU 25261000 (US$ 29590000). *Financial sources:* Private: 20%. Public: 80%.

PUBLICATIONS: *Periodicals:* Orbit (4). *Annual report. List of publications.*

EVALUATION/RESEARCH: Evaluation reports available.

PLANNED ACTIVITIES: VSO plans to raise awareness in the United Kingdom of development issues.

COMMENTS: Undertakes activities in the Commonwealth of Independent States. Information activities related to the Commonwealth of Independent States.

ACTIVITIES IN DEVELOPING REGIONS: Present in developing regions. Active in 55 country(ies). Maintains local field presence. Works through local field partners. **Sustainable Development Actions:** Children/youth/family; Democracy/good governance/institution building/participatory development; Ecology/environment/biodiversity; Education/training/literacy; Health/sanitation/water; Rural development/agriculture; Sending volunteers/experts/technical assistance; Small enterprises/informal sector/handicrafts; Urban development/habitat. **Regions:** Caribbean; Central Asia and South Asia; East Africa; East Asia; Mexico and Central America; North Africa; Oceania; South America; South East Asia; Southern Africa; West Africa.

Voir : *Comment utiliser le répertoire,* page 11.

INFORMATION AND EDUCATION ACTIVITIES: Topics: Children/youth/ family; Culture/tradition/religion; Ecology/environment/biodiversity; Education/training/literacy; Gender issues/women; Health/sanitation/water; Human rights/peace/conflicts; International relations/cooperation/development aid; Poverty/living conditions; Rural development/agriculture; Urban development/habitat. Activities: Conferences/seminars/workshops/training activities; Fund raising; Information campaigns/exhibitions; Publishing/audiovisual materials/educational materials.

GBR2536

VOLUNTEER MISSIONARY MOVEMENT, UNITED KINGDOM (VMM)

VMN Comboni House, London Road, Sunningdale, Berks SL5 OJY, United Kingdom.

Telephone: 44 (1344) 875380. Fax: 44 (1344) 875280. Contact: Maggie Prowse, General Coordinator.

OBJECTIVES: To recruit, prepare and send Christian volunteers to live and work in development projects in Africa. To promote mission awareness and development education, and encourage a Christian lifestyle in industrialized countries.

GENERAL INFORMATION: Creation: 1969. Affiliated to: AIDS Consortiun (United Kingdom) - Council of Churches for Britain and Ireland (United Kingdom) - British Overseas NGOs for Development (United Kingdom). Personnel/Total: 74. Salaried: 11. Volunteers: 63 of which: 63 in developing countries. Budget/Total 1993: ECU 180000 (US$ 210000). Financial sources: Private: 95%. Self-financing: 5%.

PUBLICATIONS: Periodicals: VMM Newsletter (3). Annual report.

ACTIVITIES IN DEVELOPING REGIONS: Present in developing regions. Active in 6 country(ies). Works through local field partners. Sustainable Development Actions: Children/youth/family; Democracy/good governance/institution building/participatory development; Education/training/literacy; Emergency relief/refugees/humanitarian assistance; Health/sanitation/water; Rural development/agriculture; Sending volunteers/experts/technical assistance; Small enterprises/informal sector/handicrafts. Regions: East Africa; Southern Africa.

INFORMATION AND EDUCATION ACTIVITIES: Topics: Children/youth/ family; Culture/tradition/religion; Gender issues/women; Health/sanitation/water; International economic relations/trade/debt/finance; International relations/cooperation/development aid; Poverty/living conditions; Racism/xenophobia/antisemitism; Rural development/agriculture; Urban development/habitat. Activities: Conferences/seminars/workshops/ training activities; Exchanges/twinning/linking; Information campaigns/ exhibitions.

GBR2537

WAR ON WANT (WOW)

37-39 Great Guildford Street, London SE1 0ES, United Kingdom.

Telephone: 44 (171) 620 1111. Fax: 44 (171) 261 9291. E-mail: WOW @gn.apc.org. Contact: Giampi Alhadeff, Director.

OBJECTIVES: To empower communities and organisations in the North and South which support practical projects aimed at building a future free from poverty and oppression.

GENERAL INFORMATION: Creation: 1953. Affiliated to: Charity Forum - UK NGO AIDS Consortium - GreenNet - Mozambique Angola Committee - GEONET - TUIREG - Development Education Association - NPC - NWN - NCVO -Industrial Society - ACENVO - BOND - IWA - EC-NGO Network - Refugee Council -IBT - Alliance for Rights of Indigenous People - NGO Finance - UNED-UK - ICFS. Personnel/Total: 14. Salaried: 8. Volunteers: 6. Budget/Total 1993: ECU 1513000 (US$ 1772000). Financial sources: Private: 83%. Public: 17%.

PUBLICATIONS: Periodicals: (3). Annual report. List of publications.

EVALUATION/RESEARCH: Undertakes research activities.

PLANNED ACTIVITIES: WOW plans to campaign for the "Human Right to Development" and against "Violence against Women". WOW will charter development education campaign materials, relating to the Third World Debt and urbanisation, in Bangladesh.

ACTIVITIES IN DEVELOPING REGIONS: Active in 8 country(ies). Works through local field partners. Sustainable Development Actions: Democracy/good governance/institution building/participatory development; Ecology/environment/biodiversity; Education/training/literacy; Gender issues/women; Health/sanitation/water; Human rights/peace/ conflicts; Rural development/agriculture; Sending volunteers/experts/ technical assistance; Small enterprises/informal sector/handicrafts; Urban development/habitat. Regions: Middle East; South America; South East Asia; Southern Africa.

INFORMATION AND EDUCATION ACTIVITIES: Topics: Ecology/environment/biodiversity; Education/training/literacy; Employment/unemployment; Gender issues/women; Health/sanitation/water; Human rights/peace/conflicts; Poverty/living conditions; Refugees/migrants/ethnic groups; Rural development/agriculture; Urban development/habitat. Activities: Conferences/seminars/workshops/training activities; Fund raising; Information and documentation services/data bases; Information campaigns/exhibitions; Lobbying/advocacy.

GBR2538

WATERAID

1 Queen Anne's Gate, London SW1H 9BT, United Kingdom.

Telephone: 44 (171) 233 4800. Fax: 44 (171) 233 3161. Contact: Jon Lane, Director.

OBJECTIVES: To support low-cost, low-technology, people-participant water and sanitation improvements in developing countries.

GENERAL INFORMATION: Creation: 1981. Personnel/Total: 75. Salaried: 40 of which: 18 in developing countries. Volunteers: 35. (US$ 7810000). Financial sources: Private: 70%. Public: 30%.

PUBLICATIONS: Periodicals: Oasis (2) - On Tap (3). Annual report. List of publications.

EVALUATION/RESEARCH: Undertakes research activities.

PLANNED ACTIVITIES: Wateraid plans to develop a new primary school resource pack and to collate a secondary school pack in collaboration with water companies.

ACTIVITIES IN DEVELOPING REGIONS: Present in developing regions. Active in 15 country(ies). Maintains local field presence. Works through local field partners. Sustainable Development Actions: Health/sanitation/water. Regions: Central Asia and South Asia; East Africa; Southern Africa; West Africa.

INFORMATION AND EDUCATION ACTIVITIES: Topics: Health/sanitation/water. Activities: Broadcasting/cultural events; Fund raising; Information and documentation services/data bases; Information campaigns/ exhibitions; Publishing/audiovisual materials/educational materials.

GBR2539

WELSH CENTRE FOR INTERNATIONAL AFFAIRS (WCIA)

Temple of Peace, Cathays Park, Cardiff CF1 3AP, United Kingdom.

Telephone: 44 (222) 228549. Contact: W.R. Davies, Director.

OBJECTIVES: To promote awareness of international issues, particularly the work of the United Nations and its agencies.

GENERAL INFORMATION: Creation: 1973. Personnel/Total: 9. Salaried: 8. Volunteers: 1. Budget/Total 1993: ECU 128000 (US$ 150000). Financial sources: Private: 7%. Public: 18%. Self-financing: 75%.

PLANNED ACTIVITIES: WCIA will help organise several events to celebrate the 50th anniversary of the United Nations.

INFORMATION AND EDUCATION ACTIVITIES: Topics: International relations/cooperation/development aid. Activities: Conferences/seminars/workshops/training activities; Lobbying/advocacy.

GBR2540

WILBERFORCE COUNCIL

Salisbury Hall Park Road, Hull HU3 1TD, United Kingdom.

Telephone: 44 (1482) 26848. Fax: 44 (1482) 568756. Contact: Jack Lennard, Co-ordinator/Executive Director.

See: How to Use the Directory, page 11.

GBR2541
WOMANKIND WORLDWIDE

122 Whitechapel High Street, London E1 7PT, United Kingdom.

Telephone: 44 (171) 247 6931. *Fax:* 44 (171) 247 3436. *E-mail:* Womankind @gn.atc.org. *Contact:* Kate Young, Executive Director.

OBJECTIVES: To finance and support women's initiatives in developing countries. To offer partnership, training and material support to a wide range of groups working to improve women's social position and to overcome their poverty, lack of education and poor health.

GENERAL INFORMATION: *Creation:* 1989. *Affiliated to:* Gender Network (United Kingdom). *Personnel/Total:* 11. *Salaried:* 8. *Volunteers:* 3. *Budget/Total 1993:* ECU 671000 (US$ 785000). *Financial sources:* Private: 81%. Public: 15%. Self-financing: 4%.

PUBLICATIONS: *Periodicals:* Newsletter (2) - Annual Review (1). *Annual report.*

EVALUATION/RESEARCH: Evaluation reports available. Undertakes research activities.

PLANNED ACTIVITIES: Womankind Worldwide plans to campaign against violence against women.

COMMENTS: Undertakes activities in the Commonwealth of Independent States.

ACTIVITIES IN DEVELOPING REGIONS: Active in 47 country(ies). Works through local field partners. **Sustainable Development Actions:** Gender issues/women. **Regions:** Caribbean; Central Africa; Central Asia and South Asia; East Africa; East Asia; Mexico and Central America; Middle East; North Africa; Oceania; South America; South East Asia; Southern Africa; West Africa.

INFORMATION AND EDUCATION ACTIVITIES: Topics: Gender issues/ women. **Activities:** Exchanges/twinning/linking; Fund raising; Information and documentation services/data bases; Information campaigns/ exhibitions; Lobbying/advocacy; Publishing/audiovisual materials/educational materials.

GBR2542
WOMEN AID / UNIFEM

3 Whitehall Court, London SW1A 2EL, United Kingdom.

Contact: Pida Ripley.

GBR2543
WOMEN WORKING WORLDWIDE

190 Upper Street, Box 92, London N1 1RQ, United Kingdom.

GBR2544
THE WOMEN'S ENVIRONMENTAL NETWORK (WEN)

Aberdeen Studios, 22 Highbury Grove, London N5 2EA, United Kingdom.

Telephone: 44 (171) 354 8823. *Fax:* 44 (171) 354 0464. *E-mail:* wenuk@gnet.apc.org.. *Contact:* Angela Mawle, Chief Executive.

OBJECTIVES: To inform, educate and empower women who care about the planet. To address environmental and health issues that specifically affect women.

GENERAL INFORMATION: *Creation:* 1988. *Affiliated to:* National Alliance of Women's Organisations - Women in Development Europe. *Personnel/Total:* 41. *Salaried:* 6. *Volunteers:* 35. *Budget/Total 1993:* ECU 231000 (US$ 270000). *Financial sources:* Private: 30%. Public: 30%. Self-financing: 40%.

PUBLICATIONS: *Periodicals:* Newsletter (4). *List of publications.*

EVALUATION/RESEARCH: Evaluation reports available. Undertakes research activities.

COMMENTS: Undertakes activities in the Commonwealth of Independent States. Information activities related to the Commonwealth of Independent States.

ACTIVITIES IN DEVELOPING REGIONS: Works through local field partners.

INFORMATION AND EDUCATION ACTIVITIES: Topics: Ecology/environment/biodiversity; Food/famine; Gender issues/women; Health/sanitation/water; International economic relations/trade/debt/finance; Population/family planning/demography. **Activities:** Broadcasting/cultural events; Conferences/seminars/workshops/training activities; Exchanges/twinning/linking; Formal education; Fund raising; Information and documentation services/data bases; Information campaigns/exhibitions; Lobbying/advocacy; Networking/electronic telecommunications; Publishing/audiovisual materials/educational materials.

GBR2545
WORDS AND PICTURES

Tudor St Anthony, Muchelney, Somerset TA10 0DL, United Kingdom.

Telephone: 44 (1458) 251727. *Fax:* 44 (1458) 251749. *Contact:* Nick Cater, Director.

OBJECTIVES: To provide consultancy services specialising in information, media and communication issues relating to the environment, development, education, health and human rights.

GENERAL INFORMATION: *Creation:* 1986. *Personnel/Total:* 2. *Salaried:* 2. *Budget/Total 1993:* ECU 128000 (US$ 150000). *Financial sources:* Self-financing: 100%.

EVALUATION/RESEARCH: Undertakes research activities.

COMMENTS: Words and Pictures works with the International Federation of Red Cross and Red Crescent Societies in gathering information on issues of development and disaster relief. Undertakes activities in the Commonwealth of Independent States. Information activities related to the Commonwealth of Independent States.

ACTIVITIES IN DEVELOPING REGIONS: Present in developing regions. Works through local field partners.

INFORMATION AND EDUCATION ACTIVITIES: Topics: Children/youth/ family; Culture/tradition/religion; Ecology/environment/biodiversity; Education/training/literacy; Emergency relief/refugees/humanitarian assistance; Employment/unemployment; Food/famine; Gender issues/ women; Health/sanitation/water; Human rights/peace/conflicts; International economic relations/trade/debt/finance; International relations/ cooperation/development aid; Peace/ethnic conflicts/armament/disarmament; Population/family planning/demography; Poverty/living conditions; Racism/xenophobia/antisemitism; Refugees/migrants/ethnic groups; Rural development/agriculture; Urban development/habitat. **Activities:** Broadcasting/cultural events; Conferences/seminars/workshops/training activities; Information and documentation services/data bases; Information campaigns/exhibitions; Lobbying/advocacy; Networking/electronic telecommunications; Publishing/audiovisual materials/educational materials.

GBR2546
WORLD ASSOCIATION FOR CHRISTIAN COMMUNICATION (WACC) ♦ Association mondiale pour la communication chrétienne

357 Kennington Lane, London SE11 5QY, United Kingdom.

Telephone: 44 (171) 582 9139. *Fax:* 44 (171) 753 0340. *E-mail:* wacc@gn.apc.org.. *Contact:* Rev. Carlos Valle, General Secretary.

OBJECTIVES: To assist churches, organisations and individuals who wish to give high priority to Christian values in the world's communication and development needs.

GENERAL INFORMATION: *Creation:* 1975. *Type of organisation:* association of NGOs. *Member organisations:* 406. *Personnel/Total:* 61. *Salaried:* 21. *Volunteers:* 40 of which: 40 in developing countries.

PUBLICATIONS: *Periodicals:* Media Development (4) - Action (10). *Annual report. List of publications.*

ACTIVITIES IN DEVELOPING REGIONS: Maintains local field presence. Works through local field partners. **Sustainable Development Actions:** Democracy/good governance/institution building/participatory development; Education/training/literacy; Human rights/peace/conflicts; Other. **Regions:** Caribbean; Central Africa; Central Asia and South Asia; East Africa; East Asia; Mexico and Central America; Middle East; North Africa; Oceania; South America; South East Asia; Southern Africa; West Africa.

Voir : *Comment utiliser le répertoire,* page 11.

INFORMATION AND EDUCATION ACTIVITIES: Topics: Culture/tradition/religion; Education/training/literacy; Human rights/peace/conflicts; Other. **Activities:** Conferences/seminars/workshops/training activities; Lobbying/advocacy; Publishing/audiovisual materials/educational materials.

GBR2547

WORLD ASSOCIATION OF GIRL GUIDES AND GIRL SCOUTS (WAGGGS) ♦ Association mondiale des Guides et des Eclaireuses

12c Lyndhurst Road, London NW3 5PQ, United Kingdom.

Telephone: 44 (171) 794 1181. *Fax:* 44 (171) 431 3764. *Contact:* Doris Riehm, Chairman.

GBR2548

WORLD DEVELOPMENT MOVEMENT (WDM)

25 Beehive Place, London SW9 7QR, United Kingdom.

Telephone: 44 (171) 737 6215. *Fax:* 44 (171) 274 8232. *Contact:* Roger Briottet, Director.

OBJECTIVES: To campaign for changes in the aid policies at the British government level, at the European Parliament and in international bodies such as the World Bank and the IMF, to protect the interests of the poor in the Third World.

GENERAL INFORMATION: *Creation:* 1969. ***Affiliated to:*** ICDA - Debt Crisis Network - Aid and Environment Group - EC-NGO Liaison Committee. ***Personnel/Total:*** 34. *Salaried:* 14. *Volunteers:* 20. ***Budget/Total 1993:*** ECU 670000 (US$ 784000). ***Financial sources:*** *Private:* 30%. *Public:* 13%. *Self-financing:* 57%.

PUBLICATIONS: *Periodicals:* SPUR (6). *Annual report. List of publications.*

PLANNED ACTIVITIES: WDM plans a new campaign on transnational companies.

INFORMATION AND EDUCATION ACTIVITIES: Topics: International relations/cooperation/development aid. **Activities:** Information campaigns/exhibitions; Lobbying/advocacy.

GBR2549

WORLD EDUCATION BERKSHIRE (WEB)

c/o Reading International Support Centre, 103 London Street, Reading, Berkshire RG1 4QA, United Kingdom.

Telephone: 44 (1734) 586692/594357.

GBR2550

WORLD ORT UNION (ORT)

ORT House, Sumpter Close, Finchley Road, London NW3 5HR, United Kingdom.

Telephone: 44 (171) 431 1333. *Fax:* 44 (171) 435 4784. *Contact:* S. Feldman, Director.

OBJECTIVES: To help the individual become self-sustaining and to participate in general social and economic development. To sponsor, operate, maintain and provide assistance for vocational and technical schools, apprenticeship programmes and adult training workshops.

GENERAL INFORMATION: *Creation:* 1880. ***Type of organisation:*** association of NGOs. ***Member organisations:*** 38. ***Personnel/Total:*** 16500. *Salaried:* 10500 of which: 2000 in developing countries. *Volunteers:* 6000 of which: 300 in developing countries. ***Budget/Total 1993:*** ECU 193791000 (US$ 227000000). ***Financial sources:*** *Private:* 9%. *Public:* 85%. *Self-financing:* 6%.

PUBLICATIONS: *Periodicals:* WORLD ORT UNION YEARBOOK (1). *Annual report.*

PLANNED ACTIVITIES: ORT will undertake programmes in training and human resources management and community-based projects for mothers and children. ORT plans to support an information technology and multi-media resource centre. ORT will provide technical assistance to the Ivory Coast Ministry of Education.

COMMENTS: Undertakes activities in the Commonwealth of Independent States. Information activities related to the Commonwealth of Independent States.

ACTIVITIES IN DEVELOPING REGIONS: Present in developing regions. Active in 18 country(ies). Maintains local field presence. Works through local field partners. **Sustainable Development Actions:** Education/training/literacy; Gender issues/women; Health/sanitation/water; Population/family planning/demography; Rural development/agriculture; Sending volunteers/experts/technical assistance; Small enterprises/informal sector/handicrafts. **Regions:** Caribbean; Central Africa; Central Asia and South Asia; East Africa; East Asia; Mexico and Central America; North Africa; South America; South East Asia; Southern Africa; West Africa.

INFORMATION AND EDUCATION ACTIVITIES: Topics: Education/training/literacy; Gender issues/women; Health/sanitation/water; International relations/cooperation/development aid; Population/family planning/demography; Rural development/agriculture. **Activities:** Conferences/seminars/workshops/training activities; Formal education; Fund raising; Networking/electronic telecommunications; Publishing/audiovisual materials/educational materials.

GBR2551

WORLD UNIVERSITY SERVICE, UNITED KINGDOM (WUS-UK)

20 Compton Terrace, London N1 2UN, United Kingdom.

Telephone: 44 (171) 226 6747. *Fax:* 44 (171) 226 0482. *Contact:* Sam Clarke, General Secretary.

OBJECTIVES: To promote development in poor, disadvantaged or oppressed communities by providing educational programmes. To work in co-operation with local partners, focusing on refugees, women and people in areas of conflict where education has been disrupted.

GENERAL INFORMATION: *Creation:* 1952. ***Member organisations:*** 200. ***Affiliated to:*** British Refugee Council - ECRE. ***Personnel/Total:*** 35. *Salaried:* 35 of which: 5 in developing countries. ***Budget/Total 1993:*** ECU 3206000 (US$ 3751000). ***Financial sources:*** *Private:* 3%. *Public:* 95%. *Self-financing:* 2%.

PUBLICATIONS: *Periodicals:* WUS Update (2). *Annual report. List of publications.*

EVALUATION/RESEARCH: Evaluation reports available.

PLANNED ACTIVITIES: WUS will undertake an NGO capacity-building programme for Africa.

ACTIVITIES IN DEVELOPING REGIONS: Present in developing regions. Active in 10 country(ies). Works through local field partners. **Sustainable Development Actions:** Democracy/good governance/institution building/participatory development; Education/training/literacy; Gender issues/women. **Regions:** East Africa; Mexico and Central America; Middle East; South America; Southern Africa.

INFORMATION AND EDUCATION ACTIVITIES: Topics: Education/training/literacy; Gender issues/women; Refugees/migrants/ethnic groups. **Activities:** Conferences/seminars/workshops/training activities; Formal education; Fund raising; Lobbying/advocacy.

GBR2552

WORLD VISION UK (WVUK)

World Vision House, 599 Avebury Boulevard, Central Milton Keynes, Bucks, MK9 3PG, United Kingdom.

Telephone: 44 (1908) 841000. *Fax:* 44 (1908) 841001. *Contact:* Charles Clayton, Executive Director.

OBJECTIVES: To work to relieve suffering and improve the quality of life among the poor, sick and underprivileged. To promote development education in the United Kingdom and raise awareness of issues affecting the poor of the Third World. To respond to situations of injustice and advocate the case of the powerless before the world's economic and political powers.

GENERAL INFORMATION: *Creation:* 1979. ***Affiliated to:*** UK NGO AIDS Consortium - NGO Forum on Cambodia - British Agencies Afghanistan Group - British Overseas NGOs in Development. ***Personnel/Total:*** 79. *Salaried:* 74 of which: 17 in developing countries. *Volunteers:*

See: *How to Use the Directory*, page 11.

5. ***Budget/Total 1993:*** ECU 16000 (US$ 19000). ***Financial sources:*** *Private: 54%. Public: 46%.*

PUBLICATIONS: *Periodicals:* World Vision Magazine (4). *Annual report. List of publications.*

EVALUATION/RESEARCH: Evaluation reports available. Undertakes research activities.

PLANNED ACTIVITIES: WVUK will undertake educational and advocacy campaigns in Mozambique.

COMMENTS: Undertakes activities in the Commonwealth of Independent States.

ACTIVITIES IN DEVELOPING REGIONS: Active in 32 country(ies). Works through local field partners. **Sustainable Development Actions:** Children/youth/family; Ecology/environment/biodiversity; Education/training/literacy; Emergency relief/refugees/humanitarian assistance; Food/famine; Health/sanitation/water; Rural development/agriculture; Small enterprises/informal sector/handicrafts; Urban development/habitat. **Regions:** Caribbean; Central Asia and South Asia; East Africa; Mexico and Central America; Oceania; South America; South East Asia; Southern Africa; West Africa.

INFORMATION AND EDUCATION ACTIVITIES: Topics: Children/youth/family; Culture/tradition/religion; Ecology/environment/biodiversity; Education/training/literacy; Emergency relief/refugees/humanitarian assistance; Food/famine; Gender issues/women; Health/sanitation/water; Human rights/peace/conflicts; International economic relations/trade/debt/finance; International relations/cooperation/development aid; Peace/ethnic conflicts/armament/disarmament; Population/family planning/demography; Poverty/living conditions; Refugees/migrants/ethnic groups; Rural development/agriculture; Urban development/habitat. **Activities:** Fund raising; Information campaigns/exhibitions; Lobbying/advocacy; Publishing/audiovisual materials/educational materials.

GBR2553
WORLD WIDE FUND FOR NATURE, UNITED KINGDOM (WWF UK)

Panda House, Weyside Park, Catteshall Lane, Godalming, Surrey GU7 1XR, United Kingdom.

Telephone: 44 (1483) 426444. ***Fax:*** 44 (1483) 426409. ***Contact:*** Robin Pellew, Director.

OBJECTIVES: To achieve the conservation of nature and ecological processes. To stop, and eventually reverse, the degradation of the planet's natural environment and help build a future in which humans live in harmony with nature.

GENERAL INFORMATION: *Creation:* 1961.

EVALUATION/RESEARCH: Evaluation reports available. Undertakes research activities.

COMMENTS: Undertakes activities in the Commonwealth of Independent States.

ACTIVITIES IN DEVELOPING REGIONS: Present in developing regions. Maintains local field presence. Works through local field partners. **Sustainable Development Actions:** Debt/finance/trade; Democracy/good governance/institution building/participatory development; Ecology/environment/biodiversity; Education/training/literacy; Energy/transport; Gender issues/women; Health/sanitation/water; Population/family planning/demography; Rural development/agriculture; Sending volunteers/experts/technical assistance; Small enterprises/informal sector/handicrafts; Urban development/habitat. **Regions:** Caribbean; Central Africa; Central Asia and South Asia; East Africa; East Asia; Mexico and Central America; Oceania; South America; South East Asia; Southern Africa; West Africa.

INFORMATION AND EDUCATION ACTIVITIES: Topics: Children/youth/family; Culture/tradition/religion; Ecology/environment/biodiversity; Education/training/literacy; Employment/unemployment; Gender issues/women; Health/sanitation/water; Human rights/peace/conflicts; International economic relations/trade/debt/finance; International relations/cooperation/development aid; Population/family planning/demography; Poverty/living conditions; Refugees/migrants/ethnic groups; Rural development/agriculture; Urban development/habitat. **Activities:** Broadcasting/cultural events; Conferences/seminars/workshops/training activities; Exchanges/twinning/linking; Formal education; Fund raising; Information

campaigns/exhibitions; Lobbying/advocacy; Networking/electronic telecommunications.

GBR2554
WORLDAWARE

1 Catton Street, London WC1R 4AB, United Kingdom.

Telephone: 44 (171) 831 3844. ***Fax:*** 44 (171) 831 1746. ***Contact:*** Derek Walker, Director.

OBJECTIVES: To increase understanding in the United Kingdom of world development issues, the need for sustainable development and the interdependence of developed and developing countries.

GENERAL INFORMATION: *Creation:* 1977. ***Affiliated to:*** Development Education Association (United Kingdom) - International Broadcasting Trust (United Kingdom) - Education for Sustainability Forum (United Kingdom). ***Personnel/Total:*** 12. *Salaried:* 7. *Volunteers:* 5. ***Budget/Total 1993:*** ECU 422000 (US$ 495000). ***Financial sources:*** *Private: 24%. Public: 56%. Self-financing: 20%.*

PUBLICATIONS: *Periodicals:* WORLDAWARE Update (3) - Business WORLDAWARE (4). *Annual report. List of publications.*

EVALUATION/RESEARCH: Undertakes research activities.

PLANNED ACTIVITIES: WORLDAWARE will publish resources for schools and will begin a new series of "Development Leadership visits" and seminars for the business community. WORLDAWARE will launch new travel grants for a project for local radio journalists and a "North-South connections" service for local media.

INFORMATION AND EDUCATION ACTIVITIES: Topics: Children/youth/family; Ecology/environment/biodiversity; Education/training/literacy; Employment/unemployment; Food/famine; Gender issues/women; Health/sanitation/water; International economic relations/trade/debt/finance; International relations/cooperation/development aid; Population/family planning/demography; Poverty/living conditions; Rural development/agriculture; Urban development/habitat. **Activities:** Conferences/seminars/workshops/training activities; Exchanges/twinning/linking; Formal education; Networking/electronic telecommunications; Publishing/audiovisual materials/educational materials.

GBR2555
WRITERS IN PRISON COMMITTEE OF INTERNATIONAL PEN (PEN)

9/10 Charterhouse BLDGS, Goswell Road, London EC1M 7AT, United Kingdom.

Telephone: 44 (171) 253 3226. ***Fax:*** 44 (171) 253 5711. ***E-mail:*** intpen@gn.apc.org.. ***Contact:*** Joanne Leedom-Ackerman, Chair.

OBJECTIVES: To work towards the release of writers and journalists detained for the peaceful expression of their views and activities worldwide. To try to end killing and torture as a form of censorship.

GENERAL INFORMATION: *Creation:* 1960. ***Type of organisation:*** network. ***Member organisations:*** 117. ***Personnel/Total:*** 5. *Salaried:* 4. *Volunteers:* 1. ***Budget/Total 1993:*** ECU 90000 (US$ 105000). ***Financial sources:*** *Private: 37%. Public: 25%. Self-financing: 38%.*

PUBLICATIONS: *Periodicals:* (2) - Centre to Centre (6). *Annual report.*

EVALUATION/RESEARCH: Undertakes research activities.

COMMENTS: Undertakes activities in the Commonwealth of Independent States. Information activities related to the Commonwealth of Independent States.

ACTIVITIES IN DEVELOPING REGIONS: Present in developing regions. Active in 25 country(ies). Maintains local field presence. Works through local field partners. **Sustainable Development Actions:** Emergency relief/refugees/humanitarian assistance; Human rights/peace/conflicts. **Regions:** Caribbean; Central Africa; Central Asia and South Asia; East Africa; East Asia; Mexico and Central America; Middle East; North Africa; Oceania; South America; South East Asia; Southern Africa; West Africa.

INFORMATION AND EDUCATION ACTIVITIES: Topics: Emergency relief/refugees/humanitarian assistance; Human rights/peace/conflicts. **Activities:** Conferences/seminars/workshops/training activities; Fund raising; Information and documentation services/data bases; Information

Voir : *Comment utiliser le répertoire,* page 11.

campaigns/exhibitions; Lobbying/advocacy; Publishing/audiovisual materials/educational materials.

GBR2556

Y CARE INTERNATIONAL

640 Forest Road, National Council of YMCAs, London E17 9RY, United Kingdom.

Telephone: 44 (181) 520 5599. *Fax:* 44 (181) 503 7461. *Contact:* Angus Sageant.

OBJECTIVES: To provide financial support to long-term development projects which are initiated and managed by overseas YMCAs and to provide emergency and disaster relief when necessary.

GENERAL INFORMATION: *Creation:* 1984. *Personnel/Total:* 14. *Salaried:* 13. *Volunteers:* 1. *Budget/Total 1993:* ECU 4488000 (US$ 5257000). *Financial sources:* Private: 83%. Public: 17%.

PUBLICATIONS: *Periodicals:* Annual Review (1) - Quaterly Newsletter (4). *Annual report. List of publications.*

EVALUATION/RESEARCH: Evaluation reports available.

PLANNED ACTIVITIES: Focusing on the 1995-1996, the International Year of Women and on women's programmes.

COMMENTS: Undertakes activities in the Commonwealth of Independent States. Information activities related to the Commonwealth of Independent States.

ACTIVITIES IN DEVELOPING REGIONS: Active in 38 country(ies). Works through local field partners. **Sustainable Development Actions:** Children/youth/family; Democracy/good governance/institution building/participatory development; Emergency relief/refugees/humanitarian assistance; Gender issues/women; Health/sanitation/water; Rural development/agriculture; Urban development/habitat. **Regions:** Central Asia and South Asia; East Africa; East Asia; Mexico and Central America; Middle East; South America; South East Asia; Southern Africa; West Africa.

GBR2557

YOUTH AGAINST RACISM IN EUROPE

P.O. Box 858, London E2 7RR, United Kingdom.

Telephone: 44 (181) 533 4533.

GBR2558

YOUTH ENTERPRISE SERVICES INTERNATIONAL (YES INTERNATIONAL)

Hobart House, 40 Grosvenor Place, 4th Floor, London SW1X 7AE, United Kingdom.

Telephone: 44 (171) 201 4375. *Fax:* 44 (171) 201 4402. *Contact:* Julie Misselbrook, Director.

OBJECTIVES: To promote and assist the development of effective youth enterprise programmes. To develop a strategy from youth motivation and personal development to business training through the provision of start-up credit and continuing advice for small and micro-businesses.

GENERAL INFORMATION: *Creation:* 1993. *Type of organisation:* coordinating body. *Member organisations:* 7. *Affiliated to:* British Overseas NGOs in Development (United Kingdom) - EC NGO Network. *Personnel/Total:* 12. *Salaried:* 5 of which: 1 in developing countries. *Volunteers:* 7 of which: 4 in developing countries. *Budget/Total 1993:* ECU 641000 (US$ 751000). *Financial sources:* Private: 75%. Public: 25%.

PUBLICATIONS: *Periodicals:* YES News (1). *Annual report.*

EVALUATION/RESEARCH: Evaluation reports available.

PLANNED ACTIVITIES: YES International plans to establish a model project in every operating region which involves setting up national youth business trusts, supported by business training and life skills programmes.

COMMENTS: Undertakes activities in the Commonwealth of Independent States. Information activities related to the Commonwealth of Independent States.

ACTIVITIES IN DEVELOPING REGIONS: Present in developing regions. Active in 15 country(ies). Works through local field partners. **Sustainable Development Actions:** Children/youth/family; Education/training/literacy; Sending volunteers/experts/technical assistance; Small enterprises/informal sector/handicrafts. **Regions:** Caribbean; Central Asia and South Asia; East Africa; South America; Southern Africa; West Africa.

INFORMATION AND EDUCATION ACTIVITIES: Topics: Children/youth/family; Employment/unemployment. **Activities:** Conferences/seminars/workshops/training activities; Fund raising; Information and documentation services/data bases.

GBR2559

YOUTH WITH A MISSION

13 Highfield Oval, Ambrose Lane, Harpenden, Herts AL5 4BX, United Kingdom.

GBR2560

YWCA OF GREAT BRITAIN

Clarendon House, 52 Cornmarket Street, Oxford 0X1 3EJ, United Kingdom.

Telephone: 44 (865) 726110.

GBR2561

ZIMBABWE TRUST (ZIMTRUST)

The Old Lodge, Christchurch Road, Epsom, Surrey KT19 8NE, United Kingdom.

Telephone: 44 (1372) 741237. *Fax:* 44 (1372) 725604. *Contact:* K.A. Madders, Chief Executive Director.

OBJECTIVES: To help relieve poverty. To promote sustainable economic activities, primarily in the communal areas of Zimbabwe, by facilitating and assisting rural communities to develop their organisational, management and skills capacity.

GENERAL INFORMATION: *Creation:* 1980. *Affiliated to:* World Conservation Union - Campfire Collaborative Group (Zimbabwe) - Zimbabwe National Conservation Trust (Zimbabwe) - Community Action Network. *Personnel/Total:* 48. *Salaried:* 45 of which: 42 in developing countries. *Volunteers:* 3 of which: 3 in developing countries. *Budget/Total 1993:* ECU 1870000 (US$ 2191000). *Financial sources:* Private: 17%. Public: 63%. Self-financing: 20%.

PUBLICATIONS: *Periodicals:* Miscellaneous Research Papers (6). *Annual report. List of publications.*

EVALUATION/RESEARCH: Evaluation reports available. Undertakes research activities.

PLANNED ACTIVITIES: ZIMTRUST will try to raise public awareness of the importance of the sustainable use of natural resources to indigenous communities.

ACTIVITIES IN DEVELOPING REGIONS: Present in developing regions. Active in 1 country(ies). Maintains local field presence. Works through local field partners. **Sustainable Development Actions:** Children/youth/family; Democracy/good governance/institution building/participatory development; Ecology/environment/biodiversity; Education/training/literacy; Gender issues/women; Health/sanitation/water; Human rights/peace/conflicts; Rural development/agriculture; Sending volunteers/experts/technical assistance; Small enterprises/informal sector/handicrafts; Urban development/habitat. **Regions:** Southern Africa.

INFORMATION AND EDUCATION ACTIVITIES: Topics: Culture/tradition/religion; Ecology/environment/biodiversity; Education/training/literacy; Employment/unemployment; Gender issues/women; Health/sanitation/water; Human rights/peace/conflicts; International relations/cooperation/development aid; Peace/ethnic conflicts/armament/disarmament; Poverty/living conditions; Racism/xenophobia/antisemitism; Rural development/agriculture; Urban development/habitat. **Activities:** Conferences/seminars/workshops/training activities; Fund raising; Information and documentation services/data bases; Information campaigns/

See: *How to Use the Directory*, page 11.

exhibitions; Lobbying/advocacy; Networking/electronic telecommunications; Publishing/audiovisual materials/educational materials.

GBR2562

ZOOLOGICAL SOCIETY OF LONDON (ZSL)

Regents Park, London NW1 4NY, United Kingdom.

Telephone: 44 (171) 722 3333. *Fax:* 44 (171) 483 4436. *Contact:* Alexandra Dixon, Director Conservation and Consultancy.

OBJECTIVES: To promote the worldwide conservation of species and their habitats by stimulating public awareness and concern through the presentation of living collections, relevant research and direct action in the field.

GENERAL INFORMATION: *Creation:* 1826. *Affiliated to:* Wildlife and Countryside Link (United Kingdom) - Federation of Zoos (United Kingdom) - IUCN (Switzerland and United Kingdom). *Personnel/Total:* 350. *Salaried:* 350 of which: 50 in developing countries. *Budget/*

Total 1993: ECU 18000000 (US$ 21000000). *Financial sources:* Private: 30%. *Self-financing:* 70%.

PUBLICATIONS: *Annual report. List of publications.*

EVALUATION/RESEARCH: Undertakes research activities.

COMMENTS: Information activities related to the Commonwealth of Independent States.

ACTIVITIES IN DEVELOPING REGIONS: Present in developing regions. Active in 15 country(ies). Maintains local field presence. Works through local field partners. **Sustainable Development Actions:** Ecology/environment/biodiversity; Sending volunteers/experts/technical assistance. **Regions:** Central Asia and South Asia; East Africa; Middle East; North Africa; South East Asia; Southern Africa; West Africa.

INFORMATION AND EDUCATION ACTIVITIES: Topics: Ecology/environment/biodiversity. **Activities:** Conferences/seminars/workshops/training activities; Fund raising; Information and documentation services/data bases; Publishing/audiovisual materials/educational materials.

GRC2563

AMNESTY INTERNATIONAL, GREEK SECTION

30 Sina Street, 106 72 Athens, Greece.

GRC2564

APOSTOLIKI DIAKONIA TIS EKLISSIAS TIS ELLADOS ♦ Apostolic Diakonia of the Church of Greece

14 I. Gennadiou Street, 115 21 Athens, Greece.

Telephone: 30 (1) 72 44 108. *Contact:* Bishop Anastasios Yannoulatos.

GRC2565

CARITAS HELLAS

Capodistriou 52, 104 32 Athènes, Grèce.

Téléphone: 30 (1) 52 47 879. *Contact:* Mgr Nicolas Foscolos.

GRC2566

CENTER OF RURAL WOMEN

Lekka 12, 105 62 Athens, Grèce.

Telephone: 30 (1) 32 23 048. *Contact:* Krinanthi Ioannidou.

GRC2567

CENTRE EUROPEEN D'ETUDES POUR LE DEVELOPPEMENT ET L'ENVIRONNEMENT (EKAPEM)

chez M.G. Tsaltas 3, rue Sfakion, 166 72 Athènes, Grèce.

Téléphone: 30 (1) 89 70 036. *Contact:* Tsaltas Grigoris, Président.

OBJECTIFS: Réaliser des études scientifiques et des projets de développement ou de protection de l'environnement. Organiser des colloques, des séminaires, des conférences sur les méthodes et moyens de coopération sur le développement et l'environnement. Sensibiliser l'opinion publique sur les questions du développement et de l'environnement.

INFORMATIONS GENERALES: *Création:* 1991. *Personnel/Total:* 11. *Bénévoles:* 11. *Budget/Total 1993:* ECU 74000 (US$ 86000). *Sources financières:* Public: 85%. Autofinancement: 15%.

PUBLICATIONS: *Rapport annuel. Liste des publications.*

EVALUATION/RECHERCHE: Rapports d'évaluation disponibles. Entreprend des activités de recherche.

COMMENTAIRES: Intervient dans la Communauté des Etats indépendants. Activités d'information concernant la Communauté des Etats indépendants.

ACTIVITES DANS LES REGIONS EN DEVELOPPEMENT: Intervient directement dans les régions en développement. Intervient dans 6 pays. **Actions de Développement durable:** Développement rural/agriculture; Envoi de volontaires/experts/assistance technique; Petites entreprises/secteur informel/artisanat; Questions relatives aux femmes; Santé/assainissement/eau; Secours d'urgence/réfugiés/aide humanitaire; Écologie/environnement/biodiversité; Éducation/formation/alphabétisation. **Régions:** Afrique centrale; Afrique de l'Ouest; Afrique du Nord.

ACTIVITES D'INFORMATION ET D'EDUCATION: Domaines: Développement rural/agriculture; Pauvreté/conditions de vie; Questions relatives aux femmes; Écologie/environnement/biodiversité. **Activités:** Campagnes d'information/expositions; Collecte de fonds; Conférences/séminaires/ateliers/activités de formation; Services d'information et de documentation/bases de données; Échanges/parrainage/jumelage; Édition/documents audiovisuels/documents éducatifs; Éducation formelle.

GRC2568

CHRISTIANIKI ENOSSI NEANIDON ELLADOS (CHEN) ♦ Young Women's Christian Association of Greece

11 Amerikis Street, 106 72 Athens, Greece.

Telephone: 30 (1) 36 26 180. *Fax:* 30 (1) 36 22 400. *Contact:* Athena Athanasiou.

GRC2569

DIETHNIS ETERIA OIKISTIKIS ♦ World Society for Ekistics

P.O. Box 3471, 102 10 Athens, Greece.

Telephone: 30 (1) 36 23 216. *Fax:* 30 (1) 36 33 395. *Contact:* Panayotis Psomopoulos, Secretary General.

GRC2570

DIORTHODOXO KENDRO "POREFTHENDES" ♦ Centre international "Porefthendes"

Zalongou 13-15, 106 78 Athènes, Grèce.

Téléphone: 30 (1) 36 33 792. *Fax:* 30 (1) 36 02 145. *Contact:* Alexandros Stavropoulos.

GRC2571

ELLENIKO INSTITUTO ALLILENGYIS KE SYNERGASIAS ME TIS ANAPTYSSOMENES CHORES (HELINAS) ♦ Hellenic Institute of Solidarity and Co-operation with the Developing Countries

9 Orminioy Street, 115 28 Athens, Greece.

Telephone: 30 (1) 72 34 456. *Fax:* 30 (1) 72 17 455. *Contact:* Mara Levidi, General Director.

OBJECTIVES: To increase solidarity and co-operation between the people of Greece and the peoples of the Third World as the first step toward achieving justice in the relations between the countries of the North and South.

GENERAL INFORMATION: *Creation:* 1986. *Affiliated to:* YDC (Netherlands) - EUROSTEP (Belgium) - SATIS (Senegal) - ICDA (Belgium) -EURODEBT - Towns and Development. *Personnel/Total:* 18. *Salaried:* 15 of which: 5 in developing countries. *Volunteers:* 3. *Financial sources:* Private: 25%. Public: 65%. Self-financing: 10%.

PUBLICATIONS: *Periodicals:* SYNERGASIA (5).

EVALUATION/RESEARCH: Undertakes research activities.

COMMENTS: Undertakes activities in the Commonwealth of Independent States.

ACTIVITIES IN DEVELOPING REGIONS: Active in 4 country(ies). Maintains local field presence. Works through local field partners. **Sustainable Development Actions:** Democracy/good governance/institution building/participatory development; Education/training/literacy; Food/famine; Gender issues/women; Health/sanitation/water; Rural development/agriculture; Small enterprises/informal sector/handicrafts. **Regions:** Central Africa; Central Asia and South Asia; East Africa; Southern Africa.

INFORMATION AND EDUCATION ACTIVITIES: Topics: Culture/tradition/religion; Ecology/environment/biodiversity; Emergency relief/refugees/humanitarian assistance; Food/famine; Health/sanitation/water; International relations/cooperation/development aid; Poverty/living conditions; Racism/xenophobia/antisemitism; Refugees/migrants/ethnic groups; Rural development/agriculture; Urban development/habitat. **Activities:** Broadcasting/cultural events; Conferences/seminars/workshops/training activities; Exchanges/twinning/linking; Formal education; Fund raising; Information and documentation services/data bases; Information campaigns/exhibitions; Lobbying/advocacy.

GRC2572

ELLINIKI EPITROPI DIETHNOUS DIMOCRATIKIS ALLILEGHISIS (EEDDA) ♦ Greek Committee for International Democratic Solidarity (GCIDS)

25 Spyridonos Trikoupi Street, 106 83 Athens, Greece.

Telephone: 30 (1) 36 13 052. *Fax:* 30 (1) 36 31 603. *Contact:* Theocharis Papamargaris, President.

OBJECTIVES: To promote solidarity between peoples. To plan, promote and implement development projects in developing countries, in partnership with local NGOs. To inform and mobilise the Greek people to offer moral, political and economic support to the people in developing countries.

GENERAL INFORMATION: *Creation:* 1981. *Affiliated to:* Afro-Asian People's Solidarity Organisation (Egypt) - The liaison Committee of NGDOs to the European Union - Liaison Group of National Anti-

See: *How to Use the Directory,* page 11.

Apartheid Movements in the European Union. *Personnel/Total:* 26. *Salaried:* 2. *Volunteers:* 24. *Budget/Total 1993:* ECU 1791000 (US$ 2094000). *Financial sources:* Private: 10%. Public: 85%. Self-financing: 5%.

PUBLICATIONS: *Periodicals:* International Solidarity (4). *Annual report.*

EVALUATION/RESEARCH: Evaluation reports available.

COMMENTS: Undertakes activities in the Commonwealth of Independent States.

ACTIVITIES IN DEVELOPING REGIONS: Active in 8 country(ies). Works through local field partners. **Sustainable Development Actions:** Children/youth/family; Education/training/literacy; Health/sanitation/water; Rural development/agriculture; Small enterprises/informal sector/handicrafts; Urban development/habitat. **Regions:** Caribbean; Middle East; South America; Southern Africa;

INFORMATION AND EDUCATION ACTIVITIES: Topics: Children/youth/family; Ecology/environment/biodiversity; Education/training/literacy; Emergency relief/refugees/humanitarian assistance; Human rights/peace/conflicts; International relations/cooperation/development aid; Peace/ethnic conflicts/armament/disarmament; Poverty/living conditions; Racism/xenophobia/antisemitism; Refugees/migrants/ethnic groups. **Activities:** Broadcasting/cultural events; Conferences/seminars/workshops/training activities; Exchanges/twinning/linking; Fund raising; Information and documentation services/data bases; Information campaigns/exhibitions; Lobbying/advocacy; Publishing/audiovisual materials/educational materials.

GRC2573

ELLINIKOS ERITHROS STAVROS (EES) ♦ Hellenic Red Cross

1 Lycavittou Street, 106 72 Athens, Greece.

Telephone: 30 (1) 36 21 681. *Fax:* 30 (1) 36 15 606. *Contact:* Andreas Martinis, President.

OBJECTIVES: To provide assistance in times of war and desaster. To foster humanitarian ideals among the general public through community programmes. To implement special programmes on drugs, alcohol and cancer care.

GENERAL INFORMATION: *Creation:* 1877. *Affiliated to:* LRCS (Switzerland) - International Red Cross Committee (Switzerland). *Personnel/Total:* 20450. Salaried: 450. Volunteers: 20000. *Financial sources:* Private: 56%. Public: 28%. Self-financing: 16%.

PUBLICATIONS: *Periodicals:* The Hellenic Red Cross - Red Cross News. *Annual report.*

EVALUATION/RESEARCH: Undertakes research activities.

COMMENTS: Undertakes activities in the Commonwealth of Independent States.

INFORMATION AND EDUCATION ACTIVITIES: Topics: Children/youth/family; Emergency relief/refugees/humanitarian assistance; Employment/unemployment; Food/famine; Health/sanitation/water; Racism/xenophobia/antisemitism; Refugees/migrants/ethnic groups. **Activities:** Conferences/seminars/workshops/training activities; Formal education; Fund raising; Information and documentation services/data bases; Lobbying/advocacy; Networking/electronic telecommunications.

GRC2574

ETERIA SPOUDIS TIS PAGOSMIAS ANAPTIXIS - EDECN-HELLAS (ESPA) ♦ Society for the Study of World Development - EDECN-Greece

c/o C. Christidis, Zach. Papantoniou 13, 546 46 Depot, Thessaloniki, Greece.

Telephone: 30 (31) 42 06 74. *Fax:* 30 (31) 42 06 74. *Contact:* Christos Christidis.

GRC2575

EUROMARE

101 Syngrou Avenue, 117 45 Athens, Greece.

Telephone: 30 (1) 92 21 254. *Fax:* 30 (1) 92 21 589. *Contact:* Alexis Caniaris, President.

OBJECTIVES: To provide information on environmental issues. To develop human resources and promote profesional training on issues related to environment, development and communication. To study and research the protection and development of the environment.

GENERAL INFORMATION: *Creation:* 1994. *Personnel/Total:* 6. Salaried: 2. Volunteers: 4. *Budget/Total 1993:* ECU 112000 (US$ 131000). *Financial sources:* Private: 20%. Public: 60%. Self-financing: 20%.

PUBLICATIONS: *Periodicals:* EUROMARE Newsletter (3). *Annual report.*

EVALUATION/RESEARCH: Evaluation reports available. Undertakes research activities.

PLANNED ACTIVITIES: Exhibitions and conferences on "Mediterrenean and the Environment," Eastern Europe and the Environment" and "Subcontracting the Balkans Region."

COMMENTS: Budget for 1994: 131000 US$; 112000 ECU. Undertakes activities in the Commonwealth of Independent States. Information activities related to the Commonwealth of Independent States.

ACTIVITIES IN DEVELOPING REGIONS: Active in 3 country(ies). Works through local field partners. **Sustainable Development Actions:** Ecology/environment/biodiversity; Rural development/agriculture; Small enterprises/informal sector/handicrafts. **Regions:** Central Asia and South Asia; Middle East; North Africa.

INFORMATION AND EDUCATION ACTIVITIES: Topics: Ecology/environment/biodiversity; Rural development/agriculture. **Activities:** Broadcasting/cultural events; Conferences/seminars/workshops/training activities; Exchanges/twinning/linking; Formal education; Fund raising; Information and documentation services/data bases; Information campaigns/exhibitions; Publishing/audiovisual materials/educational materials.

GRC2576

FAMILY PLANNING ASSOCIATION OF GREECE

Solonos 121, 106 78 Athens, Greece.

Telephone: 30 (1) 36 06 390. *Fax:* 30 (1) 36 06 390. *Contact:* Sophia Apostolopovlov, Vice-President.

OBJECTIVES: To increase awareness about family planning issues and improve family planning services. To help create and implement population policies at a national level. To fight for safe abortion, aids prevention and women's empowerment.

GENERAL INFORMATION: *Creation:* 1976. *Affiliated to:* National European Women's Lobby (Greece) - International Planned Parenthood Federation (United Kingdom). *Personnel/Total:* 742. Salaried: 2. Volunteers: 740. *Budget/Total 1993:* ECU 45000 (US$ 52000). *Financial sources:* Private: 85%. Self-financing: 15%.

PUBLICATIONS: *Periodicals:* Planned Parenthood in Europe (4). *Annual report.* List of publications.

EVALUATION/RESEARCH: Undertakes research activities.

COMMENTS: Undertakes activities in the Commonwealth of Independent States. Information activities related to the Commonwealth of Independent States.

INFORMATION AND EDUCATION ACTIVITIES: Topics: Children/youth/family; Emergency relief/refugees/humanitarian assistance; Gender issues/women; Human rights/peace/conflicts; International relations/cooperation/development aid; Population/family planning/demography; Refugees/migrants/ethnic groups. **Activities:** Broadcasting/cultural events; Conferences/seminars/workshops/training activities; Exchanges/twinning/linking; Formal education; Fund raising; Information and documentation services/data bases; Information campaigns/exhibitions; Lobbying/advocacy; Networking/electronic telecommunications; Publishing/audiovisual materials/educational materials.

GRC2577

GIATRI TOV KOSMOV ♦ Médecins du Monde

Stadiov 5 - Bureau 104, 105 62 Athènes, Grèce.

GRC2578

GREEK ASSOCIATION FOR THE UNITED NATIONS

Megaron "Parnassos", Plateia Karytsi 8, Athens, Greece.

Telephone: 30 (1) 80 80 905.

GRC2579

GREEK COUNCIL FOR REFUGEES ♦ Conseil Grec pour les Réfugiés

39, Arahovis Street, 106 81 Athens, Greece.

Telephone: 30 (1) 36 00 059. *Fax:* 30 (1) 36 03 774. *Contact:* Chariklia Hari Brissimi, President.

OBJECTIVES: To examine requests of asylum seekers. To offer phsyco-social, legal and material assistance to refugees. To advocate in favour of measures for the protection of refugees and for the provision of the assistance they require. To train persons responsible for dealing with refugees and asylum seekers in Greece and abroad.

GENERAL INFORMATION: *Creation:* 1989. *Affiliated to:* European Council on Refugges and Exiles (United Kingdom) - HURIDOCS (Norway). *Personnel/Total:* 25. *Salaried:* 19. *Volunteers:* 6. *Budget/Total 1993:* ECU 702000 (US$ 821000). *Financial sources:* Private: 4%. Public: 96%.

PUBLICATIONS: *Annual report.*

EVALUATION/RESEARCH: Evaluation reports available. Undertakes research activities.

PLANNED ACTIVITIES: A symposium for persons who play a key role in refugee protection.

COMMENTS: Information activities related to the Commonwealth of Independent States.

INFORMATION AND EDUCATION ACTIVITIES: Topics: Emergency relief/refugees/humanitarian assistance; Human rights/peace/conflicts; International relations/cooperation/development aid; Racism/xenophobia/antisemitism; Refugees/migrants/ethnic groups. **Activities:** Broadcasting/cultural events; Conferences/seminars/workshops/training activities; Exchanges/twinning/linking; Formal education; Fund raising; Information and documentation services/data bases; Information campaigns/exhibitions; Lobbying/advocacy.

GRC2580

GREEK GIRL GUIDES ASSOCIATION (SEO)

10 Xenofondos Street, 105 57 Athens, Greece.

Telephone: 30 (1) 32 35 794. *Fax:* 30 (1) 32 35 526. *Contact:* Nelly Kouskoleka, Liaison NGO.

GRC2581

HELLENIC ASSOCIATION OF UNIVERSITY WOMEN

44A Voulis Street, Platia Syntagamatos, 105 57 Athens, Greece.

Contact: Mrs Nicolaou.

GRC2582

HELLENIC MARINE ENVIRONMENT PROTECTION ASSOCIATION (HELMEPA)

5 Pergamon Street, 171 21 Athens, Greece.

Telephone: 30 (1) 93 43 088. *Fax:* 30 (1) 93 53 847. *Contact:* Dimitri Mitsatsos, Director General.

GRC2583

HELLENIC YOUTH FOR DEVELOPMENT (ENEA)

22 Mykonou Street, 15772 Athens, Greece.

Telephone: 30 (1) 77 06 988.

GRC2584

IATRICO KENTRO APOKATASTASIS THYMATON VASSANISTIRION ♦ Medical Rehabilitation Centre for Torture Victims

9 Lycabettous Street, Kolonakki, 106 72 Athens, Greece.

Telephone: 30 (1) 36 04 967. *Fax:* 30 (1) 36 12 273. *Contact:* Maria Piniou-Kalli, Medical Director.

OBJECTIVES: To work for the prevention of torture. To promote the ratification of the International Convention for Human Rights. To provide medical and psychological assistance to victims of torture. To research medical aspects of torture and educate the public about human rights.

GENERAL INFORMATION: *Creation:* 1989. *Affiliated to:* International Rehabilitation Council for Torture Victims (Denmark). *Personnel/Total:* 150. *Salaried:* 10. *Volunteers:* 140. *Budget/Total 1993:* ECU 149000 (US$ 174000). *Financial sources:* Private: 10%. Public: 90%.

EVALUATION/RESEARCH: Undertakes research activities.

PLANNED ACTIVITIES: Development of a Balkan Network for the prevention of torture. "Children in Crisis" project for the provision of medical and psychological assistance to Kurdish children.

COMMENTS: Undertakes activities in the Commonwealth of Independent States. Information activities related to the Commonwealth of Independent States.

ACTIVITIES IN DEVELOPING REGIONS: Present in developing regions. Active in 5 country(ies). Works through local field partners. **Sustainable Development Actions:** Other. **Regions:** Caribbean; Central Africa; Central Asia and South Asia; East Africa; East Asia; Mexico and Central America; Middle East; North Africa; Oceania; South America; South East Asia; Southern Africa; West Africa.

INFORMATION AND EDUCATION ACTIVITIES: Topics: Emergency relief/refugees/humanitarian assistance; Human rights/peace/conflicts; International relations/cooperation/development aid; Racism/xenophobia/antisemitism; Refugees/migrants/ethnic groups. **Activities:** Conferences/seminars/workshops/training activities; Exchanges/twinning/linking; Formal education; Information and documentation services/data bases; Information campaigns/exhibitions; Lobbying/advocacy; Publishing/audiovisual materials/educational materials.

GRC2585

IDRIMA MARANGOPOULOU GIA TA DIKEOMATA TOU ANTROPOU ♦ Marangopoulos Foundation for Human Rights

1 Lycavittou Street, 10672 Athens, Greece.

Telephone: 30 (1) 36 37 455. *Fax:* 30 (1) 36 22 454. *Contact:* Alice Yotopoulos-Marangopoulos, President.

OBJECTIVES: To research, study, defend and promote fundamental human rights and freedoms.

GENERAL INFORMATION: *Creation:* 1978. *Personnel/Total:* 8. *Salaried:* 7. *Volunteers:* 1. *Budget/Total 1993:* ECU 169000 (US$ 198000). *Financial sources:* Public: 15%. Self-financing: 85%.

PUBLICATIONS: *List of publications.*

EVALUATION/RESEARCH: Undertakes research activities.

COMMENTS: Undertakes activities in the Commonwealth of Independent States. Information activities related to the Commonwealth of Independent States.

INFORMATION AND EDUCATION ACTIVITIES: Topics: Children/youth/family; Education/training/literacy; Emergency relief/refugees/humanitarian assistance; Human rights/peace/conflicts; Racism/xenophobia/antisemitism; Refugees/migrants/ethnic groups. **Activities:** Conferences/seminars/workshops/training activities; Fund raising; Information and documentation services/data bases; Information campaigns/exhibitions; Lobbying/advocacy; Publishing/audiovisual materials/educational materials.

GRC2586

INSTITUTE OF INTERNATIONAL SOCIAL AFFAIRS (IISA)

19, Erehthiou and 6, Tzireon, 117 42 Athens, Greece.

Telephone: 30 (1) 92 31 559. *Fax:* 30 (1) 92 27 472. *Contact:* Very Rev. Nicholas Psarombas.

See: *How to Use the Directory,* page 11.

OBJECTIVES: To promote international relations free of discrimination. To disseminate information, mobilize and co-operate with institutions and organisations. To offer developing countries solidarity and co-operation.

GENERAL INFORMATION: *Creation:* 1984. *Affiliated to:* Liaison Committee of NGDOs of the European Communities. *Personnel/Total:* 87. *Salaried:* 29 of which: 25 in developing countries. *Volunteers:* 58 of which: 12 in developing countries. *Budget/Total 1993:* ECU 418000 (US$ 489000). *Financial sources:* Private: 61%. Self-financing: 39%.

PUBLICATIONS: *Periodicals:* Journal of Oriental and African Studies (4).

EVALUATION/RESEARCH: Undertakes research activities.

COMMENTS: The IAA is an institution of the "Order of the Orthodox Hospitallers" with representation offices in London, Bon, Moscow, New York, Lagas, Cotonou and Addis Ababa. The IAA works in co-operation with local churches in those areas. Undertakes activities in the Commonwealth of Independent States. Information activities related to the Commonwealth of Independent States.

ACTIVITIES IN DEVELOPING REGIONS: Present in developing regions. Active in 4 country(ies). Maintains local field presence. Works through local field partners. **Sustainable Development Actions:** Children/youth/family; Ecology/environment/biodiversity; Education/training/literacy; Emergency relief/refugees/humanitarian assistance; Food/famine; Health/sanitation/water; Population/family planning/demography; Rural development/agriculture; Sending volunteers/experts/technical assistance; Small enterprises/informal sector/handicrafts. **Regions:** Central Africa; East Africa; North Africa; West Africa.

INFORMATION AND EDUCATION ACTIVITIES: Topics: Children/youth/family; Culture/tradition/religion; Education/training/literacy; Emergency relief/refugees/humanitarian assistance; Food/famine; Health/sanitation/water; Human rights/peace/conflicts; International relations/cooperation/development aid; Peace/ethnic conflicts/armament/disarmament; Population/family planning/demography; Poverty/living conditions; Refugees/migrants/ethnic groups; Rural development/agriculture. **Activities:** Broadcasting/cultural events; Conferences/seminars/workshops/training activities; Formal education; Fund raising; Information campaigns/exhibitions; Lobbying/advocacy.

GRC2587
INTERNATIONAL ALLIANCE OF WOMEN

1 Lycaultton 57, Athens, Greece.

Telephone: 30 (1) 36 26 111.

GRC2588
KENDRO EREVNON YA TIS GINEKES TIS MESOYIOU (KEGME) ♦ Mediterranean Women's Studies

115, Har. TriKoupi Street, 114 73 Athens, Greece.

Telephone: 30 (1) 64 36 436. *Contact:* Ketty Lazaris, President.

GRC2589
MEDECINS SANS FRONTIERES, GRECE

11A rue Paioniou, 104 40 Athènes, Grèce.

Contact: Docteur Sotiris Papaspyropoulos, Président.

GRC2590
MEDITERRANEAN CENTRE FOR ENVIRONMENT (CME)

Polynikous 2, 174 55 Alimos, Greece.

Téléphone: 30 (1) 98 87 630. *Fax:* 30 (1) 98 87 565. *Contact:* Isabelle Bouchy, Manager.

OBJECTIFS: Sensibiliser l'opinion et mener des études sur les problèmes de l'environnement. Rechercher et aider au développement de formes de tourisme alternatives, compatibles avec l'environnement.

INFORMATIONS GENERALES: *Création:* 1992. *Affiliée à:* Groupement Européen des Campus de l'Environnement (France). *Personnel/Total:* 4. *Bénévoles:* 4. *Budget/Total 1993:* ECU 6000 (US$ 7000). *Sources financières:* Privé: 30%. Public: 70%.

PUBLICATIONS: *Liste des publications.*

EVALUATION/RECHERCHE: Rapports d'évaluation disponibles. Entreprend des activités de recherche.

COMMENTAIRES: Intervient dans la Communauté des Etats indépendants. Activités d'information concernant la Communauté des Etats indépendants.

ACTIVITES D'INFORMATION ET D'EDUCATION: Domaines: Développement rural/agriculture; Écologie/environnement/biodiversité. **Activités:** Collecte de fonds; Conférences/séminaires/ateliers/activités de formation; Échanges/parrainage/jumelage; Éducation formelle.

GRC2591
NATIONAL COUNCIL OF HELLENIC YOUTH ORGANISATIONS (ESONE)

Amerikis Street 11, 106 79 Athens, Greece.

Telephone: 30 (1) 36 11 596. *Fax:* 30 (1) 36 22 400. *Contact:* Anastasia Diamandakoy.

GRC2592
ORTHODOX ACADEMIA OF CRETE

Kalliga 69, 152 37 Filothei, Grèce.

Telephone: 30 (x) 68 12 643. *Fax:* 30 (x) 77 09 024. *Contact:* Lena Angelopoulou.

GRC2593
SOCIAL WORK FOUNDATION

6 Mantzapou Street, 106 72 Athens, Greece.

Telephone: 30 (1) 36 35 881. *Fax:* 30 (1) 36 00 786. *Contact:* Anastasia Christakis, Director.

GRC2594
SOS RATSISMOS

9 Euripidou Street. P.O. Box 3724, 10210 Athènes, Grèce.

Téléphone: 30 (1) 32 50 665.

GRC2595
SOSTE TA PAIDIA ♦ Save the Children

Papadiamandopoulou 54, 157 71 Zografou, Greece.

Telephone: 30 (1) 77 58 732. *Fax:* 30 (1) 77 99 481. *Contact:* Esa Kyrimi, Director.

OBJECTIVES: To improve the lives of needy children. To stress community development projects which build self-help skills. To help people build a better life for themselves and for their children.

GENERAL INFORMATION: *Creation:* 1974. *Affiliated to:* ISCA (Switzerland). *Personnel/Total:* 17. *Salaried:* 10. *Volunteers:* 7. *Budget/Total 1993:* ECU 261000 (US$ 305000). *Financial sources:* Private: 30%. Public: 65%. Self-financing: 5%.

PUBLICATIONS: *Annual report. List of publications.*

COMMENTS: Undertakes activities in the Commonwealth of Independent States.

ACTIVITIES IN DEVELOPING REGIONS: Present in developing regions. Active in 3 country(ies). Maintains local field presence. Works through local field partners. **Sustainable Development Actions:** Children/youth/family; Education/training/literacy. **Regions:** Southern Africa; West Africa.

INFORMATION AND EDUCATION ACTIVITIES: Topics: Children/youth/family; Education/training/literacy; Health/sanitation/water; Population/family planning/demography. **Activities:** Conferences/seminars/workshops/training activities.

GRC2596
XAN ♦ YMCA

36 Akadimias Street, 106 72 Athens, Greece.

Telephone: 30 (1) 36 26 970. *Fax:* 30 (1) 36 44 901. *Contact:* Ionnais Xydias.

Voir : *Comment utiliser le répertoire,* page 11.

HUN2597

ACT UP AGAINST HATRED FOUNDATION AND MOVEMENT

Madarasz Viktor u. 22-24, 1131 Budapest, Hungary.

HUN2598

AGRAR ES FALUSI IFJUSAG SZOVETSEGE (AGRYA) ♦ Agricultural and Rural Youth Association

Üllöi út 66/b, 1447 Budapest Pf. 518, Hungary.

Telephone: 36 (6) 1 133 0743. *Fax:* 36 (6) 1 133 0743. *Contact:* Lajos Mikula, President.

OBJECTIVES: To represent rural youth. To provide financial, moral and technical help for rural and agricultural organisations active in the following areas: promotion of agricultural professions, cultural preservation, unemployment and rural community-building.

GENERAL INFORMATION: *Creation:* 1989. *Affiliated to:* Hungarian Child and Youth Council (MAGYIT) (Hungary) - European Committee for Young Farmers and 4 H Clubs. *Personnel/Total:* 14. *Salaried:* 2. *Volunteers:* 12. *Budget/Total 1993:* ECU 25000 (US$ 33000). *Financial sources:* Private: 35%. Public: 60%. Self-financing: 5%.

PUBLICATIONS: *Periodicals:* Hirharang (10).

EVALUATION/RESEARCH: Evaluation reports available.

COMMENTS: Undertakes activities in the Commonwealth of Independent States. Information activities related to the Commonwealth of Independent States.

ACTIVITIES IN DEVELOPING REGIONS: Present in developing regions.

INFORMATION AND EDUCATION ACTIVITIES: Topics: Children/youth/family; Culture/tradition/religion; Education/training/literacy; Employment/unemployment; Health/sanitation/water; International relations/cooperation/development aid; Racism/xenophobia/antisemitism; Rural development/agriculture. Activities: Broadcasting/cultural events; Conferences/seminars/workshops/training activities; Exchanges/twinning/linking; Formal education; Fund raising; Information and documentation services/data bases; Information campaigns/exhibitions; Lobbying/advocacy; Publishing/audiovisual materials/educational materials.

HUN2599

AIESEC

Alkotmany u. 9-11, 1054 Budapest, Hungary.

HUN2600

ALBA CIRCLE - NONVIOLENT MOVEMENT FOR PEACE

Pf. 225, 1461 Budapest, Hungary.

HUN2601

AMNESTY INTERNATIONAL, MAGYARORSZAG ♦ Amnesty International Hungary

Pf. 701/343, 1399 Budapest, Hungary.

Telephone: 36 (1) 134 2400. *Fax:* 36 (1) 134 2400. *Contact:* Jànos Malina, Chairperson.

OBJECTIVES: To support the Universal Declaration of Human Rights. To fight for the fair trial and release of all political prisoners of conscience. To fight for the abolition of the death penalty, torture and other cruel and inhuman treatment of prisoners. To fight for the abolition of "disappearances" and extrajudicial executions.

GENERAL INFORMATION: *Creation:* 1989. *Member organisations:* 2. *Personnel/Total:* 4. *Volunteers:* 4. *Budget/Total 1993:* ECU 2500 (US$ 3000). *Financial sources:* Private: 20%. Public: 70%. Self-financing: 10%.

PUBLICATIONS: *Annual report. List of publications.*

PLANNED ACTIVITIES: A.I. Hungary will provide Hungarian versions of existing Amnesty International materials to strengthen their human rights education activity. They are also planning to set up a nationwide network of Amnesty International groups in Hungary.

COMMENTS: Undertakes activities in the Commonwealth of Independent States. Information activities related to the Commonwealth of Independent States.

INFORMATION AND EDUCATION ACTIVITIES: Topics: Human rights/peace/conflicts; Refugees/migrants/ethnic groups. Activities: Broadcasting/cultural events; Exchanges/twinning/linking; Formal education; Fund raising; Information and documentation services/data bases; Information campaigns/exhibitions; Lobbying/advocacy; Publishing/audiovisual materials/educational materials.

HUN2602

ANTI-FASCIST ACTION

Pf. 13, 1360 Budapest, Hungary.

HUN2603

ANTI-RACIST COMMITTEE

Pf. 701/647, 1399 Budapest, Hungary.

HUN2604

ANTI-VIOLENCE FORUM

Baross u. 61 V. em. 516, 1082 Budapest, Hungary.

HUN2605

ASSOCIATION OF VICTIMS OF VIOLATION OF RIGHTS

Nagymezo ut. 38, Fszt. 17, 1065 Budapest, Hungary.

HUN2606

BDTK-KOTAK

Karolyi Gaspdr. ter 4, 9701 Szombutholy, Hungary.

HUN2607

BEM JOZSEF ALT ISK HERMAN OTTO KOR ♦ Herman Ottó Environmentalist Ring Bem Jozsef Elementary Schoo

Termv. Kor, Hungaria krt. 5-7, 6dp1/1, 1101 Budapest, Hungary.

Telephone: 36 (2) 616 786. *Fax:* 36 (2) 616 786. *Contact:* Naginé Honath Emilia.

OBJECTIVES: To fight for the protection of the environment. To promote environmentally-friendly products.

GENERAL INFORMATION: *Creation:* 1985. *Affiliated to:* Association of Hungarian Conservationists (Hungary) - Air Team (Hungary). *Personnel/Total:* 60. *Volunteers:* 60. *Budget/Total 1993:* ECU 420 (US$ 540). *Financial sources:* Private: 20%. Public: 40%. Self-financing: 40%.

PUBLICATIONS: *Annual report. List of publications.*

EVALUATION/RESEARCH: Evaluation reports available.

PLANNED ACTIVITIES: The Organisation plans to publish a newsletter twice a year.

COMMENTS: Undertakes activities in the Commonwealth of Independent States. Information activities related to the Commonwealth of Independent States.

INFORMATION AND EDUCATION ACTIVITIES: Topics: Ecology/environment/biodiversity; Education/training/literacy; Rural development/agriculture. Activities: Conferences/seminars/workshops/training activities; Formal education; Information campaigns/exhibitions; Publishing/audiovisual materials/educational materials.

HUN2608

BIOCEN ENVIRONMENT AND NATURE PROTECTION CLUB

Bzedn anna u. 26, 4024 Dobrecen, Hungary.

HUN2609

BOCS ALAPITVANY ♦ BOCS Foundation

Pf.7, 8003 Székerfehérvár, Hungary.

See: *How to Use the Directory*, page 11.

Telephone: 36 (22) 32 72 63. *Fax:* 36 (22) 31 97 01. *E-mail:* GYULA@SIMONYI.ZPOK.HU. *Contact:* Gyula Simonyi, President.

OBJECTIVES: To focus on ecological and environmental issues. To promote peace, non-violence and conflict resolution.

GENERAL INFORMATION: *Creation:* 1945. *Type of organisation:* coordinating body. *Affiliated to:* KAIROS EUROPE - Church and Peace - International Fellowship of Reconciliation -BOKOR Basecommunity Network (Hungary). *Personnel/Total:* 6. *Volunteers:* 6. *Budget/Total 1993:* ECU 840 (US$ 1100). *Financial sources: Self-financing:* 100%.

PUBLICATIONS: *Periodicals:* Justice, Peace and Integrity of Creation Newsletter (4). *Annual report. List of publications.*

EVALUATION/RESEARCH: Undertakes research activities.

COMMENTS: Undertakes activities in the Commonwealth of Independent States. Information activities related to the Commonwealth of Independent States.

INFORMATION AND EDUCATION ACTIVITIES: Topics: Children/youth/family; Culture/tradition/religion; Ecology/environment/biodiversity; Education/training/literacy; Food/famine; Human rights/peace/conflicts; International economic relations/trade/debt/finance; Peace/ethnic conflicts/armament/disarmament; Population/family planning/demography. **Activities:** Conferences/seminars/workshops/training activities; Fund raising; Information and documentation services/data bases; Information campaigns/exhibitions; Lobbying/advocacy; Networking/electronic telecommunications; Publishing/audiovisual materials/educational materials.

HUN2610
BOKOR OKO-CSOPORT ♦ Eco-Group of 'Bokor'

Mandula u. 7-9, 2000 Szentendre, Hungary.

Telephone: 36 (26) 313 823. *Fax:* 36 (26) 313 823. *E-mail:* DI @BOK.ZPOK.HU. *Contact:* Istvan Döry, Secretary.

OBJECTIVES: To undertake ecological, cultural and educational activities.

GENERAL INFORMATION: *Creation:* 1977. *Affiliated to:* BOKOR Basecommunity Network (Hungary). *Personnel/Total:* 5. *Volunteers:* 5. *Budget/Total 1993:* ECU 2500 (US$ 3300). *Financial sources: Private:* 100%.

PUBLICATIONS: *Periodicals:* Erted vagyok (6). *Annual report. List of publications.*

EVALUATION/RESEARCH: Evaluation reports available. Undertakes research activities.

COMMENTS: Undertakes activities in the Commonwealth of Independent States. Information activities related to the Commonwealth of Independent States.

INFORMATION AND EDUCATION ACTIVITIES: Topics: Culture/tradition/religion; Ecology/environment/biodiversity; Education/training/literacy. **Activities:** Conferences/seminars/workshops/training activities; Formal education; Fund raising; Information and documentation services/data bases; Lobbying/advocacy; Networking/electronic telecommunications; Publishing/audiovisual materials/educational materials.

HUN2611
CATHOLIC YOUTH MOVEMENT

Dohany u. 20, 1077 Budapest, Hungary.

HUN2612
DEMOCRATIC GYPSIES FEDERATION OF HUNGARY - NATIONAL YOUTH BRANCH

Zagrabi u. 5, 1107 Budapest, Hungary.

Telephone: 36 (1) 263 22 81. *Fax:* 36 (1) 263 22 81. *Contact:* Naday Gyula, President.

OBJECTIVES: To represent the interests of gypsies and help them achieve equal rights.

GENERAL INFORMATION: *Creation:* 1988. *Personnel/Total:* 400. *Salaried:* 416. *Volunteers:* 16.

EVALUATION/RESEARCH: Undertakes research activities.

COMMENTS: Undertakes activities in the Commonwealth of Independent States. Information activities related to the Commonwealth of Independent States.

ACTIVITIES IN DEVELOPING REGIONS: Works through local field partners.

HUN2613
E-MISSZIO ♦ E-Mission

Sóstó-erdei Szabadidö Park, 4430 Sóstófürdö, Hungary.

Telephone: 36 (42) 311 799. *Contact:* Légany András, President.

OBJECTIVES: To raise environmental awareness among citizens of Szabolcs County through: lectures at schools, information dissemination and designation of environmentally protected areas.

GENERAL INFORMATION: *Creation:* 1988. *Personnel/Total:* 4. *Salaried:* 3. *Volunteers:* 1. *Budget/Total 1993:* ECU 15000 (US$ 20000). *Financial sources: Private:* 58%. *Public:* 40%. *Self-financing:* 2%.

PUBLICATIONS: *Periodicals:* Süvöltö (6) - Eletjel (6).

EVALUATION/RESEARCH: Undertakes research activities.

COMMENTS: Undertakes activities in the Commonwealth of Independent States. Information activities related to the Commonwealth of Independent States.

INFORMATION AND EDUCATION ACTIVITIES: Topics: Ecology/environment/biodiversity. **Activities:** Information and documentation services/data bases; Information campaigns/exhibitions; Publishing/audiovisual materials/educational materials.

HUN2614
ENCIAN ENVIRONMENTAL EDUCATION CENTRE

Soto u.1, 1052 Budapest V, Hungary.

HUN2615
ENVIRONMENTAL EDUCATION CENTRE OF FOLOPHAZA

Pf. 186, 6001 Kocskemel, Hungary.

HUN2616
ENVIRONMENTAL GROUP OF THE DEMOCRATIC TRADE UNION OF THE SCIENTIFIC WORKERS (TDDSZ)

Jagello Ut 42/b, 1124 Budapest, Hungary.

HUN2617
FIGHT FOR EUROPE MOVEMENT

Narcisz 56, 1124 Budapest, Hungary.

HUN2618
FOUNDATION FOR HUNGARIAN WOMEN

Tatra u. 30/b, 1136 Budapest, Hungary.

HUN2619
FOUNDATION FOR SCHOOL DEVELOPMENT LASZLO HORVATH

Gyalin ut 22, 1097 Budapest, Hungary.

HUN2620
GAJA KORNYEZETVEDO EGYESULET ♦ Gaja Environmental Society

Box: Pf. 40, Petöfi s.u.5, 8008 Székesfehérvar, Hungary.

Telephone: 36 (22) 343 669. *Contact:* Szili Istvan.

OBJECTIVES: To help solve environmental problems of Székesfehérvar and its surroundings. To promote warnings for the protection of the environment.

Voir : *Comment utiliser le répertoire,* page 11.

GENERAL INFORMATION: *Creation:* 1991. *Personnel/Total:* 30. *Volunteers:* 30. *Budget/Total 1993:* ECU 4200 (US$ 5400). *Financial sources:* Private: 30%. Public: 50%. Self-financing: 20%.

EVALUATION/RESEARCH: Evaluation reports available. Undertakes research activities.

COMMENTS: Undertakes activities in the Commonwealth of Independent States. Information activities related to the Commonwealth of Independent States.

INFORMATION AND EDUCATION ACTIVITIES: Topics: Ecology/environment/biodiversity; Education/training/literacy; Health/sanitation/water; Rural development/agriculture; Urban development/habitat. **Activities:** Conferences/seminars/workshops/training activities; Exchanges/twinning/linking; Information and documentation services/data bases; Information campaigns/exhibitions; Networking/electronic telecommunications; Publishing/audiovisual materials/educational materials.

HUN2621
GEMEINSCHAFT JUNGER UNGARNDEUTSCHER (GJU)

Solymar, Marcibanyi u.10, 2083 Budapest, Hungary.

HUN2622
GEO-ENVIRON

Pf. 653, 6701 Szeged, Hungary.

Telephone: 36 (62) 310 865. *Fax:* 36 (62) 310 865. *E-mail:* j66b002.huszeg 11.bitnet. *Contact:* Imre Tóth.

OBJECTIVES: To undertake environmental education in schools and collect and publish information. To carry out lobbying activities to help preserve the environment, notably the springs in the Mecsek mountains in southern Hungary.

GENERAL INFORMATION: *Creation:* 1990. *Affiliated to:* National Society of Nature Conservationists (Hungary). *Budget/Total 1993:* ECU 800 (US$ 1100). *Financial sources:* Private: 30%. Public: 60%. Self-financing: 10%.

PUBLICATIONS: *Annual report. List of publications.*

EVALUATION/RESEARCH: Undertakes research activities.

COMMENTS: Undertakes activities in the Commonwealth of Independent States. Information activities related to the Commonwealth of Independent States.

INFORMATION AND EDUCATION ACTIVITIES: Topics: Culture/tradition/religion; Ecology/environment/biodiversity; Education/training/literacy; Health/sanitation/water; Human rights/peace/conflicts; Peace/ethnic conflicts/armament/disarmament. **Activities:** Exchanges/twinning/linking; Formal education; Information and documentation services/data bases; Information campaigns/exhibitions; Lobbying/advocacy; Publishing/audiovisual materials/educational materials.

HUN2623
GONCOL FOUNDATION

lloma u. 3 Pf. 184, 2600 Vao, Hungary.

HUN2624
GREEN ACTION NGO

Kossuth u.13, 3525 Miskolc, Hungary.

Telephone: 36 (46) 349 806. *Fax:* 36 (46) 352 010. *Contact:* Dezsö Nagy, Secretary.

OBJECTIVES: To protect and conserve nature. To initiate social action and act on behalf of environmental laws. To undertake international networking with other NGOs and governments. To work for the conservation and protection of natural energy sources and of environmentally damaged areas.

GENERAL INFORMATION: *Creation:* 1990. *Personnel/Total:* 114. *Salaried:* 4. *Volunteers:* 110. *Budget/Total 1993:* ECU 46000 (US$ 60000). *Financial sources:* Public: 83%. Self-financing: 17%.

PUBLICATIONS: *List of publications.*

EVALUATION/RESEARCH: Evaluation reports available. Undertakes research activities.

PLANNED ACTIVITIES: GREEN ACTION NGO plans to increase its network by contacting factories and expanding its environmental education programme to the local school system and camps.

COMMENTS: Undertakes activities in the Commonwealth of Independent States. Information activities related to the Commonwealth of Independent States.

INFORMATION AND EDUCATION ACTIVITIES: Topics: Ecology/environment/biodiversity; Education/training/literacy; Health/sanitation/water; Rural development/agriculture; Urban development/habitat. **Activities:** Information and documentation services/data bases; Information campaigns/exhibitions; Networking/electronic telecommunications; Publishing/audiovisual materials/educational materials.

HUN2625
GYERMEKERDEKEK MAGYARORSZAGI FORUMA ♦ Hungarian Forum for Children's Interests

Kontyfa u. 5, 1156 Budapest, Hungary.

Telephone: 36 (1) 164 3280. *Fax:* 36 (1) 164 3280. *Contact:* György Papp, Co-President.

OBJECTIVES: To raise awareness of children's rights and cases of their violations. To lobby for children's interests and for compliance in Hungary with the United Nation's Declaration of the Rights of the Child.

GENERAL INFORMATION: *Creation:* 1989. *Personnel/Total:* 2. *Volunteers:* 2. *Budget/Total 1993:* ECU 17000 (US$ 22000). *Financial sources:* Public: 95%. Self-financing: 5%.

PUBLICATIONS: *Periodicals:* Tájékoztató (8). *Annual report.*

PLANNED ACTIVITIES: The Hungarian Forum plans to organise international workshops with participants from other Central European countries and the former Soviet Union to promote advocacy for children's rights.

COMMENTS: Information activities related to the Commonwealth of Independent States.

INFORMATION AND EDUCATION ACTIVITIES: Topics: Children/youth/family; Human rights/peace/conflicts. **Activities:** Conferences/seminars/workshops/training activities; Information and documentation services/data bases; Lobbying/advocacy; Publishing/audiovisual materials/educational materials.

HUN2626
H. YOUTH ENVIRONMENTALIST ORGANIZATION

Bocskai ter 2/125, 4220 Hajduboszormeny, Hungary.

Telephone: 36 (52) 371 200/2. *Fax:* 36 (52) 371 200/21. *Contact:* Attila Molnar, President.

OBJECTIVES: To undertake environmental education. To promote the protection of nature in the town of Hajduboszormeny.

GENERAL INFORMATION: *Creation:* 1991. *Affiliated to:* Alliance of Environmentalists (Hungary) - Alliance of Environmentalists in the Tisza-Region (Hungary). *Personnel/Total:* 42. *Salaried:* 2. *Volunteers:* 40. *Budget/Total 1993:* ECU 8000 (US$ 11000). *Financial sources:* Public: 98%. Self-financing: 2%.

PUBLICATIONS: *Annual report.*

EVALUATION/RESEARCH: Evaluation reports available. Undertakes research activities.

COMMENTS: Undertakes activities in the Commonwealth of Independent States. Information activities related to the Commonwealth of Independent States.

INFORMATION AND EDUCATION ACTIVITIES: Topics: Ecology/environment/biodiversity; Urban development/habitat. **Activities:** Formal education; Information and documentation services/data bases; Information campaigns/exhibitions; Lobbying/advocacy; Publishing/audiovisual materials/educational materials.

HUN2627
HARMADIK VILAG ALAPITRANY ♦ Third World Foundation
Pf. 40, 1476 Budapest, Hungary.

Telephone: 36 (1) 271 04 10. *Fax:* 36 (1) 271 04 10. *Contact:* György Bisztrai, Secretary.

OBJECTIVES: To provide aid to the Third World.

GENERAL INFORMATION: *Creation:* 1968. *Type of organisation:* coordinating body. *Affiliated to:* BOKOR Basecommunity Network. *Personnel/Total:* 1. *Volunteers:* 1. *Budget/Total 1993:* ECU 43000 (US$ 44000). *Financial sources:* Self-financing: 100%.

PUBLICATIONS: *Annual report. List of publications.*

EVALUATION/RESEARCH: Evaluation reports available. Undertakes research activities.

COMMENTS: Undertakes activities in the Commonwealth of Independent States. Information activities related to the Commonwealth of Independent States.

ACTIVITIES IN DEVELOPING REGIONS: Active in 1 country(ies). Works through local field partners. **Sustainable Development Actions:** Children/youth/family; Education/training/literacy; Food/famine. **Regions:** Central Asia and South Asia.

INFORMATION AND EDUCATION ACTIVITIES: Topics: Children/youth/family; Education/training/literacy; Food/famine. **Activities:** Fund raising; Publishing/audiovisual materials/educational materials.

HUN2628
HELSINKI COMMITTEE
c/o AB - Bcszelo Kiado, Pf.573, 1447 Budapest, Hungary.

HUN2629
HERMANN OTTO ENVIRONMENTAL SCHOOL TEAM
Fo u. 95, 4066 Tiszacogo, Hungary.

HUN2630
HUNGARIAN CENTRE FOR FOUNDATION
Belgrad rakpart 24, III emelet, 1056 Budapest, Hungary.

HUN2631
HUNGARIAN INTERCHURCH AID
Tomaj u. 4, 1116 Budapest XI, Hungary.

Telephone: 36 (1) 186 54 53. *Fax:* 36 (1) 186 89 13. *Contact:* Rev. László Lehel, Director.

OBJECTIVES: To provide assistance to the needy regardless of their faith. To undertake refugee relief, international aid programmes and programmes that address Hungarian social needs.

GENERAL INFORMATION: *Creation:* 1991. *Affiliated to:* ECRE (United Kingdom) - APRODEV (Belgium). *Personnel/Total:* 135. *Salaried:* 35 of which: 3 in developing countries. *Volunteers:* 100. *Budget/Total 1993:* ECU 3263000 (US$ 4232000). *Financial sources:* Private: 1%. Public: 97%.

PUBLICATIONS: *Annual report. List of publications.*

EVALUATION/RESEARCH: Evaluation reports available. Undertakes research activities.

COMMENTS: Undertakes activities in the Commonwealth of Independent States. Information activities related to the Commonwealth of Independent States.

ACTIVITIES IN DEVELOPING REGIONS: Active in 1 country(ies). Maintains local field presence. Works through local field partners. **Sustainable Development Actions:** Emergency relief/refugees/humanitarian assistance. **Regions:** Central Africa.

INFORMATION AND EDUCATION ACTIVITIES: Topics: Children/youth/family; Emergency relief/refugees/humanitarian assistance; Employment/unemployment; Food/famine; Gender issues/women; Health/sanitation/water; Human rights/peace/conflicts; International relations/coop-eration/development aid; Poverty/living conditions; Racism/xenophobia/antisemitism; Refugees/migrants/ethnic groups. **Activities:** Broadcasting/cultural events; Conferences/seminars/workshops/training activities; Exchanges/twinning/linking; Formal education; Fund raising; Information and documentation services/data bases; Information campaigns/exhibitions; Lobbying/advocacy; Networking/electronic telecommunications; Publishing/audiovisual materials/educational materials.

HUN2632
HUNGARIAN LEAGUE OF HUMAN RIGHTS
Nador u.7, 1051 Budapest, Hungary.

HUN2633
HUNGARIAN NORTH-SOUTH ASSOCIATION
Kinizsi u. 1-7, room 145, 1093 Budapest, Hungary.

HUN2634
HUNGARIAN YOUTH COUNCIL (MISZOT)
Rosenberg hp. u. 1, 1054 Budapest, Hungary.

HUN2635
INDEPENDENT ECOLOGICAL CENTRE
Miklos ter 1, 1035 Budapest, Hungary.

HUN2636
INTERNATIONAL COMMITTEE OF CHILDREN'S AND ADOLESCENTS MOVEMENT
P.O. Box 147, 1389 Budapest, Hungary.

HUN2637
IPOLY UNIO KORNYEZETVEDELMI ES KULTURALIS EGYESULET ♦ Ipoly Union Environmental and Cultural Association
Rákóczi ut 12, 2660 Balassagyarmat, Hungary.

Telephone: 36 (27) 314 983. *Fax:* 36 (27) 311 179. *E-mail:* vkiszel@goncol.zpok.hu. *Contact:* Vilmos Kiszel, Hungarian Co-Chairman, Endre Szkladanyi, Slovakian Co-Chairman.

OBJECTIVES: To revitalise the region of Ipoly by restoring transportation structures and promoting professional and cultural activities. To preserve natural heritage and promote environmental protection in the region.

GENERAL INFORMATION: *Creation:* 1992. *Affiliated to:* Göncöl Allience (Hungary) - International Rivers Network - Slovalian Rivers Network (Slovakia) - Hungarian Transportation Club (Hungary). *Personnel/Total:* 51. *Salaried:* 1. *Volunteers:* 50. *Budget/Total 1993:* ECU 10000 (US$ 14000). *Financial sources:* Private: 20%. Public: 75%. *Self-financing:* 5%.

PUBLICATIONS: *Periodicals:* IPOLY FÜZETEK (4).

EVALUATION/RESEARCH: Undertakes research activities.

COMMENTS: Undertakes activities in the Commonwealth of Independent States. Information activities related to the Commonwealth of Independent States.

INFORMATION AND EDUCATION ACTIVITIES: Topics: Culture/tradition/religion; Ecology/environment/biodiversity; Education/training/literacy; Health/sanitation/water; Human rights/peace/conflicts; International relations/cooperation/development aid; Peace/ethnic conflicts/armament/disarmament; Rural development/agriculture; Urban development/habitat. **Activities:** Conferences/seminars/workshops/training activities; Exchanges/twinning/linking; Fund raising; Information and documentation services/data bases; Information campaigns/exhibitions; Lobbying/advocacy; Networking/electronic telecommunications; Publishing/audiovisual materials/educational materials.

HUN2638
THE JOINT EASTERN EUROPE CENTER FOR DEMOCRATIC EDUCATION AND GOVERNANCE
Pf. 427, Victor Hugo u.18.22, 1395 Budapest, XIII-Ker, Hungary.

Voir : *Comment utiliser le répertoire*, page 11.

HUN2639

KISS FORENO ENVIRONMENTAL ASSOCIATION OF CAONGRAD COUNTY

Ag u. 4 II/8, 6723 Szeged, Hungary.

HUN2640

MAGTAR IFJUSAGI KAMARA ♦ Junior Chamber Hungary

Ruthen U. 28, 1025 Budapest, Hungary.

Telephone: 36 (1) 250 14 66. *Fax:* 36 (1) 167 11 33. *Contact:* Attila Karvalics, president.

OBJECTIVES: To undertake personal and leadership development training programmes and community, social and youth projects.

GENERAL INFORMATION: *Creation:* 1990. *Affiliated to:* Junior Chamber International (USA). *Personnel/Total:* 1. *Budget/Total 1993:* ECU 4000 (US$ 5000). *Financial sources:* Private: 40%. Public: 30%. Self-financing: 30%.

PUBLICATIONS: *Periodicals:* JCI News (12) - Jaycee News (4). *List of publications.*

EVALUATION/RESEARCH: Evaluation reports available. Undertakes research activities.

PLANNED ACTIVITIES: The Junior Chamber plans to carry out small-business education, management training, environmental projects and an international trainee exchange.

COMMENTS: Undertakes activities in the Commonwealth of Independent States. Information activities related to the Commonwealth of Independent States.

INFORMATION AND EDUCATION ACTIVITIES: Topics: Children/youth/family; Culture/tradition/religion; Ecology/environment/biodiversity; International economic relations/trade/debt/finance; International relations/cooperation/development aid; Other; Urban development/habitat. **Activities:** Conferences/seminars/workshops/training activities; Exchanges/twinning/linking; Formal education; Information and documentation services/data bases; Information campaigns/exhibitions; Lobbying/advocacy; Networking/electronic telecommunications; Publishing/audiovisual materials/educational materials.

HUN2641

MAGYAR CSERKESZLEANY SZOVETSEG ♦ League of the Hungarian Girl Scouts

Pf. 433, 1371 Budapest, Hungary.

Telephone: 36 (1) 201 2011 138.

HUN2642

MAGYAR EMBERI JOGUEDO KOZPONT-MARTIN LUTHER KING PROJECT ♦ Centre for Defense of Human Rights-Martin Luther King Project

Pf. 562, 1447 Budapest, Hungary.

Telephone: 36 (11) 387 84. *Fax:* 36 (11) 438 62. *Contact:* Martin III, Executive Director.

OBJECTIVES: To provide assistance, legal advice and representation, and to disseminate information to victims of human rights abuses.

GENERAL INFORMATION: *Creation:* 1993. *Type of organisation:* network. *Personnel/Total:* 52. *Salaried:* 7. *Volunteers:* 45. *Financial sources:* Private: 100%.

PUBLICATIONS: *Periodicals:* Colors of Reality. *Annual report. List of publications.*

COMMENTS: Undertakes activities in the Commonwealth of Independent States. Information activities related to the Commonwealth of Independent States.

INFORMATION AND EDUCATION ACTIVITIES: Topics: Racism/xenophobia/antisemitism; Refugees/migrants/ethnic groups. **Activities:** Conferences/seminars/workshops/training activities; Fund raising; Information and documentation services/data bases; Lobbying/advocacy.

HUN2643

MAGYARORSZAGI GYERMEKBARATOK MOZGALMA ♦
Movement of Hungarian Childfriends

Zrinyi u. 97, 1196 Budapest, Hungary.

Telephone: 36 (1) 282 38 52. *Fax:* 36 (1) 282 38 52. *Contact:* Hanti Vilmos.

OBJECTIVES: To represent the interests of children. To provide social assistance to children to ensure their proper physical and mental education. To prepare children to become successfully integrated into the Hungarian society and workforce.

GENERAL INFORMATION: *Creation:* 1992. *Type of organisation:* network. *Affiliated to:* Hungarian Civil Chamber - Non-Profit Human Chamber - Hungarian Anti-Fascists' Organisation - Hungarian Child and Youth Council. *Personnel/Total:* 101. *Salaried:* 1. *Volunteers:* 100. *Budget/Total 1993:* ECU 13000 (US$ 17000). *Financial sources:* Private: 30%. Public: 60%. Self-financing: 10%.

PUBLICATIONS: *Periodicals:* Childfriend (4).

EVALUATION/RESEARCH: Evaluation reports available.

COMMENTS: Undertakes activities in the Commonwealth of Independent States. Information activities related to the Commonwealth of Independent States.

INFORMATION AND EDUCATION ACTIVITIES: Topics: Children/youth/family; Culture/tradition/religion; Ecology/environment/biodiversity; Education/training/literacy; Gender issues/women; Health/sanitation/water; Human rights/peace/conflicts; Peace/ethnic conflicts/armament/disarmament; Population/family planning/demography; Racism/xenophobia/antisemitism. **Activities:** Conferences/seminars/workshops/training activities; Exchanges/twinning/linking; Formal education; Information and documentation services/data bases; Information campaigns/exhibitions; Lobbying/advocacy; Publishing/audiovisual materials/educational materials.

HUN2644

MARTIN LUTHER KING ORGANIZATION

Zsombolyai u. 3, 1113 Budapest, Hungary.

Telephone: 36 (1) 135 68 65. *Fax:* 36 (1) 135 68 65. *Contact:* Mester Csaba, President.

OBJECTIVES: To provide legal advice and representation for victims of human rights violations. To bring together children of inter-racial marriages. To provide legal visits to refugees in camps through Eastern and Central Europe. To promote educational and multi-cultural programmes for non-European refugees.

GENERAL INFORMATION: *Creation:* 1991. *Personnel/Total:* 14. *Salaried:* 4. *Volunteers:* 10. *Budget/Total 1993:* ECU 25000 (US$ 33000). *Financial sources:* Private: 98%. Self-financing: 2%.

PUBLICATIONS: *Periodicals:* Colourful News (12) - Information on MLKO (6). *Annual report. List of publications.*

EVALUATION/RESEARCH: Evaluation reports available. Undertakes research activities.

COMMENTS: Undertakes activities in the Commonwealth of Independent States. Information activities related to the Commonwealth of Independent States.

INFORMATION AND EDUCATION ACTIVITIES: Topics: Emergency relief/refugees/humanitarian assistance; Human rights/peace/conflicts; Peace/ethnic conflicts/armament/disarmament; Racism/xenophobia/antisemitism; Refugees/migrants/ethnic groups. **Activities:** Broadcasting/cultural events; Conferences/seminars/workshops/training activities; Exchanges/twinning/linking; Formal education; Fund raising; Information and documentation services/data bases; Information campaigns/exhibitions; Lobbying/advocacy; Networking/electronic telecommunications; Publishing/audiovisual materials/educational materials.

HUN2645

MASSAG ALAPITVANY - NMZETI ES ETNIKAI KISEBBSEGI JOGVEDO IRODA ♦ Otherness Foundation - Legal Aid Office for National and Ethnic Minorities

See: *How to Use the Directory,* page 11.

Pf. 453/269, 1537 Budapest, Hungary.

Telephone: 36 (1) 131 11 63. **Fax:** 36 (1) 131 11 63. **Contact:** Andras Bíró, President of the Board.

OBJECTIVES: To provide legal defence of national and ethnic minorities in cases of injuries due to ethnic discrimination.

GENERAL INFORMATION: *Creation:* 1993. *Personnel/Total:* 32. *Salaried:* 4. *Volunteers:* 28. *Financial sources:* *Private:* 80%. *Public:* 20%.

PUBLICATIONS: *Annual report. List of publications.*

EVALUATION/RESEARCH: Evaluation reports available. Undertakes research activities.

COMMENTS: Undertakes activities in the Commonwealth of Independent States. Information activities related to the Commonwealth of Independent States.

INFORMATION AND EDUCATION ACTIVITIES: Topics: Human rights/peace/conflicts; Racism/xenophobia/antisemitism; Refugees/migrants/ethnic groups. **Activities:** Information and documentation services/data bases; Lobbying/advocacy.

HUN2646
MOVEMENT FOR A GLOBAL PARLIAMENT

P.O. Box 118, 5540 Szarvas, Hungary.

HUN2647
MOVEMENT OF YOUNG SOCIALISTS

Bp. VII Erzsebet Krt 40-42, 1073 Budapest, Hungary.

HUN2648
NATIONAL CONFEDERATION OF HUNGARIAN TRADE UNIONS (MSZOSZ)

Dosza Gyorgy ut. 84/B, 1415 Budapest VI, Hungary.

HUN2649
NATIONAL COUNCIL OF YOUTH ORGANISATIONS

Hold utca 1, 1054 Budapest, Hungary.

HUN2650
NATIONAL SOCIETY OF CONSERVATIONISTS

Kolto u 21, 1121 Budapest, Hungary.

HUN2651
ORCHID ASSOCIATION FOR NATURE CONSERVATION

Egystem Idr, 4010 Dobrecen, Hungary.

HUN2652
OXYGEN ENVIRONMENTAL CLUB

Simondly u. 21, 1025 Dobrecen, Hungary.

HUN2653
P. CULTURAL ASSOCIATION, ENVIRONMENTAL SECTION

Doberdo u. 13, 4032 Dobrecen, Hungary.

HUN2654
PROGRESSIVE YOUTH FOUNDATION

Koztarsasag ter 27, 1081 Budapest, Hungary.

HUN2655
RAOUL WALLENBERG ASSOCIATION

Baross u. 61, 1082 Budapest, Hungary.

Telephone: 36 (1) 113 54 39. **Fax:** 36 (1) 113 54 39.

OBJECTIVES: To protect the rights of religious, ethnic, racial and other minorities in Hungary. To cultivate the memory of Raoul Wallenberg, the saviour of tens of thousands of Jews during his stay in Hungary in 1944-1945.

GENERAL INFORMATION: *Creation:* 1988. **Affiliated to:** LICRA. **Personnel/Total:** 6. *Salaried:* 1. *Volunteers:* 5. **Budget/Total 1993:** ECU 7000 (US$ 9000). **Financial sources:** *Private:* 32%. *Public:* 63%. *Self-financing:* 5%.

PUBLICATIONS: *Periodicals:* Többesszám (8). *Annual report.*

EVALUATION/RESEARCH: Evaluation reports available.

PLANNED ACTIVITIES: The Association plans to publish a series of Wallenberg notebooks in Hungarian dealing with inter-ethnic relations and conflicts, to set up its own team of civil rights lawyers and a network of lawyers to defend civil rights and penal cases affecting minorities.

COMMENTS: Undertakes activities in the Commonwealth of Independent States.

INFORMATION AND EDUCATION ACTIVITIES: Topics: Peace/ethnic conflicts/armament/disarmament; Racism/xenophobia/antisemitism; Refugees/migrants/ethnic groups. **Activities:** Conferences/seminars/workshops/training activities; Information campaigns/exhibitions; Networking/electronic telecommunications.

HUN2656
REFLEX ENVIRONMENTAL PROTECTION SOCIETY

Bartok Bela u. 7, 9024 Gyor, Hungary.

HUN2657
REGIONAL ENVIRONMENTAL CENTRE FOR CENTRAL AND EASTERN EUROPE

Miklos ter 1, 1035 Budapest, Hungary.

Telephone: 36 (1) 250 34 01. **Fax:** 36 (1) 250 34 03. **E-mail:** REC-INFO REC.HU. **Contact:** Stanislav Sitnicki, Executive Director.

OBJECTIVES: To promote co-operation among diverse environmental groups in Central and Eastern Europe. To act as a catalyst for developing solutions to environmental problems in this region. To promote public participation in environmental decision-making.

GENERAL INFORMATION: *Creation:* 1990. *Personnel/Total:* 56. *Salaried:* 53. *Volunteers:* 3. **Budget/Total 1993:** ECU 3000000 (US$ 3890000). **Financial sources:** *Public:* 100%.

PUBLICATIONS: *Annual report. List of publications.*

EVALUATION/RESEARCH: Evaluation reports available. Undertakes research activities.

PLANNED ACTIVITIES: REC will strengthen NGO assistance at the local level, will establish an electronic communication link with Budapest and start a reference library collection.

COMMENTS: Undertakes activities in the Commonwealth of Independent States. Information activities related to the Commonwealth of Independent States.

INFORMATION AND EDUCATION ACTIVITIES: Topics: Ecology/environment/biodiversity; Health/sanitation/water; Rural development/agriculture. **Activities:** Conferences/seminars/workshops/training activities; Exchanges/twinning/linking; Formal education; Fund raising; Information and documentation services/data bases; Information campaigns/exhibitions; Networking/electronic telecommunications; Publishing/audiovisual materials/educational materials.

HUN2658
ROMA CIVIL RIGHTS MOVEMENT

Pannonia u. 22 fszt. 1.a, 1136 Budapest, Hungary.

HUN2659
SOCIETY OF NATURE PROTECTIONISTS

Gagarin u. 2 4/4, 3524 Miskolo, Hungary.

HUN2660
STUDENT CO-OPERATIVE GROUP "UNIVERSITAS"

Kinizsi u. 1-7, 1092 Budapest, Hungary.

Voir : *Comment utiliser le répertoire,* page 11.

2>

HUN2661
SUN DIAL CLUB
Karpat u. 56, 1133 Budapest, Hungary.

HUN2662
THIRD SHORE
Nemetvolgyi ut. 120, 1124 Budapest, Hungary.

HUN2663
TRADE UNION COOPERATION FORUM
Corkij fasor 10, 1071 Budapest, Hungary.

HUN2664
TRADE UNION YOUTH FEDERATION
Dozsa Gyorgy ut 84/B, 1415 Budapest, Hungary.

HUN2665
TRANSDANUBIAN LIFE AND ENVIRONMENTAL PROTECTIONISTS
Fo u. 35, 2475 Kapodnasnyck, Hungary.

HUN2666
UNION FOR ENVIRONMENT IN REGION OF ILOVES
Bajcay Zsilbansy u.9, 3300 Eger, Hungary.

HUN2667
UNION OF CALVINIST YOUTH
Arpad Fejedelem utja 49, 1036 Budapest, Hungary.

HUN2668
UNION OF HUNGARIAN PIONEERS
Konkoly thege M. ut. 21, 1121 Budapest, Hungary.

HUN2669
UNITED WAY OF HUNGARY
Csersznye u.1, 1112 Budapest, Hungary.

HUN2670
WORLD FEDERATION OF DEMOCRATIC YOUTH (WFDY)
XIII Frangepan ut. 16, POB 147, 1139 Budapest, Hungary.

Telephone: 36 (1) 129.5226. *Fax:* 36 (1) 129.5226. *Contact:* Rasheed Kh. Ali, Vice-President.

HUN2671
WWF FOUNDATION FOR THE HUNGARIAN ENVIRONMENTAL EDUCATION
Nmetvlgyi ut 78/b, 1124 Budapest, Hungary.

HUN2672
YOUTH DEMOCRATIC FORUM
O-utca 8-10, 1066 Budapest, Hungary.

HUN2673
YOUTH ENVIRONMENTAL ASSOCIATION
Bajcsy-Zsilinszky u. 31.11/3, 1065 Budapest, Hungary.

HUN2674
YOUTH FOREST ACTION
Pf. 72, 2000 Szenlendro, Hungary.

HUN2675
YOUTH ORGANISATION OF THE ALLIANCE OF FREE DEMOCRATS
Bp. V., Merleg u.6, 1051 Budapest, Hungary.

HUN2676
YOUTH UNION
Szolo u. 88 IX/50, 1032 Budapest, Hungary.

HUN2677
YWCA OF HUNGARY
Deovai B.M. teor 1, 1034 Budapest, Hungary.

HUN2678
ZOLD SZIV IFJUSAGI TERMESZETVEDO MOZGALAM ♦ Green Heart Youth Movement for Nature Conservation
Matyas Kir. u.2., 2013 Pomaz, Hungary.

Telephone: 36 (26) 325 957. *E-mail:* aniko@zsziv.zpok.hu. *Contact:* Aniko' Orgova'nyi, President.

OBJECTIVES: To promote the appreciation of nature. To protect and monitor natural habitats and fauna. To teach children to respect nature and the environment. To conduct environmental workshops for teachers.

GENERAL INFORMATION: *Creation:* 1989. *Personnel/Total:* 13. *Salaried:* 3. *Volunteers:* 10.

PUBLICATIONS: *Periodicals:* Zöldszivküldi (2). *Annual report. List of publications.*

EVALUATION/RESEARCH: Evaluation reports available. Undertakes research activities.

PLANNED ACTIVITIES: The organisation plans to begin a summer camp programme for children.

COMMENTS: Undertakes activities in the Commonwealth of Independent States. Information activities related to the Commonwealth of Independent States.

INFORMATION AND EDUCATION ACTIVITIES: Topics: Ecology/environment/biodiversity; Urban development/habitat. **Activities:** Conferences/seminars/workshops/training activities; Formal education; Fund raising; Information campaigns/exhibitions; Lobbying/advocacy; Networking/electronic telecommunications; Publishing/audiovisual materials/educational materials.

2>

IRL2679
ACTION FROM IRELAND (AFRI)

2nd fl. Harcourt Rd., Dublin 2, Ireland.

Telephone: 353 (1) 478 51 00. *Fax:* 353 (1) 478 51 42. *Contact:* Joe Murray, Co-ordinator.

OBJECTIVES: To develop a clearer understanding of the causes of poverty and hunger in the world. To draw parallels between Ireland's colonial experience and that of the Third World countries today. To raise awareness of the major causes of poverty and hunger.

GENERAL INFORMATION: *Creation:* 1975. *Type of organisation:* association of NGOs. *Affiliated to:* International Peace Bureau (Switzerland) - Dóchas (Ireland) - Debt and Development Coalition (Ireland) - Dolgon Pork (Ireland). *Personnel/Total:* 5. *Salaried:* 3. *Volunteers:* 2. *Budget/Total 1993:* ECU 125000 (US$ 147000). *Financial sources:* Private: 35%. Self-financing: 65%.

PUBLICATIONS: *Periodicals:* Peace Maker (2). *Annual report.*

PLANNED ACTIVITIES: AFRI is planning a series of 'Famine Walks' to commemorate the 150th anniversary of Ireland's great 'famine' and to draw the links between this and famine throughout the world today.

ACTIVITIES IN DEVELOPING REGIONS: Works through local field partners.

INFORMATION AND EDUCATION ACTIVITIES: Topics: Ecology/environment/biodiversity; Food/famine; Health/sanitation/water; Human rights/peace/conflicts; International economic relations/trade/debt/finance; Peace/ethnic conflicts/armament/disarmament; Urban development/habitat. Activities: Conferences/seminars/workshops/training activities; Fund raising; Information campaigns/exhibitions; Lobbying/advocacy; Publishing/audiovisual materials/educational materials.

IRL2680
AL-SADAQA IRELAND-PALESTINE FRIENDSHIP

86 Marian Crescent, Dublin 14, Ireland.

Telephone: 353 (1) 494 38 60. *Fax:* 353 (1) 493 73 41. *Contact:* Seán T. Ryan.

OBJECTIVES: To co-ordinate the work of individuals and groups in Ireland concerned by human rights, justice and peace in Israel/Palestine and to seek their co-operation towards achieving this objective.

GENERAL INFORMATION: *Personnel/Total:* 4. *Volunteers:* 4. *Budget/Total 1993:* ECU 313 (US$ 367). *Financial sources:* Self-financing: 100%.

PUBLICATIONS: *Periodicals:* Al-Sadâqa (4). *Annual report.*

PLANNED ACTIVITIES: The organisation is planning to develop links with local Palestinian groups in the Middle East that are involved in human rights activities and women's affairs.

ACTIVITIES IN DEVELOPING REGIONS: Works through local field partners. Sustainable Development Actions: Gender issues/women; Human rights/peace/conflicts; Rural development/agriculture. Regions: Middle East.

INFORMATION AND EDUCATION ACTIVITIES: Topics: Health/sanitation/water; Human rights/peace/conflicts; Peace/ethnic conflicts/armament/disarmament. Activities: Exchanges/twinning/linking; Fund raising; Information campaigns/exhibitions; Lobbying/advocacy.

IRL2681
AMNESTY INTERNATIONAL, IRISH SECTION

Sean MacBride House, 8 Shaw Street, Dublin 2, Ireland.

IRL2682
ASSOCIATION OF MISSIONARY SOCIETIES (AMS)

Overseas House, 3 Belgrave Road, Rathmines, Dublin 6, Ireland.

Telephone: 353 (1) 970.931. *Fax:* 353 (1) 970.939. *Contact:* Rev. Declan Smith.

IRL2683
BOTHAR

99 O'Connell Street, Limerick, Ireland.

Telephone: 353 (61) 414 142. *Fax:* 353 (61) 315 833. *Contact:* Peter Ireton, Chief Executive Officer.

OBJECTIVES: To assist needy families to overcome hunger, malnutrition and poverty through the development of animal production, improved farming systems and local self-sustainable organisations in East Africa. To promote the empowerment of women, environmental protection and agricultural/economic self-sufficiency.

GENERAL INFORMATION: *Creation:* 1991. *Affiliated to:* Heifer Project International (United States). *Personnel/Total:* 2. *Salaried:* 2. *Budget/Total 1993:* ECU 363000 (US$ 425000). *Financial sources:* Private: 80%. Public: 10%. Self-financing: 10%.

PUBLICATIONS: *Periodicals:* The Bo Vine (6). *Annual report.*

EVALUATION/RESEARCH: Evaluation reports available. Undertakes research activities.

COMMENTS: Undertakes activities in the Commonwealth of Independent States. Information activities related to the Commonwealth of Independent States.

ACTIVITIES IN DEVELOPING REGIONS: Active in 1 country(ies). Works through local field partners. Sustainable Development Actions: Education/training/literacy; Food/famine; Gender issues/women; Rural development/agriculture; Sending volunteers/experts/technical assistance. Regions: East Africa; West Africa.

INFORMATION AND EDUCATION ACTIVITIES: Topics: Rural development/agriculture. Activities: Conferences/seminars/workshops/training activities; Fund raising; Information campaigns/exhibitions; Publishing/audiovisual materials/educational materials.

IRL2684
CAMBODIA SOLIDARITY GROUP

c/o 55 Grand Parade, Cork, Ireland.

Telephone: 353 (21) 275 881. *Contact:* Helen O'Doherty.

OBJECTIVES: To support the right of the Cambodian people to self-determination. To campaign for the isolation of the Khmer Rouge and to stop military support for them. To press for the trial of the Khmer Rouge leaders for their crimes of genocide. To raise awareness of the Cambodian situation within Ireland.

GENERAL INFORMATION: *Type of organisation:* network. *Budget/Total 1993:* ECU 250 (US$ 300). *Financial sources:* Private: 50%. Self-financing: 50%.

INFORMATION AND EDUCATION ACTIVITIES: Topics: Culture/tradition/religion; Education/training/literacy; Human rights/peace/conflicts; International relations/cooperation/development aid; Peace/ethnic conflicts/armament/disarmament. Activities: Broadcasting/cultural events; Conferences/seminars/workshops/training activities; Exchanges/twinning/linking; Fund raising; Information and documentation services/data bases; Information campaigns/exhibitions; Lobbying/advocacy.

IRL2685
CAMPAIGN AID

61 Lower Camden Street, Dublin 2, Ireland.

Telephone: 353 (1) 478.3490. *Contact:* Bairbre Hand.

IRL2686
CENTRE FOR INTERNATIONAL CO-OPERATION

1 Tower Bock, Shannon Airport, Co. Clare, Ireland.

Telephone: 353 (61) 475 352. *Fax:* 353 (61) 472 349. *Contact:* Brendan O'Regan, President.

OBJECTIVES: To increase international understanding and co-operation by creating people-to-people contacts and by developing these contacts into managed programmes of co-operation.

GENERAL INFORMATION: *Creation:* 1987. *Type of organisation:* association of NGOs. *Personnel/Total:* 9. *Salaried:* 4. *Volunteers:*

5. *Budget/Total 1993:* ECU 100000 (US$ 117000). *Financial sources:* Private: 8%. Public: 72%. Self-financing: 20%.

PUBLICATIONS: *Periodicals:* Newsletter (1). *Annual report.*

EVALUATION/RESEARCH: Undertakes research activities.

PLANNED ACTIVITIES: The organisation is planning to submit various proposals, under the PHARE/TACIS programmes for technical assistance to the countries of the former Soviet Union including the Baltic Republics.

COMMENTS: The Centre for International Co-operation is in association with the United Nations Department of Public Information. Undertakes activities in the Commonwealth of Independent States. Information activities related to the Commonwealth of Independent States.

INFORMATION AND EDUCATION ACTIVITIES: Topics: Culture/tradition/religion; Education/training/literacy; Employment/unemployment; Human rights/peace/conflicts; International economic relations/trade/debt/finance; International relations/cooperation/development aid; Peace/ethnic conflicts/armament/disarmament; Rural development/agriculture; Urban development/habitat. Activities: Broadcasting/cultural events; Conferences/seminars/workshops/training activities; Exchanges/twinning/linking; Formal education; Information and documentation services/data bases; Information campaigns/exhibitions.

IRL2687

CHRISTIAN AID, IRELAND

Christ Church, Rathgar Road, Dublin 6, Ireland.

Telephone: 353 (1) 496 61 84. *Fax:* 353 (1) 497 38 80. *Contact:* Coordinator.

OBJECTIVES: To channel the gifts of Christians and others to those areas of the world where human needs are great and local resources inadequate, enabling the churches overseas to serve the needy without regard to race, religion or politics.

GENERAL INFORMATION: *Creation:* 1949. *Affiliated to:* Dochas - Debt and Development Coalition - Irish Refugee Council. *Personnel/Total:* 18. *Salaried:* 3. *Volunteers:* 15. *Budget/Total 1993:* ECU 673000 (US$ 789000). *Financial sources:* Private: 19%. Public: 81%.

PUBLICATIONS: *Periodicals:* Jubilee (4). *Annual report. List of publications.*

COMMENTS: Many of the activities are carried out by Christian Aid UK. Undertakes activities in the Commonwealth of Independent States.

ACTIVITIES IN DEVELOPING REGIONS: Active in 20 country(ies). Works through local field partners. Sustainable Development Actions: Ecology/environment/biodiversity; Education/training/literacy; Emergency relief/refugees/humanitarian assistance; Food/famine; Health/sanitation/water; Human rights/peace/conflicts; Rural development/agriculture; Urban development/habitat. Regions: Caribbean; Central Africa; East Africa; Middle East; South East Asia; Southern Africa.

INFORMATION AND EDUCATION ACTIVITIES: Topics: Emergency relief/refugees/humanitarian assistance; Human rights/peace/conflicts; International economic relations/trade/debt/finance. Activities: Conferences/seminars/workshops/training activities; Information campaigns/exhibitions; Lobbying/advocacy.

IRL2688

CHURCH MISSIONARY SOCIETY IRELAND (CMSI) ◆ Societé missionaire de l'Eglise d'Irlande

Overseas House, 3 Belgrave Road, Dublin 6, Ireland.

Telephone: 353 (1) 497 09 31. *Fax:* 353 (1) 497 09 39. *Contact:* Rev. Cecil Wilson, General Secretary.

OBJECTIVES: To assist the Church in carrying out its mission of development and to share resources with the needy. To inform members about missionary activities and to encourage new volunteers to take part in them.

GENERAL INFORMATION: *Creation:* 1814. *Affiliated to:* Association of Housing Societies (Ireland) - DOCHAS (Ireland). *Personnel/Total:* 33. *Salaried:* 7. *Volunteers:* 26 of which: 26 in developing

countries. *Budget/Total 1993:* ECU 840000 (US$ 984000). *Financial sources:* Private: 17%. Public: 25%. Self-financing: 49%.

PUBLICATIONS: *Periodicals:* Yes Magazine (4) - Transmission (3). *Annual report. List of publications.*

PLANNED ACTIVITIES: Education project for Irish primary school children about life in a Nairobi Shanty town. Supporting health projects in India, Nepal and Uganda. Promoting understanding between Islam and Christianity.

ACTIVITIES IN DEVELOPING REGIONS: Works through local field partners. Sustainable Development Actions: Children/youth/family; Ecology/environment/biodiversity; Education/training/literacy; Food/famine; Gender issues/women; Health/sanitation/water; Human rights/peace/conflicts; Rural development/agriculture; Sending volunteers/experts/technical assistance; Small enterprises/informal sector/handicrafts; Urban development/habitat. Regions: Central Africa; Central Asia and South Asia; East Africa; North Africa.

INFORMATION AND EDUCATION ACTIVITIES: Topics: Children/youth/family; Culture/tradition/religion; Education/training/literacy; Emergency relief/refugees/humanitarian assistance; Food/famine; Gender issues/women; Health/sanitation/water; Human rights/peace/conflicts; International relations/cooperation/development aid; Peace/ethnic conflicts/armament/disarmament; Refugees/migrants/ethnic groups; Rural development/agriculture; Urban development/habitat. Activities: Conferences/seminars/workshops/training activities; Formal education; Fund raising; Information campaigns/exhibitions.

IRL2689

CHURCH OF IRELAND BISHOPS' APPEAL: WORLD DEVELOPMENT COMMITTEE

Church of Ireland House, Church Avenue, Rathmines, Dublin 6, Ireland.

Telephone: 353 (1) 497 84 22. *Fax:* 353 (1) 497 88 21. *Contact:* Bishop Robert Warue, Chairman.

OBJECTIVES: To raise awareness of development issues in the context of the Anglican Church of Ireland. To raise and allocate funds for projects amd emergency relief in co-operation with other NGOs and local churches.

GENERAL INFORMATION: *Creation:* 1971. *Affiliated to:* DOCHAS (Ireland). *Personnel/Total:* 22. *Salaried:* 2. *Volunteers:* 20. *Budget/Total 1993:* ECU 438000 (US$ 513000). *Financial sources:* Private: 92%. Public: 8%.

PUBLICATIONS: *Annual report.*

COMMENTS: Undertakes activities in the Commonwealth of Independent States. Information activities related to the Commonwealth of Independent States.

ACTIVITIES IN DEVELOPING REGIONS: Active in 26 country(ies). Works through local field partners.

INFORMATION AND EDUCATION ACTIVITIES: Topics: Education/training/literacy; Emergency relief/refugees/humanitarian assistance; Food/famine; Health/sanitation/water; International economic relations/trade/debt/finance; Refugees/migrants/ethnic groups; Rural development/agriculture. Activities: Conferences/seminars/workshops/training activities; Formal education; Fund raising; Information campaigns/exhibitions; Lobbying/advocacy.

IRL2690

COMHLAMH, THE ASSOCIATION OF IRISH RETURNED DEVELOPMENT WORKERS ◆ Mutual Cooperation

10 Upper Camden Street, Dublin 2, Ireland.

Telephone: 353 (1) 478 34 90. *Fax:* 353 (1) 478 37 38. *Contact:* Robin Hanan, Coordinator.

OBJECTIVES: To enable persons who have rendered services overseas in developing countries to share their experiences upon their return to Ireland and continue to further international development co-operation from Ireland.

GENERAL INFORMATION: *Creation:* 1976. *Affiliated to:* Irish Association of Development NGOs - Irish Fair Trade Network - Debt and Development Coalition - Network of Irish Environment and Development

Organisations. . *Personnel/Total:* 52. *Salaried:* 12. *Volunteers:* 40. *Budget/Total 1993:* ECU 188000 (US$ 220000). *Financial sources:* Private: 30%. Public: 60%. Self-financing: 10%.

PUBLICATIONS: *Periodicals:* Focus on Ireland in the Wider World (3) - NODE News (5). *Annual report.*

EVALUATION/RESEARCH: Undertakes research activities.

INFORMATION AND EDUCATION ACTIVITIES: Topics: Ecology/environment/biodiversity; Food/famine; Gender issues/women; Human rights/peace/conflicts; International economic relations/trade/debt/finance; International relations/cooperation/development aid; Peace/ethnic conflicts/armament/disarmament; Population/family planning/demography; Poverty/living conditions; Racism/xenophobia/antisemitism; Refugees/migrants/ethnic groups; Rural development/agriculture. **Activities:** Broadcasting/cultural events; Conferences/seminars/workshops/training activities; Formal education; Information and documentation services/data bases; Information campaigns/exhibitions; Lobbying/advocacy; Publishing/audiovisual materials/educational materials.

IRL2691
CONCERN WORLDWIDE

Camden Street, Dublin 2, Ireland.

Telephone: 353 (1) 475 41 62. *Fax:* 353 (1) 475 73 62. *Contact:* Aengus Finucane, Chief Executive.

OBJECTIVES: To be devoted to the relief, assistance and advancement of peoples in need in less developed areas of the world.

GENERAL INFORMATION: *Creation:* 1968. *Affiliated to:* DOCHAS (Ireland) - EURONAID - NGO-Liaison Committee - VOICE - Euro Step. *Personnel/Total:* 4767. *Salaried:* 4664 of which: 4572 in developing countries. *Volunteers:* 103 of which: 88 in developing countries. *Budget/Total 1993:* ECU 41452000 (US$ 48598000). *Financial sources:* Private: 38%. Public: 58%. Self-financing: 4%.

PUBLICATIONS: *Periodicals:* Education News (3). *Annual report.*

EVALUATION/RESEARCH: Evaluation reports available. Undertakes research activities.

PLANNED ACTIVITIES: Campaigning on debt and environmental issues. Promoting development education in the youth sector.

ACTIVITIES IN DEVELOPING REGIONS: Present in developing regions. Active in 12 country(ies). Maintains local field presence. Works through local field partners. **Sustainable Development Actions:** Children/youth/family; Democracy/good governance/institution building/participatory development; Education/training/literacy; Emergency relief/refugees/humanitarian assistance; Food/famine; Gender issues/women; Health/sanitation/water; Population/family planning/demography; Rural development/agriculture; Sending volunteers/experts/technical assistance; Small enterprises/informal sector/handicrafts; Urban development/habitat. **Regions:** East Africa; South East Asia; Southern Africa.

INFORMATION AND EDUCATION ACTIVITIES: Topics: Children/youth/family; Culture/tradition/religion; Ecology/environment/biodiversity; Education/training/literacy; Emergency relief/refugees/humanitarian assistance; Food/famine; Gender issues/women; Health/sanitation/water; Human rights/peace/conflicts; International economic relations/trade/debt/finance; International relations/cooperation/development aid; Peace/ethnic conflicts/armament/disarmament; Population/family planning/demography; Poverty/living conditions; Racism/xenophobia/antisemitism; Refugees/migrants/ethnic groups; Rural development/agriculture; Urban development/habitat. **Activities:** Conferences/seminars/workshops/training activities; Formal education; Fund raising; Lobbying/advocacy; Publishing/audiovisual materials/educational materials.

IRL2692
DEBT AND DEVELOPMENT COALITION IRELAND

Dalgan Park Navan, Co. Meath, Ireland.

Telephone: 353 (46) 215 25. *Fax:* 353 (46) 227 99. *Contact:* Jean Somers, Co-ordinator.

OBJECTIVES: To raise awareness in Ireland of the continuing burden of debt on the peoples of the South and to motivate people to take action. To lobby Irish politicians to support debt relief.

GENERAL INFORMATION: *Creation:* 1993. *Affiliated to:* European Network on Debt and Development (Belgium). *Personnel/Total:* 2. *Salaried:* 2. *Budget/Total 1993:* ECU 54000 (US$ 64000). *Financial sources:* Public: 50%. Self-financing: 50%.

PUBLICATIONS: *Periodicals:* Update (3). *Annual report. List of publications.*

EVALUATION/RESEARCH: Undertakes research activities.

PLANNED ACTIVITIES: The coalition will produce educational materials on debt.

INFORMATION AND EDUCATION ACTIVITIES: Topics: International economic relations/trade/debt/finance. **Activities:** Broadcasting/cultural events; Conferences/seminars/workshops/training activities; Information and documentation services/data bases; Information campaigns/exhibitions; Lobbying/advocacy; Publishing/audiovisual materials/educational materials.

IRL2693
DEVELOPMENT EDUCATION FOR YOUTH (DEFY)

c/o National Youth Council of Ireland, 3 Montague Street, Dublin 2, Ireland.

Telephone: 353 (1) 478 41 22. *Fax:* 353 (1) 478 39 74. *Contact:* Liam Wegimont, Co-ordinator.

OBJECTIVES: To integrate development education into the programmes and policies of non-formal youth organisations through training, programme development, production of educational materials and networking.

GENERAL INFORMATION: *Creation:* 1985. *Type of organisation:* coordinating body. *Member organisations:* 5. *Affiliated to:* DOCHAS (Ireland) - EC-NGO Liaison Committee - Youth Forum of the EC. *Personnel/Total:* 43. *Salaried:* 3. *Volunteers:* 40 of which: 3 in developing countries. *Budget/Total 1993:* ECU 94000 (US$ 110000). *Financial sources:* Private: 50%. Public: 50%.

PUBLICATIONS: *Annual report. List of publications.*

EVALUATION/RESEARCH: Evaluation reports available. Undertakes research activities.

PLANNED ACTIVITIES: The coalition will work on the institutionalisation of development education in youth sectors, will organise an exchange programme aimed at "learning from Latin America" and will develop new models of development education.

ACTIVITIES IN DEVELOPING REGIONS: Active in 2 country(ies). Works through local field partners. **Sustainable Development Actions:** Children/youth/family; Education/training/literacy. **Regions:** South America.

INFORMATION AND EDUCATION ACTIVITIES: Topics: Children/youth/family; Culture/tradition/religion; Employment/unemployment; Food/famine; Gender issues/women; International economic relations/trade/debt/finance; International relations/cooperation/development aid; Peace/ethnic conflicts/armament/disarmament; Poverty/living conditions; Racism/xenophobia/antisemitism; Refugees/migrants/ethnic groups; Rural development/agriculture; Urban development/habitat. **Activities:** Broadcasting/cultural events; Conferences/seminars/workshops/training activities; Exchanges/twinning/linking; Formal education; Information and documentation services/data bases; Information campaigns/exhibitions; Lobbying/advocacy; Publishing/audiovisual materials/educational materials.

IRL2694
DR. TOM DOOLEY FUND

Cuala, Greenfield Road, Sutton, Dublin 13, Ireland.

Telephone: 353 (1) 832 22 09. *Contact:* Dr. Joseph Barnes, President.

OBJECTIVES: To send medical personnel to developing countries and to sponser the training of local nurses in mission hospitals.

GENERAL INFORMATION: *Creation:* 1961. *Personnel/Total:* 8. *Volunteers:* 8 of which: 1 in developing countries. *Budget/Total 1993:* ECU 19000 (US$ 22000). *Financial sources:* Private: 40%. Public: 60%.

PUBLICATIONS: *Annual report.*

ACTIVITIES IN DEVELOPING REGIONS: Active in 2 country(ies). **Sustainable Development Actions:** Sending volunteers/experts/technical assistance. **Regions:** East Africa.

IRL2695

EAST TIMOR - IRELAND SOLIDARITY CAMPAIGN

210 Le Fanu Road, Ballyfermot, Dublin 10, Ireland.

Telephone: 353 (1) 623 31 48. *Fax:* 353 (1) 623 31 48. *E-mail:* etisc@toppsi.gn.APC.ORG.. *Contact:* Tom Hyland.

OBJECTIVES: To improve the human rights situation in East Timor. To raise awarenes of the occupation of East Timor. To lobby for the withdrawal of the Indonesian Armed Forces from East Timor.

GENERAL INFORMATION: *Creation:* 1992. *Member organisations:* 3. *Affiliated to:* Debt and Development Coalition (Ireland). *Personnel/Total:* 5. *Volunteers:* 5. *Budget/Total 1993:* ECU 8000 (US$ 9000). *Financial sources:* Private: 30%. Public: 50%. Self-financing: 20%.

PUBLICATIONS: *Periodicals:* Maubere (4). *Annual report. List of publications.*

EVALUATION/RESEARCH: Evaluation reports available. Undertakes research activities.

PLANNED ACTIVITIES: The Organisation is planning a seminar on East Timor in 1996.

ACTIVITIES IN DEVELOPING REGIONS: **Sustainable Development Actions:** Human rights/peace/conflicts. **Regions:** South East Asia.

INFORMATION AND EDUCATION ACTIVITIES: **Topics:** Culture/tradition/religion; Human rights/peace/conflicts; Racism/xenophobia/antisemitism; Refugees/migrants/ethnic groups. **Activities:** Conferences/seminars/workshops/training activities; Formal education; Fund raising; Information and documentation services/data bases; Information campaigns/exhibitions; Lobbying/advocacy; Publishing/audiovisual materials/educational materials.

IRL2696

ECO - UNESCO CLUBS (ECO)

39 Fleet Street, Dublin 2, Ireland.

Telephone: 353 (1) 679 96 73. *Fax:* 353 (1) 679 41 29. *Contact:* Michael Murphy, Director.

OBJECTIVES: To teach young people about development through practical environmental activities. To promote the protection and conservation of the environment and raise awareness and understanding of environmental issues.

GENERAL INFORMATION: *Creation:* 1984. *Type of organisation:* network, coordinating body. *Affiliated to:* National Youth Council of Ireland (Ireland) - Tree Council of Ireland (Ireland) - Youth Environment Europe (Netherlands) - World Federation of Unesco Clubs. *Budget/Total 1993:* ECU 38000 (US$ 44000). *Financial sources:* Private: 20%. Public: 70%. Self-financing: 10%.

PUBLICATIONS: *Periodicals:* ECO News (2).

EVALUATION/RESEARCH: Evaluation reports available. Undertakes research activities.

PLANNED ACTIVITIES: ECO is planning a research report on Urban Forestry in Ireland.

INFORMATION AND EDUCATION ACTIVITIES: **Topics:** Children/youth/family; Ecology/environment/biodiversity. **Activities:** Conferences/seminars/workshops/training activities; Exchanges/twinning/linking; Fund raising; Information and documentation services/data bases; Information campaigns/exhibitions; Networking/electronic telecommunications; Publishing/audiovisual materials/educational materials.

IRL2697

EL SALVADOR AWARENESS

Romero Room, St. Clare's Convent, 101 Harold's Cross Road, Dublin 6W, Ireland.

Telephone: 353 (1) 496 41 38. *Fax:* 353 (1) 496 41 38. *Contact:* Sister Mary Peter Coleman, Co-ordinator.

OBJECTIVES: To raise awareness about El Salvador. To provide and promote development education. To sell artifacts and crafts made in El Salvador. To make links with projects in El Salvador. To serve as a resource centre for El Salvador.

GENERAL INFORMATION: *Creation:* 1990. *Type of organisation:* network. *Affiliated to:* Central America Week Committee (Ireland) - Irish Brazil Support Co. (Ireland) -Trócaire (Ireland) - AFRI (Ireland) - Comhlámh (Ireland) - Project El-Salvador (USA). *Personnel/Total:* 6. *Volunteers:* 6. *Budget/Total 1993:* ECU 3000 (US$ 4000). *Financial sources:* Private: 5%. Public: 85%. Self-financing: 10%.

PUBLICATIONS: *Periodicals:* El Salvador Awareness (10). *Annual report. List of publications.*

EVALUATION/RESEARCH: Undertakes research activities.

PLANNED ACTIVITIES: El Salvador Awareness is planning to publish and dissiminate an educational pack with a focus on El Salvador. There is a plan to visit El Salvador for updating information and the creation of new links.

ACTIVITIES IN DEVELOPING REGIONS: Present in developing regions. Active in 1 country(ies). Maintains local field presence. Works through local field partners. **Sustainable Development Actions:** Children/youth/family; Debt/finance/trade; Democracy/good governance/institution building/participatory development; Ecology/environment/biodiversity; Education/training/literacy; Food/famine; Gender issues/women; Health/sanitation/water; Human rights/peace/conflicts; Population/family planning/demography; Rural development/agriculture; Small enterprises/informal sector/handicrafts; Urban development/habitat. **Regions:** Mexico and Central America.

INFORMATION AND EDUCATION ACTIVITIES: **Topics:** Children/youth/family; Culture/tradition/religion; Ecology/environment/biodiversity; Education/training/literacy; Employment/unemployment; Food/famine; Gender issues/women; Health/sanitation/water; Human rights/peace/conflicts; International economic relations/trade/debt/finance; Poverty/living conditions; Refugees/migrants/ethnic groups; Rural development/agriculture; Urban development/habitat. **Activities:** Broadcasting/cultural events; Conferences/seminars/workshops/training activities; Exchanges/twinning/linking; Formal education; Fund raising; Information and documentation services/data bases; Information campaigns/exhibitions; Publishing/audiovisual materials/educational materials.

IRL2698

GALWAY ONE WORLD CENTRE

Canavan House, Nun's island, Galway, Ireland.

Telephone: 353 (91) 655 89. *Contact:* Heike Vornhagen, Marian Monaghan, Sean Connealy, Joan O'Connor, Ann Donnellan, Coordinating Committee.

OBJECTIVES: To raise awareness of the connections between the so-called underdeveloped and developed parts of the world and of marginalized groups at home and abroad. To promote action and to take part in selected national and worldwide campaigns.

GENERAL INFORMATION: *Creation:* 1993. *Affiliated to:* Network for Outreach Development Education (Ireland) - Debt and Development Coalition (Ireland) - Central America Work Committee (Ireland). *Personnel/Total:* 2. *Salaried:* 2. *Budget/Total 1993:* ECU 14000 (US$ 16000). *Financial sources:* Public: 98%. Self-financing: 2%.

PUBLICATIONS: *Periodicals:* One World (3). *List of publications.*

INFORMATION AND EDUCATION ACTIVITIES: **Topics:** Children/youth/family; Culture/tradition/religion; Ecology/environment/biodiversity; Education/training/literacy; Employment/unemployment; Food/famine; Gender issues/women; Health/sanitation/water; Human rights/peace/conflicts; International economic relations/trade/debt/finance; International relations/cooperation/development aid; Peace/ethnic conflicts/armament/disarmament; Population/family planning/demography; Poverty/living conditions; Racism/xenophobia/antisemitism; Refugees/migrants/ethnic groups; Rural development/agriculture; Urban development/habitat. **Activities:** Conferences/seminars/workshops/training activities; Exchanges/twinning/linking; Formal education; Information and docu-

See: *How to Use the Directory,* page 11.

mentation services/data bases; Information campaigns/exhibitions; Networking/electronic telecommunications; Publishing/audiovisual materials/educational materials.

IRL2699
GOAL

P.O. Box 19, Dunlaoghaire, Co Dublin, Ireland.

Telephone: 353 (1) 280 97 79. *Fax:* 353 (1) 280 92 15. *Contact:* John O'Shea, Director.

OBJECTIVES: To alleviate the suffering of people irrespective of nationality, race or religion.

GENERAL INFORMATION: *Creation:* 1977. *Personnel/Total:* 75. *Salaried:* 15 of which: 5 in developing countries. *Volunteers:* 60 of which: 60 in developing countries. *Budget/Total 1993:* ECU 4380000 (US$ 5135000). *Financial sources:* Private: 33%. Public: 65%. Self-financing: 2%.

PUBLICATIONS: *Annual report.*

ACTIVITIES IN DEVELOPING REGIONS: Active in 12 country(ies). Maintains local field presence. Works through local field partners. **Sustainable Development Actions:** Children/youth/family; Education/training/literacy; Emergency relief/refugees/humanitarian assistance; Energy/transport; Food/famine; Gender issues/women; Health/sanitation/water; Population/family planning/demography; Rural development/agriculture; Sending volunteers/experts/technical assistance. **Regions:** Central Asia and South Asia; East Africa.

IRL2700
GORTA

12 Herbert Street, Dublin 2, Ireland.

Telephone: 353 (1) 661 55 22. *Fax:* 353 (1) 661 26 27. *Contact:* James Coughlan, Chief Executive Officer.

OBJECTIVES: To help alleviate world hunger through long-term self-help development programmes in developing countries. To promote these objectives within Ireland by disseminating information about world hunger and by collecting funds.

GENERAL INFORMATION: *Creation:* 1965. *Affiliated to:* Dochas (Ireland). *Personnel/Total:* 18. *Salaried:* 7. *Volunteers:* 11 of which: 11 in developing countries. *Budget/Total 1993:* ECU 1090000 (US$ 1278000). *Financial sources:* Private: 83%. Public: 17%.

PUBLICATIONS: *Periodicals:* Newsletter (6). *Annual report.*

EVALUATION/RESEARCH: Evaluation reports available.

PLANNED ACTIVITIES: Radio campaigns highlighting world development needs.

ACTIVITIES IN DEVELOPING REGIONS: Present in developing regions. Active in 18 country(ies). Maintains local field presence. Works through local field partners. **Sustainable Development Actions:** Rural development/agriculture; Sending volunteers/experts/technical assistance. **Regions:** Central Africa; Central Asia and South Asia; East Africa; North Africa; South America; South East Asia; Southern Africa; West Africa.

INFORMATION AND EDUCATION ACTIVITIES: Topics: Food/famine; Rural development/agriculture. **Activities:** Broadcasting/cultural events; Conferences/seminars/workshops/training activities; Exchanges/twinning/linking; Fund raising; Information and documentation services/data bases; Information campaigns/exhibitions; Lobbying/advocacy.

IRL2701
GREENPEACE IRELAND

44 Upper Mount Street, Dublin 2, Ireland.

Telephone: 353 (1) 661.9836. *Fax:* 353 (1) 660.5258. *Contact:* Andrew Booth, Director.

IRL2702
HIGHER EDUCATION FOR DEVELOPMENT COOPERATION (HEDCO)

65 Fitzwilliam Square, Dublin 2, Ireland.

Telephone: 353 (1) 661 20 85. *Fax:* 353 (1) 676 86 32. *Contact:* Colm Mc Grady, Chief Executive.

OBJECTIVES: To promote and implement education programmes in co-operation with other countries. To establish and further institutions of learning in developing countries. To promote human resources related activities through development co-operation.

GENERAL INFORMATION: *Creation:* 1975. *Affiliated to:* Donors to African Education (France) - Northern Policy Research Review & Advisory Network on Education & Training (Switzerland). *Personnel/Total:* 25. *Salaried:* 25 of which: 17 in developing countries. *Budget/Total 1993:* ECU 438000 (US$ 513000). *Financial sources:* Self-financing: 100%.

PUBLICATIONS: *Annual report.*

EVALUATION/RESEARCH: Undertakes research activities.

PLANNED ACTIVITIES: HEDCO plans to work on capacity-building of the third level educational sector in South Africa, Uganda, Jordan and Tanzania.

COMMENTS: HEDCO also organises inter-institutional linkages between North and South and arranges fellowships and training programmes. Undertakes activities in the Commonwealth of Independent States. Information activities related to the Commonwealth of Independent States.

ACTIVITIES IN DEVELOPING REGIONS: Present in developing regions. Active in 12 country(ies). Maintains local field presence. Works through local field partners. **Sustainable Development Actions:** Education/training/literacy; Gender issues/women; Rural development/agriculture; Small enterprises/informal sector/handicrafts. **Regions:** Central Africa; East Africa; East Asia; Middle East; Southern Africa.

INFORMATION AND EDUCATION ACTIVITIES: Topics: Education/training/literacy; Employment/unemployment; Gender issues/women; International relations/cooperation/development aid; Rural development/agriculture. **Activities:** Conferences/seminars/workshops/training activities; Exchanges/twinning/linking; Formal education; Information and documentation services/data bases; Publishing/audiovisual materials/educational materials.

IRL2703
ICTU THIRD WORLD COMMITTEE

31 Parnell Square, Dublin 1, Ireland.

Telephone: 353 (1) 748221. *Fax:* 353 (1) 722765. *Contact:* Joan O'Connell, Deputy Education & Training Officer.

IRL2704
IRELAND AND THE WIDER WORLD

The Wider World, 55 Grand Parade, Cork, Ireland.

Telephone: 353 (21) 275881. *Contact:* John Walsh, Honorary Secretary.

IRL2705
IRISH ASSOCIATION OF NON-GOVERNMENTAL DEVELOPMENT ORGANISATIONS (DOCHAS) ♦ Hope

59 Deerpark Road, Mount Merrion, Dublin, Ireland.

Telephone: 353 (1) 288 61 41. *Fax:* 353 (1) 288 61 41. *Contact:* Jerome Connolly, Chairperson.

OBJECTIVES: To bring together the Irish Voluntary agencies with the Third World. To promote closer co-operation between its member agencies. To act as the Irish Assembly of development and relief organisations in relation to the Liaison Committee of Development NGOs to the European Communities.

GENERAL INFORMATION: *Creation:* 1993. *Type of organisation:* coordinating body. *Member organisations:* 16. *Affiliated to:* EC NGDO Liason Committee (Brussels) - ICDA (Belgium). *Personnel/Total:* 1. *Salaried:* 1. *Budget/Total 1993:* ECU 35000 (US$ 41000). *Financial sources:* Self-financing: 100%.

PUBLICATIONS: *Periodicals:* DOCHAS Newsletter (12). *Annual report. List of publications.*

EVALUATION/RESEARCH: Undertakes research activities.

Voir : *Comment utiliser le répertoire,* page 11.

PLANNED ACTIVITIES: DOCHAS is planning the publication of an updated version of 75:25 Ireland in a Still Unequal World.

COMMENTS: DOCHAS elects a National Delegate to the EU/NGDO LC and National Representatives to each of its working groups. It elects representatives to the General Assembly as well, and keeps Irish NGDOs and other agencies and groups informed on the work of the LC. Dochas also circulates LC documents to its member agencies on a regular basis.

INFORMATION AND EDUCATION ACTIVITIES: Topics: Education/training/literacy; Emergency relief/refugees/humanitarian assistance; Food/famine; Gender issues/women; Health/sanitation/water; Human rights/peace/conflicts; International economic relations/trade/debt/finance; International relations/cooperation/development aid; Peace/ethnic conflicts/armament/disarmament; Population/family planning/demography; Poverty/living conditions; Urban development/habitat. **Activities:** Conferences/seminars/workshops/training activities; Information and documentation services/data bases; Lobbying/advocacy.

IRL2706
IRISH COMMISSION FOR JUSTICE AND PEACE (ICJP)

169 Booterstown Avenue, Blackrock, Co. Dublin, Ireland.

Telephone: 353 (1) 288 48 53. **Fax:** 353 (1) 283 41 61. **Contact:** Jerome Connolly, Executive Secretary.

OBJECTIVES: To promote and educate on issues of justice, peace, human rights and development in relation to Ireland and developing countries.

GENERAL INFORMATION: Creation: 1970. **Affiliated to:** Women and Development Europe - Joint Body of Europe and Justice Confederation of Irish NGOs (Ireland) - Irish Environment and Development Network and Peace Organizations (Ireland) - DOCHAS (Ireland) - Conference of European Justice and Peace Commissions (Belgium). **Personnel/Total:** 6. Salaried: 5. Volunteers: 1. **Financial sources:** Private: 10%. Public: 20%. Self-financing: 70%.

PUBLICATIONS: List of publications.

EVALUATION/RESEARCH: Undertakes research activities.

INFORMATION AND EDUCATION ACTIVITIES: Topics: Gender issues/women; Human rights/peace/conflicts; International relations/cooperation/development aid; Peace/ethnic conflicts/armament/disarmament; Racism/xenophobia/antisemitism; Refugees/migrants/ethnic groups. **Activities:** Conferences/seminars/workshops/training activities; Formal education; Information and documentation services/data bases; Lobbying/advocacy; Publishing/audiovisual materials/educational materials.

IRL2707
IRISH EL SALVADOR SUPPORT COMMITTEE

Pennock Hill, Swords, Dublin, Ireland.

Telephone: 353 (1) 840 54 69. **Contact:** Brendan Butler, Chairman.

OBJECTIVES: To increase awareness of the problems of El Salvador among Irish people with an emphasis on human rights, self-determination and the necessity for a negotiated settlement involving all sections of society. To help in alleviating the immediate distress of Salvadorian refugees and displaced persons.

GENERAL INFORMATION: Creation: 1979. **Type of organisation:** coordinating body. **Member organisations:** 3. **Personnel/Total:** 23. Volunteers: 23 of which: 3 in developing countries. **Financial sources:** Public: 10%. Self-financing: 90%.

PUBLICATIONS: List of publications.

EVALUATION/RESEARCH: Evaluation reports available. Undertakes research activities.

ACTIVITIES IN DEVELOPING REGIONS: Present in developing regions. Active in 1 country(ies). Works through local field partners. **Sustainable Development Actions:** Education/training/literacy; Emergency relief/refugees/humanitarian assistance; Energy/transport; Health/sanitation/water; Human rights/peace/conflicts; Rural development/agriculture; Urban development/habitat. **Regions:** Mexico and Central America.

INFORMATION AND EDUCATION ACTIVITIES: Topics: Education/training/literacy; Emergency relief/refugees/humanitarian assistance; Health/

sanitation/water; Human rights/peace/conflicts; International economic relations/trade/debt/finance; International relations/cooperation/development aid; Peace/ethnic conflicts/armament/disarmament; Poverty/living conditions; Rural development/agriculture; Urban development/habitat. **Activities:** Information and documentation services/data bases; Information campaigns/exhibitions; Lobbying/advocacy.

IRL2708
IRISH FAIR TRADE NETWORK (IFTN)

New Orchard, Newpark, Kilkenny, Ireland.

Telephone: 353 (56) 637 33. **Fax:** 353 (56) 632 20. **Contact:** Carol Bergin.

OBJECTIVES: To help Third World producers by providing marketing and trading information in order to improve the quality of their products and to develop markets for their products in Europe. To mobilise consumer power by the introduction of a consumer guarantee that products conform to the standards and criteria of Fair Trading.

GENERAL INFORMATION: Creation: 1991. **Type of organisation:** network. **Affiliated to:** International Federation for Alternative Trade (United States) - European Fair Trade Association - Transfair (Germany) - Comhlamh (Ireland). **Personnel/Total:** 24. Salaried: 4. Volunteers: 20. **Budget/Total 1993:** ECU 106000 (US$ 125000). **Financial sources:** Private: 10%. Public: 50%. Self-financing: 40%.

PUBLICATIONS: Periodicals: Fair Trader (4). Annual report. List of publications.

EVALUATION/RESEARCH: Evaluation reports available. Undertakes research activities.

PLANNED ACTIVITIES: IFTN is planning to develop high quality products and markets for Nigerian producers, and to research the importation of tea, coffee and bananas into Ireland.

ACTIVITIES IN DEVELOPING REGIONS: Present in developing regions. Active in 2 country(ies). Works through local field partners. **Sustainable Development Actions:** Small enterprises/informal sector/handicrafts. **Regions:** South America; South East Asia; West Africa.

INFORMATION AND EDUCATION ACTIVITIES: Topics: International economic relations/trade/debt/finance. **Activities:** Broadcasting/cultural events; Conferences/seminars/workshops/training activities; Exchanges/twinning/linking; Formal education; Fund raising; Information and documentation services/data bases; Information campaigns/exhibitions; Lobbying/advocacy; Networking/electronic telecommunications; Publishing/audiovisual materials/educational materials.

IRL2709
IRISH FOUNDATION FOR CO-OPERATIVE DEVELOPMENT (IFCD)

The Plunkett House, 84 Merrion Square, Dublin 2, Ireland.

Telephone: 353 (1) 676 47 83. **Fax:** 353 (1) 688 17 84. **Contact:** Malachy Prunty, Director.

OBJECTIVES: To harness the resources of the Irish Agriculture Co-operative Movement for the purpose of promoting and assisting co-operative development in developing countries.

GENERAL INFORMATION: Creation: 1978. **Type of organisation:** network. **Member organisations:** 50. **Affiliated to:** DOCHAS (Ireland). **Personnel/Total:** 1. Salaried: 1 of which: 1 in developing countries. **Budget/Total 1993:** ECU 113000 (US$ 132000). **Financial sources:** Private: 75%. Public: 25%.

PLANNED ACTIVITIES: The extension of involvement, from local to regional level, in Tanzania.

COMMENTS: Undertakes activities in the Commonwealth of Independent States.

ACTIVITIES IN DEVELOPING REGIONS: Present in developing regions. Active in 3 country(ies). Maintains local field presence. Works through local field partners. **Sustainable Development Actions:** Democracy/good governance/institution building/participatory development; Rural development/agriculture; Sending volunteers/experts/technical assis-

                                          See: *How to Use the Directory,* page 11.

tance; Small enterprises/informal sector/handicrafts. **Regions:** East Africa.

INFORMATION AND EDUCATION ACTIVITIES: Topics: International relations/cooperation/development aid; Rural development/agriculture. **Activities:** Fund raising.

IRL2710
IRISH INFANT FORMULA ACTION GROUP

7 Greenpark Road, Bray, Co. Wicklow., Ireland.

Telephone: 353 (1) 28 66 106. **Contact:** Cliona Mc Longhlin.

IRL2711
IRISH MISSIONARY UNION (IMU)

Orwell Park, Rathgar, Dublin 6, Ireland.

Telephone: 353 (1) 496 54 33. **Fax:** 353 (1) 496 50 29. **Contact:** Father Tom Kiggins, Executive Secretary.

OBJECTIVES: To co-ordinate, support and evaluate the development activities of Irish missionaries working in developing countries.

GENERAL INFORMATION: Creation: 1970. **Type of organisation:** association of NGOs. **Member organisations:** 75. **Affiliated to:** DOCHAS (Ireland). **Personnel/Total:** 8. Salaried: 4. Volunteers: 4. **Budget/Total 1993:** ECU 113000 (US$ 132000). **Financial sources:** Private: 100%.

PUBLICATIONS: Periodicals: IMU Report (6). Annual report.

EVALUATION/RESEARCH: Undertakes research activities.

COMMENTS: Member organisations are working in most of the other categories of activities mentioned in this survey. Information activities related to the Commonwealth of Independent States.

ACTIVITIES IN DEVELOPING REGIONS: Active in 90 country(ies). **Sustainable Development Actions:** Education/training/literacy; Health/sanitation/water. **Regions:** Caribbean; Central Africa; Central Asia and South Asia; East Africa; East Asia; Mexico and Central America; Middle East; North Africa; Oceania; South America; South East Asia; Southern Africa; West Africa.

IRL2712
IRISH MOZAMBIQUE SOCIETY

13 Carlisle Street, Dublin 8, Ireland.

Telephone: 353 (1) 454 12 02. **Fax:** 353 (1) 874 26 26. **Contact:** Niall Crowley, Chairperson.

OBJECTIVES: To inform our members and the general public about the situation in Mozambique. To promote political and material solidarity and develop relationships between the institutions, organisations and people of Ireland and Mozambique. To influence Irish foreign policy towards Mozambique and Southern Africa.

GENERAL INFORMATION: Creation: 1988. **Affiliated to:** Joint Solidarity Forum (Ireland) - NODE network (Ireland) - ECASAAMA (Ireland). **Personnel/Total:** 5. Salaried: 1. Volunteers: 4. **Budget/Total 1993:** ECU 13000 (US$ 15000). **Financial sources:** Private: 70%. Public: 25%. Self-financing: 5%.

PUBLICATIONS: Periodicals: Mozambique News (2). Annual report. List of publications.

EVALUATION/RESEARCH: Evaluation reports available. Undertakes research activities.

PLANNED ACTIVITIES: The organisation plans to undertake a campaign to improve the quality of development and emergency aid to Mozambique.

INFORMATION AND EDUCATION ACTIVITIES: Topics: Emergency relief/refugees/humanitarian assistance; Human rights/peace/conflicts; International economic relations/trade/debt/finance; International relations/cooperation/development aid; Racism/xenophobia/antisemitism; Refugees/migrants/ethnic groups. **Activities:** Conferences/seminars/workshops/training activities; Information and documentation services/data bases; Information campaigns/exhibitions; Lobbying/advocacy; Publishing/audiovisual materials/educational materials.

IRL2713
IRISH NATIONAL COMMITTEE FOR UNICEF

4 St. Andrew Street, Dublin 2, Ireland.

Telephone: 353 (1) 770843.

IRL2714
IRISH NICARAGUA SUPPORT GROUP

61 Lower Camden Street, Dublin 2, Ireland.

Telephone: 353 (1) 478 03 21. **Fax:** 353 (1) 478 37 38. **Contact:** Robin Hanan, Chairperson.

OBJECTIVES: To develop solidarity between Ireland and Nicaragua. To support and defend the achievements of the Sandinista Revolution.

GENERAL INFORMATION: Creation: 1984. **Affiliated to:** European Co-ordination of Nicaragua Solidarity Groups - Central America Week (Ireland) - Joint Solidarity Forum (Ireland) - Debt and Development Coalition (Ireland) - Network on Development Education. **Personnel/Total:** 16. Salaried: 4 of which: 1 in developing countries. Volunteers: 12 of which: 2 in developing countries. **Budget/Total 1993:** ECU 8000 (US$ 10000). **Financial sources:** Public: 20%. Self-financing: 80%.

PUBLICATIONS: Periodicals: NICANEWS (3) - Update (10). Annual report. List of publications.

EVALUATION/RESEARCH: Evaluation reports available. Undertakes research activities.

PLANNED ACTIVITIES: Establishing a resource centre for Ireland-Latin American solidarity groups. Publishing bulletins on the effects of structural adjustments on Latin America. Supporting Nicaragua's popular organisations.

ACTIVITIES IN DEVELOPING REGIONS: Present in developing regions. Active in 1 country(ies). Maintains local field presence. Works through local field partners. **Sustainable Development Actions:** Children/youth/family; Democracy/good governance/institution building/participatory development; Gender issues/women; Rural development/agriculture. **Regions:** Mexico and Central America.

INFORMATION AND EDUCATION ACTIVITIES: Topics: Culture/tradition/religion; Ecology/environment/biodiversity; Education/training/literacy; Emergency relief/refugees/humanitarian assistance; Employment/unemployment; Food/famine; Gender issues/women; Human rights/peace/conflicts; International economic relations/trade/debt/finance; International relations/cooperation/development aid; Peace/ethnic conflicts/armament/disarmament; Poverty/living conditions; Racism/xenophobia/antisemitism; Refugees/migrants/ethnic groups; Rural development/agriculture; Urban development/habitat. **Activities:** Broadcasting/cultural events; Conferences/seminars/workshops/training activities; Exchanges/twinning/linking; Fund raising; Information and documentation services/data bases; Information campaigns/exhibitions; Lobbying/advocacy; Networking/electronic telecommunications; Publishing/audiovisual materials/educational materials.

IRL2715
IRISH PEACE COUNCIL

c/o ECO, 39 Fleet Street, Dublin 2, Ireland.

Telephone: 353 (1) 679 9673. **Contact:** Ken McCue, Co-ordinator.

IRL2716
IRISH RED CROSS SOCIETY

16 Merrion Square, P.O. Box 1312, Dublin 2, Ireland.

Telephone: 353 (1) 676 51 35. **Fax:** 353 (1) 661 44 61. **Contact:** Martin Good, Secretary General.

OBJECTIVES: To provide volunteer aid to the sick, the wounded and the shipwrecked at sea, and to armed forces in times of war. To undertake and assist in work for the improvement of health, the prevention of disease and the mitigation of suffering throughout the world.

GENERAL INFORMATION: Creation: 1939. **Affiliated to:** International Federation of Red Cross and Red Crescent Societies (Switzerland). **Personnel/Total:** 3054. Salaried: 54 of which: 21 in developing countries. Volunteers: 3000. **Budget/Total 1993:**

Voir : *Comment utiliser le répertoire*, page 11.

ECU 2376000 (US$ 2785000). *Financial sources: Private:* 76%. *Public:* 20%. *Self-financing:* 4%.

PUBLICATIONS: *Periodicals:* Newsletter (20000).

COMMENTS: Undertakes activities in the Commonwealth of Independent States. Information activities related to the Commonwealth of Independent States.

ACTIVITIES IN DEVELOPING REGIONS: Active in 7 country(ies). Works through local field partners. **Sustainable Development Actions:** Food/famine; Health/sanitation/water; Rural development/agriculture; Sending volunteers/experts/technical assistance. **Regions:** Central Africa; Central Asia and South Asia; East Africa; North Africa; Southern Africa.

INFORMATION AND EDUCATION ACTIVITIES: Topics: Children/youth/family; Emergency relief/refugees/humanitarian assistance. **Activities:** Conferences/seminars/workshops/training activities; Formal education; Fund raising.

IRL2717
IRISH REFUGEE COUNCIL

Arran House, 35-36 Arran Quay, Dublin 7, Ireland.

Telephone: 353 (1) 872 44 24. *Fax:* 353 (1) 872 44 11. *Contact:* Nadette Foley, Co-ordinator.

OBJECTIVES: To co-ordinate the work of member NGOs with refugees. To raise awareness of the causes of and solutions to the worldwide refugee crisis. To ensure the incorporation and implementation in Irish law of the principles of the 1951 UN Convention on the status of refugees. To provide direct assistance, legal advice and a referral service for asylum seekers and refugees in Ireland.

GENERAL INFORMATION: *Creation:* 1990. *Type of organisation:* coordinating body. *Member organisations:* 53. *Affiliated to:* ECRE (United Kingdom) - EAPN (Ireland) - ILPA (United Kingdom). *Personnel/Total:* 7. *Salaried:* 1. *Volunteers:* 6. *Budget/Total 1993:* ECU 34000 (US$ 40000). *Financial sources: Private:* 5%. *Public:* 56%. *Self-financing:* 39%.

PUBLICATIONS: *Annual report.*

PLANNED ACTIVITIES: Setting-up a newsletter for Irish NGOs on refugee issues. Producing an explanatory briefing for Irish asylum lawyers on the Irish Refugee legislation when it is enacted.

COMMENTS: The member NGOs of the Council carry out activities in developing countries but not the Council itself.

INFORMATION AND EDUCATION ACTIVITIES: Topics: Children/youth/family; Ecology/environment/biodiversity; Education/training/literacy; Emergency relief/refugees/humanitarian assistance; Food/famine; Gender issues/women; Human rights/peace/conflicts; International economic relations/trade/debt/finance; International relations/cooperation/development aid; Poverty/living conditions; Racism/xenophobia/antisemitism; Refugees/migrants/ethnic groups. **Activities:** Broadcasting/cultural events; Conferences/seminars/workshops/training activities; Exchanges/twinning/linking; Formal education; Fund raising; Information and documentation services/data bases; Information campaigns/exhibitions; Lobbying/advocacy; Networking/electronic telecommunications; Publishing/audiovisual materials/educational materials.

IRL2718
IRISH UNITED NATIONS ASSOCIATION (IUNA)

3/4 South Leinster Street, Dublin 2, Ireland.

Telephone: 353 (1) 772941 (ext. 1917). *Contact:* Hilda Tweedy, President.

IRL2719
IRISH WILDLIFE FEDERATION

Conservation Centre, 132A East Wall Road, Dublin 3, Ireland.

Telephone: 353 (1) 636 68 21. *Fax:* 353 (1) 636 68 21. *Contact:* Fergus O'Gorman, President.

OBJECTIVES: To conserve wildlife habitats and species including genetic resources.

GENERAL INFORMATION: *Creation:* 1979. *Affiliated to:* Network of Irish Environment and Development Organisations (Ireland) - European Environment Bureau (Belgium). *Personnel/Total:* 26. *Salaried:* 1. *Volunteers:* 25. *Budget/Total 1993:* ECU 56000 (US$ 66000). *Financial sources: Private:* 10%. *Self-financing:* 90%.

PUBLICATIONS: *Periodicals:* The Badger (4).

COMMENTS: Undertakes activities in the Commonwealth of Independent States. Information activities related to the Commonwealth of Independent States.

ACTIVITIES IN DEVELOPING REGIONS: Active in 3 country(ies). Works through local field partners. **Sustainable Development Actions:** Ecology/environment/biodiversity; Education/training/literacy; Sending volunteers/experts/technical assistance. **Regions:** South America; Southern Africa.

INFORMATION AND EDUCATION ACTIVITIES: Topics: Ecology/environment/biodiversity. **Activities:** Conferences/seminars/workshops/training activities; Exchanges/twinning/linking; Formal education; Information campaigns/exhibitions; Publishing/audiovisual materials/educational materials.

IRL2720
KERRY ACTION FOR DEVELOPMENT EDUCATION (KADE)

103 Balloonagh Estate, Tralee, Ireland.

Telephone: 353 (66) 280 36. *Contact:* Mary McGillicuddy-Sheehy, Chairperson.

OBJECTIVES: To initiate local projects and to create international links related to development issues.

GENERAL INFORMATION: *Creation:* 1993. *Type of organisation:* coordinating body. *Affiliated to:* Comhlamh (Ireland) - Irish Environment and Develpment Organisations (Ireland). *Personnel/Total:* 1. *Volunteers:* 1. *Budget/Total 1993:* ECU 2500 (US$ 3000). *Financial sources: Private:* 5%. *Public:* 95%.

PUBLICATIONS: *List of publications.*

PLANNED ACTIVITIES: Sending development education experts to local primary schools and to work with local women's groups.

INFORMATION AND EDUCATION ACTIVITIES: Topics: Children/youth/family; Culture/tradition/religion; Ecology/environment/biodiversity; Education/training/literacy; Food/famine; Gender issues/women; Health/sanitation/water; Human rights/peace/conflicts; International economic relations/trade/debt/finance; International relations/cooperation/development aid; Peace/ethnic conflicts/armament/disarmament; Population/family planning/demography; Poverty/living conditions; Racism/xenophobia/antisemitism; Refugees/migrants/ethnic groups; Rural development/agriculture; Urban development/habitat. **Activities:** Broadcasting/cultural events; Conferences/seminars/workshops/training activities; Exchanges/twinning/linking; Formal education; Information and documentation services/data bases; Information campaigns/exhibitions; Lobbying/advocacy; Publishing/audiovisual materials/educational materials.

IRL2721
THE LEPROSY MISSION

5 St. James Terrace, Clonskeagh Road, Dublin 6, Ireland.

Telephone: 353 (1) 269 88 04. *Contact:* Rev. Jack Teggin, National Director.

OBJECTIVES: To preach the gospel and heal the sick.

GENERAL INFORMATION: *Creation:* 1874. *Affiliated to:* World Wide Leprosy Mission. *Personnel/Total:* 15. *Salaried:* 3. *Volunteers:* 12. *Budget/Total 1993:* ECU 188000 (US$ 220000). *Financial sources: Private:* 99%. *Self-financing:* 1%.

PUBLICATIONS: *Periodicals:* New Day (2). *Annual report.*

EVALUATION/RESEARCH: Evaluation reports available. Undertakes research activities.

COMMENTS: The organization undertakes projects under the guidance of the World Wide Leprosy Mission, which operates in 39 countries in the Third World.

See: *How to Use the Directory,* page 11.

IRL2722
OXFAM-IN-IRELAND

202 Lower Rathmines Road, Dublin 6, Ireland.

Telephone: 353 (1) 972195. *Contact:* Ciaran O'Donovan.

IRL2723
PAX CHRISTI IRELAND

52 Lower Rathmines Road, Dublin 6, Ireland.

Contact: Bishop Dermot O'Mahony, National President.

IRL2724
REFUGEE TRUST

4, Dublin Road, Stillorgan, County Dublin, Ireland.

Telephone: 353 (1) 283 42 56. *Fax:* 353 (1) 283 51 55. *Contact:* E. Norman Fitzgerald, Executive Director.

OBJECTIVES: To provide emergency relief, long term assistance and rehabilitation programmes for refugees and displaced people. To raise public and government awareness to improve understanding of the worldwide refugee crisis.

GENERAL INFORMATION: *Creation:* 1990. *Personnel/Total:* 16. *Salaried:* 5. *Volunteers:* 11 of which: 11 in developing countries. *Budget/Total 1993:* ECU 1502000 (US$ 1761000). *Financial sources:* Private: 95%. *Public:* 5%.

PUBLICATIONS: *Periodicals:* Refugee Trust Newsletter (4).

PLANNED ACTIVITIES: New programmes with Somali refugees in Kenya. War trauma physical and psychological help to elderly, disabled and blind people in Bosnia.

COMMENTS: Undertakes activities in the Commonwealth of Independent States. Information activities related to the Commonwealth of Independent States.

ACTIVITIES IN DEVELOPING REGIONS: Present in developing regions. Active in 4 country(ies). Maintains local field presence. **Sustainable Development Actions:** Education/training/literacy; Health/sanitation/water; Rural development/agriculture; Small enterprises/informal sector/handicrafts. **Regions:** Central Africa; East Africa; West Africa.

INFORMATION AND EDUCATION ACTIVITIES: Topics: Emergency relief/refugees/humanitarian assistance; International relations/cooperation/development aid; Refugees/migrants/ethnic groups. **Activities:** Information campaigns/exhibitions; Lobbying/advocacy.

IRL2725
SELF HELP DEVELOPMENT INTERNATIONAL

Main Street, Hacketstown Co, Carlow, Ireland.

Telephone: 353 (508) 711 75. *Fax:* 353 (508) 712 92. *Contact:* Michael Lambert, Chief Executive.

OBJECTIVES: To provide the means of combating the long term causes of famine through self-help programmes.

GENERAL INFORMATION: *Creation:* 1984. *Affiliated to:* Christian Relief and Development Association (Ethiopia). *Personnel/Total:* 86. *Salaried:* 6 of which: 3 in developing countries. *Volunteers:* 80. *Financial sources:* Private: 25%. *Public:* 75%.

PUBLICATIONS: *Periodicals:* Newsletter (1).

EVALUATION/RESEARCH: Evaluation reports available. Undertakes research activities.

ACTIVITIES IN DEVELOPING REGIONS: Present in developing regions. Active in 1 country(ies). Maintains local field presence. Works through local field partners. **Sustainable Development Actions:** Ecology/environment/biodiversity; Education/training/literacy; Emergency relief/refugees/humanitarian assistance; Food/famine; Gender issues/women; Rural development/agriculture. **Regions:** East Africa.

INFORMATION AND EDUCATION ACTIVITIES: Topics: Food/famine; Rural development/agriculture. **Activities:** Fund raising; Publishing/audiovisual materials/educational materials.

IRL2726
TROCAIRE

169 Booterstown Avenue, Blackrock, Co. Dublin, Ireland.

Telephone: 353 (1) 288 53 85. *Fax:* 353 (1) 288 35 77. *Contact:* Justin Kilcullen, Director.

OBJECTIVES: To support small-scale, community-based, local projects which work to alleviate poverty and foster self-reliant development and human dignity.

GENERAL INFORMATION: *Creation:* 1973. *Affiliated to:* CIDSE - Dóchas - The Asian Partnership for Human Development. *Personnel/Total:* 56. *Salaried:* 56 of which: 6 in developing countries. *Budget/Total 1993:* ECU 11301000 (US$ 13200000). *Financial sources:* Private: 66%. *Public:* 34%.

ACTIVITIES IN DEVELOPING REGIONS: Active in 50 country(ies). Works through local field partners. **Sustainable Development Actions:** Children/youth/family; Ecology/environment/biodiversity; Education/training/literacy; Emergency relief/refugees/humanitarian assistance; Food/famine; Gender issues/women; Health/sanitation/water; Human rights/peace/conflicts; Rural development/agriculture; Sending volunteers/experts/technical assistance; Small enterprises/informal sector/handicrafts; Urban development/habitat. **Regions:** Caribbean; Central Asia and South Asia; East Africa; East Asia; Mexico and Central America; South America; South East Asia; Southern Africa; West Africa.

INFORMATION AND EDUCATION ACTIVITIES: Topics: Culture/tradition/religion; Ecology/environment/biodiversity; Emergency relief/refugees/humanitarian assistance; Gender issues/women; Health/sanitation/water; Human rights/peace/conflicts; International economic relations/trade/debt/finance; Peace/ethnic conflicts/armament/disarmament; Poverty/living conditions; Refugees/migrants/ethnic groups; Rural development/agriculture. **Activities:** Conferences/seminars/workshops/training activities; Formal education; Fund raising; Information and documentation services/data bases; Information campaigns/exhibitions; Lobbying/advocacy.

IRL2727
VIATORES CHRISTI ♦ Travellers for Christ

38/39 Upper Gardiner Street, Dublin 1, Ireland.

Telephone: 353 (1) 8728027. *Fax:* 353 (1) 8745731. *Contact:* Andrew Fanthom, President.

IRL2728
VOLUNTARY SERVICE INTERNATIONAL (VSI)

30 Mountjoy Square, Dublin 1, Ireland.

Telephone: 353 (1) 855 10 11. *Fax:* 353 (1) 855 10 12. *Contact:* Tom Ryder, Co-ordinator.

OBJECTIVES: To work for peace and international understanding through the medium of practical voluntary service, international exchanges, and education and awareness programmes.

GENERAL INFORMATION: *Creation:* 1965. *Budget/Total 1993:* ECU 119000 (US$ 139000). *Financial sources:* Private: 24%. *Public:* 56%. *Self-financing:* 20%.

PUBLICATIONS: *Periodicals:* VSI Newsletter (4) (1). *Annual report.*

COMMENTS: Undertakes activities in the Commonwealth of Independent States. Information activities related to the Commonwealth of Independent States.

ACTIVITIES IN DEVELOPING REGIONS: Present in developing regions. Works through local field partners.

INFORMATION AND EDUCATION ACTIVITIES: Topics: Children/youth/family; Other; Peace/ethnic conflicts/armament/disarmament; Refugees/migrants/ethnic groups. **Activities:** Broadcasting/cultural events; Conferences/seminars/workshops/training activities; Exchanges/twinning/linking; Information campaigns/exhibitions; Lobbying/advocacy; Publishing/audiovisual materials/educational materials.

IRL2729
VOLUNTEER MISSIONARY MOVEMENT, IRELAND (VMM)

High Park, Grace Park Road, Drumcondra, Dublin 9, Ireland.

Voir : *Comment utiliser le répertoire,* page 11.

Telephone: 353 (1) 837 65 65. *Fax:* 353 (1) 836 71 12. *Contact:* Catherine Furlong.

OBJECTIVES: To recruit and prepare people to work with communities in developing countries. To help people help themselves and to be concerned with the causes as well as the conditions of poverty and injustice.

GENERAL INFORMATION: *Creation:* 1972. *Personnel/Total:* 68. *Salaried:* 3. *Volunteers:* 65 of which: 65 in developing countries. *Financial sources:* Private: 40%. Public: 60%.

PUBLICATIONS: *Periodicals:* VMM Newsletter (4). *Annual report.*

ACTIVITIES IN DEVELOPING REGIONS: Active in 6 country(ies). Works through local field partners. **Sustainable Development Actions:** Children/youth/family; Education/training/literacy; Gender issues/women; Health/sanitation/water; Rural development/agriculture; Sending volunteers/experts/technical assistance; Urban development/habitat. **Regions:** East Africa; Southern Africa.

INFORMATION AND EDUCATION ACTIVITIES: Topics: Culture/tradition/religion; Education/training/literacy; Employment/unemployment; Gender issues/women; Health/sanitation/water; International economic relations/trade/debt/finance; Poverty/living conditions; Rural development/agriculture. **Activities:** Conferences/seminars/workshops/training activities.

IRL2730
WATERFORD-KITUI PARTNERSHIP

World Development Centre, St. John's Way, Parnell Street, Waterford, Ireland.

Telephone: 353 (51) 730 64. *Fax:* 353 (51) 539 79. *Contact:* Roger Green, Development Officer.

OBJECTIVES: To promote understanding of the culture and conditions of life in Kitui, Kenya. To participate in development projects carried out by people in Kitui. To promote an increase in Overseas Development Assistance by the Irish government.

GENERAL INFORMATION: *Creation:* 1976. *Affiliated to:* Campaign Aid (Ireland). *Personnel/Total:* 4. *Salaried:* 2. *Volunteers:* 2. *Budget/ Total 1993:* ECU 59000 (US$ 69000). *Financial sources:* Private: 80%. Public: 18%. Self-financing: 2%.

PUBLICATIONS: *Periodicals:* (4) (4). *Annual report.*

EVALUATION/RESEARCH: Evaluation reports available.

PLANNED ACTIVITIES: The creation of awareness in Waterford of the new partnership with schools for the mentally handicapped in Kitui.

ACTIVITIES IN DEVELOPING REGIONS: Active in 1 country(ies). Maintains local field presence. Works through local field partners. **Sustainable Development Actions:** Children/youth/family; Education/training/literacy; Emergency relief/refugees/humanitarian assistance; Food/famine; Gender issues/women; Health/sanitation/water; Other; Rural development/agriculture; Small enterprises/informal sector/handicrafts. **Regions:** East Africa.

INFORMATION AND EDUCATION ACTIVITIES: Topics: Children/youth/family; Culture/tradition/religion; Ecology/environment/biodiversity; Education/training/literacy; Employment/unemployment; Food/famine; Gender issues/women; Health/sanitation/water; Human rights/peace/conflicts; International economic relations/trade/debt/finance; International relations/cooperation/development aid; Peace/ethnic conflicts/armament/disarmament; Population/family planning/demography; Poverty/living conditions; Racism/xenophobia/antisemitism; Refugees/migrants/ethnic groups; Rural development/agriculture; Urban development/habitat. **Activities:** Conferences/seminars/workshops/training activities; Exchanges/twinning/linking; Fund raising; Information and documentation services/data bases; Information campaigns/exhibitions; Publishing/audiovisual materials/educational materials.

IRL2731
WORLD EDUCATION PROJECT

St. Angela's College, Lough Gill, Sligo, Ireland.

Telephone: 353 (71) 45485. *Contact:* Aengus Cantwell.

IRL2732
WORLD MERCY FUND

Nagor House, Dundrum Road, Dublin 14, Ireland.

Telephone: 353 (1) 296 13 60. *Fax:* 353 (1) 296 13 72. *Contact:* Fr. Patrick Leonard, President.

OBJECTIVES: To alleviate suffering throughout the developing world with particular emphasis on the funding of Primary Health, Agricultural and Educational programmes.

GENERAL INFORMATION: *Creation:* 1969. *Personnel/Total:* 18. *Salaried:* 8 of which: 2 in developing countries. *Volunteers:* 10 of which: 10 in developing countries. *Budget/Total 1993:* ECU 6257000 (US$ 7336000). *Financial sources:* Public: 5%. Self-financing: 95%.

PUBLICATIONS: *Annual report.*

EVALUATION/RESEARCH: Evaluation reports available.

COMMENTS: Undertakes activities in the Commonwealth of Independent States.

ACTIVITIES IN DEVELOPING REGIONS: Present in developing regions. Active in 25 country(ies). Maintains local field presence. Works through local field partners. **Sustainable Development Actions:** Children/youth/family; Education/training/literacy; Emergency relief/refugees/humanitarian assistance; Energy/transport; Gender issues/women; Health/sanitation/water; Rural development/agriculture; Small enterprises/informal sector/handicrafts; Urban development/habitat. **Regions:** Central Africa; East Africa; Mexico and Central America; Oceania; South America; Southern Africa; West Africa.

INFORMATION AND EDUCATION ACTIVITIES: Topics: Children/youth/family; Education/training/literacy; Food/famine; Gender issues/women; Health/sanitation/water; Poverty/living conditions; Refugees/migrants/ethnic groups; Rural development/agriculture; Urban development/habitat. **Activities:** Fund raising.

IRL2733
WORLD VISION OF IRELAND

10 Main Street, Donnybrook, Dublin 4, Ireland.

Telephone: 353 (1) 283 78 00. *Fax:* 353 (1) 283 76 73. *Contact:* Thora Mackey, Director.

OBJECTIVES: To raise funds for its relief and development projects. To heighten awareness in Ireland of the problems facing the underdeveloped countries.

GENERAL INFORMATION: *Creation:* 1986. *Personnel/Total:* 9. *Salaried:* 9 of which: 4 in developing countries. *Budget/Total 1993:* ECU 876000 (US$ 1027000). *Financial sources:* Private: 70%. Public: 30%.

PUBLICATIONS: *Periodicals:* Window on the World (4).

EVALUATION/RESEARCH: Evaluation reports available.

PLANNED ACTIVITIES: Campaigning against river blindness and undertaking development education in schools.

COMMENTS: Undertakes activities in the Commonwealth of Independent States.

ACTIVITIES IN DEVELOPING REGIONS: Present in developing regions. Active in 8 country(ies). Maintains local field presence. Works through local field partners. **Sustainable Development Actions:** Children/youth/family; Democracy/good governance/institution building/participatory development; Ecology/environment/biodiversity; Education/training/literacy; Emergency relief/refugees/humanitarian assistance; Food/famine; Gender issues/women; Health/sanitation/water; Human rights/peace/conflicts; Population/family planning/demography; Rural development/agriculture; Sending volunteers/experts/technical assistance; Small enterprises/informal sector/handicrafts; Urban development/habitat. **Regions:** Central Asia and South Asia; East Africa; Middle East; South East Asia; Southern Africa; West Africa.

INFORMATION AND EDUCATION ACTIVITIES: Topics: Children/youth/family; Education/training/literacy; Emergency relief/refugees/humanitarian assistance; Food/famine; Gender issues/women; Health/sanitation/water; International relations/cooperation/development aid; Peace/eth-

See: How to Use the Directory, page 11.

nic conflicts/armament/disarmament; Poverty/living conditions; Racism/ xenophobia/antisemitism; Refugees/migrants/ethnic groups; Rural development/agriculture; Urban development/habitat. **Activities:** Conferences/seminars/workshops/training activities; Exchanges/twinning/ linking; Formal education; Fund raising; Information and documentation services/data bases; Information campaigns/exhibitions; Publishing/ audiovisual materials/educational materials.

ISL2734

AMNESTY INTERNATIONAL, ICELANDIC SECTION

P.O. Box 618, 121 Reykjavík, Iceland.

Telephone: 354 (1) 16940. *Fax:* 354 (1) 616 940. *Contact:* Sigurdur A. Magnusson, Chairman.

ISL2735

HJALPARSTARF ADVENTISTA

Suëurhifë 36, 105 Reykjávik, Iceland.

Contact: Erik Guömundsson.

ISL2736

HJALPARSTOFNUN KIRKJUNNAR ♦ Icelandic Church Aid

Tjarnargata 10, 150 Reykjavik, Iceland.

Telephone: 354 (1) 62 4400. *Fax:* 354 (1) 62 4495. *Contact:* Jónas Thórisson, Director.

OBJECTIVES: To provide assistance to distressed populations in developing countries.

GENERAL INFORMATION: *Creation:* 1969. *Affiliated to:* LWF (Switzerland) - World Council of Churches (Switzerland). *Personnel/Total:* 3. *Salaried:* 3 of which: 1 in developing countries. *Budget/Total 1993:* ECU 578000 (US$ 750000). *Financial sources: Private:* 75%. *Public:* 15%. *Self-financing:* 10%.

PUBLICATIONS: *Periodicals:* Fréttabréf Hjálparstofnunar Kirkjunnar (4). *Annual report.*

ACTIVITIES IN DEVELOPING REGIONS: Present in developing regions. Maintains local field presence. **Sustainable Development Actions:** Children/youth/family; Emergency relief/refugees/humanitarian assistance; Gender issues/women; Health/sanitation/water; Urban development/habitat. **Regions:** Central Asia and South Asia; East Africa; Middle East.

INFORMATION AND EDUCATION ACTIVITIES: Topics: Children/youth/family; Emergency relief/refugees/humanitarian assistance; Gender issues/women; Health/sanitation/water; Urban development/habitat. **Activities:** Conferences/seminars/workshops/training activities; Information and documentation services/data bases; Publishing/audiovisual materials/educational materials.

ISL2737

HVITASUNNUSSOFNUDURINN

Hátúni 2, 105 Reykjavík, Iceland.

Contact: Haflibi Kristinsson.

ISL2738

INSTITUTE FOR ENVIRONMENTAL ISSUES AND DEVELOPMENT

Hedi, Rangarvallahreppi, 851 Hella, Iceland.

Telephone: 354 (98) 75179.

ISL2739

RAUDI KROSS ISLANDS ♦ Icelandic Red Cross

Rauòarástíg 18, P.O. Box 5450, 105 Reykjavik, Iceland.

Telephone: 354 (1) 62 6722. *Fax:* 354 (1) 62 3150. *Contact:* Sigrúm Arnadòttir, Secretary General.

OBJECTIVES: To prevent or alleviate suffering, protect life and health, and ensure respect for human rights. To work towards mutual understanding, friendship, co-operation and lasting peace in co-operation with other Red Cross and Red Crescent Societies.

GENERAL INFORMATION: *Creation:* 1924. *Affiliated to:* International Federation of Red Cross and Red Crescent Societies (Switzerland). *Personnel/Total:* 937. *Salaried:* 35 of which: 11 in developing countries. *Volunteers:* 902 of which: 2 in developing countries. *Budget/*

Total 1993: ECU 4184000 (US$ 5426000). *Financial sources: Private:* 94%. *Public:* 2%. *Self-financing:* 4%.

PUBLICATIONS: *Periodicals:* Rki Tidindi (10) - Hjàlpum (2). *Annual report.*

EVALUATION/RESEARCH: Evaluation reports available.

COMMENTS: Undertakes activities in the Commonwealth of Independent States. Information activities related to the Commonwealth of Independent States.

ACTIVITIES IN DEVELOPING REGIONS: Present in developing regions. Maintains local field presence. Works through local field partners. **Sustainable Development Actions:** Children/youth/family; Ecology/environment/biodiversity; Education/training/literacy; Emergency relief/refugees/humanitarian assistance; Food/famine; Gender issues/women; Health/sanitation/water; Human rights/peace/conflicts; Rural development/agriculture; Sending volunteers/experts/technical assistance. **Regions:** Caribbean; Central Africa; Central Asia and South Asia; East Africa; East Asia; Mexico and Central America; Middle East; North Africa; South America; South East Asia; Southern Africa; West Africa.

INFORMATION AND EDUCATION ACTIVITIES: Topics: Children/youth/family; Ecology/environment/biodiversity; Health/sanitation/water; Rural development/agriculture. **Activities:** Exchanges/twinning/linking; Publishing/audiovisual materials/educational materials.

ISL2740

SAMBAND ISLENSKRA KRISTNIBODSFELAGA (SIK) ♦ Icelandic Mission Society

P.O. Box 4060 IS-124, 105 Reykjavik, Iceland.

Telephone: 354 (1) 88 8899. *Fax:* 354 (1) 88 8840. *Contact:* Skuli Svavarsson, General Secretary.

OBJECTIVES: To help needy people both spiritually and materially.

GENERAL INFORMATION: *Creation:* 1929. *Type of organisation:* association of NGOs. *Member organisations:* 18. *Affiliated to:* Norwegian Lutheran Mission (Norway) - Ethiopian Evangelical Church Mekane Yesus (Ethiopia) - Evangelical Lutheran Church in Kenya (Kenya). *Personnel/Total:* 14. *Salaried:* 14 of which: 11 in developing countries. *Budget/Total 1993:* ECU 180000 (US$ 233000). *Financial sources: Private:* 100%.

PUBLICATIONS: *Periodicals:* BJARMI (8) (6). *Annual report.*

ACTIVITIES IN DEVELOPING REGIONS: Active in 2 country(ies). Maintains local field presence. Works through local field partners. **Sustainable Development Actions:** Children/youth/family; Education/training/literacy; Emergency relief/refugees/humanitarian assistance; Food/famine; Gender issues/women; Health/sanitation/water; Rural development/agriculture; Sending volunteers/experts/technical assistance; Small enterprises/informal sector/handicrafts; Urban development/habitat. **Regions:** East Africa.

INFORMATION AND EDUCATION ACTIVITIES: Topics: Children/youth/family; Culture/tradition/religion; Education/training/literacy; Food/famine; Gender issues/women; Health/sanitation/water; Rural development/agriculture; Urban development/habitat. **Activities:** Formal education; Fund raising.

ISL2741

SOS BARNAPORPIN

Hamtaborg 1, 200 Kópavogur, Iceland.

Telephone: 354 - 64 29 10. *Fax:* 354 - 64 29 07. *Contact:* Ulla Magnússon, President.

ISL2742

UNICEF IN ICELAND

Storagerdi 30, 108 Reykjavik, Iceland.

ISL2743

UNITED NATIONS ASSOCIATION OF ICELAND

Postbox 679, Reykjavik, Iceland.

See: *How to Use the Directory,* page 11.

ITA2744
AFRICA (70)

Viale Monza 48, 20127 Milano, Italie.

Téléphone: 39 (2) 26825228. *Fax:* 39 (2) 26146229. *Contact:* Donatella Vergari, Présidente.

OBJECTIFS: Soutenir les pays en développement, en les représentant auprès de l'opinion publique italienne et auprès des institutions. Apporter une aide financière et une assistance technique à ces pays. Sensibiliser l'opinion publique italienne sur les thèmes du dialogue Nord-Sud, grâce à des activités d'information éditoriale.

INFORMATIONS GENERALES: *Création:* 1970. *Affiliée à:* Coordinamento delle ONG per la cooperazione internazionale allo sviluppo (Italie). *Personnel/Total:* 45. *Salariés:* 29 dont: 21 dans les pays en développement. *Bénévoles:* 16 dont: 12 dans les pays en développement. *Budget/Total 1993:* ECU 2546000 (US\$ 2980000). *Sources financières:* Privé: 8%. Public: 90%. *Autofinancement:* 2%.

PUBLICATIONS: *Liste des publications.*

EVALUATION/RECHERCHE: Rapports d'évaluation disponibles. Entreprend des activités de recherche.

ACTIVITES DANS LES REGIONS EN DEVELOPPEMENT: Intervient directement dans les régions en développement. Intervient dans 12 pays. Maintient une présence locale sur le terrain. Intervient par l'intermédiaire d'organisations locales partenaires. **Actions de Développement durable:** Démocratie/bonne gestion publique/création d'institutions/développement participatif; Développement rural/agriculture; Développement urbain/habitat; Envoi de volontaires/experts/assistance technique; Petites entreprises/secteur informel/artisanat; Santé/assainissement/eau; Secours d'urgence/réfugiés/aide humanitaire; Écologie/environnement/biodiversité. **Régions:** Afrique centrale; Afrique de l'Est; Afrique de l'Ouest; Amérique du Sud; Asie du Sud-Est; Mexique et Amerique centrale.

ACTIVITES D'INFORMATION ET D'EDUCATION: Domaines: Culture/tradition/religion; Développement rural/agriculture; Développement urbain/habitat; Enfants/jeunesse/famille; Relations internationales/coopération/aide au développement; Santé/assainissement/eau; Écologie/environnement/biodiversité. **Activités:** Radiodiffusion/manifestations culturelles; Services d'information et de documentation/bases de données; Édition/documents audiovisuels/documents éducatifs.

ITA2745
AGENZIA INTERNAZIONALE DI INFORMAZIONE (AGINT)

Via Buonarroti N° 51, 00185 Roma, Italie.

Téléphone: 39 (6) 732769. *Fax:* 39 (6) 734006.

ITA2746
L'ALTRITALIA, CENTRO STUDI

Via Duomo, 255, 80138 Napoli, Italy.

Telephone: 39 (81) 5538349. *Fax:* 39 (81) 5538349.

ITA2747
AMICI DEI POPOLI

Via Genova 7, 40139 Bologna, Italie.

Téléphone: 39 (51) 460381. *Fax:* 39 (51) 451928. *Contact:* Stefano Carati, Secrétaire général.

OBJECTIFS: Mener des actions de développement dans les pays du Tiers Monde. Sensibiliser et éduquer au développement. Apporter une aide aux réfugiés.

INFORMATIONS GENERALES: *Création:* 1978. *Affiliée à:* Fédération Organismes Chrétiens Service International Volontaire.. *Personnel/Total:* 310. *Salariés:* 10 dont: 6 dans les pays en développement. *Bénévoles:* 300 dont: 40 dans les pays en développement. *Budget/Total 1993:* ECU 580000 (US\$ 678000). *Sources financières:* Privé: 33%. Public: 37%. *Autofinancement:* 30%.

PUBLICATIONS: *Périodiques:* Un Solo mondo (2) - Revue de Presse (12). *Liste des publications.*

PREVISIONS D'ACTIVITES: Formation professionnelle au Vietnam, en Amérique du Sud et aux Caraïbes. Soutien aux enfants des orphelinats rwandais.

ACTIVITES DANS LES REGIONS EN DEVELOPPEMENT: Intervient directement dans les régions en développement. Intervient dans 3 pays. Maintient une présence locale sur le terrain. Intervient par l'intermédiaire d'organisations locales partenaires. **Actions de Développement durable:** Aliments/famine; Développement rural/agriculture; Enfants/jeunesse/famille; Envoi de volontaires/experts/assistance technique; Petites entreprises/secteur informel/artisanat; Santé/assainissement/eau; Secours d'urgence/réfugiés/aide humanitaire; Éducation/formation/alphabétisation. **Régions:** Afrique centrale; Asie du Sud-Est.

ACTIVITES D'INFORMATION ET D'EDUCATION: Domaines: Enfants/jeunesse/famille; Paix/conflits ethniques/armement/désarmement; Pauvreté/conditions de vie; Relations internationales/coopération/aide au développement; Réfugiés/migrants/groupes ethniques; Secours d'urgence/réfugiés/aide humanitaire; Éducation/formation/alphabétisation. **Activités:** Collecte de fonds; Conférences/séminaires/ateliers/activités de formation; Radiodiffusion/manifestations culturelles; Services d'information et de documentation/bases de données.

ITA2748
AMICI DELLA TERRA ♦ Friends of the Earth

Via di Torre Argentina 18, 00186 Roma, Italy.

Telephone: 39 (6) 6868289. *Fax:* 39 (6) 68308610. *E-mail:* foeitaly@igc.apc.org. *Contact:* Mario Signorino, President.

OBJECTIVES: To organise groups of people to protect the environment and promote a harmonious relationship between nature and humankind. To fight against injustice and insecurity in the international community.

GENERAL INFORMATION: *Creation:* 1977. *Affiliated to:* Friends of the Earth International (the Netherlands) - European Environmental Bureau (Belgium). *Personnel/Total:* 173. *Salaried:* 15 of which: 3 in developing countries. *Volunteers:* 158. *Budget/Total 1993:* ECU 585000 (US\$ 684000). *Financial sources:* Private: 5%. Public: 38%. *Self-financing:* 57%.

PUBLICATIONS: *Periodicals:* ADT Newsletter (12). *Annual report.*

EVALUATION/RESEARCH: Undertakes research activities.

ACTIVITIES IN DEVELOPING REGIONS: Present in developing regions. Active in 1 country(ies). Maintains local field presence. Works through local field partners. **Sustainable Development Actions:** Democracy/good governance/institution building/participatory development; Ecology/environment/biodiversity; Education/training/literacy; Human rights/peace/conflicts; Sending volunteers/experts/technical assistance; Small enterprises/informal sector/handicrafts. **Regions:** South America.

INFORMATION AND EDUCATION ACTIVITIES: Topics: Ecology/environment/biodiversity; International economic relations/trade/debt/finance; International relations/cooperation/development aid. **Activities:** Broadcasting/cultural events; Conferences/seminars/workshops/training activities; Fund raising; Information and documentation services/data bases; Information campaigns/exhibitions; Lobbying/advocacy; Networking/electronic telecommunications; Publishing/audiovisual materials/educational materials.

ITA2749
AMICI DELLO STATO BRASILIANO DELL'ESPIRITO SANTO - CENTRO DI COLLABORAZIONE COMUNITARIA (AES-CCC)
♦ Friends of the Brazilian State of Espirito Santo - Community Collaboration Centre

Via Locatelli 5 - C.P. 447, 35123 Padova, Italy .

Telephone: 39 (49) 8753266. *Fax:* 39 (49) 8753641. *Contact:* Giovanni Michelotto, President.

ITA2750
AMNESTY INTERNATIONAL CENTRO PER L'EDUCAZIONE AI DIRITTI UMANI (CEDU) ♦ Centre pour l'éducation aux Droits de l'Homme

Via Castiglione 25, 40124 Bologna, Italie.

Voir : *Comment utiliser le répertoire,* page 11.

Téléphone: 39 (51) 225186. *Fax:* 39 (51) 260090. *Contact:* Giuseppe Giliberti.

OBJECTIFS: Fournir une documentation concernant les droits de l'Homme. Organiser des cours sur les droits de l'Homme. Proposer une consultation pédagogique aux enseignants.

INFORMATIONS GENERALES: *Création:* 1991. *Personnel/Total:* 10. *Bénévoles:* 10. *Budget/Total 1993:* ECU 2700 (US$ 3000). *Sources financières:* Privé: 90%. Autofinancement: 10%.

PUBLICATIONS: *Rapport annuel. Liste des publications.*

EVALUATION/RECHERCHE: Rapports d'évaluation disponibles. Entreprend des activités de recherche.

ACTIVITES D'INFORMATION ET D'EDUCATION: Domaines: Droits de l'Homme/paix/conflits. **Activités:** Conférences/séminaires/ateliers/activités de formation; Services d'information et de documentation/bases de données; Échanges/parrainage/jumelage; Éducation formelle.

ITA2751

AMNESTY INTERNATIONAL, ITALIAN SECTION

Viale Mazzini 146, 00195 Roma, Italy.

ITA2752

ARCI - CULTURA E SVILUPPO (ARCI-CS) ♦ ARCI - Culture and Development

23 Via dei Mille, 00196 Roma, Italy.

Telephone: 39 (6) 4958620. *Fax:* 39 (6) 4465735. *Contact:* Domenico Pinto, President.

ITA2753

ASSOCIATION INTERNATIONALE CONTRA LA TORTURA

CP 1487, 20100 Milano, Italie.

ITA2754

ASSOCIAZIONE AAM TERRA NUOVA

C.P. 199, 50032 Borgo S. Lorenzo (FI), Italie.

Téléphone: 39 (55) 8456116.

ITA2755

ASSOCIAZIONE AMICI DEI BAMBINI (AIBI)

Via G. Frassi 19, 20077 Melegnano (MI), Italy.

Telephone: 39 (2) 98232102. *Fax:* 39 (2) 98232611. *Contact:* Dr. Marco Griffini, President.

OBJECTIVES: To help minors in difficulty in Italy and abroad. To promote the rights of children and help them grow up and become educated within their own family and society.

GENERAL INFORMATION: *Creation:* 1986. *Affiliated to:* Federazione Organismi Cristiani di Servizio Internationale Volontario - Union Internationale des Organismes Familiaux - Bureau International Catholique de l'Enfance - Voluntary Organisations in Cooperation in Emergencies - Movimento di Volontariato Italiano.. *Personnel/Total:* 86. *Salaried:* 9 of which: 2 in developing countries. *Volunteers:* 77 of which: 17 in developing countries. *Budget/Total 1993:* ECU 498000 (US$ 582000). *Financial sources:* Private: 4%. Public: 6%. Self-financing: 90%.

PUBLICATIONS: *Periodicals:* Il Foglio dell'Ai.Bi (4). *Annual report. List of publications.*

EVALUATION/RESEARCH: Evaluation reports available. Undertakes research activities.

COMMENTS: Undertakes activities in the Commonwealth of Independent States. Information activities related to the Commonwealth of Independent States.

ACTIVITIES IN DEVELOPING REGIONS: Present in developing regions. Active in 8 country(ies). Maintains local field presence. Works through local field partners. **Sustainable Development Actions:** Children/youth/family; Human rights/peace/conflicts; Other. **Regions:** Mexico and Central America; Middle East; North Africa; South America; West Africa.

INFORMATION AND EDUCATION ACTIVITIES: Topics: Children/youth/family; Emergency relief/refugees/humanitarian assistance; Human rights/peace/conflicts; International relations/cooperation/development aid; Peace/ethnic conflicts/armament/disarmament. **Activities:** Conferences/seminars/workshops/training activities; Fund raising; Information and documentation services/data bases; Information campaigns/exhibitions; Lobbying/advocacy; Publishing/audiovisual materials/educational materials.

ITA2756

ASSOCIAZIONE AZIONE PER UN MONDO UNITO (AMU) ♦ Action for a United World

Corso V. Colonna, 78/B, 00047 Marino (RM), Italy.

Telephone: 39 (6) 9367071. *Fax:* 39 (6) 9367071. *Contact:* Pier Giorgio Colonnetti, President.

OBJECTIVES: To support development projects and voluntary services in developing countries. To inform and educate the Italian public about development co-operation.

GENERAL INFORMATION: *Creation:* 1986. *Personnel/Total:* 11. *Salaried:* 7 of which: 5 in developing countries. *Volunteers:* 4. *Budget/Total 1993:* ECU 761000 (US$ 891000). *Financial sources:* Private: 80%. *Public:* 20%.

PUBLICATIONS: *Periodicals:* AMU Notizie (3). *Annual report.*

COMMENTS: Undertakes activities in the Commonwealth of Independent States.

ACTIVITIES IN DEVELOPING REGIONS: Present in developing regions. Active in 25 country(ies). Maintains local field presence. Works through local field partners. **Sustainable Development Actions:** Children/youth/family; Democracy/good governance/institution building/participatory development; Education/training/literacy; Gender issues/women; Health/sanitation/water; Population/family planning/demography; Rural development/agriculture; Sending volunteers/experts/technical assistance; Small enterprises/informal sector/handicrafts. **Regions:** Central Africa; Mexico and Central America; Middle East; South America; South East Asia; West Africa.

INFORMATION AND EDUCATION ACTIVITIES: Topics: Children/youth/family; Ecology/environment/biodiversity; Emergency relief/refugees/humanitarian assistance; International economic relations/trade/debt/finance; International relations/cooperation/development aid; Rural development/agriculture. **Activities:** Conferences/seminars/workshops/training activities; Fund raising; Publishing/audiovisual materials/educational materials.

ITA2757

ASSOCIAZIONE CENTRO AIUTI VOLONTARI COOPERAZIONE SVILUPPO TERZO MONDO (ACAV)

Via Giusti 40, 38100 Trento, Italy.

Telephone: 39 (461) 935893. *Fax:* 39 (461) 935893. *Contact:* Carlo Bridi, President.

OBJECTIVES: To improve living conditions through self-development initiatives within the developing world. To mobilize and sensitize public opinion about the problems of developing countries.

GENERAL INFORMATION: *Creation:* 1986. *Personnel/Total:* 18. *Salaried:* 14 of which: 12 in developing countries. *Volunteers:* 4 of which: 2 in developing countries. *Budget/Total 1993:* ECU 513000 (US$ 600000). *Financial sources:* Private: 21%. Public: 46%. Self-financing: 4%.

PUBLICATIONS: *Periodicals:* ACAV INFORMA - Newsletters (9).

EVALUATION/RESEARCH: Evaluation reports available.

ACTIVITIES IN DEVELOPING REGIONS: Present in developing regions. Active in 6 country(ies). Maintains local field presence. Works through local field partners. **Sustainable Development Actions:** Education/training/literacy; Health/sanitation/water; Rural development/agriculture. **Regions:** Central Africa; East Africa; Southern Africa.

INFORMATION AND EDUCATION ACTIVITIES: **Topics:** Education/training/literacy; Health/sanitation/water; Rural development/agriculture. **Activities:** Conferences/seminars/workshops/training activities; Publishing/audiovisual materials/educational materials.

ITA2758

ASSOCIAZIONE CENTRO ELIS ♦ Centro Ellis Association

Via Sandro Sandri, 45, 00159 Roma, Italy.

Telephone: 39 (6) 4394661. *Fax:* 39 (6) 4394681. *Contact:* Bruno Agostino Picker, Director.

OBJECTIVES: To develop and establish technical educational centers. To promote educational and training activities for youth and workers in Italy and developing countries.

GENERAL INFORMATION: *Creation:* 1964. ***Personnel/Total:*** 101. *Salaried:* 84 of which: 1 in developing countries. *Volunteers:* 17 of which: 3 in developing countries. ***Budget/Total 1993:*** ECU 3937000 (US$ 4607000). *Financial sources: Private:* 32%. *Public:* 19%. *Self-financing:* 49%.

PUBLICATIONS: *Periodicals:* Elis Notizie (2).

EVALUATION/RESEARCH: Undertakes research activities.

ACTIVITIES IN DEVELOPING REGIONS: Present in developing regions. Active in 3 country(ies). Maintains local field presence. Works through local field partners. **Sustainable Development Actions:** Education/training/literacy; Health/sanitation/water; Sending volunteers/experts/technical assistance; Small enterprises/informal sector/handicrafts. **Regions:** South America; South East Asia.

INFORMATION AND EDUCATION ACTIVITIES: Topics: Education/training/literacy; Employment/unemployment; International relations/cooperation/development aid. **Activities:** Conferences/seminars/workshops/training activities; Exchanges/twinning/linking; Formal education; Fund raising; Information campaigns/exhibitions; Publishing/audiovisual materials/educational materials.

ITA2759

ASSOCIAZIONE COOPERATIVA INTERNAZIONALE PER LO SVILUPPO ♦ Association coopérative internationale pour le développement

Piazza Borgo Dora 61, 10152 Torino, Italie.

Téléphone: 39 (11) 5213770. *Contact:* Ernesto Olivero, Président.

ITA2760

ASSOCIAZIONE DALLA PARTE DEGLI ULTIMI (DPU)

Via 24 Maggio 8, 86100 Campobasso, Italy.

Telephone: 39 (874) 698571. *Fax:* 39 (874) 698571. *Contact:* Raffaele De Angelis, President.

OBJECTIVES: To support development projects in developing countries. To inform and educate the Italian public about development co-operation. To maintain a reception centre for university students from developing countries.

GENERAL INFORMATION: *Creation:* 1987. ***Affiliated to:*** CIPSI. ***Personnel/Total:*** 9. *Volunteers:* 9. ***Budget/Total 1993:*** ECU 576000 (US$ 674000). *Financial sources: Private:* 80%. *Public:* 20%.

ACTIVITIES IN DEVELOPING REGIONS: Active in 2 country(ies). **Sustainable Development Actions:** Education/training/literacy; Health/sanitation/water. **Regions:** Central Africa.

INFORMATION AND EDUCATION ACTIVITIES: Topics: Culture/tradition/religion; International relations/cooperation/development aid; Urban development/habitat. **Activities:** Conferences/seminars/workshops/training activities; Publishing/audiovisual materials/educational materials.

ITA2761

ASSOCIAZIONE DI COOPERAZIONE CRISTIANA INTERNAZIONALE (ACCRI) ♦ International Christian Co-operation Association

Via Cavana 16/A, 34124 Trieste, Italy.

Telephone: 39 (40) 307899. *Fax:* 39 (40) 391666. *Contact:* Nives

OBJECTIVES: To educate the public about the problems of developing countries. To promote programmes in developing countries and initiatives that focus on the professional formation of local groups and individuals.

GENERAL INFORMATION: *Creation:* 1987. ***Affiliated to:*** Federation of Christian Organisations of Volunteer International Service. ***Personnel/Total:*** 32. *Salaried:* 3. *Volunteers:* 29 of which: 11 in developing countries. ***Budget/Total 1993:*** ECU 92000 (US$ 108000). *Financial sources: Private:* 30%. *Public:* 35%. *Self-financing:* 35%.

PUBLICATIONS: *Periodicals:* "Missione una Chiesa in cammino" (4). *List of publications.*

EVALUATION/RESEARCH: Evaluation reports available.

ACTIVITIES IN DEVELOPING REGIONS: Present in developing regions. Maintains local field presence. Works through local field partners. **Sustainable Development Actions:** Children/youth/family; Education/training/literacy; Rural development/agriculture; Sending volunteers/experts/technical assistance. **Regions:** East Africa; South America; West Africa.

INFORMATION AND EDUCATION ACTIVITIES: Topics: Culture/tradition/religion; Food/famine; International relations/cooperation/development aid; Poverty/living conditions; Racism/xenophobia/antisemitism; Refugees/migrants/ethnic groups; Rural development/agriculture. **Activities:** Formal education; Information and documentation services/data bases; Information campaigns/exhibitions.

ITA2762

ASSOCIAZIONE DI COOPERAZIONE RURALE IN AFRICA E AMERICA LATINA (ACRA) ♦ Association of Rural Co-operation in Africa and Latin America

Via Breda 54, 20126 Milano, Italy.

Telephone: 39 (2) 27000291. *Fax:* 39 (2) 2552270. *Contact:* Giuseppe Biella, President.

OBJECTIVES: To fight against the exploitation and injustice characteristic of economic and political relations between nations. To develop public awareness about the problems of underdevelopment and to undertake concrete multisectoral rural development programmes.

GENERAL INFORMATION: *Creation:* 1968. ***Affiliated to:*** COCIS (Italy). ***Personnel/Total:*** 39. *Salaried:* 17 of which: 7 in developing countries. *Volunteers:* 22 of which: 10 in developing countries. ***Budget/Total 1993:*** ECU 1629000 (US$ 1906000). *Financial sources: Private:* 15%. *Public:* 70%. *Self-financing:* 15%.

PUBLICATIONS: *Periodicals:* A.C.R.A Notizie (10). *List of publications.*

ACTIVITIES IN DEVELOPING REGIONS: Present in developing regions. Active in 13 country(ies). Maintains local field presence. Works through local field partners. **Sustainable Development Actions:** Children/youth/family; Debt/finance/trade; Ecology/environment/biodiversity; Education/training/literacy; Emergency relief/refugees/humanitarian assistance; Energy/transport; Food/famine; Gender issues/women; Health/sanitation/water; Rural development/agriculture; Sending volunteers/experts/technical assistance; Small enterprises/informal sector/handicrafts; Urban development/habitat. **Regions:** Central Africa; East Africa; Mexico and Central America; South America; Southern Africa; West Africa.

INFORMATION AND EDUCATION ACTIVITIES: Topics: Children/youth/family; Culture/tradition/religion; Ecology/environment/biodiversity; Education/training/literacy; Emergency relief/refugees/humanitarian assistance; Employment/unemployment; Food/famine; Gender issues/women; Health/sanitation/water; Human rights/peace/conflicts; International economic relations/trade/debt/finance; International relations/cooperation/development aid; Peace/ethnic conflicts/armament/disarmament; Population/family planning/demography; Poverty/living conditions; Racism/xenophobia/antisemitism; Refugees/migrants/ethnic groups; Rural development/agriculture; Urban development/habitat. **Activities:** Broadcasting/cultural events; Conferences/seminars/workshops/training activities; Exchanges/twinning/linking; Formal education; Fund raising; Information and documentation services/data bases; Information campaigns/exhibitions; Lobbying/advocacy; Publishing/audiovisual materials/educational materials.

ITA2763

ASSOCIAZIONE DI TECNICI PER LA SOLIDARIETA E COOPERAZIONE INTERNAZIONALE (RE.TE)

Via Rodi, 45, 10095 Grugliasco (TO), Italy.

Telephone: 39 (11) 7707388. *Fax:* 39 (11) 7707410.

ITA2764

ASSOCIAZIONE DI-SVI DISARMO E SVILUPPO (DISVI) ◆
Désarmement et développement

Via Rossini 13, 14100 Asti, Italie.

Téléphone: 39 (141) 593407. *Fax:* 39 (141) 355893. *Contact:* Dr. Angelo Casabianca, Président.

OBJECTIFS: Réaliser des projets de coopération socio-sanitaire dans les pays en développement. Organiser des programmes d'information et d'éducation en Italie.

INFORMATIONS GENERALES: *Création:* 1982. ***Affiliée à:*** COCIS (Italie) - Coordinamento Formazione Sanitaria (Italie). ***Personnel/Total:*** 28. *Salariés:* 13 dont: 10 dans les pays en développement. *Bénévoles:* 15. ***Budget/Total 1993:*** ECU 1090000 (US$ 1276000). ***Sources financières:*** Privé: 5%. *Public:* 90%. *Autofinancement:* 5%.

PUBLICATIONS: *Périodiques:* Bulletin d'Information interne (4). *Rapport annuel. Liste des publications.*

EVALUATION/RECHERCHE: Entreprend des activités de recherche.

COMMENTAIRES: L'organisation travaille actuellement en Inde, au Népal, à Bhoutan, en Palestine (Hebron), au Yemen, au Mozambique et au Soudan.

ACTIVITES DANS LES REGIONS EN DEVELOPPEMENT: Intervient directement dans les régions en développement. Intervient dans 6 pays. Maintient une présence locale sur le terrain. Intervient par l'intermédiaire d'organisations locales partenaires. **Actions de Développement durable:** Enfants/jeunesse/famille; Population/planning familial/démographie; Santé/assainissement/eau; Éducation/formation/alphabétisation. **Régions:** Afrique australe; Asie centrale et Asie du Sud; Moyen-Orient.

ACTIVITES D'INFORMATION ET D'EDUCATION: Domaines: Enfants/jeunesse/famille; Paix/conflits ethniques/armement/désarmement; Racisme/xénophobie/antisémitisme; Santé/assainissement/eau. **Activités:** Campagnes d'information/expositions; Collecte de fonds; Conférences/séminaires/ateliers/activités de formation; Réseaux/télécommunications électroniques; Services d'information et de documentation/bases de données; Échanges/parrainage/jumelage; Édition/documents audiovisuels/documents éducatifs; Éducation formelle.

ITA2765

ASSOCIAZIONE GUIDE E SCOUTS CATTOLICI ITALIANI (AGESCI) ◆ Association of Italian Catholic Guides and Scouts

Piazza P. Paoli 18, 00186 Roma, Italy.

Telephone: 39 (6) 6872841. *Fax:* 39 (6) 6871376. *Contact:* Dr Gianni dei Bufalo, Director.

OBJECTIVES: To educate youth according to the principles of the Scout Movement.

GENERAL INFORMATION: *Creation:* 1974. ***Affiliated to:*** WAGGGS (United Kingdom) - World Organisation of the Scout Movement (Switzerland). ***Personnel/Total:*** 125. *Salaried:* 25. *Volunteers:* 100. ***Financial sources:*** Private: 1%. Public: 1%. Self-financing: 98%.

PUBLICATIONS: *Periodicals:* SCOUT (10). *List of publications.*

EVALUATION/RESEARCH: Evaluation reports available.

COMMENTS: Undertakes activities in the Commonwealth of Independent States. Information activities related to the Commonwealth of Independent States.

ACTIVITIES IN DEVELOPING REGIONS: Active in 4 country(ies). Works through local field partners. **Sustainable Development Actions:** Emergency relief/refugees/humanitarian assistance; Health/sanitation/water; Rural development/agriculture; Sending volunteers/experts/technical assistance. **Regions:** West Africa.

INFORMATION AND EDUCATION ACTIVITIES: Topics: Children/youth/family; Emergency relief/refugees/humanitarian assistance; Gender issues/women; Health/sanitation/water; Population/family planning/demography; Poverty/living conditions; Racism/xenophobia/antisemitism; Refugees/migrants/ethnic groups. **Activities:** Conferences/seminars/workshops/training activities; Exchanges/twinning/linking; Formal education; Information campaigns/exhibitions; Publishing/audiovisual materials/educational materials.

ITA2766

ASSOCIAZIONE ITALIANA ''AMICI DI RAOUL FOLLEREAU'' (AIFO) ◆ Italian Leprosy Relief Association - Raoul Follereau Foundation

Via Borselli 4, 40135 Bologna, Italy.

Telephone: 39 (51) 433402. *Fax:* 39 (51) 434046. *Contact:* Enzo VENZA, President.

OBJECTIVES: To finance and support leprosy treatment and community based rehabilitation projects. To educate and inform the Italian public about leprosy and development education. To provide scientific training and information to health workers.

GENERAL INFORMATION: *Creation:* 1961. ***Affiliated to:*** CIPSI (Italy) - International Federation of Anti-Leprosy Association (United Kingdom) - Association Internationale des Fondations Raoul Follereau (France). ***Personnel/Total:*** 119. *Salaried:* 59 of which: 15 in developing countries. *Volunteers:* 60. ***Budget/Total 1993:*** ECU 7350000 (US$ 8601000). ***Financial sources:*** Private: 87%. Public: 13%.

PUBLICATIONS: *Periodicals:* Amici dei Lebrosi (11) - Health Cooperation Papers (1). *Annual report. List of publications.*

EVALUATION/RESEARCH: Evaluation reports available.

ACTIVITIES IN DEVELOPING REGIONS: Present in developing regions. Active in 50 country(ies). Maintains local field presence. Works through local field partners. **Sustainable Development Actions:** Children/youth/family; Debt/finance/trade; Democracy/good governance/institution building/participatory development; Education/training/literacy; Emergency relief/refugees/humanitarian assistance; Food/famine; Gender issues/women; Health/sanitation/water; Sending volunteers/experts/technical assistance; Small enterprises/informal sector/handicrafts. **Regions:** Caribbean; Central Africa; Central Asia and South Asia; East Africa; East Asia; Mexico and Central America; Middle East; North Africa; Oceania; South America; South East Asia; Southern Africa; West Africa.

INFORMATION AND EDUCATION ACTIVITIES: Topics: Children/youth/family; Emergency relief/refugees/humanitarian assistance; Food/famine; Health/sanitation/water; International relations/cooperation/development aid; Poverty/living conditions; Racism/xenophobia/antisemitism. **Activities:** Conferences/seminars/workshops/training activities; Exchanges/twinning/linking; Formal education; Fund raising; Information and documentation services/data bases; Information campaigns/exhibitions; Lobbying/advocacy; Publishing/audiovisual materials/educational materials.

ITA2767

ASSOCIAZIONE ITALIANA DONNE PER LO SVILUPPO (AIDOS) ◆ Italian Association for Women in Development

Via dei Giubbonari 30, int.6, 00186 Roma, Italy.

Telephone: 39 (6) 6873214/6873196. *Fax:* 39 (6) 6872549. *Contact:* Daniela Colombo, President.

OBJECTIVES: To improve women's role and participation in the development process in Third World countries. To empower women's organisations.

GENERAL INFORMATION: *Creation:* 1981. ***Affiliated to:*** COCIS (Italy) - INSTRAW (United Nations) - UNIFEM (United Nations) - WIDE (Europe). ***Personnel/Total:*** 14. *Salaried:* 9 of which: 2 in developing countries. *Volunteers:* 5. ***Budget/Total 1993:*** ECU 228000 (US$ 266000). ***Financial sources:*** Public: 85%. Self-financing: 15%.

PUBLICATIONS: *Periodicals:* AIDOS NEWS (6). *Annual report. List of publications.*

See: *How to Use the Directory,* page 11.

EVALUATION/RESEARCH: Undertakes research activities.

PLANNED ACTIVITIES: Undertaking an information campaign on female genital mutilations. Researching a gender strategy paper for the occupied Palestinian territories. Reinforcing institution-building in Tanzania to improve conditions for women.

COMMENTS: Undertakes activities in the Commonwealth of Independent States.

ACTIVITIES IN DEVELOPING REGIONS: Active in 8 country(ies). Works through local field partners. Sustainable Development Actions: Emergency relief/refugees/humanitarian assistance; Gender issues/women; Health/sanitation/water; Small enterprises/informal sector/handicrafts. Regions: Caribbean; East Africa; Middle East; South America; South East Asia; Southern Africa.

INFORMATION AND EDUCATION ACTIVITIES: Topics: Emergency relief/refugees/humanitarian assistance; Gender issues/women; International relations/cooperation/development aid. Activities: Broadcasting/cultural events; Conferences/seminars/workshops/training activities; Exchanges/twinning/linking; Formal education; Fund raising; Information and documentation services/data bases; Information campaigns/exhibitions; Lobbying/advocacy; Networking/electronic telecommunications; Publishing/audiovisual materials/educational materials.

ITA2768

ASSOCIAZIONE ITALIANA PER LA SOLIDARIETA TRA I POPOLI (AISPO) ♦ Italian Association for Solidarity Among Peoples

Via Olgettina N. 60, 20132 Milano, Italy.

Telephone: 39 (2) 23434481. Fax: 39 (2) 23434484. Contact: Enrico Pianetta, General Manager.

ITA2769

ASSOCIAZIONE ITALIANA PER LO SVILUPPO INTERNAZIONALE (AISI-SID) ♦ Italian Association for International Development

Via L.Lilio, 19, 00142 Roma, Italy.

Telephone: 39 (6) 5190011. Fax: 39 (6) 5191323. Contact: Roberto Vanore, President.

OBJECTIVES: To promote activities for sustainable development through such activities as conducting seminars and research. To develop projects funded by bilateral and multilateral organisations in the areas of agriculture, environment and technical assistance training for developing and former Soviet Union countries.

GENERAL INFORMATION: Creation: 1977. Affiliated to: Society for International Development (Italy). Personnel/Total: 6. Salaried: 1. Volunteers: 5. Budget/Total 1993: ECU 14000 (US$ 16000). Financial sources: Self-financing: 100%.

PUBLICATIONS: Periodicals: AISI Newsletter (4). Annual report. List of publications.

EVALUATION/RESEARCH: Evaluation reports available. Undertakes research activities.

ACTIVITIES IN DEVELOPING REGIONS: Sustainable Development Actions: Education/training/literacy; Rural development/agriculture. Regions: Middle East; North Africa.

ITA2770

ASSOCIAZIONE ITALIANA SOCI COSTRUTTORI ♦ Association italienne des compagnons-bâtisseurs

Via Smeraldina, 35, 44044 Cassana- Ferrara, Italie.

Téléphone: 39 (532) 730079. Fax: 39 (532) 730545. Contact: Marcandeus B. padre Angelo, Président..

OBJECTIFS: Apporter une aide concrète et gratuite à ceux qui sont dans le besoinpar l'envoi de volontaires. Contribuer à la promotion et au développement des pays du Tiers-Monde. Témoigner sa foi en Dieu et dans l'Homme.

INFORMATIONS GENERALES: Création: 1957. Type d'organisation: regroupement d'ONG. Organisations membres: 14. Personnel/Total: 17. Salariés: 5 dont: 2 dans les pays en développement. Bénévoles:

12 dont: 5 dans les pays en développement. Budget/Total 1993: ECU 462000 (US$ 541000).

PUBLICATIONS: Périodiques: Incontri (2) - Notizie IBO (3). Rapport annuel.

COMMENTAIRES: Intervient dans la Communauté des Etats indépendants.

ACTIVITES DANS LES REGIONS EN DEVELOPPEMENT: Intervient directement dans les régions en développement. Maintient une présence locale sur le terrain. Intervient par l'intermédiaire d'organisations locales partenaires. Actions de Développement durable: Aliments/famine; Développement rural/agriculture; Développement urbain/habitat; Enfants/jeunesse/famille; Envoi de volontaires/experts/assistance technique; Population/planning familial/démographie; Questions relatives aux femmes; Santé/assainissement/eau; Éducation/formation/alphabétisation. Régions: Afrique centrale; Afrique de l'Ouest; Amérique du Sud; Asie centrale et Asie du Sud.

ACTIVITES D'INFORMATION ET D'EDUCATION: Domaines: Aliments/famine; Développement rural/agriculture; Développement urbain/habitat; Enfants/jeunesse/famille; Pauvreté/conditions de vie; Questions relatives aux femmes; Relations internationales/coopération/aide au développement; Réfugiés/migrants/groupes ethniques; Santé/assainissement/eau; Éducation/formation/alphabétisation. Activités: Campagnes d'information/expositions; Collecte de fonds; Échanges/parrainage/jumelage; Éducation formelle.

ITA2771

ASSOCIAZIONE LAICALE MISSIONARIA (ALM) ♦ Association of Lay Missionaries

Via le Quattro Venti 166/2, 00152 Roma, Italy.

Telephone: 39 (6) 5897752. Fax: 39 (6) 584856. Contact: Margherita Gallo.

OBJECTIVES: To undertake evangelical activities and promote the development of people in developing countries. To train leaders and animators to assist in this work.

GENERAL INFORMATION: Creation: 1976. Affiliated to: FOCSIV (Italy). Personnel/Total: 24. Volunteers: 24 of which: 12 in developing countries. Budget/Total 1993: ECU 112000 (US$ 131000). Financial sources: Private: 25%. Public: 24%. Self-financing: 51%.

PUBLICATIONS: Periodicals: ALM (4).

EVALUATION/RESEARCH: Evaluation reports available.

PLANNED ACTIVITIES: Undertaking an AIDS campaign aimed at the youth in Zambia.

ACTIVITIES IN DEVELOPING REGIONS: Present in developing regions. Active in 4 country(ies). Maintains local field presence. Works through local field partners. Sustainable Development Actions: Children/youth/family; Democracy/good governance/institution building/participatory development; Education/training/literacy; Gender issues/women; Health/sanitation/water; Human rights/peace/conflicts; Population/family planning/demography; Rural development/agriculture; Sending volunteers/experts/technical assistance. Regions: East Africa; Mexico and Central America; Southern Africa.

INFORMATION AND EDUCATION ACTIVITIES: Topics: Children/youth/family; Education/training/literacy; Gender issues/women; Human rights/peace/conflicts; Population/family planning/demography. Activities: Conferences/seminars/workshops/training activities; Formal education.

ITA2772

ASSOCIAZIONE MONDO GIUSTO ♦ Right World Association

Via Zanella 5, 22053 Lecco, Italy.

Telephone: 39 (341) 363696. Fax: 39 (341) 360491. Contact: Domenico Colombo, President.

OBJECTIVES: To train and send volunteers to work on development projects in developing countries.

GENERAL INFORMATION: Creation: 1972. Type of organisation: association of NGOs. Member organisations: 100. Affiliated to: FOCSIV (Italy). Personnel/Total: 13. Volunteers: 13 of which: 7 in develop-

ing countries. *Financial sources:* Private: 20%. Public: 70%. Self-financing: 10%.

PUBLICATIONS: *Periodicals:* Mondo Giusto Notizie (6). *Annual report.*

ACTIVITIES IN DEVELOPING REGIONS: Active in 1 country(ies). Maintains local field presence. Works through local field partners. **Sustainable Development Actions:** Children/youth/family; Ecology/environment/biodiversity; Education/training/literacy; Emergency relief/refugees/humanitarian assistance; Food/famine; Gender issues/women; Health/sanitation/water; Rural development/agriculture; Sending volunteers/experts/technical assistance. **Regions:** East Africa.

ITA2773

ASSOCIAZIONE PER GLI INTERVENTI DI COOPERAZIONE ALLO SVILUPPO (AICOS) ◆ Association for Development Co-operation Interventions

Via Martiri Oscuri 5, 20125 Milano, Italy.

Telephone: 39 (2) 2841423. *Fax:* 39 (2) 26143638. *Contact:* Roberto Girola, Director.

OBJECTIVES: To strengthen scientific and technical co-operation between institutions in developing and industrialized countries. To support emergency programmes in developing countries.

GENERAL INFORMATION: *Creation:* 1985. *Affiliated to:* COCIS (Italy) - CIPEO. *Personnel/Total:* 47. *Salaried:* 15 of which: 11 in developing countries. *Volunteers:* 32 of which: 7 in developing countries. *Budget/Total 1993:* ECU 769000 (US$ 900000). *Financial sources:* Private: 30%. Public: 50%. Self-financing: 20%.

PUBLICATIONS: *Annual report. List of publications.*

EVALUATION/RESEARCH: Evaluation reports available. Undertakes research activities.

ACTIVITIES IN DEVELOPING REGIONS: Present in developing regions. Maintains local field presence. Works through local field partners. **Sustainable Development Actions:** Children/youth/family; Debt/finance/trade; Democracy/good governance/institution building/participatory development; Ecology/environment/biodiversity; Education/training/literacy; Emergency relief/refugees/humanitarian assistance; Energy/transport; Food/famine; Gender issues/women; Health/sanitation/water; Human rights/peace/conflicts; Population/family planning/demography; Rural development/agriculture; Sending volunteers/experts/technical assistance; Small enterprises/informal sector/handicrafts; Urban development/habitat. **Regions:** Caribbean; Central Asia and South Asia; East Africa; Mexico and Central America; Middle East; South America; West Africa.

INFORMATION AND EDUCATION ACTIVITIES: **Topics:** Children/youth/family; Culture/tradition/religion; Ecology/environment/biodiversity; Education/training/literacy; Emergency relief/refugees/humanitarian assistance; Employment/unemployment; Food/famine; Gender issues/women; Health/sanitation/water; Human rights/peace/conflicts; International economic relations/trade/debt/finance; International relations/cooperation/development aid; Peace/ethnic conflicts/armament/disarmament; Population/family planning/demography; Poverty/living conditions; Racism/xenophobia/antisemitism; Refugees/migrants/ethnic groups; Rural development/agriculture; Urban development/habitat. **Activities:** Broadcasting/cultural events; Conferences/seminars/workshops/training activities; Exchanges/twinning/linking; Formal education; Fund raising; Information and documentation services/data bases; Information campaigns/exhibitions; Networking/electronic telecommunications; Publishing/audiovisual materials/educational materials.

ITA2774

ASSOCIAZIONE PER LA COOPERAZIONE MISSIONARIA (ASCOM) ◆ Association for Missionary Co-operation

Galleria Risorgimento 3, 37045 Legnano, Italy.

Telephone: 39 (4) 4228333. *Fax:* 39 (4) 4228333. *Contact:* Enzo Ziviani, Chairman.

OBJECTIVES: To undertake projects to supply basic necessities in developing countries.

GENERAL INFORMATION: *Creation:* 1982. *Personnel/Total:* 10. *Volunteers:* 10 of which: 4 in developing countries. *Budget/Total 1993:*

ECU 380000 (US$ 445000). *Financial sources:* Private: 17%. Public: 80%. Self-financing: 3%.

PUBLICATIONS: *Periodicals:* ASCOM Notizie (5). *Annual report.*

ACTIVITIES IN DEVELOPING REGIONS: Present in developing regions. Active in 2 country(ies). Works through local field partners. **Sustainable Development Actions:** Education/training/literacy; Emergency relief/refugees/humanitarian assistance; Food/famine; Health/sanitation/water; Rural development/agriculture; Sending volunteers/experts/technical assistance. **Regions:** Central Africa; West Africa.

INFORMATION AND EDUCATION ACTIVITIES: **Topics:** Emergency relief/refugees/humanitarian assistance; Food/famine. **Activities:** Broadcasting/cultural events; Fund raising; Networking/electronic telecommunications.

ITA2775

ASSOCIAZIONE PER LA PARTECIPAZIONE ALLO SVILUPPO (APS) ◆ Association for Participation in Development

163 Corso Regina Margherita, 10144 Torino, Italy.

Telephone: 39 (11) 4374936. *Fax:* 39 (11) 4375267. *Contact:* Renato Forte, President.

OBJECTIVES: To work with South American, Asian and African groups to improve the living conditions of the poor. To provide the Italian and European public with better information on underdevelopment.

GENERAL INFORMATION: *Creation:* 1985. *Affiliated to:* Coordinamento delle Organizzazioni non Governative per la Cooperazione Internazionale allo Sviluppo (Italy) - International Workers' Aid. *Personnel/Total:* 40. *Salaried:* 32 of which: 25 in developing countries. *Volunteers:* 8 of which: 1 in developing countries. *Budget/Total 1993:* ECU 975 (US$ 1000). *Financial sources:* Private: 19%. Public: 76%. Self-financing: 5%.

PUBLICATIONS: *Annual report.*

EVALUATION/RESEARCH: Evaluation reports available. Undertakes research activities.

PLANNED ACTIVITIES: APS plans to include Bolivia, Mongolia and the Sudan into their development, rehabilitation and humanitarian programmes.

COMMENTS: APS is participating in the development of citizens' associations in Eastern Europe. Undertakes activities in the Commonwealth of Independent States. Information activities related to the Commonwealth of Independent States.

ACTIVITIES IN DEVELOPING REGIONS: Present in developing regions. Active in 10 country(ies). Maintains local field presence. Works through local field partners. **Sustainable Development Actions:** Children/youth/family; Democracy/good governance/institution building/participatory development; Ecology/environment/biodiversity; Education/training/literacy; Emergency relief/refugees/humanitarian assistance; Gender issues/women; Health/sanitation/water; Human rights/peace/conflicts; Population/family planning/demography; Rural development/agriculture; Sending volunteers/experts/technical assistance; Small enterprises/informal sector/handicrafts. **Regions:** Central Asia and South Asia; Mexico and Central America; Middle East; South America; South East Asia.

INFORMATION AND EDUCATION ACTIVITIES: **Topics:** Culture/tradition/religion; Ecology/environment/biodiversity; Emergency relief/refugees/humanitarian assistance; Employment/unemployment; Food/famine; Gender issues/women; Health/sanitation/water; Human rights/peace/conflicts; International economic relations/trade/debt/finance; International relations/cooperation/development aid; Peace/ethnic conflicts/armament/disarmament; Population/family planning/demography; Poverty/living conditions; Racism/xenophobia/antisemitism; Refugees/migrants/ethnic groups; Rural development/agriculture. **Activities:** Conferences/seminars/workshops/training activities; Exchanges/twinning/linking; Formal education; Fund raising; Information and documentation services/data bases; Information campaigns/exhibitions; Lobbying/advocacy.

ITA2776

ASSOCIAZIONE SANITARIA INTERNAZIONALE (ASI) ◆ International Health Association

See: *How to Use the Directory,* page 11.

Via Terme di Deciane 5/A, 00153 Roma, Italy.
Telephone: 39 (6) 573482.

ITA2777

ASSOCIAZIONE SOLIDARIETA PAESI EMERGENTI (ASPEM)
♦ Association solidarité avec les pays en développement

Via per Alzate 1, 22063 Cantù (Como), Italie.

Téléphone: 39 (31) 711394. *Fax:* 39 (31) 713411. *Contact:* Stefano Girgi, Président.

OBJECTIFS: Former, envoyer des volontaires et réaliser des projets dans les pays en développement. Sensibiliser l'opinion publique italienne aux problèmes du Tiers-Monde.

INFORMATIONS GENERALES: *Création:* 1979. *Affiliée à:* Federazione Organismi Cristiani Servizio Internazionale Volontario (Italie). *Personnel/Total:* 75. *Salariés:* 25 dont: 10 dans les pays en développement. *Bénévoles:* 50. *Sources financières:* Privé: 20%. Public: 60%. Autofinancement: 10%.

PUBLICATIONS: *Périodiques:* Volontari per lo Sviluppo (5). *Rapport annuel. Liste des publications.*

PREVISIONS D'ACTIVITES: Présentation de films des pays en développement dans les écoles italiennes.

ACTIVITES DANS LES REGIONS EN DEVELOPPEMENT: Intervient directement dans les régions en développement. Intervient dans 3 pays. Maintient une présence locale sur le terrain. Intervient par l'intermédiaire d'organisations locales partenaires. **Actions de Développement durable:** Droits de l'Homme/paix/conflits; Démocratie/bonne gestion publique/création d'institutions/développement participatif; Développement rural/agriculture; Développement urbain/habitat; Enfants/jeunesse/famille; Envoi de volontaires/experts/assistance technique; Petites entreprises/secteur informel/artisanat; Santé/assainissement/eau; Éducation/formation/alphabétisation. **Régions:** Afrique centrale; Amérique du Sud; Caraïbes.

ACTIVITES D'INFORMATION ET D'EDUCATION: Domaines: Culture/tradition/religion; Développement rural/agriculture; Développement urbain/habitat; Enfants/jeunesse/famille; Pauvreté/conditions de vie; Réfugiés/migrants/groupes ethniques; Santé/assainissement/eau. **Activités:** Campagnes d'information/expositions; Collecte de fonds; Conférences/séminaires/ateliers/activités de formation; Radiodiffusion/manifestations culturelles; Éducation formelle.

ITA2778

ASSOCIAZIONE SOLIDARIETA PER LO SVILUPPO

Via A. Costa, 20, 30172 Mestre (VE), Italy.

Telephone: 39 (41) 983058. *Fax:* 39 (41) 981679.

ITA2779

ASSOCIAZIONE SOLIDARIETA' PACE E SVILUPPO

c/o Gianni Bertone Localita' Frazione Piscine, 1, 11100 Aosta, Italie.

Téléphone: 39 (165) 250411.

OBJECTIFS: Soutenir au Nord du Cameroun, un projet de femmes dans le domaine du développement agricole.

INFORMATIONS GENERALES: *Affiliée à:* CIPSI (Italie). *Personnel/Total:* 15. *Bénévoles:* 15. *Budget/Total 1993:* ECU 14000 (US$ 16000). *Sources financières:* Public: 30%. Autofinancement: 70%.

PUBLICATIONS: *Rapport annuel.*

EVALUATION/RECHERCHE: Rapports d'évaluation disponibles. Entreprend des activités de recherche.

PREVISIONS D'ACTIVITES: Mise en place d'une banque alimentaire en Côte d'Ivoire.

ACTIVITES DANS LES REGIONS EN DEVELOPPEMENT: Intervient directement dans les régions en développement. Intervient dans 1 pays. Intervient par l'intermédiaire d'organisations locales partenaires. **Actions de Développement durable:** Dette/finances/commerce; Développement rural/agriculture; Envoi de volontaires/experts/assistance technique; Petites entreprises/secteur informel/arti-

sanat; Questions relatives aux femmes; Éducation/formation/alphabétisation. **Régions:** Afrique centrale.

ITA2780

ASSOCIAZIONE STUDI AMERICA LATINA (ASAL) ♦ Association d'études sur l'Amérique latine

Via Tacito 10, 00193 Roma, Italie.

Téléphone: 39 (6) 3235389. *Fax:* 39 (6) 3235388. *Contact:* Cesare Taviani, Directeur.

OBJECTIFS: Réaliser des projets de coopération dans les pays en développement, en particulier dans les domaines de la culture, de l'information et de l'éducation populaire.

INFORMATIONS GENERALES: *Création:* 1966. *Affiliée à:* Assemblea ONG Italiane di Sviluppo - CEDAG (Belgique) - EURODAD (Belgique) - Concertación Relaciones Europa-America latina.. *Personnel/Total:* 14. *Salariés:* 7. *Bénévoles:* 7. *Budget/Total 1993:* ECU 163000 (US$ 191000). *Sources financières:* Privé: 49%. Public: 41%. Autofinancement: 10%.

PUBLICATIONS: *Périodiques:* ONG-CE Notizie (24). *Liste des publications.*

EVALUATION/RECHERCHE: Rapports d'évaluation disponibles.

COMMENTAIRES: Intervient dans la Communauté des Etats indépendants. Activités d'information concernant la Communauté des Etats indépendants.

ACTIVITES DANS LES REGIONS EN DEVELOPPEMENT: Intervient directement dans les régions en développement. Intervient dans 7 pays. Intervient par l'intermédiaire d'organisations locales partenaires. **Actions de Développement durable:** Dette/finances/commerce; Droits de l'Homme/paix/conflits; Petites entreprises/secteur informel/artisanat; Éducation/formation/alphabétisation. **Régions:** Amérique du Sud; Caraïbes; Mexique et Amerique centrale.

ACTIVITES D'INFORMATION ET D'EDUCATION: Domaines: Culture/tradition/religion; Droits de l'Homme/paix/conflits; Questions relatives aux femmes; Relations internationales/coopération/aide au développement; Relations économiques internationales/commerce/dette/finances; Réfugiés/migrants/groupes ethniques; Secours d'urgence/réfugiés/aide humanitaire; Éducation/formation/alphabétisation. **Activités:** Campagnes d'information/expositions; Collecte de fonds; Conférences/séminaires/ateliers/activités de formation; Lobbying/plaidoyer; Réseaux/télécommunications électroniques; Services d'information et de documentation/bases de données; Échanges/parrainage/jumelage; Édition/documents audiovisuels/documents éducatifs.

ITA2781

ASSOCIAZIONE UNIVERSITARIA PER LA COOPERAZIONE INTERNAZIONALE (AUCI)

Largo Francesco Vito, 1, 00168 Roma, Italy.

Telephone: 39 (6) 30154538.

ITA2782

ASSOCIAZIONE VOLONTARI PER IL SERVIZIO INTERNAZIONALE (AVSI) ♦ International Service Volunteers' Association

Viale Carducci 85, 47023 Cesena (Forli), Italy.

Telephone: 39 (547) 24054. *Fax:* 39 (547) 611290. *Contact:* Arturo Alberti.

OBJECTIVES: To raise awareness of development issues and funds among people and institutions in the North, encouraging their participation in development co-operation with NGOs from the South. To support and implement development projects in the South providing human, material and financial resources.

GENERAL INFORMATION: *Creation:* 1972. *Affiliated to:* FOCSIV (Italy) - VIOCE (Belgium) - SYNERGY (Italy). *Personnel/Total:* 67. *Salaried:* 7. *Volunteers:* 60 of which: 52 in developing countries. *Budget/Total 1993:* ECU 4856000 (US$ 5683000). *Financial sources:* Private: 24%. Public: 74%. Self-financing: 2%.

PUBLICATIONS: *Periodicals:* Dimensioni dello Sviluppo (4) - Nuone Notizie (3). *Annual report. List of publications.*

EVALUATION/RESEARCH: Evaluation reports available. Undertakes research activities.

PLANNED ACTIVITIES: AVSI will be promoting the creation of an international research and training centre on suburban areas development.

COMMENTS: Undertakes activities in the Commonwealth of Independent States. Information activities related to the Commonwealth of Independent States.

ACTIVITIES IN DEVELOPING REGIONS: Present in developing regions. Active in 19 country(ies). Maintains local field presence. Works through local field partners. **Sustainable Development Actions:** Children/ youth/family; Democracy/good governance/institution building/participatory development; Ecology/environment/biodiversity; Education/ training/literacy; Emergency relief/refugees/humanitarian assistance; Food/famine; Gender issues/women; Health/sanitation/water; Population/family planning/demography; Rural development/agriculture; Sending volunteers/experts/technical assistance; Small enterprises/informal sector/handicrafts; Urban development/habitat. **Regions:** East Africa; Mexico and Central America; Middle East; South America; West Africa.

INFORMATION AND EDUCATION ACTIVITIES: Topics: Children/youth/ family; Ecology/environment/biodiversity; Education/training/literacy; Emergency relief/refugees/humanitarian assistance; Food/famine; Health/sanitation/water; International economic relations/trade/debt/ finance; International relations/cooperation/development aid; Poverty/ living conditions; Rural development/agriculture; Urban development/ habitat. **Activities:** Conferences/seminars/workshops/training activities; Exchanges/twinning/linking; Formal education; Fund raising; Information and documentation services/data bases; Information campaigns/exhibitions; Lobbying/advocacy; Publishing/audiovisual materials/educational materials.

ITA2783
CARE ITALIE

Via Raffaele Cadorna, 29, 00187 Rome, Italie.

Contact: Alvaro Merli, Directeur National.

ITA2784

CARITAS INTERNATIONALIS ♦ Confédération internationale d'organismes catholiques d'action charitable et sociale

Palazzo San Calisto, 00120 Citta' del Vaticano, Italie.

Téléphone: 39 (6) 69887197. *Fax:* 39 (6) 69887237. *Contact:* Gerhard Meier, Secrétaire général.

OBJECTIFS: Inciter les organisations membres à participer, par une charité active, à la promotion de l'homme et au développement des plus défavorisés, dans une optique pastorale. Coordonner leurs actions en vue d'établir des programmes de développement à long et moyen terme.

INFORMATIONS GENERALES: *Création:* 1950. *Type d'organisation:* regroupement d'ONG. *Organisations membres:* 125. *Personnel/ Total:* 20. *Salariés:* 20. *Sources financières:* Privé: 100%.

COMMENTAIRES: Intervient dans la Communauté des Etats indépendants.

ACTIVITES DANS LES REGIONS EN DEVELOPPEMENT: Intervient directement dans les régions en développement. Intervient dans 150 pays. Maintient une présence locale sur le terrain. **Actions de Développement durable:** Aliments/famine; Droits de l'Homme/paix/conflits; Développement rural/agriculture; Développement urbain/habitat; Enfants/jeunesse/famille; Petites entreprises/secteur informel/artisanat; Questions relatives aux femmes; Santé/assainissement/eau; Secours d'urgence/réfugiés/aide humanitaire; Écologie/environnement/biodiversité; Éducation/formation/alphabétisation. **Régions:** Afrique australe; Afrique centrale; Afrique de l'Est; Afrique de l'Ouest; Afrique du Nord; Amérique du Sud; Asie centrale et Asie du Sud; Asie de l'Est; Asie du Sud-Est; Caraïbes; Mexique et Amerique centrale; Moyen-Orient; Océanie.

ITA2785

CARITAS ITALIANA ♦ CARITAS Italy

Viale F. Baldelli 41, 00146 Roma, Italy.

Telephone: 39 (6) 541921. *Fax:* 39 (6) 5410300. *Contact:* H.E. Mgr Armando Franco, President.

OBJECTIVES: To foster and encourage the sense of charity towards communities and people in need. To co-ordinate charitable actions and assistance interventions of Christian inspiration. To contribute to the human and social development in developing countries and coordinate the initiatives of the various groups and movments inspires by Christian values.

GENERAL INFORMATION: *Creation:* 1971. *Type of organisation:* coordinating body. *Affiliated to:* CARITAS INTERNATIONALIS (Italy). *Personnel/Total:* 47. Salaried: 35. Volunteers: 12 of which: 5 in developing countries. *Budget/Total 1993:* ECU 23509000 (US$ 275110000). *Financial sources:* Private: 96%. *Public:* 4%.

PUBLICATIONS: *Periodicals:* ITALIA CARITAS (11) (22) (4) (6). *Annual report. List of publications.*

EVALUATION/RESEARCH: Evaluation reports available. Undertakes research activities.

COMMENTS: Undertakes activities in the Commonwealth of Independent States. Information activities related to the Commonwealth of Independent States.

ACTIVITIES IN DEVELOPING REGIONS: Present in developing regions. Active in 89 country(ies). Maintains local field presence. Works through local field partners. **Sustainable Development Actions:** Democracy/ good governance/institution building/participatory development; Education/training/literacy; Emergency relief/refugees/humanitarian assistance; Food/famine; Gender issues/women; Health/sanitation/water; Rural development/agriculture; Small enterprises/informal sector/handicrafts. **Regions:** Central Africa; East Africa; East Asia; Mexico and Central America; Middle East; North Africa; South America; South East Asia; Southern Africa; West Africa.

INFORMATION AND EDUCATION ACTIVITIES: Topics: Children/youth/ family; Culture/tradition/religion; Emergency relief/refugees/humanitarian assistance; Employment/unemployment; Food/famine; Health/sanitation/water; Human rights/peace/conflicts; International economic relations/trade/debt/finance; International relations/cooperation/ development aid; Peace/ethnic conflicts/armament/disarmament; Poverty/living conditions; Racism/xenophobia/antisemitism; Refugees/ migrants/ethnic groups. **Activities:** Broadcasting/cultural events; Conferences/seminars/workshops/training activities; Exchanges/twinning/ linking; Fund raising; Information and documentation services/data bases; Information campaigns/exhibitions; Lobbying/advocacy; Publishing/audiovisual materials/educational materials.

ITA2786

CELIM BERGAMO - ORGANIZZAZIONE DI VOLONTARIATO INTERNAZIONALE CRISTIANO ♦ Organisation de volontariat international chrétien - Celim Bergamo

Via M. Gavazzeni 3, 24100 Bergamo, Italie.

Téléphone: 39 (35) 319457. *Fax:* 39 (35) 319239. *Contact:* Costantino Zanda, President.

OBJECTIFS: Aider à la formation des communautés locales pour la prise en charge de laur propre développement. Réaliser des projets avec envoi de volontaires préparés.

INFORMATIONS GENERALES: *Création:* 1964. *Affiliée à:* Fédération des Organismes de Volontariat International Chrétien (Italie). *Personnel/Total:* 18. *Salariés:* 6 dont: 5 dans les pays en développement. *Bénévoles:* 12. *Budget/Total 1993:* ECU 945000 (US$ 111000). *Sources financières:* Public: 30%. Autofinancement: 70%.

PUBLICATIONS: *Périodiques:* Quaderni (1). *Liste des publications.*

EVALUATION/RECHERCHE: Rapports d'évaluation disponibles. Entreprend des activités de recherche.

ACTIVITES DANS LES REGIONS EN DEVELOPPEMENT: Intervient directement dans les régions en développement. Intervient dans 3 pays. Maintient une présence locale sur le terrain. **Actions de Développement durable:** Démocratie/bonne gestion publique/création d'institutions/développement participatif; Développement rural/agriculture; Envoi de volontaires/experts/assistance technique; Petites entreprises/secteur

See: *How to Use the Directory,* page 11.

informel/artisanat; Santé/assainissement/eau; Éducation/formation/
alphabétisation. **Régions:** Afrique de l'Ouest.

ACTIVITES D'INFORMATION ET D'EDUCATION: Domaines: Culture/
tradition/religion; Droits de l'Homme/paix/conflits; Développement rural/
agriculture; Enfants/jeunesse/famille; Population/planning familial/démo-
graphie; Questions relatives aux femmes; Relations internationales/
coopération/aide au développement; Réfugiés/migrants/groupes ethniques; Santé/assainissement/eau; Éducation/formation/alphabétisation.
Activités: Conférences/séminaires/ateliers/activités de formation; Services d'information et de documentation/bases de données; Édition/
documents audiovisuels/documents éducatifs.

ITA2787
CENTRO AIUTI MONDIALI (CAM)

Piazza Medaglie d'Oro 20, 00136 Rome, Italy.

Telephone: 39 (6) 348176. **Fax:** 39 (6) 3420720. **Contact:** Anselmo
Previdi, President.

OBJECTIVES: To provide food and development aid to countries in Latin
America, Africa and Asia.

GENERAL INFORMATION: Creation: 1977. **Affiliated to:** EuronAid (the
Netherlands). **Personnel/Total:** 3. **Volunteers:** 3. **Budget/Total 1993:**
ECU 22000 (US$ 25000). **Financial sources:** Self-financing: 100%.

PUBLICATIONS: Annual report.

EVALUATION/RESEARCH: Evaluation reports available. Undertakes
research activities.

ACTIVITIES IN DEVELOPING REGIONS: Active in 10 country(ies). Works
through local field partners. **Sustainable Development Actions:** Edu-
cation/training/literacy; Emergency relief/refugees/humanitarian assistance; Food/famine; Rural development/agriculture. **Regions:** Caribbean; Central Asia and South Asia; East Africa; Mexico and Central
America; South America; Southern Africa.

ITA2788
CENTRO BERTRAND RUSSELL

Via Cernaia, 30, 10122 Torino, Italy.

Telephone: 39 (11) 533345. **Fax:** 39 (11) 544023.

ITA2789
CENTRO COMUNITARIO SERVIZIO CRISTIANO (CCSC)

Via Montalbano, 758, 51034 Casalguidi (PT), Italy.

Telephone: 39 (573) 527259. **Fax:** 39 (573) 527259.

ITA2790
CENTRO DI ADDESTRAMENTO PER L'AZIONE SOCIALE NELLE REGIONI IN VIA DI SVILUPPO (CESTA) ♦ Centre for
Social Training and Action in Developing Regions

c/o Pontificia Università San Tommaso d'Aquino, Largo Angelicum 1,
00184 Roma, Italie.

Téléphone: 39 (6) 6790407. **Contact:** Andor Sigmond, Président.

ITA2791
CENTRO DI EDUCAZIONE SANITARIA E TECNOLOGIE APPROPRIATE SANITARIE (CESTAS) ♦ Centre for Health Edu-
cation and Appropriate Health Technologies

Via G.A. Magini, 6, 40139 Bologna, Italy.

Telephone: 39 (51) 6240955. **Fax:** 39 (51) 6240980. **Contact:** Luigi
Orlandi, Chairman.

OBJECTIVES: To promote projects in developing countries and raise
awareness in Italy as to the problems of these countries.

GENERAL INFORMATION: Creation: 1979. **Affiliated to:** COCIS (Italy) -
CFS (Italy). **Personnel/Total:** 30. Salaried: 20 of which: 16 in developing countries. Volunteers: 10 of which: 2 in developing
countries. **Budget/Total 1993:** ECU 1623000 (US$ 1899000). **Finan-
cial sources:** Private: 20%. Public: 70%. Self-financing: 10%.

PUBLICATIONS: Periodicals: Sahara News (12). Annual report.

EVALUATION/RESEARCH: Evaluation reports available. Undertakes
research activities.

ACTIVITIES IN DEVELOPING REGIONS: Present in developing regions.
Active in 8 country(ies). Maintains local field presence. Works through
local field partners. **Sustainable Development Actions:** Children/
youth/family; Ecology/environment/biodiversity; Education/training/liter-
acy; Emergency relief/refugees/humanitarian assistance; Food/famine;
Gender issues/women; Health/sanitation/water; Human rights/peace/
conflicts; Rural development/agriculture; Sending volunteers/experts/
technical assistance; Small enterprises/informal sector/handicrafts.
Regions: Central Africa; North Africa; South America; Southern Africa;
West Africa.

INFORMATION AND EDUCATION ACTIVITIES: Topics: Children/youth/
family; Education/training/literacy; Emergency relief/refugees/humanita-
rian assistance; Health/sanitation/water; Human rights/peace/conflicts;
Peace/ethnic conflicts/armament/disarmament; Population/family plan-
ning/demography; Racism/xenophobia/antisemitism; Refugees/
migrants/ethnic groups; Rural development/agriculture. **Activities:** Con-
ferences/seminars/workshops/training activities; Exchanges/twinning/
linking; Formal education; Fund raising; Information campaigns/exhibi-
tions; Publishing/audiovisual materials/educational materials.

ITA2792
CENTRO DI VOLONTARIATO INTERNAZIONALE (CEVI) ♦ Cen-
tre de volontariat international

Via Tiberio Deciani, 17, 33100 Udine, Italie.

Téléphone: 39 (432) 504712. **Fax:** 39 (432) 504712. **Contact:** Francesco
Alessandrini, Directeur.

OBJECTIFS: Promouvoir l'éducation au développement, la solidarité et
diffuser une culture de paix.

INFORMATIONS GENERALES: Création: 1985. **Type d'organisation:**
collectif. **Affiliée à:** Coordinamento di Iniziative Popolari di Solidarietà
Internazionale (Italie). **Personnel/Total:** 23. Salariés: 1 dont: 1 dans les
pays en développement. Bénévoles: 22 dont: 2 dans les pays en
développement. **Budget/Total 1993:**
ECU 73000 (US$ 86000). **Sources financières:** Privé: 19%. Public:
48%. Autofinancement: 33%.

PUBLICATIONS: Périodiques: Ho un sogno (12). Liste des publications.

COMMENTAIRES: Activités d'information concernant la Communauté des
Etats indépendants.

ACTIVITES DANS LES REGIONS EN DEVELOPPEMENT: Intervient
directement dans les régions en développement. Intervient dans 1 pays.
Maintient une présence locale sur le terrain. Intervient par l'intermédiaire
d'organisations locales partenaires. **Actions de Développement durable:** Développement rural/agriculture; Envoi de volontaires/experts/
assistance technique; Questions relatives aux femmes; Éducation/for-
mation/alphabétisation. **Régions:** Amérique du Sud.

ACTIVITES D'INFORMATION ET D'EDUCATION: Domaines: Culture/
tradition/religion; Développement rural/agriculture; Racisme/xénopho-
bie/antisémitisme. **Activités:** Campagnes d'information/expositions;
Collecte de fonds; Conférences/séminaires/ateliers/activités de formation; Services d'information et de documentation/bases de données;
Édition/documents audiovisuels/documents éducatifs; Éducation
formelle.

ITA2793
CENTRO DOCUMENTAZIONE OSCAR ROMERO (CEDOR) ♦
Centre de documentation Oscar Romero

Bacilieri 1/A, 37139 Verona, Italie.

Téléphone: 39 (45) 565944.

ITA2794
CENTRO ECCLESIALE ITALIANO AMERICA LATINA (CEIAL)
♦ Centre ecclésiastique italien pour l'Amérique latine

Bacilieri 1/A, 37139 Verona, Italie.

Téléphone: 39 (45) 8900329. **Contact:** Mario Agazzi, Directeur.

Voir : *Comment utiliser le répertoire,* page 11.

ITA2795

CENTRO ECCLESIALE ITALIANO PER L'AFRICA I ASIA (CEIAS) ♦ Italian Ecclesiastic Centre for Africa and Asia

Via Bacilieri 1/A, 37139 Verona, Italy.

Telephone: 39 (45) 8900329. *Contact:* Zecchin Renzo.

ITA2796

CENTRO EDUCAZIONE ALLA MONDIALITA

Viale San Martino 8, 43100 Parma, Italy.

ITA2797

CENTRO INFORMAZIONE DOCUMENTAZIONE E INIZIATIVE PER LO SVILUPPO (CIDIS)

Via della Viola, 1, 06122 Perugia, Italy.

Telephone: 39 (75) 5722221. *Fax:* 39 (75) 5721234.

ITA2798

CENTRO INFORMAZIONE E EDUCAZIONE ALLO SVI-LUPPO (CIES) ♦ Centre for Information and Education on Development

Via Palermo 36, 00184 Roma, Italy.

Telephone: 39 (6) 4820464. *Fax:* 39 (6) 486419. *Contact:* Elisabetta B. Melandri, Chairperson.

OBJECTIVES: To contribute to the establishment of a culture founded on solidarity and co-operation, and committed to eliminating the imbalance between industrialized and developing countries. To implement develop-ment education programmes in Italy and projects in developing countries.

GENERAL INFORMATION: *Creation:* 1983. *Affiliated to:* COCIS (Italy) - National Association for a Democratic South Africa (Italy) -Forum Filip-pine - Immigration Service of the Province of Rome (Italy). *Personnel/ Total:* 8. *Salaried:* 8. *Budget/Total 1993:* ECU 1162000 (US$ 1360000). *Financial sources:* Private: 1%. Public: 94%. Self-financing: 5%.

PUBLICATIONS: *Periodicals:* Tam Tam Video News (3). *Annual report.* List of publications.

EVALUATION/RESEARCH: Evaluation reports available. Undertakes research activities.

PLANNED ACTIVITIES: Holding of an international campaign to ban landmines.

ACTIVITIES IN DEVELOPING REGIONS: Present in developing regions. Active in 11 country(ies). Maintains local field presence. Works through local field partners. **Sustainable Development Actions:** Children/ youth/family; Democracy/good governance/institution building/par-ticipatory development; Ecology/environment/biodiversity; Education/ training/literacy; Food/famine; Gender issues/women; Health/sanitation/ water; Human rights/peace/conflicts; Rural development/agriculture; Sending volunteers/experts/technical assistance; Small enterprises/ informal sector/handicrafts. **Regions:** South America; South East Asia; Southern Africa.

INFORMATION AND EDUCATION ACTIVITIES: Topics: Children/youth/ family; Culture/tradition/religion; Ecology/environment/biodiversity; Edu-cation/training/literacy; Emergency relief/refugees/humanitarian assis-tance; Employment/unemployment; Food/famine; Gender issues/ women; Health/sanitation/water; Human rights/peace/conflicts; Interna-tional economic relations/trade/debt/finance; International relations/ cooperation/development aid; Peace/ethnic conflicts/armament/dis-armament; Population/family planning/demography; Poverty/living con-ditions; Racism/xenophobia/antisemitism; Refugees/migrants/ethnic groups; Rural development/agriculture; Urban development/habitat. **Activities:** Broadcasting/cultural events; Conferences/seminars/work-shops/training activities; Exchanges/twinning/linking; Formal education; Fund raising; Information and documentation services/data bases; Infor-mation campaigns/exhibitions; Lobbying/advocacy; Networking/elec-tronic telecommunications; Publishing/audiovisual materials/educational materials.

ITA2799

CENTRO INTERNAZIONALE CROCEVIA (CIC)

Via Ferraironi 88/G, 00172 Roma, Italie.

Téléphone: 39 (6) 2413976. *Fax:* 39 (6) 2424177. *Courrier électronique:* CROCEVIA@OX.apc.org.. *Contact:* Antonio Onorati, Président.

OBJECTIFS: Renforcer la solidarité entre les peuples engagés dans la lutte pour la sauvegarde de leur indépendance et pour l'exploitation autonome de leurs richesses.

INFORMATIONS GENERALES: *Création:* 1958. *Affiliée à:* COCIS (Italie) - ZEBRA - VIDEAZIMUT (Canada) - SOLAGRAL (France) - RONGEAD (France) - RIDAAM (France) - GRAIN (Espagne) - AMARC (Canada) - FORUM PHILIPPINES (Pays-Bas) - INFID (Pays-Bas). *Personnel/Total:* 31. *Salariés:* 6. *Bénévoles:* 25 dont: 3 dans les pays en développement. *Budget/Total 1993:* ECU 3137000 (US$ 3671000). *Sources financières:* Privé: 4%. Public: 95%. Autofinancement: 1%.

PUBLICATIONS: *Périodiques:* SEMI (4). *Rapport annuel. Liste des publications.*

EVALUATION/RECHERCHE: Rapports d'évaluation disponibles. Entre-prend des activités de recherche.

COMMENTAIRES: L'ONG produit des ouvrages juridiques et des vidéos.

ACTIVITES DANS LES REGIONS EN DEVELOPPEMENT: Intervient directement dans les régions en développement. Intervient dans 14 pays. Maintient une présence locale sur le terrain. Intervient par l'inter-médiaire d'organisations locales partenaires. **Actions de Développe-ment durable:** Droits de l'Homme/paix/conflits; Développement rural/ agriculture; Développement urbain/habitat; Envoi de volontaires/experts/ assistance technique; Écologie/environnement/biodiversité; Éducation/ formation/alphabétisation. **Régions:** Afrique australe; Afrique de l'Ouest; Amérique du Sud; Asie du Sud-Est; Mexique et Amerique cen-trale; Moyen-Orient.

ACTIVITES D'INFORMATION ET D'EDUCATION: Domaines: Culture/ tradition/religion; Droits de l'Homme/paix/conflits; Développement rural/ agriculture; Racisme/xénophobie/antisémitisme; Relations internatio-nales/coopération/aide au développement; Relations économiques internationales/commerce/dette/finances; Réfugiés/migrants/groupes ethniques; Écologie/environnement/biodiversité; Éducation/formation/ alphabétisation. **Activités:** Campagnes d'information/expositions; Col-lecte de fonds; Conférences/séminaires/ateliers/activités de formation; Lobbying/plaidoyer; Radiodiffusion/manifestations culturelles; Réseaux/ télécommunications électroniques; Services d'information et de docu-mentation/bases de données; Échanges/parrainage/jumelage; Édition/ documents audiovisuels/documents éducatifs; Éducation formelle.

ITA2800

CENTRO INTERNAZIONALE DI COOPERAZIONE ALLO SVI-LUPPO (CICS) ♦ International Centre for Development Co-operation

Via Crescenzio 82, 00193 Roma, Italy.

Telephone: 39 (6) 6874328. *Fax:* 39 (6) 68307508 . *Contact:* Emidio Totaro, Administrative Advisor.

ITA2801

CENTRO ITALIANO DI COLLABORAZIONE PER LO SVILUPPO EDILIZIO DELLE NAZIONI EMERGENTI (CIC-SENE) ♦ Centre italien de collaboration pour le développement de la construction dans les pays en développement

Via Borgosesia 30, 10145 Torino, Italie.

Téléphone: 39 (11) 7412435. *Fax:* 39 (11) 745261. *Contact:* Mario Moiso, Président.

OBJECTIFS: Offrir une assistance technique au Tiers-Monde dans les domaines de la construction, des nouvelles technologies et de l'écolo-gie, avec une référence particulière à l'habitat. Fournir des documents sur les technologies et l'environnement dans le Tiers-Monde.

INFORMATIONS GENERALES: *Création:* 1972. *Affiliée à:* Habitat Inter-national Coalition (Belgique) - Fédération Européenne pour la Promo-tion et l'Insertion par le Logement et son Environnement (France) - ASTAC (Italie). *Personnel/Total:* 8. *Salariés:* 3 dont: 1 dans les pays en développement. *Bénévoles:* 5. *Budget/Total 1993:*

See: *How to Use the Directory,* page 11.

ECU 217000 (US$ 254000). *Sources financières: Privé:* 30%. *Public:* 50%. *Autofinancement:* 20%.

PUBLICATIONS: *Périodiques:* Habitat et Sviluppo (12). *Liste des publications.*

EVALUATION/RECHERCHE: Rapports d'évaluation disponibles. Entreprend des activités de recherche.

PREVISIONS D'ACTIVITES: Projet de promotion de la culture de la joint-venture entre les PME du Nord et les pays en développement. Projet logement pour les immigrés au Piémont.

ACTIVITES DANS LES REGIONS EN DEVELOPPEMENT: Intervient directement dans les régions en développement. Intervient dans 2 pays. Maintient une présence locale sur le terrain. **Actions de Développement durable:** Démocratie/bonne gestion publique/création d'institutions/développement participatif; Développement urbain/habitat; Enfants/jeunesse/famille; Envoi de volontaires/experts/assistance technique; Petites entreprises/secteur informel/artisanat; Population/planning familial/démographie; Santé/assainissement/eau; Écologie/environnement/biodiversité; Éducation/formation/alphabétisation. **Régions:** Afrique de l'Ouest; Amérique du Sud; Mexique et Amerique centrale.

ACTIVITES D'INFORMATION ET D'EDUCATION: **Domaines:** Aliments/famine; Culture/tradition/religion; Droits de l'Homme/paix/conflits; Développement rural/agriculture; Développement urbain/habitat; Emploi/chômage; Enfants/jeunesse/famille; Paix/conflits ethniques/armement/désarmement; Pauvreté/conditions de vie; Population/planning familial/démographie; Questions relatives aux femmes; Racisme/xénophobie/antisémitisme; Relations internationales/coopération/aide au développement; Réfugiés/migrants/groupes ethniques; Santé/assainissement/eau; Secours d'urgence/réfugiés/aide humanitaire; Écologie/environnement/biodiversité; Éducation/formation/alphabétisation. **Activités:** Campagnes d'information/expositions; Conférences/séminaires/ateliers/activités de formation; Lobbying/plaidoyer; Radiodiffusion/manifestations culturelles; Réseaux/télécommunications électroniques; Services d'information et de documentation/bases de données; Échanges/parrainage/jumelage; Édition/documents audiovisuels/documents éducatifs; Éducation formelle.

ITA2802

CENTRO ITALIANO DI SOLIDARIETA (CEIS) ♦ Italian Centre of Solidarity

Via Attilio Ambrosini 129, 00147 Roma, Italy.

Telephone: 39 (6) 541951. *Fax:* 39 (6) 5407304. *Contact:* Mario Picchi, President.

OBJECTIVES: To support community development programmes focusing on health care and social development. To undertake drug rehabilitation projects and staff training.

GENERAL INFORMATION: *Creation:* 1971. *Affiliated to:* Italian Federation of Therapeutic Communities (Italy) - Confederación de programas Terapeuticos del Estado Español (Spain) - International Council of Alcohol and Addictions (Switzerland) - World Federation of Therapeutic Communities. *Personnel/Total:* 300. *Salaried:* 180 of which: 60 in developing countries. *Volunteers:* 120. *Budget/Total 1993:* ECU 3801000 (US$ 4448000). *Financial sources: Private:* 45%. *Public:* 45%. *Self-financing:* 10%.

PUBLICATIONS: *Periodicals:* Il Delfino (6). *Annual report. List of publications.*

EVALUATION/RESEARCH: Evaluation reports available. Undertakes research activities.

COMMENTS: Undertakes activities in the Commonwealth of Independent States. Information activities related to the Commonwealth of Independent States.

ACTIVITIES IN DEVELOPING REGIONS: Present in developing regions. Active in 5 country(ies). Maintains local field presence. Works through local field partners. **Sustainable Development Actions:** Children/youth/family; Education/training/literacy; Gender issues/women; Health/sanitation/water; Rural development/agriculture; Urban development/habitat. **Regions:** South America.

INFORMATION AND EDUCATION ACTIVITIES: **Topics:** Children/youth/family; Education/training/literacy; Gender issues/women; Health/sanitation/water; International relations/cooperation/development aid. **Activi-**

ties: Conferences/seminars/workshops/training activities; Exchanges/twinning/linking.

ITA2803

CENTRO LAICI ITALIANI PER LE MISSIONI - VOLONTARI PER UN SERVIZIO INTERNAZIONALE (CELIM) ♦ Center of Italian Laymen for Missions - Volunteers for International service.

Via S. Calimero 11/13, 20122 Milano, Italy.

Telephone: 39 (2) 58316324. *Fax:* 39 (2) 58317213. *Contact:* Gian Matteo Crovetto, President.

OBJECTIVES: To implement projects in developing countries that both aid and involve the local population and organisations. To organise educational programmes in Italy about multi-racial and development issues that involve schools and communities.

GENERAL INFORMATION: *Creation:* 1954. *Affiliated to:* Federazione Organismi Cristiani di Servizio Internazionale Volontario (Italy). *Personnel/Total:* 15. *Salaried:* 2 of which: in developing countries. *Volunteers:* 13 of which: 11 in developing countries. *Budget/Total 1993:* ECU 504000 (US$ 590000). *Financial sources: Private:* 9%. *Public:* 51%. *Self-financing:* 40%.

PUBLICATIONS: *Periodicals:* Ad Lucem (6). *Annual report.*

ACTIVITIES IN DEVELOPING REGIONS: Present in developing regions. Active in 3 country(ies). Maintains local field presence. Works through local field partners. **Sustainable Development Actions:** Children/youth/family; Education/training/literacy; Health/sanitation/water; Rural development/agriculture; Sending volunteers/experts/technical assistance; Small enterprises/informal sector/handicrafts. **Regions:** East Africa; Southern Africa; West Africa.

INFORMATION AND EDUCATION ACTIVITIES: **Topics:** Children/youth/family; Education/training/literacy; Health/sanitation/water; Refugees/migrants/ethnic groups; Rural development/agriculture. **Activities:** Conferences/seminars/workshops/training activities; Formal education; Fund raising; Information campaigns/exhibitions; Publishing/audiovisual materials/educational materials.

ITA2804

CENTRO MONDIALITA' SVILUPPO RECIPROCO (CMSR)

Via della Madonna, 32, 57123 Livorno, Italy.

Telephone: 39 (586) 887350. *Fax:* 39 (586) 882132. *Contact:* Giorgi Alessandro, President.

OBJECTIVES: To undertake projects and activities of multicultural education to remove structural causes of inequality between the North and South

GENERAL INFORMATION: *Creation:* 1979. *Affiliated to:* FOCSIV. *Personnel/Total:* 24. *Salaried:* 14 of which: 5 in developing countries. *Volunteers:* 10. *Budget/Total 1993:* ECU 396000 (US$ 464000). *Financial sources: Private:* 66%. *Public:* 19%. *Self-financing:* 15%.

PUBLICATIONS: *Periodicals:* KARIBU (6) - Epoké (4). *Annual report. List of publications.*

EVALUATION/RESEARCH: Undertakes research activities.

COMMENTS: Undertakes activities in the Commonwealth of Independent States. Information activities related to the Commonwealth of Independent States.

ACTIVITIES IN DEVELOPING REGIONS: Present in developing regions. Active in 1 country(ies). Maintains local field presence. Works through local field partners. **Sustainable Development Actions:** Education/training/literacy; Gender issues/women; Health/sanitation/water; Rural development/agriculture; Sending volunteers/experts/technical assistance; Small enterprises/informal sector/handicrafts. **Regions:** East Africa.

INFORMATION AND EDUCATION ACTIVITIES: **Topics:** Culture/tradition/religion; Education/training/literacy; Gender issues/women; Health/sanitation/water; Human rights/peace/conflicts; International relations/cooperation/development aid; Racism/xenophobia/antisemitism; Rural development/agriculture. **Activities:** Conferences/seminars/workshops/training activities; Exchanges/twinning/linking; Formal education; Fund raising; Information and documentation services/data bases; Information

campaigns/exhibitions; Publishing/audiovisual materials/educational materials.

ITA2805

CENTRO NUOVO MODELLO DI SVILUPPO ◆ New Model of Development Centre

Via della Barra 32, 56019 Vecchiano (Pisa), Italy.

Telephone: 39 (50) 826354. **Fax:** 39 (50) 827165. **Contact:** Francesco Gesualdi.

OBJECTIVES: To undertake development education. To search for the causes of underdevelopment and to further the understanding of the responsibilities of people in developed countries. To define defence strategies for the rights of the lowest on the social scale. To seek new economic formulae able to guarantee the vital needs of all human beings without violating the environment.

GENERAL INFORMATION: Creation: 1985. **Type of organisation:** network. **Affiliated to:** Coordinamento Educazione allo Sviluppo, SATIS (the Netherlands). **Personnel/Total:** 5. Volunteers: 5. **Budget/ Total 1993:** ECU 16000 (US$ 19000). **Financial sources:** Private: 90%. Self-financing: 10%.

PUBLICATIONS: List of publications.

EVALUATION/RESEARCH: Undertakes research activities.

PLANNED ACTIVITIES: Publication of a "Guide to an Ethical Consume".

INFORMATION AND EDUCATION ACTIVITIES: Topics: Children/youth/ family; Ecology/environment/biodiversity; Employment/unemployment; Food/famine; International economic relations/trade/debt/finance; International relations/cooperation/development aid; Poverty/living conditions; Rural development/agriculture; Urban development/habitat. **Activities:** Conferences/seminars/workshops/training activities; Information and documentation services/data bases; Information campaigns/exhibitions; Publishing/audiovisual materials/educational materials.

ITA2806

CENTRO ORIENTAMENTO EDUCATIVO (COE) ◆ Centre d'orientation éducatif

Via Milano 4, 22040 Barzio (Como), Italie.

Téléphone: 39 (341) 996453. **Fax:** 39 (341) 910311. **Contact:** Airoldi Carla, Présidente.

OBJECTIFS: Réaliser des projets de volontariat international dans l'esprit de la promotion humaine et sociale et des programmes plurisectoriels (santé, éducation, art et culture, etc.) répondant aux exigences et aux demandes du milieu.

INFORMATIONS GENERALES: Création: 1959. **Affiliée à:** Federazione Organismi Cristiani Servizio Internazionale Volontaria (Italie). **Personnel/Total:** 103. Salariés: 23 dont: 15 dans les pays en développement. Bénévoles: 80 dont: 30 dans les pays en développement. **Budget/Total 1993:** ECU 3801000 (US$ 4448000). **Sources financières:** Privé: 33%. Public: 36%. Autofinancement: 31%.

PUBLICATIONS: Périodiques: Centro Orientamento Educativo. Liste des publications.

PREVISIONS D'ACTIVITES: Education à la mondialité à travers l'audiovisuel dans les écoles.

ACTIVITES DANS LES REGIONS EN DEVELOPPEMENT: Intervient directement dans les régions en développement. Intervient dans 6 pays. Maintient une présence locale sur le terrain. Intervient par l'intermédiaire d'organisations locales partenaires. **Actions de Développement durable:** Développement rural/agriculture; Envoi de volontaires/experts/ assistance technique; Petites entreprises/secteur informel/artisanat; Questions relatives aux femmes; Santé/assainissement/eau; Écologie/ environnement/biodiversité; Éducation/formation/alphabétisation. **Régions:** Afrique australe; Afrique centrale; Amérique du Sud.

ACTIVITES D'INFORMATION ET D'EDUCATION: Domaines: Culture/ tradition/religion; Développement urbain/habitat; Enfants/jeunesse/ famille; Pauvreté/conditions de vie; Relations internationales/coopération/aide au développement; Santé/assainissement/eau; Écologie/environnement/biodiversité; Éducation/formation/alphabétisation. **Activités:**

Campagnes d'information/expositions; Collecte de fonds; Conférences/ séminaires/ateliers/activités de formation; Radiodiffusion/manifestations culturelles; Édition/documents audiovisuels/documents éducatifs.

ITA2807

CENTRO PER UN APPROPRIATO SVILUPPO TECNOLOGICO (CAST) ◆ Centre pour un développement technologique approprié

Viale dei Tigli 32, 21014 Laveno Mombello, Italie.

Téléphone: 39 (332) 667082. **Fax:** 39 (332) 667082. **Contact:** Stoppa Adriana, Président.

OBJECTIFS: Effectuer des recherches sur les technologies appropriées et les énergies renouvelables et introduire ces technologies dans les régions rurales du Tiers-Monde

INFORMATIONS GENERALES: Création: 1980. **Personnel/Total:** 10. Salariés: 2 dont: 2 dans les pays en développement. Bénévoles: 8. **Budget/Total 1993:** ECU 157000 (US$ 184000). **Sources financières:** Privé: 30%. Public: 50%. Autofinancement: 20%.

PUBLICATIONS: Liste des publications.

EVALUATION/RECHERCHE: Rapports d'évaluation disponibles. Entreprend des activités de recherche.

ACTIVITES DANS LES REGIONS EN DEVELOPPEMENT: Intervient directement dans les régions en développement. Intervient dans 5 pays. Maintient une présence locale sur le terrain. Intervient par l'intermédiaire d'organisations locales partenaires. **Actions de Développement durable:** Envoi de volontaires/experts/assistance technique; Petites entreprises/secteur informel/artisanat; Santé/assainissement/eau; Éducation/ formation/alphabétisation; Énergie/transport. **Régions:** Afrique centrale; Afrique de l'Ouest; Amérique du Sud; Mexique et Amerique centrale.

ACTIVITES D'INFORMATION ET D'EDUCATION: Domaines: Santé/ assainissement/eau. **Activités:** Radiodiffusion/manifestations culturelles; Édition/documents audiovisuels/documents éducatifs.

ITA2808

CENTRO PER UN FUTURO SOSTENIBILE (CFS) ◆ Centre for a Sustainable Future

Viale Giulio Cesare 49, 00192 Roma, Italy.

Telephone: 39 (6) 3215491. **Fax:** 39 (6) 3215493. **Contact:** Roberto Giachetti, Co-ordinator.

OBJECTIVES: To improve the global environment through research and awareness-raising activities.

GENERAL INFORMATION: Creation: 1990. **Personnel/Total:** 2. Salaried: 2. **Financial sources:** Self-financing: 100%.

PUBLICATIONS: Periodicals: Futuro Sostenibile (40). List of publications.

EVALUATION/RESEARCH: Undertakes research activities.

INFORMATION AND EDUCATION ACTIVITIES: Topics: Ecology/environment/biodiversity; Food/famine; Gender issues/women; Health/sanitation/water; International economic relations/trade/debt/finance; International relations/cooperation/development aid; Population/family planning/demography; Rural development/agriculture; Urban development/habitat. **Activities:** Information and documentation services/data bases.

ITA2809

CENTRO REGIONALE D'INTERVENTO PER LA COOPERAZIONE (CRIC) ◆ Centre régional d'intervention pour la coopération

Via Monsolini 12, 89100 Reggio Calabria, Italie.

Téléphone: 39 (965) 812345. **Fax:** 39 (965) 812560. **Contact:** Antonietta Cammarota, Présidente.

OBJECTIFS: Apporter une aide aux pays en développement par la mise en place de projets de coopération.

INFORMATIONS GENERALES: Création: 1983. **Affiliée à:** Coodinamento delle Organizzazioni non-governative per la Cooperazione Internazionale allo Sviluppo (Italie). **Personnel/Total:** 56. Salariés:

See: *How to Use the Directory,* page 11.

26 dont: 15 dans les pays en développement. *Bénévoles:* 30 dont: 10 dans les pays en développement. ***Budget/Total 1993:*** ECU 6159000 (US$ 7207000). ***Sources financières:*** *Privé:* 2%. *Public:* 97%. *Autofinancement:* 1%.

PUBLICATIONS: *Périodiques:* Sud/Sud (3). *Rapport annuel. Liste des publications.*

EVALUATION/RECHERCHE: Rapports d'évaluation disponibles. Entreprend des activités de recherche.

COMMENTAIRES: Intervient dans la Communauté des Etats indépendants. Activités d'information concernant la Communauté des Etats indépendants.

ACTIVITES DANS LES REGIONS EN DEVELOPPEMENT: Intervient directement dans les régions en développement. Intervient dans 11 pays. Maintient une présence locale sur le terrain. Intervient par l'intermédiaire d'organisations locales partenaires. **Actions de Développement durable:** Droits de l'Homme/paix/conflits; Développement rural/agriculture; Enfants/jeunesse/famille; Envoi de volontaires/experts/assistance technique; Questions relatives aux femmes; Santé/assainissement/eau; Secours d'urgence/réfugiés/aide humanitaire; Écologie/environnement/biodiversité; Éducation/formation/alphabétisation. **Régions:** Afrique de l'Ouest; Afrique du Nord; Amérique du Sud; Mexique et Amerique centrale; Moyen-Orient.

ACTIVITES D'INFORMATION ET D'EDUCATION: Domaines: Culture/tradition/religion; Droits de l'Homme/paix/conflits; Développement rural/agriculture; Enfants/jeunesse/famille; Paix/conflits ethniques/armement/désarmement; Pauvreté/conditions de vie; Questions relatives aux femmes; Racisme/xénophobie/antisémitisme; Relations internationales/coopération/aide au développement; Relations économiques internationales/commerce/dette/finances; Réfugiés/migrants/groupes ethniques; Santé/assainissement/eau; Secours d'urgence/réfugiés/aide humanitaire; Écologie/environnement/biodiversité; Éducation/formation/alphabétisation. **Activités:** Campagnes d'information/expositions; Collecte de fonds; Conférences/séminaires/ateliers/activités de formation; Radiodiffusion/manifestations culturelles; Services d'information et de documentation/bases de données; Échanges/parrainage/jumelage; Édition/documents audiovisuels/documents éducatifs.

ITA2810

CENTRO STUDI TERZO MONDO ♦ Centre d'études pour le Tiers monde

Via G.B. Morgagni 39, 20129 Milano, Italie.

Téléphone: 39 (2) 29409041. *Fax:* 39 (2) 29409041. *Contact:* Umberto Melotti.

OBJECTIFS: Former des techniciens et des volontaires pour travailler dans les paya en développement. Réaliser des études et des recherches sur ces pays.

INFORMATIONS GENERALES: *Création:* 1964. *Personnel/Total:* 17. *Salariés:* 7 dont: 3 dans les pays en développement. *Bénévoles:* 10 dont: 1 dans les pays en développement. ***Budget/Total 1993:*** ECU 54000 (US$ 63000). ***Sources financières:*** *Privé:* 80%. *Autofinancement:* 20%.

PUBLICATIONS: *Périodiques:* Terzo Mondo (4) - Quaderni di Terzo Mondo (2) - Corso di Sociologia a Dispense (12). *Liste des publications.*

EVALUATION/RECHERCHE: Entreprend des activités de recherche.

ACTIVITES DANS LES REGIONS EN DEVELOPPEMENT: Intervient directement dans les régions en développement. Intervient dans 4 pays. Intervient par l'intermédiaire d'organisations locales partenaires. **Actions de Développement durable:** Aliments/famine; Droits de l'Homme/paix/conflits; Démocratie/bonne gestion publique/création d'institutions/développement participatif; Développement rural/agriculture; Développement urbain/habitat; Enfants/jeunesse/famille; Envoi de volontaires/experts/assistance technique; Population/planning familial/démographie; Questions relatives aux femmes; Santé/assainissement/eau; Écologie/environnement/biodiversité; Éducation/formation/alphabétisation. **Régions:** Afrique de l'Est; Afrique du Nord; Amérique du Sud.

ACTIVITES D'INFORMATION ET D'EDUCATION: Domaines: Aliments/famine; Culture/tradition/religion; Droits de l'Homme/paix/conflits; Développement rural/agriculture; Développement urbain/habitat; Enfants/jeu-

nesse/famille; Paix/conflits ethniques/armement/désarmement; Pauvreté/conditions de vie; Population/planning familial/démographie; Questions relatives aux femmes; Racisme/xénophobie/antisémitisme; Relations internationales/coopération/aide au développement; Relations économiques internationales/commerce/dette/finances; Réfugiés/migrants/groupes ethniques; Santé/assainissement/eau; Écologie/environnement/biodiversité; Éducation/formation/alphabétisation. **Activités:** Campagnes d'information/expositions; Collecte de fonds; Conférences/séminaires/ateliers/activités de formation; Lobbying/plaidoyer; Services d'information et de documentation/bases de données; Édition/documents audiovisuels/documents éducatifs; Éducation formelle.

ITA2811

CENTRO SVILUPPO TERZO MONDO (CESVITEM) ♦ Centre de Développement du Tiers monde

Via L. Mariutto 36, 30035 Mirano (VE), Italie.

Téléphone: 39 (41) 5700843. *Fax:* 39 (41) 5702226. *Contact:* Simone Naletto, Présidente.

OBJECTIFS: Promouvoir et favoriser l'éducation au développement. Soutenir des activités et des projets de formation professionnelle et sociale dans les pays en développement. Sélectionner, former et envoyer des volontaires et des coopérants. Connaitre et faire connaitre la réalité du Tiers-Monde.

INFORMATIONS GENERALES: *Création:* 1987. *Affiliée à:* Coordinamento Iniziative Popolari di Solidarieta Internazionale (Italie) -Coordinamento Associazioni di Solidarieta Internazionale del Veneto (italie). *Personnel/Total:* 11. *Salariés:* 1. *Bénévoles:* 10. ***Budget/Total 1993:*** ECU 356000 (US$ 417000). ***Sources financières:*** *Public:* 69%. *Autofinancement:* 31%.

PUBLICATIONS: *Périodiques:* Il Girotondo (4).

EVALUATION/RECHERCHE: Rapports d'évaluation disponibles. Entreprend des activités de recherche.

ACTIVITES DANS LES REGIONS EN DEVELOPPEMENT: Intervient directement dans les régions en développement. Intervient dans 4 pays. Maintient une présence locale sur le terrain. Intervient par l'intermédiaire d'organisations locales partenaires. **Actions de Développement durable:** Dette/finances/commerce; Développement rural/agriculture; Enfants/jeunesse/famille; Questions relatives aux femmes; Santé/assainissement/eau; Secours d'urgence/réfugiés/aide humanitaire; Écologie/environnement/biodiversité; Éducation/formation/alphabétisation. **Régions:** Afrique australe; Afrique centrale; Amérique du Sud; Asie de l'Est.

ACTIVITES D'INFORMATION ET D'EDUCATION: Domaines: Droits de l'Homme/paix/conflits; Population/planning familial/démographie; Questions relatives aux femmes; Santé/assainissement/eau; Éducation/formation/alphabétisation. **Activités:** Campagnes d'information/expositions; Radiodiffusion/manifestations culturelles; Édition/documents audiovisuels/documents éducatifs.

ITA2812

CENTRO VOLONTARI COOPERAZIONE ALLO SVILUPPO (CVCS) ♦ Volunteers Centre for Development Co-operation

Via Bellinzona 4, C.P. 91, 34170 Gorizia, Italy.

Telephone: 39 (481) 34170. *Fax:* 39 (481) 536305. *Contact:* Luigi Caccia, President.

OBJECTIVES: To support development projects in Third World countries through financial investments and the service of volunteers.

GENERAL INFORMATION: *Creation:* 1980. *Affiliated to:* Federazione Organismi Cristiani di Servizio Interazionale Volontario (Italy). *Personnel/Total:* 36. *Salaried:* 16 of which: 11 in developing countries. *Volunteers:* 20. *Financial sources:* *Private:* 20%. *Public:* 75%. *Self-financing:* 5%.

ACTIVITIES IN DEVELOPING REGIONS: Active in 5 country(ies). Maintains local field presence. Works through local field partners. **Sustainable Development Actions:** Health/sanitation/water; Rural development/agriculture; Sending volunteers/experts/technical assistance; Urban development/habitat. **Regions:** East Africa; South America; West Africa.

INFORMATION AND EDUCATION ACTIVITIES: Topics: Culture/tradition/religion; Health/sanitation/water; International economic relations/

Voir : *Comment utiliser le répertoire,* page 11.

trade/debt/finance; International relations/cooperation/development aid; Rural development/agriculture. **Activities:** Conferences/seminars/workshops/training activities; Formal education; Fund raising; Publishing/audiovisual materials/educational materials.

ITA2813

CENTRO VOLONTARI MARCHIGIANI (CVM) ♦ Volunteers' Centre in the Marche Region

Via de Bosis 3, 60123 Ancona , Italy.

Telephone: 39 (71) 202074. *Fax:* 39 (71) 57358. *Contact:* Walter Farella, President.

OBJECTIVES: To undertake development projects in Africa and Asia. To promote development education activities in Italy.

GENERAL INFORMATION: *Creation:* 1978. *Affiliated to:* FOCSIV (Italy). *Personnel/Total:* 41. *Salaried:* 11 of which: 9 in developing countries. *Volunteers:* 30. *Budget/Total 1993:* ECU 760000 (US$ 890000). *Financial sources:* Private: 15%. Public: 85%.

PUBLICATIONS: *Periodicals:* CVM Flash (4). *Annual report. List of publications.*

EVALUATION/RESEARCH: Evaluation reports available. Undertakes research activities.

PLANNED ACTIVITIES: AIDS prevention and control programmes in Ethiopia.

ACTIVITIES IN DEVELOPING REGIONS: Present in developing regions. Active in 5 country(ies). Maintains local field presence. Works through local field partners. **Sustainable Development Actions:** Children/youth/family; Ecology/environment/biodiversity; Education/training/literacy; Emergency relief/refugees/humanitarian assistance; Food/famine; Gender issues/women; Health/sanitation/water; Human rights/peace/conflicts; Rural development/agriculture; Sending volunteers/experts/technical assistance; Small enterprises/informal sector/handicrafts. **Regions:** Central Africa; Central Asia and South Asia; East Africa; East Asia; South East Asia; Southern Africa.

INFORMATION AND EDUCATION ACTIVITIES: Topics: Children/youth/family; Ecology/environment/biodiversity; Emergency relief/refugees/humanitarian assistance; Food/famine; Gender issues/women; Health/sanitation/water; Human rights/peace/conflicts; International relations/cooperation/development aid; Peace/ethnic conflicts/armament/disarmament; Rural development/agriculture. **Activities:** Broadcasting/cultural events; Conferences/seminars/workshops/training activities; Exchanges/twinning/linking; Formal education; Fund raising; Information and documentation services/data bases; Information campaigns/exhibitions; Lobbying/advocacy; Publishing/audiovisual materials/educational materials.

ITA2814

CENTROINFORMAZIONE TERZO MONDO (CTM) ♦ Third World Counter Information

F. De Mura, 3, 73100 Lecce, Italy.

Telephone: 39 (832) 315519. *Fax:* 39 (832) 315606. *Contact:* Vinicio Russo, President.

OBJECTIVES: To undertake programmes supporting immigrants from non-European Union countries. To promote the spread of fair trade in Italy. To undertake development projects in collaboration with governments and local NGOs in developing countries.

GENERAL INFORMATION: *Creation:* 1985. *Affiliated to:* MOVIMONDO (Italy) - FOCSIV (Italy). *Personnel/Total:* 14. *Salaried:* 9 of which: 4 in developing countries. *Volunteers:* 5. *Budget/Total 1993:* ECU 632000 (US$ 740000). *Financial sources:* Private: 3%. Public: 88%. *Self-financing:* 9%.

PUBLICATIONS: *List of publications.*

COMMENTS: CTM belongs to the MOVIMONDO association. Undertakes activities in the Commonwealth of Independent States. Information activities related to the Commonwealth of Independent States.

ACTIVITIES IN DEVELOPING REGIONS: Present in developing regions. Active in 5 country(ies). Maintains local field presence. Works through

local field partners. **Sustainable Development Actions:** Children/youth/family; Education/training/literacy; Rural development/agriculture; Sending volunteers/experts/technical assistance; Small enterprises/informal sector/handicrafts; Urban development/habitat. **Regions:** Caribbean; Mexico and Central America; Middle East; South America.

INFORMATION AND EDUCATION ACTIVITIES: Topics: Children/youth/family; Culture/tradition/religion; Ecology/environment/biodiversity; Education/training/literacy; Emergency relief/refugees/humanitarian assistance; Employment/unemployment; Food/famine; Health/sanitation/water; Human rights/peace/conflicts; International economic relations/trade/debt/finance; International relations/cooperation/development aid; Poverty/living conditions; Racism/xenophobia/antisemitism; Refugees/migrants/ethnic groups; Rural development/agriculture; Urban development/habitat. **Activities:** Broadcasting/cultural events; Conferences/seminars/workshops/training activities; Formal education; Fund raising; Information and documentation services/data bases; Information campaigns/exhibitions; Lobbying/advocacy; Publishing/audiovisual materials/educational materials.

ITA2815

CITTASTUDI/CLESAV

Via Bazzini 24, 20131 Milano, Italy.

Telephone: 39 (2) 2664168. *Contact:* Dr. Gianni Di Domenico.

ITA2816

COLLEGIO UNIVERSITARIO ASPIRANTI MEDICI MISSIONARI (CUAMM) ♦ International College for Health Co-operation in Developing Countries

Via S. Francesco 126, 35121 Padova, Italy.

Telephone: 39 (49) 8751649. *Fax:* 39 (49) 8754738. *Contact:* Luigi Mazzucato, Director.

OBJECTIVES: To prepare and send medical and paramedical volunteers and specialized personnel to developing countries. To develop health programmes, especially in the field of primary health care and training of local personnel. To promote integrated development projects with other NGOs.

GENERAL INFORMATION: *Creation:* 1950. *Affiliated to:* FOCSIV (Italy). *Personnel/Total:* 73. *Salaried:* 13. *Volunteers:* 60 of which: 55 in developing countries. *Budget/Total 1993:* ECU 5430000 (US$ 6354000). *Financial sources:* Private: 9%. Public: 90%. *Self-financing:* 1%.

PUBLICATIONS: *Periodicals:* Cuamm Notizie Salute E Sviluppo (3) - Cumm Quaderni (3). *Annual report. List of publications.*

EVALUATION/RESEARCH: Evaluation reports available.

ACTIVITIES IN DEVELOPING REGIONS: Present in developing regions. Active in 6 country(ies). Maintains local field presence. Works through local field partners. **Sustainable Development Actions:** Emergency relief/refugees/humanitarian assistance; Health/sanitation/water; Sending volunteers/experts/technical assistance. **Regions:** Central Africa; East Africa; Southern Africa; West Africa.

INFORMATION AND EDUCATION ACTIVITIES: Topics: Culture/tradition/religion; Emergency relief/refugees/humanitarian assistance; Health/sanitation/water; Human rights/peace/conflicts; International relations/cooperation/development aid; Poverty/living conditions; Refugees/migrants/ethnic groups. **Activities:** Conferences/seminars/workshops/training activities; Formal education; Fund raising; Information and documentation services/data bases.

ITA2817

COME NOI

Via Saluzzo, 58, 10125 Torino, Italy.

Telephone: 39 (11) 655866. *Fax:* 39 (11) 6698096.

ITA2818

COMITATO COLLABORAZIONE MEDICA (CCM) ♦ Doctors for Developing Countries

Corso Giovanni Lanza 100, 10133 Torino, Italie.

See: *How to Use the Directory,* page 11.

Téléphone: 39 (11) 6602793 . *Fax:* 39 (11) 6602798. *Contact:* Pier Carlo Micheletti, Président.

OBJECTIFS: Favoriser, par l'envoi de volontaires spécialisés, le développement technique de la médecine traitante, la formation du personnel local et l'éducation sanitaire de la population. Promouvoir des programmes de soins de santé primaires et d'aide d'urgence.

INFORMATIONS GENERALES: *Création:* 1968. *Type d'organisation:* réseau. *Affiliée à:* Coordinamento Formazione Sanitaria - CFS - VOICE - Coordinamento di Iniziative Popolari di Solidarietà Internazionale - CIPSI. *Personnel/Total:* 18. *Salariés:* 6 dont: 3 dans les pays en développement. *Bénévoles:* 12. *Budget/Total 1993:* ECU 855000 (US$ 1000000). *Sources financières:* Privé: 43%. Public: 57%.

PUBLICATIONS: *Périodiques:* Volontari per lo Sviluppo (5). *Liste des publications.*

COMMENTAIRES: L'association a reçu 524449000 Lit de matériel et d'équipement sous forme de don, en plus du budget mentionné.

ACTIVITES DANS LES REGIONS EN DEVELOPPEMENT: Intervient directement dans les régions en développement. Intervient dans 4 pays. Maintient une présence locale sur le terrain. **Actions de Développement durable:** Envoi de volontaires/experts/assistance technique; Santé/assainissement/eau; Secours d'urgence/réfugiés/aide humanitaire; Éducation/formation/alphabétisation. **Régions:** Afrique centrale; Afrique de l'Est.

ACTIVITES D'INFORMATION ET D'EDUCATION: Domaines: Réfugiés/migrants/groupes ethniques; Santé/assainissement/eau. **Activités:** Collecte de fonds; Conférences/séminaires/ateliers/activités de formation; Services d'information et de documentation/bases de données; Édition/documents audiovisuels/documents éducatifs.

ITA2819

COMITATO DI COORDINAMENTO DELLE ORGANIZZAZIONI PER IL SERVIZIO VOLONTARIO (COSV) ♦ Co-ordinating Committee of Voluntary Service Organisations

Via Iglesias 33, 20128 Milano, Italy.

Telephone: 39 (2) 2552067. *Fax:* 39 (2) 2552281. *Contact:* Cinzia Giudici, President.

ITA2820

COMITATO EUROPEO DI FORMAZIONE AGRARIA (CEFA) ♦
Comité européen de formation agricole

Via Lame 118, 40122 Bologna, Italie.

Téléphone: 39 (51) 520285. *Fax:* 39 (51) 520712. *Contact:* Giovanni Bersani, Président.

OBJECTIFS: Oeuvrer, dans un but humanitaire, à des programmes de développement rural intégré dans le Tiers-Monde, à la promotion du respect de la justice, des droits et libertés fondamentales de la personne et des peuples.

INFORMATIONS GENERALES: *Création:* 1968. *Affiliée à:* FOCSIV (Italie) - MCL (Italie) - EURONAID (Pays-Bas) - VOICE/ONGDE (Belgique) -NGO Consortium (Kenya). *Personnel/Total:* 3350. *Salariés:* 350 dont: 345 dans les pays en développement. *Bénévoles:* 3100 dont: 3000 dans les pays en développement. *Budget/Total 1993:* ECU 3495000 (US$ 4090000). *Sources financières:* Privé: 20%. Public: 32%. Autofinancement: 6%.

PUBLICATIONS: *Périodiques:* Notiziario CEFA (12) - Supplemento Notiziario (2). *Rapport annuel. Liste des publications.*

EVALUATION/RECHERCHE: Rapports d'évaluation disponibles. Entreprend des activités de recherche.

COMMENTAIRES: Intervient dans la Communauté des Etats indépendants. Activités d'information concernant la Communauté des Etats indépendants.

ACTIVITES DANS LES REGIONS EN DEVELOPPEMENT: Intervient directement dans les régions en développement. Intervient dans 10 pays. Maintient une présence locale sur le terrain. Intervient par l'intermédiaire d'organisations locales partenaires. **Actions de Développement durable:** Aliments/famine; Droits de l'Homme/paix/conflits; Démo-

cratie/bonne gestion publique/création d'institutions/développement participatif; Développement rural/agriculture; Développement urbain/habitat; Enfants/jeunesse/famille; Envoi de volontaires/experts/assistance technique; Petites entreprises/secteur informel/artisanat; Questions relatives aux femmes; Santé/assainissement/eau; Secours d'urgence/réfugiés/aide humanitaire; Écologie/environnement/biodiversité; Éducation/formation/alphabétisation; Énergie/transport. **Régions:** Afrique de l'Est; Amérique du Sud.

ACTIVITES D'INFORMATION ET D'EDUCATION: Domaines: Aliments/famine; Culture/tradition/religion; Droits de l'Homme/paix/conflits; Développement rural/agriculture; Enfants/jeunesse/famille; Paix/conflits ethniques/armement/désarmement; Pauvreté/conditions de vie; Population/planning familial/démographie; Questions relatives aux femmes; Racisme/xénophobie/antisémitisme; Relations internationales/coopération/aide au développement; Relations économiques internationales/commerce/dette/finances; Réfugiés/migrants/groupes ethniques; Santé/assainissement/eau; Secours d'urgence/réfugiés/aide humanitaire; Écologie/environnement/biodiversité; Éducation/formation/alphabétisation. **Activités:** Campagnes d'information/expositions; Collecte de fonds; Conférences/séminaires/ateliers/activités de formation; Lobbying/plaidoyer; Radiodiffusion/manifestations culturelles; Services d'information et de documentation/bases de données; Édition/documents audiovisuels/documents éducatifs.

ITA2821

COMITATO HARAMBEE - VOLONTARI PER IL TERZO MONDO ♦ Comité Harambee - Volontaires pour le Tiers monde

Viale Mazzini 22, 12032 Barge (Cuneo), Italie.

Téléphone: 39 (175) 36507. *Contact:* Domenico Aimar.

ITA2822

COMITATO INTERNAZIONALE PER LO SVILUPPO DEI POPOLI (CISP) ♦ International Committee for the Development of Peoples

Via Marianna Dionigi, 57, 00193 Roma, Italy.

Telephone: 39 (6) 3215498. *Fax:* 39 (6) 3216163. *Contact:* Maura Viezzoli, Director.

OBJECTIVES: To undertake development projects in collaboration with governments and local NGOs in developing countries. To promote development education in Italy and throughout Europe.

GENERAL INFORMATION: *Creation:* 1982. *Affiliated to:* VOICE - MOVIMONDO (Italy). *Personnel/Total:* 38. *Salaried:* 32 of which: 20 in developing countries. *Volunteers:* 6 of which: 1 in developing countries. *Budget/Total 1993:* ECU 4129000 (US$ 4832000). *Financial sources:* Private: 3%. Public: 97%.

PUBLICATIONS: *Periodicals:* Forum Volutazione (2). *List of publications.*

EVALUATION/RESEARCH: Evaluation reports available. Undertakes research activities.

PLANNED ACTIVITIES: The implementation of an emergency relief workshop.

COMMENTS: CISP established an associacion of NGOs, MOVIMONDO, in 1993 with CTM and MOLISV. The association is present in 25 countries and undertakes development, relief and educational programmes. Undertakes activities in the Commonwealth of Independent States. Information activities related to the Commonwealth of Independent States.

ACTIVITIES IN DEVELOPING REGIONS: Present in developing regions. Active in 10 country(ies). Maintains local field presence. Works through local field partners. **Sustainable Development Actions:** Children/youth/family; Debt/finance/trade; Democracy/good governance/institution building/participatory development; Ecology/environment/biodiversity; Education/training/literacy; Emergency relief/refugees/humanitarian assistance; Energy/transport; Food/famine; Gender issues/women; Health/sanitation/water; Human rights/peace/conflicts; Other; Rural development/agriculture; Sending volunteers/experts/technical assistance; Small enterprises/informal sector/handicrafts. **Regions:** Caribbean; East Africa; East Asia; North Africa; South America; Southern Africa.

Voir : *Comment utiliser le répertoire,* page 11.

INFORMATION AND EDUCATION ACTIVITIES: Topics: Children/youth/family; Culture/tradition/religion; Ecology/environment/biodiversity; Education/training/literacy; Emergency relief/refugees/humanitarian assistance; Employment/unemployment; Food/famine; Gender issues/women; Health/sanitation/water; Human rights/peace/conflicts; International economic relations/trade/debt/finance; International relations/cooperation/development aid; Peace/ethnic conflicts/armament/disarmament; Poverty/living conditions; Racism/xenophobia/antisemitism; Refugees/migrants/ethnic groups; Rural development/agriculture. **Activities:** Conferences/seminars/workshops/training activities; Formal education; Fund raising; Information and documentation services/data bases; Information campaigns/exhibitions; Lobbying/advocacy; Networking/electronic telecommunications; Publishing/audiovisual materials/educational materials.

ITA2823
COMMUNITA DI AGAPE
10060 Prali, Italie.

ITA2824
COMUNITA DI SANT'EGIDIO-ACAP ♦ Community of Sant'Egidio-ACAP
Piazza S. Egidio 3/a, 00153 Rome, Italie.

Téléphone: 39 (6) 585661. **Fax:** 39 (6) 5800197. **Contact:** Matteo Maria Zuppi, Serétaire général.

OBJECTIFS: Apporter une aide aux pauvres dans les grandes villes d'Europe. Contribuer au développement, à la paix (Mozambique). Sensibiliser l'opinion aux problèmes Nord-Sud.

INFORMATIONS GENERALES: Création: 1968. **Affiliée à:** Fédération Européenne des Communautés de S.Egidio (Belgique.). **Personnel/Total:** 1004. **Salariés:** 4 dont: 2 dans les pays en développement. **Bénévoles:** 1000. **Sources financières:** Privé: 75%. Public: 15%. Autofinancement: 10%.

COMMENTAIRES: Intervient dans la Communauté des Etats indépendants. Activités d'information concernant la Communauté des Etats indépendants.

ACTIVITES DANS LES REGIONS EN DEVELOPPEMENT: Intervient directement dans les régions en développement. Maintient une présence locale sur le terrain. Intervient par l'intermédiaire d'organisations locales partenaires. **Actions de Développement durable:** Droits de l'Homme/paix/conflits; Enfants/jeunesse/famille; Envoi de volontaires/experts/assistance technique; Santé/assainissement/eau; Secours d'urgence/réfugiés/aide humanitaire; Éducation/formation/alphabétisation. **Régions:** Afrique australe; Afrique centrale; Afrique de l'Ouest; Amérique du Sud; Asie centrale et Asie du Sud; Asie du Sud-Est; Mexique et Amerique centrale; Moyen-Orient.

ACTIVITES D'INFORMATION ET D'EDUCATION: Domaines: Droits de l'Homme/paix/conflits; Paix/conflits ethniques/armement/désarmement; Pauvreté/conditions de vie; Racisme/xénophobie/antisémitisme; Relations internationales/coopération/aide au développement; Secours d'urgence/réfugiés/aide humanitaire; Éducation/formation/alphabétisation. **Activités:** Campagnes d'information/expositions; Collecte de fonds; Conférences/séminaires/ateliers/activités de formation; Lobbying/plaidoyer; Services d'information et de documentation/bases de données; Échanges/parrainage/jumelage.

ITA2825
COMUNITA EMMAUS ♦ Communauté Emmaüs
Via la Luna 1, 52020 Pergine (Arezzo), Italie.

Téléphone: 39 (575) 896558. **Fax:** 39 (575) 896086. **Contact:** Franco Bettoli.

ITA2826
COMUNITA IMPEGNO SERVIZIO VOLONTARIATO (CISV) ♦
Communauté engagement service volontariat
Corso Chieri 121/6, 10132 Torino, Italie.

Téléphone: 39 (11) 8993823. **Fax:** 39 (11) 8994700. **Contact:** Rosa Maria Rondelli, Présidente.

OBJECTIFS: Soutenir des projets de développement en Afrique francophone à travers le travail des volontaires. Organiser des activités d'éducation au développement en Italie.

INFORMATIONS GENERALES: Création: 1972. **Affiliée à:** Fédération des Organismes Chrétiens du Service International des Volontaires (Italie). **Personnel/Total:** 98. Salariés: 8. Bénévoles: 90 dont: 13 dans les pays en développement. **Budget/Total 1993:** ECU 2034000 (US$ 2380000). **Sources financières:** Public: 50%.

PUBLICATIONS: Périodiques: Volontari per lo Sviluppo (6). Rapport annuel. Liste des publications.

EVALUATION/RECHERCHE: Rapports d'évaluation disponibles. Entreprend des activités de recherche.

PREVISIONS D'ACTIVITES: Participation à la journée mondiale de l'alimentation

ACTIVITES DANS LES REGIONS EN DEVELOPPEMENT: Intervient directement dans les régions en développement. Intervient dans 4 pays. Maintient une présence locale sur le terrain. Intervient par l'intermédiaire d'organisations locales partenaires. **Actions de Développement durable:** Démocratie/bonne gestion publique/création d'institutions/développement participatif; Développement rural/agriculture; Développement urbain/habitat; Envoi de volontaires/experts/assistance technique; Petites entreprises/secteur informel/artisanat; Questions relatives aux femmes; Santé/assainissement/eau; Éducation/formation/alphabétisation. **Régions:** Afrique centrale; Afrique de l'Ouest.

ACTIVITES D'INFORMATION ET D'EDUCATION: Domaines: Aliments/famine; Culture/tradition/religion; Droits de l'Homme/paix/conflits; Développement rural/agriculture; Développement urbain/habitat; Emploi/chômage; Enfants/jeunesse/famille; Paix/conflits ethniques/armement/désarmement; Pauvreté/conditions de vie; Population/planning familial/démographie; Questions relatives aux femmes; Racisme/xénophobie/antisémitisme; Relations internationales/coopération/aide au développement; Relations économiques internationales/commerce/dette/finances; Réfugiés/migrants/groupes ethniques; Santé/assainissement/eau; Secours d'urgence/réfugiés/aide humanitaire; Écologie/environnement/biodiversité; Éducation/formation/alphabétisation. **Activités:** Campagnes d'information/expositions; Collecte de fonds; Conférences/séminaires/ateliers/activités de formation; Radiodiffusion/manifestations culturelles; Réseaux/télécommunications électroniques; Édition/documents audiovisuels/documents éducatifs; Éducation formelle.

ITA2827
COMUNITA LAICI MISSIONARI CATTOLICI (CLMC) ♦ Communauté des laïcs missionaires catholiques
Via B. Buozzi 19 A/3, 16126 Genes, Italy.

Telephone: 39 (10) 256628. **Fax:** 39 (10) 252740. **Contact:** Chiara Cavalcante, President.

OBJECTIVES: To promote the self development of the rural populations, provide aid to agricultural co-operatives and stop urban migration.

GENERAL INFORMATION: Creation: 1968. **Affiliated to:** FOCSIV (Italy). **Personnel/Total:** 24. Salaried: 4. Volunteers: 20 of which: 5 in developing countries. **Budget/Total 1993:** ECU 163000 (US$ 191000). **Financial sources:** Private: 20%. Public: 50%. Self-financing: 30%.

PUBLICATIONS: Periodicals: CLMC Informazioni (12).

EVALUATION/RESEARCH: Evaluation reports available.

ACTIVITIES IN DEVELOPING REGIONS: Present in developing regions. Active in 1 country(ies). Maintains local field presence. **Sustainable Development Actions:** Education/training/literacy; Gender issues/women; Health/sanitation/water; Rural development/agriculture; Sending volunteers/experts/technical assistance; Small enterprises/informal sector/handicrafts. **Regions:** West Africa.

INFORMATION AND EDUCATION ACTIVITIES: Topics: Culture/tradition/religion; Human rights/peace/conflicts; International economic relations/trade/debt/finance; Poverty/living conditions; Racism/xenophobia/antisemitism; Refugees/migrants/ethnic groups. **Activities:** Conferences/seminars/workshops/training activities; Formal education; Information and documentation services/data bases; Information campaigns/exhibitions; Publishing/audiovisual materials/educational materials.

See: *How to Use the Directory*, page 11.

ITA2828

COMUNITA PROMOZIONE E SVILUPPO (CPS) ♦ Communauté promotion et développement

Corso Vittorio Emanuele 93, 80053 Castellamare di Stabia (NA), Italie.

Téléphone: 39 (81) 8704180. *Fax:* 39 (81) 8704180. *Contact:* Francesco Rivoli, Président.

OBJECTIFS: Aider à la promotion des pays en développement en choisissant d'autres voies que l'assistance, source de dépendance à l'égard des pays industrialisés.

INFORMATIONS GENERALES: *Création:* 1974. *Affiliée à:* FOCSIV. *Personnel/Total:* 9. *Salariés:* 1. *Bénévoles:* 8 dont: 4 dans les pays en développement. *Budget/Total 1993:* ECU 142000 (US$ 166000). *Sources financières:* Privé: 30%. Public: 55%. Autofinancement: 15%.

PUBLICATIONS: *Rapport annuel. Liste des publications.*

EVALUATION/RECHERCHE: Rapports d'évaluation disponibles.

ACTIVITES DANS LES REGIONS EN DEVELOPPEMENT: Intervient directement dans les régions en développement. Intervient dans 2 pays. Maintient une présence locale sur le terrain. Intervient par l'intermédiaire d'organisations locales partenaires. **Actions de Développement durable:** Développement rural/agriculture; Envoi de volontaires/experts/assistance technique; Petites entreprises/secteur informel/artisanat; Santé/assainissement/eau; Éducation/formation/alphabétisation. **Régions:** Afrique de l'Ouest; Amérique du Sud.

ACTIVITES D'INFORMATION ET D'EDUCATION: Domaines: Paix/conflits ethniques/armement/désarmement; Relations internationales/coopération/aide au développement. **Activités:** Campagnes d'information/expositions; Conférences/séminaires/ateliers/activités de formation; Services d'information et de documentation/bases de données; Édition/documents audiovisuels/documents éducatifs.

ITA2829

COMUNITA' INTERNAZIONALE VOLONTARI LAICI ♦ Association Internationale Laics Volontaires

Corso IV Novembre 28, 12100 Cuneo, Italie.

Téléphone: 39 (171) 696975. *Fax:* 39 (171) 602558. *Contact:* Aldo Benevelli, Président.

OBJECTIFS: Promouvoir une coopération technique avec les pays en voie de développement.

INFORMATIONS GENERALES: *Création:* 1966. *Affiliée à:* Fédération des Organismes Chrétiens pour le Service International de Volontariat (Italie). *Personnel/Total:* 97. *Salariés:* 17 dont: 50 dans les pays en développement. *Bénévoles:* 80 dont: 45 dans les pays en développement. *Budget/Total 1993:* ECU 3964000 (US$ 4639000).

PUBLICATIONS: *Périodiques:* "Volontari" (6). *Liste des publications.*

EVALUATION/RECHERCHE: Rapports d'évaluation disponibles. Entreprend des activités de recherche.

COMMENTAIRES: Intervient dans la Communauté des Etats indépendants.

ACTIVITES DANS LES REGIONS EN DEVELOPPEMENT: Intervient directement dans les régions en développement. Intervient dans 11 pays. Maintient une présence locale sur le terrain. **Actions de Développement durable:** Aliments/famine; Développement rural/agriculture; Développement urbain/habitat; Enfants/jeunesse/famille; Envoi de volontaires/experts/assistance technique; Petites entreprises/secteur informel/artisanat; Questions relatives aux femmes; Santé/assainissement/eau; Secours d'urgence/réfugiés/aide humanitaire; Éducation/formation/alphabétisation. **Régions:** Afrique centrale; Afrique de l'Est; Afrique de l'Ouest.

ACTIVITES D'INFORMATION ET D'EDUCATION: Domaines: Aliments/famine; Droits de l'Homme/paix/conflits; Développement rural/agriculture; Développement urbain/habitat; Enfants/jeunesse/famille; Paix/conflits ethniques/armement/désarmement; Pauvreté/conditions de vie; Questions relatives aux femmes; Racisme/xénophobie/antisémitisme; Relations internationales/coopération/aide au développement; Relations économiques internationales/commerce/dette/finances; Réfugiés/migrants/groupes ethniques; Santé/assainissement/eau; Secours d'urgence/réfugiés/aide humanitaire; Écologie/environnement/biodiversité. **Activités:** Campagnes d'information/expositions; Collecte de fonds; Conférences/séminaires/ateliers/activités de formation; Services d'information et de documentation/bases de données; Édition/documents audiovisuels/documents éducatifs.

ITA2830

CONFEDERAZIONE COOPERATIVE ITALIANE (CONFCOOPERATIVE-CCI) ♦ Confédération des coopératives italiennes

Borgo Santo Spirito 78, 00193 Roma, Italie.

Téléphone: 39 (6) 680001. *Fax:* 39 (6) 6868595. *Contact:* Luigi Marino, Président.

OBJECTIFS: Fournir des informations aux coopératives membres et les amener à s'intéresser à des projets d'envergure internationale. Encourager l'esprit d'entreprise des petits producteurs des pays en développement en leur montrant les avantages des systèmes associatifs ou coopératifs adaptés aux conditions locales.

INFORMATIONS GENERALES: *Création:* 1919. *Organisations membres:* 4. *Personnel/Total:* 68. *Salariés:* 68. *Sources financières:* Privé: 50%. Public: 50%.

PUBLICATIONS: *Périodiques:* Italia Cooperativa (6) - Notizie Confcooperative/Speciale Esteri (6).

EVALUATION/RECHERCHE: Entreprend des activités de recherche.

COMMENTAIRES: Activités d'information concernant la Communauté des Etats indépendants.

ACTIVITES DANS LES REGIONS EN DEVELOPPEMENT: Intervient dans 6 pays. **Actions de Développement durable:** Développement rural/agriculture; Envoi de volontaires/experts/assistance technique; Éducation/formation/alphabétisation. **Régions:** Afrique du Nord; Amérique du Sud; Asie du Sud-Est; Caraïbes; Mexique et Amerique centrale.

ACTIVITES D'INFORMATION ET D'EDUCATION: Domaines: Développement rural/agriculture; Relations internationales/coopération/aide au développement. **Activités:** Conférences/séminaires/ateliers/activités de formation; Lobbying/plaidoyer; Services d'information et de documentation/bases de données; Édition/documents audiovisuels/documents éducatifs.

ITA2831

CONSEIL ITALIEN POUR LES REFUGIES

Via S. Tommaso D'Aquino 116, 00136 Rome, Italie.

Contact: Pietro Scoppola, Président.

ITA2832

COOPERAZIONE E SVILUPPO (CESVI) ♦ Cooperation and Development

Via Pignolo 50, 24121 Bergamo, Italy.

Telephone: 39 (35) 243990. *Fax:* 39 (35) 229046. *E-mail:* CESVI.COOPERAZIONE@AGORA.STM.IT. *Contact:* Paolo Caroli, Director.

OBJECTIVES: To promote development programmes in developing countries. To promote development education in Italy.

GENERAL INFORMATION: *Creation:* 1985. *Affiliated to:* UNA (Italy) - COCIS (Italy). *Personnel/Total:* 34. *Salaried:* 14 of which: 8 in developing countries. *Volunteers:* 20. *Budget/Total 1993:* ECU 1135000 (US$ 1328000). *Financial sources:* Private: 5%. Public: 90%. Self-financing: 5%.

PUBLICATIONS: *Periodicals:* Cooperando (12). *Annual report. List of publications.*

EVALUATION/RESEARCH: Evaluation reports available. Undertakes research activities.

COMMENTS: Undertakes activities in the Commonwealth of Independent States.

ACTIVITIES IN DEVELOPING REGIONS: Active in 6 country(ies). Maintains local field presence. Works through local field partners. **Sustainable Development Actions:** Children/youth/family; Ecology/environment/biodiversity; Education/training/literacy; Health/sanitation/water;

Rural development/agriculture; Sending volunteers/experts/technical assistance; Small enterprises/informal sector/handicrafts. **Regions:** East Asia; South America.

INFORMATION AND EDUCATION ACTIVITIES: Topics: Children/youth/family; Culture/tradition/religion; Ecology/environment/biodiversity; Emergency relief/refugees/humanitarian assistance; Food/famine; Gender issues/women; Health/sanitation/water; Human rights/peace/conflicts; International economic relations/trade/debt/finance; International relations/cooperation/development aid; Peace/ethnic conflicts/armament/disarmament; Population/family planning/demography; Poverty/living conditions; Racism/xenophobia/antisemitism; Refugees/migrants/ethnic groups; Rural development/agriculture. **Activities:** Broadcasting/cultural events; Conferences/seminars/workshops/training activities; Formal education; Fund raising; Information and documentation services/data bases; Information campaigns/exhibitions; Publishing/audiovisual materials/educational materials.

ITA2833

COOPERAZIONE E SVILUPPO   (C&D)   ♦ Coopération et développement

Via Talamoni 1/F, 29100 Piacenza, Italie.

Téléphone: 39 (523) 44924.

ITA2834

COOPERAZIONE INTERNATIONALE SUD-SUD (CISS) ♦ International Cooperation South-South

Via Benedetto d'Acquisto 30, 90141 Palermo, Italy.

Telephone: 39 (91) 6111062. *Fax:* 39 (91) 332739. *Contact:* Sergio Cipolla, President.

OBJECTIVES: To promote programmes of co-operation with developing countries. To promote international solidarity and co-operation. To connect the South of Italy (Sicily) with the South of the world, given the realities between these two worlds that make communication necessary between them.

GENERAL INFORMATION: *Creation:* 1985. *Affiliated to:* COCIS - RONGEAD. *Personnel/Total:* 22. *Salaried:* 16 of which: 8 in developing countries. *Volunteers:* 6. *Budget/Total 1993:* ECU 869000 (US$ 1017000). *Financial sources:* Private: 7%. Public: 83%. Self-financing: 10%.

PUBLICATIONS: *Periodicals:* SUD (5). *List of publications.*

EVALUATION/RESEARCH: Undertakes research activities.

PLANNED ACTIVITIES: Undertaking a water co-operation project in the Gaza Strip.

ACTIVITIES IN DEVELOPING REGIONS: Active in 8 country(ies). Maintains local field presence. Works through local field partners. **Sustainable Development Actions:** Children/youth/family; Ecology/environment/biodiversity; Education/training/literacy; Emergency relief/refugees/humanitarian assistance; Gender issues/women; Health/sanitation/water; Human rights/peace/conflicts; Rural development/agriculture; Sending volunteers/experts/technical assistance; Small enterprises/informal sector/handicrafts. **Regions:** Mexico and Central America; Middle East; North Africa; South America.

INFORMATION AND EDUCATION ACTIVITIES: Topics: Children/youth/family; Culture/tradition/religion; Ecology/environment/biodiversity; Emergency relief/refugees/humanitarian assistance; Employment/unemployment; Food/famine; Gender issues/women; Health/sanitation/water; Human rights/peace/conflicts; International economic relations/trade/debt/finance; International relations/cooperation/development aid; Peace/ethnic conflicts/armament/disarmament; Poverty/living conditions; Racism/xenophobia/antisemitism; Refugees/migrants/ethnic groups; Rural development/agriculture; Urban development/habitat. **Activities:** Broadcasting/cultural events; Conferences/seminars/workshops/training activities; Exchanges/twinning/linking; Formal education; Fund raising; Information and documentation services/data bases; Information campaigns/exhibitions; Lobbying/advocacy; Publishing/audiovisual materials/educational materials.

ITA2835

COOPERAZIONE INTERNAZIONALE   (COOPI)   ♦ Coopération internationale

Via De Lemene 50, 20151 Milano, Italie.

Téléphone: 39 (2) 3085057. *Fax:* 39 (2) 33403570. *Contact:* Paolo Giorgi, Directeur.

OBJECTIFS: Apporter une assistance pour la réalisation de projets dans les pays en développement, notamment par l'envoi de volontaires. Réfléchir aux problèmes du sous-développement et de la paix dans le monde.

INFORMATIONS GENERALES: *Création:* 1961. *Personnel/Total:* 121. *Salariés:* 45 dont: 30 dans les pays en développement. *Bénévoles:* 76 dont: 43 dans les pays en développement. *Budget/Total 1993:* ECU 5756000 (US$ 6736000). *Sources financières:* Privé: 40%. Public: 45%. Autofinancement: 15%.

PUBLICATIONS: *Rapport annuel. Liste des publications.*

EVALUATION/RECHERCHE: Rapports d'évaluation disponibles. Entreprend des activités de recherche.

ACTIVITES DANS LES REGIONS EN DEVELOPPEMENT: Intervient directement dans les régions en développement. Intervient dans 7 pays. Maintient une présence locale sur le terrain. Intervient par l'intermédiaire d'organisations locales partenaires. **Actions de Développement durable:** Développement rural/agriculture; Enfants/jeunesse/famille; Envoi de volontaires/experts/assistance technique; Petites entreprises/secteur informel/artisanat; Questions relatives aux femmes; Santé/assainissement/eau; Secours d'urgence/réfugiés/aide humanitaire; Éducation/formation/alphabétisation. **Régions:** Afrique centrale; Afrique de l'Est; Amérique du Sud.

ACTIVITES D'INFORMATION ET D'EDUCATION: Domaines: Culture/tradition/religion; Développement rural/agriculture; Développement urbain/habitat; Enfants/jeunesse/famille; Pauvreté/conditions de vie; Questions relatives aux femmes; Relations internationales/coopération/aide au développement; Réfugiés/migrants/groupes ethniques; Santé/assainissement/eau; Secours d'urgence/réfugiés/aide humanitaire; Écologie/environnement/biodiversité; Éducation/formation/alphabétisation. **Activités:** Campagnes d'information/expositions; Collecte de fonds; Conférences/séminaires/ateliers/activités de formation; Radiodiffusion/manifestations culturelles; Services d'information et de documentation/bases de données; Échanges/parrainage/jumelage; Édition/documents audiovisuels/documents éducatifs; Éducation formelle.

ITA2836

COOPERAZIONE INTERNAZIONALE   (GAO)

Via Giorgio de Chirico, 217, 87036 Saporito di Rende (CS), Italy.

Telephone: 39 (984) 462052. *Fax:* 39 (984) 461554.

ITA2837

COOPERAZIONE PAESI EMERGENTI   (COPE)   ♦ CO-OPERATION WITH DEVELOPING COUNTRIES

Via Crociferi, 38, 95124 Catania, Italy.

Telephone: 39 (95) 321288. *Fax:* 39 (95) 321288. *Contact:* Dr. Eleonora Caltabiano, President.

OBJECTIVES: To raise awareness among public opinion in Italy of development problems. To organise programmes of intervention and of technical co-operation in favour of communities in developing countries. To promote the selection and training of volunteers to be sent to developing countries.

GENERAL INFORMATION: *Creation:* 1983. *Affiliated to:* Fedazione di organismi cristiani di servizio internazionale volontario (Italy). *Personnel/Total:* 41. *Salaried:* 1. *Volunteers:* 40 of which: 3 in developing countries. *Budget/Total 1993:* ECU 1629000 (US$ 1906000). *Financial sources:* Private: 38%. Public: 2%. Self-financing: 60%.

PUBLICATIONS: *List of publications.*

EVALUATION/RESEARCH: Evaluation reports available.

ACTIVITIES IN DEVELOPING REGIONS: Active in 2 country(ies). Maintains local field presence. Works through local field partners. **Sustainable Development Actions:** Children/youth/family; Education/training/lit-

eracy; Health/sanitation/water; Population/family planning/demography; Rural development/agriculture. **Regions:** Central Africa; East Africa.

INFORMATION AND EDUCATION ACTIVITIES: Topics: Children/youth/family; Culture/tradition/religion; Education/training/literacy; Health/sanitation/water; International economic relations/trade/debt/finance; International relations/cooperation/development aid; Peace/ethnic conflicts/armament/disarmament; Population/family planning/demography; Refugees/migrants/ethnic groups; Rural development/agriculture. **Activities:** Conferences/seminars/workshops/training activities; Fund raising; Information and documentation services/data bases; Information campaigns/exhibitions; Publishing/audiovisual materials/educational materials.

ITA2838

COOPERAZIONE PER LO SVILUPPO DEI PAESI EMER-GENTI (COSPE) ♦ Coopération pour l'aide aux pays en développement

Via della Colonna 25, 50121 Firenze, Italie.

Téléphone: 39 (55) 2346511. *Fax:* 39 (55) 2346514. *Courrier électronique:* MC 8008@MCLINK.IT. *Contact:* Luciana Sassatelli, Présidente .

OBJECTIFS: Soutenir les organisations de base situées dans les pays en développement, et encourager leur autonomie dans la gestion de projets. Développer la solidarité entre les peuples, sensibiliser l'opinion publique. Soutenir la réalisation de projets de développement.

INFORMATIONS GENERALES: *Création:* 1983. *Affiliée à:* COCIS (Italie) - Coordination européenne pour le peuple Sahraoui. *Personnel/Total:* 43. *Salariés:* 23 dont: 20 dans les pays en développement. *Bénévoles:* 20. *Budget/Total 1993:* ECU 2715000 (US$ 3177000). *Sources financières:* Privé: 10%. *Public:* 85%. *Autofinancement:* 5%.

PUBLICATIONS: *Périodiques:* COSPE News (4). *Rapport annuel. Liste des publications.*

EVALUATION/RECHERCHE: Rapports d'évaluation disponibles. Entreprend des activités de recherche.

PREVISIONS D'ACTIVITES: De 1995 à 1997: Activités de recherche et de lobbying sur le développement durable et pacifique.

COMMENTAIRES: Intervient dans la Communauté des Etats indépendants.

ACTIVITES DANS LES REGIONS EN DEVELOPPEMENT: Intervient dans 20 pays. Intervient par l'intermédiaire d'organisations locales partenaires. **Actions de Développement durable:** Droits de l'Homme/paix/conflits; Démocratie/bonne gestion publique/création d'institutions/développement participatif; Développement rural/agriculture; Développement urbain/habitat; Enfants/jeunesse/famille; Envoi de volontaires/experts/assistance technique; Petites entreprises/secteur informel/artisanat; Questions relatives aux femmes; Santé/assainissement/eau; Secours d'urgence/réfugiés/aide humanitaire; Écologie/environnement/biodiversité; Éducation/formation/alphabétisation. **Régions:** Afrique australe; Afrique de l'Ouest; Afrique du Nord; Amérique du Sud; Asie du Sud-Est; Mexique et Amerique centrale; Moyen-Orient.

ACTIVITES D'INFORMATION ET D'EDUCATION: Domaines: Culture/tradition/religion; Droits de l'Homme/paix/conflits; Développement urbain/habitat; Enfants/jeunesse/famille; Paix/conflits ethniques/armement/désarmement; Pauvreté/conditions de vie; Questions relatives aux femmes; Racisme/xénophobie/antisémitisme; Relations internationales/coopération/aide au développement; Relations économiques internationales/commerce/dette/finances; Réfugiés/migrants/groupes ethniques; Santé/assainissement/eau; Secours d'urgence/réfugiés/aide humanitaire; Écologie/environnement/biodiversité. **Activités:** Campagnes d'information/expositions; Collecte de fonds; Conférences/séminaires/ateliers/activités de formation; Lobbying/plaidoyer; Radiodiffusion/manifestations culturelles; Échanges/parrainage/jumelage; Édition/documents audiovisuels/documents éducatifs; Éducation formelle.

ITA2839

COORDINAMENTO DELLE ONG PER LA COOPERAZIONE INTERNAZIONALE ALLO SVILUPPO (COCIS) ♦ Coordination des ONG de coopération internationale pour le développement

Via Giosue' Borsi 5, 20143 Milano, Italie.

Téléphone: 39 (2) 89401602. *Fax:* 39 (2) 58102285. *Contact:* Raffaele K. Salinari, Président.

OBJECTIFS: Servir de lieu de coordination pour les ONG membres, leur apporter un soutien logistique et les représenter auprès des administrations italiennes et étrangères. Effectuer des recherches dans le domaine de la coopération non-gouvernementale. Faire de l'éducation au développement auprès du public italien.

INFORMATIONS GENERALES: *Création:* 1986. *Personnel/Total:* 2. *Salariés:* 1. *Bénévoles:* 1. *Budget/Total 1993:* ECU 741000 (US$ 867000). *Sources financières:* Privé: 45%. *Public:* 50%. *Autofinancement:* 5%.

PUBLICATIONS: *Périodiques:* COCIS INFORM (4). *Rapport annuel.*

EVALUATION/RECHERCHE: Rapports d'évaluation disponibles. Entreprend des activités de recherche.

ACTIVITES DANS LES REGIONS EN DEVELOPPEMENT: Intervient directement dans les régions en développement. Intervient dans 4 pays. Maintient une présence locale sur le terrain. **Actions de Développement durable:** Envoi de volontaires/experts/assistance technique; Écologie/environnement/biodiversité. **Régions:** Amérique du Sud; Moyen-Orient.

ACTIVITES D'INFORMATION ET D'EDUCATION: Domaines: Relations internationales/coopération/aide au développement. **Activités:** Conférences/séminaires/ateliers/activités de formation; Services d'information et de documentation/bases de données; Édition/documents audiovisuels/documents éducatifs.

ITA2840

COORDINAMENTO DI INIZIATIVE POPOLARI DI SOLIDARIETA INTERNAZIONALE (CIPSI) ♦ Coordination d'initiatives populaires de solidarité internationale

Viale Ferdinando Baldelli 41, 00146 Roma, Italie.

Téléphone: 39 (6) 5414894. *Fax:* 39 (6) 59600533. *Contact:* Rosario Lembo, Président.

OBJECTIFS: Etre une structure de coordination pour les organisations non-gouvernementales italiennes qui travaillent dans le domaine de la coopération au développement, notamment par la fourniture de services et l'organisation de manifestations culturelles et de campagnes d'opinion.

INFORMATIONS GENERALES: *Création:* 1985. *Type d'organisation:* regroupement d'ONG. *Organisations membres:* 26. *Personnel/Total:* 8. *Salariés:* 5. *Bénévoles:* 3. *Budget/Total 1993:* ECU 1195000 (US$ 1398000). *Sources financières:* Privé: 30%. *Public:* 70%.

PUBLICATIONS: *Périodiques:* "Solidarieta internationale" (4). *Rapport annuel. Liste des publications.*

EVALUATION/RECHERCHE: Rapports d'évaluation disponibles. Entreprend des activités de recherche.

ACTIVITES DANS LES REGIONS EN DEVELOPPEMENT: Intervient directement dans les régions en développement. Intervient dans 4 pays. Maintient une présence locale sur le terrain. Intervient par l'intermédiaire d'organisations locales partenaires. **Actions de Développement durable:** Démocratie/bonne gestion publique/création d'institutions/développement participatif; Petites entreprises/secteur informel/artisanat; Secours d'urgence/réfugiés/aide humanitaire; Éducation/formation/alphabétisation. **Régions:** Afrique de l'Est; Afrique de l'Ouest; Asie centrale et Asie du Sud.

ACTIVITES D'INFORMATION ET D'EDUCATION: Domaines: Droits de l'Homme/paix/conflits; Développement rural/agriculture; Paix/conflits ethniques/armement/désarmement; Pauvreté/conditions de vie; Racisme/xénophobie/antisémitisme; Relations internationales/coopération/aide au développement; Relations économiques internationales/commerce/dette/finances; Santé/assainissement/eau; Écologie/environnement/biodiversité; Éducation/formation/alphabétisation. **Activités:** Campagnes d'information/expositions; Collecte de fonds; Conférences/séminaires/ateliers/activités de formation; Lobbying/plaidoyer; Radiodiffusion/manifestations culturelles; Services d'information et de documentation/bases de données; Édition/documents audiovisuels/documents éducatifs; Éducation formelle.

Voir : *Comment utiliser le répertoire,* page 11.

ITA2841

CROCE ROSSA ITALIANA ♦ Croix Rouge italienne

Via Toscana 12, 00187 Roma, Italie.

Téléphone: 39 (6) 47591. *Fax:* 39 (6) 4883541. *Contact:* Luigi Giannico.

OBJECTIFS: Aider, à l'intérieur ou à l'extérieur, les victimes des catastrophes ou de conflits. Diffuser le droit international humanitaire et les principes de la Croix-Rouge. Apporter une assistance aux handicapés, aux écoles d'infirmiers et assurer des services sanitaires d'intérêt public.

INFORMATIONS GENERALES: *Création:* 1864. *Affiliée à:* Fédération Internationale des Sociétés de Croix-Rouge et du Croissant-Rouge (Suisse). *Salariés:* 2316. *Bénévoles:* 65000. *Budget/Total 1993:* ECU 157472000 (US$ 184279000). *Sources financières:* *Privé:* 6%. *Public:* 67%. *Autofinancement:* 27%.

PUBLICATIONS: *Périodiques:* ERASMO (6). *Rapport annuel.*

EVALUATION/RECHERCHE: Entreprend des activités de recherche.

COMMENTAIRES: L'organisation agit comme auxiliaire des pouvoirs publics dans le domaine humanitaire. Intervient dans la Communauté des Etats indépendants.

ACTIVITES DANS LES REGIONS EN DEVELOPPEMENT: Intervient directement dans les régions en développement. Intervient dans 3 pays. Maintient une présence locale sur le terrain. Intervient par l'intermédiaire d'organisations locales partenaires. **Actions de Développement durable:** Santé/assainissement/eau; Secours d'urgence/réfugiés/aide humanitaire. **Régions:** Afrique de l'Est; Afrique de l'Ouest.

ACTIVITES D'INFORMATION ET D'EDUCATION: Domaines: Droits de l'Homme/paix/conflits; Paix/conflits ethniques/armement/désarmement; Relations économiques internationales/commerce/dette/finances; Réfugiés/migrants/groupes ethniques; Santé/assainissement/eau; Secours d'urgence/réfugiés/aide humanitaire. **Activités:** Campagnes d'information/expositions; Collecte de fonds; Conférences/séminaires/ateliers/activités de formation; Radiodiffusion/manifestations culturelles; Réseaux/télécommunications électroniques; Échanges/parrainage/jumelage; Édition/documents audiovisuels/documents éducatifs.

ITA2842

ENTE NAZIONALE GIUSEPPINI DEL MURIALDO (ENGIM)

Via degli Etruschi, 7, 00185 Rome, Italy.

Telephone: 39 (6) 4441688. *Fax:* 39 (6) 4441672. *Contact:* Luigi Pierini.

OBJECTIVES: To promote activities concerning vocational training and the improvement of human resources. To provide technical and professional education. To support centres studying labour problems and offering job orientation.

GENERAL INFORMATION: *Creation:* 1977. *Affiliated to:* CONFAP (Italy). *Personnel/Total:* 324. *Salaried:* 320 of which: 20 in developing countries. *Volunteers:* 4 of which: 4 in developing countries. *Budget/Total 1993:* ECU 10589000 (US$ 12391000). *Financial sources:* Private: 8%. Public: 90%. Self-financing: 2%.

PUBLICATIONS: *Periodicals:* Sierra Leone Notizie - Guinea Bissau Notizie. *Annual report. List of publications.*

PLANNED ACTIVITIES: Opening a new vocational centre in Guinea Bissau, Argentina, Albania and Ukraine.

COMMENTS: Undertakes activities in the Commonwealth of Independent States. Information activities related to the Commonwealth of Independent States.

ACTIVITIES IN DEVELOPING REGIONS: Present in developing regions. Active in 7 country(ies). Maintains local field presence. Works through local field partners. **Sustainable Development Actions:** Children/youth/family; Education/training/literacy; Health/sanitation/water; Rural development/agriculture; Sending volunteers/experts/technical assistance. **Regions:** Mexico and Central America; South America; West Africa.

INFORMATION AND EDUCATION ACTIVITIES: Topics: Education/training/literacy; Employment/unemployment; International relations/cooperation/development aid; Rural development/agriculture. **Activities:** Conferences/seminars/workshops/training activities; Exchanges/twinning/

linking; Formal education; Publishing/audiovisual materials/educational materials.

ITA2843

FEDERAZIONE ITALIANA DEI CLUB UNESCO

Casella Postale n° 1519, 7 Firenze, Italie.

Téléphone: 39 (55) 572676.

ITA2844

FEDERAZIONE ORGANISMI CRISTIANI DI SERVIZIO INTERNAZIONALE VOLONTARIO (FOCSIV) ♦ Fédération des Organismes Chrétiens de Service International Volontaire

Via Conservatorio, 1, 00186 Roma, Italie.

Téléphone: 39 (6) 6877796. *Fax:* 39 (6) 6872373. *Contact:* Luca Jahier, Président.

OBJECTIFS: Coordonner et représenter au niveau international les ONG d'inspiration chrétienne membres. Favoriser la collaboration entre des organismes en ce qui concerne l'information, l'éducation au développement, les projets dans le Sud, la formation, l'emploi et la réinsertion des volontaires.

INFORMATIONS GENERALES: *Création:* 1969. *Type d'organisation:* collectif. *Organisations membres:* 52. *Affiliée à:* EECOD (Belgique) - CIDSE (Belgique) - Conférence des Organisations Catholiques Internationales (France) - Forum (Allemagne). *Personnel/Total:* 22. *Salariés:* 10 dont: 1 dans les pays en développement. *Bénévoles:* 12. *Budget/Total 1993:* ECU 49473000 (US$ 57895000). *Sources financières:* Privé: 47%. Public: 53%.

PUBLICATIONS: *Périodiques:* Piccolo Pianeta - Volontari e Terzo Mondo. *Liste des publications.*

EVALUATION/RECHERCHE: Rapports d'évaluation disponibles. Entreprend des activités de recherche.

COMMENTAIRES: FOCSIV intervient dans les domaines de la santé, de l'agriculture, de l'éducation, de la production artisanale et de l'aide d'urgence en Afrique, en Asie et en Amérique Latine. Intervient dans la Communauté des Etats indépendants.

ACTIVITES DANS LES REGIONS EN DEVELOPPEMENT: Intervient dans 60 pays. Maintient une présence locale sur le terrain. Intervient par l'intermédiaire d'organisations locales partenaires.

ITA2845

FERRARA TERZO MUNDO (FTM)..

Corso Porta Po', 72/a, 44100 Ferrara, Italy.

Telephone: 39 (532) 205472.

ITA2846

FONDATION FRANCO VERGA

Via Anfiteatro 14, 20121 Milan, Italie.

Téléphone: 39 (2) 8693194. *Fax:* 39 (2) 86460052. *Contact:* Giampiero Bartolucci, Président.

OBJECTIFS: Favoriser l'insertion sociale et culturelle de émigrés et des réfugiés.

INFORMATIONS GENERALES: *Création:* 1978. *Personnel/Total:* 43. *Salariés:* 18. *Bénévoles:* 25. *Budget/Total 1993:* ECU 81000 (US$ 95000). *Sources financières:* Privé: 2%. Public: 98%.

PUBLICATIONS: *Périodiques:* "Incontro e Solidarietà" (4). *Liste des publications.*

ACTIVITES D'INFORMATION ET D'EDUCATION: Domaines: Droits de l'Homme/paix/conflits; Emploi/chômage; Relations internationales/coopération/aide au développement; Réfugiés/migrants/groupes ethniques; Secours d'urgence/réfugiés/aide humanitaire; Éducation/formation/alphabétisation. **Activités:** Conférences/séminaires/ateliers/activités de formation; Services d'information et de documentation/bases de données; Édition/documents audiovisuels/documents éducatifs; Éducation formelle.

ITA2847

FONDATION INTERNATIONALE E. BALZAN

Piazzetta V. Giordano 4, 20122 Milan, Italie.

Contact: Son Excellence, M. Cesidio Guazzaroni, Président.

ITA2848

FONDAZIONE BROWNSEA ♦ Brownsea Foundation

Via Burigozzo II, 20122 Milano, Italy.

Telephone: 39 (2) 58314760. *Contact:* Alberto Lucchesini, President.

OBJECTIVES: To promote self-development in Kenya in collaboration with the Kenya Scouts Association and run a community centre that carries out development projects in Kenya.

GENERAL INFORMATION: *Creation:* 1961. *Affiliated to:* CIPSI (Italy). *Personnel/Total:* 24. *Salaried:* 4 of which: 4 in developing countries. *Volunteers:* 20. *Budget/Total 1993:* ECU 150000 (US$ 176000). *Financial sources: Public:* 40%. *Self-financing:* 60%.

PUBLICATIONS: *Periodicals:* Marambee (6).

ACTIVITIES IN DEVELOPING REGIONS: Present in developing regions. Active in 1 country(ies). Maintains local field presence. Works through local field partners. **Sustainable Development Actions:** Children/youth/family; Food/famine; Health/sanitation/water; Rural development/agriculture. **Regions:** East Africa.

INFORMATION AND EDUCATION ACTIVITIES: Topics: Children/youth/family; Food/famine; Health/sanitation/water; Rural development/agriculture. **Activities:** Conferences/seminars/workshops/training activities; Formal education; Fund raising.

ITA2849

FONDAZIONE GIUSEPPE TOVINI ♦ Giuseppe Tovini Foundation

Via Martinengo da Barco 2, 25121 Brescia, Italy.

Telephone: 39 (30) 295737. *Fax:* 39 (30)3757498. *Contact:* Luciano Silveri, Secretary.

OBJECTIVES: To promote co-operation by undertaking development, information and educational activities.

GENERAL INFORMATION: *Creation:* 1957. *Affiliated to:* FOCSIV (Italy). *Personnel/Total:* 22. *Salaried:* 7. *Volunteers:* 15 of which: 5 in developing countries. *Budget/Total 1993:* ECU 1632000 (US$ 1910000). *Financial sources: Private:* 5%. *Public:* 95%.

ACTIVITIES IN DEVELOPING REGIONS: Active in 3 country(ies). Maintains local field presence. Works through local field partners. **Sustainable Development Actions:** Education/training/literacy; Health/sanitation/water; Rural development/agriculture. **Regions:** Central Africa; South America; South East Asia.

INFORMATION AND EDUCATION ACTIVITIES: Topics: International relations/cooperation/development aid. **Activities:** Conferences/seminars/workshops/training activities; Publishing/audiovisual materials/educational materials.

ITA2850

FONDAZIONE SIPEC

Via Collebeato, 26, 25127 Brescia, Italy.

Telephone: 39 (30) 306730. *Fax:* 39 (30) 380706.

ITA2851

FORUM DELLO SVILUPPO ♦ Development Forum

Palazzo Chiablese, Piazza S. Giovanni, 2, 10122 Torino, Italy.

Telephone: 39 (11) 501329. *Fax:* 39 (11) 503701.

ITA2852

FRATELLI DELL'UOMO ♦ Frères des Hommes

Via Varesina 214, 20156 Milano, Italie.

Téléphone: 39 (2) 33404091. *Fax:* 39 (2) 38009194. *Contact:* Adolfo Soldini, Président.

OBJECTIFS: Soutenir les initiatives des organisations populaires dans les pays en développement. Informer et sensibiliser l'opinion publique européenne aux problèmes de ces pays.

INFORMATIONS GENERALES: *Création:* 1969. *Affiliée à:* Frères des Hommes (France) - Coordinamento di Iniziative Popolari di Solidarietà Internazionale (Italie). *Personnel/Total:* 8. *Salariés:* 5. *Bénévoles:* 3. *Budget/Total 1993:* ECU 652000 (US$ 763000). *Sources financières: Privé:* 35%. *Public:* 65%.

PUBLICATIONS: *Périodiques:* Fratelli dell'Uomo (4). *Rapport annuel. Liste des publications.*

EVALUATION/RECHERCHE: Rapports d'évaluation disponibles.

ACTIVITES DANS LES REGIONS EN DEVELOPPEMENT: Intervient dans 8 pays. Intervient par l'intermédiaire d'organisations locales partenaires. **Actions de Développement durable:** Droits de l'Homme/paix/conflits; Démocratie/bonne gestion publique/création d'institutions/développement participatif; Développement rural/agriculture; Développement urbain/habitat; Enfants/jeunesse/famille; Petites entreprises/secteur informel/artisanat; Questions relatives aux femmes. **Régions:** Afrique centrale; Afrique de l'Ouest; Amérique du Sud; Asie du Sud-Est; Caraïbes; Mexique et Amerique centrale.

ACTIVITES D'INFORMATION ET D'EDUCATION: Domaines: Aliments/famine; Culture/tradition/religion; Droits de l'Homme/paix/conflits; Développement rural/agriculture; Développement urbain/habitat; Enfants/jeunesse/famille; Paix/conflits ethniques/armement/désarmement; Racisme/xénophobie/antisémitisme; Relations économiques internationales/commerce/dette/finances; Réfugiés/migrants/groupes ethniques. **Activités:** Campagnes d'information/expositions; Collecte de fonds; Conférences/séminaires/ateliers/activités de formation; Lobbying/plaidoyer; Services d'information et de documentation/bases de données; Édition/documents audiovisuels/documents éducatifs.

ITA2853

GRUPPO ABELE ♦ Groupe Abele

Via Giolitti 21, 10121 Torino, Italie.

Téléphone: 39 (11) 8395444. *Fax:* 39 (11) 8395577. *Contact:* Roberto Maurizio.

ITA2854

GRUPPO DI RICERCA SULLE TECNOLOGIE APPROPRIATE - CENTRO DI INFORMAZIONE NONVIOLENTA (GRTA-CIN) ♦

Appropriate Technologies Research Group - Non-violence Information Centre

Via D.Giovanni Verita 25 C.P. 78, 47023 Cesena (FO), Italy.

Telephone: 39 (547) 23018. *Contact:* Lonardo Belli.

ITA2855

GRUPPO DI VOLONTARIATO CIVILE (GVC) ♦ Groupe de volontariat civil

Villa Aldini, Via dell'Osservanza 35/2, 40136 Bologna, Italie.

Téléphone: 39 (51) 585604. *Fax:* 39 (51) 582225. *Contact:* Dr. Raffele Salinari, Président.

OBJECTIFS: Aider les pays en développement à améliorer leur situation sanitaire, agricole, technique et socio-éducative, par l'envoi de volontaires.

INFORMATIONS GENERALES: *Création:* 1975. *Affiliée à:* Coordinamento delle ONG per la Cooperazione Internazionale allo Sviluppo (Italie). *Personnel/Total:* 20. *Salariés:* 9. *Bénévoles:* 11 dont: 11 dans les pays en développement. *Budget/Total 1993:* ECU 3369000 (US$ 3943000). *Sources financières: Privé:* 10%. *Public:* 80%. *Autofinancement:* 10%.

PUBLICATIONS: *Rapport annuel. Liste des publications.*

EVALUATION/RECHERCHE: Rapports d'évaluation disponibles. Entreprend des activités de recherche.

COMMENTAIRES: Intervient dans la Communauté des Etats indépendants.

Voir : *Comment utiliser le répertoire*, page 11.

ACTIVITES DANS LES REGIONS EN DEVELOPPEMENT: Intervient directement dans les régions en développement. Intervient dans 15 pays. Maintient une présence locale sur le terrain. Intervient par l'intermédiaire d'organisations locales partenaires. **Actions de Développement durable:** Dette/finances/commerce; Développement rural/agriculture; Envoi de volontaires/experts/assistance technique; Questions relatives aux femmes; Santé/assainissement/eau; Secours d'urgence/réfugiés/aide humanitaire; Écologie/environnement/biodiversité. **Régions:** Afrique australe; Afrique centrale; Afrique de l'Est; Afrique de l'Ouest; Amérique du Sud; Asie de l'Est; Asie du Sud-Est; Mexique et Amerique centrale; Moyen-Orient.

ACTIVITES D'INFORMATION ET D'EDUCATION: Domaines: Développement rural/agriculture; Paix/conflits ethniques/armement/désarmement; Questions relatives aux femmes; Relations internationales/coopération/aide au développement; Santé/assainissement/eau; Secours d'urgence/réfugiés/aide humanitaire; Écologie/environnement/biodiversité. **Activités:** Campagnes d'information/expositions; Collecte de fonds; Conférences/séminaires/ateliers/activités de formation; Lobbying/plaidoyer; Radiodiffusion/manifestations culturelles; Services d'information et de documentation/bases de données; Édition/documents audiovisuels/documents éducatifs; Éducation formelle.

ITA2856

GRUPPO LAICI TERZO MONDO (LTM) ♦ Groupe de laïcs pour le Tiers monde

Via Marechiaro 42/46, 80123 Napoli, Italie.

Téléphone: 39 (81) 7691852.

ITA2857

GRUPPO MISSIONI ASMARA (GMA)

c/o Istituto Sacchieri, Via Luppia Alberi, 3, 35044 Montagnana (PD), Italie.

Téléphone: 39 (429) 800830. **Fax:** 39 (429) 804040. **Contact:** Vitali P. Vitale, Président.

OBJECTIFS: Promouvoir la solidarité entre les peuples, pour aider au développement démocratique dans les pays en voie de développement. Organiser un vaste réseau d'adoptions à distance en Eritrée. Assurer une formation scolaire et/ou professionnelle aux jeunes Eritréens.

INFORMATIONS GENERALES: Création: 1986. **Type d'organisation:** collectif. **Affiliée à:** Coordination des Initiatives Populaires de Solidarité internationale (Italie) -Coordination des Associations de Solidarité Internationale du Veneto (Italie). **Personnel/Total:** 35. **Bénévoles:** 35. **Budget/Total 1993:** ECU 815000 (US$ 953000). **Sources financières:** Privé: 98%. Public: 2%.

PUBLICATIONS: Périodiques: Notiziario GMA-PSC (4). Liste des publications.

ACTIVITES DANS LES REGIONS EN DEVELOPPEMENT: Intervient directement dans les régions en développement. Intervient dans 1 pays. Maintient une présence locale sur le terrain. Intervient par l'intermédiaire d'organisations locales partenaires. **Actions de Développement durable:** Aliments/famine; Enfants/jeunesse/famille; Questions relatives aux femmes; Secours d'urgence/réfugiés/aide humanitaire; Éducation/formation/alphabétisation. **Régions:** Afrique de l'Est.

ACTIVITES D'INFORMATION ET D'EDUCATION: Domaines: Aliments/famine; Culture/tradition/religion; Droits de l'Homme/paix/conflits; Emploi/chômage; Enfants/jeunesse/famille; Paix/conflits ethniques/armement/désarmement; Pauvreté/conditions de vie; Questions relatives aux femmes; Racisme/xénophobie/antisémitisme; Relations internationales/coopération/aide au développement; Relations économiques internationales/commerce/dette/finances; Santé/assainissement/eau; Secours d'urgence/réfugiés/aide humanitaire; Éducation/formation/alphabétisation. **Activités:** Campagnes d'information/expositions; Collecte de fonds; Conférences/séminaires/ateliers/activités de formation; Services d'information et de documentation/bases de données; Édition/documents audiovisuels/documents éducatifs; Éducation formelle.

ITA2858

GRUPPO PER LE RELAZIONI TRANSCULTURALI (GRT) ♦
Groupe pour les relations transculturelles

Via Borsi, 5, 20143 Milano, Italie.

Téléphone: 39 (2) 89400371. **Fax:** 39 (2) 89407274. **Contact:** Loris Panzeri, Président.

OBJECTIFS: Réaliser des projets socio-sanitaires dans les pays en voie de développement. Former des volontaires. Sensibiliser à la solidarité internationale et favoriser de meilleures relations interculturelles.

INFORMATIONS GENERALES: Création: 1968. **Affiliée à:** Coordinamento delle Organizzazioni non governative per la Cooperazione allo Ssviluppo (Italie). **Personnel/Total:** 28. Salariés: 8 dont: 6 dans les pays en développement. Bénévoles: 20 dont: 5 dans les pays en développement. **Budget/Total 1993:** ECU 700000 (US$ 819000). **Sources financières:** Privé: 25%. Public: 50%. Autofinancement: 25%.

PUBLICATIONS: Liste des publications.

EVALUATION/RECHERCHE: Rapports d'évaluation disponibles. Entreprend des activités de recherche.

ACTIVITES DANS LES REGIONS EN DEVELOPPEMENT: Intervient directement dans les régions en développement. Intervient dans 2 pays. Maintient une présence locale sur le terrain. Intervient par l'intermédiaire d'organisations locales partenaires. **Actions de Développement durable:** Enfants/jeunesse/famille; Envoi de volontaires/experts/assistance technique; Questions relatives aux femmes; Santé/assainissement/eau; Éducation/formation/alphabétisation. **Régions:** Mexique et Amerique centrale.

ACTIVITES D'INFORMATION ET D'EDUCATION: Domaines: Culture/tradition/religion; Enfants/jeunesse/famille; Pauvreté/conditions de vie; Questions relatives aux femmes; Racisme/xénophobie/antisémitisme; Relations internationales/coopération/aide au développement; Santé/assainissement/eau; Éducation/formation/alphabétisation. **Activités:** Campagnes d'information/expositions; Collecte de fonds; Conférences/séminaires/ateliers/activités de formation; Édition/documents audiovisuels/documents éducatifs.

ITA2859

INSEDIAMENTI UMANI E TERRITORIO (ITER) ♦ Human Settlements and Environment

Via Pacini 28, 20131 Milano, Italy.

Telephone: 39 (2) 230676.

ITA2860

INTER PRESS SERVICE (IPS)

Via Panisperna 207, 00184 Roma, Italy.

Telephone: 39 (6) 485692. **Fax:** 39 (6) 4817877. **E-mail:** IPSROM@gn.apc.org. **Contact:** Roberto Savio, Director General.

OBJECTIVES: To foster communication between southern countries. To disseminate information in the North about the South. To promote sustainable development and democracy.

GENERAL INFORMATION: Creation: 1964. **Type of organisation:** association of NGOs. **Member organisations:** 22. **Personnel/Total:** 387. Salaried: 387 of which: 296 in developing countries. **Budget/Total 1993:** ECU 9874000 (US$ 11555000). **Financial sources:** Private: 40%. Public: 35%. Self-financing: 25%.

PUBLICATIONS: Periodicals: IPS Daily News Service by Satellite (250) - IPS Daily Journal "Terra Viva" (250) - IPS UN Conference Newspaper "Terra Viva" (25). Annual report.

EVALUATION/RESEARCH: Evaluation reports available. Undertakes research activities.

COMMENTS: Undertakes activities in the Commonwealth of Independent States. Information activities related to the Commonwealth of Independent States.

ACTIVITIES IN DEVELOPING REGIONS: Present in developing regions. Active in 67 country(ies). Maintains local field presence. Works through local field partners. **Sustainable Development Actions:** Children/youth/family; Debt/finance/trade; Democracy/good governance/institution building/participatory development; Ecology/environment/biodiversity; Education/training/literacy; Emergency relief/refugees/humanitarian assistance; Energy/transport; Food/famine; Gender issues/women; Health/sanitation/water; Human rights/peace/conflicts; Population/family

See: *How to Use the Directory,* page 11.

planning/demography; Rural development/agriculture; Sending volunteers/experts/technical assistance; Small enterprises/informal sector/handicrafts; Urban development/habitat. **Regions:** Caribbean; Central Africa; Central Asia and South Asia; East Africa; East Asia; Mexico and Central America; Middle East; North Africa; Oceania; South America; South East Asia; Southern Africa; West Africa.

INFORMATION AND EDUCATION ACTIVITIES: Topics: Children/youth/family; Culture/tradition/religion; Ecology/environment/biodiversity; Education/training/literacy; Emergency relief/refugees/humanitarian assistance; Employment/unemployment; Food/famine; Gender issues/women; Health/sanitation/water; Human rights/peace/conflicts; International economic relations/trade/debt/finance; International relations/cooperation/development aid; Other; Peace/ethnic conflicts/armament/disarmament; Population/family planning/demography; Poverty/living conditions; Racism/xenophobia/antisemitism; Refugees/migrants/ethnic groups; Rural development/agriculture; Urban development/habitat. **Activities:** Broadcasting/cultural events; Conferences/seminars/workshops/training activities; Information and documentation services/data bases; Information campaigns/exhibitions; Networking/electronic telecommunications; Publishing/audiovisual materials/educational materials.

ITA2861

INTERNATIONAL DOCUMENTATION AND COMMUNICATION CENTRE (IDOC)

Via S. Maria dell'Anima 30, 00186 Roma, Italy.

Telephone: 39 (6) 6868332. *Fax:* 39 (6) 6832766. *E-mail:* idoc@gn.apc.org. *Contact:* Heinz Hunke, Executive Director.

OBJECTIVES: To collect and disseminate information and documentation on North-South relations with a special focus on Africa, in the areas of development, trade, debt, human rights, information and communication systems and labour issues.

GENERAL INFORMATION: *Creation:* 1965. *Personnel/Total:* 6. *Salaried:* 6. *Budget/Total 1993:* ECU 190 (US$ 220). *Financial sources:* Private: 90%. Self-financing: 10%.

PUBLICATIONS: *Periodicals:* (4) - Africa Dossiers (5). *Annual report. List of publications.*

EVALUATION/RESEARCH: Undertakes research activities.

INFORMATION AND EDUCATION ACTIVITIES: Topics: Culture/tradition/religion; Ecology/environment/biodiversity; Gender issues/women; Human rights/peace/conflicts; International economic relations/trade/debt/finance; Other; Peace/ethnic conflicts/armament/disarmament; Racism/xenophobia/antisemitism; Refugees/migrants/ethnic groups. **Activities:** Conferences/seminars/workshops/training activities; Information and documentation services/data bases; Publishing/audiovisual materials/educational materials.

ITA2862

INTERNATIONAL JURIDICAL ORGANIZATION FOR ENVIRONMENT AND DEVELOPMENT (IJO)

Via Barberini 3, 00187 Roma, Italy.

Telephone: 39 (6) 4742117. *Fax:* 39 (6) 4745779. *Contact:* Mario Guttieres, President.

OBJECTIVES: To promote and study the legal aspects of environmental protection and the development of the international community.

GENERAL INFORMATION: *Creation:* 1964. *Affiliated to:* CONGO (Switzerland) - Centre for our Common Future (Switzerland). *Personnel/Total:* 10. *Salaried:* 6. *Volunteers:* 4. *Budget/Total 1993:* ECU 119000 (US$ 139000). *Financial sources:* Private: 20%. Self-financing: 80%.

PUBLICATIONS: *Periodicals:* IJO Newsletter (4). *Annual report. List of publications.*

EVALUATION/RESEARCH: Undertakes research activities.

COMMENTS: Undertakes activities in the Commonwealth of Independent States. Information activities related to the Commonwealth of Independent States.

ACTIVITIES IN DEVELOPING REGIONS: Present in developing regions. Works through local field partners. **Sustainable Development Actions:** Ecology/environment/biodiversity. **Regions:** Middle East; North Africa; Southern Africa; West Africa.

INFORMATION AND EDUCATION ACTIVITIES: Topics: Ecology/environment/biodiversity; Gender issues/women; Human rights/peace/conflicts; International relations/cooperation/development aid. **Activities:** Conferences/seminars/workshops/training activities; Exchanges/twinning/linking; Information and documentation services/data bases; Lobbying/advocacy; Publishing/audiovisual materials/educational materials.

ITA2863

ISES - PROGETTO MARCO POLO ♦ Italian Senior Expert Service - Marco Polo Project

Via Carena 3, 10144 Torino, Italy.

Telephone: 39 (11) 481677. *Contact:* Prof. Abele Giovanni Rangoni.

ITA2864

ISIS INTERNATIONAL WOMEN'S INFORMATION AND COMMUNICATION SERVICE

Via San Saba 5, 00153 Roma, Italy.

Telephone: 39 (6) 5746479.

ITA2865

ISPA NORD/SUD

14 via Cesare Correnti, 20123 Milano, Italie.

Téléphone: 39 (2) 8057789.

ITA2866

ISTITUTO COOPERAZIONE ECONOMICA INTERNAZIONALE (ICEI) ♦ Institute for International Economic Co-operation

Via de Amicis, 17, 20123 Milano, Italy.

Telephone: 39 (2) 58107673. *Fax:* 39 (2) 58107543. *E-mail:* PN:ICEI.. *Contact:* Lucia Lanzanova, Director.

OBJECTIVES: To raise public awareness of international economic co-operation and politics. To promote professional debate and research in matters of international co-operation. To support development projects in Third World countries.

GENERAL INFORMATION: *Creation:* 1977. *Affiliated to:* COCIS (Italy). *Personnel/Total:* 13. *Salaried:* 3. *Volunteers:* 10 of which: 1 in developing countries. *Budget/Total 1993:* ECU 434000 (US$ 508000). *Financial sources:* Private: 20%. Public: 70%. Self-financing: 10%.

PUBLICATIONS: *Periodicals:* (4). *List of publications.*

EVALUATION/RESEARCH: Undertakes research activities.

PLANNED ACTIVITIES: Undertaking an educational campaign on North-South trade and economic interdependence.

COMMENTS: Information activities related to the Commonwealth of Independent States.

INFORMATION AND EDUCATION ACTIVITIES: Topics: Culture/tradition/religion; Ecology/environment/biodiversity; Emergency relief/refugees/humanitarian assistance; Gender issues/women; Human rights/peace/conflicts; International economic relations/trade/debt/finance; International relations/cooperation/development aid; Peace/ethnic conflicts/armament/disarmament; Population/family planning/demography; Poverty/living conditions; Racism/xenophobia/antisemitism; Refugees/migrants/ethnic groups. **Activities:** Conferences/seminars/workshops/training activities; Information and documentation services/data bases; Information campaigns/exhibitions; Networking/electronic telecommunications; Publishing/audiovisual materials/educational materials.

ITA2867

ISTITUTO PACE SVILUPPO INNOVAZIONE (IPSIA-ACLI) ♦ Institut pour la paix, le développement et l'innovation

Via Marcora 18/20, 00153 Roma, Italie.

Téléphone: 39 (6) 58401. *Contact:* Aldo de Matteo, Président.

Voir : *Comment utiliser le répertoire,* page 11.

ITA2868

ISTITUTO PER LA COOPERAZIONE UNIVERSITARIA (ICU) ♦
Institute for University Co-operation

Viale G. Rossini 26, 00198 Roma, Italy.

Telephone: 39 (6) 85300722. **Fax:** 39 (6) 8554646. **Contact:** Raffaello Cortesini, President.

OBJECTIVES: To undertake development co-operation programmes aimed at strengthening the local participation of developing countries. To foster a culture of solidarity and international co-operation, particularly within the university environment of industrialized nations.

GENERAL INFORMATION: Creation: 1966. **Affiliated to:** ICU-CINDA-CICSEULA - EADI (Switzerland). **Personnel/Total:** 27. Salaried: 22 of which: 8 in developing countries. Volunteers: 5 of which: 2 in developing countries. **Budget/Total 1993:** ECU 4073000 (US$ 4766000). **Financial sources:** Private: 10%. Public: 85%. Self-financing: 5%.

PUBLICATIONS: Periodicals: SIPE (12) - Educazione e Sviluppo (3). List of publications.

EVALUATION/RESEARCH: Undertakes research activities.

PLANNED ACTIVITIES: Undertaking emergency aid programmes in Albania, Armenia, Peru. Planning congresses on Mediterranean development, youth employment and development co-operation.

COMMENTS: Undertakes activities in the Commonwealth of Independent States.

ACTIVITIES IN DEVELOPING REGIONS: Present in developing regions. Maintains local field presence. Works through local field partners. **Sustainable Development Actions:** Children/youth/family; Democracy/good governance/institution building/participatory development; Ecology/environment/biodiversity; Education/training/literacy; Emergency relief/refugees/humanitarian assistance; Gender issues/women; Health/sanitation/water; Rural development/agriculture; Sending volunteers/experts/technical assistance. **Regions:** Central Africa; Central Asia and South Asia; East Africa; East Asia; Mexico and Central America; North Africa; South America; South East Asia.

INFORMATION AND EDUCATION ACTIVITIES: Topics: Children/youth/family; Culture/tradition/religion; Ecology/environment/biodiversity; Education/training/literacy; Emergency relief/refugees/humanitarian assistance; Employment/unemployment; Gender issues/women; Health/sanitation/water; Human rights/peace/conflicts; International relations/cooperation/development aid; Rural development/agriculture. **Activities:** Conferences/seminars/workshops/training activities; Formal education; Fund raising; Information and documentation services/data bases; Information campaigns/exhibitions; Publishing/audiovisual materials/educational materials.

ITA2869

ISTITUTO SINDACALE PER LA COOPERAZIONE CON I PAESI IN VIA DI SVILUPPO (ISCOS) ♦ Institut syndical pour la coopération au développement

Via Boncompagni 19, 00187 Roma, Italie.

Téléphone: 39 (6) 4817100. **Fax:** 39 (6) 4821995. **Contact:** Pietro Merli Brandini, Président.

ITA2870

ITALIAN UNITED NATIONS ASSOCIATION (SIOI)

Via San Marco 3, 00186 Roma, Italy.

Telephone: 39 (6) 6789102.

ITA2871

LEGA ITALIANA PER I DIRITTI E LA LIBERAZIONE DEI POPOLI ♦ Ligue italienne pour les droits et la libération des peuples

Via della Dogana Vecchia, 5, 00186 Roma, Italie.

Téléphone: 39 (6) 6864640. **Fax:** 39 (2) 6864640. **Contact:** Luciano Ardesi, Secrétaire national.

ITA2872

LEGAMBIENTE ♦ Environmental League

Via Salaria 280, 00199 Rome, Italy.

Telephone: 39 (6) 8841552. **Fax:** 39 (6) 8552976. **Contact:** Giovanna Melandri, International Program Director.

ITA2873

MANI TESE '76 ♦ Mains tendues '76

Via Cavenaghi 4, 20149 Milano, Italie.

Téléphone: 39 (2) 48008617. **Fax:** 39 (2) 4812296. **Contact:** Giovanni Mozzi, Président.

OBJECTIFS: Connaître et faire connaître la réalité des pays en développement par des initiatives culturelles et par la sensibilisation de l'opinion publique. Réaliser des projets de promotion humaine et favoriser l'autosuffisance alimentaire des populations dans les pays en développement.

INFORMATIONS GENERALES: Création: 1964. **Affiliée à:** ACORD (Royaume-Uni) - EUROSTEP - CIPEO (Italie) - Forum des ONG au Cambodge -Working Group for the Horn of Affrica. **Personnel/Total:** 460. Salariés: 10. Bénévoles: 450. **Budget/Total 1993:** ECU 3034000 (US$ 3550000). **Sources financières:** Privé: 43%. Public: 35%. Autofinancement: 22%.

PUBLICATIONS: Périodiques: Mani Tese (12). Rapport annuel. Liste des publications.

EVALUATION/RECHERCHE: Rapports d'évaluation disponibles. Entreprend des activités de recherche.

PREVISIONS D'ACTIVITES: Campagne contre le travail des mineurs. Campagne sur le thème du Sommet Mondial sur le Développement Social.

ACTIVITES DANS LES REGIONS EN DEVELOPPEMENT: Intervient par l'intermédiaire d'organisations locales partenaires. **Actions de Développement durable:** Droits de l'Homme/paix/conflits; Démocratie/bonne gestion publique/création d'institutions/développement participatif; Développement rural/agriculture; Développement urbain/habitat; Enfants/jeunesse/famille; Envoi de volontaires/experts/assistance technique; Petites entreprises/secteur informel/artisanat; Questions relatives aux femmes; Santé/assainissement/eau; Secours d'urgence/réfugiés/aide humanitaire; Écologie/environnement/biodiversité; Éducation/formation/alphabétisation. **Régions:** Afrique australe; Afrique centrale; Afrique de l'Est; Afrique de l'Ouest; Amérique du Sud; Asie centrale et Asie du Sud; Asie du Sud-Est; Caraïbes; Mexique et Amerique centrale.

ACTIVITES D'INFORMATION ET D'EDUCATION: Domaines: Aliments/famine; Culture/tradition/religion; Droits de l'Homme/paix/conflits; Développement rural/agriculture; Développement urbain/habitat; Enfants/jeunesse/famille; Paix/conflits ethniques/armement/désarmement; Pauvreté/conditions de vie; Questions relatives aux femmes; Racisme/xénophobie/antisémitisme; Relations internationales/coopération/aide au développement; Relations économiques internationales/commerce/dette/finances; Réfugiés/migrants/groupes ethniques; Santé/assainissement/eau; Secours d'urgence/réfugiés/aide humanitaire; Écologie/environnement/biodiversité; Éducation/formation/alphabétisation. **Activités:** Campagnes d'information/expositions; Collecte de fonds; Conférences/séminaires/ateliers/activités de formation; Lobbying/plaidoyer; Services d'information et de documentation/bases de données; Édition/documents audiovisuels/documents éducatifs.

ITA2874

MEDICUS MUNDI, ITALIA (MMIt)

Via Martinengo da Barco, 6/a, 25121 Brescia, Italy.

Telephone: 39 (30) 3752517. **Fax:** 39 (30) 43266. **Contact:** Enrico Cavalli, President.

OBJECTIVES: To promote co-operation in social and health programmes in Africa with medical physicians and provide training.

GENERAL INFORMATION: Creation: 1971. **Affiliated to:** Medicus Mundi International (Belgium) - CIPSI (Italy). **Personnel/Total:** 17. Salaried: 2. Volunteers: 15 of which: 5 in developing countries. **Budget/Total 1993:** ECU 953000 (US$ 1115000). **Financial sources:** Private: 23%. Public: 47%. Self-financing: 29%.

See: *How to Use the Directory*, page 11.

PUBLICATIONS: *Periodicals:* Bollettino Della Medicus Mundi Italia (3).

ACTIVITIES IN DEVELOPING REGIONS: Present in developing regions. Active in 5 country(ies). Works through local field partners. **Sustainable Development Actions:** Children/youth/family; Education/training/literacy; Emergency relief/refugees/humanitarian assistance; Health/sanitation/water; Sending volunteers/experts/technical assistance. **Regions:** Central Africa; East Africa; West Africa.

INFORMATION AND EDUCATION ACTIVITIES: Topics: Emergency relief/refugees/humanitarian assistance; Health/sanitation/water. Activities: Conferences/seminars/workshops/training activities; Fund raising.

ITA2875
MIGRANTES

17, Via delle Zoccolette, 00186 Rome, Italie.

Contact: Rev. Msgr. A. Cantisani, Président.

ITA2876

MOVIMENTO APOSTOLICO CIECHI (MAC) ♦ Mouvement apostolique pour les aveugles

Via Porta Angelica 63, 00139 Roma, Italie.

Téléphone: 39 (6) 6561977.

ITA2877

MOVIMENTO COOPERAZIONE E SVILUPPO

Via Stefano Gallina 42, 12030 Marene (CN), Italy.

Telephone: 39 (172) 742314. *Fax:* 39 (172) 742818.

OBJECTIVES: To support development projects and voluntary services in developing countries. To inform and educate the Italian public about development co-operation.

GENERAL INFORMATION: *Creation:* 1987. *Affiliated to:* CIPSI (Italy). *Personnel/Total:* 12. *Volunteers:* 12. *Budget/Total 1993:* ECU 26000 (US$ 30000). *Financial sources:* Public: 10%. Self-financing: 90%.

EVALUATION/RESEARCH: Evaluation reports available.

PLANNED ACTIVITIES: The organization is planning an integrated development project focusing on agriculture, health and education in Tanzania.

ACTIVITIES IN DEVELOPING REGIONS: Active in 2 country(ies). Works through local field partners. **Sustainable Development Actions:** Children/youth/family; Emergency relief/refugees/humanitarian assistance; Health/sanitation/water; Rural development/agriculture. **Regions:** East Africa.

ITA2878

MOVIMENTO DI COOPERAZIONE EDUCATIVA (MCE)

Via dei Piceni, 16, 00185 Roma, Italy.

Telephone: 39 (6) 4457228.

ITA2879

MOVIMENTO E AZIONE DEI GESUITI ITALIANI PER LO SVILUPPO (MAGIS) ♦ Movement and Action of Italian Jesuits for Development

c/o Residenza Gesuiti S. Fedele, Piazza S. Fedele, 4, 20121 Milano, Italy.

Telephone: 39 (2) 86352226 . *Fax:* 39 (2) 86352224. *Contact:* Arch. Rosario Bomdì, President.

OBJECTIVES: To co-ordinate the development co-operation activities related to the "Society of Jesus." To carry out projects of human, cultural, socio-economic development in co-operation with local social bodies. To organise educational and training programmes in developing countries.

GENERAL INFORMATION: *Creation:* 1988. *Type of organisation:* coordinating body. *Member organisations:* 17. *Affiliated to:* FOC-SIV (Italy). *Personnel/Total:* 7. *Volunteers:* 7. *Budget/Total 1993:* ECU 1176000 (US$ 1377000). *Financial sources:* Private: 80%. Public: 19%. Self-financing: 1%.

PUBLICATIONS: *Periodicals:* Popoli (10) - Gesuiti Italiani Missionari (4).

COMMENTS: Undertakes activities in the Commonwealth of Independent States.

ACTIVITIES IN DEVELOPING REGIONS: Present in developing regions. Active in 15 country(ies). Maintains local field presence. Works through local field partners. **Sustainable Development Actions:** Children/youth/family; Democracy/good governance/institution building/participatory development; Education/training/literacy; Emergency relief/refugees/humanitarian assistance; Energy/transport; Food/famine; Health/sanitation/water; Human rights/peace/conflicts; Population/family planning/demography; Rural development/agriculture; Sending volunteers/experts/technical assistance; Urban development/habitat. **Regions:** Central Asia and South Asia; East Africa; South America; Southern Africa.

INFORMATION AND EDUCATION ACTIVITIES: Topics: Children/youth/family; Culture/tradition/religion; Education/training/literacy; Emergency relief/refugees/humanitarian assistance; Employment/unemployment; Food/famine; Health/sanitation/water; Poverty/living conditions; Refugees/migrants/ethnic groups; Rural development/agriculture; Urban development/habitat. **Activities:** Fund raising.

ITA2880

MOVIMENTO LAICI AMERICA LATINA (MLAL) ♦ Mouvement laïque pour l'Amérique latine

San Domenico, 11, 37122 Verona, Italie.

Téléphone: 39 (45) 8003538. *Fax:* 39 (45) 8000930. *Contact:* Anna Rosa Fioretta.

OBJECTIFS: Promouvoir des projets de coopération et organiser des campagnes de solidarité en Italie.

INFORMATIONS GENERALES: *Création:* 1966. *Affiliée à:* FOC-SIV (Italie). *Personnel/Total:* 56. *Salariés:* 41 dont: 38 dans les pays en développement. *Bénévoles:* 15 dont: 15 dans les pays en développement. *Budget/Total 1993:* ECU 3801000 (US$ 4448000). *Sources financières:* Privé: 10%. Public: 90%.

PUBLICATIONS: *Périodiques:* Lettera agli Amici (6). *Liste des publications.*

EVALUATION/RECHERCHE: Rapports d'évaluation disponibles.

ACTIVITES DANS LES REGIONS EN DEVELOPPEMENT: Intervient directement dans les régions en développement. Maintient une présence locale sur le terrain. Intervient par l'intermédiaire d'organisations locales partenaires. **Actions de Développement durable:** Droits de l'Homme/paix/conflits; Démocratie/bonne gestion publique/création d'institutions/développement participatif; Développement rural/agriculture; Développement urbain/habitat; Enfants/jeunesse/famille; Envoi de volontaires/experts/assistance technique; Questions relatives aux femmes; Santé/assainissement/eau; Écologie/environnement/biodiversité; Éducation/formation/alphabétisation. **Régions:** Amérique du Sud.

ACTIVITES D'INFORMATION ET D'EDUCATION: Domaines: Droits de l'Homme/paix/conflits; Développement rural/agriculture; Enfants/jeunesse/famille; Questions relatives aux femmes; Racisme/xénophobie/antisémitisme; Relations internationales/coopération/aide au développement; Relations économiques internationales/commerce/dette/finances; Réfugiés/migrants/groupes ethniques; Santé/assainissement/eau; Écologie/environnement/biodiversité; Éducation/formation/alphabétisation. **Activités:** Collecte de fonds; Conférences/séminaires/ateliers/activités de formation; Services d'information et de documentation/bases de données; Édition/documents audiovisuels/documents éducatifs.

ITA2881

MOVIMENTO LIBERAZIONE E SVILUPPO (MOLISV) ♦ Mouvement pour la libération et le développement

Piazza Albania 10, 00153 Roma, Italie.

Téléphone: 39 (6) 57300330. *Fax:* 39 (6) 5744869. *Contact:* Claudio Bernabucci, Président.

OBJECTIFS: Promouvoir et réaliser des actions de lobbying pour adapter le plus possible la législation sur la coopération au développement aux

Voir : *Comment utiliser le répertoire,* page 11.

besoins des pays du Tiers-Monde. Sensibiliser et informer le public en matière de développement. Réaliser des actions basées sur la solidarité et la participation populaire.

INFORMATIONS GENERALES: *Création:* 1971. *Affiliée à:* COCIS - Wide - Eurostep - Grupo Sur - Sanam - CREAL. *Personnel/Total:* 45. *Salariés:* 45 dont: 30 dans les pays en développement. *Budget/Total 1993:* ECU 3258000 (US$ 3812000). *Sources financières:* Privé: 5%. *Public:* 85%. *Autofinancement:* 10%.

PUBLICATIONS: *Liste des publications.*

PREVISIONS D'ACTIVITES: Activités d'information, de sensibilisation et solidarité sur le thème "Gens âgés et développement" avec des organisations syndicales de retraités.

COMMENTAIRES: Intervient dans la Communauté des Etats indépendants. Activités d'information concernant la Communauté des Etats indépendants.

ACTIVITES DANS LES REGIONS EN DEVELOPPEMENT: Intervient directement dans les régions en développement. Maintient une présence locale sur le terrain. Intervient par l'intermédiaire d'organisations locales partenaires. **Actions de Développement durable:** Aliments/famine; Droits de l'Homme/paix/conflits; Démocratie/bonne gestion publique/création d'institutions/développement participatif; Développement rural/agriculture; Envoi de volontaires/experts/assistance technique; Petites entreprises/secteur informel/artisanat; Questions relatives aux femmes; Santé/assainissement/eau; Secours d'urgence/réfugiés/aide humanitaire; Écologie/environnement/biodiversité; Éducation/formation/alphabétisation. **Régions:** Afrique australe; Amérique du Sud; Caraïbes; Mexique et Amerique centrale.

ACTIVITES D'INFORMATION ET D'EDUCATION: Domaines: Droits de l'Homme/paix/conflits; Développement rural/agriculture; Population/planning familial/démographie; Questions relatives aux femmes; Réfugiés/migrants/groupes ethniques; Santé/assainissement/eau; Écologie/environnement/biodiversité. **Activités:** Campagnes d'information/expositions; Collecte de fonds; Conférences/séminaires/ateliers/activités de formation; Lobbying/plaidoyer; Radiodiffusion/manifestations culturelles; Réseaux/télécommunications électroniques; Édition/documents audiovisuels/documents éducatifs.

ITA2882

MOVIMENTO PER L'AUTOSVILUPPO, L'INTERSCAMBIO E LA SOLIDARIETA' (MAIS)

Via Saluzzo, 23, 10125 Torino, Italy.

Telephone: 39 (11) 655737. *Fax:* 39 (11) 655959. *Contact:* Chiaffredo Olivero, President.

OBJECTIVES: To support the self-development of developing countries. To raise awareness in Italy about development, international relations and immigration. To support the exchange of knowledge and activities between organizations in developing and developed countries, especially those working on children's and rural issues.

GENERAL INFORMATION: *Creation:* 1990. *Affiliated to:* COCIS (Italy). *Personnel/Total:* 14. *Salaried:* 8 of which: 4 in developing countries. *Volunteers:* 6 of which: 2 in developing countries. *Budget/Total 1993:* ECU 299000 (US$ 349000). *Financial sources:* Private: 31%. *Public:* 58%. *Self-financing:* 11%.

PUBLICATIONS: *List of publications.*

EVALUATION/RESEARCH: Evaluation reports available.

ACTIVITIES IN DEVELOPING REGIONS: Active in 3 country(ies). Maintains local field presence. Works through local field partners. **Sustainable Development Actions:** Children/youth/family; Rural development/agriculture; Sending volunteers/experts/technical assistance. **Regions:** Mexico and Central America; South America.

INFORMATION AND EDUCATION ACTIVITIES: Topics: Children/youth/family; International relations/cooperation/development aid; Refugees/migrants/ethnic groups; Rural development/agriculture. **Activities:** Conferences/seminars/workshops/training activities; Fund raising; Information and documentation services/data bases; Information campaigns/exhibitions; Lobbying/advocacy; Publishing/audiovisual materials/educational materials.

ITA2883

MOVIMENTO PER LA COOPERAZIONE INTERNAZIONALE (MOCI) ♦ Mouvement pour la Coopération Internationale

Via Pio XI, Tr. Putorti 18, 89133 Reggio Calabria, Italie.

Téléphone: 39 (965) 331329. *Fax:* 39 (965) 331329. *Contact:* Santo Caserta, Président.

OBJECTIFS: Organiser, en Italie, des activités d'information et d'éducation au développement. Accueillir des immigrés en provenance de pays en voie de développement. Apporter une aide aux pays en développement.

INFORMATIONS GENERALES: *Création:* 1983. *Affiliée à:* FOCSIV. *Personnel/Total:* 20. *Salariés:* 6 dont: 6 dans les pays en développement. *Bénévoles:* 14 dont: 4 dans les pays en développement. *Budget/Total 1993:* ECU 227000 (US$ 266000). *Sources financières:* Privé: 11%. *Public:* 35%. *Autofinancement:* 54%.

PUBLICATIONS: *Périodiques:* Moci Mondialita (12).

ACTIVITES DANS LES REGIONS EN DEVELOPPEMENT: Intervient directement dans les régions en développement. Intervient dans 1 pays. Maintient une présence locale sur le terrain. **Actions de Développement durable:** Envoi de volontaires/experts/assistance technique; Questions relatives aux femmes; Éducation/formation/alphabétisation. **Régions:** Afrique centrale.

ACTIVITES D'INFORMATION ET D'EDUCATION: Domaines: Culture/tradition/religion; Droits de l'Homme/paix/conflits; Paix/conflits ethniques/armement/désarmement; Pauvreté/conditions de vie; Racisme/xénophobie/antisémitisme; Relations internationales/coopération/aide au développement; Réfugiés/migrants/groupes ethniques; Écologie/environnement/biodiversité; Éducation/formation/alphabétisation. **Activités:** Conférences/séminaires/ateliers/activités de formation; Échanges/parrainage/jumelage; Éducation formelle.

ITA2884

MOVIMENTO PER LA LOTTA CONTRO LA FAME NEL MONDO ♦ Mouvement pour la lutte contre la faim dans le monde

Via Cavour 73, 22075 Lodi (Milano), Italie.

Téléphone: 39 (371) 420766. *Fax:* 39 (371) 420766. *Contact:* Aldo Garzia, Président.

OBJECTIFS: Promouvoir, grâce à l'envoi de volontaires, le développement des pays du Tiers monde, dans les domaines de la santé, de la nutrition et de l'éducation.

INFORMATIONS GENERALES: *Création:* 1965. *Personnel/Total:* 4. *Salariés:* 1 dont: 1 dans les pays en développement. *Bénévoles:* 3 dont: 1 dans les pays en développement. *Budget/Total 1993:* ECU 272000 (US$ 318000). *Sources financières:* Privé: 54%. *Public:* 36%. *Autofinancement:* 10%.

PUBLICATIONS: *Périodiques:* Circolare informativa (4). *Rapport annuel.* Liste des publications.

EVALUATION/RECHERCHE: Rapports d'évaluation disponibles.

ACTIVITES DANS LES REGIONS EN DEVELOPPEMENT: Intervient directement dans les régions en développement. Intervient dans 4 pays. Maintient une présence locale sur le terrain. Intervient par l'intermédiaire d'organisations locales partenaires. **Actions de Développement durable:** Développement rural/agriculture; Enfants/jeunesse/famille; Santé/assainissement/eau. **Régions:** Afrique australe; Afrique centrale; Afrique de l'Ouest.

ITA2885

MOVIMENTO SVILUPPO E PACE (MSP) ♦ Mouvement Développement et Paix

Via Saluzzo 58, 10128 Torino, Italie.

Téléphone: 39 (11) 655866. *Fax:* 39 (11) 6698096. *Contact:* Dr. Pierre Monkam, Vice-Président.

OBJECTIFS: Eduquer et informer l'opinion italienne sur les problèmes des pays en développement. Soutenir la réalisation de projets de développement dans les pays en développement et les pays de l'Est.

See: *How to Use the Directory,* page 11.

INFORMATIONS GENERALES: *Création:* 1968. *Affiliée à:* Coordinamento di Iniziative Popolari di Solidarietà Internazionale (Italie) -Rete Educazione Allo Sviluppo (Italie) - Comitato oltre il Razzismo (Italie). *Personnel/Total:* 76. *Salariés:* 6 dont: 2 dans les pays en développement. *Bénévoles:* 70 dont: 4 dans les pays en développement. *Budget/Total 1993:* ECU 2151000 (US$ 2518000). *Sources financières:* Privé: 30%. *Public:* 60%. *Autofinancement:* 10%.

PUBLICATIONS: *Périodiques:* Terzo Mondo Informzioni (12). *Liste des publications.*

COMMENTAIRES: Intervient dans la Communauté des Etats indépendants.

ACTIVITES DANS LES REGIONS EN DEVELOPPEMENT: Intervient dans 30 pays. Intervient par l'intermédiaire d'organisations locales partenaires. **Actions de Développement durable:** Développement rural/agriculture; Enfants/jeunesse/famille; Envoi de volontaires/experts/assistance technique; Petites entreprises/secteur informel/artisanat; Questions relatives aux femmes; Santé/assainissement/eau; Éducation/formation/alphabétisation. **Régions:** Afrique australe; Afrique centrale; Afrique de l'Est; Afrique de l'Ouest; Amérique du Sud; Asie centrale et Asie du Sud; Mexique et Amerique centrale.

ACTIVITES D'INFORMATION ET D'EDUCATION: Domaines: Développement rural/agriculture; Enfants/jeunesse/famille; Pauvreté/conditions de vie; Questions relatives aux femmes; Racisme/xénophobie/antisémitisme; Relations internationales/coopération/aide au développement; Relations économiques internationales/commerce/dette/finances; Réfugiés/migrants/groupes ethniques; Santé/assainissement/eau. **Activités:** Campagnes d'information/expositions; Collecte de fonds; Conférences/séminaires/ateliers/activités de formation; Radiodiffusion/manifestations culturelles; Édition/documents audiovisuels/documents éducatifs.

ITA2886

NAPOLI EUROPA AFRICA (NEA)

Via Michelangelo Schipa, 115, 80122 Napoli, Italy.

Telephone: 39 (81) 660606. *Fax:* 39 (81) 664638. *Contact:* Fabrizio Carola, President.

OBJECTIVES: To educate the Italian people about African culture. To foster integration of immigrants in the city of Naples, Italy.

GENERAL INFORMATION: *Creation:* 1987. *Affiliated to:* FISA (Italy). *Personnel/Total:* 23. *Salaried:* 3. *Volunteers:* 20. *Financial sources:* Public: 60%. *Self-financing:* 40%.

PUBLICATIONS: *Annual report. List of publications.*

EVALUATION/RESEARCH: Evaluation reports available. Undertakes research activities.

ACTIVITIES IN DEVELOPING REGIONS: Present in developing regions. Active in 1 country(ies). Maintains local field presence. **Sustainable Development Actions:** Education/training/literacy; Urban development/habitat. **Regions:** Central Africa.

INFORMATION AND EDUCATION ACTIVITIES: Topics: Culture/tradition/religion; Education/training/literacy; Human rights/peace/conflicts; Refugees/migrants/ethnic groups. **Activities:** Broadcasting/cultural events; Conferences/seminars/workshops/training activities; Formal education; Fund raising; Information campaigns/exhibitions; Publishing/audiovisual materials/educational materials.

ITA2887

NOVA T-INIZIATIVE PER LA CONOSCENZA E LA SOLIDARIETA' TRA I POPOLI

Via Cardinal Massaia, 92, 10147 Torino, Italy.

ITA2888

OPERA DI PROMOZIONE DELL'ALFABETIZZAZIONE DEL MONDO (OPAM) ♦ Organization for the Promotion of World Literacy

Via Monte della Farina 64, 00186 Roma, Italy.

Telephone: 39 (6) 6875351. *Fax:* 39 (6) 6893738. *Contact:* Msgr Carlo Muratore, President.

OBJECTIVES: To inform the public about the problem of illiteracy and its consequences in developing countries. To promote the creation of centres active in the fields of literacy, hygiene, agronomy and crafts. To lobby official authorities to take the appropriate measures against illiteracy.

GENERAL INFORMATION: *Creation:* 1972. *Affiliated to:* FOCSIV (Italy). *Personnel/Total:* 46. *Salaried:* 6. *Volunteers:* 40 of which: 6 in developing countries. *Budget/Total 1993:* ECU 554000 (US$ 649000). *Financial sources:* Private: 61%. *Public:* 23%. *Self-financing:* 16%.

PUBLICATIONS: *Periodicals:* OPAM. *List of publications.*

EVALUATION/RESEARCH: Evaluation reports available.

ACTIVITIES IN DEVELOPING REGIONS: Present in developing regions. Active in 41 country(ies). Maintains local field presence. Works through local field partners. **Sustainable Development Actions:** Children/youth/family; Education/training/literacy; Emergency relief/refugees/humanitarian assistance; Food/famine; Gender issues/women; Health/sanitation/water; Human rights/peace/conflicts; Population/family planning/demography; Rural development/agriculture; Sending volunteers/experts/technical assistance; Small enterprises/informal sector/handicrafts. **Regions:** Caribbean; Central Africa; Central Asia and South Asia; East Africa; Mexico and Central America; North Africa; South America; South East Asia; Southern Africa; West Africa.

INFORMATION AND EDUCATION ACTIVITIES: Topics: Children/youth/family; Culture/tradition/religion; Education/training/literacy; Emergency relief/refugees/humanitarian assistance; Food/famine; Gender issues/women; Human rights/peace/conflicts; International relations/cooperation/development aid; Population/family planning/demography; Poverty/living conditions; Rural development/agriculture. **Activities:** Broadcasting/cultural events; Conferences/seminars/workshops/training activities; Exchanges/twinning/linking; Fund raising; Information and documentation services/data bases; Information campaigns/exhibitions; Lobbying/advocacy; Publishing/audiovisual materials/educational materials.

ITA2889

ORGANISMO DI VOLONTARIATO PER LA COOPERAZIONE INTERNAZIONALE "LA NOSTRA FAMIGLIA" (OVCI) ♦ Organisme de volontariat pour la coopération internationale "La Nostra Famiglia"

Via Don Luigi Monza 1, 22037 Ponte Lambro (CO), Italie.

Téléphone: 39 (31) 625111. *Fax:* 39 (31) 625275. *Contact:* Elio Cerini, President.

OBJECTIFS: Participer à la mise en place de projets inspirés par la charité chrétienne et favorisant la promotion sociale des peuples du Tiers-Monde. Encourager les interventions qui ont pour objet les soins et la réhabilitation des enfants handicapés mentaux et physiques.

INFORMATIONS GENERALES: *Création:* 1983. *Affiliée à:* FOCSIV. *Budget/Total 1993:* ECU 490000 (US$ 573000). *Sources financières:* Public: 20%.

PUBLICATIONS: *Périodiques:* Notiziario La Nostra Famiglia (4). *Liste des publications.*

ACTIVITES DANS LES REGIONS EN DEVELOPPEMENT: Intervient directement dans les régions en développement. Intervient dans 4 pays. Maintient une présence locale sur le terrain. Intervient par l'intermédiaire d'organisations locales partenaires. **Actions de Développement durable:** Aliments/famine; Enfants/jeunesse/famille; Envoi de volontaires/experts/assistance technique; Questions relatives aux femmes; Santé/assainissement/eau; Secours d'urgence/réfugiés/aide humanitaire; Éducation/formation/alphabétisation. **Régions:** Afrique de l'Est; Amérique du Sud.

ACTIVITES D'INFORMATION ET D'EDUCATION: Domaines: Aliments/famine; Culture/tradition/religion; Droits de l'Homme/paix/conflits; Enfants/jeunesse/famille; Pauvreté/conditions de vie; Questions relatives aux femmes; Relations internationales/coopération/aide au développement; Relations économiques internationales/commerce/dette/finances; Réfugiés/migrants/groupes ethniques; Santé/assainissement/eau; Secours d'urgence/réfugiés/aide humanitaire; Éducation/formation/alphabétisation. **Activités:** Campagnes d'information/expositions; Collecte de fonds; Conférences/séminaires/ateliers/activités de formation;

Voir : *Comment utiliser le répertoire*, page 11.

Services d'information et de documentation/bases de données; Éducation formelle.

ITA2890

ORGANISMO SARDO DI VOLONTARIATO INTERNAZIONALE CRISTIANO (OSVIC) ♦ Organisme Sarde de Volontariat International Chrétien

Via Goito, 25, 09170 Oristano, Italie.

Téléphone: 39 (783) 71817. *Contact:* Maria Colomba Cabras, President.

OBJECTIFS: Apporter une contribution personnelle, inspirée par la charité chrétienne, au développement des peuples du Tiers-Monde. Collaborer avec la population locale et les institutions laïques et religieuses, à des projets de développement.

INFORMATIONS GENERALES: *Création:* 1981. *Affiliée à:* Fédération des Organismes Chrétiens de Service International Volontaire (Italie). *Personnel/Total:* 22. *Salariés:* 1. *Bénévoles:* 21 dont: 6 dans les pays en développement. *Budget/Total 1993:* ECU 330000 (US\$ 386000). *Sources financières:* Privé: 21%. Public: 33%. Autofinancement: 46%.

PUBLICATIONS: *Liste des publications.*

ACTIVITES DANS LES REGIONS EN DEVELOPPEMENT: Intervient directement dans les régions en développement. Intervient dans 3 pays. Maintient une présence locale sur le terrain. Intervient par l'intermédiaire d'organisations locales partenaires. **Actions de Développement durable:** Démocratie/bonne gestion publique/création d'institutions/développement participatif; Développement rural/agriculture; Développement urbain/habitat; Enfants/jeunesse/famille; Envoi de volontaires/experts/assistance technique; Petites entreprises/secteur informel/artisanat; Questions relatives aux femmes; Santé/assainissement/eau; Secours d'urgence/réfugiés/aide humanitaire; Éducation/formation/alphabétisation. **Régions:** Afrique centrale; Afrique de l'Est.

ACTIVITES D'INFORMATION ET D'EDUCATION: Domaines: Culture/tradition/religion; Droits de l'Homme/paix/conflits; Développement rural/agriculture; Enfants/jeunesse/famille; Pauvreté/conditions de vie; Questions relatives aux femmes; Racisme/xénophobie/antisémitisme; Relations internationales/coopération/aide au développement; Relations économiques internationales/commerce/dette/finances; Réfugiés/migrants/groupes ethniques; Santé/assainissement/eau; Secours d'urgence/réfugiés/aide humanitaire; Éducation/formation/alphabétisation. **Activités:** Campagnes d'information/expositions; Collecte de fonds; Conférences/séminaires/ateliers/activités de formation; Radiodiffusion/manifestations culturelles; Services d'information et de documentation/bases de données; Échanges/parrainage/jumelage; Éducation formelle.

ITA2891

ORGANIZZAZIONE PER LO SVILUPPO GLOBALE DI COMUNITA IN PAESI EXTRAEUROPEI (OVERSEAS) ♦ Organization for the Global Development of Communities in Extraeuropean Countries

Via Castelnuovo R., 96/3, 41057 Spilamberto (Modena), Italy.

Telephone: 39 (59) 784464. *Fax:* 39 (59) 785468. *Contact:* Mario Cavani.

ITA2892

PADRI BIANCHI-MISSIONARI DI AFRICA

269 via Aurelia, Casella Postale 9078, 00165 Roma, Italie.

Téléphone: 39 (6) 632314.

ITA2893

PAX CHRISTI

Via A. Giudice 5, 84100 Salerno, Italie.

ITA2894

PROGETTO CONTINENTI

Viale Baldelli, 41, 00146 Roma, Italy.

Telephone: 39 (6) 59600319. *Fax:* 39 (6) 59600533. *Contact:* Giuseppe Florio, President.

OBJECTIVES: To undertake projects in the field of health and education in developing countries.

GENERAL INFORMATION: *Creation:* 1989. *Affiliated to:* CIPSI (Italy). *Personnel/Total:* 7. *Salaried:* 1. *Volunteers:* 6. *Budget/Total 1993:* ECU 243000 (US\$ 285000). *Financial sources:* Private: 31%. Public: 37%. Self-financing: 32%.

PUBLICATIONS: *Periodicals:* Progetto Continenti (4) - Progetto Continenti Flash (12).

EVALUATION/RESEARCH: Evaluation reports available. Undertakes research activities.

PLANNED ACTIVITIES: Progetto Continenti will hold campaigns on human rights in Cambodia and Italy and also plans to create six peace schools in Italy.

ACTIVITIES IN DEVELOPING REGIONS: Active in 5 country(ies). Works through local field partners. **Sustainable Development Actions:** Children/youth/family; Education/training/literacy; Gender issues/women; Health/sanitation/water; Human rights/peace/conflicts; Rural development/agriculture; Small enterprises/informal sector/handicrafts. **Regions:** Mexico and Central America; South East Asia.

INFORMATION AND EDUCATION ACTIVITIES: Topics: Children/youth/family; Ecology/environment/biodiversity; Education/training/literacy; Food/famine; Gender issues/women; Health/sanitation/water; Human rights/peace/conflicts; International economic relations/trade/debt/finance; International relations/cooperation/development aid; Peace/ethnic conflicts/armament/disarmament; Rural development/agriculture; Urban development/habitat. **Activities:** Conferences/seminars/workshops/training activities; Formal education; Fund raising; Information and documentation services/data bases; Information campaigns/exhibitions; Publishing/audiovisual materials/educational materials.

ITA2895

PROGETTO DOMANI: CULTURA E SOLIDARIETA (PRODOCS) ♦ Tomorrow Project: Culture and Solidarity

Via Etruria 14/C, 00183 Roma, Italy.

Telephone: 39 (6) 7081172. *Fax:* 39 (6) 7003710. *Contact:* Annamaria Donnarumma, President.

OBJECTIVES: To promote the use of culture as an instrument of human solidarity. To promote pluralism and cultural dialogue at local, national and international levels. To promote, elaborate and manage with Southern partners projects of international co-operation.

GENERAL INFORMATION: *Creation:* 1981. *Affiliated to:* FOCSIV (Italy). *Personnel/Total:* 57. *Salaried:* 12 of which: 10 in developing countries. *Volunteers:* 45 of which: 7 in developing countries. *Budget/Total 1993:* ECU 513000 (US\$ 600000). *Financial sources:* Private: 20%. Public: 50%. Self-financing: 30%.

PUBLICATIONS: *Periodicals:* Cultura E Solidarieta (4). *List of publications.*

EVALUATION/RESEARCH: Evaluation reports available. Undertakes research activities.

COMMENTS: PRODOCS has a documentation centre named ALDEA. PRODOCS is an associated member at the department of Public Information of the UN.

ACTIVITIES IN DEVELOPING REGIONS: Present in developing regions. Active in 3 country(ies). Maintains local field presence. Works through local field partners. **Sustainable Development Actions:** Democracy/good governance/institution building/participatory development; Education/training/literacy; Health/sanitation/water; Human rights/peace/conflicts; Rural development/agriculture; Sending volunteers/experts/technical assistance. **Regions:** South America.

INFORMATION AND EDUCATION ACTIVITIES: Topics: Culture/tradition/religion; Gender issues/women; Human rights/peace/conflicts; International economic relations/trade/debt/finance; International relations/cooperation/development aid; Peace/ethnic conflicts/armament/disarmament; Population/family planning/demography; Racism/xenophobia/antisemitism; Urban development/habitat. **Activities:** Broadcasting/cultural events; Conferences/seminars/workshops/training activities; Formal education; Information and documentation services/data bases;

See: *How to Use the Directory,* page 11.

Information campaigns/exhibitions; Lobbying/advocacy; Publishing/audiovisual materials/educational materials.

ITA2896

PROGETTO MONDIALITA ♦ Projet "un seul monde"

Piazza Garibaldi 67, 70122 Bari, Italie.

Téléphone: 39 (80) 5212811. *Fax:* 39 (80) 5211817. *Contact:* Felice Parisi, Président.

OBJECTIFS: Entreprendre des projets dans les domaines sociaux, de l'artisanat et de l'eau, dans les pays en développement. Former des volontaires. Accueillir les étrangers auprès du centre de Bitonto.

INFORMATIONS GENERALES: *Création:* 1980. *Affiliée à:* FOCSIV (Italie). *Personnel/Total:* 8. *Bénévoles:* 8. *Budget/Total 1993:* ECU 458000 (US$ 536000). *Sources financières:* Privé: 40%. Public: 50%. *Autofinancement:* 10%.

PUBLICATIONS: *Rapport annuel. Liste des publications.*

EVALUATION/RECHERCHE: Rapports d'évaluation disponibles.

ACTIVITES DANS LES REGIONS EN DEVELOPPEMENT: Intervient directement dans les régions en développement. Intervient dans 4 pays. Maintient une présence locale sur le terrain. Intervient par l'intermédiaire d'organisations locales partenaires. **Actions de Développement durable:** Développement rural/agriculture; Enfants/jeunesse/famille; Envoi de volontaires/experts/assistance technique; Petites entreprises/secteur informel/artisanat; Questions relatives aux femmes; Santé/assainissement/eau; Éducation/formation/alphabétisation. **Régions:** Afrique centrale; Afrique de l'Est; Amérique du Sud.

ACTIVITES D'INFORMATION ET D'EDUCATION: Domaines: Développement rural/agriculture; Enfants/jeunesse/famille; Questions relatives aux femmes; Éducation/formation/alphabétisation. **Activités:** Campagnes d'information/expositions; Conférences/séminaires/ateliers/activités de formation; Services d'information et de documentation/bases de données; Édition/documents audiovisuels/documents éducatifs; Éducation formelle.

ITA2897

PROGETTO SVILUPPO - CONFEDERAZIONE GENERALE ITALIANA DEL LAVORO ♦ Development Project - Italian General Confederation of Labour

Via Goito 39, 00185 Roma, Italy.

Telephone: 39 (6) 4041408. *Fax:* 39 (6) 421941 - 222. *Contact:* Alvaro Agrumi, President.

ITA2898

UNA PROPOSTA DIVERSA (UPD) ♦ Une proposition différente

Via Cristo, 29 - C.P. 62, 35013 Cittadella (PD), Italie.

Téléphone: 39 (49) 9400748. *Contact:* Emanuela Pinton, Présidente.

OBJECTIFS: Soutenir et promouvoir des activités pour favoriser l'autodéveloppement dans les pays du Sud ainsi que des activités d'information et de sensibilisation en Italie.

INFORMATIONS GENERALES: *Création:* 1980. *Affiliée à:* Coordination des Initiatives Populaires de Solidarité Internationale (Italie). *Personnel/Total:* 21. *Salariés:* 1. *Bénévoles:* 20. *Budget/Total 1993:* ECU 73000 (US$ 85000). *Sources financières:* Privé: 27%. Public: 9%. *Autofinancement:* 64%.

PUBLICATIONS: *Périodiques:* Una proposta diversa (6). *Rapport annuel.*

EVALUATION/RECHERCHE: Rapports d'évaluation disponibles.

ACTIVITES DANS LES REGIONS EN DEVELOPPEMENT: Intervient directement dans les régions en développement. Intervient dans 10 pays. Intervient par l'intermédiaire d'organisations locales partenaires. **Actions de Développement durable:** Droits de l'Homme/paix/conflits; Démocratie/bonne gestion publique/création d'institutions/développement participatif; Développement rural/agriculture; Enfants/jeunesse/famille; Population/planning familial/démographie; Questions relatives aux femmes; Santé/assainissement/eau; Secours d'urgence/réfugiés/aide humanitaire; Éducation/formation/alphabétisation. **Régions:** Afrique australe; Afrique centrale; Afrique de l'Est; Afrique de

l'Ouest; Afrique du Nord; Amérique du Sud; Asie centrale et Asie du Sud; Asie du Sud-Est.

ACTIVITES D'INFORMATION ET D'EDUCATION: Domaines: Droits de l'Homme/paix/conflits; Développement rural/agriculture; Enfants/jeunesse/famille; Paix/conflits ethniques/armement/désarmement; Population/planning familial/démographie; Questions relatives aux femmes; Racisme/xénophobie/antisémitisme; Réfugiés/migrants/groupes ethniques; Santé/assainissement/eau; Secours d'urgence/réfugiés/aide humanitaire. **Activités:** Campagnes d'information/expositions; Conférences/séminaires/ateliers/activités de formation; Lobbying/plaidoyer; Radiodiffusion/manifestations culturelles; Éducation formelle.

ITA2899

PUNTO DI FRATERNITA (PF) ♦ Lieu de Fraternité

Piazza N. Barabino 2/6, 16149 Genova, Italie.

Téléphone: 39 (10) 412393. *Fax:* 39 (10) 412393. *Contact:* Pietro Gambaro, Directeur général.

OBJECTIFS: Apporter une aide aux pays en développement.

INFORMATIONS GENERALES: *Création:* 1984. *Organisations membres:* 23. *Affiliée à:* CIPSI (Italie). *Personnel/Total:* 39. *Salariés:* 3 dont: 2 dans les pays en développement. *Bénévoles:* 36 dont: 20 dans les pays en développement. *Budget/Total 1993:* ECU 2258000 (US$ 2642000). *Sources financières:* Public: 75%.

PUBLICATIONS: *Périodiques:* Punto News (4). *Rapport annuel. Liste des publications.*

EVALUATION/RECHERCHE: Rapports d'évaluation disponibles.

ACTIVITES DANS LES REGIONS EN DEVELOPPEMENT: Intervient directement dans les régions en développement. Intervient dans 6 pays. Maintient une présence locale sur le terrain. **Actions de Développement durable:** Aliments/famine; Développement rural/agriculture; Développement urbain/habitat; Envoi de volontaires/experts/assistance technique; Questions relatives aux femmes; Santé/assainissement/eau. **Régions:** Afrique australe; Afrique centrale; Amérique du Sud.

ACTIVITES D'INFORMATION ET D'EDUCATION: Domaines: Aliments/famine; Développement rural/agriculture; Développement urbain/habitat; Enfants/jeunesse/famille; Pauvreté/conditions de vie; Questions relatives aux femmes; Santé/assainissement/eau; Éducation/formation/alphabétisation. **Activités:** Collecte de fonds; Conférences/séminaires/ateliers/activités de formation.

ITA2900

REGGIO - TERZO MONDO (RTM) ♦ Reggio - Third World

Via Ferrari Bonini 3, 42100 Reggio Emilia, Italy.

Telephone: 39 (522) 436840. *Fax:* 39 (522) 438657. *Contact:* Angelo Grazzi, President.

OBJECTIVES: To recruit, prepare and send volunteers to work in developing countries. To undertake development projects with local churches in developing countries.

GENERAL INFORMATION: *Creation:* 1973. *Affiliated to:* FOCSIV (Italy). *Personnel/Total:* 42. *Salaried:* 8 of which: 3 in developing countries. *Volunteers:* 34 of which: 12 in developing countries. *Budget/Total 1993:* ECU 2140000 (US$ 2505000). *Financial sources:* Private: 46%. Public: 43%. Self-financing: 11%.

PUBLICATIONS: *Periodicals:* Reggio Missioni (10). *Annual report. List of publications.*

EVALUATION/RESEARCH: Evaluation reports available.

COMMENTS: Undertakes activities in the Commonwealth of Independent States.

ACTIVITIES IN DEVELOPING REGIONS: Present in developing regions. Active in 7 country(ies). Maintains local field presence. Works through local field partners. **Sustainable Development Actions:** Children/youth/family; Debt/finance/trade; Democracy/good governance/institution building/participatory development; Ecology/environment/biodiversity; Education/training/literacy; Emergency relief/refugees/humanitarian assistance; Energy/transport; Food/famine; Gender issues/women; Health/sanitation/water; Population/family planning/demography; Rural development/agriculture; Sending volunteers/experts/technical assis-

Voir : *Comment utiliser le répertoire,* page 11.

tance; Small enterprises/informal sector/handicrafts; Urban development/habitat. **Regions:** Central Africa; Central Asia and South Asia; East Africa; South America; Southern Africa.

INFORMATION AND EDUCATION ACTIVITIES: Topics: Children/youth/family; Culture/tradition/religion; Ecology/environment/biodiversity; Education/training/literacy; Emergency relief/refugees/humanitarian assistance; Employment/unemployment; Food/famine; Gender issues/women; Health/sanitation/water; Human rights/peace/conflicts; International economic relations/trade/debt/finance; International relations/cooperation/development aid; Peace/ethnic conflicts/armament/disarmament; Population/family planning/demography; Poverty/living conditions; Racism/xenophobia/antisemitism; Refugees/migrants/ethnic groups; Rural development/agriculture; Urban development/habitat. **Activities:** Broadcasting/cultural events; Conferences/seminars/workshops/training activities; Exchanges/twinning/linking; Formal education; Fund raising; Information and documentation services/data bases; Information campaigns/exhibitions; Lobbying/advocacy; Publishing/audiovisual materials/educational materials.

ITA2901

RICERCA E COOPERAZIONE-ORGANIZZAZIONE PER LA RICERCA, LA DOCUMENTAZIONE E IL LAVORO VOLONTARIO NELLA COOPERAZIONE INTERNAZIONALE (RC) ♦ Research and Co-operation-Association for Research, Documentation and Voluntary Work in International Cooperation

Via Latina 276, 00179 Roma, Italy.

Telephone: 39 (6) 78346432. **Fax:** 39 (6) 78346447. **Contact:** Arturo Parolini, President.

OBJECTIVES: To promote, plan and implement development programmes in developing countries. To promote and implement initiatives for development education and information in Italy.

GENERAL INFORMATION: Creation: 1985. **Affiliated to:** COCIS (Italy). **Personnel/Total:** 21. *Salaried:* 16 of which: 8 in developing countries. *Volunteers:* 5. **Budget/Total 1993:** ECU 1358000 (US$ 1589000). **Financial sources:** *Private:* 15%. *Public:* 80%. *Self-financing:* 5%.

PUBLICATIONS: Periodicals: RC News (2). *List of publications.*

EVALUATION/RESEARCH: Evaluation reports available. Undertakes research activities.

ACTIVITIES IN DEVELOPING REGIONS: Present in developing regions. Active in 9 country(ies). Maintains local field presence. Works through local field partners. **Sustainable Development Actions:** Children/youth/family; Democracy/good governance/institution building/participatory development; Ecology/environment/biodiversity; Education/training/literacy; Gender issues/women; Health/sanitation/water; Rural development/agriculture; Sending volunteers/experts/technical assistance; Small enterprises/informal sector/handicrafts; Urban development/habitat. **Regions:** East Africa; Middle East; North Africa; South America; West Africa.

INFORMATION AND EDUCATION ACTIVITIES: Topics: Ecology/environment/biodiversity; Emergency relief/refugees/humanitarian assistance; Gender issues/women; International relations/cooperation/development aid; Population/family planning/demography; Racism/xenophobia/antisemitism; Refugees/migrants/ethnic groups; Rural development/agriculture. **Activities:** Conferences/seminars/workshops/training activities; Fund raising; Information and documentation services/data bases; Information campaigns/exhibitions; Publishing/audiovisual materials/educational materials.

ITA2902

SERVICIO JESUITA A REFUGIADOS (JRS) ♦ Jesuit Refugee Service

Borgo S. Spirito 4, C.P. 6139 , 00195 Roma, Italy.

Telephone: 39 (6) 68977386. **Fax:** 39 (6) 6879283. **E-mail:** jrsrome.@gn.apc.org. **Contact:** Mark Raper, Director.

OBJECTIVES: To work with refugees worldwide. To provide pastoral services and undertake a wide variety of development programmes, emergency relief and training activities.

GENERAL INFORMATION: Creation: 1981. **Affiliated to:** ICVA (Switzerland). **Personnel/Total:** 400. *Salaried:* 80 of which: 50 in developing countries. *Volunteers:* 320 of which: 100 in developing countries. **Financial sources:** *Private:* 80%. *Public:* 20%.

PUBLICATIONS: Periodicals: Servir-Bulletin of the Jesuit Refugee Service (4). *Annual report. List of publications.*

EVALUATION/RESEARCH: Undertakes research activities.

PLANNED ACTIVITIES: JRS plans to activate their Jesuit network on an international campaign to ban the use of landmines.

COMMENTS: Undertakes activities in the Commonwealth of Independent States. Information activities related to the Commonwealth of Independent States.

ACTIVITIES IN DEVELOPING REGIONS: Present in developing regions. Maintains local field presence. Works through local field partners. **Sustainable Development Actions:** Children/youth/family; Democracy/good governance/institution building/participatory development; Education/training/literacy; Emergency relief/refugees/humanitarian assistance; Food/famine; Gender issues/women; Human rights/peace/conflicts; Rural development/agriculture; Sending volunteers/experts/technical assistance; Small enterprises/informal sector/handicrafts; Urban development/habitat. **Regions:** Central Africa; Central Asia and South Asia; East Africa; Mexico and Central America; South East Asia; Southern Africa; West Africa.

INFORMATION AND EDUCATION ACTIVITIES: Topics: Emergency relief/refugees/humanitarian assistance; Peace/ethnic conflicts/armament/disarmament; Racism/xenophobia/antisemitism; Refugees/migrants/ethnic groups. **Activities:** Conferences/seminars/workshops/training activities; Formal education; Fund raising; Information and documentation services/data bases; Information campaigns/exhibitions; Lobbying/advocacy; Networking/electronic telecommunications; Publishing/audiovisual materials/educational materials.

ITA2903

SERVIZIO CIVILE INTERNAZIONALE - ITALIE (SCI) ♦ Service Civil International - Italie

Via dei Laterani, 28, 00184 Roma, Italy.

Telephone: 39 (6) 7005994. **Fax:** 39 (6) 7005472. **Contact:** Renzo Sabatini, President.

OBJECTIVES: To promote peace, international understanding, education for development, human rights and antiracism efforts. To support and organise relief, solidarity and voluntary projects.

GENERAL INFORMATION: Creation: 1948. **Affiliated to:** COCIS (Italy) - European Civil Service International (Belgium) - Italian Consortium of Solidarity (Italy). **Personnel/Total:** 11. *Salaried:* 7. *Volunteers:* 4. **Budget/Total 1993:** ECU 217000 (US$ 254000). **Financial sources:** *Private:* 35%. *Public:* 50%. *Self-financing:* 15%.

PUBLICATIONS: Periodicals: Centofiori (4) - Agenzia (24). *Annual report. List of publications.*

EVALUATION/RESEARCH: Evaluation reports available.

COMMENTS: Undertakes activities in the Commonwealth of Independent States. Information activities related to the Commonwealth of Independent States.

ACTIVITIES IN DEVELOPING REGIONS: Present in developing regions. Works through local field partners. **Sustainable Development Actions:** Education/training/literacy; Human rights/peace/conflicts; Rural development/agriculture; Sending volunteers/experts/technical assistance. **Regions:** Central Asia and South Asia; Mexico and Central America; North Africa; Southern Africa.

INFORMATION AND EDUCATION ACTIVITIES: Topics: Emergency relief/refugees/humanitarian assistance; Employment/unemployment; Human rights/peace/conflicts; International relations/cooperation/development aid; Peace/ethnic conflicts/armament/disarmament; Racism/xenophobia/antisemitism; Refugees/migrants/ethnic groups; Rural development/agriculture. **Activities:** Conferences/seminars/workshops/training activities; Exchanges/twinning/linking; Fund raising; Information campaigns/exhibitions; Lobbying/advocacy.

See: How to Use the Directory, page 11.

ITA2904

SERVIZIO COOPERAZIONE AIUTO INTERNAZIONALE PIA-MARTINO (SCAIP) ♦ Service international de coopération du Père Piamartino

Via Veronica Gambara, 6/B, 25121 Brescia, Italie.

Téléphone: 39 (30) 46584. *Contact:* Gianantonio Galanti, Président.

ITA2905

SERVIZIO RIFUGIATI E MIGRANTI DELLA FEDERATIONE DELLE CHIESE EVANGELICHE IN ITALIA (SRM/FCEI) ♦ Service des Réfugiés et Migrants de la Fédération des Eglises Protestantes en Italie

38, Via Firenze, 00184 Rome, Italie.

Téléphone: 39 (6) 483188. *Fax:* 39 (6) 4828728. *Contact:* Anne-Marie Dupré, Responsable.

OBJECTIFS: Apporter une aide concrète aux immigrés et aux réfugiés (assistance légale et sociale). Sensibiliser l'opinion publique sur ce problème.

INFORMATIONS GENERALES: *Création:* 1984. ***Organisations membres:*** 7. ***Affiliée à:*** Commission Européenne pour les Migrants en Europe. ***Personnel/Total:*** 154. *Salariés:* 4. *Bénévoles:* 150. ***Sources financières:*** *Privé:* 50%. *Public:* 50%.

PUBLICATIONS: *Périodiques:* SRM-materiali (3). *Rapport annuel.*

EVALUATION/RECHERCHE: Rapports d'évaluation disponibles.

COMMENTAIRES: Intervient dans la Communauté des Etats indépendants. Activités d'information concernant la Communauté des Etats indépendants.

ACTIVITES DANS LES REGIONS EN DEVELOPPEMENT: Intervient directement dans les régions en développement. Intervient dans 2 pays. Intervient par l'intermédiaire d'organisations locales partenaires.

ACTIVITES D'INFORMATION ET D'EDUCATION: Domaines: Culture/tradition/religion; Droits de l'Homme/paix/conflits; Enfants/jeunesse/famille; Paix/conflits ethniques/armement/désarmement; Questions relatives aux femmes; Racisme/xénophobie/antisémitisme; Réfugiés/migrants/groupes ethniques; Secours d'urgence/réfugiés/aide humanitaire. **Activités:** Campagnes d'information/expositions; Collecte de fonds; Conférences/séminaires/ateliers/activités de formation; Lobbying/plaidoyer; Services d'information et de documentation/bases de données; Échanges/parrainage/jumelage; Édition/documents audiovisuels/documents éducatifs; Éducation formelle.

ITA2906

SERVIZIO SOCIALE INTERNAZIONALE - SEZIONE ITALIANA ♦ Service Social International - Section Italienne

Via Veneto 96, 00187 Rome, Italie.

Téléphone: 39 (6) 48810910. *Fax:* 39 (6) 4817605. *Contact:* Adriana Loreti Begh, Présidente.

ITA2907

SERVIZIO VOLONTARIO INTERNAZIONALE (SVI) ♦ Service volontaire international

Via Tosio 1, 25121 Brescia, Italie.

Téléphone: 39 (30) 295621. *Fax:* 39 (30) 3771675. *Contact:* Ungari Aldo, Président.

OBJECTIFS: Favoriser l'auto-développement des peuples du Tiers monde par l'envoi de volontaires, selon l'enseignement chrétien.

INFORMATIONS GENERALES: *Création:* 1963. ***Affiliée à:*** FOCSIV. ***Personnel/Total:*** 48. *Salariés:* 18 dont: 14 dans les pays en développement. *Bénévoles:* 30. ***Budget/Total 1993:*** ECU 1074 (US$ 1257). ***Sources financières:*** *Privé:* 66%. *Public:* 18%. *Autofinancement:* 16%.

PUBLICATIONS: *Périodiques:* SVINOTIZIE (6). *Rapport annuel. Liste des publications.*

PREVISIONS D'ACTIVITES: Organisation de tables rondes sur leRwanda et le Burundi.

ACTIVITES DANS LES REGIONS EN DEVELOPPEMENT: Intervient directement dans les régions en développement. Intervient dans 4 pays. Maintient une présence locale sur le terrain. Intervient par l'intermédiaire d'organisations locales partenaires. **Actions de Développement durable:** Aliments; Dette/finances/commerce; Développement rural/agriculture; Développement urbain/habitat; Enfants/jeunesse/famille; Envoi de volontaires/experts/assistance technique; Petites entreprises/secteur informel/artisanat; Questions relatives aux femmes; Santé/assainissement/eau; Éducation/formation/alphabétisation; Énergie/transport. **Régions:** Afrique centrale; Afrique de l'Est; Amérique du Sud.

ACTIVITES D'INFORMATION ET D'EDUCATION: Domaines: Aliments/famine; Culture/tradition/religion; Droits de l'Homme/paix/conflits; Développement rural/agriculture; Développement urbain/habitat; Emploi/chômage; Enfants/jeunesse/famille; Paix/conflits ethniques/armement/désarmement; Pauvreté/conditions de vie; Population/planning familial/démographie; Questions relatives aux femmes; Racisme/xénophobie/antisémitisme; Relations internationales/coopération/aide au développement; Relations économiques internationales/commerce/dette/finances; Réfugiés/migrants/groupes ethniques; Santé/assainissement/eau; Secours d'urgence/réfugiés/aide humanitaire; Écologie/environnement/biodiversité; Éducation/formation/alphabétisation. **Activités:** Campagnes d'information/expositions; Collecte de fonds; Conférences/séminaires/ateliers/activités de formation; Radiodiffusion/manifestations culturelles; Services d'information et de documentation/bases de données; Échanges/parrainage/jumelage; Édition/documents audiovisuels/documents éducatifs.

ITA2908

SOCIETY FOR INTERNATIONAL DEVELOPMENT (SID) ♦ Société Internationale pour le Développement

Palazzo Civiltà del Lavoro, 00144 Roma, Italy.

Telephone: 39 (6) 5925506. *Fax:* 39 (6) 5919836. *E-mail:* S.I.D.@agora.stm.it. *Contact:* Robert Cassani, Executive Director.

OBJECTIVES: To encourage, support and facilitate a sense of community among individuals and organisations committed to development. To promote international dialogue, understanding and co-operation for social and economic development. To advance the science, processes and art of sustainable social and economic development through educational means.

GENERAL INFORMATION: *Creation:* 1957. ***Personnel/Total:*** 17. *Salaried:* 14. *Volunteers:* 3. ***Budget/Total 1993:*** ECU 920000 (US$ 1077000). ***Financial sources:*** *Private:* 2%. *Public:* 90%. *Self-financing:* 8%.

PUBLICATIONS: *Periodicals:* Development (4) - Development Hotline (24). *Annual report.*

EVALUATION/RESEARCH: Evaluation reports available. Undertakes research activities.

INFORMATION AND EDUCATION ACTIVITIES: Topics: Children/youth/family; Culture/tradition/religion; Ecology/environment/biodiversity; Education/training/literacy; Employment/unemployment; Food/famine; Gender issues/women; Health/sanitation/water; Human rights/peace/conflicts; International economic relations/trade/debt/finance; International relations/cooperation/development aid; Peace/ethnic conflicts/armament/disarmament; Population/family planning/demography; Poverty/living conditions; Racism/xenophobia/antisemitism; Refugees/migrants/ethnic groups; Rural development/agriculture; Urban development/habitat. **Activities:** Conferences/seminars/workshops/training activities; Information and documentation services/data bases; Publishing/audiovisual materials/educational materials.

ITA2909

SOLIDARIETA E COOPERAZIONE SENZA FRONTIERE (SCSF) ♦ Solidarité et coopération sans frontières

Via Marescalchi 4, 40123 Bologna, Italie.

Téléphone: 39 (51) 220637.

ITA2910

SOLIDARIETA UOMO COOPERAZIONE ALLO SVILUPPO (SUCOS) ♦ Human Solidarity and Co-operation for Development

Voir : *Comment utiliser le répertoire,* page 11.

Via Don Gaetano Boschi, 28, 56126 Pisa, Italy.

Telephone: 39 (50) 554920. *Fax:* 39 (50) 554920. *Contact:* Gino Niccodemi.

OBJECTIVES: To provide assistance to children and populations unable to satisfy their primary needs. To support the self-development of local peoples. To promote cultural exchanges with national and international institutions with similar aims.

GENERAL INFORMATION: *Creation:* 1989. *Personnel/Total:* 13. *Salaried:* 3 of which: 3 in developing countries. *Volunteers:* 10. *Budget/Total 1993:* ECU 21000 (US$ 24000). *Financial sources:* Private: 20%. Self-financing: 80%.

EVALUATION/RESEARCH: Evaluation reports available. Undertakes research activities.

ACTIVITIES IN DEVELOPING REGIONS: Present in developing regions. Active in 2 country(ies). Maintains local field presence. Works through local field partners. **Sustainable Development Actions:** Children/youth/family; Democracy/good governance/institution building/participatory development; Ecology/environment/biodiversity; Education/training/literacy; Gender issues/women; Health/sanitation/water; Human rights/peace/conflicts; Population/family planning/demography; Rural development/agriculture; Sending volunteers/experts/technical assistance; Small enterprises/informal sector/handicrafts; Urban development/habitat. **Regions:** East Africa; South America.

ITA2911

SOLIDARIETA' CON IL TERZO MONDO ♦ Solidarity with the Third World

Vicolo del Cinque, 59, 00153 Roma, Italy.

Telephone: 39 (6) 585661. *Fax:* 39 (6) 5883625. *Contact:* Matteo Maria Zuppi, President.

OBJECTIVES: To undertake emergency relief and development programmes to help the poor and refugees in the Third World and in the countries of the former Soviet Union. To carry out awareness-raising and educational programmes on development issues in Europe.

GENERAL INFORMATION: *Creation:* 1983. *Personnel/Total:* 301. *Salaried:* 1 of which: 1 in developing countries. *Volunteers:* 300. *Budget/Total 1993:* ECU 114000 (US$ 1334000). *Financial sources:* Private: 65%. Public: 20%. Self-financing: 15%.

PUBLICATIONS: *Annual report.*

EVALUATION/RESEARCH: Evaluation reports available. Undertakes research activities.

PLANNED ACTIVITIES: Fostering the institutional building of the Southern NGOs.

COMMENTS: Undertakes activities in the Commonwealth of Independent States.

ACTIVITIES IN DEVELOPING REGIONS: Present in developing regions. Maintains local field presence. Works through local field partners. **Sustainable Development Actions:** Children/youth/family; Democracy/good governance/institution building/participatory development; Education/training/literacy; Emergency relief/refugees/humanitarian assistance; Food/famine; Health/sanitation/water; Human rights/peace/conflicts; Rural development/agriculture; Sending volunteers/experts/technical assistance. **Regions:** Caribbean; Central Asia and South Asia; Mexico and Central America; Middle East; North Africa; South East Asia; Southern Africa.

INFORMATION AND EDUCATION ACTIVITIES: Topics: Children/youth/family; Education/training/literacy; Emergency relief/refugees/humanitarian assistance; Health/sanitation/water; Human rights/peace/conflicts; International relations/cooperation/development aid; Peace/ethnic conflicts/armament/disarmament; Racism/xenophobia/antisemitism. **Activities:** Conferences/seminars/workshops/training activities; Exchanges/twinning/linking; Fund raising; Information and documentation services/data bases; Information campaigns/exhibitions; Lobbying/advocacy; Publishing/audiovisual materials/educational materials.

ITA2912

SOS MISSIONARIO

Via Giovanni XXIII 23, P.O. Box 218, 63039 San Benedetto del Tronto, Italy.

Telephone: 39 (735) 585037. *Fax:* 39 (735) 585037. *Contact:* Antonio Monieri, President.

OBJECTIVES: To promote economic and social activities in developing countries. To raise awareness of development problems among the Italian public.

GENERAL INFORMATION: *Creation:* 1983. *Affiliated to:* CIPSI (Italy). *Personnel/Total:* 16. *Salaried:* 1. *Volunteers:* 15. *Budget/Total 1993:* ECU 240000 (US$ 280000). *Financial sources:* Private: 99%. Self-financing: 1%.

PUBLICATIONS: *Periodicals:* Notiziario SOS Missionario (2). *List of publications.*

ACTIVITIES IN DEVELOPING REGIONS: Present in developing regions. Active in 5 country(ies). Works through local field partners. **Sustainable Development Actions:** Children/youth/family; Democracy/good governance/institution building/participatory development; Education/training/literacy; Food/famine; Gender issues/women; Health/sanitation/water; Rural development/agriculture. **Regions:** Central Africa; Central Asia and South Asia; South East Asia.

INFORMATION AND EDUCATION ACTIVITIES: Topics: Children/youth/family; Culture/tradition/religion; Emergency relief/refugees/humanitarian assistance; Food/famine; Gender issues/women; Health/sanitation/water; International economic relations/trade/debt/finance; International relations/cooperation/development aid; Peace/ethnic conflicts/armament/disarmament; Poverty/living conditions; Racism/xenophobia/antisemitism; Refugees/migrants/ethnic groups; Rural development/agriculture. **Activities:** Broadcasting/cultural events; Conferences/seminars/workshops/training activities; Formal education; Fund raising; Information and documentation services/data bases; Information campaigns/exhibitions; Lobbying/advocacy.

ITA2913

TERRA NUOVA - CENTRO PER IL VOLONTARIATO ♦ New Earth - Volunteer Centre

Via Urbana 156, 00184 Roma, Italy.

Telephone: 39 (6) 485534. *Fax:* 39 (6) 4747599. *Contact:* Caterina Imbastari, Chairman.

OBJECTIVES: To promote activities in developing countries. To increase mutually beneficial exchanges between the North and the South. To increase awareness among the Italian public through development education activities.

GENERAL INFORMATION: *Creation:* 1972. *Affiliated to:* COCIS (Italy). *Personnel/Total:* 20. *Salaried:* 16 of which: 9 in developing countries. *Volunteers:* 4 of which: 4 in developing countries. *Budget/Total 1993:* ECU 3258000 (US$ 3813000). *Financial sources:* Private: 20%. Public: 75%. Self-financing: 5%.

PUBLICATIONS: *Periodicals:* Terra Nuova-Forum (4). *List of publications.*

ACTIVITIES IN DEVELOPING REGIONS: Present in developing regions. Active in 12 country(ies). Maintains local field presence. Works through local field partners. **Sustainable Development Actions:** Children/youth/family; Democracy/good governance/institution building/participatory development; Ecology/environment/biodiversity; Education/training/literacy; Gender issues/women; Health/sanitation/water; Other; Rural development/agriculture; Sending volunteers/experts/technical assistance; Small enterprises/informal sector/handicrafts. **Regions:** Caribbean; East Africa; Mexico and Central America; Middle East; South America; West Africa.

INFORMATION AND EDUCATION ACTIVITIES: Topics: Children/youth/family; Culture/tradition/religion; Ecology/environment/biodiversity; Education/training/literacy; Employment/unemployment; Gender issues/women; Health/sanitation/water; Human rights/peace/conflicts; International economic relations/trade/debt/finance; International relations/cooperation/development aid; Peace/ethnic conflicts/armament/disarmament; Population/family planning/demography; Racism/xenophobia/antisemitism; Refugees/migrants/ethnic groups; Rural development/

          See: *How to Use the Directory,* page 11.

agriculture; Urban development/habitat. **Activities:** Conferences/seminars/workshops/training activities; Formal education; Fund raising; Information and documentation services/data bases; Information campaigns/exhibitions; Lobbying/advocacy; Publishing/audiovisual materials/educational materials.

ITA2914

THIRD WORLD ACADEMY OF SCIENCES (TWAS)

Strada Costiera 11, P.O. Box 586, 34100 Trieste, Italy.

Telephone: 39 (40) 2240327. *Fax:* 39 (40) 224559. *E-mail:* TWAS@ictp.trieste.it. *Contact:* Abdus Salam, President.

OBJECTIVES: To recognize, support and promote excellence in scientific research in the South. To provide promising scientists in the South with research facilities necessary for the advancement of their work. To facilitate contacts between individual scientists and institutions in the South. To encourage South-North co-operation between individuals and centres of scholarship. To encourage scientific research on major Third World problems.

GENERAL INFORMATION: *Creation:* 1983. *Type of organisation:* association of NGOs. *Personnel/Total:* 10. *Salaried:* 10. *Budget/Total 1993:* ECU 1588000 (US$ 1800000). *Financial sources:* Private: 5%. *Public:* 85%. *Self-financing:* 10%.

PUBLICATIONS: *Periodicals:* Newsletter (4) - Journal on Science and Technology Policy in the South (2). *Annual report. List of publications.*

EVALUATION/RESEARCH: Undertakes research activities.

PLANNED ACTIVITIES: The establishment of a network of international science and technology research and training centres of excellence for sustainable development.

ACTIVITIES IN DEVELOPING REGIONS: Present in developing regions. Active in 57 country(ies). Maintains local field presence. Works through local field partners. **Sustainable Development Actions:** Ecology/environment/biodiversity; Education/training/literacy; Gender issues/women. **Regions:** Caribbean; Central Africa; Central Asia and South Asia; East Africa; East Asia; Mexico and Central America; Middle East; North Africa; Oceania; South America; South East Asia; Southern Africa; West Africa.

INFORMATION AND EDUCATION ACTIVITIES: Topics: Ecology/environment/biodiversity; Education/training/literacy; Other. **Activities:** Broadcasting/cultural events; Conferences/seminars/workshops/training activities; Exchanges/twinning/linking; Formal education; Fund raising; Information and documentation services/data bases; Information campaigns/exhibitions; Lobbying/advocacy; Networking/electronic telecommunications; Publishing/audiovisual materials/educational materials.

ITA2915

UFFICIO CENTRALE STUDENTI ESTERI IN ITALIA (UCSEI)

Lungotevere dei Vallati 14 , 00186 Roma , Italie.

Téléphone: 39 (6) 8804062. *Fax:* 39 (6) 8804063. *Contact:* Monsignor Remigio Musaragno, Président.

OBJECTIFS: Promouvoir l'insertion des étudiants étrangers sur le plan social et culturel.

INFORMATIONS GENERALES: *Création:* 1968. *Personnel/Total:* 12. *Bénévoles:* 12. *Budget/Total 1993:* ECU 434000 (US$ 508000).

PUBLICATIONS: *Périodiques:* Amicizia/Studenti esteri (12). *Rapport annuel. Liste des publications.*

EVALUATION/RECHERCHE: Rapports d'évaluation disponibles. Entreprend des activités de recherche.

COMMENTAIRES: L'organisation projette d'ouvrir une galerie d'art pour les artistes des pays en développement qui étudient en Italie. Activités d'information concernant la Communauté des Etats indépandans. **Actions de Développement durable:** Éducation/formation/alphabétisation. **Régions:** Afrique de l'Ouest.

ACTIVITES D'INFORMATION ET D'EDUCATION: Domaines: Culture/tradition/religion; Relations internationales/coopération/aide au développement; Réfugiés/migrants/groupes ethniques; Éducation/formation/alphabétisation. **Activités:** Conférences/séminaires/ateliers/activités de formation.

ITA2916

UNIONE MEDICO MISSIONARIA ITALIANA (UMMI) ♦ Union médicale missionnaire italienne

Viale Rizzardi 3, 37024 Negrar (Verona), Italy.

Telephone: 39 (45) 7500501. *Fax:* 39 (45) 7500501. *Contact:* Giuseppe Brunelli, President.

OBJECTIVES: To inform and train people from developed and developing countries on the problem of "full and total health". To formulate social and health programmes for the promotion of development. To collect and ship efficient medical structures and material to operators in developing countries.

GENERAL INFORMATION: *Creation:* 1933. *Affiliated to:* FOCSIV (Italy) - Foundation for Tropical Diseases (Italy). *Personnel/Total:* 16. *Salaried:* 6 of which: 3 in developing countries. *Volunteers:* 10 of which: 2 in developing countries. *Budget/Total 1993:* ECU 239000 (US$ 279000). *Financial sources:* Private: 48%. Public: 47%. *Self-financing:* 5%.

PUBLICATIONS: *Periodicals:* Medicina e Missioni (12). *Annual report. List of publications.*

EVALUATION/RESEARCH: Evaluation reports available. Undertakes research activities.

COMMENTS: Undertakes activities in the Commonwealth of Independent States.

ACTIVITIES IN DEVELOPING REGIONS: Present in developing regions. Active in 4 country(ies). Maintains local field presence. Works through local field partners. **Sustainable Development Actions:** Children/youth/family; Emergency relief/refugees/humanitarian assistance; Health/sanitation/water; Sending volunteers/experts/technical assistance. **Regions:** Central Africa; Middle East; South America; Southern Africa; West Africa.

INFORMATION AND EDUCATION ACTIVITIES: Topics: Children/youth/family; Culture/tradition/religion; Ecology/environment/biodiversity; Education/training/literacy; Emergency relief/refugees/humanitarian assistance; Food/famine; Gender issues/women; Health/sanitation/water; Human rights/peace/conflicts; International relations/cooperation/development aid; Peace/ethnic conflicts/armament/disarmament; Population/family planning/demography; Poverty/living conditions; Refugees/migrants/ethnic groups; Urban development/habitat. **Activities:** Conferences/seminars/workshops/training activities; Formal education; Fund raising; Publishing/audiovisual materials/educational materials.

ITA2917

UNIONE VOLONTARIATO INTERNAZIONALE PER LO SVILUPPO E LA PACE (UVISP-ASSISI) ♦ Union of International Volunteers for Development and Peace

Piazza Porziuncola 1, C.P. 32, 06088 Santa Maria degli Angeli (PG), Italy.

Telephone: 39 (75) 8004667. *Fax:* 39 (75) 8004728. *Contact:* Ruggero de Grisogono, Program Officer.

ITA2918

UNIVERSITA DELLA PACE GIORGIO LA PIRA ♦ Université de la Paix Giorgio La Pira

Corso IV Novembre 28, 12100 Cuneo, Italie.

Téléphone: 39 (171) 696975. *Fax:* 39 (171) 602558. *Contact:* Père Aldo Benevelli, Vice-président.

ITA2919

VELLETRI PER IL MALI (VPM)

Via del Comune, 41, 00049 Velletri RM, Italy.

Telephone: 39 (6) 9635660.

ITA2920

VOLONTARI INTERNAZIONALI DELLA SCUOLA BEATO ANGELICO (VISBA) ♦ Volontaires Internationaux de l'Ecole Beato Angelico

Beato Angelico, Via S. Gimignano, 19, 20146 Milano, Italy.

Telephone: 39 (2) 48302857. *Fax:* 39 (2) 48301954. *Contact:* Vittore Rizzi, President.

OBJECTIVES: To co-operate with developing countries in order to develop education and professional training programmes in the areas of environmental protection, habitat, craftmanship and the arts.

GENERAL INFORMATION: *Creation:* 1972. *Type of organisation:* coordinating body. *Affiliated to:* FOCSIV. *Personnel/Total:* 21. *Volunteers:* 21 of which: 4 in developing countries. *Budget/Total 1993:* ECU 465400 (US$ 545000). *Financial sources:* *Private:* 64%. *Public:* 21%. *Self-financing:* 15%.

PUBLICATIONS: *Periodicals:* "L'Amico dell'Arte Cristiana" (2).

EVALUATION/RESEARCH: Evaluation reports available. Undertakes research activities.

COMMENTS: The organisation has a sponsorship/distant adoption programme for approximately 2000 school children to provide financial support for the children to attend school.

ACTIVITIES IN DEVELOPING REGIONS: Present in developing regions. Active in 6 country(ies). Maintains local field presence. Works through local field partners. **Sustainable Development Actions:** Children/youth/family; Education/training/literacy; Health/sanitation/water; Urban development/habitat. **Regions:** Central Africa; East Africa; South East Asia.

INFORMATION AND EDUCATION ACTIVITIES: Topics: Education/training/literacy; Health/sanitation/water; Urban development/habitat. **Activities:** Conferences/seminars/workshops/training activities; Exchanges/twinning/linking; Fund raising; Information and documentation services/data bases; Information campaigns/exhibitions; Publishing/audiovisual materials/educational materials.

ITA2921

VOLONTARI ITALIANI PER LA SOLIDARIETA' AI PAESI EMERGENTI (VISPE) ♦ Volontaires italiens pour la solidarité avec les pays en développement

Via della Chiesa 3, 20084 Cassirate Olona di Lacchiarella - Milano, Italie.

Téléphone: 39 (2) 57602941. *Fax:* 39 (2) 57604754. *Contact:* Luigi Bettinelli, Président.

OBJECTIFS: Réaliser des projets de développement animés par des volontaires.

INFORMATIONS GENERALES: *Création:* 1978. *Affiliée à:* FOCSIV. *Personnel/Total:* 123. *Bénévoles:* 123 dont: 38 dans les pays en développement. *Budget/Total 1993:* ECU 1629000 (US$ 1906000). *Sources financières:* *Privé:* 85%. *Public:* 10%. *Autofinancement:* 5%.

ACTIVITES DANS LES REGIONS EN DEVELOPPEMENT: Intervient directement dans les régions en développement. Intervient dans 2 pays. Maintient une présence locale sur le terrain. **Actions de Développement durable:** Aliments/famine; Dette/finances/commerce; Développement rural/agriculture; Enfants/jeunesse/famille; Envoi de volontaires/experts/assistance technique; Petites entreprises/secteur informel/artisanat; Santé/assainissement/eau; Secours d'urgence/réfugiés/aide humanitaire; Éducation/formation/alphabétisation; Énergie/transport. **Régions:** Afrique centrale; Amérique du Sud.

ACTIVITES D'INFORMATION ET D'EDUCATION: Domaines: Développement rural/agriculture; Enfants/jeunesse/famille; Pauvreté/conditions de vie; Réfugiés/migrants/groupes ethniques; Santé/assainissement/eau; Secours d'urgence/réfugiés/aide humanitaire; Éducation/formation/alphabétisation. **Activités:** Collecte de fonds; Édition/documents audiovisuels/documents éducatifs.

ITA2922

VOLONTARIATO INTERNAZIONALE DONNA EDUCAZIONE E SVILUPPO (VIDES)

Via dell'Ateneo Salesiano, 81, 00153 Roma, Italy.

Telephone: 39 (6) 5750048. *Fax:* 39 (6) 5750904. *Contact:* Maria Grazia Caputo, President.

OBJECTIVES: To promote the study of women's rights in developing countries. To promote development education and voluntary social programmes for marginalized young people. To promote and organise volunteer youth activities. To represent member organisations within the European Community institutions.

GENERAL INFORMATION: *Creation:* 1987. *Type of organisation:* network, coordinating body. *Member organisations:* 14. *Personnel/Total:* 36. *Salaried:* 10 of which: 2 in developing countries. *Volunteers:* 26 of which: 10 in developing countries.

PUBLICATIONS: *Periodicals:* VIDES Review (4). *Annual report.*

EVALUATION/RESEARCH: Evaluation reports available. Undertakes research activities.

COMMENTS: Undertakes activities in the Commonwealth of Independent States. Information activities related to the Commonwealth of Independent States.

ACTIVITIES IN DEVELOPING REGIONS: Present in developing regions. Active in 18 country(ies). Works through local field partners. **Sustainable Development Actions:** Children/youth/family; Education/training/literacy; Gender issues/women; Health/sanitation/water; Sending volunteers/experts/technical assistance. **Regions:** Caribbean; Central Africa; Central Asia and South Asia; East Africa; East Asia; Mexico and Central America; North Africa; South America; South East Asia; Southern Africa; West Africa.

INFORMATION AND EDUCATION ACTIVITIES: Topics: Children/youth/family; Education/training/literacy; Gender issues/women; International relations/cooperation/development aid; Peace/ethnic conflicts/armament/disarmament. **Activities:** Conferences/seminars/workshops/training activities; Exchanges/twinning/linking; Publishing/audiovisual materials/educational materials.

ITA2923

VOLONTARIATO INTERNAZIONALE PER LO SVILUPPO (VIS)
♦ Volontariat international pour le développement

Via Appia Antica, 126, 00179 Roma, Italie.

Téléphone: 39 (06) 5130253. *Fax:* 39 (06) 5130276. *Contact:* Antonio Raimondi, Président.

OBJECTIFS: Former et envoyer des volontaires dans le Tiers monde. Eduquer au développement en Italie.

INFORMATIONS GENERALES: *Création:* 1986. *Affiliée à:* FOCSIV. *Personnel/Total:* 26. *Salariés:* 5. *Bénévoles:* 21 dont: 18 dans les pays en développement. *Budget/Total 1993:* ECU 283000 (US$ 332000). *Sources financières:* *Privé:* 25%. *Public:* 72%. *Autofinancement:* 3%.

PUBLICATIONS: *Périodiques:* VISNOTIZIE (4). *Liste des publications.*

EVALUATION/RECHERCHE: Entreprend des activités de recherche.

COMMENTAIRES: Intervient dans la Communauté des Etats indépendants.

ACTIVITES DANS LES REGIONS EN DEVELOPPEMENT: Intervient directement dans les régions en développement. Maintient une présence locale sur le terrain. Intervient par l'intermédiaire d'organisations locales partenaires. **Actions de Développement durable:** Enfants/jeunesse/famille; Envoi de volontaires/experts/assistance technique; Questions relatives aux femmes; Éducation/formation/alphabétisation. **Régions:** Afrique australe; Afrique centrale; Afrique de l'Est; Afrique de l'Ouest; Afrique du Nord; Amérique du Sud; Asie du Sud-Est; Mexique et Amerique centrale; Moyen-Orient.

ACTIVITES D'INFORMATION ET D'EDUCATION: Domaines: Culture/tradition/religion; Droits de l'Homme/paix/conflits; Enfants/jeunesse/famille; Paix/conflits ethniques/armement/désarmement; Pauvreté/conditions de vie; Questions relatives aux femmes; Racisme/xénophobie/antisémitisme; Relations internationales/coopération/aide au développement; Relations économiques internationales/commerce/dette/finances; Réfugiés/migrants/groupes ethniques; Éducation/formation/alphabétisation. **Activités:** Campagnes d'information/expositions; Collecte de fonds; Conférences/séminaires/ateliers/activités de formation; Radiodiffusion/manifestations culturelles; Services d'information et de documentation/bases de données; Édition/documents audiovisuels/documents éducatifs.

See: *How to Use the Directory,* page 11.

LIE2924

CARITAS LIECHTENSTEIN

Binzastrasse 72, 9493 Mauren, Liechtenstein.

Contact: Marina Kieber.

LIE2925

HILFSWERK LIECHTENSTEIN ♦ Oeuvre d'assistance Liechtenstein

Dorfstrasse 27, 9495 Triesen, Liechtenstein.

Téléphone: 41 (75) 384 14 42. *Fax:* 41 (75) 41751444. *Contact:* Inge Büchel, Présidente.

OBJECTIFS: Collecter des fonds et des produits de première nécessité et les envoyer dans des pays en situation d'urgence.

INFORMATIONS GENERALES: *Création:* 1988. *Personnel/Total:* 200. *Bénévoles:* 200. *Budget/Total 1993:* ECU 354000 (US$ 459000). *Sources financières:* Privé: 34%. Public: 63%. Autofinancement: 3%.

PUBLICATIONS: *Rapport annuel.*

PREVISIONS D'ACTIVITES: Assistance aux réfugiés en Ex-Yougoslavie.

COMMENTAIRES: L'association envisage la coopération avec d'autres organisations en particulier lors des activités d'urgence. Intervient dans la Communauté des Etats indépendants.

ACTIVITES DANS LES REGIONS EN DEVELOPPEMENT: Intervient directement dans les régions en développement. Intervient dans 15 pays. Intervient par l'intermédiaire d'organisations locales partenaires. **Actions de Développement durable:** Développement urbain/habitat; Enfants/jeunesse/famille; Secours d'urgence/réfugiés/aide humanitaire. **Régions:** Afrique australe; Amérique du Sud; Asie centrale et Asie du Sud.

LIE2926

INDIEN HILFSWERK "HILFE ZUR SELBSTHILFE" ♦ Aid Organisation "Help to Help Yourselves"

Mitteldorf 1, 9490 Vaduz, Liechtenstein.

Telephone: 41 (75) 232 71 04. *Fax:* 41 (75) 232 38 76. *Contact:* Erich Ospelt.

OBJECTIVES: To provide financial aid to schools, orphanages and health care centres through Indian NGOs.

GENERAL INFORMATION: *Creation:* 1987. *Budget/Total 1993:* ECU 52000 (US$ 68000). *Financial sources:* Private: 80%. Public: 20%.

PUBLICATIONS: *Periodicals:* Rundschreiben (4). *Annual report. List of publications.*

ACTIVITIES IN DEVELOPING REGIONS: Present in developing regions. Active in 1 country(ies). Works through local field partners. **Sustainable Development Actions:** Children/youth/family; Education/training/literacy; Gender issues/women; Health/sanitation/water; Population/family planning/demography; Rural development/agriculture; Sending volunteers/experts/technical assistance. **Regions:** Central Asia and South Asia.

LIE2927

JUSTITIA ET PAX ♦ Justice et paix

BP 63, 9487 Bendern, Liechtenstein.

Téléphone: 41 (75) 373 50 61. *Fax:* 41 (75) 373 53 61. *Contact:* Pieter Allaart, Président.

OBJECTIFS: Aider les personnes en détresse, en particulier les réfugiés, en leur donnant un appui administratif et social.

INFORMATIONS GENERALES: *Création:* 1984. *Type d'organisation:* collectif. *Personnel/Total:* 10. *Salariés:* 1. *Bénévoles:* 9. *Sources financières:* Privé: 100%.

ACTIVITES D'INFORMATION ET D'EDUCATION: Domaines: Droits de l'Homme/paix/conflits; Enfants/jeunesse/famille; Questions relatives aux femmes; Racisme/xénophobie/antisémitisme; Réfugiés/migrants/groupes ethniques; Secours d'urgence/réfugiés/aide humanitaire. **Activités:** Lobbying/plaidoyer; Échanges/parrainage/jumelage.

LIE2928

LIECHTENSTEINISCHER ENTWICKLUNGSDIENST

Marianumstrasse 45, Postfach 386, 9490 Vaduz, Liechtenstein.

LIE2929

LIECHTENSTEINISCHER FASTENOPFER

Rtelti 537, 9497 Triesenberg, Liechtenstein.

Contact: Helmut Gassner.

LIE2930

LIECHTENSTEINISCHES ROTES KREUZ ♦ Liechtenstein Red Cross Society

Heiligkreuz 25, 9490 Vaduz, Liechtenstein.

Telephone: 41 (75) 232 22 94. *Fax:* 41 (75) 232 22 40. *Contact:* Marianne Marxer, Secretary General.

OBJECTIVES: To provide disaster relief in cases of natural disasters and armed conflicts.

GENERAL INFORMATION: *Creation:* 1945. *Affiliated to:* Federation of Red Cross and Red Crescent Societies. *Personnel/Total:* 15. *Salaried:* 15.

PUBLICATIONS: *Annual report.*

COMMENTS: Undertakes activities in the Commonwealth of Independent States.

ACTIVITIES IN DEVELOPING REGIONS: Active in 4 country(ies). Works through local field partners. **Sustainable Development Actions:** Emergency relief/refugees/humanitarian assistance; Health/sanitation/water; Human rights/peace/conflicts. **Regions:** Central Africa.

INFORMATION AND EDUCATION ACTIVITIES: Topics: Emergency relief/refugees/humanitarian assistance; Food/famine; International relations/cooperation/development aid; Poverty/living conditions. **Activities:** Fund raising.

LIE2931

TERRE DES HOMMES

Guler 411, 9493 Mauren, Liechtenstein.

Contact: Ursula Matt.

LIE2932

TIBET UNTERSTTZUNG LIECHTENST.

Im Quderle 9, 9490 Vaduz, Liechtenstein.

Contact: Hansjrg Quaderer.

LIE2933

VEREIN HILFSWERK EZIOHA-MMAKU NIGERIA

Feldkircherstrasse 52, 9494 Schaan, Liechtenstein.

Contact: Helga Netzer.

LIE2934

VEREIN WELT UND HEIMAT

Herrengasse 45, 9490 Vaduz, Liechtenstein.

Contact: Gerda Bicker.

LUX2935

ACTION DES CHRETIENS POUR L'ABOLITION DE LA TORTURE, LUXEMBOURG (ACAT LUXEMBOURG)

23 Avenue Gaston Diderich, 1420 Luxembourg, Luxembourg.

Téléphone: 352 - 25 04 57. *Fax:* 352 - 25 18 20 . *Contact:* Paule de Marcillac, Présidente.

OBJECTIFS: S'engager aux côtés de tous ceux qui luttent pour l'abolition de la torture et des exécutions capitales.

INFORMATIONS GENERALES: *Création:* 1985. *Personnel/Total:* 12. Bénévoles: 12. Budget/Total 1993: ECU 10000 (US$ 12000). *Sources financières:* Privé: 10%. Autofinancement: 90%.

PUBLICATIONS: *Rapport annuel.*

COMMENTAIRES: Agir en tant que relais des campagnes d'Amnesty international au Luxembourg. **Actions de Développement durable:** Droits de l'Homme/paix/conflits. **Régions:** Afrique australe; Afrique centrale; Afrique de l'Est; Afrique de l'Ouest; Afrique du Nord; Amérique du Sud; Asie centrale et Asie du Sud; Asie de l'Est; Asie du Sud-Est; Caraïbes; Mexique et Amerique centrale; Moyen-Orient; Océanie.

ACTIVITES D'INFORMATION ET D'EDUCATION: Domaines: Droits de l'Homme/paix/conflits. **Activités:** Campagnes d'information/expositions; Conférences/séminaires/ateliers/activités de formation; Édition/documents audiovisuels/documents éducatifs.

LUX2936

ACTION POUR UN MONDE UNI

30, rue des Aubépines, 1145 Luxembourg, Luxembourg.

Téléphone: 352 - 44 69 74. *Fax:* 352 - 44 69 74. *Contact:* Marie-Anne Thommes.

OBJECTIFS: Favoriser toutes les initiatives qui contribuent à créer un monde de justice et de paix. Diffuser la culture du dialogue entre les peuples. Contribuer au développement économique et social des peuples. Apporter une aide sanitaire, sociale, culturelle et technique aux pays en développement. Promouvoir la formation professionnelle et l'éducation.

INFORMATIONS GENERALES: *Création:* 1993. *Budget/Total 1993:* ECU 11000 (US$ 13000). *Sources financières:* Privé: 50%. Public: 49%. Autofinancement: 1%.

PREVISIONS D'ACTIVITES: Soutenir un projet en Argentine et au Mexique. Organiser des conférences et des rencontres pour promouvoir l'éducation à la paix et à la solidarité.

COMMENTAIRES: Intervient dans la Communauté des Etats indépendants.

ACTIVITES DANS LES REGIONS EN DEVELOPPEMENT: Intervient par l'intermédiaire d'organisations locales partenaires.

ACTIVITES D'INFORMATION ET D'EDUCATION: Domaines: Aliments/famine; Questions relatives aux femmes; Réfugiés/migrants/groupes ethniques; Secours d'urgence/réfugiés/aide humanitaire. **Activités:** Collecte de fonds.

LUX2937

ACTION SOLIDARITE TIERS MONDE (ASTM) ♦ Third World Solidarity Action

39, rue du Fort Neipperg, 2230 Luxembourg, Luxembourg.

Téléphone: 352 - 40 04 27. *Fax:* 352 - 40 58 49. *Contact:* Mike Mathias.

OBJECTIFS: Soutenir des projets de développement. Lier ce soutien au travail de sensibilisation de la population luxembourgeoise (revue, centre d'information, agence culturelle, campagnes).

INFORMATIONS GENERALES: *Création:* 1969. *Affiliée à:* CLONG (Belgique) - Cercle des ONG (Luxembourg) - Eurodad (Belgique). *Personnel/Total:* 64. Salariés: 4. Bénévoles: 60. *Budget/Total 1993:* ECU 494000 (US$ 578000). *Sources financières:* Privé: 25%. Public: 70%. Autofinancement: 5%.

PUBLICATIONS: *Périodiques:* Brennpunkt Drëtt Welt (10). *Liste des publications.*

EVALUATION/RECHERCHE: Rapports d'évaluation disponibles.

ACTIVITES DANS LES REGIONS EN DEVELOPPEMENT: Intervient dans 10 pays. Intervient par l'intermédiaire d'organisations locales partenaires. **Actions de Développement durable:** Développement rural/agriculture; Petites entreprises/secteur informel/artisanat; Questions relatives aux femmes; Écologie/environnement/biodiversité; Éducation/formation/alphabétisation. **Régions:** Afrique de l'Ouest; Amérique du Sud; Asie centrale et Asie du Sud; Mexique et Amerique centrale; Moyen-Orient.

ACTIVITES D'INFORMATION ET D'EDUCATION: Domaines: Aliments/famine; Culture/tradition/religion; Droits de l'Homme/paix/conflits; Développement rural/agriculture; Développement urbain/habitat; Emploi/chômage; Enfants/jeunesse/famille; Paix/conflits ethniques/armement/désarmement; Pauvreté/conditions de vie; Population/planning familial/démographie; Questions relatives aux femmes; Racisme/xénophobie/antisémitisme; Relations internationales/coopération/aide au développement; Relations économiques internationales/commerce/dette/finances; Réfugiés/migrants/groupes ethniques; Santé/assainissement/eau; Secours d'urgence/réfugiés/aide humanitaire; Écologie/environnement/biodiversité; Éducation/formation/alphabétisation. **Activités:** Campagnes d'information/expositions; Collecte de fonds; Conférences/séminaires/ateliers/activités de formation; Lobbying/plaidoyer; Radiodiffusion/manifestations culturelles; Services d'information et de documentation/bases de données; Échanges/parrainage/jumelage.

LUX2938

ADOPTION FAMILY INTERNATIONAL

13, Avenue Guillaume, 1651 Luxembourg, Luxembourg.

Contact: Anny-Regina Siebens, Initiator.

LUX2939

AKTIOUN A-B-C FIR BILDUNG A GESONDHEET AM TIERS-MONDE ♦ Action A-B-C en faveur de l'éducation et de la santé dans le Tiers monde

157 avenue Pasteur, B.P. 1744, 1017 Luxembourg, Luxembourg.

Téléphone: 352 - 48 33 54. *Contact:* Jean Hierzig.

LUX2940

AKTIOUN BANKOUOP

8 rue de l'Ecole, 8352 Dahlem, Luxembourg.

Téléphone: 352 - 3 85 23. *Contact:* Renée Lippert.

LUX2941

AMICALE INTERNATIONALE D'AIDE A L'ENFANCE LA PLUS MEURTRIE

92, bld. de la Pétrusse, 2320 Luxembourg, Luxembourg.

Téléphone: 352 - 50 72 98. *Contact:* Irène Dauphin, Présidente.

OBJECTIFS: Soutenir des projets d'investissement et de développement, dans le domaine social et éducatif, afin de secourir l'enfance la plus meurtrie, à l'échelle internationale, par une aide sur place ou par l'adoption au Luxembourg.

INFORMATIONS GENERALES: *Personnel/Total:* 9. Salariés: 1. Bénévoles: 8. *Budget/Total 1993:* ECU 214000 (US$ 251000). *Sources financières:* Privé: 68%. Public: 12%. Autofinancement: 20%.

EVALUATION/RECHERCHE: Rapports d'évaluation disponibles.

ACTIVITES DANS LES REGIONS EN DEVELOPPEMENT: Intervient dans 3 pays. Intervient par l'intermédiaire d'organisations locales partenaires. **Actions de Développement durable:** Enfants/jeunesse/famille. **Régions:** Amérique du Sud; Asie centrale et Asie du Sud; Asie de l'Est.

ACTIVITES D'INFORMATION ET D'EDUCATION: Domaines: Enfants/jeunesse/famille. **Activités:** Collecte de fonds.

LUX2942

AMICALE RWANDA-LUXEMBOURG

47, rue de Limpach, 3932 Mondercange, Luxembourg.

See: *How to Use the Directory,* page 11.

Téléphone: 352 - 55 30 35. *Contact:* Antonia Kinnen.

OBJECTIFS: Collecter des fonds pour la construction, l'aménagement et le bon fonctionnement d'un hôpital à Musasa. Etre solidaire du peuple rwandais.

INFORMATIONS GENERALES: *Création:* 1983. *Type d'organisation:* regroupement d'ONG. *Organisations membres:* 36. *Affiliée à:* Cercle de Coopération des Organisations Non-Gouvernementales de Développement du Luxembourg (Luxemboug). *Personnel/Total:* 12. *Bénévoles:* 12 dont: 4 dans les pays en développement. *Budget/Total 1993:* ECU 249000 (US$ 292000). *Sources financières:* Privé: 90%. Public: 6%. Autofinancement: 4%.

PUBLICATIONS: *Périodiques:* Un hôpital va être construit (1) - Nos activités (2). *Rapport annuel.*

EVALUATION/RECHERCHE: Rapports d'évaluation disponibles.

PREVISIONS D'ACTIVITES: En raison de la situation actuelle au Rwanda, l'organisation va renforcer ses activités d'accueil des réfugiés, d'aide médicale et humanitaire et l'assistance aux orphelins.

ACTIVITES DANS LES REGIONS EN DEVELOPPEMENT: Intervient directement dans les régions en développement. Maintient une présence locale sur le terrain. Intervient par l'intermédiaire d'organisations locales partenaires. **Actions de Développement durable:** Aliments/famine; Enfants/jeunesse/famille; Envoi de volontaires/experts/assistance technique; Santé/assainissement/eau; Secours d'urgence/réfugiés/aide humanitaire. **Régions:** Afrique centrale.

ACTIVITES D'INFORMATION ET D'EDUCATION: Domaines: Aliments/famine; Réfugiés/migrants/groupes ethniques; Santé/assainissement/eau; Secours d'urgence/réfugiés/aide humanitaire. **Activités:** Campagnes d'information/expositions; Collecte de fonds; Conférences/séminaires/ateliers/activités de formation; Échanges/parrainage/jumelage; Édition/documents audiovisuels/documents éducatifs; Éducation formelle.

LUX2943

LES AMIS "AYUDAME"-LUXEMBOURG ♦ Aide-nous

2, rue des Sports, 5322 Contern, Luxembourg.

Téléphone: 352 - 35 88 42. *Contact:* Reuter Gusty, Secrétaire.

OBJECTIFS: Apporter un soutien au Père Emilio Wagner qui aide les plus démunis au Brésil.

INFORMATIONS GENERALES: *Création:* 1981. *Affiliée à:* Cercle de coopération des organisations non-gouvernementales de Développement du Luxembourg.. *Personnel/Total:* 10. *Bénévoles:* 10. *Budget/Total 1993:* ECU 22000 (US$ 26000). *Sources financières:* Privé: 25%. Autofinancement: 75%.

ACTIVITES DANS LES REGIONS EN DEVELOPPEMENT: Intervient directement dans les régions en développement. Intervient dans 1 pays. Intervient par l'intermédiaire d'organisations locales partenaires. **Actions de Développement durable:** Enfants/jeunesse/famille; Santé/assainissement/eau; Éducation/formation/alphabétisation. **Régions:** Amérique du Sud.

LUX2944

AMITIES LUXEMBOURG-EQUATEUR

28 rue Alfred de Musset, 2175 Luxembourg, Luxembourg.

Téléphone: 352 - 47 47 38. *Contact:* Patrick Hoss.

LUX2945

AMNESTY INTERNATIONAL, SECTION LUXEMBOURGEOISE

BP 1914, 1019 Luxembourg, Luxembourg.

Téléphone: 352 - 48 16 87. *Fax:* 352 - 48 36 80.

LUX2946

APPUI AU DEVELOPPEMENT AUTONOME (ADA)

9 Am Beieblerg, 6973 Rameldange, Luxembourg.

Téléphone: 352 - 34 08 69. *Fax:* 352 - 34 08 47. *Contact:* Mia Adams, Présidente.

OBJECTIFS: Encourager le développement autonome dans le Tiers monde, par des ressources humaines économiques, financières propres, notamment par l'appui aux systèmes d'épargne, les crédits locaux, les garanties bancaires, etc. Lancer des programmes de suivi et de formation permettant de mieux identifier et de rentabiliser les ressources propres, puis d'assurer l'apprentissage par les bénéficiaires des outils utilisés.

INFORMATIONS GENERALES: *Création:* 1994. *Type d'organisation:* collectif. *Personnel/Total:* 11. *Salariés:* 1. *Bénévoles:* 10.

PUBLICATIONS: *Périodiques:* Dialogue (4). *Rapport annuel. Liste des publications.*

EVALUATION/RECHERCHE: Rapports d'évaluation disponibles. Entreprend des activités de recherche.

ACTIVITES DANS LES REGIONS EN DEVELOPPEMENT: Intervient directement dans les régions en développement. Intervient par l'intermédiaire d'organisations locales partenaires. **Actions de Développement durable:** Dette/finances/commerce; Démocratie/bonne gestion publique/création d'institutions/développement participatif; Développement rural/agriculture; Développement urbain/habitat; Petites entreprises/secteur informel/artisanat; Questions relatives aux femmes; Éducation/formation/alphabétisation. **Régions:** Afrique australe; Afrique de l'Ouest; Amérique du Sud.

ACTIVITES D'INFORMATION ET D'EDUCATION: Domaines: Développement rural/agriculture; Développement urbain/habitat; Questions relatives aux femmes; Relations internationales/coopération/aide au développement; Relations économiques internationales/commerce/dette/finances; Éducation/formation/alphabétisation. **Activités:** Collecte de fonds; Conférences/séminaires/ateliers/activités de formation; Services d'information et de documentation/bases de données.

LUX2947

ASSOCIATION D'AMITIE AVEC LE PEUPLE CAPVERDIEN ♦
Association for Friendship with the People of Cape Verdean

11 rue Michel Engels, 1465 Luxembourg, Luxembourg.

Téléphone: 352 - 44 86 57. *Fax:* 352 - 45 47 94. *Contact:* Carlo Back, Président.

LUX2948

ASSOCIATION DES GIRL GUIDES LUXEMBOURGEOISES (AGGL)

B.P. 2331, 1023 Luxembourg, Luxembourg.

Téléphone: 352 - 43 34 66. *Contact:* Jacqueline Ahnen, Commissaire Internationale.

OBJECTIFS: Sensibiliser les membres de l'associatioon aux problèmes des pays du tiers monde. Financer des projets de développement qui concernent les jeunes femmes et les jeunes filles de ces pays.

INFORMATIONS GENERALES: *Création:* 1915. *Personnel/Total:* 1. *Bénévoles:* 1. *Budget/Total 1993:* ECU 6000 (US$ 7000). *Sources financières:* Privé: 5%. Public: 95%.

PUBLICATIONS: *Périodiques:* Solidarité (4).

ACTIVITES DANS LES REGIONS EN DEVELOPPEMENT: Intervient dans 1 pays. Intervient par l'intermédiaire d'organisations locales partenaires. **Actions de Développement durable:** Éducation/formation/alphabétisation. **Régions:** Afrique de l'Ouest.

ACTIVITES D'INFORMATION ET D'EDUCATION: Domaines: Éducation/formation/alphabétisation. **Activités:** Collecte de fonds.

LUX2949

ASSOCIATION LUXEMBOURG-PEROU

13A, cité du Kiem, 3393 Roedgen, Luxembourg.

Téléphone: 352 - 44 42 93. *Fax:* 352 - 76 91 07. *Contact:* Boever Raymond, Président.

OBJECTIFS: Aider les enfants nécessiteux de la région de Ayalucho (Pérou), par la construction d'orphelinats, l'équipement des maisons, l'aide à l'éducation, etc. Faire adopter des enfants selon les normes du Ministère de la Famille du Luxembourg.

Voir : *Comment utiliser le répertoire,* page 11.

INFORMATIONS GENERALES: *Création:* 1991. *Personnel/Total:* 101. *Salariés:* 1. *Bénévoles:* 100. *Budget/Total 1993:* ECU 25000 (US$ 29000). *Sources financières:* Privé: 35%. Public: 50%. Autofinancement: 15%.

PUBLICATIONS: *Rapport annuel.*

PREVISIONS D'ACTIVITES: Lutte contre la tuberculose.

ACTIVITES DANS LES REGIONS EN DEVELOPPEMENT: Intervient dans 1 pays. **Actions de Développement durable:** Enfants/jeunesse/famille; Petites entreprises/secteur informel/artisanat; Santé/assainissement/eau; Secours d'urgence/réfugiés/aide humanitaire. **Régions:** Amérique du Sud.

ACTIVITES D'INFORMATION ET D'EDUCATION: **Domaines:** Aliments/famine; Emploi/chômage; Enfants/jeunesse/famille; Pauvreté/conditions de vie; Relations internationales/coopération/aide au développement; Santé/assainissement/eau. **Activités:** Campagnes d'information/expositions; Radiodiffusion/manifestations culturelles; Services d'information et de documentation/bases de données; Échanges/parrainage/jumelage.

LUX2950

ASSOCIATION POUR LA PROMOTION DES ILES DE PAIX

33C rue de la Forêt, 7227 Béreldange, Luxembourg.

Téléphone: 352 - 33 21 86. *Contact:* Gaby Faber-Hurt.

OBJECTIFS: Accompagner les gens qui veulent prendre en main leur avenir. Former de bons techniciens.

INFORMATIONS GENERALES: *Création:* 1962. *Personnel/Total:* 17. *Bénévoles:* 17. *Budget/Total 1993:* ECU 107000 (US$ 125000). *Sources financières:* Privé: 40%. Public: 50%. Autofinancement: 10%.

PUBLICATIONS: *Périodiques:* Transitions (4). *Rapport annuel.*

PREVISIONS D'ACTIVITES: Création d'un nouveau projet au Népal: formation des classes d'accueil et création d'une école professionnelle, à Itakari.

ACTIVITES DANS LES REGIONS EN DEVELOPPEMENT: Intervient directement dans les régions en développement. Maintient une présence locale sur le terrain. Intervient par l'intermédiaire d'organisations locales partenaires. **Actions de Développement durable:** Développement rural/agriculture; Éducation/formation/alphabétisation. **Régions:** Afrique de l'Ouest; Asie de l'Est.

ACTIVITES D'INFORMATION ET D'EDUCATION: **Domaines:** Pauvreté/conditions de vie. **Activités:** Campagnes d'information/expositions; Collecte de fonds.

LUX2951

ASSOCIATION SOLIDARITE LUXEMBOURG-NICARAGUA - AIDE AU DEVELOPPEMENT (ASLN)

93 rue de Strasbourg, B.P. 1766, 1017 Luxembourg, Luxembourg.

Téléphone: 352 - 48 23 73. *Contact:* G. Stoos.

LUX2952

ATD QUART MONDE ♦ ATD Fourth World

1 boulevard Royal, 2449 Luxembourg, Luxembourg.

Téléphone: 352 - 2 35 85. *Contact:* Soeur Véronique Hutsch, Présidente.

LUX2953

LA BERGERIE - SOS ENFANTS EN DETRESSE

Rue de Warken 173, 9088 Ettelbruck, Luxembourg.

Téléphone: 352 - 8 27 77. *Fax:* 352 - 81 64 10. *Contact:* René Foulqier, Président.

OBJECTIFS: Aider les enfants des rues et des bidonvilles de Bogota, en Colombie.

INFORMATIONS GENERALES: *Création:* 1985. *Affiliée à:* Cercle de Coopération des ONG du Luxembourg. *Personnel/Total:* 13. *Salariés:* 3 dont: 3 dans les pays en développement. *Bénévoles:* 10. *Sources financières:* Privé: 25%. Public: 75%.

PUBLICATIONS: *Rapport annuel.*

ACTIVITES DANS LES REGIONS EN DEVELOPPEMENT: Intervient directement dans les régions en développement. Maintient une présence locale sur le terrain. Intervient par l'intermédiaire d'organisations locales partenaires. **Actions de Développement durable:** Droits de l'Homme/paix/conflits; Développement rural/agriculture; Enfants/jeunesse/famille; Envoi de volontaires/experts/assistance technique; Petites entreprises/secteur informel/artisanat; Éducation/formation/alphabétisation. **Régions:** Amérique du Sud.

LUX2954

BRIDDERLECH DELEN ♦ Partager fraternellement

5 avenue Marie-Thérèse, 2132 Luxembourg, Luxembourg.

Téléphone: 352 - 4 47 43 - 2 58. *Fax:* 352 - 4 47 43 - 2 58. *Contact:* L'Abbé Henri Hamus, Vice- président.

OBJECTIFS: Réliser des projets de développement dans les pays du Tiers monde. Promouvoir le développement dans divers domaines: agriculture, éducation, santé, émancipation de la femme.

INFORMATIONS GENERALES: *Création:* 1968. *Personnel/Total:* 2. *Salariés:* 2. *Budget/Total 1993:* ECU 840000 (US$ 983000). *Sources financières:* Privé: 54%. Public: 45%. Autofinancement: 1%.

PUBLICATIONS: *Rapport annuel.*

EVALUATION/RECHERCHE: Rapports d'évaluation disponibles.

ACTIVITES DANS LES REGIONS EN DEVELOPPEMENT: Intervient dans 25 pays. Intervient par l'intermédiaire d'organisations locales partenaires. **Actions de Développement durable:** Développement rural/agriculture; Développement urbain/habitat; Enfants/jeunesse/famille; Questions relatives aux femmes; Santé/assainissement/eau; Éducation/formation/alphabétisation; Énergie/transport. **Régions:** Afrique australe; Afrique centrale; Afrique de l'Ouest; Amérique du Sud; Asie du Sud-Est.

ACTIVITES D'INFORMATION ET D'EDUCATION: **Domaines:** Culture/tradition/religion; Droits de l'Homme/paix/conflits; Développement rural/agriculture; Développement urbain/habitat; Enfants/jeunesse/famille; Paix/conflits ethniques/armement/désarmement; Pauvreté/conditions de vie; Questions relatives aux femmes; Racisme/xénophobie/antisémitisme; Relations internationales/coopération/aide au développement; Santé/assainissement/eau; Écologie/environnement/biodiversité; Éducation/formation/alphabétisation. **Activités:** Campagnes d'information/expositions; Conférences/séminaires/ateliers/activités de formation; Radiodiffusion/manifestations culturelles.

LUX2955

CARITAS LUXEMBOURG

B.P.1721, 1017 Luxembourg, Luxembourg.

Fax: 352 - 40 21 31. *Contact:* François Jacobs, Chef du Département Secours International.

OBJECTIFS: Organiser des secours d'urgence internationaux. Promouvoir des projets de développement éducatif, scolaire, socio-culturel, socio-économique, agricole et alimentaire destinés à venir en aide à des populations en détresse.

INFORMATIONS GENERALES: *Création:* 1992. *Type d'organisation:* regroupement d'ONG. *Organisations membres:* 13. *Affiliée à:* Caritas europe - Caritas Internationalis - Cercle de Coopération des Organisations Non-Gouvernementales de Développement. *Personnel/Total:* 74. *Salariés:* 30. *Bénévoles:* 40. *Budget/Total 1993:* ECU 1082000 (US$ 1266000). *Sources financières:* Privé: 30%. Public: 55%. Autofinancement: 15%.

PUBLICATIONS: *Rapport annuel.*

COMMENTAIRES: Intervient dans la Communauté des Etats indépendants.

ACTIVITES DANS LES REGIONS EN DEVELOPPEMENT: Intervient dans 11 pays. Intervient par l'intermédiaire d'organisations locales partenaires. **Actions de Développement durable:** Aliments/famine; Enfants/jeunesse/famille; Santé/assainissement/eau; Secours d'urgence/réfugiés/aide humanitaire. **Régions:** Afrique australe; Afrique

See: *How to Use the Directory,* page 11.

centrale; Afrique de l'Est; Afrique de l'Ouest; Afrique du Nord; Amérique du Sud; Asie centrale et Asie du Sud; Moyen-Orient.

ACTIVITES D'INFORMATION ET D'EDUCATION: Domaines: Aliments/famine; Développement rural/agriculture; Développement urbain/habitat; Enfants/jeunesse/famille; Pauvreté/conditions de vie; Relations internationales/coopération/aide au développement; Réfugiés/migrants/groupes ethniques; Santé/assainissement/eau; Secours d'urgence/réfugiés/aide humanitaire. **Activités:** Campagnes d'information/expositions; Collecte de fonds; Conférences/séminaires/ateliers/activités de formation; Lobbying/plaidoyer; Radiodiffusion/manifestations culturelles.

LUX2956
CARITAS SERVICE REFUGIES ET AIDE INTERNATIONALE
B.P. 1721, 1017 Luxembourg, Luxembourg.

Téléphone: 352 - 40 21 31-1. *Fax:* 352 - 40 21 31 309. *Contact:* Agnès Rausch, Responsable Service Réfugiés.

OBJECTIFS: Lutter contre toutes les formes de pauvreté, les fléaux sociaux, les maladies et les misères humaines au Luxembourg et à l'étranger.

INFORMATIONS GENERALES: *Création:* 1991. *Type d'organisation:* collectif. *Organisations membres:* 15. *Affiliée à:* Collectif Réfugiés du Luxembourg (Luxembourg) - Caritas-Europe - Cercle des ONG luxembourgeoises - ECRE - Caritas Internationalis. *Personnel/Total:* 6. *Salariés:* 6. *Budget/Total 1993:* ECU 1470000 (US$ 1720000). *Sources financières:* Privé: 60%. Public: 40%.

PUBLICATIONS: *Périodiques:* Caritas-News (2). *Rapport annuel.*

COMMENTAIRES: Intervient dans la Communauté des Etats indépendants.

ACTIVITES DANS LES REGIONS EN DEVELOPPEMENT: Intervient directement dans les régions en développement. Intervient dans 12 pays. Intervient par l'intermédiaire d'organisations locales partenaires. **Actions de Développement durable:** Aliments/famine; Développement urbain/habitat; Enfants/jeunesse/famille; Santé/assainissement/eau; Secours d'urgence/réfugiés/aide humanitaire; Éducation/formation/alphabétisation. **Régions:** Afrique centrale; Afrique de l'Est; Afrique de l'Ouest; Afrique du Nord; Amérique du Sud; Asie centrale et Asie du Sud; Moyen-Orient.

ACTIVITES D'INFORMATION ET D'EDUCATION: Domaines: Aliments/famine; Développement urbain/habitat; Secours d'urgence/réfugiés/aide humanitaire. **Activités:** Campagnes d'information/expositions; Collecte de fonds; Conférences/séminaires/ateliers/activités de formation; Lobbying/plaidoyer; Radiodiffusion/manifestations culturelles.

LUX2957
CERCLE DE COOPERATION DES ORGANISATIONS NON GOUVERNEMENTALES DE DEVELOPPEMENT DU LUXEMBOURG
5, avenue Marie-Thérèse, 2132 Luxembourg, Luxembourg.

Téléphone: 352 - 44743. *Fax:* 352 - 40 58 49. *Contact:* Gaston Kemp, Président.

OBJECTIFS: Coordonner et former les ONG luxembourgeoises.

INFORMATIONS GENERALES: *Création:* 1984. *Type d'organisation:* regroupement d'ONG. *Organisations membres:* 42. *Personnel/Total:* 11. *Salariés:* 1. *Bénévoles:* 10. *Budget/Total 1993:* ECU 15000 (US$ 17000). *Sources financières:* Public: 54%. Autofinancement: 46%.

PUBLICATIONS: *Périodiques:* Bulletin de liaison des ONG (5).

PREVISIONS D'ACTIVITES: Organisation de cours à la gestion de projets.

ACTIVITES D'INFORMATION ET D'EDUCATION: Domaines: Aliments/famine; Culture/tradition/religion; Droits de l'Homme/paix/conflits; Développement rural/agriculture; Développement urbain/habitat; Emploi/chômage; Enfants/jeunesse/famille; Paix/conflits ethniques/armement/désarmement; Pauvreté/conditions de vie; Population/planning familial/démographie; Questions relatives aux femmes; Racisme/xénophobie/antisémitisme; Relations internationales/coopération/aide au développement; Relations économiques internationales/commerce/dette/finances;

Réfugiés/migrants/groupes ethniques; Santé/assainissement/eau; Secours d'urgence/réfugiés/aide humanitaire; Écologie/environnement/biodiversité; Éducation/formation/alphabétisation. **Activités:** Conférences/séminaires/ateliers/activités de formation; Lobbying/plaidoyer.

LUX2958
CHILES KINDER ♦ Enfants du Chili
20, rue des Champs, 3327 Crauthem, Luxembourg.

Téléphone: 352 - 36 93 37. *Contact:* Michel Schaack, Président.

OBJECTIFS: Agir en faveur de la promotion des personnes démunies au Chili, en aidant des organisations et des œuvres sociales locales. Sensibiliser l'opinion publique luxembourgeoise aux problèmes du Chili.

INFORMATIONS GENERALES: *Création:* 1987. *Affiliée à:* Cercle de Coopération des ONG du Luxembourg. *Personnel/Total:* 14. *Bénévoles:* 14. *Budget/Total 1993:* ECU 148000 (US$ 173000). *Sources financières:* Privé: 44%. Public: 56%.

PUBLICATIONS: *Périodiques:* Chiles Kinder Info (3). *Rapport annuel.* Liste des publications.

ACTIVITES DANS LES REGIONS EN DEVELOPPEMENT: Intervient par l'intermédiaire d'organisations locales partenaires. **Actions de Développement durable:** Droits de l'Homme/paix/conflits; Démocratie/bonne gestion publique/création d'institutions/développement participatif; Développement rural/agriculture; Enfants/jeunesse/famille; Population/planning familial/démographie; Questions relatives aux femmes; Écologie/environnement/biodiversité; Éducation/formation/alphabétisation. **Régions:** Amérique du Sud.

ACTIVITES D'INFORMATION ET D'EDUCATION: Domaines: Aliments/famine; Culture/tradition/religion; Droits de l'Homme/paix/conflits; Développement rural/agriculture; Développement urbain/habitat; Emploi/chômage; Enfants/jeunesse/famille; Paix/conflits ethniques/armement/désarmement; Pauvreté/conditions de vie; Questions relatives aux femmes; Relations économiques internationales/commerce/dette/finances; Secours d'urgence/réfugiés/aide humanitaire; Écologie/environnement/biodiversité. **Activités:** Campagnes d'information/expositions; Collecte de fonds; Conférences/séminaires/ateliers/activités de formation; Lobbying/plaidoyer; Radiodiffusion/manifestations culturelles; Édition/documents audiovisuels/documents éducatifs.

LUX2959
CHRESCHTE MAM SAHEL ♦ Chrétiens pour le Sahel
23, boulevard Dr. Charles Marx, 2130 Luxembourg, Luxembourg.

Téléphone: 352 - 49 27 87. *Contact:* M. Roger Hoffman.

OBJECTIFS: Soutenir financièrement des projets de développement en Afrique et au Sahel.

INFORMATIONS GENERALES: *Création:* 1984. *Affiliée à:* Cercle de Coopération des ONG de Développement. *Personnel/Total:* 50. *Bénévoles:* 50. *Budget/Total 1993:* ECU 1483000 (US$ 1734000). *Sources financières:* Privé: 20%. Public: 75%. Autofinancement: 5%.

PUBLICATIONS: *Périodiques:* Chrétiens pour le Sahel (2).

ACTIVITES DANS LES REGIONS EN DEVELOPPEMENT: Intervient dans 4 pays. Intervient par l'intermédiaire d'organisations locales partenaires. **Actions de Développement durable:** Développement rural/agriculture; Enfants/jeunesse/famille; Petites entreprises/secteur informel/artisanat; Population/planning familial/démographie; Questions relatives aux femmes; Santé/assainissement/eau; Secours d'urgence/réfugiés/aide humanitaire; Écologie/environnement/biodiversité; Éducation/formation/alphabétisation; Énergie/transport. **Régions:** Afrique de l'Ouest.

ACTIVITES D'INFORMATION ET D'EDUCATION: Domaines: Aliments/famine; Culture/tradition/religion; Développement rural/agriculture; Enfants/jeunesse/famille; Population/planning familial/démographie; Questions relatives aux femmes; Relations économiques internationales/commerce/dette/finances; Santé/assainissement/eau; Écologie/environnement/biodiversité. **Activités:** Collecte de fonds.

LUX2960
CHRISTIAN SOLIDARITY INTERNATIONAL
21 boulevard Jules Salentiny, 2511 Luxembourg, Luxembourg.

Voir : *Comment utiliser le répertoire,* page 11.

Contact: Robert Brosius.

LUX2961

COMITE LUXEMBOURGEOIS POUR L'UNICEF ♦ Luxembourg
Committee for UNICEF

99 route d'Arlon, 1140 Luxembourg, Luxembourg.

Téléphone: 352 - 44 87 15. *Fax:* 352 - 44 53 14. *Contact:* Roger Conrad, Secrétaire général.

OBJECTIFS: Engager et poursuivre une action d'appui à l'œuvre de l'UNICEF.

INFORMATIONS GENERALES: *Création:* 1979. *Personnel/Total:* 44. *Salariés:* 4. *Bénévoles:* 40. *Budget/Total 1993:* ECU 1374000 (US\$ 1607000). *Sources financières:* Privé: 15%. Public: 5%. Autofinancement: 80%.

PUBLICATIONS: *Rapport annuel.*

PREVISIONS D'ACTIVITES: Convention relative aux droits de l'enfant. Enfants dans des situations de conflits (guerres). Problème des mines terrestres.

COMMENTAIRES: Intervient dans la Communauté des Etats indépendants. Activités d'information concernant la Communauté des Etats indépendants.

ACTIVITES DANS LES REGIONS EN DEVELOPPEMENT: Intervient dans 138 pays. Intervient par l'intermédiaire d'organisations locales partenaires.

ACTIVITES D'INFORMATION ET D'EDUCATION: Domaines: Enfants/jeunesse/famille; Santé/assainissement/eau. **Activités:** Campagnes d'information/expositions; Collecte de fonds; Conférences/séminaires/ateliers/activités de formation; Radiodiffusion/manifestations culturelles; Services d'information et de documentation/bases de données; Édition/documents audiovisuels/documents éducatifs.

LUX2962

COMMISSION JUSTICE ET PAIX

52 rue Jules Wilhelm, 2728 Luxembourg, Luxembourg.

Téléphone: 352 - 43 60 51 40. *Fax:* 352 - 42 31 03. *Contact:* Georges Hellinghausen, Président.

OBJECTIFS: Sensibiliser la population et lutter pour la justice sociale, la paix, l'environnement et les droits de l'homme.

INFORMATIONS GENERALES: *Création:* 1970. *Affiliée à:* Conférence des Commissions "Justice et Paix" d'Europe.. *Personnel/Total:* 1. *Salariés:* 1.

PUBLICATIONS: *Liste des publications.*

ACTIVITES D'INFORMATION ET D'EDUCATION: Domaines: Aliments/famine; Culture/tradition/religion; Droits de l'Homme/paix/conflits; Développement rural/agriculture; Développement urbain/habitat; Emploi/chômage; Enfants/jeunesse/famille; Paix/conflits ethniques/armement/désarmement; Pauvreté/conditions de vie; Population/planning familial/démographie; Questions relatives aux femmes; Racisme/xénophobie/antisémitisme; Relations internationales/coopération/aide au développement; Relations économiques internationales/commerce/dette/finances; Réfugiés/migrants/groupes ethniques; Santé/assainissement/eau; Secours d'urgence/réfugiés/aide humanitaire; Écologie/environnement/biodiversité; Éducation/formation/alphabétisation. **Activités:** Lobbying/plaidoyer; Services d'information et de documentation/bases de données; Édition/documents audiovisuels/documents éducatifs.

LUX2963

CONFERENCE ST. VINCENT DE PAUL

B.P. 138, 2011 Luxembourg, Luxembourg.

Contact: Mathias Thinnes.

LUX2964

CROIX ROUGE LUXEMBOURGEOISE

B.P. 404, 2014 Luxembourg, Luxembourg.

Téléphone: 352 - 45 02 02. *Fax:* 352 - 45 72 69. *Contact:* Jacques Hansen, Directeur général.

OBJECTIFS: Travailler au Luxembourg pour le bien-être social et sanitaire de la population. Soutenir des missions et opérations de la Croix-Rouge sur le plan international.

INFORMATIONS GENERALES: *Création:* 1914. *Affiliée à:* Fédération Internationale des Sociétés de la Croix-Rouge et du Croissant Rouge (Suisse) - Bureau de Liaison Croix-Rouge. *Personnel/Total:* 240. *Salariés:* 230 dont: 1 dans les pays en développement. *Bénévoles:* 10. *Budget/Total 1993:* ECU 13740000 (US\$ 16070000). *Sources financières:* Privé: 7%. Public: 20%. Autofinancement: 73%.

PUBLICATIONS: *Rapport annuel.*

COMMENTAIRES: Intervient dans la Communauté des Etats indépendants.

ACTIVITES DANS LES REGIONS EN DEVELOPPEMENT: Intervient directement dans les régions en développement. Intervient dans 7 pays. Maintient une présence locale sur le terrain. Intervient par l'intermédiaire d'organisations locales partenaires. **Actions de Développement durable:** Aliments/famine; Envoi de volontaires/experts/assistance technique; Santé/assainissement/eau; Secours d'urgence/réfugiés/aide humanitaire. **Régions:** Afrique de l'Ouest; Amérique du Sud; Asie centrale et Asie du Sud; Asie du Sud-Est.

LUX2965

ECLAIREURS ET ECLAIREUSES POUR LE DEVELOPPEMENT COMMUNAUTAIRE (FNEL)

B.P. 2676, 1026 Luxembourg, Luxembourg.

Téléphone: 352 - 48 49 55. *Fax:* 352 - 49 46 47. *Contact:* Paul Geditz.

OBJECTIFS: Proposer des projets de développement économique, social, technique et culturel en faveur des pays en voie de développement et envoyer des coopérants dans le cadre de ces projets. Fournir une aide à des organisations, institutions et habitants de ces pays, notamment aux organisations "guides et scouts".

INFORMATIONS GENERALES: *Création:* 1989. *Personnel/Total:* 1. *Bénévoles:* 1. *Budget/Total 1993:* ECU 247000 (US\$ 289000). *Sources financières:* Privé: 50%. Public: 50%.

PUBLICATIONS: *Rapport annuel.*

EVALUATION/RECHERCHE: Rapports d'évaluation disponibles.

ACTIVITES DANS LES REGIONS EN DEVELOPPEMENT: Intervient directement dans les régions en développement. Intervient dans 1 pays. Maintient une présence locale sur le terrain. Intervient par l'intermédiaire d'organisations locales partenaires. **Actions de Développement durable:** Enfants/jeunesse/famille; Santé/assainissement/eau; Écologie/environnement/biodiversité; Éducation/formation/alphabétisation. **Régions:** Asie centrale et Asie du Sud.

LUX2966

ECOLE SANS FRONTIERES

3 montée de l'Abbaye, 9713 Clervaux, Luxembourg.

Contact: Rita Reuter.

LUX2967

ENFANTS DE L'ESPOIR - NINOS DE LA ESPERANZA

53 rue de Pétange, 4645 Niederkorn, Luxembourg.

Téléphone: 352 - 58 98 99. *Fax:* 352 - 39 78 20. *Contact:* Francine Lippert, Présidente.

OBJECTIFS: Aider les familles nécessiteuses des bidonvilles de Bogota par l'intermédiaire de parrainages (prise en charge scolaire, alimentaire,etc). Assurer une formation aux mères seules. Soutenir toute initiative dans les domaines de l'éducation et de la formation.

INFORMATIONS GENERALES: *Création:* 1991. *Personnel/Total:* 21. *Salariés:* 12 dont: 12 dans les pays en développement. *Bénévoles:* 9 dont: 1 dans les pays en développement. *Budget/Total 1993:* ECU 91000 (US\$ 109000). *Sources financières:* Privé: 52%. Public: 36%. Autofinancement: 12%.

See: *How to Use the Directory,* page 11.

PUBLICATIONS: *Rapport annuel.*

EVALUATION/RECHERCHE: Rapports d'évaluation disponibles.

PREVISIONS D'ACTIVITES: Développer des ateliers de couture et d'artisanat.

ACTIVITES DANS LES REGIONS EN DEVELOPPEMENT: Intervient directement dans les régions en développement. Intervient dans 1 pays. Maintient une présence locale sur le terrain. Intervient par l'intermédiaire d'organisations locales partenaires. **Actions de Développement durable:** Enfants/jeunesse/famille; Petites entreprises/secteur informel/artisanat; Questions relatives aux femmes; Éducation/formation/alphabétisation. **Régions:** Amérique du Sud.

ACTIVITES D'INFORMATION ET D'EDUCATION: Domaines: Enfants/jeunesse/famille; Questions relatives aux femmes; Éducation/formation/alphabétisation. **Activités:** Campagnes d'information/expositions; Collecte de fonds; Conférences/séminaires/ateliers/activités de formation; Échanges/parrainage/jumelage; Éducation formelle.

LUX2968

ENG BRECK MAT LATAINAMERIKA ♦ Un pont avec l'Amérique latine

17, rue Jean l'Aveugle, 9208 Diekirch, Luxembourg.

Téléphone: 352 - 80 80 71. **Fax:** 352 - 80 80 71. **Contact:** Jacques Dahm, Président.

OBJECTIFS: Favoriser le développement dans les pays d'Amérique latine. Organiser des voyages d'étude, et sensibiliser les Luxembourgeois aux problèmes de l'Amérique latine.

INFORMATIONS GENERALES: Création: 1986. **Type d'organisation:** réseau. **Affiliée à:** Cercle des ONG (Luxembourg). **Personnel/Total:** 8. *Salariés:* 8 dont: 8 dans les pays en développement. **Budget/Total 1993:** ECU 1532000 (US$ 1792000). **Sources financières:** Privé: 20%. Public: 76%. Autofinancement: 4%.

PUBLICATIONS: Périodiques: Eng mat Latäinamerika (5). *Rapport annuel.*

EVALUATION/RECHERCHE: Rapports d'évaluation disponibles.

PREVISIONS D'ACTIVITES: projet d'aide aux enfants de la rue à, Medellin.

ACTIVITES DANS LES REGIONS EN DEVELOPPEMENT: Intervient directement dans les régions en développement. Intervient dans 6 pays. Maintient une présence locale sur le terrain. Intervient par l'intermédiaire d'organisations locales partenaires. **Actions de Développement durable:** Développement rural/agriculture; Développement urbain/habitat; Enfants/jeunesse/famille; Petites entreprises/secteur informel/artisanat; Questions relatives aux femmes; Santé/assainissement/eau; Secours d'urgence/réfugiés/aide humanitaire; Écologie/environnement/biodiversité; Éducation/formation/alphabétisation. **Régions:** Amérique du Sud; Mexique et Amerique centrale.

ACTIVITES D'INFORMATION ET D'EDUCATION: Domaines: Développement rural/agriculture; Santé/assainissement/eau; Éducation/formation/alphabétisation. **Activités:** Campagnes d'information/expositions; Collecte de fonds; Conférences/séminaires/ateliers/activités de formation; Radiodiffusion/manifestations culturelles.

LUX2969

ENTWECKLONG DURCH GERECHTEN HANDEL

30 rue Béatrix, 1225 Luxembourg, Luxembourg.

Téléphone: 352 - 433664. **Contact:** Renée Estgen.

OBJECTIFS: Participer à la création, au développement et au fonctionnement de communautés artisanales dans les pays en développement. Assurer à leurs membres un revenu juste et durable leur permettant de rester dans leur milieu traditionnel.

INFORMATIONS GENERALES: Création: 1987. **Personnel/Total:** 31. *Bénévoles:* 31. **Budget/Total 1993:** ECU 47000 (US$ 55000). **Sources financières:** Privé: 50%. Autofinancement: 50%.

ACTIVITES DANS LES REGIONS EN DEVELOPPEMENT: Intervient directement dans les régions en développement. Intervient dans 3 pays.

Intervient par l'intermédiaire d'organisations locales partenaires. **Actions de Développement durable:** Développement rural/agriculture; Développement urbain/habitat; Enfants/jeunesse/famille; Éducation/formation/alphabétisation. **Régions:** Amérique du Sud; Mexique et Amerique centrale; Moyen-Orient.

ACTIVITES D'INFORMATION ET D'EDUCATION: Domaines: Développement rural/agriculture; Développement urbain/habitat; Enfants/jeunesse/famille; Éducation/formation/alphabétisation. **Activités:** Collecte de fonds.

LUX2970

ENVIRONMENTALLY SUSTAINABLE FORESTRY

10 rue Schrobilgen, 2526 Luxembourg, Luxembourg.

Contact: Jup Weber.

LUX2971

ETAL - FIR E BESSERT LIEWEN AN LATEINAMERIKA

14 rue de Kayl, 3385 Noertzange, Luxembourg.

Contact: Antoine Bohnert.

LUX2972

EUROPE TIERS-MONDE

Rue Alcide de Gasperi, Bâtiment Jean Monnet, Bureau B2/82, 2920 Luxembourg, Luxembourg.

Téléphone: 352 - 43 01 33. **Fax:** 352 - 43 01 34. **Contact:** Gérard Brémaud, Président.

OBJECTIFS: Aider, sans considération raciale, religieuse ou politique, les populations du Tiers-Monde en soutenant les initiatives locales concernant le développement.

INFORMATIONS GENERALES: Création: 1986. **Affiliée à:** Cercle des ONG du Luxembourg (Luxembourg). **Personnel/Total:** 7. *Bénévoles:* 7. **Budget/Total 1993:** ECU 45000 (US$ 53000). **Sources financières:** Autofinancement: 100%.

PUBLICATIONS: *Rapport annuel.*

EVALUATION/RECHERCHE: Rapports d'évaluation disponibles.

ACTIVITES DANS LES REGIONS EN DEVELOPPEMENT: Intervient dans 6 pays. Intervient par l'intermédiaire d'organisations locales partenaires. **Actions de Développement durable:** Dette/finances/commerce; Développement rural/agriculture; Santé/assainissement/eau; Éducation/formation/alphabétisation. **Régions:** Afrique centrale; Afrique de l'Est; Afrique de l'Ouest; Amérique du Sud; Mexique et Amerique centrale.

ACTIVITES D'INFORMATION ET D'EDUCATION: Domaines: Développement rural/agriculture; Santé/assainissement/eau. **Activités:** Collecte de fonds.

LUX2973

FONDATION LUXEMBOURGEOISE RAOUL FOLLEREAU (FFL)

151 avenue du X Septembre, 2551 Luxembourg, Luxembourg.

Téléphone: 352 - 44 66 06/ 45 78 07. **Fax:** 352 - 45 96 53. **Contact:** Mr. Jos Hilger, Président.

OBJECTIFS: Promouvoir la fraternité et la solidarité entre les hommes. Entreprendre des missions charitables et humanitaires, en particulier dans les domaines de la lutte contre la lèpre et du secours aux pays en voie de développement, ceci conformément à la pensée de Raoul Follereau, et dans un esprit d'indépendance absolue vis-à-vis de toute opinion religieuse, publique et sociale.

INFORMATIONS GENERALES: Création: 1966. **Affiliée à:** Fédération Internationale des Associations contre la lèpre (Royaume Uni) -Union internationale des Associations Raoul Follereau (France). **Personnel/Total:** 12. *Salariés:* 2. *Bénévoles:* 10. **Budget/Total 1993:** ECU 2051000 (US$ 2399000).

PUBLICATIONS: Périodiques: La Lèpre se guérit (2). *Liste des publications.*

Voir : *Comment utiliser le répertoire,* page 11.

ACTIVITES DANS LES REGIONS EN DEVELOPPEMENT: Intervient directement dans les régions en développement. Intervient dans 26 pays. Maintient une présence locale sur le terrain. Intervient par l'intermédiaire d'organisations locales partenaires. **Actions de Développement durable:** Aliments/famine; Développement rural/agriculture; Développement urbain/habitat; Enfants/jeunesse/famille; Petites entreprises/secteur informel/artisanat; Questions relatives aux femmes; Santé/assainissement/eau; Éducation/formation/alphabétisation. **Régions:** Afrique australe; Afrique centrale; Afrique de l'Est; Afrique de l'Ouest; Amérique du Sud; Asie centrale et Asie du Sud; Asie de l'Est; Asie du Sud-Est; Mexique et Amerique centrale; Moyen-Orient.

LUX2974
FONDS DE SOLIDARITE MONDIALE

11 rue du Commerce, 1351 Luxembourg, Luxembourg.

Contact: Robert Schadeck.

LUX2975
FONDS POUR LES VILLAGES D'ENFANTS SOS DANS LE MONDE (SOS-INTERFONDS) ♦ Fund for SOS-Children's Villages throughout the World

Rue Glesener 37, 1631 Luxembourg, Luxembourg.

Téléphone: 352 - 49 04 30. *Fax:* 352 - 40 75 30. *Contact:* Barbara François, présidente.

OBJECTIFS: Participer à la création, au développement et au fonctionnement des Villages d'Enfants SOS dans le Tiers monde.

INFORMATIONS GENERALES: *Création:* 1974. *Type d'organisation:* regroupement d'ONG. *Affiliée à:* SOS Kinderdorf International (Autriche). *Personnel/Total:* 9. *Salariés:* 3. *Bénévoles:* 6. *Budget/Total 1993:* ECU 840000 (US$ 983000). *Sources financières:* Privé: 88%. Public: 6%. Autofinancement: 6%.

PUBLICATIONS: *Périodiques:* Bulletin SOS-Interfonfs (4). *Rapport annuel.*

COMMENTAIRES: Les activités mentionnées ci-dessus sont entreprises par l'intermédiaire de SOS Kinderdorf International. Intervient dans la Communauté des Etats indépendants.

ACTIVITES DANS LES REGIONS EN DEVELOPPEMENT: Intervient dans 60 pays. Intervient par l'intermédiaire d'organisations locales partenaires. **Actions de Développement durable:** Enfants/jeunesse/famille; Secours d'urgence/réfugiés/aide humanitaire; Éducation/formation/alphabétisation. **Régions:** Afrique australe; Afrique centrale; Afrique de l'Est; Afrique de l'Ouest; Afrique du Nord; Amérique du Sud; Asie centrale et Asie du Sud; Asie de l'Est; Asie du Sud-Est; Caraïbes; Mexique et Amerique centrale; Moyen-Orient.

LUX2976
FRERES DES HOMMES, LUXEMBOURG (FDH-LUX)

11, rue des Bains, 1212 Luxembourg, Luxembourg.

Téléphone: 352 - 46 62 38. *Fax:* 352 - 22 19 55. *Contact:* Fabienne Reding, Secrétaire générale.

OBJECTIFS: Contribuer au développement dans les pays du Tiers monde. Soutenir des projets de toutes sortes (agriculture, femmes, formation, sensibilisation, actions économiques et sociales), en Amérique latine, en Afrique et en Asie.

INFORMATIONS GENERALES: *Création:* 1974. *Type d'organisation:* regroupement d'ONG. *Organisations membres:* 5. *Personnel/Total:* 7. *Salariés:* 4.

PUBLICATIONS: *Rapport annuel.*

EVALUATION/RECHERCHE: Rapports d'évaluation disponibles.

ACTIVITES DANS LES REGIONS EN DEVELOPPEMENT: Intervient directement dans les régions en développement. Intervient dans 7 pays. Intervient par l'intermédiaire d'organisations locales partenaires. **Actions de Développement durable:** Aliments/famine; Droits de l'Homme/paix/conflits; Démocratie/bonne gestion publique/création d'institutions/développement participatif; Développement rural/agriculture; Développement urbain/habitat; Enfants/jeunesse/famille; Petites entreprises/secteur informel/artisanat; Questions relatives aux

femmes; Santé/assainissement/eau; Écologie/environnement/biodiversité; Éducation/formation/alphabétisation. **Régions:** Afrique australe; Afrique de l'Ouest; Amérique du Sud; Mexique et Amerique centrale.

ACTIVITES D'INFORMATION ET D'EDUCATION: Domaines: Culture/tradition/religion; Droits de l'Homme/paix/conflits; Développement rural/agriculture; Développement urbain/habitat; Enfants/jeunesse/famille; Population/planning familial/démographie; Relations internationales/coopération/aide au développement; Secours d'urgence/réfugiés/aide humanitaire; Éducation/formation/alphabétisation. **Activités:** Campagnes d'information/expositions; Collecte de fonds; Conférences/séminaires/ateliers/activités de formation; Lobbying/plaidoyer; Radiodiffusion/manifestations culturelles; Échanges/parrainage/jumelage; Édition/documents audiovisuels/documents éducatifs; Éducation formelle.

LUX2977
GROUPE NORD-SUD

19 rue Epernay, 1490 Luxembourg, Luxembourg.

Contact: José Balaguer.

LUX2978
GUIDEN A SCOUTEN MAT DER DRETTER WELT ♦ Guides et Scouts avec le Tiers monde

5 avenue Marie-Thérèse, B.P. 313, 2013 Luxembourg, Luxembourg.

Téléphone: 352 - 44 74 32 56. *Fax:* 352 - 44 74 32 49. *Contact:* Jos Loos, Président.

OBJECTIFS: Réaliser des projets de développement économique, social, technique et culturel dans des pays du Tiers monde, en apportant une aide à des organisations locales de Guides et de Scouts. Envoyer des coopérants dans le cadre de ces projets. Collaborer, au Luxembourg, avec les institutions qui poursuivent des buts similaires.

INFORMATIONS GENERALES: *Création:* 1987. *Personnel/Total:* 26. *Salariés:* 5 dont: 5 dans les pays en développement. *Bénévoles:* 21. *Sources financières:* Privé: 15%. Public: 75%. Autofinancement: 10%.

ACTIVITES DANS LES REGIONS EN DEVELOPPEMENT: Intervient directement dans les régions en développement. Intervient dans 1 pays. Maintient une présence locale sur le terrain. **Actions de Développement durable:** Développement rural/agriculture; Développement urbain/habitat; Enfants/jeunesse/famille; Envoi de volontaires/experts/assistance technique; Petites entreprises/secteur informel/artisanat; Population/planning familial/démographie; Questions relatives aux femmes; Santé/assainissement/eau; Secours d'urgence/réfugiés/aide humanitaire; Écologie/environnement/biodiversité; Éducation/formation/alphabétisation. **Régions:** Afrique de l'Ouest.

LUX2979
HAND AN HAND, KANNER, ELTEREN, DRETT WELT ♦ Mains serrées, enfants-parents, Tiers monde

19, rue Léon Metz, 4238 Esch-sur-Alzette, Luxembourg.

Téléphone: 352 - 55 64 90. *Contact:* Monique Philippart, Présidente.

OBJECTIFS: Aider les enfants en détresse, dans les pays en développement.

INFORMATIONS GENERALES: *Création:* 1986. *Personnel/Total:* 12. *Bénévoles:* 12. *Budget/Total 1993:* ECU 33000 (US$ 39000). *Sources financières:* Privé: 98%. Autofinancement: 2%.

PUBLICATIONS: *Rapport annuel. Liste des publications.*

COMMENTAIRES: Intervient dans la Communauté des Etats indépendants.

ACTIVITES DANS LES REGIONS EN DEVELOPPEMENT: Intervient directement dans les régions en développement. Intervient dans 5 pays. Intervient par l'intermédiaire d'organisations locales partenaires. **Actions de Développement durable:** Enfants/jeunesse/famille; Santé/assainissement/eau. **Régions:** Amérique du Sud.

ACTIVITES D'INFORMATION ET D'EDUCATION: Domaines: Enfants/jeunesse/famille. **Activités:** Services d'information et de documentation/bases de données.

LUX2980

HELLEF FIR TAPIRAI

1 Michelshof, 6251 Scheidgen, Luxembourg.

Téléphone: 352 - 7 90 63. *Contact:* Marie-Louise Tibesart.

OBJECTIFS: Apporter une aide aux habitants de la région de Tapirai, notamment dans le domaine de l'éducation.

INFORMATIONS GENERALES: *Création:* 1993. *Personnel/Total:* var. *Salariés:* 1 dont: 1 dans les pays en développement. *Bénévoles:* var. *Budget/Total 1993:* ECU 111000 (US$ 130000). *Sources financières:* Privé: 30%. Public: 22%. Autofinancement: 48%.

PUBLICATIONS: *Périodiques:* Hellef fir Tapirai. *Rapport annuel.*

EVALUATION/RECHERCHE: Rapports d'évaluation disponibles.

ACTIVITES DANS LES REGIONS EN DEVELOPPEMENT: Intervient directement dans les régions en développement. Intervient dans 1 pays. Maintient une présence locale sur le terrain. Intervient par l'intermédiaire d'organisations locales partenaires. **Actions de Développement durable:** Aliments/famine; Développement rural/agriculture; Enfants/jeunesse/famille; Envoi de volontaires/experts/assistance technique; Santé/assainissement/eau; Éducation/formation/alphabétisation. **Régions:** Amérique du Sud.

ACTIVITES D'INFORMATION ET D'EDUCATION: Domaines: Aliments/famine; Enfants/jeunesse/famille; Pauvreté/conditions de vie; Éducation/formation/alphabétisation. **Activités:** Campagnes d'information/expositions; Collecte de fonds; Radiodiffusion/manifestations culturelles; Services d'information et de documentation/bases de données; Édition/documents audiovisuels/documents éducatifs; Éducation formelle.

LUX2981

HOGAR DE CHRISTO

35 allée Scheffer, 2520 Luxembourg, Luxembourg.

Contact: Adolphe Sunnen.

LUX2982

INDESCH PATENSCHAFTEN

13, rue Michel Lentz, 6944 Niederanven, Luxembourg.

Telephone: 352 - 34 04 34. *Fax:* 352 - 34 63 85. *Contact:* Marc Weitzel, Trésorier.

OBJECTIVES: To undertake and support medical, educational and social projects in India, such as constructing schools and maintaining dispensaries.

GENERAL INFORMATION: *Creation:* 1987. *Personnel/Total:* 6. *Volunteers:* 6. *Budget/Total 1993:* ECU 321000 (US$ 375000). *Financial sources:* Private: 70%. Public: 30%.

PUBLICATIONS: *Annual report.*

ACTIVITIES IN DEVELOPING REGIONS: Active in 1 country(ies). Works through local field partners. **Sustainable Development Actions:** Children/youth/family; Democracy/good governance/institution building/participatory development; Ecology/environment/biodiversity; Education/training/literacy; Emergency relief/refugees/humanitarian assistance; Food/famine; Gender issues/women; Health/sanitation/water; Human rights/peace/conflicts; Rural development/agriculture; Small enterprises/informal sector/handicrafts; Urban development/habitat. **Regions:** Central Asia and South Asia.

INFORMATION AND EDUCATION ACTIVITIES: Topics: Children/youth/family; Ecology/environment/biodiversity; Education/training/literacy; Emergency relief/refugees/humanitarian assistance; Gender issues/women; Health/sanitation/water; Human rights/peace/conflicts; International economic relations/trade/debt/finance; Poverty/living conditions; Refugees/migrants/ethnic groups; Rural development/agriculture; Urban development/habitat. **Activities:** Broadcasting/cultural events; Formal education; Fund raising; Information campaigns/exhibitions.

LUX2983

INITIATIV FIR MEI GERECHTEGKEET MAT DER DRETTER WELT ♦ Initiative pour plus de justice avec le Tiers monde

39, rue du Fosse, 4123 Esch-sur-Alzette, Luxembourg.

Téléphone: 352 - 54 33 77. *Fax:* 352 - 56 69 99. *Contact:* Guy Reger, Secrétaire.

OBJECTIFS: Favoriser tout ce qui améliore les conditions de vie des hommes, femmes et enfants dans les pays en voie de développement. Promouvoir des projets qui favorisent la production et le commerce équitable.

INFORMATIONS GENERALES: *Création:* 1992. *Affiliée à:* Cercle de Coopération des ONGD du Luxembourg (Luxembourg) - Trans-Fair Minka (Luxembourg) - ARA-Radio socio-culturelle des ONG. *Personnel/Total:* 35. *Bénévoles:* 35. *Budget/Total 1993:* ECU 37000 (US$ 43000). *Sources financières:* Privé: 15%. Public: 25%. Autofinancement: 60%.

ACTIVITES DANS LES REGIONS EN DEVELOPPEMENT: Intervient directement dans les régions en développement. Intervient dans 3 pays. Intervient par l'intermédiaire d'organisations locales partenaires. **Actions de Développement durable:** Petites entreprises/secteur informel/artisanat; Éducation/formation/alphabétisation. **Régions:** Amérique du Sud; Asie du Sud-Est; Mexique et Amerique centrale.

ACTIVITES D'INFORMATION ET D'EDUCATION: Domaines: Aliments/famine; Pauvreté/conditions de vie; Questions relatives aux femmes; Relations économiques internationales/commerce/dette/finances; Écologie/environnement/biodiversité; Éducation/formation/alphabétisation. **Activités:** Campagnes d'information/expositions; Collecte de fonds; Conférences/séminaires/ateliers/activités de formation; Lobbying/plaidoyer; Radiodiffusion/manifestations culturelles; Services d'information et de documentation/bases de données; Éducation formelle.

LUX2984

IWERLIEWEN FIR BEDREETE VOLLEKER ♦ Societé pour les peuples menacés

1, rue Heldenstein, 1723 Luxembourg, Luxembourg.

Téléphone: 352 - 40 32 91. *Fax:* 352 - 40 32 49. *Contact:* André Rollinger, Président.

OBJECTIFS: Lutter contre toute tentative de détruire un peuple et de porter atteinte à sa sécurité, à son identité et à son droit à la terre. Aider les peuples menacés, en diffusant des informations au Luxembourg, et en soutenant des actions humanitaires en leur faveur. Soutenir les projets d'auto-développement des peuples.

INFORMATIONS GENERALES: *Création:* 1982. *Affiliée à:* International Gesellschaft für Bedrohte Völker (Allemagne). *Personnel/Total:* 8. *Bénévoles:* 8. *Budget/Total 1993:* ECU 42000 (US$ 49000). *Sources financières:* Privé: 20%. Public: 60%. Autofinancement: 20%.

PUBLICATIONS: *Périodiques:* Iwerliewen Info (5). *Rapport annuel.*

ACTIVITES DANS LES REGIONS EN DEVELOPPEMENT: Intervient dans 4 pays. Intervient par l'intermédiaire d'organisations locales partenaires. **Actions de Développement durable:** Autres; Droits de l'Homme/paix/conflits; Développement rural/agriculture; Santé/assainissement/eau; Éducation/formation/alphabétisation. **Régions:** Afrique centrale; Amérique du Sud.

ACTIVITES D'INFORMATION ET D'EDUCATION: Domaines: Culture/tradition/religion; Droits de l'Homme/paix/conflits; Paix/conflits ethniques/armement/désarmement; Pauvreté/conditions de vie; Réfugiés/migrants/groupes ethniques; Écologie/environnement/biodiversité. **Activités:** Campagnes d'information/expositions; Collecte de fonds; Conférences/séminaires/ateliers/activités de formation; Lobbying/plaidoyer.

LUX2985

JEUNESSE OUVRIERE CHRETIENNE-SOLIDARITE INTERNATIONALE (JOC)

5, avenue Marie-Thérèse, 2132 Luxembourg, Luxembourg.

Téléphone: 352 - 4 47 43. *Contact:* Paul Schalz.

OBJECTIFS: Favoriser toute action en faveur du Tiers monde, notamment en appuyant les efforts des groupes JOC. Promouvoir ces actions par l'éducation au développement.

Voir : *Comment utiliser le répertoire,* page 11.

INFORMATIONS GENERALES: *Création:* 1983. *Personnel/Total:* 1. *Bénévoles:* 1. *Budget/Total 1993:* ECU 1600 (US$ 2000). *Sources financières:* Privé: 50%. Public: 40%. Autofinancement: 10%.

ACTIVITES DANS LES REGIONS EN DEVELOPPEMENT: Intervient par l'intermédiaire d'organisations locales partenaires. **Actions de Développement durable:** Éducation/formation/alphabétisation. **Régions:** Amérique du Sud.

ACTIVITES D'INFORMATION ET D'EDUCATION: **Domaines:** Enfants/jeunesse/famille; Pauvreté/conditions de vie; Racisme/xénophobie/antisémitisme. **Activités:** Campagnes d'information/expositions; Conférences/séminaires/ateliers/activités de formation.

LUX2986

JONGBAUEREN & JONGWENZER - SERVICE TIERS-MONDE

5, avenue Marie-Thérèse, 2132 Luxembourg, Luxembourg.

Téléphone: 352 - 44 74 32. *Fax:* 352 - 44 74 51. *Contact:* M. l'Abbé Léon Wagener, Administrateur délégué.

OBJECTIFS: Promouvoir l'agriculture, l'éducation scolaire et sanitaire en milieu rural, dans le Tiers monde.

INFORMATIONS GENERALES: *Création:* 1959. *Type d'organisation:* regroupement d'ONG. *Salariés:* 1 dont: 1 dans les pays en développement. *Bénévoles:* 20. *Budget/Total 1993:* ECU 49000 (US$ 58000). *Sources financières:* Privé: 80%. Public: 10%. Autofinancement: 10%.

PUBLICATIONS: *Périodiques:* "Lëtzebuerger DVERF" (12).

ACTIVITES DANS LES REGIONS EN DEVELOPPEMENT: Intervient directement dans les régions en développement. Intervient dans 1 pays. Maintient une présence locale sur le terrain. Intervient par l'intermédiaire d'organisations locales partenaires. **Actions de Développement durable:** Développement rural/agriculture; Enfants/jeunesse/famille; Envoi de volontaires/experts/assistance technique; Population/planning familial/démographie; Questions relatives aux femmes; Santé/assainissement/eau; Écologie/environnement/biodiversité; Éducation/formation/alphabétisation. **Régions:** Afrique de l'Ouest.

ACTIVITES D'INFORMATION ET D'EDUCATION: **Domaines:** Développement rural/agriculture; Population/planning familial/démographie; Questions relatives aux femmes; Écologie/environnement/biodiversité; Éducation/formation/alphabétisation. **Activités:** Campagnes d'information/expositions; Collecte de fonds; Édition/documents audiovisuels/documents éducatifs; Éducation formelle.

LUX2987

KATHOULESCH MANNERAKTIOUN (KMA) ♦ Action Catholique des Hommes

5 avenue Marie-Thérèse, 2132 Luxembourg, Luxembourg.

Téléphone: 352 - 4 47 43-251. *Contact:* Lonidas Munyans, Président.

LUX2988

KIWANIS- ESCH-SUR-ALZETTE SOLIDARITE TIERS MONDE

28 rue Alfred de Musset, 2175 Luxembourg, Luxembourg.

Contact: M. Patrick Hoss.

LUX2989

LIESEN A SCHREIWEN

B.P. 209, 4003 Esch-sur-Alzette, Luxembourg.

Contact: M. Fernand Reding.

LUX2990

LIONS CLUB LUXEMBOURG

28 rue Marie-Adelaïde, 2128 Luxembourg, Luxembourg.

Téléphone: 352 - 44 35 08. *Contact:* R. Munhowen.

LUX2991

MEDAFRICA

18, rue de la Piscine, 8508 Redange/Attert, Luxembourg.

Téléphone: 352 - 62 05 32. *Fax:* 352 - 62 08 41. *Contact:* Marc Zigrand.

OBJECTIFS: Fournir en médicaments et matériel les hôpitaux et dispensaires du Zaïre.

INFORMATIONS GENERALES: *Création:* 1993. *Personnel/Total:* 2. *Bénévoles:* 2. *Budget/Total 1993:* ECU 2000 (US$ 3000). *Sources financières:* Privé: 65%. Autofinancement: 35%.

PUBLICATIONS: *Rapport annuel.*

ACTIVITES DANS LES REGIONS EN DEVELOPPEMENT: Intervient dans 1 pays. Intervient par l'intermédiaire d'organisations locales partenaires. **Actions de Développement durable:** Santé/assainissement/eau. **Régions:** Afrique centrale.

ACTIVITES D'INFORMATION ET D'EDUCATION: **Domaines:** Enfants/jeunesse/famille; Santé/assainissement/eau. **Activités:** Collecte de fonds.

LUX2992

MEDECINS SANS FRONTIERES, LUXEMBOURG

B.P 38, 7201 Walferdange, Luxembourg.

Téléphone: 352 - 33 25 15. *Fax:* 352 - 33 51 33. *Contact:* Docteur Bechara Ziade, Directeur.

OBJECTIFS: Apporter une assistance médicale.

INFORMATIONS GENERALES: *Création:* 1986. *Type d'organisation:* réseau. *Organisations membres:* 7. *Personnel/Total:* 42. *Salariés:* 37 dont: 31 dans les pays en développement. *Bénévoles:* 5 dont: 4 dans les pays en développement. *Budget/Total 1993:* ECU 2735000 (US$ 3199000). *Sources financières:* Privé: 77%. Public: 22%. Autofinancement: 1%.

PUBLICATIONS: *Périodiques:* Reflets (4). *Rapport annuel. Liste des publications.*

ACTIVITES DANS LES REGIONS EN DEVELOPPEMENT: Intervient directement dans les régions en développement. Intervient dans 11 pays. Intervient par l'intermédiaire d'organisations locales partenaires. **Actions de Développement durable:** Aliments/famine; Enfants/jeunesse/famille; Santé/assainissement/eau; Secours d'urgence/réfugiés/aide humanitaire; Éducation/formation/alphabétisation. **Régions:** Afrique de l'Ouest; Amérique du Sud; Caraïbes; Moyen-Orient.

ACTIVITES D'INFORMATION ET D'EDUCATION: **Domaines:** Droits de l'Homme/paix/conflits; Enfants/jeunesse/famille; Réfugiés/migrants/groupes ethniques; Santé/assainissement/eau; Secours d'urgence/réfugiés/aide humanitaire. **Activités:** Campagnes d'information/expositions; Collecte de fonds; Conférences/séminaires/ateliers/activités de formation; Lobbying/plaidoyer; Radiodiffusion/manifestations culturelles.

LUX2993

OBJECTIF TIERS MONDE (OTM) ♦ Objective Third World

Rue Nic Martha 33, 2133 Luxembourg, Luxembourg.

Téléphone: 352 - 49 53 02. *Contact:* Camille Schneider, Président.

OBJECTIFS: Soutenir des projets de développement du Tiers-Monde, notamment en Haïti. Sensibiliser l'opinion publique du Luxembourg aux problèmes de développement. Entretenir des contacts directs avec des organisations partenaires en Haïti.

INFORMATIONS GENERALES: *Création:* 1975. *Type d'organisation:* collectif. *Affiliée à:* Centre de Coopération des ONG luxembourgeoises d'aide au développement du Tiers-Monde (Luxembourg) - Coordination francophone des comités belges pour Haïti (Belgique.). *Personnel/Total:* 18. *Bénévoles:* 18. *Budget/Total 1993:* ECU 185000 (US$ 217000). *Sources financières:* Privé: 15%. Public: 73%. Autofinancement: 12%.

PUBLICATIONS: *Périodiques:* OTM-Aktuell (1). *Rapport annuel.*

ACTIVITES DANS LES REGIONS EN DEVELOPPEMENT: Intervient directement dans les régions en développement. Intervient dans 1 pays. Intervient par l'intermédiaire d'organisations locales partenaires. **Actions de Développement durable:** Aliments/famine; Développement rural/agriculture; Enfants/jeunesse/famille; Envoi de volontaires/experts/assistance technique; Petites entreprises/secteur

See: *How to Use the Directory*, page 11.

informel/artisanat; Questions relatives aux femmes; Santé/assainissement/eau; Secours d'urgence/réfugiés/aide humanitaire; Écologie/environnement/biodiversité; Éducation/formation/alphabétisation. **Régions:** Caraïbes.

ACTIVITES D'INFORMATION ET D'EDUCATION: Domaines: Aliments/famine; Développement rural/agriculture; Enfants/jeunesse/famille; Pauvreté/conditions de vie; Questions relatives aux femmes; Santé/assainissement/eau; Secours d'urgence/réfugiés/aide humanitaire; Écologie/environnement/biodiversité; Éducation/formation/alphabétisation. **Activités:** Campagnes d'information/expositions; Collecte de fonds; Conférences/séminaires/ateliers/activités de formation.

LUX2994

OEUVRE DE MERE TERESA LUXEMBOURG ♦ Work of Mother Teresa Luxembourg

1 rue de la Montagne, 6136 Junglinster, Luxembourg.

Téléphone: 352 - 7 80 71. *Contact:* Mathias Thinnes.

LUX2995

ENG OPPEN HAND FIR MALAWI ♦ An Open Hand for Malawi

32 rue Zithe, 2763 Luxembourg, Luxembourg.

Telephone: 352 - 4 97 76 . *Fax:* 352 - 4 97 76. *Contact:* Sr. Marie-Bernard Schäfer, General Superior.

OBJECTIVES: To provide aid to certain regions of Malawi to help them become self-efficient. To undertake development projects on health, economy and education for children and adults.

GENERAL INFORMATION: Creation: 1989. **Affiliated to:** Cercle de Coopération des ONGD du Luxembourg. **Personnel/Total:** 19. *Salaried:* 14 of which: 14 in developing countries. *Volunteers:* 5. **Financial sources:** *Private:* 33%. *Public:* 7%. *Self-financing:* 60%.

PUBLICATIONS: *Annual report.*

EVALUATION/RESEARCH: Undertakes research activities.

ACTIVITIES IN DEVELOPING REGIONS: Present in developing regions. Active in 1 country(ies). Maintains local field presence. **Sustainable Development Actions:** Children/youth/family; Democracy/good governance/institution building/participatory development; Ecology/environment/biodiversity; Education/training/literacy; Emergency relief/refugees/humanitarian assistance; Energy/transport; Food/famine; Gender issues/women; Health/sanitation/water; Population/family planning/demography; Rural development/agriculture; Sending volunteers/experts/technical assistance; Small enterprises/informal sector/handicrafts; Urban development/habitat. **Regions:** Southern Africa.

INFORMATION AND EDUCATION ACTIVITIES: Topics: Children/youth/family; Culture/tradition/religion; Ecology/environment/biodiversity; Education/training/literacy; Emergency relief/refugees/humanitarian assistance; Employment/unemployment; Food/famine; Gender issues/women; Health/sanitation/water; Human rights/peace/conflicts; Population/family planning/demography; Poverty/living conditions; Refugees/migrants/ethnic groups; Rural development/agriculture; Urban development/habitat. **Activities:** Conferences/seminars/workshops/training activities; Exchanges/twinning/linking; Formal education; Fund raising; Information campaigns/exhibitions; Lobbying/advocacy; Networking/electronic telecommunications; Publishing/audiovisual materials/educational materials.

LUX2996

ORDRE MILITAIRE ET HOSPITALIER DE ST. LAZARE DE JERUSALEM

19 rue Théodore Eberhard, 1451 Luxembourg, Luxembourg.

Téléphone: 352 - 44 97 20. *Contact:* Fernand Lavandier.

LUX2997

ORT LUXEMBOURG

9 rue de la Corniche, 5956 Itzig, Luxembourg.

Téléphone: 352 - 36 52 52. *Fax:* 352 - 36 52 52. *Contact:* Jean Hertz, Président.

OBJECTIFS: Travailler dans le domaine de la formation professionnelle et de l'éducation dans le monde. Entreprendre également, en dehors des écoles propres et affiliées de ORT, des projets de coopération internationale dans les domaines de la formation, la santé, etc.

INFORMATIONS GENERALES: Création: 1989. **Type d'organisation:** réseau. **Organisations membres:** 35. **Personnel/Total:** 400. *Salariés:* 200 dont: 100 dans les pays en développement. *Bénévoles:* 200. **Budget/Total 1993:** ECU 211165000 (US$ 247000000). **Sources financières:** *Privé:* 20%. *Public:* 70%. *Autofinancement:* 10%.

PUBLICATIONS: *Périodiques:* World ORT Union Yearbook (1). *Rapport annuel. Liste des publications.*

EVALUATION/RECHERCHE: Entreprend des activités de recherche.

COMMENTAIRES: Intervient dans la Communauté des Etats indépendants. Activités d'information concernant la Communauté des Etats indépendants.

ACTIVITES DANS LES REGIONS EN DEVELOPPEMENT: Intervient directement dans les régions en développement. Intervient dans 40 pays. Maintient une présence locale sur le terrain. Intervient par l'intermédiaire d'organisations locales partenaires. **Actions de Développement durable:** Développement rural/agriculture; Envoi de volontaires/experts/assistance technique; Petites entreprises/secteur informel/artisanat; Population/planning familial/démographie; Santé/assainissement/eau; Éducation/formation/alphabétisation. **Régions:** Afrique australe; Afrique centrale; Afrique de l'Est; Afrique de l'Ouest; Afrique du Nord; Amérique du Sud; Asie centrale et Asie du Sud; Asie de l'Est; Asie du Sud-Est; Mexique et Amerique centrale; Moyen-Orient.

ACTIVITES D'INFORMATION ET D'EDUCATION: Domaines: Développement rural/agriculture; Enfants/jeunesse/famille; Population/planning familial/démographie; Questions relatives aux femmes; Secours d'urgence/réfugiés/aide humanitaire; Éducation/formation/alphabétisation. **Activités:** Collecte de fonds; Conférences/séminaires/ateliers/activités de formation; Lobbying/plaidoyer; Réseaux/télécommunications électroniques; Services d'information et de documentation/bases de données; Édition/documents audiovisuels/documents éducatifs; Éducation formelle.

LUX2998

PHARMACIENS SANS FRONTIERES

62 rue Gaaschtbierg, 8230 Mamer, Luxembourg.

Contact: M. Camille Groos.

LUX2999

PRO NINOS POBRES (PNP) ♦ Pour les enfants pauvres

12 bd J.F. Kennedy, B.P. 100, 4901 Bascharage, Luxembourg.

Téléphone: 352 - 50 23 67. *Fax:* 352 - 50 49 59. *Contact:* Aloyse Mirkes, Président Responsable des Projets.

OBJECTIFS: Contribuer financièrement à la gestion d'œuvres et d'institutions situées en Amérique du Sud et ayant pour objet d'accueillir et de prendre soin des enfants vivant dans des conditions sociales défavorables à leur développement.

INFORMATIONS GENERALES: Création: 1965. **Affiliée à:** Cercle de Coopération des ONG du Luxembourg. **Personnel/Total:** 13. *Salariés:* 1. *Bénévoles:* 12. **Budget/Total 1993:** ECU 769000 (US$ 899000). **Sources financières:** *Privé:* 40%. *Public:* 57%. *Autofinancement:* 3%.

PUBLICATIONS: *Périodiques:* PNP Aktuell (4).

ACTIVITES DANS LES REGIONS EN DEVELOPPEMENT: Intervient par l'intermédiaire d'organisations locales partenaires. **Actions de Développement durable:** Développement rural/agriculture; Développement urbain/habitat; Enfants/jeunesse/famille; Petites entreprises/secteur informel/artisanat; Questions relatives aux femmes; Éducation/formation/alphabétisation. **Régions:** Amérique du Sud.

LUX3000

ROTARY INTERNATIONAL

5 place du Marché, 6460 Echternach, Luxembourg.

Contact: Will Decker.

Voir : *Comment utiliser le répertoire,* page 11.

LUX3001

SEMEURS DE JOIE

114c, route de Fischbach, 7447 Lintgen, Luxembourg.

Téléphone: 352 - 3 24 84. *Contact:* Jeanne Thies, Présidente.

OBJECTIFS: Soutenir financièrement des projets dans les pays du Tiers monde, principalement l'Inde.

INFORMATIONS GENERALES: *Création:* 1984. *Personnel/Total:* 30. *Bénévoles:* 30. *Sources financières:* Privé: 1%. Autofinancement: 99%.

ACTIVITES DANS LES REGIONS EN DEVELOPPEMENT: Intervient directement dans les régions en développement. Intervient dans 3 pays. Intervient par l'intermédiaire d'organisations locales partenaires. **Actions de Développement durable:** Développement rural/agriculture; Enfants/jeunesse/famille; Santé/assainissement/eau; Éducation/formation/alphabétisation. **Régions:** Afrique de l'Ouest; Amérique du Sud; Asie centrale et Asie du Sud.

LUX3002

SOCIETE KOLPING DU GRAND-DUCHE DE LUXEMBOURG ♦
Kolping Society of Luxembourg

40 rue des Champs, 7218 Walferdange, Luxembourg.

Téléphone: 352 - 33 96 48. *Contact:* Paul Schroeder, Président.

OBJECTIFS: Améliorer le niveau de vie des populations des pays en développement par une solide formation professionnelle.

INFORMATIONS GENERALES: *Création:* 1961. *Affiliée à:* Sozial une Entwicklungshilfe des Kolpingwerkes (Allemagne). *Personnel/Total:* 100. *Bénévoles:* 100. *Budget/Total 1993:* ECU 37000 (US$ 43000). *Sources financières:* Autofinancement: 100%.

ACTIVITES DANS LES REGIONS EN DEVELOPPEMENT: Intervient dans 3 pays. Intervient par l'intermédiaire d'organisations locales partenaires. **Actions de Développement durable:** Développement rural/agriculture; Enfants/jeunesse/famille; Questions relatives aux femmes. **Régions:** Afrique centrale; Amérique du Sud.

LUX3003

SOLIDARESCH HELLEF-REISERBANN ♦ Aide solidaire du Roeserbann

B.P 8 3326 Roeser, Luxembourg.

Contact: KRAUS Léon, Président.

OBJECTIFS: Agir en faveur des êtres humains démunis dans le Tiers monde. Fournir une aide directe ou indirecte à des organisations, institutions et habitants des pays en développpement. Sensibiliser l'opinion publique sur les problèmes du Tiers monde.

INFORMATIONS GENERALES: *Création:* 1990. *Affiliée à:* Cercle des ONG (Luxembourg). *Budget/Total 1993:* ECU 28000 (US$ 33000). *Sources financières:* Privé: 30%. Public: 50%. Autofinancement: 20%.

PUBLICATIONS: *Périodiques:* Info Aktuell (1).

COMMENTAIRES: Intervient dans la Communauté des Etats indépendants.

ACTIVITES DANS LES REGIONS EN DEVELOPPEMENT: Intervient directement dans les régions en développement. Intervient dans 3 pays. Maintient une présence locale sur le terrain. Intervient par l'intermédiaire d'organisations locales partenaires. **Actions de Développement durable:** Droits de l'Homme/paix/conflits; Démocratie/bonne gestion publique/création d'institutions/développement participatif; Écologie/environnement/biodiversité; Éducation/formation/alphabétisation. **Régions:** Amérique du Sud.

LUX3004

SOLIDARITE LUXEMBOURG TIERS MONDE

B.P. 138, 4002 Esch-sur-Alzette, Luxembourg.

Téléphone: 352 - 55 47 82. *Contact:* Serge Allegrezza.

LUX3005

SOS ENFANTS EN DETRESSE MERSCH

12 rue Belle-vue, 7516 Rollingen, Luxembourg.

Téléphone: 352 - 32 76 84. *Contact:* Silvia Palazzari.

LUX3006

SOS FAIM - ACTION POUR LE DEVELOPPEMENT

46 rue Théodore Eberhard, 1452 Luxembourg, Luxembourg.

Téléphone: 352 - 25 26 81. *Fax:* 352 - 25 26 81. *Contact:* Laurence Demaeght, Responsable projets.

OBJECTIFS: Appuyer des initiatives de développement dans les pays du Tiers monde. Informer et sensibiliser l'opinion publique au Grand-Duché de Luxembourg.

INFORMATIONS GENERALES: *Création:* 1993. *Personnel/Total:* 7. *Salariés:* 1. *Bénévoles:* 6. *Budget/Total 1993:* ECU 69000 (US$ 81000). *Sources financières:* Privé: 46%. Public: 52%. Autofinancement: 2%.

PUBLICATIONS: *Périodiques:* Bulletin d'Information (2) - Défis-Sud (4). Rapport annuel. Liste des publications.

ACTIVITES DANS LES REGIONS EN DEVELOPPEMENT: Intervient dans 1 pays. Intervient par l'intermédiaire d'organisations locales partenaires. **Actions de Développement durable:** Démocratie/bonne gestion publique/création d'institutions/développement participatif; Développement rural/agriculture; Développement urbain/habitat; Petites entreprises/secteur informel/artisanat; Questions relatives aux femmes; Santé/assainissement/eau; Écologie/environnement/biodiversité; Éducation/formation/alphabétisation. **Régions:** Afrique centrale; Afrique de l'Ouest.

ACTIVITES D'INFORMATION ET D'EDUCATION: Domaines: Aliments/famine; Culture/tradition/religion; Droits de l'Homme/paix/conflits; Développement rural/agriculture; Développement urbain/habitat; Emploi/chômage; Enfants/jeunesse/famille; Paix/conflits ethniques/armement/désarmement; Pauvreté/conditions de vie; Population/planning familial/démographie; Questions relatives aux femmes; Racisme/xénophobie/antisémitisme; Relations internationales/coopération/aide au développement; Relations économiques internationales/commerce/dette/finances; Réfugiés/migrants/groupes ethniques; Santé/assainissement/eau; Secours d'urgence/réfugiés/aide humanitaire; Écologie/environnement/biodiversité; Éducation/formation/alphabétisation. **Activités:** Campagnes d'information/expositions; Collecte de fonds; Radiodiffusion/manifestations culturelles; Édition/documents audiovisuels/documents éducatifs.

LUX3007

SOS-SAHEL INTERNATIONAL

B.P. 388, 2018 Luxembourg, Luxembourg.

Contact: Henri Guillaume.

LUX3008

TRANSFAIR-MINKA

3, rue des Vergers, 7338 Heisdorf, Luxembourg.

Téléphone: 352 - 33 22 76. *Fax:* 352 - 33 22 76. *Contact:* Jean-Louis Zeien, Président.

OBJECTIFS: Coopérer au développement des populations défavorisées du Tiers monde. Promouvoir un commerce plus juste entre les petits producteurs du Tiers monde et les consommateurs du Luxembourg. Informer le public luxembourgeois sur les conditions inéquitables que subissent les producteurs du Tiers monde et sur le lien qui existe entre cette situation et leur style de vie.

INFORMATIONS GENERALES: *Création:* 1990. *Type d'organisation:* regroupement d'ONG. *Organisations membres:* 16. *Personnel/Total:* 20. *Bénévoles:* 20. *Budget/Total 1993:* ECU 7000 (US$ 9000). *Sources financières:* Privé: 30%. Public: 35%. Autofinancement: 35%.

PUBLICATIONS: *Rapport annuel. Liste des publications.*

ACTIVITES DANS LES REGIONS EN DEVELOPPEMENT: Intervient dans 16 pays. Intervient par l'intermédiaire d'organisations locales

See: *How to Use the Directory*, page 11.

partenaires. **Actions de Développement durable:** Dette/finances/ commerce; Écologie/environnement/biodiversité. **Régions:** Afrique australe; Afrique centrale; Afrique de l'Est; Afrique de l'Ouest; Amérique du Sud; Caraïbes; Mexique et Amerique centrale.

ACTIVITES D'INFORMATION ET D'EDUCATION: Domaines: Pauvreté/ conditions de vie; Relations économiques internationales/commerce/ dette/finances; Écologie/environnement/biodiversité. **Activités:** Campagnes d'information/expositions; Conférences/séminaires/ateliers/activités de formation; Lobbying/plaidoyer; Radiodiffusion/manifestations culturelles; Services d'information et de documentation/bases de données; Éducation formelle.

LUX3009

UNION INTERNATIONALE HUMANISTE ET LAIQUE

39 rue de Hollerich, 1741 Luxembourg, Luxembourg.
Contact: A.M. Dees de Sterio.

LUX3010

UNITY FOUNDATION

17 allée Léopold Goebel, 1635 Luxembourg, Luxembourg.
Téléphone: 352 - 44 22 20. *Contact:* Farzin Dustdar.

MLT3011
AIESEC NATIONAL COMMITTEE
Humanities Building, University of Malta, Tal Qroqq, Malta.

MLT3012
BRIGATA LABURISTA ♦ Labour Brigade
P.O. Box 403, Valletta CMR 01, Malta.

Telephone: 356 - 690 129/33. *Fax:* 356 - 690 145.

OBJECTIVES: To educate children and youth on issues of world peace, democracy, socialism, justice and solidarity.

GENERAL INFORMATION: *Creation:* 1959. *Affiliated to:* Federation of Youth Organisations in Malta (Malta). *Budget/Total 1993:* ECU 300 (US$ 400). *Financial sources:* Private: 90%. Self-financing: 10%.

PUBLICATIONS: *Annual report.*

EVALUATION/RESEARCH: Evaluation reports available.

PLANNED ACTIVITIES: Undertaking a campaign on the protection of the environment.

COMMENTS: Undertakes activities in the Commonwealth of Independent States.

INFORMATION AND EDUCATION ACTIVITIES: Topics: Children/youth/family; Ecology/environment/biodiversity; Human rights/peace/conflicts; Peace/ethnic conflicts/armament/disarmament. **Activities:** Broadcasting/cultural events; Exchanges/twinning/linking; Formal education.

MLT3013
CARITAS MALTA
5 Lion Street, Floriana, Malta.

MLT3014
CATHOLIC YOUTH LEADERS ORGANISATION
c/o St Aloysius' College, Birkirkara, Malta.

MLT3015
CENTRU ANIMAZZJONI MISSJUNARJA
St Josephs Home, St Venera, Malta.

MLT3016
ECO, THE MALTA ECOLOGICAL SOCIETY (ECO)
P.O. Box 322, Valletta CMR 01, Malta.

Telephone: 356 - 338 780. *Fax:* 356 - 320 983. *Contact:* Dunstan Hamilton, Education Officer.

OBJECTIVES: To raise awareness of the protection of the environment. To promote global environmental action and the study of the local environment.

GENERAL INFORMATION: *Creation:* 1991. *Personnel/Total:* 7. *Volunteers:* 7. *Budget/Total 1993:* ECU 9000 (US$ 12000). *Financial sources:* Private: 18%. Self-financing: 82%.

PUBLICATIONS: *Periodicals:* ECO Hearing Reports (1) - Information Sheets (var). *Annual report. List of publications.*

EVALUATION/RESEARCH: Evaluation reports available. Undertakes research activities.

COMMENTS: Undertakes activities in the Commonwealth of Independent States. Information activities related to the Commonwealth of Independent States.

ACTIVITIES IN DEVELOPING REGIONS: Present in developing regions. Active in 7 country(ies). Works through local field partners. **Sustainable Development Actions:** Children/youth/family; Ecology/environment/biodiversity; Education/training/literacy; Gender issues/women; Health/sanitation/water; Human rights/peace/conflicts. **Regions:** Caribbean; Central Africa; Central Asia and South Asia; East Africa; East Asia; Mexico and Central America; Middle East; North Africa; Oceania; South America; South East Asia; Southern Africa; West Africa.

INFORMATION AND EDUCATION ACTIVITIES: Topics: Children/youth/family; Culture/tradition/religion; Ecology/environment/biodiversity; Education/training/literacy; Employment/unemployment; Food/famine; Gender issues/women; Health/sanitation/water; Human rights/peace/conflicts; International economic relations/trade/debt/finance; International relations/cooperation/development aid; Peace/ethnic conflicts/armament/disarmament; Population/family planning/demography; Poverty/living conditions; Racism/xenophobia/antisemitism; Refugees/migrants/ethnic groups; Rural development/agriculture; Urban development/habitat. **Activities:** Broadcasting/cultural events; Conferences/seminars/workshops/training activities; Exchanges/twinning/linking; Formal education; Information and documentation services/data bases; Information campaigns/exhibitions; Lobbying/advocacy; Publishing/audiovisual materials/educational materials.

MLT3017
FORUM ZGHAZAGH LABURISTI (FZL) ♦ Labour Youth Forum
General Headquarters Workers' Party, 31st March 1979 Street, Senglea CSP 06, Malta.

Telephone: 356 - 690 129-33. *Fax:* 356 - 690 145. *Contact:* Mario Azzopardi, President.

OBJECTIVES: To encourage local youth to take an interest in national politics and educate them in democratic socialism. To represent youth's interests in Malta and abroad.

GENERAL INFORMATION: *Creation:* 1951. *Type of organisation:* coordinating body. *Affiliated to:* National Youth Council of Malta (Malta) - International Union of Socialist Youth (Austria) - European Community Organisation of Socialist Youth (Belgium). *Personnel/Total:* 16. *Volunteers:* 16. *Budget/Total 1993:* ECU 10000 (US$ 13000). *Financial sources:* Private: 75%. Self-financing: 25%.

PUBLICATIONS: *Periodicals:* IS-SENS (6) - Vizjoni Zaghzugha (var.). *Annual report.*

EVALUATION/RESEARCH: Evaluation reports available. Undertakes research activities.

PLANNED ACTIVITIES: Anti-drug abuse campaigns.

COMMENTS: Undertakes activities in the Commonwealth of Independent States. Information activities related to the Commonwealth of Independent States.

ACTIVITIES IN DEVELOPING REGIONS: Works through local field partners. **Sustainable Development Actions:** Children/youth/family; Democracy/good governance/institution building/participatory development; Gender issues/women; Human rights/peace/conflicts. **Regions:** Middle East; North Africa.

INFORMATION AND EDUCATION ACTIVITIES: Topics: Children/youth/family; Culture/tradition/religion; Ecology/environment/biodiversity; Education/training/literacy; Employment/unemployment; Gender issues/women; Human rights/peace/conflicts; International relations/cooperation/development aid; Peace/ethnic conflicts/armament/disarmament; Racism/xenophobia/antisemitism. **Activities:** Broadcasting/cultural events; Conferences/seminars/workshops/training activities; Exchanges/twinning/linking; Formal education; Information and documentation services/data bases; Information campaigns/exhibitions; Lobbying/advocacy; Publishing/audiovisual materials/educational materials.

MLT3018
FOUNDATION FOR INTERNATIONAL STUDIES (FIS)
University of Malta, St. Paul Street, Valletta, Malta.

Telephone: 356 - 234 121/2. *Fax:* 356 - 220 551. *Contact:* Salvino Busuttil.

OBJECTIVES: To promote and support institutes, centres or other units of the University of Malta that have an international character.

GENERAL INFORMATION: *Creation:* 1986. *Affiliated to:* International Peace Research Association (USA) - World Conservation Union -IUCN - Mediterranean Action Plan - Society for the Study and Conservation of Nature - MareVivo - FIELD - Institute for the Integrated Study of Future Generations. *Personnel/Total:* 34. *Salaried:* 34. *Budget/Total 1993:* ECU 605000 (US$ 785000). *Financial sources:* Private: 20%. Public: 70%. Self-financing: 10%.

PUBLICATIONS: *Periodicals:* Future Generations Journal (3) - Mediterranean Social Sciences Review (2). *Annual report. List of publications.*

EVALUATION/RESEARCH: Evaluation reports available. Undertakes research activities.

PLANNED ACTIVITIES: Organising training courses in human rights education.

ACTIVITIES IN DEVELOPING REGIONS: Present in developing regions. Maintains local field presence. Works through local field partners. **Sustainable Development Actions:** Children/youth/family; Democracy/good governance/institution building/participatory development; Ecology/environment/biodiversity; Education/training/literacy; Energy/transport; Human rights/peace/conflicts; Rural development/agriculture; Sending volunteers/experts/technical assistance; Urban development/habitat. **Regions:** Middle East; North Africa.

INFORMATION AND EDUCATION ACTIVITIES: Topics: Culture/tradition/religion; Ecology/environment/biodiversity; Human rights/peace/conflicts; International economic relations/trade/debt/finance; International relations/cooperation/development aid; Peace/ethnic conflicts/armament/disarmament; Refugees/migrants/ethnic groups; Urban development/habitat. **Activities:** Broadcasting/cultural events; Conferences/seminars/workshops/training activities; Exchanges/twinning/linking; Formal education; Fund raising; Information and documentation services/data bases; Information campaigns/exhibitions; Lobbying/advocacy; Networking/electronic telecommunications; Publishing/audiovisual materials/educational materials.

MLT3019
GIRL GUIDES ASSOCIATION
85 Capuchins Street, Floriana, Malta.

MLT3020
GLOBAL RESPONSIBILITIES TO FUTURE GENERATIONS
c/o FIS, University of Malta, St Paul's Street, Valletta, Malta.

MLT3021
INTERNATIONAL OCEAN INSTITUTE
P.O. Box 3, Gzira GZR 01, Malta.

Telephone: 356 - 346 528/9. *Fax:* 356 - 346 502. *Contact:* Kristan Saigal, Executive Director.

OBJECTIVES: To promote education, training and research with the goal of fostering the peaceful use of the ocean and its resources.

GENERAL INFORMATION: Creation: 1972. *Type of organisation:* network. *Affiliated to:* Earth Council (Costa Rica). *Personnel/Total:* 30. *Salaried:* 5. *Volunteers:* 25 of which: 23 in developing countries. *Budget/Total 1993:* ECU 2159000 (US$ 2800000). *Financial sources:* Private: 25%. Public - 50%. Self-financing: 25%.

PUBLICATIONS: *Periodicals:* Ocean Year Book (1) (2). *Annual report. List of publications.*

EVALUATION/RESEARCH: Undertakes research activities.

COMMENTS: Undertakes activities in the Commonwealth of Independent States. Information activities related to the Commonwealth of Independent States.

ACTIVITIES IN DEVELOPING REGIONS: Present in developing regions. Active in 50 country(ies). Maintains local field presence. Works through local field partners. **Sustainable Development Actions:** Ecology/environment/biodiversity; Education/training/literacy. **Regions:** Caribbean; Central Africa; Central Asia and South Asia; East Africa; East Asia; Mexico and Central America; Middle East; North Africa; Oceania; South America; South East Asia; Southern Africa; West Africa.

INFORMATION AND EDUCATION ACTIVITIES: Topics: Ecology/environment/biodiversity; Education/training/literacy. **Activities:** Conferences/seminars/workshops/training activities; Exchanges/twinning/linking; Fund raising; Networking/electronic telecommunications; Publishing/audiovisual materials/educational materials.

MLT3022
INTERNATIONAL YOUNG NATURE FRIENDS
138 Triq. L-Antinni, Mosta, Malta.

MLT3023
KUNSILL NAZZJONALI TAZ-ZGHAZAGH ♦ National Youth Council (Malta)
St Francis Ravelin, Floriana VLT 15, Malta.

Telephone: 356 - 234 305. *Fax:* 356 - 245 376. *Contact:* Ian Micallef, Secretary General.

OBJECTIVES: To bring together National Youth NGOs and to promote co-operation among them. To work on topics such as youth employment and equal opportunities, the environnment, education and family.

GENERAL INFORMATION: Creation: 1992. *Type of organisation:* association of NGOs. *Member organisations:* 40. *Affiliated to:* Council of European National Youth Committees. *Budget/Total 1993:* ECU 8000 (US$ 11000). *Financial sources:* Public: 100%.

PUBLICATIONS: *Periodicals:* In Touch (2). *Annual report.*

EVALUATION/RESEARCH: Evaluation reports available.

PLANNED ACTIVITIES: Undertaking an AIDS awareness campaign.

INFORMATION AND EDUCATION ACTIVITIES: Topics: Children/youth/family; Culture/tradition/religion; Ecology/environment/biodiversity; Employment/unemployment; Gender issues/women; Health/sanitation/water; Human rights/peace/conflicts; International relations/cooperation/development aid; Peace/ethnic conflicts/armament/disarmament; Racism/xenophobia/antisemitism; Urban development/habitat. **Activities:** Broadcasting/cultural events; Conferences/seminars/workshops/training activities; Formal education; Information and documentation services/data bases; Information campaigns/exhibitions; Lobbying/advocacy; Publishing/audiovisual materials/educational materials.

MLT3024
MISSION FUND
19 Summer Street, Mosta, Malta.

MLT3025
MOVIMENT GHALL-AMBJENT (MGHA) ♦ Friends of the Earth Malta
P.O. Box 13, Valletta CMR 01, Malta.

Telephone: 356 - 235 306. *Fax:* 356 - 235 306. *Contact:* E.A. Mallla.

OBJECTIVES: To promote environment-conservation action. To find and promote solutions to land use conflicts and waste management problems.

GENERAL INFORMATION: Creation: 1984. *Member organisations:* 1. *Affiliated to:* Youth and Environment - Europe. *Personnel/Total:* 7. *Salaried:* 1. *Volunteers:* 6. *Budget/Total 1993:* ECU 4000 (US$ 5000). *Financial sources:* Private: 80%. Public: 15%. Self-financing: 5%.

PUBLICATIONS: *Periodicals:* Ecoforum (4) - Ambjent (1).

EVALUATION/RESEARCH: Undertakes research activities.

COMMENTS: Friends of the Earth Malta is focused on Mediterranean issues within the Mediterranean network of Friends of the Earth.

INFORMATION AND EDUCATION ACTIVITIES: Topics: Culture/tradition/religion; Ecology/environment/biodiversity; Other; Rural development/agriculture; Urban development/habitat. **Activities:** Conferences/seminars/workshops/training activities; Fund raising; Information and documentation services/data bases; Information campaigns/exhibitions; Lobbying/advocacy; Networking/electronic telecommunications.

MLT3026
MOVIMENT GHALL-AMBJENT, FRIENDS OF THE EARTH, MALTA ♦ Movement for the Environment, Friends of the Earth, Malta
P.O. Box 13, Valletta CMR 01, Malta.

Voir : *Comment utiliser le répertoire,* page 11.

Telephone: 356 - 235306. *Fax:* 356 - 235306. *E-mail:* julian@unimt.mt. *Contact:* E.A. Mallia, Chairperson.

MLT3027
MOVIMENT ZGHAZAGH PARTIT NAZZJONALISTA (MZPN)

Dar Centrall, Pleta, Malta.

MLT3028
NATIONAL STUDENT TRAVEL FOUNDATION

220 Saint Paul Street, Valletta VLT 07, Malta.

Telephone: 356 - 244 983. *Fax:* 356 - 230 330. *Contact:* Francis Stivala, Secretary General.

OBJECTIVES: To encourage, develop and support youth exchanges to generate greater international understanding, broaden education opportunities and expand cultural and linguistic appreciation.

GENERAL INFORMATION: *Creation:* 1954. *Affiliated to:* International Student Travel Confederation (Denmark) - International Student Identity Card (Denmark) - International Association for Educational and Work Exchanges (Canada) - Federation of International Youth Travel Organisations (Denmark). *Personnel/Total:* 40. *Salaried:* 40. *Budget/ Total 1993:* ECU 3027000 (US$ 3926000). *Financial sources: Self-financing:* 100%.

PUBLICATIONS: *Periodicals:* Newsflash (6).

PLANNED ACTIVITIES: A training campaign in management, finance and accounting, marketing and sales, and business English directed towards the emerging business community in Eastern Europe and the former Soviet Union.

COMMENTS: Undertakes activities in the Commonwealth of Independent States. Information activities related to the Commonwealth of Independent States.

ACTIVITIES IN DEVELOPING REGIONS: Works through local field partners. **Sustainable Development Actions:** Education/training/literacy. **Regions:** Middle East; North Africa.

INFORMATION AND EDUCATION ACTIVITIES: Topics: Education/training/literacy. **Activities:** Conferences/seminars/workshops/training activities; Exchanges/twinning/linking; Formal education.

MLT3029
PEACE LAB - YOUTH MOVEMENT

5 Old Mint Street, Valletta, Malta.

MLT3030
SCOUT ASSOCIATION

Island Headquarters, Floriana, Malta.

Telephone: 356 - 346 631/224 334. *Fax:* 356 - 342 273. *Contact:* Joseph G. Grech, Chief Commissioner.

OBJECTIVES: To foster the mental, physical and spiritual development of the members.

GENERAL INFORMATION: *Creation:* 1908. *Type of organisation:* association of NGOs, network. *Member organisations:* 31. *Personnel/ Total:* 18. *Volunteers:* 18. *Financial sources: Private:* 10%. *Self-financing:* 90%.

EVALUATION/RESEARCH: Evaluation reports available.

COMMENTS: Undertakes activities in the Commonwealth of Independent States.

INFORMATION AND EDUCATION ACTIVITIES: Topics: Ecology/environment/biodiversity. **Activities:** Information campaigns/exhibitions.

MLT3031
SOCIETY FOR THE PROTECTION OF TREES (ARBOR)

P.O. Box 121, Valletta, Malta.

MLT3032
SOCIETY FOR THE STUDY AND CONSERVATION OF NATURE (SSCN)

P.O. Box 459, Valletta, Malta.

MLT3033
SONNENBERG ASSOCIATION

46D St Julian Court, Sur Fons Street, St. Julians, Malta.

MLT3034
YOUNG CHRISTIAN WORKERS

11 Filippo Sciberras Street, Floriana, Malta.

MLT3035
YOUNG EUROPEAN FEDERALISTS

Champignon, Triq il-Gladjoli, San Gwann, Malta.

MLT3036
YOUNG MEN'S CHRISTIAN ASSOCIATION (YMCA)

41 Merchant Street, Valletta, Malta.

Telephone: 356 - 240 680. *Fax:* 356 - 236 119. *Contact:* Albert Degiorgio.

OBJECTIVES: To provide assistance to the socially underprivileged.

GENERAL INFORMATION: *Creation:* 1976. *Personnel/Total:* 8. *Volunteers:* 8 of which: 3 in developing countries. *Budget/Total 1993:* ECU 4000 (US$ 5000). *Financial sources: Private:* 50%. *Public:* 10%. *Self-financing:* 40%.

PUBLICATIONS: *Periodicals:* YMCA Valletta Newsletter (3). *Annual report.*

ACTIVITIES IN DEVELOPING REGIONS: Present in developing regions. Active in 1 country(ies). Maintains local field presence. Works through local field partners. **Sustainable Development Actions:** Children/youth/family; Ecology/environment/biodiversity; Education/training/literacy; Emergency relief/refugees/humanitarian assistance; Human rights/peace/conflicts. **Regions:** North Africa.

INFORMATION AND EDUCATION ACTIVITIES: Topics: Children/youth/family; Ecology/environment/biodiversity; Education/training/literacy; Emergency relief/refugees/humanitarian assistance; Employment/unemployment; Peace/ethnic conflicts/armament/disarmament; Poverty/living conditions. **Activities:** Conferences/seminars/workshops/training activities; Formal education; Fund raising; Information campaigns/exhibitions; Lobbying/advocacy.

MLT3037
YOUTH FOR EXCHANGE AND UNDERSTANDING

c/o "Merlin", Sir Paul Boffa Avenue, Paoloa, Malta.

MLT3038
ZGHAZAGH AZZJONI KATTOLIKA

Catholic Institute, Floriana, Malta.

MLT3039
ZGHAZAGH HBIEB IN-NATURA

P.O. Box 339, Valletta, Malta.

MLT3040
ZGHAZAGH TAHT L-ART

P.O. Box 28, Old Bakery Street, Valletta, Malta.

See: *How to Use the Directory,* page 11.

NLD3041
ADVIES- EN INFORMATIEBUREAU LATIJNS-AMERIKA (AILA)

Nieuwegracht 47, 3512 LE Utrecht, The Netherlands.

Telephone: 31 (30) 31 96 75. *Fax:* 31 (30) 36 71 85.

NLD3042
AFRICAN EUROPEAN INSTITUTE

Prins Hendrikkade 48, 1012 AC Amsterdam, The Netherlands.

Telephone: 31 (20) 62 28 751. *Fax:* 31 (20) 62 21 30. *Contact:* Jan Nico Scholten, Executive President.

NLD3043
AFRICAN MEDICAL AND RESEARCH FOUNDATION, NEDERLAND (AMREF)

Jan Van Brakelplantsoen 5, 2253 TD Voorschoten, The Netherlands.

Telephone: 31 (71) 57 62 480. *Contact:* Dr. J.T. Braaksma, Chairman.

NLD3044
AFRICAN NETWORK

Europalaan 5, Postbus 90, 5250 AB Vlijmen, The Netherlands.

Telephone: 31 (41) 08 17 777. *Fax:* 31 (41) 08 18 338.

NLD3045
AFRIKA CENTRUM ♦ Africa Centre

Rijksweg 15, 6267 AC Maastricht, The Netherlands.

Telephone: 31 (43) 40 71 226. *Fax:* 31 (44) 07 32 33. *Contact:* Jo Demarteau.

OBJECTIVES: To provide information about development in Africa. To encourage dialogue between people in Africa and in the Netherlands.

GENERAL INFORMATION: *Creation:* 1959. *Personnel/Total:* 8. *Salaried:* 4. *Volunteers:* 4. *Financial sources:* Private: 85%. Public: 10%. Self-financing: 5%.

PUBLICATIONS: *Periodicals:* Africadier (4) - Afrihaarse Opinies (4).

ACTIVITIES IN DEVELOPING REGIONS: Present in developing regions. **Sustainable Development Actions:** Children/youth/family; Debt/finance/trade; Democracy/good governance/institution building/participatory development; Ecology/environment/biodiversity; Education/training/literacy; Food/famine; Gender issues/women; Health/sanitation/water; Human rights/peace/conflicts; Rural development/agriculture; Small enterprises/informal sector/handicrafts; Urban development/habitat. **Regions:** Central Africa; East Africa; Southern Africa; West Africa.

NLD3046
AFRIPROJEKT

Nieuwe Keizersgracht 56, 1018 DT Amsterdam, The Netherlands.

Telephone: 31 (20) 62 02 862. *Fax:* 31 (20) 63 90 046. *Contact:* Paul A.J. Staal, Director.

NLD3047
AKTIE STROHALM ♦ Grassroot Campaign "The Last Straw"

Oudegracht 42, 3511 AR Utrecht, The Netherlands.

Telephone: 31 (30) 23 14 314. *Fax:* 31 (30) 23 43 986. *Contact:* Henk van Arhel.

OBJECTIVES: To increase public awareness of the degradation of the environment and to find the root causes of the problems. To disseminate information, undertake education and research. To stimulate public debate on these matters in Holland and abroad.

GENERAL INFORMATION: *Creation:* 1970. *Personnel/Total:* 21. *Salaried:* 6. *Volunteers:* 15. *Budget/Total 1993:* ECU 70000 (US$ 81000). *Financial sources:* Private: 10%. Public: 20%. Self-financing: 70%.

PUBLICATIONS: *Periodicals:* Strohaln Nieuws (4-6). *List of publications.*

EVALUATION/RESEARCH: Undertakes research activities.

ACTIVITIES IN DEVELOPING REGIONS: Present in developing regions. Active in 3 country(ies). Works through local field partners. **Sustainable Development Actions:** Debt/finance/trade; Ecology/environment/biodiversity; Rural development/agriculture; Small enterprises/informal sector/handicrafts; Urban development/habitat. **Regions:** Central Asia and South Asia; North Africa; Southern Africa.

INFORMATION AND EDUCATION ACTIVITIES: Topics: Ecology/environment/biodiversity; International economic relations/trade/debt/finance; International relations/cooperation/development aid; Poverty/living conditions; Rural development/agriculture; Urban development/habitat. **Activities:** Conferences/seminars/workshops/training activities; Fund raising; Information and documentation services/data bases; Information campaigns/exhibitions; Lobbying/advocacy.

NLD3048
ALLIANCE OF NORTHERN PEOPLE ON ENVIRONMENT AND DEVELOPMENT (ANPED)

c/o WISE, P.O. Box 18185, 1001 ZB Amsterdam, The Netherlands.

Telephone: 31 (20) 63 92 681. *Fax:* 31 (20) 63 91 379. *Contact:* Anna Syomina co-chair.

OBJECTIVES: To change consumption and production patterns in the North by encouraging debate on the issues of environment, development and participatory democracy. To link activities, exchange experiences and enhance mutual learning.

GENERAL INFORMATION: *Creation:* 1991. *Type of organisation:* association of NGOs. *Member organisations:* 64. *Personnel/Total:* 1. *Salaried:* 1. *Budget/Total 1993:* ECU 56000 (US$ 65000). *Financial sources:* Private: 5%. Public: 90%. Self-financing: 5%.

PUBLICATIONS: *Periodicals:* Northen Lights (4) - CAP-an interactive newsletter on changing consumption and production patterns. *Annual report. List of publications.*

PLANNED ACTIVITIES: Campaign on consumption and production patterns; debate on the role of social movements in sustainable development and new strategies for civil society.

INFORMATION AND EDUCATION ACTIVITIES: Topics: Ecology/environment/biodiversity; **Activities:** Lobbying/advocacy; Publishing/audiovisual materials/educational materials.

NLD3049
AMNESTY INTERNATIONAL, AFDELING NEDERLAND ♦
Amnesty International, Dutch Section

Keizersgracht 620, 1017 ER Amsterdam, The Netherlands.

Telephone: 31 (20) 62 64 436. *Fax:* 31 (20) 62 40 889.

OBJECTIVES: To work worldwide for the release of prisoners of conscience, fair and prompt trials for all political prisoners, the abolition of torture and the death penalty. To oppose extrajudicial executions and "disappearances".

GENERAL INFORMATION: *Creation:* 1968. *Personnel/Total:* 160. *Salaried:* 40. *Volunteers:* 120. *Budget/Total 1993:* ECU 6905000 (US$ 8076000). *Financial sources:* Private: 40%. Self-financing: 60%.

PUBLICATIONS: *Periodicals:* Wordt Vervolgd (11). *Annual report. List of publications.*

EVALUATION/RESEARCH: Undertakes research activities.

INFORMATION AND EDUCATION ACTIVITIES: Topics: Human rights/peace/conflicts; Refugees/migrants/ethnic groups. **Activities:** Conferences/seminars/workshops/training activities; Fund raising; Information and documentation services/data bases; Information campaigns/exhibitions; Lobbying/advocacy; Publishing/audiovisual materials/educational materials.

NLD3050
ARTSEN ZONDER GRENZEN NEDERLAND ♦ Doctors without Borders

Max Euweplein 40, Postbus 10014, 1001 EA Amsterdam, The Netherlands.

Telephone: 31 (20) 52 08 700. *Fax:* 31 (20) 62 05 170. *Contact:* Dr. Jacques de Milliano, Director.

OBJECTIVES: To provide emergency medical aid to victims of natural disasters, man-made catastrophes or war. To provide aid on a humanitarian basis, without distinction as to race, creed or political beliefs.

GENERAL INFORMATION: *Creation:* 1984. *Type of organisation:* network. *Personnel/Total:* 332. *Salaried:* 187 of which: 81 in developing countries. *Volunteers:* 145 of which: 139 in developing countries. *Budget/Total 1993:* ECU 41126000 (US$ 48100000). *Financial sources:* *Private:* 43%. *Public:* 56%. *Self-financing:* 1%.

PUBLICATIONS: *Periodicals:* Medical News. *Annual report. List of publications.*

EVALUATION/RESEARCH: Evaluation reports available. Undertakes research activities.

COMMENTS: Undertakes activities in the Commonwealth of Independent States.

ACTIVITIES IN DEVELOPING REGIONS: Present in developing regions. Active in 31 country(ies). Maintains local field presence. Works through local field partners. **Sustainable Development Actions:** Education/training/literacy; Emergency relief/refugees/humanitarian assistance; Food/famine; Health/sanitation/water; Human rights/peace/conflicts. **Regions:** Caribbean; Central Africa; Central Asia and South Asia; East Africa; Middle East; South America; South East Asia; Southern Africa; West Africa.

INFORMATION AND EDUCATION ACTIVITIES: Topics: Emergency relief/refugees/humanitarian assistance; Health/sanitation/water; Human rights/peace/conflicts; Peace/ethnic conflicts/armament/disarmament; Refugees/migrants/ethnic groups. **Activities:** Conferences/seminars/workshops/training activities; Formal education; Fund raising; Information and documentation services/data bases; Information campaigns/exhibitions; Lobbying/advocacy; Publishing/audiovisual materials/educational materials.

NLD3051

ASIAN STUDIES, INFORMATION & AUDIOVISUALS (ASIA)

Himalayan Research Institute, Postbus 53143, 1007 RC Amsterdam, The Netherlands.

Telephone: 31 (20) 68 31 175. *Contact:* Hans G. Ponse, Director.

OBJECTIVES: To disseminate information on Asia. To produce audiovisual programs (slides/music/text). To fundraise for small-scale development projects mainly in the Himalayas.

GENERAL INFORMATION: *Creation:* 1975. *Personnel/Total:* 3. *Volunteers:* 3. *Budget/Total 1993:* ECU 4000 (US$ 5000). *Financial sources:* *Private:* 50%. *Self-financing:* 50%.

PUBLICATIONS: *Periodicals:* ASIA Catalogus (4). *List of publications.*

EVALUATION/RESEARCH: Undertakes research activities.

ACTIVITIES IN DEVELOPING REGIONS: Present in developing regions. Active in 2 country(ies). Maintains local field presence. Works through local field partners. **Sustainable Development Actions:** Children/youth/family; Education/training/literacy; Emergency relief/refugees/humanitarian assistance; Small enterprises/informal sector/handicrafts. **Regions:** Central Asia and South Asia; South East Asia.

INFORMATION AND EDUCATION ACTIVITIES: Topics: Children/youth/family; Culture/tradition/religion; Ecology/environment/biodiversity; Education/training/literacy; Emergency relief/refugees/humanitarian assistance; Gender issues/women; Human rights/peace/conflicts; International economic relations/trade/debt/finance; International relations/cooperation/development aid; Peace/ethnic conflicts/armament/disarmament; Population/family planning/demography; Poverty/living conditions; Refugees/migrants/ethnic groups; Rural development/agriculture; Urban development/habitat. **Activities:** Broadcasting/cultural events; Fund raising; Information and documentation services/data bases; Information campaigns/exhibitions; Publishing/audiovisual materials/educational materials.

NLD3052

ASSOCIATION INTERNATIONALE DES URBANISTES

Mauritskade 23, 2514 HD Den Haag, The Netherlands.

Contact: E.C. Poventud.

NLD3053

ASSOCIATION OF EUROPEAN PARLIAMENTARIANS FOR AFRICA (AWEPA)

Prins Hendrikkade 48, 1012 AC Amsterdam, The Netherlands.

Telephone: 31 (20) 62 66 639. *Fax:* 31 (20) 62 20 130.

NLD3054

AYUBOWAN

Statenjachtstraat 240, 1034 EL Amsterdam, Pays-Bas.

Téléphone: 31 (20) 633 59 67. *Contact:* Rosine Elst-Vijlbrief.

NLD3055

BANGLADESH GROEP NEDERLAND

Postbus 11699, 1001 GR Amsterdam, The Netherlands.

Telephone: 31 (20) 66 29 953. *Fax:* 31 (20) 66 29 953.

NLD3056

BASHATI - STICHTING VOOR BANGLADESH ♦ Bashati - Trust for Bangladesh

Belterwijdestraat 41, 1316 JS Almere, The Netherlands.

Telephone: 31 (36) 53 37 051. *Fax:* 31 (20) 68 36 622. *Contact:* Roel van Nek, Chairman.

OBJECTIVES: To set up small-scale projects for the poor in co-operation with Bengali NGOs in the fields of education, healthcare, development and gender issues.

GENERAL INFORMATION: *Creation:* 1990. *Personnel/Total:* 4. *Volunteers:* 4 of which: 2 in developing countries. *Budget/Total 1993:* ECU 23000 (US$ 27000). *Financial sources:* *Private:* 10%. *Public:* 10%. *Self-financing:* 80%.

PUBLICATIONS: *Periodicals:* Newsletter (1). *Annual report. List of publications.*

EVALUATION/RESEARCH: Evaluation reports available. Undertakes research activities.

PLANNED ACTIVITIES: Establishing a primary school. Setting up women's paramedical programmes.

ACTIVITIES IN DEVELOPING REGIONS: Active in 1 country(ies). Maintains local field presence. Works through local field partners. **Sustainable Development Actions:** Education/training/literacy; Energy/transport; Gender issues/women; Health/sanitation/water; Rural development/agriculture; Sending volunteers/experts/technical assistance; Urban development/habitat. **Regions:** Central Asia and South Asia.

INFORMATION AND EDUCATION ACTIVITIES: Topics: Education/training/literacy; Gender issues/women; Health/sanitation/water; Rural development/agriculture; Urban development/habitat. **Activities:** Exchanges/twinning/linking; Formal education; Fund raising; Information and documentation services/data bases; Information campaigns/exhibitions; Publishing/audiovisual materials/educational materials.

NLD3057

BERNARD VAN LEER FOUNDATION

Postbus 82334, 2508 EH Den Haag, The Netherlands.

Telephone: 31 (70) 35 12 040. *Fax:* 31 (70) 35 02 373. *Contact:* Dr. M.C.E. van Gendt, Executive Director.

NLD3058

BIJEEN DERDE WERELD INFORMATIEHUIS ♦ Bijeen Third World Information Centre

See: *How to Use the Directory*, page 11.

Simon Stevinweg 17, Postbus 750, 5201 AT's-Hertogenbosch, The Netherlands.

Telephone: 31 (73) 62 18 970. *Fax:* 31 (73) 62 18 512. *Contact:* Joep Brouwers.

OBJECTIVES: To disseminate information via computerised bibliographic searches and publications about the Third World and our society.

GENERAL INFORMATION: *Creation:* 1968. *Personnel/Total:* 18. *Salaried:* 18. *Budget/Total 1993:* ECU 1151000 (US$ 1346000). *Financial sources:* Private: 2%. Public: 5%. Self-financing: 93%.

PUBLICATIONS: *Periodicals:* Magazine Bijeen (11).

INFORMATION AND EDUCATION ACTIVITIES: Topics: Children/youth/family; Culture/tradition/religion; Ecology/environment/biodiversity; Education/training/literacy; Emergency relief/refugees/humanitarian assistance; Employment/unemployment; Food/famine; Gender issues/women; Health/sanitation/water; Human rights/peace/conflicts; International economic relations/trade/debt/finance; International relations/cooperation/development aid; Peace/ethnic conflicts/armament/disarmament; Population/family planning/demography; Poverty/living conditions; Racism/xenophobia/antisemitism; Refugees/migrants/ethnic groups; Rural development/agriculture; Urban development/habitat. **Activities:** Information and documentation services/data bases.

NLD3059

BISSCHOP BEKKERS INSTITUUT (BBI) ♦ Bishop Bekkers Institute

Postbus 415, Korte Elisabethstraat 6, 3500 AK Utrecht, The Netherlands.

Telephone: 31 (30) 23 33 504. *Fax:* 31 (30) 23 40 026. *Contact:* M.G.M. Schuurman.

OBJECTIVES: To advise on research in the field of care for the mentally handicapped. To stimulate research and improve care for the mentally handicapped in developing countries by encouraging the exchange of information about Third World projects.

GENERAL INFORMATION: *Creation:* 1972. *Affiliated to:* International League of Societies for Persons with Mental Handicaps -International Association for the Scientific Study of Mental Deficiency. *Personnel/Total:* 9. *Salaried:* 9 of which: 2 in developing countries.

PUBLICATIONS: *Periodicals:* Literatuurattendering & Bibliotneekacnwinsten (12) - NTZ (4) - Nieuwsbrief Informatiecentrum (2) - ZORG, Care in Development (2). *Annual report.*

EVALUATION/RESEARCH: Evaluation reports available. Undertakes research activities.

PLANNED ACTIVITIES: Compiling literature on the mentally handicapped in the Third World

ACTIVITIES IN DEVELOPING REGIONS: Active in 22 country(ies). **Sustainable Development Actions:** Other. **Regions:** Caribbean; Central Africa; Central Asia and South Asia; East Africa; Middle East; South America; South East Asia; Southern Africa; West Africa.

INFORMATION AND EDUCATION ACTIVITIES: Topics: Other. **Activities:** Conferences/seminars/workshops/training activities; Exchanges/twinning/linking; Formal education; Information and documentation services/data bases; Lobbying/advocacy.

NLD3060

BISSCHOPPELIJKE VASTENACTIE

Postbus 587, 3800 AN Amersfoort, The Netherlands.

Telephone: 31 (33) 61 29 57. *Contact:* F. Meeus.

NLD3061

BOERENGROEP ♦ Farmers' Group

Duivendaal 2-b, Postbus 265, 6700 AG Wageningen, The Netherlands.

Telephone: 31 (31) 74 10 500. *Fax:* 31 (31) 74 21 500. *Contact:* W. Verhaak.

OBJECTIVES: To support groups of progressive Dutch farmers by undertaking research on agricultural policy alternatives. To encourage Dutch farmers to think in global terms and university students to think critically about development in agriculture.

GENERAL INFORMATION: *Creation:* 1971. *Affiliated to:* Food for the Future (Netherlands) - PERMAGOON (Netherlands). *Personnel/Total:* 13. *Salaried:* 1. *Volunteers:* 12 of which: 3 in developing countries. *Budget/Total 1993:* ECU 16000 (US$ 19000). *Financial sources:* Public: 100%.

PUBLICATIONS: *List of publications.*

EVALUATION/RESEARCH: Evaluation reports available. Undertakes research activities.

INFORMATION AND EDUCATION ACTIVITIES: Topics: International economic relations/trade/debt/finance; International relations/cooperation/development aid; Rural development/agriculture. **Activities:** Conferences/seminars/workshops/training activities; Publishing/audiovisual materials/educational materials.

NLD3062

BOTH ENDS

Damrak 28-30, 1012 LJ Amsterdam, The Netherlands.

Telephone: 31 (20) 62 30 823. *Fax:* 31 (20) 62 08 049. *E-mail:* BOTHENDS@Geo2.Geonet.De. *Contact:* Wiert Wiertsema, Policy Coordinator.

OBJECTIVES: To support NGOs working for the protection of the environment and for social justice through dialogue, exchange and collaboration in gathering information and fund-raising for campaigns.

GENERAL INFORMATION: *Creation:* 1990. *Affiliated to:* World Rainforest Movement (Malaysia) - Environmental Liason Centre International (Kenya) - El Taller (Tunisia) - South-North Federation (Netherlands). *Personnel/Total:* 20. *Salaried:* 13 of which: 1 in developing countries. *Volunteers:* 7. *Budget/Total 1993:* ECU 414000 (US$ 485000). *Financial sources:* Private: 10%. Public: 75%. Self-financing: 15%.

PUBLICATIONS: *Annual report. List of publications.*

EVALUATION/RESEARCH: Undertakes research activities.

PLANNED ACTIVITIES: Exchanging information on multilateral funding institions. Organising a survey on sustainable forest management practices. Networking on environment and development.

COMMENTS: Undertakes activities in the Commonwealth of Independent States.

ACTIVITIES IN DEVELOPING REGIONS: Active in 1 country(ies). Maintains local field presence. Works through local field partners. **Sustainable Development Actions:** Ecology/environment/biodiversity; Gender issues/women; Rural development/agriculture; Urban development/habitat. **Regions:** Caribbean; Central Africa; Central Asia and South Asia; East Africa; East Asia; Mexico and Central America; Middle East; North Africa; Oceania; South America; South East Asia; Southern Africa; West Africa.

INFORMATION AND EDUCATION ACTIVITIES: Topics: Ecology/environment/biodiversity; Gender issues/women; Population/family planning/demography; Urban development/habitat. **Activities:** Conferences/seminars/workshops/training activities; Exchanges/twinning/linking; Fund raising; Information and documentation services/data bases; Information campaigns/exhibitions; Lobbying/advocacy; Networking/electronic telecommunications; Publishing/audiovisual materials/educational materials.

NLD3063

BREED OVERLEG VROUWEN EN ONTWIKKELING (BOVO)

FC Donderstraat 23, 3572 JB Utrecht, Netherlands.

Telephone: 31 (30) 27 15 525.

NLD3064

BUREAU BELEIDSVORMIG ONTWIKKELINGSSAMENWERKING (BBO) ♦ Christian Institute for Development Policy

Plein 9, 2511 CR Den Haag, The Netherlands.

Telephone: 31 (70) 345 22 06. *Fax:* 31 (70) 356 14 96. *Contact:* G. van Oord, Director.

OBJECTIVES: To lobby the Dutch Parliament, Dutch members of the European parliament, ministries and economic actors on trade and development on behalf of 11 church related development organisations.

GENERAL INFORMATION: *Creation:* 1992. *Member organisations:* 11. *Affiliated to:* ICCO - Cebemo - Interchurch Aid - Catholic Miss Council - Catholic Lent Campaign - Solidaridad - Missionary Department of Protestant Churches - OIKOS -CMC. *Personnel/Total:* 5. *Salaried:* 3. *Volunteers:* 2. *Budget/Total 1993:* ECU 184000 (US$ 215000). *Financial sources:* Self-financing: 100%.

PUBLICATIONS: *Periodicals:* Briefing (6). *Annual report.*

EVALUATION/RESEARCH: Evaluation reports available. Undertakes research activities.

COMMENTS: Information activities related to the Commonwealth of Independent States.

INFORMATION AND EDUCATION ACTIVITIES: Topics: Emergency relief/refugees/humanitarian assistance; Food/famine; Human rights/peace/conflicts; International economic relations/trade/debt/finance; International relations/cooperation/development aid; Peace/ethnic conflicts/armament/disarmament; Poverty/living conditions; Rural development/agriculture. **Activities:** Conferences/seminars/workshops/training activities; Information and documentation services/data bases; Lobbying/advocacy.

NLD3065
BUREAU VROUWEN EN AIDS

Predikheren Kerkhof 2, 3512 TK Utrecht, The Netherlands.

NLD3066
CARITAS NEERLANDICA - STICHTING MENSEN IN NOOD ♦
Caritas Netherlands

Rompertsebaan 50, P.O. Box 1041, 5200 BA Hertogenbosch, The Netherlands.
Telephone: 31 (73) 61 44 544. *Fax:* 31 (73) 61 32 115. *E-mail:* caritas neerlandica@tool.nl. *Contact:* J.J. van Soest, Director.

OBJECTIVES: To provide help to people in need, both in emergencies and in structural marginalization. To work on the basis of Christian values. To render services to people in need, including refugees and victims of disasters, especially in developing countries.

GENERAL INFORMATION: *Creation:* 1914. *Affiliated to:* Caritas Internationalis (Italy) - Euronaid (the Netherlands) - VOICE (Belgium). *Personnel/Total:* 47. *Salaried:* 45. *Volunteers:* 2. *Budget/Total 1993:* ECU 29002000 (US$ 33920000). *Financial sources:* Private: 58%. Public: 34%. Self-financing: 8%.

PUBLICATIONS: *Periodicals:* Plan and Action (2) - Clamavi (3) - Clamavi Special (3). *Annual report.*

COMMENTS: The organisation undertakes a variety of field activities and information projects except programmes concerning health and purely pastoral projects. Undertakes activities in the Commonwealth of Independent States.

ACTIVITIES IN DEVELOPING REGIONS: Active in 73 country(ies). Works through local field partners.

NLD3067
CEBEMO/VASTENAKTIE

Rhijngeesterstraatweg 40, Postbus 77, 2341 BV Oegstgeest, The Netherlands.
Telephone: 31 (71) 15 91 59. *Fax:* 31 (71) 17 53 91. *E-mail:* Cebemo@ANTENNA.NL. *Contact:* H.A.J. Kruÿssen, General Director.

OBJECTIVES: To finance and support socio-economic development initiatives of grassroots groups and organisations in the South. To lobby the Dutch government and other institutions to bring these initiatives to the forefront.

GENERAL INFORMATION: *Creation:* 1980. *Affiliated to:* Coopération Internationale pour le Développement et la Solidarité (Belgium) -NGO-EU Network (the Netherlands). *Personnel/Total:* 125. *Salaried:*

108. *Budget/Total 1993:* ECU 75496000 (US$ 88300000). *Financial sources:* Private: 10%. Public: 90%.

PUBLICATIONS: *Annual report. List of publications.*

EVALUATION/RESEARCH: Evaluation reports available. Undertakes research activities.

PLANNED ACTIVITIES: Focusing on capacity building especially in Africa.

COMMENTS: Undertakes activities in the Commonwealth of Independent States. Information activities related to the Commonwealth of Independent States.

ACTIVITIES IN DEVELOPING REGIONS: Active in 80 country(ies). Maintains local field presence. Works through local field partners. **Sustainable Development Actions:** Children/youth/family; Debt/finance/trade; Democracy/good governance/institution building/participatory development; Ecology/environment/biodiversity; Education/training/literacy; Energy/transport; Gender issues/women; Health/sanitation/water; Human rights/peace/conflicts; Population/family planning/demography; Rural development/agriculture; Small enterprises/informal sector/handicrafts; Urban development/habitat. **Regions:** Caribbean; Central Africa; Central Asia and South Asia; East Africa; East Asia; Mexico and Central America; Middle East; North Africa; Oceania; South America; South East Asia; Southern Africa; West Africa.

INFORMATION AND EDUCATION ACTIVITIES: Topics: Children/youth/family; Culture/tradition/religion; Ecology/environment/biodiversity; Education/training/literacy; Employment/unemployment; Gender issues/women; Health/sanitation/water; Human rights/peace/conflicts; International economic relations/trade/debt/finance; International relations/cooperation/development aid; Peace/ethnic conflicts/armament/disarmament; Population/family planning/demography; Poverty/living conditions; Racism/xenophobia/antisemitism; Refugees/migrants/ethnic groups; Rural development/agriculture; Urban development/habitat. **Activities:** Broadcasting/cultural events; Conferences/seminars/workshops/training activities; Exchanges/twinning/linking; Formal education; Fund raising; Information and documentation services/data bases; Information campaigns/exhibitions; Lobbying/advocacy; Networking/electronic telecommunications; Publishing/audiovisual materials/educational materials.

NLD3068
CENTRAAL MISSIE COMMISSARIAAT (CMC) ♦ Central Mission Board

Rhijngeesterstraatweg 40, Postbus 75, 2340 AB Oegstgeest, The Netherlands.
Telephone: 31 (71) 51 71 771. *Fax:* 31 (71) 51 75 391. *Contact:* J. Naron, Director.

OBJECTIVES: To act as an intermediary for the recruitment of Dutch personnel in the field of development and pastoral work. To advise religious orders and congregations on sending funds to support pastoral projects in the Third World.

GENERAL INFORMATION: *Creation:* 1945. *Type of organisation:* coordinating body. *Member organisations:* 50. *Affiliated to:* PSO - Dutch Missionary Council (Netherlands) - Organismes Chrétiens de Coopération Internationale. *Personnel/Total:* 185. *Salaried:* 35. *Volunteers:* 150 of which: 150 in developing countries. *Budget/Total 1993:* ECU 2072000 (US$ 2423000). *Financial sources:* Private: 70%. Public: 30%.

PUBLICATIONS: *Periodicals:* Verder Gekeken (4).

EVALUATION/RESEARCH: Evaluation reports available.

PLANNED ACTIVITIES: Organising exchanges between organisations in the North and in the South.

COMMENTS: Undertakes activities in the Commonwealth of Independent States.

ACTIVITIES IN DEVELOPING REGIONS: Active in 30 country(ies). Maintains local field presence. Works through local field partners. **Sustainable Development Actions:** Children/youth/family; Democracy/good governance/institution building/participatory development; Ecology/environment/biodiversity; Education/training/literacy; Emergency relief/refugees/humanitarian assistance; Food/famine; Gender issues/women; Health/sanitation/water; Human rights/peace/conflicts; Rural develop-

ment/agriculture; Sending volunteers/experts/technical assistance; Small enterprises/informal sector/handicrafts. **Regions:** Caribbean; Central Africa; East Africa; East Asia; Mexico and Central America; South America; South East Asia; Southern Africa; West Africa.

INFORMATION AND EDUCATION ACTIVITIES: Topics: Culture/tradition/religion; Human rights/peace/conflicts; International relations/cooperation/development aid; Peace/ethnic conflicts/armament/disarmament; Poverty/living conditions; Refugees/migrants/ethnic groups. **Activities:** Fund raising; Lobbying/advocacy.

NLD3069

CENTRE FOR DEVELOPMENT COOPERATION SERVICES (CDCS)

Vrije Univ. Amsterdam, 1081 HV Amsterdam, The Netherlands.

Telephone: 31 (20) 444 9090. *Fax:* 31 (20) 444 9095. *E-mail:* mp.van der laan@dienst.vu.nl. *Contact:* J.H.P. van Weeren.

OBJECTIVES: To facilitate development co-operation between Vrije University Amsterdam and counterpart institutions. To encourage human resource development and capacity building in the field of education and research.

GENERAL INFORMATION: *Creation:* 1966. *Personnel/Total:* 65. *Salaried:* 65 of which: 20 in developing countries. *Budget/Total 1993:* ECU 5524000 (US$ 6461000). *Financial sources:* Private: 2%. Public: 90%. *Self-financing:* 8%.

PUBLICATIONS: *Annual report.*

EVALUATION/RESEARCH: Undertakes research activities.

ACTIVITIES IN DEVELOPING REGIONS: Present in developing regions. Active in 13 country(ies). Maintains local field presence. Works through local field partners. **Sustainable Development Actions:** Ecology/environment/biodiversity; Education/training/literacy; Food/famine; Health/sanitation/water; Rural development/agriculture; Small enterprises/informal sector/handicrafts. **Regions:** Central Africa; East Africa; East Asia; South East Asia; Southern Africa; West Africa.

INFORMATION AND EDUCATION ACTIVITIES: Topics: Ecology/environment/biodiversity; Education/training/literacy; Food/famine; Health/sanitation/water; International relations/cooperation/development aid; Other; Rural development/agriculture. **Activities:** Conferences/seminars/workshops/training activities; Formal education; Fund raising; Information and documentation services/data bases; Lobbying/advocacy; Networking/electronic telecommunications; Other; Publishing/audiovisual materials/educational materials.

NLD3070

CENTRE FOR INTERNATIONAL CO-OPERATION ACTIVITIES (CICA)

Eindhoven University of Technology, Building W-hoog 2.108, P.O. Box 513, 5600 MB Eindhoven, The Netherlands.

Telephone: 31 (40) 24 72 802. *Fax:* 31 (40) 24 49 171. *E-mail:* L. PENNINKS@WMW.TUE.NL. *Contact:* Jan Van Cranenbroek, Head.

OBJECTIVES: To contribute to the development of developing countries through its projects, research and training programmes.

GENERAL INFORMATION: *Creation:* 1968. *Affiliated to:* Netherlands Universities Foundation for International Cooperation (Netherlands) . *Personnel/Total:* 10. *Budget/Total 1993:* ECU 1703000 (US$ 1992000). *Financial sources:* Public: 88%. Self-financing: 12%.

PUBLICATIONS: *Annual report.*

EVALUATION/RESEARCH: Evaluation reports available. Undertakes research activities.

PLANNED ACTIVITIES: Undertaking telecommunication research in collaboration with universities in Uganda, Tanzania, Zambia and Cameroon. Links with universities in Benin and Costa Rica.

COMMENTS: Undertakes activities in the Commonwealth of Independent States. Information activities related to the Commonwealth of Independent States.

ACTIVITIES IN DEVELOPING REGIONS: Present in developing regions. Active in 7 country(ies). Maintains local field presence. Works through local field partners. **Sustainable Development Actions:** Ecology/environment/biodiversity; Education/training/literacy; Sending volunteers/experts/technical assistance; Small enterprises/informal sector/handicrafts. **Regions:** Central Africa; East Africa; South East Asia; Southern Africa.

INFORMATION AND EDUCATION ACTIVITIES: Topics: Ecology/environment/biodiversity; Education/training/literacy. **Activities:** Conferences/seminars/workshops/training activities; Exchanges/twinning/linking; Formal education; Fund raising; Information and documentation services/data bases; Lobbying/advocacy; Networking/electronic telecommunications; Publishing/audiovisual materials/educational materials.

NLD3071

CENTRE FOR INTERNATIONAL CO-OPERATION AND APPROPRIATE TECHNOLOGY OF THE DELFT UNIVERSITY OF TECHNOLOGY (CICAT) ♦ Centre pour la coopération internationale et la technologie appropriée de l'Université de technologie de Delft

Postbus 5048, 2600 GA Delft, The Netherlands.

Telephone: 31 (15) 27 83 612. *Fax:* 31 (15) 27 81 179. *E-mail:* CICAT@CT.TUDelft.NL. *Contact:* H.P.S. Althuis.

OBJECTIVES: To organise and co-ordinate the development co-operation efforts of the DELFT University of Technology (DUT). To mobilize the expertise of DUT in the field of development co-operation, in order to provide research consultants and to maintain ties with universities and research institutions in developing countries.

GENERAL INFORMATION: *Creation:* 1978. *Personnel/Total:* 33. *Salaried:* 32 of which: 5 in developing countries. *Volunteers:* 1. *Budget/Total 1993:* ECU 690000 (US$ 808000). *Financial sources:* Public: 80%. *Self-financing:* 20%.

PUBLICATIONS: *Annual report. List of publications.*

EVALUATION/RESEARCH: Evaluation reports available. Undertakes research activities.

COMMENTS: Undertakes activities in the Commonwealth of Independent States. Information activities related to the Commonwealth of Independent States.

ACTIVITIES IN DEVELOPING REGIONS: Present in developing regions. **Sustainable Development Actions:** Ecology/environment/biodiversity; Health/sanitation/water; Sending volunteers/experts/technical assistance; Urban development/habitat. **Regions:** Central Asia and South Asia; East Africa; East Asia; Mexico and Central America; South America; South East Asia; Southern Africa; West Africa.

INFORMATION AND EDUCATION ACTIVITIES: Topics: Ecology/environment/biodiversity; Health/sanitation/water; Urban development/habitat. **Activities:** Exchanges/twinning/linking; Networking/electronic telecommunications; Other.

NLD3072

THE CENTRE ON HOUSING RIGHTS AND EVICTIONS (COHRE)

Postbus 15100, 3501 BC Utrecht, The Netherlands.

Telephone: 31 (30) 27 31 976. *Fax:* 31 (30) 27 21 453. *Contact:* Scott Leckie and Miloon Kothari, Co-Directors.

OBJECTIVES: To promote the right for adequate housing for everyone. To oppose and condemn forced and arbitrary evictions. To carry out academic research on various housing rights issues, including housing rights indicators and structural adjustment programmes.

GENERAL INFORMATION: *Creation:* 1991. *Affiliated to:* Habitat International Coalition (Mexico). *Personnel/Total:* 2. *Salaried:* 2 of which: 1 in developing countries. *Budget/Total 1993:* ECU 46000 (US$ 54000). *Financial sources:* Private: 60%. Public: 30%. *Self-financing:* 10%.

PUBLICATIONS: *Periodicals:* Sources Series (1) - Global Survey on Forced Evictions (1). *Annual report. List of publications.*

Voir : *Comment utiliser le répertoire,* page 11.

EVALUATION/RESEARCH: Evaluation reports available. Undertakes research activities.

ACTIVITIES IN DEVELOPING REGIONS: Present in developing regions. Active in 19 country(ies). Works through local field partners. **Sustainable Development Actions:** Children/youth/family; Education/training/literacy; Gender issues/women; Human rights/peace/conflicts; Urban development/habitat. **Regions:** Caribbean; Central Africa; Central Asia and South Asia; East Africa; East Asia; Mexico and Central America; Middle East; North Africa; Oceania; South America; South East Asia; Southern Africa; West Africa.

INFORMATION AND EDUCATION ACTIVITIES: Topics: Human rights/peace/conflicts; Poverty/living conditions; Urban development/habitat. **Activities:** Conferences/seminars/workshops/training activities; Exchanges/twinning/linking; Formal education; Fund raising; Information and documentation services/data bases; Information campaigns/exhibitions; Lobbying/advocacy; Networking/electronic telecommunications; Publishing/audiovisual materials/educational materials.

NLD3073

CENTRE VOOR ONTWIKKELINGSSAMENWERKING (COS-NOORD-HOLLAND-ZUM) ♦ Centre for International Co-operation

Hoofdweg 671, Postbus 271, 2130 AG Hoofddorp, The Netherlands.

Telephone: 31 (23) 56 16 560. **Fax:** 31 (23) 56 23 818. **Contact:** Léon Werry.

OBJECTIVES: To promote and encourage people, organisations, institutions and local governments in pursuing activities in the field of international co-operation, especially North-South relations.

GENERAL INFORMATION: Creation: 1981. **Affiliated to:** Association of regional COSses (Netherlands). **Personnel/Total:** 6. Salaried: 4. Volunteers: 2. **Budget/Total 1993:** ECU 111000 (US$ 130000). **Financial sources:** Public: 100%.

PUBLICATIONS: Annual report.

EVALUATION/RESEARCH: Evaluation reports available. Undertakes research activities.

COMMENTS: Information activities related to the Commonwealth of Independent States.

INFORMATION AND EDUCATION ACTIVITIES: Topics: Gender issues/women; Racism/xenophobia/antisemitism; Refugees/migrants/ethnic groups; Urban development/habitat. **Activities:** Broadcasting/cultural events; Conferences/seminars/workshops/training activities; Exchanges/twinning/linking; Formal education; Fund raising; Information and documentation services/data bases; Information campaigns/exhibitions; Lobbying/advocacy; Publishing/audiovisual materials/educational materials.

NLD3074

CENTRUM MISSIONAIRE PARTICIPATIE AFRIKA (CMPA) ♦ Centre for Missionary Participation in Africa

Schandelerstraat 49, 6412 XM Heerlen, The Netherlands.

Telephone: 31 (45) 57 24 171.

OBJECTIVES: To promote development in Ghana, Tanzania and Morocco through small-scale projects focusing on women, primary health care, street children and agriculture by sending young volunteers as lay missionaries. To provide pastoral care for African refugees in Holland.

GENERAL INFORMATION: Creation: 1985. **Personnel/Total:** 12. Salaried: 3. Volunteers: 9 of which: 8 in developing countries. **Financial sources:** Self-financing: 100%.

ACTIVITIES IN DEVELOPING REGIONS: Present in developing regions. Active in 3 country(ies). Maintains local field presence. Works through local field partners. **Sustainable Development Actions:** Children/youth/family; Democracy/good governance/institution building/participatory development; Ecology/environment/biodiversity; Education/training/literacy; Gender issues/women; Health/sanitation/water; Human rights/peace/conflicts; Population/family planning/demography; Rural development/agriculture; Sending volunteers/experts/technical assistance; Small enterprises/informal sector/handicrafts; Urban development/habitat. **Regions:** East Africa; West Africa.

NLD3075

CENTRUM ONTMOETING DER VOLKEREN ♦ Centre de rencontre des peuples pour développement, paix et justice

Rijksweg 8, 6267 AG Cadier en Keer, Pays-Bas.

Téléphone: 31 (43) 40 72 333. **Fax:** 31 (43) 40 73 183. **Contact:** F. van Lieshout, Directeur.

OBJECTIFS: Offrir une formation aux coopérants sur la culture, l'histoire et la situation économique et sociale des pays en développement. Donner une vision réaliste du développement. Collaborer avec des organisations homologues dans les pays en développement par l'envoi des coopérants.

INFORMATIONS GENERALES: Création: 1967. **Affiliée à:** PSO. **Personnel/Total:** 51. Salariés: 20 dont: 2 dans les pays en développement. Bénévoles: 31 dont: 6 dans les pays en développement. **Budget/Total 1993:** ECU 92000 (US$ 108000). **Sources financières:** Privé: 85%. Public: 10%. Autofinancement: 5%.

PUBLICATIONS: Périodiques: Keerkring (2).

EVALUATION/RECHERCHE: Entreprend des activités de recherche.

ACTIVITES DANS LES REGIONS EN DEVELOPPEMENT: Intervient par l'intermédiaire d'organisations locales partenaires. **Actions de Développement durable:** Droits de l'Homme/paix/conflits; Développement rural/agriculture; Enfants/jeunesse/famille; Envoi de volontaires/experts/assistance technique; Population/planning familial/démographie; Questions relatives aux femmes; Santé/assainissement/eau; Secours d'urgence/réfugiés/aide humanitaire; Écologie/environnement/biodiversité; Éducation/formation/alphabétisation. **Régions:** Afrique de l'Est; Afrique de l'Ouest; Amérique du Sud.

NLD3076

CENTRUM VOOR DE STUDIE VAN HET ONDERWIJS IN ONTWIKKELINGSLANDEN ♦ Centre for the Study of Education in Developing Countries

Kortenaerkade 11, Postbus 29777, 2502 LT Den Haag, The Netherlands.

Telephone: 31 (70) 42 60 291. **Fax:** 31 (70) 42 60 299. **E-mail:** cesosecr@nufficcs.nl. **Contact:** L.F.B. Dubbeldam.

OBJECTIVES: To contribute in a scientific and practical way to the improvement of education in developing countries and development co-operation.

GENERAL INFORMATION: Creation: 1963. **Affiliated to:** Nuffic (Netherlands). **Personnel/Total:** 19. Salaried: 19 of which: 10 in developing countries. **Budget/Total 1993:** ECU 1428000 (US$ 1670000). **Financial sources:** Private: 8%. Public: 47%. Self-financing: 45%.

PUBLICATIONS: Annual report. List of publications.

EVALUATION/RESEARCH: Evaluation reports available. Undertakes research activities.

PLANNED ACTIVITIES: Developing educational systems and processes.

COMMENTS: Information activities related to the Commonwealth of Independent States.

ACTIVITIES IN DEVELOPING REGIONS: Present in developing regions. Works through local field partners. **Sustainable Development Actions:** Education/training/literacy; Gender issues/women. **Regions:** Caribbean; Central Africa; Central Asia and South Asia; East Africa; East Asia; Mexico and Central America; Middle East; North Africa; South America; South East Asia; Southern Africa; West Africa.

NLD3077

CENTRUM VOOR MONDIAAL ONDERWIJS ♦ Centre for Global Education

Postbus 9108, 6500 HK Nijmegen, The Netherlands.

Telephone: 31 (24) 36 13 074. **Fax:** 31 (24) 36 13 014.

OBJECTIVES: To make available to a large public Dutch language educational materials on the environment, development, peace, human rights and intercultural education.

GENERAL INFORMATION: *Creation:* 1967. *Personnel/Total:* 12. *Salaried:* 4. *Volunteers:* 8.

PUBLICATIONS: *Annual report. List of publications.*

EVALUATION/RESEARCH: Evaluation reports available.

COMMENTS: Information activities related to the Commonwealth of Independent States.

NLD3078

CHRISTELIJK NATIONAAL VAKVERBOND (CNV) ♦ National Federation of Christian Trade Unions

Postbus 2475, 3500 GL Utrecht, The Netherlands.

Telephone: 31 (30) 29 13 911. *Fax:* 31 (30) 29 33 806. *Contact:* G. Pruim, project Co-ordinator.

OBJECTIVES: To raise awareness in the Netherlands about the trade union movements in developing countries. To provide financial assistance to trade unions and to promote the existance of vital, independent and strong trade unionism.

GENERAL INFORMATION: *Creation:* 1967. *Type of organisation:* coordinating body. *Member organisations:* 15. *Affiliated to:* World Confederation of Labour (Belgium). *Personnel/Total:* 7. *Salaried:* 7 of which: 1 in developing countries. *Budget/Total 1993:* ECU 2302000 (US$ 2692000). *Financial sources:* Private: 15%. Public: 80%. Self-financing: 5%.

PUBLICATIONS: *Periodicals:* KomOver Magazine (4). *Annual report.*

EVALUATION/RESEARCH: Evaluation reports available. Undertakes research activities.

PLANNED ACTIVITIES: Campaigning on Madagascar Trade Unions and the globalisation of labour.

COMMENTS: Undertakes activities in the Commonwealth of Independent States. Information activities related to the Commonwealth of Independent States.

ACTIVITIES IN DEVELOPING REGIONS: Present in developing regions. Works through local field partners. **Sustainable Development Actions:** Democracy/good governance/institution building/participatory development; Education/training/literacy; Energy/transport; Gender issues/women; Human rights/peace/conflicts; Other; Rural development/agriculture; Sending volunteers/experts/technical assistance; Small enterprises/informal sector/handicrafts; Urban development/habitat. **Regions:** Caribbean; Central Africa; Central Asia and South Asia; East Africa; East Asia; Mexico and Central America; North Africa; South America; South East Asia; Southern Africa; West Africa.

INFORMATION AND EDUCATION ACTIVITIES: **Topics:** Education/training/literacy; Emergency relief/refugees/humanitarian assistance; Employment/unemployment; Gender issues/women; Human rights/peace/conflicts; International economic relations/trade/debt/finance; International relations/cooperation/development aid; Poverty/living conditions; Rural development/agriculture; Urban development/habitat. **Activities:** Conferences/seminars/workshops/training activities; Exchanges/twinning/linking; Formal education; Fund raising; Information and documentation services/data bases; Information campaigns/exhibitions; Lobbying/advocacy; Publishing/audiovisual materials/educational materials.

NLD3079

CHRISTELYK PLATTELANDSVROUWEN BOND (CPB) ♦ Christian Countrywomen Alliance

Bergstraat 33-A, 3811 NG Amersfoort, The Netherlands.

Telephone: 31 (33) 46 53 492. *Fax:* 31 (33) 46 53 988. *Contact:* K. Eisses-Timmerman, President.

OBJECTIVES: To raise consciousness of, provide education for and contribute to the welfare of their members, women farmers. To promote the interests of women farmers.

GENERAL INFORMATION: *Creation:* 1938. *Affiliated to:* Associated Country Women of the World (United Kingdom). *Personnel/Total:* 22. *Salaried:* 7. *Volunteers:* 15. *Budget/Total 1993:* ECU 276000 (US$ 323000). *Financial sources:* Public: 25%. Self-financing: 75%.

PUBLICATIONS: *Annual report.*

EVALUATION/RESEARCH: Evaluation reports available.

PLANNED ACTIVITIES: Undertaking exchanges with women farmers in Nicaragua and Sierra Leone.

ACTIVITIES IN DEVELOPING REGIONS: Works through local field partners. **Sustainable Development Actions:** Ecology/environment/biodiversity; Gender issues/women; Rural development/agriculture; Small enterprises/informal sector/handicrafts. **Regions:** Mexico and Central America; West Africa.

INFORMATION AND EDUCATION ACTIVITIES: **Topics:** Culture/tradition/religion; Ecology/environment/biodiversity; Gender issues/women; Racism/xenophobia/antisemitism; Rural development/agriculture. **Activities:** Conferences/seminars/workshops/training activities; Exchanges/twinning/linking; Information campaigns/exhibitions; Lobbying/advocacy.

NLD3080

CLAT NEDERLAND ♦ Latin American Central of Workers - Dutch Section

Nieuwegracht 47, 3512 LE Utrecht, The Netherlands.

Telephone: 31 (30) 23 19 675. *Fax:* 31 (30) 23 67 185 . *Contact:* Cor Kavelaars, Director.

NLD3081

CNV JONGERENORGANISATIE ♦ Youth Organisation of the CNV

Ravellaan 1, Postbus 2475, 3500 GL Utrecht, The Netherlands.

Telephone: 31 (30) 29 13 911. *Fax:* 31 (30) 29 46 544. *Contact:* Theo Nelissen.

NLD3082

COMMISSIE JUSTITIA ET PAX - NEDERLAND ♦ Justice and Peace Commission - Netherlands

Rhijngeesterstraatweg 40, Postbus 1031, 2340 BA Oegstgeest, The Netherlands.

Telephone: 31 (71) 51 75 901. *Fax:* 31 (71) 51 75 391. *Contact:* V. M. Scheffers, General Secretary.

OBJECTIVES: To persuade the members of the Roman Catholic Church that it is everybody's responsibility to try to bring about more justice and peace in the Netherlands and abroad. To call for special attention to individuals and groups of people whose rights are not respected.

GENERAL INFORMATION: *Creation:* 1968. *Type of organisation:* association of NGOs. *Member organisations:* 11. *Affiliated to:* Europe Justice and Peace Network. *Personnel/Total:* 5. *Salaried:* 5. *Budget/Total 1993:* ECU 170000 (US$ 199000). *Financial sources:* Private: 100%.

PUBLICATIONS: *Periodicals:* Nieuwsbrief (4) - Bulletin (4). *Annual report. List of publications.*

EVALUATION/RESEARCH: Undertakes research activities.

PLANNED ACTIVITIES: Focusing on Human Rights in South Afica, East Timor and Haiti.

COMMENTS: Undertakes activities in the Commonwealth of Independent States. Information activities related to the Commonwealth of Independent States.

INFORMATION AND EDUCATION ACTIVITIES: **Topics:** Employment/unemployment; Human rights/peace/conflicts; Peace/ethnic conflicts/armament/disarmament; Population/family planning/demography; Poverty/living conditions; Racism/xenophobia/antisemitism; Refugees/migrants/ethnic groups. **Activities:** Conferences/seminars/workshops/training activities; Exchanges/twinning/linking; Lobbying/advocacy; Networking/electronic telecommunications; Publishing/audiovisual materials/educational materials.

NLD3083

COMPUPLAN - INSTITUUT VOOR TOEGEPASTE RUIMTELIJKE INFORMATICA (CP) ♦ COMPUPLAN - Institute for Applied Spatial Informatics

Postbus 102, 5450 AC Mill & St Hubert, The Netherlands.

Voir : *Comment utiliser le répertoire,* page 11.

Telephone: 31 (48) 54 52 724. *Fax:* 31 (48) 54 55 011. *Contact:* George G. van der Meulen, Chairman.

OBJECTIVES: To supply and support innovations in computer aided urban planning, management, civil engineering and cartography. To develop and promote software applications of those methodologies and techniques for design implementation. To establish international contacts directed at problem solving by computerisation in developing countries.

GENERAL INFORMATION: *Creation:* 1984. *Personnel/Total:* 14. *Salaried:* 5 of which: 1 in developing countries. *Volunteers:* 9 of which: 2 in developing countries. *Budget/Total 1993:* ECU 1111000 (US$ 1300000). *Financial sources:* Public: 50%. Self-financing: 50%.

PUBLICATIONS: *List of publications.*

EVALUATION/RESEARCH: Evaluation reports available. Undertakes research activities.

COMMENTS: Information activities related to the Commonwealth of Independent States.

ACTIVITIES IN DEVELOPING REGIONS: Present in developing regions. Active in 2 country(ies). Maintains local field presence. Works through local field partners. **Sustainable Development Actions:** Democracy/good governance/institution building/participatory development; Ecology/environment/biodiversity; Emergency relief/refugees/humanitarian assistance; Energy/transport; Health/sanitation/water; Human rights/peace/conflicts; Urban development/habitat. **Regions:** South East Asia.

INFORMATION AND EDUCATION ACTIVITIES: Topics: Ecology/environment/biodiversity; Education/training/literacy; Emergency relief/refugees/humanitarian assistance; Health/sanitation/water; Human rights/peace/conflicts; International relations/cooperation/development aid; Poverty/living conditions; Urban development/habitat. **Activities:** Conferences/seminars/workshops/training activities; Formal education; Information and documentation services/data bases; Information campaigns/exhibitions; Publishing/audiovisual materials/educational materials.

NLD3084

COOPERATIEVE ADVIESGROEP VOOR MELKVEEHOUDERIJ EN MELKERWERKING (SDTG) ♦
Small-scale Dairy Technology Group

Wildforster 37, 6713 KA Ede, The Netherlands.

Telephone: 31 (13) 86 23 245. *Fax:* 31 (13) 86 23 245. *Contact:* F. Kool.

OBJECTIVES: To give guidance and support the development of small-scale dairy farms. To promote ecologically sound animal husbandry.

GENERAL INFORMATION: *Creation:* 1990. *Personnel/Total:* 20. *Volunteers:* 20. *Financial sources:* Self-financing: 100%.

PUBLICATIONS: *Periodicals:* Dairy Technology Papers (2). *Annual report. List of publications.*

EVALUATION/RESEARCH: Evaluation reports available. Undertakes research activities.

PLANNED ACTIVITIES: Developing databases and software on technologies of dairy farming.

COMMENTS: Information activities related to the Commonwealth of Independent States.

INFORMATION AND EDUCATION ACTIVITIES: Topics: Ecology/environment/biodiversity; Food/famine; Rural development/agriculture. **Activities:** Information and documentation services/data bases.

NLD3085

COORDINATIEPIMS MONDIAAL VROUWENWERK ♦ Service Point on Gender and Development

Zonnenberg 3, 3512 NL Utrecht, The Netherlands.

Telephone: 31 (30) 23 33 937. *Fax:* 31 (30) 23 43 839. *Contact:* Jel Engelen.

OBJECTIVES: To raise awareness of gender issues in the information and education sector of development co-operation.

GENERAL INFORMATION: *Creation:* 1991. *Personnel/Total:* 2. *Salaried:* 2. *Budget/Total 1993:* ECU 138000 (US$ 162000). *Financial sources:* Public: 100%.

PUBLICATIONS: *Annual report.*

EVALUATION/RESEARCH: Evaluation reports available. Undertakes research activities.

PLANNED ACTIVITIES: Offering training and consultation for men and women on the implementation of gender sensitive programmes and activities.

NLD3086

DEFENCE FOR CHILDREN INTERNATIONAL - AFDELING NEDERLAND

Postbus 75297, 1070 AG Amsterdam, Netherlands.

Telephone: 31 (20) 42 03 771. *Fax:* 31 (20) 42 03 832.

NLD3087

DERDE WERELD CENTRUM DEN HAAG ♦ Third World Centre of The Hague

Prinsegracht 38, 2512 GA Den Haag, The Netherlands.

Telephone: 31 (70) 45 61 54. *Fax:* 31 (70) 36 04 736. *Contact:* Gijs van Seters, Director.

OBJECTIVES: To strengthen support for development co-operation by supporting development education

GENERAL INFORMATION: *Creation:* 1987. *Affiliated to:* ORC (the Netherlands). *Personnel/Total:* 10. *Salaried:* 6. *Volunteers:* 4. *Budget/Total 1993:* ECU 207000 (US$ 242000). *Financial sources:* Private: 10%. Public: 85%. Self-financing: 5%.

PUBLICATIONS: *Periodicals:* Derde Wereld Couramt (4). *Annual report. List of publications.*

INFORMATION AND EDUCATION ACTIVITIES: Topics: Children/youth/family; Culture/tradition/religion; Ecology/environment/biodiversity; Gender issues/women; Human rights/peace/conflicts; International relations/cooperation/development aid; Racism/xenophobia/antisemitism; Refugees/migrants/ethnic groups. **Activities:** Broadcasting/cultural events; Conferences/seminars/workshops/training activities; Formal education; Information and documentation services/data bases; Information campaigns/exhibitions; Lobbying/advocacy; Publishing/audiovisual materials/educational materials.

NLD3088

DERDE WERELD CENTRUM ONTWIKKELINGSSTUDIES

Thomas van Aquinostraat 4, Postbus 9104, 6500 HE Nijmegen, The Netherlands.

Telephone: 31 (024) 36 13 058. *Fax:* 31 (024) 36 15 564.

NLD3089

DERDE WERELDGROEP SOEST

Valeriaanstraat 77, 3765 EK Soest, The Netherlands.

Telephone: 31 (35) 60 17 629. *Contact:* C. Smit, President.

OBJECTIVES: To support small projects in Third World countries which are planned and implemented by the local population, with particular emphasis on women. To raise awareness of Third World issues among the Dutch public.

GENERAL INFORMATION: *Creation:* 1983. *Personnel/Total:* 12. *Volunteers:* 12. *Budget/Total 1993:* ECU 23000 (US$ 27000). *Financial sources:* Private: 60%. Public: 40%.

PUBLICATIONS: *Annual report. List of publications.*

PLANNED ACTIVITIES: Giving lectures on their projects in primary and secondary schools in Soest.

ACTIVITIES IN DEVELOPING REGIONS: Active in 3 country(ies). Maintains local field presence. Works through local field partners. **Sustainable Development Actions:** Education/training/literacy; Gender issues/women; Small enterprises/informal sector/handicrafts. **Regions:** East Africa; South America; Southern Africa.

See: *How to Use the Directory,* page 11.

INFORMATION AND EDUCATION ACTIVITIES: **Topics:** Education/training/literacy; Gender issues/women. **Activities:** Broadcasting/cultural events; Formal education; Fund raising; Information and documentation services/data bases; Information campaigns/exhibitions; Publishing/audiovisual materials/educational materials;

NLD3090

DICK SCHERPENZEEL STICHTING ♦ Dick Scherpenzeel Foundation

p/a School voor Journalistiek en Voorlichting, Postbus 30001, 3503 AB Utrecht, The Netherlands.

Telephone: 31 (30) 29 10 273. *Fax:* 31 (30) 29 43 093. *Contact:* N. Kussendrager, Chairman of the Board.

OBJECTIVES: To increase the quality of news on Third World subjects in the Dutch media.

GENERAL INFORMATION: *Creation:* 1991. *Personnel/Total:* 13. *Volunteers:* 13. *Budget/Total 1993:* ECU 92000 (US$ 108000). *Financial sources:* Public: 100%.

PUBLICATIONS: *Annual report. List of publications.*

EVALUATION/RESEARCH: Evaluation reports available. Undertakes research activities.

INFORMATION AND EDUCATION ACTIVITIES: Topics: Other. **Activities:** Conferences/seminars/workshops/training activities; Publishing/audiovisual materials/educational materials.

NLD3091

DIENST OVER GRENZEN (DOG) ♦ Service Abroad

Zusterplein 22A, Postbus 177, 3700 AD Zeist, The Netherlands.

Telephone: 31 (30) 69 24 884. *Fax:* 31 (30) 69 24 855. *Contact:* J.L.A. van Melle, Director.

OBJECTIVES: To promote a more human and just distribution of resources between the rich and the poor. To serve as an intermediary for staffing development projects in developing countries.

GENERAL INFORMATION: *Creation:* 1962. *Type of organisation:* association of NGOs. *Member organisations:* 25. *Affiliated to:* World Council of Churches (Switzerland). *Personnel/Total:* 210. *Salaried:* 10. *Volunteers:* 200 of which: 150 in developing countries. *Budget/Total 1993:* ECU 5754000 (US$ 6730000). *Financial sources: Private:* 70%. *Public:* 15%. *Self-financing:* 15%.

PUBLICATIONS: *Periodicals:* Doggersbank (4). *Annual report.*

EVALUATION/RESEARCH: Evaluation reports available.

COMMENTS: Undertakes activities in the Commonwealth of Independent States.

ACTIVITIES IN DEVELOPING REGIONS: Active in 38 country(ies). Works through local field partners. **Sustainable Development Actions:** Children/youth/family; Education/training/literacy; Emergency relief/refugees/humanitarian assistance; Food/famine; Gender issues/women; Health/sanitation/water; Human rights/peace/conflicts; Rural development/agriculture; Sending volunteers/experts/technical assistance; Small enterprises/informal sector/handicrafts; Urban development/habitat. **Regions:** Caribbean; Central Africa; Central Asia and South Asia; East Africa; East Asia; Mexico and Central America; Middle East; Oceania; South America; South East Asia; Southern Africa; West Africa.

INFORMATION AND EDUCATION ACTIVITIES: Topics: Other. **Activities:** Exchanges/twinning/linking; Fund raising.

NLD3092

DIENSTENCENTRUM VOOR AKTIEGROEPEN DE BRANDNETEL (BRANDNETEL)

Burg. Engelkenslaan 53, 9671 LL Winschoten, The Netherlands.

Telephone: 31 (597) 424 226.

NLD3093

DIERGENEESKUNDE IN ONTWIKKELINGSSAMENWERKING (DIO) ♦ Veterinary Science in Development Cooperation

Yalelaan 17, 3584 CL Utrecht, The Netherlands.

Telephone: 31 (30) 25 32 032. *Fax:* 31 (30) 25 32 032. *Contact:* Hans de Smit.

OBJECTIVES: To promote and improve the practice of veterinary science in developing countries by acting as an intermediary between local NGOs and veterinarians, and by providing technical and financial assistance.

GENERAL INFORMATION: *Creation:* 1987. *Affiliated to:* Vétérinaires sans Frontières (France) - VSF (Belgium) - VSF (Switzerland) - VetAid (United Kingdon) - Vetermon/VSF (Spain) - Sivtro (Italy) - TEO (Germany) - Vetug (Norway). *Personnel/Total:* 17. *Salaried:* 1. *Volunteers:* 16. *Budget/Total 1993:* ECU 28000 (US$ 32000). *Financial sources:* Private: 80%. Public: 15%. Self-financing: 5%.

PUBLICATIONS: *Periodicals:* DIO Dialog (4). *Annual report.*

ACTIVITIES IN DEVELOPING REGIONS: Present in developing regions. Active in 4 country(ies). Works through local field partners. **Sustainable Development Actions:** Rural development/agriculture. **Regions:** Central Asia and South Asia; East Africa; South East Asia.

INFORMATION AND EDUCATION ACTIVITIES: Topics: Rural development/agriculture. **Activities:** Conferences/seminars/workshops/training activities; Fund raising; Information and documentation services/data bases; Information campaigns/exhibitions; Networking/electronic telecommunications.

NLD3094

DISASTER AND EMERGENCY REFERENCE CENTRE (DERC)

TU Delft, Stevinweg 1, Gebouw Civiele Techniek, kamer 488, Postbus 5048, 2600 GA Delft, The Netherlands.

Telephone: 31 (15) 27 84 408. *Fax:* 31 (15) 26 28 126.

NLD3095

DISASTER RELIEF AGENCY

Van Meerdervoort Laan 192, 2517 BH Den Haag, The Netherlands.

Telephone: 31 (70) 34 52 255. *Fax:* 31 (70) 35 60 753. *Contact:* P.M.J. Meijs.

OBJECTIVES: To bridge the gap between emergency relief and sustainable aid. To assist local organisations in planning for emergencies. To help victims of natural disasters after emergency relief has ended.

GENERAL INFORMATION: *Creation:* 1994. *Type of organisation:* association of NGOs. *Member organisations:* 4. *Personnel/Total:* 3. *Salaried:* 3. *Budget/Total 1993:* ECU 173000 (US$ 202000). *Financial sources:* Private: 60%. Public: 25%. Self-financing: 15%.

PUBLICATIONS: *Annual report.*

EVALUATION/RESEARCH: Evaluation reports available. Undertakes research activities.

COMMENTS: Undertakes activities in the Commonwealth of Independent States.

ACTIVITIES IN DEVELOPING REGIONS: Present in developing regions. Maintains local presence. Works through local field partners. **Sustainable Development Actions:** Children/youth/family; Education/training/literacy; Emergency relief/refugees/humanitarian assistance; Food/famine; Health/sanitation/water; Human rights/peace/conflicts; Rural development/agriculture; Sending volunteers/experts/technical assistance. **Regions:** Central Africa; Central Asia and South Asia; East Africa; Mexico and Central America; Southern Africa.

INFORMATION AND EDUCATION ACTIVITIES: Topics: Culture/tradition/religion; Education/training/literacy; Emergency relief/refugees/humanitarian assistance; Employment/unemployment; Food/famine; Health/sanitation/water; Human rights/peace/conflicts; International economic relations/trade/debt/finance; Peace/ethnic conflicts/armament/disarmament; Refugees/migrants/ethnic groups; Rural development/agriculture. **Activities:** Information and documentation services/data bases.

Voir : *Comment utiliser le répertoire,* page 11.

NLD3096

ECUMENICAL DEVELOPMENT CO-OPERATIVE SOCI-ETY (EDCS) ♦ Société coopérative oecuménique pour le développement

PC Hooftlaan 3, 3010 HG Amersfoort, The Netherlands .

Telephone: 31 (33) 46 33 122. **Fax:** 31 (33) 46 50 336. **Contact:** G.H.O. van Maanen, General Manager.

OBJECTIVES: To mobilize financial credit from churches and individuals. To promote development as a liberating process aimed at economic growth, social justice and self-reliance.

GENERAL INFORMATION: Creation: 1975. **Member organisations:** 307. **Personnel/Total:** 24. Salaried: 24 of which: 12 in developing countries. **Budget/Total 1993:** ECU 5224000 (US$ 64610000). **Financial sources:** Private: 5%. Public: 2%. Self-financing: 93%.

PUBLICATIONS: Periodicals: Newsletter (4). Annual report.

EVALUATION/RESEARCH: Evaluation reports available.

COMMENTS: Undertakes activities in the Commonwealth of Independent States. Information activities related to the Commonwealth of Independent States.

ACTIVITIES IN DEVELOPING REGIONS: Present in developing regions. Active in 61 country(ies). Maintains local field presence. Works through local field partners. **Sustainable Development Actions:** Ecology/environment/biodiversity; Education/training/literacy; Gender issues/women; Health/sanitation/water; Rural development/agriculture; Small enterprises/informal sector/handicrafts. **Regions:** Central Africa; Central Asia and South Asia; East Africa; East Asia; Mexico and Central America; Oceania; South America; South East Asia; Southern Africa; West Africa.

INFORMATION AND EDUCATION ACTIVITIES: Topics: Ecology/environment/biodiversity; Education/training/literacy; Employment/unemployment; Food/famine; Gender issues/women; Health/sanitation/water; International relations/cooperation/development aid; Poverty/living conditions; Rural development/agriculture; Urban development/habitat. **Activities:** Exchanges/twinning/linking; Information and documentation services/data bases; Lobbying/advocacy; Other.

NLD3097

EDUARDO FREI STICHTING ♦ Eduard Frei Foundation for International Solidarity

Dr. Kuyperstraat 5, 2514 BA Den Haag, The Netherlands.

Telephone: 31 (70) 34 24 845. **Fax:** 31 (70) 35 61 501. **Contact:** J.W. Wiggers.

OBJECTIVES: To promote Christian democratic ideology. To show solidarity with Christian democratic sister parties in Central and Eastern Europe and in the Third World.

GENERAL INFORMATION: Creation: 1990. **Personnel/Total:** 1. Salaried: 1. **Budget/Total 1993:** ECU 276000 (US$ 323000). **Financial sources:** Public: 98%. Self-financing: 2%.

PUBLICATIONS: Annual report.

EVALUATION/RESEARCH: Evaluation reports available. Undertakes research activities.

COMMENTS: This NGO works primarily in Central and Eastern Europe. Undertakes activities in the Commonwealth of Independent States. Information activities related to the Commonwealth of Independent States.

ACTIVITIES IN DEVELOPING REGIONS: Present in developing regions. Maintains local field presence. Works through local field partners. **Sustainable Development Actions:** Human rights/peace/conflicts. **Regions:** South America.

INFORMATION AND EDUCATION ACTIVITIES: Topics: Gender issues/women; Human rights/peace/conflicts. **Activities:** Conferences/seminars/workshops/training activities.

NLD3098

EDUARDO MONDLANE STICHTING (EMS) ♦ Eduardo Mondlane Foundation

Hoogte Kadyk 145, 1018 BH Amsterdam, The Netherlands.

Telephone: 31 (20) 62 37 263. **Fax:** 31 (20) 62 42 721. **Contact:** Gerrit Berkelder, General Co-ordinator.

OBJECTIVES: To support progressive developments in Southern Africa and Cape Verde through the recruitment and training of development workers, financial and material support for development projects and emergency aid and information.

GENERAL INFORMATION: Creation: 1969. **Affiliated to:** South-North Federation (Netherlands) - European Committee Against South African Agression Against Mozambique and Angola - Institute for Southern Africa. **Personnel/Total:** 28. Salaried: 8 of which: 4 in developing countries. Volunteers: 16 of which: 8 in developing countries. **Budget/Total 1993:** ECU 875000 (US$ 1023000). **Financial sources:** Private: 40%. Public: 5%. Self-financing: 55%.

PUBLICATIONS: Periodicals: Informatiekrant (4). Annual report.

EVALUATION/RESEARCH: Undertakes research activities.

PLANNED ACTIVITIES: Organising seminars on traumatised children and on the role of NGOs.

ACTIVITIES IN DEVELOPING REGIONS: Present in developing regions. Active in 3 country(ies). Maintains local field presence. Works through local field partners. **Sustainable Development Actions:** Democracy/good governance/institution building/participatory development; Ecology/environment/biodiversity; Education/training/literacy; Emergency relief/refugees/humanitarian assistance; Gender issues/women; Health/sanitation/water; Human rights/peace/conflicts; Rural development/agriculture; Sending volunteers/experts/technical assistance; Urban development/habitat. **Regions:** Southern Africa.

INFORMATION AND EDUCATION ACTIVITIES: Topics: Children/youth/family; Culture/tradition/religion; Education/training/literacy; Gender issues/women; Health/sanitation/water; Human rights/peace/conflicts; International economic relations/trade/debt/finance; International relations/cooperation/development aid; Peace/ethnic conflicts/armament/disarmament; Poverty/living conditions; Rural development/agriculture; Urban development/habitat. **Activities:** Broadcasting/cultural events; Conferences/seminars/workshops/training activities; Exchanges/twinning/linking; Information and documentation services/data bases; Information campaigns/exhibitions; Lobbying/advocacy; Publishing/audiovisual materials/educational materials.

NLD3099

ENVIRONMENTAL AWARENESS FOUNDATION

Postbus 772, 1200 AT Hilversum, The Netherlands.

Telephone: 31 (35) 62 35 908. **Fax:** 31 (35) 62 36 258. **Contact:** Ludo Van Oyen, Director.

OBJECTIVES: To promote environmental awareness among young people and to encourage environmentally friendly building construction.

GENERAL INFORMATION: Creation: 1989. **Personnel/Total:** 3. Salaried: 3. **Financial sources:** Private: 100%.

PUBLICATIONS: Annual report.

EVALUATION/RESEARCH: Undertakes research activities.

COMMENTS: Undertakes activities in the Commonwealth of Independent States.

INFORMATION AND EDUCATION ACTIVITIES: Topics: Ecology/environment/biodiversity. **Activities:** Information campaigns/exhibitions; Lobbying/advocacy.

NLD3100

EPILEPSY CARE DEVELOPING COUNTRIES (EPICADEC)

Achterweg 5, Postbus 21, 2100 AA Heemstede, The Netherlands.

Telephone: 31 (23) 52 37 175. **Fax:** 31 (23) 54 70 119. **Contact:** Dr. P.H.A. Voskuil, President.

OBJECTIVES: To promote care for people with epilepsy in developing countries. To act as a go-between for organisations or persons in developing countries involved in epilepsy care and international support organisations. To provide information about new developments in epilepsy care to health workers in developing countries.

See: *How to Use the Directory*, page 11.

GENERAL INFORMATION: *Creation:* 1990. *Personnel/Total:* 2. *Salaried:* 1. *Volunteers:* 1. *Budget/Total 1993:* ECU 23000 (US$ 27000). *Financial sources:* Self-financing: 100%.

PUBLICATIONS: *Periodicals:* Epicadec News (2). *Annual report.*

EVALUATION/RESEARCH: Evaluation reports available.

ACTIVITIES IN DEVELOPING REGIONS: Active in 6 country(ies). Works through local field partners. **Sustainable Development Actions:** Health/sanitation/water. **Regions:** Central Asia and South Asia; East Africa; South East Asia; Southern Africa; West Africa.

NLD3101
ETC INTERNATIONAL (ETC)

Kastanjelaan 5, P.O. Box 64, 3830 AB Leusden, The Netherlands.

Telephone: 31 (33) 49 43 086. *Fax:* 31 (33) 49 40 791. *E-mail:* ETC@ANTENNA.NL. *Contact:* Harry Buikema, Manager.

OBJECTIVES: To encourage and support local initiatives for sustainable development in developing countries.

GENERAL INFORMATION: *Creation:* 1974. *Personnel/Total:* 200. *Salaried:* 200 of which: 150 in developing countries. *Budget/Total 1993:* ECU 5205000 (US$ 6088000). *Financial sources:* Self-financing: 100%.

PUBLICATIONS: *Periodicals:* ILEIA Newsletter (4).

EVALUATION/RESEARCH: Evaluation reports available. Undertakes research activities.

COMMENTS: Undertakes activities in the Commonwealth of Independent States. Information activities related to the Commonwealth of Independent States.

ACTIVITIES IN DEVELOPING REGIONS: Present in developing regions. Active in 30 country(ies). Maintains local field presence. Works through local field partners. **Sustainable Development Actions:** Democracy/good governance/institution building/participatory development; Ecology/environment/biodiversity; Education/training/literacy; Energy/transport; Gender issues/women; Health/sanitation/water; Population/family planning/demography; Rural development/agriculture; Small enterprises/informal sector/handicrafts; Urban development/habitat. **Regions:** Central Africa; Central Asia and South Asia; East Africa; Mexico and Central America; Middle East; North Africa; South America; South East Asia; Southern Africa; West Africa.

INFORMATION AND EDUCATION ACTIVITIES: Topics: Culture/tradition/religion; Gender issues/women; International economic relations/trade/debt/finance; Rural development/agriculture. **Activities:** Conferences/seminars/workshops/training activities; Information and documentation services/data bases; Networking/electronic telecommunications.

NLD3102
EUROPEAN ASSOCIATION OF NON GOVERNMENTAL ORGANISATIONS FOR FOOD AID AND EMERGENCY AID (EURONAID)

Houtweg 60, Postbus 12, 2501 CA Den Haag, The Netherlands.

Telephone: 31 (70) 33 05 757. *Fax:* 31 (70) 36 41 701. *Contact:* B. Dreesmann, Secretary General.

OBJECTIVES: To facilitate the planning and execution of programmes and projects providing food or emergency aid, mainly from the European Union, to people in need, particularly in developing countries, according to the principles of the Universal Declaration of Human Rights.

GENERAL INFORMATION: *Creation:* 1980. *Type of organisation:* association of NGOs. *Member organisations:* 26. *Personnel/Total:* 18. *Salaried:* 18.

PUBLICATIONS: *Annual report.*

EVALUATION/RESEARCH: Evaluation reports available. Undertakes research activities.

COMMENTS: Undertakes activities in the Commonwealth of Independent States.

ACTIVITIES IN DEVELOPING REGIONS: Maintains local field presence. Works through local field partners. **Sustainable Development Actions:** Emergency relief/refugees/humanitarian assistance; Food/famine. **Regions:** Caribbean; Central Africa; Central Asia and South Asia; East Africa; East Asia; Mexico and Central America; Middle East; North Africa; South America; South East Asia; Southern Africa; West Africa.

INFORMATION AND EDUCATION ACTIVITIES: Topics: Emergency relief/refugees/humanitarian assistance; Food/famine; International relations/cooperation/development aid. **Activities:** Conferences/seminars/workshops/training activities; Exchanges/twinning/linking; Formal education; Fund raising; Information and documentation services/data bases; Information campaigns/exhibitions; Lobbying/advocacy; Networking/electronic telecommunications; Publishing/audiovisual materials/educational materials.

NLD3103
EUROPEAN FAIR TRADE ASSOCIATION

Witmakersstraat 10, 6211 JB Maastricht, The Netherlands.

Telephone: 31 (43) 32 56 917. *Fax:* 31 (43) 32 58 433. *Contact:* M. Kocken.

OBJECTIVES: To stimulate practical co-operation among members, develop common policies and offer joint support to producers. To work for the adoption of fair trade principles in commercial trading among the general public and on a political level in Europe.

GENERAL INFORMATION: *Creation:* 1990. *Type of organisation:* association of NGOs. *Member organisations:* 11. *Salaried:* 2. *Budget/Total 1993:* ECU 92000 (US$ 108000). *Financial sources:* Self-financing: 100%.

PUBLICATIONS: *List of publications.*

EVALUATION/RESEARCH: Undertakes research activities.

PLANNED ACTIVITIES: Campaigns regarding fair trade in cocoa and textiles. Publishing a bi-annual yearbook.

INFORMATION AND EDUCATION ACTIVITIES: Topics: Other. **Activities:** Conferences/seminars/workshops/training activities; Exchanges/twinning/linking; Formal education; Information and documentation services/data bases; Information campaigns/exhibitions; Lobbying/advocacy.

NLD3104
EUROPEAN YOUTH FOREST ACTION (EYFA)

P.O. Box 94115, 1090 GC Amsterdam, The Netherlands.

Telephone: 31 (20) 66 57 743. *Fax:* 31 (20) 66 57 743. *E-mail:* EYFA@antenna.nl. *Contact:* Ann Vikkelso, International Co-ordination Team.

OBJECTIVES: To secure a common future for generations to come by finding new methods of economic, cultural and ecological development and redefining social relationships on the planet.

GENERAL INFORMATION: *Creation:* 1985. *Type of organisation:* network. *Member organisations:* 400. *Personnel/Total:* 5. *Volunteers:* 5. *Budget/Total 1993:* ECU 161000 (US$ 189000). *Financial sources:* Private: 5%. Public: 90%. Self-financing: 5%.

PUBLICATIONS: *Periodicals:* The Verge (5). *Annual report. List of publications.*

PLANNED ACTIVITIES: Networking among environmental youth NGOs.

COMMENTS: Undertakes activities in the Commonwealth of Independent States. Information activities related to the Commonwealth of Independent States.

INFORMATION AND EDUCATION ACTIVITIES: Topics: Children/youth/family; Culture/tradition/religion; Ecology/environment/biodiversity; Emergency relief/refugees/humanitarian assistance; Gender issues/women; Human rights/peace/conflicts; International economic relations/trade/debt/finance; Peace/ethnic conflicts/armament/disarmament; Racism/xenophobia/antisemitism. **Activities:** Broadcasting/cultural events; Conferences/seminars/workshops/training activities; Exchanges/twinning/linking; Formal education; Fund raising; Information and documentation services/data bases; Information campaigns/exhibi-

Voir : *Comment utiliser le répertoire,* page 11.

tions; Lobbying/advocacy; Networking/electronic telecommunications; Publishing/audiovisual materials/educational materials.

NLD3105
EUROPEES PLATFORM ♦ European Platform
Nassauplein 8, 1815 GM Alkmaar, The Netherlands.

Telephone: 31 (72) 51 18 502. *Fax:* 31 (72) 51 51 221. *Contact:* G.H. Oonk.

OBJECTIVES: To promote school partnerships between Dutch schools and their conterparts in developing countries. To inform Dutch schools about international topics, including development issues.

GENERAL INFORMATION: *Creation:* 1961. *Personnel/Total:* 27. *Salaried:* 15. *Volunteers:* 12. *Budget/Total 1993:* ECU 3130000 (US$ 3661000). *Financial sources:* Private: 20%. Public: 70%. Self-financing: 10%.

PUBLICATIONS: *Periodicals:* Europa en hef Onderwigs (3) - Europa Ohderwigs Bericht (6). *Annual report. List of publications.*

EVALUATION/RESEARCH: Evaluation reports available. Undertakes research activities.

COMMENTS: Undertakes activities in the Commonwealth of Independent States. Information activities related to the Commonwealth of Independent States.

INFORMATION AND EDUCATION ACTIVITIES: Topics: Culture/tradition/religion; Education/training/literacy; Human rights/peace/conflicts; Racism/xenophobia/antisemitism. Activities: Conferences/seminars/workshops/training activities; Exchanges/twinning/linking; Formal education; Fund raising; Information and documentation services/data bases; Information campaigns/exhibitions; Lobbying/advocacy; Networking/electronic telecommunications; Publishing/audiovisual materials/educational materials.

NLD3106
EVERT VERMEER STICHTING (EVS) ♦ Evert Vermeer Foundation
Nicolaas Witsenkade 30, Postbus 1310, 1000 BH Amsterdam, The Netherlands.

Telephone: 31 (20) 55 12 453. *Fax:* 31 (20) 55 12 330.

NLD3107
FAIR TRADE ORGANISATIE ♦ Fair Trade Organisation
Postbus 115, 4100 AC Culemborg, Pays-Bas.

Téléphone: 31 (345) 513 744. *Fax:* 31 (345) 521 423. *Contact:* Stefan Durwael, Directeur Général.

OBJECTIFS: Aider directement les producteurs des pays en développement en vendant leurs produits aux Pays-Bas et en Belgique. Informer l'opinion publique néerlandaise et belge sur les problèmes du Tiers-Monde.

INFORMATIONS GENERALES: *Création:* 1959. *Affiliée à:* EFTA. *Personnel/Total:* 240. *Salariés:* 90. *Bénévoles:* 150. *Budget/Total 1993:* ECU 13534000 (US$ 15829000). *Sources financières:* Privé: 2%. Autofinancement: 98%.

PUBLICATIONS: *Périodiques:* Handelskraut (4) - Handelswijzer (3). *Rapport annuel. Liste des publications.*

EVALUATION/RECHERCHE: Rapports d'évaluation disponibles. Entreprend des activités de recherche.

ACTIVITES DANS LES REGIONS EN DEVELOPPEMENT: Intervient directement dans les régions en développement. Intervient dans 40 pays. Intervient par l'intermédiaire d'organisations locales partenaires. Actions de Développement durable: Autres. Régions: Afrique australe; Afrique de l'Est; Amérique du Sud; Asie centrale et Asie du Sud; Asie du Sud-Est; Caraïbes; Mexique et Amerique centrale.

ACTIVITES D'INFORMATION ET D'EDUCATION: Domaines: Autres. Activités: Campagnes d'information/expositions; Collecte de fonds; Lobbying/plaidoyer; Radiodiffusion/manifestations culturelles; Services d'information et de documentation/bases de données; Édition/documents audiovisuels/documents éducatifs.

NLD3108
FAMILY HELP PROGRAMME HOLLAND - SRI LANKA (FHP-SRI LANKA)
Oosteinde 15, Postbus 27, 1474 ZG Oosthuizen, The Netherlands.

Telephone: 31 (29) 91 13 42. *Fax:* 31 (29) 91 38 66. *Contact:* Drs. Th. Koning, Chairperson.

NLD3109
FEDERATIE NEDERLANDSE VAKBEWEGING (FNV) ♦ International Solidarity Fund
Postbus 8456, 1005 AL Amsterdam, The Netherlands.

Telephone: 31 (20) 58 16 300. *Fax:* 31 (20) 68 44 541. *Contact:* Johan Stekelenburg, President.

NLD3110
FILIPIJNEN INFORMATIE-EN DOCUMENTATIE CENTRUM (FIDOC) ♦ Philippines Information and Documentation Centre
Nolensweg 8, 3317 LE Dordrecht, The Netherlands.

Telephone: 31 (78) 61 85 652. *Fax:* 31 (78) 61 85 578. *Contact:* Edgar Koning, Director.

OBJECTIVES: To provide information on the Philippines to all interested parties on various issues including rural development, the environment and women movements.

GENERAL INFORMATION: *Creation:* 1987. *Personnel/Total:* 7. *Salaried:* 5 of which: 5 in developing countries. *Volunteers:* 2. *Budget/Total 1993:* ECU 18000 (US$ 22000). *Financial sources:* Private: 100%.

PUBLICATIONS: *Periodicals:* Fidoc Bulletin (10). *Annual report. List of publications.*

PLANNED ACTIVITIES: Undertaking a project on human rights and development in 1996 and a project on the environment and development in 1997.

COMMENTS: FIDOC is a documentation centre on the Philippines containing a library with over 2000 titles and subscriptions to 150 Philippino magazines. FIDOC also maintains a sub-office in Manila.

INFORMATION AND EDUCATION ACTIVITIES: Topics: Ecology/environment/biodiversity; Gender issues/women; Rural development/agriculture. Activities: Information and documentation services/data bases.

NLD3111
FILIPPIJNENGROEP NEDERLAND (FGN) ♦ Philippines Solidarity Group of the Netherlands
Korte Jansstraat 2A, 3512 GN Utrecht, The Netherlands.

Telephone: 31 (30) 23 19 323.

NLD3112
FORUM ON DEBT AND DEVELOPMENT (FONDAD)
Noordeinde 107A, 2514 GE Den Haag, The Netherlands.

Telephone: 31 (70) 36 53 820. *Fax:* 31 (70) 34 63 939. *Contact:* Jan Joost Teunissen, Director.

OBJECTIVES: To provide policy-oriented research on a range of North-South problems, with particular emphasis on international financial issues.

GENERAL INFORMATION: *Creation:* 1987. *Personnel/Total:* 2. *Salaried:* 2. *Financial sources:* Public: 100%.

PUBLICATIONS: *List of publications.*

EVALUATION/RESEARCH: Undertakes research activities.

PLANNED ACTIVITIES: Undertaking a research programme on regional economic co-operation.

COMMENTS: Information activities related to the Commonwealth of Independent States.

INFORMATION AND EDUCATION ACTIVITIES: Topics: International economic relations/trade/debt/finance; International relations/coopera-

See: *How to Use the Directory,* page 11.

tion/development aid. **Activities:** Conferences/seminars/workshops/ training activities; Publishing/audiovisual materials/educational materials.

NLD3113

FOSTER PARENTS PLAN NEDERLAND (FPPN)

Van Boshuizenstr. 12, 1083 BA Amsterdam, The Netherlands.

Telephone: 31 (20) 67 67 676. *Fax:* 31 (20) 64 44 065. *Contact:* H.P. Kolk, National Director.

NLD3114

FOUNDATION TO PROMOTE WOMEN'S WORLD BANKING, NEDERLAND (WWB)

p/a Triodos Bank NV, Postbus 55, 3700 AB Zeist, The Netherlands.

Telephone: 31 (30) 69 16 544. *Fax:* 31 (30) 69 12 524.

NLD3115

FRIENDS OF THE EARTH INTERNATIONAL (FOEI)

Postbus 19199, 1000 GD Amsterdam, The Netherlands.

Telephone: 31 (20) 62 21 369. *Fax:* 31 (20) 63 92 181. *E-mail:* foeint@Xs4ll.nl or foeintsecr@gn.apc.org. *Contact:* John Hontelez, Chairman.

OBJECTIVES: To protect the earth against further deterioration and restore damage inflicted upon the environment as a result of human activity and negligence. To promote environmentally sound sustainable development, on a local, national and global level.

GENERAL INFORMATION: *Creation:* 1971. *Type of organisation:* network. *Member organisations:* 52. *Affiliated to:* ELCI - IUCN. *Personnel/Total:* 4. *Salaried:* 4. *Budget/Total 1993:* ECU 333000 (US$ 390000).

PUBLICATIONS: *Periodicals:* FOE Link (6). *Annual report.*

COMMENTS: FOEI is a Federation of 52 independent member groups. FOEI is the secretariat for the federation.

INFORMATION AND EDUCATION ACTIVITIES: Topics: Ecology/environment/biodiversity. **Activities:** Conferences/seminars/workshops/ training activities; Fund raising; Information and documentation services/ data bases; Information campaigns/exhibitions; Lobbying/advocacy.

NLD3116

GEMEENSCHAPPELIJK OVERLEG MEDEFINANCIER-ING (GOM) ♦ Co-financing Consultative Body

Rhijngeesterstraatweg 40, Postbus 77, 2340 AB Oegstgeest, The Netherlands.

Telephone: 31 (71) 51 59 231. *Fax:* 31 (71) 51 75 391. *Contact:* Marÿke Priester, Secretary General.

OBJECTIVES: To represent the four Dutch co-financing organisations : CEBEMO, ICCO, NOVIB and HIVOS, and co-ordinate their activities with the Dutch government which include providing financial assistance to developing countries.

GENERAL INFORMATION: *Creation:* 1972. *Type of organisation:* coordinating body. *Member organisations:* 4. *Affiliated to:* CEBEMO (Netherlands) - ICCO (Netherlands) - NOVIB (Netherlands) - HIVOS (Netherlands). *Personnel/Total:* 3. *Salaried:* 3. *Budget/ Total 1993:* ECU 161000 (US$ 188000). *Financial sources: Self-financing:* 100%.

COMMENTS: GOM does not itself undertake activities in developing regions but through its member organisations.

NLD3117

GENOOTSCHAP VOOR ENERGIE ONTWIKKELING & PLAN-NING (EDP) ♦ Association for Energy Development & Planning

Rotterdamsedijk 248 a, 3112 BP Schiedam, The Netherlands.

Telephone: 31 (10) 42 65 751. *Fax:* 31 (10) 47 35 248. *Contact:* T. Hans Jansen.

OBJECTIVES: To provide an independent forum for energy planners from the developed and developing world, whose main concern is the creation of opportunities for sustainable development.

GENERAL INFORMATION: *Creation:* 1989. *Personnel/Total:* 21. *Volunteers:* 21 of which: 5 in developing countries. *Budget/Total 1993:* ECU 10000 (US$ 12000). *Financial sources: Private:* 30%. *Public:* 10%. *Self-financing:* 60%.

PUBLICATIONS: *Periodicals:* Energy Development News (4).

EVALUATION/RESEARCH: Evaluation reports available. Undertakes research activities.

COMMENTS: Undertakes activities in the Commonwealth of Independent States. Information activities related to the Commonwealth of Independent States.

ACTIVITIES IN DEVELOPING REGIONS: Present in developing regions. Active in 50 country(ies). Maintains local field presence. Works through local field partners. **Sustainable Development Actions:** Democracy/ good governance/institution building/participatory development; Ecology/environment/biodiversity; Education/training/literacy; Energy/transport; Gender issues/women; Other; Sending volunteers/experts/technical assistance. **Regions:** Central Africa; East Africa; Middle East; North Africa; South East Asia; Southern Africa; West Africa.

INFORMATION AND EDUCATION ACTIVITIES: Topics: Ecology/environment/biodiversity; Education/training/literacy; Gender issues/women; Human rights/peace/conflicts; International economic relations/trade/ debt/finance; International relations/cooperation/development aid; Other; Poverty/living conditions; Rural development/agriculture; Urban development/habitat. **Activities:** Conferences/seminars/workshops/ training activities; Exchanges/twinning/linking; Formal education; Fund raising; Information and documentation services/data bases; Information campaigns/exhibitions; Lobbying/advocacy; Networking/electronic telecommunications; Other; Publishing/audiovisual materials/educational materials.

NLD3118

GEZONDHEIDSZORG IN ONTWIKKELINGSLANDEN ♦ Health Care in Developing Countries

Henri Dunantstr. 5, Postbus 4446, 6401 CX Heerlen, The Netherlands.

Telephone: 31 (45) 76 60 88.

NLD3119

GLOBAL COALITION FOR AFRICA, DUTCH OFFICE (GCA)

c/o DGIS, Postbus 20061, 2500 EB Den Haag, The Netherlands.

Telephone: 31 (70) 34 86 105/34 84 427. *Fax:* 31 (70) 34 86 080. *Contact:* M. van Hulten, Head.

OBJECTIVES: To bring together representatives of African governments, bilateral donors, regional and multilateral agencies and other development partners in Africa to examine long-term development issues and to promote consensus on objectives and programmes of action.

GENERAL INFORMATION: *Creation:* 1990. *Personnel/Total:* 2. *Salaried:* 2. *Budget/Total 1993:* ECU 414000 (US$ 484000). *Financial sources: Public:* 100%.

PUBLICATIONS: *Annual report. List of publications.*

EVALUATION/RESEARCH: Undertakes research activities.

COMMENTS: Secretariat - Global Coalition for Africa: 1850 K Street N.W. Suite 295 Washington D.C. 20006 USA tel:1 202 676 0845 fax:1 202 676-1014

ACTIVITIES IN DEVELOPING REGIONS: Active in 54 country(ies). **Sustainable Development Actions:** Democracy/good governance/institution building/participatory development; Human rights/peace/conflicts. **Regions:** Central Africa; East Africa; North Africa; Southern Africa; West Africa.

INFORMATION AND EDUCATION ACTIVITIES: Topics: Human rights/ peace/conflicts. **Activities:** Conferences/seminars/workshops/training activities; Lobbying/advocacy.

Voir : *Comment utiliser le répertoire*, page 11.

NLD3120

GOED WERK ♦ Good Work

Industrieweg Noord 6-A, Postbus 87, 3958 ZV Amerongen, The Netherlands.

Telephone: 31 (34) 34 53 434. *Fax:* 31 (34) 34 57 743. *Contact:* Piet Hopman, Director.

OBJECTIVES: To promote job creation activities and provide training to people with no income. To import products from projects in developing countries. To work with organisations with a Christian leadership.

GENERAL INFORMATION: *Creation:* 1985. *Affiliated to:* European Christian Alternative Trading Association (Netherlands) - TEAR Craft (United Kingdom) - SEL Atisanat (France). *Personnel/Total:* 8. *Salaried:* 5. *Volunteers:* 3. *Budget/Total 1993:* ECU 598000 (US$ 670000). *Financial sources:* Private: 1%. Self-financing: 99%.

PUBLICATIONS: *Periodicals:* Goed Werk Nieuws (4) - STUW Kracht Info (8). *Annual report.*

EVALUATION/RESEARCH: Evaluation reports available.

PLANNED ACTIVITIES: Raising awareness among the Dutch public of "trading" with people in other parts of the world to enable them to earn a living.

ACTIVITIES IN DEVELOPING REGIONS: Active in 13 country(ies). Works through local field partners. **Sustainable Development Actions:** Debt/finance/trade; Small enterprises/informal sector/handicrafts. **Regions:** Central Africa; Central Asia and South Asia; South America; South East Asia.

NLD3121

GRAPHIC MEDIA DEVELOPMENT CENTRE (GMDC)

P.O. Box 14090, 2501 GB Den Haag, The Netherlands.

Telephone: 31 (70) 36 46 400. *Fax:* 31 (70) 36 16 230.

OBJECTIVES: To support the expansion and strengthening of communication infrastructures via printed/graphic media in developing countries. To encourage media facilitated communication for development with an emphasis on non-urban areas.

GENERAL INFORMATION: *Personnel/Total:* 9. Salaried: 9 of which: 4 in developing countries. *Budget/Total 1993:* ECU 921000 (US$ 1077000). *Financial sources:* Private: 10%. Public: 90%.

PUBLICATIONS: *Annual report.*

PLANNED ACTIVITIES: Undertaking a communication campaign entitled "Basic education for all".

COMMENTS: GMDC is an international development institute in the field of graphic communication which mainly provides training courses for participants from developing countries. It also provides consultancy services.

ACTIVITIES IN DEVELOPING REGIONS: Present in developing regions. Maintains local field presence. **Sustainable Development Actions:** Education/training/literacy; Sending volunteers/experts/technical assistance. **Regions:** Central Africa; Central Asia and South Asia; East Africa.

NLD3122

GREENPEACE INTERNATIONAL

Keizersgracht 176, 1016 DW Amsterdam, The Netherlands.

Telephone: 31 (20) 52 36 222. *Fax:* 31 (20) 52 36 200. *E-mail:* Greenpeace.International@green2.greenpeace.org. *Contact:* Steve d'Esposito, Executive Director.

OBJECTIVES: To protect the environment through peaceful means.

GENERAL INFORMATION: *Creation:* 1971. *Affiliated to:* IUCN (Switzerland) - EarthAction (United Kingdom) - CAN (Belgium). *Budget/Total 1993:* ECU 33300100 (US$ 39000000). *Financial sources:* Self-financing: 100%.

PUBLICATIONS: *Periodicals:* Campaign Report (4) - International Newsletter (4). *Annual report.* List of publications.

EVALUATION/RESEARCH: Undertakes research activities.

PLANNED ACTIVITIES: Undertaking campaigns on biodiversity, the atmosphere in crisis, nuclear disarmament and on killer chemicals.

COMMENTS: Undertakes activities in the Commonwealth of Independent States.

ACTIVITIES IN DEVELOPING REGIONS: Works through local field partners. **Sustainable Development Actions:** Ecology/environment/biodiversity. **Regions:** Central Asia and South Asia; East Asia; Mexico and Central America; Middle East; South America; South East Asia.

INFORMATION AND EDUCATION ACTIVITIES: Topics: Ecology/environment/biodiversity; Health/sanitation/water; International economic relations/trade/debt/finance; Peace/ethnic conflicts/armament/disarmament; Rural development/agriculture; Urban development/habitat. **Activities:** Conferences/seminars/workshops/training activities; Exchanges/twinning/linking; Fund raising; Information and documentation services/data bases; Information campaigns/exhibitions; Lobbying/advocacy; Publishing/audiovisual materials/educational materials.

NLD3123

HEALTH ACTION INTERNATIONAL (HAI)

Jacob van Lennepkade 334 - T, 1053 NJ Amsterdam, The Netherlands.

Telephone: 31 (20) 68 33 684. *Fax:* 31 (20) 68 55 002. *E-mail:* HAI@HAI.ANTENNA.NL. *Contact:* Catherine Hodgkin.

OBJECTIVES: To promote the rational use of medicines in conjunction with the World Health Organisation's (WHO) essential drug concept.

GENERAL INFORMATION: *Creation:* 1981. *Type of organisation:* network. *Member organisations:* 40.

PUBLICATIONS: *Periodicals:* HAI News (6). List of publications.

COMMENTS: Undertakes activities in the Commonwealth of Independent States. Information activities related to the Commonwealth of Independent States.

ACTIVITIES IN DEVELOPING REGIONS: Active in 70 country(ies). Works through local field partners. **Sustainable Development Actions:** Health/sanitation/water; Population/family planning/demography. **Regions:** Caribbean; Central Africa; Central Asia and South Asia; East Africa; East Asia; Mexico and Central America; Middle East; North Africa; Oceania; South America; South East Asia; Southern Africa; West Africa.

INFORMATION AND EDUCATION ACTIVITIES: Topics: Health/sanitation/water; Population/family planning/demography. **Activities:** Information and documentation services/data bases.

NLD3124

HEALTH PERFECT INTERNATIONAL

Herenweg 68, 1718 AG Hoogwoud, The Netherlands.

Telephone: 31 (22) 63 55 658. *Fax:* 31 (22) 63 55 658. *Contact:* Balthasar Schaap, Director.

OBJECTIVES: To provide consultancy services and training on health care, mother and child health and family planning in Third World countries.

GENERAL INFORMATION: *Creation:* 1993. *Personnel/Total:* 1. *Salaried:* 1. *Budget/Total 1993:* ECU 14000 (US$ 16000). *Financial sources:* Self-financing: 100%.

EVALUATION/RESEARCH: Undertakes research activities.

ACTIVITIES IN DEVELOPING REGIONS: Active in 1 country(ies). **Sustainable Development Actions:** Children/youth/family; Health/sanitation/water; Population/family planning/demography. **Regions:** Central Asia and South Asia.

INFORMATION AND EDUCATION ACTIVITIES: Topics: Population/family planning/demography. **Activities:** Lobbying/advocacy; Networking/electronic telecommunications.

See: How to Use the Directory, page 11.

NLD3125

HENDRIK KRAEMER INSTITUUT (HKI)

Leidsestraatweg 11, Postbus 12, 2340 AA Oegstgeest, The Netherlands.

Telephone: 31 (71) 51 77 900. *Fax:* 31 (71) 51 53 601. *Contact:* J.J. Visser.

OBJECTIVES: To train volunteers for development projects undertaken by agencies of the Protestant Churches.

GENERAL INFORMATION: *Creation:* 1971. *Affiliated to:* Netherlands Missionary Council (Netherlands) - Vereniging voor personele Samenwerking in Ontwikkelingslanden (Netherlands). *Personnel/Total:* 6. *Salaried:* 6. *Budget/Total 1993:* ECU 230000 (US$ 269000). *Financial sources: Self-financing:* 100%.

PUBLICATIONS: *Periodicals:* Oven en Weer Bulletin (1). *Annual report. List of publications.*

INFORMATION AND EDUCATION ACTIVITIES: Topics: International relations/cooperation/development aid. **Activities:** Conferences/seminars/workshops/training activities.

NLD3126

HINDOE-MOSLIMS ORGANISATIE VOOR MEDEFINANCIERING VAN ONTWIKKELINGSPROGRAMMA'S (HIMOS) ♦ Hindu-Muslim Organisation for Joint Financing of Development Programmes

p/a Cebemo, Rhijngeesterstraatweg 40, Postbus 77, 2340 AB Oegstgeest, The Netherlands.

Telephone: 31 (71) 15 285. *Fax:* 31 (71) 17 53 91.

OBJECTIVES: To co-finance development projects in the Third World.

GENERAL INFORMATION: *Creation:* 1988. *Personnel/Total:* 28. *Salaried:* 3. *Volunteers:* 25 of which: 7 in developing countries. *Budget/ Total 1993:* ECU 1059000 (US$ 1238000). *Financial sources: Private:* 2%. *Public:* 98%.

PUBLICATIONS: *Annual report.*

EVALUATION/RESEARCH: Evaluation reports available.

COMMENTS: Undertakes activities in the Commonwealth of Independent States.

ACTIVITIES IN DEVELOPING REGIONS: Active in 3 country(ies). Works through local field partners. **Sustainable Development Actions:** Education/training/literacy; Gender issues/women; Rural development/agriculture. **Regions:** Caribbean; Central Asia and South Asia.

INFORMATION AND EDUCATION ACTIVITIES: Topics: Gender issues/women; Health/sanitation/water; Poverty/living conditions; Rural development/agriculture. **Activities:** Conferences/seminars/workshops/training activities; Fund raising.

NLD3127

HOLLAND WORLD YOUTH (HWY)

Postbus 19318, Godebaldkwatier 74, 3501 OH Utrecht, The Netherlands.

Telephone: 31 (30) 23 60 448. *Fax:* 31 (30) 23 60 199. *Contact:* Ellen Meyer, Co-ordinator.

OBJECTIVES: To present a more balanced image of each other's culture to as great a number of young people as possible from the Netherlands and developing countries.

GENERAL INFORMATION: *Creation:* 1990. *Personnel/Total:* 16. *Salaried:* 6 of which: 2 in developing countries. *Volunteers:* 10. *Budget/ Total 1993:* ECU 304000 (US$ 355000). *Financial sources: Private:* 3%. *Public:* 95%. *Self-financing:* 2%.

PUBLICATIONS: *Annual report.*

EVALUATION/RESEARCH: Evaluation reports available.

PLANNED ACTIVITIES: Undertaking an exchange programme with with Benin and South Africa.

ACTIVITIES IN DEVELOPING REGIONS: Active in 2 country(ies). **Sustainable Development Actions:** Children/youth/family. **Regions:** East Africa; Southern Africa.

INFORMATION AND EDUCATION ACTIVITIES: Topics: Children/youth/family. **Activities:** Exchanges/twinning/linking; Publishing/audiovisual materials/educational materials.

NLD3128

HONGER HOEFT NIET (HHN) ♦ There Need Be No Hunger

Oude Gracht 42, 3511 AR Utrecht, The Netherlands.

Telephone: 31 (30) 23 16 566. *Contact:* Campaign Co-ordinator.

NLD3129

HONGERSTICHTING - DERDE WERELD ORGANISATIE ♦ Hunger Foundation - Third World Organisation

Bergstraat 30, Postbus 27, 3800 AA Amersfoort, The Netherlands.

Telephone: 31 (33) 46 50 840.

NLD3130

HORIZON HOLLAND STICHTING ♦ Holland Horizon Foundation

Conradkade 63, 2517 BS Den Haag, The Netherlands.

Telephone: 31 (70) 34 52 300. *Fax:* 31 (70) 34 52 301.

NLD3131

HULP AAN MEDISCHE LABORATORIA IN ONTWIKKELING-SLANDEN (HAMLO) ♦ Aid to Medical Laboratories in Developing Countries

Wilhelminapark 52, 3581 NM Utrecht, The Netherlands.

Telephone: 31 (30) 25 23 792.

OBJECTIVES: To assist medical laboratories in developing countries

GENERAL INFORMATION: *Personnel/Total:* 5. *Volunteers:* 5. *Budget/ Total 1993:* ECU 14000 (US$ 16000). *Financial sources: Private:* 90%. *Self-financing:* 10%.

PUBLICATIONS: *Annual report. List of publications.*

COMMENTS: HAMLO sends laboratory equipment (second-hand mainly) to laboratories that request aid in developing countries Undertakes activities in the Commonwealth of Independent States.

ACTIVITIES IN DEVELOPING REGIONS: Active in 18 country(ies). **Sustainable Development Actions:** Health/sanitation/water. **Regions:** Caribbean; Central Africa; Central Asia and South Asia; East Africa; South America; Southern Africa; West Africa.

INFORMATION AND EDUCATION ACTIVITIES: Topics: Health/sanitation/water. **Activities:** Fund raising; Information campaigns/exhibitions.

NLD3132

HUMANISTISCH INSTITUUT VOOR ONTWIKKELING-SSAMENWERKING (HIVOS) ♦ Humanistic Institute for Co-operation with Developing Countries

Raamweg 16, 2596 HL Den Haag, The Netherlands.

Telephone: 31 (70) 36 36 907. *Fax:* 31 (70) 36 17 447. *Contact:* Drs. J.J. Dijkstra, General Director.

NLD3133

HUMANISTISCH OVERLEG MENSENRECHTEN (HOM) ♦ Humanist Committee on Human Rights

Postbus 114, 3500 AC Utrecht, The Netherlands.

Telephone: 31 (30) 23 92 134. *Fax:* 31 (30) 23 67 104. *Contact:* M. Meijer.

OBJECTIVES: To promote an active human rights policy in the Foreign Affairs and Development Co-operation Departments and in the European Union. To protect and promote the rights of women. To raise public awareness of all human rights and thereby increase political action.

GENERAL INFORMATION: *Creation:* 1981. *Affiliated to:* Vrouwenberaad Outwikkelingssamenwerking (Netherlands) - Women in Develop-

ment Europe (Netherlands) - Breed Meusenrechtenoverleg (Netherlands) - National Platform of Women's Human Rights Beijing (Netherlands) - NGDO-EC-Network (Netherlands). *Personnel/ Total:* 3. *Salaried:* 3. *Budget/Total 1993:* ECU 138000 (US$ 162000). *Financial sources:* Private: 50%. Public: 40%. Self-financing: 10%.

PUBLICATIONS: *Periodicals:* HOM Newsletter (2). *Annual report. List of publications.*

PLANNED ACTIVITIES: Undertaking a campaign on the "Violence against women in conflict situations". Organising public debates, seminars and publications on the human rights situation in China.

COMMENTS: Undertakes activities in the Commonwealth of Independent States. Information activities related to the Commonwealth of Independent States.

INFORMATION AND EDUCATION ACTIVITIES: Topics: Gender issues/ women; Human rights/peace/conflicts; International relations/cooperation/development aid; Peace/ethnic conflicts/armament/disarmament; Racism/xenophobia/antisemitism; Refugees/migrants/ethnic groups. **Activities:** Conferences/seminars/workshops/training activities; Lobbying/advocacy; Other; Publishing/audiovisual materials/educational materials.

NLD3134

HUN DAGELIJKS BROOD

Neuhuyskade 17, 2596 XJ Den Haag, The Netherlands.

Telephone: 31 (70) 32 82 477.

NLD3135

INDONESISCH DOCUMENTATIE-EN INFORMATIE CENTRUM (INDOC) ♦ Indonesian Documentation and Information Centre

Postbus 11250, 2301 EG Leiden, The Netherlands.

Telephone: 31 (71) 51 24 739. *Fax:* 31 (71) 51 27 233. *E-mail:* indoc@antenna.nl. *Contact:* M. van Kanten, Co-ordinator.

OBJECTIVES: To inform the general public about present day developments in Indonesia, specifically about human rights, labour conditions and environmental issues.

GENERAL INFORMATION: *Creation:* 1979. *Personnel/Total:* 24. *Salaried:* 4 of which: 3 in developing countries. *Volunteers:* 20. *Budget/ Total 1993:* ECU 43000 (US$ 50000). *Financial sources:* Private: 25%. Public: 65%. Self-financing: 10%.

PUBLICATIONS: *Periodicals:* Mensenredite in Indonesie (1) - Minidoc (3) - Indoc Nieuws (4). *Annual report. List of publications.*

EVALUATION/RESEARCH: Evaluation reports available. Undertakes research activities.

INFORMATION AND EDUCATION ACTIVITIES: Topics: Children/youth/ family; Culture/tradition/religion; Ecology/environment/biodiversity; Education/training/literacy; Emergency relief/refugees/humanitarian assistance; Employment/unemployment; Gender issues/women; Health/sanitation/water; Human rights/peace/conflicts; International economic relations/trade/debt/finance; International relations/cooperation/development aid; Other; Peace/ethnic conflicts/armament/disarmament; Population/family planning/demography; Poverty/living conditions; Racism/ xenophobia/antisemitism; Refugees/migrants/ethnic groups; Rural development/agriculture; Urban development/habitat. **Activities:** Broadcasting/cultural events; Conferences/seminars/workshops/training activities; Exchanges/twinning/linking; Formal education; Fund raising; Information and documentation services/data bases; Information campaigns/ exhibitions; Lobbying/advocacy; Networking/electronic telecommunications; Publishing/audiovisual materials/educational materials.

NLD3136

INFORMATION CENTRE FOR LOW EXTERNAL INPUT AND SUSTAINABLE AGRICULTURE (ILEIA)

Postbus 64 Kastanjelaan 5, 3830 AB Leusden, The Netherlands.

Telephone: 31 (33) 49 43 086. *Fax:* 31 (33) 49 40 791. *E-mail:* ileia@antenna.nl.

OBJECTIVES: To promote the acceptance and adoption of the Low External Input and Sustainable Agriculture (LEISA) as a valid approach to agricultural development in areas not suited to the use of high levels of external inputs.

GENERAL INFORMATION: *Creation:* 1982. *Personnel/Total:* 8. *Salaried:* 8. *Financial sources:* Public: 100%.

PUBLICATIONS: *Periodicals:* ILEIA Newsletter (4). *List of publications.*

INFORMATION AND EDUCATION ACTIVITIES: Topics: Ecology/environment/biodiversity; Rural development/agriculture. **Activities:** Information and documentation services/data bases; Networking/electronic telecommunications; Publishing/audiovisual materials/educational materials.

NLD3137

INSTITUTE FOR EUROPEAN MARKETING AND DEVELOPMENT ASSOCIATION (EMDA INSTITUTE)

Postbus 100, 7590 AC Denekamp, The Netherlands.

Telephone: 31 (541) 35 50 00. *Fax:* 31 (541) 35 49 73. *E-mail:* DATANET 25. *Contact:* P.J. Ijben, President.

OBJECTIVES: To work with target developing countries (those who have signed an association agreement with the EU) on micro-development projects. To conduct on-going monitoring and evaluations of NGO projects, evaluations and report to the European Commission.

GENERAL INFORMATION: *Creation:* 1987. *Affiliated to:* NGO-EC Network (Netherlands) - World Bank (USA). *Personnel/Total:* 67. *Salaried:* 36 of which: 5 in developing countries. *Volunteers:* 31 of which: 26 in developing countries. *Budget/Total 1993:* ECU 1565000 (US$ 1831000). *Financial sources:* Private: 30%. Public: 50%. Self-financing: 20%.

PUBLICATIONS: *Annual report.*

EVALUATION/RESEARCH: Evaluation reports available. Undertakes research activities.

PLANNED ACTIVITIES: Supporting credit facilities for micro-lending. Implementation of micro-scale projects in associated countries. Supporting marketing, training and institutional development in 20 ACP countries.

COMMENTS: Undertakes activities in the Commonwealth of Independent States. Information activities related to the Commonwealth of Independent States.

ACTIVITIES IN DEVELOPING REGIONS: Present in developing regions. Active in 42 country(ies). Maintains local field presence. Works through local field partners. **Sustainable Development Actions:** Debt/finance/ trade; Democracy/good governance/institution building/participatory development; Ecology/environment/biodiversity; Education/training/literacy; Emergency relief/refugees/humanitarian assistance; Energy/transport; Food/famine; Gender issues/women; Health/sanitation/water; Other; Population/family planning/demography; Rural development/agriculture; Sending volunteers/experts/technical assistance; Small enterprises/informal sector/handicrafts; Urban development/habitat. **Regions:** Caribbean; Central Africa; Central Asia and South Asia; East Africa; Mexico and Central America; Oceania; South America; South East Asia; Southern Africa; West Africa.

INFORMATION AND EDUCATION ACTIVITIES: Topics: Ecology/environment/biodiversity; Emergency relief/refugees/humanitarian assistance; Employment/unemployment; Food/famine; Gender issues/ women; Health/sanitation/water; International economic relations/trade/ debt/finance; International relations/cooperation/development aid; Population/family planning/demography; Refugees/migrants/ethnic groups; Rural development/agriculture; Urban development/habitat. **Activities:** Conferences/seminars/workshops/training activities; Exchanges/twinning/linking; Fund raising; Information and documentation services/data bases; Information campaigns/exhibitions; Lobbying/advocacy; Networking/electronic telecommunications; Other; Publishing/audiovisual materials/educational materials.

See: *How to Use the Directory,* page 11.

NLD3138

INSTITUTE FOR HOUSING AND URBAN DEVELOPMENT STUDIES (IHS)

Postbus 1935, Weena 718, 3000 BX Rotterdam, The Netherlands.

Telephone: 31 (10) 40 21 523. *Fax:* 31 (10) 40 45 671. *Contact:* C. Dijkgraaf, Director.

OBJECTIVES: To acquire and transfer knowledge in the field of urban development through research, education and advisory work.

GENERAL INFORMATION: *Creation:* 1958. *Affiliated to:* Federation of International Education Institutes (Netherlands) - UrbaNeth -Habitat Stad - Habitat International Coalition. *Personnel/Total:* 59. *Salaried:* 59 of which: 13 in developing countries. *Budget/Total 1993:* ECU 4143000 (US$ 4846000). *Financial sources: Public:* 30%. *Self-financing:* 70%.

PUBLICATIONS: *Periodicals:* IHS Newspaper (3) - IHS Working Papers (3). *Annual report. List of publications.*

EVALUATION/RESEARCH: Evaluation reports available. Undertakes research activities.

COMMENTS: IHS is an educational institution which offers a variety of courses in the fields of planning, urban development and environmental management mainly to students from developing countries. Undertakes activities in the Commonwealth of Independent States. Information activities related to the Commonwealth of Independent States.

ACTIVITIES IN DEVELOPING REGIONS: Present in developing regions. Active in 15 country(ies). Maintains local field presence. Works through local field partners. **Sustainable Development Actions:** Ecology/environment/biodiversity; Education/training/literacy; Gender issues/women; Health/sanitation/water; Sending volunteers/experts/technical assistance; Small enterprises/informal sector/handicrafts; Urban development/habitat. **Regions:** Caribbean; Central Africa; Central Asia and South Asia; East Africa; East Asia; Mexico and Central America; Middle East; North Africa; South America; South East Asia; Southern Africa; West Africa.

INFORMATION AND EDUCATION ACTIVITIES: Topics: Ecology/environment/biodiversity; Education/training/literacy; Employment/unemployment; International relations/cooperation/development aid; Poverty/living conditions; Urban development/habitat. **Activities:** Conferences/seminars/workshops/training activities; Exchanges/twinning/linking; Formal education; Information and documentation services/data bases; Information campaigns/exhibitions; Publishing/audiovisual materials/educational materials.

NLD3139

INSTITUTE FOR SOUTHERN AFRICA

P.O. Box 11275, 1001GG Amsterdam, The Netherlands.

Telephone: 31 (20) 62 67 525. *Fax:* 31 (20) 62 37 335. *Contact:* Peter Hermes, Director.

OBJECTIVES: To maintain an information archive on Southern Africa. To facilitate projects, seminars, exchanges in the field of human rights, democratisation, culture and education. To conduct research.

GENERAL INFORMATION: *Creation:* 1994. *Type of organisation:* coordinating body. *Personnel/Total:* 16. *Salaried:* 6. *Volunteers:* 10. *Budget/Total 1993:* ECU 262000 (US$ 307000). *Financial sources: Private:* 20%. *Public:* 80%.

PUBLICATIONS: *Annual report. List of publications.*

EVALUATION/RESEARCH: Evaluation reports available. Undertakes research activities.

ACTIVITIES IN DEVELOPING REGIONS: Present in developing regions. Active in 4 country(ies). Works through local field partners. **Sustainable Development Actions:** Children/youth/family; Democracy/good governance/institution building/participatory development; Education/training/literacy; Gender issues/women; Human rights/peace/conflicts. **Regions:** Southern Africa.

INFORMATION AND EDUCATION ACTIVITIES: Topics: Children/youth/family; Culture/tradition/religion; Ecology/environment/biodiversity; Education/training/literacy; Emergency relief/refugees/humanitarian assis-

tance; Employment/unemployment; Food/famine; Gender issues/women; Health/sanitation/water; Human rights/peace/conflicts; International economic relations/trade/debt/finance; International relations/cooperation/development aid; Peace/ethnic conflicts/armament/disarmament; Population/family planning/demography; Poverty/living conditions; Racism/xenophobia/antisemitism; Refugees/migrants/ethnic groups; Rural development/agriculture; Urban development/habitat. **Activities:** Broadcasting/cultural events; Conferences/seminars/workshops/training activities; Exchanges/twinning/linking; Formal education; Fund raising; Information and documentation services/data bases; Information campaigns/exhibitions; Lobbying/advocacy; Networking/electronic telecommunications; Publishing/audiovisual materials/educational materials.

NLD3140

INSTITUTE OF CULTURAL AFFAIRS (ICA)

Postbus 11143, 1001 GC Amsterdam, The Netherlands.

Telephone: 31 (20) 90 65 17.

NLD3141

INSTITUUT VOOR EUROPEES LATIJNS-AMERIKAANSE BETREKKINGEN (IELAB) ♦ Indonesian European Latin American Relations

Postbus 85397, 3508 AJ Utrecht, The Netherlands.

Telephone: 31 (30) 25 85 222. *Fax:* 31 (30) 25 85 225. *Contact:* Th. J. de Hosson.

OBJECTIVES: To mount an exchange programme for students and professionals.

GENERAL INFORMATION: *Creation:* 1988. *Personnel/Total:* 7. *Salaried:* 7 of which: 4 in developing countries. *Budget/Total 1993:* ECU 598000 (US$ 670000). *Financial sources: Public:* 20%. *Self-financing:* 80%.

EVALUATION/RESEARCH: Evaluation reports available. Undertakes research activities.

PLANNED ACTIVITIES: Organising an exchange between low-budget experts.

ACTIVITIES IN DEVELOPING REGIONS: Active in 6 country(ies). Maintains local field presence. Works through local field partners. **Sustainable Development Actions:** Children/youth/family; Education/training/literacy; Health/sanitation/water; Rural development/agriculture; Sending volunteers/experts/technical assistance; Small enterprises/informal sector/handicrafts. **Regions:** Mexico and Central America; South East Asia.

INFORMATION AND EDUCATION ACTIVITIES: Topics: Children/youth/family; Education/training/literacy; Health/sanitation/water; International economic relations/trade/debt/finance; Rural development/agriculture. **Activities:** Conferences/seminars/workshops/training activities; Exchanges/twinning/linking; Formal education.

NLD3142

INSTITUUT VOOR LEERPLAN ONTWIKKELING (SLO) ♦ National Institute for Curriculum Development

Postbus 2041 / Boulevard 1945 nr. 3, 7511 AA Enschede, The Netherlands.

Telephone: 31 (53) 48 40 840. *Fax:* 31 (53) 43 07 692. *Contact:* P.A. de Bruijne, Managing Director.

OBJECTIVES: To support education with adaptation to changing societal circumstances by means of developing curricula and examples for teaching materials and giving information.

GENERAL INFORMATION: *Creation:* 1976. *Affiliated to:* Consortium of Institutions for Development and Research in Education in Europe. *Personnel/Total:* 250. *Salaried:* 250. *Budget/Total 1993:* ECU 16112000 (US$ 18845000). *Financial sources: Public:* 80%. *Self-financing:* 20%.

PUBLICATIONS: *Annual report. List of publications.*

EVALUATION/RESEARCH: Evaluation reports available. Undertakes research activities.

Voir : *Comment utiliser le répertoire,* page 11.

COMMENTS: Undertakes activities in the Commonwealth of Independent States. Information activities related to the Commonwealth of Independent States.

ACTIVITIES IN DEVELOPING REGIONS: Present in developing regions. Active in 10 country(ies). Works through local field partners. **Sustainable Development Actions:** Education/training/literacy. **Regions:** Caribbean; East Africa; Middle East; North Africa; South America; South East Asia; Southern Africa.

INFORMATION AND EDUCATION ACTIVITIES: Topics: Education/training/literacy. **Activities:** Conferences/seminars/workshops/training activities; Exchanges/twinning/linking; Formal education; Information and documentation services/data bases; Lobbying/advocacy; Networking/electronic telecommunications; Publishing/audiovisual materials/educational materials.

NLD3143

INTER PRESS SERVICE - NEDERLANDSE AFDELING (IPS-NEDERLAND) ♦ IPS-Third World News Agency

Van Eeghenstraat 77, 1071 EX Amsterdam, The Netherlands.

Telephone: 31 (20) 662 64 16. *Fax:* 31 (20) 676 14 01.

NLD3144

INTERKERKELIJKE ORGANISATIE VOOR ONTWIKKELINGSSAMENWERKING (ICCO) ♦ Interchurch Organisation for Development Co-operation

Zusterplein 22a, Postbus 151, 3700 AD Zeist, The Netherlands.

Telephone: 31 (30) 69 27 811. *Fax:* 31 (30) 69 25 614. *Contact:* J.J. van Es, Director.

OBJECTIVES: To provide assistance for development activities through financial support and advice for projects in developing countries.

GENERAL INFORMATION: *Creation:* 1964. *Affiliated to:* Gemeenschappelijke Overleg Medefinanciering (the Netherlands) - Association of Protestant Development Agencies (Belgium). *Personnel/Total:* 110. *Salaried:* 110 of which: 1 in developing countries. *Budget/Total 1993:* ECU 68399000 (US$ 80000000). *Financial sources:* Private: 1%. Public: 98%. Self-financing: 1%.

PUBLICATIONS: *Periodicals:* Vandar (10). *Annual report.*

EVALUATION/RESEARCH: Evaluation reports available.

COMMENTS: Information dissemination is undertaken in co-operation with the Protestant Churches and Christian Organisations in the Netherlands. Undertakes activities in the Commonwealth of Independent States.

ACTIVITIES IN DEVELOPING REGIONS: Active in 72 country(ies). Works through local field partners. **Sustainable Development Actions:** Education/training/literacy; Emergency relief/refugees/humanitarian assistance; Health/sanitation/water; Human rights/peace/conflicts; Rural development/agriculture. **Regions:** Caribbean; Central Africa; Central Asia and South Asia; East Africa; East Asia; Mexico and Central America; Middle East; North Africa; Oceania; South America; South East Asia; Southern Africa; West Africa.

NLD3145

INTERKERKELIJKE STICHTING ETHIOPIE (ETHIOPIE)

Wijk 4-77, 8321 GG Urk, The Netherlands.

Telephone: 31 (52) 76 82 123. *Fax:* 31 (52) 76 86 071. *Contact:* Jaap Bakler, Chairman.

OBJECTIVES: To support small-scale development projects in Ethiopia.

GENERAL INFORMATION: *Creation:* 1973. *Personnel/Total:* 53. *Salaried:* 3 of which: 1 in developing countries. *Volunteers:* 50. *Budget/Total 1993:* ECU 460000 (US$ 538000). *Financial sources:* Private: 80%. Public: 15%. Self-financing: 5%.

PUBLICATIONS: *Annual report.*

EVALUATION/RESEARCH: Evaluation reports available. Undertakes research activities.

COMMENTS: Information activities related to the Commonwealth of Independent States.

ACTIVITIES IN DEVELOPING REGIONS: Present in developing regions. Active in 2 country(ies). Maintains local field presence. Works through local field partners. **Sustainable Development Actions:** Children/youth/family; Education/training/literacy; Rural development/agriculture; Sending volunteers/experts/technical assistance. **Regions:** East Africa.

INFORMATION AND EDUCATION ACTIVITIES: Topics: Children/youth/family; Gender issues/women; Rural development/agriculture. **Activities:** Fund raising; Publishing/audiovisual materials/educational materials.

NLD3146

INTERNATIONAAL CHRISTELIJK STEUNFONDS (ICS)

Postbus 2480, 1200 CL Hilversum, The Netherlands.

Telephone: 31 (35) 62 84 984. *Fax:* 31 (35) 62 37 610. *Contact:* J. Huizinga.

OBJECTIVES: To give aid to persons in need in any part of the world.

GENERAL INFORMATION: *Creation:* 1980. *Personnel/Total:* 14. *Salaried:* 14 of which: 7 in developing countries. *Budget/Total 1993:* ECU 1289000 (US$ 1508000). *Financial sources:* Private: 90%. Public: 10%.

PUBLICATIONS: *Periodicals:* Weldoen (4). *Annual report. List of publications.*

EVALUATION/RESEARCH: Evaluation reports available. Undertakes research activities.

ACTIVITIES IN DEVELOPING REGIONS: Present in developing regions. Active in 7 country(ies). Maintains local field presence. Works through local field partners. **Sustainable Development Actions:** Children/youth/family; Education/training/literacy; Rural development/agriculture. **Regions:** East Africa; South East Asia.

INFORMATION AND EDUCATION ACTIVITIES: Topics: Children/youth/family; Rural development/agriculture. **Activities:** Fund raising; Information campaigns/exhibitions.

NLD3147

INTERNATIONAL ALLIANCE OF WOMEN (IAW) ♦ Alliance Internationale des Femmes

Kerklaan 43, 1251 JS Laren, The Netherlands.

Telephone: 31 (35) 53 82 193. *Fax:* 31 (35) 53 80 477. *E-mail:* RRBJIFI@CC.RUU.NL. *Contact:* Alice Marangopoulos, President.

OBJECTIVES: To establish equality of liberties, status and opportunities between men and women and to work for equal partnership between men and women in all spheres of life. To promote a better quality of life and better understanding among peoples.

GENERAL INFORMATION: *Creation:* 1904. *Type of organisation:* network. *Budget/Total 1993:* ECU 12000 (US$ 14000). *Financial sources:* Private: 30%. Self-financing: 70%.

PUBLICATIONS: *Periodicals:* International Women's News (4). *Annual report.*

PLANNED ACTIVITIES: Undertaking a worldwide legal literacy campaign. Disseminating the results of the Beijing conference on women.

COMMENTS: Undertakes activities in the Commonwealth of Independent States.

ACTIVITIES IN DEVELOPING REGIONS: Active in 10 country(ies). Works through local field partners. **Sustainable Development Actions:** Democracy/good governance/institution building/participatory development; Ecology/environment/biodiversity; Education/training/literacy; Food/famine; Gender issues/women; Health/sanitation/water; Population/family planning/demography; Small enterprises/informal sector/handicrafts; Urban development/habitat. **Regions:** Central Africa; Central Asia and South Asia; Middle East; North Africa; Southern Africa; West Africa.

INFORMATION AND EDUCATION ACTIVITIES: Topics: Children/youth/family; Ecology/environment/biodiversity; Education/training/literacy; Employment/unemployment; Gender issues/women; Health/sanitation/water; Human rights/peace/conflicts; International relations/cooperation/development aid; Peace/ethnic conflicts/armament/disarmament; Popu-

See: *How to Use the Directory,* page 11.

lation/family planning/demography; Urban development/habitat. **Activities:** Conferences/seminars/workshops/training activities; Formal education; Information and documentation services/data bases; Lobbying/advocacy.

NLD3148

INTERNATIONAL CHILDREN WELFARE FOUNDATION (KARTINI)

Watermolenweg 17, 1611 XN Bovenkarspel, The Netherlands.

Telephone: 31 (228) 51 18 61.

NLD3149

INTERNATIONAL COUNCIL FOR FRIENDS OF NEPAL - THE NETHERLANDS (ICFON-NETH)

Zeeweg 6, 2586 AK Den Haag, The Netherlands.

Telephone: 31 (70) 35 52 989. *Fax:* 31 (70) 35 14 362. *Contact:* Rudi J.M. de Groot, Chairman.

OBJECTIVES: To support development projects initiated by a local rural community in Nepal. To supply information about development issues in Nepal.

GENERAL INFORMATION: *Creation:* 1991. *Personnel/Total:* 4. *Volunteers:* 4. *Budget/Total 1993:* ECU 50000 (US$ 58000). *Financial sources:* Private: 100%.

PUBLICATIONS: *Periodicals:* Samachar (4). *Annual report.*

PLANNED ACTIVITIES: Undertaking an income generation programme.

ACTIVITIES IN DEVELOPING REGIONS: Active in 1 country(ies). Works through local field partners. **Sustainable Development Actions:** Children/youth/family; Education/training/literacy; Gender issues/women; Health/sanitation/water; Rural development/agriculture. **Regions:** Central Asia and South Asia.

INFORMATION AND EDUCATION ACTIVITIES: Topics: Children/youth/family; Education/training/literacy; Gender issues/women; Health/sanitation/water; Poverty/living conditions; Rural development/agriculture. **Activities:** Fund raising.

NLD3150

INTERNATIONAL DISPENSARY ASSOCIATION (IDA)

Postbus 37098, 1030 AB Amsterdam, The Netherlands.

Telephone: 31 (29) 03 30 51. *Fax:* 31 (29) 03 18 54. *Contact:* H.W.A. den Besten, Managing Director.

OBJECTIVES: To improve the availability, quality and correct selection of essential drugs and medical supplies in developing countries.

GENERAL INFORMATION: *Creation:* 1972. *Personnel/Total:* 100. *Salaried:* 100. *Budget/Total 1993:* ECU 64124000 (US$ 75000000). *Financial sources:* Self-financing: 100%.

PUBLICATIONS: *Periodicals:* Info Bulletin (2).

EVALUATION/RESEARCH: Undertakes research activities.

ACTIVITIES IN DEVELOPING REGIONS: Active in 160 country(ies). **Sustainable Development Actions:** Health/sanitation/water. **Regions:** Caribbean; Central Africa; Central Asia and South Asia; East Africa; East Asia; Mexico and Central America; Middle East; North Africa; Oceania; South America; South East Asia; Southern Africa; West Africa.

INFORMATION AND EDUCATION ACTIVITIES: Topics: Health/sanitation/water. **Activities:** Broadcasting/cultural events; Conferences/seminars/workshops/training activities; Exchanges/twinning/linking; Formal education; Fund raising; Information and documentation services/data bases; Information campaigns/exhibitions; Lobbying/advocacy; Networking/electronic telecommunications; Publishing/audiovisual materials/educational materials.

NLD3151

INTERNATIONAL FEDERATION CALCUTTA RESCUE

Spreiweg 95, 311 GT Dordrecht, The Netherlands.

Contact: Alice van Essen.

NLD3152

INTERNATIONAL FEDERATION FOR HOUSING AND PLANNING (IFHP)

Wassenaarseweg 43, 2596 CG Den Haag, The Netherlands.

Telephone: 31 (70) 24 45 57. *Fax:* 31 (70) 49 69 16. *Contact:* IFHP Secretariat.

NLD3153

INTERNATIONAL HUMANIST & ETHICAL UNION (IHEU)

Nieuwegracht 69A, 3512 LG Utrecht, The Netherlands.

Telephone: 31 (30) 23 12 155. *Fax:* 31 (30) 23 64 169. *Contact:* R. Tielman.

OBJECTIVES: To bring together groups and individuals throughout the world interested in promoting humanism - the dedication to and responsibility for human life by the maintenance and development of human values.

GENERAL INFORMATION: *Creation:* 1959. *Type of organisation:* association of NGOs. *Member organisations:* 97. *Personnel/Total:* 13. *Salaried:* 3. *Volunteers:* 19. *Budget/Total 1993:* ECU 161000 (US$ 188000). *Financial sources:* Private: 30%. Self-financing: 70%.

PUBLICATIONS: *Periodicals:* International Humanist News (4).

EVALUATION/RESEARCH: Undertakes research activities.

PLANNED ACTIVITIES: Undertaking a partnership programme to facilitate 'twinning' between humanist groups in different countries especially between the North and South.

COMMENTS: Undertakes activities in the Commonwealth of Independent States. Information activities related to the Commonwealth of Independent States.

ACTIVITIES IN DEVELOPING REGIONS: Active in 11 country(ies). Works through local field partners. **Sustainable Development Actions:** Children/youth/family; Democracy/good governance/institution building/participatory development; Ecology/environment/biodiversity; Education/training/literacy; Gender issues/women; Human rights/peace/conflicts; Population/family planning/demography. **Regions:** Central Asia and South Asia; Mexico and Central America; West Africa.

INFORMATION AND EDUCATION ACTIVITIES: Topics: Children/youth/family; Culture/tradition/religion; Education/training/literacy; Gender issues/women; Human rights/peace/conflicts; International relations/cooperation/development aid; Peace/ethnic conflicts/armament/disarmament; Population/family planning/demography. **Activities:** Conferences/seminars/workshops/training activities; Exchanges/twinning/linking; Formal education; Lobbying/advocacy; Publishing/audiovisual materials/educational materials.

NLD3154

INTERNATIONAL INSTITUTE FOR AEROSPACE SURVEY AND EARTH SCIENCES (ITC)

350 Boulevard 1945, Postbus 6, 7500 AA Enschede, The Netherlands.

Telephone: 31 (53) 48 74 444. *Fax:* 31 (53) 48 74 400. *Contact:* K.J. Beek, Rector.

OBJECTIVES: To assist developing countries in human resource development in areospace surveys, remote sensing applications, the establishment of geoinformation systems and the management of geoinformation.

GENERAL INFORMATION: *Creation:* 1950. *Type of organisation:* coordinating body. *Member organisations:* 5. *Affiliated to:* Indian institute of Remote Sensing (India) - Department of Education and Investigation at the Instituto Geografico 'Agustin Codazzi' (Bogota) - Regional Centre for Training in Aerial Survey (Nigeria). *Personnel/Total:* 350. *Budget/Total 1993:* ECU 20255000 (US$ 23690000). *Financial sources:* Private: 7%. Public: 76%. Self-financing: 17%.

PUBLICATIONS: *Periodicals:* ITC Journal (4). *Annual report.*

EVALUATION/RESEARCH: Evaluation reports available. Undertakes research activities.

Voir : *Comment utiliser le répertoire,* page 11.

COMMENTS: Undertakes activities in the Commonwealth of Independent States. Information activities related to the Commonwealth of Independent States.

ACTIVITIES IN DEVELOPING REGIONS: Present in developing regions. Works through local field partners. **Sustainable Development Actions:** Ecology/environment/biodiversity; Education/training/literacy; Health/sanitation/water; Rural development/agriculture; Sending volunteers/experts/technical assistance; Urban development/habitat. **Regions:** Caribbean; Central Africa; Central Asia and South Asia; East Africa; East Asia; Mexico and Central America; Middle East; North Africa; Oceania; South America; South East Asia; Southern Africa; West Africa.

INFORMATION AND EDUCATION ACTIVITIES: Topics: Ecology/environment/biodiversity; Education/training/literacy; Health/sanitation/water; International relations/cooperation/development aid; Rural development/agriculture; Urban development/habitat. **Activities:** Conferences/seminars/workshops/training activities; Exchanges/twinning/linking; Formal education; Fund raising; Information and documentation services/data bases; Networking/electronic telecommunications; Publishing/audiovisual materials/educational materials.

NLD3155

INTERNATIONAL INSTITUTE FOR INFRASTRUCTURAL HYDRAULIC AND ENVIRONMENTAL ENGINEERING (IHE)

Postbus 3015, 2601 DA Delft, The Netherlands.

Telephone: 31 (15) 21 51 715. **Fax:** 31 (15) 21 22 921. **E-mail:** asr@ieh.nl. **Contact:** W. A. Segeren.

OBJECTIVES: To contribute to the international transfer and exchange of knowledge and skills in science and technology among professionals in the fields of infrastructural, hydraulic and environmental engineering.

GENERAL INFORMATION: Creation: 1957. **Affiliated to:** Federation of International Education Institute (Netherlands) - Geoscience Network with the Netherlands - Urban Network with the Netherlands (Netherlands) - TECHWARE - ARMADA. **Personnel/Total:** 122. Salaried: 122 of which: 4 in developing countries. **Budget/Total 1993:** ECU 14501000 (US$ 16960000). **Financial sources:** Private: 6%. Public: 80%. Self-financing: 14%.

PUBLICATIONS: Periodicals: Newsletter (3) - IEH Scientific Report Series (4). Annual report. List of publications.

EVALUATION/RESEARCH: Evaluation reports available. Undertakes research activities.

PLANNED ACTIVITIES: Establishment of Msc programmes in Columbia, Yemen, Indonesia, Kenya, Ghana, Zimbabwe, Bangladesh and the Palestinian territories.

COMMENTS: Undertakes activities in the Commonwealth of Independent States. Information activities related to the Commonwealth of Independent States.

ACTIVITIES IN DEVELOPING REGIONS: Present in developing regions. Maintains local field presence. Works through local field partners. **Sustainable Development Actions:** Democracy/good governance/institution building/participatory development; Ecology/environment/biodiversity; Education/training/literacy; Energy/transport; Health/sanitation/water; Other; Urban development/habitat. **Regions:** Central Asia and South Asia; East Africa; Middle East; North Africa; South America; South East Asia; Southern Africa; West Africa.

INFORMATION AND EDUCATION ACTIVITIES: Topics: Ecology/environment/biodiversity; Education/training/literacy; Health/sanitation/water; International relations/cooperation/development aid; Poverty/living conditions; Urban development/habitat. **Activities:** Conferences/seminars/workshops/training activities; Exchanges/twinning/linking; Formal education; Fund raising; Information and documentation services/data bases; Information campaigns/exhibitions; Lobbying/advocacy; Networking/electronic telecommunications; Publishing/audiovisual materials/educational materials.

NLD3156

INTERNATIONAL NGO FORUM ON INDONESIAN DEVELOPMENT

PO Box 11609, 2502 AP Den Haag, The Netherlands.

Telephone: 31 (70) 34 21 621. **Fax:** 31 (70) 36 14 461. **E-mail:** infidnl@antenna.nl. **Contact:** Peter van Tuijl, INFID Secretary.

OBJECTIVES: To ensure the implementation of policy in disbursement of aid, investment and trade in the interests of the poor and disadvantaged and based on the principals of peace, justice and human rights. To strengthen democracy in Indonesia.

GENERAL INFORMATION: Creation: 1985. **Type of organisation:** network. **Member organisations:** 125. **Personnel/Total:** 9. Salaried: 9 of which: 6 in developing countries. **Budget/Total 1993:** ECU 354000 (US$ 415000). **Financial sources:** Private: 15%. Self-financing: 85%.

PUBLICATIONS: List of publications.

EVALUATION/RESEARCH: Evaluation reports available. Undertakes research activities.

ACTIVITIES IN DEVELOPING REGIONS: Active in 1 country(ies). Maintains local field presence. **Sustainable Development Actions:** Democracy/good governance/institution building/participatory development; Human rights/peace/conflicts; Other. **Regions:** South East Asia.

INFORMATION AND EDUCATION ACTIVITIES: Topics: Ecology/environment/biodiversity; Employment/unemployment; Gender issues/women; Human rights/peace/conflicts; International economic relations/trade/debt/finance; International relations/cooperation/development aid; Poverty/living conditions. **Activities:** Conferences/seminars/workshops/training activities; Information and documentation services/data bases; Lobbying/advocacy; Networking/electronic telecommunications; Publishing/audiovisual materials/educational materials.

NLD3157

INTERNATIONAL RESTRUCTURING EDUCATION NETWORK EUROPE (IRENE)

Stationsstraat 39, 5038 EC Tilburg, The Netherlands.

Telephone: 31 (13) 53 51 523. **Fax:** 31 (13) 53 50 253. **E-mail:** IRENE@ANTENNA. **Contact:** P. Pennartz, Executive Secretary.

OBJECTIVES: To stimulate the exchange of information between organisations working in development education and the international division of labour. To publish research and educational materials on North-South relations.

GENERAL INFORMATION: Creation: 1981. **Type of organisation:** network. **Member organisations:** 6. **Personnel/Total:** 2. Salaried: 2. **Budget/Total 1993:** ECU 92000 (US$ 108000). **Financial sources:** Public: 85%. Self-financing: 15%.

PUBLICATIONS: Periodicals: News from IRENE (3). List of publications.

EVALUATION/RESEARCH: Undertakes research activities.

PLANNED ACTIVITIES: Organising international workshops on the position of women in the economy, transnational companies, their codes of conduct and the effects of their relocation on North and South workers.

INFORMATION AND EDUCATION ACTIVITIES: Topics: Employment/unemployment; International economic relations/trade/debt/finance. **Activities:** Conferences/seminars/workshops/training activities; Fund raising; Information and documentation services/data bases; Networking/electronic telecommunications.

NLD3158

INTERNATIONAL SOIL REFERENCE AND INFORMATION CENTRE (ISRIC)

Postbus 353, 6700 AJ Wageningen, The Netherlands.

Telephone: 31 (31) 74 71 711. **Fax:** 31 (31) 74 24 460. **E-mail:** ISRIC@RCL.WAK.NL. **Contact:** Roel Oldeman.

OBJECTIVES: To serve as a documentation centre on land and resources. To improve methods of soil analysis and contribute to new developments in soil science. To provide consultancy and training in soil science and agroclimatology.

GENERAL INFORMATION: Creation: 1966. **Affiliated to:** Environmental Liaison Centre International (Kenya). **Personnel/Total:** 30. Salaried: 28 of which: 2 in developing countries. Volunteers: 2. **Budget/**

Total 1993: ECU 1381000 (US$ 1615000). *Financial sources: Public:* 60%. *Self-financing:* 40%.

PUBLICATIONS: *Periodicals:* Newsletter (var). *Annual report. List of publications.*

EVALUATION/RESEARCH: Undertakes research activities.

PLANNED ACTIVITIES: Developing and implementing the Soils and Terrain Digital Database (SOTER).

COMMENTS: Undertakes activities in the Commonwealth of Independent States.

ACTIVITIES IN DEVELOPING REGIONS: Active in 20 country(ies). Works through local field partners. **Sustainable Development Actions:** Ecology/environment/biodiversity; Education/training/literacy; Rural development/agriculture. **Regions:** Caribbean; Central Asia and South Asia; East Africa; Mexico and Central America; Middle East; South America; South East Asia; Southern Africa; West Africa.

INFORMATION AND EDUCATION ACTIVITIES: Topics: Ecology/environment/biodiversity; Rural development/agriculture. **Activities:** Conferences/seminars/workshops/training activities; Information and documentation services/data bases; Information campaigns/exhibitions.

NLD3159
INTERNATIONAL TREE FUND (ITF)

Markweg 1a, Postbus 160, 6870 AD Renkum, The Netherlands.

Telephone: 31 (317) 31 36 16. *Fax:* 31 (317) 31 80 40. *Contact:* Wouter van Dam, President of the Board.

OBJECTIVES: To preserve and restore the forest, in particular the tropical forest in order to protect the economic, social and cultural development of those who live within and around the rainforest.

GENERAL INFORMATION: *Creation:* 1987. *Affiliated to:* Both Ends (Denmark). *Personnel/Total:* 72. *Volunteers:* 72 of which: 2 in developing countries. *Budget/Total 1993:* ECU 104000 (US$ 121000). *Financial sources: Private:* 80%. *Public:* 20%.

PUBLICATIONS: *Annual report.*

EVALUATION/RESEARCH: Evaluation reports available.

ACTIVITIES IN DEVELOPING REGIONS: Present in developing regions. Active in 3 country(ies). Maintains local field presence. Works through local field partners. **Sustainable Development Actions:** Children/youth/family; Debt/finance/trade; Democracy/good governance/institution building/participatory development; Ecology/environment/biodiversity; Education/training/literacy; Gender issues/women; Health/sanitation/water; Rural development/agriculture; Small enterprises/informal sector/handicrafts; Urban development/habitat. **Regions:** Mexico and Central America.

INFORMATION AND EDUCATION ACTIVITIES: Topics: Children/youth/family; Culture/tradition/religion; Ecology/environment/biodiversity; Education/training/literacy; Employment/unemployment; Gender issues/women; Health/sanitation/water; Poverty/living conditions; Refugees/migrants/ethnic groups; Rural development/agriculture; Urban development/habitat. **Activities:** Conferences/seminars/workshops/training activities; Exchanges/twinning/linking; Formal education; Fund raising; Information campaigns/exhibitions; Publishing/audiovisual materials/educational materials.

NLD3160
INTERNATIONAL UNION OF LOCAL AUTHORITIES (IULA) ♦
Union internationale des villes et pouvoirs locaux

Wassenaarseweg 39, Postbus 90646, 2596 CG Den Haag, The Netherlands.

Telephone: 31 (70) 32 44 032. *Fax:* 31 (70) 32 46 916. *Contact:* Riccardo Triglia, President.

OBJECTIVES: To raise the standards of local administration and services. To promote the welfare of citizens and foster citizen involvement in local government affairs. To defend the interests of local governement in international governmental organisations.

GENERAL INFORMATION: *Creation:* 1913. *Member organisations:* 218. *Personnel/Total:* 8. *Salaried:* 8. *Budget/Total 1993:* ECU 691000 (US$ 808000). *Financial sources: Self-financing:* 100%.

PUBLICATIONS: *Periodicals:* IULA 1994 (4). *Annual report.*

EVALUATION/RESEARCH: Evaluation reports available.

PLANNED ACTIVITIES: Planning the 1997 33rd Annual World Congress, Mauritius.

COMMENTS: Undertakes activities in the Commonwealth of Independent States.

ACTIVITIES IN DEVELOPING REGIONS: Present in developing regions. Active in 30 country(ies). Maintains local field presence. Works through local field partners. **Sustainable Development Actions:** Democracy/good governance/institution building/participatory development; Urban development/habitat. **Regions:** Caribbean; Central Africa; Central Asia and South Asia; East Africa; East Asia; Mexico and Central America; Middle East; North Africa; Oceania; South America; South East Asia; Southern Africa; West Africa.

INFORMATION AND EDUCATION ACTIVITIES: Topics: Ecology/environment/biodiversity; Human rights/peace/conflicts; International relations/cooperation/development aid; Urban development/habitat. **Activities:** Conferences/seminars/workshops/training activities; Exchanges/twinning/linking; Fund raising; Information and documentation services/data bases; Lobbying/advocacy.

NLD3161
INTERNATIONAL YOUTH FEDERATION FOR ENVIRONMENTAL STUDIES AND CONSERVATION

Oude Gracht 42, 3511 AR Utrecht, The Netherlands.
Telephone: 31 (30) 23 11 537.

NLD3162
INTERNATIONALE VRIJWILLIGERSPROJEKTEN (SIW)

Willemstraat 7, 3511 RJ Utrecht, The Netherlands.
Telephone: 31 (30) 23 17 721.

NLD3163
INTERSERVE-NEDERLAND

Krakelingweg 10a, 3707 HV Zeist, The Netherlands.

Telephone: 31 (30) 69 13 741. *Fax:* 31 (30) 69 56 878. *E-mail:* 100121 1477. *Contact:* H.J. Blom.

OBJECTIVES: To send personnel to assist in development work, especially in the administrative, technical, agricultural, medical and educational fields. To provide financial assistance for development projects.

GENERAL INFORMATION: *Creation:* 1969. *Affiliated to:* Personnel Services Overseas - United Mission to Nepal (Netherlands) -International Assistance Mission (Afghanistan) - Association de coopération en Tunisie (Tunisia) - Joint Christian Services (Mongolia). *Personnel/Total:* 32. *Salaried:* 2. *Volunteers:* 30 of which: 22 in developing countries. *Budget/Total 1993:* ECU 691000 (US$ 808000). *Financial sources: Private:* 80%. *Public:* 15%. *Self-financing:* 5%.

PUBLICATIONS: *Periodicals:* DIENEN (4). *Annual report. List of publications.*

ACTIVITIES IN DEVELOPING REGIONS: Maintains local field presence. Works through local field partners. **Sustainable Development Actions:** Children/youth/family; Education/training/literacy; Health/sanitation/water. **Regions:** Central Asia and South Asia; East Asia; Middle East; North Africa.

INFORMATION AND EDUCATION ACTIVITIES: Topics: Children/youth/family; Education/training/literacy; Health/sanitation/water. **Activities:** Conferences/seminars/workshops/training activities; Formal education; Fund raising; Publishing/audiovisual materials/educational materials.

NLD3164
INZET - VERENINGING VOOR NOORD-ZUID CAMPAGNES ♦
INZET - Association for North-South Campaigns

Keizersgracht 132, 1015 CW Amsterdam, The Netherlands.

Telephone: 31 (20) 62 73 339. *Fax:* 31 (20) 62 73 839. *Contact:* P. Gelauff, Director.

OBJECTIVES: To achieve sustainable development in the North and South by influencing policy-makers in the Netherlands and in the European Union through information campaigns.

GENERAL INFORMATION: *Creation:* 1992. *Affiliated to:* South North Federation (Netherlands) - Platform Sustainable Development (Netherlands). *Personnel/Total:* 130. *Salaried:* 10. *Volunteers:* 120. *Budget/Total 1993:* ECU 506000 (US$ 592000). *Financial sources:* Private: 30%. Public: 60%. Self-financing: 10%.

PUBLICATIONS: *Periodicals:* INZET Magazine (6) - Stand van Zahun (4). *Annual report. List of publications.*

EVALUATION/RESEARCH: Undertakes research activities.

PLANNED ACTIVITIES: Lobbying and undertaking an information campaign: "Invest in Africa", Developing a "European Action Plan on Africa".

INFORMATION AND EDUCATION ACTIVITIES: Topics: Ecology/environment/biodiversity; Gender issues/women; Human rights/peace/conflicts; International economic relations/trade/debt/finance; International relations/cooperation/development aid; Peace/ethnic conflicts/armament/disarmament; Racism/xenophobia/antisemitism; Rural development/agriculture. **Activities:** Conferences/seminars/workshops/training activities; Information campaigns/exhibitions; Lobbying/advocacy; Publishing/audiovisual materials/educational materials.

NLD3165

IRC INTERNATIONAL WATER AND SANITATION CENTRE

Prinses Margrietplantsoen 20, Postbus 93190, 2509 AD Den Haag, The Netherlands.

Telephone: 31 (70) 33 14 133. *Fax:* 31 (70) 38 14 034. *E-mail:* IRCWATER@ANTENNA.NL. *Contact:* Drs. J.M.G. van Damme.

OBJECTIVES: To foster the generation and transfer of knowledge on water supply, sanitation, water resources and solid waste managmement in developing countries. To emphasize innovative approaches to prevailing problems.

GENERAL INFORMATION: *Creation:* 1968. *Personnel/Total:* 40. *Salaried:* 40. *Budget/Total 1993:* ECU 1749000 (US$ 2046000). *Financial sources:* Public: 40%. Self-financing: 60%.

PUBLICATIONS: *Periodicals:* Water Newsletter (10) - Faits Nouveaux (6) - Highlights (6). *Annual report. List of publications.*

EVALUATION/RESEARCH: Evaluation reports available. Undertakes research activities.

PLANNED ACTIVITIES: Supporting national campaigns advocating change for improved performance and on the impact of water supply and sanitation services.

COMMENTS: Undertakes activities in the Commonwealth of Independent States.

ACTIVITIES IN DEVELOPING REGIONS: Active in 34 country(ies). Works through local field partners. **Sustainable Development Actions:** Democracy/good governance/institution building/participatory development; Education/training/literacy; Gender issues/women; Health/sanitation/water; Other; Urban development/habitat. **Regions:** Central Africa; Central Asia and South Asia; East Africa; Mexico and Central America; Middle East; North Africa; Oceania; South America; South East Asia; Southern Africa; West Africa.

INFORMATION AND EDUCATION ACTIVITIES: Topics: Gender issues/women; Health/sanitation/water; Urban development/habitat. **Activities:** Conferences/seminars/workshops/training activities; Information and documentation services/data bases; Lobbying/advocacy; Networking/electronic telecommunications; Other; Publishing/audiovisual materials/educational materials.

NLD3166

IVN. VERENIGING VOOR NATUUR-EN MILIEUEDUCATIE ♦
IVN. Association for Environmental Education

Plantage Middenlaan 2c, P.O. Box 20123, NL 1000 HC Amsterdam, The Netherlands.

Telephone: 31 (20) 62 28 115. *Fax:* 31 (20) 62 66 091. *Contact:* G.J. Jutten.

OBJECTIVES: To promote the idea that the environment needs protection and to foster environmental awareness.

GENERAL INFORMATION: *Creation:* 1960. *Type of organisation:* association of NGOs. *Affiliated to:* Landelyk Milieu Overleg - Stichting Natuur Milieu - IUCN. *Personnel/Total:* 16070. *Salaried:* 70. *Volunteers:* 16000. *Budget/Total 1993:* ECU 2762000 (US$ 3230000). *Financial sources:* Private: 8%. Public: 85%. Self-financing: 7%.

PUBLICATIONS: *Periodicals:* Mens en Natuur (4) - Muurpaper (4). *Annual report. List of publications.*

COMMENTS: Undertakes activities in the Commonwealth of Independent States.

INFORMATION AND EDUCATION ACTIVITIES: Topics: Ecology/environment/biodiversity. **Activities:** Conferences/seminars/workshops/training activities; Formal education; Information and documentation services/data bases; Information campaigns/exhibitions; Publishing/audiovisual materials/educational materials.

NLD3167

KAIROS - OECUMENISCH ADVIES- EN INFORMATIECENTRUM ZUID-AFRIKA ♦ KAIROS - Ecumenical Advice and Information Centre on South Africa

Pauwstraat 7, 3512 TG Utrecht, The Netherlands.

Telephone: 31 (30) 23 19 714. *Fax:* 31 (30) 23 16 518. *E-mail:* KAIROS@ANTENNA.NL.

OBJECTIVES: To inform people in the Netherlands about events in South Africa and follow closely the economic relations between South Africa and Western Europe.

GENERAL INFORMATION: *Creation:* 1970. *Personnel/Total:* 16. *Salaried:* 4. *Volunteers:* 12.

PUBLICATIONS: *Periodicals:* Amandla (6). *Annual report.*

PLANNED ACTIVITIES: Focusing on issues concerning children and South Africa, domestic workers and the living conditions of farm workers.

INFORMATION AND EDUCATION ACTIVITIES: Topics: Children/youth/family; Culture/tradition/religion; Gender issues/women; Human rights/peace/conflicts; International economic relations/trade/debt/finance; International relations/cooperation/development aid; Peace/ethnic conflicts/armament/disarmament; Poverty/living conditions; Racism/xenophobia/antisemitism; Rural development/agriculture. **Activities:** Information and documentation services/data bases; Lobbying/advocacy.

NLD3168

KIND EN TOEKOMST

Tuinstraat 1, 6971 BG Brummen, The Netherlands.

Telephone: 31 (575) 56 24 93.

NLD3169

DE KLEINE AARDE ♦ The Small Earth - Exhibition Centre for Sustainable Development

Het Klaverblad 1, P.O. Box 151, 5280 AD Boxtel, The Netherlands.

Telephone: 31 (41) 16 84 921. *Fax:* 31 (41) 16 83 407. *Contact:* Petra Souwerbren and Martin van Meurs, Directors.

OBJECTIVES: To promote sustainable lifestyles based on organic farming, ecological food, solar energy and a reduced consumption of raw materials.

GENERAL INFORMATION: *Creation:* 1972. *Personnel/Total:* 41. *Salaried:* 23. *Volunteers:* 18. *Budget/Total 1993:* ECU 679000 (US$ 794000). *Financial sources:* Public: 30%. Self-financing: 70%.

PUBLICATIONS: *Periodicals:* DE Kleine AArde (4). *Annual report. List of publications.*

EVALUATION/RESEARCH: Undertakes research activities.

ACTIVITIES IN DEVELOPING REGIONS: Present in developing regions. Works through local field partners. **Sustainable Development Actions:** Ecology/environment/biodiversity; Energy/transport; Food/famine; Rural development/agriculture. **Regions:** East Africa.

INFORMATION AND EDUCATION ACTIVITIES: Topics: Ecology/environment/biodiversity; International relations/cooperation/development aid; Rural development/agriculture; Urban development/habitat. **Activities:** Broadcasting/cultural events; Conferences/seminars/workshops/training activities; Exchanges/twinning/linking; Information campaigns/exhibitions; Publishing/audiovisual materials/educational materials.

NLD3170

KOMITEE INDONESIE (INDONESIE)

Postbus 92066, Minahassastraat 1, 1090 AB Amsterdam, The Netherlands.

Telephone: 31 (20) 69 36 050. *Fax:* 31 (20) 66 84 085.

OBJECTIVES: To provide the Dutch public with information on human rights issues in Indonesia and East Timor.

GENERAL INFORMATION: Creation: 1968. **Affiliated to:** International Federation for East Timor. **Personnel/Total:** 12. Salaried: 2. Volunteers: 10. **Budget/Total 1993:** ECU 41000 (US$ 48000). **Financial sources:** Private: 10%. Public: 75%. Self-financing: 15%.

PUBLICATIONS: Periodicals: Indonesia Feiten en Meningen (6). *Annual report. List of publications.*

EVALUATION/RESEARCH: Undertakes research activities.

PLANNED ACTIVITIES: Undertaking campaigns on: "Stop arming Indonesia" and "Women's Labour rights in shoe industries".

INFORMATION AND EDUCATION ACTIVITIES: Topics: Ecology/environment/biodiversity; Food/famine; Gender issues/women; Human rights/peace/conflicts; International relations/cooperation/development aid; Peace/ethnic conflicts/armament/disarmament; Poverty/living conditions. **Activities:** Conferences/seminars/workshops/training activities; Exchanges/twinning/linking; Information and documentation services/data bases; Information campaigns/exhibitions; Lobbying/advocacy.

NLD3171

KOMITEE TWEE ♦ Committee Two

Postbus 4300 , 2003 EH Haarlem, The Netherlands.

Telephone: 31 (23) 54 02 223. *Fax:* 31 (23) 53 67 518. *Contact:* R. Knippenberg.

NLD3172

KOMITEE WETENSCHAP EN TECHNIEK VOOR VIETNAM

Prinseneiland 13-15, 1013 LL Amsterdam, The Netherlands.

Telephone: 31 (20) 52 56 355. *Contact:* Dhr. P. de Goeje.

NLD3173

KONINKLIJK INSTITUUT VOOR DE TROPEN (KIT) ♦ Royal Tropical Institute

63 Mauritskade, 1092 AD Amsterdam, The Netherlands.

Telephone: 31 (20) 56 88 711. *Fax:* 31 (20) 66 84 579. *Contact:* N.H. Vink, Director General.

OBJECTIVES: To contribute to the sustainable development of non-Western countries and to inform the Dutch public on the tropics and subtropics. To disseminate research on health, rural development and culture.

GENERAL INFORMATION: Creation: 1910. **Affiliated to:** European Consortium for Agricultural Research in the Tropics. **Personnel/Total:** 488. Salaried: 488 of which: 55 in developing countries. **Budget/Total 1993:** ECU 27620000 (US$ 32305000). **Financial sources:** Public: 45%. Self-financing: 55%.

PUBLICATIONS: Periodicals: KIT Newsletter (2) - AIDS Promotional Health Exchange (4). *Annual report. List of publications.*

EVALUATION/RESEARCH: Evaluation reports available. Undertakes research activities.

PLANNED ACTIVITIES: Organising an exhibition in the Tropenmuseum on puppet theatre in Africa and Asia. Undertaking an integrated health programme in Namibia to support national and district health care.

COMMENTS: Undertakes activities in the Commonwealth of Independent States. Information activities related to the Commonwealth of Independent States.

ACTIVITIES IN DEVELOPING REGIONS: Present in developing regions. Active in 79 country(ies). Maintains local field presence. Works through local field partners. **Sustainable Development Actions:** Children/youth/family; Ecology/environment/biodiversity; Education/training/literacy; Gender issues/women; Health/sanitation/water; Other; Rural development/agriculture; Sending volunteers/experts/technical assistance; Small enterprises/informal sector/handicrafts; Urban development/habitat. **Regions:** Caribbean; Central Africa; Central Asia and South Asia; East Africa; Mexico and Central America; Middle East; North Africa; South America; South East Asia; Southern Africa; West Africa.

INFORMATION AND EDUCATION ACTIVITIES: Topics: Children/youth/family; Culture/tradition/religion; Ecology/environment/biodiversity; Gender issues/women; Health/sanitation/water; International economic relations/trade/debt/finance; International relations/cooperation/development aid; Population/family planning/demography; Poverty/living conditions; Rural development/agriculture; Urban development/habitat. **Activities:** Broadcasting/cultural events; Conferences/seminars/workshops/training activities; Exchanges/twinning/linking; Formal education; Information and documentation services/data bases; Information campaigns/exhibitions; Networking/electronic telecommunications; Publishing/audiovisual materials/educational materials.

NLD3174

KONTAKT DER KONTINENTEN (KDK)

Amersfoortsestraat 20, 3769 AS Soesterberg, The Netherlands.

Telephone: 31 (34) 63 51 755. *Fax:* 31 (34) 63 54 735. *Contact:* Wico Bunskoek.

OBJECTIVES: To accelerate the development process aimed at promoting equality of opportunity among the rich and the poor. To reduce the intolerable poverty in developing countries. To evoke in the Netherlands society an interest in development co-operation.

GENERAL INFORMATION: Creation: 1961. **Affiliated to:** PSO (Netherlands) - FORUM. **Personnel/Total:** 65. Salaried: 65. **Budget/Total 1993:** ECU 2302000 (US$ 2692000). **Financial sources:** Public: 27%. Self-financing: 73%.

PUBLICATIONS: *Annual report.*

EVALUATION/RESEARCH: Evaluation reports available.

COMMENTS: Undertakes activities in the Commonwealth of Independent States. Information activities related to the Commonwealth of Independent States.

INFORMATION AND EDUCATION ACTIVITIES: Topics: Children/youth/family; Culture/tradition/religion; Ecology/environment/biodiversity; Education/training/literacy; Emergency relief/refugees/humanitarian assistance; Employment/unemployment; Food/famine; Gender issues/women; Health/sanitation/water; Human rights/peace/conflicts; International economic relations/trade/debt/finance; International relations/cooperation/development aid; Peace/ethnic conflicts/armament/disarmament; Population/family planning/demography; Poverty/living conditions; Racism/xenophobia/antisemitism; Refugees/migrants/ethnic groups; Rural development/agriculture; Urban development/habitat. **Activities:** Conferences/seminars/workshops/training activities.

NLD3175

KONTAKTGROEP NEDERLANDSE VRIJWILLIGERS (KNV) ♦ Dutch Volunteers Liaison Committee

Keizersgracht 181, 1016 DR Amsterdam, The Netherlands.

Telephone: 31 (20) 25 72 12 . *Contact:* Mrs. Berentsen, Chairperson.

NLD3176

KWALITEITS CENTRUM HGZO, LEIDSE HOGESCHOOL (HGZO-OC/GZ) ♦ Centre for Quality Improvement of Public Health Services

Leidse Hogeschool, Sector Hoger Gezondheidsorg Onderwijs, Endegeesterwatering 22, 2333 CG Leiden, The Netherlands.

Telephone: 31 (71) 51 71 121. *Fax:* 31 (71) 51 54 041. *Contact:* A.C. Voordouw.

OBJECTIVES: To improve the quality of public health care by offering post-graduate courses and in-company training, both national and international, for nurses and paramedical officers.

GENERAL INFORMATION: *Creation:* 1991. *Personnel/Total:* 3. *Salaried:* 3. *Budget/Total 1993:* ECU 230000 (US$ 269000). *Financial sources:* Public: 40%. Self-financing: 60%.

EVALUATION/RESEARCH: Evaluation reports available. Undertakes research activities.

PLANNED ACTIVITIES: Undertaking a project for management of health care institutions in St. Petersburg, Russia. Improving public health education in Costa Rica.

COMMENTS: Undertakes activities in the Commonwealth of Independent States. Information activities related to the Commonwealth of Independent States.

ACTIVITIES IN DEVELOPING REGIONS: Present in developing regions. Active in 1 country(ies). Works through local field partners. **Sustainable Development Actions:** Education/training/literacy; Health/sanitation/water. **Regions:** West Africa.

INFORMATION AND EDUCATION ACTIVITIES: Topics: Health/sanitation/water. **Activities:** Conferences/seminars/workshops/training activities; Formal education.

NLD3177

LANDELIJK BERAAD STEDENBANDEN NEDERLAND-NICARAGUA (LBSNN)

Postbus 202, 1000 AE Amsterdam, The Netherlands.

Telephone: 31 (20) 55 22 505. *Fax:* 31 (20) 55 23 426.

NLD3178

LANDELIJK NETWERK ONTWIKKELINGSEDUCATIE (LNO) ♦
National Development Education Network

Heresingel 13, 9711 ER Groningen, The Netherlands.

Telephone: 31 (50) 36 35 655. *Contact:* C. Bartelds.

NLD3179

LANDELIJK SERVICEBUREAU ONTWIKKELINGSEDUCATIE (LSO) ♦ National Centre for Global Education in Schools

Oostenburgervoorstraat 90, 1018 MR Amsterdam, The Netherlands.

Telephone: 31 (20) 62 04 815. *Fax:* 31 (20) 63 91 499. *E-mail:* LSO@antenna.nl. *Contact:* G.A. Lommerse, Co-ordinator.

OBJECTIVES: To advise teachers from all types of schools about training on development issues. To offer information on good teaching material, classified according to age, target group, theme and classroom use.

GENERAL INFORMATION: *Creation:* 1986. *Personnel/Total:* 5. *Salaried:* 5. *Budget/Total 1993:* ECU 276000 (US$ 323000). *Financial sources:* Public: 90%. Self-financing: 10%.

PUBLICATIONS: *Periodicals:* Newsletter (4) - Onze Wereld Spiegel (1) - Catalogue (1). *Annual report. List of publications.*

EVALUATION/RESEARCH: Evaluation reports available. Undertakes research activities.

PLANNED ACTIVITIES: Organising an international educational exchange to explore the possibilities of integrating issues of development, environment and peace in education.

COMMENTS: Undertakes activities in the Commonwealth of Independent States. Information activities related to the Commonwealth of Independent States.

INFORMATION AND EDUCATION ACTIVITIES: Topics: Children/youth/family; Culture/tradition/religion; Ecology/environment/biodiversity; Food/famine; Gender issues/women; Health/sanitation/water; Human rights/peace/conflicts; International relations/cooperation/development

aid; Population/family planning/demography; Poverty/living conditions; Refugees/migrants/ethnic groups. **Activities:** Conferences/seminars/workshops/training activities; Exchanges/twinning/linking; Formal education; Fund raising; Information and documentation services/data bases; Publishing/audiovisual materials/educational materials.

NLD3180

LANDELIJKE INDIA WERKGROEP (LIW) ♦ India Committee of the Netherlands

Oudegracht 36, 3511 AP Utrecht, The Netherlands.

Telephone: 31 (30) 23 21 340. *Fax:* 31 (30) 23 22 246. *Contact:* Gerard Oonk.

NLD3181

LATYNS AMERIKA CENTRUM (LAC) ♦ Latin America Centre

Nieuwe Herengracht 29, 1011 RL Amsterdam, The Netherlands.

Telephone: 31 (20) 62 70 307. *Fax:* 31 (20) 62 65 258. *E-mail:* Lac@Lac.Lacktic.nl. *Contact:* W. Langedÿk.

OBJECTIVES: To inform the Dutch population on the most recent political, socio-economic and cultural processes in Latin America.

GENERAL INFORMATION: *Creation:* 1994. *Personnel/Total:* 44. *Salaried:* 4. *Volunteers:* 40 of which: 5 in developing countries. *Budget/Total 1993:* ECU 69000 (US$ 80000). *Financial sources:* Private: 30%. Public: 60%. Self-financing: 5%.

PUBLICATIONS: *Periodicals:* Alerta (10) - Revista Latina (6). *Annual report. List of publications.*

EVALUATION/RESEARCH: Evaluation reports available.

PLANNED ACTIVITIES: Organising seminars on multiculturalism and youth exchange programmes.

ACTIVITIES IN DEVELOPING REGIONS: Works through local field partners. **Sustainable Development Actions:** Debt/finance/trade; Democracy/good governance/institution building/participatory development; Energy/transport; Gender issues/women; Human rights/peace/conflicts; Population/family planning/demography; Rural development/agriculture; Sending volunteers/experts/technical assistance; Small enterprises/informal sector/handicrafts; Urban development/habitat. **Regions:** South America.

INFORMATION AND EDUCATION ACTIVITIES: Topics: Culture/tradition/religion; Education/training/literacy; Emergency relief/refugees/humanitarian assistance; Employment/unemployment; Gender issues/women; Human rights/peace/conflicts; International economic relations/trade/debt/finance; International relations/cooperation/development aid; Peace/ethnic conflicts/armament/disarmament; Population/family planning/demography; Poverty/living conditions; Racism/xenophobia/antisemitism; Rural development/agriculture; Urban development/habitat. **Activities:** Broadcasting/cultural events; Conferences/seminars/workshops/training activities; Exchanges/twinning/linking; Fund raising; Information and documentation services/data bases; Information campaigns/exhibitions; Lobbying/advocacy; Networking/electronic telecommunications; Publishing/audiovisual materials/educational materials.

NLD3182

MANAGEMENT FOR DEVELOPMENT FOUNDATION (MDF)

Postbus 430, 6710 BK Ede, The Netherlands.

Telephone: 31 (318) 65 00 60. *Fax:* 31 (318) 61 45 03. *Contact:* Drs. H. L. van Loo, Executive Director.

NLD3183

MATRIX CONSULTANTS IN DEVELOPMENT MANAGEMENT (MATRIX) ♦ Matrix Consultants en gestion du développement

Korte Jansstraat 7, 3512 GM Utrecht, The Netherlands.

Telephone: 31 (30) 23 10 784. *Fax:* 31 (30) 23 22 568. *Contact:* Ir. A. Hordijk.

OBJECTIVES: To contribute to the improvement of project management in the fields of renewable energy, water and sanitation, women and development, NGOs and technology transfer.

GENERAL INFORMATION: *Creation:* 1986. *Personnel/Total:* 24. *Salaried:* 24. *Financial sources: Self-financing:* 100%.

PUBLICATIONS: *Annual report.*

EVALUATION/RESEARCH: Undertakes research activities.

COMMENTS: Matrix consultants is an independent group of professionals with the aim of improving the quality of international development cooperation by helping institutions develop their capacities to manage change. Undertakes activities in the Commonwealth of Independent States.

ACTIVITIES IN DEVELOPING REGIONS: Active in 31 country(ies). Works through local field partners. **Sustainable Development Actions:** Debt/finance/trade; Democracy/good governance/institution building/participatory development; Ecology/environment/biodiversity; Education/training/literacy; Emergency relief/refugees/humanitarian assistance; Energy/transport; Food/famine; Gender issues/women; Health/sanitation/water; Rural development/agriculture; Small enterprises/informal sector/handicrafts. **Regions:** Caribbean; Central Asia and South Asia; East Africa; East Asia; Mexico and Central America; Middle East; North Africa; South America; South East Asia; Southern Africa; West Africa.

INFORMATION AND EDUCATION ACTIVITIES: Topics: Ecology/environment/biodiversity; Education/training/literacy; Emergency relief/refugees/humanitarian assistance; Employment/unemployment; Food/famine; Gender issues/women; Health/sanitation/water; Human rights/peace/conflicts; International economic relations/trade/debt/finance; International relations/cooperation/development aid; Refugees/migrants/ethnic groups; Rural development/agriculture; Urban development/habitat. **Activities:** Other.

NLD3184

MEDISCH COMITE NEDERLAND VIETNAM (MCNV) ♦ Medical Committee Netherlands Vietnam

Postbus 75701, Weteringschans 32, 1070 AS Amsterdam, The Netherlands.

Telephone: 31 (20) 62 70 411. *Fax:* 31 (20) 62 50 147. *E-mail:* MCNW@TOOL.NL.

OBJECTIVES: To prevent major public health problems and strengthen the health care system in Vietnam. To advance accessibility of health care for the most vulnerable groups and support local initiatives and existing programmes. To create sustainable projects which can be transferred to the responsibility of local authorities. To inform the Dutch public about Vietnam.

GENERAL INFORMATION: *Creation:* 1968. *Personnel/Total:* 8. *Salaried:* 5. *Volunteers:* 3. *Budget/Total 1993:* ECU 1151000 (US$ 1346000). *Financial sources: Private:* 85%. *Self-financing:* 15%.

PUBLICATIONS: *Periodicals:* MCNV-Krant (6) - Reiskrant (1). *Annual report. List of publications.*

EVALUATION/RESEARCH: Evaluation reports available. Undertakes research activities.

PLANNED ACTIVITIES: Support to national tuberculosis programme in Vietnam, malaria control, Dengue prevention project, support to Dong Ha Hospital, Primary Health Care project

ACTIVITIES IN DEVELOPING REGIONS: Present in developing regions. Active in 1 country(ies). Works through local field partners. **Sustainable Development Actions:** Health/sanitation/water. **Regions:** South East Asia.

INFORMATION AND EDUCATION ACTIVITIES: Topics: Culture/tradition/religion; Gender issues/women; Health/sanitation/water. **Activities:** Conferences/seminars/workshops/training activities; Formal education; Fund raising; Information and documentation services/data bases; Information campaigns/exhibitions; Lobbying/advocacy.

NLD3185

MEDISCH COORDINATIE SECRETARIAAT (MCS) ♦ Medical Coordination Secretariat

Postbus 12, 2340 AA Oegstgeest, The Netherlands.

Telephone: 31 (71) 51 77 900. *Fax:* 31 (71) 51 53 601. *Contact:* J. N. Breevelt.

OBJECTIVES: To serve as an advisory board for participating protestant organisations in the Netherlands concerning their health and development activities in the Third World. To select and recruit medical personnel for such programmes.

GENERAL INFORMATION: *Creation:* 1978. *Personnel/Total:* 4. *Salaried:* 4. *Budget/Total 1993:* ECU 184000 (US$ 215000). *Financial sources: Private:* 100%.

ACTIVITIES IN DEVELOPING REGIONS: Works through local field partners. **Sustainable Development Actions:** Health/sanitation/water; Population/family planning/demography. **Regions:** Caribbean; Central Africa; Central Asia and South Asia; East Africa; Mexico and Central America; South America; South East Asia; Southern Africa; West Africa.

NLD3186

MEMISA MEDICUS MUNDI

Eendrachtsweg 48, Postbus 61, 3000 AB Rotterdam, The Netherlands.

Telephone: 31 (10) 41 44 888. *Fax:* 31 (10) 40 47 319. *E-mail:* operations@memisa.nl. *Contact:* Johan Rademaker, General Manager.

OBJECTIVES: To promote primary health care in developing countries.

GENERAL INFORMATION: *Creation:* 1925. *Affiliated to:* Medicus Mundi Internationalis. *Personnel/Total:* 205. *Salaried:* 200 of which: 150 in developing countries. *Volunteers:* 5. *Budget/Total 1993:* ECU 22298000 (US$ 26079000). *Financial sources: Private:* 52%. *Public:* 45%. *Self-financing:* 3%.

PUBLICATIONS: *Periodicals:* Memisma Nieuws (4) - Memisma Mgisch (6). *Annual report. List of publications.*

EVALUATION/RESEARCH: Evaluation reports available. Undertakes research activities.

ACTIVITIES IN DEVELOPING REGIONS: Present in developing regions. Active in 60 country(ies). Maintains local field presence. Works through local field partners. **Sustainable Development Actions:** Emergency relief/refugees/humanitarian assistance; Health/sanitation/water; Sending volunteers/experts/technical assistance. **Regions:** Caribbean; Central Africa; Central Asia and South Asia; East Africa; East Asia; Mexico and Central America; Oceania; South America; South East Asia; West Africa.

INFORMATION AND EDUCATION ACTIVITIES: Topics: Emergency relief/refugees/humanitarian assistance; Health/sanitation/water. **Activities:** Conferences/seminars/workshops/training activities; Fund raising; Lobbying/advocacy; Networking/electronic telecommunications.

NLD3187

MISSIE EN JONGEREN ♦ Mission and Youth

Dr. Peelenstraat 8, 5831 EG Boxmeer, The Netherlands.

Telephone: 31 (48) 55 75 530. *Fax:* 31 (48) 55 78 987. *Contact:* Willem van Beek.

OBJECTIVES: To encourage young people to become interested in Third World issues and the mission movement. To give them an opportunity to experience living in a developing country.

GENERAL INFORMATION: *Creation:* 1988. *Personnel/Total:* 28. *Salaried:* 3. *Volunteers:* 25 of which: 25 in developing countries. *Budget/Total 1993:* ECU 207000 (US$ 284000). *Financial sources: Private:* 95%. *Public:* 5%.

PUBLICATIONS: *Annual report. List of publications.*

COMMENTS: Undertakes activities in the Commonwealth of Independent States. Information activities related to the Commonwealth of Independent States.

ACTIVITIES IN DEVELOPING REGIONS: Active in 12 country(ies). Maintains local field presence. Works through local field partners. **Sustainable Development Actions:** Children/youth/family; Education/training/literacy; Health/sanitation/water; Small enterprises/informal sector/handicrafts. **Regions:** East Africa; Mexico and Central America; South America; South East Asia; West Africa.

Voir : *Comment utiliser le répertoire,* page 11.

INFORMATION AND EDUCATION ACTIVITIES: **Topics:** Children/youth/family; Culture/tradition/religion; International relations/cooperation/development aid; Peace/ethnic conflicts/armament/disarmament; Poverty/living conditions; Racism/xenophobia/antisemitism; Refugees/migrants/ethnic groups. **Activities:** Conferences/seminars/workshops/training activities; Exchanges/twinning/linking; Information campaigns/exhibitions.

NLD3188

MISSIONAIR CENTRUM (MC) ♦ Missionary Centre

Gasthuisstraat 19, 6411 KD Heerlen, The Netherlands.

Telephone: 31 (45) 57 11 980. *Contact:* Meindert Muller, Director.

NLD3189

MONDIALE WERKPLAATS (MW) ♦ World Workshop

Bilstraat 449, 3572 AW Utrecht, The Netherlands.

Telephone: 31 (30) 23 33 154. *Fax:* 31 (30) 23 31 055. *Contact:* M.A. Van Grafhorst, Director.

OBJECTIVES: To help children become aware that they too have a growing responsibility for the world.

GENERAL INFORMATION: *Creation:* 1979. *Member organisations:* 4. *Personnel/Total:* 2. *Salaried:* 1. *Volunteers:* 1. *Budget/Total 1993:* ECU 138000 (US$ 162000). *Financial sources:* Private: 90%. *Self-financing:* 10%.

PUBLICATIONS: *Periodicals:* Tambura (6) - Marimba (6) - Docent (6). *Annual report. List of publications.*

EVALUATION/RESEARCH: Evaluation reports available. Undertakes research activities.

COMMENTS: Undertakes activities in the Commonwealth of Independent States. Information activities related to the Commonwealth of Independent States.

ACTIVITIES IN DEVELOPING REGIONS: Active in 3 country(ies). Works through local field partners. **Sustainable Development Actions:** Children/youth/family; Education/training/literacy. **Regions:** South America; West Africa.

INFORMATION AND EDUCATION ACTIVITIES: Topics: Children/youth/family; Culture/tradition/religion. **Activities:** Broadcasting/cultural events; Formal education; Information and documentation services/data bases; Information campaigns/exhibitions; Publishing/audiovisual materials/educational materials.

NLD3190

NATIONALE COMMISSIE VOORLICHTING EN BEWUSTWORDING ONTWIKKELINGSSAMENWERK-ING (NCO) ♦ National Committee for Development Education

Postbus 18184, 1001 ZB Amsterdam, The Netherlands.

Telephone: 31 (20) 55 03 555. *Fax:* 31 (20) 62 08 716. *Contact:* Ton Waarts, Director.

OBJECTIVES: To encourage and to sponsor information and education activities in the Netherlands on international development.

GENERAL INFORMATION: *Creation:* 1970. *Type of organisation:* association of NGOs. *Member organisations:* 32. *Personnel/Total:* 15. *Salaried:* 15. *Budget/Total 1993:* ECU 9069000 (US$ 10607000). *Financial sources:* Public: 100%.

PUBLICATIONS: *Periodicals:* NCO Informatre (3). *Annual report. List of publications.*

EVALUATION/RESEARCH: Evaluation reports available. Undertakes research activities.

PLANNED ACTIVITIES: Holding a human rights survey in 1996.

COMMENTS: NCO's 1995 budget consists of 17.2 for education and inforamtion activities in Holland and 2.5 for financial support to small development projects in developing countries adopted by local communities in the Netherlands. Information activities related to the Commonwealth of Independent States.

INFORMATION AND EDUCATION ACTIVITIES: **Topics:** Children/youth/family; Culture/tradition/religion; Ecology/environment/biodiversity; Education/training/literacy; Emergency relief/refugees/humanitarian assistance; Employment/unemployment; Food/famine; Gender issues/women; Health/sanitation/water; Human rights/peace/conflicts; International economic relations/trade/debt/finance; International relations/cooperation/development aid; Peace/ethnic conflicts/armament/disarmament; Population/family planning/demography; Poverty/living conditions; Racism/xenophobia/antisemitism; Refugees/migrants/ethnic groups; Rural development/agriculture; Urban development/habitat. **Activities:** Broadcasting/cultural events; Conferences/seminars/workshops/training activities; Formal education; Information and documentation services/data bases; Information campaigns/exhibitions; Networking/electronic telecommunications; Publishing/audiovisual materials/educational materials.

NLD3191

NEDERLANDS CENTRUM VOOR INHEEMSE VOLKEN (NCIV)

Postbus 4098, 1009 AB Amsterdam, The Netherlands.

Telephone: 31 (20) 69 38 625. *Fax:* 31 (20) 66 52 818.

NLD3192

NEDERLANDS COMITE VAN WORLD UNIVERSITY SERVICE (WUS-NETHERLANDS) ♦ Dutch Committee of World University Service

Oranje Nassaulaan 5, 1075 AH Amsterdam, The Netherlands.

Telephone: 31 (20) 71 59 15. *Contact:* F.H. Tunnissen, Secretary.

NLD3193

NEDERLANDS FAO COMITE

Prinsevinkenpark 19, 2585 HK Den Haag, The Netherlands.

Telephone: 31 (70) 35 26 666. *Fax:* 31 (70) 35 22 701.

NLD3194

NEDERLANDS INSTITUUT VOOR INTERNATIONALE BETREKKINGEN, CLINGENDAEL ♦ Netherlands Institute of International Relations, Clingendael

Postbus 93080, 2509 AB Den Haag, The Netherlands.

Telephone: 31 (70) 32 45 384. *Fax:* 31 (70) 32 82 002. *E-mail:* info@clingendael.nl. *Contact:* F. van Staden.

OBJECTIVES: To promote the understanding of international affairs with special attention devoted to NATO, the European Community, the United Nations and other international organisations.

GENERAL INFORMATION: *Creation:* 1983. *Personnel/Total:* 50. *Salaried:* 42. *Budget/Total 1993:* ECU 230000 (US$ 269000). *Financial sources:* Public: 60%. Self-financing: 40%.

PUBLICATIONS: *Periodicals:* Internationale Spectator (12). *Annual report. List of publications.*

EVALUATION/RESEARCH: Evaluation reports available. Undertakes research activities.

COMMENTS: Undertakes activities in the Commonwealth of Independent States. Information activities related to the Commonwealth of Independent States.

INFORMATION AND EDUCATION ACTIVITIES: **Topics:** International economic relations/trade/debt/finance; International relations/cooperation/development aid; Peace/ethnic conflicts/armament/disarmament. **Activities:** Conferences/seminars/workshops/training activities; Information and documentation services/data bases; Publishing/audiovisual materials/educational materials.

NLD3195

NEDERLANDS JURISTEN COMITE VOOR DE MENSENRECHTEN (NJCM) ♦ Dutch Commission of Jurists for Human Rights

Hugo De Grootstraat 27, P.O. Box 9520, 2300 RA Leiden, The Netherlands.

See: *How to Use the Directory,* page 11.

Telephone: 31 (71) 52 77 748. *Fax:* 31 (71) 52 77 748. *E-mail:* njcm@rulsur.leiden.univ.nl. *Contact:* H.C. Wiersinga.

OBJECTIVES: To promote human rights and the Rule of Law in the Netherlands and in Dutch foreign policy.

GENERAL INFORMATION: *Creation:* 1974. *Type of organisation:* network. *Affiliated to:* The International Commission of Jurists. *Personnel/Total:* 102. *Salaried:* 2. *Volunteers:* 100. *Budget/Total 1993:* ECU 63000 (US$ 253000). *Financial sources:* Private: 2%. Public: 45%. Self-financing: 53%.

PUBLICATIONS: *Periodicals:* NJCM Bulletin Nederland Tijdschirft (8) - Voor de Mensenrechten/Dutch Review of H.R.. *Annual report. List of publications.*

EVALUATION/RESEARCH: Evaluation reports available. Undertakes research activities.

NLD3196

NEDERLANDSE BOND VAN PLATTELANDSVROUWEN ♦
Dutch Association of Country Women

Postbus 90652, 2509 LR Den Haag, The Netherlands.

Telephone: 31 (70) 32 44 429. *Fax:* 31 (70) 32 64 227. *Contact:* E.A.M. de Zwaan-Heymans, President.

OBJECTIVES: To provide information on the situation of rural women in developing countries. To increase awareness of these topics and to prepare members for social activity. To fundraise for projects initiated by women in developing countries.

GENERAL INFORMATION: *Creation:* 1930. *Type of organisation:* association of NGOs, coordinating body. *Affiliated to:* ACWW (United Kingdom) - Confédération européenne de l'agriculture. *Personnel/Total:* 15022. *Salaried:* 22. *Volunteers:* 15000. *Budget/Total 1993:* ECU 1979000 (US$ 2315000). *Financial sources:* Private: 3%. Public: 19%. Self-financing: 78%.

PUBLICATIONS: *Periodicals:* Plattelandsvrouw Magazine (10). *Annual report. List of publications.*

EVALUATION/RESEARCH: Evaluation reports available.

INFORMATION AND EDUCATION ACTIVITIES: Topics: Culture/tradition/religion; Ecology/environment/biodiversity; Education/training/literacy; Food/famine; Gender issues/women; International economic relations/trade/debt/finance; International relations/cooperation/development aid; Racism/xenophobia/antisemitism; Rural development/agriculture. **Activities:** Conferences/seminars/workshops/training activities; Exchanges/twinning/linking; Information and documentation services/data bases; Information campaigns/exhibitions; Lobbying/advocacy; Publishing/audiovisual materials/educational materials.

NLD3197

NEDERLANDSE FINANCIERINGSMAATSCHAPPIJ VOOR ONTWIKKELINGSLANDEN (FMO) ♦ Dutch Financing Corporation for Developing Countries

Koningskade 40, Postbus 93060, 2509 AB Den Haag, The Netherlands.

Telephone: 31 (70) 31 49 632. *Fax:* 31 (70) 32 46 187. *Contact:* L.B.M. Mennes.

OBJECTIVES: To support the development of private sector entrepreneurship in the industrial and rural sectors of developing countries. To create employment and income generation as well as export opportunities.

GENERAL INFORMATION: *Creation:* 1970. *Affiliated to:* INTERACT (Belgium). *Personnel/Total:* 74. *Salaried:* 74. *Budget/Total 1993:* ECU 760310000 (US$ 188450000). *Financial sources:* Public: 30%. Self-financing: 70%.

PUBLICATIONS: *Annual report.*

COMMENTS: Undertakes activities in the Commonwealth of Independent States.

ACTIVITIES IN DEVELOPING REGIONS: Present in developing regions. Active in 4 country(ies). **Sustainable Development Actions:** Other. **Regions:** Caribbean; Central Africa; Central Asia and South Asia; East Africa; East Asia; Mexico and Central America; Middle East; North

Africa; Oceania; South America; South East Asia; Southern Africa; West Africa.

NLD3198

NEDERLANDSE HERVORMDE KERK (NHK)

Postbus 12, 2340 AA Oegstgeest, The Netherlands.

Telephone: 31 (71) 51 77 900. *Fax:* 31 (71) 51 53 601. *Contact:* Rev. D.C. Nicolai, General Secretary.

OBJECTIVES: To co-operate with churches and Christian organisations mainly in developing countries.

GENERAL INFORMATION: *Creation:* 1951. *Type of organisation:* coordinating body. *Affiliated to:* Network for Mission (Netherlands) - Diaconate (Netherlands) - ZWO (Netherlands) . *Personnel/Total:* 2650. *Salaried:* 150 of which: 75 in developing countries. *Volunteers:* 2500. *Budget/Total 1993:* ECU 6905000 (US$ 8076000). *Financial sources:* Private: 70%. Public: 5%. Self-financing: 25%.

PUBLICATIONS: *Periodicals:* Vandaar (10) - Omkeer (3). *Annual report.*

EVALUATION/RESEARCH: Undertakes research activities.

ACTIVITIES IN DEVELOPING REGIONS: Active in 31 country(ies). Works through local field partners. **Sustainable Development Actions:** Children/youth/family; Democracy/good governance/institution building/participatory development; Education/training/literacy; Gender issues/women; Health/sanitation/water; Human rights/peace/conflicts; Population/family planning/demography; Rural development/agriculture; Sending volunteers/experts/technical assistance; Small enterprises/informal sector/handicrafts. **Regions:** Caribbean; Central Asia and South Asia; East Africa; East Asia; Mexico and Central America; North Africa; South America; South East Asia; Southern Africa; West Africa.

INFORMATION AND EDUCATION ACTIVITIES: Topics: Children/youth/family; Culture/tradition/religion; Education/training/literacy; Gender issues/women; Health/sanitation/water; Human rights/peace/conflicts; International relations/cooperation/development aid; Population/family planning/demography; Rural development/agriculture. **Activities:** Conferences/seminars/workshops/training activities; Exchanges/twinning/linking; Fund raising; Information and documentation services/data bases; Information campaigns/exhibitions; Lobbying/advocacy; Publishing/audiovisual materials/educational materials.

NLD3199

NEDERLANDSE ORGANISATIE VOOR INTERNATIONALE ONTWIKKELINGSSAMENWERKING (NOVIB) ♦ Netherlands Organisation for International Development Co-operation

Amaliastraat 7, 2514 JC Den Haag, The Netherlands.

Telephone: 31 (70) 34 21 625. *Fax:* 31 (70) 36 14 461. *E-mail:* ADMIN@NOVIB.ANTENNA.NL. *Contact:* M. van den Berg, Secretary General.

OBJECTIVES: To provide aid to partners and the underprivileged in developing countries and to exert political pressure in their favour. To involve as many people and organisations as possible in the joint responsability for world development.

GENERAL INFORMATION: *Creation:* 1956. *Member organisations:* 50. *Affiliated to:* SID (The Netherlands) - ICVA (Switzerland) - SANAM (Belgium) - Acord (United Kingdom) - Eurostep (Belgium). *Personnel/Total:* 250. *Budget/Total 1993:* ECU 78258000 (US$ 91531000). *Financial sources:* Public: 69%.

PUBLICATIONS: *Periodicals:* Novib News (6). *Annual report. List of publications.*

EVALUATION/RESEARCH: Evaluation reports available. Undertakes research activities.

COMMENTS: Undertakes activities in the Commonwealth of Independent States. Information activities related to the Commonwealth of Independent States.

ACTIVITIES IN DEVELOPING REGIONS: Active in 48 country(ies). Works through local field partners. **Sustainable Development Actions:** Democracy/good governance/institution building/participatory development; Ecology/environment/biodiversity; Education/training/literacy; Emergency relief/refugees/humanitarian assistance; Food/famine; Gen-

der issues/women; Health/sanitation/water; Human rights/peace/conflicts; Population/family planning/demography; Rural development/agriculture; Small enterprises/informal sector/handicrafts; Urban development/habitat. **Regions:** Central Africa; Central Asia and South Asia; East Africa; Mexico and Central America; Middle East; North Africa; South America; South East Asia; Southern Africa; West Africa.

INFORMATION AND EDUCATION ACTIVITIES: Topics: Culture/tradition/religion; Ecology/environment/biodiversity; Education/training/literacy; Emergency relief/refugees/humanitarian assistance; Food/famine; Gender issues/women; Human rights/peace/conflicts; International economic relations/trade/debt/finance; International relations/cooperation/development aid; Peace/ethnic conflicts/armament/disarmament; Poverty/living conditions; Rural development/agriculture; Urban development/habitat. **Activities:** Broadcasting/cultural events; Conferences/seminars/workshops/training activities; Exchanges/twinning/linking; Formal education; Fund raising; Information campaigns/exhibitions; Lobbying/advocacy; Networking/electronic telecommunications; Publishing/audiovisual materials/educational materials.

NLD3200

NEDERLANDSE PALESTINA KOMITEE

Postbus 10520, Lauriergracht 116, 1001 EM Amsterdam, The Netherlands.

Telephone: 31 (20) 62 46 046. *Fax:* 31 (20) 62 68 857.

NLD3201

NEDERLANDSE RODE KRUIS ♦ Netherlands Red Cross

27 Leeghwaterplein, Postbus 28120, 2502 KC Den Haag, The Netherlands.

Telephone: 31 (70) 38 46 868. *Fax:* 31 (70) 38 46 643. *Contact:* W.H. Cense, Director General.

OBJECTIVES: To offer relief without discrimination on any grounds to the wounded, the sick, and all others in need of aid, both in times of peace and war. To participate in all attempts to alleviate or prevent human suffering, wherever found.

GENERAL INFORMATION: *Creation:* 1867. *Affiliated to:* International Federation of Red Cross and Red Crescent Societies (Switzerland). *Personnel/Total:* 32780. *Salaried:* 280 of which: 2 in developing countries. *Volunteers:* 32500 of which: 141 in developing countries. *Budget/Total 1993:* ECU 78258000 (US$ 91531000). *Financial sources:* Private: 72%. Public: 8%. Self-financing: 20%.

PUBLICATIONS: *Periodicals:* Red Cross Courier (6). *Annual report. List of publications.*

EVALUATION/RESEARCH: Evaluation reports available.

COMMENTS: Undertakes activities in the Commonwealth of Independent States.

ACTIVITIES IN DEVELOPING REGIONS: Present in developing regions. Active in 52 country(ies). Maintains local field presence. Works through local field partners. **Sustainable Development Actions:** Democracy/good governance/institution building/participatory development; Emergency relief/refugees/humanitarian assistance; Food/famine; Health/sanitation/water; Rural development/agriculture; Sending volunteers/experts/technical assistance. **Regions:** Caribbean; Central Africa; Central Asia and South Asia; East Africa; East Asia; Middle East; North Africa; South East Asia; Southern Africa; West Africa.

INFORMATION AND EDUCATION ACTIVITIES: Topics: Emergency relief/refugees/humanitarian assistance; Health/sanitation/water; Human rights/peace/conflicts; International relations/cooperation/development aid; Peace/ethnic conflicts/armament/disarmament; Poverty/living conditions; Refugees/migrants/ethnic groups. **Activities:** Formal education; Fund raising; Information and documentation services/data bases; Information campaigns/exhibitions; Lobbying/advocacy; Publishing/audiovisual materials/educational materials.

NLD3202

NEDERLANDSE STICHTING VOOR LEPRABESTRIJDING (NSL) ♦ Netherlands Leprosy Relief Association

Wibautstraat 135, 1097 DN Amsterdam, The Netherlands.

Telephone: 31 (20) 59 50 500. *Fax:* 31 (20) 66 80 823. *Contact:* K.L. Braber.

OBJECTIVES: To directly as well as indirectly promote and render assistance in the prevention of leprosy and its effects in developing countries, irrespective of race, politics or religion.

GENERAL INFORMATION: *Creation:* 1967. *Affiliated to:* ILEP (United Kingdom) - PSO (Netherlands). *Personnel/Total:* 32. *Salaried:* 32 of which: 17 in developing countries. *Budget/Total 1993:* ECU 7343000 (US$ 8588000). *Financial sources:* Private: 80%. Public: 10%. Self-financing: 10%.

PUBLICATIONS: *Periodicals:* De Klepper. *Annual report. List of publications.*

EVALUATION/RESEARCH: Evaluation reports available. Undertakes research activities.

ACTIVITIES IN DEVELOPING REGIONS: Present in developing regions. Active in 17 country(ies). Maintains local field presence. Works through local field partners. **Sustainable Development Actions:** Health/sanitation/water; Sending volunteers/experts/technical assistance. **Regions:** Caribbean; Central Asia and South Asia; East Africa; East Asia; South America; South East Asia; West Africa.

INFORMATION AND EDUCATION ACTIVITIES: Topics: Health/sanitation/water. **Activities:** Conferences/seminars/workshops/training activities; Formal education; Fund raising; Information and documentation services/data bases; Information campaigns/exhibitions; Publishing/audiovisual materials/educational materials.

NLD3203

NEDERLANDSE VERENIGING TOT STEUN AAN DE OECUMENISCHE OWTWIKKELINGSCOOPERATIE (NVOC) ♦ Dutch Support Association for the Ecumenical Development Cooperative Society

Postbus 19120, 3501 DC Utrecht, The Netherlands.

Telephone: 31 (30) 234 10 69. *Contact:* A.H. Verdonk, President.

OBJECTIVES: To promote the activities of the Ecumenical Development Cooperative Society (EDCS) which provides loans at acceptable conditions to co-operative groups in need of capital investment for development projects in developing countries.

GENERAL INFORMATION: *Creation:* 1976. *Personnel/Total:* 26. *Salaried:* 1. *Volunteers:* 25. *Budget/Total 1993:* ECU 129000 (US$ 151000). *Financial sources:* Private: 45%. Self-financing: 55%.

PUBLICATIONS: *Periodicals:* AndersOm (4). *Annual report. List of publications.*

COMMENTS: NVOC's activities are restricted to promotion and advocacy on behalf of EDCS in the Netherlands to encourage people to buy share certificates in the Ecumenical Development Cooperative Society (EDCS). Information activities related to the Commonwealth of Independent States.

INFORMATION AND EDUCATION ACTIVITIES: Topics: Other. **Activities:** Publishing/audiovisual materials/educational materials.

NLD3204

NEDERLANDSE VERENIGING VOOR CULTUUR EN ONTWIKKELING (NVCO) ♦ Dutch Association for Culture and Development

Amersfoortsestraat 20, 3769 AS Soesterberg, The Netherlands.

Telephone: 31 (346) 351 755. *Fax:* 31 (346) 354 735. *Contact:* Dr. C. Hamelink, President.

OBJECTIVES: To bring about critical reflection on various forms of international co-operation from a cultural perspective.

GENERAL INFORMATION: *Creation:* 1987. *Member organisations:* 40. *Affiliated to:* South-North Network on Cultural Development (Belgium). *Volunteers:* 5. *Budget/Total 1993:* ECU 18000 (US$ 22000). *Financial sources:* Private: 94%. Public: 1%. Self-financing: 5%.

PUBLICATIONS: *Periodicals:* Tussenijdsbericht (3). *Annual report. List of publications.*

INFORMATION AND EDUCATION ACTIVITIES: **Topics:** Culture/tradition/religion; Human rights/peace/conflicts; International relations/cooperation/development aid. **Activities:** Conferences/seminars/workshops/training activities; Information and documentation services/data bases; Lobbying/advocacy.

NLD3205

NEDERLANDSE VERENIGING VOOR EEN NIEUW INTERNATIONAAL ONTWIKKELINGSBELEID (NIO) ♦ Dutch Association for a New Development Co-operation Policy

Wilhelmina Gasthuisplein 61, 1054 RB Amsterdam, Netherlands.

Telephone: 31 (20) 61 21 220. *Fax:* 31 (20) 61 65 726. *Contact:* Arjen Alberts.

NLD3206

NETHERLANDS ASSOCIATION FOR THE UNITED NATIONS (NVUN)

Alexanderstraat 20-2, 2514 JM Den Haag, The Netherlands.

Telephone: 31 (70) 34 20 351. *Fax:* 31 (70) 34 20 359. *Contact:* G. Ringnalda, Chairman.

OBJECTIVES: To inform the Dutch public on the work of the United Nations. To organise symposia and publish a quarterly "UN Forum".

GENERAL INFORMATION: *Creation:* 1987. *Affiliated to:* World Federation of United Nations Associations. *Volunteers:* 300. *Budget/Total 1993:* ECU 9000 (US$ 11000). *Financial sources:* Self-financing: 100%.

PUBLICATIONS: *Periodicals:* UN Forum (4). *Annual report.*

NLD3207

THE NETHERLANDS COMMITTEE OF THE INTERNATIONAL COUNCIL ON SOCIAL WELFARE (ICSW-NEDERLAND)

P.O. Box 110, 2280 AC Rijswijk, The Netherlands.

Telephone: 31 (70) 39 49 349. *Fax:* 31 (70) 39 64 308. *Contact:* Drs L.M. Horn.

OBJECTIVES: To exchange information nationally and internationally on social welfare issues. To develop an international policy on welfare.

GENERAL INFORMATION: *Type of organisation:* association of NGOs. *Affiliated to:* The Netherlands Foundation for Rehabilitation (Netherlands) - Consultative Council on the Disabled (Netherlands) - Social and Planning Office (Netherlands) - Employers'Organisation of Social Welfare and Care Services (Netherlands) - Union of Local Authorities (Netherlands). *Salaried:* 2. *Financial sources:* Public: 100%.

PUBLICATIONS: *Periodicals:* PIW Bulletin (4). *Annual report.*

COMMENTS: Information activities related to the Commonwealth of Independent States.

INFORMATION AND EDUCATION ACTIVITIES: Topics: Other. **Activities:** Conferences/seminars/workshops/training activities.

NLD3208

NETHERLANDS NETWORK FOR URBAN DEVELOPMENT (URBANETH)

Postbus 1935, Weena 718, 3000 BX Rotterdam, The Netherlands.

Telephone: 31 (10) 40 21 558. *Fax:* 31 (10) 40 45 671.

NLD3209

NETHERLANDS ORGANISATION FOR MANPOWER DEVELOPMENT ASSISTANCE (NOMDA)

Postbus 17477, 1001 JL Amsterdam, The Netherlands.

Telephone: 31 (20) 62 25 446. *Fax:* 31 (20) 63 86 763. *Contact:* L. Nanta.

OBJECTIVES: To assist in the development of formal vocational training/education in the fields of health, agriculture and technical subjects.

GENERAL INFORMATION: *Creation:* 1990. *Personnel/Total:* 13. *Salaried:* 1. *Volunteers:* 12 of which: 3 in developing countries. *Budget/*

Total 1993: ECU 14000 (US$ 16000). *Financial sources:* Private: 36%. Public: 4%. Self-financing: 60%.

PUBLICATIONS: *Annual report.*

EVALUATION/RESEARCH: Undertakes research activities.

ACTIVITIES IN DEVELOPING REGIONS: Present in developing regions. Active in 6 country(ies). Maintains local field presence. **Sustainable Development Actions:** Education/training/literacy; Sending volunteers/experts/technical assistance. **Regions:** East Africa; Southern Africa.

INFORMATION AND EDUCATION ACTIVITIES: Topics: Education/training/literacy. **Activities:** Exchanges/twinning/linking; Formal education; Fund raising; Information campaigns/exhibitions; Lobbying/advocacy.

NLD3210

NICARAGUA KOMITEE NEDERLAND

Minahassastraat 1, 1094 RS Amsterdam, The Netherlands.

Telephone: 31 (575) 51 10 94. *Contact:* B. Prins.

NLD3211

OIKOS ♦ Interchurch Development Organisation for Research, Education and Campaign in the Netherlands

Mariahoek 16/17, Postbus 19170, 3501 DD Utrecht, The Netherlands.

Telephone: 31 (30) 23 19 424. *Fax:* 31 (30) 23 64 903. *Contact:* A. Leeuwis.

OBJECTIVES: To investigate issues with root causes in Northern countries. To educate people on these issues and to initiate political campaigns.

GENERAL INFORMATION: *Creation:* 1972. *Affiliated to:* Food for the Future (the Netherlands) - Development Education Network of the World Council of Churches (Switzerland) - Eurodad (Belgium) - European Eucumenical Cooperation on Development (Belgium). *Personnel/Total:* 20. *Budget/Total 1993:* ECU 598000 (US$ 700000). *Financial sources:* Private: 55%. Public: 45%.

PUBLICATIONS: *Periodicals:* OIKOS Nieuws (4). *Annual report. List of publications.*

EVALUATION/RESEARCH: Undertakes research activities.

INFORMATION AND EDUCATION ACTIVITIES: Topics: Children/youth/family; Food/famine; Gender issues/women; International economic relations/trade/debt/finance; International relations/cooperation/development aid; Peace/ethnic conflicts/armament/disarmament; Population/family planning/demography; Refugees/migrants/ethnic groups; Rural development/agriculture. **Activities:** Conferences/seminars/workshops/training activities; Information and documentation services/data bases; Information campaigns/exhibitions; Lobbying/advocacy; Networking/electronic telecommunications; Publishing/audiovisual materials/educational materials.

NLD3212

ONDERWIJS PROJEKT AMSTERDAM-MANAGUA (OPAM) ♦ Education Project Amsterdam-Managua

Nieuwe Herengracht 29, 1011 RL Amsterdam, The Netherlands.

Telephone: 31 (20) 62 29 953. *Fax:* 31 (20) 62 65 258. *Contact:* Ralf Maslowski.

OBJECTIVES: To promote exchange of information between schools in Amsterdam and Managua. To stimulate and support development education in primary and secondary schools in Amsterdam.

GENERAL INFORMATION: *Creation:* 1985. *Affiliated to:* Landelijk Beraad Stedenbanden Nederland -Nicaragua (The NEtherlands). *Personnel/Total:* 2. *Salaried:* 1 of which: 1 in developing countries. *Volunteers:* 1 of which: 1 in developing countries. *Budget/Total 1993:* ECU 22000 (US$ 26000). *Financial sources:* Private: 10%. Public: 85%. Self-financing: 5%.

PUBLICATIONS: *Annual report. List of publications.*

EVALUATION/RESEARCH: Evaluation reports available.

PLANNED ACTIVITIES: Setting up an inventory of educational materials about Nicaragua.

Voir : *Comment utiliser le répertoire*, page 11.

ACTIVITIES IN DEVELOPING REGIONS: Present in developing regions. Active in 1 country(ies). Maintains local field presence. **Sustainable Development Actions:** Education/training/literacy. **Regions:** Mexico and Central America.

INFORMATION AND EDUCATION ACTIVITIES: Topics: Children/youth/family; Culture/tradition/religion; Ecology/environment/biodiversity; Education/training/literacy; Food/famine; Health/sanitation/water; International economic relations/trade/debt/finance; International relations/cooperation/development aid; Urban development/habitat. **Activities:** Formal education; Fund raising; Publishing/audiovisual materials/educational materials.

NLD3213

OOGKAMP HIMALAYA

Postbus 174, 2110 AD Aerdenhout, The Netherlands.

Telephone: 31 (23) 52 90 073. **Fax:** 31 (23) 52 86 922. **Contact:** Peter de Boer, President.

OBJECTIVES: To support financially programmes for the prevention of blindness in the Himalayan region.

GENERAL INFORMATION: Creation: 1984. **Affiliated to:** International Association for the Prevention of Blindness. **Personnel/Total:** 46. Salaried: 40 of which: 40 in developing countries. Volunteers: 6. **Budget/Total 1993:** ECU 460000 (US$ 538000). **Financial sources:** Private: 90%. Self-financing: 10%.

PUBLICATIONS: Periodicals: Op Ooghoogte (2). Annual report.

EVALUATION/RESEARCH: Evaluation reports available.

PLANNED ACTIVITIES: Starting an eye care programme in Tibet, Bhutan and Sikkim. Establishing an eye care training centre in Nepal.

ACTIVITIES IN DEVELOPING REGIONS: Present in developing regions. Active in 2 country(ies). Maintains local field presence. **Sustainable Development Actions:** Health/sanitation/water. **Regions:** Central Asia and South Asia.

INFORMATION AND EDUCATION ACTIVITIES: Topics: Health/sanitation/water. **Activities:** Conferences/seminars/workshops/training activities; Fund raising; Information and documentation services/data bases; Information campaigns/exhibitions; Publishing/audiovisual materials/educational materials.

NLD3214

OPLEIDINGSCENTRUM VOOR DIERVEREDELING, DIERVERZORGING EN DE MENGVOEDER INDUSTRIE BARNEVELD ♦ International Training Centre on Animal Husbandry and Milling Technology, IPC Livestock Barneveld College

32 Wesselseweg, Postbus 64, 3770 AB Barneveld, The Netherlands.

Telephone: 31 (3420) 14 881. **Fax:** 31 (3420) 92 813. **Contact:** P.J. van Rees, Managing Director.

OBJECTIVES: To provide courses and seminars in animal husbandry and care, veterinary nursing and milling technology. To assist local organisations to set up, strengthen and intensify practical training. To provide consultation and backup services.

GENERAL INFORMATION: Creation: 1961. **Type of organisation:** association of NGOs. **Member organisations:** 3. **Personnel/Total:** 110. Salaried: 110 of which: 2 in developing countries. **Budget/Total 1993:** ECU 6905000 (US$ 8076000). **Financial sources:** Private: 20%. Public: 60%. Self-financing: 20%.

PLANNED ACTIVITIES: Developing a series of short courses for the commercial sector.

COMMENTS: Undertakes activities in the Commonwealth of Independent States. Information activities related to the Commonwealth of Independent States.

ACTIVITIES IN DEVELOPING REGIONS: Present in developing regions. Active in 4 country(ies). Maintains local field presence. Works through local field partners. **Sustainable Development Actions:** Democracy/good governance/institution building/participatory development; Education/training/literacy; Rural development/agriculture; Sending volunteers/experts/technical assistance. **Regions:** Caribbean; Central Africa; Central Asia and South Asia; East Africa; East Asia; Mexico and Central

America; Middle East; North Africa; Oceania; South America; South East Asia; Southern Africa; West Africa.

INFORMATION AND EDUCATION ACTIVITIES: Topics: Rural development/agriculture. **Activities:** Conferences/seminars/workshops/training activities; Exchanges/twinning/linking; Formal education; Fund raising; Information and documentation services/data bases; Lobbying/advocacy; Publishing/audiovisual materials/educational materials.

NLD3215

ORGANISATIE VOOR ONDERWIJS OVER LATIJNS-AMERIKA (SLA) ♦ Organisation for Education on Latin America

Nieuwe Herengracht 29-1, 1011 RL Amsterdam, The Netherlands.

Telephone: 31 (20) 623 15 54. **Fax:** 31 (20) 626 52 58. **Contact:** Miriam Gribling.

OBJECTIVES: To enhance solidarity between countries in the North and in the South specifically Central and South America by modifying existing images of the South and organising formal development education in the Netherlands. To encourage innovation within formal education by producing multi-media educational materials.

GENERAL INFORMATION: Creation: 1972. **Affiliated to:** National Service Bureau Development Education (The Netherlands) - Latin America Centre (The Netherlands) - Organisation of Latin American Committees (The Netherlands). **Personnel/Total:** 19. Salaried: 4. Volunteers: 15. **Budget/Total 1993:** ECU 91000 (US$ 106000). **Financial sources:** Private: 25%. Public: 75%.

PUBLICATIONS: Annual report. List of publications.

EVALUATION/RESEARCH: Evaluation reports available.

PLANNED ACTIVITIES: Undertaking an educational campaign for senior high school students on the sustainable development contract between the Netherlands and Costa Rica.

INFORMATION AND EDUCATION ACTIVITIES: Topics: Children/youth/family; Culture/tradition/religion; Ecology/environment/biodiversity; Education/training/literacy; Employment/unemployment; Gender issues/women; Human rights/peace/conflicts; International economic relations/trade/debt/finance; International relations/cooperation/development aid; Poverty/living conditions; Racism/xenophobia/antisemitism. **Activities:** Exchanges/twinning/linking; Formal education; Networking/electronic telecommunications; Publishing/audiovisual materials/educational materials.

NLD3216

OROMO KOMITEE NEDERLAND (OKN) ♦ Oromo Committee of the Netherlands

Postbus 26, 3500 AA Utrecht, The Netherlands.

OBJECTIVES: To raise awareness about the problems faced by the Oromo people, living in the Horn of Africa (Ethiopia). To raise funds in support of the Oromo Relief Association in Addis Ababa.

GENERAL INFORMATION: Creation: 1979. **Affiliated to:** The Oromo Relief Association (Ethiopia). **Financial sources:** Self-financing: 100%.

PUBLICATIONS: Periodicals: Oromo Bulletin (2).

ACTIVITIES IN DEVELOPING REGIONS: Active in 1 country(ies). Works through local field partners. **Sustainable Development Actions:** Children/youth/family; Democracy/good governance/institution building/participatory development; Ecology/environment/biodiversity; Education/training/literacy; Emergency relief/refugees/humanitarian assistance; Energy/transport; Food/famine; Gender issues/women; Health/sanitation/water; Human rights/peace/conflicts; Rural development/agriculture; Small enterprises/informal sector/handicrafts. **Regions:** East Africa.

INFORMATION AND EDUCATION ACTIVITIES: Topics: Children/youth/family; Culture/tradition/religion; Ecology/environment/biodiversity; Education/training/literacy; Emergency relief/refugees/humanitarian assistance; Food/famine; Gender issues/women; Health/sanitation/water; Human rights/peace/conflicts; International relations/cooperation/development aid; Peace/ethnic conflicts/armament/disarmament; Poverty/living conditions; Refugees/migrants/ethnic groups; Rural development/agriculture. **Activities:** Publishing/audiovisual materials/educational materials.

See: How to Use the Directory, page 11.

NLD3217

OVERLEG REGIONALE CENTRA (ORC) ♦ Platform of Regional Centers for Development Education

c/o Demer 38, 5611 AS Eindhoven, The Netherlands.

Telephone: 31 (40) 24 40 699. *Fax:* 31 (40) 24 51 668. *Contact:* Kees Nauta, Secretary.

OBJECTIVES: To support and promote the activities of development education centres in the Netherlands.

GENERAL INFORMATION: *Creation:* 1982. *Personnel/Total:* 102. *Salaried:* 52. *Volunteers:* 50. *Budget/Total 1993:* ECU 104000 (US$ 121000). *Financial sources:* Private: 1%. Public: 84%. *Self-financing:* 10%.

PUBLICATIONS: *Annual report.*

INFORMATION AND EDUCATION ACTIVITIES: Topics: Culture/tradition/religion; Ecology/environment/biodiversity; Gender issues/women; Human rights/peace/conflicts; International relations/cooperation/development aid; Racism/xenophobia/antisemitism; Refugees/migrants/ethnic groups. **Activities:** Broadcasting/cultural events; Conferences/seminars/workshops/training activities; Exchanges/twinning/linking; Formal education; Information and documentation services/data bases; Information campaigns/exhibitions.

NLD3218

DE PACIFIC WERKGROEP (Pacific) ♦ The Pacific Working Group

Zusterplein 22a, Postbus 151, 3700 AD Zeist, The Netherlands.

Telephone: 31 (30) 69 27 827. *Fax:* 31 (30) 69 25 614. *E-mail:* esciep@gn.apc.org. *Contact:* Madeleen Helmer, Co-ordinator.

OBJECTIVES: To inform the Dutch public about environment and development issues in the Pacific, and to network with Dutch NGOs and policy makers on these issues.

GENERAL INFORMATION: *Creation:* 1904. *Member organisations:* 8. *Affiliated to:* Europe-Pacific Solidarity Network - European Centre on Studies, Information and Education on Pacific Issues. *Personnel/Total:* 4. *Salaried:* 2. *Volunteers:* 2. *Budget/Total 1993:* ECU 69000 (US$ 81000). *Financial sources:* Private: 5%. Public: 95%.

PUBLICATIONS: *Periodicals:* EPS Bulletin (10). *Annual report.*

PLANNED ACTIVITIES: Producing two films on the impact of global warming in the Pacific.

INFORMATION AND EDUCATION ACTIVITIES: Topics: Ecology/environment/biodiversity; Human rights/peace/conflicts; International relations/cooperation/development aid; Peace/ethnic conflicts/armament/disarmament. **Activities:** Broadcasting/cultural events; Conferences/seminars/workshops/training activities; Exchanges/twinning/linking; Formal education; Information and documentation services/data bases; Information campaigns/exhibitions; Lobbying/advocacy; Networking/electronic telecommunications; Publishing/audiovisual materials/educational materials.

NLD3219

PAULO FREIRE STICHTING (PFS) ♦ Paulo Freire Foundation

Onstein 75, 7006 JR Doetinchem, The Netherlands.

Telephone: 31 (26) 44 55 445. *Fax:* 31 (26) 44 55 978. *E-mail:* pfs@antenna.nl. *Contact:* N. Verbree, Co-ordinator.

OBJECTIVES: To stimulate worldwide agrarian development co-operation and development education through information and exchange programmes aimed at awareness raising, self-determination and continuing education.

GENERAL INFORMATION: *Creation:* 1983. *Affiliated to:* La Via Campesina (the Netherlands). *Personnel/Total:* 7. Salaried: 4. *Volunteers:* 3 of which: 1 in developing countries. *Budget/Total 1993:* ECU 230000 (US$ 269000). *Financial sources:* Private: 25%. Public: 65%. *Self-financing:* 10%.

PUBLICATIONS: *Periodicals:* Intercambio (6).

EVALUATION/RESEARCH: Evaluation reports available. Undertakes research activities.

PLANNED ACTIVITIES: Organising exchanges and twinnings of grassroots rural groups and of agricultural educational institutes.

COMMENTS: Undertakes activities in the Commonwealth of Independent States. Information activities related to the Commonwealth of Independent States.

ACTIVITIES IN DEVELOPING REGIONS: Active in 1 country(ies). Maintains local field presence. Works through local field partners. **Sustainable Development Actions:** Democracy/good governance/institution building/participatory development; Ecology/environment/biodiversity; Education/training/literacy; Gender issues/women; Rural development/agriculture; Sending volunteers/experts/technical assistance. **Regions:** Caribbean; Mexico and Central America; South America; South East Asia; Southern Africa.

INFORMATION AND EDUCATION ACTIVITIES: Topics: Ecology/environment/biodiversity; Education/training/literacy; Gender issues/women; Rural development/agriculture. **Activities:** Conferences/seminars/workshops/training activities; Exchanges/twinning/linking; Formal education; Fund raising; Information campaigns/exhibitions; Lobbying/advocacy; Networking/electronic telecommunications; Publishing/audiovisual materials/educational materials.

NLD3220

PAUSELIJKE MISSIEWERKEN ♦ Oeuvres Pontificales Missionnaires

Laan van N.O. Indie 191, Postbus 93140, 2509 AC Den Haag, Pays-Bas.

Téléphone: 31 (70) 82 54 84. *Contact:* Harrie Verhoeven, Directeur.

NLD3221

PAX CHRISTI NEDERLAND

P.O. Box 19318, 3501 DH Utrecht, The Netherlands.

Telephone: 31 (30) 23 33 346. *Fax:* 31 (30) 23 68 199.

NLD3222

PEACE AND APPROPRIATE DEVELOPMENT FOR THE HORN OF AFRICA (PADA)

Postbus 857, 2300 AW Leiden, The Netherlands.

Telephone: 31 (71) 51 48 117. *Fax:* 31 (71) 51 47 550. *Contact:* T.M. Gubena, Director.

OBJECTIVES: To increase public awareness of issues that confront the Horn of Africa and influence policy-makers. To facilitate a process of reconciliation among opposing groups and government representatives in the region of the Horn.

GENERAL INFORMATION: *Creation:* 1991. *Personnel/Total:* 8. *Salaried:* 1. *Volunteers:* 7. *Budget/Total 1993:* ECU 46000 (US$ 54000). *Financial sources:* Private: 15%. Public: 70%. *Self-financing:* 15%.

PUBLICATIONS: *Periodicals:* New Horn of Africa (12). *Annual report. List of publications.*

EVALUATION/RESEARCH: Evaluation reports available.

PLANNED ACTIVITIES: Carrying out education in primary schools on peace, famine and war.

INFORMATION AND EDUCATION ACTIVITIES: Topics: Children/youth/family; Culture/tradition/religion; Emergency relief/refugees/humanitarian assistance; Food/famine; Gender issues/women; Human rights/peace/conflicts; Peace/ethnic conflicts/armament/disarmament; Poverty/living conditions; Refugees/migrants/ethnic groups. **Activities:** Broadcasting/cultural events; Conferences/seminars/workshops/training activities; Fund raising; Information and documentation services/data bases; Information campaigns/exhibitions; Lobbying/advocacy; Publishing/audiovisual materials/educational materials.

NLD3223

PEACE BRIGADES INTERNATIONAL (PBI-NEDERLAND)

Hardesteinstraat 6, 8012 ET Zwolle, The Netherlands.

Telephone: 31 (38) 42 16 587. *Fax:* 31 (252) 216 467. *Contact:* E.A. Huisman.

Voir : *Comment utiliser le répertoire,* page 11.

OBJECTIVES: To provide non-violent protection to peaceful individuals in danger in countries suffering violent conflict by providing peace brigade volunteers to act as witnesses.

GENERAL INFORMATION: *Creation:* 1988. *Affiliated to:* Peace Brigades International (United Kingdom). *Personnel/Total:* 12. *Volunteers:* 12 of which: 2 in developing countries. *Budget/Total 1993:* ECU 35000 (US$ 41000). *Financial sources:* Private: 75%. Self-financing: 25%.

PUBLICATIONS: *Periodicals:* Nieuwsbrief (2). *Annual report. List of publications.*

INFORMATION AND EDUCATION ACTIVITIES: Topics: Human rights/peace/conflicts; International relations/cooperation/development aid; Peace/ethnic conflicts/armament/disarmament. **Activities:** Conferences/seminars/workshops/training activities; Formal education; Fund raising; Lobbying/advocacy; Other; Publishing/audiovisual materials/educational materials.

NLD3224

PERU KOMITEE NEDERLAND

Nieuwe Herengracht 29-1, 1011 RL Amsterdam, The Netherlands.

Telephone: 31 (20) 62 66 717. *Fax:* 31 (20) 62 65 258.

NLD3225

PHARMACIE & ONTWIKKELINGSSAMENWERKING ♦ Foundation for Pharmacy and Development Co-operation

Alexanderstraat 11, Postbus 30460, 2500 GL Den Haag, The Netherlands.

Telephone: 31 (70) 36 24 111. *Fax:* 31 (70) 31 06 530. *Contact:* F.W.J. van Mansvelt, President.

OBJECTIVES: To stimulate and support pharmaceutical supply in developing countries and help improve their health care system. To encourage pharmacists and pharmacy technicians to take a central position in the drug supply system.

GENERAL INFORMATION: *Creation:* 1984. *Personnel/Total:* 11. *Salaried:* 1. *Volunteers:* 10. *Budget/Total 1993:* ECU 23000 (US$ 27000). *Financial sources:* Private: 50%. Self-financing: 50%.

PUBLICATIONS: *Annual report. List of publications.*

EVALUATION/RESEARCH: Evaluation reports available.

COMMENTS: Undertakes activities in the Commonwealth of Independent States.

ACTIVITIES IN DEVELOPING REGIONS: Present in developing regions. Active in 5 country(ies). Works through local field partners. **Sustainable Development Actions:** Health/sanitation/water. **Regions:** Caribbean; Central Africa; Central Asia and South Asia; East Africa; East Asia; Mexico and Central America; North Africa; South America; South East Asia; Southern Africa; West Africa.

INFORMATION AND EDUCATION ACTIVITIES: Topics: Health/sanitation/water. **Activities:** Conferences/seminars/workshops/training activities; Formal education; Information and documentation services/data bases; Lobbying/advocacy; Publishing/audiovisual materials/educational materials.

NLD3226

PROGRAMMA INTERDISCIPLINAIR ONDERZOEK OORZAKEN MENSENRECHT SCHENDINGEN (PIOOM) ♦ Interdisciplinary Research Program on Root Causes of Human Rights Violations

Leiden University, Wassenaarseweg 52, 2333 AK Leiden, The Netherlands.

Telephone: 31 (71) 52 73 848. *Fax:* 31 (71) 52 73 619. *E-mail:* PIOOM@RULFSW.LEIDEN UNIV.NL.. *Contact:* Alex P. Schmid, Research Director.

OBJECTIVES: To utilise the intellectual resources of the academic world for the analysis of the root causes and circumstances of human rights violations. To produce useful knowledge of human rights organisations

and inter-governmental agencies fighting against violations of fundamental human rights.

GENERAL INFORMATION: *Creation:* 1988. *Personnel/Total:* 8. *Salaried:* 4. *Volunteers:* 4. *Budget/Total 1993:* ECU 92000 (US$ 108000). *Financial sources:* Private: 30%. Public: 70%.

PUBLICATIONS: *Periodicals:* PIOOM Newsletter Progress Report (1). *Annual report. List of publications.*

EVALUATION/RESEARCH: Evaluation reports available. Undertakes research activities.

COMMENTS: Undertakes activities in the Commonwealth of Independent States. Information activities related to the Commonwealth of Independent States.

ACTIVITIES IN DEVELOPING REGIONS: Active in 50 country(ies). **Sustainable Development Actions:** Democracy/good governance/institution building/participatory development; Human rights/peace/conflicts. **Regions:** Caribbean; Central Africa; Central Asia and South Asia; East Africa; East Asia; Mexico and Central America; Middle East; North Africa; Oceania; South America; South East Asia; Southern Africa; West Africa.

INFORMATION AND EDUCATION ACTIVITIES: Topics: Human rights/peace/conflicts; Peace/ethnic conflicts/armament/disarmament; Refugees/migrants/ethnic groups. **Activities:** Conferences/seminars/workshops/training activities; Fund raising; Information and documentation services/data bases; Networking/electronic telecommunications; Publishing/audiovisual materials/educational materials.

NLD3227

PROGRAMMA UITZENDING MANAGERS (PUM) ♦ Programme néerlandais de conseils en matière de gestion pour les pays en développement

Postbus 84100, 2508 AC Den Haag, Pays-Bas.

Téléphone: 31 (70) 35 19 620. *Fax:* 31 (70) 35 19 590. *Contact:* Wa Zuidhof, Coordinateur.

NLD3228

RAAD VAN ADVIES VOOR HET WETENSCHAPPELIJK ONDERZOEK IN HET KADER VAN ONTWIKKELINGSSAMENWERKING (RAWOO)

p/a NUFFIC, Postbus 29777, 2502 LT Den Haag, Netherlands.

Telephone: 31 (70) 42 60 331. *Fax:* 31 (70) 42 60 329.

NLD3229

RAAD VOOR DE ZENDING DER NEDERLANDSE HERVORMDE KERK ♦ Board of Mission of the Dutch Reformed Church

Leidsestraatweg 11, Postbus 12, 2340 AA Oegstgeest, The Netherlands.

Telephone: 31 (71) 51 77 900. *Fax:* 31 (71) 51 53 601. *Contact:* D.C. Nicolai, Acting Secretary General.

OBJECTIVES: To support, through the provision of personnel and financial assistance, sister churches overseas in their missionary calling in church and society.

GENERAL INFORMATION: *Creation:* 1951. *Personnel/Total:* 131. *Salaried:* 98 of which: 34 in developing countries. *Volunteers:* 33. *Budget/Total 1993:* ECU 6905000 (US$ 8076000). *Financial sources:* Private: 100%.

PUBLICATIONS: *Periodicals:* Missive (11) - Vardoor (10). *Annual report.*

PLANNED ACTIVITIES: Focusing on women in development. Organising interreligious dialogue especially between Muslims and Christians.

NLD3230

RADIO NEDERLAND TRAINING CENTRE (RNTC)

Postbus 222, 1200 JG Hilversum, The Netherlands.

Telephone: 31 (35) 62 47 779. *Fax:* 31 (35) 67 24 532. *Contact:* Jaap R. Swart, General Manager.

OBJECTIVES: To support the use of the media in developing countries for informative and educational purposes.

GENERAL INFORMATION: *Creation:* 1968. *Affiliated to:* Federation of International Education (Netherlands) - The Education Network (Netherlands) - Communication Development International (Costa Rica) -Foundation Working with Young People (Netherlands). *Personnel/Total:* 18. *Salaried:* 18 of which: 2 in developing countries. *Budget/Total 1993:* ECU 1657000 (US$ 1938000). *Financial sources:* Public: 95%. *Self-financing:* 5%.

PUBLICATIONS: *Annual report. List of publications.*

EVALUATION/RESEARCH: Undertakes research activities.

COMMENTS: Undertakes activities in the Commonwealth of Independent States. Information activities related to the Commonwealth of Independent States.

ACTIVITIES IN DEVELOPING REGIONS: Present in developing regions. Active in 14 country(ies). Maintains local field presence. Works through local field partners. **Sustainable Development Actions:** Children/youth/family; Democracy/good governance/institution building/participatory development; Ecology/environment/biodiversity; Education/training/literacy; Gender issues/women; Human rights/peace/conflicts; Other; Population/family planning/demography; Rural development/agriculture; Sending volunteers/experts/technical assistance. **Regions:** Caribbean; Central Africa; Central Asia and South Asia; East Africa; East Asia; Mexico and Central America; Middle East; North Africa; Oceania; South America; South East Asia; Southern Africa; West Africa.

INFORMATION AND EDUCATION ACTIVITIES: Topics: Children/youth/family; Culture/tradition/religion; Ecology/environment/biodiversity; Education/training/literacy; Employment/unemployment; Gender issues/women; Health/sanitation/water; Human rights/peace/conflicts; International relations/cooperation/development aid; Other; Population/family planning/demography; Rural development/agriculture; Urban development/habitat. **Activities:** Broadcasting/cultural events; Conferences/seminars/workshops/training activities; Formal education; Fund raising; Information and documentation services/data bases; Information campaigns/exhibitions; Lobbying/advocacy; Publishing/audiovisual materials/educational materials.

NLD3231

REFORMATORISCHE HULPAKTIE WOORD EN DAAD ♦
Reformed Relief Organisation Word and Deed

Postbus 560, 4200 AN Gorinchem, The Netherlands.

Telephone: 31 (18) 36 24 288. *Fax:* 31 (18) 36 25 575. *Contact:* J. Lock, Managing Director.

OBJECTIVES: To give help to the needy in any circumstances irrespective of race, colour or religion, according to the teachings of the Holy Scripture.

GENERAL INFORMATION: *Creation:* 1973. *Affiliated to:* Overlegorgaan Christelgtu Hubiporganisaties in Nederland - PSO. *Personnel/Total:* 18. *Salaried:* 16 of which: 8 in developing countries. *Volunteers:* 2. *Budget/Total 1993:* ECU 7319000 (US$ 8561000). *Financial sources:* Private: 96%. Public: 1%. Self-financing: 3%.

PUBLICATIONS: *Periodicals:* Word en Daad (4). *Annual report.*

PLANNED ACTIVITIES: Setting up of scholarship funds in several parts of the world.

ACTIVITIES IN DEVELOPING REGIONS: Present in developing regions. Active in 14 country(ies). Maintains local field presence. Works through local field partners. **Sustainable Development Actions:** Children/youth/family; Debt/finance/trade; Democracy/good governance/institution building/participatory development; Ecology/environment/biodiversity; Education/training/literacy; Emergency relief/refugees/humanitarian assistance; Food/famine; Gender issues/women; Health/sanitation/water; Rural development/agriculture; Sending volunteers/experts/technical assistance; Small enterprises/informal sector/handicrafts; Urban development/habitat. **Regions:** Caribbean; Central Asia and South Asia; East Africa; Mexico and Central America; South America; South East Asia; Southern Africa; West Africa.

INFORMATION AND EDUCATION ACTIVITIES: Topics: Children/youth/family; Culture/tradition/religion; Ecology/environment/biodiversity; Education/training/literacy; Emergency relief/refugees/humanitarian assis-

tance; Employment/unemployment; Food/famine; Gender issues/women; Health/sanitation/water; International economic relations/trade/debt/finance; Poverty/living conditions; Rural development/agriculture; Urban development/habitat. **Activities:** Fund raising.

NLD3232

REFUGEE CARE NETHERLANDS (ZOA)

P.O.Box 10343, 7301 GH Apeldoorn, The Netherlands.

Telephone: 31 (55) 36 63 339. *Fax:* 31 (55) 36 68 799. *Contact:* Hendrik Huberts, Director.

OBJECTIVES: To lend aid to refugees, displaced persons and victims of disasters regardless of race, sex, religion and political affiliation.

GENERAL INFORMATION: *Creation:* 1973. *Personnel/Total:* 155. *Salaried:* 135 of which: 101 in developing countries. *Volunteers:* 20. *Budget/Total 1993:* ECU 3301000 (US$ 3860000). *Financial sources:* Private: 88%. Public: 12%.

PUBLICATIONS: *Periodicals:* ZOA Nieuws (9). *Annual report. List of publications.*

EVALUATION/RESEARCH: Evaluation reports available. Undertakes research activities.

PLANNED ACTIVITIES: Undertaking re-integration projects in Laos, Cambodia, Vietnam and Mozambique.

INFORMATION AND EDUCATION ACTIVITIES: Topics: Children/youth/family; Culture/tradition/religion; Ecology/environment/biodiversity; Education/training/literacy; Emergency relief/refugees/humanitarian assistance; Food/famine; Gender issues/women; Health/sanitation/water; Population/family planning/demography; Poverty/living conditions; Refugees/migrants/ethnic groups; Rural development/agriculture; Urban development/habitat. **Activities:** Broadcasting/cultural events; Conferences/seminars/workshops/training activities; Exchanges/twinning/linking; Formal education; Fund raising; Information and documentation services/data bases; Information campaigns/exhibitions; Lobbying/advocacy; Networking/electronic telecommunications; Other; Publishing/audiovisual materials/educational materials.

NLD3233

SAHELP ♦ Aid the Sahel

Postbus 466, 5340 AL Oss, The Netherlands.

Telephone: 31 (41) 28 14 52.

NLD3234

SATIS

Entrepôt dok 68 a, 1018 AD Amsterdam, The Netherlands.

Telephone: 31 (20) 26 44 09. *Contact:* Paul Osborn, General Secretary.

NLD3235

SAWA

Beukenlaan 2-B, 6711 NH Ede, The Netherlands.

Telephone: 31 (31) 86 55 380. *Fax:* 31 (31) 86 51 636. *Contact:* Henk J. van Dijk, Director.

OBJECTIVES: To improve the position of the poor and disadvantaged, with a particular focus on women, and to assist them in increasing their independence.

GENERAL INFORMATION: *Creation:* 1983. *Affiliated to:* CERDPAD (Vietnam) - Solidami (Guinea Bissau) - BCA (Rwanda/Zaire) - SAWA (Cambodia). *Personnel/Total:* 41. *Salaried:* 40 of which: 29 in developing countries. *Volunteers:* 1. *Budget/Total 1993:* ECU 1937000 (US$ 2265000). *Financial sources:* Self-financing: 100%.

PUBLICATIONS: *Annual report. List of publications.*

EVALUATION/RESEARCH: Undertakes research activities.

COMMENTS: SAWA develops local consultancy capacity in developing countries in the fields of rural development, agriculture, land and water management. Undertakes activities in the Commonwealth of Indepen-

dent States. Information activities related to the Commonwealth of Independent States.

ACTIVITIES IN DEVELOPING REGIONS: Present in developing regions. Active in 13 country(ies). Maintains local field presence. Works through local field partners. **Sustainable Development Actions:** Ecology/environment/biodiversity; Emergency relief/refugees/humanitarian assistance; Gender issues/women; Health/sanitation/water; Rural development/agriculture; Sending volunteers/experts/technical assistance; Small enterprises/informal sector/handicrafts; Urban development/habitat. **Regions:** Central Africa; East Africa; South America; South East Asia; Southern Africa; West Africa.

INFORMATION AND EDUCATION ACTIVITIES: Topics: Gender issues/women; Health/sanitation/water; Rural development/agriculture. **Activities:** Conferences/seminars/workshops/training activities; Exchanges/twinning/linking; Fund raising; Information and documentation services/data bases.

NLD3236
A SEED

Begÿnenstraat 34-36, 6511 WP Nÿjmegen, The Netherlands.

Telephone: 31 (24) 36 02 939. **Fax:** 31 (24) 32 31 708. **E-mail:** aseednl@antenna.

OBJECTIVES: To raise public awareness about the necessity for fundamental changes in economics and lifestyles. To achieve a sustainable, just and peaceful world.

GENERAL INFORMATION: Creation: 1991. **Personnel/Total:** 60. *Salaried:* 0. *Volunteers:* 60. **Budget/Total 1993:** ECU 32000 (US$ 38000). **Financial sources:** *Private:* 32%. *Public:* 60%. *Self-financing:* 8%.

PUBLICATIONS: Periodicals: Ongehoord (5).

EVALUATION/RESEARCH: Undertakes research activities.

COMMENTS: Information activities related to the Commonwealth of Independent States.

INFORMATION AND EDUCATION ACTIVITIES: Topics: Culture/tradition/religion; Ecology/environment/biodiversity; Employment/unemployment; Food/famine; Gender issues/women; Human rights/peace/conflicts; International economic relations/trade/debt/finance; International relations/cooperation/development aid; Peace/ethnic conflicts/armament/disarmament; Poverty/living conditions; Racism/xenophobia/antisemitism; Refugees/migrants/ethnic groups; Rural development/agriculture. **Activities:** Broadcasting/cultural events; Conferences/seminars/workshops/training activities; Exchanges/twinning/linking; Information and documentation services/data bases; Information campaigns/exhibitions; Lobbying/advocacy; Networking/electronic telecommunications.

NLD3237
SIMAVI

Spruitenbosstraat 6, 2012 LK Haarlem, The Netherlands.

Telephone: 31 (23) 53 18 055. **Fax:** 31 (23) 53 28 538. **Contact:** S. Keuning, Managing Director.

OBJECTIVES: To support health related and medical projects and institutions in developing countries. To provide assistance irrespective of race, religion or political conviction.

GENERAL INFORMATION: Creation: 1925. **Personnel/Total:** 11. *Salaried:* 11. **Budget/Total 1993:** ECU 2256000 (US$ 2638000). **Financial sources:** *Private:* 100%.

PUBLICATIONS: *Annual report.*

EVALUATION/RESEARCH: Evaluation reports available.

PLANNED ACTIVITIES: Developing educational computer software.

ACTIVITIES IN DEVELOPING REGIONS: Present in developing regions. Active in 24 country(ies). Works through local field partners. **Sustainable Development Actions:** Children/youth/family; Education/training/literacy; Gender issues/women; Health/sanitation/water; Population/family planning/demography. **Regions:** Central Asia and South Asia; East Africa; South East Asia; Southern Africa; West Africa.

INFORMATION AND EDUCATION ACTIVITIES: Topics: Children/youth/family; Gender issues/women; Health/sanitation/water; Population/family planning/demography. **Activities:** Fund raising.

NLD3238
THE SOCIETY FOR INTERNATIONAL EDUCATION, TRAINING AND RESEARCH (SIETAR)

The Haarlem Business School, P.O. Box 614, 2003 RP Haarlem, The Netherlands.

Telephone: 31 (23) 52 77 345. **Fax:** 31 (23) 52 77 384.

NLD3239
SOLIDARIDAD

Goedestraat 2, 3572 RT Utrecht, The Netherlands.

Telephone: 31 (30) 27 20 313. **Fax:** 31 (30) 27 20 194.

NLD3240
SOS KINDERDORPEN ♦ SOS Children's Villages

Postbus 74032, 1070 BA Amsterdam, The Netherlands.

Telephone: 31 (20) 67 11 411. **Fax:** 31 (20) 61 92 081. **Contact:** D. Vriesendorp, Director.

NLD3241
ST. IUCN LEDEN-CONTACT ♦ Netherlands Committee for IUCN

Plantage Middenlaan 2-B, 1018 DD Amsterdam, The Netherlands.

Telephone: 31 (20) 62 61 732. **Fax:** 31 (20) 62 79 349. **E-mail:** IUCNNETHCOMM@gn.apc org. **Contact:** Simone Bilderbeck, Legal Project Officer.

NLD3242
STICHTING & VERENIGING ALVADAM ♦ Alvadam Foundation and Association

Bernard van Beeklaan 8, 1241 AH Kortenhoef, The Netherlands.

Telephone: 31 (35) 65 61 378. **Fax:** 31 (35) 65 61 378. **Contact:** Rev. A.A. van Daalen, President.

OBJECTIVES: To raise funds to support educational projects carried out by partner organisations of Alvadam. To promote and defend the rights of ministers of religion and other personnel in developing countries. To represent partner organisations in the South at EC committees and in other (inter)national government agencies.

GENERAL INFORMATION: Creation: 1987. **Type of organisation:** association of NGOs. **Member organisations:** 60. **Affiliated to:** NGO-EC Network. **Personnel/Total:** 5. *Salaried:* 2. *Volunteers:* 3. **Budget/Total 1993:** ECU 173000 (US$ 202000). **Financial sources:** *Private:* 20%. *Self-financing:* 80%.

PUBLICATIONS: Periodicals: Pax Ecclesia (4).

PLANNED ACTIVITIES: Giving priority to human rights, peace and conflicts worldwide.

ACTIVITIES IN DEVELOPING REGIONS: Active in 30 country(ies). Works through local field partners. **Sustainable Development Actions:** Children/youth/family; Education/training/literacy; Food/famine; Health/sanitation/water; Sending volunteers/experts/technical assistance; Urban development/habitat. **Regions:** Central Asia and South Asia; East Africa.

INFORMATION AND EDUCATION ACTIVITIES: Topics: Culture/tradition/religion; Education/training/literacy; Human rights/peace/conflicts; International relations/cooperation/development aid; Other; Poverty/living conditions; Racism/xenophobia/antisemitism. **Activities:** Conferences/seminars/workshops/training activities; Information and documentation services/data bases; Lobbying/advocacy.

NLD3243
STICHTING ACTIE AFGHANEN IN NOOD ♦ Action for Afghans in Need Foundation

Gravenstraat 8, 1012 NM Amsterdam, The Netherlands.

Telephone: 31 (20) 23 75 09.

NLD3244

STICHTING ACTIE CALCUTTA ♦ Foundation Actie Calcutta

Hazelaar 112, 5664 VL Geldrop, The Netherlands.

Telephone: 31 (40) 25 73 18. *Contact:* J. Zuidgeest, Chairman.

OBJECTIVES: To sponsor the education of poor children in India

GENERAL INFORMATION: *Creation:* 1972. *Personnel/Total:* 9. *Volunteers:* 9. *Budget/Total 1993:* ECU 691000 (US$ 808000). *Financial sources:* Private: 100%.

PUBLICATIONS: *Periodicals:* Newsletter (2). *Annual report.*

ACTIVITIES IN DEVELOPING REGIONS: Active in 1 country(ies). Works through local field partners. **Sustainable Development Actions:** Children/youth/family; Education/training/literacy. **Regions:** Central Asia and South Asia.

INFORMATION AND EDUCATION ACTIVITIES: Topics: Children/youth/family; Education/training/literacy. **Activities:** Fund raising.

NLD3245

STICHTING ASHOKA NEDERLAND ♦ Ashoka : Innovators for the Public-Netherlands

P.O. Box 93125, 1090 BC Amsterdam, The Netherlands.

Telephone: 31 (20) 66 58 743. *Fax:* 31 (20) 66 58 743. *Contact:* Ir. F.E. Six, Chairwoman.

OBJECTIVES: To change world systems through individual empowerment. To raise funds from private individuals and businesses for the support of Asoka fellows in the South and in Eastern Europe and spread their stories in funding countries and elsewhere.

GENERAL INFORMATION: *Creation:* 1993. *Affiliated to:* Ashoka Global Network (USA). *Personnel/Total:* 5. Volunteers: 5. *Budget/Total 1993:* ECU 14000 (US$ 16000). *Financial sources:* Private: 100%.

PUBLICATIONS: *Annual report.*

EVALUATION/RESEARCH: Evaluation reports available.

COMMENTS: Undertakes activities in the Commonwealth of Independent States.

ACTIVITIES IN DEVELOPING REGIONS: Maintains local field presence. Works through local field partners. **Sustainable Development Actions:** Children/youth/family; Ecology/environment/biodiversity; Education/training/literacy. **Regions:** South East Asia.

INFORMATION AND EDUCATION ACTIVITIES: Topics: Children/youth/family; Culture/tradition/religion; Ecology/environment/biodiversity; Education/training/literacy. **Activities:** Exchanges/twinning/linking; Fund raising.

NLD3246

STICHTING BLINDHEIDBESTRIJDING ONTWIKKELING-SLANDEN (SBO) ♦ Society Against Blindness Overseas

Aetsveld 57, 3645 XN Vinkeveen, The Netherlands.

Telephone: 31 (29) 72 37 36. *Contact:* J.P. van der Reijden, President.

NLD3247

STICHTING BRASIL OP WEG ♦ Foundation for Brazil

Domstraat 29, Postbus 380, 3500 AJ Utrecht, The Netherlands.

Telephone: 31 (30) 23 11 870.

NLD3248

STICHTING COLOMBIA KOMITEE NEDERLAND ♦ Foundation Colombia Committee of the Netherlands

Postbus 10717, 1001 ES Amsterdam, The Netherlands.

Telephone: 31 (20) 38 03 10. *Contact:* Drs. Monika Mulder.

NLD3249

STICHTING COMMUNICATIE ONTWIKKELINGSSAMENWERKING (SCO)

Eisenhowerlaan 128, 2517 KM Den Haag, The Netherlands.

Telephone: 31 (70) 35 21 811. *Fax:* 31 (70) 35 54 465. *Contact:* J.W. Le Grand, Secretary of Projects.

OBJECTIVES: To support media related activities in developing countries. To promote democracy through freedom of the press.

GENERAL INFORMATION: *Creation:* 1986. *Personnel/Total:* 5. *Salaried:* 3. *Volunteers:* 2. *Budget/Total 1993:* ECU 1151000 (US$ 1346000). *Financial sources:* Private: 10%. Public: 90%.

PUBLICATIONS: *Annual report.*

EVALUATION/RESEARCH: Evaluation reports available.

ACTIVITIES IN DEVELOPING REGIONS: Active in 30 country(ies). Works through local field partners. **Sustainable Development Actions:** Other. **Regions:** Caribbean; Central Africa; Central Asia and South Asia; East Africa; Mexico and Central America; South America; South East Asia; Southern Africa; West Africa.

INFORMATION AND EDUCATION ACTIVITIES: Topics: Gender issues/women; Human rights/peace/conflicts; Other. **Activities:** Broadcasting/cultural events; Conferences/seminars/workshops/training activities; Fund raising.

NLD3250

STICHTING DE WAAL (DWF) ♦ De Waal Foundation

Maliebaan 32, 3581 CR Utrecht, The Netherlands.

Telephone: 31 (30) 23 10 494. *Fax:* 31 (30) 23 40 904. *Contact:* Kees de Waal, President.

OBJECTIVES: To help socially and physically disabled youth in South America.

GENERAL INFORMATION: *Creation:* 1985. *Personnel/Total:* 4. *Salaried:* 2 of which: 2 in developing countries. *Financial sources:* Self-financing: 100%.

PLANNED ACTIVITIES: Exploring new areas in employment projects.

ACTIVITIES IN DEVELOPING REGIONS: Present in developing regions. Active in 6 country(ies). Maintains local field presence. Works through local field partners. **Sustainable Development Actions:** Children/youth/family; Education/training/literacy; Health/sanitation/water; Small enterprises/informal sector/handicrafts. **Regions:** South America.

INFORMATION AND EDUCATION ACTIVITIES: Topics: Children/youth/family; Education/training/literacy. **Activities:** Formal education.

NLD3251

STICHTING DENTAL HEALTH INTERNATIONAL NEDERLAND (DHIN)

Postbus 186, 6560 AD Groesbeek, The Netherlands.

Telephone: 31 (35) 60 19 495. *Fax:* 31 (26) 47 42 800. *Contact:* Drs. A.Ch.H.M. Veraart, President.

OBJECTIVES: To assist developing countries in the field of dentistry.

GENERAL INFORMATION: *Creation:* 1973. *Personnel/Total:* 14. *Volunteers:* 14. *Budget/Total 1993:* ECU 83000 (US$ 97000). *Financial sources:* Private: 20%. Public: 20%. Self-financing: 60%.

PUBLICATIONS: *Periodicals:* DHIN Review (4).

EVALUATION/RESEARCH: Evaluation reports available. Undertakes research activities.

COMMENTS: Undertakes activities in the Commonwealth of Independent States.

ACTIVITIES IN DEVELOPING REGIONS: Present in developing regions. Maintains local field presence. Works through local field partners. **Sustainable Development Actions:** Health/sanitation/water. **Regions:** Caribbean; Central Africa; Central Asia and South Asia; East Africa; East Asia; Mexico and Central America; South East Asia; West Africa.

INFORMATION AND EDUCATION ACTIVITIES: Topics: Health/sanitation/water. **Activities:** Fund raising; Information and documentation services/data bases; Lobbying/advocacy.

Voir : *Comment utiliser le répertoire,* page 11.

NLD3252

STICHTING DERDE WERELD COMMUNICATIE ♦ Foundation Third World Communication

Kanaalweg 94A, Postbus 840 42, 2584 CN Den Haag, The Netherlands.

Telephone: 31 (70) 55 76 11. *Contact:* B. den Ronden.

NLD3253

STICHTING DOEN ♦ DOEN Foundation

P.O. Box 1070AP Van Eeghenstraat 70, AP Amsterdam, The Netherlands.

Telephone: 31 (20) 573 73 33. *Fax:* 31 (20) 675 73 97. *E-mail:* DOEN@ANTENNA NL. *Contact:* B.C. Van Oven.

OBJECTIVES: To undertake subsidy, credit and communications programmes.

GENERAL INFORMATION: *Creation:* 1991. *Affiliated to:* EFC. *Personnel/Total:* 7. *Salaried:* 7. *Budget/Total 1993:* ECU 18414000 (US$ 21537000). *Financial sources:* Private: 100%.

PUBLICATIONS: *Periodicals:* Buitenhaus (4). *Annual report.*

EVALUATION/RESEARCH: Undertakes research activities.

COMMENTS: Undertakes activities in the Commonwealth of Independent States. Information activities related to the Commonwealth of Independent States.

ACTIVITIES IN DEVELOPING REGIONS: Present in developing regions. Active in 36 country(ies). Works through local field partners. **Sustainable Development Actions:** Children/youth/family; Debt/finance/trade; Democracy/good governance/institution building/participatory development; Ecology/environment/biodiversity; Education/training/literacy; Emergency relief/refugees/humanitarian assistance; Energy/transport; Food/famine; Gender issues/women; Human rights/peace/conflicts; Rural development/agriculture; Sending volunteers/experts/technical assistance; Small enterprises/informal sector/handicrafts; Urban development/habitat. **Regions:** Caribbean; Central Africa; Central Asia and South Asia; East Africa; Mexico and Central America; North Africa; South America; South East Asia; Southern Africa; West Africa.

INFORMATION AND EDUCATION ACTIVITIES: Topics: Children/youth/family; Ecology/environment/biodiversity; Emergency relief/refugees/humanitarian assistance; Gender issues/women; Human rights/peace/conflicts; International economic relations/trade/debt/finance; International relations/cooperation/development aid; Other; Peace/ethnic conflicts/armament/disarmament; Poverty/living conditions; Racism/xenophobia/antisemitism; Refugees/migrants/ethnic groups; Rural development/agriculture; Urban development/habitat. **Activities:** Broadcasting/cultural events; Exchanges/twinning/linking; Fund raising.

NLD3254

STICHTING ECOLOGISCHE LANDBOUWPROJECTEN GHANA ♦ Foundation for Organic Agricultural Projects in Ghana

Den Broekweg 1, 6971 LT Brummen, The Netherlands.

Telephone: 31 (35) 53 15 723. *Fax:* 31 (35) 53 15 723. *Contact:* J.G. Spee, President.

OBJECTIVES: To support environmentally and ecologically sustainable agricultural projects in Ghana.

GENERAL INFORMATION: *Creation:* 1979. *Personnel/Total:* 17. *Salaried:* 1 of which: 1 in developing countries. *Volunteers:* 16 of which: 10 in developing countries. *Budget/Total 1993:* ECU 21000 (US$ 24000). *Financial sources:* Private: 100%.

PUBLICATIONS: *Periodicals:* Rondzendbrief (2).

PLANNED ACTIVITIES: Creating a model garden for sustainable model farming. Undertaking a riverbank rehabilitation project.

ACTIVITIES IN DEVELOPING REGIONS: Present in developing regions. Active in 1 country(ies). Maintains local field presence. **Sustainable Development Actions:** Ecology/environment/biodiversity; Education/training/literacy; Food/famine; Health/sanitation/water; Rural development/agriculture; Sending volunteers/experts/technical assistance. **Regions:** West Africa.

INFORMATION AND EDUCATION ACTIVITIES: Topics: Ecology/environment/biodiversity; Emergency relief/refugees/humanitarian assistance; Food/famine; Health/sanitation/water; Poverty/living conditions; Rural development/agriculture. **Activities:** Formal education; Fund raising; Information and documentation services/data bases; Lobbying/advocacy.

NLD3255

STICHTING ECOPLAN ♦ The Ecoplan Foundation

Langenhorst 919, 6714 LN Ede, The Netherlands.

Telephone: 31 (318) 63 58 53. *Fax:* 31 (318) 63 29 07. *Contact:* Oscar J.A. Martijn.

OBJECTIVES: To provide sustainable housing for urban fringe citizens by providing lot allocation and basic services.

GENERAL INFORMATION: *Creation:* 1990. *Personnel/Total:* 3. *Volunteers:* 3 of which: 1 in developing countries. *Budget/Total 1993:* ECU 7000 (US$ 8000). *Financial sources:* Private: 25%. Public: 25%. Self-financing: 50%.

PUBLICATIONS: *Periodicals:* Nieuwsbrief (4). *Annual report.*

EVALUATION/RESEARCH: Evaluation reports available. Undertakes research activities.

ACTIVITIES IN DEVELOPING REGIONS: Present in developing regions. Active in 1 country(ies). Maintains local field presence. Works through local field partners. **Sustainable Development Actions:** Health/sanitation/water; Small enterprises/informal sector/handicrafts; Urban development/habitat. **Regions:** West Africa.

INFORMATION AND EDUCATION ACTIVITIES: Topics: Health/sanitation/water; Urban development/habitat. **Activities:** Fund raising; Information and documentation services/data bases; Information campaigns/exhibitions; Publishing/audiovisual materials/educational materials.

NLD3256

STICHTING EMMAUS NEDERLAND ♦ Emmaüs Foundation of the Netherlands

Julianalaan 25, 3722 GD Bilthoven, The Netherlands.

Telephone: 31 (30) 22 90 780. *Fax:* 31 (30) 22 90 780.

OBJECTIVES: To collect and recycle second-hand goods for people in developing countries and for the poor in the Netherlands. To inform Dutch people about Third World issues. To strive for a society based on justice and equity.

GENERAL INFORMATION: *Creation:* 1967. *Type of organisation:* network. *Member organisations:* 24. *Affiliated to:* Emmaüs International (France). *Personnel/Total:* 4. *Salaried:* 4. *Budget/Total 1993:* ECU 29000 (US$ 34000). *Financial sources:* Self-financing: 100%.

PUBLICATIONS: *Periodicals:* Hongen en Dorst (3).

PLANNED ACTIVITIES: Finding ways of becoming more involved with the problems of the poor in the Netherlands.

ACTIVITIES IN DEVELOPING REGIONS: Works through local field partners.

INFORMATION AND EDUCATION ACTIVITIES: Topics: Children/youth/family; Ecology/environment/biodiversity; Education/training/literacy; Emergency relief/refugees/humanitarian assistance; Employment/unemployment; Food/famine; Gender issues/women; Health/sanitation/water; Human rights/peace/conflicts; Peace/ethnic conflicts/armament/disarmament; Poverty/living conditions; Racism/xenophobia/antisemitism; Refugees/migrants/ethnic groups; Rural development/agriculture; Urban development/habitat. **Activities:** Fund raising.

NLD3257

STICHTING GERED GEREEDSCHAP ♦ Foundation for Saved Tools

Postbus 3767, 1001 AN Amsterdam, The Netherlands.

Telephone: 31 (20) 83 96 09. *Contact:* Laura Dols, Chairperson.

OBJECTIVES: To collect and refurbish hand tools and supply them to people in developing countries.

                                See: *How to Use the Directory*, page 11.

GENERAL INFORMATION: *Creation:* 1982. *Type of organisation:* network. *Affiliated to:* Tools for Self-Reliance (United Kingdom) - Tools for Solidarity (Ireland) -Gesellschaft für Arbeits und Berufsbeforderung (Germany) - ELEOS (Austria) - MS Reroverings Vaerksted (Denmark). *Personnel/Total:* 403. *Salaried:* 3. *Volunteers:* 400. *Budget/Total 1993:* ECU 127000 (US$ 148000). *Financial sources:* Private: 64%. Public: 30%. Self-financing: 6%.

PUBLICATIONS: *Periodicals:* Gazet (4) (12). *Annual report. List of publications.*

ACTIVITIES IN DEVELOPING REGIONS: Works through local field partners. **Sustainable Development Actions:** Education/training/literacy; Gender issues/women; Health/sanitation/water; Rural development/agriculture; Small enterprises/informal sector/handicrafts. **Regions:** Caribbean; Central Africa; Central Asia and South Asia; East Africa; Mexico and Central America; South America; Southern Africa; West Africa.

INFORMATION AND EDUCATION ACTIVITIES: Topics: Employment/unemployment; Gender issues/women; Health/sanitation/water; International relations/cooperation/development aid; Rural development/agriculture; Urban development/habitat. **Activities:** Exchanges/twinning/linking; Information campaigns/exhibitions; Networking/electronic telecommunications; Publishing/audiovisual materials/educational materials.

NLD3258

STICHTING GUATEMALA KOMITEE NEDERLAND (GUATEMALA) ♦ Dutch Guatemala Solidarity Committee

Domstraat 29, 3512 JA Utrecht, The Netherlands.

Telephone: 31 (30) 23 21 112. *Fax:* 31 (30) 23 17 278. *E-mail:* GKN@ANTENNA.NL. *Contact:* P. Bellemakers.

OBJECTIVES: To support popular organisations in Guatemala in order for Guatemala to become a truly democratic country.

GENERAL INFORMATION: *Creation:* 1979. *Affiliated to:* European Co-ordinating Body for Guatemalan Solidarity Groups. *Personnel/Total:* 11. *Volunteers:* 11. *Budget/Total 1993:* ECU 16000 (US$ 19000). *Financial sources:* Private: 78%. Self-financing: 22%.

PUBLICATIONS: *Periodicals:* La Jentana (5). *Annual report. List of publications.*

ACTIVITIES IN DEVELOPING REGIONS: Active in 1 country(ies). Works through local field partners. **Sustainable Development Actions:** Democracy/good governance/institution building/participatory development; Gender issues/women; Human rights/peace/conflicts. **Regions:** Mexico and Central America.

INFORMATION AND EDUCATION ACTIVITIES: Topics: Human rights/peace/conflicts; International relations/cooperation/development aid; Refugees/migrants/ethnic groups. **Activities:** Fund raising; Information campaigns/exhibitions; Lobbying/advocacy; Networking/electronic telecommunications.

NLD3259

STICHTING HELP BANGLADESH ♦ Aid Bangladesh Foundation

c/o COS, Godsweerdersingel 17, 6041 GJ Roermond, The Netherlands.
Telephone: 31 (475) 31 50 55.

NLD3260

STICHTING HULP AAN TIBETANEN (SHAT)

Dr. Beguinlaan 70, 2272 AL Voorburg, The Netherlands.

Telephone: 31 (70) 38 63 644. *Contact:* E. Rose, LLM.

OBJECTIVES: To give aid to Tibetans outside Tibet, especially children.

GENERAL INFORMATION: *Creation:* 1963. *Personnel/Total:* 6. *Volunteers:* 6. *Budget/Total 1993:* ECU 74000 (US$ 86000). *Financial sources:* Private: 100%.

PUBLICATIONS: *Periodicals:* Tibet News (3). *Annual report.*

EVALUATION/RESEARCH: Evaluation reports available.

PLANNED ACTIVITIES: Providing assistance for the education and care of children.

ACTIVITIES IN DEVELOPING REGIONS: Present in developing regions. Active in 1 country(ies). Works through local field partners. **Sustainable Development Actions:** Children/youth/family; Ecology/environment/biodiversity; Education/training/literacy; Emergency relief/refugees/humanitarian assistance; Energy/transport; Food/famine; Gender issues/women; Health/sanitation/water; Small enterprises/informal sector/handicrafts; Urban development/habitat. **Regions:** Central Asia and South Asia.

INFORMATION AND EDUCATION ACTIVITIES: Topics: Children/youth/family. **Activities:** Fund raising.

NLD3261

STICHTING IDEELE IMPORT

Herengracht 142, 1015 BW Amsterdam, The Netherlands.

NLD3262

STICHTING KINDERPOSTZEGELS NEDERLAND (SKN) ♦
Foundation for Children's Stamps Netherlands

Stationsweg 25, 2312 AS Leiden, The Netherlands.

Telephone: 31 (71) 52 59 800. *Fax:* 31 (71) 51 30 147. *Contact:* D. Rijkers, Executive Director.

OBJECTIVES: To improve the living conditions of children in Holland as well as in countries of Africa, Latin America, Asia and parts of Eastern Europe. To give financial support to projects benefitting handicapped children.

GENERAL INFORMATION: *Creation:* 1924. *Personnel/Total:* 20. *Salaried:* 20. *Budget/Total 1993:* ECU 4603000 (US$ 5384000). *Financial sources:* Private: 100%.

PUBLICATIONS: *Periodicals:* De Nieuve Serie (1). *Annual report.*

COMMENTS: Undertakes activities in the Commonwealth of Independent States.

ACTIVITIES IN DEVELOPING REGIONS: Active in 54 country(ies). Works through local field partners. **Sustainable Development Actions:** Children/youth/family. **Regions:** Caribbean; Central Africa; Central Asia and South Asia; East Africa; Mexico and Central America; Middle East; North Africa; South America; South East Asia; Southern Africa; West Africa.

INFORMATION AND EDUCATION ACTIVITIES: Topics: Children/youth/family. **Activities:** Fund raising.

NLD3263

STICHTING KLEINSCHALIGE ONTWIKKELINGSPROJECTEN
♦ Foundation for Small-Scale Development Projects

Postbus 1514, 6501 BM Nijmegen, The Netherlands.

Telephone: 31 (24) 32 29 196. *Fax:* 31 (24) 32 20 796. *Contact:* Jeanne Baggen.

OBJECTIVES: To improve infrastructural conditions for the poorest people in developing countries.

GENERAL INFORMATION: *Creation:* 1981. *Personnel/Total:* 3. *Salaried:* 1 of which: 1 in developing countries. *Volunteers:* 2. *Budget/Total 1993:* ECU 69000 (US$ 81000). *Financial sources:* Private: 15%. Public: 80%. Self-financing: 5%.

EVALUATION/RESEARCH: Evaluation reports available. Undertakes research activities.

PLANNED ACTIVITIES: Supporting the development of a former war zone in El Salvador in the domain of agriculture and reconstruction.

ACTIVITIES IN DEVELOPING REGIONS: Present in developing regions. Active in 1 country(ies). Maintains local field presence. Works through local field partners. **Sustainable Development Actions:** Democracy/good governance/institution building/participatory development; Ecology/environment/biodiversity; Emergency relief/refugees/humanitarian assistance; Energy/transport; Human rights/peace/conflicts; Rural development/agriculture; Sending volunteers/experts/technical assis-

tance; Small enterprises/informal sector/handicrafts; Urban development/habitat. **Regions:** Mexico and Central America.

INFORMATION AND EDUCATION ACTIVITIES: Topics: Ecology/environment/biodiversity; Emergency relief/refugees/humanitarian assistance; International relations/cooperation/development aid; Peace/ethnic conflicts/armament/disarmament; Refugees/migrants/ethnic groups; Rural development/agriculture; Urban development/habitat. **Activities:** Fund raising; Information campaigns/exhibitions.

NLD3264

STICHTING KOPPELGEMEENTE WAGENINGEN-NYABIKENKE ♦ Foundation Community-Twinning Wageningen-Nyabikenke

Postbus 200, 6700 AE Wageningen, The Netherlands.

Telephone: 31 (31) 74 14 407. **Fax:** 31 (31) 74 14 407. **Contact:** J. Blok.

OBJECTIVES: To maintain and expand ties between the communities of Wagemnga, the Netherlands and Nyabikenke, Central Rwanda.

GENERAL INFORMATION: Creation: 1979. **Personnel/Total:** var. *Volunteers:* var. **Budget/Total 1993:** ECU 9000 (US$ 11000). **Financial sources:** *Private:* 25%. *Public:* 50%. *Self-financing:* 25%.

PUBLICATIONS: Periodicals: Umubano (4).

ACTIVITIES IN DEVELOPING REGIONS: Active in 1 country(ies). Works through local field partners. **Sustainable Development Actions:** Ecology/environment/biodiversity; Education/training/literacy; Gender issues/women; Rural development/agriculture. **Regions:** Central Africa.

NLD3265

STICHTING LILIANE FONDS ♦ La Fondation Liliane

St. Catharinastraat 1, Postbus 75, 5250 AB Vlijmen, Pays-Bas.

Téléphone: 31 (41) 08 90 29. **Fax:** 31 (41) 08 17 354. **Contact:** G. Dollevoet, Directeur.

OBJECTIFS: Apporter un secours financier et matériel aux enfants handicappés physiques et/ou mentaux dans les pays en développement.

INFORMATIONS GENERALES: Création: 1980. **Affiliée à:** European Rehabilitation Partners (Pays-Bas) - Bureau International catolique de l'enfance (Suisse). **Personnel/Total:** 1073. *Salariés:* 13. *Bénévoles:* 1060 dont: 1000 dans les pays en développement. **Budget/Total 1993:** ECU 2992000 (US$ 3500000). **Sources financières:** *Privé:* 100%.

PUBLICATIONS: Périodiques: Lettre de Nouvelles (2). *Rapport annuel. Liste des publications.*

ACTIVITES DANS LES REGIONS EN DEVELOPPEMENT: Intervient directement dans les régions en développement. Intervient dans 69 pays. Maintient une présence locale sur le terrain. Intervient par l'intermédiaire d'organisations locales partenaires. **Actions de Développement durable:** Enfants/jeunesse/famille. **Régions:** Afrique australe; Afrique centrale; Afrique de l'Est; Afrique de l'Ouest; Afrique du Nord; Amérique du Sud; Asie centrale et Asie du Sud; Asie de l'Est; Asie du Sud-Est; Caraïbes; Mexique et Amerique centrale; Moyen-Orient; Océanie.

ACTIVITES D'INFORMATION ET D'EDUCATION: Domaines: Enfants/jeunesse/famille; Santé/assainissement/eau. **Activités:** Collecte de fonds.

NLD3266

STICHTING LITTLE PHILIPPINES (SLP) ♦ Little Philippines Foundation

Velserstraat 3, 2023 EA Haarlem, The Netherlands.

Telephone: 31 (23) 52 50 932.

NLD3267

STICHTING MAX HAVELAAR ♦ Max Havelaar Foundation

Postbus 1252, 3500 BG Utrecht, The Netherlands.

Telephone: 31 (30) 23 34 602. **Fax:** 31 (30) 23 32 992. **Contact:** A. Abbema, Chairman.

OBJECTIVES: To promote fair trade and influence world trade conditions. To establish direct relations between Third world producers and consumers in the North. To mobilize consumers in order to reach a more just world economic order.

GENERAL INFORMATION: Creation: 1988. **Personnel/Total:** 11. *Salaried:* 11. **Budget/Total 1993:** ECU 921000 (US$ 1077000). **Financial sources:** *Private:* 25%. *Public:* 25%. *Self-financing:* 50%.

PUBLICATIONS: Periodicals: Max Havelaar Nieuws (2) - Max Havelaar Post (6). *Annual report. List of publications.*

EVALUATION/RESEARCH: Evaluation reports available. Undertakes research activities.

PLANNED ACTIVITIES: Undertaking group campaigns targetted at young people, women and the catering establishment.

ACTIVITIES IN DEVELOPING REGIONS: Present in developing regions. Active in 20 country(ies). **Sustainable Development Actions:** Debt/finance/trade. **Regions:** Caribbean; Central Africa; Central Asia and South Asia; East Africa; Mexico and Central America; South America; South East Asia; Southern Africa; West Africa.

INFORMATION AND EDUCATION ACTIVITIES: Topics: International economic relations/trade/debt/finance. **Activities:** Broadcasting/cultural events; Conferences/seminars/workshops/training activities; Exchanges/twinning/linking; Fund raising; Information and documentation services/data bases; Information campaigns/exhibitions; Networking/electronic telecommunications; Publishing/audiovisual materials/educational materials.

NLD3268

STICHTING MEDISCHE HULP KENYA (SMHK)

Meibergdreef 9, p/a AMC, 1105 AZ Amsterdam, The Netherlands.

Telephone: 31 (20) 56 69 111. **Fax:** 31 (20) 69 68 833.

NLD3269

STICHTING MENA (MENA) ♦ MENA FOUNDATION

Postbus 6549, 1005 EM Amsterdam, The Netherlands.

Telephone: 31 (20) 68 94 068. **Fax:** 31 (20) 68 94 068. **Contact:** Jeanette H. Eggengoor, President.

OBJECTIVES: To build and to maintain in conjunction with their partners a 50 bed health clinic in Ghana.

GENERAL INFORMATION: Personnel/Total: 7. *Volunteers:* 7. **Budget/Total 1993:** ECU 28000 (US$ 32000). **Financial sources:** *Private:* 95%. *Public:* 5%.

PUBLICATIONS: Periodicals: News Bulletin (2). *Annual report.*

EVALUATION/RESEARCH: Evaluation reports available. Undertakes research activities.

ACTIVITIES IN DEVELOPING REGIONS: Present in developing regions. Active in 1 country(ies). Maintains local field presence. **Sustainable Development Actions:** Children/youth/family; Debt/finance/trade; Education/training/literacy; Energy/transport; Food/famine; Gender issues/women; Health/sanitation/water; Population/family planning/demography; Rural development/agriculture; Sending volunteers/experts/technical assistance; Small enterprises/informal sector/handicrafts; Urban development/habitat. **Regions:** West Africa.

INFORMATION AND EDUCATION ACTIVITIES: Topics: Children/youth/family; Culture/tradition/religion; Education/training/literacy; Employment/unemployment; Food/famine; Gender issues/women; Health/sanitation/water; International economic relations/trade/debt/finance; Population/family planning/demography; Poverty/living conditions; Rural development/agriculture. **Activities:** Broadcasting/cultural events; Conferences/seminars/workshops/training activities; Formal education; Fund raising; Information campaigns/exhibitions.

NLD3270

STICHTING MILIEU EDUCATIE (SME) ♦ Institute of Environmental Communication

Australiëlaan 14, Postbus 13030, 3507 LA Utrecht, The Netherlands.

See: *How to Use the Directory,* page 11.

Telephone: 31 (30) 28 02 444. *Fax:* 31 (30) 28 01 345. *Contact:* F.J. Hesselink, Director.

OBJECTIVES: To provide consultancy services in communication management and attitude change in respect to the environment.

GENERAL INFORMATION: *Creation:* 1975. *Affiliated to:* World Conservation Union. *Salaried:* 30. *Budget/Total 1993:* ECU 2302000 (US$ 2692000). *Financial sources:* Private: 2%. Public: 12%. *Self-financing:* 86%.

PUBLICATIONS: *List of publications.*

EVALUATION/RESEARCH: Undertakes research activities.

PLANNED ACTIVITIES: Promoting primary environmental education in schools and a motivation campaign with public authorities for public participation. Developing mass media and feedback mechanisms for environmental participation.

COMMENTS: Undertakes activities in the Commonwealth of Independent States. Information activities related to the Commonwealth of Independent States.

INFORMATION AND EDUCATION ACTIVITIES: Topics: Education/training/literacy; International relations/cooperation/development aid. **Activities:** Conferences/seminars/workshops/training activities; Exchanges/twinning/linking; Formal education; Information and documentation services/data bases; Publishing/audiovisual materials/educational materials.

NLD3271

STICHTING MISSIE VERKEERSMIDDELEN AKTIE (MIVA-NEDERLAND) ♦ Missionary Vehicle Association

Vijverstraat 12, 4818 ST Breda, The Netherlands.

Telephone: 31 (76) 52 17 150. *Fax:* 31 (76) 52 03 530. *Contact:* H.B.A.M. van Peer.

OBJECTIVES: To co-finance the acquisition of means of transport for missionary and development organisations in the South.

GENERAL INFORMATION: *Creation:* 1935. *Personnel/Total:* 9. *Salaried:* 9. *Budget/Total 1993:* ECU 3453000 (US$ 4038000). *Financial sources:* Private: 100%.

PUBLICATIONS: *Periodicals:* MIVA Bulletin (1). *Annual report.*

ACTIVITIES IN DEVELOPING REGIONS: Active in 50 country(ies). Works through local field partners. **Sustainable Development Actions:** Energy/transport. **Regions:** Caribbean; Central Africa; Central Asia and South Asia; East Africa; Mexico and Central America; Middle East; North Africa; Oceania; South America; South East Asia; Southern Africa; West Africa.

NLD3272

STICHTING MONDIAAL ALTERNATIEF (SMA) ♦ Foundation for Ecological Development Alternatives

Korsholm 36, Postbus 151, 2130 AD Hoofddorp, The Netherlands.

Telephone: 31 (23) 56 32 305. *Contact:* Th. J. Henrar, R. Gerrits.

NLD3273

STICHTING MUNDELNINO

Torenlaan 25, 5328 CL Rossum, The Netherlands.

Telephone: 31 (418) 66 15 00.

NLD3274

STICHTING NATUUR EN MILIEU (SNM) ♦ Netherlands Society for Nature and Environment

Donkerstraat 17, 3511 KB Utrecht, The Netherlands.

Telephone: 31 (30) 23 31 328. *Fax:* 31 (30) 23 31 311. *E-mail:* SNM@gn.apc.org. *Contact:* Peter Nijhoff, Director.

OBJECTIVES: To promote environmental protection and the sustainable use of nature, landscape and natural resources.

GENERAL INFORMATION: *Creation:* 1972. *Member organisations:* 21. *Affiliated to:* European Environmental Bureau (Belgium) - Climate

Network Europe (Belgium) -European Federation for Transport and Environment (Brussels) - IUCN. *Personnel/Total:* 60. *Salaried:* 60. *Budget/Total 1993:* ECU 3337000 (US$ 3904000). *Financial sources:* Private: 20%. Public: 60%. Self-financing: 20%.

PUBLICATIONS: *Periodicals:* Natuur en Milieu (11). *Annual report. List of publications.*

EVALUATION/RESEARCH: Undertakes research activities.

COMMENTS: Undertakes activities in the Commonwealth of Independent States.

INFORMATION AND EDUCATION ACTIVITIES: Topics: Ecology/environment/biodiversity. **Activities:** Conferences/seminars/workshops/training activities; Exchanges/twinning/linking; Information and documentation services/data bases; Information campaigns/exhibitions; Lobbying/advocacy; Publishing/audiovisual materials/educational materials.

NLD3275

STICHTING NEDERLAND-SRI LANKA ♦ Netherlands-Sri Lanka Foundation

Rigolettostraat 55, 2555 VN Den Haag, The Netherlands.

Telephone: 31 (70) 32 52 381.

NLD3276

STICHTING NEDERLANDS COMITE UNICEF ♦ Dutch National Committee for UNICEF

Postbus 30603, St. Barbaraweg 4, 2500 GP Den Haag, The Netherlands.

Telephone: 31 (70) 33 39 333. *Fax:* 31 (70) 38 24 774.

NLD3277

STICHTING OECUMENISCHE HULP (SOH) ♦ Dutch Interchurch Aid

Cornelis Houtmanstraat 17, Postbus 13077, 3507 LB Utrecht, The Netherlands.

Telephone: 31 (30) 27 10 614. *Fax:* 31 (30) 27 17 814. *E-mail:* DIA@Antenna.nl. *Contact:* H. Zomer, General Secretary.

OBJECTIVES: To enable local organisations to provide aid to refugees. To undertake and support emergency relief activities in situations of natural or man-made disasters. To support projects and programmes aimed at food security for vunerable groups.

GENERAL INFORMATION: *Creation:* 1952. *Member organisations:* 15. *Affiliated to:* Vluchtelingen Werk (Netherlands) - Stichting Vluchteling (Netherlands) - WCC (Switzerland) - Aprodev (Belgium) - Euronaid. *Personnel/Total:* 52. *Salaried:* 44 of which: 5 in developing countries. *Volunteers:* 8. *Budget/Total 1993:* ECU 29922000 (US$ 34997000). *Financial sources:* Private: 33%. Public: 67%.

PUBLICATIONS: *Periodicals:* Direct mail newsletter (6). *Annual report.*

EVALUATION/RESEARCH: Evaluation reports available. Undertakes research activities.

PLANNED ACTIVITIES: Campaigning on reconstruction of "communities in transition".

COMMENTS: Undertakes activities in the Commonwealth of Independent States. Information activities related to the Commonwealth of Independent States.

ACTIVITIES IN DEVELOPING REGIONS: Active in 65 country(ies). Works through local field partners. **Sustainable Development Actions:** Children/youth/family; Democracy/good governance/institution building/participatory development; Emergency relief/refugees/humanitarian assistance; Food/famine; Gender issues/women; Health/sanitation/water; Human rights/peace/conflicts; Rural development/agriculture; Sending volunteers/experts/technical assistance. **Regions:** Caribbean; Central Africa; Central Asia and South Asia; East Africa; East Asia; Mexico and Central America; Middle East; North Africa; Oceania; South America; South East Asia; Southern Africa; West Africa.

INFORMATION AND EDUCATION ACTIVITIES: Topics: Children/youth/family; Emergency relief/refugees/humanitarian assistance; Food/fam-

ine; Human rights/peace/conflicts; Peace/ethnic conflicts/armament/disarmament; Racism/xenophobia/antisemitism; Refugees/migrants/ethnic groups. **Activities:** Conferences/seminars/workshops/training activities; Fund raising; Information and documentation services/data bases; Information campaigns/exhibitions; Publishing/audiovisual materials/educational materials.

NLD3278

STICHTING ONDERZOEK EN VOORLICHTING BEVOLKINGS POLITIEK ♦ Foundation for Research and Information on Population Policy

Amstellaan 25, 2105 VD Heemstede, The Netherlands.

Telephone: 31 (23) 52 82 891. **Fax:** 31 (23) 52 82 891. **Contact:** Thea Wuest-Zaremba, Co-ordinator.

OBJECTIVES: To raise consciousness in the Netherlands about the complex relations between population issues, women's rights and development programmes. To encourage critical research about the effects of family planning programmes on the position of women.

GENERAL INFORMATION: *Creation:* 1991. *Affiliated to:* WGNRR (the Netherlands). *Personnel/Total:* var. *Volunteers:* 10. *Budget/Total 1993:* ECU 920 (US$ 1000). *Financial sources:* Private: 50%. Self-financing: 50%.

EVALUATION/RESEARCH: Undertakes research activities.

PLANNED ACTIVITIES: Publishing a book on women's personal experience with sexual and reproductive health care services.

COMMENTS: Information activities related to the Commonwealth of Independent States.

INFORMATION AND EDUCATION ACTIVITIES: Topics: Gender issues/women; Health/sanitation/water; Population/family planning/demography. **Activities:** Conferences/seminars/workshops/training activities; Lobbying/advocacy; Publishing/audiovisual materials/educational materials.

NLD3279

STICHTING ONDERZOEK MULTINATIONALE ONDERNEMINGEN (SOMO) ♦ Centre for Research on Multinational Corporations

Keizersgracht 132, 1015 CW Amsterdam, The Netherlands.

Telephone: 31 (20) 63 91 291. **Fax:** 31 (20) 63 91 321. **E-mail:** GEO2:SOMO. **Contact:** S. Van Slageren, Chairman.

OBJECTIVES: To contribute to a more just international division of labour between the industrialised and developing countries. To support sustainable development in local, regional, national and international economies. To increase workers' role in corporate decision-making.

GENERAL INFORMATION: *Creation:* 1973. *Personnel/Total:* 16. *Salaried:* 12. *Volunteers:* 4. *Budget/Total 1993:* ECU 414000 (US$ 485000). *Financial sources:* Public: 10%. Self-financing: 90%.

PUBLICATIONS: *Periodicals:* (var). *Annual report. List of publications.*

EVALUATION/RESEARCH: Evaluation reports available. Undertakes research activities.

PLANNED ACTIVITIES: Conducting research on campaigns: on fair trade and working conditions in East Asia and trade relations in Africa.

INFORMATION AND EDUCATION ACTIVITIES: Topics: Ecology/environment/biodiversity; Gender issues/women; International economic relations/trade/debt/finance; International relations/cooperation/development aid; Rural development/agriculture. **Activities:** Conferences/seminars/workshops/training activities; Information and documentation services/data bases; Information campaigns/exhibitions; Networking/electronic telecommunications; Publishing/audiovisual materials/educational materials.

NLD3280

STICHTING ONTWIKKELINGSHULP ZUID-AZIE (SOZA) ♦ Foundation for Development Aid to South Asia

Schoolstraat 3, 6102 AD Echt, The Netherlands.

Telephone: 31 (47) 54 18 98.

NLD3281

STICHTING ONTWIKKELINGSSAMENWERKING BREDA (SOB) ♦ Foundation for Development Co-operation

Kortenaerlaan 49, 4819 AP Breda, The Netherlands.

Telephone: 31 (76) 51 45 360. **Fax:** 31 (76) 51 45 360. **Contact:** J. Hipke.

OBJECTIVES: To support small projects in developing countries.

GENERAL INFORMATION: *Creation:* 1984. *Type of organisation:* coordinating body. *Personnel/Total:* 8. *Volunteers:* 8. *Budget/Total 1993:* ECU 57000 (US$ 66000). *Financial sources:* Public: 100%.

PUBLICATIONS: *Annual report.*

ACTIVITIES IN DEVELOPING REGIONS: Sustainable Development Actions: Children/youth/family; Gender issues/women; Health/sanitation/water; Rural development/agriculture; Small enterprises/informal sector/handicrafts. **Regions:** Central Africa; Central Asia and South Asia; East Africa; Mexico and Central America; South America; West Africa.

NLD3282

STICHTING ONTWIKKELINGSSAMENWERKING NEDERLAND-TUNESIE (SONT) ♦ Development Co-operation between the Netherlands and Tunisia

De Twee Gebroeders 35, 9207 CL Drachten, The Netherlands.

Telephone: 31 (512) 52 12 95.

NLD3283

STICHTING ONTWIKKELINGSSAMENWERKING UGANDA (SOU)

Postbus 1623, 8901 BX Leeuwarden, The Netherlands.

Telephone: 31 (513) 41 76 16.

NLD3284

STICHTING ORTHOPEDIE EN REVALIDATIE IN ONTWIKKELINGSLANDEN (ORION)

Prinses Marijkelaan 8, 3155 VG Maasland, The Netherlands.

Telephone: 31 (10) 59 14 677.

NLD3285

STICHTING OVERAL (OVERAL)

Bredestraat 52, 6542 SW Nijmegen, The Netherlands.

Telephone: 31 (24) 37 71 744.

OBJECTIVES: To support financially small scale projects initiated by local organisations and directed at lasting improvements in the lives of people who live in very disadvantageous conditions.

GENERAL INFORMATION: *Creation:* 1975. *Volunteers:* 20. *Budget/Total 1993:* ECU 28000 (US$ 32000). *Financial sources:* Private: 10%. Self-financing: 90%.

PUBLICATIONS: *Annual report.*

PLANNED ACTIVITIES: Giving priority to working in Eritrea over the next two years.

COMMENTS: Undertakes activities in the Commonwealth of Independent States.

ACTIVITIES IN DEVELOPING REGIONS: Active in 8 country(ies). Works through local field partners. **Sustainable Development Actions:** Democracy/good governance/institution building/participatory development; Ecology/environment/biodiversity; Education/training/literacy; Gender issues/women; Health/sanitation/water; Human rights/peace/conflicts; Rural development/agriculture. **Regions:** Mexico and Central America; Middle East; Oceania; South America; South East Asia.

NLD3286

STICHTING PLATFORM VOOR DUURZAME ONTWIKKELING (PDO) ♦ Platform for Sustainable Development

Mariaplaats 3-I, Postbus 19245, 3501 DE Utrecht, The Netherlands.

See: *How to Use the Directory,* page 11.

Telephone: 31 (30) 23 67 997. *Fax:* 31 (30) 23 67 998. *Contact:* Ken Waagmeester, Director.

OBJECTIVES: To foster debate between its 50 member organisations on issues of sustainable development, including trade, environment, development, women, youth, religion, science, agriculture, peace and security and human rights.

GENERAL INFORMATION: *Member organisations:* 50. *Personnel/Total:* 7. *Salaried:* 7. *Budget/Total 1993:* ECU 230000 (US$ 269000). *Financial sources: Public:* 100%.

PUBLICATIONS: *Periodicals:* Diurzaam (15). *Annual report.*

EVALUATION/RESEARCH: Undertakes research activities.

PLANNED ACTIVITIES: Publishing a book on sustainable development in the Netherlands.

COMMENTS: This organisation is primarily involved in development education in the Netherlands. It also co-ordinates the dutch non-governmental input to the sustainable development agreements between the Netherlands and Benin, Bhutan and Costa Rica.

INFORMATION AND EDUCATION ACTIVITIES: Topics: Ecology/environment/biodiversity; International economic relations/trade/debt/finance; International relations/cooperation/development aid; Rural development/agriculture; Urban development/habitat. Activities: Conferences/seminars/workshops/training activities.

NLD3287

STICHTING PROJECTEN VOOR KINDEREN IN SRI LANKA

Postbus 43538, Leyweg 525h, 2504 AM Den Haag, The Netherlands.

Telephone: 31 (70) 32 99 510.

NLD3288

STICHTING REDT DE KINDEREN ♦ Save the Children Foundation - Netherlands

Postbus 30470, 2500 GL Den Haag, The Netherlands.

Telephone: 31 (70) 35 05 967. *Fax:* 31 (70) 35 01 279. *Contact:* B.Y. Eysink.

OBJECTIVES: To improve the living conditions of children all over the world.

GENERAL INFORMATION: *Personnel/Total:* 10. *Salaried:* 9 of which: 2 in developing countries. *Volunteers:* 1. *Budget/Total 1993:* ECU 1898000 (US$ 2220000). *Financial sources: Private:* 84%. *Public:* 16%.

PUBLICATIONS: *Annual report.*

ACTIVITIES IN DEVELOPING REGIONS: Present in developing regions. Active in 6 country(ies). Maintains local field presence. Works through local field partners. Sustainable Development Actions: Children/youth/family; Education/training/literacy; Gender issues/women; Health/sanitation/water; Population/family planning/demography; Rural development/agriculture; Sending volunteers/experts/technical assistance. Regions: Caribbean; Mexico and Central America; West Africa.

INFORMATION AND EDUCATION ACTIVITIES: Topics: Children/youth/family; Gender issues/women; Health/sanitation/water; International relations/cooperation/development aid; Population/family planning/demography; Rural development/agriculture. Activities: Fund raising.

NLD3289

STICHTING REFORMATORISCHE HULPAKTIE WOORD EN DAAD (Woord en Daad)

Postbus 560, 4200 AN Gorinchem, Netherlands.

Telephone: 31 (183) 62 42 88. *Fax:* 31 (183) 62 55 75.

NLD3290

STICHTING REVALIDATIE HULP (ICRS) ♦ Foundation for Rehabilitation Aid Projects

Willem de Zwijgerlaan 17, 2012 SB Haarlem, The Netherlands.

Telephone: 31 (23) 52 85 939. *Fax:* 31 (23) 54 71 615. *Contact:* H.C. Holst, President.

OBJECTIVES: To collect second hand orthopedic and rehabilitation equipment and materials in the Netherlands to send to special hospital projects in developing countries.

GENERAL INFORMATION: *Creation:* 1987. *Personnel/Total:* 7. *Volunteers:* 7. *Budget/Total 1993:* ECU 28000 (US$ 32000). *Financial sources: Private:* 95%. *Public:* 5%.

PUBLICATIONS: *Annual report.*

EVALUATION/RESEARCH: Evaluation reports available. Undertakes research activities.

ACTIVITIES IN DEVELOPING REGIONS: Present in developing regions. Active in 1 country(ies). Works through local field partners. Sustainable Development Actions: Health/sanitation/water. Regions: North Africa; South America; South East Asia; Southern Africa.

NLD3291

STICHTING RWANDA ONDERWIJS 2000 (SRO 2000) ♦ Rwanda Education Foundation 2000

Postbus 93375, 2509 AJ Den Haag, The Netherlands.

Telephone: 31 (70) 34 96 151. *Fax:* 31 (70) 38 19 677. *Contact:* Rudolf B. Contant, Chairman.

OBJECTIVES: To support and strengthen education in Rwanda especially technical and secondary education. To advise on national policies for development and rehabilitation, financing and administration of the educational system at all levels.

GENERAL INFORMATION: *Creation:* 1992. *Personnel/Total:* 15. *Volunteers:* 15 of which: 9 in developing countries. *Budget/Total 1993:* ECU 580000 (US$ 678000). *Financial sources: Private:* 13%. *Public:* 84%. *Self-financing:* 3%.

PUBLICATIONS: *Annual report.*

EVALUATION/RESEARCH: Evaluation reports available.

PLANNED ACTIVITIES: Assisting Rwandan schools with the reinsertion of pupils.

ACTIVITIES IN DEVELOPING REGIONS: Present in developing regions. Active in 1 country(ies). Maintains local field presence. Works through local field partners. Sustainable Development Actions: Children/youth/family; Education/training/literacy. Regions: Central Africa.

INFORMATION AND EDUCATION ACTIVITIES: Topics: Children/youth/family; Education/training/literacy. Activities: Exchanges/twinning/linking; Formal education; Fund raising; Information campaigns/exhibitions; Lobbying/advocacy.

NLD3292

STICHTING SAWA ♦ SAWA Foundation

Beukenlaan 2B, 6711 NH Ede, The Netherlands.

Telephone: 31 (318) 65 33 80. *Fax:* 31 (318) 65 16 36. *Contact:* H.J. van Dijk.

OBJECTIVES: To support rural development through institutional support with an emphasis on water supply, sanitation, integrated agriculture and NGOs.

GENERAL INFORMATION: *Creation:* 1983. *Personnel/Total:* 38. *Salaried:* 36 of which: 25 in developing countries. *Volunteers:* 2. *Budget/Total 1993:* ECU 1841000 (US$ 2154000). *Financial sources: Self-financing:* 100%.

PUBLICATIONS: *Annual report. List of publications.*

EVALUATION/RESEARCH: Undertakes research activities.

PLANNED ACTIVITIES: Establishing local consultancy organisations in developing regions such as Central Africa, Southern Africa, South East Asia and Western Africa.

COMMENTS: Undertakes activities in the Commonwealth of Independent States.

ACTIVITIES IN DEVELOPING REGIONS: Present in developing regions. Maintains local field presence. Works through local field partners. Sustainable Development Actions: Democracy/good governance/institution building/participatory development; Education/training/literacy; Gen-

Voir : *Comment utiliser le répertoire,* page 11.

der issues/women; Health/sanitation/water; Rural development/ agriculture; Sending volunteers/experts/technical assistance; Small enterprises/informal sector/handicrafts; Urban development/habitat. **Regions:** Central Africa; Central Asia and South Asia; East Africa; South East Asia; Southern Africa; West Africa.

INFORMATION AND EDUCATION ACTIVITIES: Topics: Gender issues/ women; Health/sanitation/water; Rural development/agriculture. **Activities:** Conferences/seminars/workshops/training activities; Exchanges/ twinning/linking; Fund raising; Networking/electronic telecommunications.

NLD3293

STICHTING SCHOOL & WERELD ♦ School and World Foundation

Wulverderlaan 1A, 2071 BG Santpoort, The Netherlands.

Telephone: 31 (23) 53 82 724. *Contact:* Rolf Schmidt.

NLD3294

STICHTING STEDENBAND AMSTERDAM-MANAGUA (SAM)

Niewe Herengracht 29, 1011 RL Amsterdam, The Netherlands.

Telephone: 31 (20) 62 29 953. *Fax:* 31 (20) 62 65 258.

NLD3295

STICHTING SUWA SETHA NEDERLAND (SSN)

Woldzoom 9, 9301 RA Roden, The Netherlands.

Telephone: 31 (50) 50 16 481. *Contact:* K.J. Brouwer, Chairman of the Board.

OBJECTIVES: To support children in developing countries with an emphasis on education, development of rural villages, water and agriculture.

GENERAL INFORMATION: *Creation:* 1983. *Personnel/Total:* 28. *Volunteers:* 28 of which: 20 in developing countries. *Budget/Total 1993:* ECU 44000 (US$ 52000). *Financial sources:* Private: 68%. Public: 12%. Self-financing: 20%.

PUBLICATIONS: *Annual report.*

PLANNED ACTIVITIES: Fundraising for a major project concerning approximately 50 villages in Tamil Nadu.

ACTIVITIES IN DEVELOPING REGIONS: Active in 2 country(ies). Works through local field partners. **Sustainable Development Actions:** Children/youth/family; Education/training/literacy; Health/sanitation/water; Rural development/agriculture. **Regions:** Central Asia and South Asia.

INFORMATION AND EDUCATION ACTIVITIES: Topics: Children/youth/ family; Education/training/literacy; Health/sanitation/water; Rural development/agriculture. **Activities:** Fund raising; Information and documentation services/data bases.

NLD3296

STICHTING TER BEVORDERING VAN INTERNATIONALE SOLIDARITEIT UTRECHT (SISU) ♦ Foundation for the Advancement of International Solidarity Utrecht

Stadhuis, Postbus 16200, 3500 CE Utrecht, The Netherlands.

Telephone: 31 (30) 23 28 511. *Contact:* C. Jonker, Chairman.

NLD3297

STICHTING TERRE DES HOMMES NEDERLAND ♦ Foundation Terre des Hommes Netherlands

Van Speykstraat 3, 2518 EV Den Haag, The Netherlands.

Telephone: 31 (70) 36 37 940. *Fax:* 31 (70) 36 52 160. *Contact:* Ron van Huizen, General Director.

OBJECTIVES: To provide financial support to needy children up to the age of 18. To assist groups of children rather than individuals.

GENERAL INFORMATION: *Creation:* 1965. *Affiliated to:* Fédération Internationale Terre des Hommes (Switzerland). *Personnel/Total:* 23. *Salaried:* 23 of which: 4 in developing countries. *Budget/Total 1993:* ECU 6445000 (US$ 7538000). *Financial sources:* Private: 100%.

PUBLICATIONS: *Periodicals:* Terre des Hommes Bulletin (4). *Annual report.*

PLANNED ACTIVITIES: Giving special attention to the support of formal and non-formal education for children in developing countries.

ACTIVITIES IN DEVELOPING REGIONS: Active in 20 country(ies). Maintains local field presence. Works through local field partners. **Sustainable Development Actions:** Children/youth/family; Education/training/literacy; Emergency relief/refugees/humanitarian assistance; Food/ famine; Urban development/habitat. **Regions:** Central Asia and South Asia; East Africa; South America; South East Asia.

INFORMATION AND EDUCATION ACTIVITIES: Topics: Children/youth/ family; Education/training/literacy; Emergency relief/refugees/humanitarian assistance; Food/famine; Urban development/habitat. **Activities:** Fund raising.

NLD3298

STICHTING TOT BEVORDERING VAN DE GEZONDHEIDSZORG IN ONTWIKKELINGSLANDEN/ SAMEN PETER - SAMEN STERK

Postbus 4446, 6401 CX Heerlen, The Netherlands.

Telephone: 31 (13) 76 66 66.

NLD3299

STICHTING TOT BEVORDERING VAN SAMENWERKING MET LANDEN IN ONTWIKKELING (SLO) ♦ S.L.O. Foundation

Bergstraat 28, 5051 HC Goirle, The Netherlands.

Telephone: 31 (13) 53 42 155. *Fax:* 31 (13) 54 40 695. *Contact:* T. van Puijenbroek-Vroom, Chairman.

NLD3300

STICHTING VLUCHTELING ♦ Netherlands Refugee Foundation

Stadhouderslaan 28, 2517 HZ Den Haag, The Netherlands.

Telephone: 31 (70) 34 68 946. *Fax:* 31 (70) 36 15 740. *Contact:* Klaas Keuning, Director.

OBJECTIVES: To provide assistance and raise funds for refugees in developing countries and inform people in the Netherlands about their situation.

GENERAL INFORMATION: *Creation:* 1982. *Personnel/Total:* 7. *Salaried:* 7. *Budget/Total 1993:* ECU 10588000 (US$ 12384000). *Financial sources:* Private: 75%. Public: 18%. Self-financing: 7%.

PUBLICATIONS: *Annual report. List of publications.*

EVALUATION/RESEARCH: Evaluation reports available.

COMMENTS: Undertakes activities in the Commonwealth of Independent States. Information activities related to the Commonwealth of Independent States.

ACTIVITIES IN DEVELOPING REGIONS: Active in 35 country(ies). Works through local field partners. **Sustainable Development Actions:** Children/youth/family; Ecology/environment/biodiversity; Education/training/ literacy; Emergency relief/refugees/humanitarian assistance; Health/ sanitation/water; Rural development/agriculture. **Regions:** Central Africa; Central Asia and South Asia; East Africa; Mexico and Central America; Middle East; North Africa; South East Asia; Southern Africa; West Africa.

INFORMATION AND EDUCATION ACTIVITIES: Topics: Children/youth/ family; Ecology/environment/biodiversity; Education/training/literacy; Emergency relief/refugees/humanitarian assistance; Gender issues/ women; Health/sanitation/water; Refugees/migrants/ethnic groups; Rural development/agriculture. **Activities:** Exchanges/twinning/linking; Fund raising; Information campaigns/exhibitions; Publishing/audiovisual materials/educational materials.

NLD3301

STICHTING VOLUNTARY SERVICE OVERSEAS NEDERLAND (VSO-NEDERLAND)

Hooghiemstraplein 142, 3514 AZ Utrecht, The Netherlands.

Telephone: 31 (30) 27 69 231. *Fax:* 31 (30) 27 20 922. *Contact:* Drs. G.M. Eekhout, Director.

See: How to Use the Directory, page 11.

OBJECTIVES: To contribute to the development of Third World nations in accordance with the needs as formulated by local development agencies and governments.

GENERAL INFORMATION: *Creation:* 1989. *Type of organisation:* association of NGOs. *Affiliated to:* Voluntary Service International. *Personnel/Total:* 3. *Salaried:* 3. *Volunteers:* 120 of which: 114 in developing countries. *Budget/Total 1993:* ECU 154000 (US$ 180000). *Financial sources:* Public: 95%. Self-financing: 5%.

PUBLICATIONS: *Periodicals:* VSO NL Newsletter (4). *Annual report. List of publications.*

EVALUATION/RESEARCH: Undertakes research activities.

ACTIVITIES IN DEVELOPING REGIONS: Present in developing regions. Active in 55 country(ies). Works through local field partners. **Sustainable Development Actions:** Children/youth/family; Democracy/good governance/institution building/participatory development; Education/training/literacy; Gender issues/women; Health/sanitation/water; Population/family planning/demography; Rural development/agriculture; Sending volunteers/experts/technical assistance; Small enterprises/informal sector/handicrafts; Urban development/habitat. **Regions:** Caribbean; Central Africa; Central Asia and South Asia; East Africa; Middle East; North Africa; Oceania; South East Asia; Southern Africa; West Africa.

INFORMATION AND EDUCATION ACTIVITIES: Topics: Children/youth/family; Culture/tradition/religion; Ecology/environment/biodiversity; Education/training/literacy; Emergency relief/refugees/humanitarian assistance; Employment/unemployment; Food/famine; Gender issues/women; Health/sanitation/water; Human rights/peace/conflicts; International economic relations/trade/debt/finance; International relations/cooperation/development aid; Peace/ethnic conflicts/armament/disarmament; Population/family planning/demography; Poverty/living conditions; Racism/xenophobia/antisemitism; Refugees/migrants/ethnic groups; Rural development/agriculture; Urban development/habitat. **Activities:** Conferences/seminars/workshops/training activities; Fund raising; Information and documentation services/data bases; Lobbying/advocacy; Publishing/audiovisual materials/educational materials.

NLD3302

STICHTING VOOR GEMEENSCHAPSONTWIKKELING IN SRI LANKA (PALM) ◆ Foundation for Community Development at Sri Lanka

Postbus 423, 8300 AK Emmeloord, The Netherlands.

Telephone: 31 (527) 61 71 80. *Contact:* S. Oppewal.

OBJECTIVES: To support community based development programmes. To raise awarenesss in the Netherlands of the situation in developing countries.

GENERAL INFORMATION: *Creation:* 1984. *Member organisations:* 1. *Affiliated to:* PALM Foundation (Sri Lanka). *Personnel/Total:* 11. *Salaried:* 6 of which: 6 in developing countries. *Volunteers:* 5. *Budget/Total 1993:* ECU 92000 (US$ 108000). *Financial sources:* Private: 70%. Public: 10%. Self-financing: 20%.

PUBLICATIONS: *Periodicals:* PALM Magazine (4). *Annual report.*

EVALUATION/RESEARCH: Evaluation reports available.

ACTIVITIES IN DEVELOPING REGIONS: Present in developing regions. Active in 1 country(ies). Maintains local field presence. Works through local field partners. **Sustainable Development Actions:** Children/youth/family; Democracy/good governance/institution building/participatory development; Education/training/literacy; Gender issues/women; Health/sanitation/water; Rural development/agriculture; Small enterprises/informal sector/handicrafts. **Regions:** Central Asia and South Asia.

INFORMATION AND EDUCATION ACTIVITIES: Topics: Children/youth/family; Education/training/literacy; Employment/unemployment; Gender issues/women; Health/sanitation/water; Poverty/living conditions; Rural development/agriculture. **Activities:** Fund raising; Information and documentation services/data bases; Publishing/audiovisual materials/educational materials.

NLD3303

STICHTING VOOR GEZONDHEID EN BEVRIJDING IN MIDDEN-AMERIKA (YAMILET) ◆ Organisation for Health and Liberation in Central America

Postbus 8105, Stationsstraat 39, 5004 GC Tilburg, The Netherlands.

Telephone: 31 (13) 54 30 947. *Fax:* 31 (13) 54 37 096. *E-mail:* Yamilet@Yamilet.Hacktie.NL. *Contact:* Chris Huinder, President.

OBJECTIVES: To provide medical supplies to partner NGOs in Central America. To lobby in Holland/Europe in support of partners in Central America. To conduct development education activites in Holland about health and liberation in Central America.

GENERAL INFORMATION: *Creation:* 1992. *Affiliated to:* International Public Health Council (Nicaragua/USA). *Personnel/Total:* 18. *Salaried:* 3. *Volunteers:* 15 of which: 2 in developing countries. *Budget/Total 1993:* ECU 78000 (US$ 92000). *Financial sources:* Private: 40%. Public: 55%. Self-financing: 5%.

PUBLICATIONS: *Periodicals:* La Ventana (6). *Annual report. List of publications.*

EVALUATION/RESEARCH: Evaluation reports available. Undertakes research activities.

PLANNED ACTIVITIES: Giving priority to basic health and dental care in Central America; refugees in Guatemala; democracy in El Salvador; production and health of workers on banana plantations in Costa Rica.

ACTIVITIES IN DEVELOPING REGIONS: Present in developing regions. Active in 5 country(ies). Maintains local field presence. Works through local field partners. **Sustainable Development Actions:** Children/youth/family; Democracy/good governance/institution building/participatory development; Ecology/environment/biodiversity; Education/training/literacy; Emergency relief/refugees/humanitarian assistance; Food/famine; Gender issues/women; Health/sanitation/water; Human rights/peace/conflicts; Population/family planning/demography; Rural development/agriculture; Sending volunteers/experts/technical assistance; Urban development/habitat. **Regions:** Mexico and Central America.

INFORMATION AND EDUCATION ACTIVITIES: Topics: Children/youth/family; Culture/tradition/religion; Ecology/environment/biodiversity; Emergency relief/refugees/humanitarian assistance; Employment/unemployment; Food/famine; Gender issues/women; Health/sanitation/water; Human rights/peace/conflicts; International economic relations/trade/debt/finance; International relations/cooperation/development aid; Peace/ethnic conflicts/armament/disarmament; Population/family planning/demography; Poverty/living conditions; Refugees/migrants/ethnic groups; Rural development/agriculture; Urban development/habitat. **Activities:** Broadcasting/cultural events; Conferences/seminars/workshops/training activities; Exchanges/twinning/linking; Fund raising; Information and documentation services/data bases; Information campaigns/exhibitions; Lobbying/advocacy; Networking/electronic telecommunications; Other; Publishing/audiovisual materials/educational materials.

NLD3304

STICHTING VOOR HERGEBRUIK VAN MEDISCHE HULPMIDDELEN (HERMED)

H. de Ruyter de Wildt, KNO-arts, Nassaulaan 4, 3851 XZ Ermelo, The Netherlands.

Telephone: 31 (3417) 55 72 29. *Contact:* H. de Ruyter de Wildt.

OBJECTIVES: To collect used hearing aids and eye glasses in Holland and distribute them in Sri Lanka.

GENERAL INFORMATION: *Creation:* 1991. *Personnel/Total:* 3. *Volunteers:* 3.

ACTIVITIES IN DEVELOPING REGIONS: Active in 1 country(ies). **Sustainable Development Actions:** Health/sanitation/water. **Regions:** South East Asia.

NLD3305

STICHTING VOOR LATIJNS AMERIKAANS SOCIAAL ONDERZOEK (LASO) ◆ Foundation for Latin American Social Research

Postbus 40088, 6504 AB Nijmegen, The Netherlands.

Telephone: 31 (80) 32 37 093. *Contact:* M.L. Malaver Ruiz.

OBJECTIVES: To promote scientific exchanges and inter-institutional contacts between Latin America and Europe. To carry out social research, development policy analyses, evaluation studies, consultancy to development programmes, information and dissemination activities and training.

GENERAL INFORMATION: *Creation:* 1984. *Type of organisation:* network. *Member organisations:* 15. *Personnel/Total:* 9. *Salaried:* 4 of which: 1 in developing countries. *Volunteers:* 5 of which: 3 in developing countries. *Financial sources:* Private: 10%. Public: 30%. *Self-financing:* 60%.

PUBLICATIONS: *Annual report. List of publications.*

EVALUATION/RESEARCH: Evaluation reports available. Undertakes research activities.

PLANNED ACTIVITIES: Undertaking research on: cultural and social changes among Indian peoples of the Amazon region; development co-operation policies and local participation in rural development in several countries. Organising a conference on scientific co-operation between Latin America and Europe.

ACTIVITIES IN DEVELOPING REGIONS: Present in developing regions. Active in 4 country(ies). Maintains local field presence. Works through local field partners. **Sustainable Development Actions:** Children/youth/family; Debt/finance/trade; Democracy/good governance/institution building/participatory development; Ecology/environment/biodiversity; Education/training/literacy; Food/famine; Gender issues/women; Human rights/peace/conflicts; Population/family planning/demography; Rural development/agriculture; Sending volunteers/experts/technical assistance; Small enterprises/informal sector/handicrafts; Urban development/habitat. **Regions:** Mexico and Central America; South America.

INFORMATION AND EDUCATION ACTIVITIES: Topics: Children/youth/family; Culture/tradition/religion; Ecology/environment/biodiversity; Education/training/literacy; Employment/unemployment; Food/famine; Gender issues/women; Health/sanitation/water; Human rights/peace/conflicts; International economic relations/trade/debt/finance; International relations/cooperation/development aid; Other; Peace/ethnic conflicts/armament/disarmament; Population/family planning/demography; Poverty/living conditions; Racism/xenophobia/antisemitism; Refugees/migrants/ethnic groups; Rural development/agriculture; Urban development/habitat. **Activities:** Conferences/seminars/workshops/training activities; Exchanges/twinning/linking; Formal education; Fund raising; Information and documentation services/data bases; Information campaigns/exhibitions; Lobbying/advocacy; Publishing/audiovisual materials/educational materials.

NLD3306
STICHTING VOOR LEPRABESTRIJDING IN THAILAND
De Sperwer 7, 9231 KL Surhuisterveen, The Netherlands.

Telephone: 31 (512) 36 26 94. *Contact:* Dhr. E. van Hofwegen.

NLD3307
STICHTING VOOR NEDERLANDSE BOSBOUW-ONTWIKKEL-INGSSAMENWERKING (BOS) ♦ Foundation for Dutch Forestry Development Co-operation
c/o De Dorschkamp, 20 Bosrandweg, Postbus 23, 6700 AA Wageningen, The Netherlands.

Telephone: 31 (83) 70 95 353. *Contact:* Dr. A.G. Voorhoeve.

NLD3308
STICHTING VRIENDEN MEDISCHE MISSIEZUSTERS ♦ Foundation Friends of the Medical Mission Sisters
Witte Vrouwensingel 55, 3572 CB Utrecht, The Netherlands.

Telephone: 31 (30) 27 32 503. *Fax:* 31 (30) 27 23 000. *Contact:* C.W.M. Muskens.

OBJECTIVES: To provide information on the aims and work of the Society of Medical Mission Sisters and especially on the Netherlands branch. To obtain moral and financial support for the promotion of health care, preventative and curative medical care projects of the Sisters, in developing countries.

GENERAL INFORMATION: *Creation:* 1977. *Personnel/Total:* 3. *Salaried:* 2. *Volunteers:* 1. *Budget/Total 1993:* ECU 921000 (US$ 1077000). *Financial sources:* Private: 100%.

PUBLICATIONS: *Periodicals:* Medische Missiezusters (3). *Annual report.*

ACTIVITIES IN DEVELOPING REGIONS: Active in 14 country(ies). **Sustainable Development Actions:** Health/sanitation/water. **Regions:** Central Africa; Central Asia and South Asia; East Africa; East Asia; South America; South East Asia; West Africa.

NLD3309
STICHTING VRIENDEN VAN ADESA - ASOCIACION DESARROLLO DE LA SALUD (ADESA)
Ter Weerlaan 108, Postbus 490, 2240 AL Wassenaar, The Netherlands.

Telephone: 31 (70) 51 78 477. *Fax:* 31 (70) 51 76 852.

NLD3310
STICHTING VRIENDEN VAN RWANDA
Van Zijldreef 14, 3981 GX Bunnik, The Netherlands.

Telephone: 31 (3405) 65 63 632.

NLD3311
STICHTING VRONESTEIN ♦ Vronestein Foundation
Postbus 1176, 2260 BD Leidschendam, The Netherlands.

Telephone: 31 (70) 32 01 737. *Contact:* L.B.M. van der Knaap, Chairman of the Board.

OBJECTIVES: To provide financial aid to developing countries for the training of nursing staff and co-workers in the field of health care.

GENERAL INFORMATION: *Creation:* 1937. *Personnel/Total:* 8. *Salaried:* 1. *Volunteers:* 7. *Budget/Total 1993:* ECU 231000 (US$ 27000). *Financial sources:* Private: 100%.

PUBLICATIONS: *Annual report.*

ACTIVITIES IN DEVELOPING REGIONS: Active in 8 country(ies). Works through local field partners. **Sustainable Development Actions:** Education/training/literacy; Health/sanitation/water. **Regions:** Central Africa; Central Asia and South Asia; East Africa; Southern Africa; West Africa.

NLD3312
STICHTING WERKGROEP AVISE (AVISE)
Rooseveltlaan 197, 1079 AP Amsterdam, Pays-Bas.

Téléphone: 31 (20) 64 22 788. *Fax:* 31 (20) 64 64 247. *Contact:* Luis Artigas de Quadras, Responsable des projets.

NLD3313
STICHTING WERKGROEP ECUADOR-NEDERLAND
Nieuwe Herengracht 29-I, 1011 RL Amsterdam, Netherlands.

Telephone: 31 (20) 69 46 350. *Fax:* 31 (20) 69 46 350.

NLD3314
STICHTING WERKGROEP INHEEMSE VOLKEN (WIP) ♦ Working Group Indigenous Peoples
Minahassastraat 1, Postbus 40066, 1009 AB Amsterdam, The Netherlands.

Telephone: 31 (20) 69 38 625. *Contact:* Drs. A.H.M. Goossens.

NLD3315
STUDIO 3
Doeldijk 22, 3417 ZG Montfoort, The Netherlands .

Telephone: 31 (34) 84 15 93. *Contact:* Dr. P.J.F. Pennarts.

NLD3316
TALLTREE
Van Eeghenstraat 78, 1071 GK Amsterdam, The Netherlands.

See: *How to Use the Directory,* page 11.

Telephone: 31 (20) 67 58 774. *Fax:* 31 (20) 67 58 935. *Contact:* Drs. A. Hoogenboom.

NLD3317
TEAR FUND, NEDERLAND ♦ Tear Fund of the Netherlands

Hoofdstraat 55-I, Postbus 104, 3970 AC Driebergen-Rijsenburg, The Netherlands.
Telephone: 31 (343) 51 48 44. *Fax:* 31 (343) 51 60 89. *Contact:* J.N. Bogaards, Director.

OBJECTIVES: To assist churches and Christian organisations in developing countries in relief and development programmes and projects. To raise awareness and funds among Christians in the Netherlands.

GENERAL INFORMATION: *Creation:* 1973. *Affiliated to:* Interchurch Relief and Development Alliance (Netherlands). *Personnel/Total:* 245. *Salaried:* 45 of which: 31 in developing countries. *Volunteers:* 200. *Budget/Total 1993:* ECU 3241000 (US$ 3791000). *Financial sources:* Private: 88%. Public: 12%.

PUBLICATIONS: *Periodicals:* Tear fund Nieuws (10). *Annual report. List of publications.*

ACTIVITIES IN DEVELOPING REGIONS: Active in 46 country(ies). Works through local field partners. Sustainable Development Actions: Children/youth/family; Education/training/literacy; Emergency relief/refugees/humanitarian assistance; Food/famine; Gender issues/women; Health/sanitation/water; Human rights/peace/conflicts; Rural development/agriculture; Sending volunteers/experts/technical assistance; Small enterprises/informal sector/handicrafts; Urban development/habitat. Regions: Caribbean; Central Africa; Central Asia and South Asia; East Africa; Mexico and Central America; Middle East; North Africa; South America; South East Asia; Southern Africa; West Africa.

NLD3318
TECHNOLOGIE OVERDRACHT ONTWIKKELING-SLANDEN (TOOL) ♦ Technology Transfer for Development

Sarphatistraat 650, 1018 AV Amsterdam, The Netherlands.
Telephone: 31 (20) 62 64 409. *Fax:* 31 (20) 62 77 489. *E-mail:* toolnet2:2882. *Contact:* R.J. Engelhard, Director.

OBJECTIVES: To strengthen small industrial enterprises in developing countries through technology transfer.

GENERAL INFORMATION: *Creation:* 1974. *Affiliated to:* European Appropriate Technology Consortium. *Personnel/Total:* 33. *Salaried:* 28. *Volunteers:* 5 of which: 2 in developing countries. *Budget/Total 1993:* ECU 1289000 (US$ 1508000). *Financial sources:* Private: 1%. Public: 99%.

PUBLICATIONS: *Annual report. List of publications.*

EVALUATION/RESEARCH: Evaluation reports available. Undertakes research activities.

ACTIVITIES IN DEVELOPING REGIONS: Active in 17 country(ies). Maintains local field presence. Works through local field partners. Sustainable Development Actions: Energy/transport; Gender issues/women; Health/sanitation/water; Rural development/agriculture; Sending volunteers/experts/technical assistance; Small enterprises/informal sector/handicrafts. Regions: Central Asia and South Asia; East Africa; South America; South East Asia; Southern Africa; West Africa.

INFORMATION AND EDUCATION ACTIVITIES: Topics: Ecology/environment/biodiversity; Food/famine; Gender issues/women; Health/sanitation/water; Rural development/agriculture. Activities: Conferences/seminars/workshops/training activities; Exchanges/twinning/linking; Information and documentation services/data bases; Networking/electronic telecommunications; Publishing/audiovisual materials/educational materials.

NLD3319
TELDERS STICHTING

Koninginnegracht 55a, 2514 AE Den Haag, The Netherlands.
Telephone: 31 (70) 363 19 48. *Fax:* 31 (70) 363 19 51.

NLD3320
TEMAGROEP ONDERONTWIKKELING (TEGON) ♦ Theme Group Underdevelopment

Postbus 269, Costerweg 27, 6700 AG Wageningen, The Netherlands.
Telephone: 31 (8370) 42 35 90.

OBJECTIVES: To support organisations through research that aims to improve the conditions of the poor in rural areas of developing countries.

GENERAL INFORMATION: *Creation:* 1982. *Personnel/Total:* 7. *Salaried:* 1. *Volunteers:* 6. *Budget/Total 1993:* ECU 11000 (US$ 13000). *Financial sources:* Public: 100%.

PUBLICATIONS: *Annual report. List of publications.*

NLD3321
TOWNS AND DEVELOPMENT

P.O Box 90646, 2509 LP the Hague, The Netherlands.
Telephone: 31 (70) 32 44 032. *Fax:* 31 (70) 32 46 916. *Contact:* Joane Knight, Chairperson.

NLD3322
TRANSNATIONAL INSTITUTE

Paulus Potterstraat 20, 1071 DA Amsterdam, The Netherlands.
Telephone: 31 (20) 66 26 608.

NLD3323
UNDUGU VRIENDENKRING NEDERLAND - KENYA (UVN) ♦ Undugu Friends' Society Netherlands

Postbus 668, 3000 AR Rotterdam, The Netherlands.
Telephone: 31 (10) 47 41 842. *Contact:* Peter A. Erkelens.

OBJECTIVES: To support the aims of the Undugu Society of Kenya. To improve relations between our members. To inform the Dutch public about UVN's activities and fundraising activities.

GENERAL INFORMATION: *Creation:* 1986. *Personnel/Total:* 10. *Volunteers:* 10. *Budget/Total 1993:* ECU 41000 (US$ 48000). *Financial sources:* Private: 90%. Self-financing: 10%.

PUBLICATIONS: *Periodicals:* Undugu Bulletin (3). *List of publications.*

ACTIVITIES IN DEVELOPING REGIONS: Active in 1 country(ies). Works through local field partners. Sustainable Development Actions: Children/youth/family; Education/training/literacy; Food/famine; Gender issues/women; Health/sanitation/water; Rural development/agriculture; Small enterprises/informal sector/handicrafts; Urban development/habitat. Regions: East Africa.

INFORMATION AND EDUCATION ACTIVITIES: Topics: Children/youth/family; Education/training/literacy; Food/famine; Gender issues/women; Health/sanitation/water; International relations/cooperation/development aid; Poverty/living conditions; Rural development/agriculture; Urban development/habitat. Activities: Fund raising; Information campaigns/exhibitions; Publishing/audiovisual materials/educational materials.

NLD3324
UNESCO CENTRUM NEDERLAND ♦ UNESCO Centre in the Netherlands

Oranje Nassaulaan 5, 1075 AH Amsterdam, The Netherlands.
Telephone: 31 (20) 67 30 100. *Fax:* 31 (20) 67 39 531.

NLD3325
UNIE VOOR CHRISTELIJK ONDERWIJS ♦ Foundation for Christian Schools

Postbus 1492, 3800 BL Amersfoort, The Netherlands.
Telephone: 31 (33) 46 51 272. *Fax:* 31 (33) 46 50 519. *Contact:* Ron Rÿnbende, Director.

OBJECTIVES: To promote Christian schools in the Netherlands. To assist Christian schools and their education abroad.

Voir : *Comment utiliser le répertoire*, page 11.

GENERAL INFORMATION: *Creation:* 1879. *Personnel/Total:* 16. *Salaried:* 16. *Budget/Total 1993:* ECU 1748000 (US$ 2045000). *Financial sources:* Private: 50%. Self-financing: 50%.

PUBLICATIONS: *Periodicals:* Bulletin (4). *Annual report. List of publications.*

COMMENTS: Undertakes activities in the Commonwealth of Independent States.

ACTIVITIES IN DEVELOPING REGIONS: Active in 37 country(ies). **Sustainable Development Actions:** Children/youth/family; Education/training/literacy. **Regions:** Caribbean; Central Africa; Central Asia and South Asia; East Africa; Mexico and Central America; Middle East; South America; South East Asia; West Africa.

INFORMATION AND EDUCATION ACTIVITIES: Topics: Children/youth/family; Education/training/literacy. **Activities:** Conferences/seminars/workshops/training activities; Exchanges/twinning/linking; Formal education; Fund raising; Information and documentation services/data bases; Information campaigns/exhibitions; Lobbying/advocacy; Publishing/audiovisual materials/educational materials.

NLD3326
UNITED FOR INTERCULTURAL ACTION

Postbus 413, 1000 AK Amsterdam, The Netherlands.

Telephone: 31 (20) 68 34 778. *Fax:* 31 (20) 68 34 582. *E-mail:* united@aps.hacktic.nl.

OBJECTIVES: To support anti-racist, anti-facist and anti-nationalist activities in Europe. To work to protect the rights of migrants and refugees.

GENERAL INFORMATION: *Creation:* 1992. *Personnel/Total:* 3. *Salaried:* 3.

PUBLICATIONS: *Periodicals:* Calendar of Internationalism (8) - Directory of Internationalism (1). *List of publications.*

EVALUATION/RESEARCH: Evaluation reports available. Undertakes research activities.

COMMENTS: Undertakes activities in the Commonwealth of Independent States. Information activities related to the Commonwealth of Independent States.

ACTIVITIES IN DEVELOPING REGIONS: Works through local field partners.

INFORMATION AND EDUCATION ACTIVITIES: Topics: Human rights/peace/conflicts; Peace/ethnic conflicts/armament/disarmament; Racism/xenophobia/antisemitism; Refugees/migrants/ethnic groups. **Activities:** Broadcasting/cultural events; Conferences/seminars/workshops/training activities; Exchanges/twinning/linking; Formal education; Fund raising; Information and documentation services/data bases; Information campaigns/exhibitions; Lobbying/advocacy; Networking/electronic telecommunications; Publishing/audiovisual materials/educational materials.

NLD3327
UNITED NATIONS VOLUNTEERS (UNV)

p/a SNV, Bezuidenhoutseweg 161, 2594 AG Den Haag, The Netherlands.

Telephone: 31 (70) 34 40 129. *Fax:* 31 (70) 34 40 212.

NLD3328
UNIVERSITY ASSISTANCE FUND

Wilhelminapark 38, 3581 NJ Utrecht, The Netherlands.

Contact: K.Bleichrodt, Director.

NLD3329
UNIVERSITY WOMEN OF EUROPE (UWE) ♦ Groupe Européen Femmes Diplômées des Universités

250 Sportlaan, 2566 LK Dan Haag, The Netherlands.

Telephone: 31 (70) 36 51 009.

OBJECTIVES: To promote understanding and friendship among women university graduates throughout the world. To encourage international co-operation. To further development of education. To represent women

graduates in international organisations. To encourage women graduates to apply their knowledge and skills to the problems which arise at all levels of public life.

GENERAL INFORMATION: *Creation:* 1981. *Member organisations:* 12. *Affiliated to:* European Women's Lobby - International Federation of University Women. *Financial sources:* Self-financing: 100%.

EVALUATION/RESEARCH: Undertakes research activities.

COMMENTS: Undertakes activities in the Commonwealth of Independent States. Information activities related to the Commonwealth of Independent States.

ACTIVITIES IN DEVELOPING REGIONS: Works through local field partners.

INFORMATION AND EDUCATION ACTIVITIES: Topics: Education/training/literacy; Human rights/peace/conflicts; Population/family planning/demography. **Activities:** Conferences/seminars/workshops/training activities; Formal education; Information and documentation services/data bases.

NLD3330
UNREPRESENTED NATIONS AND PEOPLES ORGANIZATION (UNPO)

Postbus 85878, 2508 CN Den Haag, The Netherlands.

Telephone: 31 (70) 360 33 18. *Fax:* 31 (70) 360 33 46. *E-mail:* unponl@antenna.nl. *Contact:* Michiel van Walt van Praag.

OBJECTIVES: To assist members to express their needs and grievances in legitimate forums. To provide a community of support to advance the aspirations of members by effective non-violent means.

GENERAL INFORMATION: *Creation:* 1991. *Personnel/Total:* 30. *Salaried:* 2. *Volunteers:* 28 of which: 3 in developing countries.

PUBLICATIONS: *Periodicals:* UNPO News (6). *Annual report. List of publications.*

EVALUATION/RESEARCH: Evaluation reports available. Undertakes research activities.

COMMENTS: Undertakes activities in the Commonwealth of Independent States. Information activities related to the Commonwealth of Independent States.

ACTIVITIES IN DEVELOPING REGIONS: **Sustainable Development Actions:** Ecology/environment/biodiversity; Human rights/peace/conflicts. **Regions:** Central Africa; Central Asia and South Asia; East Africa; East Asia; Oceania; South East Asia; West Africa.

INFORMATION AND EDUCATION ACTIVITIES: Topics: Ecology/environment/biodiversity; Human rights/peace/conflicts; International relations/cooperation/development aid; Peace/ethnic conflicts/armament/disarmament; Refugees/migrants/ethnic groups. **Activities:** Conferences/seminars/workshops/training activities; Exchanges/twinning/linking; Fund raising; Information and documentation services/data bases; Lobbying/advocacy.

NLD3331
UTRECHTS PLATTELAND EN DERDE WERELD

Postbus 74, 6700 AB Wageningen, The Netherlands.

Telephone: 31 (8370) 41 25 15.

NLD3332
VAN VOLLENHOVEN INSTITUUT VOOR RECHT EN BESTUUR IN NIET-WESTERSE LANDEN

Rapenburg 33, 2311 GG Leiden, The Netherlands.

Telephone: 31 (71) 52 77 260.

NLD3333
VENCEREMOS - SOLIDARITEIT MET CUBA ♦ Venceremos - Solidarity with Cuba

Postbus 4709, 1009 AS Amsterdam, The Netherlands.

Telephone: 31 (20) 66 56 838.

See: *How to Use the Directory,* page 11.

NLD3334

VERENIGING 31 ♦ Netherlands' Committee for Multilateral Youthwork

Prof. Tulpstraat 2, 1018 HA Amsterdam, The Netherlands.

Telephone: 31 (20) 62 62 664. *Fax:* 31 (20) 62 28 590. *Contact:* Gert-Jan Rietveld.

OBJECTIVES: To participate in multilateral forums such as the Council of Europe and UNESCO and build a link between international youth work and national youth work.

GENERAL INFORMATION: *Creation:* 1988. *Member organisations:* 33. *Affiliated to:* Council of European National Youth Committees - Youth Forum of European Communities - European Youth Centre (France) - Platform all European Youth and Student Cooperation - Platform for Sustainable Development (Netherlands). *Personnel/Total:* 22. *Salaried:* 2. *Volunteers:* 20. *Budget/Total 1993:* ECU 29000 (US$ 34000). *Financial sources:* Public: 90%. Self-financing: 10%.

PUBLICATIONS: *Periodicals:* 31 Nieuws (6). *Annual report.*

EVALUATION/RESEARCH: Evaluation reports available. Undertakes research activities.

COMMENTS: Undertakes activities in the Commonwealth of Independent States.

ACTIVITIES IN DEVELOPING REGIONS: Active in 1 country(ies). Works through local field partners. **Sustainable Development Actions:** Children/youth/family; Population/family planning/demography. **Regions:** North Africa; West Africa.

INFORMATION AND EDUCATION ACTIVITIES: Topics: Children/youth/family; Ecology/environment/biodiversity; Education/training/literacy; Gender issues/women; International economic relations/trade/debt/finance; International relations/cooperation/development aid; Peace/ethnic conflicts/armament/disarmament; Population/family planning/demography; Racism/xenophobia/antisemitism. **Activities:** Conferences/seminars/workshops/training activities; Exchanges/twinning/linking; Fund raising; Information and documentation services/data bases; Information campaigns/exhibitions; Lobbying/advocacy; Networking/electronic telecommunications.

NLD3335

VERENIGING DE VERRE NAASTEN (DVN)

Oosterlaan 22, Postbus 372, 8000 AJ Zwolle, The Netherlands.

Telephone: 31 (38) 42 10 555. *Fax:* 31 (38) 42 11 021.

NLD3336

VERENIGING HUMANA (HUMANA) ♦ Association Humana

Schoudermantel 15, 3981 AE Bunik, The Netherlands.

Telephone: 31 (30) 65 70 998. *Fax:* 31 (30) 65 62 804. *Contact:* P.E. Knudsen, Chairman.

OBJECTIVES: To provide development aid to the peoples of the Third World.

GENERAL INFORMATION: *Creation:* 1987. *Financial sources:* Self-financing: 100%.

PUBLICATIONS: *Periodicals:* Humana Nieuwsbrief (4). *Annual report.*

ACTIVITIES IN DEVELOPING REGIONS: Active in 4 country(ies). Works through local field partners. **Sustainable Development Actions:** Children/youth/family; Ecology/environment/biodiversity; Education/training/literacy; Emergency relief/refugees/humanitarian assistance; Food/famine; Health/sanitation/water; Rural development/agriculture; Sending volunteers/experts/technical assistance; Small enterprises/informal sector/handicrafts. **Regions:** Caribbean; South East Asia; Southern Africa.

NLD3337

VERENIGING MILIEUDEFENSIE (VMD) ♦ Friends of the Earth Netherlands

Postbus 19199, Damrak 26, 1000 GD Amsterdam, The Netherlands.

Telephone: 31 (20) 62 21 366. *Fax:* 31 (20) 62 75 287. *E-mail:* foen@antenna.nl. *Contact:* Teo Wams, Director.

OBJECTIVES: To support the search for solutions to environmental problems. To promote sustainable development in the Netherlands and around the world.

GENERAL INFORMATION: *Affiliated to:* Friends of the Earth International. *Personnel/Total:* 100. *Salaried:* 50. *Volunteers:* 50. *Budget/Total 1993:* ECU 2676000 (US$ 3130000). *Financial sources:* Private: 20%. Public: 40%. Self-financing: 40%.

PUBLICATIONS: *Periodicals:* Milieudefensie (10) - Danateurskrant (2). *Annual report. List of publications.*

EVALUATION/RESEARCH: Evaluation reports available. Undertakes research activities.

PLANNED ACTIVITIES: Undertaking research and dialogue projects involving other environmental NGOs on developing a vision of sustainability based on global equity and on Southern perspectives.

INFORMATION AND EDUCATION ACTIVITIES: Topics: Ecology/environment/biodiversity. **Activities:** Conferences/seminars/workshops/training activities; Formal education; Fund raising; Information and documentation services/data bases; Information campaigns/exhibitions; Lobbying/advocacy; Networking/electronic telecommunications; Publishing/audiovisual materials/educational materials.

NLD3338

VERENIGING VAN NEDERLANDSE GEMEENTEN - DIREKTIE SEKRETARIAAT INTERNATIONALE SAMENWERKING (VNG)

Postbus 30435, 2500 GK Den Haag, The Netherlands.

Telephone: 31 (70) 37 38 393. *Fax:* 31 (70) 36 35 682. *Contact:* Klaas de Vries, Director-General.

OBJECTIVES: To represent members' interests. To render services (advice, library and archives, administrative and sociographic research). To provide information for members. To offer members a forum for the exchange of experiences.

GENERAL INFORMATION: *Creation:* 1912. *Type of organisation:* association of NGOs. *Affiliated to:* International Union of local Authorities (The Netherlands) - Council of European Municipalities and Regions (France) - Congress of Local and Regional Authorities of Europe. *Personnel/Total:* 478. *Salaried:* 476. *Volunteers:* 2. *Budget/Total 1993:* ECU 23017000 (US$ 26921000). *Financial sources:* Self-financing: 100%.

PUBLICATIONS: *Periodicals:* NG Magazine (45) - Lokaal & Mondiaal/Vakmatig (4). *Annual report. List of publications.*

EVALUATION/RESEARCH: Evaluation reports available. Undertakes research activities.

PLANNED ACTIVITIES: Municipal network for Southern Africa and a municipal peace platform for Central and Eastern Europe.

COMMENTS: VNG is an association of all the local municipalities in the Netherlands. Undertakes activities in the Commonwealth of Independent States. Information activities related to the Commonwealth of Independent States.

ACTIVITIES IN DEVELOPING REGIONS: Present in developing regions. Active in 50 country(ies). Works through local field partners. **Sustainable Development Actions:** Democracy/good governance/institution building/participatory development; Health/sanitation/water; Sending volunteers/experts/technical assistance; Urban development/habitat. **Regions:** Caribbean; Central Africa; Central Asia and South Asia; East Africa; East Asia; Mexico and Central America; Middle East; North Africa; South America; South East Asia; Southern Africa; West Africa.

INFORMATION AND EDUCATION ACTIVITIES: Topics: Health/sanitation/water; Human rights/peace/conflicts; International relations/cooperation/development aid; Urban development/habitat. **Activities:** Conferences/seminars/workshops/training activities; Exchanges/twinning/linking; Information and documentation services/data bases.

NLD3339

VERENIGING VLUCHTELINGENWERK NEDERLAND ♦ Dutch Refugee Council

3ᵉ Hugo de Grootstraat 7, 1052 LJ Amsterdam, The Netherlands.

Telephone: 31 (20) 68 81 311. *Fax:* 31 (20) 68 82 181. *Contact:* F. Florin, Senior Policy Advisor on Protection.

OBJECTIVES: To promote a just refugee policy in the Netherlands. To assist refugees to integrate into Dutch society.

GENERAL INFORMATION: *Creation:* 1979. *Type of organisation:* coordinating body. *Affiliated to:* European Council on Refugees and Exiles. *Personnel/Total:* 7480. *Salaried:* 180. *Volunteers:* 7300. *Budget/Total 1993:* ECU 12337000 (US$ 14430000). *Financial sources:* Private: 57%. Public: 35%. Self-financing: 7%.

PUBLICATIONS: *Periodicals:* Status (3) - Infobulletin (10). *Annual report. List of publications.*

EVALUATION/RESEARCH: Evaluation reports available. Undertakes research activities.

COMMENTS: The Dutch refugee Council is an umbrella organisation which comprises nine developmental, church, human rights, refugee and social welfare organisations.

INFORMATION AND EDUCATION ACTIVITIES: Topics: Refugees/migrants/ethnic groups. **Activities:** Broadcasting/cultural events; Conferences/seminars/workshops/training activities; Exchanges/twinning/linking; Formal education; Information and documentation services/data bases; Information campaigns/exhibitions; Lobbying/advocacy; Networking/electronic telecommunications; Publishing/audiovisual materials/educational materials.

NLD3340

VERENIGING VOOR EEN NIEUW INTERNATIONAAL ONTWIKKELINGSBELEID (NIO) ♦ Association for a New International Development Policy

Wilhelmina Gasthuisplein 61, 1054 RB Amsterdam, The Netherlands.

Telephone: 31 (20) 61 21 220. *Fax:* 31 (20) 61 65 726.

NLD3341

VERENIGING VOOR PERSONELE SAMENWERKING MET ONTWIKKELINGSLANDEN (PSO) ♦ Association de coopération en matière de personnel avec les pays en développement

Willem Witsenplein 2, 2596 BK Den Haag, Pays-Bas.

Téléphone: 31 (70) 32 45 008. *Fax:* 31 (70) 32 82 430. *Contact:* M.H.M van Hulten.

OBJECTIFS: Pourvoir les ONG néerlandaises d'organes de concertation. Coordonner des activités communes et des relations avec les pouvoirs publics néerlandais. Co-financer un certain nombre de prestations complémentaires pour les coopérants ONG envoyés dans un pays en développement.

INFORMATIONS GENERALES: *Création:* 1985. *Type d'organisation:* regroupement d'ONG. *Organisations membres:* 30. *Personnel/Total:* 15. *Salariés:* 15. *Budget/Total 1993:* ECU 13719000 (US$ 16045000). *Sources financières:* Public: 100%.

PUBLICATIONS: *Rapport annuel. Liste des publications.*

COMMENTAIRES: Intervient dans la Communauté des Etats indépendants.

ACTIVITES DANS LES REGIONS EN DEVELOPPEMENT: Intervient dans 52 pays. Intervient par l'intermédiaire d'organisations locales partenaires. **Actions de Développement durable:** Envoi de volontaires/experts/assistance technique. **Régions:** Afrique australe; Afrique centrale; Afrique de l'Est; Afrique de l'Ouest; Afrique du Nord; Amérique du Sud; Asie centrale et Asie du Sud; Asie du Sud-Est; Caraïbes; Mexique et Amerique centrale; Océanie.

ACTIVITES D'INFORMATION ET D'EDUCATION: Domaines: Droits de l'Homme/paix/conflits; Questions relatives aux femmes; Relations internationales/coopération/aide au développement. **Activités:** Conférences/séminaires/ateliers/activités de formation.

NLD3342

VERENING WERELDKINDEREN ♦ Netherlands Intercountry Child Welfare Organisation

Riouwstraat 191, 2585 HT Den Haag, The Netherlands.

Telephone: 31 (70) 35 06 699. *Fax:* 31 (70) 35 47 867. *Contact:* A.F.C.J. Hendriks, Executive Director.

OBJECTIVES: To provide help for destitute children in developing countries through project aid, sponsorship or adoptions.

GENERAL INFORMATION: *Creation:* 1971. *Affiliated to:* Federation of European Adoption Agencies - Platform Adoptions (Netherlands) - Euradopt. *Personnel/Total:* 440. *Salaried:* 40 of which: 3 in developing countries. *Volunteers:* 400 of which: 20 in developing countries. *Budget/Total 1993:* ECU 3682000 (US$ 4307000). *Financial sources:* Private: 20%. Public: 60%. Self-financing: 20%.

PUBLICATIONS: *Periodicals:* Wereld Kinderen (6). *Annual report.*

COMMENTS: Undertakes activities in the Commonwealth of Independent States.

ACTIVITIES IN DEVELOPING REGIONS: Present in developing regions. Active in 15 country(ies). Maintains local field presence. Works through local field partners. **Sustainable Development Actions:** Children/youth/family. **Regions:** Caribbean; Central Asia and South Asia; East Africa; East Asia; Middle East; South America; South East Asia.

INFORMATION AND EDUCATION ACTIVITIES: Topics: Children/youth/family. **Activities:** Fund raising.

NLD3343

VINCENTIUS VERENIGING NEDERLAND ♦ Vincentius Association of the Netherlands

Westeinde 99, 2512 GV Den Haag, The Netherlands.

Telephone: 31 (70) 38 00 011.

NLD3344

VRAAG EN AANBOD INTERNATIONAAL

Postbus 1354, 5004 BJ Tilburg, The Netherlands.

Telephone: 31 (13) 54 32 592. *Fax:* 31 (13) 54 41 405.

NLD3345

VRIENDEN VAN JOHAN WACHTERS ♦ Friends of Johan Wachters

Putterschoeksestraat 33, 3114 PJ Schiedam, The Netherlands.

Telephone: 31 (10) 42 63 910. *Contact:* H.J. Povel.

OBJECTIVES: To help the poorest in Mali.

GENERAL INFORMATION: *Creation:* 1981. *Personnel/Total:* 5. *Volunteers:* 5 of which: 1 in developing countries. *Budget/Total 1993:* ECU 4600 (US$ 5300). *Financial sources:* Private: 100%.

PUBLICATIONS: *Periodicals:* Rondzeudbrief (1).

ACTIVITIES IN DEVELOPING REGIONS: Present in developing regions. Active in 1 country(ies). Maintains local field presence. **Sustainable Development Actions:** Ecology/environment/biodiversity; Health/sanitation/water; Rural development/agriculture; Small enterprises/informal sector/handicrafts. **Regions:** West Africa.

INFORMATION AND EDUCATION ACTIVITIES: Topics: Health/sanitation/water. **Activities:** Formal education; Fund raising; Lobbying/advocacy.

NLD3346

VRIENDSCHAPSVERENIGING NEDERLAND-CHINA (VNC) ♦ Friendship Society Netherlands-China

Postbus 79, 3500 AB Utrecht, The Netherlands.

Telephone: 31 (30) 26 11 846. *Fax:* 31 (30) 26 27 734. *Contact:* A.A.C.M. Leenders.

OBJECTIVES: To provide information and to promote knowledge and understanding about China and its people. To foster friendly relations between the people of China and the Netherlands.

GENERAL INFORMATION: *Creation:* 1977. *Personnel/Total:* 4. *Volunteers:* 4. *Budget/Total 1993:* ECU 40000 (US$ 46000). *Financial sources:* Self-financing: 100%.

PUBLICATIONS: *Periodicals:* China Nu (4) - Nieuwsbrief (5). *Annual report.*

INFORMATION AND EDUCATION ACTIVITIES: Topics: Culture/tradition/religion. **Activities:** Exchanges/twinning/linking; Information and documentation services/data bases; Information campaigns/exhibitions; Publishing/audiovisual materials/educational materials.

NLD3347

VROUWENBERAAD ONTWIKKELINGSSAMENWERKING ♦
Network of Gender Experts in Development Agencies in the Netherlands

Postbus 77, 2340 AB Oegstgeest, The Netherlands.

Telephone: 31 (71) 51 59 392. *Fax:* 31 (71) 51 75 391. *Contact:* E.J.E. Schoustra van Beukering, President.

OBJECTIVES: To improve the living and working conditions of women in developing countries. To promote the right of women to make autonomous decisions about their lives. To promote development co-operation between NGOs, governments and research and educational institutions.

GENERAL INFORMATION: *Creation:* 1978. *Type of organisation:* network. *Member organisations:* 35. *Affiliated to:* Women in Development Europe (Belgium). *Salaried:* 4. *Budget/Total 1993:* ECU 152000 (US$ 178000). *Financial sources:* Private: 40%. Public: 50%. *Self-financing:* 10%.

PUBLICATIONS: *Periodicals:* Vrouwenberaad Nieuws (4). *Annual report. List of publications.*

EVALUATION/RESEARCH: Undertakes research activities.

INFORMATION AND EDUCATION ACTIVITIES: Topics: Gender issues/women. **Activities:** Conferences/seminars/workshops/training activities; Information and documentation services/data bases; Information campaigns/exhibitions; Lobbying/advocacy; Networking/electronic telecommunications; Publishing/audiovisual materials/educational materials.

NLD3348

WERELDWINKELS ♦ Dutch Association of Third World Shops

Catharijnesingel 82, 3511 GP Utrecht, The Netherlands.

Telephone: 31 (30) 23 16 312. *Fax:* 31 (30) 23 00 440. *Contact:* H. Jansen, General Director.

OBJECTIVES: To sell "clean" products bought directly from small-scale producers of the Third World and to expand the alternative trade system. To increase awareness among the Dutch population and promote their involvement in development issues, particularly with regard to the matter of unfair trade structures.

GENERAL INFORMATION: *Creation:* 1972. *Affiliated to:* Stichting Max Havelaar (Netherlands) - NOVIB - NIO - SOMO - IKVOS - Fair Trade Organisate - Zuid-Nord Federatie. *Personnel/Total:* 7012. *Salaried:* 12. *Volunteers:* 7000. *Budget/Total 1993:* ECU 506000 (US$ 592000). *Financial sources:* Private: 5%. Public: 90%. *Self-financing:* 5%.

PUBLICATIONS: *Periodicals:* Ontzet (10). *Annual report. List of publications.*

EVALUATION/RESEARCH: Evaluation reports available. Undertakes research activities.

INFORMATION AND EDUCATION ACTIVITIES: Topics: Gender issues/women; International economic relations/trade/debt/finance. **Activities:** Broadcasting/cultural events; Conferences/seminars/workshops/training activities; Exchanges/twinning/linking; Information campaigns/exhibitions; Lobbying/advocacy; Publishing/audiovisual materials/educational materials.

NLD3349

WERKGROEP ARBEIDSVERHOUDINGEN EN WERKGELEGENHEID IN HET CARAIBISCH GEBEID (AWIC)

OZ Achterburgwal 185, 1012 DK Amsterdam, Netherlands.

Telephone: 31 (20) 525 26 20. *Fax:* 31 (20) 525 30 10.

NLD3350

WERKGROEP FYSIOTHERAPIE EN DERDE WERELD (FDW) ♦
Dutch Committee of Physiotherapy in Third World Countries

Nolensstraat 32b, 3039 PV Rotterdam, The Netherlands.

Telephone: 31 (10) 26 50 708. *Contact:* I. van Hemert, Chairman.

OBJECTIVES: To supply information to physiotherapists who are preparing to work in a developing country. To provide a platform for rehabilitation workers to exchange information and experiences.

GENERAL INFORMATION: *Creation:* 1981. *Affiliated to:* Dutch Association of Physiotherapy (the Netherlands). *Personnel/Total:* 12. *Volunteers:* 12. *Budget/Total 1993:* ECU 2000 (US$ 3000). *Financial sources:* Private: 80%. Self-financing: 20%.

PUBLICATIONS: *Periodicals:* Network Newsletter (2). *Annual report. List of publications.*

PLANNED ACTIVITIES: Developing an international network for rehabilitation workers in developing countries.

INFORMATION AND EDUCATION ACTIVITIES: Topics: Other. **Activities:** Broadcasting/cultural events; Conferences/seminars/workshops/training activities; Exchanges/twinning/linking; Formal education; Fund raising; Information and documentation services/data bases; Information campaigns/exhibitions; Lobbying/advocacy; Networking/electronic telecommunications; Publishing/audiovisual materials/educational materials.

NLD3351

WERKGROEP INCA PIRCA NEDERLAND (INCA PIRCA)

Postbus 3930, 1001 AS Amsterdam, Netherlands.

Telephone: 31 (20) 67 69 748. *Contact:* M. Dekker.

NLD3352

WERKGROEP MEDISCHE ONTWIKKELINGSSAMENWERK-ING (WEMOS) ♦ Working Group on Health and Development Issues

Postbus 1693, 1000 BR Amsterdam, The Netherlands.

Telephone: 31 (20) 42 02 222. *Fax:* 31 (20) 62 05 094. *E-mail:* wemos@antenna.nl. *Contact:* Jaap Kemkes.

OBJECTIVES: To inform the Dutch and European public about topics concerning health, politics and the Third World. To influence, from a consumer's viewpoint, EEC policies on these issues.

GENERAL INFORMATION: *Creation:* 1981. *Affiliated to:* Health Action International (Malaysia) - International Organisation of Consumers Unions (Malaysia) - International Baby Food Action Network (USA) - Women's Global Network on Reproductive Rights (United Kingdom). *Personnel/Total:* 55. *Salaried:* 9. *Volunteers:* 46. *Budget/Total 1993:* ECU 237000 (US$ 277000). *Financial sources:* Private: 5%. Public: 86%. *Self-financing:* 9%.

PUBLICATIONS: *Periodicals:* WEMOS Bulletin (6). *Annual report. List of publications.*

EVALUATION/RESEARCH: Evaluation reports available. Undertakes research activities.

PLANNED ACTIVITIES: Organising an orientation course on working in the health sector in developing countries.

COMMENTS: Information activities related to the Commonwealth of Independent States.

INFORMATION AND EDUCATION ACTIVITIES: Topics: Culture/tradition/religion; Ecology/environment/biodiversity; Education/training/literacy; Emergency relief/refugees/humanitarian assistance; Food/famine; Gender issues/women; Health/sanitation/water; International economic relations/trade/debt/finance; International relations/cooperation/development aid; Population/family planning/demography; Poverty/living conditions; Refugees/migrants/ethnic groups; Rural development/agriculture. **Activities:** Conferences/seminars/workshops/training activities; Formal education; Information and documentation services/data bases; Information campaigns/exhibitions; Lobbying/advocacy; Publishing/audiovisual materials/educational materials.

NLD3353

WERKGROEP ONTWIKKELINGSTECHNIEKEN (WOT) ♦ Working Group on Development Techniques

Vryhof 207, Postbus 217, 7500 AE Enschede, The Netherlands.

Telephone: 31 (53) 48 92 845. *Fax:* 31 (53) 43 57 042. *E-mail:* WOT@TOOL.NL. *Contact:* W.E. Klunne.

OBJECTIVES: To improve the economic and social conditions of the poor in developing countries. To support development workers through training, advice, information, documentation and research in the fields of solar energy, wind energy and micro hydro-power.

GENERAL INFORMATION: *Creation:* 1969. *Affiliated to:* TOOL. *Personnel/Total:* 102. *Salaried:* 2. *Volunteers:* 100. *Financial sources:* Public: 95%. *Self-financing:* 5%.

PUBLICATIONS: *Periodicals:* SOWOT (2). *Annual report. List of publications.*

EVALUATION/RESEARCH: Undertakes research activities.

COMMENTS: Undertakes activities in the Commonwealth of Independent States.

ACTIVITIES IN DEVELOPING REGIONS: Works through local field partners. **Sustainable Development Actions:** Energy/transport. **Regions:** Caribbean; Central Africa; Central Asia and South Asia; East Africa; East Asia; Mexico and Central America; Middle East; North Africa; Oceania; South America; South East Asia; Southern Africa; West Africa.

INFORMATION AND EDUCATION ACTIVITIES: Topics: Ecology/environment/biodiversity. **Activities:** Information and documentation services/data bases; Networking/electronic telecommunications; Publishing/audiovisual materials/educational materials.

NLD3354

WERKGROEP PAPUA NEW GUINEA ♦ Workgroup Papua New Guinea

Eekelerweg 7, 7102 ES Winterswijk, The Netherlands.

Telephone: 31 (543) 51 56 10. *Contact:* F. van der Werf, Secretary.

OBJECTIVES: To foster knowledge about Papua New Guinea in the Netherlands. To supervise and channel project funds to various agencies in Papua New Guinea.

GENERAL INFORMATION: *Creation:* 1973. *Personnel/Total:* 12. *Volunteers:* 12. *Budget/Total 1993:* ECU 1100 (US$ 1300). *Financial sources:* Private: 60%. *Self-financing:* 40%.

PUBLICATIONS: *Periodicals:* Papua New Guinea Newsletter (5) (3).

PLANNED ACTIVITIES: Organising three exhibitions with artifacts about Papua New Guinea. Preparing educational material for high schools on Papua New Guinea.

INFORMATION AND EDUCATION ACTIVITIES: Topics: Culture/tradition/religion; Ecology/environment/biodiversity; Education/training/literacy; Emergency relief/refugees/humanitarian assistance; Human rights/peace/conflicts; International relations/cooperation/development aid; Peace/ethnic conflicts/armament/disarmament; Poverty/living conditions; Refugees/migrants/ethnic groups; Rural development/agriculture; Urban development/habitat. **Activities:** Publishing/audiovisual materials/educational materials.

NLD3355

WERKGROEP ZAMBIA ♦ Dutch Committee on Zambia

Lombokstraat 8, 3818 CV Amersfoort, The Netherlands.

Telephone: 31 (33) 46 51 718.

OBJECTIVES: To contribute to the development of Zambia into a democratic society in which the most deprived groups can flourish through activities in the Netherlands.

GENERAL INFORMATION: *Creation:* 1980. *Personnel/Total:* 13. *Volunteers:* 13. *Budget/Total 1993:* ECU 230 (US$ 270). *Financial sources:* Private: 1%. *Self-financing:* 99%.

PUBLICATIONS: *Periodicals:* Zambia Nieuwsbrief (4).

INFORMATION AND EDUCATION ACTIVITIES: Topics: Children/youth/family; Culture/tradition/religion; Ecology/environment/biodiversity; Education/training/literacy; Employment/unemployment; Food/famine; Gender issues/women; Health/sanitation/water; Human rights/peace/conflicts; International economic relations/trade/debt/finance; International relations/cooperation/development aid; Poverty/living conditions; Refugees/migrants/ethnic groups; Rural development/agriculture; Urban development/habitat. **Activities:** Information and documentation services/data bases.

NLD3356

WILDE GANZEN ♦ Oies sauvages

Heuvellaan 36, 1217 JN Hilversum, Pays-Bas.

Téléphone: 31 (35) 62 46 622. *Fax:* 31 (35) 62 46 677. *Contact:* M. Th.K. de Vries, Secrétaire général.

OBJECTIFS: Faciliter le travail pastoral et diaconal en apportant une aide financière aux personnes et organisations qui en ont besoin sur le terrain, suivant en cela le devoir d'entraide oecuménique.

INFORMATIONS GENERALES: *Création:* 1957. *Affiliée à:* Interkerkelijke Omroep Nederland (Pays-Bas). *Personnel/Total:* 7. *Salariés:* 7. *Budget/Total 1993:* ECU 3222000 (US$ 3769000). *Sources financières:* Privé: 100%.

PUBLICATIONS: *Rapport annuel.*

COMMENTAIRES: Intervient dans la Communauté des Etats indépendants.

ACTIVITES DANS LES REGIONS EN DEVELOPPEMENT: Intervient par l'intermédiaire d'organisations locales partenaires. **Actions de Développement durable:** Développement rural/agriculture; Enfants/jeunesse/famille; Petites entreprises/secteur informel/artisanat; Santé/assainissement/eau; Secours d'urgence/réfugiés/aide humanitaire; Education/formation/alphabétisation. **Régions:** Afrique australe; Afrique centrale; Afrique de l'Est; Afrique de l'Ouest; Afrique du Nord; Amérique du Sud; Asie centrale et Asie du Sud; Asie de l'Est; Asie du Sud-Est; Caraïbes; Mexique et Amerique centrale; Moyen-Orient; Océanie.

NLD3357

WOMEN'S GLOBAL NETWORK FOR REPRODUCTIVE RIGHTS (WGNRR)

Nw. Z. Voorburgwal 32, 1012 RZ Amsterdam, The Netherlands.

Telephone: 31 (20) 62 09 672. *Fax:* 31 (20) 62 22 450. *Contact:* Martha de la Fuente, Co-ordinator.

OBJECTIVES: To promote women's reproductive rights including access to good quality, comprehensive reproductive health services and information on sexuality and reproduction.

GENERAL INFORMATION: *Creation:* 1978. *Type of organisation:* network. *Personnel/Total:* 6. *Salaried:* 6. *Budget/Total 1993:* ECU 322000 (US$ 377000).

PUBLICATIONS: *Periodicals:* WGNRR Newsletter (4). *Annual report. List of publications.*

EVALUATION/RESEARCH: Evaluation reports available. Undertakes research activities.

PLANNED ACTIVITIES: Undertaking campaigns on maternal mortality and morbidity and against the anti-fertility "vaccine".

COMMENTS: WGNRR does not undertake development activities itself. The members of the network carry out activities in developing regions in the fields of health, gender, population and human rights. Information activities related to the Commonwealth of Independent States.

INFORMATION AND EDUCATION ACTIVITIES: Topics: Culture/tradition/religion; Gender issues/women; Health/sanitation/water; Human rights/peace/conflicts; Population/family planning/demography; Poverty/living conditions; Racism/xenophobia/antisemitism; Refugees/migrants/ethnic groups. **Activities:** Conferences/seminars/workshops/training activities; Exchanges/twinning/linking; Fund raising; Information and documentation services/data bases; Information campaigns/exhibitions; Networking/electronic telecommunications; Publishing/audiovisual materials/educational materials.

See: *How to Use the Directory,* page 11.

NLD3358

WORLD INFORMATION SERVICE ON ENERGY (WISE)

Postbus 18185, 1001 ZB Amsterdam, The Netherlands.

Telephone: 31 (20) 63 92 681. *Fax:* 31 (20) 63 91 379. *Contact:* Thijs de la Court.

NLD3359

WORLD POPULATION FOUNDATION

Derkinderenlaan 14, 1251 EM Laren, The Netherlands.

Telephone: 31 (35) 53 82 551. *Fax:* 31 (35) 53 89 443. *Contact:* H. Rolink, Programme Officer.

NLD3360

WORLD RUNNERS NEDERLAND

Industriestraat 39, 9744 BP Hoogkerk, The Netherlands.

Telephone: 31 (50) 55 66 738.

NLD3361

WORLD VISION NEDERLAND

Joh. van Oldenbarneveltlaan 44, 3818 HB Amersfoort, The Netherlands.

Telephone: 31 (33) 46 55 111. *Fax:* 31 (33) 46 54 551. *Contact:* A.H. Delmaas-Van Dyk, Director.

OBJECTIVES: To follow our Lord and Saviour Jesus Christ in working with the poor and oppressed. To promote human transformation, to seek justice and to bear witness to the good news of the kingdom of God.

GENERAL INFORMATION: *Creation:* 1981. *Affiliated to:* World Vision International (USA). *Personnel/Total:* 207. *Salaried:* 7. *Volunteers:* 200. *Budget/Total 1993:* ECU 6491000 (US$ 7592000). *Financial sources:* Private: 17%. Public: 83%.

PUBLICATIONS: *Periodicals:* World Vision Nieuws (4) - Together Magazine/WVI (4). *Annual report.*

EVALUATION/RESEARCH: Evaluation reports available. Undertakes research activities.

COMMENTS: Undertakes activities in the Commonwealth of Independent States. Information activities related to the Commonwealth of Independent States.

ACTIVITIES IN DEVELOPING REGIONS: Present in developing regions. Active in 90 country(ies). Maintains local field presence. Works through local field partners. **Sustainable Development Actions:** Children/youth/family; Democracy/good governance/institution building/participatory development; Ecology/environment/biodiversity; Education/training/literacy; Emergency relief/refugees/humanitarian assistance; Energy/transport; Food/famine; Gender issues/women; Health/sanitation/water; Human rights/peace/conflicts; Population/family planning/demography; Rural development/agriculture; Sending volunteers/experts/technical assistance; Small enterprises/informal sector/handicrafts; Urban development/habitat. **Regions:** Caribbean; Central Africa; Central Asia and South Asia; East Africa; East Asia; Mexico and Central America; Middle East; Oceania; South America; South East Asia; Southern Africa; West Africa.

INFORMATION AND EDUCATION ACTIVITIES: Topics: Children/youth/family; Culture/tradition/religion; Ecology/environment/biodiversity; Education/training/literacy; Emergency relief/refugees/humanitarian assistance; Employment/unemployment; Food/famine; Gender issues/women; Health/sanitation/water; Human rights/peace/conflicts; International economic relations/trade/debt/finance; Peace/ethnic conflicts/armament/disarmament; Population/family planning/demography; Poverty/living conditions; Racism/xenophobia/antisemitism; Refugees/migrants/ethnic groups; Rural development/agriculture; Urban development/habitat. **Activities:** Broadcasting/cultural events; Conferences/seminars/workshops/training activities; Exchanges/twinning/linking; Fund raising; Information and documentation services/data bases; Information campaigns/exhibitions; Lobbying/advocacy; Publishing/audiovisual materials/educational materials.

NLD3362

X MIN Y ♦ X Minus Y

Keizersgracht 132-II, 1015 CW Amsterdam, The Netherlands.

Telephone: 31 (20) 627 96 61. *Fax:* 31 (20) 622 82 29. *Contact:* Chris Huinder.

OBJECTIVES: To provide political and financial support for grass-roots movements in Third World countries and organisations that fight for fundamental changes in their own countries or act internationally.

GENERAL INFORMATION: *Creation:* 1968. *Personnel/Total:* 50. *Salaried:* 5. *Volunteers:* 45. *Budget/Total 1993:* ECU 322000 (US$ 377000). *Financial sources:* Private: 100%.

PUBLICATIONS: *Periodicals:* XminY Bulletin (3). *Annual report. List of publications.*

PLANNED ACTIVITIES: Campaigning for equal rights and access to public services for (illegal) immigrants in the Netherlands.

COMMENTS: Undertakes activities in the Commonwealth of Independent States.

ACTIVITIES IN DEVELOPING REGIONS: Active in 30 country(ies). **Sustainable Development Actions:** Democracy/good governance/institution building/participatory development; Ecology/environment/biodiversity; Human rights/peace/conflicts. **Regions:** Caribbean; Central Africa; Central Asia and South Asia; East Africa; East Asia; Mexico and Central America; Middle East; North Africa; Oceania; South America; South East Asia; Southern Africa; West Africa.

INFORMATION AND EDUCATION ACTIVITIES: Topics: Ecology/environment/biodiversity; Human rights/peace/conflicts; International economic relations/trade/debt/finance; International relations/cooperation/development aid; Peace/ethnic conflicts/armament/disarmament; Racism/xenophobia/antisemitism; Refugees/migrants/ethnic groups. **Activities:** Fund raising; Lobbying/advocacy.

NLD3363

YMCA NEDERLAND ♦ YMCA Netherlands

Postbus 115, 3970 AC Driebergen, The Netherlands.

Telephone: 31 (343) 52 32 33. *Fax:* 31 (343) 52 01 70. *Contact:* Willem Hoornstra, President.

OBJECTIVES: To help people, particularly the young, to become responsible citizens of the world.

GENERAL INFORMATION: *Creation:* 1853. *Personnel/Total:* 732. *Salaried:* 32. *Volunteers:* 700. *Budget/Total 1993:* ECU 690000 (US$ 808000). *Financial sources:* Public: 75%. Self-financing: 25%.

PUBLICATIONS: *Periodicals:* Inklusief (6) - Komby (10). *Annual report. List of publications.*

COMMENTS: YMCA Nederland participates in a wide variety of sustainable development actions undertaken by the World Alliance of YMCAs. It also undertakes an integrated programme of information and education activities in the Netherlands on sustainable development issues. Information activities related to the Commonwealth of Independent States.

NLD3364

YOUNG WOMEN'S CHRISTIAN ASSOCIATION OF NEDERLAND (YWCA-NEDERLAND)

F.C. Dondersstraat 23, 3572 JB Utrecht, The Netherlands.

Telephone: 31 (30) 27 15 525. *Fax:* 31 (30) 27 15 525. *Contact:* Dinie Donze, President.

OBJECTIVES: To promote the protection of human rights internationally and nationally with special emphasis on women.

GENERAL INFORMATION: *Creation:* 1920. *Type of organisation:* association of NGOs. *Personnel/Total:* 2. *Salaried:* 2.

PUBLICATIONS: *Periodicals:* Contour (8). *Annual report.*

COMMENTS: Information activities related to the Commonwealth of Independent States.

ACTIVITIES IN DEVELOPING REGIONS: Sustainable Development Actions: Emergency relief/refugees/humanitarian assistance; Health/sanitation/water; Human rights/peace/conflicts; Population/family planning/demography; Rural development/agriculture; Small enterprises/informal sector/handicrafts. **Regions:** Caribbean; Central Africa; Central Asia and South Asia; East Africa; East Asia; Mexico and Central America; Middle East; North Africa; Oceania; South America; South East Asia; Southern Africa; West Africa.

INFORMATION AND EDUCATION ACTIVITIES: Topics: Ecology/environment/biodiversity; Gender issues/women; Human rights/peace/conflicts; International economic relations/trade/debt/finance; International relations/cooperation/development aid; Racism/xenophobia/antisemitism; Refugees/migrants/ethnic groups. **Activities:** Conferences/seminars/workshops/training activities; Exchanges/twinning/linking; Fund raising; Information and documentation services/data bases; Information campaigns/exhibitions; Lobbying/advocacy; Networking/electronic telecommunications; Publishing/audiovisual materials/educational materials.

NLD3365

YOUTH AND ENVIRONMENT EUROPE (YEE)

Oudegracht 42, 3511 AR Utrecht, The Netherlands.

Telephone: 31 (30) 23 11 537. **Fax:** 31 (30) 23 43 986. **E-mail:** YEE@antenna.nl. **Contact:** Victor Jonsson.

OBJECTIVES: To conserve the natural environment. To support member organisations in lobbying and raising public awareness for a better environment and a sustainable society.

GENERAL INFORMATION: Creation: 1983. **Type of organisation:** coordinating body. **Member organisations:** 31. **Affiliated to:** European Environmental Bureau (Belgium) - International Youth Federation for Environmental Studies and Conservation (India) - Umbrella of European Youth Organisations (Belgium). **Personnel/Total:** 2. **Salaried:** 1. **Volunteers:** 1. **Budget/Total 1993:** ECU 87000 (US$ 102000). **Financial sources:** Private: 20%. Public: 60%. Self-financing: 10%.

PUBLICATIONS: Periodicals: Youth & Environment (4). *Annual report. List of publications.*

COMMENTS: Undertakes activities in the Commonwealth of Independent States. Information activities related to the Commonwealth of Independent States.

INFORMATION AND EDUCATION ACTIVITIES: Topics: Ecology/environment/biodiversity; International economic relations/trade/debt/finance; International relations/cooperation/development aid; Rural development/agriculture; Urban development/habitat. **Activities:** Conferences/seminars/workshops/training activities; Exchanges/twinning/linking; Fund raising; Information campaigns/exhibitions; Lobbying/advocacy; Networking/electronic telecommunications.

NLD3366

YOUTH FOR DEVELOPMENT AND COOPERATION (YDC)

Overschiestraat 9, 1062 HN Amsterdam, The Netherlands.

Telephone: 31 (20) 61 42 510. **Fax:** 31 (20) 61 75 545. **E-mail:** YDC@GEO2.GEONET.DE. **Contact:** Bas Auer, Secretary General.

OBJECTIVES: To strengthen youth structures that aim to forge new cooperation between young people in the North and South to support sustainable development, economic equity, protection of the environment and social justice.

GENERAL INFORMATION: Creation: 1947. **Member organisations:** 52. **Affiliated to:** European Coordination Bureau (Belgium) - European Youth Forum (Belgium). **Personnel/Total:** 9. Salaried: 3. Volunteers: 6. **Budget/Total 1993:** ECU 55000 (US$ 65000). **Financial sources:** Private: 5%. Public: 80%. Self-financing: 15%.

PUBLICATIONS: Periodicals: Flash (6) - Focus (2). *List of publications.*

EVALUATION/RESEARCH: Evaluation reports available. Undertakes research activities.

COMMENTS: Undertakes activities in the Commonwealth of Independent States. Information activities related to the Commonwealth of Independent States.

ACTIVITIES IN DEVELOPING REGIONS: Works through local field partners. **Sustainable Development Actions:** Debt/finance/trade; Democracy/good governance/institution building/participatory development; Energy/transport; Gender issues/women. **Regions:** Central Africa; East Africa; Mexico and Central America; South America; South East Asia; West Africa.

INFORMATION AND EDUCATION ACTIVITIES: Topics: Ecology/environment/biodiversity; Gender issues/women; Human rights/peace/conflicts; International economic relations/trade/debt/finance; Racism/xenophobia/antisemitism; Refugees/migrants/ethnic groups. **Activities:** Conferences/seminars/workshops/training activities; Exchanges/twinning/linking; Formal education; Fund raising; Information campaigns/exhibitions; Lobbying/advocacy; Networking/electronic telecommunications; Publishing/audiovisual materials/educational materials.

NLD3367

ZEISTER ZENDINGSGENOOTSCHAP ♦ Zeist Missionary Society

Postbus 19, 3700 AA Zeist, The Netherlands.

Telephone: 31 (30) 69 17 424. **Fax:** 31 (30) 69 17 622. **Contact:** Ole van Luyn, General Secretary.

OBJECTIVES: To support Moravian churches in their missionary and social responsibilities. To participate in the eucumenical mandate of the churches worldwide.

GENERAL INFORMATION: Creation: 1793. **Personnel/Total:** 30. Salaried: 20. Volunteers: 10. **Budget/Total 1993:** ECU 2394000 (US$ 2800000). **Financial sources:** Private: 90%. Self-financing: 10%.

PUBLICATIONS: Periodicals: Suriname Zending (4). *Annual report.*

ACTIVITIES IN DEVELOPING REGIONS: Active in 9 country(ies). Works through local field partners.

NLD3368

ZOA VLUCHTELINGENZORG ♦ ZOA Refugee Care

Postbus 10343, 7301 GH Apeldoorn, The Netherlands.

Telephone: 31 (55) 66 38 33. **Fax:** 31 (55) 66 87 99. **Contact:** H. Huberts, Executive Director.

NOR3369

ADOPSJONSFORUM ♦ Adoption Forum

Inkognitogt. 17, 0256 Oslo, Norway.

Telephone: 47 (22) 55 78 60. **Fax:** 47 (22) 44 62 60. **Contact:** Ketil Lehland, Director.

OBJECTIVES: To mediate international adoptions. To provide assistance to children who are not for adoption.

GENERAL INFORMATION: Creation: 1970. **Personnel/Total:** 17. Salaried: 17. **Budget/Total 1993:** ECU 1266000 (US$ 1490000). **Financial sources:** Private: 87%. Public: 5%. Self-financing: 8%.

PUBLICATIONS: Periodicals: Adopsjonsforum (6). Annual report.

COMMENTS: Undertakes activities in the Commonwealth of Independent States. Information activities related to the Commonwealth of Independent States.

ACTIVITIES IN DEVELOPING REGIONS: Present in developing regions. Active in 15 country(ies). Works through local field partners. **Sustainable Development Actions:** Children/youth/family; Emergency relief/refugees/humanitarian assistance; Rural development/agriculture. **Regions:** Central Asia and South Asia; East Africa; East Asia; Mexico and Central America; South America; South East Asia.

INFORMATION AND EDUCATION ACTIVITIES: Topics: Children/youth/family; Rural development/agriculture. **Activities:** Conferences/seminars/workshops/training activities; Fund raising; Information campaigns/exhibitions; Lobbying/advocacy; Other.

NOR3370

ADVENTISTSAMFUNNET, NORGE ♦ Seventh Day Adventist Church of Norway

John E Mattensons Vei 13, 0687 Oslo, Norway.

Telephone: 47 (22) 27 01 80. **Fax:** 47 (22) 26 83 66. **Contact:** Roger Robertsen.

NOR3371

AFGHANISTANKOMITEEN I NORGE (AIN) ♦ Norwegian Committee for Afghanistan

Chr. Kroghsgt 34, 0168 Oslo, Norway.

Telephone: 47 (22) 20 10 65. **Fax:** 47 (22) 20 10 68. **Contact:** Terrie Skanfiord, President.

OBJECTIVES: To support Afgans through emergency and development aid. To disseminate information on Afganistan in Norway.

GENERAL INFORMATION: Creation: 1979. **Personnel/Total:** 100. Salaried: 100 of which: 97 in developing countries. **Budget/Total 1993:** ECU 1916000 (US$ 2255000). **Financial sources:** Private: 10%. Public: 88%. Self-financing: 2%.

PUBLICATIONS: Periodicals: Afghanistanytt (4). Annual report.

EVALUATION/RESEARCH: Evaluation reports available. Undertakes research activities.

ACTIVITIES IN DEVELOPING REGIONS: Present in developing regions. Active in 1 country(ies). Maintains local field presence. Works through local field partners. **Sustainable Development Actions:** Children/youth/family; Democracy/good governance/institution building/participatory development; Ecology/environment/biodiversity; Education/training/literacy; Emergency relief/refugees/humanitarian assistance; Energy/transport; Food/famine; Gender issues/women; Health/sanitation/water; Human rights/peace/conflicts; Rural development/agriculture; Sending volunteers/experts/technical assistance; Small enterprises/informal sector/handicrafts. **Regions:** Central Asia and South Asia.

INFORMATION AND EDUCATION ACTIVITIES: Topics: Children/youth/family; Culture/tradition/religion; Ecology/environment/biodiversity; Education/training/literacy; Emergency relief/refugees/humanitarian assistance; Food/famine; Gender issues/women; Health/sanitation/water; Human rights/peace/conflicts; International relations/cooperation/development aid; Peace/ethnic conflicts/armament/disarmament; Poverty/living conditions; Racism/xenophobia/antisemitism; Refugees/migrants/ethnic groups; Rural development/agriculture. **Activities:** Conferences/seminars/workshops/training activities; Fund raising; Information and documentation services/data bases; Information campaigns/exhibitions.

NOR3372

ALL BURMA STUDENTS' DEMOCRATIC FRONT - EUROPE OFFICE (ABSDF)

P.O.Box 6720, St. Olavs Plass, 0130 Oslo, Norway.

Telephone: 47 (22) 41 41 43. **Fax:** 47 (22) 41 41 43. **E-mail:** absdf@pns.apc.org. **Contact:** Aye Chan Naing, European Representative.

OBJECTIVES: To disseminate information on Burma. To lobby government officials, organisations and NGOs. To act as a liaison office.

GENERAL INFORMATION: Creation: 1988. **Type of organisation:** network. **Affiliated to:** Human Rights Information and Documentation Centre - Asia Student Association. **Personnel/Total:** 2000. Volunteers: 2000 of which: 2000 in developing countries. **Budget/Total 1993:** ECU 7000 (US$ 8000). **Financial sources:** Private: 100%.

PUBLICATIONS: Periodicals: DAWN (12) - Burma Focus (24). Annual report. List of publications.

COMMENTS: The ABSDF (Europe office) works on behalf of the organisation in Burma. Most of its 2000 volunteers/members are in Burma border camps.

ACTIVITIES IN DEVELOPING REGIONS: Present in developing regions. Active in 1 country(ies). Maintains local field presence. Works through local field partners. **Sustainable Development Actions:** Children/youth/family; Democracy/good governance/institution building/participatory development; Ecology/environment/biodiversity; Education/training/literacy; Emergency relief/refugees/humanitarian assistance; Food/famine; Gender issues/women; Health/sanitation/water; Human rights/peace/conflicts; Rural development/agriculture; Small enterprises/informal sector/handicrafts. **Regions:** South East Asia.

INFORMATION AND EDUCATION ACTIVITIES: Topics: Ecology/environment/biodiversity; Education/training/literacy; Emergency relief/refugees/humanitarian assistance; Human rights/peace/conflicts; Refugees/migrants/ethnic groups; Rural development/agriculture. **Activities:** Broadcasting/cultural events; Conferences/seminars/workshops/training activities; Exchanges/twinning/linking; Formal education; Fund raising; Information and documentation services/data bases; Information campaigns/exhibitions; Lobbying/advocacy; Networking/electronic telecommunications; Publishing/audiovisual materials/educational materials.

NOR3373

AMMEHJELPEN ♦ Breast Feeding Mothers Support Group

Ammehjelpens Secretariat, v/brit Oyehaug, 2423 Ostby, Norway.

Telephone: 47 (62) 45 52 51. **Contact:** Anne Lise Krogh Robak Chairperson.

NOR3374

AMMEHJELPENS INTERNASJONALE GRUPPE (IBFAN) ♦ International Group of the Norwegian Breastfeeding Mothers' Support Group

c/o Ammehjelpens Sekretariat, 2423 Oestby, Norway.

Telephone: 47 (62) 45 52 51. **Contact:** Ann Karin Paulsen, Co-ordinator.

OBJECTIVES: To promote, support and protect breastfeeding.

GENERAL INFORMATION: Creation: 1968. **Affiliated to:** International Baby Food Action Network - World Alliance of Breastfeeding Associations - Internaitonal Nestle Boycott Committee. **Personnel/Total:** 512. Volunteers: 512.

PUBLICATIONS: Periodicals: Ammenytt(Breastfeeding News) (4). Annual report. List of publications.

EVALUATION/RESEARCH: Evaluation reports available.

ACTIVITIES IN DEVELOPING REGIONS: Active in 3 country(ies). Works through local field partners. **Sustainable Development Actions:** Children/youth/family; Health/sanitation/water. **Regions:** Mexico and Central America; South America.

INFORMATION AND EDUCATION ACTIVITIES: **Topics:** Children/youth/family; Health/sanitation/water; Other. **Activities:** Broadcasting/cultural events; Conferences/seminars/workshops/training activities; Exchanges/twinning/linking; Information and documentation services/data bases; Information campaigns/exhibitions; Networking/electronic telecommunications; Publishing/audiovisual materials/educational materials.

NOR3375

AMNESTY INTERNATIONAL, NORWEGIAN SECTION

Madridalsveien 87, 0461 Oslo 4, Norway.

NOR3376

ARBEIDERBEVEGELSENS INTERNASJONALE STOT-TEKOMITE ♦ The International Solidarity Committee of the Norwegian Labour Movement

Youngsgate 11, 0181 Oslo, Norway.

Telephone: 47 (22) 40 10 50.

NOR3377

ARBEIDERBEVEGELSENS UNGDOMSORGANISASJON ♦

Norwegian Labour Youth League

Arbeidersammfunnets plass 1, 0181 Oslo, Norway.

Telephone: 47 (22) 20 15 79.

NOR3378

ARBEIDERNES OPPLYSNINGSFORBUND ♦ Worker's Educational Association of Norway

Storgt 23C, 0184 Oslo, Norway.

Telephone: 47 (22) 03 10 50. **Fax:** 47 (22) 03 12 70.

NOR3379

BLA KORS I NORGE (BKIN) ♦ The Blue Cross of Norway

PO Box 4793, Sofienberg, 0506 Oslo, Norway.

Telephone: 47 (22) 20 42 69. **Fax:** 47 (22) 36 31 01. **Contact:** Finn Kristian Marthinsen, General Secretary.

OBJECTIVES: To work towards the prevention of alcohol and drug related problems in society. To rehabilitate alcohol and drug dependents and aid their famalies. To spread the good news of God's love for mankind. To encourage a lifestyle of abstinence.

GENERAL INFORMATION: *Type of organisation:* association of NGOs. *Affiliated to:* The Blue Cross Federation (Switzerland) - Avholdfolkets Landsnemnd (Norway) -Kristenfolkets Edruskapsråd (Norway). *Personnel/Total:* 700. *Salaried:* 700 of which: 1 in developing countries. ***Budget/Total 1993:*** ECU 35926000 (US$ 42289000). *Financial sources:* Public: 97%. Self-financing: 3%.

PUBLICATIONS: *Periodicals:* Blåkorsbladet (7). *Annual report. List of publications.*

EVALUATION/RESEARCH: Evaluation reports available. Undertakes research activities.

ACTIVITIES IN DEVELOPING REGIONS: Present in developing regions. Active in 2 country(ies). Maintains local field presence. Works through local field partners. **Sustainable Development Actions:** Children/youth/family; Gender issues/women; Health/sanitation/water. **Regions:** Southern Africa.

INFORMATION AND EDUCATION ACTIVITIES: Topics: Children/youth/family; Gender issues/women; Health/sanitation/water. **Activities:** Conferences/seminars/workshops/training activities; Fund raising; Information and documentation services/data bases; Information campaigns/exhibitions; Lobbying/advocacy; Publishing/audiovisual materials/educational materials.

NOR3380

CARE NORGE ♦ Care Norway

Kirkegaten 10, P.O. Box 180 Sentrum, 0102 Oslo 1, Norway.

Telephone: 47 (22) 42 52 18. **Fax:** 47 (22) 42 45 77. **Contact:** Torkild Skallerud, National Director.

NOR3381

CARITAS NORGE ♦ Caritas Norway

Fagerborggt. 17, 0360 Oslo, Norway.

Telephone: 47 (22) 60 77 75. **Fax:** 47 (22) 56 83 06. **Contact:** Bernt Gulbrandsen, Secretary General.

OBJECTIVES: To act as a reliable and effective organisation for the development and emergency aid involvement of the Norwegian Catholic Church.

GENERAL INFORMATION: *Creation:* 1965. *Affiliated to:* Caritas Internationalis - International Catholic Migration Commission. *Personnel/Total:* 7. *Salaried:* 6. *Volunteers:* 1. ***Budget/Total 1993:*** ECU 2322000 (US$ 2733000). *Financial sources:* Private: 18%. Public: 82%.

PUBLICATIONS: *Periodicals:* Caritas Info (5). *Annual report.*

COMMENTS: Undertakes activities in the Commonwealth of Independent States.

ACTIVITIES IN DEVELOPING REGIONS: Active in 15 country(ies). Works through local field partners. **Sustainable Development Actions:** Children/youth/family; Democracy/good governance/institution building/participatory development; Education/training/literacy; Emergency relief/refugees/humanitarian assistance; Food/famine; Health/sanitation/water; Human rights/peace/conflicts; Rural development/agriculture; Small enterprises/informal sector/handicrafts. **Regions:** Caribbean; East Africa; Mexico and Central America; Middle East; South America; South East Asia; Southern Africa.

INFORMATION AND EDUCATION ACTIVITIES: Topics: Children/youth/family; Emergency relief/refugees/humanitarian assistance; Food/famine; Health/sanitation/water; Human rights/peace/conflicts; International economic relations/trade/debt/finance; Poverty/living conditions; Rural development/agriculture. **Activities:** Conferences/seminars/workshops/training activities; Fund raising; Information campaigns/exhibitions.

NOR3382

CENTRE FOR INTERNATIONAL WOMEN'S ISSUES (CEWI)

Fr. Nansenspl. 6, 4 ltg, 0160 Oslo, Norway.

Telephone: 47 (22) 42 62 45. **Fax:** 47 (22) 42 32 05.

NOR3383

COUNCIL OF FREE CHURCHES

Christian Krohgsgt. 34, 0186 Oslo, Norway.

NOR3384

DELTA INTERNASJONALT KFUK-KFUM ♦ International Partnerships YWCA-YMCA

P.O.Box 6814, St. Olav pl., 0130 Oslo, Norway.

Telephone: 47 (22) 11 56 90. **Fax:** 47 (22) 20 47 59. **Contact:** Eilert Rostrup, Director.

OBJECTIVES: To provide financial assistance for projects in developing countries that aim to improve the educational and living standards of children and youth.

GENERAL INFORMATION: *Creation:* 1948. *Affiliated to:* National Council YMCA/YWCA (Norway) - World Alliance of YMCAs (Switzerland) - World YWCA (Switzerland). *Personnel/Total:* 33. *Salaried:* 3. *Volunteers:* 30. *Financial sources:* Private: 95%. Public: 5%.

PUBLICATIONS: *Periodicals:* Sponsor Information (2).

ACTIVITIES IN DEVELOPING REGIONS: Active in 10 country(ies). Works through local field partners. **Sustainable Development Actions:** Children/youth/family; Democracy/good governance/institution building/participatory development; Education/training/literacy; Emergency relief/refugees/humanitarian assistance; Food/famine; Gender issues/women; Health/sanitation/water; Human rights/peace/conflicts; Small enterprises/informal sector/handicrafts; Urban development/habitat.

See: *How to Use the Directory*, page 11.

Regions: Central Asia and South Asia; East Africa; Middle East; South America; Southern Africa.

NOR3385

DET NORSKE TIBETMISJON ♦ Norwegian Himal-Asian Mission

PO Box 9111, Grönland, 0133 Oslo, Norway.

Telephone: 47 (22) 36 33 10. *Fax:* 47 (22) 11 02 91.

NOR3386

DIAKONHJEMMETS INTERNASJONALE SENTER (DIS) ♦ Centre for Partnership in Development

Vinderen, P.O. Box 23, 0319 Oslo, Norway.

Telephone: 47 (22) 45 18 18. *Fax:* 47 (22) 45 18 10. *Contact:* Sigrun Møgedal, Director.

OBJECTIVES: To contribute to the dialogue on North/South issues. To incorporate Third World learning and perspectives into all activities. To facilitate discussions and reflections related to global justice and global development with specific reference to social issues.

GENERAL INFORMATION: *Creation:* 1987. *Personnel/Total:* 14. *Salaried:* 14. *Budget/Total 1993:* ECU 599000 (US$ 705000). *Financial sources:* Private: 10%. Public: 10%. Self-financing: 80%.

PUBLICATIONS: *Periodicals:* Working Notes (2). *Annual report. List of publications.*

EVALUATION/RESEARCH: Undertakes research activities.

ACTIVITIES IN DEVELOPING REGIONS: Active in 20 country(ies). **Sustainable Development Actions:** Democracy/good governance/institution building/participatory development; Health/sanitation/water; Human rights/peace/conflicts. **Regions:** Central Asia and South Asia; East Africa; Middle East; Southern Africa; West Africa.

INFORMATION AND EDUCATION ACTIVITIES: Topics: Children/youth/family; Culture/tradition/religion; Gender issues/women; Health/sanitation/water; Human rights/peace/conflicts; International economic relations/trade/debt/finance; International relations/cooperation/development aid; Population/family planning/demography. **Activities:** Conferences/seminars/workshops/training activities; Formal education; Information and documentation services/data bases; Lobbying/advocacy; Networking/electronic telecommunications; Publishing/audiovisual materials/educational materials.

NOR3387

DEN EVANGELISKE LUTHERSKE FRIKIRKE, YTREMIS-JONEN ♦ The Lutheran Free Church of Norway

P.O. Box 23, Bekkelagshogda, 1109 Oslo, Norway.

Telephone: 47 (22) 74 50 90. *Fax:* 47 (22) 74 75 05. *Contact:* Anne May Stavenes.

OBJECTIVES: To promote a wholistic Christian mission through church "plantings", leadership training, media and communication, and development work.

GENERAL INFORMATION: *Creation:* 1917. *Type of organisation:* coordinating body. *Member organisations:* 78. *Affiliated to:* Norwegian Missionary Council (Norway) - Norwegian Institute for Christian and Islamic Studies (Norway). *Personnel/Total:* 26. *Salaried:* 26 of which: 9 in developing countries. *Budget/Total 1993:* ECU 1307000 (US$ 1539000). *Financial sources:* Public: 3%. Self-financing: 97%.

PUBLICATIONS: *Periodicals:* Be os Alberd (4). *Annual report.*

EVALUATION/RESEARCH: Evaluation reports available. Undertakes research activities.

ACTIVITIES IN DEVELOPING REGIONS: Present in developing regions. Active in 3 country(ies). Maintains local field presence. Works through local field partners. **Sustainable Development Actions:** Debt/finance/trade; Democracy/good governance/institution building/participatory development; Education/training/literacy; Food/famine; Health/sanitation/water; Rural development/agriculture; Sending volunteers/experts/technical assistance. **Regions:** East Asia; West Africa.

INFORMATION AND EDUCATION ACTIVITIES: Topics: Children/youth/family; Culture/tradition/religion; Education/training/literacy; Food/famine; Health/sanitation/water; Human rights/peace/conflicts; Peace/ethnic conflicts/armament/disarmament; Poverty/living conditions; Rural development/agriculture; Urban development/habitat. **Activities:** Broadcasting/cultural events; Exchanges/twinning/linking; Fund raising; Information campaigns/exhibitions.

NOR3388

FELLESKAMPANJEN FOR JORDAS MILJO OG UTVIKLING (NCED) ♦ Norwegian Campaign for Environment and Development

Langesgate 4, 0165 Oslo 1, Norway.

Telephone: 47 (2) 36 20 35. *Fax:* 47 (2) 36 14 54. *Contact:* Elin Enge, Executive Director.

NOR3389

FELLESRADET FOR AFRIKA ♦ The Norwegian Council for Africa

Fredenborgveien 39, 0177 Oslo, Norway.

Telephone: 47 (22) 36 22 00. *Fax:* 47 (22) 36 22 80. *Contact:* Kristina Medin, President.

OBJECTIVES: To support the promotion of participatory democracy, respect for human rights and equity in Sub-Saharan Africa. To create consciousness and a sense of solidarity towards Africa among the Norwegian population, member organisations, the media, politicians, businesses, etc...

GENERAL INFORMATION: *Creation:* 1967. *Type of organisation:* coordinating body. *Member organisations:* 35. *Affiliated to:* FN-Sambandet (Norway) - Forum for Utviklingsjournalistkik (Norway) - European Anti-Apartheid Movements (United Kingdom) - Interfund (South Africa). *Personnel/Total:* 15. *Salaried:* 5 of which: 1 in developing countries. *Volunteers:* 10. *Budget/Total 1993:* ECU 173000 (US$ 204000). *Financial sources:* Private: 10%. Public: 73%. Self-financing: 17%.

PUBLICATIONS: *Periodicals:* 3.World Magazine (6) - Det Sørlige Afrika (20). *Annual report.*

EVALUATION/RESEARCH: Evaluation reports available. Undertakes research activities.

ACTIVITIES IN DEVELOPING REGIONS: Present in developing regions. Active in 3 country(ies). Maintains local field presence. Works through local field partners. **Sustainable Development Actions:** Democracy/good governance/institution building/participatory development; Education/training/literacy; Gender issues/women; Sending volunteers/experts/technical assistance. **Regions:** Southern Africa.

INFORMATION AND EDUCATION ACTIVITIES: Topics: Children/youth/family; Education/training/literacy; Gender issues/women; Human rights/peace/conflicts; International economic relations/trade/debt/finance; International relations/cooperation/development aid; Peace/ethnic conflicts/armament/disarmament; Poverty/living conditions. **Activities:** Conferences/seminars/workshops/training activities; Exchanges/twinning/linking; Fund raising; Information and documentation services/data bases; Information campaigns/exhibitions; Lobbying/advocacy; Publishing/audiovisual materials/educational materials.

NOR3390

FLYKTNINGERADET ♦ Norwegian Refugee Council (NRC)

Pilestredet 15B, Postboks 6758 St. Olav's plass, 0130 Oslo , Norway.

Telephone: 47 (22) 11 65 00. *Fax:* 47 (22) 11 65 01. *Contact:* Gunnar F. Andersen, Secretary General.

OBJECTIVES: To defend human rights of refugees and internally displaced persons. To contribute to international protection for refugees and internally displaced persons. To act as an advising and co-ordinating body for international refugee work.

GENERAL INFORMATION: *Creation:* 1952. *Member organisations:* 16. *Affiliated to:* Nordic Assistance to repatriated Vietnamese (Vietnam) - Project Counseling Services (Costa Rica). *Personnel/Total:* 268. *Salaried:* 268 of which: 233 in developing countries. *Budget/Total 1993:* ECU 23160000 (US$ 27261000). *Financial sources:* Private: 16%. Public: 84%.

Voir : *Comment utiliser le répertoire*, page 11.

PUBLICATIONS: *Periodicals:* PÅ Flukt Nyheter (11) - PÅ Flukt Tema (6). *Annual report. List of publications.*

EVALUATION/RESEARCH: Evaluation reports available. Undertakes research activities.

COMMENTS: Undertakes activities in the Commonwealth of Independent States.

ACTIVITIES IN DEVELOPING REGIONS: Active in 8 country(ies). Maintains local field presence. Works through local field partners. **Sustainable Development Actions:** Democracy/good governance/institution building/participatory development; Education/training/literacy; Emergency relief/refugees/humanitarian assistance; Human rights/peace/conflicts; Rural development/agriculture; Sending volunteers/experts/technical assistance; Small enterprises/informal sector/handicrafts. **Regions:** Central Asia and South Asia; Mexico and Central America; Middle East; South East Asia; Southern Africa.

INFORMATION AND EDUCATION ACTIVITIES: Topics: Education/training/literacy; Emergency relief/refugees/humanitarian assistance; Gender issues/women; Human rights/peace/conflicts; International relations/cooperation/development aid; Peace/ethnic conflicts/armament/disarmament; Racism/xenophobia/antisemitism; Refugees/migrants/ethnic groups. **Activities:** Broadcasting/cultural events; Conferences/seminars/workshops/training activities; Exchanges/twinning/linking; Formal education; Fund raising; Information and documentation services/data bases; Information campaigns/exhibitions; Lobbying/advocacy; Networking/electronic telecommunications; Publishing/audiovisual materials/educational materials.

NOR3391

FN - SAMBANDET I NORGE ♦ United Nations Association of Norway

Storgt. 33 A, 0184 Oslo, Norway.

Telephone: 47 (22) 20 91 70. *Fax:* 47 (22) 20 81 42. *Contact:* Svein-Erik Odden, Secretary General.

OBJECTIVES: To circulate information concerning the United Nations' ideas, organisation and activities in order to create interest in and discussion on international matters.

GENERAL INFORMATION: Creation: 1946. **Type of organisation:** network. **Member organisations:** 80. **Affiliated to:** World Federation of UN Associations. **Personnel/Total:** 35. *Salaried:* 28. *Volunteers:* 7. **Budget/Total 1993:** ECU 1437000 (US$ 1692000). **Financial sources:** *Public:* 96%. *Self-financing:* 4%.

PUBLICATIONS: *Periodicals:* Brennpunkt (11) - Alternativ (3) - ILO-nytt (4). *Annual report. List of publications.*

EVALUATION/RESEARCH: Evaluation reports available.

INFORMATION AND EDUCATION ACTIVITIES: Topics: Ecology/environment/biodiversity; Human rights/peace/conflicts; International relations/cooperation/development aid. **Activities:** Conferences/seminars/workshops/training activities; Information and documentation services/data bases; Publishing/audiovisual materials/educational materials.

NOR3392

FORUT-SOLIDARITETSAKSJON FOR UTVIKLING ♦ Forut-Campaign for Development and Solidarity

P.O. Box 300, 2800 Gjøvik, Norway.

Telephone: 47 (61) 17 74 22. *Fax:* 47 (61) 17 99 53. *Contact:* Thor Ostby, Programme Director.

NOR3393

FRAMTIDEN I VARE HENDER (FIVH) ♦ Future in Our Hands

Arenfeldtsvei 39, 4630 Kristiansand, Norway.

Telephone: 47 (42) 91 390.

NOR3394

FRELSESARMEEN ♦ The Salvation Army

PO Box 6866 St Olavs plass, 0130 Oslo, Norway.

Telephone: 47 (22) 11 20 50. *Fax:* 47 (22) 20 84 49. *Contact:* John Ord, Territorial Commander.

OBJECTIVES: To preach the gospel, disseminate Christian truths and supply basic human necessities. To provide personal counselling and undertake the spiritual and moral regeneration and physical rehabilitation of all persons in need within its sphere of influence.

GENERAL INFORMATION: Creation: 1865. **Affiliated to:** The Salvation Army Internaional (United Kingdom) - Norwegian Missionary Council for International Development Cooperation (Norway). **Personnel/Total:** 83. *Salaried:* 83 of which: 13 in developing countries. **Budget/Total 1993:** ECU 1078000 (US$ 1269000). **Financial sources:** *Private:* 56%. *Public:* 44%.

PUBLICATIONS: *Periodicals:* Krigsropet (51).

EVALUATION/RESEARCH: Evaluation reports available.

COMMENTS: Each project is run locally by the National Territory. The Salvation Army International provides financial and technical assistance and co-ordinates development activities.

ACTIVITIES IN DEVELOPING REGIONS: Active in 23 country(ies). Maintains local field presence. Works through local field partners. **Sustainable Development Actions:** Children/youth/family; Democracy/good governance/institution building/participatory development; Education/training/literacy; Health/sanitation/water; Population/family planning/demography. **Regions:** Central Asia and South Asia; East Africa; South America; South East Asia; Southern Africa.

INFORMATION AND EDUCATION ACTIVITIES: Topics: Children/youth/family; Culture/tradition/religion; Education/training/literacy; Emergency relief/refugees/humanitarian assistance; Gender issues/women; Health/sanitation/water; International relations/cooperation/development aid. **Activities:** Conferences/seminars/workshops/training activities; Formal education; Fund raising; Publishing/audiovisual materials/educational materials.

NOR3395

DE FRIE EVANGELISKE FORSAMLINGERS MISJON-SUTVALG ♦ The Free Evangelical Assemblies of Norway

Mollergt. 40, 0179 Oslo, Norway.

Telephone: 47 (22) 36 22 78. *Fax:* 47 (22) 36 22 78. *Contact:* Olav Fjalestad, Secretary.

OBJECTIVES: To provide spiritual and material support to needy people, following the gospel of Jesus Christ.

GENERAL INFORMATION: Creation: 1935. **Personnel/Total:** 39. *Salaried:* 37 of which: 25 in developing countries. *Volunteers:* 2 of which: 2 in developing countries. **Budget/Total 1993:** ECU 539000 (US$ 634000). **Financial sources:** *Private:* 98%. *Public:* 2%.

COMMENTS: Undertakes activities in the Commonwealth of Independent States.

ACTIVITIES IN DEVELOPING REGIONS: Present in developing regions. Active in 7 country(ies). Maintains local field presence. Works through local field partners. **Sustainable Development Actions:** Children/youth/family; Education/training/literacy; Health/sanitation/water. **Regions:** Central Africa; South America; South East Asia; Southern Africa.

INFORMATION AND EDUCATION ACTIVITIES: Topics: Education/training/literacy. **Activities:** Formal education.

NOR3396

FUNKSJONSHEMMEDES FELLESORGANISASJON (FFO) ♦ Norwegian Federation of Organisations of Disabled People

PO Box 114, Kjelsås, 0411 Oslo, Norway.

Telephone: 47 (22) 23 50 50. *Fax:* 47 (22) 23 57 00. *Contact:* Finn Grønseth.

OBJECTIVES: To promote the social equality and particiaption of disabled people in society.

GENERAL INFORMATION: Creation: 1950. **Type of organisation:** association of NGOs, coordinating body. **Member organisations:** 45. **Affiliated to:** Disabled Peoples' International. **Personnel/Total:** 12. *Salaried:* 12. **Budget/Total 1993:**

See: *How to Use the Directory,* page 11.

ECU 983000 (US$ 1157000). *Financial sources:* Public: 88%. Self-financing: 12%.

PUBLICATIONS: *Periodicals:* Weekly Report (50). *Annual report. List of publications.*

INFORMATION AND EDUCATION ACTIVITIES: **Topics:** Health/sanitation/water. **Activities:** Lobbying/advocacy.

NOR3397
HUNGERSHJELPEN I NORGE ♦ Food for the Hungry International

Furumo 4, 2743 Harestua, Norway.

Telephone: 47 (63) 23 3 98. *Fax:* 47 (63) 55 9 20.

NOR3398
DET HVITE BAND ♦ White Ribbon in Norway

Møllergt. 38, 0179 Oslo, Norway.

NOR3399
INDIGENOUS PEOPLES FUND

FAFO INTERNATIONAL, Fossveien 19, 0551 Oslo 5, Norway.

NOR3400
INTERNATIONAL FEDERATION OF SOCIAL WORKERS (IFSW)

Box 4649 Sofienberg, 0506 Oslo, Norway.

Telephone: 47 (22) 03 11 52. *Fax:* 47 (22) 03 11 14. *Contact:* Tom Johannesen, Secretary General.

OBJECTIVES: To promote social work as a profession. To support national organisations of social workers. To facilitate contacts between social workers in all countries. To represent the viewpoints of the profession on an international level.

GENERAL INFORMATION: *Creation:* 1956. *Type of organisation:* association of NGOs. *Member organisations:* 55. *Salaried:* 1. *Volunteers:* 41 of which: 12 in developing countries. *Budget/Total 1993:* ECU 118000 (US$ 139000). *Financial sources:* Private: 6%. Self-financing: 94%.

PUBLICATIONS: *Periodicals:* IFSW Newsletter (3) - International Social Work (4). *List of publications.*

COMMENTS: Undertakes activities in the Commonwealth of Independent States. Information activities related to the Commonwealth of Independent States.

ACTIVITIES IN DEVELOPING REGIONS: Present in developing regions. Active in 22 country(ies). Maintains local field presence. Works through local field partners. **Sustainable Development Actions:** Children/youth/family; Democracy/good governance/institution building/participatory development; Education/training/literacy; Health/sanitation/water; Human rights/peace/conflicts. **Regions:** Central Asia and South Asia; Southern Africa.

INFORMATION AND EDUCATION ACTIVITIES: **Topics:** Children/youth/family; Employment/unemployment; Gender issues/women; Health/sanitation/water; Human rights/peace/conflicts; International relations/cooperation/development aid; Peace/ethnic conflicts/armament/disarmament; Population/family planning/demography; Poverty/living conditions; Racism/xenophobia/antisemitism; Refugees/migrants/ethnic groups; Rural development/agriculture. **Activities:** Conferences/seminars/workshops/training activities; Exchanges/twinning/linking; Information and documentation services/data bases; Lobbying/advocacy; Publishing/audiovisual materials/educational materials.

NOR3401
KIRKENS NODHJELP (KN) ♦ Norwegian Church Aid

PO Box 4544, Torshov, 0404 Oslo, Norway.

Telephone: 47 (22) 22 22 99. *Fax:* 47 (22) 22 24 20. *Contact:* Mr. Stein Villumstad, Director of Emergencies and Refugee Affairs.

NOR3402
KIRKENS U-LANDSINFORMASJON ♦ Church of Norway Development Education Service

Postboks 5913, Majorstua, 0380 Oslo 3, Norway.

Telephone: 47 (22) 60 46 90. *Fax:* 47 (22) 69 72 80. *Contact:* Berit Hagen Agøy.

OBJECTIVES: To undertake development education activities on behalf of the church of Norway.

GENERAL INFORMATION: *Creation:* 1977. *Type of organisation:* network. *Member organisations:* 4. *Affiliated to:* Network of Norwegian NGOs Working with Development Education (Norway) -European Development Education Network. *Personnel/Total:* 3. *Salaried:* 3. *Budget/Total 1993:* ECU 108000 (US$ 127000). *Financial sources:* Public: 95%.

PUBLICATIONS: *Periodicals:* U-landsavisa (1) - FFR-permen (3). *Annual report. List of publications.*

EVALUATION/RESEARCH: Evaluation reports available.

INFORMATION AND EDUCATION ACTIVITIES: **Topics:** Children/youth/family; Culture/tradition/religion; Ecology/environment/biodiversity; Gender issues/women; Human rights/peace/conflicts; International economic relations/trade/debt/finance; International relations/cooperation/development aid; Population/family planning/demography; Racism/xenophobia/antisemitism. **Activities:** Broadcasting/cultural events; Conferences/seminars/workshops/training activities; Exchanges/twinning/linking; Information and documentation services/data bases; Information campaigns/exhibitions; Lobbying/advocacy; Networking/electronic telecommunications; Publishing/audiovisual materials/educational materials.

NOR3403
DET KONGELIGE SELSKAP FOR NORGES VEL (SNV) ♦ Royal Norwegian Society for Rural Development

Bråteveien, P.O. Box 115, 2013 Skjetten, Norway.

Telephone: 47 (63) 84 50 00. *Fax:* 47 (63) 84 51 30. *Contact:* Per Dæhlen, Managing Director.

OBJECTIVES: To support the development of vibrant local communities in Norway and in developing countries.

GENERAL INFORMATION: *Creation:* 1809. *Type of organisation:* association of NGOs. *Member organisations:* 35. *Affiliated to:* Nordic Consortium for Co-operative Development. *Personnel/Total:* 71. *Salaried:* 71 of which: 2 in developing countries. *Budget/Total 1993:* ECU 4790000 (US$ 5638000). *Financial sources:* Private: 10%. Public: 7%. Self-financing: 83%.

PUBLICATIONS: *Periodicals:* Norcoop (2). *Annual report. List of publications.*

EVALUATION/RESEARCH: Evaluation reports available. Undertakes research activities.

COMMENTS: Undertakes activities in the Commonwealth of Independent States. Information activities related to the Commonwealth of Independent States.

ACTIVITIES IN DEVELOPING REGIONS: Present in developing regions. Active in 26 country(ies). Maintains local field presence. Works through local field partners. **Sustainable Development Actions:** Children/youth/family; Education/training/literacy; Gender issues/women; Rural development/agriculture; Sending volunteers/experts/technical assistance; Urban development/habitat. **Regions:** Caribbean; East Africa; Mexico and Central America; South America; West Africa.

INFORMATION AND EDUCATION ACTIVITIES: **Topics:** Children/youth/family; Education/training/literacy; Gender issues/women. **Activities:** Conferences/seminars/workshops/training activities.

NOR3404
KVEKERHJELP ♦ Quaker Service Norway

Skovveien 20, 0257 Oslo, Norway.

Telephone: 47 (22) 43 45 60. *Fax:* 47 (22) 43 63 01. *Contact:* Faith Ann Sevilä, Director.

OBJECTIVES: To improve the quality of life of people in developing countries by meeting their material and non-material needs, and by making it possible for them to achieve control over their lives. To promote development by people and to foster peace and justice.

GENERAL INFORMATION: *Creation:* 1963. *Affiliated to:* Quaker Services Europe - Quaker Services (USA). *Personnel/Total:* 7. *Salaried:* 1. *Volunteers:* 6. *Budget/Total 1993:* ECU 51000 (US$ 593000). *Financial sources:* Private: 9%. Public: 80%. Self-financing: 11%.

PUBLICATIONS: *Periodicals:* Kvekerhjelp Nytt (2). *Annual report.*

EVALUATION/RESEARCH: Evaluation reports available.

ACTIVITIES IN DEVELOPING REGIONS: Present in developing regions. Active in 6 country(ies). Maintains local field presence. Works through local field partners. **Sustainable Development Actions:** Children/youth/family; Ecology/environment/biodiversity; Education/training/literacy; Gender issues/women; Health/sanitation/water; Human rights/peace/conflicts; Rural development/agriculture. **Regions:** East Africa; Middle East; South America; Southern Africa.

INFORMATION AND EDUCATION ACTIVITIES: Topics: Children/youth/family; Ecology/environment/biodiversity; Education/training/literacy; Gender issues/women; Health/sanitation/water; Human rights/peace/conflicts; Peace/ethnic conflicts/armament/disarmament; Refugees/migrants/ethnic groups; Rural development/agriculture. **Activities:** Fund raising; Lobbying/advocacy; Publishing/audiovisual materials/educational materials.

NOR3405

LANDSFORENINGEN FOR HJERTE- OG LUNGESYKE ♦ Norwegian Heart and Lung Association

Sandakerveien 78, P.O. Box 4375, Torshov, 0402 Oslo, Norway.

Telephone: 47 (22) 22 24 50. *Fax:* 47 (22) 22 38 33. *Contact:* Lise Berit Johannessen, Consultant.

NOR3406

LANDSLAGET FOR NORGES SYKEPLEIERSTUDENTER ♦ Norwegian Nursing Student Association

PO Box 9326 Grønland, 0135 Oslo, Norway.

Telephone: 47 (22) 17 22 82.

NOR3407

LANDSORGANISASJONEN I NORGE (LO) ♦ Norwegian Federation of Trade Unions

Youngsgt. 11, 0181 Oslo, Norway.

Telephone: 47 (22) 03 10 50. *Fax:* 47 (22) 03 11 00. *Contact:* Yngre Hågensen.

OBJECTIVES: To strengthen trade unions in developing countries through education and management development. To promote sustainable self-development of trade unions. To train men and women in trade unions and provide equipment for trade union offices and organisations.

GENERAL INFORMATION: *Creation:* 1899. *Affiliated to:* Council of Nordic Trade Unions (Belgium) - European Trade Union Confederation (Belgium). *Personnel/Total:* 197. *Salaried:* 7 of which: 1 in developing countries. *Budget/Total 1993:* ECU 3832000 (US$ 4511000). *Financial sources:* Public: 80%. Self-financing: 20%.

PUBLICATIONS: *Periodicals:* Lo-Aktuelt (15). *Annual report.*

EVALUATION/RESEARCH: Evaluation reports available.

ACTIVITIES IN DEVELOPING REGIONS: Active in 21 country(ies). Maintains local field presence. Works through local field partners. **Sustainable Development Actions:** Democracy/good governance/institution building/participatory development; Education/training/literacy. **Regions:** Caribbean; East Africa; Mexico and Central America; Middle East; South America; South East Asia; Southern Africa.

NOR3408

LANDSRADET FOR NORSKE BARNE-OG UNGDOMSOR-GANISASJONER (LNU) ♦ Norwegian Youth Council

Rolf Hofmosgt 18, 0655 Oslo, Norway.

Telephone: 47 (22) 67 00 43. *Fax:* 47 (22) 68 68 08.

NOR3409

LATIN AMERIKA HELSEFOND ♦ Latin America Health Foundation

Maridalsvn. 232, 0467 Oslo, Norway.

Telephone: 47 (22) 23 60 62. *Fax:* 47 (22) 26 59 86. *Contact:* Hector Carvallo.

OBJECTIVES: To support the development of the health and social sectors in Latin America. To support human rights in the region. To raise awareness in Norway on events in Latin America.

GENERAL INFORMATION: *Creation:* 1989. *Personnel/Total:* 6. *Salaried:* 1 of which: 1 in developing countries. *Volunteers:* 20 of which: var in developing countries. *Budget/Total 1993:* ECU 108000 (US$ 127000). *Financial sources:* Private: 30%. Public: 60%. Self-financing: 10%.

PUBLICATIONS: *Annual report.*

EVALUATION/RESEARCH: Evaluation reports available.

PLANNED ACTIVITIES: Establishing a women's centre for indigenous peoples. Undertaking a sanitary development project in Nicaragua.

ACTIVITIES IN DEVELOPING REGIONS: Present in developing regions. Active in 4 country(ies). Maintains local field presence. Works through local field partners. **Sustainable Development Actions:** Education/training/literacy; Gender issues/women; Health/sanitation/water; Human rights/peace/conflicts; Sending volunteers/experts/technical assistance. **Regions:** Mexico and Central America; South America.

NOR3410

LATINAMERIKAGRUPPENE I NORGE (LAG) ♦ Latin American Solidarity Group of Norway

Fredensborgv 39, 0177 Oslo, Norway.

Telephone: 47 (22) 36 22 00. *Fax:* 47 (22) 36 22 80. *Contact:* Jan Thomas Odegard, President.

OBJECTIVES: To provide information about the situation in Latin America. To support liberation movements.

GENERAL INFORMATION: *Creation:* 1977. *Type of organisation:* coordinating body. *Affiliated to:* Forum for Sustainable Development. *Personnel/Total:* 779. *Salaried:* 2 of which: 1 in developing countries. *Volunteers:* 777 of which: 50 in developing countries. *Budget/Total 1993:* ECU 120000 (US$ 141000). *Financial sources:* Private: 20%. Public: 60%. Self-financing: 20%.

PUBLICATIONS: *Periodicals:* X-3Vernen Magasin (6) - Lag-Kontakt (6). *Annual report. List of publications.*

EVALUATION/RESEARCH: Evaluation reports available.

ACTIVITIES IN DEVELOPING REGIONS: Present in developing regions. Active in 4 country(ies). Maintains local field presence. Works through local field partners. **Sustainable Development Actions:** Democracy/good governance/institution building/participatory development; Ecology/environment/biodiversity; Gender issues/women; Health/sanitation/water; Human rights/peace/conflicts; Rural development/agriculture; Sending volunteers/experts/technical assistance; Small enterprises/informal sector/handicrafts; Urban development/habitat. **Regions:** Mexico and Central America; South America.

INFORMATION AND EDUCATION ACTIVITIES: Topics: Ecology/environment/biodiversity; Gender issues/women; Health/sanitation/water; Human rights/peace/conflicts; International economic relations/trade/debt/finance; International relations/cooperation/development aid; Peace/ethnic conflicts/armament/disarmament; Poverty/living conditions; Racism/xenophobia/antisemitism; Refugees/migrants/ethnic groups; Rural development/agriculture; Urban development/habitat. **Activities:** Fund raising; Information and documentation services/data bases; Information campaigns/exhibitions; Lobbying/advocacy; Publishing/audiovisual materials/educational materials.

NOR3411

LERERFORBUNDET ♦ Teachers' Union, Norway

Wergelandsveien 15, 0167 Oslo 1, Norway.

See: *How to Use the Directory*, page 11.

Telephone: 47 (22) 03 00 00. *Fax:* 47 (22) 11 05 42. *Contact:* Anders Folkestad, President.

NOR3412
LIONS INTERNATIONAL SECRETARY

Eric Evang, Djupdalsfaret 18, 2200 Kongsvinger, Norway.

Telephone: 47 (62) 81 37 43. *Fax:* 47 (62) 81 37 43. *Contact:* Steinar Gjertsen, Chairman.

OBJECTIVES: To support development through a variety of activities in developing countries.

GENERAL INFORMATION: *Creation:* 1949. *Personnel/Total:* 19. *Salaried:* 5 of which: 5 in developing countries. *Volunteers:* 14 of which: 14 in developing countries. *Budget/Total 1993:* ECU 719000 (US$ 846000). *Financial sources:* Private: 75%. Self-financing: 25%.

PUBLICATIONS: *Periodicals:* The-Lion-Norwegian-Edition (8). *Annual report. List of publications.*

EVALUATION/RESEARCH: Evaluation reports available.

PLANNED ACTIVITIES: Eye care project in Uganda 95-98 together with NORAD. Agricultural project in Nepal 95-97.

COMMENTS: Undertakes activities in the Commonwealth of Independent States. Information activities related to the Commonwealth of Independent States.

ACTIVITIES IN DEVELOPING REGIONS: Present in developing regions. Active in 4 country(ies). Maintains local field presence. Works through local field partners. **Sustainable Development Actions:** Children/youth/family; Ecology/environment/biodiversity; Education/training/literacy; Emergency relief/refugees/humanitarian assistance; Food/famine; Gender issues/women; Health/sanitation/water; Rural development/agriculture; Urban development/habitat. **Regions:** Central Africa; Central Asia and South Asia; East Africa.

INFORMATION AND EDUCATION ACTIVITIES: Topics: Children/youth/family; Ecology/environment/biodiversity; Education/training/literacy; Emergency relief/refugees/humanitarian assistance; Food/famine; Health/sanitation/water; International relations/cooperation/development aid; Refugees/migrants/ethnic groups; Rural development/agriculture; Urban development/habitat. **Activities:** Conferences/seminars/workshops/training activities; Exchanges/twinning/linking; Formal education; Fund raising; Information campaigns/exhibitions.

NOR3413
LIONS SEKRETARIAT ♦ Lions Clubs International

Tvetenvn 152, 0671 Oslo, Norway.

Telephone: 47 (22) 27 29 80. *Fax:* 47 (22) 27 29 27.

NOR3414
MARY'S VENNER ♦ Mary's Friends

v/ Viggo Jørgensen, Postboks 3045, Elisenberg, 0207 Oslo, Norway.

NOR3415
MEDISINERNES ERITREA-AKSJON

P.B. 81, Ullevål Sykehus, 0407 Oslo, Norway.

NOR3416
MELLOMKIRKELIG RAD FOR DEN NORSKE KIRKE ♦ Church of Norway, Council on Ecumenical and International Relations

Underhaugsvn. 15, Majorstua, P.O. Box 5816, 0308 Oslo, Norway.

Telephone: 47 (22) 6O 46 90. *Fax:* 47 (22) 56 58 64. *Contact:* Stig Utnem, General Secretary.

OBJECTIVES: To increase public awareness of development issues. To carry out political lobbying on development aid and North-South issues. To participate, on behalf of the Church of Norway, in the ecumenical co-operation movement.

GENERAL INFORMATION: *Creation:* 1970. *Affiliated to:* World Council of Churches (Switzerland) - Conference of European Churches

(Switzerland). *Personnel/Total:* 49. *Salaried:* 9. *Volunteers:* 40. *Financial sources:* Private: 5%. Public: 90%. Self-financing: 5%.

PUBLICATIONS: *Annual report. List of publications.*

PLANNED ACTIVITIES: The mobilization of public support and political will for sustainable production and consumption patterns.

COMMENTS: Undertakes activities in the Commonwealth of Independent States. Information activities related to the Commonwealth of Independent States.

ACTIVITIES IN DEVELOPING REGIONS: Present in developing regions. Works through local field partners. **Sustainable Development Actions:** Democracy/good governance/institution building/participatory development; Gender issues/women; Human rights/peace/conflicts. **Regions:** Central Africa; Mexico and Central America; Southern Africa.

INFORMATION AND EDUCATION ACTIVITIES: Topics: Gender issues/women; Human rights/peace/conflicts; International economic relations/trade/debt/finance; International relations/cooperation/development aid; Peace/ethnic conflicts/armament/disarmament; Racism/xenophobia/antisemitism; Refugees/migrants/ethnic groups. **Activities:** Conferences/seminars/workshops/training activities; Formal education; Fund raising; Information and documentation services/data bases; Lobbying/advocacy.

NOR3417
METODISTKIRKENS MISJONSSELSKAP - METODISTKIRKENS INTERNASJONALE UTVALG ♦ United Methodist Church in Norway - Board of International Relations

St. Olavs gt. 28, 0166 Oslo 1, Norway.

Telephone: 47 (22) 36 44 50. *Contact:* Tove Odland, Executive Secretary.

NOR3418
NAMIBIA FORENINGEN ♦ The Namibia Association of Norway

P.B. 369, 2401 Elverum, Norway.

Telephone: 47 (62) 41 36 22. *Fax:* 47 (62) 41 30 42. *Contact:* Hallvard Holøyen, Secretary General.

OBJECTIVES: To assist Namibia to implement education reform. To provide advice and teachers at the secondary level.

GENERAL INFORMATION: *Creation:* 1980. *Type of organisation:* coordinating body. *Personnel/Total:* 12. *Salaried:* 4. *Volunteers:* 8 of which: 8 in developing countries. *Budget/Total 1993:* ECU 1198000 (US$ 1410000). *Financial sources:* Private: 26%. Public: 74%.

PUBLICATIONS: *Annual report.*

EVALUATION/RESEARCH: Evaluation reports available.

ACTIVITIES IN DEVELOPING REGIONS: Present in developing regions. Active in 1 country(ies). Maintains local field presence. Works through local field partners. **Sustainable Development Actions:** Children/youth/family; Democracy/good governance/institution building/participatory development; Ecology/environment/biodiversity; Education/training/literacy; Gender issues/women; Human rights/peace/conflicts; Sending volunteers/experts/technical assistance. **Regions:** Southern Africa.

INFORMATION AND EDUCATION ACTIVITIES: Topics: Children/youth/family; Culture/tradition/religion; Education/training/literacy; International economic relations/trade/debt/finance. **Activities:** Conferences/seminars/workshops/training activities; Information campaigns/exhibitions; Publishing/audiovisual materials/educational materials.

NOR3419
NANSEN CHILDWATCH

Ingar Nilsens vei 3B, 0268 Oslo, Norway.

Telephone: 47 (22) 43 18 41. *Fax:* 47 (22) 43 40 96. *Contact:* Margaret Ellson Davies, Secretary General.

OBJECTIVES: To promote and protect children's rights around the world. To assist refugees and asylum seeking children in Norway.

Voir : *Comment utiliser le répertoire,* page 11.

GENERAL INFORMATION: *Creation:* 1991. *Personnel/Total:* 3. *Volunteers:* 3. *Budget/Total 1993:* ECU 2000 (US$ 3000). *Financial sources:* Private: 100%.

PUBLICATIONS: *Periodicals:* Reports. *Annual report.*

EVALUATION/RESEARCH: Evaluation reports available. Undertakes research activities.

COMMENTS: Undertakes activities in the Commonwealth of Independent States.

INFORMATION AND EDUCATION ACTIVITIES: Topics: Children/youth/family; Human rights/peace/conflicts; International relations/cooperation/development aid; Racism/xenophobia/antisemitism; Refugees/migrants/ethnic groups. **Activities:** Lobbying/advocacy.

NOR3420

NASJONALFORENINGEN FOR FOLKEHELSEN ♦ Norwegian National Health Association

Inkognitogt 1, P.O. Box 7139, Homansbyen, 0307 Oslo 3, Norway.

Telephone: 47 (22) 44 19 10. *Contact:* Vidar G. Wilberg, Secretary General.

NOR3421

NASJONALT ANDELIG RAD FOR BAHA'IER I NORGE ♦
National Spriritual Assembly for the Baha'is of Norway

Drammensvn 110A, 0273 Oslo, Norway.

Telephone: 47 (22) 55 95 85. *Fax:* 47 (22) 55 19 77. *Contact:* Thorhenning Lerstad, Chairman.

OBJECTIVES: To apply more systematically the priniciples in the teachings of the Bahai faith to achieve spiritual and material progress in expanding the quality of human life.

GENERAL INFORMATION: *Creation:* 1972. *Personnel/Total:* 3. *Salaried:* 2 of which: 1 in developing countries. *Volunteers:* 1. *Budget/Total 1993:* ECU 60000 (US$ 70000). *Financial sources:* Public: 80%. Self-financing: 20%.

PUBLICATIONS: *Annual report.*

EVALUATION/RESEARCH: Evaluation reports available.

PLANNED ACTIVITIES: A community capacity building project in 1996.

ACTIVITIES IN DEVELOPING REGIONS: Present in developing regions. Active in 1 country(ies). Maintains local field presence. Works through local field partners. **Sustainable Development Actions:** Rural development/agriculture. **Regions:** Central Asia and South Asia.

NOR3422

NATUR OG UNGDOM ♦ Nature and Youth

Torggata 34, 0183 Oslo, Norway.

Telephone: 47 (22) 36 42 18. *Fax:* 47 (22) 20 45 94.

OBJECTIVES: To promote sustainable development in society based upon respect and solidarity for all human beings. To protect nature by reducing the consumption of non-renewable resources.

GENERAL INFORMATION: *Creation:* 1967. *Affiliated to:* Friends of the Earth - Action for Solidarity, Environment, Equality and Development (Netherlands). *Personnel/Total:* 25. *Salaried:* 5. *Volunteers:* 15. *Budget/Total 1993:* ECU 479000 (US$ 564000). *Financial sources:* Private: 20%. Public: 47%. Self-financing: 33%.

PUBLICATIONS: *Periodicals:* Nature and Society (6) - News from Nature and youth (8). *List of publications.*

EVALUATION/RESEARCH: Evaluation reports available. Undertakes research activities.

COMMENTS: Undertakes activities in the Commonwealth of Independent States. Information activities related to the Commonwealth of Independent States.

INFORMATION AND EDUCATION ACTIVITIES: Topics: Ecology/environment/biodiversity. **Activities:** Conferences/seminars/workshops/training activities; Information and documentation services/data bases; Information campaigns/exhibitions; Lobbying/advocacy; Networking/

electronic telecommunications; Publishing/audiovisual materials/educational materials.

NOR3423

NERINGSLIVETS HOVEDORGANISASJON (NHO) ♦ Confederation of Norwegian Business and Industry

Postboks 5250, Middelthunsgt 27, Majorstua, 0303 Oslo 3, Norway.

Telephone: 47 (22) 60 32 90. *Fax:* 47 (22) 69 55 93. *Contact:* Ragnar Halvorsen, President.

NOR3424

NEW LIFE MISSION

Wm. Thranesgt 86, 0175 Oslo, Norway.

Telephone: 47 (22) 38 45 30.

NOR3425

NORGES BLINDEFORBUND ♦ Norwegian Association of the Blind and Partially Sighted

Sporveisgt. 10, P.O. Box 5900, Majorstuen, 0308 Oslo, Norway.

Telephone: 47 (22) 46 69 90. *Fax:* 47 (22) 56 40 47. *Contact:* Helen Aareskjold, Leader.

OBJECTIVES: To achieve equal opportunity for the visually handicapped in society.

GENERAL INFORMATION: *Creation:* 1909. *Affiliated to:* European Blind Union - World Blind Union - Nordic Co-operation Committee - Norwegian Federation of the Disabled People. *Personnel/Total:* 293. *Salaried:* 233 of which: 6 in developing countries. *Volunteers:* 60 of which: 1 in developing countries. *Budget/Total 1993:* ECU 16344000 (US$ 19238000). *Financial sources:* Private: 20%. Public: 35%. Self-financing: 45%.

PUBLICATIONS: *Periodicals:* Norges Blinde (23). *Annual report. List of publications.*

PLANNED ACTIVITIES: Undertaking eye-health projects. Rehabilitating women and institutions for the visually handicapped. Establishing Braille-presses and print shops.

ACTIVITIES IN DEVELOPING REGIONS: Present in developing regions. Active in 11 country(ies). Maintains local field presence. Works through local field partners. **Sustainable Development Actions:** Children/youth/family; Democracy/good governance/institution building/participatory development; Education/training/literacy; Gender issues/women; Health/sanitation/water; Population/family planning/demography; Rural development/agriculture; Sending volunteers/experts/technical assistance; Small enterprises/informal sector/handicrafts. **Regions:** Caribbean; Central Asia and South Asia; East Africa; Mexico and Central America; South America; South East Asia; Southern Africa.

NOR3426

NORGES BONDELAG ♦ Norwegian Farmers Union

PO Box 9354 Grønland, 0135 Oslo, Norway.

Telephone: 47 (22) 17 34 00. *Fax:* 47 (22) 17 17 87. *Contact:* Amund Venger, Secretary General.

OBJECTIVES: To safeguard and preserve the economic, social and cultural interests of rural areas. To protect sustainable development, secure food production, the environment and the vitality of rural communities.

GENERAL INFORMATION: *Creation:* 1896. *Affiliated to:* International Federation of Agricultural Producers (France) - European Cofederation of Agriculture (Belgium) - Conseil Internationale de la Chasse (France). *Personnel/Total:* 137. *Salaried:* 137. *Budget/Total 1993:* ECU 11460000 (US$ 13490000). *Financial sources:* Private: 4%. Self-financing: 96%.

COMMENTS: Undertakes activities in the Commonwealth of Independent States.

ACTIVITIES IN DEVELOPING REGIONS: Present in developing regions. Active in 1 country(ies). Maintains local field presence. Works through local field partners. **Sustainable Development Actions:** Debt/finance/trade; Democracy/good governance/institution building/participatory

See: *How to Use the Directory*, page 11.

development; Gender issues/women; Rural development/agriculture; Small enterprises/informal sector/handicrafts. **Regions:** Mexico and Central America.

NOR3427

NORGES DIABETESFORBUND ◆ Norwegian Diabetes Association

Ostensjøvn 29, 0661 Oslo, Norway.

Telephone: 47 (22) 65 45 50.

NOR3428

NORGES DOVEFORBUND (NDF) ◆ Norwegian Association of the Deaf

Sven Bruns Gate 7, P.O. Box 6850, 0130 Oslo 1, Norway.

Telephone: 47 (2) 11 17 75. *Fax:* 47 (2) 11 16 33. *Contact:* Toralf Ringsø, President.

NOR3429

NORGES FREDSLAG ◆ Norwegian Peace Society

Eikstubben 6B, 1343 Eiksmarka, Norway.

Telephone: 47 (22) 67 14 03 29. *Fax:* 47 (22) 67 14 67 17. *Contact:* Ivar Teigen, President.

OBJECTIVES: To work for lasting world peace built on the security of individuals and peoples.

GENERAL INFORMATION: *Creation:* 1885. *Affiliated to:* The Norwegian Forum for Environment and Developpment (Norway) - Korn Peace Centre (Norway) - International Coalition for Non-Proliferation and Nuclear Disarmament (Switzerland). *Personnel/Total:* 2. *Volunteers:* 2. *Budget/Total 1993:* ECU 9000 (US$ 10000). *Financial sources:* Public: 30%. *Self-financing:* 70%.

PUBLICATIONS: *Periodicals:* Fredsviljen (4). *Annual report.*

EVALUATION/RESEARCH: Evaluation reports available.

PLANNED ACTIVITIES: A campaign for the elimination of nuclear weapons.

COMMENTS: Undertakes activities in the Commonwealth of Independent States. Information activities related to the Commonwealth of Independent States.

INFORMATION AND EDUCATION ACTIVITIES: Topics: Children/youth/family; Education/training/literacy; Human rights/peace/conflicts; International relations/cooperation/development aid; Peace/ethnic conflicts/armament/disarmament. **Activities:** Conferences/seminars/workshops/training activities; Exchanges/twinning/linking; Information campaigns/exhibitions; Lobbying/advocacy; Networking/electronic telecommunications; Publishing/audiovisual materials/educational materials.

NOR3430

NORGES HANDIKAPFORBUND ◆ Norwegian Association of the Disabled

Schweigaardsgt. 12, P.O. Box 9217 Grønland, 0134 Oslo, Norway.

Telephone: 47 (22) 17 02 55. *Fax:* 46 (22) 17 61 77. *Contact:* Lars Odegaard, President.

OBJECTIVES: To foster the creation of organisations which provide care for the disabled. To support programmes aimed at training the disabled to manage on their own. To promote projects fostering appropriate technology.

GENERAL INFORMATION: *Creation:* 1931. *Member organisations:* 8. *Affiliated to:* FIMITIC (Germany). *Personnel/Total:* var. *Salaried:* 75 of which: 15 in developing countries. *Volunteers:* var. *Budget/Total 1993:* ECU 5988000 (US$ 705000). *Financial sources:* Private: 1%. *Public:* 20%. *Self-financing:* 79%.

PUBLICATIONS: *Periodicals:* Handikapnyth (10) - Afrolink (4). *Annual report. List of publications.*

EVALUATION/RESEARCH: Evaluation reports available.

COMMENTS: Undertakes activities in the Commonwealth of Independent States.

ACTIVITIES IN DEVELOPING REGIONS: Present in developing regions. Active in 8 country(ies). Maintains local field presence. Works through local field partners. **Sustainable Development Actions:** Democracy/good governance/institution building/participatory development; Health/sanitation/water. **Regions:** East Africa; Middle East; West Africa.

INFORMATION AND EDUCATION ACTIVITIES: Topics: Health/sanitation/water. **Activities:** Conferences/seminars/workshops/training activities; Formal education.

NOR3431

NORGES HUSMORFORBUND (NH) ◆ Norwegian Housewives Association

Oscarsgt. 43, 0258 Oslo, Norway.

Telephone: 47 (22) 55 79 07. *Fax:* 47 (22) 55 82 94. *Contact:* Anne Marit Hovstad.

OBJECTIVES: To support women and in particular rural women, in their struggle for a better future for themselves and for their children. To spread knowledge and information amongst housewives on cultural, professional and economic issues as well as the rights of the family and international affairs.

GENERAL INFORMATION: *Creation:* 1915. *Affiliated to:* ACWW (United Kingdom). *Personnel/Total:* 36. *Salaried:* 1. *Volunteers:* 35. *Budget/Total 1993:* ECU 734000 (US$ 964000). *Financial sources:* Private: 73%. *Public:* 27%.

PUBLICATIONS: *Periodicals:* Husmorbladet (6). *Annual report. List of publications.*

PLANNED ACTIVITIES: Water supply projects planned for rural women's groups in Kenya; forming rural women's groups into an NGO organisation in Kenya.

COMMENTS: Undertakes activities in the Commonwealth of Independent States. Information activities related to the Commonwealth of Independent States.

ACTIVITIES IN DEVELOPING REGIONS: Active in 9 country(ies). Works through local field partners. **Sustainable Development Actions:** Education/training/literacy; Emergency relief/refugees/humanitarian assistance; Health/sanitation/water; Rural development/agriculture; Small enterprises/informal sector/handicrafts. **Regions:** Central Asia and South Asia; East Africa; North Africa; South East Asia; Southern Africa.

INFORMATION AND EDUCATION ACTIVITIES: Topics: Education/training/literacy; Other; Rural development/agriculture. **Activities:** Conferences/seminars/workshops/training activities.

NOR3432

NORGES IDRETTSFORBUND (NIF) ◆ Norwegian Confederation of Sports

Hauger Skolevei 1, 1351 Rud, Norway.

Telephone: 47 (2) 51 88 00. *Fax:* 47 (2) 13 29 89. *Contact:* Hans B. Skanset, President.

NOR3433

NORGES KFUK-KFUM ◆ Norwegian YWCA-YMCA

Pilestredet 38, P.O. Box 6905, St. Olavs Plass, 0130 Oslo 1, Norway.

Telephone: 47 (22) 20 44 75. *Fax:* 47 (22) 20 47 59. *Contact:* Irene Wenaas Holte, General Secretary.

NOR3434

NORGES KOOPERATIVE LANDSFORENING (NKL) ◆ Norwegian Cooperative Union and Wholesale Union

Revierstredet 2, Postbox 1173 Sentrum, 0107 Oslo 1, Norway.

Telephone: 47 (22) 20 62 90. *Fax:* 47 (22) 41 14 42. *Contact:* Jarle Benum, Chairman.

NOR3435

NORGES RODE KORS ◆ Norwegian Red Cross

Holberggt 1, P.O. Box 6875, St. Olavs pl., 0130 Oslo 1, Norway.

Voir : *Comment utiliser le répertoire,* page 11.

Telephone: 47 (22) 94 30 30. *Fax:* 47 (22) 20 68 40. *Contact:* Sven Mol-lekle, Secretary General.

OBJECTIVES: To prevent and alleviate human suffering. To protect life and health and insure respect for human beings, in particular in times of armed conflict and other emergencies. To work for the prevention of disease and for the promotion of health and social welfare. To encourage voluntary service.

GENERAL INFORMATION: *Creation:* 1865. *Affiliated to:* International Federation of Red Cross and Red Crescent Societies (Switzerland). *Personnel/Total:* 10150. *Salaried:* 150 of which: 40 in developing countries. *Volunteers:* 10000. *Budget/Total 1993:* ECU 39858000 (US$ 46917000). *Financial sources:* Private: 21%. Public: 31%. Self-financing: 48%.

PUBLICATIONS: *Periodicals:* Tankekors (7). *Annual report. List of publications.*

EVALUATION/RESEARCH: Evaluation reports available. Undertakes research activities.

COMMENTS: Undertakes activities in the Commonwealth of Independent States. Information activities related to the Commonwealth of Independent States.

ACTIVITIES IN DEVELOPING REGIONS: Active in 50 country(ies). Maintains local field presence. Works through local field partners. **Sustainable Development Actions:** Children/youth/family; Emergency relief/refugees/humanitarian assistance; Food/famine; Gender issues/women; Health/sanitation/water; Human rights/peace/conflicts; Sending volunteers/experts/technical assistance. **Regions:** Caribbean; Central Africa; Central Asia and South Asia; East Africa; East Asia; Mexico and Central America; Middle East; Oceania; South America; South East Asia; Southern Africa; West Africa.

INFORMATION AND EDUCATION ACTIVITIES: Topics: Children/youth/family; Emergency relief/refugees/humanitarian assistance; Food/famine; Health/sanitation/water; Human rights/peace/conflicts; International relations/cooperation/development aid; Peace/ethnic conflicts/armament/disarmament; Poverty/living conditions; Racism/xenophobia/antisemitism; Refugees/migrants/ethnic groups. **Activities:** Conferences/seminars/workshops/training activities; Fund raising; Information and documentation services/data bases; Information campaigns/exhibitions; Publishing/audiovisual materials/educational materials.

NOR3436

NORSK ARBEIDSMANDSFORBUND ♦ Norwegian Union of General Workers

Mollergata 3, 0179 Oslo, Norway.

Telephone: 47 (22) 03 10 50. *Fax:* 47 (22) 03 10 92. *Contact:* Odd Arne Olafsen.

NOR3437

NORSK BANGLADESHFORENING ♦ Norwegian Bangladesh Association

Tollbugt 4, 0154 Oslo, Norway.

Telephone: 47 (22) 41 31 82. *Contact:* Jens Pether Homleid, President.

OBJECTIVES: To educate underpriveledged children living in institutions in Bangladesh.

GENERAL INFORMATION: *Creation:* 1972. *Personnel/Total:* 8. *Salaried:* 1. *Volunteers:* 7. *Budget/Total 1993:* ECU 84000 (US$ 99000). *Financial sources:* Private: 1%. Self-financing: 99%.

PUBLICATIONS: *Periodicals:* Fadderkontakten (2). *Annual report.*

EVALUATION/RESEARCH: Evaluation reports available.

COMMENTS: Information activities related to the Commonwealth of Independent States.

ACTIVITIES IN DEVELOPING REGIONS: Present in developing regions. Active in 1 country(ies). Works through local field partners. **Sustainable Development Actions:** Children/youth/family; Education/training/literacy; Urban development/habitat. **Regions:** South East Asia.

INFORMATION AND EDUCATION ACTIVITIES: Topics: Children/youth/family. **Activities:** Formal education; Fund raising.

NOR3438

NORSK FOLKEHJELP ♦ Norwegian People's Aid

Youngstorget 2a, P.O. Box 8844, 0028 Oslo 1, Norway.

Telephone: 47 (22) 33 15 90. *Fax:* 47 (22) 33 33 53. *Contact:* J.E.Linstad, Head of International Department.

NOR3439

NORSK FORBUND FOR PSYKISK UTVIKLINGS-HEM-MEDE (NFPU) ♦ Norwegian Association for the Mentally Retarded

Rosenkrantzgt. 16, 0160 Oslo, Norway.

Telephone: 47 (22) 33 05 85. *Fax:* 47 (22) 33 29 04. *Contact:* Kjell Lorentzen, Secretary General.

OBJECTIVES: To act as an advocacy organisation for mentally retarded people in Norway and their families. To support the development of similar organisations in developing countries. To promote the establishment of services for mentally retarded people.

GENERAL INFORMATION: *Creation:* 1967. *Affiliated to:* Funkslonskemmedes Fellesorganisasion - ILSMH (Belgium). *Personnel/Total:* 16. *Salaried:* 12 of which: 1 in developing countries. *Volunteers:* 4 of which: 1 in developing countries. *Financial sources:* Private: 20%. Public: 80%.

PUBLICATIONS: *Periodicals:* Samfunn For Alle (10). *Annual report.*

ACTIVITIES IN DEVELOPING REGIONS: Active in 7 country(ies). Maintains local field presence. Works through local field partners. **Sustainable Development Actions:** Children/youth/family; Democracy/good governance/institution building/participatory development; Education/training/literacy; Sending volunteers/experts/technical assistance. **Regions:** Caribbean; Central Asia and South Asia; East Africa; Mexico and Central America.

NOR3440

NORSK FREDSKORPSSAMBAND ♦ Norwegian Ex-Volunteer Association

Postboks 220, Sentrum , 0103 Oslo, Norway.

Telephone: 47 (22) 33 30 53. *Fax:* 47 (22) 33 30 51. *Contact:* Rune Henriksen, Chairperson.

OBJECTIVES: To educate the Norwegian public about developing countries. To train volunteers in preparation for working in the South.

GENERAL INFORMATION: *Creation:* 1967. *Affiliated to:* Ex-Volunteer International - United Nations Association of Norway (Norway) -The Norwegian Forum for Environment and Development (Norway). *Personnel/Total:* 12. *Salaried:* 12. *Budget/Total 1993:* ECU 1028000 (US$ 1210000). *Financial sources:* Public: 96%. Self-financing: 4%.

PUBLICATIONS: *Periodicals:* Fredskorpsforum (4) - Nytt fra Sambandet (6). *Annual report. List of publications.*

EVALUATION/RESEARCH: Evaluation reports available.

PLANNED ACTIVITIES: The Association plans to begin a school exchange programmme and produce an informational handbook.

INFORMATION AND EDUCATION ACTIVITIES: Topics: Children/youth/family; Education/training/literacy; Gender issues/women; Health/sanitation/water; Human rights/peace/conflicts; International economic relations/trade/debt/finance; International relations/cooperation/development aid; Population/family planning/demography; Rural development/agriculture. **Activities:** Conferences/seminars/workshops/training activities; Information campaigns/exhibitions; Publishing/audiovisual materials/educational materials.

NOR3441

NORSK KVINNEFORBUND ♦ Norwegian Women Association

Thygesonvei 11, 0667 Oslo, Norway.

Telephone: 47 (22) 26 59 86. *Fax:* 47 (22) 26 59 86. *Contact:* Grethe Haldorsen, Journalist.

                                   See: *How to Use the Directory,* page 11.

OBJECTIVES: To raise awareness of gender issues, women's rights, anti-racism and solidarity with women in the Third World. To work for peace in the world, anti-militarism and against nuclear weapons.

GENERAL INFORMATION: *Creation:* 1954. *Affiliated to:* Peace Council (Norway) - Women's International Democratic Federation (France). *Personnel/Total:* 10. *Volunteers:* 10 of which: 1 in developing countries. *Budget/Total 1993:* ECU 7000 (US$ 8000). *Financial sources:* Private: 25%. Public: 43%. Self-financing: 32%.

PUBLICATIONS: *Periodicals:* Kvinner I Tiden (Women in our Time) (6).

EVALUATION/RESEARCH: Evaluation reports available. Undertakes research activities.

ACTIVITIES IN DEVELOPING REGIONS: Present in developing regions. Works through local field partners. **Sustainable Development Actions:** Gender issues/women; Other. **Regions:** Mexico and Central America.

INFORMATION AND EDUCATION ACTIVITIES: Topics: Ecology/environment/biodiversity; Food/famine; Gender issues/women; Health/sanitation/water; Human rights/peace/conflicts; International economic relations/trade/debt/finance; Other; Poverty/living conditions. **Activities:** Publishing/audiovisual materials/educational materials.

NOR3442

NORSK LERERLAG (NL) ♦ Norwegian Union of Teachers

Rosenkrantzgt. 15, 0160 Oslo, Norway.

Telephone: 47 (22) 41 58 75. *Fax:* 47 (22) 33 67 74. *Contact:* Per Wøien, President.

NOR3443

NORSK LUTHERSK MISJONSSAMBAND ♦ Norwegian Lutheran Mission

Grensen 19, 0159 Oslo 1, Norway.

Telephone: 47 (22) 42 91 30. *Fax:* 47 (22) 42 10 49. *Contact:* Egil Grandhagen, General Secretary.

OBJECTIVES: To undertake the management of hospitals and clinics, agricultural projects and programmes in technical and training schools.

GENERAL INFORMATION: *Creation:* 1891. *Type of organisation:* coordinating body. *Member organisations:* 3. *Affiliated to:* Norwegian Missionary Council (Norway). *Personnel/Total:* 1074. *Salaried:* 785 of which: 287 in developing countries. *Volunteers:* 289. *Budget/Total 1993:* ECU 14370000 (US$ 16915000). *Financial sources:* Private: 85%. Public: 15%.

PUBLICATIONS: *Periodicals:* Utsyn (38) - Ungdom & Tiden (10) - Blaaveisen (16). *Annual report.*

EVALUATION/RESEARCH: Evaluation reports available.

ACTIVITIES IN DEVELOPING REGIONS: Present in developing regions. Active in 8 country(ies). Maintains local field presence. Works through local field partners. **Sustainable Development Actions:** Education/training/literacy; Emergency relief/refugees/humanitarian assistance; Health/sanitation/water; Other; Rural development/agriculture; Sending volunteers/experts/technical assistance. **Regions:** Central Asia and South Asia; East Africa; South America; West Africa.

INFORMATION AND EDUCATION ACTIVITIES: Topics: Culture/tradition/religion; Health/sanitation/water; Rural development/agriculture. **Activities:** Broadcasting/cultural events; Conferences/seminars/workshops/training activities; Formal education; Fund raising; Information campaigns/exhibitions; Publishing/audiovisual materials/educational materials.

NOR3444

NORSK MEDISINSK KOMITE FOR MIDTOSTEN ♦ Norwegian Medical Committee for the Middle East

Postboks 5126, Majorstua, 0301 Oslo, Norway.

Contact: Ragnhild Beck.

OBJECTIVES: To provide humanitarian health care support to groups in difficult situations in the Middle East. To promote the interests of these

groups by providing resources and medical treatment to the population and by sharing professional experience.

GENERAL INFORMATION: *Creation:* 1983. *Personnel/Total:* 7. *Salaried:* 3 of which: 3 in developing countries. *Volunteers:* 4. *Budget/Total 1993:* ECU 164000 (US$ 193000). *Financial sources:* Private: 20%. Public: 80%.

PUBLICATIONS: *Annual report.*

PLANNED ACTIVITIES: The committee plans to initiate a home nursing programme with local partners and will have nurses to provide information and training to families of patients with special needs.

ACTIVITIES IN DEVELOPING REGIONS: Present in developing regions. Active in 1 country(ies). Maintains local field presence. Works through local field partners. **Sustainable Development Actions:** Health/sanitation/water. **Regions:** Middle East.

INFORMATION AND EDUCATION ACTIVITIES: Topics: Health/sanitation/water. **Activities:** Fund raising.

NOR3445

NORSK MISJONSRADS BISTANDSNEMND ♦ Norwegian Missionary Council

P.O. Box 2347, Solli, 0201 Oslo 2, Norway.

Telephone: 47 (22) 43 81 10. *Fax:* 47 (22) 43 87 30. *Contact:* Viggo Koch, Chairman of the Board.

OBJECTIVES: To handle applications from member organisations for governmnet funding of development projects in developing countries.

GENERAL INFORMATION: *Creation:* 1983. *Type of organisation:* network. *Member organisations:* 13. *Personnel/Total:* 5. *Budget/Total 1993:* ECU 8383000 (US$ 9867000). *Financial sources:* Public: 100%.

EVALUATION/RESEARCH: Undertakes research activities.

NOR3446

NORSK ORGANISASJON FOR ASYLSOKERE (NOAS) ♦ Norwegian Organisation for Asylum Seekers

PO Box 8893 Yongstorget, 0028 Oslo , Norway.

Telephone: 47 (22) 20 84 40. *Fax:* 47 (22) 20 84 44. *Contact:* Annette A. Thommessen, Secretary General.

OBJECTIVES: To promote human rights and improve civil rights for asylum seekers and refugees. To inform and influence the media and public opinion on refugee-related issues.

GENERAL INFORMATION: *Creation:* 1984. *Affiliated to:* Norwegian Refugee Council (Norway) - European Consultants on Refugees and Exiles. *Personnel/Total:* 11. *Salaried:* 6. *Volunteers:* 5. *Budget/Total 1993:* ECU 228000 (US$ 268000). *Financial sources:* Private: 8%. Public: 60%. Self-financing: 32%.

PUBLICATIONS: *Periodicals:* Noas Ark (4). *Annual report. List of publications.*

EVALUATION/RESEARCH: Evaluation reports available. Undertakes research activities.

COMMENTS: Undertakes activities in the Commonwealth of Independent States. Information activities related to the Commonwealth of Independent States.

ACTIVITIES IN DEVELOPING REGIONS: Works through local field partners.

INFORMATION AND EDUCATION ACTIVITIES: Topics: Culture/tradition/religion; Human rights/peace/conflicts; International relations/cooperation/development aid; Racism/xenophobia/antisemitism; Refugees/migrants/ethnic groups. **Activities:** Broadcasting/cultural events; Conferences/seminars/workshops/training activities; Exchanges/twinning/linking; Formal education; Fund raising; Information and documentation services/data bases; Information campaigns/exhibitions; Lobbying/advocacy; Publishing/audiovisual materials/educational materials.

Voir : *Comment utiliser le répertoire,* page 11.

NOR3447

NORSK SYKEPLEIERFORBUND (NSF) ♦ Norwegian Nurses Association

Collett GT 54, P.O. Box 2633 St. Hanshaugen, 0131 Oslo 1, Norway.

Telephone: 47 (22) 04 33 04. *Fax:* 47 (22) 71 60 96. *Contact:* Laila Dåvøy, President.

OBJECTIVES: To develop the nursing profession and nursing education nationally and internationally. To collaborate with other nursing organisations throughout the world. To negotiate salaries and all aspects of socio-economic welfare on behalf of its members.

GENERAL INFORMATION: *Creation:* 1912. *Affiliated to:* Internation Council of Nurses (Switzerland) - Northern Nurses Federation (Norway) - Norwegian Federation of Professional Associations (Norway). *Personnel/Total:* 143. *Salaried:* 143 of which: 12 in developing countries. *Budget/Total 1993:* ECU 13652000 (US$ 16070000). *Financial sources:* Public: 5%. Self-financing: 95%.

PUBLICATIONS: *Periodicals:* Sykepleien (28). *Annual report. List of publications.*

EVALUATION/RESEARCH: Evaluation reports available. Undertakes research activities.

PLANNED ACTIVITIES: The organisation will establish new activities in Northern Russia

COMMENTS: Undertakes activities in the Commonwealth of Independent States. Information activities related to the Commonwealth of Independent States.

ACTIVITIES IN DEVELOPING REGIONS: Present in developing regions. Active in 5 country(ies). Works through local field partners. **Sustainable Development Actions:** Democracy/good governance/institution building/participatory development; Education/training/literacy; Health/sanitation/water; Population/family planning/demography; Sending volunteers/experts/technical assistance. **Regions:** Central Asia and South Asia; East Africa; Middle East; Southern Africa.

INFORMATION AND EDUCATION ACTIVITIES: Topics: Education/training/literacy; International relations/cooperation/development aid. **Activities:** Conferences/seminars/workshops/training activities; Exchanges/twinning/linking.

NOR3448

DEN NORSKE ADVOKATFORENING ♦ The Norwegian Bar Association

Kongensgt 6, 0153 Oslo, Norway.

Telephone: 47 (22) 42 06 20.

NOR3449

DET NORSKE BAPTISTSAMFUNN ♦ Baptist Union of Norway

Micheletsvei 62, 1320 Stabekk, Norway.

Telephone: 47 (2) 53 35 90. *Fax:* 47 (2) 12 30 44. *Contact:* Jan Arnth Larssen, General Secretary.

NOR3450

DET NORSKE MENNESKERETTIGHETSFOND ♦ The Norwegian Human Rights Fund

Youngsgate 11, 0181 Oslo, Norway.

Telephone: 47 (22) 40 11 04. *Fax:* 47 (22) 40 11 00. *Contact:* Ellinor Kolstad, Acting Director.

NOR3451

DEN NORSKE MISJONSALLIANSE ♦ Norwegian Missionary Alliance

Munchsgt. 9, P.O. Box 6863, St. Olavs Plass, 0130 Oslo 1, Norway.

Telephone: 47 (22) 20 06 46 / 20 62 65. *Fax:* 47 (22) 11 17 83.

NOR3452

DET NORSKE MISJONSFORBUND (DNM) ♦ Mission Covenant Church of Norway

Chr. Krohgsgt 34, 0186 Oslo 1, Norway.

Telephone: 47 (22) 11 33 30. *Fax:* 47 (22) 20 54 53. *Contact:* Bjørn Oyvind Fjeld, President.

OBJECTIVES: To support local churches' initiatives in development activities. To work for the extension of Evangelical Free Churches in Norway and overseas.

GENERAL INFORMATION: *Creation:* 1884. *Affiliated to:* International Federation of Free Evangelical Churches. *Personnel/Total:* 117. *Salaried:* 117 of which: 20 in developing countries. *Budget/Total 1993:* ECU 21562000 (US$ 2537000). *Financial sources:* Private: 65%. Public: 24%. Self-financing: 11%.

PUBLICATIONS: *Periodicals:* Misjonsbladet (20). *Annual report.*

EVALUATION/RESEARCH: Undertakes research activities.

COMMENTS: Undertakes activities in the Commonwealth of Independent States.

ACTIVITIES IN DEVELOPING REGIONS: Present in developing regions. Active in 2 country(ies). Maintains local field presence. Works through local field partners. **Sustainable Development Actions:** Children/youth/family; Education/training/literacy; Health/sanitation/water; Other; Sending volunteers/experts/technical assistance. **Regions:** Central Africa; South America.

NOR3453

DEN NORSKE MUHAMMEDANERMISJON (NMM) ♦ Norwegian Christian Mission

Ovregaten 10, 5003 Bergen, Norway.

Telephone: 47 (55) 32 29 90. *Fax:* 47 (55) 32 37 85. *Contact:* Eivind Olav Flå.

OBJECTIVES: To bring the gospel of Jesus Christ to Muslims all over the world.

GENERAL INFORMATION: *Creation:* 1940. *Type of organisation:* coordinating body. *Affiliated to:* Norwegian Missionary Council (Norway) - Norwegian Missionary Council office for International Development Cooperation (Norway). *Personnel/Total:* 93. *Salaried:* 13 of which: 4 in developing countries. *Volunteers:* 80. *Budget/Total 1993:* ECU 313000 (US$ 369000). *Financial sources:* Private: 44%. Public: 56%.

PUBLICATIONS: *Periodicals:* Lys Over Land (10) - Misbah ul Haqq (6). *Annual report.*

EVALUATION/RESEARCH: Evaluation reports available.

ACTIVITIES IN DEVELOPING REGIONS: Present in developing regions. Active in 4 country(ies). Maintains local field presence. Works through local field partners. **Sustainable Development Actions:** Children/youth/family; Democracy/good governance/institution building/participatory development; Ecology/environment/biodiversity; Education/training/literacy; Emergency relief/refugees/humanitarian assistance; Gender issues/women; Health/sanitation/water; Population/family planning/demography; Rural development/agriculture; Sending volunteers/experts/technical assistance. **Regions:** Central Asia and South Asia; West Africa.

INFORMATION AND EDUCATION ACTIVITIES: Topics: Children/youth/family; Culture/tradition/religion; Ecology/environment/biodiversity; Education/training/literacy; Food/famine; Gender issues/women; Health/sanitation/water; International relations/cooperation/development aid; Population/family planning/demography; Rural development/agriculture. **Activities:** Conferences/seminars/workshops/training activities; Formal education; Fund raising; Publishing/audiovisual materials/educational materials.

NOR3454

DET NORSKE SKOGSELSKAP ♦ The Norwegian Forestry Society

Wergelandsveien 23B, 0167 Oslo, Norway.

Telephone: 47 (22) 46 98 57.

See: *How to Use the Directory*, page 11.

NOR3455
NORTH-SOUTH COALITION

c/o PRIO, Fuglehauggt. 11, 0260 Oslo , Norway.

Telephone: 47 (22) 55 71 50. **Fax:** 47 (22) 55 84 22. **Contact:** Dan Smith, Co-ordinator.

OBJECTIVES: To lobby the Norwegian government on North-South development issues. To act as a forum for discussion of new government proposals affecting official Norwegian development policy.

GENERAL INFORMATION: Creation: 1976. **Type of organisation:** network. **Affiliated to:** International Coalition for Development Action (Belgium) - Forum for Environment and Development (Norway). **Personnel/Total:** 10. *Salaried:* 1. *Volunteers:* 9. **Budget/Total 1993:** ECU 51000 (US$ 60000). **Financial sources:** Public: 100%.

PUBLICATIONS: Periodicals: Information Bulletin (2). *Annual report. List of publications.*

INFORMATION AND EDUCATION ACTIVITIES: Topics: Emergency relief/refugees/humanitarian assistance; International economic relations/trade/debt/finance; International relations/cooperation/development aid; Peace/ethnic conflicts/armament/disarmament; Poverty/living conditions. **Activities:** Conferences/seminars/workshops/training activities; Information and documentation services/data bases; Lobbying/advocacy.

NOR3456
NORWAC ♦ Norwegian Aid Committee

P.O. Box 93, Ullevål Sykehus, 0407 Oslo, Norway.

Telephone: 47 (22) 71 28 67. **Fax:** 47 (22) 71 30 75. **Contact:** Erik Fosse, Secretary General.

OBJECTIVES: To procure medical supplies and other help for countries and regions where it is needed. To help develop the health sectors together with the health service plan. To educate the general public on development issues.

GENERAL INFORMATION: Creation: 1983. **Type of organisation:** coordinating body. **Personnel/Total:** 9. *Salaried:* 1. *Volunteers:* 8 of which: 8 in developing countries. **Budget/Total 1993:** ECU 619000 (US$ 728000). **Financial sources:** Public: 80%. Self-financing: 20%.

PLANNED ACTIVITIES: A theatre nurse training programme. Training teachers in the health sectors and training of public health nurses.

ACTIVITIES IN DEVELOPING REGIONS: Present in developing regions. Active in 4 country(ies). Maintains local field presence. Works through local field partners. **Sustainable Development Actions:** Education/training/literacy; Health/sanitation/water; Sending volunteers/experts/technical assistance. **Regions:** East Africa; Middle East; North Africa.

NOR3457
THE NORWEGIAN CANCER ASSOCIATION ♦ Landsforeningen mot kreft

Huitfeldtsgate 49, 0253 Oslo, Norway.

Telephone: 47 (22) 20 05 18.

NOR3458
THE NORWEGIAN FORUM FOR ENVIRONMENT AND DEVELOPMENT

P.O. Box 3894, 0805 Oslo, Norway.

Telephone: 47 (22) 95 10 22. **Fax:** 47 (22) 95 10 22. **Contact:** Vegard Bye, Executive Director.

OBJECTIVES: To co-ordinate Norwegian NGOs and UNCED follow-up activities.

GENERAL INFORMATION: Creation: 1993. **Type of organisation:** coordinating body. **Member organisations:** 55. **Affiliated to:** Alliance of Northern People for Environment and Development. **Personnel/Total:** 5. *Salaried:* 5. **Budget/Total 1993:** ECU 2635000 (US$ 3101000). **Financial sources:** Public: 98%. Self-financing: 2%.

PUBLICATIONS: Periodicals: Eco-Bulletin (4). *Annual report.*

EVALUATION/RESEARCH: Evaluation reports available.

COMMENTS: This organisation evolved from the Norwegian Campaign for the Environment and Development, which no longer exists.

NOR3459
NORWEGIAN HIMAL-ASIA MISSION (NHAM)

Postboks 9111, Vaterland, 0134 Oslo, Norway.

Telephone: 47 (22) 36 33 10. **Contact:** Einar Kippenes, Secretary General.

OBJECTIVES: To help people in the Himalayan region of Nepal and Central Asia. To bring the Gospel to Tibetians, Nepalis and other peoples in the Himalayas.

GENERAL INFORMATION: Creation: 1938. **Affiliated to:** United Mission to Nepal (Nepal) - Norsk Misjonsråds Bistandsnemnd (Norway). **Personnel/Total:** 19. *Salaried:* 17 of which: 13 in developing countries. *Volunteers:* 2. **Budget/Total 1993:** ECU 390000 (US$ 459000). **Financial sources:** Private: 55%. Public: 38%. Self-financing: 7%.

PUBLICATIONS: Periodicals: Tibetaneren (10). *Annual report.*

EVALUATION/RESEARCH: Evaluation reports available.

ACTIVITIES IN DEVELOPING REGIONS: Present in developing regions. Active in 2 country(ies). Maintains local field presence. Works through local field partners. **Sustainable Development Actions:** Education/training/literacy; Energy/transport; Health/sanitation/water; Sending volunteers/experts/technical assistance; Small enterprises/informal sector/handicrafts. **Regions:** Central Asia and South Asia.

NOR3460
THE NORWEGIAN SANTAL MISSION

PO Box 9219 Grønland, 0134 Oslo, Norway.

Telephone: 47 (22) 67 94 00. **Fax:** 47 (22) 67 93 35. **Contact:** Torbjörn Lied, General Secretary.

OBJECTIVES: To spread the word of God and build His church among the peoples of the world.

GENERAL INFORMATION: Creation: 1867. **Personnel/Total:** 210. *Salaried:* 210 of which: 130 in developing countries. **Budget/Total 1993:** ECU 6706000 (US$ 8000000). **Financial sources:** Public: 20%.

PUBLICATIONS: Periodicals: Santalen (22). *Annual report. List of publications.*

EVALUATION/RESEARCH: Evaluation reports available. Undertakes research activities.

COMMENTS: Undertakes activities in the Commonwealth of Independent States.

ACTIVITIES IN DEVELOPING REGIONS: Present in developing regions. Active in 7 country(ies). Maintains local field presence. Works through local field partners. **Sustainable Development Actions:** Debt/finance/trade; Democracy/good governance/institution building/participatory development; Ecology/environment/biodiversity; Education/training/literacy; Emergency relief/refugees/humanitarian assistance; Gender issues/women; Health/sanitation/water; Rural development/agriculture; Small enterprises/informal sector/handicrafts. **Regions:** Caribbean; Central Asia and South Asia; Middle East; South America; West Africa.

INFORMATION AND EDUCATION ACTIVITIES: Topics: Children/youth/family; Education/training/literacy; Gender issues/women; Health/sanitation/water; Human rights/peace/conflicts; Refugees/migrants/ethnic groups; Rural development/agriculture. **Activities:** Broadcasting/cultural events; Conferences/seminars/workshops/training activities; Exchanges/twinning/linking; Formal education; Fund raising; Information and documentation services/data bases; Lobbying/advocacy; Publishing/audiovisual materials/educational materials.

NOR3461
THE NORWEGIAN SOCIETY FOR TRAINED SOCIAL WORKERS (FO)

PO Box 4693, Sofienberg, 0506 Oslo, Norway.

Voir : *Comment utiliser le répertoire*, page 11.

Telephone: 47 (22) 40 11 70.

NOR3462

THE NORWEGIAN UNION OF JOURNALISTS

Postboks 8793, Youngstorget, 0028 Oslo, Norway.

Telephone: 47 (22) 17 01 17. Fax: 47 (22) 17 17 82.

NOR3463

PALESTINAGRUPPENE I NORGE ♦ The Palestine Group of Norway

PO Box 1808 Vika, 0123 Oslo, Norway.

Telephone: 47 (22) 33 26 72.

NOR3464

PALESTINAKOMITEEN I NORGE (PALKOM) ♦ Palestine Committee of Norway

Box 6876 St. Olavsplass, 0130 Oslo, Norway.

Telephone: 47 (2) 71 29 33. Contact: Egil Fossum.

NOR3465

PASTOR STROMMES MINNESTIFTELSE (PSM) ♦ Strømme Memorial Foundation

P.O. Box 414, 4601 Kristiansand, Norway.

Telephone: 47 (38) 02 85 75. Fax: 47 (38) 02 57 10. Contact: Oistein Garcia de Presno, General Secretary.

OBJECTIVES: To support development projects in several of the least developed countries in Africa, Asia and Latin America. To care for material and spiritual needs viewing man as a whole.

GENERAL INFORMATION: Creation: 1976. Personnel/Total: 35. Salaried: 30 of which: 3 in developing countries. Volunteers: 5. Budget/Total 1993: ECU 7904000 (US$ 9304000). Financial sources: Private: 70%. Public: 27%. Self-financing: 3%.

PUBLICATIONS: Periodicals: Hjelp Til Selv Hjelp (5). Annual report.

EVALUATION/RESEARCH: Evaluation reports available.

ACTIVITIES IN DEVELOPING REGIONS: Active in 15 country(ies). Maintains local field presence. Works through local field partners. Sustainable Development Actions: Children/youth/family; Democracy/good governance/institution building/participatory development; Ecology/environment/biodiversity; Education/training/literacy; Emergency relief/refugees/humanitarian assistance; Food/famine; Gender issues/women; Health/sanitation/water; Human rights/peace/conflicts; Population/family planning/demography; Rural development/agriculture; Sending volunteers/experts/technical assistance; Small enterprises/informal sector/handicrafts; Urban development/habitat. Regions: Central Africa; Central Asia and South Asia; East Africa; East Asia; South America; South East Asia; West Africa.

INFORMATION AND EDUCATION ACTIVITIES: Topics: Children/youth/family; Education/training/literacy; Gender issues/women; Health/sanitation/water; International relations/cooperation/development aid; Rural development/agriculture. Activities: Formal education.

NOR3466

PINSEVENNENES YTRE MISJON ♦ Pentecostal Foreign Mission

Haraldrudvn. 5, P.O. Box 25, 0508 Oslo 5, Norway.

Telephone: 47 (22) 64 64 00. Fax: 47 (22) 64 74 69. Contact: Reinert O. Innvær, Mission Secretary.

NOR3467

REDD BARNA ♦ Norwegian Save the Children

Grensesvingen 7, Box 6200, Etterstad, 0602 Olso 6, Norway.

Telephone: 47 (22) 57 00 80. Fax: 47 (22) 67 48 84. Contact: Tor Elden, General Secretary.

OBJECTIVES: To participate in national and international work for children in need. To work for better understanding and friendship between peo-

ples. To seek to develop public opinion on national and international problems related to the objectives of the organisation.

GENERAL INFORMATION: Creation: 1946. Affiliated to: International Save the Children Alliance. Personnel/Total: 1200. of which: 1100 in developing countries. Budget/Total 1993: ECU 4467000 (US$ 5258000). Financial sources: Private: 59%. Public: 41%.

PUBLICATIONS: Periodicals: Redd Barna Newspaper (8). Annual report.

EVALUATION/RESEARCH: Evaluation reports available. Undertakes research activities.

ACTIVITIES IN DEVELOPING REGIONS: Present in developing regions. Active in 20 country(ies). Maintains local field presence. Works through local field partners. Sustainable Development Actions: Children/youth/family; Debt/finance/trade; Democracy/good governance/institution building/participatory development; Ecology/environment/biodiversity; Education/training/literacy; Emergency relief/refugees/humanitarian assistance; Food/famine; Gender issues/women; Health/sanitation/water; Human rights/peace/conflicts; Population/family planning/demography; Rural development/agriculture; Small enterprises/informal sector/handicrafts; Urban development/habitat. Regions: Central Asia and South Asia; East Africa; East Asia; Mexico and Central America; Middle East; South East Asia; Southern Africa.

INFORMATION AND EDUCATION ACTIVITIES: Topics: Children/youth/family; Ecology/environment/biodiversity; Education/training/literacy; Emergency relief/refugees/humanitarian assistance; Employment/unemployment; Food/famine; Gender issues/women; Health/sanitation/water; Human rights/peace/conflicts; International economic relations/trade/debt/finance; International relations/cooperation/development aid; Peace/ethnic conflicts/armament/disarmament; Population/family planning/demography; Poverty/living conditions; Racism/xenophobia/antisemitism; Refugees/migrants/ethnic groups; Rural development/agriculture; Urban development/habitat. Activities: Broadcasting/cultural events; Conferences/seminars/workshops/training activities; Exchanges/twinning/linking; Formal education; Fund raising; Information and documentation services/data bases; Information campaigns/exhibitions; Lobbying/advocacy; Networking/electronic telecommunications; Publishing/audiovisual materials/educational materials.

NOR3468

SKOLENES U-LANDSAKSJON ♦ The Norwegian School Agency for International Development and Co-operation

P.B. 1600, Kjelvene, 4004 Stavanger, Norway.

Telephone: 47 (51) 53 92 30. Fax: 47 (51) 53 92 35. Contact: Holger Susort, Executive Officer.

NOR3469

SRI LANKA RESOURCE CENTRE

Grensen 18, 0159 Oslo 1, Norway.

NOR3470

STIFTELSEN INTER-FOLK ♦ The Inter-Folk Foundation

v/ Håkon Olav Aandstad, Kolstad, Solbergfossvn 95, 1800 Askim, Norway.

Telephone: 47 (9) 88 31 12.

NOR3471

TAMIL DEVELOPMENT NETWORK OF NORWAY

Sondre Tollbugt. 2, 9008 Tromso, Norway.

Telephone: 47 (776) 10 344. Contact: Kanapathipillai Sivarajah, Coordinator.

OBJECTIVES: To work for the recognition by Norway that the Tamils of Sri Lanka are a nation with the right to self-determination. To work for the socio-economic cultural development of Tamils living in the Tamil homelands of Sri Lanka. To work for the socio-economic-cultural development of Tamils living in Norway.

GENERAL INFORMATION: Personnel/Total: 3. Salaried: 1. Volunteers: 2. Budget/Total 1993: ECU 10000 (US$ 11000). Financial sources: Private: 10%. Public: 80%. Self-financing: 10%.

PUBLICATIONS: *Periodicals:* Tamil Development (2). *Annual report.*

ACTIVITIES IN DEVELOPING REGIONS: Active in 1 country(ies). Works through local field partners. **Sustainable Development Actions:** Debt/finance/trade; Democracy/good governance/institution building/participatory development; Small enterprises/informal sector/handicrafts. **Regions:** Central Asia and South Asia.

INFORMATION AND EDUCATION ACTIVITIES: Topics: International relations/cooperation/development aid; Refugees/migrants/ethnic groups. **Activities:** Conferences/seminars/workshops/training activities; Fund raising; Information and documentation services/data bases; Lobbying/advocacy.

NOR3472

U-ASSIST-SAS-NORGE ♦ U-ASSIST NORWAY

OSL TSE, SAS Fornebu, 1335 Snarøya, Norway.

Telephone: 47 (2) 59 68 88. *Contact:* Helge Andersen, Chairman.

NOR3473

U-LANDSFORENINGEN SVALENE ♦ Swallows Development Organisation

Herman Fossgt. 9, 5007 Bergen, Norway.

Telephone: 47 (55) 93 49 08. *Fax:* 47 (55) 32 02 37. *Contact:* Marthe Kvarteig de Ibanez.

OBJECTIVES: To promote the education and training of young women from disadvantaged areas in Latin America.

GENERAL INFORMATION: *Creation:* 1960. *Affiliated to:* Emmaüs International (France). *Personnel/Total:* 8. *Volunteers:* 8. *Budget/Total 1993:* ECU 34000 (US$ 39000). *Financial sources:* Private: 100%.

PUBLICATIONS: *Periodicals:* Svalene (4). *Annual report.*

EVALUATION/RESEARCH: Evaluation reports available.

ACTIVITIES IN DEVELOPING REGIONS: Active in 1 country(ies). Maintains local field presence. Works through local field partners. **Sustainable Development Actions:** Education/training/literacy; Urban development/habitat. **Regions:** South America.

INFORMATION AND EDUCATION ACTIVITIES: Topics: Education/training/literacy; Gender issues/women; Urban development/habitat. **Activities:** Conferences/seminars/workshops/training activities; Formal education.

NOR3474

UNICEF KOMITEEN I NORGE ♦ Norwegian Committee for UNICEF

Langesgt 4, P.O. Box 6877 St. Olavs Plass, 0165 Oslo 1, Norway.

Telephone: 47 (22) 36 33 40. *Fax:* 47 (22) 36 30 10. *Contact:* Annie Kirsten Søgaard, Secretary General.

NOR3475

UTVIKLINGSFONDET - FREMTIDEN I VARE HENDER ♦ Fonds de développement - L'avenir entre nos mains

Kristian Augustsgt 7A, 0164 Oslo, Norvège.

Téléphone: 47 (22) 20 05 71. *Contact:* Andrew Kroglund, Coordinateur de projets.

OBJECTIFS: Soutenir des initiatives menées par des organisations locales dans les pays en développement et qui ont comme objectifs de promouvoir l'autosuffisance, le respect de l'environnement, l'autodétermination des populations, la justice sociale et le renforcement des traditions locales.

INFORMATIONS GENERALES: *Création:* 1978. *Personnel/Total:* 6. *Salariés:* 6. *Budget/Total 1993:* ECU 2754000 (US$ 3242000). *Sources financières:* Privé: 20%. *Public:* 80%.

PUBLICATIONS: *Périodiques:* Future (1) - X (24). *Rapport annuel.*

EVALUATION/RECHERCHE: Rapports d'évaluation disponibles.

PREVISIONS D'ACTIVITES: Campagne sur l'importance de la biodiversité, de l'intégration du développement et de l'environnement. Pour que l'aide apportée mène à un développement durable.

ACTIVITES DANS LES REGIONS EN DEVELOPPEMENT: Intervient dans 9 pays. Intervient par l'intermédiaire d'organisations locales partenaires. **Actions de Développement durable:** Aliments/famine; Développement rural/agriculture; Questions relatives aux femmes; Écologie/environnement/biodiversité; Éducation/formation/alphabétisation. **Régions:** Afrique de l'Est; Asie centrale et Asie du Sud; Asie du Sud-Est; Mexique et Amerique centrale.

ACTIVITES D'INFORMATION ET D'EDUCATION: Domaines: Développement rural/agriculture; Questions relatives aux femmes; Écologie/environnement/biodiversité. **Activités:** Collecte de fonds; Conférences/séminaires/ateliers/activités de formation; Lobbying/plaidoyer.

NOR3476

VOKSENOPPLERINGSFORBUNDET (VOFO) ♦ Norwegian Association for Adult Education

Dronningens Gate 17, P.O. Box 560 Sentrum, 0105 Oslo 1, Norway.

Telephone: 47 (22) 41 00 00. *Fax:* 47 (22) 33 40 85. *Contact:* Ole Ormseth, Secretary General.

OBJECTIVES: To act as a contact point and co-ordinating unit for Norwegian organisations engaged in the field of adult education. To promote contact between adult education organisations in developing countries and in Norway. To support adult education projects in developing countries and provide information about developing countries to people in Norway.

GENERAL INFORMATION: *Creation:* 1932. *Type of organisation:* association of NGOs. *Member organisations:* 331. *Affiliated to:* International Council for Adult Education (Canada). *Personnel/Total:* 8. *Salaried:* 8. *Budget/Total 1993:* ECU 425000 (US$ 500000). *Financial sources:* Public: 90%. *Self-financing:* 10%.

PUBLICATIONS: *Periodicals:* Studienytt (4). *Annual report.*

PLANNED ACTIVITIES: Strengthen international co-operation. Assist the development of adult education in eastern Europe and the Baltics.

ACTIVITIES IN DEVELOPING REGIONS: Works through local field partners. **Sustainable Development Actions:** Education/training/literacy. **Regions:** East Africa; Mexico and Central America; Middle East; South America; Southern Africa.

NOR3477

WOMEN FOR PEACE NORWAY (KFF)

BOX 389, 7001 Trondheim, Norway.

Telephone: 47 (3) 47 38 75. *Fax:* 47 (3) 47 38 75. *Contact:* Tulle Elster, Editor/Board Member.

NOR3478

WORLDVIEW INTERNATIONAL FOUNDATION

Wellhavensgt. 1, 0166 Oslo 1, Norway.

Telephone: 47 (22) 11 49 80. *Fax:* 47 (22) 11 49 88.

Voir : *Comment utiliser le répertoire,* page 11.

POL3479
AKADEMICKI KLUB EKOLOGICZNY "OIKOS"

Akademia Ekonomiczna, ul. Nowowiejska 3/99, 58-500 Jelenia Gora, Poland.

POL3480
ALL-POLAND ALLIANCE OF CATHOLIC ORGANISATIONS (OPOKA)

Krakowskie Przedmiescie 68, 00-322 Warszawa, Poland.

Telephone: 48 (22) 268991. **Contact:** Robert Kuraszkiewicz, President.

OBJECTIVES: To foster co-operation among member organisations and co-ordinate their activities.

GENERAL INFORMATION: Creation: 1991. **Type of organisation:** coordinating body. **Member organisations:** 17. **Affiliated to:** Polish Council of Youth (Poland).

PUBLICATIONS: Periodicals: Vademecum.

EVALUATION/RESEARCH: Evaluation reports available.

COMMENTS: Undertakes activities in the Commonwealth of Independent States. Information activities related to the Commonwealth of Independent States.

ACTIVITIES IN DEVELOPING REGIONS: Works through local field partners.

INFORMATION AND EDUCATION ACTIVITIES: Topics: Children/youth/family; Culture/tradition/religion; Human rights/peace/conflicts; Population/family planning/demography. **Activities:** Broadcasting/cultural events; Conferences/seminars/workshops/training activities; Exchanges/twinning/linking; Information campaigns/exhibitions.

POL3481
ARKADIA

Lodzki Dom Kultury, ul. Traugutta 18, 90-113 Lodz, Poland.

POL3482
BALTYCKI SEKRETARIAT POLSCE (BSSP) ♦ Baltic Sea Secretariat in Poland

ul. Wyspianskiego 5, 80-434 Gdansk-Wrezeszcz, Poland.

Telephone: 48 (58) 472860. **Fax:** 48 (58) 471651. **Contact:** Marek Maciejowski.

OBJECTIVES: To promote public awareness and environmental education in the Baltic Sea region.

GENERAL INFORMATION: Creation: 1991. **Affiliated to:** Coalition Clean Baltic (Sweden) - Helsinki Commission (Finland). **Personnel/Total:** 3. Salaried: 2. Volunteers: 1. **Budget/Total 1993:** ECU 9600 (US$ 12500). **Financial sources:** Private: 85%. Public: 10%. Self-financing: 5%.

PUBLICATIONS: Periodicals: CCB Newsletter (6). Annual report.

EVALUATION/RESEARCH: Evaluation reports available. Undertakes research activities.

PLANNED ACTIVITIES: Disseminating information on anti-phosphates.

COMMENTS: Undertakes activities in the Commonwealth of Independent States. Information activities related to the Commonwealth of Independent States.

INFORMATION AND EDUCATION ACTIVITIES: Topics: Ecology/environment/biodiversity; Health/sanitation/water; Human rights/peace/conflicts; International economic relations/trade/debt/finance; International relations/cooperation/development aid; Rural development/agriculture. **Activities:** Broadcasting/cultural events; Conferences/seminars/workshops/training activities; Exchanges/twinning/linking; Formal education; Fund raising; Information and documentation services/data bases; Information campaigns/exhibitions; Lobbying/advocacy; Networking/electronic telecommunications; Publishing/audiovisual materials/educational materials.

POL3483
BIFIS-FISE

Jasna 22, 00-054 Warszawa, Poland.

POL3484
BIURO PRASOWE POROZUMIENIA CENTRUM ♦ Young Christian Democrats Union

ul. Nowy Swiat, Warszawa, Poland.

POL3485
CATHOLIC SCOUTING ASSOCIATION - GLOWNA KWATERA SHK "ZAWISZA"

ul. Droga Meczennikow Majdanka 27, Dublin, Poland.

POL3486
CENTRE FOR ENVIRONMENT AND DEVELOPMENT

c/o Centre for Environmental Protection, 5/11 Kruckza Str, 00-548 Warszawa, Poland.

POL3487
CENTRUM EDUKACJI EKOLOGICZNEJ

ul. Mikolwska 26, Palak Mlodziety, 40-066 Katowice, Poland.

POL3488
CENTRUM SRODOWISKA I ROZWOJU

ul. Chmielna 15, 00-117 Warszawa, Poland.

POL3489
CHRISTIAN CHILDREN'S FUND - NATIONAL OFFICE

Kredytowa 4/18, 00-062 Warszawa, Poland.

POL3490
CIVIC DIALOGUE NGO PROGRAMME (PHARE)

ul. Zurwia 4, Pokoj 617, 00-503 Warszawa, Poland.

POL3491
CLEAN AIR FOUNDATION

ul. Jakuba Kubickiego 17/23, 02-954 Warszawa, Poland.

POL3492
COOPERATION FUND

ul. Zurawia 4A/617, Warszawa, Poland.

POL3493
DEMOCRATIC YOUTH UNION

ul. Chmielna 9, 00-950 Warszawa, Poland.

POL3494
ECOLOGICAL CLUB "PANDA"

Wydz. Hydrotechniki Politechnik, ul Szara 27 m 4, 80-116 Gdansk, Poland.

POL3495
ECOVAST, POLSKA SEKCJA EUROPESJSKIEGO RUCHU ODNOWY WSI

Malyck Miast, ul. Mickiewicza 121, 87-100 Torun, Poland.

POL3496
EKOLOGICZNY RUCH STUDENCKI

Uniwersytet Szczecinski, Wydzial Ekonomiczny, ul. Mickiewicza 66, 71-101 Szczecin, Poland.

See: How to Use the Directory, page 11.

POL3497
EUROPEJSKIE STOWARZYSZENIE

Ekonomistow Srodowiska i Zasobow Naturalnych, Akademia Ekonomiczna, ul. Sownskiego 17/21, 99-300 Kutno, Poland.

POL3498
FELLOWSHIP OF ORTHODOX YOUTH

ul. Liniarskiego 2, 15-420 Bialystok, Poland.

POL3499
FUNDACJA WSPIERANIA INICJATYW EKO-LOGICZNYCH (FWIE) ♦ Foundation for the Support of Ecological Initiatives

ul. Stawhowska 12, 31-014 Kraków, Poland.

Telephone: 48 (12) 222264. *Fax:* 48 (12) 222264. *E-mail:*
zielbryg@gn.apc.org. *Contact:* Iwona Walerowska, Manager.

OBJECTIVES: To improve the state of the environment.

GENERAL INFORMATION: *Creation:* 1989. *Type of organisation:*
network. *Member organisations:* 30. *Affiliated to:* Alliance for
Northern People for Environment and Development (Germany) - Action
for Solidarity Equality Environment Development (the Netherlands).
Personnel/Total: 610. *Salaried:* 10. *Volunteers:* 600. *Budget/
Total 1993:* ECU 43000 (US$ 55000). *Financial sources:* Private:
40%. *Public:* 20%. *Self-financing:* 40%.

PUBLICATIONS: *Periodicals:* Green Brigades Ecologists' Paper (4) -
Zielone Brygady Pismo Ekologiczne (12) - Grasshopper Environment
NGOs Quarterly of the East Carpathians Region (4). *List of publications.*

EVALUATION/RESEARCH: Evaluation reports available.

COMMENTS: Undertakes activities in the Commonwealth of Independent
States. Information activities related to the Commonwealth of Independent States.

INFORMATION AND EDUCATION ACTIVITIES: Topics: Ecology/envi-
ronment/biodiversity; Education/training/literacy; Health/sanitation/
water; International economic relations/trade/debt/finance; International
relations/cooperation/development aid; Rural development/agriculture;
Urban development/habitat. **Activities:** Conferences/seminars/work-
shops/training activities; Exchanges/twinning/linking; Information and
documentation services/data bases; Information campaigns/exhibitions;
Lobbying/advocacy; Networking/electronic telecommunications; Pub-
lishing/audiovisual materials/educational materials.

POL3500
GREEN EARTH

ul. Prybyszewskiego 41, 51-151 Wroclaw, Poland.

POL3501
INSTITUTE FOR ENVIRONMENTAL MANAGEMENT AND PROTECTION

ul. Mickiewicza 30 Pawilon c-4, 30-059 Krakow, Poland.

POL3502
INSTYTUT NA NEOZ EKOROZWOJU (INE) ♦ Institute for Sustain-able Development

ul. Krzywickiego 9, 02-078 Warszawa, Poland.

Telephone: 48 (22) 250378. *Fax:* 48 (22) 253461. *E-mail:*
INE@PLEARN.EDV.PL. *Contact:* Andrzej Kassenberg, President.

OBJECTIVES: To implement sustainable development projects and disseminate information about sustainable development in Poland. To provide the local government, municipalities and NGOs with policy-oriented
and multi-disciplinary expertise.

GENERAL INFORMATION: *Creation:* 1991. *Personnel/Total:* 11. *Salaried:* 10. *Volunteers:* 1. *Financial sources:* Private: 48%. *Public:*
37%. *Self-financing:* 15%.

PUBLICATIONS: *List of publications.*

EVALUATION/RESEARCH: Undertakes research activities.

PLANNED ACTIVITIES: A two year pilot programme, teaching the local
authorities and society how to jointly prepare an action programme for
environmental protection. A study on Environmental Awareness and
Consumerism of the Poles.

COMMENTS: Undertakes activities in the Commonwealth of Independent
States. Information activities related to the Commonwealth of Independent States.

INFORMATION AND EDUCATION ACTIVITIES: Topics: Ecology/envi-
ronment/biodiversity; Employment/unemployment; Human rights/peace/
conflicts; International economic relations/trade/debt/finance. **Activities:**
Conferences/seminars/workshops/training activities; Information cam-
paigns/exhibitions; Publishing/audiovisual materials/educational
materials.

POL3503
INTERNATIONAL ENVIRONMENTAL SERVICE CENTRE

ul. Czackiego 3/5, 00-043 Warszawa, Poland.

POL3504
INTERSCHOOL SOLIDARITY COMMITTEE (MKS)

ul. Pasteura 4/6 m. 54, Warszawa, Poland.

POL3505
KLUB EKOLOGICZNY "MALOPOLSKA"

ul. Spokojna 26m 3, 30-054 Krakow, Poland.

POL3506
KRAJOWA RADA EKOLOGICZNA ZMW

ul. Nowy Swiat 18/20, 00-920 Warszawa, Poland.

POL3507
KRAJOWE CENTRUM EDUKACJI EKOLOGICZNEJ (KCEE) ♦
National Environmental Education Centre

ul. Dubois 9, 00-182 Warszawa, Poland.

Telephone: 48 (2) 635 6468. *Fax:* 48 (2) 635 6468. *E-mail:*
kceekol@plearn. *Contact:* Jan Bogdanowicz, Director.

OBJECTIVES: To inspire, encourage and develop environmental education activities. To promote the idea of sustainable development.

GENERAL INFORMATION: *Creation:* 1992. *Type of organisation:* net-
work, coordinating body. *Member organisations:* 20. *Affiliated to:*
National Network of Environmental Education Centres (Poland) - EE-
NET (Latvia). *Personnel/Total:* 13. *Salaried:* 13. *Budget/Total 1993:*
ECU 204000 (US$ 265000). *Financial sources:* Private: 30%. *Public:*
70%.

PUBLICATIONS: *Periodicals:* EE Network Newsletter (4). *Annual report.*
List of publications.

EVALUATION/RESEARCH: Evaluation reports available.

PLANNED ACTIVITIES: Holding campaigns on waste segregation and
ozone.

COMMENTS: Undertakes activities in the Commonwealth of Independent
States. Information activities related to the Commonwealth of Independent States.

INFORMATION AND EDUCATION ACTIVITIES: Topics: Ecology/envi-
ronment/biodiversity; Education/training/literacy. **Activities:** Confer-
ences/seminars/workshops/training activities; Exchanges/twinning/link-
ing; Formal education; Fund raising; Information and documentation
services/data bases; Information campaigns/exhibitions; Lobbying/advo-
cacy; Networking/electronic telecommunications; Publishing/audiovisual
materials/educational materials.

POL3508
LEAGUE FOR THE PROTECTION OF NATURE - YOUTH ORGANISATION (LNP-YO)

ul. Tamka 37/2, 00-355 Warszawa, Poland.

Voir : *Comment utiliser le répertoire*, page 11.

Telephone: 48 (2) 635 8171. *Fax:* 48 (2) 635 8171. *Contact:* Tomasz Cieslik, Chairman.

OBJECTIVES: To promote education on the ecology through camps, training programmes and sessions.

GENERAL INFORMATION: *Creation:* 1990. *Personnel/Total:* 1. *Salaried:* 1. *Budget/Total 1993:* ECU 2000 (US$ 2500).

PUBLICATIONS: *Periodicals:* Wiadomosci Omlop (6). *Annual report. List of publications.*

EVALUATION/RESEARCH: Evaluation reports available. Undertakes research activities.

COMMENTS: Undertakes activities in the Commonwealth of Independent States. Information activities related to the Commonwealth of Independent States.

ACTIVITIES IN DEVELOPING REGIONS: Present in developing regions. Maintains local field presence. Works through local field partners. **Sustainable Development Actions:** Children/youth/family; Debt/finance/trade; Democracy/good governance/institution building/participatory development; Ecology/environment/biodiversity; Education/training/literacy; Emergency relief/refugees/humanitarian assistance; Energy/transport; Gender issues/women; Health/sanitation/water; Human rights/peace/conflicts; Population/family planning/demography; Rural development/agriculture; Sending volunteers/experts/technical assistance; Small enterprises/informal sector/handicrafts; Urban development/habitat. **Regions:** Caribbean; Central Africa; Central Asia and South Asia; East Africa; East Asia; Mexico and Central America; Middle East; North Africa; Oceania; South America; South East Asia; Southern Africa; West Africa.

INFORMATION AND EDUCATION ACTIVITIES: Topics: Children/youth/family; Culture/tradition/religion; Ecology/environment/biodiversity; Education/training/literacy; Emergency relief/refugees/humanitarian assistance; Employment/unemployment; Gender issues/women; Health/sanitation/water; Human rights/peace/conflicts; International economic relations/trade/debt/finance; International relations/cooperation/development aid; Peace/ethnic conflicts/armament/disarmament; Population/family planning/demography; Poverty/living conditions; Refugees/migrants/ethnic groups; Rural development/agriculture; Urban development/habitat. **Activities:** Broadcasting/cultural events; Conferences/seminars/workshops/training activities; Exchanges/twinning/linking; Formal education; Information and documentation services/data bases; Networking/electronic telecommunications; Publishing/audiovisual materials/educational materials.

POL3509

LIGA OCHRONY PRZYRODY - ZARZAD GLOWNY (LOP) ♦
Polish League for Nature Protection - Headquarters

ul. Tamka 37/2, 00-355 Warszawa, Poland.

Telephone: 48 (2) 635 8171. *Fax:* 48 (2) 635 8171. *Contact:* Janusz Janecki.

OBJECTIVES: To prevent the degradation of the environment, to provide environmental education and to collect and publish information.

GENERAL INFORMATION: *Creation:* 1928. *Affiliated to:* IUCN. *Personnel/Total:* 170. *Salaried:* 20. *Volunteers:* 150. *Financial sources:* Self-financing: 100%.

PUBLICATIONS: *Periodicals:* Polish Nature (12) - The Bulletin (12). *Annual report.*

EVALUATION/RESEARCH: Evaluation reports available.

COMMENTS: Undertakes activities in the Commonwealth of Independent States. Information activities related to the Commonwealth of Independent States.

INFORMATION AND EDUCATION ACTIVITIES: Topics: Ecology/environment/biodiversity; Urban development/habitat. **Activities:** Broadcasting/cultural events; Conferences/seminars/workshops/training activities; Exchanges/twinning/linking; Formal education; Fund raising; Information and documentation services/data bases; Information campaigns/exhibitions; Lobbying/advocacy; Networking/electronic telecommunications; Publishing/audiovisual materials/educational materials.

POL3510

NATIONAL FOUNDATION FOR ENVIRONMENTAL PROTECTION

ul. Krzywickiego 9, 02-078 Warszawa, Poland.

POL3511

NIEZALEZNE ZRZESZENIE STUDENTOW ♦ Independent Students Union

ul. Okolnik 11, 00-386 Warszawa, Poland.

POL3512

ORGANIZATION OF LAOTIAN STUDENTS FIGHTING FOR INDEPENDENCE AND DEMOCRACY

ul. Nowy Swiat 18/20, Warszawa, Poland.

Contact: Bounthanh Thammavong.

OBJECTIVES: To help restore democracy in Laos, defend political prisoners and promote the respect of human rights. To disseminate information about problems and human rights violations in Laos. To make the Laos people aware of their rights to freedom and democracy.

GENERAL INFORMATION: *Creation:* 1990. *Personnel/Total:* 215. *Volunteers:* 215 of which: 112 in developing countries. *Budget/Total 1993:* ECU 5000 (US$ 7000). *Financial sources:* Private: 59%. Self-financing: 41%.

PUBLICATIONS: *Periodicals:* My Homeland-Laos (6) - Freedom for Laos (12). *List of publications.*

COMMENTS: Undertakes activities in the Commonwealth of Independent States.

ACTIVITIES IN DEVELOPING REGIONS: Active in 4 country(ies). Maintains local field presence. **Sustainable Development Actions:** Democracy/good governance/institution building/participatory development; Emergency relief/refugees/humanitarian assistance; Human rights/peace/conflicts. **Regions:** South East Asia.

INFORMATION AND EDUCATION ACTIVITIES: Topics: Human rights/peace/conflicts; International relations/cooperation/development aid; Refugees/migrants/ethnic groups. **Activities:** Conferences/seminars/workshops/training activities; Information and documentation services/data bases; Publishing/audiovisual materials/educational materials.

POL3513

OSRODEK EDUKACJI EKOLGICZNEJ "EKO-OKO"

ul. Grojecka 75, 02-094 Warszawa, Poland.

POL3514

POLISH ASSOCIATION OF AFRICAN STUDIES (PTAFR)

c/o Dept. of African languages and cultures, University of Warsz, ul. Krakowskie Przedmiescie 26/28, 00-927 Warszawa, Poland.

Telephone: 48 (22) 20 03 81. *Contact:* Stanislaw Pilaszewics, President.

POL3515

POLISH COMMITTEE FOR COOPERATION WITH UNICEF

Ul Mokotowska 39, 00-551 Warszawa, Poland.

POL3516

POLISH ECOLOGICAL CLUB

ul. Armii Ludoweh 82, 05-200 Wolomin, Poland.

POL3517

POLISH PEACE COALITION

ul. Rajcow 10, 00-220 Warszawa, Poland.

POL3518

POLISH YOUTH COUNCIL

Okolnik 11, 00-368 Warszawa, Poland.

See: *How to Use the Directory,* page 11.

POL3519

POLISH-AFRICAN FRIENDSHIP SOCIETY

Rajców 1, 00-220 Warszawa, Poland.

Telephone: 48 (22) 314 168. *Fax:* 48 (22) 319 694. *Contact:* B. Winid, President.

OBJECTIVES: To develop relations and co-operate with social and political organisations in Eastern Europe and in developing countries. To co-operate with NGOs in northern America and Western Europe.

GENERAL INFORMATION: *Creation:* 1962. *Personnel/Total:* 11. *Salaried:* 1. *Volunteers:* 10. *Budget/Total 1993:* ECU 12000 (US$ 15000). *Financial sources:* Private: 80%. Public: 10%. Self-financing: 10%.

PUBLICATIONS: *Periodicals:* Africana Bulletin. *List of publications.*

EVALUATION/RESEARCH: Undertakes research activities.

COMMENTS: Undertakes activities in the Commonwealth of Independent States. Information activities related to the Commonwealth of Independent States.

ACTIVITIES IN DEVELOPING REGIONS: Present in developing regions. Active in 10 country(ies). Maintains local field presence. Works through local field partners. **Sustainable Development Actions:** Children/youth/family; Debt/finance/trade; Democracy/good governance/institution building/participatory development; Ecology/environment/biodiversity; Education/training/literacy; Emergency relief/refugees/humanitarian assistance; Energy/transport; Food/famine; Gender issues/women; Health/sanitation/water; Human rights/peace/conflicts; Population/family planning/demography; Rural development/agriculture; Sending volunteers/experts/technical assistance; Small enterprises/informal sector/handicrafts; Urban development/habitat. **Regions:** Caribbean; Central Africa; Central Asia and South Asia; East Africa; Mexico and Central America; Middle East; North Africa; South America; South East Asia; Southern Africa; West Africa.

INFORMATION AND EDUCATION ACTIVITIES: Topics: Children/youth/family; Culture/tradition/religion; Ecology/environment/biodiversity; Education/training/literacy; Emergency relief/refugees/humanitarian assistance; Employment/unemployment; Food/famine; Gender issues/women; Health/sanitation/water; Human rights/peace/conflicts; International economic relations/trade/debt/finance; International relations/cooperation/development aid; Peace/ethnic conflicts/armament/disarmament; Population/family planning/demography; Poverty/living conditions; Racism/xenophobia/antisemitism; Refugees/migrants/ethnic groups; Rural development/agriculture; Urban development/habitat. **Activities:** Conferences/seminars/workshops/training activities; Exchanges/twinning/linking; Information and documentation services/data bases; Information campaigns/exhibitions; Publishing/audiovisual materials/educational materials.

POL3520

POLSKA ASOCJACJA EKOLOGH KRAJOBRAZU (PAEK) ♦
Polish Association for Landscape Ecology

ul. Krakowskie Przedmiescie 30, 00-927 Warszawa, Poland.

Telephone: 48 (22) 200301. *Fax:* 48 (22) 261965. *E-mail:* GZKO1@plearn.bitnet. *Contact:* Andrzej Richling, President.

OBJECTIVES: To support the development of landscape ecology.

GENERAL INFORMATION: *Creation:* 1993. *Personnel/Total:* 7. Volunteers: 7. *Financial sources:* Self-financing: 100%.

PUBLICATIONS: *Periodicals:* Biuletyn Paek (2).

EVALUATION/RESEARCH: Undertakes research activities.

COMMENTS: Undertakes activities in the Commonwealth of Independent States.

INFORMATION AND EDUCATION ACTIVITIES: Topics: Ecology/environment/biodiversity; Rural development/agriculture; Urban development/habitat. **Activities:** Conferences/seminars/workshops/training activities.

POL3521

POLSKA YMCA ♦ The Polish YMCA

Konopnicka 6, 00-590 Warszawa, Poland.

Telephone: 48 (2) 621 9848. *Fax:* 48 (2) 628 9037. *Contact:* Jerzy Kieli, President.

OBJECTIVES: To foster the physical, mental and spiritual development of the Polish youth. To promote the spirit of volunterism. To maintain relations with the youth organisations abroad that pursue similar aims.

GENERAL INFORMATION: *Creation:* 1923. *Affiliated to:* Polish Youth Council (Poland) - World Alliance of YMCA's (Switzerland). *Personnel/Total:* 406. *Salaried:* 27 of which: 5 in developing countries. *Volunteers:* 379 of which: 70 in developing countries.

PUBLICATIONS: *Periodicals:* WATRA (4). *Annual report.*

EVALUATION/RESEARCH: Undertakes research activities.

PLANNED ACTIVITIES: Undertaking programmes for handicapped children and promoting education for tolerance.

COMMENTS: Information activities related to the Commonwealth of Independent States.

ACTIVITIES IN DEVELOPING REGIONS: Active in 1 country(ies). **Sustainable Development Actions:** Emergency relief/refugees/humanitarian assistance. **Regions:** Central Asia and South Asia.

INFORMATION AND EDUCATION ACTIVITIES: Topics: Culture/tradition/religion; Ecology/environment/biodiversity; Emergency relief/refugees/humanitarian assistance; Employment/unemployment; Human rights/peace/conflicts; Racism/xenophobia/antisemitism; Refugees/migrants/ethnic groups. **Activities:** Conferences/seminars/workshops/training activities; Exchanges/twinning/linking; Formal education; Fund raising; Information and documentation services/data bases; Information campaigns/exhibitions; Lobbying/advocacy; Networking/electronic telecommunications; Publishing/audiovisual materials/educational materials.

POL3522

POLSKI CZERWONY KRZYZ ♦ Polish Red Cross

ul. Mokotowska 1, Warszawa, Poland.

POL3523

POLSKI KLUB EKOLOGICZNY - ZARZAD GLOWNY

ul. Garbarska 9, 31-031 Krakow, Poland.

POL3524

POLSKI KLUBEKOLOGICZNY, OKREG GORNOSLASKI (PKE)
♦ Information Centre for Air Protection - Polish Ecological Club, Upper Sileasian Branch (ICAP)

Pl. Grunwaldzki 8/10, p. 243, 40-950 Katowice, Poland.

Telephone: 48 (32) 594315. *Fax:* 48 (32) 594315. *Contact:* Piotr Poborski, President.

OBJECTIVES: To minimize health threats to inhabitants of upper Silesia. To protect and restore the natural environment, and to create conditions for sustainable economic development.

GENERAL INFORMATION: *Creation:* 1981. *Type of organisation:* network, coordinating body. *Personnel/Total:* 5. *Salaried:* 4. *Volunteers:* 1. *Budget/Total 1993:* ECU 17000 (US$ 22000). *Financial sources:* Private: 67%. Public: 30%. Self-financing: 3%.

PUBLICATIONS: *Periodicals:* Ecological Bulletin (12). *Annual report. List of publications.*

COMMENTS: PKE Upper Silesian Branch is an independent NGO co-operating with a network of 17 other PKE regional branch offices. PKE Upper Silesian Branch has over 506 members, and is organised into 16 local chapters. PKE works on a local, regional and national level. Undertakes activities in the Commonwealth of Independent States. Information activities related to the Commonwealth of Independent States.

INFORMATION AND EDUCATION ACTIVITIES: Topics: Ecology/environment/biodiversity. **Activities:** Conferences/seminars/workshops/

training activities; Fund raising; Information and documentation services/ data bases; Information campaigns/exhibitions; Lobbying/advocacy; Networking/electronic telecommunications; Publishing/audiovisual materials/educational materials.

POL3525

POLSKIE TOWARZYSTWO PRZYJACIOL PRZYRODY 'PRO-NATURA' (PTPP) ♦ Polish Society of Wildlife Friends 'Pro-Natura'

ul. Podwale 75, 50-449 Wroclaw, Poland.

Telephone: 48 (71) 445055. *Fax:* 48 (71) 446135. *Contact:* Wojciech Jankowski.

OBJECTIVES: To promote and support the preservation and restoration of the values of nature.

GENERAL INFORMATION: *Creation:* 1990. *Affiliated to:* Central and Eastern European Working Group for Enhancement of Biodiversity (Hungary) - Earth Action (Belgium). *Personnel/Total:* 8. *Salaried:* 3. *Volunteers:* 5. *Financial sources: Private:* 70%. *Public:* 10%. *Self-financing:* 20%.

PUBLICATIONS: *Periodicals:* Biuletyn PTPP "Pro Natura" (4).

EVALUATION/RESEARCH: Undertakes research activities.

PLANNED ACTIVITIES: Undertaking programmes for the protection of species and the conservation of river valleys.

COMMENTS: Undertakes activities in the Commonwealth of Independent States. Information activities related to the Commonwealth of Independent States.

INFORMATION AND EDUCATION ACTIVITIES: Topics: Ecology/environment/biodiversity. **Activities:** Conferences/seminars/workshops/ training activities; Exchanges/twinning/linking; Fund raising; Information and documentation services/data bases; Information campaigns/exhibitions; Publishing/audiovisual materials/educational materials.

POL3526

POLSKIE TOWARZYSTWO PRZYRODNIKOW IM. KOPERNIKA ♦ Polish "Copernicus" Society of Naturalists

ul. Rakowiecka 36p. F25, 02-532 Warszawa, Poland.

Telephone: 48 (2) 490171. *Contact:* Henryk Sandner, President.

OBJECTIVES: To spread the knowledge of natural science and ecology in Poland.

GENERAL INFORMATION: *Creation:* 1875. *Personnel/Total:* 26. *Salaried:* 6. *Volunteers:* 20. *Budget/Total 1993:* ECU 34000 (US$ 44200). *Financial sources: Private:* 2%. *Public:* 90%. *Self-financing:* 8%.

PUBLICATIONS: *Periodicals:* Kosmos (4) - Wszechswiat (12) - Entomonematologia (4).

COMMENTS: Undertakes activities in the Commonwealth of Independent States. Information activities related to the Commonwealth of Independent States.

INFORMATION AND EDUCATION ACTIVITIES: Topics: Ecology/environment/biodiversity. **Activities:** Conferences/seminars/workshops/ training activities; Formal education; Information campaigns/exhibitions; Lobbying/advocacy; Publishing/audiovisual materials/educational materials.

POL3527

POLSKIE TOWRZYSTWO EKOLOGICZNE

ul. Krakowskie Przedmiescie 30, 00-927 Warszawa, Poland.

POL3528

RUCH EKOLOGICZNO-OKOJOWY "WOLE BYC" ♦ Being-over-Having Ecology and Peace Movement

ul. Konopnickiej 6, pokoj 355, 00-491 Warszawa, Poland.

POL3529

RURAL YOUTH UNION - ZARZAD KRAJOWY ZMW

ul. Nowy Swiat 18/20, 00-373 Warszawa, Poland.

POL3530

SOCIAL ECOLOGICAL INSTITUTE

ul. Irlandzka 9 a, 00-909 Warszawa, Poland.

POL3531

SOS-EKO

ul. Sierakowska 1, 42-780 Dobrodzien, Poland.

POL3532

SPOLECSNY INSTYTUT EKOLOGICSNY (SIE) ♦ Social Institute for Ecology

Zielenieycka 6/8, 03-127 Warszawa, Poland.

Telephone: 48 (2) 618 3781. *Fax:* 48 (2) 618 2884. *E-mail:* bore@plearn.edu.pl. *Contact:* Justyna Krynacka, President.

OBJECTIVES: To initiate support and promote research and projects in environmental protection. To collect and disseminate information on the state of the environment in Poland. To provide services and advice to citizens and NGOs in all matters concerning the protection of the environment.

GENERAL INFORMATION: *Creation:* 1990.

PUBLICATIONS: *Periodicals:* Biuletyn Niecodzienny (12).

INFORMATION AND EDUCATION ACTIVITIES: Topics: Ecology/environment/biodiversity. **Activities:** Broadcasting/cultural events; Information and documentation services/data bases; Information campaigns/ exhibitions; Publishing/audiovisual materials/educational materials.

POL3533

SPOLECZNA KOMISJA EKOURBANISTYCZNA

Pl. Bankowy 3/5, 00-950 Warszawa, Poland.

POL3534

SPOLECZNE CENTRUM INFORMACYJNE

Ochrony Srodowiska, skr. poczt 645, 00-950 Warszawa, Poland.

POL3535

SPOLECZNY INSTYTUT EKOLOGICZNY

ul. Szara 14m 34, 00-420 Warszawa, Poland.

POL3536

THE STEFAN BATORY FOUNDATION

ul. Flory 9, 00-586 Warszawa, Poland.

Telephone: 48 (22) 488055. *Fax:* 48 (22) 493561. *Contact:* Aleksander Smolar, Chairman of the Board.

OBJECTIVES: To allocate grants to support education, health, the protection of the environment, science, charity, culture and the development of civil society.

GENERAL INFORMATION: *Creation:* 1988. *Affiliated to:* European Foundation Centre - Polish Foundations Forum. *Personnel/Total:* 28. *Salaried:* 28. *Budget/Total 1993:* ECU 2686000 (US$ 3484000). *Financial sources: Private:* 100%.

PUBLICATIONS: *Periodicals:* Stefan Batory Foundation Bulletin (12). *Annual report. List of publications.*

COMMENTS: Undertakes activities in the Commonwealth of Independent States. Information activities related to the Commonwealth of Independent States.

ACTIVITIES IN DEVELOPING REGIONS: Works through local field partners.

INFORMATION AND EDUCATION ACTIVITIES: Topics: Children/youth/ family; Culture/tradition/religion; Emergency relief/refugees/humanita-

See: *How to Use the Directory,* page 11.

rian assistance; Employment/unemployment; Gender issues/women; Health/sanitation/water; Human rights/peace/conflicts; International economic relations/trade/debt/finance; Peace/ethnic conflicts/armament/disarmament; Refugees/migrants/ethnic groups. **Activities:** Conferences/seminars/workshops/training activities; Information campaigns/exhibitions; Lobbying/advocacy; Publishing/audiovisual materials/educational materials.

POL3537

STUDENCKI KLUB EKOLGICZNY

pok. 265, ul. Majakowskiego 11, 80-952 Gdansk, Poland.

POL3538

SZKOLNE KOLO EKOLOGICZNE, 53 LO SW AUGUSTYNA

al. Niedpodleglosci 52, 02-626 Warszawa, Poland.

POL3539

WORKSHOP FOR ALL BEINGS

ul. Urie 5m 23, 02-43? Warszawa, Poland.

POL3540

YWCA OF POLAND

Spalska 3/4, 02-934 Warszawa, Poland.

POL3541

ZIELONE BRYGADY ♦ Green Brigades

Andrej Zwawa, Wydzial Chemii UJ, Ingardena 3/100, 30-060 Krakow, Poland.

Telephone: 48 (12) 33 63 77 (ext 234). **Fax:** 48 (12) 34 05 15. **Contact:** Andrej Zwawa, Editor.

POL3542

ZRZESZENIS STUDENTOW POLSKICH ♦ Polish Student Association

ul. Ordynacka 9, 00-950 Warszawa, Poland.

POL3543

ZWIAZEK HARCERSTWA POLSKIEGO (ZHP) ♦ Polish Scout Association

Glowna Kwatera ZHP, Konopnickiej 6, 00-491 Warszawa, Poland.

Telephone: 48 (2) 628 8921. **Fax:** 48 (2) 621 1757. **Contact:** Stefan Mirowski, President.

OBJECTIVES: To contribute to the spiritual and physical development of young people and spread the basic Scout values. To promote the protection of the environment.

GENERAL INFORMATION: Creation: 1910. **Personnel/Total:** 27600. *Salaried:* 600. *Volunteers:* 27000. **Budget/Total 1993:** ECU 17666000 (US$ 22909000). **Financial sources:** *Private:* 15%. *Public:* 25%. *Self-financing:* 65%.

PUBLICATIONS: Periodicals: Scouting (12) - Be Prepared12 - Cub Scout News (4) - Proposals (4) - On the Trail (12). *List of publications.*

EVALUATION/RESEARCH: Evaluation reports available. Undertakes research activities.

PLANNED ACTIVITIES: Undertaking the ZHP national programme "My Homelands".

COMMENTS: Undertakes activities in the Commonwealth of Independent States. Information activities related to the Commonwealth of Independent States.

INFORMATION AND EDUCATION ACTIVITIES: Topics: Children/youth/family; Culture/tradition/religion; Ecology/environment/biodiversity; Gender issues/women; Health/sanitation/water; Human rights/peace/conflicts; International relations/cooperation/development aid; Peace/ethnic conflicts/armament/disarmament; Poverty/living conditions; Refugees/migrants/ethnic groups; Rural development/agriculture; Urban development/habitat. **Activities:** Broadcasting/cultural events; Conferences/seminars/workshops/training activities; Exchanges/twinning/linking; Fund raising; Information and documentation services/data bases; Information campaigns/exhibitions; Lobbying/advocacy; Other; Publishing/audiovisual materials/educational materials.

POL3544

ZWIAZEK HARCERSTWA RZECZYPOSPOLITEJ (ZHR) ♦

Scouting and Guiding Association of the Polish Republic

ul. Krakowskie Przedmiescie 64, 00-322 Warszawa, Poland.

Telephone: 48 (2) 635 9882. **Fax:** 48 (2) 635 9882. **Contact:** Wojciech Hausner, President.

OBJECTIVES: To develop scouting methods among the youth in Poland. To prepare young people for future social activities.

GENERAL INFORMATION: Creation: 1989. **Type of organisation:** association of NGOs. **Affiliated to:** The Polish Youth Council. **Personnel/Total:** 748. *Salaried:* 8. *Volunteers:* 740. **Budget/Total 1993:** ECU 170 (US$ 200). **Financial sources:** *Private:* 10%. *Public:* 30%. *Self-financing:* 60%.

PUBLICATIONS: Periodicals: Instructor (12) - The Guide (12) - The Brownie-Leader (12). *Annual report. List of publications.*

EVALUATION/RESEARCH: Evaluation reports available.

PLANNED ACTIVITIES: Supporting scouting in ethnic minorities in the former Soviet Union.

COMMENTS: Undertakes activities in the Commonwealth of Independent States. Information activities related to the Commonwealth of Independent States.

INFORMATION AND EDUCATION ACTIVITIES: Topics: Children/youth/family; Education/training/literacy; Emergency relief/refugees/humanitarian assistance; International relations/cooperation/development aid; Peace/ethnic conflicts/armament/disarmament. **Activities:** Conferences/seminars/workshops/training activities; Exchanges/twinning/linking; Fund raising.

POL3545

ZYCIE WRSZAWY ♦ Life of Warszawa

Marszalkowska 3/5/7, 00-624 Warszawa, Poland.

Voir : *Comment utiliser le répertoire,* page 11.

PRT3546
ACM-YMCA

Rua da Beira 11, Carcavelos, 2775 Parede, Portugal.

Téléphone: 351 - 247 07 61.

PRT3547
AMIGOS DA TERRA / ASSOCIACAO PORTUGUESA DE ECOLOGISTAS ♦ Friends of the Earth Portugal

Travessa da Laranjeira 1-A, 1200 Lisboa, Portugal.

Telephone: 351 (3) 47 07 88. *Fax:* 351 (3) 47 35 86. *Contact:* Antonio Eloy, Director.

PRT3548
AMNESTY INTERNATIONAL, PORTUGUESE SECTION

Apartado 12081, 1057 Lisboa Codex, Portugal.

Telephone: 351 (1) 38 61 652. *Fax:* 351 (1) 38 61 782 . *Contact:* Victor Nogueira, President .

OBJECTIVES: To work for the release of prisoners of conscience, fair trials for political prisoners, the abolition of the death penalty, and an end to torture, extrajudicial executions, disapperances and other forms of unusually cruel treatment.

GENERAL INFORMATION: *Creation:* 1981. *Personnel/Total:* 3. *Salaried:* 3. *Financial sources:* Private: 34%. Self-financing: 40%.

PUBLICATIONS: *Periodicals:* Amnista Internacional Informação (6). *Annual report. List of publications.*

ACTIVITIES IN DEVELOPING REGIONS: Sustainable Development Actions: Human rights/peace/conflicts. **Regions:** Caribbean; Central Africa; Central Asia and South Asia; East Africa; East Asia; Mexico and Central America; Middle East; North Africa; Oceania; South America; South East Asia; Southern Africa; West Africa.

PRT3549
ASSISTENCIA MEDICA INTERNACIONAL (AMI-FUNDAÇAO) ♦
International Medical Assistance

R. José do Patrocínio, 49- Marvila, 1900 Lisboa, Portugal.

Téléphone: 351 (1) 837 15 63. *Fax:* 351 (1) 859 23 62. *Contact:* Dr. Fernando Nobre, Président.

OBJECTIFS: Apporter un secours médical à toutes les victimes de catastrophes naturelles, d'accidents collectifs, de guerres ou de graves carences en services médicaux dans le monde entier. Mener des actions à caractère social au Portugal.

INFORMATIONS GENERALES: *Création:* 1984. *Affiliée à:* VOICE (Belgique) - EURONAID (Pays-Bas) - Plataforma Nacional das ONGD's (Portugal) - Comité de Liaison (Belgique). *Budget/Total 1993:* ECU 2997000 (US$ 3500000). *Sources financières:* Privé: 66%. Public: 24%. Autofinancement: 10%.

PUBLICATIONS: *Périodiques:* AMI Noticias (4).

ACTIVITES DANS LES REGIONS EN DEVELOPPEMENT: Intervient directement dans les régions en développement. Intervient dans 11 pays. Maintient une présence locale sur le terrain. Intervient par l'intermédiaire d'organisations locales partenaires. **Actions de Développement durable:** Aliments/famine; Envoi de volontaires/experts/assistance technique; Population/planning familial/démographie; Santé/assainissement/eau; Secours d'urgence/réfugiés/aide humanitaire; Éducation/formation/alphabétisation. **Régions:** Afrique australe; Afrique centrale; Afrique de l'Ouest; Amérique du Sud; Asie centrale et Asie du Sud.

ACTIVITES D'INFORMATION ET D'EDUCATION: Domaines: Aliments/famine; Droits de l'Homme/paix/conflits; Paix/conflits ethniques/armement/désarmement; Pauvreté/conditions de vie; Relations internationales/coopération/aide au développement; Réfugiés/migrants/groupes ethniques; Santé/assainissement/eau; Secours d'urgence/réfugiés/aide humanitaire. **Activités:** Campagnes d'information/expositions; Collecte de fonds; Conférences/séminaires/ateliers/activités de formation; Lobbying/plaidoyer.

PRT3550
ASSOCIACAO AFRICA SOLIDARIEDADE ♦ Solidarity Africa Association

R. Anibal Cunha, 193, 4000 Porto, Portugal.

Telephone: 351 (2) 20 86 926. *Fax:* 351 (2) 20 86 926. *Contact:* Levi Guerra.

OBJECTIVES: To increase solidarity between Portugal and the African Portugeuse speaking countries and between Portuguese Catholic Churches and the Churches in these African communities.

GENERAL INFORMATION: *Creation:* 1989. *Type of organisation:* association of NGOs. *Affiliated to:* Plataforma Das ONG Portuguesas (Portugal). *Personnel/Total:* 21. *Volunteers:* 21 of which: 2 in developing countries. *Budget/Total 1993:* ECU 3201000 (US$ 3738000). *Financial sources:* Private: 11%. Public: 39%. Self-financing: 20%.

PUBLICATIONS: *Periodicals:* (1). *Annual report.*

COMMENTS: The organisation is a full supporter of the Catholic University in Mozambique in collaboration with the Portuguese Catholic University.

ACTIVITIES IN DEVELOPING REGIONS: Active in 2 country(ies). Maintains local field presence. Works through local field partners. **Sustainable Development Actions:** Children/youth/family; Education/training/literacy; Gender issues/women; Health/sanitation/water; Small enterprises/informal sector/handicrafts; Urban development/habitat. **Regions:** East Africa.

INFORMATION AND EDUCATION ACTIVITIES: Topics: Children/youth/family; Gender issues/women; Health/sanitation/water; International relations/cooperation/development aid; Poverty/living conditions; Urban development/habitat. **Activities:** Conferences/seminars/workshops/training activities; Information and documentation services/data bases.

PRT3551
ASSOCIACAO CRISTA DA MOCIDADE (ACM)

Estrada Nacional 6, ao Km/4 Caxias, 2780 Oeiras, Portugal.

PRT3552
ASSOCIACAO DE BENEFICENCIA LUSO-ALEMA (ABLA) ♦
Portuguese German Aid Organization

Apartado 1073, 2725 Parede, Portugal.

Telephone: 351 - 45 74 387. *Fax:* 351 - 45 66 541. *Contact:* Heinrich Floreck, President.

OBJECTIVES: To provide aid to African children. To provide food and health care to refugees in Angola.

GENERAL INFORMATION: *Creation:* 1983. *Type of organisation:* network. *Affiliated to:* IPPS (Portugal) - Deutscher Hilfsfonds (Germany) - ORA International (Angola). *Personnel/Total:* 367. *Salaried:* 67 of which: 30 in developing countries. *Volunteers:* 300 of which: 300 in developing countries. *Budget/Total 1993:* ECU 639000 (US$ 746000). *Financial sources:* Private: 60%. Public: 20%. Self-financing: 20%.

PUBLICATIONS: *Periodicals:* ABLA-Actualidades (3).

ACTIVITIES IN DEVELOPING REGIONS: Present in developing regions. Active in 2 country(ies). Maintains local field presence. Works through local field partners. **Sustainable Development Actions:** Children/youth/family; Education/training/literacy; Emergency relief/refugees/humanitarian assistance; Food/famine. **Regions:** South America; Southern Africa.

INFORMATION AND EDUCATION ACTIVITIES: Topics: Children/youth/family; Emergency relief/refugees/humanitarian assistance; Poverty/living conditions; Refugees/migrants/ethnic groups. **Activities:** Formal education; Fund raising; Information campaigns/exhibitions.

PRT3553
ASSOCIACAO NACIONAL DE CONSERVACAO DA NATUREZA (QUERCUS-ANCN)

Rua Bernardo Santareno, lote 10, 1° esq, 7800 Beja, Portugal.

See: *How to Use the Directory,* page 11.

Telephone: 351 (84) 32 89 30. *Fax:* 351 (2) 200 33 90. *Contact:* José Paulo Martins, Secretario Nacional.

PRT3554
ASSOCIACAO PARA A COOPERACAO ENTRE OS POVOS (ACEP)
R. Esperança, 63 R/C DTO, 1200 Lisboa, Portugal.

Téléphone: 351 396 55 45. *Fax:* 351 347 86 55. *Contact:* Maria De Fatima Belo, President.

OBJECTIFS: Assister les migrants d'origine Africaine au Portugal.

INFORMATIONS GENERALES: *Création:* 1990. *Affiliée à:* Plataforma das ONGD's portuguesa. *Personnel/Total:* 16. *Salariés:* 1. *Bénévoles:* 15.

PUBLICATIONS: *Rapport annuel.*

EVALUATION/RECHERCHE: Rapports d'évaluation disponibles.

PREVISIONS D'ACTIVITES: Projets de terrain au Mozambique.

ACTIVITES D'INFORMATION ET D'EDUCATION: **Domaines:** Réfugiés/migrants/groupes ethniques. **Activités:** Conférences/séminaires/ateliers/activités de formation; Lobbying/plaidoyer; Services d'information et de documentation/bases de données.

PRT3555
ASSOCIACAO PARA A COOPERACAO INTERCAMBIO E CULTURA (CIC) ♦ Association pour la coopération, Echange et Culture
R. Sabino de Sousa, nº 66 R/C Esq, 1900 Lisboa, Portugal.

Téléphone: 351 (01) 815 11 00. *Contact:* Ramos Eugénio Santos, Président.

OBJECTIFS: Développer des actions humanitaires d'urgence médicale et d'éducation, sans but lucratif, dans les pays d'Afrique où la langue officielle est le portugais (PALOP).

INFORMATIONS GENERALES: *Création:* 1992. *Affiliée à:* Plate-forme des ONG Portugaises.. *Personnel/Total:* 27. *Salariés:* 13 dont: 8 dans les pays en développement. *Bénévoles:* 14 dont: 11 dans les pays en développement. *Budget/Total 1993:* ECU 62839000 (US$ 73000000). *Sources financières:* Privé: 20%. Public: 70%. Autofinancement: 10%.

PUBLICATIONS: *Périodiques:* Relatório de Actividados (1) - Informação/CIC-News (3). *Rapport annuel.*

EVALUATION/RECHERCHE: Rapports d'évaluation disponibles. Entreprend des activités de recherche.

ACTIVITES DANS LES REGIONS EN DEVELOPPEMENT: Intervient directement dans les régions en développement. Intervient dans 5 pays. Maintient une présence locale sur le terrain. Intervient par l'intermédiaire d'organisations locales partenaires. **Actions de Développement durable:** Aliments/famine; Envoi de volontaires/experts/assistance technique; Santé/assainissement/eau; Secours d'urgence/réfugiés/aide humanitaire; Éducation/formation/alphabétisation. **Régions:** Afrique australe; Afrique centrale; Afrique de l'Ouest.

ACTIVITES D'INFORMATION ET D'EDUCATION: **Domaines:** Aliments/famine; Enfants/jeunesse/famille; Réfugiés/migrants/groupes ethniques; Santé/assainissement/eau; Secours d'urgence/réfugiés/aide humanitaire; Éducation/formation/alphabétisation. **Activités:** Collecte de fonds; Radiodiffusion/manifestations culturelles; Éducation formelle.

PRT3556
ASSOCIACAO PARA O DESENVOLVIMENTO ECONOMICO E SOCIAL ♦ Association pour le développement économique et social
Rua Duque de Palmela 2, 4º D, 1200 Lisboa, Portugal.

Téléphone: 351 (1) 54 38 30. *Fax:* 351 (1) 54 38 30. *Contact:* Guilherme Oliveira Martins.

PRT3557
ASSOCIACAO PORTUGUESA AMIGOS DE RAOUL FOLLEREAU (APARF)
Rue da Rosa, 177 - 2º Esq., 1200 Lisboa, Portugal.

Téléphone: 351 (3) 42 99 14. *Fax:* 351 (3) 42 83 37. *Contact:* Mario Nogueira.

OBJECTIFS: Lutter contre la lèpre et toutes les lèpres.

INFORMATIONS GENERALES: *Création:* 1987. *Affiliée à:* UIARF - Union Internationale des Associations Raoul Follreau. *Sources financières:* Privé: 80%. Public: 3%. Autofinancement: 17%.

PUBLICATIONS: *Périodiques:* O Amigo Dos Leprosos (4). *Liste des publications.*

ACTIVITES DANS LES REGIONS EN DEVELOPPEMENT: Intervient dans 11 pays. Maintient une présence locale sur le terrain. Intervient par l'intermédiaire d'organisations locales partenaires.

PRT3558
ASSOCIACAO PORTUGUESA DE CONSULTORES SENIORES (APCS)
Praça das Industrias, 1399 Lisboa CODEX, Portugal.

Telephone: 351 (1) 362 01 00. *Fax:* 351 (1) 363 56 08. *Contact:* Ernesto Almeida Freire, President.

OBJECTIVES: To provide specialized assistance in technical and managerial fields; in agriculture, architecture, economy, engineering, teaching and human resources.

GENERAL INFORMATION: *Creation:* 1988. *Affiliated to:* National Platform of Portuguese NGOs (Portugal). *Budget/Total 1993:* ECU 16000 (US$ 19000). *Financial sources:* Private: 51%. Self-financing: 49%.

PUBLICATIONS: *Periodicals:* Consulta Senior (1). *Annual report.*

EVALUATION/RESEARCH: Evaluation reports available.

INFORMATION AND EDUCATION ACTIVITIES: **Topics:** International relations/cooperation/development aid. **Activities:** Other.

PRT3559
ASSOCIACAO PORTUGUESA PARA O ESTUDO DAS RELACOES INTERNACIONAIS (APRI)
R. Rodrigo da Fonseca, 17-1§, 1200 Lisboa, Portugal.

PRT3560
CARITAS PORTUGUESA ♦ Caritas portugaise
Estrada do Forte da Ameixoeira 19, 1700 Lisboa, Portugal.

Téléphone: 351 (1) 759 60 46. *Contact:* Acácio F. Catarino, Président.

PRT3561
CENTRO DE CULTURA E ESTUDOS RURAIS (CERCOOP) ♦
Centre pour la culture et les études rurales
Av. Sidónio Pais, 20, 4º D, 1200 Lisboa, Portugal.

Téléphone: 351 (1) 54 97 52. *Contact:* Josi Miranda Magalhas.

PRT3562
CENTRO DE ESTUDOS DA CULTURA E ENSINO DOS PAISES DE EXPRESSAO PORTUGUESA (CECEPEP) ♦ Centre d'études sur la culture et l'enseignement des pays d'expression portugaise
Saudade 59 - Salas 31 e 39, 4000 Porto, Portugal.

Téléphone: 351 (2) 69 31 63. *Contact:* Prof. Abel Mendes, Président.

PRT3563
CENTRO DE ESTUDOS, DOCUMENTACAO E INFORMACAO DAS REGIOES POLARES
Rua Conselheiro Veloso Cruz 149, 4400 Vila Nova de Gaia, Portugal.
Téléphone: 351 (3) 399392.

Voir : *Comment utiliser le répertoire,* page 11.

PRT3564

CENTRO DE INFORMACAO E DOCUMENTACAO AMILCAR CABRAL (CIDAC) ♦ Amilcar Cabral Information and Documentation Centre

Rua Pinheiro Chagas 77 2° Esq., 1000 Lisboa, Portugal.

Téléphone: 351 (1) 35 28 718. *Fax:* 351 (1) 35 34 009. *Contact:* Luisa Teotónio Pereira, Directrice.

OBJECTIFS: Rassembler de la documentation sur les ex-colonies portugaises. Entreprendre des activités d'information et d'éducation au développement. Former des coopérants et mettre en place des projets de développement.

INFORMATIONS GENERALES: *Création:* 1974. *Personnel/Total:* 18. *Salariés:* 18. *Budget/Total 1993:* ECU 453000 (US$ 529000). *Sources financières:* *Privé:* 10%. *Public:* 20%. *Autofinancement:* 70%.

PUBLICATIONS: *Périodiques:* CIDAC(Newsletter) (4) - Information bibliographique (3). *Rapport annuel. Liste des publications.*

EVALUATION/RECHERCHE: Entreprend des activités de recherche.

PREVISIONS D'ACTIVITES: Campagne sur la coopération au développement

ACTIVITES DANS LES REGIONS EN DEVELOPPEMENT: Intervient directement dans les régions en développement. Intervient dans 5 pays. Intervient par l'intermédiaire d'organisations locales partenaires. **Actions de Développement durable:** Démocratie/bonne gestion publique/création d'institutions/développement participatif; Développement rural/agriculture; Enfants/jeunesse/famille; Petites entreprises/secteur informel/artisanat; Questions relatives aux femmes; Santé/assainissement/eau; Éducation/formation/alphabétisation. **Régions:** Afrique australe; Afrique de l'Ouest; Afrique du Nord.

ACTIVITES D'INFORMATION ET D'EDUCATION: Domaines: Droits de l'Homme/paix/conflits; Population/planning familial/démographie; Racisme/xénophobie/antisémitisme; Relations internationales/coopération/aide au développement; Relations économiques internationales/commerce/dette/finances; Réfugiés/migrants/groupes ethniques; Écologie/environnement/biodiversité. **Activités:** Campagnes d'information/expositions; Conférences/séminaires/ateliers/activités de formation; Lobbying/plaidoyer; Services d'information et de documentation/bases de données; Édition/documents audiovisuels/documents éducatifs.

PRT3565

CENTRO DE SOLIDARIEDADE CRISTA MARANATHA ♦ Centre de Solidarité Chrétienne "Maranatha"

Av. S.Salvador, 1200 Grijo, 4415 Carvalhos, Portugal.

Téléphone: 351 (2) 764 01 24. *Contact:* Bernardino de Queiros Alves, Directeur.

PRT3566

CENTRO INTERNACIONAL PARA A COOPERACAO E DESENVOLVIMIENTO (CIDC)

Rua de S. Nicolau, n° 105-1° , 1100 Lisboa, Portugal.

PRT3567

CENTRO NACIONAL DE CULTURA (CNC) ♦ National Cultural Center

Rua Antonio Maria Cardoso 68, 1200 Lisboa, Portugal.

Telephone: 351 (1) 34 66 722. *Fax:* 351 (1) 34 28 250. *Contact:* Helena Vaz da Silva.

OBJECTIVES: To organise and promote study tours, courses and activities related to the environment, cultural heritage and the arts.

GENERAL INFORMATION: *Creation:* 1945. *Affiliated to:* Forum of European Networks - European Forum of Arts and Heritage - Euro-South Network - Centers in Historical Monuments and Sites Network. *Personnel/Total:* 35. *Salaried:* 25. *Volunteers:* 10. *Budget/Total 1993:* ECU 1065000 (US$ 1244000). *Financial sources:* *Private:* 30%. *Public:* 30%. *Self-financing:* 40%.

PUBLICATIONS: *Periodicals:* Descoberms (4). *Annual report. List of publications.*

EVALUATION/RESEARCH: Evaluation reports available.

ACTIVITIES IN DEVELOPING REGIONS: Works through local field partners.

INFORMATION AND EDUCATION ACTIVITIES: Topics: Culture/tradition/religion. **Activities:** Fund raising.

PRT3568

COLECTIVIDADE CULTURAL E RECREATIVA DE SANTA CATARINA (CHAPITO) ♦ Collectivité Culturelle et Récréative de Santa Catarina

R. Costa do Castelo, n§1, 1100 Lisboa, Portugal.

Telephone: 351 (8) 86 14 10. *Fax:* 351 (8) 86 14 63. *Contact:* Teresa Ricov, Présidente.

PRT3569

COMITE PORTUGUES PARA A UNICEF

Rua António Augusto de Aguiar, 56-3§, Esq, 1000 Lisboa, Portugal.

Telephone: 351 (1) 54 78 43. *Fax:* 351 (1) 54 79 13.

PRT3570

COMMISSION NATIONALE DE L'UNESCO - CENTRE NATIONAL DE CULTURE

Av. Infante Santo 42, 5§, 1300 Lisboa, Portugal.

Téléphone: 351 (1) 396 90 61. *Fax:* 351 (1) 396 90 64. *Contact:* Helena Vaz da Silva, Presidente.

PRT3571

CONSELHO PORTUGUES DE COOPERACAO E INTERCAMBIO DE SERVICIOS SOCIAIS

Largo Trindade Coelho, 1200 Lisboa, Portugal.

Téléphone: 351 - 3460361. *Fax:* 351 - 3472655.

PRT3572

CONSELHO PORTUGUES PARA A PAZ E COOPERACAO (CPPC)

R. Rodrigo da Fonseca, 56-2° , 1200 Lisboa, Portugal.

PRT3573

CONSELHO PORTUGUES PARA OS REFUGIADOS (CPR) ♦ Conseil portugais pour les réfugiés (CPR)

Rua Viriato, 27-2° A, 1000 Lisboa, Portugal.

Téléphone: 351 (1) 315 98 47. *Fax:* 351 (1) 353 76 92. *Contact:* Marie Teresa Tito de Morais Mendes, Présidente.

OBJECTIFS: Apporter un soutien humanitaire à des réfugiés, exilés, apatrides, minorités ethniques persécutées, délogés ou aux personnes en difficulté qui ont besoin d'aide.

INFORMATIONS GENERALES: *Création:* 1991. *Affiliée à:* Conseil Européen sur les Réfugiés et les Exilés (Royaume-Uni) - Partenaires en Action - International Council of Voluntary Agencies. *Personnel/Total:* 11. *Salariés:* 4. *Bénévoles:* 7. *Budget/Total 1993:* ECU 49000 (US$ 57000).

PUBLICATIONS: *Rapport annuel.*

EVALUATION/RECHERCHE: Rapports d'évaluation disponibles. Entreprend des activités de recherche.

COMMENTAIRES: Intervient dans la Communauté des Etats indépendants.

ACTIVITES DANS LES REGIONS EN DEVELOPPEMENT: Intervient dans 2 pays. Intervient par l'intermédiaire d'organisations locales partenaires. **Actions de Développement durable:** Droits de l'Homme/paix/conflits. **Régions:** Afrique australe.

ACTIVITES D'INFORMATION ET D'EDUCATION: Domaines: Réfugiés/migrants/groupes ethniques; Secours d'urgence/réfugiés/aide humanitaire; Éducation/formation/alphabétisation. **Activités:** Campagnes d'information/expositions; Conférences/séminaires/ateliers/activités de

See: *How to Use the Directory,* page 11.

formation; Lobbying/plaidoyer; Services d'information et de documentation/bases de données.

PRT3574

COOPAFRICA - ASSOCIACAO PARA A COOPERACAO E DESENVOLVIMENTO ♦ CoopAfrica - Association pour la Coopération et le Développement

Rua Maria Pia 445, 1300 Lisboa, Portugal.

Téléphone: 351 (1) 437 32 87. *Contact:* Dr. Fernando Ferreira da Costa, Président.

PRT3575

COOPERACAO, SAUDE E DESENVOLVIMENTO - FUNDACAO (CSD) ♦ Coopération, Santé et Développement

R. José Afonso, 7-1° Esq, 2800 Almada, Portugal.

Téléphone: 351 (1) 25 90 499. *Fax:* 351 (1) 25 90 476. *Contact:* Manuel Henrique Pedro, President.

PRT3576

CRUZ VERMELHA PORTUGUESA (CVP) ♦ Portuguese Red Cross

Jardim 9 de Abril, 1 a 5, 1293 Lisboa CODEX, Portugal.

Telephone: 351 (1) 39 62 127. *Fax:* 351 (1) 39 51 045.

OBJECTIVES: To support the principles of the Red Cross

GENERAL INFORMATION: *Creation:* 1865. *Member organisations:* 163. *Affiliated to:* International Federation of the Red Cross and of the Red Crescent Societies (Switzerland). *Personnel/Total:* 3. *Volunteers:* 3 of which: 3 in developing countries. *Budget/Total 1993:* ECU 487560000 (US$ 569420000). *Financial sources:* Private: 40%. *Public:* 45%. *Self-financing:* 15%.

PUBLICATIONS: *Periodicals:* Boletim Informativo (4). *Annual report.*

EVALUATION/RESEARCH: Evaluation reports available.

PLANNED ACTIVITIES:

COMMENTS: All support to emergency and development programmes is provided through the International Federation and/or the International Committee. Undertakes activities in the Commonwealth of Independent States.

ACTIVITIES IN DEVELOPING REGIONS: Active in 5 country(ies). Works through local field partners. **Sustainable Development Actions:** Emergency relief/refugees/humanitarian assistance; Rural development/agriculture; Sending volunteers/experts/technical assistance. **Regions:** East Africa; Southern Africa.

INFORMATION AND EDUCATION ACTIVITIES: **Topics:** Food/famine; Gender issues/women; Health/sanitation/water; Human rights/peace/conflicts; Refugees/migrants/ethnic groups. **Activities:** Conferences/seminars/workshops/training activities; Exchanges/twinning/linking; Formal education; Fund raising; Information and documentation services/data bases; Lobbying/advocacy.

PRT3577

FUNDACAO ANTERO DE QUENTAL

Av. das Descobertas, 17, 1400 Lisboa, Portugal.

PRT3578

FUNDACAO OLIVEIRA MARTINS

R. Rodrigo da Fonseca,17-1§, 1200 Lisboa, Portugal.

PRT3579

GRAAL ♦ Le Graal

Rua Luciano Cordeiro, 24-6° A, 1100 Lisboa, Portugal.

Téléphone: 351 (1) 54 68 31. *Fax:* 351 (1) 52 25 14. *Contact:* Teresa Santa Clara Gomes.

OBJECTIFS: Promouvoir des activités de sensibilisation et d'éducation sur les questions liées à la coopération pour le développement, surtout parmi les femmes. Assurer la formation de cadres locaux.

INFORMATIONS GENERALES: *Création:* 1977. *Affiliée à:* Plataforma das ONG para Cooperaçao e Desenvolvimento (Portugal) - Union Fraternelle entre les Races et les Peuples (Suisse). *Personnel/Total:* 32. *Salariés:* 7 dont: 3 dans les pays en développement. *Bénévoles:* 25 dont: 10 dans les pays en développement. *Budget/Total 1993:* ECU 111000 (US$ 130000). *Sources financières:* Privé: 80%. *Autofinancement:* 20%.

PUBLICATIONS: *Périodiques:* Lien (4) - Folha Informativa-Terraco (2) - Folha De Noticias-Graal (2). *Rapport annuel.*

EVALUATION/RECHERCHE: Rapports d'évaluation disponibles.

ACTIVITES DANS LES REGIONS EN DEVELOPPEMENT: Intervient dans 4 pays. Intervient par l'intermédiaire d'organisations locales partenaires. **Actions de Développement durable:** Envoi de volontaires/experts/assistance technique; Questions relatives aux femmes; Écologie/environnement/biodiversité; Éducation/formation/alphabétisation. **Régions:** Afrique australe; Afrique de l'Ouest; Amérique du Sud.

ACTIVITES D'INFORMATION ET D'EDUCATION: **Domaines:** Culture/tradition/religion; Droits de l'Homme/paix/conflits; Questions relatives aux femmes; Écologie/environnement/biodiversité; Éducation/formation/alphabétisation. **Activités:** Campagnes d'information/expositions; Conférences/séminaires/ateliers/activités de formation; Lobbying/plaidoyer; Radiodiffusion/manifestations culturelles; Échanges/parrainage/jumelage; Édition/documents audiovisuels/documents éducatifs; Éducation formelle.

PRT3580

GRUPO DE ESTUDOS E SOLIDARIEDADE COM A AMERICA LATINA (GSAL)

Rua Pinheiro Chagas 77-2.ET, 1000 Lisboa, Portugal.

PRT3581

INSTITUTO 1° DE MAIO

Trav. da Boa Hora 46-1° , 1200 Lisboa, Portugal.

Téléphone: 351 (1) 37 24 03.

PRT3582

INSTITUTO AGRARIO PARA A FORMACAO, COOPERACAO E DESENVOLVIMENTO SOCIAL (SETAAFOC)

Largo Rafael Bordalo Pinheiro, 29 - 2§, 1294 Lisboa CODEX, Portugal.

PRT3583

INSTITUTO AMARO DA COSTA ♦ Amaro da Costa Institute

R. de Sao Marcal 77-79, 1200 Lisboa, Portugal.

Telephone: 351 (1) 36 05 54. *Contact:* Eugenio A. Correia.

PRT3584

INSTITUTO DE APOIO A CRIANCA (IAC) ♦ L'INSTITUT D'AIDE A L'ENFANCE

Largo da Memoria, 14 (à Calçada do Galvaô), 1300 Lisboa, Portugal.

Téléphone: 351 (1) 362 17 93. *Fax:* 351 (1) 362 47 56. *Contact:* DRA. Manuela Ramalho Eanes, Président.

OBJECTIFS: Contribuer au développement global de l'enfant, en défendant tous ses droits: santé, éducation et loisirs.

INFORMATIONS GENERALES: *Création:* 1983. *Type d'organisation:* regroupement d'ONG. *Organisations membres:* 3. *Affiliée à:* Bureau International Catholique de l'Enfance (Suisse) - International Play Association - Confedacâo National Accao sobre o Trabacho Infantil (Portugal). *Personnel/Total:* 65. *Salariés:* 65. *Sources financières:* Privé: 30%. *Public:* 50%. *Autofinancement:* 20%.

PUBLICATIONS: *Périodiques:* Boletin Do IAC (6). *Rapport annuel. Liste des publications.*

EVALUATION/RECHERCHE: Rapports d'évaluation disponibles. Entreprend des activités de recherche.

COMMENTAIRES: Activités d'information concernant la Communauté des Etats indépendants.

Voir : *Comment utiliser le répertoire,* page 11.

ACTIVITES DANS LES REGIONS EN DEVELOPPEMENT: Intervient par l'intermédiaire d'organisations locales partenaires. **Actions de Développement durable:** Enfants/jeunesse/famille. **Régions:** Afrique de l'Est; Afrique de l'Ouest.

ACTIVITES D'INFORMATION ET D'EDUCATION: Domaines: Autres; Enfants/jeunesse/famille; Pauvreté/conditions de vie; Éducation/formation/alphabétisation. **Activités:** Campagnes d'information/expositions; Conférences/séminaires/ateliers/activités de formation; Lobbying/plaidoyer; Édition/documents audiovisuels/documents éducatifs.

PRT3585

INSTITUTO DE ESTUDOS ESTRATEGICOS E INTERNACIONAIS (IEEI) ♦ Institute for Strategic and International Studies

Largo de S. Sebastiao, 8-Paço do Lumiar, 1600 Lisboa, Portugal.

Telephone: 351 (1) 75 72 701. **Fax:** 351 (1) 75 93 983. **Contact:** Alvaro de Vasconcelos, Director.

OBJECTIVES: To research, provide information and foster debate on international affairs, defence and security matters.

GENERAL INFORMATION: Creation: 1980. **Personnel/Total:** 13. **Budget/Total 1993:** ECU 479000 (US$ 560000). **Financial sources:** Private: 35%. Public: 33%. Self-financing: 12%.

PUBLICATIONS: Periodicals: Estratégia (2).

EVALUATION/RESEARCH: Undertakes research activities.

COMMENTS: The IEEI is primarily a research centre which does not, therefore, engage in educational and humanitarian activities.

INFORMATION AND EDUCATION ACTIVITIES: Topics: Human rights/peace/conflicts; International economic relations/trade/debt/finance; International relations/cooperation/development aid; Peace/ethnic conflicts/armament/disarmament. **Activities:** Conferences/seminars/workshops/training activities; Information and documentation services/data bases; Publishing/audiovisual materials/educational materials.

PRT3586

INSTITUTO DE ESTUDOS PARA O DESENVOLVIMENTO (IED) ♦ Institut d'Etudes pour le Développement

S. Domingos à Lapa 111-3°, 1200 Lisbonne, Portugal.

Téléphone: 351 (1) 60 96 38. **Fax:** 351 (1) 395 15 70. **Contact:** A. Trigo de Abreu, Directeur.

OBJECTIFS: Assurer une éducation et une formation sur le développement. Développer la recherche, les études et projets sur la coopération et le développement durable.

INFORMATIONS GENERALES: Création: 1979. **Affiliée à:** Entraide Ouvrière Internationale (réseau) (Allemagne). **Personnel/Total:** 12. **Salariés:** 10. **Bénévoles:** 2. **Budget/Total 1993:** ECU 654000 (US$ 764000). **Sources financières:** Privé: 40%. Public: 50%. Autofinancement: 10%.

PUBLICATIONS: Périodiques: Desenvolvimento (2). **Rapport annuel.** Liste des publications.

EVALUATION/RECHERCHE: Rapports d'évaluation disponibles. Entreprend des activités de recherche.

PREVISIONS D'ACTIVITES: Campagne publique européanne sur l'interdépendance et la solidarité Nord-Sud.

ACTIVITES DANS LES REGIONS EN DEVELOPPEMENT: Intervient directement dans les régions en développement. Intervient dans 3 pays. Maintient une présence locale sur le terrain. Intervient par l'intermédiaire d'organisations locales partenaires. **Actions de Développement durable:** Dette/finances/commerce; Droits de l'Homme/paix/conflits; Développement rural/agriculture; Envoi de volontaires/experts/assistance technique; Éducation/formation/alphabétisation. **Régions:** Afrique australe; Afrique de l'Ouest.

ACTIVITES D'INFORMATION ET D'EDUCATION: Domaines: Aliments/famine; Droits de l'Homme/paix/conflits; Développement rural/agriculture; Développement urbain/habitat; Paix/conflits ethniques/armement/désarmement; Population/planning familial/démographie; Questions relatives aux femmes; Racisme/xénophobie/antisémitisme; Relations internationales/coopération/aide au développement; Réfugiés/migrants/

groupes ethniques; Santé/assainissement/eau; Écologie/environnement/biodiversité; Éducation/formation/alphabétisation. **Activités:** Campagnes d'information/expositions; Conférences/séminaires/ateliers/activités de formation; Lobbying/plaidoyer; Services d'information et de documentation/bases de données; Échanges/parrainage/jumelage; Édition/documents audiovisuels/documents éducatifs.

PRT3587

INSTITUTO DE INVESTIGACAO PARA O DESENVOLVIMENTO, COOPERACAO E FORMACAO 1° DE MAIO ♦ Institut de recherche pour le développement, la coopération et la formation 1er Mai

Av. Almirante Reis, 74F-5§, 1000 Lisboa, Portugal.

Téléphone: 351 (1) 387 80 18. **Fax:** 351 (1) 352 29 61. **Contact:** Alvaro Fernandes Rana, Président.

PRT3588

INSTITUTO DE SOLIDARIEDADE E COOPERACAO UNIVERSITARIA (ISU) ♦ Institut de Solidarité et de Coopération Universitaire

Tv. do Possolo, 11 3°, 1200 Lisboa, Portugal.

Téléphone: 351 (1) 60 72 06. **Fax:** 351 (1) 39 79 681. **Contact:** Antonio José da Costa Malheiro Sarmento.

OBJECTIFS: Aider les étudiants du Tiers-Monde qui poursuivent des études dans les universités portugaises. Contribuer à l'intégration des immigrés dans la société portugaise. Sensibiliser aux problèmes du développement dans le Tiers-Monde. Réaliser des projets de développement, notamment d'éducation, dans les pays du Tiers-Monde.

INFORMATIONS GENERALES: Création: 1989. **Affiliée à:** Plate-forme des ONG Portugaises pour le Développement (Portugal). **Personnel/Total:** 37. **Salariés:** 2. **Bénévoles:** 35 dont: 2 dans les pays en développement. **Budget/Total 1993:** ECU 43000 (US$ 50000). **Sources financières:** Privé: 23%. Public: 77%.

PUBLICATIONS: Rapport annuel.

ACTIVITES DANS LES REGIONS EN DEVELOPPEMENT: Intervient directement dans les régions en développement. Intervient dans 3 pays. Maintient une présence locale sur le terrain. Intervient par l'intermédiaire d'organisations locales partenaires. **Actions de Développement durable:** Questions relatives aux femmes; Éducation/formation/alphabétisation. **Régions:** Afrique australe; Afrique de l'Ouest.

ACTIVITES D'INFORMATION ET D'EDUCATION: Domaines: Questions relatives aux femmes; Réfugiés/migrants/groupes ethniques; Éducation/formation/alphabétisation. **Activités:** Collecte de fonds; Radiodiffusion/manifestations culturelles; Éducation formelle.

PRT3589

INSTITUTO LUSO-AFRICANO PARA O DESENVOLVIMIENTO E ACTIVIDADES DA POPULACAO (ILADAP)

R. Coronel Ribeiro, Viana 15-4° dto, 1300 Lisboa, Portugal.

Contact: Aleixo Luis Leonetti Terra-da-Motta, Presidente.

PRT3590

INSTITUTO MARQUES DE VALLE FLOR

Rua de Sao Nicolau 105, 1100 Lisboa, Portugal.

Téléphone: 351 - 347 08 45. **Fax:** 351 - 346 59 73. **Contact:** Paulo Telles de Freitas, Président du Conseil d'Administration.

OBJECTIFS: Réaliser des programmes humanitaires, des programmes de développement et des études scientifiques dans divers domaines, au Portugal et dans les pays africains lusophones (PALOP).

INFORMATIONS GENERALES: Création: 1951. **Type d'organisation:** collectif. **Personnel/Total:** 22. **Salariés:** 11 dont: 9 dans les pays en développement. **Bénévoles:** 11. **Budget/Total 1993:** ECU 735000 (US$ 858000). **Sources financières:** Public: 56%. Autofinancement: 44%.

PUBLICATIONS: Rapport annuel. Liste des publications.

EVALUATION/RECHERCHE: Rapports d'évaluation disponibles.

See: *How to Use the Directory,* page 11.

ACTIVITES DANS LES REGIONS EN DEVELOPPEMENT: Intervient directement dans les régions en développement. Intervient dans 2 pays. Maintient une présence locale sur le terrain. Intervient par l'intermédiaire d'organisations locales partenaires. **Actions de Développement durable:** Aliments/famine; Droits de l'Homme/paix/conflits; Démocratie/ bonne gestion publique/création d'institutions/développement participatif; Développement urbain/habitat; Enfants/jeunesse/famille; Envoi de volontaires/experts/assistance technique; Petites entreprises/secteur informel/artisanat; Population/planning familial/démographie; Questions relatives aux femmes; Santé/assainissement/eau; Secours d'urgence/ réfugiés/aide humanitaire; Éducation/formation/alphabétisation. **Régions:** Afrique australe; Afrique de l'Ouest.

ACTIVITES D'INFORMATION ET D'EDUCATION: Domaines: Aliments/ famine; Développement rural/agriculture; Emploi/chômage; Paix/conflits ethniques/armement/désarmement; Pauvreté/conditions de vie; Population/planning familial/démographie; Relations internationales/coopération/aide au développement; Réfugiés/migrants/groupes ethniques; Santé/assainissement/eau; Secours d'urgence/réfugiés/aide humanitaire; Éducation/formation/alphabétisation. **Activités:** Collecte de fonds; Conférences/séminaires/ateliers/activités de formation; Lobbying/plaidoyer; Services d'information et de documentation/bases de données; Échanges/parrainage/jumelage; Édition/documents audiovisuels/documents éducatifs; Éducation formelle.

PRT3591

INSTITUTO PROGRESSO SOCIAL E DEMOCRACIA FRANCISCO SA CARNEIRO (IPSD)

R. Ricardo Espiritu Santo,1, R/C Esq, 1200 Lisboa, Portugal.

PRT3592

INSTITUTO SINDICAL DE ESTUDOS, FORMACAO E COOPERACAO (ISEFOC)

Rua da Cintura do Porto de Lisboa, lote B-3° , 1900 Lisboa, Portugal.

Téléphone: 351 (1) 858 24 16. **Fax:** 351 (1) 32 70 54. **Contact:** Joaquim Coelho.

PRT3593

INTERNATIONAL FRIENDSHIP LEAGUE

Calçada da Baleia, 9, 2655 Ericeira, Portugal.

PRT3594

LEIGOS PARA O DESENVOLVIMENTO (LD) ♦ Laïcs pour le Développement

Estrada da Torre 26, 1700 Lisboa, Portugal.

Téléphone: 351 (1) 7590516. **Fax:** 351 (1) 7599615. **Contact:** Artur Paulo Araújo, Secrétaire de Direction.

OBJECTIFS: Contribuer au développement des populations du Tiers monde, notamment dans les pays lusophones.

INFORMATIONS GENERALES: Création: 1986. **Affiliée à:** Organisme Chrétien de Coopération Internationale - Plate-forme Nationale des ONG Portugaises (Portugal) - Comité de Liaison des ONG Européennes. **Personnel/Total:** 34. **Salariés:** 4. **Bénévoles:** 30 dont: 16 dans les pays en développement. **Budget/Total 1993:** ECU 106000 (US$ 124000). **Sources financières:** Privé: 25%. Public: 70%. Autofinancement: 5%.

PUBLICATIONS: Périodiques: Jornal Dos Leigos (12). Rapport annuel.

ACTIVITES DANS LES REGIONS EN DEVELOPPEMENT: Intervient directement dans les régions en développement. Intervient dans 4 pays. Maintient une présence locale sur le terrain. Intervient par l'intermédiaire d'organisations locales partenaires. **Actions de Développement durable:** Démocratie/bonne gestion publique/création d'institutions/développement participatif; Développement rural/agriculture; Développement urbain/habitat; Enfants/jeunesse/famille; Envoi de volontaires/experts/ assistance technique; Petites entreprises/secteur informel/artisanat; Population/planning familial/démographie; Questions relatives aux femmes; Santé/assainissement/eau; Éducation/formation/alphabétisation. **Régions:** Afrique australe; Afrique centrale.

ACTIVITES D'INFORMATION ET D'EDUCATION: Domaines: Aliments/ famine; Culture/tradition/religion; Développement rural/agriculture;

Développement urbain/habitat; Enfants/jeunesse/famille; Paix/conflits ethniques/armement/désarmement; Pauvreté/conditions de vie; Population/planning familial/démographie; Questions relatives aux femmes; Relations internationales/coopération/aide au développement; Relations économiques internationales/commerce/dette/finances; Réfugiés/ migrants/groupes ethniques; Santé/assainissement/eau; Écologie/environnement/biodiversité; Éducation/formation/alphabétisation. **Activités:** Campagnes d'information/expositions; Collecte de fonds; Conférences/ séminaires/ateliers/activités de formation; Lobbying/plaidoyer; Éducation formelle.

PRT3595

LIGA DOS AFRICANOS E AMIGOS DE AFRICA (LIAFRICA)

R. Forno do Tijolo, 46 - 2° dto, 1100 Lisboa, Portugal.

PRT3596

LIGA PERMANENTE INTERNACIONAL DE COMBATE A FAME ♦ Ligue internationale permanente de lutte contre la faim

Rua da Constituiçao, 656, 2° (s/216), 4200 Porto, Portugal.

Téléphone: 351 (2) 52 11 88. **Fax:** 351 (2) 52 11 88. **Contact:** Manuel António Chandikua.

OBJECTIFS: Apporter du secours alimentaire aux populations du Tiers monde qui sont dans le besoin, afin de les inserrer dans la vie active.

INFORMATIONS GENERALES: Création: 1987. **Salariés:** 39 dont: 27 dans les pays en développement. **Bénévoles:** var. **Budget/ Total 1993:** ECU 12843000 (US$ 15000000). **Sources financières:** Privé: 10%. Autofinancement: 90%.

PUBLICATIONS: Rapport annuel.

EVALUATION/RECHERCHE: Rapports d'évaluation disponibles. Entreprend des activités de recherche.

PREVISIONS D'ACTIVITES: Apporter une aide humanitaire à l'Europe de l'Est.

ACTIVITES DANS LES REGIONS EN DEVELOPPEMENT: Intervient directement dans les régions en développement. Intervient dans 2 pays. Maintient une présence locale sur le terrain. Intervient par l'intermédiaire d'organisations locales partenaires. **Actions de Développement durable:** Aliments/famine; Démocratie/bonne gestion publique/création d'institutions/développement participatif; Développement rural/agriculture; Envoi de volontaires/experts/assistance technique; Santé/assainissement/eau; Secours d'urgence/réfugiés/aide humanitaire. **Régions:** Afrique australe.

ACTIVITES D'INFORMATION ET D'EDUCATION: Domaines: Aliments/ famine; Développement rural/agriculture; Enfants/jeunesse/famille; Pauvreté/conditions de vie; Relations internationales/coopération/aide au développement; Secours d'urgence/réfugiés/aide humanitaire. **Activités:** Campagnes d'information/expositions; Collecte de fonds; Conférences/séminaires/ateliers/activités de formation; Services d'information et de documentation/bases de données; Éducation formelle.

PRT3597

MISSAO DE ESTUDOS PARA O DESENVOLVIMENTO E COOPERACAO (MEDEC) ♦ Mission of Study for Development and Cooperation

Praceta Gonçalves Crespo, 1-4§Dto, 2795 Carnaxide, Portugal.

Telephone: 351 (1) 41 85 076. **Fax:** 351 (1) 41 85 076. **Contact:** Esmeraldo Rosa Monteiro de Azevedo.

OBJECTIVES: To improve the life conditions in developing countries through co-operation and solidarity.

GENERAL INFORMATION: Creation: 1980. **Personnel/Total:** 16. Volunteers: 16 of which: 2 in developing countries.

PUBLICATIONS: Annual report. List of publications.

EVALUATION/RESEARCH: Evaluation reports available. Undertakes research activities.

ACTIVITIES IN DEVELOPING REGIONS: Present in developing regions. Active in 1 country(ies). Maintains local field presence. Works through local field partners. **Sustainable Development Actions:** Education/

training/literacy; Emergency relief/refugees/humanitarian assistance. **Regions:** East Africa; West Africa.

INFORMATION AND EDUCATION ACTIVITIES: Topics: Education/training/literacy; Emergency relief/refugees/humanitarian assistance; International relations/cooperation/development aid. **Activities:** Conferences/seminars/workshops/training activities; Formal education.

PRT3598

MOVIMENTO SOS RACISMO

Av. Guerra Junqueiro 19, 5 Esq., 1000 Lisboa, Portugal.

Telephone: 351 (1) 84 64 055. *Fax:* 351 (1) 80 96 28.

OBJECTIVES: To fight against racism.

GENERAL INFORMATION: Creation: 1990. *Type of organisation:* network. *Affiliated to:* Pror Europeia Para a Igualdado na Europa (Belgium) - Fédéracion des SOS Racismo (France). *Budget/ Total 1993:* ECU 21000 (US$ 25000). *Financial sources: Public:* 20%. *Self-financing:* 80%.

PUBLICATIONS: Periodicals: Boletim do SOS Racismo (6). *Annual report. List of publications.*

EVALUATION/RESEARCH: Evaluation reports available. Undertakes research activities.

INFORMATION AND EDUCATION ACTIVITIES: Topics: Racism/xenophobia/antisemitism; Refugees/migrants/ethnic groups. **Activities:** Conferences/seminars/workshops/training activities; Information and documentation services/data bases; Information campaigns/exhibitions; Networking/electronic telecommunications; Publishing/audiovisual materials/educational materials.

PRT3599

OBRA PONTIFICIA DA PROPAGACAO DA FE ♦ Oeuvre pontificale de la propagation de la foi

Rua da Ilha do Principe 19, 1100 Lisboa, Portugal.

Téléphone: 351 (1) 814 84 28. *Contact:* Msgr. Joaquim Luís Cupertino, Directeur.

OBJECTIFS: Fournir une aide financière et matérielle aux pays en développement.

INFORMATIONS GENERALES: Création: 1880. *Personnel/Total:* 6. *Salariés:* 2. *Bénévoles:* 4. *Budget/Total 1993:* ECU 522000 (US$ 609000). *Sources financières: Privé:* 100%.

PUBLICATIONS: Périodiques: Anais Das Obras Missonárias Pontificias (4).

ACTIVITES DANS LES REGIONS EN DEVELOPPEMENT: Intervient directement dans les régions en développement. Intervient dans 1 pays. **Actions de Développement durable:** Enfants/jeunesse/famille; Éducation/formation/alphabétisation. **Régions:** Afrique de l'Ouest.

ACTIVITES D'INFORMATION ET D'EDUCATION: Domaines: Enfants/jeunesse/famille; Éducation/formation/alphabétisation. **Activités:** Collecte de fonds.

PRT3600

OIKOS - COOPERACAO E DESENVOLVIMENTO ♦ OIKOS - Coopération et Développement

Avenida Visconde Valmor, 35, 3° Dt, 1000 Lisboa, Portugal.

Téléphone: 351 (1) 79 64 719. *Fax:* 351 (1) 79 39 791. *Contact:* Agostinho Jardim Gonçalves, Secrétaire général.

OBJECTIFS: Soutenir le développement des pays du Tiers monde par la coopération et la solidarité. Promouvoir le développement des couches sociales les plus marginalisées au Portugal. Entreprendre des activités d'éducation et d'information, axées sur la problématique du développement et de la coopération dans le monde.

INFORMATIONS GENERALES: Création: 1988. *Affiliée à:* EECOD (Belgique) - ZEBRA (Hollande) - EUROSTEP (Belgique) - CREAL (France.). *Personnel/Total:* 25. *Salariés:* 45 dont: 15 dans les pays en développement. *Budget/Total 1993:*

ECU 2569000 (US$ 3000000). *Sources financières: Privé:* 20%. *Public:* 60%. *Autofinancement:* 20%.

PUBLICATIONS: Périodiques: OIKOS (6). *Rapport annuel. Liste des publications.*

EVALUATION/RECHERCHE: Entreprend des activités de recherche.

ACTIVITES DANS LES REGIONS EN DEVELOPPEMENT: Intervient directement dans les régions en développement. Intervient dans 7 pays. Maintient une présence locale sur le terrain. Intervient par l'intermédiaire d'organisations locales partenaires. **Actions de Développement durable:** Aliments/famine; Droits de l'Homme/paix/conflits; Démocratie/bonne gestion publique/création d'institutions/développement participatif; Développement rural/agriculture; Développement urbain/habitat; Enfants/jeunesse/famille; Questions relatives aux femmes; Santé/assainissement/eau; Secours d'urgence/réfugiés/aide humanitaire; Écologie/environnement/biodiversité; Éducation/formation/alphabétisation. **Régions:** Afrique australe; Amérique du Sud; Caraïbes; Mexique et Amerique centrale.

ACTIVITES D'INFORMATION ET D'EDUCATION: Domaines: Culture/tradition/religion; Droits de l'Homme/paix/conflits; Développement rural/agriculture; Développement urbain/habitat; Enfants/jeunesse/famille; Paix/conflits ethniques/armement/désarmement; Pauvreté/conditions de vie; Population/planning familial/démographie; Questions relatives aux femmes; Racisme/xénophobie/antisémitisme; Relations internationales/coopération/aide au développement; Relations économiques internationales/commerce/dette/finances; Réfugiés/migrants/groupes ethniques; Santé/assainissement/eau; Secours d'urgence/réfugiés/aide humanitaire; Écologie/environnement/biodiversité. **Activités:** Campagnes d'information/expositions; Conférences/séminaires/ateliers/activités de formation; Lobbying/plaidoyer; Radiodiffusion/manifestations culturelles; Services d'information et de documentation/bases de données; Édition/documents audiovisuels/documents éducatifs; Éducation formelle.

PRT3601

SERVICOS DE ASSISTENCIA ORGANIZACAO DE MARIA (SAOM)

R. das Virtudes 11, 4000 Porto, Portugal.

Téléphone: 351 (2) 20 02 424. *Contact:* Joao Rebello de Carvalho, Présidente.

PRT3602

SUL - ASSOCIACAO DE COOPERACAO PARA O DESENVOLVIMENTO (SUL/ACD) ♦ SUD - Association de Coopération pour le Développement

Travessa Maria da Fonte, n§5 (Esguiera), 3800 Aveiro, Portugal.

Téléphone: 351 (34) 31 52 92. *Fax:* 351 (34) 22 787. *Contact:* Rui Correia, Président de la Commission éxecutive.

OBJECTIFS: Mener des projets de coopération directe et décentralisée avec les pays du Sud, dans les domaines de l'environnement et des droits de l'Homme. Sensibiliser la population portugaise aux problèmes de développement.

INFORMATIONS GENERALES: Création: 1990. *Type d'organisation:* collectif. *Affiliée à:* Federaçao de Associaçaoes de Juventud de Distrito Aveiro (Portugal) -Platáforma Nacional de ONGD's (Portugal) - Asian Human Rights Commission (Hong-Kong) - United Nations Conference on Environment and Development (USA) -Youth for Development and Cooperation (Pays-Bas). *Personnel/Total:* 20. *Salariés:* 4. *Bénévoles:* 16 dont: 7 dans les pays en développement. *Budget/Total 1993:* ECU 43000 (US$ 50000). *Sources financières: Privé:* 10%. *Public:* 60%. *Autofinancement:* 10%.

PUBLICATIONS: Périodiques: Meridialis (2). *Rapport annuel. Liste des publications.*

EVALUATION/RECHERCHE: Rapports d'évaluation disponibles. Entreprend des activités de recherche.

ACTIVITES DANS LES REGIONS EN DEVELOPPEMENT: Intervient directement dans les régions en développement. Intervient dans 5 pays. Maintient une présence locale sur le terrain. Intervient par l'intermédiaire d'organisations locales partenaires. **Actions de Développement durable:** Droits de l'Homme/paix/conflits; Démocratie/bonne gestion publique/création d'institutions/développement participatif; Développement

         See: How to Use the Directory, page 11.

rural/agriculture; Développement urbain/habitat; Enfants/jeunesse/ famille; Envoi de volontaires/experts/assistance technique; Petites entreprises/secteur informel/artisanat; Population/planning familial/ démographie; Questions relatives aux femmes; Santé/assainissement/ eau; Secours d'urgence/réfugiés/aide humanitaire; Écologie/environne-ment/biodiversité; Éducation/formation/alphabétisation. **Régions:** Afri-que australe; Afrique centrale; Afrique du Nord; Amérique du Sud; Asie de l'Est; Asie du Sud-Est.

ACTIVITES D'INFORMATION ET D'EDUCATION: Domaines: Droits de l'Homme/paix/conflits; Développement urbain/habitat; Enfants/jeunesse/ famille; Paix/conflits ethniques/armement/désarmement; Questions relatives aux femmes; Racisme/xénophobie/antisémitisme; Relations internationales/coopération/aide au développement; Réfugiés/migrants/ groupes ethniques; Santé/assainissement/eau; Écologie/environne-ment/biodiversité. **Activités:** Campagnes d'information/expositions; Collecte de fonds; Conférences/séminaires/ateliers/activités de forma-tion; Lobbying/plaidoyer; Réseaux/télécommunications électroniques; Services d'information et de documentation/bases de données; Échanges/parrainage/jumelage; Édition/documents audiovisuels/docu-ments éducatifs.

PRT3603

UNIAO DAS CIDADES CAPITAIS DE LINGUA POR-TUGUESA (UCCLA) ♦ Union of Portuguese-Speaking Capital Cities

Avenida 24 de Julho, 118 - B/C/D, 1300 Lisboa, Portugal.

Telephone: 351 (1) 39 55 309. **Fax:** 351 (1) 60 81 55. **E-mail:** 351 1 60311 UCPPLA - P. **Contact:** Jorge Sampaio, President.

OBJECTIVES: To stimulate the understanding and co-operation between the Portuguese-speaking people. To promote the rights of good neighbouring and citizens' participation in public affairs. To provide infor-mation on economics, culture, tourism and the professional sector.

GENERAL INFORMATION: Creation: 1985. **Type of organisation:** network. **Affiliated to:** Union of Iberoamerican Capital Cities - The United Cities World Federation -The United Cities Development - The Portuguese Co-Operation Institute (Portugal) - The Portugal/Angola Chamber of Trade and Industry - The Club of the Portuguese Managers and Undertakers from Guinea-Bissau - The National Union of Writters and Artists of S. Tomé and Prince. **Personnel/Total:** 13. Salaried: 12. Volunteers: 1. **Financial sources:** Public: 30%. Self-financing: 70%.

PUBLICATIONS: Periodicals: (6). Annual report.

ACTIVITIES IN DEVELOPING REGIONS: Present in developing regions. Active in 5 country(ies). Works through local field partners. **Sustainable Development Actions:** Education/training/literacy; Emergency relief/ refugees/humanitarian assistance; Food/famine; Health/sanitation/ water; Human rights/peace/conflicts; Sending volunteers/experts/techni-cal assistance; Urban development/habitat. **Regions:** Central Africa; Southern Africa; West Africa.

INFORMATION AND EDUCATION ACTIVITIES: Topics: Culture/tradi-tion/religion; Education/training/literacy; Emergency relief/refugees/ humanitarian assistance; Health/sanitation/water; International relations/ cooperation/development aid; Urban development/habitat. **Activities:** Broadcasting/cultural events; Conferences/seminars/workshops/training activities; Exchanges/twinning/linking; Formal education; Fund raising.

PRT3604

UNIAO DAS MISERICORDIAS PORTUGUESAS (UMP)

Calçada das Lages, n° 12 A, 1900 Lisboa, Portugal.

Telephone: 351 (1) 81 55 342. **Fax:** 351 (1) 82 13 24. **Contact:** Dr, Vitor Melicias, Président.

PRT3605

VOLUNTARIADO INTERNACIONAL PARA O DESENVOLVIMENTO AFRICANO (VIDA) ♦ International Volun-teer Service for African Development

Rua das Pedras Negras, n° 3 - R/C Esq° , 1100 Lisboa, Portugal.

Telephone: 351 (1) 88 83 979. **Fax:** 351 (1) 88 82 819. **Contact:** Maria da Luz Vasconcelos e Souza, President.

OBJECTIVES: To improve the living conditions of the population in devel-oping countries. To provide basic education and vocational training through volunteer work. To improve women's conditions.

GENERAL INFORMATION: Creation: 1992. **Affiliated to:** Plataforma Nacional de ONGD (Portugal). **Personnel/Total:** 39. Salaried: 21 of which: 21 in developing countries. Volunteers: 18 of which: 4 in develop-ing countries. **Budget/Total 1993:** ECU 101000 (US$ 118000). **Finan-cial sources:** Private: 72%. Public: 21%. Self-financing: 7%.

PUBLICATIONS: Annual report.

EVALUATION/RESEARCH: Evaluation reports available.

PLANNED ACTIVITIES: The creation of a national volunteer training cen-tre. The creation of a vocational training centre in Boane, Mozambique for demobilized soldiers.

ACTIVITIES IN DEVELOPING REGIONS: Present in developing regions. Active in 1 country(ies). Maintains local field presence. Works through local field partners. **Sustainable Development Actions:** Children/ youth/family; Education/training/literacy; Food/famine; Gender issues/ women; Health/sanitation/water; Rural development/agriculture; Send-ing volunteers/experts/technical assistance; Small enterprises/informal sector/handicrafts. **Regions:** Southern Africa.

INFORMATION AND EDUCATION ACTIVITIES: Topics: Children/youth/ family; Education/training/literacy; Food/famine; Gender issues/women; Health/sanitation/water; Poverty/living conditions; Rural development/ agriculture. **Activities:** Formal education; Fund raising; Information campaigns/exhibitions; Lobbying/advocacy.

SVK3606
ANDREJ KMET FOUNDATION

Dolna 23, 969 00 Banska Stiavnica, Slovakia.

SVK3607
ASSOCIATION FOR YOUTH, SCIENCE AND TECHNOLOGY (AMAVET)

M. Majerovej 40, 841 04 Bratislava, Slovakia.

SVK3608
CHARTER 77 FOUNDATION

Staromestská 6, 811 03 Bratislava, Slovakia.

Telephone: 42 (7) 31 64 48. *Fax:* 42 (7) 31 63 41. *Contact:* Zuzana Szatmary, Director.

OBJECTIVES: To promote the protection and education of human rights. To provide legal aid in cases of human rights violations.

GENERAL INFORMATION: *Creation:* 1978. *Affiliated to:* Association of Slovak NGOs - ECRE - ELENA. *Personnel/Total:* 33. *Salaried:* 3. *Volunteers:* 30. *Budget/Total 1993:* ECU 8000 (US$ 11000). *Financial sources:* Private: 70%. Self-financing: 30%.

PUBLICATIONS: *Annual report. List of publications.*

EVALUATION/RESEARCH: Evaluation reports available. Undertakes research activities.

COMMENTS: Undertakes activities in the Commonwealth of Independent States. Information activities related to the Commonwealth of Independent States.

INFORMATION AND EDUCATION ACTIVITIES: Topics: Children/youth/family; Culture/tradition/religion; Education/training/literacy; Emergency relief/refugees/humanitarian assistance; Human rights/peace/conflicts; Racism/xenophobia/antisemitism; Refugees/migrants/ethnic groups. **Activities:** Broadcasting/cultural events; Conferences/seminars/workshops/training activities; Exchanges/twinning/linking; Fund raising; Information and documentation services/data bases; Information campaigns/exhibitions; Lobbying/advocacy; Publishing/audiovisual materials/educational materials.

SVK3609
COMMITTEE OF THE EUROPEAN CULTURAL FOUNDATION

Safarikovo Namestie 6, 818 06 Bratislava, Slovakia.

SVK3610
DEMOCRACY FOUNDATION

Wilsonovo Nabrezie 112, 949 01 Nitra, Slovakia.

SVK3611
THE FEDERATION DEFENDING THE INTERESTS OF THE HUNGARIAN YOUTH (FDIHY-MIESZ)

Bucinova 6, 821 07 Bratislava, Slovakia.

Telephone: 42 (813) 210 22. *Fax:* 42 (813) 210 22. *Contact:* Geonczeol Zsuzsanna, President.

OBJECTIVES: To help young people get a better education and by maintaining relations with international organisations.

GENERAL INFORMATION: *Creation:* 1990. *Personnel/Total:* 38. *Salaried:* 3 of which: 3 in developing countries. *Volunteers:* 35. *Budget/Total 1993:* ECU 9000 (US$ 12000). *Financial sources:* Public: 76%. Self-financing: 24%.

PUBLICATIONS: *Periodicals:* MIÉSZ HIRADO (5). *Annual report. List of publications.*

EVALUATION/RESEARCH: Evaluation reports available. Undertakes research activities.

COMMENTS: Undertakes activities in the Commonwealth of Independent States. Information activities related to the Commonwealth of Independent States.

INFORMATION AND EDUCATION ACTIVITIES: Topics: Children/youth/family; Culture/tradition/religion; Ecology/environment/biodiversity; Education/training/literacy; Employment/unemployment; Food/famine; Health/sanitation/water; Human rights/peace/conflicts; International relations/cooperation/development aid; Poverty/living conditions; Refugees/migrants/ethnic groups; Rural development/agriculture; Urban development/habitat. **Activities:** Broadcasting/cultural events; Conferences/seminars/workshops/training activities; Exchanges/twinning/linking; Formal education; Fund raising; Information and documentation services/data bases; Information campaigns/exhibitions; Networking/electronic telecommunications; Publishing/audiovisual materials/educational materials.

SVK3612
FOUNDATION ECOLOGY AND LIFE

Starkova 12, 010 01 Zilina, Slovakia.

Telephone: 42 (89) 62 17 44. *Fax:* 42 (89) 62 17 44. *Contact:* Dusan Mellner.

OBJECTIVES: To educate the public on environmental science, preventive medicine, philosophy, aesthetics and sociology.

GENERAL INFORMATION: *Creation:* 1991. *Personnel/Total:* 92. *Salaried:* 2. *Volunteers:* 90. *Budget/Total 1993:* ECU 6000 (US$ 8000). *Financial sources:* Private: 100%.

PUBLICATIONS: *Periodicals:* Ecology and Life (6). *Annual report. List of publications.*

EVALUATION/RESEARCH: Evaluation reports available.

COMMENTS: Undertakes activities in the Commonwealth of Independent States. Information activities related to the Commonwealth of Independent States.

ACTIVITIES IN DEVELOPING REGIONS: Present in developing regions. Active in 4 country(ies). Maintains local field presence. Works through local field partners.

INFORMATION AND EDUCATION ACTIVITIES: Topics: Children/youth/family; Culture/tradition/religion; Ecology/environment/biodiversity; Education/training/literacy; Emergency relief/refugees/humanitarian assistance; Food/famine; Gender issues/women; Health/sanitation/water; Human rights/peace/conflicts; International relations/cooperation/development aid; Peace/ethnic conflicts/armament/disarmament; Population/family planning/demography; Rural development/agriculture; Urban development/habitat. **Activities:** Conferences/seminars/workshops/training activities; Exchanges/twinning/linking; Formal education; Information campaigns/exhibitions.

SVK3613
FOUNDATION PROMETHEUS

USS pre mladez, Krasna Ulica 1083, 924 00 Galanta, Slovakia.

SVK3614
FRIENDS OF THE EARTH - EASTERN EUROPE (FOE)

PO Box 163, 814 99 Bratislava, Slovakia.

SVK3615
GEOEKO FOUNDATION

Sturova 1, 811 02 Bratislava, Slovakia.

SVK3616
HELSINKI CITIZENS' ASSEMBLY

Civic Secretariat, Staromestsk 6 a, 811 03 Bratislava, Slovakia.

SVK3617
HUMAN

Civic Secretariat, Staromestsk 6 a, 811 03 Bratislava, Slovakia.

SVK3618
HUNGARIAN SCOUTS UNION

Malinovskeho 2, 811 04 Bratislava, Slovakia.

SVK3619

INFORMACNE CENTRUM NADACII ♦ NGO Information Centre

Samova 9, 949 01 Nitra, Slovakia.

SVK3620

MINORITY RIGHTS GROUP SLOVAKIA

Safarikovo nam. 6, 818 06 Bratislava, Slovakia.

SVK3621

MOVEMENT OF THE CHRISTIAN ASSOCIATIONS OF YOUTH

Ceskoslovenskej Armady 7, 811 08 Bratislava, Slovakia.

SVK3622

NADACIA MILANA SIMECKU (MSF) ♦ MILAN SIMECKA FOUNDATION

Hviezdoslavovo nam. 17, 811 02 Bratislava, Slovakia.

Telephone: 42 (7) 33 15 93. *Fax:* 42 (7) 33 35 52. *Contact:* Miroslav Kusy, Chariman of the Board of Directors.

OBJECTIVES: To initiate and promote activities strengthening the development of democratic, cultural, humanitarian and civil values in society.

GENERAL INFORMATION: *Creation:* 1991. *Affiliated to:* Institute for Democracy in Eastern Europe Network. *Personnel/Total:* 3. *Salaried:* 3. *Budget/Total 1993:* ECU 81000 (US$ 105000). *Financial sources: Private:* 95%. *Self-financing:* 5%.

PUBLICATIONS: *Annual report. List of publications.*

EVALUATION/RESEARCH: Evaluation reports available. Undertakes research activities.

COMMENTS: Information activities related to the Commonwealth of Independent States.

INFORMATION AND EDUCATION ACTIVITIES: Topics: Culture/tradition/religion; Education/training/literacy; Human rights/peace/conflicts; International relations/cooperation/development aid; Peace/ethnic conflicts/armament/disarmament; Racism/xenophobia/antisemitism. **Activities:** Broadcasting/cultural events; Conferences/seminars/workshops/training activities; Exchanges/twinning/linking; Formal education; Fund raising; Information and documentation services/data bases; Lobbying/advocacy; Networking/electronic telecommunications; Publishing/audiovisual materials/educational materials.

SVK3623

OBCIANSKY INSTITUT BRATISLAVA

Dostojevskho rad 7, 811 09 Bratislava, Slovakia.

SVK3624

OPEN SOCIETY FUND

Staromestska 6, 811 03 Bratislava, Slovakia.

SVK3625

PARTNERSHIP FOUNDATION (EPCE SR)

Skuteckeho 30, 974 00 Banska Bystrica, Slovakia.

Telephone: 42 (88) 29 42 59. *Fax:* 42 (88) 29 42 59. *Contact:* Juraj Mesik.

OBJECTIVES: To allocate grants and provide services for NGOs.

GENERAL INFORMATION: *Creation:* 1991. *Type of organisation:* coordinating body. *Personnel/Total:* 3. *Salaried:* 3. *Budget/Total 1993:* ECU 139000 (US$ 180000). *Financial sources: Private:* 100%.

PUBLICATIONS: *Annual report.*

EVALUATION/RESEARCH: Evaluation reports available.

COMMENTS: Undertakes activities in the Commonwealth of Independent States.

SVK3626

PIONIER ♦ Pioneer

Prazska 11, 816 36 Bratislava, Slovakia.

Telephone: 42 (427) 49 55 97. *Fax:* 42 (427) 49 55 97. *Contact:* Milan Varhol, President.

OBJECTIVES: To support socially oriented projects in accordance with other organisations and promote children's rights based on the UN's Children Right Convention.

GENERAL INFORMATION: *Creation:* 1990. *Affiliated to:* Youth Council of Slovakia (Slovakia) - CENYC - WAY (Denmark) - Youth Forum. *Personnel/Total:* 852. *Salaried:* 2. *Volunteers:* 850. *Budget/Total 1993:* ECU 47000 (US$ 62000). *Financial sources: Private:* 10%. *Public:* 70%. *Self-financing:* 20%.

PUBLICATIONS: *Periodicals:* Spravodaj (4). *List of publications.*

EVALUATION/RESEARCH: Evaluation reports available. Undertakes research activities.

COMMENTS: Information activities related to the Commonwealth of Independent States.

INFORMATION AND EDUCATION ACTIVITIES: Topics: Children/youth/family; Emergency relief/refugees/humanitarian assistance; Human rights/peace/conflicts; International relations/cooperation/development aid. **Activities:** Conferences/seminars/workshops/training activities; Exchanges/twinning/linking; Fund raising.

SVK3627

RADA MLADEZE SLOVENSKA (RMS) ♦ Youth Council of Slovakia

Prazska 11, 811 04 Bratislava, Slovakia.

Telephone: 42 (27) 49 33 01. *Fax:* 42 (27) 49 33 01. *Contact:* Brano Ondrus.

OBJECTIVES: To serve as an umbrella for 40 youth organisations.

GENERAL INFORMATION: *Creation:* 1990. *Type of organisation:* coordinating body. *Member organisations:* 39. *Affiliated to:* CENYC (Belgium) - WAY (Denmark) - United (Germany). *Personnel/Total:* 11. *Salaried:* 1. *Volunteers:* 10. *Budget/Total 1993:* ECU 20000 (US$ 26000). *Financial sources: Private:* 24%. *Public:* 76%.

EVALUATION/RESEARCH: Evaluation reports available.

COMMENTS: Undertakes activities in the Commonwealth of Independent States.

SVK3628

RAINBOW - ASSOCIATION FOR LEISURE TIME AND NATURE

Csl. Parasutustov 5, 831 03 Bratislava, Slovakia.

SVK3629

SANDOR MARAI FOUNDATION

Hviezdoslavovo nam. 17, 811 02 Bratislava, Slovakia.

SVK3630

SASAKAWA PEACE FOUNDATION

Iveta Mozsnyakova, Romanova 46, 851 02 Bratislava, Slovakia.

SVK3631

SCOTT VIATOR FOUNDATION FOR NEW EUROPE

PO 34, 830 04 Bratislava, Slovakia.

SVK3632

SLAVOMIR STRACAR FOUNDATION

Hlavna 68, 040 01 Kosice, Slovakia.

Voir : *Comment utiliser le répertoire,* page 11.

SVK3633
SLOVAK CHILDREN'S FUND

Z padn 2, 821 02 Bratislava, Slovakia.

SVK3634
SLOVAK COMMITTEE FOR UNICEF

Grösslingova 6, P.O. Box 52, 810 00 Bratislava, Slovakia.

Telephone: 42 (7) 36 50 82. *Fax:* 42 (7) 36 50 84. *Contact:* Blazej Slaby.

OBJECTIVES: To improve the social status of women and children. To prevent the deterioration of the health care and education systems.

GENERAL INFORMATION: *Creation:* 1993. *Member organisations:* 4. *Personnel/Total:* 17. *Salaried:* 6. *Volunteers:* 11. *Budget/Total 1993:* ECU 40000 (US$ 51000). *Financial sources: Private:* 5%. *Public:* 20%. *Self-financing:* 75%.

PUBLICATIONS: *Periodicals:* Introduction "Up Date" (4).

EVALUATION/RESEARCH: Evaluation reports available.

INFORMATION AND EDUCATION ACTIVITIES: Topics: Children/youth/family; Culture/tradition/religion; Ecology/environment/biodiversity; Education/training/literacy; Emergency relief/refugees/humanitarian assistance; Food/famine; Gender issues/women; Human rights/peace/conflicts; International relations/cooperation/development aid; Peace/ethnic conflicts/armament/disarmament; Population/family planning/demography; Poverty/living conditions; Racism/xenophobia/antisemitism. **Activities:** Broadcasting/cultural events; Conferences/seminars/workshops/training activities; Formal education; Fund raising; Information campaigns/exhibitions; Lobbying/advocacy.

SVK3635
SLOVAK HELSINKI COMMITTE

Zabotova 2, 814 04 Bratislava, Slovakia.

SVK3636
SLOVAK UNION FOR PEACE AND HUMAN RIGHTS

Stefanikova 8, 811 05 Bratislava, Slovakia.

SVK3637
SLOVAK UNION OF NATURE AND LANDSCAPE PROTECTORS (SZOPK)

Gorkého 6, 811 01 Bratislava, Slovakia.

Telephone: 42 (7) 506 65. *Fax:* 42 (7) 506 65. *Contact:* Elena Vartikova, International Contacts.

SVK3638
SLOVENSKA ADADEMICKA INFORMACNA AGENTURA (SAIA) ♦ Slovak Academic Information Agency

Hviezdoslavovo nam. 14, PO Box 108, 810 00 Bratislava, Slovakia.

Telephone: 42 (7) 33 37 62. *Fax:* 42 (7) 33 21 92. *Contact:* David Paul Daniel, Director.

OBJECTIVES: To advice and provide information about study opportunities. To provide foreign assistance and service programmes for Third Sector Organisations.

GENERAL INFORMATION: *Creation:* 1992. *Type of organisation:* coordinating body. *Personnel/Total:* 20. *Salaried:* 17. *Volunteers:* 3. *Budget/Total 1993:* ECU 281000 (US$ 364000). *Financial sources: Private:* 37%. *Public:* 23%. *Self-financing:* 40%.

PUBLICATIONS: *Periodicals:* Bulletin SAIA (11) - Nonprofit (12). *Annual report. List of publications.*

EVALUATION/RESEARCH: Evaluation reports available. Undertakes research activities.

COMMENTS: Undertakes activities in the Commonwealth of Independent States. Information activities related to the Commonwealth of Independent States.

INFORMATION AND EDUCATION ACTIVITIES: Topics: Education/training/literacy; Human rights/peace/conflicts; International relations/cooperation/development aid; Other. **Activities:** Broadcasting/cultural events; Conferences/seminars/workshops/training activities; Exchanges/twinning/linking; Formal education; Fund raising; Information and documentation services/data bases; Information campaigns/exhibitions; Lobbying/advocacy; Networking/electronic telecommunications; Publishing/audiovisual materials/educational materials.

SVK3639
STEFANKA STUDENTSKA NADACIA A ♦ Student Foundation A

Safarikova nam. 6, 811 02 Bratislava, Slovakia.

SVK3640
STROM ZIVOTA ♦ Tree of Life

Prazská 11, 816 36 Bratislava, Slovakia.

Telephone: 42 (7) 49 87 03. *Fax:* 42 (7) 49 87 03. *Contact:* Oto Makys, Chairman.

OBJECTIVES: To promote environmental education and the saving of cultural heritage.

GENERAL INFORMATION: *Creation:* 1979. *Affiliated to:* Youth Council of Slovakia (Slovakia) - Global Network of Environmental Education Centers. *Personnel/Total:* 625. *Salaried:* 25. *Volunteers:* 600. *Financial sources: Private:* 30%. *Public:* 60%. *Self-financing:* 10%.

PUBLICATIONS: *Periodicals:* STROM (4). *Annual report. List of publications.*

EVALUATION/RESEARCH: Evaluation reports available.

COMMENTS: Undertakes activities in the Commonwealth of Independent States. Information activities related to the Commonwealth of Independent States.

INFORMATION AND EDUCATION ACTIVITIES: Topics: Children/youth/family; Culture/tradition/religion; Education/training/literacy; International relations/cooperation/development aid. **Activities:** Broadcasting/cultural events; Conferences/seminars/workshops/training activities; Exchanges/twinning/linking; Formal education; Fund raising; Information campaigns/exhibitions; Lobbying/advocacy; Networking/electronic telecommunications; Publishing/audiovisual materials/educational materials.

SVK3641
TREE OF LIFE CLUBS ASSOCIATION (ZKSZ)

Hronska 30, 976 13 Slovenska' Lupca, Slovakia.

Telephone: 42 (7) 72 55 50. *Fax:* 42 (7) 49 33 01. *Contact:* Jana Slobodova, International Relations.

SVK3642
UNION OF PROTECTION OF INTEREST OF HUNGARIAN YOUTH

Bucinova 6 VI/54, 821 07 Bratislava, Slovakia.

SVK3643
UNION OF YOUNG SLOVAK CULTURE

Dunajska 35, 811 08 Bratislava, Slovakia.

SVK3644
YOUNG PIONEERS

Children Org. Pionier, Prazska 11, 811 04 Bratislava, Slovakia.

SVK3645
ZELENA NADEJ ♦ Green Hope Foundation

Levocska 5, 080 01 Presov, Slovakia.

SWE3646

ADOPTIONSCENTRUM (AC) ♦ Adoption Centre, Swedish Society for International Child Welfare

Smidesvägen 1, Box 1520, 172 29 Sundbyberg, Sweden.

Telephone: 46 (8) 627 44 00. *Fax:* 46 (8) 29 69 28. *Contact:* Elisabet Sandberg, Director.

OBJECTIVES: To promote adoption. To prevent children from being abandoned. To support and protect abandoned children.

GENERAL INFORMATION: *Creation:* 1969. *Affiliated to:* Euroadopt - The committee for the Nordic authorized adoption organisations. *Personnel/Total:* 665. *Salaried:* 65 of which: 25 in developing countries. *Volunteers:* 600. *Budget/Total 1993:* ECU 3511000 (US$ 4111000). *Financial sources: Public:* 3%. *Self-financing:* 97%.

PUBLICATIONS: *Periodicals:* Att Adoptera (6) - Newsletter (2). *Annual report.*

PLANNED ACTIVITIES: Providing services to teenage and adult adoptees and a new development programme to implement the UN convention on the Rights of the Child.

COMMENTS: Undertakes activities in the Commonwealth of Independent States. Information activities related to the Commonwealth of Independent States.

ACTIVITIES IN DEVELOPING REGIONS: Present in developing regions. Active in 22 country(ies). Maintains local field presence. Works through local field partners. **Sustainable Development Actions:** Children/youth/family. **Regions:** Central Asia and South Asia; East Asia; Middle East; North Africa; South America; West Africa.

INFORMATION AND EDUCATION ACTIVITIES: Topics: Children/youth/family. **Activities:** Conferences/seminars/workshops/training activities; Fund raising.

SWE3647

AFRIKA IMPORT/TANZANIA IMPORT EKONOMISK FORENING

Box 211, Matrosg. 6, 613 10 Oxelösund, Sweden.

Telephone: 46 (155) 36 020. *Fax:* 46 (155) 37 525.

SWE3648

AFRIKAGRUPPERNA ♦ Africa Groups of Sweden

Barnängsgatan 23, 116 41 Stockholm, Sweden.

Telephone: 46 (8) 644 04 25. *Fax:* 46 (8) 640 36 60. *Contact:* Sören Lindh, Chairman of the Board.

OBJECTIVES: To support national reconstruction and development towards genuine independence and self-determination in independent countries in Southern Africa and in Cape Verde. To establish closer relations with the peoples of these countries and to exchange information and experience in order to improve and broaden solidarity work in Sweden.

GENERAL INFORMATION: *Creation:* 1992. *Affiliated to:* Practical Solidarity (Sweden) - Swedish Voluntary Service (Sweden) - BIFO (Sweden). *Personnel/Total:* 86. *Salaried:* 86 of which: 65 in developing countries. *Budget/Total 1993:* ECU 6583000 (US$ 7709000). *Financial sources: Private:* 5%. *Public:* 90%. *Self-financing:* 5%.

PUBLICATIONS: *Periodicals:* Södra Afrika (11). *Annual report. List of publications.*

EVALUATION/RESEARCH: Evaluation reports available.

PLANNED ACTIVITIES: A campaign on debt and development.

ACTIVITIES IN DEVELOPING REGIONS: Present in developing regions. Active in 6 country(ies). Maintains local field presence. Works through local field partners. **Sustainable Development Actions:** Children/youth/family; Democracy/good governance/institution building/participatory development; Ecology/environment/biodiversity; Education/training/literacy; Emergency relief/refugees/humanitarian assistance; Gender issues/women; Health/sanitation/water; Human rights/peace/conflicts; Rural development/agriculture; Sending volunteers/experts/

technical assistance; Small enterprises/informal sector/handicrafts; Urban development/habitat. **Regions:** Southern Africa; West Africa.

INFORMATION AND EDUCATION ACTIVITIES: Topics: Children/youth/family; Culture/tradition/religion; Ecology/environment/biodiversity; Education/training/literacy; Emergency relief/refugees/humanitarian assistance; Gender issues/women; Health/sanitation/water; Human rights/peace/conflicts; International economic relations/trade/debt/finance; International relations/cooperation/development aid; Peace/ethnic conflicts/armament/disarmament; Poverty/living conditions; Racism/xenophobia/antisemitism; Refugees/migrants/ethnic groups; Rural development/agriculture; Urban development/habitat. **Activities:** Broadcasting/cultural events; Conferences/seminars/workshops/training activities; Exchanges/twinning/linking; Formal education; Fund raising; Information and documentation services/data bases; Information campaigns/exhibitions; Lobbying/advocacy; Networking/electronic telecommunications; Other; Publishing/audiovisual materials/educational materials.

SWE3649

AFS INTERKULTURELL UTBILDNING (AFSIU) ♦ AFS Intercultural Programs - AFS Associated Field Service

Timmermansgatan 8, Box 17517, 118 91 Stockholm, Sweden.

Telephone: 46 (8) 668 89 56. *Fax:* 46 (8) 668 40 18. *Contact:* Bettan Carlsson, Chairperson.

SWE3650

ALTERNATIV HANDEL ♦ Alternative Trading

Linnégatan 13-21, 413 04 Göteborg, Sweden.

Telephone: 46 (31) 12 97 21. *Fax:* 46 (31) 14 90 75. *Contact:* Dag Fredriksson.

OBJECTIVES: To act as an alternative trading organisation, fostering trade with producers in Third World countries in order to show that fair trade between North and South is possible, and can lead to development.

GENERAL INFORMATION: *Creation:* 1968. *Affiliated to:* International Federation for Alternative Trade (USA) - Swedish World Shop Association (Sweden). *Personnel/Total:* 39. *Salaried:* 4. *Volunteers:* 35. *Budget/Total 1993:* ECU 329000 (US$ 385000). *Financial sources: Public:* 5%. *Self-financing:* 95%.

PUBLICATIONS: *Periodicals:* Alternativ Handel-nyheter (4). *List of publications.*

ACTIVITIES IN DEVELOPING REGIONS: Active in 10 country(ies). Works through local field partners. **Sustainable Development Actions:** Ecology/environment/biodiversity; Gender issues/women; Rural development/agriculture; Small enterprises/informal sector/handicrafts. **Regions:** Central Asia and South Asia; East Africa; Mexico and Central America; Middle East; South America; South East Asia; Southern Africa.

INFORMATION AND EDUCATION ACTIVITIES: Topics: Other; Rural development/agriculture. **Activities:** Conferences/seminars/workshops/training activities; Information campaigns/exhibitions; Lobbying/advocacy; Networking/electronic telecommunications; Publishing/audiovisual materials/educational materials.

SWE3651

AMAZONAS-STIFTELSEN (AMAZSWED) ♦ Amazonico Foundation

Box 71, 643 00 Vingåker, Sweden.

Telephone: 46 (151) 122 23.

SWE3652

AMAZONASFORENINGEN ♦ Amazonas Association

Box 200, 435 38 Mölnlycke, Sweden.

Telephone: 46 (31) 12 29 09. *Fax:* 46 (31) 12 29 09. *Contact:* Ulrika Eriksson, President.

SWE3653

ANTROPOSOFISKA SALLSKAPET ♦ The Anthroposophical Society

c/o Arbetsgruppen för landsbygdsutveckling, Pipblåsarg. 28, 412 71 Göteborg, Sweden.

Telephone: 46 (31) 40 81 72. *Fax:* 46 (31) 40 58 77. *Contact:* Håkan Blomberg.

OBJECTIVES: To convert agricultural practices from industrial or slash and burn techniques to biodynamic, self-sufficient methods. To create 'cultural islands' around the new agriculture with an emphasis on health, education and small business activities.

GENERAL INFORMATION: *Creation:* 1913. *Personnel/Total:* 11. *Salaried:* 4. *Volunteers:* 7 of which: 6 in developing countries. *Budget/ Total 1993:* ECU 241000 (US$ 283000). *Financial sources: Private:* 45%. *Public:* 50%. *Self-financing:* 5%.

PUBLICATIONS: *Periodicals:* Aktuellt (4). *Annual report.*

EVALUATION/RESEARCH: Evaluation reports available. Undertakes research activities.

COMMENTS: Undertakes activities in the Commonwealth of Independent States. Information activities related to the Commonwealth of Independent States.

ACTIVITIES IN DEVELOPING REGIONS: Present in developing regions. Active in 4 country(ies). Maintains local field presence. Works through local field partners. **Sustainable Development Actions:** Children/ youth/family; Debt/finance/trade; Ecology/environment/biodiversity; Education/training/literacy; Gender issues/women; Health/sanitation/water; Rural development/agriculture; Sending volunteers/experts/technical assistance; Small enterprises/informal sector/handicrafts. **Regions:** Caribbean; Mexico and Central America.

INFORMATION AND EDUCATION ACTIVITIES: Topics: Ecology/environment/biodiversity; Education/training/literacy; Health/sanitation/ water; Rural development/agriculture. **Activities:** Formal education; Fund raising.

SWE3654

BALSTA JORDVANNER ♦ Friends of the Earth - Bålsta

Norra Villavägen 7, 198 00 Bålsta, Sweden.

Telephone: 46 (171) 56 296. *Contact:* Monica Bjurström.

SWE3655

BARNENS REGNSKOG ♦ The Children's Rainforest of Sweden

c/o Kern, P2 4471 Hagadal, 137 94 Västerhaninge, Sweden.

Telephone: 46 (8) 530 231 73. *Fax:* 46 (8) 530 231 73. *Contact:* Eha and Bernd Kern.

OBJECTIVES: To preserve rainforests and raise awareness of the importance of nature conservation.

GENERAL INFORMATION: *Creation:* 1987. *Affiliated to:* International Children's Rainforest Network. *Personnel/Total:* 1. *Salaried:* 1. *Budget/Total 1993:* ECU 280000 (US$ 328000). *Financial sources: Private:* 82%. *Public:* 8%. *Self-financing:* 10%.

PUBLICATIONS: *Periodicals:* Frogchirps (6). *Annual report. List of publications.*

EVALUATION/RESEARCH: Evaluation reports available.

ACTIVITIES IN DEVELOPING REGIONS: Present in developing regions. Active in 3 country(ies). Works through local field partners. **Sustainable Development Actions:** Ecology/environment/biodiversity; Education/ training/literacy; Rural development/agriculture. **Regions:** Mexico and Central America; South America.

INFORMATION AND EDUCATION ACTIVITIES: Topics: Ecology/environment/biodiversity; Education/training/literacy; Rural development/ agriculture. **Activities:** Formal education; Fund raising; Information and documentation services/data bases; Information campaigns/exhibitions; Lobbying/advocacy; Networking/electronic telecommunications; Publishing/audiovisual materials/educational materials.

SWE3656

BARNFONDEN INSAMLINGSSTIFTELSE   (BARNfonden) ♦ Children's Fund

Box 4100, 203 12 Malmö, Sweden.

Telephone: 46 (40) 12 18 85. *Fax:* 46 (40) 97 24 04. *Contact:* Margareta Westergård, Secretary General.

OBJECTIVES: To mediate personal sponsorship of children and their families in developing countries. To provide the children with schooling, health care, medical treatment and a balanced diet. To offer the parents education and assistacne in starting income generating activities to become self-sufficient in the long term.

GENERAL INFORMATION: *Creation:* 1990. *Type of organisation:* association of NGOs. *Affiliated to:* World Alliance of Christian Children's Fund. *Personnel/Total:* 5. *Salaried:* 4. *Volunteers:* 1. *Budget/Total 1993:* ECU 892000 (US$ 1045000). *Financial sources: Private:* 100%.

PUBLICATIONS: *Periodicals:* BARNfonden (4) - Fadderhälswingar (1). *Annual report.*

COMMENTS: BARNfonden is not involved directly in activities in developing countries. It transfers funds to support the work of BORNEfonder in Denmark and Christian Children's Fund in the US.

ACTIVITIES IN DEVELOPING REGIONS: Active in 24 country(ies). **Sustainable Development Actions:** Children/youth/family; Ecology/environment/biodiversity; Education/training/literacy; Food/famine; Health/ sanitation/water; Population/family planning/demography; Rural development/agriculture; Small enterprises/informal sector/handicrafts. **Regions:** Caribbean; Central Africa; Central Asia and South Asia; East Africa; Mexico and Central America; South America; South East Asia; Southern Africa; West Africa.

SWE3657

BHARATBISTAND ♦ Bharat Aid

S:a Pitholms väg 31, 941 43 Piteå, Sweden.

Contact: Claes-Åke Carlsson.

SWE3658

BIFO, FORENINGEN BISTAND OCH INFORMATION GENOM FRIVILLIGA ORGANISATIONER ♦ BIFO, NGO Information Centre

Hornsgatan 54, 118 21 Stockholm, Sweden.

Telephone: 46 (8) 702 77 00. *Fax:* 46 (8) 642 70 77.

OBJECTIVES: To encourage and to work as a gathering point for the exchange of experiences and information between organisations on questions relating to aid and development co-operation. To assist and represent member NGOs and to act as a forum for non-member NGOs.

GENERAL INFORMATION: *Creation:* 1972. *Type of organisation:* coordinating body. *Member organisations:* 60. *Personnel/Total:* 11. *Salaried:* 11. *Budget/Total 1993:* ECU 812000 (US$ 951000). *Financial sources: Private:* 5%. *Public:* 95%.

PUBLICATIONS: *Annual report. List of publications.*

EVALUATION/RESEARCH: Evaluation reports available.

COMMENTS: In July 1995 BIFO joined with SVS to form a new NGO, Forum South.

INFORMATION AND EDUCATION ACTIVITIES: Topics: Children/youth/ family; Culture/tradition/religion; Ecology/environment/biodiversity; Education/training/literacy; Emergency relief/refugees/humanitarian assistance; Employment/unemployment; Food/famine; Gender issues/ women; Health/sanitation/water; Human rights/peace/conflicts; International economic relations/trade/debt/finance; International relations/ cooperation/development aid; Peace/ethnic conflicts/armament/disarmament; Population/family planning/demography; Poverty/living conditions; Racism/xenophobia/antisemitism; Refugees/migrants/ethnic groups; Rural development/agriculture; Urban development/habitat. **Activities:** Conferences/seminars/workshops/training activities; Exchanges/twinning/linking; Formal education; Information and documentation services/data bases; Lobbying/advocacy.

SWE3659

BISTANDSFORUM ♦ Forum for Development

Box 89, 668 00 Ed, Sweden.

Telephone: 46 (534) 11 807. *Contact:* Leif Thybell.

SWE3660

BLABANDSRORELSEN ♦ The Swedish Blue Ribbon Movement

Köpmangatan 3, 702 10 Örebro, Sweden.

Telephone: 46 (19) 13 05 75. *Fax:* 46 (19) 12 11 36. *Contact:* Gun-Britt Karlsson.

SWE3661

BLLF SWEDEN - FRONT MOT LIVEGENSKAP OCH SLAVERI (BLLF SWEDEN) ♦ Bonded Labour Liberation Front-Sweden

Lindmätarv. 53, 141 37 Huddinge, Sweden.

Telephone: 46 (8) 711 65 34. *Fax:* 46 (8) 711 65 04. *Contact:* Anna-Karin Wilmenius.

OBJECTIVES: To work for the abolition of bondage through information, networking, advocacy and financial support to NGOs in developing countries.

GENERAL INFORMATION: *Creation:* 1991. *Affiliated to:* Anti-Slavery International (United Kingdom). *Personnel/Total:* 2. *Volunteers:* 2 of which: 1 in developing countries. *Budget/Total 1993:* ECU 4800 (US$ 5700). *Financial sources:* Private: 70%. Self-financing: 30%.

PUBLICATIONS: *Periodicals:* BLLF Nyhetsbrev (4). *Annual report.*

PLANNED ACTIVITIES: A campaign against child labour and bonded child labour especially in handknotted carpets.

ACTIVITIES IN DEVELOPING REGIONS: Active in 3 country(ies). Maintains local field presence. Works through local field partners. **Sustainable Development Actions:** Children/youth/family; Democracy/good governance/institution building/participatory development; Education/training/literacy; Gender issues/women; Human rights/peace/conflicts; Other. **Regions:** Central Asia and South Asia.

INFORMATION AND EDUCATION ACTIVITIES: Topics: Children/youth/family; Education/training/literacy; Gender issues/women; Human rights/peace/conflicts; Other; Poverty/living conditions. **Activities:** Formal education; Fund raising; Information campaigns/exhibitions; Lobbying/advocacy.

SWE3662

BOLIVIA-GRUPPEN - U-GRUPPEN ♦ Bolivia Group

Linnégatan 13-21, 413 04 Göteborg, Sweden.

Telephone: 46 (31) 24 94 58. *Contact:* Astrid Möller.

SWE3663

BOTILDA-UNIFEM SVERIGE ♦ Botilda-Unifem Sweden

Box 2158, 103 14 Stockholm, Sweden.

Contact: Ulla Jonsdotter.

SWE3664

BRODET & FISKARNA ♦ Bread and Fish

Brandthovdagatan 14 , 723 50 Västerås, Sweden.

Telephone: 46 (21) 11 40 07. *Contact:* Mats Brenner, President.

OBJECTIVES: To support liberation movements in South Africa, Namibia, El Salvador and Eritrea as well as democratic processes in Angola, Mozambique and Nicaragua.

GENERAL INFORMATION: *Creation:* 1972. *Type of organisation:* network. *Member organisations:* 6. *Personnel/Total:* 35. Salaried: 15. *Volunteers:* 20. *Budget/Total 1993:* ECU 1097000 (US$ 1285000). *Financial sources:* Public: 60%. Self-financing: 40%.

PUBLICATIONS: *Annual report.*

EVALUATION/RESEARCH: Evaluation reports available.

ACTIVITIES IN DEVELOPING REGIONS: Present in developing regions. Maintains local field presence. Works through local field partners. **Sus-**

tainable Development Actions: Emergency relief/refugees/humanitarian assistance; Gender issues/women; Human rights/peace/conflicts; Rural development/agriculture. **Regions:** Mexico and Central America; North Africa; Southern Africa.

INFORMATION AND EDUCATION ACTIVITIES: Topics: Emergency relief/refugees/humanitarian assistance; Gender issues/women; Human rights/peace/conflicts; International economic relations/trade/debt/finance; International relations/cooperation/development aid. **Activities:** Conferences/seminars/workshops/training activities; Information campaigns/exhibitions.

SWE3665

BYSKOGSINSAMLINGEN ♦ Village Forestry Funds

Solängsvägen 63, 191 54 Sollentuna, Sweden.

Telephone: 46 (8) 754 38 07. *Fax:* 46 (8) 754 56 99. *E-mail:* Hans.Johansson@ncr.se. *Contact:* Hans Johansson.

OBJECTIVES: To support village forestation projects in Tanzania, in collaboration with the Tanzania Association of Foresters.

GENERAL INFORMATION: *Creation:* 1983. *Personnel/Total:* 1. *Volunteers:* 1 of which: 1 in developing countries. *Budget/Total 1993:* ECU 22000 (US$ 26000). *Financial sources:* Private: 100%.

PUBLICATIONS: *Annual report.*

ACTIVITIES IN DEVELOPING REGIONS: Active in 1 country(ies). Works through local field partners. **Sustainable Development Actions:** Rural development/agriculture. **Regions:** East Africa.

INFORMATION AND EDUCATION ACTIVITIES: Topics: Rural development/agriculture. **Activities:** Fund raising.

SWE3666

CARITAS SVERIGE ♦ CARITAS Sweden

Box 4098, 102 62 Stockholm, Sweden.

Telephone: 46 (8) 21 55 35. *Fax:* 46 (8) 21 55 85. *Contact:* Bishop William Kenney, President.

OBJECTIVES: To awaken interest in aid and development work. To support development initiatives in developing countries. To co-ordinate the international aid within the Catholic diocese. To carry out charitable work in Sweden.

GENERAL INFORMATION: *Creation:* 1946. *Type of organisation:* network, coordinating body. *Member organisations:* 73. *Affiliated to:* Caritas Internationalis (Vatican State) - SVS (Sweden) - Swedish Christian Council (Sweden) - Swedish Mission Council (Sweden) - Swedish Council for Refugees (Sweden). *Personnel/Total:* 17. Salaried: 13. *Volunteers:* 4 of which: 2 in developing countries. *Budget/Total 1993:* ECU 5595000 (US$ 6552000). *Financial sources:* Private: 11%. Public: 88%. Self-financing: 1%.

PUBLICATIONS: *Periodicals:* CARITAS-NYTT (6) - Baltic Report (2) - Liberia Report (4). *Annual report.*

COMMENTS: Undertakes activities in the Commonwealth of Independent States. Information activities related to the Commonwealth of Independent States.

ACTIVITIES IN DEVELOPING REGIONS: Present in developing regions. Active in 26 country(ies). Works through local field partners. **Sustainable Development Actions:** Children/youth/family; Education/training/literacy; Emergency relief/refugees/humanitarian assistance; Gender issues/women; Health/sanitation/water; Human rights/peace/conflicts; Rural development/agriculture; Sending volunteers/experts/technical assistance; Small enterprises/informal sector/handicrafts; Urban development/habitat. **Regions:** Central Asia and South Asia; East Africa; Mexico and Central America; Middle East; South America; Southern Africa; West Africa.

INFORMATION AND EDUCATION ACTIVITIES: Topics: Children/youth/family; Gender issues/women; Health/sanitation/water; International relations/cooperation/development aid; Poverty/living conditions. **Activities:** Conferences/seminars/workshops/training activities; Other.

Voir : *Comment utiliser le répertoire,* page 11.

SWE3667

CENTERKVINNORNA (CKF) ♦ The Centerwomen

Box 22039, 104 22 Stockholm, Sweden.

Telephone: 46 (8) 617 38 00. *Fax:* 46 (8) 654 25 90. *Contact:* Karin Starrin, President.

OBJECTIVES: To offer education/training which increases womens knowledge and interests in questions concerning society. To work actively for equality between women and men.

GENERAL INFORMATION: *Creation:* 1933. *Salaried:* 9. *Budget/ Total 1993:* ECU 549000 (US$ 642000). *Financial sources:* Private: 14%. Public: 54%. Self-financing: 32%.

PUBLICATIONS: *Periodicals:* Nya Budkavle (6) - Focus (12). *Annual report.*

COMMENTS: Undertakes activities in the Commonwealth of Independent States. Information activities related to the Commonwealth of Independent States.

ACTIVITIES IN DEVELOPING REGIONS: Active in 3 country(ies). Works through local field partners. **Sustainable Development Actions:** Health/sanitation/water; Small enterprises/informal sector/handicrafts. **Regions:** Central Africa; North Africa; South America.

INFORMATION AND EDUCATION ACTIVITIES: Topics: Ecology/environment/biodiversity; Gender issues/women; Health/sanitation/water; Human rights/peace/conflicts; Peace/ethnic conflicts/armament/disarmament. **Activities:** Conferences/seminars/workshops/training activities; Exchanges/twinning/linking; Fund raising; Information and documentation services/data bases; Information campaigns/exhibitions; Lobbying/advocacy; Publishing/audiovisual materials/educational materials.

SWE3668

CENTRUM FOR KOOPERATIVA STUDIER OCH VERKSAMHET "COMUNIDAD" ♦ Centre for Cooperative Studies and Activities "Comunidad"

Tjärhovsgatan 44, Box 151 28, 104 65 Stockholm, Sweden.

Telephone: 46 (8) 714 78 58. *Fax:* 46 (8) 644 59 85. *Contact:* Silvia Ribeiro, Member of the Board.

SWE3669

COLOMBIA VIVE

Box 13018, 580 13 Linköping, Sweden.

Telephone: 46 (42) 59 245. *Contact:* Karina Avila.

SWE3670

COOPERATION FOR PEACE

Fjällgatan 23, Stockholm, Sweden.

Telephone: 46 (8) 640 14 41. *Fax:* 46 (8) 642 25 21.

SWE3671

DAG HAMMARSKJOLD FOUNDATION

Övre Slottsgatan 2, 753 10 Uppsala, Sweden.

Telephone: 46 (18) 12 88 72. *Fax:* 46 (18) 12 20 72. *Contact:* Olle Nordberg, Executive Director.

OBJECTIVES: To organise seminars, conferences and courses on the political, social, economic, legal and cultural issues facing the Third World.

GENERAL INFORMATION: *Creation:* 1962. *Personnel/Total:* 5. *Salaried:* 5.

PUBLICATIONS: *Periodicals:* Development Dialogue (2). *List of publications.*

INFORMATION AND EDUCATION ACTIVITIES: Topics: Ecology/environment/biodiversity; Health/sanitation/water. **Activities:** Conferences/seminars/workshops/training activities.

SWE3672

DALANGSSKOLANS TANZANIAGRUPP ♦ The Tanzanian Group of Dalängsskolan

Dalängsskolan, 531 53 Lidköping, Sweden.

Telephone: 46 (510) 83 600. *Fax:* 46 (510) 26 181. *Contact:* Inghar Främberg.

OBJECTIVES: To support a secondary school in Nzezu, Tanzania.

GENERAL INFORMATION: *Creation:* 1982. *Budget/Total 1993:* ECU 11000 (US$ 13000). *Financial sources:* Public: 80%. Self-financing: 20%.

PLANNED ACTIVITIES: A water-drilling project for fresh water for a sister secondary school and the surrounding villages.

ACTIVITIES IN DEVELOPING REGIONS: Present in developing regions. Active in 1 country(ies). Works through local field partners. **Sustainable Development Actions:** Education/training/literacy; Rural development/ agriculture. **Regions:** East Africa.

INFORMATION AND EDUCATION ACTIVITIES: Topics: Education/training/literacy. **Activities:** Exchanges/twinning/linking.

SWE3673

DALARNAS FORSKNINGSROD

Svärdsjögatan 19, 791 31 Falun, Sweden.

Telephone: N6 (23) 86 296. *Fax:* 46 (23) 86 398.

SWE3674

DIAKONIA

P.O.Box 1774, 111 87 Stockholm, Sweden.

Telephone: 46 (8) 453 69 00. *Fax:* 46 (8) 453 69 29. *E-mail:* DIAKONIA@MM.apc.org. *Contact:* Bo Forsberg, Director.

OBJECTIVES: To act on behalf of the Swedish free churches, together with other Christians, for united efforts for and with people in need, above all in developing countries. To support projects which contribute to the development of more just and humanitarian conditions of life.

GENERAL INFORMATION: *Creation:* 1966. *Affiliated to:* International Council of Voluntary Agencies (Switzerland) - APRODEV (Belgium). *Personnel/Total:* 50. *Salaried:* 50 of which: 30 in developing countries. *Budget/Total 1993:* ECU 23039000 (US$ 26980000). *Financial sources:* Private: 10%. Public: 90%.

PUBLICATIONS: *Periodicals:* Dela Med (6). *Annual report. List of publications.*

EVALUATION/RESEARCH: Evaluation reports available.

ACTIVITIES IN DEVELOPING REGIONS: Active in 48 country(ies). Maintains local field presence. Works through local field partners. **Sustainable Development Actions:** Children/youth/family; Democracy/good governance/institution building/participatory development; Education/ training/literacy; Emergency relief/refugees/humanitarian assistance; Food/famine; Gender issues/women; Health/sanitation/water; Human rights/peace/conflicts; Rural development/agriculture; Small enterprises/ informal sector/handicrafts; Urban development/habitat. **Regions:** Central Africa; Central Asia and South Asia; East Africa; Mexico and Central America; Middle East; South America; South East Asia; Southern Africa; West Africa.

INFORMATION AND EDUCATION ACTIVITIES: Topics: Children/youth/ family; Emergency relief/refugees/humanitarian assistance; Gender issues/women; Health/sanitation/water; Human rights/peace/conflicts; Peace/ethnic conflicts/armament/disarmament; Refugees/migrants/ethnic groups; Rural development/agriculture. **Activities:** Conferences/ seminars/workshops/training activities; Fund raising; Lobbying/ advocacy.

SWE3675

DOVAS AFRIKA MISSION (DAM) ♦ Deaf Africa Mission

c/o Godvig, Soderv 46V, 183 64 Taby, Sweden.

Telephone: 46 (8) 756 09 05. *Fax:* 46 (8) 756 09 05. *Contact:* Hans Godvig, Chairman.

See: *How to Use the Directory,* page 11.

OBJECTIVES: To support school and other institutions for deaf people in Eritrea, Ethiopia, Tanzania and other African countries. To establish links with organisations in Sweden, Finalnd and Germany that share the objective of helping organisations assisting the deaf in Africa.

GENERAL INFORMATION: *Creation:* 1951. *Affiliated to:* Kuurojen Lähetys Åbo (Finland) - Deutsche Arbeitsgemeinschaft für Ev. Gehörlosenseelsorger (Germany). *Personnel/Total:* 2. *Salaried:* 2 of which: 2 in developing countries. *Budget/Total 1993:* ECU 69000 (US$ 81000). *Financial sources:* Private: 25%. Public: 75%.

PUBLICATIONS: *Annual report.*

PLANNED ACTIVITIES: Vocational training in schools in Eritrea and Tanzania.

ACTIVITIES IN DEVELOPING REGIONS: Active in 3 country(ies). Works through local field partners. **Sustainable Development Actions:** Education/training/literacy; Sending volunteers/experts/technical assistance. **Regions:** East Africa.

INFORMATION AND EDUCATION ACTIVITIES: Topics: Education/training/literacy. **Activities:** Conferences/seminars/workshops/training activities; Formal education.

SWE3676

EMMAUS STOCKHOLM ♦ Emmaüs Stockholm

Vretensborgv. 6, 126 30 Hägersten, Sweden.

Telephone: 46 (8) 744 20 01. *Fax:* 46 (8) 744 98 10.

OBJECTIVES: To collect and donate materials to various liberations movements and progressive countries in the Third World.

GENERAL INFORMATION: *Creation:* 1970. *Affiliated to:* Emmaus International (France) - Praktisk Solidaritet (Sweden) - South Africa Committee (Sweden).

PUBLICATIONS: *Annual report.*

EVALUATION/RESEARCH: Evaluation reports available.

ACTIVITIES IN DEVELOPING REGIONS: Active in 8 country(ies). Works through local field partners. **Sustainable Development Actions:** Emergency relief/refugees/humanitarian assistance; Other; Rural development/agriculture; Small enterprises/informal sector/handicrafts; Urban development/habitat. **Regions:** Mexico and Central America; Middle East; North Africa; South East Asia; Southern Africa.

SWE3677

EMMAUS SUNDSVALL ♦ Sundsvall Emmaüs Association

Enhörningsv. 26, 854 62 Sundsvall, Sweden.

Telephone: 46 (60) 11 82 20. *Fax:* 46 (60) 11 39 20.

SWE3678

ERIKSHJALPEN ♦ Uncle Erik's Relief Organisation

570 15 Holsbybrunn, Sweden.

Telephone: 46 (38) 35 04 00. *Fax:* 46 (38) 35 06 56. *Contact:* Bernt Einarsson.

SWE3679

EVANGELISKA FOSTERLANDS-STIFTELSEN (EFS) ♦ Swedish Evangelical Mission (SEM)

von Bahrs Väg 3, Box 23045, 750 23 Uppsala, Sweden.

Telephone: 46 (18) 16 98 00. *Fax:* 46 (18) 25 86 75. *Contact:* Rev. Bertil Johansson.

OBJECTIVES: To minister to the whole man body, mind and spirit. To meet the needs of all people in its sphere of influence regardless of their religion or ethnic background.

GENERAL INFORMATION: *Creation:* 1856. *Personnel/Total:* 562. *Salaried:* 562 of which: 65 in developing countries. *Budget/Total 1993:* ECU 10203000 (US$ 11949000). *Financial sources:* Private: 40%. Public: 39%. Self-financing: 17%.

PUBLICATIONS: *Periodicals:* Budbäraren (45). *Annual report.*

EVALUATION/RESEARCH: Evaluation reports available. Undertakes research activities.

ACTIVITIES IN DEVELOPING REGIONS: Active in 6 country(ies). Maintains local field presence. Works through local field partners. **Sustainable Development Actions:** Children/youth/family; Ecology/environment/biodiversity; Education/training/literacy; Emergency relief/refugees/humanitarian assistance; Food/famine; Gender issues/women; Health/sanitation/water; Population/family planning/demography; Rural development/agriculture; Sending volunteers/experts/technical assistance; Urban development/habitat. **Regions:** Central Asia and South Asia; East Africa.

INFORMATION AND EDUCATION ACTIVITIES: Topics: Children/youth/family; Culture/tradition/religion; Ecology/environment/biodiversity; Education/training/literacy; Emergency relief/refugees/humanitarian assistance; Food/famine; Gender issues/women; Health/sanitation/water; Population/family planning/demography; Refugees/migrants/ethnic groups; Rural development/agriculture; Urban development/habitat. **Activities:** Conferences/seminars/workshops/training activities; Formal education; Fund raising.

SWE3680

FADDERBARNSVERKSAMHETEN I KENYA

c/o G. Jägare, Vaksalag. 47, 753 31 Uppsala, Sweden.

Telephone: 46 (18) 14 89 52.

SWE3681

FALTBIOLOGERNA ♦ The Swedish Youth Association for Nature Studies and Environmental Protection

Box 6022, 191 06 Sollentuna, Sweden.

Telephone: 46 (8) 754 46 40. *Fax:* 46 (8) 754 53 63. *Contact:* Marie-Louise Bengtsson.

SWE3682

FOODFIRST INFORMATION AND ACTION NETWORK, SVERIGE (FIAN-SVERIGE)

Box 31021, 400 32 Göteborg, Sweden.

Fax: 46 (31) 773 49 10. *Contact:* Lisa Fredriksson, Chairman.

OBJECTIVES: To support the right to food as a fundamental human right as stated in the Universal Declaration of Human Rights. To work for sustainable access to adequate food in states where hunger can be seen as a consequence of the states violation of the right to feed oneself.

GENERAL INFORMATION: *Creation:* 1990. *Affiliated to:* FIAN International. *Budget/Total 1993:* ECU 5400 (US$ 6300). *Financial sources:* Private: 2%. Public: 75%. Self-financing: 23%.

PUBLICATIONS: *Periodicals:* Membership Letter (6) - Hungry for What is Right (3).

EVALUATION/RESEARCH: Undertakes research activities.

ACTIVITIES IN DEVELOPING REGIONS: Active in 5 country(ies). Works through local field partners. **Sustainable Development Actions:** Food/famine; Human rights/peace/conflicts. **Regions:** Central Asia and South Asia; East Africa; South America; South East Asia.

INFORMATION AND EDUCATION ACTIVITIES: Topics: Food/famine; Human rights/peace/conflicts. **Activities:** Conferences/seminars/workshops/training activities; Fund raising; Information and documentation services/data bases; Information campaigns/exhibitions; Lobbying/advocacy; Publishing/audiovisual materials/educational materials.

SWE3683

FORBUNDET VI UNGA ♦ Young Folks' Association

Box 255, 151 23 Södertälje, Sweden.

Telephone: 46 (8) 550 342 90. *Fax:* 46 (8) 550 606 79.

SWE3684

FORENINGEN 6:E DECEMBER ♦ The Association 6th December

Box 2031 Björksätrav. 22, 127 02 Skärholmen, Sweden.

Voir : *Comment utiliser le répertoire,* page 11.

Contact: Oscar Montenegro.

SWE3685

FORENINGEN BADZA

c/o S-E Pettersson, Ryktareg. 2, 273 33 Tomelilla, Sweden.

Telephone: 46 (417) 12 905. *Contact:* Sven-Erik Pettersson.

OBJECTIVES: To create knowledge and understanding through studies, cultural exchange and solidarity, especially concerning farmworkers in rural Zimbabwe.

GENERAL INFORMATION: *Creation:* 1987. *Personnel/Total:* 1. *Volunteers:* 1. *Budget/Total 1993:* ECU 10000 (US$ 12000). *Financial sources:* Public: 70%. Self-financing: 30%.

PUBLICATIONS: *Periodicals:* Badzanews (4). *Annual report.*

ACTIVITIES IN DEVELOPING REGIONS: Present in developing regions. Active in 1 country(ies). Maintains local field presence. Works through local field partners. **Sustainable Development Actions:** Ecology/environment/biodiversity; Education/training/literacy; Health/sanitation/water; Rural development/agriculture. **Regions:** Southern Africa.

INFORMATION AND EDUCATION ACTIVITIES: Topics: Ecology/environment/biodiversity; Education/training/literacy; Health/sanitation/water; International relations/cooperation/development aid; Rural development/agriculture. **Activities:** Conferences/seminars/workshops/training activities; Exchanges/twinning/linking; Formal education; Fund raising; Information and documentation services/data bases; Information campaigns/exhibitions.

SWE3686

FORENINGEN CARMENCITA ♦ The Association Carmencita

Sunnanvägen 235:115, 220 70 Lund, Sweden.

Telephone: 46 (46) 35 56 42. *Contact:* Ann-Christin Ubelacker.

SWE3687

FORENINGEN COLCHAJ NAC LUUM ♦ The Cooperative Land and Freedom

Foderv. 6, 616 90 Åby, Sweden.

Telephone: 46 (11) 64 260. *Fax:* 46 (11) 64 260. *Contact:* Per Bylund.

OBJECTIVES: To support co-operatives of Guatemalan refugees living in Southern Mexico. To assist them to build up their societies through schools, medical care, agriculture, energy systems etc.

GENERAL INFORMATION: *Creation:* 1982. *Personnel/Total:* 10. *Volunteers:* 10. *Budget/Total 1993:* ECU 44000 (US$ 51000). *Financial sources:* Private: 90%. Self-financing: 10%.

PUBLICATIONS: *Periodicals:* News from the Cooperatives Land and Freedom (5).

EVALUATION/RESEARCH: Evaluation reports available.

ACTIVITIES IN DEVELOPING REGIONS: Present in developing regions. Active in 1 country(ies). **Sustainable Development Actions:** Children/youth/family; Democracy/good governance/institution building/participatory development; Ecology/environment/biodiversity; Education/training/literacy; Emergency relief/refugees/humanitarian assistance; Energy/transport; Food/famine; Gender issues/women; Health/sanitation/water; Human rights/peace/conflicts; Rural development/agriculture; Sending volunteers/experts/technical assistance; Small enterprises/informal sector/handicrafts. **Regions:** Mexico and Central America.

INFORMATION AND EDUCATION ACTIVITIES: Topics: Refugees/migrants/ethnic groups. **Activities:** Conferences/seminars/workshops/training activities; Exchanges/twinning/linking; Formal education; Fund raising; Information and documentation services/data bases; Information campaigns/exhibitions; Publishing/audiovisual materials/educational materials.

SWE3688

FORENINGEN EMMAUS BJORKA ♦ Emmaüs Björkå Association

Björkå, 360 70 Åseda, Sweden.

Telephone: 46 (481) 63 330. *Fax:* 46 (481) 63 514.

OBJECTIVES: To work in solidarity with the poor and oppressed in deeveloping countries for a more equitable distribution of wealth. To provide material assistance to democratic organisations and institutions in developing countries struggling for a better society.

GENERAL INFORMATION: *Creation:* 1965. *Affiliated to:* Emmaüs International (France). *Personnel/Total:* 72. Salaried: 66. Volunteers: 6. *Budget/Total 1993:* ECU 1975000 (US$ 2313000). *Financial sources:* Private: 1%. Public: 72%. Self-financing: 27%.

PUBLICATIONS: *Annual report.*

EVALUATION/RESEARCH: Undertakes research activities.

ACTIVITIES IN DEVELOPING REGIONS: Active in 6 country(ies). Works through local field partners. **Sustainable Development Actions:** Democracy/good governance/institution building/participatory development; Education/training/literacy; Gender issues/women; Health/sanitation/water; Rural development/agriculture; Small enterprises/informal sector/handicrafts. **Regions:** East Africa; Mexico and Central America; North Africa; Southern Africa.

SWE3689

FORENINGEN ETT FRITT PAPUA (FFP)

c/o Mats Sjögren, Korng. 4A, 212 20 Malmö, Sweden.

Telephone: 46 (40) 11 76 02. *Contact:* Mats Sjögren.

SWE3690

FORENINGEN FOLKBILDNING NORDEN LATINAMERIKA (FONOLA)

c/o Jan-Erik Perneman, Almv. 4, 459 31 Ljungskile, Sweden.

Telephone: 46 (10) 287 33 37. *Fax:* 46 (522) 221 19. *Contact:* Jan-Erik Perneman.

SWE3691

FORENINGEN FOR REHABILITERING I U-LANDER ♦ The Association for Rehabilitation in Developing Countries

c/o Christina Norén, Meijerfeldtsväg 10, 183 50 Täby, Sweden.

Telephone: 46 (8) 768 74 76. *Contact:* Christina Norén.

OBJECTIVES: To stimulate and encourage rehabilitation for people with disabilities in particular through Community-Based Rehabilitation (CBR) in developing countries.

GENERAL INFORMATION: *Creation:* 1991. *Personnel/Total:* 150. *Volunteers:* 150 of which: 10 in developing countries. *Budget/Total 1993:* ECU 1000 (US$ 1200). *Financial sources:* Public: 50%. Self-financing: 50%.

PUBLICATIONS: *Annual report. List of publications.*

COMMENTS: This organisation does not undertake any projects itself.

INFORMATION AND EDUCATION ACTIVITIES: Topics: Other. **Activities:** Conferences/seminars/workshops/training activities; Information and documentation services/data bases; Information campaigns/exhibitions; Lobbying/advocacy; Networking/electronic telecommunications.

SWE3692

FORENINGEN FOR UTVECKLINGS-JOURNALISTIK ♦ Association for Development Journalism

Box 15068, 104 65 Stockholm, Sweden.

Telephone: 46 (8) 43 11 73. *Contact:* Madi Gray.

SWE3693

FORENINGEN GATUBARN ♦ The Streetchildren Association

Vikingagatan 6, 360 51 Hovmantorp, Sweden.

Telephone: 46 (478) 41 277. *Fax:* 46 (478) 41 303. *Contact:* Maude Malmström, Chairman.

OBJECTIVES: To increase awareness of the plight of street children. To work towards the provision of basic needs for all street children.

GENERAL INFORMATION: *Creation:* 1991. *Affiliated to:* BIFO (Sweden). *Personnel/Total:* 3. Salaried: 2. Volunteers: 1 of

which: 1 in developing countries. *Budget/Total 1993:* ECU 176000 (US$ 206000). *Financial sources:* Public: 62%. *Self-financing:* 38%.

PUBLICATIONS: *Annual report.*

ACTIVITIES IN DEVELOPING REGIONS: Present in developing regions. Active in 1 country(ies). Maintains local field presence. Works through local field partners. **Sustainable Development Actions:** Children/youth/family; Democracy/good governance/institution building/participatory development; Education/training/literacy; Emergency relief/refugees/humanitarian assistance; Food/famine; Gender issues/women; Health/sanitation/water; Human rights/peace/conflicts; Population/family planning/demography; Rural development/agriculture; Sending volunteers/experts/technical assistance; Small enterprises/informal sector/handicrafts. **Regions:** South America.

INFORMATION AND EDUCATION ACTIVITIES: **Topics:** Children/youth/family; Emergency relief/refugees/humanitarian assistance; Food/famine; Gender issues/women; Health/sanitation/water; Human rights/peace/conflicts; Population/family planning/demography; Poverty/living conditions; Rural development/agriculture; Urban development/habitat. **Activities:** Information and documentation services/data bases.

SWE3694

FORENINGEN GREENPEACE - SVERIGE ♦ Greenpeace

Box 8913, 402 73 Göteborg, Sweden.

Telephone: 46 (31) 22 22 55. *Fax:* 46 (31) 23 24 29.

SWE3695

FORENINGEN INTERNATIONELLA FOLKHOGSKOLAN ♦ The Association International Folkhighschool

Box 2059, 403 11 Göteborg, Sweden.

Telephone: 46 (31) 11 82 53. *Fax:* 46 (31) 11 28 25. *Contact:* Preben Laursen, Education Manager.

OBJECTIVES: To undertake information activities on international subjects. To organise education and training activities in order to increase the understanding among peoples' cultures and religions. To carry out aid projects abroad, intended to create employment.

GENERAL INFORMATION: *Creation:* 1959. *Type of organisation:* association of NGOs. *Member organisations:* 90. *Personnel/Total:* 4. *Salaried:* 3. *Volunteers:* 1 of which: 1 in developing countries. *Budget/Total 1993:* ECU 98000 (US$ 116000). *Financial sources:* Public: 50%. *Self-financing:* 50%.

PUBLICATIONS: *Annual report.*

ACTIVITIES IN DEVELOPING REGIONS: Active in 3 country(ies). Maintains local field presence. Works through local field partners. **Sustainable Development Actions:** Children/youth/family; Education/training/literacy; Energy/transport; Food/famine; Gender issues/women; Population/family planning/demography; Rural development/agriculture; Sending volunteers/experts/technical assistance; Small enterprises/informal sector/handicrafts. **Regions:** South America; West Africa.

INFORMATION AND EDUCATION ACTIVITIES: **Topics:** Children/youth/family; Culture/tradition/religion; Ecology/environment/biodiversity; Education/training/literacy; Employment/unemployment; Food/famine; Gender issues/women; Human rights/peace/conflicts; International economic relations/trade/debt/finance; International relations/cooperation/development aid; Peace/ethnic conflicts/armament/disarmament; Population/family planning/demography; Poverty/living conditions; Racism/xenophobia/antisemitism; Refugees/migrants/ethnic groups; Rural development/agriculture. **Activities:** Conferences/seminars/workshops/training activities; Information and documentation services/data bases; Information campaigns/exhibitions; Other; Publishing/audiovisual materials/educational materials.

SWE3696

FORENINGEN SKOVDESKOLOR - KIBAHA

c/o UllaBritt Lindblom, Södra Bergv. 23, 541 31 Skövde, Sweden.

Telephone: 46 (500) 48 09 37. *Contact:* UllaBritt Lindblom.

SWE3697

FORENINGEN SVALORNA / INDIEN-BANGLADESH SEKTIONEN ♦ Swallows in Sweden / India-Bangladesh Section

Spolegatan 5, 222 20 Lund, Sweden.

Telephone: 46 (46) 12 10 05. *Contact:* Olof Sahlström, Chairman.

SWE3698

FORENINGEN SVENSKA U-LANDSVOLONTARER (UV) ♦ Swedish Volunteer Association

Box 2059, 403 11 Göteborg, Sweden.

Telephone: 46 (31) 13 86 53. *Contact:* Lars Jung.

SWE3699

FORENINGEN VASTSAHARA ♦ The Western Sahara Committee

Box 31 154, 400 32 Göteborg, Sweden.

Telephone: 46 (31) 24 72 30. *Contact:* Lena Thunberg.

OBJECTIVES: To spread information about the conflict in the Western Sahara.

GENERAL INFORMATION: *Creation:* 1978. *Type of organisation:* association of NGOs. *Member organisations:* 2. *Budget/Total 1993:* ECU 10000 (US$ 11000). *Financial sources:* Private: 10%. Public: 40%. *Self-financing:* 50%.

PUBLICATIONS: *Periodicals:* Sahara Bulletin (4). *Annual report. List of publications.*

EVALUATION/RESEARCH: Evaluation reports available.

ACTIVITIES IN DEVELOPING REGIONS: Present in developing regions. Active in 1 country(ies). Works through local field partners. **Sustainable Development Actions:** Human rights/peace/conflicts. **Regions:** North Africa.

INFORMATION AND EDUCATION ACTIVITIES: **Topics:** Human rights/peace/conflicts; International relations/cooperation/development aid; Peace/ethnic conflicts/armament/disarmament; Refugees/migrants/ethnic groups. **Activities:** Conferences/seminars/workshops/training activities; Fund raising; Information and documentation services/data bases; Information campaigns/exhibitions; Lobbying/advocacy; Publishing/audiovisual materials/educational materials.

SWE3700

FRAMTIDEN I VARA HANDER ♦ The Future in our Hands

Västmannagatan 34, 113 25 Stockholm, Sweden.

Telephone: 46 (8) 31 00 01.

SWE3701

FRAMTIDEN I VARA HANDER - GAMBIAGRUPPERNA ♦ The Future in our Hands - Gambia Groups

Smedstigen 1, 564 35 Bankeryd, Sweden.

Telephone: 46 (36) 37 74 82. *Fax:* 46 (36) 37 72 39. *Contact:* Eva Noreborg, Chairman of the Swedish Board.

OBJECTIVES: To build schools in the Gambia and to provide them with necessary supplies. To support the Gambian College by providing teacher training and education.

GENERAL INFORMATION: *Creation:* 1978. *Member organisations:* 65. *Affiliated to:* BIFO (Sweden). *Personnel/Total:* 7. *Salaried:* 4 of which: 4 in developing countries. *Volunteers:* 3 of which: 3 in developing countries. *Budget/Total 1993:* ECU 549000 (US$ 642000). *Financial sources:* Public: 80%. *Self-financing:* 20%.

PUBLICATIONS: *Annual report.*

ACTIVITIES IN DEVELOPING REGIONS: Present in developing regions. Active in 1 country(ies). Maintains local field presence. Works through local field partners. **Sustainable Development Actions:** Education/training/literacy; Gender issues/women. **Regions:** West Africa.

Voir : *Comment utiliser le répertoire,* page 11.

SWE3702

FRAMTIDSJORDEN ♦ The Future Earth

Tideliusgatan 36, 118 69 Stockholm, Sweden.

Telephone: 46 (8) 720 65 68. *Fax:* 46 (8) 720 65 81. *E-mail:* futurearth@nordnet.se. *Contact:* Ralph Monö, Coordinator.

OBJECTIVES: To develop an information network for sustainable development and to support such projects in developing countries.

GENERAL INFORMATION: *Creation:* 1988. *Member organisations:* 45. *Personnel/Total:* 10. *Salaried:* 9 of which: 5 in developing countries. *Budget/Total 1993:* ECU 823000 (US$ 964000).

PUBLICATIONS: *Periodicals:* Newsletters (4). *Annual report. List of publications.*

EVALUATION/RESEARCH: Evaluation reports available. Undertakes research activities.

ACTIVITIES IN DEVELOPING REGIONS: Present in developing regions. Active in 14 country(ies). Maintains local field presence. Works through local field partners. **Sustainable Development Actions:** Children/youth/family; Ecology/environment/biodiversity; Education/training/literacy; Gender issues/women; Health/sanitation/water; Rural development/agriculture; Sending volunteers/experts/technical assistance. **Regions:** Central Asia and South Asia; Mexico and Central America; South America; West Africa.

INFORMATION AND EDUCATION ACTIVITIES: Topics: Culture/tradition/religion; Ecology/environment/biodiversity; Education/training/literacy; Food/famine; Health/sanitation/water; Human rights/peace/conflicts; International economic relations/trade/debt/finance; International relations/cooperation/development aid; Other; Poverty/living conditions; Rural development/agriculture; Urban development/habitat. **Activities:** Broadcasting/cultural events; Conferences/seminars/workshops/training activities; Fund raising; Information and documentation services/data bases; Information campaigns/exhibitions; Networking/electronic telecommunications.

SWE3703

FREDAGSGRUPPEN

c/o Hellquist, Hvitfeldtsg. 13, 302 34 Halmstad, Sweden.

Telephone: 46 (35) 10 46 04.

SWE3704

FREDLIGT ARBETE TILL INSIKT, MEDMANSKLIGHET, ANSVAR-UNIONEN (FATIMA) ♦ Union for Peace Service through Human Responsibility

Lillåvägen 47, Box 2078, 103 12 Stockholm, Sweden.

Telephone: 46 (8) 659 85 21. *Contact:* Sam Dahlgren, Chief Representative.

OBJECTIVES: To assist in raising awareness of young people about humanity, social responsibility, justice, internaitonal solidarity and non-violence. To provide information about the world and what can be done to improve it. To work for homeless and lonely people in Sweden and abroad.

GENERAL INFORMATION: *Creation:* 1951. *Affiliated to:* LSU-The national council of Swedish youth (Sweden) - Forum Syd - Swedish Volunteer Service (Sweden) - Föreningen Norden (Sweden) - United Nations Association of Sweden (Sweden). *Personnel/Total:* 63. *Volunteers:* 63. *Budget/Total 1993:* ECU 118000 (US$ 138000). *Financial sources:* Private: 14%. Public: 41%. Self-financing: 45%.

ACTIVITIES IN DEVELOPING REGIONS: Sustainable Development Actions: Children/youth/family. **Regions:** Central Africa; South America.

INFORMATION AND EDUCATION ACTIVITIES: Topics: Education/training/literacy; Refugees/migrants/ethnic groups. **Activities:** Information and documentation services/data bases; Information campaigns/exhibitions.

SWE3705

FRIVILLIGORGANISATIONERNAS FOND FOR MANSKLIGA RATTIGHETER ♦ The Swedish NGO Foundation for Human Rights

Drottinggatan 101, 113 60 Stockholm, Sweden.

Telephone: 46 (8) 30 31 50. *Fax:* 46 (8) 30 30 31. *E-mail:* Seehr@nn.apc.org. *Contact:* Birgitta Berggren, Secretary General.

OBJECTIVES: To provide support to organisations defending human rights in the Third World. To raise awareness in Sweden regarding the importance of human rights.

GENERAL INFORMATION: *Creation:* 1991. *Personnel/Total:* 4. *Salaried:* 4. *Budget/Total 1993:* ECU 1213000 (US$ 1420000). *Financial sources:* Public: 90%. Self-financing: 10%.

PUBLICATIONS: *Periodicals:* MR-INFO (6). *Annual report.*

ACTIVITIES IN DEVELOPING REGIONS: Active in 20 country(ies). Works through local field partners. **Sustainable Development Actions:** Democracy/good governance/institution building/participatory development; Gender issues/women; Human rights/peace/conflicts. **Regions:** Caribbean; Central Africa; East Africa; North Africa; South America; South East Asia; Southern Africa; West Africa.

INFORMATION AND EDUCATION ACTIVITIES: Topics: Human rights/peace/conflicts. **Activities:** Conferences/seminars/workshops/training activities; Exchanges/twinning/linking; Information and documentation services/data bases; Lobbying/advocacy; Networking/electronic telecommunications; Publishing/audiovisual materials/educational materials.

SWE3706

GAVLEBORGS BISTANDSGRUPP ♦ Gävleborg's Aid Group

Telev. 2, 818 33 Valbo, Sweden.

Telephone: 46 (26) 13 29 85. *Fax:* 46 (26) 13 28 33.

SWE3707

GLOBAL HELP GHANA FUND

Box 170 26, 104 62 Stockholm, Sweden.

Telephone: 46 (8) 16 70 37. *Fax:* 46 (8) 16 70 37. *Contact:* Henry Broni Amponsah.

OBJECTIVES: To help institutions (such as hospitals and schools) and individuals (principally children) in Ghana. To provide care for orphans and the disabled in rural areas. To increase environmental understanding so as to limit the use of dangerous chemicals.

GENERAL INFORMATION: *Creation:* 1990. *Personnel/Total:* 27. *Salaried:* 9 of which: 9 in developing countries. *Volunteers:* 18 of which: 18 in developing countries. *Financial sources:* Private: 7%. Public: 93%.

PUBLICATIONS: *Annual report.*

EVALUATION/RESEARCH: Evaluation reports available. Undertakes research activities.

ACTIVITIES IN DEVELOPING REGIONS: Present in developing regions. Active in 1 country(ies). Works through local field partners. **Sustainable Development Actions:** Children/youth/family; Ecology/environment/biodiversity; Education/training/literacy; Emergency relief/refugees/humanitarian assistance; Food/famine; Gender issues/women; Rural development/agriculture; Sending volunteers/experts/technical assistance. **Regions:** West Africa.

INFORMATION AND EDUCATION ACTIVITIES: Topics: Children/youth/family; Culture/tradition/religion; Ecology/environment/biodiversity; Emergency relief/refugees/humanitarian assistance; Health/sanitation/water; Poverty/living conditions. **Activities:** Conferences/seminars/workshops/training activities; Fund raising; Information campaigns/exhibitions.

SWE3708

GUATEMALAGRUPPERNA I SVERIGE (GGS) ♦ The Guatemala Groups in Sweden

Brevia 423, Frejg. 13, 114 20 Stockholm, Sweden.

Telephone: 46 (8) 14 50 38. *Contact:* Kerstin Sumelius.

SWE3709
HAND IN HAND
c/o Blomqvist, Karlsruhev. 11, 134 32 Gustavsberg, Sweden.

Telephone: 46 (8) 570 349 40. *Fax:* 46 (8) 570 359 56. *Contact:* Gunnel Blomqvist.

SWE3710
HARNOSAND INDIA DEVELOPMENT COLLABORATION AGENCY (HIDCA)
Runstensv 12, 871 40 Härnösand, Sweden.

Telephone: 46 (611) 29 640. *Contact:* Adir Ragnar Holmberg, Chairman.

SWE3711
HJALPANDE HANDER ♦ Helping Hands
Box 9101, 580 09 Linköping, Sweden.

Telephone: 46 (13) 17 38 25. *Fax:* 46 (13) 17 38 25. *Contact:* Jagannath and Margareta Gautam.

SWE3712
HOPPETS STJARNA ♦ Star of Hope International
Kärrsjö , 890 54 Trehörningsjö, Sweden.

Telephone: 46 (660) 108 80. *Fax:* 46 (662) 410 39. *E-mail:* lennart.eriksson@postcan.postnet.se. *Contact:* Lennart Eriksson, Executive Director.

OBJECTIVES: To provide humanitarian development assistance to mothers and children, physically handicapped persons and victims of emergencies and disasters. To follow up this help through training and the promotion of self-help activities. To assist single mothers in supporting their children.

GENERAL INFORMATION: *Creation:* 1966. *Type of organisation:* network. *Affiliated to:* Swedish Missionary Council (Sweden). *Personnel/Total:* 35. *Salaried:* 25 of which: 5 in developing countries. *Volunteers:* 10 of which: 5 in developing countries. *Budget/Total 1993:* ECU 5551000 (US$ 6501000). *Financial sources: Private:* 70%. *Public:* 30%.

PUBLICATIONS: *Periodicals:* Världens Bam (2) - Månadsbevet (12). *Annual report.*

EVALUATION/RESEARCH: Evaluation reports available. Undertakes research activities.

COMMENTS: Undertakes activities in the Commonwealth of Independent States. Information activities related to the Commonwealth of Independent States.

ACTIVITIES IN DEVELOPING REGIONS: Present in developing regions. Active in 15 country(ies). Works through local field partners. **Sustainable Development Actions:** Children/youth/family; Education/training/literacy; Emergency relief/refugees/humanitarian assistance; Food/famine; Gender issues/women; Health/sanitation/water; Population/family planning/demography; Rural development/agriculture; Urban development/habitat. **Regions:** Caribbean; East Africa; East Asia; South America; South East Asia; West Africa.

INFORMATION AND EDUCATION ACTIVITIES: Topics: Children/youth/family; Education/training/literacy; Emergency relief/refugees/humanitarian assistance; Employment/unemployment; Food/famine; Gender issues/women; Health/sanitation/water; International relations/cooperation/development aid; Population/family planning/demography; Poverty/living conditions; Refugees/migrants/ethnic groups; Rural development/agriculture. **Activities:** Conferences/seminars/workshops/training activities; Formal education; Fund raising; Information campaigns/exhibitions; Networking/electronic telecommunications; Publishing/audiovisual materials/educational materials.

SWE3713
HUNGERPROJEKTET ♦ The Hunger Project
Västmannag. 17C, 1 tr., 113 25 Stockholm, Sweden.

Telephone: 46 (8) 30 23 00. *Fax:* 46 (8) 32 84 62.

SWE3714
HUSMODERSFORBUNDET HEM OCH SAMHALLE ♦ The Swedish Housewives' Association Home and Society
Box 19109, 104 32 Stockholm, Sweden.

Telephone: 46 (8) 612 28 20. *Fax:* 46 (8) 612 72 14. *Contact:* Ethel Floren-Winther, President.

OBJECTIVES: To promote increased equality for women in society, the well-being of children, teenagers and the family, and quality care for the aged. To work for enlightened consumer policies. Nordic and international co-operation and world peace.

GENERAL INFORMATION: *Creation:* 1919. *Affiliated to:* Associated Country Women of the World. *Personnel/Total:* 4. *Budget/Total 1993:* ECU 227000 (US$ 265000). *Financial sources: Self-financing:* 70%.

PUBLICATIONS: *Periodicals:* Hem Och Samhälle (4). *Annual report.*

EVALUATION/RESEARCH: Evaluation reports available.

ACTIVITIES IN DEVELOPING REGIONS: Works through local field partners. **Sustainable Development Actions:** Education/training/literacy; Gender issues/women; Health/sanitation/water. **Regions:** East Africa.

INFORMATION AND EDUCATION ACTIVITIES: Topics: Gender issues/women. **Activities:** Fund raising.

SWE3715
INDIVIDUELL MANNISKOHJALP (IM) ♦ Swedish Organisation for Individual Relief
Spolegatan 12B, Box 45, 221 00 Lund, Sweden.

Telephone: 46 (46) 11 79 80. *Fax:* 46 (46) 15 83 09. *Contact:* Örjan Ekman, Chairman.

SWE3716
INTERNATIONAL CHRISTIAN YOUTH EXCHANGE (ICYE)
Storsvängen 30, 126 58 Hägersten, Sweden.

Telephone: 46 (8) 88 98 86. *Fax:* 46 (8) 494 210 09.

SWE3717
INTERNATIONAL FOUNDATION FOR SCIENCE (IFS) ♦ Fondation internationale pour la science
Grev Turegatan 19, 114 38 Stockholm, Sweden.

Telephone: 46 (8) 791 29 00. *Contact:* Dr. Jaan Teär, Director.

SWE3718
INTERNATIONAL WORK GROUP FOR INDIGENOUS AFFAIRS (IWGIA)
Socialantropologiska Institutionen, Brog. 4, 413 01 Göteborg, Sweden.

Telephone: 46 (31) 13 42 70. *Fax:* 46 (31) 733 46 07. *Contact:* Heidi Moksnes.

SWE3719
INTERNATIONELLA ARBETSLAG ♦ Service Civil International - Sweden
Barnängsgatan 23, 116 41 Stockholm, Sweden.

Telephone: 46 (8) 643 08 89.

SWE3720
INTERNATIONELLA KVINNOFORBUNDET FOR FRED OCH FRIHET (IKFF)
Tjärhovsg. 9, 116 21 Stockholm, Sweden.

Telephone: 46 (8) 702 98 10. *Fax:* 46 (8) 702 19 73. *Contact:* Kerstin Grebäck.

SWE3721
INTI WAWA-BOCKER AT AYMARAINDIANER
c/o Maria Ohldin, Jonstorpsv. 9, 263 71 Jonstorp, Sweden.

Voir : *Comment utiliser le répertoire,* page 11.

Telephone: 46 (42) 36 73 03.

SWE3722

JAMSHOG ASSOCIATION FOR INTERNATIONAL COOPERATION (JAFIC)

Jämshögs Folkhögskola, 293 02 Jämshög , Sweden.

Telephone: 46 (454) 46 340. *Contact:* Peter Ekdahl.

SWE3723

JAMTLANDSGRUPPEN FOR INTERNATIONELLT SAMARBETE (JIDCA) ◆ Jämtland International Development Collaboration Agency

c\o Gun Olsén, Frösöv. 23, 832 43 Frösön, Sweden.

Telephone: 46 (63) 12 33 51. *Contact:* Ewy England, Chairman of the Board.

OBJECTIVES: To provide assistance to villages in developing countries with a focus on women and children. To assist self-help and other small projects in accordance with the needs and traditions of the villagers themselves. To promote contacts between the developed and the developing world and provide up-to-date information on developing countries.

GENERAL INFORMATION: *Creation:* 1984. *Budget/Total 1993:* ECU 36000 (US$ 42000). *Financial sources:* Private: 60%. Public: 40%.

PUBLICATIONS: *Annual report.*

EVALUATION/RESEARCH: Evaluation reports available.

COMMENTS: Undertakes activities in the Commonwealth of Independent States. Information activities related to the Commonwealth of Independent States.

ACTIVITIES IN DEVELOPING REGIONS: Present in developing regions. Active in 1 country(ies). Maintains local field presence. Works through local field partners. **Sustainable Development Actions:** Children/youth/family; Education/training/literacy; Gender issues/women; Health/sanitation/water; Rural development/agriculture. **Regions:** Central Asia and South Asia.

INFORMATION AND EDUCATION ACTIVITIES: Topics: Children/youth/family. **Activities:** Fund raising.

SWE3724

JORDENS VANNER ◆ Friends of the Earth - Sweden

Fjällgatan 23 A, 116 28 Stockholm, Sweden.

Telephone: 46 (8) 702 20 17. *Fax:* 46 (8) 714 01 54. *E-mail:* foesweden@pns.apc.org. *Contact:* Magnus Eriksson, Chairman.

OBJECTIVES: To promote the protection of the environment through an equitable and sustainable use of the Earth's resources.

GENERAL INFORMATION: *Creation:* 1971. *Affiliated to:* Friends of the Earth International (Netherlands) - Underverbet (Sweden) -Folknöretsenmot (Sweden) — Värlasbanksforum (Sweden). *Personnel/Total:* 6. *Salaried:* 2. *Volunteers:* 4. *Budget/Total 1993:* ECU 55000 (US$ 64000). *Financial sources:* Public: 35%. Self-financing: 65%.

PUBLICATIONS: *Periodicals:* Jordvännen (4). *Annual report. List of publications.*

EVALUATION/RESEARCH: Undertakes research activities.

COMMENTS: Information activities related to the Commonwealth of Independent States.

ACTIVITIES IN DEVELOPING REGIONS: Active in 1 country(ies). Works through local field partners. **Sustainable Development Actions:** Ecology/environment/biodiversity; Rural development/agriculture. **Regions:** South America.

INFORMATION AND EDUCATION ACTIVITIES: Topics: Ecology/environment/biodiversity; International economic relations/trade/debt/finance; Rural development/agriculture. **Activities:** Conferences/seminars/workshops/training activities; Exchanges/twinning/linking; Fund

raising; Information campaigns/exhibitions; Lobbying/advocacy; Networking/electronic telecommunications; Publishing/audiovisual materials/educational materials.

SWE3725

KAMPANJEN EL SALVADOR SKA SEGRA (KESSS)

Solidaritetshuset, Barnängsg. 23, 116 41 Stockholm, Sweden.

Telephone: 46 (8) 644 15 16. *Fax:* 46 (8) 641 11 35. *Contact:* Jan Czahowski.

OBJECTIVES: To support popular mouvements and NGOs in El Salvador. To inform the Swedish public about El Salvador.

GENERAL INFORMATION: *Creation:* 1988. *Budget/Total 1993:* ECU 27000 (US$ 32000). *Financial sources:* Self-financing: 100%.

PUBLICATIONS: *Periodicals:* El Salvador Information (5). *Annual report.*

ACTIVITIES IN DEVELOPING REGIONS: Active in 1 country(ies). Works through local field partners. **Sustainable Development Actions:** Democracy/good governance/institution building/participatory development; Education/training/literacy; Human rights/peace/conflicts; Rural development/agriculture. **Regions:** Mexico and Central America.

INFORMATION AND EDUCATION ACTIVITIES: Topics: Other. **Activities:** Broadcasting/cultural events; Conferences/seminars/workshops/training activities; Information and documentation services/data bases; Information campaigns/exhibitions; Publishing/audiovisual materials/educational materials.

SWE3726

KAMPANJEN NICARAGUA MASTE OVERLEVA ◆ The Campaign Nicaragua Must Survive

Hornsg. 54, 3tr, 118 21 Stockholm, Sweden.

Telephone: 46 (8) 641 73 87. *Fax:* 46 (8) 702 90 99. *Contact:* Rodrigo Arce.

SWE3727

KARAGWE-FORENINGEN ◆ Karagwe Association in Sweden

Frostbo 261, 781 96 Borlänge, Sweden.

Telephone: 46 (243) 35 297. *Contact:* Irina Blid, Chairperson.

OBJECTIVES: To provide adult education in Tanzania focusing particularly on women in the Karagwe District. To work in co-operation with Karadea, the Karagwe Development Association.

GENERAL INFORMATION: *Creation:* 1981. *Type of organisation:* network. *Member organisations:* 15. *Affiliated to:* Workers' Study Organisation in Sweden (Sweden) - Future Earth Foundation (Sweden) - Swedish-Tanzanian Association (Sweden) - Karibu Association (Sweden) - Swedish Folkhighschool Teachers' Association (Sweden) - Volvo Workers Aid (Sweden) - Emmaüs (France) - Borlänge - St. Erik's Friends of Africa. *Personnel/Total:* 2. *Salaried:* 2 of which: 2 in developing countries. *Budget/Total 1993:* ECU 66000 (US$ 77000). *Financial sources:* Private: 4%. Public: 73%. Self-financing: 23%.

PUBLICATIONS: *Periodicals:* Newsletter (4). *Annual report.*

EVALUATION/RESEARCH: Evaluation reports available.

ACTIVITIES IN DEVELOPING REGIONS: Active in 1 country(ies). Works through local field partners. **Sustainable Development Actions:** Children/youth/family; Debt/finance/trade; Democracy/good governance/institution building/participatory development; Ecology/environment/biodiversity; Education/training/literacy; Energy/transport; Gender issues/women; Health/sanitation/water; Rural development/agriculture; Small enterprises/informal sector/handicrafts. **Regions:** East Africa.

INFORMATION AND EDUCATION ACTIVITIES: Topics: Ecology/environment/biodiversity; Gender issues/women; International economic relations/trade/debt/finance; International relations/cooperation/development aid; Rural development/agriculture. **Activities:** Conferences/seminars/workshops/training activities; Fund raising; Information campaigns/exhibitions.

See: *How to Use the Directory,* page 11.

SWE3728
KARIBU

Boksta Skola, 610 60 Tystberga, Sweden.

Telephone: 46 (155) 26 10 97. *Fax:* 46 (155) 26 10 97. *Contact:* Per Andersson.

OBJECTIVES: To work for co-operation between folk development colleges in Tanzania and folk high schools in Sweden by providing advice and facilitating contacts.

GENERAL INFORMATION: *Creation:* 1980. *Budget/Total 1993:* ECU 11000 (US$ 13000). *Financial sources: Self-financing:* 100%.

PUBLICATIONS: *Periodicals:* Karibu Kontakt (2). *Annual report.*

ACTIVITIES IN DEVELOPING REGIONS: Active in 1 country(ies). Works through local field partners. **Sustainable Development Actions:** Democracy/good governance/institution building/participatory development; Education/training/literacy; Gender issues/women; Rural development/agriculture; Small enterprises/informal sector/handicrafts. **Regions:** East Africa.

INFORMATION AND EDUCATION ACTIVITIES: Topics: Education/training/literacy. **Activities:** Conferences/seminars/workshops/training activities; Exchanges/twinning/linking; Information and documentation services/data bases; Information campaigns/exhibitions; Publishing/audiovisual materials/educational materials.

SWE3729
KENYA-SWEDEN FRIENDSHIP ASSOCIATION (KESFA)

c/o Majrut Kivistö, Gällerstagränd 11 nb 101, 124 76 Bandhagen, Sweden.

Telephone: 46 (16) 13 60 75. *Contact:* Klaus-Jurgen Schmidt.

SWE3730
KFUK-KFUMS RIKSFORBUND ♦ National Council of YWCA-YMCA of Sweden

Box 2054, 103 12 Stockholm, Sweden.

Telephone: 46 (8) 14 53 30. *Fax:* 46 (8) 21 75 22. *Contact:* Jan Olov Söderberg, National General Secretary.

OBJECTIVES: To help individuals develop a personal Christian faith. To inspire personal responsibility in issues concerning the society in which we live. To encourage and promote fellowship within our movement and work for Christian unity. To promote international solidarity and justice.

GENERAL INFORMATION: *Creation:* 1887. *Affiliated to:* World Alliance of YMCAs (Switzerland) - World YWCA (Switzerland).

PUBLICATIONS: *Periodicals:* WHY (6).

EVALUATION/RESEARCH: Undertakes research activities.

PLANNED ACTIVITIES: A "democracy through Sport" campaign linking the East Jerrusalem YMCA, the Palestinian Sports Club and the Swedish YMCA-YWCA sports club.

COMMENTS: Undertakes activities in the Commonwealth of Independent States. Information activities related to the Commonwealth of Independent States.

ACTIVITIES IN DEVELOPING REGIONS: Works through local field partners. **Sustainable Development Actions:** Children/youth/family; Democracy/good governance/institution building/participatory development; Education/training/literacy; Emergency relief/refugees/humanitarian assistance; Food/famine; Gender issues/women; Health/sanitation/water; Human rights/peace/conflicts; Rural development/agriculture; Sending volunteers/experts/technical assistance; Small enterprises/informal sector/handicrafts. **Regions:** East Africa; Middle East; Oceania; South America; South East Asia; Southern Africa; West Africa.

INFORMATION AND EDUCATION ACTIVITIES: Topics: Children/youth/family; Education/training/literacy; Gender issues/women; Human rights/peace/conflicts; International relations/cooperation/development aid; Peace/ethnic conflicts/armament/disarmament; Refugees/migrants/ethnic groups; Rural development/agriculture. **Activities:** Conferences/seminars/workshops/training activities; Exchanges/twinning/linking; Fund raising; Information campaigns/exhibitions.

SWE3731
KONSTNARER MOT APARTHEID (KMA) ♦ Artists Against Apartheid

c/o Anshelm, Högbergsg. 32A, 1 tr, 116 20 Stockholm, Sweden.

Telephone: 46 (8) 640 44 56. *Fax:* 46 (8) 93 81 44. *Contact:* Albio Gonzalez.

OBJECTIVES: To encourage cultural exchange between institutions and workers in South Africa and Sweden. To train cultural workers in all artistic disciplines. To promote South African art in Sweden and vice versa.

GENERAL INFORMATION: *Creation:* 1984. *Personnel/Total:* 7. *Volunteers:* 7. *Financial sources: Public:* 95%. *Self-financing:* 5%.

PUBLICATIONS: *Annual report.*

EVALUATION/RESEARCH: Evaluation reports available. Undertakes research activities.

ACTIVITIES IN DEVELOPING REGIONS: Present in developing regions. Active in 1 country(ies). Works through local field partners. **Sustainable Development Actions:** Education/training/literacy; Other; Sending volunteers/experts/technical assistance. **Regions:** Southern Africa.

INFORMATION AND EDUCATION ACTIVITIES: Topics: Children/youth/family; Culture/tradition/religion; Gender issues/women; Human rights/peace/conflicts; International relations/cooperation/development aid; Peace/ethnic conflicts/armament/disarmament; Racism/xenophobia/antisemitism; Refugees/migrants/ethnic groups. **Activities:** Conferences/seminars/workshops/training activities; Exchanges/twinning/linking; Fund raising; Information campaigns/exhibitions; Publishing/audiovisual materials/educational materials.

SWE3732
KOOPERATIVA FORBUNDET (KF)

Box 15200, 10465 Stockholm, Sweden.

Telephone: 46 (8) 743 10 00.

SWE3733
KRISTDEMOKRATISKA UNGDOMSFORBUNDET (KDU) ♦ Young Christian Democrats of Sweden

Box 451, 101 29 Stockholm, Sweden.

Telephone: 46 (8) 24 38 29. *Fax:* 46 (8) 20 17 07. *Contact:* Cecilia Hjort-Pedersen.

SWE3734
KRISTNA FREDSRORELSEN ♦ Swedish Fellowship of Reconciliation

P.O. Box 1768 Lästmakargatan 18, 111 87 Stockholm, Sweden.

Telephone: 46 (8) 453 68 40. *Fax:* 46 (8) 453 68 41. *Contact:* Urban Hermansson, General Secretary.

OBJECTIVES: To support and encourage the churches' work for peace, justice and the environment. To promote non-violent conflict resolution. To support and promote the ideal of social justice between North and South and between people inside nations. To provide peace volunteers to countries in need. To support the choice of conscientious objectors.

GENERAL INFORMATION: *Creation:* 1919. *Affiliated to:* Swedish Peace Council (Sweden) - International Fellowship of Reconciliation - International Peace Bureau - War Resisters International - Kairos Europe Network. *Personnel/Total:* 4. *Salaried:* 4 of which: 1 in developing countries. *Budget/Total 1993:* ECU 219000 (US$ 257000). *Financial sources: Private:* 30%. *Public:* 30%. *Self-financing:* 30%.

PUBLICATIONS: *Periodicals:* One World (10). *Annual report. List of publications.*

EVALUATION/RESEARCH: Evaluation reports available. Undertakes research activities.

COMMENTS: Undertakes activities in the Commonwealth of Independent States. Information activities related to the Commonwealth of Independent States.

Voir : *Comment utiliser le répertoire,* page 11.

ACTIVITIES IN DEVELOPING REGIONS: Present in developing regions. Active in 3 country(ies). Maintains local field presence. Works through local field partners. **Sustainable Development Actions:** Human rights/peace/conflicts. **Regions:** Mexico and Central America; Middle East; Southern Africa.

INFORMATION AND EDUCATION ACTIVITIES: Topics: Ecology/environment/biodiversity; Employment/unemployment; Human rights/peace/conflicts; International economic relations/trade/debt/finance; International relations/cooperation/development aid; Peace/ethnic conflicts/armament/disarmament; Racism/xenophobia/antisemitism; Refugees/migrants/ethnic groups. **Activities:** Conferences/seminars/workshops/training activities; Exchanges/twinning/linking; Fund raising; Information and documentation services/data bases; Lobbying/advocacy; Networking/electronic telecommunications; Publishing/audiovisual materials/educational materials.

SWE3735

KRISTNA SOCIALDEMOKRATERNA - BRODERSKAP-SRORELSEN (SKSF) ♦ The Christian Social Democrats in Sweden

Box 70403, 107 25 Stockholm, Sweden.

Telephone: 46 (8) 700 26 00. **Fax:** 46 (8) 411 17 95. **Contact:** Berndt Ekholm, M.P..

OBJECTIVES: To influence political policies at the national and local level especially on social issues, cultural affairs, environment-development and international solidarity. To raise awareness of development assistance. To exchange information with other organisations.

GENERAL INFORMATION: Creation: 1929. **Affiliated to:** International League of Religious Socialists (Netherlands). **Personnel/Total:** 8. **Salaried:** 8. **Budget/Total 1993:** ECU 658000 (US$ 771000). **Financial sources:** Private: 69%. Public: 24%. Self-financing: 7%.

PUBLICATIONS: Periodicals: Tidningan Broderskap (52). Annual report. List of publications.

EVALUATION/RESEARCH: Undertakes research activities.

COMMENTS: Undertakes activities in the Commonwealth of Independent States. Information activities related to the Commonwealth of Independent States.

ACTIVITIES IN DEVELOPING REGIONS: Active in 3 country(ies). Works through local field partners. **Sustainable Development Actions:** Democracy/good governance/institution building/participatory development; Education/training/literacy. **Regions:** Central Africa; East Africa; Mexico and Central America.

INFORMATION AND EDUCATION ACTIVITIES: Topics: Culture/tradition/religion; Education/training/literacy; Human rights/peace/conflicts; International economic relations/trade/debt/finance; International relations/cooperation/development aid; Peace/ethnic conflicts/armament/disarmament; Racism/xenophobia/antisemitism; Refugees/migrants/ethnic groups. **Activities:** Conferences/seminars/workshops/training activities; Exchanges/twinning/linking; Information and documentation services/data bases; Information campaigns/exhibitions; Lobbying/advocacy; Publishing/audiovisual materials/educational materials.

SWE3736

KRISTNA STUDENTRORELSEN I SVERIGE (KRISS) ♦ Christian Student Movement of Sweden

Götgatan 3, 753 15 Uppsala, Sweden.

Telephone: 46 (18) 52 12 19. **Fax:** 46 (18) 55 00 42. **Contact:** Anders Wesslund, Chairperson.

SWE3737

KULTURFORENINGEN MISTELN ♦ Culture Association in Misteln

c/o Hans Ljungqvist, Smältverksg. 117, 724 74 Västerås, Sweden.

Telephone: 46 (21) 35 27 91. **Contact:** Kjell Gustavsson, Chairman.

OBJECTIVES: To work in solidarity with our Indian counterpart organisation to promote development.

GENERAL INFORMATION: Creation: 1984. **Budget/Total 1993:** ECU 78000 (US$ 90000). **Financial sources:** Private: 25%. Public: 70%. Self-financing: 5%.

PUBLICATIONS: Annual report.

EVALUATION/RESEARCH: Evaluation reports available.

ACTIVITIES IN DEVELOPING REGIONS: Present in developing regions. Active in 1 country(ies). Maintains local field presence. Works through local field partners. **Sustainable Development Actions:** Children/youth/family; Education/training/literacy; Health/sanitation/water; Rural development/agriculture; Small enterprises/informal sector/handicrafts. **Regions:** Central Asia and South Asia.

INFORMATION AND EDUCATION ACTIVITIES: Topics: Children/youth/family; Education/training/literacy; Poverty/living conditions; Rural development/agriculture. **Activities:** Conferences/seminars/workshops/training activities; Formal education; Fund raising; Information and documentation services/data bases; Information campaigns/exhibitions; Publishing/audiovisual materials/educational materials.

SWE3738

KVINNOR FOR FRED (KFF) ♦ Women for Peace (WFP)

Box 10098, 100 55 Stockholm, Sweden.

Telephone: 46 (8) 667 97 27. **Fax:** 46 (8) 667 97 27. **Contact:** Bibbi Steinertz, Executive Secretary.

OBJECTIVES: To support disarmament. To encourage ecological balance through the use of renewable sources of energy. To promote social and economic justice. To eradicate all violence against women and to achieve the full realization of human rights for women.

GENERAL INFORMATION: Creation: 1978. **Type of organisation:** network. **Affiliated to:** The Swedish Peace Council (Sweden) - North Atlantic Network - European Nuclear Disarmament - Helsinki Citizens Assembly (Finland) - Solidarity for Ecology, Equality and Development - Alliance of Northern People for Environment and Development - The Latin American Network - The Swedish UN Federation (Sweden) - Democracy in South Africa. **Budget/Total 1993:** ECU 44000 (US$ 51000). **Financial sources:** Private: 10%. Public: 70%. Self-financing: 20%.

PUBLICATIONS: Periodicals: Women for Peace (4). Annual report.

EVALUATION/RESEARCH: Evaluation reports available. Undertakes research activities.

PLANNED ACTIVITIES: Fund raising for women and children in the former Yugoslavia and Israel-Palestine peace work.

COMMENTS: Undertakes activities in the Commonwealth of Independent States. Information activities related to the Commonwealth of Independent States.

ACTIVITIES IN DEVELOPING REGIONS: Sustainable Development Actions: Democracy/good governance/institution building/participatory development; Gender issues/women; Human rights/peace/conflicts. **Regions:** Middle East.

INFORMATION AND EDUCATION ACTIVITIES: Topics: Children/youth/family; Culture/tradition/religion; Ecology/environment/biodiversity; Emergency relief/refugees/humanitarian assistance; Gender issues/women; Human rights/peace/conflicts; International economic relations/trade/debt/finance; International relations/cooperation/development aid; Peace/ethnic conflicts/armament/disarmament; Population/family planning/demography; Racism/xenophobia/antisemitism; Refugees/migrants/ethnic groups. **Activities:** Broadcasting/cultural events; Conferences/seminars/workshops/training activities; Fund raising; Information campaigns/exhibitions; Lobbying/advocacy; Publishing/audiovisual materials/educational materials.

SWE3739

KYRKORNAS VARLDSFORUM ♦ World Forum of the Swedish Churches

Box 1764, 111 87 Stockholm, Sweden.

Telephone: 46 (8) 45 36 800. **Fax:** 46 (8) 45 36 829. **Contact:** Peter Weiderud.

See: *How to Use the Directory*, page 11.

SWE3740

LANDSRADET FOR SVERIGES UNGDOMSORGANISA-TIONER (LSU) ♦ National Council of Swedish Youth

Kungsgatan 48, 3tr, 111 35 Stockholm, Sweden.

Telephone: 46 (8) 20 11 22. *Fax:* 46 (8) 20 35 30. *Contact:* Björn Mellstrand.

SWE3741

LANKA SARANA SWEDEN

c/o Birgitta Berg Salmi, Ortv. 166, 760 49 Herräng, Sweden.

Telephone: 46 (175) 13 347. *Contact:* Lena Larsson.

SWE3742

LANTBRUKARNAS RIKSFORBUND (LRF) ♦ Federation of Swedish Farmers

Klara Östra Kyrkogata 12, 105 33 Stockholm, Sweden.

Telephone: 46 (8) 787 50 00 . *Fax:* 46 (8) 14 91 66. *Contact:* Bo Dockered, President.

OBJECTIVES: To promote the interests of Swedish farmers and their co-operatives. To promote sustainable agriculture between farmers in Sweden and in developing countries.

GENERAL INFORMATION: *Creation:* 1970.

PUBLICATIONS: *Periodicals:* Land (50). *Annual report.*

EVALUATION/RESEARCH: Undertakes research activities.

COMMENTS: Undertakes activities in the Commonwealth of Independent States. Information activities related to the Commonwealth of Independent States.

ACTIVITIES IN DEVELOPING REGIONS: Present in developing regions. Maintains local field presence. Works through local field partners. **Sustainable Development Actions:** Rural development/agriculture. **Regions:** East Africa.

INFORMATION AND EDUCATION ACTIVITIES: Topics: Ecology/environment/biodiversity; Rural development/agriculture. **Activities:** Information campaigns/exhibitions; Lobbying/advocacy.

SWE3743

LARARE FOR FRED I NORRKOPING ♦ Teachers for Peace in Norrköping

c/o Eklund, Vårfruv. 20, 618 30 Kolmården, Sweden.

Telephone: 46 (11) 91 560. *Fax:* 46 (11) 14 50 52. *Contact:* Helen Eklund.

SWE3744

LATINA - LATINAMERIKANSKA KOOPERATIONSFOREN-INGEN ♦ Latin-Association of Latinamerican Cooperation

Norra Stationsgatan 121, 4th Floor, 113 64 Stockholm, Sweden.

Telephone: 46 (8) 34 52 66. *Fax:* 46 (8) 728 47 66. *Contact:* Jorge Jeraci.

OBJECTIVES: To promote co-operation and exchange for sustainable social, cultural, economic and environmental development between the North and the South. To promote a just policy for refugees in Europe.

GENERAL INFORMATION: *Creation:* 1986. *Affiliated to:* Biståndsinformation (Sweden) - Amnesty (Sweden). *Personnel/Total:* 218. *Salaried:* 25 of which: 21. in developing countries. *Volunteers:* 193 of which: 151 in developing countries. *Budget/Total 1993:* ECU 267757 (US$ 314000). *Financial sources:* Private: 3%. Public: 87%. *Self-financing:* 10%.

PUBLICATIONS: *Periodicals:* Info-Sol (4). *Annual report. List of publications.*

EVALUATION/RESEARCH: Evaluation reports available.

PLANNED ACTIVITIES: The establishment of a regional centre for co-ordination in South America.

ACTIVITIES IN DEVELOPING REGIONS: Present in developing regions. Active in 5 country(ies). Maintains local field presence. Works through local field partners. **Sustainable Development Actions:** Children/youth/family; Debt/finance/trade; Democracy/good governance/institution building/participatory development; Ecology/environment/biodiversity; Education/training/literacy; Emergency relief/refugees/humanitarian assistance; Energy/transport; Food/famine; Gender issues/women; Health/sanitation/water; Human rights/peace/conflicts; Population/family planning/demography; Rural development/agriculture; Sending volunteers/experts/technical assistance; Small enterprises/informal sector/handicrafts; Urban development/habitat. **Regions:** South America.

INFORMATION AND EDUCATION ACTIVITIES: Topics: Children/youth/family; Culture/tradition/religion; Ecology/environment/biodiversity; Education/training/literacy; Emergency relief/refugees/humanitarian assistance; Employment/unemployment; Food/famine; Gender issues/women; Health/sanitation/water; Human rights/peace/conflicts; International economic relations/trade/debt/finance; International relations/cooperation/development aid; Peace/ethnic conflicts/armament/disarmament; Population/family planning/demography; Poverty/living conditions; Racism/xenophobia/antisemitism; Refugees/migrants/ethnic groups; Rural development/agriculture; Urban development/habitat. **Activities:** Broadcasting/cultural events; Conferences/seminars/workshops/training activities; Exchanges/twinning/linking; Fund raising; Information and documentation services/data bases; Information campaigns/exhibitions; Lobbying/advocacy; Publishing/audiovisual materials/educational materials.

SWE3745

LEPRAMISSIONEN ♦ The Leprosy Mission in Sweden

Box 145, 692 23 Kumla, Sweden.

Telephone: 46 (19) 58 37 90. *Fax:* 46 (19) 58 14 50. *Contact:* Håkan Wistrand.

OBJECTIVES: To minister in the name of Jesus Christ to the physical, mental and spiritual needs of the leprosy sufferers and to work towards the eradication of the disease. To spread information about leprosy to the Swedish community.

GENERAL INFORMATION: *Creation:* 1984. *Affiliated to:* The Leprosy Mission International (United Kingdom). *Personnel/Total:* 3. *Salaried:* 2. *Volunteers:* 1. *Budget/Total 1993:* ECU 263000 (US$ 308000). *Financial sources:* Private: 77%. Public: 22%. *Self-financing:* 1%.

PUBLICATIONS: *Periodicals:* Lepra Nytt (4). *Annual report.*

PLANNED ACTIVITIES: Medical seminars focusing on different aspects of leprosy and visits to secondary schools and nursing colleges to give information on leprosy.

COMMENTS: Undertakes activities in the Commonwealth of Independent States.

ACTIVITIES IN DEVELOPING REGIONS: Present in developing regions. Maintains local field presence. Works through local field partners. **Sustainable Development Actions:** Education/training/literacy; Health/sanitation/water; Small enterprises/informal sector/handicrafts. **Regions:** Central Africa; Central Asia and South Asia; East Africa; East Asia; South East Asia; Southern Africa; West Africa.

INFORMATION AND EDUCATION ACTIVITIES: Topics: Health/sanitation/water. **Activities:** Conferences/seminars/workshops/training activities; Formal education; Fund raising; Information campaigns/exhibitions; Publishing/audiovisual materials/educational materials.

SWE3746

LIFE & PEACE INSTITUTE (LPI)

Sysslomanse 7, 751 70 Uppsala, Sweden.

Telephone: 46 (18) 16 95 00. *Fax:* 46 (18) 69 30 59. *E-mail:* bjonsson@nniapc.org. *Contact:* Bernt Jonsson, Director.

OBJECTIVES: To support the Church's work for justice, peace and reconciliation. To develop research projects and means of communication at the local, regional and global levels, for the improvement of understanding about the roots of conflict.

GENERAL INFORMATION: *Creation:* 1985. *Personnel/Total:* 17. *Salaried:* 14 of which: 3 in developing countries. *Volunteers:* 3 of which: 3 in

Voir : *Comment utiliser le répertoire,* page 11.

developing countries. *Budget/Total 1993:* ECU 1426000 (US$ 1670000). *Financial sources: Private:* 15%. *Public:* 80%. *Self-financing:* 5%.

PUBLICATIONS: *Periodicals:* Life and Peace Review (4) - Horn of Africa Bulletin (6). *Annual report. List of publications.*

EVALUATION/RESEARCH: Evaluation reports available. Undertakes research activities.

ACTIVITIES IN DEVELOPING REGIONS: Present in developing regions. Active in 4 country(ies). Maintains local field presence. Works through local field partners. **Sustainable Development Actions:** Democracy/good governance/institution building/participatory development; Gender issues/women; Human rights/peace/conflicts; Other. **Regions:** East Africa.

INFORMATION AND EDUCATION ACTIVITIES: Topics: Emergency relief/refugees/humanitarian assistance; Gender issues/women; Human rights/peace/conflicts; International economic relations/trade/debt/finance; Peace/ethnic conflicts/armament/disarmament; Population/family planning/demography; Refugees/migrants/ethnic groups. **Activities:** Conferences/seminars/workshops/training activities; Fund raising; Information and documentation services/data bases; Information campaigns/exhibitions; Lobbying/advocacy; Networking/electronic telecommunications; Publishing/audiovisual materials/educational materials.

SWE3747
LIONS CLUBS INTERNATIONAL, MD 101-SWEDEN

Sjöbjörnsv. 5, 117 67 Stockholm, Sweden.

Telephone: 46 (8) 744 59 00. *Fax:* 46 (8) 726 92 00.

SWE3748
LO/TCO BISTANDSNAMND ♦ LO/TCO Council for International Trade Union Co-operation

Barnhusg. 16, 111 23 Stockholm, Sweden.

Telephone: 46 (8) 10 95 24. *Fax:* 46 (8) 24 97 94. *Contact:* Hans Fogelström, Director.

SWE3749
LUTHERHJALPEN ♦ Church of Sweden Aid

Sysslomansgatan 70, 751 70 Uppsala, Sweden.

Telephone: 46 (18) 16 95 00. *Fax:* 46 (18) 16 97 07. *Contact:* Margaretha Ringström, Director.

OBJECTIVES: To help create a better global society through emergency aid and long-term development programmes in impoverished areas of the world. To promote, in Sweden, the idea of the just sharing of resources.

GENERAL INFORMATION: *Creation:* 1947. *Type of organisation:* network. *Affiliated to:* Lutheran World Federation (Switzerland) - World Council of Churches (Switzerland). *Personnel/Total:* 40. *Salaried:* 40 of which: 6 in developing countries. *Budget/Total 1993:* ECU 28526000 (US$ 33404000). *Financial sources: Private:* 70%. *Public:* 30%.

PUBLICATIONS: *Periodicals:* Lutherhjälpem (4). *Annual report.*

EVALUATION/RESEARCH: Evaluation reports available.

COMMENTS: Undertakes activities in the Commonwealth of Independent States. Information activities related to the Commonwealth of Independent States.

ACTIVITIES IN DEVELOPING REGIONS: Active in 60 country(ies). Works through local field partners. **Sustainable Development Actions:** Children/youth/family; Democracy/good governance/institution building/participatory development; Ecology/environment/biodiversity; Education/training/literacy; Emergency relief/refugees/humanitarian assistance; Energy/transport; Food/famine; Gender issues/women; Health/sanitation/water; Human rights/peace/conflicts; Population/family planning/demography; Rural development/agriculture; Small enterprises/informal sector/handicrafts; Urban development/habitat. **Regions:** Caribbean; Central Africa; Central Asia and South Asia; East Africa; East Asia; Mexico and Central America; Middle East; North Africa; Oceania; South America; South East Asia; Southern Africa; West Africa.

INFORMATION AND EDUCATION ACTIVITIES: Topics: Children/youth/family; Culture/tradition/religion; Ecology/environment/biodiversity; Education/training/literacy; Emergency relief/refugees/humanitarian assistance; Employment/unemployment; Food/famine; Gender issues/women; Health/sanitation/water; Human rights/peace/conflicts; International economic relations/trade/debt/finance; International relations/cooperation/development aid; Peace/ethnic conflicts/armament/disarmament; Population/family planning/demography; Poverty/living conditions; Racism/xenophobia/antisemitism; Refugees/migrants/ethnic groups; Rural development/agriculture; Urban development/habitat. **Activities:** Conferences/seminars/workshops/training activities; Exchanges/twinning/linking; Fund raising; Information campaigns/exhibitions; Lobbying/advocacy; Publishing/audiovisual materials/educational materials.

SWE3750
MARGIT NYLANDERS STIFTELSE FOR HANDIKAPPADE PA SRI LANKA ♦ The Foundation Margit Nylander's Home for Handicapped in Sri Lanka

c/o Carin Boalt, Kommendörsg. 8c, 114 48 Stockholm, Sweden.

Telephone: 46 (8) 662 23 78. *Contact:* Gösta Rehn.

SWE3751
MARIAHJALPEN

c/o Ann Marie Johansson, Bryngelsrud 2167, 660 52 Edsvalla, Sweden.

Telephone: 46 (54) 54 41 43. *Contact:* Gunilla Ström-Eriksson.

SWE3752
MEDSYSTRARNA - TETRA LAVAL ♦ Kinsisters - Tetra Laval

Box 64, 221 00 Lund, Sweden.

Telephone: 46 (46) 36 50 00. *Fax:* 46 (46) 13 78 86. *Contact:* Madeleine Wisenborn.

OBJECTIVES: To offer support to women in developing countries, especially by encouraging small-scale projects in the field of food processing. To give women access to technology and education adapted to their capabilities and their country's needs.

GENERAL INFORMATION: *Creation:* 1984. *Personnel/Total:* 10. *Financial sources: Private:* 50%. *Self-financing:* 50%.

PUBLICATIONS: *Periodicals:* Alma (2). *Annual report.*

ACTIVITIES IN DEVELOPING REGIONS: Present in developing regions. Works through local field partners. **Sustainable Development Actions:** Education/training/literacy; Food/famine; Gender issues/women; Small enterprises/informal sector/handicrafts. **Regions:** East Africa.

SWE3753
METODISTKYRKANS UNGDOMSFORBUND ♦ Youth Department of the United Methodist Church

Älvsjö Gårdsväg 3, 125 30 Älvsjö, Sweden.

Telephone: 46 (8) 749 15 00. *Fax:* 46 (8) 749 55 60. *Contact:* Ulf Rickardsson, Chairman.

OBJECTIVES: To spread the message of the gospel to the people of all nations. To undertake activities which seek to improve the social and economic living conditions of people in developing countries. To make young people aware of the causes behind human suffering.

GENERAL INFORMATION: *Creation:* 1892. *Affiliated to:* Swedish Christian Youth Council (Sweden) - Methodist Youth Board for Northern Europe - European Methodist Youth Council - World Methodist Council Youth Committee. *Personnel/Total:* 2. *Salaried:* 2. *Budget/Total 1993:* ECU 75000 (US$ 87000). *Financial sources: Private:* 55%. *Public:* 12%. *Self-financing:* 33%.

PUBLICATIONS: *Periodicals:* Trikå (4). *Annual report. List of publications.*

EVALUATION/RESEARCH: Evaluation reports available.

COMMENTS: Undertakes activities in the Commonwealth of Independent States. Information activities related to the Commonwealth of Independent States.

See: *How to Use the Directory*, page 11.

ACTIVITIES IN DEVELOPING REGIONS: Active in 2 country(ies). Works through local field partners. **Sustainable Development Actions:** Children/youth/family; Education/training/literacy. **Regions:** Southern Africa; West Africa.

INFORMATION AND EDUCATION ACTIVITIES: **Topics:** Children/youth/family; Education/training/literacy. **Activities:** Formal education; Fund raising; Information campaigns/exhibitions.

SWE3754

MILJOFORBUNDET ♦ The Environmental Federation of Sweden

Box 7048, 402 31 Göteborg, Sweden.

Telephone: 46 (31) 12 18 08. *Fax:* 46 (31) 12 18 17. *Contact:* Anna Mattsson.

OBJECTIVES: To work for a resource saving society built on solidarity.

GENERAL INFORMATION: *Creation:* 1976. *Member organisations:* 40. *Affiliated to:* EYFA - ANPED - ASEED (Netherlands) - ELCI (Kenya). *Personnel/Total:* 203. *Salaried:* 2. *Volunteers:* 201 of which: 1 in developing countries. *Budget/Total 1993:* ECU 22000 (US$ 26000). *Financial sources:* Public: 20%. Self-financing: 80%.

PUBLICATIONS: *Periodicals:* Miljötidning (8). *Annual report. List of publications.*

EVALUATION/RESEARCH: Evaluation reports available. Undertakes research activities.

PLANNED ACTIVITIES: Campaigns on climate issues, green consumerism, fair trade and anti-nuclear work.

COMMENTS: Undertakes activities in the Commonwealth of Independent States. Information activities related to the Commonwealth of Independent States.

ACTIVITIES IN DEVELOPING REGIONS: Present in developing regions. Active in 1 country(ies). Maintains local field presence. Works through local field partners. **Sustainable Development Actions:** Ecology/environment/biodiversity; Education/training/literacy; Human rights/peace/conflicts. **Regions:** South America.

INFORMATION AND EDUCATION ACTIVITIES: **Topics:** Ecology/environment/biodiversity; Employment/unemployment; Human rights/peace/conflicts; International economic relations/trade/debt/finance; International relations/cooperation/development aid; Poverty/living conditions; Refugees/migrants/ethnic groups. **Activities:** Broadcasting/cultural events; Conferences/seminars/workshops/training activities; Exchanges/twinning/linking; Information and documentation services/data bases; Information campaigns/exhibitions; Lobbying/advocacy; Networking/electronic telecommunications; Publishing/audiovisual materials/educational materials.

SWE3755

MISSION AVIATION FELLOWSHIPS-SWEDEN (MAF)

Flygfältet, 577 91 Hultsfred, Sweden.

Telephone: 46 (495) 11 558. *Fax:* 46 (495) 13 303. *Contact:* Tord Bergroth, Lars-Erik Wallhagen.

SWE3756

MISSIONSSALLSKAPET BIBELTROGNA VANNER ♦ The Missionary Society

Box 6160, 102 33 Stockholm, Sweden.

Telephone: 46 (8) 33 25 23. *Fax:* 46 (8) 34 58 18.

SWE3757

NATURSKYDDSFORENINGEN, BISTANDSSEKRETARIATET ♦ Swedish Society for Nature Conservation

Box 4625, 116 91 Stockholm, Sweden.

Telephone: 46 (8) 702 65 00. *Fax:* 46 (8) 702 08 55. *Contact:* Lilian Bellander.

SWE3758

NORDANSTIGS U-LANDSGRUPP (NULAG) ♦ Nordanstig Group for Developing Countries

Bergsvägen 2, Box 27, 820 78 Hassela, Sweden.

Telephone: 46 (652) 40 015. *Contact:* Karl Åkerblom.

SWE3759

NORDISKA ARBETSGRUPPEN FOR INTERNATIONELLA AMNINGSFRAGOR (NAFIA) ♦ The Nordic Group for International Breastfeeding Issues

c/o Ann-Margret Yngve, Lavalv. 5, 131 41 Nacka, Sweden.

Telephone: 46 (8) 716 03 64. *Contact:* Ann-Margret Yngve.

SWE3760

NORTH & SOUTH EXCHANGE

Wrångebäck, 544 94 Hjo, Sweden.

Telephone: 46 (503) 20 001. *Fax:* 46 (503) 20 165. *Contact:* Nicolas Berglund, Managing Director.

OBJECTIVES: To contribute to and stimulate local economic development in developing countries by importing and selling food and handicrafts in Sweden.

GENERAL INFORMATION: *Creation:* 1990. *Affiliated to:* International Federation of Alternative Trade (USA). *Salaried:* 3. *Volunteers:* var. *Budget/Total 1993:* ECU 219000 (US$ 257000). *Financial sources:* Private: 5%. Self-financing: 95%.

PUBLICATIONS: *Annual report. List of publications.*

EVALUATION/RESEARCH: Undertakes research activities.

ACTIVITIES IN DEVELOPING REGIONS: Present in developing regions. Active in 14 country(ies). Works through local field partners. **Sustainable Development Actions:** Debt/finance/trade; Sending volunteers/experts/technical assistance; Small enterprises/informal sector/handicrafts. **Regions:** Central Asia and South Asia; East Africa; East Asia; Mexico and Central America; South America.

INFORMATION AND EDUCATION ACTIVITIES: **Topics:** Children/youth/family; Ecology/environment/biodiversity; Gender issues/women; International relations/cooperation/development aid; Rural development/agriculture; Urban development/habitat. **Activities:** Broadcasting/cultural events; Exchanges/twinning/linking; Information and documentation services/data bases; Information campaigns/exhibitions; Publishing/audiovisual materials/educational materials.

SWE3761

NYBRO U-LANDS OCH FN-FORENING (NUFF) ♦ Nybro UN-Development Association

Gummemåla 3312 B, 382 90 Nybro, Sweden.

Telephone: 46 (481) 40 192. *Fax:* 46 (481) 45 505. *Contact:* Thomas Dahlgren.

OBJECTIVES: To initiate dialogue between people in Nybro and developing countries. To initiate and carry out development projects in developing countries. To initiate and maintain a dialogue between people in Nybro and refugees to encourage mutual understanding.

GENERAL INFORMATION: *Creation:* 1979. *Type of organisation:* association of NGOs. *Member organisations:* 15. *Affiliated to:* World Federation of United Nations Associations. *Volunteers:* 1. *Budget/Total 1993:* ECU 27000 (US$ 32000). *Financial sources:* Private: 15%. Public: 80%. Self-financing: 5%.

PUBLICATIONS: *Periodicals:* Inforamtion Bulletine NUFF (2). *Annual report.*

EVALUATION/RESEARCH: Evaluation reports available.

ACTIVITIES IN DEVELOPING REGIONS: Active in 1 country(ies). Works through local field partners. **Sustainable Development Actions:** Education/training/literacy. **Regions:** East Africa.

INFORMATION AND EDUCATION ACTIVITIES: **Topics:** Education/training/literacy; Emergency relief/refugees/humanitarian assistance; Human rights/peace/conflicts; International relations/cooperation/development

aid; Refugees/migrants/ethnic groups. **Activities:** Broadcasting/cultural events; Formal education; Fund raising; Information campaigns/exhibitions.

SWE3762

OLOF PALMES INTERNATIONELLA CENTRUM ◆ The Olof Palme International Centre

Box 3221, 103 64 Stockholm, Sweden.

Telephone: 46 (8) 21 07 39. *Fax:* 46 (8) 10 23 75. *Contact:* Birgitta Silén.

SWE3763

OREBROMISSIONEN ◆ Örebro Mission

Box 1623, 701 16 Örebro, Sweden.

Telephone: 46 (19) 11 93 60. *Fax:* 46 (19) 611 73 58. *Contact:* Gustav Sundström, Head of Mission.

OBJECTIVES: To undertake evangelism and social services in Asia, Africa and Latin America.

GENERAL INFORMATION: *Creation:* 1892. *Type of organisation:* network, coordinating body. *Affiliated to:* United Mission to Nepal (Nepal) - International Assistance Mission (Afganistan) - L'Association de Cooperation (Tunisie) - JCS International (Mongolia). *Salaried:* 184 of which: 128 in developing countries. *Budget/Total 1993:* ECU 9832000 (US$ 11514000). *Financial sources: Private:* 38%. *Public:* 30%. *Self-financing:* 32%.

PUBLICATIONS: *Periodicals:* Petrus (46). *Annual report.*

EVALUATION/RESEARCH: Evaluation reports available. Undertakes research activities.

COMMENTS: Undertakes activities in the Commonwealth of Independent States. Information activities related to the Commonwealth of Independent States.

ACTIVITIES IN DEVELOPING REGIONS: Active in 16 country(ies). Maintains local field presence. Works through local field partners. **Sustainable Development Actions:** Children/youth/family; Debt/finance/trade; Democracy/good governance/institution building/participatory development; Education/training/literacy; Emergency relief/refugees/humanitarian assistance; Energy/transport; Food/famine; Gender issues/women; Health/sanitation/water; Human rights/peace/conflicts; Population/family planning/demography; Rural development/agriculture; Sending volunteers/experts/technical assistance; Small enterprises/informal sector/handicrafts. **Regions:** Central Africa; Central Asia and South Asia; East Asia; Middle East; North Africa; South America.

INFORMATION AND EDUCATION ACTIVITIES: Topics: Children/youth/family; Culture/tradition/religion; Education/training/literacy; Emergency relief/refugees/humanitarian assistance; Food/famine; Health/sanitation/water; Human rights/peace/conflicts; Population/family planning/demography; Refugees/migrants/ethnic groups; Rural development/agriculture. **Activities:** Fund raising; Information campaigns/exhibitions; Publishing/audiovisual materials/educational materials.

SWE3764

ORJANSGARDEN AGNI ◆ AGNI Association

Box 1528, 751 45 Uppsala, Sweden.

Telephone: 46 (18) 10 37 82.

SWE3765

PALESTINAGRUPPERNA I SVERIGE ◆ The Palestine Solidarity Association in Sweden

Solidaritetshuset, Barnängsg. 23, 116 41 Stockholm, Sweden.

Telephone: 46 (8) 641 72 88. *Contact:* Yvonne Fredriksson.

SWE3766

PALMERAS VANNER ◆ Friends of Palmera

c/o Jan Sondér, Filipstadsbacken 48, 123 43 Farsta, Sweden.

Telephone: 46 (8) 605 25 25.

SWE3767

PAN-ASIA COOPERATION SOCIETY (PACS)

Box 1010, Pedagogen, Göteborgs Universitet, 431 26 Mölndal, Sweden.

Telephone: 46 (31) 14 15 42. *Fax:* 46 (31) 29 50 87. *Contact:* Allan Norlander.

SWE3768

PEACE BRIDGES INTERNATIONAL, SVERIGE (PBI) ◆ Peace Bridges International, Sweden

Kungsgatan 30, 75321 Uppsala, Sweden.

Telephone: 46 (18) 10 08 93. *Fax:* 46 (18) 10 08 92. *E-mail:* pbiswe@nn.apc.org.

OBJECTIVES: To recruit, train and support volunteers of Peace Bridges who are sent to work in developing countries experiencing political upheaval. To raise awareness of Peace bridges'projects.

GENERAL INFORMATION: *Type of organisation:* network, coordinating body. *Affiliated to:* Peace Brigades International (United Kingdom). *Personnel/Total:* 1. *Volunteers:* 1. *Budget/Total 1993:* ECU 31000 (US$ 37000). *Financial sources: Private:* 10%. *Public:* 84%. *Self-financing:* 6%.

PUBLICATIONS: *Periodicals:* PBI-Sverige Nyhetsblad (4).

EVALUATION/RESEARCH: Evaluation reports available.

ACTIVITIES IN DEVELOPING REGIONS: Present in developing regions. Active in 3 country(ies). Maintains local field presence. **Sustainable Development Actions:** Democracy/good governance/institution building/participatory development; Education/training/literacy; Human rights/peace/conflicts. **Regions:** Central Asia and South Asia; Mexico and Central America.

INFORMATION AND EDUCATION ACTIVITIES: Topics: Culture/tradition/religion; Education/training/literacy; Human rights/peace/conflicts; International relations/cooperation/development aid; Peace/ethnic conflicts/armament/disarmament; Poverty/living conditions; Racism/xenophobia/antisemitism. **Activities:** Conferences/seminars/workshops/training activities; Fund raising; Information and documentation services/data bases; Information campaigns/exhibitions; Lobbying/advocacy; Publishing/audiovisual materials/educational materials.

SWE3769

PINGST MISSIONENS U-LANDSHJALP (PMU-INTERLIFE) ◆ Swedish Pentecostal International Relief and Development Agency

Regulatorvägen 11, Box 4093, 141 04 Huddinge, Sweden.

Telephone: 46 (8) 608 96 00. *Fax:* 46 (8) 608 96 50. *Contact:* Roland Stenlund, Director.

OBJECTIVES: To co-ordinate emergency relief and development programmes carried out by the Swedish Pentecostal Movement in developing countries.

GENERAL INFORMATION: *Creation:* 1964. *Affiliated to:* VOICE (Belgium) - Swedish Mission Council (Sweden) - Forum Syd (Sweden). *Personnel/Total:* 290. *Salaried:* 240 of which: 200 in developing countries. *Volunteers:* 50. *Budget/Total 1993:* ECU 23369000 (US$ 27366000). *Financial sources: Private:* 9%. *Public:* 83%. *Self-financing:* 8%.

PUBLICATIONS: *Periodicals:* Nödbromsen (4) - Till Alla Folk (4). *Annual report.*

EVALUATION/RESEARCH: Evaluation reports available. Undertakes research activities.

COMMENTS: Undertakes activities in the Commonwealth of Independent States. Information activities related to the Commonwealth of Independent States.

ACTIVITIES IN DEVELOPING REGIONS: Active in 42 country(ies). Maintains local field presence. Works through local field partners. **Sustainable Development Actions:** Education/training/literacy; Emergency relief/refugees/humanitarian assistance; Energy/transport; Food/famine; Health/sanitation/water; Rural development/agriculture; Sending volunteers/experts/technical assistance. **Regions:** Central Africa; Central

Asia and South Asia; East Africa; Mexico and Central America; Middle East; South America; South East Asia; Southern Africa; West Africa.

INFORMATION AND EDUCATION ACTIVITIES: Topics: Education/training/literacy; Emergency relief/refugees/humanitarian assistance; Food/famine; Health/sanitation/water; Poverty/living conditions; Refugees/migrants/ethnic groups; Rural development/agriculture. Activities: Conferences/seminars/workshops/training activities; Fund raising; Information and documentation services/data bases; Information campaigns/exhibitions; Publishing/audiovisual materials/educational materials.

SWE3770

PRAKTISK SOLIDARITET

Box 8037, 402 77 Göteborg, Sweden.

Telephone: 46 (31) 51 77 59. Fax: 46 (31) 51 98 24. Contact: Göran Larsson, Chairman.

OBJECTIVES: To provide material support, mainly second hand clothes to poor people and refugees. To support activities initiated by the receiving organisation aiming to improve their situation.

GENERAL INFORMATION: Creation: 1989. Member organisations: 6. Personnel/Total: 100. Salaried: 100 of which: 1 in developing countries. Budget/Total 1993: ECU 4937000 (US$ 5782000). Financial sources: Private: 5%. Public: 50%. Self-financing: 45%.

PUBLICATIONS: Annual report.

EVALUATION/RESEARCH: Evaluation reports available. Undertakes research activities.

ACTIVITIES IN DEVELOPING REGIONS: Active in 5 country(ies). Works through local field partners. Sustainable Development Actions: Debt/finance/trade; Democracy/good governance/institution building/participatory development; Education/training/literacy; Emergency relief/refugees/humanitarian assistance; Gender issues/women; Health/sanitation/water; Human rights/peace/conflicts; Rural development/agriculture; Small enterprises/informal sector/handicrafts; Urban development/habitat. Regions: Mexico and Central America; North Africa; Southern Africa.

SWE3771

RADDA BARNEN ♦ Swedish Save the Children

Torsgatan 4, 107 88 Stockholm, Sweden.

Telephone: 46 (8) 698 90 00. Fax: 46 (8) 698 90 12. Contact: Lennart Lindgren, Secretary General.

OBJECTIVES: To promote and protect the rights of children in accordance with the UN Convention on the Rights of the Child. To improve living conditions for children at risk.

GENERAL INFORMATION: Creation: 1919. Affiliated to: International Save the Children (Switzerland). Personnel/Total: 142. Salaried: 142 of which: 24 in developing countries. Budget/Total 1993: ECU 30720000 (US$ 35974000). Financial sources: Private: 47%. Public: 39%. Self-financing: 14%.

PUBLICATIONS: Periodicals: Barnen & Vi (7). Annual report. List of publications.

EVALUATION/RESEARCH: Evaluation reports available.

COMMENTS: Undertakes activities in the Commonwealth of Independent States. Information activities related to the Commonwealth of Independent States.

ACTIVITIES IN DEVELOPING REGIONS: Present in developing regions. Active in 10 country(ies). Maintains local field presence. Works through local field partners. Sustainable Development Actions: Children/youth/family; Democracy/good governance/institution building/participatory development; Education/training/literacy; Emergency relief/refugees/humanitarian assistance; Gender issues/women; Health/sanitation/water; Human rights/peace/conflicts; Other; Population/family planning/demography; Rural development/agriculture; Sending volunteers/experts/technical assistance; Small enterprises/informal sector/handicrafts; Urban development/habitat. Regions: Central Asia and South Asia; East Africa; Mexico and Central America; Middle East; North Africa; South America; South East Asia; Southern Africa; West Africa.

INFORMATION AND EDUCATION ACTIVITIES: Topics: Children/youth/family; Culture/tradition/religion; Education/training/literacy; Emergency relief/refugees/humanitarian assistance; Gender issues/women; Health/sanitation/water; Human rights/peace/conflicts; International economic relations/trade/debt/finance; Other; Peace/ethnic conflicts/armament/disarmament; Poverty/living conditions; Refugees/migrants/ethnic groups; Urban development/habitat. Activities: Broadcasting/cultural events; Conferences/seminars/workshops/training activities; Exchanges/twinning/linking; Formal education; Information and documentation services/data bases; Information campaigns/exhibitions; Lobbying/advocacy; Publishing/audiovisual materials/educational materials.

SWE3772

RAOUL WALLENBERG INSTITUTET FOR MANSKILIGA RATTGHETER OCH HUMANITAR RATT (RWI) ♦ Raoul Wallenberg Institute of Human Rights and Humanitarian Law

Sankt Annegatan 4, 223 50 Lund, Sweden.

Telephone: 46 (46) 10 43 10. Fax: 46 (46) 10 44 55. Contact: Gran Melander, Director.

OBJECTIVES: To promote research on human rights and humanitarian law by establishing a research library containing works on international law, as well as to initiate, develop and support research and scholarly/scientific tuition in the field.

GENERAL INFORMATION: Creation: 1984. Affiliated to: Network of the Nordic Institutes of Human Rights - Coucil of Europe Network for Human Rights Institutes. Personnel/Total: 6. Salaried: 6. Financial sources: Private: 5%. Public: 95%.

PUBLICATIONS: Annual report. List of publications.

EVALUATION/RESEARCH: Undertakes research activities.

COMMENTS: Undertakes activities in the Commonwealth of Independent States. Information activities related to the Commonwealth of Independent States.

ACTIVITIES IN DEVELOPING REGIONS: Present in developing regions. Active in 10 country(ies). Works through local field partners. Sustainable Development Actions: Education/training/literacy; Gender issues/women; Human rights/peace/conflicts. Regions: Central Africa; East Africa; North Africa; South East Asia; Southern Africa; West Africa.

INFORMATION AND EDUCATION ACTIVITIES: Topics: Gender issues/women; Human rights/peace/conflicts; Refugees/migrants/ethnic groups. Activities: Conferences/seminars/workshops/training activities; Information and documentation services/data bases.

SWE3773

RAVARUGRUPPEN ♦ Raw Materials Group

Box 90103, 120 21 Stockholm, Sweden.

Telephone: 46 (8) 642 86 77. Fax: 46 (8) 640 11 87. Contact: Magnus Ericsson.

OBJECTIVES: To provide information and technical assistance on mining and minerals.

GENERAL INFORMATION: Creation: 1971. Personnel/Total: 5. Salaried: 5.

PUBLICATIONS: Periodicals: Raw Materials Report (4). Annual report. List of publications.

EVALUATION/RESEARCH: Undertakes research activities.

ACTIVITIES IN DEVELOPING REGIONS: Maintains local field presence. Works through local field partners. Sustainable Development Actions: Sending volunteers/experts/technical assistance. Regions: Southern Africa.

INFORMATION AND EDUCATION ACTIVITIES: Topics: International economic relations/trade/debt/finance. Activities: Information and documentation services/data bases.

SWE3774

RIGHT LIVELIHOOD AWARDS FOUNDATION

P.O. Box 15072, 104 65 Stockholm, Sweden.

Voir : Comment utiliser le répertoire, page 11.

Telephone: 46 (8) 702 03 40. *Fax:* 46 (8) 702 03 38. *Contact:* Jakob von Vexkull.

OBJECTIVES: To give four prizes annually to individuals who have found practical solutions to development problems. To support those who work to alleviate material poverty in the Third World and to combat spiritual poverty in the North.

GENERAL INFORMATION: *Creation:* 1989. *Personnel/Total:* 2. *Salaried:* 2.

PUBLICATIONS: *Periodicals:* Cornerstones (2). *List of publications.*

EVALUATION/RESEARCH: Undertakes research activities.

COMMENTS: Undertakes activities in the Commonwealth of Independent States.

ACTIVITIES IN DEVELOPING REGIONS: Works through local field partners.

INFORMATION AND EDUCATION ACTIVITIES: Topics: Culture/tradition/religion; Ecology/environment/biodiversity; Education/training/literacy; Food/famine; Health/sanitation/water; Human rights/peace/conflicts; Peace/ethnic conflicts/armament/disarmament; Rural development/agriculture. **Activities:** Broadcasting/cultural events; Conferences/seminars/workshops/training activities; Information and documentation services/data bases; Information campaigns/exhibitions.

SWE3775
RIKSFORBUNDET FOR SEXUELL UPPLYSINING/SWEDEN ♦
Swedish Association for Sex Education

Box 12 128, 102 24 Stockholm, Sweden.

Telephone: 46 (8) 692 07 00. *Fax:* 46 (8) 653 08 23.

OBJECTIVES: To promote sexual and reproductive health.

GENERAL INFORMATION: *Creation:* 1933. *Affiliated to:* International Planned Parenthood Federation - The United Nations Association of Sweden. *Personnel/Total:* 1515. *Salaried:* 15. *Volunteers:* 1500. *Budget/Total 1993:* ECU 1536000 (US$ 1799000).

PUBLICATIONS: *Annual report. List of publications.*

EVALUATION/RESEARCH: Evaluation reports available. Undertakes research activities.

COMMENTS: Undertakes activities in the Commonwealth of Independent States. Information activities related to the Commonwealth of Independent States.

ACTIVITIES IN DEVELOPING REGIONS: Present in developing regions. Active in 3 country(ies). Maintains local field presence. Works through local field partners. **Sustainable Development Actions:** Children/youth/family; Education/training/literacy; Gender issues/women; Population/family planning/demography. **Regions:** East Africa.

INFORMATION AND EDUCATION ACTIVITIES: Topics: Children/youth/family; Gender issues/women; Population/family planning/demography. **Activities:** Conferences/seminars/workshops/training activities.

SWE3776
RODA KORSETS UNGDOMSFORBUND ♦ Red Cross Youth

Östhammarsgatan 70, Box 27316, 102 54 Stockholm, Sweden.

Telephone: 46 (8) 665 56 00. *Fax:* 46 (8) 783 66 92. *Contact:* A. Odelius.

OBJECTIVES: To work for a humanitarian world. To prevent human suffering and to undertake health projects where needed.

GENERAL INFORMATION: *Creation:* 1921. *Affiliated to:* International Federation of the Red Cross. *Personnel/Total:* 13. *Salaried:* 8. *Volunteers:* 5 of which: 5 in developing countries. *Budget/Total 1993:* ECU 625000 (US$ 732000). *Financial sources:* Private: 40%. Public: 60%.

PUBLICATIONS: *Periodicals:* Med Mera (4).

EVALUATION/RESEARCH: Evaluation reports available.

PLANNED ACTIVITIES: A campaign against xenophobia and racism in Sweden and educating the public on the UN Convention on the Rights of the Child.

ACTIVITIES IN DEVELOPING REGIONS: Active in 3 country(ies). Maintains local field presence. Works through local field partners. **Sustainable Development Actions:** Children/youth/family; Health/sanitation/water; Rural development/agriculture; Sending volunteers/experts/technical assistance; Small enterprises/informal sector/handicrafts. **Regions:** East Africa; Southern Africa; West Africa.

INFORMATION AND EDUCATION ACTIVITIES: Topics: Children/youth/family; Emergency relief/refugees/humanitarian assistance; Health/sanitation/water; Human rights/peace/conflicts; International relations/cooperation/development aid; Peace/ethnic conflicts/armament/disarmament; Racism/xenophobia/antisemitism; Refugees/migrants/ethnic groups; Rural development/agriculture. **Activities:** Conferences/seminars/workshops/training activities; Exchanges/twinning/linking; Fund raising; Information and documentation services/data bases; Information campaigns/exhibitions; Lobbying/advocacy.

SWE3777
ROTARY INTERNATIONAL - DISTRIKT 2320

Helsingforsg 11, 921 92 Lycksele, Sweden.

Telephone: 46 (950) 150 15. *Fax:* 46 (950) 152 31. *Contact:* M.P.Rune Ångström.

OBJECTIVES: To promote international understanding through scholarships and youth programmes. To support educational and training activities in developing countries. To replant trees in Kenya and to promote education in support of reforestation projects.

GENERAL INFORMATION: *Creation:* 1925. *Affiliated to:* Rotary International (USA). *Personnel/Total:* 39. *Salaried:* 1 of which: 1 in developing countries. *Volunteers:* 38 of which: 30 in developing countries. *Budget/Total 1993:* ECU 38000 (US$ 45000). *Financial sources:* Public: 70%. *Self-financing:* 30%.

PUBLICATIONS: *Annual report. List of publications.*

EVALUATION/RESEARCH: Evaluation reports available.

ACTIVITIES IN DEVELOPING REGIONS: Present in developing regions. Maintains local field presence. Works through local field partners. **Sustainable Development Actions:** Education/training/literacy; Rural development/agriculture; Sending volunteers/experts/technical assistance. **Regions:** East Africa.

INFORMATION AND EDUCATION ACTIVITIES: Topics: Education/training/literacy; Rural development/agriculture. **Activities:** Publishing/audiovisual materials/educational materials.

SWE3778
S-KVINNOR, SVERIGES SOCIALDEMOKRATISKA KVINNOFORBUND ♦ National Federation of Social Democratic Women in Sweden

Box 70458, 107 26 Stockholm, Sweden.

Telephone: 46 (8) 700 26 00. *Fax:* 46 (8) 676 09 26.

SWE3779
SABS KOMMITTE FOR U-LANDSFRAGOR ♦ The Swedish Library Association Standing Committee on Information about Developing Countries

Uppsala Universitetsbibliotek, Box 510, 751 20 Uppsala, Sweden.

Telephone: 46 (18) 18 39 22. *Fax:* 46 (18) 18 39 13. *Contact:* Astrid Kiselman.

SWE3780
SAMARBETE FOR FRED (SAM) ♦ Co-operation for Peace

Lundagatan 56, 117 27 Stockholm, Sweden.

Telephone: 46 (8) 669 75 20. *Fax:* 46 (8) 84 90 16. *E-mail:* PeaceQuestSto@.apc.org. *Contact:* Valentin Sevéus, Secretary General.

OBJECTIVES: To actively contribute in association with peace organisations around the globe to the peaceful development of our world.

GENERAL INFORMATION: *Creation:* 1983. *Affiliated to:* International Peace Bureau (Switzerland). *Personnel/Total:* 20. *Salaried:* 10 of which: 3 in developing countries. *Volunteers:* 10 of which: 2 in develop-

See: *How to Use the Directory*, page 11.

ing countries. *Budget/Total 1993:* ECU 219000 (US$ 257000). *Financial sources:* Private: 20%. Public: 60%. Self-financing: 20%.

COMMENTS: Undertakes activities in the Commonwealth of Independent States. Information activities related to the Commonwealth of Independent States.

ACTIVITIES IN DEVELOPING REGIONS: Maintains local field presence. Works through local field partners. **Sustainable Development Actions:** Human rights/peace/conflicts. **Regions:** Central Asia and South Asia.

INFORMATION AND EDUCATION ACTIVITIES: Topics: Ecology/environment/biodiversity; Human rights/peace/conflicts. **Activities:** Conferences/seminars/workshops/training activities.

SWE3781
SCANDINAVIAN ASSOCIATION FOR DEVELOPMENT, RESTORATION AND AID ♦ SADRA

Röseg. 16, 784 54 Borlänge, Sweden.

Telephone: 46 (243) 83 346. *Fax:* 46 (243) 85 777. *Contact:* Urban Näslund.

OBJECTIVES: To promote democracy and the protection of local culture. To promote the development of communities through the formation of trade unions, social organisations and cultural activities.

GENERAL INFORMATION: Creation: 1990. **Personnel/Total:** 1. Volunteers: 1. **Financial sources:** Public: 80%. Self-financing: 20%.

PUBLICATIONS: Annual report.

EVALUATION/RESEARCH: Evaluation reports available.

ACTIVITIES IN DEVELOPING REGIONS: Present in developing regions. Active in 4 country(ies). Works through local field partners. **Sustainable Development Actions:** Democracy/good governance/institution building/participatory development; Ecology/environment/biodiversity; Education/training/literacy; Human rights/peace/conflicts; Other. **Regions:** Mexico and Central America; South America.

INFORMATION AND EDUCATION ACTIVITIES: Topics: Culture/tradition/religion; Human rights/peace/conflicts. **Activities:** Fund raising; Lobbying/advocacy; Publishing/audiovisual materials/educational materials.

SWE3782
SKANDINAVISKA BARNMISSIONEN ♦ Scandinavian Children's Mission

Virkesv. 2, 230 30 Oxie, Sweden.

Telephone: 46 (40) 54 53 30. *Fax:* 46 (40) 54 50 88. *Contact:* Sigvard Wallenberg.

SWE3783
STIFTELSEN EMMAUS I UPPSALA ♦ Emmaüs Foundation - Uppsala

Stövarvägen 7, 756 46 Uppsala, Sweden.

Telephone: 46 (18) 30 38 36/ 37 10 09. *Fax:* 46 (18) 30 38 37. *Contact:* Lars Mellgren, President.

OBJECTIVES: To promote the rehabilitation of disabled children in Gambia, the Baltic States and Russia.

GENERAL INFORMATION: Creation: 1961. **Affiliated to:** Emmaüs International (France). **Personnel/Total:** 21. Salaried: 13 of which: 4 in developing countries. Volunteers: 8. **Budget/Total 1993:** ECU 383000 (US$ 450000). **Financial sources:** Private: 50%. Public: 50%.

COMMENTS: Undertakes activities in the Commonwealth of Independent States. Information activities related to the Commonwealth of Independent States.

ACTIVITIES IN DEVELOPING REGIONS: Present in developing regions. Active in 1 country(ies). Maintains local field presence. Works through local field partners. **Sustainable Development Actions:** Children/youth/family; Education/training/literacy; Health/sanitation/water; Sending volunteers/experts/technical assistance. **Regions:** West Africa.

INFORMATION AND EDUCATION ACTIVITIES: Topics: Children/youth/family; Education/training/literacy; Health/sanitation/water. **Activities:** Conferences/seminars/workshops/training activities; Fund raising.

SWE3784
STIFTELSEN ESTHER AXENES BARNHJALP

c/o Lars-Göran Svensson, Brageg. 12, 386 93 Färjestaden, Sweden.

Telephone: 46 (485) 38 529. *Fax:* 46 (485) 34 753. *Contact:* Lars-Göran and Solveig Svensson.

SWE3785
STIFTELSEN FOR GLOBALA BEFOLKNINGSFRAGOR ♦
World Population Foundation, Sweden

Rådmansgatan 22, 3rd floor, 114 25 Stockholm, Sweden.

Telephone: 46 (8) 24 81 41. *Fax:* 46 (8) 792 31 66. *Contact:* Rigmor Allbäck, Director.

OBJECTIVES: To raise funds to stimulate solutions to global problems of population and development. To create understanding concerning the nature, size and complexity of world population, in particular with regard to the social and economic development of humanity.

GENERAL INFORMATION: Creation: 1993. **Personnel/Total:** 9. Salaried: 4. Volunteers: 5. **Budget/Total 1993:** ECU 38000 (US$ 45000). **Financial sources:** Private: 33%. Public: 66%. Self-financing: 1%.

PUBLICATIONS: Periodicals: Newsletter (4). Annual report. List of publications.

EVALUATION/RESEARCH: Evaluation reports available. Undertakes research activities.

PLANNED ACTIVITIES: Undertaking several advocacy activities including developing an information centre for students and journalists, training communicators and youth and conducting study days for teachers.

COMMENTS: The World Population Foundation has a sister organisation in Laren, Netherlands.

ACTIVITIES IN DEVELOPING REGIONS: Active in 1 country(ies). Works through local field partners. **Sustainable Development Actions:** Children/youth/family; Population/family planning/demography. **Regions:** Mexico and Central America.

INFORMATION AND EDUCATION ACTIVITIES: Topics: Children/youth/family; Ecology/environment/biodiversity; Gender issues/women; Human rights/peace/conflicts; International relations/cooperation/development aid; Population/family planning/demography; Poverty/living conditions; Refugees/migrants/ethnic groups. **Activities:** Conferences/seminars/workshops/training activities; Exchanges/twinning/linking; Fund raising; Information and documentation services/data bases; Information campaigns/exhibitions; Lobbying/advocacy; Networking/electronic telecommunications; Publishing/audiovisual materials/educational materials.

SWE3786
STIFTELSEN FOR INTERNATIONELLT UNGDOMSUTBYTE ♦
The Swedish Foundation for International Youth Exchange

Kungsg. 48, 111 35 Stockholm, Sweden.

Telephone: 46 (8) 20 01 90. *Fax:* 46 (8) 20 35 30. *E-mail:* Internet:Bengt-Persson@ETT.se. *Contact:* Bengt Persson, Director.

OBJECTIVES: To promote mobility among young people.

GENERAL INFORMATION: Creation: 1990. **Personnel/Total:** 13. Salaried: 8. Volunteers: 5 of which: 5 in developing countries. **Budget/Total 1993:** ECU 1097000 (US$ 1285000). **Financial sources:** Public: 95%. Self-financing: 5%.

PUBLICATIONS: Periodicals: UFE - News (4) - WYS - News (2). Annual report. List of publications.

EVALUATION/RESEARCH: Evaluation reports available. Undertakes research activities.

PLANNED ACTIVITIES: Preparing a CD-ROM guide and publishing a book on youth mobility.

COMMENTS: SIU is a semi governmental foundation. Information activities related to the Commonwealth of Independent States.

ACTIVITIES IN DEVELOPING REGIONS: Present in developing regions. Maintains local field presence. Works through local field partners. **Sustainable Development Actions:** Children/youth/family; Rural development/agriculture; Sending volunteers/experts/technical assistance; Urban development/habitat. **Regions:** Mexico and Central America; South East Asia.

INFORMATION AND EDUCATION ACTIVITIES: Topics: Culture/tradition/religion; Education/training/literacy; Racism/xenophobia/antisemitism. **Activities:** Exchanges/twinning/linking; Information campaigns/exhibitions.

SWE3787

STIFTELSEN GLOBTRADET ♦ The Globetree Foundation

P.O. Box 22206, 104 22 Stockholm, Sweden.

Telephone: 46 (8) 652 35 27. *Fax:* 46 (8) 652 21 77. *E-mail:* globetree@nn.apc.org. *Contact:* Kajsa B. Dahlström, Chairperson.

OBJECTIVES: To support the development of teaching and education. To promote scientific research and teaching through cultural expression. To support the education of children and adults about their environment within an international perspective.

GENERAL INFORMATION: *Creation:* 1982. *Affiliated to:* SONBO (Keynia) - Sasana Daya Cipta (Indonesia) - Kahoy ny Bahay (Philippines). *Volunteers:* 33 of which: 19 in developing countries. *Budget/Total 1993:* ECU 148000 (US$ 173000). *Financial sources:* Private: 10%. Public: 60%. Self-financing: 30%.

PUBLICATIONS: *Periodicals:* Meeting in the Globetree (4) (6). *Annual report. List of publications.*

EVALUATION/RESEARCH: Evaluation reports available. Undertakes research activities.

PLANNED ACTIVITIES: An international programme for children aged 6-16 and their teachers on water and the environment and a programme designed to help children deal with complex social problems such as racism and xenophobia.

ACTIVITIES IN DEVELOPING REGIONS: Active in 4 country(ies). Works through local field partners. **Sustainable Development Actions:** Children/youth/family; Democracy/good governance/institution building/participatory development; Ecology/environment/biodiversity; Education/training/literacy; Energy/transport; Gender issues/women; Health/sanitation/water; Rural development/agriculture; Sending volunteers/experts/technical assistance; Urban development/habitat. **Regions:** Central Asia and South Asia; East Africa; Mexico and Central America; South America; South East Asia.

INFORMATION AND EDUCATION ACTIVITIES: Topics: Children/youth/family; Culture/tradition/religion; Ecology/environment/biodiversity; Education/training/literacy; Gender issues/women; Health/sanitation/water; Racism/xenophobia/antisemitism; Rural development/agriculture; Urban development/habitat. **Activities:** Broadcasting/cultural events; Conferences/seminars/workshops/training activities; Fund raising; Networking/electronic telecommunications; Publishing/audiovisual materials/educational materials.

SWE3788

STIFTELSEN SVENSK INTERNATIONELL BARNHJALP - BARN I NOD

Box 2038, 431 02 Mölndal, Sweden.

Telephone: 46 (31) 16 72 94. *Contact:* Ingegerd Norin.

SWE3789

STOCKHOLM ENVIRONMENT INSTITUTE (SEI)

P.O. Box 2142, 103 14 Stockholm, Sweden.

Telephone: 46 (8) 723 02 60. *Fax:* 46 (8) 723 03 48. *E-mail:* seihq@nordnet.se. *Contact:* Michael J. Chadwick, Director.

OBJECTIVES: To conduct global research of environmental and development issues.

GENERAL INFORMATION: *Creation:* 1989. *Personnel/Total:* 60. *Budget/Total 1993:* ECU 5486000 (US$ 6424000). *Financial sources:* Private: 25%. Public: 75%.

PUBLICATIONS: *Periodicals:* SEI International Environmental Bulletin (4) - Renewable Energy for Devlopment (3). *List of publications.*

EVALUATION/RESEARCH: Undertakes research activities.

COMMENTS: Undertakes activities in the Commonwealth of Independent States. Information activities related to the Commonwealth of Independent States.

ACTIVITIES IN DEVELOPING REGIONS: Present in developing regions. Active in 15 country(ies). Maintains local field presence. **Sustainable Development Actions:** Ecology/environment/biodiversity; Energy/transport; Health/sanitation/water; Rural development/agriculture. **Regions:** Caribbean; Central Africa; Central Asia and South Asia; East Africa; East Asia; Mexico and Central America; Middle East; North Africa; Oceania; South America; South East Asia; Southern Africa; West Africa.

INFORMATION AND EDUCATION ACTIVITIES: Topics: Ecology/environment/biodiversity; Health/sanitation/water; Poverty/living conditions; Rural development/agriculture; Urban development/habitat. **Activities:** Conferences/seminars/workshops/training activities; Information and documentation services/data bases; Information campaigns/exhibitions; Networking/electronic telecommunications; Publishing/audiovisual materials/educational materials.

SWE3790

STODFORENING TILL REST I SVERIGE ♦ Swedish Support Committee of the Relief Society of Tigray

Runsligan 24A, 223 53 Lund, Sweden.

Telephone: 46 (46) 13 25 60/14 66 48. *Contact:* Aberra Fekadu, Chairman.

SWE3791

STODFORENINGEN FOR PRAKTIKANTUTBYTE TOREBODABYGDEN - KIBAHA ♦ Support Organisation for Trainee Exchange Törebodabygden - Kibaha

Prästgården, Flistad, 540 18 Tidan, Sweden.

Telephone: 46 (500) 70 395. *Contact:* Rut Aronson.

SWE3792

STODKOMMITTEN FOR CENTRALAMERIKAS FOLK ♦ Support Committee for the Support of the Peoples of Central America

Box 2151, 220 02 Lund, Sweden.

Telephone: 46 (46) 14 50 38. *Contact:* Maria Dahmén.

SWE3793

SUSILA DHARMA SVERIGE

c/o Vivianne Trumén, Sätraängsv. 122, 182 37 Danderyd, Sweden.
Telephone: 46 (8) 622 53 92.

SWE3794

SVALORNA - INDIEN-BANGLADESHSEKTIONEN

Spoleg. 5, 222 20 Lund, Sweden.

Telephone: 46 (46) 12 10 05. *Fax:* 46 (46) 14 54 43.

SWE3795

SVALORNA I GOTEBORG ♦ The Swallows in Gothenburg

Box 72 82, 402 35 Göteborg, Sweden.

Telephone: 46 (31) 42 40 33. *Fax:* 46 (31) 42 50 09. *Contact:* Barbro von Krusenstierna, Chairman.

OBJECTIVES: To work for social and economic justice in the world in solidarity with and support for neglected people.

GENERAL INFORMATION: *Creation:* 1976. *Type of organisation:* association of NGOs. *Affiliated to:* Emmaüs Interna-

See: *How to Use the Directory,* page 11.

tional (France). *Personnel/Total:* var.. *Salaried:* 1. *Volunteers:* 15. *Financial sources:* Private: 20%. Self-financing: 80%.

PUBLICATIONS: *Periodicals:* Svalorna (2). *Annual report.*

ACTIVITIES IN DEVELOPING REGIONS: Present in developing regions. Active in 5 country(ies). Maintains local field presence. Works through local field partners. **Sustainable Development Actions:** Children/ youth/family; Democracy/good governance/institution building/participatory development; Ecology/environment/biodiversity; Education/ training/literacy; Gender issues/women; Health/sanitation/water; Human rights/peace/conflicts; Rural development/agriculture; Sending volunteers/experts/technical assistance; Small enterprises/informal sector/ handicrafts; Urban development/habitat. **Regions:** Central Asia and South Asia; Mexico and Central America; South America.

INFORMATION AND EDUCATION ACTIVITIES: **Topics:** Children/youth/ family; Culture/tradition/religion; Ecology/environment/biodiversity; Employment/unemployment; Gender issues/women; International economic relations/trade/debt/finance; International relations/cooperation/ development aid; Poverty/living conditions. **Activities:** Fund raising; Information campaigns/exhibitions.

SWE3796

SVALORNA I SVERIGE - LATINAMERIKASEKTIONEN ♦ The Swallows in Sweden - Latin America Section

Barnängsgatan 23, 116 41 Stockholm, Sweden.

Telephone: 46 (8) 642 16 96. *Fax:* 46 (8) 640 36 60.

OBJECTIVES: To work for and with the most disadvantaged peoples in the world not only to reduce their suffering but to destroy the underlying causes of underdevelopment.

GENERAL INFORMATION: *Creation:* 1959. *Affiliated to:* Emmaüs International (France) - Svensk Voluntärsamreckan (Sweden) -Biståndsinformation (Sweden). *Personnel/Total:* 28. *Salaried:* 18 of which: 15 in developing countries. *Volunteers:* 10. *Budget/Total 1993:* ECU 79000 (US$ 93000).

PUBLICATIONS: *Periodicals:* Svalorna (2). *Annual report. List of publications.*

ACTIVITIES IN DEVELOPING REGIONS: Active in 5 country(ies). Maintains local field presence. Works through local field partners. **Sustainable Development Actions:** Children/youth/family; Democracy/good governance/institution building/participatory development; Ecology/environment/biodiversity; Education/training/literacy; Gender issues/women; Health/sanitation/water; Rural development/agriculture; Sending volunteers/experts/technical assistance; Small enterprises/informal sector/ handicrafts; Urban development/habitat. **Regions:** Mexico and Central America; South America.

INFORMATION AND EDUCATION ACTIVITIES: **Topics:** Children/youth/ family; Culture/tradition/religion; Ecology/environment/biodiversity; Education/training/literacy; Gender issues/women; Health/sanitation/water; International relations/cooperation/development aid; Poverty/living conditions; Refugees/migrants/ethnic groups; Rural development/agriculture; Urban development/habitat. **Activities:** Conferences/seminars/ workshops/training activities; Exchanges/twinning/linking; Formal education; Fund raising; Information campaigns/exhibitions.

SWE3797

SVENSK UTVECKLINGSHJALP I HONDURAS

c/o Eriksson, Kimsta, Skånela, 195 96 Rosersberg, Sweden.

Telephone: 46 (8) 591 440 60.

SWE3798

SVENSK VOLONTARSAMVERKAN (SVS) ♦ Swedish Volunteer Service

Box 17510, Hornsgatan 54, III, 118 91 Stockholm, Sweden.

Telephone: 46 (8) 702 77 20. *Fax:* 46 (8) 702 90 99. *Contact:* Svante Sandberg, Executive Secretary.

OBJECTIVES: To recruit and train skilled volunteers to work in developing countries in order to support the local people in their endeavours to develop their resources, achieve economic and political independence and work towards a democratic social order.

GENERAL INFORMATION: *Creation:* 1981. *Type of organisation:* association of NGOs. *Member organisations:* 65. *Affiliated to:* European Forum on Development Service - Eurostep (Belgium) - El Taller (Tunisia). *Personnel/Total:* 86. *Salaried:* 11. *Volunteers:* 75 of which: 75 in developing countries. *Budget/Total 1993:* ECU 3291000 (US$ 3854000). *Financial sources:* Private: 1%. Public: 98%. Self-financing: 1%.

PUBLICATIONS: *Periodicals:* Volontären (4). *Annual report. List of publications.*

PLANNED ACTIVITIES: Constitution of an "emergency corps" of ex-volunteers for emergencies, election surveillance etc.

COMMENTS: In July 1995, SVS joined with BIFO to form a new NGO, Forum South.

ACTIVITIES IN DEVELOPING REGIONS: Present in developing regions. Active in 5 country(ies). Maintains local field presence. Works through local field partners. **Sustainable Development Actions:** Children/ youth/family; Ecology/environment/biodiversity; Education/training/literacy; Food/famine; Health/sanitation/water; Rural development/agriculture; Sending volunteers/experts/technical assistance. **Regions:** East Africa; Mexico and Central America; South East Asia; Southern Africa.

INFORMATION AND EDUCATION ACTIVITIES: **Topics:** Children/youth/ family; International relations/cooperation/development aid. **Activities:** Conferences/seminars/workshops/training activities; Exchanges/twinning/linking; Formal education; Information and documentation services/ data bases; Information campaigns/exhibitions; Lobbying/advocacy; Publishing/audiovisual materials/educational materials.

SWE3799

SVENSK-ETIOPISKA LANDSBYGDSUTVECKLINGSFORENINGEN (SELUF) ♦ Swedish Ethiopian Rural Development Association

P.O. Box 1159, 141 60 Huddinge, Sweden.

Telephone: 46 (8) 608 21 42. *Fax:* 46 (8) 608 21 41. *Contact:* Birgit Negussie.

OBJECTIVES: To promote rural development in south-west Ethiopia in collaboration with the people of the area and to support the development of local resources. To promote the use of medicinal and useful plants in Ethiopia and Africa.

GENERAL INFORMATION: *Creation:* 1984. *Personnel/Total:* 13. *Salaried:* 12 of which: 12 in developing countries. *Volunteers:* 1 of which: 1 in developing countries. *Budget/Total 1993:* ECU 109000 (US$ 128000). *Financial sources:* Private: 20%. Public: 80%.

PUBLICATIONS: *Periodicals:* Bulletins (1) - Newsletter (4). *Annual report.*

EVALUATION/RESEARCH: Evaluation reports available. Undertakes research activities.

PLANNED ACTIVITIES: The organisation plans to build up infastructure in their projects concerning health care for children, building a primary and secondary school, a bridge and managing a mill.

ACTIVITIES IN DEVELOPING REGIONS: Present in developing regions. Active in 1 country(ies). Maintains local field presence. Works through local field partners. **Sustainable Development Actions:** Children/ youth/family; Ecology/environment/biodiversity; Education/training/literacy; Gender issues/women; Health/sanitation/water; Population/family planning/demography; Rural development/agriculture; Sending volunteers/experts/technical assistance; Small enterprises/informal sector/ handicrafts. **Regions:** East Africa.

INFORMATION AND EDUCATION ACTIVITIES: **Topics:** Children/youth/ family; Culture/tradition/religion; Ecology/environment/biodiversity; Education/training/literacy; Gender issues/women; Health/sanitation/water; Rural development/agriculture. **Activities:** Conferences/seminars/workshops/training activities; Lobbying/advocacy.

SWE3800

SVENSK-FILIPPINSKA FORENINGEN (SFF) ♦ Swedish Filipino Association

Barnängsgatan 23, 3tr, 116 41 Stockholm, Sweden.

Voir : *Comment utiliser le répertoire,* page 11.

Telephone: 46 (8) 642 97 26. *Fax:* 46 (8) 641 11 35. *Contact:* Krister Holm, Chairperson.

SWE3801

SVENSK-GAMBIANSKA FORENINGEN ♦ Swedish Gambian Society

Bergsgatan 18, Box 22 556, 104 22 Stockholm, Sweden.

Telephone: 46 (8) 653 27 32. *Contact:* Ebrima Jawara, President.

SWE3802

SVENSK-INDIANSKA FORBUNDET ♦ Swedish-American Indian Association

Solidaritetshuset, Barnängsg. 23, 116 41 Stockholm, Sweden.

Telephone: 46 (8) 640 73 98. *Contact:* Monika Johnsson.

SWE3803

SVENSK-KUBANSKA FORENINGEN ♦ Swedish-Cuban Association

Box 45065, 104 30 Stockholm, Sweden.

Telephone: 46 (8) 31 95 30.

SWE3804

SVENSK-LATINAMERIKANSKA KVINNOGRUPPEN

Box 1615, 221 01 Lund, Sweden.

Telephone: 46 (46) 32 30 80. *Fax:* 46 (46) 18 49 40. *Contact:* Helena Persson.

SWE3805

SVENSK-SEYCHELLISKA FORENINGEN ♦ Swedish-Seychellois Association

Nässelstigen 2, 181 31 Lidingö, Sweden.

Telephone: 46 (8) 767 66 88. *Contact:* Pär Gunnartz, Secretary.

SWE3806

SVENSK-SUDANSKA FORENINGEN ♦ Swedish Sudanese Association

c/o Herne Nordlund, Jakob Westinsgatan 4, 112 20 Stockholm, Sweden.

Telephone: 46 (8) 652 74 35. *Fax:* 46 (8) 652 55 12. *Contact:* Gunvor Herne Nordlund, President.

OBJECTIVES: To increase understanding and improve relations between Sweden and Sudan. To support village development projects in desert areas of Sudan. To promote self-help activities and to teach children both ordinary school subjects and topics related to projects.

GENERAL INFORMATION: *Creation:* 1970. *Personnel/Total:* 10. *Salaried:* 2 of which: 2 in developing countries. *Volunteers:* 8. *Budget/Total 1993:* ECU 411000 (US$ 482000). *Financial sources: Private:* 11%. *Public:* 80%. *Self-financing:* 9%.

PUBLICATIONS: *Annual report.*

EVALUATION/RESEARCH: Evaluation reports available.

ACTIVITIES IN DEVELOPING REGIONS: Present in developing regions. Active in 1 country(ies). Maintains local field presence. **Sustainable Development Actions:** Democracy/good governance/institution building/participatory development; Education/training/literacy; Energy/transport; Health/sanitation/water; Rural development/agriculture. **Regions:** East Africa.

SWE3807

SVENSK-TANZANISKA FORENINGEN (SVETAN) ♦ Swedish Tanzanian Association

Box 22003, 104 22 Stockholm, Sweden.

Telephone: 46 (8) 785 88 15. *Contact:* Folke Strömberg, Chairman.

OBJECTIVES: To promote co-operation between Sweden and Tanzania. To inform the Swedish public about the situation in Tanzania and support local development efforts.

GENERAL INFORMATION: *Creation:* 1968. *Member organisations:* 15. *Affiliated to:* Swedish Volunteer Service (Sweden) - BIFO. *Budget/Total 1993:* ECU 11000 (US$ 13000). *Financial sources: Private:* 5%. *Self-financing:* 95%.

PUBLICATIONS: *Periodicals:* Habari (4). *Annual report. List of publications.*

PLANNED ACTIVITIES: Supporting a Mottessori Teacher Training Centre and a school of sculpture in Bagamoyo Tanzania.

ACTIVITIES IN DEVELOPING REGIONS: Present in developing regions. Active in 1 country(ies). Works through local field partners. **Sustainable Development Actions:** Gender issues/women; Health/sanitation/water; Rural development/agriculture. **Regions:** East Africa.

INFORMATION AND EDUCATION ACTIVITIES: Topics: Children/youth/family; Culture/tradition/religion; Ecology/environment/biodiversity; Education/training/literacy; Emergency relief/refugees/humanitarian assistance; Employment/unemployment; Food/famine; Gender issues/women; Health/sanitation/water; Human rights/peace/conflicts; International economic relations/trade/debt/finance; International relations/cooperation/development aid; Peace/ethnic conflicts/armament/disarmament; Population/family planning/demography; Poverty/living conditions; Racism/xenophobia/antisemitism; Refugees/migrants/ethnic groups; Rural development/agriculture; Urban development/habitat. **Activities:** Conferences/seminars/workshops/training activities; Fund raising; Information and documentation services/data bases; Lobbying/advocacy.

SWE3808

SVENSK-THAILANDSKA FORENINGEN ♦ Swedish Thai Society

c/o Söderlund, Tottvägen 18, 171 35 Solna, Sweden.

Telephone: 46 (8) 83 24 83. *Contact:* Captain L.A. Nilsson, Chairman.

SWE3809

SVENSK-TIBETANSKA SKOL-OCH KULTURFORENINGEN ♦ Swedish-Tibetan Society for School and Culture

Box 153, 127 23 Skärholmen, Sweden.

Telephone: 46 (8) 740 66 63. *Fax:* 46 (8) 710 60 11. *Contact:* Sonam T. Jamyangling, Chairman.

OBJECTIVES: To build a primary school in the village of Katsel Lhasa, Tibet.

GENERAL INFORMATION: *Creation:* 1989. *Personnel/Total:* 8. *Volunteers:* 8. *Financial sources: Private:* 20%. *Public:* 80%.

PUBLICATIONS: *Periodicals:* Norbu (4).

ACTIVITIES IN DEVELOPING REGIONS: Present in developing regions. Active in 2 country(ies). Maintains local field presence. Works through local field partners. **Sustainable Development Actions:** Education/training/literacy; Food/famine; Health/sanitation/water; Sending volunteers/experts/technical assistance. **Regions:** Central Asia and South Asia; East Asia.

INFORMATION AND EDUCATION ACTIVITIES: Topics: Culture/tradition/religion; Education/training/literacy; Health/sanitation/water. **Activities:** Formal education.

SWE3810

SVENSK-TUNISISKA FORENINGEN ♦ Swedish-Tunisian Association

c/o Seth Schultz, Huvudstag. 16, 592 30 Vadstena, Sweden.

Telephone: 46 (143) 10 673.

SWE3811

SVENSK-ZAMBISKA FORENINGEN ♦ Swedish Zambian Association

P.O. Box 16236, 103 25 Stockholm, Sweden.

Contact: Lennart Lindholm, Chairman.

OBJECTIVES: To promote relations between Sweden and Zambia.

See: *How to Use the Directory,* page 11.

GENERAL INFORMATION: *Creation:* 1975. *Budget/Total 1993:* ECU 3300 (US$ 3800). *Financial sources:* Self-financing: 100%.

PUBLICATIONS: *Periodicals:* Newsletter (3).

EVALUATION/RESEARCH: Undertakes research activities.

INFORMATION AND EDUCATION ACTIVITIES: Topics: International economic relations/trade/debt/finance; Rural development/agriculture. **Activities:** Fund raising; Lobbying/advocacy; Publishing/audiovisual materials/educational materials;

SWE3812

SVENSKA AFGHANISTANKOMMITTEN (SAK) ♦ Swedish Committee for Afghanistan

Essingeringen 90, 112 64 Stockholm, Sweden.

Telephone: 46 (8) 13 30 00. *Fax:* 46 (8) 130 11. *Contact:* Sven Johnsson, Office Manager.

SWE3813

SVENSKA ALLIANSMISSIONEN ♦ Swedish Alliance Mission

V. Storgatan 14, Box 615, 551 18 Jönköping, Sweden.

Telephone: 46 (36) 71 91 30. *Fax:* 46 (36) 71 58 22. *Contact:* Eskil Albertsson, General Secretary.

OBJECTIVES: To support development projects that give dignity to human beings and promote social participation, acting in the spirit of Christian Gospel teachings.

GENERAL INFORMATION: *Creation:* 1853. *Affiliated to:* International Federation of Free Evangelical Churches. *Personnel/Total:* 218. *Salaried:* 218 of which: 40 in developing countries. *Budget/Total 1993:* ECU 3855000 (US$ 4515000). *Financial sources:* Private: 30%. Public: 22%. Self-financing: 48%.

PUBLICATIONS: *Periodicals:* Petrus (39). *Annual report.*

EVALUATION/RESEARCH: Evaluation reports available.

COMMENTS: Undertakes activities in the Commonwealth of Independent States. Information activities related to the Commonwealth of Independent States.

ACTIVITIES IN DEVELOPING REGIONS: Present in developing regions. Active in 14 country(ies). Maintains local field presence. Works through local field partners. **Sustainable Development Actions:** Children/youth/family; Education/training/literacy; Food/famine; Health/sanitation/water; Other; Rural development/agriculture; Sending volunteers/experts/technical assistance; Small enterprises/informal sector/handicrafts; Urban development/habitat. **Regions:** Central Africa; Central Asia and South Asia; East Asia; North Africa; Oceania; South America; Southern Africa.

INFORMATION AND EDUCATION ACTIVITIES: Topics: Education/training/literacy; Emergency relief/refugees/humanitarian assistance; Food/famine; Health/sanitation/water; Refugees/migrants/ethnic groups; Rural development/agriculture. **Activities:** Fund raising.

SWE3814

SVENSKA AMBOSELIFORENINGEN ♦ Swedish Amboseli Association

c/o Bo Fredriksson, Gullbergsv. 59, 511 59 Kinna, Sweden.

Telephone: 46 (320) 31 837. *Fax:* 46 (320) 15 326. *Contact:* Dick Windle, Chairman of the Board.

OBJECTIVES: To install solar water pumps in the surroundings of Amboseli National Park in southern Kenya.

GENERAL INFORMATION: *Creation:* 1991. *Personnel/Total:* 2. Volunteers: 2 of which: 2 in developing countries. *Budget/Total 1993:* ECU 100000 (US$ 118000). *Financial sources:* Public: 80%. Self-financing: 20%.

PUBLICATIONS: *Periodicals:* Amboseli News (4). *Annual report.*

EVALUATION/RESEARCH: Evaluation reports available. Undertakes research activities.

ACTIVITIES IN DEVELOPING REGIONS: Present in developing regions. Active in 1 country(ies). Maintains local field presence. **Sustainable Development Actions:** Ecology/environment/biodiversity; Education/training/literacy; Gender issues/women; Health/sanitation/water; Rural development/agriculture; Sending volunteers/experts/technical assistance. **Regions:** East Africa.

INFORMATION AND EDUCATION ACTIVITIES: Topics: Ecology/environment/biodiversity; Health/sanitation/water; Rural development/agriculture. **Activities:** Information campaigns/exhibitions.

SWE3815

SVENSKA FLYKTINGRADET ♦ Swedish Refugee Council

Torstenssonsgatan 6, 114 56 Stockholm, Sweden.

Telephone: 46 (08) 667 68 99. *Fax:* 46 (08) 667 44 26. *Contact:* Eva Norström.

OBJECTIVES: To work for a humane refugee policy and good ethnic relations.

GENERAL INFORMATION: *Creation:* 1971. *Affiliated to:* European Council of Refugees and Exiles. *Personnel/Total:* 1. Salaried: 1. *Budget/Total 1993:* ECU 110000 (US$ 128000). *Financial sources:* Private: 25%. Public: 25%. Self-financing: 50%.

PUBLICATIONS: *Annual report.*

COMMENTS: Undertakes activities in the Commonwealth of Independent States. Information activities related to the Commonwealth of Independent States.

INFORMATION AND EDUCATION ACTIVITIES: Topics: Human rights/peace/conflicts; International relations/cooperation/development aid; Refugees/migrants/ethnic groups. **Activities:** Conferences/seminars/workshops/training activities; Fund raising; Information and documentation services/data bases; Information campaigns/exhibitions; Lobbying/advocacy.

SWE3816

SVENSKA FN-FORBUNDET (SFN) ♦ United Nations Association of Sweden

Skolgränd 2, Box 15115, 104 65 Stockholm, Sweden.

Telephone: 46 (8) 644 98 35. *Fax:* 46 (8) 641 88 76. *Contact:* Ove Johansson, Secretary General.

OBJECTIVES: To disseminate information to the Swedish public on the United Nations and its specialized agencies and institutions.

GENERAL INFORMATION: *Creation:* 1957. *Affiliated to:* World Federation of United Nations Association. *Personnel/Total:* 11. Salaried: 11. *Budget/Total 1993:* ECU 877712 (US$ 1027828). *Financial sources:* Public: 90%. Self-financing: 10%.

PUBLICATIONS: *Periodicals:* Världshonsent (6). *Annual report. List of publications.*

PLANNED ACTIVITIES: Events based on forthcoming UN conferences.

COMMENTS: Information activities related to the Commonwealth of Independent States.

INFORMATION AND EDUCATION ACTIVITIES: Topics: Children/youth/family; Culture/tradition/religion; Ecology/environment/biodiversity; Education/training/literacy; Emergency relief/refugees/humanitarian assistance; Employment/unemployment; Food/famine; Gender issues/women; Health/sanitation/water; Human rights/peace/conflicts; International economic relations/trade/debt/finance; International relations/cooperation/development aid; Peace/ethnic conflicts/armament/disarmament; Population/family planning/demography; Poverty/living conditions; Racism/xenophobia/antisemitism; Refugees/migrants/ethnic groups; Rural development/agriculture; Urban development/habitat. **Activities:** Conferences/seminars/workshops/training activities; Information and documentation services/data bases; Information campaigns/exhibitions; Publishing/audiovisual materials/educational materials.

SWE3817

SVENSKA FORBUNDET FOR INTERNATIONELLA BARNBYAR (CISV)

Vallonv. 12, 735 00 Surahammar, Sweden.

Telephone: 46 (220) 33 696. *Fax:* 46 (220) 36 810. *Contact:* Lisbeth Wernerson.

SWE3818

SVENSKA FORENINGEN FOR INDISK BYFOLKHOGSKOLA ♦
Swedish Society for Indian Village Folk High Schools

Ljungskile folkhögskola, 45980 Ljungskile, Sweden.

Telephone: 46 (522) 29 195. *Fax:* 46 (522) 22 119. *Contact:* Sten Larsson.

OBJECTIVES: To provide financial asisstance to Jagriti Vihara, centre for education for rural reconstruction in Bihar state, India.

GENERAL INFORMATION: *Creation:* 1972. *Volunteers:* 7. *Budget/Total 1993:* ECU 84000 (US$ 99000). *Financial sources:* Private: 50%. *Public:* 40%. *Self-financing:* 10%.

PUBLICATIONS: *Periodicals:* Newsletters (4).

EVALUATION/RESEARCH: Evaluation reports available. Undertakes research activities.

ACTIVITIES IN DEVELOPING REGIONS: Active in 1 country(ies). Works through local field partners. **Sustainable Development Actions:** Children/youth/family; Democracy/good governance/institution building/participatory development; Ecology/environment/biodiversity; Education/training/literacy; Emergency relief/refugees/humanitarian assistance; Energy/transport; Food/famine; Gender issues/women; Health/sanitation/water; Human rights/peace/conflicts; Rural development/agriculture; Sending volunteers/experts/technical assistance; Small enterprises/informal sector/handicrafts. **Regions:** Central Asia and South Asia.

SWE3819

SVENSKA FREDS- OCH SKILJEDOMSFORENINGEN (SPAS)
♦ The Swedish Peace and Arbitration Society

Box 17515, 118 91 Stockholm, Sweden.

Telephone: 46 (8) 668 02 00. *Fax:* 46 (8) 668 18 70. *E-mail:* SPAS@nn.apc.org. *Contact:* Lars Ångström, Chairman.

OBJECTIVES: To promote "Secure-Community" as an alternative to traditional security policies which tend to focus too much on militarism. To stop the arms trade. To help conscientious objectors. To support democracy in Eastern Europe.

GENERAL INFORMATION: *Creation:* 1883. *Affiliated to:* International Peace Bureau (Switzerland) - War Resisters International (United Kingdom) - European Network Against the Arms Trade. *Personnel/Total:* 15. *Salaried:* 10. *Volunteers:* 5. *Budget/Total 1993:* ECU 329000 (US$ 385000). *Financial sources:* Private: 33%. *Public:* 33%. *Self-financing:* 33%.

PUBLICATIONS: *Periodicals:* PAX (6). *Annual report. List of publications.*

EVALUATION/RESEARCH: Evaluation reports available. Undertakes research activities.

PLANNED ACTIVITIES: Lobbying the Swedish government for the creation of a new Swedish and European Defence policy not based on military defence. Supporting democratic organisations in Russia and the conversion of the arms industry, and the cleaning up of anti-personnel mines in Iraqi Kurdistan.

COMMENTS: This organisation works strictly in Sweden but has contacts with organisations in India and Pakistan. Undertakes activities in the Commonwealth of Independent States. Information activities related to the Commonwealth of Independent States.

ACTIVITIES IN DEVELOPING REGIONS: Works through local field partners. **Sustainable Development Actions:** Education/training/literacy; Health/sanitation/water; Human rights/peace/conflicts; Urban development/habitat. **Regions:** Central Asia and South Asia; East Asia; Middle East; South East Asia.

INFORMATION AND EDUCATION ACTIVITIES: Topics: Ecology/environment/biodiversity; Gender issues/women; Health/sanitation/water; Human rights/peace/conflicts; International economic relations/trade/debt/finance; Peace/ethnic conflicts/armament/disarmament; Urban development/habitat. **Activities:** Broadcasting/cultural events; Conferences/seminars/workshops/training activities; Exchanges/twinning/linking; Formal education; Fund raising; Information and documentation services/data bases; Information campaigns/exhibitions; Lobbying/advocacy; Networking/electronic telecommunications; Publishing/audiovisual materials/educational materials.

SWE3820

SVENSKA FREDSKOMMITTEN ♦ The Peace Committee

Solidaritetshuset, Barnängsg. 23, 116 41 Stockholm, Sweden.

Telephone: 46 (8) 644 78 68. *Fax:* 46 (8) 643 46 76.

SWE3821

SVENSKA HANDIKAPPORGANISATIONERNAS INTERNATIONELLA BISTANDSSTIFTELSE (SHIA) ♦ Swedish Organisations of Handicapped - International Aid Foundation

Magnus Ladulåsgatan 63, P.O. Box 4060, 102 61 Stockholm, Sweden.

Telephone: 46 (8) 643 73 80. *Fax:* 46 (8) 714 59 22. *Contact:* Barbro Carlsson, Secretary General.

OBJECTIVES: To support organisations of persons with disabilities in devloping countries and to participate in devlopment programmes and projects aimed at improving the situation of persons with disabilities in those countries.

GENERAL INFORMATION: *Creation:* 1981. *Type of organisation:* association of NGOs. *Member organisations:* 14. *Personnel/Total:* 14. *Salaried:* 14 of which: 4 in developing countries. *Budget/Total 1993:* ECU 2743000 (US$ 3212000). *Financial sources:* Public: 90%. *Self-financing:* 10%.

PUBLICATIONS: *Periodicals:* Handling (4). *Annual report.*

EVALUATION/RESEARCH: Evaluation reports available.

PLANNED ACTIVITIES: Working for the implememntion of the UN standard rules for equalization of opportunities for persons with disabilities.

ACTIVITIES IN DEVELOPING REGIONS: Present in developing regions. Active in 18 country(ies). Maintains local field presence. Works through local field partners. **Sustainable Development Actions:** Children/youth/family; Democracy/good governance/institution building/participatory development; Education/training/literacy; Gender issues/women; Human rights/peace/conflicts. **Regions:** Central Asia and South Asia; East Africa; Mexico and Central America; South America; South East Asia; Southern Africa; West Africa.

INFORMATION AND EDUCATION ACTIVITIES: Topics: Children/youth/family; Education/training/literacy; Employment/unemployment; Gender issues/women; Human rights/peace/conflicts. **Activities:** Conferences/seminars/workshops/training activities; Information and documentation services/data bases; Information campaigns/exhibitions; Lobbying/advocacy; Publishing/audiovisual materials/educational materials.

SWE3822

SVENSKA JERUSALEMSFORENINGEN ♦ Swedish Jerusalem Society

c/o Jan-Olof Johansson, Skogsv. 2, 360 44 Ingelstad, Sweden.

Telephone: 46 (470) 309 45. *Contact:* Bishop Sven Lindegård.

OBJECTIVES: To educate the children of the Bethlehem area. To provide health services to the people of the Betlehem area through a local hospital supported by the Society and administered by the local authorities.

GENERAL INFORMATION: *Creation:* 1900. *Affiliated to:* Swedish Mission Council (Sweden). *Budget/Total 1993:* ECU 144000 (US$ 168000). *Financial sources:* Private: 65%. *Public:* 5%. *Self-financing:* 30%.

PUBLICATIONS: *Periodicals:* Svenska Jerusalemsföreningens Tidskrift (4). *Annual report.*

PLANNED ACTIVITIES: Building a operating theatre for the hospital.

See: *How to Use the Directory,* page 11.

COMMENTS: The organisation has staff and volunteers in Bethlehem but chose not to list them.

ACTIVITIES IN DEVELOPING REGIONS: Present in developing regions. Active in 1 country(ies). Works through local field partners. **Sustainable Development Actions:** Education/training/literacy; Health/sanitation/ water. **Regions:** Middle East.

INFORMATION AND EDUCATION ACTIVITIES: Topics: Education/training/literacy; Health/sanitation/water. **Activities:** Fund raising; Information campaigns/exhibitions.

SWE3823

SVENSKA KOREAFORENINGEN ♦ Swedish Korean Society

Box 3259, 103 65 Stockholm 3, Sweden.

Telephone: 46 (8) 38 90 95. *Fax:* 46 (8) 759 59 75. *Contact:* Carl E. Svensson, President.

OBJECTIVES: To provide information about Korea. To allocate scholarships to students in Korea and to Korean students in Sweden.

GENERAL INFORMATION: *Creation:* 1951. *Personnel/Total:* 3. *Volunteers:* 3. *Budget/Total 1993:* ECU 5000 (US$ 6000). *Financial sources:* Self-financing: 100%.

PUBLICATIONS: *Periodicals:* Koreansk Journal (4). *Annual report.*

EVALUATION/RESEARCH: Evaluation reports available.

ACTIVITIES IN DEVELOPING REGIONS: Active in 1 country(ies). **Sustainable Development Actions:** Children/youth/family; Education/training/literacy; Health/sanitation/water; Urban development/habitat. **Regions:** East Asia.

INFORMATION AND EDUCATION ACTIVITIES: Topics: Children/youth/ family; Culture/tradition/religion; Education/training/literacy; Health/sanitation/water; International relations/cooperation/development aid; Urban development/habitat. **Activities:** Formal education.

SWE3824

SVENSKA KRISTNA UNGDOMSRAD (SKU)

Box 9215, 102 73 Stockholm, Sweden.

Telephone: 46 (8) 669 75 20. *Fax:* 46 (8) 84 90 16.

SWE3825

SVENSKA KVINNORS VANSTERFORBUND (SKV) ♦ Left Association of Swedish Women

Linnégatan 21, 413 04 Gothenburg, Sweden.

Telephone: 46 (31) 14 40 28. *Fax:* 46 (31) 14 40 28. *Contact:* Zaida Hagman, Secretary.

SWE3826

SVENSKA KYRKANS MISSION (SKM) ♦ Church of Sweden Mission

Sysslomansgatan 4, 751 70 Uppsala, Sweden.

Telephone: 46 (18) 16 95 00. *Fax:* 46 (18) 16 96 40. *Contact:* Birgitta Larsson, Mission Director.

OBJECTIVES: To support local churches and organisations in the Third World in their evangelical activities and efforts to promote development, economic justice and human rights.

GENERAL INFORMATION: *Creation:* 1874. *Affiliated to:* Swedish Mission Council (Sweden) - Christian Council of Sweden (Sweden). *Personnel/Total:* 175. *Salaried:* 175 of which: 125 in developing countries. *Budget/Total 1993:* ECU 14811000 (US$ 17345000). *Financial sources:* Private: 55%. Public: 35%. Self-financing: 10%.

PUBLICATIONS: *Periodicals:* Church of Sweden Mission Yearbook (1) - Missionsaktuellt (6). *Annual report.*

EVALUATION/RESEARCH: Evaluation reports available.

ACTIVITIES IN DEVELOPING REGIONS: Active in 33 country(ies). Maintains local field presence. Works through local field partners. **Sustainable Development Actions:** Children/youth/family; Debt/finance/trade; Democracy/good governance/institution building/participatory development; Education/training/literacy; Emergency relief/refugees/humanita-

rian assistance; Gender issues/women; Health/sanitation/water; Human rights/peace/conflicts; Rural development/agriculture; Sending volunteers/experts/technical assistance; Small enterprises/informal sector/ handicrafts. **Regions:** Central Asia and South Asia; East Africa; East Asia; Mexico and Central America; Middle East; South America; South East Asia; Southern Africa; West Africa.

INFORMATION AND EDUCATION ACTIVITIES: Topics: Children/youth/ family; Culture/tradition/religion; Education/training/literacy; Emergency relief/refugees/humanitarian assistance; Food/famine; Gender issues/ women; Health/sanitation/water; Human rights/peace/conflicts; International economic relations/trade/debt/finance; International relations/ cooperation/development aid; Poverty/living conditions; Rural development/agriculture. **Activities:** Conferences/seminars/workshops/training activities; Fund raising; Information and documentation services/data bases; Information campaigns/exhibitions; Publishing/audiovisual materials/educational materials.

SWE3827

SVENSKA MISSIONSFORBUNDET (SMF) ♦ Mission Covenant Church of Sweden

Tegnérgatan 8, Box 6302, 113 81 Stockholm, Sweden.

Telephone: 46 (8) 15 18 30. *Fax:* 46 (8) 15 87 57. *Contact:* Rev. Bertil Svensson, General Secretary of World Missions.

OBJECTIVES: To undertake projects in developing countries, focusing on health, education, water supply and forest conservation as part of the organisation's overall mission activities.

GENERAL INFORMATION: *Creation:* 1878. *Affiliated to:* World Alliance of Reformed Churches (Switzerland). *Personnel/Total:* 150. *Salaried:* 150 of which: 80 in developing countries. *Budget/Total 1993:* ECU 11410000 (US$ 13362000). *Financial sources:* Private: 60%. Public: 40%.

PUBLICATIONS: *Periodicals:* Sändaren (40). *Annual report.*

EVALUATION/RESEARCH: Evaluation reports available.

COMMENTS: Undertakes activities in the Commonwealth of Independent States. Information activities related to the Commonwealth of Independent States.

ACTIVITIES IN DEVELOPING REGIONS: Present in developing regions. Active in 7 country(ies). Maintains local field presence. Works through local field partners. **Sustainable Development Actions:** Children/ youth/family; Ecology/environment/biodiversity; Education/training/literacy; Emergency relief/refugees/humanitarian assistance; Gender issues/women; Health/sanitation/water; Population/family planning/ demography; Rural development/agriculture; Sending volunteers/ experts/technical assistance. **Regions:** Central Africa; Central Asia and South Asia; Mexico and Central America; South America.

INFORMATION AND EDUCATION ACTIVITIES: Topics: Culture/tradition/religion; Education/training/literacy; Emergency relief/refugees/ humanitarian assistance; Employment/unemployment; Health/sanitation/water; Human rights/peace/conflicts; International relations/cooperation/development aid; Racism/xenophobia/antisemitism; Refugees/ migrants/ethnic groups; Rural development/agriculture. **Activities:** Conferences/seminars/workshops/training activities; Formal education; Information and documentation services/data bases; Publishing/audiovisual materials/educational materials.

SWE3828

SVENSKA MISSIONSRADET (SMR) ♦ Swedish Mission Council

Box 1767, 111 87 Stockholm, Sweden.

Telephone: 46 (8) 453 68 80. *Fax:* 46 (8) 21 51 30. *Contact:* Rolf Berglund, General Secretary.

OBJECTIVES: To enable church organisations to participate more fully in development work. To allocate government funds for projects and personnel of member organisations.

GENERAL INFORMATION: *Creation:* 1980. *Type of organisation:* coordinating body. *Member organisations:* 23. *Personnel/Total:* 10. *Salaried:* 10. *Budget/Total 1993:* ECU 21943000 (US$ 25696000). *Financial sources:* Public: 100%.

PUBLICATIONS: *Periodicals:* Halsa OCS Mission (2) - Tekuik OCS Bistånd (2) - Svensk Missionstidskrift (4). *Annual report. List of publications.*

EVALUATION/RESEARCH: Evaluation reports available.

COMMENTS: Undertakes activities in the Commonwealth of Independent States.

ACTIVITIES IN DEVELOPING REGIONS: Active in 75 country(ies). Works through local field partners. **Sustainable Development Actions:** Children/youth/family; Democracy/good governance/institution building/participatory development; Education/training/literacy; Emergency relief/refugees/humanitarian assistance; Energy/transport; Food/famine; Health/sanitation/water; Human rights/peace/conflicts; Population/family planning/demography; Rural development/agriculture; Sending volunteers/experts/technical assistance; Urban development/habitat. **Regions:** Central Africa; Central Asia and South Asia; East Africa; East Asia; Mexico and Central America; Middle East; North Africa; South America; South East Asia; Southern Africa; West Africa.

SWE3829

SVENSKA MOUNT ELGONFORENINGEN ♦ Swedish Mount Elgon Association

c/o Erik Björklund, Axhult, 590 40 Kisa, Sweden.

SWE3830

SVENSKA RODA KORSET ♦ Swedish Red Cross

Östhammarsgatan 70, Box 27316, 102 54 Stockholm, Sweden.

Telephone: 46 (8) 665 56 00. *Fax:* 46 (8) 783 66 92. *Contact:* Peter Öru, Secretary General.

OBJECTIVES: To work for the improvement of health, to defend the Geneva conventions and furnish aid to the sick and wounded in time of war. To help in the prevention of diseases and the mitigation of suffering throughout the world.

GENERAL INFORMATION: *Creation:* 1865. *Affiliated to:* International Federation of the Red Cross and Red Crescent Societies (Switzerland). *Personnel/Total:* 40408. *Salaried:* 408 of which: 265 in developing countries. *Volunteers:* 40000. *Budget/Total 1993:* ECU 107311000 (US$ 1256645000). *Financial sources:* Private: 25%. Public: 49%. Self-financing: 26%.

PUBLICATIONS: *Periodicals:* Röda Kors-tidniugen (4) - RK -Nytt i text och bild (6). *Annual report. List of publications.*

EVALUATION/RESEARCH: Evaluation reports available.

COMMENTS: Undertakes activities in the Commonwealth of Independent States. Information activities related to the Commonwealth of Independent States.

ACTIVITIES IN DEVELOPING REGIONS: Present in developing regions. Active in 20 country(ies). Maintains local field presence. Works through local field partners. **Sustainable Development Actions:** Democracy/good governance/institution building/participatory development; Education/training/literacy; Emergency relief/refugees/humanitarian assistance; Gender issues/women; Health/sanitation/water; Human rights/peace/conflicts; Sending volunteers/experts/technical assistance; Small enterprises/informal sector/handicrafts. **Regions:** Caribbean; Central Africa; Central Asia and South Asia; East Africa; East Asia; Mexico and Central America; Middle East; North Africa; Oceania; South America; South East Asia; Southern Africa; West Africa.

INFORMATION AND EDUCATION ACTIVITIES: **Topics:** Emergency relief/refugees/humanitarian assistance; International relations/cooperation/development aid; Racism/xenophobia/antisemitism; Refugees/migrants/ethnic groups. **Activities:** Broadcasting/cultural events; Conferences/seminars/workshops/training activities; Exchanges/twinning/linking; Formal education; Fund raising; Information and documentation services/data bases; Information campaigns/exhibitions; Lobbying/advocacy; Networking/electronic telecommunications; Publishing/audiovisual materials/educational materials.

SWE3831

SVENSKA ROTARIANERS FOND FOR INTERNATIONELLT UTVECKLINGSARBETE, U-FONDEN ♦ The Swedish Rotarians Fund for International Development Work

Andv. 20 Nybrostrand, 27022 Köpingebro, Sweden.

Telephone: 46 (411) 50 090. *Fax:* 46 (411) 50 090. *Contact:* Sven Karud.

OBJECTIVES: To support the nutrition, education and training of children and youth in developing countries.

GENERAL INFORMATION: *Creation:* 1968. *Type of organisation:* coordinating body. *Personnel/Total:* 4. *Volunteers:* 4. *Budget/Total 1993:* ECU 143000 (US$ 167000). *Financial sources:* Private: 29%. Public: 2%. Self-financing: 69%.

PUBLICATIONS: *Annual report.*

EVALUATION/RESEARCH: Evaluation reports available.

COMMENTS: Undertakes activities in the Commonwealth of Independent States. Information activities related to the Commonwealth of Independent States.

ACTIVITIES IN DEVELOPING REGIONS: Present in developing regions. Active in 22 country(ies). Works through local field partners. **Sustainable Development Actions:** Children/youth/family; Education/training/literacy; Energy/transport; Food/famine; Health/sanitation/water; Sending volunteers/experts/technical assistance; Urban development/habitat. **Regions:** Central Asia and South Asia; East Africa; Mexico and Central America; South America; South East Asia; Southern Africa; West Africa.

SWE3832

SVENSKA SCOUTRADET (SSR) ♦ The Swedish Guide and Scout Council

Igeldammsgatan 22, Box 49005, 100 28 Stockholm, Sweden.

Telephone: 46 (8) 650 35 35. *Fax:* 46 (8) 653 07 43. *Contact:* Christer Persson, President.

OBJECTIVES: To contribute to the development of individuals, encouraging them to take responsibility for their local and national societies. To promote an awareness of international development issues.

GENERAL INFORMATION: *Creation:* 1960. *Member organisations:* 5. *Affiliated to:* World Association of the Scout Movement (Switzerland) - World Association of Girl Guides and Girl Scouts (United Kingdom). *Personnel/Total:* 150200. *Salaried:* 200. *Volunteers:* 150000. *Budget/Total 1993:* ECU 209000 (US$ 245000). *Financial sources:* Private: 20%. Public: 60%. Self-financing: 20%.

PUBLICATIONS: *Annual report. List of publications.*

EVALUATION/RESEARCH: Evaluation reports available.

PLANNED ACTIVITIES: Participating in inernational events, World Scout Jamboree; to organise the World Moot in 1996 in Sweden.

COMMENTS: Undertakes activities in the Commonwealth of Independent States. Information activities related to the Commonwealth of Independent States.

INFORMATION AND EDUCATION ACTIVITIES: **Topics:** Children/youth/family; Ecology/environment/biodiversity; Emergency relief/refugees/humanitarian assistance; Human rights/peace/conflicts; International economic relations/trade/debt/finance. **Activities:** Information and documentation services/data bases; Publishing/audiovisual materials/educational materials.

SWE3833

SVENSKA SEKTIONEN AV AMNESTY INTERNATIONAL ♦ Amnesty International - Swedish Section

Gyllenstiernsgata 18, Box 27 827, 115 93 Stockholm, Sweden.

Telephone: 46 (8) 670 62 00. *Fax:* 46 (8) 662 73 22.

SWE3834

SVENSKA TIBETKOMMITTEN ♦ The Swedish Tibet Committee

P.O. Box 2032, 103 11 Stockholm, Sweden.

See: *How to Use the Directory,* page 11.

Telephone: 46 (8) 702 94 95. *Fax:* 46 (9) 24 42 25. *Contact:* Anneli Gunnar.

OBJECTIVES: To spread information on the history, culture and religion of Tibet. To give humanitarian aid to the Tibetan refugees in India and defend the Tibetan people's right to live in peace and independence as well as influence Swedish politicians and government to engage positively in the Tibetan Question's solution.

GENERAL INFORMATION: *Creation:* 1968. *Personnel/Total:* 13. *Volunteers:* 13. *Budget/Total 1993:* ECU 7400 (US$ 8700). *Financial sources:* Private: 7%. Self-financing: 93%.

PUBLICATIONS: *Periodicals:* Tibet (4). *Annual report. List of publications.*

EVALUATION/RESEARCH: Evaluation reports available.

ACTIVITIES IN DEVELOPING REGIONS: Active in 1 country(ies). Works through local field partners. **Sustainable Development Actions:** Children/youth/family; Education/training/literacy; Emergency relief/refugees/humanitarian assistance; Gender issues/women; Human rights/peace/conflicts; Urban development/habitat. **Regions:** Central Asia and South Asia.

INFORMATION AND EDUCATION ACTIVITIES: Topics: Children/youth/family; Culture/tradition/religion; Ecology/environment/biodiversity; Education/training/literacy; Gender issues/women; Human rights/peace/conflicts; Peace/ethnic conflicts/armament/disarmament; Refugees/migrants/ethnic groups; Urban development/habitat. **Activities:** Conferences/seminars/workshops/training activities; Formal education; Fund raising; Information and documentation services/data bases; Information campaigns/exhibitions; Lobbying/advocacy.

SWE3835
SVENSKA TOGOFORENINGEN ♦ Swedish Togo Association

c/o Håkan Franklin, Molkoms Folkhögskola, Box 66, 660 60 Molkom, Sweden.

Contact: Johan Snögren, Président.

SWE3836
SVENSKA UNICEF-KOMMITTEN ♦ Swedish National Committee for UNICEF

Box 22223, 104 22 Stockholm, Sweden.

Telephone: 46 (8) 692 25 10. *Fax:* 46 (8) 651 20 21.

SWE3837
SVERIGES BLABANDSUNGDOM (SBU) ♦ Swedish Blue Ribbon Youth

Köpmangatan 3, 702 10 Örebro, Sweden.

Telephone: 46 (19) 13 05 75. *Contact:* Erica Cyrillus, President.

SWE3838
SVERIGES FORENADE STUDENTKARER ♦ Swedish National Union of Students

St. Eriksplan 2, 113 20 Stockholm, Sweden.

Telephone: 46 (8) 34 09 10. *Fax:* 46 (8) 30 42 93. *Contact:* Johan Rockström, Vice President.

SWE3839
SVERIGES RIKSIDROTTSFORBUND ♦ Swedish Sports Confederation

Storforsplan 44, 123 87 Farsta, Sweden.

Telephone: 46 (8) 605 60 00. *Fax:* 46 (8) 605 61 25. *Contact:* Bengt Sevelius, General Secretary.

OBJECTIVES: To sponsor the international development of the sports movement. To promote sports as a vehicle for international contacts and respect for the equality of all people.

GENERAL INFORMATION: *Creation:* 1903. *Type of organisation:* association of NGOs. *Member organisations:* 63. *Personnel/Total:* 72. *Salaried:* 72. *Budget/Total 1993:* ECU 62098000 (US$ 72719000). *Financial sources:* Public: 100%.

PUBLICATIONS: *Periodicals:* Svensk Idrott (11) - News from the Swedish Sports Scene (3). *Annual report. List of publications.*

EVALUATION/RESEARCH: Evaluation reports available.

PLANNED ACTIVITIES: Supporting sports development in the Baltic Republics, South Africa and Zimbabwe.

COMMENTS: Undertakes activities in the Commonwealth of Independent States. Information activities related to the Commonwealth of Independent States.

ACTIVITIES IN DEVELOPING REGIONS: Present in developing regions. Active in 2 country(ies). Works through local field partners. **Sustainable Development Actions:** Other; Sending volunteers/experts/technical assistance. **Regions:** East Africa; Southern Africa.

INFORMATION AND EDUCATION ACTIVITIES: Topics: International relations/cooperation/development aid; Other. **Activities:** Conferences/seminars/workshops/training activities; Exchanges/twinning/linking; Information and documentation services/data bases.

SWE3840
SWEDISH ASSOCIATION FOR DEVELOPMENT OF LOW-COST HOUSING (SADEL)

Sölvegatan 24, Box 118, 221 00 Lund, Sweden.

Telephone: 46 (46) 10 92 44. *Contact:* Johnny Åstrand.

SWE3841
SWEDISH CHURCH RELIEF

Box 110, 751 03 Uppsala, Sweden.

Contact: Birger Olsson, Secretary General.

SWE3842
SWEDISH COMMITTEE FOR THE HUMAN RIGHTS OF KURDISH PEOPLE

Box 27320, 102 54 Stockholm, Sweden.

SWE3843
SWEDISH COMMITTEE FOR UNICEF

Box 11114, 100 61 Stockholm, Sweden.

Telephone: 46 (8) 714 54 60.

SWE3844
SWEDISH IRAN COMMITEE

Gunnarbovägen 2B, 171 65 Solna, Sweden.

SWE3845
SWEDISH MEDICAL STUDENTS' INTERNATIONAL COMMITTEE (SWEMSIC)

Locus Medicus, Tunav. 5, 223 62 Lund, Sweden.

Telephone: 46 (46) 14 27 32. *Fax:* 46 (46) 10 41 70.

SWE3846
SWEDISH NORTH-SOUTH COALITION

Körsbärsvägen 21 B, 510 45 Sparsör, Sweden.

Telephone: 46 (33) 16 78 63. *Fax:* 46 (33) 16 58 29.

SWE3847
SWEDISH NURSING MOTHERS ASSOCIATION

c/o Sandbyvägen 208, 240 10 Dalby, Sweden.

SWE3848
SWEDISH PEACE & ARBITRATION SOCIETY (SPAS)

Box 17515, 118 91 Stockholm, Sweden.

Voir : *Comment utiliser le répertoire,* page 11.

SWE3849

SYDASIENKOMMITTEERNA I SVERIGE (SAKS) ♦ South Asia Committees of Sweden

Box 1142, 221 05 Lund, Sweden.

Telephone: 46 (46) 13 35 68. *Contact:* Eva Johansson, Chairman.

SWE3850

SYNSKADADES RIKSFORBUND (SRF) ♦ Swedish Federation of the Visually Handicapped

Sandsborgsvägen 52, 122 88 Enskede (Stockholm), Sweden.

Telephone: 46 (8) 39 90 00. *Contact:* Lennart Nolte, President.

OBJECTIVES: To promote the interests of blind and partially sighted people in Sweden. To co-operate in forming associations of the blind in developing countries and in conveying technical know-how for the establishment of braille printing houses.

GENERAL INFORMATION: *Creation:* 1889. *Affiliated to:* Central Committee of the National Federation of the Disabled - European Blind Union - World Blind Union. *Personnel/Total:* 86. *Salaried:* 86. *Financial sources:* Public: 90%. Self-financing: 10%.

PUBLICATIONS: *Periodicals:* Perspektiv (12). *Annual report. List of publications.*

EVALUATION/RESEARCH: Evaluation reports available. Undertakes research activities.

COMMENTS: Undertakes activities in the Commonwealth of Independent States. Information activities related to the Commonwealth of Independent States.

ACTIVITIES IN DEVELOPING REGIONS: Active in 15 country(ies). Works through local field partners.

INFORMATION AND EDUCATION ACTIVITIES: Topics: Health/sanitation/water. **Activities:** Conferences/seminars/workshops/training activities.

SWE3851

TEATER UNO

Stampg. 4, 411 01 Göteborg, Sweden.

Telephone: 46 (31) 15 99 90.

SWE3852

TIBETAN COMMUNITY IN SWEDEN

c/o Lobsan T. Kyaga, Bastuv. 53, 138 00 Älta, Sweden.

Telephone: 46 (8) 773 43 14. *Fax:* 46 (8) 773 43 14.

SWE3853

TIGRAY DEVELOPMENT ASSOCIATION (TDA)

Nygärdsvagen 22, 143 45 Vårby, Sweden.

Telephone: 46 (8) 710 91 37. *Contact:* Michael Giezahegn.

OBJECTIVES: To support development activities in Tigray, Northern Ethiopia. To organise Tigrian professionals. To promote cultural exchange among people.

GENERAL INFORMATION: *Creation:* 1988. *Affiliated to:* Tigray Development Association (Ethiopia) - Bistånds information (Sweden). *Personnel/Total:* 7. *Volunteers:* 7. *Budget/Total 1993:* ECU 329000 (US$ 385000). *Financial sources:* Private: 60%. Public: 10%. Self-financing: 30%.

PUBLICATIONS: *Periodicals:* Development Platform (4). *Annual report. List of publications.*

EVALUATION/RESEARCH: Evaluation reports available.

ACTIVITIES IN DEVELOPING REGIONS: Present in developing regions. Active in 1 country(ies). Maintains local field presence. Works through local field partners. **Sustainable Development Actions:** Children/youth/family; Ecology/environment/biodiversity; Education/training/literacy; Energy/transport; Gender issues/women; Health/sanitation/water; Other; Population/family planning/demography; Rural development/agri-

culture; Sending volunteers/experts/technical assistance; Urban development/habitat. **Regions:** East Africa.

INFORMATION AND EDUCATION ACTIVITIES: Topics: Children/youth/family; Culture/tradition/religion; Education/training/literacy; Emergency relief/refugees/humanitarian assistance; Gender issues/women; Health/sanitation/water; Other; Population/family planning/demography; Poverty/living conditions; Rural development/agriculture; Urban development/habitat. **Activities:** Conferences/seminars/workshops/training activities; Formal education; Fund raising; Information and documentation services/data bases; Lobbying/advocacy; Publishing/audiovisual materials/educational materials.

SWE3854

TROSGNISTANS MISSION ♦ Bethel Faith Ministries

Söderhamnsvägen 2, Box 3014, 821 50 Bollnäs, Sweden.

Telephone: 46 (278) 13 010. *Fax:* 46 (278) 24 888. *Contact:* Curt Johansson, Director.

OBJECTIVES: To care for neglected children by supporting children's homes, food distribution and medical care. To build schools, set up literacy programmes, promote women's education and provide help for the sick and suffering.

GENERAL INFORMATION: *Creation:* 1969. *Affiliated to:* SMR. *Personnel/Total:* 19. *Salaried:* 4. *Volunteers:* 15 of which: 15 in developing countries. *Budget/Total 1993:* ECU 1163000 (US$ 1362000). *Financial sources:* Private: 55%. Public: 40%. Self-financing: 5%.

PUBLICATIONS: *Periodicals:* Trons Gnista (4). *Annual report.*

COMMENTS: Undertakes activities in the Commonwealth of Independent States.

ACTIVITIES IN DEVELOPING REGIONS: Present in developing regions. Active in 6 country(ies). Maintains local field presence. Works through local field partners. **Sustainable Development Actions:** Children/youth/family; Democracy/good governance/institution building/participatory development; Education/training/literacy; Emergency relief/refugees/humanitarian assistance; Food/famine; Gender issues/women; Health/sanitation/water; Population/family planning/demography; Rural development/agriculture; Sending volunteers/experts/technical assistance; Urban development/habitat. **Regions:** Central Asia and South Asia; East Africa; South East Asia.

INFORMATION AND EDUCATION ACTIVITIES: Topics: Children/youth/family; Emergency relief/refugees/humanitarian assistance; Food/famine; Gender issues/women; Health/sanitation/water; Rural development/agriculture; Urban development/habitat. **Activities:** Conferences/seminars/workshops/training activities; Fund raising; Information and documentation services/data bases; Information campaigns/exhibitions; Publishing/audiovisual materials/educational materials.

SWE3855

TRYGG-HANSA PERSONALENS U-HJALPSFORENING (TH U) ♦ Trygg-Hansa Staff Development Aid Organization

106 26 Stockholm, Sweden.

Telephone: 46 (8) 758 29 57. *Fax:* 46 (8) 758 29 57. *Contact:* Carl Olof Odehammar, President.

OBJECTIVES: To give correct information about developing countries in order to increase willingness to help.

GENERAL INFORMATION: *Creation:* 1970. *Type of organisation:* coordinating body. *Budget/Total 1993:* ECU 149000 (US$ 175000). *Financial sources:* Private: 86%. Public: 14%.

PUBLICATIONS: *Periodicals:* Vår Livbos Till U-land (3). *Annual report.*

PLANNED ACTIVITIES: The installation of radios between hospitals in Zambia. The improvement of a youth hostel in Brazil. Helping a mental hospital in Albania and building an SOS children's village in Estonia.

ACTIVITIES IN DEVELOPING REGIONS: Active in 16 country(ies). **Sustainable Development Actions:** Children/youth/family; Ecology/environment/biodiversity; Education/training/literacy; Health/sanitation/water. **Regions:** Central Asia and South Asia; East Africa; Middle East; South America; South East Asia; West Africa.

INFORMATION AND EDUCATION ACTIVITIES: Topics: Children/youth/family; Ecology/environment/biodiversity; Education/training/literacy; Health/sanitation/water. **Activities:** Fund raising.

SWE3856

TYRESO ULANDS-OCH FREDS FORENING (TUFF) ♦ Tyresö
Organisation for Peace and Third World Development

Granängsringen 50B, Box 58, 135 21 Tyresö, Sweden.

Contact: Monica Schelin, Chairman.

SWE3857

U-ASSIST

19 587 Stockholm, Sweden.

Telephone: 46 (8) 797 16 06. *Contact:* K.G. Eriksson, Chairman.

OBJECTIVES: To provide economic support for aid projects in developing countries.

GENERAL INFORMATION: *Creation:* 1979. *Affiliated to:* BIFO (Sweden). *Personnel/Total:* 1. *Volunteers:* 1. *Budget/Total 1993:* ECU 165000 (US$ 193000). *Financial sources: Public:* 33%. *Self-financing:* 67%.

PUBLICATIONS: *Periodicals:* Information to Members (3).

COMMENTS: Undertakes activities in the Commonwealth of Independent States.

ACTIVITIES IN DEVELOPING REGIONS: Active in 18 country(ies). Works through local field partners. **Sustainable Development Actions:** Children/youth/family; Ecology/environment/biodiversity; Education/training/literacy; Emergency relief/refugees/humanitarian assistance; Energy/transport; Food/famine; Gender issues/women; Health/sanitation/water; Population/family planning/demography; Rural development/agriculture; Small enterprises/informal sector/handicrafts; Urban development/habitat. **Regions:** Central Asia and South Asia; East Africa; Mexico and Central America; South America; South East Asia; West Africa.

INFORMATION AND EDUCATION ACTIVITIES: Topics: Children/youth/family; Ecology/environment/biodiversity; Education/training/literacy; Emergency relief/refugees/humanitarian assistance; Food/famine; Gender issues/women; Health/sanitation/water; Other; Population/family planning/demography; Refugees/migrants/ethnic groups; Rural development/agriculture; Urban development/habitat. **Activities:** Exchanges/twinning/linking; Fund raising.

SWE3858

U-LANDSGRUPPERS SAMARBETSFORENING (U-SAM)

c/o Anna Axberg, Vadmalsv. 9, 161 36 Bromma, Sweden.

Telephone: 46 (8) 25 75 46.

SWE3859

U-LANDSHJALP FRAN FOLK TILL FOLK I SVERIGE (UFF) ♦
Development Aid from People to People in Sweden (DAPP)

P.O. Box 37, 101 20 Stockholm, Sweden.

Telephone: 46 (8) 735 75 00. *Fax:* 46 (8) 735 75 25. *Contact:* Michael Grönborg, Chairman.

OBJECTIVES: To undertake development projects in developing countries.

GENERAL INFORMATION: *Creation:* 1979. *Personnel/Total:* 55. *Salaried:* 15 of which: 10 in developing countries. *Volunteers:* 40 of which: 12 in developing countries. *Budget/Total 1993:* ECU 2271000 (US$ 2659000). *Financial sources: Self-financing:* 100%.

PUBLICATIONS: *Periodicals:* DAPP Newsletter (12). *Annual report.*

EVALUATION/RESEARCH: Evaluation reports available.

ACTIVITIES IN DEVELOPING REGIONS: Active in 6 country(ies). Works through local field partners. **Sustainable Development Actions:** Children/youth/family; Ecology/environment/biodiversity; Education/training/literacy; Emergency relief/refugees/humanitarian assistance; Food/famine; Health/sanitation/water; Rural development/agriculture; Sending

volunteers/experts/technical assistance; Small enterprises/informal sector/handicrafts. **Regions:** Southern Africa.

INFORMATION AND EDUCATION ACTIVITIES: Topics: Children/youth/family; Ecology/environment/biodiversity; Education/training/literacy; Emergency relief/refugees/humanitarian assistance; Employment/unemployment; Food/famine; Health/sanitation/water; Population/family planning/demography; Poverty/living conditions; Refugees/migrants/ethnic groups; Rural development/agriculture; Urban development/habitat. **Activities:** Formal education; Fund raising; Information and documentation services/data bases; Information campaigns/exhibitions; Publishing/audiovisual materials/educational materials.

SWE3860

UNG VANSTER ♦ Young Left

Box 12660, 112 93 Stockholm, Sweden.

Telephone: 46 (8) 654 31 00. *Fax:* 46 (8) 650 85 57.

SWE3861

UNGA ORNARS RIKSFORBUND

Box 11540, 100 61 Stockholm, Sweden.

Telephone: 46 (8) 714 48 50. *Fax:* 46 (8) 714 95 08. *Contact:* Sanna Johnsson.

SWE3862

UNGDOM MED UPPGIFT (UMU) ♦ Youth With A Mission

Restenäs 32200, 459 93 Ljungskile, Sweden.

Telephone: 46 (522) 21 020. *Fax:* 46 (522) 20 245. *Contact:* Randy and Karen Purves, Directors.

SWE3863

UNGDOMENS OCH STUDENTERNAS FN-FORBUND I SVERIGE - UTRIKESPOLITISKA FORENINGARNAS FN-FORBUND (UFFN) ♦ United Nations Youth and Student Association of Sweden

Box 15073, 104 65 Stockholm, Sweden.

Telephone: 46 (18) 55 64 57. *Fax:* 46 (18) 55 79 98. *Contact:* Karin Kruse, Chairperson.

SWE3864

UTAN GRANSER (UG) ♦ Swedish Cooperative Centre

Box 30214, 104 25 Stockholm, Sweden.

Telephone: 46 (8) 657 47 00. *Fax:* 46 (8) 657 85 15. *E-mail:* swecoopns.apc.org. *Contact:* Eidi Genfors, Executive Director.

OBJECTIVES: To contribute towards positive changes in the living conditions of the poorest people in developing countries by supporting the activities of co-o peratives and similar organisations working for economic and social development and independence.

GENERAL INFORMATION: *Creation:* 1958. *Member organisations:* 8. *Personnel/Total:* 26. *Salaried:* 26. *Budget/Total 1993:* ECU 15909000 (US$ 18629000). *Financial sources: Private:* 10%. *Public:* 90%.

PUBLICATIONS: *Periodicals:* UG-NYTT (6). *Annual report.*

EVALUATION/RESEARCH: Evaluation reports available. Undertakes research activities.

ACTIVITIES IN DEVELOPING REGIONS: Present in developing regions. Active in 12 country(ies). Maintains local field presence. Works through local field partners. **Sustainable Development Actions:** Debt/finance/trade; Democracy/good governance/institution building/participatory development; Ecology/environment/biodiversity; Emergency relief/refugees/humanitarian assistance; Gender issues/women; Rural development/agriculture; Sending volunteers/experts/technical assistance; Small enterprises/informal sector/handicrafts; Urban development/habitat. **Regions:** Central Asia and South Asia; East Africa; Mexico and Central America; South America; Southern Africa.

INFORMATION AND EDUCATION ACTIVITIES: Topics: Ecology/environment/biodiversity; Emergency relief/refugees/humanitarian assis-

Voir : *Comment utiliser le répertoire*, page 11.

tance; Employment/unemployment; Gender issues/women; Human rights/peace/conflicts; International economic relations/trade/debt/ finance; Poverty/living conditions; Rural development/agriculture; Urban development/habitat. **Activities:** Conferences/seminars/workshops/ training activities; Exchanges/twinning/linking; Fund raising; Information and documentation services/data bases; Information campaigns/exhibitions; Lobbying/advocacy; Networking/electronic telecommunications; Publishing/audiovisual materials/educational materials.

SWE3865

UTBILDNING FOR BISTANDSVERKSAMHET ♦ Training for Development Assistance

Barnängsgatan 23, 116 41 Stockholm, Sweden.

Telephone: 46 (8) 714 09 85. **Fax:** 46 (8) 702 94 17. **E-mail:** PNS:NFLA. **Contact:** Inger Björk, President.

OBJECTIVES: To send volunteers to participate in development projects in Latin America.

GENERAL INFORMATION: Creation: 1968. **Personnel/Total:** 62. Salaried: 12. Volunteers: 50. **Budget/Total 1993:** ECU 1755000 (US$ 2056000). **Financial sources:** Public: 95%. Self-financing: 5%.

PUBLICATIONS: Periodicals: Nyheter från Latinamerika (9). List of publications.

PLANNED ACTIVITIES: Publishing books on Colombia and Ecuador.

ACTIVITIES IN DEVELOPING REGIONS: Active in 6 country(ies). Maintains local field presence. Works through local field partners. **Sustainable Development Actions:** Children/youth/family; Democracy/good governance/institution building/participatory development; Ecology/environment/biodiversity; Education/training/literacy; Emergency relief/refugees/humanitarian assistance; Food/famine; Gender issues/women; Health/sanitation/water; Human rights/peace/conflicts; Population/family planning/demography; Rural development/agriculture; Sending volunteers/experts/technical assistance; Small enterprises/informal sector/ handicrafts; Urban development/habitat. **Regions:** Mexico and Central America; South America.

INFORMATION AND EDUCATION ACTIVITIES: Topics: Children/youth/ family; Culture/tradition/religion; Ecology/environment/biodiversity; Education/training/literacy; Employment/unemployment; Gender issues/ women; Health/sanitation/water; Human rights/peace/conflicts; International economic relations/trade/debt/finance; Population/family planning/ demography; Poverty/living conditions; Racism/xenophobia/antisemitism; Refugees/migrants/ethnic groups; Rural development/agriculture; Urban development/habitat. **Activities:** Conferences/seminars/workshops/training activities; Exchanges/twinning/linking; Information and documentation services/data bases; Information campaigns/exhibitions; Publishing/audiovisual materials/educational materials.

SWE3866

VADDO BISTANDSFORENING ♦ Väddö Development Association

c/o N-S Brandt, Björkö-Arholma skola, 760 42 Björkö, Sweden.

Telephone: 46 (176) 91 518. **Fax:** 46 (176) 91 386.

SWE3867

VANORTSFORENINGEN EKSJO-BANGLADESH ♦ The Sister Community Association Eksjö-Bangladesh

c/o Jona Eriksson, Soläng 580, 575 91 Eksjö, Sweden.

Telephone: 46 (381) 12 514. **Contact:** Stig Dahnielson.

SWE3868

VANORTSFORENINGEN JONKOPING-BANGLADESH

c/o Lars Forsberg, Stigby, 560 34 Visingsö, Sweden.

Telephone: 46 (390) 40 464. **Fax:** 46 (390) 40 563.

SWE3869

VANORTSFORENINGEN STRANGNAS-KIBAYA-LOIBORSOIT (SKL)

c/o Karlsson, Utsiktsv. 11, 645 42 Strängnäs, Sweden.

Telephone: 46 (159) 10 969. **Fax:** 46 (159) 11 766. **Contact:** Ulf Haake.

SWE3870

VANSKAPSFORENINGEN BURKINA FASO-SVERIGE, ASSAMBUS ♦ Friendship Association Burkina Faso-Sweden, ASSAMBUS

c/o Staffan Söderholm, Gullmarsv. 117, 120 39 Årsta, Sweden.

Telephone: 46 (8) 81 46 32. **Contact:** Hans Eriksson.

SWE3871

VANSKAPSFORENINGEN SVERIGE-FRIA BURMA

Burma Centre, Box 4034, 181 04 Lidingö, Sweden.

Telephone: 46 (8) 765 59 03. **Fax:** 46 (8) 765 59 03. **Contact:** Bosse Olson.

SWE3872

VANSKAPSFORENINGEN SVERIGE-URUGUAY

Brevia 414, Frejg. 6, 114 49 Stockholm, Sweden.

Telephone: 46 (8) 580 387 24. **Fax:** 46 (8) 740 68 02.

SWE3873

VANSKAPSFORENINGEN SVERIGE-ZIMBABWE ♦ Sweden-Zimbabwe Friendship Association

c/o Rolf Pearson, Bruksförvaltarg. 14, 740 33 Vattholma, Sweden.

Telephone: 46 (18) 35 08 65/44 02 76. **Contact:** Björn Andreasson, Chairman.

SWE3874

VANSKAPSKLUBBEN KANIMAMBO ♦ Kanimambo Friendship Club

Skärbäcksvägen 13, 270 59 Vitaby, Sweden.

Telephone: 46 (414) 72 331. **Contact:** Lena Holmgren, Chairman.

SWE3875

VANSKOLEFORENINGEN DJURO-LOS RINCONES ♦ The Friend-School Association Djurö-Los Rincones

Djurö Skola, 130 40 Djurhamn, Sweden.

Telephone: 46 (8) 571 502 16. **Contact:** Kjell Göransson.

SWE3876

VARLDSNATURFONDEN (WWF) ♦ World Wide Fund for Nature

Ulriksdals slott, 170 71 Solna, Sweden.

Telephone: 46 (8) 624 74 00. **Fax:** 46 (8) 85 13 29. **Contact:** Jens Wahlstedt, Secretary General.

OBJECTIVES: To protect and conserve biodiversity globally and nationally. To promote sustainable use of natural resources. To minimize pollution and wasteful consumption.

GENERAL INFORMATION: Creation: 1971. **Type of organisation:** association of NGOs. **Member organisations:** 28. **Personnel/Total:** 35. Salaried: 35. **Budget/Total 1993:** ECU 8777000 (US$ 10278000). **Financial sources:** Private: 46%. Public: 4%. Self-financing: 50%.

PUBLICATIONS: Periodicals: WWF EKO (4) - Panda (6). Annual report. List of publications.

EVALUATION/RESEARCH: Evaluation reports available. Undertakes research activities.

COMMENTS: Undertakes activities in the Commonwealth of Independent States. Information activities related to the Commonwealth of Independent States.

ACTIVITIES IN DEVELOPING REGIONS: Works through local field partners. **Sustainable Development Actions:** Democracy/good governance/institution building/participatory development; Ecology/environment/biodiversity; Education/training/literacy; Gender issues/women; Rural development/agriculture; Small enterprises/informal sector/handi-

See: How to Use the Directory, page 11.

crafts. **Regions:** East Africa; South America; South East Asia; West Africa.

INFORMATION AND EDUCATION ACTIVITIES: Topics: Ecology/environment/biodiversity; Rural development/agriculture; Urban development/habitat. **Activities:** Conferences/seminars/workshops/training activities; Formal education; Fund raising; Information and documentation services/data bases; Information campaigns/exhibitions; Lobbying/advocacy; Publishing/audiovisual materials/educational materials.

SWE3877
VATTEN AT ALLA ◆ Water for All

c/o Atlas Copco AB, 105 23 Stockholm, Sweden.

Telephone: 46 (8) 743 85 22. **Fax:** 46 (8) 644 11 51. **Contact:** Torgny Rogert.

OBJECTIVES: To help to improve the quality of life for people who suffer from a shortage of drinking water, primarily by drilling wells and installing hand pumps.

GENERAL INFORMATION: Creation: 1984. **Personnel/Total:** 6. Volunteers: 6. **Budget/Total 1993:** ECU 27000 (US$ 32000). **Financial sources:** Self-financing: 100%.

PUBLICATIONS: Periodicals: Nyhetsbrev (2). Annual report.

ACTIVITIES IN DEVELOPING REGIONS: Active in 3 country(ies). Works through local field partners. **Sustainable Development Actions:** Education/training/literacy; Health/sanitation/water. **Regions:** East Africa; South America.

SWE3878
VI PLANTERAR TRAD ◆ Tree Planting Project

Box 15210, 104 65 Stockholm, Sweden.

Telephone: 46 (8) 743 24 58.

SWE3879
VIDEOCENTRUM FOR U-LANDSFRAGOR ◆ The Video Centre for Third World Issues

Hornsg. 54, 4 tr, 118 21 Stockholm, Suède.

Téléphone: 46 (8) 640 06 49. **Fax:** 46 (8) 702 90 99. **Contact:** Marc Davin.

OBJECTIFS: Mettre à la disposition des ONGs des moyens techniques du production vidéo, afin de développer une autre image du Tiers Monde.

INFORMATIONS GENERALES: Création: 1989. **Type d'organisation:** regroupement d'ONG. **Organisations membres:** 11. **Affiliée à:** Bistándsinformation Fo (Suède) - ZEBRA - Fircentrum (Suède). **Personnel/Total:** var.. Salariés: 2. **Budget/Total 1993:** ECU 165000 (US$ 193000). **Sources financières:** Autofinancement: 100%.

PUBLICATIONS: Rapport annuel. Liste des publications.

EVALUATION/RECHERCHE: Rapports d'évaluation disponibles. Entreprend des activités de recherche.

COMMENTAIRES: Activités d'information concernant la Communauté des Etats indépendants.

ACTIVITES DANS LES REGIONS EN DEVELOPPEMENT: Intervient dans 10 pays. Intervient par l'intermédiaire d'organisations locales partenaires. **Actions de Développement durable:** Développement rural/agriculture; Éducation/formation/alphabétisation. **Régions:** Afrique de l'Est; Afrique de l'Ouest.

ACTIVITES D'INFORMATION ET D'EDUCATION: Domaines: Culture/tradition/religion; Développement rural/agriculture; Développement urbain/habitat; Enfants/jeunesse/famille; Population/planning familial/démographie; Questions relatives aux femmes; Racisme/xénophobie/antisémitisme; Réfugiés/migrants/groupes ethniques; Santé/assainissement/eau; Écologie/environnement/biodiversité. **Activités:** Campagnes d'information/expositions; Conférences/séminaires/ateliers/activités de formation; Échanges/parrainage/jumelage; Édition/documents audiovisuels/documents éducatifs; Éducation formelle.

SWE3880
VIKINGASKOLANS BISTANDSPROJEKT I HUAYRA KHASA, BOLIVIA ◆ Viking School Aid Project in Huayra Khasa, Bolivia

Sleipnervägen 2, 136 81 Haninge, Sweden.

Telephone: 46 (8) 745 80 00. **Fax:** 46 (8) 777 35 22 . **Contact:** Torsten Arvidsson.

SWE3881
VOLVOANSTALLDAS U-HJALPSFORENING

VLH 5 Rum 5401, 405 08 Göteborg, Sweden.

Telephone: 46 (31) 66 12 02. **Fax:** 46 (31) 23 89 78. **Contact:** Sigvard Kunni.

TUR3882

ANADOLU KALKINMA VAKFI ♦ Anatolian Development Foundation

Atatürk Bulvari No. 121/182, 06640 Ankara, Turkey.

Telephone: 90 (312) 418 26 68. *Fax:* 90 (312) 417 67 28. *Contact:* Ahmet Akyurek, President of the Board.

OBJECTIVES: To support rural development projects in Anatolia, Turkey. To support local organisations' economic and social projects, disaster relief, refugee assistance and rehabilitation.

GENERAL INFORMATION: *Creation:* 1981. *Personnel/Total:* 26. *Salaried:* 15. *Volunteers:* 11. *Budget/Total 1993:* ECU 1121000 (US$ 1455000). *Financial sources:* Private: 2%. Public: 95%. *Self-financing:* 3%.

PUBLICATIONS: *Annual report.*

COMMENTS: The Anatolian Development Fund is active mainly in Turkey.

INFORMATION AND EDUCATION ACTIVITIES: Topics: Emergency relief/refugees/humanitarian assistance; Peace/ethnic conflicts/armament/disarmament; Refugees/migrants/ethnic groups; Rural development/agriculture. **Activities:** Information and documentation services/data bases; Lobbying/advocacy.

TUR3883

ARKADAS ♦ Friends

ilhan Akgü C. 12/C, 33960 Silifke, Turkey.

Telephone: 90 (324) 714 37 26. *Fax:* 90 (324) 714 37 26. *E-mail:* u.ozturk@bradford.ac.uk. *Contact:* Yasar Öztürk, Chairman and Chief Editor.

OBJECTIVES: To raise awareness, through media, of issues such as environmental problems, sustainable development and peace. To monitor and encourage youth environmental activism.

GENERAL INFORMATION: *Creation:* 1987. *Type of organisation:* network. *Member organisations:* 1. *Affiliated to:* Youth for Development and Co-operation (the Netherlands) - World Constitution and Parliament Association (USA) - Youth and Environment Europe (the Netherlands) - International Young Nature Friends (Belgium) - Young Meditarrenean Ecologists' Network - European Youth Forest Action (the Netherlands) - International Federation of Environmental Journalists (France) -United Nations of Youth (the Netherlands) - Taiga Rescue Network (Spain) -UNITED for Intercultural Action (the Netherlands). *Personnel/Total:* 904. *Salaried:* 4. *Volunteers:* 900 of which: 2 in developing countries. *Budget/Total 1993:* ECU 2100 (US$ 2700). *Financial sources:* Private: 10%. *Self-financing:* 90%.

PUBLICATIONS: *Periodicals:* ARKADAS (12) - Green Screen (52). *Annual report. List of publications.*

EVALUATION/RESEARCH: Evaluation reports available. Undertakes research activities.

PLANNED ACTIVITIES: Building a "Nature Friend's House" for eco-friendly youth tourism and leisure. International training course on nuclear energy, in collaboration with YEE. International workshop on environmental education. Setting up the first-ever nationwide electronic data network on environment.

COMMENTS: Information activities related to the Commonwealth of Independent States.

ACTIVITIES IN DEVELOPING REGIONS: Active in 1 country(ies). Maintains local field presence. Works through local field partners. **Sustainable Development Actions:** Children/youth/family; Debt/finance/trade; Democracy/good governance/institution building/participatory development; Ecology/environment/biodiversity; Education/training/literacy; Emergency relief/refugees/humanitarian assistance; Energy/transport; Food/famine; Gender issues/women; Health/sanitation/water; Human rights/peace/conflicts; Other; Population/family planning/demography; Rural development/agriculture; Small enterprises/informal sector/handicrafts; Urban development/habitat. **Regions:** Caribbean; Central Africa; Central Asia and South Asia; East Africa; East Asia; Mexico and Central America; Middle East; North Africa; Oceania; South America; South East Asia; Southern Africa; West Africa.

INFORMATION AND EDUCATION ACTIVITIES: Topics: Children/youth/family; Culture/tradition/religion; Ecology/environment/biodiversity; Education/training/literacy; Emergency relief/refugees/humanitarian assistance; Employment/unemployment; Food/famine; Gender issues/women; Health/sanitation/water; Human rights/peace/conflicts; International economic relations/trade/debt/finance; International relations/cooperation/development aid; Peace/ethnic conflicts/armament/disarmament; Population/family planning/demography; Poverty/living conditions; Racism/xenophobia/antisemitism; Refugees/migrants/ethnic groups; Rural development/agriculture; Urban development/habitat. **Activities:** Broadcasting/cultural events; Conferences/seminars/workshops/training activities; Exchanges/twinning/linking; Information and documentation services/data bases; Information campaigns/exhibitions; Lobbying/advocacy; Networking/electronic telecommunications; Publishing/audiovisual materials/educational materials.

TUR3884

ÇEVRE MUHENDISLERI ODASI (ÇMO) ♦ Chamber of Environmental Engineers

Selanik Cad. No 19/1 Kizilay, 06650 Ankara, Turkey.

Telephone: 90 (312) 418 47 12. *Fax:* 90 (312) 417 06 32. *Contact:* Ayhan Kizilates, Chairman of the Board.

OBJECTIVES: To ensure the rights of Environmental Engineers. To study and research scientific and political views on environmental problems. To apply environmental technology and to lobby for the development of human rights and democracy in Turkey.

GENERAL INFORMATION: *Creation:* 1992. *Affiliated to:* Union of the Chambers of Turkish Engineers and Architects (Turkey). *Budget/Total 1993:* ECU 17000 (US$ 23000). *Financial sources:* Self-financing: 100%.

PUBLICATIONS: *Periodicals:* Environment and Engineers (4).

EVALUATION/RESEARCH: Undertakes research activities.

INFORMATION AND EDUCATION ACTIVITIES: Topics: Ecology/environment/biodiversity; Health/sanitation/water; Human rights/peace/conflicts. **Activities:** Conferences/seminars/workshops/training activities.

TUR3885

DOGAL HAYATI KORUMA DERNEGI

Kelaynak Sok. Aygül Apt. 50/1, 80600 Ulus, Istanbul, Turkey.

Telephone: 90 (212) 279 01 40. *Fax:* 90 (212) 279 55 44. *Contact:* Nergis Yazgan, Director General.

OBJECTIVES: To promote long term protection of natural habitats and species in Turkey.

GENERAL INFORMATION: *Creation:* 1975. *Personnel/Total:* 42. *Salaried:* 22. *Volunteers:* 20. *Budget/Total 1993:* ECU 557000 (US$ 722000). *Financial sources:* Private: 42%. Public: 44%. *Self-financing:* 14%.

PUBLICATIONS: *Periodicals:* Kelaynaktan Haberler (4). *Annual report. List of publications.*

EVALUATION/RESEARCH: Evaluation reports available. Undertakes research activities.

ACTIVITIES IN DEVELOPING REGIONS: Present in developing regions. Maintains local field presence.

INFORMATION AND EDUCATION ACTIVITIES: Topics: Ecology/environment/biodiversity; Rural development/agriculture; Urban development/habitat. **Activities:** Broadcasting/cultural events; Conferences/seminars/workshops/training activities; Formal education; Fund raising; Information and documentation services/data bases; Information campaigns/exhibitions; Lobbying/advocacy; Publishing/audiovisual materials/educational materials.

TUR3886

INSAN HAKLARI DERNEGI ♦ Human Rights Association

Yüksel Caddesi 29/13, 06420 Ankara, Turkey.

Telephone: 90 (312) 425 95 47. *Fax:* 90 (312) 425 95 47. *Contact:* Akin Birdal, Chairman.

See: *How to Use the Directory,* page 11.

TUR3887
INSAN KAYNAGINI CELISTIRME VAKFI ♦ The Human Resource Development Foundation

Yenicarsi Caddesi n° 54, Beyoglu 80050 Istanbul, Turkey.

Telephone: 90 (212) 293 16 05. *Fax:* 90 (212) 293 10 09. *Contact:* Nuray Fincancioglu, Executive Director.

TUR3888
INTERNATIONAL CATHOLIC MIGRATION COMMISSION (ICMC)

146/2 Kalipci Sok. Tesvikiye, Istanbul, Turkey.

Contact: Viviane Dumezic.

TUR3889
LEAGUE OF TURKISH WOMEN

Eczane ik, Apt 336/9 Bebek, Konur kokak 4, Turkey.

Telephone: 90 (1) 163 67 39.

TUR3890
MATERNAL, CHILD CARE AND FAMILY PLANNING FOUNDATION OF TURKEY

Ataç Sokak n° : 13/10, Ankara, Turkey.

TUR3891
TURKIYE AILE PLANLAMASI DERNEGI (TAPD) ♦ FAMILY PLANNING ASSOCIATION OF TURKEY

Ataç Sokak 73/3, 06420 Ankara, Turkey.

Telephone: 90 (312) 431 18 78. *Fax:* 90 (312) 434 29 46. *Contact:* Dr. Semra Koral, Executive Director.

TUR3892
TURKIYE AILE SAGLIGI VE PLANLAMASI VAKFI (TAP-VAKFI) ♦ Turkish Family Health and Planning Foundation

Güzel Konutlar Sitesi A Blok D. 3-4 Ulus Mahallesi, B0600 Etiler Istanbul, Turkey.

Telephone: 90 (212) 257 79 41. *Fax:* 90 (212) 257 79 43. *Contact:* Yaser Yasar, Executive Director.

OBJECTIVES: To undertake information and education activities which raise awareness of family planning services. To support family planning services clinics and to facilitate access to contraceptives.

GENERAL INFORMATION: *Creation:* 1985. *Personnel/Total:* 34. *Salaried:* 26. *Volunteers:* 8. *Budget/Total 1993:* ECU 872000 (US$ 1131000). *Financial sources:* Private: 60%. Public: 30%. Self-financing: 10%.

PUBLICATIONS: *Annual report. List of publications.*

EVALUATION/RESEARCH: Undertakes research activities.

INFORMATION AND EDUCATION ACTIVITIES: Topics: Population/family planning/demography. **Activities:** Broadcasting/cultural events; Conferences/seminars/workshops/training activities; Fund raising; Information campaigns/exhibitions; Lobbying/advocacy.

TUR3893
TURKIYE CEVRE KORUMA VE YESILLENDIRME DERNEGI

Muhurdarbagi sk. No:6, Kadikoy/Istanbul, Turkey.

Telephone: 90 (212) 338 00 17. *Fax:* 90 (212) 338 55 92 .

TUR3894
TURKIYE CEVRE VAKFI (TÇV) ♦ Environment Foundation of Turkey (EFT)

Tunali Hilmi Caddesi 50/20, Kavaklidere 06660 Ankara, Turkey.

Telephone: 90 (312) 425 55 08. *Fax:* 90 (312) 418 51 18. *Contact:* Necmi Sonmez, Chairman Board of Trustees.

OBJECTIVES: To research and raise awareness of environmental issues. To advise and assist government officials and the public on sustainable development policies. To co-operate with Central Asian and Black Sea countries to create an environmental network.

GENERAL INFORMATION: *Creation:* 1978. *Personnel/Total:* 8. *Salaried:* 8. *Budget/Total 1993:* ECU 281000 (US$ 364000). *Financial sources:* Private: 65%. Public: 15%. Self-financing: 20%.

PUBLICATIONS: *Periodicals:* ÇEVRE (4) - Newsletter (3). *List of publications.*

EVALUATION/RESEARCH: Evaluation reports available. Undertakes research activities.

COMMENTS: Undertakes activities in the Commonwealth of Independent States. Information activities related to the Commonwealth of Independent States.

ACTIVITIES IN DEVELOPING REGIONS: Active in 10 country(ies). **Sustainable Development Actions:** Ecology/environment/biodiversity. **Regions:** Central Asia and South Asia.

INFORMATION AND EDUCATION ACTIVITIES: Topics: Ecology/environment/biodiversity. **Activities:** Broadcasting/cultural events; Conferences/seminars/workshops/training activities; Information and documentation services/data bases; Lobbying/advocacy; Networking/electronic telecommunications; Publishing/audiovisual materials/educational materials.

TUR3895
TURKIYE INSAN HAKLARI VAKFI ♦ Human Rights Foundation of Turkey

Menekse 2 Sokak 16/6, 06640 Kizilay, Ankara, Turkey.

Telephone: 90 (312) 417 71 80. *Fax:* 90 (312) 425 45 52. *Contact:* Yavuz Önen, President.

OBJECTIVES: To undertake projects for the defence of human rights and the treatment of torture victims. To issue publications and documentation on human rights and democracy. To carry out scientific and educational research.

GENERAL INFORMATION: *Creation:* 1990. *Personnel/Total:* 26. *Salaried:* 18. *Volunteers:* 8. *Budget/Total 1993:* ECU 330000 (US$ 428000). *Financial sources:* Public: 88%. Self-financing: 12%.

PUBLICATIONS: *Annual report. List of publications.*

EVALUATION/RESEARCH: Evaluation reports available. Undertakes research activities.

PLANNED ACTIVITIES: Undertaking a project for job searching and training. Setting-up various centres for education, communications and research.

INFORMATION AND EDUCATION ACTIVITIES: Topics: Emergency relief/refugees/humanitarian assistance; Human rights/peace/conflicts; Peace/ethnic conflicts/armament/disarmament. **Activities:** Conferences/seminars/workshops/training activities; Information and documentation services/data bases; Information campaigns/exhibitions; Publishing/audiovisual materials/educational materials.

TUR3896
TURKIYE KALKINMA VAKFI (TKV) ♦ Development Foundation of Turkey (DFT)

Tunali Hilmi Caddesi 22, K. Esat, 06660 Ankara, Turkey.

Telephone: 90 (312) 417 86 85. *Fax:* 90 (312) 417 10 87. *Contact:* Necmi Sonmez, Chairman Board of Trustees.

OBJECTIVES: To promote rural and agricultural development among Turkey's rural poor. To undertake projects in Turkey focusing on community organisation and on raising the income of small farmers. To advocate policies and programmes consistent with the ultimate objectives of development.

GENERAL INFORMATION: *Creation:* 1969. *Personnel/Total:* 106. *Salaried:* 104. *Volunteers:* 2. *Budget/Total 1993:* ECU 11232000 (US$ 14566000). *Financial sources:* Private: 5%. Public: 20%. Self-financing: 75%.

PUBLICATIONS: *Periodicals:* Practical Beekeeping (6). *Annual report. List of publications.*

EVALUATION/RESEARCH: Evaluation reports available. Undertakes research activities.

PLANNED ACTIVITIES: Providing training to technical personnel from the Central Asian Republics in such fields as: project design, management, monitoring and evaluation, poultry farming and beekeeping.

INFORMATION AND EDUCATION ACTIVITIES: Topics: Children/youth/family; Ecology/environment/biodiversity; Education/training/literacy; Employment/unemployment; Gender issues/women; Health/sanitation/water; International relations/cooperation/development aid; Rural development/agriculture. **Activities:** Conferences/seminars/workshops/training activities; Fund raising; Information and documentation services/data bases; Lobbying/advocacy; Publishing/audiovisual materials/educational materials.

TUR3897

TURKIYE KIZILAY DERNEGI ♦ Turkish Red Crescent Society

Genel Baskanligi, Karanfil Sokak No.7, 06650 Wizilay-Ankara, Turkey.

Telephone: 90 (312) 431 76 80. **Fax:** 90 (312) 418 06 10. **Contact:** Dr. Kemal Demir, President.

OBJECTIVES: To follow and help with the implementation of international agreements that have been signed by the Turkish government. To provide assistance and services to disaster victims in Turkey and abroad. To assist the improvement of social welfare.

GENERAL INFORMATION: Creation: 1868. **Personnel/Total:** 1830. Salaried: 1830. **Budget/Total 1993:** ECU 34000 (US$ 44000). **Financial sources:** Private: 13%. Public: 17%. Self-financing: 70%.

PUBLICATIONS: Periodicals: Turkish Red Crescent - Red Crescent Magazine. Annual report.

EVALUATION/RESEARCH: Evaluation reports available. Undertakes research activities.

INFORMATION AND EDUCATION ACTIVITIES: Topics: Emergency relief/refugees/humanitarian assistance; Health/sanitation/water; Human rights/peace/conflicts; International relations/cooperation/development aid; Peace/ethnic conflicts/armament/disarmament; Poverty/living conditions. **Activities:** Lobbying/advocacy.

TUR3898

TURKIYE TABIATINI KORUMA DERNEGI ♦ Turkish Association for the Protection of Nature

Menekse sk. 29/4, 06540 Kizilay/Ankara, Turkey.

Telephone: 90 (312) 425 19 44. **Fax:** 90 (312) 417 95 52. **Contact:** Hasan Asmaz.

OBJECTIVES: To protect the environment including wildlife, natural resources and wild habitats. To foster a harmonious relationship between nature and humankind. To find solutions to environmental problems caused by industrialisation.

GENERAL INFORMATION: Creation: 1955. **Type of organisation:** association of NGOs. **Member organisations:** 14. **Affiliated to:** IUCN - Naturopa-National Agency. **Personnel/Total:** 28. Salaried: 3. Volunteers: 25. **Budget/Total 1993:** ECU 30000 (US$ 39000). **Financial sources:** Private: 50%. Public: 30%. Self-financing: 20%.

PUBLICATIONS: Periodicals: Nature and Men (4).

EVALUATION/RESEARCH: Evaluation reports available. Undertakes research activities.

PLANNED ACTIVITIES: Undertaking similar activities in the former Soviet Union countries.

COMMENTS: The association would like to co-operate with similar NGOs around the world.

INFORMATION AND EDUCATION ACTIVITIES: Topics: Children/youth/family; Ecology/environment/biodiversity; Health/sanitation/water; Rural development/agriculture; Urban development/habitat. **Activities:** Broadcasting/cultural events; Conferences/seminars/workshops/training activities; Fund raising; Information and documentation services/data bases; Information campaigns/exhibitions; Lobbying/advocacy; Publishing/audiovisual materials/educational materials.

TUR3899

UNICEF TURKIYE MILLI KOMITESI ♦ Turkish National Committee for UNICEF

Abdullah Cevdet Sokak 20/10, Cankaya, Ankara, Turkey.

Telephone: 90 (41) 138 17 45 / 139 02 50. **Contact:** Dr. Ihsan Dogramaci.

TUR3900

WORLD COUNCIL OF CHURCHES

Siracevizler CAD, Marmara Apartments 116/3, Sisli, Istanbul, Turkey.

Contact: Reuben Colley.

See: *How to Use the Directory,* page 11.

Index 1: SUSTAINABLE DEVELOPMENT ACTIONS IN DEVELOPING COUNTRIES
by Subject and Region

Index 1 : ACTIONS DE DÉVELOPPEMENT DURABLE DANS LES RÉGIONS EN DÉVELOPPEMENT
par thème et par région

ISO Codes / Codes ISO

AUT	Austria	Autriche
BEL	Belgium	Belgique
CHE	Switzerland	Suisse
CYP	Cyprus	Chypre
CZE	Czech Republic	République tchèque
DEU	Germany	Allemagne
DNK	Denmark	Danemark
ESP	Spain	Espagne
FIN	Finland	Finlande
FRA	France	France
GBR	United Kingdom	Royaume-Uni
GRC	Greece	Grèce
HUN	Hungary	Hongrie
IRL	Ireland	Irlande
ISL	Iceland	Islande
ITA	Italy	Italie
LIE	Liechtenstein	Liechtenstein
LUX	Luxembourg	Luxembourg
MLT	Malta	Malte
NLD	Netherlands	Pays-Bas
NOR	Norway	Norvège
POL	Poland	Pologne
PRT	Portugal	Portugal
SVK	Slovac Republic	République slovaque
SWE	Sweden	Suède
TUR	Turkey	Turquie

Subjects

Thèmes

CHILDREN, YOUTH, FAMILY ------------------- ENFANTS, JEUNESSE, FAMILLE
DEBT, FINANCE, TRADE --------------------- DETTE, FINANCES, COMMERCE
DEMOCRACY, GOOD GOVERNANCE, INSTITUTION - - - DEMOCRATIE, BONNE GESTION PUBLIQUE, CREATION
    BUILDING, PARTICIPATORY DEVELOPMENT   D'INSTITUTIONS, DEVELOPPEMENT PARTICIPATIF
ECOLOGY, ENVIRONMENT, BIODIVERSITY ------- ECOLOGIE, ENVIRONNEMENT, BIODIVERSITE
EDUCATION, TRAINING, LITERACY ------------ EDUCATION, FORMATION, ALPHABETISATION
EMERGENCY RELIEF, REFUGEES, HUMANITARIAN -- SECOURS D'URGENCE, REFUGIES, AIDE HUMANITAIRE
    ASSISTANCE
ENERGY, TRANSPORT --------------------- ENERGIE, TRANSPORT
FOOD, FAMINE ------------------------- ALIMENTS, FAMINE
GENDER ISSUES, WOMEN ------------------ QUESTIONS RELATIVES AUX FEMMES
HEALTH, SANITATION, WATER -------------- SANTE, ASSAINISSEMENT, EAU
HUMAN RIGHTS, PEACE, CONFLICTS ----------- DROITS DE L'HOMME, PAIX, CONFLITS
OTHER ----------------------------- AUTRES
POPULATION, FAMILY PLANNING, DEMOGRAPHY - - - POPULATION, PLANNING FAMILIAL, DEMOGRAPHIE
RURAL DEVELOPMENT, AGRICULTURE --------- DEVELOPPEMENT RURAL, AGRICULTURE
SENDING VOLUNTEERS, EXPERTS, TECHNICAL----- ENVOI DE VOLONTAIRES, EXPERTS, ASSISTANCE
    ASSISTANCE   TECHNIQUE
SMALL ENTERPRISES, INFORMAL SECTOR, ------- PETITES ENTREPRISES, SECTEUR INFORMEL,
    HANDICRAFTS   ARTISANAT
URBAN DEVELOPMENT, HABITAT ------------- DEVELOPPEMENT URBAIN, HABITAT

Regions

Régions

CARIBBEAN ---------------------------- CARAÏBES
CENTRAL AFRICA ----------------------- AFRIQUE CENTRALE
CENTRAL ASIA AND SOUTH ASIA ------------- ASIE CENTRALE ET DU SUD
EAST AFRICA -------------------------- AFRIQUE DE L'EST
EAST ASIA --------------------------- ASIE DE L'EST
MEXICO AND CENTRAL AMERICA ------------- MEXIQUE ET AMÉRIQUE CENTRALE
THE MIDDLE EAST ---------------------- MOYEN-ORIENT
NORTH AFRICA ------------------------- AFRIQUE DU NORD
OCEANIA ----------------------------- OCÉANIE
SOUTHERN AFRICA ---------------------- AFRIQUE AUSTRALE
SOUTH AMERICA ----------------------- AMÉRIQUE DU SUD
SOUTH EAST ASIA---------------------- ASIE DU SUD-EST
WEST AFRICA ------------------------- AFRIQUE DE L'OUEST

CHILDREN, YOUTH, FAMILY - ENFANTS, JEUNESSE, FAMILLE

CARIBBEAN - CARAIBES

AUT0003	AUT0076	BEL0123	BEL0129
BEL0144	BEL0173	BEL0186	BEL0198
BEL0199	BEL0218	BEL0224	BEL0260
BEL0327	BEL0335	BEL0336	BEL0351
BEL0353	BEL0355	BEL0358	BEL0361
BEL0362	BEL0368	BEL0399	CHE0420
CHE0432	CHE0434	CHE0558	CHE0559
CHE0568	CHE0570	CHE0582	CHE0586
CHE0587	CHE0640	CHE0643	CHE0655
CHE0689	CHE0711	CHE0712	CHE0730
CHE0785	CHE0798	CHE0814	CHE0817
CHE0819	CYP0832	DEU0944	DEU0965
DEU0967	DEU0972	DEU0983	DEU0989
DEU0991	DEU1053	DEU1078	DEU1106
DEU1127	DEU1128	DEU1164	DNK1288
DNK1366	DNK1402	ESP1435	ESP1442
ESP1455	ESP1461	ESP1486	ESP1488
ESP1491	ESP1492	ESP1496	ESP1507
ESP1517	ESP1525	FIN1567	FIN1611
FRA1644	FRA1672	FRA1675	FRA1685
FRA1726	FRA1796	FRA1824	FRA1843
FRA1865	FRA1905	FRA1934	FRA1946
FRA2023	FRA2034	FRA2060	FRA2062
FRA2081	FRA2096	FRA2116	FRA2119
FRA2137	FRA2159	FRA2168	GBR2175
GBR2218	GBR2238	GBR2242	GBR2247
GBR2266	GBR2280	GBR2293	GBR2351
GBR2359	GBR2371	GBR2403	GBR2436
GBR2445	GBR2463	GBR2464	GBR2481
GBR2489	GBR2500	GBR2501	GBR2535
GBR2552	GBR2558	IRL2726	ITA2766
ITA2773	ITA2777	ITA2784	ITA2860
ITA2922	LUX2975	LUX2993	MLT3016
NLD3067	NLD3072	NLD3173	NLD3230
NLD3231	NLD3253	NLD3262	NLD3265
NLD3288	NLD3325	NLD3336	NLD3342
NLD3356	NLD3361	NOR3439	POL3519
SWE3653	SWE3656	SWE3712	SWE3749
TUR3883			

CENTRAL AFRICA - AFRIQUE CENTRALE

AUT0013	AUT0024	AUT0026	AUT0076
BEL0097	BEL0105	BEL0110	BEL0120
BEL0123	BEL0133	BEL0148	BEL0148
BEL0153	BEL0155	BEL0156	BEL0158
BEL0169	BEL0173	BEL0186	BEL0192
BEL0198	BEL0199	BEL0201	BEL0202
BEL0203	BEL0218	BEL0258	BEL0318
BEL0323	BEL0327	BEL0328	BEL0342
BEL0351	BEL0352	BEL0353	BEL0355
BEL0358	BEL0359	BEL0361	BEL0381
BEL0390	BEL0396	BEL0399	CHE0420
CHE0421	CHE0432	CHE0434	CHE0444
CHE0521	CHE0524	CHE0535	CHE0541
CHE0550	CHE0559	CHE0562	CHE0566
CHE0568	CHE0569	CHE0570	CHE0582
CHE0598	CHE0604	CHE0628	CHE0630
CHE0636	CHE0643	CHE0645	CHE0655
CHE0687	CHE0689	CHE0711	CHE0712
CHE0730	CHE0750	CHE0757	CHE0762
CHE0796	CHE0805	CHE0814	CHE0817
CHE0819	DEU0942	DEU0942	DEU0944
DEU0968	DEU0972	DEU0978	DEU0989
DEU1006	DEU1053	DEU1078	DEU1106
DEU1114	DEU1128	DEU1131	DEU1149
DNK1227	DNK1272	DNK1358	DNK1360
DNK1366	DNK1392	DNK1402	ESP1486
ESP1492	ESP1513	ESP1517	FIN1594
FRA1611	FRA1671	FRA1675	FRA1704
FRA1715	FRA1727	FRA1740	FRA1774
FRA1787	FRA1796	FRA1815	FRA1824
FRA1832	FRA1876	FRA1880	FRA1885
FRA1887	FRA1905	FRA1934	FRA1946
FRA1956	FRA1966	FRA2032	FRA2034
FRA2039	FRA2042	FRA2055	FRA2060
FRA2061	FRA2062	FRA2080	FRA2081
FRA2086	FRA2096	FRA2097	FRA2107
FRA2114	FRA2116	FRA2117	FRA2119
FRA2123	FRA2145	FRA2159	FRA2168
GBR2174	GBR2175	GBR2185	GBR2218
GBR2238	GBR2240	GBR2259	GBR2274
GBR2280	GBR2289	GBR2350	GBR2351
GBR2359	GBR2371	GBR2390	GBR2445
GBR2460	GBR2464	GBR2481	GBR2500

GBR2501	IRL2732	ITA2747	ITA2756
ITA2762	ITA2766	ITA2770	ITA2784
ITA2813	ITA2835	ITA2860	ITA2874
ITA2885	ITA2888	ITA2890	ITA2896
ITA2898	ITA2902	ITA2920	ITA2921
ITA2922	LUX2942	LUX2954	LUX2973
LUX2975	MLT3016	NLD3045	NLD3067
NLD3095	NLD3173	NLD3262	NLD3265
NLD3277	NLD3291	NLD3301	NLD3325
NLD3356	NLD3361	NOR3395	NOR3452
NOR3465	POL3508	POL3519	PRT3594
PRT3602	SWE3656	SWE3704	SWE3749
SWE3763	SWE3827	SWE3828	TUR3883

CENTRAL ASIA AND SOUTH ASIA - ASIE CENTRALE ET ASIE DU SUD

AUT0013	AUT0024	AUT0026	AUT0051
AUT0052	AUT0076	AUT0089	AUT0091
BEL0097	BEL0104	BEL0123	BEL0129
BEL0144	BEL0148	BEL0173	BEL0186
BEL0198	BEL0199	BEL0201	BEL0202
BEL0203	BEL0245	BEL0270	BEL0275
BEL0327	BEL0341	BEL0351	BEL0352
BEL0355	BEL0358	BEL0361	BEL0368
CHE0406	CHE0412	CHE0417	CHE0420
CHE0432	CHE0434	CHE0472	CHE0550
CHE0558	CHE0559	CHE0566	CHE0568
CHE0569	CHE0582	CHE0586	CHE0628
CHE0636	CHE0643	CHE0645	CHE0655
CHE0687	CHE0689	CHE0711	CHE0712
CHE0730	CHE0742	CHE0757	CHE0785
CHE0796	CHE0798	CHE0814	CHE0817
CHE0819	DEU0927	DEU0942	DEU0944
DEU0954	DEU0965	DEU0971	DEU0972
DEU0983	DEU0985	DEU0989	DEU0991
DEU0993	DEU1006	DEU1053	DEU1066
DEU1078	DEU1086	DEU1106	DEU1110
DEU1115	DEU1121	DEU1127	DEU1128
DEU1129	DEU1131	DEU1132	DEU1141
DEU1142	DEU1149	DEU1178	DEU1187
DNK1216	DNK1222	DNK1229	DNK1244
DNK1259	DNK1260	DNK1275	DNK1292
DNK1304	DNK1339	DNK1358	DNK1360
DNK1366	DNK1384	DNK1402	ESP1435
ESP1486	ESP1491	ESP1492	ESP1513
ESP1517	FIN1567	FIN1580	FIN1591
FRA1611	FRA1642	FRA1644	FRA1658
FRA1661	FRA1677	FRA1824	FRA1866
FRA1887	FRA1905	FRA1934	FRA1966
FRA1980	FRA1990	FRA1991	FRA2023
FRA2032	FRA2034	FRA2039	FRA2041
FRA2042	FRA2057	FRA2060	FRA2062
FRA2081	FRA2096	FRA2096	FRA2116
FRA2119	FRA2131	FRA2150	FRA2159
FRA2168	GBR2172	GBR2174	GBR2175
GBR2186	GBR2197	GBR2201	GBR2218
GBR2236	GBR2238	GBR2259	GBR2260
GBR2264	GBR2266	GBR2274	GBR2280
GBR2302	GBR2307	GBR2321	GBR2330
GBR2334	GBR2348	GBR2349	GBR2351
GBR2358	GBR2359	GBR2371	GBR2372
GBR2375	GBR2385	GBR2390	GBR2410
GBR2413	GBR2436	GBR2439	GBR2440
GBR2445	GBR2463	GBR2464	GBR2467
GBR2481	GBR2492	GBR2500	GBR2501
GBR2506	GBR2509	GBR2532	GBR2535
GBR2552	GBR2556	GBR2558	HUN2627
IRL2726	ISL2736	ITA2764	ITA2766
ITA2770	ITA2784	ITA2813	ITA2860
ITA2888	ITA2898	ITA2902	ITA2912
ITA2922	LIE2926	LUX2941	LUX2965
LUX2975	LUX2982	LUX3001	MLT3016
NLD3051	NLD3067	NLD3072	NLD3124
NLD3149	NLD3153	NLD3163	NLD3173
NLD3231	NLD3237	NLD3242	NLD3244
NLD3253	NLD3260	NLD3262	NLD3265
NLD3277	NLD3295	NLD3297	NLD3302
NLD3317	NLD3325	NLD3342	NLD3356
NLD3361	NOR3369	NOR3371	NOR3384
NOR3412	NOR3439	NOR3453	NOR3465
NOR3467	POL3508	POL3519	SWE3646
SWE3656	SWE3661	SWE3666	SWE3674
SWE3679	SWE3723	SWE3737	SWE3749
SWE3763	SWE3771	SWE3787	SWE3795
SWE3818	SWE3826	SWE3827	SWE3828
SWE3831	SWE3834	SWE3854	SWE3857
TUR3883			

EAST AFRICA - AFRIQUE DE L'EST

AUT0003	AUT0013	AUT0024	AUT0067
AUT0076	AUT0085	AUT0091	BEL0123
BEL0129	BEL0144	BEL0148	BEL0173
BEL0186	BEL0198	BEL0199	BEL0224
BEL0269	BEL0270	BEL0275	BEL0318
BEL0327	BEL0351	BEL0358	BEL0361
BEL0368	BEL0381	BEL0399	CHE0420
CHE0432	CHE0434	CHE0448	CHE0462
CHE0491	CHE0521	CHE0550	CHE0566
CHE0569	CHE0570	CHE0582	CHE0586
CHE0620	CHE0630	CHE0643	CHE0645
CHE0649	CHE0660	CHE0687	CHE0689
CHE0711	CHE0712	CHE0730	CHE0754
CHE0764	CHE0772	CHE0785	CHE0796
CHE0798	CHE0814	CHE0817	CHE0819
CHE0823	DEU0936	DEU0942	DEU0944
DEU0947	DEU0968	DEU0972	DEU0983
DEU0989	DEU0991	DEU1002	DEU1006
DEU1012	DEU1053	DEU1066	DEU1069
DEU1078	DEU1106	DEU1128	DEU1129
DEU1131	DEU1142	DEU1145	DEU1149
DEU1176	DEU1178	DEU1181	DNK1229
DNK1244	DNK1245	DNK1259	DNK1275
DNK1285	DNK1316	DNK1328	DNK1339
DNK1342	DNK1358	DNK1360	DNK1366
DNK1377	DNK1391	DNK1392	DNK1402
DNK1405	ESP1432	ESP1486	ESP1491
ESP1492	ESP1510	ESP1524	FIN1549
FIN1556	FIN1567	FIN1572	FIN1580
FIN1585	FIN1591	FRA1611	FRA1617
FRA1644	FRA1658	FRA1672	FRA1675
FRA1717	FRA1727	FRA1796	FRA1824
FRA1855	FRA1887	FRA1930	FRA1934
FRA1956	FRA2032	FRA2039	FRA2060
FRA2062	FRA2080	FRA2081	FRA2096
FRA2107	FRA2116	FRA2119	FRA2123
FRA2159	FRA2168	GBR2172	GBR2174
GBR2175	GBR2179	GBR2183	GBR2185
GBR2186	GBR2218	GBR2224	GBR2228
GBR2238	GBR2240	GBR2241	GBR2247
GBR2259	GBR2262	GBR2274	GBR2278
GBR2280	GBR2282	GBR2292	GBR2293
GBR2307	GBR2321	GBR2338	GBR2348
GBR2350	GBR2351	GBR2359	GBR2371
GBR2383	GBR2385	GBR2390	GBR2396
GBR2409	GBR2410	GBR2436	GBR2439
GBR2445	GBR2459	GBR2460	GBR2463
GBR2464	GBR2467	GBR2471	GBR2474
GBR2481	GBR2489	GBR2500	GBR2501
GBR2502	GBR2521	GBR2535	GBR2536
GBR2552	GBR2556	GBR2558	IRL2688
IRL2691	IRL2699	IRL2726	IRL2729
IRL2730	IRL2732	IRL2733	ISL2739
ISL2740	ITA2762	ITA2766	ITA2771
ITA2772	ITA2782	ITA2784	ITA2810
ITA2813	ITA2820	ITA2822	ITA2835
ITA2837	ITA2848	ITA2857	ITA2860
ITA2877	ITA2885	ITA2888	ITA2889
ITA2890	ITA2898	ITA2902	ITA2910
ITA2922	ITA2922	ITA2923	LUX2975
MLT3016	NLD3045	NLD3067	NLD3068
NLD3074	NLD3075	NLD3127	NLD3145
NLD3146	NLD3198	NLD3216	NLD3231
NLD3237	NLD3262	NLD3265	NLD3277
NLD3297	NLD3301	NLD3317	NLD3323
NLD3325	NLD3342	NLD3356	NLD3361
NOR3369	NOR3381	NOR3384	NOR3404
NOR3435	NOR3439	NOR3465	NOR3467
POL3508	POL3519	PRT3550	PRT3584
SWE3656	SWE3679	SWE3712	SWE3727
SWE3730	SWE3749	SWE3771	SWE3775
SWE3779	SWE3787	SWE3799	SWE3821
SWE3826	SWE3828	SWE3853	SWE3854
SWE3855	TUR3883		

EAST ASIA - ASIE DE L'EST

AUT0013	AUT0024	AUT0076	BEL0123
BEL0129	BEL0144	BEL0173	BEL0186
BEL0198	BEL0199	BEL0275	BEL0351
BEL0358	BEL0359	BEL0361	CHE0420
CHE0432	CHE0434	CHE0550	CHE0570
CHE0582	CHE0586	CHE0636	CHE0643
CHE0645	CHE0649	CHE0655	CHE0689
CHE0711	CHE0712	CHE0730	CHE0796
CHE0814	CHE0817	CHE0819	DEU0944
DEU0972	DEU0989	DEU1006	DEU1078
DEU1106	DEU1128	DEU1129	DEU1131

DEU1142	DEU1143	DEU1149	DNK1244
DNK1275	DNK1292	DNK1366	DNK1402
ESP1432	ESP1492	ESP1508	ESP1510
FIN1567	FRA1611	FRA1658	FRA1672
FRA1871	FRA2032	FRA2062	FRA2096
FRA2114	FRA2116	FRA2149	FRA2159
FRA2168	GBR2175	GBR2218	GBR2238
GBR2260	GBR2264	GBR2266	GBR2280
GBR2351	GBR2359	GBR2371	GBR2445
GBR2464	GBR2481	GBR2500	GBR2501
GBR2535	GBR2556	IRL2726	ITA2766
ITA2784	ITA2832	ITA2860	ITA2922
LUX2941	LUX2975	MLT3016	NLD3067
NLD3163	NLD3198	NLD3265	NLD3277
NLD3342	NLD3356	NLD3361	NOR3369
NOR3465	POL3508	SWE3646	SWE3712
SWE3823	SWE3826	SWE3828	TUR3883

MEXICO AND CENTRAL AMERICA - MEXIQUE ET AMERIQUE CENTRALE

AUT0003	AUT0013	AUT0024	AUT0067
AUT0076	AUT0091	BEL0123	BEL0129
BEL0144	BEL0148	BEL0173	BEL0186
BEL0198	BEL0199	BEL0201	BEL0203
BEL0224	BEL0269	BEL0275	BEL0318
BEL0327	BEL0335	BEL0336	BEL0351
BEL0353	BEL0358	BEL0359	BEL0361
BEL0381	BEL0396	CHE0420	CHE0432
CHE0434	CHE0485	CHE0486	CHE0491
CHE0493	CHE0517	CHE0550	CHE0557
CHE0559	CHE0566	CHE0566	CHE0568
CHE0570	CHE0582	CHE0586	CHE0630
CHE0636	CHE0640	CHE0645	CHE0649
CHE0689	CHE0711	CHE0712	CHE0730
CHE0735	CHE0757	CHE0772	CHE0785
CHE0788	CHE0789	CHE0800	CHE0814
CHE0817	CHE0819	CYP0832	DEU0933
DEU0942	DEU0944	DEU0954	DEU0967
DEU0968	DEU0972	DEU0983	DEU0989
DEU1002	DEU1053	DEU1078	DEU1114
DEU1128	DEU1129	DEU1138	DEU1142
DEU1149	DEU1176	DEU1177	DEU1178
DEU1187	DNK1229	DNK1283	DNK1312
DNK1317	DNK1339	DNK1358	DNK1360
DNK1366	DNK1402	ESP1413	ESP1432
ESP1435	ESP1442	ESP1455	ESP1461
ESP1474	ESP1486	ESP1488	ESP1491
ESP1492	ESP1496	ESP1506	ESP1510
ESP1517	ESP1524	ESP1525	FIN1544
FIN1546	FIN1549	FIN1567	FIN1580
FIN1591	FIN1599	FIN1602	FRA1611
FRA1658	FRA1671	FRA1672	FRA1675
FRA1677	FRA1685	FRA1824	FRA1843
FRA1905	FRA1934	FRA1938	FRA1942
FRA1967	FRA1975	FRA1978	FRA1991
FRA2032	FRA2034	FRA2041	FRA2042
FRA2057	FRA2060	FRA2062	FRA2081
FRA2090	FRA2096	FRA2116	FRA2119
FRA2152	FRA2159	FRA2168	GBR2174
GBR2175	GBR2201	GBR2218	GBR2228
GBR2236	GBR2238	GBR2242	GBR2247
GBR2259	GBR2280	GBR2293	GBR2306
GBR2321	GBR2349	GBR2351	GBR2359
GBR2371	GBR2385	GBR2390	GBR2436
GBR2439	GBR2445	GBR2463	GBR2464
GBR2467	GBR2481	GBR2500	GBR2501
GBR2535	GBR2552	GBR2556	IRL2697
IRL2714	IRL2726	IRL2732	ITA2755
ITA2756	ITA2762	ITA2771	ITA2773
ITA2775	ITA2784	ITA2824	ITA2838
ITA2842	ITA2858	ITA2860	ITA2868
ITA2873	ITA2894	ITA2902	ITA2911
ITA2913	ITA2922	ITA2923	LUX2968
LUX2973	LUX2975	MLT3016	NLD3067
NLD3068	NLD3141	NLD3153	NLD3159
NLD3198	NLD3230	NLD3231	NLD3262
NLD3265	NLD3277	NLD3288	NLD3300
NLD3303	NLD3305	NLD3325	NLD3356
NLD3361	NOR3369	NOR3374	NOR3381
NOR3439	NOR3467	POL3519	SWE3656
SWE3666	SWE3687	SWE3749	SWE3771
SWE3785	SWE3786	SWE3787	SWE3795
SWE3796	SWE3798	SWE3828	SWE3831
SWE3857	SWE3865	TUR3883	

MIDDLE EAST - MOYEN-ORIENT

AUT0021	AUT0076	AUT0091	BEL0105
BEL0129	BEL0133	BEL0148	BEL0173
BEL0186	BEL0198	BEL0270	BEL0275
BEL0303	BEL0306	BEL0318	BEL0342
BEL0353	BEL0358	BEL0359	BEL0361
BEL0399	CHE0406	CHE0410	CHE0420
CHE0434	CHE0506	CHE0550	CHE0559
CHE0568	CHE0570	CHE0582	CHE0600
CHE0640	CHE0645	CHE0649	CHE0655
CHE0664	CHE0682	CHE0687	CHE0689
CHE0711	CHE0712	CHE0730	CHE0739
CHE0796	CHE0814	CHE0817	CHE0819
CHE0823	CYP0832	DEU0927	DEU0942
DEU0944	DEU0972	DEU0989	DEU0991
DEU1065	DEU1078	DEU1106	DEU1128
DEU1131	DEU1176	DNK1275	DNK1292
DNK1304	DNK1360	DNK1366	DNK1372
DNK1402	FIN1567	FIN1570	FIN1588
FRA1611	FRA1675	FRA1724	FRA1791
FRA1793	FRA1824	FRA1832	FRA1942
FRA1948	FRA2016	FRA2032	FRA2041
FRA2057	FRA2081	FRA2096	FRA2114
FRA2116	FRA2149	FRA2159	GBR2175
GBR2218	GBR2228	GBR2238	GBR2260
GBR2280	GBR2351	GBR2359	GBR2371
GBR2378	GBR2385	GBR2396	GBR2445
GBR2464	GBR2500	GBR2501	GBR2525
GBR2556	GRC2572	IRL2733	ITA2755
ITA2756	ITA2766	ITA2773	ITA2784
ITA2814	ITA2860	LUX2955	LUX2956
LUX2969	LUX2975	LUX2992	MLT3016
MLT3017	MLT3018	NLD3067	NLD3091
NLD3163	NLD3173	NLD3262	NLD3265
NLD3300	NLD3317	NLD3325	NLD3342
NLD3356	NLD3361	NOR3384	NOR3404
POL3508	POL3519	SWE3646	SWE3730
SWE3749	SWE3828	TUR3883	

NORTH AFRICA - AFRIQUE DU NORD

AUT0013	AUT0066	AUT0076	BEL0097
BEL0123	BEL0129	BEL0148	BEL0173
BEL0186	BEL0198	BEL0199	BEL0269
BEL0270	BEL0275	BEL0303	BEL0323
BEL0342	BEL0355	BEL0358	BEL0359
BEL0361	BEL0399	CHE0409	CHE0420
CHE0432	CHE0434	CHE0491	CHE0506
CHE0550	CHE0568	CHE0570	CHE0582
CHE0655	CHE0687	CHE0689	CHE0711
CHE0712	CHE0730	CHE0796	CHE0814
CHE0817	DEU0944	DEU0972	DEU0989
DEU1078	DEU1106	DEU1128	DEU1131
DEU1142	DEU1176	DEU1177	DEU1191
DNK1275	DNK1304	DNK1358	DNK1360
DNK1366	DNK1402	ESP1406	ESP1442
ESP1486	ESP1491	ESP1492	FIN1567
FRA1611	FRA1675	FRA1715	FRA1726
FRA1768	FRA1796	FRA1815	FRA1846
FRA1871	FRA1887	FRA1942	FRA1946
FRA1956	FRA1966	FRA2034	FRA2057
FRA2061	FRA2062	FRA2096	FRA2107
FRA2111	FRA2114	FRA2116	FRA2159
GBR2175	GBR2185	GBR2218	GBR2238
GBR2280	GBR2359	GBR2371	GBR2385
GBR2445	GBR2464	GBR2501	GBR2535
GRC2586	ITA2755	ITA2766	ITA2784
ITA2791	ITA2810	ITA2822	ITA2838
ITA2860	ITA2898	ITA2922	LUX2975
MLT3016	MLT3017	MLT3036	
NLD3067	NLD3198	NLD3262	NLD3265
NLD3317	NLD3334	NLD3356	POL3508
POL3519	SWE3646	SWE3763	SWE3813
SWE3828	TUR3883		

OCEANIA - OCEANIE

AUT0024	AUT0067	BEL0123	BEL0129
BEL0173	BEL0186	BEL0198	BEL0199
BEL0361	BEL0399	CHE0420	CHE0432
CHE0434	CHE0550	CHE0582	CHE0640
CHE0645	CHE0711	CHE0712	CHE0730
CHE0772	CHE0814	CHE0819	DEU0944
DEU0972	DEU0989	DEU0992	DEU1078
DEU1128	DEU1149	DNK1402	ESP1492
FIN1567	FRA1672	FRA2032	FRA2041
FRA2096	FRA2116	FRA2168	GBR2175
GBR2218	GBR2247	GBR2266	GBR2280
GBR2312	GBR2351	GBR2359	GBR2371
GBR2445	GBR2481	GBR2489	GBR2501

GBR2524	GBR2535	ITA2784	ITA2860
MLT3016	NLD3067	NLD3265	NLD3356
SWE3749	TUR3883		

SOUTH AMERICA - AMERIQUE DU SUD

AUT0009	AUT0013	AUT0022	AUT0024
AUT0026	AUT0052	AUT0067	AUT0076
AUT0091	BEL0105	BEL0119	BEL0123
BEL0129	BEL0132	BEL0139	BEL0144
BEL0148	BEL0155	BEL0173	BEL0184
BEL0186	BEL0198	BEL0199	BEL0201
BEL0203	BEL0226	BEL0269	BEL0270
BEL0275	BEL0282	BEL0303	BEL0306
BEL0314	BEL0318	BEL0323	BEL0352
BEL0335	BEL0336	BEL0351	BEL0352
BEL0353	BEL0355	BEL0358	BEL0359
BEL0361	BEL0368	BEL0381	BEL0399
CHE0420	CHE0432	CHE0434	CHE0438
CHE0443	CHE0475	CHE0486	CHE0491
CHE0510	CHE0550	CHE0559	CHE0566
CHE0568	CHE0569	CHE0570	CHE0581
CHE0582	CHE0586	CHE0596	CHE0598
CHE0604	CHE0628	CHE0636	CHE0640
CHE0643	CHE0645	CHE0649	CHE0669
CHE0681	CHE0689	CHE0701	CHE0711
CHE0712	CHE0730	CHE0750	CHE0757
CHE0764	CHE0772	CHE0785	CHE0789
CHE0796	CHE0798	CHE0800	CHE0806
CHE0814	CHE0817	CHE0819	DEU0927
DEU0933	DEU0942	DEU0944	DEU0967
DEU0968	DEU0972	DEU0983	DEU0989
DEU0991	DEU1006	DEU1031	DEU1066
DEU1078	DEU1110	DEU1114	DEU1115
DEU1127	DEU1128	DEU1129	DEU1131
DEU1138	DEU1142	DEU1143	DEU1149
DEU1178	DEU1187	DNK1218	DNK1244
DNK1288	DNK1304	DNK1312	DNK1317
DNK1358	DNK1360	DNK1366	DNK1402
ESP1407	ESP1413	ESP1432	ESP1435
ESP1442	ESP1452	ESP1455	ESP1461
ESP1474	ESP1475	ESP1486	ESP1488
ESP1492	ESP1496	ESP1502	ESP1505
ESP1507	ESP1508	ESP1510	ESP1511
ESP1513	ESP1517	ESP1521	ESP1525
FIN1549	FIN1558	FRA1611	FRA1615
FRA1658	FRA1672	FRA1675	FRA1710
FRA1726	FRA1741	FRA1815	FRA1824
FRA1832	FRA1843	FRA1905	FRA1926
FRA1930	FRA1932	FRA1934	FRA1938
FRA1946	FRA1975	FRA1991	FRA2023
FRA2032	FRA2034	FRA2042	FRA2057
FRA2060	FRA2062	FRA2081	FRA2086
FRA2096	FRA2107	FRA2111	FRA2114
FRA2116	FRA2119	FRA2131	FRA2149
FRA2152	FRA2159	FRA2168	GBR2174
GBR2175	GBR2201	GBR2218	GBR2228
GBR2229	GBR2236	GBR2238	GBR2259
GBR2266	GBR2280	GBR2290	GBR2293
GBR2303	GBR2306	GBR2321	GBR2351
GBR2359	GBR2371	GBR2383	GBR2390
GBR2436	GBR2445	GBR2454	GBR2464
GBR2464	GBR2467	GBR2481	GBR2485
GBR2489	GBR2500	GBR2501	GBR2525
GBR2535	GBR2552	GBR2558	IRL2693
IRL2726	IRL2732	ITA2755	ITA2756
ITA2762	ITA2766	ITA2773	ITA2775
ITA2777	ITA2782	ITA2784	ITA2791
ITA2802	ITA2809	ITA2810	ITA2811
ITA2824	ITA2834	ITA2838	ITA2842
ITA2860	ITA2868	ITA2880	ITA2882
ITA2885	ITA2889	ITA2898	ITA2900
ITA2907	ITA2910	ITA2913	ITA2922
ITA2923	LIE2925	LUX2943	
LUX2949	LUX2953	LUX2954	LUX2958
LUX2967	LUX2968	LUX2973	LUX2975
LUX2979	LUX2980	LUX2992	LUX2999
LUX3002	MLT3016	NLD3067	NLD3068
NLD3072	NLD3075	NLD3091	NLD3113
NLD3187	NLD3198	NLD3230	NLD3231
NLD3250	NLD3253	NLD3262	NLD3265
NLD3277	NLD3281	NLD3297	NLD3305
NLD3317	NLD3325	NLD3342	NLD3356
NLD3361	NOR3369	NOR3374	NOR3381
NOR3384	NOR3394	NOR3395	NOR3425
NOR3452	NOR3465	POL3519	PRT3552
PRT3600	SWE3646	SWE3656	SWE3666
SWE3693	SWE3695	SWE3702	SWE3704
SWE3712	SWE3730	SWE3744	SWE3749

See: *How to Use the Directory*, page 11.

SWE3763 SWE3771 SWE3787 SWE3795
SWE3796 SWE3827 SWE3828 SWE3831
SWE3855 SWE3857 SWE3865 TUR3883

SOUTH EAST ASIA - ASIE DU SUD-EST

AUT0013 AUT0024 AUT0036 AUT0076
AUT0091 BEL0123 BEL0129 BEL0173
BEL0186 BEL0198 BEL0199 BEL0203
BEL0224 BEL0269 BEL0275 BEL0297
BEL0318 BEL0327 BEL0340 BEL0342
BEL0351 BEL0358 BEL0359 BEL0361
BEL0368 CHE0420 CHE0432 CHE0434
CHE0524 CHE0550 CHE0559 CHE0566
CHE0568 CHE0570 CHE0582 CHE0586
CHE0598 CHE0604 CHE0630 CHE0636
CHE0637 CHE0643 CHE0645 CHE0649
CHE0689 CHE0711 CHE0712 CHE0730
CHE0749 CHE0757 CHE0785 CHE0796
CHE0798 CHE0814 CHE0817 CHE0819
DEU0944 DEU0954 DEU0972 DEU0983
DEU0989 DEU1006 DEU1053 DEU1078
DEU1082 DEU1106 DEU1110 DEU1128
DEU1129 DEU1132 DEU1149 DEU1176
DEU1178 DEU1186 DEU1187 DNK1229
DNK1248 DNK1259 DNK1288 DNK1292
DNK1316 DNK1360 DNK1366 DNK1402
ESP1420 ESP1492 ESP1510 FIN1549
FIN1567 FIN1580 FIN1599 FRA1611
FRA1615 FRA1617 FRA1638 FRA1671
FRA1672 FRA1675 FRA1715 FRA1726
FRA1824 FRA1850 FRA1865 FRA1871
FRA1891 FRA1905 FRA1930 FRA1934
FRA1937 FRA1938 FRA1941 FRA1946
FRA1967 FRA1978 FRA1979 FRA2016
FRA2023 FRA2032 FRA2034 FRA2039
FRA2060 FRA2062 FRA2065 FRA2080
FRA2081 FRA2096 FRA2097 FRA2114
FRA2116 FRA2119 FRA2137 FRA2140
FRA2150 FRA2159 FRA2168 GBR2175
GBR2201 GBR2236 GBR2238 GBR2238
GBR2240 GBR2242 GBR2260 GBR2264
GBR2266 GBR2280 GBR2293 GBR2303
GBR2310 GBR2321 GBR2330 GBR2349
GBR2350 GBR2351 GBR2359 GBR2371
GBR2385 GBR2390 GBR2410 GBR2413
GBR2436 GBR2445 GBR2464 GBR2467
GBR2481 GBR2500 GBR2501 GBR2508
GBR2535 GBR2552 GBR2556 IRL2691
IRL2726 IRL2733 ITA2756 ITA2766
ITA2784 ITA2860 ITA2888 ITA2894
ITA2902 ITA2920 ITA2922 LUX2954
LUX2975 MLT3016 NLD3067 NLD3068
NLD3141 NLD3146 NLD3187 NLD3198
NLD3231 NLD3237 NLD3245 NLD3262
NLD3265 NLD3277 NLD3297 NLD3317
NLD3325 NLD3336 NLD3342 NLD3356
NLD3361 NOR3369 NOR3372 NOR3381
NOR3395 NOR3437 NOR3465 NOR3467
POL3508 POL3519 SWE3656 SWE3674
SWE3749 SWE3771 SWE3787 SWE3821
SWE3826 SWE3828 SWE3831 SWE3854
SWE3855 SWE3857 TUR3883

SOUTHERN AFRICA - AFRIQUE AUSTRALE

AUT0013 AUT0022 AUT0024 AUT0034
AUT0052 AUT0067 AUT0076 AUT0091
BEL0097 BEL0123 BEL0129 BEL0148
BEL0173 BEL0186 BEL0198 BEL0199
BEL0203 BEL0260 BEL0275 BEL0327
BEL0351 BEL0355 BEL0358 BEL0361
BEL0399 CHE0414 CHE0420 CHE0432
CHE0434 CHE0506 CHE0559 CHE0566
CHE0569 CHE0570 CHE0582 CHE0586
CHE0628 CHE0640 CHE0645 CHE0649
CHE0689 CHE0693 CHE0711 CHE0712
CHE0730 CHE0734 CHE0750 CHE0796
CHE0798 CHE0814 CHE0817 CHE0819
DEU0927 DEU0931 DEU0942 DEU0944
DEU0968 DEU0972 DEU0989 DEU0991
DEU1006 DEU1031 DEU1038 DEU1069
DEU1078 DEU1082 DEU1106 DEU1127
DEU1128 DEU1129 DEU1131 DEU1142
DEU1143 DEU1149 DEU1161 DEU1176
DEU1181 DEU1187 DNK1245 DNK1259
DNK1275 DNK1288 DNK1292 DNK1312
DNK1339 DNK1358 DNK1360 DNK1366
DNK1375 DNK1388 DNK1391 DNK1402
ESP1420 ESP1454 ESP1486 ESP1491

ESP1502 FIN1549 FIN1556 FIN1557
FIN1567 FIN1580 FRA1611 FRA1657
FRA1658 FRA1659 FRA1671 FRA1672
FRA1675 FRA1691 FRA1715 FRA1726
FRA1727 FRA1738 FRA1768 FRA1769
FRA1794 FRA1824 FRA1849 FRA1871
FRA1876 FRA1887 FRA1930 FRA1946
FRA1956 FRA1966 FRA2018 FRA2032
FRA2062 FRA2080 FRA2096 FRA2107
FRA2114 FRA2116 FRA2119 FRA2123
FRA2159 FRA2168 GBR2174 GBR2175
GBR2178 GBR2181 GBR2185 GBR2201
GBR2202 GBR2218 GBR2222 GBR2228
GBR2229 GBR2236 GBR2238 GBR2240
GBR2242 GBR2247 GBR2259 GBR2266
GBR2277 GBR2280 GBR2292 GBR2293
GBR2318 GBR2319 GBR2321 GBR2348
GBR2349 GBR2359 GBR2371 GBR2385
GBR2390 GBR2402 GBR2436 GBR2445
GBR2460 GBR2463 GBR2464 GBR2467
GBR2471 GBR2481 GBR2489 GBR2492
GBR2500 GBR2501 GBR2509 GBR2535
GBR2536 GBR2552 GBR2556 GBR2558
GBR2561 IRL2691 IRL2726 IRL2729
IRL2732 IRL2733 ISL2739 ITA2766
ITA2771 ITA2784 ITA2798 ITA2803
ITA2811 ITA2813 ITA2824 ITA2860
ITA2879 ITA2884 ITA2888 ITA2900
ITA2902 ITA2911 ITA2916 ITA2922
ITA2923 ITA2973 ITA2975 LUX2995
MLT3016 NLD3045 NLD3067 NLD3127
NLD3139 NLD3173 NLD3198 NLD3231
NLD3265 NLD3277 NLD3336
NLD3356 NLD3361 NOR3379 NOR3384
NOR3400 NOR3418 NOR3467 POL3508
POL3519 PRT3564 PRT3590 PRT3594
PRT3600 PRT3602 PRT3605 SWE3648
SWE3656 SWE3730 SWE3749 SWE3753
SWE3771 SWE3776 SWE3813 SWE3826
SWE3828 SWE3859 TUR3883

WEST AFRICA - AFRIQUE DE L'OUEST

AUT0003 AUT0013 AUT0024 AUT0076
AUT0086 AUT0091 BEL0097 BEL0123
BEL0129 BEL0133 BEL0144 BEL0148
BEL0153 BEL0173 BEL0186 BEL0198
BEL0199 BEL0201 BEL0203 BEL0269
BEL0270 BEL0275 BEL0297 BEL0318
BEL0327 BEL0328 BEL0342 BEL0351
BEL0353 BEL0355 BEL0358 BEL0359
BEL0361 BEL0368 BEL0381 BEL0390
BEL0399 CHE0402 CHE0420 CHE0432
CHE0434 CHE0435 CHE0444 CHE0479
CHE0490 CHE0510 CHE0521 CHE0542
CHE0550 CHE0558 CHE0559 CHE0566
CHE0568 CHE0569 CHE0570 CHE0582
CHE0598 CHE0604 CHE0636 CHE0643
CHE0645 CHE0649 CHE0687 CHE0689
CHE0707 CHE0711 CHE0712 CHE0730
CHE0734 CHE0757 CHE0762 CHE0764
CHE0772 CHE0796 CHE0798 CHE0806
CHE0814 CHE0817 CHE0819 DEU0922
DEU0933 DEU0944 DEU0968 DEU0972
DEU0983 DEU0989 DEU0991 DEU1006
DEU1053 DEU1069 DEU1078 DEU1106
DEU1110 DEU1114 DEU1115 DEU1127
DEU1128 DEU1131 DEU1142 DEU1149
DEU1178 DEU1181 DEU1215 DNK1227
DNK1244 DNK1259 DNK1266 DNK1292
DNK1304 DNK1360 DNK1366 DNK1374
DNK1402 ESP1435 ESP1468 ESP1486
ESP1488 ESP1492 ESP1502 ESP1510
ESP1517 FIN1563 FIN1567 FIN1580
FRA1607 FRA1611 FRA1615 FRA1619
FRA1644 FRA1651 FRA1658 FRA1664
FRA1672 FRA1675 FRA1679 FRA1690
FRA1691 FRA1715 FRA1726 FRA1727
FRA1739 FRA1746 FRA1768 FRA1778
FRA1785 FRA1786 FRA1787 FRA1789
FRA1796 FRA1824 FRA1832 FRA1846
FRA1848 FRA1871 FRA1876 FRA1880
FRA1885 FRA1887 FRA1905 FRA1907
FRA1913 FRA1914 FRA1926 FRA1929
FRA1930 FRA1932 FRA1934 FRA1935
FRA1946 FRA1956 FRA1967 FRA1978
FRA2009 FRA2032 FRA2034 FRA2037
FRA2039 FRA2042 FRA2043 FRA2057
FRA2060 FRA2061 FRA2062 FRA2065

FRA2074 FRA2084 FRA2086 FRA2096
FRA2107 FRA2114 FRA2116 FRA2119
FRA2123 FRA2131 FRA2138 FRA2148
FRA2149 FRA2150 FRA2159 FRA2168
GBR2174 GBR2175 GBR2185 GBR2201
GBR2218 GBR2238 GBR2247 GBR2256
GBR2259 GBR2274 GBR2280 GBR2351
GBR2359 GBR2371 GBR2383 GBR2385
GBR2390 GBR2392 GBR2436 GBR2439
GBR2445 GBR2460 GBR2463 GBR2464
GBR2472 GBR2481 GBR2489 GBR2500
GBR2501 GBR2525 GBR2529 GBR2535
GBR2552 GBR2556 GBR2558 GRC2586
GRC2595 IRL2726 IRL2732 IRL2733
ISL2739 ITA2755 ITA2756 ITA2761
ITA2766 ITA2773 ITA2782 ITA2784
ITA2791 ITA2801 ITA2803 ITA2829
ITA2838 ITA2842 ITA2852 ITA2860
ITA2888 ITA2898 ITA2901 ITA2913
ITA2922 ITA2923 LUX2954 LUX2959
LUX2973 LUX2975 LUX2976 LUX2978
LUX2986 LUX3001 MLT3016 NLD3045
NLD3067 NLD3068 NLD3074 NLD3153
NLD3187 NLD3189 NLD3198 NLD3231
NLD3237 NLD3253 NLD3262 NLD3265
NLD3269 NLD3277 NLD3288 NLD3301
NLD3325 NLD3334 NLD3356 NLD3361
NOR3403 NOR3453 NOR3465 POL3508
POL3519 PRT3564 PRT3584 PRT3599
SWE3646 SWE3648 SWE3656 SWE3666
SWE3695 SWE3707 SWE3712 SWE3730
SWE3749 SWE3753 SWE3771 SWE3776
SWE3783 SWE3821 SWE3828 TUR3883

DEBT, FINANCE, TRADE - DETTE, FINANCES, COMMERCE

CARIBBEAN - CARAIBES

AUT0029 BEL0123 BEL0198 BEL0289
BEL0322 BEL0353 BEL0397 CHE0403
CHE0568 CHE0655 CHE0689 CHE0814
CHE0820 DEU1047 DEU1055 DEU1074
DEU1083 DNK1314 ESP1455 ESP1522
FRA1629 FRA1843 FRA1917 FRA2096
GBR2212 GBR2218 GBR2238 GBR2266
GBR2294 GBR2371 GBR2422 GBR2423
GBR2501 GBR2518 GBR2553 ITA2773
ITA2780 ITA2860 LUX3008 NLD3067
NLD3137 NLD3231 NLD3267 POL3519
SWE3653

CENTRAL AFRICA - AFRIQUE CENTRALE

BEL0123 BEL0158 BEL0198 BEL0203
BEL0322 BEL0353 BEL0378 BEL0397
CHE0403 CHE0541 CHE0562 CHE0568
CHE0626 CHE0632 CHE0655 CHE0688
CHE0691 CHE0762 CHE0814 CHE0820
CZE0905 DEU1035 DEU1047 DEU1055
DEU1106 DEU1167 DNK1230 DNK1314
DNK1392 FIN1531 FRA1629 FRA1636
FRA1830 FRA1835 FRA1879 FRA1880
FRA1917 FRA1947 FRA1956 FRA2012
FRA2096 FRA2105 GBR2180 GBR2185
GBR2218 GBR2337 GBR2371 GBR2390
GBR2402 GBR2422 GBR2491 GBR2501
GBR2553 ITA2779 ITA2860 ITA2907
ITA2921 LUX3008 NLD3045 NLD3067
NLD3120 NLD3137 NLD3267 NLD3366
POL3519

CENTRAL ASIA AND SOUTH ASIA - ASIE CENTRALE ET ASIE DU SUD

AUT0029 BEL0123 BEL0198 BEL0203
BEL0341 BEL0353 BEL0397 CHE0403
CHE0559 CHE0568 CHE0632 CHE0655
CHE0689 CHE0814 DEU0990 DEU1035
DEU1047 DEU1055 DEU1106 DEU1132
DNK1229 DNK1230 DNK1314 FIN1596
FRA1661 FRA1830 FRA1917 FRA2044
FRA2096 GBR2174 GBR2195 GBR2212
GBR2218 GBR2266 GBR2297 GBR2371
GBR2390 GBR2402 GBR2423 GBR2501
GBR2553 ITA2860 NLD3047 NLD3067
NLD3120 NLD3137 NLD3231 NLD3267
NOR3460 NOR3467 NOR3471 POL3519
SWE3760 SWE3763

EAST AFRICA - AFRIQUE DE L'EST

AUT0029	BEL0123	BEL0198	BEL0322
BEL0353	BEL0397	CHE0403	CHE0626
CHE0689	CHE0691	CHE0814	CHE0820
CZE0905	DEU1035	DEU1047	DEU1055
DEU1106	DEU1211	DNK1229	DNK1230
DNK1275	DNK1285	DNK1314	DNK1392
DNK1403	FIN1531	FIN1596	FRA1636
FRA1830	FRA1835	FRA1843	FRA1879
FRA1917	FRA1947	FRA1956	FRA2096
GBR2174	GBR2180	GBR2185	GBR2212
GBR2218	GBR2241	GBR2259	GBR2337
GBR2338	GBR2371	GBR2388	GBR2390
GBR2402	GBR2422	GBR2423	GBR2501
GBR2518	GBR2553	ITA2860	ITA2907
LUX2972	LUX3008	NLD3045	NLD3067
NLD3137	NLD3183	NLD3267	NLD3366
NOR3467	POL3508	POL3519	SWE3727
SWE3760	SWE3826	SWE3864	

EAST ASIA - ASIE DE L'EST

BEL0123	BEL0198	BEL0322	BEL0353
BEL0397	CHE0403	CHE0655	CHE0689
CHE0814	CHE0820	DEU1035	DEU1047
DEU1055	DEU1211	DNK1230	DNK1314
FRA1917	FRA2070	FRA2096	GBR2218
GBR2266	GBR2371	GBR2402	GBR2422
GBR2423	GBR2501	GBR2553	ITA2860
NLD3067	SWE3760		

MEXICO AND CENTRAL AMERICA - MEXIQUE ET AMERIQUE CENTRALE

AUT0029	BEL0123	BEL0198	BEL0203
BEL0289	BEL0322	BEL0353	BEL0378
BEL0397	CHE0403	CHE0568	CHE0602
CHE0626	CHE0632	CHE0689	CHE0720
CHE0804	CHE0814	CHE0820	DEU1035
DEU1047	DEU1055	DEU1083	DEU1167
DNK1229	DNK1230	DNK1314	ESP1409
ESP1437	ESP1455	ESP1506	ESP1522
FIN1596	FRA1636	FRA1852	FRA1917
FRA1947	FRA2012	FRA2096	FRA2116
FRA2150	GBR2174	GBR2201	GBR2212
GBR2218	GBR2371	GBR2402	GBR2413
GBR2422	GBR2423	GBR2501	GBR2518
GBR2553	IRL2697	ITA2762	ITA2780
ITA2860	LUX3008	NLD3067	NLD3137
NLD3159	NLD3253	NLD3267	NLD3305
NLD3366	NOR3426	NOR3467	POL3508
POL3519	SWE3760	SWE3864	

MIDDLE EAST - MOYEN-ORIENT

BEL0198	BEL0322	BEL0353	BEL0397
CHE0403	CHE0568	CHE0655	CHE0689
CHE0814	CZE0906	DEU1047	DEU1055
DEU1065	DEU1106	DEU1150	DNK1314
ESP1522	FRA1629	FRA1636	FRA1917
FRA2044	FRA2096	GBR2218	GBR2371
GBR2423	GBR2501	ITA2860	NLD3067
POL3519	TUR3883		

NORTH AFRICA - AFRIQUE DU NORD

BEL0123	BEL0198	BEL0322	BEL0353
BEL0397	CHE0403	CHE0568	CHE0655
CHE0689	CHE0814	CHE0820	CZE0905
DEU1047	DEU1055	DNK1230	DNK1314
ESP1406	FIN1531	FRA1629	FRA1636
FRA1917	FRA1947	FRA1956	FRA2096
GBR2185	GBR2218	GBR2371	GBR2402
GBR2423	GBR2501	ITA2766	ITA2860
NLD3067	POL3519		

OCEANIA - OCEANIE

BEL0123	BEL0198	BEL0397	CHE0403
CHE0814	CHE0820	DEU1047	DEU1055
DNK1314	FRA1917	FRA2096	GBR2218
GBR2264	GBR2266	GBR2294	GBR2371
GBR2422	GBR2501	GBR2553	ITA2860
NLD3067	NLD3137		

SOUTH AMERICA - AMERIQUE DU SUD

AUT0029	BEL0123	BEL0198	BEL0203
BEL0289	BEL0322	BEL0353	BEL0359
BEL0397	CHE0403	CHE0455	CHE0568
CHE0602	CHE0604	CHE0626	CHE0689
CHE0720	CHE0727	CHE0814	CHE0820
DEU1035	DEU1047	DEU1055	DEU1074

DEU1083	DEU1143	DEU1211	DNK1230
DNK1314	ESP1437	ESP1452	ESP1455
ESP1457	ESP1474	ESP1522	FIN1531
FIN1549	FIN1596	FRA1636	FRA1828
FRA1843	FRA1917	FRA1947	FRA2070
FRA2086	FRA2096	FRA2116	FRA2150
GBR2174	GBR2201	GBR2212	GBR2218
GBR2264	GBR2266	GBR2294	GBR2371
GBR2390	GBR2402	GBR2422	GBR2423
GBR2501	GBR2518	GBR2553	ITA2762
ITA2773	ITA2780	ITA2811	ITA2822
ITA2855	ITA2860	ITA2900	ITA2907
LUX2946	LUX3008	NLD3067	NLD3120
NLD3137	NLD3181	NLD3267	NLD3305
NLD3366	POL3519	SWE3744	SWE3760
SWE3864			

SOUTH EAST ASIA - ASIE DU SUD-EST

AUT0029	BEL0123	BEL0198	BEL0203
BEL0322	BEL0353	BEL0359	BEL0397
CHE0403	CHE0568	CHE0626	CHE0632
CHE0689	CHE0814	CHE0820	DEU1035
DEU1047	DEU1055	DEU1106	DEU1132
DNK1229	DNK1230	DNK1238	DNK1314
FRA1629	FRA1917	FRA2012	FRA2044
FRA2070	FRA2096	GBR2212	GBR2218
GBR2266	GBR2371	GBR2390	GBR2402
GBR2413	GBR2422	GBR2423	GBR2498
GBR2501	GBR2553	ITA2860	NLD3067
NLD3120	NLD3137	NLD3253	NLD3267
NLD3366	NOR3467	POL3519	SWE3826

SOUTHERN AFRICA - AFRIQUE AUSTRALE

AUT0029	BEL0123	BEL0198	BEL0203
BEL0322	BEL0353	BEL0397	CHE0403
CHE0626	CHE0689	CHE0727	CHE0762
CHE0814	CHE0820	CZE0905	DEU1047
DEU1055	DEU1065	DEU1106	DEU1143
DEU1187	DEU1211	DNK1229	DNK1230
DNK1314	DNK1403	FIN1531	FRA1830
FRA1879	FRA1917	FRA1947	FRA1956
FRA2096	GBR2174	GBR2185	GBR2201
GBR2212	GBR2218	GBR2222	GBR2259
GBR2266	GBR2294	GBR2318	GBR2337
GBR2371	GBR2390	GBR2402	GBR2413
GBR2422	GBR2423	GBR2501	GBR2553
ITA2860	ITA2900	LUX2946	LUX3008
NLD3045	NLD3047	NLD3067	NLD3137
NLD3253	NLD3267	NOR3467	POL3519
SWE3770	SWE3826	SWE3864	

WEST AFRICA - AFRIQUE DE L'OUEST

AUT0029	BEL0118	BEL0123	BEL0198
BEL0203	BEL0322	BEL0353	BEL0397
CHE0403	CHE0435	CHE0559	CHE0568
CHE0604	CHE0626	CHE0689	CHE0762
CHE0814	CHE0820	CZE0905	DEU1035
DEU1047	DEU1055	DEU1074	DEU1106
DEU1143	DEU1211	DNK1314	FIN1531
FIN1596	FRA1624	FRA1629	FRA1636
FRA1760	FRA1785	FRA1787	FRA1830
FRA1835	FRA1879	FRA1917	FRA1947
FRA1956	FRA2012	FRA2086	FRA2096
FRA2105	GBR2174	GBR2180	GBR2185
GBR2218	GBR2294	GBR2337	GBR2371
GBR2390	GBR2402	GBR2422	GBR2423
GBR2501	GBR2518	GBR2553	ITA2762
ITA2860	LUX2946	LUX3008	NLD3045
NLD3067	NLD3137	NLD3231	NLD3267
NLD3269	NLD3366	NOR3387	POL3519
PRT3586			

DEMOCRACY, GOOD GOVERNANCE, INSTITUTION BUILDING, PARTICIPATORY DEVELOPMENT - DEMOCRATIE, BONNE GESTION PUBLIQUE, CREATION D'INSTITUTIONS, DEVELOPPEMENT PARTICIPATIF

CARIBBEAN - CARAIBES

BEL0123	BEL0129	BEL0186	BEL0198
BEL0199	BEL0218	BEL0221	BEL0265
BEL0289	BEL0306	BEL0327	BEL0335
BEL0336	BEL0351	BEL0353	BEL0361
BEL0392	BEL0396	BEL0397	BEL0399
CHE0420	CHE0434	CHE0454	CHE0465

CHE0501	CHE0564	CHE0568	CHE0619
CHE0622	CHE0643	CHE0655	CHE0682
CHE0689	CHE0711	CHE0721	CHE0814
CHE0817	CHE0819	CHE0820	DEU0972
DEU0983	DEU1047	DEU1055	DEU1056
DEU1074	DEU1097	DEU1106	DEU1110
DEU1161	DEU1209	DNK1292	DNK1300
ESP1435	ESP1442	ESP1461	ESP1472
ESP1475	ESP1486	ESP1517	ESP1524
ESP1525	FIN1574	FIN1604	FRA1629
FRA1675	FRA1817	FRA1827	FRA1843
FRA1946	FRA1975	FRA2012	FRA2034
FRA2062	FRA2069	FRA2096	FRA2101
FRA2103	FRA2126	FRA2161	GBR2212
GBR2228	GBR2229	GBR2238	GBR2242
GBR2247	GBR2256	GBR2278	GBR2281
GBR2294	GBR2332	GBR2359	GBR2419
GBR2423	GBR2436	GBR2437	GBR2501
GBR2535	GBR2546	GBR2553	ITA2766
ITA2773	ITA2860	NLD3067	NLD3078
NLD3137	NLD3160	NLD3219	NLD3226
NLD3231	NLD3253	NLD3338	NLD3361
NLD3362	NOR3407	NOR3439	NOR3460
POL3508	POL3519	SWE3705	SWE3830

CENTRAL AFRICA - AFRIQUE CENTRALE

BEL0120	BEL0123	BEL0128	BEL0129
BEL0152	BEL0155	BEL0158	BEL0186
BEL0198	BEL0199	BEL0201	BEL0203
BEL0218	BEL0221	BEL0265	BEL0289
BEL0306	BEL0327	BEL0328	BEL0351
BEL0352	BEL0353	BEL0356	BEL0361
BEL0390	BEL0392	BEL0397	BEL0399
CHE0420	CHE0434	CHE0456	CHE0541
CHE0562	CHE0568	CHE0604	CHE0619
CHE0622	CHE0626	CHE0632	CHE0638
CHE0639	CHE0643	CHE0645	CHE0655
CHE0687	CHE0689	CHE0711	CHE0750
CHE0757	CHE0814	CHE0817	CHE0819
CHE0820	DEU0972	DEU1006	DEU1027
DEU1047	DEU1055	DEU1056	DEU1097
DEU1106	DEU1110	DEU1114	DEU1131
DEU1209	DNK1227	DNK1272	DNK1300
ESP1486	ESP1517	FIN1594	FIN1604
FRA1629	FRA1636	FRA1649	FRA1675
FRA1727	FRA1776	FRA1787	FRA1815
FRA1817	FRA1819	FRA1827	FRA1836
FRA1863	FRA1879	FRA1885	FRA1946
FRA1956	FRA1974	FRA1980	FRA1988
FRA2011	FRA2012	FRA2032	FRA2034
FRA2062	FRA2069	FRA2092	FRA2096
FRA2101	FRA2103	FRA2105	FRA2126
GBR2173	GBR2174	GBR2185	GBR2238
GBR2278	GBR2332	GBR2337	GBR2359
GBR2396	GBR2422	GBR2423	GBR2437
GBR2460	GBR2501	GBR2546	GBR2553
ITA2744	ITA2777	ITA2826	ITA2860
ITA2890	ITA2898	LUX3006	NLD3045
NLD3067	NLD3068	NLD3078	NLD3101
NLD3117	NLD3119	NLD3137	NLD3160
NLD3165	NLD3199	NLD3226	NLD3230
NLD3277	NLD3292	NLD3301	NLD3338
NLD3361	NLD3362	NLD3366	POL3519
PRT3594	PRT3602	SWE3705	SWE3735
SWE3749	SWE3763	SWE3828	SWE3830

CENTRAL ASIA AND SOUTH ASIA - ASIE CENTRALE ET ASIE DU SUD

AUT0021	AUT0026	AUT0051	AUT0091
BEL0123	BEL0129	BEL0186	BEL0198
BEL0199	BEL0201	BEL0203	BEL0221
BEL0265	BEL0270	BEL0306	BEL0327
BEL0340	BEL0351	BEL0361	BEL0378
BEL0392	BEL0397	CHE0420	CHE0434
CHE0467	CHE0568	CHE0586	CHE0619
CHE0622	CHE0632	CHE0638	CHE0643
CHE0645	CHE0655	CHE0682	CHE0689
CHE0711	CHE0721	CHE0757	CHE0814
CHE0817	CHE0819	CHE0820	DEU0918
DEU0971	DEU0972	DEU0983	DEU0991
DEU1006	DEU1047	DEU1055	DEU1056
DEU1074	DEU1086	DEU1097	DEU1106
DEU1110	DEU1121	DEU1151	DEU1178
DEU1187	DEU1209	DNK1255	DNK1259
DNK1275	DNK1292	DNK1300	DNK1339
DNK1384	ESP1486	FIN1549	FIN1587
FIN1604	FRA1817	FRA1862	FRA1910
FRA1921	FRA1990	FRA2034	FRA2096

See: *How to Use the Directory*, page 11.

FRA2101	GBR2173	GBR2174	GBR2176
GBR2186	GBR2197	GBR2201	GBR2212
GBR2213	GBR2222	GBR2228	GBR2232
GBR2238	GBR2256	GBR2264	GBR2273
GBR2278	GBR2281	GBR2297	GBR2302
GBR2321	GBR2323	GBR2334	GBR2358
GBR2359	GBR2364	GBR2375	GBR2413
GBR2419	GBR2422	GBR2423	GBR2436
GBR2437	GBR2464	GBR2467	GBR2490
GBR2500	GBR2501	GBR2530	GBR2532
GBR2535	GBR2546	GBR2553	GRC2571
ITA2766	ITA2840	ITA2860	LUX2982
NLD3067	NLD3078	NLD3101	NLD3137
NLD3147	NLD3153	NLD3155	NLD3160
NLD3165	NLD3183	NLD3199	NLD3226
NLD3231	NLD3253	NLD3277	NLD3302
NLD3338	NLD3361	NLD3362	NOR3371
NOR3386	NOR3425	NOR3439	NOR3443
NOR3447	NOR3460	NOR3465	NOR3467
NOR3471	POL3519	SWE3661	SWE3674
SWE3743	SWE3763	SWE3768	SWE3787
SWE3795	SWE3818	SWE3821	SWE3828
SWE3830	SWE3854	SWE3864	

EAST AFRICA - AFRIQUE DE L'EST

AUT0003	AUT0041	AUT0058	AUT0063
AUT0091	BEL0123	BEL0129	BEL0186
BEL0198	BEL0199	BEL0221	BEL0265
BEL0269	BEL0270	BEL0289	BEL0306
BEL0327	BEL0351	BEL0353	BEL0356
BEL0361	BEL0392	BEL0397	BEL0399
CHE0420	CHE0434	CHE0448	CHE0586
CHE0622	CHE0626	CHE0638	CHE0639
CHE0643	CHE0655	CHE0660	CHE0682
CHE0687	CHE0689	CHE0691	CHE0711
CHE0814	CHE0817	CHE0819	CHE0820
DEU0936	DEU0972	DEU0983	DEU0991
DEU1006	DEU1047	DEU1055	DEU1056
DEU1066	DEU1074	DEU1097	DEU1106
DEU1131	DEU1178	DEU1209	DNK1255
DNK1259	DNK1275	DNK1285	DNK1292
DNK1300	DNK1302	DNK1339	DNK1351
DNK1405	ESP1432	ESP1486	FIN1544
FIN1549	FIN1572	FIN1587	FIN1604
FRA1636	FRA1675	FRA1727	FRA1817
FRA1843	FRA1879	FRA1956	FRA2032
FRA2062	FRA2069	FRA2096	FRA2101
FRA2126	FRA2159	GBR2173	GBR2174
GBR2185	GBR2186	GBR2198	GBR2199
GBR2212	GBR2222	GBR2228	GBR2232
GBR2238	GBR2240	GBR2241	GBR2247
GBR2256	GBR2259	GBR2273	GBR2278
GBR2280	GBR2281	GBR2303	GBR2321
GBR2332	GBR2337	GBR2339	GBR2359
GBR2419	GBR2422	GBR2423	GBR2436
GBR2437	GBR2459	GBR2460	GBR2464
GBR2467	GBR2474	GBR2483	GBR2497
GBR2501	GBR2530	GBR2535	GBR2536
GBR2546	GBR2551	GBR2553	GBR2556
IRL2691	IRL2709	IRL2733	ITA2744
ITA2766	ITA2810	ITA2822	ITA2822
ITA2860	ITA2868	ITA2901	ITA2910
ITA2913	NLD3045	NLD3067	NLD3068
NLD3074	NLD3101	NLD3117	NLD3119
NLD3137	NLD3155	NLD3160	NLD3165
NLD3183	NLD3199	NLD3201	NLD3216
NLD3231	NLD3253	NLD3277	NLD3292
NLD3301	NLD3338	NLD3361	NLD3362
NLD3366	NOR3381	NOR3386	NOR3394
NOR3407	NOR3425	NOR3430	NOR3439
NOR3447	NOR3465	NOR3467	POL3519
SWE3688	SWE3705	SWE3727	SWE3728
SWE3746	SWE3749	SWE3771	SWE3787
SWE3806	SWE3821	SWE3828	SWE3830
SWE3854	SWE3864		

EAST ASIA - ASIE DE L'EST

BEL0123	BEL0129	BEL0186	BEL0198
BEL0199	BEL0221	BEL0265	BEL0289
BEL0327	BEL0351	BEL0361	BEL0392
BEL0397	CHE0420	CHE0434	CHE0570
CHE0622	CHE0638	CHE0643	CHE0655
CHE0689	CHE0711	CHE0721	CHE0814
CHE0817	CHE0819	CHE0820	DEU0972
DEU1006	DEU1047	DEU1055	DEU1056
DEU1097	DEU1106	DEU1149	DEU1209
DNK1275	DNK1292	DNK1300	ESP1432
FIN1604	FRA1817	FRA2096	FRA2101

FRA2159	GBR2199	GBR2228	GBR2238
GBR2264	GBR2278	GBR2332	GBR2359
GBR2423	GBR2464	GBR2490	GBR2501
GBR2535	GBR2546	GBR2553	GBR2556
ITA2766	ITA2860	NLD3067	NLD3078
NLD3160	NLD3226	NLD3322	NLD3338
NLD3361	NLD3362	NOR3387	NOR3465
SWE3826	SWE3828	SWE3830	

MEXICO AND CENTRAL AMERICA - MEXIQUE ET AMERIQUE CENTRALE

AUT0003	AUT0041	AUT0051	AUT0052
AUT0058	AUT0063	AUT0091	BEL0123
BEL0129	BEL0148	BEL0186	BEL0198
BEL0199	BEL0201	BEL0203	BEL0221
BEL0265	BEL0269	BEL0270	BEL0289
BEL0327	BEL0335	BEL0336	BEL0340
BEL0351	BEL0353	BEL0361	BEL0378
BEL0392	BEL0397	CHE0420	CHE0434
CHE0446	CHE0456	CHE0465	CHE0559
CHE0568	CHE0602	CHE0619	CHE0622
CHE0626	CHE0632	CHE0638	CHE0682
CHE0689	CHE0711	CHE0721	CHE0755
CHE0773	CHE0814	CHE0817	CHE0819
CHE0820	DEU0972	DEU0983	DEU0991
DEU1047	DEU1055	DEU1056	DEU1074
DEU1097	DEU1110	DEU1114	DEU1149
DEU1161	DEU1178	DEU1187	DEU1209
DNK1226	DNK1274	DNK1283	DNK1292
DNK1300	DNK1312	DNK1317	DNK1339
DNK1351	DNK1367	ESP1409	ESP1432
ESP1435	ESP1442	ESP1461	ESP1475
ESP1486	ESP1506	ESP1517	ESP1521
ESP1525	FIN1544	FIN1546	FIN1574
FIN1578	FIN1587	FIN1603	FIN1604
FRA1636	FRA1675	FRA1701	FRA1703
FRA1817	FRA1827	FRA1843	FRA1964
FRA1974	FRA1975	FRA1985	FRA2012
FRA2032	FRA2034	FRA2062	FRA2069
FRA2092	FRA2096	FRA2101	FRA2103
FRA2150	FRA2165	GBR2174	GBR2201
GBR2212	GBR2228	GBR2229	GBR2232
GBR2238	GBR2256	GBR2256	GBR2273
GBR2278	GBR2303	GBR2321	GBR2332
GBR2359	GBR2396	GBR2402	GBR2413
GBR2419	GBR2436	GBR2437	
GBR2467	GBR2490	GBR2501	GBR2535
GBR2546	GBR2551	GBR2553	GBR2556
IRL2697	IRL2714	ITA2744	ITA2838
ITA2852	ITA2860	ITA2881	LUX2976
NLD3067	NLD3068	NLD3078	NLD3101
NLD3137	NLD3160	NLD3165	NLD3165
NLD3199	NLD3219	NLD3226	NLD3230
NLD3231	NLD3253	NLD3258	NLD3263
NLD3277	NLD3305	NLD3305	NLD3338
NLD3361	NLD3362	NLD3366	NOR3407
NOR3410	NOR3425	NOR3426	NOR3439
NOR3447	POL3519	SWE3674	SWE3687
SWE3688	SWE3725	SWE3735	SWE3749
SWE3768	SWE3770	SWE3771	SWE3787
SWE3795	SWE3796	SWE3821	SWE3826
SWE3828	SWE3830	SWE3864	

MIDDLE EAST - MOYEN-ORIENT

BEL0129	BEL0186	BEL0198	BEL0199
BEL0221	BEL0270	BEL0275	BEL0306
BEL0351	BEL0353	BEL0361	BEL0397
CHE0420	CHE0434	CHE0456	CHE0568
CHE0622	CHE0640	CHE0655	CHE0687
CHE0689	CHE0711	CHE0814	CHE0817
CHE0819	DEU0972	DEU0991	DEU1047
DEU1055	DEU1056	DEU1065	DEU1106
DEU1131	DNK1300	DNK1304	DNK1367
FIN1604	FRA1629	FRA1636	FRA1675
FRA1791	FRA1793	FRA1817	FRA1827
FRA1843	FRA1974	FRA2057	FRA2069
FRA2096	FRA2101	FRA2103	FRA2159
GBR2199	GBR2229	GBR2232	GBR2238
GBR2244	GBR2273	GBR2278	GBR2303
GBR2332	GBR2359	GBR2396	GBR2402
GBR2423	GBR2501	GBR2525	GBR2537
GBR2546	GBR2551	ITA2860	MLT3017
MLT3018	NLD3067	NLD3155	NLD3160
NLD3165	NLD3199	NLD3201	NLD3226
NLD3338	NLD3361	NLD3362	NOR3381
NOR3407	NOR3430	POL3519	SWE3674
SWE3730	SWE3738	SWE3749	SWE3771
SWE3826	SWE3828	SWE3830	TUR3883

NORTH AFRICA - AFRIQUE DU NORD

BEL0118	BEL0123	BEL0129	BEL0186
BEL0198	BEL0199	BEL0221	BEL0265
BEL0269	BEL0270	BEL0275	BEL0289
BEL0353	BEL0361	BEL0397	CHE0420
CHE0434	CHE0456	CHE0491	CHE0568
CHE0622	CHE0655	CHE0682	CHE0687
CHE0689	CHE0711	CHE0814	CHE0817
DEU0972	DEU0990	DEU1047	DEU1055
DEU1106	DEU1191	DEU1209	
DNK1255	DNK1275	DNK1300	ESP1435
ESP1475	ESP1486	FIN1604	FRA1629
FRA1636	FRA1759	FRA1759	FRA1817
FRA1843	FRA1846	FRA1871	FRA1946
FRA1956	FRA1974	FRA2034	FRA2057
FRA2062	FRA2069	FRA2096	FRA2101
FRA2126	FRA2159	GBR2185	GBR2199
GBR2238	GBR2278	GBR2281	GBR2332
GBR2359	GBR2413	GBR2422	GBR2423
GBR2437	GBR2490	GBR2501	GBR2535
GBR2546	ITA2838	ITA2860	ITA2901
MLT3017	MLT3018	NLD3067	NLD3078
NLD3101	NLD3117	NLD3119	NLD3160
NLD3165	NLD3199	NLD3214	NLD3226
NLD3253	NLD3277	NLD3338	NLD3362
POL3519	SWE3688	SWE3705	SWE3828
SWE3830			

OCEANIA - OCEANIE

BEL0123	BEL0129	BEL0186	BEL0198
BEL0199	BEL0361	BEL0397	BEL0399
CHE0420	CHE0434	CHE0645	CHE0711
CHE0721	CHE0814	CHE0817	CHE0819
CHE0820	DEU0972	DEU1047	DEU1055
DEU1097	DEU1106	DEU1110	DEU1131
DEU1149	DNK1300	FIN1604	FRA2096
FRA2126	GBR2228	GBR2256	GBR2278
GBR2294	GBR2312	GBR2332	GBR2359
GBR2437	GBR2490	GBR2501	GBR2524
GBR2535	GBR2546	GBR2553	ITA2860
NLD3067	NLD3137	NLD3160	NLD3226
NLD3361	NLD3362	POL3508	SWE3830

SOUTH AMERICA - AMERIQUE DU SUD

AUT0003	AUT0051	AUT0091	BEL0119
BEL0123	BEL0129	BEL0139	BEL0148
BEL0155	BEL0186	BEL0198	BEL0199
BEL0203	BEL0221	BEL0241	BEL0265
BEL0269	BEL0270	BEL0289	BEL0306
BEL0327	BEL0335	BEL0336	BEL0351
BEL0352	BEL0353	BEL0356	BEL0359
BEL0361	BEL0392	BEL0397	CHE0420
CHE0434	CHE0456	CHE0465	CHE0479
CHE0559	CHE0568	CHE0570	CHE0602
CHE0604	CHE0613	CHE0619	CHE0622
CHE0626	CHE0632	CHE0638	CHE0643
CHE0682	CHE0689	CHE0701	CHE0711
CHE0721	CHE0750	CHE0798	CHE0814
CHE0817	CHE0819	CHE0820	DEU0972
DEU0983	DEU0990	DEU0991	DEU1006
DEU1031	DEU1047	DEU1055	DEU1056
DEU1066	DEU1074	DEU1097	DEU1109
DEU1114	DEU1129	DEU1131	DEU1149
DEU1161	DEU1178	DEU1187	DEU1209
DNK1238	DNK1248	DNK1289	DNK1292
DNK1300	DNK1304	DNK1312	DNK1317
DNK1319	DNK1351	DNK1367	DNK1403
ESP1407	ESP1410	ESP1410	ESP1432
ESP1435	ESP1437	ESP1442	ESP1452
ESP1461	ESP1472	ESP1475	ESP1486
ESP1510	ESP1515	ESP1521	ESP1525
FIN1574	FIN1587	FIN1604	FRA1615
FRA1636	FRA1675	FRA1701	FRA1703
FRA1817	FRA1827	FRA1836	FRA1930
FRA1946	FRA1964	FRA1974	FRA1975
FRA1980	FRA2012	FRA2018	FRA2032
FRA2034	FRA2062	FRA2069	FRA2092
FRA2096	FRA2101	FRA2103	FRA2159
GBR2174	GBR2201	GBR2212	GBR2228
GBR2229	GBR2232	GBR2238	GBR2273
GBR2278	GBR2303	GBR2321	GBR2332
GBR2339	GBR2359	GBR2383	GBR2402
GBR2419	GBR2423	GBR2436	GBR2437
GBR2467	GBR2490	GBR2501	GBR2525
GBR2535	GBR2537	GBR2546	GBR2551
GBR2553	ITA2748	ITA2756	ITA2766
ITA2773	ITA2775	ITA2777	ITA2782
ITA2785	ITA2798	ITA2820	ITA2838

Voir : *Comment utiliser le répertoire*, page 11.

ITA2852	ITA2860	ITA2880	ITA2881
ITA2895	ITA2901	ITA2910	ITA2913
LUX2946	LUX2958	LUX3003	NLD3067
NLD3068	NLD3160	NLD3101	NLD3137
NLD3155	NLD3160	NLD3165	NLD3181
NLD3183	NLD3199	NLD3219	NLD3226
NLD3231	NLD3277	NLD3285	NLD3305
NLD3361	NLD3362	NLD3366	NOR3407
NOR3460	NOR3465	POL3508	POL3519
SWE3674	SWE3693	SWE3705	SWE3730
SWE3744	SWE3749	SWE3771	SWE3781
SWE3787	SWE3795	SWE3796	SWE3821
SWE3826	SWE3828	SWE3830	SWE3864
SWE3865	SWE3876		

SOUTH EAST ASIA - ASIE DU SUD-EST

AUT0051	AUT0091	BEL0123	BEL0129
BEL0186	BEL0198	BEL0199	BEL0203
BEL0221	BEL0269	BEL0289	BEL0306
BEL0327	BEL0351	BEL0361	BEL0392
BEL0397	CHE0420	CHE0434	CHE0456
CHE0568	CHE0570	CHE0586	CHE0604
CHE0619	CHE0622	CHE0626	CHE0632
CHE0638	CHE0643	CHE0682	CHE0689
CHE0711	CHE0721	CHE0749	CHE0757
CHE0773	CHE0814	CHE0817	CHE0819
CHE0820	DEU0918	DEU0971	DEU0972
DEU0983	DEU0990	DEU1006	DEU1047
DEU1055	DEU1056	DEU1074	DEU1097
DEU1106	DEU1110	DEU1149	DEU1178
DEU1187	DEU1209	DNK1238	DNK1259
DNK1292	DNK1300	DNK1403	FIN1587
FIN1603	FIN1604	FRA1615	FRA1629
FRA1701	FRA1817	FRA1850	FRA1871
FRA1917	FRA1946	FRA1974	FRA1980
FRA2012	FRA2034	FRA2062	FRA2069
FRA2096	FRA2101	FRA2126	FRA2140
GBR2199	GBR2201	GBR2212	GBR2222
GBR2228	GBR2232	GBR2238	GBR2240
GBR2242	GBR2256	GBR2264	GBR2266
GBR2272	GBR2278	GBR2294	GBR2303
GBR2321	GBR2332	GBR2339	GBR2359
GBR2396	GBR2413	GBR2419	GBR2423
GBR2436	GBR2437	GBR2467	GBR2490
GBR2498	GBR2500	GBR2501	GBR2508
GBR2535	GBR2537	GBR2546	GBR2553
IRL2691	IRL2733	ITA2766	ITA2838
ITA2860	ITA2902	ITA2912	NLD3067
NLD3068	NLD3078	NLD3083	NLD3117
NLD3137	NLD3155	NLD3156	NLD3160
NLD3165	NLD3199	NLD3214	NLD3219
NLD3226	NLD3253	NLD3277	NLD3362
NLD3338	NLD3361	NLD3362	NLD3366
NOR3372	NOR3407	NOR3465	NOR3467
POL3519	POL3519	SWE3674	SWE3705
SWE3771	SWE3787	SWE3821	SWE3828
SWE3830	SWE3876		

SOUTHERN AFRICA - AFRIQUE AUSTRALE

AUT0022	AUT0058	AUT0091	BEL0123
BEL0129	BEL0186	BEL0198	BEL0199
BEL0203	BEL0221	BEL0241	BEL0265
BEL0269	BEL0275	BEL0289	BEL0327
BEL0351	BEL0361	BEL0392	BEL0397
BEL0399	CHE0420	CHE0434	CHE0491
CHE0619	CHE0622	CHE0626	CHE0632
CHE0638	CHE0639	CHE0643	CHE0645
CHE0682	CHE0687	CHE0689	CHE0711
CHE0721	CHE0750	CHE0755	CHE0814
CHE0817	CHE0819	CHE0820	DEU0972
DEU0991	DEU1006	DEU1047	DEU1055
DEU1056	DEU1065	DEU1074	DEU1097
DEU1106	DEU1110	DEU1131	DEU1149
DEU1187	DEU1209	DNK1243	DNK1259
DNK1273	DNK1274	DNK1275	DNK1289
DNK1292	DNK1300	DNK1312	DNK1339
DNK1351	DNK1367	DNK1375	DNK1403
ESP1486	FIN1546	FIN1549	FIN1554
FIN1557	FIN1559	FIN1574	FIN1577
FIN1587	FIN1603	FIN1604	FIN1659
FRA1675	FRA1691	FRA1727	FRA1738
FRA1756	FRA1817	FRA1827	FRA1843
FRA1879	FRA1917	FRA1956	FRA1980
FRA2005	FRA2018	FRA2096	FRA2101
FRA2103	FRA2126	FRA2159	GBR2173
GBR2174	GBR2181	GBR2185	GBR2198
GBR2199	GBR2201	GBR2212	GBR2222
GBR2228	GBR2229	GBR2238	GBR2242

GBR2244	GBR2247	GBR2256	GBR2259
GBR2266	GBR2273	GBR2277	GBR2278
GBR2281	GBR2294	GBR2321	GBR2332
GBR2337	GBR2339	GBR2351	GBR2359
GBR2364	GBR2402	GBR2413	GBR2419
GBR2423	GBR2436	GBR2437	GBR2460
GBR2464	GBR2467	GBR2478	GBR2490
GBR2500	GBR2501	GBR2530	GBR2535
GBR2536	GBR2537	GBR2546	GBR2551
GBR2553	GBR2556	GBR2561	IRL2691
IRL2733	ITA2771	ITA2798	ITA2838
ITA2860	ITA2873	ITA2879	ITA2881
ITA2900	ITA2902	ITA2911	LUX2946
LUX2995	NLD3045	NLD3067	NLD3078
NLD3098	NLD3101	NLD3117	NLD3119
NLD3137	NLD3139	NLD3155	NLD3160
NLD3165	NLD3183	NLD3198	NLD3199
NLD3201	NLD3214	NLD3219	NLD3226
NLD3230	NLD3231	NLD3277	NLD3338
NLD3361	NLD3362	NOR3384	NOR3386
NOR3389	NOR3390	NOR3394	NOR3400
NOR3407	NOR3416	NOR3418	NOR3447
NOR3467	POL3519	PRT3564	PRT3590
PRT3594	PRT3596	PRT3600	SWE3648
SWE3674	SWE3688	SWE3705	SWE3730
SWE3749	SWE3771	SWE3821	SWE3826
SWE3828	SWE3830	SWE3864	

WEST AFRICA - AFRIQUE DE L'OUEST

AUT0003	AUT0021	AUT0028	AUT0041
AUT0086	AUT0091	BEL0118	BEL0123
BEL0129	BEL0152	BEL0186	BEL0198
BEL0199	BEL0201	BEL0203	BEL0206
BEL0221	BEL0265	BEL0269	BEL0270
BEL0289	BEL0306	BEL0327	BEL0328
BEL0351	BEL0353	BEL0356	BEL0361
BEL0390	BEL0392	BEL0397	BEL0399
CHE0420	CHE0434	CHE0435	CHE0439
CHE0456	CHE0479	CHE0490	CHE0498
CHE0568	CHE0570	CHE0604	CHE0619
CHE0622	CHE0626	CHE0638	CHE0639
CHE0643	CHE0645	CHE0682	CHE0687
CHE0689	CHE0711	CHE0757	CHE0814
CHE0817	CHE0819	CHE0820	CHE0823
DEU0972	DEU0983	DEU0991	DEU1006
DEU1047	DEU1055	DEU1056	DEU1074
DEU1097	DEU1106	DEU1110	DEU1114
DEU1131	DEU1178	DEU1209	DNK1215
DNK1227	DNK1238	DNK1255	DNK1259
DNK1300	DNK1307	DNK1366	DNK1403
ESP1472	ESP1486	ESP1517	FIN1587
FIN1604	FRA1607	FRA1629	FRA1636
FRA1649	FRA1675	FRA1690	FRA1691
FRA1727	FRA1739	FRA1746	FRA1756
FRA1760	FRA1776	FRA1785	FRA1787
FRA1799	FRA1817	FRA1818	FRA1827
FRA1836	FRA1843	FRA1846	FRA1879
FRA1885	FRA1907	FRA1913	FRA1946
FRA1956	FRA1964	FRA1974	FRA1980
FRA1988	FRA1991	FRA2009	FRA2012
FRA2018	FRA2032	FRA2034	FRA2043
FRA2057	FRA2062	FRA2069	FRA2086
FRA2092	FRA2096	FRA2101	FRA2103
FRA2105	FRA2126	FRA2150	FRA2159
FRA2161	GBR2173	GBR2174	GBR2185
GBR2198	GBR2201	GBR2222	GBR2232
GBR2238	GBR2241	GBR2247	GBR2256
GBR2273	GBR2278	GBR2303	GBR2332
GBR2337	GBR2351	GBR2359	GBR2383
GBR2396	GBR2413	GBR2419	GBR2422
GBR2423	GBR2436	GBR2437	GBR2460
GBR2464	GBR2483	GBR2490	GBR2501
GBR2515	GBR2525	GBR2535	GBR2546
GBR2553	GBR2556	IRL2733	ITA2766
ITA2786	ITA2801	ITA2826	ITA2838
ITA2860	ITA2901	ITA2902	ITA2913
LUX2946	NLD3045	NLD3067	NLD3068
NLD3074	NLD3078	NLD3101	NLD3117
NLD3119	NLD3137	NLD3147	NLD3155
NLD3160	NLD3165	NLD3183	NLD3198
NLD3199	NLD3226	NLD3231	NLD3277
NLD3292	NLD3301	NLD3338	NLD3361
NLD3362	NLD3366	NOR3386	NOR3430
NOR3453	NOR3460	NOR3465	POL3519
PRT3564	SWE3705	SWE3771	SWE3821
SWE3828	SWE3830		

ECOLOGY, ENVIRONMENT, BIODIVERSITY - ECOLOGIE, ENVIRONNEMENT, BIODIVERSITE

CARIBBEAN - CARAIBES

AUT0045	BEL0123	BEL0124	BEL0129
BEL0144	BEL0186	BEL0198	BEL0218
BEL0221	BEL0306	BEL0327	BEL0335
BEL0336	BEL0351	BEL0359	BEL0361
BEL0397	CHE0403	CHE0434	CHE0465
CHE0564	CHE0568	CHE0619	CHE0629
CHE0655	CHE0682	CHE0689	CHE0712
CHE0730	CHE0798	CHE0813	CHE0814
CHE0817	CHE0819	CHE0820	DEU0972
DEU0983	DEU1055	DEU1107	DNK1291
DNK1292	DNK1300	DNK1314	ESP1435
ESP1442	ESP1455	ESP1472	ESP1486
ESP1492	ESP1522	ESP1525	ESP1529
FIN1584	FRA1610	FRA1629	FRA1644
FRA1744	FRA1796	FRA1827	FRA1860
FRA1934	FRA1946	FRA1964	FRA1967
FRA2062	FRA2069	FRA2096	FRA2103
FRA2109	FRA2117	FRA2126	FRA2153
FRA2158	FRA2161	FRA2168	FRA2170
GBR2218	GBR2229	GBR2238	GBR2244
GBR2278	GBR2294	GBR2346	GBR2365
GBR2371	GBR2386	GBR2422	GBR2423
GBR2434	GBR2436	GBR2481	GBR2501
GBR2535	GBR2552	GBR2553	ITA2773
ITA2784	ITA2822	ITA2860	ITA2914
LUX2993	LUX3008	MLT3021	NLD3062
NLD3067	NLD3137	NLD3138	NLD3154
NLD3183	NLD3230	NLD3231	NLD3362
POL3519	SWE3653	SWE3656	SWE3789
TUR3883			

CENTRAL AFRICA - AFRIQUE CENTRALE

AUT0041	AUT0045	BEL0123	BEL0124
BEL0129	BEL0144	BEL0148	BEL0153
BEL0155	BEL0156	BEL0186	BEL0198
BEL0200	BEL0203	BEL0218	BEL0221
BEL0237	BEL0261	BEL0327	BEL0342
BEL0351	BEL0352	BEL0359	BEL0361
BEL0381	BEL0395	BEL0397	CHE0403
CHE0434	CHE0444	CHE0562	CHE0568
CHE0619	CHE0626	CHE0629	CHE0630
CHE0632	CHE0645	CHE0655	CHE0689
CHE0712	CHE0730	CHE0762	CHE0778
CHE0813	CHE0814	CHE0817	CHE0819
CHE0820	CZE0905	DEU0972	DEU1006
DEU1055	DEU1106	DEU1107	DEU1114
DEU1116	DEU1131	DEU1167	DNK1255
DNK1300	DNK1314	ESP1492	ESP1517
ESP1529	FRA1610	FRA1629	FRA1636
FRA1727	FRA1740	FRA1744	FRA1757
FRA1787	FRA1815	FRA1827	FRA1865
FRA1887	FRA1934	FRA1946	FRA1956
FRA2012	FRA2020	FRA2039	FRA2069
FRA2092	FRA2096	FRA2103	FRA2105
FRA2109	FRA2126	FRA2168	FRA2170
GBR2174	GBR2175	GBR2185	GBR2218
GBR2238	GBR2259	GBR2278	GBR2298
GBR2337	GBR2346	GBR2351	GBR2365
GBR2370	GBR2371	GBR2392	GBR2422
GBR2423	GBR2434	GBR2460	GBR2481
GBR2501	GBR2553	GRC2567	ITA2762
ITA2784	ITA2806	ITA2860	ITA2900
ITA2914	LUX3006	LUX3008	NLD3045
NLD3062	NLD3067	NLD3096	NLD3101
NLD3117	NLD3137	NLD3138	NLD3147
NLD3154	NLD3235	NLD3264	NLD3362
POL3519	SWE3656	SWE3749	SWE3789
TUR3883			

CENTRAL ASIA AND SOUTH ASIA - ASIE CENTRALE ET ASIE DU SUD

AUT0024	AUT0026	AUT0045	AUT0051
AUT0063	AUT0091	BEL0123	BEL0124
BEL0129	BEL0144	BEL0186	BEL0192
BEL0198	BEL0203	BEL0221	BEL0261
BEL0270	BEL0273	BEL0306	BEL0327
BEL0340	BEL0341	BEL0359	BEL0361
BEL0397	CHE0403	CHE0422	CHE0434
CHE0568	CHE0619	CHE0632	CHE0638
CHE0645	CHE0655	CHE0682	CHE0689
CHE0712	CHE0730	CHE0798	CHE0813
CHE0814	CHE0817	CHE0819	CHE0820
DEU0918	DEU0971	DEU0972	DEU0983

See: *How to Use the Directory*, page 11.

DEU1006 DEU1055 DEU1066 DEU1086
DEU1107 DEU1116 DEU1121 DEU1131
DEU1149 DEU1151 DEU1167 DEU1187
DNK1259 DNK1291 DNK1292 DNK1300
DNK1314 DNK1339 DNK1384 ESP1492
FIN1591 FRA1610 FRA1642 FRA1644
FRA1661 FRA1744 FRA1757 FRA1862
FRA1887 FRA1921 FRA1934 FRA1990
FRA2062 FRA2096 FRA2109 FRA2131
FRA2158 FRA2168 FRA2170 GBR2174
GBR2176 GBR2186 GBR2197 GBR2201
GBR2218 GBR2226 GBR2227 GBR2228
GBR2238 GBR2260 GBR2264 GBR2278
GBR2297 GBR2318 GBR2333 GBR2334
GBR2348 GBR2351 GBR2358
GBR2370 GBR2371 GBR2372 GBR2376
GBR2422 GBR2423 GBR2434 GBR2436
GBR2475 GBR2480 GBR2481 GBR2501
GBR2535 GBR2553 GBR2562 GRC2575
ITA2784 ITA2813 ITA2860 ITA2914
LUX2937 LUX2965 LUX2982 MLT3021
NLD3047 NLD3062 NLD3067 NLD3071
NLD3096 NLD3101 NLD3122 NLD3137
NLD3153 NLD3154 NLD3158
NLD3183 NLD3199 NLD3253 NLD3260
NLD3361 NLD3362 NOR3371 NOR3412
NOR3465 NOR3467 NOR3475 POL3519
SWE3656 SWE3702 SWE3749 SWE3787
SWE3789 SWE3795 SWE3818 SWE3857
SWE3864 TUR3883 TUR3894

EAST AFRICA - AFRIQUE DE L'EST

AUT0003 AUT0024 AUT0026 AUT0041
AUT0045 AUT0085 AUT0091 BEL0123
BEL0124 BEL0129 BEL0144 BEL0148
BEL0186 BEL0198 BEL0221 BEL0270
BEL0306 BEL0327 BEL0340 BEL0361
BEL0381 BEL0397 CHE0403 CHE0434
CHE0491 CHE0586 CHE0629 CHE0630
CHE0645 CHE0649 CHE0660 CHE0682
CHE0689 CHE0691 CHE0712 CHE0730
CHE0813 CHE0814 CHE0817 CHE0819
CHE0820 CZE0905 DEU0972 DEU0983
DEU1006 DEU1032 DEU1055 DEU1066
DEU1074 DEU1097 DEU1106 DEU1107
DEU1116 DEU1131 DEU1178 DEU1202
DNK1255 DNK1259 DNK1291 DNK1300
DNK1302 DNK1314 DNK1339 DNK1377
ESP1432 ESP1492 ESP1509 ESP1514
FIN1549 FIN1572 FIN1584 FRA1610
FRA1636 FRA1644 FRA1727 FRA1744
FRA1796 FRA1887 FRA1934 FRA1956
FRA2039 FRA2062 FRA2069 FRA2096
FRA2109 FRA2126 FRA2168 FRA2170
GBR2174 GBR2175 GBR2185 GBR2187
GBR2218 GBR2226 GBR2227 GBR2232
GBR2238 GBR2259 GBR2262 GBR2264
GBR2278 GBR2292 GBR2293 GBR2298
GBR2337 GBR2346 GBR2350 GBR2351
GBR2365 GBR2370 GBR2371 GBR2383
GBR2392 GBR2422 GBR2423 GBR2434
GBR2436 GBR2460 GBR2474 GBR2480
GBR2481 GBR2483 GBR2500 GBR2501
GBR2518 GBR2535 GBR2552 GBR2553
GBR2562 IRL2688 IRL2725 IRL2733
ITA2772 ITA2784 ITA2820
ITA2860 ITA2910 ITA2914 LUX3008
MLT3021 NLD3045 NLD3062 NLD3067
NLD3068 NLD3070 NLD3071 NLD3074
NLD3096 NLD3101 NLD3117 NLD3137
NLD3138 NLD3154 NLD3155 NLD3158
NLD3169 NLD3189 NLD3199 NLD3216
NLD3235 NLD3253 NLD3362 NOR3465
NOR3475 POL3519 SWE3656 SWE3679
SWE3727 SWE3749 SWE3787 SWE3789
SWE3798 SWE3799 SWE3814 SWE3853
SWE3857 SWE3864 SWE3876 TUR3883

EAST ASIA - ASIE DE L'EST

AUT0024 AUT0045 AUT0090 BEL0123
BEL0124 BEL0129 BEL0144 BEL0186
BEL0198 BEL0221 BEL0273 BEL0327
BEL0361 BEL0397 CHE0403 CHE0422
CHE0434 CHE0570 CHE0638 CHE0649
CHE0655 CHE0689 CHE0712 CHE0730
CHE0795 CHE0814 CHE0817 CHE0819
CHE0820 DEU0971 DEU0972 DEU1006
DEU1055 DEU1107 DEU1116 DEU1131

DEU1149 DEU1167 DNK1292 DNK1300
DNK1314 ESP1432 ESP1492 ESP1508
FRA1610 FRA1744 FRA1757 FRA1992
FRA2096 FRA2109 FRA2168 FRA2170
GBR2218 GBR2228 GBR2238 GBR2260
GBR2264 GBR2278 GBR2294 GBR2351
GBR2370 GBR2371 GBR2422 GBR2423
GBR2434 GBR2481 GBR2501 GBR2535
GBR2553 ITA2784 ITA2832 ITA2860
ITA2914 MLT3021 NLD3062 NLD3067
NLD3071 NLD3096 NLD3122 NLD3138
NLD3154 NLD3362 NOR3465 SWE3789
TUR3883

MEXICO AND CENTRAL AMERICA - MEXIQUE ET AMERIQUE CENTRALE

AUT0003 AUT0029 AUT0034 AUT0041
AUT0045 AUT0051 AUT0063 AUT0091
BEL0123 BEL0124 BEL0129 BEL0144
BEL0148 BEL0164 BEL0186 BEL0198
BEL0203 BEL0221 BEL0270 BEL0273
BEL0327 BEL0335 BEL0336 BEL0340
BEL0353 BEL0361 BEL0381 BEL0387
BEL0397 CHE0403 CHE0427 CHE0434
CHE0465 CHE0557 CHE0559 CHE0568
CHE0613 CHE0619 CHE0632 CHE0649
CHE0682 CHE0689 CHE0712 CHE0730
CHE0755 CHE0789 CHE0793 CHE0804
CHE0813 CHE0814 CHE0817 CHE0819
CHE0820 DEU0948 DEU0972 DEU0983
DEU1031 DEU1055 DEU1074 DEU1106
DEU1107 DEU1114 DEU1131 DEU1149
DEU1167 DEU1187 DEU1202 DNK1226
DNK1283 DNK1292 DNK1300 DNK1312
DNK1314 DNK1317 DNK1339 DNK1359
ESP1409 ESP1413 ESP1427 ESP1432
ESP1435 ESP1437 ESP1442 ESP1453
ESP1455 ESP1457 ESP1475 ESP1485
ESP1486 ESP1492 ESP1506 ESP1517
ESP1521 ESP1522 ESP1525 ESP1529
FIN1544 FIN1546 FIN1591 FRA1610
FRA1636 FRA1707 FRA1744 FRA1757
FRA1827 FRA1934 FRA1964 FRA1985
FRA2012 FRA2062 FRA2069 FRA2090
FRA2092 FRA2096 FRA2103 FRA2109
FRA2158 FRA2168 FRA2170 GBR2174
GBR2201 GBR2218 GBR2226 GBR2228
GBR2229 GBR2238 GBR2278 GBR2351
GBR2371 GBR2413 GBR2422 GBR2423
GBR2434 GBR2436 GBR2480 GBR2481
GBR2500 GBR2501 GBR2518 GBR2535
GBR2553 IRL2697 ITA2762 ITA2775
ITA2784 ITA2799 ITA2809 ITA2855
ITA2860 ITA2881 ITA2913 ITA2914
LUX3008 NLD3062 NLD3067 NLD3068
NLD3071 NLD3079 NLD3096 NLD3101
NLD3122 NLD3137 NLD3138 NLD3154
NLD3158 NLD3159 NLD3183 NLD3199
NLD3219 NLD3230 NLD3253 NLD3263
NLD3285 NLD3303 NLD3305 NLD3361
NLD3362 NOR3410 NOR3475 POL3508
POL3519 SWE3650 SWE3655 SWE3656
SWE3687 SWE3702 SWE3749 SWE3787
SWE3789 SWE3795 SWE3827 SWE3864
SWE3865 TUR3883

MIDDLE EAST - MOYEN-ORIENT

AUT0035 AUT0045 BEL0124 BEL0129
BEL0144 BEL0186 BEL0198 BEL0221
BEL0306 BEL0361 BEL0397 CHE0403
CHE0410 CHE0434 CHE0568 CHE0649
CHE0655 CHE0689 CHE0712 CHE0730
CHE0813 CHE0814 CHE0817 CHE0819
CHE0820 DEU0972 DEU1055 DEU1065
DEU1107 DEU1116 DEU1150 DNK1300
DNK1314 ESP1514 ESP1522 FRA1610
FRA1629 FRA1636 FRA1744 FRA1791
FRA1794 FRA1827 FRA1964 FRA2041
FRA2057 FRA2069 FRA2096 FRA2103
FRA2109 FRA2158 FRA2170 GBR2218
GBR2232 GBR2238 GBR2260 GBR2278
GBR2365 GBR2371 GBR2422 GBR2423
GBR2434 GBR2500 GBR2501 GBR2525
GBR2562 GRC2575 ITA2773 ITA2784
ITA2860 ITA2862 ITA2914 MLT3016
MLT3018 MLT3021 NLD3062 NLD3067

NLD3122 NLD3138 NLD3154 NLD3155
NLD3158 NLD3362 POL3519 SWE3789
TUR3883

NORTH AFRICA - AFRIQUE DU NORD

AUT0045 BEL0123 BEL0124 BEL0129
BEL0144 BEL0148 BEL0186 BEL0198
BEL0221 BEL0340 BEL0361 BEL0395
BEL0397 CHE0403 CHE0434 CHE0568
CHE0655 CHE0682 CHE0689 CHE0712
CHE0730 CHE0813 CHE0814 CHE0817
CHE0820 CZE0905 DEU0972 DEU1055
DEU1106 DEU1107 DEU1111 DEU1116
DNK1255 DNK1300 DNK1314 ESP1442
ESP1486 ESP1492 FRA1610 FRA1629
FRA1636 FRA1719 FRA1744 FRA1757
FRA1794 FRA1796 FRA1836 FRA1887
FRA1946 FRA1956 FRA1964 FRA1985
FRA1992 FRA2018 FRA2057 FRA2069
FRA2096 FRA2109 FRA2126 FRA2158
FRA2170 GBR2185 GBR2218 GBR2278
GBR2365 GBR2370 GBR2371 GBR2422
GBR2434 GBR2501 GBR2535 GBR2562
GRC2567 GRC2575 ITA2784 ITA2791
ITA2810 ITA2860 ITA2862 ITA2901
ITA2914 MLT3016 MLT3018 MLT3021
MLT3036 NLD3062 NLD3067 NLD3101
NLD3117 NLD3138 NLD3154 NLD3362
POL3519 SWE3789 TUR3883

OCEANIA - OCEANIE

AUT0024 AUT0045 BEL0123 BEL0124
BEL0129 BEL0186 BEL0198 BEL0273
BEL0361 BEL0397 CHE0403 CHE0434
CHE0640 CHE0712 CHE0730 CHE0813
CHE0814 CHE0817 CHE0819 CHE0820
DEU0972 DEU0992 DEU1055 DEU1107
DEU1149 DNK1300 DNK1314 ESP1492
FRA1610 FRA1744 FRA2041 FRA2096
FRA2109 FRA2126 FRA2168 FRA2170
GBR2218 GBR2228 GBR2264 GBR2266
GBR2278 GBR2294 GBR2312 GBR2351
GBR2370 GBR2371 GBR2422 GBR2434
GBR2480 GBR2481 GBR2501 GBR2524
GBR2535 GBR2553 ITA2784 ITA2860
ITA2914 MLT3021 NLD3062 NLD3067
NLD3096 NLD3137 NLD3154 NLD3362
POL3508 SWE3789 TUR3883

SOUTH AMERICA - AMERIQUE DU SUD

AUT0003 AUT0022 AUT0024 AUT0026
AUT0030 AUT0041 AUT0045 AUT0051
AUT0052 AUT0090 AUT0091 BEL0119
BEL0123 BEL0124 BEL0126 BEL0129
BEL0133 BEL0139 BEL0144 BEL0148
BEL0155 BEL0186 BEL0198 BEL0203
BEL0221 BEL0241 BEL0258 BEL0270
BEL0273 BEL0306 BEL0327 BEL0335
BEL0336 BEL0340 BEL0351 BEL0353
BEL0359 BEL0361 BEL0381 BEL0392
BEL0395 BEL0396 BEL0397 CHE0403
CHE0434 CHE0438 CHE0455 CHE0465
CHE0479 CHE0491 CHE0559 CHE0568
CHE0570 CHE0581 CHE0602 CHE0604
CHE0619 CHE0632 CHE0640 CHE0649
CHE0654 CHE0682 CHE0689 CHE0693
CHE0712 CHE0730 CHE0755 CHE0789
CHE0798 CHE0813 CHE0814 CHE0817
CHE0819 CHE0820 DEU0948 DEU0972
DEU0983 DEU1006 DEU1055 DEU1066
DEU1074 DEU1097 DEU1107 DEU1111
DEU1114 DEU1131 DEU1132 DEU1137
DEU1138 DEU1149 DEU1167 DEU1187
DNK1255 DNK1291 DNK1292 DNK1300
DNK1304 DNK1314 DNK1403 ESP1409
ESP1419 ESP1432 ESP1435 ESP1437
ESP1442 ESP1452 ESP1455 ESP1457
ESP1474 ESP1475 ESP1484 ESP1485
ESP1486 ESP1488 ESP1492 ESP1517
ESP1522 ESP1525 ESP1529 FIN1549
FRA1610 FRA1616 FRA1636 FRA1703
FRA1744 FRA1815 FRA1827 FRA1828
FRA1926 FRA1927 FRA1934 FRA1946
FRA1964 FRA1980 FRA2041 FRA2062
FRA2069 FRA2092 FRA2096 FRA2103
FRA2109 FRA2117 FRA2131 FRA2158
FRA2163 FRA2168 FRA2170 GBR2174
GBR2201 GBR2218 GBR2226 GBR2228

Voir : *Comment utiliser le répertoire*, page 11.

GBR2229 GBR2238 GBR2244 GBR2264
GBR2278 GBR2351 GBR2365 GBR2371
GBR2383 GBR2422 GBR2423 GBR2434
GBR2436 GBR2456 GBR2480 GBR2481
GBR2500 GBR2501 GBR2525 GBR2535
GBR2552 GBR2553 IRL2719 IRL2726
ITA2748 ITA2762 ITA2773 ITA2782
ITA2784 ITA2809 ITA2810 ITA2811
ITA2822 ITA2832 ITA2834
ITA2838 ITA2839 ITA2860 ITA2868
ITA2873 ITA2880 ITA2881 ITA2901
ITA2910 ITA2913 ITA2914 LUX2937
LUX2958 LUX2968 LUX2976 LUX3003
LUX3008 NLD3062 NLD3067 NLD3071
NLD3096 NLD3101 NLD3122 NLD3137
NLD3138 NLD3154 NLD3158 NLD3199
NLD3253 NLD3305 NLD3361 NLD3362
NOR3404 NOR3460 NOR3465 POL3508
POL3519 PRT3579 PRT3602 SWE3655
SWE3656 SWE3702 SWE3724 SWE3744
SWE3749 SWE3754 SWE3781 SWE3787
SWE3789 SWE3795 SWE3796 SWE3855
SWE3865 SWE3876 TUR3883

SOUTH EAST ASIA - ASIE DU SUD-EST

AUT0024 AUT0045 AUT0051 AUT0063
AUT0091 BEL0123 BEL0124 BEL0128
BEL0129 BEL0144 BEL0186 BEL0198
BEL0203 BEL0211 BEL0221 BEL0261
BEL0273 BEL0306 BEL0327 BEL0340
BEL0342 BEL0361 BEL0396 BEL0397
CHE0403 CHE0434 CHE0479 CHE0568
CHE0570 CHE0604 CHE0619 CHE0630
CHE0638 CHE0649 CHE0682 CHE0689
CHE0693 CHE0712 CHE0730 CHE0798
CHE0813 CHE0814 CHE0817 CHE0819
CHE0820 DEU0948 DEU0971 DEU0972
DEU0983 DEU0990 DEU1006 DEU1037
DEU1055 DEU1097 DEU1107 DEU1116
DEU1149 DEU1167 DEU1178 DEU1187
DNK1259 DNK1292 DNK1300 DNK1314
DNK1403 ESP1492 FIN1584 FIN1599
FRA1610 FRA1629 FRA1744 FRA1860
FRA1934 FRA1946 FRA1964 FRA1979
FRA1992 FRA2069 FRA2096 FRA2109
FRA2126 FRA2140 FRA2168 FRA2170
GBR2201 GBR2218 GBR2228 GBR2238
GBR2260 GBR2264 GBR2278 GBR2346
GBR2351 GBR2370 GBR2371 GBR2413
GBR2422 GBR2423 GBR2434 GBR2436
GBR2481 GBR2501 GBR2535 GBR2537
GBR2553 GBR2562 IRL2687 IRL2726
ITA2744 ITA2784 ITA2799 ITA2860
ITA2914 MLT3021 NLD3062 NLD3067
NLD3068 NLD3071 NLD3083 NLD3096
NLD3117 NLD3122 NLD3137 NLD3138
NLD3154 NLD3155 NLD3199 NLD3235
NLD3245 NLD3362 NOR3332 NOR3465
NOR3475 POL3519 SWE3656 SWE3787
SWE3789 SWE3876 TUR3883

SOUTHERN AFRICA - AFRIQUE AUSTRALE

AUT0024 AUT0045 AUT0091 BEL0123
BEL0124 BEL0129 BEL0144 BEL0148
BEL0186 BEL0198 BEL0203 BEL0211
BEL0221 BEL0260 BEL0273 BEL0327
BEL0340 BEL0359 BEL0361 BEL0397
CHE0434 CHE0454 CHE0498 CHE0570
CHE0619 CHE0632 CHE0682 CHE0689
CHE0712 CHE0730 CHE0778 CHE0813
CHE0814 CHE0819 CHE0820 CZE0905
CZE0905 DEU0972 DEU1006 DEU1055
DEU1082 DEU1097 DEU1106 DEU1107
DEU1111 DEU1116 DEU1131 DEU1149
DEU1202 DNK1259 DNK1275 DNK1288
DNK1292 DNK1300 DNK1312 DNK1314
DNK1339 DNK1388 DNK1403 ESP1420
ESP1450 ESP1486 ESP1509 FIN1546
FIN1557 FRA1610 FRA1738 FRA1744
FRA1796 FRA1827 FRA1887 FRA1956
FRA2096 FRA2103 FRA2109 FRA2126
FRA2163 FRA2168 FRA2170 GBR2174
GBR2181 GBR2185 GBR2201 GBR2218
GBR2222 GBR2226 GBR2229 GBR2238
GBR2259 GBR2264 GBR2277 GBR2278
GBR2292 GBR2294 GBR2318 GBR2337
GBR2346 GBR2365 GBR2370 GBR2371
GBR2392 GBR2422 GBR2423 GBR2434

GBR2436 GBR2460 GBR2480 GBR2481
GBR2483 GBR2500 GBR2501 GBR2535
GBR2553 GBR2561 GBR2562 IRL2719
IRL2726 ITA2784 ITA2798 ITA2799
ITA2860 ITA2862 ITA2881 ITA2900
ITA2914 LUX2995 LUX3008 MLT3021
NLD3045 NLD3047 NLD3062 NLD3067
NLD3069 NLD3071 NLD3096 NLD3098
NLD3101 NLD3117 NLD3137 NLD3138
NLD3147 NLD3154 NLD3155 NLD3183
NLD3199 NLD3235 NLD3253 NLD3300
NLD3336 NLD3362 NOR3418 NOR3467
POL3519 PRT3600 SWE3648 SWE3656
SWE3685 SWE3749 SWE3789 SWE3859
SWE3864 TUR3883

WEST AFRICA - AFRIQUE DE L'OUEST

AUT0003 AUT0024 AUT0028 AUT0041
AUT0045 AUT0091 BEL0118 BEL0123
BEL0124 BEL0129 BEL0144 BEL0148
BEL0186 BEL0198 BEL0203 BEL0211
BEL0221 BEL0261 BEL0270 BEL0273
BEL0275 BEL0327 BEL0340 BEL0342
BEL0353 BEL0359 BEL0361 BEL0381
BEL0390 BEL0392 BEL0395 BEL0397
CHE0402 CHE0403 CHE0434 CHE0435
CHE0439 CHE0444 CHE0463 CHE0491
CHE0498 CHE0510 CHE0542 CHE0568
CHE0570 CHE0604 CHE0619 CHE0629
CHE0645 CHE0649 CHE0659 CHE0682
CHE0689 CHE0707 CHE0712 CHE0730
CHE0762 CHE0798 CHE0813 CHE0814
CHE0817 CHE0819 CHE0820 CHE0823
CZE0905 DEU0971 DEU0972 DEU0983
DEU0991 DEU1006 DEU1055 DEU1074
DEU1106 DEU1107 DEU1114 DEU1116
DEU1131 DEU1151 DNK1215 DNK1255
DNK1259 DNK1291 DNK1292 DNK1300
DNK1306 DNK1308 DNK1314 DNK1403
ESP1486 ESP1492 ESP1514 ESP1517
FRA1610 FRA1629 FRA1634 FRA1636
FRA1644 FRA1651 FRA1663 FRA1679
FRA1690 FRA1699 FRA1727 FRA1737
FRA1739 FRA1744 FRA1756 FRA1760
FRA1778 FRA1785 FRA1787 FRA1794
FRA1796 FRA1827 FRA1836 FRA1880
FRA1887 FRA1907 FRA1913 FRA1914
FRA1926 FRA1934 FRA1946 FRA1956
FRA1967 FRA1988 FRA2005 FRA2012
FRA2020 FRA2039 FRA2057 FRA2062
FRA2069 FRA2086 FRA2088 FRA2092
FRA2096 FRA2103 FRA2105 FRA2109
FRA2117 FRA2126 FRA2150 FRA2158
FRA2161 FRA2162 FRA2163 FRA2168
FRA2170 FRA2174 FRA2175 FRA2185
GBR2201 GBR2218 GBR2226 GBR2238
GBR2259 GBR2264 GBR2278 GBR2337
GBR2346 GBR2351 GBR2365 GBR2370
GBR2371 GBR2383 GBR2392 GBR2422
GBR2423 GBR2434 GBR2436 GBR2460
GBR2481 GBR2483 GBR2500 GBR2501
GBR2515 GBR2518 GBR2525 GBR2535
GBR2552 GBR2553 GBR2562 GRC2567
GRC2586 ISL2739 ITA2744 ITA2773
ITA2784 ITA2791 ITA2799 ITA2801
ITA2838 ITA2860 ITA2862 ITA2914
LUX2959 LUX2978 LUX2986 LUX3008
MLT3021 NLD3045 NLD3062 NLD3067
NLD3071 NLD3074 NLD3075 NLD3079
NLD3096 NLD3101 NLD3117 NLD3137
NLD3138 NLD3147 NLD3154 NLD3173
NLD3183 NLD3199 NLD3235 NLD3253
NLD3254 NLD3330 NLD3345 NLD3362
NOR3453 NOR3460 NOR3465 POL3508
POL3519 SWE3656 SWE3702 SWE3707
SWE3789 SWE3855 SWE3876 TUR3883

EDUCATION, TRAINING, LITERACY - EDUCATION, FORMATION, ALPHABETISATION

CARIBBEAN - CARAIBES

AUT0076 BEL0107 BEL0123 BEL0129
BEL0144 BEL0186 BEL0199 BEL0218
BEL0221 BEL0245 BEL0254 BEL0289
BEL0299 BEL0306 BEL0316 BEL0327
BEL0331 BEL0335 BEL0336 BEL0341

BEL0351 BEL0353 BEL0358 BEL0359
BEL0361 BEL0368 BEL0392 BEL0394
CHE0411 CHE0432 CHE0434 CHE0454
CHE0466 CHE0501 CHE0546 CHE0558
CHE0559 CHE0564 CHE0568 CHE0570
CHE0586 CHE0587 CHE0619 CHE0622
CHE0643 CHE0655 CHE0682 CHE0689
CHE0712 CHE0730 CHE0773 CHE0785
CHE0798 CHE0814 CHE0819 DEU0944
DEU0968 DEU0972 DEU0983 DEU0989
DEU0991 DEU1016 DEU1047 DEU1055
DEU1097 DEU1103 DEU1106 DEU1128
DEU1142 DEU1164 DEU1174 DEU1209
DNK1320 ESP1435 ESP1442 ESP1455
ESP1461 ESP1486 ESP1488 ESP1492
ESP1496 ESP1507 ESP1517 ESP1522
ESP1524 ESP1525 ESP1529 FIN1567
FIN1574 FIN1604 FRA1610 FRA1629
FRA1644 FRA1672 FRA1796 FRA1817
FRA1824 FRA1827 FRA1843 FRA1865
FRA1903 FRA1904 FRA1905 FRA1917
FRA1934 FRA1939 FRA1946 FRA1975
FRA1980 FRA1993 FRA2023 FRA2026
FRA2032 FRA2034 FRA2060 FRA2062
FRA2069 FRA2081 FRA2086 FRA2096
FRA2102 FRA2103 FRA2106 FRA2116
FRA2119 FRA2126 FRA2137 FRA2158
FRA2159 FRA2161 FRA2168 FRA2170
GBR2198 GBR2210 GBR2212 GBR2218
GBR2228 GBR2229 GBR2232 GBR2238
GBR2241 GBR2242 GBR2247 GBR2266
GBR2278 GBR2281 GBR2293 GBR2324
GBR2341 GBR2346 GBR2351 GBR2371
GBR2392 GBR2423 GBR2436 GBR2437
GBR2439 GBR2441 GBR2445 GBR2463
GBR2464 GBR2477 GBR2481 GBR2500
GBR2501 GBR2513 GBR2518 GBR2535
GBR2546 GBR2550 GBR2553 GBR2558
IRL2687 IRL2711 IRL2726 ITA2766
ITA2773 ITA2777 ITA2780 ITA2784
ITA2787 ITA2814 ITA2822 ITA2860
ITA2888 ITA2914 ITA2922 LUX2992
LUX2993 MLT3021 NLD3067 NLD3072
NLD3076 NLD3078 NLD3126 NLD3137
NLD3138 NLD3142 NLD3144 NLD3158
NLD3158 NLD3214 NLD3231 NLD3288
NLD3325 NLD3356 NLD3361 NOR3403
NOR3407 NOR3425 NOR3439 POL3508
POL3519 SWE3653 SWE3656 SWE3712
SWE3749 SWE3830

CENTRAL AFRICA - AFRIQUE CENTRALE

AUT0013 AUT0024 AUT0040 AUT0076
BEL0097 BEL0105 BEL0107 BEL0110
BEL0120 BEL0123 BEL0126 BEL0129
BEL0133 BEL0144 BEL0145 BEL0148
BEL0152 BEL0153 BEL0155 BEL0158
BEL0169 BEL0184 BEL0186 BEL0192
BEL0199 BEL0200 BEL0201 BEL0202
BEL0203 BEL0218 BEL0221 BEL0231
BEL0233 BEL0234 BEL0237 BEL0258
BEL0284 BEL0289 BEL0299 BEL0306
BEL0315 BEL0316 BEL0327 BEL0328
BEL0341 BEL0342 BEL0347 BEL0351
BEL0352 BEL0358 BEL0359 BEL0361
BEL0378 BEL0392 BEL0396 CHE0432
CHE0434 CHE0444 CHE0456 CHE0477
CHE0483 CHE0535 CHE0541 CHE0559
CHE0562 CHE0566 CHE0568 CHE0570
CHE0613 CHE0619 CHE0622 CHE0626
CHE0628 CHE0629 CHE0630 CHE0632
CHE0638 CHE0643 CHE0645 CHE0655
CHE0681 CHE0687 CHE0689 CHE0691
CHE0712 CHE0730 CHE0750 CHE0762
CHE0796 CHE0805 CHE0806 CHE0814
CHE0819 CZE0905 DEU0918 DEU0944
DEU0968 DEU0972 DEU0978 DEU0986
DEU0989 DEU0995 DEU1015 DEU1016
DEU1017 DEU1027 DEU1047 DEU1055
DEU1097 DEU1103 DEU1106 DEU1114
DEU1116 DEU1118 DEU1128 DEU1131
DEU1146 DEU1149 DEU1174 DEU1209
DNK1214 DNK1227 DNK1255 DNK1272
DNK1287 DNK1360 DNK1366 DNK1392
ESP1486 ESP1489 ESP1492 ESP1507
ESP1513 ESP1517 ESP1529 FIN1531
FIN1549 FIN1604 FRA1610 FRA1614
FRA1616 FRA1629 FRA1634 FRA1636
FRA1645 FRA1647 FRA1675 FRA1704

See: *How to Use the Directory*, page 11.

FRA1715	FRA1727	FRA1731	FRA1740
FRA1769	FRA1774	FRA1787	FRA1815
FRA1817	FRA1820	FRA1824	FRA1827
FRA1835	FRA1863	FRA1876	FRA1879
FRA1880	FRA1885	FRA1886	FRA1887
FRA1893	FRA1903	FRA1904	FRA1905
FRA1917	FRA1928	FRA1934	FRA1939
FRA1946	FRA1956	FRA1978	FRA1980
FRA1993	FRA2005	FRA2011	FRA2012
FRA2015	FRA2021	FRA2032	FRA2034
FRA2039	FRA2042	FRA2051	FRA2054
FRA2055	FRA2060	FRA2061	FRA2069
FRA2080	FRA2081	FRA2086	FRA2096
FRA2097	FRA2102	FRA2103	FRA2105
FRA2106	FRA2107	FRA2108	FRA2116
FRA2122	FRA2123	FRA2126	FRA2137
FRA2145	FRA2159	FRA2162	FRA2168
FRA2170	GBR2174	GBR2175	GBR2178
GBR2180	GBR2183	GBR2185	GBR2187
GBR2210	GBR2218	GBR2232	GBR2238
GBR2240	GBR2259	GBR2274	GBR2278
GBR2337	GBR2340	GBR2346	GBR2350
GBR2351	GBR2369	GBR2371	GBR2382
GBR2390	GBR2392	GBR2402	GBR2403
GBR2423	GBR2437	GBR2445	GBR2454
GBR2460	GBR2477	GBR2481	GBR2500
GBR2501	GBR2517	GBR2546	GBR2550
GBR2553	IRL2702	IRL2711	IRL2732
ITA2747	ITA2756	ITA2757	ITA2760
ITA2762	ITA2766	ITA2770	ITA2774
ITA2777	ITA2779	ITA2784	ITA2791
ITA2806	ITA2807	ITA2813	ITA2824
ITA2826	ITA2835	ITA2837	ITA2860
ITA2868	ITA2883	ITA2885	ITA2886
ITA2888	ITA2890	ITA2896	ITA2898
ITA2900	ITA2907	ITA2912	ITA2914
ITA2920	ITA2921	ITA2922	ITA2923
LUX2954	LUX2975	LUX2997	LUX3006
MLT3021	NLD3045	NLD3050	NLD3067
NLD3068	NLD3070	NLD3072	NLD3076
NLD3078	NLD3095	NLD3096	NLD3101
NLD3121	NLD3137	NLD3138	NLD3144
NLD3154	NLD3199	NLD3214	NLD3230
NLD3257	NLD3264	NLD3291	NLD3292
NLD3301	NLD3311	NLD3317	NLD3325
NLD3356	NLD3361	NOR3452	NOR3465
POL3508	POL3519	PRT3549	PRT3555
PRT3594	PRT3602	PRT3603	SWE3656
SWE3674	SWE3749	SWE3763	SWE3769
SWE3772	SWE3827	SWE3828	SWE3830

CENTRAL ASIA AND SOUTH ASIA - ASIE CENTRALE ET ASIE DU SUD

AUT0013	AUT0024	AUT0026	AUT0051
AUT0063	AUT0076	AUT0089	AUT0091
BEL0097	BEL0104	BEL0107	BEL0123
BEL0144	BEL0186	BEL0192	BEL0199
BEL0201	BEL0203	BEL0221	BEL0231
BEL0254	BEL0258	BEL0270	BEL0284
BEL0299	BEL0306	BEL0315	BEL0327
BEL0340	BEL0341	BEL0351	BEL0352
BEL0358	BEL0361	BEL0368	BEL0378
BEL0392	CHE0406	CHE0412	CHE0417
CHE0432	CHE0434	CHE0467	CHE0472
CHE0477	CHE0491	CHE0558	CHE0559
CHE0566	CHE0568	CHE0586	CHE0619
CHE0622	CHE0628	CHE0632	CHE0634
CHE0638	CHE0643	CHE0645	CHE0655
CHE0665	CHE0682	CHE0689	CHE0712
CHE0730	CHE0742	CHE0757	CHE0785
CHE0793	CHE0796	CHE0798	CHE0814
CHE0819	DEU0918	DEU0928	DEU0940
DEU0944	DEU0954	DEU0968	DEU0971
DEU0972	DEU0980	DEU0983	DEU0985
DEU0989	DEU0990	DEU0991	DEU0995
DEU1005	DEU1015	DEU1016	DEU1017
DEU1038	DEU1047	DEU1055	DEU1086
DEU1097	DEU1103	DEU1106	DEU1116
DEU1118	DEU1121	DEU1127	DEU1128
DEU1129	DEU1131	DEU1132	DEU1142
DEU1146	DEU1149	DEU1174	DEU1178
DEU1187	DEU1209	DNK1216	DNK1218
DNK1222	DNK1229	DNK1244	DNK1248
DNK1255	DNK1259	DNK1260	DNK1275
DNK1287	DNK1292	DNK1304	DNK1339
DNK1360	DNK1366	DNK1369	DNK1384
ESP1486	ESP1492	ESP1510	ESP1513
ESP1517	ESP1523	FIN1549	FIN1567
FIN1574	FIN1580	FIN1591	FIN1604

FRA1610	FRA1642	FRA1644	FRA1645
FRA1647	FRA1655	FRA1658	FRA1661
FRA1817	FRA1824	FRA1831	FRA1866
FRA1886	FRA1887	FRA1904	FRA1905
FRA1917	FRA1929	FRA1934	FRA1939
FRA1966	FRA1978	FRA1980	FRA1990
FRA2023	FRA2026	FRA2032	FRA2034
FRA2039	FRA2042	FRA2044	FRA2054
FRA2081	FRA2086	FRA2096	FRA2102
FRA2116	FRA2117	FRA2131	FRA2159
FRA2168	FRA2170	GBR2172	GBR2174
GBR2175	GBR2176	GBR2186	GBR2197
GBR2201	GBR2202	GBR2210	GBR2212
GBR2213	GBR2218	GBR2228	GBR2232
GBR2238	GBR2241	GBR2242	GBR2259
GBR2260	GBR2264	GBR2266	GBR2274
GBR2278	GBR2281	GBR2290	GBR2297
GBR2302	GBR2306	GBR2307	GBR2321
GBR2333	GBR2334	GBR2341	GBR2346
GBR2348	GBR2349	GBR2351	GBR2353
GBR2358	GBR2364	GBR2369	GBR2371
GBR2372	GBR2375	GBR2376	GBR2382
GBR2385	GBR2390	GBR2392	GBR2396
GBR2409	GBR2410	GBR2423	GBR2432
GBR2436	GBR2437	GBR2439	GBR2440
GBR2445	GBR2463	GBR2464	GBR2467
GBR2475	GBR2477	GBR2481	GBR2492
GBR2500	GBR2501	GBR2506	GBR2509
GBR2517	GBR2532	GBR2535	GBR2546
GBR2550	GBR2552	GBR2553	GBR2558
GRC2571	HUN2627	IRL2688	IRL2699
IRL2711	IRL2726	ITA2764	ITA2766
ITA2770	ITA2775	ITA2784	ITA2787
ITA2813	ITA2860	ITA2873	ITA2888
ITA2903	ITA2912	ITA2914	ITA2922
LIE2926	LUX2965	LUX2973	LUX2982
LUX2997	LUX3001	MLT3021	NLD3051
NLD3056	NLD3067	NLD3072	NLD3076
NLD3078	NLD3095	NLD3096	NLD3101
NLD3121	NLD3126	NLD3137	NLD3138
NLD3144	NLD3147	NLD3149	NLD3153
NLD3154	NLD3155	NLD3163	NLD3165
NLD3199	NLD3214	NLD3231	NLD3237
NLD3242	NLD3253	NLD3263	NLD3260
NLD3295	NLD3297	NLD3300	NLD3301
NLD3302	NLD3311	NLD3317	NLD3325
NLD3356	NLD3361	NOR3371	NOR3384
NOR3390	NOR3394	NOR3400	NOR3412
NOR3425	NOR3431	NOR3439	NOR3447
NOR3459	NOR3460	NOR3465	NOR3476
POL3519	PRT3549	SWE3656	SWE3661
SWE3666	SWE3674	SWE3679	SWE3723
SWE3737	SWE3745	SWE3749	SWE3763
SWE3768	SWE3769	SWE3771	SWE3787
SWE3795	SWE3809	SWE3813	SWE3818
SWE3819	SWE3821	SWE3826	SWE3827
SWE3828	SWE3830	SWE3834	SWE3854
SWE3857			

EAST AFRICA - AFRIQUE DE L'EST

AUT0003	AUT0013	AUT0024	AUT0041
AUT0052	AUT0061	AUT0063	AUT0067
AUT0076	AUT0085	AUT0091	BEL0097
BEL0107	BEL0123	BEL0129	BEL0133
BEL0144	BEL0148	BEL0186	BEL0199
BEL0221	BEL0224	BEL0231	BEL0269
BEL0270	BEL0284	BEL0289	BEL0299
BEL0316	BEL0327	BEL0341	BEL0351
BEL0358	BEL0361	BEL0392	CHE0432
CHE0434	CHE0448	CHE0462	CHE0483
CHE0559	CHE0566	CHE0570	CHE0586
CHE0620	CHE0622	CHE0626	CHE0630
CHE0634	CHE0638	CHE0643	CHE0645
CHE0649	CHE0660	CHE0661	CHE0682
CHE0687	CHE0689	CHE0691	CHE0693
CHE0712	CHE0730	CHE0754	CHE0772
CHE0796	CHE0798	CHE0814	CHE0819
CHE0823	CZE0905	DEU0918	DEU0928
DEU0936	DEU0940	DEU0944	DEU0965
DEU0968	DEU0972	DEU0980	DEU0983
DEU0989	DEU0991	DEU0995	DEU1002
DEU1005	DEU1016	DEU1017	DEU1031
DEU1047	DEU1055	DEU1066	DEU1069
DEU1074	DEU1097	DEU1103	DEU1106
DEU1116	DEU1118	DEU1128	DEU1129
DEU1131	DEU1142	DEU1145	DEU1146
DEU1149	DEU1174	DEU1178	DEU1181
DEU1202	DEU1209	DNK1214	DNK1218
DNK1229	DNK1244	DNK1245	DNK1255

DNK1259	DNK1274	DNK1275	DNK1285
DNK1287	DNK1292	DNK1316	DNK1339
DNK1342	DNK1351	DNK1358	DNK1360
DNK1369	DNK1377	DNK1391	DNK1392
DNK1405	ESP1432	ESP1435	ESP1486
ESP1491	ESP1492	ESP1509	ESP1510
ESP1514	ESP1524	FIN1531	FIN1539
FIN1544	FIN1547	FIN1549	FIN1556
FIN1567	FIN1580	FIN1591	FIN1604
FRA1610	FRA1636	FRA1644	FRA1645
FRA1658	FRA1675	FRA1683	FRA1717
FRA1727	FRA1731	FRA1796	FRA1817
FRA1824	FRA1835	FRA1843	FRA1855
FRA1879	FRA1886	FRA1887	FRA1903
FRA1917	FRA1930	FRA1934	FRA1956
FRA2032	FRA2039	FRA2051	FRA2054
FRA2060	FRA2062	FRA2069	FRA2080
FRA2081	FRA2096	FRA2106	FRA2107
FRA2116	FRA2123	FRA2126	FRA2159
FRA2168	FRA2170	GBR2172	GBR2174
GBR2175	GBR2178	GBR2179	GBR2180
GBR2183	GBR2185	GBR2186	GBR2187
GBR2198	GBR2212	GBR2212	GBR2214
GBR2218	GBR2232	GBR2238	GBR2242
GBR2247	GBR2259	GBR2262	GBR2264
GBR2274	GBR2278	GBR2281	GBR2282
GBR2292	GBR2293	GBR2298	GBR2307
GBR2321	GBR2337	GBR2338	GBR2340
GBR2341	GBR2346	GBR2348	GBR2350
GBR2351	GBR2353	GBR2369	GBR2371
GBR2382	GBR2383	GBR2385	GBR2390
GBR2392	GBR2409	GBR2410	GBR2423
GBR2436	GBR2437	GBR2439	GBR2441
GBR2445	GBR2459	GBR2460	GBR2463
GBR2464	GBR2467	GBR2471	GBR2474
GBR2477	GBR2481	GBR2483	GBR2497
GBR2500	GBR2501	GBR2513	GBR2517
GBR2518	GBR2533	GBR2535	GBR2536
GBR2546	GBR2550	GBR2551	GBR2552
GBR2553	GBR2558	GRC2571	IRL2683
IRL2688	IRL2691	IRL2699	IRL2702
IRL2711	IRL2724	IRL2725	IRL2726
IRL2729	IRL2730	IRL2732	IRL2733
ISL2739	ISL2740	ITA2757	ITA2762
ITA2766	ITA2772	ITA2782	ITA2784
ITA2785	ITA2804	ITA2810	ITA2818
ITA2820	ITA2822	ITA2829	ITA2836
ITA2837	ITA2840	ITA2857	ITA2860
ITA2868	ITA2873	ITA2874	ITA2879
ITA2885	ITA2888	ITA2889	ITA2890
ITA2896	ITA2902	ITA2907	ITA2910
ITA2914	ITA2922	ITA2923	LUX2975
LUX2997	MLT3021	NLD3045	NLD3050
NLD3067	NLD3068	NLD3070	NLD3072
NLD3074	NLD3076	NLD3096	NLD3101
NLD3121	NLD3137	NLD3138	NLD3142
NLD3144	NLD3145	NLD3146	NLD3154
NLD3155	NLD3158	NLD3165	NLD3173
NLD3183	NLD3199	NLD3209	NLD3214
NLD3216	NLD3231	NLD3237	NLD3242
NLD3257	NLD3297	NLD3300	NLD3301
NLD3311	NLD3317	NLD3323	NLD3325
NLD3356	NLD3361	NOR3384	NOR3404
NOR3407	NOR3425	NOR3439	NOR3443
NOR3447	NOR3465	NOR3467	NOR3476
POL3508	POL3519	PRT3550	PRT3597
SWE3656	SWE3672	SWE3675	SWE3679
SWE3688	SWE3712	SWE3714	SWE3727
SWE3728	SWE3735	SWE3749	SWE3752
SWE3761	SWE3769	SWE3771	SWE3772
SWE3775	SWE3777	SWE3787	SWE3798
SWE3799	SWE3806	SWE3814	SWE3821
SWE3826	SWE3828	SWE3830	SWE3831
SWE3853	SWE3854	SWE3855	SWE3877
SWE3879			

EAST ASIA - ASIE DE L'EST

AUT0013	AUT0021	AUT0024	AUT0076
BEL0107	BEL0123	BEL0144	BEL0186
BEL0199	BEL0221	BEL0231	BEL0254
BEL0284	BEL0289	BEL0327	BEL0351
BEL0358	BEL0359	BEL0361	BEL0392
CHE0432	CHE0434	CHE0570	CHE0622
CHE0638	CHE0643	CHE0645	CHE0649
CHE0650	CHE0655	CHE0674	CHE0689
CHE0693	CHE0712	CHE0713	CHE0730
CHE0796	CHE0814	CHE0819	DEU0944
DEU0968	DEU0972	DEU0980	DEU0989
DEU0994	DEU0995	DEU1005	DEU1015

Voir : *Comment utiliser le répertoire*, page 11.

DEU1016 DEU1017 DEU1047 DEU1055
DEU1097 DEU1103 DEU1106 DEU1116
DEU1118 DEU1128 DEU1129 DEU1131
DEU1142 DEU1146 DEU1149 DEU1174
DEU1209 DNK1244 DNK1251 DNK1275
DNK1287 DNK1292 ESP1432 ESP1492
ESP1508 FIN1549 FIN1567 FIN1604
FRA1610 FRA1817 FRA1833 FRA1917
FRA1966 FRA1992 FRA2026 FRA2032
FRA2054 FRA2062 FRA2096 FRA2116
FRA2149 FRA2159 FRA2168 FRA2170
GBR2175 GBR2210 GBR2218 GBR2228
GBR2232 GBR2238 GBR2260 GBR2264
GBR2266 GBR2278 GBR2306 GBR2351
GBR2369 GBR2371 GBR2382 GBR2392
GBR2423 GBR2441 GBR2445 GBR2464
GBR2477 GBR2481 GBR2501 GBR2535
GBR2546 GBR2550 GBR2553 IRL2711
IRL2726 ITA2766 ITA2784 ITA2811
ITA2822 ITA2832 ITA2860 ITA2868
ITA2914 ITA2922 LUX2950 LUX2973
LUX2997 MLT3021 NLD3067 NLD3072
NLD3076 NLD3078 NLD3091 NLD3096
NLD3138 NLD3154 NLD3163 NLD3183
NLD3183 NLD3198 NLD3214 NLD3356
NOR3387 NOR3465 SWE3712 SWE3809
SWE3823 SWE3826 SWE3828 SWE3830

MEXICO AND CENTRAL AMERICA - MEXIQUE ET AMERIQUE CENTRALE

AUT0003 AUT0013 AUT0021 AUT0024
AUT0026 AUT0029 AUT0030 AUT0034
AUT0040 AUT0041 AUT0051 AUT0052
AUT0058 AUT0067 AUT0076 AUT0091
BEL0107 BEL0123 BEL0129 BEL0144
BEL0148 BEL0182 BEL0184 BEL0186
BEL0199 BEL0201 BEL0203 BEL0221
BEL0224 BEL0231 BEL0254 BEL0269
BEL0270 BEL0275 BEL0284 BEL0289
BEL0299 BEL0306 BEL0316 BEL0323
BEL0327 BEL0335 BEL0336 BEL0340
BEL0341 BEL0351 BEL0353 BEL0358
BEL0359 BEL0361 BEL0378 BEL0392
CHE0427 CHE0432 CHE0434 CHE0446
CHE0456 CHE0483 CHE0491 CHE0517
CHE0557 CHE0558 CHE0559 CHE0566
CHE0568 CHE0570 CHE0586 CHE0602
CHE0609 CHE0613 CHE0619 CHE0622
CHE0626 CHE0630 CHE0632 CHE0634
CHE0638 CHE0640 CHE0645 CHE0649
CHE0650 CHE0665 CHE0682 CHE0689
CHE0712 CHE0713 CHE0730 CHE0755
CHE0772 CHE0785 CHE0788 CHE0789
CHE0793 CHE0794 CHE0796 CHE0800
CHE0804 CHE0814 CHE0819 DEU0933
DEU0944 DEU0954 DEU0968 DEU0972
DEU0980 DEU0983 DEU0989 DEU0991
DEU0995 DEU1002 DEU1005 DEU1015
DEU1016 DEU1025 DEU1031 DEU1047
DEU1055 DEU1081 DEU1097 DEU1103
DEU1114 DEU1118 DEU1128 DEU1129
DEU1131 DEU1132 DEU1138 DEU1142
DEU1149 DEU1167 DEU1174 DEU1178
DEU1187 DEU1209 DNK1226 DNK1229
DNK1283 DNK1287 DNK1312 DNK1317
DNK1321 DNK1339 DNK1351 DNK1359
DNK1360 DNK1369 ESP1409 ESP1413
ESP1427 ESP1431 ESP1432 ESP1435
ESP1442 ESP1450 ESP1455 ESP1461
ESP1475 ESP1484 ESP1485 ESP1486
ESP1488 ESP1489 ESP1492 ESP1496
ESP1505 ESP1506 ESP1510 ESP1511
ESP1517 ESP1521 ESP1522 ESP1523
ESP1524 ESP1525 ESP1529 FIN1544
FIN1546 FIN1549 FIN1567 FIN1574
FIN1578 FIN1591 FIN1603 FIN1604
FRA1610 FRA1636 FRA1645 FRA1658
FRA1673 FRA1675 FRA1817 FRA1824
FRA1827 FRA1831 FRA1843 FRA1852
FRA1856 FRA1904 FRA1905 FRA1917
FRA1920 FRA1934 FRA1938 FRA1939
FRA1942 FRA1967 FRA1975 FRA1978
FRA1980 FRA2026 FRA2032 FRA2034
FRA2041 FRA2047 FRA2044 FRA2047
FRA2053 FRA2060 FRA2062 FRA2069
FRA2081 FRA2090 FRA2092 FRA2096
FRA2102 FRA2103 FRA2116 FRA2117
FRA2119 FRA2152 FRA2159 FRA2168
FRA2170 GBR2174 GBR2201 GBR2212

GBR2218 GBR2228 GBR2229 GBR2231
GBR2232 GBR2238 GBR2247 GBR2259
GBR2278 GBR2293 GBR2306 GBR2321
GBR2349 GBR2351 GBR2353 GBR2371
GBR2385 GBR2390 GBR2392 GBR2411
GBR2423 GBR2436 GBR2437 GBR2439
GBR2441 GBR2445 GBR2463 GBR2464
GBR2467 GBR2481 GBR2500 GBR2501
GBR2513 GBR2518 GBR2535 GBR2546
GBR2550 GBR2551 GBR2552 GBR2553
IRL2697 IRL2707 IRL2711 IRL2726
IRL2732 ITA2756 ITA2762 ITA2780
ITA2782 ITA2784 ITA2787 ITA2809
ITA2824 ITA2834 ITA2838 ITA2842
ITA2858 ITA2860 ITA2868 ITA2881
ITA2885 ITA2888 ITA2894 ITA2902
ITA2911 ITA2914 ITA2922 ITA2923
LUX2968 LUX2973 LUX2983 LUX2997
MLT3021 NLD3067 NLD3068 NLD3072
NLD3076 NLD3078 NLD3095 NLD3096
NLD3101 NLD3137 NLD3138 NLD3141
NLD3144 NLD3154 NLD3158 NLD3159
NLD3165 NLD3198 NLD3199 NLD3212
NLD3214 NLD3219 NLD3230 NLD3231
NLD3253 NLD3257 NLD3285 NLD3288
NLD3300 NLD3303 NLD3305 NLD3325
NLD3356 NLD3361 NOR3381 NOR3390
NOR3403 NOR3407 NOR3409 NOR3425
NOR3439 NOR3467 NOR3475 NOR3476
POL3519 SWE3655 SWE3656 SWE3666
SWE3674 SWE3687 SWE3688 SWE3702
SWE3725 SWE3749 SWE3768 SWE3769
SWE3770 SWE3771 SWE3787 SWE3795
SWE3796 SWE3798 SWE3821 SWE3826
SWE3828 SWE3830 SWE3831 SWE3865

MIDDLE EAST - MOYEN-ORIENT

AUT0002 AUT0021 AUT0035 AUT0076
AUT0091 BEL0105 BEL0144 BEL0186
BEL0199 BEL0221 BEL0270 BEL0275
BEL0306 BEL0315 BEL0316 BEL0317
BEL0342 BEL0353 BEL0358 BEL0361
CHE0403 CHE0406 CHE0410 CHE0434
CHE0456 CHE0493 CHE0568 CHE0570
CHE0600 CHE0622 CHE0634 CHE0640
CHE0645 CHE0649 CHE0650 CHE0655
CHE0664 CHE0689 CHE0709
CHE0712 CHE0713 CHE0730 CHE0796
CHE0814 CHE0819 CZE0906 DEU0944
DEU0968 DEU0972 DEU0980 DEU0989
DEU0991 DEU0995 DEU1005 DEU1015
DEU1016 DEU1017 DEU1047 DEU1055
DEU1065 DEU1097 DEU1103 DEU1106
DEU1116 DEU1128 DEU1131 DEU1146
DEU1150 DEU1174 DNK1275 DNK1292
DNK1304 DNK1320 DNK1360 DNK1372
ESP1450 ESP1455 ESP1514 FIN1549
FIN1567 FIN1570 FIN1588 FIN1604
FRA1610 FRA1628 FRA1629 FRA1636
FRA1645 FRA1675 FRA1683 FRA1696
FRA1724 FRA1749 FRA1791 FRA1793
FRA1794 FRA1817 FRA1824 FRA1827
FRA1843 FRA1865 FRA1886 FRA1917
FRA1942 FRA1948 FRA1978 FRA2026
FRA2032 FRA2044 FRA2057 FRA2069
FRA2081 FRA2096 FRA2103 FRA2116
FRA2117 FRA2137 FRA2159 FRA2170
GBR2218 GBR2229 GBR2230 GBR2232
GBR2238 GBR2241 GBR2260 GBR2278
GBR2281 GBR2351 GBR2369 GBR2371
GBR2378 GBR2385 GBR2392 GBR2396
GBR2423 GBR2441 GBR2445 GBR2455
GBR2464 GBR2500 GBR2501 GBR2525
GBR2546 GBR2551 GRC2572 IRL2702
IRL2711 IRL2733 ITA2756 ITA2773
ITA2784 ITA2785 ITA2799 ITA2860
ITA2914 ITA2923 LUX2956 LUX2969
LUX2997 MLT3016 MLT3018 MLT3021
MLT3028 NLD3050 NLD3067 NLD3072
NLD3076 NLD3138 NLD3142 NLD3144
NLD3147 NLD3154 NLD3163 NLD3183
NLD3199 NLD3214 NLD3325 NLD3356
NLD3361 NOR3384 NOR3404 NOR3407
NOR3447 NOR3456 NOR3476 POL3508
POL3519 SWE3674 SWE3749 SWE3763
SWE3769 SWE3771 SWE3822 SWE3826
SWE3828 SWE3830 TUR3883

NORTH AFRICA - AFRIQUE DU NORD

AUT0013 AUT0076 BEL0097 BEL0118
BEL0123 BEL0144 BEL0148 BEL0186
BEL0199 BEL0221 BEL0269 BEL0270
BEL0275 BEL0289 BEL0316 BEL0323
BEL0358 BEL0361 CHE0403 CHE0409
CHE0432 CHE0434 CHE0456 CHE0477
CHE0506 CHE0568 CHE0570 CHE0622
CHE0634 CHE0645 CHE0650 CHE0655
CHE0682 CHE0687 CHE0689 CHE0712
CHE0730 CHE0753 CHE0796 CHE0814
CZE0905 DEU0944 DEU0968 DEU0972
DEU0980 DEU0989 DEU0990 DEU0995
DEU1005 DEU1017 DEU1047 DEU1055
DEU1063 DEU1103 DEU1106 DEU1116
DEU1128 DEU1131 DEU1146 DEU1174
DEU1209 DNK1255 DNK1275 DNK1304
DNK1318 DNK1360 ESP1406 ESP1442
ESP1455 ESP1475 ESP1486 ESP1492
ESP1505 ESP1521 ESP1523 FIN1531
FIN1567 FIN1604 FRA1610 FRA1629
FRA1636 FRA1675 FRA1683 FRA1696
FRA1731 FRA1749 FRA1759 FRA1794
FRA1796 FRA1817 FRA1831 FRA1833
FRA1836 FRA1846 FRA1886 FRA1887
FRA1917 FRA1942 FRA1946 FRA1956
FRA1966 FRA1992 FRA1993 FRA2018
FRA2026 FRA2034 FRA2057 FRA2061
FRA2069 FRA2096 FRA2107 FRA2111
FRA2116 FRA2117 FRA2126 FRA2129
FRA2150 FRA2159 FRA2170 FRA2185
GBR2210 GBR2218 GBR2231 GBR2232
GBR2238 GBR2278 GBR2281 GBR2369
GBR2371 GBR2385 GBR2392 GBR2423
GBR2437 GBR2445 GBR2464 GBR2501
GBR2535 GBR2546 GBR2550 IRL2711
ITA2766 ITA2769 ITA2784 ITA2809
ITA2822 ITA2834 ITA2860 ITA2868
ITA2888 ITA2901 ITA2903 ITA2914
ITA2922 LUX2975 LUX2997 MLT3016
MLT3018 MLT3021 MLT3028 MLT3036
NLD3067 NLD3072 NLD3076 NLD3078
NLD3101 NLD3138 NLD3142 NLD3144
NLD3147 NLD3154 NLD3163 NLD3173
NLD3198 NLD3214 NLD3253 NLD3317
NLD3356 NOR3431 NOR3456 POL3508
POL3519 PRT3564 SWE3688 SWE3763
SWE3772 SWE3828 SWE3830

OCEANIA - OCEANIE

AUT0024 BEL0107 BEL0123 BEL0129
BEL0186 BEL0199 BEL0270 BEL0361
CHE0432 CHE0434 CHE0640 CHE0645
CHE0687 CHE0712 CHE0730 CHE0772
CHE0814 CHE0819 DEU0944 DEU0968
DEU0972 DEU0989 DEU0992 DEU0995
DEU1015 DEU1016 DEU1017 DEU1047
DEU1055 DEU1097 DEU1103 DEU1106
DEU1128 DEU1131 DEU1146 DEU1174
DNK1292 ESP1492 FIN1567 FIN1604
FRA1610 FRA1672 FRA1817 FRA1917
FRA2026 FRA2032 FRA2041 FRA2086
FRA2096 FRA2116 FRA2117 FRA2126
FRA2159 FRA2168 FRA2170 GBR2210
GBR2218 GBR2232 GBR2247 GBR2264
GBR2266 GBR2278 GBR2312 GBR2351
GBR2369 GBR2371 GBR2382 GBR2392
GBR2437 GBR2445 GBR2477 GBR2481
GBR2501 GBR2524 GBR2535 GBR2546
GBR2553 IRL2711 ITA2784 ITA2860
ITA2914 MLT3021 NLD3067 NLD3072
NLD3096 NLD3137 NLD3144 NLD3154
NLD3214 NLD3356 NLD3361 POL3508
SWE3749 SWE3813 SWE3830

SOUTH AMERICA - AMERIQUE DU SUD

AUT0003 AUT0009 AUT0013 AUT0022
AUT0024 AUT0026 AUT0051 AUT0052
AUT0067 AUT0076 AUT0091 BEL0105
BEL0107 BEL0119 BEL0123 BEL0126
BEL0129 BEL0133 BEL0139 BEL0144
BEL0148 BEL0155 BEL0157 BEL0169
BEL0182 BEL0186 BEL0199 BEL0201
BEL0203 BEL0221 BEL0226 BEL0231
BEL0254 BEL0258 BEL0269 BEL0270
BEL0275 BEL0282 BEL0289 BEL0299
BEL0314 BEL0316 BEL0323 BEL0327
BEL0335 BEL0336 BEL0341 BEL0347

See: *How to Use the Directory*, page 11.

BEL0351	BEL0352	BEL0353	BEL0358
BEL0359	BEL0361	BEL0387	BEL0392
CHE0432	CHE0434	CHE0438	CHE0443
CHE0455	CHE0456	CHE0475	CHE0477
CHE0479	CHE0483	CHE0491	CHE0515
CHE0559	CHE0566	CHE0568	CHE0570
CHE0581	CHE0586	CHE0596	CHE0602
CHE0604	CHE0619	CHE0622	CHE0626
CHE0628	CHE0634	CHE0640	CHE0643
CHE0645	CHE0649	CHE0650	CHE0667
CHE0669	CHE0682	CHE0687	CHE0689
CHE0693	CHE0701	CHE0712	CHE0730
CHE0742	CHE0750	CHE0755	CHE0772
CHE0785	CHE0789	CHE0793	CHE0796
CHE0798	CHE0800	CHE0806	CHE0814
CHE0819	DEU0926	DEU0928	DEU0931
DEU0933	DEU0940	DEU0944	DEU0965
DEU0968	DEU0972	DEU0980	DEU0983
DEU0989	DEU0991	DEU0994	DEU0995
DEU1005	DEU1015	DEU1016	DEU1017
DEU1031	DEU1038	DEU1047	DEU1055
DEU1066	DEU1097	DEU1098	DEU1103
DEU1114	DEU1127	DEU1128	DEU1129
DEU1131	DEU1132	DEU1138	DEU1142
DEU1149	DEU1161	DEU1167	DEU1174
DEU1178	DEU1186	DEU1187	DEU1209
DNK1244	DNK1248	DNK1251	DNK1287
DNK1304	DNK1312	DNK1319	DNK1351
DNK1366	DNK1369	DNK1403	
ESP1410	ESP1413	ESP1431	ESP1432
ESP1435	ESP1437	ESP1442	ESP1450
ESP1455	ESP1457	ESP1461	ESP1475
ESP1485	ESP1486	ESP1488	ESP1489
ESP1491	ESP1492	ESP1496	ESP1502
ESP1503	ESP1505	ESP1507	ESP1508
ESP1510	ESP1511	ESP1513	ESP1517
ESP1521	ESP1522	ESP1523	ESP1525
ESP1529	FIN1549	FIN1558	FIN1559
FIN1569	FIN1574	FIN1604	FRA1610
FRA1615	FRA1636	FRA1645	FRA1647
FRA1655	FRA1658	FRA1672	FRA1673
FRA1675	FRA1703	FRA1710	FRA1741
FRA1749	FRA1815	FRA1817	FRA1824
FRA1827	FRA1831	FRA1836	FRA1843
FRA1869	FRA1886	FRA1903	FRA1904
FRA1905	FRA1917	FRA1926	FRA1928
FRA1930	FRA1932	FRA1934	FRA1938
FRA1939	FRA1946	FRA1975	FRA1978
FRA1980	FRA1991	FRA2016	FRA2018
FRA2023	FRA2026	FRA2032	FRA2034
FRA2042	FRA2044	FRA2047	FRA2060
FRA2062	FRA2069	FRA2081	FRA2086
FRA2096	FRA2102	FRA2103	FRA2107
FRA2111	FRA2116	FRA2117	FRA2119
FRA2131	FRA2137	FRA2149	FRA2152
FRA2159	FRA2168	FRA2170	GBR2174
GBR2201	GBR2212	GBR2218	GBR2228
GBR2229	GBR2231	GBR2232	GBR2238
GBR2259	GBR2264	GBR2266	GBR2278
GBR2293	GBR2303	GBR2306	GBR2321
GBR2324	GBR2351	GBR2369	GBR2371
GBR2383	GBR2390	GBR2392	GBR2411
GBR2423	GBR2436	GBR2437	GBR2439
GBR2445	GBR2445	GBR2454	GBR2456
GBR2463	GBR2464	GBR2467	GBR2481
GBR2485	GBR2500	GBR2501	GBR2518
GBR2525	GBR2535	GBR2537	GBR2546
GBR2550	GBR2551	GBR2552	GBR2553
GBR2558	IRL2693	IRL2711	IRL2719
IRL2726	IRL2732	ITA2748	ITA2756
ITA2758	ITA2761	ITA2762	ITA2766
ITA2770	ITA2773	ITA2775	ITA2777
ITA2782	ITA2784	ITA2787	ITA2787
ITA2791	ITA2792	ITA2798	ITA2799
ITA2801	ITA2802	ITA2806	ITA2807
ITA2809	ITA2820	ITA2822	ITA2824
ITA2828	ITA2832	ITA2834	ITA2835
ITA2838	ITA2842	ITA2860	ITA2868
ITA2879	ITA2879	ITA2880	ITA2885
ITA2888	ITA2889	ITA2895	ITA2896
ITA2898	ITA2900	ITA2901	ITA2907
ITA2910	ITA2913	ITA2914	ITA2921
ITA2922	ITA2923	LUX2937	LUX2943
LUX2946	LUX2953	LUX2954	LUX2958
LUX2967	LUX2968	LUX2972	LUX2973
LUX2975	LUX2980	LUX2984	LUX2985
LUX2997	LUX2999	LUX3003	MLT3021
NLD3050	NLD3067	NLD3068	NLD3072
NLD3075	NLD3076	NLD3078	NLD3089

NLD3096	NLD3101	NLD3137	NLD3138
NLD3142	NLD3144	NLD3154	NLD3155
NLD3158	NLD3187	NLD3189	NLD3198
NLD3199	NLD3214	NLD3231	NLD3250
NLD3253	NLD3297	NLD3305	NLD3325
NLD3356	NLD3361	NOR3381	NOR3384
NOR3394	NOR3404	NOR3407	NOR3409
NOR3425	NOR3460	NOR3465	NOR3473
NOR3476	POL3508	POL3519	PRT3549
PRT3552	PRT3600	SWE3656	SWE3666
SWE3674	SWE3693	SWE3695	SWE3702
SWE3712	SWE3730	SWE3744	SWE3749
SWE3754	SWE3763	SWE3769	SWE3771
SWE3781	SWE3795	SWE3796	SWE3821
SWE3826	SWE3828	SWE3830	SWE3831
SWE3855	SWE3857	SWE3865	SWE3876
SWE3877			

SOUTH EAST ASIA - ASIE DU SUD-EST

AUT0013	AUT0024	AUT0051	AUT0052
AUT0076	AUT0091	BEL0097	BEL0107
BEL0123	BEL0144	BEL0186	BEL0199
BEL0203	BEL0221	BEL0231	BEL0254
BEL0269	BEL0284	BEL0289	BEL0299
BEL0306	BEL0315	BEL0316	BEL0327
BEL0340	BEL0341	BEL0342	BEL0351
BEL0358	BEL0359	BEL0361	BEL0392
CHE0432	CHE0434	CHE0456	CHE0477
CHE0479	CHE0559	CHE0566	CHE0568
CHE0570	CHE0586	CHE0604	CHE0619
CHE0622	CHE0626	CHE0630	CHE0634
CHE0637	CHE0638	CHE0643	CHE0645
CHE0649	CHE0665	CHE0669	CHE0681
CHE0682	CHE0689	CHE0712	CHE0730
CHE0749	CHE0773	CHE0785	CHE0793
CHE0796	CHE0798	CHE0814	CHE0819
DEU0928	DEU0940	DEU0944	DEU0947
DEU0954	DEU0968	DEU0972	DEU0980
DEU0983	DEU0986	DEU0989	DEU0994
DEU0995	DEU1005	DEU1015	DEU1016
DEU1017	DEU1047	DEU1055	DEU1097
DEU1103	DEU1106	DEU1116	DEU1127
DEU1128	DEU1129	DEU1132	DEU1146
DEU1149	DEU1174	DEU1178	DEU1186
DEU1187	DEU1209	DNK1229	DNK1238
DNK1287	DNK1292	DNK1316	DNK1360
ESP1420	ESP1435	ESP1492	ESP1510
FIN1549	FIN1567	FIN1599	FIN1603
FIN1604	FRA1610	FRA1614	FRA1615
FRA1628	FRA1629	FRA1634	FRA1638
FRA1640	FRA1645	FRA1647	FRA1667
FRA1672	FRA1683	FRA1715	FRA1749
FRA1817	FRA1820	FRA1824	FRA1850
FRA1869	FRA1871	FRA1886	FRA1891
FRA1905	FRA1917	FRA1920	FRA1928
FRA1930	FRA1934	FRA1937	FRA1938
FRA1939	FRA1941	FRA1946	FRA1966
FRA1967	FRA1978	FRA1979	FRA1980
FRA1983	FRA1992	FRA2005	FRA2023
FRA2026	FRA2032	FRA2034	FRA2039
FRA2041	FRA2044	FRA2053	FRA2054
FRA2060	FRA2062	FRA2069	FRA2076
FRA2080	FRA2081	FRA2096	FRA2097
FRA2116	FRA2117	FRA2119	FRA2126
FRA2140	FRA2159	FRA2162	FRA2168
FRA2170	GBR2175	GBR2201	GBR2210
GBR2212	GBR2218	GBR2228	GBR2232
GBR2238	GBR2240	GBR2242	GBR2260
GBR2264	GBR2266	GBR2278	GBR2293
GBR2306	GBR2310	GBR2321	GBR2324
GBR2346	GBR2349	GBR2350	GBR2351
GBR2353	GBR2369	GBR2371	GBR2382
GBR2385	GBR2390	GBR2392	GBR2410
GBR2411	GBR2423	GBR2435	GBR2436
GBR2437	GBR2441	GBR2445	GBR2467
GBR2477	GBR2481	GBR2494	GBR2498
GBR2500	GBR2501	GBR2508	GBR2533
GBR2535	GBR2537	GBR2546	GBR2553
IRL2687	IRL2691	IRL2711	IRL2726
IRL2733	ITA2756	ITA2758	ITA2766
ITA2775	ITA2784	ITA2785	ITA2798
ITA2824	ITA2830	ITA2849	ITA2860
ITA2868	ITA2888	ITA2894	ITA2898
ITA2902	ITA2912	ITA2914	ITA2920
ITA2922	ITA2923	LUX2954	LUX2973
LUX2997	MLT3021	NLD3050	NLD3067
NLD3068	NLD3069	NLD3070	NLD3072
NLD3076	NLD3078	NLD3096	NLD3117
NLD3137	NLD3138	NLD3141	NLD3142

NLD3144	NLD3146	NLD3154	NLD3155
NLD3158	NLD3183	NLD3198	NLD3199
NLD3214	NLD3231	NLD3237	NLD3245
NLD3253	NLD3292	NLD3297	NLD3300
NLD3325	NLD3356	NOR3372	NOR3381
NOR3390	NOR3395	NOR3407	NOR3425
NOR3431	NOR3437	NOR3465	NOR3467
POL3519	SWE3656	SWE3674	SWE3749
SWE3769	SWE3771	SWE3772	SWE3787
SWE3798	SWE3821	SWE3826	SWE3828
SWE3830	SWE3857		

SOUTHERN AFRICA - AFRIQUE AUSTRALE

AUT0002	AUT0013	AUT0022	AUT0024
AUT0026	AUT0051	AUT0052	AUT0067
AUT0076	AUT0091	BEL0097	BEL0123
BEL0129	BEL0144	BEL0148	BEL0186
BEL0199	BEL0203	BEL0221	BEL0260
BEL0269	BEL0289	BEL0299	BEL0323
BEL0327	BEL0341	BEL0358	BEL0359
BEL0361	BEL0392	CHE0432	CHE0434
CHE0483	CHE0559	CHE0566	CHE0570
CHE0586	CHE0619	CHE0622	CHE0626
CHE0628	CHE0632	CHE0634	CHE0638
CHE0640	CHE0643	CHE0645	CHE0665
CHE0671	CHE0682	CHE0687	CHE0689
CHE0693	CHE0709	CHE0712	CHE0730
CHE0734	CHE0750	CHE0755	CHE0796
CHE0798	CHE0814	CHE0819	CZE0905
DEU0931	DEU0944	DEU0968	DEU0972
DEU0980	DEU0989	DEU0991	DEU0995
DEU1005	DEU1015	DEU1016	DEU1031
DEU1038	DEU1047	DEU1055	DEU1065
DEU1069	DEU1081	DEU1082	DEU1097
DEU1103	DEU1106	DEU1116	DEU1127
DEU1128	DEU1129	DEU1131	DEU1142
DEU1146	DEU1149	DEU1174	DEU1181
DEU1187	DEU1202	DEU1209	DNK1218
DNK1229	DNK1238	DNK1243	DNK1245
DNK1259	DNK1273	DNK1275	DNK1288
DNK1292	DNK1312	DNK1339	DNK1351
DNK1360	DNK1375	DNK1388	ESP1420
ESP1445	ESP1486	ESP1502	ESP1509
ESP1523	FIN1531	FIN1546	FIN1549
FIN1554	FIN1557	FIN1559	FIN1567
FIN1569	FIN1574	FIN1577	FIN1579
FIN1580	FIN1603	FIN1604	FRA1610
FRA1615	FRA1645	FRA1657	FRA1658	FRA1659
FRA1672	FRA1675	FRA1677	FRA1691
FRA1715	FRA1727	FRA1738	FRA1769
FRA1796	FRA1817	FRA1820	FRA1824
FRA1827	FRA1843	FRA1849	FRA1865
FRA1876	FRA1879	FRA1887	FRA1903
FRA1917	FRA1930	FRA1948	FRA1956
FRA1966	FRA1978	FRA1980	FRA2005
FRA2023	FRA2026	FRA2032	FRA2044
FRA2047	FRA2054	FRA2080	FRA2096
FRA2103	FRA2107	FRA2116	FRA2117
FRA2119	FRA2123	FRA2126	FRA2159
FRA2162	FRA2168	FRA2170	GBR2174
GBR2178	GBR2181	GBR2183	GBR2185
GBR2187	GBR2198	GBR2201	GBR2210
GBR2212	GBR2218	GBR2228	GBR2229
GBR2232	GBR2238	GBR2240	GBR2242
GBR2247	GBR2259	GBR2264	GBR2266
GBR2277	GBR2278	GBR2281	GBR2290
GBR2292	GBR2306	GBR2318	GBR2321
GBR2324	GBR2337	GBR2340	GBR2341
GBR2346	GBR2348	GBR2349	GBR2351
GBR2353	GBR2364	GBR2369	GBR2371
GBR2382	GBR2385	GBR2390	GBR2392
GBR2402	GBR2413	GBR2423	GBR2432
GBR2436	GBR2437	GBR2441	GBR2445
GBR2460	GBR2463	GBR2464	GBR2467
GBR2471	GBR2477	GBR2478	GBR2481
GBR2492	GBR2500	GBR2501	GBR2513
GBR2535	GBR2536	GBR2546	GBR2550
GBR2551	GBR2552	GBR2553	GBR2558
GBR2561	GRC2571	GRC2572	GRC2595
IRL2691	IRL2702	IRL2711	IRL2719
IRL2726	IRL2729	IRL2732	ISL2739
ITA2757	ITA2771	ITA2784	ITA2787
ITA2791	ITA2798	ITA2799	ITA2803
ITA2806	ITA2811	ITA2824	ITA2838
ITA2860	ITA2879	ITA2885	ITA2888
ITA2900	ITA2902	ITA2911	ITA2914
ITA2922	ITA2923	LUX2946	LUX2954
LUX2975	LUX2995	LUX2997	MLT3021
NLD3045	NLD3050	NLD3067	NLD3069

NLD3070	NLD3072	NLD3076	NLD3078
NLD3091	NLD3095	NLD3096	NLD3098
NLD3101	NLD3137	NLD3138	NLD3139
NLD3142	NLD3144	NLD3147	NLD3154
NLD3155	NLD3158	NLD3183	NLD3198
NLD3199	NLD3209	NLD3214	NLD3231
NLD3253	NLD3257	NLD3292	NLD3301
NLD3311	NLD3336	NLD3356	NLD3361
NOR3389	NOR3390	NOR3394	NOR3395
NOR3400	NOR3407	NOR3418	NOR3431
NOR3447	NOR3467	NOR3476	POL3508
POL3519	PRT3549	PRT3564	PRT3579
PRT3586	PRT3588	PRT3590	PRT3594
PRT3600	PRT3605	SWE3648	SWE3656
SWE3674	SWE3685	SWE3688	SWE3730
SWE3731	SWE3749	SWE3753	SWE3769
SWE3771	SWE3772	SWE3798	SWE3813
SWE3821	SWE3826	SWE3828	SWE3830
SWE3831	SWE3859		

WEST AFRICA - AFRIQUE DE L'OUEST

AUT0003	AUT0013	AUT0021	AUT0024
AUT0028	AUT0033	AUT0041	AUT0076
AUT0086	AUT0091	BEL0097	BEL0107
BEL0118	BEL0123	BEL0129	BEL0133
BEL0144	BEL0148	BEL0152	BEL0186
BEL0192	BEL0199	BEL0201	BEL0203
BEL0206	BEL0221	BEL0231	BEL0254
BEL0269	BEL0270	BEL0275	BEL0289
BEL0299	BEL0316	BEL0327	BEL0328
BEL0342	BEL0351	BEL0353	BEL0358
BEL0359	BEL0361	BEL0362	BEL0368
BEL0390	BEL0392	CHE0402	CHE0432
CHE0434	CHE0435	CHE0439	CHE0444
CHE0456	CHE0479	CHE0483	CHE0490
CHE0498	CHE0519	CHE0542	CHE0558
CHE0559	CHE0566	CHE0568	CHE0570
CHE0604	CHE0609	CHE0619	CHE0622
CHE0626	CHE0634	CHE0637	CHE0638
CHE0643	CHE0645	CHE0649	CHE0650
CHE0659	CHE0682	CHE0687	CHE0689
CHE0707	CHE0712	CHE0730	CHE0734
CHE0742	CHE0755	CHE0762	CHE0772
CHE0793	CHE0796	CHE0798	CHE0806
CHE0814	CHE0819	CHE0823	CZE0905
DEU0928	DEU0933	DEU0940	DEU0944
DEU0968	DEU0972	DEU0980	DEU0983
DEU0989	DEU0991	DEU0995	DEU1005
DEU1016	DEU1017	DEU1038	DEU1047
DEU1055	DEU1069	DEU1074	DEU1097
DEU1098	DEU1103	DEU1106	DEU1114
DEU1116	DEU1118	DEU1128	DEU1131
DEU1142	DEU1146	DEU1149	DEU1174
DEU1178	DEU1181	DEU1187	DEU1209
DNK1214	DNK1215	DNK1218	DNK1227
DNK1244	DNK1255	DNK1259	DNK1266
DNK1287	DNK1304	DNK1306	DNK1307
DNK1318	DNK1320	DNK1360	DNK1366
DNK1369	DNK1374	DNK1397	ESP1468
ESP1486	ESP1488	ESP1492	ESP1502
ESP1507	ESP1510	ESP1514	ESP1517
FIN1531	FIN1549	FIN1563	FIN1567
FIN1580	FIN1604	FRA1607	FRA1610
FRA1612	FRA1614	FRA1615	FRA1619
FRA1621	FRA1624	FRA1629	FRA1632
FRA1634	FRA1636	FRA1644	FRA1645
FRA1651	FRA1655	FRA1658	FRA1663
FRA1664	FRA1672	FRA1675	FRA1677
FRA1679	FRA1683	FRA1690	FRA1699
FRA1715	FRA1727	FRA1731	FRA1737
FRA1739	FRA1746	FRA1752	FRA1760
FRA1761	FRA1778	FRA1785	FRA1786
FRA1787	FRA1789	FRA1794	FRA1796
FRA1799	FRA1815	FRA1817	FRA1820
FRA1824	FRA1827	FRA1835	FRA1836
FRA1843	FRA1844	FRA1846	FRA1848
FRA1869	FRA1871	FRA1876	FRA1879
FRA1880	FRA1885	FRA1886	FRA1887
FRA1893	FRA1903	FRA1905	FRA1907
FRA1913	FRA1914	FRA1917	FRA1926
FRA1929	FRA1930	FRA1932	
FRA1934	FRA1935	FRA1939	FRA1946
FRA1956	FRA1966	FRA1967	FRA1978
FRA1980	FRA1986	FRA1991	FRA1992
FRA1993	FRA2005	FRA2006	FRA2009
FRA2012	FRA2018	FRA2021	FRA2026
FRA2032	FRA2034	FRA2039	FRA2042
FRA2043	FRA2044	FRA2051	FRA2054

FRA2060	FRA2061	FRA2062	FRA2069
FRA2077	FRA2084	FRA2086	FRA2096
FRA2103	FRA2105	FRA2106	FRA2107
FRA2108	FRA2114	FRA2116	FRA2117
FRA2119	FRA2122	FRA2123	FRA2126
FRA2131	FRA2137	FRA2138	FRA2149
FRA2150	FRA2159	FRA2161	FRA2162
FRA2168	FRA2170	GBR2174	GBR2175
GBR2178	GBR2180	GBR2183	GBR2185
GBR2187	GBR2198	GBR2201	GBR2210
GBR2218	GBR2228	GBR2232	GBR2238
GBR2242	GBR2247	GBR2259	GBR2264
GBR2274	GBR2278	GBR2303	GBR2337
GBR2340	GBR2341	GBR2346	GBR2351
GBR2353	GBR2369	GBR2371	GBR2382
GBR2383	GBR2385	GBR2390	GBR2392
GBR2423	GBR2436	GBR2437	GBR2439
GBR2445	GBR2460	GBR2463	GBR2464
GBR2472	GBR2477	GBR2481	GBR2483
GBR2500	GBR2501	GBR2513	GBR2515
GBR2517	GBR2518	GBR2525	GBR2533
GBR2535	GBR2546	GBR2550	GBR2552
GBR2553	GBR2558	GRC2567	GRC2586
IRL2711	IRL2726	IRL2732	IRL2733
ISL2739	ITA2756	ITA2761	ITA2762
ITA2766	ITA2770	ITA2773	ITA2774
ITA2782	ITA2784	ITA2786	ITA2791
ITA2801	ITA2803	ITA2824	ITA2826
ITA2827	ITA2829	ITA2838	ITA2840
ITA2842	ITA2860	ITA2873	ITA2885
ITA2888	ITA2898	ITA2901	ITA2902
ITA2914	ITA2915	ITA2922	ITA2923
LUX2937	LUX2946	LUX2948	LUX2954
LUX2959	LUX2973	LUX2975	LUX2976
LUX2978	LUX2986	LUX2997	LUX3006
MLT3021	NLD3045	NLD3067	NLD3068
NLD3072	NLD3074	NLD3075	NLD3076
NLD3078	NLD3096	NLD3101	NLD3137
NLD3138	NLD3144	NLD3147	NLD3153
NLD3154	NLD3155	NLD3158	NLD3165
NLD3173	NLD3176	NLD3187	NLD3189
NLD3198	NLD3199	NLD3214	NLD3231
NLD3254	NLD3257	NLD3269	NLD3288
NLD3292	NLD3300	NLD3301	NLD3311
NLD3325	NLD3356	NLD3361	NOR3387
NOR3403	NOR3443	NOR3453	NOR3460
NOR3465	POL3508	POL3519	PRT3549
PRT3564	PRT3579	PRT3597	PRT3599
PRT3603	SWE3648	SWE3656	SWE3666
SWE3674	SWE3695	SWE3701	SWE3702
SWE3707	SWE3712	SWE3749	SWE3753
SWE3769	SWE3772	SWE3783	SWE3821
SWE3828	SWE3830	SWE3831	SWE3879

EMERGENCY RELIEF, REFUGEES, HUMANITARIAN ASSISTANCE - SECOURS D'URGENCE, REFUGIES, AIDE HUMANITAIRE

CARIBBEAN - CARAIBES

BEL0097	BEL0107	BEL0124	BEL0144
BEL0198	BEL0224	BEL0316	BEL0323
BEL0338	BEL0358	BEL0362	CHE0420
CHE0434	CHE0510	CHE0580	CHE0655
CHE0689	CHE0711	CHE0730	CHE0757
CHE0798	CHE0814	CHE0819	DEU0944
DEU0983	DEU0989	DEU1053	DEU1108
DEU1131	ESP1451	ESP1475	FIN1587
FRA1610	FRA1614	FRA1676	FRA1685
FRA1824	FRA1904	FRA1934	FRA1975
FRA2062	FRA2096	FRA2102	FRA2116
FRA2154	GBR2175	GBR2238	GBR2266
GBR2361	GBR2371	GBR2392	GBR2463
GBR2489	GBR2500	GBR2501	GBR2552
GBR2555	ISL2739	ITA2766	ITA2773
ITA2784	ITA2860	ITA2911	LUX2992
LUX2993	NLD3050	NLD3102	NLD3144
NLD3231	NLD3277	NLD3356	NLD3361
NLD3364	NOR3381	POL3519	PRT3600
SWE3712	SWE3749	SWE3830	

CENTRAL AFRICA - AFRIQUE CENTRALE

AUT0076	BEL0097	BEL0105	BEL0107
BEL0124	BEL0128	BEL0129	BEL0144
BEL0148	BEL0152	BEL0158	BEL0169
BEL0192	BEL0198	BEL0201	BEL0218

BEL0284	BEL0297	BEL0299	BEL0301
BEL0315	BEL0316	BEL0318	BEL0328
BEL0338	BEL0350	BEL0352	BEL0358
BEL0359	CHE0420	CHE0434	CHE0477
CHE0510	CHE0541	CHE0559	CHE0562
CHE0580	CHE0637	CHE0643	CHE0655
CHE0683	CHE0684	CHE0687	CHE0689
CHE0711	CHE0730	CHE0750	CHE0755
CHE0759	CHE0796	CHE0814	CHE0817
CHE0819	DEU0928	DEU0944	DEU0968
DEU0978	DEU0989	DEU0991	DEU1006
DEU1017	DEU1053	DEU1108	DEU1110
DEU1131	DEU1141	DEU1146	DNK1214
DNK1227	DNK1248	DNK1272	DNK1292
DNK1358	ESP1435	ESP1451	ESP1486
ESP1493	ESP1513	ESP1528	FIN1549
FIN1587	FRA1610	FRA1614	FRA1617
FRA1647	FRA1715	FRA1740	FRA1771
FRA1819	FRA1824	FRA1904	FRA1928
FRA1934	FRA1948	FRA1956	FRA1978
FRA1991	FRA2012	FRA2047	FRA2080
FRA2091	FRA2097	FRA2102	FRA2116
FRA2117	FRA2119	FRA2149	FRA2154
FRA2164	GBR2174	GBR2175	GBR2185
GBR2187	GBR2222	GBR2238	GBR2240
GBR2259	GBR2280	GBR2289	GBR2293
GBR2361	GBR2371	GBR2392	GBR2422
GBR2423	GBR2464	GBR2467	GBR2500
GBR2525	GBR2555	GRC2586	HUN2631
IRL2732	ISL2739	ITA2747	ITA2766
ITA2774	ITA2784	ITA2785	ITA2816
ITA2818	ITA2855	ITA2860	ITA2873
ITA2874	ITA2888	ITA2890	ITA2898
ITA2902	ITA2916	ITA2921	LIE2930
LUX2942	LUX2955	LUX2956	NLD3050
NLD3068	NLD3095	NLD3102	NLD3137
NLD3144	NLD3186	NLD3199	NLD3201
NLD3277	NLD3300	NLD3356	NLD3361
NLD3364	NOR3412	NOR3435	NOR3465
POL3519	PRT3549	PRT3555	PRT3602
SWE3749	SWE3769	SWE3827	SWE3828
SWE3830			

CENTRAL ASIA AND SOUTH ASIA - ASIE CENTRALE ET ASIE DU SUD

AUT0063	AUT0091	BEL0097	BEL0107
BEL0124	BEL0144	BEL0192	BEL0198
BEL0201	BEL0207	BEL0306	BEL0315
BEL0338	BEL0340	BEL0358	BEL0359
BEL0368	CHE0412	CHE0417	CHE0420
CHE0434	CHE0467	CHE0477	CHE0491
CHE0510	CHE0558	CHE0559	CHE0580
CHE0637	CHE0655	CHE0682	CHE0689
CHE0711	CHE0730	CHE0757	CHE0814
CHE0817	CHE0819	DEU0944	DEU0968
DEU0983	DEU0985	DEU0989	DEU0993
DEU1006	DEU1017	DEU1066	DEU1086
DEU1086	DEU1108	DEU1121	DEU1131
DEU1146	DEU1149	DEU1187	DNK1260
DNK1304	DNK1451	ESP1435	ESP1451
FIN1549	FIN1587	FRA1610	FRA1647
FRA1661	FRA1715	FRA1824	FRA1862
FRA1866	FRA1904	FRA1934	FRA1978
FRA2047	FRA2102	FRA2116	FRA2117
FRA2119	FRA2154	GBR2174	GBR2175
GBR2176	GBR2186	GBR2197	GBR2222
GBR2226	GBR2228	GBR2238	GBR2266
GBR2280	GBR2303	GBR2358	GBR2361
GBR2371	GBR2385	GBR2392	GBR2410
GBR2413	GBR2423	GBR2436	GBR2463
GBR2464	GBR2467	GBR2475	GBR2500
GBR2501	GBR2506	GBR2509	GBR2555
IRL2726	IRL2733	ISL2739	ITA2766
ITA2784	ITA2824	ITA2860	ITA2868
ITA2873	ITA2902	ITA2911	LUX2955
LUX2959	LUX2964	LUX2982	NLD3050
NLD3051	NLD3091	NLD3095	NLD3102
NLD3144	NLD3199	NLD3201	NLD3253
NLD3260	NLD3277	NLD3297	NLD3300
NLD3317	NLD3356	NLD3361	NLD3364
NOR3371	NOR3384	NOR3390	NOR3431
NOR3435	NOR3460	NOR3465	NOR3467
POL3508	POL3519	POL3521	SWE3674
SWE3749	SWE3763	SWE3769	SWE3771
SWE3818	SWE3827	SWE3828	SWE3830
SWE3834	SWE3854		

See: *How to Use the Directory*, page 11.

EAST AFRICA - AFRIQUE DE L'EST

AUT0033	AUT0076	AUT0085	BEL0097
BEL0107	BEL0124	BEL0144	BEL0198
BEL0224	BEL0284	BEL0297	BEL0299
BEL0301	BEL0316	BEL0318	BEL0323
BEL0338	BEL0353	BEL0358	BEL0359
CHE0420	CHE0434	CHE0448	CHE0510
CHE0559	CHE0570	CHE0580	CHE0586
CHE0620	CHE0630	CHE0637	CHE0660
CHE0682	CHE0683	CHE0684	CHE0687
CHE0689	CHE0711	CHE0730	CHE0755
CHE0757	CHE0759	CHE0764	CHE0798
CHE0814	CHE0817	CHE0819	CHE0823
DEU0918	DEU0922	DEU0936	DEU0939
DEU0944	DEU0965	DEU0968	DEU0978
DEU0983	DEU0989	DEU0991	DEU0994
DEU1006	DEU1017	DEU1053	DEU1108
DEU1109	DEU1129	DEU1131	DEU1141
DEU1145	DEU1146	DEU1181	DNK1214
DNK1245	DNK1259	DNK1275	DNK1292
DNK1339	DNK1351	DNK1358	ESP1432
ESP1435	ESP1451	ESP1486	ESP1493
ESP1510	ESP1528	FIN1956	FIN1587
FRA1610	FRA1614	FRA1644	FRA1651
FRA1715	FRA1824	FRA1855	FRA1887
FRA1934	FRA1956	FRA1967	FRA2041
FRA2046	FRA2047	FRA2062	FRA2080
FRA2087	FRA2096	FRA2116	FRA2117
FRA2154	GBR2174	GBR2175	GBR2179
GBR2183	GBR2185	GBR2187	GBR2226
GBR2228	GBR2238	GBR2240	GBR2259
GBR2280	GBR2282	GBR2292	GBR2293
GBR2303	GBR2324	GBR2348	GBR2350
GBR2353	GBR2361	GBR2371	GBR2390
GBR2392	GBR2410	GBR2422	GBR2423
GBR2459	GBR2463	GBR2464	GBR2467
GBR2483	GBR2489	GBR2500	GBR2501
GBR2502	GBR2523	GBR2552	GBR2555
GBR2556	GRC2586	IRL2687	IRL2691
IRL2699	IRL2725	IRL2726	IRL2730
IRL2732	IRL2733	ISL2736	ISL2739
ISL2740	ITA2766	ITA2767	ITA2772
ITA2782	ITA2784	ITA2785	ITA2787
ITA2813	ITA2816	ITA2818	ITA2820
ITA2822	ITA2829	ITA2835	ITA2840
ITA2841	ITA2857	ITA2860	ITA2873
ITA2877	ITA2879	ITA2888	ITA2889
ITA2890	ITA2898	ITA2902	LUX2955
LUX2956	LUX2975	NLD3050	NLD3068
NLD3075	NLD3091	NLD3102	NLD3137
NLD3144	NLD3186	NLD3199	NLD3201
NLD3216	NLD3231	NLD3253	NLD3253
NLD3277	NLD3297	NLD3300	NLD3317
NLD3356	NLD3361	NLD3364	NOR3381
NOR3412	NOR3435	NOR3443	NOR3465
NOR3467	POL3519	PRT3576	PRT3597
SWE3666	SWE3679	SWE3712	SWE3749
SWE3769	SWE3771	SWE3826	SWE3828
SWE3830	SWE3854	SWE3857	SWE3864

EAST ASIA - ASIE DE L'EST

BEL0097	BEL0107	BEL0124	BEL0144
BEL0198	BEL0338	BEL0358	CHE0420
CHE0434	CHE0510	CHE0570	CHE0637
CHE0655	CHE0689	CHE0711	CHE0730
CHE0814	CHE0819	DEU0944	DEU0989
DEU0994	DEU1006	DEU1108	DEU1146
ESP1451	FRA1610	FRA2047	FRA2116
FRA2154	GBR2175	GBR2222	GBR2228
GBR2266	GBR2361	GBR2371	GBR2392
GBR2464	GBR2467	GBR2501	GBR2555
GBR2556	IRL2726	ISL2739	ITA2766
ITA2784	ITA2785	ITA2860	NLD3102
NLD3144	NLD3201	NLD3277	NLD3356
NLD3364	NOR3435	NOR3465	SWE3712
SWE3749	SWE3830		

MEXICO AND CENTRAL AMERICA - MEXIQUE ET AMERIQUE CENTRALE

AUT0076	BEL0097	BEL0107	BEL0124
BEL0129	BEL0144	BEL0198	BEL0201
BEL0315	BEL0316	BEL0318	BEL0338
BEL0358	CHE0420	CHE0434	CHE0510
CHE0559	CHE0570	CHE0580	CHE0637
CHE0683	CHE0689	CHE0711	CHE0730
CHE0757	CHE0814	CHE0819	DEU0944
DEU0968	DEU0983	DEU0989	DEU1053
DEU1108	DEU1109	DEU1131	DEU1143

DEU1149	DEU1187	DNK1226	DNK1292
DNK1317	ESP1427	ESP1450	ESP1451
ESP1475	ESP1486	ESP1493	ESP1506
ESP1521	ESP1528	FIN1549	FIN1587
FRA1610	FRA1685	FRA1824	FRA1904
FRA1934	FRA1938	FRA1942	FRA2041
FRA2080	FRA2102	FRA2116	FRA2117
FRA2150	FRA2154	GBR2174	GBR2175
GBR2228	GBR2229	GBR2238	GBR2244
GBR2280	GBR2293	GBR2303	GBR2361
GBR2371	GBR2373	GBR2392	GBR2463
GBR2500	GBR2501	GBR2552	GBR2555
IRL2707	ISL2739	ITA2762	ITA2766
ITA2773	ITA2784	ITA2785	ITA2809
ITA2834	ITA2838	ITA2855	ITA2860
ITA2881	ITA2902	NLD3095	NLD3102
NLD3144	NLD3263	NLD3277	NLD3300
NLD3303	NLD3356	NLD3361	NLD3364
NOR3390	NOR3467	POL3508	POL3519
PRT3600	SWE3664	SWE3666	SWE3674
SWE3676	SWE3687	SWE3749	SWE3771
SWE3830	SWE3864	SWE3865	

MIDDLE EAST - MOYEN-ORIENT

AUT0035	BEL0105	BEL0124	BEL0129
BEL0144	BEL0198	BEL0297	BEL0299
BEL0306	BEL0316	BEL0318	BEL0323
BEL0338	BEL0353	BEL0358	CHE0410
CHE0420	CHE0434	CHE0510	CHE0559
CHE0580	CHE0640	CHE0655	CHE0684
CHE0689	CHE0711	CHE0730	CHE0741
CHE0757	CHE0796	CHE0814	CHE0819
CZE0906	DEU0918	DEU0939	DEU0944
DEU0983	DEU0989	DEU1017	DEU1108
DEU1131	DEU1141	DEU1146	DNK1292
DNK1304	ESP1435	ESP1450	ESP1451
FIN1570	FIN1587	FRA1610	FRA1617
FRA1651	FRA1715	FRA1771	FRA1791
FRA1793	FRA1942	FRA1948	
FRA1978	FRA2116	FRA2117	FRA2154
GBR2229	GBR2230	GBR2238	GBR2244
GBR2303	GBR2361	GBR2371	GBR2378
GBR2392	GBR2422	GBR2464	GBR2500
GBR2501	GBR2555	GBR2556	ISL2736
ISL2739	ITA2773	ITA2775	ITA2782
ITA2784	ITA2809	ITA2824	ITA2855
ITA2860	ITA2911	ITA2916	LUX2955
LUX2992	NLD3050	NLD3102	NLD3144
NLD3183	NLD3201	NLD3277	NLD3300
NLD3356	NLD3364	NOR3435	NOR3460
POL3519	SWE3666	SWE3674	SWE3730
SWE3749	SWE3771	SWE3828	SWE3830
TUR3883			

NORTH AFRICA - AFRIQUE DU NORD

AUT0058	BEL0097	BEL0124	BEL0144
BEL0198	BEL0316	BEL0338	BEL0353
BEL0358	CHE0409	CHE0420	CHE0434
CHE0477	CHE0506	CHE0510	CHE0570
CHE0655	CHE0682	CHE0689	CHE0711
CHE0730	CHE0753	CHE0814	DEU0944
DEU0989	DEU1017	DEU1063	DEU1108
DEU1146	DEU1191	DNK1275	DNK1304
DNK1358	DNK1366	ESP1435	ESP1451
ESP1493	ESP1521	FIN1587	FRA1610
FRA1715	FRA1926	FRA1956	FRA2057
FRA2116	FRA2154	GBR2185	GBR2361
GBR2371	GBR2392	GBR2413	GBR2501
GBR2555	ISL2739	ITA2766	ITA2784
ITA2785	ITA2822	ITA2838	ITA2860
ITA2911	LUX2955	MLT3036	NLD3102
NLD3144	NLD3201	NLD3277	NLD3356
NLD3364	POL3519	SWE3664	SWE3676
SWE3749	SWE3770	SWE3771	SWE3830

OCEANIA - OCEANIE

BEL0107	BEL0124	BEL0198	BEL0358
CHE0420	CHE0434	CHE0510	CHE0711
CHE0730	CHE0814	CHE0819	DEU0944
DEU0989	DEU0992	DEU1108	DEU1146
ESP1451	FRA1610	FRA2096	FRA2116
FRA2154	GBR2266	GBR2361	GBR2371
GBR2392	GBR2489	GBR2501	GBR2524
GBR2555	ITA2766	ITA2784	ITA2860
NLD3144	NLD3277	NLD3356	NLD3361
NLD3364	NOR3435	SWE3830	

SOUTH AMERICA - AMERIQUE DU SUD

AUT0076	BEL0097	BEL0105	BEL0107
BEL0124	BEL0129	BEL0144	BEL0198
BEL0201	BEL0316	BEL0318	BEL0338
BEL0358	CHE0420	CHE0434	CHE0438
CHE0475	CHE0477	CHE0510	CHE0515
CHE0559	CHE0580	CHE0637	CHE0689
CHE0711	CHE0720	CHE0730	CHE0757
CHE0814	CHE0819	DEU0944	DEU0983
DEU0989	DEU1006	DEU1108	DEU1129
DEU1187	DNK1248	DNK1304	ESP1435
ESP1450	ESP1451	ESP1461	ESP1493
ESP1508	ESP1521	ESP1528	FIN1549
FIN1587	FRA1610	FRA1685	FRA1824
FRA1904	FRA1930	FRA1934	FRA1938
FRA1978	FRA2062	FRA2102	FRA2116
FRA2154	GBR2174	GBR2175	GBR2228
GBR2238	GBR2280	GBR2361	GBR2371
GBR2392	GBR2463	GBR2489	GBR2500
GBR2501	GBR2555	ISL2739	ITA2766
ITA2773	ITA2784	ITA2785	ITA2835
ITA2860	ITA2916	LUX2949	LUX2955
LUX2956	LUX2968	LUX2992	NLD3050
NLD3102	NLD3144	NLD3277	NLD3356
NLD3364	NOR3381	NOR3435	NOR3465
POL3519	SWE3693	SWE3712	SWE3730
SWE3744	SWE3749	SWE3763	SWE3771
SWE3827	SWE3828	SWE3830	SWE3865

SOUTH EAST ASIA - ASIE DU SUD-EST

BEL0107	BEL0124	BEL0144	BEL0198
BEL0297	BEL0306	BEL0315	BEL0316
BEL0318	BEL0338	BEL0358	CHE0420
CHE0434	CHE0477	CHE0479	CHE0491
CHE0510	CHE0559	CHE0570	CHE0580
CHE0637	CHE0682	CHE0689	CHE0711
CHE0730	CHE0757	CHE0814	CHE0819
DEU0944	DEU0983	DEU0989	DEU1006
DEU1053	DEU1108	DEU1110	DEU1132
DEU1146	DEU1187	DNK1292	ESP1435
ESP1451	FIN1549	FIN1587	FRA1610
FRA1614	FRA1615	FRA1638	FRA1640
FRA1647	FRA1667	FRA1715	FRA1824
FRA1850	FRA1934	FRA1937	FRA1967
FRA1978	FRA1979	FRA2041	FRA2047
FRA2080	FRA2116	FRA2140	FRA2154
GBR2175	GBR2222	GBR2228	GBR2238
GBR2240	GBR2293	GBR2324	GBR2361
GBR2371	GBR2392	GBR2422	GBR2423
GBR2436	GBR2467	GBR2498	GBR2500
GBR2501	GBR2552	GBR2555	IRL2687
IRL2691	IRL2726	ISL2739	ITA2766
ITA2784	ITA2785	ITA2860	ITA2902
NLD3050	NLD3051	NLD3083	NLD3091
NLD3102	NLD3137	NLD3144	NLD3235
NLD3253	NLD3277	NLD3297	NLD3300
NLD3317	NLD3356	NLD3364	NOR3369
NOR3372	NOR3390	NOR3435	NOR3465
NOR3467	POL3512	POL3519	SWE3674
SWE3749	SWE3771	SWE3830	SWE3857

SOUTHERN AFRICA - AFRIQUE AUSTRALE

AUT0091	BEL0097	BEL0124	BEL0129
BEL0144	BEL0198	BEL0260	BEL0297
BEL0338	BEL0358	BEL0359	CHE0414
CHE0420	CHE0434	CHE0510	CHE0559
CHE0580	CHE0586	CHE0628	CHE0637
CHE0682	CHE0683	CHE0687	CHE0689
CHE0711	CHE0730	CHE0755	CHE0757
CHE0759	CHE0796	CHE0814	CHE0817
CHE0819	DEU0944	DEU0965	DEU0989
DEU1006	DEU1082	DEU1108	DEU1109
DEU1131	DEU1146	DEU1181	DEU1187
DNK1245	DNK1248	DNK1259	DNK1275
DNK1288	DNK1292	DNK1339	DNK1366
DNK1388	ESP1420	ESP1435	ESP1450
ESP1451	ESP1486	ESP1493	FIN1549
FIN1587	FRA1610	FRA1614	FRA1651
FRA1657	FRA1715	FRA1771	FRA1824
FRA1876	FRA1956	FRA2047	FRA2080
FRA2116	FRA2154	GBR2174	GBR2185
GBR2187	GBR2226	GBR2228	GBR2238
GBR2240	GBR2244	GBR2259	GBR2266
GBR2293	GBR2303	GBR2324	GBR2353
GBR2361	GBR2371	GBR2385	GBR2390
GBR2392	GBR2413	GBR2422	GBR2423
GBR2436	GBR2463	GBR2464	GBR2467
GBR2489	GBR2500	GBR2501	GBR2536

GBR2552	GBR2555	GBR2556	IRL2691
IRL2726	ISL2739	ITA2766	ITA2784
ITA2785	ITA2791	ITA2811	ITA2816
ITA2838	ITA2860	ITA2881	ITA2898
ITA2900	ITA2902	ITA2911	ITA2916
LIE2925	LUX2995	NLD3050	NLD3091
NLD3095	NLD3098	NLD3102	NLD3137
NLD3144	NLD3183	NLD3199	NLD3201
NLD3277	NLD3300	NLD3317	NLD3336
NLD3356	NLD3361	NLD3364	NOR3381
NOR3390	NOR3435	NOR3467	POL3519
PRT3549	PRT3552	PRT3555	PRT3576
PRT3590	PRT3596	PRT3600	PRT3603
SWE3648	SWE3664	SWE3666	SWE3674
SWE3676	SWE3730	SWE3749	SWE3769
SWE3826	SWE3828	SWE3830	SWE3859
SWE3864			

WEST AFRICA - AFRIQUE DE L'OUEST

AUT0063	AUT0076	BEL0107	BEL0124
BEL0144	BEL0152	BEL0198	BEL0201
BEL0297	BEL0316	BEL0318	BEL0328
BEL0338	BEL0352	BEL0353	BEL0358
CHE0420	CHE0434	CHE0510	CHE0519
CHE0580	CHE0629	CHE0637	CHE0682
CHE0684	CHE0686	CHE0687	CHE0689
CHE0711	CHE0730	CHE0734	CHE0757
CHE0759	CHE0764	CHE0814	CHE0819
DEU0918	DEU0939	DEU0944	DEU0983
DEU0989	DEU0994	DEU1006	DEU1017
DEU1053	DEU1108	DEU1131	DEU1146
DEU1181	DEU1187	DNK1214	DNK1266
DNK1304	DNK1307	DNK1374	ESP1451
ESP1486	ESP1493	ESP1524	ESP1528
FIN1549	FIN1587	FRA1610	FRA1614
FRA1615	FRA1651	FRA1664	FRA1715
FRA1739	FRA1771	FRA1778	FRA1785
FRA1787	FRA1824	FRA1880	FRA1887
FRA1929	FRA1934	FRA1948	FRA1956
FRA1967	FRA1978	FRA2047	FRA2077
FRA2087	FRA2116	FRA2119	FRA2148
FRA2154	GBR2174	GBR2175	GBR2185
GBR2187	GBR2226	GBR2228	GBR2238
GBR2259	GBR2280	GBR2361	GBR2371
GBR2385	GBR2392	GBR2422	GBR2436
GBR2463	GBR2464	GBR2472	GBR2489
GBR2500	GBR2521	GBR2552	GBR2555
GRC2567	GRC2586	IRL2726	IRL2732
ISL2739	ITA2744	ITA2765	ITA2766
ITA2773	ITA2784	ITA2785	ITA2791
ITA2809	ITA2841	ITA2855	ITA2860
ITA2873	ITA2898	ITA2902	ITA2916
LUX2955	LUX2964	LUX2969	LUX2964
LUX2978	LUX2992	NLD3050	NLD3091
NLD3102	NLD3137	NLD3144	NLD3201
NLD3277	NLD3300	NLD3356	NLD3361
NLD3364	NOR3435	NOR3453	NOR3465
POL3519	PRT3549	PRT3555	PRT3597
SWE3666	SWE3674	SWE3707	SWE3712
SWE3749	SWE3769	SWE3828	SWE3830

ENERGY, TRANSPORT - ENERGIE, TRANSPORT

CARIBBEAN - CARAIBES

BEL0198	BEL0218	BEL0265	BEL0323
BEL0359	BEL0397	CHE0434	CHE0465
CHE0568	CHE0655	CHE0689	DEU1174
DNK1291	DNK1300	DNK1314	ESP1419
ESP1442	ESP1475	ESP1492	ESP1522
ESP1525	FRA1860	FRA1917	FRA2062
FRA2096	GBR2218	GBR2221	GBR2266
GBR2294	GBR2361	GBR2371	GBR2501
GBR2553	ITA2773	ITA2822	ITA2860
NLD3067	NLD3078	NLD3137	NLD3271
NLD3353	POL3508	POL3519	SWE3789

CENTRAL AFRICA - AFRIQUE CENTRALE

BEL0158	BEL0198	BEL0218	BEL0265
BEL0359	BEL0397	CHE0434	CHE0459
CHE0541	CHE0562	CHE0568	CHE0604
CHE0655	CHE0689	CHE0778	DEU0919
DEU0965	DEU0968	DEU1131	DEU1174
DNK1214	DNK1255	DNK1300	DNK1314
ESP1492	FRA1731	FRA1781	FRA1879
FRA1917	FRA1948	FRA1956	FRA1992

CENTRAL ASIA AND SOUTH ASIA - ASIE CENTRALE ET ASIE DU SUD

BEL0198	BEL0265	BEL0340	BEL0341
BEL0397	CHE0403	CHE0434	CHE0568
CHE0619	CHE0655	CHE0689	DEU0965
DEU0971	DEU0990	DEU1086	DEU1149
DEU1151	DEU1174	DNK1248	DNK1291
DNK1300	DNK1314	ESP1492	FIN1594
FRA1917	FRA1927	FRA2096	FRA2144
GBR2186	GBR2197	GBR2218	GBR2221
GBR2238	GBR2266	GBR2278	GBR2333
GBR2358	GBR2361	GBR2371	GBR2475
GBR2501	GBR2553	ITA2773	ITA2860
NLD3056	NLD3067	NLD3260	NLD3271
NLD3318	NLD3353	NLD3361	NOR3371
NOR3459	POL3519	SWE3749	SWE3763
SWE3769	SWE3789	SWE3818	

EAST AFRICA - AFRIQUE DE L'EST

AUT0063	AUT0085	BEL0198	BEL0265
BEL0397	CHE0434	CHE0459	CHE0682
CHE0684	CHE0689	CHE0754	DEU0919
DEU0965	DEU0968	DEU1131	DEU1174
DNK1255	DNK1275	DNK1285	DNK1291
DNK1300	DNK1314	DNK1342	ESP1492
FIN1580	FRA1731	FRA1879	FRA1917
FRA1956	FRA1992	FRA2062	FRA2096
FRA2144	GBR2185	GBR2214	GBR2218
GBR2221	GBR2238	GBR2278	GBR2339
GBR2361	GBR2371	GBR2460	GBR2464
GBR2497	GBR2500	GBR2501	GBR2553
IRL2699	IRL2732	ITA2820	ITA2860
NLD3067	NLD3101	NLD3107	NLD3137
NLD3155	NLD3169	NLD3183	NLD3216
NLD3271	NLD3353	NLD3366	POL3519
SWE3727	SWE3749	SWE3789	SWE3806
SWE3828	SWE3853		

EAST ASIA - ASIE DE L'EST

BEL0198	BEL0265	BEL0397	CHE0434
CHE0655	CHE0689	DEU0971	DEU1174
DNK1300	DNK1314	ESP1492	ESP1508
FRA1917	FRA1992	FRA2096	GBR2218
GBR2221	GBR2278	GBR2361	GBR2371
GBR2464	GBR2501	GBR2553	ITA2860
NLD3067	NLD3353	SWE3763	SWE3789

MEXICO AND CENTRAL AMERICA - MEXIQUE ET AMERIQUE CENTRALE

AUT0040	BEL0198	BEL0265	BEL0397
CHE0434	CHE0465	CHE0568	CHE0689
DEU1129	DEU1149	DEU1174	DEU1202
DNK1300	DNK1314	ESP1409	ESP1413
ESP1442	ESP1475	ESP1485	ESP1492
ESP1506	ESP1525	FRA1917	FRA2062
FRA2096	GBR2218	GBR2221	GBR2361
GBR2371	GBR2501	GBR2553	IRL2707
ITA2762	ITA2773	ITA2860	NLD3067
NLD3101	NLD3263	NLD3271	NLD3353
NLD3361	NLD3366	POL3508	POL3519
SWE3687	SWE3789		

MIDDLE EAST - MOYEN-ORIENT

BEL0198	BEL0306	BEL0397	CHE0434
CHE0568	CHE0655	CHE0684	CHE0689
DEU1065	DEU1143	DEU1150	DEU1174
DNK1300	DNK1314	ESP1522	FRA1917
FRA2096	GBR2218	GBR2221	GBR2361
GBR2371	GBR2501	ITA2860	MLT3018
NLD3067	NLD3271	NLD3353	POL3519
SWE3789	TUR3883		

NORTH AFRICA - AFRIQUE DU NORD

BEL0198	BEL0265	BEL0397	CHE0434
CHE0565	CHE0568	CHE0655	CHE0682
CHE0689	DEU0919	DEU1174	DEU1191
DNK1255	DNK1300	DNK1314	ESP1442

ESP1492	FRA1846	FRA1917	FRA1927
FRA1956	FRA1992	FRA2096	GBR2185
GBR2218	GBR2221	GBR2361	GBR2371
GBR2501	GBR2553	MLT3018	NLD3067
NLD3117	NLD3271	NLD3353	POL3508
POL3519	SWE3789		

OCEANIA - OCEANIE

BEL0198	BEL0397	CHE0434	CHE0565
DNK1300	DNK1314	FRA1917	FRA2096
GBR2218	GBR2221	GBR2266	GBR2361
GBR2371	GBR2501	GBR2553	ITA2860
NLD3067	NLD3137	NLD3271	NLD3353
SWE3789			

SOUTH AMERICA - AMERIQUE DU SUD

BEL0119	BEL0133	BEL0198	BEL0265
BEL0331	BEL0359	BEL0397	CHE0434
CHE0465	CHE0565	CHE0568	CHE0602
CHE0689	CHE0806	DEU0965	DEU0990
DEU1129	DEU1149	DEU1174	DNK1291
DNK1300	DNK1314	ESP1409	ESP1442
ESP1452	ESP1485	ESP1488	ESP1492
ESP1525	FRA1917	FRA1927	FRA2062
FRA2096	GBR2201	GBR2218	GBR2221
GBR2266	GBR2361	GBR2371	GBR2383
GBR2501	GBR2553	ITA2773	ITA2807
ITA2820	ITA2860	NLD3067	NLD3101
NLD3137	NLD3181	NLD3253	NLD3271
NLD3318	NLD3353	NLD3366	POL3508
POL3519	SWE3695	SWE3744	SWE3789

SOUTH EAST ASIA - ASIE DU SUD-EST

BEL0198	BEL0397	CHE0434	CHE0568
CHE0632	CHE0689	DEU0971	DEU0990
DEU1149	DEU1174	DNK1300	DNK1314
ESP1492	FRA1781	FRA1850	FRA1860
FRA1917	FRA1946	FRA2005	FRA2062
FRA2096	FRA2097	GBR2201	GBR2218
GBR2221	GBR2278	GBR2361	GBR2371
GBR2501	GBR2553	ITA2860	LUX2954
NLD3067	NLD3083	NLD3101	NLD3117
NLD3271	NLD3318	NLD3353	NLD3366
POL3519	SWE3787	SWE3789	SWE3857

SOUTHERN AFRICA - AFRIQUE AUSTRALE

AUT0063	BEL0198	BEL0265	BEL0359
BEL0397	CHE0434	CHE0682	CHE0689
CHE0727	DEU0919	DEU0965	DEU1131
DEU1174	DNK1245	DNK1248	DNK1300
DNK1314	DNK1375	DNK1403	FRA1731
FRA1738	FRA1781	FRA1849	FRA1879
FRA1917	FRA1946	FRA1956	FRA1988
FRA2005	FRA2096	GBR2185	GBR2218
GBR2221	GBR2266	GBR2277	GBR2278
GBR2318	GBR2361	GBR2371	GBR2460
GBR2464	GBR2500	GBR2501	GBR2553
ITA2860	ITA2879	ITA2900	LUX2954
LUX2995	NLD3067	NLD3101	NLD3117
NLD3137	NLD3155	NLD3271	NLD3353
NLD3361	POL3519	SWE3789	

WEST AFRICA - AFRIQUE DE L'OUEST

AUT0086	BEL0198	BEL0201	BEL0265
BEL0359	BEL0397	CHE0402	CHE0434
CHE0519	CHE0568	CHE0669	CHE0682
CHE0689	CHE0778	DEU0919	DEU0965
DEU0968	DEU0971	DEU1131	DEU1174
DNK1291	DNK1300	DNK1308	DNK1314
ESP1492	ESP1524	FRA1731	FRA1778
FRA1785	FRA1787	FRA1846	FRA1865
FRA1879	FRA1917	FRA1927	FRA1946
FRA1956	FRA1984	FRA1988	FRA1992
FRA2005	FRA2014	FRA2021	FRA2062
FRA2096	FRA2144	GBR2185	GBR2218
GBR2221	GBR2228	GBR2361	GBR2371
GBR2383	GBR2460	GBR2464	GBR2501
GBR2553	IRL2732	ITA2773	ITA2807
ITA2860	LUX2954	LUX2959	NLD3067
NLD3101	NLD3117	NLD3253	NLD3269

See: *How to Use the Directory*, page 11.

NLD3271 NLD3318 NLD3353 NLD3366
POL3508 POL3519 SWE3789 SWE3831

FOOD, FAMINE - ALIMENTS, FAMINE

CARIBBEAN - CARAIBES

BEL0124 BEL0144 BEL0198 BEL0224
BEL0331 BEL0338 BEL0355 BEL0358
CHE0434 CHE0491 CHE0559 CHE0568
CHE0655 CHE0682 CHE0689 CHE0712
CHE0798 CHE0814 CHE0819 CZE0859
DEU0944 DEU0983 DEU1106 DEU1128
ESP1455 ESP1472 ESP1475 ESP1491
FRA1614 FRA1644 FRA1672 FRA1685
FRA1824 FRA1934 FRA1978 FRA2116
FRA2137 GBR2218 GBR2361 GBR2371
GBR2501 ITA2773 ITA2784 ITA2787
ITA2822 ITA2860 ITA2911 LUX2992
LUX2993 NLD3102 NLD3277 POL3519
SWE3656 SWE3712

CENTRAL AFRICA - AFRIQUE CENTRALE

AUT0013 BEL0097 BEL0110 BEL0120
BEL0124 BEL0144 BEL0152 BEL0156
BEL0158 BEL0198 BEL0237 BEL0258
BEL0261 BEL0297 BEL0338 BEL0341
BEL0350 BEL0352 BEL0355 BEL0358
CHE0422 CHE0434 CHE0444 CHE0491
CHE0541 CHE0562 CHE0568 CHE0570
CHE0655 CHE0683 CHE0684 CHE0689
CHE0712 CHE0750 CHE0796 CHE0805
CHE0814 CHE0817 CHE0819 CYP0832
DEU0922 DEU0944 DEU0968 DEU1006
DEU1106 DEU1128 DEU1131 DEU1141
DNK1259 ESP1435 ESP1467 ESP1486
ESP1491 ESP1493 FIN1587 FRA1614
FRA1704 FRA1715 FRA1747 FRA1771
FRA1819 FRA1824 FRA1904 FRA1934
FRA1956 FRA1966 FRA2005 FRA2047
FRA2055 FRA2056 FRA2080 FRA2097
FRA2102 FRA2116 FRA2147 FRA2148
FRA2168 GBR2174 GBR2175 GBR2180
GBR2218 GBR2222 GBR2238 GBR2240
GBR2289 GBR2293 GBR2361 GBR2371
GBR2390 GBR2392 GBR2422 GBR2423
GBR2460 GBR2467 GBR2500 GBR2501
IRL2716 ISL2739 ITA2747 ITA2770
ITA2774 ITA2784 ITA2785 ITA2860
ITA2888 ITA2907 ITA2921 LUX2942
LUX2955 LUX2956 NLD3045 NLD3050
NLD3102 NLD3137 NLD3199 NLD3201
NLD3277 NLD3361 NOR3435 NOR3465
POL3519 PRT3549 PRT3555 SWE3656
SWE3749 SWE3763 SWE3769 SWE3813

CENTRAL ASIA AND SOUTH ASIA - ASIE CENTRALE ET ASIE DU SUD

AUT0013 BEL0097 BEL0104 BEL0124
BEL0144 BEL0158 BEL0201 BEL0297
BEL0338 BEL0340 BEL0355 BEL0358
CHE0434 CHE0467 CHE0529 CHE0568
CHE0655 CHE0689 CHE0712 CHE0796
CHE0798 CHE0814 CHE0819 CZE0859
DEU0944 DEU0954 DEU0968 DEU0983
DEU0993 DEU1016 DEU1106 DEU1118
DEU1128 DEU1132 DEU1141 DEU1149
DNK1216 DNK1244 DNK1259 FRA1644
FRA1661 FRA1747 FRA1824 FRA1904
FRA1934 FRA1978 FRA1990 FRA2102
FRA2116 GBR2174 GBR2175 GBR2176
GBR2186 GBR2218 GBR2260 GBR2318
GBR2339 GBR2348 GBR2358 GBR2361
GBR2371 GBR2372 GBR2392 GBR2436
GBR2475 GBR2500 GBR2501 HUN2627
IRL2716 ITA2773 ITA2784 ITA2787
ITA2860 ITA2879 ITA2888 ITA2912
LUX2964 LUX2982 NLD3102 NLD3199
NLD3201 NLD3242 NLD3260 NLD3277
NLD3297 NOR3371 NOR3435 NOR3465
NOR3467 POL3519 PRT3549 SWE3656
SWE3682 SWE3749 SWE3763 SWE3809
SWE3818

EAST AFRICA - AFRIQUE DE L'EST

AUT0013 AUT0085 BEL0097 BEL0124
BEL0144 BEL0198 BEL0224 BEL0270
BEL0297 BEL0338 BEL0358 BEL0368
CHE0434 CHE0448 CHE0491 CHE0570
CHE0586 CHE0630 CHE0660 CHE0682
CHE0683 CHE0684 CHE0689 CHE0712
CHE0757 CHE0764 CHE0796 CHE0814
CHE0817 CHE0819 CYP0832 DEU0922
DEU0939 DEU0944 DEU0968 DEU0983
DEU1006 DEU1017 DEU1032 DEU1106
DEU1128 DEU1131 DEU1141 DEU1145
DEU1149 DNK1222 DNK1244 DNK1245
DNK1259 DNK1292 DNK1316 DNK1358
ESP1432 ESP1435 ESP1486 ESP1491
ESP1493 FIN1549 FIN1572 FIN1580
FRA1614 FRA1617 FRA1644 FRA1717
FRA1824 FRA1855 FRA1934 FRA1956
FRA2046 FRA2047 FRA2080 FRA2116
FRA2147 FRA2168 GBR2174 GBR2175
GBR2180 GBR2218 GBR2222 GBR2226
GBR2228 GBR2238 GBR2240 GBR2264
GBR2282 GBR2292 GBR2293 GBR2303
GBR2339 GBR2348 GBR2350 GBR2361
GBR2371 GBR2390 GBR2392 GBR2423
GBR2436 GBR2460 GBR2464 GBR2467
GBR2483 GBR2500 GBR2501 GBR2502
GBR2552 GRC2571 GRC2586 IRL2683
IRL2687 IRL2688 IRL2691 IRL2699
IRL2716 IRL2725 IRL2726 IRL2730
IRL2733 ITA2739 ISL2740 ITA2772
ITA2773 ITA2782 ITA2784 ITA2785
ITA2787 ITA2813 ITA2820 ITA2822
ITA2829 ITA2848 ITA2857 ITA2860
ITA2889 ITA2907 LUX2956 NLD3045
NLD3050 NLD3068 NLD3095 NLD3102
NLD3137 NLD3169 NLD3199 NLD3216
NLD3231 NLD3253 NLD3277 NLD3297
NLD3317 NLD3323 NLD3361 NOR3381
NOR3384 NOR3412 NOR3435 NOR3465
NOR3467 NOR3475 POL3519 SWE3656
SWE3674 SWE3679 SWE3682 SWE3712
SWE3749 SWE3752 SWE3828 SWE3854

EAST ASIA - ASIE DE L'EST

AUT0013 BEL0124 BEL0144 BEL0198
BEL0338 BEL0358 CHE0434 CHE0529
CHE0655 CHE0689 CHE0712 CHE0814
CHE0819 DEU0944 DEU0968 DEU1006
DEU1106 DEU1128 DEU1149 DNK1244
FRA1747 FRA2116 GBR2218 GBR2260
GBR2361 GBR2371 GBR2392 GBR2501
ITA2784 ITA2860 NLD3102 NLD3277
NOR3465 SWE3712 SWE3809

MEXICO AND CENTRAL AMERICA - MEXIQUE ET AMERIQUE CENTRALE

AUT0013 BEL0124 BEL0144 BEL0198
BEL0224 BEL0338 BEL0358 CHE0434
CHE0485 CHE0568 CHE0570 CHE0689
CHE0712 CHE0788 CHE0814 CHE0819
DEU0944 DEU0954 DEU0983 DEU1128
DEU1149 DNK1317 ESP1455 ESP1475
ESP1493 ESP1506 FIN1554 FIN1599
FRA1672 FRA1747 FRA1824 FRA1904
FRA1934 FRA1938 FRA2102 FRA2116
GBR2174 GBR2175 GBR2218 GBR2361
GBR2371 GBR2392 GBR2501 IRL2697
ITA2762 ITA2773 ITA2784 ITA2787
ITA2860 NLD3068 NLD3102 NLD3277
NLD3303 NOR3435 POL3519 SWE3687
SWE3687 SWE3831 SWE3865

MIDDLE EAST - MOYEN-ORIENT

BEL0124 BEL0144 BEL0198 BEL0297
BEL0306 BEL0338 BEL0358 CHE0434
CHE0568 CHE0655 CHE0664 CHE0684
CHE0689 CHE0712 CHE0814 CHE0819
DEU0939 DEU0944 DEU1106 DEU1128
DEU1141 DEU1143 FIN1588 FRA1724
FRA1771 FRA1791 FRA1793 FRA1824
FRA1978 FRA2116 GBR2218 GBR2260
GBR2361 GBR2371 GBR2500 GBR2501
ITA2773 ITA2784 ITA2860 NLD3102
NLD3277 NLD3317 POL3519 SWE3730
TUR3883

NORTH AFRICA - AFRIQUE DU NORD

AUT0013 BEL0124 BEL0144 BEL0198
BEL0323 BEL0338 BEL0355 BEL0358
CHE0434 CHE0568 CHE0655 CHE0682
CHE0689 CHE0712 CHE0753 CHE0814
CYP0832 DEU0918 DEU0944 DEU1106
DEU1128 DNK1366 ESP1435 ESP1493
FRA1956 FRA2116 GBR2218 GBR2222
GBR2361 GBR2371 GBR2392 GBR2501
IRL2716 ITA2784 ITA2822 ITA2860
NLD3102 NLD3183 NLD3277 POL3519
SWE3763

OCEANIA - OCEANIE

BEL0124 BEL0198 BEL0358 CHE0434
CHE0689 CHE0712 CHE0814 CHE0819
DEU0944 DEU0992 DEU1128 DEU1149
FRA1672 FRA2116 GBR2218 GBR2264
GBR2361 GBR2371 GBR2501 GBR2524
ITA2784 ITA2860 NLD3277

SOUTH AMERICA - AMERIQUE DU SUD

AUT0013 BEL0097 BEL0124 BEL0144
BEL0198 BEL0338 BEL0341 BEL0355
BEL0358 CHE0434 CHE0475 CHE0568
CHE0570 CHE0681 CHE0689 CHE0712
CHE0798 CHE0806 CHE0814 CHE0819
DEU0918 DEU0944 DEU0983 DEU1006
DEU1128 DEU1143 DEU1149 DNK1244
ESP1435 ESP1455 ESP1488 ESP1493
ESP1502 ESP1508 FRA1685 FRA1747
FRA1824 FRA1904 FRA1932 FRA1934
FRA2086 FRA2102 FRA2116 FRA2174
GBR2175 GBR2218 GBR2264 GBR2293
GBR2303 GBR2339 GBR2361 GBR2371
GBR2392 GBR2485 GBR2501 ITA2762
ITA2773 ITA2784 ITA2787 ITA2810
ITA2860 ITA2899 ITA2907 LUX2980
LUX2992 NLD3068 NLD3091 NLD3102
NLD3277 NLD3305 NOR3465 POL3519
PRT3549 SWE3656 SWE3682 SWE3693
SWE3695 SWE3712 SWE3744 SWE3763
SWE3857 SWE3865

SOUTH EAST ASIA - ASIE DU SUD-EST

AUT0013 BEL0124 BEL0144 BEL0198
BEL0338 BEL0358 CHE0434 CHE0559
CHE0655 CHE0598 CHE0689 CHE0712
CHE0796 CHE0814 CHE0817 CHE0819
DEU0944 DEU0954 DEU0968 DEU0983
DEU1006 DEU1016 DEU1128 DEU1132
DEU1149 DEU1187 DNK1259 DNK1316
FRA1747 FRA1824 FRA1850 FRA1891
FRA1934 FRA1937 FRA1941 FRA1979
FRA1992 FRA2065 FRA2080 FRA2097
FRA2116 FRA2137 FRA2140 GBR2175
GBR2218 GBR2260 GBR2339 GBR2361
GBR2371 GBR2392 GBR2467 GBR2501
GBR2552 IRL2691 ITA2766 ITA2784
ITA2888 ITA2888 NLD3050 NLD3102
NLD3277 NLD3297 NOR3372 NOR3381
NOR3465 NOR3467 POL3519 SWE3656
SWE3674 SWE3682 SWE3857

SOUTHERN AFRICA - AFRIQUE AUSTRALE

AUT0013 AUT0091 BEL0097 BEL0124
BEL0144 BEL0152 BEL0198 BEL0260
BEL0297 BEL0338 BEL0355 BEL0358
CHE0434 CHE0491 CHE0498 CHE0586
CHE0682 CHE0689 CHE0693 CHE0712
CHE0734 CHE0798 CHE0814 CHE0817
CHE0819 CYP0832 DEU0944 DEU1006
DEU1082 DEU1106 DEU1128 DEU1131
DEU1176 DNK1259 DNK1288 DNK1292
DNK1366 DNK1388 ESP1420 ESP1486
ESP1493 FIN1557 FRA1659 FRA1672
FRA1691 FRA1715 FRA1738 FRA1769
FRA1771 FRA1824 FRA1956 FRA2047
FRA2056 FRA2080 FRA2116 GBR2174
GBR2218 GBR2222 GBR2228 GBR2238
GBR2240 GBR2242 GBR2264 GBR2266
GBR2277 GBR2293 GBR2303 GBR2318
GBR2339 GBR2361 GBR2371 GBR2422
GBR2423 GBR2436 GBR2460 GBR2464
GBR2500 GBR2501 GBR2552 IRL2691
IRL2716 IRL2726 ISL2739 ITA2766
ITA2784 ITA2787 ITA2791 ITA2798

Voir : *Comment utiliser le répertoire*, page 11.

ITA2860	ITA2879	ITA2881	ITA2888
ITA2899	ITA2900	ITA2911	LUX2955
LUX2995	NLD3045	NLD3050	NLD3069
NLD3095	NLD3102	NLD3137	NLD3147
NLD3199	NLD3201	NLD3277	NLD3317
NLD3336	NLD3361	NOR3435	NOR3467
POL3519	PRT3549	PRT3552	PRT3555
PRT3590	PRT3596	PRT3600	PRT3603
PRT3605	SWE3656	SWE3749	SWE3798
SWE3828	SWE3859		

WEST AFRICA - AFRIQUE DE L'OUEST

AUT0013	BEL0097	BEL0118	BEL0124
BEL0144	BEL0152	BEL0156	BEL0198
BEL0270	BEL0297	BEL0338	BEL0355
BEL0358	CHE0402	CHE0434	CHE0444
CHE0491	CHE0498	CHE0510	CHE0568
CHE0570	CHE0598	CHE0682	CHE0684
CHE0686	CHE0712	CHE0734	CHE0757
CHE0764	CHE0796	CHE0814	CHE0817
CHE0819	CYP0832	DEU0922	DEU0944
DEU0968	DEU0983	DEU1006	DEU1106
DEU1128	DEU1131	DEU1149	DEU1187
DNK1244	DNK1259	DNK1374	ESP1407
ESP1468	ESP1493	ESP1502	FIN1587
FRA1612	FRA1614	FRA1624	FRA1644
FRA1664	FRA1672	FRA1679	FRA1683
FRA1715	FRA1739	FRA1747	FRA1771
FRA1778	FRA1785	FRA1787	FRA1824
FRA1865	FRA1929	FRA1932	FRA1934
FRA1956	FRA2005	FRA2047	FRA2056
FRA2065	FRA2100	FRA2116	FRA2119
FRA2138	FRA2147	FRA2148	GBR2174
GBR2175	GBR2218	GBR2222	GBR2238
GBR2259	GBR2264	GBR2303	GBR2361
GBR2371	GBR2392	GBR2423	GBR2460
GBR2464	GBR2472	GBR2500	GBR2501
GBR2515	GRC2586	ISL2739	ITA2766
ITA2773	ITA2784	ITA2791	ITA2860
ITA2902	LUX2964	LUX2973	LUX2976
LUX2992	NLD3045	NLD3102	NLD3137
NLD3199	NLD3254	NLD3269	NLD3277
NLD3361	NOR3387	NOR3465	POL3519
PRT3549	PRT3555	SWE3656	SWE3695
SWE3707	SWE3712	SWE3749	SWE3769

GENDER ISSUES, WOMEN - QUESTIONS RELATIVES AUX FEMMES

CARIBBEAN - CARAIBES

BEL0123	BEL0124	BEL0129	BEL0144
BEL0186	BEL0198	BEL0199	BEL0221
BEL0254	BEL0306	BEL0327	BEL0335
BEL0336	BEL0351	BEL0353	BEL0358
BEL0361	CHE0420	CHE0434	CHE0564
CHE0568	CHE0587	CHE0614	CHE0619
CHE0640	CHE0655	CHE0682	CHE0689
CHE0711	CHE0712	CHE0721	CHE0798
CHE0814	CHE0819	DEU0944	DEU0972
DEU0983	DEU0989	DEU1047	DEU1055
DEU1106	DNK1292	ESP1435	ESP1442
ESP1455	ESP1461	ESP1472	ESP1484
ESP1486	ESP1491	ESP1492	ESP1507
ESP1517	ESP1522	FIN1584	FRA1644
FRA1672	FRA1817	FRA1827	FRA1843
FRA1946	FRA2023	FRA2034	FRA2081
FRA2086	FRA2096	FRA2102	FRA2103
FRA2116	FRA2117	FRA2126	FRA2159
FRA2168	FRA2170	GBR2212	GBR2218
GBR2228	GBR2229	GBR2235	GBR2238
GBR2242	GBR2244	GBR2256	GBR2266
GBR2281	GBR2324	GBR2326	GBR2332
GBR2351	GBR2359	GBR2371	GBR2392
GBR2419	GBR2423	GBR2436	GBR2445
GBR2481	GBR2501	GBR2541	GBR2553
IRL2726	ITA2773	ITA2784	ITA2822
ITA2852	ITA2860	ITA2881	ITA2913
ITA2914	ITA2922	LUX2993	NLD3067
NLD3078	NLD3091	NLD3126	NLD3137
NLD3183	NLD3230	NLD3288	NLD3361
NOR3403	POL3519	SWE3653	SWE3705
SWE3712	SWE3830	TUR3883	

CENTRAL AFRICA - AFRIQUE CENTRALE

AUT0013	AUT0041	BEL0097	BEL0110
BEL0123	BEL0124	BEL0129	BEL0144
BEL0148	BEL0155	BEL0156	BEL0158
BEL0186	BEL0189	BEL0198	BEL0199
BEL0200	BEL0203	BEL0221	BEL0245
BEL0254	BEL0261	BEL0265	BEL0289
BEL0306	BEL0327	BEL0342	BEL0351
BEL0352	BEL0353	BEL0358	BEL0359
BEL0361	BEL0367	BEL0381	BEL0390
BEL0392	CHE0420	CHE0434	CHE0444
CHE0521	CHE0535	CHE0541	CHE0562
CHE0566	CHE0568	CHE0570	CHE0598
CHE0604	CHE0619	CHE0628	CHE0638
CHE0645	CHE0655	CHE0681	CHE0687
CHE0689	CHE0711	CHE0712	CHE0727
CHE0762	CHE0805	CHE0814	CHE0819
DEU0944	DEU0968	DEU0972	DEU0978
DEU0989	DEU1006	DEU1047	DEU1055
DEU1106	DEU1114	DEU1131	DEU1146
DNK1227	DNK1238	DNK1255	DNK1272
DNK1392	ESP1475	ESP1486	ESP1492
ESP1513	ESP1517	FRA1671	FRA1704
FRA1715	FRA1727	FRA1774	FRA1787
FRA1817	FRA1827	FRA1861	FRA1865
FRA1876	FRA1946	FRA1956	FRA2005
FRA2011	FRA2012	FRA2032	FRA2034
FRA2042	FRA2061	FRA2062	FRA2080
FRA2081	FRA2086	FRA2096	FRA2102
FRA2103	FRA2107	FRA2114	FRA2116
FRA2119	FRA2126	FRA2159	FRA2168
FRA2170	GBR2173	GBR2174	GBR2175
GBR2180	GBR2185	GBR2187	GBR2199
GBR2218	GBR2235	GBR2238	GBR2241
GBR2259	GBR2289	GBR2332	GBR2337
GBR2351	GBR2359	GBR2371	GBR2390
GBR2392	GBR2423	GBR2445	GBR2460
GBR2481	GBR2500	GBR2501	GBR2541
GBR2550	GBR2553	IRL2702	ITA2762
ITA2770	ITA2779	ITA2784	ITA2806
ITA2811	ITA2813	ITA2829	ITA2835
ITA2860	ITA2868	ITA2883	ITA2885
ITA2888	ITA2890	ITA2896	ITA2898
ITA2899	ITA2907	ITA2914	ITA2922
LUX2954	LUX3002	LUX3006	NLD3045
NLD3067	NLD3078	NLD3096	NLD3101
NLD3117	NLD3137	NLD3199	NLD3257
NLD3264	NLD3277	NLD3301	NLD3361
NLD3366	POL3519	PRT3594	PRT3602
SWE3763	SWE3827	SWE3830	TUR3883

CENTRAL ASIA AND SOUTH ASIA - ASIE CENTRALE ET ASIE DU SUD

AUT0013	AUT0024	AUT0026	AUT0051
AUT0089	AUT0091	BEL0097	BEL0104
BEL0123	BEL0124	BEL0129	BEL0144
BEL0148	BEL0186	BEL0192	BEL0198
BEL0199	BEL0203	BEL0221	BEL0254
BEL0261	BEL0265	BEL0269	BEL0270
BEL0273	BEL0297	BEL0306	BEL0327
BEL0340	BEL0341	BEL0351	BEL0355
BEL0358	BEL0361	BEL0368	BEL0392
CHE0406	CHE0417	CHE0420	CHE0434
CHE0472	CHE0510	CHE0558	CHE0559
CHE0566	CHE0568	CHE0570	CHE0586
CHE0619	CHE0628	CHE0632	CHE0638
CHE0645	CHE0655	CHE0682	CHE0687
CHE0689	CHE0711	CHE0712	CHE0721
CHE0727	CHE0742	CHE0757	CHE0758
CHE0798	CHE0809	CHE0814	CHE0819
DEU0940	DEU0944	DEU0954	DEU0965
DEU0971	DEU0972	DEU0983	DEU0989
DEU1006	DEU1047	DEU1055	DEU1074
DEU1086	DEU1106	DEU1110	DEU1121
DEU1129	DEU1131	DEU1132	DEU1142
DEU1146	DEU1178	DEU1186	DEU1187
DNK1222	DNK1229	DNK1238	DNK1255
DNK1259	DNK1275	DNK1292	DNK1339
DNK1358	DNK1384	ESP1486	ESP1491
ESP1492	ESP1513	ESP1517	FIN1580
FIN1591	FRA1642	FRA1644	FRA1647
FRA1661	FRA1817	FRA1862	FRA1866
FRA1887	FRA1939	FRA1990	FRA2023
FRA2034	FRA2041	FRA2081	FRA2086
FRA2096	FRA2102	FRA2116	FRA2131
FRA2150	FRA2159	FRA2168	FRA2170
GBR2172	GBR2173	GBR2174	GBR2175
GBR2176	GBR2186	GBR2197	GBR2201

GBR2212	GBR2213	GBR2218	GBR2226
GBR2228	GBR2235	GBR2238	GBR2256
GBR2259	GBR2262	GBR2264	GBR2266
GBR2273	GBR2274	GBR2281	GBR2290
GBR2297	GBR2302	GBR2321	GBR2324
GBR2326	GBR2332	GBR2333	GBR2348
GBR2351	GBR2353	GBR2358	GBR2369
GBR2371	GBR2372	GBR2375	GBR2385
GBR2390	GBR2392	GBR2402	GBR2410
GBR2413	GBR2419	GBR2423	GBR2436
GBR2439	GBR2445	GBR2464	GBR2467
GBR2481	GBR2500	GBR2501	GBR2506
GBR2532	GBR2541	GBR2553	GBR2556
GRC2571	IRL2688	IRL2699	IRL2726
ITA2766	ITA2770	ITA2775	ITA2784
ITA2813	ITA2860	ITA2873	ITA2888
ITA2898	ITA2912	ITA2914	ITA2922
LIE2926	LUX2982	NLD3056	NLD3067
NLD3076	NLD3078	NLD3096	NLD3101
NLD3126	NLD3137	NLD3138	NLD3147
NLD3149	NLD3153	NLD3165	NLD3183
NLD3199	NLD3237	NLD3253	NLD3260
NLD3277	NLD3292	NLD3302	NLD3317
NLD3361	NOR3371	NOR3384	NOR3412
NOR3453	NOR3460	NOR3465	NOR3467
NOR3475	POL3508	POL3519	SWE3650
SWE3661	SWE3666	SWE3674	SWE3679
SWE3723	SWE3749	SWE3763	SWE3771
SWE3787	SWE3795	SWE3818	SWE3821
SWE3826	SWE3830	SWE3834	SWE3854
SWE3857	SWE3864	TUR3883	

EAST AFRICA - AFRIQUE DE L'EST

AUT0003	AUT0013	AUT0024	AUT0026
AUT0033	AUT0041	AUT0085	AUT0091
BEL0123	BEL0124	BEL0129	BEL0133
BEL0144	BEL0148	BEL0167	BEL0186
BEL0198	BEL0199	BEL0221	BEL0254
BEL0269	BEL0270	BEL0289	BEL0297
BEL0306	BEL0327	BEL0341	BEL0351
BEL0353	BEL0358	BEL0361	BEL0381
BEL0392	CHE0420	CHE0434	CHE0521
CHE0566	CHE0570	CHE0586	CHE0619
CHE0620	CHE0630	CHE0638	CHE0645
CHE0660	CHE0681	CHE0682	CHE0683
CHE0684	CHE0687	CHE0689	CHE0711
CHE0712	CHE0754	CHE0758	CHE0764
CHE0772	CHE0814	CHE0819	DEU0936
DEU0940	DEU0944	DEU0968	DEU0972
DEU0983	DEU0989	DEU1006	DEU1032
DEU1047	DEU1055	DEU1066	DEU1069
DEU1106	DEU1129	DEU1131	DEU1142
DEU1145	DEU1146	DEU1178	DNK1229
DNK1238	DNK1255	DNK1259	DNK1275
DNK1285	DNK1302	DNK1316	DNK1339
DNK1342	DNK1377	DNK1392	DNK1405
ESP1432	ESP1435	ESP1486	ESP1491
ESP1492	ESP1510	ESP1524	FIN1544
FIN1572	FIN1580	FIN1584	FIN1585
FIN1587	FIN1591	FRA1644	FRA1668
FRA1672	FRA1727	FRA1817	FRA1843
FRA1855	FRA1887	FRA1947	FRA1956
FRA2023	FRA2062	FRA2080	FRA2081
FRA2096	FRA2107	FRA2116	FRA2126
FRA2159	FRA2168	FRA2170	GBR2172
GBR2173	GBR2174	GBR2175	GBR2178
GBR2180	GBR2183	GBR2185	GBR2186
GBR2187	GBR2199	GBR2212	GBR2218
GBR2226	GBR2228	GBR2235	GBR2238
GBR2256	GBR2259	GBR2273	GBR2281
GBR2282	GBR2292	GBR2303	GBR2321
GBR2324	GBR2332	GBR2337	GBR2338
GBR2348	GBR2351	GBR2353	GBR2359
GBR2371	GBR2385	GBR2390	GBR2396
GBR2410	GBR2419	GBR2423	GBR2436
GBR2439	GBR2445	GBR2460	GBR2464
GBR2467	GBR2474	GBR2481	GBR2483
GBR2500	GBR2501	GBR2521	GBR2530
GBR2541	GBR2550	GBR2551	GBR2553
GBR2556	GRC2571	IRL2683	IRL2688
IRL2691	IRL2699	IRL2702	IRL2725
IRL2726	IRL2729	IRL2730	IRL2732
IRL2733	ISL2736	ISL2739	ISL2740
ITA2762	ITA2767	ITA2771	ITA2772
ITA2773	ITA2782	ITA2784	ITA2804
ITA2857	ITA2860	ITA2868	ITA2888
ITA2889	ITA2890	ITA2896	ITA2898
ITA2901	ITA2902	ITA2910	ITA2914

See: *How to Use the Directory*, page 11.

ITA2922	NLD3045	NLD3062	NLD3067
NLD3068	NLD3072	NLD3074	NLD3076
NLD3096	NLD3101	NLD3117	NLD3137
NLD3165	NLD3183	NLD3189	NLD3199
NLD3216	NLD3237	NLD3257	NLD3277
NLD3301	NLD3323	NLD3361	NLD3366
NOR3403	NOR3404	NOR3435	NOR3465
NOR3467	NOR3475	POL3519	PRT3550
SWE3679	SWE3688	SWE3712	SWE3714
SWE3727	SWE3728	SWE3730	SWE3746
SWE3749	SWE3752	SWE3771	SWE3775
SWE3787	SWE3799	SWE3807	SWE3814
SWE3821	SWE3826	SWE3830	SWE3853
SWE3854	SWE3864	TUR3883	

EAST ASIA - ASIE DE L'EST

AUT0013	BEL0123	BEL0124	BEL0129
BEL0144	BEL0186	BEL0198	BEL0199
BEL0221	BEL0254	BEL0265	BEL0273
BEL0289	BEL0351	BEL0358	BEL0361
CHE0420	CHE0550	CHE0570	
CHE0638	CHE0645	CHE0655	CHE0689
CHE0711	CHE0712	CHE0721	CHE0814
CHE0819	DEU0944	DEU0972	DEU0989
DEU1006	DEU1047	DEU1055	DEU1106
DEU1129	DEU1131	DEU1142	DEU1146
DNK1292	ESP1432	ESP1492	FRA1817
FRA2096	FRA2114	FRA2116	FRA2159
FRA2168	FRA2170	GBR2199	GBR2218
GBR2226	GBR2228	GBR2235	GBR2238
GBR2260	GBR2264	GBR2266	GBR2332
GBR2351	GBR2359	GBR2371	GBR2423
GBR2445	GBR2481	GBR2501	GBR2541
GBR2550	GBR2553	GBR2556	IRL2726
ITA2784	ITA2860	ITA2914	ITA2922
NLD3067	NLD3078	NLD3096	NLD3198
NLD3277	NLD3361	NOR3465	POL3508
SWE3826	SWE3830	TUR3883	

MEXICO AND CENTRAL AMERICA - MEXIQUE ET AMERIQUE CENTRALE

AUT0003	AUT0013	AUT0026	AUT0030
AUT0034	AUT0058	AUT0091	BEL0123
BEL0124	BEL0129	BEL0144	BEL0148
BEL0186	BEL0189	BEL0198	BEL0199
BEL0203	BEL0221	BEL0254	BEL0269
BEL0270	BEL0273	BEL0297	BEL0327
BEL0335	BEL0336	BEL0340	BEL0351
BEL0353	BEL0358	BEL0361	BEL0362
BEL0381	CHE0420	CHE0427	CHE0434
CHE0446	CHE0491	CHE0493	CHE0517
CHE0558	CHE0559	CHE0566	CHE0568
CHE0570	CHE0613	CHE0619	CHE0632
CHE0638	CHE0640	CHE0645	CHE0682
CHE0689	CHE0711	CHE0712	CHE0721
CHE0735	CHE0755	CHE0757	CHE0772
CHE0789	CHE0809	CHE0814	
CHE0819	DEU0944	DEU0954	DEU0972
DEU0983	DEU0989	DEU1047	DEU1055
DEU1074	DEU1097	DEU1106	DEU1114
DEU1129	DEU1138	DEU1142	DEU1149
DEU1161	DEU1176	DEU1178	DEU1187
DNK1283	DNK1292	DNK1312	DNK1317
DNK1339	ESP1413	ESP1427	ESP1431
ESP1432	ESP1435	ESP1437	ESP1442
ESP1450	ESP1455	ESP1461	ESP1475
ESP1486	ESP1491	ESP1492	ESP1506
ESP1510	ESP1517	ESP1521	ESP1522
FIN1546	FIN1558	FIN1602	FRA1671
FRA1672	FRA1701	FRA1703	FRA1817
FRA1827	FRA1843	FRA1852	FRA1975
FRA1978	FRA2034	FRA2041	FRA2042
FRA2081	FRA2096	FRA2102	FRA2103
FRA2116	FRA2117	FRA2159	FRA2163
FRA2168	FRA2170	GBR2174	GBR2199
GBR2201	GBR2212	GBR2218	GBR2226
GBR2228	GBR2229	GBR2238	GBR2242
GBR2244	GBR2256	GBR2259	GBR2321
GBR2324	GBR2332	GBR2351	GBR2359
GBR2371	GBR2373	GBR2385	GBR2390
GBR2392	GBR2396	GBR2413	GBR2419
GBR2423	GBR2436	GBR2439	GBR2445
GBR2467	GBR2481	GBR2500	GBR2501
GBR2541	GBR2551	GBR2553	GBR2556
IRL2697	IRL2714	IRL2726	ITA2762
ITA2771	ITA2773	ITA2775	ITA2784
ITA2834	ITA2838	ITA2858	ITA2860
ITA2868	ITA2881	ITA2888	ITA2894

ITA2902	ITA2913	ITA2914	ITA2922
ITA2923	LUX2976	NLD3067	NLD3068
NLD3078	NLD3079	NLD3096	NLD3101
NLD3137	NLD3159	NLD3165	
NLD3198	NLD3199	NLD3219	NLD3230
NLD3253	NLD3257	NLD3258	NLD3277
NLD3285	NLD3288	NLD3303	NLD3305
NLD3361	NLD3366	NOR3403	NOR3409
NOR3410	NOR3425	NOR3426	NOR3441
NOR3467	NOR3475	POL3519	SWE3674
SWE3687	SWE3749	SWE3771	SWE3795
SWE3830	SWE3864	SWE3865	TUR3883

MIDDLE EAST - MOYEN-ORIENT

AUT0035	BEL0124	BEL0129	BEL0144
BEL0186	BEL0198	BEL0199	BEL0221
BEL0241	BEL0270	BEL0306	BEL0317
BEL0353	BEL0358	BEL0361	CHE0406
CHE0420	CHE0434	CHE0493	CHE0506
CHE0559	CHE0568	CHE0640	CHE0645
CHE0655	CHE0664	CHE0682	CHE0687
CHE0689	CHE0711	CHE0712	CHE0773
CHE0809	CHE0814	CHE0819	DEU0944
DEU0972	DEU0989	DEU1047	DEU1055
DEU1065	DEU1106	DEU1146	DEU1200
ESP1450	ESP1522	ESP1524	FRA1724
FRA1791	FRA1793	FRA1794	FRA1817
FRA1827	FRA1865	FRA1967	FRA2016
FRA2041	FRA2057	FRA2081	FRA2096
FRA2103	FRA2114	FRA2116	FRA2159
FRA2170	GBR2199	GBR2218	GBR2228
GBR2229	GBR2238	GBR2244	GBR2260
GBR2273	GBR2303	GBR2332	GBR2351
GBR2359	GBR2371	GBR2378	GBR2385
GBR2396	GBR2423	GBR2445	GBR2464
GBR2501	GBR2525	GBR2541	GBR2551
GBR2556	IRL2680	ITA2767	ITA2773
ITA2784	ITA2838	ITA2860	ITA2914
LUX2937	MLT3016	MLT3017	NLD3067
NLD3076	NLD3101	NLD3173	NLD3199
NLD3361	POL3519	SWE3674	SWE3730
SWE3738	SWE3830	TUR3883	

NORTH AFRICA - AFRIQUE DU NORD

AUT0013	BEL0097	BEL0118	BEL0123
BEL0124	BEL0129	BEL0144	BEL0148
BEL0186	BEL0198	BEL0199	BEL0221
BEL0265	BEL0269	BEL0270	BEL0289
BEL0340	BEL0353	BEL0358	BEL0361
CHE0409	CHE0420	CHE0434	CHE0506
CHE0568	CHE0655	CHE0682	CHE0687
CHE0689	CHE0711	CHE0712	CHE0753
CHE0814	DEU0944	DEU0972	DEU0989
DEU1047	DEU1055	DEU1106	DEU1142
DEU1146	DEU1176	DEU1191	DNK1255
ESP1442	ESP1486	ESP1492	ESP1505
ESP1521	FRA1683	FRA1701	FRA1715
FRA1768	FRA1794	FRA1817	FRA1846
FRA1887	FRA1946	FRA1956	FRA1978
FRA2034	FRA2057	FRA2061	FRA2096
FRA2107	FRA2114	FRA2116	FRA2117
FRA2159	FRA2170	GBR2185	GBR2218
GBR2226	GBR2238	GBR2281	GBR2332
GBR2359	GBR2371	GBR2385	GBR2392
GBR2413	GBR2423	GBR2501	GBR2541
ITA2784	ITA2791	ITA2809	ITA2810
ITA2834	ITA2838	ITA2860	ITA2901
ITA2914	ITA2922	MLT3016	MLT3017
NLD3067	NLD3078	NLD3101	NLD3117
NLD3183	NLD3198	NLD3277	POL3519
SWE3688	SWE3763	SWE3770	SWE3830
TUR3883			

OCEANIA - OCEANIE

BEL0123	BEL0124	BEL0129	BEL0186
BEL0198	BEL0199	BEL0270	BEL0273
BEL0361	BEL0362	CHE0420	CHE0434
CHE0640	CHE0645	CHE0711	CHE0712
CHE0721	CHE0772	CHE0814	CHE0819
DEU0944	DEU0972	DEU0989	DEU0992
DEU1047	DEU1055	DEU1106	DEU1146
FRA1672	FRA1817	FRA2041	FRA2096
FRA2116	FRA2168	FRA2170	GBR2218
GBR2228	GBR2235	GBR2256	GBR2266
GBR2312	GBR2332	GBR2351	GBR2359
GBR2371	GBR2445	GBR2481	GBR2501

GBR2524	GBR2541	GBR2553	ITA2784
ITA2860	ITA2914	NLD3067	NLD3096
NLD3137	SWE3749	SWE3830	TUR3883

SOUTH AMERICA - AMERIQUE DU SUD

AUT0003	AUT0013	AUT0022	AUT0024
AUT0051	AUT0052	AUT0091	BEL0119
BEL0123	BEL0124	BEL0129	BEL0139
BEL0144	BEL0148	BEL0155	BEL0186
BEL0189	BEL0198	BEL0199	BEL0203
BEL0221	BEL0241	BEL0245	BEL0254
BEL0265	BEL0269	BEL0270	BEL0273
BEL0282	BEL0297	BEL0306	BEL0327
BEL0335	BEL0336	BEL0341	BEL0351
BEL0353	BEL0358	BEL0359	BEL0361
BEL0381	BEL0392	CHE0420	CHE0434
CHE0438	CHE0443	CHE0455	CHE0475
CHE0479	CHE0491	CHE0510	CHE0515
CHE0559	CHE0566	CHE0568	CHE0570
CHE0596	CHE0598	CHE0604	CHE0614
CHE0619	CHE0628	CHE0629	CHE0640
CHE0645	CHE0669	CHE0671	CHE0681
CHE0682	CHE0687	CHE0689	CHE0711
CHE0712	CHE0721	CHE0727	CHE0755
CHE0757	CHE0764	CHE0772	CHE0789
CHE0798	CHE0809	CHE0814	CHE0819
DEU0940	DEU0944	DEU0972	DEU0983
DEU0989	DEU1006	DEU1038	DEU1047
DEU1055	DEU1097	DEU1114	DEU1129
DEU1131	DEU1138	DEU1142	DEU1149
DEU1161	DEU1177	DEU1178	DEU1186
DEU1187	DNK1218	DNK1292	DNK1312
DNK1403	ESP1413	ESP1431	ESP1432
ESP1435	ESP1437	ESP1442	ESP1450
ESP1452	ESP1455	ESP1461	ESP1472
ESP1475	ESP1484	ESP1486	ESP1491
ESP1492	ESP1503	ESP1505	ESP1508
ESP1510	ESP1512	ESP1513	ESP1517
ESP1521	ESP1522	FIN1558	FRA1672
FRA1701	FRA1710	FRA1815	FRA1817
FRA1827	FRA1828	FRA1843	FRA1865
FRA1932	FRA1946	FRA1978	FRA2016
FRA2023	FRA2034	FRA2041	FRA2042
FRA2081	FRA2081	FRA2086	FRA2096
FRA2102	FRA2103	FRA2107	FRA2114
FRA2116	FRA2131	FRA2159	FRA2168
FRA2170	GBR2174	GBR2175	GBR2201
GBR2212	GBR2218	GBR2226	GBR2228
GBR2229	GBR2235	GBR2238	GBR2244
GBR2259	GBR2266	GBR2273	GBR2303
GBR2321	GBR2324	GBR2332	GBR2351
GBR2359	GBR2371	GBR2390	GBR2392
GBR2419	GBR2423	GBR2436	GBR2445
GBR2467	GBR2481	GBR2500	GBR2501
GBR2537	GBR2541	GBR2551	GBR2553
ITA2773	ITA2775	ITA2782	ITA2784
ITA2791	ITA2792	ITA2798	ITA2802
ITA2806	ITA2809	ITA2810	ITA2811
ITA2820	ITA2822	ITA2835	ITA2860
ITA2868	ITA2880	ITA2881	ITA2885
ITA2888	ITA2889	ITA2896	ITA2900
ITA2901	ITA2907	ITA2913	ITA2914
ITA2922	ITA2923	ITA2946	LUX2954
LUX2958	LUX2967	LUX2968	LUX2999
NLD3067	NLD3076	NLD3078	NLD3096
NLD3137	NLD3181	NLD3198	
NLD3199	NLD3219	NLD3230	NLD3277
NLD3281	NLD3305	NLD3361	NLD3366
NOR3460	NOR3465	POL3519	PRT3600
SWE3666	SWE3674	SWE3693	SWE3695
SWE3712	SWE3744	SWE3749	SWE3763
SWE3787	SWE3795	SWE3796	SWE3821
SWE3826	SWE3830	SWE3864	SWE3865
TUR3883			

SOUTH EAST ASIA - ASIE DU SUD-EST

AUT0013	AUT0051	AUT0091	BEL0123
BEL0124	BEL0129	BEL0144	BEL0186
BEL0198	BEL0199	BEL0203	
BEL0221	BEL0254	BEL0261	BEL0269
BEL0273	BEL0275	BEL0289	BEL0306
BEL0342	BEL0351	BEL0358	
BEL0361	BEL0392	CHE0420	CHE0434
CHE0479	CHE0491	CHE0550	CHE0559
CHE0566	CHE0568	CHE0570	CHE0598
CHE0604	CHE0619	CHE0637	CHE0638
CHE0640	CHE0645	CHE0681	CHE0682

Voir : *Comment utiliser le répertoire*, page 11.

CHE0683	CHE0689	CHE0711	CHE0712
CHE0721	CHE0798	CHE0809	CHE0814
CHE0819	DEU0940	DEU0944	DEU0954
DEU0971	DEU0972	DEU0983	DEU0989
DEU1006	DEU1047	DEU1055	DEU1074
DEU1097	DEU1106	DEU1110	DEU1129
DEU1132	DEU1146	DEU1174	DEU1176
DEU1178	DEU1186	DEU1187	DNK1259
DNK1292	DNK1298	ESP1492	FIN1580
FIN1584	FIN1587	FIN1599	FRA1647
FRA1671	FRA1672	FRA1701	FRA1715
FRA1817	FRA1941	FRA1946	FRA1979
FRA1991	FRA2023	FRA2034	FRA2080
FRA2081	FRA2096	FRA2097	FRA2114
FRA2170	GBR2175	GBR2199	GBR2201
GBR2212	GBR2218	GBR2226	GBR2228
GBR2235	GBR2238	GBR2240	GBR2242
GBR2256	GBR2262	GBR2264	GBR2266
GBR2321	GBR2324	GBR2326	GBR2332
GBR2351	GBR2359	GBR2371	GBR2385
GBR2390	GBR2413	GBR2419	GBR2423
GBR2436	GBR2445	GBR2464	GBR2467
GBR2481	GBR2500	GBR2501	GBR2508
GBR2537	GBR2541	GBR2553	GBR2556
IRL2691	IRL2726	IRL2733	ITA2775
ITA2784	ITA2785	ITA2798	ITA2860
ITA2868	ITA2894	ITA2902	ITA2914
ITA2922	LUX2954	NLD3067	NLD3068
NLD3076	NLD3078	NLD3096	NLD3117
NLD3137	NLD3198	NLD3199	NLD3235
NLD3237	NLD3253	NLD3277	NLD3292
NLD3363	NLD3366	NOR3372	NOR3465
NOR3467	POL3508	POL3519	SWE3712
SWE3730	SWE3749	SWE3826	SWE3830
SWE3876	TUR3883		

SOUTHERN AFRICA - AFRIQUE AUSTRALE

AUT0013	AUT0022	AUT0024	AUT0034
AUT0058	AUT0091	BEL0097	BEL0123
BEL0124	BEL0129	BEL0144	BEL0148
BEL0186	BEL0189	BEL0198	BEL0199
BEL0203	BEL0221	BEL0241	BEL0252
BEL0265	BEL0269	BEL0273	BEL0289
BEL0327	BEL0351	BEL0358	BEL0361
BEL0392	CHE0420	CHE0434	CHE0506
CHE0566	CHE0570	CHE0584	CHE0619
CHE0628	CHE0638	CHE0645	CHE0682
CHE0687	CHE0689	CHE0711	CHE0712
CHE0721	CHE0727	CHE0755	CHE0798
CHE0814	CHE0819	DEU0931	DEU0944
DEU0972	DEU0989	DEU1006	DEU1047
DEU1055	DEU1106	DEU1129	DEU1131
DEU1142	DEU1146	DEU1149	DEU1176
DEU1200	DNK1238	DNK1259	DNK1275
DNK1292	DNK1312	DNK1339	DNK1375
DNK1403	ESP1450	ESP1486	ESP1491
FIN1546	FIN1554	FIN1557	FIN1580
FIN1587	FIN1603	FRA1671	FRA1672
FRA1691	FRA1715	FRA1727	FRA1738
FRA1768	FRA1817	FRA1827	FRA1849
FRA1876	FRA1887	FRA1946	FRA1947
FRA1948	FRA1956	FRA2023	FRA2032
FRA2041	FRA2080	FRA2096	FRA2103
FRA2107	FRA2114	FRA2116	FRA2119
FRA2126	FRA2159	FRA2168	FRA2170
GBR2173	GBR2174	GBR2178	GBR2181
GBR2185	GBR2187	GBR2198	GBR2201
GBR2212	GBR2218	GBR2226	GBR2228
GBR2229	GBR2235	GBR2238	GBR2244
GBR2256	GBR2259	GBR2260	GBR2266
GBR2273	GBR2277	GBR2281	GBR2292
GBR2318	GBR2319	GBR2321	GBR2324
GBR2332	GBR2337	GBR2359	GBR2371
GBR2385	GBR2390	GBR2413	GBR2419
GBR2423	GBR2436	GBR2445	GBR2460
GBR2464	GBR2467	GBR2478	GBR2481
GBR2500	GBR2501	GBR2530	GBR2537
GBR2541	GBR2550	GBR2551	GBR2553
GBR2556	GBR2561	IRL2691	IRL2726
IRL2733	ISL2739	ITA2771	ITA2784
ITA2798	ITA2813	ITA2860	ITA2873
ITA2881	ITA2888	ITA2900	ITA2914
ITA2922	ITA2923	LUX2946	LUX2954
LUX2995	NLD3045	NLD3067	NLD3078
NLD3089	NLD3091	NLD3096	NLD3098
NLD3101	NLD3117	NLD3137	NLD3139
NLD3147	NLD3165	NLD3173	NLD3198
NLD3199	NLD3235	NLD3253	NLD3277

NLD3292	NLD3317	NLD3361	NOR3379
NOR3384	NOR3389	NOR3416	NOR3418
NOR3425	NOR3435	NOR3467	POL3519
PRT3564	PRT3579	PRT3590	PRT3594
PRT3605	SWE3648	SWE3650	SWE3664
SWE3674	SWE3688	SWE3705	SWE3749
SWE3772	SWE3821	SWE3826	SWE3830
SWE3864	TUR3883		

WEST AFRICA - AFRIQUE DE L'OUEST

AUT0003	AUT0013	AUT0021	AUT0041
AUT0086	AUT0091	BEL0118	BEL0123
BEL0124	BEL0129	BEL0133	BEL0144
BEL0148	BEL0152	BEL0186	BEL0192
BEL0198	BEL0199	BEL0203	BEL0221
BEL0245	BEL0254	BEL0261	BEL0269
BEL0270	BEL0273	BEL0289	BEL0327
BEL0341	BEL0342	BEL0351	BEL0352
BEL0353	BEL0355	BEL0358	BEL0359
BEL0361	BEL0367	BEL0381	BEL0390
BEL0392	CHE0420	CHE0434	CHE0435
CHE0439	CHE0444	CHE0479	CHE0491
CHE0519	CHE0521	CHE0542	CHE0558
CHE0566	CHE0568	CHE0570	CHE0598
CHE0604	CHE0619	CHE0637	CHE0638
CHE0645	CHE0659	CHE0671	CHE0682
CHE0687	CHE0689	CHE0707	CHE0711
CHE0712	CHE0721	CHE0727	CHE0755
CHE0757	CHE0758	CHE0762	CHE0764
CHE0772	CHE0798	CHE0810	CHE0814
CHE0819	CHE0823	DEU0940	DEU0944
DEU0968	DEU0971	DEU0972	DEU0983
DEU0989	DEU1006	DEU1047	DEU1055
DEU1069	DEU1097	DEU1106	DEU1110
DEU1114	DEU1131	DEU1142	DEU1146
DEU1178	DEU1186	DEU1187	DEU1200
DNK1227	DNK1248	DNK1255	DNK1259
DNK1307	DNK1374	ESP1468	ESP1486
ESP1491	ESP1492	ESP1502	ESP1510
ESP1517	FIN1580	FIN1587	FRA1607
FRA1644	FRA1664	FRA1672	FRA1690
FRA1691	FRA1715	FRA1727	FRA1737
FRA1739	FRA1746	FRA1760	FRA1761
FRA1762	FRA1768	FRA1778	FRA1785
FRA1787	FRA1789	FRA1794	FRA1799
FRA1817	FRA1827	FRA1843	FRA1846
FRA1848	FRA1865	FRA1876	FRA1880
FRA1887	FRA1907	FRA1913	FRA1914
FRA1929	FRA1935	FRA1939	FRA1946
FRA1947	FRA1956	FRA1967	FRA1978
FRA1992	FRA2005	FRA2012	FRA2016
FRA2032	FRA2034	FRA2037	FRA2042
FRA2061	FRA2062	FRA2084	FRA2086
FRA2096	FRA2103	FRA2107	FRA2114
FRA2116	FRA2117	FRA2119	FRA2126
FRA2131	FRA2138	FRA2150	FRA2159
FRA2163	FRA2168	FRA2170	GBR2173
GBR2174	GBR2175	GBR2180	GBR2185
GBR2187	GBR2199	GBR2201	GBR2218
GBR2226	GBR2228	GBR2235	GBR2238
GBR2244	GBR2256	GBR2259	GBR2303
GBR2324	GBR2332	GBR2337	GBR2351
GBR2359	GBR2371	GBR2385	GBR2390
GBR2392	GBR2413	GBR2419	GBR2423
GBR2436	GBR2439	GBR2445	GBR2460
GBR2464	GBR2481	GBR2483	GBR2500
GBR2501	GBR2513	GBR2515	GBR2525
GBR2529	GBR2541	GBR2550	GBR2553
GBR2556	GRC2567	IRL2726	IRL2732
IRL2733	ISL2739	ITA2756	ITA2762
ITA2770	ITA2773	ITA2782	ITA2784
ITA2791	ITA2826	ITA2827	ITA2838
ITA2855	ITA2860	ITA2873	ITA2885
ITA2888	ITA2898	ITA2901	ITA2914
ITA2922	LUX2937	LUX2946	LUX2954
LUX2959	LUX2973	LUX2976	LUX2978
LUX2986	LUX3006	NLD3045	NLD3067
NLD3068	NLD3074	NLD3075	NLD3078
NLD3079	NLD3096	NLD3101	NLD3117
NLD3137	NLD3147	NLD3153	NLD3183
NLD3198	NLD3199	NLD3230	NLD3231
NLD3235	NLD3257	NLD3269	NLD3277
NLD3288	NLD3296	NLD3301	NLD3303
NLD3318	NLD3361	NLD3366	NOR3403
NOR3453	NOR3460	NOR3465	POL3519
PRT3564	PRT3579	PRT3588	SWE3648
SWE3666	SWE3674	SWE3695	SWE3701

SWE3702	SWE3705	SWE3707	SWE3712
SWE3771	SWE3830	SWE3857	TUR3883

HEALTH, SANITATION, WATER - SANTE, ASSAINISSEMENT, EAU

CARIBBEAN - CARAIBES

AUT0076	BEL0107	BEL0124	BEL0144
BEL0186	BEL0194	BEL0198	BEL0218
BEL0221	BEL0224	BEL0265	BEL0299
BEL0301	BEL0316	BEL0323	BEL0327
BEL0331	BEL0335	BEL0336	BEL0351
BEL0358	BEL0359	BEL0361	BEL0362
BEL0368	BEL0394	CHE0434	CHE0501
CHE0558	CHE0564	CHE0568	CHE0586
CHE0614	CHE0619	CHE0655	CHE0682
CHE0689	CHE0712	CHE0730	CHE0798
CHE0814	CHE0819	DEU0944	DEU0965
DEU0968	DEU0972	DEU0983	DEU0989
DEU1023	DEU1031	DEU1053	DEU1105
DEU1106	DEU1128	DEU1131	DEU1185
DNK1292	DNK1314	DNK1402	ESP1419
ESP1435	ESP1442	ESP1455	ESP1472
ESP1475	ESP1486	ESP1488	ESP1492
ESP1496	ESP1507	ESP1522	ESP1525
FRA1610	FRA1614	FRA1629	FRA1644
FRA1670	FRA1672	FRA1676	FRA1685
FRA1744	FRA1843	FRA1903	FRA1904
FRA2023	FRA2047	FRA2056	FRA2060
FRA2062	FRA2069	FRA2070	FRA2081
FRA2087	FRA2096	FRA2102	FRA2116
FRA2117	FRA2137	FRA2154	FRA2159
FRA2168	GBR2175	GBR2196	GBR2218
GBR2221	GBR2228	GBR2229	GBR2256
GBR2278	GBR2280	GBR2293	GBR2361
GBR2371	GBR2392	GBR2423	GBR2434
GBR2436	GBR2454	GBR2477	GBR2481
GBR2500	GBR2501	GBR2535	GBR2553
IRL2711	IRL2726	ITA2766	ITA2784
ITA2860	ITA2911	ITA2913	ITA2922
LUX2992	LUX2993	NLD3050	NLD3067
NLD3091	NLD3123	NLD3131	NLD3144
NLD3150	NLD3154	NLD3185	NLD3186
NLD3201	NLD3202	NLD3225	NLD3231
NLD3251	NLD3288	NLD3317	NLD3338
NLD3356	NLD3361	NLD3364	NOR3435
POL3519	PRT3600	SWE3653	SWE3656
SWE3712	SWE3830		

CENTRAL AFRICA - AFRIQUE CENTRALE

AUT0013	AUT0026	AUT0051	AUT0076
BEL0097	BEL0107	BEL0110	BEL0120
BEL0124	BEL0126	BEL0128	BEL0132
BEL0133	BEL0144	BEL0145	BEL0148
BEL0152	BEL0153	BEL0155	BEL0156
BEL0158	BEL0184	BEL0186	BEL0192
BEL0194	BEL0198	BEL0200	BEL0201
BEL0202	BEL0203	BEL0218	BEL0221
BEL0233	BEL0234	BEL0237	BEL0258
BEL0265	BEL0297	BEL0299	BEL0301
BEL0306	BEL0316	BEL0318	BEL0327
BEL0328	BEL0331	BEL0341	BEL0342
BEL0347	BEL0352	BEL0353	BEL0358
BEL0359	BEL0361	BEL0368	BEL0390
BEL0392	BEL0396	CHE0422	CHE0434
CHE0444	CHE0463	CHE0477	CHE0486
CHE0491	CHE0510	CHE0521	CHE0522
CHE0541	CHE0562	CHE0565	CHE0568
CHE0569	CHE0570	CHE0583	CHE0598
CHE0619	CHE0628	CHE0630	CHE0643
CHE0655	CHE0660	CHE0683	CHE0684
CHE0687	CHE0688	CHE0689	CHE0691
CHE0692	CHE0707	CHE0712	CHE0730
CHE0750	CHE0757	CHE0759	CHE0796
CHE0805	CHE0814	CHE0817	CHE0819
CZE0905	DEU0918	DEU0922	DEU0928
DEU0944	DEU0968	DEU0972	DEU0978
DEU0986	DEU0989	DEU0995	DEU1017
DEU1023	DEU1027	DEU1053	DEU1105
DEU1106	DEU1128	DEU1131	DEU1141
DEU1149	DEU1185	DNK1214	DNK1227
DNK1255	DNK1272	DNK1310	DNK1314
DNK1366	DNK1402	ESP1439	ESP1467
ESP1486	ESP1492	ESP1493	ESP1495
ESP1513	FIN1587	FRA1610	FRA1614
FRA1629	FRA1634	FRA1649	FRA1671

See: *How to Use the Directory*, page 11.

FRA1677	FRA1684	FRA1694	FRA1704
FRA1715	FRA1727	FRA1731	FRA1740
FRA1744	FRA1769	FRA1771	FRA1774
FRA1815	FRA1820	FRA1832	FRA1863
FRA1865	FRA1880	FRA1903	FRA1904
FRA1917	FRA1926	FRA1934	FRA1946
FRA1956	FRA1966	FRA1993	FRA2005
FRA2011	FRA2016	FRA2042	FRA2047
FRA2051	FRA2054	FRA2055	FRA2056
FRA2060	FRA2069	FRA2070	FRA2074
FRA2080	FRA2081	FRA2086	FRA2087
FRA2093	FRA2096	FRA2102	FRA2107
FRA2114	FRA2116	FRA2117	FRA2119
FRA2123	FRA2145	FRA2148	FRA2150
FRA2154	FRA2159	FRA2164	FRA2168
GBR2173	GBR2174	GBR2175	GBR2185
GBR2187	GBR2196	GBR2202	GBR2218
GBR2221	GBR2238	GBR2240	GBR2259
GBR2274	GBR2278	GBR2280	GBR2289
GBR2330	GBR2350	GBR2361	GBR2369
GBR2371	GBR2382	GBR2390	GBR2392
GBR2422	GBR2423	GBR2434	GBR2454
GBR2460	GBR2464	GBR2477	GBR2481
GBR2500	GBR2501	GBR2517	GBR2550
GBR2553	IRL2711	IRL2724	IRL2732
ITA2744	ITA2747	ITA2760	ITA2762
ITA2766	ITA2770	ITA2774	ITA2777
ITA2784	ITA2785	ITA2806	ITA2807
ITA2813	ITA2818	ITA2826	ITA2829
ITA2835	ITA2849	ITA2855	ITA2860
ITA2868	ITA2874	ITA2884	ITA2888
ITA2890	ITA2896	ITA2898	ITA2899
ITA2900	ITA2907	ITA2921	LIE2930
LUX2942	LUX2954	LUX2955	LUX2972
LUX2973	LUX2984	LUX2991	LUX2997
LUX3006	NLD3045	NLD3050	NLD3067
NLD3091	NLD3095	NLD3096	NLD3123
NLD3131	NLD3137	NLD3144	NLD3150
NLD3154	NLD3165	NLD3185	NLD3186
NLD3199	NLD3225	NLD3235	NLD3251
NLD3257	NLD3277	NLD3281	NLD3292
NLD3301	NLD3308	NLD3311	NLD3338
NLD3356	NLD3361	NLD3364	NOR3395
NOR3435	NOR3452	NOR3465	POL3508
POL3519	PRT3549	PRT3555	PRT3594
PRT3602	PRT3603	SWE3656	SWE3674
SWE3745	SWE3749	SWE3763	SWE3769
SWE3813	SWE3827	SWE3828	SWE3830

CENTRAL ASIA AND SOUTH ASIA - ASIE CENTRALE ET ASIE DU SUD

AUT0013	AUT0022	AUT0026	AUT0076
AUT0089	AUT0091	BEL0097	BEL0104
BEL0107	BEL0124	BEL0144	BEL0145
BEL0148	BEL0156	BEL0158	BEL0186
BEL0192	BEL0194	BEL0198	BEL0201
BEL0202	BEL0203	BEL0221	BEL0265
BEL0297	BEL0297	BEL0299	BEL0301
BEL0303	BEL0306	BEL0315	BEL0327
BEL0340	BEL0341	BEL0351	BEL0352
BEL0358	BEL0359	BEL0361	BEL0368
BEL0396	CHE0412	CHE0417	CHE0434
CHE0467	CHE0472	CHE0477	CHE0486
CHE0491	CHE0510	CHE0522	CHE0529
CHE0565	CHE0568	CHE0569	CHE0570
CHE0586	CHE0619	CHE0628	CHE0655
CHE0660	CHE0669	CHE0682	CHE0687
CHE0688	CHE0689	CHE0692	CHE0712
CHE0730	CHE0742	CHE0757	CHE0758
CHE0764	CHE0796	CHE0798	CHE0814
CHE0819	DEU0922	DEU0928	DEU0940
DEU0944	DEU0954	DEU0965	DEU0968
DEU0971	DEU0972	DEU0983	DEU0985
DEU0989	DEU0993	DEU0995	DEU1017
DEU1023	DEU1053	DEU1066	DEU1086
DEU1105	DEU1106	DEU1121	DEU1128
DEU1129	DEU1131	DEU1132	DEU1141
DEU1142	DEU1149	DEU1151	DEU1178
DEU1185	DEU1187	DNK1216	DNK1218
DNK1248	DNK1259	DNK1260	DNK1275
DNK1292	DNK1310	DNK1314	DNK1339
DNK1366	DNK1369	DNK1384	DNK1402
ESP1486	ESP1492	ESP1513	FIN1549
FIN1580	FIN1581	FIN1591	FRA1610
FRA1642	FRA1644	FRA1655	FRA1658
FRA1661	FRA1670	FRA1744	FRA1831
FRA1843	FRA1866	FRA1887	FRA1904
FRA1921	FRA1934	FRA1939	FRA1966
FRA1978	FRA1990	FRA2023	FRA2047

FRA2053	FRA2054	FRA2057	FRA2062
FRA2074	FRA2081	FRA2086	FRA2096
FRA2131	FRA2151	FRA2154	FRA2159
FRA2168	GBR2172	GBR2173	GBR2174
GBR2175	GBR2186	GBR2196	GBR2197
GBR2201	GBR2202	GBR2213	GBR2218
GBR2219	GBR2221	GBR2226	GBR2228
GBR2238	GBR2242	GBR2256	GBR2259
GBR2260	GBR2266	GBR2278	GBR2280
GBR2297	GBR2302	GBR2306	GBR2321
GBR2324	GBR2325	GBR2330	GBR2333
GBR2334	GBR2348	GBR2351	GBR2358
GBR2361	GBR2369	GBR2371	GBR2372
GBR2375	GBR2382	GBR2385	GBR2390
GBR2392	GBR2413	GBR2422	GBR2423
GBR2434	GBR2436	GBR2439	GBR2445
GBR2464	GBR2467	GBR2475	GBR2477
GBR2481	GBR2492	GBR2500	GBR2501
GBR2509	GBR2532	GBR2535	GBR2538
GBR2552	GBR2553	GRC2571	IRL2688
IRL2699	IRL2711	IRL2726	ISL2736
ITA2764	ITA2766	ITA2784	ITA2813
ITA2860	ITA2879	ITA2888	ITA2900
ITA2912	LIE2926	LUX2965	LUX2973
LUX2982	LUX2997	NLD3050	NLD3056
NLD3067	NLD3091	NLD3091	NLD3096
NLD3100	NLD3101	NLD3123	NLD3124
NLD3131	NLD3138	NLD3144	NLD3147
NLD3149	NLD3150	NLD3154	NLD3163
NLD3165	NLD3173	NLD3185	NLD3186
NLD3199	NLD3202	NLD3213	NLD3225
NLD3231	NLD3237	NLD3242	NLD3251
NLD3257	NLD3260	NLD3277	NLD3281
NLD3292	NLD3295	NLD3300	NLD3302
NLD3308	NLD3317	NLD3317	NLD3338
NLD3356	NLD3361	NLD3364	NOR3371
NOR3384	NOR3386	NOR3394	NOR3425
NOR3435	NOR3447	NOR3453	NOR3459
NOR3460	NOR3465	NOR3467	POL3519
PRT3549	SWE3656	SWE3666	SWE3679
SWE3723	SWE3737	SWE3747	SWE3749
SWE3763	SWE3769	SWE3771	SWE3787
SWE3809	SWE3813	SWE3818	SWE3819
SWE3826	SWE3827	SWE3828	SWE3830
SWE3831	SWE3854	SWE3855	SWE3857

EAST AFRICA - AFRIQUE DE L'EST

AUT0003	AUT0013	AUT0024	AUT0026
AUT0030	AUT0041	AUT0063	AUT0067
AUT0076	AUT0085	AUT0091	BEL0097
BEL0107	BEL0124	BEL0133	BEL0144
BEL0148	BEL0167	BEL0186	BEL0192
BEL0198	BEL0221	BEL0224	BEL0265
BEL0269	BEL0270	BEL0275	BEL0297
BEL0299	BEL0301	BEL0306	BEL0316
BEL0318	BEL0327	BEL0340	BEL0341
BEL0353	BEL0358	BEL0361	CHE0434
CHE0448	CHE0486	CHE0493	CHE0510
CHE0521	CHE0522	CHE0559	CHE0565
CHE0569	CHE0570	CHE0586	CHE0598
CHE0620	CHE0629	CHE0630	CHE0632
CHE0643	CHE0660	CHE0682	CHE0683
CHE0684	CHE0687	CHE0688	CHE0689
CHE0691	CHE0692	CHE0707	CHE0712
CHE0730	CHE0754	CHE0758	CHE0759
CHE0764	CHE0776	CHE0796	CHE0814
CHE0817	CHE0819	CHE0823	CZE0905
DEU0918	DEU0928	DEU0928	DEU0936
DEU0939	DEU0944	DEU0968	DEU0972
DEU0978	DEU0983	DEU0986	DEU0989
DEU0995	DEU1002	DEU1017	DEU1023
DEU1053	DEU1069	DEU1081	DEU1105
DEU1106	DEU1128	DEU1129	DEU1131
DEU1141	DEU1142	DEU1145	DEU1149
DEU1178	DEU1181	DEU1185	DNK1214
DNK1242	DNK1245	DNK1255	DNK1259
DNK1275	DNK1285	DNK1292	DNK1310
DNK1314	DNK1316	DNK1339	DNK1342
DNK1358	DNK1369	DNK1377	DNK1391
DNK1402	DNK1405	ESP1432	ESP1486
ESP1492	ESP1493	ESP1510	ESP1524
FIN1549	FIN1551	FIN1556	FIN1580
FIN1585	FIN1587	FIN1591	FRA1610
FRA1614	FRA1617	FRA1644	FRA1658
FRA1668	FRA1672	FRA1717	FRA1731
FRA1744	FRA1843	FRA1887	FRA1903
FRA1934	FRA1939	FRA1956	FRA2023
FRA2046	FRA2047	FRA2051	FRA2054

FRA2060	FRA2069	FRA2075	FRA2080
FRA2081	FRA2087	FRA2093	FRA2096
FRA2107	FRA2116	FRA2117	FRA2123
FRA2154	FRA2159	FRA2168	GBR2172
GBR2173	GBR2174	GBR2175	GBR2179
GBR2180	GBR2183	GBR2185	GBR2186
GBR2187	GBR2196	GBR2202	GBR2214
GBR2218	GBR2219	GBR2221	GBR2222
GBR2224	GBR2226	GBR2228	GBR2238
GBR2240	GBR2242	GBR2256	GBR2259
GBR2264	GBR2274	GBR2278	GBR2280
GBR2282	GBR2292	GBR2293	GBR2303
GBR2307	GBR2320	GBR2321	GBR2324
GBR2330	GBR2338	GBR2348	GBR2350
GBR2361	GBR2369	GBR2371	GBR2382
GBR2385	GBR2390	GBR2392	GBR2413
GBR2422	GBR2423	GBR2426	GBR2434
GBR2436	GBR2439	GBR2459	GBR2460
GBR2464	GBR2467	GBR2477	GBR2481
GBR2483	GBR2489	GBR2497	GBR2500
GBR2501	GBR2502	GBR2517	GBR2521
GBR2523	GBR2533	GBR2535	GBR2536
GBR2538	GBR2550	GBR2552	GBR2553
GBR2556	GRC2571	IRL2687	IRL2688
IRL2691	IRL2699	IRL2711	IRL2716
IRL2724	IRL2726	IRL2729	IRL2730
IRL2732	IRL2733	ISL2736	ISL2739
ISL2740	ITA2744	ITA2757	ITA2766
ITA2767	ITA2771	ITA2772	ITA2782
ITA2784	ITA2785	ITA2803	ITA2804
ITA2810	ITA2812	ITA2813	ITA2816
ITA2818	ITA2820	ITA2822	ITA2829
ITA2835	ITA2837	ITA2841	ITA2848
ITA2860	ITA2868	ITA2874	ITA2877
ITA2888	ITA2889	ITA2890	ITA2900
ITA2901	ITA2907	ITA2910	ITA2920
LUX2955	LUX2956	LUX2973	LUX2997
NLD3045	NLD3050	NLD3067	NLD3068
NLD3071	NLD3074	NLD3075	NLD3091
NLD3096	NLD3100	NLD3101	NLD3123
NLD3131	NLD3137	NLD3144	NLD3150
NLD3154	NLD3155	NLD3165	NLD3173
NLD3185	NLD3186	NLD3187	NLD3198
NLD3201	NLD3202	NLD3216	NLD3225
NLD3231	NLD3235	NLD3237	NLD3251
NLD3257	NLD3277	NLD3281	NLD3292
NLD3300	NLD3301	NLD3308	NLD3311
NLD3317	NLD3318	NLD3323	NLD3338
NLD3356	NLD3361	NLD3364	NOR3381
NOR3384	NOR3386	NOR3404	NOR3412
NOR3425	NOR3430	NOR3431	NOR3435
NOR3443	NOR3447	NOR3456	NOR3465
NOR3467	POL3508	POL3519	PRT3550
SWE3656	SWE3666	SWE3679	SWE3688
SWE3712	SWE3714	SWE3727	SWE3745
SWE3749	SWE3769	SWE3771	SWE3776
SWE3787	SWE3798	SWE3799	SWE3806
SWE3807	SWE3814	SWE3826	SWE3828
SWE3830	SWE3831	SWE3853	SWE3854
SWE3855	SWE3877		

EAST ASIA - ASIE DE L'EST

AUT0013	AUT0024	AUT0076	BEL0107
BEL0124	BEL0133	BEL0144	BEL0145
BEL0186	BEL0198	BEL0221	BEL0265
BEL0351	BEL0358	BEL0359	BEL0361
CHE0434	CHE0510	CHE0565	CHE0570
CHE0655	CHE0660	CHE0689	CHE0692
CHE0693	CHE0712	CHE0730	CHE0796
CHE0814	CHE0817	CHE0819	DEU0944
DEU0968	DEU0971	DEU0972	DEU0989
DEU0994	DEU0995	DEU1017	DEU1023
DEU1129	DEU1131	DEU1149	DEU1185
DNK1292	DNK1310	DNK1314	DNK1402
ESP1432	ESP1435	ESP1492	ESP1508
FRA1610	FRA1672	FRA1744	FRA1749
FRA1865	FRA1921	FRA1992	FRA2047
FRA2054	FRA2075	FRA2087	FRA2096
FRA2114	FRA2116	FRA2123	FRA2149
FRA2154	FRA2159	FRA2168	GBR2175
GBR2196	GBR2202	GBR2218	GBR2221
GBR2232	GBR2238	GBR2260	GBR2278
GBR2280	GBR2306	GBR2361	GBR2369
GBR2371	GBR2382	GBR2392	GBR2422
GBR2423	GBR2426	GBR2434	GBR2445
GBR2464	GBR2477	GBR2481	GBR2501
GBR2525	GBR2550	GBR2553	IRL2711
IRL2726	ITA2766	ITA2784	ITA2822
ITA2832	ITA2855	ITA2860	LUX2973

NLD3067	NLD3069	NLD3071	NLD3096
NLD3123	NLD3138	NLD3144	NLD3150
NLD3154	NLD3186	NLD3198	NLD3202
NLD3225	NLD3251	NLD3277	NLD3308
NLD3338	NLD3356	NLD3361	NLD3364
NOR3387	NOR3435	NOR3465	SWE3712
SWE3745	SWE3763	SWE3809	SWE3813
SWE3823	SWE3826	SWE3828	SWE3830

MEXICO AND CENTRAL AMERICA - MEXIQUE ET AMERIQUE CENTRALE

AUT0003	AUT0013	AUT0026	AUT0030
AUT0040	AUT0041	AUT0058	AUT0067
AUT0076	AUT0090	AUT0097	BEL0097
BEL0107	BEL0124	BEL0133	BEL0144
BEL0148	BEL0184	BEL0186	BEL0189
BEL0198	BEL0201	BEL0203	BEL0221
BEL0224	BEL0241	BEL0265	BEL0269
BEL0270	BEL0297	BEL0299	BEL0301
BEL0316	BEL0318	BEL0323	BEL0327
BEL0335	BEL0336	BEL0340	BEL0351
BEL0353	BEL0358	BEL0359	BEL0361
BEL0362	CHE0427	CHE0434	CHE0485
CHE0493	CHE0510	CHE0517	CHE0558
CHE0568	CHE0570	CHE0586	CHE0613
CHE0619	CHE0630	CHE0682	CHE0683
CHE0689	CHE0712	CHE0730	CHE0735
CHE0755	CHE0757	CHE0788	CHE0789
CHE0804	CHE0818	CHE0819	DEU0944
DEU0947	DEU0954	DEU0968	DEU0972
DEU0983	DEU0989	DEU0995	DEU1012
DEU1023	DEU1031	DEU1053	DEU1128
DEU1129	DEU1131	DEU1138	DEU1141
DEU1142	DEU1149	DEU1174	DEU1176
DEU1178	DEU1185	DEU1187	DEU1202
DNK1226	DNK1283	DNK1292	DNK1310
DNK1312	DNK1317	DNK1317	DNK1339
DNK1359	DNK1369	DNK1402	ESP1409
ESP1427	ESP1432	ESP1435	ESP1442
ESP1450	ESP1455	ESP1475	ESP1484
ESP1485	ESP1486	ESP1492	ESP1493
ESP1495	ESP1496	ESP1503	ESP1505
ESP1506	ESP1510	ESP1521	ESP1522
ESP1525	FIN1546	FIN1580	FIN1591
FIN1603	FRA1610	FRA1671	FRA1672
FRA1744	FRA1815	FRA1831	FRA1843
FRA1856	FRA1904	FRA1928	FRA1934
FRA1938	FRA1939	FRA2042	FRA2044
FRA2047	FRA2060	FRA2062	FRA2069
FRA2074	FRA2081	FRA2093	FRA2096
FRA2102	FRA2116	FRA2123	FRA2154
FRA2159	FRA2175	GBR2174	GBR2175
GBR2196	GBR2201	GBR2218	GBR2221
GBR2226	GBR2228	GBR2229	GBR2238
GBR2256	GBR2259	GBR2264	GBR2278
GBR2280	GBR2293	GBR2321	GBR2361
GBR2371	GBR2373	GBR2385	GBR2390
GBR2392	GBR2422	GBR2422	GBR2423
GBR2434	GBR2436	GBR2439	GBR2467
GBR2481	GBR2500	GBR2501	GBR2535
GBR2553	GBR2556	IRL2687	IRL2707
IRL2711	IRL2726	IRL2732	ITA2744
ITA2762	ITA2766	ITA2771	ITA2773
ITA2784	ITA2781	ITA2834	ITA2858
ITA2860	ITA2873	ITA2881	ITA2888
ITA2894	ITA2913	ITA2922	LUX2973
LUX2976	LUX2997	NLD3068	NLD3068
NLD3071	NLD3091	NLD3096	NLD3123
NLD3141	NLD3144	NLD3150	NLD3154
NLD3159	NLD3165	NLD3173	NLD3185
NLD3186	NLD3198	NLD3199	NLD3225
NLD3231	NLD3251	NLD3277	NLD3285
NLD3288	NLD3300	NLD3303	NLD3338
NLD3356	NLD3361	NLD3364	NOR3374
NOR3381	NOR3409	NOR3425	NOR3435
NOR3467	POL3513	SWE3656	SWE3687
SWE3688	SWE3749	SWE3770	SWE3771
SWE3796	SWE3798	SWE3826	SWE3828
SWE3830	SWE3857	SWE3865	

MIDDLE EAST - MOYEN-ORIENT

AUT0035	AUT0076	AUT0091	BEL0124
BEL0133	BEL0144	BEL0186	BEL0198
BEL0221	BEL0241	BEL0270	BEL0297
BEL0301	BEL0306	BEL0316	BEL0318
BEL0323	BEL0353	BEL0358	BEL0361
BEL0362	CHE0403	CHE0410	CHE0434
CHE0491	CHE0493	CHE0506	CHE0568

CHE0570	CHE0655	CHE0660	CHE0664
CHE0684	CHE0687	CHE0689	CHE0712
CHE0730	CHE0757	CHE0796	CHE0814
CHE0817	CHE0819	CHE0823	CHE0825
DEU0939	DEU0944	DEU0968	DEU0972
DEU0989	DEU0995	DEU1017	DEU1023
DEU1065	DEU1106	DEU1131	DEU1176
DEU1185	DNK1292	DNK1310	DNK1314
DNK1372	DNK1402	ESP1435	ESP1522
ESP1524	FRA1610	FRA1629	FRA1731
FRA1744	FRA1749	FRA1771	FRA1791
FRA1793	FRA1794	FRA1832	FRA1843
FRA1865	FRA1904	FRA1964	FRA2047
FRA2056	FRA2069	FRA2070	FRA2081
FRA2096	FRA2114	FRA2116	FRA2117
FRA2145	FRA2150	FRA2154	FRA2159
FRA2163	GBR2175	GBR2196	GBR2218
GBR2221	GBR2229	GBR2232	GBR2238
GBR2260	GBR2280	GBR2361	GBR2369
GBR2371	GBR2385	GBR2392	GBR2423
GBR2434	GBR2445	GBR2489	GBR2500
GBR2501	GBR2556	GRC2572	IRL2687
IRL2711	ITA2764	ITA2766	ITA2773
ITA2775	ITA2784	ITA2785	ITA2809
ITA2834	ITA2860	ITA2901	LUX2973
LUX2992	MLT3016	NLD3067	NLD3101
NLD3123	NLD3144	NLD3150	NLD3154
NLD3155	NLD3165	NLD3173	NLD3199
NLD3201	NLD3338	NLD3356	NLD3364
NOR3386	NOR3430	NOR3435	NOR3444
NOR3447	NOR3456	POL3508	POL3519
SWE3749	SWE3822	SWE3826	SWE3828
SWE3830	SWE3855	TUR3883	

NORTH AFRICA - AFRIQUE DU NORD

AUT0013	AUT0051	AUT0076	BEL0097
BEL0124	BEL0133	BEL0144	BEL0148
BEL0153	BEL0186	BEL0198	BEL0221
BEL0265	BEL0269	BEL0270	BEL0301
BEL0316	BEL0340	BEL0342	BEL0352
BEL0358	BEL0361	CHE0434	CHE0477
CHE0522	CHE0568	CHE0570	CHE0598
CHE0655	CHE0682	CHE0687	CHE0688
CHE0689	CHE0712	CHE0730	CHE0796
CHE0814	CZE0905	DEU0918	DEU0944
DEU0968	DEU0972	DEU0989	DEU0995
DEU1017	DEU1023	DEU1063	DEU1111
DEU1131	DEU1185	DEU1191	DNK1255
DNK1310	DNK1314	DNK1442	ESP1442
ESP1486	ESP1492	ESP1493	ESP1495
ESP1505	ESP1521	FRA1610	FRA1629
FRA1683	FRA1731	FRA1766	FRA1832
FRA1766	FRA1794	FRA1831	FRA1832
FRA1846	FRA1887	FRA1917	FRA1946
FRA1956	FRA1964	FRA1970	FRA1993
FRA2047	FRA2069	FRA2075	FRA2087
FRA2093	FRA2096	FRA2107	FRA2114
FRA2116	FRA2117	FRA2154	FRA2159
GBR2175	GBR2185	GBR2196	GBR2218
GBR2221	GBR2238	GBR2280	GBR2361
GBR2369	GBR2371	GBR2385	GBR2392
GBR2422	GBR2423	GBR2434	GBR2500
GBR2501	GBR2535	IRL2711	ITA2766
ITA2784	ITA2785	ITA2791	ITA2810
ITA2822	ITA2860	MLT3016	NLD3067
NLD3123	NLD3144	NLD3150	NLD3154
NLD3155	NLD3163	NLD3165	NLD3173
NLD3183	NLD3198	NLD3225	NLD3277
NLD3290	NLD3300	NLD3301	NLD3338
NLD3356	NLD3364	POL3508	POL3519
SWE3667	SWE3688	SWE3763	SWE3813
SWE3828	SWE3830		

OCEANIA - OCEANIE

AUT0067	BEL0107	BEL0124	BEL0186
BEL0198	BEL0361	CHE0434	CHE0687
CHE0712	CHE0730	CHE0814	CHE0819
DEU0944	DEU0968	DEU0972	DEU0989
DEU0992	DEU0995	DEU1017	DEU1023
DEU1149	DEU1185	DNK1292	DNK1310
DNK1314	DNK1402	ESP1492	FRA1610
FRA1670	FRA1672	FRA1744	FRA2047
FRA2096	FRA2116	FRA2151	FRA2154
FRA2168	GBR2175	GBR2202	GBR2218
GBR2221	GBR2256	GBR2264	GBR2278
GBR2280	GBR2344	GBR2351	GBR2361
GBR2369	GBR2371	GBR2382	GBR2392
GBR2434	GBR2477	GBR2481	GBR2501

GBR2524	GBR2535	GBR2552	GBR2553
IRL2711	ITA2766	ITA2784	ITA2860
NLD3067	NLD3096	NLD3123	NLD3137
NLD3144	NLD3150	NLD3154	NLD3186
NLD3356	NLD3361	NLD3364	SWE3749
SWE3830			

SOUTH AMERICA - AMERIQUE DU SUD

AUT0003	AUT0013	AUT0026	AUT0030
AUT0051	AUT0052	AUT0067	AUT0076
AUT0091	BEL0107	BEL0119	BEL0124
BEL0133	BEL0139	BEL0144	BEL0148
BEL0155	BEL0164	BEL0186	BEL0198
BEL0201	BEL0203	BEL0221	BEL0258
BEL0265	BEL0269	BEL0270	BEL0282
BEL0297	BEL0299	BEL0301	BEL0314
BEL0316	BEL0318	BEL0323	BEL0327
BEL0335	BEL0336	BEL0341	BEL0347
BEL0352	BEL0353	BEL0358	BEL0359
BEL0361	BEL0368	BEL0371	BEL0392
CHE0434	CHE0438	CHE0455	CHE0465
CHE0475	CHE0477	CHE0479	CHE0510
CHE0522	CHE0565	CHE0568	CHE0569
CHE0570	CHE0581	CHE0586	CHE0596
CHE0598	CHE0602	CHE0613	CHE0614
CHE0628	CHE0660	CHE0669	CHE0682
CHE0683	CHE0687	CHE0688	CHE0689
CHE0693	CHE0712	CHE0730	CHE0750
CHE0757	CHE0764	CHE0789	CHE0796
CHE0798	CHE0806	CHE0814	CHE0819
CHE0825	DEU0926	DEU0928	DEU0944
DEU0947	DEU0948	DEU0968	DEU0972
DEU0983	DEU0989	DEU0991	DEU0994
DEU0995	DEU1012	DEU1017	DEU1023
DEU1066	DEU1105	DEU1128	DEU1129
DEU1131	DEU1132	DEU1138	DEU1141
DEU1142	DEU1149	DEU1176	DEU1185
DEU1187	DNK1292	DNK1310	DNK1314
DNK1319	DNK1358	DNK1369	DNK1402
DNK1403	ESP1407	ESP1409	ESP1413
ESP1432	ESP1435	ESP1439	ESP1442
ESP1452	ESP1455	ESP1485	ESP1486
ESP1488	ESP1491	ESP1492	ESP1493
ESP1495	ESP1496	ESP1502	ESP1505
ESP1507	ESP1508	ESP1510	ESP1513
ESP1521	ESP1522	ESP1525	FIN1551
FIN1558	FRA1610	FRA1617	FRA1655
FRA1670	FRA1672	FRA1677	FRA1683
FRA1710	FRA1741	FRA1744	FRA1749
FRA1766	FRA1815	FRA1831	FRA1832
FRA1843	FRA1903	FRA1904	FRA1917
FRA1926	FRA1928	FRA1932	FRA1934
FRA1938	FRA1946	FRA1978	FRA2005
FRA2023	FRA2042	FRA2047	FRA2056
FRA2060	FRA2062	FRA2069	FRA2074
FRA2081	FRA2086	FRA2087	FRA2093
FRA2096	FRA2102	FRA2107	FRA2114
FRA2116	FRA2123	FRA2131	FRA2154
FRA2159	FRA2168	GBR2174	GBR2175
GBR2196	GBR2201	GBR2202	GBR2218
GBR2219	GBR2221	GBR2226	GBR2228
GBR2229	GBR2238	GBR2264	GBR2266
GBR2278	GBR2280	GBR2293	GBR2321
GBR2325	GBR2344	GBR2361	GBR2369
GBR2371	GBR2383	GBR2390	GBR2392
GBR2422	GBR2423	GBR2434	GBR2436
GBR2454	GBR2467	GBR2481	GBR2485
GBR2500	GBR2501	GBR2525	GBR2535
GBR2537	GBR2550	GBR2553	IRL2711
IRL2726	IRL2732	ITA2756	ITA2762
ITA2766	ITA2767	ITA2770	ITA2775
ITA2777	ITA2782	ITA2784	ITA2785
ITA2791	ITA2798	ITA2801	ITA2802
ITA2806	ITA2807	ITA2809	ITA2810
ITA2812	ITA2820	ITA2822	ITA2828
ITA2832	ITA2834	ITA2835	ITA2842
ITA2855	ITA2860	ITA2868	ITA2873
ITA2882	ITA2885	ITA2888	ITA2889
ITA2895	ITA2898	ITA2899	ITA2901
ITA2907	ITA2910	ITA2913	ITA2921
ITA2922	LUX2943	LUX2949	LUX2954
LUX2964	LUX2968	LUX2973	LUX2979
LUX2980	LUX2992	LUX2997	NLD3050
NLD3067	NLD3068	NLD3071	NLD3091
NLD3096	NLD3123	NLD3131	NLD3144
NLD3150	NLD3154	NLD3155	NLD3165
NLD3173	NLD3185	NLD3186	NLD3198
NLD3199	NLD3202	NLD3225	NLD3250
NLD3277	NLD3290	NLD3308	NLD3317

See: *How to Use the Directory*, page 11.

NLD3356	NLD3361	NLD3364	NOR3374
NOR3381	NOR3394	NOR3409	NOR3410
NOR3425	NOR3443	NOR3452	NOR3460
NOR3465	POL3519	PRT3600	SWE3656
SWE3666	SWE3667	SWE3674	SWE3693
SWE3702	SWE3712	SWE3744	SWE3749
SWE3763	SWE3769	SWE3771	SWE3787
SWE3789	SWE3795	SWE3796	SWE3813
SWE3827	SWE3828	SWE3830	SWE3865
SWE3877			

SOUTH EAST ASIA - ASIE DU SUD-EST

AUT0013	AUT0026	AUT0052	AUT0076
AUT0091	BEL0097	BEL0107	BEL0124
BEL0128	BEL0133	BEL0144	BEL0156
BEL0186	BEL0192	BEL0198	BEL0203
BEL0221	BEL0224	BEL0269	BEL0297
BEL0299	BEL0301	BEL0306	BEL0315
BEL0316	BEL0318	BEL0323	BEL0327
BEL0341	BEL0342	BEL0351	BEL0358
BEL0359	BEL0361	BEL0362	BEL0368
CHE0434	CHE0477	CHE0479	CHE0486
CHE0493	CHE0510	CHE0522	CHE0524
CHE0559	CHE0565	CHE0568	CHE0570
CHE0586	CHE0598	CHE0604	CHE0619
CHE0630	CHE0637	CHE0660	CHE0682
CHE0683	CHE0688	CHE0689	CHE0692
CHE0693	CHE0712	CHE0730	CHE0749
CHE0757	CHE0758	CHE0796	CHE0798
CHE0814	CHE0819	CHE0825	DEU0918
DEU0940	DEU0944	DEU0954	DEU0968
DEU0972	DEU0978	DEU0983	DEU0989
DEU0990	DEU0995	DEU1017	DEU1023
DEU1053	DEU1081	DEU1105	DEU1106
DEU1128	DEU1129	DEU1132	DEU1141
DEU1149	DEU1176	DEU1178	DEU1185
DEU1187	DNK1259	DNK1292	DNK1310
DNK1314	DNK1316	DNK1402	ESP1492
FIN1551	FIN1580	FRA1610	FRA1614
FRA1617	FRA1629	FRA1638	FRA1640
FRA1648	FRA1667	FRA1670	FRA1671
FRA1701	FRA1715	FRA1744	FRA1766
FRA1820	FRA1832	FRA1843	FRA1850
FRA1860	FRA1921	FRA1928	FRA1934
FRA1938	FRA1941	FRA1946	FRA1970
FRA1979	FRA2005	FRA2023	FRA2047
FRA2054	FRA2056	FRA2060	FRA2065
FRA2069	FRA2074	FRA2075	FRA2080
FRA2081	FRA2087	FRA2093	FRA2096
FRA2097	FRA2114	FRA2116	FRA2117
FRA2123	FRA2134	FRA2137	FRA2140
FRA2150	FRA2154	FRA2159	FRA2168
GBR2175	GBR2196	GBR2201	GBR2202
GBR2218	GBR2221	GBR2226	GBR2228
GBR2238	GBR2240	GBR2242	GBR2256
GBR2260	GBR2278	GBR2280	GBR2293
GBR2303	GBR2310	GBR2321	GBR2324
GBR2330	GBR2344	GBR2350	GBR2361
GBR2369	GBR2371	GBR2382	GBR2385
GBR2390	GBR2392	GBR2423	GBR2426
GBR2434	GBR2436	GBR2464	GBR2464
GBR2467	GBR2477	GBR2481	GBR2486
GBR2500	GBR2501	GBR2533	GBR2535
GBR2537	GBR2552	GBR2553	IRL2687
IRL2691	IRL2711	IRL2726	IRL2733
ITA2758	ITA2766	ITA2784	ITA2785
ITA2798	ITA2824	ITA2855	ITA2860
ITA2894	ITA2898	ITA2911	ITA2912
LUX2954	LUX2973	LUX2997	NLD3050
NLD3067	NLD3068	NLD3071	NLD3083
NLD3091	NLD3096	NLD3100	NLD3123
NLD3137	NLD3138	NLD3141	NLD3144
NLD3150	NLD3154	NLD3155	NLD3165
NLD3173	NLD3184	NLD3185	NLD3186
NLD3198	NLD3202	NLD3225	NLD3235
NLD3237	NLD3251	NLD3277	NLD3285
NLD3290	NLD3292	NLD3304	NLD3308
NLD3317	NLD3338	NLD3356	NLD3361
NLD3364	NOR3372	NOR3381	NOR3394
NOR3395	NOR3425	NOR3435	NOR3465
NOR3467	POL3508	POL3519	SWE3656
SWE3674	SWE3730	SWE3745	SWE3749
SWE3787	SWE3789	SWE3798	SWE3826
SWE3828	SWE3830	SWE3854	SWE3855
SWE3857			

SOUTHERN AFRICA - AFRIQUE AUSTRALE

AUT0013	AUT0024	AUT0067	AUT0076
AUT0091	BEL0097	BEL0124	BEL0144
BEL0148	BEL0186	BEL0198	BEL0203
BEL0221	BEL0260	BEL0269	BEL0297
BEL0299	BEL0301	BEL0323	BEL0327
BEL0340	BEL0341	BEL0358	BEL0359
BEL0361	BEL0368	BEL0414	CHE0434
CHE0486	CHE0506	CHE0510	CHE0565
CHE0569	CHE0570	CHE0619	CHE0628
CHE0682	CHE0683	CHE0687	CHE0689
CHE0692	CHE0693	CHE0707	CHE0712
CHE0730	CHE0734	CHE0750	CHE0755
CHE0757	CHE0758	CHE0759	CHE0762
CHE0776	CHE0778	CHE0796	CHE0798
CHE0814	CHE0817	CHE0819	CZE0905
DEU0922	DEU0944	DEU0968	DEU0972
DEU0989	DEU0995	DEU1023	DEU1069
DEU1081	DEU1082	DEU1106	DEU1128
DEU1129	DEU1131	DEU1141	DEU1143
DEU1149	DEU1181	DEU1185	DEU1187
DNK1218	DNK1222	DNK1255	DNK1259
DNK1275	DNK1288	DNK1292	DNK1312
DNK1314	DNK1339	DNK1388	DNK1402
ESP1420	ESP1445	ESP1450	ESP1453
ESP1454	ESP1486	ESP1493	ESP1495
ESP1502	FIN1546	FIN1549	FIN1556
FIN1559	FIN1568	FIN1579	FIN1580
FIN1587	FRA1610	FRA1614	FRA1657
FRA1658	FRA1671	FRA1672	FRA1677
FRA1691	FRA1715	FRA1738	FRA1744
FRA1766	FRA1769	FRA1771	FRA1819
FRA1820	FRA1849	FRA1887	FRA1903
FRA1917	FRA1946	FRA1956	FRA1993
FRA2047	FRA2054	FRA2056	FRA2074
FRA2075	FRA2080	FRA2096	FRA2107
FRA2114	FRA2116	FRA2117	FRA2119
FRA2123	FRA2151	FRA2154	FRA2159
FRA2168	GBR2173	GBR2174	GBR2175
GBR2183	GBR2185	GBR2187	GBR2196
GBR2201	GBR2202	GBR2218	GBR2221
GBR2222	GBR2228	GBR2229	GBR2238
GBR2240	GBR2242	GBR2256	GBR2259
GBR2264	GBR2266	GBR2277	GBR2280
GBR2293	GBR2303	GBR2318	GBR2319
GBR2321	GBR2324	GBR2348	GBR2361
GBR2369	GBR2371	GBR2382	GBR2385
GBR2390	GBR2392	GBR2413	GBR2422
GBR2423	GBR2426	GBR2434	GBR2436
GBR2460	GBR2464	GBR2467	GBR2477
GBR2478	GBR2481	GBR2489	GBR2492
GBR2500	GBR2501	GBR2509	GBR2523
GBR2535	GBR2536	GBR2537	GBR2538
GBR2553	GBR2556	GBR2561	IRL2691
IRL2711	IRL2726	IRL2732	ISL2739
ITA2757	ITA2764	ITA2766	ITA2771
ITA2784	ITA2785	ITA2791	ITA2798
ITA2803	ITA2811	ITA2813	ITA2816
ITA2838	ITA2860	ITA2879	ITA2881
ITA2888	ITA2898	ITA2900	ITA2911
ITA2916	LUX2954	LUX2973	LUX2995
NLD3045	NLD3050	NLD3067	NLD3069
NLD3071	NLD3091	NLD3096	NLD3098
NLD3100	NLD3101	NLD3123	NLD3131
NLD3137	NLD3144	NLD3150	NLD3154
NLD3155	NLD3165	NLD3173	NLD3183
NLD3185	NLD3198	NLD3225	NLD3231
NLD3235	NLD3237	NLD3257	NLD3277
NLD3290	NLD3292	NLD3300	NLD3301
NLD3311	NLD3317	NLD3336	NLD3338
NLD3356	NLD3361	NLD3364	NOR3379
NOR3386	NOR3400	NOR3425	NOR3435
NOR3447	NOR3467	POL3508	POL3519
PRT3549	PRT3555	PRT3590	PRT3594
PRT3596	PRT3600	PRT3603	PRT3605
SWE3648	SWE3656	SWE3685	SWE3688
SWE3745	SWE3749	SWE3798	SWE3813
SWE3826	SWE3828	SWE3830	SWE3831
SWE3859			

WEST AFRICA - AFRIQUE DE L'OUEST

AUT0003	AUT0013	AUT0026	AUT0033
AUT0041	AUT0052	AUT0063	AUT0076
AUT0086	AUT0091	BEL0097	BEL0107
BEL0118	BEL0124	BEL0133	BEL0144
BEL0148	BEL0152	BEL0153	BEL0156
BEL0184	BEL0186	BEL0194	BEL0198
BEL0201	BEL0202	BEL0203	BEL0221

BEL0265	BEL0269	BEL0270	BEL0297
BEL0299	BEL0301	BEL0306	BEL0316
BEL0318	BEL0327	BEL0328	BEL0340
BEL0341	BEL0342	BEL0352	BEL0353
BEL0358	BEL0359	BEL0361	BEL0368
BEL0390	BEL0392	CHE0402	CHE0434
CHE0435	CHE0444	CHE0463	CHE0479
CHE0486	CHE0490	CHE0498	CHE0510
CHE0519	CHE0521	CHE0522	CHE0542
CHE0558	CHE0559	CHE0565	CHE0568
CHE0569	CHE0570	CHE0598	CHE0604
CHE0619	CHE0629	CHE0643	CHE0659
CHE0682	CHE0684	CHE0686	CHE0687
CHE0688	CHE0689	CHE0692	CHE0707
CHE0712	CHE0730	CHE0734	CHE0755
CHE0757	CHE0758	CHE0759	CHE0764
CHE0778	CHE0796	CHE0798	CHE0814
CHE0817	CHE0819	CHE0823	CZE0905
DEU0922	DEU0928	DEU0933	DEU0939
DEU0944	DEU0968	DEU0972	DEU0983
DEU0986	DEU0989	DEU0995	DEU1017
DEU1023	DEU1053	DEU1069	DEU1081
DEU1105	DEU1106	DEU1127	DEU1128
DEU1131	DEU1142	DEU1149	DEU1178
DEU1181	DEU1185	DEU1186	DEU1187
DNK1214	DNK1227	DNK1244	DNK1255
DNK1259	DNK1266	DNK1292	DNK1307
DNK1308	DNK1310	DNK1314	DNK1366
DNK1369	DNK1374	DNK1402	ESP1407
ESP1468	ESP1486	ESP1488	ESP1492
ESP1493	ESP1495	ESP1502	ESP1510
FIN1549	FIN1563	FIN1580	FIN1587
FRA1607	FRA1610	FRA1612	FRA1614
FRA1619	FRA1629	FRA1632	FRA1634
FRA1644	FRA1648	FRA1649	FRA1655
FRA1658	FRA1663	FRA1664	FRA1670
FRA1672	FRA1677	FRA1684	FRA1690
FRA1691	FRA1699	FRA1715	FRA1718
FRA1727	FRA1731	FRA1737	FRA1739
FRA1744	FRA1746	FRA1760	FRA1761
FRA1766	FRA1771	FRA1778	FRA1785
FRA1786	FRA1787	FRA1789	FRA1794
FRA1815	FRA1820	FRA1832	FRA1843
FRA1846	FRA1848	FRA1861	FRA1876
FRA1880	FRA1887	FRA1903	FRA1913
FRA1914	FRA1917	FRA1926	FRA1929
FRA1930	FRA1932	FRA1934	FRA1935
FRA1939	FRA1944	FRA1946	FRA1948
FRA1956	FRA1966	FRA1967	FRA1970
FRA1978	FRA1991	FRA1993	FRA2005
FRA2037	FRA2042	FRA2043	FRA2047
FRA2051	FRA2054	FRA2056	FRA2070
FRA2062	FRA2065	FRA2069	FRA2070
FRA2074	FRA2075	FRA2077	FRA2086
FRA2087	FRA2093	FRA2096	FRA2100
FRA2107	FRA2114	FRA2116	FRA2117
FRA2119	FRA2123	FRA2134	FRA2138
FRA2142	FRA2148	FRA2151	FRA2154
FRA2159	FRA2162	FRA2168	GBR2173
GBR2174	GBR2175	GBR2180	GBR2185
GBR2187	GBR2196	GBR2201	GBR2202
GBR2218	GBR2221	GBR2222	GBR2226
GBR2228	GBR2238	GBR2241	GBR2242
GBR2256	GBR2259	GBR2264	GBR2274
GBR2278	GBR2280	GBR2324	GBR2361
GBR2369	GBR2371	GBR2382	GBR2383
GBR2385	GBR2390	GBR2392	GBR2413
GBR2423	GBR2434	GBR2436	GBR2439
GBR2460	GBR2464	GBR2477	GBR2481
GBR2483	GBR2489	GBR2500	GBR2501
GBR2513	GBR2517	GBR2525	GBR2529
GBR2533	GBR2535	GBR2538	GBR2550
GBR2552	GBR2553	GBR2556	GRC2567
GRC2586	IRL2711	IRL2724	IRL2726
IRL2732	IRL2733	ISL2739	ITA2747
ITA2756	ITA2765	ITA2766	ITA2770
ITA2773	ITA2774	ITA2782	ITA2784
ITA2786	ITA2791	ITA2801	ITA2803
ITA2809	ITA2812	ITA2816	ITA2826
ITA2827	ITA2828	ITA2829	ITA2838
ITA2841	ITA2842	ITA2855	ITA2860
ITA2873	ITA2874	ITA2884	ITA2888
ITA2898	ITA2901	ITA2916	LUX2954
LUX2959	LUX2973	LUX2976	LUX2978
LUX2986	LUX2992	LUX2997	LUX3001
NLD3045	NLD3050	NLD3067	NLD3071
NLD3074	NLD3075	NLD3091	NLD3096
NLD3100	NLD3123	NLD3131	NLD3137
NLD3138	NLD3144	NLD3150	NLD3154

Voir : *Comment utiliser le répertoire*, page 11.

NLD3155 NLD3165 NLD3173 NLD3176
NLD3183 NLD3185 NLD3186 NLD3198
NLD3201 NLD3202 NLD3225 NLD3231
NLD3235 NLD3251 NLD3254 NLD3255
NLD3257 NLD3269 NLD3277 NLD3281
NLD3288 NLD3301 NLD3308 NLD3311
NLD3317 NLD3338 NLD3345 NLD3356
NLD3361 NLD3364 NOR3386 NOR3387
NOR3430 NOR3435 NOR3443 NOR3453
NOR3460 NOR3465 POL3508 POL3519
PRT3549 PRT3555 PRT3564 PRT3590
PRT3603 SWE3648 SWE3656 SWE3666
SWE3712 SWE3745 SWE3749 SWE3769
SWE3771 SWE3776 SWE3783 SWE3789
SWE3826 SWE3828 SWE3830 SWE3855

HUMAN RIGHTS, PEACE, CONFLICTS - DROITS DE L'HOMME, PAIX, CONFLITS

CARIBBEAN - CARAIBES

BEL0123 BEL0186 BEL0198 BEL0199
BEL0218 BEL0221 BEL0254 BEL0265
BEL0306 BEL0335 BEL0336 BEL0351
BEL0353 BEL0361 BEL0364 CHE0415
CHE0420 CHE0434 CHE0452 CHE0465
CHE0491 CHE0501 CHE0568 CHE0605
CHE0622 CHE0639 CHE0643 CHE0655
CHE0682 CHE0689 CHE0693 CHE0711
CHE0712 CHE0721 CHE0773 CHE0814
CHE0817 CHE0819 DEU0944 DEU0972
DEU0983 DEU1055 DEU1056 DEU1064
DEU1106 DEU1110 DEU1131 DNK1292
DNK1317 ESP1442 ESP1461 ESP1475
ESP1489 ESP1490 ESP1522 ESP1525
FIN1532 FIN1574 FIN1604 FRA1611
FRA1629 FRA1651 FRA1805 FRA1817
FRA1843 FRA1905 FRA1923 FRA1946
FRA1975 FRA1980 FRA2034 FRA2035
FRA2062 FRA2096 FRA2101 FRA2168
FRA2170 GBR2193 GBR2238 GBR2256
GBR2328 GBR2332 GBR2347 GBR2351
GBR2371 GBR2392 GBR2411 GBR2423
GBR2445 GBR2501 GBR2546 GBR2555
IRL2726 ITA2773 ITA2780 ITA2784
ITA2860 LUX2935 NLD3067 NLD3072
NLD3078 NLD3091 NLD3144 NLD3226
NLD3361 NLD3362 NLD3364 POL3508
POL3519 PRT3548 SWE3705 SWE3830

CENTRAL AFRICA - AFRIQUE CENTRALE

AUT0024 AUT0040 BEL0120 BEL0123
BEL0129 BEL0155 BEL0186 BEL0197
BEL0198 BEL0199 BEL0203 BEL0218
BEL0221 BEL0254 BEL0265 BEL0297
BEL0306 BEL0328 BEL0350 BEL0351
BEL0361 BEL0364 BEL0392 CHE0415
CHE0420 CHE0434 CHE0452 CHE0456
CHE0483 CHE0524 CHE0550 CHE0559
CHE0562 CHE0566 CHE0568 CHE0605
CHE0622 CHE0629 CHE0639 CHE0643
CHE0645 CHE0655 CHE0689 CHE0711
CHE0712 CHE0721 CHE0814 CHE0817
CHE0819 CZE0905 DEU0944 DEU0972
DEU1027 DEU1055 DEU1056 DEU1064
DEU1097 DEU1106 DEU1110 DEU1114
DEU1131 DEU1146 DEU1149 DNK1287
DNK1360 ESP1489 ESP1490 ESP1493
FIN1532 FIN1594 FIN1604 FRA1611
FRA1629 FRA1651 FRA1805 FRA1817
FRA1843 FRA1876 FRA1880 FRA1905
FRA1923 FRA1946 FRA1955 FRA1956
FRA1960 FRA1974 FRA1978 FRA2013
FRA2032 FRA2034 FRA2035 FRA2042
FRA2047 FRA2084 FRA2096 FRA2101
FRA2123 FRA2143 FRA2168 FRA2170
GBR2174 GBR2185 GBR2193 GBR2195
GBR2199 GBR2238 GBR2328 GBR2332
GBR2337 GBR2347 GBR2351 GBR2371
GBR2392 GBR2396 GBR2402 GBR2411
GBR2423 GBR2445 GBR2464 GBR2493
GBR2500 GBR2501 GBR2546 GBR2555
ITA2784 ITA2860 ITA2888 ITA2898
ITA2902 LIE2930 LUX2935 NLD3045
NLD3067 NLD3072 NLD3078 NLD3095
NLD3119 NLD3144 NLD3199 NLD3226
NLD3277 NLD3330 NLD3362 NLD3364

CENTRAL ASIA AND SOUTH ASIA - ASIE CENTRALE ET ASIE DU SUD

AUT0024 AUT0026 BEL0123 BEL0129
BEL0186 BEL0198 BEL0199 BEL0203
BEL0221 BEL0254 BEL0265 BEL0284
BEL0297 BEL0306 BEL0340 BEL0351
BEL0361 BEL0364 CHE0406 CHE0415
CHE0417 CHE0420 CHE0421 CHE0434
CHE0452 CHE0550 CHE0559 CHE0566
CHE0568 CHE0605 CHE0622 CHE0639
CHE0643 CHE0645 CHE0655 CHE0682
CHE0689 CHE0711 CHE0712 CHE0721
CHE0809 CHE0814 CHE0817 CHE0819
DEU0944 DEU0954 DEU0972 DEU0983
DEU1055 DEU1056 DEU1064 DEU1074
DEU1086 DEU1106 DEU1110 DEU1131
DEU1132 DEU1142 DEU1146 DEU1149
DEU1167 DEU1178 DEU1187 DNK1255
DNK1287 DNK1292 DNK1360 DNK1384
ESP1489 ESP1490 ESP1513 ESP1523
FIN1532 FIN1604 FRA1611 FRA1651
FRA1805 FRA1817 FRA1862 FRA1905
FRA1910 FRA1923 FRA1978 FRA1990
FRA1991 FRA2032 FRA2034 FRA2035
FRA2053 FRA2086 FRA2096 FRA2101
FRA2123 FRA2131 FRA2143 FRA2168
FRA2170 GBR2174 GBR2193 GBR2195
GBR2201 GBR2228 GBR2236 GBR2238
GBR2256 GBR2260 GBR2297 GBR2303
GBR2321 GBR2328 GBR2332 GBR2334
GBR2347 GBR2351 GBR2371 GBR2372
GBR2392 GBR2396 GBR2402 GBR2411
GBR2413 GBR2423 GBR2445 GBR2464
GBR2467 GBR2490 GBR2493 GBR2501
GBR2506 GBR2546 GBR2555 ITA2784
ITA2813 ITA2860 ITA2903 LUX2935
LUX2982 NLD3067 NLD3072 NLD3078
NLD3095 NLD3144 NLD3153 NLD3199
NLD3226 NLD3277 NLD3330 NLD3361
NLD3362 NLD3364 NOR3371 NOR3384
NOR3390 NOR3400 NOR3435 NOR3467
POL3519 PRT3548 SWE3661 SWE3674
SWE3682 SWE3749 SWE3768 SWE3771
SWE3780 SWE3795 SWE3818 SWE3819
SWE3821 SWE3826 SWE3830 SWE3834

EAST AFRICA - AFRIQUE DE L'EST

AUT0003 AUT0024 BEL0123 BEL0186
BEL0197 BEL0198 BEL0199 BEL0221
BEL0254 BEL0265 BEL0297 BEL0306
BEL0351 BEL0361 BEL0406 CHE0415
CHE0420 CHE0434 CHE0448 CHE0452
CHE0483 CHE0486 CHE0550 CHE0566
CHE0605 CHE0622 CHE0639 CHE0643
CHE0645 CHE0660 CHE0682 CHE0689
CHE0711 CHE0712 CHE0772 CHE0814
CHE0817 CHE0819 CZE0905 DEU0944
DEU0972 DEU0983 DEU1055 DEU1056
DEU1064 DEU1074 DEU1106 DEU1108
DEU1131 DEU1142 DEU1146 DEU1149
DEU1178 DNK1273 DNK1287 DNK1292
DNK1360 DNK1405 ESP1486 ESP1489
ESP1490 ESP1493 FIN1532 FIN1549
FIN1604 FRA1611 FRA1651 FRA1717
FRA1805 FRA1817 FRA1843 FRA1855
FRA1923 FRA1956 FRA2013 FRA2032
FRA2035 FRA2062 FRA2096 FRA2101
FRA2123 FRA2143 FRA2168 FRA2170
GBR2174 GBR2185 GBR2193 GBR2199
GBR2228 GBR2238 GBR2242 GBR2256
GBR2303 GBR2321 GBR2328 GBR2332
GBR2337 GBR2347 GBR2351 GBR2371
GBR2392 GBR2396 GBR2411 GBR2423
GBR2445 GBR2464 GBR2467 GBR2493
GBR2501 GBR2546 GBR2555 IRL2688
ITA2784 ITA2810 ITA2820 ITA2822
ITA2860 ITA2888 ITA2902 ITA2910
LUX2935 NLD3045 NLD3067 NLD3068
NLD3072 NLD3074 NLD3075 NLD3095
NLD3119 NLD3144 NLD3198 NLD3199
NLD3216 NLD3226 NLD3253 NLD3277
NLD3317 NLD3330 NLD3362 NLD3364
NOR3435 NOR3467 POL3519 PRT3548

NOR3416 NOR3435 NOR3465 POL3519
PRT3548 PRT3603 SWE3674 SWE3705
SWE3749 SWE3772 SWE3830

SWE3682 SWE3705 SWE3746 SWE3749
SWE3771 SWE3772 SWE3821 SWE3826
SWE3830

EAST ASIA - ASIE DE L'EST

AUT0024 BEL0123 BEL0129 BEL0186
BEL0198 BEL0199 BEL0221 BEL0254
BEL0265 BEL0284 BEL0351 BEL0361
BEL0364 CHE0415 CHE0420 CHE0434
CHE0452 CHE0550 CHE0570 CHE0605
CHE0622 CHE0639 CHE0643 CHE0645
CHE0655 CHE0689 CHE0693 CHE0711
CHE0712 CHE0721 CHE0814 CHE0817
CHE0819 DEU0944 DEU0972 DEU1055
DEU1056 DEU1064 DEU1106 DEU1131
DEU1142 DEU1146 DEU1149 DEU1167
DNK1287 DNK1292 DNK1317 ESP1490
ESP1508 FIN1532 FIN1604 FRA1611
FRA1651 FRA1805 FRA1817 FRA1978
FRA2032 FRA2035 FRA2096 FRA2101
FRA2123 FRA2159 FRA2168 FRA2170
GBR2193 GBR2199 GBR2228 GBR2260
GBR2266 GBR2328 GBR2332 GBR2351
GBR2371 GBR2392 GBR2411 GBR2423
GBR2445 GBR2464 GBR2490 GBR2501
GBR2546 GBR2555 ITA2784 ITA2813
ITA2860 LUX2935 NLD3067 NLD3072
NLD3078 NLD3144 NLD3198 NLD3226
NLD3277 NLD3330 NLD3362 NLD3364
NOR3435 PRT3548 PRT3602 SWE3819
SWE3826 SWE3830

MEXICO AND CENTRAL AMERICA - MEXIQUE ET AMERIQUE CENTRALE

AUT0003 AUT0024 AUT0041 BEL0123
BEL0129 BEL0133 BEL0148 BEL0186
BEL0198 BEL0199 BEL0203 BEL0221
BEL0254 BEL0265 BEL0275 BEL0284
BEL0297 BEL0335 BEL0336 BEL0340
BEL0351 BEL0361 BEL0364 CHE0415
CHE0420 CHE0427 CHE0434 CHE0446
CHE0452 CHE0456 CHE0465 CHE0483
CHE0486 CHE0550 CHE0559 CHE0566
CHE0568 CHE0570 CHE0605 CHE0622
CHE0626 CHE0638 CHE0639 CHE0640
CHE0645 CHE0654 CHE0682 CHE0689
CHE0711 CHE0712 CHE0721 CHE0755
CHE0772 CHE0773 CHE0800 CHE0809
CHE0814 CHE0817 CHE0819 DEU0920
DEU0944 DEU0948 DEU0968 DEU0972
DEU0983 DEU1055 DEU1056 DEU1064
DEU1108 DEU1114 DEU1114 DEU1131
DEU1132 DEU1142 DEU1149 DEU1167
DEU1178 DEU1187 DNK1287 DNK1292
DNK1312 DNK1317 DNK1339 DNK1360
ESP1407 ESP1442 ESP1457 ESP1472
ESP1475 ESP1486 ESP1489 ESP1490
ESP1493 ESP1505 ESP1506 ESP1522
ESP1523 ESP1525 FIN1532 FIN1549
FIN1574 FIN1604 FRA1611 FRA1651
FRA1675 FRA1703 FRA1805 FRA1817
FRA1843 FRA1852 FRA1905 FRA1923
FRA1938 FRA1960 FRA1974 FRA1975
FRA1978 FRA1985 FRA2013 FRA2032
FRA2034 FRA2035 FRA2041 FRA2042
FRA2053 FRA2057 FRA2062 FRA2096
FRA2101 FRA2123 FRA2143 FRA2150
FRA2152 FRA2159 FRA2168 FRA2170
GBR2174 GBR2193 GBR2195 GBR2201
GBR2228 GBR2236 GBR2238 GBR2242
GBR2256 GBR2303 GBR2321 GBR2328
GBR2332 GBR2351 GBR2371 GBR2392
GBR2396 GBR2402 GBR2411 GBR2413
GBR2423 GBR2445 GBR2464 GBR2467
GBR2490 GBR2493 GBR2501 GBR2546
GBR2555 IRL2697 IRL2707 IRL2726
ITA2755 ITA2780 ITA2784 ITA2809
ITA2834 ITA2838 ITA2852 ITA2860
ITA2881 ITA2894 ITA2902 LUX2935
NLD3067 NLD3068 NLD3072 NLD3078
NLD3091 NLD3144 NLD3153 NLD3198
NLD3199 NLD3226 NLD3230 NLD3253
NLD3263 NLD3277 NLD3303 NLD3305
NLD3361 NLD3362 NLD3364 NOR3381
NOR3390 NOR3410 NOR3416 NOR3467
POL3508 POL3519 PRT3548 SWE3664
SWE3666 SWE3674 SWE3687 SWE3725

See: *How to Use the Directory*, page 11.

SWE3734 SWE3749 SWE3768 SWE3770
SWE3821 SWE3826 SWE3828 SWE3830
SWE3865

MIDDLE EAST - MOYEN-ORIENT

BEL0129 BEL0186 BEL0197 BEL0198
BEL0199 BEL0221 BEL0254 BEL0275
BEL0306 BEL0353 BEL0361 BEL0364
CHE0403 CHE0406 CHE0415 CHE0420
CHE0434 CHE0452 CHE0456 CHE0493
CHE0506 CHE0550 CHE0568 CHE0605
CHE0622 CHE0639 CHE0640 CHE0645
CHE0655 CHE0689 CHE0711 CHE0712
CHE0773 CHE0809 CHE0814 CHE0817
CHE0819 CYP0832 CZE0906 DEU0944
DEU0972 DEU1055 DEU1056 DEU1064
DEU1065 DEU1106 DEU1131 DEU1143
DEU1146 DNK1292 DNK1304 DNK1317
DNK1360 ESP1490 ESP1522 ESP1524
FIN1532 FIN1570 FIN1588 FIN1604
FRA1611 FRA1629 FRA1651 FRA1791
FRA1793 FRA1805 FRA1817 FRA1843
FRA1923 FRA1938 FRA1955 FRA1974
FRA2013 FRA2032 FRA2035 FRA2041
FRA2047 FRA2053 FRA2057 FRA2096
FRA2101 FRA2159 FRA2170 GBR2193
GBR2199 GBR2228 GBR2238 GBR2260
GBR2303 GBR2328 GBR2332 GBR2347
GBR2351 GBR2371 GBR2378 GBR2392
GBR2396 GBR2411 GBR2423 GBR2445
GBR2455 GBR2500 GBR2501 GBR2525
GBR2537 GBR2546 GBR2555 IRL2680
IRL2687 IRL2733 ITA2773 ITA2775
ITA2784 ITA2799 ITA2809 ITA2834
ITA2838 ITA2860 LUX2935 MLT3016
MLT3017 MLT3018 NLD3067 NLD3072
NLD3144 NLD3199 NLD3226 NLD3277
NLD3285 NLD3361 NLD3362 NLD3364
NOR3404 NOR3435 POL3519 PRT3548
SWE3666 SWE3674 SWE3730 SWE3734
SWE3738 SWE3749 SWE3771 SWE3819
SWE3826 SWE3828 SWE3830 TUR3883

NORTH AFRICA - AFRIQUE DU NORD

BEL0123 BEL0186 BEL0197 BEL0198
BEL0199 BEL0221 BEL0254 BEL0265
BEL0275 BEL0361 CHE0403 CHE0415
CHE0420 CHE0434 CHE0452 CHE0456
CHE0491 CHE0550 CHE0568 CHE0570
CHE0605 CHE0622 CHE0639 CHE0655
CHE0682 CHE0689 CHE0711 CHE0712
CHE0814 CHE0817 CZE0905 DEU0944
DEU0972 DEU0990 DEU1055 DEU1056
DEU1064 DEU1106 DEU1114 DEU1142
DEU1146 DNK1255 DNK1304 DNK1360
ESP1475 ESP1490 ESP1493 ESP1505
ESP1522 FIN1532 FIN1604 FRA1611
FRA1629 FRA1651 FRA1768 FRA1805
FRA1817 FRA1843 FRA1923 FRA1938
FRA1946 FRA1955 FRA1958 FRA1974
FRA1978 FRA2013 FRA2034 FRA2035
FRA2057 FRA2096 FRA2101 FRA2117
FRA2143 FRA2159 FRA2170 GBR2185
GBR2193 GBR2195 GBR2199 GBR2332
GBR2347 GBR2351 GBR2371 GBR2392
GBR2411 GBR2413 GBR2423 GBR2445
GBR2490 GBR2501 GBR2546 GBR2555
ITA2755 ITA2784 ITA2791 ITA2810
ITA2822 ITA2860 ITA2903 LUX2935
MLT3016 MLT3017 MLT3018 MLT3036
NLD3067 NLD3072 NLD3078 NLD3119
NLD3144 NLD3198 NLD3226 NLD3277
NLD3362 NLD3364 POL3519 PRT3548
PRT3602 SWE3699 SWE3705 SWE3772
SWE3830

OCEANIA - OCEANIE

AUT0024 BEL0123 BEL0186 BEL0198
BEL0199 BEL0361 BEL0364 CHE0415
CHE0420 CHE0434 CHE0452 CHE0550
CHE0605 CHE0639 CHE0640 CHE0645
CHE0711 CHE0712 CHE0721 CHE0772
CHE0809 CHE0814 CHE0817 CHE0819
DEU0944 DEU0972 DEU0992 DEU1055
DEU1064 DEU1106 DEU1131 DEU1142
DEU1146 DEU1149 ESP1490 FIN1532
FIN1604 FRA1651 FRA1805 FRA1817
FRA1923 FRA2013 FRA2032 FRA2035

FRA2041 FRA2096 FRA2143 FRA2168
FRA2170 GBR2193 GBR2256 GBR2266
GBR2312 GBR2332 GBR2351 GBR2371
GBR2392 GBR2411 GBR2445 GBR2490
GBR2501 GBR2524 GBR2546 GBR2555
ITA2784 ITA2860 LUX2935 NLD3067
NLD3072 NLD3144 NLD3226 NLD3285
NLD3330 NLD3362 NLD3364 PRT3548
SWE3830

SOUTH AMERICA - AMERIQUE DU SUD

AUT0003 AUT0009 AUT0022 AUT0024
AUT0026 AUT0047 AUT0052 BEL0123
BEL0129 BEL0139 BEL0148 BEL0155
BEL0184 BEL0186 BEL0198 BEL0199
BEL0203 BEL0221 BEL0254 BEL0265
BEL0275 BEL0306 BEL0335 BEL0336
BEL0351 BEL0361 BEL0364 CHE0415
CHE0420 CHE0434 CHE0452 CHE0456
CHE0465 CHE0479 CHE0483 CHE0486
CHE0515 CHE0550 CHE0559 CHE0566
CHE0568 CHE0570 CHE0605 CHE0622
CHE0645 CHE0654 CHE0669 CHE0682
CHE0689 CHE0693 CHE0711 CHE0712
CHE0721 CHE0772 CHE0773 CHE0798
CHE0800 CHE0809 CHE0814 CHE0817
CHE0819 DEU0920 DEU0944 DEU0968
DEU0983 DEU1055 DEU1056 DEU1064
DEU1110 DEU1114 DEU1129 DEU1131
DEU1132 DEU1142 DEU1149 DEU1161
DEU1167 DEU1178 DEU1187 DNK1287
DNK1289 DNK1292 DNK1304 DNK1312
DNK1317 DNK1360 DNK1403 ESP1410
ESP1442 ESP1452 ESP1457 ESP1472
ESP1475 ESP1489 ESP1490 ESP1493
ESP1503 ESP1505 ESP1508 ESP1511
ESP1517 ESP1522 ESP1523 ESP1525
FIN1532 FIN1549 FIN1574 FIN1604
FRA1611 FRA1615 FRA1651 FRA1675
FRA1703 FRA1741 FRA1805 FRA1741
FRA1817 FRA1905 FRA1923 FRA1938
FRA1946 FRA1960 FRA1974 FRA1975
FRA1978 FRA2013 FRA2032 FRA2034
FRA2035 FRA2041 FRA2042 FRA2057
FRA2062 FRA2084 FRA2096 FRA2101
FRA2123 FRA2131 FRA2143 FRA2150
FRA2152 FRA2159 FRA2168 FRA2170
GBR2174 GBR2193 GBR2195 GBR2201
GBR2228 GBR2229 GBR2236 GBR2238
GBR2303 GBR2321 GBR2328 GBR2332
GBR2351 GBR2371 GBR2392 GBR2402
GBR2411 GBR2423 GBR2445 GBR2467
GBR2490 GBR2493 GBR2500 GBR2501
GBR2537 GBR2546 GBR2555 IRL2726
ITA2748 ITA2755 ITA2773 ITA2777
ITA2780 ITA2784 ITA2798 ITA2809
ITA2810 ITA2820 ITA2822 ITA2860
ITA2873 ITA2879 ITA2880 ITA2895
ITA2910 LUX2935 LUX2953 LUX2958
LUX2976 LUX2984 LUX3003 NLD3050
NLD3068 NLD3078 NLD3078 NLD3078
NLD3097 NLD3144 NLD3181 NLD3198
NLD3199 NLD3226 NLD3277 NLD3305
NLD3361 NLD3362 NLD3364 NOR3381
NOR3409 POL3519 PRT3548 PRT3600
SWE3666 SWE3674 SWE3682 SWE3693
SWE3705 SWE3730 SWE3749 SWE3754
SWE3763 SWE3781 SWE3821 SWE3826
SWE3830 SWE3865

SOUTH EAST ASIA - ASIE DU SUD-EST

AUT0024 AUT0052 BEL0123 BEL0129
BEL0186 BEL0198 BEL0199 BEL0203
BEL0221 BEL0254 BEL0275 BEL0306
BEL0341 BEL0351 BEL0361 BEL0364
CHE0415 CHE0420 CHE0434 CHE0452
CHE0456 CHE0479 CHE0524 CHE0550
CHE0559 CHE0566 CHE0568 CHE0570
CHE0605 CHE0622 CHE0639 CHE0643
CHE0645 CHE0669 CHE0682 CHE0689
CHE0693 CHE0711 CHE0712 CHE0721
CHE0773 CHE0798 CHE0809 CHE0814
CHE0817 CHE0819 DEU0944 DEU0972
DEU0983 DEU1055 DEU1056 DEU1064
DEU1074 DEU1097 DEU1106 DEU1108
DEU1132 DEU1146 DEU1149 DEU1167
DEU1178 DEU1187 DNK1287 DNK1292

DNK1317 DNK1360 ESP1489 ESP1490
FIN1532 FIN1604 FRA1611 FRA1615
FRA1629 FRA1651 FRA1805 FRA1817
FRA1843 FRA1905 FRA1923 FRA1938
FRA1946 FRA1960 FRA1974 FRA1978
FRA2013 FRA2032 FRA2034 FRA2035
FRA2041 FRA2062 FRA2084 FRA2096
FRA2101 FRA2123 FRA2143 FRA2150
FRA2168 FRA2170 GBR2193 GBR2195
GBR2199 GBR2201 GBR2228 GBR2236
GBR2238 GBR2242 GBR2256 GBR2260
GBR2266 GBR2303 GBR2321 GBR2328
GBR2332 GBR2351 GBR2371 GBR2392
GBR2396 GBR2411 GBR2413 GBR2423
GBR2445 GBR2467 GBR2490 GBR2493
GBR2498 GBR2501 GBR2537 GBR2546
GBR2555 IRL2695 IRL2726 ITA2784
ITA2798 ITA2813 ITA2838 ITA2860
ITA2894 ITA2902 LUX2935 NLD3067
NLD3068 NLD3072 NLD3078 NLD3083
NLD3144 NLD3156 NLD3198 NLD3199
NLD3277 NLD3330 NLD3362 NLD3364
POL3512 POL3519 PRT3548 PRT3602
SWE3674 SWE3682 SWE3705 SWE3772
SWE3819 SWE3821 SWE3826 SWE3830

SOUTHERN AFRICA - AFRIQUE AUSTRALE

AUT0022 AUT0052 AUT0033 AUT0052
AUT0058 BEL0123 BEL0129 BEL0186
BEL0197 BEL0198 BEL0199 BEL0203
BEL0221 BEL0254 BEL0265 BEL0265
BEL0275 BEL0351 BEL0361 BEL0364
CHE0415 CHE0420 CHE0434 CHE0452
CHE0483 CHE0486 CHE0491 CHE0506
CHE0559 CHE0566 CHE0570 CHE0584
CHE0605 CHE0619 CHE0622 CHE0639
CHE0643 CHE0645 CHE0682 CHE0689
CHE0693 CHE0711 CHE0712 CHE0721
CHE0755 CHE0809 CHE0814 CHE0817
CHE0819 CZE0906 DEU0944 DEU0972
DEU1055 DEU1056 DEU1064 DEU1106
DEU1108 DEU1110 DEU1131 DEU1142
DEU1143 DEU1146 DEU1149 DEU1187
DNK1259 DNK1273 DNK1289 DNK1292
DNK1339 DNK1360 DNK1375 ESP1445
ESP1486 ESP1490 ESP1493 ESP1523
FIN1532 FIN1547 FIN1549 FIN1554
FIN1574 FIN1604 FRA1611 FRA1651
FRA1768 FRA1805 FRA1817 FRA1843
FRA1876 FRA1923 FRA1956 FRA1978
FRA2032 FRA2035 FRA2041 FRA2096
FRA2101 FRA2123 FRA2143 FRA2168
FRA2170 GBR2174 GBR2181 GBR2185
GBR2193 GBR2195 GBR2199 GBR2201
GBR2228 GBR2236 GBR2238 GBR2242
GBR2256 GBR2259 GBR2260 GBR2266
GBR2281 GBR2303 GBR2321 GBR2328
GBR2332 GBR2337 GBR2347 GBR2351
GBR2371 GBR2392 GBR2402 GBR2411
GBR2413 GBR2423 GBR2445 GBR2464
GBR2467 GBR2490 GBR2493 GBR2501
GBR2537 GBR2546 GBR2555 GBR2561
IRL2726 ITA2771 ITA2784 ITA2798
ITA2894 ITA2838 ITA2860 ITA2903
ITA2911 LUX2935 NLD3045 NLD3067
NLD3072 NLD3078 NLD3095 NLD3098
NLD3119 NLD3139 NLD3144 NLD3198
NLD3199 NLD3226 NLD3230 NLD3277
NLD3361 NLD3362 NLD3364 NOR3384
NOR3386 NOR3390 NOR3400 NOR3404
NOR3416 NOR3418 NOR3435 NOR3467
POL3519 PRT3548 PRT3573 PRT3586
PRT3590 PRT3603 SWE3648 SWE3664
SWE3674 SWE3705 SWE3730 SWE3734
SWE3749 SWE3771 SWE3772 SWE3821
SWE3826 SWE3828 SWE3830

WEST AFRICA - AFRIQUE DE L'OUEST

AUT0003 AUT0024 BEL0118 BEL0123
BEL0186 BEL0197 BEL0198 BEL0199
BEL0203 BEL0221 BEL0254 BEL0265
BEL0275 BEL0328 BEL0351 BEL0361
BEL0364 CHE0415 CHE0420 CHE0434
CHE0452 CHE0456 CHE0479 CHE0483
CHE0519 CHE0550 CHE0566 CHE0568
CHE0605 CHE0622 CHE0639 CHE0643
CHE0645 CHE0650 CHE0682 CHE0689

Voir : *Comment utiliser le répertoire*, page 11.

CHE0712	CHE0721	CHE0755	CHE0814
CHE0817	CHE0819	CZE0905	DEU0944
DEU0972	DEU0983	DEU1055	DEU1056
DEU1064	DEU1074	DEU1097	DEU1106
DEU1110	DEU1114	DEU1131	DEU1142
DEU1146	DEU1149	DEU1178	DEU1187
DNK1287	DNK1307	DNK1360	ESP1472
ESP1490	ESP1493	ESP1524	FIN1532
FIN1604	FRA1611	FRA1615	FRA1629
FRA1651	FRA1768	FRA1778	FRA1805
FRA1817	FRA1843	FRA1876	FRA1880
FRA1905	FRA1923	FRA1946	FRA1955
FRA1956	FRA1960	FRA1964	FRA1974
FRA1978	FRA1991	FRA2013	FRA2032
FRA2034	FRA2035	FRA2042	FRA2043
FRA2047	FRA2062	FRA2084	FRA2096
FRA2101	FRA2123	FRA2143	FRA2150
FRA2159	FRA2168	FRA2170	GBR2174
GBR2185	GBR2193	GBR2195	GBR2201
GBR2238	GBR2256	GBR2328	GBR2332
GBR2337	GBR2347	GBR2351	GBR2371
GBR2392	GBR2411	GBR2423	GBR2445
GBR2464	GBR2490	GBR2501	GBR2546
GBR2555	ISL2739	ITA2784	ITA2791
ITA2860	ITA2902	LUX2935	NLD3045
NLD3050	NLD3067	NLD3072	NLD3074
NLD3078	NLD3119	NLD3144	NLD3153
NLD3198	NLD3228	NLD3277	NLD3330
NLD3362	NLD3364	POL3519	PRT3548
PRT3603	SWE3666	SWE3705	SWE3772
SWE3821	SWE3830		

OTHER - AUTRE

CARIBBEAN - CARAIBES

BEL0218	BEL0254	CHE0454	CHE0578
DEU0920	DEU0967	DEU1056	DEU1083
DEU1190	FIN1574	FIN1604	FRA1929
FRA2060	FRA2126	GBR2247	GBR2324
GBR2438	GBR2477	GBR2546	GRC2584
ITA2822	NLD3059	NLD3078	NLD3107
NLD3137	NLD3197	NLD3230	NLD3249
TUR3883			

CENTRAL AFRICA - AFRIQUE CENTRALE

BEL0156	BEL0218	BEL0254	CHE0645
CHE0709	DEU0956	DEU1056	DEU1146
DNK1218	FIN1604	FRA1627	FRA1636
FRA1756	FRA1795	FRA1837	FRA2012
FRA2014	FRA2015	FRA2060	FRA2126
GBR2313	GBR2438	GBR2477	GBR2546
GRC2584	NLD3059	NLD3078	NLD3117
NLD3137	NLD3197	NLD3230	NLD3249
TUR3883			

CENTRAL ASIA AND SOUTH ASIA - ASIE CENTRALE ET ASIE DU SUD

BEL0156	BEL0254	BEL0273	CHE0406
CHE0578	CHE0645	DEU0918	DEU0956
DEU1056	DEU1146	DEU1190	DNK1218
DNK1275	FIN1574	FIN1604	FRA1795
FRA1910	FRA1929	FRA2060	GBR2299
GBR2313	GBR2324	GBR2358	GBR2438
GBR2477	GBR2523	GBR2546	GRC2584
NLD3059	NLD3078	NLD3107	NLD3137
NLD3165	NLD3173	NLD3197	NLD3230
NLD3249	NOR3443	SWE3661	SWE3771
TUR3883			

EAST AFRICA - AFRIQUE DE L'EST

BEL0254	BEL0273	CHE0578	CHE0645
DEU0956	DEU1056	DEU1146	DEU1190
DNK1274	DNK1275	FIN1604	FRA1636
FRA1756	FRA1762	FRA1837	FRA2060
FRA2072	FRA2126	GBR2179	GBR2247
GBR2313	GBR2324	GBR2426	GBR2438
GBR2477	GBR2483	GBR2510	GBR2530
GBR2546	GRC2584	IRL2730	NLD3059
NLD3078	NLD3107	NLD3117	NLD3137
NLD3155	NLD3165	NLD3197	NLD3230
NLD3249	NOR3443	SWE3746	SWE3771
SWE3839	SWE3853	TUR3883	

EAST ASIA - ASIE DE L'EST

BEL0254	BEL0273	CHE0578	CHE0645
DEU0956	DEU1056	DEU1146	DNK1275
FIN1604	FRA1929	FRA2060	FRA2072
GBR2313	GBR2426	GBR2438	GBR2477
GBR2546	GRC2584	NLD3078	NLD3197
NLD3230	TUR3883		

MEXICO AND CENTRAL AMERICA - MEXIQUE ET AMERIQUE CENTRALE

BEL0254	BEL0273	CHE0578	CHE0645
CHE0755	DEU0920	DEU0967	DEU1056
DEU1083	DEU1190	DNK1274	DNK1367
ESP1511	FIN1546	FIN1574	FIN1603
FIN1604	FRA1636	FRA1795	FRA1837
FRA2060	FRA2072	GBR2247	GBR2313
GBR2324	GBR2438	GBR2510	GBR2546
GRC2584	ITA2755	NLD3078	NLD3107
NLD3137	NLD3197	NLD3230	NLD3249
NOR3441	SWE3676	SWE3771	SWE3781
TUR3883			

MIDDLE EAST - MOYEN-ORIENT

AUT0035	BEL0254	CHE0406	CHE0578
CHE0645	CHE0709	DEU0956	DEU1056
DEU1146	DNK1275	DNK1367	FIN1604
FRA1636	FRA2060	GBR2313	GBR2394
GBR2438	GBR2546	GRC2584	NLD3059
NLD3155	NLD3165	NLD3197	NLD3230
SWE3676	SWE3771	TUR3883	

NORTH AFRICA - AFRIQUE DU NORD

BEL0254	BEL0273	CHE0753	DEU0956
DEU1056	DEU1146	DNK1275	FIN1604
FRA1636	FRA1762	FRA1768	FRA1837
FRA2015	FRA2060	FRA2126	GBR2313
GBR2438	GBR2546	GRC2584	ITA2755
NLD3078	NLD3117	NLD3155	NLD3197
NLD3230	SWE3676	SWE3813	TUR3883

OCEANIA - OCEANIE

BEL0273	CHE0645	DEU0956	DEU1146
FIN1604	FRA2060	FRA2126	GBR2438
GBR2477	GBR2546	GRC2584	NLD3137
NLD3165	NLD3197	NLD3230	TUR3883

SOUTH AMERICA - AMERIQUE DU SUD

AUT0046	BEL0254	BEL0273	CHE0578
CHE0645	CHE0755	DEU0918	DEU0920
DEU0967	DEU1056	DEU1083	DEU1190
DNK1367	ESP1511	FIN1574	FIN1604
FRA1636	FRA1837	FRA2060	FRA2072
GBR2324	GBR2438	GBR2546	GRC2584
ITA2755	ITA2822	ITA2913	LUX2984
NLD3059	NLD3078	NLD3107	NLD3137
NLD3155	NLD3165	NLD3173	NLD3197
NLD3230	NLD3249	NOR3443	NOR3452
SWE3771	SWE3781	TUR3883	

SOUTH EAST ASIA - ASIE DU SUD-EST

AUT0046	BEL0141	BEL0156	BEL0254
BEL0273	CHE0578	CHE0645	DEU0956
DEU1056	DEU1146	DEU1190	DNK1274
FIN1603	FIN1604	FRA2060	FRA2072
FRA2126	GBR2313	GBR2324	GBR2394
GBR2426	GBR2438	GBR2477	GBR2546
GRC2584	NLD3059	NLD3078	NLD3107
NLD3117	NLD3137	NLD3155	NLD3156
NLD3165	NLD3197	NLD3230	NLD3249
SWE3676	SWE3771	TUR3883	

SOUTHERN AFRICA - AFRIQUE AUSTRALE

BEL0254	BEL0273	CHE0498	CHE0645
CHE0709	CHE0755	DEU0956	DEU1056
DEU1146	DEU1190	DNK1218	DNK1274
DNK1275	DNK1367	FIN1546	FIN1559
FIN1574	FIN1603	FIN1604	FRA1756
FRA1768	FRA1795	FRA1837	FRA2060
FRA2126	GBR2181	GBR2247	GBR2313
GBR2324	GBR2394	GBR2426	GBR2438
GBR2477	GBR2483	GBR2510	GBR2530
GBR2546	GRC2584	NLD3059	NLD3078
NLD3107	NLD3117	NLD3137	NLD3155
NLD3165	NLD3197	NLD3230	NLD3249
SWE3676	SWE3731	SWE3771	SWE3839
TUR3883			

WEST AFRICA - AFRIQUE DE L'OUEST

BEL0141	BEL0254	BEL0273	CHE0435
CHE0498	CHE0578	CHE0604	CHE0624
CHE0645	CHE0755	DEU0918	DEU0956
DEU0971	DEU1056	DEU1146	DEU1190
FIN1604	FRA1627	FRA1636	FRA1756
FRA1762	FRA1768	FRA1795	FRA1818
FRA1837	FRA1929	FRA1986	FRA2012
FRA2014	FRA2015	FRA2060	FRA2072
FRA2077	FRA2088	FRA2126	GBR2247
GBR2313	GBR2324	GBR2438	GBR2477
GBR2483	GBR2510	GBR2546	GRC2584
NLD3059	NLD3078	NLD3117	NLD3137
NLD3155	NLD3197	NLD3230	NLD3249
NOR3443	SWE3771	TUR3883	

POPULATION, FAMILY PLANNING, DEMOGRAPHY - POPULATION, PLANNING FAMILIAL, DEMOGRAPHIE

CARIBBEAN - CARAIBES

BEL0123	BEL0144	BEL0186	BEL0198
BEL0299	BEL0327	BEL0336	BEL0353
BEL0358	BEL0397	CHE0403	CHE0434
CHE0568	CHE0655	CHE0682	CHE0689
CHE0712	CHE0819	DEU0983	DEU1106
ESP1442	FRA1629	FRA1827	FRA2023
FRA2034	FRA2103	FRA2137	GBR2218
GBR2238	GBR2256	GBR2359	GBR2371
GBR2385	GBR2423	GBR2439	GBR2458
GBR2501	GBR2553	ITA2773	ITA2860
NLD3067	NLD3123	NLD3185	NLD3288
NLD3361	NLD3364	POL3508	POL3519
SWE3656	SWE3712		

CENTRAL AFRICA - AFRIQUE CENTRALE

BEL0123	BEL0144	BEL0148	BEL0155
BEL0158	BEL0186	BEL0198	BEL0200
BEL0297	BEL0299	BEL0327	BEL0342
BEL0351	BEL0358	BEL0397	CHE0403
CHE0434	CHE0444	CHE0562	CHE0568
CHE0628	CHE0655	CHE0689	CHE0712
CHE0750	CHE0805	CHE0817	CHE0819
DEU0968	DEU1106	DEU1131	DNK1227
DNK1272	ESP1467	ESP1493	FRA1629
FRA1671	FRA1715	FRA1740	FRA1787
FRA1787	FRA1827	FRA1956	FRA2034
FRA2080	FRA2103	FRA2107	GBR2174
GBR2175	GBR2185	GBR2199	GBR2218
GBR2238	GBR2359	GBR2371	GBR2390
GBR2423	GBR2458	GBR2501	GBR2550
GBR2553	ITA2860	LUX2997	NLD3067
NLD3123	NLD3185	NLD3230	NLD3301
NLD3361	NLD3364	POL3508	POL3519
PRT3549	PRT3594	PRT3602	SWE3656
SWE3749	SWE3827	SWE3828	

CENTRAL ASIA AND SOUTH ASIA - ASIE CENTRALE ET ASIE DU SUD

AUT0051	AUT0089	AUT0091	BEL0123
BEL0144	BEL0158	BEL0186	BEL0198
BEL0299	BEL0327	BEL0340	BEL0341
BEL0351	BEL0358	BEL0397	CHE0403
CHE0417	CHE0434	CHE0558	CHE0568
CHE0628	CHE0655	CHE0682	CHE0689
CHE0712	CHE0798	CHE0819	DEU0954
DEU0968	DEU0983	DEU1086	DEU1106
DEU1131	DEU1132	DEU1141	DEU1142
DNK1259	DNK1292	FIN1580	FRA1642
FRA1990	FRA2023	FRA2034	FRA2131
GBR2172	GBR2174	GBR2202	GBR2218
GBR2226	GBR2238	GBR2256	GBR2260
GBR2278	GBR2302	GBR2321	GBR2333
GBR2334	GBR2359	GBR2371	GBR2372
GBR2385	GBR2390	GBR2423	GBR2436
GBR2439	GBR2445	GBR2458	GBR2464
GBR2500	GBR2501	GBR2509	GBR2553
IRL2699	ITA2764	ITA2770	ITA2860
ITA2879	LIE2926	LUX2997	NLD3067
NLD3101	NLD3123	NLD3124	NLD3147
NLD3153	NLD3185	NLD3237	NLD3361
NLD3364	NOR3447	NOR3453	NOR3465
POL3519	PRT3549	SWE3656	SWE3679
SWE3749	SWE3763	SWE3771	SWE3828

See: *How to Use the Directory*, page 11.

EAST AFRICA - AFRIQUE DE L'EST

AUT0085	AUT0091	BEL0123	BEL0144
BEL0148	BEL0186	BEL0198	BEL0224
BEL0269	BEL0297	BEL0299	BEL0327
BEL0353	BEL0358	BEL0397	CHE0403
CHE0434	CHE0598	CHE0682	CHE0689
CHE0712	CHE0758	CHE0817	CHE0819
DEU0936	DEU0968	DEU0983	DEU0991
DEU1002	DEU1106	DEU1131	DEU1142
DEU1145	DNK1259	DNK1316	DNK1402
ESP1493	FIN1556	FIN1580	FRA1617
FRA1956	FRA2023	FRA2046	FRA2062
FRA2080	FRA2107	GBR2172	GBR2174
GBR2175	GBR2179	GBR2183	GBR2185
GBR2199	GBR2218	GBR2226	GBR2238
GBR2240	GBR2242	GBR2256	GBR2259
GBR2278	GBR2282	GBR2292	GBR2321
GBR2359	GBR2371	GBR2385	GBR2390
GBR2423	GBR2436	GBR2439	GBR2458
GBR2500	GBR2501	GBR2517	GBR2550
GBR2553	IRL2699	IRL2733	ITA2782
ITA2810	ITA2837	ITA2860	ITA2910
LUX2997	NLD3067	NLD3074	NLD3075
NLD3101	NLD3123	NLD3185	NLD3198
NLD3237	NLD3301	NLD3361	NLD3364
NOR3465	NOR3467	POL3508	POL3519
SWE3656	SWE3679	SWE3712	SWE3749
SWE3775	SWE3799	SWE3828	SWE3853
SWE3854	SWE3857		

EAST ASIA - ASIE DE L'EST

BEL0123	BEL0144	BEL0186	BEL0198
BEL0327	BEL0351	BEL0358	BEL0397
CHE0403	CHE0434	CHE0655	CHE0689
CHE0712	CHE0817	CHE0819	DEU1106
DEU1142	FRA2149	FRA2159	GBR2199
GBR2218	GBR2238	GBR2260	GBR2359
GBR2371	GBR2423	GBR2458	GBR2501
GBR2550	GBR2553	ITA2860	LUX2997
NLD3067	NLD3123	NLD3198	NLD3361
NLD3364	NOR3465	NOR3467	SWE3712

MEXICO AND CENTRAL AMERICA - MEXIQUE ET AMERIQUE CENTRALE

AUT0091	BEL0123	BEL0144	BEL0148
BEL0186	BEL0198	BEL0224	BEL0269
BEL0299	BEL0327	BEL0336	BEL0353
BEL0358	BEL0397	CHE0403	CHE0434
CHE0559	CHE0568	CHE0682	CHE0689
CHE0712	CHE0789	CHE0819	DEU0954
DEU0968	DEU0983	DEU1002	DEU1106
DEU1132	DEU1142	DEU1143	DEU1149
DEU1187	DNK1312	ESP1442	ESP1475
ESP1493	FIN1580	FIN1602	FRA1827
FRA1975	FRA2034	FRA2103	FRA2149
GBR2174	GBR2175	GBR2199	GBR2218
GBR2226	GBR2238	GBR2256	GBR2321
GBR2359	GBR2371	GBR2385	GBR2390
GBR2423	GBR2439	GBR2458	GBR2501
GBR2553	IRL2697	ITA2773	ITA2775
ITA2860	LUX2997	NLD3067	NLD3123
NLD3153	NLD3185	NLD3198	NLD3230
NLD3288	NLD3303	NLD3305	NLD3361
NLD3364	NOR3425	POL3519	SWE3656
SWE3785	SWE3865		

MIDDLE EAST - MOYEN-ORIENT

AUT0091	BEL0186	BEL0198	BEL0306
BEL0358	BEL0397	CHE0403	CHE0434
CHE0568	CHE0640	CHE0655	CHE0682
CHE0689	CHE0712	CHE0819	DEU1106
FRA1629	FRA1791	FRA1793	FRA1827
FRA2103	FRA2117	FRA2149	FRA2159
GBR2199	GBR2218	GBR2238	GBR2260
GBR2281	GBR2359	GBR2371	GBR2385
GBR2423	GBR2458	GBR2501	ITA2773
ITA2860	NLD3067	NLD3101	NLD3123
NLD3199	NLD3364	NOR3447	NOR3467
POL3519	SWE3771	TUR3883	

NORTH AFRICA - AFRIQUE DU NORD

BEL0123	BEL0148	BEL0186	BEL0198
BEL0269	BEL0358	BEL0397	CHE0403
CHE0434	CHE0568	CHE0655	CHE0682
CHE0689	CHE0712	DEU1106	DEU1142
DEU1191	ESP1442	ESP1493	FRA1629
FRA1768	FRA1846	FRA1946	FRA1956
FRA2034	FRA2107	FRA2159	GBR2185
GBR2218	GBR2238	GBR2359	GBR2371
GBR2385	GBR2423	GBR2458	GBR2501
ITA2810	ITA2860	NLD3067	NLD3123
NLD3198	NLD3334	NLD3364	POL3508
POL3519			

OCEANIA - OCEANIE

BEL0123	BEL0186	BEL0198	BEL0397
CHE0403	CHE0434	CHE0689	CHE0712
CHE0819	DEU0992	DEU1142	GBR2218
GBR2256	GBR2312	GBR2359	GBR2371
GBR2458	GBR2501	GBR2524	GBR2553
ITA2860	NLD3067	NLD3123	NLD3361
NLD3364			

SOUTH AMERICA - AMERIQUE DU SUD

AUT0091	BEL0123	BEL0144	BEL0148
BEL0155	BEL0186	BEL0198	BEL0269
BEL0299	BEL0327	BEL0336	BEL0353
BEL0358	BEL0397	CHE0403	CHE0434
CHE0475	CHE0559	CHE0568	CHE0598
CHE0604	CHE0613	CHE0628	CHE0682
CHE0689	CHE0712	CHE0750	CHE0789
CHE0798	CHE0819	DEU0926	DEU0968
DEU0983	DEU0990	DEU1131	DEU1132
DEU1142	DEU1149	DEU1187	DNK1319
ESP1442	ESP1452	ESP1455	ESP1493
ESP1502	FIN1558	FRA1946	FRA2018
FRA2034	FRA2062	FRA2103	FRA2107
FRA2149	FRA2159	GBR2174	GBR2175
GBR2218	GBR2226	GBR2238	GBR2321
GBR2359	GBR2371	GBR2390	GBR2423
GBR2458	GBR2501	GBR2550	GBR2553
ITA2773	ITA2810	ITA2860	ITA2879
ITA2910	LUX2958	LUX2997	NLD3067
NLD3123	NLD3181	NLD3185	NLD3198
NLD3305	NLD3361	NLD3364	NOR3465
POL3519	SWE3656	SWE3693	SWE3695
SWE3712	SWE3744	SWE3749	SWE3828
SWE3865			

SOUTH EAST ASIA - ASIE DU SUD-EST

AUT0051	AUT0091	BEL0123	BEL0144
BEL0186	BEL0198	BEL0297	BEL0299
BEL0327	BEL0342	BEL0351	BEL0358
BEL0397	CHE0403	CHE0434	CHE0491
CHE0568	CHE0598	CHE0682	CHE0689
CHE0712	CHE0749	CHE0817	CHE0819
DEU0954	DEU0983	DEU1106	DEU1132
DEU1149	DEU1187	DNK1259	DNK1316
FIN1580	FIN1587	FRA1617	FRA1628
FRA1629	FRA1671	FRA1917	FRA1941
FRA1970	FRA2034	FRA2080	GBR2199
GBR2218	GBR2226	GBR2238	GBR2240
GBR2242	GBR2256	GBR2260	GBR2321
GBR2351	GBR2359	GBR2371	GBR2385
GBR2390	GBR2423	GBR2436	GBR2458
GBR2500	GBR2501	GBR2508	GBR2553
IRL2691	ITA2756	ITA2860	ITA2898
LUX2997	NLD3067	NLD3123	NLD3185
NLD3198	NLD3237	NLD3361	NLD3364
NOR3394	NOR3465	POL3519	SWE3656

SOUTHERN AFRICA - AFRIQUE AUSTRALE

AUT0091	BEL0123	BEL0144	BEL0148
BEL0186	BEL0198	BEL0269	BEL0299
BEL0327	BEL0358	BEL0397	CHE0403
CHE0434	CHE0628	CHE0682	CHE0689
CHE0712	CHE0734	CHE0750	CHE0819
DEU1106	DEU1131	DEU1142	DNK1259
DNK1312	ESP1493	FIN1556	FIN1580
FRA1671	FRA1672	FRA1691	FRA1715
FRA1769	FRA1827	FRA1917	FRA1956
FRA2080	FRA2103	FRA2107	FRA2159
GBR2174	GBR2185	GBR2218	GBR2238
GBR2242	GBR2256	GBR2259	GBR2292
GBR2318	GBR2319	GBR2321	GBR2359
GBR2371	GBR2385	GBR2390	GBR2423
GBR2436	GBR2458	GBR2500	GBR2501
GBR2553	ITA2771	ITA2860	ITA2879
ITA2888	ITA2900	LUX2995	NLD3067
NLD3101	NLD3123	NLD3137	NLD3147
NLD3185	NLD3198	NLD3361	NLD3364
NOR3467	POL3508	POL3519	PRT3549
PRT3594	SWE3656	SWE3749	SWE3828

WEST AFRICA - AFRIQUE DE L'OUEST

AUT0091	BEL0123	BEL0144	BEL0148
BEL0186	BEL0198	BEL0269	BEL0297
BEL0299	BEL0327	BEL0342	BEL0353
BEL0358	BEL0397	CHE0402	CHE0403
CHE0434	CHE0444	CHE0479	CHE0568
CHE0598	CHE0682	CHE0707	CHE0712
CHE0734	CHE0758	CHE0817	CHE0819
DEU0926	DEU0968	DEU0983	DEU1106
DEU1131	DEU1142	DNK1227	DNK1259
DNK1374	DNK1402	ESP1493	ESP1502
FIN1563	FIN1580	FRA1607	FRA1629
FRA1690	FRA1715	FRA1739	FRA1760
FRA1768	FRA1785	FRA1787	FRA1827
FRA1846	FRA1929	FRA1935	FRA1946
FRA1949	FRA1956	FRA1970	FRA2034
FRA2062	FRA2074	FRA2103	FRA2107
FRA2138	FRA2149	FRA2159	GBR2174
GBR2175	GBR2180	GBR2185	GBR2218
GBR2226	GBR2238	GBR2242	GBR2256
GBR2278	GBR2359	GBR2371	GBR2385
GBR2390	GBR2423	GBR2436	GBR2439
GBR2458	GBR2501	GBR2529	GBR2550
GBR2553	GRC2586	IRL2733	ITA2773
ITA2801	ITA2860	ITA2888	LUX2959
LUX2978	LUX2986	LUX2997	NLD3067
NLD3074	NLD3075	NLD3123	NLD3147
NLD3153	NLD3185	NLD3198	NLD3230
NLD3269	NLD3288	NLD3301	NLD3361
NLD3364	NOR3465	POL3508	POL3519
PRT3549	PRT3590	SWE3656	SWE3712
SWE3828			

RURAL DEVELOPMENT, AGRICULTURE - DEVELOPPEMENT RURAL, AGRICULTURE

CARIBBEAN - CARAIBES

AUT0045	BEL0124	BEL0144	BEL0186
BEL0198	BEL0218	BEL0221	BEL0224
BEL0327	BEL0331	BEL0335	BEL0336
BEL0341	BEL0351	BEL0353	BEL0358
BEL0361	BEL0394	BEL0396	BEL0397
CHE0434	CHE0454	CHE0486	CHE0491
CHE0501	CHE0559	CHE0564	CHE0568
CHE0598	CHE0613	CHE0619	CHE0655
CHE0682	CHE0689	CHE0693	CHE0712
CHE0730	CHE0798	CHE0814	CHE0817
CHE0819	CHE0820	DEU0944	DEU0968
DEU0972	DEU0983	DEU0989	DEU1047
DEU1107	DEU1131	DEU1174	DNK1292
DNK1314	DNK1389	ESP1435	ESP1442
ESP1455	ESP1461	ESP1472	ESP1474
ESP1486	ESP1492	ESP1507	ESP1517
ESP1522	ESP1529	FIN1584	FRA1628
FRA1629	FRA1644	FRA1672	FRA1685
FRA1827	FRA1843	FRA1846	FRA1903
FRA1917	FRA1946	FRA1967	FRA1980
FRA2012	FRA2023	FRA2034	FRA2062
FRA2081	FRA2103	FRA2106	FRA2109
FRA2116	FRA2117	FRA2126	FRA2150
FRA2168	GBR2175	GBR2218	GBR2221
GBR2228	GBR2229	GBR2238	GBR2244
GBR2278	GBR2281	GBR2293	GBR2324
GBR2341	GBR2350	GBR2371	GBR2373
GBR2392	GBR2419	GBR2423	GBR2434
GBR2436	GBR2437	GBR2501	GBR2518
GBR2552	GBR2553	GRC2572	IRL2687
IRL2726	ITA2773	ITA2784	ITA2787
ITA2822	ITA2830	ITA2860	ITA2873
ITA2881	LUX2993	NLD3067	NLD3068
NLD3126	NLD3137	NLD3144	NLD3154
NLD3214	NLD3219	NLD3231	NLD3257
NLD3288	NLD3356	NLD3361	NLD3364
POL3519	SWE3653	SWE3656	SWE3712

CENTRAL AFRICA - AFRIQUE CENTRALE

AUT0013	AUT0026	AUT0040	AUT0041
AUT0045	BEL0097	BEL0102	BEL0110
BEL0120	BEL0124	BEL0128	BEL0132
BEL0133	BEL0144	BEL0145	BEL0148
BEL0155	BEL0156	BEL0158	BEL0169
BEL0184	BEL0186	BEL0189	BEL0198
BEL0200	BEL0201	BEL0203	BEL0218
BEL0221	BEL0234	BEL0237	BEL0241
BEL0245	BEL0249	BEL0258	BEL0261
BEL0306	BEL0315	BEL0323	BEL0327

BEL0331	BEL0341	BEL0342	BEL0343
BEL0351	BEL0352	BEL0353	BEL0356
BEL0358	BEL0359	BEL0361	BEL0378
BEL0381	BEL0390	BEL0396	BEL0397
CHE0422	CHE0434	CHE0444	CHE0486
CHE0491	CHE0535	CHE0541	CHE0544
CHE0559	CHE0562	CHE0566	CHE0568
CHE0570	CHE0604	CHE0619	CHE0629
CHE0630	CHE0655	CHE0660	CHE0684
CHE0689	CHE0712	CHE0727	CHE0730
CHE0750	CHE0762	CHE0805	CHE0814
CHE0817	CHE0819	CHE0820	CZE0905
DEU0944	DEU0965	DEU0968	DEU0972
DEU0978	DEU0989	DEU0995	DEU1006
DEU1027	DEU1047	DEU1097	DEU1099
DEU1107	DEU1114	DEU1131	DEU1149
DEU1167	DEU1174	DNK1227	DNK1232
DNK1255	DNK1272	DNK1314	DNK1392
ESP1453	ESP1475	ESP1486	ESP1492
ESP1517	ESP1529	FIN1549	FRA1616
FRA1629	FRA1634	FRA1636	FRA1649
FRA1704	FRA1715	FRA1727	FRA1731
FRA1740	FRA1745	FRA1769	FRA1774
FRA1776	FRA1815	FRA1827	FRA1830
FRA1836	FRA1861	FRA1879	FRA1880
FRA1897	FRA1903	FRA1917	FRA1926
FRA1946	FRA1956	FRA1966	FRA1978
FRA1980	FRA1984	FRA1988	FRA1991
FRA2005	FRA2011	FRA2012	FRA2015
FRA2032	FRA2034	FRA2055	FRA2062
FRA2069	FRA2080	FRA2086	FRA2092
FRA2093	FRA2097	FRA2103	FRA2106
FRA2107	FRA2109	FRA2116	FRA2117
FRA2119	FRA2126	FRA2147	FRA2150
FRA2163	FRA2168	GBR2173	GBR2174
GBR2175	GBR2180	GBR2185	GBR2187
GBR2190	GBR2202	GBR2218	GBR2221
GBR2238	GBR2259	GBR2274	GBR2278
GBR2337	GBR2350	GBR2351	GBR2364
GBR2371	GBR2390	GBR2392	GBR2422
GBR2423	GBR2434	GBR2437	GBR2460
GBR2500	GBR2501	GBR2553	GRC2567
GRC2571	GRC2586	IRL2687	IRL2700
IRL2732	ITA2744	ITA2747	ITA2762
ITA2770	ITA2777	ITA2779	ITA2784
ITA2785	ITA2791	ITA2806	ITA2813
ITA2826	ITA2835	ITA2837	ITA2852
ITA2855	ITA2860	ITA2884	ITA2885
ITA2888	ITA2890	ITA2896	ITA2898
ITA2899	ITA2900	ITA2907	ITA2921
LUX2954	LUX2972	LUX2984	LUX2997
LUX3002	LUX3006	NLD3045	NLD3062
NLD3067	NLD3068	NLD3069	NLD3096
NLD3101	NLD3137	NLD3144	NLD3154
NLD3214	NLD3230	NLD3235	
NLD3257	NLD3264	NLD3277	NLD3292
NLD3301	NLD3317	NLD3356	NLD3361
NLD3364	NOR3465	POL3519	PRT3594
PRT3602	SWE3656	SWE3749	SWE3763
SWE3789	SWE3827	SWE3828	

CENTRAL ASIA AND SOUTH ASIA - ASIE CENTRALE ET ASIE DU SUD

AUT0013	AUT0026	AUT0045	AUT0051
AUT0091	BEL0097	BEL0104	BEL0124
BEL0144	BEL0186	BEL0198	BEL0201
BEL0203	BEL0221	BEL0258	BEL0261
BEL0269	BEL0270	BEL0306	BEL0327
BEL0340	BEL0341	BEL0343	BEL0351
BEL0355	BEL0358	BEL0359	BEL0361
BEL0368	BEL0397	CHE0417	CHE0422
CHE0434	CHE0467	CHE0472	CHE0486
CHE0491	CHE0495	CHE0529	CHE0558
CHE0559	CHE0566	CHE0568	CHE0570
CHE0586	CHE0619	CHE0632	CHE0638
CHE0655	CHE0660	CHE0682	CHE0689
CHE0712	CHE0727	CHE0730	CHE0742
CHE0798	CHE0809	CHE0814	CHE0817
CHE0819	CHE0820	DEU0918	DEU0928
DEU0940	DEU0944	DEU0965	DEU0968
DEU0971	DEU0972	DEU0983	DEU0985
DEU0989	DEU0990	DEU0991	DEU0993
DEU0995	DEU1006	DEU1047	DEU1066
DEU1086	DEU1097	DEU1099	DEU1100
DEU1106	DEU1107	DEU1111	DEU1118
DEU1121	DEU1127	DEU1129	DEU1131
DEU1132	DEU1149	DEU1151	DEU1174
DEU1178	DEU1187	DNK1216	DNK1232
DNK1248	DNK1255	DNK1259	DNK1292

DNK1314	DNK1339	DNK1358	DNK1384
DNK1389	ESP1486	ESP1492	ESP1513
ESP1517	FIN1549	FIN1591	FRA1642
FRA1644	FRA1655	FRA1661	FRA1830
FRA1866	FRA1887	FRA1917	FRA1926
FRA1939	FRA1980	FRA1988	FRA1990
FRA1991	FRA2034	FRA2057	FRA2062
FRA2070	FRA2081	FRA2109	FRA2116
FRA2117	FRA2131	FRA2163	FRA2168
GBR2173	GBR2174	GBR2175	GBR2176
GBR2186	GBR2190	GBR2197	GBR2201
GBR2202	GBR2213	GBR2218	GBR2222
GBR2226	GBR2228	GBR2238	GBR2242
GBR2266	GBR2274	GBR2278	GBR2281
GBR2290	GBR2297	GBR2302	GBR2303
GBR2318	GBR2321	GBR2324	GBR2333
GBR2334	GBR2341	GBR2348	GBR2351
GBR2358	GBR2364	GBR2371	GBR2372
GBR2390	GBR2392	GBR2413	GBR2419
GBR2422	GBR2423	GBR2434	GBR2436
GBR2437	GBR2464	GBR2467	GBR2475
GBR2480	GBR2500	GBR2501	GBR2506
GBR2532	GBR2535	GBR2552	GBR2553
GRC2571	GRC2575	IRL2688	IRL2699
IRL2700	IRL2726	ITA2775	ITA2784
ITA2787	ITA2813	ITA2860	ITA2873
ITA2879	ITA2885	ITA2888	ITA2903
LIE2926	LUX2937	LUX2982	NLD3056
NLD3067	NLD3078	NLD3091	NLD3093
NLD3096	NLD3101	NLD3126	NLD3137
NLD3144	NLD3149	NLD3154	NLD3158
NLD3173	NLD3183	NLD3199	NLD3214
NLD3231	NLD3257	NLD3277	NLD3292
NLD3295	NLD3300	NLD3302	NLD3317
NLD3318	NLD3356	NLD3361	NLD3364
NOR3371	NOR3390	NOR3412	NOR3421
NOR3431	NOR3443	NOR3460	NOR3465
NOR3475	POL3519	SWE3656	SWE3666
SWE3674	SWE3679	SWE3702	SWE3723
SWE3737	SWE3749	SWE3763	SWE3769
SWE3787	SWE3795	SWE3818	SWE3826
SWE3827	SWE3828	SWE3854	SWE3857
SWE3864			

EAST AFRICA - AFRIQUE DE L'EST

AUT0003	AUT0013	AUT0026	AUT0030
AUT0041	AUT0045	AUT0067	AUT0085
AUT0091	BEL0097	BEL0124	BEL0144
BEL0148	BEL0167	BEL0186	BEL0198
BEL0221	BEL0224	BEL0269	BEL0270
BEL0306	BEL0323	BEL0327	BEL0340
BEL0341	BEL0343	BEL0356	BEL0358
BEL0361	BEL0381	BEL0397	CHE0434
CHE0448	CHE0462	CHE0486	CHE0491
CHE0510	CHE0559	CHE0566	CHE0570
CHE0586	CHE0598	CHE0630	CHE0660
CHE0682	CHE0684	CHE0689	CHE0693
CHE0712	CHE0730	CHE0764	CHE0772
CHE0810	CHE0814	CHE0817	CHE0819
CHE0820	CHE0823	CZE0905	DEU0928
DEU0940	DEU0944	DEU0965	DEU0968
DEU0972	DEU0983	DEU0986	DEU0989
DEU0991	DEU0995	DEU1006	DEU1032
DEU1047	DEU1066	DEU1069	DEU1074
DEU1106	DEU1107	DEU1111	DEU1121
DEU1129	DEU1131	DEU1145	DEU1149
DEU1174	DEU1178	DNK1214	DNK1222
DNK1245	DNK1255	DNK1259	DNK1274
DNK1275	DNK1285	DNK1291	DNK1292
DNK1314	DNK1339	DNK1358	DNK1389
DNK1392	DNK1405	ESP1432	ESP1486
ESP1492	ESP1509	ESP1510	ESP1514
ESP1524	ESP1529	FIN1572	FIN1584
FIN1587	FIN1591	FIN1628	FRA1636
FRA1644	FRA1653	FRA1668	FRA1731
FRA1830	FRA1843	FRA1849	FRA1879
FRA1887	FRA1903	FRA1917	FRA1947
FRA1956	FRA1978	FRA1991	FRA2012
FRA2023	FRA2032	FRA2062	FRA2069
FRA2080	FRA2093	FRA2106	FRA2107
FRA2109	FRA2116	FRA2119	FRA2126
FRA2147	FRA2163	FRA2168	GBR2173
GBR2174	GBR2175	GBR2179	GBR2180
GBR2185	GBR2187	GBR2190	GBR2198
GBR2202	GBR2214	GBR2218	GBR2221
GBR2226	GBR2228	GBR2229	GBR2232
GBR2238	GBR2240	GBR2242	GBR2259
GBR2262	GBR2274	GBR2278	GBR2281
GBR2292	GBR2293	GBR2298	GBR2303

GBR2324	GBR2337	GBR2338	GBR2339
GBR2341	GBR2348	GBR2350	GBR2351
GBR2371	GBR2390	GBR2392	GBR2419
GBR2422	GBR2423	GBR2434	GBR2436
GBR2437	GBR2459	GBR2460	GBR2467
GBR2471	GBR2474	GBR2480	GBR2483
GBR2497	GBR2500	GBR2501	GBR2502
GBR2510	GBR2518	GBR2521	GBR2535
GBR2536	GBR2550	GBR2552	GBR2553
GBR2556	GRC2571	GRC2586	IRL2687
IRL2688	IRL2691	IRL2700	IRL2702
IRL2709	IRL2716	IRL2725	IRL2726
IRL2729	IRL2730	IRL2732	IRL2733
ISL2739	ISL2740	ITA2744	ITA2757
ITA2761	ITA2771	ITA2772	ITA2773
ITA2782	ITA2784	ITA2785	ITA2787
ITA2804	ITA2810	ITA2813	ITA2820
ITA2822	ITA2829	ITA2835	ITA2848
ITA2860	ITA2868	ITA2873	ITA2877
ITA2885	ITA2888	ITA2896	ITA2901
ITA2902	ITA2907	ITA2910	LUX2997
NLD3045	NLD3062	NLD3067	NLD3068
NLD3069	NLD3074	NLD3091	NLD3093
NLD3095	NLD3096	NLD3101	NLD3137
NLD3144	NLD3145	NLD3146	NLD3154
NLD3158	NLD3169	NLD3173	NLD3183
NLD3198	NLD3199	NLD3214	NLD3216
NLD3231	NLD3235	NLD3257	NLD3277
NLD3292	NLD3301	NLD3317	NLD3318
NLD3323	NLD3356	NLD3361	NLD3364
NOR3431	NOR3443	NOR3465	NOR3467
NOR3475	POL3519	SWE3656	SWE3665
SWE3666	SWE3672	SWE3679	SWE3688
SWE3712	SWE3727	SWE3728	SWE3742
SWE3749	SWE3776	SWE3777	SWE3787
SWE3789	SWE3798	SWE3799	SWE3806
SWE3807	SWE3814	SWE3826	SWE3828
SWE3853	SWE3854	SWE3864	SWE3879

EAST ASIA - ASIE DE L'EST

AUT0013	AUT0045	BEL0124	BEL0144
BEL0186	BEL0198	BEL0221	BEL0340
BEL0351	BEL0358	BEL0361	BEL0397
CHE0422	CHE0434	CHE0495	CHE0570
CHE0638	CHE0655	CHE0660	CHE0689
CHE0712	CHE0730	CHE0749	CHE0764
CHE0817	CHE0819	CHE0820	
DEU0944	DEU0968	DEU0971	DEU0972
DEU0989	DEU0995	DEU1006	DEU1047
DEU1100	DEU1107	DEU1129	DEU1149
DEU1149	DEU1174	DNK1260	DNK1292
DNK1314	ESP1432	ESP1492	ESP1508
FRA1917	FRA1992	FRA2062	FRA2109
FRA2116	FRA2159	FRA2168	GBR2175
GBR2218	GBR2221	GBR2238	GBR2278
GBR2351	GBR2371	GBR2392	GBR2423
GBR2434	GBR2501	GBR2535	GBR2553
GBR2556	IRL2702	IRL2726	ITA2784
ITA2860	LUX2997	NLD3067	NLD3096
NLD3144	NLD3154	NLD3198	NLD3214
NLD3277	NLD3356	NLD3361	NLD3364
NOR3465	SWE3749	SWE3828	

MEXICO AND CENTRAL AMERICA - MEXIQUE ET AMERIQUE CENTRALE

AUT0003	AUT0013	AUT0026	AUT0030
AUT0040	AUT0041	AUT0045	AUT0061
AUT0067	AUT0091	BEL0097	BEL0124
BEL0132	BEL0144	BEL0164	BEL0184
BEL0186	BEL0189	BEL0198	BEL0201
BEL0203	BEL0221	BEL0224	BEL0230
BEL0241	BEL0245	BEL0269	BEL0270
BEL0306	BEL0323	BEL0327	BEL0335
BEL0336	BEL0340	BEL0351	BEL0353
BEL0358	BEL0359	BEL0361	BEL0378
BEL0381	BEL0396	BEL0397	CHE0434
CHE0446	CHE0486	CHE0491	CHE0517
CHE0558	CHE0559	CHE0566	CHE0568
CHE0570	CHE0586	CHE0619	CHE0630
CHE0632	CHE0682	CHE0689	CHE0712
CHE0730	CHE0735	CHE0755	CHE0772
CHE0788	CHE0804	CHE0809	CHE0814
CHE0819	CHE0820	DEU0944	DEU0947
DEU0968	DEU0972	DEU0983	DEU0989
DEU0995	DEU1012	DEU1031	DEU1047
DEU1074	DEU1097	DEU1107	DEU1111
DEU1114	DEU1129	DEU1131	DEU1138
DEU1143	DEU1149	DEU1163	DEU1167

See: *How to Use the Directory*, page 11.

DEU1174	DEU1178	DEU1187	DEU1202
DNK1226	DNK1232	DNK1292	DNK1312
DNK1314	DNK1339	DNK1358	DNK1359
DNK1389	ESP1407	ESP1409	ESP1413
ESP1427	ESP1431	ESP1432	ESP1435
ESP1437	ESP1439	ESP1442	ESP1450
ESP1453	ESP1455	ESP1457	ESP1461
ESP1474	ESP1475	ESP1484	ESP1486
ESP1492	ESP1506	ESP1510	ESP1511
ESP1517	ESP1521	ESP1522	ESP1524
ESP1528	ESP1529	FIN1544	FIN1546
FIN1549	FIN1587	FIN1591	FRA1636
FRA1645	FRA1672	FRA1703	FRA1827
FRA1843	FRA1846	FRA1852	FRA1856
FRA1917	FRA1938	FRA1939	FRA1967
FRA1978	FRA1985	FRA1988	FRA2012
FRA2034	FRA2057	FRA2062	FRA2069
FRA2081	FRA2090	FRA2092	FRA2093
FRA2103	FRA2109	FRA2116	FRA2117
FRA2149	FRA2150	FRA2159	FRA2163
FRA2168	GBR2174	GBR2175	GBR2190
GBR2201	GBR2218	GBR2221	GBR2226
GBR2228	GBR2229	GBR2238	GBR2244
GBR2278	GBR2293	GBR2321	GBR2324
GBR2351	GBR2373	GBR2383	GBR2392
GBR2413	GBR2419	GBR2422	GBR2423
GBR2434	GBR2436	GBR2437	GBR2467
GBR2480	GBR2500	GBR2501	GBR2510
GBR2518	GBR2535	GBR2552	GBR2553
GBR2556	IRL2697	IRL2707	IRL2714
IRL2726	IRL2732	ITA2744	ITA2762
ITA2773	ITA2784	ITA2787	ITA2799
ITA2809	ITA2814	ITA2830	ITA2834
ITA2838	ITA2855	ITA2860	ITA2868
ITA2873	ITA2881	ITA2882	ITA2894
ITA2911	LUX2937	LUX2969	LUX2972
LUX2973	LUX2976	LUX2997	NLD3067
NLD3068	NLD3078	NLD3079	NLD3091
NLD3095	NLD3096	NLD3101	NLD3137
NLD3141	NLD3144	NLD3154	NLD3158
NLD3159	NLD3173	NLD3198	NLD3199
NLD3214	NLD3219	NLD3231	NLD3253
NLD3257	NLD3263	NLD3277	NLD3281
NLD3285	NLD3288	NLD3303	NLD3305
NLD3356	NLD3361	NLD3364	NOR3381
NOR3390	NOR3403	NOR3410	NOR3425
NOR3426	NOR3467	NOR3475	POL3508
POL3519	SWE3650	SWE3653	SWE3655
SWE3656	SWE3666	SWE3674	SWE3676
SWE3687	SWE3688	SWE3725	SWE3749
SWE3770	SWE3771	SWE3796	SWE3798
SWE3864	SWE3865		

MIDDLE EAST - MOYEN-ORIENT

AUT0035	AUT0045	BEL0124	BEL0186
BEL0198	BEL0221	BEL0241	BEL0270
BEL0306	BEL0340	BEL0353	BEL0358
BEL0361	BEL0397	CHE0434	CHE0486
CHE0568	CHE0655	CHE0660	
CHE0671	CHE0684	CHE0689	CHE0712
CHE0730	CHE0814	CHE0819	DEU0918
DEU0939	DEU0944	DEU0968	DEU0972
DEU0989	DEU0995	DEU1047	DEU1097
DEU1107	DEU1143	DEU1150	DEU1174
DEU1200	DNK1314	ESP1435	ESP1455
ESP1514	ESP1522	FRA1629	FRA1636
FRA1794	FRA1827	FRA1843	FRA1846
FRA1917	FRA1978	FRA2057	FRA2069
FRA2103	FRA2109	FRA2116	FRA2159
FRA2163	GBR2175	GBR2218	GBR2221
GBR2238	GBR2244	GBR2278	GBR2371
GBR2392	GBR2423	GBR2434	GBR2500
GBR2501	GBR2525	GRC2575	IRL2680
IRL2687	ITA2726	ITA2769	ITA2784
ITA2799	ITA2834	ITA2860	MLT3018
NLD3067	NLD3144	NLD3154	NLD3158
NLD3173	NLD3214	NLD3356	NLD3364
POL3519	SWE3674	SWE3749	SWE3826
TUR3883			

NORTH AFRICA - AFRIQUE DU NORD

AUT0013	AUT0045	BEL0118	BEL0124
BEL0132	BEL0144	BEL0148	BEL0186
BEL0198	BEL0221	BEL0249	BEL0269
BEL0270	BEL0340	BEL0353	BEL0358
BEL0361	BEL0397	CHE0434	CHE0557
CHE0568	CHE0570	CHE0655	CHE0682
CHE0689	CHE0712	CHE0730	CHE0814

CZE0905	DEU0944	DEU0968	DEU0972
DEU0989	DEU0995	DEU0999	DEU1047
DEU1107	DEU1111	DEU1131	DEU1174
DNK1255	DNK1314	DNK1358	DNK1359
ESP1455	ESP1486	ESP1492	FRA1629
FRA1636	FRA1719	FRA1745	FRA1794
FRA1846	FRA1887	FRA1917	FRA1946
FRA1947	FRA1956	FRA1985	FRA2012
FRA2018	FRA2034	FRA2057	FRA2062
FRA2069	FRA2093	FRA2107	FRA2109
FRA2116	FRA2126	FRA2150	FRA2159
GBR2175	GBR2185	GBR2218	GBR2221
GBR2226	GBR2278	GBR2281	GBR2371
GBR2392	GBR2413	GBR2423	GBR2434
GBR2437	GBR2501	GBR2535	GRC2575
IRL2769	ITA2769	ITA2784	ITA2791
ITA2810	ITA2830	ITA2834	ITA2860
ITA2901	MLT3018	NLD3047	NLD3062
NLD3067	NLD3101	NLD3144	NLD3154
NLD3198	NLD3199	NLD3214	NLD3277
NLD3301	NLD3356	NLD3364	POL3519
SWE3688	SWE3813	SWE3828	

OCEANIA - OCEANIE

AUT0045	AUT0067	BEL0124	BEL0186
BEL0198	BEL0361	BEL0397	CHE0434
CHE0712	CHE0730	CHE0772	CHE0814
CHE0819	CHE0820	DEU0944	DEU0968
DEU0972	DEU0989	DEU0995	DEU0999
DEU1047	DEU1107	DEU1149	DNK1314
FRA1672	FRA1917	FRA1967	FRA2109
FRA2116	FRA2126	FRA2168	GBR2175
GBR2218	GBR2221	GBR2266	GBR2278
GBR2306	GBR2312	GBR2351	GBR2371
GBR2392	GBR2422	GBR2434	GBR2437
GBR2501	GBR2524	GBR2535	GBR2553
IRL2732	ITA2784	ITA2860	NLD3067
NLD3091	NLD3096	NLD3137	NLD3144
NLD3154	NLD3214	NLD3356	NLD3361
NLD3364	SWE3749		

SOUTH AMERICA - AMERIQUE DU SUD

AUT0003	AUT0013	AUT0022	AUT0026
AUT0030	AUT0041	AUT0045	AUT0051
AUT0052	AUT0067	AUT0091	BEL0097
BEL0119	BEL0124	BEL0126	BEL0132
BEL0139	BEL0144	BEL0155	BEL0169
BEL0182	BEL0184	BEL0186	BEL0189
BEL0198	BEL0201	BEL0203	BEL0221
BEL0226	BEL0241	BEL0249	BEL0258
BEL0269	BEL0270	BEL0282	BEL0306
BEL0323	BEL0327	BEL0335	BEL0336
BEL0340	BEL0341	BEL0351	BEL0353
BEL0358	BEL0358	BEL0359	BEL0361
BEL0368	BEL0371	BEL0381	BEL0396
BEL0397	CHE0434	CHE0455	CHE0465
CHE0479	CHE0486	CHE0491	CHE0515
CHE0559	CHE0566	CHE0568	CHE0570
CHE0581	CHE0586	CHE0619	CHE0628
CHE0632	CHE0638	CHE0660	CHE0669
CHE0681	CHE0682	CHE0689	CHE0693
CHE0712	CHE0727	CHE0730	CHE0755
CHE0764	CHE0772	CHE0798	CHE0809
CHE0814	CHE0819	CHE0820	DEU0928
DEU0933	DEU0940	DEU0944	DEU0968
DEU0972	DEU0983	DEU0989	DEU0995
DEU1006	DEU1031	DEU1047	DEU1074
DEU1097	DEU1107	DEU1111	DEU1114
DEU1118	DEU1128	DEU1129	DEU1131
DEU1138	DEU1143	DEU1149	DEU1163
DEU1167	DEU1174	DEU1178	DEU1187
DNK1232	DNK1291	DNK1292	DNK1314
DNK1312	DNK1314	DNK1389	DNK1403
ESP1409	ESP1432	ESP1435	ESP1442
ESP1452	ESP1453	ESP1455	ESP1457
ESP1475	ESP1486	ESP1488	ESP1492
ESP1503	ESP1505	ESP1508	ESP1510
ESP1517	ESP1521	ESP1522	ESP1529
FIN1549	FIN1594	FRA1616	FRA1634
FRA1636	FRA1655	FRA1672	FRA1703
FRA1710	FRA1731	FRA1741	FRA1827
FRA1828	FRA1832	FRA1836	FRA1843
FRA1846	FRA1903	FRA1917	FRA1939
FRA1946	FRA1980	FRA1988	FRA1988
FRA1991	FRA2012	FRA2018	FRA2034
FRA2057	FRA2062	FRA2069	FRA2081
FRA2086	FRA2092	FRA2093	FRA2103
FRA2107	FRA2109	FRA2116	FRA2117

FRA2131	FRA2159	FRA2163	FRA2168
GBR2174	GBR2175	GBR2190	GBR2201
GBR2218	GBR2221	GBR2226	GBR2228
GBR2229	GBR2238	GBR2244	GBR2278
GBR2293	GBR2303	GBR2321	GBR2324
GBR2371	GBR2373	GBR2383	GBR2392
GBR2419	GBR2422	GBR2423	GBR2434
GBR2436	GBR2437	GBR2456	GBR2464
GBR2467	GBR2480	GBR2485	GBR2500
GBR2501	GBR2518	GBR2525	GBR2535
GBR2537	GBR2550	GBR2552	GBR2553
IRL2700	IRL2726	IRL2732	ITA2744
ITA2762	ITA2770	ITA2770	ITA2773
ITA2775	ITA2782	ITA2784	ITA2787
ITA2792	ITA2799	ITA2802	ITA2806
ITA2809	ITA2810	ITA2811	ITA2814
ITA2820	ITA2822	ITA2832	ITA2834
ITA2835	ITA2838	ITA2842	ITA2849
ITA2852	ITA2860	ITA2868	ITA2873
ITA2879	ITA2880	ITA2881	ITA2882
ITA2885	ITA2888	ITA2895	ITA2900
ITA2901	ITA2907	ITA2910	ITA2913
ITA2921	LUX2937	LUX2946	LUX2953
LUX2954	LUX2958	LUX2968	LUX2973
LUX2979	LUX2980	LUX2997	LUX2999
LUX3001	NLD3067	NLD3068	NLD3075
NLD3091	NLD3096	NLD3101	NLD3137
NLD3144	NLD3154	NLD3158	NLD3181
NLD3198	NLD3199	NLD3214	NLD3219
NLD3235	NLD3253	NLD3257	NLD3277
NLD3305	NLD3317	NLD3318	NLD3356
NLD3361	NLD3364	NOR3381	NOR3403
NOR3404	NOR3443	NOR3460	NOR3465
POL3508	POL3519	PRT3600	SWE3655
SWE3656	SWE3666	SWE3674	SWE3693
SWE3695	SWE3702	SWE3712	SWE3724
SWE3730	SWE3747	SWE3749	SWE3763
SWE3787	SWE3796	SWE3828	SWE3857
SWE3865	SWE3876		

SOUTH EAST ASIA - ASIE DU SUD-EST

AUT0013	AUT0026	AUT0045	AUT0051
AUT0091	BEL0124	BEL0128	BEL0144
BEL0186	BEL0198	BEL0203	BEL0221
BEL0224	BEL0226	BEL0241	BEL0261
BEL0275	BEL0306	BEL0323	BEL0327
BEL0340	BEL0342	BEL0351	BEL0358
BEL0361	BEL0362	BEL0368	BEL0396
BEL0397	CHE0422	CHE0434	CHE0479
CHE0486	CHE0491	CHE0559	CHE0566
CHE0568	CHE0570	CHE0586	CHE0598
CHE0604	CHE0619	CHE0630	CHE0637
CHE0638	CHE0660	CHE0682	CHE0689
CHE0693	CHE0712	CHE0730	CHE0749
CHE0794	CHE0798	CHE0814	CHE0817
CHE0819	CHE0820	DEU0918	DEU0940
DEU0944	DEU0968	DEU0971	DEU0972
DEU0983	DEU0989	DEU0990	DEU0995
DEU1006	DEU1037	DEU1047	DEU1097
DEU1099	DEU1107	DEU1129	DEU1132
DEU1149	DEU1163	DEU1174	DEU1178
DEU1186	DEU1187	DNK1232	DNK1238
DNK1260	DNK1292	DNK1314	DNK1316
DNK1403	ESP1492	FIN1549	FIN1584
FIN1587	FRA1614	FRA1617	FRA1629
FRA1634	FRA1647	FRA1653	FRA1731
FRA1745	FRA1846	FRA1860	FRA1917
FRA1937	FRA1946	FRA1967	FRA1978
FRA1979	FRA1980	FRA1988	FRA1992
FRA2005	FRA2012	FRA2023	FRA2034
FRA2062	FRA2069	FRA2080	FRA2093
FRA2097	FRA2109	FRA2116	FRA2117
FRA2126	FRA2140	FRA2163	FRA2168
GBR2175	GBR2201	GBR2218	GBR2221
GBR2226	GBR2228	GBR2238	GBR2240
GBR2242	GBR2278	GBR2293	GBR2303
GBR2324	GBR2349	GBR2350	GBR2351
GBR2371	GBR2390	GBR2392	GBR2413
GBR2419	GBR2422	GBR2423	GBR2434
GBR2436	GBR2437	GBR2464	GBR2467
GBR2486	GBR2500	GBR2501	GBR2508
GBR2535	GBR2552	GBR2553	IRL2687
IRL2691	IRL2700	IRL2726	IRL2733
ITA2744	ITA2775	ITA2784	ITA2785
ITA2798	ITA2799	ITA2838	ITA2852
ITA2860	ITA2873	ITA2888	ITA2902
ITA2912	LUX2954	LUX2997	NLD3067
NLD3068	NLD3069	NLD3091	NLD3093
NLD3096	NLD3137	NLD3144	NLD3146

Voir : *Comment utiliser le répertoire*, page 11.

NLD3154	NLD3198	NLD3199	NLD3201
NLD3214	NLD3219	NLD3235	NLD3253
NLD3277	NLD3285	NLD3292	NLD3317
NLD3356	NLD3361	NLD3364	NOR3369
NOR3372	NOR3381	NOR3390	NOR3465
NOR3467	NOR3475	POL3519	SWE3656
SWE3674	SWE3749	SWE3786	SWE3798
SWE3828	SWE3854	SWE3857	SWE3876

SOUTHERN AFRICA - AFRIQUE AUSTRALE

AUT0013	AUT0045	AUT0067	AUT0091
BEL0097	BEL0124	BEL0144	BEL0148
BEL0186	BEL0189	BEL0198	BEL0203
BEL0211	BEL0221	BEL0241	BEL0260
BEL0269	BEL0323	BEL0327	BEL0340
BEL0358	BEL0359	BEL0361	BEL0397
CHE0434	CHE0486	CHE0498	CHE0506
CHE0566	CHE0570	CHE0584	CHE0586
CHE0598	CHE0619	CHE0632	CHE0682
CHE0689	CHE0693	CHE0712	CHE0727
CHE0730	CHE0755	CHE0762	CHE0798
CHE0814	CHE0817	CHE0819	CHE0820
CZE0905	DEU0931	DEU0931	DEU0944
DEU0965	DEU0968	DEU0972	DEU0986
DEU0989	DEU0995	DEU1006	DEU1031
DEU1038	DEU1074	DEU1082	DEU1097
DEU1107	DEU1111	DEU1129	DEU1131
DEU1143	DEU1149	DEU1174	DEU1187
DEU1200	DEU1202	DNK1218	DNK1248
DNK1255	DNK1259	DNK1275	DNK1288
DNK1292	DNK1312	DNK1314	DNK1339
DNK1388	DNK1389	DNK1403	ESP1420
ESP1450	ESP1453	ESP1486	ESP1509
FIN1546	FIN1549	FIN1557	FIN1580
FIN1584	FIN1587	FRA1614	FRA1657
FRA1659	FRA1691	FRA1715	FRA1727
FRA1756	FRA1769	FRA1819	FRA1827
FRA1830	FRA1843	FRA1849	FRA1879
FRA1887	FRA1903	FRA1917	FRA1946
FRA1947	FRA1948	FRA1956	FRA2005
FRA2012	FRA2018	FRA2032	FRA2044
FRA2070	FRA2080	FRA2103	FRA2107
FRA2109	FRA2116	FRA2117	FRA2119
FRA2126	FRA2159	FRA2163	FRA2168
GBR2173	GBR2174	GBR2175	GBR2181
GBR2185	GBR2187	GBR2190	GBR2198
GBR2201	GBR2202	GBR2218	GBR2221
GBR2226	GBR2228	GBR2229	GBR2238
GBR2242	GBR2244	GBR2259	GBR2266
GBR2277	GBR2278	GBR2281	GBR2292
GBR2293	GBR2303	GBR2318	GBR2324
GBR2337	GBR2339	GBR2348	GBR2349
GBR2364	GBR2371	GBR2392	GBR2413
GBR2419	GBR2422	GBR2423	GBR2434
GBR2436	GBR2437	GBR2460	GBR2464
GBR2467	GBR2478	GBR2480	GBR2500
GBR2501	GBR2510	GBR2535	GBR2536
GBR2537	GBR2552	GBR2553	GBR2556
GBR2561	GRC2571	IRL2687	IRL2691
IRL2700	IRL2726	IRL2732	IRL2733
ITA2757	ITA2762	ITA2771	ITA2784
ITA2787	ITA2791	ITA2799	ITA2803
ITA2811	ITA2813	ITA2838	ITA2855
ITA2860	ITA2873	ITA2879	ITA2881
ITA2885	ITA2888	ITA2899	ITA2900
ITA2902	LUX2946	LUX2954	LUX2995
NLD3045	NLD3062	NLD3067	NLD3068
NLD3069	NLD3091	NLD3095	NLD3096
NLD3098	NLD3101	NLD3137	NLD3144
NLD3154	NLD3173	NLD3198	NLD3199
NLD3214	NLD3219	NLD3235	NLD3257
NLD3277	NLD3292	NLD3317	NLD3336
NLD3356	NLD3361	NLD3364	NOR3390
NOR3467	POL3519	PRT3564	PRT3576
PRT3594	PRT3596	PRT3600	PRT3605
SWE3648	SWE3656	SWE3664	SWE3676
SWE3685	SWE3688	SWE3749	SWE3770
SWE3776	SWE3789	SWE3798	SWE3813
SWE3828	SWE3859	SWE3864	

WEST AFRICA - AFRIQUE DE L'OUEST

AUT0003	AUT0013	AUT0028	AUT0041
AUT0045	AUT0063	AUT0086	AUT0091
BEL0097	BEL0118	BEL0124	BEL0132
BEL0144	BEL0148	BEL0152	BEL0184
BEL0186	BEL0192	BEL0198	BEL0201
BEL0203	BEL0221	BEL0237	BEL0245
BEL0249	BEL0261	BEL0269	BEL0270

BEL0306	BEL0323	BEL0327	BEL0331
BEL0340	BEL0342	BEL0343	BEL0351
BEL0352	BEL0353	BEL0356	BEL0358
BEL0359	BEL0361	BEL0368	BEL0381
BEL0390	BEL0392	BEL0396	BEL0397
CHE0402	CHE0434	CHE0435	CHE0439
CHE0444	CHE0463	CHE0479	CHE0486
CHE0491	CHE0498	CHE0510	CHE0540
CHE0557	CHE0559	CHE0566	CHE0568
CHE0570	CHE0598	CHE0604	CHE0619
CHE0659	CHE0682	CHE0689	CHE0707
CHE0712	CHE0727	CHE0730	CHE0734
CHE0755	CHE0762	CHE0764	CHE0772
CHE0798	CHE0814	CHE0817	CHE0819
CHE0820	CHE0823	CZE0905	DEU0944
DEU0968	DEU0971	DEU0972	DEU0983
DEU0986	DEU0989	DEU0991	DEU0995
DEU1006	DEU1037	DEU1038	DEU1047
DEU1069	DEU1074	DEU1097	DEU1107
DEU1111	DEU1114	DEU1131	DEU1143
DEU1149	DEU1163	DEU1174	DEU1178
DEU1187	DEU1200	DNK1227	DNK1255
DNK1259	DNK1292	DNK1306	DNK1307
DNK1308	DNK1314	DNK1374	DNK1403
ESP1430	ESP1468	ESP1486	ESP1488
ESP1492	ESP1502	ESP1510	ESP1514
ESP1517	ESP1528	FIN1549	FIN1587
FRA1612	FRA1614	FRA1624	FRA1629
FRA1632	FRA1634	FRA1636	FRA1644
FRA1645	FRA1649	FRA1651	FRA1655
FRA1663	FRA1664	FRA1679	FRA1690
FRA1691	FRA1699	FRA1715	FRA1727
FRA1731	FRA1737	FRA1739	FRA1745
FRA1746	FRA1756	FRA1760	FRA1761
FRA1776	FRA1778	FRA1785	FRA1787
FRA1789	FRA1794	FRA1799	FRA1815
FRA1818	FRA1827	FRA1830	FRA1836
FRA1843	FRA1846	FRA1849	FRA1861
FRA1876	FRA1879	FRA1880	FRA1887
FRA1897	FRA1903	FRA1907	FRA1913
FRA1917	FRA1926	FRA1930	FRA1939
FRA1946	FRA1947	FRA1956	FRA1966
FRA1967	FRA1978	FRA1980	FRA1984
FRA1988	FRA1991	FRA1992	FRA2005
FRA2012	FRA2016	FRA2018	FRA2032
FRA2034	FRA2037	FRA2039	FRA2043
FRA2044	FRA2047	FRA2062	FRA2069
FRA2086	FRA2092	FRA2093	FRA2100
FRA2103	FRA2106	FRA2107	FRA2109
FRA2116	FRA2117	FRA2119	FRA2126
FRA2131	FRA2138	FRA2142	FRA2147
FRA2159	FRA2163	FRA2168	GBR2173
GBR2174	GBR2175	GBR2180	GBR2185
GBR2187	GBR2190	GBR2198	GBR2201
GBR2202	GBR2218	GBR2221	GBR2226
GBR2228	GBR2238	GBR2241	GBR2244
GBR2259	GBR2274	GBR2278	GBR2303
GBR2324	GBR2337	GBR2341	GBR2351
GBR2371	GBR2383	GBR2390	GBR2392
GBR2419	GBR2422	GBR2423	GBR2434
GBR2436	GBR2437	GBR2460	GBR2483
GBR2500	GBR2501	GBR2510	GBR2515
GBR2518	GBR2525	GBR2535	GBR2550
GBR2552	GBR2553	GBR2556	GRC2567
GRC2586	IRL2683	IRL2700	IRL2724
IRL2726	IRL2732	IRL2733	ISL2739
ITA2744	ITA2762	ITA2765	ITA2774
ITA2784	ITA2786	ITA2791	ITA2799
ITA2803	ITA2812	ITA2826	ITA2827
ITA2828	ITA2829	ITA2838	ITA2842
ITA2852	ITA2860	ITA2873	ITA2885
ITA2888	ITA2898	ITA2901	ITA2913
LUX2937	LUX2946	LUX2950	LUX2954
LUX2959	LUX2972	LUX2973	LUX2976
LUX2978	LUX2986	LUX2997	NLD3045
NLD3062	NLD3067	NLD3069	NLD3074
NLD3075	NLD3078	NLD3079	NLD3091
NLD3096	NLD3101	NLD3137	NLD3144
NLD3154	NLD3173	NLD3183	NLD3198
NLD3199	NLD3214	NLD3231	NLD3235
NLD3254	NLD3257	NLD3269	NLD3277
NLD3288	NLD3292	NLD3301	NLD3317
NLD3318	NLD3345	NLD3356	NLD3361
NLD3364	NOR3387	NOR3403	NOR3443
NOR3453	NOR3460	NOR3465	POL3519
PRT3564	PRT3586	SWE3656	SWE3666
SWE3674	SWE3695	SWE3707	SWE3712
SWE3749	SWE3789	SWE3828	SWE3879

CARIBBEAN - CARAIBES

BEL0129	BEL0144	BEL0161	BEL0199
BEL0331	BEL0336	BEL0359	BEL0361
BEL0388	BEL0396	BEL0397	CHE0434
CHE0614	CHE0619	CHE0655	CHE0689
CHE0693	CHE0712	CHE0730	CHE0793
CYP0832	DEU0944	DEU0983	DEU0986
DEU0989	DEU1029	DEU1047	DEU1055
DEU1074	DEU1174	DEU1185	DNK1314
ESP1442	ESP1455	ESP1461	ESP1474
ESP1486	ESP1488	ESP1491	ESP1496
ESP1507	ESP1517	ESP1525	ESP1529
FRA1610	FRA1629	FRA1672	FRA1676
FRA1685	FRA1817	FRA1860	FRA1898
FRA1903	FRA1904	FRA1917	FRA1975
FRA2012	FRA2096	FRA2102	FRA2106
FRA2137	FRA2163	GBR2175	GBR2212
GBR2218	GBR2229	GBR2238	GBR2241
GBR2242	GBR2244	GBR2256	GBR2266
GBR2278	GBR2341	GBR2359	GBR2361
GBR2391	GBR2422	GBR2423	GBR2441
GBR2445	GBR2458	GBR2501	GBR2535
GBR2550	GBR2553	GBR2558	ITA2773
ITA2814	ITA2822	ITA2860	ITA2911
ITA2913	ITA2922	LUX2993	NLD3068
NLD3091	NLD3137	NLD3138	NLD3154
NLD3201	NLD3202	NLD3214	NLD3231
NLD3301	NLD3317	NLD3338	NLD3341
NLD3361	POL3508	POL3519	SWE3653
SWE3830			

CENTRAL AFRICA - AFRIQUE CENTRALE

AUT0021	AUT0041	AUT0063	BEL0097
BEL0110	BEL0120	BEL0128	BEL0129
BEL0132	BEL0133	BEL0144	BEL0148
BEL0153	BEL0156	BEL0158	BEL0161
BEL0184	BEL0189	BEL0192	BEL0197
BEL0200	BEL0201	BEL0218	BEL0233
BEL0234	BEL0237	BEL0261	BEL0265
BEL0297	BEL0299	BEL0328	BEL0342
BEL0347	BEL0350	BEL0352	BEL0359
BEL0361	BEL0367	BEL0368	BEL0378
BEL0388	BEL0388	BEL0396	BEL0397
CHE0434	CHE0562	CHE0619	CHE0632
CHE0655	CHE0684	CHE0687	CHE0689
CHE0691	CHE0693	CHE0712	CHE0727
CHE0730	CHE0750	CHE0796	CHE0805
CHE0817	DEU0919	DEU0922	DEU0944
DEU0968	DEU0986	DEU0989	DEU1006
DEU1017	DEU1029	DEU1047	DEU1055
DEU1097	DEU1110	DEU1114	DEU1131
DEU1141	DEU1174	DEU1185	DNK1255
DNK1272	DNK1287	DNK1314	DNK1358
DNK1360	ESP1486	ESP1491	ESP1493
ESP1513	ESP1517	ESP1529	FIN1587
FRA1610	FRA1617	FRA1629	FRA1634
FRA1636	FRA1645	FRA1704	FRA1727
FRA1769	FRA1774	FRA1776	FRA1795
FRA1796	FRA1815	FRA1817	FRA1819
FRA1830	FRA1863	FRA1876	FRA1879
FRA1886	FRA1898	FRA1903	FRA1904
FRA1917	FRA1948	FRA1956	FRA1966
FRA1988	FRA1992	FRA2012	FRA2039
FRA2047	FRA2054	FRA2070	FRA2074
FRA2092	FRA2093	FRA2096	FRA2102
FRA2105	FRA2106	FRA2114	FRA2123
FRA2145	FRA2163	GBR2175	GBR2180
GBR2185	GBR2218	GBR2238	GBR2240
GBR2241	GBR2259	GBR2278	GBR2359
GBR2361	GBR2382	GBR2390	GBR2391
GBR2422	GBR2423	GBR2445	GBR2448
GBR2454	GBR2458	GBR2460	GBR2464
GBR2500	GBR2501	GBR2550	GBR2553
GRC2567	GRC2586	IRL2688	IRL2700
IRL2716	ISL2739	ITA2744	ITA2747
ITA2762	ITA2770	ITA2774	ITA2777
ITA2779	ITA2791	ITA2806	ITA2807
ITA2813	ITA2816	ITA2818	ITA2824
ITA2826	ITA2829	ITA2835	ITA2855
ITA2860	ITA2868	ITA2874	ITA2883
ITA2890	ITA2896	ITA2899	ITA2900
ITA2902	ITA2907	ITA2921	ITA2922
ITA2923	LUX2942	LUX2997	NLD3068

See: *How to Use the Directory*, page 11.

NLD3070 NLD3078 NLD3091 NLD3095
NLD3117 NLD3121 NLD3137 NLD3138
NLD3154 NLD3186 NLD3214 NLD3230
NLD3235 NLD3277 NLD3292 NLD3301
NLD3317 NLD3338 NLD3341 NLD3361
NOR3435 NOR3452 POL3519 PRT3549
PRT3594 PRT3602 PRT3603 SWE3763
SWE3769 SWE3813 SWE3827 SWE3828
SWE3830

CENTRAL ASIA AND SOUTH ASIA - ASIE CENTRALE ET ASIE DU SUD

AUT0063 BEL0129 BEL0133 BEL0144
BEL0148 BEL0156 BEL0158 BEL0161
BEL0199 BEL0261 BEL0297 BEL0303
BEL0340 BEL0359 BEL0361 BEL0368
BEL0378 BEL0397 CHE0417 CHE0434
CHE0510 CHE0586 CHE0619 CHE0632
CHE0655 CHE0689 CHE0712 CHE0727
CHE0730 CHE0757 CHE0793 CZE0859
DEU0944 DEU0954 DEU0971 DEU0983
DEU0989 DEU1017 DEU1029 DEU1047
DEU1055 DEU1066 DEU1074 DEU1086
DEU1100 DEU1111 DEU1131 DEU1132
DEU1141 DEU1142 DEU1174 DEU1175
DEU1185 DNK1259 DNK1275 DNK1287
DNK1291 DNK1292 DNK1314 DNK1360
ESP1491 ESP1517 FIN1580 FIN1581
FIN1582 FIN1587 FRA1610 FRA1645
FRA1677 FRA1795 FRA1817 FRA1830
FRA1831 FRA1898 FRA1904 FRA1917
FRA1966 FRA2044 FRA2047 FRA2054
FRA2057 FRA2074 FRA2096 FRA2102
FRA2123 FRA2131 GBR2172 GBR2174
GBR2176 GBR2178 GBR2186 GBR2197
GBR2212 GBR2213 GBR2218 GBR2219
GBR2222 GBR2226 GBR2238 GBR2241
GBR2242 GBR2256 GBR2259 GBR2266
GBR2274 GBR2278 GBR2281 GBR2302
GBR2303 GBR2307 GBR2321 GBR2325
GBR2333 GBR2334 GBR2341 GBR2348
GBR2353 GBR2358 GBR2359 GBR2361
GBR2364 GBR2382 GBR2390 GBR2391
GBR2409 GBR2423 GBR2445 GBR2448
GBR2458 GBR2464 GBR2475 GBR2500
GBR2501 GBR2535 GBR2550 GBR2553
GBR2558 GBR2562 IRL2688 IRL2699
IRL2700 IRL2716 ISL2739 ITA2766
ITA2770 ITA2773 ITA2775 ITA2860
ITA2868 ITA2879 ITA2888 ITA2902
ITA2903 ITA2922 LIE2926 LUX2997
NLD3056 NLD3071 NLD3091 NLD3095
NLD3121 NLD3137 NLD3138 NLD3154
NLD3173 NLD3186 NLD3201 NLD3202
NLD3214 NLD3242 NLD3253 NLD3292
NLD3301 NLD3317 NLD3338 NLD3341
NLD3361 NOR3371 NOR3390 NOR3425
NOR3435 NOR3439 NOR3443 NOR3447
NOR3453 NOR3459 NOR3465 POL3519
SWE3666 SWE3763 SWE3769 SWE3771
SWE3787 SWE3795 SWE3809 SWE3818
SWE3826 SWE3827 SWE3828 SWE3830
SWE3864

EAST AFRICA - AFRIQUE DE L'EST

AUT0033 AUT0041 AUT0063 AUT0067
AUT0085 AUT0090 BEL0129 BEL0133
BEL0144 BEL0148 BEL0161 BEL0192
BEL0199 BEL0269 BEL0297 BEL0299
BEL0340 BEL0359 BEL0361 BEL0381
BEL0388 BEL0397 CHE0434 CHE0491
CHE0510 CHE0586 CHE0630 CHE0655
CHE0684 CHE0687 CHE0689 CHE0691
CHE0693 CHE0712 CHE0730 CHE0757
CHE0758 CHE0793 CHE0796 CHE0823
CZE0859 DEU0918 DEU0919 DEU0936
DEU0944 DEU0968 DEU0983 DEU0986
DEU0989 DEU1006 DEU1016 DEU1017
DEU1029 DEU1047 DEU1055 DEU1066
DEU1069 DEU1074 DEU1097 DEU1111
DEU1131 DEU1141 DEU1142 DEU1174
DEU1175 DEU1178 DEU1185 DNK1242
DNK1245 DNK1255 DNK1259 DNK1273
DNK1275 DNK1287 DNK1291 DNK1292
DNK1314 DNK1339 DNK1358 DNK1360
DNK1377 DNK1391 DNK1402 ESP1486
ESP1491 ESP1493 ESP1524 FIN1544
FIN1549 FIN1556 FIN1572 FIN1580

FIN1587 FIN1596 FIN1604 FRA1610
FRA1617 FRA1628 FRA1636 FRA1645
FRA1677 FRA1717 FRA1727 FRA1762
FRA1817 FRA1879 FRA1886 FRA1898
FRA1898 FRA1903 FRA1917 FRA1956
FRA1966 FRA1984 FRA1988 FRA1992
FRA2039 FRA2047 FRA2054 FRA2070
FRA2087 FRA2093 FRA2096 FRA2106
FRA2123 FRA2163 GBR2172 GBR2174
GBR2175 GBR2178 GBR2179 GBR2180
GBR2183 GBR2185 GBR2186 GBR2198
GBR2212 GBR2218 GBR2219 GBR2222
GBR2226 GBR2238 GBR2240 GBR2241
GBR2242 GBR2256 GBR2259 GBR2278
GBR2292 GBR2293 GBR2307 GBR2320
GBR2321 GBR2341 GBR2348 GBR2353
GBR2359 GBR2361 GBR2382 GBR2390
GBR2391 GBR2409 GBR2422 GBR2423
GBR2441 GBR2445 GBR2448 GBR2458
GBR2460 GBR2464 GBR2471 GBR2483
GBR2500 GBR2501 GBR2502 GBR2517
GBR2530 GBR2533 GBR2535 GBR2536
GBR2550 GBR2553 GBR2558 GBR2562
GRC2586 IRL2683 IRL2688 IRL2691
IRL2694 IRL2699 IRL2700 IRL2709
IRL2716 IRL2726 IRL2729 IRL2733
ISL2739 ISL2740 ITA2744 ITA2761
ITA2766 ITA2771 ITA2772 ITA2782
ITA2804 ITA2810 ITA2812 ITA2813
ITA2816 ITA2818 ITA2820 ITA2822
ITA2829 ITA2835 ITA2855 ITA2860
ITA2868 ITA2874 ITA2888 ITA2889
ITA2890 ITA2896 ITA2901 ITA2902
ITA2907 ITA2910 ITA2913 ITA2922
ITA2923 LUX2997 NLD3068 NLD3070
NLD3071 NLD3074 NLD3075 NLD3091
NLD3095 NLD3117 NLD3121 NLD3137
NLD3138 NLD3145 NLD3154 NLD3173
NLD3186 NLD3198 NLD3201 NLD3202
NLD3209 NLD3214 NLD3231 NLD3235
NLD3242 NLD3277 NLD3292 NLD3301
NLD3317 NLD3338 NLD3341 NLD3361
NOR3425 NOR3435 NOR3439 NOR3443
NOR3447 NOR3465 POL3508 POL3519
SWE3675 SWE3679 SWE3730 SWE3760
SWE3769 SWE3771 SWE3776 SWE3777
SWE3787 SWE3798 SWE3799 SWE3814
SWE3826 SWE3828 SWE3830 SWE3853
SWE3854 SWE3864

EAST ASIA - ASIE DE L'EST

BEL0129 BEL0144 BEL0161 BEL0199
BEL0340 BEL0361 BEL0388 BEL0397
CHE0434 CHE0510 CHE0586 CHE0655
CHE0689 CHE0693 CHE0712 CHE0730
CHE0749 DEU0944 DEU0971 DEU0989
DEU1029 DEU1047 DEU1055 DEU1142
DEU1174 DEU1185 DNK1251 DNK1275
DNK1287 DNK1292 DNK1314 DNK1358
FRA1610 FRA1817 FRA1898 FRA1917
FRA1966 FRA1992 FRA2047 FRA2054
FRA2096 FRA2114 FRA2123 FRA2159
GBR2175 GBR2218 GBR2238 GBR2266
GBR2278 GBR2323 GBR2361 GBR2391
GBR2423 GBR2441 GBR2445 GBR2448
GBR2458 GBR2464 GBR2501 GBR2535
GBR2550 GBR2553 ITA2766 ITA2822
ITA2832 ITA2860 ITA2868 ITA2922
LUX2997 NLD3068 NLD3071 NLD3091
NLD3138 NLD3154 NLD3186 NLD3198
NLD3202 NLD3214 NLD3338 NLD3361
NOR3387 NOR3435 NOR3465 SWE3809
SWE3826 SWE3828 SWE3830

MEXICO AND CENTRAL AMERICA - MEXIQUE ET AMERIQUE CENTRALE

AUT0021 AUT0029 AUT0041 AUT0058
AUT0063 AUT0067 BEL0129 BEL0132
BEL0133 BEL0144 BEL0148 BEL0161
BEL0164 BEL0184 BEL0189 BEL0199
BEL0201 BEL0241 BEL0269 BEL0297
BEL0336 BEL0340 BEL0353 BEL0361
BEL0362 BEL0371 BEL0378 BEL0381
BEL0388 BEL0396 BEL0397 CHE0434
CHE0485 CHE0510 CHE0557 CHE0602
CHE0619 CHE0632 CHE0655 CHE0689
CHE0712 CHE0727 CHE0730 CHE0788
CHE0793 DEU0944 DEU0954 DEU0968

DEU0983 DEU0989 DEU1016 DEU1029
DEU1047 DEU1055 DEU1097 DEU1111
DEU1114 DEU1131 DEU1132 DEU1142
DEU1167 DEU1174 DEU1175 DEU1185
DEU1202 DNK1226 DNK1283 DNK1287
DNK1292 DNK1312 DNK1314 DNK1317
DNK1339 DNK1360 ESP1413 ESP1427
ESP1431 ESP1435 ESP1442 ESP1450
ESP1455 ESP1461 ESP1474 ESP1475
ESP1485 ESP1486 ESP1491 ESP1493
ESP1496 ESP1503 ESP1505 ESP1506
ESP1517 ESP1517 ESP1521 ESP1525
ESP1529 FIN1544 FIN1546 FIN1578
FIN1580 FIN1582 FIN1587 FRA1610
FRA1636 FRA1673 FRA1795 FRA1815
FRA1817 FRA1831 FRA1856 FRA1898
FRA1904 FRA1917 FRA1938 FRA1942
FRA1975 FRA1980 FRA1985 FRA1988
FRA2012 FRA2044 FRA2057 FRA2074
FRA2090 FRA2092 FRA2096 FRA2102
FRA2123 FRA2163 GBR2174 GBR2175
GBR2212 GBR2218 GBR2226 GBR2229
GBR2238 GBR2242 GBR2244 GBR2256
GBR2259 GBR2278 GBR2306 GBR2321
GBR2353 GBR2359 GBR2361 GBR2391
GBR2419 GBR2423 GBR2441 GBR2445
GBR2458 GBR2500 GBR2501 GBR2535
GBR2550 GBR2553 ITA2744 ITA2756
ITA2762 ITA2771 ITA2773 ITA2775
ITA2782 ITA2799 ITA2809 ITA2814
ITA2824 ITA2834 ITA2838 ITA2842
ITA2855 ITA2858 ITA2860 ITA2868
ITA2881 ITA2882 ITA2902 ITA2903
ITA2911 ITA2913 ITA2922 LUX2997
NLD3068 NLD3071 NLD3078 NLD3091
NLD3137 NLD3138 NLD3141 NLD3154
NLD3198 NLD3214 NLD3219 NLD3253
NLD3263 NLD3303 NLD3305 NLD3338
NLD3341 NLD3361 NOR3390 NOR3403
NOR3409 NOR3410 NOR3425 POL3519
SWE3687 SWE3769 SWE3786 SWE3795
SWE3796 SWE3798 SWE3826 SWE3828
SWE3830 SWE3864 SWE3865

MIDDLE EAST - MOYEN-ORIENT

AUT0035 BEL0129 BEL0132 BEL0133
BEL0144 BEL0161 BEL0270 BEL0297
BEL0303 BEL0306 BEL0340 BEL0342
BEL0361 BEL0362 BEL0397 CHE0434
CHE0491 CHE0550 CHE0655 CHE0664
CHE0684 CHE0689 CHE0712 CHE0730
CHE0757 DEU0944 DEU0989 DEU1029
DEU1047 DEU1055 DEU1065 DEU1150
DEU1174 DEU1185 DNK1275 DNK1292
DNK1304 DNK1314 DNK1360 DNK1450
ESP1455 FIN1582 FIN1587 FRA1610
FRA1628 FRA1629 FRA1636 FRA1677
FRA1683 FRA1724 FRA1749 FRA1794
FRA1817 FRA1886 FRA1898 FRA1917
FRA1942 FRA1948 FRA1988 FRA2016
FRA2041 FRA2044 FRA2047 FRA2057
FRA2096 FRA2114 FRA2123 FRA2159
FRA2163 GBR2175 GBR2218 GBR2226
GBR2229 GBR2238 GBR2241 GBR2244
GBR2278 GBR2303 GBR2359 GBR2361
GBR2378 GBR2391 GBR2423 GBR2441
GBR2445 GBR2458 GBR2464 GBR2464
GBR2500 GBR2501 GBR2525 GBR2537
GBR2562 ITA2773 ITA2782 ITA2799
ITA2824 ITA2834 ITA2839 ITA2855
ITA2860 ITA2913 ITA2923 LUX2997
MLT3018 NLD3091 NLD3117 NLD3138
NLD3154 NLD3173 NLD3201 NLD3214
NLD3301 NLD3338 NLD3361 NOR3390
NOR3435 NOR3447 NOR3456 POL3519
SWE3769 SWE3771 SWE3826 SWE3828
SWE3830

NORTH AFRICA - AFRIQUE DU NORD

BEL0097 BEL0129 BEL0132 BEL0133
BEL0144 BEL0148 BEL0153 BEL0161
BEL0199 BEL0269 BEL0270 BEL0303
BEL0340 BEL0352 BEL0361 BEL0397
CHE0434 CHE0557 CHE0655 CHE0687
CHE0689 CHE0712 CHE0727 CHE0730
CHE0796 DEU0919 DEU0944 DEU0989
DEU0999 DEU1029 DEU1047 DEU1055
DEU1063 DEU1111 DEU1174 DEU1175

Voir : *Comment utiliser le répertoire*, page 11.

DEU1185	DNK1275	DNK1304	DNK1314
DNK1360	ESP1442	ESP1455	ESP1486
ESP1491	ESP1493	ESP1505	ESP1512
ESP1521	FRA1610	FRA1629	FRA1636
FRA1683	FRA1749	FRA1759	FRA1762
FRA1794	FRA1815	FRA1817	FRA1831
FRA1846	FRA1886	FRA1898	FRA1917
FRA1942	FRA1956	FRA1966	FRA1985
FRA1988	FRA1992	FRA2012	FRA2018
FRA2047	FRA2057	FRA2070	FRA2096
FRA2114	FRA2159	GBR2175	GBR2185
GBR2359	GBR2226	GBR2229	GBR2278
GBR2359	GBR2361	GBR2391	GBR2423
GBR2445	GBR2448	GBR2458	GBR2464
GBR2501	GBR2535	GBR2562	GRC2567
GRC2586	IRL2688	IRL2700	IRL2716
ITA2766	ITA2791	ITA2809	ITA2810
ITA2822	ITA2834	ITA2868	ITA2888
ITA2901	ITA2903	ITA2922	ITA2923
LUX2997	MLT3018	NLD3078	NLD3117
NLD3138	NLD3154	NLD3198	NLD3201
NLD3214	NLD3301	NLD3338	NLD3341
NOR3456	POL3519	SWE3763	SWE3813
SWE3828	SWE3830		

OCEANIA - OCEANIE

AUT0067	BEL0129	BEL0161	BEL0199
BEL0270	BEL0361	BEL0388	BEL0397
CHE0434	CHE0655	CHE0712	CHE0730
DEU0944	DEU0989	DEU1029	DEU1047
DEU1055	DEU1185	DNK1314	FRA1610
FRA1672	FRA1817	FRA1898	FRA1917
FRA2047	FRA2096	GBR2175	GBR2218
GBR2256	GBR2266	GBR2278	GBR2312
GBR2359	GBR2361	GBR2382	GBR2391
GBR2422	GBR2423	GBR2445	GBR2458
GBR2501	GBR2535	GBR2553	GBR2553
ITA2860	NLD3091	NLD3137	NLD3154
NLD3214	NLD3301	NLD3341	NLD3361
POL3508	SWE3730	SWE3813	SWE3830

SOUTH AMERICA - AMERIQUE DU SUD

AUT0067	AUT0090	BEL0119	BEL0129
BEL0132	BEL0133	BEL0148	BEL0148
BEL0161	BEL0164	BEL0184	BEL0189
BEL0199	BEL0201	BEL0226	BEL0241
BEL0265	BEL0269	BEL0297	BEL0303
BEL0336	BEL0340	BEL0347	BEL0352
BEL0353	BEL0359	BEL0361	BEL0368
BEL0381	BEL0388	BEL0396	BEL0396
CHE0434	CHE0479	CHE0510	CHE0550
CHE0586	CHE0602	CHE0614	CHE0619
CHE0632	CHE0655	CHE0687	CHE0689
CHE0693	CHE0712	CHE0727	CHE0730
CHE0742	CHE0750	CHE0757	CHE0793
DEU0968	DEU0986	DEU0983	DEU0986
DEU0989	DEU0991	DEU1016	DEU1017
DEU1029	DEU1047	DEU1055	DEU1074
DEU1097	DEU1111	DEU1114	DEU1131
DEU1132	DEU1141	DEU1142	DEU1167
DEU1174	DEU1175	DEU1178	DEU1185
DEU1211	DNK1238	DNK1251	DNK1287
DNK1291	DNK1312	DNK1314	DNK1317
DNK1319	DNK1358	DNK1360	ESP1431
ESP1435	ESP1442	ESP1450	ESP1452
ESP1455	ESP1457	ESP1461	ESP1474
ESP1475	ESP1485	ESP1486	ESP1488
ESP1491	ESP1493	ESP1496	ESP1502
ESP1503	ESP1505	ESP1507	ESP1508
ESP1510	ESP1512	ESP1513	ESP1517
ESP1521	ESP1525	ESP1529	FIN1582
FIN1587	FIN1604	FRA1610	FRA1615
FRA1617	FRA1636	FRA1672	FRA1673
FRA1715	FRA1749	FRA1815	FRA1817
FRA1828	FRA1831	FRA1886	FRA1898
FRA1903	FRA1904	FRA1917	FRA1938
FRA1975	FRA1988	FRA2012	FRA2018
FRA2041	FRA2044	FRA2057	FRA2070
FRA2074	FRA2092	FRA2096	FRA2102
FRA2114	FRA2123	FRA2131	FRA2159
FRA2163	GBR2174	GBR2175	GBR2212
GBR2218	GBR2226	GBR2229	GBR2238
GBR2278	GBR2278	GBR2293	GBR2321
GBR2325	GBR2359	GBR2361	GBR2391
GBR2423	GBR2441	GBR2445	GBR2454
GBR2456	GBR2458	GBR2464	GBR2485
GBR2500	GBR2501	GBR2525	GBR2535
GBR2550	GBR2553	GBR2558	IRL2700

IRL2719	ITA2744	ITA2748	ITA2756
ITA2758	ITA2761	ITA2762	ITA2766
ITA2779	ITA2773	ITA2775	ITA2777
ITA2782	ITA2792	ITA2798	ITA2799
ITA2807	ITA2809	ITA2810	ITA2812
ITA2814	ITA2822	ITA2824	ITA2830
ITA2832	ITA2834	ITA2835	ITA2838
ITA2842	ITA2855	ITA2860	ITA2868
ITA2873	ITA2880	ITA2881	ITA2882
ITA2888	ITA2889	ITA2895	ITA2896
ITA2899	ITA2900	ITA2901	ITA2907
ITA2913	ITA2922	ITA2923	LUX2953
LUX2980	LUX2997	NLD3068	NLD3071
NLD3075	NLD3091	NLD3137	NLD3138
NLD3154	NLD3181	NLD3198	NLD3202
NLD3214	NLD3235	NLD3253	NLD3305
NLD3317	NLD3338	NLD3341	NLD3361
NOR3409	NOR3443	NOR3465	POL3508
POL3519	SWE3693	SWE3695	SWE3702
SWE3730	SWE3744	SWE3760	SWE3763
SWE3769	SWE3787	SWE3795	SWE3796
SWE3826	SWE3827	SWE3828	SWE3830
SWE3864	SWE3865		

SOUTH EAST ASIA - ASIE DU SUD-EST

AUT0063	BEL0128	BEL0129	BEL0133
BEL0144	BEL0156	BEL0161	BEL0192
BEL0199	BEL0226	BEL0241	BEL0261
BEL0269	BEL0270	BEL0297	BEL0306
BEL0340	BEL0342	BEL0361	BEL0362
BEL0368	BEL0381	BEL0388	BEL0396
BEL0397	CHE0434	CHE0479	CHE0510
CHE0550	CHE0586	CHE0619	CHE0630
CHE0632	CHE0655	CHE0689	CHE0693
CHE0712	CHE0727	CHE0730	CHE0749
CHE0757	CHE0785	CHE0793	CHE0796
DEU0944	DEU0954	DEU0971	DEU0983
DEU0989	DEU1029	DEU1047	DEU1055
DEU1074	DEU1132	DEU1141	DEU1167
DEU1174	DEU1175	DEU1185	DNK1238
DNK1259	DNK1287	DNK1314	DNK1360
FIN1580	FIN1587	FRA1610	FRA1615
FRA1617	FRA1628	FRA1629	FRA1640
FRA1672	FRA1683	FRA1715	FRA1749
FRA1817	FRA1820	FRA1850	FRA1860
FRA1886	FRA1898	FRA1917	FRA1928
FRA1937	FRA1938	FRA1941	FRA1966
FRA1979	FRA1980	FRA1983	FRA1988
FRA1992	FRA2012	FRA2018	FRA2044
FRA2047	FRA2054	FRA2057	FRA2074
FRA2096	FRA2114	FRA2123	FRA2134
FRA2140	FRA2163	GBR2175	GBR2198
GBR2212	GBR2218	GBR2222	GBR2238
GBR2240	GBR2242	GBR2256	GBR2278
GBR2293	GBR2303	GBR2321	GBR2353
GBR2359	GBR2361	GBR2382	GBR2390
GBR2391	GBR2419	GBR2423	GBR2441
GBR2445	GBR2448	GBR2458	GBR2486
GBR2500	GBR2501	GBR2508	GBR2533
GBR2535	GBR2550	GBR2553	IRL2691
IRL2700	IRL2726	ITA2744	ITA2758
ITA2766	ITA2775	ITA2798	ITA2799
ITA2813	ITA2824	ITA2860	ITA2868
ITA2873	ITA2902	ITA2911	ITA2922
LUX2964	LUX2997	NLD3068	NLD3070
NLD3071	NLD3091	NLD3117	NLD3137
NLD3138	NLD3141	NLD3154	NLD3186
NLD3198	NLD3201	NLD3202	NLD3214
NLD3235	NLD3253	NLD3277	NLD3292
NLD3303	NLD3338	NLD3341	NLD3361
NOR3390	NOR3425	NOR3435	NOR3465
POL3519	SWE3771	SWE3786	SWE3787
SWE3798	SWE3826	SWE3828	SWE3830
SWE3854			

SOUTHERN AFRICA - AFRIQUE AUSTRALE

AUT0033	AUT0058	AUT0063	AUT0067
BEL0129	BEL0144	BEL0148	BEL0161
BEL0189	BEL0192	BEL0199	BEL0241
BEL0260	BEL0265	BEL0269	BEL0297
BEL0299	BEL0303	BEL0340	BEL0359
BEL0361	BEL0368	BEL0388	BEL0397
CHE0434	CHE0510	CHE0619	CHE0632
CHE0655	CHE0687	CHE0689	CHE0693
CHE0712	CHE0727	CHE0730	CHE0734
CHE0758	DEU0919	DEU0944	DEU0989
DEU1006	DEU1016	DEU1029	DEU1047
DEU1055	DEU1082	DEU1097	DEU1111

WEST AFRICA - AFRIQUE DE L'OUEST

DEU1131	DEU1142	DEU1174	DEU1175
DEU1185	DEU1200	DEU1211	DNK1218
DNK1238	DNK1245	DNK1259	DNK1275
DNK1288	DNK1292	DNK1312	DNK1314
DNK1339	DNK1360	DNK1375	DNK1388
DNK1391	DNK1403	ESP1420	ESP1445
ESP1450	ESP1454	ESP1486	ESP1491
ESP1493	FIN1544	FIN1546	FIN1556
FIN1559	FIN1579	FIN1580	FIN1587
FIN1603	FRA1610	FRA1645	FRA1672
FRA1677	FRA1727	FRA1738	FRA1769
FRA1795	FRA1817	FRA1830	FRA1849
FRA1876	FRA1879	FRA1898	FRA1903
FRA1917	FRA1948	FRA1956	FRA1966
FRA2012	FRA2018	FRA2041	FRA2044
FRA2047	FRA2054	FRA2070	FRA2096
FRA2114	FRA2123	FRA2159	FRA2163
GBR2174	GBR2175	GBR2178	GBR2183
GBR2185	GBR2198	GBR2212	GBR2218
GBR2222	GBR2226	GBR2229	GBR2238
GBR2240	GBR2242	GBR2244	GBR2256
GBR2259	GBR2266	GBR2277	GBR2278
GBR2292	GBR2303	GBR2318	GBR2321
GBR2341	GBR2348	GBR2349	GBR2353
GBR2359	GBR2361	GBR2364	GBR2390
GBR2391	GBR2402	GBR2422	GBR2423
GBR2441	GBR2445	GBR2448	GBR2460
GBR2464	GBR2471	GBR2478	GBR2501
GBR2523	GBR2530	GBR2535	GBR2536
GBR2550	GBR2553	GBR2558	GBR2561
GBR2562	IRL2691	IRL2700	IRL2716
IRL2719	IRL2729	ITA2766	ITA2771
ITA2798	ITA2798	ITA2799	ITA2803
ITA2806	ITA2813	ITA2816	ITA2822
ITA2824	ITA2838	ITA2855	ITA2860
ITA2881	ITA2885	ITA2900	ITA2902
ITA2903	ITA2911	ITA2916	ITA2922
ITA2923	LUX2995	NLD3068	NLD3070
NLD3071	NLD3078	NLD3091	NLD3095
NLD3098	NLD3117	NLD3137	NLD3138
NLD3154	NLD3173	NLD3198	NLD3201
NLD3209	NLD3214	NLD3231	NLD3235
NLD3253	NLD3292	NLD3301	NLD3317
NLD3318	NLD3336	NLD3338	NLD3341
NLD3363	NOR3389	NOR3390	NOR3418
NOR3425	NOR3435	NOR3447	POL3519
PRT3549	PRT3555	PRT3576	PRT3579
PRT3586	PRT3590	PRT3594	PRT3596
PRT3603	PRT3605	SWE3648	SWE3731
SWE3769	SWE3773	SWE3776	SWE3798
SWE3813	SWE3826	SWE3828	SWE3830
SWE3839	SWE3859	SWE3864	

WEST AFRICA - AFRIQUE DE L'OUEST

AUT0021	AUT0028	AUT0033	AUT0041
AUT0063	AUT0086	BEL0118	BEL0129
BEL0132	BEL0133	BEL0144	BEL0148
BEL0153	BEL0156	BEL0161	BEL0184
BEL0192	BEL0199	BEL0201	BEL0269
BEL0297	BEL0299	BEL0328	BEL0340
BEL0342	BEL0353	BEL0359	BEL0361
BEL0367	BEL0368	BEL0381	BEL0388
BEL0396	BEL0397	CHE0402	CHE0434
CHE0479	CHE0498	CHE0510	CHE0557
CHE0619	CHE0637	CHE0655	CHE0684
CHE0687	CHE0689	CHE0707	CHE0712
CHE0727	CHE0730	CHE0734	CHE0757
CHE0758	CHE0793	CHE0796	CHE0817
CHE0823	DEU0918	DEU0919	DEU0944
DEU0968	DEU0971	DEU0983	DEU0986
DEU0989	DEU0991	DEU1006	DEU1017
DEU1029	DEU1047	DEU1055	DEU1069
DEU1074	DEU1097	DEU1106	DEU1110
DEU1111	DEU1114	DEU1131	DEU1142
DEU1174	DEU1178	DEU1185	DEU1200
DNK1215	DNK1238	DNK1259	DNK1287
DNK1307	DNK1314	DNK1360	DNK1374
DNK1402	ESP1468	ESP1486	ESP1488
ESP1491	ESP1493	ESP1502	ESP1510
ESP1517	ESP1524	FIN1580	FIN1587
FIN1604	FRA1610	FRA1615	FRA1624
FRA1629	FRA1634	FRA1636	FRA1645
FRA1677	FRA1715	FRA1727	FRA1752
FRA1762	FRA1776	FRA1778	FRA1785
FRA1787	FRA1789	FRA1794	FRA1795
FRA1796	FRA1815	FRA1817	FRA1820
FRA1830	FRA1846	FRA1848	FRA1876
FRA1879	FRA1880	FRA1886	FRA1898
FRA1903	FRA1907	FRA1914	FRA1917

See: *How to Use the Directory*, page 11.

FRA1944	FRA1948	FRA1956	FRA1966
FRA1984	FRA1988	FRA1992	FRA2012
FRA2016	FRA2018	FRA2039	FRA2044
FRA2047	FRA2054	FRA2057	FRA2070
FRA2074	FRA2086	FRA2087	FRA2092
FRA2093	FRA2096	FRA2105	FRA2106
FRA2114	FRA2116	FRA2123	FRA2131
FRA2134	FRA2159	FRA2161	FRA2163
GBR2174	GBR2175	GBR2180	GBR2185
GBR2198	GBR2218	GBR2222	GBR2226
GBR2238	GBR2241	GBR2242	GBR2244
GBR2256	GBR2259	GBR2274	GBR2278
GBR2341	GBR2353	GBR2359	GBR2361
GBR2371	GBR2382	GBR2390	GBR2391
GBR2422	GBR2423	GBR2445	GBR2448
GBR2458	GBR2460	GBR2464	GBR2483
GBR2500	GBR2501	GBR2515	GBR2517
GBR2525	GBR2533	GBR2535	GBR2550
GBR2553	GBR2558	GBR2562	GRC2567
GRC2586	IRL2700	ISL2739	ITA2744
ITA2756	ITA2761	ITA2762	ITA2765
ITA2766	ITA2770	ITA2773	ITA2774
ITA2782	ITA2786	ITA2791	ITA2799
ITA2801	ITA2803	ITA2807	ITA2809
ITA2812	ITA2816	ITA2824	ITA2826
ITA2827	ITA2828	ITA2829	ITA2838
ITA2842	ITA2855	ITA2860	ITA2873
ITA2874	ITA2901	ITA2902	ITA2913
ITA2916	ITA2922	ITA2923	LUX2978
LUX2986	LUX2997	NLD3068	NLD3074
NLD3075	NLD3091	NLD3091	NLD3117
NLD3137	NLD3138	NLD3154	NLD3173
NLD3186	NLD3198	NLD3201	NLD3202
NLD3214	NLD3230	NLD3231	NLD3235
NLD3254	NLD3269	NLD3277	NLD3288
NLD3292	NLD3301	NLD3338	NLD3341
NLD3361	NOR3387	NOR3403	NOR3435
NOR3443	NOR3453	NOR3465	POL3519
PRT3549	PRT3555	PRT3579	PRT3586
PRT3590	PRT3603	SWE3648	SWE3707
SWE3769	SWE3771	SWE3776	SWE3783
SWE3828	SWE3830	SWE3831	

SMALL ENTERPRISES, INFORMAL SECTOR, HANDICRAFTS - PETITES ENTREPRISES, SECTEUR INFORMEL, ARTISANAT

CARIBBEAN - CARAIBES

BEL0123	BEL0124	BEL0129	BEL0144
BEL0186	BEL0218	BEL0221	BEL0224
BEL0289	BEL0327	BEL0336	BEL0336
BEL0351	BEL0353	BEL0358	BEL0361
BEL0397	CHE0434	CHE0568	CHE0570
CHE0586	CHE0614	CHE0643	CHE0655
CHE0682	CHE0689	CHE0712	CHE0730
CHE0793	CHE0819	DEU0968	DEU0972
DEU0983	DEU0989	DEU0991	DEU1047
DEU1055	DEU1083	DEU1128	DEU1174
DEU1209	DNK1300	DNK1314	ESP1442
ESP1455	ESP1472	ESP1486	ESP1492
ESP1525	ESP1529	FIN1584	FRA1629
FRA1644	FRA1672	FRA1676	FRA1709
FRA1827	FRA1903	FRA1917	FRA1934
FRA1946	FRA2062	FRA2103	FRA2106
FRA2116	FRA2168	GBR2198	GBR2212
GBR2218	GBR2228	GBR2238	GBR2244
GBR2266	GBR2324	GBR2371	GBR2392
GBR2419	GBR2423	GBR2436	GBR2437
GBR2481	GBR2500	GBR2501	GBR2518
GBR2535	GBR2553	GBR2558	IRL2726
ITA2767	ITA2773	ITA2780	ITA2784
ITA2852	ITA2860	LUX2993	NLD3067
NLD3078	NLD3137	NLD3173	NLD3198
NLD3231	NLD3257	NLD3356	NLD3361
NLD3364	NOR3425	POL3519	SWE3653
SWE3656	SWE3830		

CENTRAL AFRICA - AFRIQUE CENTRALE

BEL0097	BEL0110	BEL0120	BEL0123
BEL0124	BEL0128	BEL0129	BEL0133
BEL0144	BEL0148	BEL0153	BEL0155
BEL0158	BEL0186	BEL0203	BEL0218
BEL0221	BEL0230	BEL0261	BEL0289
BEL0297	BEL0306	BEL0327	BEL0342
BEL0351	BEL0352	BEL0353	BEL0356
BEL0358	BEL0359	BEL0361	BEL0367

BEL0378	BEL0381	BEL0397	CHE0434
CHE0444	CHE0491	CHE0535	CHE0541
CHE0562	CHE0565	CHE0568	CHE0626
CHE0643	CHE0655	CHE0689	CHE0712
CHE0727	CHE0730	CHE0805	CHE0814
CHE0819	DEU0919	DEU0968	DEU0972
DEU0978	DEU0989	DEU0995	DEU1006
DEU1047	DEU1055	DEU1106	DEU1114
DEU1118	DEU1128	DEU1131	DEU1174
DEU1209	DNK1227	DNK1272	DNK1300
DNK1314	DNK1392	ESP1474	ESP1492
ESP1517	ESP1529	FIN1549	FRA1629
FRA1636	FRA1649	FRA1677	FRA1709
FRA1727	FRA1740	FRA1765	FRA1769
FRA1774	FRA1815	FRA1819	FRA1827
FRA1830	FRA1833	FRA1879	FRA1903
FRA1917	FRA1934	FRA1946	FRA1947
FRA1956	FRA1980	FRA1984	FRA1988
FRA1991	FRA2021	FRA2062	FRA2070
FRA2092	FRA2103	FRA2106	FRA2116
FRA2147	FRA2168	GBR2173	GBR2175
GBR2185	GBR2187	GBR2218	GBR2238
GBR2259	GBR2351	GBR2371	GBR2390
GBR2437	GBR2460	GBR2481	GBR2501
GBR2520	GBR2550	GBR2553	GRC2567
IRL2732	ITA2744	ITA2747	ITA2762
ITA2777	ITA2779	ITA2784	ITA2791
ITA2813	ITA2835	ITA2835	ITA2880
ITA2885	ITA2890	ITA2896	ITA2907
ITA2921	LUX2997	NLD3045	NLD3067
NLD3070	NLD3096	NLD3101	NLD3120
NLD3137	NLD3253	NLD3257	NLD3281
NLD3301	NLD3356	NLD3361	NLD3364
POL3519	PRT3594	PRT3602	SWE3656
SWE3667	SWE3749	SWE3763	SWE3830

CENTRAL ASIA AND SOUTH ASIA - ASIE CENTRALE ET ASIE DU SUD

AUT0051	AUT0091	BEL0097	BEL0123
BEL0124	BEL0129	BEL0144	BEL0186
BEL0192	BEL0203	BEL0221	BEL0261
BEL0270	BEL0327	BEL0340	BEL0341
BEL0351	BEL0353	BEL0358	BEL0359
BEL0361	BEL0368	BEL0378	BEL0397
CHE0417	CHE0434	CHE0467	CHE0491
CHE0559	CHE0565	CHE0568	CHE0586
CHE0619	CHE0638	CHE0643	CHE0655
CHE0682	CHE0689	CHE0712	CHE0727
CHE0730	CHE0742	CHE0785	CHE0793
CHE0814	CHE0819	DEU0940	DEU0968
DEU0972	DEU0983	DEU0985	DEU0989
DEU0990	DEU0995	DEU1006	DEU1015
DEU1038	DEU1047	DEU1055	DEU1066
DEU1086	DEU1106	DEU1118	DEU1128
DEU1129	DEU1131	DEU1132	DEU1149
DEU1151	DEU1174	DEU1174	DEU1187
DEU1209	DNK1229	DNK1244	DNK1248
DNK1260	DNK1275	DNK1291	DNK1292
DNK1300	DNK1314	DNK1339	DNK1366
DNK1369	DNK1384	ESP1492	ESP1513
FIN1574	FIN1591	FRA1642	FRA1644
FRA1655	FRA1658	FRA1661	FRA1681
FRA1709	FRA1830	FRA1917	FRA1934
FRA1939	FRA1988	FRA1990	FRA1991
FRA2023	FRA2116	FRA2117	FRA2131
FRA2168	GBR2173	GBR2174	GBR2175
GBR2176	GBR2186	GBR2197	GBR2201
GBR2212	GBR2218	GBR2226	GBR2228
GBR2238	GBR2266	GBR2281	GBR2297
GBR2302	GBR2324	GBR2333	GBR2334
GBR2339	GBR2348	GBR2351	GBR2358
GBR2371	GBR2372	GBR2375	GBR2376
GBR2382	GBR2390	GBR2392	GBR2409
GBR2410	GBR2419	GBR2423	GBR2436
GBR2437	GBR2464	GBR2467	GBR2475
GBR2481	GBR2492	GBR2500	GBR2501
GBR2506	GBR2509	GBR2514	GBR2532
GBR2535	GBR2553	GBR2558	GRC2571
GRC2575	IRL2726	ITA2773	ITA2775
ITA2784	ITA2840	ITA2860	ITA2873
ITA2885	ITA2888	LUX2973	LUX2982
LUX2997	NLD3051	NLD3067	NLD3078
NLD3096	NLD3101	NLD3120	NLD3137
NLD3138	NLD3173	NLD3183	NLD3198
NLD3199	NLD3231	NLD3253	NLD3257
NLD3260	NLD3281	NLD3302	NLD3317
NLD3318	NLD3356	NLD3361	NLD3364

NOR3371	NOR3384	NOR3390	NOR3459
NOR3460	NOR3465	NOR3467	NOR3471
POL3519	SWE3650	SWE3656	SWE3666
SWE3674	SWE3737	SWE3745	SWE3749
SWE3760	SWE3763	SWE3795	SWE3818
SWE3830	SWE3857	SWE3864	

EAST AFRICA - AFRIQUE DE L'EST

AUT0003	AUT0041	AUT0063	AUT0067
AUT0085	AUT0091	BEL0123	BEL0124
BEL0129	BEL0133	BEL0144	BEL0148
BEL0167	BEL0186	BEL0221	BEL0224
BEL0269	BEL0270	BEL0289	BEL0306
BEL0327	BEL0351	BEL0353	BEL0356
BEL0358	BEL0361	BEL0381	BEL0397
CHE0434	CHE0448	CHE0491	CHE0565
CHE0570	CHE0586	CHE0619	CHE0620
CHE0626	CHE0629	CHE0630	CHE0643
CHE0682	CHE0689	CHE0691	CHE0693
CHE0712	CHE0727	CHE0730	CHE0772
CHE0785	CHE0793	CHE0814	CHE0817
CHE0823	DEU0919	DEU0936	DEU0968
DEU0972	DEU0983	DEU0989	DEU0995
DEU1006	DEU1047	DEU1055	DEU1066
DEU1069	DEU1106	DEU1114	DEU1118
DEU1129	DEU1131	DEU1145	DEU1149
DEU1174	DEU1176	DEU1178	DEU1209
DNK1229	DNK1242	DNK1255	DNK1274
DNK1275	DNK1285	DNK1292	DNK1300
DNK1314	DNK1316	DNK1339	DNK1342
DNK1369	DNK1392	DNK1405	ESP1432
ESP1492	FIN1544	FIN1572	FIN1584
FIN1591	FIN1596	FRA1636	FRA1644
FRA1658	FRA1709	FRA1727	FRA1762
FRA1833	FRA1879	FRA1903	FRA1917
FRA1934	FRA1947	FRA1956	FRA1988
FRA2062	FRA2106	FRA2116	FRA2147
FRA2168	GBR2173	GBR2175	GBR2179
GBR2183	GBR2185	GBR2187	GBR2198
GBR2202	GBR2212	GBR2214	GBR2218
GBR2226	GBR2228	GBR2238	GBR2240
GBR2259	GBR2282	GBR2292	GBR2324
GBR2339	GBR2348	GBR2351	GBR2371
GBR2390	GBR2419	GBR2436	GBR2437
GBR2460	GBR2464	GBR2467	GBR2481
GBR2483	GBR2500	GBR2501	GBR2510
GBR2514	GBR2518	GBR2533	GBR2535
GBR2536	GBR2550	GBR2553	GBR2558
GRC2571	IRL2688	IRL2702	IRL2709
IRL2724	IRL2730	IRL2732	IRL2733
ISL2740	ITA2744	ITA2782	ITA2784
ITA2835	ITA2840	ITA2822	ITA2829
ITA2896	ITA2902	ITA2910	LUX2997
NLD3045	NLD3067	NLD3070	NLD3074
NLD3089	NLD3096	NLD3101	NLD3137
NLD3183	NLD3198	NLD3216	NLD3253
NLD3257	NLD3281	NLD3301	NLD3323
NLD3356	NLD3361	NLD3364	NOR3381
NOR3431	NOR3465	NOR3467	POL3519
PRT3550	SWE3650	SWE3656	SWE3666
SWE3688	SWE3727	SWE3728	SWE3730
SWE3749	SWE3752	SWE3771	SWE3799
SWE3830	SWE3864		

EAST ASIA - ASIE DE L'EST

BEL0123	BEL0124	BEL0129	BEL0144
BEL0186	BEL0221	BEL0289	BEL0327
BEL0351	BEL0353	BEL0358	BEL0361
BEL0397	CHE0434	CHE0565	CHE0586
CHE0638	CHE0643	CHE0655	CHE0689
CHE0693	CHE0712	CHE0730	CHE0795
CHE0814	CHE0819	DEU0972	DEU0989
DEU0995	DEU1006	DEU1015	DEU1047
DEU1055	DEU1118	DEU1128	DEU1129
DEU1143	DEU1149	DEU1167	DEU1174
DEU1209	DNK1244	DNK1300	DNK1314
ESP1432	ESP1492	FRA1681	FRA1709
FRA1917	FRA2070	FRA2116	FRA2168
GBR2175	GBR2218	GBR2228	GBR2238
GBR2351	GBR2371	GBR2481	GBR2501
GBR2535	GBR2550	GBR2553	IRL2726
ITA2784	ITA2860	LUX2973	LUX2997
NLD3067	NLD3078	NLD3096	NLD3198
NLD3356	NLD3364	NOR3465	SWE3760
SWE3830			

Voir : *Comment utiliser le répertoire,* page 11.

MEXICO AND CENTRAL AMERICA - MEXIQUE ET AMERIQUE CENTRALE

AUT0003	AUT0041	AUT0051	AUT0052
AUT0058	AUT0063	AUT0067	AUT0091
BEL0123	BEL0124	BEL0129	BEL0144
BEL0148	BEL0186	BEL0203	BEL0221
BEL0224	BEL0241	BEL0245	BEL0261
BEL0269	BEL0289	BEL0327	BEL0336
BEL0351	BEL0353	BEL0358	BEL0359
BEL0361	BEL0371	BEL0378	BEL0381
BEL0396	BEL0397	CHE0434	CHE0446
CHE0485	CHE0491	CHE0559	CHE0568
CHE0602	CHE0626	CHE0682	CHE0689
CHE0712	CHE0720	CHE0727	CHE0730
CHE0735	CHE0772	CHE0785	CHE0786
CHE0789	CHE0793	CHE0804	CHE0814
CHE0819	DEU0968	DEU0972	DEU0983
DEU0989	DEU0995	DEU1015	DEU1031
DEU1047	DEU1055	DEU1083	DEU1114
DEU1118	DEU1128	DEU1129	DEU1132
DEU1143	DEU1149	DEU1167	DEU1174
DEU1178	DEU1187	DEU1202	DEU1209
DNK1226	DNK1229	DNK1300	DNK1312
DNK1314	DNK1369	ESP1407	ESP1409
ESP1427	ESP1432	ESP1435	ESP1442
ESP1450	ESP1455	ESP1457	ESP1461
ESP1486	ESP1492	ESP1506	ESP1510
ESP1521	ESP1525	ESP1529	FIN1544
FIN1591	FRA1636	FRA1658	FRA1672
FRA1703	FRA1709	FRA1827	FRA1917
FRA1934	FRA1942	FRA1947	FRA2047
FRA2062	FRA2092	FRA2103	FRA2116
FRA2117	FRA2150	FRA2168	GBR2175
GBR2201	GBR2202	GBR2212	GBR2218
GBR2226	GBR2228	GBR2238	GBR2244
GBR2321	GBR2324	GBR2351	GBR2371
GBR2392	GBR2419	GBR2423	GBR2436
GBR2437	GBR2467	GBR2481	GBR2500
GBR2501	GBR2510	GBR2518	GBR2535
GBR2553	IRL2697	IRL2726	IRL2732
ITA2756	ITA2762	ITA2773	ITA2775
ITA2780	ITA2782	ITA2784	ITA2807
ITA2814	ITA2834	ITA2838	ITA2860
ITA2881	ITA2894	ITA2913	LUX2937
LUX2968	LUX2997	NLD3067	NLD3078
NLD3096	NLD3101	NLD3137	NLD3187
NLD3198	NLD3199	NLD3253	NLD3257
NLD3263	NLD3281	NLD3305	NLD3317
NLD3356	NLD3361	NLD3364	NOR3390
NOR3425	NOR3426	NOR3467	POL3508
POL3519	SWE3650	SWE3656	SWE3666
SWE3687	SWE3688	SWE3749	SWE3760
SWE3770	SWE3795	SWE3796	SWE3826
SWE3830	SWE3864	SWE3865	

MIDDLE EAST - MOYEN-ORIENT

AUT0091	BEL0129	BEL0129	BEL0144
BEL0186	BEL0221	BEL0270	BEL0306
BEL0317	BEL0353	BEL0358	BEL0361
BEL0397	CHE0434	CHE0565	CHE0568
CHE0655	CHE0689	CHE0712	CHE0730
CHE0819	CHE0823	DEU0972	DEU0989
DEU0995	DEU1015	DEU1047	DEU1055
DEU1065	DEU1106	DEU1128	DEU1131
DEU1150	DEU1174	DNK1292	DNK1300
DNK1314	ESP1450	ESP1455	FRA1629
FRA1636	FRA1683	FRA1709	FRA1724
FRA1827	FRA1917	FRA1926	FRA1942
FRA1988	FRA2023	FRA2103	FRA2116
FRA2150	GBR2218	GBR2238	GBR2244
GBR2371	GBR2500	GBR2501	GBR2525
GRC2573	ITA2773	ITA2782	ITA2784
ITA2838	ITA2860	ITA2913	NLD3067
NLD3356	NLD3361	NLD3364	POL3519
SWE3650	SWE3749	SWE3763	SWE3830
TUR3883			

NORTH AFRICA - AFRIQUE DU NORD

BEL0097	BEL0123	BEL0124	BEL0129
BEL0144	BEL0148	BEL0153	BEL0186
BEL0221	BEL0269	BEL0270	BEL0289
BEL0353	BEL0358	BEL0361	BEL0397
CHE0434	CHE0565	CHE0568	CHE0655
CHE0682	CHE0689	CHE0712	CHE0727
CHE0730	CHE0814	DEU0919	DEU0972
DEU0989	DEU0995	DEU1047	DEU1055
DEU1063	DEU1128	DEU1174	DEU1191

DEU1209	DNK1300	DNK1314	ESP1406
ESP1435	ESP1455	ESP1486	ESP1492
ESP1512	FRA1629	FRA1636	FRA1683
FRA1709	FRA1759	FRA1762	FRA1765
FRA1846	FRA1886	FRA1917	FRA1946
FRA1947	FRA1956	FRA1988	FRA1992
FRA2057	FRA2116	FRA2150	GBR2185
GBR2218	GBR2226	GBR2238	GBR2371
GBR2437	GBR2501	GBR2535	GRC2575
ITA2766	ITA2784	ITA2860	ITA2901
LUX2997	NLD3067	NLD3078	NLD3198
NLD3317	NLD3356	NLD3364	POL3519
PRT3564	SWE3688	SWE3763	SWE3813
SWE3830			

OCEANIA - OCEANIE

AUT0067	BEL0123	BEL0124	BEL0129
BEL0186	BEL0358	BEL0361	BEL0397
CHE0434	CHE0565	CHE0712	CHE0730
CHE0772	CHE0819	DEU0968	DEU0972
DEU0989	DEU0995	DEU1015	DEU1047
DEU1055	DEU1128	DEU1149	DNK1300
DNK1314	FRA1672	FRA1709	FRA1917
FRA2116	FRA2168	GBR2202	GBR2218
GBR2228	GBR2266	GBR2312	GBR2371
GBR2392	GBR2437	GBR2481	GBR2501
GBR2524	GBR2535	GBR2553	ITA2784
ITA2860	NLD3067	NLD3096	NLD3137
NLD3356	NLD3361	NLD3364	SWE3830

SOUTH AMERICA - AMERIQUE DU SUD

AUT0003	AUT0051	AUT0052	AUT0067
AUT0091	BEL0119	BEL0123	BEL0124
BEL0126	BEL0129	BEL0139	BEL0144
BEL0148	BEL0153	BEL0155	BEL0186
BEL0203	BEL0221	BEL0226	BEL0241
BEL0245	BEL0258	BEL0261	BEL0269
BEL0270	BEL0282	BEL0289	BEL0327
BEL0336	BEL0341	BEL0351	BEL0353
BEL0356	BEL0358	BEL0359	BEL0361
BEL0381	BEL0397	CHE0434	CHE0438
CHE0455	CHE0465	CHE0491	CHE0510
CHE0559	CHE0568	CHE0570	CHE0586
CHE0602	CHE0604	CHE0613	CHE0614
CHE0626	CHE0638	CHE0643	CHE0665
CHE0681	CHE0682	CHE0689	CHE0693
CHE0701	CHE0712	CHE0720	CHE0727
CHE0730	CHE0772	CHE0786	CHE0789
CHE0793	CHE0798	CHE0806	CHE0814
CHE0819	DEU0918	DEU0920	DEU0968
DEU0972	DEU0983	DEU0989	DEU0991
DEU0995	DEU1006	DEU1015	DEU1031
DEU1047	DEU1055	DEU1066	DEU1083
DEU1114	DEU1128	DEU1129	DEU1132
DEU1149	DEU1174	DEU1178	DEU1187
DEU1209	DNK1248	DNK1251	DNK1300
DNK1314	DNK1369	DNK1403	ESP1431
ESP1432	ESP1435	ESP1437	ESP1442
ESP1450	ESP1455	ESP1457	ESP1472
ESP1475	ESP1484	ESP1486	ESP1492
ESP1510	ESP1512	ESP1513	ESP1521
ESP1525	ESP1529	FIN1549	FRA1636
FRA1655	FRA1672	FRA1681	FRA1703
FRA1709	FRA1710	FRA1827	FRA1903
FRA1917	FRA1930	FRA1934	FRA1946
FRA1947	FRA1980	FRA1991	FRA2018
FRA2023	FRA2047	FRA2057	FRA2062
FRA2070	FRA2086	FRA2092	FRA2103
FRA2116	FRA2117	FRA2131	FRA2150
FRA2168	GBR2175	GBR2201	GBR2212
GBR2218	GBR2226	GBR2228	GBR2238
GBR2244	GBR2266	GBR2303	GBR2324
GBR2339	GBR2351	GBR2371	GBR2383
GBR2390	GBR2419	GBR2423	GBR2436
GBR2437	GBR2467	GBR2481	GBR2485
GBR2500	GBR2501	GBR2518	GBR2537
GBR2550	GBR2553	GBR2558	IRL2708
IRL2726	IRL2732	ITA2744	ITA2748
ITA2756	ITA2758	ITA2762	ITA2773
ITA2775	ITA2780	ITA2782	ITA2784
ITA2785	ITA2798	ITA2820	ITA2822
ITA2832	ITA2834	ITA2835	ITA2838
ITA2852	ITA2860	ITA2873	ITA2881
ITA2888	ITA2896	ITA2900	ITA2901
ITA2907	ITA2913	LUX2937	LUX2946
LUX2949	LUX2953	LUX2967	LUX2968
LUX2976	LUX2983	LUX2997	LUX2999
NLD3067	NLD3068	NLD3078	NLD3096

SOUTH EAST ASIA - ASIE DU SUD-EST

AUT0026	AUT0051	AUT0091	BEL0123
BEL0124	BEL0129	BEL0144	BEL0186
BEL0192	BEL0203	BEL0221	BEL0224
BEL0261	BEL0269	BEL0275	BEL0289
BEL0306	BEL0327	BEL0341	BEL0342
BEL0351	BEL0353	BEL0358	BEL0359
BEL0361	BEL0381	BEL0397	CHE0434
CHE0491	CHE0559	CHE0565	CHE0568
CHE0586	CHE0604	CHE0626	CHE0637
CHE0638	CHE0643	CHE0682	CHE0689
CHE0712	CHE0727	CHE0730	CHE0749
CHE0785	CHE0793	CHE0795	CHE0798
CHE0814	CHE0819	DEU0972	DEU0983
DEU0989	DEU0990	DEU0995	DEU1006
DEU1015	DEU1047	DEU1055	DEU1106
DEU1118	DEU1128	DEU1129	DEU1132
DEU1149	DEU1167	DEU1174	DEU1177
DEU1178	DEU1187	DEU1209	DNK1238
DNK1248	DNK1292	DNK1300	DNK1314
DNK1316	ESP1492	FIN1580	FIN1584
FRA1629	FRA1681	FRA1683	FRA1709
FRA1820	FRA1850	FRA1917	FRA1934
FRA1937	FRA1946	FRA1992	FRA2023
FRA2070	FRA2097	FRA2116	FRA2168
GBR2175	GBR2201	GBR2212	GBR2218
GBR2226	GBR2228	GBR2238	GBR2240
GBR2303	GBR2324	GBR2339	GBR2351
GBR2371	GBR2382	GBR2390	GBR2419
GBR2423	GBR2436	GBR2437	GBR2467
GBR2481	GBR2498	GBR2500	GBR2501
GBR2508	GBR2514	GBR2535	GBR2552
GBR2553	IRL2691	IRL2708	IRL2726
IRL2733	ITA2744	ITA2747	ITA2756
ITA2758	ITA2766	ITA2767	ITA2784
ITA2785	ITA2798	ITA2860	ITA2894
ITA2902	LUX2973	LUX2983	LUX2997
NLD3067	NLD3069	NLD3078	NLD3096
NLD3120	NLD3137	NLD3198	NLD3199
NLD3317	NLD3356	NLD3364	NOR3372
NOR3381	NOR3390	NOR3465	NOR3467
POL3519	SWE3650	SWE3656	SWE3830
SWE3876			

(continued from OCEANIA section)

NLD3101	NLD3120	NLD3137	NLD3181
NLD3198	NLD3250	NLD3253	NLD3257
NLD3305	NLD3318	NLD3356	NLD3361
NLD3364	NOR3410	NOR3465	POL3508
POL3519	SWE3650	SWE3656	SWE3666
SWE3674	SWE3693	SWE3695	SWE3730
SWE3744	SWE3749	SWE3760	SWE3763
SWE3771	SWE3795	SWE3796	SWE3830
SWE3864	SWE3865	SWE3876	

SOUTHERN AFRICA - AFRIQUE AUSTRALE

AUT0022	AUT0052	AUT0058	AUT0063
AUT0067	AUT0091	BEL0097	BEL0123
BEL0124	BEL0129	BEL0144	BEL0148
BEL0186	BEL0203	BEL0221	BEL0241
BEL0260	BEL0269	BEL0289	BEL0327
BEL0351	BEL0353	BEL0358	BEL0361
BEL0397	CHE0434	CHE0498	CHE0506
CHE0559	CHE0584	CHE0586	CHE0626
CHE0682	CHE0689	CHE0693	CHE0712
CHE0727	CHE0730	CHE0755	CHE0793
CHE0814	CHE0819	DEU0919	DEU0931
DEU0972	DEU0989	DEU0995	DEU1006
DEU1015	DEU1031	DEU1038	DEU1047
DEU1055	DEU1065	DEU1082	DEU1106
DEU1128	DEU1129	DEU1131	DEU1174
DEU1187	DEU1200	DEU1202	DEU1209
DEU1211	DNK1229	DNK1238	DNK1288
DNK1292	DNK1300	DNK1312	DNK1314
DNK1339	DNK1388	ESP1420	ESP1450
ESP1454	ESP1486	FIN1531	FIN1546
FIN1549	FIN1554	FIN1557	FIN1603
FRA1658	FRA1659	FRA1672	FRA1677
FRA1681	FRA1709	FRA1769	FRA1820
FRA1827	FRA1830	FRA1849	FRA1865
FRA1879	FRA1903	FRA1917	FRA1924
FRA1946	FRA1947	FRA1948	FRA1956
FRA1988	FRA2023	FRA2070	FRA2103
FRA2116	FRA2117	FRA2130	FRA2168
GBR2173	GBR2185	GBR2187	GBR2198
GBR2201	GBR2212	GBR2218	GBR2226
GBR2228	GBR2238	GBR2244	GBR2259
GBR2266	GBR2277	GBR2292	GBR2318
GBR2324	GBR2339	GBR2348	GBR2371

See: How to Use the Directory, page 11.

GBR2382 GBR2390 GBR2392 GBR2413
GBR2419 GBR2436 GBR2437 GBR2460
GBR2467 GBR2478 GBR2481 GBR2492
GBR2500 GBR2501 GBR2510 GBR2514
GBR2530 GBR2535 GBR2536 GBR2537
GBR2553 GBR2558 GBR2561 GRC2571
IRL2702 IRL2726 IRL2732 ITA2762
ITA2767 ITA2784 ITA2791 ITA2798
ITA2803 ITA2806 ITA2813 ITA2822
ITA2838 ITA2860 ITA2881 ITA2885
ITA2900 LUX2946 LUX2995 NLD3045
NLD3047 NLD3067 NLD3068 NLD3078
NLD3091 NLD3096 NLD3101 NLD3137
NLD3173 NLD3198 NLD3257 NLD3336
NLD3356 NLD3361 NLD3364 NOR3390
NOR3425 NOR3467 POL3519 PRT3564
PRT3590 PRT3594 PRT3605 SWE3648
SWE3650 SWE3656 SWE3676 SWE3688
SWE3749 SWE3776 SWE3826 SWE3830
SWE3859 SWE3864

WEST AFRICA - AFRIQUE DE L'OUEST

AUT0003 AUT0026 AUT0028 AUT0041
AUT0086 AUT0091 BEL0097 BEL0123
BEL0124 BEL0129 BEL0133 BEL0144
BEL0148 BEL0153 BEL0186 BEL0203
BEL0221 BEL0261 BEL0269 BEL0270
BEL0289 BEL0327 BEL0341 BEL0342
BEL0351 BEL0353 BEL0356 BEL0358
BEL0359 BEL0361 BEL0367 BEL0371
BEL0381 BEL0390 BEL0397 CHE0434
CHE0435 CHE0439 CHE0444 CHE0479
CHE0491 CHE0498 CHE0540 CHE0558
CHE0559 CHE0565 CHE0568 CHE0604
CHE0626 CHE0637 CHE0638 CHE0643
CHE0669 CHE0682 CHE0689 CHE0707
CHE0712 CHE0727 CHE0814 CHE0817
CHE0819 DEU0819 DEU0940 DEU0968
DEU0972 DEU0983 DEU0989 DEU0995
DEU1006 DEU1047 DEU1055 DEU1069
DEU1106 DEU1114 DEU1118 DEU1128
DEU1131 DEU1174 DEU1178 DEU1187
DEU1200 DEU1209 DNK1215 DNK1227
DNK1300 DNK1306 DNK1307 DNK1314
DNK1369 ESP1468 ESP1486 ESP1492
ESP1517 FRA1612 FRA1621 FRA1629
FRA1636 FRA1644 FRA1649 FRA1658
FRA1664 FRA1677 FRA1681 FRA1690
FRA1699 FRA1700 FRA1709 FRA1727
FRA1739 FRA1746 FRA1760 FRA1762
FRA1765 FRA1778 FRA1785 FRA1787
FRA1789 FRA1799 FRA1820 FRA1827
FRA1830 FRA1833 FRA1836 FRA1846
FRA1848 FRA1861 FRA1865 FRA1879
FRA1880 FRA1886 FRA1903 FRA1907
FRA1913 FRA1917 FRA1924 FRA1934
FRA1946 FRA1947 FRA1956 FRA1967
FRA1984 FRA1988 FRA1991 FRA1992
FRA2005 FRA2009 FRA2012 FRA2021
FRA2043 FRA2057 FRA2062 FRA2070
FRA2086 FRA2092 FRA2103 FRA2106
FRA2116 FRA2117 FRA2131 FRA2138
FRA2147 FRA2150 FRA2161 FRA2168
GBR2173 GBR2175 GBR2185 GBR2187
GBR2198 GBR2202 GBR2218 GBR2226
GBR2228 GBR2238 GBR2244 GBR2259
GBR3203 GBR2324 GBR2351 GBR2371
GBR2382 GBR2383 GBR2390 GBR2413
GBR2419 GBR2436 GBR2437 GBR2460
GBR2481 GBR2483 GBR2501 GBR2510
GBR2515 GBR2518 GBR2525 GBR2530
GBR2533 GBR2535 GBR2550 GBR2553
GBR2558 GRC2567 GRC2586 IRL2708
IRL2724 IRL2732 ITA2744 ITA2756
ITA2762 ITA2773 ITA2784 ITA2786
ITA2791 ITA2801 ITA2826 ITA2827
ITA2828 ITA2829 ITA2838 ITA2852
ITA2860 ITA2873 ITA2885 LUX2937
LUX2946 LUX2959 LUX2973 LUX2976
LUX2978 LUX2997 LUX3006 NLD3045
NLD3067 NLD3074 NLD3078 NLD3079
NLD3096 NLD3101 NLD3137 NLD3147
NLD3173 NLD3198 NLD3231 NLD3235
NLD3255 NLD3257 NLD3269 NLD3281
NLD3292 NLD3301 NLD3318 NLD3345
NLD3356 NLD3361 NLD3364 NOR3465

POL3519 PRT3564 SWE3656 SWE3674
SWE3749 SWE3830 SWE3857

URBAN DEVELOPMENT, HABITAT - DEVELOPPEMENT URBAIN, HABITAT

CARIBBEAN - CARAIBES

BEL0124 BEL0186 BEL0198 BEL0218
BEL0254 BEL0327 BEL0335 BEL0336
BEL0351 BEL0353 BEL0359 BEL0361
CHE0434 CHE0501 CHE0559 CHE0564
CHE0568 CHE0570 CHE0586 CHE0614
CHE0629 CHE0655 CHE0682 CHE0689
CHE0712 CHE0730 CHE0798 CHE0817
CHE0819 DEU0965 DEU0972 DEU0983
DEU0989 DEU1047 DNK1314 ESP1442
ESP1455 ESP1486 ESP1492 ESP1517
ESP1524 ESP1525 FRA1610 FRA1614
FRA1676 FRA1709 FRA1744 FRA1796
FRA1827 FRA1860 FRA1865 FRA1917
FRA1946 FRA1964 FRA1967 FRA2023
FRA2034 FRA2086 FRA2103 FRA2116
FRA2159 GBR2175 GBR2218 GBR2229
GBR2238 GBR2242 GBR2266 GBR2273
GBR2324 GBR2325 GBR2371 GBR2434
GBR2436 GBR2464 GBR2500 GBR2501
GBR2535 GBR2553 IRL2687 ITA2784
ITA2852 ITA2860 NLD3067 NLD3072
NLD3138 NLD3154 NLD3160 NLD3361
POL3508 POL3519

CENTRAL AFRICA - AFRIQUE CENTRALE

AUT0024 AUT0045 BEL0124 BEL0148
BEL0155 BEL0158 BEL0186 BEL0198
BEL0201 BEL0218 BEL0234 BEL0254
BEL0306 BEL0327 BEL0351 BEL0353
BEL0361 BEL0378 CHE0434 CHE0541
CHE0562 CHE0565 CHE0568 CHE0628
CHE0655 CHE0689 CHE0712 CHE0727
CHE0730 CHE0819 DEU0968 DEU0972
DEU0989 DEU0995 DEU1047 DEU1114
DEU1131 DNK1227 DNK1314 DNK1392
ESP1435 ESP1486 ESP1492 ESP1517
FRA1610 FRA1709 FRA1715 FRA1727
FRA1731 FRA1744 FRA1756 FRA1769
FRA1796 FRA1815 FRA1827 FRA1843
FRA1904 FRA1917 FRA1946 FRA1956
FRA1978 FRA1984 FRA1988 FRA2011
FRA2034 FRA2086 FRA2103 FRA2107
FRA2116 FRA2147 FRA2159 GBR2173
GBR2174 GBR2185 GBR2218 GBR2371
GBR2434 GBR2460 GBR2500 GBR2553
IRL2732 ITA2744 ITA2770 ITA2777
ITA2784 ITA2826 ITA2860 ITA2886
ITA2890 ITA2907 ITA2920 NLD3045
NLD3067 NLD3072 NLD3078 NLD3138
NLD3154 NLD3160 NLD3338 NLD3361
POL3519 PRT3594 PRT3602 PRT3603
SWE3828

CENTRAL ASIA AND SOUTH ASIA - ASIE CENTRALE ET ASIE DU SUD

AUT0022 AUT0024 AUT0026 AUT0045
AUT0091 BEL0097 BEL0124 BEL0144
BEL0186 BEL0201 BEL0207 BEL0254
BEL0315 BEL0327 BEL0340 BEL0359
BEL0361 CHE0406 CHE0412 CHE0417
CHE0434 CHE0472 CHE0491 CHE0529
CHE0559 CHE0565 CHE0568 CHE0586
CHE0619 CHE0628 CHE0655 CHE0682
CHE0689 CHE0712 CHE0730 CHE0785
CHE0798 CHE0819 DEU0918 DEU0971
DEU0972 DEU0983 DEU0989 DEU0990
DEU0991 DEU0993 DEU0995 DEU1047
DEU1066 DEU1128 DEU1131 DEU1132
DEU1187 DNK1216 DNK1248 DNK1260
DNK1314 DNK1339 DNK1486 ESP1492
ESP1517 FIN1549 FIN1591 FRA1610
FRA1642 FRA1661 FRA1709 FRA1744
FRA1887 FRA1917 FRA1921 FRA1939
FRA2023 FRA2034 FRA2044 FRA2053
FRA2057 FRA2116 FRA2131 FRA2159
GBR2173 GBR2174 GBR2176 GBR2197
GBR2201 GBR2218 GBR2226 GBR2238
GBR2242 GBR2260 GBR2264 GBR2266
GBR2273 GBR2324 GBR2325 GBR2371
GBR2375 GBR2392 GBR2434 GBR2436

GBR2467 GBR2475 GBR2500 GBR2501
GBR2535 GBR2552 GBR2553 ISL2736
ITA2784 ITA2860 ITA2873 LIE2925
LUX2956 LUX2973 LUX2982 NLD3056
NLD3062 NLD3067 NLD3071 NLD3072
NLD3078 NLD3101 NLD3138 NLD3147
NLD3154 NLD3160 NLD3165 NLD3231
NLD3242 NLD3260 NLD3297 NLD3317
NLD3338 NLD3361 NOR3384 NOR3412
NOR3465 POL3519 SWE3679 SWE3749
SWE3819 SWE3828 SWE3834 SWE3854

EAST AFRICA - AFRIQUE DE L'EST

AUT0024 AUT0045 AUT0085 BEL0124
BEL0144 BEL0148 BEL0186 BEL0198
BEL0254 BEL0269 BEL0327 BEL0340
BEL0351 CHE0434 CHE0462 CHE0565
CHE0570 CHE0586 CHE0598 CHE0630
CHE0632 CHE0682 CHE0687 CHE0689
CHE0712 CHE0730 CHE0819 DEU0968
DEU0972 DEU0983 DEU0989 DEU0991
DEU0995 DEU1047 DEU1114 DNK1314
DNK1339 DNK1377 DNK1392 ESP1432
ESP1486 ESP1492 FIN1591 FRA1610
FRA1617 FRA1731 FRA1744 FRA1855
FRA1796 FRA1833 FRA1843 FRA1855
FRA1917 FRA1947 FRA1956 FRA1978
FRA2017 FRA2116 FRA2147 FRA2159
GBR2173 GBR2174 GBR2179 GBR2180
GBR2185 GBR2198 GBR2214 GBR2218
GBR2226 GBR2228 GBR2238 GBR2259
GBR2273 GBR2282 GBR2293 GBR2324
GBR2325 GBR2339 GBR2371 GBR2390
GBR2434 GBR2436 GBR2460 GBR2467
GBR2500 GBR2501 GBR2535 GBR2552
GBR2553 IRL2688 IRL2691 IRL2729
IRL2733 IRL2733 ISL2740 ITA2744
ITA2762 ITA2784 ITA2820 ITA2829
ITA2860 ITA2910 NLD3045 NLD3067
NLD3071 NLD3072 NLD3091 NLD3101
NLD3138 NLD3154 NLD3160 NLD3165
NLD3199 NLD3235 NLD3297 NLD3317
NLD3323 NLD3338 NLD3361 NOR3403
NOR3465 POL3519 PRT3550 SWE3679
SWE3749 SWE3771 SWE3828 SWE3853
SWE3854 SWE3857 SWE3864

EAST ASIA - ASIE DE L'EST

AUT0024 BEL0124 BEL0186 BEL0198
BEL0254 BEL0361 CHE0434 CHE0565
CHE0655 CHE0689 CHE0712 CHE0730
CHE0795 CHE0819 DEU0972 DEU0989
DEU0995 DEU1047 DEU1114 DNK1251
DNK1314 ESP1432 ESP1492 FRA1610
FRA1709 FRA1744 FRA1833 FRA1917
FRA1921 FRA1992 FRA2116 FRA2159
GBR2218 GBR2260 GBR2264 GBR2266
GBR2371 GBR2434 GBR2500 GBR2501
GBR2535 GBR2553 ITA2784 ITA2860
NLD3067 NLD3071 NLD3072 NLD3078
NLD3138 NLD3154 NLD3160 NLD3338
NLD3361 NOR3465 SWE3712 SWE3823
SWE3828

MEXICO AND CENTRAL AMERICA - MEXIQUE ET AMERIQUE CENTRALE

AUT0024 AUT0045 AUT0058 AUT0091
BEL0124 BEL0164 BEL0186 BEL0198
BEL0201 BEL0254 BEL0269 BEL0323
BEL0327 BEL0335 BEL0336 BEL0340
BEL0353 BEL0361 BEL0378 CHE0434
CHE0517 CHE0565 CHE0568 CHE0682
CHE0689 CHE0712 CHE0730 CHE0817
CHE0819 DEU0972 DEU0983 DEU0989
DEU0995 DEU1031 DEU1047 DEU1074
DEU1114 DEU1131 DEU1138 DEU1149
DEU1187 DEU1202 DNK1226 DNK1312
DNK1314 DNK1317 DNK1339 DNK1358
ESP1407 ESP1413 ESP1427 ESP1435
ESP1442 ESP1450 ESP1453 ESP1455
ESP1485 ESP1486 ESP1492 ESP1506
ESP1517 ESP1525 FRA1610 FRA1677
FRA1701 FRA1709 FRA1744 FRA1827
FRA1833 FRA1843 FRA1852 FRA1904
FRA1917 FRA1939 FRA1964 FRA1967
FRA1978 FRA1991 FRA2016 FRA2034
FRA2103 FRA2116 FRA2150 FRA2159
GBR2174 GBR2201 GBR2218 GBR2226

GBR2228 GBR2229 GBR2238 GBR2273
GBR2303 GBR2324 GBR2371 GBR2373
GBR2434 GBR2436 GBR2467 GBR2500
GBR2501 GBR2553 GBR2556 IRL2697
IRL2707 IRL2732 ITA2744 ITA2784
ITA2801 ITA2860 NLD3067 NLD3072
NLD3078 NLD3101 NLD3138 NLD3154
NLD3159 NLD3160 NLD3199 NLD3231
NLD3263 NLD3303 NLD3305 NLD3338
NLD3361 NOR3410 POL3519 SWE3676
SWE3749 SWE3770 SWE3786 SWE3795
SWE3796 SWE3864 SWE3865

MIDDLE EAST - MOYEN-ORIENT

AUT0091 BEL0097 BEL0124 BEL0133
BEL0186 BEL0198 BEL0254 BEL0306
BEL0340 BEL0361 CHE0406 CHE0434
CHE0568 CHE0655 CHE0682 CHE0689
CHE0712 CHE0730 CHE0819 DEU0972
DEU0989 DEU0991 DEU0995 DEU1047
DEU1065 DEU1150 DNK1314 ESP1435
ESP1455 FRA1610 FRA1677 FRA1709
FRA1744 FRA1827 FRA1832 FRA1843
FRA1917 FRA1948 FRA1964 FRA1967
FRA1978 FRA1991 FRA2057 FRA2103
FRA2116 FRA2159 GBR2218 GBR2238
GBR2260 GBR2273 GBR2303 GBR2371
GBR2392 GBR2434 GBR2501 GBR2537
ITA2784 ITA2814 ITA2860 LUX2956
MLT3018 NLD3067 NLD3072 NLD3138
NLD3154 NLD3160 NLD3338 NLD3361
POL3519 SWE3666 SWE3828 TUR3883

NORTH AFRICA - AFRIQUE DU NORD

AUT0045 BEL0124 BEL0148 BEL0186
BEL0198 BEL0202 BEL0254 BEL0340
BEL0361 CHE0434 CHE0568 CHE0655
CHE0682 CHE0689 CHE0712 CHE0730
DEU0972 DEU0989 DEU0990 DEU0995
DEU1047 ESP1406 ESP1435 ESP1455 ESP1486
ESP1492 ESP1505 FRA1610 FRA1701
FRA1709 FRA1731 FRA1744 FRA1796
FRA1833 FRA1846 FRA1887 FRA1917
FRA1946 FRA1956 FRA1964 FRA1991
FRA1992 FRA2034 FRA2107 FRA2116
FRA2159 GBR2185 GBR2218 GBR2238
GBR2303 GBR2371 GBR2434 GBR2501
ITA2784 ITA2810 ITA2860 LUX2956
MLT3018 NLD3047 NLD3067 NLD3072
NLD3101 NLD3138 NLD3154 NLD3160
NLD3165 NLD3173 NLD3301 NLD3317
NLD3338 POL3508 POL3519 SWE3813
SWE3828

OCEANIA - OCEANIE

AUT0024 BEL0124 BEL0186 BEL0198
BEL0269 BEL0361 CHE0434 CHE0712
CHE0730 CHE0819 DEU0972 DEU0989
DEU0992 DEU0995 DEU1047 DNK1314
FRA1610 FRA1709 FRA1744 FRA1917
FRA2116 GBR2218 GBR2371 GBR2434
GBR2501 GBR2535 GBR2553 ITA2784
ITA2860 NLD3067 NLD3072 NLD3137
NLD3154 NLD3160 NLD3361 POL3508

SOUTH AMERICA - AMERIQUE DU SUD

AUT0024 AUT0045 AUT0091 BEL0119
BEL0124 BEL0139 BEL0144 BEL0155
BEL0186 BEL0198 BEL0201 BEL0241
BEL0245 BEL0254 BEL0269 BEL0282
BEL0327 BEL0335 BEL0336 BEL0340
BEL0341 BEL0352 BEL0353 BEL0359
BEL0361 CHE0434 CHE0479 CHE0565
CHE0568 CHE0570 CHE0586 CHE0604

CHE0613 CHE0614 CHE0619 CHE0628
CHE0682 CHE0689 CHE0693 CHE0712
CHE0730 CHE0755 CHE0798 CHE0806
CHE0817 CHE0819 DEU0972 DEU0983
DEU0989 DEU0990 DEU0995 DEU1031
DEU1047 DEU1066 DEU1097 DEU1109
DEU1114 DEU1129 DEU1131 DEU1132
DEU1138 DEU1149 DEU1187 DNK1251
DNK1314 ESP1410 ESP1432 ESP1435
ESP1437 ESP1442 ESP1450 ESP1455
ESP1457 ESP1474 ESP1485 ESP1486
ESP1488 ESP1492 ESP1502 ESP1505
ESP1507 ESP1517 ESP1525 ESP1528
FRA1610 FRA1677 FRA1701 FRA1709
FRA1731 FRA1744 FRA1827 FRA1832
FRA1843 FRA1865 FRA1904 FRA1917
FRA1926 FRA1930 FRA1939 FRA1946
FRA1964 FRA1978 FRA1988 FRA2018
FRA2023 FRA2034 FRA2103 FRA2107
FRA2116 FRA2150 FRA2159 GBR2174
GBR2175 GBR2218 GBR2226 GBR2228
GBR2229 GBR2238 GBR2259 GBR2266
GBR2273 GBR2293 GBR2303 GBR2324
GBR2325 GBR2339 GBR2371 GBR2390
GBR2434 GBR2436 GBR2464 GBR2467
GBR2500 GBR2501 GBR2525 GBR2535
GBR2553 GBR2556 GRC2572
IRL2726 IRL2732 ITA2762 ITA2773
ITA2777 ITA2782 ITA2784 ITA2799
ITA2802 ITA2810 ITA2812 ITA2820
ITA2838 ITA2852 ITA2860 ITA2873
ITA2879 ITA2880 ITA2899 ITA2901
ITA2910 LUX2946 LUX2954 LUX2968
LUX2969 LUX2999 NLD3067 NLD3072
NLD3078 NLD3101 NLD3138 NLD3154
NLD3160 NLD3181 NLD3199 NLD3231
NLD3253 NLD3297 NLD3305 NLD3317
NLD3338 NLD3361 NOR3465 NOR3473
POL3519 POL3519 PRT3600 SWE3666
SWE3674 SWE3712 SWE3744 SWE3749
SWE3787 SWE3795 SWE3796 SWE3828
SWE3857 SWE3864 SWE3865

SOUTH EAST ASIA - ASIE DU SUD-EST

AUT0024 AUT0045 AUT0091 BEL0124
BEL0186 BEL0198 BEL0254 BEL0269
BEL0315 BEL0327 BEL0340 BEL0342
BEL0351 BEL0361 BEL0381 CHE0434
CHE0479 CHE0491 CHE0559 CHE0565
CHE0568 CHE0586 CHE0598 CHE0630
CHE0682 CHE0689 CHE0712 CHE0730
CHE0785 CHE0798 CHE0819 DEU0971
DEU0972 DEU0983 DEU0986 DEU0989
DEU0990 DEU0995 DEU1047 DEU1097
DEU1149 DEU1187 DNK1259
DNK1314 DNK1316 ESP1492 FRA1610
FRA1617 FRA1683 FRA1701 FRA1709
FRA1731 FRA1744 FRA1850 FRA1865
FRA1917 FRA1921 FRA1946 FRA1964
FRA1967 FRA1978 FRA1979 FRA2023
FRA2034 FRA2035 FRA2097 FRA2116
FRA2134 FRA2140 FRA2159 GBR2201
GBR2218 GBR2238 GBR2260 GBR2264
GBR2273 GBR2293 GBR2324 GBR2371
GBR2390 GBR2419 GBR2434 GBR2436
GBR2464 GBR2467 GBR2498 GBR2500
GBR2501 GBR2535 GBR2537 GBR2553
IRL2687 IRL2691 ITA2784 ITA2860
NLD3067 NLD3071 NLD3072 NLD3078
NLD3083 NLD3138 NLD3154 NLD3155
NLD3160 NLD3235 NLD3253 NLD3292
NLD3297 NLD3317 NLD3338 NLD3361
NOR3437 NOR3465 NOR3467 POL3519
SWE3674 SWE3787 SWE3828 SWE3831
SWE3857

SOUTHERN AFRICA - AFRIQUE AUSTRALE

AUT0024 AUT0058 BEL0124 BEL0148
BEL0186 BEL0189 BEL0198 BEL0203
BEL0254 BEL0297 BEL0327 BEL0340
BEL0351 BEL0361 CHE0434 CHE0506
CHE0570 CHE0584 CHE0619 CHE0628
CHE0682 CHE0689 CHE0712 CHE0730
CHE0819 DEU0931 DEU0972 DEU0989
DEU0995 DEU1047 DEU1131 DEU1187
DNK1245 DNK1312 DNK1314 DNK1339
DNK1375 ESP1450 ESP1486 FIN1544
FRA1610 FRA1709 FRA1715 FRA1727
FRA1738 FRA1744 FRA1769 FRA1819
FRA1827 FRA1833 FRA1843 FRA1865
FRA1887 FRA1917 FRA1946 FRA1947
FRA1956 FRA1980 FRA2014 FRA2023
FRA2103 FRA2107 FRA2116 FRA2159
GBR2173 GBR2174 GBR2181 GBR2185
GBR2187 GBR2198 GBR2201 GBR2218
GBR2226 GBR2228 GBR2229 GBR2238
GBR2259 GBR2266 GBR2273 GBR2324
GBR2325 GBR2371 GBR2392 GBR2413
GBR2434 GBR2436 GBR2460 GBR2464
GBR2467 GBR2500 GBR2501 GBR2535
GBR2553 GBR2561 IRL2726 IRL2732
ITA2784 ITA2860 ITA2873 ITA2879
ITA2900 ITA2902 LUX2946 LUX2976
LUX2995 NLD3045 NLD3067 NLD3072
NLD3078 NLD3098 NLD3101 NLD3137
NLD3138 NLD3147 NLD3154 NLD3160
NLD3199 NLD3231 NLD3253 NLD3301
NLD3338 NLD3361 NOR3467 POL3508
POL3519 PRT3590 PRT3594 PRT3600
PRT3603 SWE3648 SWE3676 SWE3749
SWE3828 SWE3864

WEST AFRICA - AFRIQUE DE L'OUEST

AUT0024 AUT0045 AUT0086 BEL0124
BEL0133 BEL0148 BEL0152 BEL0186
BEL0198 BEL0201 BEL0254 BEL0327
BEL0340 BEL0353 BEL0361 BEL0390
CHE0434 CHE0439 CHE0479 CHE0498
CHE0557 CHE0565 CHE0568 CHE0604
CHE0682 CHE0689 CHE0712 CHE0730
CHE0819 CHE0823 DEU0968 DEU0972
DEU0983 DEU0989 DEU0991 DEU0995
DEU1047 DEU1106 DEU1109 DEU1114
DEU1131 DNK1215 DNK1227 DNK1314
DNK1374 ESP1430 ESP1486 ESP1488
ESP1492 ESP1517 FRA1610 FRA1614
FRA1709 FRA1715 FRA1727 FRA1731
FRA1744 FRA1746 FRA1756 FRA1778
FRA1785 FRA1787 FRA1796 FRA1799
FRA1827 FRA1833 FRA1836 FRA1843
FRA1846 FRA1865 FRA1917 FRA1926
FRA1946 FRA1947 FRA1956 FRA1967
FRA1978 FRA1988 FRA1991 FRA2005
FRA2012 FRA2034 FRA2043 FRA2044
FRA2057 FRA2086 FRA2103 FRA2107
FRA2116 FRA2131 FRA2134 FRA2147
FRA2150 FRA2159 FRA2161 FRA2162
GBR2173 GBR2174 GBR2185 GBR2198
GBR2218 GBR2273 GBR2324 GBR2351
GBR2371 GBR2413 GBR2434 GBR2436
GBR2460 GBR2501 GBR2535 GBR2553
IRL2732 ITA2744 ITA2770 ITA2784
ITA2801 ITA2829 ITA2838 ITA2852
ITA2860 ITA2873 ITA2901 LUX2946
LUX2978 LUX3006 NLD3045 NLD3067
NLD3072 NLD3074 NLD3078 NLD3138
NLD3154 NLD3160 NLD3255 NLD3269
NLD3338 NLD3361 NOR3465 POL3519
PRT3603 SWE3648 SWE3828

See: *How to Use the Directory*, page 11.

Index 2: INFORMATION AND EDUCATIONAL ACTIVITIES
by Subject and Activity

Index 2 : ACTIVITÉS D'INFORMATION ET D'ÉDUCATION
par thème et par activité

ISO Codes / Codes ISO

AUT	Austria	Autriche
BEL	Belgium	Belgique
CHE	Switzerland	Suisse
CYP	Cyprus	Chypre
CZE	Czech Republic	République tchèque
DEU	Germany	Allemagne
DNK	Denmark	Danemark
ESP	Spain	Espagne
FIN	Finland	Finlande
FRA	France	France
GBR	United Kingdom	Royaume-Uni
GRC	Greece	Grèce
HUN	Hungary	Hongrie
IRL	Ireland	Irlande
ISL	Iceland	Islande
ITA	Italy	Italie
LIE	Liechtenstein	Liechtenstein
LUX	Luxembourg	Luxembourg
MLT	Malta	Malte
NLD	Netherlands	Pays-Bas
NOR	Norway	Norvège
POL	Poland	Pologne
PRT	Portugal	Portugal
SVK	Slovac Republic	République slovaque
SWE	Sweden	Suède
TUR	Turkey	Turquie

Subjects

Thèmes

CHILDREN, YOUTH, FAMILY ------------------ ENFANTS, JEUNESSE, FAMILLE
CULTURE, TRADITION, RELIGION -------------- CULTURE, TRADITION, RELIGION
ECOLOGY, ENVIRONMENT, BIODIVERSITY -------- ECOLOGIE, ENVIRONNEMENT, BIODIVERSITE
EDUCATION, LITERACY --------------------- EDUCATION, FORMATION, ALPHABETISATION
EMERGENCY RELIEF, HUMANITARIAN ----------- SECOURS D'URGENCE, REFUGIES, AIDE HUMANITAIRE
    ASSISTANCE, ASSISTANCE TO REFUGEES
EMPLOYMENT, UNEMPLOYMENT ------------- EMPLOI, CHOMAGE
FOOD, FAMINE ------------------------- ALIMENTS, FAMINE
GENDER ISSUES, WOMEN ------------------ QUESTIONS RELATIVES AUX FEMMES
HEALTH, SANITATION, WATER --------------- SANTE, ASSAINISSEMENT, EAU
HUMAN RIGHTS, DEMOCRACY, POLITICS ------- DROITS DE L'HOMME, PAIX, CONFLITS
INTERNATIONAL ECONOMIC RELATIONS, TRADE, --- RELATIONS ECONOMIQUES INTERNATIONALES,
    DEBT, FINANCE   COMMERCE, DETTE, FINANCES
INTERNATIONAL RELATIONS, COOPERATION, ------ RELATIONS INTERNATIONALES, COOPERATION,
    DEVELOPMENT AID   AIDE AU DEVELOPPEMENT
OTHER ------------------------------- AUTRES
PEACE, ETHNIC, CONFLICTS, ARMAMENTS, ------- PAIX, CONFLITS ETHNIQUES, ARMEMENT,
    DISARMAMENT   DESARMEMENT
POPULATION, FAMILY PLANNING, DEMOGRAPHY --- POPULATION, PLANNING FAMILIAL, DEMOGRAPHIE
POVERTY, LIVING CONDITIONS -------------- PAUVRETE, CONDITIONS DE VIE
RACISM, XENOPHOBIA, ANTISEMITISM --------- RACISME, XENOPHOBIE, ANTISEMITISME
REFUGEES, MIGRANTS, ETHNIC GROUPS-------- REFUGIES, MIGRANTS, GROUPES ETHNIQUES
RURAL DEVELOPMENT, AGRICULTURE --------- DEVELOPPEMENT RURAL, AGRICULTURE
URBAN DEVELOPMENT, HABITAT ------------- DEVELOPPEMENT URBAIN, HABITAT

Activities

Activités

BROADCASTING, CULTURAL EVENTS ---------- RADIODIFFUSION, MANIFESTATIONS CULTURELLES
CONFERENCES, SEMINARS, WORKSHOPS, -------- CONFERENCES, SEMINAIRES, ATELIERS, ACTIVITES
    TRAINING   DE FORMATION
EXCHANGES, TWINNING, LINKING------------- ECHANGES, PARRAINAGE, JUMELAGE
FORMAL EDUCATION--------------------- EDUCATION FORMELLE
FUND RAISING ------------------------- COLLECTE DE FONDS
INFORMATION CAMPAIGNS, EXHIBITIONS ------- CAMPAGNE D'INFORMATION, EXPOSITIONS
INFORMATION & DOCUMENTATION SERVICES, ----- SERVICES D'INFORMATION ET DE DOCUMENTATION,
    DATA BASES   BASES DE DONNEES
LOBBYING, ADVOCACY -------------------- LOBBYING, PLAIDOYER
NETWORKING, ELECTRONIC TELECOMMUNICATIONS RESEAUX, TELECOMMUNICATIONS ELECTRONIQUES
OTHER ------------------------------- AUTRES
PUBLISHING, AUDIOVISUAL MATERIALS,--------- EDITION, DOCUMENTS AUDIOVISUELS, DOCUMENTS
    EDUCATIONAL MATERIALS   EDUCATIFS

CHILDREN, YOUTH, FAMILY - ENFANTS, JEUNESSE, FAMILLE

BROADCASTING, CULTURAL EVENTS - RADIODIFFUSION, MANIFESTATIONS CULTURELLES

AUT0021	AUT0052	AUT0086	BEL0123
BEL0129	BEL0203	BEL0226	BEL0275
BEL0327	BEL0358	CHE0434	CHE0524
CHE0534	CHE0566	CHE0568	CHE0569
CHE0598	CHE0604	CHE0624	CHE0689
CHE0819	CYP0832	CZE0859	CZE0904
DEU0918	DEU0975	DEU1004	DEU1022
DEU1053	DEU1142	DEU1203	DNK1215
DNK1283	DNK1304	DNK1307	DNK1366
DNK1405	ESP1406	ESP1430	ESP1455
ESP1486	ESP1507	ESP1510	FIN1536
FIN1560	FIN1567	FIN1582	FRA1615
FRA1621	FRA1675	FRA1704	FRA1726
FRA1768	FRA1785	FRA1787	FRA1824
FRA1871	FRA1889	FRA1937	FRA1956
FRA2002	FRA2060	FRA2062	FRA2065
FRA2117	FRA2159	GBR2194	GBR2238
GBR2325	GBR2371	GBR2378	GBR2383
GBR2416	GBR2436	GBR2464	GBR2466
GBR2501	GBR2521	GBR2545	GRC2576
HUN2631	IRL2693	IRL2717	IRL2720
ITA2747	ITA2798	ITA2801	ITA2809
ITA2820	ITA2834	ITA2838	ITA2888
ITA2890	ITA2907	ITA2923	LUX2949
LUX2961	LUX2982	MLT3012	MLT3016
MLT3023	NLD3067	NLD3135	NLD3173
NLD3222	NLD3230	NLD3253	NOR3374
NOR3460	NOR3467	POL3508	POL3543
PRT3555	SVK3611	SVK3634	SVK3640
SWE3760	SWE3771	TUR3883	

CONFERENCES, SEMINARS, WORKSHOPS, TRAINING ACTIVITIES - CONFERENCES, SEMINAIRES, ATELIERS, ACTIVITES DE FORMATION

AUT0002	AUT0010	AUT0021	AUT0024
AUT0033	AUT0052	AUT0056	AUT0076
AUT0086	AUT0089	BEL0096	BEL0123
BEL0129	BEL0133	BEL0148	BEL0156
BEL0160	BEL0168	BEL0173	BEL0177
BEL0191	BEL0199	BEL0202	BEL0203
BEL0270	BEL0275	BEL0282	BEL0287
BEL0290	BEL0297	BEL0314	BEL0318
BEL0322	BEL0335	BEL0351	BEL0353
BEL0368	BEL0379	BEL0394	BEL0399
CHE0402	CHE0406	CHE0417	CHE0434
CHE0461	CHE0462	CHE0464	CHE0521
CHE0524	CHE0549	CHE0550	CHE0562
CHE0566	CHE0568	CHE0569	CHE0604
CHE0628	CHE0642	CHE0645	CHE0649
CHE0651	CHE0655	CHE0681	CHE0689
CHE0701	CHE0711	CHE0712	CHE0730
CHE0734	CHE0747	CHE0749	CHE0750
CHE0751	CHE0756	CHE0765	CHE0772
CHE0798	CHE0814	CHE0817	CHE0819
CYP0832	CZE0897	DEU0921	DEU0942
DEU0944	DEU0947	DEU0954	DEU0975
DEU0979	DEU0983	DEU0989	DEU0990
DEU0991	DEU0992	DEU1002	DEU1004
DEU1012	DEU1019	DEU1025	DEU1031
DEU1053	DEU1066	DEU1074	DEU1090
DEU1106	DEU1114	DEU1142	DEU1149
DEU1178	DEU1180	DEU1187	DEU1193
DEU1198	DEU1203	DNK1215	DNK1227
DNK1248	DNK1272	DNK1275	DNK1283
DNK1304	DNK1305	DNK1307	DNK1312
DNK1335	DNK1358	DNK1360	DNK1361
DNK1366	DNK1391	DNK1398	ESP1406
ESP1413	ESP1430	ESP1455	ESP1472
ESP1474	ESP1488	ESP1502	ESP1505
ESP1506	ESP1507	ESP1508	ESP1510
ESP1517	FIN1544	FIN1552	FIN1553
FIN1554	FIN1555	FIN1556	FIN1557
FIN1560	FIN1567	FIN1572	FIN1577
FIN1578	FIN1582	FIN1589	FIN1592
FIN1594	FIN1602	FIN1604	FRA1619
FRA1627	FRA1642	FRA1661	FRA1672
FRA1675	FRA1679	FRA1690	FRA1704
FRA1731	FRA1785	FRA1787	FRA1800
FRA1815	FRA1832	FRA1841	FRA1846
FRA1848	FRA1849	FRA1871	FRA1885
FRA1889	FRA1907	FRA1930	FRA1935

FRA1946	FRA1956	FRA1975	FRA1990
FRA2004	FRA2009	FRA2016	FRA2019
FRA2029	FRA2032	FRA2039	FRA2040
FRA2041	FRA2042	FRA2044	FRA2047
FRA2057	FRA2060	FRA2061	FRA2062
FRA2076	FRA2086	FRA2096	FRA2117
FRA2122	FRA2123	FRA2131	FRA2140
FRA2151	FRA2159	GBR2172	GBR2174
GBR2175	GBR2183	GBR2185	GBR2186
GBR2194	GBR2195	GBR2202	GBR2217
GBR2224	GBR2238	GBR2256	GBR2264
GBR2265	GBR2266	GBR2269	GBR2277
GBR2279	GBR2292	GBR2302	GBR2303
GBR2307	GBR2312	GBR2334	GBR2348
GBR2350	GBR2355	GBR2358	GBR2359
GBR2371	GBR2378	GBR2380	GBR2383
GBR2387	GBR2390	GBR2403	GBR2408
GBR2415	GBR2416	GBR2435	GBR2436
GBR2445	GBR2452	GBR2454	GBR2460
GBR2463	GBR2464	GBR2466	GBR2471
GBR2474	GBR2481	GBR2492	GBR2500
GBR2503	GBR2510	GBR2535	GBR2545
GBR2558	GRC2572	GRC2573	GRC2576
GRC2586	GRC2595	HUN2598	HUN2609
HUN2625	HUN2643	IRL2693	IRL2696
IRL2698	IRL2717	IRL2720	IRL2730
ISL2736	ITA2747	ITA2755	ITA2762
ITA2764	ITA2771	ITA2773	ITA2777
ITA2782	ITA2798	ITA2801	ITA2802
ITA2803	ITA2805	ITA2809	ITA2810
ITA2813	ITA2814	ITA2820	ITA2826
ITA2829	ITA2834	ITA2835	ITA2838
ITA2848	ITA2857	ITA2873	ITA2880
ITA2882	ITA2890	ITA2896	ITA2898
ITA2899	ITA2900	ITA2905	ITA2907
ITA2908	ITA2913	ITA2916	ITA2922
ITA2923	LUX2955	LUX2958	LUX2961
LUX2967	LUX2985	LUX2993	MLT3016
MLT3017	MLT3023	MLT3036	NLD3067
NLD3104	NLD3139	NLD3141	NLD3153
NLD3163	NLD3174	NLD3187	NLD3198
NLD3211	NLD3222	NLD3230	NLD3232
NLD3269	NLD3277	NLD3301	NLD3305
NLD3325	NLD3334	NOR3371	NOR3374
NOR3379	NOR3386	NOR3400	NOR3402
NOR3403	NOR3429	NOR3435	NOR3440
NOR3460	NOR3467	POL3480	POL3508
POL3519	POL3543	POL3544	PRT3584
PRT3594	PRT3596	PRT3600	SVK3611
SVK3612	SVK3640	SWE3646	SWE3679
SWE3695	SWE3707	SWE3712	SWE3730
SWE3731	SWE3749	SWE3771	SWE3775
SWE3776	SWE3787	SWE3799	SWE3807
SWE3816	SWE3821	SWE3826	SWE3853
SWE3854	SWE3865	SWE3879	TUR3883

EXCHANGES, TWINNING, LINKING - ECHANGES, PARRAINAGE, JUMELAGE

AUT0010	AUT0066	AUT0086	BEL0104
BEL0105	BEL0120	BEL0123	BEL0129
BEL0177	BEL0191	BEL0198	BEL0201
BEL0203	BEL0224	BEL0275	BEL0303
BEL0322	BEL0327	BEL0335	BEL0355
BEL0358	BEL0390	BEL0399	CHE0434
CHE0443	CHE0444	CHE0448	CHE0524
CHE0557	CHE0562	CHE0564	CHE0566
CHE0595	CHE0600	CHE0604	CHE0640
CHE0643	CHE0645	CHE0649	CHE0661
CHE0674	CHE0683	CHE0689	CHE0712
CHE0730	CHE0785	CHE0798	CHE0819
CZE0839	DEU0942	DEU0975	DEU0983
DEU0990	DEU1004	DEU1065	DEU1066
DEU1074	DEU1149	DEU1175	DEU1178
DEU1193	DNK1215	DNK1259	DNK1283
DNK1304	DNK1339	DNK1391	ESP1406
ESP1517	FIN1555	FIN1556	FIN1567
FIN1572	FIN1582	FIN1602	FRA1638
FRA1642	FRA1658	FRA1661	FRA1704
FRA1715	FRA1746	FRA1785	FRA1787
FRA1787	FRA1824	FRA1846	FRA1850
FRA1871	FRA1876	FRA1885	FRA1889
FRA1907	FRA1913	FRA1928	FRA1929
FRA1937	FRA1938	FRA1942	FRA1946
FRA1956	FRA1979	FRA2009	FRA2016
FRA2032	FRA2039	FRA2044	FRA2057
FRA2060	FRA2062	FRA2065	FRA2081
FRA2117	FRA2119	FRA2131	FRA2140
FRA2145	FRA2159	GBR2186	GBR2224
GBR2231	GBR2266	GBR2274	GBR2307

GBR2334	GBR2355	GBR2359	GBR2371
GBR2379	GBR2383	GBR2390	GBR2396
GBR2416	GBR2445	GBR2481	GBR2489
GBR2536	GRC2572	HUN2640	HUN2643
IRL2693	IRL2696	IRL2698	IRL2717
IRL2720	IRL2728	IRL2730	IRL2733
ISL2739	ITA2765	ITA2766	ITA2770
ITA2782	ITA2798	ITA2801	ITA2809
ITA2834	ITA2838	ITA2888	ITA2905
ITA2907	ITA2911	ITA2922	LUX2949
LUX2976	MLT3012	MLT3016	NLD3067
NLD3127	NLD3141	NLD3159	NLD3173
NLD3187	NLD3198	NLD3215	NLD3245
NLD3325	NLD3334	NOR3374	NOR3387
NOR3400	NOR3429	NOR3467	POL3480
POL3519	POL3543	POL3544	PRT3602
SVK3611	SVK3612	SVK3626	SWE3648
SWE3785	SWE3798	SWE3865	SWE3879
TUR3883			

FORMAL EDUCATION - EDUCATION FORMELLE

AUT0021	AUT0076	AUT0086	AUT0089
BEL0123	BEL0129	BEL0177	BEL0202
BEL0224	BEL0323	BEL0351	BEL0353
BEL0359	BEL0368	BEL0390	CHE0432
CHE0434	CHE0521	CHE0549	CHE0562
CHE0566	CHE0570	CHE0600	CHE0628
CHE0640	CHE0645	CHE0649	CHE0655
CHE0660	CHE0681	CHE0687	CHE0689
CHE0730	CHE0739	CHE0747	CHE0756
CHE0759	CHE0772	CHE0805	CHE0814
CHE0819	CZE0839	CZE0859	CZE0904
DEU0954	DEU0975	DEU0983	DEU1001
DEU1132	DEU1149	DEU1178	DNK1214
DNK1218	DNK1222	DNK1227	DNK1262
DNK1272	DNK1275	DNK1283	DNK1339
DNK1360	DNK1405	ESP1406	ESP1427
ESP1455	ESP1468	ESP1479	ESP1486
ESP1502	ESP1508	ESP1510	FIN1555
FIN1560	FIN1585	FRA1607	FRA1627
FRA1661	FRA1664	FRA1672	FRA1675
FRA1704	FRA1738	FRA1739	FRA1785
FRA1787	FRA1848	FRA1849	FRA1889
FRA1935	FRA1937	FRA1946	FRA1956
FRA2016	FRA2019	FRA2032	FRA2039
FRA2044	FRA2062	FRA2123	FRA2131
FRA2140	FRA2150	FRA2151	FRA2159
GBR2175	GBR2178	GBR2181	GBR2185
GBR2194	GBR2231	GBR2238	GBR2265
GBR2266	GBR2269	GBR2334	GBR2348
GBR2349	GBR2350	GBR2359	GBR2371
GBR2378	GBR2379	GBR2380	GBR2383
GBR2390	GBR2396	GBR2408	GBR2415
GBR2432	GBR2436	GBR2439	GBR2445
GBR2452	GBR2463	GBR2464	GBR2466
GBR2467	GBR2468	GBR2474	GBR2481
GBR2522	GBR2553	HUN2643	IRL2688
IRL2691	IRL2693	IRL2697	IRL2698
IRL2716	IRL2720	ISL2740	ITA2762
ITA2770	ITA2771	ITA2777	ITA2782
ITA2798	ITA2801	ITA2803	ITA2810
ITA2813	ITA2822	ITA2826	ITA2857
ITA2889	ITA2890	ITA2896	ITA2898
ITA2907	ITA2916	LUX2967	LUX2995
LUX2997	MLT3012	MLT3016	MLT3017
MLT3023	MLT3036	NLD3067	NLD3087
NLD3104	NLD3141	NLD3147	NLD3159
NLD3163	NLD3189	NLD3190	NLD3212
NLD3215	NLD3232	NLD3250	NLD3291
NLD3325	NOR3386	NOR3394	NOR3437
NOR3465	NOR3467	POL3508	PRT3552
PRT3555	PRT3594	PRT3596	PRT3600
PRT3605	SVK3611	SVK3612	SVK3634
SWE3661	SWE3679	SWE3712	SWE3737
SWE3753	SWE3771	SWE3823	SWE3834
SWE3879			

FUND RAISING - COLLECTE DE FONDS

AUT0003	AUT0021	AUT0022	AUT0024
AUT0026	AUT0036	AUT0051	AUT0072
AUT0076	AUT0085	AUT0086	AUT0089
AUT0091	BEL0096	BEL0104	BEL0105
BEL0110	BEL0120	BEL0132	BEL0148
BEL0155	BEL0168	BEL0169	BEL0173
BEL0191	BEL0198	BEL0201	BEL0203
BEL0224	BEL0245	BEL0270	BEL0282
BEL0297	BEL0314	BEL0318	BEL0323

Voir : *Comment utiliser le répertoire,* page 11.

BEL0327	BEL0328	BEL0335	BEL0341
BEL0351	BEL0353	BEL0355	BEL0358
BEL0359	BEL0368	BEL0381	BEL0390
CHE0409	CHE0417	CHE0434	CHE0438
CHE0443	CHE0444	CHE0448	CHE0462
CHE0475	CHE0485	CHE0486	CHE0506
CHE0515	CHE0521	CHE0524	CHE0558
CHE0562	CHE0564	CHE0566	CHE0569
CHE0570	CHE0586	CHE0598	CHE0600
CHE0604	CHE0630	CHE0643	CHE0687
CHE0689	CHE0691	CHE0701	CHE0707
CHE0730	CHE0734	CHE0739	CHE0742
CHE0747	CHE0749	CHE0750	CHE0754
CHE0756	CHE0764	CHE0785	CHE0788
CHE0789	CHE0796	CHE0798	CHE0800
CHE0806	CHE0814	CHE0819	CHE0823
CYP0832	CZE0839	DEU0922	DEU0942
DEU0954	DEU0957	DEU0968	DEU0975
DEU0978	DEU0983	DEU0989	DEU0991
DEU0993	DEU1001	DEU1002	DEU1004
DEU1006	DEU1022	DEU1066	DEU1078
DEU1086	DEU1110	DEU1114	DEU1115
DEU1128	DEU1132	DEU1138	DEU1149
DEU1176	DEU1178	DEU1187	DEU1193
DNK1216	DNK1227	DNK1222	DNK1227
DNK1245	DNK1262	DNK1266	DNK1283
DNK1304	DNK1305	DNK1360	DNK1366
DNK1392	DNK1405	ESP1413	
ESP1442	ESP1455	ESP1486	ESP1491
ESP1505	ESP1506	ESP1507	ESP1508
ESP1510	ESP1517	FIN1544	FIN1549
FIN1554	FIN1555	FIN1567	FIN1572
FIN1575	FIN1583	FIN1585	FIN1591
FIN1599	FRA1611	FRA1644	FRA1661
FRA1664	FRA1672	FRA1690	FRA1691
FRA1704	FRA1726	FRA1737	FRA1738
FRA1739	FRA1741	FRA1785	FRA1786
FRA1787	FRA1789	FRA1824	FRA1843
FRA1849	FRA1850	FRA1855	FRA1866
FRA1871	FRA1889	FRA1891	FRA1913
FRA1914	FRA1928	FRA1929	FRA1930
FRA1937	FRA1938	FRA1939	FRA1946
FRA1966	FRA1978	FRA1990	FRA1991
FRA2016	FRA2037	FRA2041	FRA2047
FRA2060	FRA2080	FRA2081	FRA2086
FRA2091	FRA2116	FRA2117	FRA2119
FRA2131	FRA2137	FRA2140	FRA2145
FRA2149	FRA2152	FRA2159	GBR2172
GBR2174	GBR2175	GBR2180	GBR2183
GBR2186	GBR2197	GBR2201	GBR2224
GBR2228	GBR2238	GBR2240	GBR2242
GBR2247	GBR2265	GBR2274	GBR2277
GBR2289	GBR2292	GBR2302	GBR2310
GBR2318	GBR2319	GBR2321	GBR2334
GBR2348	GBR2349	GBR2350	GBR2358
GBR2359	GBR2371	GBR2375	GBR2378
GBR2383	GBR2385	GBR2390	GBR2396
GBR2436	GBR2439	GBR2445	GBR2464
GBR2466	GBR2474	GBR2481	GBR2489
GBR2492	GBR2500	GBR2508	GBR2509
GBR2521	GBR2522	GBR2524	GBR2525
GBR2526	GBR2532	GBR2535	GBR2552
GBR2558	GRC2572	GRC2576	GRC2586
HUN2609	HUN2627	HUN2643	IRL2691
IRL2697	IRL2730	IRL2732	IRL2733
ISL2740	ITA2747	ITA2755	ITA2756
ITA2762	ITA2766	ITA2770	ITA2773
ITA2777	ITA2782	ITA2810	ITA2813
ITA2814	ITA2820	ITA2822	ITA2826
ITA2829	ITA2832	ITA2834	ITA2837
ITA2838	ITA2848	ITA2852	ITA2857
ITA2858	ITA2868	ITA2873	ITA2879
ITA2882	ITA2885	ITA2888	ITA2888
ITA2889	ITA2890	ITA2894	ITA2899
ITA2900	ITA2907	ITA2912	ITA2913
ITA2921	ITA2923	LUX2941	LUX2955
LUX2958	LUX2959	LUX2961	LUX2967
LUX2969	LUX2980	LUX2982	LUX2991
LUX2992	LUX2993	MLT3036	NLD3051
NLD3067	NLD3104	NLD3135	NLD3146
NLD3149	NLD3159	NLD3163	NLD3198
NLD3222	NLD3232	NLD3232	NLD3237
NLD3244	NLD3245	NLD3253	NLD3256
NLD3260	NLD3262	NLD3265	NLD3269
NLD3288	NLD3291	NLD3295	NLD3297
NLD3300	NLD3301	NLD3302	NLD3323
NLD3325	NLD3334	NLD3342	NLD3361
NOR3371	NOR3379	NOR3381	NOR3404
NOR3412	NOR3435	NOR3437	NOR3453

NOR3460	NOR3467	POL3543	PRT3594
PRT3599	PRT3605	SVK3608	SVK3611
SVK3626	SVK3640	SWE3646	SWE3648
SWE3661	SWE3674	SWE3679	SWE3707
SWE3712	SWE3723	SWE3730	SWE3731
SWE3737	SWE3738	SWE3749	SWE3753
SWE3763	SWE3783	SWE3787	SWE3795
SWE3796	SWE3826	SWE3853	SWE3854
SWE3855	SWE3857	TUR3896	

INFORMATION AND DOCUMENTATION SERVICES, DATA BASES - SERVICES D'INFORMATION ET DE DOCUMENTATION, BASES DE DONNEES

AUT0010	AUT0020	AUT0024	AUT0026
AUT0056	AUT0060	AUT0079	AUT0085
AUT0086	BEL0123	BEL0129	BEL0141
BEL0155	BEL0168	BEL0173	BEL0177
BEL0191	BEL0203	BEL0226	BEL0237
BEL0267	BEL0275	BEL0290	BEL0297
BEL0303	BEL0318	BEL0335	BEL0358
BEL0359	BEL0379	BEL0390	BEL0393
BEL0399	BEL0399	CHE0406	CHE0420
CHE0429	CHE0432	CHE0434	CHE0464
CHE0503	CHE0506	CHE0521	CHE0524
CHE0534	CHE0549	CHE0550	CHE0562
CHE0566	CHE0568	CHE0624	CHE0640
CHE0645	CHE0649	CHE0651	CHE0664
CHE0668	CHE0689	CHE0711	CHE0742
CHE0747	CHE0751	CHE0756	CHE0759
CHE0762	CHE0763	CHE0796	CHE0800
CHE0814	CHE0819	CZE0859	DEU0922
DEU0942	DEU0944	DEU0968	DEU0975
DEU0989	DEU0990	DEU1002	DEU1019
DEU1025	DEU1074	DEU1076	DEU1086
DEU1088	DEU1090	DEU1091	DEU1129
DEU1138	DEU1149	DEU1184	DEU1192
DEU1193	DEU1203	DNK1215	DNK1248
DNK1262	DNK1283	DNK1292	DNK1305
DNK1339	DNK1358	DNK1360	DNK1398
ESP1407	ESP1413	ESP1430	ESP1434
ESP1436	ESP1441	ESP1455	ESP1479
ESP1486	ESP1502	ESP1506	ESP1507
FIN1548	FIN1552	FIN1555	FIN1560
FIN1567	FIN1572	FIN1582	FIN1585
FIN1591	FIN1592	FIN1599	FIN1602
FIN1604	FRA1672	FRA1675	FRA1726
FRA1737	FRA1785	FRA1787	FRA1797
FRA1800	FRA1808	FRA1811	FRA1818
FRA1832	FRA1839	FRA1841	FRA1846
FRA1871	FRA1889	FRA1930	FRA1935
FRA1946	FRA1956	FRA1990	FRA1991
FRA2002	FRA2004	FRA2009	FRA2018
FRA2029	FRA2039	FRA2062	FRA2076
FRA2096	FRA2103	FRA2104	FRA2122
FRA2123	FRA2131	FRA2140	FRA2151
FRA2152	FRA2159	GBR2194	GBR2238
GBR2265	GBR2307	GBR2326	GBR2359
GBR2371	GBR2378	GBR2379	GBR2383
GBR2387	GBR2396	GBR2408	GBR2415
GBR2416	GBR2435	GBR2438	GBR2445
GBR2452	GBR2464	GBR2466	GBR2522
GBR2545	GBR2558	GRC2576	HUN2598
HUN2609	HUN2625	HUN2643	IRL2696
IRL2697	IRL2717	IRL2720	
IRL2730	ISL2736	ITA2747	ITA2755
ITA2762	ITA2773	ITA2785	ITA2786
ITA2798	ITA2801	ITA2805	ITA2809
ITA2810	ITA2813	ITA2820	ITA2822
ITA2834	ITA2852	ITA2857	ITA2860
ITA2873	ITA2882	ITA2882	ITA2889
ITA2890	ITA2896	ITA2900	ITA2907
ITA2908	ITA2913	ITA2923	LUX2937
LUX2949	LUX2961	LUX2962	LUX2979
MLT3016	MLT3023	NLD3051	NLD3058
NLD3067	NLD3077	NLD3135	NLD3139
NLD3147	NLD3167	NLD3173	NLD3179
NLD3198	NLD3211	NLD3222	NLD3232
NLD3295	NLD3301	NLD3302	NLD3303
NLD3325	NLD3334	NLD3355	NLD3361
NOR3374	NOR3379	NOR3400	NOR3402
NOR3435	NOR3467	POL3519	PRT3550
PRT3600	SVK3611	SWE3658	SWE3693
SWE3737	SWE3744	SWE3760	SWE3771
SWE3785	SWE3807	SWE3816	SWE3821
SWE3826	SWE3853	SWE3854	SWE3859
SWE3865	TUR3883	TUR3896	

INFORMATION CAMPAIGNS, EXHIBITIONS - CAMPAGNES D'INFORMATION, EXPOSITIONS

AUT0010	AUT0020	AUT0052	AUT0085
AUT0086	AUT0091	BEL0096	BEL0123
BEL0129	BEL0148	BEL0168	BEL0173
BEL0191	BEL0192	BEL0198	BEL0202
BEL0203	BEL0224	BEL0226	BEL0267
BEL0275	BEL0282	BEL0303	BEL0318
BEL0322	BEL0327	BEL0335	BEL0351
BEL0353	BEL0358	BEL0381	BEL0390
BEL0399	CHE0406	CHE0420	CHE0432
CHE0434	CHE0444	CHE0521	CHE0524
CHE0541	CHE0549	CHE0558	CHE0562
CHE0566	CHE0568	CHE0570	CHE0598
CHE0604	CHE0664	CHE0669	CHE0689
CHE0701	CHE0711	CHE0712	CHE0747
CHE0751	CHE0756	CHE0765	CHE0796
CHE0798	CHE0800	CHE0805	CHE0819
CYP0832	CZE0839	DEU0917	DEU0940
DEU0942	DEU0955	DEU0975	DEU0983
DEU1004	DEU1022	DEU1025	DEU1031
DEU1053	DEU1066	DEU1110	DEU1129
DEU1141	DEU1142	DEU1149	DEU1164
DEU1178	DEU1187	DEU1193	DEU1198
DEU1203	DNK1214	DNK1245	DNK1248
DNK1262	DNK1262	DNK1283	DNK1285
DNK1304	DNK1305	DNK1317	DNK1335
DNK1342	DNK1358	DNK1366	DNK1375
DNK1387	DNK1398	ESP1407	ESP1413
ESP1436	ESP1478	ESP1486	ESP1488
ESP1502	ESP1505	ESP1506	ESP1507
ESP1517	ESP1524	FIN1544	
FIN1549	FIN1552	FIN1553	FIN1555
FIN1556	FIN1560	FIN1567	FIN1572
FIN1575	FIN1577	FIN1582	FIN1591
FIN1592	FIN1594	FIN1599	FIN1602
FRA1607	FRA1615	FRA1619	FRA1633
FRA1642	FRA1651	FRA1675	FRA1726
FRA1737	FRA1738	FRA1739	FRA1741
FRA1785	FRA1787	FRA1797	FRA1811
FRA1843	FRA1848	FRA1849	FRA1850
FRA1876	FRA1885	FRA1889	FRA1928
FRA1929	FRA1930	FRA1938	FRA1939
FRA1942	FRA1946	FRA1956	FRA1990
FRA2002	FRA2039	FRA2060	FRA2062
FRA2076	FRA2116	FRA2151	FRA2152
FRA2159	GBR2172	GBR2175	GBR2186
GBR2194	GBR2195	GBR2228	GBR2238
GBR2259	GBR2265	GBR2269	GBR2277
GBR2289	GBR2307	GBR2312	GBR2328
GBR2350	GBR2358	GBR2359	GBR2371
GBR2378	GBR2383	GBR2387	GBR2416
GBR2445	GBR2452	GBR2464	GBR2466
GBR2474	GBR2477	GBR2503	GBR2522
GBR2535	GBR2536	GBR2545	GBR2552
GBR2553	GRC2572	HUN2643	IRL2693
IRL2697	IRL2720	IRL2730	ITA2755
ITA2766	ITA2770	ITA2777	ITA2791
ITA2798	ITA2801	ITA2803	ITA2805
ITA2810	ITA2813	ITA2822	ITA2826
ITA2834	ITA2857	ITA2858	ITA2873
ITA2888	ITA2889	ITA2890	ITA2894
ITA2896	ITA2898	ITA2900	ITA2913
LUX2949	LUX2954	LUX2961	LUX2967
LUX2985	LUX2993	LUX2995	MLT3016
MLT3017	MLT3023	NLD3051	NLD3067
NLD3098	NLD3135	NLD3146	NLD3173
NLD3187	NLD3190	NLD3198	NLD3211
NLD3222	NLD3232	NLD3269	NLD3291
NLD3303	NLD3305	NLD3323	NLD3325
NLD3334	NOR3369	NOR3371	NOR3374
NOR3379	NOR3402	NOR3418	NOR3440
NOR3467	POL3519	POL3543	PRT3594
PRT3596	PRT3605	SVK3611	SVK3612
SVK3634	SVK3640	SWE3648	SWE3661
SWE3707	SWE3712	SWE3730	SWE3737
SWE3749	SWE3753	SWE3760	SWE3763
SWE3771	SWE3796	SWE3816	SWE3826
SWE3865	TUR3883		

LOBBYING, ADVOCACY - LOBBYING, PLAIDOYER

AUT0010	AUT0021	AUT0024	AUT0033
AUT0056	AUT0076	AUT0086	AUT0089
BEL0096	BEL0119	BEL0131	BEL0160
BEL0168	BEL0177	BEL0186	BEL0191
BEL0198	BEL0203	BEL0218	BEL0224
BEL0267	BEL0275	BEL0282	BEL0318
BEL0323	BEL0327	BEL0351	BEL0353

See: *How to Use the Directory*, page 11.

BEL0399 CHE0420 CHE0434 CHE0464
CHE0503 CHE0521 CHE0524 CHE0534
CHE0549 CHE0562 CHE0566 CHE0568
CHE0570 CHE0603 CHE0604 CHE0642
CHE0643 CHE0645 CHE0687 CHE0689
CHE0711 CHE0747 CHE0751 CHE0765
CHE0814 CHE0817 CHE0819 CZE0896
CZE0904 DEU0942 DEU0954 DEU0975
DEU0983 DEU1002 DEU1004 DEU1066
DEU1074 DEU1128 DEU1141 DEU1142
DEU1149 DEU1164 DEU1187 DEU1193
DEU1203 DNK1262 DNK1283 DNK1304
DNK1335 DNK1358 DNK1366 DNK1375
DNK1405 ESP1505 FIN1552 FIN1555
FIN1560 FIN1567 FIN1572 FIN1582
FIN1594 FIN1604 FRA1633 FRA1661
FRA1785 FRA1808 FRA1818 FRA1824
FRA1841 FRA1843 FRA1850 FRA1876
FRA1889 FRA1946 FRA1956 FRA1991
FRA2002 FRA2004 FRA2032 FRA2039
FRA2047 FRA2057 FRA2060 FRA2062
FRA2110 FRA2151 FRA2159 GBR2174
GBR2186 GBR2194 GBR2195 GBR2202
GBR2217 GBR2228 GBR2238 GBR2242
GBR2256 GBR2264 GBR2269 GBR2303
GBR2307 GBR2319 GBR2328 GBR2355
GBR2359 GBR2371 GBR2378 GBR2383
GBR2390 GBR2396 GBR2439 GBR2445
GBR2464 GBR2466 GBR2481 GBR2510
GBR2522 GBR2529 GBR2545 GBR2553
GRC2586 HUN2598 HUN2625 HUN2643
IRL2691 IRL2693 ITA2755 ITA2798
ITA2801 ITA2810 ITA2820 ITA2834
ITA2873 ITA2882 ITA2898 ITA2913
LIE2927 LUX2955 LUX2957 LUX2958
LUX2997 MLT3016 MLT3017 MLT3023
NLD3067 NLD3139 NLD3147 NLD3167
NLD3198 NLD3211 NLD3230 NLD3232
NLD3301 NLD3303 NLD3305 NLD3325
NOR3379 NOR3386 NOR3402 NOR3419
NOR3467 POL3543 PRT3594 PRT3605
SVK3634 SVK3640 SWE3661 SWE3738
SWE3749 SWE3771 SWE3799 SWE3853
TUR3883 TUR3896

NETWORKING, ELECTRONIC TELECOMMUNICATIONS - RESEAUX, TELECOMMUNICATIONS ELECTRONIQUES

AUT0010 AUT0020 BEL0177 BEL0191
BEL0198 BEL0224 BEL0318 CHE0434
CHE0524 CHE0562 CHE0568 CHE0586
CHE0642 CHE0689 CHE0711 CHE0747
CHE0751 CHE0819 DEU0955 DEU0975
DEU0990 DEU1002 DEU1004 DEU1065
DEU1187 DEU1203 DNK1283 DNK1360
ESP1434 FIN1555 FIN1572 FIN1582
FIN1591 FRA1629 FRA1889 FRA2060
FRA2159 GBR2265 GBR2285 GBR2313
GBR2328 GBR2348 GBR2359 GBR2371
GBR2378 GBR2383 GBR2387 GBR2416
GBR2438 GBR2464 GBR2522 GBR2545
GRC2576 HUN2640 IRL2696 IRL2717
ITA2773 ITA2801 ITA2860 NLD3067
NLD3077 NLD3104 NLD3215 NLD3334
NOR3374 NOR3467 SVK3611 SWE3648
SWE3785 SWE3787 TUR3883

OTHER - AUTRE

CHE0434 FIN1536 FIN1555 FRA1966
FRA2111 GBR2194 GBR2240 GBR2326
GBR2358 GBR2371 GBR2387 GBR2510
NOR3369 POL3543 SWE3666

PUBLISHING, AUDIOVISUAL MATERIALS, EDUCATIONAL MATERIALS - EDITION, DOCUMENTS AUDIOVISUELS, DOCUMENTS EDUCATIFS

AUT0009 AUT0010 AUT0020 AUT0024
AUT0026 AUT0085 AUT0086 BEL0096
BEL0120 BEL0123 BEL0155 BEL0168
BEL0177 BEL0191 BEL0203 BEL0224
BEL0226 BEL0245 BEL0275 BEL0282
BEL0290 BEL0297 BEL0306 BEL0314
BEL0318 BEL0322 BEL0323 BEL0335
BEL0351 BEL0353 BEL0368 BEL0381
BEL0390 BEL0393 BEL0396 BEL0399
CHE0406 CHE0420 CHE0429 CHE0432
CHE0434 CHE0444 CHE0499 CHE0503
CHE0511 CHE0521 CHE0549 CHE0550
CHE0562 CHE0566 CHE0568 CHE0569
CHE0604 CHE0638 CHE0649 CHE0651
CHE0689 CHE0693 CHE0711 CHE0734
CHE0747 CHE0750 CHE0751 CHE0756
CHE0759 CHE0763 CHE0819 CZE0859
DEU0942 DEU0944 DEU0975 DEU0989
DEU1004 DEU1019 DEU1022 DEU1025
DEU1038 DEU1066 DEU1076 DEU1110
DEU1115 DEU1128 DEU1142 DEU1149
DEU1180 DEU1187 DEU1193 DEU1198
DEU1203 DNK1214 DNK1215 DNK1216
DNK1248 DNK1260 DNK1262 DNK1283
DNK1292 DNK1304 DNK1312 DNK1317
DNK1335 DNK1339 DNK1351 DNK1358
DNK1360 ESP1407 ESP1413 ESP1430
ESP1434 ESP1435 ESP1455 ESP1461
ESP1491 ESP1505 ESP1506 ESP1507
ESP1510 ESP1517 FIN1536 FIN1544
FIN1548 FIN1552 FIN1555 FIN1556
FIN1560 FIN1567 FIN1572 FIN1577
FIN1580 FIN1582 FIN1585 FIN1591
FIN1592 FIN1602 FRA1607 FRA1611
FRA1615 FRA1627 FRA1642 FRA1644
FRA1661 FRA1668 FRA1672 FRA1704
FRA1713 FRA1715 FRA1737 FRA1768
FRA1785 FRA1787 FRA1795 FRA1813
FRA1832 FRA1836 FRA1843 FRA1849
FRA1889 FRA1920 FRA1929 FRA1935
FRA1938 FRA1956 FRA1986 FRA1990
FRA1991 FRA2001 FRA2002 FRA2004
FRA2018 FRA2032 FRA2039 FRA2042
FRA2047 FRA2060 FRA2062 FRA2072
FRA2076 FRA2096 FRA2104 FRA2116
FRA2119 FRA2123 FRA2131 FRA2140
FRA2151 FRA2159 GBR2175 GBR2181
GBR2183 GBR2185 GBR2186 GBR2194
GBR2195 GBR2231 GBR2238 GBR2265
GBR2266 GBR2271 GBR2289 GBR2303
GBR2307 GBR2312 GBR2326 GBR2334
GBR2358 GBR2359 GBR2371 GBR2378
GBR2380 GBR2383 GBR2387 GBR2396
GBR2416 GBR2435 GBR2436 GBR2445
GBR2452 GBR2464 GBR2466 GBR2467
GBR2474 GBR2485 GBR2489 GBR2500
GBR2501 GBR2503 GBR2510 GBR2522
GBR2525 GBR2535 GBR2545 GBR2552
GBR2554 GRC2572 GRC2585 HUN2609
HUN2625 HUN2627 IRL2693 IRL2696
IRL2697 IRL2698 IRL2717 IRL2720
IRL2730 IRL2733 ISL2736 ITA2744
ITA2755 ITA2762 ITA2764 ITA2773
ITA2785 ITA2798 ITA2801 ITA2805
ITA2806 ITA2809 ITA2810 ITA2813
ITA2814 ITA2822 ITA2826 ITA2834
ITA2838 ITA2852 ITA2857 ITA2858
ITA2873 ITA2880 ITA2882 ITA2888
ITA2896 ITA2907 ITA2908 ITA2913
ITA2916 ITA2922 ITA2923 LUX2958
LUX2961 LUX2962 LUX3006 MLT3016
MLT3023 NLD3051 NLD3067 NLD3077
NLD3087 NLD3127 NLD3135 NLD3139
NLD3145 NLD3163 NLD3173 NLD3189
NLD3190 NLD3198 NLD3211 NLD3212
NLD3215 NLD3216 NLD3222 NLD3230
NLD3232 NLD3277 NLD3301 NLD3302
NLD3305 NLD3325 NLD3361 NOR3374
NOR3379 NOR3389 NOR3394 NOR3402
NOR3418 NOR3435 NOR3440 NOR3460
NOR3467 POL3508 POL3519 POL3536
POL3543 PRT3600 SVK3611 SVK3640
SWE3648 SWE3712 SWE3737 SWE3749
SWE3760 SWE3763 SWE3787 SWE3816
SWE3826 SWE3832 SWE3854 SWE3865
SWE3879 TUR3883 TUR3898

CULTURE, TRADITION, RELIGION - CULTURE, TRADITION, RELIGION

BROADCASTING, CULTURAL EVENTS - RADIODIFFUSION, MANIFESTATIONS CULTURELLES

AUT0035 AUT0052 AUT0067 AUT0090
BEL0123 BEL0129 BEL0226 BEL0303
BEL0359 BEL0361 BEL0390 CHE0434
CHE0534 CHE0560 CHE0566 CHE0568
CHE0624 CHE0667 CHE0687 CHE0689
CHE0693 CHE0720 CHE0740 CHE0756
CHE0799 CHE0819 CZE0891 CZE0905
CZE0906 DEU0918 DEU0920 DEU0931
DEU0989 DEU1031 DEU1149 DNK1215
DNK1250 DNK1256 DNK1283 DNK1339
DNK1376 ESP1436 ESP1439 ESP1475
ESP1478 ESP1486 ESP1507 ESP1510
FIN1531 FIN1545 FIN1546 FIN1549
FIN1553 FIN1559 FIN1563 FIN1577
FIN1604 FRA1615 FRA1619 FRA1621
FRA1676 FRA1696 FRA1703 FRA1704
FRA1737 FRA1768 FRA1785 FRA1787
FRA1844 FRA1850 FRA1855 FRA1862
FRA1880 FRA1889 FRA1893 FRA1956
FRA1990 FRA2002 FRA2025 FRA2062
FRA2090 FRA2092 FRA2122 FRA2159
GBR2194 GBR2229 GBR2238 GBR2251
GBR2278 GBR2345 GBR2371 GBR2378
GBR2390 GBR2406 GBR2463 GBR2498
GBR2501 GBR2545 GBR2553 GRC2571
GRC2586 HUN2598 IRL2684 IRL2686
IRL2714 IRL2720 ITA2744 ITA2762
ITA2777 ITA2798 ITA2799 ITA2809
ITA2814 ITA2820 ITA2834 ITA2886
ITA2890 ITA2895 ITA2900 ITA2907
ITA2912 ITA2923 LUX2937 LUX2954
LUX2976 MLT3023 NLD3051 NLD3067
NLD3087 NLD3098 NLD3104 NLD3135
NLD3139 NLD3173 NLD3181 NLD3189
NLD3190 NLD3199 NLD3217 NLD3222
NLD3230 NLD3269 NLD3303 NOR3402
NOR3443 POL3480 POL3508 POL3543
PRT3600 PRT3603 SVK3611 SVK3634
SWE3774 SWE3787 TUR3883

CONFERENCES, SEMINARS, WORKSHOPS, TRAINING ACTIVITIES - CONFERENCES, SEMINAIRES, ATELIERS, ACTIVITES DE FORMATION

AUT0002 AUT0010 AUT0020 AUT0024
AUT0051 AUT0052 AUT0074 AUT0090
BEL0101 BEL0123 BEL0127 BEL0129
BEL0133 BEL0148 BEL0155 BEL0156
BEL0188 BEL0197 BEL0214 BEL0221
BEL0237 BEL0270 BEL0275 BEL0287
BEL0303 BEL0333 BEL0340 BEL0359
BEL0361 BEL0379 CHE0406 CHE0417
CHE0431 CHE0434 CHE0461 CHE0467
CHE0479 CHE0496 CHE0534 CHE0537
CHE0562 CHE0566 CHE0568 CHE0596
CHE0605 CHE0613 CHE0636 CHE0639
CHE0642 CHE0654 CHE0655 CHE0667
CHE0669 CHE0682 CHE0687 CHE0689
CHE0693 CHE0718 CHE0720 CHE0734
CHE0741 CHE0750 CHE0758 CHE0762
CHE0766 CHE0771 CHE0799 CHE0814
CHE0819 CYP0831 CZE0839 CZE0865
CZE0897 CZE0905 CZE0906 DEU0918
DEU0920 DEU0921 DEU0942 DEU0944
DEU0979 DEU0983 DEU0989 DEU0990
DEU0991 DEU0992 DEU1004 DEU1019
DEU1055 DEU1064 DEU1065 DEU1066
DEU1074 DEU1090 DEU1098 DEU1100
DEU1111 DEU1114 DEU1124 DEU1141
DEU1146 DEU1149 DEU1167 DEU1178
DEU1179 DEU1180 DEU1184 DEU1193
DEU1210 DNK1215 DNK1243 DNK1248
DNK1273 DNK1305 DNK1307 DNK1324
DNK1335 DNK1339 DNK1375 DNK1376
DNK1397 DNK1398 ESP1406 ESP1436
ESP1439 ESP1478 ESP1479 ESP1502
ESP1507 ESP1508 ESP1510 ESP1517
FIN1536 FIN1543 FIN1545 FIN1546
FIN1553 FIN1557 FIN1559 FIN1563
FIN1572 FIN1577 FIN1578 FIN1583
FIN1585 FIN1592 FIN1594 FIN1604
FIN1605 FRA1615 FRA1621 FRA1627
FRA1645 FRA1675 FRA1690 FRA1696
FRA1701 FRA1704 FRA1709 FRA1813
FRA1815 FRA1838 FRA1841 FRA1844
FRA1862 FRA1889 FRA1893 FRA1897
FRA1956 FRA1975 FRA2002 FRA2004
FRA2005 FRA2013 FRA2015 FRA2018
FRA2042 FRA2044 FRA2057 FRA2061
FRA2122 FRA2123 FRA2131 FRA2151
FRA2159 FRA2161 FRA2165 GBR2185
GBR2194 GBR2214 GBR2229 GBR2238
GBR2242 GBR2247 GBR2251 GBR2265
GBR2266 GBR2269 GBR2278 GBR2279
GBR2284 GBR2290 GBR2312 GBR2320

Voir : *Comment utiliser le répertoire*, page 11.

GBR2346	GBR2355	GBR2371	GBR2378
GBR2390	GBR2391	GBR2406	GBR2408
GBR2409	GBR2415	GBR2416	GBR2423
GBR2445	GBR2455	GBR2460	GBR2463
GBR2471	GBR2483	GBR2500	GBR2503
GBR2535	GBR2536	GBR2545	GBR2546
GBR2553	GRC2586	HUN2598	HUN2609
HUN2610	HUN2637	IRL2686	IRL2688
IRL2693	IRL2695	IRL2697	IRL2714
IRL2720	IRL2726	IRL2729	IRL2730
ITA2762	ITA2780	ITA2785	ITA2786
ITA2792	ITA2798	ITA2799	ITA2804
ITA2809	ITA2810	ITA2816	ITA2820
ITA2826	ITA2827	ITA2834	ITA2837
ITA2838	ITA2852	ITA2858	ITA2868
ITA2873	ITA2883	ITA2888	ITA2889
ITA2890	ITA2895	ITA2900	ITA2905
ITA2907	ITA2908	ITA2912	ITA2913
ITA2915	ITA2923	LUX2957	LUX2958
LUX2984	LUX2995	MLT3018	MLT3023
NLD3067	NLD3079	NLD3087	NLD3101
NLD3104	NLD3139	NLD3153	NLD3159
NLD3173	NLD3174	NLD3187	NLD3196
NLD3198	NLD3204	NLD3230	NLD3232
NLD3242	NLD3301	NLD3305	NLD3357
NOR3371	NOR3386	NOR3394	NOR3402
NOR3443	NOR3453	POL3480	POL3519
POL3543	PRT3594	PRT3594	PRT3600
SVK3611	SVK3612	SVK3622	SVK3640
SWE3648	SWE3679	SWE3695	SWE3702
SWE3707	SWE3731	SWE3735	SWE3738
SWE3744	SWE3749	SWE3768	SWE3771
SWE3774	SWE3787	SWE3799	SWE3807
SWE3816	SWE3826	SWE3865	SWE3879

EXCHANGES, TWINNING, LINKING - ECHANGES, PARRAINAGE, JUMELAGE

AUT0033	AUT0090	BEL0123	BEL0129
BEL0156	BEL0198	BEL0221	BEL0303
BEL0361	BEL0390	CHE0434	CHE0448
CHE0479	CHE0560	CHE0562	CHE0566
CHE0596	CHE0640	CHE0643	CHE0674
CHE0687	CHE0689	CHE0730	CHE0749
CHE0819	CZE0839	CZE0859	DEU0920
DEU0942	DEU0983	DEU0990	DEU0991
DEU1038	DEU1055	DEU1074	DEU1111
DEU1146	DEU1149	DEU1175	DEU1178
DEU1210	DNK1215	DNK1243	DNK1250
DNK1283	DNK1307	DNK1339	DNK1342
DNK1376	ESP1409	ESP1517	FIN1543
FIN1546	FIN1605	FRA1696	FRA1704
FRA1724	FRA1746	FRA1787	FRA1850
FRA1876	FRA1889	FRA1938	FRA1956
FRA2057	FRA2062	FRA2090	FRA2159
GBR2229	GBR2266	GBR2278	GBR2284
GBR2312	GBR2334	GBR2371	GBR2379
GBR2390	GBR2391	GBR2406	GBR2415
GBR2445	GBR2536	GRC2571	HUN2598
HUN2622	HUN2637	HUN2640	IRL2686
ITA2780	ITA2799	ITA2804	ITA2809
ITA2835	ITA2890	LUX2995	NLD3067
NLD3079	NLD3098	NLD3104	NLD3139
NLD3173	NLD3198	NLD3215	NLD3217
NLD3236	NLD3245	NLD3305	NLD3346
NLD3357	NOR3402	POL3519	POL3521
POL3543	SVK3611	SVK3612	SWE3731
SWE3749	SWE3771	SWE3786	SWE3796
SWE3865	SWE3879		

FORMAL EDUCATION - EDUCATION FORMELLE

AUT0024	AUT0052	BEL0123	BEL0129
BEL0156	BEL0157	BEL0359	BEL0361
BEL0390	CHE0434	CHE0479	CHE0537
CHE0560	CHE0562	CHE0566	CHE0640
CHE0660	CHE0687	CHE0673	CHE0734
CHE0687	CHE0689	CHE0693	CHE0734
CHE0819	CZE0839	CZE0894	DEU0983
DEU1141	DEU1178	DNK1243	DNK1339
DNK1376	ESP1409	ESP1427	ESP1486
ESP1502	ESP1517	FIN1559	FRA1627
FRA1645	FRA1675	FRA1704	FRA1724
FRA1827	FRA1841	FRA1889	FRA1956
FRA1966	FRA2002	FRA2005	FRA2044
FRA2062	FRA2103	FRA2123	FRA2131
FRA2143	FRA2159	GBR2194	GBR2238
GBR2265	GBR2266	GBR2269	GBR2278
GBR2345	GBR2371	GBR2378	GBR2379
GBR2390	GBR2406	GBR2408	GBR2415

GBR2445	GBR2448	GBR2455	GBR2463
GBR2467	GBR2468	GBR2471	GBR2553
GRC2586	HUN2643	IRL2686	IRL2688
IRL2691	IRL2695	IRL2697	IRL2720
ISL2740	ITA2761	ITA2762	ITA2775
ITA2798	ITA2799	ITA2804	ITA2810
ITA2812	ITA2822	ITA2826	ITA2834
ITA2838	ITA2883	ITA2900	ITA2905
ITA2912	ITA2916	LUX2995	MLT3017
NLD3067	NLD3104	NLD3105	NLD3139
NLD3159	NLD3179	NLD3189	NLD3190
NLD3199	NLD3212	NLD3215	NLD3305
NOR3443	NOR3453	POL3508	POL3521
PRT3594	PRT3600	SVK3611	SVK3612
SWE3679	SWE3771	SWE3796	SWE3809
SWE3823	SWE3827	SWE3879	

FUND RAISING - COLLECTE DE FONDS

AUT0024	AUT0033	AUT0051	AUT0091
BEL0148	BEL0197	BEL0198	BEL0270
BEL0359	BEL0361	BEL0387	BEL0390
CHE0417	CHE0434	CHE0448	CHE0562
CHE0566	CHE0584	CHE0619	CHE0689
CHE0693	CHE0734	CHE0749	CHE0750
CHE0800	CHE0819	CHE0820	CYP0832
CZE0839	DEU0918	DEU0957	DEU0983
DEU0989	DEU0991	DEU1004	DEU1064
DEU1114	DEU1138	DEU1146	DEU1149
DEU1167	DEU1178	DNK1215	DNK1243
DNK1248	DNK1305	DNK1316	DNK1375
DNK1377	DNK1399	ESP1409	ESP1507
ESP1508	FIN1546	FIN1549	FIN1559
FIN1591	FRA1645	FRA1724	FRA1737
FRA1739	FRA1787	FRA1789	FRA1843
FRA1850	FRA1855	FRA1880	FRA1889
FRA1939	FRA1978	FRA2025	FRA2092
FRA2131	FRA2151	FRA2152	FRA2159
GBR2175	GBR2186	GBR2194	GBR2197
GBR2201	GBR2229	GBR2230	GBR2247
GBR2266	GBR2278	GBR2289	GBR2290
GBR2312	GBR2321	GBR2371	GBR2375
GBR2378	GBR2391	GBR2406	GBR2445
GBR2463	GBR2483	GBR2535	GBR2552
GRC2586	HUN2598	HUN2609	HUN2610
HUN2637	IRL2688	IRL2695	IRL2697
ISL2740	ITA2762	ITA2799	ITA2804
ITA2809	ITA2810	ITA2820	ITA2826
ITA2879	ITA2905	LUX2959	LUX2984
LUX2995	NLD3067	NLD3068	NLD3104
NLD3139	NLD3159	NLD3198	NLD3232
NLD3245	NLD3301	NOR3371	NOR3387
NOR3443	NOR3453	PRT3567	PRT3594
SVK3608	SVK3611	SVK3622	SVK3634
SVK3640	SWE3648	SWE3679	SWE3702
SWE3707	SWE3731	SWE3744	SWE3763
SWE3768	SWE3781	SWE3787	SWE3796
SWE3853			

INFORMATION AND DOCUMENTATION SERVICES, DATA BASES - SERVICES D'INFORMATION ET DE DOCUMENTATION, BASES DE DONNEES

AUT0002	AUT0010	AUT0020	AUT0026
AUT0060	AUT0074	AUT0079	AUT0085
BEL0123	BEL0127	BEL0129	BEL0141
BEL0149	BEL0156	BEL0197	BEL0206
BEL0214	BEL0226	BEL0237	BEL0267
BEL0303	BEL0335	BEL0359	BEL0361
BEL0379	BEL0387	BEL0393	BEL0396
CHE0406	CHE0434	CHE0479	CHE0496
CHE0501	CHE0534	CHE0537	CHE0562
CHE0566	CHE0584	CHE0596	CHE0605
CHE0609	CHE0624	CHE0640	CHE0654
CHE0668	CHE0673	CHE0687	CHE0689
CHE0720	CHE0734	CHE0750	CHE0762
CHE0763	CHE0766	CHE0771	CHE0799
CHE0800	CHE0819	CYP0831	CZE0839
DEU0920	DEU0942	DEU0944	DEU0968
DEU0990	DEU1002	DEU1019	DEU1064
DEU1074	DEU1076	DEU1086	DEU1090
DEU1091	DEU1103	DEU1111	DEU1114
DEU1138	DEU1146	DEU1149	DEU1179
DEU1184	DEU1192	DNK1215	DNK1248
DNK1256	DNK1292	DNK1305	DNK1306
DNK1318	DNK1339	DNK1375	DNK1376
DNK1398	ESP1407	ESP1417	ESP1430
ESP1434	ESP1436	ESP1479	ESP1486
ESP1502	ESP1507	ESP1522	ESP1525

FIN1546	FIN1548	FIN1559	FIN1585
FIN1591	FIN1592	FIN1604	FRA1615
FRA1701	FRA1703	FRA1709	FRA1737
FRA1787	FRA1797	FRA1808	FRA1811
FRA1818	FRA1827	FRA1838	FRA1839
FRA1841	FRA1849	FRA1889	FRA1908
FRA1956	FRA2002	FRA2004	FRA2005
FRA2013	FRA2018	FRA2103	FRA2104
FRA2122	FRA2131	FRA2140	FRA2151
FRA2152	FRA2159	GBR2185	GBR2194
GBR2229	GBR2238	GBR2239	GBR2265
GBR2266	GBR2278	GBR2284	GBR2371
GBR2378	GBR2379	GBR2391	GBR2406
GBR2408	GBR2415	GBR2435	GBR2438
GBR2445	GBR2455	GBR2483	GBR2545
HUN2598	HUN2609	HUN2610	HUN2637
IRL2686	IRL2695	IRL2697	IRL2698
IRL2714	IRL2720	IRL2730	ITA2744
ITA2762	ITA2773	ITA2780	ITA2785
ITA2792	ITA2798	ITA2799	ITA2801
ITA2804	ITA2809	ITA2810	ITA2814
ITA2820	ITA2834	ITA2852	ITA2857
ITA2860	ITA2861	ITA2866	ITA2873
ITA2900	ITA2905	ITA2907	ITA2908
ITA2912	ITA2913	ITA2923	LUX2937
LUX2962	MLT3018	NLD3051	NLD3058
NLD3067	NLD3077	NLD3095	NLD3098
NLD3104	NLD3105	NLD3135	NLD3139
NLD3167	NLD3173	NLD3181	NLD3184
NLD3189	NLD3198	NLD3217	NLD3232
NLD3242	NLD3301	NLD3305	NLD3346
NLD3352	NLD3355	NLD3357	NLD3361
NOR3386	NOR3402	POL3508	POL3519
PRT3600	SVK3611	SWE3648	SWE3658
SWE3744	SWE3768	SWE3774	SWE3807
SWE3816	SWE3826	SWE3834	SWE3865
TUR3883			

INFORMATION CAMPAIGNS, EXHIBITIONS - CAMPAGNES D'INFORMATION, EXPOSITIONS

AUT0002	AUT0020	AUT0052	AUT0063
BEL0101	BEL0123	BEL0129	BEL0148
BEL0156	BEL0197	BEL0198	BEL0206
BEL0226	BEL0267	BEL0303	BEL0359
BEL0361	BEL0387	BEL0390	BEL0394
CHE0431	CHE0434	CHE0461	CHE0467
CHE0479	CHE0496	CHE0501	CHE0534
CHE0537	CHE0541	CHE0560	CHE0562
CHE0566	CHE0568	CHE0584	CHE0605
CHE0654	CHE0669	CHE0687	CHE0689
CHE0693	CHE0718	CHE0720	CHE0771
CHE0799	CHE0800	CHE0807	CHE0819
CYP0831	CZE0839	CZE0891	CZE0905
CZE0906	DEU0917	DEU0920	DEU0929
DEU0931	DEU0942	DEU0955	DEU0983
DEU1019	DEU1031	DEU1038	DEU1064
DEU1086	DEU1098	DEU1142	DEU1146
DEU1149	DEU1178	DNK1215	DNK1248
DNK1260	DNK1305	DNK1307	DNK1312
DNK1317	DNK1339	DNK1375	DNK1376
DNK1398	DNK1405	ESP1436	ESP1486
ESP1502	ESP1507	ESP1508	ESP1517
FIN1531	FIN1543	FIN1546	FIN1553
FIN1559	FIN1577	FIN1583	FIN1594
FIN1599	FIN1604	FRA1615	FRA1638
FRA1676	FRA1696	FRA1703	FRA1704
FRA1709	FRA1785	FRA1797	FRA1841
FRA1844	FRA1849	FRA1850	FRA1852
FRA1862	FRA1876	FRA1889	FRA1942
FRA1956	FRA2002	FRA2005	FRA2126
FRA2131	FRA2140	FRA2152	FRA2159
GBR2194	GBR2238	GBR2239	GBR2265
GBR2269	GBR2278	GBR2279	GBR2290
GBR2312	GBR2321	GBR2371	GBR2378
GBR2406	GBR2415	GBR2445	GBR2483
GBR2498	GBR2503	GBR2535	GBR2536
GBR2545	GBR2552	GBR2553	GBR2561
GRC2571	GRC2586	IRL2686	IRL2688
IRL2695	IRL2720	ITA2761	ITA2762
ITA2780	ITA2792	ITA2799	ITA2804
ITA2806	ITA2809	ITA2810	ITA2832
ITA2834	ITA2838	ITA2858	ITA2873
ITA2886	ITA2890	ITA2895	ITA2905
ITA2912	LUX2954	LUX2984	LUX2995
MLT3025	NLD3067	NLD3079	NLD3087
NLD3135	NLD3139	NLD3173	NLD3181
NLD3184	NLD3189	NLD3196	NLD3198
NLD3217	NLD3305	NLD3320	NLD3346
NLD3357	NOR3371	NOR3387	NOR3402

See: *How to Use the Directory*, page 11.

NOR3418	NOR3443	NOR3446	POL3480
POL3519	POL3536	POL3543	PRT3594
PRT3600	SVK3611	SVK3612	SWE3648
SWE3702	SWE3707	SWE3731	SWE3735
SWE3738	SWE3744	SWE3763	SWE3768
SWE3771	SWE3774	SWE3795	SWE3796
SWE3816	SWE3865	SWE3879	TUR3883

LOBBYING, ADVOCACY - LOBBYING, PLAIDOYER

AUT0024	BEL0131	BEL0156	BEL0197
BEL0198	BEL0214	BEL0218	BEL0267
BEL0359	BEL0361	CHE0431	CHE0434
CHE0479	CHE0534	CHE0537	CHE0562
CHE0566	CHE0568	CHE0605	CHE0619
CHE0639	CHE0643	CHE0654	CHE0668
CHE0687	CHE0689	CHE0693	CHE0749
CHE0785	CHE0819	CHE0820	CZE0891
DEU0920	DEU0929	DEU0942	DEU0983
DEU0989	DEU1004	DEU1055	DEU1064
DEU1074	DEU1131	DEU1142	DEU1146
DEU1149	DEU1167	DEU1179	DNK1248
DNK1339	DNK1376	DNK1399	DNK1405
ESP1436	ESP1437	ESP1438	ESP1525
FIN1545	FIN1546	FIN1559	FIN1577
FIN1594	FIN1604	FRA1797	FRA1841
FRA1843	FRA1850	FRA1862	FRA1889
FRA1956	FRA2002	FRA2004	FRA2126
FRA2131	FRA2159	GBR2194	GBR2239
GBR2266	GBR2269	GBR2371	GBR2378
GBR2390	GBR2391	GBR2396	GBR2406
GBR2423	GBR2445	GBR2483	GBR2545
GBR2546	GBR2553	GRC2586	HUN2609
HUN2622	HUN2637	HUN2643	IRL2691
IRL2695	ITA2799	ITA2810	ITA2820
ITA2905	ITA2913	LUX2957	LUX2958
LUX2984	MLT3016	MLT3023	MLT3025
NLD3067	NLD3068	NLD3079	NLD3104
NLD3139	NLD3153	NLD3198	NLD3204
NLD3232	NLD3236	NLD3242	NLD3301
NLD3305	NOR3386	NOR3402	PRT3594
PRT3600	SVK3634	SVK3640	SWE3648
SWE3735	SWE3749	SWE3771	SWE3781
SWE3799	SWE3807	SWE3853	TUR3883

NETWORKING, ELECTRONIC TELECOMMUNICATIONS - RESEAUX, TELECOMMUNICATIONS ELECTRONIQUES

AUT0020	BEL0198	BEL0303	BEL0361
CHE0434	CHE0562	CHE0568	CHE0596
CHE0689	CHE0817	CHE0819	DEU0955
DEU0990	DEU1002	DEU1065	DEU1149
DEU1167	DEU1210	DNK1215	ESP1434
ESP1522	FIN1546	FIN1591	FIN1604
FIN1605	FRA1862	FRA1889	FRA1908
FRA2159	GBR2265	GBR2278	GBR2284
GBR2285	GBR2313	GBR2351	GBR2371
GBR2406	GBR2438	GBR2498	GBR2545
GBR2553	HUN2609	HUN2637	ITA2773
ITA2798	ITA2799	ITA2860	MLT3025
NLD3067	NLD3077	NLD3104	NLD3139
NLD3215	NLD3357	NOR3402	POL3508
SVK3611	SWE3787	TUR3883	

OTHER - AUTRE

CHE0434	FRA1966	GBR2194	GBR2240
GBR2371			

PUBLISHING, AUDIOVISUAL MATERIALS, EDUCATIONAL MATERIALS - EDITION, DOCUMENTS AUDIOVISUELS, DOCUMENTS EDUCATIFS

AUT0010	AUT0020	AUT0026	AUT0051
AUT0052	BEL0101	BEL0123	BEL0127
BEL0155	BEL0188	BEL0206	BEL0214
BEL0226	BEL0268	BEL0303	BEL0306
BEL0340	BEL0359	BEL0361	BEL0387
BEL0390	BEL0393	BEL0396	CHE0406
CHE0431	CHE0434	CHE0483	CHE0496
CHE0501	CHE0511	CHE0534	CHE0537
CHE0560	CHE0562	CHE0566	CHE0568
CHE0687	CHE0689	CHE0693	CHE0709
CHE0738	CHE0740	CHE0750	CHE0756
CHE0763	CHE0799	CHE0819	CZE0839
CZE0906	DEU0920	DEU0931	DEU0942
DEU0944	DEU0989	DEU1019	DEU1055
DEU1064	DEU1074	DEU1076	DEU1086
DEU1095	DEU1098	DEU1103	DEU1146
DEU1149	DEU1167	DEU1180	DNK1215

DNK1243	DNK1248	DNK1260	DNK1273
DNK1283	DNK1316	DNK1317	DNK1318
DNK1339	DNK1351	DNK1375	DNK1376
DNK1399	DNK1405	ESP1409	ESP1417
ESP1434	ESP1435	ESP1436	ESP1457
ESP1468	ESP1475	ESP1486	ESP1491
ESP1510	ESP1517	ESP1522	FIN1536
FIN1546	FIN1548	FIN1549	FIN1557
FIN1559	FIN1563	FIN1572	FIN1577
FIN1585	FIN1591	FIN1604	FIN1615
FRA1627	FRA1638	FRA1645	FRA1668
FRA1703	FRA1704	FRA1709	FRA1713
FRA1768	FRA1787	FRA1795	FRA1813
FRA1827	FRA1836	FRA1849	FRA1852
FRA1889	FRA1893	FRA1897	FRA1908
FRA1920	FRA1956	FRA1986	FRA2002
FRA2004	FRA2005	FRA2013	FRA2018
FRA2042	FRA2072	FRA2122	FRA2131
FRA2151	FRA2159	FRA2161	FRA2165
GBR2181	GBR2185	GBR2194	GBR2229
GBR2238	GBR2239	GBR2247	GBR2251
GBR2265	GBR2266	GBR2271	GBR2278
GBR2279	GBR2312	GBR2345	GBR2346
GBR2371	GBR2378	GBR2391	GBR2406
GBR2415	GBR2455	GBR2463	GBR2463
GBR2467	GBR2471	GBR2483	GBR2485
GBR2501	GBR2535	GBR2545	GBR2546
HUN2609	HUN2610	HUN2637	IRL2693
IRL2695	IRL2697	IRL2698	IRL2720
ITA2760	ITA2762	ITA2780	ITA2786
ITA2792	ITA2798	ITA2799	ITA2804
ITA2806	ITA2809	ITA2810	ITA2827
ITA2835	ITA2837	ITA2852	ITA2857
ITA2858	ITA2868	ITA2873	ITA2900
ITA2905	ITA2907	ITA2908	ITA2913
ITA2916	LUX2958	LUX3006	NLD3051
NLD3067	NLD3067	NLD3105	NLD3105
NLD3139	NLD3153	NLD3173	NLD3189
NLD3196	NLD3198	NLD3212	NLD3215
NLD3226	NLD3230	NLD3232	NLD3301
NLD3305	NLD3320	NLD3346	NLD3354
NLD3357	NOR3402	NOR3443	NOR3453
POL3508	POL3519	POL3533	PRT3600
SVK3611	SVK3622	SVK3640	SWE3648
SWE3763	SWE3768	SWE3771	SWE3781
SWE3787	SWE3816	SWE3865	SWE3879
TUR3883			

ECOLOGY, ENVIRONMENT, BIODIVERSITY - ECOLOGIE, ENVIRONNEMENT, BIODIVERSITE

BROADCASTING, CULTURAL EVENTS - RADIODIFFUSION, MANIFESTATIONS CULTURELLES

AUT0020	AUT0052	AUT0090	BEL0111
BEL0123	BEL0129	BEL0165	BEL0203
BEL0226	BEL0353	BEL0359	BEL0361
CHE0434	CHE0534	CHE0566	CHE0568
CHE0604	CHE0624	CHE0689	CHE0819
CHE0820	CYP0828	CYP0830	CYP0833
CZE0891	CZE0894	CZE0916	DEU1151
DEU1157	DEU1200	DNK1215	DNK1283
DNK1403	ESP1410	ESP1430	ESP1452
ESP1455	ESP1457	ESP1486	ESP1490
ESP1506	FIN1536	FIN1545	FIN1546
FIN1553	FIN1555	FIN1563	FRA1621
FRA1631	FRA1760	FRA1785	FRA1794
FRA1862	FRA1889	FRA1956	FRA1988
FRA2002	FRA2062	FRA2092	FRA2117
FRA2126	GBR2185	GBR2186	GBR2227
GBR2238	GBR2278	GBR2345	GBR2365
GBR2371	GBR2383	GBR2406	GBR2423
GBR2436	GBR2439	GBR2501	GBR2511
GBR2515	GBR2544	GBR2545	GBR2553
GRC2575	IRL2714	ITA2798	ITA2799
ITA2809	ITA2813	ITA2832	ITA2855
ITA2907	ITA2914	LUX2954	MLT3016
MLT3018	NLD3067	NLD3104	NLD3135
NLD3169	NLD3173	NLD3217	NLD3218
NLD3236	NLD3253	NOR3372	NOR3402
POL3482	POL3509	POL3532	PRT3600
SVK3611	SWE3702	SWE3738	SWE3754
SWE3760	SWE3774	TUR3883	TUR3885
TUR3894	TUR3898		

CONFERENCES, SEMINARS, WORKSHOPS, TRAINING ACTIVITIES - CONFERENCES, SEMINAIRES, ATELIERS, ACTIVITES DE FORMATION

AUT0010	AUT0011	AUT0020	AUT0032
AUT0045	AUT0052	AUT0063	AUT0074
AUT0085	BEL0101	BEL0111	BEL0123
BEL0128	BEL0129	BEL0133	BEL0142
BEL0148	BEL0155	BEL0165	BEL0168
BEL0171	BEL0174	BEL0177	BEL0188
BEL0191	BEL0203	BEL0211	BEL0214
BEL0221	BEL0248	BEL0254	BEL0270
BEL0273	BEL0287	BEL0322	BEL0333
BEL0340	BEL0353	BEL0359	BEL0361
BEL0395	BEL0397	BEL0399	CHE0402
CHE0403	CHE0417	CHE0434	CHE0439
CHE0461	CHE0494	CHE0500	CHE0534
CHE0549	CHE0555	CHE0560	CHE0562
CHE0566	CHE0568	CHE0571	CHE0604
CHE0629	CHE0632	CHE0638	CHE0642
CHE0645	CHE0649	CHE0654	CHE0655
CHE0669	CHE0680	CHE0682	CHE0689
CHE0693	CHE0726	CHE0730	CHE0762
CHE0765	CHE0766	CHE0767	CHE0778
CHE0787	CHE0793	CHE0813	CHE0814
CHE0817	CHE0819	CHE0820	CYP0828
CYP0830	CYP0831	CYP0833	CZE0839
CZE0865	CZE0879	CZE0882	CZE0891
CZE0897	CZE0905	CZE0915	CZE0916
DEU0921	DEU0942	DEU0944	DEU0948
DEU0975	DEU0977	DEU0983	DEU0990
DEU0992	DEU0996	DEU1002	DEU1004
DEU1020	DEU1025	DEU1032	DEU1034
DEU1037	DEU1055	DEU1062	DEU1065
DEU1066	DEU1074	DEU1090	DEU1097
DEU1100	DEU1106	DEU1111	DEU1114
DEU1129	DEU1149	DEU1151	DEU1157
DEU1163	DEU1167	DEU1178	DEU1180
DEU1184	DEU1210	DEU1211	DNK1215
DNK1226	DNK1283	DNK1300	DNK1312
DNK1335	DNK1339	DNK1345	DNK1353
DNK1361	DNK1398	DNK1403	ESP1407
ESP1410	ESP1413	ESP1430	ESP1437
ESP1438	ESP1441	ESP1452	ESP1455
ESP1457	ESP1472	ESP1479	ESP1482
ESP1485	ESP1486	ESP1490	ESP1506
ESP1508	ESP1509	ESP1511	ESP1517
ESP1525	ESP1528	FIN1536	FIN1544
FIN1545	FIN1546	FIN1547	FIN1548
FIN1551	FIN1553	FIN1555	FIN1557
FIN1560	FIN1563	FIN1572	FIN1577
FIN1578	FIN1582	FIN1583	FIN1594
FIN1605	FRA1610	FRA1616	FRA1627
FRA1629	FRA1634	FRA1636	FRA1651
FRA1656	FRA1661	FRA1679	FRA1690
FRA1712	FRA1719	FRA1727	FRA1756
FRA1757	FRA1785	FRA1787	FRA1794
FRA1797	FRA1816	FRA1818	FRA1838
FRA1841	FRA1846	FRA1860	FRA1862
FRA1883	FRA1887	FRA1889	FRA1897
FRA1907	FRA1917	FRA1921	FRA1927
FRA1949	FRA1956	FRA1964	FRA1980
FRA1985	FRA1990	FRA1992	FRA2004
FRA2005	FRA2012	FRA2020	FRA2029
FRA2032	FRA2039	FRA2044	FRA2057
FRA2062	FRA2069	FRA2076	FRA2096
FRA2105	FRA2109	FRA2126	FRA2129
FRA2131	FRA2158	FRA2161	FRA2162
FRA2163	FRA2167	GBR2174	GBR2176
GBR2185	GBR2186	GBR2197	GBR2214
GBR2226	GBR2232	GBR2238	GBR2244
GBR2262	GBR2264	GBR2265	GBR2266
GBR2269	GBR2278	GBR2279	GBR2292
GBR2294	GBR2298	GBR2303	GBR2312
GBR2337	GBR2346	GBR2351	GBR2365
GBR2366	GBR2370	GBR2371	GBR2380
GBR2383	GBR2386	GBR2387	GBR2390
GBR2406	GBR2408	GBR2415	GBR2416
GBR2422	GBR2423	GBR2426	GBR2428
GBR2435	GBR2436	GBR2439	GBR2445
GBR2458	GBR2460	GBR2480	GBR2481
GBR2483	GBR2495	GBR2503	GBR2511
GBR2515	GBR2524	GBR2526	GBR2527
GBR2535	GBR2544	GBR2545	GBR2553
GBR2561	GBR2562	GRC2567	GRC2572
GRC2575	GRC2590	HUN2607	HUN2609
HUN2610	HUN2637	HUN2643	HUN2657
HUN2678	IRL2679	IRL2690	IRL2691

IRL2696	IRL2719	IRL2720	IRL2726
ITA2748	ITA2762	ITA2782	ITA2799
ITA2801	ITA2806	ITA2809	ITA2810
ITA2813	ITA2820	ITA2826	ITA2829
ITA2832	ITA2834	ITA2855	ITA2860
ITA2862	ITA2866	ITA2868	ITA2873
ITA2883	ITA2894	ITA2901	ITA2907
ITA2908	ITA2913	ITA2914	LUX2984
LUX2993	LUX3008	MLT3016	MLT3017
MLT3018	MLT3021	MLT3023	NLD3047
NLD3062	NLD3067	NLD3069	NLD3070
NLD3079	NLD3083	NLD3087	NLD3104
NLD3115	NLD3117	NLD3122	NLD3135
NLD3137	NLD3138	NLD3147	NLD3154
NLD3155	NLD3158	NLD3160	NLD3164
NLD3166	NLD3169	NLD3173	NLD3174
NLD3179	NLD3190	NLD3196	NLD3217
NLD3218	NLD3230	NLD3232	NLD3236
NLD3274	NLD3279	NLD3286	NLD3301
NLD3303	NLD3305	NLD3318	NLD3330
NLD3334	NLD3337	NLD3352	NLD3364
NLD3365	NLD3366	NOR3371	NOR3391
NOR3402	NOR3422	NOR3453	NOR3467
NOR3475	POL3482	POL3499	POL3502
POL3507	POL3508	POL3509	POL3519
POL3520	POL3521	POL3524	POL3525
POL3526	POL3543	PRT3564	PRT3579
PRT3586	PRT3600	PRT3602	SVK3611
SVK3612	SVK3634	SWE3667	SWE3671
SWE3679	SWE3685	SWE3695	SWE3702
SWE3707	SWE3724	SWE3727	SWE3738
SWE3749	SWE3754	SWE3774	SWE3780
SWE3787	SWE3789	SWE3799	SWE3807
SWE3816	SWE3834	SWE3864	SWE3865
SWE3876	SWE3879	TUR3883	TUR3884
TUR3885	TUR3894	TUR3896	TUR3898

EXCHANGES, TWINNING, LINKING - ECHANGES, PARRAINAGE, JUMELAGE

AUT0010	AUT0020	AUT0085	BEL0123
BEL0129	BEL0165	BEL0198	BEL0203
BEL0221	BEL0248	BEL0273	BEL0340
BEL0361	BEL0390	BEL0395	CHE0403
CHE0434	CHE0448	CHE0479	CHE0500
CHE0557	CHE0562	CHE0566	CHE0649
CHE0689	CHE0730	CHE0778	CHE0804
CHE0819	CHE0825	CYP0831	CYP0833
CZE0839	CZE0865	CZE0882	DEU0975
DEU0983	DEU0990	DEU1037	DEU1055
DEU1062	DEU1066	DEU1074	DEU1111
DEU1149	DEU1163	DEU1167	DEU1178
DEU1180	DEU1200	DEU1210	DNK1291
DNK1306	DNK1339	ESP1452	ESP1457
ESP1517	ESP1525	FIN1546	FRA1616
FRA1746	FRA1785	FRA1846	FRA1860
FRA1889	FRA1891	FRA1907	FRA1913
FRA1956	FRA1964	FRA1985	FRA2029
FRA2039	FRA2057	FRA2062	FRA2068
FRA2092	FRA2167	GBR2181	GBR2262
GBR2278	GBR2365	GBR2370	GBR2371
GBR2379	GBR2383	GBR2390	GBR2406
GBR2423	GBR2435	GBR2439	GBR2480
GBR2515	GBR2544	GBR2553	GRC2572
GRC2575	GRC2590	HUN2620	HUN2622
HUN2643	HUN2657	IRL2714	
IRL2719	ISL2739	ITA2762	ITA2799
ITA2809	ITA2813	ITA2914	MLT3016
MLT3018	NLD3062	NLD3067	NLD3071
NLD3079	NLD3104	NLD3117	NLD3122
NLD3137	NLD3138	NLD3154	NLD3155
NLD3169	NLD3173	NLD3179	NLD3196
NLD3199	NLD3215	NLD3218	NLD3219
NLD3236	NLD3245	NLD3274	NLD3305
NLD3318	NLD3334	NLD3361	NLD3365
NLD3366	NOR3467	POL3482	POL3499
POL3507	POL3508	POL3509	POL3519
POL3521	POL3525	POL3543	SVK3611
SVK3612	SWE3685	SWE3724	SWE3734
SWE3749	SWE3754	SWE3760	SWE3785
SWE3865	SWE3879	TUR3883	

FORMAL EDUCATION - EDUCATION FORMELLE

AUT0020	AUT0052	AUT0065	AUT0085
BEL0111	BEL0123	BEL0129	BEL0177
BEL0211	BEL0322	BEL0353	BEL0359
BEL0361	BEL0390	BEL0395	CHE0422
CHE0434	CHE0549	CHE0554	CHE0562
CHE0566	CHE0645	CHE0649	CHE0673

CHE0680	CHE0682	CHE0687	CHE0689
CHE0730	CHE0787	CHE0804	CHE0809
CHE0813	CHE0819	CHE0820	CYP0828
CYP0833	CZE0839	CZE0865	CZE0882
CZE0894	CZE0915	CZE0916	DEU0975
DEU0983	DEU1100	DEU1151	DEU1176
DEU1178	DNK1226	DNK1275	DNK1339
DNK1345	DNK1403	ESP1427	ESP1437
ESP1452	ESP1455	ESP1457	ESP1479
ESP1486	ESP1490	ESP1492	ESP1508
ESP1517	FIN1555	FRA1627	FRA1661
FRA1738	FRA1757	FRA1785	FRA1787
FRA1794	FRA1827	FRA1841	FRA1889
FRA1956	FRA1992	FRA2002	FRA2039
FRA2044	FRA2062	FRA2088	FRA2103
FRA2105	FRA2131	FRA2150	GBR2174
GBR2181	GBR2238	GBR2265	GBR2269
GBR2278	GBR2294	GBR2315	GBR2333
GBR2337	GBR2345	GBR2371	GBR2379
GBR2380	GBR2383	GBR2386	GBR2390
GBR2406	GBR2408	GBR2415	GBR2423
GBR2424	GBR2428	GBR2436	GBR2439
GBR2467	GBR2468	GBR2481	GBR2511
GBR2544	GBR2553	GRC2567	GRC2571
GRC2575	GRC2590	HUN2607	HUN2610
HUN2622	HUN2626	HUN2643	HUN2657
HUN2678	IRL2690	IRL2691	IRL2697
IRL2698	IRL2719	IRL2720	ITA2762
ITA2775	ITA2782	ITA2798	ITA2810
ITA2813	ITA2826	ITA2838	ITA2855
ITA2868	ITA2883	ITA2914	LUX2982
LUX2986	MLT3016	MLT3017	MLT3018
NLD3067	NLD3070	NLD3083	NLD3104
NLD3117	NLD3138	NLD3154	NLD3155
NLD3166	NLD3179	NLD3199	NLD3212
NLD3215	NLD3217	NLD3218	NLD3219
NLD3254	NLD3337	NOR3467	POL3482
POL3507	POL3508	POL3509	POL3521
POL3526	PRT3600	SVK3611	SVK3612
SWE3653	SWE3655	SWE3679	SWE3796
SWE3859	SWE3876	SWE3879	TUR3885

FUND RAISING - COLLECTE DE FONDS

AUT0003	AUT0026	AUT0029	AUT0051
AUT0085	AUT0091	BEL0111	BEL0118
BEL0142	BEL0148	BEL0153	BEL0155
BEL0168	BEL0198	BEL0203	BEL0211
BEL0248	BEL0254	BEL0270	BEL0272
BEL0327	BEL0351	BEL0359	BEL0361
BEL0390	CHE0410	CHE0417	CHE0434
CHE0438	CHE0463	CHE0479	CHE0549
CHE0562	CHE0564	CHE0566	CHE0584
CHE0586	CHE0602	CHE0604	CHE0619
CHE0630	CHE0659	CHE0687	CHE0689
CHE0693	CHE0707	CHE0730	CHE0755
CHE0756	CHE0767	CHE0778	CHE0789
CHE0804	CHE0814	CHE0819	CHE0820
CYP0830	CZE0839	CZE0865	CZE0882
CZE0916	DEU0948	DEU0957	DEU0968
DEU0975	DEU0983	DEU1001	DEU1006
DEU1044	DEU1062	DEU1066	DEU1086
DEU1100	DEU1114	DEU1149	DEU1151
DEU1167	DEU1178	DEU1200	DEU1202
DNK1222	DNK1226	DNK1283	DNK1291
DNK1302	DNK1306	DNK1403	ESP1409
ESP1442	ESP1452	ESP1455	ESP1457
ESP1470	ESP1486	ESP1506	ESP1508
ESP1517	FIN1544	FIN1549	FIN1591
FIN1599	FRA1610	FRA1636	FRA1644
FRA1663	FRA1690	FRA1703	FRA1738
FRA1739	FRA1757	FRA1760	FRA1785
FRA1787	FRA1889	FRA1913	FRA1914
FRA1939	FRA1980	FRA1990	FRA1990
FRA2086	FRA2092	FRA2117	FRA2131
FRA2163	GBR2176	GBR2185	GBR2186
GBR2197	GBR2201	GBR2226	GBR2227
GBR2229	GBR2238	GBR2259	GBR2264
GBR2277	GBR2278	GBR2292	GBR2298
GBR2312	GBR2318	GBR2333	GBR2337
GBR2348	GBR2350	GBR2351	GBR2358
GBR2365	GBR2370	GBR2371	GBR2372
GBR2376	GBR2383	GBR2386	GBR2390
GBR2406	GBR2423	GBR2428	GBR2436
GBR2439	GBR2445	GBR2456	GBR2480
GBR2481	GBR2483	GBR2500	GBR2511
GBR2515	GBR2524	GBR2525	GBR2535
GBR2537	GBR2544	GBR2552	GBR2553
GBR2562	GRC2567	GRC2572	GRC2575
GRC2590	HUN2609	HUN2610	HUN2637

HUN2657	HUN2678	IRL2691	IRL2696
IRL2714	ITA2748	ITA2762	ITA2773
ITA2799	ITA2809	ITA2810	ITA2813
ITA2820	ITA2822	ITA2826	ITA2832
ITA2855	ITA2900	ITA2901	ITA2913
ITA2914	LUX2959	LUX2982	LUX2984
LUX2986	LUX2993	LUX2995	LUX3006
MLT3018	MLT3021	MLT3025	NLD3062
NLD3067	NLD3070	NLD3104	NLD3115
NLD3122	NLD3137	NLD3154	NLD3159
NLD3199	NLD3219	NLD3231	NLD3245
NLD3253	NLD3254	NLD3256	NLD3263
NLD3300	NLD3301	NLD3337	NLD3362
NLD3364	NLD3365	NLD3366	NOR3371
NOR3404	NOR3410	NOR3412	NOR3453
NOR3467	NOR3475	POL3482	POL3507
POL3509	POL3524	POL3525	SVK3611
SWE3648	SWE3653	SWE3655	SWE3679
SWE3685	SWE3702	SWE3707	SWE3724
SWE3749	SWE3787	SWE3795	SWE3796
SWE3855	SWE3857	SWE3859	SWE3864
SWE3876	TUR3885	TUR3896	TUR3898

INFORMATION AND DOCUMENTATION SERVICES, DATA BASES - SERVICES D'INFORMATION ET DE DOCUMENTATION, BASES DE DONNEES

AUT0020	AUT0026	AUT0032	AUT0045
AUT0060	AUT0067	AUT0074	AUT0079
AUT0085	BEL0118	BEL0123	BEL0129
BEL0142	BEL0155	BEL0164	BEL0165
BEL0168	BEL0171	BEL0177	BEL0203
BEL0211	BEL0214	BEL0226	BEL0237
BEL0248	BEL0267	BEL0273	BEL0335
BEL0359	BEL0361	BEL0365	BEL0390
BEL0393	BEL0395	BEL0396	CHE0403
CHE0429	CHE0434	CHE0479	CHE0494
CHE0500	CHE0534	CHE0549	CHE0554
CHE0562	CHE0566	CHE0568	CHE0571
CHE0604	CHE0609	CHE0624	CHE0632
CHE0638	CHE0645	CHE0649	CHE0673
CHE0687	CHE0689	CHE0756	CHE0762
CHE0763	CHE0767	CHE0787	CHE0813
CHE0819	CHE0820	CYP0828	CYP0831
CYP0831	CYP0833	CZE0839	CZE0879
CZE0915	CZE0916	DEU0944	DEU0948
DEU0968	DEU0975	DEU0977	DEU0990
DEU0996	DEU1001	DEU1002	DEU1004
DEU1020	DEU1025	DEU1037	DEU1062
DEU1074	DEU1076	DEU1086	DEU1090
DEU1091	DEU1097	DEU1114	DEU1137
DEU1138	DEU1151	DEU1151	DEU1157
DEU1163	DEU1167	DEU1180	DEU1184
DEU1192	DEU1200	DEU1211	DNK1215
DNK1226	DNK1259	DNK1283	DNK1292
DNK1300	DNK1302	DNK1306	DNK1339
DNK1398	DNK1403	ESP1407	ESP1413
ESP1417	ESP1430	ESP1431	ESP1434
ESP1437	ESP1438	ESP1441	ESP1452
ESP1455	ESP1457	ESP1470	ESP1479
ESP1482	ESP1486	ESP1490	ESP1506
ESP1508	ESP1509	ESP1521	FIN1546
FIN1547	FIN1548	FIN1555	FIN1560
FIN1591	FIN1591	FIN1599	FRA1610
FRA1629	FRA1631	FRA1636	FRA1656
FRA1703	FRA1712	FRA1719	FRA1727
FRA1737	FRA1784	FRA1785	FRA1794
FRA1797	FRA1808	FRA1810	FRA1811
FRA1816	FRA1818	FRA1827	FRA1833
FRA1838	FRA1839	FRA1841	FRA1846
FRA1860	FRA1889	FRA1907	FRA1927
FRA1956	FRA1985	FRA1988	FRA1990
FRA2002	FRA2004	FRA2018	FRA2020
FRA2029	FRA2039	FRA2062	FRA2069
FRA2096	FRA2103	FRA2104	FRA2105
FRA2120	FRA2122	FRA2126	FRA2131
FRA2163	GBR2174	GBR2185	GBR2197
GBR2226	GBR2232	GBR2238	GBR2239
GBR2264	GBR2265	GBR2266	GBR2278
GBR2279	GBR2298	GBR2326	GBR2339
GBR2365	GBR2370	GBR2371	GBR2379
GBR2383	GBR2386	GBR2387	GBR2400
GBR2406	GBR2408	GBR2415	GBR2423
GBR2434	GBR2435	GBR2438	GBR2439
GBR2445	GBR2456	GBR2480	GBR2483
GBR2495	GBR2511	GBR2515	GBR2537
GBR2544	GBR2545	GBR2562	GRC2567
GRC2571	GRC2575	HUN2609	HUN2610
HUN2613	HUN2622	HUN2624	HUN2626

HUN2637	HUN2657	IRL2696	IRL2698
IRL2714	IRL2717	IRL2720	IRL2726
IRL2730	ITA2744	ITA2748	ITA2762
ITA2773	ITA2799	ITA2799	ITA2801
ITA2805	ITA2808	ITA2809	ITA2810
ITA2813	ITA2822	ITA2829	ITA2834
ITA2840	ITA2855	ITA2860	ITA2861
ITA2862	ITA2866	ITA2873	ITA2880
ITA2900	ITA2901	ITA2907	ITA2908
ITA2913	ITA2914	LUX2937	LUX2962
LUX2983	MLT3016	MLT3018	NLD3047
NLD3051	NLD3058	NLD3062	NLD3067
NLD3070	NLD3077	NLD3083	NLD3084
NLD3096	NLD3104	NLD3110	NLD3115
NLD3117	NLD3122	NLD3135	NLD3136
NLD3137	NLD3138	NLD3139	NLD3147
NLD3154	NLD3155	NLD3158	NLD3160
NLD3166	NLD3170	NLD3173	NLD3179
NLD3217	NLD3218	NLD3232	NLD3236
NLD3254	NLD3274	NLD3279	NLD3301
NLD3303	NLD3305	NLD3318	NLD3334
NLD3337	NLD3352	NLD3353	NLD3355
NLD3361	NLD3364	NOR3372	NOR3391
NOR3402	NOR3422	NOR3467	POL3482
POL3499	POL3507	POL3508	POL3509
POL3519	POL3521	POL3524	POL3525
POL3532	PRT3600	SVK3611	SWE3648
SWE3655	SWE3659	SWE3744	SWE3747
SWE3754	SWE3760	SWE3774	SWE3789
SWE3807	SWE3816	SWE3832	SWE3859
SWE3864	SWE3865	SWE3876	TUR3883
TUR3885	TUR3894	TUR3896	TUR3898

INFORMATION CAMPAIGNS, EXHIBITIONS - CAMPAGNES D'INFORMATION, EXPOSITIONS

AUT0006	AUT0010	AUT0020	AUT0024
AUT0032	AUT0052	AUT0068	AUT0085
AUT0091	BEL0101	BEL0111	BEL0123
BEL0129	BEL0139	BEL0148	BEL0155
BEL0165	BEL0168	BEL0198	BEL0203
BEL0211	BEL0226	BEL0241	BEL0248
BEL0254	BEL0267	BEL0273	BEL0275
BEL0322	BEL0335	BEL0353	BEL0359
BEL0361	BEL0365	BEL0390	BEL0392
BEL0395	BEL0397	CHE0403	CHE0434
CHE0461	CHE0479	CHE0486	CHE0500
CHE0534	CHE0549	CHE0554	CHE0557
CHE0560	CHE0562	CHE0566	CHE0568
CHE0571	CHE0584	CHE0604	CHE0659
CHE0669	CHE0680	CHE0689	CHE0756
CHE0765	CHE0804	CHE0819	CHE0820
CHE0828	CYP0828	CYP0830	CYP0831
CYP0832	CYP0833	CZE0839	CZE0865
CZE0882	CZE0891	CZE0916	DEU0917
DEU0931	DEU0948	DEU0955	DEU0975
DEU0977	DEU0983	DEU1002	DEU1004
DEU1025	DEU1034	DEU1037	DEU1062
DEU1066	DEU1137	DEU1149	DEU1151
DEU1163	DEU1167	DEU1178	DEU1200
DEU1202	DNK1215	DNK1226	DNK1283
DNK1300	DNK1306	DNK1312	DNK1339
DNK1345	DNK1398	DNK1403	ESP1407
ESP1410	ESP1413	ESP1437	ESP1438
ESP1452	ESP1457	ESP1475	ESP1485
ESP1486	ESP1490	ESP1506	ESP1508
ESP1517	ESP1521	ESP1528	FIN1546
FIN1547	FIN1553	FIN1557	FIN1557
FIN1560	FIN1572	FIN1577	FIN1592
FIN1594	FIN1599	FRA1610	FRA1619
FRA1633	FRA1651	FRA1656	FRA1663
FRA1738	FRA1739	FRA1757	FRA1785
FRA1797	FRA1816	FRA1841	FRA1862
FRA1889	FRA1956	FRA1990	FRA1991
FRA1992	FRA2002	FRA2005	FRA2020
FRA2039	FRA2057	FRA2062	FRA2068
FRA2076	FRA2086	FRA2088	FRA2096
FRA2104	FRA2126	FRA2131	FRA2158
FRA2163	GBR2181	GBR2186	GBR2238
GBR2239	GBR2259	GBR2264	GBR2265
GBR2269	GBR2277	GBR2278	GBR2279
GBR2312	GBR2339	GBR2350	GBR2365
GBR2371	GBR2383	GBR2386	GBR2387
GBR2406	GBR2408	GBR2415	GBR2423
GBR2434	GBR2435	GBR2439	GBR2483
GBR2495	GBR2503	GBR2511	GBR2515
GBR2524	GBR2526	GBR2527	GBR2535
GBR2537	GBR2544	GBR2545	GBR2553
GBR2561	GRC2567	GRC2572	GRC2575
HUN2607	HUN2609	HUN2613	HUN2620

HUN2624	HUN2626	HUN2637	HUN2657
HUN2678	IRL2690	IRL2696	IRL2719
IRL2720	IRL2726	ITA2748	ITA2762
ITA2775	ITA2799	ITA2801	ITA2809
ITA2810	ITA2813	ITA2832	ITA2838
ITA2855	ITA2860	ITA2866	ITA2901
ITA2914	LUX2937	LUX2954	LUX2984
LUX2986	LUX2993	LUX3006	MLT3016
MLT3018	MLT3025	MLT3030	MLT3036
NLD3047	NLD3062	NLD3067	NLD3079
NLD3083	NLD3087	NLD3099	NLD3104
NLD3115	NLD3117	NLD3122	NLD3135
NLD3137	NLD3158	NLD3159	NLD3164
NLD3166	NLD3169	NLD3173	NLD3190
NLD3196	NLD3217	NLD3218	NLD3232
NLD3236	NLD3263	NLD3274	NLD3303
NLD3305	NLD3320	NLD3337	NLD3352
NLD3361	NLD3364	NLD3365	NLD3366
NOR3371	NOR3372	NOR3402	NOR3422
POL3482	POL3499	POL3502	POL3507
POL3509	POL3519	POL3524	POL3525
POL3526	POL3532	POL3543	PRT3594
PRT3600	SVK3611	SVK3612	SWE3648
SWE3655	SWE3685	SWE3695	SWE3702
SWE3707	SWE3724	SWE3738	SWE3742
SWE3749	SWE3754	SWE3760	SWE3774
SWE3789	SWE3796	SWE3814	SWE3816
SWE3819	SWE3869	SWE3865	SWE3876
SWE3879	TUR3883	TUR3885	TUR3898

LOBBYING, ADVOCACY - LOBBYING, PLAIDOYER

AUT0020	AUT0024	AUT0051	BEL0099
BEL0111	BEL0118	BEL0131	BEL0142
BEL0155	BEL0165	BEL0168	BEL0174
BEL0177	BEL0186	BEL0191	BEL0198
BEL0203	BEL0211	BEL0214	BEL0216
BEL0218	BEL0248	BEL0254	BEL0272
BEL0273	BEL0351	BEL0359	BEL0361
BEL0397	BEL0399	CHE0429	CHE0434
CHE0479	CHE0486	CHE0491	CHE0534
CHE0549	CHE0554	CHE0560	CHE0562
CHE0566	CHE0568	CHE0604	CHE0642
CHE0645	CHE0654	CHE0680	CHE0689
CHE0765	CHE0767	CHE0778	CHE0787
CHE0809	CHE0814	CHE0819	CHE0820
CYP0828	CYP0830	CYP0831	CYP0833
CZE0879	CZE0882	CZE0891	CZE0916
DEU0942	DEU0948	DEU0975	DEU0983
DEU0998	DEU1004	DEU1032	DEU1037
DEU1055	DEU1062	DEU1066	DEU1074
DEU1097	DEU1100	DEU1114	DEU1149
DEU1151	DEU1167	DEU1176	DEU1184
DEU1200	DEU1211	DNK1226	DNK1283
DNK1291	DNK1300	DNK1302	DNK1306
DNK1335	DNK1339	DNK1345	DNK1399
DNK1403	ESP1410	ESP1438	ESP1452
ESP1457	ESP1486	ESP1525	ESP1528
FIN1546	FIN1551	FIN1555	FIN1582
FIN1594	FRA1633	FRA1636	FRA1757
FRA1785	FRA1794	FRA1797	FRA1816
FRA1841	FRA1862	FRA1876	FRA1889
FRA1946	FRA1949	FRA1956	FRA2002
FRA2004	FRA2032	FRA2039	FRA2057
FRA2062	FRA2096	FRA2105	FRA2110
FRA2126	FRA2131	FRA2167	GBR2174
GBR2181	GBR2202	GBR2215	GBR2238
GBR2239	GBR2242	GBR2245	GBR2266
GBR2269	GBR2294	GBR2303	GBR2337
GBR2351	GBR2365	GBR2366	GBR2371
GBR2376	GBR2383	GBR2385	GBR2390
GBR2406	GBR2423	GBR2434	GBR2435
GBR2439	GBR2481	GBR2483	GBR2495
GBR2503	GBR2511	GBR2526	GBR2527
GBR2537	GBR2544	GBR2545	GBR2552
GBR2553	GBR2561	GRC2572	HUN2609
HUN2610	HUN2622	HUN2626	HUN2637
HUN2640	HUN2643	HUN2678	IRL2690
IRL2691	ITA2748	ITA2799	ITA2801
ITA2810	ITA2813	ITA2820	ITA2838
ITA2855	ITA2862	ITA2881	ITA2913
ITA2914	LUX2957	LUX2958	LUX2984
MLT3016	MLT3017	MLT3018	MLT3023
MLT3025	MLT3036	NLD3047	NLD3048
NLD3062	NLD3067	NLD3079	NLD3087
NLD3099	NLD3104	NLD3115	NLD3117
NLD3122	NLD3135	NLD3137	NLD3147
NLD3155	NLD3156	NLD3160	NLD3164
NLD3196	NLD3199	NLD3218	NLD3219
NLD3232	NLD3236	NLD3254	NLD3274

NLD3301	NLD3303	NLD3305	NLD3330
NLD3334	NLD3337	NLD3362	NLD3364
NLD3365	NLD3366	NOR3402	NOR3422
NOR3467	NOR3475	POL3482	POL3499
POL3507	POL3509	POL3524	POL3526
POL3543	PRT3600	SVK3634	SWE3648
SWE3655	SWE3724	SWE3742	SWE3749
SWE3754	SWE3799	SWE3864	SWE3876
TUR3883	TUR3885	TUR3894	TUR3896
TUR3898			

NETWORKING, ELECTRONIC TELECOMMUNICATIONS - RESEAUX, TELECOMMUNICATIONS ELECTRONIQUES

AUT0020	BEL0165	BEL0177	BEL0198
BEL0254	BEL0272	BEL0361	BEL0395
CHE0403	CHE0434	CHE0500	CHE0562
CHE0568	CHE0586	CHE0602	CHE0642
CHE0689	CHE0813	CHE0819	CZE0894
CZE0915	DEU0955	DEU0990	DEU1002
DEU1055	DEU1062	DEU1065	DEU1097
DEU1149	DEU1167	DEU1180	DEU1210
DNK1300	DNK1359	ESP1434	ESP1452
ESP1457	ESP1522	FIN1546	FIN1555
FIN1583	FIN1591	FIN1599	FRA1629
FRA1816	FRA1889	FRA1985	FRA2068
FRA2105	FRA2109	FRA2126	GBR2174
GBR2181	GBR2226	GBR2262	GBR2265
GBR2278	GBR2285	GBR2313	GBR2337
GBR2351	GBR2365	GBR2370	GBR2371
GBR2383	GBR2387	GBR2400	GBR2406
GBR2434	GBR2438	GBR2495	GBR2544
GBR2545	GBR2553	GBR2561	HUN2609
HUN2610	HUN2620	HUN2624	HUN2637
HUN2657	HUN2678	IRL2696	ITA2748
ITA2773	ITA2799	ITA2860	ITA2866
ITA2881	ITA2914	MLT3018	NLD3062
NLD3067	NLD3071	NLD3077	NLD3104
NLD3117	NLD3135	NLD3136	NLD3137
NLD3154	NLD3155	NLD3215	NLD3218
NLD3236	NLD3279	NLD3318	NLD3337
NLD3353	NLD3364	NLD3365	NLD3366
NOR3372	NOR3402	NOR3422	NOR3467
POL3482	POL3499	POL3507	POL3508
POL3509	POL3524	PRT3602	SVK3611
SWE3655	SWE3702	SWE3724	SWE3754
SWE3785	SWE3787	SWE3789	SWE3864
TUR3883	TUR3894		

OTHER - AUTRE

CHE0434	FIN1555	FRA1631	FRA2012
GBR2371	GBR2387	NLD3071	NLD3096
NLD3117	NLD3137	NLD3183	

PUBLISHING, AUDIOVISUAL MATERIALS, EDUCATIONAL MATERIALS - EDITION, DOCUMENTS AUDIOVISUELS, DOCUMENTS EDUCATIFS

AUT0010	AUT0020	AUT0026	AUT0051
AUT0052	AUT0068	AUT0085	AUT0090
BEL0101	BEL0111	BEL0123	BEL0139
BEL0142	BEL0148	BEL0155	BEL0165
BEL0168	BEL0174	BEL0177	BEL0188
BEL0203	BEL0214	BEL0248	BEL0254
BEL0268	BEL0273	BEL0306	BEL0322
BEL0335	BEL0340	BEL0353	BEL0359
BEL0361	BEL0365	BEL0390	BEL0392
BEL0393	BEL0395	CHE0403	CHE0429
CHE0434	CHE0479	CHE0499	CHE0500
CHE0501	CHE0534	CHE0549	CHE0554
CHE0560	CHE0562	CHE0564	CHE0566
CHE0568	CHE0604	CHE0609	CHE0638
CHE0649	CHE0680	CHE0689	CHE0693
CHE0730	CHE0738	CHE0756	CHE0762
CHE0763	CHE0767	CHE0813	CHE0819
CHE0820	CYP0828	CYP0830	CYP0831
CYP0833	CZE0839	CZE0879	CZE0882
CZE0894	CZE0915	CZE0916	DEU0942
DEU0944	DEU0948	DEU0972	DEU0975
DEU0977	DEU1004	DEU1020	DEU1022
DEU1025	DEU1031	DEU1034	DEU1037
DEU1055	DEU1062	DEU1066	DEU1074
DEU1076	DEU1097	DEU1137	DEU1149
DEU1151	DEU1157	DEU1167	DEU1180
DEU1184	DEU1198	DEU1200	DNK1215
DNK1259	DNK1283	DNK1291	DNK1292
DNK1302	DNK1339	DNK1345	DNK1403
ESP1407	ESP1409	ESP1410	ESP1413

Voir : *Comment utiliser le répertoire*, page 11.

ESP1417	ESP1430	ESP1434	ESP1435
ESP1436	ESP1452	ESP1455	ESP1457
ESP1485	ESP1490	ESP1506	ESP1521
ESP1522	FIN1536	FIN1544	FIN1546
FIN1548	FIN1551	FIN1555	FIN1557
FIN1563	FIN1572	FRA1610	FRA1627
FRA1629	FRA1631	FRA1656	FRA1661
FRA1668	FRA1712	FRA1713	FRA1719
FRA1757	FRA1785	FRA1787	FRA1794
FRA1795	FRA1810	FRA1813	FRA1816
FRA1818	FRA1827	FRA1828	FRA1833
FRA1836	FRA1860	FRA1862	FRA1883
FRA1889	FRA1897	FRA1956	FRA1985
FRA1986	FRA1990	FRA1992	FRA2001
FRA2002	FRA2004	FRA2020	FRA2032
FRA2039	FRA2062	FRA2068	FRA2069
FRA2072	FRA2076	FRA2086	FRA2104
FRA2105	FRA2109	FRA2126	FRA2131
FRA2167	GBR2174	GBR2181	GBR2185
GBR2227	GBR2229	GBR2232	GBR2238
GBR2239	GBR2264	GBR2265	GBR2271
GBR2278	GBR2279	GBR2294	GBR2303
GBR2312	GBR2318	GBR2326	GBR2337
GBR2345	GBR2346	GBR2358	GBR2365
GBR2366	GBR2370	GBR2371	GBR2380
GBR2383	GBR2386	GBR2387	GBR2400
GBR2406	GBR2415	GBR2422	GBR2423
GBR2424	GBR2434	GBR2435	GBR2436
GBR2439	GBR2456	GBR2480	GBR2483
GBR2500	GBR2501	GBR2503	GBR2511
GBR2515	GBR2524	GBR2525	GBR2526
GBR2527	GBR2535	GBR2544	GBR2545
GBR2552	GBR2554	GBR2561	GBR2562
GRC2567	GRC2572	GRC2575	HUN2607
HUN2609	HUN2610	HUN2613	HUN2620
HUN2624	HUN2626	HUN2637	HUN2643
HUN2657	HUN2678	IRL2696	IRL2697
IRL2698	IRL2719	IRL2720	ITA2744
ITA2748	ITA2756	ITA2762	ITA2798
ITA2799	ITA2809	ITA2810	ITA2813
ITA2814	ITA2822	ITA2826	ITA2834
ITA2835	ITA2855	ITA2860	ITA2861
ITA2862	ITA2866	ITA2868	ITA2873
ITA2881	ITA2900	ITA2901	ITA2907
ITA2908	ITA2913	ITA2914	ITA2916
LUX3006	MLT3016	MLT3018	MLT3021
NLD3062	NLD3067	NLD3077	NLD3083
NLD3087	NLD3104	NLD3117	NLD3122
NLD3135	NLD3136	NLD3138	NLD3154
NLD3155	NLD3159	NLD3164	NLD3166
NLD3169	NLD3173	NLD3190	NLD3196
NLD3212	NLD3215	NLD3216	NLD3218
NLD3230	NLD3274	NLD3279	NLD3301
NLD3303	NLD3305	NLD3318	NLD3320
NLD3337	NLD3352	NLD3353	NLD3354
NLD3361	NLD3364	NOR3391	NOR3402
NOR3404	NOR3422	NOR3441	NOR3467
POL3482	POL3499	POL3502	POL3507
POL3508	POL3509	POL3519	POL3524
POL3525	POL3526	POL3532	POL3543
PRT3564	PRT3600	SVK3611	SWE3648
SWE3655	SWE3667	SWE3724	SWE3749
SWE3754	SWE3760	SWE3787	SWE3789
SWE3816	SWE3832	SWE3865	SWE3876
SWE3879	TUR3883	TUR3885	TUR3894
TUR3896	TUR3898		

EDUCATION, TRAINING, LITERACY - EDUCATION, FORMATION, ALPHABETISATION

BROADCASTING, CULTURAL EVENTS - RADIODIFFUSION, MANIFESTATIONS CULTURELLES

AUT0021	AUT0086	BEL0123	BEL0129
BEL0359	BEL0361	CHE0434	CHE0534
CHE0566	CHE0568	CHE0624	CHE0645
CHE0689	CHE0819	DEU1022	DEU1074
DNK1215	DNK1307	ESP1455	ESP1486
ESP1507	FIN1536	FIN1545	FIN1553
FIN1577	FRA1612	FRA1621	FRA1644
FRA1651	FRA1672	FRA1778	FRA1785
FRA1787	FRA1889	FRA1893	FRA1920
FRA1956	FRA2002	FRA2092	FRA2106
FRA2117	FRA2122	FRA2159	FRA2170
GBR2231	GBR2238	GBR2248	GBR2278
GBR2371	GBR2378	GBR2383	GBR2423

GBR2466	GBR2501	GBR2545	GBR2553
IRL2686	IRL2697	ITA2798	ITA2799
ITA2801	ITA2806	ITA2809	ITA2820
ITA2888	ITA2914	LUX2954	LUX2976
LUX2980	LUX2982	LUX2983	LUX3006
MLT3016	NLD3067	NLD3139	NLD3181
NLD3230	NOR3387	NOR3467	POL3508
PRT3555	PRT3588	SVK3611	SVK3638
SVK3640	SWE3702	SWE3761	SWE3774

CONFERENCES, SEMINARS, WORKSHOPS, TRAINING ACTIVITIES - CONFERENCES, SEMINAIRES, ATELIERS, ACTIVITES DE FORMATION

AUT0020	AUT0021	AUT0032	AUT0033
AUT0056	AUT0076	AUT0085	AUT0086
AUT0089	BEL0096	BEL0101	BEL0123
BEL0127	BEL0129	BEL0133	BEL0148
BEL0152	BEL0156	BEL0221	BEL0231
BEL0237	BEL0270	BEL0275	BEL0282
BEL0287	BEL0289	BEL0317	BEL0359
BEL0361	BEL0379	BEL0388	BEL0399
CHE0403	CHE0406	CHE0417	CHE0434
CHE0456	CHE0462	CHE0467	CHE0494
CHE0550	CHE0562	CHE0564	CHE0566
CHE0568	CHE0586	CHE0604	CHE0628
CHE0645	CHE0649	CHE0655	CHE0665
CHE0669	CHE0682	CHE0689	CHE0693
CHE0730	CHE0734	CHE0750	CHE0765
CHE0772	CHE0814	CHE0817	CHE0819
CZE0897	CZE0905	DEU0921	DEU0933
DEU0944	DEU0968	DEU0980	DEU0983
DEU0990	DEU0992	DEU1004	DEU1016
DEU1017	DEU1020	DEU1055	DEU1065
DEU1090	DEU1097	DEU1098	DEU1106
DEU1149	DEU1178	DEU1180	DEU1210
DNK1218	DNK1243	DNK1248	DNK1273
DNK1281	DNK1287	DNK1307	DNK1312
DNK1335	DNK1375	DNK1376	DNK1397
DNK1398	ESP1407	ESP1455	ESP1457
ESP1461	ESP1479	ESP1505	ESP1507
ESP1517	ESP1525	FIN1536	FIN1545
FIN1553	FIN1554	FIN1557
FIN1559	FIN1563	FIN1577	FIN1578
FIN1588	FIN1604	FRA1619	FRA1627
FRA1644	FRA1645	FRA1661	FRA1672
FRA1675	FRA1690	FRA1701	FRA1731
FRA1778	FRA1785	FRA1787	FRA1797
FRA1800	FRA1815	FRA1841	FRA1846
FRA1848	FRA1849	FRA1869	FRA1886
FRA1889	FRA1893	FRA1897	FRA1907
FRA1917	FRA1930	FRA1935	FRA1946
FRA1956	FRA1957	FRA1980	FRA1990
FRA2004	FRA2006	FRA2016	FRA2018
FRA2021	FRA2039	FRA2042	FRA2076
FRA2106	FRA2122	FRA2129	FRA2131
FRA2140	FRA2158	FRA2159	GBR2174
GBR2178	GBR2185	GBR2186	GBR2202
GBR2213	GBR2214	GBR2231	GBR2238
GBR2242	GBR2247	GBR2248	GBR2264
GBR2265	GBR2266	GBR2269	GBR2274
GBR2277	GBR2278	GBR2279	GBR2281
GBR2284	GBR2292	GBR2302	GBR2303
GBR2312	GBR2340	GBR2341	GBR2344
GBR2351	GBR2353	GBR2355	GBR2358
GBR2371	GBR2378	GBR2380	GBR2383
GBR2387	GBR2390	GBR2396	GBR2402
GBR2415	GBR2423	GBR2424	GBR2428
GBR2436	GBR2440	GBR2445	GBR2452
GBR2455	GBR2460	GBR2463	GBR2464
GBR2466	GBR2471	GBR2477	GBR2481
GBR2492	GBR2503	GBR2513	GBR2517
GBR2522	GBR2535	GBR2545	GBR2546
GBR2550	GBR2551	GBR2553	GRC2572
GRC2586	GRC2595	HUN2598	HUN2607
HUN2610	HUN2637	HUN2643	IRL2686
IRL2688	IRL2689	IRL2702	IRL2717
IRL2729	ITA2747	ITA2757	ITA2758
ITA2762	ITA2771	ITA2780	ITA2786
ITA2791	ITA2799	ITA2801	ITA2803
ITA2804	ITA2810	ITA2820	ITA2826
ITA2842	ITA2846	ITA2857	ITA2858
ITA2868	ITA2883	ITA2886	ITA2888
ITA2890	ITA2894	ITA2896	ITA2899
ITA2900	ITA2908	ITA2913	ITA2914
ITA2915	ITA2920	ITA2922	LUX2946
LUX2967	LUX2968	LUX2993	LUX2995
MLT3016	MLT3017	MLT3021	MLT3028
NLD3067	NLD3069	NLD3070	NLD3078

NLD3083	NLD3105	NLD3117	NLD3138
NLD3139	NLD3142	NLD3153	NLD3154
NLD3155	NLD3163	NLD3174	NLD3196
NLD3198	NLD3230	NLD3232	NLD3242
NLD3269	NLD3270	NLD3301	NLD3325
NLD3329	NLD3334	NOR3371	NOR3389
NOR3390	NOR3394	NOR3403	NOR3418
NOR3429	NOR3431	NOR3440	NOR3447
NOR3453	NOR3467	NOR3473	POL3499
POL3507	POL3519	POL3544	PRT3573
PRT3579	PRT3586	PRT3594	PRT3597
PRT3603	SVK3611	SVK3612	SVK3622
SVK3638	SVK3640	SWE3675	SWE3679
SWE3685	SWE3695	SWE3702	SWE3712
SWE3728	SWE3737	SWE3749	SWE3768
SWE3769	SWE3774	SWE3787	SWE3799
SWE3807	SWE3816	SWE3821	SWE3853
SWE3865	TUR3883	TUR3896	

EXCHANGES, TWINNING, LINKING - ECHANGES, PARRAINAGE, JUMELAGE

AUT0033	AUT0086	BEL0104	BEL0105
BEL0123	BEL0129	BEL0221
BEL0224	BEL0289	BEL0355	BEL0361
BEL0390	CHE0434	CHE0448	CHE0456
CHE0546	CHE0557	CHE0562	CHE0566
CHE0600	CHE0634	CHE0640	CHE0645
CHE0649	CHE0661	CHE0674	CHE0689
CHE0730	CHE0798	CHE0819	CZE0839
CZE0857	DEU0980	DEU0983	DEU0990
DEU1015	DEU1055	DEU1149	DEU1178
DEU1219	DNK1215	DNK1243	DNK1342
DNK1375	ESP1406	ESP1517	ESP1525
FIN1545	FRA1642	FRA1644	FRA1655
FRA1658	FRA1661	FRA1691
FRA1699	FRA1715	FRA1724	FRA1746
FRA1778	FRA1785	FRA1787	FRA1824
FRA1846	FRA1850	FRA1855	FRA1869
FRA1876	FRA1886	FRA1889	FRA1907
FRA1920	FRA1928	FRA1938	FRA1942
FRA1946	FRA1956	FRA2039	FRA2068
FRA2081	FRA2086	FRA2106	FRA2117
FRA2140	FRA2145	FRA2159	FRA2170
GBR2181	GBR2214	GBR2231	GBR2266
GBR2274	GBR2278	GBR2281	GBR2306
GBR2371	GBR2379	GBR2383	GBR2396
GBR2423	GBR2424	GBR2445	GBR2452
GBR2515	GBR2517	GRC2572	HUN2620
HUN2637	IRL2684	IRL2686	IRL2698
IRL2702	IRL2714	ITA2758	ITA2770
ITA2780	ITA2798	ITA2801	ITA2802
ITA2809	ITA2824	ITA2835	ITA2842
ITA2907	ITA2914	ITA2920	LUX2967
LUX2995	MLT3021	MLT3028	NLD3056
NLD3067	NLD3070	NLD3078	NLD3098
NLD3105	NLD3117	NLD3138	NLD3139
NLD3141	NLD3142	NLD3154	NLD3198
NLD3209	NLD3215	NLD3219	NLD3245
NLD3270	NLD3291	NLD3305	NLD3325
NOR3390	NOR3447	POL3499	POL3507
POL3508	POL3519	POL3544	PRT3579
SVK3611	SVK3612	SVK3638	SVK3640
SWE3648	SWE3658	SWE3672	SWE3728
SWE3749	SWE3771	SWE3786	SWE3796
SWE3865			

FORMAL EDUCATION - EDUCATION FORMELLE

AUT0021	AUT0024	AUT0033	AUT0056
AUT0085	AUT0086	AUT0089	BEL0123
BEL0129	BEL0145	BEL0156	BEL0224
BEL0317	BEL0323	BEL0341	BEL0359
BEL0361	BEL0390	CHE0432	CHE0434
CHE0456	CHE0562	CHE0566	CHE0570
CHE0586	CHE0600	CHE0628	CHE0640
CHE0645	CHE0649	CHE0655	CHE0660
CHE0665	CHE0673	CHE0681	CHE0682
CHE0689	CHE0713	CHE0730	CHE0753
CHE0772	CHE0799	CHE0804	CHE0805
CHE0819	DEU0928	DEU0933	DEU0954
DEU0980	DEU0983	DEU1017	DEU1063
DEU1065	DEU1129	DEU1149	DEU1178
DNK1214	DNK1218	DNK1227	DNK1243
DNK1275	DNK1281	DNK1283	DNK1312
DNK1335	DNK1342	DNK1405	ESP1406
ESP1427	ESP1437	ESP1455	ESP1479
ESP1486	ESP1510	ESP1517	FIN1545
FIN1559	FIN1580	FRA1627	FRA1645
FRA1647	FRA1651	FRA1661	FRA1664

See: *How to Use the Directory*, page 11.

FRA1672	FRA1675	FRA1699	FRA1724
FRA1731	FRA1738	FRA1752	FRA1761
FRA1769	FRA1785	FRA1787	FRA1825
FRA1827	FRA1841	FRA1848	FRA1849
FRA1856	FRA1869	FRA1879	FRA1886
FRA1889	FRA1930	FRA1935	FRA1937
FRA1946	FRA1966	FRA1957	FRA1966
FRA1992	FRA2016	FRA2021	FRA2039
FRA2062	FRA2100	FRA2103	FRA2106
FRA2131	FRA2140	FRA2145	FRA2150
FRA2159	FRA2170	GBR2174	GBR2178
GBR2181	GBR2186	GBR2228	GBR2231
GBR2233	GBR2238	GBR2242	GBR2264
GBR2265	GBR2269	GBR2277	GBR2278
GBR2281	GBR2306	GBR2341	GBR2349
GBR2371	GBR2378	GBR2379	GBR2380
GBR2382	GBR2383	GBR2415	GBR2423
GBR2428	GBR2436	GBR2445	GBR2452
GBR2455	GBR2463	GBR2464	GBR2466
GBR2467	GBR2468	GBR2471	GBR2481
GBR2522	GBR2550	GBR2551	GBR2553
GRC2586	HUN2607	HUN2610	HUN2643
IRL2686	IRL2688	IRL2689	IRL2691
IRL2697	IRL2702	IRL2717	IRL2720
ITA2758	ITA2762	ITA2782	ITA2799
ITA2801	ITA2810	ITA2826	ITA2840
ITA2842	ITA2846	ITA2857	ITA2868
ITA2883	ITA2889	ITA2896	ITA2914
ITA2900	ITA2914	LUX2976	LUX2980
LUX2983	LUX2995	LUX2997	MLT3016
MLT3017	MLT3028	NLD3056	NLD3067
NLD3069	NLD3070	NLD3078	NLD3083
NLD3089	NLD3105	NLD3117	NLD3138
NLD3139	NLD3142	NLD3147	NLD3153
NLD3154	NLD3159	NLD3163	NLD3209
NLD3212	NLD3215	NLD3219	NLD3230
NLD3250	NLD3269	NLD3280	NLD3270
NLD3291	NLD3325	NLD3329	NOR3390
NOR3395	NOR3460	NOR3465	NOR3467
NOR3473	POL3507	POL3508	PRT3579
PRT3588	PRT3590	PRT3594	PRT3597
PRT3603	PRT3605	SVK3611	SVK3612
SVK3622	SVK3638	SVK3640	SWE3653
SWE3661	SWE3675	SWE3679	SWE3712
SWE3737	SWE3761	SWE3771	SWE3796
SWE3809	SWE3823	SWE3827	SWE3853
SWE3859			

FUND RAISING - COLLECTE DE FONDS

AUT0003	AUT0021	AUT0022	AUT0026
AUT0030	AUT0033	AUT0051	AUT0072
AUT0076	AUT0085	AUT0086	AUT0091
BEL0096	BEL0104	BEL0105	BEL0110
BEL0145	BEL0148	BEL0155	BEL0169
BEL0182	BEL0201	BEL0224	BEL0233
BEL0245	BEL0270	BEL0282	BEL0314
BEL0323	BEL0341	BEL0351	BEL0352
BEL0353	BEL0358	BEL0359	BEL0361
BEL0390	CHE0410	CHE0411	CHE0417
CHE0434	CHE0438	CHE0455	CHE0462
CHE0467	CHE0475	CHE0506	CHE0515
CHE0519	CHE0546	CHE0562	CHE0566
CHE0570	CHE0586	CHE0600	CHE0602
CHE0604	CHE0619	CHE0630	CHE0637
CHE0645	CHE0659	CHE0687	CHE0689
CHE0691	CHE0693	CHE0701	CHE0707
CHE0713	CHE0730	CHE0734	CHE0742
CHE0750	CHE0754	CHE0755	CHE0756
CHE0772	CHE0788	CHE0789	CHE0796
CHE0809	CYP0832	CZE0839	DEU0933
DEU0954	DEU0957	DEU0968	DEU0983
DEU0989	DEU0993	DEU1001	DEU1002
DEU1004	DEU1017	DEU1022	DEU1038
DEU1044	DEU1063	DEU1114	DEU1138
DEU1143	DEU1149	DEU1167	DEU1178
DEU1187	DNK1214	DNK1216	DNK1218
DNK1222	DNK1227	DNK1243	DNK1245
DNK1266	DNK1304	DNK1316	DNK1351
DNK1366	DNK1372	DNK1405	ESP1413
ESP1435	ESP1442	ESP1455	ESP1457
ESP1486	ESP1491	ESP1505	ESP1507
ESP1510	ESP1517	FIN1544	FIN1545
FIN1549	FIN1554	FIN1559	FIN1570
FIN1585	FIN1588	FIN1591	
FIN1599	FRA1612	FRA1614	FRA1644
FRA1645	FRA1647	FRA1661	FRA1663
FRA1664	FRA1667	FRA1672	FRA1690
FRA1691	FRA1703	FRA1724	FRA1738

FRA1739	FRA1760	FRA1761	FRA1769
FRA1771	FRA1778	FRA1785	FRA1786
FRA1787	FRA1789	FRA1824	FRA1843
FRA1849	FRA1850	FRA1855	FRA1871
FRA1880	FRA1889	FRA1891	FRA1914
FRA1928	FRA1929	FRA1930	FRA1938
FRA1939	FRA1957	FRA1957	FRA1978
FRA1980	FRA1990	FRA2016	FRA2053
FRA2080	FRA2081	FRA2086	FRA2092
FRA2096	FRA2116	FRA2117	FRA2119
FRA2131	FRA2137	FRA2140	FRA2145
FRA2149	FRA2152	FRA2159	FRA2170
GBR2175	GBR2178	GBR2180	GBR2185
GBR2186	GBR2197	GBR2201	GBR2210
GBR2213	GBR2226	GBR2228	GBR2230
GBR2238	GBR2247	GBR2248	GBR2259
GBR2264	GBR2266	GBR2274	GBR2277
GBR2278	GBR2289	GBR2290	GBR2297
GBR2302	GBR2310	GBR2312	GBR2318
GBR2321	GBR2333	GBR2346	GBR2348
GBR2349	GBR2350	GBR2351	GBR2353
GBR2358	GBR2371	GBR2372	GBR2375
GBR2376	GBR2378	GBR2382	GBR2383
GBR2385	GBR2390	GBR2396	GBR2413
GBR2423	GBR2428	GBR2436	GBR2445
GBR2456	GBR2464	GBR2466	GBR2477
GBR2481	GBR2483	GBR2492	GBR2500
GBR2508	GBR2509	GBR2513	GBR2517
GBR2522	GBR2524	GBR2525	GBR2532
GBR2535	GBR2537	GBR2550	GBR2551
GRC2572	GRC2586	HUN2609	HUN2610
HUN2627	HUN2637	IRL2688	IRL2689
IRL2691	IRL2697	IRL2714	IRL2730
IRL2732	IRL2733	ISL2740	ITA2758
ITA2762	ITA2770	ITA2803	ITA2810
ITA2835	ITA2837	ITA2857	ITA2858
ITA2879	ITA2886	ITA2888	ITA2889
ITA2894	ITA2900	ITA2907	ITA2911
ITA2914	ITA2920	ITA2921	ITA2923
LUX2946	LUX2948	LUX2967	LUX2968
LUX2969	LUX2982	LUX2983	LUX2986
LUX2993	LUX2995	LUX2997	LUX3006
MLT3021	NLD3051	NLD3056	NLD3067
NLD3070	NLD3078	NLD3089	NLD3105
NLD3117	NLD3149	NLD3154	NLD3159
NLD3198	NLD3199	NLD3209	NLD3212
NLD3231	NLD3232	NLD3244	NLD3245
NLD3256	NLD3269	NLD3291	NLD3295
NLD3297	NLD3300	NLD3301	NLD3302
NLD3323	NLD3325	NLD3361	NOR3371
NOR3372	NOR3387	NOR3404	NOR3412
NOR3453	NOR3460	NOR3467	PRT3588
PRT3594	PRT3599	PRT3605	SVK3608
SVK3611	SVK3622	SVK3638	SVK3640
SWE3648	SWE3653	SWE3655	SWE3661
SWE3679	SWE3685	SWE3702	SWE3712
SWE3730	SWE3737	SWE3749	SWE3753
SWE3761	SWE3763	SWE3768	SWE3769
SWE3783	SWE3787	SWE3796	SWE3813
SWE3822	SWE3826	SWE3834	SWE3853
SWE3855	SWE3857		

INFORMATION AND DOCUMENTATION SERVICES, DATA BASES - SERVICES D'INFORMATION ET DE DOCUMENTATION, BASES DE DONNEES

AUT0020	AUT0026	AUT0056	AUT0060
AUT0079	AUT0085	AUT0086	BEL0123
BEL0127	BEL0129	BEL0149	BEL0155
BEL0164	BEL0237	BEL0267	BEL0335
BEL0359	BEL0361	BEL0379	BEL0390
BEL0393	BEL0396	CHE0406	CHE0432
CHE0434	CHE0456	CHE0494	CHE0501
CHE0506	CHE0534	CHE0550	CHE0562
CHE0566	CHE0568	CHE0609	CHE0624
CHE0640	CHE0645	CHE0649	CHE0664
CHE0665	CHE0673	CHE0689	CHE0742
CHE0753	CHE0756	CHE0763	CHE0796
CHE0800	CHE0819	DEU0944	DEU0968
DEU0975	DEU0980	DEU0989	DEU0990
DEU1002	DEU1020	DEU1063	DEU1076
DEU1086	DEU1090	DEU1091	DEU1097
DEU1103	DEU1129	DEU1138	DEU1149
DEU1184	DEU1192	DNK1218	DNK1248
DNK1281	DNK1287	DNK1292	DNK1335
DNK1375	DNK1376	DNK1398	ESP1407
ESP1430	ESP1431	ESP1434	ESP1455
ESP1461	ESP1479	ESP1486	ESP1507
ESP1511	FIN1545	FIN1546	FIN1548

FIN1559	FIN1591	FIN1604	FRA1647
FRA1672	FRA1701	FRA1737	FRA1752
FRA1785	FRA1787	FRA1797	FRA1800
FRA1808	FRA1810	FRA1811	FRA1818
FRA1827	FRA1841	FRA1846	FRA1871
FRA1889	FRA1907	FRA1935	FRA1956
FRA1988	FRA1990	FRA2002	FRA2004
FRA2018	FRA2021	FRA2039	FRA2076
FRA2103	FRA2104	FRA2106	FRA2122
FRA2131	FRA2140	FRA2152	FRA2159
GBR2174	GBR2178	GBR2185	GBR2226
GBR2231	GBR2238	GBR2264	GBR2265
GBR2278	GBR2281	GBR2340	GBR2346
GBR2353	GBR2371	GBR2378	GBR2379
GBR2383	GBR2387	GBR2396	GBR2402
GBR2415	GBR2423	GBR2435	GBR2438
GBR2445	GBR2452	GBR2455	GBR2456
GBR2464	GBR2466	GBR2477	GBR2522
GBR2537	GRC2572	HUN2598	
HUN2610	HUN2620	HUN2622	HUN2624
HUN2637	HUN2643	IRL2686	IRL2697
IRL2698	IRL2702	IRL2705	IRL2714
IRL2730	ITA2762	ITA2773	ITA2780
ITA2798	ITA2799	ITA2801	ITA2804
ITA2810	ITA2814	ITA2822	ITA2840
ITA2857	ITA2860	ITA2868	ITA2873
ITA2880	ITA2888	ITA2889	ITA2890
ITA2896	ITA2900	ITA2907	ITA2908
ITA2911	ITA2913	ITA2914	ITA2923
LUX2937	LUX2962	LUX2980	LUX2983
LUX2997	NLD3051	NLD3056	NLD3058
NLD3067	NLD3069	NLD3070	NLD3077
NLD3078	NLD3083	NLD3089	NLD3095
NLD3096	NLD3105	NLD3135	NLD3138
NLD3139	NLD3142	NLD3147	NLD3154
NLD3155	NLD3198	NLD3230	NLD3232
NLD3252	NLD3270	NLD3295	NLD3301
NLD3302	NLD3305	NLD3325	NLD3334
NLD3352	NLD3355	NLD3361	NOR3390
NOR3467	POL3499	POL3507	POL3508
POL3519	SVK3611	SVK3638	SWE3648
SWE3658	SWE3728	SWE3735	SWE3744
SWE3768	SWE3769	SWE3774	SWE3807
SWE3816	SWE3821	SWE3826	SWE3865
TUR3883			

INFORMATION CAMPAIGNS, EXHIBITIONS - CAMPAGNES D'INFORMATION, EXPOSITIONS

AUT0020	AUT0030	AUT0033	AUT0085
AUT0086	AUT0091	BEL0096	BEL0101
BEL0123	BEL0129	BEL0148	BEL0192
BEL0267	BEL0282	BEL0289	BEL0323
BEL0351	BEL0352	BEL0361	BEL0390
BEL0392	CHE0432	CHE0434	CHE0456
CHE0466	CHE0467	CHE0501	CHE0541
CHE0546	CHE0562	CHE0566	CHE0568
CHE0645	CHE0659	CHE0664	CHE0669
CHE0689	CHE0756	CHE0765	CHE0796
CHE0800	CHE0804	CHE0805	CHE0819
CZE0905	DEU0917	DEU0955	DEU0980
DEU0983	DEU1019	DEU1022	DEU1063
DEU1149	DEU1164	DEU1178	DEU1187
DNK1214	DNK1245	DNK1260	DNK1275
DNK1281	DNK1285	DNK1287	DNK1304
DNK1307	DNK1312	DNK1317	DNK1351
DNK1372	DNK1375	DNK1376	DNK1398
DNK1405	ESP1407	ESP1436	ESP1457
ESP1486	ESP1505	ESP1507	ESP1510
ESP1517	ESP1524	FIN1545	FIN1549
FIN1553	FIN1559	FIN1577	FIN1591
FIN1604	FRA1619	FRA1647	FRA1651
FRA1672	FRA1738	FRA1739	FRA1785
FRA1787	FRA1797	FRA1848	FRA1869
FRA1876	FRA1889	FRA1920	FRA1928
FRA1938	FRA1956	FRA1957	FRA1990
FRA1992	FRA2002	FRA2021	FRA2039
FRA2068	FRA2106	FRA2116	FRA2131
FRA2140	FRA2152	FRA2158	FRA2159
FRA2170	GBR2210	GBR2231	GBR2238
GBR2248	GBR2259	GBR2264	GBR2265
GBR2269	GBR2277	GBR2278	GBR2281
GBR2290	GBR2312	GBR2350	GBR2353
GBR2358	GBR2371	GBR2378	GBR2383
GBR2387	GBR2396	GBR2402	GBR2423
GBR2445	GBR2452	GBR2466	GBR2471
GBR2477	GBR2498	GBR2503	GBR2535
GBR2545	GBR2553	GRC2572	HUN2607
HUN2620	HUN2622	HUN2624	IRL2686
IRL2688	IRL2697	IRL2707	IRL2714

IRL2730	ITA2758	ITA2770	ITA2780
ITA2791	ITA2799	ITA2801	ITA2804
ITA2810	ITA2820	ITA2837	ITA2886
ITA2888	ITA2890	ITA2896	ITA2900
ITA2911	ITA2914	ITA2920	LUX2954
LUX2968	LUX2980	LUX2982	LUX2993
LUX2995	LUX3006	MLT3016	MLT3017
NLD3051	NLD3056	NLD3067	NLD3078
NLD3083	NLD3089	NLD3105	NLD3138
NLD3198	NLD3209	NLD3232	NLD3291
NLD3320	NLD3323	NLD3325	NOR3371
NOR3390	NOR3418	NOR3440	NOR3467
POL3499	POL3507	POL3519	PRT3579
PRT3586	PRT3594	PRT3605	SVK3611
SVK3612	SVK3638	SVK3640	SWE3661
SWE3685	SWE3702	SWE3704	SWE3728
SWE3730	SWE3737	SWE3749	SWE3753
SWE3761	SWE3763	SWE3768	SWE3769
SWE3774	SWE3816	SWE3821	SWE3822
SWE3865	TUR3883		

LOBBYING, ADVOCACY - LOBBYING, PLAIDOYER

AUT0020	AUT0024	AUT0033	AUT0056
AUT0086	BEL0096	BEL0156	BEL0186
BEL0199	BEL0218	BEL0224	BEL0267
BEL0282	BEL0323	BEL0351	BEL0361
BEL0399	CHE0434	CHE0467	CHE0479
CHE0534	CHE0550	CHE0562	CHE0566
CHE0568	CHE0570	CHE0604	CHE0642
CHE0645	CHE0687	CHE0689	CHE0755
CHE0765	CHE0819	DEU0954	DEU0983
DEU1002	DEU1004	DEU1055	DEU1097
DEU1149	DEU1164	DNK1281	DNK1312
DNK1335	DNK1375	DNK1376	DNK1405
ESP1455	ESP1479	ESP1505	FIN1545
FIN1559	FIN1570	FIN1577	FIN1588
FRA1661	FRA1785	FRA1797	FRA1824
FRA1841	FRA1843	FRA1876	FRA1889
FRA1946	FRA1956	FRA1957	FRA2002
FRA2004	FRA2039	FRA2106	FRA2116
FRA2126	FRA2159	GBR2174	GBR2178
GBR2202	GBR2210	GBR2215	GBR2222
GBR2238	GBR2242	GBR2264	GBR2269
GBR2281	GBR2371	GBR2376	GBR2383
GBR2390	GBR2396	GBR2423	GBR2445
GBR2464	GBR2481	GBR2503	GBR2517
GBR2522	GBR2537	GBR2545	GBR2546
GBR2551	GBR2553	GRC2572	GRC2586
HUN2610	HUN2643	IRL2689	IRL2691
IRL2705	IRL2707	IRL2714	ITA2782
ITA2810	ITA2820	ITA2888	ITA2888
ITA2913	ITA2914	LUX2957	LUX2997
MLT3016	MLT3017	MLT3036	NLD3067
NLD3070	NLD3078	NLD3105	NLD3117
NLD3139	NLD3142	NLD3147	NLD3198
NLD3199	NLD3209	NLD3230	NLD3232
NLD3242	NLD3291	NLD3301	NLD3305
NLD3325	NOR3372	NOR3390	NOR3467
POL3499	PRT3584	PRT3594	PRT3605
SVK3634	SVK3638	SWE3655	SWE3655
SWE3661	SWE3749	SWE3771	SWE3799
SWE3821	SWE3853	TUR3883	

NETWORKING, ELECTRONIC TELECOMMUNICATIONS - RESEAUX, TELECOMMUNICATIONS ELECTRONIQUES

AUT0020	BEL0224	BEL0361	CHE0434
CHE0562	CHE0568	CHE0586	CHE0642
CHE0645	CHE0689	CHE0817	CHE0819
DEU0955	DEU0990	DEU1002	DEU1065
DEU1097	DEU1149	DEU1210	DNK1281
DNK1375	ESP1434	FIN1545	FIN1570
FIN1591	FIN1604	FRA1644	FRA1889
FRA2068	FRA2106	FRA2159	GBR2174
GBR2226	GBR2231	GBR2265	GBR2278
GBR2285	GBR2313	GBR2340	GBR2346
GBR2348	GBR2351	GBR2371	GBR2378
GBR2383	GBR2387	GBR2424	GBR2438
GBR2498	GBR2545	GBR2550	GBR2553
GBR2554	HUN2610	HUN2620	HUN2624
HUN2637	ITA2773	ITA2798	ITA2826
ITA2860	ITA2914	LUX2997	MLT3021
NLD3067	NLD3070	NLD3077	NLD3105
NLD3139	NLD3142	NLD3154	NLD3215
NOR3390	NOR3467	POL3499	POL3507
POL3508	SVK3611	SVK3622	SVK3638
SVK3640	SWE3702	SWE3787	TUR3883

OTHER - AUTRE

CHE0434	FRA1629	FRA1785	FRA1966
FRA2111	GBR2240	GBR2358	GBR2371
GBR2387	NLD3096	NLD3117	NLD3183

PUBLISHING, AUDIOVISUAL MATERIALS, EDUCATIONAL MATERIALS - EDITION, DOCUMENTS AUDIOVISUELS, DOCUMENTS EDUCATIFS

AUT0020	AUT0026	AUT0032	AUT0051
AUT0056	AUT0076	AUT0085	AUT0086
BEL0096	BEL0101	BEL0120	BEL0123
BEL0127	BEL0148	BEL0149	BEL0155
BEL0224	BEL0245	BEL0282	BEL0284
BEL0306	BEL0314	BEL0323	BEL0361
BEL0390	BEL0392	BEL0393	BEL0396
CHE0403	CHE0406	CHE0432	CHE0434
CHE0456	CHE0483	CHE0501	CHE0562
CHE0566	CHE0568	CHE0638	CHE0645
CHE0649	CHE0689	CHE0693	CHE0730
CHE0756	CHE0763	CHE0817	CHE0819
DEU0944	DEU0968	DEU0975	DEU0980
DEU0989	DEU1016	DEU1017	DEU1020
DEU1022	DEU1055	DEU1076	DEU1095
DEU1097	DEU1103	DEU1129	DEU1149
DEU1180	DEU1187	DEU1198	DNK1214
DNK1216	DNK1218	DNK1243	DNK1260
DNK1273	DNK1281	DNK1304	DNK1316
DNK1317	DNK1335	DNK1375	DNK1376
DNK1397	DNK1405	ESP1434	ESP1435
ESP1455	ESP1457	ESP1461	ESP1468
ESP1475	ESP1479	ESP1488	ESP1491
ESP1505	ESP1507	ESP1510	ESP1517
FIN1536	FIN1545	FIN1546	FIN1548
FIN1557	FIN1559	FIN1604	FRA1612
FRA1627	FRA1642	FRA1644	FRA1645
FRA1661	FRA1667	FRA1668	FRA1713
FRA1715	FRA1752	FRA1778	FRA1787
FRA1795	FRA1810	FRA1836	FRA1843
FRA1869	FRA1886	FRA1889	FRA1893
FRA1897	FRA1907	FRA1920	FRA1935
FRA1938	FRA1956	FRA1957	FRA1983
FRA1986	FRA1990	FRA2002	FRA2004
FRA2039	FRA2042	FRA2068	FRA2076
FRA2086	FRA2104	FRA2106	FRA2131
FRA2140	FRA2159	GBR2174	GBR2178
GBR2181	GBR2185	GBR2226	GBR2231
GBR2238	GBR2247	GBR2248	GBR2264
GBR2265	GBR2271	GBR2278	GBR2281
GBR2312	GBR2318	GBR2340	GBR2341
GBR2353	GBR2358	GBR2371	GBR2378
GBR2380	GBR2383	GBR2387	GBR2402
GBR2415	GBR2423	GBR2424	GBR2436
GBR2445	GBR2452	GBR2455	GBR2464
GBR2466	GBR2467	GBR2471	GBR2477
GBR2485	GBR2499	GBR2501	GBR2503
GBR2517	GBR2522	GBR2525	GBR2535
GBR2545	GBR2546	GBR2550	GBR2552
GBR2554	GBR2561	GRC2572	GRC2585
HUN2607	HUN2610	HUN2620	HUN2620
HUN2622	HUN2624	HUN2627	HUN2637
IRL2697	IRL2698	IRL2702	IRL2730
IRL2733	IRL2757	ITA2758	ITA2762
ITA2780	ITA2782	ITA2786	ITA2798
ITA2799	ITA2801	ITA2803	ITA2810
ITA2811	ITA2835	ITA2837	ITA2840
ITA2842	ITA2846	ITA2858	ITA2868
ITA2886	ITA2888	ITA2896	ITA2900
ITA2907	ITA2908	ITA2914	ITA2916
LUX2976	LUX2980	LUX2997	LUX3006
MLT3016	MLT3021	NLD3056	NLD3067
NLD3069	NLD3070	NLD3077	NLD3078
NLD3083	NLD3089	NLD3105	NLD3138
NLD3142	NLD3154	NLD3163	NLD3190
NLD3196	NLD3198	NLD3212	NLD3215
NLD3216	NLD3219	NLD3230	NLD3232
NLD3270	NLD3301	NLD3302	NLD3305
NLD3320	NLD3325	NLD3354	NOR3389
NOR3390	NOR3418	NOR3429	NOR3440
NOR3467	POL3499	POL3507	POL3508
POL3519	SVK3611	SVK3622	SVK3638
SVK3640	SWE3648	SWE3712	SWE3728
SWE3737	SWE3763	SWE3768	SWE3769
SWE3777	SWE3787	SWE3816	SWE3821
SWE3826	SWE3865	TUR3883	

EMERGENCY RELIEF, REFUGEES, HUMANITARIAN ASSISTANCE - SECOURS D'URGENCE, REFUGIES, AIDE HUMANITAIRE

BROADCASTING, CULTURAL EVENTS - RADIODIFFUSION, MANIFESTATIONS CULTURELLES

BEL0123	BEL0129	BEL0147	BEL0192
BEL0340	CHE0434	CHE0491	CHE0524
CHE0534	CHE0624	CHE0689	CHE0819
CZE0904	DEU1022	DEU1053	DNK1376
ESP1475	ESP1475	ESP1506	FIN1553
FRA1614	FRA1615	FRA1631	FRA1676
FRA1771	FRA1778	FRA1785	FRA1791
FRA1793	FRA1808	FRA1889	FRA1904
FRA1910	FRA1956	FRA1957	FRA2002
FRA2047	FRA2102	FRA2159	GBR2175
GBR2222	GBR2226	GBR2238	GBR2248
GBR2345	GBR2371	GBR2378	GBR2423
GBR2464	GBR2498	GBR2501	GBR2545
GRC2586	HUN2631	HUN2644	ITA2773
ITA2774	ITA2785	ITA2798	ITA2820
ITA2826	ITA2838	ITA2841	ITA2855
ITA2907	LUX2955	LUX2956	LUX2976
LUX2992	NLD3190	NLD3232	NLD3253
NOR3372	NOR3390	NOR3467	SVK3634
SWE3761	SWE3830		

CONFERENCES, SEMINARS, WORKSHOPS, TRAINING ACTIVITIES - CONFERENCES, SEMINAIRES, ATELIERS, ACTIVITES DE FORMATION

BEL0107	BEL0123	BEL0129	BEL0133
BEL0152	BEL0155	BEL0168	BEL0192
BEL0237	BEL0297	BEL0318	BEL0338
BEL0340	BEL0345	CHE0417	CHE0420
CHE0434	CHE0467	CHE0494	CHE0562
CHE0586	CHE0603	CHE0637	CHE0642
CHE0651	CHE0669	CHE0682	CHE0684
CHE0687	CHE0689	CHE0711	CHE0741
CHE0755	CHE0814	CHE0819	CHE0823
CZE0859	CZE0897	CZE0904	DEU0939
DEU0944	DEU0983	DEU0990	DEU1004
DEU1006	DEU1053	DEU1054	DEU1063
DEU1064	DEU1110	DEU1141	DEU1198
DNK1248	DNK1304	DNK1305	DNK1376
DNK1398	ESP1430	ESP1435	ESP1441
ESP1443	ESP1445	ESP1450	ESP1451
ESP1456	ESP1475	ESP1493	ESP1506
FIN1536	FIN1553	FIN1572	FIN1594
FRA1610	FRA1614	FRA1615	FRA1619
FRA1640	FRA1647	FRA1661	FRA1685
FRA1778	FRA1785	FRA1788	FRA1791
FRA1793	FRA1808	FRA1813	FRA1833
FRA1850	FRA1862	FRA1887	FRA1888
FRA1889	FRA1904	FRA1957	FRA2002
FRA2004	FRA2044	FRA2047	FRA2053
FRA2057	FRA2070	FRA2102	FRA2117
FRA2159	GBR2174	GBR2175	GBR2176
GBR2185	GBR2222	GBR2238	GBR2242
GBR2248	GBR2265	GBR2269	GBR2279
GBR2292	GBR2303	GBR2325	GBR2356
GBR2371	GBR2378	GBR2387	GBR2388
GBR2392	GBR2396	GBR2408	GBR2422
GBR2423	GBR2445	GBR2448	GBR2464
GBR2481	GBR2498	GBR2500	GBR2503
GBR2545	GRC2576	GRC2579	GRC2584
GRC2586	HUN2631	HUN2644	IRL2688
IRL2689	IRL2712	IRL2716	IRL2717
ISL2736	ITA2747	ITA2766	ITA2773
ITA2780	ITA2791	ITA2798	ITA2801
ITA2809	ITA2816	ITA2820	ITA2824
ITA2826	ITA2835	ITA2841	ITA2855
ITA2857	ITA2860	ITA2866	ITA2898
ITA2900	ITA2901	ITA2902	ITA2905
ITA2907	ITA2911	ITA2916	ITA2942
LUX2955	LUX2956	LUX2992	LUX2997
NLD3050	NLD3064	NLD3078	NLD3083
NLD3102	NLD3104	NLD3174	NLD3232
NLD3277	NLD3301	NOR3371	NOR3390
NOR3435	NOR3455	NOR3467	POL3508
POL3519	PRT3549	PRT3573	PRT3590
SVK3608	SVK3612	SWE3648	SWE3679
SWE3707	SWE3744	SWE3749	SWE3769
SWE3776	SWE3807	SWE3816	SWE3830
TUR3883			

See: *How to Use the Directory*, page 11.

EXCHANGES, TWINNING, LINKING - ECHANGES, PARRAINAGE, JUMELAGE

AUT0033	BEL0123	BEL0129	BEL0147
BEL0192	BEL0198	BEL0303	BEL0340
CHE0448	CHE0444	CHE0562	CHE0595
CHE0689	CHE0730	CHE0819	CZE0857
CZE0904	DEU0939	DEU0983	DEU0990
DEU1141	DNK1304	DNK1307	ESP1445
ESP1451	FRA1638	FRA1661	FRA1715
FRA1746	FRA1778	FRA1785	FRA1791
FRA1793	FRA1850	FRA1855	FRA1887
FRA1889	FRA1904	FRA1938	FRA1956
FRA2044	FRA2047	FRA2057	FRA2081
FRA2102	FRA2140	FRA2159	GBR2371
GBR2379	GBR2423	GBR2445	GBR2448
GBR2481	GRC2579	GRC2584	HUN2644
ITA2765	ITA2775	ITA2785	ITA2791
ITA2838	ITA2903	ITA2905	LIE2927
NLD3078	NLD3102	NLD3137	NLD3232
NOR3390	NOR3467	POL3508	POL3519
SVK3612	SVK3626	SWE3744	SWE3749
SWE3771	SWE3830	SWE3864	

FORMAL EDUCATION - EDUCATION FORMELLE

BEL0123	BEL0129	BEL0192	CHE0434
CHE0562	CHE0660	CHE0682	CHE0689
CHE0759	CHE0819	CZE0896	CZE0904
CZE0907	DEU0954	DEU0983	DEU1141
DNK1222	DNK1262	ESP1451	ESP1486
FRA1661	FRA1769	FRA1825	FRA1889
FRA1889	FRA1904	FRA1937	FRA1956
FRA1957	FRA2044	FRA2102	GBR2238
GBR2265	GBR2269	GBR2371	GBR2378
GBR2379	GBR2392	GBR2408	GBR2423
GBR2436	GBR2445	GBR2448	GBR2464
GBR2467	GBR2468	GBR2484	GRC2579
GRC2584	HUN2644	IRL2688	IRL2689
IRL2691	IRL2716	IRL2717	IRL2726
ITA2773	ITA2782	ITA2798	ITA2813
ITA2816	ITA2826	ITA2855	ITA2857
ITA2868	ITA2902	NLD3050	NLD3078
NLD3083	NLD3102	NLD3232	NOR3390
NOR3467	POL3521	PRT3590	PRT3597
SVK3612	SWE3679	SWE3712	SWE3771
SWE3830			

FUND RAISING - COLLECTE DE FONDS

AUT0033	AUT0035	AUT0076	AUT0085
AUT0089	AUT0091	BEL0107	BEL0123
BEL0147	BEL0168	BEL0169	BEL0192
BEL0198	BEL0201	BEL0224	BEL0297
BEL0299	BEL0316	BEL0318	BEL0323
BEL0328	BEL0338	BEL0350	BEL0352
BEL0353	BEL0355	BEL0358	BEL0359
BEL0362	BEL0368	CHE0409	CHE0410
CHE0417	CHE0420	CHE0434	CHE0448
CHE0467	CHE0477	CHE0485	CHE0491
CHE0506	CHE0519	CHE0524	CHE0562
CHE0586	CHE0630	CHE0637	CHE0684
CHE0687	CHE0689	CHE0693	CHE0711
CHE0730	CHE0750	CHE0755	CHE0756
CHE0764	CHE0796	CHE0814	CHE0819
CHE0823	CYP0832	CZE0859	CZE0896
CZE0904	DEU0918	DEU0922	DEU0954
DEU0957	DEU0968	DEU0978	DEU0983
DEU0989	DEU0991	DEU0993	DEU0994
DEU1001	DEU1004	DEU1006	DEU1022
DEU1063	DEU1064	DEU1066	DEU1106
DEU1110	DEU1132	DEU1141	DEU1149
DEU1176	DNK1214	DNK1218	DNK1222
DNK1227	DNK1248	DNK1259	DNK1262
DNK1266	DNK1292	DNK1304	DNK1305
DNK1366	ESP1435	ESP1445	ESP1450
ESP1451	ESP1486	ESP1491	ESP1506
ESP1510	ESP1528	FIN1549	FIN1580
FIN1585	FIN1591	FRA1610	FRA1614
FRA1615	FRA1617	FRA1647	FRA1651
FRA1661	FRA1664	FRA1667	FRA1685
FRA1691	FRA1704	FRA1739	FRA1741
FRA1769	FRA1771	FRA1778	FRA1785
FRA1787	FRA1793	FRA1808	FRA1808
FRA1811	FRA1824	FRA1825	FRA1850
FRA1855	FRA1866	FRA1871	FRA1880
FRA1888	FRA1889	FRA1904	FRA1910
FRA1929	FRA1938	FRA1942	FRA1957
FRA1991	FRA2041	FRA2047	FRA2053
FRA2077	FRA2080	FRA2081	FRA2086
FRA2091	FRA2102	FRA2116	FRA2117

FRA2119	FRA2137	FRA2140	FRA2148
FRA2149	FRA2159	FRA2164	GBR2174
GBR2175	GBR2176	GBR2183	GBR2186
GBR2197	GBR2213	GBR2222	GBR2226
GBR2228	GBR2230	GBR2238	GBR2240
GBR2242	GBR2244	GBR2248	GBR2259
GBR2266	GBR2276	GBR2282	GBR2289
GBR2292	GBR2310	GBR2324	GBR2325
GBR2348	GBR2350	GBR2371	GBR2372
GBR2378	GBR2385	GBR2390	GBR2392
GBR2419	GBR2423	GBR2436	GBR2445
GBR2463	GBR2464	GBR2475	GBR2481
GBR2483	GBR2493	GBR2498	GBR2500
GBR2522	GBR2523	GBR2524	GBR2526
GBR2530	GBR2552	GBR2555	GRC2571
GRC2572	GRC2573	GRC2579	GRC2585
GRC2586	HUN2631	HUN2644	IRL2688
IRL2689	IRL2691	IRL2714	IRL2716
IRL2726	IRL2733	ITA2747	ITA2755
ITA2756	ITA2766	ITA2767	ITA2773
ITA2774	ITA2775	ITA2782	ITA2785
ITA2791	ITA2809	ITA2813	ITA2814
ITA2816	ITA2820	ITA2822	ITA2824
ITA2826	ITA2829	ITA2832	ITA2834
ITA2835	ITA2838	ITA2841	ITA2855
ITA2857	ITA2873	ITA2874	ITA2879
ITA2888	ITA2889	ITA2890	ITA2900
ITA2901	ITA2902	ITA2905	ITA2911
ITA2912	ITA2916	ITA2921	LIE2930
LUX2936	LUX2942	LUX2955	LUX2956
LUX2958	LUX2959	LUX2982	LUX2992
LUX2993	LUX2995	LUX2997	MLT3036
NLD3050	NLD3078	NLD3102	NLD3104
NLD3137	NLD3186	NLD3199	NLD3201
NLD3231	NLD3232	NLD3253	NLD3254
NLD3256	NLD3263	NLD3277	NLD3297
NLD3300	NLD3301	NLD3303	NLD3361
NOR3371	NOR3372	NOR3381	NOR3390
NOR3394	NOR3412	NOR3435	NOR3467
POL3544	PRT3549	PRT3552	PRT3555
PRT3596	PRT3603	SVK3608	SVK3626
SVK3634	SWE3648	SWE3674	SWE3679
SWE3707	SWE3712	SWE3738	SWE3744
SWE3749	SWE3761	SWE3763	SWE3769
SWE3813	SWE3826	SWE3830	SWE3853
SWE3854	SWE3857	SWE3859	SWE3864

INFORMATION AND DOCUMENTATION SERVICES, DATA BASES - SERVICES D'INFORMATION ET DE DOCUMENTATION, BASES DE DONNEES

AUT0020	AUT0035	AUT0060	AUT0079
AUT0085	BEL0107	BEL0116	BEL0123
BEL0129	BEL0155	BEL0164	BEL0168
BEL0192	BEL0237	BEL0297	BEL0299
BEL0316	BEL0318	BEL0338	BEL0345
BEL0390	BEL0393	CHE0420	CHE0434
CHE0494	CHE0506	CHE0534	CHE0562
CHE0603	CHE0624	CHE0687	CHE0689
CHE0711	CHE0756	CHE0759	CHE0763
CHE0796	CHE0814	CZE0857	CZE0904
DEU0944	DEU0968	DEU0990	DEU1063
DEU1064	DEU1076	DEU1086	DEU1091
DEU1141	DEU1207	DNK1248	DNK1259
DNK1262	DNK1292	DNK1305	DNK1358
DNK1376	DNK1398	ESP1413	ESP1430
ESP1431	ESP1434	ESP1441	ESP1443
ESP1450	ESP1451	ESP1479	ESP1486
ESP1493	ESP1506	FIN1546	FIN1572
FIN1578	FIN1591	FRA1610	FRA1614
FRA1617	FRA1631	FRA1647	FRA1737
FRA1785	FRA1787	FRA1797	FRA1808
FRA1811	FRA1818	FRA1825	FRA1839
FRA1841	FRA1871	FRA1889	FRA1904
FRA1908	FRA1956	FRA2002	FRA2004
FRA2047	FRA2102	FRA2104	FRA2131
FRA2140	FRA2159	GBR2185	GBR2197
GBR2223	GBR2226	GBR2238	GBR2265
GBR2266	GBR2323	GBR2348	GBR2356
GBR2371	GBR2378	GBR2379	GBR2387
GBR2388	GBR2392	GBR2408	GBR2422
GBR2423	GBR2425	GBR2438	GBR2445
GBR2448	GBR2464	GBR2498	GBR2522
GBR2545	GRC2579	GRC2584	HUN2631
HUN2644	IRL2705	IRL2712	IRL2714
IRL2717	IRL2726	ISL2736	ITA2755
ITA2762	ITA2773	ITA2780	ITA2785
ITA2798	ITA2801	ITA2809	ITA2813
ITA2822	ITA2824	ITA2834	ITA2846

ITA2855	ITA2860	ITA2866	ITA2873
ITA2889	ITA2900	ITA2901	ITA2902
ITA2905	ITA2907	ITA2911	LUX2937
LUX2962	NLD3050	NLD3051	NLD3058
NLD3077	NLD3078	NLD3083	NLD3095
NLD3102	NLD3135	NLD3137	NLD3139
NLD3181	NLD3201	NLD3222	NLD3232
NLD3254	NLD3301	NLD3352	NLD3361
NOR3390	NOR3435	NOR3455	NOR3467
POL3519	PRT3573	PRT3590	SVK3608
SWE3648	SWE3658	SWE3693	SWE3744
SWE3769	SWE3807	SWE3816	SWE3826
SWE3827	SWE3830	SWE3859	TUR3882
TUR3883			

INFORMATION CAMPAIGNS, EXHIBITIONS - CAMPAGNES D'INFORMATION, EXPOSITIONS

AUT0033	AUT0085	BEL0123	BEL0129
BEL0168	BEL0192	BEL0198	BEL0297
BEL0299	BEL0303	BEL0306	BEL0318
BEL0350	BEL0352	CHE0434	CHE0467
CHE0477	CHE0491	CHE0541	CHE0562
CHE0669	CHE0684	CHE0687	CHE0689
CHE0689	CHE0750	CHE0756	CHE0796
CHE0807	CHE0819	CYP0832	CZE0859
CZE0897	DEU0917	DEU0955	DEU0983
DEU1006	DEU1053	DEU1063	DEU1064
DEU1110	DEU1132	DEU1141	DEU1149
DNK1214	DNK1245	DNK1248	DNK1259
DNK1262	DNK1292	DNK1304	DNK1305
DNK1376	DNK1398	ESP1435	ESP1450
ESP1451	ESP1486	ESP1506	ESP1521
FIN1553	FIN1572	FIN1585	FIN1594
FRA1610	FRA1615	FRA1619	FRA1647
FRA1685	FRA1704	FRA1769	FRA1771
FRA1785	FRA1787	FRA1791	FRA1793
FRA1862	FRA1888	FRA1889	FRA1904
FRA1910	FRA1937	FRA1938	FRA1956
FRA1957	FRA2002	FRA2047	FRA2053
FRA2057	FRA2102	FRA2116	FRA2159
GBR2175	GBR2222	GBR2223	GBR2238
GBR2248	GBR2259	GBR2265	GBR2269
GBR2276	GBR2350	GBR2371	GBR2378
GBR2387	GBR2423	GBR2445	GBR2464
GBR2475	GBR2498	GBR2503	GBR2526
GBR2545	GRC2572	GRC2579	GRC2584
GRC2585	HUN2631	HUN2644	IRL2707
IRL2712	IRL2717	IRL2724	ITA2755
ITA2766	ITA2780	ITA2782	ITA2785
ITA2791	ITA2814	ITA2820	ITA2829
ITA2834	ITA2841	ITA2855	ITA2860
ITA2873	ITA2889	ITA2890	ITA2901
ITA2902	LUX2942	LUX2955	LUX2956
LUX2992	LUX2995	NLD3050	NLD3078
NLD3199	NLD3102	NLD3137	NLD3190
NLD3277	NLD3201	NLD3232	NLD3263
NOR3390	NLD3300	NLD3303	NOR3371
PRT3549	NOR3467	POL3519	POL3521
SVK3612	PRT3552	PRT3573	PRT3600
SWE3763	SWE3648	SWE3664	SWE3707
SWE3816	SWE3744	SWE3749	SWE3761
TUR3883	SWE3769	SWE3771	SWE3776
	SWE3830	SWE3854	SWE3864
	TUR3895		

LOBBYING, ADVOCACY - LOBBYING, PLAIDOYER

AUT0033	AUT0035	AUT0089	BEL0116
BEL0131	BEL0155	BEL0168	BEL0192
BEL0198	BEL0216	BEL0218	BEL0284
BEL0299	BEL0318	BEL0345	BEL0353
BEL0359	CHE0420	CHE0434	CHE0467
CHE0519	CHE0524	CHE0534	CHE0562
CHE0603	CHE0637	CHE0642	CHE0668
CHE0684	CHE0687	CHE0689	CHE0711
CHE0755	CHE0780	CHE0814	CHE0819
CZE0857	CZE0891	CZE0896	CZE0904
DEU0954	DEU0983	DEU1006	DEU1063
DEU1064	DEU1066	DEU1110	DEU1141
DEU1176	DNK1259	DNK1262	DNK1292
DNK1304	DNK1335	DNK1339	DNK1376
ESP1451	ESP1475	ESP1506	FIN1594
FRA1614	FRA1661	FRA1685	FRA1740
FRA1785	FRA1791	FRA1862	FRA1876
FRA1888	FRA1889	FRA1904	FRA1910
FRA1956	FRA1957	FRA1991	FRA2002
FRA2004	FRA2047	FRA2057	FRA2102
FRA2116	FRA2159	GBR2174	GBR2175
GBR2223	GBR2228	GBR2238	GBR2242

GBR2266 GBR2269 GBR2303 GBR2371
GBR2378 GBR2390 GBR2392 GBR2396
GBR2423 GBR2445 GBR2464 GBR2467
GBR2481 GBR2493 GBR2498 GBR2503
GBR2522 GBR2523 GBR2526 GBR2545
GRC2572 GRC2579 GRC2584 GRC2586
HUN2644 IRL2687 IRL2689 IRL2691
IRL2705 IRL2707 IRL2712 IRL2717
IRL2724 IRL2726 ITA2782 ITA2813
ITA2814 ITA2820 ITA2822 ITA2855
ITA2873 ITA2902 ITA2905 LIE2927
LUX2955 LUX2956 LUX2976 LUX2993
LUX2995 LUX2997 MLT3036 NLD3050
NLD3064 NLD3078 NLD3102 NLD3137
NLD3186 NLD3199 NLD3201 NLD3222
NLD3232 NLD3254 NLD3301 NLD3303
NOR3372 NOR3390 NOR3455 NOR3467
POL3521 POL3536 PRT3549 PRT3573
PRT3600 SVK3608 SVK3634 SWE3648
SWE3744 SWE3749 SWE3771 SWE3830
SWE3853 TUR3882 TUR3883 TUR3897

NETWORKING, ELECTRONIC TELECOMMUNICATIONS - RESEAUX, TELECOMMUNICATIONS ELECTRONIQUES

AUT0020 BEL0107 BEL0198 BEL0224
BEL0318 CHE0434 CHE0491 CHE0524
CHE0562 CHE0586 CHE0689 CHE0817
CHE0819 CZE0904 DEU0955 DEU0990
DEU1002 DNK1248 DNK1292 ESP1434
FIN1591 FRA1644 FRA1889 FRA1904
FRA1908 FRA1910 FRA2047 FRA2102
FRA2159 GBR2174 GBR2226 GBR2265
GBR2285 GBR2313 GBR2325 GBR2348
GBR2371 GBR2378 GBR2387 GBR2422
GBR2438 GBR2448 GBR2498 GBR2522
GBR2545 HUN2631 HUN2644 IRL2717
ITA2773 ITA2774 ITA2822 ITA2841
ITA2860 ITA2902 LUX2997 NLD3077
NLD3102 NLD3104 NLD3137 NLD3232
NOR3390 NOR3467 SWE3830 TUR3883

OTHER - AUTRE

CHE0434 FRA1631 GBR2240 GBR2371
GBR2387 NLD3137 NLD3183

PUBLISHING, AUDIOVISUAL MATERIALS, EDUCATIONAL MATERIALS - EDITION, DOCUMENTS AUDIOVISUELS, DOCUMENTS EDUCATIFS

AUT0020 AUT0085 BEL0123 BEL0155
BEL0168 BEL0224 BEL0297 BEL0299
BEL0303 BEL0306 BEL0318 BEL0340
BEL0345 BEL0393 CHE0434 CHE0506
CHE0562 CHE0651 CHE0684 CHE0687
CHE0689 CHE0730 CHE0750 CHE0759
CHE0763 CHE0819 CZE0859 DEU0944
DEU1022 DEU1063 DEU1064 DEU1076
DEU1110 DEU1141 DEU1176 DEU1198
DNK1214 DNK1259 DNK1262 DNK1292
DNK1304 DNK1376 ESP1434 ESP1443
ESP1450 ESP1451 ESP1506 FIN1549
FIN1585 FRA1610 FRA1614 FRA1615
FRA1631 FRA1647 FRA1661 FRA1713
FRA1715 FRA1747 FRA1785 FRA1787
FRA1813 FRA1889 FRA1904 FRA1908
FRA2002 FRA2004 FRA2047 FRA2053
FRA2102 FRA2104 FRA2159 GBR2175
GBR2185 GBR2222 GBR2226 GBR2238
GBR2248 GBR2265 GBR2289 GBR2325
GBR2345 GBR2371 GBR2378 GBR2387
GBR2392 GBR2422 GBR2423 GBR2445
GBR2448 GBR2464 GBR2467 GBR2498
GBR2500 GBR2501 GBR2503 GBR2545
GBR2552 GRC2572 GRC2576 GRC2584
HUN2644 IRL2712 IRL2717 IRL2733
ISL2736 ITA2755 ITA2762 ITA2766
ITA2780 ITA2785 ITA2798 ITA2809
ITA2820 ITA2822 ITA2826 ITA2832
ITA2838 ITA2841 ITA2855 ITA2857
ITA2860 ITA2901 ITA2902 ITA2911
ITA2916 LUX2995 LUX3006 NLD3050
NLD3077 NLD3078 NLD3083 NLD3102
NLD3201 NLD3216 NLD3232 NLD3300
NLD3301 NLD3352 NLD3354 NLD3361
NOR3390 NOR3435 NOR3467 POL3508
POL3519 PRT3590 PRT3600 SWE3648
SWE3712 SWE3744 SWE3746 SWE3749

SWE3763 SWE3769 SWE3771 SWE3816
SWE3830 SWE3832 TUR3883

EMPLOYMENT, UNEMPLOYMENT - EMPLOI, CHOMAGE

BROADCASTING, CULTURAL EVENTS - RADIODIFFUSION, MANIFESTATIONS CULTURELLES

AUT0010 AUT0021 BEL0123 BEL0177
CHE0434 CHE0534 CHE0566 CHE0568
CHE0602 CHE0624 CHE0689 CHE0819
DEU1074 DNK1283 ESP1455 ESP1486
FIN1545 FRA1621 FRA1791 FRA1793
FRA1794 FRA1889 FRA1957 FRA2062
FRA2092 FRA2106 FRA2117 GBR2238
GBR2371 GBR2406 GBR2419 GBR2498
GBR2501 GBR2545 IRL2686 IRL2693
ITA2801 ITA2907 LUX3006 MLT3017
NLD3067 NLD3135 NLD3190 NLD3236
NLD3269 SVK3611

CONFERENCES, SEMINARS, WORKSHOPS, TRAINING ACTIVITIES - CONFERENCES, SEMINAIRES, ATELIERS, ACTIVITES DE FORMATION

AUT0010 AUT0020 AUT0021 AUT0056
BEL0096 BEL0123 BEL0148 BEL0155
BEL0174 BEL0176 BEL0177 BEL0188
BEL0221 BEL0248 BEL0252 BEL0265
BEL0270 BEL0275 BEL0289 BEL0309
BEL0345 BEL0351 BEL0359 BEL0392
CHE0417 CHE0434 CHE0460 CHE0496
CHE0549 CHE0562 CHE0566 CHE0568
CHE0602 CHE0629 CHE0642 CHE0689
CHE0730 CHE0755 CHE0765 CHE0772
CHE0794 CHE0814 CHE0819 CYP0832
CZE0904 DEU0919 DEU0921 DEU0928
DEU0944 DEU0983 DEU0989 DEU0990
DEU0991 DEU0998 DEU1013 DEU1015
DEU1025 DEU1044 DEU1055 DEU1065
DEU1090 DEU1149 DEU1180 DEU1187
DEU1198 DEU1203 DEU1210 DNK1248
DNK1283 DNK1289 DNK1312 DNK1335
DNK1369 DNK1375 DNK1398 ESP1406
ESP1430 ESP1455 ESP1472 ESP1474
ESP1490 ESP1512 ESP1525 FIN1545
FIN1547 FIN1551 FIN1572 FIN1574
FIN1578 FIN1594 FIN1604 FRA1791
FRA1793 FRA1794 FRA1797 FRA1799
FRA1818 FRA1846 FRA1849 FRA1860
FRA1886 FRA1889 FRA1897 FRA1917
FRA1921 FRA1946 FRA1957 FRA1980
FRA2004 FRA2009 FRA2018 FRA2021
FRA2044 FRA2057 FRA2062 FRA2076
FRA2096 FRA2106 FRA2117 FRA2165
GBR2175 GBR2185 GBR2238 GBR2265
GBR2269 GBR2279 GBR2284 GBR2371
GBR2400 GBR2406 GBR2408 GBR2415
GBR2419 GBR2428 GBR2445 GBR2481
GBR2498 GBR2510 GBR2513 GBR2527
GBR2545 GBR2553 GBR2558 GRC2573
HUN2598 IRL2686 IRL2693 IRL2698
IRL2729 IRL2730 IRL2758 IRL2773
ITA2785 ITA2801 ITA2805 ITA2814
ITA2826 ITA2842 ITA2868 ITA2908
ITA2913 LUX2958 MLT3016 MLT3017
MLT3023 NLD3067 NLD3078 NLD3082
NLD3135 NLD3138 NLD3156 NLD3157
NLD3159 NLD3174 NLD3181 NLD3190
NLD3230 NLD3236 NLD3301 NLD3305
NOR3400 NOR3467 POL3519 POL3521
PRT3590 SVK3611 SWE3695 SWE3749
SWE3754 SWE3807 SWE3816 SWE3821
SWE3827 SWE3865 TUR3896

EXCHANGES, TWINNING, LINKING - ECHANGES, PARRAINAGE, JUMELAGE

AUT0010 BEL0123 BEL0129 BEL0198
BEL0221 BEL0248 BEL0275 BEL0289
BEL0390 CHE0434 CHE0448 CHE0562
CHE0566 CHE0689 CHE0819 CZE0904
DEU0983 DEU0990 DEU1038 DEU1055
DEU1149 DEU1210 FRA1699 FRA1746
FRA1759 FRA1791 FRA1793 FRA1846
FRA1889 FRA1921 FRA1946 FRA1980
FRA2009 FRA2057 FRA2062 FRA2106

GBR2231 GBR2284 GBR2371 GBR2379
GBR2406 GBR2445 GBR2481 HUN2631
IRL2686 IRL2697 ITA2773 ITA2801
NLD3067 NLD3078 NLD3082 NLD3096
NLD3137 NLD3138 NLD3215 NLD3236
NOR3400 POL3508 POL3519 SVK3611
SWE3734 SWE3749 SWE3754 SWE3864
SWE3865

FORMAL EDUCATION - EDUCATION FORMELLE

AUT0021 BEL0123 BEL0176 BEL0177
BEL0351 BEL0359 BEL0390 CHE0434
CHE0562 CHE0566 CHE0602 CHE0681
CHE0689 CHE0772 CHE0819 CZE0894
CZE0904 DEU0954 DEU0983 DEU1149
DNK1289 ESP1406 ESP1437 ESP1482
ESP1486 ESP1490 ESP1512 FRA1672
FRA1699 FRA1759 FRA1794 FRA1849
FRA1886 FRA1889 FRA1946 FRA2021
FRA2044 FRA2057 FRA2062 FRA2106
GBR2238 GBR2265 GBR2269 GBR2333
GBR2371 GBR2378 GBR2379 GBR2390
GBR2404 GBR2408 GBR2415 GBR2424
GBR2428 GBR2436 GBR2445 GBR2468
GBR2481 GBR2553 HUN2598 IRL2686
IRL2693 IRL2702 ITA2814 ITA2842
ITA2868 MLT3017 NLD3067 NLD3078
NLD3138 NLD3215 NLD3230 NLD3269
POL3508 POL3521 SVK3611 SWE3712

FUND RAISING - COLLECTE DE FONDS

AUT0003 AUT0021 AUT0051 AUT0091
BEL0096 BEL0104 BEL0148 BEL0155
BEL0198 BEL0351 BEL0352 BEL0353
BEL0358 BEL0359 BEL0390 CHE0417
CHE0434 CHE0562 CHE0566 CHE0584
CHE0586 CHE0602 CHE0689 CHE0755
CHE0756 CHE0772 CHE0786 CHE0819
DEU0957 DEU0968 DEU0983 DEU0989
DEU0993 DEU1038 DEU1044 DEU1065
DEU1118 DEU1149 DEU1149 DEU1202
DNK1227 DNK1283 ESP1442 ESP1455
ESP1486 FIN1549 FIN1572 FIN1591
FRA1667 FRA1691 FRA1739 FRA1791
FRA1793 FRA1849 FRA1889 FRA1929
FRA1946 FRA1957 FRA1980 FRA2086
FRA2092 FRA2116 FRA2117 FRA2131
GBR2175 GBR2197 GBR2238 GBR2259
GBR2297 GBR2325 GBR2333 GBR2348
GBR2371 GBR2400 GBR2406 GBR2409
GBR2419 GBR2424 GBR2428 GBR2436
GBR2445 GBR2475 GBR2481 GBR2498
GBR2513 GBR2532 GBR2545 GBR2558
HUN2598 IRL2730 ITA2773 ITA2879
ITA2900 ITA2907 LUX2958 LUX2995
LUX3006 NLD3078 NLD3135
NLD3137 NLD3157 NLD3159 NLD3181
NLD3231 NLD3256 NLD3269 NLD3301
NLD3302 SVK3611 SWE3712 SWE3795
SWE3859 SWE3864

INFORMATION AND DOCUMENTATION SERVICES, DATA BASES - SERVICES D'INFORMATION ET DE DOCUMENTATION, BASES DE DONNEES

AUT0010 AUT0020 AUT0026 AUT0060
AUT0079 BEL0123 BEL0141 BEL0149
BEL0155 BEL0177 BEL0252 BEL0267
BEL0303 BEL0345 BEL0359 BEL0390
BEL0392 BEL0393 BEL0396 CHE0434
CHE0496 CHE0534 CHE0549 CHE0554
CHE0562 CHE0566 CHE0568 CHE0602
CHE0624 CHE0689 CHE0751 CHE0756
CHE0763 CHE0819 CZE0904 DEU0919
DEU0921 DEU0944 DEU0968 DEU0990
DEU0998 DEU1013 DEU1015 DEU1020
DEU1025 DEU1076 DEU1090 DEU1091
DEU1192 DEU1138 DEU1149 DEU1184
DEU1192 DEU1203 DNK1248 DNK1283
DNK1289 DNK1375 DNK1398 ESP1430
ESP1431 ESP1434 ESP1455 ESP1482
ESP1486 ESP1490 FIN1545 FIN1547
FIN1572 FIN1591 FIN1604 FRA1673
FRA1794 FRA1797 FRA1811 FRA1818
FRA1825 FRA1839 FRA1841 FRA1846
FRA1860 FRA1889 FRA2004 FRA2009
FRA2015 FRA2018 FRA2021 FRA2096
FRA2104 FRA2106 FRA2131 GBR2185

See: *How to Use the Directory*, page 11.

GBR2238	GBR2265	GBR2284	GBR2371
GBR2378	GBR2379	GBR2406	GBR2408
GBR2415	GBR2435	GBR2438	GBR2445
GBR2498	GBR2513	GBR2537	GBR2545
GBR2558	GBR2561	HUN2598	HUN2631
IRL2686	IRL2693	IRL2698	IRL2714
IRL2730	ITA2773	ITA2798	ITA2801
ITA2805	ITA2814	ITA2822	ITA2834
ITA2846	ITA2857	ITA2860	ITA2900
ITA2907	ITA2908	LUX2937	LUX2949
LUX2962	NLD3058	NLD3067	NLD3077
NLD3078	NLD3095	NLD3096	NLD3135
NLD3137	NLD3138	NLD3139	NLD3147
NLD3156	NLD3157	NLD3181	NLD3301
NLD3302	NLD3305	NLD3355	NLD3361
POL3508	POL3519	SWE3611	SWE3658
SWE3744	SWE3807	SWE3816	SWE3821
SWE3864	SWE3865	TUR3883	

INFORMATION CAMPAIGNS, EXHIBITIONS - CAMPAGNES D'INFORMATION, EXPOSITIONS

AUT0010	AUT0020	BEL0096	BEL0123
BEL0155	BEL0176	BEL0177	BEL0198
BEL0248	BEL0252	BEL0267	BEL0275
BEL0289	BEL0351	BEL0352	BEL0390
BEL0392	CHE0434	CHE0460	CHE0496
CHE0541	CHE0549	CHE0562	CHE0566
CHE0568	CHE0584	CHE0669	CHE0689
CHE0756	CHE0765	CHE0819	DEU0917
DEU0955	DEU0983	DEU1013	DEU1025
DEU1149	DEU1187	DEU1202	DEU1203
DNK1283	DNK1317	DNK1398	ESP1457
ESP1486	ESP1490	ESP1517	FIN1545
FIN1582	FIN1594	FIN1604	FRA1642
FRA1672	FRA1791	FRA1793	FRA1797
FRA1889	FRA1957	FRA1991	FRA2021
FRA2068	FRA2076	FRA2096	FRA2106
FRA2116	GBR2231	GBR2238	GBR2259
GBR2265	GBR2269	GBR2279	GBR2371
GBR2406	GBR2419	GBR2445	GBR2498
GBR2510	GBR2527	GBR2545	GBR2553
IRL2686	IRL2693	ITA2775	ITA2903
LUX3006	MLT3017	NLD3067	NLD3078
NLD3138	NLD3181	NLD3236	NLD3257
NLD3303	POL3519	POL3521	SVK3611
SWE3749	SWE3754	SWE3795	SWE3816
SWE3864	SWE3865	TUR3883	

LOBBYING, ADVOCACY - LOBBYING, PLAIDOYER

AUT0010	AUT0021	AUT0056	BEL0096
BEL0131	BEL0174	BEL0176	BEL0177
BEL0198	BEL0265	BEL0267	BEL0345
BEL0351	BEL0353	CHE0434	CHE0460
CHE0479	CHE0491	CHE0534	CHE0549
CHE0562	CHE0566	CHE0568	CHE0602
CHE0642	CHE0689	CHE0751	CHE0755
CHE0765	CHE0794	CHE0819	CYP0832
CZE0896	CZE0904	DEU0919	DEU0954
DEU0983	DEU0998	DEU1013	DEU1015
DEU1038	DEU1055	DEU1149	DNK1283
DNK1289	DNK1335	DNK1375	ESP1455
ESP1457	ESP1490	FIN1551	FIN1572
FIN1582	FIN1594	FRA1791	FRA1793
FRA1794	FRA1797	FRA1799	FRA1841
FRA1946	FRA2004	FRA2057	FRA2062
FRA2096	FRA2106	FRA2110	FRA2116
GBR2269	GBR2284	GBR2355	GBR2371
GBR2390	GBR2396	GBR2400	GBR2406
GBR2419	GBR2445	GBR2481	GBR2498
GBR2510	GBR2527	GBR2537	GBR2545
HUN2598	HUN2631	IRL2693	ITA2913
LUX2957	LUX2958	LUX2995	MLT3017
MLT3023	MLT3036	NLD3067	NLD3078
NLD3135	NLD3147	NLD3156	NLD3230
NLD3236	NLD3301	NOR3467	POL3536
SWE3749	SWE3821	SWE3864	TUR3883
TUR3896			

NETWORKING, ELECTRONIC TELECOMMUNICATIONS - RESEAUX, TELECOMMUNICATIONS ELECTRONIQUES

AUT0020	BEL0177	BEL0198	BEL0252
CHE0434	CHE0562	CHE0568	CHE0586
CHE0642	CHE0689	CHE0819	CZE0904
DEU0955	DEU0990	DEU1002	DEU1065
DEU1149	ESP1434	FIN1545	FIN1591
FIN1604	FRA1889	FRA2018	FRA2068

FRA2106	GBR2265	GBR2284	GBR2285
GBR2313	GBR2348	GBR2371	GBR2400
GBR2406	GBR2438	GBR2498	GBR2545
IRL2698	ITA2773	ITA2860	NLD3067
NLD3077	NLD3082	NLD3135	NLD3137
NLD3156	NLD3157	NLD3181	NLD3215
NLD3236	POL3521	SVK3611	SWE3864
TUR3883			

OTHER - AUTRE

CHE0434	DEU1106	FRA1700	FRA1825
GBR2240	GBR2371	GBR2510	NLD3096
NLD3137	NLD3183	SWE3695	

PUBLISHING, AUDIOVISUAL MATERIALS, EDUCATIONAL MATERIALS - EDITION, DOCUMENTS AUDIOVISUELS, DOCUMENTS EDUCATIFS

AUT0010	AUT0020	AUT0051	BEL0096
BEL0123	BEL0148	BEL0155	BEL0174
BEL0176	BEL0177	BEL0188	BEL0252
BEL0306	BEL0345	BEL0390	BEL0392
BEL0393	BEL0396	CHE0434	CHE0496
CHE0499	CHE0549	CHE0562	CHE0566
CHE0568	CHE0602	CHE0638	CHE0689
CHE0738	CHE0751	CHE0763	CHE0794
CHE0819	DEU0944	DEU1013	DEU1020
DEU1025	DEU1055	DEU1076	DEU1095
DEU1129	DEU1149	DEU1180	DEU1187
DNK1283	DNK1289	DNK1317	DNK1375
ESP1434	ESP1435	ESP1455	ESP1457
ESP1490	FIN1545	FRA1642	FRA1713
FRA1759	FRA1794	FRA1813	FRA1860
FRA1889	FRA1897	FRA2004	FRA2018
FRA2021	FRA2057	FRA2076	FRA2086
FRA2096	FRA2106	FRA2116	FRA2165
GBR2175	GBR2185	GBR2231	GBR2238
GBR2265	GBR2271	GBR2279	GBR2371
GBR2406	GBR2415	GBR2419	GBR2445
GBR2501	GBR2510	GBR2513	GBR2527
GBR2545	GBR2554	HUN2598	IRL2693
IRL2698	ITA2762	ITA2773	ITA2785
ITA2798	ITA2907	ITA2908	LUX3006
NLD3067	NLD3077	NLD3078	NLD3082
NLD3135	NLD3138	NLD3190	NLD3215
NLD3230	NLD3301	NLD3302	NLD3305
NOR3467	POL3502	POL3508	POL3519
SVK3611	SWE3816	SWE3865	TUR3883
TUR3896			

FOOD, FAMINE - ALIMENTS, FAMINE

BROADCASTING, CULTURAL EVENTS - RADIODIFFUSION, MANIFESTATIONS CULTURELLES

BEL0156	CHE0434	CHE0491	CHE0534
CHE0624	CHE0689	CHE0819	DNK1366
ESP1486	ESP1506	ESP1510	FRA1612
FRA1614	FRA1621	FRA1631	FRA1791
FRA1793	FRA1889	FRA1956	FRA1992
FRA2002	FRA2047	FRA2092	GBR2229
GBR2238	GBR2248	GBR2345	GBR2371
GBR2415	GBR2423	GBR2464	GBR2467
GBR2501	GBR2545	IRL2714	ITA2774
ITA2785	ITA2798	ITA2813	ITA2826
ITA2907	LUX2937	LUX2955	MLT3016
NLD3190	NLD3222	NLD3269	NLD3361
SVK3611	SWE3774		

CONFERENCES, SEMINARS, WORKSHOPS, TRAINING ACTIVITIES - CONFERENCES, SEMINAIRES, ATELIERS, ACTIVITES DE FORMATION

BEL0133	BEL0152	BEL0156	BEL0168
BEL0214	BEL0224	BEL0241	BEL0261
BEL0282	BEL0290	BEL0297	BEL0306
BEL0318	CHE0417	CHE0434	CHE0461
CHE0467	CHE0562	CHE0642	CHE0682
CHE0684	CHE0689	CHE0730	CHE0766
CHE0817	CHE0819	DEU0921	DEU0944
DEU0983	DEU0990	DEU1020	DEU1032
DEU1037	DEU1064	DEU1090	DEU1141
DEU1149	DEU1163	DEU1180	DEU1210
DNK1339	DNK1361	DNK1398	ESP1407
ESP1430	ESP1479	ESP1493	ESP1502
ESP1506	ESP1510	ESP1528	FIN1531
FIN1553	FIN1557	FRA1614	FRA1619

FRA1627	FRA1640	FRA1661	FRA1679
FRA1685	FRA1747	FRA1791	FRA1793
FRA1797	FRA1818	FRA1832	FRA1841
FRA1846	FRA1889	FRA1904	FRA1937
FRA1949	FRA1956	FRA1990	FRA2002
FRA2004	FRA2029	FRA2044	FRA2047
FRA2076	FRA2102	FRA2122	GBR2174
GBR2175	GBR2185	GBR2205	GBR2226
GBR2229	GBR2238	GBR2264	GBR2265
GBR2269	GBR2279	GBR2303	GBR2371
GBR2387	GBR2390	GBR2408	GBR2415
GBR2416	GBR2423	GBR2445	GBR2448
GBR2452	GBR2460	GBR2464	GBR2483
GBR2495	GBR2500	GBR2503	GBR2544
GBR2545	GRC2586	HUN2631	IRL2679
IRL2689	IRL2691	IRL2693	IRL2700
IRL2705	IRL2717	IRL2720	ITA2773
ITA2805	ITA2810	ITA2813	ITA2820
ITA2826	ITA2829	ITA2848	ITA2857
ITA2873	ITA2894	ITA2899	ITA2900
ITA2907	ITA2908	LUX2942	LUX2955
LUX2956	LUX2958	MLT3016	NLD3064
NLD3102	NLD3174	NLD3190	NLD3196
NLD3199	NLD3211	NLD3222	NLD3232
NLD3269	NLD3277	NLD3301	NLD3305
NLD3318	NLD3361	NOR3371	NOR3453
NOR3467	POL3519	PRT3549	PRT3586
SVK3611	SVK3612	SVK3634	SWE3682
SWE3695	SWE3702	SWE3749	SWE3769
SWE3774	SWE3807	SWE3816	

EXCHANGES, TWINNING, LINKING - ECHANGES, PARRAINAGE, JUMELAGE

BEL0120	BEL0129	BEL0156	BEL0198
BEL0306	BEL0355	BEL0390	CHE0434
CHE0448	CHE0562	CHE0595	CHE0689
CHE0730	CHE0819	DEU0983	DEU0990
DEU1037	DEU1149	DEU1163	FRA1661
FRA1715	FRA1746	FRA1785	FRA1787
FRA1846	FRA1855	FRA1889	FRA1938
FRA1956	FRA2029	FRA2092	FRA2140
GBR2229	GBR2264	GBR2371	GBR2379
GBR2390	GBR2423	GBR2435	GBR2445
IRL2714	ITA2785	ITA2813	LUX2942
NLD3096	NLD3102	NLD3137	NLD3196
NLD3361	POL3519	PRT3576	SVK3611
SVK3612	SWE3749		

FORMAL EDUCATION - EDUCATION FORMELLE

BEL0156	BEL0306	BEL0323	BEL0390
CHE0434	CHE0549	CHE0562	CHE0660
CHE0682	CHE0687	CHE0689	CHE0730
CHE0819	DEU0954	DEU0983	DEU1132
DNK1339	ESP1427	ESP1455	ESP1479
ESP1502	FRA1607	FRA1627	FRA1661
FRA1672	FRA1704	FRA1738	FRA1785
FRA1889	FRA1904	FRA1956	FRA1992
FRA2002	FRA2044	FRA2102	GBR2238
GBR2265	GBR2269	GBR2345	GBR2371
GBR2379	GBR2390	GBR2408	GBR2415
GBR2423	GBR2424	GBR2436	GBR2445
GBR2448	GBR2452	GBR2464	GBR2467
GBR2468	GBR2522	IRL2688	IRL2689
IRL2690	IRL2691	IRL2698	IRL2720
ITA2761	ITA2770	ITA2782	ITA2810
ITA2813	ITA2826	ITA2857	LUX2995
NLD3212	NLD3232	NLD3254	NLD3269
NLD3352	NOR3467	SVK3611	SVK3612
SVK3634	SWE3712	SWE3859	

FUND RAISING - COLLECTE DE FONDS

AUT0036	AUT0076	AUT0085	AUT0089
BEL0104	BEL0118	BEL0168	BEL0198
BEL0224	BEL0261	BEL0282	
BEL0297	BEL0314	BEL0318	BEL0323
BEL0352	BEL0355	BEL0358	BEL0381
BEL0390	CHE0417	CHE0434	CHE0438
CHE0444	CHE0448	CHE0467	CHE0475
CHE0485	CHE0486	CHE0491	CHE0529
CHE0562	CHE0586	CHE0630	CHE0664
CHE0684	CHE0687	CHE0689	CHE0693
CHE0730	CHE0734	CHE0750	CHE0756
CHE0764	CHE0788	CHE0796	CHE0806
CHE0819	CHE0823	CYP0832	CZE0859
DEU0918	DEU0922	DEU0954	DEU0957
DEU0968	DEU0983	DEU0991	DEU0993
DEU1006	DEU1132	DEU1141	DEU1143
DEU1149	DNK1216	DNK1222	DNK1245

DNK1292	DNK1366	ESP1439	ESP1455
ESP1470	ESP1506	ESP1510	ESP1528
FIN1544	FIN1549	FIN1580	FIN1591
FIN1599	FRA1612	FRA1614	FRA1661
FRA1664	FRA1672	FRA1685	FRA1704
FRA1738	FRA1739	FRA1769	FRA1771
FRA1785	FRA1787	FRA1791	FRA1793
FRA1824	FRA1855	FRA1876	FRA1889
FRA1891	FRA1929	FRA1938	FRA1978
FRA1990	FRA2047	FRA2053	FRA2080
FRA2091	FRA2092	FRA2116	FRA2119
FRA2137	FRA2140	FRA2148	GBR2174
GBR2175	GBR2176	GBR2180	GBR2222
GBR2226	GBR2228	GBR2230	GBR2238
GBR2242	GBR2248	GBR2259	GBR2264
GBR2266	GBR2277	GBR2289	GBR2292
GBR2318	GBR2324	GBR2348	GBR2350
GBR2358	GBR2371	GBR2372	GBR2373
GBR2390	GBR2392	GBR2423	GBR2436
GBR2445	GBR2464	GBR2475	GBR2483
GBR2500	GBR2515	GBR2522	GBR2524
GBR2552	GRC2573	GRC2573	GRC2586
HUN2609	HUN2627	HUN2631	IRL2679
IRL2688	IRL2689	IRL2691	IRL2697
IRL2700	IRL2725	IRL2730	IRL2732
IRL2733	ISL2740	ITA2766	ITA2770
ITA2773	ITA2774	ITA2782	ITA2785
ITA2810	ITA2813	ITA2820	ITA2826
ITA2832	ITA2848	ITA2852	ITA2857
ITA2873	ITA2879	ITA2888	ITA2889
ITA2900	ITA2912	LIE2930	LUX2936
LUX2942	LUX2955	LUX2956	LUX2958
LUX2959	LUX2980	LUX2993	LUX2995
NLD3137	NLD3199	NLD3231	NLD3232
NLD3254	NLD3256	NLD3269	NLD3277
NLD3297	NLD3301	NLD3323	NLD3361
NOR3371	NOR3381	NOR3412	NOR3412
NOR3435	NOR3453	NOR3467	PRT3549
PRT3555	PRT3576	PRT3596	PRT3605
SVK3611	SWE3679	SWE3682	SWE3702
SWE3712	SWE3749	SWE3763	SWE3769
SWE3813	SWE3854	SWE3857	SWE3859

INFORMATION AND DOCUMENTATION SERVICES, DATA BASES - SERVICES D'INFORMATION ET DE DOCUMENTATION, BASES DE DONNEES

AUT0020	AUT0026	AUT0060	AUT0079
AUT0085	BEL0118	BEL0155	BEL0156
BEL0164	BEL0168	BEL0192	BEL0214
BEL0237	BEL0297	BEL0306	BEL0318
BEL0335	BEL0365	BEL0390	BEL0393
BEL0396	CHE0429	CHE0434	CHE0534
CHE0549	CHE0562	CHE0624	CHE0664
CHE0683	CHE0687	CHE0689	CHE0756
CHE0763	CHE0767	CHE0796	CHE0819
DEU0944	DEU0968	DEU0975	DEU0990
DEU1002	DEU1020	DEU1031	DEU1037
DEU1064	DEU1076	DEU1086	DEU1090
DEU1091	DEU1141	DEU1149	DEU1163
DEU1184	DNK1259	DNK1292	DNK1292
DNK1339	DNK1398	ESP1407	ESP1430
ESP1431	ESP1434	ESP1441	ESP1455
ESP1479	ESP1479	ESP1486	ESP1493
ESP1502	ESP1506	FIN1548	FIN1578
FIN1591	FRA1631	FRA1737	FRA1747
FRA1785	FRA1787	FRA1797	FRA1808
FRA1811	FRA1818	FRA1820	FRA1832
FRA1839	FRA1841	FRA1846	FRA1889
FRA1956	FRA1990	FRA2002	FRA2004
FRA2018	FRA2029	FRA2076	FRA2103
FRA2104	FRA2122	FRA2131	FRA2140
GBR2205	GBR2222	GBR2226	GBR2229
GBR2238	GBR2239	GBR2264	GBR2265
GBR2266	GBR2279	GBR2371	GBR2379
GBR2387	GBR2408	GBR2415	GBR2422
GBR2423	GBR2435	GBR2438	GBR2445
GBR2452	GBR2464	GBR2475	GBR2483
GBR2495	GBR2522	GBR2544	GBR2545
HUN2631	IRL2698	IRL2700	IRL2705
IRL2717	IRL2720	IRL2730	ITA2762
ITA2773	ITA2785	ITA2798	ITA2801
ITA2805	ITA2808	ITA2810	ITA2813
ITA2814	ITA2820	ITA2822	ITA2834
ITA2852	ITA2857	ITA2860	ITA2873
ITA2900	ITA2907	ITA2908	LUX2937
LUX2949	LUX2962	LUX2983	NLD3058
NLD3077	NLD3084	NLD3095	NLD3096
NLD3102	NLD3137	NLD3139	NLD3170

NLD3179	NLD3211	NLD3222	NLD3254
NLD3301	NLD3352	NLD3355	NLD3361
NOR3435	NOR3467	POL3519	SVK3611
SWE3658	SWE3682	SWE3693	SWE3695
SWE3744	SWE3769	SWE3774	SWE3807
SWE3816	TUR3883		

INFORMATION CAMPAIGNS, EXHIBITIONS - CAMPAGNES D'INFORMATION, EXPOSITIONS

BEL0168	BEL0198	BEL0224	BEL0261
BEL0282	BEL0306	BEL0318	BEL0323
BEL0352	BEL0381	BEL0390	CHE0434
CHE0444	CHE0461	CHE0467	CHE0541
CHE0549	CHE0562	CHE0664	CHE0669
CHE0684	CHE0689	CHE0756	CHE0796
CHE0807	CHE0819	DEU0917	DEU0922
DEU0955	DEU0983	DEU1037	DEU1064
DEU1141	DEU1149	DEU1163	DNK1245
DNK1260	DNK1292	DNK1339	DNK1366
DNK1398	ESP1407	ESP1486	ESP1493
ESP1502	ESP1506	ESP1528	FIN1531
FIN1544	FIN1553	FIN1557	FRA1607
FRA1624	FRA1704	FRA1738	FRA1785
FRA1787	FRA1791	FRA1793	FRA1797
FRA1889	FRA1904	FRA1938	FRA1956
FRA1990	FRA1992	FRA2002	FRA2076
FRA2102	FRA2116	FRA2138	GBR2205
GBR2222	GBR2229	GBR2238	GBR2239
GBR2248	GBR2259	GBR2264	GBR2265
GBR2269	GBR2277	GBR2279	GBR2350
GBR2371	GBR2387	GBR2408	GBR2415
GBR2423	GBR2445	GBR2452	GBR2464
GBR2467	GBR2483	GBR2495	GBR2503
GBR2544	GBR2545	GRC2571	HUN2631
IRL2679	IRL2688	IRL2690	IRL2693
IRL2698	IRL2700	IRL2717	IRL2720
ITA2761	ITA2766	ITA2770	ITA2775
ITA2785	ITA2805	ITA2810	ITA2813
ITA2820	ITA2826	ITA2873	LUX2955
LUX2956	LUX2958	LUX2995	NLD3102
NLD3190	NLD3196	NLD3199	NLD3211
NLD3222	NLD3269	NLD3277	NLD3323
NLD3352	NLD3361	NOR3371	NOR3467
POL3519	PRT3549	PRT3594	SVK3611
SVK3612	SWE3682	SWE3695	SWE3712
SWE3749	SWE3763	SWE3769	SWE3774
SWE3816	SWE3826	SWE3854	SWE3859
TUR3883			

LOBBYING, ADVOCACY - LOBBYING, PLAIDOYER

BEL0118	BEL0131	BEL0156	BEL0165
BEL0168	BEL0198	BEL0214	BEL0224
BEL0282	BEL0306	BEL0318	BEL0351
BEL0353	CHE0434	CHE0460	CHE0467
CHE0491	CHE0534	CHE0562	CHE0642
CHE0683	CHE0684	CHE0689	CHE0780
CHE0819	DEU0954	DEU0975	DEU0983
DEU1032	DEU1037	DEU1064	DEU1131
DEU1141	DEU1149	DNK1339	ESP1528
FIN1531	FRA1685	FRA1791	FRA1793
FRA1797	FRA1818	FRA1889	FRA1949
FRA1956	FRA2002	FRA2004	FRA2047
FRA2116	GBR2174	GBR2186	GBR2202
GBR2205	GBR2228	GBR2229	GBR2238
GBR2239	GBR2242	GBR2264	GBR2266
GBR2269	GBR2371	GBR2390	GBR2392
GBR2423	GBR2445	GBR2464	GBR2467
GBR2483	GBR2495	GBR2503	GBR2522
GBR2545	GRC2586	IRL2679	IRL2689
IRL2690	IRL2691	IRL2700	IRL2705
IRL2714	ITA2810	ITA2813	ITA2820
LUX2955	LUX2956	LUX2957	LUX2958
MLT3016	NLD3064	NLD3096	NLD3102
NLD3137	NLD3196	NLD3199	NLD3211
NLD3222	NLD3232	NLD3236	NLD3254
NLD3301	NLD3352	NLD3361	NOR3467
PRT3549	PRT3590	SVK3634	SWE3682
SWE3749	TUR3883		

NETWORKING, ELECTRONIC TELECOMMUNICATIONS - RESEAUX, TELECOMMUNICATIONS ELECTRONIQUES

AUT0020	BEL0198	BEL0224	BEL0318
CHE0434	CHE0491	CHE0562	CHE0586
CHE0642	CHE0689	CHE0819	DEU0955
DEU0990	DEU1002	DEU1149	ESP1434
FIN1531	FIN1591	FRA1889	GBR2174
GBR2205	GBR2226	GBR2229	GBR2265

GBR2285	GBR2313	GBR2348	GBR2371
GBR2387	GBR2438	GBR2495	GBR2545
HUN2631	IRL2717	ITA2773	ITA2774
ITA2860	NLD3077	NLD3102	NLD3137
NLD3199	NLD3303	NLD3318	NOR3467
SVK3611	TUR3883		

OTHER - AUTRE

CHE0434	FRA1631	FRA2056	GBR2240
GBR2358	GBR2371	GBR2387	NLD3069
NLD3096	NLD3137	NLD3183	

PUBLISHING, AUDIOVISUAL MATERIALS, EDUCATIONAL MATERIALS - EDITION, DOCUMENTS AUDIOVISUELS, DOCUMENTS EDUCATIFS

AUT0020	AUT0085	BEL0120	BEL0155
BEL0156	BEL0168	BEL0214	BEL0224
BEL0241	BEL0261	BEL0282	BEL0297
BEL0306	BEL0318	BEL0323	BEL0365
BEL0381	BEL0390	BEL0393	CHE0434
CHE0444	CHE0517	CHE0549	CHE0562
CHE0684	CHE0689	CHE0730	CHE0756
CHE0763	CHE0767	CHE0819	DEU0944
DEU0975	DEU1020	DEU1022	DEU1031
DEU1037	DEU1064	DEU1076	DEU1095
DEU1119	DEU1180	DNK1216	DNK1259
DNK1260	DNK1292	DNK1339	ESP1434
ESP1435	ESP1488	ESP1506	ESP1510
FIN1531	FIN1536	FIN1544	FIN1545
FIN1548	FIN1549	FIN1557	FRA1607
FRA1612	FRA1614	FRA1624	FRA1627
FRA1631	FRA1685	FRA1713	FRA1715
FRA1787	FRA1813	FRA1832	FRA1836
FRA1889	FRA1920	FRA1938	FRA1956
FRA1986	FRA1990	FRA2002	FRA2004
FRA2047	FRA2076	FRA2096	FRA2104
FRA2116	FRA2131	FRA2138	GBR2175
GBR2181	GBR2185	GBR2205	GBR2222
GBR2229	GBR2238	GBR2239	GBR2248
GBR2264	GBR2265	GBR2271	GBR2279
GBR2289	GBR2318	GBR2345	GBR2346
GBR2371	GBR2387	GBR2415	GBR2423
GBR2436	GBR2445	GBR2452	GBR2464
GBR2467	GBR2483	GBR2500	GBR2501
GBR2503	GBR2522	GBR2544	GBR2545
GBR2552	GBR2554	HUN2609	HUN2627
IRL2679	IRL2693	IRL2698	IRL2720
IRL2733	ITA2762	ITA2785	ITA2798
ITA2805	ITA2810	ITA2813	ITA2820
ITA2826	ITA2852	ITA2857	ITA2907
ITA2908	ITA2916	LUX3006	MLT3016
NLD3077	NLD3102	NLD3190	NLD3196
NLD3199	NLD3211	NLD3212	NLD3216
NLD3222	NLD3301	NLD3352	NLD3361
NOR3435	NOR3441	NOR3467	POL3519
SVK3611	SWE3682	SWE3712	SWE3749
SWE3763	SWE3769	SWE3816	TUR3883

GENDER ISSUES, WOMEN - QUESTIONS RELATIVES AUX FEMMES

BROADCASTING, CULTURAL EVENTS - RADIODIFFUSION, MANIFESTATIONS CULTURELLES

BEL0123	BEL0129	BEL0148	BEL0203
BEL0361	CHE0434	CHE0506	CHE0534
CHE0556	CHE0568	CHE0596	CHE0598
CHE0604	CHE0624	CHE0689	CHE0810
CHE0819	DEU1022	DEU1109	DEU1142
DEU1200	DNK1405	ESP1431	ESP1455
ESP1479	ESP1486	ESP1506	FIN1545
FIN1546	FIN1553	FIN1563	FRA1621
FRA1760	FRA1768	FRA1778	FRA1785
FRA1787	FRA1791	FRA1793	FRA1862
FRA1889	FRA1956	FRA2002	FRA2117
FRA2159	FRA2170	FRA2229	GBR2235
GBR2238	GBR2248	GBR2251	GBR2345
GBR2359	GBR2371	GBR2378	GBR2416
GBR2423	GBR2469	GBR2501	GBR2511
GBR2544	GBR2545	GRC2576	IRL2714
IRL2717	ITA2767	ITA2798	ITA2809
ITA2811	ITA2834	ITA2855	ITA2881
ITA2898	ITA2923	LUX2937	LUX2982
LUX2983	MLT3016	NLD3067	NLD3073
NLD3087	NLD3089	NLD3139	NLD3181
NLD3190	NLD3217	NLD3222	NLD3230

See: *How to Use the Directory*, page 11.

NLD3236 NLD3253 NLD3269 NOR3460
POL3508 PRT3579 SWE3738 SWE3760
TUR3883

CONFERENCES, SEMINARS, WORKSHOPS, TRAINING ACTIVITIES - CONFERENCES, SEMINAIRES, ATELIERS, ACTIVITES DE FORMATION

AUT0002 AUT0010 AUT0024 AUT0030
AUT0034 AUT0051 AUT0056 AUT0067
AUT0068 AUT0074 AUT0085 AUT0089
AUT0090 BEL0101 BEL0123 BEL0127
BEL0129 BEL0133 BEL0148 BEL0152
BEL0156 BEL0160 BEL0168 BEL0177
BEL0188 BEL0191 BEL0192 BEL0199
BEL0203 BEL0214 BEL0221 BEL0231
BEL0237 BEL0254 BEL0261 BEL0265
BEL0270 BEL0272 BEL0273 BEL0275
BEL0282 BEL0306 BEL0308 BEL0309
BEL0317 BEL0335 BEL0340 BEL0345
BEL0351 BEL0353 BEL0361 BEL0399
CHE0406 CHE0416 CHE0417 CHE0434
CHE0439 CHE0461 CHE0464 CHE0479
CHE0486 CHE0491 CHE0506 CHE0519
CHE0521 CHE0562 CHE0566 CHE0568
CHE0596 CHE0604 CHE0614 CHE0619
CHE0628 CHE0629 CHE0632 CHE0637
CHE0638 CHE0642 CHE0645 CHE0655
CHE0661 CHE0669 CHE0682 CHE0689
CHE0711 CHE0753 CHE0754 CHE0755
CHE0758 CHE0762 CHE0765 CHE0771
CHE0772 CHE0773 CHE0794 CHE0809
CHE0814 CHE0819 CYP0831 CYP0832
CZE0897 DEU0942 DEU0944 DEU0968
DEU0977 DEU0983 DEU0990 DEU0992
DEU1002 DEU1004 DEU1010 DEU1013
DEU1019 DEU1020 DEU1025 DEU1032
DEU1047 DEU1055 DEU1065 DEU1066
DEU1074 DEU1090 DEU1097 DEU1106
DEU1109 DEU1131 DEU1142 DEU1149
DEU1178 DEU1180 DEU1184 DEU1186
DEU1187 DEU1193 DEU1198 DNK1227
DNK1243 DNK1272 DNK1273
DNK1275 DNK1281 DNK1283 DNK1289
DNK1298 DNK1305 DNK1307 DNK1312
DNK1339 DNK1361 DNK1375
DNK1398 ESP1407 ESP1413 ESP1430
ESP1431 ESP1437 ESP1443 ESP1456
ESP1457 ESP1472 ESP1474 ESP1479
ESP1486 ESP1506 ESP1513 ESP1517
ESP1521 ESP1522 ESP1524 ESP1528
FIN1545 FIN1546 FIN1553
FIN1557 FIN1574 FIN1577 FIN1578
FIN1582 FIN1583 FIN1592 FIN1602
FIN1604 FRA1661 FRA1672
FRA1690 FRA1701 FRA1704 FRA1731
FRA1778 FRA1785 FRA1787 FRA1799
FRA1818 FRA1831 FRA1846 FRA1848
FRA1849 FRA1861 FRA1862 FRA1889
FRA1907 FRA1946 FRA1947 FRA1949
FRA1956 FRA1975 FRA1978 FRA1990
FRA2004 FRA2005 FRA2012 FRA2016
FRA2019 FRA2040 FRA2041 FRA2044
FRA2057 FRA2061 FRA2062 FRA2096
FRA2107 FRA2117 FRA2122 FRA2126
FRA2129 FRA2131 FRA2159 FRA2170
GBR2172 GBR2174 GBR2175 GBR2176
GBR2181 GBR2183 GBR2185 GBR2186
GBR2195 GBR2197 GBR2199 GBR2202
GBR2205 GBR2213 GBR2217 GBR2226
GBR2229 GBR2235 GBR2238 GBR2251
GBR2256 GBR2260 GBR2264 GBR2265
GBR2266 GBR2269 GBR2279 GBR2281
GBR2284 GBR2292 GBR2302 GBR2303
GBR2312 GBR2326 GBR2341 GBR2346
GBR2351 GBR2353 GBR2355 GBR2358
GBR2359 GBR2371 GBR2378 GBR2380
GBR2387 GBR2390 GBR2402 GBR2408
GBR2413 GBR2416 GBR2423
GBR2437 GBR2445 GBR2452 GBR2453
GBR2455 GBR2460 GBR2469 GBR2481
GBR2483 GBR2500 GBR2503 GBR2511
GBR2513 GBR2515 GBR2535 GBR2536
GBR2537 GBR2544 GBR2545 GBR2550
GBR2551 GBR2553 GBR2561 GRC2567
GRC2576 HUN2631 IRL2690 IRL2693
IRL2698 IRL2702 IRL2706 IRL2714
IRL2717 IRL2720 IRL2726 IRL2729
ISL2736 ITA2762 ITA2767 ITA2771

ITA2773 ITA2775 ITA2798 ITA2810
ITA2813 ITA2820 ITA2826 ITA2829
ITA2832 ITA2834 ITA2835 ITA2838
ITA2855 ITA2860 ITA2866 ITA2881
ITA2890 ITA2895 ITA2896 ITA2898
ITA2899 ITA2901 ITA2905 ITA2908
ITA2913 ITA2916 ITA2922 LUX2946
LUX2958 LUX2967 LUX2983 LUX2993
MLT3016 MLT3017 MLT3023 NLD3067
NLD3073 NLD3078 NLD3079 NLD3085
NLD3087 NLD3097 NLD3101 NLD3104
NLD3117 NLD3126 NLD3133 NLD3135
NLD3139 NLD3153 NLD3156 NLD3164
NLD3165 NLD3170 NLD3173 NLD3174
NLD3181 NLD3190 NLD3196 NLD3198
NLD3199 NLD3211 NLD3217 NLD3219
NLD3222 NLD3230 NLD3232 NLD3235
NLD3236 NLD3249 NLD3269 NLD3278
NLD3279 NLD3292 NLD3301 NLD3305
NLD3318 NLD3341 NLD3347 NLD3348
NLD3357 NLD3364 NLD3366 NOR3371
NOR3379 NOR3386 NOR3390 NOR3400
NOR3402 NOR3403 NOR3416 NOR3440
NOR3467 NOR3473 POL3508 POL3519
POL3536 POL3543 PRT3576 PRT3579
PRT3586 PRT3594 PRT3600 PRT3602
SVK3612 SVK3634 SWE3648 SWE3658
SWE3667 SWE3679 SWE3695 SWE3727
SWE3731 SWE3738 SWE3744 SWE3749
SWE3771 SWE3772 SWE3775 SWE3787
SWE3799 SWE3807 SWE3816 SWE3821
SWE3826 SWE3853 SWE3864 SWE3865
SWE3879 TUR3883

EXCHANGES, TWINNING, LINKING - ECHANGES, PARRAINAGE, JUMELAGE

AUT0034 AUT0051 BEL0120 BEL0123
BEL0129 BEL0198 BEL0203 BEL0221
BEL0254 BEL0273 BEL0309 BEL0335
BEL0340 BEL0361 BEL0390 CHE0434
CHE0448 CHE0479 CHE0562 CHE0566
CHE0596 CHE0604 CHE0640 CHE0645
CHE0681 CHE0687 CHE0689 CHE0753
CHE0754 CHE0758 CHE0798 CHE0809
CHE0819 CYP0831 DEU0983 DEU0990
DEU1047 DEU1055 DEU1066 DEU1074
DEU1178 DEU1186 DEU1193 DEU1198
DEU1200 DNK1243 DNK1275 DNK1375
ESP1517 ESP1521 FIN1545 FIN1546
FRA1661 FRA1724 FRA1746 FRA1778
FRA1785 FRA1787 FRA1791 FRA1793
FRA1831 FRA1846 FRA1889 FRA1907
FRA1913 FRA1956 FRA2029 FRA2057
FRA2062 FRA2081 FRA2086 FRA2107
FRA2117 FRA2159 FRA2170 GBR2266
GBR2274 GBR2284 GBR2325 GBR2355
GBR2359 GBR2371 GBR2379 GBR2390
GBR2396 GBR2402 GBR2415 GBR2416
GBR2423 GBR2439 GBR2445 GBR2469
GBR2481 GBR2536 GBR2541 GBR2544
GRC2567 GRC2576 IRL2714 IRL2717
IRL2720 ITA2765 ITA2767 ITA2770
ITA2802 ITA2804 ITA2809 ITA2834
ITA2838 ITA2862 ITA2905 MLT3017
NLD3056 NLD3067 NLD3073 NLD3077
NLD3078 NLD3079 NLD3096 NLD3137
NLD3139 NLD3173 NLD3181 NLD3198
NLD3199 NLD3236 NLD3357 NLD3364
NLD3366 NOR3389 POL3519 POL3543
PRT3579 SVK3612 SWE3667 SWE3731
SWE3744 SWE3749 SWE3760 SWE3771
SWE3785 SWE3865 SWE3879 TUR3883

FORMAL EDUCATION - EDUCATION FORMELLE

AUT0065 AUT0085 BEL0123 BEL0148
BEL0177 BEL0273 BEL0303 BEL0317
BEL0323 BEL0351 BEL0353 BEL0359
BEL0361 BEL0390 BEL0392 CHE0434
CHE0521 CHE0562 CHE0566 CHE0570
CHE0628 CHE0640 CHE0645 CHE0660
CHE0681 CHE0682 CHE0687 CHE0689
CHE0753 CHE0772 CHE0805 CHE0809
CHE0819 DEU0954 DEU0983 DEU1132
DEU1178 DNK1227 DNK1243 DNK1262
DNK1272 DNK1289 DNK1298 DNK1405
ESP1407 ESP1427 ESP1431 ESP1437
ESP1455 ESP1468 ESP1479 ESP1486
FRA1607 FRA1627 FRA1647 FRA1661

FRA1664 FRA1724 FRA1738 FRA1739
FRA1761 FRA1785 FRA1787 FRA1827
FRA1848 FRA1849 FRA1889 FRA1946
FRA1956 FRA1992 FRA2016 FRA2019
FRA2044 FRA2062 FRA2103 FRA2107
FRA2150 FRA2159 FRA2170 GBR2174
GBR2175 GBR2178 GBR2181 GBR2185
GBR2233 GBR2238 GBR2265 GBR2269
GBR2273 GBR2333 GBR2345 GBR2359
GBR2371 GBR2378 GBR2379 GBR2380
GBR2390 GBR2396 GBR2408 GBR2415
GBR2423 GBR2424 GBR2436 GBR2445
GBR2452 GBR2455 GBR2467 GBR2468
GBR2481 GBR2511 GBR2522 GBR2544
GBR2551 GBR2553 GRC2567 HUN2643
IRL2690 IRL2691 IRL2697 IRL2698
IRL2702 IRL2706 IRL2720 IRL2726
ISL2740 ITA2762 ITA2767 ITA2771
ITA2798 ITA2810 ITA2813 ITA2822
ITA2826 ITA2855 ITA2857 ITA2868
ITA2889 ITA2894 ITA2896 ITA2898
ITA2916 LUX2986 LUX2995 LUX2997
MLT3016 MLT3017 MLT3023 NLD3056
NLD3067 NLD3078 NLD3089 NLD3104
NLD3153 NLD3179 NLD3190 NLD3199
NLD3215 NLD3269 NLD3352 NOR3416
NOR3460 NOR3465 NOR3467 NOR3473
POL3508 PRT3588 PRT3594 PRT3605
SVK3612 SWE3661 SWE3679 SWE3712
SWE3796 SWE3879

FUND RAISING - COLLECTE DE FONDS

AUT0003 AUT0022 AUT0026 AUT0034
AUT0051 AUT0085 AUT0091 BEL0104
BEL0110 BEL0118 BEL0148 BEL0155
BEL0167 BEL0168 BEL0198 BEL0199
BEL0201 BEL0203 BEL0245 BEL0254
BEL0282 BEL0308 BEL0309 BEL0327
BEL0335 BEL0351 BEL0352 BEL0353
BEL0355 BEL0359 BEL0361 BEL0381
BEL0390 CHE0409 CHE0417 CHE0434
CHE0438 CHE0444 CHE0446 CHE0455
CHE0475 CHE0479 CHE0491 CHE0493
CHE0506 CHE0519 CHE0521 CHE0558
CHE0562 CHE0566 CHE0584 CHE0598
CHE0604 CHE0619 CHE0630 CHE0659
CHE0687 CHE0689 CHE0691 CHE0707
CHE0742 CHE0754 CHE0755 CHE0756
CHE0764 CHE0767 CHE0789 CHE0798
CHE0804 CHE0810 CHE0814 CHE0819
CHE0823 DEU0954 DEU0957 DEU0968
DEU0983 DEU0993 DEU1002 DEU1006
DEU1022 DEU1038 DEU1044 DEU1065
DEU1066 DEU1086 DEU1132 DEU1138
DEU1149 DEU1178 DEU1186 DEU1187
DEU1193 DEU1200 DNK1222 DNK1227
DNK1305 DNK1392 DNK1405 ESP1442
ESP1450 ESP1455 ESP1486 ESP1491
ESP1506 ESP1510 ESP1517 FIN1544
FIN1549 FIN1585 FIN1591 FIN1599
FRA1661 FRA1664 FRA1690 FRA1703
FRA1724 FRA1738 FRA1739 FRA1760
FRA1761 FRA1778 FRA1785 FRA1787
FRA1789 FRA1791 FRA1793 FRA1831
FRA1843 FRA1849 FRA1852 FRA1861
FRA1866 FRA1889 FRA1913 FRA1914
FRA1930 FRA1939 FRA1946 FRA1990
FRA1991 FRA2016 FRA2037 FRA2041
FRA2080 FRA2081 FRA2086 FRA2116
FRA2117 FRA2119 FRA2131 FRA2138
FRA2159 FRA2170 GBR2172 GBR2175
GBR2176 GBR2180 GBR2183 GBR2197
GBR2201 GBR2213 GBR2226 GBR2228
GBR2229 GBR2238 GBR2242 GBR2244
GBR2248 GBR2259 GBR2264 GBR2274
GBR2277 GBR2289 GBR2292 GBR2297
GBR2302 GBR2312 GBR2318 GBR2319
GBR2321 GBR2324 GBR2325 GBR2326
GBR2333 GBR2348 GBR2353 GBR2358
GBR2359 GBR2371 GBR2372 GBR2373
GBR2375 GBR2378 GBR2385 GBR2390
GBR2396 GBR2413 GBR2419 GBR2436
GBR2439 GBR2445 GBR2469 GBR2481
GBR2483 GBR2500 GBR2503 GBR2508
GBR2511 GBR2513 GBR2515 GBR2521
GBR2522 GBR2524 GBR2525 GBR2532
GBR2535 GBR2537 GBR2541 GBR2544
GBR2550 GBR2551 GRC2576 IRL2691
IRL2697 IRL2714 IRL2732 IRL2733

Voir : *Comment utiliser le répertoire*, page 11.

ISL2740 ITA2762 ITA2767 ITA2770
ITA2773 ITA2775 ITA2804 ITA2810
ITA2813 ITA2820 ITA2822 ITA2826
ITA2834 ITA2855 ITA2857 ITA2858
ITA2868 ITA2881 ITA2885 ITA2888
ITA2889 ITA2894 ITA2899 ITA2901
ITA2907 ITA2912 ITA2913 LUX2936
LUX2946 LUX2958 LUX2959 LUX2967
LUX2982 LUX2983 LUX2986 LUX2993
LUX3006 NLD3056 NLD3062 NLD3067
NLD3073 NLD3078 NLD3089 NLD3104
NLD3135 NLD3137 NLD3145 NLD3149
NLD3159 NLD3181 NLD3184 NLD3198
NLD3199 NLD3219 NLD3222 NLD3231
NLD3237 NLD3249 NLD3253 NLD3256
NLD3269 NLD3288 NLD3292 NLD3300
NLD3301 NLD3302 NLD3323 NLD3357
NLD3361 NLD3364 NLD3366 NOR3371
NOR3379 NOR3404 NOR3410 NOR3453
NOR3460 NOR3467 NOR3475 PRT3588
PRT3594 PRT3605 SWE3648 SWE3661
SWE3674 SWE3679 SWE3712 SWE3714
SWE3727 SWE3730 SWE3731 SWE3738
SWE3744 SWE3749 SWE3787 SWE3795
SWE3796 SWE3807 SWE3819 SWE3826
SWE3834 SWE3853 SWE3854 SWE3857
SWE3864

INFORMATION AND DOCUMENTATION SERVICES, DATA BASES - SERVICES D'INFORMATION ET DE DOCUMENTATION, BASES DE DONNEES

AUT0020 AUT0024 AUT0026 AUT0034
AUT0056 AUT0060 AUT0074 AUT0079
AUT0085 BEL0123 BEL0127 BEL0129
BEL0149 BEL0155 BEL0164 BEL0167
BEL0168 BEL0177 BEL0191 BEL0192
BEL0199 BEL0203 BEL0214 BEL0237
BEL0267 BEL0273 BEL0303 BEL0306
BEL0308 BEL0309 BEL0335 BEL0345
BEL0359 BEL0361 BEL0365 BEL0390
BEL0392 BEL0393 BEL0396 BEL0399
CHE0406 CHE0420 CHE0429 CHE0434
CHE0464 CHE0479 CHE0501 CHE0506
CHE0521 CHE0534 CHE0554 CHE0562
CHE0566 CHE0590 CHE0596 CHE0624
CHE0632 CHE0638 CHE0640 CHE0645
CHE0664 CHE0668 CHE0689 CHE0742
CHE0756 CHE0762 CHE0763 CHE0771
CHE0771 CHE0809 CHE0814 CHE0819
CYP0831 DEU0944 DEU0968 DEU0977
DEU0990 DEU1002 DEU1013 DEU1019
DEU1020 DEU1022 DEU1025 DEU1031
DEU1076 DEU1086 DEU1090 DEU1091
DEU1109 DEU1129 DEU1178 DEU1186
DEU1149 DEU1184 DEU1186 DEU1192
DEU1193 DEU1200 DNK1238 DNK1248
DNK1262 DNK1281 DNK1292 DNK1298
DNK1305 DNK1339 DNK1358 DNK1375
DNK1398 ESP1407 ESP1413 ESP1430
ESP1431 ESP1434 ESP1437 ESP1441
ESP1457 ESP1479 ESP1482 ESP1486
ESP1506 ESP1521 ESP1522 FIN1546
FIN1548 FIN1582 FIN1585 FIN1591
FIN1592 FIN1602 FIN1604 FRA1701
FRA1737 FRA1785 FRA1787 FRA1797
FRA1810 FRA1811 FRA1815 FRA1818
FRA1827 FRA1831 FRA1839 FRA1841
FRA1846 FRA1889 FRA1907 FRA1935
FRA1946 FRA1947 FRA1956 FRA1990
FRA2002 FRA2004 FRA2018 FRA2035
FRA2041 FRA2076 FRA2096 FRA2103
FRA2104 FRA2107 FRA2122 FRA2131
FRA2159 FRA2170 GBR2197 GBR2205
GBR2226 GBR2235 GBR2238 GBR2239
GBR2264 GBR2265 GBR2266 GBR2284
GBR2326 GBR2339 GBR2359 GBR2371
GBR2378 GBR2379 GBR2387 GBR2392
GBR2396 GBR2402 GBR2408 GBR2413
GBR2415 GBR2416 GBR2423 GBR2435
GBR2437 GBR2438 GBR2439 GBR2445
GBR2452 GBR2453 GBR2455 GBR2464
GBR2469 GBR2483 GBR2511 GBR2522
GBR2537 GBR2541 GBR2544 GBR2545
GRC2576 HUN2631 IRL2698 IRL2705
IRL2714 IRL2720 IRL2730 ISL2736
ITA2762 ITA2767 ITA2773 ITA2780
ITA2786 ITA2798 ITA2801 ITA2808
ITA2810 ITA2813 ITA2820 ITA2822

ITA2834 ITA2855 ITA2857 ITA2860
ITA2873 ITA2880 ITA2889 ITA2890
ITA2894 ITA2895 ITA2896 ITA2900
ITA2901 ITA2907 ITA2908 ITA2913
LUX2937 LUX2962 NLD3051 NLD3056
NLD3058 NLD3067 NLD3073 NLD3077
NLD3078 NLD3085 NLD3087 NLD3089
NLD3096 NLD3110 NLD3135 NLD3137
NLD3139 NLD3147 NLD3165 NLD3167
NLD3170 NLD3173 NLD3181 NLD3190
NLD3196 NLD3198 NLD3211 NLD3217
NLD3222 NLD3235 NLD3279 NLD3301
NLD3302 NLD3305 NLD3318 NLD3334
NLD3347 NLD3352 NLD3355 NLD3357
NLD3361 NLD3364 NOR3379 NOR3390
NOR3400 NOR3402 NOR3467 POL3519
PRT3550 PRT3600 SWE3648 SWE3658
SWE3667 SWE3693 SWE3744 SWE3746
SWE3760 SWE3772 SWE3807 SWE3816
SWE3821 SWE3826 SWE3853 SWE3864
SWE3865 TUR3883 TUR3896

INFORMATION CAMPAIGNS, EXHIBITIONS - CAMPAGNES D'INFORMATION, EXPOSITIONS

AUT0020 AUT0034 AUT0051 AUT0067
AUT0068 AUT0085 AUT0091 BEL0101
BEL0123 BEL0129 BEL0139 BEL0148
BEL0167 BEL0168 BEL0192 BEL0198
BEL0199 BEL0203 BEL0267 BEL0273
BEL0282 BEL0289 BEL0303 BEL0335
BEL0340 BEL0345 BEL0351 BEL0352
BEL0353 BEL0361 BEL0381 BEL0390
BEL0392 CHE0406 CHE0416 CHE0420
CHE0434 CHE0444 CHE0446 CHE0455
CHE0461 CHE0479 CHE0486 CHE0491
CHE0506 CHE0521 CHE0534 CHE0541
CHE0560 CHE0562 CHE0566 CHE0568
CHE0584 CHE0596 CHE0598 CHE0604
CHE0659 CHE0664 CHE0669 CHE0683
CHE0689 CHE0756 CHE0765 CHE0771
CHE0805 CHE0809 CHE0814 CHE0819
CYP0831 CYP0832 DEU0917 DEU0940
DEU0942 DEU0955 DEU0977 DEU0983
DEU1010 DEU1013 DEU1019 DEU1022
DEU1025 DEU1066 DEU1109 DEU1110
DEU1142 DEU1149 DEU1178 DEU1186
DEU1193 DEU1198 DEU1200 DNK1260
DNK1262 DNK1272 DNK1281 DNK1283
DNK1285 DNK1292 DNK1305 DNK1335
DNK1342 DNK1375 DNK1398 DNK1403
DNK1405 ESP1407 ESP1413 ESP1431
ESP1457 ESP1486 ESP1491 ESP1506
ESP1517 ESP1521 ESP1524 ESP1528
FIN1545 FIN1546 FIN1553 FIN1591
FIN1592 FRA1607 FRA1647 FRA1738
FRA1739 FRA1761 FRA1785 FRA1787
FRA1791 FRA1793 FRA1797 FRA1848
FRA1849 FRA1852 FRA1861 FRA1862
FRA1876 FRA1889 FRA1939 FRA1947
FRA1956 FRA1990 FRA2002 FRA2005
FRA2062 FRA2096 FRA2107 FRA2116
FRA2126 FRA2138 FRA2159 FRA2170
GBR2172 GBR2195 GBR2205 GBR2229
GBR2235 GBR2238 GBR2239 GBR2248
GBR2259 GBR2265 GBR2269 GBR2277
GBR2279 GBR2303 GBR2312 GBR2326
GBR2328 GBR2339 GBR2351 GBR2359
GBR2371 GBR2378 GBR2387 GBR2402
GBR2408 GBR2415 GBR2416 GBR2423
GBR2439 GBR2445 GBR2452 GBR2469
GBR2483 GBR2503 GBR2511 GBR2535
GBR2536 GBR2537 GBR2541 GBR2544
GBR2545 GBR2553 GBR2561 GBR2567
GRC2576 IRL2688 IRL2690 IRL2693
IRL2714 IRL2720 ITA2767 ITA2770
ITA2775 ITA2810 ITA2813 ITA2834
ITA2838 ITA2855 ITA2858 ITA2860
ITA2890 ITA2894 ITA2896 ITA2898
ITA2901 ITA2913 LUX2954 LUX2958
LUX2967 LUX2986 LUX2993 LUX2995
LUX3006 MLT3017 NLD3056 NLD3067
NLD3073 NLD3078 NLD3079 NLD3087
NLD3089 NLD3117 NLD3137 NLD3139
NLD3170 NLD3173 NLD3181 NLD3190
NLD3196 NLD3198 NLD3199 NLD3211
NLD3217 NLD3219 NLD3222 NLD3232
NLD3236 NLD3257 NLD3269 NLD3303
NLD3305 NLD3320 NLD3323 NLD3347
NLD3348 NLD3352 NLD3357 NLD3361

NLD3366 NOR3371 NOR3379 NOR3402
NOR3440 NOR3467 POL3519 PRT3579
PRT3594 PRT3605 SVK3612 SWE3648
SWE3661 SWE3664 SWE3667 SWE3727
SWE3730 SWE3731 SWE3738 SWE3744
SWE3749 SWE3760 SWE3795 SWE3796
SWE3816 SWE3821 SWE3864 SWE3865
SWE3879 TUR3883

LOBBYING, ADVOCACY - LOBBYING, PLAIDOYER

AUT0008 AUT0024 AUT0033 AUT0034
AUT0051 AUT0056 AUT0067 AUT0068
AUT0090 BEL0118 BEL0131 BEL0160
BEL0167 BEL0168 BEL0177 BEL0186
BEL0191 BEL0198 BEL0199 BEL0203
BEL0214 BEL0216 BEL0254 BEL0265
BEL0267 BEL0282 BEL0306 BEL0308
BEL0309 BEL0335 BEL0345 BEL0351
BEL0353 BEL0361 BEL0399 CHE0416
CHE0420 CHE0429 CHE0434 CHE0464
CHE0479 CHE0486 CHE0506 CHE0519
CHE0521 CHE0534 CHE0550 CHE0560
CHE0562 CHE0566 CHE0568 CHE0596
CHE0603 CHE0604 CHE0637 CHE0642
CHE0645 CHE0668 CHE0687 CHE0689
CHE0711 CHE0765 CHE0794 CHE0809
CHE0814 CHE0819 CYP0831 CYP0832
DEU0942 DEU0954 DEU0983 DEU1002
DEU1004 DEU1006 DEU1010 DEU1013
DEU1032 DEU1055 DEU1066 DEU1074
DEU1097 DEU1109 DEU1131 DEU1142
DEU1149 DEU1186 DEU1193 DEU1200
DNK1262 DNK1281 DNK1283 DNK1289
DNK1298 DNK1335 DNK1339 DNK1399
DNK1403 DNK1405 ESP1407 ESP1431
ESP1456 ESP1457 ESP1479 ESP1521
ESP1528 FIN1544 FIN1545 FIN1602
FIN1604 FRA1661 FRA1785 FRA1797
FRA1831 FRA1841 FRA1843 FRA1862
FRA1876 FRA1889 FRA1946 FRA1949
FRA1956 FRA2002 FRA2004 FRA2035
FRA2041 FRA2057 FRA2096 FRA2110
FRA2159 FRA2170 GBR2174 GBR2181
GBR2186 GBR2194 GBR2195 GBR2199
GBR2202 GBR2205 GBR2215 GBR2217
GBR2228 GBR2229 GBR2235 GBR2238
GBR2239 GBR2242 GBR2256 GBR2264
GBR2266 GBR2269 GBR2284 GBR2303
GBR2319 GBR2328 GBR2351 GBR2355
GBR2359 GBR2371 GBR2378 GBR2390
GBR2392 GBR2396 GBR2413 GBR2423
GBR2445 GBR2464 GBR2469 GBR2481
GBR2498 GBR2503 GBR2511 GBR2522
GBR2529 GBR2537 GBR2541 GBR2544
GBR2545 GBR2551 GBR2552 GBR2553
GRC2576 HUN2643 IRL2690 IRL2691
IRL2706 IRL2714 IRL2717 ITA2767
ITA2775 ITA2798 ITA2810 ITA2820
ITA2822 ITA2834 ITA2855 ITA2862
ITA2881 ITA2895 ITA2898 ITA2913
LIE2927 LUX2957 LUX2958 LUX2997
MLT3016 MLT3017 MLT3023 NLD3062
NLD3067 NLD3078 NLD3079 NLD3096
NLD3104 NLD3117 NLD3133 NLD3137
NLD3139 NLD3147 NLD3153 NLD3156
NLD3164 NLD3167 NLD3181 NLD3198
NLD3199 NLD3211 NLD3219 NLD3222
NLD3230 NLD3232 NLD3236 NLD3278
NLD3301 NLD3303 NLD3305 NLD3347
NLD3348 NLD3352 NLD3364 NLD3366
NOR3379 NOR3390 NOR3402 NOR3467
POL3536 POL3543 PRT3576 PRT3579
PRT3594 PRT3600 PRT3602 PRT3605
SVK3634 SWE3648 SWE3661 SWE3667
SWE3674 SWE3738 SWE3749 SWE3771
SWE3799 SWE3807 SWE3853 SWE3864
TUR3883

NETWORKING, ELECTRONIC TELECOMMUNICATIONS - RESEAUX, TELECOMMUNICATIONS ELECTRONIQUES

AUT0020 AUT0034 AUT0051 BEL0177
BEL0198 BEL0254 BEL0309 BEL0335
BEL0361 CHE0434 CHE0506 CHE0562
CHE0568 CHE0596 CHE0642 CHE0689
CHE0809 CHE0819 DEU0955 DEU0990
DEU1002 DEU1065 DEU1186 ESP1434
ESP1457 ESP1479 ESP1522 FIN1591

See: *How to Use the Directory*, page 11.

FRA1785 FRA1889 FRA1956 FRA2159
FRA2170 GBR2199 GBR2205 GBR2226
GBR2265 GBR2279 GBR2284 GBR2285
GBR2313 GBR2328 GBR2351 GBR2359
GBR2371 GBR2378 GBR2387 GBR2413
GBR2416 GBR2438 GBR2469 GBR2544
GBR2545 GRC2576 IRL2714 IRL2717
ITA2767 ITA2773 ITA2822 ITA2860
ITA2881 NLD3067 NLD3104 NLD3137
NLD3139 NLD3181 NLD3199 NLD3236
NLD3279 NLD3292 NLD3318 NLD3347
NLD3357 NLD3366 NOR3467 SWE3785
SWE3787 SWE3864 TUR3883

OTHER - AUTRE

CHE0434 FRA1700 FRA2012 GBR2240
GBR2326 GBR2358 GBR2371 GBR2387
NLD3096 NLD3117 NLD3133 NLD3137
NLD3183 SWE3648 SWE3666

PUBLISHING, AUDIOVISUAL MATERIALS,
EDUCATIONAL MATERIALS - EDITION,
DOCUMENTS AUDIOVISUELS, DOCUMENTS
EDUCATIFS

AUT0010 AUT0020 AUT0026 AUT0034
AUT0051 AUT0056 AUT0085 BEL0101
BEL0120 BEL0123 BEL0127 BEL0139
BEL0155 BEL0167 BEL0168 BEL0177
BEL0188 BEL0203 BEL0214 BEL0245
BEL0254 BEL0261 BEL0282 BEL0306
BEL0309 BEL0323 BEL0335 BEL0340
BEL0345 BEL0351 BEL0361 BEL0381
BEL0390 BEL0393 CHE0406 CHE0429
CHE0434 CHE0444 CHE0499 CHE0506
CHE0521 CHE0534 CHE0549 CHE0560
CHE0562 CHE0564 CHE0566 CHE0568
CHE0596 CHE0638 CHE0689 CHE0756
CHE0762 CHE0763 CHE0794 CHE0804
CHE0809 CHE0819 CYP0831 DEU0942
DEU0944 DEU0972 DEU0977 DEU1004
DEU1013 DEU1019 DEU1020 DEU1022
DEU1025 DEU1038 DEU1047 DEU1055
DEU1062 DEU1066 DEU1074 DEU1076
DEU1097 DEU1109 DEU1110 DEU1142
DEU1180 DEU1186 DEU1187 DEU1193
DEU1198 DNK1243 DNK1248 DNK1260
DNK1262 DNK1273 DNK1289 DNK1335
DNK1339 ESP1407 ESP1413 ESP1430
ESP1434 ESP1435 ESP1437 ESP1457
ESP1491 ESP1506 ESP1517 ESP1521
ESP1522 FIN1536 FIN1544 FIN1545
FIN1546 FIN1548 FIN1580 FIN1585
FIN1591 FRA1607 FRA1627 FRA1642
FRA1661 FRA1668 FRA1672 FRA1704
FRA1713 FRA1768 FRA1778 FRA1785
FRA1787 FRA1799 FRA1810 FRA1828
FRA1836 FRA1843 FRA1849 FRA1862
FRA1889 FRA1907 FRA1920 FRA1935
FRA1956 FRA1986 FRA1990 FRA2001
FRA2002 FRA2004 FRA2005 FRA2072
FRA2096 FRA2116 FRA2131 FRA2138
FRA2159 FRA2170 GBR2181 GBR2183
GBR2185 GBR2186 GBR2195 GBR2199
GBR2205 GBR2229 GBR2235 GBR2238
GBR2239 GBR2248 GBR2264 GBR2265
GBR2266 GBR2271 GBR2279 GBR2281
GBR2303 GBR2312 GBR2326 GBR2345
GBR2358 GBR2359 GBR2371 GBR2378
GBR2380 GBR2387 GBR2390 GBR2396
GBR2402 GBR2413 GBR2415 GBR2416
GBR2423 GBR2445 GBR2452 GBR2453
GBR2455 GBR2467 GBR2469 GBR2483
GBR2500 GBR2501 GBR2503 GBR2511
GBR2525 GBR2535 GBR2541 GBR2544
GBR2545 GBR2552 GBR2554 IRL2690
IRL2693 IRL2698 IRL2717 IRL2720
IRL2733 ISL2736 ITA2762 ITA2767
ITA2773 ITA2780 ITA2798 ITA2810
ITA2813 ITA2820 ITA2822 ITA2826
ITA2834 ITA2838 ITA2855 ITA2857
ITA2858 ITA2860 ITA2861 ITA2862
ITA2880 ITA2896 ITA2901 ITA2908
ITA2913 ITA2916 ITA2923 LUX2958
LUX3006 MLT3016 NLD3056 NLD3067
NLD3077 NLD3078 NLD3085 NLD3089
NLD3098 NLD3133 NLD3135 NLD3139
NLD3145 NLD3164 NLD3165 NLD3173
NLD3181 NLD3190 NLD3198 NLD3199

NLD3211 NLD3215 NLD3216 NLD3222
NLD3230 NLD3257 NLD3278 NLD3279
NLD3301 NLD3302 NLD3305 NLD3318
NLD3320 NLD3347 NLD3348 NLD3352
NLD3357 NLD3361 NLD3364 NOR3379
NOR3389 NOR3390 NOR3394 NOR3402
NOR3440 NOR3441 NOR3467 POL3519
POL3543 PRT3579 PRT3600 SWE3667
SWE3731 SWE3746 SWE3749 SWE3760
SWE3816 SWE3821 SWE3865 SWE3879
TUR3883

HEALTH, SANITATION, WATER - SANTE, ASSAINISSEMENT, EAU

BROADCASTING, CULTURAL EVENTS -
RADIODIFFUSION, MANIFESTATIONS
CULTURELLES

AUT0052 BEL0194 BEL0203 BEL0347
BEL0358 BEL0361 CHE0434 CHE0517
CHE0524 CHE0534 CHE0568 CHE0569
CHE0598 CHE0604 CHE0624 CHE0687
CHE0689 CHE0819 DEU0918 DEU1022
DEU1053 DEU1142 DNK1310 DNK1376
ESP1455 ESP1486 ESP1506 ESP1507
ESP1510 FIN1579 FRA1612 FRA1614
FRA1621 FRA1676 FRA1760 FRA1771
FRA1774 FRA1778 FRA1785 FRA1791
FRA1793 FRA1889 FRA1904 FRA1956
FRA1988 FRA2002 FRA2047 FRA2054
FRA2062 FRA2069 FRA2102 FRA2117
FRA2151 FRA2159 GBR2229 GBR2238
GBR2248 GBR2278 GBR2345 GBR2371
GBR2382 GBR2383 GBR2423 GBR2501
GBR2511 GBR2538 GBR2545 ITA2798
ITA2801 ITA2807 ITA2813 ITA2835
ITA2855 ITA2898 ITA2907 LUX2954
LUX2961 LUX2982 MLT3016 MLT3023
NLD3067 NLD3135 NLD3150 NLD3269
NLD3303 NOR3374 POL3508 SVK3611
SWE3774 TUR3883

CONFERENCES, SEMINARS, WORKSHOPS,
TRAINING ACTIVITIES - CONFERENCES,
SEMINAIRES, ATELIERS, ACTIVITES DE
FORMATION

AUT0002 AUT0035 AUT0052 AUT0085
AUT0089 BEL0101 BEL0107 BEL0111
BEL0127 BEL0133 BEL0142 BEL0148
BEL0152 BEL0156 BEL0168 BEL0188
BEL0192 BEL0194 BEL0202 BEL0203
BEL0221 BEL0224 BEL0265 BEL0270
BEL0282 BEL0297 BEL0299 BEL0301
BEL0318 BEL0347 BEL0359 BEL0361
BEL0362 BEL0392 CHE0402 CHE0417
CHE0434 CHE0467 CHE0494 CHE0510
CHE0521 CHE0524 CHE0549 CHE0562
CHE0565 CHE0568 CHE0569 CHE0586
CHE0618 CHE0619 CHE0628 CHE0629
CHE0642 CHE0655 CHE0660 CHE0669
CHE0682 CHE0687 CHE0689 CHE0692
CHE0693 CHE0730 CHE0734 CHE0749
CHE0758 CHE0765 CHE0767 CHE0814
CHE0817 CHE0819 CHE0823 CHE0825
CYP0831 CZE0859 DEU0921 DEU0939
DEU0944 DEU0954 DEU0968 DEU0974
DEU0983 DEU0989 DEU0990 DEU1017
DEU1019 DEU1020 DEU1023 DEU1053
DEU1066 DEU1090 DEU1106 DEU1132
DEU1141 DEU1142 DEU1149 DEU1151
DEU1178 DEU1186 DNK1218 DNK1227
DNK1242 DNK1272 DNK1275 DNK1307
DNK1310 DNK1312 DNK1319 DNK1361
DNK1391 DNK1392 DNK1398 ESP1409
ESP1455 ESP1472 ESP1478 ESP1486
ESP1488 ESP1495 ESP1502 ESP1506
ESP1507 ESP1510 ESP1517 ESP1525
FIN1539 FIN1546 FIN1551 FIN1553
FIN1556 FIN1559 FIN1574 FIN1579
FIN1580 FIN1581 FIN1603 FRA1610
FRA1616 FRA1617 FRA1619 FRA1627
FRA1629 FRA1634 FRA1640 FRA1648
FRA1661 FRA1670 FRA1671 FRA1672
FRA1704 FRA1717 FRA1727 FRA1731
FRA1774 FRA1778 FRA1785 FRA1787
FRA1788 FRA1789 FRA1797 FRA1815
FRA1818 FRA1820 FRA1832 FRA1841

FRA1846 FRA1848 FRA1849 FRA1850
FRA1860 FRA1889 FRA1904 FRA1917
FRA1921 FRA1935 FRA1944 FRA1946
FRA1956 FRA1964 FRA1970 FRA1978
FRA1988 FRA1990 FRA2004 FRA2016
FRA2044 FRA2047 FRA2054 FRA2062
FRA2069 FRA2070 FRA2074 FRA2086
FRA2093 FRA2096 FRA2102 FRA2114
FRA2122 FRA2131 FRA2151 FRA2159
FRA2162 GBR2172 GBR2174 GBR2175
GBR2181 GBR2183 GBR2185 GBR2186
GBR2196 GBR2202 GBR2205 GBR2213
GBR2214 GBR2224 GBR2226 GBR2229
GBR2232 GBR2238 GBR2242 GBR2248
GBR2256 GBR2260 GBR2264 GBR2265
GBR2269 GBR2274 GBR2278 GBR2279
GBR2281 GBR2302 GBR2303 GBR2321
GBR2344 GBR2348 GBR2350 GBR2353
GBR2356 GBR2358 GBR2369 GBR2371
GBR2382 GBR2383 GBR2387 GBR2390
GBR2392 GBR2402 GBR2408 GBR2413
GBR2415 GBR2423 GBR2426 GBR2436
GBR2445 GBR2452 GBR2454 GBR2455
GBR2458 GBR2460 GBR2464 GBR2474
GBR2475 GBR2477 GBR2481 GBR2492
GBR2500 GBR2503 GBR2511 GBR2513
GBR2517 GBR2522 GBR2527 GBR2533
GBR2535 GBR2536 GBR2544 GBR2545
GBR2550 GBR2561 GRC2573 GRC2586
GRC2595 HUN2620 HUN2637 IRL2679
IRL2689 IRL2720 IRL2729 ISL2736
ITA2757 ITA2762 ITA2764 ITA2766
ITA2773 ITA2775 ITA2782 ITA2785
ITA2791 ITA2802 ITA2803 ITA2809
ITA2810 ITA2813 ITA2814 ITA2816
ITA2818 ITA2820 ITA2822 ITA2826
ITA2829 ITA2834 ITA2835 ITA2841
ITA2848 ITA2855 ITA2858 ITA2868
ITA2874 ITA2881 ITA2890 ITA2894
ITA2898 ITA2899 ITA2900 ITA2908
ITA2913 ITA2916 ITA2920 LUX2961
LUX2968 LUX2993 MLT3016 MLT3023
NLD3050 NLD3067 NLD3083 NLD3137
NLD3150 NLD3154 NLD3155 NLD3163
NLD3165 NLD3173 NLD3174 NLD3176
NLD3184 NLD3186 NLD3198 NLD3202
NLD3213 NLD3225 NLD3230 NLD3232
NLD3235 NLD3269 NLD3278 NLD3292
NLD3301 NLD3303 NLD3305 NLD3338
NLD3352 NLD3357 NOR3374 NOR3379
NOR3381 NOR3386 NOR3400 NOR3412
NOR3430 NOR3440 NOR3443 NOR3467
POL3482 POL3499 POL3519 POL3536
POL3543 PRT3549 PRT3576 PRT3586
PRT3590 PRT3594 PRT3600 PRT3603
SVK3611 SVK3612 SWE3648 SWE3658
SWE3666 SWE3671 SWE3674 SWE3679
SWE3685 SWE3702 SWE3707 SWE3712
SWE3745 SWE3749 SWE3769 SWE3771
SWE3776 SWE3778 SWE3783 SWE3787
SWE3789 SWE3796 SWE3799 SWE3807
SWE3816 SWE3827 SWE3850 SWE3853
SWE3865 SWE3879 TUR3884 TUR3896

EXCHANGES, TWINNING, LINKING - ECHANGES,
PARRAINAGE, JUMELAGE

BEL0120 BEL0129 BEL0156 BEL0198
BEL0203 BEL0221 BEL0303 BEL0358
BEL0361 BEL0390 CHE0434 CHE0444
CHE0448 CHE0524 CHE0562 CHE0565
CHE0595 CHE0687 CHE0689 CHE0730
CHE0758 CHE0798 CHE0819 CHE0825
CYP0831 DEU0939 DEU0951 DEU0983
DEU0990 DEU1023 DEU1066 DEU1141
DEU1149 DEU1178 DNK1391 ESP1495
ESP1525 FIN1551 FIN1556 FIN1603
FRA1616 FRA1642 FRA1655 FRA1661
FRA1671 FRA1691 FRA1699 FRA1746
FRA1778 FRA1785 FRA1787 FRA1791
FRA1793 FRA1846 FRA1855 FRA1889
FRA1904 FRA1913 FRA1928 FRA1938
FRA1941 FRA1946 FRA1956 FRA1964
FRA2047 FRA2057 FRA2062 FRA2065
FRA2069 FRA2081 FRA2086 FRA2102
FRA2114 FRA2140 FRA2145 FRA2151
FRA2159 GBR2186 GBR2224 GBR2274
GBR2278 GBR2325 GBR2371 GBR2379
GBR2383 GBR2390 GBR2396 GBR2481
GBR2489 GBR2515 GBR2517 GBR2536

Voir : *Comment utiliser le répertoire*, page 11.

HUN2620 IRL2698 ITA2765 ITA2766
ITA2775 ITA2785 ITA2791 ITA2802
ITA2804 ITA2813 ITA2838 ITA2900
LUX2942 NLD3056 NLD3067 NLD3071
NLD3096 NLD3098 NLD3100 NLD3137
NLD3141 NLD3150 NLD3154 NLD3155
NLD3173 NLD3198 NLD3303 NLD3338
NLD3357 NOR3374 NOR3400 NOR3412
POL3499 POL3508 POL3519 PRT3602
PRT3603 SVK3611 SVK3612 SWE3648
SWE3685 SWE3749 SWE3771 SWE3865
SWE3879

FORMAL EDUCATION - EDUCATION FORMELLE

AUT0052 AUT0065 AUT0085 AUT0086
BEL0145 BEL0148 BEL0156 BEL0299
BEL0316 BEL0323 BEL0341 BEL0347
BEL0359 BEL0361 BEL0390 CHE0434
CHE0510 CHE0521 CHE0560 CHE0562
CHE0628 CHE0660 CHE0682 CHE0683
CHE0687 CHE0688 CHE0689 CHE0730
CHE0734 CHE0749 CHE0759 CHE0805
CHE0814 CHE0819 CYP0828 CYP0833
CZE0859 DEU0954 DEU0983 DEU0989
DEU1017 DEU1132 DEU1141 DEU1149
DNK1214 DNK1218 DNK1222 DNK1227
DNK1262 DNK1272 DNK1310 ESP1427
ESP1455 ESP1472 ESP1486 ESP1492
ESP1495 ESP1502 ESP1508 FRA1607
FRA1627 FRA1628 FRA1647 FRA1649
FRA1661 FRA1664 FRA1672 FRA1694
FRA1699 FRA1704 FRA1731 FRA1738
FRA1739 FRA1740 FRA1769 FRA1785
FRA1787 FRA1789 FRA1848 FRA1849
FRA1856 FRA1889 FRA1904 FRA1935
FRA1941 FRA1946 FRA1956 FRA1966
FRA1992 FRA2002 FRA2004 FRA2016
FRA2062 FRA2069 FRA2102 FRA2131
FRA2151 FRA2159 GBR2174 GBR2175
GBR2181 GBR2238 GBR2264 GBR2265
GBR2266 GBR2269 GBR2278 GBR2333
GBR2345 GBR2371 GBR2379 GBR2382
GBR2383 GBR2390 GBR2408 GBR2415
GBR2423 GBR2424 GBR2436 GBR2452
GBR2455 GBR2467 GBR2468 GBR2474
GBR2475 GBR2481 GBR2511 GBR2522
GBR2533 GBR2544 GBR2553 GRC2573
HUN2643 IRL2689 IRL2691 IRL2697
IRL2720 IRL2726 IRL2733 ISL2740
ITA2762 ITA2764 ITA2766 ITA2770
ITA2773 ITA2782 ITA2791 ITA2803
ITA2810 ITA2813 ITA2816 ITA2822
ITA2832 ITA2835 ITA2868 ITA2894
ITA2898 ITA2900 ITA2916 LUX2942
LUX2995 MLT3016 MLT3023 NLD3050
NLD3056 NLD3067 NLD3083 NLD3150
NLD3154 NLD3155 NLD3163 NLD3173
NLD3176 NLD3184 NLD3202 NLD3212
NLD3225 NLD3232 NLD3254 NLD3269
NLD3345 NLD3352 NOR3386 NOR3394
NOR3412 NOR3430 NOR3443 NOR3460
NOR3465 NOR3467 POL3508 PRT3576
PRT3590 PRT3594 SVK3611 SVK3612
SWE3653 SWE3679 SWE3712 SWE3745
SWE3771 SWE3796 SWE3809 SWE3823
SWE3859 SWE3879

FUND RAISING - COLLECTE DE FONDS

AUT0003 AUT0026 AUT0030 AUT0033
AUT0051 AUT0076 AUT0085 AUT0086
AUT0089 AUT0091 BEL0104 BEL0107
BEL0110 BEL0132 BEL0145 BEL0148
BEL0153 BEL0155 BEL0156 BEL0167
BEL0168 BEL0194 BEL0198 BEL0201
BEL0203 BEL0224 BEL0233 BEL0270
BEL0282 BEL0297 BEL0299 BEL0301
BEL0316 BEL0331 BEL0323 BEL0327
BEL0328 BEL0341 BEL0351 BEL0352
BEL0353 BEL0355 BEL0358 BEL0359
BEL0361 BEL0362 BEL0368 BEL0390
CHE0410 CHE0417 CHE0422 CHE0434
CHE0438 CHE0444 CHE0446 CHE0448
CHE0463 CHE0467 CHE0475 CHE0477
CHE0479 CHE0485 CHE0486 CHE0493
CHE0506 CHE0521 CHE0524 CHE0529
CHE0562 CHE0564 CHE0569 CHE0583
CHE0586 CHE0598 CHE0604 CHE0619
CHE0630 CHE0659 CHE0664 CHE0686

CHE0687 CHE0688 CHE0689 CHE0691
CHE0692 CHE0693 CHE0707 CHE0730
CHE0734 CHE0742 CHE0749 CHE0754
CHE0755 CHE0756 CHE0764 CHE0767
CHE0778 CHE0788 CHE0789 CHE0796
CHE0798 CHE0804 CHE0806 CHE0814
CHE0819 CHE0823 DEU0922 DEU0926
DEU0928 DEU0933 DEU0954 DEU0957
DEU0968 DEU0978 DEU0983 DEU0989
DEU0991 DEU0993 DEU0994 DEU1001
DEU1002 DEU1006 DEU1017 DEU1022
DEU1023 DEU1027 DEU1063 DEU1066
DEU1086 DEU1132 DEU1138 DEU1141
DEU1149 DEU1176 DEU1187 DNK1214
DNK1216 DNK1218 DNK1222 DNK1227
DNK1242 DNK1245 DNK1262 DNK1266
DNK1310 DNK1316 DNK1366 DNK1372
DNK1376 DNK1377 DNK1391 DNK1405
ESP1409 ESP1442 ESP1455 ESP1470
ESP1486 ESP1491 ESP1495 ESP1502
ESP1505 ESP1506 ESP1507 ESP1510
ESP1517 ESP1549 FIN1551 FIN1575
FIN1580 FIN1581 FIN1585 FIN1591
FRA1610 FRA1612 FRA1614 FRA1617
FRA1632 FRA1644 FRA1648 FRA1661
FRA1663 FRA1664 FRA1672 FRA1684
FRA1685 FRA1690 FRA1691 FRA1694
FRA1704 FRA1718 FRA1738 FRA1739
FRA1741 FRA1760 FRA1761 FRA1769
FRA1771 FRA1774 FRA1778 FRA1785
FRA1786 FRA1787 FRA1789 FRA1791
FRA1793 FRA1820 FRA1843 FRA1849
FRA1850 FRA1855 FRA1861 FRA1866
FRA1889 FRA1913 FRA1914 FRA1928
FRA1938 FRA1939 FRA1944 FRA1946
FRA1966 FRA1978 FRA1990 FRA1991
FRA2016 FRA2027 FRA2047 FRA2054
FRA2056 FRA2069 FRA2080 FRA2081
FRA2086 FRA2116 FRA2117 FRA2119
FRA2131 FRA2137 FRA2138 FRA2145
FRA2151 FRA2159 FRA2164 GBR2172
GBR2174 GBR2175 GBR2180 GBR2183
GBR2186 GBR2197 GBR2201 GBR2213
GBR2222 GBR2224 GBR2226 GBR2228
GBR2229 GBR2238 GBR2240 GBR2242
GBR2248 GBR2259 GBR2264 GBR2274
GBR2277 GBR2278 GBR2280 GBR2289
GBR2292 GBR2297 GBR2302 GBR2310
GBR2318 GBR2319 GBR2321 GBR2324
GBR2325 GBR2333 GBR2348 GBR2350
GBR2358 GBR2371 GBR2372 GBR2373
GBR2375 GBR2382 GBR2383 GBR2385
GBR2390 GBR2392 GBR2413 GBR2423
GBR2436 GBR2445 GBR2464 GBR2474
GBR2475 GBR2477 GBR2481 GBR2483
GBR2489 GBR2492 GBR2500 GBR2509
GBR2511 GBR2513 GBR2517 GBR2522
GBR2524 GBR2525 GBR2532 GBR2535
GBR2537 GBR2538 GBR2550 GBR2552
GRC2586 HUN2598 IRL2680 IRL2688
IRL2689 IRL2691 IRL2726 IRL2730
IRL2732 IRL2733 ISL2740 ITA2762
ITA2764 ITA2766 ITA2770 ITA2773
ITA2775 ITA2782 ITA2803 ITA2804
ITA2806 ITA2809 ITA2810 ITA2812
ITA2813 ITA2814 ITA2816 ITA2818
ITA2820 ITA2822 ITA2826 ITA2829
ITA2832 ITA2834 ITA2835 ITA2837
ITA2848 ITA2855 ITA2868 ITA2873
ITA2874 ITA2879 ITA2880 ITA2881
ITA2885 ITA2889 ITA2890 ITA2894
ITA2899 ITA2900 ITA2907 ITA2911
ITA2912 ITA2913 ITA2916 ITA2920
ITA2921 LUX2942 LUX2955 LUX2959
LUX2961 LUX2968 LUX2972 LUX2982
LUX2991 LUX2992 LUX2993 LUX2995
NLD3050 NLD3056 NLD3067 NLD3100
NLD3126 NLD3131 NLD3137 NLD3149
NLD3150 NLD3154 NLD3159 NLD3163
NLD3184 NLD3186 NLD3198 NLD3201
NLD3202 NLD3213 NLD3231 NLD3232
NLD3235 NLD3237 NLD3251 NLD3254
NLD3255 NLD3256 NLD3265 NLD3269
NLD3288 NLD3292 NLD3295 NLD3300
NLD3301 NLD3302 NLD3303 NLD3308
NLD3323 NLD3345 NLD3361 NOR3371
NOR3379 NOR3381 NOR3387 NOR3404
NOR3410 NOR3412 NOR3435 NOR3443
NOR3444 NOR3453 NOR3460 NOR3467

POL3482 PRT3549 PRT3555 PRT3590
PRT3594 PRT3605 SVK3611 SWE3648
SWE3653 SWE3667 SWE3679 SWE3685
SWE3702 SWE3707 SWE3712 SWE3745
SWE3749 SWE3763 SWE3769 SWE3783
SWE3787 SWE3796 SWE3807 SWE3813
SWE3819 SWE3822 SWE3826 SWE3853
SWE3855 SWE3857 SWE3859 TUR3896

INFORMATION AND DOCUMENTATION SERVICES, DATA BASES - SERVICES D'INFORMATION ET DE DOCUMENTATION, BASES DE DONNEES

AUT0020 AUT0026 AUT0060 AUT0067
AUT0079 AUT0085 BEL0127 BEL0141
BEL0156 BEL0164 BEL0167 BEL0168
BEL0192 BEL0194 BEL0203 BEL0237
BEL0265 BEL0297 BEL0301 BEL0316
BEL0318 BEL0335 BEL0358 BEL0359
BEL0361 BEL0362 BEL0365 BEL0390
BEL0392 BEL0393 CHE0494 CHE0494
CHE0501 CHE0506 CHE0521 CHE0524
CHE0534 CHE0549 CHE0562 CHE0565
CHE0568 CHE0624 CHE0664 CHE0687
CHE0688 CHE0689 CHE0692 CHE0734
CHE0742 CHE0751 CHE0756 CHE0758
CHE0759 CHE0763 CHE0767 CHE0796
CHE0814 CHE0819 CHE0825 CYP0831
DEU0944 DEU0968 DEU0989 DEU0990
DEU1002 DEU1006 DEU1017 DEU1020
DEU1023 DEU1076 DEU1086 DEU1090
DEU1091 DEU1129 DEU1138 DEU1141
DEU1149 DEU1176 DEU1184 DEU1187
DNK1242 DNK1262 DNK1292 DNK1310
DNK1339 DNK1358 DNK1398 ESP1407
ESP1430 ESP1431 ESP1434 ESP1441
ESP1455 ESP1470 ESP1479 ESP1486
ESP1495 ESP1502 ESP1506 ESP1507
ESP1522 FIN1548 FIN1559 FIN1578
FIN1579 FIN1585 FIN1591 FIN1603
FRA1610 FRA1617 FRA1629 FRA1670
FRA1727 FRA1737 FRA1761 FRA1785
FRA1787 FRA1797 FRA1808 FRA1810
FRA1811 FRA1815 FRA1818 FRA1820
FRA1832 FRA1839 FRA1841 FRA1846
FRA1860 FRA1889 FRA1935 FRA1946
FRA1956 FRA1988 FRA1990 FRA2002
FRA2004 FRA2018 FRA2047 FRA2054
FRA2069 FRA2076 FRA2093 FRA2096
FRA2103 FRA2104 FRA2122 FRA2131
FRA2140 FRA2151 FRA2159 GBR2174
GBR2196 GBR2205 GBR2224 GBR2226
GBR2229 GBR2238 GBR2239 GBR2264
GBR2265 GBR2278 GBR2356 GBR2369
GBR2371 GBR2379 GBR2382 GBR2383
GBR2387 GBR2402 GBR2408 GBR2413
GBR2415 GBR2434 GBR2435 GBR2438
GBR2445 GBR2452 GBR2455 GBR2464
GBR2477 GBR2511 GBR2522 GBR2527
GBR2538 GBR2544 GBR2545 GRC2573
HUN2620 HUN2624 HUN2637 HUN2657
IRL2698 IRL2705 IRL2720 IRL2730
IRL2733 ISL2736 ITA2744 ITA2762
ITA2766 ITA2773 ITA2785 ITA2786
ITA2798 ITA2801 ITA2808 ITA2809
ITA2810 ITA2813 ITA2814 ITA2816
ITA2818 ITA2820 ITA2822 ITA2829
ITA2834 ITA2840 ITA2855
ITA2857 ITA2860 ITA2873 ITA2880
ITA2890 ITA2900 ITA2907 ITA2908
ITA2913 ITA2920 LUX2937 LUX2949
LUX2961 LUX2962 NLD3050 NLD3056
NLD3058 NLD3067 NLD3077 NLD3083
NLD3095 NLD3122 NLD3123 NLD3135
NLD3137 NLD3139 NLD3150 NLD3154
NLD3155 NLD3165 NLD3173 NLD3179
NLD3184 NLD3198 NLD3202 NLD3213
NLD3225 NLD3232 NLD3251 NLD3254
NLD3295 NLD3301 NLD3302 NLD3303
NLD3338 NLD3352 NLD3355 NLD3357
NLD3361 NOR3374 NOR3379 NOR3386
NOR3400 NOR3435 NOR3467 POL3482
POL3499 POL3519 PRT3550 PRT3600
SVK3611 SWE3648 SWE3658 SWE3685
SWE3693 SWE3744 SWE3769 SWE3774
SWE3776 SWE3789 SWE3807 SWE3816
SWE3826 SWE3827 SWE3853 SWE3854
SWE3865 TUR3883

See: *How to Use the Directory*, page 11.

INFORMATION CAMPAIGNS, EXHIBITIONS - CAMPAGNES D'INFORMATION, EXPOSITIONS

```
AUT0033   AUT0051   AUT0052   AUT0085
AUT0091   BEL0101   BEL0111   BEL0142
BEL0148   BEL0156   BEL0167   BEL0168
BEL0189   BEL0194   BEL0198   BEL0203
BEL0282   BEL0301   BEL0318   BEL0323
BEL0331   BEL0347   BEL0352   BEL0358
BEL0359   BEL0361   BEL0362   BEL0365
BEL0390   BEL0392   CHE0410   CHE0434
CHE0444   CHE0446   CHE0467   CHE0477
CHE0519   CHE0521   CHE0524   CHE0541
CHE0549   CHE0560   CHE0562   CHE0568
CHE0598   CHE0604   CHE0618   CHE0659
CHE0660   CHE0664   CHE0669   CHE0683
CHE0687   CHE0689   CHE0692   CHE0751
CHE0754   CHE0756   CHE0765   CHE0767
CHE0796   CHE0804   CHE0805   CHE0819
CYP0831   DEU0917   DEU0922   DEU0940
DEU0955   DEU0972   DEU0974   DEU0983
DEU1017   DEU1019   DEU1022   DEU1023
DEU1053   DEU1063   DEU1066   DEU1129
DEU1132   DEU1141   DEU1142   DEU1149
DEU1149   DEU1151   DEU1178   DNK1214
DNK1245   DNK1259   DNK1260   DNK1262
DNK1272   DNK1275   DNK1285   DNK1310
DNK1319   DNK1342   DNK1391   DNK1398
ESP1407   ESP1409   ESP1457   ESP1478
ESP1486   ESP1495   ESP1502   ESP1506
ESP1507   ESP1508   ESP1524   FIN1553
FIN1556   FIN1559   FIN1575   FIN1579
FIN1581   FIN1603   FRA1607   FRA1610
FRA1619   FRA1633   FRA1647   FRA1648
FRA1663   FRA1671   FRA1672   FRA1694
FRA1718   FRA1727   FRA1738   FRA1739
FRA1741   FRA1766   FRA1771   FRA1774
FRA1785   FRA1787   FRA1791   FRA1793
FRA1797   FRA1808   FRA1811   FRA1839
FRA1841   FRA1848   FRA1849   FRA1850
FRA1876   FRA1889   FRA1904   FRA1928
FRA1938   FRA1939   FRA1946   FRA1956
FRA1990   FRA1992   FRA2002   FRA2047
FRA2054   FRA2062   FRA2068   FRA2069
FRA2093   FRA2096   FRA2102   FRA2116
FRA2122   FRA2131   FRA2138   FRA2151
FRA2159   GBR2172   GBR2186
GBR2205   GBR2229   GBR2238   GBR2239
GBR2248   GBR2259   GBR2264   GBR2265
GBR2269   GBR2277   GBR2278   GBR2279
GBR2321   GBR2350   GBR2358   GBR2371
GBR2382   GBR2383   GBR2387   GBR2402
GBR2423   GBR2434   GBR2452   GBR2454
GBR2474   GBR2477   GBR2503   GBR2511
GBR2527   GBR2535   GBR2536   GBR2538
GBR2544   GBR2545   GBR2552   GBR2553
GBR2561   GRC2571   HUN2620   HUN2624
IRL2697   IRL2707   IRL2720   IRL2733
ITA2766   ITA2770   ITA2773   ITA2777
ITA2782   ITA2791   ITA2803   ITA2804
ITA2809   ITA2810   ITA2811   ITA2813
ITA2822   ITA2829   ITA2834   ITA2855
ITA2858   ITA2890   ITA2894   ITA2898
ITA2900   ITA2920   LUX2942   LUX2954
LUX2961   LUX2993   LUX2995   MLT3016
MLT3023   NLD3056   NLD3067   NLD3083
NLD3131   NLD3137   NLD3150   NLD3173
NLD3184   NLD3190   NLD3198   NLD3202
NLD3213   NLD3232   NLD3269   NLD3303
NLD3305   NLD3323   NLD3352   NLD3357
NOR3371   NOR3374   NOR3379   NOR3412
NOR3440   NOR3443   POL3482   POL3499
POL3519   POL3543   PRT3549   PRT3594
SVK3611   SVK3612   SWE3667   SWE3685
SWE3707   SWE3745   SWE3749   SWE3763
SWE3769   SWE3774   SWE3776   SWE3789
SWE3796   SWE3814   SWE3816   SWE3822
SWE3826   SWE3859   SWE3865   SWE3879
TUR3883
```

LOBBYING, ADVOCACY - LOBBYING, PLAIDOYER

```
AUT0033   AUT0086   AUT0089   BEL0111
BEL0131   BEL0156   BEL0167   BEL0168
BEL0186   BEL0198   BEL0203   BEL0224
BEL0265   BEL0282   BEL0299   BEL0301
BEL0318   BEL0351   BEL0361   CHE0434
CHE0521   CHE0534   CHE0549   CHE0560
CHE0562   CHE0568   CHE0603   CHE0604
CHE0618   CHE0642   CHE0683   CHE0687
```

```
CHE0689   CHE0751   CHE0765   CHE0767
CHE0780   CHE0814   CHE0819   CYP0828
CYP0831   CYP0833   CZE0896   DEU0926
DEU0954   DEU0974   DEU0983
DEU0989   DEU1006   DEU1023   DEU1066
DEU1132   DEU1141   DEU1142   DEU1149
DEU1151   DNK1310   DNK1376   DNK1399
ESP1410   ESP1457   ESP1502   FIN1551
FIN1574   FIN1603   FRA1633   FRA1661
FRA1740   FRA1785   FRA1787   FRA1797
FRA1841   FRA1843   FRA1850   FRA1876
FRA1889   FRA1946   FRA1956   FRA2002
FRA2004   FRA2047   FRA2069   FRA2093
FRA2096   FRA2110   FRA2151   FRA2159
GBR2174   GBR2186   GBR2202   GBR2205
GBR2224   GBR2228   GBR2229   GBR2238
GBR2239   GBR2242   GBR2256   GBR2264
GBR2269   GBR2319   GBR2348   GBR2356
GBR2371   GBR2383   GBR2390   GBR2392
GBR2413   GBR2423   GBR2434   GBR2445
GBR2464   GBR2481   GBR2511   GBR2517
GBR2522   GBR2527   GBR2529   GBR2544
GBR2545   GBR2553   GRC2586   HUN2598
HUN2637   HUN2643   HUN2680
IRL2689   IRL2691   IRL2707   ITA2766
ITA2775   ITA2801   ITA2810   ITA2820
ITA2855   ITA2898   ITA2913   LUX2957
MLT3016   MLT3023   NLD3067   NLD3137
NLD3147   NLD3150   NLD3155   NLD3165
NLD3184   NLD3186   NLD3198   NLD3225
NLD3232   NLD3251   NLD3254   NLD3278
NLD3301   NLD3303   NLD3305   NLD3345
NLD3352   NOR3379   NOR3386   NOR3396
NOR3467   POL3482   POL3499   POL3543
PRT3549   PRT3594   PRT3605   SWE3749
SWE3771   SWE3799   SWE3807   SWE3853
TUR3896   TUR3897
```

NETWORKING, ELECTRONIC TELECOMMUNICATIONS - RESEAUX, TELECOMMUNICATIONS ELECTRONIQUES

```
AUT0020   AUT0051   BEL0107   BEL0198
BEL0224   BEL0265   BEL0301   BEL0318
BEL0361   CHE0434   CHE0524   CHE0562
CHE0565   CHE0568   CHE0586   CHE0642
CHE0689   CHE0819   CHE0951   DEU0955
DEU0974   DEU0990   DEU1002   DEU1019
ESP1434   ESP1522   FIN1579   FIN1591
FRA1629   FRA1785   FRA1889   FRA1904
FRA1956   FRA2069   FRA2096   FRA2102
FRA2159   GBR2205   GBR2213   GBR2226
GBR2264   GBR2278   GBR2285
GBR2313   GBR2321   GBR2348   GBR2371
GBR2383   GBR2387   GBR2413   GBR2434
GBR2438   GBR2545   GRC2573   HUN2620
HUN2624   HUN2631   HUN2637   ITA2764
ITA2773   ITA2860   LUX2995   NLD3067
NLD3071   NLD3077   NLD3137   NLD3150
NLD3154   NLD3155   NLD3165   NLD3186
NLD3190   NLD3303   NLD3318   NLD3357
NOR3374   NOR3467   POL3482   POL3499
POL3508   SVK3611   SWE3787   SWE3789
TUR3883
```

OTHER - AUTRE

```
CHE0403   CHE0422   CHE0434   CHE0477
FRA1966   FRA2056   GBR2240   GBR2358
GBR2371   GBR2387   NLD3069   NLD3071
NLD3096   NLD3137   NLD3165   NLD3183
SWE3666
```

PUBLISHING, AUDIOVISUAL MATERIALS, EDUCATIONAL MATERIALS - EDITION, DOCUMENTS AUDIOVISUELS, DOCUMENTS EDUCATIFS

```
AUT0020   AUT0026   AUT0051   AUT0052
AUT0076   BEL0101   BEL0111   BEL0120
BEL0127   BEL0148   BEL0156   BEL0167
BEL0168   BEL0188   BEL0194   BEL0203
BEL0224   BEL0265   BEL0282   BEL0301
BEL0306   BEL0316   BEL0318   BEL0323
BEL0331   BEL0347   BEL0359   BEL0361
BEL0362   BEL0365   BEL0368   BEL0390
BEL0393   CHE0434   CHE0444   CHE0501
CHE0517   CHE0521   CHE0549   CHE0560
CHE0562   CHE0565   CHE0568   CHE0569
CHE0660   CHE0664   CHE0687   CHE0689
CHE0692   CHE0693   CHE0749   CHE0751
```

```
CHE0756   CHE0758   CHE0759   CHE0763
CHE0767   CHE0819   CYP0831   CZE0859
DEU0922   DEU0944   DEU0968   DEU0972
DEU0974   DEU0989   DEU1017   DEU1019
DEU1020   DEU1022   DEU1023   DEU1066
DEU1076   DEU1141   DEU1142   DEU1149
DEU1151   DEU1180   DEU1187   DNK1214
DNK1216   DNK1255   DNK1259   DNK1260
DNK1262   DNK1275   DNK1292   DNK1310
DNK1312   DNK1316   DNK1319   DNK1339
DNK1342   DNK1391   ESP1407   ESP1409
ESP1434   ESP1435   ESP1455   ESP1457
ESP1478   ESP1495   ESP1506   ESP1507
ESP1522   FIN1536   FIN1548   FIN1551
FIN1556   FIN1568   FIN1579   FIN1581
FIN1585   FIN1603   FIN1607   FRA1610
FRA1612   FRA1617   FRA1627   FRA1629
FRA1642   FRA1644   FRA1648   FRA1661
FRA1668   FRA1670   FRA1671   FRA1713
FRA1727   FRA1774   FRA1778   FRA1785
FRA1787   FRA1795   FRA1810   FRA1813
FRA1820   FRA1832   FRA1836   FRA1839
FRA1843   FRA1849   FRA1860   FRA1889
FRA1904   FRA1913   FRA1920   FRA1935
FRA1938   FRA1941   FRA1956   FRA1970
FRA1986   FRA1990   FRA2002   FRA2004
FRA2047   FRA2054   FRA2062   FRA2068
FRA2069   FRA2076   FRA2086   FRA2093
FRA2096   FRA2102   FRA2104   FRA2114
FRA2116   FRA2122   FRA2131   FRA2138
FRA2145   FRA2149   FRA2151   FRA2159
GBR2174   GBR2175   GBR2181   GBR2183
GBR2185   GBR2186   GBR2196   GBR2205
GBR2224   GBR2229   GBR2238   GBR2239
GBR2248   GBR2264   GBR2265   GBR2271
GBR2278   GBR2279   GBR2303   GBR2318
GBR2321   GBR2325   GBR2344   GBR2345
GBR2358   GBR2371   GBR2382   GBR2383
GBR2386   GBR2387   GBR2390   GBR2392
GBR2402   GBR2413   GBR2415   GBR2423
GBR2426   GBR2434   GBR2436   GBR2452
GBR2455   GBR2464   GBR2467   GBR2474
GBR2475   GBR2477   GBR2489   GBR2499
GBR2500   GBR2501   GBR2503   GBR2511
GBR2513   GBR2517   GBR2522   GBR2525
GBR2527   GBR2533   GBR2535   GBR2538
GBR2544   GBR2545   GBR2550   GBR2552
GBR2554   HUN2624   IRL2697   IRL2698
IRL2720   IRL2733   ISL2736   ISL2739
ITA2744   ITA2757   ITA2762   ITA2764
ITA2766   ITA2773   ITA2782   ITA2785
ITA2791   ITA2798   ITA2801   ITA2803
ITA2807   ITA2809   ITA2810   ITA2811
ITA2813   ITA2818   ITA2820
ITA2822   ITA2829   ITA2834   ITA2835
ITA2837   ITA2855   ITA2858   ITA2868
ITA2881   ITA2894   ITA2900
ITA2907   ITA2908   ITA2913   ITA2916
ITA2921   LUX2942   LUX2961   LUX3006
MLT3016   NLD3056   NLD3067   NLD3077
NLD3083   NLD3135   NLD3150   NLD3154
NLD3155   NLD3163   NLD3165   NLD3173
NLD3190   NLD3198   NLD3202   NLD3212
NLD3213   NLD3216   NLD3225   NLD3230
NLD3257   NLD3278   NLD3301   NLD3302
NLD3303   NLD3305   NLD3318   NLD3352
NLD3357   NOR3374   NOR3379   NOR3394
NOR3400   NOR3404   NOR3435   NOR3440
NOR3441   NOR3443   NOR3460   NOR3467
POL3482   POL3499   POL3519   POL3543
PRT3586   PRT3590   PRT3600   SVK3611
SWE3745   SWE3749   SWE3763   SWE3769
SWE3787   SWE3789   SWE3816   SWE3826
SWE3827   SWE3859   SWE3865   SWE3879
TUR3883   TUR3898
```

HUMAN RIGHTS, PEACE, CONFLICTS - DROITS DE L'HOMME, PAIX, CONFLITS

BROADCASTING, CULTURAL EVENTS - RADIODIFFUSION, MANIFESTATIONS CULTURELLES

```
BEL0115   BEL0116   BEL0123   BEL0129
BEL0203   BEL0303   BEL0304   BEL0361
CHE0420   CHE0434   CHE0452   CHE0524
CHE0534   CHE0560   CHE0568   CHE0624
CHE0689   CHE0711   CHE0715   CHE0744
CHE0819   CZE0891   CZE0904   DEU0920
```

Voir : *Comment utiliser le répertoire*, page 11.

DEU1022 DEU1110 DEU1149 DNK1274
DNK1283 DNK1375 DNK1376 DNK1405
ESP1430 ESP1437 ESP1486 ESP1490
ESP1506 ESP1507 ESP1523 FIN1532
FIN1545 FIN1553 FRA1621 FRA1768
FRA1791 FRA1793 FRA1794 FRA1808
FRA1862 FRA1889 FRA1910 FRA1923
FRA1938 FRA1957 FRA1974 FRA2002
FRA2040 FRA2047 FRA2062 FRA2117
FRA2159 GBR2185 GBR2193 GBR2194
GBR2215 GBR2229 GBR2235 GBR2238
GBR2332 GBR2345 GBR2371 GBR2378
GBR2423 GBR2423 GBR2493 GBR2498
GBR2501 GBR2511 GBR2545 GRC2579
HUN2601 HUN2644 IRL2686 IRL2714
ITA2798 ITA2820 ITA2834 ITA2838
ITA2895 ITA2907 ITA2923 MLT3016
NLD3067 NLD3098 NLD3135 NLD3139
NLD3181 NLD3236 NLD3249 NLD3253
NLD3326 NOR3372 NOR3390 NOR3402
NOR3467 POL3480 SVK3608 SVK3611
SVK3634 SWE3648 SWE3761 SWE3774
TUR3883

CONFERENCES, SEMINARS, WORKSHOPS, TRAINING ACTIVITIES - CONFERENCES, SEMINAIRES, ATELIERS, ACTIVITES DE FORMATION

AUT0002 AUT0011 AUT0020 AUT0024
AUT0032 AUT0044 AUT0047 AUT0058
AUT0074 AUT0090 BEL0096 BEL0115
BEL0116 BEL0123 BEL0127 BEL0129
BEL0147 BEL0148 BEL0155 BEL0156
BEL0160 BEL0174 BEL0176 BEL0177
BEL0188 BEL0191 BEL0197 BEL0199
BEL0203 BEL0214 BEL0221 BEL0231
BEL0248 BEL0252 BEL0254 BEL0265
BEL0272 BEL0275 BEL0303 BEL0304
BEL0306 BEL0309 BEL0335 BEL0345
BEL0353 BEL0361 BEL0362 BEL0392
CHE0406 CHE0415 CHE0417 CHE0420
CHE0421 CHE0434 CHE0452 CHE0456
CHE0461 CHE0494 CHE0519 CHE0524
CHE0534 CHE0550 CHE0562 CHE0566
CHE0568 CHE0596 CHE0605 CHE0622
CHE0638 CHE0639 CHE0642 CHE0645
CHE0650 CHE0654 CHE0655 CHE0661
CHE0669 CHE0671 CHE0682 CHE0689
CHE0693 CHE0711 CHE0715 CHE0718
CHE0741 CHE0744 CHE0747 CHE0751
CHE0755 CHE0756 CHE0765 CHE0772
CHE0809 CHE0810 CHE0814 CHE0817
CHE0819 CYP0831 CZE0859 CZE0865
CZE0897 CZE0904 CZE0905 CZE0906
DEU0920 DEU0944 DEU0954 DEU0968
DEU0983 DEU0990 DEU0996 DEU0998
DEU1006 DEU1010 DEU1013 DEU1019
DEU1020 DEU1025 DEU1027 DEU1030
DEU1038 DEU1047 DEU1054 DEU1055
DEU1056 DEU1062 DEU1063 DEU1064
DEU1065 DEU1074 DEU1090 DEU1106
DEU1110 DEU1114 DEU1131 DEU1142
DEU1146 DEU1149 DEU1167 DEU1178
DEU1180 DEU1184 DEU1186 DEU1187
DEU1193 DEU1198 DEU1210 DNK1248
DNK1273 DNK1283 DNK1287 DNK1289
DNK1305 DNK1307 DNK1312 DNK1335
DNK1339 DNK1360 DNK1361 DNK1375
DNK1376 DNK1398 DNK1405 ESP1430
ESP1436 ESP1441 ESP1450 ESP1451
ESP1472 ESP1478 ESP1479 ESP1484
ESP1486 ESP1490 ESP1493 ESP1505
ESP1506 ESP1508 ESP1511 ESP1517
ESP1523 ESP1524 ESP1525 ESP1528
FIN1532 FIN1536 FIN1540 FIN1543
FIN1544 FIN1549 FIN1552 FIN1552
FIN1553 FIN1554 FIN1560 FIN1570
FIN1574 FIN1578 FIN1585 FIN1588
FIN1592 FIN1594 FIN1604 FIN1605
FRA1611 FRA1619 FRA1632 FRA1651
FRA1675 FRA1701 FRA1791 FRA1793
FRA1794 FRA1797 FRA1799 FRA1808
FRA1815 FRA1818 FRA1838 FRA1841
FRA1846 FRA1852 FRA1862 FRA1889
FRA1938 FRA1946 FRA1957 FRA1960
FRA1964 FRA1974 FRA1978 FRA1990
FRA2002 FRA2004 FRA2009 FRA2013
FRA2015 FRA2017 FRA2019 FRA2032
FRA2034 FRA2035 FRA2039 FRA2040

FRA2041 FRA2042 FRA2044 FRA2047
FRA2057 FRA2062 FRA2084 FRA2096
FRA2101 FRA2131 FRA2143 FRA2150
FRA2159 FRA2165 GBR2181 GBR2185
GBR2193 GBR2194 GBR2195 GBR2199
GBR2215 GBR2229 GBR2235 GBR2238
GBR2256 GBR2260 GBR2265 GBR2269
GBR2279 GBR2303 GBR2312 GBR2327
GBR2328 GBR2332 GBR2337 GBR2347
GBR2351 GBR2353 GBR2355 GBR2371
GBR2374 GBR2378 GBR2387 GBR2390
GBR2392 GBR2396 GBR2401 GBR2402
GBR2408 GBR2411 GBR2413 GBR2415
GBR2416 GBR2423 GBR2424 GBR2435
GBR2445 GBR2448 GBR2455 GBR2460
GBR2464 GBR2481 GBR2490 GBR2495
GBR2498 GBR2503 GBR2511 GBR2513
GBR2522 GBR2526 GBR2535 GBR2545
GBR2546 GBR2555 GBR2561 GRC2572
GRC2579 GRC2584 GRC2585 GRC2586
HUN2625 HUN2637 HUN2643 HUN2644
IRL2679 IRL2684 IRL2686 IRL2688
IRL2695 IRL2706 IRL2712 IRL2714
IRL2717 IRL2720 IRL2726 ITA2750
ITA2771 ITA2780 ITA2786 ITA2791
ITA2798 ITA2799 ITA2801 ITA2804
ITA2809 ITA2810 ITA2816 ITA2820
ITA2826 ITA2829 ITA2834 ITA2834
ITA2841 ITA2860 ITA2866 ITA2868
ITA2873 ITA2881 ITA2883 ITA2888
ITA2889 ITA2890 ITA2894 ITA2895
ITA2898 ITA2900 ITA2903 ITA2905
ITA2907 ITA2908 ITA2916 ITA2923
LUX2935 LUX2954 LUX2984 LUX2992
MLT3016 MLT3017 MLT3018 MLT3023
NLD3049 NLD3050 NLD3064 NLD3067
NLD3072 NLD3078 NLD3082 NLD3083
NLD3087 NLD3097 NLD3098 NLD3104
NLD3119 NLD3133 NLD3135 NLD3139
NLD3147 NLD3153 NLD3156 NLD3160
NLD3164 NLD3170 NLD3174 NLD3179
NLD3181 NLD3190 NLD3198 NLD3199
NLD3204 NLD3218 NLD3222 NLD3223
NLD3226 NLD3230 NLD3236 NLD3242
NLD3249 NLD3277 NLD3301 NLD3303
NLD3326 NLD3329 NLD3330 NLD3338
NLD3341 NLD3357 NLD3364 NLD3366
NOR3371 NOR3372 NOR3386 NOR3389
NOR3390 NOR3391 NOR3400 NOR3402
NOR3416 NOR3429 NOR3435 NOR3440
NOR3446 NOR3467 POL3482 POL3508
POL3512 POL3519 POL3521 POL3536
POL3543 PRT3549 PRT3564 PRT3576
PRT3579 PRT3585 PRT3586 PRT3600
PRT3602 SVK3608 SVK3611 SVK3612
SVK3622 SVK3626 SVK3634 SVK3638
SWE3648 SWE3664 SWE3667 SWE3682
SWE3695 SWE3699 SWE3702 SWE3705
SWE3731 SWE3734 SWE3735 SWE3738
SWE3744 SWE3749 SWE3754 SWE3768
SWE3771 SWE3772 SWE3774 SWE3776
SWE3780 SWE3807 SWE3815 SWE3816
SWE3819 SWE3821 SWE3827 SWE3864
SWE3865 TUR3883 TUR3884 TUR3895

EXCHANGES, TWINNING, LINKING - ECHANGES, PARRAINAGE, JUMELAGE

AUT0047 BEL0115 BEL0120 BEL0123
BEL0129 BEL0147 BEL0198 BEL0203
BEL0206 BEL0221 BEL0303 BEL0361
BEL0390 CHE0415 CHE0420 CHE0434
CHE0448 CHE0452 CHE0456 CHE0506
CHE0524 CHE0562 CHE0566 CHE0596
CHE0622 CHE0639 CHE0640 CHE0650
CHE0689 CHE0809 CHE0819 CZE0857
CZE0904 CZE0920 DEU0983 DEU0990
DEU1055 DEU1056 DEU1074 DEU1110
DEU1149 DEU1167 DEU1178 DEU1186
DEU1210 DNK1274 DNK1283 DNK1375
ESP1451 ESP1475 ESP1523 ESP1525
FIN1543 FIN1605 FRA1746 FRA1791
FRA1793 FRA1846 FRA1862 FRA1889
FRA1921 FRA1938 FRA1942 FRA1960
FRA1964 FRA1974 FRA1985 FRA2009
FRA2034 FRA2039 FRA2057 FRA2062
FRA2081 FRA2101 FRA2117 FRA2150
FRA2159 FRA2165 GBR2199 GBR2332
GBR2347 GBR2371 GBR2379 GBR2396
GBR2415 GBR2445 GBR2481 GBR2490

GRC2584 HUN2601 HUN2622 HUN2637
HUN2644 IRL2680 IRL2686 ITA2750
ITA2775 ITA2780 ITA2798 ITA2801
ITA2809 ITA2834 ITA2838 LUX2937
MLT3017 NLD3067 NLD3072 NLD3078
NLD3082 NLD3098 NLD3135 NLD3139
NLD3170 NLD3179 NLD3181 NLD3198
NLD3215 NLD3218 NLD3236 NLD3326
NLD3338 NLD3357 NLD3366 NOR3372
NOR3390 NOR3400 NOR3402 NOR3460
POL3480 POL3482 POL3508 POL3519
PRT3579 SVK3608 SVK3611 SVK3612
SVK3622 SVK3626 SWE3705 SWE3730
SWE3731 SWE3734 SWE3735 SWE3749
SWE3754 SWE3771 SWE3785 SWE3819
SWE3864 SWE3865 TUR3883

FORMAL EDUCATION - EDUCATION FORMELLE

AUT0044 AUT0065 BEL0115 BEL0123
BEL0129 BEL0156 BEL0176 BEL0248
BEL0265 BEL0359 BEL0361 BEL0362
BEL0390 CHE0420 CHE0434 CHE0452
CHE0456 CHE0562 CHE0566 CHE0640
CHE0645 CHE0660 CHE0682 CHE0689
CHE0711 CHE0747 CHE0809 CHE0819
CZE0894 CZE0904 DEU0954 DEU0983
DEU1074 DEU1110 DEU1149 DEU1178
DNK1262 DNK1273 DNK1283 DNK1289
DNK1335 DNK1339 DNK1360 DNK1375
ESP1436 ESP1450 ESP1451 ESP1479
ESP1486 ESP1490 ESP1517 ESP1523
FIN1540 FIN1545 FIN1560 FIN1585
FRA1675 FRA1794 FRA1841 FRA1889
FRA1938 FRA1946 FRA1957 FRA1960
FRA2002 FRA2017 FRA2019 FRA2039
FRA2044 FRA2062 FRA2084 FRA2131
FRA2143 FRA2150 GBR2178 GBR2181
GBR2193 GBR2194 GBR2199 GBR2233
GBR2238 GBR2265 GBR2269 GBR2332
GBR2337 GBR2347 GBR2371 GBR2379
GBR2392 GBR2399 GBR2408 GBR2411
GBR2415 GBR2424 GBR2445 GBR2448
GBR2455 GBR2464 GBR2468 GBR2481
GBR2511 GBR2522 GBR2553 GBR2584
HUN2601 HUN2643 HUN2644 IRL2686
IRL2688 IRL2690 IRL2691 IRL2697
IRL2706 IRL2720 IRL2726 ITA2750
ITA2775 ITA2798 ITA2810 ITA2822
ITA2826 ITA2827 ITA2883 ITA2890
ITA2894 ITA2895 ITA2898 ITA2905
ITA2905 ITA2916 LUX2982 LUX2995
MLT3012 MLT3017 MLT3023 NLD3067
NLD3072 NLD3083 NLD3083 NLD3104
NLD3105 NLD3135 NLD3139 NLD3147
NLD3153 NLD3201 NLD3215 NLD3218
NLD3223 NLD3326 NLD3329 NLD3372
NOR3390 NOR3416 NOR3467 POL3482
POL3508 POL3521 SVK3611 SVK3612
SVK3622 SWE3648 SWE3771 SWE3819

FUND RAISING - COLLECTE DE FONDS

AUT0003 AUT0022 AUT0024 AUT0026
AUT0044 AUT0051 AUT0072 BEL0096
BEL0115 BEL0116 BEL0147 BEL0148
BEL0155 BEL0197 BEL0198 BEL0199
BEL0203 BEL0248 BEL0254 BEL0272
BEL0306 BEL0351 BEL0353 BEL0361
BEL0362 BEL0387 CHE0415 CHE0417
CHE0420 CHE0434 CHE0446 CHE0448
CHE0452 CHE0486 CHE0506 CHE0515
CHE0524 CHE0562 CHE0566 CHE0584
CHE0650 CHE0689 CHE0693 CHE0711
CHE0715 CHE0744 CHE0755 CHE0772
CHE0796 CHE0800 CHE0814 CHE0819
DEU0954 DEU0957 DEU0968 DEU0983
DEU1001 DEU1022 DEU1025 DEU1030
DEU1064 DEU1110 DEU1114 DEU1146
DEU1149 DEU1167 DEU1178 DEU1186
DEU1187 DNK1222 DNK1273 DNK1283
DNK1305 DNK1360 DNK1375 DNK1405
ESP1442 ESP1445 ESP1451 ESP1505
ESP1506 ESP1508 ESP1523 FIN1532
FIN1540 FIN1544 FIN1554 FRA1611
FRA1791 FRA1793 FRA1843 FRA1855
FRA1871 FRA1880 FRA1889 FRA1910
FRA1938 FRA1946 FRA1957 FRA1960
FRA1978 FRA1990 FRA1991 FRA2017
FRA2041 FRA2047 FRA2081 FRA2086

See: *How to Use the Directory*, page 11.

FRA2101	FRA2117	FRA2131	FRA2152
FRA2159	GBR2185	GBR2193	GBR2194
GBR2201	GBR2229	GBR2238	GBR2312
GBR2328	GBR2332	GBR2337	GBR2351
GBR2353	GBR2371	GBR2372	GBR2385
GBR2396	GBR2411	GBR2413	GBR2424
GBR2445	GBR2481	GBR2493	GBR2498
GBR2511	GBR2513	GBR2522	GBR2525
GBR2535	GBR2537	HUN2601	HUN2609
HUN2644	IRL2680	IRL2684	IRL2688
IRL2695	IRL2726	ITA2755	ITA2780
ITA2791	ITA2809	ITA2820	ITA2826
ITA2838	ITA2852	ITA2886	ITA2894
LUX2984	NLD3049	NLD3067	NLD3068
NLD3072	NLD3078	NLD3135	NLD3160
NLD3179	NLD3181	NLD3198	NLD3201
NLD3223	NLD3226	NLD3249	NLD3253
NLD3256	NLD3258	NLD3277	NLD3301
NLD3303	NLD3326	NLD3330	NLD3361
NLD3362	NLD3366	NOR3372	NOR3381
NOR3389	NOR3390	NOR3404	NOR3460
NOR3467	POL3482	PRT3549	PRT3602
SVK3608	SVK3611	SVK3622	SVK3626
SVK3638	SWE3648	SWE3661	SWE3674
SWE3682	SWE3699	SWE3702	SWE3730
SWE3731	SWE3744	SWE3749	SWE3761
SWE3768	SWE3819	SWE3826	SWE3864

INFORMATION AND DOCUMENTATION SERVICES, DATA BASES - SERVICES D'INFORMATION ET DE DOCUMENTATION, BASES DE DONNEES

AUT0020	AUT0026	AUT0032	AUT0035
AUT0044	AUT0060	AUT0074	AUT0079
AUT0093	BEL0115	BEL0116	BEL0123
BEL0127	BEL0129	BEL0149	BEL0155
BEL0199	BEL0203	BEL0214	
BEL0226	BEL0237	BEL0254	BEL0265
BEL0267	BEL0272	BEL0281	BEL0303
BEL0304	BEL0306	BEL0335	BEL0345
BEL0361	BEL0362	BEL0365	BEL0390
BEL0392	BEL0393	BEL0396	CHE0406
CHE0415	CHE0420	CHE0421	CHE0434
CHE0452	CHE0456	CHE0494	CHE0501
CHE0503	CHE0506	CHE0524	CHE0534
CHE0550	CHE0562	CHE0566	CHE0568
CHE0605	CHE0622	CHE0624	CHE0640
CHE0650	CHE0654	CHE0668	CHE0689
CHE0711	CHE0715	CHE0741	CHE0744
CHE0747	CHE0751	CHE0756	CHE0763
CHE0766	CHE0796	CHE0800	CHE0809
CHE0819	CYP0831	CZE0904	DEU0920
DEU0921	DEU0944	DEU0968	DEU0990
DEU0996	DEU0998	DEU1004	DEU1013
DEU1019	DEU1020	DEU1025	DEU1030
DEU1063	DEU1064	DEU1074	DEU1076
DEU1086	DEU1090	DEU1091	DEU1110
DEU1146	DEU1149	DEU1180	DEU1184
DEU1186	DEU1192	DEU1193	DEU1207
DNK1229	DNK1248	DNK1262	DNK1283
DNK1287	DNK1289	DNK1292	DNK1305
DNK1317	DNK1339	DNK1358	DNK1360
DNK1375	DNK1398	DNK1405	ESP1407
ESP1430	ESP1431	ESP1434	ESP1441
ESP1450	ESP1451	ESP1452	ESP1478
ESP1479	ESP1486	ESP1490	ESP1493
ESP1506	ESP1508	ESP1522	ESP1523
FIN1532	FIN1540	FIN1546	FIN1548
FIN1552	FIN1560	FIN1572	FIN1585
FIN1604	FIN1605	FRA1701	FRA1703
FRA1737	FRA1794	FRA1797	FRA1808
FRA1810	FRA1811	FRA1818	FRA1838
FRA1839	FRA1841	FRA1846	FRA1849
FRA1889	FRA1908	FRA1938	FRA1990
FRA2002	FRA2004	FRA2009	FRA2013
FRA2017	FRA2018	FRA2019	FRA2034
FRA2035	FRA2039	FRA2076	FRA2096
FRA2104	FRA2131	FRA2143	FRA2152
FRA2152	FRA2159	GBR2185	GBR2193
GBR2194	GBR2195	GBR2199	GBR2222
GBR2229	GBR2235	GBR2238	GBR2265
GBR2266	GBR2328	GBR2332	GBR2347
GBR2353	GBR2371	GBR2378	GBR2379
GBR2387	GBR2396	GBR2408	GBR2411
GBR2413	GBR2415	GBR2423	GBR2435
GBR2438	GBR2445	GBR2455	GBR2464
GBR2490	GBR2493	GBR2495	GBR2498
GBR2511	GBR2513	GBR2522	GBR2537
GBR2545	GBR2555	GRC2579	GRC2584

GRC2585	HUN2601	HUN2625	HUN2644
HUN2645	IRL2684	IRL2686	IRL2695
IRL2698	IRL2705	IRL2706	IRL2707
IRL2712	IRL2714	IRL2717	IRL2720
IRL2726	IRL2730	ITA2750	ITA2762
ITA2773	ITA2780	ITA2798	ITA2799
ITA2801	ITA2804	ITA2809	ITA2813
ITA2820	ITA2822	ITA2824	ITA2827
ITA2834	ITA2840	ITA2846	ITA2852
ITA2857	ITA2860	ITA2861	ITA2862
ITA2866	ITA2873	ITA2880	ITA2889
ITA2894	ITA2895	ITA2900	ITA2905
ITA2907	ITA2908	ITA2911	ITA2923
LUX2937	LUX2962	NLD3049	NLD3050
NLD3051	NLD3058	NLD3067	NLD3072
NLD3077	NLD3078	NLD3083	NLD3095
NLD3098	NLD3105	NLD3135	NLD3139
NLD3147	NLD3156	NLD3160	NLD3167
NLD3170	NLD3179	NLD3181	NLD3198
NLD3201	NLD3217	NLD3218	NLD3222
NLD3226	NLD3242	NLD3277	NLD3301
NLD3303	NLD3305	NLD3326	NLD3329
NLD3338	NLD3355	NLD3357	NLD3361
NLD3364	NOR3372	NOR3389	NOR3390
NOR3391	NOR3400	NOR3402	NOR3410
NOR3435	NOR3467	POL3482	POL3508
POL3512	POL3519	POL3521	PRT3564
PRT3576	PRT3585	PRT3600	PRT3602
SVK3608	SVK3611	SVK3622	SVK3638
SWE3648	SWE3658	SWE3682	SWE3693
SWE3699	SWE3705	SWE3744	SWE3746
SWE3768	SWE3771	SWE3772	SWE3774
SWE3807	SWE3816	SWE3821	SWE3826
SWE3832	SWE3864	SWE3865	TUR3883
TUR3895			

INFORMATION CAMPAIGNS, EXHIBITIONS - CAMPAGNES D'INFORMATION, EXPOSITIONS

AUT0020	AUT0032	AUT0044	AUT0047
AUT0067	AUT0068	BEL0096	BEL0099
BEL0115	BEL0116	BEL0123	BEL0129
BEL0148	BEL0155	BEL0176	BEL0191
BEL0192	BEL0197	BEL0198	BEL0203
BEL0254	BEL0267	BEL0272	BEL0289
BEL0303	BEL0304	BEL0327	BEL0335
BEL0359	BEL0361	BEL0362	BEL0387
BEL0390	BEL0392	CHE0415	CHE0420
CHE0434	CHE0446	CHE0452	CHE0456
CHE0461	CHE0501	CHE0506	CHE0515
CHE0519	CHE0524	CHE0534	CHE0562
CHE0566	CHE0568	CHE0584	CHE0605
CHE0654	CHE0667	CHE0669	CHE0689
CHE0711	CHE0715	CHE0718	CHE0744
CHE0751	CHE0756	CHE0765	CHE0773
CHE0796	CHE0798	CHE0800	CHE0809
CHE0819	CYP0831	CYP0832	CZE0897
DEU0917	DEU0920	DEU0955	DEU0983
DEU1010	DEU1013	DEU1019	DEU1022
DEU1025	DEU1062	DEU1063	DEU1064
DEU1110	DEU1142	DEU1143	DEU1149
DEU1167	DEU1178	DEU1186	DEU1187
DNK1262	DNK1273	DNK1283	DNK1287
DNK1304	DNK1305	DNK1307	DNK1312
DNK1317	DNK1375	DNK1376	DNK1398
DNK1405	ESP1407	ESP1437	ESP1451
ESP1452	ESP1457	ESP1478	ESP1486
ESP1490	ESP1493	ESP1503	ESP1505
ESP1506	ESP1508	ESP1517	ESP1523
ESP1524	ESP1528	FIN1532	FIN1540
FIN1543	FIN1546	FIN1552	FIN1553
FIN1560	FIN1592	FIN1594	FIN1604
FRA1633	FRA1651	FRA1793	FRA1793
FRA1797	FRA1808	FRA1843	FRA1849
FRA1852	FRA1862	FRA1889	FRA1910
FRA1923	FRA1938	FRA1957	FRA1960
FRA1985	FRA1990	FRA2002	FRA2035
FRA2039	FRA2040	FRA2086	FRA2096
FRA2104	FRA2121	FRA2143	FRA2150
FRA2152	FRA2159	GBR2193	GBR2194
GBR2195	GBR2199	GBR2222	GBR2229
GBR2235	GBR2238	GBR2265	GBR2269
GBR2279	GBR2312	GBR2328	GBR2332
GBR2354	GBR2371	GBR2374	GBR2378
GBR2387	GBR2411	GBR2415	GBR2423
GBR2445	GBR2455	GBR2464	GBR2493
GBR2495	GBR2498	GBR2503	GBR2511
GBR2526	GBR2537	GBR2545	GBR2555
GBR2561	GRC2572	GRC2576	GRC2579
GRC2584	GRC2586	HUN2601	HUN2637

HUN2644	IRL2679	IRL2680	IRL2684
IRL2686	IRL2688	IRL2695	IRL2697
IRL2707	IRL2712	IRL2717	IRL2720
IRL2726	IRL2730	ITA2780	ITA2785
ITA2791	ITA2798	ITA2799	ITA2809
ITA2811	ITA2813	ITA2814	ITA2820
ITA2826	ITA2829	ITA2832	ITA2834
ITA2860	ITA2866	ITA2873	ITA2881
ITA2888	ITA2894	ITA2895	ITA2923
ITA2900	ITA2903	ITA2907	ITA2923
LUX2935	LUX2984	MLT3016	MLT3017
NLD3049	NLD3051	NLD3067	NLD3072
NLD3078	NLD3083	NLD3098	NLD3135
NLD3139	NLD3170	NLD3181	NLD3198
NLD3217	NLD3218	NLD3236	NLD3258
NLD3277	NLD3303	NLD3320	NLD3326
NLD3357	NLD3364	NLD3366	NOR3371
NOR3372	NOR3387	NOR3389	NOR3390
NOR3402	NOR3440	NOR3467	POL3482
POL3519	POL3543	PRT3549	PRT3600
PRT3602	SVK3608	SVK3611	SVK3612
SWE3648	SWE3661	SWE3664	SWE3682
SWE3699	SWE3702	SWE3730	SWE3731
SWE3738	SWE3744	SWE3746	SWE3749
SWE3754	SWE3761	SWE3763	SWE3768
SWE3771	SWE3774	SWE3776	SWE3816
SWE3819	SWE3826	SWE3834	SWE3865
TUR3883			

LOBBYING, ADVOCACY - LOBBYING, PLAIDOYER

AUT0003	AUT0008	AUT0020	AUT0024
AUT0033	AUT0035	AUT0044	AUT0058
AUT0093	BEL0096	BEL0099	BEL0115
BEL0116	BEL0131	BEL0147	BEL0155
BEL0156	BEL0160	BEL0174	BEL0176
BEL0177	BEL0186	BEL0191	BEL0197
BEL0198	BEL0199	BEL0203	BEL0214
BEL0218	BEL0241	BEL0248	BEL0252
BEL0254	BEL0265	BEL0267	BEL0272
BEL0284	BEL0295	BEL0297	BEL0306
BEL0309	BEL0327	BEL0335	BEL0345
BEL0351	BEL0353	BEL0359	BEL0361
BEL0392	CHE0415	CHE0420	CHE0421
CHE0427	CHE0434	CHE0452	CHE0479
CHE0491	CHE0503	CHE0519	CHE0524
CHE0534	CHE0550	CHE0562	CHE0566
CHE0568	CHE0570	CHE0605	CHE0639
CHE0642	CHE0645	CHE0650	CHE0654
CHE0661	CHE0668	CHE0689	CHE0711
CHE0715	CHE0718	CHE0744	CHE0747
CHE0751	CHE0755	CHE0756	CHE0765
CHE0809	CHE0814	CHE0819	CYP0832
CZE0891	CZE0904	DEU0920	DEU0929
DEU0954	DEU0968	DEU0972	DEU0983
DEU0996	DEU0998	DEU1004	DEU1006
DEU1010	DEU1013	DEU1038	DEU1055
DEU1056	DEU1062	DEU1063	DEU1064
DEU1074	DEU1110	DEU1114	DEU1131
DEU1142	DEU1149	DEU1164	DEU1167
DEU1177	DEU1186	DEU1186	DEU1187
DEU1193	DNK1227	DNK1262	DNK1283
DNK1289	DNK1292	DNK1312	DNK1335
DNK1339	DNK1358	DNK1375	DNK1376
DNK1399	DNK1403	DNK1405	ESP1407
ESP1436	ESP1451	ESP1452	ESP1457
ESP1475	ESP1479	ESP1486	ESP1490
ESP1505	ESP1506	ESP1528	FIN1532
FIN1540	FIN1543	FIN1544	FIN1549
FIN1552	FIN1560	FIN1570	FIN1574
FIN1582	FIN1585	FIN1588	FIN1594
FIN1604	FRA1633	FRA1651	FRA1703
FRA1791	FRA1793	FRA1794	FRA1797
FRA1799	FRA1808	FRA1818	FRA1841
FRA1843	FRA1862	FRA1876	FRA1889
FRA1910	FRA1946	FRA1956	FRA1957
FRA1960	FRA1980	FRA1985	FRA1991
FRA2002	FRA2004	FRA2017	FRA2032
FRA2035	FRA2039	FRA2041	FRA2047
FRA2057	FRA2062	FRA2086	FRA2096
FRA2110	FRA2116	FRA2123	FRA2131
FRA2142	FRA2143	FRA2150	FRA2159
GBR2181	GBR2193	GBR2194	GBR2195
GBR2199	GBR2202	GBR2215	GBR2228
GBR2229	GBR2235	GBR2238	GBR2256
GBR2266	GBR2269	GBR2303	GBR2328
GBR2332	GBR2337	GBR2347	GBR2351
GBR2355	GBR2371	GBR2374	GBR2378
GBR2390	GBR2392	GBR2396	GBR2401
GBR2411	GBR2413	GBR2423	GBR2445

Voir : *Comment utiliser le répertoire*, page 11.

GBR2455	GBR2464	GBR2466	GBR2467
GBR2481	GBR2493	GBR2495	GBR2498
GBR2500	GBR2503	GBR2511	GBR2522
GBR2526	GBR2537	GBR2545	GBR2546
GBR2552	GBR2553	GBR2555	GRC2572
GRC2576	GRC2579	GRC2584	GRC2585
GRC2586	HUN2601	HUN2609	HUN2625
HUN2631	HUN2637	HUN2643	HUN2644
HUN2645	IRL2679	IRL2680	IRL2684
IRL2687	IRL2690	IRL2691	IRL2695
IRL2705	IRL2706	IRL2707	IRL2712
IRL2714	IRL2717	IRL2726	ITA2775
ITA2780	ITA2785	ITA2798	ITA2799
ITA2801	ITA2810	ITA2813	ITA2814
ITA2820	ITA2824	ITA2834	ITA2838
ITA2862	ITA2873	ITA2888	ITA2895
ITA2900	ITA2905	ITA2911	ITA2913
LIE2927	LUX2957	LUX2958	LUX2962
LUX2976	LUX2984	LUX2992	MLT3016
MLT3017	MLT3023	NLD3049	NLD3050
NLD3064	NLD3067	NLD3068	NLD3072
NLD3078	NLD3082	NLD3098	NLD3119
NLD3133	NLD3135	NLD3139	NLD3147
NLD3153	NLD3156	NLD3160	NLD3164
NLD3170	NLD3181	NLD3198	NLD3199
NLD3201	NLD3204	NLD3218	NLD3223
NLD3230	NLD3236	NLD3242	NLD3258
NLD3301	NLD3303	NLD3305	NLD3326
NLD3330	NLD3362	NLD3364	NLD3366
NOR3372	NOR3386	NOR3389	NOR3390
NOR3400	NOR3402	NOR3416	NOR3419
NOR3429	NOR3467	POL3536	POL3543
PRT3549	PRT3564	PRT3586	PRT3600
SVK3608	SVK3622	SVK3634	SVK3638
SWE3648	SWE3661	SWE3674	SWE3682
SWE3699	SWE3705	SWE3735	SWE3738
SWE3744	SWE3749	SWE3768	SWE3771
SWE3781	SWE3819	SWE3821	SWE3834
SWE3864	TUR3883	TUR3897	

NETWORKING, ELECTRONIC TELECOMMUNICATIONS - RESEAUX, TELECOMMUNICATIONS ELECTRONIQUES

AUT0020	BEL0115	BEL0198	BEL0254
BEL0265	BEL0272	BEL0303	BEL0335
BEL0361	CHE0420	CHE0434	CHE0452
CHE0524	CHE0562	CHE0568	CHE0596
CHE0622	CHE0642	CHE0689	CHE0711
CHE0809	CHE0817	CZE0904	
DEU0955	DEU0990	DEU0996	DEU1002
DEU1019	DEU1030	DEU1055	DEU1065
DEU1110	DEU1149	DEU1167	DEU1186
DEU1187	DNK1248	DNK1283	DNK1317
DNK1360	DNK1375	ESP1434	FIN1546
FIN1570	FIN1604	FRA1862	FRA1889
FRA1908	FRA1910	FRA1985	FRA2159
GBR2193	GBR2199	GBR2229	GBR2265
GBR2285	GBR2313	GBR2332	GBR2337
GBR2351	GBR2371	GBR2378	GBR2387
GBR2392	GBR2401	GBR2411	GBR2413
GBR2415	GBR2438	GBR2455	GBR2490
GBR2495	GBR2498	GBR2545	GRC2576
HUN2609	HUN2637	HUN2644	IRL2698
IRL2714	IRL2717	ITA2773	ITA2860
ITA2866	ITA2881	NLD3067	NLD3072
NLD3077	NLD3082	NLD3104	NLD3135
NLD3139	NLD3156	NLD3181	NLD3199
NLD3215	NLD3218	NLD3226	NLD3236
NLD3258	NLD3303	NLD3326	NLD3357
NLD3364	NLD3366	NOR3372	NOR3390
NOR3402	NOR3467	PRT3602	SVK3611
SVK3622	SWE3705	SWE3785	SWE3864
TUR3883			

OTHER - AUTRE

CHE0434	GBR2193	GBR2194	GBR2371
GBR2378	GBR2387	NLD3117	NLD3133
NLD3183	NLD3223	NLD3303	

PUBLISHING, AUDIOVISUAL MATERIALS, EDUCATIONAL MATERIALS - EDITION, DOCUMENTS AUDIOVISUELS, DOCUMENTS EDUCATIFS

AUT0009	AUT0020	AUT0026	AUT0044
AUT0051	AUT0068	BEL0096	BEL0115
BEL0116	BEL0120	BEL0123	BEL0127
BEL0149	BEL0155	BEL0174	BEL0176
BEL0188	BEL0203	BEL0206	BEL0214
BEL0248	BEL0254	BEL0272	BEL0281
BEL0303	BEL0304	BEL0306	BEL0335
BEL0345	BEL0353	BEL0359	BEL0361
BEL0362	BEL0390	BEL0392	BEL0393
CHE0406	CHE0420	CHE0434	CHE0452
CHE0456	CHE0499	CHE0501	CHE0534
CHE0562	CHE0566	CHE0568	CHE0622
CHE0638	CHE0639	CHE0667	CHE0689
CHE0693	CHE0711	CHE0715	CHE0738
CHE0741	CHE0744	CHE0751	CHE0756
CHE0763	CHE0809	CHE0810	CHE0819
CYP0832	CZE0859	CZE0904	CZE0906
DEU0920	DEU0944	DEU1013	DEU1019
DEU1020	DEU1022	DEU1025	DEU1038
DEU1055	DEU1062	DEU1063	DEU1064
DEU1074	DEU1076	DEU1095	DEU1110
DEU1146	DEU1149	DEU1180	DEU1184
DEU1186	DEU1187	DEU1193	DEU1198
DNK1248	DNK1262	DNK1273	DNK1274
DNK1283	DNK1289	DNK1304	DNK1317
DNK1339	DNK1351	DNK1358	DNK1360
DNK1375	DNK1405	ESP1407	ESP1430
ESP1434	ESP1435	ESP1436	ESP1451
ESP1452	ESP1457	ESP1475	ESP1490
ESP1505	ESP1506	ESP1523	FIN1532
FIN1536	FIN1540	FIN1546	FIN1548
FIN1552	FIN1560	FIN1585	FRA1611
FRA1668	FRA1703	FRA1713	FRA1768
FRA1794	FRA1810	FRA1843	FRA1849
FRA1852	FRA1862	FRA1889	FRA1908
FRA1923	FRA1938	FRA1946	FRA1957
FRA1986	FRA1990	FRA2001	FRA2002
FRA2004	FRA2013	FRA2032	FRA2034
FRA2039	FRA2040	FRA2042	FRA2076
FRA2096	FRA2101	FRA2104	FRA2131
FRA2143	FRA2159	FRA2165	GBR2181
GBR2185	GBR2193	GBR2194	GBR2195
GBR2199	GBR2222	GBR2229	GBR2235
GBR2238	GBR2265	GBR2266	GBR2271
GBR2312	GBR2328	GBR2332	GBR2337
GBR2345	GBR2347	GBR2353	GBR2371
GBR2374	GBR2378	GBR2387	GBR2401
GBR2411	GBR2413	GBR2415	GBR2423
GBR2435	GBR2445	GBR2455	GBR2464
GBR2467	GBR2490	GBR2493	GBR2498
GBR2501	GBR2503	GBR2511	GBR2522
GBR2525	GBR2526	GBR2545	GBR2546
GBR2552	GBR2555	GRC2584	GRC2585
HUN2601	HUN2609	HUN2625	HUN2644
IRL2679	IRL2690	IRL2695	IRL2697
IRL2698	IRL2706	IRL2712	IRL2720
ITA2762	ITA2780	ITA2785	ITA2786
ITA2798	ITA2799	ITA2804	ITA2809
ITA2813	ITA2814	ITA2822	ITA2826
ITA2834	ITA2838	ITA2840	ITA2857
ITA2860	ITA2861	ITA2866	ITA2880
ITA2895	ITA2900	ITA2907	ITA2908
ITA2916	ITA2923	LUX2935	LUX3006
MLT3016	MLT3017	NLD3049	NLD3051
NLD3067	NLD3072	NLD3077	NLD3078
NLD3082	NLD3083	NLD3105	NLD3133
NLD3135	NLD3139	NLD3153	NLD3156
NLD3179	NLD3198	NLD3201	NLD3215
NLD3216	NLD3218	NLD3222	NLD3223
NLD3226	NLD3277	NLD3301	NLD3303
NLD3320	NLD3326	NLD3354	NLD3357
NLD3364	NLD3372	NOR3389	NOR3390
NOR3391	NOR3400	NOR3402	NOR3435
NOR3440	NOR3441	NOR3467	POL3482
POL3502	POL3508	POL3512	POL3519
POL3521	POL3543	PRT3564	PRT3579

PRT3585	PRT3600	PRT3602	SVK3608
SVK3611	SVK3622	SWE3648	SWE3682
SWE3699	SWE3705	SWE3738	SWE3744
SWE3746	SWE3749	SWE3763	SWE3768
SWE3771	SWE3816	SWE3826	SWE3832
SWE3865	TUR3883	TUR3895	

INTERNATIONAL ECONOMIC RELATIONS, TRADE, DEBT, FINANCE - RELATIONS ECONOMIQUES INTERNATIONALES, COMMERCE, DETTE, FINANCES

BROADCASTING, CULTURAL EVENTS - RADIODIFFUSION, MANIFESTATIONS CULTURELLES

AUT0029	BEL0123	BEL0165	BEL0203
BEL0340	BEL0361	BEL0390	CHE0534
CHE0566	CHE0568	CHE0624	CHE0689
CHE0720	CHE0819	DNK1250	DNK1389
ESP1437	ESP1455	ESP1457	ESP1486
ESP1490	ESP1507	FIN1545	FRA1621
FRA1794	FRA1889	FRA2002	GBR2229
GBR2238	GBR2248	GBR2345	GBR2371
GBR2406	GBR2415	GBR2423	GBR2467
GBR2498	GBR2501	GBR2518	GBR2545
IRL2686	IRL2692	IRL2708	IRL2714
ITA2820	ITA2841	ITA2885	ITA2907
ITA2923	LUX2937	LUX2958	LUX2983
LUX3008	MLT3016	NLD3067	NLD3236
NLD3253	NLD3267	NLD3348	NOR3467
POL3508	SWE3648	SWE3738	TUR3883

CONFERENCES, SEMINARS, WORKSHOPS, TRAINING ACTIVITIES - CONFERENCES, SEMINAIRES, ATELIERS, ACTIVITES DE FORMATION

AUT0010	AUT0011	AUT0029	AUT0051
AUT0068	AUT0074	AUT0090	
BEL0101	BEL0123	BEL0155	BEL0164
BEL0165	BEL0168	BEL0174	BEL0176
BEL0188	BEL0199	BEL0203	BEL0214
BEL0215	BEL0221	BEL0241	BEL0248
BEL0252	BEL0272	BEL0290	BEL0303
BEL0306	BEL0309	BEL0322	BEL0340
BEL0345	BEL0351	BEL0359	BEL0361
BEL0362	BEL0378	BEL0381	BEL0396
BEL0397	CHE0403	CHE0416	CHE0427
CHE0429	CHE0455	CHE0460	CHE0461
CHE0534	CHE0549	CHE0566	CHE0568
CHE0602	CHE0613	CHE0626	CHE0632
CHE0642	CHE0661	CHE0669	CHE0689
CHE0693	CHE0711	CHE0720	CHE0755
CHE0765	CHE0773	CHE0809	CHE0814
CHE0819	CHE0820	CZE0905	CZE0906
DEU0919	DEU0921	DEU0944	DEU0968
DEU0975	DEU0977	DEU0990	DEU0996
DEU1013	DEU1015	DEU1019	DEU1020
DEU1025	DEU1032	DEU1037	DEU1038
DEU1044	DEU1047	DEU1055	DEU1062
DEU1065	DEU1066	DEU1074	DEU1083
DEU1090	DEU1100	DEU1116	DEU1124
DEU1131	DEU1149	DEU1150	DEU1167
DEU1174	DEU1180	DEU1184	DEU1198
DEU1203	DEU1210	DEU1211	DNK1229
DNK1230	DNK1238	DNK1275	DNK1312
DNK1335	DNK1339	DNK1361	DNK1389
DNK1398	ESP1407	ESP1410	ESP1417
ESP1430	ESP1437	ESP1438	ESP1441
ESP1455	ESP1456	ESP1457	ESP1474
ESP1479	ESP1482	ESP1486	ESP1490
ESP1507	ESP1511	ESP1517	ESP1522
ESP1528	FIN1544	FIN1545	FIN1547
FIN1548	FIN1549	FIN1553	FIN1578
FIN1596	FRA1629	FRA1636	FRA1647
FRA1690	FRA1703	FRA1788	FRA1794
FRA1797	FRA1799	FRA1800	FRA1813
FRA1815	FRA1816	FRA1818	FRA1820
FRA1838	FRA1841	FRA1862	FRA1879
FRA1889	FRA1917	FRA1921	FRA1947
FRA1990	FRA2002	FRA2004	FRA2005
FRA2012	FRA2018	FRA2021	FRA2029
FRA2044	FRA2057	FRA2062	FRA2076
FRA2086	FRA2096	FRA2105	FRA2122
FRA2129	FRA2131	GBR2185	GBR2214
GBR2229	GBR2238	GBR2242	GBR2251
GBR2264	GBR2265	GBR2266	GBR2269
GBR2279	GBR2294	GBR2337	GBR2371

See: *How to Use the Directory*, page 11.

GBR2380 GBR2387 GBR2390 GBR2392
GBR2406 GBR2408 GBR2413 GBR2415
GBR2416 GBR2422 GBR2423 GBR2424
GBR2435 GBR2437 GBR2445 GBR2452
GBR2453 GBR2495 GBR2498 GBR2503
GBR2513 GBR2514 GBR2518 GBR2527
GBR2536 GBR2545 GBR2553 GBR2554
HUN2609 HUN2640 IRL2679 IRL2686
IRL2687 IRL2689 IRL2692 IRL2693
IRL2708 IRL2712 IRL2714 IRL2720
IRL2726 IRL2729 ITA2756 ITA2762
ITA2780 ITA2782 ITA2785 ITA2798
ITA2805 ITA2809 ITA2810 ITA2814
ITA2820 ITA2826 ITA2827 ITA2829
ITA2837 ITA2840 ITA2841 ITA2852
ITA2866 ITA2873 ITA2885 ITA2889
ITA2890 ITA2894 ITA2900 ITA2907
ITA2908 ITA2912 ITA2913 LUX2937
LUX2946 LUX2983 LUX3008 MLT3016
MLT3018 NLD3047 NLD3061 NLD3064
NLD3067 NLD3078 NLD3101 NLD3104
NLD3112 NLD3122 NLD3137 NLD3157
NLD3164 NLD3174 NLD3194 NLD3196
NLD3199 NLD3211 NLD3236 NLD3267
NLD3279 NLD3286 NLD3301 NLD3303
NLD3305 NLD3334 NLD3348 NLD3366
NOR3389 NOR3402 NOR3416 NOR3440
NOR3455 NOR3467 POL3482 POL3499
POL3519 POL3536 PRT3564 SWE3648
SWE3658 SWE3664 SWE3695 SWE3702
SWE3724 SWE3727 SWE3734 SWE3735
SWE3738 SWE3749 SWE3754 SWE3807
SWE3816 SWE3826 SWE3864 SWE3865
TUR3883

EXCHANGES, TWINNING, LINKING - ECHANGES,
PARRAINAGE, JUMELAGE

AUT0029 AUT0033 BEL0123 BEL0129
BEL0165 BEL0198 BEL0203 BEL0221
BEL0272 BEL0309 BEL0340 BEL0361
BEL0381 BEL0390 CHE0448 CHE0566
CHE0626 CHE0632 CHE0689 CHE0819
DEU0942 DEU0990 DEU1020 DEU1037
DEU1055 DEU1074 DEU1149 DEU1167
DEU1198 DEU1203 DEU1211 DNK1238
DNK1250 DNK1339 ESP1406 ESP1522
FIN1547 FRA1647 FRA1746 FRA1787
FRA1889 FRA1956 FRA2029 GBR2242
GBR2371 GBR2379 GBR2390 GBR2406
GBR2423 GBR2435 GBR2437 GBR2518
GBR2553 HUN2640 IRL2686 IRL2708
ITA2841 NLD3067 NLD3078 NLD3098
NLD3122 NLD3137 NLD3141 NLD3236
NLD3267 NLD3334 NLD3348 NLD3366
POL3499 POL3508 POL3519 SWE3724
SWE3734 SWE3749 SWE3754 SWE3771
SWE3864 SWE3865 TUR3883

FORMAL EDUCATION - EDUCATION FORMELLE

AUT0065 BEL0123 BEL0129 BEL0176
BEL0306 BEL0322 BEL0323 BEL0351
BEL0359 BEL0361 BEL0362 BEL0378
BEL0390 CHE0566 CHE0673 CHE0689
CHE0809 CHE0819 CZE0894 DEU0975
DEU1116 DEU1203 DNK1339 ESP1407
ESP1409 ESP1427 ESP1437 ESP1455
ESP1482 ESP1486 ESP1490 ESP1528
FRA1647 FRA1794 FRA1827 FRA1841
FRA1889 FRA2005 FRA2021 FRA2044
FRA2062 FRA2103 FRA2105 FRA2150
GBR2238 GBR2265 GBR2269 GBR2294
GBR2337 GBR2371 GBR2379 GBR2380
GBR2406 GBR2408 GBR2415 GBR2423
GBR2424 GBR2452 GBR2467 GBR2468
GBR2518 GBR2553 GBR2554
HUN2640 IRL2686 IRL2689 IRL2690
IRL2691 IRL2693 IRL2697 IRL2708
IRL2720 IRL2726 ITA2762 ITA2773
ITA2782 ITA2798 ITA2810 ITA2812
ITA2814 ITA2822 ITA2826 ITA2827
ITA2900 ITA2912 LUX3008 MLT3016
NLD3067 NLD3078 NLD3104 NLD3212
NLD3215 NLD3366 POL3508 SWE3648

FUND RAISING - COLLECTE DE FONDS

AUT0051 BEL0155 BEL0168 BEL0198
BEL0203 BEL0248 BEL0272 BEL0322
BEL0323 BEL0352 BEL0361 BEL0362
BEL0390 CHE0549 CHE0566 CHE0584
CHE0602 CHE0689 CHE0727 CHE0804
CHE0814 CHE0819 CHE0820 DEU0957
DEU1044 DEU1187 DEU2841 DNK1306
ESP1409 ESP1455 ESP1507 FIN1596
FRA1636 FRA1647 FRA1703 FRA1785
FRA1787 FRA1843 FRA1889 FRA1990
FRA2053 GBR2185 GBR2229 GBR2238
GBR2248 GBR2337 GBR2371 GBR2406
GBR2413 GBR2445 GBR2498 GBR2503
GBR2513 GBR2514 GBR2518 GBR2544
HUN2609 IRL2689 IRL2708 ITA2748
ITA2762 ITA2773 ITA2841 ITA2900
LUX2946 LUX2959 LUX2982 LUX2983
MLT3018 NLD3067 NLD3078 NLD3122
NLD3137 NLD3157 NLD3231 NLD3253
NLD3267 NLD3269 NLD3301 NLD3362
NLD3366 SWE3648 SWE3702 SWE3724
SWE3749 SWE3811 SWE3826 SWE3864

INFORMATION AND DOCUMENTATION
SERVICES, DATA BASES - SERVICES
D'INFORMATION ET DE DOCUMENTATION,
BASES DE DONNEES

AUT0010 AUT0020 AUT0029 AUT0074
AUT0079 AUT0085 BEL0118 BEL0123
BEL0149 BEL0155 BEL0164 BEL0165
BEL0168 BEL0199 BEL0203 BEL0214
BEL0215 BEL0237 BEL0252 BEL0267
BEL0272 BEL0281 BEL0306 BEL0335
BEL0345 BEL0353 BEL0359 BEL0361
BEL0362 BEL0365 BEL0390 BEL0393
BEL0396 CHE0429 CHE0501 CHE0506
CHE0534 CHE0549 CHE0566 CHE0568
CHE0596 CHE0624 CHE0626 CHE0629
CHE0673 CHE0687 CHE0689 CHE0720
CHE0727 CHE0763 CHE0767 CHE0809
CHE0819 CYP0832 CZE0906 DEU0919
DEU0942 DEU0944 DEU0968 DEU0975
DEU0977 DEU0990 DEU0996 DEU1002
DEU1013 DEU1015 DEU1019 DEU1020
DEU1025 DEU1031 DEU1037 DEU1074
DEU1076 DEU1083 DEU1086 DEU1090
DEU1091 DEU1129 DEU1149 DEU1167
DEU1184 DEU1192 DEU1203 DEU1211
DNK1230 DNK1238 DNK1292 DNK1306
DNK1317 DNK1335 DNK1339 DNK1358
DNK1389 DNK1398 DNK1403 ESP1407
ESP1417 ESP1430 ESP1431 ESP1434
ESP1437 ESP1438 ESP1441 ESP1455
ESP1457 ESP1479 ESP1482 ESP1486
ESP1490 ESP1506 ESP1507 ESP1511
ESP1522 FIN1546 FIN1548 FRA1629
FRA1636 FRA1647 FRA1703 FRA1737
FRA1794 FRA1797 FRA1800 FRA1808
FRA1810 FRA1811 FRA1818 FRA1820
FRA1827 FRA1838 FRA1839 FRA1841
FRA1889 FRA1947 FRA1956 FRA1990
FRA2002 FRA2004 FRA2018 FRA2021
FRA2029 FRA2076 FRA2096 FRA2103
FRA2104 FRA2105 FRA2116 FRA2122
FRA2131 GBR2185 GBR2229 GBR2238
GBR2239 GBR2242 GBR2264 GBR2265
GBR2266 GBR2279 GBR2326 GBR2371
GBR2379 GBR2387 GBR2392 GBR2406
GBR2408 GBR2413 GBR2415 GBR2423
GBR2435 GBR2437 GBR2438 GBR2445
GBR2452 GBR2453 GBR2495 GBR2498
GBR2513 GBR2514 GBR2518 GBR2522
GBR2544 GBR2545 HUN2640 IRL2686
IRL2692 IRL2697 IRL2698 IRL2705
IRL2708 IRL2712 IRL2714 IRL2717
IRL2720 IRL2726 IRL2730 ITA2748
ITA2762 ITA2773 ITA2780 ITA2782
ITA2798 ITA2805 ITA2808 ITA2809
ITA2810 ITA2814 ITA2820 ITA2822
ITA2827 ITA2829 ITA2834 ITA2840
ITA2852 ITA2857 ITA2860 ITA2861
ITA2866 ITA2873 ITA2880 ITA2894
ITA2895 ITA2900 ITA2907 ITA2908
ITA2912 ITA2913 ITA2923 LUX2937
LUX2946 LUX2962 LUX2983 LUX3008
MLT3016 MLT3018 NLD3047 NLD3051
NLD3058 NLD3064 NLD3067 NLD3077

NLD3078 NLD3095 NLD3122 NLD3135
NLD3137 NLD3139 NLD3156 NLD3157
NLD3167 NLD3173 NLD3181 NLD3194
NLD3211 NLD3236 NLD3267 NLD3279
NLD3301 NLD3305 NLD3334 NLD3352
NLD3355 NLD3361 NOR3402 NOR3410
NOR3416 NOR3455 NOR3467 POL3499
POL3508 POL3519 PRT3585 PRT3600
SWE3648 SWE3658 SWE3734 SWE3744
SWE3746 SWE3773 SWE3807 SWE3816
SWE3826 SWE3832 SWE3864 SWE3865
TUR3883

INFORMATION CAMPAIGNS, EXHIBITIONS -
CAMPAGNES D'INFORMATION, EXPOSITIONS

AUT0029 AUT0051 AUT0067 AUT0068
BEL0099 BEL0101 BEL0111 BEL0123
BEL0155 BEL0165 BEL0168 BEL0176
BEL0192 BEL0198 BEL0203 BEL0215
BEL0248 BEL0252 BEL0267 BEL0272
BEL0290 BEL0306 BEL0322 BEL0323
BEL0340 BEL0351 BEL0352 BEL0353
BEL0361 BEL0362 BEL0381 BEL0390
BEL0397 CHE0416 CHE0427 CHE0455
CHE0460 CHE0461 CHE0479 CHE0486
CHE0506 CHE0534 CHE0549 CHE0560
CHE0566 CHE0568 CHE0584 CHE0596
CHE0669 CHE0689 CHE0720 CHE0765
CHE0819 CHE0820 DEU0917 DEU0955
DEU0972 DEU0975 DEU0977 DEU1013
DEU1019 DEU1025 DEU1031 DEU1037
DEU1062 DEU1083 DEU1149 DEU1150
DEU1151 DEU1198 DEU1203 DEU1211
DNK1229 DNK1230 DNK1304 DNK1306
DNK1317 DNK1339 DNK1389 DNK1398
DNK1403 ESP1407 ESP1437 ESP1438
ESP1457 ESP1486 ESP1490 ESP1506
ESP1507 ESP1511 ESP1522 ESP1528
FIN1546 FIN1547 FIN1553 FIN1596
FIN1599 FRA1624 FRA1633 FRA1647
FRA1703 FRA1797 FRA1813 FRA1841
FRA1843 FRA1889 FRA1947 FRA1956
FRA1990 FRA2002 FRA2005 FRA2021
FRA2096 FRA2104 FRA2116 GBR2195
GBR2229 GBR2238 GBR2239 GBR2242
GBR2248 GBR2264 GBR2265 GBR2269
GBR2279 GBR2339 GBR2371 GBR2387
GBR2392 GBR2406 GBR2408 GBR2415
GBR2423 GBR2435 GBR2452 GBR2495
GBR2498 GBR2503 GBR2510 GBR2518
GBR2527 GBR2544 GBR2545 GBR2553
HUN2640 IRL2679 IRL2686 IRL2687
IRL2689 IRL2692 IRL2693 IRL2707
IRL2708 IRL2712 IRL2720 ITA2748
ITA2762 ITA2780 ITA2799 ITA2810
ITA2820 ITA2826 ITA2832 ITA2841
ITA2866 ITA2873 ITA2885 ITA2890
ITA2894 ITA2900 ITA2912 LUX2937
LUX2983 LUX3008 MLT3018 NLD3047
NLD3067 NLD3078 NLD3122 NLD3137
NLD3164 NLD3173 NLD3181 NLD3190
NLD3211 NLD3236 NLD3267 NLD3279
NLD3303 NLD3320 NLD3348 NLD3364
NLD3365 NLD3366 NOR3381 NOR3402
NOR3416 NOR3440 NOR3467 POL3499
POL3519 PRT3594 PRT3600 SWE3648
SWE3664 SWE3702 SWE3724 SWE3738
SWE3749 SWE3754 SWE3795 SWE3816
SWE3819 SWE3826 SWE3865 TUR3883

LOBBYING, ADVOCACY - LOBBYING, PLAIDOYER

AUT0010 AUT0029 AUT0033 AUT0051
AUT0068 BEL0099 BEL0118 BEL0131
BEL0155 BEL0165 BEL0168 BEL0174
BEL0176 BEL0177 BEL0186 BEL0198
BEL0199 BEL0203 BEL0214 BEL0215
BEL0216 BEL0218 BEL0241 BEL0248
BEL0272 BEL0306 BEL0309 BEL0322
BEL0323 BEL0345 BEL0353 BEL0361
BEL0381 BEL0397 CHE0416 CHE0429
CHE0455 CHE0460 CHE0479 CHE0486
CHE0534 CHE0549 CHE0560 CHE0566
CHE0568 CHE0602 CHE0619 CHE0626
CHE0642 CHE0689 CHE0693 CHE0711
CHE0718 CHE0727 CHE0755 CHE0765
CHE0814 CHE0819 CHE0820 DEU0919
DEU0942 DEU0972 DEU0975 DEU0998
DEU1013 DEU1015 DEU1032 DEU1037

INTERNATIONAL RELATIONS, COOPERATION, DEVELOPMENT AID

```
DEU1044  DEU1055  DEU1062  DEU1074
DEU1083  DEU1131  DEU1149  DEU1151
DEU1167  DEU1211  DNK1306  DNK1312
DNK1335  DNK1339  DNK1389  DNK1403
ESP1437  ESP1438  ESP1457  ESP1479
ESP1486  ESP1490  ESP1528  FIN1544
FIN1546  FIN1596  FIN1599  FRA1624
FRA1633  FRA1636  FRA1703  FRA1794
FRA1797  FRA1799  FRA1808  FRA1818
FRA1841  FRA1843  FRA1862  FRA1889
FRA2002  FRA2004  FRA2086  FRA2096
FRA2105  FRA2110  FRA2116  FRA2131
FRA2142  GBR2195  GBR2228  GBR2229
GBR2238  GBR2239  GBR2242  GBR2251
GBR2264  GBR2266  GBR2269  GBR2294
GBR2303  GBR2337  GBR2371  GBR2376
GBR2388  GBR2390  GBR2392  GBR2406
GBR2413  GBR2423  GBR2435  GBR2445
GBR2464  GBR2467  GBR2474  GBR2495
GBR2498  GBR2500  GBR2503  GBR2518
GBR2522  GBR2527  GBR2544  GBR2545
GBR2552  GBR2553  IRL2679  IRL2687
IRL2689  IRL2690  IRL2691  IRL2692
IRL2693  IRL2707  IRL2708  IRL2712
IRL2714  IRL2720  IRL2726  IRL2748
ITA2775  ITA2799  ITA2810  ITA2820
ITA2838  ITA2840  ITA2873  ITA2900
ITA2912  ITA2913  LUX2937  LUX2957
LUX2958  LUX2983  LUX3008  MLT3016
MLT3018  NLD3047  NLD3064  NLD3067
NLD3078  NLD3104  NLD3122  NLD3137
NLD3156  NLD3164  NLD3199  NLD3211
NLD3236  NLD3301  NLD3305  NLD3334
NLD3348  NLD3362  NLD3364  NLD3366
NOR3389  NOR3402  NOR3410  NOR3416
NOR3455  NOR3467  POL3499  PRT3600
SWE3648  SWE3724  SWE3738  SWE3749
SWE3807  SWE3864  TUR3883
```

*NETWORKING, ELECTRONIC
TELECOMMUNICATIONS - RESEAUX,
TELECOMMUNICATIONS ELECTRONIQUES*

```
AUT0020  BEL0165  BEL0198  BEL0248
BEL0252  BEL0272  BEL0361  BEL0568
CHE0596  CHE0626  CHE0642  CHE0689
CHE0819  DEU0955  DEU0975  DEU0990
DEU1002  DEU1019  DEU1065  DEU1149
DEU1167  DEU1187  DNK1389  ESP1434
ESP1457  ESP1479  ESP1522  FIN1546
FIN1583  FIN1596  FRA1629  FRA1889
FRA2105  GBR2229  GBR2242  GBR2264
GBR2265  GBR2285  GBR2313  GBR2337
GBR2371  GBR2387  GBR2406  GBR2413
GBR2438  GBR2495  GBR2498  GBR2518
GBR2545  GBR2553  HUN2640  IRL2698
IRL2708  IRL2714  ITA2773  ITA2780
ITA2860  NLD3067  NLD3077  NLD3104
NLD3137  NLD3157  NLD3199  NLD3236
NLD3267  NLD3279  NLD3364  NLD3366
NOR3386  NOR3402  NOR3467  POL3499
POL3508  SWE3724  TUR3883
```

OTHER - AUTRE

```
BEL0129  CHE0460  DEU1106  FRA1700
FRA2012  GBR2371  GBR2387  GBR2518
NLD3117  NLD3137  NLD3183
```

*PUBLISHING, AUDIOVISUAL MATERIALS,
EDUCATIONAL MATERIALS - EDITION,
DOCUMENTS AUDIOVISUELS, DOCUMENTS
EDUCATIFS*

```
AUT0010  AUT0020  AUT0029  AUT0051
AUT0068  BEL0101  BEL0123  BEL0149
BEL0155  BEL0164  BEL0165  BEL0168
BEL0174  BEL0176  BEL0188  BEL0203
BEL0214  BEL0248  BEL0252  BEL0272
BEL0281  BEL0306  BEL0322  BEL0323
BEL0340  BEL0345  BEL0353  BEL0361
BEL0362  BEL0381  BEL0390  BEL0393
CHE0429  CHE0499  CHE0534  CHE0549
CHE0560  CHE0566  CHE0568  CHE0602
CHE0626  CHE0638  CHE0689  CHE0711
CHE0727  CHE0738  CHE0763  CHE0767
CHE0819  CHE0820  CZE0894  DEU0944
DEU0975  DEU0977  DEU1013  DEU1020
DEU1022  DEU1025  DEU1031  DEU1037
DEU1038  DEU1044  DEU1055  DEU1062
DEU1074  DEU1076  DEU1095  DEU1143
```

```
DEU1149  DEU1150  DEU1167  DEU1180
DEU1187  DEU1198  DNK1238  DNK1304
DNK1312  DNK1317  DNK1339  DNK1389
DNK1403  DNK1410  ESP1417  ESP1430
ESP1434  ESP1437  ESP1455  ESP1456
ESP1457  ESP1474  ESP1475  ESP1486
ESP1490  ESP1507  ESP1522  ESP1528
FIN1536  FIN1546  FIN1548  FIN1549
FIN1596  FRA1624  FRA1629  FRA1647
FRA1668  FRA1703  FRA1713  FRA1794
FRA1799  FRA1810  FRA1813  FRA1836
FRA1843  FRA1889  FRA1956  FRA1986
FRA1990  FRA2002  FRA2004  FRA2021
FRA2076  FRA2086  FRA2096  FRA2104
FRA2105  FRA2131  GBR2185  GBR2229
GBR2238  GBR2239  GBR2248  GBR2264
GBR2265  GBR2266  GBR2271  GBR2279
GBR2294  GBR2326  GBR2337  GBR2345
GBR2371  GBR2380  GBR2387  GBR2392
GBR2406  GBR2408  GBR2413  GBR2415
GBR2423  GBR2424  GBR2437  GBR2452
GBR2453  GBR2498  GBR2500  GBR2501
GBR2503  GBR2513  GBR2514  GBR2518
GBR2522  GBR2527  GBR2544  GBR2545
GBR2552  GBR2553  HUN2609  IRL2679
IRL2692  IRL2693  IRL2697  IRL2698
IRL2708  IRL2712  IRL2714  IRL2720
ITA2748  ITA2762  ITA2773  ITA2780
ITA2798  ITA2799  ITA2805  ITA2809
ITA2810  ITA2820  ITA2822  ITA2834
ITA2837  ITA2838  ITA2840  ITA2857
ITA2861  ITA2866  ITA2873  ITA2885
ITA2894  ITA2900  ITA2908  ITA2913
LUX3006  MLT3016  NLD3061  NLD3067
NLD3077  NLD3078  NLD3112  NLD3135
NLD3137  NLD3164  NLD3173  NLD3190
NLD3194  NLD3211  NLD3212  NLD3215
NLD3267  NLD3279  NLD3301  NLD3305
NLD3320  NLD3348  NLD3352  NLD3364
NLD3366  NLD3386  NOR3389  NOR3402
NOR3440  NOR3441  NOR3467  POL3499
POL3502  POL3508  POL3519  PRT3564
SWE3648  SWE3695  SWE3724  SWE3749
SWE3816  SWE3826  SWE3832  SWE3865
TUR3883
```

INTERNATIONAL RELATIONS, COOPERATION, DEVELOPMENT AID - RELATIONS INTERNATIONALES, COOPERATION, AIDE AU DEVELOPPEMENT

*BROADCASTING, CULTURAL EVENTS -
RADIODIFFUSION, MANIFESTATIONS
CULTURELLES*

```
BEL0123  BEL0129  BEL0165  BEL0203
BEL0353  BEL0359  BEL0361  CHE0434
CHE0534  CHE0566  CHE0568  CHE0604
CHE0619  CHE0624  CHE0629  CHE0689
CHE0715  CHE0720  CHE0744  CHE0819
CZE0891  DNK1215  DNK1250  DNK1283
ESP1413  ESP1430  ESP1436  ESP1437
ESP1450  ESP1455  ESP1478  ESP1486
ESP1490  ESP1506  ESP1510  ESP1523
ESP1525  FIN1531  FIN1545  FIN1546
FIN1553  FIN1563  FIN1577  FRA1621
FRA1704  FRA1768  FRA1778  FRA1785
FRA1791  FRA1793  FRA1794  FRA1889
FRA1956  FRA1974  FRA2002  FRA2062
FRA2090  FRA2092  FRA2106  FRA2122
FRA2126  FRA2159  GBR2229  GBR2238
GBR2248  GBR2345  GBR2371  GBR2378
GBR2383  GBR2406  GBR2423  GBR2498
GBR2501  GBR2511  GBR2545  GRC2576
GRC2586  IRL2686  IRL2693  ITA2744
ITA2748  ITA2799  ITA2806  ITA2814
ITA2820  ITA2834  ITA2835  ITA2840
ITA2855  ITA2888  ITA2895  ITA2907
ITA2923  LUX2937  LUX2949  LUX2955
LUX2976  MLT3016  NLD3067  NLD3098
NLD3169  NLD3173  NLD3190  NLD3199
NLD3217  NLD3236  NLD3253  NLD3303
NOR3390  NOR3402  NOR3467  POL3482
POL3543  PRT3603  SVK3611  SVK3634
SWE3760  SWE3761  SWE3830  TUR3883
```

*CONFERENCES, SEMINARS, WORKSHOPS,
TRAINING ACTIVITIES - CONFERENCES,
SEMINAIRES, ATELIERS, ACTIVITES DE
FORMATION*

```
AUT0008  AUT0021  AUT0033  AUT0051
AUT0068  AUT0074  AUT0090  BEL0123
BEL0128  BEL0129  BEL0133  BEL0142
BEL0148  BEL0149  BEL0152  BEL0155
BEL0156  BEL0165  BEL0168  BEL0174
BEL0176  BEL0188  BEL0191  BEL0199
BEL0203  BEL0214  BEL0221  BEL0231
BEL0237  BEL0252  BEL0261  BEL0265
BEL0272  BEL0275  BEL0297  BEL0306
BEL0309  BEL0340  BEL0345  BEL0353
BEL0359  BEL0361  BEL0362  BEL0368
BEL0378  BEL0388  BEL0392  BEL0397
BEL0399  CHE0403  CHE0406  CHE0434
CHE0456  CHE0461  CHE0464  CHE0479
CHE0494  CHE0496  CHE0549  CHE0560
CHE0562  CHE0566  CHE0568  CHE0602
CHE0604  CHE0613  CHE0619  CHE0632
CHE0639  CHE0642  CHE0649  CHE0654
CHE0669  CHE0687  CHE0689  CHE0711
CHE0715  CHE0720  CHE0727  CHE0744
CHE0750  CHE0755  CHE0758  CHE0765
CHE0772  CHE0773  CHE0793  CHE0809
CHE0814  CHE0819  CHE0820  CYP0832
CZE0839  CZE0897  DEU0919  DEU0944
DEU0963  DEU0975  DEU0977  DEU0983
DEU0989  DEU0990  DEU0996  DEU0998
DEU0999  DEU1006  DEU1015  DEU1020
DEU1025  DEU1032  DEU1038  DEU1047
DEU1055  DEU1056  DEU1062  DEU1065
DEU1074  DEU1090  DEU1097  DEU1100
DEU1111  DEU1116  DEU1143  DEU1149
DEU1150  DEU1174  DEU1178  DEU1179
DEU1180  DEU1187  DEU1198  DNK1229
DNK1238  DNK1243  DNK1273  DNK1281
DNK1283  DNK1289  DNK1300  DNK1305
DNK1307  DNK1312  DNK1339  DNK1361
DNK1369  DNK1375  DNK1391  DNK1398
DNK1405  ESP1407  ESP1409  ESP1413
ESP1417  ESP1430  ESP1435  ESP1437
ESP1438  ESP1439  ESP1441  ESP1443
ESP1450  ESP1455  ESP1456  ESP1472
ESP1478  ESP1479  ESP1485  ESP1486
ESP1490  ESP1493  ESP1505  ESP1506
ESP1508  ESP1510  ESP1511  ESP1517
ESP1521  ESP1522  ESP1525  ESP1528
FIN1536  FIN1544  FIN1545  FIN1546
FIN1547  FIN1548  FIN1549  FIN1551
FIN1553  FIN1554  FIN1555  FIN1557
FIN1560  FIN1570  FIN1572  FIN1577
FIN1578  FIN1582  FIN1583  FIN1585
FIN1588  FIN1594  FIN1599  FIN1604
FRA1610  FRA1616  FRA1619  FRA1634
FRA1636  FRA1640  FRA1675  FRA1690
FRA1704  FRA1709  FRA1731  FRA1737
FRA1776  FRA1778  FRA1785  FRA1791
FRA1793  FRA1794  FRA1797  FRA1799
FRA1813  FRA1815  FRA1818  FRA1838
FRA1841  FRA1846  FRA1860  FRA1861
FRA1885  FRA1886  FRA1887  FRA1888
FRA1889  FRA1893  FRA1897  FRA1898
FRA1904  FRA1907  FRA1917  FRA1921
FRA1946  FRA1949  FRA1964  FRA1974
FRA1985  FRA1990  FRA2002  FRA2004
FRA2005  FRA2009  FRA2012  FRA2014
FRA2015  FRA2016  FRA2018  FRA2035
FRA2039  FRA2042  FRA2044  FRA2057
FRA2062  FRA2069  FRA2070  FRA2074
FRA2086  FRA2096  FRA2105  FRA2106
FRA2109  FRA2117  FRA2122  FRA2123
FRA2126  FRA2129  FRA2130  FRA2131
FRA2142  FRA2159  FRA2163  FRA2165
GBR2185  GBR2186  GBR2214  GBR2217
GBR2229  GBR2231  GBR2238  GBR2242
GBR2247  GBR2251  GBR2262  GBR2264
GBR2265  GBR2266  GBR2269  GBR2279
GBR2302  GBR2303  GBR2327  GBR2333
GBR2337  GBR2351  GBR2355  GBR2371
GBR2378  GBR2387  GBR2396  GBR2401
GBR2406  GBR2408  GBR2413  GBR2415
GBR2416  GBR2422  GBR2423  GBR2435
GBR2445  GBR2452  GBR2453  GBR2455
GBR2463  GBR2467  GBR2495  GBR2498
GBR2500  GBR2503  GBR2511  GBR2526
GBR2527  GBR2535  GBR2536  GBR2539
```

See: *How to Use the Directory*, page 11.

GBR2545	GBR2550	GBR2553	GBR2554
GRC2571	GRC2572	GRC2576	GRC2579
GRC2584	GRC2586	HUN2598	HUN2631
HUN2637	IRL2684	IRL2686	IRL2688
IRL2690	IRL2693	IRL2712	IRL2714
IRL2717	ITA2747	ITA2748	ITA2755
ITA2756	ITA2760	ITA2762	ITA2766
ITA2767	ITA2775	ITA2780	ITA2786
ITA2798	ITA2799	ITA2801	ITA2804
ITA2805	ITA2809	ITA2810	ITA2812
ITA2813	ITA2820	ITA2826	ITA2828
ITA2829	ITA2830	ITA2834	ITA2835
ITA2838	ITA2839	ITA2840	ITA2842
ITA2849	ITA2855	ITA2857	ITA2866
ITA2868	ITA2873	ITA2880	ITA2883
ITA2885	ITA2888	ITA2889	ITA2890
ITA2895	ITA2900	ITA2901	ITA2903
ITA2907	ITA2908	ITA2911	ITA2912
ITA2913	ITA2915	ITA2922	ITA2923
LUX2946	LUX2954	LUX2976	MLT3017
MLT3018	MLT3023	NLD3061	NLD3064
NLD3067	NLD3078	NLD3083	NLD3087
NLD3102	NLD3112	NLD3125	NLD3133
NLD3137	NLD3138	NLD3154	NLD3155
NLD3156	NLD3160	NLD3164	NLD3169
NLD3170	NLD3173	NLD3174	NLD3179
NLD3187	NLD3190	NLD3194	NLD3198
NLD3199	NLD3204	NLD3211	NLD3217
NLD3218	NLD3223	NLD3230	NLD3236
NLD3242	NLD3270	NLD3279	NLD3286
NLD3301	NLD3303	NLD3305	NLD3330
NLD3338	NLD3341	NLD3364	NOR3371
NOR3386	NOR3390	NOR3391	NOR3394
NOR3400	NOR3402	NOR3416	NOR3435
NOR3440	NOR3446	NOR3447	NOR3453
NOR3455	NOR3465	NOR3471	POL3482
POL3499	POL3508	POL3512	POL3519
POL3543	POL3544	PRT3549	PRT3564
PRT3585	PRT3586	PRT3590	PRT3594
PRT3596	PRT3597	PRT3602	PRT3603
SVK3611	SVK3612	SVK3622	SVK3638
SVK3640	SWE3648	SWE3658	SWE3664
SWE3685	SWE3695	SWE3699	SWE3702
SWE3727	SWE3730	SWE3731	SWE3735
SWE3738	SWE3744	SWE3749	SWE3754
SWE3768	SWE3776	SWE3785	SWE3798
SWE3807	SWE3815	SWE3816	SWE3826
SWE3827	SWE3830	SWE3839	TUR3883

EXCHANGES, TWINNING, LINKING - ECHANGES, PARRAINAGE, JUMELAGE

BEL0123	BEL0129	BEL0147	BEL0156
BEL0165	BEL0198	BEL0203	BEL0221
BEL0272	BEL0309	BEL0340	BEL0353
BEL0361	BEL0390	BEL0399	CHE0434
CHE0448	CHE0456	CHE0479	CHE0562
CHE0566	CHE0643	CHE0649	CHE0687
CHE0689	CHE0730	CHE0809	CHE0819
CZE0839	CZE0904	DEU0983	DEU0990
DEU0999	DEU1038	DEU1047
DEU1055	DEU1074	DEU1149	DEU1167
DEU1178	DEU1198	DNK1238	DNK1243
DNK1250	DNK1259	DNK1283	DNK1339
ESP1436	ESP1447	ESP1517	ESP1521
ESP1522	ESP1523	ESP1525	FIN1546
FIN1551	FIN1551	FIN1552	FIN1577
FIN1582	FIN1587	FRA1607	FRA1616
FRA1715	FRA1746	FRA1765	FRA1778
FRA1785	FRA1791	FRA1793	FRA1846
FRA1850	FRA1860	FRA1885	FRA1886
FRA1887	FRA1889	FRA1907	FRA1928
FRA1956	FRA1964	FRA1974	FRA1985
FRA2009	FRA2029	FRA2039	FRA2044
FRA2057	FRA2062	FRA2068	FRA2092
FRA2126	FRA2126	FRA2145	FRA2152
FRA2165	GBR2231	GBR2262	GBR2266
GBR2355	GBR2371	GBR2379	GBR2383
GBR2406	GBR2424	GBR2435	GBR2445
GBR2536	GBR2553	GBR2554	HUN2631
HUN2637	HUN2640	IRL2686	ITA2770
ITA2798	ITA2799	ITA2802	ITA2804
ITA2834	ITA2838	ITA2842	ITA2900
MLT3017	NLD3067	NLD3078	NLD3096
NLD3098	NLD3102	NLD3137	NLD3138
NLD3153	NLD3154	NLD3155	NLD3169
NLD3173	NLD3198	NLD3215	NLD3217
NLD3338	NLD3236	NLD3257	NLD3270
NLD3338	NOR3390	NOR3400	NOR3402
NOR3447	NOR3467	POL3482	POL3499

POL3508	POL3519	POL3543	PRT3590
PRT3603	SVK3611	SVK3612	SVK3622
SVK3626	SWE3658	SWE3685	SWE3731
SWE3734	SWE3735	SWE3744	SWE3749
SWE3754	SWE3760	SWE3776	SWE3785
SWE3830	SWE3839	TUR3883

FORMAL EDUCATION - EDUCATION FORMELLE

AUT0065	BEL0123	BEL0129	BEL0156
BEL0176	BEL0323	BEL0353	BEL0359
BEL0361	BEL0362	BEL0368	BEL0390
BEL0392	CHE0434	CHE0456	CHE0562
CHE0566	CHE0649	CHE0660	CHE0665
CHE0673	CHE0687	CHE0689	CHE0759
CHE0772	CHE0805	CHE0809	CHE0819
CZE0894	DEU0983	DEU1116	DEU1149
DEU1176	DEU1178	DNK1262	DNK1289
DNK1339	ESP1409	ESP1427	ESP1437
ESP1482	ESP1486	ESP1490	ESP1513
ESP1521	ESP1522	ESP1528	FIN1585
FRA1607	FRA1649	FRA1675	FRA1731
FRA1769	FRA1785	FRA1794	FRA1827
FRA1841	FRA1886	FRA1889	FRA1904
FRA1946	FRA1956	FRA2015	FRA2016
FRA2039	FRA2044	FRA2057	FRA2062
FRA2102	FRA2103	FRA2106	FRA2123
FRA2131	FRA2145	FRA2150	FRA2159
GBR2228	GBR2231	GBR2238	GBR2265
GBR2269	GBR2337	GBR2355	GBR2371
GBR2379	GBR2406	GBR2408	GBR2415
GBR2423	GBR2424	GBR2445	GBR2448
GBR2452	GBR2455	GBR2467	GBR2468
GBR2511	GBR2550	GBR2553	GBR2554
HUN2631	IRL2686	IRL2690	IRL2691
IRL2702	IRL2720	ITA2761	ITA2762
ITA2767	ITA2770	ITA2782	ITA2798
ITA2799	ITA2804	ITA2810	ITA2812
ITA2814	ITA2816	ITA2822	ITA2826
ITA2838	ITA2842	ITA2855	ITA2857
ITA2868	ITA2883	ITA2890	ITA2900
ITA2912	MLT3016	MLT3017	NLD3067
NLD3078	NLD3083	NLD3138	NLD3154
NLD3155	NLD3179	NLD3190	NLD3212
NLD3215	NLD3217	NLD3223	NLD3270
NLD3305	NOR3465	NOR3467	PRT3594
PRT3597	SVK3611	SVK3612	SWE3648
SWE3658	SWE3796	SWE3798	SWE3823
SWE3827	SWE3830

FUND RAISING - COLLECTE DE FONDS

AUT0021	AUT0035	BEL0128	BEL0142
BEL0148	BEL0155	BEL0156	BEL0168
BEL0198	BEL0199	BEL0203	BEL0224
BEL0261	BEL0272	BEL0297	BEL0306
BEL0323	BEL0327	BEL0351	BEL0353
BEL0359	BEL0361	BEL0362	BEL0381
BEL0390	CHE0434	CHE0448	CHE0549
CHE0562	CHE0566	CHE0570	CHE0584
CHE0586	CHE0602	CHE0604	CHE0619
CHE0687	CHE0689	CHE0715	CHE0727
CHE0744	CHE0749	CHE0755	CHE0756
CHE0772	CHE0785	CHE0786	CHE0800
CHE0810	CHE0814	CHE0819	CHE0820
CZE0839	DEU0957	DEU0968	DEU0983
DEU0994	DEU0999	DEU1006	DEU1044
DEU1065	DEU1111	DEU1149	DEU1167
DEU1175	DEU1178	DEU1187	DNK1222
DNK1227	DNK1238	DNK1243	DNK1259
DNK1262	DNK1283	DNK1305	DNK1377
DNK1405	ESP1409	ESP1410	ESP1413
ESP1435	ESP1447	ESP1450	ESP1452
ESP1455	ESP1505	ESP1506	ESP1508
FIN1549	FIN1551	FIN1554	FIN1557
FIN1570	FIN1572	FIN1588	FIN1591
FRA1607	FRA1610	FRA1636	FRA1664
FRA1690	FRA1710	FRA1769	FRA1778
FRA1785	FRA1787	FRA1791	FRA1793
FRA1843	FRA1861	FRA1880	FRA1889
FRA1928	FRA1946	FRA1966	FRA1978
FRA1990	FRA2015	FRA2016	FRA2053
FRA2086	FRA2092	FRA2131	FRA2152
FRA2159	GBR2185	GBR2222	GBR2226
GBR2228	GBR2229	GBR2238	GBR2247
GBR2248	GBR2277	GBR2302	GBR2333
GBR2337	GBR2371	GBR2383	GBR2406
GBR2413	GBR2424	GBR2445	GBR2493
GBR2498	GBR2500	GBR2511	GBR2530
GBR2532	GBR2550	GBR2553	GRC2572

GRC2586	HUN2598	HUN2631	HUN2637
IRL2684	IRL2709	IRL2714	IRL2733
ITA2748	ITA2755	ITA2758	ITA2762
ITA2770	ITA2785	ITA2799	ITA2804
ITA2809	ITA2820	ITA2822	ITA2824
ITA2826	ITA2829	ITA2834	ITA2840
ITA2855	ITA2857	ITA2901	ITA2907
ITA2911	LIE2930	LUX2937	LUX2946
LUX2955	NLD3067	NLD3069	NLD3078
NLD3135	NLD3137	NLD3154	NLD3155
NLD3160	NLD3179	NLD3198	NLD3201
NLD3223	NLD3230	NLD3253	NLD3258
NLD3263	NLD3288	NLD3301	NLD3303
NLD3362	NOR3371	NOR3390	NOR3412
NOR3416	NOR3435	NOR3453	NOR3467
NOR3471	POL3482	POL3543	PRT3549
PRT3590	PRT3594	PRT3596	PRT3603
SVK3611	SVK3622	SVK3626	SVK3640
SWE3648	SWE3699	SWE3702	SWE3727
SWE3731	SWE3744	SWE3761	SWE3768
SWE3785	SWE3796	SWE3826	SWE3830
TUR3896

INFORMATION AND DOCUMENTATION SERVICES, DATA BASES - SERVICES D'INFORMATION ET DE DOCUMENTATION, BASES DE DONNEES

AUT0020	AUT0026	AUT0035	AUT0060
AUT0074	AUT0079	BEL0118	BEL0123
BEL0129	BEL0141	BEL0142	BEL0149
BEL0155	BEL0164	BEL0165	BEL0168
BEL0191	BEL0199	BEL0203	BEL0214
BEL0226	BEL0237	BEL0252	BEL0267
BEL0272	BEL0281	BEL0297	BEL0306
BEL0327	BEL0335	BEL0345	BEL0353
BEL0359	BEL0361	BEL0362	BEL0365
BEL0390	BEL0392	BEL0393	BEL0396
BEL0399	CHE0406	CHE0429	CHE0434
CHE0456	CHE0464	CHE0494	CHE0496
CHE0501	CHE0534	CHE0549	CHE0550
CHE0554	CHE0562	CHE0566	CHE0568
CHE0619	CHE0624	CHE0629	CHE0649
CHE0654	CHE0665	CHE0673	CHE0687
CHE0689	CHE0715	CHE0720	CHE0727
CHE0744	CHE0756	CHE0758	CHE0759
CHE0763	CHE0800	CHE0809	CHE0819
CZE0839	DEU0918	DEU0919	DEU0921
DEU0968	DEU0968	DEU0975	DEU0977
DEU0989	DEU0990	DEU0996	DEU0998
DEU1015	DEU1020	DEU1025	DEU1031
DEU1074	DEU1076	DEU1086	DEU1090
DEU1091	DEU1111	DEU1149	DEU1179
DEU1184	DEU1192	DNK1238	DNK1248
DNK1259	DNK1262	DNK1283	DNK1292
DNK1300	DNK1305	DNK1306	DNK1318
DNK1339	DNK1358	DNK1375	DNK1398
ESP1407	ESP1413	ESP1417	ESP1430
ESP1431	ESP1434	ESP1435	ESP1437
ESP1438	ESP1441	ESP1443	ESP1447
ESP1450	ESP1455	ESP1479	ESP1482
ESP1486	ESP1490	ESP1493	ESP1506
ESP1511	ESP1521	ESP1522	FIN1546
FIN1547	FIN1548	FIN1552	FIN1572
FIN1577	FIN1582	FIN1588	FIN1591
FIN1602	FIN1604	FRA1610	FRA1617
FRA1636	FRA1672	FRA1703	FRA1709
FRA1737	FRA1785	FRA1787	FRA1794
FRA1797	FRA1808	FRA1810	FRA1811
FRA1818	FRA1827	FRA1838	FRA1839
FRA1841	FRA1846	FRA1849	FRA1860
FRA1886	FRA1889	FRA1956	FRA1988
FRA1990	FRA2002	FRA2004	FRA2009
FRA2018	FRA2035	FRA2039	FRA2069
FRA2096	FRA2103	FRA2104	FRA2105
FRA2106	FRA2109	FRA2116	FRA2122
FRA2126	FRA2130	FRA2131	FRA2140
FRA2152	FRA2159	GBR2185	GBR2226
GBR2238	GBR2239	GBR2265	GBR2279
GBR2326	GBR2355	GBR2371	GBR2378
GBR2379	GBR2383	GBR2387	GBR2406
GBR2408	GBR2413	GBR2415	GBR2423
GBR2435	GBR2438	GBR2445	GBR2452
GBR2453	GBR2455	GBR2495	GBR2498
GBR2511	GBR2522	GBR2545	GRC2571
GRC2576	GRC2579	GRC2584	HUN2631
HUN2637	IRL2684	IRL2686	IRL2698
IRL2705	IRL2712	IRL2714	IRL2717
IRL2730	ITA2744	ITA2748	ITA2762
ITA2773	ITA2775	ITA2780	ITA2782

ITA2785 ITA2798 ITA2799 ITA2801
ITA2805 ITA2808 ITA2809 ITA2810
ITA2813 ITA2814 ITA2820 ITA2822
ITA2824 ITA2834 ITA2839 ITA2840
ITA2846 ITA2855 ITA2857 ITA2860
ITA2862 ITA2866 ITA2873 ITA2880
ITA2889 ITA2894 ITA2895 ITA2900
ITA2901 ITA2907 ITA2908 ITA2911
ITA2912 ITA2913 ITA2923 LUX2937
LUX2949 LUX2962 NLD3051 NLD3058
NLD3067 NLD3077 NLD3078 NLD3083
NLD3096 NLD3102 NLD3135 NLD3137
NLD3138 NLD3153 NLD3147 NLD3154
NLD3155 NLD3156 NLD3160 NLD3167
NLD3170 NLD3173 NLD3179 NLD3181
NLD3190 NLD3194 NLD3196 NLD3198
NLD3201 NLD3204 NLD3211 NLD3217
NLD3218 NLD3230 NLD3236 NLD3242
NLD3270 NLD3279 NLD3301 NLD3303
NLD3305 NLD3334 NLD3338 NLD3352
NLD3355 NLD3364 NOR3386 NOR3390
NOR3391 NOR3402 NOR3410 NOR3435
NOR3455 NOR3467 NOR3471 POL3482
POL3499 POL3512 POL3519 PRT3550
PRT3564 PRT3585 SVK3611 SVK3622
SVK3638 SWE3648 SWE3658 SWE3699
SWE3744 SWE3760 SWE3768 SWE3798
SWE3807 SWE3815 SWE3816 SWE3826
SWE3830 TUR3883

INFORMATION CAMPAIGNS, EXHIBITIONS - CAMPAGNES D'INFORMATION, EXPOSITIONS

AUT0020 AUT0068 BEL0099 BEL0123
BEL0128 BEL0129 BEL0148 BEL0155
BEL0156 BEL0165 BEL0168 BEL0176
BEL0191 BEL0198 BEL0203 BEL0261
BEL0267 BEL0272 BEL0297 BEL0306
BEL0323 BEL0340 BEL0351 BEL0353
BEL0361 BEL0362 BEL0390 BEL0392
BEL0397 CHE0434 CHE0455 CHE0456
CHE0461 CHE0479 CHE0486 CHE0496
CHE0501 CHE0506 CHE0541 CHE0560
CHE0562 CHE0566 CHE0568 CHE0584
CHE0619 CHE0669 CHE0687 CHE0689
CHE0715 CHE0720 CHE0744 CHE0756
CHE0765 CHE0800 CHE0807 CHE0809
CHE0819 CHE0820 CZE0839 DEU0917
DEU0918 DEU0931 DEU0955 DEU0963
DEU0975 DEU0977 DEU0983 DEU0996
DEU0998 DEU0999 DEU1006 DEU1025
DEU1062 DEU1110 DEU1149 DEU1167
DEU1176 DEU1177 DEU1178 DNK1229
DNK1262 DNK1281 DNK1283 DNK1300
DNK1305 DNK1306 DNK1307 DNK1317
DNK1318 DNK1339 DNK1398 DNK1403
ESP1407 ESP1413 ESP1437 ESP1438
ESP1439 ESP1441 ESP1443 ESP1452
ESP1456 ESP1457 ESP1475 ESP1485
ESP1486 ESP1490 ESP1493 ESP1505
ESP1506 ESP1508 ESP1510 ESP1511
ESP1517 ESP1521 ESP1522 ESP1523
ESP1528 FIN1531 FIN1546 FIN1549
FIN1551 FIN1553 FIN1557 FIN1560
FIN1570 FIN1588 FIN1592 FIN1594
FIN1599 FIN1602 FIN1604 FRA1610
FRA1633 FRA1634 FRA1709 FRA1785
FRA1787 FRA1791 FRA1793 FRA1797
FRA1841 FRA1843 FRA1849 FRA1852
FRA1861 FRA1885 FRA1888 FRA1889
FRA1904 FRA1928 FRA1956 FRA1990
FRA2002 FRA2005 FRA2035 FRA2039
FRA2102 FRA2104 FRA2106 FRA2126
FRA2142 FRA2152 FRA2159 GBR2228
GBR2231 GBR2238 GBR2239 GBR2242
GBR2247 GBR2248 GBR2264 GBR2265
GBR2269 GBR2277 GBR2279 GBR2355
GBR2371 GBR2378 GBR2387 GBR2406
GBR2423 GBR2435 GBR2445 GBR2452
GBR2477 GBR2495 GBR2498 GBR2503
GBR2510 GBR2511 GBR2526 GBR2527
GBR2536 GBR2545 GBR2548 GBR2553
GBR2561 GRC2572 GRC2576 GRC2579
HUN2598 HUN2637 IRL2686 IRL2688
IRL2690 IRL2693 IRL2707 IRL2712
IRL2724 ITA2748 ITA2755 ITA2761
ITA2762 ITA2766 ITA2770 ITA2775
ITA2780 ITA2785 ITA2799 ITA2801
ITA2804 ITA2813 ITA2820 ITA2828
ITA2829 ITA2832 ITA2834 ITA2835

ITA2838 ITA2840 ITA2855 ITA2860
ITA2868 ITA2885 ITA2890 ITA2895
ITA2900 ITA2901 ITA2912 ITA2923
LUX2976 MLT3017 NLD3067 NLD3078
NLD3083 NLD3102 NLD3137 NLD3138
NLD3155 NLD3164 NLD3169 NLD3170
NLD3173 NLD3181 NLD3190 NLD3196
NLD3198 NLD3199 NLD3211 NLD3217
NLD3236 NLD3258 NLD3263 NLD3303
NLD3305 NLD3320 NLD3323 NLD3364
NLD3365 NLD3371 NOR3390 NOR3402
NOR3440 NOR3467 POL3482 POL3499
POL3519 POL3543 PRT3549 PRT3564
PRT3594 PRT3596 PRT3600 SVK3611
SVK3612 SWE3648 SWE3664 SWE3699
SWE3702 SWE3727 SWE3731 SWE3738
SWE3744 SWE3749 SWE3754 SWE3760
SWE3761 SWE3768 SWE3776 SWE3795
SWE3796 SWE3798 SWE3816 SWE3830
TUR3883

LOBBYING, ADVOCACY - LOBBYING, PLAIDOYER

AUT0008 AUT0021 AUT0033 AUT0035
AUT0068 AUT0086 AUT0089 BEL0099
BEL0118 BEL0131 BEL0142 BEL0147
BEL0155 BEL0156 BEL0165 BEL0168
BEL0174 BEL0176 BEL0177 BEL0186
BEL0191 BEL0198 BEL0199 BEL0203
BEL0214 BEL0216 BEL0218 BEL0224
BEL0241 BEL0263 BEL0265 BEL0267
BEL0272 BEL0306 BEL0309 BEL0323
BEL0345 BEL0351 BEL0353 BEL0359
BEL0361 BEL0381 BEL0392 BEL0397
BEL0399 CHE0420 CHE0427 CHE0429
CHE0434 CHE0448 CHE0464 CHE0479
CHE0486 CHE0491 CHE0524 CHE0534
CHE0549 CHE0554 CHE0560 CHE0562
CHE0566 CHE0568 CHE0602 CHE0604
CHE0619 CHE0639 CHE0642 CHE0643
CHE0654 CHE0687 CHE0689 CHE0711
CHE0715 CHE0727 CHE0744 CHE0749
CHE0754 CHE0755 CHE0765 CHE0785
CHE0814 CHE0819 CHE0820 CZE0891
DEU0919 DEU0963 DEU0983 DEU0996
DEU0998 DEU0999 DEU1002 DEU1006
DEU1015 DEU1032 DEU1055 DEU1062
DEU1074 DEU1097 DEU1110 DEU1142
DEU1143 DEU1149 DEU1167 DEU1179
DEU1187 DEU1238 DNK1262 DNK1283
DNK1289 DNK1292 DNK1300 DNK1312
DNK1335 DNK1339 DNK1375 DNK1403
DNK1405 ESP1407 ESP1437 ESP1438
ESP1455 ESP1456 ESP1457 ESP1475
ESP1479 ESP1486 ESP1490 ESP1505
ESP1506 ESP1521 ESP1522 ESP1525
ESP1528 FIN1531 FIN1544 FIN1546
FIN1549 FIN1551 FIN1552 FIN1570
FIN1572 FIN1577 FIN1582 FIN1602
FIN1588 FIN1594 FIN1599 FIN1602
FRA1633 FRA1636 FRA1703 FRA1785
FRA1791 FRA1793 FRA1794 FRA1797
FRA1799 FRA1808 FRA1818 FRA1841
FRA1843 FRA1850 FRA1876 FRA1879
FRA1888 FRA1926 FRA1946 FRA1949
FRA1956 FRA1985 FRA1991 FRA2002
FRA2004 FRA2035 FRA2039 FRA2047
FRA2062 FRA2096 FRA2102 FRA2112
FRA2105 FRA2106 FRA2116 FRA2117
FRA2123 FRA2126 FRA2131 FRA2142
FRA2159 FRA2163 GBR2214 GBR2217
GBR2228 GBR2229 GBR2238 GBR2239
GBR2242 GBR2248 GBR2251 GBR2264
GBR2266 GBR2269 GBR2337 GBR2355
GBR2371 GBR2378 GBR2390 GBR2396
GBR2401 GBR2406 GBR2413 GBR2423
GBR2435 GBR2445 GBR2453 GBR2464
GBR2467 GBR2495 GBR2498 GBR2500
GBR2503 GBR2510 GBR2511 GBR2522
GBR2526 GBR2527 GBR2539 GBR2545
GBR2548 GBR2552 GBR2553 GBR2561
GRC2571 GRC2572 GRC2576 GRC2579
GRC2586 HUN2598 HUN2637 IRL2684
IRL2690 IRL2691 IRL2693 IRL2705
IRL2706 IRL2707 IRL2712 IRL2714
IRL2717 IRL2724 ITA2748 ITA2775
ITA2810 ITA2813 ITA2820 ITA2834
ITA2838 ITA2840 ITA2855 ITA2862
ITA2873 ITA2882 ITA2911 ITA2913

LUX2937 LUX2955 LUX2957 LUX2976
MLT3016 MLT3017 MLT3023 NLD3047
NLD3064 NLD3067 NLD3068 NLD3069
NLD3078 NLD3096 NLD3098 NLD3102
NLD3133 NLD3137 NLD3156 NLD3160
NLD3164 NLD3170 NLD3198 NLD3199
NLD3204 NLD3211 NLD3218 NLD3223
NLD3230 NLD3236 NLD3242 NLD3258
NLD3301 NLD3303 NLD3305 NLD3330
NLD3334 NLD3362 NLD3364 NOR3386
NOR3389 NOR3390 NOR3402 NOR3416
NOR3419 NOR3429 NOR3455 NOR3467
NOR3471 POL3482 POL3499 PRT3549
PRT3564 PRT3590 PRT3594 PRT3600
SVK3634 SVK3638 SWE3648 SWE3658
SWE3699 SWE3735 SWE3741 SWE3749
SWE3768 SWE3785 SWE3798 SWE3807
SWE3815 SWE3830 TUR3883 TUR3896
TUR3897

NETWORKING, ELECTRONIC TELECOMMUNICATIONS - RESEAUX, TELECOMMUNICATIONS ELECTRONIQUES

AUT0010 AUT0020 BEL0165 BEL0198
BEL0224 BEL0272 BEL0361 CHE0434
CHE0479 CHE0562 CHE0568 CHE0586
CHE0642 CHE0689 CHE0809 CHE0819
CZE0859 CZE0904 DEU0955 DEU0990
DEU1002 DEU1065 DEU1097 DEU1149
DEU1167 DEU1187 DNK1248 DNK1281
DNK1300 DNK1375 ESP1434 ESP1457
ESP1479 ESP1522 FIN1531 FIN1546
FIN1552 FIN1570 FIN1582 FIN1583
FIN1591 FIN1599 FIN1604 FRA1673
FRA1889 FRA1956 FRA1985 FRA2106
FRA2109 FRA2126 FRA2159 GBR2226
GBR2252 GBR2265 GBR2285 GBR2313
GBR2337 GBR2351 GBR2355 GBR2371
GBR2387 GBR2401 GBR2406 GBR2413
GBR2438 GBR2495 GBR2498 GBR2545
GBR2553 GRC2576 HUN2631 HUN2637
IRL2698 IRL2714 ITA2748 ITA2773
ITA2780 ITA2799 ITA2860 NLD3067
NLD3077 NLD3102 NLD3137 NLD3154
NLD3156 NLD3181 NLD3199 NLD3215
NLD3218 NLD3236 NLD3257 NLD3279
NLD3303 NLD3364 NOR3390 NOR3402
NOR3467 POL3482 POL3499 SVK3611
SVK3622 SWE3712 SWE3785 SWE3830
TUR3883

OTHER - AUTRE

CHE0434 CHE0568 DEU1106 FIN1555
FRA1700 FRA1966 FRA2012 GBR2371
GBR2387 GBR2435 GBR2510 NLD3117
NLD3133 NLD3137 NLD3183 NLD3223
PRT3558 SWE3666

PUBLISHING, AUDIOVISUAL MATERIALS, EDUCATIONAL MATERIALS - EDITION, DOCUMENTS AUDIOVISUELS, DOCUMENTS EDUCATIFS

AUT0020 AUT0051 AUT0068 BEL0123
BEL0142 BEL0149 BEL0155 BEL0164
BEL0165 BEL0168 BEL0174 BEL0176
BEL0188 BEL0203 BEL0214 BEL0252
BEL0261 BEL0272 BEL0281 BEL0297
BEL0306 BEL0323 BEL0327 BEL0340
BEL0345 BEL0353 BEL0361 BEL0362
BEL0365 BEL0390 BEL0392 BEL0393
BEL0396 CHE0406 CHE0434 CHE0456
CHE0496 CHE0501 CHE0517 CHE0549
CHE0560 CHE0562 CHE0566 CHE0568
CHE0619 CHE0638 CHE0639 CHE0649
CHE0687 CHE0689 CHE0715 CHE0738
CHE0744 CHE0750 CHE0756 CHE0759
CHE0763 CHE0772 CHE0809 CHE0819
CHE0820 CYP0832 CZE0894 DEU0944
DEU0975 DEU0977 DEU0989 DEU1020
DEU1022 DEU1025 DEU1055 DEU1062
DEU1074 DEU1076 DEU1095 DEU1097
DEU1110 DEU1149 DEU1176 DEU1180
DEU1187 DEU1198 DNK1238 DNK1259
DNK1262 DNK1273 DNK1283 DNK1289
DNK1317 DNK1339 DNK1375 DNK1403
ESP1407 ESP1409 ESP1413 ESP1417
ESP1430 ESP1431 ESP1434 ESP1435
ESP1437 ESP1438 ESP1455 ESP1456

See: *How to Use the Directory*, page 11.

ESP1474 ESP1475 ESP1486 ESP1490
ESP1505 ESP1506 ESP1521 ESP1522
FIN1536 FIN1544 FIN1546 FIN1547
FIN1548 FIN1549 FIN1551 FIN1552
FIN1557 FIN1570 FIN1577 FIN1588
FIN1604 FRA1610 FRA1668 FRA1673
FRA1709 FRA1713 FRA1715 FRA1768
FRA1778 FRA1785 FRA1794 FRA1810
FRA1813 FRA1816 FRA1836 FRA1849
FRA1852 FRA1860 FRA1886 FRA1889
FRA1893 FRA1897 FRA1956 FRA1986
FRA1990 FRA2002 FRA2004 FRA2039
FRA2069 FRA2086 FRA2096 FRA2104
FRA2106 FRA2109 FRA2126 FRA2131
FRA2142 FRA2159 FRA2165 GBR2185
GBR2226 GBR2229 GBR2231 GBR2238
GBR2239 GBR2247 GBR2248 GBR2265
GBR2266 GBR2271 GBR2279 GBR2337
GBR2345 GBR2355 GBR2371 GBR2378
GBR2387 GBR2401 GBR2406 GBR2413
GBR2415 GBR2422 GBR2423 GBR2445
GBR2452 GBR2453 GBR2455 GBR2467
GBR2498 GBR2500 GBR2501 GBR2503
GBR2510 GBR2511 GBR2526 GBR2527
GBR2545 GBR2554 GRC2572 GRC2576
HUN2631 HUN2637 IRL2698 IRL2712
ITA2748 ITA2755 ITA2756 ITA2762
ITA2766 ITA2780 ITA2785 ITA2786
ITA2798 ITA2799 ITA2801 ITA2805
ITA2809 ITA2810 ITA2813 ITA2822
ITA2826 ITA2828 ITA2837 ITA2839
ITA2840 ITA2849 ITA2855 ITA2857
ITA2858 ITA2866 ITA2873 ITA2900
ITA2901 ITA2907 ITA2908 ITA2911
ITA2913 ITA2916 LUX3006 NLD3051
NLD3061 NLD3067 NLD3077 NLD3078
NLD3083 NLD3102 NLD3112 NLD3133
NLD3135 NLD3137 NLD3138 NLD3139
NLD3154 NLD3156 NLD3164 NLD3169
NLD3173 NLD3190 NLD3194 NLD3198
NLD3201 NLD3211 NLD3212 NLD3215
NLD3216 NLD3223 NLD3270 NLD3279
NLD3301 NLD3303 NLD3305 NLD3320
NLD3354 NLD3364 NLD3305 NOR3390
NOR3391 NOR3423 NOR3435 NOR3440
NOR3467 POL3482 POL3499 POL3512
POL3519 POL3543 PRT3564 PRT3585
PRT3586 PRT3600 PRT3602 SVK3611
SVK3622 SVK3638 SVK3640 SWE3648
SWE3699 SWE3735 SWE3744 SWE3749
SWE3760 SWE3768 SWE3798 SWE3816
SWE3830 TUR3883

OTHER - AUTRE

BROADCASTING, CULTURAL EVENTS - RADIODIFFUSION, MANIFESTATIONS CULTURELLES

BEL0263 BEL0390 CHE0433 CHE0434
CHE0604 CHE0683 CHE0917 DEU0956
DEU1005 DEU1144 DNK1274 FIN1604
FRA1910 FRA1992 GBR2229 GBR2241
GBR2311 GBR2345 GBR2355 GBR2466
GBR2511 IRL2728 ITA2860 ITA2914
NLD3107 NLD3249 NLD3350 NOR3374
SWE3725 SWE3771

CONFERENCES, SEMINARS, WORKSHOPS, TRAINING ACTIVITIES - CONFERENCES, SEMINAIRES, ATELIERS, ACTIVITES DE FORMATION

BEL0199 BEL0218 BEL0263 BEL0273
BEL0306 CHE0433 CHE0434 CHE0446
CHE0448 CHE0549 CHE0550 CHE0565
CHE0578 CHE0589 CHE0604 CHE0650
CHE0683 CHE0755 DEU0917 DEU0974
DEU1005 DEU1019 DEU1022 DEU1029
DEU1106 DEU1144 DEU1209 DNK1218
DNK1248 DNK1274 DNK1300 DNK1320
DNK1324 ESP1410 ESP1453 ESP1486
ESP1511 FIN1536 FIN1557 FIN1559
FIN1569 FIN1574 FIN1587 FIN1604
FIN1605 FRA1633 FRA1756 FRA1788
FRA1818 FRA1837 FRA1883 FRA1888
FRA1946 FRA1992 FRA2018 FRA2126
FRA2144 GBR2172 GBR2181 GBR2229
GBR2241 GBR2244 GBR2247 GBR2251

GBR2311 GBR2324 GBR2325 GBR2355
GBR2363 GBR2384 GBR2394 GBR2426
GBR2435 GBR2437 GBR2445 GBR2453
GBR2466 GBR2477 GBR2511 GBR2546
HUN2640 ITA2860 ITA2861 ITA2914
MLT3025 NLD3059 NLD3069 NLD3090
NLD3103 NLD3117 NLD3207 NLD3230
NLD3242 NLD3249 NLD3305 NLD3350
NOR3374 NOR3431 PRT3584 SVK3638
SWE3650 SWE3691 SWE3702 SWE3725
SWE3771 SWE3839

EXCHANGES, TWINNING, LINKING - ECHANGES, PARRAINAGE, JUMELAGE

BEL0218 BEL0263 BEL0273 BEL0390
CHE0434 CHE0550 CHE0565 CHE0589
CHE0650 CHE0795 DEU0917 DEU1005
ESP1486 FIN1587 FIN1604 FIN1605
FRA1818 FRA1946 GBR2229 GBR2325
GBR2355 GBR2435 GBR2437 ITA2914
NLD3059 NLD3091 NLD3103 NLD3117
NLD3203 NLD3305 NLD3350 NOR3374
SVK3638 SWE3771 SWE3839 SWE3857

FORMAL EDUCATION - EDUCATION FORMELLE

BEL0218 CHE0433 CHE0434 CHE0448
CHE0578 CHE0589 DEU1019 DEU1144
DEU1158 DEU1209 DNK1218 FIN1559
FIN1569 FRA1946 GBR2178 GBR2345
GBR2355 GBR2445 GBR2466 GBR2511
ITA2914 NLD3059 NLD3103 NLD3117
NLD3305 NLD3350 SVK3638 SWE3661
SWE3771

FUND RAISING - COLLECTE DE FONDS

BEL0199 BEL0273 BEL0306 CHE0434
CHE0446 CHE0550 CHE0586 CHE0604
CHE0650 CHE0755 DEU1019 DEU1209
DNK1218 FIN1559 FIN1604 FRA1825
FRA1910 FRA1946 FRA2103 GBR2172
GBR2178 GBR2198 GBR2229 GBR2244
GBR2247 GBR2324 GBR2325 GBR2355
GBR2384 GBR2400 GBR2445 GBR2477
GBR2511 ITA2914 MLT3025 NLD3091
NLD3107 NLD3117 NLD3249 NLD3350
SVK3638 SWE3661 SWE3702 SWE3853

INFORMATION AND DOCUMENTATION SERVICES, DATA BASES - SERVICES D'INFORMATION ET DE DOCUMENTATION, BASES DE DONNEES

AUT0067 BEL0139 BEL0199 BEL0263
BEL0273 BEL0306 BEL0390 CHE0433
CHE0434 CHE0459 CHE0549 CHE0550
CHE0565 CHE0589 CHE0650 DEU0956
DEU1019 DEU1144 DEU1209 DNK1218
DNK1248 DNK1300 ESP1434 ESP1453
ESP1486 ESP1511 FIN1559 FIN1569
FIN1574 FIN1604 FRA1673 FRA1756
FRA1762 FRA1818 FRA1825 FRA1837
FRA2018 FRA2126 GBR2178 GBR2229
GBR2241 GBR2324 GBR2355 GBR2363
GBR2394 GBR2400 GBR2435 GBR2437
GBR2445 GBR2453 GBR2466 GBR2477
GBR2511 HUN2640 ITA2860 ITA2861
ITA2914 MLT3025 NLD3059 NLD3103
NLD3107 NLD3117 NLD3135 NLD3242
NLD3305 NLD3350 NOR3374 SVK3638
SWE3691 SWE3702 SWE3725 SWE3771
SWE3839

INFORMATION CAMPAIGNS, EXHIBITIONS - CAMPAGNES D'INFORMATION, EXPOSITIONS

BEL0218 BEL0263 BEL0273 BEL0390
CHE0433 CHE0434 CHE0459 CHE0550
CHE0589 CHE0683 CHE0773 DEU0917
DEU0974 DEU1019 DEU1144 DEU1209
DNK1218 DNK1248 DNK1300 ESP1486
FIN1559 FIN1574 FIN1604 FRA1633
FRA1818 FRA1888 FRA1910 FRA1992
FRA2088 FRA2126 GBR2172 GBR2229
GBR2241 GBR2311 GBR2324 GBR2355
GBR2363 GBR2394 GBR2435 GBR2437
GBR2445 GBR2466 GBR2477 GBR2511
ITA2860 ITA2914 MLT3025 NLD3103

NLD3107 NLD3117 NLD3135 NLD3350
NOR3374 PRT3584 SVK3638 SWE3650
SWE3661 SWE3691 SWE3725 SWE3771

LOBBYING, ADVOCACY - LOBBYING, PLAIDOYER

BEL0199 BEL0263 BEL0273 BEL0306
CHE0433 CHE0434 CHE0549 CHE0550
CHE0589 CHE0604 CHE0650 CHE0755
DEU0974 DEU1209 DNK1248 DNK1300
ESP1453 FIN1559 FIN1574 FIN1604
FRA1633 FRA1756 FRA1818 FRA1888
FRA1910 FRA1946 FRA2126 GBR2181
GBR2229 GBR2311 GBR2324 GBR2323
GBR2355 GBR2363 GBR2384 GBR2394
GBR2400 GBR2445 GBR2453 GBR2466
GBR2511 GBR2530 GBR2546 ITA2914
MLT3025 NLD3059 NLD3103 NLD3107
NLD3117 NLD3305 NLD3350 SVK3638
SWE3650 SWE3661 SWE3691 SWE3771
SWE3853

NETWORKING, ELECTRONIC TELECOMMUNICATIONS - RESEAUX, TELECOMMUNICATIONS ELECTRONIQUES

BEL0218 CHE0434 CHE0550 CHE0565
DEU0917 DEU0956 DEU0974 DEU1019
DEU1144 DNK1300 ESP1434 ESP1486
FIN1604 FIN1605 FRA1837 FRA1910
FRA2126 GBR2229 GBR2324 GBR2355
GBR2435 GBR2437 GBR2530 ITA2860
ITA2914 MLT3025 NLD3069 NLD3117
NLD3305 NOR3374 SVK3638 SWE3650
SWE3691 SWE3702

PUBLISHING, AUDIOVISUAL MATERIALS, EDUCATIONAL MATERIALS - EDITION, DOCUMENTS AUDIOVISUELS, DOCUMENTS EDUCATIFS

BEL0218 BEL0263 BEL0273 BEL0306
BEL0390 CHE0433 CHE0434 CHE0549
CHE0550 CHE0565 CHE0589 CHE0604
CHE0683 DEU0917 DEU0956 DEU0974
DEU1005 DEU1019 DEU1022 DEU1209
DNK1218 DNK1248 DNK1255 DNK1274
ESP1410 ESP1434 ESP1453 ESP1486
FIN1536 FIN1557 FIN1559 FIN1569
FIN1587 FRA1673 FRA1756 FRA1818
FRA1837 FRA1883 FRA1992 FRA2018
FRA2126 GBR2178 GBR2185 GBR2198
GBR2229 GBR2241 GBR2244 GBR2251
GBR2311 GBR2324 GBR2325 GBR2345
GBR2355 GBR2394 GBR2400 GBR2435
GBR2437 GBR2445 GBR2453 GBR2466
GBR2477 GBR2511 GBR2530 GBR2546
HUN2640 IRL2728 ITA2860 ITA2861
ITA2914 NLD3090 NLD3107 NLD3117
NLD3350 NLD3203 NLD3230 NLD3305
NLD3350 NOR3374 NOR3441 SVK3638
SWE3650 SWE3725 SWE3771

PEACE, ETHNIC CONFLICTS, ARMAMENT, DISARMAMENT - PAIX, CONFLITS ETHNIQUES, ARMEMENT, DESARMEMENT

BROADCASTING, CULTURAL EVENTS - RADIODIFFUSION, MANIFESTATIONS CULTURELLES

AUT0020 BEL0123 BEL0129 BEL0147
BEL0148 BEL0226 BEL0275 BEL0303
BEL0340 BEL0361 CHE0434 CHE0534
CHE0566 CHE0568 CHE0624 CHE0689
CHE0819 CYP0832 CZE0906 DEU0920
DEU1022 DEU1110 DEU1114 DNK1375
DNK1376 ESP1430 ESP1457 ESP1486
ESP1490 ESP1506 ESP1523 FIN1536
FIN1545 FIN1553 FRA1621 FRA1631
FRA1791 FRA1793 FRA1889 FRA1910
FRA1923 FRA1956 FRA2002 FRA2047
FRA2057 FRA2159 GBR2238 GBR2345
GBR2371 GBR2378 GBR2411 GBR2423
GBR2498 GBR2501 GBR2545 HUN2644
IRL2686 IRL2714 ITA2785 ITA2798
ITA2809 ITA2820 ITA2826 ITA2838
ITA2838 ITA2923 LUX2937 LUX2954
MLT3018 NLD3067 NLD3181 NLD3222

NLD3253 NLD3326 NOR3390 POL3508
SVK3622 SWE3738 SWE3774 SWE3819
TUR3883

CONFERENCES, SEMINARS, WORKSHOPS, TRAINING ACTIVITIES - CONFERENCES, SEMINAIRES, ATELIERS, ACTIVITES DE FORMATION

AUT0010	AUT0020	AUT0047	AUT0074
BEL0123	BEL0127	BEL0128	BEL0129
BEL0147	BEL0168	BEL0174	BEL0176
BEL0177	BEL0188	BEL0191	BEL0192
BEL0197	BEL0199	BEL0214	BEL0221
BEL0275	BEL0297	BEL0303	BEL0306
BEL0340	BEL0345	BEL0353	BEL0361
BEL0362	BEL0368	BEL0378	BEL0379
CHE0420	CHE0426	CHE0417	CHE0420
CHE0426	CHE0434	CHE0456	CHE0461
CHE0494	CHE0519	CHE0534	CHE0553
CHE0566	CHE0568	CHE0642	CHE0654
CHE0655	CHE0682	CHE0689	CHE0693
CHE0711	CHE0718	CHE0730	CHE0755
CHE0809	CHE0814	CHE0817	CHE0819
CYP0831	CYP0832	CYP0833	CZE0897
CZE0905	CZE0906	DEU0920	DEU0929
DEU0942	DEU0944	DEU0977	DEU0983
DEU0990	DEU0992	DEU0996	DEU0998
DEU1004	DEU1034	DEU1038	DEU1054
DEU1055	DEU1056	DEU1062	DEU1064
DEU1090	DEU1097	DEU1110	DEU1114
DEU1131	DEU1146	DEU1149	DEU1175
DEU1179	DEU1180	DEU1184	DEU1193
DEU1198	DEU1210	DNK1273	DNK1289
DNK1305	DNK1312	DNK1339	DNK1358
DNK1375	DNK1398	DNK1398	ESP1407
ESP1430	ESP1436	ESP1441	ESP1445
ESP1450	ESP1457	ESP1461	ESP1472
ESP1486	ESP1490	ESP1493	ESP1505
ESP1506	ESP1508	ESP1511	ESP1517
ESP1522	ESP1523	ESP1528	FIN1536
FIN1543	FIN1545	FIN1551	FIN1553
FIN1560	FIN1570	FIN1577	FIN1578
FIN1583	FIN1588	FIN1592	FIN1594
FIN1605	FRA1675	FRA1791	FRA1793
FRA1797	FRA1811	FRA1841	FRA1862
FRA1887	FRA1889	FRA1917	FRA1946
FRA1955	FRA1956	FRA1975	FRA2002
FRA2004	FRA2019	FRA2032	FRA2034
FRA2041	FRA2042	FRA2044	FRA2047
FRA2053	FRA2057	FRA2062	FRA2086
FRA2159	GBR2174	GBR2185	GBR2238
GBR2251	GBR2260	GBR2265	GBR2266
GBR2269	GBR2279	GBR2303	GBR2312
GBR2337	GBR2371	GBR2378	GBR2387
GBR2388	GBR2396	GBR2401	GBR2408
GBR2411	GBR2415	GBR2416	GBR2423
GBR2424	GBR2435	GBR2445	GBR2455
GBR2498	GBR2503	GBR2526	GBR2545
GBR2561	GRC2572	GRC2586	HUN2609
HUN2644	HUN2655	IRL2679	IRL2684
IRL2686	IRL2688	IRL2690	IRL2693
IRL2714	IRL2720	IRL2728	ITA2747
ITA2764	ITA2773	ITA2785	ITA2798
ITA2809	ITA2810	ITA2813	ITA2820
ITA2822	ITA2824	ITA2826	ITA2828
ITA2829	ITA2832	ITA2834	ITA2837
ITA2838	ITA2840	ITA2841	ITA2860
ITA2866	ITA2883	ITA2894	ITA2898
ITA2900	ITA2903	ITA2905	ITA2907
ITA2908	ITA2911	ITA2912	ITA2922
LUX2984	MLT3016	MLT3017	MLT3018
MLT3023	MLT3036	NLD3050	NLD3064
NLD3082	NLD3098	NLD3098	NLD3104
NLD3122	NLD3133	NLD3139	NLD3164
NLD3170	NLD3174	NLD3190	NLD3194
NLD3199	NLD3211	NLD3218	NLD3222
NLD3223	NLD3226	NLD3277	NLD3301
NLD3303	NLD3326	NLD3330	NOR3371
NOR3389	NOR3390	NOR3400	NOR3429
NOR3455	NOR3467	POL3508	POL3519
POL3536	POL3543	POL3544	PRT3549
PRT3585	PRT3586	PRT3600	SVK3612
SVK3622	SWE3667	SWE3695	SWE3699
SWE3730	SWE3731	SWE3734	SWE3735
SWE3738	SWE3746	SWE3749	SWE3768
SWE3771	SWE3774	SWE3776	SWE3807
SWE3816	SWE3819	TUR3883	

EXCHANGES, TWINNING, LINKING - ECHANGES, PARRAINAGE, JUMELAGE

AUT0020	AUT0047	BEL0120	BEL0123
BEL0129	BEL0147	BEL0198	BEL0221
BEL0303	BEL0340	BEL0361	BEL0390
CHE0434	CHE0448	CHE0456	CHE0566
CHE0595	CHE0643	CHE0689	CHE0730
CHE0809	CHE0819	CYP0831	DEU0920
DEU0983	DEU0990	DEU1055	DEU1056
DEU1114	DEU1149	DEU1175	DNK1339
DNK1375	ESP1445	ESP1517	ESP1523
FIN1543	FIN1605	FRA1746	FRA1791
FRA1793	FRA1887	FRA1889	FRA1955
FRA1956	FRA1985	FRA2034	FRA2057
FRA2062	FRA2159	GBR2371	GBR2379
GBR2390	GBR2396	GBR2445	HUN2622
HUN2637	IRL2680	IRL2686	IRL2728
ITA2764	ITA2775	ITA2785	ITA2834
ITA2838	ITA2883	ITA2903	ITA2905
MLT3018	NLD3067	NLD3082	NLD3098
NLD3122	NLD3218	NLD3236	NLD3326
NLD3330	NOR3390	NOR3400	POL3519
POL3544	SVK3612	SWE3730	SWE3731
SWE3734	SWE3749	SWE3819	TUR3883

FORMAL EDUCATION - EDUCATION FORMELLE

AUT0020	BEL0123	BEL0129	BEL0147
BEL0176	BEL0323	BEL0361	BEL0362
BEL0390	CHE0434	CHE0456	CHE0566
CHE0660	CHE0682	CHE0687	CHE0689
CHE0809	CHE0819	CYP0833	DEU0983
DEU1114	DNK1262	DNK1339	ESP1427
ESP1436	ESP1479	ESP1486	ESP1490
ESP1508	ESP1517	ESP1523	FRA1675
FRA1841	FRA1889	FRA1946	FRA1956
FRA2019	FRA2044	FRA2062	FRA2159
GBR2185	GBR2233	GBR2238	GBR2265
GBR2269	GBR2337	GBR2345	GBR2371
GBR2379	GBR2390	GBR2396	GBR2408
GBR2411	GBR2415	GBR2424	GBR2436
GBR2445	GBR2467	GBR2468	GBR2522
HUN2643	HUN2644	IRL2686	IRL2690
IRL2691	IRL2706	IRL2720	IRL2726
ITA2764	ITA2798	ITA2810	ITA2813
ITA2822	ITA2826	ITA2840	ITA2883
ITA2900	ITA2912	MLT3012	MLT3016
MLT3017	MLT3018	NLD3067	NLD3104
NLD3201	NLD3218	NLD3223	NLD3326
NOR3390	POL3508	PRT3600	SVK3612
SWE3819			

FUND RAISING - COLLECTE DE FONDS

AUT0003	AUT0020	AUT0033	BEL0147
BEL0168	BEL0197	BEL0198	BEL0361
BEL0362	CHE0417	CHE0434	CHE0446
CHE0448	CHE0562	CHE0566	CHE0570
CHE0584	CHE0687	CHE0689	CHE0755
CHE0756	CHE0800	CHE0814	CHE0819
DEU0929	DEU0957	DEU0968	DEU0983
DEU0993	DEU1027	DEU1054	DEU1062
DEU1064	DEU1110	DEU1114	DEU1187
DNK1222	DNK1227	DNK1305	DNK1375
DNK1405	ESP1442	ESP1445	ESP1461
ESP1486	ESP1505	ESP1506	ESP1508
FIN1551	FIN1570	FIN1588	FRA1791
FRA1793	FRA1811	FRA1843	FRA1855
FRA1889	FRA1910	FRA1942	FRA1946
FRA1978	FRA1991	FRA2041	FRA2047
FRA2053	FRA2086	FRA2091	FRA2152
FRA2159	GBR2185	GBR2201	GBR2222
GBR2238	GBR2321	GBR2337	GBR2371
GBR2388	GBR2396	GBR2411	GBR2424
GBR2436	GBR2445	GBR2464	GBR2498
GBR2506	GBR2522	GBR2524	HUN2609
HUN2644	IRL2679	IRL2680	IRL2684
IRL2726	ITA2755	ITA2773	ITA2785
ITA2809	ITA2810	ITA2820	ITA2822
ITA2824	ITA2826	ITA2834	ITA2855
ITA2900	ITA2903	ITA2905	ITA2911
LUX2984	MLT3018	NLD3067	NLD3104
NLD3222	NLD3223	NLD3226	NLD3253
NLD3256	NLD3263	NLD3301	NLD3326
NLD3330	NLD3362	NOR3371	NOR3390
NOR3404	NOR3416	PRT3549	SWE3648
SWE3667	SWE3674	SWE3699	SWE3730
SWE3731	SWE3734	SWE3738	SWE3744
SWE3746	SWE3749	SWE3768	SWE3819

INFORMATION AND DOCUMENTATION SERVICES, DATA BASES - SERVICES D'INFORMATION ET DE DOCUMENTATION, BASES DE DONNEES

AUT0010	AUT0020	AUT0026	AUT0060
AUT0074	AUT0079	BEL0123	BEL0127
BEL0129	BEL0167	BEL0168	BEL0192
BEL0197	BEL0214	BEL0226	BEL0237
BEL0267	BEL0268	BEL0281	BEL0297
BEL0303	BEL0306	BEL0335	BEL0345
BEL0361	BEL0362	BEL0365	BEL0379
BEL0390	BEL0393	CHE0406	CHE0420
CHE0426	CHE0429	CHE0434	CHE0456
CHE0494	CHE0503	CHE0506	CHE0563
CHE0566	CHE0568	CHE0624	CHE0668
CHE0687	CHE0689	CHE0711	CHE0756
CHE0763	CHE0800	CHE0809	CHE0814
CHE0819	CYP0831	CZE0906	DEU0920
DEU0929	DEU0944	DEU0968	DEU0977
DEU0990	DEU0996	DEU0998	DEU1001
DEU1002	DEU1027	DEU1054	DEU1062
DEU1064	DEU1076	DEU1086	DEU1090
DEU1091	DEU1114	DEU1146	DEU1149
DEU1179	DEU1180	DEU1184	DEU1192
DEU1207	DNK1283	DNK1292	DNK1305
DNK1339	DNK1375	DNK1376	DNK1398
ESP1407	ESP1430	ESP1431	ESP1434
ESP1441	ESP1450	ESP1457	ESP1479
ESP1486	ESP1490	ESP1493	ESP1506
ESP1508	ESP1522	ESP1523	FIN1548
FIN1588	FRA1631	FRA1703	FRA1737
FRA1797	FRA1808	FRA1810	FRA1811
FRA1818	FRA1839	FRA1841	FRA1889
FRA1908	FRA1942	FRA1955	FRA1956
FRA2002	FRA2004	FRA2018	FRA2034
FRA2041	FRA2047	FRA2103	FRA2104
FRA2122	FRA2131	FRA2152	FRA2159
GBR2185	GBR2222	GBR2238	GBR2239
GBR2265	GBR2266	GBR2371	GBR2378
GBR2379	GBR2387	GBR2388	GBR2396
GBR2402	GBR2408	GBR2411	GBR2415
GBR2435	GBR2438	GBR2445	GBR2498
GBR2522	GBR2545	HUN2609	HUN2643
HUN2644	IRL2684	IRL2686	IRL2698
IRL2705	IRL2706	IRL2714	IRL2720
IRL2730	ITA2755	ITA2762	ITA2773
ITA2785	ITA2798	ITA2801	ITA2809
ITA2810	ITA2813	ITA2820	ITA2822
ITA2828	ITA2829	ITA2834	ITA2840
ITA2852	ITA2857	ITA2860	ITA2861
ITA2866	ITA2873	ITA2894	ITA2895
ITA2900	ITA2902	ITA2907	ITA2908
ITA2911	ITA2912	ITA2923	LUX2937
LUX2962	MLT3017	MLT3018	NLD3051
NLD3058	NLD3067	NLD3077	NLD3095
NLD3098	NLD3122	NLD3135	NLD3139
NLD3147	NLD3167	NLD3170	NLD3181
NLD3194	NLD3211	NLD3218	NLD3222
NLD3226	NLD3301	NLD3303	NLD3305
NLD3326	NLD3330	NLD3334	NLD3361
NOR3371	NOR3390	NOR3400	NOR3410
NOR3455	POL3519	PRT3585	PRT3600
SWE3648	SWE3658	SWE3695	SWE3699
SWE3734	SWE3744	SWE3746	SWE3768
SWE3771	SWE3774	SWE3807	SWE3816
SWE3819	TUR3882	TUR3883	TUR3895

INFORMATION CAMPAIGNS, EXHIBITIONS - CAMPAGNES D'INFORMATION, EXPOSITIONS

AUT0010	AUT0020	AUT0024	BEL0123
BEL0129	BEL0168	BEL0176	BEL0192
BEL0197	BEL0198	BEL0226	BEL0248
BEL0267	BEL0275	BEL0303	BEL0323
BEL0340	BEL0361	BEL0362	BEL0390
BEL0394	CHE0426	CHE0434	CHE0446
CHE0456	CHE0461	CHE0486	CHE0506
CHE0519	CHE0534	CHE0553	CHE0557
CHE0566	CHE0568	CHE0570	CHE0584
CHE0669	CHE0689	CHE0711	CHE0718
CHE0756	CHE0800	CHE0809	CHE0814
CHE0819	CYP0831	CYP0832	CZE0905
CZE0906	DEU0917	DEU0920	DEU0929
DEU0955	DEU0977	DEU0983	DEU1022
DEU1034	DEU1062	DEU1064	DEU1065
DEU1110	DEU1149	DEU1187	DNK1245
DNK1262	DNK1283	DNK1289	DNK1292
DNK1305	DNK1307	DNK1312	DNK1375
DNK1376	DNK1398	ESP1407	ESP1436

See: *How to Use the Directory*, page 11.

ESP1441	ESP1450	ESP1457	ESP1461
ESP1475	ESP1486	ESP1490	ESP1493
ESP1505	ESP1506	ESP1508	ESP1517
ESP1522	ESP1523	ESP1528	FIN1553
FIN1560	FIN1570	FIN1577	FIN1588
FIN1592	FIN1594	FRA1633	FRA1675
FRA1791	FRA1793	FRA1797	FRA1808
FRA1811	FRA1862	FRA1889	FRA1910
FRA1923	FRA1938	FRA1942	FRA1955
FRA1956	FRA1985	FRA2002	FRA2047
FRA2053	FRA2057	FRA2086	FRA2152
FRA2159	GBR2222	GBR2238	GBR2239
GBR2265	GBR2269	GBR2279	GBR2312
GBR2321	GBR2328	GBR2345	GBR2371
GBR2378	GBR2387	GBR2388	GBR2408
GBR2411	GBR2423	GBR2445	GBR2498
GBR2526	GBR2545	GBR2552	HUN2609
HUN2637	HUN2644	HUN2655	IRL2679
IRL2680	IRL2684	IRL2686	IRL2693
IRL2707	IRL2714	IRL2720	IRL2726
IRL2728	ITA2755	ITA2775	ITA2785
ITA2791	ITA2809	ITA2810	ITA2813
ITA2820	ITA2824	ITA2832	ITA2834
ITA2838	ITA2841	ITA2857	ITA2873
ITA2894	ITA2900	ITA2903	ITA2912
ITA2923	LUX2954	LUX2984	MLT3017
MLT3018	NLD3067	NLD3098	NLD3122
NLD3170	NLD3187	NLD3211	
NLD3218	NLD3222	NLD3263	NLD3277
NLD3303	NLD3326	NOR3371	NOR3387
NOR3390	NOR3410	NOR3429	POL3519
POL3543	PRT3549	PRT3594	PRT3602
SVK3612	SWE3648	SWE3695	SWE3730
SWE3731	SWE3738	SWE3746	SWE3749
SWE3768	SWE3771	SWE3774	SWE3776
SWE3816	SWE3819	SWE3834	TUR3883

LOBBYING, ADVOCACY - LOBBYING, PLAIDOYER

AUT0010	AUT0020	AUT0024	BEL0099
BEL0131	BEL0147	BEL0168	BEL0174
BEL0176	BEL0177	BEL0186	BEL0191
BEL0197	BEL0198	BEL0199	BEL0214
BEL0218	BEL0248	BEL0267	BEL0284
BEL0306	BEL0323	BEL0345	BEL0353
BEL0361	CHE0420	CHE0426	CHE0434
CHE0448	CHE0486	CHE0503	CHE0519
CHE0524	CHE0534	CHE0553	CHE0566
CHE0568	CHE0570	CHE0642	CHE0654
CHE0668	CHE0689	CHE0689	CHE0693
CHE0711	CHE0718	CHE0755	CHE0785
CHE0809	CHE0814	CHE0819	CYP0831
CYP0831	DEU0920	DEU0929	DEU0942
DEU0983	DEU0998	DEU1004	DEU1054
DEU1055	DEU1056	DEU1062	DEU1064
DEU1110	DEU1114	DEU1131	
DEU1149	DEU1179	DEU1193	DNK1283
DNK1289	DNK1292	DNK1339	DNK1375
DNK1376	DNK1405	ESP1407	ESP1457
ESP1475	ESP1486	ESP1490	ESP1505
ESP1522	ESP1528	FIN1543	FIN1551
FIN1560	FIN1570	FIN1588	FIN1594
FRA1633	FRA1703	FRA1797	FRA1808
FRA1818	FRA1841	FRA1843	FRA1862
FRA1876	FRA1889	FRA1910	FRA1946
FRA1956	FRA1985	FRA1991	FRA2002
FRA2004	FRA2032	FRA2041	FRA2047
FRA2057	FRA2062	FRA2086	FRA2096
FRA2142	FRA2143	FRA2159	GBR2174
GBR2185	GBR2215	GBR2238	GBR2239
GBR2242	GBR2251	GBR2266	GBR2269
GBR2303	GBR2328	GBR2337	GBR2371
GBR2378	GBR2388	GBR2390	GBR2392
GBR2396	GBR2401	GBR2411	GBR2423
GBR2445	GBR2464	GBR2467	GBR2498
GBR2500	GBR2522	GBR2526	GBR2545
GBR2552	GRC2572	GRC2586	HUN2609
HUN2637	HUN2643	IRL2679	IRL2680
IRL2684	IRL2690	IRL2691	IRL2706
IRL2707	IRL2714	IRL2726	ITA2775
ITA2785	ITA2798	ITA2810	ITA2820
ITA2822	ITA2824	ITA2834	ITA2838
ITA2855	ITA2873	ITA2900	ITA2902
ITA2905	ITA2911	ITA2912	ITA2913
LUX2957	LUX2958	LUX2962	LUX2984
MLT3017	MLT3023	NLD3064	NLD3067
NLD3068	NLD3098	NLD3122	NLD3133
NLD3139	NLD3147	NLD3153	NLD3164
NLD3167	NLD3170	NLD3181	NLD3199
NLD3211	NLD3218	NLD3222	NLD3223

NLD3236	NLD3301	NLD3303	NLD3326
NLD3330	NLD3362	NOR3389	NOR3390
NOR3410	NOR3416	NOR3429	NOR3455
NOR3467	POL3433	PRT3549	PRT3586
PRT3590	PRT3600	SVK3634	SWE3648
SWE3674	SWE3699	SWE3734	SWE3738
SWE3744	SWE3746	SWE3749	SWE3768
SWE3771	SWE3776	SWE3819	TUR3882
TUR3883	TUR3897		

NETWORKING, ELECTRONIC TELECOMMUNICATIONS - RESEAUX, TELECOMMUNICATIONS ELECTRONIQUES

AUT0010	AUT0020	BEL0198	BEL0303
BEL0361	CHE0434	CHE0568	CHE0642
CHE0689	CHE0711	CHE0809	CHE0819
DEU0955	DEU0990	DEU1002	DEU1062
DEU1065	DEU1149	DNK1375	ESP1434
ESP1522	FIN1543	FIN1570	FIN1583
FIN1588	FRA1862	FRA1889	FRA1908
FRA1910	FRA2159	GBR2174	GBR2265
GBR2285	GBR2313	GBR2328	GBR2337
GBR2371	GBR2378	GBR2387	GBR2392
GBR2401	GBR2411	GBR2438	GBR2498
GBR2545	HUN2609	HUN2637	HUN2644
HUN2655	ITA2773	ITA2826	ITA2860
ITA2866	MLT3018	NLD3067	NLD3077
NLD3082	NLD3104	NLD3199	NLD3218
NLD3226	NLD3303	NLD3326	NOR3390
NOR3429	NOR3467	SWE3734	SWE3819
TUR3883			

OTHER - AUTRE

CHE0434	DEU1106	FRA1631	GBR2371
GBR2378	GBR2387	NLD3133	NLD3223

PUBLISHING, AUDIOVISUAL MATERIALS, EDUCATIONAL MATERIALS - EDITION, DOCUMENTS AUDIOVISUELS, DOCUMENTS EDUCATIFS

AUT0010	AUT0020	AUT0024	BEL0120
BEL0123	BEL0167	BEL0167	BEL0168
BEL0174	BEL0176	BEL0188	BEL0192
BEL0214	BEL0268	BEL0281	BEL0303
BEL0306	BEL0323	BEL0340	BEL0345
BEL0361	BEL0362	BEL0390	BEL0393
CHE0403	CHE0406	CHE0426	CHE0434
CHE0456	CHE0499	CHE0503	CHE0511
CHE0534	CHE0566	CHE0568	CHE0689
CHE0693	CHE0711	CHE0730	CHE0738
CHE0756	CHE0763	CHE0809	CHE0819
CYP0831	CYP0832	CZE0859	DEU0920
DEU0944	DEU0977	DEU1022	DEU1027
DEU1034	DEU1055	DEU1062	DEU1064
DEU1076	DEU1095	DEU1097	DEU1110
DEU1146	DEU1149	DEU1180	DEU1198
DNK1262	DNK1273	DNK1283	DNK1289
DNK1292	DNK1375	ESP1407	ESP1409
ESP1430	ESP1434	ESP1435	ESP1436
ESP1457	ESP1486	ESP1490	ESP1505
ESP1506	ESP1522	ESP1523	FIN1536
FIN1548	FIN1549	FIN1551	FIN1570
FIN1572	FIN1588	FRA1631	FRA1668
FRA1713	FRA1795	FRA1810	FRA1813
FRA1889	FRA1908	FRA1923	FRA1942
FRA1955	FRA1956	FRA1986	FRA2002
FRA2004	FRA2032	FRA2034	FRA2041
FRA2042	FRA2047	FRA2053	FRA2057
FRA2086	FRA2131	FRA2159	GBR2185
GBR2222	GBR2238	GBR2239	GBR2251
GBR2265	GBR2266	GBR2271	GBR2303
GBR2312	GBR2337	GBR2345	GBR2371
GBR2378	GBR2387	GBR2388	GBR2401
GBR2411	GBR2415	GBR2435	GBR2445
GBR2464	GBR2467	GBR2498	GBR2500
GBR2501	GBR2503	GBR2522	GBR2526
GBR2545	GBR2552	GRC2572	HUN2609
HUN2644	IRL2679	IRL2693	IRL2698
IRL2706	IRL2714	IRL2720	IRL2728
IRL2733	ITA2762	ITA2764	ITA2785
ITA2798	ITA2809	ITA2810	ITA2820
ITA2822	ITA2826	ITA2832	ITA2837
ITA2838	ITA2857	ITA2861	ITA2900
ITA2907	ITA2908	ITA2916	LUX3006
MLT3016	MLT3018	NLD3067	NLD3077
NLD3122	NLD3133	NLD3164	NLD3194
NLD3201	NLD3211	NLD3216	NLD3218
NLD3222	NLD3223	NLD3226	NLD3301

NLD3326	NLD3354	NOR3389	NOR3390
NOR3410	NOR3435	NOR3467	POL3508
POL3519	POL3543	PRT3585	PRT3600
SVK3622	SWE3648	SWE3695	SWE3699
SWE3734	SWE3746	SWE3768	SWE3816
SWE3819	TUR3883	TUR3895	

POPULATION, FAMILY PLANNING, DEMOGRAPHY - POPULATION, PLANNING FAMILIAL, DEMOGRAPHIE

BROADCASTING, CULTURAL EVENTS - RADIODIFFUSION, MANIFESTATIONS CULTURELLES

AUT0090	BEL0123	BEL0129	CHE0434
CHE0534	CHE0568	CHE0598	CHE0689
CHE0819	DEU1022	DEU1142	ESP1455
ESP1486	FIN1553	FRA1621	FRA1760
FRA1785	FRA1787	FRA1889	FRA1956
FRA2002	FRA2159	GBR2238	GBR2248
GBR2359	GBR2371	GBR2384	GBR2423
GBR2439	GBR2501	GBR2545	GRC2576
ITA2798	LUX2937	MLT3016	NLD3067
NLD3173	NLD3230	POL3508	SWE3738
TUR3883	TUR3892		

CONFERENCES, SEMINARS, WORKSHOPS, TRAINING ACTIVITIES - CONFERENCES, SEMINAIRES, ATELIERS, ACTIVITES DE FORMATION

AUT0002	AUT0011	AUT0033	AUT0051
AUT0067	AUT0074	AUT0085	AUT0089
AUT0090	BEL0123	BEL0129	BEL0133
BEL0148	BEL0168	BEL0174	BEL0191
BEL0214	BEL0275	BEL0309	BEL0351
BEL0353	BEL0397	CHE0403	CHE0417
CHE0434	CHE0464	CHE0491	CHE0554
CHE0562	CHE0568	CHE0628	CHE0642
CHE0655	CHE0682	CHE0689	CHE0693
CHE0734	CHE0765	CHE0817	CHE0819
CYP0831	DEU0926	DEU0944	DEU0954
DEU0968	DEU0974	DEU0977	DEU0983
DEU0990	DEU0996	DEU1002	DEU1019
DEU1022	DEU1034	DEU1090	DEU1106
DEU1131	DEU1141	DEU1142	DEU1146
DEU1149	DEU1180	DEU1210	DNK1227
DNK1298	DNK1305	DNK1312	DNK1319
DNK1339	DNK1361	ESP1430	ESP1455
ESP1456	ESP1457	ESP1479	ESP1502
ESP1528	FIN1553	FIN1557	FIN1580
FIN1589	FIN1602	FRA1627	FRA1629
FRA1671	FRA1672	FRA1690	FRA1731
FRA1785	FRA1787	FRA1816	FRA1846
FRA1862	FRA1889	FRA1917	FRA1946
FRA1949	FRA1956	FRA1970	FRA1990
FRA2005	FRA2019	FRA2062	FRA2122
FRA2159	GBR2172	GBR2183	GBR2185
GBR2199	GBR2217	GBR2226	GBR2238
GBR2256	GBR2265	GBR2269	GBR2279
GBR2281	GBR2292	GBR2302	GBR2351
GBR2359	GBR2371	GBR2384	GBR2385
GBR2387	GBR2390	GBR2408	GBR2415
GBR2423	GBR2439	GBR2445	GBR2452
GBR2458	GBR2500	GBR2503	GBR2544
GBR2545	GBR2550	GBR2553	GRC2576
GRC2586	GRC2595	HUN2609	IRL2698
IRL2720	ITA2771	ITA2810	ITA2820
ITA2826	ITA2860	ITA2866	ITA2898
ITA2901	ITA2908	MLT3016	NLD3062
NLD3067	NLD3153	NLD3174	NLD3190
NLD3198	NLD3211	NLD3232	NLD3269
NLD3278	NLD3301	NLD3305	NLD3309
NLD3334	NLD3352	NLD3357	NOR3386
NOR3400	NOR3402	NOR3440	NOR3453
NOR3467	POL3508	POL3508	POL3519
PRT3564	PRT3590	PRT3594	PRT3600
SVK3612	SWE3679	SWE3695	SWE3712
SWE3738	SWE3749	SWE3775	SWE3785
SWE3807	SWE3816	SWE3853	SWE3865
SWE3879	TUR3883	TUR3892	

EXCHANGES, TWINNING, LINKING - ECHANGES, PARRAINAGE, JUMELAGE

BEL0123	BEL0129	BEL0198	BEL0390
CHE0434	CHE0448	CHE0562	CHE0683
CHE0689	CHE0819	CYP0831	DEU0951
DEU0983	DEU0990	DNK1259	ESP1525

FIN1602	FRA1661	FRA1746	FRA1785
FRA1787	FRA1846	FRA1889	FRA1956
FRA2081	FRA2159	GBR2359	GBR2371
GBR2379	GBR2384	GBR2390	GBR2423
GBR2439	GBR2445	GRC2576	ITA2765
ITA2775	NLD3067	NLD3082	NLD3137
NLD3198	NLD3357	POL3508	POL3519
SVK3612	SWE3749	SWE3785	SWE3865
SWE3879			

FORMAL EDUCATION - EDUCATION FORMELLE

AUT0065	AUT0085	BEL0123	BEL0129
BEL0351	BEL0353	BEL0390	CHE0434
CHE0554	CHE0562	CHE0628	CHE0682
CHE0687	CHE0689	CHE0805	CHE0819
CZE0859	DEU0954	DEU0983	DEU1002
DEU1132	DNK1227	DNK1272	DNK1298
DNK1339	ESP1455	ESP1479	ESP1502
FRA1607	FRA1627	FRA1628	FRA1672
FRA1739	FRA1785	FRA1787	FRA1827
FRA1889	FRA1935	FRA1946	FRA1956
FRA2019	FRA2062	FRA2103	FRA2131
FRA2159	GBR2181	GBR2238	GBR2265
GBR2269	GBR2333	GBR2359	GBR2371
GBR2379	GBR2384	GBR2390	GBR2408
GBR2415	GBR2423	GBR2424	GBR2436
GBR2439	GBR2452	GBR2468	GBR2553
GRC2576	HUN2643	IRL2690	IRL2691
IRL2720	ITA2810	ITA2826	ITA2898
ITA2900	LUX2976	LUX2986	LUX2995
LUX2997	NLD3067	NLD3232	NLD3269
NOR3467	POL3508	PRT3594	PRT3600
SVK3612	SVK3634	SWE3879	

FUND RAISING - COLLECTE DE FONDS

AUT0085	AUT0091	BEL0148	BEL0168
BEL0198	BEL0297	BEL0327	BEL0351
BEL0353	BEL0358	BEL0390	CHE0417
CHE0434	CHE0475	CHE0562	CHE0598
CHE0689	CHE0707	CHE0749	CHE0789
CHE0819	DEU0926	DEU0954	DEU0957
DEU0968	DEU0983	DEU1002	DEU1022
DEU1132	DNK1222	DNK1227	DNK1305
DNK1316	ESP1442	ESP1455	FIN1591
FRA1614	FRA1690	FRA1691	FRA1739
FRA1760	FRA1785	FRA1787	FRA1889
FRA1929	FRA1946	FRA1990	FRA2081
FRA2131	FRA2138	FRA2159	GBR2172
GBR2180	GBR2183	GBR2226	GBR2238
GBR2242	GBR2248	GBR2292	GBR2302
GBR2318	GBR2321	GBR2333	GBR2359
GBR2371	GBR2372	GBR2384	GBR2385
GBR2392	GBR2436	GBR2439	GBR2445
GBR2500	GBR2508	GBR2522	GBR2524
GBR2550	GRC2576	HUN2609	ITA2810
ITA2837	ITA2888	ITA2901	LUX2959
LUX2986	NLD3067	NLD3198	NLD3232
NLD3237	NLD3288	NLD3301	NLD3361
NOR3467	PRT3594	SWE3785	SWE3853
SWE3857	SWE3859	TUR3892	

INFORMATION AND DOCUMENTATION SERVICES, DATA BASES - SERVICES D'INFORMATION ET DE DOCUMENTATION, BASES DE DONNEES

AUT0010	AUT0020	AUT0026	AUT0060
AUT0074	AUT0079	AUT0085	BEL0123
BEL0129	BEL0141	BEL0168	BEL0214
BEL0237	BEL0275	BEL0297	BEL0335
BEL0358	BEL0359	BEL0365	BEL0390
BEL0393	BEL0396	CHE0429	CHE0434
CHE0464	CHE0534	CHE0554	CHE0562
CHE0568	CHE0687	CHE0689	CHE0756
CHE0762	CHE0763	CHE0819	CYP0831
DEU0926	DEU0944	DEU0968	DEU0977
DEU0990	DEU0996	DEU1002	DEU1019
DEU1020	DEU1022	DEU1076	DEU1086
DEU1090	DEU1091	DEU1146	DEU1149
DEU1184	DEU1192	DNK1262	DNK1298
DNK1305	DNK1339	ESP1407	ESP1430
ESP1431	ESP1434	ESP1441	ESP1455
ESP1457	ESP1479	ESP1482	ESP1486
ESP1502	ESP1525	FIN1548	FIN1578
FIN1591	FIN1592	FIN1602	FRA1617
FRA1629	FRA1672	FRA1737	FRA1785
FRA1787	FRA1797	FRA1808	FRA1811
FRA1827	FRA1839	FRA1841	FRA1846
FRA1889	FRA1935	FRA1956	FRA1990

FRA2002	FRA2018	FRA2035	FRA2103
FRA2104	FRA2122	FRA2131	FRA2159
GBR2226	GBR2238	GBR2265	GBR2359
GBR2371	GBR2379	GBR2384	GBR2385
GBR2387	GBR2390	GBR2408	GBR2415
GBR2423	GBR2435	GBR2438	GBR2439
GBR2445	GBR2452	GBR2458	GBR2464
GBR2498	GBR2522	GBR2545	GRC2576
IRL2698	IRL2705	IRL2720	IRL2730
ITA2762	ITA2773	ITA2786	ITA2798
ITA2801	ITA2808	ITA2810	ITA2820
ITA2832	ITA2860	ITA2895	ITA2900
ITA2901	ITA2907	ITA2908	LUX2937
LUX2962	NLD3051	NLD3058	NLD3067
NLD3077	NLD3123	NLD3135	NLD3137
NLD3139	NLD3147	NLD3173	NLD3179
NLD3190	NLD3198	NLD3211	NLD3232
NLD3301	NLD3305	NLD3334	NLD3352
NLD3357	NLD3361	NOR3402	NOR3467
POL3519	PRT3600	SWE3658	SWE3693
SWE3744	SWE3785	SWE3807	SWE3816
SWE3853	SWE3859	SWE3865	TUR3883

INFORMATION CAMPAIGNS, EXHIBITIONS - CAMPAGNES D'INFORMATION, EXPOSITIONS

AUT0020	AUT0067	AUT0068	BEL0123
BEL0129	BEL0148	BEL0168	BEL0198
BEL0275	BEL0368	BEL0390	BEL0397
CHE0434	CHE0486	CHE0554	CHE0560
CHE0562	CHE0568	CHE0598	CHE0669
CHE0683	CHE0689	CHE0765	CHE0805
CHE0819	CYP0831	CYP0832	CZE0891
DEU0917	DEU0926	DEU0955	DEU0974
DEU0977	DEU0983	DEU0996	DEU1002
DEU1019	DEU1034	DEU1141	DEU1142
DEU1176	DNK1262	DNK1298	DNK1305
DNK1319	DNK1351	DNK1403	ESP1486
ESP1502	ESP1528	FIN1553	FIN1592
FIN1602	FRA1607	FRA1633	FRA1739
FRA1785	FRA1787	FRA1797	FRA1862
FRA1889	FRA1956	FRA1990	FRA2002
FRA2122	FRA2131	FRA2138	FRA2159
GBR2172	GBR2238	GBR2248	GBR2265
GBR2269	GBR2279	GBR2351	GBR2359
GBR2371	GBR2384	GBR2385	GBR2387
GBR2423	GBR2439	GBR2445	GBR2452
GBR2458	GBR2498	GBR2545	GBR2553
GRC2576	IRL2720	ITA2791	ITA2810
ITA2811	ITA2860	ITA2898	ITA2901
LUX2986	LUX2995	NLD3067	NLD3173
NLD3181	NLD3198	NLD3211	NLD3230
NLD3232	NLD3303	NLD3357	NLD3361
POL3519	PRT3594	PRT3600	SVK3612
SWE3738	SWE3749	SWE3763	SWE3785
SWE3816	SWE3859	SWE3865	SWE3879
TUR3883	TUR3892		

LOBBYING, ADVOCACY - LOBBYING, PLAIDOYER

AUT0051	AUT0067	AUT0068	AUT0090
BEL0131	BEL0168	BEL0174	BEL0186
BEL0191	BEL0198	BEL0214	BEL0216
BEL0309	BEL0351	BEL0353	BEL0397
CHE0429	CHE0434	CHE0464	CHE0486
CHE0534	CHE0554	CHE0560	CHE0562
CHE0568	CHE0642	CHE0687	CHE0689
CHE0693	CHE0765	CHE0819	DEU0926
DEU0951	DEU0954	DEU0974	DEU0983
DEU0996	DEU1002	DEU1131	DEU1141
DEU1142	DNK1262	DNK1339	DNK1399
DNK1403	ESP1457	ESP1528	FIN1602
FRA1633	FRA1785	FRA1797	FRA1841
FRA1862	FRA1889	FRA1946	FRA1949
FRA1956	FRA2002	FRA2035	FRA2159
GBR2174	GBR2199	GBR2202	GBR2217
GBR2238	GBR2242	GBR2256	GBR2269
GBR2355	GBR2359	GBR2371	GBR2384
GBR2390	GBR2423	GBR2439	GBR2445
GBR2464	GBR2498	GBR2522	GBR2529
GBR2544	GBR2545	GBR2553	GRC2576
GRC2586	HUN2643	IRL2691	ITA2775
ITA2810	ITA2881	ITA2898	ITA2913
LUX2957	LUX2997	NLD3067	NLD3082
NLD3124	NLD3147	NLD3153	NLD3198
NLD3211	NLD3232	NLD3278	NLD3278
NLD3301	NLD3334	NLD3352	NOR3386
NOR3402	NOR3467	PRT3594	PRT3600
SVK3634	SWE3749	SWE3785	SWE3853
TUR3883	TUR3892		

NETWORKING, ELECTRONIC TELECOMMUNICATIONS - RESEAUX, TELECOMMUNICATIONS ELECTRONIQUES

AUT0020	BEL0198	CHE0434	CHE0562
CHE0568	CHE0642	CHE0689	CHE0819
DEU0951	DEU0955	DEU0974	DEU0990
DEU0996	DEU1002	ESP1434	FIN1591
FRA1629	FRA1785	FRA1889	FRA2159
GBR2174	GBR2199	GBR2226	GBR2265
GBR2285	GBR2313	GBR2359	GBR2371
GBR2387	GBR2438	GBR2498	GBR2545
GRC2576	ITA2773	ITA2860	ITA2881
NLD3067	NLD3077	NLD3082	NLD3124
NLD3137	NLD3357	NOR3467	SWE3746
SWE3785	TUR3883		

OTHER - AUTRE

CHE0434	GBR2240	GBR2371	GBR2384
GBR2387	NLD3137		

PUBLISHING, AUDIOVISUAL MATERIALS, EDUCATIONAL MATERIALS - EDITION, DOCUMENTS AUDIOVISUELS, DOCUMENTS EDUCATIFS

AUT0020	AUT0051	AUT0068	AUT0085
BEL0123	BEL0168	BEL0174	BEL0214
BEL0306	BEL0365	BEL0390	BEL0393
CHE0429	CHE0434	CHE0510	CHE0554
CHE0560	CHE0562	CHE0568	CHE0689
CHE0693	CHE0763	CHE0819	CYP0831
CZE0859	DEU0944	DEU0974	DEU0977
DEU1002	DEU1019	DEU1022	DEU1031
DEU1034	DEU1062	DEU1076	DEU1142
DEU1146	DEU1180	DEU1198	DNK1262
DNK1298	DNK1316	DNK1319	DNK1339
DNK1351	DNK1358	ESP1430	ESP1434
ESP1435	ESP1455	ESP1456	ESP1457
ESP1475	FIN1548	FIN1602	FRA1607
FRA1627	FRA1629	FRA1671	FRA1713
FRA1785	FRA1787	FRA1836	FRA1889
FRA1920	FRA1929	FRA1935	FRA1956
FRA1986	FRA1990	FRA2001	FRA2002
FRA2072	FRA2131	FRA2138	FRA2159
GBR2181	GBR2183	GBR2185	GBR2199
GBR2238	GBR2248	GBR2265	GBR2271
GBR2318	GBR2359	GBR2371	GBR2384
GBR2387	GBR2390	GBR2415	GBR2439
GBR2445	GBR2452	GBR2458	GBR2500
GBR2501	GBR2503	GBR2545	GBR2552
GBR2554	GRC2576	HUN2609	IRL2698
IRL2720	ITA2762	ITA2798	ITA2810
ITA2901	ITA2908	ITA2916	LUX3006
MLT3016	NLD3051	NLD3067	NLD3077
NLD3082	NLD3173	NLD3198	NLD3211
NLD3230	NLD3278	NLD3301	NLD3305
NLD3352	NLD3357	NOR3402	NOR3467
POL3519	PRT3564	PRT3586	SWE3785
SWE3816	SWE3865	SWE3879	TUR3883

POVERTY, LIVING CONDITIONS - PAUVRETE, CONDITIONS DE VIE

BROADCASTING, CULTURAL EVENTS - RADIODIFFUSION, MANIFESTATIONS CULTURELLES

BEL0123	BEL0203	BEL0226	BEL0275
BEL0358	CHE0434	CHE0534	CHE0566
CHE0568	CHE0624	CHE0689	CHE0720
CHE0819	DEU1022	DNK1250	DNK1283
ESP1437	ESP1439	ESP1455	ESP1486
ESP1490	ESP1506	ESP1507	ESP1510
ESP1513	FIN1545	FRA1614	FRA1621
FRA1631	FRA1672	FRA1785	FRA1791
FRA1793	FRA1794	FRA1889	FRA1956
FRA2002	FRA2060	FRA2092	FRA2117
FRA2159	GBR2229	GBR2235	GBR2238
GBR2248	GBR2278	GBR2345	GBR2371
GBR2383	GBR2423	GBR2436	GBR2439
GBR2469	GBR2498	GBR2501	GBR2545
IRL2714	ITA2777	ITA2798	ITA2801
ITA2806	ITA2820	ITA2826	ITA2907
LUX2954	LUX2958	LUX2982	LUX2983
LUX3006	LUX3008	MLT3016	NLD3067
NLD3181	NLD3190	NLD3199	NLD3253
NOR3467	SWE3648		

See: *How to Use the Directory*, page 11.

CONFERENCES, SEMINARS, WORKSHOPS, TRAINING ACTIVITIES - CONFERENCES, SEMINAIRES, ATELIERS, ACTIVITES DE FORMATION

AUT0002	AUT0010	AUT0020	BEL0096
BEL0123	BEL0128	BEL0148	BEL0149
BEL0168	BEL0174	BEL0176	BEL0177
BEL0188	BEL0203	BEL0219	BEL0221
BEL0224	BEL0231	BEL0237	BEL0254
BEL0270	BEL0275	BEL0282	BEL0289
BEL0303	BEL0345	BEL0351	BEL0359
BEL0362	BEL0378	BEL0394	BEL0396
CHE0402	CHE0417	CHE0434	CHE0461
CHE0534	CHE0549	CHE0562	CHE0566
CHE0568	CHE0604	CHE0613	CHE0618
CHE0632	CHE0642	CHE0655	CHE0669
CHE0687	CHE0689	CHE0693	CHE0718
CHE0720	CHE0730	CHE0758	CHE0765
CHE0772	CHE0773	CHE0794	CHE0809
CHE0814	CHE0817	CHE0819	CHE0820
CHE0823	DEU0921	DEU0928	DEU0942
DEU0944	DEU0975	DEU0983	DEU0990
DEU0991	DEU1013	DEU1019	DEU1020
DEU1025	DEU1034	DEU1044	DEU1055
DEU1064	DEU1066	DEU1090	DEU1097
DEU1100	DEU1114	DEU1131	DEU1141
DEU1142	DEU1146	DEU1149	DEU1180
DEU1187	DEU1198	DEU1210	DNK1229
DNK1281	DNK1283	DNK1289	DNK1305
DNK1312	DNK1319	DNK1335	DNK1339
DNK1398	ESP1407	ESP1413	ESP1435
ESP1439	ESP1450	ESP1452	ESP1455
ESP1457	ESP1479	ESP1488	ESP1490
ESP1491	ESP1493	ESP1502	ESP1506
ESP1507	ESP1508	ESP1510	ESP1511
ESP1517	ESP1522	ESP1525	ESP1528
FIN1536	FIN1544	FIN1545	FIN1546
FIN1553	FIN1574	FIN1582	FRA1610
FRA1615	FRA1619	FRA1627	FRA1636
FRA1642	FRA1661	FRA1672	FRA1685
FRA1701	FRA1704	FRA1785	FRA1791
FRA1793	FRA1794	FRA1797	FRA1799
FRA1813	FRA1815	FRA1818	FRA1846
FRA1889	FRA1930	FRA1946	FRA1949
FRA1956	FRA1980	FRA1990	FRA2002
FRA2004	FRA2018	FRA2044	FRA2047
FRA2057	FRA2060	FRA2062	FRA2069
FRA2096	FRA2117	FRA2122	FRA2123
FRA2131	FRA2159	GBR2174	GBR2181
GBR2185	GBR2186	GBR2214	GBR2215
GBR2226	GBR2229	GBR2235	GBR2238
GBR2242	GBR2251	GBR2264	GBR2265
GBR2266	GBR2269	GBR2278	GBR2279
GBR2284	GBR2292	GBR2302	GBR2326
GBR2334	GBR2337	GBR2350	GBR2351
GBR2355	GBR2358	GBR2364	GBR2371
GBR2387	GBR2390	GBR2392	GBR2402
GBR2408	GBR2413	GBR2415	GBR2416
GBR2423	GBR2424	GBR2436	GBR2439
GBR2445	GBR2448	GBR2452	GBR2460
GBR2469	GBR2474	GBR2492	GBR2495
GBR2500	GBR2503	GBR2513	GBR2527
GBR2535	GBR2536	GBR2537	GBR2545
GBR2554	GBR2561	GRC2567	GRC2586
HUN2631	IRL2693	IRL2697	IRL2714
IRL2717	IRL2720	IRL2726	IRL2729
ITA2747	ITA2762	ITA2766	ITA2785
ITA2798	ITA2801	ITA2805	ITA2810
ITA2820	ITA2824	ITA2826	ITA2829
ITA2835	ITA2838	ITA2840	ITA2883
ITA2889	ITA2890	ITA2899	ITA2900
ITA2908	ITA2912	ITA2916	LUX2954
LUX2984	LUX2985	LUX2993	LUX3008
MLT3016	NLD3047	NLD3064	NLD3067
NLD3072	NLD3078	NLD3082	NLD3083
NLD3126	NLD3138	NLD3155	NLD3156
NLD3174	NLD3181	NLD3199	NLD3222
NLD3232	NLD3301	NLD3303	NLD3305
NLD3357	NOR3371	NOR3400	NOR3455
NOR3467	POL3519	PRT3549	PRT3550
PRT3584	PRT3594	PRT3600	SWE3695
SWE3702	SWE3707	SWE3737	SWE3749
SWE3754	SWE3768	SWE3769	SWE3771
SWE3789	SWE3807	SWE3816	SWE3865

EXCHANGES, TWINNING, LINKING - ECHANGES, PARRAINAGE, JUMELAGE

BEL0104	BEL0120	BEL0123	BEL0129
BEL0198	BEL0203	BEL0219	BEL0221
BEL0303	BEL0309	BEL0355	BEL0358
BEL0390	CHE0434	CHE0448	CHE0562
CHE0566	CHE0596	CHE0689	CHE0730
CHE0798	CHE0819	DEU0983	DEU0990
DEU1055	DEU1149	DNK1283	DNK1289
DNK1304	ESP1522	FIN1587	FRA1655
FRA1661	FRA1672	FRA1685	FRA1715
FRA1746	FRA1785	FRA1787	FRA1791
FRA1793	FRA1846	FRA1889	FRA1929
FRA1938	FRA1946	FRA1956	FRA1980
FRA2057	FRA2060	FRA2081	FRA2092
FRA2140	FRA2159	GBR2278	GBR2284
GBR2325	GBR2355	GBR2371	GBR2379
GBR2390	GBR2423	GBR2439	GBR2445
GBR2469	IRL2717	IRL2730	ITA2765
ITA2770	NLD3067	NLD3072	NLD3078
NLD3082	NLD3096	NLD3098	NLD3138
NLD3215	NLD3357	NOR3400	POL3519
SWE3744	SWE3749	SWE3754	SWE3771
SWE3785	SWE3864	SWE3865	

FORMAL EDUCATION - EDUCATION FORMELLE

BEL0123	BEL0176	BEL0323	BEL0351
BEL0359	BEL0362	BEL0390	CHE0434
CHE0460	CHE0479	CHE0549	CHE0562
CHE0566	CHE0640	CHE0660	CHE0689
CHE0730	CHE0805	CHE0809	CHE0819
DEU0928	DEU0954	DEU0983	DEU1146
DNK1226	DNK1227	DNK1262	DNK1283
DNK1289	DNK1335	DNK1339	DNK1405
ESP1409	ESP1437	ESP1455	ESP1486
ESP1490	ESP1502	ESP1506	ESP1508
ESP1517	ESP1528	FRA1627	FRA1661
FRA1672	FRA1704	FRA1731	FRA1769
FRA1785	FRA1794	FRA1889	FRA1930
FRA1946	FRA1956	FRA2044	FRA2057
FRA2062	FRA2123	FRA2131	FRA2150
FRA2159	GBR2181	GBR2238	GBR2242
GBR2265	GBR2269	GBR2278	GBR2337
GBR2345	GBR2371	GBR2379	GBR2383
GBR2390	GBR2408	GBR2415	GBR2423
GBR2424	GBR2436	GBR2439	GBR2445
GBR2448	GBR2452	GBR2467	GBR2469
GBR2474	GBR2553	GBR2554	GRC2567
IRL2690	IRL2691	IRL2697	IRL2720
IRL2726	IRL2761	ITA2762	ITA2782
ITA2798	ITA2810	ITA2822	ITA2826
ITA2827	ITA2838	ITA2883	ITA2900
ITA2912	LUX2995	LUX3008	NLD3067
NLD3072	NLD3078	NLD3083	NLD3138
NLD3155	NLD3179	NLD3199	NLD3215
NLD3254	NOR3467	POL3508	PRT3594
SWE3712	SWE3737	SWE3796	

FUND RAISING - COLLECTE DE FONDS

AUT0003	AUT0051	AUT0085	AUT0086
AUT0091	BEL0096	BEL0104	BEL0110
BEL0129	BEL0148	BEL0155	BEL0168
BEL0182	BEL0198	BEL0201	BEL0203
BEL0224	BEL0254	BEL0270	BEL0282
BEL0297	BEL0314	BEL0327	BEL0328
BEL0350	BEL0351	BEL0355	BEL0358
BEL0359	BEL0362	BEL0368	BEL0381
BEL0390	CHE0417	CHE0434	CHE0444
CHE0446	CHE0448	CHE0475	CHE0479
CHE0515	CHE0524	CHE0562	CHE0566
CHE0570	CHE0584	CHE0586	CHE0604
CHE0619	CHE0630	CHE0664	CHE0684
CHE0687	CHE0689	CHE0693	CHE0730
CHE0750	CHE0754	CHE0756	CHE0772
CHE0785	CHE0788	CHE0789	CHE0796
CHE0798	CHE0806	CHE0810	CHE0814
CHE0819	CHE0820	CYP0832	DEU0922
DEU0954	DEU0957	DEU0968	DEU0983
DEU0989	DEU0993	DEU1006	DEU1022
DEU1044	DEU1066	DEU1086	DEU1114
DEU1132	DEU1138	DEU1141	DEU1146
DEU1149	DEU1187	DNK1216	DNK1222
DNK1227	DNK1251	DNK1283	DNK1292
DNK1304	DNK1305	DNK1316	DNK1405
ESP1409	ESP1435	ESP1442	ESP1452
ESP1455	ESP1457	ESP1486	ESP1491
ESP1506	ESP1508	ESP1510	FIN1544
FIN1549	FIN1581	FIN1583	FIN1591

FIN1599	FRA1610	FRA1614	FRA1615
FRA1636	FRA1661	FRA1664	FRA1672
FRA1685	FRA1691	FRA1703	FRA1739
FRA1769	FRA1785	FRA1787	FRA1791
FRA1793	FRA1824	FRA1843	FRA1849
FRA1855	FRA1880	FRA1889	FRA1891
FRA1929	FRA1930	FRA1939	FRA1946
FRA1978	FRA1980	FRA1990	FRA2047
FRA2053	FRA2060	FRA2080	FRA2081
FRA2086	FRA2092	FRA2116	FRA2117
FRA2131	FRA2140	FRA2159	GBR2175
GBR2176	GBR2180	GBR2181	GBR2185
GBR2186	GBR2197	GBR2201	GBR2226
GBR2228	GBR2229	GBR2238	GBR2248
GBR2277	GBR2278	GBR2280	GBR2289
GBR2292	GBR2297	GBR2302	GBR2318
GBR2321	GBR2324	GBR2325	GBR2334
GBR2337	GBR2348	GBR2350	GBR2351
GBR2358	GBR2371	GBR2372	GBR2375
GBR2376	GBR2385	GBR2390	GBR2392
GBR2413	GBR2419	GBR2423	GBR2424
GBR2436	GBR2439	GBR2445	GBR2464
GBR2469	GBR2474	GBR2475	GBR2492
GBR2498	GBR2500	GBR2503	GBR2509
GBR2513	GBR2524	GBR2525	GBR2530
GBR2532	GBR2535	GBR2537	GBR2561
GRC2586	HUN2631	IRL2691	IRL2697
IRL2714	IRL2726	IRL2730	IRL2732
IRL2733	ITA2747	ITA2762	ITA2766
ITA2770	ITA2810	ITA2816	ITA2820
ITA2822	ITA2824	ITA2826	ITA2832
ITA2838	ITA2873	ITA2879	ITA2885
ITA2888	ITA2900	ITA2921	ITA2923
LIE2930	LUX2950	LUX2955	LUX2980
LUX2982	LUX2984	LUX2993	LUX2995
LUX3006	MLT3036	NLD3047	NLD3067
NLD3072	NLD3078	NLD3126	NLD3149
NLD3159	NLD3181	NLD3199	NLD3201
NLD3231	NLD3232	NLD3253	NLD3254
NLD3256	NLD3269	NLD3301	NLD3302
NLD3323	NLD3361	NOR3371	NOR3381
NOR3467	POL3543	PRT3549	PRT3552
PRT3594	PRT3605	SVK3611	SWE3648
SWE3702	SWE3707	SWE3712	SWE3737
SWE3744	SWE3749	SWE3768	SWE3769
SWE3796	SWE3826	SWE3853	SWE3864

INFORMATION AND DOCUMENTATION SERVICES, DATA BASES - SERVICES D'INFORMATION ET DE DOCUMENTATION, BASES DE DONNEES

AUT0010	AUT0020	AUT0026	AUT0060
AUT0079	AUT0085	BEL0123	BEL0149
BEL0155	BEL0164	BEL0168	BEL0177
BEL0203	BEL0219	BEL0226	BEL0237
BEL0254	BEL0267	BEL0297	BEL0335
BEL0345	BEL0358	BEL0359	BEL0362
BEL0365	BEL0390	BEL0393	BEL0396
CHE0434	CHE0479	CHE0501	CHE0534
CHE0549	CHE0562	CHE0566	CHE0568
CHE0596	CHE0624	CHE0640	CHE0664
CHE0687	CHE0689	CHE0720	CHE0756
CHE0763	CHE0796	CHE0809	CHE0817
CHE0819	CYP0832	DEU0944	DEU0968
DEU0975	DEU0990	DEU1002	DEU1013
DEU1019	DEU1020	DEU1025	DEU1031
DEU1064	DEU1076	DEU1086	DEU1090
DEU1091	DEU1097	DEU1114	DEU1129
DEU1138	DEU1146	DEU1149	DEU1184
DEU1192	DNK1251	DNK1259	DNK1262
DNK1281	DNK1283	DNK1289	DNK1292
DNK1305	DNK1335	DNK1339	DNK1358
DNK1375	DNK1398	ESP1407	ESP1413
ESP1430	ESP1431	ESP1434	ESP1437
ESP1441	ESP1455	ESP1457	ESP1479
ESP1486	ESP1490	ESP1493	ESP1502
ESP1506	ESP1507	ESP1508	ESP1522
ESP1525	FIN1546	FIN1548	FIN1578
FIN1582	FIN1591	FRA1610	FRA1631
FRA1636	FRA1701	FRA1737	FRA1785
FRA1787	FRA1794	FRA1797	FRA1808
FRA1810	FRA1811	FRA1818	FRA1839
FRA1841	FRA1846	FRA1889	FRA1930
FRA1956	FRA1990	FRA2002	FRA2004
FRA2018	FRA2076	FRA2096	FRA2104
FRA2122	FRA2131	FRA2140	FRA2159
GBR2185	GBR2226	GBR2235	GBR2238
GBR2239	GBR2265	GBR2266	GBR2278
GBR2284	GBR2326	GBR2355	GBR2371

GBR2379 GBR2383 GBR2387 GBR2402
GBR2408 GBR2413 GBR2415 GBR2423
GBR2435 GBR2438 GBR2439 GBR2445
GBR2452 GBR2486 GBR2495 GBR2498
GBR2513 GBR2522 GBR2537 GBR2545
GBR2561 GRC2567 GRC2571 IRL2698
IRL2705 IRL2714 IRL2717 IRL2720
IRL2726 IRL2730 ITA2762 ITA2773
ITA2785 ITA2798 ITA2801 ITA2805
ITA2809 ITA2810 ITA2814 ITA2820
ITA2822 ITA2824 ITA2827 ITA2829
ITA2834 ITA2840 ITA2857 ITA2860
ITA2866 ITA2873 ITA2900 ITA2907
ITA2908 ITA2912 ITA2923 LUX2937
LUX2949 LUX2962 LUX2983 LUX3008
NLD3047 NLD3051 NLD3058 NLD3067
NLD3072 NLD3077 NLD3078 NLD3083
NLD3096 NLD3135 NLD3138 NLD3139
NLD3156 NLD3167 NLD3170 NLD3173
NLD3179 NLD3181 NLD3222 NLD3254
NLD3301 NLD3302 NLD3305 NLD3352
NLD3355 NLD3357 NLD3361 NOR3400
NOR3410 NOR3435 NOR3455 NOR3467
POL3519 PRT3590 PRT3596 PRT3600
SWE3648 SWE3658 SWE3693 SWE3737
SWE3744 SWE3768 SWE3769 SWE3789
SWE3807 SWE3816 SWE3826 SWE3859
SWE3864 SWE3865 TUR3883

INFORMATION CAMPAIGNS, EXHIBITIONS - CAMPAGNES D'INFORMATION, EXPOSITIONS

AUT0020 AUT0091 BEL0096 BEL0123
BEL0139 BEL0148 BEL0168 BEL0176
BEL0177 BEL0192 BEL0198 BEL0203
BEL0219 BEL0226 BEL0254 BEL0267
BEL0282 BEL0350 BEL0351 BEL0358
BEL0359 BEL0362 BEL0381 BEL0390
CHE0434 CHE0444 CHE0446 CHE0460
CHE0461 CHE0479 CHE0534 CHE0541
CHE0562 CHE0566 CHE0568 CHE0584
CHE0604 CHE0618 CHE0664 CHE0669
CHE0684 CHE0689 CHE0718 CHE0720
CHE0756 CHE0765 CHE0796 CHE0807
CHE0819 CHE0820 DEU0917 DEU0940
DEU0955 DEU0983 DEU1013 DEU1019
DEU1022 DEU1025 DEU1034 DEU1064
DEU1114 DEU1129 DEU1141 DEU1146
DEU1149 DEU1187 DNK1245 DNK1251
DNK1260 DNK1262 DNK1281 DNK1283
DNK1289 DNK1292 DNK1304 DNK1305
DNK1317 DNK1319 DNK1339 DNK1375
DNK1398 DNK1405 ESP1407 ESP1413
ESP1437 ESP1457 ESP1486 ESP1488
ESP1491 ESP1493 ESP1502 ESP1503
ESP1506 ESP1507 ESP1508 ESP1513
ESP1522 ESP1528 FIN1553 FIN1581
FIN1592 FRA1610 FRA1615 FRA1619
FRA1642 FRA1651 FRA1657 FRA1672
FRA1685 FRA1704 FRA1737 FRA1785
FRA1791 FRA1793 FRA1797 FRA1843
FRA1849 FRA1852 FRA1889 FRA1929
FRA1938 FRA1939 FRA1956 FRA1990
FRA2002 FRA2047 FRA2057 FRA2060
FRA2096 FRA2116 FRA2117 FRA2131
FRA2159 GBR2229 GBR2235 GBR2238
GBR2239 GBR2248 GBR2264 GBR2265
GBR2269 GBR2277 GBR2278 GBR2279
GBR2321 GBR2326 GBR2350 GBR2355
GBR2371 GBR2387 GBR2402 GBR2423
GBR2439 GBR2445 GBR2452 GBR2467
GBR2469 GBR2474 GBR2495 GBR2498
GBR2503 GBR2527 GBR2535 GBR2545
GBR2552 GBR2553 GBR2561 GRC2567
GRC2571 IRL2693 IRL2707 IRL2717
IRL2720 IRL2726 ITA2761 ITA2762
ITA2766 ITA2770 ITA2775 ITA2785
ITA2805 ITA2810 ITA2820 ITA2824
ITA2832 ITA2838 ITA2858 ITA2873
ITA2890 ITA2912 LUX2950 LUX2954
LUX2982 LUX2984 LUX2985 LUX2993
LUX3006 LUX3008 NLD3047 NLD3067
NLD3072 NLD3078 NLD3083 NLD3173
NLD3181 NLD3187 NLD3190 NLD3199
NLD3222 NLD3303 NLD3320 NLD3357
NLD3361 NOR3371 NOR3381 NOR3387
NOR3467 POL3519 PRT3549 PRT3594
PRT3600 PRT3605 SWE3648 SWE3661
SWE3707 SWE3712 SWE3737 SWE3749
SWE3754 SWE3768 SWE3769 SWE3789
SWE3795 SWE3816 SWE3864 SWE3865
TUR3883

LOBBYING, ADVOCACY - LOBBYING, PLAIDOYER

AUT0010 AUT0020 AUT0033 AUT0086
BEL0096 BEL0099 BEL0131 BEL0160
BEL0168 BEL0174 BEL0176 BEL0177
BEL0186 BEL0198 BEL0203 BEL0216
BEL0218 BEL0219 BEL0252 BEL0254
BEL0267 BEL0282 BEL0323 BEL0345
BEL0351 BEL0353 BEL0392 CHE0434
CHE0460 CHE0479 CHE0524 CHE0549
CHE0562 CHE0566 CHE0568 CHE0570
CHE0604 CHE0618 CHE0619 CHE0642
CHE0687 CHE0689 CHE0718 CHE0755
CHE0765 CHE0778 CHE0785 CHE0794
CHE0814 CHE0819 CHE0820 DEU0942
DEU0954 DEU0963 DEU0975 DEU0983
DEU0998 DEU1013 DEU1055 DEU1062
DEU1064 DEU1066 DEU1097 DEU1114
DEU1141 DEU1142 DEU1146 DEU1149
DEU1151 DEU1187 DNK1281 DNK1283
DNK1289 DNK1304 DNK1312 DNK1335
DNK1339 DNK1375 DNK1403 ESP1437
ESP1457 ESP1486 ESP1490 ESP1528
FIN1546 FIN1582 FRA1636 FRA1661
FRA1685 FRA1703 FRA1785 FRA1791
FRA1793 FRA1794 FRA1797 FRA1799
FRA1808 FRA1824 FRA1841 FRA1843
FRA1876 FRA1889 FRA1946 FRA1949
FRA1956 FRA2002 FRA2004 FRA2047
FRA2057 FRA2060 FRA2096 FRA2110
FRA2116 FRA2142 FRA2159 GBR2174
GBR2202 GBR2215 GBR2228 GBR2229
GBR2235 GBR2238 GBR2239 GBR2242
GBR2251 GBR2264 GBR2266 GBR2269
GBR2337 GBR2355 GBR2364 GBR2371
GBR2376 GBR2390 GBR2392 GBR2396
GBR2413 GBR2423 GBR2439 GBR2445
GBR2464 GBR2466 GBR2467 GBR2469
GBR2495 GBR2498 GBR2500 GBR2503
GBR2522 GBR2527 GBR2537 GBR2545
GBR2552 GBR2553 GRC2572 GRC2586
IRL2690 IRL2691 IRL2693 IRL2707
IRL2714 IRL2717 IRL2726 ITA2785
ITA2801 ITA2810 ITA2820 ITA2834
ITA2873 LUX2957 LUX2984 LUX3008
MLT3016 MLT3036 NLD3047 NLD3064
NLD3067 NLD3068 NLD3072 NLD3078
NLD3082 NLD3096 NLD3156 NLD3199
NLD3232 NLD3236 NLD3242 NLD3254
NLD3301 NOR3455 NOR3467 PRT3549
PRT3584 PRT3590 PRT3594 PRT3600
SVK3634 SWE3648 SWE3749 SWE3768
SWE3771 SWE3807 SWE3853 SWE3864
TUR3883 TUR3897

NETWORKING, ELECTRONIC TELECOMMUNICATIONS - RESEAUX, TELECOMMUNICATIONS ELECTRONIQUES

AUT0020 BEL0177 BEL0198 BEL0224
BEL0254 CHE0434 CHE0562 CHE0568
CHE0586 CHE0596 CHE0642 CHE0689
CHE0817 CHE0819 DEU0955 DEU0990
DEU1002 DNK1281 ESP1434 ESP1522
FIN1546 FIN1591 FRA1785 FRA1889
FRA2060 FRA2159 GBR2174 GBR2226
GBR2229 GBR2265 GBR2278 GBR2284
GBR2285 GBR2313 GBR2337 GBR2348
GBR2351 GBR2355 GBR2364 GBR2371
GBR2387 GBR2402 GBR2413 GBR2438
GBR2469 GBR2495 GBR2498 GBR2545
GBR2561 HUN2631 IRL2717 ITA2773
ITA2860 NLD3067 NLD3072 NLD3077
NLD3082 NLD3156 NLD3199 NLD3215
NLD3357 NOR3467 SWE3785 SWE3789
SWE3864 TUR3883

OTHER - AUTRE

CHE0434 DEU1106 FRA1631 FRA1700
FRA1956 GBR2240 GBR2358 GBR2371
GBR2387 NLD3096 NLD3117 NLD3232
POL3543 SWE3666

PUBLISHING, AUDIOVISUAL MATERIALS, EDUCATIONAL MATERIALS - EDITION, DOCUMENTS AUDIOVISUELS, DOCUMENTS EDUCATIFS

AUT0010 AUT0020 AUT0026 BEL0096
BEL0120 BEL0123 BEL0139 BEL0149
BEL0155 BEL0168 BEL0174 BEL0176
BEL0177 BEL0188 BEL0203 BEL0226
BEL0254 BEL0282 BEL0297 BEL0306
BEL0323 BEL0345 BEL0359 BEL0362
BEL0381 BEL0390 BEL0393 BEL0396
CHE0429 CHE0434 CHE0444 CHE0499
CHE0501 CHE0510 CHE0534 CHE0549
CHE0562 CHE0566 CHE0568 CHE0596
CHE0604 CHE0638 CHE0683 CHE0689
CHE0693 CHE0730 CHE0738 CHE0750
CHE0756 CHE0763 CHE0794 CHE0819
CHE0820 CZE0859 DEU0922 DEU0942
DEU0944 DEU0975 DEU1013 DEU1019
DEU1020 DEU1025 DEU1031 DEU1034
DEU1038 DEU1044 DEU1055 DEU1064
DEU1066 DEU1076 DEU1095 DEU1097
DEU1114 DEU1146 DEU1180 DEU1187
DNK1216 DNK1251 DNK1259 DNK1260
DNK1262 DNK1283 DNK1289 DNK1292
DNK1304 DNK1317 DNK1319 DNK1321
DNK1321 DNK1339 DNK1351 DNK1358
DNK1375 ESP1407 ESP1413 ESP1431
ESP1434 ESP1435 ESP1437 ESP1455
ESP1457 ESP1461 ESP1475 ESP1486
ESP1488 ESP1490 ESP1503 ESP1506
ESP1507 ESP1517 ESP1522 FIN1536
FIN1546 FIN1548 FIN1581 FIN1610
FRA1615 FRA1627 FRA1631 FRA1642
FRA1644 FRA1661 FRA1685 FRA1713
FRA1715 FRA1737 FRA1787 FRA1794
FRA1813 FRA1843 FRA1849 FRA1852
FRA1889 FRA1920 FRA1929 FRA1938
FRA1946 FRA1956 FRA1986 FRA1990
FRA2002 FRA2004 FRA2018 FRA2057
FRA2060 FRA2076 FRA2086 FRA2096
FRA2104 FRA2116 FRA2122 FRA2131
FRA2159 GBR2181 GBR2185 GBR2229
GBR2235 GBR2238 GBR2239 GBR2248
GBR2264 GBR2265 GBR2266 GBR2271
GBR2278 GBR2279 GBR2289 GBR2318
GBR2325 GBR2326 GBR2334 GBR2337
GBR2345 GBR2346 GBR2351 GBR2355
GBR2358 GBR2371 GBR2387 GBR2413
GBR2415 GBR2423 GBR2424 GBR2436
GBR2439 GBR2445 GBR2452 GBR2464
GBR2467 GBR2469 GBR2474 GBR2485
GBR2498 GBR2500 GBR2501 GBR2503
GBR2513 GBR2522 GBR2525 GBR2527
GBR2535 GBR2545 GBR2552 GBR2561
GBR2561 GRC2567 IRL2693 IRL2697
IRL2698 IRL2720 IRL2733 ITA2762
ITA2785 ITA2798 ITA2805 ITA2806
ITA2809 ITA2810 ITA2814 ITA2820
ITA2822 ITA2832 ITA2834 ITA2858
ITA2866 ITA2873 ITA2900 ITA2907
ITA2908 ITA2916 LUX3006 MLT3016
NLD3067 NLD3072 NLD3077 NLD3078
NLD3083 NLD3138 NLD3156 NLD3173
NLD3199 NLD3215 NLD3216 NLD3222
NLD3301 NLD3302 NLD3320 NLD3354
NLD3357 NLD3361
NOR3389 NOR3435 NOR3441 NOR3467
POL3519 PRT3584 PRT3600 SWE3648
SWE3737 SWE3749 SWE3768 SWE3769
SWE3789 SWE3816 SWE3865
TUR3883

RACISM, XENOPHOBIA, ANTISEMITISM - RACISME, XENOPHOBIE, ANTISEMITISME

BROADCASTING, CULTURAL EVENTS - RADIODIFFUSION, MANIFESTATIONS CULTURELLES

BEL0123 BEL0129 BEL0177 BEL0203
BEL0303 BEL0304 BEL0340 BEL0361
CHE0434 CHE0534 CHE0560 CHE0566
CHE0568 CHE0624 CHE0689 CHE0715
CHE0744 CHE0819 CZE0891 CZE0904
DEU0931 DEU1149 DEU1200 DNK1283
DNK1376 ESP1455 ESP1478 ESP1490
ESP1506 ESP1507 ESP1523 FIN1545

See: How to Use the Directory, page 11.

FIN1546 FIN1553 FRA1621 FRA1791
FRA1793 FRA1889 FRA1956 FRA1957
FRA2002 FRA2025 FRA2040 FRA2062
FRA2159 FRA2170 GBR2186 GBR2194
GBR2238 GBR2311 GBR2345 GBR2371
GBR2378 GBR2501 GBR2545 GRC2572
GRC2579 HUN2644 IRL2690 IRL2693
ITA2798 ITA2799 ITA2801 ITA2832
ITA2834 ITA2838 ITA2840 ITA2885
LUX2937 LUX2954 MLT3016 MLT3023
NLD3067 NLD3087 NLD3181 NLD3217
NLD3253 NLD3326 NOR3390 NOR3446
PRT3600 SVK3608 SWE3744 SWE3787
SWE3830 TUR3883

CONFERENCES, SEMINARS, WORKSHOPS, TRAINING ACTIVITIES - CONFERENCES, SEMINAIRES, ATELIERS, ACTIVITES DE FORMATION

AUT0002 AUT0010 AUT0020 AUT0047
AUT0056 AUT0067 AUT0068 BEL0096
BEL0123 BEL0127 BEL0129 BEL0156
BEL0160 BEL0174 BEL0176 BEL0177
BEL0188 BEL0191 BEL0199 BEL0203
BEL0221 BEL0275 BEL0284 BEL0287
BEL0289 BEL0290 BEL0303 BEL0304
BEL0322 BEL0340 BEL0345 BEL0361
BEL0362 BEL0399 CHE0417 CHE0434
CHE0456 CHE0461 CHE0534 CHE0537
CHE0549 CHE0562 CHE0566 CHE0568
CHE0596 CHE0605 CHE0639 CHE0642
CHE0669 CHE0671 CHE0689 CHE0693
CHE0701 CHE0711 CHE0715 CHE0718
CHE0741 CHE0744 CHE0755 CHE0794
CHE0809 CHE0814 CHE0819 CZE0865
CZE0897 CZE0904 CZE0905 DEU0917
DEU0921 DEU0923 DEU0931 DEU0942
DEU0944 DEU0977 DEU0983 DEU0990
DEU1004 DEU1025 DEU1027 DEU1034
DEU1054 DEU1055 DEU1056 DEU1062
DEU1064 DEU1066 DEU1074 DEU1090
DEU1097 DEU1098 DEU1110 DEU1111
DEU1149 DEU1175 DEU1180 DEU1193
DEU1198 DEU1200 DEU1203 DEU1210
DNK1273 DNK1289 DNK1305 DNK1335
DNK1339 DNK1376 DNK1398 ESP1413
ESP1417 ESP1430 ESP1435 ESP1441
ESP1442 ESP1450 ESP1455 ESP1461
ESP1472 ESP1478 ESP1479 ESP1486
ESP1490 ESP1493 ESP1505 ESP1506
ESP1507 ESP1508 ESP1511 ESP1512
ESP1517 ESP1522 ESP1523 ESP1528
FIN1536 FIN1540 FIN1543 FIN1545
FIN1546 FIN1549 FIN1553 FIN1560
FIN1570 FIN1572 FIN1578 FIN1585
FIN1588 FIN1594 FRA1619 FRA1675
FRA1791 FRA1793 FRA1800 FRA1813
FRA1818 FRA1841 FRA1862 FRA1887
FRA1889 FRA1956 FRA1957 FRA1964
FRA1978 FRA2002 FRA2004 FRA2013
FRA2019 FRA2025 FRA2032 FRA2040
FRA2041 FRA2042 FRA2044 FRA2047
FRA2057 FRA2062 FRA2096 FRA2117
FRA2159 FRA2162 FRA2170 GBR2185
GBR2186 GBR2194 GBR2238 GBR2251
GBR2260 GBR2265 GBR2269 GBR2279
GBR2284 GBR2311 GBR2326 GBR2327
GBR2355 GBR2371 GBR2378 GBR2380
GBR2402 GBR2408 GBR2415 GBR2416
GBR2424 GBR2445 GBR2448 GBR2453
GBR2503 GBR2526 GBR2536 GBR2545
GRC2571 GRC2572 GRC2585 HUN2598
HUN2642 HUN2644 HUN2655 IRL2693
IRL2695 IRL2712 IRL2717 IRL2733
ITA2765 ITA2766 ITA2785 ITA2791
ITA2798 ITA2799 ITA2801 ITA2804
ITA2809 ITA2810 ITA2820 ITA2824
ITA2826 ITA2829 ITA2832 ITA2834
ITA2838 ITA2840 ITA2852 ITA2857
ITA2883 ITA2885 ITA2890 ITA2895
ITA2898 ITA2900 ITA2901 ITA2902
ITA2903 ITA2905 ITA2907 ITA2908
ITA2911 ITA2912 ITA2913 LUX2954
LUX2985 MLT3016 MLT3017 MLT3023
NLD3067 NLD3079 NLD3082 NLD3104
NLD3133 NLD3164 NLD3174 NLD3181
NLD3187 NLD3242 NLD3277 NLD3301
NLD3326 NLD3334 NLD3357 NLD3366
NOR3390 NOR3400 NOR3402 NOR3416

NOR3446 NOR3467 POL3519 PRT3564
PRT3598 PRT3600 SVK3608 SVK3622
SWE3648 SWE3658 SWE3695 SWE3731
SWE3735 SWE3738 SWE3744 SWE3749
SWE3768 SWE3776 SWE3787 SWE3807
SWE3816 SWE3827 SWE3830 SWE3865
SWE3879 TUR3883

EXCHANGES, TWINNING, LINKING - ECHANGES, PARRAINAGE, JUMELAGE

AUT0020 AUT0066 BEL0123 BEL0129
BEL0156 BEL0198 BEL0203 BEL0221
BEL0275 BEL0303 BEL0340 BEL0361
BEL0390 BEL0434 CHE0448 CHE0456
CHE0560 CHE0562 CHE0566 CHE0595
CHE0596 CHE0640 CHE0643 CHE0687
CHE0689 CHE0809 CHE0819 CZE0904
DEU0942 DEU0983 DEU0990 DEU1055
DEU1074 DEU1111 DEU1149 DEU1193
DEU1200 DNK1318 ESP1523 FIN1543
FIN1546 FIN1587 FRA1746 FRA1791
FRA1793 FRA1887 FRA1889 FRA1946
FRA1956 FRA1964 FRA2159 FRA2159
FRA2170 GBR2284 GBR2355 GBR2371
GBR2379 GBR2390 GBR2396 GBR2415
GBR2445 GRC2571 GRC2584 HUN2644
IRL2693 ITA2799 ITA2834 ITA2900
ITA2903 NLD3067 NLD3079 NLD3082
NLD3105 NLD3181 NLD3326 NLD3357
NLD3366 NOR3390 NOR3446 POL3519
SWE3731 SWE3734 SWE3749 SWE3776
SWE3830 SWE3865 SWE3879 TUR3883

FORMAL EDUCATION - EDUCATION FORMELLE

AUT0068 BEL0123 BEL0129 BEL0156
BEL0176 BEL0177 BEL0323 BEL0359
BEL0361 BEL0362 BEL0390 CHE0434
CHE0456 CHE0549 CHE0560 CHE0562
CHE0566 CHE0640 CHE0660 CHE0689
CHE0809 CHE0819 CZE0904 DEU0975
DEU0983 DEU1176 DNK1289 DNK1335
DNK1339 DNK1375 ESP1427 ESP1450
ESP1455 ESP1479 ESP1490 ESP1492
ESP1508 ESP1517 ESP1522 ESP1523
ESP1528 FIN1560 FIN1585 FRA1675
FRA1841 FRA1889 FRA1956 FRA1957
FRA2002 FRA2019 FRA2044 FRA2062
GBR2194 GBR2223 GBR2231 GBR2233
GBR2238 GBR2265 GBR2269 GBR2345
GBR2371 GBR2379 GBR2380 GBR2392
GBR2408 GBR2415 GBR2424 GBR2445
GBR2448 GBR2467 GBR2468 HUN2643
HUN2644 IRL2690 IRL2691 IRL2693
IRL2695 IRL2706 IRL2720 ITA2761
ITA2765 ITA2773 ITA2775 ITA2792
ITA2799 ITA2799 ITA2804 ITA2810
ITA2822 ITA2826 ITA2827 ITA2838
ITA2840 ITA2883 ITA2895 ITA2900
ITA2905 ITA2912 MLT3016 MLT3017
NLD3067 NLD3073 NLD3105 NLD3215
NLD3326 NOR3390 POL3521 PRT3600
SVK3622 SWE3830 SWE3879

FUND RAISING - COLLECTE DE FONDS

BEL0096 BEL0129 BEL0160 BEL0198
BEL0203 BEL0351 BEL0361 BEL0362
CHE0417 CHE0434 CHE0448 CHE0566
CHE0689 CHE0715 CHE0744 CHE0755
CHE0814 CHE0819 DEU0923 DEU0957
DEU0983 DEU1064 DEU1110 DEU1111
DEU1176 DEU1187 DEU1193 DEU1200
DNK1283 DNK1305 DNK1375 ESP1442
ESP1445 ESP1505 ESP1506 ESP1508
ESP1523 ESP1528 FIN1546 FRA1791
FRA1793 FRA1843 FRA1889 FRA1946
FRA1957 FRA1978 FRA2025 FRA2041
FRA2086 FRA2159 FRA2170 GBR2186
GBR2194 GBR2201 GBR2311 GBR2371
GBR2396 GBR2424 GBR2445 GBR2522
HUN2642 HUN2644 IRL2695 ITA2773
ITA2799 ITA2804 ITA2809 ITA2810
ITA2824 ITA2852 ITA2900 ITA2901
ITA2903 ITA2905 ITA2911 NLD3067
NLD3104 NLD3181 NLD3253 NLD3256
NLD3277 NLD3301 NLD3326 NLD3362
NLD3366 NOR3371 NOR3390 NOR3446
SVK3608 SWE3648 SWE3731 SWE3744
SWE3768 SWE3787 SWE3830

INFORMATION AND DOCUMENTATION SERVICES, DATA BASES - SERVICES D'INFORMATION ET DE DOCUMENTATION, BASES DE DONNEES

AUT0010 AUT0020 AUT0060 AUT0079
BEL0123 BEL0127 BEL0129 BEL0155
BEL0160 BEL0177 BEL0199 BEL0203
BEL0237 BEL0267 BEL0275 BEL0284
BEL0303 BEL0304 BEL0335 BEL0345
BEL0359 BEL0361 BEL0362 BEL0390
BEL0393 BEL0396 BEL0399 CHE0434
CHE0456 CHE0491 CHE0506 CHE0534
CHE0537 CHE0562 CHE0566 CHE0568
CHE0596 CHE0605 CHE0640
CHE0668 CHE0687 CHE0689 CHE0715
CHE0744 CHE0763 CHE0809 CHE0819
CZE0904 DEU0923 DEU0944 DEU0968
DEU0977 DEU0990 DEU0996 DEU1001
DEU1025 DEU1031 DEU1064 DEU1074
DEU1076 DEU1088 DEU1090 DEU1091
DEU1097 DEU1110 DEU1111 DEU1149
DEU1184 DEU1192 DEU1193 DEU1200
DEU1203 DEU1207 DNK1248 DNK1283
DNK1289 DNK1292 DNK1305 DNK1318
DNK1335 DNK1339 DNK1375 DNK1376
DNK1398 ESP1407 ESP1413 ESP1430
ESP1434 ESP1435 ESP1441 ESP1442
ESP1450 ESP1457 ESP1461 ESP1478
ESP1479 ESP1486 ESP1490 ESP1493
ESP1506 ESP1507 ESP1508 ESP1523
FIN1540 FIN1546 FIN1572 FIN1582
FIN1585 FRA1737 FRA1797 FRA1800
FRA1808 FRA1810 FRA1811 FRA1818
FRA1839 FRA1841 FRA1889 FRA1908
FRA1956 FRA2002 FRA2004 FRA2013
FRA2041 FRA2096 FRA2104 FRA2122
FRA2131 FRA2159 GBR2185 GBR2194
GBR2223 GBR2228 GBR2265 GBR2284
GBR2311 GBR2326 GBR2347 GBR2355
GBR2371 GBR2378 GBR2379 GBR2392
GBR2396 GBR2402 GBR2408 GBR2415
GBR2435 GBR2438 GBR2445 GBR2545
GRC2571 GRC2579 GRC2584 GRC2585
HUN2644 HUN2645 IRL2690
IRL2693 IRL2695 IRL2698 IRL2706
IRL2717 IRL2720 IRL2730 ITA2764
ITA2773 ITA2798 ITA2799 ITA2801
ITA2804 ITA2809 ITA2810 ITA2822
ITA2824 ITA2827 ITA2829 ITA2834
ITA2840 ITA2852 ITA2857 ITA2860
ITA2861 ITA2866 ITA2873 ITA2880
ITA2895 ITA2900 ITA2901 ITA2902
ITA2905 ITA2907 ITA2908 ITA2911
ITA2912 ITA2913 ITA2923 LUX2937
LUX2962 MLT3017 MLT3023 NLD3058
NLD3067 NLD3073 NLD3077 NLD3105
NLD3135 NLD3139 NLD3167 NLD3181
NLD3196 NLD3217 NLD3242 NLD3301
NLD3305 NLD3326 NLD3334 NLD3357
NLD3361 NLD3364 NOR3390 NOR3400
NOR3402 NOR3410 NOR3435 NOR3446
POL3519 PRT3564 PRT3598 PRT3600
SVK3608 SWE3648 SWE3658 SWE3744
SWE3768 SWE3807 SWE3816 SWE3830
SWE3865 TUR3883

INFORMATION CAMPAIGNS, EXHIBITIONS - CAMPAGNES D'INFORMATION, EXPOSITIONS

AUT0020 AUT0067 BEL0096 BEL0123
BEL0129 BEL0156 BEL0160 BEL0176
BEL0177 BEL0191 BEL0198 BEL0203
BEL0267 BEL0275 BEL0297 BEL0303
BEL0304 BEL0340 BEL0359 BEL0361
BEL0362 BEL0390 BEL0392 CHE0434
CHE0456 CHE0461 CHE0506 CHE0534
CHE0537 CHE0560 CHE0562 CHE0566
CHE0568 CHE0596 CHE0605 CHE0668
CHE0669 CHE0689 CHE0701 CHE0715
CHE0718 CHE0744 CHE0807 CHE0809
CHE0819 CYP0832 CZE0897 DEU0917
DEU0923 DEU0931 DEU0942 DEU0955
DEU0975 DEU0977 DEU0983 DEU1022
DEU1025 DEU1031 DEU1034 DEU1064
DEU1110 DEU1111 DEU1149 DEU1176
DEU1193 DEU1200 DEU1203 DNK1248
DNK1283 DNK1292 DNK1305 DNK1317
DNK1339 DNK1376 DNK1398 ESP1407
ESP1413 ESP1442 ESP1450 ESP1478

Voir : *Comment utiliser le répertoire*, page 11.

ESP1486	ESP1490	ESP1493	ESP1503
ESP1505	ESP1506	ESP1508	ESP1511
ESP1512	ESP1517	ESP1522	ESP1523
ESP1528	FIN1540	FIN1543	FIN1546
FIN1549	FIN1553	FIN1560	FIN1582
FIN1585	FIN1592	FIN1594	FRA1651
FRA1791	FRA1793	FRA1797	FRA1843
FRA1862	FRA1889	FRA1956	FRA1957
FRA2002	FRA2040	FRA2057	FRA2131
FRA2143	FRA2159	FRA2170	GBR2194
GBR2238	GBR2265	GBR2269	GBR2311
GBR2326	GBR2355	GBR2371	GBR2378
GBR2402	GBR2415	GBR2445	GBR2503
GBR2526	GBR2545	GBR2561	GRC2571
GRC2572	GRC2579	GRC2584	HUN2631
HUN2644	HUN2655	IRL2690	IRL2693
IRL2695	IRL2717	ITA2761	ITA2764
ITA2765	ITA2766	ITA2773	ITA2785
ITA2791	ITA2798	ITA2799	ITA2804
ITA2809	ITA2810	ITA2824	ITA2827
ITA2834	ITA2838	ITA2840	ITA2852
ITA2885	ITA2890	ITA2895	ITA2900
ITA2901	ITA2903	ITA2905	ITA2912
LUX2954	LUX2985	MLT3016	MLT3017
MLT3023	NLD3067	NLD3073	NLD3079
NLD3087	NLD3105	NLD3164	NLD3181
NLD3190	NLD3217	NLD3277	NLD3326
NLD3334	NLD3357	NLD3364	NLD3366
NOR3371	NOR3390	NOR3402	NOR3435
NOR3446	POL3519	PRT3598	PRT3600
SVK3608	SWE3648	SWE3731	SWE3738
SWE3744	SWE3768	SWE3776	SWE3786
SWE3816	SWE3830	SWE3865	SWE3879
TUR3883			

LOBBYING, ADVOCACY - LOBBYING, PLAIDOYER

AUT0002	AUT0008	AUT0020	AUT0033
AUT0056	AUT0067	BEL0096	BEL0129
BEL0160	BEL0174	BEL0176	BEL0177
BEL0191	BEL0198	BEL0199	BEL0203
BEL0218	BEL0248	BEL0267	BEL0284
BEL0303	BEL0345	BEL0351	BEL0359
BEL0361	BEL0399	CHE0434	CHE0448
CHE0491	CHE0503	CHE0534	CHE0537
CHE0562	CHE0566	CHE0568	CHE0605
CHE0639	CHE0642	CHE0643	CHE0661
CHE0668	CHE0689	CHE0711	CHE0715
CHE0718	CHE0744	CHE0755	CHE0785
CHE0794	CHE0809	CHE0814	CHE0819
CYP0832	CZE0891	CZE0904	DEU0923
DEU0929	DEU0942	DEU0975	DEU0983
DEU0998	DEU1004	DEU1055	DEU1062
DEU1064	DEU1074	DEU1097	DEU1110
DEU1124	DEU1131	DEU1149	DEU1164
DEU1193	DEU1200	DEU1203	DNK1283
DNK1289	DNK1292	DNK1335	DNK1339
DNK1375	DNK1407	ESP1407	ESP1437
ESP1479	ESP1490	ESP1505	ESP1528
FIN1540	FIN1543	FIN1546	FIN1560
FIN1564	FIN1570	FIN1585	FIN1588
FIN1594	FRA1791	FRA1793	FRA1797
FRA1808	FRA1841	FRA1843	FRA1862
FRA1876	FRA1889	FRA1956	FRA1957
FRA2002	FRA2004	FRA2032	FRA2041
FRA2057	FRA2062	FRA2096	FRA2143
FRA2159	GBR2186	GBR2194	GBR2215
GBR2223	GBR2251	GBR2266	GBR2269
GBR2284	GBR2347	GBR2355	GBR2371
GBR2371	GBR2374	GBR2378	GBR2390
GBR2392	GBR2396	GBR2445	GBR2503
GBR2522	GBR2526	GBR2545	GRC2571
GRC2572	GRC2573	GRC2579	GRC2584
GRC2585	HUN2642	HUN2643	HUN2645
IRL2690	IRL2691	IRL2693	IRL2695
IRL2706	IRL2714	IRL2717	ITA2785
ITA2798	ITA2799	ITA2801	ITA2810
ITA2814	ITA2820	ITA2824	ITA2834
ITA2838	ITA2852	ITA2895	ITA2900
ITA2903	ITA2905	ITA2911	ITA2913
LIE2927	LUX2957	LUX2962	MLT3016
MLT3017	MLT3023	NLD3067	NLD3079
NLD3082	NLD3133	NLD3164	NLD3181
NLD3236	NLD3242	NLD3301	NLD3326
NLD3334	NLD3362	NLD3364	NLD3366
NOR3390	NOR3416	NOR3419	NOR3446
NOR3467	PRT3586	PRT3600	PRT3602
SVK3634	SWE3648	SWE3735	SWE3744
SWE3749	SWE3807	SWE3830	TUR3883

NETWORKING, ELECTRONIC TELECOMMUNICATIONS - RESEAUX, TELECOMMUNICATIONS ELECTRONIQUES

AUT0020	AUT0066	BEL0177	BEL0198
BEL0303	BEL0361	CHE0434	CHE0506
CHE0568	CHE0642	CHE0689	CHE0809
CHE0817	CHE0819	CZE0904	DEU0923
DEU0955	DEU0990	DEU1002	DEU1097
DEU1149	ESP1434	ESP1522	FIN1543
FIN1546	FIN1570	FRA1889	FRA1956
FRA2159	GBR2265	GBR2284	GBR2285
GBR2313	GBR2351	GBR2355	GBR2371
GBR2402	GBR2438	GBR2545	HUN2644
HUN2655	IRL2717	ITA2764	ITA2773
ITA2799	ITA2860	ITA2902	NLD3067
NLD3077	NLD3082	NLD3104	NLD3181
NLD3326	NLD3357	NLD3364	NLD3366
NOR3390	PRT3598	SWE3787	SWE3830
TUR3883			

OTHER - AUTRE

CHE0434	GBR2194	GBR2371

PUBLISHING, AUDIOVISUAL MATERIALS, EDUCATIONAL MATERIALS - EDITION, DOCUMENTS AUDIOVISUELS, DOCUMENTS EDUCATIFS

AUT0010	AUT0020	AUT0068	BEL0096
BEL0123	BEL0127	BEL0155	BEL0160
BEL0174	BEL0176	BEL0177	BEL0188
BEL0203	BEL0303	BEL0304	BEL0323
BEL0340	BEL0345	BEL0359	BEL0361
BEL0362	BEL0390	BEL0393	CHE0429
CHE0434	CHE0456	CHE0499	CHE0534
CHE0537	CHE0549	CHE0560	CHE0562
CHE0566	CHE0568	CHE0596	CHE0668
CHE0689	CHE0693	CHE0715	CHE0738
CHE0744	CHE0763	CHE0794	CHE0809
CHE0819	CYP0832	CZE0904	DEU0917
DEU0923	DEU0931	DEU0942	DEU0944
DEU0977	DEU0991	DEU1004	DEU1022
DEU1025	DEU1031	DEU1034	DEU1055
DEU1064	DEU1074	DEU1076	DEU1097
DEU1110	DEU1149	DEU1176	DEU1180
DEU1193	DEU1198	DEU1200	DNK1248
DNK1273	DNK1283	DNK1292	DNK1317
DNK1339	DNK1375	ESP1430	ESP1434
ESP1435	ESP1442	ESP1450	ESP1457
ESP1461	ESP1478	ESP1490	ESP1505
ESP1506	ESP1523	FIN1536	FIN1546
FIN1549	FIN1572	FIN1585	FRA1713
FRA1813	FRA1843	FRA1862	FRA1889
FRA1908	FRA1956	FRA2002	FRA2004
FRA2013	FRA2032	FRA2040	FRA2041
FRA2042	FRA2057	FRA2096	FRA2131
FRA2159	GBR2185	GBR2194	GBR2238
GBR2265	GBR2271	GBR2311	GBR2326
GBR2345	GBR2355	GBR2371	GBR2378
GBR2380	GBR2402	GBR2415	GBR2445
GBR2453	GBR2501	GBR2503	GBR2522
GBR2545	GRC2585	HUN2598	HUN2644
IRL2690	IRL2693	IRL2695	IRL2698
IRL2712	ITA2762	ITA2765	ITA2785
ITA2798	ITA2799	ITA2804	ITA2809
ITA2810	ITA2820	ITA2822	ITA2826
ITA2832	ITA2834	ITA2838	ITA2840
ITA2852	ITA2857	ITA2858	ITA2861
ITA2885	ITA2895	ITA2900	ITA2901
ITA2902	ITA2905	ITA2908	LUX2962
LUX3006	NLD3067	NLD3073	NLD3077
NLD3082	NLD3105	NLD3164	NLD3215
NLD3301	NLD3326	NLD3357	NLD3364
NOR3390	NOR3402	NOR3435	NOR3446
POL3519	PRT3564	PRT3598	PRT3600
SVK3608	SVK3622	SWE3648	SWE3744
SWE3768	SWE3787	SWE3816	SWE3827
SWE3830	SWE3865	SWE3879	TUR3883

REFUGEES, MIGRANTS, ETHNIC GROUPS - REFUGIES, MIGRANTS, GROUPES ETHNIQUES

BROADCASTING, CULTURAL EVENTS - RADIODIFFUSION, MANIFESTATIONS CULTURELLES

AUT0021	BEL0123	BEL0129	BEL0203
BEL0303	BEL0340	BEL0359	CHE0434
CHE0534	CHE0568	CHE0604	CHE0624
CHE0654	CHE0689	CHE0715	CHE0744
CHE0799	CHE0819	CZE0904	DEU0920
DEU0921	DEU1110	DEU1143	DNK1283
DNK1339	DNK1376	ESP1430	ESP1431
ESP1478	ESP1486	ESP1490	ESP1506
ESP1507	FIN1545	FIN1553	FIN1563
FRA1615	FRA1621	FRA1631	FRA1768
FRA1778	FRA1785	FRA1787	FRA1791
FRA1793	FRA1889	FRA1910	FRA1956
FRA1957	FRA2002	FRA2025	FRA2100
GBR2194	GBR2229	GBR2238	GBR2248
GBR2311	GBR2345	GBR2371	GBR2378
GBR2423	GBR2464	GBR2493	GBR2498
GBR2501	GBR2545	GRC2579	HUN2631
HUN2644	IRL2693	IRL2717	ITA2785
ITA2799	ITA2799	ITA2801	ITA2809
ITA2820	ITA2834	ITA2886	ITA2907
ITA2923	LUX2955	LUX2992	MLT3016
NLD3051	NLD3067	NLD3073	NLD3135
NLD3217	NLD3232	NLD3236	NLD3253
NLD3303	NLD3326	NLD3339	NOR3372
NOR3390	NOR3446	NOR3467	PRT3588
PRT3600	SWE3744	SWE3761	SWE3830
TUR3883			

CONFERENCES, SEMINARS, WORKSHOPS, TRAINING ACTIVITIES - CONFERENCES, SEMINAIRES, ATELIERS, ACTIVITES DE FORMATION

AUT0020	AUT0033	AUT0034	AUT0044
AUT0047	AUT0074	BEL0096	BEL0107
BEL0123	BEL0127	BEL0129	BEL0133
BEL0147	BEL0148	BEL0152	BEL0155
BEL0160	BEL0174	BEL0176	BEL0188
BEL0191	BEL0192	BEL0197	BEL0203
BEL0221	BEL0237	BEL0284	BEL0289
BEL0290	BEL0297	BEL0303	BEL0304
BEL0318	BEL0322	BEL0340	BEL0345
BEL0359	BEL0362	CHE0417	CHE0420
CHE0434	CHE0461	CHE0464	CHE0467
CHE0491	CHE0534	CHE0537	CHE0562
CHE0568	CHE0596	CHE0604	CHE0605
CHE0618	CHE0629	CHE0636	CHE0637
CHE0642	CHE0651	CHE0654	CHE0669
CHE0682	CHE0683	CHE0689	CHE0693
CHE0711	CHE0715	CHE0718	CHE0741
CHE0744	CHE0755	CHE0758	CHE0799
CHE0809	CHE0814	CHE0819	CZE0865
CZE0897	CZE0904	DEU0920	DEU0921
DEU0931	DEU0944	DEU0977	DEU0983
DEU0990	DEU0991	DEU0996	DEU1004
DEU1013	DEU1025	DEU1027	DEU1054
DEU1055	DEU1064	DEU1074	DEU1090
DEU1097	DEU1098	DEU1100	DEU1108
DEU1110	DEU1111	DEU1141	DEU1142
DEU1143	DEU1149	DEU1167	DEU1169
DEU1175	DEU1179	DEU1180	DEU1184
DEU1186	DEU1187	DEU1193	DEU1198
DEU1210	DNK1248	DNK1273	DNK1283
DNK1289	DNK1304	DNK1305	DNK1312
DNK1339	DNK1360	DNK1375	DNK1376
DNK1393	DNK1398	ESP1413	ESP1417
ESP1430	ESP1431	ESP1435	ESP1441
ESP1450	ESP1451	ESP1461	ESP1472
ESP1478	ESP1486	ESP1490	ESP1491
ESP1493	ESP1505	ESP1506	ESP1507
ESP1511	ESP1512	ESP1517	ESP1522
ESP1528	FIN1536	FIN1540	FIN1544
FIN1545	FIN1548	FIN1549	FIN1551
FIN1553	FIN1557	FIN1560	FIN1563
FIN1564	FIN1570	FIN1577	FIN1578
FIN1583	FIN1585	FIN1588	FIN1594
FRA1621	FRA1627	FRA1675	FRA1778
FRA1791	FRA1793	FRA1800	FRA1811
FRA1813	FRA1818	FRA1832	FRA1841
FRA1846	FRA1862	FRA1887	FRA1889
FRA1946	FRA1956	FRA1957	FRA2002
FRA2004	FRA2013	FRA2019	FRA2020

See: *How to Use the Directory*, page 11.

FRA2032 FRA2041 FRA2047 FRA2057
FRA2117 FRA2123 FRA2131 FRA2140
FRA2143 GBR2176 GBR2185 GBR2186
GBR2194 GBR2215 GBR2222 GBR2228
GBR2229 GBR2238 GBR2265 GBR2269
GBR2279 GBR2284 GBR2303 GBR2311
GBR2326 GBR2347 GBR2348 GBR2350
GBR2353 GBR2355 GBR2371 GBR2378
GBR2387 GBR2388 GBR2392 GBR2396
GBR2408 GBR2415 GBR2416 GBR2423
GBR2424 GBR2435 GBR2445 GBR2447
GBR2448 GBR2455 GBR2464 GBR2481
GBR2483 GBR2500 GBR2503 GBR2526
GBR2545 GBR2551 GRC2571 GRC2572
GRC2576 GRC2579 GRC2584 GRC2585
GRC2586 HUN2631 HUN2644 HUN2655
IRL2688 IRL2689 IRL2693 IRL2695
IRL2717 IRL2726 IRL2728 ITA2747
ITA2773 ITA2785 ITA2786 ITA2791
ITA2798 ITA2799 ITA2801 ITA2803
ITA2809 ITA2810 ITA2814 ITA2816
ITA2826 ITA2827 ITA2834
ITA2835 ITA2838 ITA2841 ITA2846
ITA2852 ITA2866 ITA2873 ITA2882
ITA2883 ITA2885 ITA2886 ITA2898
ITA2900 ITA2901 ITA2902 ITA2903
ITA2905 ITA2907 ITA2908 ITA2912
ITA2913 ITA2915 LUX2955 LUX2984
LUX2992 MLT3016 MLT3018 NLD3067
NLD3073 NLD3082 NLD3087 NLD3133
NLD3179 NLD3187 NLD3190
NLD3211 NLD3226 NLD3232 NLD3236
NLD3277 NLD3301 NLD3303 NLD3305
NLD3326 NLD3339 NLD3357 NLD3364
NLD3366 NOR3371 NOR3390 NOR3400
NOR3416 NOR3446 NOR3467 NOR3471
POL3508 POL3512 POL3519 PRT3549
PRT3554 PRT3564 PRT3573 PRT3586
PRT3594 PRT3598 PRT3600 SWE3687
SWE3695 SWE3699 SWE3731 SWE3735
SWE3738 SWE3744 SWE3746 SWE3749
SWE3754 SWE3769 SWE3771 SWE3772
SWE3776 SWE3807 SWE3815 SWE3816
SWE3827 SWE3830 SWE3865 SWE3879
TUR3883

EXCHANGES, TWINNING, LINKING - ECHANGES, PARRAINAGE, JUMELAGE

AUT0020 AUT0033 AUT0034 BEL0105
BEL0123 BEL0129 BEL0160 BEL0203
BEL0221 BEL0303 BEL0340 BEL0390
CHE0434 CHE0448 CHE0595 CHE0643
CHE0689 CHE0689 CHE0758 CHE0809
CHE0819 CZE0904 DEU0920 DEU0983
DEU0990 DEU1055 DEU1074 DEU1111
DEU1186 DEU1193 DNK1283 DNK1304
DNK1339 ESP1413 ESP1447 ESP1451
FIN1587 FRA1715 FRA1746 FRA1778
FRA1791 FRA1793 FRA1846 FRA1887
FRA1889 FRA1942 FRA1956 FRA2057
FRA2140 GBR2284 GBR2355 GBR2371
GBR2379 GBR2396 GBR2423 GBR2435
GBR2445 GBR2448 GBR2481 GRC2584
HUN2601 HUN2644 ITA2765 ITA2770
ITA2775 ITA2785 ITA2799 ITA2834
ITA2838 ITA2903 LUX2942 NLD3067
NLD3082 NLD3137 NLD3232 NLD3236
NLD3300 NLD3303 NLD3326 NLD3339
NLD3357 NLD3366 NOR3390 NOR3446
POL3519 POL3521 PRT3576 SWE3687
SWE3731 SWE3734 SWE3749 SWE3754
SWE3785 SWE3830 SWE3879 TUR3883

FORMAL EDUCATION - EDUCATION FORMELLE

AUT0021 AUT0063 BEL0123 BEL0129
BEL0160 BEL0176 BEL0359 BEL0362
BEL0390 CHE0434 CHE0660 CHE0682
CHE0689 CHE0799 CHE0809 CHE0819
CZE0904 DEU0954 DEU0983 DNK1275
DNK1289 DNK1339 ESP1409 ESP1427
ESP1450 ESP1451 ESP1486 ESP1490
ESP1522 ESP1528 FIN1560 FIN1585
FIN1602 FRA1615 FRA1627 FRA1651
FRA1675 FRA1769 FRA1785 FRA1889
FRA1946 FRA1956 FRA2019 FRA2123
FRA2131 FRA2143 FRA2150 GBR2178
GBR2194 GBR2223 GBR2228 GBR2238
GBR2265 GBR2269 GBR2345 GBR2371

GBR2378 GBR2379 GBR2396 GBR2408
GBR2415 GBR2423 GBR2424 GBR2445
GBR2448 GBR2455 GBR2464 GBR2468
GBR2481 GBR2551 GBR2553 IRL2688
IRL2689 IRL2690 IRL2691 IRL2695
IRL2697 IRL2706 IRL2717 IRL2720
IRL2726 ITA2761 ITA2773 ITA2798
ITA2799 ITA2803 ITA2810 ITA2814
ITA2822 ITA2826 ITA2827 ITA2838
ITA2846 ITA2883 ITA2886 ITA2900
ITA2902 ITA2905 ITA2912 ITA2913
LUX2942 MLT3016 NLD3067 NLD3073
NLD3190 NLD3232 NLD3326 NLD3339
NOR3372 NOR3390 NOR3446 NOR3467
PRT3590 PRT3594 PRT3600 SWE3687
SWE3712 SWE3830 SWE3879

FUND RAISING - COLLECTE DE FONDS

AUT0021 AUT0026 AUT0033 AUT0072
AUT0091 BEL0096 BEL0105 BEL0107
BEL0129 BEL0147 BEL0148 BEL0160
BEL0197 BEL0198 BEL0201 BEL0203
BEL0224 BEL0297 BEL0318 BEL0350
BEL0351 BEL0355 BEL0358 BEL0359
BEL0362 BEL0368 CHE0410 CHE0417
CHE0434 CHE0467 CHE0506 CHE0515
CHE0562 CHE0570 CHE0586 CHE0604
CHE0630 CHE0637 CHE0687 CHE0689
CHE0693 CHE0744 CHE0744 CHE0755
CHE0756 CHE0764 CHE0814 CHE0819
CYP0832 CZE0859 CZE0896 CZE0904
DEU0918 DEU0922 DEU0954 DEU0957
DEU0968 DEU0983 DEU0989 DEU0991
DEU0993 DEU1001 DEU1064 DEU1108
DEU1110 DEU1111 DEU1132 DEU1141
DEU1146 DEU1167 DEU1169 DEU1176
DEU1186 DEU1187 DEU1202 DNK1214
DNK1222 DNK1248 DNK1251 DNK1283
DNK1292 DNK1304 DNK1305 DNK1316
DNK1366 ESP1409 ESP1431 ESP1442
ESP1445 ESP1447 ESP1450 ESP1451
ESP1486 ESP1491 ESP1505 ESP1506
ESP1517 ESP1528 FIN1549 FIN1585
FIN1591 FRA1769 FRA1778 FRA1785
FRA1787 FRA1791 FRA1793 FRA1811
FRA1824 FRA1843 FRA1855 FRA1880
FRA1889 FRA1910 FRA1929 FRA1939
FRA1942 FRA1946 FRA1957 FRA1978
FRA2025 FRA2041 FRA2047 FRA2086
FRA2116 FRA2117 FRA2119 FRA2131
FRA2140 FRA2163 GBR2175 GBR2176
GBR2178 GBR2185 GBR2186 GBR2194
GBR2197 GBR2222 GBR2223 GBR2230
GBR2238 GBR2244 GBR2248 GBR2259
GBR2280 GBR2289 GBR2311 GBR2321
GBR2324 GBR2326 GBR2348 GBR2350
GBR2353 GBR2371 GBR2378 GBR2385
GBR2392 GBR2396 GBR2413 GBR2419
GBR2423 GBR2445 GBR2464 GBR2475
GBR2481 GBR2483 GBR2493 GBR2500
GBR2506 GBR2523 GBR2524 GBR2526
GBR2537 GBR2551 GRC2552 GRC2572
GRC2579 GRC2586 HUN2644 IRL2688
IRL2689 IRL2691 IRL2695 IRL2697
IRL2717 IRL2732 IRL2733 ITA2747
ITA2762 ITA2770 ITA2773 ITA2777
ITA2785 ITA2791 ITA2798 ITA2799
ITA2809 ITA2810 ITA2816 ITA2818
ITA2820 ITA2822 ITA2826 ITA2829
ITA2834 ITA2838 ITA2852 ITA2879
ITA2881 ITA2885 ITA2889 ITA2890
ITA2900 ITA2901 ITA2902 ITA2903
ITA2905 ITA2907 ITA2913 ITA2921
LUX2936 LUX2942 LUX2955 LUX2982
LUX2984 LUX2992 LUX2995 NLD3050
NLD3051 NLD3067 NLD3137 NLD3159
NLD3201 NLD3228 NLD3232 NLD3253
NLD3256 NLD3258 NLD3263 NLD3277
NLD3300 NLD3301 NLD3303 NLD3362
NLD3366 NOR3371 NOR3390 NOR3404
NOR3412 NOR3435 NOR3460 NOR3467
POL3521 POL3543 PRT3549 PRT3552
PRT3555 PRT3594 SVK3611 SWE3648
SWE3674 SWE3679 SWE3687 SWE3699
SWE3712 SWE3730 SWE3731 SWE3744
SWE3749 SWE3763 SWE3769 SWE3796
SWE3813 SWE3815 SWE3830 SWE3857

INFORMATION AND DOCUMENTATION SERVICES, DATA BASES - SERVICES D'INFORMATION ET DE DOCUMENTATION, BASES DE DONNEES

AUT0010 AUT0015 AUT0020 AUT0034
AUT0060 AUT0074 AUT0079 AUT0085
AUT0093 BEL0123 BEL0127 BEL0129
BEL0149 BEL0155 BEL0160 BEL0192
BEL0197 BEL0203 BEL0237 BEL0267
BEL0284 BEL0297 BEL0303 BEL0304
BEL0318 BEL0335 BEL0345 BEL0359
BEL0362 BEL0365 BEL0390 BEL0393
BEL0396 CHE0420 CHE0434 CHE0464
CHE0491 CHE0501 CHE0506 CHE0534
CHE0537 CHE0549 CHE0554 CHE0562
CHE0568 CHE0582 CHE0596 CHE0604
CHE0605 CHE0624 CHE0654 CHE0668
CHE0687 CHE0689 CHE0715 CHE0741
CHE0744 CHE0756 CHE0758 CHE0763
CHE0766 CHE0799 CHE0809 CHE0817
CHE0819 CYP0832 CZE0859 CZE0904
DEU0917 DEU0920 DEU0921 DEU0944
DEU0968 DEU0975 DEU0977 DEU0990
DEU0996 DEU1001 DEU1002 DEU1013
DEU1020 DEU1025 DEU1031 DEU1064
DEU1074 DEU1076 DEU1086 DEU1088
DEU1090 DEU1091 DEU1097 DEU1108
DEU1111 DEU1143 DEU1169 DEU1179
DEU1184 DEU1186 DEU1192 DEU1193
DEU1207 DNK1248 DNK1251 DNK1259
DNK1283 DNK1289 DNK1292 DNK1305
DNK1335 DNK1339 DNK1358 DNK1360
DNK1375 DNK1376 DNK1398 ESP1413
ESP1430 ESP1431 ESP1434 ESP1441
ESP1447 ESP1450 ESP1451 ESP1457
ESP1478 ESP1479 ESP1486 ESP1490
ESP1493 ESP1506 ESP1507 ESP1522
FIN1540 FIN1546 FIN1548 FIN1560
FIN1564 FIN1582 FIN1585 FIN1591
FRA1631 FRA1737 FRA1785 FRA1797
FRA1800 FRA1808 FRA1810 FRA1811
FRA1818 FRA1832 FRA1839 FRA1841
FRA1846 FRA1889 FRA1908 FRA1956
FRA2002 FRA2004 FRA2013 FRA2018
FRA2020 FRA2096 FRA2104 FRA2122
FRA2131 FRA2140 FRA2143 GBR2185
GBR2193 GBR2194 GBR2197 GBR2222
GBR2223 GBR2238 GBR2239 GBR2265
GBR2284 GBR2311 GBR2326 GBR2347
GBR2353 GBR2355 GBR2371 GBR2378
GBR2379 GBR2387 GBR2388 GBR2392
GBR2396 GBR2408 GBR2415 GBR2423
GBR2435 GBR2438 GBR2445 GBR2448
GBR2455 GBR2464 GBR2483 GBR2493
GBR2498 GBR2545 GRC2571 GRC2576
GRC2579 GRC2584 GRC2585 HUN2601
HUN2631 HUN2644 HUN2645 IRL2695
IRL2698 IRL2714 IRL2717 IRL2720
IRL2730 ITA2762 ITA2773 ITA2780
ITA2785 ITA2798 ITA2799 ITA2801
ITA2809 ITA2810 ITA2814 ITA2822
ITA2827 ITA2834 ITA2837 ITA2846
ITA2852 ITA2860 ITA2861 ITA2866
ITA2873 ITA2880 ITA2900 ITA2901
ITA2902 ITA2905 ITA2907 ITA2908
ITA2912 ITA2913 LUX2937 LUX2962
MLT3018 NLD3049 NLD3050 NLD3051
NLD3058 NLD3067 NLD3073 NLD3077
NLD3095 NLD3135 NLD3137 NLD3139
NLD3211 NLD3217 NLD3222 NLD3226
NLD3232 NLD3236 NLD3301 NLD3305
NLD3326 NLD3339 NLD3352 NLD3353
NLD3357 NLD3361 NLD3364 NOR3390
NOR3400 NOR3410 NOR3435 NOR3446
NOR3460 NOR3467 NOR3471 POL3512
POL3519 POL3521 PRT3554 PRT3564
PRT3573 PRT3586 PRT3590 PRT3598
PRT3600 SVK3608 SWE3648 SWE3658
SWE3687 SWE3699 SWE3704 SWE3735
SWE3744 SWE3746 SWE3769 SWE3771
SWE3772 SWE3807 SWE3815 SWE3816
SWE3830 SWE3834 SWE3859 SWE3865
TUR3882 TUR3883

INFORMATION CAMPAIGNS, EXHIBITIONS - CAMPAGNES D'INFORMATION, EXPOSITIONS

AUT0006	AUT0010	AUT0015	AUT0020
AUT0032	AUT0034	AUT0047	BEL0096
BEL0123	BEL0129	BEL0148	BEL0176
BEL0191	BEL0192	BEL0197	BEL0198
BEL0203	BEL0267	BEL0284	BEL0289
BEL0290	BEL0303	BEL0304	BEL0318
BEL0340	BEL0350	BEL0359	BEL0362
BEL0368	BEL0390	CHE0420	CHE0434
CHE0461	CHE0467	CHE0491	CHE0506
CHE0515	CHE0534	CHE0537	CHE0541
CHE0562	CHE0568	CHE0596	CHE0605
CHE0618	CHE0654	CHE0668	CHE0669
CHE0689	CHE0715	CHE0718	CHE0744
CHE0756	CHE0799	CHE0807	CHE0809
CHE0819	CZE0897	CZE0904	DEU0920
DEU0931	DEU0955	DEU0975	DEU0977
DEU0983	DEU1013	DEU1025	DEU1064
DEU1098	DEU1110	DEU1111	DEU1129
DEU1141	DEU1142	DEU1149	DEU1169
DEU1175	DEU1176	DEU1186	DEU1187
DEU1193	DNK1248	DNK1251	DNK1259
DNK1273	DNK1283	DNK1292	DNK1304
DNK1305	DNK1307	DNK1317	DNK1339
DNK1376	DNK1391	DNK1398	DNK1403
ESP1413	ESP1431	ESP1441	ESP1450
ESP1451	ESP1478	ESP1486	ESP1490
ESP1493	ESP1503	ESP1505	ESP1506
ESP1524	ESP1528	FIN1540	FIN1549
FIN1553	FIN1560	FIN1577	FIN1582
FIN1583	FIN1585	FIN1592	FIN1594
FRA1615	FRA1633	FRA1651	FRA1785
FRA1787	FRA1791	FRA1793	FRA1797
FRA1841	FRA1843	FRA1862	FRA1889
FRA1910	FRA1942	FRA1956	FRA1957
FRA2002	FRA2020	FRA2047	FRA2057
FRA2116	FRA2131	FRA2143	GBR2193
GBR2194	GBR2222	GBR2223	GBR2228
GBR2238	GBR2239	GBR2248	GBR2259
GBR2265	GBR2269	GBR2311	GBR2321
GBR2326	GBR2328	GBR2355	GBR2371
GBR2378	GBR2387	GBR2396	GBR2423
GBR2445	GBR2464	GBR2483	GBR2493
GBR2498	GBR2503	GBR2526	GBR2545
GBR2553	GRC2572	GRC2576	GRC2579
GRC2584	HUN2631	HUN2644	HUN2655
IRL2688	IRL2693	IRL2695	IRL2698
IRL2717	IRL2724	IRL2726	ITA2761
ITA2765	ITA2770	ITA2777	ITA2780
ITA2785	ITA2791	ITA2798	ITA2799
ITA2801	ITA2803	ITA2809	ITA2810
ITA2814	ITA2827	ITA2832	ITA2834
ITA2837	ITA2852	ITA2882	ITA2885
ITA2890	ITA2901	ITA2902	ITA2903
ITA2905	ITA2912	ITA2913	LUX2942
LUX2984	LUX2992	LUX2995	NLD3051
NLD3067	NLD3073	NLD3087	NLD3135
NLD3211	NLD3217	NLD3232	NLD3236
NLD3258	NLD3263	NLD3277	NLD3300
NLD3303	NLD3305	NLD3326	NLD3339
NLD3363	NLD3364	NLD3366	NOR3371
NOR3372	NOR3390	NOR3446	NOR3467
POL3519	POL3521	POL3543	PRT3549
PRT3552	PRT3573	PRT3594	PRT3598
PRT3600	SWE3648	SWE3687	SWE3699
SWE3730	SWE3731	SWE3738	SWE3744
SWE3754	SWE3761	SWE3763	
SWE3769	SWE3771	SWE3776	SWE3796
SWE3815	SWE3816	SWE3830	SWE3879
TUR3883			

LOBBYING, ADVOCACY - LOBBYING, PLAIDOYER

AUT0010	AUT0015	AUT0020	AUT0021
AUT0033	AUT0034	AUT0044	AUT0058
AUT0089	AUT0093	BEL0096	BEL0147
BEL0160	BEL0174	BEL0176	BEL0191
BEL0197	BEL0198	BEL0203	BEL0218
BEL0267	BEL0284	BEL0309	BEL0318
BEL0345	BEL0351	BEL0359	CHE0420
CHE0434	CHE0467	CHE0491	CHE0534
CHE0537	CHE0550	CHE0562	CHE0568
CHE0570	CHE0596	CHE0604	CHE0605
CHE0613	CHE0618	CHE0619	CHE0637
CHE0642	CHE0654	CHE0661	CHE0668
CHE0683	CHE0687	CHE0689	CHE0693
CHE0711	CHE0715	CHE0718	CHE0744
CHE0755	CHE0785	CHE0809	CHE0814

CHE0819	CYP0832	CZE0891	CZE0896
CZE0904	DEU0920	DEU0929	DEU0954
DEU0983	DEU0998	DEU1004	DEU1013
DEU1019	DEU1055	DEU1062	DEU1064
DEU1074	DEU1097	DEU1110	DEU1124
DEU1131	DEU1141	DEU1142	DEU1143
DEU1149	DEU1167	DEU1169	DEU1176
DEU1179	DEU1184	DEU1186	DEU1187
DEU1193	DNK1259	DNK1275	DNK1283
DNK1289	DNK1292	DNK1304	DNK1312
DNK1335	DNK1339	DNK1376	DNK1403
DNK1405	ESP1407	ESP1431	ESP1451
ESP1479	ESP1486	ESP1490	ESP1505
ESP1528	FIN1540	FIN1549	FIN1551
FIN1560	FIN1564	FIN1570	FIN1585
FIN1588	FIN1594	FRA1633	FRA1791
FRA1793	FRA1797	FRA1808	FRA1841
FRA1843	FRA1862	FRA1889	FRA1910
FRA1946	FRA1956	FRA1957	FRA2002
FRA2004	FRA2032	FRA2041	FRA2047
FRA2057	FRA2062	FRA2096	FRA2110
FRA2116	FRA2131	FRA2140	FRA2143
FRA2163	GBR2178	GBR2194	GBR2215
GBR2223	GBR2228	GBR2238	GBR2229
GBR2266	GBR2269	GBR2311	GBR2328
GBR2347	GBR2355	GBR2371	GBR2374
GBR2378	GBR2390	GBR2392	GBR2396
GBR2423	GBR2435	GBR2445	GBR2447
GBR2464	GBR2467	GBR2481	GBR2483
GBR2493	GBR2498	GBR2503	GBR2522
GBR2523	GBR2537	GBR2545	GBR2551
GBR2552	GBR2553	GRC2572	GRC2573
GRC2579	GRC2584	GRC2585	GRC2586
HUN2601	HUN2631	HUN2642	HUN2645
IRL2689	IRL2691	IRL2693	IRL2695
IRL2706	IRL2712	IRL2717	IRL2724
IRL2726	IRL2728	ITA2780	ITA2799
ITA2801	ITA2810	ITA2820	ITA2834
ITA2852	ITA2881	ITA2882	ITA2902
ITA2903	ITA2905	ITA2913	LIE2927
LUX2955	LUX2957	LUX2962	LUX2984
LUX2992	MLT3016	NLD3049	NLD3067
NLD3068	NLD3073	NLD3082	NLD3133
NLD3137	NLD3211	NLD3222	NLD3232
NLD3236	NLD3258	NLD3301	NLD3303
NLD3305	NLD3326	NLD3330	NLD3339
NLD3362	NLD3364	NLD3366	NOR3390
NOR3404	NOR3416	NOR3419	NOR3446
NOR3460	NOR3467	NOR3471	POL3521
POL3536	PRT3549	PRT3554	PRT3573
PRT3594	PRT3600	PRT3602	SWE3648
SWE3699	SWE3735	SWE3744	SWE3749
SWE3771	SWE3815	SWE3830	TUR3882
TUR3883			

NETWORKING, ELECTRONIC TELECOMMUNICATIONS - RESEAUX, TELECOMMUNICATIONS ELECTRONIQUES

AUT0010	AUT0020	AUT0034	BEL0107
BEL0198	BEL0224	BEL0303	BEL0318
CHE0434	CHE0568	CHE0586	CHE0596
CHE0642	CHE0689	CHE0809	CHE0817
CHE0819	CZE0904	DEU0955	DEU0990
DEU1002	DEU1108	DEU1186	DNK1248
ESP1434	ESP1522	FIN1570	FIN1591
FRA1889	FRA1908	FRA1910	FRA1956
GBR2265	GBR2284	GBR2285	GBR2313
GBR2328	GBR2348	GBR2351	GBR2355
GBR2371	GBR2378	GBR2387	GBR2438
GBR2448	GBR2498	GBR2545	HUN2631
HUN2655	IRL2714	IRL2717	ITA2773
ITA2799	ITA2801	ITA2860	ITA2902
NLD3067	NLD3077	NLD3082	NLD3137
NLD3226	NLD3232	NLD3236	NLD3303
NLD3326	NLD3339	NLD3357	NLD3364
NLD3366	NOR3372	NOR3390	NOR3467
PRT3598	SWE3785	SWE3830	TUR3883

OTHER - AUTRE

CHE0434	DEU1169	FRA1631	FRA1693
FRA1825	GBR2194	GBR2240	GBR2371
GBR2378	GBR2387	NLD3133	NLD3137
NLD3183			

PUBLISHING, AUDIOVISUAL MATERIALS, EDUCATIONAL MATERIALS - EDITION, DOCUMENTS AUDIOVISUELS, DOCUMENTS EDUCATIFS

AUT0010	AUT0020	AUT0026	AUT0034
AUT0044	BEL0096	BEL0123	BEL0127
BEL0147	BEL0155	BEL0160	BEL0174
BEL0176	BEL0188	BEL0203	BEL0224
BEL0303	BEL0304	BEL0306	BEL0340
BEL0345	BEL0359	BEL0362	BEL0368
BEL0390	BEL0393	BEL0396	CHE0429
CHE0434	CHE0491	CHE0499	CHE0501
CHE0534	CHE0537	CHE0549	CHE0562
CHE0568	CHE0596	CHE0609	CHE0638
CHE0651	CHE0668	CHE0689	CHE0693
CHE0715	CHE0738	CHE0741	CHE0744
CHE0747	CHE0756	CHE0763	CHE0809
CHE0819	CYP0832	CZE0859	CZE0904
DEU0920	DEU0944	DEU0975	DEU0977
DEU0991	DEU1013	DEU1020	DEU1025
DEU1031	DEU1055	DEU1064	DEU1074
DEU1076	DEU1095	DEU1097	DEU1098
DEU1149	DEU1176	DEU1180	
DEU1186	DEU1198	DNK1248	DNK1251
DNK1259	DNK1273	DNK1283	DNK1292
DNK1304	DNK1316	DNK1317	DNK1321
DNK1339	DNK1403	ESP1430	ESP1434
ESP1435	ESP1436	ESP1451	ESP1457
ESP1461	ESP1475	ESP1478	ESP1490
ESP1505	ESP1506	ESP1522	FIN1536
FIN1548	FIN1549	FIN1577	FIN1585
FRA1615	FRA1627	FRA1631	FRA1668
FRA1713	FRA1715	FRA1768	FRA1778
FRA1795	FRA1813	FRA1843	FRA1889
FRA1897	FRA1908	FRA1920	FRA1946
FRA1956	FRA2002	FRA2004	FRA2013
FRA2032	FRA2047	FRA2096	FRA2104
FRA2116	FRA2131	FRA2143	GBR2185
GBR2193	GBR2194	GBR2222	GBR2223
GBR2228	GBR2238	GBR2239	GBR2248
GBR2265	GBR2271	GBR2289	GBR2311
GBR2326	GBR2345	GBR2353	GBR2355
GBR2371	GBR2378	GBR2387	GBR2392
GBR2396	GBR2415	GBR2423	GBR2445
GBR2455	GBR2464	GBR2467	GBR2483
GBR2493	GBR2498	GBR2500	GBR2501
GBR2503	GBR2506	GBR2526	GBR2545
GBR2552	GRC2572	GRC2585	HUN2631
HUN2644	IRL2693	IRL2695	IRL2698
IRL2717	IRL2728	IRL2733	ITA2762
ITA2780	ITA2785	ITA2786	ITA2798
ITA2799	ITA2801	ITA2803	ITA2809
ITA2810	ITA2814	ITA2822	ITA2834
ITA2837	ITA2846	ITA2852	ITA2860
ITA2861	ITA2866	ITA2873	ITA2881
ITA2890	ITA2902	ITA2905	ITA2907
ITA2908	ITA2916	LUX2962	LUX3006
NLD3049	NLD3051	NLD3067	NLD3077
NLD3082	NLD3135	NLD3211	NLD3216
NLD3226	NLD3232	NLD3277	NLD3300
NLD3301	NLD3303	NLD3305	NLD3326
NLD3333	NLD3354	NLD3357	NLD3364
NOR3390	NOR3435	NOR3446	NOR3460
NOR3467	POL3512	POL3519	POL3543
PRT3564	PRT3586	PRT3598	PRT3600
SWE3648	SWE3687	SWE3699	SWE3749
SWE3763	SWE3769	SWE3771	SWE3816
SWE3827	SWE3830	SWE3865	SWE3879
TUR3883			

RURAL DEVELOPMENT, AGRICULTURE - DEVELOPPEMENT RURAL, AGRICULTURE

BROADCASTING, CULTURAL EVENTS - RADIODIFFUSION, MANIFESTATIONS CULTURELLES

BEL0165	BEL0203	BEL0226	BEL0249
BEL0340	BEL0353	BEL0358	BEL0359
BEL0361	BEL0390	CHE0434	CHE0534
CHE0566	CHE0568	CHE0598	CHE0604
CHE0624	CHE0689	CHE0810	CHE0817
CHE0819	DEU0921	DEU1143	DEU1200
DNK1307	DNK1339	DNK1377	DNK1389
DNK1405	ESP1439	ESP1457	ESP1486
ESP1507	ESP1510	FRA1612	FRA1627
FRA1631	FRA1653	FRA1690	FRA1703

See: *How to Use the Directory*, page 11.

FRA1760	FRA1778	FRA1785	FRA1787
FRA1794	FRA1889	FRA1956	FRA1988
FRA1992	FRA2002	FRA2062	FRA2092
FRA2106	FRA2159	GBR2175	GBR2186
GBR2229	GBR2238	GBR2248	GBR2278
GBR2297	GBR2312	GBR2333	GBR2345
GBR2351	GBR2371	GBR2372	GBR2417
GBR2501	GBR2511	GBR2515	GBR2545
HUN2598	IRL2686	IRL2700	IRL2714
ITA2773	ITA2798	ITA2799	ITA2813
ITA2820	ITA2834	ITA2835	ITA2855
ITA2898	ITA2907	LUX2937	LUX2954
LUX2968	LUX2982	MLT3016	NLD3067
NLD3169	NLD3230	NLD3236	NLD3253
POL3508	POL3543	SVK3611	SWE3702
SWE3760	SWE3774	TUR3883	TUR3885

CONFERENCES, SEMINARS, WORKSHOPS, TRAINING ACTIVITIES - CONFERENCES, SEMINAIRES, ATELIERS, ACTIVITES DE FORMATION

AUT0002	AUT0010	AUT0011	AUT0035
AUT0045	AUT0085	AUT0086	BEL0101
BEL0128	BEL0148	BEL0152	BEL0156
BEL0165	BEL0203	BEL0211	BEL0214
BEL0221	BEL0224	BEL0231	BEL0237
BEL0248	BEL0261	BEL0270	BEL0282
BEL0306	BEL0333	BEL0352	BEL0353
BEL0356	BEL0359	BEL0361	BEL0368
BEL0378	BEL0394	BEL0397	CHE0402
CHE0417	CHE0422	CHE0434	CHE0439
CHE0455	CHE0461	CHE0462	CHE0467
CHE0491	CHE0495	CHE0510	CHE0562
CHE0566	CHE0568	CHE0586	CHE0604
CHE0619	CHE0628	CHE0629	CHE0632
CHE0638	CHE0642	CHE0655	CHE0669
CHE0681	CHE0682	CHE0687	CHE0689
CHE0693	CHE0727	CHE0730	CHE0734
CHE0749	CHE0762	CHE0765	CHE0766
CHE0772	CHE0810	CHE0814	CHE0817
CHE0819	CHE0823	CYP0831	CYP0832
DEU0921	DEU0942	DEU0944	DEU0968
DEU0975	DEU0977	DEU0983	DEU0989
DEU0990	DEU0999	DEU1006	DEU1020
DEU1032	DEU1037	DEU1044	DEU1047
DEU1066	DEU1074	DEU1090	DEU1097
DEU1100	DEU1106	DEU1114	DEU1143
DEU1149	DEU1151	DEU1163	DEU1167
DEU1180	DNK1227	DNK1238	DNK1242
DNK1291	DNK1307	DNK1312	DNK1339
DNK1353	DNK1361	DNK1389	DNK1398
DNK1403	ESP1409	ESP1413	ESP1439
ESP1450	ESP1455	ESP1457	ESP1472
ESP1474	ESP1482	ESP1485	ESP1486
ESP1488	ESP1506	ESP1507	ESP1509
ESP1510	ESP1517	ESP1528	ESP1529
FIN1545	FIN1546	FIN1553	FIN1572
FIN1584	FRA1616	FRA1627	FRA1629
FRA1632	FRA1634	FRA1636	FRA1653
FRA1661	FRA1672	FRA1679	FRA1690
FRA1701	FRA1703	FRA1704	FRA1709
FRA1719	FRA1727	FRA1731	FRA1737
FRA1756	FRA1776	FRA1778	FRA1785
FRA1787	FRA1794	FRA1797	FRA1799
FRA1800	FRA1811	FRA1815	FRA1818
FRA1828	FRA1832	FRA1841	FRA1846
FRA1849	FRA1856	FRA1860	FRA1861
FRA1885	FRA1889	FRA1907	FRA1917
FRA1946	FRA1947	FRA1956	FRA1980
FRA1985	FRA1988	FRA1990	FRA2004
FRA2005	FRA2012	FRA2015	FRA2016
FRA2018	FRA2039	FRA2062	FRA2069
FRA2070	FRA2093	FRA2093	FRA2105
FRA2106	FRA2108	FRA2109	FRA2122
FRA2126	FRA2131	FRA2147	FRA2159
FRA2161	FRA2163	GBR2174	GBR2175
GBR2176	GBR2181	GBR2185	GBR2186
GBR2190	GBR2197	GBR2202	GBR2213
GBR2214	GBR2226	GBR2229	GBR2232
GBR2238	GBR2240	GBR2241	GBR2242
GBR2244	GBR2265	GBR2269	GBR2274
GBR2277	GBR2278	GBR2279	GBR2281
GBR2288	GBR2292	GBR2298	GBR2302
GBR2303	GBR2312	GBR2333	GBR2334
GBR2337	GBR2341	GBR2348	GBR2350
GBR2351	GBR2353	GBR2358	GBR2364
GBR2371	GBR2387	GBR2390	GBR2392
GBR2408	GBR2417	GBR2419	GBR2422
GBR2423	GBR2428	GBR2435	GBR2436

GBR2437	GBR2452	GBR2460	GBR2463
GBR2474	GBR2475	GBR2480	GBR2483
GBR2495	GBR2500	GBR2503	GBR2511
GBR2515	GBR2527	GBR2535	GBR2545
GBR2550	GBR2553	GBR2561	GRC2567
GRC2575	GRC2586	GRC2590	HUN2598
HUN2637	HUN2657	IRL2683	IRL2686
IRL2688	IRL2689	IRL2693	IRL2700
IRL2702	IRL2720	IRL2729	IRL2730
ITA2757	ITA2762	ITA2791	ITA2799
ITA2803	ITA2804	ITA2805	ITA2810
ITA2813	ITA2820	ITA2822	ITA2826
ITA2829	ITA2830	ITA2834	ITA2835
ITA2842	ITA2848	ITA2855	ITA2881
ITA2882	ITA2890	ITA2896	ITA2898
ITA2899	ITA2900	ITA2907	ITA2908
ITA2913	LUX2946	LUX2957	LUX2958
LUX2968	LUX2993	LUX2997	MLT3016
NLD3047	NLD3061	NLD3064	NLD3067
NLD3069	NLD3078	NLD3079	NLD3093
NLD3101	NLD3122	NLD3126	NLD3137
NLD3154	NLD3158	NLD3169	NLD3173
NLD3174	NLD3196	NLD3198	NLD3211
NLD3214	NLD3219	NLD3230	NLD3232
NLD3235	NLD3236	NLD3269	NLD3279
NLD3286	NLD3301	NLD3305	NLD3318
NOR3369	NOR3381	NOR3431	NOR3440
NOR3443	NOR3453	NOR3460	NOR3467
POL3482	POL3499	POL3519	POL3520
POL3543	PRT3586	PRT3590	PRT3594
PRT3596	SVK3611	SVK3612	SWE3658
SWE3679	SWE3685	SWE3695	SWE3702
SWE3724	SWE3727	SWE3737	SWE3749
SWE3769	SWE3774	SWE3776	SWE3787
SWE3789	SWE3796	SWE3799	SWE3807
SWE3816	SWE3827	SWE3853	SWE3864
SWE3865	SWE3876	SWE3879	TUR3883
TUR3885	TUR3896	TUR3898	

EXCHANGES, TWINNING, LINKING - ECHANGES, PARRAINAGE, JUMELAGE

AUT0010	BEL0118	BEL0120	BEL0129
BEL0156	BEL0165	BEL0198	BEL0203
BEL0221	BEL0248	BEL0306	BEL0340
BEL0353	BEL0358	BEL0361	BEL0378
BEL0390	CHE0434	CHE0448	CHE0479
CHE0557	CHE0562	CHE0566	CHE0681
CHE0689	CHE0730	CHE0749	CHE0804
CHE0819	CYP0831	DEU0942	DEU0983
DEU0990	DEU0999	DEU1037	DEU1066
DEU1074	DEU1114	DEU1163	DEU1167
DNK1242	DNK1291	DNK1302	DNK1306
DNK1307	DNK1377	ESP1447	ESP1517
FIN1572	FRA1616	FRA1627	FRA1634
FRA1651	FRA1655	FRA1661	FRA1672
FRA1746	FRA1761	FRA1769	FRA1776
FRA1778	FRA1785	FRA1787	FRA1828
FRA1836	FRA1846	FRA1860	FRA1885
FRA1889	FRA1907	FRA1913	FRA1937
FRA1956	FRA1985	FRA2016	FRA2029
FRA2039	FRA2057	FRA2062	FRA2081
FRA2086	FRA2092	FRA2100	FRA2106
FRA2140	FRA2150	FRA2159	FRA2161
FRA2163	GBR2186	GBR2190	GBR2229
GBR2242	GBR2266	GBR2274	GBR2278
GBR2281	GBR2288	GBR2302	GBR2325
GBR2334	GBR2371	GBR2379	GBR2390
GBR2417	GBR2435	GBR2437	GBR2515
GBR2536	GBR2553	GRC2575	GRC2590
HUN2598	HUN2637	IRL2686	IRL2693
IRL2700	IRL2714	IRL2720	IRL2730
ISL2739	ITA2762	ITA2770	ITA2775
ITA2799	ITA2804	ITA2813	ITA2834
ITA2835	ITA2903	NLD3056	NLD3067
NLD3078	NLD3079	NLD3096	NLD3137
NLD3141	NLD3154	NLD3169	NLD3173
NLD3198	NLD3214	NLD3219	NLD3235
NLD3236	NLD3292	NLD3305	POL3482
POL3499	POL3519	PRT3586	SVK3611
SVK3612	SWE3685	SWE3730	SWE3749
SWE3760	SWE3864	SWE3865	SWE3879
TUR3883			

FORMAL EDUCATION - EDUCATION FORMELLE

AUT0065	AUT0085	BEL0148	BEL0156
BEL0189	BEL0211	BEL0249	BEL0270
BEL0306	BEL0323	BEL0341	BEL0343
BEL0353	BEL0359	BEL0361	BEL0368

BEL0378	BEL0390	CHE0422	CHE0434
CHE0439	CHE0479	CHE0495	CHE0510
CHE0562	CHE0566	CHE0586	CHE0628
CHE0655	CHE0681	CHE0682	CHE0689
CHE0730	CHE0749	CHE0772	CHE0804
CHE0805	CHE0814	CHE0819	DEU0928
DEU0933	DEU0983	DEU1132	DEU1167
DNK1218	DNK1227	DNK1275	DNK1339
DNK1377	DNK1405	ESP1427	ESP1455
ESP1472	ESP1486	ESP1508	ESP1510
ESP1529	FRA1627	FRA1628	FRA1649
FRA1661	FRA1664	FRA1672	FRA1699
FRA1731	FRA1769	FRA1785	FRA1787
FRA1794	FRA1827	FRA1849	FRA1856
FRA1889	FRA1946	FRA1956	FRA1966
FRA1992	FRA2005	FRA2016	FRA2018
FRA2039	FRA2062	FRA2090	FRA2103
FRA2106	FRA2131	FRA2150	GBR2175
GBR2181	GBR2238	GBR2242	GBR2265
GBR2266	GBR2269	GBR2278	GBR2281
GBR2315	GBR2333	GBR2337	GBR2341
GBR2345	GBR2349	GBR2371	GBR2379
GBR2408	GBR2415	GBR2417	GBR2423
GBR2424	GBR2428	GBR2436	GBR2452
GBR2467	GBR2468	GBR2471	GBR2474
GBR2475	GBR2511	GBR2553	GRC2567
GRC2575	GRC2590	HUN2598	HUN2607
HUN2657	IRL2686	IRL2688	IRL2689
IRL2691	IRL2697	IRL2702	IRL2720
IRL2726	ISL2740	ITA2761	ITA2762
ITA2782	ITA2803	ITA2810	ITA2813
ITA2832	ITA2842	ITA2848	ITA2868
ITA2896	ITA2898	ITA2900	LUX2982
LUX2986	LUX2995	LUX2997	MLT3016
NLD3056	NLD3067	NLD3078	NLD3154
NLD3199	NLD3214	NLD3219	NLD3232
NLD3254	NLD3269	NLD3305	NLD3352
NOR3465	NOR3467	POL3482	PRT3594
PRT3596	SVK3611	SVK3612	SWE3653
SWE3679	SWE3685	SWE3712	SWE3737
SWE3796	SWE3876	SWE3879	TUR3885

FUND RAISING - COLLECTE DE FONDS

AUT0003	AUT0022	AUT0026	AUT0029
AUT0030	AUT0051	AUT0085	AUT0091
BEL0104	BEL0110	BEL0118	BEL0119
BEL0132	BEL0148	BEL0155	BEL0167
BEL0169	BEL0182	BEL0192	BEL0198
BEL0203	BEL0211	BEL0224	BEL0245
BEL0248	BEL0261	BEL0270	BEL0282
BEL0306	BEL0323	BEL0327	BEL0341
BEL0351	BEL0352	BEL0353	BEL0355
BEL0356	BEL0358	BEL0359	BEL0361
BEL0362	BEL0368	BEL0381	BEL0390
CHE0417	CHE0422	CHE0434	CHE0438
CHE0444	CHE0446	CHE0448	CHE0455
CHE0462	CHE0463	CHE0467	CHE0479
CHE0486	CHE0506	CHE0515	CHE0529
CHE0562	CHE0564	CHE0566	CHE0570
CHE0584	CHE0586	CHE0598	CHE0604
CHE0619	CHE0630	CHE0659	CHE0671
CHE0684	CHE0687	CHE0689	CHE0693
CHE0707	CHE0727	CHE0730	CHE0734
CHE0742	CHE0749	CHE0755	CHE0756
CHE0764	CHE0788	CHE0798	CHE0804
CHE0809	CHE0810	CHE0814	CHE0819
CHE0820	CHE0823	DEU0918	DEU0957
DEU0968	DEU0972	DEU0978	DEU0983
DEU0989	DEU0991	DEU0999	DEU1006
DEU1027	DEU1044	DEU1066	DEU1086
DEU1114	DEU1138	DEU1143	DEU1149
DEU1151	DEU1167	DEU1178	DEU1187
DEU1200	DNK1216	DNK1222	DNK1227
DNK1232	DNK1242	DNK1245	DNK1251
DNK1306	DNK1316	DNK1377	DNK1392
DNK1405	ESP1409	ESP1435	ESP1442
ESP1447	ESP1450	ESP1455	ESP1457
ESP1470	ESP1486	ESP1505	ESP1506
ESP1507	ESP1510	ESP1517	ESP1529
FIN1544	FIN1549	FIN1572	FIN1583
FIN1591	FIN1594	FIN1599	FRA1612
FRA1624	FRA1632	FRA1636	FRA1644
FRA1645	FRA1649	FRA1661	FRA1663
FRA1664	FRA1672	FRA1679	FRA1690
FRA1703	FRA1704	FRA1737	FRA1739
FRA1741	FRA1760	FRA1761	FRA1778
FRA1785	FRA1787	FRA1789	FRA1828
FRA1843	FRA1849	FRA1852	FRA1861

Voir : *Comment utiliser le répertoire*, page 11.

FRA1866	FRA1889	FRA1913	FRA1930
FRA1939	FRA1946	FRA1966	FRA1978
FRA1980	FRA1990	FRA1991	FRA2005
FRA2016	FRA2037	FRA2041	FRA2080
FRA2081	FRA2086	FRA2092	FRA2116
FRA2117	FRA2119	FRA2131	FRA2138
FRA2159	FRA2163	GBR2175	GBR2176
GBR2180	GBR2186	GBR2190	GBR2197
GBR2201	GBR2213	GBR2222	GBR2226
GBR2228	GBR2229	GBR2238	GBR2240
GBR2242	GBR2244	GBR2248	GBR2259
GBR2274	GBR2277	GBR2278	GBR2292
GBR2297	GBR2298	GBR2302	GBR2312
GBR2318	GBR2321	GBR2324	GBR2325
GBR2333	GBR2334	GBR2337	GBR2348
GBR2349	GBR2350	GBR2358	GBR2371
GBR2372	GBR2373	GBR2390	GBR2413
GBR2419	GBR2423	GBR2428	GBR2436
GBR2445	GBR2456	GBR2474	GBR2475
GBR2480	GBR2483	GBR2500	GBR2503
GBR2508	GBR2511	GBR2515	GBR2524
GBR2525	GBR2532	GBR2535	GBR2537
GBR2550	GBR2552	GBR2561	GRC2567
GRC2586	GRC2590	HUN2598	HUN2657
IRL2683	IRL2688	IRL2689	IRL2691
IRL2697	IRL2700	IRL2709	IRL2714
IRL2725	IRL2726	IRL2730	IRL2732
IRL2733	ISL2741	ITA2762	ITA2770
ITA2773	ITA2775	ITA2782	ITA2791
ITA2792	ITA2799	ITA2803	ITA2804
ITA2809	ITA2810	ITA2812	ITA2813
ITA2820	ITA2826	ITA2829	ITA2832
ITA2834	ITA2835	ITA2837	ITA2848
ITA2852	ITA2855	ITA2873	ITA2879
ITA2880	ITA2881	ITA2882	ITA2885
ITA2888	ITA2890	ITA2894	ITA2899
ITA2900	ITA2901	ITA2903	ITA2907
ITA2912	ITA2913	ITA2921	LUX2937
LUX2946	LUX2955	LUX2958	LUX2959
LUX2968	LUX2969	LUX2972	LUX2982
LUX2986	LUX2993	LUX2995	LUX3006
MLT3025	NLD3056	NLD3067	NLD3078
NLD3093	NLD3126	NLD3137	NLD3145
NLD3146	NLD3149	NLD3154	NLD3159
NLD3181	NLD3198	NLD3199	NLD3214
NLD3219	NLD3231	NLD3232	NLD3235
NLD3253	NLD3254	NLD3256	NLD3263
NLD3269	NLD3288	NLD3292	NLD3295
NLD3300	NLD3301	NLD3302	NLD3305
NLD3323	NLD3361	NOR3369	NOR3371
NOR3372	NOR3381	NOR3387	NOR3404
NOR3410	NOR3412	NOR3414	NOR3453
NOR3460	NOR3467	NOR3475	POL3482
POL3543	PRT3594	PRT3605	SVK3611
SWE3648	SWE3653	SWE3655	SWE3665
SWE3674	SWE3679	SWE3685	SWE3702
SWE3724	SWE3730	SWE3737	SWE3749
SWE3763	SWE3769	SWE3776	SWE3787
SWE3796	SWE3807	SWE3811	SWE3813
SWE3826	SWE3853	SWE3854	SWE3857
SWE3859	SWE3864	SWE3876	TUR3896

INFORMATION AND DOCUMENTATION SERVICES, DATA BASES - SERVICES D'INFORMATION ET DE DOCUMENTATION, BASES DE DONNEES

AUT0010	AUT0011	AUT0020	AUT0026
AUT0035	AUT0045	AUT0060	AUT0079
AUT0085	BEL0118	BEL0141	BEL0149
BEL0155	BEL0156	BEL0164	BEL0165
BEL0167	BEL0192	BEL0203	BEL0211
BEL0214	BEL0226	BEL0237	BEL0249
BEL0267	BEL0306	BEL0353	BEL0356
BEL0358	BEL0359	BEL0361	BEL0365
BEL0390	BEL0393	BEL0396	CHE0434
CHE0501	CHE0534	CHE0562	CHE0566
CHE0568	CHE0609	CHE0624	CHE0638
CHE0689	CHE0727	CHE0742	CHE0756
CHE0762	CHE0763	CHE0810	CHE0819
CYP0831	DEU0944	DEU0968	DEU0975
DEU0977	DEU0989	DEU0990	DEU0999
DEU1002	DEU1020	DEU1074	DEU1086
DEU1090	DEU1091	DEU1097	DEU1114
DEU1138	DEU1143	DEU1149	DEU1163
DEU1167	DEU1184	DEU1192	DNK1251
DNK1292	DNK1306	DNK1339	DNK1389
DNK1398	ESP1407	ESP1413	ESP1430
ESP1431	ESP1434	ESP1438	ESP1441
ESP1447	ESP1455	ESP1457	ESP1470

ESP1479	ESP1482	ESP1486	ESP1506
ESP1507	ESP1509	ESP1522	ESP1529
FIN1548	FIN1578	FIN1591	FIN1599
FRA1617	FRA1629	FRA1631	FRA1636
FRA1698	FRA1701	FRA1703	FRA1709
FRA1719	FRA1727	FRA1737	FRA1756
FRA1761	FRA1785	FRA1787	FRA1794
FRA1797	FRA1800	FRA1808	FRA1810
FRA1811	FRA1815	FRA1818	FRA1827
FRA1828	FRA1832	FRA1839	FRA1841
FRA1846	FRA1860	FRA1889	FRA1907
FRA1946	FRA1947	FRA1956	FRA1985
FRA1988	FRA1990	FRA1991	FRA2002
FRA2004	FRA2015	FRA2018	FRA2039
FRA2062	FRA2069	FRA2076	FRA2093
FRA2103	FRA2104	FRA2106	FRA2109
FRA2122	FRA2131	FRA2159	FRA2163
GBR2190	GBR2197	GBR2226	GBR2229
GBR2238	GBR2241	GBR2242	GBR2265
GBR2278	GBR2298	GBR2333	GBR2339
GBR2371	GBR2379	GBR2387	GBR2408
GBR2415	GBR2422	GBR2434	GBR2435
GBR2437	GBR2438	GBR2445	GBR2452
GBR2456	GBR2480	GBR2483	GBR2495
GBR2515	GBR2515	GBR2537	GBR2545
GRC2567	GRC2571	GRC2575	HUN2598
HUN2620	HUN2637	HUN2657	IRL2686
IRL2697	IRL2698	IRL2700	IRL2720
IRL2730	ITA2744	ITA2761	ITA2762
ITA2773	ITA2786	ITA2798	ITA2799
ITA2801	ITA2805	ITA2808	ITA2809
ITA2810	ITA2813	ITA2814	ITA2820
ITA2822	ITA2829	ITA2830	ITA2834
ITA2840	ITA2852	ITA2855	ITA2860
ITA2873	ITA2880	ITA2900	ITA2901
ITA2907	ITA2908	ITA2913	LUX2937
LUX2962	NLD3047	NLD3051	NLD3056
NLD3058	NLD3067	NLD3077	NLD3078
NLD3084	NLD3093	NLD3095	NLD3096
NLD3101	NLD3110	NLD3135	NLD3136
NLD3137	NLD3139	NLD3154	NLD3158
NLD3167	NLD3173	NLD3181	NLD3196
NLD3198	NLD3211	NLD3214	NLD3232
NLD3254	NLD3279	NLD3295	NLD3301
NLD3302	NLD3305	NLD3318	NLD3355
NLD3361	NOR3372	NOR3400	NOR3467
POL3482	POL3499	POL3519	POL3543
PRT3600	SVK3611	SWE3648	SWE3658
SWE3693	SWE3702	SWE3737	SWE3744
SWE3760	SWE3769	SWE3774	SWE3789
SWE3807	SWE3816	SWE3826	SWE3827
SWE3853	SWE3859	SWE3859	SWE3864
SWE3865	SWE3876	TUR3882	TUR3883
TUR3896	TUR3898		

INFORMATION CAMPAIGNS, EXHIBITIONS - CAMPAGNES D'INFORMATION, EXPOSITIONS

AUT0020	AUT0026	AUT0068	AUT0085
AUT0091	BEL0101	BEL0102	BEL0111
BEL0119	BEL0139	BEL0148	BEL0155
BEL0165	BEL0167	BEL0189	BEL0192
BEL0198	BEL0203	BEL0211	BEL0226
BEL0248	BEL0261	BEL0267	BEL0282
BEL0306	BEL0323	BEL0331	BEL0351
BEL0352	BEL0353	BEL0358	BEL0359
BEL0361	BEL0365	BEL0381	BEL0390
BEL0392	BEL0396	BEL0397	CHE0427
CHE0434	CHE0446	CHE0455	CHE0461
CHE0467	CHE0479	CHE0541	CHE0557
CHE0560	CHE0562	CHE0566	CHE0568
CHE0584	CHE0598	CHE0604	CHE0659
CHE0669	CHE0689	CHE0756	CHE0765
CHE0804	CHE0807	CHE0819	CYP0831
CZE0882	DEU0921	DEU0940	DEU0955
DEU0975	DEU0977	DEU0983	DEU0999
DEU1006	DEU1037	DEU1066	DEU1114
DEU1132	DEU1143	DEU1149	DEU1151
DEU1163	DEU1167	DEU1200	DNK1232
DNK1260	DNK1272	DNK1285	DNK1292
DNK1306	DNK1307	DNK1339	DNK1389
DNK1398	DNK1403	DNK1405	ESP1407
ESP1409	ESP1438	ESP1439	ESP1457
ESP1485	ESP1486	ESP1506	ESP1507
ESP1508	ESP1510	ESP1517	ESP1529
FIN1544	FIN1553	FIN1572	FRA1624
FRA1632	FRA1633	FRA1634	FRA1653
FRA1663	FRA1690	FRA1703	FRA1709
FRA1727	FRA1739	FRA1741	FRA1785

FRA1787	FRA1797	FRA1799	FRA1841
FRA1843	FRA1849	FRA1861	FRA1876
FRA1885	FRA1889	FRA1939	FRA1947
FRA1956	FRA1990	FRA1992	FRA2002
FRA2005	FRA2039	FRA2062	FRA2100
FRA2106	FRA2116	FRA2122	FRA2131
FRA2138	FRA2150	FRA2159	FRA2163
GBR2175	GBR2181	GBR2186	GBR2229
GBR2238	GBR2242	GBR2248	GBR2259
GBR2265	GBR2269	GBR2277	GBR2278
GBR2279	GBR2288	GBR2297	GBR2312
GBR2325	GBR2339	GBR2350	GBR2358
GBR2371	GBR2387	GBR2408	GBR2417
GBR2419	GBR2434	GBR2452	GBR2474
GBR2483	GBR2495	GBR2511	GBR2527
GBR2535	GBR2536	GBR2545	GBR2552
GBR2553	GBR2561	GRC2567	GRC2575
IRL2683	IRL2686	IRL2690	IRL2693
IRL2697	IRL2700	IRL2707	IRL2720
IRL2730	ITA2761	ITA2762	ITA2770
ITA2773	ITA2777	ITA2799	ITA2803
ITA2804	ITA2810	ITA2813	ITA2815
ITA2820	ITA2826	ITA2834	ITA2855
ITA2898	ITA2901	LUX2937	LUX2954
LUX2976	LUX2986	LUX2993	LUX2995
LUX3006	MLT3025	NLD3056	NLD3067
NLD3078	NLD3079	NLD3093	NLD3098
NLD3137	NLD3146	NLD3158	NLD3169
NLD3173	NLD3181	NLD3190	NLD3196
NLD3198	NLD3211	NLD3219	NLD3232
NLD3236	NLD3263	NLD3303	NLD3320
NLD3323	NLD3361	NLD3365	NOR3371
NOR3372	NOR3387	NOR3440	NOR3443
POL3482	POL3499	POL3519	PRT3594
PRT3596	SVK3611	SVK3612	SWE3650
SWE3702	SWE3724	SWE3730	SWE3737
SWE3742	SWE3749	SWE3760	SWE3763
SWE3769	SWE3774	SWE3789	SWE3796
SWE3814	SWE3816	SWE3864	SWE3865
SWE3879	TUR3883	TUR3885	

LOBBYING, ADVOCACY - LOBBYING, PLAIDOYER

AUT0010	AUT0086	BEL0099	BEL0118
BEL0119	BEL0131	BEL0165	BEL0167
BEL0186	BEL0189	BEL0198	BEL0203
BEL0211	BEL0214	BEL0224	BEL0248
BEL0282	BEL0306	BEL0333	BEL0351
BEL0353	BEL0356	BEL0361	BEL0397
CHE0434	CHE0467	CHE0534	CHE0560
CHE0562	CHE0566	CHE0568	CHE0570
CHE0604	CHE0642	CHE0687	CHE0689
CHE0749	CHE0765	CHE0810	CHE0814
CHE0819	CHE0820	CYP0831	DEU0942
DEU0975	DEU0983	DEU0999	DEU1006
DEU1032	DEU1037	DEU1066	DEU1074
DEU1114	DEU1143	DEU1149	DEU1151
DEU1178	DEU1178	DEU1200	DNK1238
DNK1242	DNK1291	DNK1292	DNK1306
DNK1312	DNK1339	DNK1399	DNK1403
ESP1410	ESP1438	ESP1452	ESP1457
FIN1572	FIN1584	FRA1624	FRA1633
FRA1634	FRA1636	FRA1661	FRA1734
FRA1740	FRA1756	FRA1785	FRA1794
FRA1797	FRA1799	FRA1818	FRA1841
FRA1843	FRA1876	FRA1889	FRA1946
FRA1956	FRA2002	FRA2004	FRA2062
FRA2093	FRA2106	FRA2110	FRA2131
FRA2142	FRA2159	FRA2163	GBR2174
GBR2181	GBR2186	GBR2202	GBR2228
GBR2229	GBR2238	GBR2242	GBR2269
GBR2303	GBR2337	GBR2364	GBR2371
GBR2390	GBR2392	GBR2423	GBR2434
GBR2483	GBR2495	GBR2498	GBR2511
GBR2527	GBR2537	GBR2545	GBR2553
GBR2561	GBR2586	HUN2598	HUN2637
IRL2689	IRL2690	IRL2691	IRL2700
IRL2707	IRL2714	IRL2726	ITA2762
ITA2775	ITA2799	ITA2810	ITA2813
ITA2820	ITA2830	ITA2855	ITA2898
ITA2913	LUX2937	LUX2957	LUX2958
LUX2997	MLT3025	NLD3064	NLD3067
NLD3078	NLD3079	NLD3096	NLD3122
NLD3137	NLD3164	NLD3167	NLD3198
NLD3199	NLD3211	NLD3214	NLD3219
NLD3232	NLD3236	NLD3254	NLD3301
NLD3303	NLD3305	NOR3369	NOR3372
NOR3467	NOR3475	POL3499	POL3543
PRT3594	SWE3655	SWE3724	SWE3742

See: *How to Use the Directory*, page 11.

SWE3749	SWE3799	SWE3811	SWE3853
SWE3864	SWE3876	TUR3882	TUR3883
TUR3885	TUR3896		

NETWORKING, ELECTRONIC TELECOMMUNICATIONS - RESEAUX, TELECOMMUNICATIONS ELECTRONIQUES

AUT0020	BEL0165	BEL0198	BEL0224
BEL0361	CHE0434	CHE0562	CHE0568
CHE0586	CHE0642	CHE0689	CHE0819
DEU0955	DEU0975	DEU0990	DEU1002
DEU1149	DEU1167	DNK1307	DNK1359
ESP1434	ESP1522	FIN1572	FIN1591
FRA1629	FRA1889	FRA1985	FRA2106
FRA2109	GBR2174	GBR2181	GBR2190
GBR2213	GBR2226	GBR2242	GBR2265
GBR2285	GBR2313	GBR2337	GBR2337
GBR2348	GBR2364	GBR2371	GBR2387
GBR2422	GBR2434	GBR2435	GBR2438
GBR2495	GBR2498	GBR2545	GBR2561
HUN2620	HUN2624	HUN2637	HUN2657
ITA2773	ITA2799	ITA2822	ITA2860
NLD3077	NLD3093	NLD3093	NLD3101
NLD3136	NLD3137	NLD3154	NLD3173
NLD3181	NLD3211	NLD3219	NLD3236
NLD3279	NLD3318	NOR3467	POL3499
POL3508	SVK3611	SWE3702	SWE3724
SWE3787	SWE3789	SWE3864	TUR3883

OTHER - AUTRE

CHE0434	CHE0439	FRA1631	FRA1700
FRA1966	FRA2012	GBR2190	GBR2240
GBR2358	GBR2371	GBR2387	GBR2510
NLD3069	NLD3096	NLD3117	NLD3137
NLD3183	POL3543		

PUBLISHING, AUDIOVISUAL MATERIALS, EDUCATIONAL MATERIALS - EDITION, DOCUMENTS AUDIOVISUELS, DOCUMENTS EDUCATIFS

AUT0010	AUT0020	AUT0026	AUT0068
BEL0101	BEL0120	BEL0139	BEL0148
BEL0155	BEL0164	BEL0165	BEL0167
BEL0189	BEL0203	BEL0214	BEL0226
BEL0241	BEL0245	BEL0249	BEL0261
BEL0282	BEL0306	BEL0323	BEL0331
BEL0353	BEL0356	BEL0359	BEL0361
BEL0365	BEL0368	BEL0378	BEL0381
BEL0390	BEL0392	BEL0393	BEL0396
CHE0427	CHE0434	CHE0439	CHE0495
CHE0499	CHE0501	CHE0506	CHE0517
CHE0560	CHE0562	CHE0566	CHE0568
CHE0609	CHE0638	CHE0689	CHE0693
CHE0727	CHE0762	CHE0763	CHE0763
CHE0767	CHE0804	CHE0810	CHE0817
CHE0819	CYP0831	DEU0918	DEU0942
DEU0944	DEU0968	DEU0972	DEU0975
DEU0977	DEU0989	DEU0999	DEU1020
DEU1031	DEU1037	DEU1066	DEU1076
DEU1086	DEU1097	DEU1143	DEU1149
DEU1151	DEU1167	DEU1180	DEU1187
DEU1198	DEU1200	DNK1216	DNK1232
DNK1238	DNK1251	DNK1255	DNK1255
DNK1260	DNK1292	DNK1312	DNK1316
DNK1339	DNK1351	DNK1389	ESP1407
ESP1410	ESP1434	ESP1435	ESP1435
ESP1438	ESP1457	ESP1461	ESP1474
ESP1485	ESP1506	ESP1507	ESP1510
ESP1517	ESP1522	ESP1529	FIN1544
FIN1545	FIN1548	FIN1572	FRA1612
FRA1624	FRA1627	FRA1629	FRA1631
FRA1642	FRA1644	FRA1661	FRA1668
FRA1703	FRA1709	FRA1713	FRA1719
FRA1727	FRA1756	FRA1769	FRA1778
FRA1785	FRA1787	FRA1794	FRA1795
FRA1799	FRA1813	FRA1818	FRA1827
FRA1832	FRA1836	FRA1843	FRA1849
FRA1852	FRA1860	FRA1889	FRA1907
FRA1913	FRA1920	FRA1956	FRA1986
FRA1990	FRA1991	FRA1992	FRA2002
FRA2004	FRA2018	FRA2039	FRA2069
FRA2072	FRA2076	FRA2086	FRA2093
FRA2103	FRA2104	FRA2106	FRA2108
FRA2109	FRA2116	FRA2122	FRA2131
FRA2138	FRA2159	FRA2161	GBR2174
GBR2175	GBR2181	GBR2185	GBR2186
GBR2190	GBR2228	GBR2229	GBR2238
GBR2241	GBR2248	GBR2265	GBR2266

GBR2271	GBR2278	GBR2281	GBR2297
GBR2303	GBR2312	GBR2318	GBR2325
GBR2334	GBR2337	GBR2341	GBR2345
GBR2358	GBR2371	GBR2387	GBR2392
GBR2408	GBR2415	GBR2417	GBR2419
GBR2422	GBR2423	GBR2434	GBR2436
GBR2437	GBR2456	GBR2456	GBR2467
GBR2474	GBR2475	GBR2480	GBR2483
GBR2485	GBR2499	GBR2500	GBR2501
GBR2503	GBR2511	GBR2515	GBR2525
GBR2527	GBR2535	GBR2545	GBR2552
GBR2554	GBR2561	GRC2567	HUN2598
HUN2637	IRL2683	IRL2691	IRL2697
IRL2698	IRL2720	IRL2725	IRL2730
IRL2733	ITA2756	ITA2757	ITA2762
ITA2798	ITA2799	ITA2803	ITA2805
ITA2809	ITA2810	ITA2812	ITA2813
ITA2820	ITA2822	ITA2830	ITA2834
ITA2835	ITA2837	ITA2852	ITA2855
ITA2860	ITA2873	ITA2881	ITA2882
ITA2901	ITA2907	ITA2908	ITA2913
LUX2986	LUX3006	MLT3016	NLD3051
NLD3056	NLD3061	NLD3067	NLD3077
NLD3078	NLD3098	NLD3136	NLD3145
NLD3154	NLD3164	NLD3169	NLD3173
NLD3198	NLD3211	NLD3214	NLD3216
NLD3230	NLD3257	NLD3279	NLD3301
NLD3302	NLD3305	NLD3318	NLD3320
NLD3352	NLD3354	NOR3404	NOR3440
NOR3443	NOR3467	POL3482	POL3499
POL3519	POL3543	PRT3600	SVK3611
SWE3650	SWE3724	SWE3737	SWE3749
SWE3760	SWE3769	SWE3777	SWE3789
SWE3811	SWE3816	SWE3853	SWE3854
SWE3864	SWE3865	SWE3876	SWE3879
TUR3883	TUR3885	TUR3896	TUR3898

URBAN DEVELOPMENT, HABITAT - DEVELOPPEMENT URBAIN, HABITAT

BROADCASTING, CULTURAL EVENTS - RADIODIFFUSION, MANIFESTATIONS CULTURELLES

BEL0340	BEL0361	BEL0390	CHE0434
CHE0534	CHE0568	CHE0598	CHE0604
CHE0624	CHE0689	CHE0819	DEU1022
DNK1283	ESP1406	ESP1439	ESP1455
ESP1457	ESP1486	ESP1507	FIN1545
FRA1676	FRA1778	FRA1785	FRA1889
FRA1904	FRA1956	FRA1988	FRA1991
FRA2002	FRA2102	FRA2159	GBR2229
GBR2238	GBR2248	GBR2345	GBR2371
GBR2383	GBR2383	GBR2511	GBR2545
IRL2686	ITA2798	ITA2801	LUX2954
LUX2956	LUX2976	LUX2982	LUX3006
MLT3016	NLD3098	NLD3169	NLD3173
NLD3181	NLD3230	NLD3253	POL3509
POL3543	SVK3611	SWE3760	TUR3883

CONFERENCES, SEMINARS, WORKSHOPS, TRAINING ACTIVITIES - CONFERENCES, SEMINAIRES, ATELIERS, ACTIVITES DE FORMATION

AUT0002	AUT0045	AUT0074	AUT0090
BEL0096	BEL0148	BEL0152	BEL0188
BEL0219	BEL0248	BEL0254	BEL0282
BEL0353	BEL0359	BEL0361	BEL0378
CHE0417	CHE0422	CHE0434	CHE0439
CHE0461	CHE0462	CHE0562	CHE0565
CHE0568	CHE0628	CHE0629	CHE0629
CHE0642	CHE0655	CHE0669	CHE0682
CHE0684	CHE0687	CHE0689	CHE0727
CHE0730	CHE0766	CHE0766	CHE0819
CHE0823	CYP0831	CYP0832	DEU0944
DEU0968	DEU0983	DEU0989	DEU0990
DEU1004	DEU1065	DEU1066	DEU1090
DEU1097	DEU1100	DEU1106	DEU1114
DEU1149	DEU1151	DEU1180	DNK1226
DNK1283	DNK1312	DNK1339	DNK1353
DNK1361	DNK1375	DNK1398	ESP1410
ESP1437	ESP1439	ESP1450	ESP1455
ESP1457	ESP1482	ESP1485	ESP1486
ESP1506	ESP1517	ESP1525	FIN1545
FIN1553	FIN1572	FRA1610	FRA1627
FRA1661	FRA1701	FRA1727	FRA1731
FRA1756	FRA1778	FRA1785	FRA1797

FRA1799	FRA1815	FRA1818	FRA1832
FRA1833	FRA1841	FRA1846	FRA1850
FRA1860	FRA1885	FRA1889	FRA1897
FRA1904	FRA1917	FRA1921	FRA1946
FRA1947	FRA1956	FRA1964	FRA1980
FRA1988	FRA2004	FRA2005	FRA2014
FRA2039	FRA2044	FRA2069	FRA2086
FRA2102	FRA2122	FRA2147	FRA2159
FRA2162	GBR2175	GBR2176	GBR2178
GBR2181	GBR2185	GBR2214	GBR2226
GBR2229	GBR2238	GBR2241	GBR2242
GBR2264	GBR2265	GBR2269	GBR2274
GBR2279	GBR2284	GBR2303	GBR2325
GBR2350	GBR2355	GBR2371	GBR2383
GBR2387	GBR2408	GBR2415	GBR2423
GBR2436	GBR2452	GBR2460	GBR2475
GBR2511	GBR2527	GBR2535	GBR2545
GBR2553	GBR2561	HUN2637	IRL2679
IRL2686	IRL2688	IRL2693	IRL2720
ISL2736	ITA2760	ITA2782	ITA2801
ITA2810	ITA2826	ITA2829	ITA2899
ITA2908	ITA2920	LUX2946	LUX2958
MLT3016	MLT3018	NLD3047	NLD3067
NLD3072	NLD3078	NLD3083	NLD3138
NLD3154	NLD3155	NLD3160	NLD3169
NLD3174	NLD3199	NLD3230	NLD3232
NLD3286	NLD3301	NLD3305	NLD3338
NOR3467	NOR3473	POL3499	POL3508
POL3509	POL3519	POL3520	POL3543
PRT3550	PRT3586	PRT3594	SVK3611
SVK3612	SWE3679	SWE3702	SWE3744
SWE3749	SWE3787	SWE3789	SWE3807
SWE3816	SWE3853	SWE3864	SWE3865
SWE3876	SWE3879	TUR3885	TUR3898

EXCHANGES, TWINNING, LINKING - ECHANGES, PARRAINAGE, JUMELAGE

BEL0129	BEL0198	BEL0219	BEL0254
BEL0340	BEL0353	BEL0361	BEL0378
BEL0390	CHE0434	CHE0448	CHE0562
CHE0565	CHE0689	CHE0730	CHE0819
CYP0831	DEU0983	DEU0990	DEU1066
DEU1097	DEU1106	DEU1114	ESP1406
ESP1457	ESP1517	ESP1525	FRA1746
FRA1769	FRA1778	FRA1785	FRA1787
FRA1836	FRA1846	FRA1852	FRA1860
FRA1889	FRA1904	FRA1946	FRA1956
FRA1964	FRA1980	FRA2014	FRA2039
FRA2044	FRA2057	FRA2086	FRA2102
FRA2131	FRA2140	FRA2150	FRA2159
GBR2242	GBR2266	GBR2284	GBR2325
GBR2355	GBR2371	GBR2379	GBR2383
GBR2390	GBR2515	GBR2536	GBR2553
HUN2637	IRL2686	ITA2762	ITA2770
ITA2782	ITA2801	ITA2838	NLD3056
NLD3067	NLD3071	NLD3072	NLD3073
NLD3078	NLD3098	NLD3138	NLD3153
NLD3160	NLD3169	NLD3338	POL3499
POL3508	POL3509	POL3519	POL3543
PRT3602	PRT3603	SVK3611	SVK3612
SWE3744	SWE3749	SWE3760	SWE3771
SWE3864	SWE3865	SWE3879	

FORMAL EDUCATION - EDUCATION FORMELLE

AUT0065	BEL0148	BEL0353	BEL0359
BEL0361	BEL0378	BEL0390	CHE0434
CHE0460	CHE0479	CHE0562	CHE0586
CHE0628	CHE0682	CHE0689	CHE0730
CHE0819	CYP0833	CZE0882	DEU0983
DEU1132	DNK1226	DNK1339	ESP1406
ESP1455	ESP1486	ESP1524	FRA1627
FRA1731	FRA1738	FRA1769	FRA1785
FRA1787	FRA1827	FRA1889	FRA1904
FRA1946	FRA1956	FRA1992	FRA2005
FRA2039	FRA2044	FRA2102	FRA2103
FRA2150	FRA2159	GBR2181	GBR2238
GBR2242	GBR2265	GBR2266	GBR2269
GBR2273	GBR2315	GBR2345	GBR2350
GBR2371	GBR2379	GBR2383	GBR2408
GBR2415	GBR2424	GBR2436	GBR2452
GBR2467	GBR2468	GBR2511	GBR2553
HUN2626	HUN2678	IRL2686	IRL2691
IRL2697	IRL2720	IRL2740	ITA2773
ITA2782	ITA2801	ITA2810	ITA2835
LUX2982	MLT3016	NLD3056	NLD3067
NLD3072	NLD3078	NLD3083	NLD3138
NLD3154	NLD3212	NLD3232	NLD3305

NOR3467	NOR3473	POL3509	PRT3594
SVK3611	SVK3612	SWE3679	SWE3823
SWE3876	SWE3879	TUR3885	

FUND RAISING - COLLECTE DE FONDS

AUT0022	AUT0026	AUT0086	AUT0091
BEL0096	BEL0104	BEL0132	BEL0148
BEL0155	BEL0198	BEL0201	BEL0245
BEL0248	BEL0254	BEL0282	BEL0306
BEL0327	BEL0351	BEL0353	BEL0359
BEL0361	BEL0390	CHE0417	CHE0434
CHE0446	CHE0462	CHE0506	CHE0529
CHE0584	CHE0586	CHE0598	CHE0604
CHE0630	CHE0684	CHE0687	CHE0689
CHE0693	CHE0727	CHE0730	CHE0755
CHE0756	CHE0785	CHE0819	CHE0823
DEU0931	DEU0957	DEU0968	DEU0983
DEU0989	DEU1022	DEU1044	DEU1065
DEU1066	DEU1114	DEU1132	DEU1138
DEU1149	DEU1187	DEU1202	DNK1216
DNK1227	DNK1251	DNK1283	DNK1316
ESP1413	ESP1442	ESP1455	ESP1470
ESP1486	ESP1506	ESP1517	FIN1544
FIN1591	FRA1610	FRA1642	FRA1661
FRA1738	FRA1778	FRA1785	FRA1787
FRA1843	FRA1850	FRA1852	FRA1889
FRA1930	FRA1939	FRA1946	FRA1978
FRA1980	FRA1991	FRA2016	FRA2086
FRA2116	FRA2131	FRA2159	GBR2175
GBR2176	GBR2197	GBR2201	GBR2226
GBR2228	GBR2229	GBR2238	GBR2242
GBR2248	GBR2259	GBR2264	GBR2282
GBR2324	GBR2325	GBR2371	GBR2375
GBR2383	GBR2390	GBR2413	GBR2419
GBR2436	GBR2445	GBR2475	GBR2500
GBR2509	GBR2511	GBR2525	GBR2535
GBR2537	GBR2552	HUN2678	IRL2688
IRL2691	IRL2697	IRL2732	IRL2733
ISL2740	ITA2773	ITA2806	ITA2810
ITA2814	ITA2826	ITA2829	ITA2852
ITA2873	ITA2879	ITA2894	ITA2899
ITA2900	ITA2907	ITA2920	LUX2946
LUX2955	LUX2958	LUX2969	LUX2982
LUX2995	LUX3006	NLD3056	NLD3062
NLD3067	NLD3072	NLD3078	NLD3137
NLD3154	NLD3159	NLD3181	NLD3231
NLD3231	NLD3232	NLD3253	NLD3255
NLD3256	NLD3263	NLD3297	NLD3301
NLD3323	NLD3361	NOR3410	NOR3412
NOR3467	POL3509	POL3543	PRT3594
SVK3611	SWE3648	SWE3679	SWE3702
SWE3744	SWE3793	SWE3787	SWE3796
SWE3819	SWE3834	SWE3853	SWE3854
SWE3857	SWE3859	SWE3864	

INFORMATION AND DOCUMENTATION SERVICES, DATA BASES - SERVICES D'INFORMATION ET DE DOCUMENTATION, BASES DE DONNEES

AUT0020	AUT0026	AUT0045	AUT0060
AUT0074	AUT0079	BEL0141	BEL0149
BEL0155	BEL0164	BEL0219	BEL0237
BEL0254	BEL0267	BEL0335	BEL0359
BEL0361	BEL0365	BEL0390	BEL0393
CHE0406	CHE0434	CHE0501	CHE0506
CHE0534	CHE0562	CHE0565	CHE0568
CHE0624	CHE0638	CHE0687	CHE0689
CHE0727	CHE0742	CHE0756	CHE0763
CHE0795	CHE0819	CYP0831	CZE0915
DEU0944	DEU0968	DEU0989	DEU0990
DEU1002	DEU1004	DEU1020	DEU1076
DEU1086	DEU1090	DEU1091	DEU1097
DEU1114	DEU1138	DEU1184	DEU1192
DNK1226	DNK1251	DNK1283	DNK1339
DNK1375	DNK1398	ESP1407	ESP1430
ESP1431	ESP1450	ESP1441	ESP1450
ESP1455	ESP1457	ESP1470	ESP1486
ESP1506	ESP1522	ESP1525	FIN1548
FIN1578	FIN1591	FIN1592	FRA1610
FRA1617	FRA1701	FRA1727	FRA1737
FRA1785	FRA1787	FRA1797	FRA1810
FRA1815	FRA1818	FRA1827	FRA1832
FRA1833	FRA1839	FRA1841	FRA1846
FRA1860	FRA1889	FRA1946	FRA1947
FRA1988	FRA1991	FRA2004	FRA2004
FRA2014	FRA2018	FRA2039	FRA2069
FRA2076	FRA2103	FRA2104	FRA2122
FRA2131	FRA2159	GBR2226	GBR2238

GBR2241	GBR2242	GBR2265	GBR2284
GBR2325	GBR2355	GBR2371	GBR2379
GBR2383	GBR2387	GBR2408	GBR2413
GBR2415	GBR2434	GBR2435	GBR2438
GBR2445	GBR2452	GBR2498	GBR2511
GBR2537	GBR2545	HUN2620	HUN2624
HUN2626	HUN2637	IRL2686	IRL2698
IRL2705	IRL2720	IRL2730	ISL2736
ITA2744	ITA2762	ITA2773	ITA2782
ITA2798	ITA2801	ITA2805	ITA2808
ITA2810	ITA2834	ITA2860	ITA2873
ITA2895	ITA2900	ITA2907	ITA2908
LUX2937	LUX2962	MLT3018	NLD3047
NLD3051	NLD3056	NLD3058	NLD3067
NLD3072	NLD3077	NLD3078	NLD3083
NLD3122	NLD3135	NLD3137	NLD3138
NLD3139	NLD3154	NLD3165	NLD3181
NLD3232	NLD3255	NLD3301	NLD3305
NLD3338	NLD3355	NLD3361	NOR3467
POL3499	POL3509	POL3519	SVK3611
SWE3648	SWE3658	SWE3693	SWE3744
SWE3760	SWE3789	SWE3807	SWE3816
SWE3853	SWE3859	SWE3864	SWE3865
SWE3876	TUR3883	TUR3898	

INFORMATION CAMPAIGNS, EXHIBITIONS - CAMPAGNES D'INFORMATION, EXPOSITIONS

AUT0020	AUT0091	BEL0096	BEL0139
BEL0148	BEL0189	BEL0198	BEL0219
BEL0254	BEL0267	BEL0282	BEL0340
BEL0353	BEL0359	BEL0361	BEL0365
BEL0390	CHE0434	CHE0446	CHE0461
CHE0479	CHE0541	CHE0562	CHE0568
CHE0584	CHE0598	CHE0604	CHE0669
CHE0684	CHE0689	CHE0756	CHE0765
CHE0807	CHE0819	CYP0831	DEU0917
DEU0955	DEU0983	DEU1022	DEU1066
DEU1114	DEU1132	DEU1151	DEU1202
DNK1251	DNK1283	DNK1375	DNK1398
ESP1410	ESP1439	ESP1457	ESP1485
ESP1486	ESP1506	ESP1507	ESP1517
ESP1524	FIN1553	FRA1610	FRA1727
FRA1738	FRA1785	FRA1787	FRA1797
FRA1799	FRA1818	FRA1841	FRA1843
FRA1850	FRA1852	FRA1885	FRA1889
FRA1904	FRA1946	FRA1946	FRA1947
FRA1991	FRA1992	FRA2002	FRA2005
FRA2039	FRA2068	FRA2102	FRA2116
FRA2150	FRA2159	GBR2174	GBR2175
GBR2181	GBR2229	GBR2238	GBR2242
GBR2248	GBR2259	GBR2264	GBR2265
GBR2282	GBR2279	GBR2325	GBR2371
GBR2383	GBR2387	GBR2415	GBR2434
GBR2452	GBR2511	GBR2527	GBR2535
GBR2536	GBR2545	GBR2553	GBR2571
GRC2571	HUN2624	HUN2626	HUN2637
HUN2640	HUN2678	IRL2686	IRL2707
IRL2720	ITA2762	ITA2773	ITA2777
ITA2782	ITA2801	ITA2810	ITA2920
LUX2954	LUX3006	MLT3016	MLT3025
NLD3056	NLD3067	NLD3072	NLD3078
NLD3083	NLD3169	NLD3173	NLD3181
NLD3190	NLD3199	NLD3255	NLD3263
NLD3303	NLD3305	NLD3323	NLD3361
NLD3365	NOR3387	POL3499	POL3509
POL3519	PRT3594	SVK3611	SVK3612
SWE3744	SWE3749	SWE3760	SWE3789
SWE3796	SWE3816	SWE3865	SWE3879
TUR3883	TUR3885		

LOBBYING, ADVOCACY - LOBBYING, PLAIDOYER

AUT0086	BEL0096	BEL0131	BEL0186
BEL0198	BEL0219	BEL0248	BEL0254
BEL0282	BEL0353	BEL0361	CHE0434
CHE0460	CHE0479	CHE0534	CHE0562
CHE0568	CHE0604	CHE0687	CHE0689
CHE0765	CHE0819	CYP0828	CYP0831
CYP0833	DEU0983	DEU1004	DEU1066
DEU1149	DEU1151	DNK1283	DNK1312
ESP1410	ESP1457	FRA1661	FRA1756
FRA1797	FRA1799	FRA1841	FRA1843
FRA1850	FRA1889	FRA1946	FRA2002
FRA2004	FRA2110	FRA2131	FRA2159
GBR2174	GBR2228	GBR2229	GBR2238
GBR2241	GBR2242	GBR2264	GBR2269
GBR2325	GBR2355	GBR2371	GBR2383
GBR2390	GBR2434	GBR2498	GBR2511
GBR2527	GBR2537	GBR2545	GBR2553

HUN2626	HUN2637	HUN2640	HUN2678
IRL2691	IRL2693	IRL2707	IRL2714
ITA2801	ITA2810	ITA2913	LUX2957
MLT3023	NLD3062	NLD3067	NLD3072
NLD3078	NLD3147	NLD3160	NLD3301
NLD3303	NLD3305	NOR3467	POL3499
POL3509	POL3543	PRT3594	SWE3749
SWE3853	SWE3876	TUR3885	

NETWORKING, ELECTRONIC TELECOMMUNICATIONS - RESEAUX, TELECOMMUNICATIONS ELECTRONIQUES

AUT0020	BEL0198	BEL0254	BEL0361
CHE0434	CHE0562	CHE0565	CHE0568
CHE0586	CHE0642	CHE0689	CHE0754
CHE0819	DEU0955	DEU0990	DEU1002
DEU1065	ESP1434	ESP1522	FIN1591
FRA1785	FRA1889	FRA1904	FRA2014
FRA2102	FRA2159	GBR2174	GBR2181
GBR2226	GBR2242	GBR2265	GBR2284
GBR2285	GBR2313	GBR2325	GBR2355
GBR2371	GBR2383	GBR2387	GBR2434
GBR2438	GBR2498	GBR2545	GBR2561
HUN2620	HUN2624	HUN2637	ITA2773
ITA2860	NLD3067	NLD3071	NLD3072
NLD3077	NLD3137	NLD3154	NLD3181
NOR3467	POL3499	POL3508	SVK3611
SWE3787	SWE3789	SWE3864	TUR3883

OTHER - AUTRE

CHE0434	FRA2012	GBR2371	GBR2387
NLD3071	NLD3096	NLD3117	NLD3137
NLD3183	POL3543		

PUBLISHING, AUDIOVISUAL MATERIALS, EDUCATIONAL MATERIALS - EDITION, DOCUMENTS AUDIOVISUELS, DOCUMENTS EDUCATIFS

AUT0020	AUT0026	BEL0096	BEL0139
BEL0148	BEL0155	BEL0188	BEL0206
BEL0245	BEL0248	BEL0254	BEL0282
BEL0306	BEL0353	BEL0359	BEL0361
BEL0365	BEL0390	BEL0393	CHE0406
CHE0434	CHE0501	CHE0517	CHE0562
CHE0565	CHE0568	CHE0638	CHE0684
CHE0689	CHE0727	CHE0756	CHE0763
CHE0819	CYP0831	DEU0944	DEU0968
DEU0989	DEU1020	DEU1022	DEU1066
DEU1076	DEU1151	DEU1180	DEU1187
DNK1216	DNK1251	DNK1283	DNK1292
DNK1316	DNK1339	DNK1351	ESP1407
ESP1410	ESP1434	ESP1435	ESP1450
ESP1457	ESP1474	ESP1485	ESP1506
ESP1517	ESP1525	FIN1536	FIN1545
FIN1548	FRA1610	FRA1627	FRA1642
FRA1661	FRA1713	FRA1727	FRA1778
FRA1785	FRA1787	FRA1799	FRA1810
FRA1813	FRA1827	FRA1832	FRA1833
FRA1836	FRA1843	FRA1852	FRA1860
FRA1889	FRA1904	FRA1986	FRA1991
FRA1992	FRA2002	FRA2004	FRA2005
FRA2014	FRA2039	FRA2068	FRA2069
FRA2072	FRA2076	FRA2086	FRA2102
FRA2104	FRA2116	FRA2131	FRA2159
FRA2161	GBR2175	GBR2181	GBR2185
GBR2229	GBR2238	GBR2241	GBR2248
GBR2265	GBR2266	GBR2325	GBR2345
GBR2371	GBR2383	GBR2387	GBR2413
GBR2415	GBR2434	GBR2436	GBR2452
GBR2485	GBR2498	GBR2500	GBR2501
GBR2515	GBR2527	GBR2535	GBR2545
GBR2552	GBR2554	HUN2624	HUN2626
HUN2637	IRL2693	IRL2698	IRL2720
ISL2736	ITA2744	ITA2762	ITA2798
ITA2801	ITA2810	ITA2834	ITA2907
ITA2908	ITA2916	ITA2920	LUX2976
LUX3006	MLT3016	MLT3018	NLD3056
NLD3067	NLD3072	NLD3077	NLD3078
NLD3083	NLD3138	NLD3154	NLD3169
NLD3190	NLD3199	NLD3212	NLD3230
NLD3255	NLD3257	NLD3301	NLD3305
NLD3323	NLD3354	NOR3467	POL3499
POL3508	POL3509	POL3519	PRT3600
SVK3611	SWE3648	SWE3744	SWE3749
SWE3760	SWE3789	SWE3816	SWE3865
SWE3879	TUR3883	TUR3885	TUR3898

See: *How to Use the Directory*, page 11.

ALPHABETICAL LIST OF NGOS

LISTE ALPHABÉTIQUE DES ONG

ABEN AV-RADGIVNING OM U-LANDSSPORGSMAL §	DNK1213
ABOKOBI SOCIETY SWITZERLAND	CHE0402
ACADEMIA REMEMBER	ESP1406
ACADEMIE INTERNATIONALE DE L'ENVIRONNEMENT	CHE0403
ACAUPED-MISSION MEDICALE	FRA1607
ACCION SOLIDARIA ARAGONESA	ESP1407
ACCUEIL SANS FRONTIERES §	FRA1608
ACET §	GBR2171
ACM-YMCA §	PRT3546
ACT UP AGAINST HATRED FOUNDATION AND MOVEMENT §	HUN2597
ACTEURS ICI ET LA-BAS §	FRA1609
ACTION 365 §	AUT0001
ACTION D'URGENCE INTERNATIONALE	FRA1610
ACTION DES CHRETIENS POUR L'ABOLITION DE LA TORTURE, FRANCE	FRA1611
ACTION DES CHRETIENS POUR L'ABOLITION DE LA TORTURE, LUXEMBOURG	LUX2935
ACTION ET PARTAGE HUMANITAIRE	FRA1612
ACTION ET SOLIDARITE AVEC LES PEUPLES D'AFRIQUE CENTRALE §	FRA1613
ACTION FROM IRELAND	IRL2679
ACTION HEALTH	GBR2172
ACTION INTERNATIONALE CONTRE LA FAIM	FRA1614
ACTION INTERNATIONALE POUR LES DROITS DE L'ENFANT	FRA1615
ACTION LOCALE POUR UN DEVELOPPEMENT INTERNATIONAL SOLIDAIRE	FRA1616
ACTION MICRO BARRAGES §	BEL0094
ACTION NORD SUD §	BEL0095
ACTION NORD SUD	FRA1617
ACTION ON DISABILITY AND DEVELOPMENT	GBR2173
ACTION POUR LES ENFANTS DES LEPREUX DE CALCUTTA §	FRA1618
ACTION POUR UN MONDE UNI	LUX2936
ACTION SCOLAIRE ET SANITAIRE POUR L'AFRIQUE FRANCOPHONE	FRA1619
ACTION SOLIDARITE TIERS MONDE	LUX2937
ACTION VIVRE ENSEMBLE	BEL0096
ACTIONAID	GBR2174
ADOLF-GRIMME INSTITUT	DEU0917
ADOPSJONSFORUM	NOR3369
ADOPTION FAMILY INTERNATIONAL §	LUX2938
ADOPTION INTERNATIONAL §	CHE0404
ADOPTIONSCENTRUM	SWE3646
ADVENTINISCHE ENTWICKLUNGSUND KATASTROPHENHILFE §	CHE0405
ADVENTIST DEVELOPMENT AND RELIEF AGENCY	BEL0097
ADVENTIST DEVELOPMENT AND RELIEF AGENCY	DEU0918
ADVENTIST DEVELOPMENT AND RELIEF AGENCY	DNK1214
ADVENTIST DEVELOPMENT AND RELIEF AGENCY	GBR2175
ADVENTISTSAMFUNNET, NORGE §	NOR3370
ADVIES- EN INFORMATIEBUREAU LATIJNS-AMERIKA §	NLD3041
ADVOKATEN ZONDER GRENZEN §	BEL0098
AFGHANAID	GBR2176
AFGHANISTAN LIBRE	CHE0406
AFGHANISTANKOMITEEN I NORGE	NOR3371
AFRANE §	FRA1620
AFRICA (70)	ITA2744
AFRICA - EUROPE FAITH & JUSTICE NETWORK	BEL0099

AFRICA CENTRE §	GBR2177
AFRICA EDUCATIONAL TRUST	GBR2178
AFRICA INLAND MISSION INTERNATIONAL	GBR2179
AFRICA NOW	GBR2180
AFRICA RESOURCES TRUST	GBR2181
AFRICA WOMEN'S SUPPORT GROUP §	GBR2182
AFRICAN EUROPEAN INSTITUTE §	NLD3042
AFRICAN MEDICAL AND RESEARCH FOUNDATION - UNITED KINGDOM	GBR2183
AFRICAN MEDICAL AND RESEARCH FOUNDATION, NEDERLAND §	NLD3043
AFRICAN NETWORK §	NLD3044
AFRICAN REFUGEE HOUSING ACTION GROUP §	GBR2184
AFRICAN SOCIETY OF INTERNATIONAL AND COMPARATIVE LAW	GBR2185
AFRIKA CENTRUM	NLD3045
AFRIKA IMPORT/TANZANIA IMPORT EKONOMISK FORENING §	SWE3647
AFRIKA-KOMITEE BASEL §	CHE0407
AFRIKA-VEREIN	DEU0919
AFRIKAGRUPPERNA	SWE3648
AFRIKAN TAHTI RY	FIN1531
AFRIPROJEKT §	NLD3046
AFRIQUE CA NOUS INTERESSE	FRA1621
AFRIQUE 2000 §	FRA1622
AFRIQUE PARTENAIRES SERVICES §	FRA1623
AFRIQUE VERTE	FRA1624
AFRO-ASIATISCHES INSTITUT WIEN	AUT0002
AFS INTERKULTURELL UTBILDNING §	SWE3649
AGA KHAN FOUNDATION	GBR2186
AGENCE D'INFORMATION ET DE PRESSE HUMANITAIRE §	FRA1625
AGENCE DE COOPERATION AU DEVELOPPEMENT PAR LES SCIENCES ET LES TECHNIQUES §	BEL0100
AGENCE DES CITES POUR LA COOPERATION NORD-SUD §	CHE0408
AGENCE ENVIRONNEMENT DEVELOPPEMENT §	FRA1626
AGENCE EUROPEENNE DE PROMOTION ET DE REALISATIONS TIERS MONDE	FRA1627
AGENCE EUROPEENNE POUR DES ACTIONS DE COOPERATION TECHNIQUE	FRA1628
AGENCE FRANCOPHONE POUR L'ENSEIGNEMENT SUPERIEUR ET LA RECHERCHE	FRA1629
AGENCE INTERNATIONALE POUR LE DEVELOPPEMENT §	FRA1630
AGENCE PERISCOOP	FRA1631
AGENCIA LATINOAMERICANA DE SERVICIOS ESPECIALES DE INFORMACION -INITIATIVE PRO KULTURDIALOG LATEINAMERIKA	DEU0920
AGENCY FOR CO-OPERATION AND RESEARCH IN DEVELOPMENT	GBR2187
AGENZIA INTERNAZIONALE DI INFORMAZIONE §	ITA2745
AGIR AVEC LE TIERS MONDE	FRA1632
AGIR ICI POUR UN MONDE SOLIDAIRE	FRA1633
AGORA - VITRINE DU MONDE	BEL0101
AGORO I DANMARK	DNK1215
AGRAR ES FALUSI IFJUSAG SZOVETSEGE	HUN2598
AGRICULTEURS FRANCAIS ET DEVELOPPEMENT INTERNATIONAL	FRA1634
AGRICULTURE ET PAYS DU TIERS MONDE §	FRA1635
AGRICULTURE SANS FRONTIERES	FRA1636
AGRONOMES SANS FRONTIERES §	FRA1637

Voir : *Comment utiliser le répertoire,* page 11.

AID FOR DESTITUTE VICTIMS OF OPPRESSION §	GBR2188
AIDE A L'ENFANCE DU VIET NAM	FRA1638
AIDE A L'ENFANT REFUGIE §	FRA1639
AIDE A L'EQUIPEMENT MEDICAL DANS LE TIERS MONDE	FRA1640
AIDE ASSISTANCE RETOUR CREATIF PLUS §	FRA1641
AIDE AU DEVELOPPEMENT GEMBLOUX	BEL0102
AIDE AU TIERS MONDE §	BEL0103
AIDE AU VOLONTARIAT EN INDE	BEL0104
AIDE AU VOLONTARIAT EN INDE	FRA1642
AIDE AUX DISPENSAIRES DE KOUDOUGOU ET BOASSA §	FRA1643
AIDE AUX ENFANTS DU MAGHREB	CHE0409
AIDE AUX PERSONNES DEPLACEES	BEL0105
AIDE ET ACTION	FRA1644
AIDE ET COOPERATION AU DEVELOPPEMENT D'AREQUIPA §	BEL0106
AIDE INTER-MONASTERES	FRA1645
AIDE MEDICALE ET SANITAIRE AU NEPAL §	FRA1646
AIDE MEDICALE INTERNATIONALE	FRA1647
AIDE ODONTOLOGIQUE INTERNATIONALE	FRA1648
AIDE SANITAIRE SUISSE AUX PALESTINIENS	CHE0410
AIDE SUISSE A L'ACTION COMMUNAUTAIRE EN HAITI	CHE0411
AIDE SUISSE AUX TIBETAINS	CHE0412
AIESEC §	HUN2599
AIESEC NATIONAL COMMITTEE §	MLT3011
AIR SECOURS INTERNATIONAL	FRA1649
AIUTO MEDICO AL CENTRO AMERICA §	CHE0413
AKADEMICKI KLUB EKOLOGICZNY "OIKOS" §	POL3479
AKADEMIE KLAUSENHOF	DEU0921
AKINA MAMA WA AFRIKA §	GBR2189
THE AKLETON TRUST	GBR2190
AKTIE STROHALM	NLD3047
AKTIE VOOR SANITAIRE CENTRA IN NOOD	BEL0107
AKTION "KIRCHE WOHIN?"	CHE0414
AKTION BRUDER IN NOT INNSBRUCK	AUT0003
AKTION BiRNEHJAELP	DNK1216
AKTION CANCHANABURY, LEPRAHILFE HANS REINHARDT	DEU0922
AKTION COURAGE - SOS RASSISMUS	DEU0923
AKTION DER CHRISTEN FUR DIE ABSCHAFFUNG DER FOLTER	CHE0415
AKTION DER CHRISTEN FUR DIE ABSHAFFUNG DER FOLTER §	DEU0924
AKTION DRITTE WELT §	AUT0004
AKTION DRITTE WELT §	DEU0925
AKTION DRITTE WELT DORNBIRN §	AUT0005
AKTION DRITTE WELT ST. JOHANN	AUT0006
AKTION FAMILIENPLANUNG INTERNATIONAL	DEU0926
AKTION FINANZPLATZ SCHWEIZ - DRITTE WELT	CHE0416
AKTION KINDERHILFE MUNSTER	DEU0927
AKTION MISSION UND LEPRAHILFE SCHIEFBAHN	DEU0928
AKTIONSGEMEINSCHAFT DIENST FUR DEN FRIEDEN	DEU0929
AKTIONSGEMEINSCHAFT FRIEDENSWOCHE MINDEN §	DEU0930
AKTIONSGEMEINSCHAFT HUMANE WELT	DEU0931
AKTIONSGRUPPE KINDER IN NOT §	DEU0932
AKTIOUN A-B-C FIR BILDUNG A GESONDHEET AM TIERS-MONDE §	LUX2939
AKTIOUN BANKOUOP §	LUX2940

AL-SADAQA IRELAND-PALESTINE FRIENDSHIP	IRL2680
ALBA CIRCLE - NONVIOLENT MOVEMENT FOR PEACE §	HUN2600
ALERTE AUX REALITES INTERNATIONALES	FRA1650
ALFONS GOPPEL-STIFTUNG FONDATION	DEU0933
ALGEMEEN BELGISCH VAK VERBOND/FEDERATION GENERALE DU TRAVAIL DE BELGIQUE §	BEL0108
ALGEMENE STICHTING VOOR ONTWIKKELING §	BEL0109
ALIMENTACION Y DESARME §	ESP1408
ALL BURMA STUDENTS' DEMOCRATIC FRONT - EUROPE OFFICE	NOR3372
ALL INDIA WOMEN'S CONFERENCE	CHE0417
ALL-POLAND ALLIANCE OF CATHOLIC ORGANISATIONS	POL3480
ALLIANCE DES UNIONS CHRETIENNES DE JEUNES GENS DE FRANCE	FRA1651
ALLIANCE INTERNATIONALE DE LA COOPERATION SCOLAIRE §	FRA1652
ALLIANCE MISSIONNAIRE INTERNATIONALE §	CHE0418
ALLIANCE OF NORTHERN PEOPLE ON ENVIRONMENT AND DEVELOPMENT	NLD3048
ALLIANCE REFORMEE MONDIALE §	CHE0419
ALTAIR	FRA1653
ALTERNATIV HANDEL	SWE3650
ALTERNATIVA SOLIDARIA - PLENTY	ESP1409
ALTERNATIVE FOR INDIA DEVELOPMENT §	GBR2191
ALTERNATIVES TECHNIQUES ET SYSTEMES ALIMENTAIRES §	FRA1654
L'ALTRITALIA, CENTRO STUDI §	ITA2746
AMALA KREBSHILFE §	DEU0934
AMANI CHRISTIAN COMMUNITY §	GBR2192
AMAZONAS-STIFTELSEN §	SWE3651
AMAZONASFORENINGEN §	SWE3652
AMICALE INTERNATIONALE D'AIDE A L'ENFANCE LA PLUS MEURTRIE	LUX2941
AMICALE RWANDA-LUXEMBOURG	LUX2942
AMICI DEI POPOLI	ITA2747
AMICI DELLA TERRA	ITA2748
AMICI DELLO STATO BRASILIANO DELL'ESPIRITO SANTO - CENTRO DI COLLABORAZIONE COMUNITARIA §	ITA2749
AMIGO §	CZE0837
AMIGOS DA TERRA / ASSOCIACAO PORTUGUESA DE ECOLOGISTAS §	PRT3547
AMIGOS DE LA TIERRA	ESP1410
LES AMIS "AYUDAME"-LUXEMBOURG	LUX2943
LES AMIS D'UN COIN DE L'INDE ET DU MONDE	FRA1655
LES AMIS DE GATAGARA	BEL0110
LES AMIS DE LA TERRE	BEL0111
LES AMIS DE LA TERRE	FRA1656
LES AMIS DE TOPAZA	FRA1657
LES AMIS DES ENFANTS DU MONDE	FRA1658
LES AMIS DES PECHEURS MALGACHES	FRA1659
LES AMIS DU CESO §	FRA1660
LES AMIS DU PERE GUEZOU ET DE DON BOSCO EN INDE	FRA1661
LES AMIS DU TOGO §	FRA1662
LES AMIS SEINE ET MARNAIS DU BURKINA FASO	FRA1663
AMITIE ET DEVELOPPEMENT	FRA1664
AMITIE EURO-KHMERE §	FRA1665
AMITIE FRANCO-AFGHANE §	FRA1666
AMITIES BELGIQUE BURUNDI §	BEL0112
AMITIES BELGO-CAMBODGIENNES §	BEL0113

See: *How to Use the Directory*, page 11.

AMITIES BELGO-CHILIENNES §	BEL0114
AMITIES FRANCO-KHMERES	FRA1667
AMITIES FRANCO-TANZANIENNES	FRA1668
AMITIES LUXEMBOURG-EQUATEUR §	LUX2944
AMMEHJELPEN §	NOR3373
AMMEHJELPENS INTERNASJONALE GRUPPE	NOR3374
AMNESTY INTERNATIONAL CENTRO PER L'EDUCAZIONE AI DIRITTI UMANI	ITA2750
AMNESTY INTERNATIONAL, AFDELING NEDERLAND	NLD3049
AMNESTY INTERNATIONAL, AUSTRIAN SECTION §	AUT0007
AMNESTY INTERNATIONAL, BELGIAN SECTION	BEL0115
AMNESTY INTERNATIONAL, BRITISH SECTION	GBR2193
AMNESTY INTERNATIONAL, CZECH SECTION §	CZE0838
AMNESTY INTERNATIONAL, DANSK AFDELING §	DNK1217
AMNESTY INTERNATIONAL, FLEMISH SECTION	BEL0116
AMNESTY INTERNATIONAL, GERMAN SECTION §	DEU0935
AMNESTY INTERNATIONAL, GREEK SECTION §	GRC2563
AMNESTY INTERNATIONAL, ICELANDIC SECTION §	ISL2734
AMNESTY INTERNATIONAL, IRISH SECTION §	IRL2681
AMNESTY INTERNATIONAL, ITALIAN SECTION §	ITA2751
AMNESTY INTERNATIONAL, MAGYARORSZAG	HUN2601
AMNESTY INTERNATIONAL, NORWEGIAN SECTION §	NOR3375
AMNESTY INTERNATIONAL, PORTUGUESE SECTION	PRT3548
AMNESTY INTERNATIONAL, SCHWEIZER SEKTION	CHE0420
AMNESTY INTERNATIONAL, SECTION LUXEMBOURGEOISE §	LUX2945
AMNESTY INTERNATIONAL, SPANISH SECTION §	ESP1411
AMNESTY INTERNATIONAL, SUOMEN OSASTO	FIN1532
AMREF GESELLSCHAFT FUR MEDIZIN UND FORSCHUNG IN AFRIKA	DEU0936
ANADOLU KALKINMA VAKFI	TUR3882
ANDHERI-HILFE §	DEU0937
ANDREJ KMET FOUNDATION §	SVK3606
ANESVAD §	ESP1412
ANIMATION ET DEVELOPPEMENT §	FRA1669
ANTENNA INTERNATIONALE	CHE0421
ANTENNA TECHNOLOGY	CHE0422
ANTHROPOLOGIE MEDICALE APPLIQUEE AU DEVELOPPEMENT ET A LA SANTE	FRA1670
ANTI-FASCIST ACTION §	HUN2602
ANTI-RACISM INFORMATION SERVICE §	CHE0423
ANTI-RACIST ALLIANCE	GBR2194
ANTI-RACIST COMMITTEE §	HUN2603
ANTI-SLAVERY INTERNATIONAL	GBR2195
ANTI-VIOLENCE FORUM §	HUN2604
ANTIRASSISTISCHE INITIATIVE §	DEU0938
ANTROPOSOFISKA SALLSKAPET	SWE3653
APOSTOLIKI DIAKONIA TIS EKLISSIAS TIS ELLADOS §	GRC2564
APOSTOLSK KIRKES MISSION	DNK1218
APPEL AIDE AUX ENFANTS VICTIMES DE CONFLITS DANS LES PAYS EN VOIE DE DEVELOPPEMENT	FRA1671
APPEL DETRESSE	FRA1672
APPOGGIO POPOLAZIONE BIJAGOS §	CHE0424
APPROCHE §	BEL0117
APPROPRIATE HEALTH RESOURCES AND TECHNOLOGIES ACTION GROUP	GBR2196
APPROPRIATE TECHNOLOGY FOR TIBETANS TRUST	GBR2197
APPUI AU DEVELOPPEMENT AUTONOME	LUX2946

APPUI MUTUEL POUR UN USAGE SOCIAL DE L'INFORMATION	FRA1673
APT DESIGN AND DEVELOPMENT	GBR2198
AQUACULTURE ET DEVELOPPEMENT	BEL0118
ARBEIDERBEVEGELSENS INTERNASJONALE STOTTEKOMITE §	NOR3376
ARBEIDERBEVEGELSENS UNGDOMSORGANISASJON §	NOR3377
ARBEIDERNES OPPLYSNINGSFORBUND §	NOR3378
ARBEITER-SAMARITER-BUND DEUTSCHLAND	DEU0939
ARBEITERWOHLFAHRT BUNDESVERBAND	DEU0940
ARBEITGEMEINSCHAFT ENTWICKLUNGSZUSAMMENARBEIT	AUT0008
ARBEITGEMEINSCHAFT SPINA BIDIFA UND HYDROCEPHALUS §	DEU0941
ARBEITSGEMEINSCHAFT "BRENNPUNKT WELT" §	CHE0425
ARBEITSGEMEINSCHAFT CHRISTEN FUR CHILE	AUT0009
ARBEITSGEMEINSCHAFT DER EVANGELISCHEN JUGEND IN DER BUNDESREPUBLIK DEUTSCHLAND	DEU0942
ARBEITSGEMEINSCHAFT ENTWICKLUNGSLANDER	DEU0943
ARBEITSGEMEINSCHAFT FUR ENTWICKLUNGSHILFE	DEU0944
ARBEITSGEMEINSCHAFT FUR RUSTUNGSKONTROLLE UND EIN WAFFENAUSFUHRVERBOT	CHE0426
ARBEITSGEMEINSCHAFT GERECHTEN BANANENHANDEL	CHE0427
ARBEITSGEMEINSCHAFT INTERNATIONALE POLITIK §	DEU0945
ARBEITSGEMEINSCHAFT KATHOLISCHER JUGEND OSTERREICHS	AUT0010
ARBEITSGEMEINSCHAFT KIRCHLICHER ENTWICKLUNGSDIENST - PLANUNGS- UND GRUNDSATZABTEILUNG	DEU0946
ARBEITSGEMEINSCHAFT OSTERREICH DRITTE WELT DER SPO	AUT0011
ARBEITSGEMEINSCHAFT PRIVATER ENTWICKLUNGSDIENSTE	DEU0947
ARBEITSGEMEINSCHAFT REGENWALD UND ARTENSCHUTZ	DEU0948
ARBEITSGEMEINSCHAFT SCHWEIZERISCHER ENTWICKLUNGSDIENSTE	CHE0428
ARBEITSGEMEINSCHAFT SWISSAID/FASTENOPFER/ BROT FUR ALLE/HELVETAS/CARITAS	CHE0429
ARBEITSGRUPPE FUR ENTWICKLUNGSPOLITISCHE INFORMATION UND BILDUNG §	CHE0430
ARBEITSGRUPPE LITERATUR AUS AFRIKA, ASIEN UND LATEINAMERIKA/ERKLARUNG VON BERN	CHE0431
ARBEITSKREIS "LERNEN UND HELFEN IN UBERSEE"	DEU0949
ARBEITSKREIS ENTWICKLUNGSHILFE UND MENSCHENRECHTE §	AUT0012
ARBEITSKREIS ENTWICKLUNGSPOLITIK §	DEU0950
ARBEITSKREIS MEDIZINISCHE ENTWICKLUNGSHILFE	DEU0951
ARBEITSKREIS SEHEN UND LEBEN	CHE0432
ARBEITSKREIS TOURISMUS UND ENTWICKLUNG	CHE0433
ARBEITSKREIS WELTKIRCHE DES VIKARIATES SUD	AUT0013
ARBEITSKREIS WELTKIRCHE UND ENTWICKLUNGSFORDERUNG DER DIOZESE LINZ §	AUT0014
ARBEITSSTELLE FRIEDENSFORSCHUNG BONN §	DEU0952
ARBEJDERBEVAEGELSENS INTERNATIONALE FORUM §	DNK1219
ARBEJDERBEVAEGELSENS U-LANDSUDVALG §	DNK1220
ARCHAIA	CZE0839
L'ARCHE §	FRA1674
L'ARCHE DE LA FRATERNITE	FRA1675
ARCHITECTES ET INGENIEURS DU MONDE	FRA1676
ARCHITECTES SANS FRONTIERES	FRA1677

ARCHIV FUR POLITIK UND ZEITGESCHICHTE / DRITTE-WELT-ARCHIV GYMNASIUM WERTINGEN/SCHWABEN §	DEU0953
ARCI - CULTURA E SVILUPPO §	ITA2752
ARDESCO §	FRA1678
ARHUS-KLUNSERNE §	DNK1221
ARKADAS	TUR3883
ARKADIA §	POL3481
ARMEE DU SALUT	CHE0434
ARMOR DEVELOPPEMENT - SAHEL	FRA1679
ART CULTURE COMMUNICATION §	FRA1680
ARTICLE 19, THE INTERNATIONAL CENTRE AGAINST CENSORSHIP	GBR2199
ARTISAN TRUST §	GBR2200
ARTISANAT SERVICE	FRA1681
ARTS ET OCEANS §	FRA1682
ARTSEN ZONDER GRENZEN NEDERLAND	NLD3050
ARTZE FUR DIE DRITTE WELT	DEU0954
ASF-DANSK FOLKEHJAELP	DNK1222
ASHOKA UK TRUST	GBR2201
ASIA FRIENDSHIP ASSOCIATION §	CZE0840
ASIAN STUDIES, INFORMATION & AUDIOVISUALS	NLD3051
ASMAE-LES AMIS DE SOEUR EMMANUELLE	FRA1683
ASOCIACION ANDALUZA POR LA SOLIDARIDAD Y LA PAZ	ESP1413
ASOCIACION CATALANA DE PROFESIONALES PARA LA COOPERACION CON NICARAGUA §	ESP1414
ASOCIACION DE AMIGOS DE LA REPUBLICA ARABE SAHARAUI DEMOCRATICA DE ARAGON §	ESP1415
ASOCIACION DE COLABORACION Y AMISTAD CON MOZAMBIQUE §	ESP1416
ASOCIACION DE INVESTIGACION Y ESPECIALIZACION SOBRE TEMAS IBEROAMERICANOS	ESP1417
ASOCIACION DE TRABAJADORES INMIGRANTES EN ESPANA §	ESP1418
ASOCIACION ECOLOGISTA DE DEFENSA DE LA NATURALEZA	ESP1419
ASOCIACION HUMANA	ESP1420
ASOCIACION MALAGUENA PARA LA PROTECCION DE LA VIDA SILVESTRE §	ESP1421
ASOCIACION PARA LA COOPERACION CON EL SUR - LAS SEGOVIAS §	ESP1422
ASOCIACION PARA LA COOPERACION CON LOS PUEBLOS DE AMERICA CENTRAL §	ESP1423
ASOCIACION PARA LA DEFENSA DE LA SALUD PUBLICA §	ESP1424
ASOCIACION PARA REFUGIADOS AFRICANOS §	ESP1425
ASOCIACION PRO DERECHOS HUMANOS §	ESP1426
ASOCIACION RUBEN DARIO	ESP1427
ASOCIACION UNICEF-ESPANA §	ESP1428
ASSISTANCE MEDICALE INTER-SANITAIRE	FRA1684
ASSISTANCE TECHNIQUE INTERNATIONALE	FRA1685
ASSISTENCIA MEDICA INTERNACIONAL	PRT3549
ASSOCIACAO AFRICA SOLIDARIEDADE	PRT3550
ASSOCIACAO CRISTA DA MOCIDADE §	PRT3551
ASSOCIACAO DE BENEFICENCIA LUSO-ALEMA	PRT3552
ASSOCIACAO NACIONAL DE CONSERVACAO DA NATUREZA §	PRT3553
ASSOCIACAO PARA A COOPERACAO ENTRE OS POVOS	PRT3554
ASSOCIACAO PARA A COOPERACAO INTERCAMBIO E CULTURA	PRT3555

ASSOCIACAO PARA O DESENVOLVIMENTO ECONOMICO E SOCIAL §	PRT3556
ASSOCIACAO PORTUGUESA AMIGOS DE RAOUL FOLLEREAU	PRT3557
ASSOCIACAO PORTUGUESA DE CONSULTORES SENIORES	PRT3558
ASSOCIACAO PORTUGUESA PARA O ESTUDO DAS RELACOES INTERNACIONAIS §	PRT3559
ASSOCIACIO CATALANA DE PROFESSIONALS PER LA COOPERACIO AMB NICARAGUA §	ESP1429
ASSOCIACIO PER A LES NACIONS UNIDES A ESPANYA	ESP1430
ASSOCIATED COUNTRY WOMEN OF THE WORLD	GBR2202
ASSOCIATED HOUSING ADVISORY SERVICES FOR ALTERNATIVES IN HOUSING FOR ANOTHER SOCIETY §	GBR2203
ASSOCIATION 6-S	CHE0435
ASSOCIATION ACCUEIL TIERS-MONDE §	CHE0436
ASSOCIATION AFRICAINE D'EDUCATION POUR LE DEVELOPPEMENT §	CHE0437
ASSOCIATION ALBORADA	CHE0438
ASSOCIATION ALTER EGO	CHE0439
ASSOCIATION ARC EN CIEL §	FRA1686
ASSOCIATION ASSISTANCE EN FRANCE §	FRA1687
ASSOCIATION AUBE-GUINEE §	FRA1688
ASSOCIATION BANCAIRE POUR L'ENTREPRISE ET LE DEVELOPPEMENT §	FRA1689
ASSOCIATION BELGIQUE-BOLIVIE	BEL0119
ASSOCIATION BELGIQUE-RWANDA	BEL0120
ASSOCIATION CARABAYA-PEROU §	CHE0440
ASSOCIATION CHAMPENOISE DE COOPERATION INTER-REGIONALE	FRA1690
ASSOCIATION COLOMBIE §	CHE0441
ASSOCIATION CONTRE L'EXCLUSION, POUR LA SANTE ET LE DEVELOPPEMENT COMMUNAUTAIRE	FRA1691
ASSOCIATION COOPERATION COUP DE MAIN - JEUNES POUR L'ENTRAIDE §	CHE0442
ASSOCIATION CULTURELLE ET AMICALE DES FAMILLES D'OUTRE-MER ET MIGRANTS §	FRA1692
ASSOCIATION D'ACCUEIL AUX MEDECINS ET PERSONNELS DE SANTE REFUGIES EN FRANCE	FRA1693
ASSOCIATION D'AIDE AU DEVELOPPEMENT ECONOMICO-ECOLOGIQUE DE L'EST DE L'AFRIQUE ET DE L'OCEAN INDIEN §	BEL0121
ASSOCIATION D'ALSACE DES OEUVRES HOSPITALIERES DE SAINT LAZARE	FRA1694
ASSOCIATION D'AMITIE AVEC LE PEUPLE CAPVERDIEN §	LUX2947
ASSOCIATION D'AMITIE ET DE COOPERATION AVEC L'URUGUAY	CHE0443
ASSOCIATION D'AMITIE FRANCO-VIETNAMIENNE §	FRA1695
ASSOCIATION D'ECHANGES CULTURELS EN MEDITERRANEE	FRA1696
ASSOCIATION D'ENTRAIDE POUR LE SAHEL	CHE0444
ASSOCIATION DE COOPERATION SUISSE-PEROU §	CHE0445
ASSOCIATION DE DEFENSE DES DROITS DE L'HOMME AU MAROC §	FRA1697
ASSOCIATION DE FORMATION ET D'INFORMATION POUR LE DEVELOPPEMENT D'INITIATIVES RURALES	FRA1698
ASSOCIATION DE LIAISON D'AGNAM	FRA1699
ASSOCIATION DE PARTENAIRES DES ARTISANS DU SAHEL	FRA1700
ASSOCIATION DE RECHERCHE COOPERATIVE INTERNATIONALE	FRA1701
ASSOCIATION DE RECHERCHE EN AMENAGEMENT DU TERRITOIRE DANS LES PVD §	FRA1702

See: *How to Use the Directory*, page 11.

ASSOCIATION DE SOLIDARITE AVEC LE NICARAGUA ET EL SALVADOR	CHE0446
ASSOCIATION DE SOLIDARITE AVEC LES PAYSANS D'AMERIQUE LATINE	FRA1703
ASSOCIATION DE SOUTIEN AUX NATIONS AMERINDIENNES §	CHE0447
ASSOCIATION DE SOUTIEN DES MISSIONS DES ASSEMBLEES DE FRANCE	FRA1704
ASSOCIATION DES AMIS DE CHARLES DE FOUCAULD §	FRA1705
ASSOCIATION DES AMIS DE LA MAISON FAMILIALE DE FORMATION RURALE D'HAHOMEGBE §	FRA1706
ASSOCIATION DES AMITIES BURUNDI-SUISSE	CHE0448
ASSOCIATION DES ANALYSTES DE PROJETS INDUSTRIELS ET AGRICOLES §	FRA1707
ASSOCIATION DES CENTRES DE PREFORMATION MEDITERRANEENS §	FRA1708
ASSOCIATION DES CENTRES MEDICO-EDUCATIFS - CHILI §	CHE0449
ASSOCIATION DES CONSOMMATEURS TIERS MONDE §	BEL0122
ASSOCIATION DES CONSTRUCTEURS POUR LA REHABILITATION ET L'OPTIMALISATION DE LA TERRE	FRA1709
ASSOCIATION DES ETUDIANTS EN SCIENCES ECONOMIQUES ET COMMERCIALES	BEL0123
ASSOCIATION DES FEMMES URUGUAYENNES LOURDES PINTOS	FRA1710
ASSOCIATION DES FOYERS INTERNATIONAUX §	FRA1711
ASSOCIATION DES GIRL GUIDES LUXEMBOURGEOISES	LUX2948
ASSOCIATION DES JOURNALISTES-ECRIVAINS POUR LA NATURE ET L'ECOLOGIE	FRA1712
ASSOCIATION DES TROIS MONDES	FRA1713
ASSOCIATION DU VOLONTARIAT EN EUROPE §	FRA1714
ASSOCIATION EN SUISSE DE DEFENSE DES DROITS DE L'HOMME AU MAGHREB §	CHE0450
ASSOCIATION ENFANTS DU MONDE	FRA1715
ASSOCIATION EURO-AFRICAINE POUR L'ANTHROPOLOGIE DU CHANGEMENT SOCIAL ET DU DEVELOPPEMENT §	FRA1716
ASSOCIATION EUROPE - TIERS MONDE	BEL0124
ASSOCIATION EUROPEENNE POUR L'ETUDE DE L'ALIMENTATION ET DU DEVELOPPEMENT DE L'ENFANT	FRA1717
ASSOCIATION FEMMES D'EUROPE §	BEL0125
ASSOCIATION FOR CULTURAL, TECHNICAL AND EDUCATIONAL COOPERATION	BEL0126
ASSOCIATION FOR EASY CONNECTION §	CZE0841
ASSOCIATION FOR EUROPEAN HOUSE, HELSINKI COMMITTEE §	CZE0842
ASSOCIATION FOR PROGRESSIVE COMMUNICATIONS	DEU0955
ASSOCIATION FOR TEACHER EDUCATION IN EUROPE	BEL0127
ASSOCIATION FOR THE COOPERATION WITH THE COUNTRIES OF AFRICA, ASIA AND LATIN AMERICA §	CZE0843
ASSOCIATION FOR THE PROTECTION OF THE CYPRUS ENVIRONMENT §	CYP0827
ASSOCIATION FOR YOUTH, SCIENCE AND TECHNOLOGY §	SVK3607
ASSOCIATION FORAGES MALI	FRA1718
ASSOCIATION FORET MEDITERRANEENNE	FRA1719
ASSOCIATION FRANCAISE D'AMITIE ET DE SOLIDARITE AVEC LES PEUPLES D'AFRIQUE §	FRA1720
ASSOCIATION FRANCAISE D'ENTRAIDE §	FRA1721
ASSOCIATION FRANCAISE DE FORMATION, COOPERATION, PROMOTION ET ANIMATION D'ENTREPRISES §	FRA1722
ASSOCIATION FRANCAISE DE SOLIDARITE §	FRA1723
ASSOCIATION FRANCAISE DE SOLIDARITE INTERNATIONALE	FRA1724
ASSOCIATION FRANCAISE DES EXPERTS DE LA COOPERATION TECHNIQUE INTERNATIONALE §	FRA1725
ASSOCIATION FRANCAISE DES VILLAGES D'ENFANTS SOS DANS LE MONDE	FRA1726
ASSOCIATION FRANCAISE DES VOLONTAIRES DU PROGRES	FRA1727
ASSOCIATION FRANCAISE RAOUL FOLLEREAU §	FRA1728
ASSOCIATION FRANCE TCHAD ESPOIR §	FRA1729
ASSOCIATION FRANCE-PALESTINE §	FRA1730
ASSOCIATION FRATERNELLE INTERNATIONALE §	CHE0451
ASSOCIATION GENERALE DES INTERVENANTS RETRAITES - ACTIONS DE BENEVOLES POUR LA COOPERATION ET LE DEVELOPPEMENT	FRA1731
ASSOCIATION INDUSTRIES ET TECHNOLOGIES POUR LE DEVELOPPEMENT §	FRA1732
ASSOCIATION INTERNATIONALE CONTRA LA TORTURA §	ITA2753
ASSOCIATION INTERNATIONALE DE DEFENSE DES ARTISTES §	DNK1223
ASSOCIATION INTERNATIONALE DE DEVELOPPEMENT ET D'ACTION COMMUNAUTAIRES	BEL0128
ASSOCIATION INTERNATIONALE DE TECHNICIENS, EXPERTS ET CHERCHEURS §	FRA1733
ASSOCIATION INTERNATIONALE DES EDUCATEURS POUR LA PAIX DU MONDE	BEL0129
ASSOCIATION INTERNATIONALE DES JURISTES DEMOCRATES §	BEL0130
ASSOCIATION INTERNATIONALE DES JURISTES DEMOCRATES	CHE0452
ASSOCIATION INTERNATIONALE DES MAISONS FAMILIALES RURALES	FRA1734
ASSOCIATION INTERNATIONALE DES URBANISTES §	NLD3052
ASSOCIATION INTERNATIONALE POUR LA DEFENSE DE LA LIBERTE RELIGIEUSE §	CHE0453
ASSOCIATION INTERNATIONALE POUR LA RECHERCHE ET LE DEVELOPPEMENT EN AFRIQUE §	FRA1735
ASSOCIATION JEUNES TIERS MONDE §	FRA1736
ASSOCIATION JEUNESSE D'ACTIONS POUR LA COOPERATION ET LA SOLIDARITE	FRA1737
ASSOCIATION KOMBIT (HAITI)	CHE0454
ASSOCIATION LA FLORIDA - PEROU	CHE0455
ASSOCIATION LANGUEDOC-COMORES	FRA1738
ASSOCIATION LANGUEDOCIENNE D'AIDE AU DEVELOPPEMENT	FRA1739
ASSOCIATION LASER PRODUCTIONS - CAISSE PHARMACEUTIQUE D'ASSISTANCE SOCIALE	FRA1740
ASSOCIATION LORRAINE POUR LE DEVELOPPEMENT DES PEUPLES	FRA1741
ASSOCIATION LUXEMBOURG-PEROU	LUX2949
ASSOCIATION MEDICALE ENGHIENNOISE §	FRA1742
ASSOCIATION MEDICALE FRANCO-PALESTINIENNE §	FRA1743
ASSOCIATION MONDIALE DES GRANDES METROPOLES	FRA1744
ASSOCIATION MONDIALE POUR L'ECOLE INSTRUMENT DE PAIX	CHE0456
ASSOCIATION NATIONALE POUR LE DEVELOPPEMENT AGRICOLE	FRA1745
ASSOCIATION NIORTAISE POUR LE JUMELAGE ET LA COOPERATION AVEC ATAKPAME	FRA1746
ASSOCIATION OF EUROPEAN PARLIAMENTARIANS FOR AFRICA §	NLD3053
ASSOCIATION OF MISSIONARY SOCIETIES §	IRL2682
ASSOCIATION OF POLISH YOUTH §	CZE0844
ASSOCIATION OF PROTESTANT DEVELOPMENT ORGANISATIONS IN EUROPE	BEL0131
ASSOCIATION OF UNGANDAN YOUTH AND STUDENTS §	GBR2204
ASSOCIATION OF VICTIMS OF VIOLATION OF RIGHTS §	HUN2605

Voir : *Comment utiliser le répertoire,* page 11.

ASSOCIATION OF WOMEN'S ORGANISATIONS §	CZE0845
ASSOCIATION OF WORLD EDUCATION §	DNK1224
ASSOCIATION OF YOUNG SCIENTISTS PUGWASH §	CZE0846
ASSOCIATION ORIENT REALITES §	CHE0457
ASSOCIATION POUR COMBATTRE LA MALNUTRITION PAR ALGOCULTURE	FRA1747
ASSOCIATION POUR L'ETABLISSEMENT DES REFUGIES §	FRA1748
ASSOCIATION POUR L'UNION ENTRE LES PEUPLES JUIF ET PALESTINIEN §	CHE0458
ASSOCIATION POUR LA COOPERATION ET LE DEVELOPPEMENT DES STRUCTURES SANITAIRES	FRA1749
ASSOCIATION POUR LA DEFENSE DES DROITS DE L'HOMME EN AFRIQUE §	FRA1750
ASSOCIATION POUR LA FORMATION EN MILIEU RURAL §	FRA1751
ASSOCIATION POUR LA GERANCE DES LYCEES ET DES ECOLES DE FORMATION MARITIME ET AQUACOLE	FRA1752
ASSOCIATION POUR LA MEDECINE ET LA RECHERCHE EN AFRIQUE §	FRA1753
ASSOCIATION POUR LA PREPARATION AU VOLONTARIAT §	FRA1754
ASSOCIATION POUR LA PROMOTION DE LA MEDECINE PREVENTIVE §	FRA1755
ASSOCIATION POUR LA PROMOTION DES ILES DE PAIX	LUX2950
ASSOCIATION POUR LA PROMOTION DES RECHERCHES ET ETUDES FONCIERES EN AFRIQUE	FRA1756
ASSOCIATION POUR LA PROTECTION DES ANIMAUX SAUVAGES ET DU PATRIMOINE NATUREL	FRA1757
ASSOCIATION POUR LA VALORISATION ET LA PERFORMANCE DE L'ENCADREMENT AFRICAIN §	FRA1758
ASSOCIATION POUR LE CONSEIL A LA CREATION D'ENTREPRISES ET LA COOPERATION INTERNATIONALE	FRA1759
ASSOCIATION POUR LE DEVELOPPEMENT AGRO-INDUSTRIEL DU SAHEL	FRA1760
ASSOCIATION POUR LE DEVELOPPEMENT DE MELGA	FRA1761
ASSOCIATION POUR LE DEVELOPPEMENT DES ACTIVITES MARITIMES	FRA1762
ASSOCIATION POUR LE DEVELOPPEMENT DES ECHANGES EN TECHNOLOGIE ECONOMIQUE ET FINANCIERE §	FRA1763
ASSOCIATION POUR LE DEVELOPPEMENT DES ECHANGES INTERNATIONAUX DE PRODUITS ET TECHNIQUES AGROALIMENTAIRES §	FRA1764
ASSOCIATION POUR LE DEVELOPPEMENT DES ENERGIES RENOUVELABLES	CHE0459
ASSOCIATION POUR LE DEVELOPPEMENT PAR LA RECHERCHE ET L'ACTION INTEGREES	BEL0132
ASSOCIATION PROTESTANTE DES VOLONTAIRES DE LA COOPERATION	BEL0133
ASSOCIATION REGIONALE POUR LE DEVELOPPEMENT DE LA COOPERATION INDUSTRIELLE INTERNATIONALE	FRA1765
ASSOCIATION ROMANDE DES COMMUNAUTES EMMAUS	CHE0460
ASSOCIATION ROMANDE DES MAGASINS DU MONDE	CHE0461
ASSOCIATION SCOUTISME TIERS-MONDE	CHE0462
ASSOCIATION SOLIDARITE LUXEMBOURG-NICARAGUA - AIDE AU DEVELOPPEMENT §	LUX2951
ASSOCIATION SOLIDARITE SANTE	FRA1766
ASSOCIATION SUISSE D'AIDE A L'HOPITAL ALBERT SCHWEITZER A LAMBARENE	CHE0463
ASSOCIATION SUISSE DE PLANNING FAMILIAL ET D'EDUCATION SEXUELLE	CHE0464
ASSOCIATION SUISSE DE SOLIDARITE AVEC LES PEUPLES INDIGENES "TUPAJ KATARI"/MOUVEMENT INDIEN "TUPAJKATARI"	CHE0465
ASSOCIATION SUISSE DES AMIS D'HAITI	CHE0466
ASSOCIATION SUISSE DES AMIS DE L'AFGHANISTAN	CHE0467
ASSOCIATION SUISSE RAOUL FOLLEREAU §	CHE0468
ASSOCIATION SUISSE-CAMEROUN §	CHE0469
ASSOCIATION SUISSE-CUBA §	CHE0470
ASSOCIATION SUISSE-PARAGUAY §	CHE0471
ASSOCIATION TECHNIQUE AFRICAINE §	FRA1767
ASSOCIATION TECHNIQUE DE RECHERCHES ET D'INFORMATIONS AUDIOVISUELLES	FRA1768
ASSOCIATION TEMO	FRA1769
ASSOCIATION TERRA-BRASIL §	FRA1770
ASSOCIATION TERRE D'AMITIE	FRA1771
ASSOCIATION TIERS-MONDE §	FRA1772
ASSOCIATION TIERS-MONDE DE LA REGION DE QUINTIN §	FRA1773
ASSOCIATION TOKOMBERE	FRA1774
ASSOCIATION VITROLLES-KIFFA §	FRA1775
ASSOCIAZIONE AAM TERRA NUOVA §	ITA2754
ASSOCIAZIONE AMICI DEI BAMBINI	ITA2755
ASSOCIAZIONE AMICI DI PADRE MANTOVANI	CHE0472
ASSOCIAZIONE AZIONE PER UN MONDO UNITO	ITA2756
ASSOCIAZIONE CENTRO AIUTI VOLONTARI COOPERAZIONE SVILUPPO TERZO MONDO	ITA2757
ASSOCIAZIONE CENTRO ELIS	ITA2758
ASSOCIAZIONE COOPERATIVA INTERNAZIONALE PER LO SVILUPPO §	ITA2759
ASSOCIAZIONE DALLA PARTE DEGLI ULTIMI	ITA2760
ASSOCIAZIONE DI COOPERAZIONE CRISTIANA INTERNAZIONALE	ITA2761
ASSOCIAZIONE DI COOPERAZIONE RURALE IN AFRICA E AMERICA LATINA	ITA2762
ASSOCIAZIONE DI TECNICI PER LA SOLIDARIETA E COOPERAZIONE INTERNAZIONALE §	ITA2763
ASSOCIAZIONE DI-SVI DISARMO E SVILUPPO	ITA2764
ASSOCIAZIONE GUIDE E SCOUTS CATTOLICI ITALIANI	ITA2765
ASSOCIAZIONE ITALIANA "AMICI DI RAOUL FOLLEREAU"	ITA2766
ASSOCIAZIONE ITALIANA DONNE PER LO SVILUPPO	ITA2767
ASSOCIAZIONE ITALIANA PER LA SOLIDARIETA TRA I POPOLI §	ITA2768
ASSOCIAZIONE ITALIANA PER LO SVILUPPO INTERNAZIONALE	ITA2769
ASSOCIAZIONE ITALIANA SOCI COSTRUTTORI	ITA2770
ASSOCIAZIONE LAICALE MISSIONARIA	ITA2771
ASSOCIAZIONE MEDAGLIA MIRACOLOS §	CHE0473
ASSOCIAZIONE MONDO GIUSTO	ITA2772
ASSOCIAZIONE PER GLI INTERVENTI DI COOPERAZIONE ALLO SVILUPPO	ITA2773
ASSOCIAZIONE PER LA COOPERAZIONE MISSIONARIA	ITA2774
ASSOCIAZIONE PER LA PARTECIPAZIONE ALLO SVILUPPO	ITA2775
ASSOCIAZIONE SANITARIA INTERNAZIONALE §	ITA2776
ASSOCIAZIONE SOLIDARIETA PAESI EMERGENTI	ITA2777
ASSOCIAZIONE SOLIDARIETA PER LO SVILUPPO §	ITA2778
ASSOCIAZIONE SOLIDARIETA' PACE E SVILUPPO	ITA2779
ASSOCIAZIONE STUDI AMERICA LATINA	ITA2780
ASSOCIAZIONE UNIVERSITARIA PER LA COOPERAZIONE INTERNAZIONALE §	ITA2781
ASSOCIAZIONE VOLONTARI PER IL SERVIZIO INTERNAZIONALE	ITA2782
ASYLKOORDINATION - OSTERREICH	AUT0015
ATD QUART MONDE §	BEL0134

See: *How to Use the Directory*, page 11.

ATD QUART MONDE §	LUX2952
ATD QUART-MONDE §	CHE0474
ATELIER - ASOCIACION PARA LA COOPERACION INTERNACIONAL AL DESARROLLO	ESP1431
ATELIER DES ENFANTS LIMA	CHE0475
ATELIER PANAFRICAIN DE RECHERCHE-ACTION EN COMMUNICATION §	CHE0476
ATELIER POUR LES INITIATIVES DE DEVELOPPEMENT	FRA1776
ATELIERS VARAN §	FRA1777
ATLIK	FRA1778
AUSBILDUNGSSTATTE FUR AUSLANDISCHE FERNSEHKRAFTE BEIM SENDER FREIES BERLIN	DEU0956
AUSSATZIGENHILFE EMMAUS-SCHWEIZ	CHE0477
AUSSCHUSS DES DIOZESANRATES FUR WELTKIRCHE UND ENTWICKLUNGSFORDERUNG §	AUT0016
AUSSCHUSS FUR ENTWICKLUNGSBEZOGENE BILDUNG UND PUBLIZISTIK	DEU0957
AUSSENSTELLE DES EKD KIRCHENAMTS §	DEU0958
AUSTRIAN COMMISSION OF JURISTS §	AUT0017
AUSTRIAN FEDERATION OF UN AND UNESCO CLUBS §	AUT0018
AUSTRIAN INSTITUTE FOR HUMAN RIGHTS §	AUT0019
AUTO-JA KULJGTUSALAN TYONTEKIJALUTTO §	FIN1533
AUVERGNE MALI 87 §	FRA1779
AUX QUATRE COINS DU MONDE §	FRA1780
AUXILIUM GESELLSCHAFT FUR ENTWICKLUNGSHILFE §	DEU0959
AVEC VOUS POUR LA DEMOCRATIE CONTRE TOUTES LES EXCLUSIONS §	BEL0135
AVIATION SANS FRONTIERES	FRA1781
AVICEN §	FRA1782
AYUBOWAN §	NLD3054
AYUDA EN ACCION	ESP1432
AYUDA FRATERNA - VOLUNTARIADO INTERNACIONAL Y CRISTIANO §	ESP1433
AYUDAME-HILFE FUR PERU §	DEU0960
AZ-INTERNATIONAL TECHNICAL TEAM §	DNK1225
BABY MILK ACTION	GBR2205
BAHA'I INTERNATIONAL COMMUNITY §	CHE0478
BALSTA JORDVANNER §	SWE3654
BALTYCKI SEKRETARIAT POLSCE	POL3482
BAM §	GBR2206
BAMTARE - ASSOCIATION POUR LE DEVELOPPEMENT D'OUROSSOGUI §	FRA1783
BANGLADESH GROEP NEDERLAND §	NLD3055
BARNENS REGNSKOG	SWE3655
BARNFONDEN INSAMLINGSSTIFTELSE	SWE3656
BASHATI - STICHTING VOOR BANGLADESH	NLD3056
BASLER MISSION EVANGELISCHE MISSIONSGESELLSCHAFT IN BASEL	CHE0479
BDTK-KOTAK §	HUN2606
BECKER MOBIL §	DEU0961
BEGEGNUNGSZENTRUM FUR AKTIVE GEWALTLOSIGKEIT	AUT0020
BEHANDLUNGSZENTRUM FUR FOLTEROPFER §	DEU0962
BELGIAN INDONESIAN FOUNDATION FOR SOCIAL AIM §	BEL0136
BELGO-INDIAN VILLAGE RECONSTRUCTION ORGANISATION §	BEL0137
BELLERIVE FOUNDATION §	CHE0480
BEM JOZSEF ALT ISK HERMAN OTTO KOR	HUN2607
BENEDIKTINER MISSIONARE §	CHE0481

BENEVOLES FRANCO-MALIENS POUR L'AIDE AU DEVELOPPEMENT DE L'ARRONDISSEMENT DE MOURDIAH §	FRA1784
BENEVOLES FRANCO-MALIENS POUR L'AIDE AU DEVELOPPEMENT DE L'ARRONDISSEMENT DE OUSSOUBIDIAGNA (MALI)	FRA1785
BENEVOLES FRANCO-MALIENS POUR L'AIDE AU DEVELOPPEMENT DE SAMANTARA (MALI)	FRA1786
BENEVOLES FRANCO-MALIENS POUR L'AIDE AU DEVELOPPEMENT DES LOCALITES DE MOUSSALA ET MADIHAWAYA	FRA1787
BENSHEIMER KREIS	DEU0963
LA BERGERIE - SOS ENFANTS EN DETRESSE	LUX2953
BERLINER MISSIONSWERK §	DEU0964
BERNARD VAN LEER FOUNDATION §	NLD3057
BERTRAND RUSSELL PEACE FOUNDATION §	GBR2207
BERUFSPADAGOGISCHES INSTITUT - MODLING	AUT0021
BESCHAFFUNGSGESELLSCHAFT MIT BESCHRANKTER HAFTUNG FUR KIRCHLICHE, CARITATIVE UND SOZIALE EINRICHTUNGEN	DEU0965
BEVRIJDE WERELD §	BEL0138
BEWEGUNG FUR OFFENE, DEMOKRATISCHE UND SOLIDARISCHE SCHWEIZ §	CHE0482
BHARATBISTAND §	SWE3657
BICTIN OVERSEAS AGRICULTURAL TRUST §	GBR2208
BIFIS-FISE §	POL3483
BIFO, FORENINGEN BISTAND OCH INFORMATION GENOM FRIVILLIGA ORGANISATIONER	SWE3658
BIJEEN DERDE WERELD INFORMATIEHUIS	NLD3058
BILDUNGS - UND AKTIONS - ZENTRUM DRITTE WELT §	DEU0966
BIOCEN ENVIRONMENT AND NATURE PROTECTION CLUB §	HUN2608
BIOFORCE DEVELOPPEMENT	FRA1788
BIRMINGHAM ONE WORLD COMMITTEE §	GBR2209
BISCHOFLICHE AKTION ADVENIAT	DEU0967
BISCHOFLICHES HILFSWERK MISEREOR	DEU0968
BISSCHOP BEKKERS INSTITUUT	NLD3059
BISSCHOPPELIJKE VASTENACTIE §	NLD3060
BISTANDSFORUM §	SWE3659
BISU	DNK1226
BIURO PRASOWE POROZUMIENIA CENTRUM §	POL3484
BLA KORS I NORGE	NOR3379
BLABANDSRORELSEN §	SWE3660
BLLF SWEDEN - FRONT MOT LIVEGENSKAP OCH SLAVERI	SWE3661
BLOSSOM - ASSOCIATION OF RURAL CHILDREN CLUBS §	CZE0847
BOCS ALAPITVANY	HUN2609
BOERENGROEP	NLD3061
BOKOR OKO-CSOPORT	HUN2610
BOLETIN ONG	ESP1434
BOLIVIA-GRUPPEN - U-GRUPPEN §	SWE3662
BOLIVIACENTRUM ANTWERPEN	BEL0139
BOLIVIANISCHES KINDERHILFSWERK §	DEU0969
BONNE VOLONTE MONDIALE §	CHE0483
BOOK AID INTERNATIONAL	GBR2210
BORNEFONDEN	DNK1227
BOTH ENDS	NLD3062
BOTHAR	IRL2683
BOTILDA-UNIFEM SVERIGE §	SWE3663
BOY'S BRIGADE §	GBR2211
BRASILIENWERK DES MARTIN-LUTHER-BUNDES §	DEU0970

Voir : *Comment utiliser le répertoire*, page 11.

BREED OVERLEG VROUWEN EN ONTWIKKELING §	NLD3063
BREMER ARBEITSGEMEINSCHAFT FUR UBERSEEFORSCHUNG UND ENTWICKLUNG	DEU0971
BRENNPUNKT WELT §	CHE0484
BRIDDERLECH DELEN	LUX2954
BRIDGE PROGRAMME OF OXFAM TRADING	GBR2212
BRIGADA LATINO-BERNESA	CHE0485
BRIGATA LABURISTA	MLT3012
BRITAIN - NEPAL MEDICAL TRUST	GBR2213
BRITAIN TANZANIA SOCIETY	GBR2214
BRITISH AFRO-ASIAN SOLIDARITY ORGANIZATION	GBR2215
BRITISH AIRWAYS TRUST §	GBR2216
BRITISH ALL PARTY PARLIAMENTARY GROUP ON POPULATION AND DEVELOPMENT	GBR2217
BRITISH EXECUTIVE SERVICE OVERSEAS	GBR2218
BRITISH LEPROSY RELIEF ASSOCIATION	GBR2219
BRITISH OVERSEAS AID GROUP §	GBR2220
BRITISH PHOTOVOLTAICS ASSOCIATION	GBR2221
BRITISH RED CROSS SOCIETY	GBR2222
BRITISH REFUGEE COUNCIL	GBR2223
BRODET & FISKARNA	SWE3664
BRODREMENIGHEDENS DANSKE MISSION §	DNK1228
BROEDERLIJK DELEN §	BEL0140
BROT FUR ALLE	CHE0486
BROT FUR DIE WELT	DEU0972
BROT FUR HUNGERNDE	AUT0022
THE BROTHERHOOD FOUNDATION §	CZE0848
BRUCKE DER BRUDERHILFE §	CHE0487
BRUDERHILFE RUMANIEN §	DEU0973
BUKO PHARMA-KAMPAGNE	DEU0974
BUND DER DEUTSCHEN KATHOLISCHEN JUGEND	DEU0975
BUND FUR UMWELT UND NATURSCHUTZ DEUTSCHLAND §	DEU0976
BUNDESKONGRESS ENTWICKLUNGSPOLITISCHER AKTIONSGRUPPEN	DEU0977
BUREAU BELEIDSVORMIG ONTWIKKELINGSSAMENWERKING	NLD3064
BUREAU D'ETUDES POUR UN DEVELOPPEMENT HARMONISE	BEL0141
BUREAU EUROPEEN DE L'ENVIRONNEMENT	BEL0142
BUREAU INDEPENDANT SUR LES QUESTIONS HUMANITAIRES §	CHE0488
BUREAU INTERNATIONAL DE LA PAIX §	CHE0489
BUREAU VROUWEN EN AIDS §	NLD3065
BURKINA-87	FRA1789
BUSOGA TRUST	GBR2224
BUTIK PAPAYA	DNK1229
BUTIK SALAM	DNK1230
BYSKOGSINSAMLINGEN	SWE3665
CAABU §	BEL0143
CAFE CIKADEN §	DNK1231
CAISSE NATIONALE DU CREDIT AGRICOLE §	FRA1790
CAMBODIA SOLIDARITY GROUP	IRL2684
CAMBODIA TRUST §	GBR2225
LES CAMIONS DE L'ESPERANCE	FRA1791
CAMPAIGN AID §	IRL2685
CAP-VERT GENEVE	CHE0490
CARE BRITAIN	GBR2226
CARE DANMARK	DNK1232

CARE DEUTSCHLAND	DEU0978
CARE FOR THE WILD	GBR2227
CARE FRANCE §	FRA1792
CARE INTERNATIONAL	BEL0144
CARE ITALIE §	ITA2783
CARE NORGE §	NOR3380
CARIBIENKOMITEEN §	DNK1233
CARITAS DANMARK	DNK1234
CARITAS ESPANOLA	ESP1435
CARITAS HELLAS §	GRC2565
CARITAS INTERNATIONALIS	ITA2784
CARITAS ITALIANA	ITA2785
CARITAS KONFERENZEN DEUTSCHLANDS	DEU0979
CARITAS LIECHTENSTEIN §	LIE2924
CARITAS LUXEMBOURG	LUX2955
CARITAS MALTA §	MLT3013
CARITAS NEERLANDICA - STICHTING MENSEN IN NOOD	NLD3066
CARITAS NORGE	NOR3381
CARITAS PORTUGUESA §	PRT3560
CARITAS SCHWEIZ	CHE0491
CARITAS SERVICE REFUGIES ET AIDE INTERNATIONALE	LUX2956
CARITAS SVERIGE	SWE3666
CARITAS UNIVERSALIS	FRA1793
CARITATE AEGRORUM SERVI	BEL0145
CARL DUISBERG CENTREN GEMINNUTZIGE GESELLSCHAFT MBH	DEU0980
CARL DUISBERG GESELLSCHAFT §	DEU0981
CARL DUISBERG GESELLSCHAFT, ASA-PROGRAMM	DEU0982
CARREFOUR CHANTIERS §	BEL0146
CARREFOUR INTERNATIONAL D'ECHANGES DE PRATIQUES APPLIQUEES AU DEVELOPPEMENT	FRA1794
CATHOLIC FUND FOR OVERSEAS DEVELOPMENT	GBR2228
CATHOLIC INSTITUTE FOR INTERNATIONAL RELATIONS	GBR2229
CATHOLIC RELIEF SERVICES §	CHE0492
CATHOLIC SCOUTING ASSOCIATION - GLOWNA KWATERA SHK "ZAWISZA" §	POL3485
CATHOLIC YOUTH LEADERS ORGANISATION §	MLT3014
CATHOLIC YOUTH MOVEMENT §	HUN2611
CAUSES COMMUNES	BEL0147
CCF KINDERHILFSWERK	DEU0983
CE QU'IL FAUDRAIT DEVELOPPER	FRA1795
CEBEMO/VASTENAKTIE	NLD3067
CEKOSLOVENSKY USTAV ZAHRANICNI §	CZE0849
CELIM BERGAMO - ORGANIZZAZIONE DI VOLONTARIATO INTERNAZIONALE CRISTIANO	ITA2786
CEMEA-CLED	FRA1796
CENTER FOR ALTERNATIV SAMFUNDSANALYSE §	DNK1235
CENTER OF RURAL WOMEN §	GRC2566
CENTERKVINNORNA	SWE3667
CENTRAAL MISSIE COMMISSARIAAT	NLD3068
CENTRAL BRITISH FUND FOR WORLD JEWISH RELIEF	GBR2230
THE CENTRAL BUREAU FOR EDUCATIONAL VISITS AND EXCHANGES	GBR2231
CENTRALE SANITAIRE SUISSE	CHE0493
CENTRE AUVERGNE POUR UNE SOLIDARITE INTERNATIONALE	FRA1797
CENTRE CATHOLIQUE INTERNATIONAL DE GENEVE	CHE0494
CENTRE CATHOLIQUE INTERNATIONAL POUR L'UNESCO §	FRA1798

See: *How to Use the Directory*, page 11.

CENTRE D'AIDE AU DEVELOPPEMENT DANS LA LIBERTE ET LE PROGRES	BEL0148
CENTRE D'ECHANGES ET PROMOTION DES ARTISANS EN ZONES A EQUIPER	FRA1799
CENTRE D'ECHANGES INTERNATIONAUX DU NORD	FRA1800
CENTRE D'EDUCATION ET DE FORMATION PROFESSIONNELLE DU MARANHAO §	FRA1801
CENTRE D'ETUDE DU DEVELOPPEMENT EN AMERIQUE LATINE §	FRA1802
CENTRE D'ETUDE ET DE DEVELOPPEMENT DES RESSOURCES ECOLOGIQUES §	FRA1803
CENTRE D'ETUDE ET DE DOCUMENTATION AFRICAINES	BEL0149
CENTRE D'ETUDE RECHERCHE-ACTION POUR LE DEVELOPPEMENT DE LA ZONE SOUDANO-SAHELIENNE §	FRA1804
CENTRE D'ETUDES CONFLITS ET TIERS MONDE	FRA1805
CENTRE D'ETUDES ET D'INITIATIVES DE SOLIDARITE INTERNATIONALE §	FRA1806
CENTRE D'ETUDES TIBETAINES RABTEN CHOELING	CHE0495
CENTRE D'INFORMATION ET D'ETUDES SUR LES MIGRATIONS INTERNATIONALES §	FRA1807
CENTRE D'INFORMATION ET D'ORIENTATION POUR LES PROFESSIONS RELATIVES A LA COOPERATION AU DEVELOPPEMENT ET A L'AIDE HUMANITAIRE	CHE0496
CENTRE D'INFORMATION ET DE DOCUMENTATION - MAISON DES ASSOCIATIONS HUMANITAIRES DE TOURAINE	FRA1808
CENTRE D'INFORMATION SUR LES PRATIQUES ASSOCIATIVES §	BEL0150
CENTRE D'INITIATION POUR REFUGIES ET ETRANGERS §	BEL0151
CENTRE DE COOPERATION TECHNIQUE ET DE RECHERCHE POUR L'EDUCATION DES TRAVAILLEURS DANS LES PAYS EN VOIE DE DEVELOPPEMENT §	CHE0497
CENTRE DE CULTURE ET D'INFORMATION SUR LE MONDE ARABE §	FRA1809
CENTRE DE DOCUMENTATION INTERNATIONALE POUR LE DEVELOPPEMENT, LES LIBERTES ET LA PAIX	FRA1810
CENTRE DE DOCUMENTATION TIERS MONDE PEUPLES SOLIDAIRES	FRA1811
CENTRE DE FORMATION AUX REALITES INTERNATIONALES §	FRA1812
CENTRE DE FORMATION ET D'ECHANGES INTERNATIONAUX	FRA1813
CENTRE DE FORMATION ET DE COOPERATION INTERNATIONALE §	FRA1814
CENTRE DE FORMATION POUR LE DEVELOPPEMENT	FRA1815
CENTRE DE RECHERCHE ET D'INFORMATION POUR LE DEVELOPPEMENT	FRA1816
CENTRE DE RECHERCHE ET DE COOPERATION INTERNATIONALE	FRA1817
CENTRE DE RECHERCHE, D'INFORMATION ET DE SOLIDARITE AVEC LES PEUPLES D'AFRIQUE, D'AMERIQUE LATINE ET D'ASIE	FRA1818
CENTRE DE RECHERCHE-INFORMATION ACTION POUR LE DEVELOPPEMENT EN AFRIQUE	FRA1819
CENTRE DE RECHERCHES ET D'ETUDES POUR LE DEVELOPPEMENT DE LA SANTE	FRA1820
CENTRE DE RELATIONS INTERNATIONALES ENTRE AGRICULTEURS POUR LE DEVELOPPEMENT §	FRA1821
CENTRE ECOLOGIQUE ALBERT SCHWEITZER	CHE0498
CENTRE EUROPE-TIERS MONDE	CHE0499
CENTRE EUROPEEN D'ETUDES POUR LE DEVELOPPEMENT ET L'ENVIRONNEMENT	GRC2567
CENTRE EUROPEEN DE FORMATION DES STATISTICIENS ECONOMISTES DES PAYS EN VOIE DE DEVELOPPEMENT §	FRA1822
CENTRE FOR DEVELOPMENT COOPERATION SERVICES	NLD3069
CENTRE FOR ENVIRONMENT AND DEVELOPMENT §	POL3486
CENTRE FOR ENVIRONMENTAL MANAGEMENT AND PLANNING	GBR2232
CENTRE FOR GLOBAL EDUCATION	GBR2233
CENTRE FOR INTERNATIONAL CO-OPERATION	IRL2686
CENTRE FOR INTERNATIONAL CO-OPERATION ACTIVITIES	NLD3070
CENTRE FOR INTERNATIONAL CO-OPERATION AND APPROPRIATE TECHNOLOGY OF THE DELFT UNIVERSITY OF TECHNOLOGY	NLD3071
CENTRE FOR INTERNATIONAL STUDIES §	GBR2234
CENTRE FOR INTERNATIONAL WOMEN'S ISSUES §	NOR3382
CENTRE FOR OUR COMMON FUTURE	CHE0500
CENTRE FRANCAIS DE PROMOTION INDUSTRIELLE EN AFRIQUE §	FRA1823
CENTRE FRANCAIS DE PROTECTION DE L'ENFANCE	FRA1824
CENTRE FRANCE-ASIE	FRA1825
CENTRE FRANCO-BENINOIS D'ECHANGES CULTURELS §	FRA1826
CENTRE HAITIEN DE RECHERCHES ET DE DOCUMENTATION	CHE0501
CENTRE INTERNATIONAL D'ETUDES POUR LE DEVELOPPEMENT LOCAL	FRA1827
CENTRE INTERNATIONAL D'ETUDES, DE RECHERCHE ET D'ACTIONS POUR LE DEVELOPPEMENT	BEL0152
CENTRE INTERNATIONAL DE COOPERATION POUR LE DEVELOPPEMENT AGRICOLE	FRA1828
CENTRE INTERNATIONAL DE CULTURE POPULAIRE	FRA1829
CENTRE INTERNATIONAL DE DEVELOPPEMENT ET DE RECHERCHE	FRA1830
CENTRE INTERNATIONAL DE FORMATION DES CADRES DU DEVELOPPEMENT	BEL0153
CENTRE INTERNATIONAL DE L'EAU	FRA1831
CENTRE INTERNATIONAL DE L'ENFANCE	FRA1832
CENTRE INTERNATIONAL DE LA CONSTRUCTION EN TERRE	FRA1833
CENTRE INTERNATIONAL DE RECHERCHES ET D'ETUDES SUR LE DEVELOPPEMENT ECONOMIQUE ET COMMERCIAL NORD-SUD §	FRA1834
CENTRE INTERNATIONAL DU CREDIT MUTUEL	FRA1835
CENTRE INTERNATIONAL POUR L'EDUCATION PERMANENTE ET L'AMENAGEMENT CONCERTE	FRA1836
CENTRE INTERNATIONAL POUR LA FORMATION ET LES ECHANGES GEOLOGIQUES	FRA1837
CENTRE INTERNATIONAL POUR LA PROMOTION ET L'EDUCATION DES DROITS DE L'HOMME §	CHE0502
CENTRE LEBRET	FRA1838
CENTRE LORRAIN D'INFORMATION POUR LE DEVELOPPEMENT	FRA1839
CENTRE MARTIN LUTHER KING POUR LA NON-VIOLENCE	CHE0503
CENTRE MEDICO-PSYCHOSOCIAL POUR REFUGIES §	BEL0154
CENTRE NATIONAL DE COOPERATION AU DEVELOPPEMENT	BEL0155
CENTRE NORD-SUD DE L'INSTITUT DE L'ENTREPRISE §	FRA1840
THE CENTRE ON HOUSING RIGHTS AND EVICTIONS	NLD3072
CENTRE RENNAIS D'INFORMATION POUR LE DEVELOPPEMENT ET LA LIBERATION DES PEUPLES	FRA1841
CENTRE SCIENTIFIQUE ET MEDICAL DE L'UNIVERSITE LIBRE DE BRUXELLES POUR SES ACTIVITES DE COOPERATION	BEL0156
CENTRE TRICONTINENTAL	BEL0157
CENTRE UNESCO DE CATALUNYA	ESP1436
CENTRE VOOR ONTWIKKELINGSSAMENWERKING	NLD3073
CENTRO AIUTI MONDIALI	ITA2787

CENTRO BERTRAND RUSSELL §	ITA2788
CENTRO COMUNITARIO SERVIZIO CRISTIANO §	ITA2789
CENTRO DE COMUNICACION, INVESTIGACION Y DOCUMENTACION ENTRE EUROPA, ESPANA Y AMERICA LATINA	ESP1437
CENTRO DE CULTURA E ESTUDOS RURAIS §	PRT3561
CENTRO DE ESTUDIOS Y DESARROLLO RURAL	ESP1438
CENTRO DE ESTUDIOS Y SOLIDARIDAD CON AMERICA LATINA	ESP1439
CENTRO DE ESTUDOS DA CULTURA E ENSINO DOS PAISES DE EXPRESSAO PORTUGUESA §	PRT3562
CENTRO DE ESTUDOS, DOCUMENTACAO E INFORMACAO DAS REGIOES POLARES §	PRT3563
CENTRO DE INFORMACAO E DOCUMENTACAO AMILCAR CABRAL	PRT3564
CENTRO DE INFORMACION EDUCACION Y AUDIOVISUALES PARA EL DESARROLLO §	ESP1440
CENTRO DE INFORMACION Y DOCUMENTACION INTERNACIONALES EN BARCELONA	ESP1441
CENTRO DE INVESTIGACIONES Y PROMOCION IBEROAMERICA-EUROPA	ESP1442
CENTRO DE SOLIDARIEDADE CRISTA MARANATHA §	PRT3565
CENTRO DI ADDESTRAMENTO PER L'AZIONE SOCIALE NELLE REGIONI IN VIA DI SVILUPPO §	ITA2790
CENTRO DI EDUCAZIONE SANITARIA E TECNOLOGIE APPROPRIATE SANITARIE	ITA2791
CENTRO DI VOLONTARIATO INTERNAZIONALE	ITA2792
CENTRO DOCUMENTAZIONE OSCAR ROMERO §	ITA2793
CENTRO ECCLESIALE ITALIANO AMERICA LATINA §	ITA2794
CENTRO ECCLESIALE ITALIANO PER L'AFRICA I ASIA §	ITA2795
CENTRO EDUCAZIONE ALLA MONDIALITA §	ITA2796
CENTRO INFORMAZIONE DOCUMENTAZIONE E INIZIATIVE PER LO SVILUPPO §	ITA2797
CENTRO INFORMAZIONE E EDUCAZIONE ALLO SVILUPPO	ITA2798
CENTRO INTERNACIONAL PARA A COOPERACAO E DESENVOLVIMIENTO §	PRT3566
CENTRO INTERNAZIONALE CROCEVIA	ITA2799
CENTRO INTERNAZIONALE DI COOPERAZIONE ALLO SVILUPPO §	ITA2800
CENTRO ITALIANO DI COLLABORAZIONE PER LO SVILUPPO EDILIZIO DELLE NAZIONI EMERGENTI	ITA2801
CENTRO ITALIANO DI SOLIDARIETA	ITA2802
CENTRO LAICI ITALIANI PER LE MISSIONI - VOLONTARI PER UN SERVIZIO INTERNAZIONALE	ITA2803
CENTRO MONDIALITA' SVILUPPO RECIPROCO	ITA2804
CENTRO NACIONAL DE CULTURA	PRT3567
CENTRO NUOVO MODELLO DI SVILUPPO	ITA2805
CENTRO ORIENTAMENTO EDUCATIVO	ITA2806
CENTRO PARA EL DESARROLLO DE LA MUJER IBEROAMERICANA	ESP1443
CENTRO PER UN APPROPRIATO SVILUPPO TECNOLOGICO	ITA2807
CENTRO PER UN FUTURO SOSTENIBILE	ITA2808
CENTRO REGIONALE D'INTERVENTO PER LA COOPERAZIONE	ITA2809
CENTRO STUDI TERZO MONDO	ITA2810
CENTRO SVILUPPO TERZO MONDO	ITA2811
CENTRO VOLONTARI COOPERAZIONE ALLO SVILUPPO	ITA2812
CENTRO VOLONTARI MARCHIGIANI	ITA2813
CENTROINFORMAZIONE TERZO MONDO	ITA2814
CENTRU ANIMAZZJONI MISSJUNARJA §	MLT3015
CENTRUM EDUKACJI EKOLOGICZNEJ §	POL3487
CENTRUM FOR KOOPERATIVA STUDIER OCH VERKSAMHET "COMUNIDAD" §	SWE3668
CENTRUM FUR TECHNOLOGIETRANSFER CLAUSTHAL E.V. §	DEU0984
CENTRUM MISSIONAIRE PARTICIPATIE AFRIKA	NLD3074
CENTRUM ONTMOETING DER VOLKEREN	NLD3075
CENTRUM SRODOWISKA I ROZWOJU §	POL3488
CENTRUM VOOR DE STUDIE VAN HET ONDERWIJS IN ONTWIKKELINGSLANDEN	NLD3076
CENTRUM VOOR DORPSINTEGRATIE-BWAMANDA-BELGIE	BEL0158
CENTRUM VOOR MONDIAAL ONDERWIJS	NLD3077
CENTRUM VOOR ONTWIKKELINGSSAMENWERKING KORTRIJK §	BEL0159
CERCLE DE COOPERATION DES ORGANISATIONS NON GOUVERNEMENTALES DE DEVELOPPEMENT DU LUXEMBOURG	LUX2957
CERCLE DES PROMOTEURS DES RELATIONS AFRIQUE-EUROPE §	CHE0504
CESKA KATOLICKA CHARITA §	CZE0850
CEVRE MUHENDISLERI ODASI	TUR3884
CEYLON-DIREKTHILFE	DEU0985
CHAIRNAY'S FUND §	CZE0851
CHANGE INTERNATIONAL REPORTS	GBR2235
CHARLES UNIVERSITY FOUNDATION §	CZE0852
CHARTER 77 FOUNDATION	SVK3608
CHILD CARE INTERNATIONAL - DENMARK §	DNK1236
CHILDHOPE	GBR2236
CHILDHOPE - DEN INTERNATIONALE BEVEGELSE FOR GADEBORN §	DNK1237
CHILDREN OF THE EARTH §	CZE0853
CHILDREN'S INTERNATIONAL SUMMER VILLAGES §	GBR2237
CHILE-AMERIKA CENTRO DE ESTUDIOS, DOCUMENTACION Y PROMOCION DE AMERICA LATINA Y EL CARIBE, CILE-AMERICA §	ESP1444
CHILES KINDER	LUX2958
CHILI FLASH ESPACE LATINO-AMERICAIN §	FRA1842
CHRESCHTE MAM SAHEL	LUX2959
CHRISTELIJK NATIONAAL VAKVERBOND	NLD3078
CHRISTELYK PLATTELANDSVROUWEN BOND	NLD3079
CHRISTIAN AID	GBR2238
CHRISTIAN AID, IRELAND	IRL2687
CHRISTIAN CHILDREN'S FUND §	CHE0505
CHRISTIAN CHILDREN'S FUND - NATIONAL OFFICE §	POL3489
CHRISTIAN CONCERN FOR ONE WORLD	GBR2239
CHRISTIAN MOVEMENT FOR PEACE	CHE0506
CHRISTIAN OUTREACH	GBR2240
CHRISTIAN SOLIDARITY INTERNATIONAL §	CHE0507
CHRISTIAN SOLIDARITY INTERNATIONAL §	LUX2960
CHRISTIANIKI ENOSSI NEANIDON ELLADOS §	GRC2568
CHRISTIANS ABROAD	GBR2241
CHRISTKATHOLISCHES HILFSWERK §	CHE0508
CHRISTLICHE FACHKRAFTE INTERNATIONAL	DEU0986
CHRISTLICHER FRIEDENSDIENST §	CHE0509
CHRISTLICHER FRIEDENSDIENST §	DEU0987
CHRISTLICHES INITIATIV- UND STUDIENZENTRUM DORTMUND §	DEU0988
CHRISTOFFEL-BLINDENMISSION	DEU0989
CHURCH MISSIONARY SOCIETY IRELAND	IRL2688
CHURCH OF IRELAND BISHOPS' APPEAL: WORLD DEVELOPMENT COMMITTEE	IRL2689

CHURCH OF SCOTLAND-WORLD MISSION	GBR2242
CHURCHES COMMISSION FOR MIGRANTS IN EUROPE	BEL0160
CIBA-GEIGY STIFTUNG FUR ZUSAMMENARBEIT MIT ENTWICKLUNGSLANDERN	CHE0510
CIMADE - SERVICE OECUMENIQUE D'ENTRAIDE	FRA1843
CINEDIA	CHE0511
CINEMAS D'AFRIQUE ANGERS	FRA1844
CIRUJANOS Y ENFERMERAS EN ACCION	ESP1445
CITES UNIES DEVELOPPEMENT §	FRA1845
CITES UNIES FRANCE - VILLES JUMELEES	FRA1846
CITOYENS ET DEVELOPPEMENT §	FRA1847
CITTASTUDI/CLESAV §	ITA2815
CIVIC DIALOGUE NGO PROGRAMME §	POL3490
CIVIC FORUM FOUNDATION §	CZE0854
CLAIR-LOGIS AFRIQUE	FRA1848
CLAT NEDERLAND §	NLD3080
CLEAN AIR FOUNDATION §	POL3491
CLEARINGHOUSE FOR APPLIED FUTURES	DEU0990
CLIMATE ACTION NETWORK UK §	GBR2243
CLUB INTERNATIONAL DE COOPERATION - GENEVE §	CHE0512
CLUB TIERS MONDE DE SAINT-ADRIEN	FRA1849
CNV JONGERENORGANISATIE §	NLD3081
CO-OPERATION FOR DEVELOPMENT	GBR2244
THE CO-OPERATIVE BANK §	GBR2245
CO-OPERATIVE CENTRE DENMARK	DNK1238
CODA INTERNATIONAL TRAINING §	GBR2246
CODE EUROPE	GBR2247
CODEF - FEDERATION FRANCOPHONE DES ONG D'ENVOI DE COOPERANTS-ONG	BEL0161
CODEV-VIET-PHAP	FRA1850
COLECTIVIDADE CULTURAL E RECREATIVA DE SANTA CATARINA §	PRT3568
COLECTIVOS DE ACCION SOLIDARIA §	ESP1446
COLLABORATION MEDICALE TIERS-MONDE §	BEL0162
COLLECTIF D'ACCUEIL DES REFUGIES DU CHILI §	BEL0163
COLLECTIF D'ECHANGES POUR LA TECHNOLOGIE APPROPRIEE	BEL0164
COLLECTIF ENVIRONNEMENT DEVELOPPEMENT INTERNATIONAL	FRA1851
COLLECTIF STRATEGIES ALIMENTAIRES	BEL0165
COLLECTIF SUISSE DE SOLIDARITE AVEC LE PEUPLE ALGERIEN §	CHE0513
COLLEGIO UNIVERSITARIO ASPIRANTI MEDICI MISSIONARI	ITA2816
COLOMBIA VIVE §	SWE3669
COME NOI §	ITA2817
COMHLAMH, THE ASSOCIATION OF IRISH RETURNED DEVELOPMENT WORKERS	IRL2690
COMIC RELIEF - CHARITY PROJECTS	GBR2248
COMISION CATOLICA ESPANOLA DE MIGRACION	ESP1447
COMISION DERECHOS HUMANOS GUATEMALA §	ESP1448
COMISION ESPANOLA DE "JUSTICIA Y PAZ" §	ESP1449
COMISION ESPANOLA DE AYUDA AL REFUGIADO	ESP1450
COMITATO COLLABORAZIONE MEDICA	ITA2818
COMITATO DI COORDINAMENTO DELLE ORGANIZZAZIONI PER IL SERVIZIO VOLONTARIO §	ITA2819
COMITATO EUROPEO DI FORMAZIONE AGRARIA	ITA2820
COMITATO HARAMBEE - VOLONTARI PER IL TERZO MONDO §	ITA2821
COMITATO INTERNAZIONALE PER LO SVILUPPO DEI POPOLI	ITA2822

COMITE AMERIQUE CENTRALE DE CHABLAIS	FRA1852
COMITE BELGE D'AIDE AUX REFUGIES §	BEL0166
COMITE BELGE DE SECOURS A L'ERYTHREE	BEL0167
COMITE BELGE POUR L'UNICEF	BEL0168
COMITE CATHOLIQUE CONTRE LA FAIM ET POUR LE DEVELOPPEMENT §	FRA1853
COMITE CHILI §	CHE0514
COMITE CHRETIEN D'AIDE AU TIERS-MONDE §	FRA1854
COMITE COLOMBIE	CHE0515
COMITE COMMUN DE LA COOPERATION PEDAGOGIQUE EN AFRIQUE §	CHE0516
COMITE D'ACTION SOCIALE ET CULTURELLE JEUNESSE D'ETHIOPIE ET DE FRANCE	FRA1855
COMITE D'AIDE AUX CALAMINOIS DU TIERS MONDE	BEL0169
COMITE D'AIDE PROFONDEVILLOIS AUX PAYS EN VOIE DE DEVELOPPEMENT §	BEL0170
COMITE DE COOPERATION SCIENTIFIQUE ET TECHNIQUE FRANCE-NICARAGUA	FRA1856
COMITE DE DEFENSA DE LOS REFUGIADOS, ASILADOS E IMMIGRANTES	ESP1451
COMITE DE JUMELAGE - COMMISSION COOPERATION EPERNAY FADA N'GOURMA §	FRA1857
COMITE DE LIAISON DES ORGANISATIONS DE SOLIDARITE INTERNATIONALE §	FRA1858
COMITE DE LIAISON DES ORGANISATIONS NON GOUVERNEMENTALES DE VOLONTARIAT §	FRA1859
COMITE DE LIAISON ENERGIES RENOUVELABLES	FRA1860
COMITE DE SAINT PIERRE ET MIQUELON D'AIDE AU DEVELOPPEMENT ET DE LUTTE CONTRE LA FAIM DANS LE MONDE	FRA1861
COMITE DE SOLIDARITE AVEC L'AMERIQUE CENTRALE	CHE0517
COMITE DE SOLIDARITE AVEC LE PEUPLE BRESILIEN §	CHE0518
COMITE DE SOUTIEN AU PEUPLE SAHRAOUI	CHE0519
COMITE DE SOUTIEN AU PEUPLE TIBETAIN	FRA1862
COMITE ECHANGES ISERE-KIVU	FRA1863
COMITE EUROPEEN DE L'ASSOCIATION MONDIALE DES GUIDES ET DES ECLAIREUSES §	FRA1864
COMITE EUROPEEN POUR LA DEFENSE DES REFUGIES ET IMMIGRES §	CHE0520
COMITE EXTERIOR MAPUCHE, ENGLISH SECTION §	GBR2249
COMITE FRANCAIS CONTRE LA FAIM	FRA1865
COMITE FRANCAIS DE SOUTIEN GK-SAVAR BANGLADESH	FRA1866
COMITE FRANCAIS POUR L'ENVIRONNEMENT §	FRA1867
COMITE FRANCAIS POUR L'UNICEF §	FRA1868
COMITE INTER-AFRICAIN SUR LES PRATIQUES TRADITIONNELLES AYANT EFFET SUR LA SANTE DES FEMMES ET DES ENFANTS	CHE0521
COMITE INTERNATIONAL DE L'ORDRE DE MALTE POUR L'ASSISTANCE AUX LEPREUX	CHE0522
COMITE INTERNATIONAL DE LA CROIX ROUGE §	CHE0523
COMITE INTERNATIONAL POUR LA DIGNITE DE L'ENFANT	CHE0524
COMITE JEAN PAIN	BEL0171
COMITE LAIQUE POUR L'EDUCATION AU DEVELOPPEMENT - EDUCATEURS SANS FRONTIERES	FRA1869
COMITE LUXEMBOURGEOIS POUR L'UNICEF	LUX2961
COMITE MEDICAL POUR LES EXILES §	FRA1870
COMITE NATIONAL DE SOLIDARITE LAIQUE	FRA1871
COMITE NATIONAL POUR L'INDEPENDANCE ET LE DEVELOPPEMENT §	FRA1872
COMITE NATIONAL POUR LA PAIX ET LE DEVELOPPEMENT §	BEL0172
COMITE NICARAGUA - EL SALVADOR §	CHE0525

COMITE PAIX §	CHE0526
COMITE PATRICE LUMUMBA §	CHE0527
COMITE PORTUGUES PARA A UNICEF §	PRT3569
COMITE POUR LERE §	FRA1873
COMITE POUR LES RELATIONS INTERNATIONALES DE JEUNESSE DE LA COMMUNAUTE FRANCAISE DE BELGIQUE	BEL0173
COMITE POUR LES RELATIONS NATIONALES ET INTERNATIONALES DES ASSOCIATIONS DE JEUNESSE ET D'EDUCATION POPULAIRE §	FRA1874
COMITE SUISSE CONTRE LA TORTURE §	CHE0528
COMITE SUISSE DE SOUTIEN AU PEUPLE AFGHAN	CHE0529
COMITE SUISSE POUR LA DEFENSE DU DROIT D'ASILE §	CHE0530
COMITE TOULOUSE-BAURU/FRANCE-BRESIL §	FRA1875
COMMISSIE JUSTITIA ET PAX - NEDERLAND	NLD3082
COMMISSIE RECHTVAARDIGH. EN VREDE	BEL0174
COMMISSION AFRICAINE DES PROMOTEURS DE LA SANTE ET DES DROITS DE L'HOMME §	CHE0531
COMMISSION EUROPEENNE IMMIGRES §	BEL0175
COMMISSION FOR RACIAL EQUALITY §	GBR2250
COMMISSION JUSTICE ET PAIX	BEL0176
COMMISSION JUSTICE ET PAIX	LUX2962
COMMISSION LUTHERIENNE DES RELATIONS AVEC LES EGLISES D'OUTRE-MER	FRA1876
COMMISSION NATIONALE DE L'UNESCO - CENTRE NATIONAL DE CULTURE §	PRT3570
COMMISSION NATIONALE DE LA JEUNESSE POUR LE DEVELOPPEMENT §	FRA1877
COMMISSION ON GLOBAL GOVERNANCE §	CHE0532
COMMISSION ON THE CHURCHES' PARTICIPATION IN DEVELOPMENT OF THE WORLD COUNCIL OF CHURCHES §	CHE0533
COMMISSION PRO-AMAZONIA	ESP1452
COMMISSION TIERS-MONDE DE L'EGLISE CATHOLIQUE	CHE0534
COMMISSION TIERS-MONDE DE L'EGLISE NATIONALE PROTESTANTE DE GENEVE	CHE0535
COMMITTEE OF LIMASSOL FOR THE PROTECTION OF THE ENVIRONMENT	CYP0828
COMMITTEE OF THE EUROPEAN CULTURAL FOUNDATION §	SVK3609
COMMONWEAL	GBR2251
COMMONWEALTH ASSOCIATION OF ARCHITECTS §	GBR2252
COMMONWEALTH HUMAN ECOLOGY COUNCIL	GBR2253
COMMONWEALTH HUMAN RIGHTS INITIATIVE §	GBR2254
COMMONWEALTH INSTITUTE §	GBR2255
COMMONWEALTH MEDICAL ASSOCIATION	GBR2256
COMMONWEALTH SOCIETY FOR THE DEAF §	GBR2257
COMMONWEALTH TRADE UNION COUNCIL §	GBR2258
COMMUNAUTE DES MISSIONNAIRES LAIQUES §	CHE0536
COMMUNIST YOUTH UNION §	CZE0855
COMMUNITA DI AGAPE §	ITA2823
COMORER KOMITEEN §	DNK1239
COMPAGNONS BATISSEURS §	FRA1878
COMPUPLAN - INSTITUUT VOOR TOEGEPASTE RUIMTELIJKE INFORMATICA	NLD3083
COMUNITA DI LAVORO PER I PROBLEMI DEGLI STRANIERI	CHE0537
COMUNITA DI SANT'EGIDIO-ACAP	ITA2824
COMUNITA EMMAUS §	ITA2825
COMUNITA IMPEGNO SERVIZIO VOLONTARIATO	ITA2826
COMUNITA LAICI MISSIONARI CATTOLICI	ITA2827
COMUNITA PROMOZIONE E SVILUPPO	ITA2828

COMUNITA' INTERNAZIONALE VOLONTARI LAICI	ITA2829
CONCERN UNIVERSAL	GBR2259
CONCERN WORLDWIDE	IRL2691
CONCERTACIO N/S	ESP1453
CONCORD VIDEO AND FILM COUNCIL	GBR2260
CONFEDERATION EUROPEENNE DES SYNDICATS	BEL0177
CONFEDERATION INTERNATIONALE DES SYNDICATS LIBRES §	BEL0178
CONFEDERATION MONDIALE DU TRAVAIL §	BEL0179
CONFEDERATION OF REFUGEE GROUPS AND ETHNIC MINORITIES §	GBR2261
CONFEDERAZIONE COOPERATIVE ITALIANE	ITA2830
CONFERENCE PERMANENTE DES COMPAGNIES CONSULAIRES AFRICAINES ET FRANCAISES	FRA1879
CONFERENCE ST. VINCENT DE PAUL §	LUX2963
CONFERENZA MISSIONARIA DELLA SVIZZERA ITALIANA §	CHE0538
CONGREGATION DES MISSIONS AFRICAINES PROVINCE DE LYON	FRA1880
CONSEIL DE LA JEUNESSE CATHOLIQUE §	BEL0180
CONSEIL DES ASSOCIATIONS DES IMMIGRES EN EUROPE §	CHE0539
CONSEIL DES INVESTISSEURS FRANCAIS EN AFRIQUE §	FRA1881
CONSEIL EUROPEEN DES COMITES NATIONAUX DE JEUNESSE §	BEL0181
CONSEIL EUROPEEN DES ETUDES AFRICAINES §	FRA1882
CONSEIL INTERNATIONAL DES UNIONS SCIENTIFIQUES	FRA1883
CONSEIL INTERNATIONAL DU CINEMA, DE LA TELEVISION ET DE LA COMMUNICATION AUDIOVISUELLE §	FRA1884
CONSEIL ITALIEN POUR LES REFUGIES §	ITA2831
CONSEJO INTERHOSPITALARIO DE COOPERACION	ESP1454
CONSELHO PORTUGUES DE COOPERACAO E INTERCAMBIO DE SERVICIOS SOCIAIS §	PRT3571
CONSELHO PORTUGUES PARA A PAZ E COOPERACAO §	PRT3572
CONSELHO PORTUGUES PARA OS REFUGIADOS	PRT3573
CONSERVATION FOUNDATION	GBR2262
CONSORTIUM FOR STREET CHILDREN §	GBR2263
CONSUMERS' INTERNATIONAL	GBR2264
CONTRIBUTION A LA COMMUNICATION ET A L'ECHANGE D'EXPERIENCES POUR UN MEILLEUR DEVELOPPEMENT	FRA1885
COOP SUISSE	CHE0540
COOPAFRICA - ASSOCIACAO PARA A COOPERACAO E DESENVOLVIMENTO §	PRT3574
COOPERACAO, SAUDE E DESENVOLVIMENTO - FUNDACAO §	PRT3575
COOPERACION AL DESARROLLO Y PROMOCION DE ACTIVIDADES ASISTENCIALES	ESP1455
COOPERATIE VRIJ TECHNISCH ONDERWIJS WEST-VLAANDEREN	BEL0182
COOPERATIEVE ADVIESGROEP VOOR MELKVEEHOUDERIJ EN MELKERWERKING	NLD3084
COOPERATION DEVELOPPEMENT INDUSTRIEL ET FORMATION	FRA1886
COOPERATION DIALOGUE COMMUNICATION NORD-SUD §	BEL0183
COOPERATION ET PROGRES	BEL0184
COOPERATION ET SOLIDARITE §	BEL0185
COOPERATION FOR PEACE §	SWE3670
COOPERATION FUND §	POL3492
COOPERATION INTERNATIONALE POUR LE DEVELOPPEMENT ET LA SOLIDARITE	BEL0186

See: *How to Use the Directory*, page 11.

COOPERATION PAR L'EDUCATION ET LA CULTURE §	BEL0187
COOPERATION POUR LE BIEN-ETRE	CHE0541
COOPERATION TECHNIQUE INTERNATIONALE	BEL0188
COOPERATIVA ESSERE UMANI	CHE0542
COOPERAZIONE E SVILUPPO	ITA2832
COOPERAZIONE E SVILUPPO §	ITA2833
COOPERAZIONE INTERNATIONALE SUD-SUD	ITA2834
COOPERAZIONE INTERNAZIONALE	ITA2835
COOPERAZIONE INTERNAZIONALE §	ITA2836
COOPERAZIONE PAESI EMERGENTI	ITA2837
COOPERAZIONE PER LO SVILUPPO DEI PAESI EMERGENTI	ITA2838
COOPIBO PLATTELAND MET TOEKOMST IN NOOR EN ZUID	BEL0189
COORDINADORA DE ONG PARA EL DESARROLLO	ESP1456
COORDINADORA DE ORGANIZACIONES DE DEFENSA AMBIENTAL	ESP1457
COORDINAMENTO DELLE ONG PER LA COOPERAZIONE INTERNAZIONALE ALLO SVILUPPO	ITA2839
COORDINAMENTO DI INIZIATIVE POPOLARI DI SOLIDARIETA INTERNAZIONALE	ITA2840
COORDINATIEPIMS MONDIAAL VROUWENWERK	NLD3085
COORDINATING COMMITTEE FOR INTERNATIONAL VOLUNTARY SERVICE	FRA1887
COORDINATION D'AGEN POUR LES MISSIONS D'URGENCE ET DE COOPERATION VOLONTAIRE	FRA1888
COORDINATION INFORMATION TIERS-MONDE	FRA1889
COORDINATION INTERCOMMUNAUTAIRE CONTRE L'ANTISEMITISME ET LA DIFFAMATION §	CHE0543
COORDINATION ROMANDE DE "PAYSANS SOLIDAIRES"	CHE0544
COPROGRAM	BEL0190
CORPS AFRICAIN DE REFLEXION ET D'ACTION CONTRE LA FAIM §	CHE0545
CORPS MONDIAL DE SECOURS §	FRA1890
COUNCIL FOR EDUCATION IN WORLD CITIZENSHIP	GBR2265
THE COUNCIL FOR WORLD MISSION	GBR2266
COUNCIL OF CHURCHES FOR BRITAIN AND IRELAND	GBR2267
COUNCIL OF EUROPEAN NATIONAL YOUTH COMMITTEES	BEL0191
COUNCIL OF FREE CHURCHES §	NOR3383
COUP DE POUCE SUISSE-HAITI	CHE0546
LES COUREURS DU MONDE	FRA1891
CROCE ROSSA ITALIANA	ITA2841
CROIX ROUGE DE BELGIQUE	BEL0192
CROIX ROUGE FRANCAISE §	FRA1892
CROIX ROUGE LUXEMBOURGEOISE	LUX2964
CROIX VERTE INTERNATIONALE	CHE0547
CRUZ ROJA ESPANOLA §	ESP1458
CRUZ VERMELHA PORTUGUESA	PRT3576
CULTURE ET DEVELOPPEMENT §	BEL0193
CULTURE ET DEVELOPPEMENT	FRA1893
CULTURE ET LIBERTE §	FRA1894
CUSICHACA PROJECT TRUST §	GBR2268
CVJM - GESAMTVERBAND IN DEUTSCHLAND	DEU0991
CYFANFYD	GBR2269
CYPRUS FORESTRY ASSOCIATION §	CYP0829
CYPRUS WILDLIFE SOCIETY	CYP0830
CZECH CULTURE FOUNDATION §	CZE0856
CZECH HELSINKI COMMITTEE	CZE0857
CZECH PEACE SOCIETY §	CZE0858
CZECH RED CROSS	CZE0859
CZECH SOCIETY FOR CHILDREN'S RIGHTS §	CZE0860
CZECHOSLOVAK CHARTA 77 FOUNDATION PRAGUE §	CZE0861
CZECHOSLOVAK COMMITTEE FOR EUROPEAN SECURITY AND CO-OPERATION §	CZE0862
CZECHOSLOVAK LATINAMERICAN ASSOCIATION §	CZE0863
DAENK E MOL LADE §	CHE0548
DAG HAMMARSKJOLD FOUNDATION	SWE3671
DAKSA DEVELOPPEMENT §	FRA1895
DALANGSSKOLANS TANZANIAGRUPP	SWE3672
DALARNAS FORSKNINGSROD §	SWE3673
DAMIAANAKTIE	BEL0194
DANISH COMMITTEE FOR AID TO AFGHAN REFUGEES §	DNK1240
DANISH RESOURCE MANAGEMENT CENTRE §	DNK1241
DANSK - TANZANIANSK VENSKABSFORENING	DNK1242
DANSK AFS	DNK1243
DANSK BORNEFOND	DNK1244
DANSK ETHIOPER MISSION	DNK1245
DANSK FILIPPINSK GRUPPE §	DNK1246
DANSK FILIPPINSK KVINDEGRUPPE §	DNK1247
DANSK FLYGTNINGEHJALP	DNK1248
DANSK FOLKEOPLYSNINGS SAMRAD §	DNK1249
DANSK INDISK FORENING	DNK1250
DANSK INTERNATIONAL BOSAETNINGSSERVICE	DNK1251
DANSK INTERNATIONAL CHRISTIAN YOUTH EXCHANGE §	DNK1252
DANSK KURDISK KULTUR OG SOLIDARITETS FORENING §	DNK1253
DANSK KVINDESAMFUND §	DNK1254
DANSK MISSIONSRADS PROJEKTAFDELING	DNK1255
DANSK MONGOLSK SELSKAB	DNK1256
DANSK PALAESTINENSISK VENSKABSFORENING §	DNK1257
DANSK POLYNESISK SELSKAB §	DNK1258
DANSK RODE KORS	DNK1259
DANSK SANTALMISSION	DNK1260
DANSK SELSKAB FOR TIBETANSK KULTUR §	DNK1261
DANSK UNICEF KOMITE	DNK1262
DANSK VIETNAMESISK FORENING §	DNK1263
DANSK-ARABISK UDVALG §	DNK1264
DANSK-CUBANSK FORENING §	DNK1265
DANSK-GAMBIANSK FORENING, GAMBIAS VENNER	DNK1266
DANSK-KURDISK VENSKABSFORENING §	DNK1267
DANSK-SRI LANKA FORENING §	DNK1268
DANSK-UGANDISK VENSKABSFORENING §	DNK1269
DEN DANSKE AFGHANISTAN KOMITE §	DNK1270
DEN DANSKE BANGLADESHFORENING §	DNK1271
DET DANSKE BAPTISTSAMFUND - YDRE MISSION	DNK1272
DET DANSKE CENTER FOR MENNESKERETTIGHEDER	DNK1273
DANSKE GYMNASTIK- OG IDRAETSFORENINGER	DNK1274
DET DANSKE MISSIONSSELSKAB	DNK1275
DANSKE OG SYDAMERIKANSKE VENNER §	DNK1276
DE DANSKE PALAESTINEGRUPPER §	DNK1277
DEN DANSKE PALAESTINEKOMITE §	DNK1278
DEN DANSKE STOTTEGRUPPE FOR MENNESKERETTIGHEDSKOMMISSIONEN I CHILE §	DNK1279
DEN DANSKE STOTTEKOMITE FOR KOREAS GENFORENING §	DNK1280
DANSKE STUDERENDES FELLESRAD	DNK1281
DATA FOR DEVELOPMENT §	FRA1896

Voir : *Comment utiliser le répertoire*, page 11.

DATAFRO	FRA1897
DEBT AND DEVELOPMENT COALITION IRELAND	IRL2692
DECLARATION DE BERNE, SECRETARIAT ROMAND	CHE0549
DEFENCE FOR CHILDREN INTERNATIONAL	CHE0550
DEFENCE FOR CHILDREN INTERNATIONAL - AFDELING NEDERLAND §	NLD3086
DEFENSE FOR CHILDREN INTERNATIONAL §	CZE0864
DELEGATION CATHOLIQUE POUR LA COOPERATION	FRA1898
DELTA 7 §	FRA1899
DELTA INTERNASJONALT KFUK-KFUM	NOR3384
DEMAIN, HOPITAUX SANS FRONTIERES §	FRA1900
DEMOCRACY FOUNDATION §	SVK3610
DEMOCRATIC GYPSIES FEDERATION OF HUNGARY - NATIONAL YOUTH BRANCH	HUN2612
DEMOCRATIC YOUTH UNION §	POL3493
DEMOCRATIE POUR L'AFRIQUE §	FRA1901
DEMOS' DOKUMENTATIONSGRUPPE §	DNK1282
DENTISTES SANS FRONTIERES §	FRA1902
DEPARTEMENT EVANGELIQUE FRANCAIS D'ACTION APOSTOLIQUE	FRA1903
DEPARTEMENT MISSIONNAIRE DES EGLISES PROTESTANTES DE SUISSE ROMANDE §	CHE0551
DERDE WERELD CENTRUM DEN HAAG	NLD3087
DERDE WERELD CENTRUM ONTWIKKELINGSSTUDIES §	NLD3088
DERDE WERELDGROEP SOEST	NLD3089
DERRY DEVELOPMENT EDUCATION CENTRE §	GBR2270
DESENVOLVIMENTO INTEGRAL SUDOESTE DO PARANA-BRAZIL §	BEL0195
DET NORSKE TIBETMISJON §	NOR3385
DETACHEMENT D'INTERVENTION CONTRE LES CATASTROPHES ET DE FORMATION DE LA FEDERATION FRANCAISE DE SAUVETAGE ET DE SECOURISME	FRA1904
DEUTSCH PAZIFISCHE GESELLSCHAFT	DEU0992
DEUTSCHE AFGHANISTAN STIFTUNG	DEU0993
DEUTSCHE ARZTEGEMEINSCHAFT FUR MEDIZINISCHE ZUSAMMENARBEIT	DEU0994
DEUTSCHE ENTWICKLUNGSHILFE FUR SOZIALES WOHNUNGS- UND SIEDLUNGSWESEN	DEU0995
DEUTSCHE GESELLSCHAFT FUR DIE VEREINTEN NATIONEN	DEU0996
DEUTSCHE GESELLSCHAFT ZUR RETTUNG SCHIFFBRUCHIGER §	DEU0997
DEUTSCHE KOMMISSION JUSTITIA ET PAX	DEU0998
DEUTSCHE LANDWIRTSCHAFTS-GESELLSCHAFT	DEU0999
DEUTSCHE STIFTUNG FUR INTERNATIONALE ENTWICKLUNG §	DEU1000
DEUTSCHE STIFTUNG FUR UNO-FLUCHTLINGSHILFE	DEU1001
DEUTSCHE STIFTUNG WELTBEVOLKERUNG	DEU1002
DEUTSCHE TECHNISCHE AKADEMIE §	DEU1003
DEUTSCHE UNESCO-KOMMISSION	DEU1004
DEUTSCHE WELLE - AUSBILDUNGSZENTRUM	DEU1005
DEUTSCHE WELTHUNGERHILFE	DEU1006
DEUTSCHER BUNDESJUGENDRING §	DEU1007
DEUTSCHER CARITASVERBAND §	DEU1008
DEUTSCHER ENTWICKLUNGSDIENST §	DEU1009
DEUTSCHER FRAUENRAT - LOBBY DER FRAUEN	DEU1010
DEUTSCHER FRAUENRING §	DEU1011
DEUTSCHER FREIWILLIGENDIENST IN UBERSEE	DEU1012
DEUTSCHER GEWERKSCHAFTSBUND	DEU1013
DEUTSCHER HILFSVEREIN FUR DAS ALBERT-SCHWEITZER-SPITAL IN LAMBARENE §	DEU1014
DEUTSCHER INDUSTRIE- UND HANDELSTAG	DEU1015
DEUTSCHER VOLKSHOCHSCHUL-VERBAND	DEU1016
DEUTSCHES AUSSATZIGEN-HILFSWERK	DEU1017
DEUTSCHES BLINDENHILFSWERK §	DEU1018
DEUTSCHES INSTITUT FUR ARZTLICHE MISSION	DEU1019
DEUTSCHES INSTITUT FUR ENTWICKLUNGSPOLITIK GMBH	DEU1020
DEUTSCHES KATOLISCHES BLINDENWERK §	DEU1021
DEUTSCHES KOMITEE FUR UNICEF	DEU1022
DEUTSCHES MEDIKAMENTEN-HILFSWERK	DEU1023
DEUTSCHES ROTES KREUZ §	DEU1024
DEVELOPMENT EDUCATION ASSOCIATION	GBR2271
DEVELOPMENT EDUCATION FOR YOUTH	IRL2693
DEVELOPMENT INITIATIVES §	GBR2272
DEVELOPMENT PLANNING UNIT	GBR2273
DEVON AID	GBR2274
DGB-BUIDINGSWERK NORD-SUD-NETZ	DEU1025
DHAMMANAT FOUNDATION §	GBR2275
DIAKONHJEMMETS INTERNASJONALE SENTER	NOR3386
DIAKONIA	SWE3674
DIAKONISCHES WERK DER EVANGELISCHEN KIRCHE IN DEUTSCHLAND	DEU1026
DIALOG INTERNATIONAL, FORDERGEMEINSCHAFT FUR DEMOKRATISCHE FRIEDENS ENTWICKLUNG	DEU1027
DIALOG-BILDUNGSWERK §	DEU1028
DIALOGUE ET COOPERATION	FRA1905
DIALOGUES §	FRA1906
DIAPANTE	FRA1907
DICHIARAZIONE DI BERNA - ASSOCIAZIONE PER UNO SVILUPPO SOLIDARE §	CHE0552
DICK SCHERPENZEEL STICHTING	NLD3090
DIENST OVER GRENZEN	NLD3091
DIENSTE IN UBERSEE - ARBEITSGEMEINSCHAFT EVANGELISCHER KIRCHEN IN DEUTSCHLAND	DEU1029
DIENSTENCENTRUM VOOR AKTIEGROEPEN DE BRANDNETEL §	NLD3092
DIERGENEESKUNDE IN ONTWIKKELINGSSAMENWERKING	NLD3093
DIETHNIS ETERIA OIKISTIKIS §	GRC2569
DIORTHODOXO KENDRO "POREFTHENDES" §	GRC2570
DIOZESANKOMMISSION FUR WELTKIRCHE UND ENTWICKLUNGSFORDERUNG §	AUT0023
DIRECCION DE SERVICIOS DE COOPERACION INTERNACIONAL I AYUDA HUMANITARIA §	ESP1459
DISASTER AND EMERGENCY REFERENCE CENTRE §	NLD3094
DISASTER RELIEF AGENCY	NLD3095
DISASTERS EMERGENCY COMMITTEE	GBR2276
DOCUMENTATION-REFUGIES	FRA1908
DOGAL HAYATI KORUMA DERNEGI	TUR3885
DOKUMENTATIONS UND INFORMATIONSZENTRUM MENSCHENRECHTE IN LATEINAMERIKA	DEU1030
DON BOSCO DIENSTBETOON §	BEL0196
DONNE PER LA PACE - GRUPPO TICINO	CHE0553
DOUAR NEVEZ-TERRE NOUVELLE §	FRA1909
DOVAS AFRIKA MISSION	SWE3675
DR. TOM DOOLEY FUND	IRL2694
DREIKONIGSAKTION D. KATHOLISCHE JUNGSCHAR OSTERREICHS	AUT0024
DRITTE WELT HAUS	DEU1031
DROIT DE PAROLE	FRA1910
DROITS DE L'HOMME ET SOLIDARITE §	FRA1911

See: *How to Use the Directory,* page 11.

DROITS DE L'HOMME SANS FRONTIERES	BEL0197
DURHAM - LESOTHO DIOCESAN LINK	GBR2277
DVI- LEG OG VIRKE	DNK1283
E-MISSZIO	HUN2613
EARTH ACTION	BEL0198
EARTHLINKS	CZE0865
EARTHWATCH EUROPE	GBR2278
EARTHWISE	GBR2279
EAST TIMOR - IRELAND SOLIDARITY CAMPAIGN	IRL2695
EAU POUR LA VIE §	FRA1912
EAU VIVE	FRA1913
EAU, AGRICULTURE ET SANTE EN MILIEU TROPICAL	FRA1914
ECHANGE COOPERATION EN MILIEU RURAL §	FRA1915
ECHANGE FRANCE-COLOMBIE §	FRA1916
ECHANGES ET CONSULTATIONS TECHNIQUES INTERNATIONAUX	FRA1917
ECHANGES ET SOLIDARITE §	FRA1918
ECHO INTERNATIONAL HEALTH SERVICES LIMITED	GBR2280
ECLAIREURS ET ECLAIREUSES POUR LE DEVELOPPEMENT COMMUNAUTAIRE	LUX2965
ECLAIREUSES ET ECLAIREURS DE FRANCE §	FRA1919
ECO - UNESCO CLUBS	IRL2696
ECO, THE MALTA ECOLOGICAL SOCIETY	MLT3016
ECOLE SANS FRONTIERES §	LUX2966
ECOLES SANS FRONTIERES	FRA1920
ECOLOGICAL CLUB "PANDA" §	POL3494
THE ECOLOGICAL MOVEMENT OF CYPRUS	CYP0831
ECOLOGY AGRICULTURE DEVELOPMENT	DEU1032
ECONOMIE ET HUMANISME	FRA1921
ECOPOP	CHE0554
ECOROPA §	FRA1922
ECOSOLIDAR §	CHE0555
ECOVAST, POLSKA SEKCJA EUROPESJSKIEGO RUCHU ODNOWY WSI §	POL3495
ECUMENICAL DEVELOPMENT CO-OPERATIVE SOCIETY	NLD3096
ECUMENICAL HEARING ON THE INTERNATIONAL FINANCIAL SYSTEM §	DEU1033
EDIFICANDO-COMUNIDAD DE NAZARET §	ESP1460
EDITIONS FRANCOPHONES D'AMNESTY INTERNATIONAL	FRA1923
EDUARDO FREI STICHTING	NLD3097
EDUARDO MONDLANE STICHTING	NLD3098
EDUCACION SIN FRONTERAS	ESP1461
EDUCATION ET ECHANGES	FRA1924
EDUCATION ET LIBERATION §	CHE0556
EDUCATION FOR DEVELOPMENT	GBR2281
EDUCATION INTERNATIONAL	BEL0199
EDUCATION SANITAIRE ET NUTRITIONNELLE EN AFRIQUE CENTRALE	BEL0200
THE EDUCATIONAL PROGRAMME FOUNDATION §	CZE0866
EDVARD BENES SOCIETY §	CZE0867
EINE WELT FUR ALLE	DEU1034
EINE-WELT TEAM VERSAND	DEU1035
EIRENE - COMITE SUISSE	CHE0557
EIRENE FRANCE-SERVICE CHRETIEN INTERNATIONAL POUR LA PAIX §	FRA1925
EJF HEIMBETRIEBSGESELLSCHAFT GEMEINNUTZIGE GMBH §	DEU1036
EKOLOGICZNY RUCH STUDENCKI §	POL3496
EKUMENE §	ESP1462

EL SALVADOR AWARENESS	IRL2697
ELLENIKO INSTITUTO ALLILENGYIS KE SYNERGASIAS ME TIS ANAPTYSSOMENES CHORES	GRC2571
ELLINIKI EPITROPI DIETHNOUS DIMOCRATIKIS ALLILEGHISIS	GRC2572
ELLINIKOS ERITHROS STAVROS	GRC2573
EMMAUS DANMARK §	DNK1284
EMMAUS INTERNATIONAL	FRA1926
EMMAUS STOCKHOLM	SWE3676
EMMAUS SUNDSVALL §	SWE3677
EMMAUS-SAMFUNDET I AALBORG - ABBE PIERRES KLUNSERE	DNK1285
ENCIAN ENVIRONMENTAL EDUCATION CENTRE §	HUN2614
ENERGIE & ENVIRONNEMENT - SOLUTIONS ADAPTEES POUR UN ENVIRONNEMENT DURABLE	FRA1927
ENFANCE ESPOIR	FRA1928
ENFANCE ET PARTAGE	FRA1929
ENFANCE ET PARTAGE	FRA1930
ENFANCE ET VIE §	FRA1931
ENFANCE MEURTRIE : UN SOURIRE RETOUVE	FRA1932
ENFANCE TIERS-MONDE	BEL0201
ENFANT D'EL SALVADOR §	FRA1933
UN ENFANT PAR LA MAIN	FRA1934
L'ENFANT POUR L'ENFANT	FRA1935
ENFANTS DE L'ESPOIR - NINOS DE LA ESPERANZA	LUX2967
ENFANTS DE LA TERRE §	FRA1936
ENFANTS DU MEKONG	FRA1937
ENFANTS DU MONDE - DROITS DE L'HOMME	FRA1938
ENFANTS DU MONDE, FRANCE	FRA1939
ENFANTS DU MONDE, SUISSE	CHE0558
LES ENFANTS DU SOLEIL §	FRA1940
ENFANTS ET DEVELOPPEMENT	FRA1941
ENFANTS REFUGIES DU MONDE	FRA1942
ENG BRECK MAT LATAINAMERIKA	LUX2968
ENIEA DIMOKRATIKI ORGANOSI NEOLEAS	CYP0832
ENSEIGNANTS FRANCAIS ET DEVELOPPEMENT INTERNATIONAL §	FRA1943
ENTE NAZIONALE GIUSEPPINI DEL MURIALDO	ITA2842
ENTRAIDE ET AMITIE	BEL0202
ENTRAIDE ET FRATERNITE	BEL0203
ENTRAIDE MEDICALE INTERNATIONALE	FRA1944
ENTRAIDE PROTESTANTE SUISSE	CHE0559
ENTREPRISE ET DEVELOPPEMENT - RESEAU D'INITIATIVES DECENTRALISEES POUR LE PARTENARIAT INDUSTRIEL NORD-SUD §	FRA1945
ENTREPUEBLOS §	ESP1463
ENTWECKLONG DURCH GERECHTEN HANDEL	LUX2969
ENTWICKLUNGSHILFE DER ERZDIOZESEK WIEN - DIOZESEN INFORMATIONSSTELLE DES OED §	AUT0025
ENTWICKLUNGSHILFE-KLUB	AUT0026
ENTWICKLUNGSPOLITISCHE BILDUNGSARBEIT AUF DEM LANDE IN DER EVANGELISCHEN KIRCHE IN DEUTSCHLAND	DEU1037
ENTWICKLUNGSPOLITISCHEN BILDUNGSZENTRUM DES OED UND AAI §	AUT0027
ENTWICKLUNGSPOLITISCHEN GESELLSCHAFT BERLIN	DEU1038
ENTWICKLUNGSWERKSTATT AUSTRIA	AUT0028
ENTWICKLUNGSZUSAMMENARBEIT MIT DER DRITTEN WELT	AUT0029
ENVIRONMENT AND DEVELOPMENT RESOURCE CENTRE §	BEL0204

ENVIRONMENTAL AWARENESS FOUNDATION	NLD3099
ENVIRONMENTAL EDUCATION CENTRE OF FOLOPHAZA §	HUN2615
ENVIRONMENTAL GROUP OF THE DEMOCRATIC TRADE UNION OF THE SCIENTIFIC WORKERS §	HUN2616
ENVIRONMENTAL SOCIETY §	CZE0868
ENVIRONMENTALLY SUSTAINABLE FORESTRY §	LUX2970
ENVIRONNEMENT ET DEVELOPPEMENT DU TIERS MONDE - DELEGATION EN EUROPE	FRA1946
EPARGNE SANS FRONTIERE	FRA1947
EPILEPSY CARE DEVELOPING COUNTRIES	NLD3100
EQUILIBRE	FRA1948
EQUILIBRE - BELGIQUE §	BEL0205
EQUILIBRES ET POPULATIONS	FRA1949
EQUIPO DE COMUNICACION EDUCATIVA §	ESP1464
ERIKSHJALPEN §	SWE3678
ERITREA-HILFSWERK IN DEUTSCHLAND §	DEU1039
DEN ERITREANSKE HJAELPEORGANISATION I DANMARK §	DNK1286
ERKLARUNG VON BERN	CHE0560
ERKLARUNG VON GRAZ FUR SOLIDARISCHE ENTWICKLUNG	AUT0030
ERZEUGER-VERBRAUCHER INITIATIVEN §	AUT0031
ESPACE ET COOPERATION	BEL0206
ESPOIR POUR UN ENFANT §	FRA1950
ETAL - FIR E BESSERT LIEWEN AN LATEINAMERIKA §	LUX2971
ETC INTERNATIONAL	NLD3101
ETERIA SPOUDIS TIS PAGOSMIAS ANAPTIXIS - EDECN-HELLAS §	GRC2574
ETHIOPIAID	GBR2282
ETUDIANTS POUR LE DEVELOPPEMENT §	FRA1951
EURO CITIZEN ACTION SERVICE §	BEL0207
EURO-CARITAS - CARITAS EUROPA §	BEL0208
EURODIAKONIA §	BEL0209
EUROMARE	GRC2575
EURONAID §	BEL0210
EUROPAHAUS EISENSTADT	AUT0032
EUROPAISCHE BILDUNGS- UND AKTIONSGEMEINSCHAFT §	DEU1040
EUROPE TIERS-MONDE	LUX2972
EUROPEAN ACADEMY FOR THE ENVIRONMENT §	DEU1041
EUROPEAN ASSOCIATION FOR LEISURE TIME INSTITUTIONS OF CHILDREN AND YOUTH OF GREAT CITIES §	CZE0869
EUROPEAN ASSOCIATION OF NON GOVERNMENTAL ORGANISATIONS FOR FOOD AID AND EMERGENCY AID	NLD3102
EUROPEAN BUREAU FOR CONSERVATION AND DEVELOPMENT	BEL0211
EUROPEAN CONSULTATION ON REFUGEES AND EXILES §	BEL0212
EUROPEAN CONSULTATION ON REFUGEES AND EXILES §	GBR2283
EUROPEAN CONTACT GROUP ON URBAN INDUSTRIAL MISSION	GBR2284
EUROPEAN COORDINATION BUREAU §	BEL0213
EUROPEAN CULTURE CLUB §	CZE0870
EUROPEAN DEVELOPMENT EDUCATION NETWORK	GBR2285
EUROPEAN DIALOGUE §	GBR2286
EUROPEAN ECUMENICAL ORGANIZATION FOR DEVELOPMENT	BEL0214
EUROPEAN FAIR TRADE ASSOCIATION	NLD3103
EUROPEAN FORUM ON DEVELOPMENT SERVICE	DEU1042

EUROPEAN HOME IN BRNO §	CZE0871
EUROPEAN HUMAN RIGHTS FOUNDATION §	GBR2287
EUROPEAN MIGRATION CENTRE §	DEU1043
EUROPEAN MOVEMENT IN THE CZECH REPUBLIC §	CZE0872
EUROPEAN NETWORK ON DEBT AND DEVELOPMENT	BEL0215
EUROPEAN SOLIDARITY TOWARDS EQUAL PARTICIPATION OF PEOPLE	BEL0216
EUROPEAN SUPPORT ASSOCIATIONS OF THE ECUMENICAL DEVELOPMENT CO-OPERATIVE SOCIETY	DEU1044
EUROPEAN YOUTH FOREST ACTION	NLD3104
THE EUROPEAN YWCAS	BEL0217
EUROPEES PLATFORM	NLD3105
EUROPEJSKIE STOWARZYSZENIE §	POL3497
EVANGELISCH-METHODISTISCHE KIRCHE IN DER SCHWEIZ UND IN FRANKREICH, AUSSERE MISSION §	CHE0561
DAS EVANGELISCHE JUGENDWERK AN DER SAAR §	DEU1045
EVANGELISCHE MISSION IM KWANGO	CHE0562
EVANGELISCHE STUDENTENGEMEINDE §	DEU1046
EVANGELISCHE ZENTRALSTELLE FUR ENTWICKLUNGSHILFE	DEU1047
EVANGELISCHER ARBEITSKREIS FUR WELTMISSION IN OSTERREICH	AUT0033
EVANGELISKA FOSTERLANDS-STIFTELSEN	SWE3679
DEN EVANGELISKE LUTHERSKE FRIKIRKE, YTREMISJONEN	NOR3387
EVANGLISCHE MISSION IM TSCHAD §	CHE0563
EVERT VERMEER STICHTING §	NLD3106
EXPERIENCE RURALE ALTERNATIVE	CHE0564
FACHSTELLE DER SCHWEIZERISCHEN ENTWICKLUNGSZUSAMMENARBEIT FUR TECHNOLOGIE MANAGEMENT	CHE0565
FADDERBARNSVERKSAMHETEN I KENYA §	SWE3680
FAGBEVAEGELSENS U-LANDSSEKRETARIAT	DNK1287
FAIR TRADE ORGANISATIE	NLD3107
FALTBIOLOGERNA §	SWE3681
FAMILY HELP PROGRAMME HOLLAND - SRI LANKA §	NLD3108
FAMILY PLANNING ASSOCIATION OF GREECE	GRC2576
FARMERS' WORLD NETWORK	GBR2288
FASSODEMIN §	FRA1952
FASTENOPFER KATHOLISCHES HILFSWERK SCHWEIZ	CHE0566
FE Y ALEGRIA §	ESP1465
FEDERACION DE ORGANIZACIONES PARA REFUGIADOS Y ASILADOS §	ESP1466
FEDERACION ESPANOLA DE RELIGIOSAS SANITARIAS	ESP1467
FEDERACION ESPANOLA DE RELIGIOSOS DE ENSENANZA	ESP1468
FEDERATIE NEDERLANDSE VAKBEWEGING §	NLD3109
FEDERATION ABOLITIONISTE MONDIALE §	FRA1953
FEDERATION ARTISANS DU MONDE §	FRA1954
THE FEDERATION DEFENDING THE INTERESTS OF THE HUNGARIAN YOUTH	SVK3611
FEDERATION DES ASSOCIATIONS DE RECHERCHE ET D'EDUCATION POUR LA PAIX	FRA1955
FEDERATION DES ASSOCIATIONS FRANCO-AFRICAINES DE DEVELOPPEMENT	FRA1956
FEDERATION DES FONDATIONS POUR LA SANTE MONDIALE	CHE0567
FEDERATION DES SCOUTS CATHOLIQUES - SCOUTS BADEN POWELL DE BELGIQUE	BEL0218
FEDERATION DES TRAVAILLEURS AFRICAINS	FRA1957
FEDERATION EUROPEENNE DE PROFESSIONNELS DE L'ENVIRONNEMENT §	FRA1958

FEDERATION EUROPEENNE DES ASSOCIATIONS NATIONALES TRAVAILLANT AVEC LES SANS-ABRI	BEL0219
FEDERATION FRANCAISE DES CLUBS UNESCO §	FRA1959
FEDERATION GENEVOISE DE COOPERATION	CHE0568
FEDERATION INTERNATIONALE DE L'ACTION DES CHRETIENS POUR L'ABOLITION DE LA TORTURE	FRA1960
FEDERATION INTERNATIONALE DE LA CROIX BLEUE	CHE0569
FEDERATION INTERNATIONALE DES CENTRES D'ENTRAINEMENT AUX METHODES D'EDUCATION ACTIVES §	FRA1961
FEDERATION INTERNATIONALE DES JOURNALISTES §	BEL0220
FEDERATION INTERNATIONALE DES LIGUES DES DROITS DE L'HOMME §	FRA1962
FEDERATION INTERNATIONALE DES MOUVEMENTS D'ADULTES RURAUX CATHOLIQUES	BEL0221
FEDERATION INTERNATIONALE POUR L'ECONOMIE FAMILIALE §	FRA1963
FEDERATION INTERNATIONALE SERV. AMERIQUE LATINE ET ASIE §	BEL0222
FEDERATION INTERNATIONALE TERRE DES HOMMES	CHE0570
FEDERATION MONDIALE DES CITES UNIES ET VILLES JUMELEES	FRA1964
FEDERATION OF ENVIRONMENTAL AND ECOLOGICAL ORGANISATIONS OF CYPRUS	CYP0833
FEDERATION OF UNESCO CLUBS §	BEL0223
FEDERATION ROMANDE DES CONSOMMATRICES	CHE0571
FEDERATION VAUDOISE DE COOPERATION §	CHE0572
FEDERATIONEN FOR PROJEKTER, KNYTTET TIL DEN INTERNATIONALE FRA FOLK TIL FOLK BEVEGELSE	DNK1288
FEDERAZIONE ITALIANA DEI CLUB UNESCO §	ITA2843
FEDERAZIONE ORGANISMI CRISTIANI DI SERVIZIO INTERNAZIONALE VOLONTARIO	ITA2844
FEED THE CHILDREN EUROPE	GBR2289
FEED THE CHILDREN INTERNATIONAL	BEL0224
FEED THE MINDS	GBR2290
FELLESKAMPANJEN FOR JORDAS MILJO OG UTVIKLING §	NOR3388
FELLESRADET FOR AFRIKA	NOR3389
FELLOWSHIP OF ORTHODOX YOUTH §	POL3498
FEMMES SOUS LOIS MUSULMANES §	FRA1965
FERRARA TERZO MONDO §	ITA2845
FGM - STIFTUNG FUR INTERNATIONALE ZUSAMMENARBEIT §	CHE0573
FIDESCO	FRA1966
FIGHT FOR EUROPE MOVEMENT §	HUN2617
FILIPIJNEN INFORMATIE-EN DOCUMENTATIE CENTRUM	NLD3110
FILIPPIJNENGROEP NEDERLAND §	NLD3111
FIND YOUR FEET §	GBR2291
FINLANDS SVENSKA MARTHAFORBUND §	FIN1534
FINLANDS SVENSKA PINGSTMISSION - FILADELFIAFORSAMLINGEN I HELSINGFORS §	FIN1535
FINLANDS SVENSKA SKOLUNGDOMSFORBUND	FIN1536
FINNWID §	FIN1537
FIU-CENTRET	DNK1289
FLAMANT VERT §	CHE0574
FLEMISH KOMMISSIE RECHTVAADIGHEID EN VREDE §	BEL0225
FLEMISH ORGANIZATION FOR ASSISTANCE IN DEVELOPMENT	BEL0226
FLEMISH PLATFORM FOR INTERNATIONAL YOUTH WORK §	BEL0227
FLEMISH SUPPORT GROUP FOR INDIGENOUS PEOPLES §	BEL0228
FLORES VRIENDEN §	BEL0229
FLYKTNINGERADET	NOR3390
FN - FORBUNDET §	DNK1290
FN - SAMBANDET I NORGE	NOR3391
FOI ET ECONOMIE - BUREAU INTERCONFESSIONNEL D'INFORMATION §	CHE0575
FOLKECENTRE FOR RENEWABLE ENERGY	DNK1291
FOLKEKIRKENS NODHJELP	DNK1292
FOLKELIGT OPLYSNINGS FORBUND §	DNK1293
FOLKETEKNIK, DANSKE ABGEJDERES U- LANDSGRUPPER §	DNK1294
FOLKHASAN §	FIN1538
FONDACION PABLO IGLESIAS §	ESP1469
FONDATION ANDRE RYCKMANS	BEL0230
FONDATION CHRISTOPHE ECKENSTEIN	CHE0576
FONDATION DE FRANCE	FRA1967
FONDATION DE L'EAU §	FRA1968
FONDATION DE SOLIDARITE INTERNATIONALE	BEL0231
FONDATION DES ROTARY CLUBS BELGES POUR LA COOPERATION AU DEVELOPPEMENT A.S.B.L §	BEL0232
FONDATION FRANCO VERGA	ITA2846
FONDATION FRANZ WEBER §	CHE0577
FONDATION INTERNATIONALE E. BALZAN §	ITA2847
FONDATION INTERNATIONALE POUR LE DEVELOPPEMENT §	FRA1969
FONDATION LEILA FODIL	FRA1970
FONDATION LIBANAISE POUR LA PAIX CIVILE PERMANENTE §	FRA1971
FONDATION LUXEMBOURGEOISE RAOUL FOLLEREAU	LUX2973
FONDATION MEDICALE DE L'UNIVERSITE CATHOLIQUE DE LOUVAIN EN AFRIQUE CENTRALE	BEL0233
FONDATION NESTLE	CHE0578
FONDATION OECUMENIQUE POUR L'AIDE AUX EGLISES §	CHE0579
FONDATION PERE DAMIEN POUR LA LUTTE CONTRE LA LEPRE	BEL0234
FONDATION POUR LE MECENAT HUMANITAIRE §	FRA1972
FONDATION PRO VICTIMIS - GENEVE	CHE0580
FONDATION ROGER RIOU D'AIDE AUX PAYS EN VOIE DE DEVELOPPEMENT §	BEL0235
FONDATION ROI BAUDOUIN §	BEL0236
FONDATION SIMON I. PATINO	CHE0581
FONDATION SUISSE DU SERVICE SOCIAL INTERNATIONAL	CHE0582
FONDATION UNIVERSITAIRE POUR LA COOPERATION INTERNATIONALE AU DEVELOPPEMENT	BEL0237
FONDAZIONE BROWNSEA	ITA2848
FONDAZIONE ELVETICA OSPEDALE DI MADA - OPERA UMANITARIA DR MAGGI	CHE0583
FONDAZIONE GIUSEPPE TOVINI	ITA2849
FONDAZIONE SIPEC §	ITA2850
FONDS DE SOLIDARITE MONDIALE §	LUX2974
FONDS DE SOLIDARITE POUR LE LIBAN §	FRA1973
FONDS FUR ENTWICKLUNG UND PARTNERSCHAFT IN AFRIKA	CHE0584
FONDS INGRID RENARD §	BEL0238
FONDS MEDICAL TROPICAL §	BEL0239
FONDS POUR L'ENVIRONNEMENT ET LE DEVELOPPEMENT §	CHE0585
FONDS POUR LES VILLAGES D'ENFANTS SOS DANS LE MONDE	LUX2975
FONDS VOOR ONTWIKKELINGSHULP §	BEL0240
FONDS VOOR ONTWIKKELINGSSAMENWERKING	BEL0241

FONS DE DOCUMENTACIO DEL MEDI AMBIENT	ESP1470
FOOD AND AGRICULTURAL RESEARCH MANAGEMENT AFRICA	GBR2292
FOOD AND DISARMAMENT INTERNATIONAL §	BEL0242
FOOD FOR THE HUNGRY	GBR2293
FOOD FOR THE HUNGRY INTERNATIONAL	CHE0586
FOODFIRST INFORMATION AND ACTION NETWORK, BELGIUM §	BEL0243
FOODFIRST INFORMATION AND ACTION NETWORK, GERMANY §	DEU1048
FOODFIRST INFORMATION AND ACTION NETWORK, SVERIGE	SWE3682
FOR INDIAN - INUIT - INDIGENOUS RIGHTS EVERYWHERE §	DNK1295
FOR LIFE §	CZE0873
FORBUNDET VI UNGA §	SWE3683
FORDERKREIS "HOSPITAL ANDINO" PERU §	DEU1049
FORDERKREIS-KREBSKRANKE KINDER §	DEU1050
FORDERVEREIN BASISGESUNDHEITSDIENST IN DER PARTNERDIOZESE JABALPUR/INDIEN §	DEU1051
FORDERVEREIN FUR HUMANITARE WOHLTATIGKEIT IN KOSOVO "MUTTER THERESA" §	DEU1052
FORENINGEN 6:E DECEMBER §	SWE3684
FORENINGEN AF ZANZIBARIER I SKANDINAVIEN §	DNK1296
FORENINGEN BADZA	SWE3685
FORENINGEN CARMENCITA §	SWE3686
FORENINGEN COLCHAJ NAC LUUM	SWE3687
FORENINGEN ECUADORGRUPPEN §	DNK1297
FORENINGEN EMMAUS BJORKA	SWE3688
FORENINGEN ETT FRITT PAPUA §	SWE3689
FORENINGEN FOLKBILDNING NORDEN LATINAMERIKA §	SWE3690
FORENINGEN FOR FAMILIEPLANLAEGNING, SEX OG SAMFUND	DNK1298
FORENINGEN FOR REHABILITERING I U-LANDER	SWE3691
FORENINGEN FOR UTVECKLINGS-JOURNALISTIK §	SWE3692
FORENINGEN GATUBARN	SWE3693
FORENINGEN GREENPEACE - SVERIGE §	SWE3694
FORENINGEN INTERNATIONELLA FOLKHOGSKOLAN	SWE3695
FORENINGEN SKOVDESKOLOR - KIBAHA §	SWE3696
FORENINGEN SVALORNA / INDIEN-BANGLADESH SEKTIONEN §	SWE3697
FORENINGEN SVENSKA U-LANDSVOLONTARER §	SWE3698
FORENINGEN TIL STOTTE FOR KULTUREN I NICARAGUA §	DNK1299
FORENINGEN VASTSAHARA	SWE3699
FORMATION POUR L'AUTOPROMOTION	CHE0587
FORUM CIVIQUE EUROPEEN §	CHE0588
FORUM DELLO SVILUPPO §	ITA2851
FORUM FOR ENERGI OG UDVIKLING	DNK1300
FORUM OF EUROPEAN STUDENTS §	CZE0874
FORUM ON DEBT AND DEVELOPMENT	NLD3112
FORUM SCHULE FUR EINE WELT	CHE0589
FORUM ZGHAZAGH LABURISTI	MLT3017
FORUT-SOLIDARITETSAKSJON FOR UTVIKLING §	NOR3392
FOSTER PARENTS PLAN NEDERLAND §	NLD3113
FOUNDATION ECOLOGY AND LIFE	SVK3612
FOUNDATION FOR CHILDREN IN DANGER §	CZE0875
FOUNDATION FOR DEVELOPMENT §	BEL0244
FOUNDATION FOR ENVIRONMENTAL CONSERVATION §	CHE0590

FOUNDATION FOR ENVIRONMENTAL EDUCATION IN EUROPE §	DNK1301
FOUNDATION FOR HUNGARIAN WOMEN §	HUN2618
FOUNDATION FOR INTERNATIONAL ENVIRONMENTAL LAW AND DEVELOPMENT	GBR2294
FOUNDATION FOR INTERNATIONAL STUDIES	MLT3018
FOUNDATION FOR SCHOOL DEVELOPMENT LASZLO HORVATH §	HUN2619
FOUNDATION FOR WOMEN'S HEALTH §	GBR2295
FOUNDATION OF JOSEF PLIVA §	CZE0876
FOUNDATION PROMETHEUS §	SVK3613
FOUNDATION SIMON I. PATINO §	CHE0591
FOUNDATION TO PROMOTE WOMEN'S WORLD BANKING, NEDERLAND §	NLD3114
FOYER D'ECHANGES ET DE RENCONTRES ADMINISTRATIFS MONDIAUX	FRA1974
FRAMTIDEN I VARA HANDER §	SWE3700
FRAMTIDEN I VARA HANDER - GAMBIAGRUPPERNA	SWE3701
FRAMTIDEN I VARE HENDER §	NOR3393
FRAMTIDSJORDEN	SWE3702
FRANCE AMERIQUE LATINE	FRA1975
LA FRANCE AVEC VOUS §	FRA1976
FRANCE TERRE D'ASILE §	FRA1977
FRANCE-LIBERTES FONDATION DANIELLE MITTERRAND	FRA1978
FRANZ JORDAN-VEREIN §	CHE0592
FRANZ XAVER STIFTUNG §	CHE0593
FRANZISKANER MISSIONSSCHWESTERN VON MARIA HILFE §	CHE0594
FRATELLI DELL'UOMO	ITA2852
FRATERNITE EUROPE-ASIE	FRA1979
FRATERNITE SAINT PAUL POUR L'AIDE AU DEVELOPPEMENT	BEL0245
FRAUEN FUR DEN FRIEDEN	CHE0595
FRAUENINFORMATIONSZENTRUM DRITTE WELT	CHE0596
FRAUENSOLIDARITAT - ENTWICKLUNGSPOLITISCHE INITIATIVEN FUR DIE FRAUEN IN DER DRITTEN WELT	AUT0034
FREDAGSGRUPPEN §	SWE3703
FREDLIGT ARBETE TILL INSIKT, MEDMANSKLIGHET, ANSVAR-UNIONEN	SWE3704
FREEDOM FROM HUNGER CAMPAIGN §	GBR2296
FREIPLATZAKTION FUR ASYLSUCHENDE §	CHE0597
FRELSESARMEEN	NOR3394
FREMTIDSSKOVEN - MSITU WA KESHO	DNK1302
FRERES DE NOS FRERES	CHE0598
FRERES DES HOMMES, BELGIQUE §	BEL0246
FRERES DES HOMMES, FRANCE	FRA1980
FRERES DES HOMMES, LUXEMBOURG	LUX2976
FREUNDE DES KINDERZENTRUMS MANDIRITUBA (BRASILIEN) §	CHE0599
FREUNDE DES SCHWEIZER KINDERDORFS KIRJATH JEARIM IN ISRAEL	CHE0600
DE FRIE EVANGELISKE FORSAMLINGERS MISJONSUTVALG	NOR3395
FRIEDENSDORF INTERNATIONAL	DEU1053
FRIEDENSZENTRUM MARTIN-NIEMOLLER-HAUS	DEU1054
FRIEDRICH-EBERT-STIFTUNG §	BEL0247
FRIEDRICH-EBERT-STIFTUNG	DEU1055
FRIEDRICH-NAUMANN-STIFTUNG	DEU1056
FRIEDRICH-THIEDING-STIFTUNG §	DEU1057
FRIENDS OF ASSEFA	GBR2297

See: *How to Use the Directory*, page 11.

FRIENDS OF CONSERVATION	GBR2298
FRIENDS OF THE CENTRE FOR REHABILITATION AND PARALYSED	GBR2299
FRIENDS OF THE EARTH - EASTERN EUROPE §	SVK3614
FRIENDS OF THE EARTH - EUROPE	BEL0248
FRIENDS OF THE EARTH INTERNATIONAL	NLD3115
FRIENDS OF THE EARTH, CYPRUS §	CYP0834
FRIENDS OF THE JAIROS JIRI ASSOCIATION §	GBR2300
FRIENDS OF URAMBO AND MWANHALA §	GBR2301
FRIENDS OF VELLORE	GBR2302
FRIENDS WORLD COMMITTEE FOR CONSULTATION §	CHE0601
FRIENDS WORLD COMMITTEE FOR CONSULTATION	GBR2303
FRILUFTSRADET §	DNK1303
FRIVILLIGORGANISATIONERNAS FOND FOR MANSKLIGA RATTIGHETER	SWE3705
FRIVILLIGT DRENGE - OG PIGE-FORBUND	DNK1304
FRONTIERES OUVERTES ISERE-FERKESSEDOUGOU §	FRA1981
FUND FOR WOMEN §	GBR2304
FUNDACAO ANTERO DE QUENTAL §	PRT3577
FUNDACAO OLIVEIRA MARTINS §	PRT3578
FUNDACION ESPANOLA PARA LA COOPERACION §	ESP1471
FUNDACION HUMANISMO Y DEMOCRACIA	ESP1472
FUNDACION LARGO CABALLERO §	ESP1473
FUNDACION PARA EL DESARROLLO DEL COOPERATIVISMO Y LA ECONOMIA SOCIAL	ESP1474
FUNDACION PAZ Y SOLIDARIDAD	ESP1475
FUNDACJA WSPIERANIA INICJATYW EKOLOGICZNYCH	POL3499
FUNDES-SUISSE	CHE0602
FUNKSJONSHEMMEDES FELLESORGANISASJON	NOR3396
DET FYNSKE U-LANDSKAB	DNK1305
GAIA FOUNDATION §	GBR2305
GAJA KORNYEZETVEDO EGYESULET	HUN2620
GALWAY ONE WORLD CENTRE	IRL2698
GAP ACTIVITY PROJECTS	GBR2306
GATEWAY	GBR2307
GAVLEBORGS BISTANDSGRUPP §	SWE3706
GEMEENSCHAPPELIJK OVERLEG MEDEFINANCIERING	NLD3116
GEMEINSAN IST ES MOGLICH §	DEU1058
GEMEINSCHAFT DER VINZENZ-KONFERENZEN DEUTSCHLANDS §	DEU1059
GEMEINSCHAFT JUNGER UNGARNDEUTSCHER §	HUN2621
GEMEINSCHAFT ZUR FORDERUNG SOZIAL-MEDIZINISCHER STIFTUNGEN AMBERG §	DEU1060
GENAGRO	BEL0249
GENEVA INFANT FEEDING ASSOCIATION	CHE0603
GENEVE - TIERS-MONDE	CHE0604
GENOOTSCHAP VOOR ENERGIE ONTWIKKELING & PLANNING	NLD3117
GENVEJ TIL UDVIKLING	DNK1306
GEO-ENVIRON	HUN2622
GEOEKO FOUNDATION §	SVK3615
GEOMETRES SANS FRONTIERES §	FRA1982
GEORGE ADAMSON WILDLIFE PRESERVATION TRUST §	GBR2308
GERMAN EMERGENCY DOCTORS §	DEU1061
GERMANWATCH - NORD-SUD INITIATIVE	DEU1062
GERNIKA §	BEL0250
GESELLSCHAFT DER FREUNDE DES SAHRAUISCHEN VOLKES	DEU1063
GESELLSCHAFT FUR BEDROHTE VOLKER	DEU1064
GESELLSCHAFT FUR BEDROHTE VOLKER, SCHWEIZ §	CHE0605
GESELLSCHAFT FUR EUROPAISCHE KOMMUNIKATION	DEU1065
GESELLSCHAFT FUR OSTERREICHISCH-ARABISCHE BEZIEHUNGEN	AUT0035
GESELLSCHAFT FUR SOLIDARISCHE ENTWICKLUNGSZUSAMMENARBEIT	DEU1066
GESELLSCHAFT OSTERREICH-VIETNAM	AUT0036
GESELLSCHAFT SCHWEIZ-ISRAEL §	CHE0606
GESELLSCHAFT SCHWEIZ-SUDAFRIKA §	CHE0607
GESELLSCHAFT ZUR FORDERUNG INTERDISZIPLINARER PROJEKTE IN LATEINAMERIKA §	DEU1067
GESELLSCHAFT ZUR FORDERUNG KONKRETER ENTWICKLUNGPROJEKTE §	DEU1068
GEZONDHEIDSZORG IN ONTWIKKELINGSLANDEN §	NLD3118
GHANA VENSKABSGRUPPERNE I DANMARK/GHANAIAN DANISH COMMUNITIES ASSOCIATION	DNK1307
GHANA-AKTION	DEU1069
GIATRI TOV KOSMOV §	GRC2577
GIPZUZKOA BIDE LAGUNTZA ELKARTEA §	ESP1476
GIRL GUIDES ASSOCIATION §	MLT3019
GLOBAL COALITION FOR AFRICA, DUTCH OFFICE	NLD3119
GLOBAL HELP GHANA FUND	SWE3707
GLOBAL INK	GBR2309
GLOBAL RESPONSIBILITIES TO FUTURE GENERATIONS §	MLT3020
GOAL	IRL2699
GOED WERK	NLD3120
GONCOL FOUNDATION §	HUN2623
GOOD WILL CENTRE, HUMANITARIAN ASSOCIATION §	CZE0877
GORDON BARCLAY VIETNAM FUND	GBR2310
GORTA	IRL2700
GOTA §	CZE0878
GRAAL	PRT3579
THE GRAIL - INTERNATIONAL MOVEMENT OF CHRISTIAN WOMEN §	DEU1070
GRAPHIC MEDIA DEVELOPMENT CENTRE	NLD3121
GREATER LONDON ACTION FOR RACIAL EQUALITY	GBR2311
GREEK ASSOCIATION FOR THE UNITED NATIONS §	GRC2578
GREEK COUNCIL FOR REFUGEES	GRC2579
GREEK GIRL GUIDES ASSOCIATION §	GRC2580
GREEN ACTION NGO	HUN2624
GREEN CIRCLE	CZE0879
GREEN EARTH §	POL3500
GREEN LIGHT TRUST	GBR2312
GREEN NET FOUNDATION §	CZE0880
GREEN NETWORK FOUNDATION §	CZE0881
GREENNET	GBR2313
GREENPEACE GERMANY §	DEU1071
GREENPEACE INTERNATIONAL	NLD3122
GREENPEACE INTERNATIONAL EC UNIT §	BEL0251
GREENPEACE IRELAND §	IRL2701
GREENPEACE SCHWEIZ §	CHE0608
GRENOBLE PARTAGE	FRA1983
GRON BURKINA FASO	DNK1308
GROUPE D'ETUDES ET DE FORMATION SUR LES OUTILS SOLAIRES ET LES ALTERNATIVES TECHNOLOGIQUES	FRA1984
GROUPE D'ETUDES ET DE SERVICES POUR L'ECONOMIE DES RESSOURCES	FRA1985

Voir : *Comment utiliser le répertoire*, page 11.

GROUPE DE REALISATIONS AUDIOVISUELLES POUR LE DEVELOPPEMENT	CHE0609
GROUPE DE REALISATIONS AUDIOVISUELLES POUR LE DEVELOPPEMENT	FRA1986
GROUPE DE RECHERCHE ET D'APPUI POUR L'AUTOPROMOTION PAYSANNE §	FRA1987
GROUPE DE RECHERCHE ET D'ECHANGES TECHNOLOGIQUES	FRA1988
GROUPE DE RECHERCHE ET DE REALISATIONS POUR LE DEVELOPPEMENT RURAL DANS LE TIERS MONDE §	FRA1989
GROUPE DE RECHERCHE POUR UNE STRATEGIE ECONOMIQUE ALTERNATIVE	BEL0252
GROUPE DE SOUTIEN AUX MOUVEMENTS D'EDUCATION POPULAIRE ET DE DEVELOPPEMENT EN INDE	FRA1990
GROUPE DEVELOPPEMENT	FRA1991
GROUPE ENERGIES RENOUVELABLES ET ENVIRONNEMENT	FRA1992
GROUPE NORD-SUD §	LUX2977
GROUPE POUR LES DROITS DES MINORITES §	CHE0610
GROUPE POUR UNE COORDINATION DE LA DOCUMENTATION DES ONG SUISSES	CHE0611
GROUPE SOLIDARITE GUATEMALA §	CHE0612
GROUPE VOLONTAIRE OUTRE MER	CHE0613
GROUPEMENT DES ASSOCIATIONS DENTAIRES FRANCOPHONES	FRA1993
GROUPEMENT EUROPEEN DES CAISSES D'EPARGNE §	BEL0253
GRUPO CULTURAL LOS ANDES DEL PERU §	DNK1309
GRUPO DE ESTUDOS E SOLIDARIEDADE COM A AMERICA LATINA §	PRT3580
GRUPO ECOLOGISTA HELICA §	ESP1477
GRUPO SOFONIAS	CHE0614
GRUPPE SCHWEIZ-PHILIPPINEN - REGIONALGRUPPE BERN §	CHE0615
GRUPPO ABELE §	ITA2853
GRUPPO DI RICERCA SULLE TECNOLOGIE APPROPRIATE - CENTRO DI INFORMAZIONE NONVIOLENTA §	ITA2854
GRUPPO DI VOLONTARIATO CIVILE	ITA2855
GRUPPO LAICI TERZO MONDO §	ITA2856
GRUPPO MISSIONI ASMARA	ITA2857
GRUPPO NORD-SUD §	CHE0616
GRUPPO PER LE RELAZIONI TRANSCULTURALI	ITA2858
GRUPS DE RECERIA I ACTUACIO SOBRE MINORIES CULTURALS I TREBALLADORS ESTRANGERS	ESP1478
GUATEMALA KOMITEE §	CHE0617
GUATEMALAGRUPPERNA I SVERIGE §	SWE3708
GUIDEN A SCOUTEN MAT DER DRETTER WELT	LUX2978
LES GUIDES DE FRANCE §	FRA1994
GUILDE EUROPEENNE DU RAID §	FRA1995
GYERMEKERDEKEK MAGYARORSZAGI FORUMA	HUN2625
H. YOUTH ENVIRONMENTALIST ORGANIZATION	HUN2626
HABITAT INTERNATIONAL COALITION - EUROPEAN SECTION	BEL0254
HALO TRUST §	GBR2314
HAMPSHIRE DEVELOPMENT EDUCATION CENTRE	GBR2315
HAND AN HAND, KANNER, ELTEREN, DRETT WELT	LUX2979
HAND IN HAND §	GBR2316
HAND IN HAND §	SWE3709
HANDICAP INTERNATIONAL, BELGIQUE §	BEL0255
HANDICAP INTERNATIONAL, DANMARK	DNK1310
HANDICAP INTERNATIONAL, FRANCE §	FRA1996

HANNS SEIDEL STIFTUNG §	BEL0256
HANNS-SEIDEL-STIFTUNG - INSTITUT FUR INTERNATIONALE BEGEGNUNGEN UND ZUSAMMENARBEIT §	DEU1072
HARMADIK VILAG ALAPITRANY	HUN2627
HARNOSAND INDIA DEVELOPMENT COLLABORATION AGENCY §	SWE3710
HAROLD MACMILLAN TRUST §	GBR2317
HARVEST HELP	GBR2318
HAUS DER KULTUREN DER WELT §	DEU1073
HEALTH ACTION INTERNATIONAL	NLD3123
HEALTH ACTION INTERNATIONAL, DANMARK §	DNK1311
HEALTH AID MOYO	GBR2319
HEALTH PERFECT INTERNATIONAL	NLD3124
HEALTH PROJECTS ABROAD	GBR2320
HEALTH UNLIMITED	GBR2321
HEDLEY ROBERTS TRUST §	GBR2322
HEGOA CENTRO DE DOCUMENTACION E INVESTIGACIONES SOBRE PAISES EN DESARROLLO	ESP1479
DIE HEILSARMEE - NATIONALES HAUPTQUARTIER MISSIONSABTEILUNG	CHE0618
HEINRICH BOLL STIFTUNG	DEU1074
THE HEKIMA TRUST §	GBR2323
HELLEF FIR TAPIRAI	LUX2980
HELLENIC ASSOCIATION OF UNIVERSITY WOMEN §	GRC2581
HELLENIC MARINE ENVIRONMENT PROTECTION ASSOCIATION §	GRC2582
HELLENIC YOUTH FOR DEVELOPMENT §	GRC2583
HELP-HILFE ZUR SELBSTHILFE §	DEU1075
HELPAGE INTERNATIONAL §	BEL0257
HELPAGE INTERNATIONAL	GBR2324
HELPING HANDS - KOORDINATIONSBURO FUR FLUCHTLINGSHILFE §	AUT0037
HELSINKI CITIZENS' ASSEMBLY §	SVK3616
HELSINKI COMMITTEE §	HUN2628
HELVETAS - SCHWEIZER GESELLSCHAFT FUR ENTWICKLUNG UND ZUSAMMENARBEIT	CHE0619
HENDRIK KRAEMER INSTITUUT	NLD3125
HENGITYD JA TERVEIS RY	FIN1539
HEPD - ENTWICKLUNGSPOLITIK	DEU1076
HERBERT-THEIS-STIFTUNG §	DEU1077
HERMANDADES DEL TRABAJO §	ESP1480
HERMANN OTTO ENVIRONMENTAL SCHOOL TEAM §	HUN2629
HERMANN-GMEINER-FONDS DEUTSCHLAND	DEU1078
HIGHER EDUCATION FOR DEVELOPMENT COOPERATION	IRL2702
HILFE FUR ALLE §	AUT0038
HILFE FUR KINDER IN NOT §	DEU1079
HILFE FUR OSTEEUROPA TODTNAU SEELSCHEID §	DEU1080
HILFE FUR TOGO AUF PRIVATER BASIS	CHE0620
HILFSWERK DER DEUTSCHEN LIONS	DEU1081
HILFSWERK LIECHTENSTEIN	LIE2925
HILFSWERK MUTTER TERESA §	CHE0621
HINDOE-MOSLIMS ORGANISATIE VOOR MEDEFINANCIERING VAN ONTWIKKELINGSPROGRAMMA'S	NLD3126
HJALPANDE HANDER §	SWE3711
HJALPARSTARF ADVENTISTA §	ISL2735
HJALPARSTOFNUN KIRKJUNNAR	ISL2736
HNUTI BRONTOSAURUS	CZE0882
HNUTI OBCANSKE SOLIDARITY A TOLERANCE §	CZE0883

See: *How to Use the Directory*, page 11.

HOGAR DE CHRISTO §	LUX2981
HOLLAND WORLD YOUTH	NLD3127
HOMELESS INTERNATIONAL	GBR2325
HOMEOPATHES SANS FRONTIERES §	FRA1997
HONGER HOEFT NIET §	NLD3128
HONGERSTICHTING - DERDE WERELD ORGANISATIE §	NLD3129
HOPITAL SANS FRONTIERE §	FRA1998
HOPPETS STJARNA	SWE3712
HORIZON HOLLAND STICHTING §	NLD3130
HOUSEWIVES IN DIALOGUE	GBR2326
HULP AAN MEDISCHE LABORATORIA IN ONTWIKKELINGSLANDEN	NLD3131
HULP VAN SINT-ANDRIES AAN DE DERDE WERELD	BEL0258
HUMAN §	SVK3617
HUMAN RIGHTS ADVOCATES - GENEVA OFFICE §	FRA1999
HUMAN RIGHTS INFORMATION AND DOCUMENTATION SYSTEMS INTERNATIONAL	CHE0622
HUMAN RIGHTS NETWORK	GBR2327
HUMAN RIGHTS WATCH §	BEL0259
HUMAN RIGHTS WATCH	GBR2328
HUMANA	BEL0260
HUMANA - VEREIN ZUR FORDERUNG NOTLEIDENDER MENSCHEN IN DER DRITTEN WELT §	AUT0039
HUMANA KLEIDERHANDEL	DEU1082
HUMANISTISCH INSTITUUT VOOR ONTWIKKELINGSSAMENWERKING §	NLD3132
HUMANISTISCH OVERLEG MENSENRECHTEN	NLD3133
HUN DAGELIJKS BROOD §	NLD3134
HUNGARIAN CENTRE FOR FOUNDATION §	HUN2630
HUNGARIAN INTERCHURCH AID	HUN2631
HUNGARIAN LEAGUE OF HUMAN RIGHTS §	HUN2632
HUNGARIAN NORTH-SOUTH ASSOCIATION §	HUN2633
HUNGARIAN SCOUTS UNION §	SVK3618
HUNGARIAN YOUTH COUNCIL §	HUN2634
HUNGERPROJEKTET §	SWE3713
HUNGERSHJELPEN I NORGE §	NOR3397
HUSMODERSFORBUNDET HEM OCH SAMHALLE	SWE3714
HVITASUNNUSSOFNUDURINN §	ISL2737
DET HVITE BAND §	NOR3398
IAMANEH MUTTER + KIND SCHWEIZ	CHE0623
IATRICO KENTRO APOKATASTASIS THYMATON VASSANISTIRION	GRC2584
IBERO-AMERIKA VEREIN	DEU1083
IBIS	DNK1312
ICTU THIRD WORLD COMMITTEE §	IRL2703
IDEALS AID INTERNATIONAL §	GBR2329
IDRIMA MARANGOPOULOU GIA TA DIKEOMATA TOU ANTROPOU	GRC2585
IEDER VOOR ALLEN	BEL0261
IHMISOIKEUSLIITTO	FIN1540
ILES DE PAIX §	BEL0262
IMAGES ET SOLIDARITE §	FRA2000
IMPACT FOUNDATION	GBR2330
IMPORTE AUS AFRIKA, ASIEN, SUD- UND CENTRALAMERIKA §	DEU1084
IMPRESS - DOKUMENTATIONSCENTER OM NARKOTIKA OG UDVIKLING	BEL0263
IN-MEDIAS §	BEL0264
INCA §	GBR2331
IND-SAM, DE ETNISKE MINDRETAL I DANMARK §	DNK1313

THE INDEPENDENT COMMISSION FOR POPULATION AND QUALITY OF LIFE	FRA2001
INDEPENDENT CZECH YOUTH §	CZE0884
INDEPENDENT ECOLOGICAL CENTRE §	HUN2635
INDEPENDENT INSTITUTE FOR PEACE AND CONFLICT RESEARCH §	DEU1085
INDESCH PATENSCHAFTEN	LUX2982
INDEX ON CENSORSHIP	GBR2332
INDIA DEVELOPMENT GROUP UK	GBR2333
INDIA FRIENDSHIP ASSOCIATION §	CZE0885
INDIAN VOLUNTEERS FOR COMMUNITY SERVICE	GBR2334
INDIEN HILFSWERK "HILFE ZUR SELBSTHILFE"	LIE2926
INDIENHILFE - VEREIN FUR DEUTSCH-INDISCHE ENTWICKLUNGSZUSAMMENARBEIT	DEU1086
INDIENHILFE - VEREIN ZUR UNTERSTUTZUNG UND FORDERUNG NOTLEINDER KINDER §	DEU1087
INDIGENOUS MINORITIES RESEARCH COUNCIL §	GBR2335
INDIGENOUS PEOPLES FUND §	NOR3399
INDIVIDUELL MANNISKOHJALP §	SWE3715
INDONESIA FRIENDSHIP ASSOCIATION §	CZE0886
INDONESISCH DOCUMENTATIE-EN INFORMATIE CENTRUM	NLD3135
INDUSTRIALISERINGSFONDEN FOR UDVIKLINGSLANDENE	DNK1314
INDVANDRERNES FELLESRAD I DANMARK §	DNK1315
INFEDOP	BEL0265
INFO-SOLIDARITE BELGIQUE-TIERS MONDE §	BEL0266
INFO-TURK	BEL0267
INFOLIFE §	GBR2336
INFORMACNE CENTRUM NADACII §	SVK3619
INFORMATION ACTION TIERS MONDE EN AQUITAINE	FRA2002
INFORMATION CENTRE FOR LOW EXTERNAL INPUT AND SUSTAINABLE AGRICULTURE	NLD3136
INFORMATION PRESSE HUMANITAIRE §	FRA2003
INFORMATION-FOI-DEVELOPPEMENT	FRA2004
INFORMATIONS-, DOKUMENTATIONS- UND AKTIONSZENTRUM GEGEN AUSLAENDERFEINDLICHKEIT FUR EINE MULTIKULTURELLE ZUKUNFT	DEU1088
INFORMATIONSSTELLE LATEINAMERIKA §	DEU1089
INFORMATIONSSTELLE SUDLICHES AFRIKA	DEU1090
INFORMATIONSZENTRUM DRITTE WELT	DEU1091
INFORMATIONSZENTRUM DRITTE WELT DORTMUND §	DEU1092
INFORMATIONSZENTRUM DRITTE WELT HANNOVER §	DEU1093
INFOSUD - AGENCE DE PRESSE DOCUMENTATION	CHE0624
INGENIEURS DU MONDE - EPFL §	CHE0625
INGENIEURS SANS FRONTIERES	FRA2005
INITIATIV FIR MEI GERECHTEGKEET MAT DER DRETTER WELT	LUX2983
INITIATIVE DRITTE WELT	AUT0040
INKOTA OKUMENISCHES NETZWERK E.V. §	DEU1094
INNOVATIONS ET RESEAUX POUR LE DEVELOPPEMENT	CHE0626
INSAN HAKLARI DERNEGI §	TUR3886
INSAN KAYNAGINI CELISTIRME VAKFI §	TUR3887
INSEDIAMENTI UMANI E TERRITORIO §	ITA2859
INSERMEDIA	FRA2006
INSTITUT AFRICAIN POUR LE DEVELOPPEMENT ECONOMIQUE ET SOCIAL - FRANCE §	FRA2007
INSTITUT BELLEVILLE §	FRA2008
INSTITUT DE FORMATION ET DE COOPERATION DECENTRALISEE	FRA2009

INSTITUT DE L'ENVIRONNEMENT INTERNATIONAL §	FRA2010
INSTITUT DE RECHERCHE ET D'APPUI AU DEVELOPPEMENT INTERCONTINENTAL ENDOGENE	FRA2011
INSTITUT DE RECHERCHES ET D'APPLICATIONS DES METHODES DE DEVELOPPEMENT	FRA2012
INSTITUT DES DROITS DE L'HOMME, UNIVERSITE CATHOLIQUE DE LYON	FRA2013
INSTITUT DES SCIENCES ET DES TECHNIQUES DE L'EQUIPEMENT ET DE L'ENVIRONNEMENT POUR LE DEVELOPPEMENT	FRA2014
INSTITUT EUROPE-AFRIQUE	FRA2015
INSTITUT EUROPEEN DE COOPERATION ET DE DEVELOPPEMENT	FRA2016
INSTITUT EUROPEEN DE RECHERCHE ET D'INFORMATION SUR LA PAIX ET LA SECURITE	BEL0268
INSTITUT FUR AFRIKA-KUNDE	DEU1095
INSTITUT FUR ASIENKUNDE IM VERBAND DER STIFTUNG DEUTSCHES UBERSEE-INSTITUT §	DEU1096
INSTITUT FUR INTERNATIONALE ZUSAMMENARBEIT	AUT0041
INSTITUT FUR INTERNATIONALE ZUSAMMENARBEIT DES DEUTSCHEN VOLKSHOCHSCHUL-VERBANDES	DEU1097
INSTITUT FUR KULTURELLE WEITERBILDUNG	DEU1098
INSTITUT FUR STAATS- UND VERWALTUNGSRECHT §	AUT0042
INSTITUT FUR WISSENSCHAFTLICHE ZUSAMMENARBEIT	DEU1099
INSTITUT FUR WISSENSCHAFTLICHE ZUSAMMENARBEIT MIT ENTWICKLUNGSLANDERN	DEU1100
INSTITUT INTERNATIONAL DE LA DEMOCRATIE	FRA2017
INSTITUT INTERNATIONAL DE RECHERCHE ET DE FORMATION: EDUCATION ET DEVELOPPEMENT	FRA2018
INSTITUT INTERNATIONAL DES CAISSES D'EPARGNE §	CHE0627
INSTITUT INTERNATIONAL DES DROITS DE L'HOMME	FRA2019
INSTITUT MENZINGEN	CHE0628
INSTITUT PANOS	FRA2020
INSTITUT POUR LA RENOVATION INDUSTRIELLE DANS LES PAYS ACP - INSTITUT POUR LA RENOVATION INDUSTRIELLE EN AFRIQUE NOIRE	FRA2021
INSTITUT POUR LE DEVELOPPEMENT ECONOMIQUE, SOCIAL ET CULTUREL §	FRA2022
INSTITUT UNIVERSITAIRE D'ETUDES DU DEVELOPPEMENT	CHE0629
INSTITUTE FOR AFRICAN ALTERNATIVES	GBR2337
INSTITUTE FOR DEMOCRACY AND EUROPEAN UNITY §	CZE0887
INSTITUTE FOR ENVIRONMENTAL ISSUES AND DEVELOPMENT §	ISL2738
INSTITUTE FOR ENVIRONMENTAL MANAGEMENT AND PROTECTION §	POL3501
INSTITUTE FOR EUROPEAN MARKETING AND DEVELOPMENT ASSOCIATION	NLD3137
INSTITUTE FOR HOUSING AND URBAN DEVELOPMENT STUDIES	NLD3138
INSTITUTE FOR HUMAN RIGHTS §	FIN1541
INSTITUTE FOR SOUTHERN AFRICA	NLD3139
INSTITUTE OF CULTURAL AFFAIRS	BEL0269
INSTITUTE OF CULTURAL AFFAIRS §	DEU1101
INSTITUTE OF CULTURAL AFFAIRS §	NLD3140
INSTITUTE OF CULTURAL AFFAIRS INTERNATIONAL	BEL0270
INSTITUTE OF CULTURAL AFFAIRS, UNITED KINGDOM	GBR2338
INSTITUTE OF INTERNATIONAL SOCIAL AFFAIRS	GRC2586
INSTITUTO 1° DE MAIO §	PRT3581
INSTITUTO AGRARIO PARA A FORMACAO, COOPERACAO E DESENVOLVIMENTO SOCIAL §	PRT3582
INSTITUTO AMARO DA COSTA §	PRT3583
INSTITUTO DE APOIO A CRIANCA	PRT3584
INSTITUTO DE ESTUDIOS POLITICOS PARA AMERICA LATINA Y AFRICA §	ESP1481
INSTITUTO DE ESTUDOS ESTRATEGICOS E INTERNACIONAIS	PRT3585
INSTITUTO DE ESTUDOS PARA O DESENVOLVIMENTO	PRT3586
INSTITUTO DE INVESTIGACAO PARA O DESENVOLVIMENTO, COOPERACAO E FORMACAO 1° DE MAIO §	PRT3587
INSTITUTO DE SOLIDARIEDADE E COOPERACAO UNIVERSITARIA	PRT3588
INSTITUTO INTERCULTURAL PARA LA AUTOGESTION Y LA ACCION COMUNAL	ESP1482
INSTITUTO LUSO-AFRICANO PARA O DESENVOLVIMIENTO E ACTIVIDADES DA POPULACAO §	PRT3589
INSTITUTO MARQUES DE VALLE FLOR	PRT3590
INSTITUTO PARA LA PROMOCION Y APOYO AL DESARROLLO	ESP1483
INSTITUTO PROGRESSO SOCIAL E DEMOCRACIA FRANCISCO SA CARNEIRO §	PRT3591
INSTITUTO SINDICAL DE COOPERACION AL DESARROLLO	ESP1484
INSTITUTO SINDICAL DE ESTUDOS, FORMACAO E COOPERACAO §	PRT3592
INSTITUUT VOOR EUROPEES LATIJNS-AMERIKAANSE BETREKKINGEN	NLD3141
INSTITUUT VOOR LEERPLAN ONTWIKKELING	NLD3142
INSTYTUT NA NEOZ EKOROZWOJU	POL3502
INTEGRRAVE SCHULE FRANKFURT AM MAIN GRUND- UND SONDERSCHULE GMBH §	DEU1102
INTER AIDE	FRA2023
INTER MED ASSISTANCE §	FRA2024
INTER NATIONES	DEU1103
INTER PRESS SERVICE	ITA2860
INTER PRESS SERVICE - NEDERLANDSE AFDELING §	NLD3143
INTER-ACCION	ESP1485
INTERAID INTERNATIONAL	CHE0630
INTERANDES AG	CHE0631
INTERCOOPERATION - SCHWEIZERISCHE ORGANISATION FUR ENTWICKLUNG UND ZUSAMMENARBEIT	CHE0632
INTEREG §	DEU1104
INTERFERENCES CULTURELLES	FRA2025
INTERKERKELIJKE ORGANISATIE VOOR ONTWIKKELINGSSAMENWERKING	NLD3144
INTERKERKELIJKE STICHTING ETHIOPIE	NLD3145
INTERMEDIATE TECHNOLOGY DEVELOPMENT GROUP	GBR2339
INTERMEDICA-MEDIKAMENTENHILFE FUR ENTWICKLUNGSLANDER	DEU1105
INTERMON	ESP1486
INTERNATIONAAL CHRISTELIJK STEUNFONDS	NLD3146
INTERNATIONAL AFRICAN INSTITUTE	GBR2340
INTERNATIONAL AGRICULTURAL TRAINING PROGRAMME	GBR2341
INTERNATIONAL ALERT §	GBR2342
INTERNATIONAL ALLIANCE OF WOMEN §	CHE0633
INTERNATIONAL ALLIANCE OF WOMEN	DEU1106
INTERNATIONAL ALLIANCE OF WOMEN §	GBR2343
INTERNATIONAL ALLIANCE OF WOMEN §	GRC2587
INTERNATIONAL ALLIANCE OF WOMEN	NLD3147
INTERNATIONAL ASSOCIATION FOR THE EXCHANGE OF STUDENTS FOR TECHNICAL EXPERIENCE	CHE0634
INTERNATIONAL ASSOCIATION FOR THE EXCHANGE OF STUDENTS FOR TECHNICAL EXPERIENCE	FRA2026

See: *How to Use the Directory*, page 11.

INTERNATIONAL ASSOCIATION FOR THE PROTECTION OF HUMAN RIGHTS IN CYPRUS §	CYP0835
INTERNATIONAL ASSOCIATION ON WATER QUALITY	GBR2344
INTERNATIONAL BABY FOOD ACTION NETWORK §	CHE0635
INTERNATIONAL BORNEHJAELP	DNK1316
INTERNATIONAL BROADCASTING TRUST	GBR2345
INTERNATIONAL CATHOLIC CHILD BUREAU	CHE0636
INTERNATIONAL CATHOLIC MIGRATION COMMISSION §	BEL0271
INTERNATIONAL CATHOLIC MIGRATION COMMISSION	CHE0637
INTERNATIONAL CATHOLIC MIGRATION COMMISSION §	TUR3888
INTERNATIONAL CENTRE FOR CONSERVATION EDUCATION	GBR2346
INTERNATIONAL CENTRE FOR THE LEGAL PROTECTION OF HUMAN RIGHTS	GBR2347
INTERNATIONAL CHAMBER OF COMMERCE - COMMISSION ON ENVIRONMENT §	FRA2027
INTERNATIONAL CHILDCARE TRUST	GBR2348
INTERNATIONAL CHILDREN WELFARE FOUNDATION §	NLD3148
INTERNATIONAL CHILDRENS TRUST	GBR2349
INTERNATIONAL CHRISTIAN RELIEF	GBR2350
INTERNATIONAL CHRISTIAN YOUTH EXCHANGE §	SWE3716
INTERNATIONAL CO-OPERATIVE ALLIANCE	CHE0638
INTERNATIONAL COALITION FOR DEVELOPMENT ACTION	BEL0272
INTERNATIONAL COLLECTIVE IN SUPPORT OF FISH-WORKERS	BEL0273
INTERNATIONAL COMMISSION OF JURISTS	CHE0639
INTERNATIONAL COMMITTEE OF CHILDREN'S AND ADOLESCENTS MOVEMENT §	HUN2636
INTERNATIONAL COMMMUNITY EDUCATION ASSOCIATION	GBR2351
INTERNATIONAL CONFEDERATION OF FREE TRADE UNIONS §	BEL0274
INTERNATIONAL COUNCIL FOR BIRD PRESERVATION §	GBR2352
INTERNATIONAL COUNCIL FOR FRIENDS OF NEPAL - THE NETHERLANDS	NLD3149
INTERNATIONAL COUNCIL OF JEWISH WOMEN	CHE0640
INTERNATIONAL COUNCIL OF JEWISH WOMEN §	FRA2028
INTERNATIONAL COUNCIL OF SOCIAL WELFARE §	CHE0641
INTERNATIONAL COUNCIL OF VOLUNTARY AGENCIES	CHE0642
INTERNATIONAL DISPENSARY ASSOCIATION	NLD3150
INTERNATIONAL DOCUMENTATION AND COMMUNICATION CENTRE	ITA2861
INTERNATIONAL ENVIRONMENTAL SERVICE CENTRE §	POL3503
INTERNATIONAL EXTENSION COLLEGE	GBR2353
INTERNATIONAL FALCON MOVEMENT - SOCIALIST EDUCATIONAL INTERNATIONAL	BEL0275
INTERNATIONAL FEDERATION CALCUTTA RESCUE §	NLD3151
INTERNATIONAL FEDERATION FOR HOUSING AND PLANNING §	NLD3152
INTERNATIONAL FEDERATION OF AGRICULTURAL PRODUCERS	FRA2029
INTERNATIONAL FEDERATION OF CATHOLIC PAROCHIAL YOUTH COMMUNITIES	CHE0643
INTERNATIONAL FEDERATION OF FREE JOURNALISTS	GBR2354
INTERNATIONAL FEDERATION OF LIBERAL AND RADICAL YOUTH §	BEL0276
INTERNATIONAL FEDERATION OF MEDICAL STUDENTS' ASSOCIATIONS §	AUT0043
INTERNATIONAL FEDERATION OF ORGANIC AGRICULTURE MOVEMENTS	DEU1107
INTERNATIONAL FEDERATION OF RED CROSS AND RED CRESCENT SOCIETIES §	CHE0644
INTERNATIONAL FEDERATION OF SETTLEMENTS AND NEIGHBOURHOOD CENTRES	GBR2355
INTERNATIONAL FEDERATION OF SOCIAL WORKERS	NOR3400
INTERNATIONAL FEDERATION OF UNIVERSITY WOMEN	CHE0645
INTERNATIONAL FORUM	DNK1317
INTERNATIONAL FOUNDATION FOR SCIENCE §	SWE3717
INTERNATIONAL FRIENDSHIP LEAGUE §	PRT3593
INTERNATIONAL GRAPHICAL FEDERATION - EDUCATION DEPARTMENT §	BEL0277
INTERNATIONAL HEALTH EXCHANGE	GBR2356
INTERNATIONAL HELSINKI FEDERATION FOR HUMAN RIGHTS	AUT0044
INTERNATIONAL HUMANIST & ETHICAL UNION	NLD3153
INTERNATIONAL INSTITUTE FOR AEROSPACE SURVEY AND EARTH SCIENCES	NLD3154
INTERNATIONAL INSTITUTE FOR ENVIRONMENT AND DEVELOPMENT §	GBR2357
INTERNATIONAL INSTITUTE FOR INFRASTRUCTURAL HYDRAULIC AND ENVIRONMENTAL ENGINEERING	NLD3155
INTERNATIONAL JURIDICAL ORGANIZATION FOR ENVIRONMENT AND DEVELOPMENT	ITA2862
INTERNATIONAL KONTAKT	DNK1318
INTERNATIONAL LEAGUE OF SOCIETIES FOR PERSONS WITH MENTAL RETARDATION §	BEL0278
INTERNATIONAL MEDICAL COOPERATION COMMITTEE	DNK1319
INTERNATIONAL MOVEMENT AGAINST ALL FORMS OF DISCRIMINATION AND RACISM §	CHE0646
INTERNATIONAL MOVEMENT FOR FRATERNAL UNION AMONG RACES & PEOPLES §	BEL0279
INTERNATIONAL NEPAL FELLOWSHIP	GBR2358
INTERNATIONAL NGO FORUM ON INDONESIAN DEVELOPMENT	NLD3156
INTERNATIONAL OCEAN INSTITUTE	MLT3021
INTERNATIONAL ORGANIZATION OF CONSUMERS UNIONS §	FRA2030
INTERNATIONAL PEACE BUREAU §	CHE0647
INTERNATIONAL PLANNED PARENTHOOD FEDERATION	GBR2359
INTERNATIONAL PRESS INSTITUTE §	GBR2360
INTERNATIONAL REFUGEE DOCUMENTATION NETWORK	DEU1108
INTERNATIONAL RESCUE COMMITTEE §	ESP1487
INTERNATIONAL RESCUE CORPS	GBR2361
INTERNATIONAL RESTRUCTURING EDUCATION NETWORK EUROPE	NLD3157
INTERNATIONAL SAVE THE CHILDREN ALLIANCE §	BEL0280
INTERNATIONAL SAVE THE CHILDREN ALLIANCE §	CHE0648
INTERNATIONAL SCHOOLS ASSOCIATION	CHE0649
INTERNATIONAL SERVICE FOR HUMAN RIGHTS	CHE0650
INTERNATIONAL SOCIAL SERVICE	CHE0651
INTERNATIONAL SOCIAL SERVICE GREAT BRITAIN §	GBR2362
INTERNATIONAL SOCIETY OF SOIL SCIENCE	AUT0045
INTERNATIONAL SOIL REFERENCE AND INFORMATION CENTRE	NLD3158
INTERNATIONAL SOLAR ENERGY SOCIETY - UK SECTION	GBR2363
INTERNATIONAL SOLID WASTES ASSOCIATION	DNK1320
INTERNATIONAL SOLIDARITET	DNK1321
INTERNATIONAL TASK FORCE FOR THE RURAL POOR	GBR2364
INTERNATIONAL TREE FUND	NLD3159
INTERNATIONAL TREE PLANTING COMMITTEE	GBR2365
INTERNATIONAL UNION AGAINST TUBERCULOSIS AND LUNG DISEASE §	FRA2031
INTERNATIONAL UNION OF LOCAL AUTHORITIES	NLD3160

INTERNATIONAL UNION OF PURE AND APPLIED CHEMISTRY	GBR2366
INTERNATIONAL VOLUNTARY SERVICE - UNITED KINGDOM §	GBR2367
INTERNATIONAL WAGES FOR HOUSEWORK CAMPAIGN §	GBR2368
INTERNATIONAL WATER SUPPLY ASSOCIATION	GBR2369
INTERNATIONAL WATERFOWL AND WETLANDS RESEARCH BUREAU	GBR2370
INTERNATIONAL WORK GROUP FOR INDIGENOUS AFFAIRS §	DNK1322
INTERNATIONAL WORK GROUP FOR INDIGENOUS AFFAIRS §	SWE3718
INTERNATIONAL WORKERS AID	DEU1109
INTERNATIONAL YOUNG NATURE FRIENDS §	MLT3022
INTERNATIONAL YOUTH AND STUDENT MOVEMENT FOR THE UNITED NATIONS §	CHE0652
INTERNATIONAL YOUTH FEDERATION FOR ENVIRONMENTAL STUDIES AND CONSERVATION §	NLD3161
DEN INTERNATIONALE FOLKEHOJSKOLE §	DNK1323
INTERNATIONALE GESELLSCHAFT FUR MENSCHENRECHTE	DEU1110
DEN INTERNATIONALE HOJSKOLE	DNK1324
INTERNATIONALE JUGENDGEMEINSCHAFTSDIENSTE	DEU1111
INTERNATIONALE VREDESINFORMATIE DIENST	BEL0281
INTERNATIONALE VRIJWILLIGERSPROJEKTEN §	NLD3162
INTERNATIONALER ARBEITSKREIS §	DEU1112
INTERNATIONALER BUND FUR SOZIALARBEIT - JUGENDSOZIALWERK §	DEU1113
INTERNATIONALER CHRISTLICHER FRIEDENSDIENST	DEU1114
INTERNATIONALER VERBAND FORSTLICHER FORSCHUNGSANSTALTEN	AUT0046
INTERNATIONALER VERBAND WESTFALISCHER KINDERDORFER	DEU1115
INTERNATIONALER VERSOHNUNGSBUND OSTERREICHISCHER ZWEIG	AUT0047
INTERNATIONALES INSTITUT FUR JOURNALISMUS IN BERLIN	DEU1116
INTERNATIONALES KATHOLISCHES MISSIONSWERK §	CHE0653
INTERNATIONALES KOMITEE FUR DIE INDIANER AMERIKAS	CHE0654
INTERNATIONALT HUS §	DNK1325
INTERNATIONALT LANDSBY SAMARBEJDE §	DNK1326
INTERNATIONELLA ARBETSLAG §	SWE3719
INTERNATIONELLA KVINNOFORBUNDET FOR FRED OCH FRIHET §	SWE3720
INTERPEDIA §	FIN1542
INTERSCHOOL SOLIDARITY COMMITTEE §	POL3504
INTERSERVE-NEDERLAND	NLD3163
INTERTEAM - ENTWICKLUNGSDIENST DURCH FREIWILLIGEN-EINSATZ	CHE0655
INTERTEAM - WALLIS §	CHE0656
INTI WAWA-BOCKER AT AYMARAINDIANER §	SWE3721
INZET - VERENINGING VOOR NOORD-ZUID CAMPAGNES	NLD3164
IPOLY UNIO KORNYEZETVEDELMI ES KULTURALIS EGYESULET	HUN2637
IPS-DRITTE WELT NACHRICHTENAGENTUR §	DEU1117
IRAN DEMOCRATIQUE §	CHE0657
IRC INTERNATIONAL WATER AND SANITATION CENTRE	NLD3165
IRELAND AND THE WIDER WORLD §	IRL2704
IRISH ASSOCIATION OF NON-GOVERNMENTAL DEVELOPMENT ORGANISATIONS	IRL2705
IRISH COMMISSION FOR JUSTICE AND PEACE	IRL2706
IRISH EL SALVADOR SUPPORT COMMITTEE	IRL2707
IRISH FAIR TRADE NETWORK	IRL2708
IRISH FOUNDATION FOR CO-OPERATIVE DEVELOPMENT	IRL2709
IRISH INFANT FORMULA ACTION GROUP §	IRL2710
IRISH METHODIST WORLD DEVELOPMENT FUND	GBR2371
IRISH MISSIONARY UNION	IRL2711
IRISH MOZAMBIQUE SOCIETY	IRL2712
IRISH NATIONAL COMMITTEE FOR UNICEF §	IRL2713
IRISH NICARAGUA SUPPORT GROUP	IRL2714
IRISH PEACE COUNCIL §	IRL2715
IRISH RED CROSS SOCIETY	IRL2716
IRISH REFUGEE COUNCIL	IRL2717
IRISH UNITED NATIONS ASSOCIATION §	IRL2718
IRISH WILDLIFE FEDERATION	IRL2719
ISES - PROGETTO MARCO POLO §	ITA2863
ISIS INTERNATIONAL WOMEN'S INFORMATION AND COMMUNICATION SERVICE §	ITA2864
ISLAMIC AFRICAN RELIEF AGENCY §	AUT0048
ISPA NORD/SUD §	ITA2865
ISRAEL-PALASTINA-KOMITEE §	AUT0049
ISTITUTO COOPERAZIONE ECONOMICA INTERNAZIONALE	ITA2866
ISTITUTO ELVETICO - OPERA DON BOSCO §	CHE0658
ISTITUTO PACE SVILUPPO INNOVAZIONE §	ITA2867
ISTITUTO PER LA COOPERAZIONE UNIVERSITARIA	ITA2868
ISTITUTO SINDACALE PER LA COOPERAZIONE CON I PAESI IN VIA DI SVILUPPO §	ITA2869
ITALIAN UNITED NATIONS ASSOCIATION §	ITA2870
IVN. VERENIGING VOOR NATUUR-EN MILIEUEDUCATIE	NLD3166
IWERLIEWEN FIR BEDREETE VOLLEKER	LUX2984
JALCHATRA PROJECT	GBR2372
JAMSHOG ASSOCIATION FOR INTERNATIONAL COOPERATION §	SWE3722
JAMTLANDSGRUPPEN FOR INTERNATIONELLT SAMARBETE	SWE3723
JAN MASARYK FOUNDATION, UNIVERSITY OF ECONOMICS §	CZE0888
JAPABEL	BEL0282
LES JARDINS DE COCAGNE SOLIDARITE NORD-SUD	CHE0659
JEKA ONTWIKKELINGSSAMENWERKING §	BEL0283
JEMIAT-A-DAWAH	CHE0660
JESUIT REFUGEE SERVICE - EUROPE	BEL0284
JEUNESSE ET COOPERATION §	BEL0285
JEUNESSE ET SANTE §	BEL0286
JEUNESSE ETUDIANTE CATHOLIQUE INTERNATIONALE	FRA2032
JEUNESSE ETUDIANTE CATHOLIQUE INTERNATIONALE - MOUVEMENT INTERNATIONAL D'ETUDIANTS CATHOLIQUES - COORDINATION EUROPEENNE	BEL0287
JEUNESSE ETUDIANTE CHRETIENNE	CHE0661
JEUNESSE OUVRIERE CHRETIENNE EUROPEENNE §	BEL0288
JEUNESSE OUVRIERE CHRETIENNE INTERNATIONALE	BEL0289
JEUNESSE OUVRIERE CHRETIENNE-SOLIDARITE INTERNATIONALE	LUX2985
JOHN HUS EDUCATIONAL FOUNDATION §	CZE0889
THE JOINT EASTERN EUROPE CENTER FOR DEMOCRATIC EDUCATION AND GOVERNANCE §	HUN2638
JONGBAUEREN & JONGWENZER - SERVICE TIERS-MONDE	LUX2986
JONGEREN EN DE WERELD	BEL0290
JORDENS VANNER	SWE3724
JOSPICE INTERNATIONAL	GBR2373

JOVENES DEL TERCER MUNDO	ESP1488
JUGEND DRITTE WELT	DEU1118
JUGEND-BILDUNG-HILFE IN BOLIVIEN §	DEU1119
JUMELAGE ET RENCONTRE POUR L'ENTRAIDE MEDICALE INTERNATIONALE §	FRA2033
JURGEN-WAHN-STIFTUNG §	DEU1120
JURISTES-SOLIDARITES	FRA2034
JUSTICE	GBR2374
JUSTICE ET PAIX §	BEL0291
JUSTICE ET PAIX	FRA2035
JUSTICIA I PAU	ESP1489
JUSTICIA Y PAZ	ESP1490
JUSTITIA ET PAX	LIE2927
KAIROS - OECUMENISCH ADVIES- EN INFORMATIECENTRUM ZUID-AFRIKA	NLD3167
KAIROS EUROPA - INTERNATIONAL OFFICE §	BEL0292
KALAHARI-GRUPPEN §	DNK1327
KAMPANJEN EL SALVADOR SKA SEGRA	SWE3725
KAMPANJEN NICARAGUA MASTE OVERLEVA §	SWE3726
KANSAINVALINEN KRISTILLINEN NUORISOVAIHTORY	FIN1543
KANSAINVALINEN SOLIDAARISUUSSAATIO	FIN1544
KANSAN SIVISTYSTYON LIITTO	FIN1545
KARAGWE-FORENINGEN	SWE3727
KARIBU	SWE3728
KARL KUBEL STIFTUNG FUR KIND UND FAMILIE	DEU1121
KARTEI DER NOT-HILFSWERK DER AUGSBURGER ALLGEMEINEN UND DER ALLGAUER ZEITUNG MIT IHREN HEIMATBLATTERN §	DEU1122
THE KARUNA TRUST	GBR2375
KATHMANDU ENVIRONMENTAL EDUCATION PROJECT	GBR2376
KATHOLISCHE ARBEITNEHMERBEWEGUNG OSTERREICHS §	AUT0050
KATHOLISCHE FRAUENBEWEGUNG OSTERREICHS	AUT0051
KATHOLISCHE ZENTRALSTELLE FUR ENTWICKLUNGSHILFE §	DEU1123
KATHOLISCHER AKADEMISCHER AUSLANDER-DIENST	DEU1124
KATHOULESCH MANNERAKTIOUN §	LUX2987
KATOLIEK BEURZENFONDS VOOR AFRIKANEN §	BEL0293
KEHITYSYHTEISTYON PALVELUKESKUS	FIN1546
KEMIANLIITTO - KEMIFACKET RY	FIN1547
KENDRO EREVNON YA TIS GINEKES TIS MESOYIOU §	GRC2588
KENYA-SWEDEN FRIENDSHIP ASSOCIATION §	SWE3729
KENYANSK DANSK VENSKABSFORENING	DNK1328
KERRY ACTION FOR DEVELOPMENT EDUCATION	IRL2720
KFUK-KFUMS RIKSFORBUND	SWE3730
KIHITYSMAANTIETEEN YHDISTYS	FIN1548
KIND EN TOEKOMST §	NLD3168
KINDER IN NOT - HILFSWERK FUR HUNGERNDE KINDER §	CHE0662
KINDER INTERNATIONAL §	CHE0663
KINDER- UND LEPRAHILFE ANDHERI §	DEU1125
KINDERDORF RIO §	DEU1126
KINDERHILFE BETHLEHEM	CHE0664
KINDERHILFSWERK FUR DIE DRITTE WELT	DEU1127
KINDERMISSIONSWERK	DEU1128
KINDERNOTHILFE	DEU1129
KING GEORGE PODEBRADY FOUNDATION FOR EUROPEAN COOPERATION §	CZE0890
KING MAHENDRA TRUST §	GBR2377
KIRCHE IN NOT-OSTPRIESTERHILFE DEUTSCHLAND §	DEU1130

KIRCHLICHER ENTWICKLUNGSDIENST DER EVANGELISCHEN KIRCHE IN DEUTSCHLAND	DEU1131
KIRKENS NODHJELP §	NOR3401
KIRKENS U-LANDSINFORMASJON	NOR3402
KIRKERNES RACEPROGRAM §	DNK1329
KIRKERNES U-LANDSOPLYSNING §	DNK1330
KIRKON ULKOMAANAPU	FIN1549
KISS FORENO ENVIRONMENTAL ASSOCIATION OF CAONGRAD COUNTY §	HUN2639
KIWANIS- ESCH-SUR-ALZETTE SOLIDARITE TIERS MONDE §	LUX2988
DE KLEINE AARDE	NLD3169
KLUB EKOLOGICZNY "MALOPOLSKA" §	POL3505
KODIS-FACHSTELLE FUR BERUFSBILDUNG IN ENTWICKLUNGSLANDERN	CHE0665
KOFINANZIERUNGSSTELLE FUR ENTWICKLUNGSZUSAMMENARBEIT	AUT0052
KOGE OG OMEGNS GHANA VENSKABSFORENING §	DNK1331
KOMITEE ARZTE FUR DIE DRITTE WELT	DEU1132
KOMITEE CAP ANAMUR §	DEU1133
KOMITEE FUR DIE MENSCHENRECHTE IN KUBA §	CHE0666
KOMITEE FUR DIE VERTEIDIGUNG DER CHILENISCHE KULTUR	CHE0667
KOMITEE FUR MEDIZINISCHE UND SOZIALE HILFE FUR PALASTINENSER §	AUT0053
KOMITEE GEGEN DIE AUSHOHLUNG DES ASYLRECHTS, ARBEITSSTELLE FUR ASYLFRAGEN	CHE0668
KOMITEE INDONESIE	NLD3170
KOMITEE TWEE §	NLD3171
KOMITEE WETENSCHAP EN TECHNIEK VOOR VIETNAM §	NLD3172
KOMITEEN FOR SOLIDARITET MED BURUNDIS FOLK §	DNK1332
KOMMISSIE RECHTVAARDIGHEID EN VREDE §	BEL0294
KOMMISSION FUR ENTWICKLUNGSFRAGEN DER UNIVERSITAT UND ETH ZURICH	CHE0669
KOMMUNALES KINO §	DEU1134
DET KONGELIGE SELSKAP FOR NORGES VEL	NOR3403
KONINKLIJK INSTITUUT VOOR DE TROPEN	NLD3173
KONRAD-ADENAUER-STIFTUNG §	DEU1135
KONSTNARER MOT APARTHEID	SWE3731
KONTAKT DER KONTINENTEN	NLD3174
KONTAKTGROEP NEDERLANDSE VRIJWILLIGERS §	NLD3175
KONTINENTY	CZE0891
KOOPERATION EVANGELISCHER KIRCHEN UND MISSIONEN DER DEUTSCHEN SCHWEIZ §	CHE0670
KOOPERATIVA FORBUNDET §	SWE3732
KOORDINATIONSSTELLE FUR OEKUMENE, MISSION UND ENTWICKLUNGSZUSAMMENARBEIT	CHE0671
KOORDINIERUNGSTELLE DER OSTERREICHISCHEN BISCHOFSKONFERENZ FUR INTERNATIONALE ENTWICKLUNG UND MISSION	AUT0054
KOREAN RELIEF §	CHE0672
KRAJOWA RADA EKOLOGICZNA ZMW §	POL3506
KRAJOWE CENTRUM EDUKACJI EKOLOGICZNEJ	POL3507
KRESTANSKE SDRVZENI MLADYCH ZEN - CESKE REPUBLICE	CZE0892
KRISTDEMOKRATISKA UNGDOMSFORBUNDET §	SWE3733
KRISTNA FREDSRORELSEN	SWE3734
KRISTNA SOCIALDEMOKRATERNA - BRODERSKAPSRORELSEN	SWE3735
KRISTNA STUDENTRORELSEN I SVERIGE §	SWE3736
KULTUR UND ENTWICKLUNG ARBEITSGEMEINSCHAFT	CHE0673

KULTURBURO 3. WELT - KULTUR-COOPERATION AFRIKA, ASIEN, LATEIN AMERIKA §	DEU1136
KULTURELLE GESELLSCHAFT REPUBLIK KOREA-SCHWEIZ	CHE0674
KULTURFORENINGEN MISTELN	SWE3737
KUNSILL NAZZJONALI TAZ-ZGHAZAGH	MLT3023
KUNTA-ALAN AMMATTILIITTO KTV §	FIN1550
KURDISTAN INDEPENDANT §	CHE0675
KURDISTAN WORKERS ASSOCIATION	GBR2378
KVEKERHJELP	NOR3404
KVINDERNES U-LANDSUDVALG §	DNK1333
KVINNOR FOR FRED	SWE3738
KWALITEITS CENTRUM HGZO, LEIDSE HOGESCHOOL	NLD3176
KYRKORNAS VARLDSFORUM §	SWE3739
LAAKARIN SOSIAALINEN VASTUU	FIN1551
LAERERNES MISSIONS FORENING	DNK1334
LANCASHIRE DEVELOPMENT EDUCATION GROUP	GBR2379
LANDELIJK BERAAD STEDENBANDEN NEDERLAND-NICARAGUA §	NLD3177
LANDELIJK NETWERK ONTWIKKELINGSEDUCATIE §	NLD3178
LANDELIJK SERVICEBUREAU ONTWIKKELINGSEDUCATIE	NLD3179
LANDELIJKE INDIA WERKGROEP §	NLD3180
LANDESGEMEINSCHAFT NATURSCHUTZ UND UMWELT NORDRHEIN WESTFALEN	DEU1137
LANDSFORENINGEN FOR HJERTE- OG LUNGESYKE §	NOR3405
LANDSLAGET FOR NORGES SYKEPLEIERSTUDENTER §	NOR3406
LANDSORGANISASJONEN I NORGE	NOR3407
LANDSORGANISATIONEN I DANMARK	DNK1335
LANDSRADET FOR NORSKE BARNE-OG UNGDOMSORGANISASJONER §	NOR3408
LANDSRADET FOR SVERIGES UNGDOMSORGANISATIONER §	SWE3740
LANKA SARANA SWEDEN §	SWE3741
LANTBRUKARNAS RIKSFORBUND	SWE3742
LARARE FOR FRED I NORRKOPING §	SWE3743
LASTENSUOJELUN KESKUSLIITTO	FIN1552
LATEINAMERIKA-KOMITEE §	CHE0676
LATEINAMERIKA-ZENTRUM	DEU1138
LATEINAMERIKAKREIS DER KATHOLISCHEN STUDENTINNENGEMEINDE BERLIN §	DEU1139
LATIN AMERIKA HELSEFOND	NOR3409
LATINA - LATINAMERIKANSKA KOOPERATIONSFORENINGEN	SWE3744
LATINALAISEN AMERIKAN KULTTUURIKESKUS	FIN1553
LATINAMERIKA INFORMATION §	DNK1336
LATINAMERIKAGRUPPENE I NORGE	NOR3410
LATYNS AMERIKA CENTRUM	NLD3181
LEAGUE FOR THE PROTECTION OF NATURE - YOUTH ORGANISATION	POL3508
LEAGUE OF TURKISH WOMEN §	TUR3889
LEBENSHILFE FUR GEISTIG BEHINDERTE KREISVEREINIGUNG EHEMALIGER DILLKREIS §	DEU1140
LA LECHE LEAGUE INTERNATIONAL §	CHE0677
LEEDS DEVELOPMENT EDUCATION CENTRE	GBR2380
LEGA ITALIANA PER I DIRITTI E LA LIBERAZIONE DEI POPOLI §	ITA2871
LEGAMBIENTE §	ITA2872
LEGER UDEN GRENSER §	DNK1337
LEIGOS PARA O DESENVOLVIMENTO	PRT3594
LEONARD CHESHIRE FOUNDATION INTERNATIONAL §	GBR2381

LEPRAMISSIONEN	SWE3745
THE LEPROSY MISSION	IRL2721
THE LEPROSY MISSION INTERNATIONAL	GBR2382
LERERFORBUNDET §	NOR3411
LIAISON ET ACTION CONTRE LA FAIM	FRA2036
LIECHTENSTEINISCHER ENTWICKLUNGSDIENST §	LIE2928
LIECHTENSTEINISCHER FASTENOPFER §	LIE2929
LIECHTENSTEINISCHES ROTES KREUZ	LIE2930
LIENS-SAHEL	FRA2037
LIESEN A SCHREIWEN §	LUX2989
LIFE & PEACE INSTITUTE	SWE3746
LIGA DOS AFRICANOS E AMIGOS DE AFRICA §	PRT3595
LIGA OCHRONY PRZYRODY - ZARZAD GLOWNY	POL3509
LIGA PERMANENTE INTERNACIONAL DE COMBATE A FAME	PRT3596
LIGA VOOR MENSENRECHTEN	BEL0295
LIGUE DES DROITS DE L'HOMME §	FRA2038
LIGUE FRANCAISE DE L'ENSEIGNEMENT ET DE L'EDUCATION PERMANENTE	FRA2039
LIGUE INTERNATIONALE CONTRE LE RACISME ET L'ANTISEMITISME	FRA2040
LIGUE INTERNATIONALE DE FEMMES POUR LA PAIX ET LA LIBERTE - SECTION FRANCAISE	FRA2041
LIGUE INTERNATIONALE DE L'ENSEIGNEMENT, DE L'EDUCATION ET DE LA CULTURE POPULAIRE	FRA2042
LIGUE INTERNATIONALE DES FEMMES POUR LA PAIX ET LA LIBERTE §	CHE0678
LIGUE SUISSE DES DROITS DE L'HOMME §	CHE0679
LIGUE SUISSE POUR LA PROTECTION DE LA NATURE	CHE0680
LIIKEALAN AMMATTILIITTO	FIN1554
LIMMAT FOUNDATION	CHE0681
LIONS CLUB INTERNATIONAL §	DNK1338
LIONS CLUB LUXEMBOURG §	LUX2990
LIONS CLUBS INTERNATIONAL, MD 101-SWEDEN §	SWE3747
LIONS INTERNATIONAL SECRETARY	NOR3412
LIONS SEKRETARIAT §	NOR3413
LIVING EARTH	GBR2383
LO/TCO BISTANDSNAMND §	SWE3748
LUONTO-LIITTO	FIN1555
LUTHERAN WORLD FEDERATION - DEPARTMENT FOR WORLD SERVICE	CHE0682
LUTHERHJALPEN	SWE3749
MADRESELVA	ESP1491
MAGTAR IFJUSAGI KAMARA	HUN2640
MAGYAR CSERKESZLEANY SZOVETSEG §	HUN2641
MAGYAR EMBERI JOGUEDO KOZPONT-MARTIN LUTHER KING PROJECT	HUN2642
MAGYARORSZAGI GYERMEKBARATOK MOZGALMA	HUN2643
LA MAIN TENDUE	FRA2043
DES MAINS SANS FRONTIERE	FRA2044
MAIRES SANS FRONTIERES §	FRA2045
MALTESER AUSLANDSDIENST	DEU1141
MANAGEMENT FOR DEVELOPMENT FOUNDATION §	NLD3182
MANI TESE '76	ITA2873
MANNERHEIMIN LASTENSUOJELULIITTO	FIN1556
MANOS UNIDAS - COMITE CATOLICO DE LA CAMPANA CONTRA EL HAMBRE	ESP1492
MARGARET PYKE MEMORIAL TRUST	GBR2384
MARGIT NYLANDERS STIFTELSE FOR HANDIKAPPADE PA SRI LANKA §	SWE3750

MARIAHJALPEN §	SWE3751
MARIATER HUMANITY FOUNDATION §	CZE0893
MARIE STOPES INTERNATIONAL	GBR2385
MARINE CONSERVATION SOCIETY	GBR2386
MARINS SANS FRONTIERES	FRA2046
MARTIN LUTHER KING ORGANIZATION	HUN2644
MARTTALIITTO	FIN1557
MARY'S VENNER §	NOR3414
MASSAG ALAPITVANY - NMZETI ES ETNIKAI KISEBBSEGI JOGVEDO IRODA	HUN2645
MATERNAL, CHILD CARE AND FAMILY PLANNING FOUNDATION OF TURKEY §	TUR3890
MATRIX CONSULTANTS IN DEVELOPMENT MANAGEMENT	NLD3183
MEDAFRICA	LUX2991
MEDECINS DU MONDE	FRA2047
MEDECINS DU SECOURS POPULAIRE FRANCAIS §	FRA2048
MEDECINS POUR TOUS LES HOMMES §	FRA2049
MEDECINS SANS FRONTIERES INTERNATIONAL	BEL0296
MEDECINS SANS FRONTIERES, BELGIQUE	BEL0297
MEDECINS SANS FRONTIERES, FRANCE §	FRA2050
MEDECINS SANS FRONTIERES, GRECE §	GRC2589
MEDECINS SANS FRONTIERES, LUXEMBOURG	LUX2992
MEDECINS SANS FRONTIERES, SUISSE	CHE0683
MEDIA ANIMATION §	BEL0298
MEDIA NATURA	GBR2387
MEDICAL ACTION FOR GLOBAL SECURITY	GBR2388
MEDICAL AID FOR PALESTINIANS §	GBR2389
MEDICAL ENVIRONMENTAL DEVELOPMENT WITH AIR ASSISTANCE	CHE0684
MEDICAL MISSION SISTERS	GBR2390
MEDICAL WOMEN'S INTERNATIONAL ASSOCIATION §	CHE0685
MEDICAL WOMEN'S INTERNATIONAL ASSOCIATION	DEU1142
MEDICAMENTS POUR L'AFRIQUE	CHE0686
MEDICO INTERNATIONAL	DEU1143
MEDICO-LIONS CLUBS DE FRANCE	FRA2051
MEDICOS SIN FRONTERAS	ESP1493
MEDICUS MUNDI INTERNATIONAL	BEL0299
MEDICUS MUNDI, BELGIUM §	BEL0300
MEDICUS MUNDI, CATALOGNE §	ESP1494
MEDICUS MUNDI, ESPANA	ESP1495
MEDICUS MUNDI, ITALIA	ITA2874
MEDICUS MUNDI, SCHWEIZ	CHE0687
MEDIENPLANUNG FUR ENTWICKLUNGSLANDER	DEU1144
MEDISCH COMITE NEDERLAND VIETNAM	NLD3184
MEDISCH COORDINATIE SECRETARIAAT	NLD3185
MEDISINERNES ERITREA-AKSJON §	NOR3415
MEDISWISS	CHE0688
MEDITERRANEAN CENTRE FOR ENVIRONMENT	GRC2590
MEDSYSTRARNA - TETRA LAVAL	SWE3752
MELLEMFOLKELIGT SAMVIRKE	DNK1339
MELLOMKIRKELIG RAD FOR DEN NORSKE KIRKE	NOR3416
MEMISA BELGIQUE	BEL0301
MEMISA MEDICUS MUNDI	NLD3186
MENNESKERETTIGHEDSGRUPPEN SOL §	DNK1340
MENNONITE CENTRAL COMMITTEE	CHE0689
MENSCHEN FUR MENSCHEN	DEU1145
METHODIST CHURCH, OVERSEAS DIVISION	GBR2391
METHODIST RELIEF AND DEVELOPMENT FUND	GBR2392
METHODIST WORLD DEVELOPMENT AND RELIEF COMMITTEE	GBR2393
METODISTKIRKENS MISJONSSELSKAP - METODISTKIRKENS INTERNASJONALE UTVALG §	NOR3417
METODISTKYRKANS UNGDOMSFORBUND	SWE3753
MIGRANTES §	ITA2875
MIGRATIONS SANTE - COMITE MEDICO-SOCIAL POUR LA SANTE DES MIGRANTS §	FRA2052
MIGREUROPE §	BEL0302
MILJOFORBUNDET	SWE3754
MINES ADVISORY GROUP	GBR2394
MINEWATCH §	GBR2395
MINORITY RIGHTS GROUP - INTERNATIONAL SECRETARIAT	GBR2396
MINORITY RIGHTS GROUP SLOVAKIA §	SVK3620
MISION AMERICA	ESP1496
MISSAO DE ESTUDOS PARA O DESENVOLVIMENTO E COOPERACAO	PRT3597
MISSIE EN JONGEREN	NLD3187
MISSIO INTERNATIONALES KATHOLISCHES MISSIONSWERK - PAPSTLICHES WERK DER GLAUBENSVERBREITUNG	DEU1146
MISSION AVIATION FELLOWSHIPS-SWEDEN §	SWE3755
MISSION BIBLIQUE EN COTE D'IVOIRE §	CHE0690
MISSION DER BRUDERGEMEINE - SCHWEIZER ZWEIG	CHE0691
MISSION ENFANCE	FRA2053
MISSION EVANGELIQUE CONTRE LA LEPRE	CHE0692
MISSION EVANGELIQUE CONTRE LA LEPRE	FRA2054
MISSION FUND §	MLT3024
MISSION PROTESTANTE FRANCO SUISSE DU TCHAD	FRA2055
MISSIONAIR CENTRUM §	NLD3188
MISSIONS ET DEVELOPPEMENT	FRA2056
MISSIONSARZTLICHES INSTITUT - ARBEITSGRUPPE AIDS UND INTERNATIONALE GESUNDHEIT §	DEU1147
MISSIONSGESELLSCHAFT BETHLEHEM	CHE0693
MISSIONSKREIS WALLISELLEN	CHE0694
MISSIONSSALLSKAPET BIBELTROGNA VANNER §	SWE3756
MISSIONSWERK DER EVANGELISCHE-LUTHERISCHE KIRCHE IN BAYERN §	DEU1148
MISSIONSZENTRALE DER FRANZISKANER	DEU1149
MITTELSCHULERKONGREGATION - JUGENDZENTRUM §	AUT0055
MODRENE FRA PLAZA DE MAYO, STOTTEGRUPPE I DK §	DNK1341
MONDIALE WERKPLAATS	NLD3189
MONEY FOR MADAGASCAR §	GBR2397
MORSO U-LANDSFORENING	DNK1342
MOSQUITO §	CHE0695
MOTAMAR AL-ALAM AL-ISLAMI §	CHE0696
MOTHER AND CHILD INTERNATIONAL §	CHE0697
MOUVEMENT ANTI-APARTHEID SUISSE, SECTION DE GENEVE §	CHE0698
MOUVEMENT ATD QUART-MONDE TERRE ET HOMMES DE DEMAIN §	CHE0699
MOUVEMENT CHRETIEN POUR LA PAIX	FRA2057
MOUVEMENT CHRETIEN POUR LA PAIX INTERNATIONALE	BEL0303
MOUVEMENT CONTRE LE RACISME ET POUR L'AMITIE ENTRE LES PEUPLES §	FRA2058
MOUVEMENT CONTRE LE RACISME, L'ANTISEMITISME, LA XENOPHOBIE	BEL0304
MOUVEMENT D'ENTRAIDE POUR LE TIERS MONDE ET LA COOPERATION §	FRA2059

MOUVEMENT INTERNATIONAL ATD - AIDE A TOUTE DETRESSE - QUART MONDE	FRA2060
MOUVEMENT INTERNATIONAL DE LA JEUNESSE AGRICOLE ET RURALE CATHOLIQUE - EUROPE §	BEL0305
MOUVEMENT INTERNATIONAL POUR L'UNION FRATERNELLE ENTRE LES RACES ET LES PEUPLES §	CHE0700
MOUVEMENT MONDIAL DES MERES	FRA2061
MOUVEMENT POPULAIRE DES FAMILLES	CHE0701
MOUVEMENT RURAL DE LA JEUNESSE CHRETIENNE	FRA2062
MOUVEMENT SOS ASILE VAUD §	CHE0702
MOUVEMENT SUISSE DE LA PAIX §	CHE0703
MOVEMENT FOR A GLOBAL PARLIAMENT §	HUN2646
MOVEMENT OF THE CHRISTIAN ASSOCIATIONS OF YOUTH §	SVK3621
MOVEMENT OF YOUNG SOCIALISTS §	HUN2647
MOVIMENT GHALL-AMBJENT	MLT3025
MOVIMENT GHALL-AMBJENT, FRIENDS OF THE EARTH, MALTA §	MLT3026
MOVIMENT ZGHAZAGH PARTIT NAZZJONALISTA §	MLT3027
MOVIMENTO APOSTOLICO CIECHI §	ITA2876
MOVIMENTO COOPERAZIONE E SVILUPPO	ITA2877
MOVIMENTO DI COOPERAZIONE EDUCATIVA §	ITA2878
MOVIMENTO E AZIONE DEI GESUITI ITALIANI PER LO SVILUPPO	ITA2879
MOVIMENTO LAICI AMERICA LATINA	ITA2880
MOVIMENTO LIBERAZIONE E SVILUPPO	ITA2881
MOVIMENTO PER L'AUTOSVILUPPO, L'INTERSCAMBIO E LA SOLIDARIETA'	ITA2882
MOVIMENTO PER LA COOPERAZIONE INTERNAZIONALE	ITA2883
MOVIMENTO PER LA LOTTA CONTRO LA FAME NEL MONDO	ITA2884
MOVIMENTO SOS RACISMO	PRT3598
MOVIMENTO SVILUPPO E PACE	ITA2885
MOVIMIENTO 0.7 §	ESP1497
MOVIMIENTO POR LA PAZ, EL DESARME Y LA LIBERTAD §	ESP1498
MU'ASSAT AL-TA'AWUN §	CHE0704
MUSLIM WORLD LEAGUE §	CHE0705
NADACE EVA - NARODNI STREDISKO EKOL. VYCHOVY	CZE0894
NADACE HEINRICHE BOLLA PRAZKA KANCELAR §	CZE0895
NADACE KRESTANSKA POMOC	CZE0896
NADACE TOLERANCE	CZE0897
NADACIA MILANA SIMECKU	SVK3622
NAH - UND MITTELOST-VEREIN	DEU1150
NAIROBI - KLUBBEN, SAMMENSLUTNINGEN AF DANSKE U-LANDSJOURNALISTER §	DNK1343
NAIROBI HOSPICE CHARITABLE TRUST §	GBR2398
NAISASIALIITTO SUOMESSA RY	FIN1558
NAKOVAMMAISTEN KESKUSLIITTO	FIN1559
NAMIBIA FORENINGEN	NOR3418
NAMIBIA SUPPORT COMMITTEE §	GBR2399
NANSEN CHILDWATCH	NOR3419
NAPOLI EUROPA AFRICA	ITA2886
NASJONALFORENINGEN FOR FOLKEHELSEN §	NOR3420
NASJONALT ANDELIG RAD FOR BAHA'IER I NORGE	NOR3421
NATIONAAL CENTRUM VOOR ONTWIKKELINGSSAMENWERKING	BEL0306
NATIONAL CONFEDERATION OF HUNGARIAN TRADE UNIONS §	HUN2648
NATIONAL COUNCIL FOR VOLUNTARY ORGANISATIONS	GBR2400

NATIONAL COUNCIL OF HELLENIC YOUTH ORGANISATIONS §	GRC2591
NATIONAL COUNCIL OF YOUTH ORGANISATIONS §	HUN2649
NATIONAL FOUNDATION FOR ENVIRONMENTAL PROTECTION §	POL3510
NATIONAL PEACE COUNCIL	GBR2401
NATIONAL SOCIETY OF CONSERVATIONISTS §	HUN2650
NATIONAL STUDENT TRAVEL FOUNDATION	MLT3028
NATIONAL UNION OF STUDENTS	GBR2402
THE NATIONAL UNIONS OF STUDENTS IN EUROPE	AUT0056
NATIONALE COMMISSIE VOORLICHTING EN BEWUSTWORDING ONTWIKKELINGSSAMENWERKING	NLD3190
NATIONALE VROUWEN RAAD VAN BELGIE §	BEL0307
NATUR OG UNGDOM	NOR3422
NATURE ET PROGRES §	FRA2063
NATURSCHUTZBUND DEUTSCHLAND	DEU1151
NATURSKYDDSFORENINGEN, BISTANDSSEKRETARIATET §	SWE3757
NCH EDUCATION FOR CHILDREN	GBR2403
NEDERLANDS CENTRUM VOOR INHEEMSE VOLKEN §	NLD3191
NEDERLANDS COMITE VAN WORLD UNIVERSITY SERVICE §	NLD3192
NEDERLANDS FAO COMITE §	NLD3193
NEDERLANDS INSTITUUT VOOR INTERNATIONALE BETREKKINGEN, CLINGENDAEL	NLD3194
NEDERLANDS JURISTEN COMITE VOOR DE MENSENRECHTEN	NLD3195
NEDERLANDSE BOND VAN PLATTELANDSVROUWEN	NLD3196
NEDERLANDSE FINANCIERINGSMAATSCHAPPIJ VOOR ONTWIKKELINGSLANDEN	NLD3197
NEDERLANDSE HERVORMDE KERK	NLD3198
NEDERLANDSE ORGANISATIE VOOR INTERNATIONALE ONTWIKKELINGSSAMENWERKING	NLD3199
NEDERLANDSE PALESTINA KOMITEE §	NLD3200
NEDERLANDSE RODE KRUIS	NLD3201
NEDERLANDSE STICHTING VOOR LEPRABESTRIJDING	NLD3202
NEDERLANDSE VERENIGING TOT STEUN AAN DE OECUMENISCHE OWTWIKKELINGSCOOPERATIE	NLD3203
NEDERLANDSE VERENIGING VOOR CULTUUR EN ONTWIKKELING	NLD3204
NEDERLANDSE VERENIGING VOOR EEN NIEUW INTERNATIONAAL ONTWIKKELINGSBELEID §	NLD3205
NEDERLANDSTALGIE NATIONALE VROUWENRAAD	BEL0308
NEPALWATCH - UK §	GBR2404
NERINGSLIVETS HOVEDORGANISASJON §	NOR3423
NETHERLANDS ASSOCIATION FOR THE UNITED NATIONS	NLD3206
THE NETHERLANDS COMMITTEE OF THE INTERNATIONAL COUNCIL ON SOCIAL WELFARE	NLD3207
NETHERLANDS NETWORK FOR URBAN DEVELOPMENT §	NLD3208
NETHERLANDS ORGANISATION FOR MANPOWER DEVELOPMENT ASSISTANCE	NLD3209
NETWORK WOMEN IN DEVELOPMENT EUROPE	BEL0309
NEW AGE ACCESS §	GBR2405
NEW ECONOMICS FOUNDATION	GBR2406
THE NEW INDEPENDENT COMMISSION §	CHE0706
NEW LIFE MISSION §	NOR3424
THE NEW REFUGEE UNIT §	GBR2407
NGO PLANNING COMMITTEE §	AUT0057
NICARAGUA KOMITEE NEDERLAND §	NLD3210
NICARAGUA KOMITEEN §	DNK1344
NIEZALEZNE ZRZESZENIE STUDENTOW §	POL3511

NINAFRI §	BEL0310
NOAH - FRIENDS OF THE EARTH, DANMARK	DNK1345
NON AU DROIT D'AFFAMER - OPINION PUBLIQUE ET FAIM DANS LE MONDE §	FRA2064
NORD-SUD COOPERATION §	BEL0311
NORD-SUD INSTITUT FUR ENTWICKLUNGSZUSAMMENARBEIT	AUT0058
NORD-SUD-FORUM §	DEU1152
NORD/SYD-KOALITITONEN §	DNK1346
NORDANSTIGS U-LANDSGRUPP §	SWE3758
NORDISKA ARBETSGRUPPEN FOR INTERNATIONELLA AMNINGSFRAGOR §	SWE3759
NORDVESTJYSK FOLKECENTER FOR VEDVARENDE ENERGI §	DNK1347
NORFOLK EDUCATION AND ACTION FOR DEVELOPMENT	GBR2408
NORGES BLINDEFORBUND	NOR3425
NORGES BONDELAG	NOR3426
NORGES DIABETESFORBUND §	NOR3427
NORGES DOVEFORBUND §	NOR3428
NORGES FREDSLAG	NOR3429
NORGES HANDIKAPFORBUND	NOR3430
NORGES HUSMORFORBUND	NOR3431
NORGES IDRETTSFORBUND §	NOR3432
NORGES KFUK-KFUM §	NOR3433
NORGES KOOPERATIVE LANDSFORENING §	NOR3434
NORGES RODE KORS	NOR3435
NORSK ARBEIDSMANDSFORBUND §	NOR3436
NORSK BANGLADESHFORENING	NOR3437
NORSK FOLKEHJELP §	NOR3438
NORSK FORBUND FOR PSYKISK UTVIKLINGS- HEMMEDE	NOR3439
NORSK FREDSKORPSSAMBAND	NOR3440
NORSK KVINNEFORBUND	NOR3441
NORSK LERERLAG §	NOR3442
NORSK LUTHERSK MISJONSSAMBAND	NOR3443
NORSK MEDISINSK KOMITE FOR MIDTOSTEN	NOR3444
NORSK MISJONSRADS BISTANDSNEMND	NOR3445
NORSK ORGANISASJON FOR ASYLSOKERE	NOR3446
NORSK SYKEPLEIERFORBUND	NOR3447
DEN NORSKE ADVOKATFORENING §	NOR3448
DET NORSKE BAPTISTSAMFUNN §	NOR3449
DET NORSKE MENNESKERETTIGHETSFOND §	NOR3450
DEN NORSKE MISJONSALLIANSE §	NOR3451
DET NORSKE MISJONSFORBUND	NOR3452
DEN NORSKE MUHAMMEDANERMISJON	NOR3453
DET NORSKE SKOGSELSKAP §	NOR3454
NORTH & SOUTH EXCHANGE	SWE3760
NORTH-SOUTH COALITION	NOR3455
NORWAC	NOR3456
THE NORWEGIAN CANCER ASSOCIATION §	NOR3457
THE NORWEGIAN FORUM FOR ENVIRONMENT AND DEVELOPMENT	NOR3458
NORWEGIAN HIMAL-ASIA MISSION	NOR3459
NORWEGIAN REFUGEE COUNCIL §	BEL0312
THE NORWEGIAN SANTAL MISSION	NOR3460
THE NORWEGIAN SOCIETY FOR TRAINED SOCIAL WORKERS §	NOR3461
THE NORWEGIAN UNION OF JOURNALISTS §	NOR3462
NOTHELFERGEMEINSCHAFT DER FREUNDE §	DEU1153
NOUS CAMINS §	ESP1499
NOUVELLE PLANETE	CHE0707
NOVA T-INIZIATIVE PER LA CONOSCENZA E LA SOLIDARIETA' TRA I POPOLI §	ITA2887
NUORTEN KOTKAIN KESKUSLIITTO	FIN1560
NUORTEN NAISTEN KRISTILLISTEN YHDISTYSTEN LIITTO §	FIN1561
NYBRO U-LANDS OCH FN-FORENING	SWE3761
L'OASIS - ASSOCIATION SUISSE DE SOUTIEN A LA FONDATION DANIEL BALAVOINE §	CHE0708
OASIS - BEHANDLING OG RADGIVNING FOR FLYGTNINGE §	DNK1348
OASIS CHARITABLE TRUST	GBR2409
OBCIANSKY INSTITUT BRATISLAVA §	SVK3623
OBJECTIF TIERS MONDE	LUX2993
OBRA COOPERACION APOSTOLICA SEGLAR HISPANOAMERICANA §	ESP1500
OBRA DE COOPERACION SACERDOTAL HISPANO AMERICANA §	ESP1501
OBRA PONTIFICIA DA PROPAGACAO DA FE	PRT3599
OCIRIZ NATIONAAL §	BEL0313
THE OCKENDEN VENTURE	GBR2410
OEKUMENISCHE GESELLSCHAFT FUR GERECHTIGKEIT, FRIEDEN UND BEWAHRUNG DER SCHOPFUNG GEM. §	DEU1154
OEUVRE BELGO-COLOMBIENNE DE L'ENFANCE	BEL0314
OEUVRE DE MERE TERESA LUXEMBOURG §	LUX2994
OEUVRE DE SAINT-PAUL	CHE0709
OEUVRE SAINT JUSTIN §	CHE0710
OEUVRES DU SAHEL-ASIE	FRA2065
OEUVRES HOSPITALIERES FRANCAISES DE L'ORDRE DE MALTE §	FRA2066
OEUVRES PONTIFICALES MISSIONNAIRES §	FRA2067
OEUVRES SOCIALES ET EDUCATIVES DES JESUITES AU TIERS-MONDE	BEL0315
OFFICE FRANCAIS DE LA FONDATION POUR L'EDUCATION A L'ENVIRONNEMENT EN EUROPE	FRA2068
OFFICE INTERNATIONAL DE L'EAU	FRA2069
OFFICE TECHNIQUE D'ETUDES ET DE COOPERATION INTERNATIONALE	FRA2070
OIEW §	DEU1155
OIKOS	NLD3211
OIKOS - COOPERACAO E DESENVOLVIMENTO	PRT3600
OIKOS EINE WELT §	DEU1156
OKOMEDIA INSTITUT - INSTITUT FUR OKOLOGISCHE MEDIENARBEIT	DEU1157
OKUMENISCHES STUDIENWERK	DEU1158
DET OKUMENISKE CENTER §	DNK1349
DET OKUMENISKE FELLESRAD I DANMARK §	DNK1350
OLOF PALMES INTERNATIONELLA CENTRUM §	SWE3762
OMEGA FOUNDATION	GBR2411
ONDERWIJS PROJEKT AMSTERDAM-MANAGUA	NLD3212
ONE VILLAGE §	GBR2412
ONE WORLD ACTION	GBR2413
ONE WORLD BROADCASTING TRUST §	GBR2414
ONE WORLD CENTRE FOR NORTHERN IRELAND	GBR2415
ONE WORLD QUILT 2000	GBR2416
ONE WORLD WEEK	GBR2417
ONG PARA LA PROMOCION DE LA SALUD EN PAISES EN DESARROLLO	ESP1502
OOGKAMP HIMALAYA	NLD3213
OPEN SOCIETY FOUNDATION §	CZE0898

OPEN SOCIETY FUND §	SVK3624
OPERA DI PROMOZIONE DELL'ALFABETIZZAZIONE DEL MONDO	ITA2888
OPERATION CHRISTMAS CHILD §	GBR2418
OPERATION DAGSVERK	DNK1351
OPETTAJIEN AMMATTIJARJESTO §	FIN1562
OPHTALMO SANS FRONTIERES §	FRA2071
OPINTOTOIMINNAN KESKUSLIITTO	FIN1563
OPLEIDINGSCENTRUM VOOR DIERVEREDELING, DIERVERZORGING EN DE MENGVOEDER INDUSTRIE BARNEVELD	NLD3214
OPLYSNINGSCENTER OM DEN 3. VERDEN §	DNK1352
ENG OPPEN HAND FIR MALAWI	LUX2995
OPPORTUNITY TRUST	GBR2419
OPUS ARABICUM §	CZE0899
ORBI-PHARMA	BEL0316
ORCHID ASSOCIATION FOR NATURE CONSERVATION §	HUN2651
ORCHIDEES	FRA2072
THE ORDER OF ST. JOHN §	GBR2420
ORDRE DES CHEVALIERS DU SAINT-SEPULCRE DE JERUSALEM	BEL0317
ORDRE DES CHEVALIERS HOSPITALIERS DE SAINT-JEAN DE JERUSALEM	BEL0318
ORDRE MILITAIRE ET HOSPITALIER DE ST. LAZARE DE JERUSALEM §	LUX2996
OREBROMISSIONEN	SWE3763
ORGANISATIE VOOR ONDERWIJS OVER LATIJNS-AMERIKA	NLD3215
ORGANISATION DES TRAVAILLEURS MALIENS DU CERCLE DE DIEMA EN FRANCE §	FRA2073
ORGANISATION INTERNATIONALE DE COOPERATION POUR LA SANTE MEDICUS MUNDI, FRANCE	FRA2074
ORGANISATION MONDIALE CONTRE LA TORTURE	CHE0711
ORGANISATION MONDIALE DU MOUVEMENT SCOUT	CHE0712
ORGANISATION MONDIALE POUR L'ENFANT	CHE0713
ORGANISATION POUR LA PREVENTION DE LA CECITE	FRA2075
ORGANISATION POUR LA RECHERCHE, LA COMMUNICATION ET L'ACTION EN FAVEUR D'UN DEVELOPPEMENT SOLIDAIRE ENTRE LE NORD ET LE SUD	FRA2076
ORGANISATION SUISSE - TIERS MONDE §	CHE0714
ORGANISATION SUISSE D'AIDE AUX REFUGIES-SECRETARIAT ROMAND	CHE0715
ORGANISATIONEN FOR VEDVARENDE ENERGI	DNK1353
ORGANISMO DI VOLONTARIATO PER LA COOPERAZIONE INTERNAZIONALE ''LA NOSTRA FAMIGLIA''	ITA2889
ORGANISMO SARDO DI VOLONTARIATO INTERNAZIONALE CRISTIANO	ITA2890
ORGANIZACION DE COOPERACION Y SOLIDARIDAD INTERNACIONAL	ESP1503
ORGANIZATION OF LAOTIAN STUDENTS FIGHTING FOR INDEPENDENCE AND DEMOCRACY	POL3512
ORGANIZZAZIONE PER LO SVILUPPO GLOBALE DI COMUNITA IN PAESI EXTRAEUROPEI §	ITA2891
ORIENTALIA §	BEL0319
ORJANSGARDEN AGNI §	SWE3764
OROMO KOMITEE NEDERLAND	NLD3216
ORT DEUTSCHLAND §	DEU1159
ORT LUXEMBOURG	LUX2997
ORTHODOX ACADEMIA OF CRETE §	GRC2592
ORTHOPEDIE SANS FRONTIERES	FRA2077
OSRODEK EDUKACJI EKOLOGICZNEJ "EKO-OKO" §	POL3513
OSTASIATISCHER VEREIN E.V. §	DEU1160

OSTERREICHISCHE CARITAS-ZENTRALE §	AUT0059
OSTERREICHISCHE FORSCHUNGSSTIFTUNG FUR ENTWICKLUNGSHILFE	AUT0060
OSTERREICHISCHE GESELLSCHAFT ''RETTET DAS KIND''	AUT0061
OSTERREICHISCHE GESELLSCHAFT DER FREUNDE KENIAS §	AUT0062
OSTERREICHISCHE GESELLSCHAFT FUR ENTWICKLUNGSZUSAMMENARBEIT	AUT0063
OSTERREICHISCHE UNESCO KOMMISSION §	AUT0064
OSTERREICHISCHER AKADEMISCHER AUSTAUSCHDIENST	AUT0065
OSTERREICHISCHER BUNDESJUGENDRING	AUT0066
OSTERREICHISCHER ENTWICKLUNGSDIENST	AUT0067
OSTERREICHISCHER INFORMATIONSDIENST FUR ENTWICKLUNGSPOLITIK	AUT0068
OSTERREICHISCHES HILFSKOMITEE FUR AFGHANISTAN §	AUT0069
OSTERREICHISCHES INSTITUT FUR ENTWICKLUNGSHILFE UND TECHNISCHE ZUSAMMENARBEIT MIT DEN ENTWICKLUNGSLANDERN §	AUT0070
OSTERREICHISCHES JUGENDROTKREUZ §	AUT0071
OSTERREICHISCHES KOMITEE FUR UNICEF	AUT0072
OSTERREICHISCHES KOMITEE GEGEN DIE FOLTER §	AUT0073
OSTERREICHISCHES LATEINAMERIKA-INSTITUT	AUT0074
OSTTIMOR-KOMITEEN §	DNK1354
OUAGA-BORDEAUX PARTAGE §	FRA2078
OUTWARD BOUND INTERNATIONAL SECRETARIAT §	GBR2421
OVERLEG REGIONALE CENTRA	NLD3217
OVERSEAS DEVELOPMENT INSTITUTE	GBR2422
OVERSEAS MISSION SECRETARIAT §	BEL0320
OXFAM - MAGASINS DU MONDE §	BEL0321
OXFAM - WERELDWINKELS	BEL0322
OXFAM BELGIQUE	BEL0323
OXFAM UK	GBR2423
OXFAM-IN-IRELAND §	IRL2722
OXFORD DEVELOPMENT EDUCATION CENTRE	GBR2424
OXYGEN ENVIRONMENTAL CLUB §	HUN2652
P. CULTURAL ASSOCIATION, ENVIRONMENTAL SECTION §	HUN2653
PACE-UK INTERNATIONAL AFFAIRS §	GBR2425
DE PACIFIC WERKGROEP	NLD3218
PADRI BIANCHI-MISSIONARI DI AFRICA §	ITA2892
PAKOLAISNEUVONTA	FIN1564
PALESTINAGRUPPENE I NORGE §	NOR3463
PALESTINAGRUPPERNA I SVERIGE §	SWE3765
PALESTINAKAMPAGNEN §	DNK1355
PALESTINAKOMITEEN I NORGE §	NOR3464
PALMERAS VANNER §	SWE3766
PAN-ASIA COOPERATION SOCIETY §	SWE3767
PAN-PACIFIC SOUTH-EAST ASIAN WOMEN'S ORGANIZATION §	CHE0716
PANCYPRIAN ORGANIZATION OF ARCHITECTURAL HERITAGE §	CYP0836
PANOS LONDON	GBR2426
PARASTA LAPSILLE RY §	FIN1565
PARI DU COEUR - ANITOU §	FRA2079
PARLIAMENTARY HUMAN RIGHTS GROUP §	GBR2427
THE PARNHAM TRUST	GBR2428
PARRAINS DE L'ESPOIR	FRA2080

See: *How to Use the Directory*, page 11.

PARTAGE AVEC LES ENFANTS DU MONDE	FRA2081
PARTENAIRES DU MONDE §	FRA2082
PARTNERSHIP FOUNDATION	SVK3625
PAS §	ESP1504
PASSE-PARTOUT §	GBR2429
PASTOR STROMMES MINNESTIFTELSE	NOR3465
THE PATHFINDER FUND §	CHE0717
PATRIMUNDIA §	FRA2083
PAULO FREIRE GESELLSCHAFT	DEU1161
PAULO FREIRE STICHTING	NLD3219
PAUSELIJKE MISSIEWERKEN §	NLD3220
PAX CHRISTI §	ITA2893
PAX CHRISTI DANMARK §	DNK1356
PAX CHRISTI DEUTSCHLAND §	DEU1162
PAX CHRISTI INTERNATIONAL §	BEL0324
PAX CHRISTI IRELAND §	IRL2723
PAX CHRISTI NEDERLAND §	NLD3221
PAX CHRISTI SUISSE	CHE0718
PAX CHRISTI WALLONIE-BRUXELLES §	BEL0325
PAX ROMANA - INTERNATIONAL MOVEMENT FOR INTELLECTUAL AND CULTURAL AFFAIRS §	CHE0719
PAX ROMANA - MOUVEMENT INTERNATIONAL DES JURISTES CATHOLIQUES	FRA2084
PAZ Y COOPERACION	ESP1505
PAZ Y TERCER MUNDO	ESP1506
PEACE AND APPROPRIATE DEVELOPMENT FOR THE HORN OF AFRICA	NLD3222
PEACE BRIDGES INTERNATIONAL, INTERNATIONAL OFFICE §	GBR2430
PEACE BRIDGES INTERNATIONAL, SVERIGE	SWE3768
PEACE BRIGADES INTERNATIONAL	NLD3223
PEACE LAB - YOUTH MOVEMENT §	MLT3029
PEACE PLEDGE UNION §	GBR2431
PEHMEAN TEKNOLIGIAN SEURA / PEHMEAN KEHITYKSEN RAHASTO §	FIN1566
PELASTAKAA LAPSET RY	FIN1567
PERSONAS	ESP1507
PERU KOMITEE NEDERLAND §	NLD3224
PESTALOZZI CHILDREN'S VILLAGE TRUST	GBR2432
PESTICIDES ACTION NETWORK - EUROPE §	GBR2433
THE PESTICIDES TRUST	GBR2434
PESTIZID AKTIONS NETZWERK	DEU1163
PETER-HESSE-STIFTUNG - SOLIDARITAT IN PARTNERSCHAFT	DEU1164
PEUPLE ET CULTURE §	FRA2085
PEUPLES SOLIDAIRES	FRA2086
PHARMACIE & ONTWIKKELINGSSAMENWERKING	NLD3225
PHARMACIENS SANS FRONTIERES	FRA2087
PHARMACIENS SANS FRONTIERES §	LUX2998
PHILIPPINE INTERNATIONAL CENTRE FOR HUMAN RIGHTS §	BEL0326
PHILIPPINE RESOURCE CENTRE	GBR2435
PINGST MISSIONENS U-LANDSHJALP	SWE3769
PINSEVENNENES YTRE MISJON §	NOR3466
PIONEER CHILDREN AND YOUTH ORGANIZATION §	CZE0900
PIONIER	SVK3626
PIONYR §	CZE0901
PLAN INTERNATIONAL, BELGIUM	BEL0327
PLAN INTERNATIONAL, UK	GBR2436

PLANETE SANS FRONTIERES	FRA2088
PLEIN-CHAMP §	FRA2089
PLUNKETT FOUNDATION	GBR2437
POLISH ASSOCIATION OF AFRICAN STUDIES §	POL3514
POLISH COMMITTEE FOR COOPERATION WITH UNICEF §	POL3515
POLISH ECOLOGICAL CLUB §	POL3516
POLISH PEACE COALITION §	POL3517
POLISH YOUTH COUNCIL §	POL3518
POLISH-AFRICAN FRIENDSHIP SOCIETY	POL3519
POLSKA ASOCJACJA EKOLOGH KRAJOBRAZU	POL3520
POLSKA YMCA	POL3521
POLSKI CZERWONY KRZYZ §	POL3522
POLSKI KLUB EKOLOGICZNY - ZARZAD GLOWNY §	POL3523
POLSKI KLUBEKOLOGICZNY, OKREG GORNOSLASKI	POL3524
POLSKIE TOWARZYSTWO PRZYJACIOL PRZYRODY 'PRO-NATURA'	POL3525
POLSKIE TOWARZYSTWO PRZYRODNIKOW IM. KOPERNIKA	POL3526
POLSKIE TOWRZYSTWO EKOLOGICZNE §	POL3527
POPTEL-SOFT SOLUTION	GBR2438
POPULATION CONCERN	GBR2439
PORTO NOVO MISSIONEN §	DNK1357
THE PRAGUE FOUNDATION FOR CENTRAL EUROPEAN UNIVERSITY §	CZE0902
PRAKTISK SOLIDARITET	SWE3770
PRANAMAYA	FRA2090
PREMIERE URGENCE	FRA2091
PRIEURE D'AVALTERRE DE L'ORDRE SOUVERAIN DE SAINT-JEAN-DE-JERUSALEM	BEL0328
PRIVATINITIATIVE "SAN LUIS', ANCASH - PERU §	AUT0075
PRO ASYL, ARBEITSGEMEINSCHAFT FUR FLUCHTLINGE §	DEU1165
PRO FAMILIA: DEUTSCHE GESELLSCHAFT FUR SEXUELBERATUNG UND FAMILIENPLANNUNG §	DEU1166
PRO NINOS POBRES	LUX2999
PRO REGENWALD	DEU1167
PRO-NATURA INTERNATIONAL	FRA2092
PRODOTTI TERZO MONDO	CHE0720
PROGETTO CONTINENTI	ITA2894
PROGETTO DOMANI: CULTURA E SOLIDARIETA	ITA2895
PROGETTO MONDIALITA	ITA2896
PROGETTO SUD-UIL §	BEL0329
PROGETTO SVILUPPO - CONFEDERAZIONE GENERALE ITALIANA DEL LAVORO §	ITA2897
PROGRAMMA INTERDISCIPLINAIR ONDERZOEK OORZAKEN MENSENRECHT SCHENDINGEN	NLD3226
PROGRAMMA UITZENDING MANAGERS §	NLD3227
PROGRAMME DE RECHERCHE ET DE LIAISON UNIVERSITAIRES POUR LE DEVELOPPEMENT	BEL0330
PROGRAMME SOLIDARITE - EAU	FRA2093
PROGRAMME TO COMBAT RACISM OF THE WORLD COUNCIL OF CHURCHES	CHE0721
PROGRAMME UNIT ON JUSTICE AND PEACE §	CHE0722
PROGRESSIVE YOUTH FOUNDATION §	HUN2654
PROJECT MALA	GBR2440
THE PROJECT TRUST	GBR2441
PROJECTGROEP VOOR TECHNISCHE ONTWIKKELINGSSAMENWERKING	BEL0331
PROJEKT-SERVICE FUR MISSIONS-, SOZIAL- UND ENTWICKLUNGSHILFE §	CHE0723

Voir : *Comment utiliser le répertoire,* page 11.

PROJET DE MANILLE - OEUVRE D'ENTRAIDE DU PERE SCHWARTZ §	CHE0724
LE PROJET FAIM §	CHE0725
PROJET TOMORROW §	FRA2094
PROMOCION CLARETIANA DE DESARROLLO	ESP1508
PROMOPIC INTERNATIONAL §	FRA2095
PROPAGE	ESP1509
UNA PROPOSTA DIVERSA	ITA2898
PROYDE - PROMOCION Y DESARROLLO	ESP1510
PROYECTO CULTURA Y SOLIDARIDAD	ESP1511
PROYECTO LOCAL	ESP1512
PUBLIC SERVICES INTERNATIONAL	FRA2096
PUEBLOS HERMANOS	ESP1513
PUERTO MORAZAN - OBERHAUSENER BURGER HELFEN NICARAGUA §	DEU1168
PUNTO DI FRATERNITA	ITA2899
QUAKER COUNCIL FOR EUROPEAN AFFAIRS §	BEL0332
QUAKER PEACE AND SERVICE §	GBR2442
QUAKERS UNITED NATIONS OFFICE	CHE0726
RAAD VAN ADVIES VOOR HET WETENSCHAPPELIJK ONDERZOEK IN HET KADER VAN ONTWIKKELINGSSAMENWERKING §	NLD3228
RAAD VOOR DE ZENDING DER NEDERLANDSE HERVORMDE KERK	NLD3229
RADA MLADEZE SLOVENSKA	SVK3627
RADDA BARNEN	SWE3771
RADIO NEDERLAND TRAINING CENTRE	NLD3230
RAINBOW - ASSOCIATION FOR LEISURE TIME AND NATURE §	SVK3628
RAITTIUDEN YSTAVAT	FIN1568
RAKENNUSLIITTO	FIN1569
LES RAMEAUX VERTS	FRA2097
RAOUL WALLENBERG ASSOCIATION	HUN2655
RAOUL WALLENBERG INSTITUTET FOR MANSKILIGA RATTGHETER OCH HUMANITAR RATT	SWE3772
RAPHAELS-WERK	DEU1169
RAUDI KROSS ISLANDS	ISL2739
RAVARUGRUPPEN	SWE3773
READING INTERNATIONAL SUPPORT CENTRE §	GBR2443
RECHERCHES ET APPLICATIONS DE FINANCEMENTS ALTERNATIFS AU DEVELOPPEMENT	CHE0727
RED BARNET	DNK1358
REDD BARNA	NOR3467
REFLEX ENVIRONMENTAL PROTECTION SOCIETY §	HUN2656
REFORMATORISCHE HULPAKTIE WOORD EN DAAD	NLD3231
REFUGEE ACTION §	GBR2444
REFUGEE CARE NETHERLANDS	NLD3232
REFUGEE COUNCIL	GBR2445
REFUGEE HEALTH GROUP §	GBR2446
REFUGEE LEGAL CENTRE	GBR2447
REFUGEE POLICY GROUP §	CHE0728
REFUGEE STUDIES PROGRAMME	GBR2448
REFUGEE TRUST	IRL2724
REGARDS AFRICAINS - ASSOCIATION CULTURELLE §	CHE0729
REGARDS CROISES DIALOGUE DES CULTURES §	FRA2098
REGGIO - TERZO MONDO	ITA2900
REGIONAL ENVIRONMENTAL CENTRE FOR CENTRAL AND EASTERN EUROPE	HUN2657
REGISTER OF ENGINEERS FOR DISASTER RELIEF §	GBR2449
REGNSKOVSGRUPPEN NEPENTHES	DNK1359
REHABILITERINGS-OG FORSKNINGSCENTRET FOR TORTUROFRE & INTERNATIONAL REHABILITATION COUNCIL FOR TORTURE VICTIMS	DNK1360
RELACIONES - VEREIN ZUR FORDERUNG ENTWICKLUNGSPOLITISCHER INITIATIVEN UND ENTWICKLUNGSZUSAMMENARBEIT IN NIEDERSACHSEN §	DEU1170
RELIEF SOCIETY OF TIGRAY - UK SUPPORT COMMITTEE §	GBR2450
RENCONTRES AFRICAINES §	FRA2099
RENCONTRES AFRICAINES - MAISON DES ASSOCIATIONS	FRA2100
REPORTERS SANS FRONTIERES	FRA2101
RESCUE INTERNATIONAL ASSISTANCE LEAGUE	FRA2102
RESEAU D'APPUI AUX FORMATIONS POUR LE DEVELOPPEMENT	FRA2103
RESEAU D'INFORMATION TIERS MONDE DES CENTRES DE DOCUMENTATION POUR LE DEVELOPPEMENT	FRA2104
RESEAU DES ONG EUROPEENNES SUR LES QUESTIONS AGRO-ALIMENTAIRES ET LE DEVELOPPEMENT	FRA2105
RESEAU ENSEIGNEMENT TECHNIQUE ET DEVELOPPEMENT INDUSTRIEL	FRA2106
RESEAU FEMMES ET DEVELOPPEMENT	FRA2107
RESEAU GROUPEMENTS - ASSOCIATIONS VILLAGEOISES - ORGANISATIONS PAYSANNES	FRA2108
RESEAU PALMIER DATTIER ET OASIS	ESP1514
RESEAU RECHERCHE DEVELOPPEMENT	FRA2109
RESEAU SOLIDARITE	FRA2110
RESOURCES FOR LEARNING DEVELOPMENT UNIT §	GBR2451
RESULTS EDUCATION	GBR2452
RETURNED VOLUNTEER ACTION	GBR2453
RICERCA E COOPERAZIONE-ORGANIZZAZIONE PER LA RICERCA, LA DOCUMENTAZIONE E IL LAVORO VOLONTARIO NELLA COOPERAZIONE INTERNAZIONALE	ITA2901
THE RICHMOND FELLOWSHIP INTERNATIONAL	GBR2454
RIGHT LIVELIHOOD AWARDS FOUNDATION	SWE3774
RIGHTS AND HUMANITY	GBR2455
RIKSFORBUNDET FOR SEXUELL UPPLYSINING/SWEDEN	SWE3775
RIO MAZAN	GBR2456
RODA KORSETS UNGDOMSFORBUND	SWE3776
ROMA CIVIL RIGHTS MOVEMENT §	HUN2658
ROTARY INTERNATIONAL	CHE0730
ROTARY INTERNATIONAL §	LUX3000
ROTARY INTERNATIONAL - DISTRIKT 2320	SWE3777
ROUE LIBRE VOYAGES	FRA2111
ROYAL BOTANIC GARDENS §	GBR2457
THE ROYAL SOCIETY	GBR2458
RUCH EKOLOGICZNO-OKOJOWY "WOLE BYC" §	POL3528
RUDOLF WALTHER STIFTUNG §	DEU1171
RUFIJI LEPROSY TRUST	GBR2459
RURAL DEVELOPMENT COUNSELLORS FOR CHRISTIAN CHURCHES IN AFRICA	GBR2460
RURAL YOUTH §	CZE0903
RURAL YOUTH UNION - ZARZAD KRAJOWY ZMW §	POL3529
RURALITE-ENVIRONNEMENT-DEVELOPPEMENT	BEL0333
S-KVINNOR, SVERIGES SOCIALDEMOKRATISKA KVINNOFORBUND §	SWE3778
SABS KOMMITTE FOR U-LANDSFRAGOR §	SWE3779
SADANKOMITEALIITTO	FIN1570
SAHARA KLEIDERLADEN - SCHWEIZERISCHE ARBEITERHILFSWERK §	CHE0731
SAHEL INTER ACTIONS SERVICES §	FRA2112

See: *How to Use the Directory*, page 11.

SAHELP §	NLD3233
SAINT JOSEPH'S HOSPICE ASSOCIATION - HOSPICE INTERNATIONAL §	GBR2461
SALTLIC §	GBR2462
THE SALVATION ARMY	GBR2463
THE SALVATION ARMY, EUROPEAN OFFICE §	BEL0334
SAMARBEJDET FOR INTERNATIONALT MILJO OG UDVIKLING	DNK1361
SAMARBETE FOR FRED	SWE3780
SAMBAND ISLENSKRA KRISTNIBODSFELAGA	ISL2740
SAMEN ANDERS GAAN ONTWIKKELEN	BEL0335
SAMENWERKING LATIJNS AMERIKA	BEL0336
SAMF. OG HJEM FOR VANFORE §	DNK1362
SAMRADET FOR UNGDOMSUDVEKSLING §	DNK1363
SANABEL FRANCE §	FRA2113
SANDOR MARAI FOUNDATION §	SVK3629
SANTE SUD	FRA2114
SASAKAWA PEACE FOUNDATION §	SVK3630
SATIS §	NLD3234
THE SAVE THE CHILDREN FUND	GBR2464
SAWA	NLD3235
SCANDINAVIAN ASSOCIATION FOR DEVELOPMENT, RESTORATION AND AID	SWE3781
SCHOOL LINKS INTERNATIONAL §	GBR2465
SCHULSTELLE 3. WELT §	CHE0732
SCHWEITZER REDEMPTORISTEN §	CHE0733
SCHWEIZER ALLIANZ-MISSION	CHE0734
SCHWEIZER INDIANERHILFE	CHE0735
SCHWEIZER KOLPINGWERK VERBANDSSEKRETARIAT §	CHE0736
SCHWEIZER MISSIONS VERKEHRS AKTION §	CHE0737
SCHWEIZER NATIONALKOMMISSION JUSTITIA ET PAX	CHE0738
SCHWEIZER WIZO-FODERATION	CHE0739
SCHWEIZERISCH-CHINESISCHE GESELLSCHAFT	CHE0740
SCHWEIZERISCHE AKADEMIE FUR ENTWICKLUNG	CHE0741
SCHWEIZERISCHE EMMAUS VEREINIGUNG	CHE0742
SCHWEIZERISCHE EVANGELISCHE NILLAND-MISSION §	CHE0743
SCHWEIZERISCHE FLUCHTLINGSHILFE	CHE0744
SCHWEIZERISCHE FRIEDENSRAT - SEKRETARIAT §	CHE0745
SCHWEIZERISCHE KATHOLISCHE ARBEITSGEMEINSCHAFT FUR AUSLANDERFRAGEN	CHE0746
SCHWEIZERISCHE KINDERSCHUTZBUND	CHE0747
SCHWEIZERISCHE OEKUMENISCHE FLUCHTLINGSHILFE §	CHE0748
SCHWEIZERISCHE OSTASIEN-MISSION	CHE0749
SCHWEIZERISCHE PFINGSTMISSION	CHE0750
SCHWEIZERISCHE STIFTUNG PRO JUVENTUTE - ZENTRALSEKRETARIAT	CHE0751
SCHWEIZERISCHE STIFTUNG ZUR FORDERUNG VON KLEININDUSTRIE UND GEWERBE IN DER DRITTEN WELT §	CHE0752
SCHWEIZERISCHE UNTERSTUTZUNGSKOMITEE FUR DIE SAHARAOUIS	CHE0753
SCHWEIZERISCHE UNTERSTUTZUNGSKOMITEE FUR ERITREA	CHE0754
SCHWEIZERISCHES ARBEITERHILFSWERK	CHE0755
SCHWEIZERISCHES KOMITEE FUR UNICEF	CHE0756
SCHWEIZERISCHES ROTES KREUZ	CHE0757
SCHWEIZERISCHES TROPENINSTITUT GESUNDHEITWESEN & EPIDEMIOLOGIE	CHE0758
SCOPE	GBR2466
SCOTT VIATOR FOUNDATION FOR NEW EUROPE §	SVK3631

SCOTTISH CATHOLIC INTERNATIONAL AID FUND	GBR2467
SCOTTISH DEVELOPMENT EDUCATION CENTRE	GBR2468
SCOTTISH EDUCATION AND ACTION FOR DEVELOPMENT	GBR2469
SCOTTISH EDUCATIONAL TRUST FOR UNITED NATIONS AND INTERNATIONAL AFFAIRS §	GBR2470
SCOTTISH EUROPEAN AID §	BEL0337
SCOUT ASSOCIATION	MLT3030
SCOUTS DE FRANCE §	FRA2115
SCRIPTURE UNION, SCOTLAND	GBR2471
SCT. GEORGS GILDERNE §	DNK1364
SDB TRUSTEES	GBR2472
SDRUZENI OBCANU ZABYVAJICICH SE EMIGRANTY	CZE0904
SECOURS CATHOLIQUE - CARITAS FRANCE	FRA2116
SECOURS DENTAIRE INTERNATIONAL	CHE0759
SECOURS INTERNATIONAL CARITAS CATHOLICA, BELGIQUE	BEL0338
SECOURS POPULAIRE FRANCAIS	FRA2117
SECRETARIADO EUROPEO OSCAR ROMERO DE SOLIDARIDAD CON LOS PUEBLOS CENTROAMERICANOS §	CHE0760
SECRETARIADO LATINOAMERICANO DE LA COMPANIA DE JESUS §	ESP1515
A SEED	NLD3236
SEEDS ACTION NETWORK §	DEU1172
SEKRETARIAT FUR ENTWICKLUNGSBEZOGENE BILDUNG UND PUBLIZISTIK §	DEU1173
SELF HELP DEVELOPMENT INTERNATIONAL	IRL2725
SELLY OAK DEVELOPMENT EDUCATION CENTRE §	GBR2473
SELSKABET FOR NORD-SYD SAMARBEJDE §	DNK1365
SEMEURS DE JOIE	LUX3001
SEND A COW	GBR2474
SENIOR EXPERT CORPS §	CHE0761
SENIOR EXPERTEN SERVICE	DEU1174
SENSORIAL HANDICAP COOPERATION §	BEL0339
SERVE	GBR2475
SERVICE CHRETIEN D'ANIMATION RURALE	CHE0762
SERVICE CIVIL INTERNATIONAL	DEU1175
SERVICE CIVIL INTERNATIONAL - SOLIDARITY, EXCHANGE, EDUCATION FOR DEVELOPMENT	BEL0340
SERVICE CIVIL INTERNATIONAL, BRANCHE FRANCAISE §	FRA2118
SERVICE D'ENTRAIDE ET DE LIAISON	FRA2119
SERVICE DE COOPERATION AU DEVELOPPEMENT §	FRA2120
SERVICE DE COOPERATION MISSIONNAIRE AU DEVELOPPEMENT-DMOS	BEL0341
SERVICE ECOLE DE LA COMMUNAUTE DE TRAVAIL	CHE0763
SERVICE INTERNATIONAL D'APPUI AU DEVELOPPEMENT §	FRA2121
SERVICE INTERNATIONAL DE LIAISON D'ORGANISATION POUR UN DEVELOPPEMENT SOLIDAIRE	FRA2122
SERVICE LAIQUE DE COOPERATION AU DEVELOPPEMENT	BEL0342
SERVICE MISSIONNAIRE DES JEUNES	FRA2123
SERVICE SOCIAL D'AIDE AUX EMIGRANTS §	FRA2124
SERVICE SOCIAL DES ETRANGERS-FORMATION ET AIDE AUX ENTREPRISES-VITROBIO	BEL0343
SERVICE TECHNIQUE D'INFORMATION ET DE RECHERCHE D'EQUIPEMENTS POUR LE DEVELOPPEMENT §	FRA2125
SERVICIO DE REFUGIADOS Y MIGRANTES §	ESP1516
SERVICIO JESUITA A REFUGIADOS	ITA2902

SERVICOS DE ASSISTENCIA ORGANIZACAO DE MARIA §	PRT3601
SERVIZIO CIVILE INTERNAZIONALE - ITALIE	ITA2903
SERVIZIO COOPERAZIONE AIUTO INTERNAZIONALE PIAMARTINO §	ITA2904
SERVIZIO RIFUGIATI E MIGRANTI DELLA FEDERATIONE DELLE CHIESE EVANGELICHE IN ITALIA	ITA2905
SERVIZIO SOCIALE INTERNATIONALE - SEZIONE ITALIANA §	ITA2906
SERVIZIO VOLONTARIO INTERNAZIONALE	ITA2907
SETEM - SERVICIO TERCER MUNDO	ESP1517
SID VALE AFRICA LINK §	GBR2476
7 CAMPAIGN §	ESP1518
SIGHT SAVERS, THE ROYAL COMMONWEALTH SOCIETY FOR THE BLIND	GBR2477
SILVA, ARBRES, FORETS ET SOCIETES	FRA2126
SIMAVI	NLD3237
SKANDINAVISKA BARNMISSIONEN §	SWE3782
SKILLSHARE AFRICA	GBR2478
SKOLENES U-LANDSAKSJON §	NOR3468
SLAVOMIR STRACAR FOUNDATION §	SVK3632
SLOVAK CHILDREN'S FUND §	SVK3633
SLOVAK COMMITTEE FOR UNICEF	SVK3634
SLOVAK HELSINKI COMMITTE §	SVK3635
SLOVAK UNION FOR PEACE AND HUMAN RIGHTS §	SVK3636
SLOVAK UNION OF NATURE AND LANDSCAPE PROTECTORS §	SVK3637
SLOVENSKA ADADEMICKA INFORMACNA AGENTURA	SVK3638
SOBER VOOR ANDEREN §	BEL0344
SOCIAL ECOLOGICAL INSTITUTE §	POL3530
SOCIAL WORK FOUNDATION §	GRC2593
SOCIEDAD INTERNACIONAL PARA EL DESARROLLO §	ESP1519
SOCIETE D'INVESTISSEMENT ET DE DEVELOPPEMENT INTERNATIONAL §	FRA2127
SOCIETE DE SAINT-VINCENT DE PAUL/CONSEIL GENERAL INTERNATIONAL §	FRA2128
SOCIETE INTERNATIONALE MISSIONNAIRE	CHE0764
SOCIETE INTERNATIONALE POUR LE DEVELOPPEMENT - SECTION SUISSE	CHE0765
SOCIETE INTERNATIONALE POUR LE DEVELOPPEMENT, FRANCE	FRA2129
SOCIETE KOLPING DU GRAND-DUCHE DE LUXEMBOURG	LUX3002
SOCIETE POUR LA PROMOTION ET LA GESTION INDUSTRIELLE	FRA2130
SOCIETE SUISSE D'ETUDES AFRICAINES	CHE0766
SOCIETE SUISSE POUR LA PROTECTION DE L'ENVIRONNEMENT	CHE0767
SOCIETY FOR INTERNATIONAL DEVELOPMENT	ITA2908
SOCIETY FOR INTERNATIONAL DEVELOPMENT, FINNISH CHAPTER §	FIN1571
SOCIETY FOR INTERNATIONAL DEVELOPMENT, UK CHAPTER §	GBR2479
THE SOCIETY FOR INTERNATIONAL EDUCATION, TRAINING AND RESEARCH §	NLD3238
SOCIETY FOR THE PROTECTION OF TREES §	MLT3031
SOCIETY FOR THE STUDY AND CONSERVATION OF NATURE §	MLT3032
SOCIETY OF NATURE PROTECTIONISTS §	HUN2659
SOIL ASSOCIATION	GBR2480
SOLARAID §	CHE0768
SOLIDAR	BEL0345
SOLIDARESCH HELLEF-REISERBANN	LUX3003

SOLIDARIDAD §	NLD3239
SOLIDARIDAD DEMOCRATICA §	ESP1520
SOLIDARIDAD INTERNACIONAL - FUNDUCION ESPANOLA PARA LA COOPERACION	ESP1521
SOLIDARIDAD PARA EL DESARROLLO Y LA PAZ	ESP1522
SOLIDARIETA E COOPERAZIONE SENZA FRONTIERE §	ITA2909
SOLIDARIETA MEDICA CON IL NICARAGUA §	CHE0769
SOLIDARIETA TERZO MONDO §	CHE0770
SOLIDARIETA UOMO COOPERAZIONE ALLO SVILUPPO	ITA2910
SOLIDARIETA' CON IL TERZO MONDO	ITA2911
SOLIDARITAT MIT MOCAMBIQUE	CHE0771
SOLIDARITATSDIENST-INTERNATIONAL	DEU1176
SOLIDARITATSFONDS DES CHRISTLICHNATIONALEN GEWERKSCHAFTSBUNDES DER SCHWEIZ	CHE0772
SOLIDARITATSFONDS DRITTE WELT	DEU1177
SOLIDARITATSFONDS FUR DEN SOZIALEN BEFREIUNGSKAMPF IN DER DRITTEN WELT	CHE0773
SOLIDARITE	FRA2131
SOLIDARITE AFGHANISTAN §	BEL0346
SOLIDARITE AFRIQUE DU SUD §	CHE0774
SOLIDARITE ET COOPERATION MEDICALE AU TIERS MONDE	BEL0347
SOLIDARITE FRANCE BRESIL §	FRA2132
SOLIDARITE INTERNATIONALE DES MAISONS FAMILIALES RURALES §	BEL0348
SOLIDARITE INTERNATIONALE DES TRAVAILLEURS NORD/SUD §	BEL0349
SOLIDARITE INTERNATIONALE ET DEVELOPPEMENT RURAL	FRA2133
SOLIDARITE LIBERALE INTERNATIONALE	BEL0350
SOLIDARITE LUXEMBOURG TIERS MONDE §	LUX3004
SOLIDARITE MONDIALE	BEL0351
SOLIDARITE PROTESTANTE	BEL0352
SOLIDARITE SOCIALISTE - FONDS DE COOPERATION AU DEVELOPPEMENT	BEL0353
SOLIDARITE TIERS MONDE §	CHE0775
SOLIDARITE-VILLES	FRA2134
SOLIDARITEIT BOLIVIE §	BEL0354
SOLIDARITES AGRO-ALIMENTAIRES §	FRA2135
SOLIDARITES INTERNATIONALES §	FRA2136
SOLIDARMED - CHRISTLICHER DIENST FUR MEDIZINISCHE ZUSAMMENARBEIT	CHE0776
SONNENBERG ASSOCIATION §	MLT3033
SOROPTIMIST INTERNATIONAL §	CHE0777
SOROPTIMIST INTERNATIONAL, UNITED KINGDOM	GBR2481
SOS BARNAPORPIN §	ISL2741
SOS BOITES DE LAIT	BEL0355
SOS CHILDREN'S VILLAGES UNITED KINGDOM	GBR2482
SOS ENFANTS EN DETRESSE MERSCH §	LUX3005
SOS ENFANTS SANS FRONTIERES	FRA2137
SOS ENVIRONNEMENT A LA BASE	CHE0778
SOS FAIM - ACTION POUR LE DEVELOPPEMENT	LUX3006
SOS FAIM - COMITE BELGE POUR LA CAMPAGNE CONTRE LA FAIM	BEL0356
SOS HONGER §	BEL0357
SOS KINDERDORF INTERNATIONAL	AUT0076
SOS KINDERDORPEN §	NLD3240
SOS LAYETTES	BEL0358
SOS MISSIONARIO	ITA2912
SOS MITMENSCH §	AUT0077

See: *How to Use the Directory*, page 11.

SOS RACISME VAUD §	CHE0779
SOS RACISMO ESPANA	ESP1523
SOS RATSISMOS §	GRC2594
SOS SAHEL INTERNATIONAL, FRANCE	FRA2138
SOS SAHEL INTERNATIONAL, UNITED KINGDOM	GBR2483
SOS-BORNEBYERNE, DANMARK	DNK1366
SOS-CECITE §	FRA2139
SOS-EKO §	POL3531
SOS-PER GENTES PRO GENTIBUS	BEL0359
SOS-SAHEL INTERNATIONAL §	LUX3007
SOS-WERELDHANDEL §	BEL0360
SOSTE TA PAIDIA	GRC2595
SOUTH AFRICAN TOWNSHIPS §	GBR2484
SOUTH AMERICAN MISSIONARY SOCIETY	GBR2485
SOUTH-NORTH NETWORK CULTURES AND DEVELOPMENT	BEL0361
SOUTHEAST-ASIAN OUTREACH	GBR2486
SOUTIEN A L'INITIATIVE PRIVEE POUR L'AIDE A LA RECONSTRUCTION DES PAYS DU SUD-EST ASIATIQUE	FRA2140
SOZIAL- UND ENTWICKLUNGSHILFE DES KOLPINGWERKES	DEU1178
SOZIALWISSENSCHAFTLICHER STUDIENKREIS FUR INTERNATIONALE PROBLEME	DEU1179
SPANA §	GBR2487
SPECIALARBEJDERFORBUNDET I DANMARK	DNK1367
SPICMA §	GBR2488
SPOLECNOST PRATEL AFRIKY	CZE0905
SPOLECSNY INSTYTUT EKOLOGICSNY	POL3532
SPOLECTNOST CESKO-ARABSKA	CZE0906
SPOLECZNA KOMISJA EKOURBANISTYCZNA §	POL3533
SPOLECZNE CENTRUM INFORMACYJNE §	POL3534
SPOLECZNY INSTYTUT EKOLOGICZNY §	POL3535
SRI LANKA INFORMATIONSGRUPPE §	DNK1368
SRI LANKA RESOURCE CENTRE §	NOR3469
ST. IUCN LEDEN-CONTACT §	NLD3241
ST. JOHN AMBULANCE	GBR2489
STATES OF EMERGENCY DATABASE CENTRE	GBR2490
STATION INTERNATIONALE DE RECHERCHE CONTRE LA FAIM DANS LE MONDE §	FRA2141
STEERING COMMITTEE FOR HUMANITARIAN RESPONSE	CHE0780
THE STEFAN BATORY FOUNDATION	POL3536
STEFANKA STUDENTSKA NADACIA A §	SVK3639
STEIRISCHE ENTWICKLUNGSPOLITISCHE INITIATIVE §	AUT0078
STEUNFONDS DERDE WERELD	BEL0362
STICHTING & VERENIGING ALVADAM	NLD3242
STICHTING ACTIE AFGHANEN IN NOOD §	NLD3243
STICHTING ACTIE CALCUTTA	NLD3244
STICHTING ANTOON SPINOY §	BEL0363
STICHTING ASHOKA NEDERLAND	NLD3245
STICHTING BLINDHEIDBESTRIJDING ONTWIKKELINGSLANDEN §	NLD3246
STICHTING BRASIL OP WEG §	NLD3247
STICHTING COLOMBIA KOMITEE NEDERLAND §	NLD3248
STICHTING COMMUNICATIE ONTWIKKELINGSSAMENWERKING	NLD3249
STICHTING DE WAAL	NLD3250
STICHTING DENTAL HEALTH INTERNATIONAL NEDERLAND	NLD3251
STICHTING DERDE WERELD COMMUNICATIE §	NLD3252
STICHTING DOEN	NLD3253
STICHTING ECOLOGISCHE LANDBOUWPROJECTEN GHANA	NLD3254
STICHTING ECOPLAN	NLD3255
STICHTING EMMAUS NEDERLAND	NLD3256
STICHTING EUROPEAN HUMAN RIGHTS FOUNDATION	BEL0364
STICHTING GERED GEREEDSCHAP	NLD3257
STICHTING GUATEMALA KOMITEE NEDERLAND	NLD3258
STICHTING HELP BANGLADESH §	NLD3259
STICHTING HULP AAN TIBETANEN	NLD3260
STICHTING IDEELE IMPORT §	NLD3261
STICHTING KINDERPOSTZEGELS NEDERLAND	NLD3262
STICHTING KLEINSCHALIGE ONTWIKKELINGSPROJECTEN	NLD3263
STICHTING KOPPELGEMEENTE WAGENINGEN-NYABIKENKE	NLD3264
STICHTING LEEFMILIEU	BEL0365
STICHTING LILIANE FONDS	NLD3265
STICHTING LITTLE PHILIPPINES §	NLD3266
STICHTING MAX HAVELAAR	NLD3267
STICHTING MEDISCHE HULP KENYA §	NLD3268
STICHTING MENA	NLD3269
STICHTING MILIEU EDUCATIE	NLD3270
STICHTING MISSIE VERKEERSMIDDELEN AKTIE	NLD3271
STICHTING MONDIAAL ALTERNATIEF §	NLD3272
STICHTING MUNDELNINO §	NLD3273
STICHTING NATUUR EN MILIEU	NLD3274
STICHTING NEDERLAND-SRI LANKA §	NLD3275
STICHTING NEDERLANDS COMITE UNICEF §	NLD3276
STICHTING OECUMENISCHE HULP	NLD3277
STICHTING ONDERZOEK EN VOORLICHTING BEVOLKINGS POLITIEK	NLD3278
STICHTING ONDERZOEK MULTINATIONALE ONDERNEMINGEN	NLD3279
STICHTING ONTWIKKELINGSHULP ZUID-AZIE §	NLD3280
STICHTING ONTWIKKELINGSSAMENWERKING BREDA	NLD3281
STICHTING ONTWIKKELINGSSAMENWERKING NEDERLAND-TUNESIE §	NLD3282
STICHTING ONTWIKKELINGSSAMENWERKING UGANDA §	NLD3283
STICHTING ORTHOPEDIE EN REVALIDATIE IN ONTWIKKELINGSLANDEN §	NLD3284
STICHTING OVERAL	NLD3285
STICHTING PLATFORM VOOR DUURZAME ONTWIKKELING	NLD3286
STICHTING PROJECTEN VOOR KINDEREN IN SRI LANKA §	NLD3287
STICHTING REDT DE KINDEREN	NLD3288
STICHTING REFORMATORISCHE HULPAKTIE WOORD EN DAAD §	NLD3289
STICHTING REVALIDATIE HULP	NLD3290
STICHTING RWANDA ONDERWIJS 2000	NLD3291
STICHTING SAWA	NLD3292
STICHTING SCHOOL & WERELD §	NLD3293
STICHTING STEDENBAND AMSTERDAM-MANAGUA §	NLD3294
STICHTING SUWA SETHA NEDERLAND	NLD3295
STICHTING TER BEVORDERING VAN INTERNATIONALE SOLIDARITEIT UTRECHT §	NLD3296
STICHTING TERRE DES HOMMES NEDERLAND	NLD3297
STICHTING TOT BEVORDERING VAN DE GEZONDHEIDSZORG IN ONTWIKKELINGSLANDEN/ SAMEN PETER - SAMEN STERK §	NLD3298

Voir : *Comment utiliser le répertoire*, page 11.

STICHTING TOT BEVORDERING VAN SAMENWERKING MET LANDEN IN ONTWIKKELING §	NLD3299
STICHTING VLUCHTELING	NLD3300
STICHTING VOLUNTARY SERVICE OVERSEAS NEDERLAND	NLD3301
STICHTING VOOR GEMEENSCHAPSONTWIKKELING IN SRI LANKA	NLD3302
STICHTING VOOR GEZONDHEID EN BEVRIJDING IN MIDDEN-AMERIKA	NLD3303
STICHTING VOOR HERGEBRUIK VAN MEDISCHE HULPMIDDELEN	NLD3304
STICHTING VOOR LATIJNS AMERIKAANS SOCIAAL ONDERZOEK	NLD3305
STICHTING VOOR LEPRABESTRIJDING IN THAILAND §	NLD3306
STICHTING VOOR NEDERLANDSE BOSBOUW-ONTWIKKELINGSSAMENWERKING §	NLD3307
STICHTING VRIENDEN MEDISCHE MISSIEZUSTERS	NLD3308
STICHTING VRIENDEN VAN ADESA - ASOCIACION DESARROLLO DE LA SALUD §	NLD3309
STICHTING VRIENDEN VAN RWANDA §	NLD3310
STICHTING VRONESTEIN	NLD3311
STICHTING WERKGROEP AVISE §	NLD3312
STICHTING WERKGROEP ECUADOR-NEDERLAND §	NLD3313
STICHTING WERKGROEP INHEEMSE VOLKEN §	NLD3314
STIFTELSEN EMMAUS I UPPSALA	SWE3783
STIFTELSEN ESTHER AXENES BARNHJALP §	SWE3784
STIFTELSEN FOR GLOBALA BEFOLKNINGSFRAGOR	SWE3785
STIFTELSEN FOR INTERNATIONELLT UNGDOMSUTBYTE	SWE3786
STIFTELSEN GLOBTRADET	SWE3787
STIFTELSEN INTER-FOLK §	NOR3470
STIFTELSEN SVENSK INTERNATIONELL BARNHJALP - BARN I NOD §	SWE3788
STIFTUNG ENGAGEMENT DRITTE WELT §	CHE0781
STIFTUNG ENTWICKLUNG UND FRIEDEN	DEU1180
STIFTUNG FUR INTERNATIONAL ZUSAMMENARBEIT §	CHE0782
STIFTUNG GERTRUD KURZ §	CHE0783
STIFTUNG KINDER IN AFRIKA	DEU1181
STIFTUNG KINDERDIREKTHILFE KOLUMBIEN §	CHE0784
STIFTUNG KINDERDORF PESTALOZZI - ABTEILUNG KINDERHILFE DRITTE WELT	CHE0785
STIFTUNG OFFENE HAND	CHE0786
STIFTUNG UMWELTBILDUNG SCHWEIZ	CHE0787
STIFTUNG UNSERE KLEINEN BRUDER UND SCHWESTERN	CHE0788
STIFTUNG VIVAMOS MEJOR	CHE0789
STIFTUNG WIR BAUEN MITEINANDER §	CHE0790
STIFTUNG WIR FUR KINDER IN NOT §	DEU1182
STOCKHOLM ENVIRONMENT INSTITUTE	SWE3789
STODFORENING TILL REST I SVERIGE §	SWE3790
STODFORENINGEN FOR PRAKTIKANTUTBYTE TOREBODABYGDEN - KIBAHA §	SWE3791
STODKOMMITTEN FOR CENTRALAMERIKAS FOLK §	SWE3792
STORSTROMS AMTS U AND K FORVALTNINGEN U-LANDSPROJEKTET	DNK1369
STOTTEGRUPPE FOR BEDSTEMODRENE PA PLAZA DE MAYO, ARGENTINA §	DNK1370
STOTTEGRUPPEN FOR ANDES §	DNK1371
STOTTEKOMITEEN FOR GHASSAN KANAFANIS KULTURFOND	DNK1372
STOTTEKOMITEEN FOR TIBET, DANMARK §	DNK1373
STRAFFALLIGEN-UND BEWAHRUNGSHILFE BERLIN §	DEU1183
STREDISKO KRESTANSKE POMOCI MLADYM V KRIZI	CZE0907
STROM ZIVOTA	SVK3640
STUDENCKI KLUB EKOLGICZNY §	POL3537
STUDENT CO-OPERATIVE GROUP "UNIVERSITAS" §	HUN2660
STUDIE EN ORGANISATIE VOOR MEDISCHE AKTIE §	BEL0366
STUDIE- EN DOCUMENTATIE CENTRUM VOOR AANGEPASTE TECHNOLOGIE IN ONTWIKKELINGSLANDEN	BEL0367
STUDIO 3 §	NLD3315
SUDAFRIKA MISSION §	CHE0791
SUDAN HUMAN RIGHTS ORGANIZATION §	GBR2491
SUDAN MISSIONEN	DNK1374
SUDOSTASIEN-INFORMATIONSSTELLE	DEU1184
SUDWIND-BUCHWELT	AUT0079
SUE RYDER FOUNDATION	GBR2492
SUL - ASSOCIACAO DE COOPERACAO PARA O DESENVOLVIMENTO	PRT3602
SUN DIAL CLUB §	HUN2661
SUOMEN 4H-LIITTO	FIN1572
SUOMEN ADVENTTIKIRKKO §	FIN1573
SUOMEN AMMATTILIITTOJEN SOLIDAARISUUSKESKUS	FIN1574
SUOMEN DEMOKRATIAN PIONEERIEN LIITTO	FIN1575
SUOMEN KATILOLITTO §	FIN1576
SUOMEN KIRJASTOSEURA	FIN1577
SUOMEN KRISTILLINEN YLIOPPILASLASLIITTO	FIN1578
SUOMEN LAAKARILIITTO	FIN1579
SUOMEN LAHETYSSEURA	FIN1580
SUOMEN LEPRALAHETYS RY	FIN1581
SUOMEN NUORISOYHTEIDSTHYO ALLIANSI	FIN1582
SUOMEN NUORTEN JA OPISKELIJOIDEN YK-LUITO	FIN1583
SUOMEN OSUUSTOIMINNAN KEHITYSYHTEISTYOKEKSUS	FIN1584
SUOMEN PAKOLAISAPU	FIN1585
SUOMEN PARTIOLAISET - FINLANDS SCOUTER §	FIN1586
SUOMEN PUNAINEN RISTI	FIN1587
SUOMEN RAUHANLIITTO - YK - YHDISTYS	FIN1588
SUOMEN UNICEF-YHDISTYS	FIN1589
SUOMEN UNIFEM §	FIN1590
SUOMEN WORLD VISION	FIN1591
SUOMEN YK-LIITTO RY	FIN1592
SUOMI-NICARAGUA-SEURA §	FIN1593
SUR	ESP1524
SURVIE	FRA2142
SURVIVAL INTERNATIONAL	GBR2493
SURVIVAL INTERNATIONAL FRANCE	FRA2143
SUSILA DHARMA SVERIGE §	SWE3793
SUSSEX ALLIANCE FOR NUCLEAR DISARMAMENT §	GBR2494
SUSTAINABLE AGRICULTURE FOOD AND ENVIRONMENT ALLIANCE	GBR2495
SVALORNA - INDIEN-BANGLADESHSEKTIONEN §	SWE3794
SVALORNA I GOTEBORG	SWE3795
SVALORNA I SVERIGE - LATINAMERIKASEKTIONEN	SWE3796
SVENSK UNGDOM - SVENSKA FOLKPARTIETS UNGDOMSORGANISATION	FIN1594
SVENSK UTVECKLINGSHJALP I HONDURAS §	SWE3797
SVENSK VOLONTARSAMVERKAN	SWE3798
SVENSK-ETIOPISKA LANDSBYGDSUTVECKLINGSFORENINGEN	SWE3799
SVENSK-FILIPPINSKA FORENINGEN §	SWE3800
SVENSK-GAMBIANSKA FORENINGEN §	SWE3801

SVENSK-INDIANSKA FORBUNDET §	SWE3802
SVENSK-KUBANSKA FORENINGEN §	SWE3803
SVENSK-LATINAMERIKANSKA KVINNOGRUPPEN §	SWE3804
SVENSK-SEYCHELLISKA FORENINGEN §	SWE3805
SVENSK-SUDANSKA FORENINGEN	SWE3806
SVENSK-TANZANISKA FORENINGEN	SWE3807
SVENSK-THAILANDSKA FORENINGEN §	SWE3808
SVENSK-TIBETANSKA SKOL-OCH KULTURFORENINGEN	SWE3809
SVENSK-TUNISISKA FORENINGEN §	SWE3810
SVENSK-ZAMBISKA FORENINGEN	SWE3811
SVENSKA AFGHANISTANKOMMITTEN §	SWE3812
SVENSKA ALLIANSMISSIONEN	SWE3813
SVENSKA AMBOSELIFORENINGEN	SWE3814
SVENSKA FLYKTINGRADET	SWE3815
SVENSKA FN-FORBUNDET	SWE3816
SVENSKA FORBUNDET FOR INTERNATIONELLA BARNBYAR §	SWE3817
SVENSKA FORENINGEN FOR INDISK BYFOLKHOGSKOLA	SWE3818
SVENSKA FREDS- OCH SKILJEDOMSFORENINGEN	SWE3819
SVENSKA FREDSKOMMITTEN §	SWE3820
SVENSKA HANDIKAPPORGANISATIONERNAS INTERNATIONELLA BISTANDSSTIFTELSE	SWE3821
SVENSKA JERUSALEMSFORENINGEN	SWE3822
SVENSKA KOREAFORENINGEN	SWE3823
SVENSKA KRISTNA UNGDOMSRAD §	SWE3824
SVENSKA KVINNORS VANSTERFORBUND §	SWE3825
SVENSKA KYRKANS MISSION	SWE3826
SVENSKA MISSIONSFORBUNDET	SWE3827
SVENSKA MISSIONSRADET	SWE3828
SVENSKA MOUNT ELGONFORENINGEN §	SWE3829
SVENSKA RODA KORSET	SWE3830
SVENSKA ROTARIANERS FOND FOR INTERNATIONELLT UTVECKLINGSARBETE, U-FONDEN	SWE3831
SVENSKA SCOUTRADET	SWE3832
SVENSKA SEKTIONEN AV AMNESTY INTERNATIONAL §	SWE3833
SVENSKA TIBETKOMMITTEN	SWE3834
SVENSKA TOGOFORENINGEN §	SWE3835
SVENSKA UNICEF-KOMMITTEN §	SWE3836
SVERIGES BLABANDSUNGDOM §	SWE3837
SVERIGES FORENADE STUDENTKARER §	SWE3838
SVERIGES RIKSIDROTTSFORBUND	SWE3839
SWEDISH ASSOCIATION FOR DEVELOPMENT OF LOW-COST HOUSING §	SWE3840
SWEDISH CHURCH RELIEF §	SWE3841
SWEDISH COMMITTEE FOR THE HUMAN RIGHTS OF KURDISH PEOPLE §	SWE3842
SWEDISH COMMITTEE FOR UNICEF §	SWE3843
SWEDISH IRAN COMMITEE §	SWE3844
SWEDISH MEDICAL STUDENTS' INTERNATIONAL COMMITTEE §	SWE3845
SWEDISH NORTH-SOUTH COALITION §	SWE3846
SWEDISH NURSING MOTHERS ASSOCIATION §	SWE3847
SWEDISH PEACE & ARBITRATION SOCIETY §	SWE3848
SWISS SOCIETY FOR THE PROTECTION OF THE ENVIRONMENT §	CHE0792
SWISSCONTACT SCHWEIZERISCHE STIFTUNG FUR TECHNISCHE ENTWICKLUNGSZUSAMMENARBEIT	CHE0793
SYDAFRIKA KONTAKT	DNK1375
SYDASIENKOMMITTEERNA I SVERIGE §	SWE3849
SYNDICAT INTERPROFESSIONNEL DE TRAVAILLEUSES ET TRAVAILLEURS	CHE0794
SYNOPSIS	FRA2144
SYNSKADADES RIKSFORBUND	SWE3850
SZKOLNE KOLO EKOLOGICZNE, 53 LO SW AUGUSTYNA §	POL3538
TAKSVARKKITOIMIKUNTA-85 §	FIN1595
TALLTREE §	NLD3316
TAM-TAM DE NKOL EKONG	FRA2145
TAMIL DEVELOPMENT NETWORK OF NORWAY	NOR3471
TAMIL INFORMATION CENTRE §	GBR2496
TAMILSK DANSK VENSKABSFORENING	DNK1376
TAMPEREEN KEHITYSMAAKAUPPAVHDISTYS	FIN1596
TAN-DAN FORENING	DNK1377
TANZANIA DEVELOPMENT TRUST	GBR2497
TAPOL INDONESIA HUMAN RIGHTS CAMPAIGN	GBR2498
TCHAD, PAYS DE LA SERRE, SOLIDAIRES §	FRA2146
TEACHING AIDS AT LOW COST	GBR2499
TEAR FUND	GBR2500
TEAR FUND, BELGIUM	BEL0368
TEAR FUND, NEDERLAND	NLD3317
TEATER UNO §	SWE3851
TECHNAP	FRA2147
TECHNOLOGIE OVERDRACHT ONTWIKKELINGSLANDEN	NLD3318
TECHNOLOGIE TRANSFER MARBURG IN DIE DRITTE WELT	DEU1185
TECHNOLOGY FOR THE PEOPLE	CHE0795
TELDERS STICHTING §	NLD3319
TELEVISION TRUST FOR THE ENVIRONMENT	GBR2501
TEMAGROEP ONDERONTWIKKELING	NLD3320
TERRA NUOVA - CENTRO PER IL VOLONTARIATO	ITA2913
TERRE D'AMITIE	FRA2148
TERRE DE DEMAIN §	BEL0369
TERRE DE VIE	FRA2149
TERRE DES FEMMES, HUMAN RIGHTS FOR WOMEN	DEU1186
TERRE DES HOMMES	CHE0796
TERRE DES HOMMES §	LIE2931
TERRE DES HOMMES KINDERHILFE §	CHE0797
TERRE DES HOMMES, BELGIQUE §	BEL0370
TERRE DES HOMMES, BUNDESREPUBLIK DEUTSCHLAND	DEU1187
TERRE DES HOMMES, DENMARK §	DNK1378
TERRE DES HOMMES, FRANCE	FRA2150
TERRE DES HOMMES, OSTERREICH - HILFE FUR KINDER IN NOT §	AUT0080
TERRE DES HOMMES, SUISSE - GENEVE	CHE0798
TERRE TIERS-MONDE ET INFORMATION	BEL0371
TERRES ET VIE §	BEL0372
TERRES NOUVELLES §	BEL0373
TERVEYSKASVATUKSEN KESKUS RY §	FIN1597
TESO DEVELOPMENT TRUST	GBR2502
THIRD SHORE §	HUN2662
THIRD WORLD ACADEMY OF SCIENCES	ITA2914
THIRD WORLD FIRST	GBR2503
THIRD WORLD MEDIA §	GBR2504
THIRD WORLD NETWORK - EUROPE §	GBR2505
THIRD WORLD TRADE ASSOCIATION OF TURKU §	FIN1598
TIBET INSTITUTE	CHE0799

Voir : *Comment utiliser le répertoire,* page 11.

TIBET SOCIETY AND TIBET RELIEF FUND OF THE UNITED KINGDOM	GBR2506
TIBET UNTERSTTZUNG LIECHTENST. §	LIE2932
TIBETAN COMMUNITY IN SWEDEN §	SWE3852
TIERRA NUEVA §	DEU1188
TIGRAY DEVELOPMENT ASSOCIATION	SWE3853
TILAPIA FOOD AID ORGANIZATION §	BEL0374
TIVERTON KABALE LINK §	GBR2507
TIVERTON SUNDARBAN LINK	GBR2508
TOC H	GBR2509
TOLSTOY FOUNDATION §	DEU1189
TOOLS FOR SELF RELIANCE	GBR2510
TOURISM CONCERN	GBR2511
TOWER HAMLETS INTERNATIONAL SOLIDARITY §	GBR2512
TOWNS AND DEVELOPMENT §	NLD3321
TOXICOMANIES-COOPERATION	FRA2151
TRADE UNION COOPERATION FORUM §	HUN2663
TRADE UNION INTERNATIONAL RESEARCH AND EDUCATION GROUP	GBR2513
TRADE UNION YOUTH FEDERATION §	HUN2664
TRADITIONS POUR DEMAIN	CHE0800
TRADITIONS POUR DEMAIN	FRA2152
TRAIDCRAFT EXCHANGE	GBR2514
TRANS-AFRICA ASSOCIATION §	FRA2153
TRANSDANUBIAN LIFE AND ENVIRONMENTAL PROTECTIONISTS §	HUN2665
TRANSFAIR INTERNATIONAL	DEU1190
TRANSFAIR-MINKA	LUX3008
TRANSFERTS D'URGENCE DE L'INDUSTRIE PHARMACEUTIQUE	FRA2154
TRANSNATIONAL INSTITUTE §	NLD3322
TRANSSAHARA - CARAVANES SANS FRONTIERES §	FRA2155
TRAX PROGRAMME SUPPORT	GBR2515
DEN ; 3.=TRE VERDENS AFTENHOJSKOLE §	DNK1379
TREDJE VERDEN INFORMATION §	DNK1380
TREDJE VERDENS STEMME §	DNK1381
TREE OF LIFE CLUBS ASSOCIATION §	SVK3641
TREE TRUST §	GBR2516
TROCAIRE	IRL2726
EIN TROPFCHEN MILCH	DEU1191
TROPICAL HEALTH AND EDUCATION TRUST	GBR2517
TROSGNISTANS MISSION	SWE3854
TRYGG-HANSA PERSONALENS U-HJALPSFORENING	SWE3855
TURKIYE AILE PLANLAMASI DERNEGI §	TUR3891
TURKIYE AILE SAGLIGI VE PLANLAMASI VAKFI	TUR3892
TURKIYE CEVRE KORUMA VE YESILLENDIRME DERNEGI §	TUR3893
TURKIYE CEVRE VAKFI	TUR3894
TURKIYE INSAN HAKLARI VAKFI	TUR3895
TURKIYE KALKINMA VAKFI	TUR3896
TURKIYE KIZILAY DERNEGI	TUR3897
TURKIYE TABIATINI KORUMA DERNEGI	TUR3898
TWIN - DEVELOPMENT THROUGH TRADE	GBR2518
TYRESO ULANDS-OCH FREDS FORENING §	SWE3856
TZEDEK §	GBR2519
U-ASSIST	SWE3857
U-ASSIST-SAS-NORGE §	NOR3472
U-LANDSDEBAT 1980 §	DNK1382
U-LANDSFONDEN AF 1962 §	DNK1383

U-LANDSFORENINGEN SVALENE	NOR3473
U-LANDSFORENINGEN SVALERNE	DNK1384
U-LANDSFORENINGEN SVALORNA	FIN1599
U-LANDSGRUPPEN FOR FREDERIKSBORG AMT §	DNK1385
U-LANDSGRUPPEN PA KUL §	DNK1386
U-LANDSGRUPPEN PA LANDBOHOJSKOLEN §	DNK1387
U-LANDSGRUPPERS SAMARBETSFORENING §	SWE3858
U-LANDSHJALP FRAN FOLK TILL FOLK I SVERIGE	SWE3859
U-LANDSHJELP FRA FOLK TIL FOLK	DNK1388
U-LANDSIMPORTEN	DNK1389
U-LANDSTV §	DNK1390
UBERSEE-DOKUMENTATION IM DEUTSCHEN UBERSEE-INSTITUT	DEU1192
UFFICIO CENTRALE STUDENTI ESTERI IN ITALIA	ITA2915
UGANDA DEVELOPMENT SERVICES	GBR2520
UGANDA SOCIETY FOR DISABLED CHILDREN	GBR2521
UK COMMITTEE FOR THE UNITED NATIONS CHILDREN'S FUND	GBR2522
UK JEWISH AID	GBR2523
UN AND UNESCO CENTRE §	BEL0375
UNDUGU VRIENDENKRING NEDERLAND - KENYA	NLD3323
UNESCO CENTRUM NEDERLAND §	NLD3324
UNG VANSTER §	SWE3860
UNGA ORNARS RIKSFORBUND §	SWE3861
UNGDOM MED UPPGIFT §	SWE3862
UNGDOMENS OCH STUDENTERNAS FN-FORBUND I SVERIGE - UTRIKESPOLITISKA FORENINGARNAS FN-FORBUND §	SWE3863
UNGDOMMENS RODE KORS	DNK1391
UNIAO DAS CIDADES CAPITAIS DE LINGUA PORTUGUESA	PRT3603
UNIAO DAS MISERICORDIAS PORTUGUESAS §	PRT3604
UNICEF IN ICELAND §	ISL2742
UNICEF KOMITEEN I NORGE §	NOR3474
UNICEF TURKIYE MILLI KOMITESI §	TUR3899
UNIE VOOR CHRISTELIJK ONDERWIJS	NLD3325
UNIFEM-DANMARK, DEN DANSKE FORENING FOR FN'S UDVIKLINGSFOND FOR KVINDER	DNK1392
UNION CATHOLIQUE INTERNATIONALE DE SERVICE SOCIAL §	BEL0376
UNION DE CIUDADES CAPITALES IBEROAMERICANAS	ESP1525
UNION DE ESCUELAS FAMILIARES AGRARIAS §	ESP1526
UNION EUROPEENNE FEMININE §	FRA2156
UNION FOR ENVIRONMENT IN REGION OF ILOVES §	HUN2666
UNION FOR THE GOOD NEIGHBOURLY RELATIONS WITH THE GERMAN-SPEAKING COUNTRIES §	CZE0908
UNION INTERNATIONALE DE PROMOTION DE LA SANTE §	FRA2157
UNION INTERNATIONALE DES ASSOCIATIONS ET ORGANISMES TECHNIQUES	FRA2158
UNION INTERNATIONALE DES ORGANISMES FAMILIAUX	FRA2159
UNION INTERNATIONALE HUMANISTE ET LAIQUE §	LUX3009
UNION INTERNATIONALE POUR L'ETUDE SCIENTIFIQUE DE LA POPULATION §	BEL0377
UNION MONDIALE DES ENSEIGNANTS CATHOLIQUES §	FRA2160
UNION NATIONALE DES CENTRES PERMANENTS D'INITIATION A L'ENVIRONNEMENT	FRA2161
UNION OF ARAY YOUTH §	CZE0909
UNION OF CALVINIST YOUTH §	HUN2667
THE UNION OF HEALTH AND SOCIAL CARE SERVICES §	FIN1600
UNION OF HUNGARIAN PIONEERS §	HUN2668

UNION OF PROTECTION OF INTEREST OF HUNGARIAN YOUTH §	SVK3642
UNION OF UGANDANS §	DNK1393
UNION OF YOUNG SLOVAK CULTURE §	SVK3643
UNION OF YOUTH CLUBS §	CZE0910
UNION SOLIDARIA §	ESP1527
UNIONE MEDICO MISSIONARIA ITALIANA	ITA2916
UNIONE VOLONTARIATO INTERNAZIONALE PER LO SVILUPPO E LA PACE §	ITA2917
UNITED FOR INTERCULTURAL ACTION	NLD3326
UNITED KINGDOM FOUNDATION FOR THE PEOPLES OF THE SOUTH PACIFIC	GBR2524
UNITED NATIONS ASSOCIATION INTERNATIONAL SERVICE	GBR2525
UNITED NATIONS ASSOCIATION OF AUSTRIA §	AUT0081
UNITED NATIONS ASSOCIATION OF GREAT BRITAIN AND NORTHERN IRELAND	GBR2526
UNITED NATIONS ASSOCIATION OF ICELAND §	ISL2743
UNITED NATIONS ENVIRONMENT AND DEVELOPMENT UK COMMITTEE	GBR2527
UNITED NATIONS VOLUNTEERS §	NLD3327
UNITED NATIONS YOUTH AND STUDENT ASSOCIATION OF FINLAND §	FIN1601
UNITED WAY OF HUNGARY §	HUN2669
UNITED WORLD COLLEGES INTERNATIONAL §	GBR2528
UNITY FOUNDATION §	LUX3010
UNIVERSITA DELLA PACE GIORGIO LA PIRA §	ITA2918
UNIVERSITAIRE STICHTING VOOR ONTWIKKELINGSSAMENWERKING	BEL0378
UNIVERSITARIS PEL TERCER MON	ESP1528
UNIVERSITE DE PAIX	BEL0379
UNIVERSITE SANS FRONTIERE	FRA2162
UNIVERSITY ASSISTANCE FUND §	NLD3328
UNIVERSITY WOMEN OF EUROPE	NLD3329
UNIZEM - JUVENA §	CZE0911
UNREPRESENTED NATIONS AND PEOPLES ORGANIZATION	NLD3330
UNTERSTUZUNGSKOMITEE FUR POLITISCH VERFOLGTE AUSLANDERINNEN §	AUT0082
URBANAID	GBR2529
URUGUAY KOMITEE §	CHE0801
UTAMADUNI CENTRE FOR CULTURAL EXCHANGE §	DNK1394
UTAN GRANSER	SWE3864
UTBILDNING FOR BISTANDSVERKSAMHET	SWE3865
UTRECHTS PLATTELAND EN DERDE WERELD §	NLD3331
UTVIKLINGSFONDET - FREMTIDEN I VARE HENDER	NOR3475
VADDO BISTANDSFORENING §	SWE3866
VAESTOLIITTO	FIN1602
VAMMAISJARJESTOJEN KEHITYSYHTEISTTOYHDISTTS	FIN1603
VAN VOLLENHOVEN INSTITUUT VOOR RECHT EN BESTUUR IN NIET-WESTERSE LANDEN §	NLD3332
VANORTSFORENINGEN EKSJO-BANGLADESH §	SWE3867
VANORTSFORENINGEN JONKOPING-BANGLADESH §	SWE3868
VANORTSFORENINGEN STRANGNAS-KIBAYA-LOIBORSOIT §	SWE3869
VANSKAPSFORENINGEN BURKINA FASO-SVERIGE, ASSAMBUS §	SWE3870
VANSKAPSFORENINGEN SVERIGE-FRIA BURMA §	SWE3871
VANSKAPSFORENINGEN SVERIGE-URUGUAY §	SWE3872
VANSKAPSFORENINGEN SVERIGE-ZIMBABWE §	SWE3873
VANSKAPSKLUBBEN KANIMAMBO §	SWE3874
VANSKOLEFORENINGEN DJURO-LOS RINCONES §	SWE3875
VARLDSNATURFONDEN	SWE3876
VATTEN AT ALLA	SWE3877
VELLETRI PER IL MALI §	ITA2919
VENCEREMOS - SOLIDARITEIT MET CUBA §	NLD3333
VENSKABSFORBUNDET DANMARK-KINA §	DNK1395
VENSKABSFORENINGEN DANMARK-BHUTAN §	DNK1396
VENSKABSFORENINGEN DANMARK-BURKINA FASO	DNK1397
VENSKABSFORENINGEN DANMARK-DEN DEMOKRATISKE FOLKEREPUBLIK KOREA	DNK1398
VENSKABSFORENINGEN DANMARK-NIGER	DNK1399
VENSKABSFORENINGEN DANMARK-ZAMBIA §	DNK1400
VERBAND BI NATIONALER FAMILIEN UND PARTNERSCHAFTEN	DEU1193
VERBAND UNABHANGIG BERATENDER INGENIEURFIRMEN E.V. §	DEU1194
VERDENSVERKSTEDET §	DNK1401
VEREIN DER FREUNDE UND FORDERER DER OSTERREICHISCHEN ENTWICKLUNGSHELFER §	AUT0083
VEREIN DER SANDOZ-MITARBEITER FUR BASISHILFE IN DER DRITTEN WELT §	CHE0802
VEREIN FUR AFGHANISTAN-FORDERUNG §	DEU1195
VEREIN FUR STADTEPARTNERSCHAFT FREIBURG-WIWILI §	DEU1196
VEREIN GEMEINSAM FUR GERECHTIGKEIT §	AUT0084
VEREIN HILFSWERK EZIOHA-MMAKU NIGERIA §	LIE2933
VEREIN MENSCHEN FUR MENSCHEN	AUT0085
VEREIN SCHWEIZER KINDERHILFE §	CHE0803
VEREIN STADTEPARTNERSCHAFT BERN-ACHUAPA	CHE0804
VEREIN STADTEPARTNERSCHAFT PEDRA BADEJO-LEIBNITZ	AUT0086
VEREIN WELT UND HEIMAT §	LIE2934
VEREIN ZUR UNTERSTUTZUNG DER HUNGERNDEN, VERLASSEN UND KRANKEN KINDER INDIENS §	DEU1197
VEREIN ZUSAMMENARBEIT DRITTE WELT §	AUT0087
VEREINIGTE SUDAN MISSION	CHE0805
VEREINIGUNG DON BOSCO WERK	CHE0806
VEREINIGUNG EHEMALIGER ENTWICKLUNGSHELFERINNEN UND ENTWICKLUNGSHELFER	DEU1198
VEREINIGUNG FUR ENTWICKLUNG, GERECHTIGKEIT, SOLIDARITAT	CHE0807
VEREINIGUNG FUR INTERNATIONALE ZUSAMMENARBEIT §	DEU1199
VEREINIGUNG SCHWEIZ - ERITREA §	CHE0808
VERENIGING 31	NLD3334
VERENIGING DE VERRE NAASTEN §	NLD3335
VERENIGING HUMANA	NLD3336
VERENIGING MILIEUDEFENSIE	NLD3337
VERENIGING VAN NEDERLANDSE GEMEENTEN - DIREKTIE SEKRETARIAAT INTERNATIONALE SAMENWERKING	NLD3338
VERENIGING VLUCHTELINGENWERK NEDERLAND	NLD3339
VERENIGING VOOR DE VERENIGDE NATIES §	BEL0380
VERENIGING VOOR EEN NIEUW INTERNATIONAAL ONTWIKKELINGSBELEID §	NLD3340
VERENIGING VOOR PERSONELE SAMENWERKING MET ONTWIKKELINGSLANDEN	NLD3341
VERENIGING VOOR TECHNISCHE SAMENWERKING	BEL0381
VERENING WERELDKINDEREN	NLD3342
VERONICA - THE ECOLOGICAL CENTRE §	CZE0912
VETAID	GBR2530
VETERINAIRES SANS FRONTIERES	FRA2163

VETERINARIOS SIN FRONTERAS	ESP1529
VI PLANTERAR TRAD §	SWE3878
VIATORES CHRISTI §	IRL2727
VIDEOCENTRUM FOR U-LANDSFRAGOR	SWE3879
VIE ET LIBERTE	FRA2164
VIE FEMININE - MOUVEMENT CHRETIEN D'ACTION CULTURELLE ET SOCIALE §	BEL0382
LA VIE NOUVELLE	FRA2165
VIENNA MALAYALEE ASSOCIATION §	AUT0088
VIETNAMESE REFUGEES COMMUNITY IN LONDON §	GBR2531
VIKINGASKOLANS BISTANDSPROJEKT I HUAYRA KHASA, BOLIVIA §	SWE3880
VILLAGE SERVICE TRUST	GBR2532
VINCENTIUS VERENIGING NEDERLAND §	NLD3343
VISION AID OVERSEAS	GBR2533
VISION INTERNATIONAL HEALTHCARE §	GBR2534
VIVRE ENSEMBLE AVEC NOS DIFFERENCES §	FRA2166
VLAAMS CENTRUM INTEGRATIE MIGRANTEN §	BEL0383
VLAAMS INTERNATIONAAL CENTRUM §	BEL0384
VLAAMS OVERLEGCOMITE MIGRANTEN §	BEL0385
VLAAMSE VERENIGING VOOR OPLEIDINGSPROGRAMMA'S IN HET BUITENLAND §	BEL0386
VLAAMSE WERKGROEP INDIANEN ZUID-AMERIKA	BEL0387
VOKSENOPPLERINGSFORBUNDET	NOR3476
VOLKSHILFE OSTERREICH	AUT0089
VOLONTAIRES POUR L'ENSEIGNEMENT-VOLONTARIAT ET COOPERATION INTERNATIONALE	BEL0388
VOLONTARI INTERNAZIONALI DELLA SCUOLA BEATO ANGELICO	ITA2920
VOLONTARI ITALIANI PER LA SOLIDARIETA' AI PAESI EMERGENTI	ITA2921
VOLONTARIATO INTERNAZIONALE DONNA EDUCAZIONE E SVILUPPO	ITA2922
VOLONTARIATO INTERNAZIONALE PER LO SVILUPPO	ITA2923
VOLUNTARIADO INTERNACIONAL PARA O DESENVOLVIMENTO AFRICANO	PRT3605
VOLUNTARY SERVICE INTERNATIONAL	IRL2728
VOLUNTARY SERVICE OVERSEAS	GBR2535
VOLUNTEER MISSIONARY MOVEMENT, IRELAND	IRL2729
VOLUNTEER MISSIONARY MOVEMENT, UNITED KINGDOM	GBR2536
VOLVOANSTALLDAS U-HJALPSFORENING §	SWE3881
VRAAG EN AANBOD INTERNATIONAAL §	NLD3344
VREDE - STUDY AND INFORMATION CENTRE FOR PEACE AND DEVELOPMENT PROBLEMS §	BEL0389
VREDESEILANDEN	BEL0390
VRIENDEN VAN JOHAN WACHTERS	NLD3345
VRIENDSCHAPSVERENIGING NEDERLAND-CHINA	NLD3346
VROUWENBERAAD ONTWIKKELINGSSAMENWERKING	NLD3347
WAR ON WANT	GBR2537
WATERAID	GBR2538
WATERFORD-KITUI PARTNERSHIP	IRL2730
WELSH CENTRE FOR INTERNATIONAL AFFAIRS	GBR2539
WELTFRIEDENSDIENST	DEU1200
WELTLADEN EUPEN §	BEL0391
WELTWEITE PARTNERSCHAFT §	DEU1201
WERELDSOLIDARITEIT - SOLIDARITE MONDIALE	BEL0392
WERELDWIJD	BEL0393
WERELDWINKELS	NLD3348
WERKGROEP ARBEIDSVERHOUDINGEN EN WERKGELEGENHEID IN HET CARAIBISCH GEBIED §	NLD3349

WERKGROEP BASISPROJEKTEN HAITI	BEL0394
WERKGROEP FYSIOTHERAPIE EN DERDE WERELD	NLD3350
WERKGROEP INCA PIRCA NEDERLAND §	NLD3351
WERKGROEP MEDISCHE ONTWIKKELINGSSAMENWERKING	NLD3352
WERKGROEP ONTWIKKELINGSTECHNIEKEN	NLD3353
WERKGROEP PAPUA NEW GUINEA	NLD3354
WERKGROEP TECHNOLOGIE - DIALOOG	BEL0395
WERKGROEP ZAMBIA	NLD3355
WERKHOF DARMSTADT	DEU1202
WERKSTATT OKONOMIE	DEU1203
WIENER INSTITUT FUR ENTWICKLUNGSFRAGEN UND ZUSAMMENARBEIT	AUT0090
WILBERFORCE COUNCIL §	GBR2540
WILDE GANZEN	NLD3356
WITHUIS-VOLONTARIAAT	BEL0396
WOMANKIND WORLDWIDE	GBR2541
WOMEN AID / UNIFEM §	GBR2542
WOMEN FOR PEACE NORWAY §	NOR3477
WOMEN WORKING WORLDWIDE §	GBR2543
THE WOMEN'S ENVIRONMENTAL NETWORK	GBR2544
WOMEN'S GLOBAL NETWORK FOR REPRODUCTIVE RIGHTS	NLD3357
WOMEN'S INTERNATIONAL LEAGUE FOR PEACE AND FREEDOM	CHE0809
WOMEN'S WORLD SUMMIT FOUNDATION	CHE0810
WORDS AND PICTURES	GBR2545
WORKSHOP FOR ALL BEINGS §	POL3539
WORLD ALLIANCE OF YOUNG MEN'S CHRISTIAN ASSOCIATIONS §	CHE0811
WORLD ASSEMBLY OF YOUTH	DNK1402
WORLD ASSOCIATION FOR CHRISTIAN COMMUNICATION	GBR2546
WORLD ASSOCIATION OF GIRL GUIDES AND GIRL SCOUTS §	GBR2547
WORLD CONFERENCE ON RELIGION AND PEACE INTERNATIONAL §	CHE0812
THE WORLD CONSERVATION UNION	CHE0813
WORLD COUNCIL OF CHURCHES	CHE0814
WORLD COUNCIL OF CHURCHES §	TUR3900
WORLD DEVELOPMENT MOVEMENT	GBR2548
WORLD EDUCATION BERKSHIRE §	GBR2549
WORLD EDUCATION PROJECT §	IRL2731
WORLD FEDERATION OF DEMOCRATIC YOUTH §	HUN2670
WORLD FEDERATION OF DEVELOPMENT FINANCING INSTITUTIONS §	ESP1530
WORLD FEDERATION OF THE DEAF	FIN1604
WORLD FEDERATION OF UNITED NATIONS ASSOCIATIONS §	CHE0815
WORLD FUTURES STUDIES FEDERATION	FIN1605
WORLD INDUSTRY COUNCIL FOR THE ENVIRONMENT	FRA2167
WORLD INFORMATION SERVICE ON ENERGY §	NLD3358
WORLD JEWISH CONGRESS §	CHE0816
WORLD MERCY FUND	IRL2732
WORLD ORGANIZATION OF THE SCOUT MOVEMENT	CHE0817
WORLD ORT UNION	GBR2550
WORLD POPULATION FOUNDATION §	NLD3359
WORLD RUNNERS NEDERLAND §	NLD3360
WORLD UNION OF CATHOLIC WOMEN'S ORGANIZATIONS	FRA2168
WORLD UNIVERSITY SERVICE, DEUTSCHES KOMITEE §	DEU1204

See: *How to Use the Directory,* page 11.

WORLD UNIVERSITY SERVICE, SWITZERLAND §	CHE0818
WORLD UNIVERSITY SERVICE, UNITED KINGDOM	GBR2551
WORLD VISION INTERNATIONAL	CHE0819
WORLD VISION INTERNATIONAL §	DEU1205
WORLD VISION NEDERLAND	NLD3361
WORLD VISION OF IRELAND	IRL2733
WORLD VISION OSTERREICH - CHRISTLICHES HILFSWERK	AUT0091
WORLD VISION UK	GBR2552
WORLD WIDE FUND FOR NATURE INTERNATIONAL	CHE0820
WORLD WIDE FUND FOR NATURE, AUSTRIA §	AUT0092
WORLD WIDE FUND FOR NATURE, BELGIUM	BEL0397
WORLD WIDE FUND FOR NATURE, DENMARK	DNK1403
WORLD WIDE FUND FOR NATURE, EUROPEAN POLICY OFFICE	BEL0398
WORLD WIDE FUND FOR NATURE, UNITED KINGDOM	GBR2553
WORLD WILDLIFE FUND SUISSE §	CHE0821
WORLD YOUNG WOMEN'S CHRISTIAN ASSOCIATION §	CHE0822
WORLDAWARE	GBR2554
WORLDVIEW INTERNATIONAL FOUNDATION §	NOR3478
WORT & TAT, ALLGEMEINE MISSIONSGESELLSCHAFT §	DEU1206
WRITERS IN PRISON COMMITTEE OF INTERNATIONAL PEN	GBR2555
WWF FOUNDATION FOR THE HUNGARIAN ENVIRONMENTAL EDUCATION §	HUN2671
X MIN Y	NLD3362
XAN §	GRC2596
Y CARE INTERNATIONAL	GBR2556
YAKA §	FRA2169
YMCA NEDERLAND	NLD3363
YMPARISTO JA KEHITYS §	FIN1606
YOUNG CHRISTIAN WORKERS §	MLT3034
YOUNG EUROPEAN FEDERALISTS §	MLT3035
YOUNG EUROPEAN FEDERALISTS OF CZECH REPUBLIC §	CZE0913
YOUNG MEN'S CHRISTIAN ASSOCIATION	MLT3036
YOUNG PIONEERS §	SVK3644
YOUNG SOCIAL DEMOCRATS §	CZE0914
YOUNG WOMEN'S CHRISTIAN ASSOCIATION OF NEDERLAND	NLD3364
YOUTH AGAINST RACISM IN EUROPE §	GBR2557
YOUTH AND ENVIRONMENT EUROPE §	DNK1404
YOUTH AND ENVIRONMENT EUROPE	NLD3365
YOUTH DEMOCRATIC FORUM §	HUN2672
YOUTH ENTERPRISE SERVICES INTERNATIONAL	GBR2558
YOUTH ENVIRONMENTAL ASSOCIATION §	HUN2673
YOUTH FOR DEVELOPMENT AND COOPERATION	NLD3366

YOUTH FOR EXCHANGE AND UNDERSTANDING §	MLT3037
YOUTH FOREST ACTION §	HUN2674
YOUTH FORUM OF THE EUROPEAN COMMUNITY	BEL0399
YOUTH ORGANISATION OF THE ALLIANCE OF FREE DEMOCRATS §	HUN2675
YOUTH UNION §	HUN2676
YOUTH WITH A MISSION §	GBR2559
YOUTH WITH A MISSION - RELIEF AND DEVELOPMENT SERVICES	CHE0823
YWCA OF GREAT BRITAIN §	GBR2560
YWCA OF HUNGARY §	HUN2677
YWCA OF POLAND §	POL3540
YYE - ENVIRONMENT POLICY WG §	BEL0400
ZANZIBAR DEMOCRATIC ALTERNATIVE	DNK1405
ZEBRA - AUDIOVISUAL NETWORK FOR NORTH-SOUTH UNDERSTANDING §	BEL0401
ZEISTER ZENDINGSGENOOTSCHAP	NLD3367
ZELENA NADEJ §	SVK3645
ZELENY BOD OSTRAVA	CZE0915
ZELENY DUM LITVINOV	CZE0916
ZENTRALAMERIKA - KOMITEES DER SCHWEIZ §	CHE0824
ZENTRALE DOKUMENTATIONSSTELLE DER FREIEN WOHLFAHRTSPFLEGE FUR FLUCHTLINGE	DEU1207
ZENTRALSTELLE FUR UMWELTERZIEHUNG §	DEU1208
ZENTRALVERBAND DES DEUTSCHEN HANDWERKS	DEU1209
ZENTRUM FUR ANGEWANDTE OEKOLOGIE SCHATTWEID	CHE0825
ZENTRUM FUR ENTWICKLUNGSBEZOGENE BILDUNG	DEU1210
ZENTRUM FUR HANDELSFORUDERUNG GMBH	DEU1211
ZENTRUM ZUR SOZIALMEDIZINISCHEN, RECHTLICHEN UND KULTURELLEN BETREUUNG VON AUSLANDERINNEN IN OSTERREICH	AUT0093
ZGHAZAGH AZZJONI KATTOLIKA §	MLT3038
ZGHAZAGH HBIEB IN-NATURA §	MLT3039
ZGHAZAGH TAHT L-ART §	MLT3040
ZIELONE BRYGADY §	POL3541
ZIMBABWE HILFSAKTION §	DEU1212
ZIMBABWE TRUST	GBR2561
ZOA VLUCHTELINGENZORG §	NLD3368
ZOLD SZIV IFJUSAGI TERMESZETVEDO MOZGALAM	HUN2678
ZONTA INTERNATIONAL §	CHE0826
ZONTA INTERNATIONAL COMMITTEE	FRA2170
ZOOLOGICAL SOCIETY OF LONDON	GBR2562
ZRZESZENIS STUDENTOW POLSKICH §	POL3542
ZWIAZEK HARCERSTWA POLSKIEGO	POL3543
ZWIAZEK HARCERSTWA RZECZYPOSPOLITEJ	POL3544
ZYCIE WRSZAWY §	POL3545

Voir : *Comment utiliser le répertoire*, page 11.

LIST OF ACRONYMS OF NGOS

LISTE DES SIGLES DES ONG

3W1	GBR2503	ADDHA	FRA1750	AGIB	CHE0430	ALTERSIAL	FRA1654
6S	CHE0435	ADE	FRA1717	AGINT	ITA2745	AM87	FRA1779
A COMME AFRIQUE	FRA2098	ADECI	FRA1765	AGIR-ABCD	FRA1731	AMADES	FRA1670
A-EFJN	BEL0099	ADEPTA	FRA1764	AGKED	DEU0946	AMAVET	SVK3607
A3CI	FRA1759	ADER	CHE0459	AGPTM	FRA1635	AMAZSWED	SWE3651
A3W	AUT0004	ADESA	NLD3309	AGRYA	HUN2598	AMB	BEL0094
A3W	AUT0006	ADETEF	FRA1763	AHAS	GBR2203	AMCA	CHE0769
AAFV	FRA1695	ADKB	FRA1643	AHRTAG	GBR2196	AME	FRA1742
AAI	AUT0002	ADM	FRA1761	AI	CHE0420	AMI	FRA1647
AARC+	FRA1641	ADRA	GBR2175	AI	DNK1217	L'AMI	FRA1673
ABC	BEL0113	ADRA DENMARK	DNK1214	AI	GBR2193	AMI-FUNDAÇAO	PRT3549
ABED	FRA1689	ADRA GERMANY	DEU0918	AIBI	ITA2755	AMIS	FRA1684
ABLA	PRT3552	ADRA-CE	BEL0097	AICF	FRA1614	AMPSRF	FRA1693
ABP	DEU0957	ADRAI	BEL0132	AICOS	ITA2773	AMREF	NLD3043
ABP	DEU1173	ADVO	GBR2188	AICS	FRA1652	AMREF DEUTSCHLAND	DEU0936
ABSDF	NOR3372	ADW	DEU0925	AID	FRA1776	AMREF FRANCE	FRA1753
ABVV/FGTB	BEL0108	AEDENAT	ESP1419	AIDA	DNK1223	AMREF UK	GBR2183
AC	SWE3646	AEF	CHE0504	AIDAC	BEL0128	AMS	FRA1646
ACAFOM	FRA1692	AEGEE	CZE0874	AIDE	FRA1615	AMS	IRL2682
ACAT	CHE0415	AEJ	DEU0942	AIDE	FRA1630	AMU	ITA2756
ACAT	DEU0924	AEM	AUT0012	AIDOS	ITA2767	AMULP	FRA1710
ACAT FRANCE	FRA1611	AEM	FRA1658	AIE	CHE0403	ANDA	FRA1745
ACAT LUXEMBOURG	LUX2935	AER	FRA1639	AIESEC	BEL0123	ANIDEVELOP	FRA1669
ACAV	ITA2757	AES-CCC	ITA2749	AIETI	ESP1417	ANJCA	FRA1746
ACC	FRA1680	AESDC	FRA1691	AIF	DNK1219	ANPED	NLD3048
ACCIR	FRA1690	AET	GBR2178	AIFO	ITA2766	ANS	CHE0446
ACCRI	ITA2761	AEVN	FRA1638	AILA	NLD3041	ANS	FRA1617
ACDA	BEL0106	AFASPA	FRA1720	AIM	FRA1645	AOF	DNK1220
ACDST	BEL0100	AFCOPA	FRA1722	AIM	FRA1676	AOI	FRA1648
ACEP	PRT3554	AFDI	FRA1634	AIM	GBR2179	APAD	FRA1716
ACM	PRT3551	AFECTI	FRA1725	AIMFR	FRA1734	APARF	PRT3557
ACMA	FRA1747	AFI	CHE0451	AIN	NOR3371	APAS	FRA1700
ACNI	FRA1621	AFI	FRA1711	AIPH	FRA1625	APC/ComLink	DEU0955
ACODESS	FRA1749	AFIP	FRA1698	AISI-SID	ITA2769	APCS	PRT3558
ACORD	GBR2187	AFMR	FRA1751	AISPO	ITA2768	APD	BEL0105
ACPAHU	FRA1612	AFP	CHE0416	AITD-TIERS MONDE	FRA1732	APDH	ESP1426
ACPM	FRA1708	AFRANE	FRA1666	AITEC	FRA1733	APED	DEU0947
ACRA	ITA2762	AFRASSCA	DEU1084	AIWC	CHE0417	APIA	FRA1707
ACROTERRE	FRA1709	AFRI	IRL2679	AJACS	FRA1737	APM	FRA1659
ACSUR - LAS SEGOVIAS	ESP1422	AFS	FRA1723	AJTM	FRA1736	APMP	FRA1755
ACT	BEL0381	AFSI	FRA1724	AKE	DEU0950	APPOBI	CHE0424
ACTEC	BEL0126	AFSIU	SWE3649	AKF-UK	GBR2186	APRACOM	CHE0476
ACTION MEDEOR	DEU1023	AFT	FRA1668	AKJÖ	AUT0010	APREFA	FRA1756
ACTM	BEL0122	AFVP	FRA1727	AKM	DNK1218	APRI	PRT3559
ACUCONS-UTANSCO	CHE0408	AGDF	DEU0929	AKME	DEU0951	APRODEV	BEL0131
ACWW	GBR2202	AGE	DEU0943	AKT	FIN1533	APS	ITA2775
AD	FRA1672	AGEH	DEU0944	AKT+E	CHE0433	APTT	GBR2197
ADA	LUX2946	AGEMA	FRA1752	ALAD	FRA1739	APVC	BEL0133
ADAIS	FRA1760	AGEP TIERS MONDE	FRA1627	ALASEI-Bonn	DEU0920	AQUADEV	BEL0118
ADC AUSTRIA	AUT0063	AGESCI	ITA2765	ALDA	FRA1699	ARA	DEU0948
ADD	GBR2173	AGEZ	AUT0008	ALDIS	FRA1616	ARAT	FRA1702
		AGGL	LUX2948	ALM	ITA2771		

ARBOR	MLT3031	ATD	FRA2060	BRC	GBR2223	CED	FRA1893
ARCI	FRA1701	ATEE	BEL0127	BRCS	GBR2222	CEDAF	BEL0149
ARCI-CS	ITA2752	ATI	FRA1685	BSSP	POL3482	CEDAL	FRA1802
ARDA	FRA1735	ATIME	ESP1418	BTS UK	GBR2214	CEDEMI	ESP1443
ARHAG	GBR2184	ATM	BEL0103	BUKO	DEU0977	CEDETIM	FRA1806
ARIS	CHE0423	ATM	CHE0436	BUND	DEU0976	CEDI	FRA1851
ARM	CHE0419	ATM	FRA1713	BURUNDIKOMITEEN	DNK1332	CEDIDELP	FRA1810
ART	GBR2181	ATM	FRA1772	BW	CHE0484	CEDOR	ITA2793
ARW	CHE0426	ATOL	BEL0367	BZFO	DEU0962	CEDRE	FRA1803
ASA-FRANCE	FRA1687	ATRIA	FRA1768	C&D	ITA2833	CEDRI	CHE0520
ASAA	CHE0467	AUCI	ITA2781	CAA	GBR2252	CEDU	ITA2750
ASACH	CHE0411	AUI	FRA1610	CACTM	BEL0169	CEFA	ITA2820
ASAFED	CHE0437	AV	DEU0919	CAF	DEU0990	CEFODE	FRA1815
ASAH	CHE0466	AVE	FRA1714	CAFOD	GBR2228	CEFRI	FRA1812
ASAL	ITA2780	AVI	BEL0104	CAM	ITA2787	CEI	BEL0175
ASB	DEU0939	AVISE	NLD3312	CARAES	BEL0145	CEIAL	ITA2794
ASC	CHE0469	AVP	FRA1758	CARAF	CHE0545	CEIAS	ITA2795
ASCOM	ITA2774	AVSI	ITA2782	CARITAS	BEL0338	CEIDER	ESP1438
ASD	CHE0741	AWE	DNK1224	CASA	DNK1235	CEIK	FRA1863
ASDHM	CHE0450	AWEPA	NLD3053	CASC	FRA1855	CEIS	ITA2802
ASF	FRA1608	AWIC	NLD3349	CASI	FRA1797	CELIM	ITA2803
ASF	FRA1636	AWO	DEU0940	CAST	ITA2807	CEMP	GBR2232
ASF	FRA1637	AZITT	DNK1225	CB	FRA1878	CEMUBAC	BEL0156
ASF	FRA1677	B87	FRA1789	CBAR	BEL0166	CENYC	BEL0191
ASF	FRA1781	BARNfonden	SWE3656	CBE	CHE0541	CEPAZE	FRA1799
ASI	FRA1649	BASAID	CHE0802	CBEVE	GBR2231	CEPIA	FRA1823
ASI	GBR2195	BAZ	DEU0966	CBM	DEU0989	CEPROMAR	FRA1801
ASI	ITA2776	BBI	NLD3059	CBSE	BEL0167	CERADS	FRA1804
ASIA	NLD3051	BBO	NLD3064	CCATM	FRA1854	CERCI	FRA1817
ASLN	LUX2951	BDKJ	DEU0975	CCD	DNK1238	CERCOOP	PRT3561
ASMAE	FRA1683	BDM	DNK1228	CCF GERMANY	DEU0983	CES	BEL0177
ASMAF	FRA1704	BEDH	BEL0141	CCFD	FRA1853	CESD	FRA1822
ASN	BEL0107	BEE	BEL0142	CCIC	FRA1798	CESTA	ITA2790
ASO	BEL0109	BEGECA	DEU0965	CCIG	CHE0494	CESTAS	ITA2791
ASP	CHE0471	BESO	GBR2218	CCIVS	FRA1887	CESVI	ITA2832
ASPA	ESP1413	BFA	CHE0486	CCM	ITA2818	CESVITEM	ITA2811
ASPAC	FRA1613	BFAG	AUT0020	CCOW	GBR2239	CETIM	CHE0499
ASPAL	FRA1703	BFM-ADAO	FRA1785	CCPD-WCC	CHE0533	CETRI	BEL0157
ASPAS	FRA1757	BIFOSA	BEL0136	CCSC	ITA2789	CEU	CHE0542
ASPEM	ITA2777	BIP	CHE0489	CCSTF-N	FRA1856	CEVI	ITA2792
ASPFES	CHE0464	BIVRO	BEL0137	CDC	DEU0980	CEWC	GBR2265
ASSAF	FRA1619	BKIN	NOR3379	CDC N/S	BEL0183	CEWI	NOR3382
ASSAJVCO	FRA1741	BLLF SWEDEN	SWE3661	CDCS	NLD3069	CFBEC	FRA1826
ASSOCIATION SUISSE-AFRIQUE DU SUD	CHE0607	BMW	DEU0964	CDG	DEU0981	CFCF	FRA1865
		BNMT	GBR2213	CDI-BWAMANDA	BEL0158	CFCI	FRA1814
ASSP	CHE0410	BOAG	GBR2220	CDM	CHE0610	CFD	CHE0509
AST	CHE0412	BODS	CHE0482	CEAR	ESP1450	CFD	DEU0987
ASTM	CHE0462	BORDA	DEU0971	CEAS	CHE0498	CFE	FRA1867
ASTM	LUX2937	BOS	NLD3307	CEASM	FRA1762	CFEI	FRA1813
AT-B	FRA1770	BOVO	NLD3063	CEC	BEL0187	CFI	DEU0986
ATA	FRA1767	BPI	AUT0021	CECEPEP	PRT3562	CFPE	FRA1824
ATD	CHE0699	BRANDNETEL	NLD3092	CECOTRET	CHE0497	CFS	ITA2808

                          See: *How to Use the Directory*, page 11.

CHAPITO

DVV

CHAPITO	PRT3568	CJP	BEL0171	COTMEP	CHE0535	DEFAP	FRA1903
CHC	CZE0857	CKD	DEU0979	CP	NLD3083	DEFY	IRL2693
CHEC	GBR2253	CKF	SWE3667	CPB	NLD3079	DELIPRO	BEL0148
CHEN	GRC2568	CL	FRA1838	CPCCA & F	FRA1879	DEM	DNK1245
CHRD	CHE0501	CLED-ESF	FRA1869	CPPC	PRT3572	DERC	NLD3094
CI	GBR2255	CLER	FRA1860	CPR	PRT3573	DESWOS	DEU0995
CI-AF	CHE0521	CLID	FRA1839	CPS	ITA2828	DF	DEU1010
CIAN	FRA1881	CLMC	ITA2827	CQFD	FRA1795	DFD	FRA1896
CIC	ITA2799	CLONG-VOLONTARIAT	FRA1859	CRATERRE-EAG	FRA1833	DFG	DNK1246
CIC	PRT3555	CLOSI	FRA1858	CREDES	FRA1820	DFR	DEU1011
CICA	NLD3070	CMA	GBR2256	CRF	FRA1892	DFU	DEU1012
CICAD	CHE0543	CMC	NLD3068	CRIAA	FRA1819	DFU	DNK1305
CICAT	NLD3071	CME	GRC2590	CRIAD	FRA1821	DGB	DEU1013
CICDA	FRA1828	CMI	CHE0536	CRIC	ITA2809	DGI	DNK1274
CICM	FRA1835	CMO	TUR3884	CRID	FRA1816	DGVN	DEU0996
CICP	FRA1829	CMPA	NLD3074	CRIDEV	FRA1841	DHIN	NLD3251
CICS	ITA2800	CMS	FRA1890	CRIJ	BEL0173	DHSF	BEL0197
CICSENE	ITA2801	CMSI	CHE0538	CRISLA	FRA1818	DHSF	FRA1900
CID-MAHT	FRA1808	CMSI	IRL2688	CRS	CHE0492	DIB	DNK1251
CIDAC	PRT3564	CMSR	ITA2804	CSD	PRT3575	DICAF/FFSS	FRA1904
CIDC	PRT3566	CMT	BEL0162	CSPT	FRA1862	DIE	DEU1020
CIDE	CHE0524	CMT	BEL0179	CSS	CHE0493	DIHT	DEU1015
CIDEAL	ESP1437	CNADP	BEL0172	CSSPA	CHE0513	DIML	DEU1030
CIDIS	ITA2797	CNAJEP	FRA1874	CSUZ	CZE0849	DIO	NLD3093
CIDOB	ESP1441	CNC	PRT3567	CTB	FRA1875	DIS	NOR3386
CIDR	FRA1830	CNCA	FRA1790	CTM	FRA1849	DISOP	BEL0195
CIDSE	BEL0186	CNCD	BEL0155	CTM	ITA2814	DISVI	ITA2764
CIE	FRA1832	CNID	FRA1872	CTTC	DEU0984	DK	DNK1254
CIEDEL	FRA1827	CNJD	FRA1877	CTUC	GBR2258	DKKSF	DNK1253
CIEMI	FRA1807	CNV	NLD3078	CUAMM	ITA2816	DKV	DNK1267
CIEPAC	FRA1836	COCIS	ITA2839	CUC	ESP1436	DLG	DEU0999
CIEPAD	FRA1794	CODA	ESP1457	CVCS	ITA2812	DMR-P	DNK1255
CIES	ITA2798	CODESPA	ESP1455	CVM	ITA2813	DNM	NOR3452
CIFEG	FRA1837	CODIFOR	FRA1886	CVP	FRA1850	DOCHAS	IRL2705
CIIR	GBR2229	COE	ITA2806	CVP	PRT3576	DOF	DNK1350
CIMADE	FRA1843	COHRE	NLD3072	CWM	GBR2266	DOG	NLD3091
CINADE	ESP1440	COK	BEL0159	DACAAR	DNK1240	DOSV	DNK1276
CINTERAD	BEL0152	COLARCH-COLOCH	BEL0163	DAHW	DEU1017	DPG	DEU0992
CIOMAL	CHE0522	COLUREOM	FRA1876	DAM	SWE3675	DPU	GBR2273
CIPA	BEL0150	COMEDE	FRA1870	DANTAN	DNK1242	DPU	ITA2760
CIPEDH	CHE0502	COMIDE-DMOS	BEL0341	DAS	DEU0993	DR	FRA1908
CIPIE	ESP1442	COMRADE	ESP1451	DÄZ	DEU0994	DRK	DEU1024
CIPSI	ITA2840	CONCED	FRA1885	DB	CHE0552	DRK	DNK1259
CIS	DEU0988	CONFCOOPERATIVE-CCI	ITA2830	DCC	FRA1898	DSE	DEU1000
CISP	ITA2822	COOPI	ITA2835	DCI	CHE0550	DSF	DNK1281
CISS	ITA2834	COPE	ITA2837	DCI	CZE0864	DSW	DEU1002
CISV	GBR2237	COS-NOORD-HOLLAND-ZUM	NLD3073	DCMR	DNK1273	DU	DEU1029
CISV	ITA2826	COSPE	ITA2838	DCV	DEU1008	DUK	DEU1004
CISV	SWE3817	COSV	ITA2819	DDEC	GBR2270	DUWA	DNK1269
CIT	GBR2246	COTA	BEL0164	DDP	DNK1278	DVI	DNK1283
CITIM	FRA1889	COTMEC	CHE0534	DEA	GBR2271	DVN	NLD3335
CJC	BEL0180			DED	DEU1009	DVV	DEU1016

Voir : *Comment utiliser le répertoire,* page 11.

759

DW	DEU1006	EMS	NLD3098	FDF	DNK1304	FMO	NLD3197
DWAZ	DEU1005	EMT	CHE0563	FDH	BEL0246	FMVJ	FRA1964
DWF	NLD3250	ENDA-TM	FRA1946	FDH-LUX	LUX2976	FNEL	LUX2965
DYA	ESP1476	ENEA	GRC2583	FDI	BEL0242	FNST	DEU1056
E&L	CHE0556	ENGIM	ITA2842	FDI	ESP1408	FNV	NLD3109
EAICY	CZE0869	EPARGNEUROP	BEL0253	FDIHY-MIESZ	SVK3611	FO	NOR3461
EAST	FRA1914	EPCE SR	SVK3625	FDW	NLD3350	FOCSIV	ITA2844
EAWM	AUT0033	EPDE	FRA1951	FEA	FRA1979	FODEP	BEL0244
EBAG	DEU1040	EPER	CHE0559	FEANTSA	BEL0219	FÖE	AUT0083
EBZ	AUT0027	EPICADEC	NLD3100	FEC	CHE0590	FOE	SVK3614
ECAS	BEL0207	EPOG	DEU1038	FED	CHE0585	FOE-E	BEL0248
ECG	GBR2284	ERA	CHE0564	FEDORA	ESP1466	FOEI	NLD3115
ECMR-CIVAM	FRA1915	ERA	DNK1286	FEDUC VZW	BEL0223	FOF	DNK1293
ECO	IRL2696	ERM	FRA1942	FEEE	DNK1301	FOH	BEL0240
ECO	MLT3016	ESF	ESP1461	FERAM	FRA1974	FOMETRO	BEL0239
ECO-DEV	BEL0121	ESF	FRA1920	FERE	ESP1468	FOMULAC	BEL0233
EcoAgriDev	DEU1032	ESF	FRA1947	FERS	ESP1467	FONDAD	NLD3112
ECOE	ESP1464	ESIB	AUT0056	FETAF	FRA1957	FONOLA	SWE3690
ECONNECT	CZE0841	ESNAC	BEL0200	FEU	DNK1300	FOPERDA	BEL0234
ECRE	BEL0212	ESONE	GRC2591	FF	DNK1298	FOS	BEL0241
ECRE	GBR2283	ESPA	GRC2574	FFCU	FRA1959	FPPN	NLD3113
ECTI	FRA1917	ETC	NLD3101	FFL	LUX2973	FSC-SBPB	BEL0218
ECUME	FRA1696	ETDI	FRA2106	FFO	NOR3396	FSI	BEL0231
ED	GBR2286	ETHIOPIE	NLD3145	FFP	SWE3689	FSS	FIN1536
EDCS	NLD3096	ETM	BEL0124	FFSM	CHE0567	FTCI	BEL0224
EDEN	GBR2285	ETM	FRA2059	FGC	CHE0568	FTDA	FRA1977
EDLT	FRA1936	EUB	CHE0560	FGN	NLD3111	FTM	ITA2845
EDM	FRA1937	EURO-CARITAS	BEL0208	FHI	CHE0586	FUCID	BEL0237
EDON	CYP0832	EUROCOM	DEU1065	FHP-SRI LANKA	NLD3108	FUNDES	CHE0602
EDP	NLD3117	EURODAD	BEL0215	FIACAT	FRA1960	FUNDES	CHE0752
EDRC	BEL0204	EURONAID	NLD3102	FIAN	BEL0243	FUNDESCOOP	ESP1474
EE	FRA1924	EUROPACT	FRA1628	FIAN	DEU1048	FVC	CHE0572
EE	FRA1928	EUROSTEP	BEL0216	FIAN-SVERIGE	SWE3682	FWIE	POL3499
EECOD	BEL0214	EVG	AUT0030	FICEMEA	FRA1961	FWN	GBR2288
EEDDA	GRC2572	EVI	AUT0031	FID	FRA1969	FYF	GBR2291
EEDF	FRA1919	EVS	NLD3106	FIDH	FRA1962	FZL	MLT3017
EES	GRC2573	EWA	AUT0028	FIDIDA	FIN1603	GADEF	FRA1993
EFAI	FRA1923	EXIL	BEL0154	FIDOC	NLD3110	GAO	ITA2836
EFDI	FRA1943	EYFA	NLD3104	FIEF	FRA1963	GAP	GBR2306
EFS	SWE3679	EZA	AUT0029	FIELD	GBR2294	GBVF	GBR2310
EHD	DEU1039	EZE	DEU1047	FIJ	BEL0220	GCA	NLD3119
EHRF	BEL0364	FADO	BEL0226	FIMARC	BEL0221	GE-TM	CHE0604
EI	FRA1926	FAFRAD	FRA1956	FIMCAP	CHE0643	GEBANA	CHE0427
EIP	CHE0456	FAL	FRA1975	FIRE	DNK1295	GEFOSAT	FRA1984
EIRENE	DEU1114	FAM	FRA1954	FIS	MLT3018	GELAT	DEU1067
EIRENE-FRANCE	FRA1925	FAR	BEL0230	FITDH	CHE0570	GERES	FRA1992
EKAPEM	GRC2567	FAREP	FRA1955	FIVH	NOR3393	GEYSER	FRA1985
EM	FRA1932	FARM-AFRICA	GBR2292	FIZ	CHE0596	GFBV	CHE0605
EMDA INSTITUTE	NLD3137	FATIMA	SWE3704	FKN	DNK1292	GFBV	DEU1064
EMI	FRA1944	FCC	FIN1584	FLAPE-INAUCO	ESP1482	GFSV	DEU1063
EMIK	CHE0562	FCRP	GBR2299	FLI-AV CR	CZE0872	GGS	SWE3708
EMK	CHE0561	FDE	FRA1968	FMH	FRA1972	GIFA	CHE0603

GJU	HUN2621	IAESTE	CHE0634	IDG	GBR2333	IN	DEU1103
GLARE	GBR2311	IAESTE	FRA2026	IdM	CHE0625	INADES-FORMATION	FRA2007
GMA	ITA2857	IAF	DEU1193	IDOC	ITA2861	INCA PIRCA	NLD3351
GMDC	NLD3121	IAI	GBR2340	IEA	FRA2015	INDOC	NLD3135
GOAB	AUT0035	IAK	DEU1095	IEC	GBR2353	INDONESIE	NLD3170
GOM	NLD3116	IAK	DEU1112	IECD	FRA2016	INE	POL3502
GRAAP	FRA1987	IATMA	FRA2002	IED	PRT3586	INF	GBR2358
GRAD	CHE0609	IATP	GBR2341	IEEI	PRT3585	INFODEV	FRA2004
GRAD	FRA1986	IAV	DEU1083	IEI	FRA2010	INKOTA	DEU1094
GRAMC	ESP1478	IAW	DEU1106	IELAB	NLD3141	INTAF	GBR2364
GRDR	FRA1989	IAW	NLD3147	IEPALA	ESP1481	INTERIGHTS	GBR2347
GRESEA	BEL0252	IAWQ	GBR2344	IFA	DEU1096	INTERTEAM	CHE0655
GRET	FRA1988	IB-JSW	DEU1113	IFAP	FRA2029	IOCU	FRA2030
GRIP	BEL0268	IBFAN	CHE0635	IFCD	IRL2709	IPADE	ESP1483
GRT	ITA2858	IBFAN	NOR3374	IFCOD	FRA2009	IPH	FRA2003
GRTA-CIN	ITA2854	IBT	GBR2345	IFD	DNK1315	IPIS	BEL0281
GSAL	PRT3580	IC	CHE0632	IFFJ	GBR2354	IPPF	GBR2359
GSE	DEU1066	ICA	CHE0638	IFHP	NLD3152	IPS	ITA2860
GSF	FRA1982	ICA	NLD3140	IFLRY	BEL0276	IPS-NEDERLAND	NLD3143
GSP	CHE0615	ICA-UK	GBR2338	IFM-SEI	BEL0275	IPSD	PRT3591
GTU	DNK1306	ICAI	BEL0270	IFMSA	AUT0043	IPSIA-ACLI	ITA2867
GUATEMALA	NLD3258	ICBP	GBR2352	IFS	GBR2355	IRADIE	FRA2011
GVC	ITA2855	ICC	FRA2027	IFS	SWE3717	IRAM	FRA2012
GVOM	CHE0613	ICCB	CHE0636	IFSW	NOR3400	IRC	GBR2361
HAI	NLD3123	ICCE	GBR2346	IFTN	IRL2708	IRCT	DNK1360
HAI-DK	DNK1311	ICCO	NLD3144	IFU	DNK1314	IRDN	DEU1108
HAMAKI	DNK1405	ICDA	BEL0272	IFUW	CHE0645	IRED	CHE0626
HAMLO	NLD3131	ICEA	GBR2351	IGF	BEL0277	IRENE	NLD3157
HEDCO	IRL2702	ICEI	ITA2866	IGFM	DEU1110	IRFED	FRA2018
HEGOA	ESP1479	ICFON-NETH	NLD3149	IHE	GBR2356	IRIACP-IRIAN	FRA2021
HELINAS	GRC2571	ICFTU	BEL0274	IHE	NLD3155	ISCA	BEL0280
HELMEPA	GRC2582	ICJ	CHE0639	IHEU	NLD3153	ISCA	CHE0648
HELVETAS	CHE0619	ICJP	IRL2706	IHF	AUT0044	ISCOD	ESP1484
HERMED	NLD3304	ICJW	CHE0640	IHS	NLD3138	ISCOS	ITA2869
HGZO-OC/GZ	NLD3176	ICMC	BEL0271	IIC	DNK1282	ISD	FRA1935
HHN	NLD3128	ICMC	CHE0637	IICE	CHE0627	ISEFOC	PRT3592
HIC	BEL0254	ICMC	TUR3888	IID	FRA2017	ISF	FRA2005
HIDCA	SWE3710	ICMICA/MIIC	CHE0719	IIED	GBR2357	ISRIC	NLD3158
HIFA	AUT0038	ICR	GBR2350	IIJ	DEU1116	ISSA	DEU1090
HIMOS	NLD3126	ICRS	NLD3290	IISA	GRC2586	ISSS	AUT0045
HinD	GBR2326	ICS	NLD3146	IIZ	AUT0041	ISTED	FRA2014
HIVOS	NLD3132	ICSF	BEL0273	IIZ-DVV	DEU1097	ISU	PRT3588
HKI	NLD3125	ICSU	FRA1883	IJO	ITA2862	ISWA	DNK1320
HOM	NLD3133	ICSW	CHE0641	IK	DNK1318	ITC	NLD3154
HSF	FRA1997	ICSW-NEDERLAND	NLD3207	IKFF	SWE3720	ITDG	GBR2339
HUMANA	AUT0039	ICT	GBR2348	ILA	DEU1089	ITECO	BEL0188
HUMANA	DEU1082	ICU	ITA2868	ILADAP	PRT3589	ITER	ITA2859
HUMANA	ESP1420	ICVA	CHE0642	ILEIA	NLD3136	ITF	NLD3159
HUMANA	NLD3336	ICYE	DNK1252	ILSMH	BEL0278	ITPC	GBR2365
HURIDOCS	CHE0622	ICYE	FIN1543	IM	SWE3715	IUATLD	FRA2031
HWY	NLD3127	ICYE	SWE3716	IMCC	DNK1319	IUCN	CHE0813
IAC	PRT3584	IDA	NLD3150	IMU	IRL2711	IUED	CHE0629

IUFRO	AUT0046	KJSÖ	AUT0024	MAC	ITA2876	MSF	SVK3622
IULA	NLD3160	KKS	DEU1121	MAF	SWE3755	MSF-B	BEL0297
IUNA	IRL2718	KMA	LUX2987	MAG-UK	GBR2394	MSF-CH	CHE0683
IUPAC	GBR2366	KMA	SWE3731	MAGIS	ITA2879	MSP	CHE0703
IVB-ÖZ	AUT0047	KN	NOR3401	MAIS	ITA2882	MSP	ITA2885
IVCS	GBR2334	KNV	NLD3175	MATRIX	NLD3183	MSZOSZ	HUN2648
IVS	GBR2367	KODIS	CHE0665	MC	NLD3188	MW	NLD3189
IWA	DEU1109	KOO	AUT0054	MCE	ITA2878	MWDRC	GBR2393
IWGIA	DNK1322	KRISS	SWE3736	MCI	CHE0697	MWIA	DEU1142
IWGIA	SWE3718	KSL	FIN1545	MCNV	NLD3184	MZF	DEU1149
IWRB	GBR2370	KSM	CZE0855	MCOD	GBR2391	MZPN	MLT3027
IWZE	DEU1099	KUA	FIN1549	MCP	FRA2057	NABU	DEU1151
IWZE	DEU1100	KULU	DNK1333	MCPI	BEL0303	NAFIA	SWE3759
Iz3w	DEU1091	KVET	CZE0847	MCS	NLD3185	NAN.C.IE	FRA1831
JAFIC	SWE3722	KWA	GBR2378	MDF	NLD3182	NCED	NOR3388
JBH	DEU1119	KWIA	BEL0228	MdM	CHE0461	NCIV	NLD3191
JDW	BEL0290	LA-INFO	DNK1336	MDM-F	FRA2047	NCO	NLD3190
JEC-SUISSE	CHE0661	LAC	NLD3181	MEDACT	GBR2388	NCOS	BEL0306
JECI-MIEC	BEL0287	LACIM	FRA1655	MEDAF	CHE0686	NCVO	GBR2400
JEREMI	FRA2033	LAG	NOR3410	MEDAIR	CHE0684	NDF	NOR3428
JIDCA	SWE3723	LAI	AUT0074	MEDEC	PRT3597	NEA	ITA2886
JINT	BEL0227	LASO	NLD3305	MEDICUS MUNDI	FRA2074	NEAD	GBR2408
JNE	FRA1712	LAZ	DEU1138	MENA	NLD3269	NEF	GBR2406
JOC	LUX2985	LBSNN	NLD3177	METROPOLIS	FRA1744	NFPU	NOR3439
JOC EUROPEENNE	BEL0288	LD	PRT3594	MGHA	MLT3025	NH	NOR3431
JOCI	BEL0289	LEEDS DEC	GBR2380	MIJARC	BEL0305	NHAM	NOR3459
JRS	ITA2902	LEPRA	GBR2219	MIJC	FRA2084	NHK	NLD3198
JRS-E	BEL0284	LHÜ	DEU0949	MISSIO	CHE0653	NHO	NOR3423
JTM	ESP1488	LIA.CO.FA	FRA2036	MISZOT	HUN2634	NIF	NOR3432
KAAD	DEU1124	LIAFRICA	PRT3595	MIVA	CHE0737	NIO	NLD3205
KADE	IRL2720	LICRA	FRA2040	MIVA-NEDERLAND	NLD3271	NIO	NLD3340
KARIBU	ESP1425	LIEECP	FRA2042	MK	AUT0055	NJCM	NLD3195
KARTINI	NLD3148	LIFPL	CHE0678	MKS	POL3504	NKL	FIN1559
KBA	BEL0293	LIFPL	FRA2041	MLAL	ITA2880	NKL	NOR3434
KCEE	POL3507	LA LIGUE	FRA2039	MMB	BEL0300	NL	NOR3442
KDK	NLD3174	LIW	NLD3180	MMIt	ITA2874	NMM	NOR3453
KDU	SWE3733	LMF	DNK1334	MMM	FRA2061	NOAS	NOR3446
KED	DEU1131	LNO	NLD3178	MMS	GBR2390	NODAF	FRA2064
KEEP-UK	GBR2376	LNP-YO	POL3508	MOCI	ITA2883	NOMDA	NLD3209
KEGME	GRC2588	LNU	NOR3408	MOLISV	ITA2881	NOVIB	NLD3199
KEM	CHE0670	LO	DNK1335	MON-3	ESP1528	NPC	GBR2401
KEPA	FIN1546	LO	NOR3407	MORIJA	CHE0444	NS	CHE0616
KESFA	SWE3729	LOP	POL3509	MPDL	ESP1498	NSF	NOR3447
KESSS	SWE3725	LPI	SWE3746	MPF	CHE0701	NSL	NLD3202
KF	SWE3732	LRF	SWE3742	MPFST	FRA2055	NUFF	SWE3761
KFBÖ	AUT0051	LSO	NLD3179	MRAP	FRA2058	NULAG	SWE3758
KFE	CHE0669	LSPN	CHE0680	MRAX	BEL0304	NUMOV	DEU1150
KFF	NOR3477	LSU	SWE3740	MRJC	FRA2062	NUS	GBR2402
KFF	SWE3738	LSV	FIN1551	MS	DNK1339	NVCO	NLD3204
KFS	AUT0052	LTM	ITA2856	MSD	CZE0914	NVOC	NLD3203
KHB	CHE0664	LWF/WS	CHE0682	MSF	ESP1493	NVR	BEL0308
KIT	NLD3173	MAAS	CHE0698	MSF	FRA2050	NVUN	NLD3206

O.I.EAU	FRA2069	Pacific	NLD3218	RED GRROUND!	ESP1434	SDTG	NLD3084
O3V	DNK1352	PACS	SWE3767	RedR	GBR2449	SEAD	GBR2469
OAD	AUT0065	PADA	NLD3222	RENDAN A/S	DNK1241	SEC	CHE0761
OAJ	FIN1562	PAEK	POL3520	Réseay GAO	FRA2108	SEI	SWE3789
OAV	DEU1160	PALKOM	NOR3464	RESOPALM	ESP1514	SEL	FRA2119
OBCE	BEL0314	PALM	NLD3302	RIAL	FRA2102	SELAVIP	BEL0222
OBJR	AUT0066	PAN	DEU1163	RISC	GBR2443	SELUF	SWE3799
OBP	FRA2078	PAN-EUROPE	GBR2433	RITIMO	FRA2104	SEO	GRC2580
OCASHA	ESP1500	PBI	GBR2430	RLS	GBR2210	SEPI	AUT0078
OCC	GBR2418	PBI	SWE3768	RMS	SVK3627	SES	DEU1174
OCSHA	ESP1501	PBI-NEDERLAND	NLD3223	RNTC	NLD3230	SETAAFOC	PRT3582
OCSI/AMS	ESP1503	PDO	NLD3286	RONGEAD	FRA2105	SFB	FRA2132
OD	DNK1351	PEN	GBR2555	RSP	GBR2448	SFF	SWE3800
ODEC	GBR2424	PF	ITA2899	RTM	ITA2900	SFH	CHE0744
ODI	GBR2422	PFS	NLD3219	RURCON	GBR2460	SFN	SWE3816
OED	AUT0067	PHARE	POL3490	RVA	GBR2453	SGU	CHE0792
OEME	CHE0671	PICHR	BEL0326	RWI	SWE3772	SHAT	NLD3260
OF-FEEE	FRA2068	PIOOM	NLD3226	RY	FIN1568	SHC	BEL0339
OFSE	AUT0060	PKE	POL3524	SADEL	SWE3840	SHIA	SWE3821
OHFOM	FRA2066	PMU-INTERLIFE	SWE3769	SAFE	GBR2495	SHRO	GBR2491
OIE	AUT0068	PNP	LUX2999	SAFU	DNK1363	SI	ESP1521
OJRK	AUT0071	PRAVOSJ	BEL0328	SAGO	BEL0335	SI	FRA2136
OKN	NLD3216	PREDEP	FRA1754	SAH	CHE0755	SI	GBR2481
OKOMEDIA	DEU1157	PRELUDE	BEL0330	SAIA	SVK3638	SIAD	FRA2121
OMCT/SOS-TORTURE	CHE0711	PROCLADE	ESP1508	SAK	DNK1375	SIAS	FRA2112
OME	CHE0713	PRODOCS	ITA2895	SAK	SWE3812	SID	CHE0765
OMMS	CHE0712	PROSALUS	ESP1502	SAKS	SWE3849	SID	DNK1367
OPAM	ITA2888	PROTOS	BEL0331	SAM	CHE0791	SID	ESP1519
OPAM	NLD3212	PS-EAU	FRA2093	SAM	NLD3294	SID	ITA2908
OPC	FRA2075	PSF	FRA2087	SAM	SWE3780	SID UK	GBR2479
OPOKA	POL3480	PSF	FRA2088	SAMS	GBR2485	SID-FINLAND	FIN1571
ORC	NLD3217	PSI	FRA2096	SAN-FRG	DEU1172	SID-FRANCE	FRA2129
ORCADES	FRA2076	PSM	NOR3465	SAND	GBR2494	SIDI	FRA2127
ORION	NLD3284	PSO	FRA2086	SAOM	PRT3601	SIE	POL3532
ORT	GBR2550	PSO	NLD3341	SASK	FIN1574	SIETAR	NLD3238
OS3	CHE0714	PTAFR	POL3514	SATIMO	BEL0258	SIK	ISL2740
OSA	FRA2065	PTM	ESP1506	SBO	NLD3246	SILO	FRA2122
OSAR	CHE0715	PTPP	POL3525	SBU	SWE3837	SIM	CHE0764
OSF	FRA2071	PTS/PKR	FIN1566	SCAIP	ITA2904	SIMU	DNK1361
OSJ	BEL0318	PUM	NLD3227	SCAR	CHE0762	SIOI	ITA2870
OSL	FRA1694	PV-UK	GBR2221	SCD	FRA2120	SIPAR	FRA2140
OSVIC	ITA2890	QCEA	BEL0332	SCF	GBR2464	SIRCOFAM	FRA2141
OSW	DEU1158	QPS	GBR2442	SCI	DEU1175	SISU	NLD3296
OTECI	FRA2070	QUERCUS-ANCN	PRT3553	SCI	FRA2118	SIT	CHE0794
OTM	LUX2993	QUNO	CHE0726	SCI	ITA2903	SITNS	BEL0349
OTMCDF	FRA2073	RAFAD	CHE0727	SCI-SEED	BEL0340	SIW	NLD3162
OUK	AUT0064	RAFOD	FRA2103	SCIAF	GBR2467	SKAF	CHE0746
OVCI	ITA2889	RAM	CZE0846	SCMTM	BEL0347	SKAT	CHE0565
OVE	DNK1353	RAWOO	NLD3228	SCO	NLD3249	SKIP	CHE0785
OVERAL	NLD3285	RC	ITA2901	SCSF	ITA2909	SKL	SWE3869
OVERSEAS	ITA2891	RE.TE	ITA2763	SDI	CHE0759	SKM	CZE0910
P3M	CHE0720	RED	BEL0333	SDPL	FIN1575	SKM	SWE3826

SKN	NLD3262	SRF	SWE3850	UATI	FRA2158	VISBA	ITA2920
SKSB	CHE0747	SRK	CHE0757	UCCI	ESP1525	VISPE	ITA2921
SKSF	SWE3735	SRM/FCEI	ITA2905	UCCLA	PRT3603	VIZ	DEU1199
SKU	SWE3824	SRO 2000	NLD3291	UCISS	BEL0376	VLAAMSE WIZA	BEL0387
SKV	SWE3825	SSCN	MLT3032	UCJG	FRA1651	VMD	NLD3337
SLA	BEL0336	SSEA-SAG	CHE0766	UCSEI	ITA2915	VMM	GBR2536
SLA	NLD3215	SSI-SUISSE	CHE0582	UDS	GBR2520	VMM	IRL2729
SLCD	BEL0342	SSIP	DEU1179	UFER	CHE0700	VNC	NLD3346
SLI	GBR2465	SSN	NLD3295	UFF	DNK1388	VNG	NLD3338
SLIG	DNK1368	SSR	SWE3832	UFF	SWE3859	VOFO	NOR3476
SLO	NLD3142	SUCOS	ITA2910	UFFN	SWE3863	VOLENS	BEL0388
SLO	NLD3299	SUKE	CHE0754	UG	SWE3864	VPM	ITA2919
SLP	NLD3266	SUL/ACD	PRT3602	UIESP	BEL0377	VSF	FRA2163
SM	BEL0351	SVETAN	SWE3807	UIOF	FRA2159	VSI	IRL2728
SMA	FRA1880	SVI	ITA2907	UK-ISES	GBR2363	VSM	CHE0805
SMA	NLD3272	SVM	CZE0909	UKFSP	GBR2524	VSO	GBR2535
SMB	CHE0693	SVS	SWE3798	ULD-80	DNK1382	VSO-NEDERLAND	NLD3301
SME	FRA1990	SWEMSIC	SWE3845	UMMI	ITA2916	VUBI	DEU1194
SME	NLD3270	SWF	CHE0739	UMOFC-WUCWO	FRA2168	VVN	BEL0380
SMF	SWE3827	SWISSCONTACT	CHE0793	UMP	PRT3604	VVOB	BEL0386
SMHK	NLD3268	SWV	FIN1591	UMU	SWE3862	WACC	GBR2546
SMJ	FRA2123	SZOPK	SVK3637	UNA-UK	GBR2526	WAGGGS	GBR2547
SMR	SWE3828	TAA	FRA2153	UNAIS	GBR2525	WAY	DNK1402
SNM	NLD3274	TALC	GBR2499	UNCPIE	FRA2161	WCC	CHE0814
SNV	NOR3403	TAP-VAKFI	TUR3892	UNEFA	ESP1526	WCIA	GBR2539
SOAM	CHE0749	TAPD	TUR3891	UNIONI	FIN1558	WDM	GBR2548
SOB	NLD3281	TÇV	TUR3894	UNIS	ESP1527	WEB	GBR2549
SODEPAZ	ESP1522	TDA	SWE3853	UNITE	CHE0428	WEKEF	AUT0014
SODI	DEU1176	TDDSZ	HUN2616	UNPO	NLD3330	WEKEF	AUT0016
SOEF	CHE0748	TDH	DNK1378	UNSAF	FIN1583	WEMOS	NLD3352
SOH	NLD3277	TDHF	FRA2150	UNSAF	FIN1601	WEN	GBR2544
SOLAGRAL	FRA2135	TDHS	CHE0798	UNV	NLD3327	WFD	DEU1200
SOLAGRO	FRA1927	TEGON	NLD3320	UPD	ITA2898	WFD	FIN1604
SOLBO	BEL0354	TEHY	FIN1600	URBANETH	NLD3208	WFDFI	ESP1530
SOLIDER	FRA2133	TFAO	BEL0374	USDC	GBR2521	WFDY	HUN2670
SOLIFONDS	CHE0773	TFSR	GBR2510	USF	FRA2162	WFSF	FIN1605
SOMO	NLD3279	TFTP	CHE0795	USOS	BEL0378	WGNRR	NLD3357
SONT	NLD3282	TH U	SWE3855	UTV	DNK1390	WICE	FRA2167
SOPROGI	FRA2130	THE CONTINENTS	CZE0843	UV	SWE3698	WIDE	BEL0309
SOS ASILE	CHE0702	THET	GBR2517	UVISP-ASSISI	ITA2917	WILPF	CHE0809
SOS-INTERFONDS	LUX2975	THIS	GBR2512	UVN	NLD3323	WIP	NLD3314
SOS-UK	GBR2482	TKV	TUR3896	UWC	GBR2528	WISE	NLD3358
SOS/PG	BEL0359	TLM	GBR2382	UWE	NLD3329	Woord en Daad	NLD3289
SOU	NLD3283	TOOL	NLD3318	VAO	GBR2533	WOSM	CHE0817
SOZA	NLD3280	TTMI	BEL0371	VEGS	CHE0807	WOT	NLD3353
SOZE	CZE0904	TUFF	SWE3856	VEHEMENT	DEU1198	WOW	GBR2537
SP	BEL0352	TUIREG	GBR2513	VEN	DEU1170	WSM	BEL0392
SPAS	SWE3819	TVE	GBR2501	VESOS MONDE	FRA1726	WUS	DEU1204
SPAS	SWE3848	TVS	DNK1381	VETERMON	ESP1529	WUS-NETHERLANDS	NLD3192
SPE	CHE0767	TWAS	ITA2914	VIDA	PRT3605	WUS-SWITZERLAND	CHE0818
SPF	FRA2117	TWM	GBR2504	VIDES	ITA2922	WUS-UK	GBR2551
SPM	CHE0750	U-SAM	SWE3858	VIS	ITA2923	WVI	CHE0819

See: *How to Use the Directory*, page 11.

WVUK	GBR2552	WWF UK	GBR2553	YES INTERNATIONAL	GBR2558	ZHP	POL3543
WWB	NLD3114	WWP	DEU1201	YMCA	MLT3036	ZHR	POL3544
WWF	BEL0398	WWSF	CHE0810	YWCA	CZE0892	ZIHA	DEU1212
WWF	CHE0820	WYWCA	CHE0822	YWCA-NEDERLAND	NLD3364	ZIMTRUST	GBR2561
WWF	SWE3876	YAMILET	NLD3303	ZAK	CHE0824	ZKSZ	SVK3641
WWF AUSTRIA	AUT0092	YDC	NLD3366	ZDH	DEU1209	ZOA	NLD3232
WWF DENMARK	DNK1403	YEE	DNK1404	ZDWF	DEU1207	ZSL	GBR2562
WWF SUISSE	CHE0821	YEE	NLD3365	ZEBRA	AUT0093		

MAIN SALES OUTLETS OF OECD PUBLICATIONS
PRINCIPAUX POINTS DE VENTE DES PUBLICATIONS DE L'OCDE

ARGENTINA – ARGENTINE
Carlos Hirsch S.R.L.
Galería Güemes, Florida 165, 4° Piso
1333 Buenos Aires   Tel. (1) 331.1787 y 331.2391
Telefax: (1) 331.1787

AUSTRALIA – AUSTRALIE
D.A. Information Services
648 Whitehorse Road, P.O.B 163
Mitcham, Victoria 3132   Tel. (03) 9210.7777
Telefax: (03) 9210.7788

AUSTRIA – AUTRICHE
Gerold & Co.
Graben 31
Wien I   Tel. (0222) 533.50.14
Telefax: (0222) 512.47.31.29

BELGIUM – BELGIQUE
Jean De Lannoy
Avenue du Roi 202 Koningslaan
B-1060 Bruxelles   Tel. (02) 538.51.69/538.08.41
Telefax: (02) 538.08.41

CANADA
Renouf Publishing Company Ltd.
1294 Algoma Road
Ottawa, ON K1B 3W8   Tel. (613) 741.4333
Telefax: (613) 741.5439
Stores:
61 Sparks Street
Ottawa, ON K1P 5R1   Tel. (613) 238.8985
12 Adelaide Street West
Toronto, ON M5H 1L6   Tel. (416) 363.3171
Telefax: (416)363.59.63

Les Éditions La Liberté Inc.
3020 Chemin Sainte-Foy
Sainte-Foy, PQ G1X 3V6   Tel. (418) 658.3763
Telefax: (418) 658.3763

Federal Publications Inc.
165 University Avenue, Suite 701
Toronto, ON M5H 3B8   Tel. (416) 860.1611
Telefax: (416) 860.1608

Les Publications Fédérales
1185 Université
Montréal, QC H3B 3A7   Tel. (514) 954.1633
Telefax: (514) 954.1635

CHINA – CHINE
China National Publications Import
Export Corporation (CNPIEC)
16 Gongti E. Road, Chaoyang District
P.O. Box 88 or 50
Beijing 100704 PR   Tel. (01) 506.6688
Telefax: (01) 506.3101

CHINESE TAIPEI – TAIPEI CHINOIS
Good Faith Worldwide Int'l. Co. Ltd.
9th Floor, No. 118, Sec. 2
Chung Hsiao E. Road
Taipei   Tel. (02) 391.7396/391.7397
Telefax: (02) 394.9176

**CZECH REPUBLIC –
RÉPUBLIQUE TCHÈQUE**
Artia Pegas Press Ltd.
Narodni Trida 25
POB 825
111 21 Praha 1   Tel. (2) 242 246 04
Telefax: (2) 242 278 72

DENMARK – DANEMARK
Munksgaard Book and Subscription Service
35, Nørre Søgade, P.O. Box 2148
DK-1016 København K   Tel. (33) 12.85.70
Telefax: (33) 12.93.87

EGYPT – ÉGYPTE
Middle East Observer
41 Sherif Street
Cairo   Tel. 392.6919
Telefax: 360-6804

FINLAND – FINLANDE
Akateeminen Kirjakauppa
Keskuskatu 1, P.O. Box 128
00100 Helsinki
Subscription Services/Agence d'abonnements :
P.O. Box 23
00371 Helsinki   Tel. (358 0) 121 4416
Telefax: (358 0) 121.4450

FRANCE
OECD/OCDE
Mail Orders/Commandes par correspondance :
2, rue André-Pascal
75775 Paris Cedex 16   Tel. (33-1) 45.24.82.00
Telefax: (33-1) 49.10.42.76
Telex: 640048 OCDE
Internet: Compte.PUBSINQ @ oecd.org
Orders via Minitel, France only/
Commandes par Minitel, France exclusivement :
36 15 OCDE
OECD Bookshop/Librairie de l'OCDE :
33, rue Octave-Feuillet
75016 Paris   Tel. (33-1) 45.24.81.81
(33-1) 45.24.81.67
Dawson
B.P. 40
91121 Palaiseau Cedex   Tel. 69.10.47.00
Telefax: 64.54.83.26

Documentation Française
29, quai Voltaire
75007 Paris   Tel. 40.15.70.00

Economica
49, rue Héricart
75015 Paris   Tel. 45.78.12.92
Telefax: 40.58.15.70

Gibert Jeune (Droit-Économie)
6, place Saint-Michel
75006 Paris   Tel. 43.25.91.19

Librairie du Commerce International
10, avenue d'Iéna
75016 Paris   Tel. 40.73.34.60

Librairie Dunod
Université Paris-Dauphine
Place du Maréchal-de-Lattre-de-Tassigny
75016 Paris   Tel. 44.05.40.13

Librairie Lavoisier
11, rue Lavoisier
75008 Paris   Tel. 42.65.39.95

Librairie des Sciences Politiques
30, rue Saint-Guillaume
75007 Paris   Tel. 45.48.36.02

P.U.F.
49, boulevard Saint-Michel
75005 Paris   Tel. 43.25.83.40

Librairie de l'Université
12a, rue Nazareth
13100 Aix-en-Provence   Tel. (16) 42.26.18.08

Documentation Française
165, rue Garibaldi
69003 Lyon   Tel. (16) 78.63.32.23

Librairie Decitre
29, place Bellecour
69002 Lyon   Tel. (16) 72.40.54.54

Librairie Sauramps
Le Triangle
34967 Montpellier Cedex 2 Tel. (16) 67.58.85.15
Telefax: (16) 67.58.27.36

A la Sorbonne Actual
23, rue de l'Hôtel-des-Postes
06000 Nice   Tel. (16) 93.13.77.75
Telefax: (16) 93.80.75.69

GERMANY – ALLEMAGNE
OECD Publications and Information Centre
August-Bebel-Allee 6
D-53175 Bonn   Tel. (0228) 959.120
Telefax: (0228) 959.12.17

GREECE – GRÈCE
Librairie Kauffmann
Mavrokordatou 9
106 78 Athens   Tel. (01) 32.55.321
Telefax: (01) 32.30.320

HONG-KONG
Swindon Book Co. Ltd.
Astoria Bldg. 3F
34 Ashley Road, Tsimshatsui
Kowloon, Hong Kong   Tel. 2376.2062
Telefax: 2376.0685

HUNGARY – HONGRIE
Euro Info Service
Margitsziget, Európa Ház
1138 Budapest   Tel. (1) 111.62.16
Telefax: (1) 111.60.61

ICELAND – ISLANDE
Mál Mog Menning
Laugavegi 18, Pósthólf 392
121 Reykjavik   Tel. (1) 552.4240
Telefax: (1) 562.3523

INDIA – INDE
Oxford Book and Stationery Co.
Scindia House
New Delhi 110001   Tel. (11) 331.5896/5308
Telefax: (11) 332.5993
17 Park Street
Calcutta 700016   Tel. 240832

INDONESIA – INDONÉSIE
Pdii-Lipi
P.O. Box 4298
Jakarta 12042   Tel. (21) 573.34.67
Telefax: (21) 573.34.67

IRELAND – IRLANDE
Government Supplies Agency
Publications Section
4/5 Harcourt Road
Dublin 2   Tel. 661.31.11
Telefax: 475.27.60

ISRAEL – ISRAËL
Praedicta
5 Shatner Street
P.O. Box 34030
Jerusalem 91430   Tel. (2) 52.84.90/1/2
Telefax: (2) 52.84.93

R.O.Y. International
P.O. Box 13056
Tel Aviv 61130   Tel. (3) 546 1423
Telefax: (3) 546 1442

Palestinian Authority/Middle East:
INDEX Information Services
P.O.B. 19502
Jerusalem   Tel. (2) 27.12.19
Telefax: (2) 27.16.34

ITALY – ITALIE
Libreria Commissionaria Sansoni
Via Duca di Calabria 1/1
50125 Firenze   Tel. (055) 64.54.15
Telefax: (055) 64.12.57
Via Bartolini 29
20155 Milano   Tel. (02) 36.50.83

Editrice e Libreria Herder
Piazza Montecitorio 120
00186 Roma   Tel. 679.46.28
                                Telefax: 678.47.51

Libreria Hoepli
Via Hoepli 5
20121 Milano   Tel. (02) 86.54.46
                                Telefax: (02) 805.28.86

Libreria Scientifica
Dott. Lucio de Biasio 'Aeiou'
Via Coronelli, 6
20146 Milano   Tel. (02) 48.95.45.52
                                Telefax: (02) 48.95.45.48

JAPAN – JAPON
OECD Publications and Information Centre
Landic Akasaka Building
2-3-4 Akasaka, Minato-ku
Tokyo 107   Tel. (81.3) 3586.2016
                                Telefax: (81.3) 3584.7929

KOREA – CORÉE
Kyobo Book Centre Co. Ltd.
P.O. Box 1658, Kwang Hwa Moon
Seoul   Tel. 730.78.91
                                Telefax: 735.00.30

MALAYSIA – MALAISIE
University of Malaya Bookshop
University of Malaya
P.O. Box 1127, Jalan Pantai Baru
59700 Kuala Lumpur
Malaysia   Tel. 756.5000/756.5425
                                Telefax: 756.3246

MEXICO – MEXIQUE
OECD Publications and Information Centre
Edificio INFOTEC
Av. San Fernando no. 37
Col. Toriello Guerra
Tlalpan C.P. 14050
Mexico D.F.
                      Tel. (525) 606 00 11 Extension 100
                                Fax: (525) 606 13 07

Revistas y Periodicos Internacionales S.A. de C.V.
Florencia 57 - 1004
Mexico, D.F. 06600   Tel. 207.81.00
                                Telefax: 208.39.79

NETHERLANDS – PAYS-BAS
SDU Uitgeverij Plantijnstraat
Externe Fondsen
Postbus 20014
2500 EA's-Gravenhage   Tel. (070) 37.89.880
Voor bestellingen: Telefax: (070) 34.75.778

**NEW ZEALAND –
NOUVELLE-ZÉLANDE**
GPLegislation Services
P.O. Box 12418
Thorndon, Wellington   Tel. (04) 496.5655
                                Telefax: (04) 496.5698

NORWAY – NORVÈGE
NIC INFO A/S
Bertrand Narvesens vei 2
P.O. Box 6512 Etterstad
0606 Oslo 6   Tel. (022) 57.33.00
                                Telefax: (022) 68.19.01

PAKISTAN
Mirza Book Agency
65 Shahrah Quaid-E-Azam
Lahore 54000   Tel. (42) 353.601
                                Telefax: (42) 231.730

PHILIPPINE – PHILIPPINES
International Booksource Center Inc.
Rm 179/920 Cityland 10 Condo Tower 2
HV dela Costa Ext cor Valero St.
Makati Metro Manila   Tel. (632) 817 9676
                           Telefax: (632) 817 1741

POLAND – POLOGNE
Ars Polona
00-950 Warszawa
Krakowskie Przedmieácie 7   Tel. (22) 264760
                                Telefax: (22) 268673

PORTUGAL
Livraria Portugal
Rua do Carmo 70-74
Apart. 2681
1200 Lisboa   Tel. (01) 347.49.82/5
                                Telefax: (01) 347.02.64

SINGAPORE – SINGAPOUR
Gower Asia Pacific Pte Ltd.
Golden Wheel Building
41, Kallang Pudding Road, No. 04-03
Singapore 1334   Tel. 741.5166
                                Telefax: 742.9356

SPAIN – ESPAGNE
Mundi-Prensa Libros S.A.
Castelló 37, Apartado 1223
Madrid 28001   Tel. (91) 431.33.99
                                Telefax: (91) 575.39.98

Mundi-Prensa Barcelona
Consell de Cent No. 391
08009 – Barcelona   Tel. (93) 488.34.92
                                Telefax: (93) 487.76.59

Llibreria de la Generalitat
Palau Moja
Rambla dels Estudis, 118
08002 – Barcelona
                    (Subscripcions) Tel. (93) 318.80.12
                    (Publicacions) Tel. (93) 302.67.23
                                Telefax: (93) 412.18.54

SRI LANKA
Centre for Policy Research
c/o Colombo Agencies Ltd.
No. 300-304, Galle Road
Colombo 3   Tel. (1) 574240, 573551-2
                        Telefax: (1) 575394, 510711

SWEDEN – SUÈDE
CE Fritzes AB
S–106 47 Stockholm   Tel. (08) 690.90.90
                                Telefax: (08) 20.50.21

Subscription Agency/Agence d'abonnements :
Wennergren-Williams Info AB
P.O. Box 1305
171 25 Solna   Tel. (08) 705.97.50
                                Telefax: (08) 27.00.71

SWITZERLAND – SUISSE
Maditec S.A. (Books and Periodicals - Livres
et périodiques)
Chemin des Palettes 4
Case postale 266
1020 Renens VD 1   Tel. (021) 635.08.65
                                Telefax: (021) 635.07.80

Librairie Payot S.A.
4, place Pépinet
CP 3212
1002 Lausanne   Tel. (021) 320.25.11
                                Telefax: (021) 320.25.14

Librairie Unilivres
6, rue de Candolle
1205 Genève   Tel. (022) 320.26.23
                                Telefax: (022) 329.73.18

Subscription Agency/Agence d'abonnements :
Dynapresse Marketing S.A.
38, avenue Vibert
1227 Carouge   Tel. (022) 308.07.89
                                Telefax: (022) 308.07.99

See also – Voir aussi :
OECD Publications and Information Centre
August-Bebel-Allee 6
D-53175 Bonn (Germany)   Tel. (0228) 959.120
                           Telefax: (0228) 959.12.17

THAILAND – THAÏLANDE
Suksit Siam Co. Ltd.
113, 115 Fuang Nakhon Rd.
Opp. Wat Rajbopith
Bangkok 10200   Tel. (662) 225.9531/2
                                Telefax: (662) 222.5188

TUNISIA – TUNISIE
Grande Librairie Spécialisée
Fendri Ali
Avenue Haffouz Imm El-Intilaka
Bloc B 1 Sfax 3000   Tel. (216-4) 296 855
                                Telefax: (216-4) 298.270

TURKEY – TURQUIE
Kültür Yayinlari Is-Türk Ltd. Sti.
Atatürk Bulvari No. 191/Kat 13
Kavaklidere/Ankara
                        Tel. (312) 428.11.40 Ext. 2458
                                Telefax: (312) 417 24 90
Dolmabahce Cad. No. 29
Besiktas/Istanbul   Tel. (212) 260 7188

UNITED KINGDOM – ROYAUME-UNI
HMSO
Gen. enquiries   Tel. (171) 873 8242
Postal orders only:
P.O. Box 276, London SW8 5DT
Personal Callers HMSO Bookshop
49 High Holborn, London WC1V 6HB
                                Telefax: (171) 873 8416
Branches at: Belfast, Birmingham, Bristol,
Edinburgh, Manchester

UNITED STATES – ÉTATS-UNIS
OECD Publications and Information Center
2001 L Street N.W., Suite 650
Washington, D.C. 20036-4922 Tel. (202) 785.6323
                                Telefax: (202) 785.0350

Subscriptions to OECD periodicals may also be
placed through main subscription agencies.

Les abonnements aux publications périodiques de
l'OCDE peuvent être souscrits auprès des
principales agences d'abonnement.

Orders and inquiries from countries where Distribu-
tors have not yet been appointed should be sent to:
OECD Publications Service, 2, rue André-Pascal,
75775 Paris Cedex 16, France.

Les commandes provenant de pays où l'OCDE n'a
pas encore désigné de distributeur peuvent être
adressées à : OCDE, Service des Publications,
2, rue André-Pascal, 75775 Paris Cedex 16, France.

1-1996

OECD PUBLICATIONS, 2, rue André-Pascal, 75775 PARIS CEDEX 16
PRINTED IN FRANCE
(40 96 01 3) ISBN 92-64-04839-1 – No. 48426 1996